BESTSELLING BILINGUAL DICTIONARIES

Collins

Collins

Italian
Dictionary

Collins

HarperCollins Publishers
Westerhill Road
Bishopbriggs
Glasgow
G64 2QT
Great Britain

Second Edition 2010

Reprint 10 9 8 7 6 5 4 3 2

© HarperCollins Publishers 2008, 2010

ISBN 978-0-00-732318-0

Collins® and Bank of English® are
registered trademarks of
HarperCollins Publishers Limited

www.collinslanguage.com

A catalogue record for this book is
available from the British Library

HarperCollins Publishers, 10 East 53rd Street,
New York, NY 10022

COLLINS ITALIAN CONCISE DICTIONARY
Fifth US Edition 2010

ISBN 978-0-06-114185-0

www.harpercollins.com

HarperCollins books may be purchased for
educational, business, or sales promotional
use. For information, please write to:
Special Markets Department, HarperCollins
Publishers, 10 East 53rd Street, New York,
NY 10022

Typeset by Davidson Publishing Solutions,
Glasgow

Printed in Italy by
LEGO S.p.A., Lavis (Trento), Italy

Acknowledgements
We would like to thank those authors and
publishers who kindly gave permission for
copyright material to be used in the Collins
Word Web. We would also like to thank Times
Newspapers Ltd for providing valuable data.

MANAGING EDITOR
Gaëlle Amiot-Cadey

PROJECT MANAGEMENT
Maggie Seaton
Rachel Smith

CONTRIBUTORS
Gabriella Bacchelli
Donatella Boi
Michela Clari
Daphne Day
Genevieve Gerrard
Angela Jack
Joyce Littlejohn
Val McNulty
Elizabeth Potter
Caroline Smart
Jill Williams

TECHNICAL SUPPORT
Thomas Callan

SERIES EDITOR
Rob Scriven

Indice

Contents

William Collins' dream of knowledge for all began with the publication of his first book in 1819. A self-educated mill worker, he not only enriched millions of lives, but also founded a flourishing publishing house. Today, staying true to this spirit, Collins books are packed with inspiration, innovation, and practical expertise. They place you at the centre of a world of possibility and give you exactly what you need to explore it.

Language is the key to this exploration, and at the heart of Collins Dictionaries is language as it is really used. New words, phrases, and meanings spring up every day, and all of them are captured and analysed by the Collins Word Web. Constantly updated, and with over 2.5 billion entries, this living language resource is unique to our dictionaries.

Words are tools for life. And a Collins Dictionary makes them work for you.

Collins. Do more.

Introduzione

Se desiderate imparare l'inglese o approfondire le conoscenze già acquisite, se volete leggere o redigere dei testi in inglese, oppure conversare con interlocutori di madrelingua inglese, se siete studenti, turisti, uomini o donne d'affari avete scelto il compagno di viaggio ideale per esprimervi e comunicare in inglese sia a voce che per iscritto. Strumento pratico e moderno, il vostro dizionario dà largo spazio al linguaggio quotidiano in campi quali l'attualità, gli affari, la gestione d'ufficio, l'informatica e il turismo. Come in tutti i nostri dizionari, grande importanza è stata data alla lingua contemporanea e alle espressioni idiomatiche.

Come usare il dizionario

Troverete qui di seguito alcune spiegazioni sul modo in cui le informazioni sono state presentate nel testo. L'obiettivo del dizionario è quello di darvi il maggior numero possibile di informazioni senza tuttavia sacrificare la chiarezza all'interno delle voci.

Le voci

Qui di seguito verranno descritti i vari elementi di cui si compone una voce tipo del vostro dizionario.

La trascrizione fonetica

Come regola generale è stata data la pronuncia di tutte le parole inglesi e quella delle parole italiane che potevano presentare qualche difficoltà per il parlante inglese. Nella parte inglese-italiano, tuttavia, per la pronuncia di nomi composti formati da due parole non unite dal trattino si dovrà cercare la trascrizione di ciascuna di queste parole alla rispettiva posizione alfabetica. La pronuncia si trova tra parentesi quadra, subito dopo il lemma. Come nella maggior parte dei dizionari moderni è stato adottato il sistema noto come "alfabeto fonetico internazionale". Troverete qui di seguito, a pagina xiii e xiv, un elenco completo dei caratteri utilizzati in questo sistema.

Le categorie grammaticali

Tutte le parole appartengono ad una categoria grammaticale, cioè possono essere sostantivi, verbi, aggettivi, avverbi, pronomi, articolio o congiunzioni.

I sostantivi possono essere singolari o plurali, sia in italiano che in inglese, e maschili o femminili in italiano. I verbi possono essere transitivi o intransitivi in entrambe le lingue, ma anche riflessivi o impersonali in italiano. La categoria grammaticale è stata introdotta in *corsivo* subito dopo la pronuncia ed eventuali informazioni di tipo morfologico (plurali irregolari ecc.).

Numerose voci sono state suddivise in varie categorie grammaticali. Per esempio la parola italiana **bene** può essere sia un avverbio che un aggettivo o un sostantivo, e la parola inglese **sneeze** può essere sia un sostantivo ("starnuto") che un verbo intransitivo ("starnutire"). Analogamente il verbo italiano **correre** può essere usato sia come verbo intransitivo ("correre alla stazione") che come transitivo ("correre un rischio"). Per presentare la voce con maggiore chiarezza e permettervi di trovare rapidamente la traduzione che cercate, è stato introdotto il simbolo ■ per contrassegnare il passaggio da una categoria grammaticale ad un'altra.

Suddivisioni semantiche

La maggior parte delle parole ha più di un significato. Per esempio, la parola **fiocco** può essere sia un'annodatura di un nastro che una falda di neve. Molte parole si traducono in modo diverso a seconda del contesto in cui sono usate: per esempio **scala** si tradurrà in inglese con "staircase" o "stairs" se si tratta di una scala con gradini, con "ladder" se è una scala a pioli. Per permettervi di scegliere la traduzione giusta per ciascuno dei contesti in cui la parola si può trovare, le voci sono state suddivise in categorie di significato. Ciascuna suddivisione è introdotta da un "indicatore d'uso" tra parentesi in *corsivo*. Le voci **fiocco** e **scala** compariranno quindi nel testo nel modo seguente:

> **fiocco, chi** *sm* (*di nastro*) bow; (*di stoffa, lana*) flock; (*di neve*) flake
> **scala** *sf* (*a gradini etc*) staircase, stairs *pl*; (*a pioli, di corda*) ladder

Per segnalare la traduzione appropriata sono stati introdotti anche degli indicatori d'ambito d'uso in *corsivo* con la prima lettera maiuscola, tra parentesi, spesso in forma abbreviata, come per esempio nel caso della voce **tromba**:

> **tromba** *sf* (*Mus*) trumpet; (*Aut*) horn

L'elenco completo delle abbreviazioni adottate nel dizionario è riportato alle pagine xiii e xiv.

Le traduzioni

Per la maggior parte delle parole inglesi ed italiane ci sono traduzioni precise a seconda del significato o del contesto, come risulta dagli esempi riportati fin qui. A volte, tuttavia, le parole non hanno un preciso equivalente nella lingua d'arrivo: in questi casi è stato fornito un equivalente approssimativo, preceduto dal segno ≈, come ad esempio per l'abbreviazione **RAC**, per cui è stato dato l'equivalente italiano "A.C.I.", dato che le due associazioni svolgono nei due paesi funzioni analoghe:

> **RAC** *n abbr* (*Brit*: = *Royal Automobile Club*) ≈ A.C.I. *m* (= *Automobile Club d'Italia*)

A volte è persino impossibile trovare un equivalente approssimativo. Questo è il caso, per esempio, di piatti tipici di un certo paese, come ad esempio **pandoro**:

> **pandoro** *sm type of sponge cake eaten at Christmas*

In questi casi, al posto della traduzione, che non esiste, comparirà una spiegazione: per maggiore chiarezza, questa spiegazione o glossa è stata messa in *corsivo*.

Molto spesso la traduzione di una parola può non funzionare all'interno di una data locuzione. Ad esempio alla voce **dare**, verbo spesso tradotto con "to give" in inglese, troviamo varie locuzioni per alcune delle quali la traduzione fornita all'inizio della voce non si può utilizzare: **quanti anni mi dai?** "how old do you think I am?" **danno ancora quel film?** "is that film still showing?", **dare per certo qc** "to consider sth certain", e così via. Ed è proprio in questi casi che potrete verificare l'utilità e la completezza del dizionario, che contiene una ricca gamma di composti, locuzioni e frasi idiomatiche.

Il registro linguistico

In italiano sapete istintivamente scegliere l'espressione corretta da usare a seconda del contesto in cui vi esprimete. Per esempio saprete quando dire **Non me ne importa!** e quando invece potete dire **Chi se ne frega?** Più difficile sarà farlo in inglese, dove avete minore consapevolezza delle sfumature di registro linguistico. Per questo motivo nella parte inglese-italiano le parole ed espressioni inglesi di uso più familiare sono segnalate dall'abbreviazione *(col)*, mentre *(col!)* segnala le parole ed espressioni volgari. Nella parte italiano-inglese *(!)* dopo una traduzione segnala che si tratta di una parola od espressione volgare.

Parole chiave

Come vedrete, ad alcune voci è stato riservato un trattamento particolare sia dal punto di vista grafico che da quello linguistico. Si tratta di voci come **essere** o **fare**, o dei loro equivalenti inglesi **be** e **do**, che per la loro importanza e complessità meritano una strutturazione più articolata ed un maggior numero di locuzioni illustrative. Queste voci sono strutturate in diverse categorie di significato contrassegnate da numeri, e le costruzioni sintattiche e locuzioni che illustrano quel particolare significato sono riportate all'interno della relativa categoria.

Informazioni culturali

Le voci affiancate da una riga verticale di punti approfondiscono aspetti della cultura italiana o di quella dei paesi di lingua inglese in argomenti quali la politica, la scuola, i mass media e le festività nazionali.

Introduction

You may be starting to learn Italian, or you may wish to extend your knowledge of the language. Perhaps you want to read and study Italian books, newspapers and magazines, or perhaps simply have a conversation with Italian speakers. Whatever the reason, whether you're a student, a tourist or want to use Italian for business, this is the ideal book to help you understand and communicate. This modern, user-friendly dictionary gives priority to everyday vocabulary and the language of current affairs, business and tourism. As in all Collins dictionaries, the emphasis is firmly placed on contemporary language and expressions.

How to use the dictionary
Below you will find an outline of how information is presented in your dictionary. Our aim is to give you the maximum amount of detail in the clearest and most helpful way.

Entries
A typical entry in your dictionary will be made up of the following elements:

Phonetic transcription
Phonetics appear in square brackets immediately after the headword. They are shown using the International Phonetic Alphabet (IPA), and a complete list of the symbols used in this system can be found on pages xiii and xiv.

Grammatical information
All words belong to one of the following parts of speech: noun, verb, adjective, adverb, pronoun, article, conjunction, preposition.

Nouns can be singular or plural and, in Italian, masculine or feminine. Verbs can be transitive, intransitive, reflexive or impersonal. Parts of speech appear in *italics* immediately after the phonetic spelling of the headword.

Often a word can have more than one part of speech. Just as the English word **chemical** can be an adjective or a noun, the Italian word **fondo** can be an adjective ("deep") or a masculine noun ("bottom"). In the same way the verb **to walk** is sometimes transitive, ie it takes an object ("to walk the dog") and sometimes intransitive, ie it doesn't take an object ("to walk to school"). To help you find the meaning you are looking for quickly and for clarity of presentation, the different part of speech categories are separated by the symbol ■.

Meaning divisions
Most words have more than one meaning. Take, for example, **punch** which can be, amongst other things, a blow with the fist or an object used for making holes. Other words are translated differently depending on the context in which they are used.

The transitive verb **to roll up**, for example, can be translated by "arrotolare" or "rimboccare" depending on what it is you are rolling up. To help you select the most appropriate translation in every context, entries are divided according to meaning. Each different meaning is introduced by an "indicator" in *italics* and in brackets. Thus, the examples given above will be shown as follows:

> **punch** n (*blow*) pugno; (*tool*) punzone m
> **roll up** vt (*carpet, cloth, map*) arrotolare; (*sleeves*) rimboccare

Likewise, some words can have a different meaning when used to talk about a specific subject area or field. For example, **bishop,** which is generally used to mean a high-ranking clergyman, is also the name of a chess piece. To show English speakers which translation to use, we have added "subject field labels" in *italics*, starting with a capital letter, and in brackets, in this case (*Chess*):

> **bishop** n vescovo; (*Chess*) alfiere m

Field labels are often shortened to save space. You will find a complete list of abbreviations used in the dictionary on pages xiii and xiv.

Translations

Most English words have a direct translation in Italian and vice versa, as shown in the examples given above. Sometimes, however, no exact equivalent exists in the target language. In such cases we have given an approximate equivalent, indicated by the sign ≈. Such is the case of **National Insurance**, the Italian equivalent of which is "Previdenza Sociale". This is not an exact translation since the systems of the two countries in question are quite different:

> **National Insurance** n (*Brit*) ≈ Previdenza Sociale

On occasion it is impossible to find even an approximate equivalent. This may be the case, for example, with the names of types of food:

> **cottage pie** n *piatto a base di carne macinata in sugo e purè di patate*

Here the translation (which doesn't exist) is replaced by an explanation. For increased clarity the explanation, or "gloss", is shown in *italics*.

It is often the case that a word, or a particular meaning of a word, cannot be translated in isolation. The translation of **Dutch**, for example, is "olandese". However, the phrase **to go Dutch** is rendered by "fare alla romana". Even an expression as simple as **washing powder** needs a separate translation since it translates as "detersivo (in polvere)", not "polvere per lavare". This is where your dictionary will prove to be particularly informative and useful since it contains an abundance of compounds, phrases and idiomatic expressions.

Levels of formality and familiarity

In English you instinctively know when to say **I'm broke** *or* **I'm a bit short of cash** and when to say **I don't have any money**. When you are trying to understand someone who is speaking Italian, however, or when you yourself try to speak Italian, it is important to know what is polite and what is less so, and what you can say in a relaxed situation but not in a formal context. To help you with this, on the Italian-English side we have added the label (*fam*) to show that an Italian word or expression is colloquial, while those words or expressions which are vulgar are given an exclamation mark (*fam!*), warning you they can cause serious offence. Note also that on the English-Italian side, translations which are vulgar are followed by an exclamation mark in brackets.

Keywords

Words labelled in the text as KEYWORDS, such as **be** and **do** or their Italian equivalents **essere** and **fare**, have been given special treatment because they form the basic elements of the language. This extra help will ensure that you know how to use these complex words with confidence.

Cultural information

Entries which appear distinguished in the text by a column of dots explain aspects of culture in Italy and English-speaking countries. Subject areas covered include politics, education, media and national festivals.

Abbreviazioni

Abbreviations

abbreviazione	*abbr*	abbreviation
aggettivo	*adj*	adjective
amministrazione	*Admin*	administration
avverbio	*adv*	adverb
aeronautica, viaggi aerie	*Aer*	flying, air travel
aggettivo	*ag*	adjective
agricoltura	*Agr*	agriculture
amministrazione	*Amm*	administration
anatomia	*Anat*	anatomy
architettura	*Archit*	architecture
astronomia, astrologia	*Astr*	astronomy, astrology
l'automobile	*Aut*	the motor car and motoring
verbo ausiliare	*aux vb*	auxiliary verb
avverbio	*av*	adverb
aeronautica, viaggi aerei	*Aviat*	flying, air travel
biologia	*Biol*	biology
botanica	*Bot*	botany
inglese della Gran Bretagna	*Brit*	British English
consonante	*C*	consonant
chimica	*Chim, Chem*	chemistry
familiare (! da evitare)	*col(!)*	colloquial usage (! particularly offensive)
commercio, finanza, banca	*Comm*	commerce, finance, banking
informatica	*Comput*	computing
congiunzione	*cong*	conjunction
congiunzione	*conj*	conjunction
edilizia	*Constr*	building
sostantivo usato come aggettivo, non può essere usato nè come attributo, nè dopo il sostantivo qualificato	*cpd*	compound element: noun used as adjective and which cannot follow the noun it qualifies
cucina	*Cus, Culin*	cookery
davanti a	*dav*	before
determinante: articolo, aggettivo dimostrativo o indefinito etc	*det*	determiner: article, demonstrative etc
diritto	*Dir*	law
economia	*Econ*	economics
edilizia	*Edil*	building
elettricità, elettronica	*Elettr, Elec*	electricity, electronics
esclamazione, interiezione	*escl, excl*	exclamation, interjection
specialmente	*esp*	especially
femminile	*f*	feminine
familiare (! da evitare)	*fam(!)*	colloquial usage (! particularly offensive)
ferrovia	*Ferr*	railways
figurato	*fig*	figurative use
fisiologia	*Fisiol*	physiology
fotografia	*Fot*	photography
(verbo inglese) la cui particella è inseparabile dal verbo	*vt fus*	(phrasal verb) where the particle cannot be separated from main verb
nella maggior parte dei sensi; generalmente	*gen*	in most or all senses; generally
geografia, geologia	*Geo*	geography, geology
geometria	*Geom*	geometry
impersonale	*impers*	impersonal
informatica	*Inform*	computing

insegnamento, sistema scolastico e universitario	Ins	schooling, schools and universities
invariabile	inv	invariable
irregolare	irreg	irregular
grammatica, linguistica	Ling	grammar, linguistics
maschile	m	masculine
matematica	Mat(h)	mathematics
termine medico, medicina	Med	medical term, medicine
il tempo, meteorologia	Meteor	the weather, meteorology
maschile o femminile	m/f	either masculine or feminine depending on sex
esercito, linguaggio militare	Mil	military matters
musica	Mus	music
sostantivo	n	noun
nautical	Naut	sailing, navigation
sostantivo che non si usa al plurale	no pl	uncountable noun: not used in the plural
numerale (aggettivo, sostantivo)	num	numeral adjective or noun
	o.s.	oneself
peggiorativo	peg, pej	derogatory, pejorative
fotografia	Phot	photography
fisiologia	Physiol	physiology
plurale	pl	plural
politica	Pol	politics
participio passato	pp	past participle
preposizione	prep	preposition
pronome	pron	pronoun
psicologia, psichiatria	Psic, Psych	psychology, psychiatry
tempo passato	pt	past tense
qualcosa	qc	
qualcuno	qn	
religione, liturgia	Rel	religions, church service
sostantivo	s	noun
	sb	somebody
insegnamento, sistema scolastico e universitario	Scol	schooling, schools and universities
singolare	sg	singular
soggetto (grammaticale)	sog	(grammatical) subject
	sth	something
congiuntivo	sub	subjunctive
soggetto (grammaticale)	subj	(grammatical) subject
termine tecnico, tecnologia	Tecn, Tech	technical term, technology
telecomunicazioni	Tel	telecommunications
tipografia	Tip	typography, printing
televisione	TV	television
tipografia	Typ	typography, printing
inglese degli Stati Uniti	US	American English
vocale	v	vowel
verbo (ausiliare)	vb (aus)	(auxiliary) verb
verbo o gruppo verbale con funzione intransitiva	vi	verb or phrasal verb used intransitively
verbo riflessivo	vr	reflexive verb
verbo o gruppo verbale con funzione transitiva	vt	verb or phrasal verb used transitively
zoologia	Zool	zoology
marchio registrato	®	registered trademark
introduce un'equivalenza culturale	≈	introduces a cultural equivalent

Trascrizione Fonetica

Consonanti

NB. **p, b, t, d, k, g** sono seguite
da un'aspirazione in inglese.

Consonants

NB. **p, b, t, d, k, g** are not
aspirated in Italian.

Italiano	IPA	English
padre	p	puppy
bambino	b	baby
tutto	t	tent
dado	d	daddy
cane che	k	cork kiss chord
gola ghiro	g	gag guess
sano	s	so rice kiss
svago esame	z	cousin buzz
scena	ʃ	sheep sugar
	ʒ	pleasure beige
pece lanciare	tʃ	church
giro gioco	dʒ	judge general
afa faro	f	farm raffle
vero bravo	v	very rev
	θ	thin maths
	ð	that other
letto ala	l	little ball
gli	ʎ	
rete arco	r	rat brat
ramo madre	m	mummy comb
no fumante	n	no ran
gnomo	ɲ	
	ŋ	singing bank
	h	hat reheat
buio piacere	j	yet
uomo guaio	w	wall bewail
	x	loch

Varie

per l'inglese: la "r" finale viene
pronunciata se seguita da una
vocale   ʳ

precede la sillaba accentata   ˈ

Miscellaneous

precedes the stressed syllable

Come regola generale, in tutte le voci la trascrizione fonetica in parentesi quadra segue il termine cui si riferisce. Tuttavia, dalla parte inglese-italiano del dizionario, per la pronuncia di composti che sono formati da più parole non unite da trattino che appaiono comunque nel dizionario, si veda la trascrizione fonetica di ciascuna di queste parole alla rispettiva posizione alfabetica.

Phonetic Transcription

Vocali

NB. La messa in equivalenza di certi suoni indica solo una rassomiglianza approssimativa.

Vowels

NB. The pairing of some vowel sounds only indicates approximate equivalence.

Vocali		Vowels
vino idea	i i:	heel bead
	ɪ	hit pity
stella edera	e	
epoca eccetto	ɛ	set tent
mamma amore	a æ	apple bat
	ɑ:	after car calm
	ʌ	fun cousin
	ə	over above
	əː	urn fern work
rosa occhio	ɔ	wash pot
	ɔː	born cork
ponte ognuno	o	
utile zucca	u	full soot
	u:	boon lewd

Dittonghi

Diphthongs

	Dittonghi / Diphthongs
ɪə	beer tier
ɛə	tear fair there
eɪ	date plaice day
aɪ	life buy cry
au	owl foul now
əu	low no
ɔɪ	boil boy oily
uə	poor tour

In general, we give the pronunciation of each entry in square brackets after the word in question. However, on the English-Italian side, where the entry is composed of two or more unhyphenated words, each of which is given elsewhere in this dictionary, you will find the pronunciation of each word in its alphabetical position.

Italian Pronunciation

Vowels

Where the vowel **e** or the vowel **o** appears in a stressed syllable it can be either open [ɛ], [ɔ] or closed [e], [o]. As the open or closed pronunciation of these vowels is subject to regional variation, the distinction is of little importance to the user of this dictionary. Phonetic transcription for headwords containing these vowels will therefore only appear where other pronunciation difficulties are present.

Consonants

c before "e" or "i" is pronounced *tch*.

ch is pronounced like the "k" in "kit".

g before "e" or "i" is pronounced like the "j" in "jet".

gh is pronounced like the "g" in "get".

gl before "e" or "i" is normally pronounced like the "lli" in "million", and in a few cases only like the "gl" in "glove".

gn is pronounced like the "ny" in "canyon".

sc before "e" or "i" is pronounced *sh*.

z is pronounced like the "ts" in "stetson", or like the "d's" in "bird's eye".

Headwords containing the above consonants and consonantal groups have been given full phonetic transcription in this dictionary.

NB. All double written consonants in Italian are fully sounded: e.g. the *tt* in "tutto" is pronounced as in "hat trick".

Italian Verbs

1 Gerund 2 Past participle 3 Present 4 Imperfect 5 Past historic 6 Future 7 Conditional 8 Present subjunctive 9 Imperfect subjunctive 10 Imperative

accadere *like* **cadere**
accedere *like* **concedere**
accendere 2 acceso 5 accesi, accendesti
accludere *like* **alludere**
accogliere *like* **cogliere**
accondiscendere *like* **scendere**
accorgersi *like* **scorgere**
accorrere *like* **correre**
accrescere *like* **crescere**
addirsi *like* **dire**
addurre *like* **ridurre**
affiggere 2 affisso 5 affissi, affiggesti
affliggere 2 afflitto 5 afflissi, affliggesti
aggiungere *like* **giungere**
alludere 2 alluso 5 allusi, alludesti
ammettere *like* **mettere**
andare 3 vado, vai, va, andiamo, andate, vanno 6 andrò *etc* 8 vada 10 va'!, vada!, andate!, vadano!
annettere 2 annesso 5 annessi *o* annettei, annettesti
apparire 2 apparso 3 appaio, appari *o* apparisci, appare *o* apparisce, appaiono *o* appariscono 5 apparvi *o* apparsi, apparisti, apparve *o* apparì *o* apparse, apparvero *o* apparirono *o* apparsero 8 appaia *o* apparisca
appartenere *like* **tenere**
appendere 2 appeso 5 appesi, appendesti
apporre *like* **porre**
apprendere *like* **prendere**
aprire 2 aperto 3 apro 5 aprii *o* apersi, apristi 8 apra
ardere 2 arso 5 arsi, ardesti
ascendere *like* **scendere**
aspergere 2 asperso 5 aspersi, aspergesti
assalire *like* **salire**
assistere 2 assistito
assolvere 2 assolto 5 assolsi *o* assolvei *o* assolvetti, assolvesti
assumere 2 assunto 5 assunsi, assumesti
astenersi *like* **tenere**
attendere *like* **tendere**
attingere *like* **tingere**
AVERE 3 ho, hai, ha, abbiamo, avete, hanno 5 ebbi, avesti, ebbe, avemmo, aveste, ebbero 6 avrò *etc* 8 abbia *etc* 10 abbi!, abbia!, abbiate!, abbiano!
avvedersi *like* **vedere**
avvenire *like* **venire**
avvincere *like* **vincere**
avvolgere *like* **volgere**
benedire *like* **dire**

bere 1 bevendo 2 bevuto 3 bevo *etc* 4 bevevo *etc* 5 bevvi *o* bevetti, bevesti 6 berrò *etc* 8 beva *etc* 9 bevessi *etc*
cadere 5 caddi, cadesti 6 cadrò *etc*
chiedere 2 chiesto 5 chiesi, chiedesti
chiudere 2 chiuso 5 chiusi, chiudesti
cingere 2 cinto 5 cinsi, cingesti
cogliere 2 colto 3 colgo, colgono 5 colsi, cogliesti 8 colga
coincidere 2 coinciso 5 coincisi, coincidesti
coinvolgere *like* **volgere**
commettere *like* **mettere**
commuovere *like* **muovere**
comparire *like* **apparire**
compiacere *like* **piacere**
compiangere *like* **piangere**
comporre *like* **porre**
comprendere *like* **prendere**
comprimere 2 compresso 5 compressi, comprimesti
compromettere *like* **mettere**
concedere 2 concesso *o* conceduto 5 concessi *o* concedei *o* concedetti, concedesti
concludere *like* **alludere**
concorrere *like* **correre**
condurre *like* **ridurre**
confondere *like* **fondere**
congiungere *like* **giungere**
connettere *like* **annettere**
conoscere 2 conosciuto 5 conobbi, conoscesti
consistere *like* **assistere**
contendere *like* **tendere**
contenere *like* **tenere**
contorcere *like* **torcere**
contraddire *like* **dire**
contraffare *like* **fare**
contrarre *like* **trarre**
convenire *like* **venire**
convincere *like* **vincere**
coprire *like* **aprire**
correggere *like* **reggere**
correre 2 corso 5 corsi, corresti
corrispondere *like* **rispondere**
corrompere *like* **rompere**
costringere *like* **stringere**
costruire 5 costrussi, costruisti
crescere 2 cresciuto 5 crebbi, crescesti
cuocere 2 cotto 3 cuocio, cociamo, cuociono 5 cossi, cocesti
dare 3 do, dai, dà, diamo, date, danno 5 diedi *o* detti, desti 6 darò *etc* 8 dia *etc* 9 dessi *etc* 10 da'!, dai!, date!, diano!

decidere 2 deciso 5 decisi, decidesti
decrescere *like* crescere
dedurre *like* ridurre
deludere *like* alludere
deporre *like* porre
deprimere *like* comprimere
deridere *like* ridere
descrivere *like* scrivere
desumere *like* assumere
detergere *like* tergere
devolvere 2 devoluto
difendere 2 difeso 5 difesi, difendesti
diffondere *like* fondere
dipendere *like* appendere
dipingere *like* tingere
dire 1 dicendo 2 detto 3 dico, dici, dice,
   diciamo, dite, dicono 4 dicevo *etc* 5 dissi,
   dicesti 6 dirò *etc* 8 dica, diciamo, diciate,
   decano 9 dicessi *etc* 10 di'!, dica!, dite!,
   dicano!
dirigere 2 diretto 5 diressi, dirigesti
discendere *like* scendere
dischiudere *like* chiudere
disciogliere *like* sciogliere
discorrere *like* correre
discutere 2 discusso 5 discussi, discutesti
disfare *like* fare
disilludere *like* alludere
disperdere *like* perdere
dispiacere *like* piacere
disporre *like* porre
dissolvere 2 dissolto *o* disoluto 5 dissolsi *o*
   dissolvetti *o* dissolvei, dissolvesti
dissuadere *like* persuadere
distendere *like* tendere
distinguere 2 distinto 5 distinsi,
   distinguesti
distogliere *like* togliere
distrarre *like* trarre
distruggere *like* struggere
divenire *like* venire
dividere 2 diviso 5 divisi, dividesti
dolere 3 dolgo, duoli, duole, dolgono
   5 dolsi, dolesti 6 dorrò *etc* 8 dolga
DORMIRE 1 GERUND dormendo
2 PAST PARTICIPLE dormito
3 PRESENT dormo, dormi, dorme, dormiamo,
   dormite, dormono
4 IMPERFECT dormivo, dormivi, dormiva,
   dormivamo, dormivate, dormivano
5 PAST HISTORIC dormii, dormisti, dormì,
   dormimmo, dormiste, dormirono
6 FUTURE dormirò, dormirai, dormirà,
   dormiremo, dormirete, dormiranno
7 CONDITIONAL dormirei, dormiresti,
   dormirebbe, dormiremmo, dormireste,
   dormirebbero
8 PRESENT SUBJUNCTIVE dorma, dorma,
   dorma, dormiamo, dormiate, dormano

9 IMPERFECT SUBJUNCTIVE dormissi,
   dormissi, dormisse, dormissimo,
   dormiste, dormissero
10 IMPERATIVE dormi!, dorma!, dormite!,
   dormano!
dovere 3 devo *o* debbo, devi, deve,
   dobbiamo, dovete, devono *o* debbono
   6 dovrò *etc*
8 debba, dobbiamo, dobbiate, devano *o*
   debbano
eccellere 2 eccelso 5 eccelsi, eccellesti
eludere *like* alludere
emergere 2 emerso 5 emersi, emergesti
emettere *like* mettere
erigere *like* dirigere
escludere *like* alludere
esigere 2 esatto
esistere 2 esistito
espellere 2 espulso 5 espulsi, espellesti
esplodere 2 esploso 5 esplosi, esplodesti
esporre *like* porre
esprimere *like* comprimere
ESSERE 2 stato 3 sono, sei, è, siamo, siete,
   sono 4 ero, eri, era, eravamo, eravate,
   erano 5 fui, fosti, fu, fummo, foste, furono
   6 sarò *etc* 8 sia *etc* 9 fossi, fossi, fosse,
   fossimo, foste, fossero 10 sii!, sia!, siate!,
   siano!
estendere *like* tendere
estinguere *like* distinguere
estrarre *like* trarre
evadere 2 evaso 5 evasi, evadesti
evolvere 2 evoluto
fare 1 facendo 2 fatto 3 faccio, fai, fa,
   facciamo, fate, fanno 4 facevo *etc* 5 feci,
   facesti 6 farò *etc* 8 faccia *etc* 9 facessi *etc*
   10 fa'!, faccia!, fate!, facciano!
fingere *like* cingere
FINIRE 1 GERUND finendo
2 PAST PARTICIPLE finito
3 PRESENT finisco, finisci, finisce, finiamo,
   finite, finiscono
4 IMPERFECT finivo, finivi, finiva, finivamo,
   finivate, finivano
5 PAST HISTORIC finii, finisti, finì, finimmo,
   finiste, finirono
6 FUTURE finirò, finirai, finirà, finiremo,
   finirete, finiranno
7 CONDITIONAL finirei, finiresti, finirebbe,
   finiremmo, finireste, finirebbero
8 PRESENT SUBJUNCTIVE finisca, finisca,
   finisca, finiamo, finiate, finiscano
9 IMPERFECT SUBJUNCTIVE finissi, finissi,
   finisse, finissimo, finiste, finissero
10 IMPERATIVE finisci!, finisca!, finite!,
   finiscano!
flettere 2 flesso
fondere 2 fuso 5 fusi, fondesti
friggere 2 fritto 5 frissi, friggesti

fungere 2 funto 5 funsi, fungesti
giacere 3 giaccio, giaci, giace, giac(c)iamo, giacete, giacciono 5 giacqui, giacesti 8 giaccia *etc* 10 giaci!, giaccia!, giac(c)iamo!, giacete!, giacciano!
giungere 2 giunto 5 giunsi, giungesti
godere 6 godrò *etc*
illudere *like* **alludere**
immergere *like* **emergere**
immettere *like* **mettere**
imporre *like* **porre**
imprimere *like* **comprimere**
incidere *like* **decidere**
includere *like* **alludere**
incorrere *like* **correre**
incutere *like* **discutere**
indulgere 2 indulto 5 indulsi, indulgesti
indurre *like* **ridurre**
inferire¹ 2 inferto 5 infersi, inferisti
inferire² 2 inferito 5 inferii, inferisti
infliggere *like* **affliggere**
infrangere 2 infranto 5 infransi, infrangesti
infondere *like* **fondere**
insistere *like* **assistere**
intendere *like* **tendere**
interdire *like* **dire**
interporre *like* **porre**
interrompere *like* **rompere**
intervenire *like* **venire**
intraprendere *like* **prendere**
introdurre *like* **ridurre**
invadere *like* **evadere**
irrompere *like* **rompere**
iscrivere *like* **scrivere**
istruire *like* **costruire**
ledere 2 leso 5 lesi, ledesti
leggere 2 letto 5 lessi, leggesti
maledire *like* **dire**
mantenere *like* **tenere**
mettere 2 messo 5 misi, mettesti
mordere 2 morso 5 morsi, mordesti
morire 2 morto 3 muoio, muori, muore, moriamo, morite, muoiono 6 morirò *o* morrò *etc* 8 muoia
mungere 2 munto 5 munsi, mungesti
muovere 2 mosso 5 mossi, movesti
nascere 2 nato 5 nacqui, nascesti
nascondere 2 nascosto 5 nascosi, nascondesti
nuocere 2 nuociuto 3 nuoccio, nuoci, nuoce, nociamo *o* nuociamo, nuocete, nuocciono 4 nuocevo *etc* 5 nocqui, nuocesti 6 nuocerò *etc* 7 nuoccia
occorrere *like* **correre**
offendere *like* **difendere**
offrire 2 offerto 3 offro 5 offersi *o* offrii, offristi 8 offra
omettere *like* **mettere**

opporre *like* **porre**
opprimere *like* **comprimere**
ottenere *like* **tenere**
parere 2 parso 3 paio, paiamo, paiono 5 parvi *o* parsi, paresti 6 parrò *etc* 8 paia, paiamo, paiate, paiano
PARLARE 1 GERUND parlando
2 PAST PARTICIPLE parlato
3 PRESENT parlo, parli, parla, parliamo, parlate, parlano
4 IMPERFECT parlavo, parlavi, parlava, parlavamo, parlavate, parlavano
5 PAST HISTORIC parlai, parlasti, parlò, parlammo, parlaste, parlarono
6 FUTURE parlerò, parlerai, parlerà, parleremo, parlerete, parleranno
7 CONDITIONAL parlerei, parleresti, parlerebbe, parleremmo, parlereste, parlerebbero
8 PRESENT SUBJUNCTIVE parli, parli, parli, parliamo, parliate, parlino
9 IMPERFECT SUBJUNCTIVE parlassi, parlassi, parlasse, parlassimo, parlaste, parlassero
10 IMPERATIVE parla!, parli!, parlate!, parlino!
percorrere *like* **correre**
percuotere 2 percosso 5 percossi, percotesti
perdere 2 perso *o* perduto 5 persi *o* perdei *o* perdetti, perdesti
permettere *like* **mettere**
persuadere 2 persuaso 5 persuasi, persuadesti
pervenire *like* **venire**
piacere 2 piaciuto 3 piaccio, piacciamo, piacciono 5 piacqui, piacesti 8 piaccia *etc*
piangere 2 pianto 5 piansi, piangesti
piovere 5 piovve
porgere 2 porto 5 porsi, porgesti
porre 1 ponendo 2 posto 3 pongo, poni, pone, poniamo, ponete, pongono 4 ponevo *etc* 5 posi, ponesti 6 porrò *etc* 8 ponga, poniamo, poniate, pongano 9 ponessi *etc*
posporre *like* **porre**
possedere *like* **sedere**
potere 3 posso, puoi, può, possiamo, potete, possono 6 potrò *etc* 8 possa, possiamo, possiate, possano
prediligere 2 prediletto 5 predilessi, prediligesti
predire *like* **dire**
prefiggersi *like* **affiggere**
preludere *like* **alludere**
prendere 2 preso 5 presi, prendesti
preporre *like* **porre**
prescrivere *like* **scrivere**
presiedere *like* **sedere**
presumere *like* **assumere**
pretendere *like* **tendere**

prevalere *like* **valere**
prevedere *like* **vedere**
prevenire *like* **venire**
produrre *like* **ridurre**
proferire *like* **inferire**²
profondere *like* **fondere**
promettere *like* **mettere**
promuovere *like* **muovere**
proporre *like* **porre**
prorompere *like* **rompere**
proscrivere *like* **scrivere**
proteggere 2 protetto 5 protessi,
    proteggesti
provenire *like* **venire**
provvedere *like* **vedere**
pungere 2 punto 5 punsi, pungesti
racchiudere *like* **chiudere**
raccogliere *like* **cogliere**
radere 2 raso 5 rasi, radesti
raggiungere *like* **giungere**
rapprendere *like* **prendere**
ravvedersi *like* **vedere**
recidere *like* **decidere**
redigere 2 redatto
redimere 2 redento 5 redensi, redimesti
reggere 2 retto 5 ressi, reggesti
rendere 2 reso 5 resi, rendesti
reprimere *like* **comprimere**
rescindere *like* **scindere**
respingere *like* **spingere**
restringere *like* **stringere**
ricadere *like* **cadere**
richiedere *like* **chiedere**
riconoscere *like* **conoscere**
ricoprire *like* **coprire**
ricorrere *like* **correre**
ridere 2 riso 5 risi, ridesti
ridire *like* **dire**
ridurre 1 riducendo 2 ridotto 3 riduco *etc*
    4 riducevo *etc* 5 ridussi, riducesti 6 ridurrò
    etc 8 riduca *etc* 9 riducessi *etc*
riempire 1 riempiendo 3 riempio, riempi,
    riempie, riempiono
rifare *like* **fare**
riflettere 2 riflettuto *o* riflesso
rifrangere *like* **infrangere**
rimanere 2 rimasto 3 rimango, rimangono
    5 rimasi, rimanesti 6 rimarrò *etc*
    8 rimanga
rimettere *like* **mettere**
rimpiangere *like* **piangere**
rinchiudere *like* **chiudere**
rincrescere *like* **crescere**
rinvenire *like* **venire**
ripercuotere *like* **percuotere**
riporre *like* **porre**
riprendere *like* **prendere**
riprodurre *like* **ridurre**
riscuotere *like* **scuotere**

risolvere *like* **assolvere**
risorgere *like* **sorgere**
rispondere 2 risposto 5 risposi, rispondesti
ritenere *like* **tenere**
ritrarre *like* **trarre**
riuscire *like* **uscire**
rivedere *like* **vedere**
rivivere *like* **vivere**
rivolgere *like* **volgere**
rodere 2 roso 5 rosi, rodesti
rompere 2 rotto 5 ruppi, rompesti
salire 3 salgo, sali, salgono 8 salga
sapere 3 so, sai, sa, sappiamo, sapete, sanno
    5 seppi, sapesti 6 saprò *etc* 8 sappia *etc*
    10 sappi!, sappia!, sappiate!, sappiano!
scadere *like* **cadere**
scegliere 2 scelto 3 scelgo, scegli, sceglie,
    scegliamo, scegliete, scelgono 5 scelsi,
    scegliesti 8 scelga, scegliamo, scegliate,
    scelgano 10 scegli!, scelga!, scegliamo!,
    scegliete!, scelgano!
scendere 2 sceso 5 scesi, scendesti
schiudere *like* **chiudere**
scindere 2 scisso 5 scissi, scindesti
sciogliere 2 sciolto 3 sciolgo, sciolgi,
    scioglie, sciogliamo, sciogliete, sciolgono
    5 sciolsi, sciogliesti 8 sciolga, sciogliamo,
    sciogliate, sciolgano 10 sciogli!, sciolga!,
    sciogliamo!, sciogliete!, sciolgano!
scommettere *like* **mettere**
scomparire *like* **apparire**
scomporre *like* **porre**
sconfiggere 2 sconfitto 5 sconfissi,
    sconfiggesti
sconvolgere *like* **volgere**
scoprire *like* **aprire**
scorgere 2 scorto 5 scorsi, scorgesti
scorrere *like* **correre**
scrivere 2 scritto 5 scrissi, scrivesti
scuotere 2 scosso 3 scuoto, scuoti, scuote,
    scotiamo, scotete, scuotono 5 scossi,
    scotesti 6 scoterò *etc* 8 scuota, scotiamo,
    scotiate, scuotano 10 scuoti!, scuota!,
    scotiamo!, scotete!, scuotano!
sedere 3 siedo, siedi, siede, siedono 8 sieda
seppellire 2 sepolto
smettere *like* **mettere**
smuovere *like* **muovere**
socchiudere *like* **chiudere**
soccorrere *like* **correre**
soddisfare *like* **fare**
soffriggere *like* **friggere**
soffrire 2 sofferto 5 soffersi *o* soffrii,
    soffristi
soggiungere *like* **giungere**
solere 2 solito 3 soglio, suoli, suole,
    sogliamo, solete, sogliono 8 soglia,
    sogliamo, sogliate, sogliano
sommergere *like* **emergere**

sopprimere *like* **comprimere**
sorgere 2 sorto 3 sorsi, sorgesti
sorprendere *like* **prendere**
sorreggere *like* **reggere**
sorridere *like* **ridere**
sospendere *like* **appendere**
sospingere *like* **spingere**
sostenere *like* **tenere**
sottintendere *like* **tendere**
spandere 2 spanto
spargere 2 sparso 5 sparsi, spargesti
sparire 5 sparii *o* sparvi, sparisti
spegnere 2 spento 3 spengo, spengono
  5 spensi, spegnesti 8 spenga
spendere 2 speso 5 spesi, spendesti
spingere 2 spinto 5 spinsi, spingesti
sporgere *like* **porgere**
stare 2 stato 3 sto, stai, sta, stiamo,
  state, stanno 5 stetti, stesti 6 starò *etc*
  8 stia *etc* 9 stessi *etc* 10 sta'!, stia!, state!,
  stiano!
stendere *like* **tendere**
storcere *like* **torcere**
stringere 2 stretto 5 strinsi, stringesti
struggere 2 strutto 5 strussi, struggesti
succedere *like* **concedere**
supporre *like* **porre**
svenire *like* **venire**
svolgere *like* **volgere**
tacere 2 taciuto 3 taccio, tacciono 5 tacqui,
  tacesti 8 taccia
tendere 2 teso 5 tesi, tendesti *etc*
tenere 3 tengo, tieni, tiene, tengono
  5 tenni, tenesti 6 terrò *etc* 8 tenga
tingere 2 tinto 5 tinsi, tingesti
togliere 2 tolto 3 tolgo, togli, toglie,
  togliamo, togliete, tolgono 5 tolsi,
  togliesti 8 tolga, togliamo, togliate,
  tolgano 10 togli!, tolga!, togliamo!,
  togliete!, tolgano!
torcere 2 torto 5 torsi, torcesti
tradurre *like* **ridurre**
trafiggere *like* **sconfiggere**
transigere *like* **esigere**
trarre 1 traendo 2 tratto 3 traggo, trai, trae,
  traiamo, traete, traggono 4 traevo *etc*

5 trassi, traesti 6 trarrò *etc* 8 tragga
  9 traessi *etc*
trascorrere *like* **correre**
trascrivere *like* **scrivere**
trasmettere *like* **mettere**
trasparire *like* **apparire**
trattenere *like* **tenere**
uccidere 2 ucciso 5 uccisi, uccidesti
udire 3 odo, odi, ode, odono 8 oda
ungere 2 unto 5 unsi, ungesti
uscire 3 esco, esci, esce, escono 8 esca
valere 2 valso 3 valgo, valgono 5 valsi,
  valesti 6 varrò *etc* 8 valga
vedere 2 visto *o* veduto 5 vidi, vedesti
  6 vedrò *etc*
VENDERE 1 GERUND vendendo
2 PAST PARTICIPLE venduto
3 PRESENT vendo, vendi, vende, vendiamo,
  vendete, vendono
4 IMPERFECT vendevo, vendevi, vendeva,
  vendevamo, vendevate, vendevano
5 PAST HISTORIC vendei *o* vendetti, vendesti,
  vendé *o* vendette, vendemmo, vendeste,
  venderono *o* vendettero
6 FUTURE venderò, venderai, venderà,
  venderemo, venderete, venderanno
7 CONDITIONAL venderei, venderesti,
  venderebbe, venderemmo, vendereste,
  venderebbero
8 PRESENT SUBJUNCTIVE venda, venda, venda,
  vendiamo, vendiate, vendano
9 IMPERFECT SUBJUNCTIVE vendessi,
  vendessi, vendesse, vendessimo, vendeste,
  vendessero
10 IMPERATIVE vendi!, venda!, vendete!,
  vendano!
venire 2 venuto 3 vengo, vieni, viene,
  vengono 5 venni, venisti 6 verrò *etc*
  8 venga
vincere 2 vinto 5 vinsi, vincesti
vivere 2 vissuto 5 vissi, vivesti
volere 3 voglio, vuoi, vuole, vogliamo,
  volete, vogliono 5 volli, volesti 6 vorrò
  etc 8 voglia *etc* 10 vogli!, voglia!, vogliate!,
  vogliano!
volgere 2 volto 5 volsi, volgesti

For additional information on Italian verb formation, see pp6-125 of the Grammar section.

Verbi inglesi

present	pt	pp	present	pt	pp
arise	arose	arisen	drink	drank	drunk
awake	awoke	awoken	drive	drove	driven
be (am, is, are; being)	was, were	been	dwell	dwelt	dwelt
			eat	ate	eaten
bear	bore	born(e)	fall	fell	fallen
beat	beat	beaten	feed	fed	fed
become	became	become	feel	felt	felt
befall	befell	befallen	fight	fought	fought
begin	began	begun	find	found	found
behold	beheld	beheld	flee	fled	fled
bend	bent	bent	fling	flung	flung
beset	beset	beset	fly	flew	flown
bet	bet, betted	bet, betted	forbid	forbad(e)	forbidden
bid (at auction, cards)	bid	bid	forecast	forecast	forecast
			forget	forgot	forgotten
bid (say)	bade	bidden	forgive	forgave	forgiven
bind	bound	bound	forsake	forsook	forsaken
bite	bit	bitten	freeze	froze	frozen
bleed	bled	bled	get	got	got, (US) gotten
blow	blew	blown			
break	broke	broken	give	gave	given
breed	bred	bred	go (goes)	went	gone
bring	brought	brought	grind	ground	ground
build	built	built	grow	grew	grown
burn	burnt, burned	burnt, burned	hang	hung	hung
			hang (execute)	hanged	hanged
burst	burst	burst	have	had	had
buy	bought	bought	hear	heard	heard
can	could	(been able)	hide	hid	hidden
cast	cast	cast	hit	hit	hit
catch	caught	caught	hold	held	held
choose	chose	chosen	hurt	hurt	hurt
cling	clung	clung	keep	kept	kept
come	came	come	kneel	knelt, kneeled	knelt, kneeled
cost	cost	cost			
cost (work out price of)	costed	costed	know	knew	known
			lay	laid	laid
creep	crept	crept	lead	led	led
cut	cut	cut	lean	leant, leaned	leant, leaned
deal	dealt	dealt			
dig	dug	dug	leap	leapt, leaped	leapt, leaped
do (3rd person: he/she/it does)	did	done			
			learn	learnt, learned	learnt, learned
draw	drew	drawn	leave	left	left
dream	dreamed, dreamt	dreamed, dreamt	lend	lent	lent
			let	let	let

present	pt	pp	present	pt	pp
lie (lying)	lay	lain	sow	sowed	sown, sowed
light	lit, lighted	lit, lighted			
lose	lost	lost	speak	spoke	spoken
make	made	made	speed	sped, speeded	sped, speeded
may	might	—			
mean	meant	meant	spell	spelt, spelled	spelt, spelled
meet	met	met			
mistake	mistook	mistaken	spend	spent	spent
mow	mowed	mown, mowed	spill	spilt, spilled	spilt, spilled
must	(had to)	(had to)	spin	spun	spun
pay	paid	paid	spit	spat	spat
put	put	put	spoil	spoiled, spoilt	spoiled, spoilt
quit	quit, quitted	quit, quitted			
			spread	spread	spread
read	read	read	spring	sprang	sprung
rid	rid	rid	stand	stood	stood
ride	rode	ridden	steal	stole	stolen
ring	rang	rung	stick	stuck	stuck
rise	rose	risen	sting	stung	stung
run	ran	run	stink	stank	stunk
saw	sawed	sawed, sawn	stride	strode	stridden
			strike	struck	struck
say	said	said	strive	strove	striven
see	saw	seen	swear	swore	sworn
seek	sought	sought	sweep	swept	swept
sell	sold	sold	swell	swelled	swollen, swelled
send	sent	sent			
set	set	set	swim	swam	swum
sew	sewed	sewn	swing	swung	swung
shake	shook	shaken	take	took	taken
shear	sheared	shorn, sheared	teach	taught	taught
			tear	tore	torn
			tell	told	told
shed	shed	shed	think	thought	thought
shine	shone	shone	throw	threw	thrown
shoot	shot	shot	thrust	thrust	thrust
show	showed	shown	tread	trod	trodden
shrink	shrank	shrunk	wake	woke, waked	woken, waked
shut	shut	shut			
sing	sang	sung	wear	wore	worn
sink	sank	sunk	weave	wove	woven
sit	sat	sat	weave (wind)	weaved	weaved
slay	slew	slain	wed	wedded, wed	wedded, wed
sleep	slept	slept			
slide	slid	slid	weep	wept	wept
sling	slung	slung	win	won	won
slit	slit	slit	wind	wound	wound
smell	smelt, smelled	smelt, smelled	wring	wrung	wrung
			write	wrote	written

I numeri

uno(a)	1	one
due	2	two
tre	3	three
quattro	4	four
cinque	5	five
sei	6	six
sette	7	seven
otto	8	eight
nove	9	nine
dieci	10	ten
undici	11	eleven
dodici	12	twelve
tredici	13	thirteen
quattordici	14	fourteen
quindici	15	fifteen
sedici	16	sixteen
diciassette	17	seventeen
diciotto	18	eighteen
diciannove	19	nineteen
venti	20	twenty
ventuno	21	twenty-one
ventidue	22	twenty-two
ventitré	23	twenty-three
ventotto	28	twenty-eight
trenta	30	thirty
quaranta	40	forty
cinquanta	50	fifty
sessanta	60	sixty
settanta	70	seventy
ottanta	80	eighty
novanta	90	ninety
cento	100	a hundred, one hundred
centouno	101	a hundred and one
duecento	200	two hundred
mille	1 000	a thousand, one thousand
milleduecentodue	1 202	one thousand two hundred and two
cinquemila	5 000	five thousand
un milione	1 000 000	a million, one million

Numbers

I numeri

primo(a), 1°
secondo(a), 2°
terzo(a), 3°
quarto(a)
quinto(a)
sesto(a)
settimo(a)
ottavo(a)
nono(a)
decimo(a)
undicesimo(a)
dodicesimo(a)
tredicesimo(a)
quattordicesimo(a)
quindicesimo(a)
sedicesimo(a)
diciassettesimo(a)
diciottesimo(a)
diciannovesimo(a)
ventesimo(a)
ventunesimo(a)
ventiduesimo(a)
ventitreesimo(a)
ventottesimo(a)
trentesimo(a)
centesimo(a)
centunesimo(a)
millesimo(a)
milionesimo(a)

Numbers

first, 1st
second, 2nd
third, 3rd
fourth, 4th
fifth, 5th
sixth, 6th
seventh
eighth
ninth
tenth
eleventh
twelfth
thirteenth
fourteenth
fifteenth
sixteenth
seventeenth
eighteenth
nineteenth
twentieth
twenty-first
twenty-second
twenty-third
twenty-eighth
thirtieth
hundredth
hundred-and-first
thousandth
millionth

L'ora

che ora è ?, che ore sono?
è ..., sono ...
mezzanotte
l'una (del mattino)
l'una e cinque
l'una e dieci
l'una e un quarto, l'una e quindici
l'una e venticinque
l'una e mezzo *o* mezza, l'una e trenta
l'una e trentacinque
le due meno venti, l'una e quaranta
le due meno un quarto, l'una e
  quarantacinque
le due meno dieci, l'una e cinquanta
mezzogiorno
le tre (del pomeriggio), le quindici
le sette (di sera), le diciannove

a che ora?
a mezzanotte
alle sette at
fra venti minuti
venti minuti fa

The time

what time is it?
it's ...
midnight
one o'clock (in the morning), one (am)
five past one
ten past one
a quarter past one, one fifteen
twenty-five past one, one twenty-five
half past one, one thirty
twenty-five to two, one thirty-five
twenty to two, one forty
a quarter to two, one forty-five

ten to two, one fifty
twelve o'clock, midday, noon
three o'clock (in the afternoon), three (pm)
seven o'clock (in the evening), seven (pm)

at what time?
at midnight
seven o'clock
in twenty minutes
twenty minutes ago

La data

oggi
domani
dopodomani
ieri
l'altro ieri
il giorno prima
il giorno dopo
la mattina
la sera
stamattina
stasera
questo pomeriggio
ieri mattina
ieri sera
domani mattina

The date

today
tomorrow
the day after tomorrow
yesterday
the day before yesterday
the day before, the previous day
the next *or* following day
morning
evening
this morning
this evening
this afternoon
yesterday morning
yesterday evening
tomorrow morning

domani sera	tomorrow evening
nella notte tra sabato e domenica	during Saturday night, during the night of Saturday to Sunday
viene sabato	he's coming on Saturday
il sabato	on Saturdays
tutti i sabati	every Saturday
sabato scorso, lo scorso sabato	last Saturday
il prossimo sabato	next Saturday
fra due sabati	a week on Saturday
fra tre sabati	a fortnight or two weeks on Saturday
da lunedý a sabato	from Monday to Saturday
tutti i giorni	every day
una volta alla settimana	once a week
una volta al mese	once a month
due volte alla settimana	twice a week
una settimana fa	a week ago
quindici giorni fa	a fortnight or two weeks ago
l'anno scorso or passato	last year
fra due giorni	in two days
fra una settimana	in a week
fra quindici giorni	in a fortnight or two weeks
il mese prossimo	next month
l'anno prossimo	next year

che giorno è oggi?	***what day is it?***
il primo/24 ottobre 2010	the 1st/24th of October 2010, October 1st/24th 2010
nel 2011	in 2011
il millenovecentonovantacinque	nineteen ninety-five
44 a.C.	44 BC
14 d.C.	14 AD
nel diciannovesimo secolo, nel XIX secolo, nell'Ottocento	in the nineteenth century
negli anni trenta	in the thirties
c'era una volta ...	once upon a time ...

Aa

A, a [a] *sf o m inv* (*lettera*) A, a; **A come Ancona** ≈ A for Andrew (*Brit*), ≈ A for Able (*US*); **dalla a alla z** from a to z

A *abbr* (= *altezza*) h; (= *area*) A; (= *autostrada*) ≈ M (*Brit*)

O **PAROLA CHIAVE**

a (*a*+*il* = **al**, *a*+*lo* = **allo**, *a*+*l'* = **all'**, *a*+*la* = **alla**, *a*+*i* = **ai**, *a*+*gli* = **agli**, *a*+*le* = **alle**) *prep* **1** (*stato in luogo*) at; (: *in*) in; **essere alla stazione** to be at the station; **essere a casa/a scuola/a Roma** to be at home/at school/in Rome; **è a 10 km da qui** it's 10 km from here, it's 10 km away; **restare a cena** to stay for dinner
2 (*moto a luogo*) to; **andare a casa/a scuola/ alla stazione** to go home/to school/to the station; **andare a Roma/al mare** to go to Rome/to the seaside
3 (*tempo*) at; (*epoca, stagione*) in; **alle cinque** at five (o'clock); **a mezzanotte/Natale** at midnight/Christmas; **al mattino** in the morning; **a maggio/primavera** in May/ spring; **a cinquant'anni** at fifty (years of age); **a domani!** see you tomorrow!; **a lunedì!** see you on Monday!; **a giorni** within (a few) days
4 (*complemento di termine*) to; **dare qc a qn** to give sb sth, give sth to sb; **l'ho chiesto a lui** I asked him
5 (*mezzo, modo*) with, by; **a piedi/cavallo** on foot/horseback; **viaggiare a 100 km all'ora** to travel at 100 km an *o* per hour; **alla televisione/radio** on television/the radio; **fatto a mano** made by hand, handmade; **una barca a motore** a motorboat; **una stufa a gas** a gas heater; **a uno a uno** one by one; **a fatica** with difficulty; **all'italiana** the Italian way, in the Italian fashion
6 (*rapporto*) a, per; (: *con prezzi*) at; **due volte al giorno/mese** twice a day/month; **prendo 2000 euro al mese** I get 2000 euro a *o* per month; **pagato a ore** paid by the hour;

vendere qc a 2 euro il chilo to sell sth at 2 euro a *o* per kilo; **cinque a zero** (*punteggio*) five nil

AA *sigla* = **Alto Adige**
AAST *sigla f* = **Azienda Autonoma di Soggiorno e Turismo**
AA.VV. *abbr* = **autori vari**
ab. *abbr* = **abitante**
a'bate *sm* abbot
abbacchi'ato, -a [abbak'kjato] *ag* downhearted, in low spirits
abbacin'are [abbatʃi'nare] *vt* to dazzle
abbagli'ante [abbaʎ'ʎante] *ag* dazzling; **abbaglianti** *smpl* (*Aut*): **accendere gli abbaglianti** to put one's headlights on full (*Brit*) *o* high (*US*) beam
abbagli'are [abbaʎ'ʎare] *vt* to dazzle; (*illudere*) to delude
ab'baglio [ab'baʎʎo] *sm* blunder; **prendere un ~** to blunder, make a blunder
abbai'are *vi* to bark
abba'ino *sm* dormer window; (*soffitta*) attic room
abbando'nare *vt* to leave, abandon, desert; (*trascurare*) to neglect; (*rinunciare a*) to abandon, give up; **abbandonarsi** *vr* to let o.s. go; **~ il campo** (*Mil*) to retreat; **~ la presa** to let go; **abbandonarsi a** (*ricordi, vizio*) to give o.s. up to
abbando'nato, -a *ag* (*casa*) deserted; (*miniera*) disused; (*trascurato: terreno, podere*) neglected; (*bambino*) abandoned
abban'dono *sm* abandoning; neglecting; (*stato*) abandonment; neglect; (*Sport*) withdrawal; (*fig*) abandon; **in ~** (*edificio, giardino*) neglected
abbarbi'carsi *vr*: **~ (a)** (*anche fig*) to cling (to)
abbassa'mento *sm* lowering; (*di pressione, livello dell'acqua*) fall; (*di prezzi*) reduction; **~ di temperatura** drop in temperature
abbas'sare *vt* to lower; (*radio*) to turn down; **abbassarsi** *vr* (*chinarsi*) to stoop; (*livello, sole*)

to go down; (*fig: umiliarsi*) to demean o.s.; **~ i fari** (*Aut*) to dip (*Brit*) *o* dim (*US*) one's lights; **~ le armi** (*Mil*) to lay down one's arms

ab'basso *escl*: **~ il re!** down with the king!

abbas'tanza [abbas'tantsa] *av* (*a sufficienza*) enough; (*alquanto*) quite, rather, fairly; **non è ~ furbo** he's not shrewd enough; **un vino ~ dolce** quite a sweet wine, a fairly sweet wine; **averne ~ di qn/qc** to have had enough of sb/sth

ab'battere *vt* (*muro, casa, ostacolo*) to knock down; (*albero*) to fell; (*: vento*) to bring down; (*bestie da macello*) to slaughter; (*cane, cavallo*) to destroy, put down; (*selvaggina, aereo*) to shoot down; (*fig: malattia, disgrazia*) to lay low; **abbattersi** *vr* (*avvilirsi*) to lose heart; **abbattersi a terra** *o* **al suolo** to fall to the ground; **abbattersi su** (*maltempo*) to beat down on; (*disgrazia*) to hit, strike

abbatti'mento *sm* knocking down; felling; (*di casa*) demolition; (*prostrazione: fisica*) exhaustion; (*: morale*) despondency

abbat'tuto, -a *ag* despondent, depressed

abba'zia [abbat'tsia] *sf* abbey

abbece'dario [abbetʃe'darjo] *sm* primer

abbelli'mento *sm* embellishment

abbel'lire *vt* to make beautiful; (*ornare*) to embellish

abbeve'rare *vt* to water; **abbeverarsi** *vr* to drink

abbevera'toio *sm* drinking trough

'abbi *vb vedi* **avere**

'abbia *vb vedi* **avere**

abbi'amo *vb vedi* **avere**

'abbiano *vb vedi* **avere**

abbi'ate *vb vedi* **avere**

abbicì [abbit'ʃi] *sm inv* alphabet; (*sillabario*) primer; (*fig*) rudiments *pl*

abbi'ente *ag* well-to-do, well-off

abbi'etto, -a *ag* = **abietto**

abbiezi'one [abbjet'tsjone] *sf* = **abiezione**

abbiglia'mento [abbiʎʎa'mento] *sm* dress *no pl*; (*indumenti*) clothes *pl*; (*industria*) clothing industry

abbigli'are [abbiʎ'ʎare] *vt* to dress up

abbina'mento *sm* combination; linking; matching

abbi'nare *vt*: **~ (con** *o* **a)** (*gen*) to combine (with); (*nomi*) to link (with); **~ qc a qc** (*colori etc*) to match sth with sth

abbindo'lare *vt* (*fig*) to cheat, trick

abbocca'mento *sm* (*colloquio*) talks *pl*, meeting; (*Tecn: di tubi*) connection

abboc'care *vt* (*tubi, canali*) to connect, join up ■ *vi* (*pesce*) to bite; (*tubi*) to join; **~ (all'amo)** (*fig*) to swallow the bait

abboc'cato, -a *ag* (*vino*) sweetish

abbona'mento *sm* subscription; (*alle ferrovie etc*) season ticket; **in ~** for subscribers only; for season ticket holders only; **fare l'~ (a)** to take out a subscription (to); to buy a season ticket (for)

abbo'nare *vt* (*cifra*) to deduct; (*fig: perdonare*) to forgive; **abbonarsi** *vr*: **abbonarsi a un giornale** to take out a subscription to a newspaper; **abbonarsi al teatro/alle ferrovie** to take out a season ticket for the theatre/the train

abbo'nato, -a *sm/f* subscriber; season-ticket holder; **elenco degli abbonati** telephone directory

abbon'dante *ag* abundant, plentiful; (*giacca*) roomy

abbon'danza [abbon'dantsa] *sf* abundance; plenty

abbon'dare *vi* to abound, be plentiful; **~ in** *o* **di** to be full of, abound in

abbor'dabile *ag* (*persona*) approachable; (*prezzo*) reasonable

abbor'dare *vt* (*nave*) to board; (*persona*) to approach; (*argomento*) to tackle; **~ una curva** to take a bend

abbotto'nare *vt* to button up, do up; **abbottonarsi** *vr* to button (up)

abbotto'nato, -a *ag* (*camicia etc*) buttoned (up); (*fig*) reserved

abbottona'tura *sf* buttons *pl*; **questo cappotto ha l'~ da uomo/da donna** this coat buttons on the man's/woman's side

abboz'zare [abbot'tsare] *vt* to sketch, outline; (*Scultura*) to rough-hew; **~ un sorriso** to give a hint of a smile

ab'bozzo [ab'bɔttso] *sm* sketch, outline; (*Dir*) draft

abbracci'are [abbrat'tʃare] *vt* to embrace; (*persona*) to hug, embrace; (*professione*) to take up; (*contenere*) to include; **abbracciarsi** *vr* to hug *o* embrace (one another)

ab'braccio [ab'brattʃo] *sm* hug, embrace

abbrevi'are *vt* to shorten; (*parola*) to abbreviate, shorten

abbreviazi'one [abbrevjat'tsjone] *sf* abbreviation

abbron'zante [abbron'dzante] *ag* tanning, sun *cpd*

abbron'zare [abbron'dzare] *vt* (*pelle*) to tan; (*metalli*) to bronze; **abbronzarsi** *vr* to tan, get a tan

abbron'zato, -a [abbron'dzato] *ag* (sun)tanned

abbronza'tura [abbrondza'tura] *sf* tan, suntan

abbrusto'lire *vt* (*pane*) to toast; (*caffè*) to roast

abbruti'mento *sm* exhaustion; degradation

abbru'tire vt (snervare, stancare) to exhaust; (degradare) to degrade; **essere abbrutito dall'alcool** to be ruined by drink

abbuffarsi vr (fam): ~ **(di qc)** to stuff o.s. (with sth)

abbuffata sf (fam) nosh-up; (fig) binge; **farsi un'**~ to stuff o.s.

abbuo'nare vt = **abbonare**

abbu'ono sm (Comm) allowance, discount; (Sport) handicap

abdi'care vi to abdicate; ~ **a** to give up, renounce

abdicazi'one [abdikat'tsjone] sf abdication

aberrazi'one [aberrat'tsjone] sf aberration

abe'taia sf fir wood

a'bete sm fir (tree); ~ **bianco** silver fir; ~ **rosso** spruce

abi'etto, -a ag despicable, abject

abiezi'one [abjet'tsjone] sf abjection

'abile ag (idoneo): ~ **(a qc/a fare qc)** fit (for sth/ to do sth); (capace) able; (astuto) clever; (accorto) skilful; ~ **al servizio militare** fit for military service

abilità sf inv ability; cleverness; skill

abili'tante ag qualifying; **corsi abilitantei** (Ins) ≈ teacher training sg

abili'tare vt: ~ **qn a qc/a fare qc** to qualify sb for sth/to do sth; **è stato abilitato all'insegnamento** he has qualified as a teacher

abili'tato, -a ag qualified; (Tel) which has an outside line

abilitazi'one [abilitat'tsjone] sf qualification

abis'sale ag abysmal; (fig: senza limiti) profound

abis'sino, -a ag, sm/f Abyssinian

a'bisso sm abyss, gulf

abitabilità sf: **licenza di** ~ document stating that a property is fit for habitation

abi'tacolo sm (Aer) cockpit; (Aut) inside; (di camion) (driver's) cab

abi'tante sm/f inhabitant

abi'tare vt to live in, dwell in ■ vi: ~ **in campagna/a Roma** to live in the country/ in Rome

abi'tato, -a ag inhabited; lived in ■ sm (anche: **centro abitato**) built-up area

abitazi'one [abitat'tsjone] sf residence; house

'abito sm dress no pl; (da uomo) suit; (da donna) dress; (abitudine, disposizione, Rel) habit; **abiti** smpl (vestiti) clothes; **in** ~ **da cerimonia** in formal dress; **in** ~ **da sera** in evening dress; **"è gradito l'** ~ **scuro"** "dress formal"; ~ **mentale** way of thinking

abitu'ale ag usual, habitual; (cliente) regular

abitual'mente av usually, normally

abitu'are vt: ~ **qn a** to get sb used o accustomed to; **abituarsi a** to get used to, accustom o.s. to

abitudi'nario, -a ag of fixed habits ■ sm/f creature of habit

abi'tudine sf habit; **aver l'** ~ **di fare qc** to be in the habit of doing sth; **d'**~ usually; **per** ~ from o out of habit

abiu'rare vt to renounce

abla'tivo sm ablative

abnegazi'one [abnegat'tsjone] sf (self-) abnegation, self-denial

ab'norme ag (enorme) extraordinary; (anormale) abnormal

abo'lire vt to abolish; (Dir) to repeal

abolizi'one [abolit'tsjone] sf abolition; repeal

abomi'nevole ag abominable

abo'rigeno [abo'ridʒeno] sm aborigine

abor'rire vt to abhor, detest

abor'tire vi (Med: accidentalmente) to miscarry, have a miscarriage; (: deliberatamente) to have an abortion; (fig) to miscarry, fail

abor'tista, -i, e ag pro-choice, pro-abortion ■ sm/f pro-choicer

a'borto sm miscarriage; abortion; (fig) freak; ~ **clandestino** backstreet abortion

abrasi'one sf abrasion

abra'sivo, -a ag, sm abrasive

abro'gare vt to repeal, abrogate

abrogazi'one [abrogat'tsjone] sf repeal

abruz'zese [abrut'tsese] ag of (o from) the Abruzzi

A'bruzzo [a'bruttso] sm: **l'**~, **gli Abruzzi** the Abruzzi

ABS [abi'ɛsse] sigla m ABS (= anti-lock braking system)

'abside sf apse

'Abu 'Dhabi sf Abu Dhabi

a'bulico, -a, ci, che ag lacking in willpower

abu'sare vi: ~ **di** to abuse, misuse; (approfittare, violare) to take advantage of; ~ **dell'alcool/ dei cibi** to drink/eat to excess

abu'sivismo sm (anche: **abusivismo edilizio**) unlawful building, building without planning permission (Brit)

abu'sivo, -a ag unauthorized, unlawful; **(occupante)** ~ (di una casa) squatter

a'buso sm abuse, misuse; excessive use; **fare** ~ **di** (stupefacenti, medicine) to abuse

a.C. abbr (= avanti Cristo) BC

a'cacia, -cie [a'katʃa] sf acacia

'acca sf letter H; **non capire un'**~ not to understand a thing

ac'cadde vb vedi **accadere**

acca'demia sf (società) learned society; (scuola: d'arte, militare) academy; ~ **di Belle Arti** art school

acca'demico, -a, ci, che *ag* academic ▪ *sm*
academician

acca'dere *vi* to happen, occur

acca'duto *sm* event; **raccontare l'~** to
describe what has happened

accalappia'cani *sm inv* dog-catcher

accalappi'are *vt* to catch; *(fig)* to trick, dupe

accal'care *vt*, **accal'carsi** *vr* to crowd,
throng

accal'darsi *vr* to grow hot

accalo'rarsi *vr (fig)* to get excited

accampa'mento *sm* camp

accam'pare *vt* to encamp; *(fig)* to put
forward, advance; **accamparsi** *vr* to camp;
~ scuse to make excuses

accani'mento *sm* fury; *(tenacia)* tenacity,
perseverance

acca'nirsi *vr (infierire)* to rage; *(ostinarsi)* to
persist

accanita'mente *av* fiercely; assiduously

acca'nito, -a *ag (odio, gelosia)* fierce, bitter;
(lavoratore) assiduous; *(giocatore)* inveterate;
(tifoso, sostenitore) keen; **fumatore ~** chain
smoker

ac'canto *av* near, nearby; **~ a** *prep* near,
beside, close to; **la casa ~** the house next
door

accanto'nare *vt (problema)* to shelve; *(somma)*
to set aside

accaparra'mento *sm (Comm)* cornering,
buying up

accapar'rare *vt (Comm)* to corner, buy up;
(versare una caparra) to pay a deposit on;
accaparrarsi *vr*: **accaparrarsi qc** *(fig:
simpatia, voti)* to secure sth (for o.s.)

accapigli'arsi [akkapiʎ'ʎarsi] *vr* to come to
blows; *(fig)* to quarrel

accappa'toio *sm* bathrobe

accappo'nare *vi*: **far ~ la pelle a qn** *(fig)* to
bring sb out in goosepimples

accarez'zare [akkaret'tsare] *vt* to caress,
stroke, fondle; *(fig)* to toy with

accartocci'are [akkartot'tʃare] *vt (carta)* to
roll up, screw up; **accartocciarsi** *vr (foglie)*
to curl up

acca'sarsi *vr* to set up house; to get married

accasci'arsi [akkaʃ'ʃarsi] *vr* to collapse; *(fig)*
to lose heart

accatas'tare *vt* to stack, pile

accatto'naggio [akkatto'naddʒo] *sm*
begging

accat'tone, -a *sm/f* beggar

accaval'lare *vt (gambe)* to cross; **accavallarsi**
vr (sovrapporsi) to overlap; *(addensarsi)* to
gather

acce'care [attʃe'kare] *vt* to blind ▪ *vi* to go
blind

ac'cedere [at'tʃɛdere] *vi*: **~ a** to enter;
(richiesta) to grant, accede to; *(fonte)* to gain
access to

accele'rare [attʃele'rare] *vt* to speed up ▪ *vi*
(Aut) to accelerate; **~ il passo** to quicken
one's pace

accele'rato, -a [attʃele'rato] *ag* quick, rapid
▪ *sm (Ferr)* local train, stopping train

accelera'tore [attʃelera'tore] *sm (Aut)*
accelerator

accelerazi'one [attʃelerat'tsjone] *sf*
acceleration

ac'cendere [at'tʃendere] *vt (fuoco, sigaretta)* to
light; *(luce, televisione)* to put o switch o turn
on; *(Aut: motore)* to switch on; *(Comm: conto)*
to open; *(: debito)* to contract; *(: ipoteca)* to
raise; *(fig: suscitare)* to inflame, stir up;
accendersi *vr (luce)* to come o go on; *(legna)*
to catch fire, ignite; *(fig: lotta, conflitto)* to
break out

accen'dino [attʃen'dino], **accendi'sigaro**
[attʃendi'sigaro] *sm (cigarette)* lighter

accen'nare [attʃen'nare] *vt* to indicate, point
out; *(Mus)* to pick out the notes of; to hum
▪ *vi*: **~ a** *(fig: alludere a)* to hint at; *(: far atto di)*
to make as if; **~ un saluto** *(con la mano)* to
make as if to wave; *(col capo)* to half nod; **~ un
sorriso** to half smile; **accenna a piovere** it
looks as if it's going to rain

ac'cenno [at'tʃenno] *sm (cenno)* sign; nod;
(allusione) hint

accensi'one [attʃen'sjone] *sf (vedi accendere)*
lighting; switching on; opening; *(Aut)*
ignition

accen'tare [attʃen'tare] *vt (parlando)* to stress;
(scrivendo) to accent

accentazi'one [attʃentat'tsjone] *sf*
accentuation; stressing

ac'cento [at'tʃento] *sm* accent; *(Fonetica, fig)*
stress; *(inflessione)* tone (of voice)

accentra'mento [attʃentra'mento] *sm*
centralization

accen'trare [attʃen'trare] *vt* to centralize

accentra'tore, -'trice [attʃentra'tore] *ag*
(persona) unwilling to delegate; **politica
accentratrice** policy of centralization

accentu'are [attʃentu'are] *vt* to stress,
emphasize; **accentuarsi** *vr* to become more
noticeable

accerchi'are [attʃer'kjare] *vt* to surround,
encircle

accerta'mento [attʃerta'mento] *sm* check;
assessment

accer'tare [attʃer'tare] *vt* to ascertain;
(verificare) to check; *(reddito)* to assess;
accertarsi *vr*: **accertarsi (di qc/che)** to
make sure (of sth/that)

ac'ceso, -a [at'tʃeso] *pp di* **accendere** ■ *ag* lit; on; open; (*colore*) bright; **~ di** (*ira, entusiasmo etc*) burning with

acces'sibile [attʃes'sibile] *ag* (*luogo*) accessible; (*persona*) approachable; (*prezzo*) reasonable; (*idea*): **~ a qn** within the reach of sb

ac'cesso [at'tʃɛsso] *sm* (*anche* Inform) access; (*Med*) attack, fit; (*impulso violento*) fit, outburst; **programmi dell'~** (*TV*) educational programmes; **tempo di ~** (*Inform*) access time; **~ casuale/seriale/sequenziale** (*Inform*) random/serial/sequential access

accessori'ato, -a [attʃesso'rjato] *ag* with accessories

acces'sorio, -a [attʃes'sɔrjo] *ag* secondary, of secondary importance; **accessori** *smpl* accessories

ac'cetta [at'tʃetta] *sf* hatchet

accet'tabile [attʃet'tabile] *ag* acceptable

accet'tare [attʃet'tare] *vt* to accept; **~ di fare qc** to agree to do sth

accettazi'one [attʃettat'tsjone] *sf* acceptance; (*locale di servizio pubblico*) reception; **~ bagagli** (*Aer*) check-in (desk); **~ con riserva** qualified acceptance

ac'cetto, -a [at'tʃetto] *ag* (*persona*) welcome; **(ben) ~ a tutti** well-liked by everybody

accezi'one [attʃet'tsjone] *sf* meaning

acchiap'pare [akkjap'pare] *vt* to catch; (*afferrare*) to seize

ac'chito [ak'kito] *sm*: **a primo ~** at first sight

acciac'cato, -a [attʃak'kato] *ag* (*persona*) full of aches and pains; (*abito*) crushed

acci'acco, -chi [at'tʃakko] *sm* ailment; **acciacchi** *smpl* aches and pains

acciaie'ria [attʃaje'ria] *sf* steelworks *sg*

acci'aio [at'tʃajo] *sm* steel; **~ inossidabile** stainless steel

acciden'tale [attʃiden'tale] *ag* accidental

accidental'mente [attʃidental'mente] *av* (*per caso*) by chance; (*non deliberatamente*) accidentally, by accident

acciden'tato, -a [attʃiden'tato] *ag* (*terreno etc*) uneven

acci'dente [attʃi'dɛnte] *sm* (*caso imprevisto*) accident; (*disgrazia*) mishap; **accidenti!** (*fam: per rabbia*) damn (it)!; (*: per meraviglia*) good heavens!; **accidenti a lui!** damn him!; **non vale un ~** it's not worth a damn; **non capisco un ~** it's as clear as mud to me; **mandare un ~ a qn** to curse sb

ac'cidia [at'tʃidja] *sf* (*Rel*) sloth

accigli'ato, -a [attʃiʎ'ʎato] *ag* frowning

ac'cingersi [at'tʃindʒersi] *vr*: **~ a fare** to be about to do

acciotto'lato [attʃotto'lato] *sm* cobbles *pl*

acciuf'fare [attʃuf'fare] *vt* to seize, catch

acci'uga, -ghe [at'tʃuga] *sf* anchovy; **magro come un'~** as thin as a rake

accla'mare *vt* (*applaudire*) to applaud; (*eleggere*) to acclaim

acclamazi'one [akklamat'tsjone] *sf* applause; acclamation

acclima'tare *vt* to acclimatize; **acclimatarsi** *vr* to become acclimatized

acclimatazi'one [akklimatat'tsjone] *sf* acclimatization

ac'cludere *vt* to enclose

ac'cluso, -a *pp di* **accludere** ■ *ag* enclosed

accocco'larsi *vr* to crouch

acco'darsi *vr* to follow, tag on (behind)

accogli'ente [akkoʎ'ʎɛnte] *ag* welcoming, friendly

accogli'enza [akkoʎ'ʎɛntsa] *sf* reception; welcome; **fare una buona ~ a qn** to welcome sb

ac'cogliere [ak'kɔʎʎere] *vt* (*ricevere*) to receive; (*dare il benvenuto*) to welcome; (*approvare*) to agree to, accept; (*contenere*) to hold, accommodate

ac'colgo *etc vb vedi* **accogliere**

accol'lare *vt* (*fig*): **~ qc a qn** to force sth on sb; **accollarsi** *vr*: **accollarsi qc** to take sth upon o.s., shoulder sth

accol'lato, -a *ag* (*vestito*) high-necked

ac'colsi *etc vb vedi* **accogliere**

accoltel'lare *vt* to knife, stab

ac'colto, -a *pp di* **accogliere**

accoman'dita *sf* (*Dir*) limited partnership

accomia'tare *vt* to dismiss; **accomiatarsi (da)** to take one's leave (of)

accomoda'mento *sm* agreement, settlement

accomo'dante *ag* accommodating

accomo'dare *vt* (*aggiustare*) to repair, mend; (*riordinare*) to tidy; (*sistemare: questione, lite*) to settle; **accomodarsi** *vr* (*sedersi*) to sit down; (*fig: risolversi: situazione*) to work out; **si accomodi!** (*venga avanti*) come in!; (*si sieda*) take a seat!

accompagna'mento [akkompaɲɲa'mento] *sm* (*Mus*) accompaniment; (*Comm*): **lettera di ~** accompanying letter

accompa'gnare [akkompaɲ'ɲare] *vt* to accompany, come o go with; (*Mus*) to accompany; (*unire*) to couple; **accompagnarsi** *vr* (*armonizzarsi*) to go well together; **~ qn a casa** to see sb home; **~ qn alla porta** to show sb out; **~ un regalo con un biglietto** to put in o send a card with a present; **~ qn con lo sguardo** to follow sb with one's eyes; **~ la porta** to close the door

5

gently; **accompagnarsi a** (*frequentare*) to frequent; (*colori*) to go with, match; (*cibi*) to go with

accompagnatore, -trice [akkompaɲɲaˈtore] *sm/f* companion, escort; ~ **turistico** courier; tour guide; (*Mus*) accompanist; (*Sport*) team manager

accomunare *vt* to pool, share; (*avvicinare*) to unite

acconciatura [akkontʃaˈtura] *sf* hairstyle

accondiscendente [akkondiʃʃenˈdɛnte] *ag* affable

accondiscendere [akkondiʃʃendere] *vi*: ~ **a** to agree *o* consent to

accondisceso, -a [akkondiʃʃeso] *pp di* **accondiscendere**

acconsentire *vi*: ~ **(a)** to agree *o* consent (to); **chi tace acconsente** silence means consent

accontentare *vt* to satisfy; **accontentarsi** *vr*: **accontentarsi di** to be satisfied with, content o.s. with; **chi si accontenta gode** there's no point in complaining

acconto *sm* part payment; **pagare una somma in** ~ to pay a sum of money as a deposit; ~ **di dividendo** interim dividend

accoppiamento *sm* pairing off; mating; (*Elettr, Inform*) coupling

accoppiare *vt* to couple, pair off; (*Biol*) to mate; **accoppiarsi** *vr* to pair off; to mate

accoppiatore *sm* (*Tecn*) coupler; ~ **acustico** (*Inform*) acoustic coupler

accorato, -a *ag* heartfelt

accorciare [akkorˈtʃare] *vt* to shorten; **accorciarsi** *vr* to become shorter; (*vestiti: nel lavaggio*) to shrink

accordare *vt* to reconcile; (*colori*) to match; (*Mus*) to tune; (*Ling*): ~ **qc con qc** to make sth agree with sth; (*Dir*) to grant; **accordarsi** *vr* to agree, come to an agreement; (*colori*) to match

accordo *sm* agreement; (*armonia*) harmony; (*Mus*) chord; **essere d'**~ to agree; **andare d'**~ to get on well together; **d'**~! all right!, agreed!; **mettersi d'**~ **(con qn)** to agree *o* come to an agreement with sb; **prendere accordi con** to reach an agreement with; ~ **commerciale** trade agreement; **A~ generale sulle tariffe ed il commercio** General Agreement on Tariffs and Trade, GATT

accorgersi [akˈkɔrdʒersi] *vr*: ~ **di** to notice; (*fig*) to realize

accorgimento [akkordʒiˈmento] *sm* shrewdness *no pl*; (*espediente*) trick, device

accorrere *vi* to run up

accorsi *vb vedi* **accorgersi**; **accorrere**

accorso, -a *pp di* **accorrere**

accortezza [akkorˈtettsa] *sf* (*avvedutezza*) good sense; (*astuzia*) shrewdness

accorto, -a *pp di* **accorgersi** ▪ *ag* shrewd; **stare** ~ to be on one's guard

accostamento *sm* (*di colori etc*) combination

accostare *vt* (*avvicinarsi a*) to approach; (*socchiudere: imposte*) to half-close; (*: porta*) to leave ajar ▪ *vi*: ~ **(a)** (*Naut*) to come alongside; (*Aut*) to draw up (at); **accostarsi** *vr*: **accostarsi a** to draw near, approach; (*somigliare*) to be like, resemble; (*fede, religione*) to turn to; (*idee politiche*) to come to agree with; ~ **qc a** (*avvicinare*) to bring sth near to, put sth near to; (*colori, stili*) to match sth with; (*appoggiare: scala etc*) to lean sth against

accovacciarsi [akkovatˈtʃarsi] *vr* to crouch

accozzaglia [akkotˈtsaʎʎa] *sf* (*peg: di idee, oggetti*) jumble, hotchpotch; (*: di persone*) odd assortment

accrebbi *etc vb vedi* **accrescere**

accreditare *vt* (*notizia*) to confirm the truth of; (*Comm*) to credit; (*diplomatico*) to accredit; **accreditarsi** *vr* (*fig*) to gain credit

accredito *sm* (*Comm: atto*) crediting; (*: effetto*) credit

accrescere [akˈkreʃʃere] *vt* to increase; **accrescersi** *vr* to increase, grow

accrescimento [akkreʃʃiˈmento] *sm* increase, growth

accrescitivo, -a [akkreʃʃiˈtivo] *ag, sm* (*Ling*) augmentative

accresciuto, -a [akkreʃʃuto] *pp di* **accrescere**

accucciarsi [akkutˈtʃarsi] *vr* (*cane*) to lie down; (*persona*) to crouch down

accudire *vi*: ~ **a** to attend to ▪ *vt* to look after

acculturazione [akkulturatˈsjone] *sf* (*Sociologia*) integration

accumulare *vt* to accumulate; **accumularsi** *vr* to accumulate; (*Finanza*) to accrue

accumulatore *sm* (*Elettr*) accumulator

accumulazione [akkumulatˈsjone] *sf* accumulation

accumulo *sm* accumulation

accuratamente *av* carefully

accuratezza [akkuraˈtettsa] *sf* care; accuracy

accurato, -a *ag* (*diligente*) careful; (*preciso*) accurate

accusa *sf* accusation; (*Dir*) charge; **l'**~, **la pubblica** ~ (*Dir*) the prosecution; **mettere qn sotto** ~ to indict sb; **in stato di** ~ committed for trial

accusare *vt* (*sentire: dolore*) to feel; ~ **qn di qc** to accuse sb of sth; (*Dir*) to charge sb with sth; ~ **ricevuta di** (*Comm*) to acknowledge receipt of; ~ **la fatica** to show signs of exhaustion; **ha accusato il colpo** (*anche fig*) you could see that he had felt the blow

accusa'tivo *sm* accusative

accu'sato, -a *sm/f* accused

accusa'tore, -'trice *ag* accusing ■ *sm/f* accuser ■ *sm (Dir)* prosecutor

a'cerbo, -a [a'tʃɛrbo] *ag* bitter; *(frutta)* sour, unripe; *(persona)* immature

'acero ['atʃero] *sm* maple

a'cerrimo, -a [a'tʃɛrrimo] *ag* very fierce

ace'tato [atʃe'tato] *sm* acetate

a'ceto [a'tʃeto] *sm* vinegar; **mettere sotto ~** to pickle

ace'tone [atʃe'tone] *sm* nail varnish remover

'A.C.I. ['atʃi] *sigla m* (= *Automobile Club d'Italia*) ≈ AA *(Brit)*, ≈ AAA *(US)*

acidità [atʃidi'ta] *sf* acidity; sourness; **~ (di stomaco)** heartburn

'acido, -a ['atʃido] *ag (sapore)* acid, sour; *(Chim, colore)* acid ■ *sm (Chim)* acid

a'cidulo, -a [a'tʃidulo] *ag* slightly sour, slightly acid

'acino ['atʃino] *sm* berry; **~ d'uva** grape

'ACLI *sigla fpl* (= *Associazioni Cristiane dei Lavoratori Italiani*) *Christian Trade Union Association*

'acme *sf (fig)* acme, peak; *(Med)* crisis

'acne *sf* acne

ACNUR *sigla m* (= *Alto Commissariato delle Nazioni Unite per i Rifugiati*) UNHCR

'acqua *sf* water; *(pioggia)* rain; **acque** *sfpl* waters; **fare ~** *(Naut)* to leak, take in water; **essere con** *o* **avere l'~ alla gola** to be in great difficulty; **tirare ~ al proprio mulino** to feather one's own nest; **navigare in cattive acque** *(fig)* to be in deep water; **~ in bocca!** mum's the word!; **~ corrente** running water; **~ dolce** fresh water; **~ di mare** sea water; **~ minerale** mineral water; **~ ossigenata** hydrogen peroxide; **~ piovana** rain water; **~ potabile** drinking water; **~ salata** *o* **salmastra** salt water; **~ tonica** tonic water

acqua'forte (*pl* **acqueforti**) *sf* etching

a'cquaio *sm* sink

acqua'ragia [akkwa'radʒa] *sf* turpentine

a'cquario *sm* aquarium; *(dello zodiaco)*: **A~** Aquarius; **essere dell'A~** to be Aquarius

acquartie'rare *vt (Mil)* to quarter

acqua'santa *sf* holy water

acquas'cooter [akkwas'cuter] *sm inv* Jet Ski®

a'cquatico, -a, ci, che *ag* aquatic; *(sport, sci)* water *cpd*

acquat'tarsi *vr* to crouch (down)

acqua'vite *sf* brandy

acquaz'zone [akkwat'tsone] *sm* cloudburst, heavy shower

acque'dotto *sm* aqueduct; waterworks *pl*, water system

'acqueo, -a *ag*: **vapore ~** water vapour *(Brit)* *o* vapor *(US)*; **umore ~** aqueous humour *(Brit)* *o* humor *(US)*

acque'rello *sm* watercolour *(Brit)*, watercolor *(US)*

acque'rugiola [akkwe'rudʒola] *sf* drizzle

acquie'tare *vt* to appease; *(dolore)* to ease; **acquietarsi** *vr* to calm down

acqui'rente *sm/f* purchaser, buyer

acqui'sire *vt* to acquire

acquisizi'one [akkwizit'tsjone] *sf* acquisition

acquis'tare *vt* to purchase, buy; *(fig)* to gain ■ *vi* to improve; **~ in bellezza** to become more beautiful; **ha acquistato in salute** his health has improved

a'cquisto *sm* purchase; **fare acquisti** to go shopping; **ufficio acquisti** *(Comm)* purchasing department; **~ rateale** instalment purchase, hire purchase *(Brit)*

acqui'trino *sm* bog, marsh

acquo'lina *sf*: **far venire l'~ in bocca a qn** to make sb's mouth water

ac'quoso, -a *ag* watery

'acre *ag* acrid, pungent; *(fig)* harsh, biting

a'credine *sf (fig)* bitterness

a'crilico, -a, ci, che *ag, sm* acrylic

a'critico, -a, ci, che *ag* uncritical

a'crobata, -i, e *sm/f* acrobat

acro'batico, -a, ci, che *ag (ginnastica)* acrobatic; *(Aer)* aerobatic ■ *sf* acrobatics *sg*

acroba'zia [akrobat'tsia] *sf* acrobatic feat; **acrobazie aeree** aerobatics

a'cronimo *sm* acronym

a'cropoli *sf inv*: **l'A~** the Acropolis

acu'ire *vt* to sharpen; **acuirsi** *vr (gen)* to increase; *(crisi)* to worsen

a'culeo *sm (Zool)* sting; *(Bot)* prickle

a'cume *sm* acumen, perspicacity

acumi'nato, -a *ag* sharp

a'custico, -a, ci, che *ag* acoustic ■ *sf (scienza)* acoustics *sg*; *(di una sala)* acoustics *pl*; **apparecchio ~** hearing aid; **cornetto ~** ear trumpet

acu'tezza [aku'tettsa] *sf* sharpness; shrillness; acuteness; high pitch; intensity; keenness

acutiz'zare [akutid'dzare] *vt (fig)* to intensify; **acutizzarsi** *vr (fig: crisi, malattia)* to become worse, worsen

a'cuto, -a *ag (appuntito)* sharp, pointed; *(suono, voce)* shrill, piercing; *(Mat, Ling, Med)* acute; *(Mus)* high-pitched; *(fig: dolore, desiderio)* intense; *(: perspicace)* acute, keen ■ *sm (Mus)* high note

ad *prep (dav V)* = **a**

adagi'are [ada'dʒare] *vt* to lay *o* set down carefully; **adagiarsi** *vr* to lie down, stretch out a'dagio [a'dadʒo] av slowly ■ sm (Mus) adagio; (proverbio) adage, saying

ada'mitico, -a, ci, che ag: in costume ~ in one's birthday suit

adat'tabile ag adaptable

adattabilità sf adaptability

adatta'mento sm adaptation; avere spirito di ~ to be adaptable

adat'tare vt to adapt; (sistemare) to fit; adattarsi vr: adattarsi (a) (ambiente, tempi) to adapt (to); (essere adatto) to be suitable (for); (accontentarsi): adattarsi a qc/a fare qc to make the best of sth/of doing sth

adatta'tore sm (Elettr) adapter, adaptor

a'datto, -a ag: ~ (a) suitable (for), right (for)

addebi'tare vt: ~ qc a qn to debit sb with sth; (fig: incolpare) to blame sb for sth

ad'debito sm (Comm) debit

addensa'mento sm thickening; gathering

adden'sare vt to thicken; addensarsi vr to thicken; (nuvole) to gather

adden'tare vt to bite into

adden'trarsi vr: ~ in to penetrate, go into

ad'dentro av (fig): essere molto ~ in qc to be well-versed in sth

addestra'mento sm training; ~ aziendale company training

addes'trare vt, addes'trarsi vr to train; addestrarsi in qc to practise (Brit) o practice (US) sth

ad'detto, -a ag: ~ a (persona) assigned to; (oggetto) intended for ■ sm employee; (funzionario) attaché; ~ commerciale/ stampa commercial/press attaché; ~ al telex telex operator; gli addetti ai lavori authorized personnel; (fig) those in the know; "vietato l'ingresso ai non addetti ai lavori" "authorized personnel only"

addì av (Amm): ~ 3 luglio 1989 on the 3rd of July 1989 (Brit), on July 3rd 1989 (US)

addi'accio [ad'djattʃo] sm (Mil) bivouac; dormire all'~ to sleep in the open

addi'etro av (indietro) behind; (nel passato, prima) before, ago

ad'dio sm, escl goodbye, farewell

addirit'tura av (veramente) really, absolutely; (perfino) even; (direttamente) directly, right away

ad'dirsi vr: ~ a to suit, be suitable for

'Addis A'beba sf Addis Ababa

addi'tare vt to point out; (fig) to expose

addi'tivo sm additive

addizio'nale [addittsjo'nale] ag additional ■ sf (anche: imposta addizionale) surtax

addizio'nare [addittsjo'nare] vt (Mat) to add (up)

addizi'one [addit'tsjone] sf addition

addob'bare vt to decorate

ad'dobbo sm decoration

addol'cire [addol'tʃire] vt (caffè etc) to sweeten; (acqua, fig: carattere) to soften; addolcirsi vr (fig) to mellow, soften; ~ la pillola (fig) to sugar the pill

addolo'rare vt to pain, grieve; addolorarsi vr: addolorarsi (per) to be distressed (by)

addolo'rato, -a ag distressed, upset; l'Addolorata (Rel) Our Lady of Sorrows

ad'dome sm abdomen

addomesti'care vt to tame

addomi'nale ag abdominal; (muscoli) addominali stomach muscles

addormen'tare vt to put to sleep; addormentarsi vr to fall asleep, go to sleep

addormen'tato, -a ag sleeping, asleep; (fig: tardo) stupid, dopey

addos'sare vt (appoggiare): ~ qc a qc to lean sth against sth; (fig): ~ la colpa a qn to lay the blame on sb; addossarsi vr: addossarsi qc (responsabilità etc) to shoulder sth

ad'dosso av (sulla persona) on; ~ a prep (sopra) on; (molto vicino) right next to; mettersi ~ il cappotto to put one's coat on; andare (o venire) ~ a (Aut: altra macchina) to run into; (: pedone) to run over; non ho soldi ~ I don't have any money on me; stare ~ a qn (fig) to breathe down sb's neck; dare ~ a qn (fig) to attack sb; mettere gli occhi ~ a qn/qc to take quite a fancy to sb/sth; mettere le mani ~ a qn (picchiare) to hit sb; (catturare) to seize sb; (molestare: donna) to touch sb up

ad'dotto, -a pp di addurre

ad'duco etc vb vedi addurre

ad'durre vt (Dir) to produce; (citare) to cite

ad'dussi etc vb vedi addurre

adegu'are vt: ~ qc a to adjust sth to; adeguarsi vr to adapt

adegua'tezza [adegwa'tettsa] sf adequacy; suitability; fairness

adegu'ato, -a ag adequate; (conveniente) suitable; (equo) fair

a'dempiere vt to fulfil (Brit), fulfill (US), carry out; (comando) to carry out

adempi'mento sm fulfilment (Brit), fulfillment (US); carrying out; nell'~ del proprio dovere in the performance of one's duty

adem'pire vt = adempiere

'Aden: il golfo di ~ sm the Gulf of Aden

ade'noidi sfpl adenoids

a'depto sm disciple, follower

ade'rente ag adhesive; (vestito) close-fitting ■ sm/f follower

ade'renza [ade'rɛntsa] sf adhesion; aderenze sfpl (fig) connections, contacts ade'rire vi (stare attaccato) to adhere, stick; ~ **a** to adhere to, stick to; (fig: società, partito) to join; (: opinione) to support; (richiesta) to agree to

ades'care vt (attirare) to lure, entice; (Tecn: pompa) to prime

adesi'one sf adhesion; (fig: assenso) agreement, acceptance; (appoggio) support

ade'sivo, -a ag, sm adhesive

a'desso av (ora) now; (or ora, poco fa) just now; (tra poco) any moment now; **da ~ in poi** from now on; **per ~** for the moment, for now

adia'cente [adja'tʃɛnte] ag adjacent

adi'bire vt (usare): ~ **qc a** to turn sth into

'Adige ['adidʒe] sm: **l'~** the Adige

'adipe sm fat

adi'poso, -a ag (tessuto, zona) adipose

adi'rarsi vr: ~ **(con** o **contro qn per qc)** to get angry (with sb over sth)

adi'rato, -a ag angry

a'dire vt (Dir): ~ **le vie legali** to take legal proceedings; ~ **un'eredità** to take legal possession of an inheritance

'adito sm: **dare ~ a** (sospetti) to give rise to

adocchi'are [adok'kjare] vt (scorgere) to catch sight of; (occhieggiare) to eye

adole'scente [adoleʃʃɛnte] ag, sm/f adolescent

adole'scenza [adoleʃʃɛntsa] sf adolescence

adolescenzi'ale [adoleʃʃen'tsjale] ag adolescent

adom'brarsi vr (cavallo) to shy; (persona) to grow suspicious; (: aversene a male) to be offended

adope'rare vt to use; **adoperarsi** vr to strive; **adoperarsi per qn/qc** to do one's best for sb/sth

ado'rabile ag adorable

ado'rare vt to adore; (Rel) to adore, worship

adorazi'one [adorat'tsjone] sf adoration; worship

ador'nare vt to adorn

a'dorno, -a ag: ~ **(di)** adorned (with)

adot'tare vt to adopt; (decisione, provvedimenti) to pass

adot'tivo, -a ag (genitori) adoptive; (figlio, patria) adopted

adozi'one [adot'tsjone] sf adoption; ~ **a distanza** child sponsorship

adrena'linico, -a, ci, che ag (fig: vivace, eccitato) charged-up

adri'atico, -a, ci, che ag Adriatic ■ sm: **l'A~**, **il mare A~** the Adriatic, the Adriatic Sea

ADSL sigla m ADSL (= asymmetric digital subscriber line)

adu'lare vt to flatter

adula'tore, -'trice sm/f flatterer

adula'torio, -a ag flattering

adulazi'one [adulat'tsjone] sf flattery

adulte'rare vt to adulterate

adul'terio sm adultery

a'dultero, -a ag adulterous ■ sm/f adulterer/adulteress

a'dulto, -a ag adult; (fig) mature ■ sm adult, grown-up

adu'nanza [adu'nantsa] sf assembly, meeting

adu'nare vt, **adu'narsi** vr to assemble, gather

adu'nata sf (Mil) parade, muster

a'dunco, -a, chi, che ag hooked

aerazi'one [aerat'tsjone] sf ventilation; (Tecn) aeration

a'ereo, -a ag air cpd; (radice) aerial ■ sm aerial; (aeroplano) plane; ~ **da caccia** fighter (plane); ~ **di linea** airliner; ~ **a reazione** jet (plane)

ae'robica sf aerobics sg

aerodi'namico, -a, ci, che ag aerodynamic; (affusolato) streamlined ■ sf aerodynamics sg

aeromo'dello sm model aircraft

aero'nautica sf (scienza) aeronautics sg; ~ **militare** air force

aerona'vale ag (forze, manovre) air and sea cpd

aero'plano sm (aero)plane (Brit), (air)plane (US)

aero'porto sm airport

aeroportu'ale ag airport cpd

aeros'calo sm airstrip

aero'sol sm inv aerosol

aerospazi'ale [aerospat'tsjale] ag aerospace

aeros'tatico, -a, ci, che ag aerostatic; **pallone** ~ air balloon

ae'rostato sm aerostat

A.F. abbr (= alta frequenza) HF; (Amm) = **assegni familiari**

'afa sf sultriness

af'fabile ag affable

affabilità sf affability

affacen'darsi [affattʃen'darsi] vr: ~ **intorno a qc** to busy o.s. with sth

affacen'dato, -a [affattʃen'dato] ag busy

affacci'arsi [affat'tʃarsi] vr: ~ **(a)** to appear (at); ~ **alla vita** to come into the world

affa'mato, -a ag starving; (fig): ~ **(di)** eager (for)

affan'nare vt to leave breathless; (fig) to worry; **affannarsi** vr: **affannarsi per qn/qc** to worry about sb/sth

af'fanno sm breathlessness; (fig) anxiety, worry

affannosa'mente av with difficulty; anxiously

affan'noso, -a ag (respiro) difficult; (fig) troubled, anxious

affare *sm* (*faccenda*) matter, affair; (*Comm*) piece of business, (business) deal; (*occasione*) bargain; (*Dir*) case; (*fam: cosa*) thing; **affari** *smpl* (*Comm*) business *sg*; ~ **fatto!** done!, it's a deal!; **sono affari miei** that's my business; **bada agli affari tuoi!** mind your own business!; **uomo d'affari** businessman; **ministro degli Affari Esteri** Foreign Secretary (*Brit*), Secretary of State (*US*)

affarista, -i *sm* profiteer, unscrupulous businessman

affascinante [affaʃʃi'nante] *ag* fascinating

affascinare [affaʃʃi'nare] *vt* to bewitch; (*fig*) to charm, fascinate

affaticamento *sm* tiredness

affaticare *vt* to tire; **affaticarsi** *vr* (*durar fatica*) to tire o.s. out

affatto *av* completely; **non ... ~** not ... at all; **niente ~** not at all

affermare *vi* (*dire di sì*) to say yes ■ *vt* (*dichiarare*) to maintain, affirm; **affermarsi** *vr* to assert o.s., make one's name known

affermativamente *av* in the affirmative, affirmatively

affermativo, -a *ag* affirmative

affermato, -a *ag* established, well-known

affermazione [affermat'tsjone] *sf* affirmation, assertion; (*successo*) achievement

afferrare *vt* to seize, grasp; (*fig: idea*) to grasp; **afferrarsi** *vr*: **afferrarsi a** to cling to

Aff. Est. *abbr* = **Affari Esteri**

affettare *vt* (*tagliare a fette*) to slice; (*ostentare*) to affect

affettato, -a *ag* sliced; affected ■ *sm* sliced cold meat

affettatrice [affetta'tritʃe] *sf* meat slicer

affettazione [affettat'tsjone] *sf* affectation

affettivo, -a *ag* emotional, affective

affetto, -a *ag*: **essere ~ da** to suffer from ■ *sm* affection; **gli affetti familiari** one's nearest and dearest

affettuosamente *av* affectionately; (*nelle lettere*): (**ti saluto**) ~, **Maria** love, Maria

affettuosità *sf inv* affection; **affettuosità** *sfpl* (*manifestazioni*) demonstrations of affection

affettuoso, -a *ag* affectionate

affezionarsi [affettsjo'narsi] *vr*: ~ **a** to grow fond of

affezionato, -a [affettsjo'nato] *ag*: ~ **a qn/qc** fond of sb/sth; (*attaccato*) attached to sb/sth

affezione [affet'tsjone] *sf* (*affetto*) affection; (*Med*) ailment, disorder

affiancare *vt* to place side by side; (*Mil*) to flank; (*fig*) to support; ~ **qc a qc** to place sth next to o beside sth; **affiancarsi** *vr*: **affiancarsi a qn** to stand beside sb

affiatamento *sm* understanding

affiatato, -a *ag*: **essere affiatati** to work well together o get on; **formano una squadra affiatata** they make a good team

affibbiare *vt* to buckle, do up; (*fig: dare*) to give

affidabile *ag* reliable

affidabilità *sf* reliability

affidamento *sm* (*Dir: di bambino*) custody; (*fiducia*): **fare ~ su qn** to rely on sb; **non dà nessun ~** he's not to be trusted

affidare *vt*: ~ **qc o qn a qn** to entrust sth o sb to sb; **affidarsi** *vr*: **affidarsi a** to place one's trust in

affievolirsi *vr* to grow weak

affiggere [af'fiddʒere] *vt* to stick up, post up

affilare *vt* to sharpen

affilato, -a *ag* (*gen*) sharp; (*volto, naso*) thin

affiliare *vt* to affiliate; **affiliarsi** *vr*: **affiliarsi a** to become affiliated to

affinare *vt* to sharpen

affinché [affin'ke] *cong* in order that, so that

affine *ag* similar

affinità *sf inv* affinity

affiorare *vi* to emerge

affissi *etc vb vedi* **affiggere**

affissione *sf* billposting

affisso, -a *pp di* **affiggere** ■ *sm* bill, poster; (*Ling*) affix

affittacamere *sm/f inv* landlord/landlady

affittare *vt* (*dare in affitto*) to let, rent (out); (*prendere in affitto*) to rent

affitto *sm* rent; (*contratto*) lease; **dare in ~** to rent (out), let; **prendere in ~** to rent

affittuario *sm* lessee

affliggere [af'fliddʒere] *vt* to torment; **affliggersi** *vr* to grieve

afflissi *etc vb vedi* **affliggere**

afflitto, -a *pp di* **affliggere**

afflizione [afflit'tsjone] *sf* distress, torment

afflosciarsi [affloʃʃarsi] *vr* to go limp; (*frutta*) to go soft

affluente *sm* tributary

affluenza [afflu'entsa] *sf* flow; (*di persone*) crowd

affluire *vi* to flow; (*fig: merci, persone*) to pour in

afflusso *sm* influx

affogare *vt, vi* to drown; **affogarsi** *vr* to drown; (*deliberatamente*) to drown o.s.

affogato, -a *ag* drowned; (*Cuc: uova*) poached

affollamento *sm* crowding; (*folla*) crowd

affollare *vt*, **affollarsi** *vr* to crowd

affollato, -a *ag* crowded

affondamento *sm* (*di nave*) sinking

affondare *vt* to sink

affran'care *vt* to free, liberate; (*Amm*) to redeem; (*lettera*) to stamp; (: *meccanicamente*) to frank (*Brit*), meter (*US*); **affrancarsi** *vr* to free o.s.

affranca'trice [affranka'tritʃe] *sf* franking machine (*Brit*), postage meter (*US*)

affranca'tura *sf* (*di francobollo*) stamping; franking (*Brit*), metering (*US*); (*tassa di spedizione*) postage; **~ a carico del destinatario** postage paid

af'franto, -a *ag* (*esausto*) worn out; (*abbattuto*) overcome

af'fresco, -schi *sm* fresco

affret'tare *vt* to quicken, speed up; **affrettarsi** *vr* to hurry; **affrettarsi a fare qc** to hurry o hasten to do sth

affret'tato, -a *ag* (*veloce: passo, ritmo*) quick, fast; (*frettoloso: decisione*) hurried, hasty; (: *lavoro*) rushed

affron'tare *vt* (*pericolo etc*) to face; (*assalire: nemico*) to confront; **affrontarsi** *vr* (*reciproco*) to confront each other

af'fronto *sm* affront, insult; **fare un ~ a qn** to insult sb

affumi'care *vt* to fill with smoke; to blacken with smoke; (*alimenti*) to smoke

affuso'lato, -a *ag* tapering

af'gano, -a *ag, sm/f* Afghan

Af'ghanistan [af'ganistan] *sm*: **l'~** Afghanistan

af'ghano, -a *ag, sm/f* = **afgano**

afo'risma, -i *sm* aphorism

a'foso, -a *ag* sultry, close

'Africa *sf*: **l'~** Africa

afri'cano, -a *ag, sm/f* African

afroasi'atico, -a, ci, che *ag* Afro-Asian

afrodi'siaco, -a, ci, che *ag, sm* aphrodisiac

AG *sigla* = **Agrigento**

a'genda [a'dʒɛnda] *sf* diary; **~ tascabile/da tavolo** pocket/desk diary

a'gente [a'dʒɛnte] *sm* agent; **~ di cambio** stockbroker; **~ di custodia** prison officer; **~ marittimo** shipping agent; **~ di polizia** police officer; **~ provocatore** agent provocateur; **~ delle tasse** tax inspector; **~ di vendita** sales agent; **resistente agli agenti atmosferici** weather-resistant

agen'zia [adʒen'tsia] *sf* agency; (*succursale*) branch; **~ di collocamento** employment agency; **~ immobiliare** estate agent's (office) (*Brit*), real estate office (*US*); **A~ Internazionale per l'Energia Atomica** International Atomic Energy Agency; **~ matrimoniale** marriage bureau; **~ pubblicitaria** advertising agency; **~ di stampa** press agency; **~ viaggi** travel agency

agevo'lare [adʒevo'lare] *vt* to facilitate, make easy

agevolazi'one [adʒevolat'tsjone] *sf* (*facilitazione economica*) facility; **~ di pagamento** payment on easy terms; **agevolazioni creditizie** credit facilities; **agevolazioni fiscali** tax concessions

a'gevole [a'dʒevole] *ag* easy; (*strada*) smooth

aggan'ciare [aggan'tʃare] *vt* to hook up; (*Ferr*) to couple; **agganciarsi** *vr*: **agganciarsi a** to hook up to; (*fig: pretesto*) to seize on

ag'gancio [ag'gantʃo] *sm* (*Tecn*) coupling; (*fig: conoscenza*) contact

ag'geggio [ad'dʒeddʒo] *sm* gadget, contraption

agget'tivo [addʒet'tivo] *sm* adjective

agghiacciante [aggjat'tʃante] *ag* (*fig*) chilling

agghiacci'are [aggjat'tʃare] *vt* to freeze; (*fig*) to make one's blood run cold; **agghiacciarsi** *vr* to freeze

agghin'darsi [aggin'darsi] *vr* to deck o.s. out

aggiorna'mento [addʒorna'mento] *sm* updating; revision; postponement; **corso di ~** refresher course

aggior'nare [addʒor'nare] *vt* (*opera, manuale*) to bring up-to-date; (: *rivedere*) to revise; (*listino*) to maintain, up-date; (*seduta etc*) to postpone; **aggiornarsi** *vr* to bring (o keep) o.s. up-to-date

aggior'nato, -a [addʒor'nato] *ag* up-to-date

aggio'taggio [addʒo'taddʒo] *sm* (*Econ*) rigging the market

aggi'rare [addʒi'rare] *vt* to go round; (*fig: ingannare*) to trick; **aggirarsi** *vr* to wander about; **il prezzo s'aggira sul milione** the price is around the million mark

aggiudi'care [addʒudi'kare] *vt* to award; (*all'asta*) to knock down; **aggiudicarsi qc** to win sth

aggi'ungere [ad'dʒundʒere] *vt* to add; (*Inform*): **grazie per avermi aggiunto (come amico)** thanks for the add

aggi'unsi *etc* [ad'dʒunsi] *vb vedi* **aggiungere**

aggi'unto, -a [ad'dʒunto] *pp di* **aggiungere** ◼ *ag* assistant *cpd* ◼ *sm* assistant ◼ *sf* addition; **sindaco ~** deputy mayor; **in aggiunta ...** what's more ...

aggius'tare [addʒus'tare] *vt* (*accomodare*) to mend, repair; (*riassettare*) to adjust; (*fig: lite*) to settle; **aggiustarsi** *vr* (*arrangiarsi*) to make do; (*con senso reciproco*) to come to an agreement; **ti aggiusto io!** I'll fix you!

agglome'rato *sm* (*di rocce*) conglomerate; (*di legno*) chipboard; **~ urbano** built-up area

aggrap'parsi *vr*: **~ a** to cling to

aggrava'mento *sm* worsening

aggra'vante *ag* (*Dir*) aggravating ◼ *sf* aggravation

aggra'vare *vt* (*aumentare*) to increase; (*appesantire: anche fig*) to weigh down, make heavy; *(fig: pena)* to make worse; **aggravarsi** *vr (fig)* to worsen, become worse

ag'gravio *sm*: ~ **di costi** increase in costs

aggrazi'ato, -a [aggrat'tsjato] *ag* graceful

aggre'dire *vt* to attack, assault

aggre'gare *vt*: ~ **qn a qc** to admit sb to sth; **aggregarsi** *vr* to join; **aggregarsi a** to join, become a member of

aggre'gato, -a *ag* associated ■ *sm* aggregate; ~ **urbano** built-up area

aggressi'one *sf* aggression; *(atto)* attack; ~ **a mano armata** armed assault

aggressività *sf* aggressiveness

aggres'sivo, -a *ag* aggressive

aggres'sore *sm* aggressor, attacker

aggrot'tare *vt*: ~ **le sopracciglia** to frown

aggrovigli'are [aggroviʎ'ʎare] *vt* to tangle; **aggrovigliarsi** *vr (fig)* to become complicated

agguan'tare *vt* to catch, seize

aggu'ato *sm* trap; *(imboscata)* ambush; **tendere un ~ a qn** to set a trap for sb

agguer'rito, -a *ag (sostenitore, nemico)* fierce

agia'tezza [adʒa'tettsa] *sf* prosperity

agi'ato, -a [a'dʒato] *ag (vita)* easy; *(persona)* well-off, well-to-do

'agile ['adʒile] *ag* agile, nimble

agilità [adʒili'ta] *sf* agility, nimbleness

'agio ['adʒo] *sm* ease, comfort; **agi** *smpl* comforts; **mettersi a proprio ~** to make o.s. at home *o* comfortable; **dare ~ a qn di fare qc** to give sb the chance of doing sth

a'gire [a'dʒire] *vi* to act; *(esercitare un'azione)* to take effect; *(Tecn)* to work, function; ~ **contro qn** *(Dir)* to take action against sb

agi'tare [adʒi'tare] *vt (bottiglia)* to shake; *(mano, fazzoletto)* to wave; *(fig: turbare)* to disturb; *(: incitare)* to stir (up); **agitarsi** *vr (mare)* to be rough; *(malato, dormitore)* to toss and turn; *(bambino)* to fidget; *(emozionarsi)* to get upset; *(Pol)* to agitate

agi'tato, -a [adʒi'tato] *ag* rough; restless; fidgety; upset, perturbed

agita'tore, -'trice [adʒita'tore] *sm/f (Pol)* agitator

agitazi'one [adʒitat'tsjone] *sf* agitation; *(Pol)* unrest, agitation; **mettere in ~ qn** to upset *o* distress sb

'agli ['aʎʎi] *prep+det vedi* **a**

'aglio ['aʎʎo] *sm* garlic

a'gnello [aɲ'ɲɛllo] *sm* lamb

a'gnostico, -a, ci, che [aɲ'ɲɔstiko] *ag, sm/f* agnostic

'ago *(pl* **aghi)** *sm* needle; ~ **da calza** knitting needle

ago. *abbr (= agosto)* Aug.

ago'nia *sf* agony

ago'nistico, -a, ci, che *ag* athletic; *(fig)* competitive

agoniz'zante [agonid'dzante] *ag* dying

agoniz'zare [agonid'dzare] *vi* to be dying

agopun'tura *sf* acupuncture

agorafo'bia *sf* agoraphobia

a'gosto *sm* August; *vedi anche* **luglio**

a'grario, -a *ag* agrarian, agricultural; *(riforma)* land *cpd* ■ *sm* landowner ■ *sf* agriculture

a'gricolo, -a *ag* agricultural, farm *cpd*

agricol'tore *sm* farmer

agricol'tura *sf* agriculture, farming

agri'foglio [agri'fɔʎʎo] *sm* holly

agrimen'sore *sm* land surveyor

agritu'rismo *sm* farm holidays *pl*

agritu'ristico, -a, ci, che *ag* farm holiday *cpd*

'agro, -a *ag* sour, sharp

agro'dolce [agro'doltʃe] *ag* bittersweet; *(salsa)* sweet and sour

agrono'mia *sf* agronomy

a'gronomo *sm* agronomist

a'grume *sm (spesso al pl: pianta)* citrus; *(: frutto)* citrus fruit

agru'meto *sm* citrus grove

aguz'zare [agut'tsare] *vt* to sharpen; ~ **gli orecchi** to prick up one's ears; ~ **l'ingegno** to use one's wits

aguz'zino, -a [agud'dzino] *sm/f* jailer; *(fig)* tyrant

a'guzzo, -a [a'guttso] *ag* sharp

'ahi *escl (dolore)* ouch!

ahimè *escl* alas!

'ai *prep+det vedi* **a**

'Aia *sf*: **L'~** The Hague

'aia *sf* threshing floor

AIDDA *sigla f (= Associazione Imprenditrici Donne Dirigenti d'Azienda) association of women entrepreneurs and managers*

AIDS ['aids] *abbr m o f* AIDS

AIE *sigla f (= Associazione Italiana degli Editori) publishers' association*

AIEA *sigla f* = **Agenzia Internazionale per l'Energia Atomica**

AIED *sigla f (= Associazione Italiana Educazione Demografica)* ≈ FPA (= Family Planning Association)

AIG *sigla f (= Associazione Italiana Alberghi per la Gioventù)* ≈ YHA (Brit)

ai'ola *sf* = **aiuola**

airbag *sm inv* air bag

AIRC *abbr f* = **Associazione Italiana per la Ricerca sul Cancro**

ai'rone *sm* heron

ai'tante *ag* robust

aiu'ola *sf* flower bed

aiu'tante *sm/f* assistant ■ *sm (Mil)* adjutant; *(Naut)* master-at-arms; ~ **di campo** aide-de-camp

aiu'tare *vt* to help; ~ **qn (a fare)** to help sb
(to do)

ai'uto *sm* help, assistance, aid; *(aiutante)*
assistant; **venire in ~ di qn** to come to sb's
aid; ~ **chirurgo** assistant surgeon

aiz'zare [ait'tsare] *vt* to incite; ~ **i cani
contro qn** to set the dogs on sb

al *prep+det vedi* **a**

a.l. *abbr* = **anno luce**

'**ala** *(pl* **ali)** *sf* wing; **fare ~** to fall back, make
way; ~ **destra/sinistra** *(Sport)* right/left
wing

ala'bastro *sm* alabaster

'**alacre** *ag* quick, brisk

alacrità *sf* promptness, speed

alam'bicco, -chi *sm* still *(Chim)*

a'lano *sm* Great Dane

a'lare *ag* wing *cpd;* **alari** *smpl* firedogs

A'laska *sf:* **l'~** Alaska

a'lato, -a *ag* winged

'**alba** *sf* dawn; **all'~** at dawn

alba'nese *ag, sm/f, sm* Albanian

Alba'nia *sf:* **l'~** Albania

'**albatro** *sm* albatross

albeggi'are [albed'dʒare] *vi, vb impers* to dawn

albe'rato, -a *ag (viale, piazza)* lined with trees,
tree-lined

albera'tura *sf (Naut)* masts *pl*

alber'gare *vt (dare albergo)* to accommodate
■ *vi (poetico)* to dwell

alberga'tore, -'trice *sm/f* hotelier, hotel
owner

alberghi'ero, -a [alber'gjɛro] *ag* hotel *cpd*

al'bergo, -ghi *sm* hotel; ~ **diurno** public toilets
with washing and shaving facilities etc; ~ **della
gioventù** youth hostel

'**albero** *sm* tree; *(Naut)* mast; *(Tecn)* shaft; ~ **a
camme** camshaft; ~ **genealogico** family
tree; ~ **a gomiti** crankshaft; ~ **maestro**
mainmast; ~ **di Natale** Christmas tree; ~ **di
trasmissione** transmission shaft

albi'cocca, -che *sf* apricot

albi'cocco, -chi *sm* apricot tree

al'bino, -a *ag, sm/f* albino

'**albo** *sm (registro)* register, roll; *(Amm)* notice
board

'**album** *sm* album; ~ **da disegno** sketch book

al'bume *sm* albumen; *(bianco d'uovo)* egg
white

albu'mina *sf* albumin

'**alce** ['altʃe] *sm* elk

al'chimia [al'kimja] *sf* alchemy

alchi'mista, -i [alki'mista] *sm* alchemist

'**alcol** *sm inv* = **alcool**

alcolicità [alkolitʃi'ta] *sf* alcohol(ic) content

al'colico, -a, ci, che *ag* alcoholic ■ *sm*
alcoholic drink

alco'lismo *sm* alcoholism

alco'lista, -i, e *sm/f* alcoholic

alcoliz'zato, -a [alkolid'dzato] *sm/f* alcoholic

'**alcool** *sm inv* alcohol; ~ **denaturato**
methylated spirits *pl* (Brit), wood alcohol
(US); ~ **etilico** ethyl alcohol; ~ **metilico**
methyl alcohol

alco'olico *etc vedi* **alcolico** *etc*

alco'test *sm inv* Breathalyser® (Brit),
Breathalyzer® (US)

al'cova *sf* alcove

al'cuno, -a *det (dav sm:* **alcun**+C, V, **alcuno**+s
impura, gn, pn, ps, x, z; dav sf: **alcuna**+C, **alcun'**
+V: *nessuno):* **non ... ~** no, not any; **alcuni, e**
det pl, pron pl some, a few; **non c'è alcuna
fretta** there's no hurry, there isn't any
hurry; **senza alcun riguardo** without any
consideration

aldilà *sm inv:* **l'~** the next life, the after-life

alea'torio, -a *ag (incerto)* uncertain

aleggi'are [aled'dʒare] *vi (fig: profumo, sospetto)*
to be in the air

Ales'sandria *sf (anche:* **Alessandria d'Egitto)**
Alexandria

a'letta *sf (Tecn)* fin; tab

alet'tone *sm (Aer)* aileron

Aleu'tine *sfpl:* **le isole ~** the Aleutian Islands

alfa'betico, -a, ci, che *ag* alphabetical

alfa'beto *sm* alphabet

alfanu'merico, -a, ci, che *ag* alphanumeric

alfi'ere *sm* standard-bearer; *(Scacchi)* bishop

al'fine *av* finally, in the end

'**alga, -ghe** *sf* seaweed *no pl,* alga

'**algebra** ['aldʒebra] *sf* algebra

Al'geri [al'dʒeri] *sf* Algiers

Alge'ria [aldʒe'ria] *sf:* **l'~** Algeria

alge'rino, -a [aldʒe'rino] *ag, sm/f* Algerian

algo'ritmo *sm* algorithm

ALI *sigla f (= Associazione Librai Italiani) booksellers'*
association

ali'ante *sm (Aer)* glider

'**alibi** *sm inv* alibi

a'lice [a'litʃe] *sf* anchovy

alie'nare *vt (Dir)* to transfer; *(rendere ostile)* to
alienate; **alienarsi qn** to alienate sb

alie'nato, -a *ag* alienated; transferred;
(fuor di senno) insane ■ *sm* lunatic, insane
person

alienazi'one [aljenat'tsjone] *sf* alienation;
transfer; insanity

ali'eno, -a *ag (avverso):* ~ **(da)** opposed (to),
averse (to) ■ *sm/f* alien

alimen'tare *vt* to feed; *(Tecn)* to feed, supply;
(fig) to sustain ■ *ag* food *cpd;* **alimentari**
smpl foodstuffs; *(anche:* **negozio di
alimentari)** grocer's shop; **regime ~** diet

alimenta'tore *sm (Elettr)* feeder

alimentazi'one [alimentat'tsjone] *sf*
feeding; (*cibi*) diet; ~ **di fogli** (*Inform*) sheet
feed

ali'mento *sm* food; **alimenti** *smpl* food *sg*;
(*Dir*) alimony

a'liquota *sf* share; ~ **d'imposta** tax rate;
~ **minima** (*Fisco*) basic rate

alis'cafo *sm* hydrofoil

'alito *sm* breath

all. *abbr* (= *allegato*) enc., encl.

'alla *prep + det vedi* **a**

allaccia'mento [allattʃa'mento] *sm* (*Tecn*)
connection

allacci'are [allat'tʃare] *vt* (*scarpe*) to tie, lace
(up); (*cintura*) to do up, fasten; (*due località*) to
link; (*luce, gas*) to connect; (*amicizia*) to form;
allacciarsi *vr* (*vestito*) to fasten; ~ o
allacciarsi la cintura to fasten one's belt

allaccia'tura [allattʃa'tura] *sf* fastening

allaga'mento *sm* flooding *no pl*; flood

alla'gare *vt*, **alla'garsi** *vr* to flood

allampa'nato, -a *ag* lanky

allar'gare *vt* to widen; (*vestito*) to let out;
(*aprire*) to open; (*fig: dilatare*) to extend;
allargarsi *vr* (*gen*) to widen; (*scarpe, pantaloni*)
to stretch; (*fig: problema, fenomeno*) to spread

allar'mare *vt* to alarm; **allarmarsi** *vr* to
become alarmed

al'larme *sm* alarm; **mettere qn in** ~ to alarm
sb; ~ **aereo** air-raid warning

allar'mismo *sm* scaremongering

allar'mista, -i, e *sm/f* scaremonger, alarmist

allat'tare *vt* (*donna*) to (breast-)feed;
(*: animale*) to suckle; ~ **artificialmente** to
bottle-feed

'alle *prep + det vedi* **a**

alle'anza [alle'antsa] *sf* alliance; **A~
Democratica** (*Pol*) *moderate centre-left party*;
A~ Nazionale (*Pol*) *party on the far right*

alle'arsi *vr* to form an alliance

alle'ato, -a *ag* allied ■ *sm/f* ally

alleg. *abbr* = **all.**

alle'gare *vt* (*accludere*) to enclose; (*Dir: citare*)
to cite, adduce; (*denti*) to set on edge

alle'gato, -a *ag* enclosed ■ *sm* enclosure;
(*di e-mail*) attachment; **in** ~ enclosed; **in ~ Vi
inviamo ...** please find enclosed ...

allegge'rire [alleddʒe'rire] *vt* to lighten,
make lighter; (*fig: sofferenza*) to alleviate,
lessen; (*: lavoro, tasse*) to reduce

allego'ria *sf* allegory

alle'gorico, -a, ci, che *ag* allegorical

alle'gria *sf* gaiety, cheerfulness

al'legro, -a *ag* cheerful, merry; (*un po' brillo*)
merry, tipsy; (*vivace: colore*) bright ■ *sm* (*Mus*)
allegro

allena'mento *sm* training

alle'nare *vt*, **alle'narsi** *vr* to train

allena'tore *sm* (*Sport*) trainer, coach

allen'tare *vt* to slacken; (*disciplina*) to relax;
allentarsi *vr* to become slack; (*ingranaggio*)
to work loose

aller'gia, -'gie [aller'dʒia] *sf* allergy

al'lergico, -a, ci, che [al'lerdʒiko] *ag* allergic

allesti'mento *sm* preparation, setting up; **in
~ in preparation**

alles'tire *vt* (*cena*) to prepare; (*esercito, nave*)
to equip, fit out; (*spettacolo*) to stage

allet'tante *ag* attractive, alluring

allet'tare *vt* to lure, entice

alleva'mento *sm* breeding, rearing; (*luogo*)
stock farm; **pollo d'~** battery hen

alle'vare *vt* (*animale*) to breed, rear; (*bambino*)
to bring up

alleva'tore *sm* breeder

allevi'are *vt* to alleviate

alli'bire *vi* to turn pale; (*essere turbato*) to be
disconcerted

alli'bito, -a *ag* pale; disconcerted

allibra'tore *sm* bookmaker

allie'tare *vt* to cheer up, gladden

alli'evo *sm* pupil; (*apprendista*) apprentice;
~ **ufficiale** cadet

alliga'tore *sm* alligator

allinea'mento *sm* alignment

alline'are *vt* (*persone, cose*) to line up; (*Tip*) to
align; (*fig: economia, salari*) to adjust, align;
allinearsi *vr* to line up; (*fig: a idee*): **allinearsi
a** to come into line with

alline'ato, -a *ag* aligned, in line; **paesi non
allineati** (*Pol*) non-aligned countries

'allo *prep + det vedi* **a**

allo'care *vt* to allocate

al'locco, -a, chi, che *sm/f* oaf ■ *sm* tawny owl

allocuzi'one [allokut'tsjone] *sf* address,
solemn speech

al'lodola *sf* (sky)lark

alloggi'are [allod'dʒare] *vt* to accommodate
■ *vi* to live

al'loggio [al'lɔddʒo] *sm* lodging,
accommodation (*Brit*), accommodations
(*US*); (*appartamento*) flat (*Brit*), apartment (*US*)

allontana'mento *sm* removal; dismissal;
estrangement

allonta'nare *vt* to send away, send off;
(*impiegato*) to dismiss; (*pericolo*) to avert,
remove; (*estraniare*) to alienate; **allontanarsi**
vr: **allontanarsi (da)** to go away (from);
(*estraniarsi*) to become estranged (from)

al'lora *av* (*in quel momento*) then ■ *cong* (*in
questo caso*) well then; (*dunque*) well then, so;
la gente d'~ people then o in those days; **da ~
in poi** from then on; **e ~?** (*che fare?*) what
now?; (*e con ciò?*) so what?

allor ché [allor'ke] *cong (formale)* when, as soon as

al loro *sm* laurel; **riposare** *o* **dormire sugli allori** to rest on one's laurels

alluce ['allutʃe] *sm* big toe

alluci nante [allutʃi'nante] *ag (scena, spettacolo)* awful, terrifying; *(fam: incredibile)* amazing

alluci nato, -a [allutʃi'nato] *ag* terrified; *(fuori di sé)* bewildered, confused

allucinazi one [allutʃinat'tsjone] *sf* hallucination

al ludere *vi:* ~ **a** to allude to, hint at

allu minio *sm* aluminium (*Brit*), aluminum (*US*)

allu naggio [allu'naddʒo] *sm* moon landing

allu nare *vi* to land on the moon

allun gare *vt* to lengthen; *(distendere)* to prolong, extend; *(diluire)* to water down; **allungarsi** *vr* to lengthen; *(ragazzo)* to stretch, grow taller; *(sdraiarsi)* to lie down, stretch out; ~ **le mani** *(rubare)* to pick pockets; **gli allungò uno schiaffo** he took a swipe at him

al lusi *etc vb vedi* **alludere**

allusi one *sf* hint, allusion

al luso, -a *pp di* **alludere**

alluvi one *sf* flood

alma nacco, -chi *sm* almanac

al meno *av* at least ■ *cong:* **(se)** ~ if only; **(se)** ~ **piovesse!** if only it would rain!

a logeno, -a [a'lɔdʒeno] *ag:* **lampada alogena** halogen lamp

a lone *sm* halo

al pestre *ag (delle alpi)* alpine; *(montuoso)* mountainous

Alpi *sfpl:* **le** ~ the Alps

alpi nismo *sm* mountaineering, climbing

alpi nista, -i, e *sm/f* mountaineer, climber

al pino, -a *ag* Alpine; mountain *cpd*; **alpini** *smpl (Mil)* Italian Alpine troops

al quanto *av* rather, a little ■ *det:* ~(-a)a certain amount of, some ■ *pron* a certain amount, some; **alquanti, e** *det pl, pron pl* several, quite a few

Al sazia [al'sattsja] *sf* Alsace

alt *escl* halt!, stop! ■ *sm:* **dare l'**~ to call a halt

alta lena *sf (a funi)* swing; *(in bilico, anche fig)* seesaw

alta mente *av* extremely, highly

al tare *sm* altar

alte rare *vt* to alter, change; *(cibo)* to adulterate; *(registro)* to falsify; *(persona)* to irritate; **alterarsi** *vr* to alter; *(cibo)* to go bad; *(persona)* to lose one's temper

alterazi one [alterat'tsjone] *sf* alteration, change; adulteration; falsification; annoyance

al terco, -chi *sm* altercation, wrangle

alter nanza [alter'nantsa] *sf* alternation; *(Agr)* rotation

alter nare *vt,* **alter narsi** *vr* to alternate

alterna tivo, -a *ag* alternative ■ *sf* alternative; **non abbiamo alternative** we have no alternative

alter nato, -a *ag* alternate; *(Elettr)* alternating

alterna tore *sm* alternator

al terno, -a *ag* alternate; **a giorni alterni** on alternate days, every other day; **circolazione a targhe alterne** *(Aut) system of restricting vehicle use to odd/even registrations on alternate days*

al tero, -a *ag* proud

al tezza [al'tettsa] *sf (di edificio, persona)* height; *(di tessuto)* width, breadth; *(di acqua, pozzo)* depth; *(di suono)* pitch; *(Geo)* latitude; *(titolo)* highness; *(fig: nobiltà)* greatness; **essere all'**~ **di** to be on a level with; *(fig)* to be up to *o* equal to; **all'**~ **della farmacia** near the chemist's

altez zoso, -a [altet'tsoso] *ag* haughty

al ticcio, -a, ci, ce [al'tittʃo] *ag* tipsy

altipi ano *sm* = **altopiano**

altiso nante *ag (fig)* high-sounding, pompous

alti tudine *sf* altitude

alto, -a *ag* high; *(persona)* tall; *(tessuto)* wide, broad; *(sonno, acque)* deep; *(suono)* high (-pitched); *(Geo)* upper; *(: settentrionale)* northern ■ *sm* top (part) ■ *av* high; *(parlare)* aloud, loudly; **il palazzo è** ~ **20 metri** the building is 20 metres high; **il tessuto è** ~ **70 cm** the material is 70 cm wide; **ad alta voce** aloud; **a notte alta** in the dead of night; **in** ~ up, upwards; at the top; **mani in** ~! hands up!; **dall'**~ **in** *o* **al basso** up and down; **degli alti e bassi** *(fig)* ups and downs; **andare a testa alta** *(fig)* to carry one's head high; **essere in** ~ **mare** *(fig)* to be far from a solution; **alta definizione** *(TV)* high definition; **alta fedeltà** high fidelity, hi-fi; **alta moda** haute couture; **l'A** ~ **Medioevo** the Early Middle Ages; **l'** ~ **Po** the upper reaches of the Po; **alta velocità** *(Ferr)* high speed rail system

altoate sino, -a *ag* of (*o* from) the Alto Adige

alto forno *sm* blast furnace

altolo cato, -a *ag* of high rank, highly placed

altopar lante *sm* loudspeaker

altopi ano *(pl* **altipiani**) *sm* upland plain, plateau

Alto Volta *sm:* **l'** ~ Upper Volta

altret tanto, -a *ag, pron* as much; *(pl)* as many ■ *av* equally; **tanti auguri!** — **grazie,** ~ all the best! — thank you, the same to you '**altri** *pron inv* (*qualcuno*) somebody; (: *in espressioni negative*) anybody; (*un'altra persona*) another (person)

altri'menti *av* otherwise

 PAROLA CHIAVE

'**altro, -a** *det* **1** (*diverso*) other, different; **questa è un'altra cosa** that's another *o* a different thing; **passami l'altra penna** give me the other pen

2 (*supplementare*) other; **prendi un altro cioccolatino** have another chocolate; **hai avuto altre notizie?** have you had any more *o* any other news?; **hai altro pane?** have you got any more bread?

3 (*nel tempo*): **l'altro giorno** the other day; **l'altr'anno** last year; **l'altro ieri** the day before yesterday; **domani l'altro** the day after tomorrow; **quest'altro mese** next month

4: **d'altra parte** on the other hand

◼ *pron* **1** (*persona, cosa diversa o supplementare*): **un altro, un'altra** another (one); **lo farà un altro** someone else will do it; **altri, e** others; **gli altri** (*la gente*) others, other people; **l'uno e l'altro** both (of them); **aiutarsi l'un l'altro** to help one another; **prendine un altro** have another (one); **da un giorno all'altro** from day to day; (*nel giro di 24 ore*) from one day to the next; (*da un momento all'altro*) any day now

2 (*sostantivato: solo maschile*) something else; (: *in espressioni interrogative*) anything else; **non ho altro da dire** I have nothing else *o* I don't have anything else to say; **desidera altro?** do you want anything else?; **più che altro** above all; **se non altro** if nothing else, at least; **tra l'altro** among other things; **ci mancherebbe altro!** that's all we need!; **non faccio altro che lavorare** I do nothing but work; **contento? — altro che!** are you pleased? — I certainly am!; *vedi anche* **senza**; **noialtri**; **voialtri**; **tutto**

altroché [altro'ke] *escl* certainly!, and how!

al'tronde *av*: **d'~** on the other hand

al'trove *av* elsewhere, somewhere else

al'trui *ag inv* other people's ◼ *sm*: **l'~** other people's belongings *pl*

altru'ismo *sm* altruism

altru'ista, -i, e *ag* altruistic ◼ *sm/f* altruist

al'tura *sf* (*rialto*) height, high ground; (*alto mare*) open sea; **pesca d'~** deep-sea fishing

a'lunno, -a *sm/f* pupil

alve'are *sm* hive

'**alveo** *sm* riverbed

alzabandi'era [altsaban'djɛra] *sm inv* (*Mil*): **l'~** the raising of the flag

al'zare [al'tsare] *vt* to raise, lift; (*issare*) to hoist; (*costruire*) to build, erect; **alzarsi** *vr* to rise; (*dal letto*) to get up; (*crescere*) to grow tall (*o* taller); **~ le spalle** to shrug one's shoulders; **~ le carte** to cut the cards; **~ il gomito** to drink too much; **~ le mani su qn** to raise one's hand to sb; **~ i tacchi** to take to one's heels; **alzarsi in piedi** to stand up, get to one's feet; **alzarsi col piede sbagliato** to get out of bed on the wrong side

al'zata [al'tsata] *sf* lifting, raising; **un'~ di spalle** a shrug

A.M. *abbr* = **aeronautica militare**

a'mabile *ag* lovable; (*vino*) sweet

'**AMAC** *sigla f* = **Aeronautica Militare-Aviazione Civile**

a'maca, -che *sf* hammock

amalga'mare *vt*, **amalga'marsi** *vr* to amalgamate

a'mante *ag*: **~ di** (*musica etc*) fond of ◼ *sm/f* lover/mistress

amara'mente *av* bitterly

ama'ranto *sm* (*Bot*) love-lies-bleeding ◼ *ag inv*: **color ~** reddish purple

a'mare *vt* to love; (*amico, musica, sport*) to like

amareggi'are [amared'dʒare] *vt* to sadden, upset; **amareggiarsi** *vr* to get upset; **amareggiarsi la vita** to make one's life a misery

amareggi'ato, -a [amared'dʒato] *ag* upset, saddened

ama'rena *sf* sour black cherry

ama'retto *sm* (*dolce*) macaroon; (*liquore*) *bitter liqueur made with almonds*

ama'rezza [ama'rettsa] *sf* bitterness

a'maro, -a *ag* bitter ◼ *sm* bitterness; (*liquore*) bitters *pl*

ama'rognolo, -a [ama'roɲɲolo] *ag* slightly bitter

a'mato, -a *ag* beloved, loved, dear ◼ *sm/f* loved one

ama'tore, -trice *sm/f* (*amante*) lover; (*intenditore: di vini etc*) connoisseur; (*dilettante*) amateur

a'mazzone [a'maddzone] *sf* (*Mitologia*) Amazon; (*cavallerizza*) horsewoman; (*abito*) riding habit; **cavalcare all'~** to ride sidesaddle; **il Rio delle Amazzoni** the (river) Amazon

Amaz'zonia [amad'dzɔnja] *sf* Amazonia

amaz'zonico, -a, ci, che [amad'dzɔniko] *ag* Amazonian; Amazon *cpd*

ambasce'ria [ambaʃʃe'ria] *sf* embassy

ambasci'ata [ambaʃʃata] *sf* embassy; (*messaggio*) message

ambascia'tore, -'trice [ambaʃʃa'tore] *sm/f*
ambassador/ambassadress

ambe'due *ag inv*: ~ **i ragazzi** both boys ■ *pron
inv* both

ambi'destro, -a *ag* ambidextrous

ambien'tale *ag* (*temperatura*) ambient *cpd*;
(*problemi, tutela*) environmental

ambienta'lismo *sm* environmentalism

ambienta'lista, -i, e *ag* environmental
■ *sm/f* environmentalist

ambien'tare *vt* to acclimatize; (*romanzo, film*)
to set; **ambientarsi** *vr* to get used to one's
surroundings

ambientazi'one [ambjentat'tsjone] *sf*
setting

ambi'ente *sm* environment; (*fig: insieme di
persone*) milieu; (*stanza*) room

ambiguità *sf inv* ambiguity

am'biguo, -a *ag* ambiguous; (*persona*) shady

am'bire *vt* (*anche: vi: ambire a*) to aspire to; **un
premio molto ambito** a much sought-after
prize

'ambito *sm* sphere, field

ambiva'lente *ag* ambivalent; **questo
apparecchio è** ~ this is a dual-purpose
device

ambizi'one [ambit'tsjone] *sf* ambition

ambizi'oso, -a [ambit'tsjoso] *ag* ambitious

'ambo *ag inv* both

'ambra *sf* amber; ~ **grigia** ambergris

ambu'lante *ag* travelling, itinerant

ambu'lanza [ambu'lantsa] *sf* ambulance

ambulatori'ale *ag* (*Med*) outpatients *cpd*;
operazione ~ operation as an outpatient;
visita ~ visit to the doctor's surgery (*Brit*) o
office (*US*)

ambula'torio *sm* (*studio medico*) surgery (*Brit*),
doctor's office (*US*)

'AMDI *sigla f* = **Associazione Medici Dentisti
Italiani**

a'meba *sf* amoeba (*Brit*), ameba (*US*)

amenità *sf inv* pleasantness *no pl*; (*facezia*)
pleasantry

a'meno, -a *ag* pleasant; (*strano*) funny,
strange; (*spiritoso*) amusing

A'merica *sf*: **l'**~ America; **l'**~ **latina** Latin
America; **l'**~ **del sud** South America

america'nata *sf* (*peg*): **le Olimpiadi sono
state una vera** ~ the Olympics were a
typically vulgar American extravaganza

america'nismo *sm* Americanism;
(*ammirazione*) love of America

ameri'cano, -a *ag, sm/f* American

ame'tista *sf* amethyst

ami'anto *sm* asbestos

a'mica *sf vedi* **amico**

ami'chevole [ami'kevole] *ag* friendly

ami'cizia [ami'tʃittsja] *sf* friendship;
amicizie *sfpl* (*amici*) friends; **fare** ~ **con qn**
to make friends with sb

a'mico, -a, ci, che *sm/f* friend; (*amante*)
boyfriend/girlfriend; ~ **del cuore** o **intimo**
bosom friend; ~ **d'infanzia** childhood friend;
(*Internet*): **aggiungere come** ~ to friend

'amido *sm* starch

ammac'care *vt* (*pentola*) to dent; (*persona*) to
bruise; **ammaccarsi** *vr* to bruise

ammacca'tura *sf* dent; bruise

ammaes'trare *vt* (*animale*) to train; (*persona*)
to teach

ammai'nare *vt* to lower, haul down

amma'larsi *vr* to fall ill

amma'lato, -a *ag* ill, sick ■ *sm/f* sick person;
(*paziente*) patient

ammali'are *vt* (*fig*) to enchant, charm

ammalia'tore, -'trice *sm/f* enchanter/
enchantress

am'manco, -chi *sm* (*Econ*) deficit

ammanet'tare *vt* to handcuff

ammani'cato, -a, ammanigli'ato, -a
[ammaniʎ'ʎato] *ag* (*fig*) with friends in high
places

amman'sire *vt* (*animale*) to tame; (*fig: persona*)
to calm down, placate

amman'tarsi *vr*: ~ **di** (*persona*) to wrap o.s. in;
(*fig: prato etc*) to be covered in

amma'raggio [amma'raddʒo] *sm* (*sea*)
landing; splashdown

amma'rare *vi* (*Aer*) to make a sea landing;
(*astronave*) to splash down

ammas'sare *vt* (*ammucchiare*) to amass;
(*raccogliere*) to gather together; **ammassarsi**
vr to pile up; to gather

am'masso *sm* mass; (*mucchio*) pile, heap;
(*Econ*) stockpile

ammat'tire *vi* to go mad

ammaz'zare [ammat'tsare] *vt* to kill;
ammazzarsi *vr* (*uccidersi*) to kill o.s.; (*rimanere
ucciso*) to be killed; **ammazzarsi di lavoro** to
work o.s. to death

am'menda *sf* amends *pl*; (*Dir, Sport*) fine; **fare**
~ **di qc** to make amends for sth

am'messo, -a *pp di* **ammettere** ■ *cong*: ~ **che**
supposing that

am'mettere *vt* to admit; (*riconoscere: fatto*) to
acknowledge, admit; (*permettere*) to allow,
accept; (*supporre*) to suppose; **ammettiamo
che ...** let us suppose that ...

ammez'zato [ammed'dzato] *sm* (*anche:* **piano
ammezzato**) entresol, mezzanine

ammic'care *vi*: ~ **(a)** to wink (at)

amminis'trare *vt* to run, manage; (*Rel, Dir*)
to administer

amministra'tivo, -a *ag* administrative

amministra`tore *sm* administrator; (*Comm*) director; **~ aggiunto** associate director; **~ delegato** managing director; **~ fiduciario** trustee; **~ unico** sole director

amministrazi`one [amministrat'tsjone] *sf* management; administration; **consiglio d'~** board of directors; **l'~ comunale** local government; **~ fiduciaria** trust

ammi`raglia [ammi'raʎʎa] *sf* flagship

ammiragli`ato [ammiraʎ'ʎato] *sm* admiralty

ammi`raglio [ammi'raʎʎo] *sm* admiral

ammi`rare *vt* to admire

ammira`tore, -trice *sm/f* admirer

ammirazi`one [ammirat'tsjone] *sf* admiration

am`misi *etc vb vedi* **ammettere**

ammis`sibile *ag* admissible, acceptable

ammissi`one *sf* admission; (*approvazione*) acknowledgment

Amm.ne *abbr* = **amministrazione**

ammobili`are *vt* to furnish

ammobili`ato, -a *ag* (*camera, appartamento*) furnished

ammoder`nare *vt* to modernize

am`modo, a`modo *av* properly *ag inv* respectable, nice

ammogli`are [ammoʎ'ʎare] *vt* to find a wife for; **ammogliarsi** *vr* to marry, take a wife

am`mollo *sm*: **lasciare in ~** to leave to soak

ammo`niaca *sf* ammonia

ammoni`mento *sm* warning; admonishment

ammo`nire *vt* (*avvertire*) to warn; (*rimproverare*) to admonish; (*Dir*) to caution

ammonizi`one [ammonit'tsjone] *sf* (*monito: anche Sport*) warning; (*rimprovero*) reprimand; (*Dir*) caution

ammon`tare *vi*: **~ a** to amount to *sm* (total) amount

ammonticchi`are [ammontik'kjare] *vt* to pile up, heap up

ammor`bare *vt* (*diffondere malattia*) to infect; (*odore*) to taint, foul

ammorbi`dente *sm* fabric softener

ammorbi`dire *vt* to soften

ammorta`mento *sm* redemption; amortization; **~ fiscale** capital allowance

ammor`tare *vt* (*Finanza: debito*) to pay off, redeem; (*: spese d'impianto*) to write off

ammortiz`zare [ammortid'dzare] *vt* (*Finanza*) to pay off, redeem; (*: spese d'impianto*) to write off; (*Aut, Tecn*) to absorb, deaden

ammortizza`tore [ammortiddza'tore] *sm* (*Aut, Tecn*) shock absorber

ammucchi`are** [ammuk'kjare] *vt*, **ammucchi`arsi *vr* to pile up, accumulate

ammuf`fire *vi* to go mouldy (*Brit*) o moldy (*US*)

ammutina`mento *sm* mutiny

ammuti`narsi *vr* to mutiny

ammuti`nato, -a *ag* mutinous *sm* mutineer

ammuto`lire *vi* to be struck dumb

amne`sia *sf* amnesia

amnis`tia *sf* amnesty

`amo *sm* (*Pesca*) hook; (*fig*) bait

amo`rale *ag* amoral

a`more *sm* love; **amori** *smpl* love affairs; **il tuo bambino è un ~** your baby's a darling; **fare l'~ o all'~** to make love; **andare d'~ e d'accordo con qn** to get on like a house on fire with sb; **per ~ o per forza** by hook or by crook; **amor proprio** self-esteem, pride

amoreggi`are [amored'dʒare] *vi* to flirt

amo`revole *ag* loving, affectionate

a`morfo, -a *ag* amorphous; (*fig: persona*) lifeless

amo`rino *sm* cupid

amo`roso, -a *ag* (*affettuoso*) loving, affectionate; (*d'amore: sguardo*) amorous; (*: poesia, relazione*) love *cpd*

am`pere ['pɛr] *sm inv* amp(ère)

ampi`ezza [am'pjettsa] *sf* width, breadth; spaciousness; (*fig: importanza*) scale, size; **~ di vedute** broad-mindedness

`ampio, -a *ag* wide, broad; (*spazioso*) spacious; (*abbondante: vestito*) loose; (*: gonna*) full; (*: spiegazione*) ample, full

am`plesso *sm* (*sessuale*) intercourse

amplia`mento *sm* (*di strada*) widening; (*di aeroporto*) expansion; (*fig*) broadening

ampli`are *vt* (*allargare*) to widen; (*fig: discorso*) to enlarge on; **ampliarsi** *vr* to grow, increase; **~ la propria cultura** to broaden one's mind

amplifi`care *vt* to amplify; (*magnificare*) to extol

amplifica`tore *sm* (*Tecn, Mus*) amplifier

amplificazi`one [amplifikat'tsjone] *sf* amplification

am`polla *sf* (*vasetto*) cruet

ampol`loso, -a *ag* bombastic, pompous

ampu`tare *vt* (*Med*) to amputate

amputazi`one [amputat'tsjone] *sf* amputation

`Amsterdam *sf* Amsterdam

amu`leto *sm* lucky charm

AN *sigla* = **Ancona**

A.N. *sigla f* (*Pol*) = **Alleanza Nazionale**

anabbagli`ante [anabbaʎ'ʎante] *ag* (*Aut*) dipped (*Brit*), dimmed (*US*); **anabbaglianti** *smpl* dipped *or* dimmed headlights

anaboliz`zante [anabolid'dzante] *sm* anabolic steroid *ag* anabolic

anacro`nismo *sm* anachronism

a'nagrafe *sf* (*registro*) register of births, marriages and deaths; (*ufficio*) registry office (*Brit*), office of vital statistics (*US*)

ana'grafico, -a, ci, che *ag* (*Amm*): **dati anagrafici** personal data; **comune di residenza anagrafica** district where resident

ana'gramma, -i *sm* anagram

anal'colico, -a, ci, che *ag* non-alcoholic ▪ *sm* soft drink; **bevanda analcolica** soft drink

a'nale *ag* anal

analfa'beta, -i, e *ag, sm/f* illiterate

analfabe'tismo *sm* illiteracy

anal'gesico, -a, ci, che [anal'dʒɛziko] *ag, sm* analgesic

a'nalisi *sf inv* analysis; (*Med: esame*) test; **in ultima** ~ in conclusion, in the final analysis; ~ **grammaticale** parsing; ~ **del sangue** blood test; ~ **dei sistemi/costi** systems/cost analysis

ana'lista, -i, e *sm/f* analyst; (*Psic*) (psycho)analyst; ~ **finanziario** financial analyst; ~ **di sistemi** systems analyst

ana'litico, -a, ci, che *ag* analytic(al)

analiz'zare [analid'dzare] *vt* to analyse (*Brit*), analyze (*US*); (*Med*) to test

analo'gia, -'gie [analo'dʒia] *sf* analogy

ana'logico, -a, ci, che [ana'lɔdʒiko] *ag* analogical; (*calcolatore, orologio*) analog(ue)

a'nalogo, -a, ghi, ghe *ag* analogous

'ananas *sm inv* pineapple

anar'chia [anar'kia] *sf* anarchy

a'narchico, -a, ci, che [a'narkiko] *ag* anarchic(al) ▪ *sm/f* anarchist

anarco-insurreziona'lista [anarko,insurret-tsjona'lista] *ag* anarcho-revolutionary

'A.N.A.S. *sigla f* (= *Azienda Nazionale Autonoma delle Strade*) national roads department

ana'tema, -i *sm* anathema

anato'mia *sf* anatomy

ana'tomico, -a, ci, che *ag* anatomical; (*sedile*) contoured

'anatra *sf* duck; ~ **selvatica** mallard

ana'troccolo *sm* duckling

'ANCA *sigla f* = **Associazione Nazionale Cooperative Agricole**

'anca, -che *sf* (*Anat*) hip; (*Zool*) haunch

ANCC *sigla f* = **Associazione Nazionale Carabinieri**

'anche ['anke] *cong* also; (*perfino*) even; **vengo anch'io!** I'm coming too!; ~ **se** even if; ~ **volendo, non finiremmo in tempo** even if we wanted to, we wouldn't finish in time

ancheggi'are [anked'dʒare] *vi* to wiggle (one's hips)

anchilo'sato, -a [ankilo'zato] *ag* stiff

'ANCI ['antʃi] *sigla f* (= *Associazione Nazionale dei Comuni Italiani*) national confederation of local authorities

anconе'tano, -a *ag* of (*o* from) Ancona

an'cora *av* still; (*di nuovo*) again; (*di più*) some more; (*persino*): ~ **più forte** even stronger; **non** ~ not yet; ~ **una volta** once more, once again; ~ **un po'** a little more; (*di tempo*) a little longer

'ancora *sf* anchor; **gettare/levare l'**~ to cast/weigh anchor; ~ **di salvezza** (*fig*) last hope

anco'raggio [anko'raddʒo] *sm* anchorage

anco'rare *vt*, **anco'rarsi** *vr* to anchor

ANCR *sigla f* (= *Associazione Nazionale Combattenti e Reduci*) servicemen's and ex-servicemen's association

Andalu'sia *sf*: **l'**~ Andalusia

anda'luso, -a *ag, sm/f* Andalusian

anda'mento *sm* (*di strada, malattia*) course; (*del mercato*) state

an'dante *ag* (*corrente*) current; (*di poco pregio*) cheap, second-rate ▪ *sm* (*Mus*) andante

an'dare *sm*: **a lungo** ~ in the long run; **con l'andar del tempo** with the passing of time; **racconta storie a tutto** ~ she's forever talking rubbish ▪ *vi* (*gen*) to go; (*essere adatto*): ~ **a** to suit; (*piacere*): **il suo comportamento non mi va** I don't like the way he behaves; **ti va di** ~ **al cinema?** do you feel like going to the cinema?; ~ **a cavallo** to ride; ~ **in macchina/aereo** to go by car/plane; ~ **a fare qc** to go and do sth; ~ **a pescare/sciare** to go fishing/skiing; **andarsene** to go away; **vado e vengo** I'll be back in a minute; ~ **per i 50** (*età*) to be getting on for 50; ~ **a male** to go bad; ~ **fiero di qc/qn** to be proud of sth/sb; ~ **perduto** to be lost; **come va?** (*lavoro, progetto*) how are things?; **come va?** — **bene, grazie!** how are you? — fine, thanks!; **va fatto entro oggi** it's got to be done today; **ne va della nostra vita** our lives are at stake; **se non vado errato** if I'm not mistaken; **le mele vanno molto** apples are selling well; **va da sé** (*è naturale*) it goes without saying; **per questa volta vada** let's say no more about it this time

an'data *sf* (*viaggio*) outward journey; **biglietto di sola** ~ single (*Brit*) *o* one-way ticket; **biglietto di** ~ **e ritorno** return (*Brit*) *o* round-trip (*US*) ticket

anda'tura *sf* (*modo di andare*) walk, gait; (*Sport*) pace; (*Naut*) tack

an'dazzo [an'dattso] *sm* (*peg*): **prendere un brutto** ~ to take a turn for the worse

'Ande *sfpl*: **le** ~ the Andes

an'dino, -a *ag* Andean

andirivi'eni *sm inv* coming and going

'**andito** *sm* corridor, passage

An'dorra *sf* Andorra

andrò *etc vb vedi* **andare**

an'**drone** *sm* entrance hall

a'**neddoto** *sm* anecdote

ane'**lare** *vi*: ~ **a** (*fig*) to long for, yearn for

a'**nelito** *sm* (*fig*): ~ **di** longing *o* yearning for

a'**nello** *sm* ring; (*di catena*) link

ane'**mia** *sf* anaemia (*Brit*), anemia (*US*)

a'**nemico, -a, ci, che** *ag* anaemic (*Brit*), anemic (*US*)

a'**nemone** *sm* anemone

aneste'**sia** *sf* anaesthesia (*Brit*), anesthesia (*US*)

aneste'**sista, -i, e** *sm/f* anaesthetist (*Brit*), anesthetist (*US*)

anes'**tetico, -a, ci, che** *ag, sm* anaesthetic (*Brit*), anesthetic (*US*)

anestetiz'**zare** [anestetid'dzare] *vt* to anaesthetize (*Brit*), anesthetize (*US*)

anfeta'**mina** *sf* amphetamine

anfeta'**minico, -a, ci, che** *ag* (*fig*) hyper

an'**fibio, -a** *ag* amphibious ■ *sm* amphibian; (*Aut*) amphibious vehicle

anfite'**atro** *sm* amphitheatre (*Brit*), amphitheater (*US*)

anfitri'**one** *sm* host

'**anfora** *sf* amphora

an'**fratto** *sm* ravine

an'**gelico, -a, ci, che** [an'dʒɛliko] *ag* angelic(al)

'**angelo** ['andʒelo] *sm* angel; ~ **custode** guardian angel; **l'~ del focolare** (*fig*) the perfect housewife

anghe'**ria** [ange'ria] *sf* vexation

an'**gina** [an'dʒina] *sf* tonsillitis; ~ **pectoris** angina

angli'**cano, -a** *ag* Anglican

angli'**cismo** [angli'tʃizmo] *sm* anglicism

an'**glofilo, -a** *ag* anglophilic ■ *sm/f* anglophile

anglo'**sassone** *ag* Anglo-Saxon

An'**gola** *sf*: **l'~** Angola

ango'**lano, -a** *ag, sm/f* Angolan

ango'**lare** *ag* angular

angolazi'**one** [angolat'tsjone] *sf* (*di angolo*) angulation; (*Fot, Cine, TV, fig*) angle

'**angolo** *sm* corner; (*Mat*) angle; ~ **cottura** (*di appartamento etc*) cooking area; **fare ~ con** (*strada*) to run into; **dietro l'~** (*anche fig*) round the corner

ango'**loso, -a** *ag* (*oggetto*) angular; (*volto, corpo*) angular, bony

an'**gora** *sf*: **lana d'~** angora

an'**goscia, -sce** [an'gɔʃʃa] *sf* deep anxiety, anguish *no pl*

angosci'**are** [angoʃ'ʃare] *vt* to cause anguish to; **angosciarsi** *vr*: **angosciarsi (per)** (*preoccuparsi*) to become anxious (about); (*provare angoscia*) to get upset (about *o* over)

angosci'**oso, -a** [angoʃ'ʃoso] *ag* (*d'angoscia*) anguished; (*che dà angoscia*) distressing, painful

angu'**illa** *sf* eel

an'**guria** *sf* watermelon

an'**gustia** *sf* (*ansia*) anguish, distress; (*povertà*) poverty, want

angusti'**are** *vt* to distress; **angustiarsi** *vr*: **angustiarsi (per)** to worry (about)

an'**gusto, -a** *ag* (*stretto*) narrow; (*fig*) mean, petty

'**anice** ['anitʃe] *sm* (*Cuc*) aniseed; (*Bot*) anise; (*liquore*) anisette

ani'**dride** *sf* (*Chim*): ~ **carbonica/solforosa** carbon/sulphur dioxide

'**anima** *sf* soul; (*abitante*) inhabitant; ~ **gemella** soul mate; **un'~ in pena** (*anche fig*) a tormented soul; **non c'era ~ viva** there wasn't a living soul; **volere un bene dell'~ a qn** to be extremely fond of sb; **rompere l'~ a qn** to drive sb mad; **il nonno buon'~ ...** Grandfather, God rest his soul ...

ani'**male** *sm, ag* animal

anima'**lesco, -a, schi, sche** *ag* (*gesto, atteggiamento*) animal-like

anima'**lista, -i, e** *ag* animal rights *cpd* ■ *sm/f* animal rights activist

ani'**mare** *vt* to give life to, liven (up); (*incoraggiare*) to encourage; **animarsi** *vr* to become animated, come to life

ani'**mato, -a** *ag* animate; (*vivace*) lively, animated; (: *strada*) busy

anima'**tore, -trice** *sm/f* guiding spirit; (*Cine*) animator; (*di festa*) life and soul

animazi'**one** [animat'tsjone] *sf* liveliness; (*di strada*) bustle; (*Cine*) animation; ~ **teatrale** amateur dramatics

'**animo** *sm* (*mente*) mind; (*cuore*) heart; (*coraggio*) courage; (*disposizione*) character, disposition; **avere in ~ di fare qc** to intend *o* have a mind to do sth; **farsi ~** to pluck up courage; **fare qc di buon/mal ~** to do sth willingly/unwillingly; **perdersi d'~** to lose heart

animosità *sf* animosity

A'**NITA** *sigla f* = **Associazione Naturista Italiana**

'**anitra** *sf* = **anatra**

'**Ankara** *sf* Ankara

ANM *sigla f* (= *Associazione Nazionale dei Magistrati*) national association of Magistrates

anna'**cquare** *vt* to water down, dilute

annaffi'**are** *vt* to water

annaffia'toio *sm* watering can
an'nali *smpl* annals
annas'pare *vi* (*nell'acqua*) to flounder; (*fig: nel buio, nell'incertezza*) to grope
an'nata *sf* year; (*importo annuo*) annual amount; **vino di ~** vintage wine
annebbi'are *vt* (*fig*) to cloud; **annebbiarsi** *vr* to become foggy; (*vista*) to become dim
annega'mento *sm* drowning
anne'gare *vt, vi* to drown; **annegarsi** *vr* (*accidentalmente*) to drown; (*deliberatamente*) to drown o.s.
anne'rire *vt* to blacken ◼ *vi* to become black
annessi'one *sf* (*Pol*) annexation
an'nesso, -a *pp di* **annettere** ◼ *ag* attached; (*Pol*) annexed; **... e tutti gli annessi e connessi** ... and so on and so forth
an'nettere *vt* (*Pol*) to annex; (*accludere*) to attach
annichi'lire [anniki'lire] *vt* to annihilate
anni'darsi *vr* to nest
annienta'mento *sm* annihilation, destruction
annien'tare *vt* to annihilate, destroy
anniver'sario *sm* anniversary
'anno *sm* year; **quanti anni hai? — ho 40 anni** how old are you? — I'm 40 (years old); **gli anni 20** the 20s; **porta bene gli anni** she doesn't look her age; **porta male gli anni** she looks older than she is; **~ commerciale** business year; **~ giudiziario** legal year; **~ luce** light year; **gli anni di piombo** *the Seventies in Italy, characterized by terrorist attacks and killings*
anno'dare *vt* to knot, tie; (*fig: rapporto*) to form
annoi'are *vt* to bore; (*seccare*) to annoy; **annoiarsi** *vr* to be bored; to be annoyed
an'noso, -a *ag* (*albero*) old; (*fig: problema etc*) age-old
anno'tare *vt* (*registrare*) to note, note down (*Brit*); (*commentare*) to annotate
annotazi'one [annotat'tsjone] *sf* note; annotation
annove'rare *vt* to number
annu'ale *ag* annual
annual'mente *av* annually, yearly
annu'ario *sm* yearbook
annu'ire *vi* to nod; (*acconsentire*) to agree
annulla'mento *sm* annihilation, destruction; cancellation; annulment; quashing
annul'lare *vt* to annihilate, destroy; (*contratto, francobollo*) to cancel; (*matrimonio*) to annul; (*sentenza*) to quash; (*risultati*) to declare void
annunci'are [annun't∫are] *vt* to announce; (*dar segni rivelatori*) to herald

annuncia'tore, -'trice [annunt∫a'tore] *sm/f* (*Radio, TV*) announcer
Annunciazi'one [annunt∫at'tsjone] *sf* (*Rel*): **l'~** the Annunciation
an'nuncio [an'nunt∫o] *sm* announcement; (*fig*) sign; **~ pubblicitario** advertisement; **annunci economici** classified advertisements, small ads; **piccoli annunci** small ads, classified ads; **annunci mortuari** (*colonna*) obituary column
'annuo, -a *ag* annual, yearly
annu'sare *vt* to sniff, smell; **~ tabacco** to take snuff
annuvola'mento *sm* clouding (over)
annuvo'lare *vt* to cloud; **annuvolarsi** *vr* to become cloudy, cloud over
'ano *sm* anus
'anodo *sm* anode
anoma'lia *sf* anomaly
a'nomalo, -a *ag* anomalous
anoni'mato *sm* anonymity; **conservare l'~** to remain anonymous
a'nonimo, -a *ag* anonymous ◼ *sm* (*autore*) anonymous writer (*o painter etc*); **un tipo ~** (*peg*) a colourless (*Brit*) *o* colorless (*US*) character
anores'sia *sf* anorexia; **~ nervosa** anorexia nervosa
ano'ressico, -a, ci, che *ag* anorexic
anor'male *ag* abnormal ◼ *sm/f* subnormal person; (*eufemismo*) homosexual
anormalità *sf inv* abnormality
'ANSA *sigla f* (= *Agenzia Nazionale Stampa Associata*) national press agency
'ansa *sf* (*manico*) handle; (*di fiume*) bend, loop
an'sante *ag* out of breath, panting
'ANSEA *sigla f* (= *Associazione delle Nazioni del Sud-Est asiatico*) ASEAN
'ansia *sf* anxiety; **stare in ~ (per qn/qc)** to be anxious (about sb/sth)
ansietà *sf* anxiety
ansi'mare *vi* to pant
ansi'oso, -a *ag* anxious
'anta *sf* (*di finestra*) shutter; (*di armadio*) door
antago'nismo *sm* antagonism
antago'nista, -i, e *sm/f* antagonist
an'tartico, -a, ci, che *ag* Antarctic ◼ *sm*: **l'A~** the Antarctic
An'tartide *sf*: **l'~** Antarctica
ante'bellico, -a, ci, che *ag* prewar *cpd*
antece'dente [antet∫e'dɛnte] *ag* preceding, previous
ante'fatto *sm* previous events *pl*; previous history
ante'guerra *sm* pre-war period
ante'nato *sm* ancestor, forefather

an'tenna *sf* (*Radio, TV*) aerial; (*Zool*) antenna, feeler; **rizzare le antenne** (*fig*) to prick up one's ears; **~ parabolica** (*TV*) satellite dish

ante'porre *vt*: ~ qc a qc to place *o* put sth before sth

ante'posto, -a *pp di* **anteporre**

ante'prima *sf* preview; **~ di stampa** (*Inform*) print preview

anteri'ore *ag* (*ruota, zampa*) front *cpd*; (*fatti*) previous, preceding

antesi'gnano [antesiɲˈɲano] *sm* (*Storia*) standard-bearer; (*fig*) forerunner

antiade'rente *ag* non-stick

antia'ereo, -a *ag* anti-aircraft *cpd*

antial'lergico, -a [antialˈlɛrdʒiko] *ag, sm* hypoallergenic

antia'tomico, -a, ci, che *ag* anti-nuclear; **rifugio ~** fallout shelter

antibi'otico, -a, ci, che *ag, sm* antibiotic

anti'caglia [antiˈkaʎʎa] *sf* junk *no pl*

antical'care *ag* (*prodotto, detersivo*) anti-limescale

anti'camera *sf* anteroom; **fare ~** to be kept waiting; **non mi passerebbe neanche per l'~ del cervello** it wouldn't even cross my mind

anti'carie *ag inv* which fights tooth decay

antichità [antikiˈta] *sf inv* antiquity; (*oggetto*) antique

antici'clone [antitʃiˈklone] *sm* anticyclone

antici'pare [antitʃiˈpare] *vt* (*consegna, visita*) to bring forward, anticipate; (*somma di denaro*) to pay in advance; (*notizia*) to disclose ■ *vi* to be ahead of time

antici'pato, -a [antitʃiˈpato] *ag* (*prima del previsto*) early; **pagamento ~** payment in advance

anticipazi'one [antitʃipatˈtsjone] *sf* anticipation; (*di notizia*) advance information; (*somma di denaro*) advance

an'ticipo [anˈtitʃipo] *sm* anticipation; (*di denaro*) advance; **in ~** early, in advance; **con un sensibile ~** well in advance

anti'clan *ag inv* (*magistrato, processo*) anti-Mafia

an'tico, -a, chi, che *ag* (*quadro, mobili*) antique; (*dell'antichità*) ancient; **all'antica** old-fashioned

anticoncezio'nale [antikontʃetsjoˈnale] *sm* contraceptive

anticonfor'mista, -i, e *ag, sm/f* nonconformist

anticonge'lante [antikondʒeˈlante] *ag, sm* antifreeze

anticongiuntu'rale [antikondʒuntuˈrale] *ag* (*Econ*): **misure anticongiunturali** measures to remedy the economic situation

anti'corpo *sm* antibody

anticostituzio'nale [antikostituttsjoˈnale] *ag* unconstitutional

antidepres'sivo, -a *ag, sm* antidepressant

antidiluvi'ano, -a *ag* (*fig: antiquato*) ancient

antidolo'rifico, -ci *sm* painkiller

anti'doping *sm inv* (*Sport*) dope test ■ *ag inv* drug testing; **test ~** drugs (*Brit*) *o* drug (*US*) test

an'tidoto *sm* antidote

anti'droga *ag inv* anti-drugs *cpd*

antie'stetico, -a, ci, che *ag* unsightly

an'tifona *sf* (*Mus, Rel*) antiphon; **capire l'~** (*fig*) to take the hint

anti'forfora *ag inv* anti-dandruff

anti'furto *sm* anti-theft device

anti'gelo [antiˈdʒɛlo] *ag inv* antifreeze *cpd* ■ *sm* (*per motore*) antifreeze; (*per cristalli*) de-icer

an'tigene [anˈtidʒene] *sm* antigen

antigi'enico, -a, ci, che [antiˈdʒɛniko] *ag* unhygienic

antiglobalizza'zione [antiglobaliddzaˈtsjone] *ag* anti-globalization

An'tille *sfpl*: **le ~** the West Indies

an'tilope *sf* antelope

anti'mafia *ag inv* anti-mafia *cpd*

antin'cendio [antinˈtʃendjo] *ag inv* fire *cpd*; **bombola ~** fire extinguisher

anti'nebbia *sm inv* (*anche:* **faro antinebbia**: *Aut*) fog lamp

antine'vralgico, -a, ci, che [antineˈvraldʒiko] *ag* painkilling ■ *sm* painkiller

antin'fiammatorio, -a *ag, sm* anti-inflammatory

antio'rario *ag*: **in senso ~** in an anticlockwise (*Brit*) *o* counterclockwise (*US*) direction, anticlockwise, counterclockwise

anti'pasto *sm* hors d'œuvre

antipa'tia *sf* antipathy, dislike

anti'patico, -a, ci, che *ag* unpleasant, disagreeable

anti'placca *ag inv* (*dentifricio*) anti-plaque

an'tipodi *smpl*: **essere agli ~** (*fig: di idee opposte*) to be poles apart

antipro'iettile *ag inv* bulletproof

antiquari'ato *sm* antique trade; **un pezzo d'~** an antique

anti'quario *sm* antique dealer

anti'quato, -a *ag* antiquated, old-fashioned

antirici'claggio [antiritʃiˈkladdʒo] *ag* (*attività, operazioni*) anti-laundering

antiri'flesso *ag inv* (*schermo*) non-glare *cpd*

anti'ruggine [antiˈruddʒine] *ag* anti-rust *cpd* ■ *sm inv* rust-preventer

anti'rughe [antiˈruge] *ag inv* anti-wrinkle

antise'mita, -i, e *ag* anti-semitic

antisemi'tismo *sm* anti-semitism
anti'settico, -a, ci, che *ag, sm* antiseptic
antista'minico, -a, ci, che *ag, sm* antihistamine
anti'stante *ag* opposite
anti'tartaro *ag inv* anti-tartar
antiterro'rismo *sm* anti-terrorist measures *pl*
an'titesi *sf* antithesis
antitraspi'rante *ag* antiperspirant
anti'vipera *ag inv*: **siero ~** remedy for snake bites
antivi'rale *adj* antiviral
anti'virus [anti'virus] *sm inv* antivirus software *no pl*
antolo'gia, -gie [antolo'dʒia] *sf* anthology
antono'masia *sf* antonomasia; **per ~** par excellence
antra'cite [antra'tʃite] *sf* anthracite
'antro *sm* cavern
antro'pofago, -gi *sm* cannibal
antropolo'gia [antropolo'dʒia] *sf* anthropology
antropo'logico, -a, ci, che [antropo'lɔdʒiko] *ag* anthropological
antro'pologo, -a, gi, ghe *sm/f* anthropologist
anu'lare *ag* ring *cpd* ■ *sm* ring finger
An'versa *sf* Antwerp
'anzi ['antsi] *av* (*invece*) on the contrary; (*o meglio*) or rather, or better still
anzianità [antsjani'ta] *sf* old age; (*Amm*) seniority
anzi'ano, -a [an'tsjano] *ag* old; (*Amm*) senior ■ *sm/f* old person; senior member
anziché [antsi'ke] *cong* rather than
anzi'tempo [antsi'tɛmpo] *av* (*in anticipo*) early
anzi'tutto [antsi'tutto] *av* first of all
AO *sigla* = **Aosta**
a'orta *sf* aorta
aos'tano, -a *ag* of (*o* from) Aosta
AP *sigla* = **Ascoli Piceno**
apar'titico, -a, ci, che *ag* (*Pol*) non-party *cpd*
apa'tia *sf* apathy, indifference
a'patico, -a, ci, che *ag* apathetic, indifferent
a.p.c. *abbr* = **a pronta cassa**
'ape *sf* bee
aperi'tivo *sm* apéritif
aperta'mente *av* openly
a'perto, -a *pp di* **aprire** ■ *ag* open ■ *sm*: **all'~** in the open (air); **rimanere a bocca aperta** (*fig*) to be taken aback
aper'tura *sf* opening; (*ampiezza*) width, spread; (*Pol*) approach; (*Fot*) aperture; **~ alare** wing span; **~ mentale** open-mindedness; **~ di credito** (*Comm*) granting of credit
API *sigla f* = **Associazione Piccole e Medie Industrie**
'apice ['apitʃe] *sm* apex; (*fig*) height

apicol'tore *sm* beekeeper
apicol'tura *sf* beekeeping
ap'nea *sf*: **immergersi in ~** to dive without breathing apparatus
apoca'lisse *sf* apocalypse
apo'geo [apo'dʒɛo] *sm* (*Astr*) apogee; (*fig*: *culmine*) zenith
a'polide *ag* stateless
apo'litico, -a, ci, che *ag* (*neutrale*) nonpolitical; (*indifferente*) apolitical
apolo'gia, -gie [apolo'dʒia] *sf* (*difesa*) apologia; (*esaltazione*) praise; **~ di reato** attempt to defend criminal acts
apoples'sia *sf* (*Med*) apoplexy
apop'lettico, -a, ci, che *ag* apoplectic; **colpo ~** apoplectic fit
a'postolo *sm* apostle
apostro'fare *vt* (*parola*) to write with an apostrophe; (*persona*) to address
a'postrofo *sm* apostrophe
app. *abbr* (= *appendice*) app.
appaga'mento *sm* satisfaction; fulfilment
appa'gare *vt* to satisfy; (*desiderio*) to fulfil; **appagarsi** *vr*: **appagarsi di** to be satisfied with
appa'gato, -a *ag* satisfied
appai'are *vt* to couple, pair
ap'paio *etc vb vedi* **apparire**
appallotto'lare *vt* (*carta, foglio*) to screw into a ball; **appallottolarsi** *vr* (*gatto*) to roll up into a ball
appalta'tore *sm* contractor
ap'palto *sm* (*Comm*) contract; **dare/prendere in ~ un lavoro** to let out/undertake a job on contract
appan'naggio [appan'naddʒo] *sm* (*compenso*) annuity; (*fig*) privilege, prerogative
appan'nare *vt* (*vetro*) to mist; (*metallo*) to tarnish; (*vista*) to dim; **appannarsi** *vr* to mist over; to tarnish; to grow dim
appa'rato *sm* equipment, machinery; (*Anat*) apparatus; **~ scenico** (*Teat*) props *pl*
apparecchi'are [apparek'kjare] *vt* to prepare; (*tavola*) to set ■ *vi* to set the table
apparecchia'tura [apparekkja'tura] *sf* equipment; (*macchina*) machine, device
appa'recchio [appa'rekkjo] *sm* piece of apparatus, device; (*aeroplano*) aircraft *inv*; **apparecchi sanitari** bathroom *o* sanitary appliances; **~ televisivo/telefonico** television set/telephone
appa'rente *ag* apparent
apparente'mente *av* apparently
appa'renza [appa'rentsa] *sf* appearance; **in** *o* **all'~** apparently, to all appearances
appa'rire *vi* to appear; (*sembrare*) to seem, appear

23

appari'scente [appariʃʃɛnte] *ag* (*colore*) garish, gaudy; (*bellezza*) striking

apparizi'one [apparit'tsjone] *sf* apparition

ap'parso, -a *pp di* **apparire**

apparta'mento *sm* flat (*Brit*), apartment (*US*)

appar'tarsi *vr* to withdraw

appar'tato, -a *ag* (*luogo*) secluded

apparte'nenza [apparte'nentsa] *sf*: ~ **(a)** (*gen*) belonging (to); (*a un partito, club*) membership (of)

apparte'nere *vi*: ~ **a** to belong to

ap'parvi *etc vb vedi* **apparire**

appassio'nante *ag* thrilling, exciting

appassio'nare *vt* to thrill; (*commuovere*) to move; **appassionarsi** *vr*: **appassionarsi a qc** to take a great interest in sth; to be deeply moved by sth

appassio'nato, -a *ag* passionate; (*entusiasta*): ~ **(di)** keen (on)

appas'sire *vi* to wither

appel'larsi *vr* (*ricorrere*): ~ **a** to appeal to; (*Dir*): ~ **contro** to appeal against

ap'pello *sm* roll-call; (*implorazione, Dir*) appeal; (*sessione d'esame*) exam session; **fare ~ a** to appeal to; **fare l'~** (*Ins*) to call the register *o* roll; (*Mil*) to call the roll

ap'pena *av* (*a stento*) hardly, scarcely; (*solamente, da poco*) just ■ *cong* as soon as; **(non) ~ furono arrivati ...** as soon as they had arrived ...; **basta ~ a sfamarli** it's scarcely enough to feed them; **ho ~ finito** I've just finished

ap'pendere *vt* to hang (up)

appendi'abiti *sm inv* hook, peg; (*mobile*) hall stand (*Brit*), hall tree (*US*)

appen'dice [appen'ditʃe] *sf* appendix; **romanzo d'~** popular serial

appendi'cite [appendi'tʃite] *sf* appendicitis

appen'dino *sm* (*coat*) hook

Appen'nini *smpl*: **gli ~** the Apennines

appesan'tire *vt* to make heavy; **appesantirsi** *vr* to grow stout

ap'peso, -a *pp di* **appendere**

appe'tito *sm* appetite

appeti'toso, -a *ag* appetising; (*fig*) attractive, desirable

appezza'mento [appettsa'mento] *sm* (*anche*: **appezzamento di terreno**) plot, piece of ground

appia'nare *vt* to level; (*fig*) to smooth away, iron out; **appianarsi** *vr* (*divergenze*) to be ironed out

appiat'tire *vt* to flatten; **appiattirsi** *vr* to become flatter; (*farsi piatto*) to flatten o.s.; **appiattirsi al suolo** to lie flat on the ground

appic'care *vt*: ~ **il fuoco a** to set fire to, set on fire

appicci'care [appittʃi'kare] *vt* to stick; (*fig*): ~ **qc a qn** to palm sth off on sb; **appiccicarsi** *vr* to stick; (*fig: persona*) to cling

appiccica'ticcio, -a, ci, ce [appittʃika'tittʃo], **appicci'coso, -a** [appittʃi'koso] *ag* sticky; (*fig: persona*): **essere ~** to cling like a leech

appie'dato, -a *ag*: **rimanere ~** to be left without means of transport

appi'eno *av* fully

appigli'arsi [appiʎʎarsi] *vr*: ~ **a** (*afferrarsi*) to take hold of; (*fig*) to cling to

ap'piglio [ap'piʎʎo] *sm* hold; (*fig*) pretext

appiop'pare *vt*: ~ **qc a qn** (*nomignolo*) to pin sth on sb; (*compito difficile*) to saddle sb with sth; **gli ha appioppato un pugno sul muso** he punched him in the face

appiso'larsi *vr* to doze off

applau'dire *vt, vi* to applaud

ap'plauso *sm* applause *no pl*

appli'cabile *ag*: ~ **(a)** applicable (to)

appli'care *vt* to apply; (*regolamento*) to enforce; **applicarsi** *vr* to apply o.s.

appli'cato, -a *ag* (*arte, scienze*) applied ■ *sm* (*Amm*) clerk

applica'tore *sm* applicator

applicazi'one [applikat'tsjone] *sf* application; enforcement; **applicazioni tecniche** (*Ins*) practical subjects

appoggi'are [appod'dʒare] *vt* (*mettere contro*): ~ **qc a qc** to lean *o* rest sth against sth; (*fig: sostenere*) to support; **appoggiarsi** *vr*: **appoggiarsi a** to lean against; (*fig*) to rely upon

ap'poggio [ap'poddʒo] *sm* support

appollai'arsi *vr* (*anche fig*) to perch

ap'pongo, ap'poni *etc vb vedi* **apporre**

ap'porre *vt* to affix

appor'tare *vt* to bring

ap'porto *sm* (*gen, Finanza*) contribution

ap'posi *etc vb vedi* **apporre**

apposita'mente *av* (*apposta*) on purpose; (*specialmente*) specially

ap'posito, -a *ag* appropriate

ap'posta *av* on purpose, deliberately; **neanche a farlo ~, ...** by sheer coincidence, ...

appos'tarsi *vr* to lie in wait

ap'posto, -a *pp di* **apporre**

ap'prendere *vt* (*imparare*) to learn; (*comprendere*) to grasp

apprendi'mento *sm* learning

appren'dista, -i, e *sm/f* apprentice

apprendi'stato *sm* apprenticeship

apprensi'one *sf* apprehension

appren'sivo, -a *ag* apprehensive

ap'preso, -a *pp di* **apprendere**

ap'presso *av* (*accanto, vicino*) close by, near; (*dietro*) behind; (*dopo, più tardi*) after, later

■ *ag inv* (*dopo*): **il giorno** ~ the next day; **~ a** *prep* (*vicino a*) near, close to

appres'tare *vt* to prepare, get ready; **apprestarsi** *vr*: **apprestarsi a fare qc** to prepare *o* get ready to do sth

ap'pretto *sm* starch

apprez'zabile [appret'tsabile] *ag* (*notevole*) noteworthy, significant; (*percepibile*) appreciable

apprezza'mento [apprettsa'mento] *sm* appreciation; (*giudizio*) opinion; (*commento*) comment

apprez'zare [appret'tsare] *vt* to appreciate

ap'proccio [ap'prɔttʃo] *sm* approach

appro'dare *vi* (*Naut*) to land; (*fig*): **non ~ a nulla** to come to nothing

ap'prodo *sm* landing; (*luogo*) landing place

approfit'tare *vi*: **~ di** (*persona, situazione*) to take advantage of; (*occasione, opportunità*) to make the most of, profit by

approfon'dire *vt* to deepen; (*fig*) to study in depth; **approfondirsi** *vr* (*gen, fig*) to deepen; (*peggiorare*) to get worse

appron'tare *vt* to prepare, get ready

appropri'arsi *vr*: **~ di qc** to appropriate sth, take possession of sth; **~ indebitamente di** to embezzle

appropri'ato, -a *ag* appropriate

appropriazi'one [approprjat'tsjone] *sf* appropriation; **~ indebita** (*Dir*) embezzlement

approssi'mare *vt* (*cifra*): **~ per eccesso/per difetto** to round up/down; **approssimarsi** *vr*: **approssimarsi a** to approach, draw near

approssima'tivo, -a *ag* approximate, rough; (*impreciso*) inexact, imprecise

approssimazi'one [approssimat'tsjone] *sf* approximation; **per ~** approximately, roughly

appro'vare *vt* (*condotta, azione*) to approve of; (*candidato*) to pass; (*progetto di legge*) to approve

approvazi'one [approvat'tsjone] *sf* approval

approvvigiona'mento [approvvidʒona'mento] *sm* supplying; stocking up; **approvvigionamenti** *smpl* (*Mil*) supplies

approvvigio'nare [approvvidʒo'nare] *vt* to supply; **approvvigionarsi** *vr* to lay in provisions, stock up; **~ qn di qc** to supply sb with sth

appunta'mento *sm* appointment; (*amoroso*) date; **darsi** ~ to arrange to meet (one another)

appun'tare *vt* (*rendere aguzzo*) to sharpen; (*fissare*) to pin, fix; (*annotare*) to note down

appun'tato *sm* (*Carabinieri*) corporal

appun'tino *av* perfectly

appun'tire *vt* to sharpen

ap'punto *sm* note; (*rimprovero*) reproach; (*Inform*): **Appunti** Clipboard *sg* ■ *av* (*proprio*) exactly, just; **per l'~!, ~!** exactly!

appu'rare *vt* to check, verify

apr. *abbr* (= *aprile*) Apr.

apribot'tiglie [apribot'tiʎʎe] *sm inv* bottleopener

a'prile *sm* April; **pesce d'~!** April Fool!; *vedi anche* **luglio**

a'prire *vt* to open; (*via, cadavere*) to open up; (*gas, luce, acqua*) to turn on ■ *vi* to open; **aprirsi** *vr* to open; **~ le ostilità** (*Mil*) to start up *o* begin hostilities; **~ una sessione** (*Inform*) to log on; **aprirsi a qn** to confide in sb, open one's heart to sb; **mi si è aperto lo stomaco** I feel rather peckish; **apriti cielo!** heaven forbid!

apris'catole *sm inv* tin (*Brit*) *o* can opener

APT *sigla f* (= *Azienda di Promozione*) ≈ tourist board

AQ *sigla* = **L'Aquila**

aquagym [akwa'dʒim] *sf* aquarobics

a'quario *sm* = **acquario**

'aquila *sf* (*Zool*) eagle; (*fig*) genius

aqui'lino, -a *ag* aquiline

aqui'lone *sm* (*giocattolo*) kite; (*vento*) North wind

AR *sigla* = **Arezzo**

A/R *abbr* (= *andata e ritorno*) return

ara'besco *sm* (*decorazione*) arabesque

A'rabia Sau'dita *sf*: **l'~** Saudi Arabia

a'rabico, -a, ci, che *ag*: **il Deserto ~** the Arabian Desert

a'rabile *ag* arable

'arabo, -a *ag, sm/f* Arab ■ *sm* (*Ling*) Arabic; **parlare ~** (*fig*) to speak double Dutch (*Brit*)

a'rachide [a'rakide] *sf* peanut

ara'gosta *sf* spiny lobster

a'raldica *sf* heraldry

a'raldo *sm* herald

aran'ceto [aran'tʃeto] *sm* orange grove

a'rancia, -ce [a'rantʃa] *sf* orange

aranci'ata [aran'tʃata] *sf* orangeade

a'rancio [a'rantʃo] *sm* (*Bot*) orange tree; (*colore*) orange ■ *ag inv* (*colore*) orange; **fiori di** ~ orange blossom *sg*

aranci'one [aran'tʃone] *ag inv*: (**color**) ~ bright orange

a'rare *vt* to plough (*Brit*), plow (*US*)

ara'tore *sm* ploughman (*Brit*), plowman (*US*)

a'ratro *sm* plough (*Brit*), plow (*US*)

ara'tura *sf* ploughing (*Brit*), plowing (*US*)

a'razzo [a'rattso] *sm* tapestry

arbi'traggio [arbi'traddʒo] *sm* (*Sport*) refereeing; umpiring; (*Dir*) arbitration; (*Comm*) arbitrage

arbi'trare vt (Sport) to referee; to umpire; (Dir) to arbitrate

arbi'trario, -a ag arbitrary

arbi'trato sm arbitration

ar'bitrio sm will; (abuso, sopruso) arbitrary act

'arbitro sm arbiter, judge; (Dir) arbitrator; (Sport) referee; (: Tennis, Cricket) umpire

ar'busto sm shrub

'arca, -che sf (sarcofago) sarcophagus; **l'~ di Noè** Noah's ark

ar'caico, -a, ci, che ag archaic

arca'ismo sm (Ling) archaism

ar'cangelo [ar'kandʒelo] sm archangel

ar'cano, -a ag arcane, mysterious ■ sm mystery

ar'cata sf (Archit, Anat) arch; (ordine di archi) arcade

archeolo'gia [arkeolo'dʒia] sf arch(a)eology

archeo'logico, -a, ci, che [arkeo'lɔdʒiko] ag arch(a)eological

arche'ologo, -a, gi, ghe [arke'ɔlogo] sm/f arch(a)eologist

ar'chetipo [ar'kɛtipo] sm archetype

ar'chetto [ar'ketto] sm (Mus) bow

architet'tare [arkitet'tare] vt (fig: ideare) to devise; (: macchinare) to plan, concoct

archi'tetto [arki'tetto] sm architect

architet'tonico, -a, ci, che [arkitet'tɔniko] ag architectural

architet'tura [arkitet'tura] sf architecture

archivi'are [arki'vjare] vt (documenti) to file; (Dir) to dismiss

archiviazi'one [arkivjat'tsjone] sf filing; dismissal

ar'chivio [ar'kivjo] sm archives pl; (Inform) file; **~ principale** (Inform) master file

archi'vista, -i, e [arki'vista] sm/f (Amm) archivist; (in ufficio) filing clerk

'ARCI ['artʃi] sigla f (= Associazione Ricreativa Culturale Italiana) cultural society

arci'duca, -chi [artʃi'duka] sm archduke

arci'ere [ar'tʃɛre] sm archer

ar'cigno, -a [ar'tʃiɲɲo] ag grim, severe

arci'pelago, -ghi [artʃi'pɛlago] sm archipelago

arci'vescovo [artʃi'veskovo] sm archbishop

'arco, -chi sm (arma, Mus) bow; (Archit) arch; (Mat) arc; **nell'~ di 3 settimane** within the space of 3 weeks; **~ costituzionale** political parties involved in formulating Italy's post-war constitution

arcoba'leno sm rainbow

arcu'ato, -a ag curved, bent; **dalle gambe arcuate** bow-legged

ar'dente ag burning; (fig) burning, ardent

'ardere vt, vi to burn; **legna da ~** firewood

ar'desia sf slate

ardi'mento sm daring

ar'dire vi to dare ■ sm daring

ar'dito, -a ag brave, daring, bold; (sfacciato) bold

ar'dore sm blazing heat; (fig) ardour, fervour

'arduo, -a ag arduous, difficult

'area sf area; (Edil) land, ground; **nell'~ dei partiti di sinistra** among the parties of the left; **~ fabbricabile** building land; **~ di rigore** (Sport) penalty area; **~ di servizio** (Aut) service area

a'rena sf arena; (per corride) bullring; (sabbia) sand

are'naria sf sandstone

are'narsi vr to run aground; (fig: trattative) to come to a standstill

areo'plano sm = **aeroplano**

are'tino, -a ag of (o from) Arezzo

'argano sm winch

argen'tato, -a [ardʒen'tato] ag silver-plated; (colore) silver, silvery; (capelli) silver(-grey)

ar'genteo, -a [ar'dʒenteo] ag silver, silvery

argente'ria [ardʒente'ria] sf silverware, silver

Argen'tina [ardʒen'tina] sf: **l'~** Argentina

argen'tino, -a [ardʒen'tino] ag, sm/f (dell'Argentina) Argentinian ■ sf crewneck sweater

ar'gento [ar'dʒento] sm silver; **~ vivo** quicksilver; **avere l'~ (vivo) addosso** (fig) to be fidgety

ar'gilla [ar'dʒilla] sf clay

argil'loso, -a [ardʒil'loso] ag (contenente argilla) clayey; (simile ad argilla) clay-like

argi'nare [ardʒi'nare] vt (fiume, acque) to embank; (: con diga) to dyke up; (fig: inflazione, corruzione) to check; (: spese) to limit

'argine ['ardʒine] sm embankment, bank; (diga) dyke, dike; **far ~ a, porre un ~ a** (fig) to check, hold back

argomen'tare vi to argue

argo'mento sm argument; (materia, tema) subject; **tornare sull'~** to bring the matter up again

argu'ire vt to deduce

ar'guto, -a ag sharp, quick-witted; (spiritoso) witty

ar'guzia [ar'guttsja] sf wit; (battuta) witty remark

'aria sf air; (espressione, aspetto) air, look; (Mus: melodia) tune; (: di opera) aria; **all'~ aperta** in the open (air); **manca l'~** it's stuffy; **andare all'~** (piano, progetto) to come to nothing; **mandare all'~ qc** to ruin o upset sth; **darsi delle arie** to put on airs and graces; **ha la testa per ~** his head is in the clouds; **che ~ tira?** (fig: atmosfera) what's the atmosphere like?

aridità *sf* aridity, dryness; (*fig*) lack of feeling

'**arido, -a** *ag* arid

arieggi'are [arjed'dʒare] *vt* (*cambiare aria*) to air; (*imitare*) to imitate

ari'ete *sm* ram; (*Mil*) battering ram; (*dello zodiaco*): **A~** Aries; **essere dell'A~** to be Aries

a'**ringa, -ghe** *sf* herring *inv*; ~ **affumicata** smoked herring, kipper; ~ **marinata** pickled herring

ari'oso, -a *ag* (*ambiente, stanza*) airy; (*Mus*) ariose

'**arista** *sf* (*Cuc*) chine of pork

aristo'cratico, -a, ci, che *ag* aristocratic

aristocra'zia [aristokrat'tsia] *sf* aristocracy

arit'metica *sf* arithmetic

arit'metico, -a, ci, che *ag* arithmetical

arlec'chino [arlek'kino] *sm* harlequin

'**arma, -i** *sf* weapon, arm; (*parte dell'esercito*) arm; **alle armi!** to arms!; **chiamare alle armi** to call up (*Brit*), draft (*US*); **sotto le armi** in the army (*o* forces); **combattere ad armi pari** (*anche fig*) to fight on equal terms; **essere alle prime armi** (*fig*) to be a novice; **passare qn per le armi** to execute sb; ~ **a doppio taglio** (*anche fig*) double-edged weapon; ~ **da fuoco** firearm; **armi convenzionali/non convenzionali** conventional/unconventional weapons; **armi di distruzione de massa** weapons of mass destruction

ar'madio *sm* cupboard; (*per abiti*) wardrobe; ~ **a muro** built-in cupboard

armamen'tario *sm* equipment, instruments *pl*

arma'mento *sm* (*Mil*) armament; (: *materiale*) arms *pl*, weapons *pl*; (*Naut*) fitting out; manning; **la corsa agli armamenti** the arms race

ar'mare *vt* to arm; (*arma da fuoco*) to cock; (*Naut: nave*) to rig, fit out; to man; (*Edil: volta, galleria*) to prop up, shore up; **armarsi** *vr* to arm o.s.; (*Mil*) to take up arms

ar'mato, -a *ag:* ~ (**di**) (*anche fig*) armed (with) ■ *sf* (*Mil*) army; (*Naut*) fleet; **rapina a mano armata** armed robbery

arma'tore *sm* shipowner

arma'tura *sf* (*struttura di sostegno*) framework; (*impalcatura*) scaffolding; (*Storia*) armour *no pl* (*Brit*), armor *no pl* (*US*)

armeggi'are [armed'dʒare] *vi* (*affaccendarsi*): ~ (**intorno a qc**) to mess about (with sth)

ar'meno, -a *ag, sm/f, sm* Armenian

arme'ria *sf* (*deposito*) armoury (*Brit*), armory (*US*); (*collezione*) collection of arms

armis'tizio [armis'tittsjo] *sm* armistice

armo'nia *sf* harmony

ar'monico, -a, ci, che *ag* harmonic; (*fig*) harmonious ■ *sf* (*Mus*) harmonica; **armonica a bocca** mouth organ

armoni'oso, -a *ag* harmonious

armoniz'zare [armonid'dzare] *vt* to harmonize; (*colori, abiti*) to match ■ *vi* to be in harmony; to match

ar'nese *sm* tool, implement; (*oggetto indeterminato*) thing, contraption; **male in** ~ (*malvestito*) badly dressed; (*di salute malferma*) in poor health; (*di condizioni economiche*) down-at-heel

'**arnia** *sf* hive

a'**roma, -i** *sm* aroma; fragrance; **aromi** *smpl* herbs and spices; **aromi naturali/ artificiali** natural/artificial flavouring *sg* (*Brit*) *o* flavoring *sg* (*US*)

aromatera'pia *sf* aromatherapy

aro'matico, -a, ci, che *ag* aromatic; (*cibo*) spicy

aromatiz'zare [aromatid'dzare] *vt* to season, flavour (*Brit*), flavor (*US*)

'**arpa** *sf* (*Mus*) harp

ar'peggio [ar'peddʒo] *sm* (*Mus*) arpeggio

ar'pia *sf* (*anche fig*) harpy

arpi'one *sm* (*gancio*) hook; (*cardine*) hinge; (*Pesca*) harpoon

arrabat'tarsi *vr* to do all one can, strive

arrabbi'are *vi* (*cane*) to be affected with rabies; **arrabbiarsi** *vr* (*essere preso dall'ira*) to get angry, fly into a rage

arrabbi'ato, -a *ag* (*cane*) rabid, with rabies; (*persona*) furious, angry

arrabbia'tura *sf*: **prendersi un'~ (per qc)** to become furious (over sth)

arraf'fare *vt* to snatch, seize; (*sottrarre*) to pinch

arrampi'carsi *vr* to climb (up); ~ **sui vetri** *o* **sugli specchi** (*fig*) to clutch at straws

arrampi'cata *sf* climb

arrampica'tore, -trice *sm/f* (*gen, Sport*) climber; ~ **sociale** (*fig*) social climber

arran'care *vi* to limp, hobble; (*fig*) to struggle along

arrangia'mento [arrandʒa'mento] *sm* (*Mus*) arrangement

arran'giare [arran'dʒare] *vt* to arrange; **arrangiarsi** *vr* to manage, do the best one can

arre'care *vt* to bring; (*causare*) to cause

arreda'mento *sm* (*studio*) interior design; (*mobili etc*) furnishings *pl*

arre'dare *vt* to furnish

arreda'tore, -trice *sm/f* interior designer

ar'redo *sm* fittings *pl*, furnishings *pl*; ~ **per uffici** office furnishings

arrem'baggio [arrem'baddʒo] *sm* (*Naut*) boarding

27

ar'rendersi *vr* to surrender; **~ all'evidenza (dei fatti)** to face (the) facts

arren'devole *ag* (*persona*) yielding, compliant

arrendevo'lezza [arrendevo'lettsa] *sf* compliancy

ar'reso, -a *pp di* **arrendersi**

arres'tare *vt* (*fermare*) to stop, halt; (*catturare*) to arrest; **arrestarsi** *vr* (*fermarsi*) to stop

arres'tato, -a *sm/f* person under arrest

ar'resto *sm* (*cessazione*) stopping; (*fermata*) stop; (*cattura, Med*) arrest; (*Comm: in produzione*) stoppage; **subire un ~** to come to a stop *o* standstill; **mettere agli arresti** to place under arrest; **arresti domiciliari** (*Dir*) house arrest

arre'trare *vt, vi* to withdraw

arre'trato, -a *ag* (*lavoro*) behind schedule; (*paese, bambino*) backward; (*numero di giornale*) back *cpd*; **arretrati** *smpl* arrears; **gli arretrati dello stipendio** back pay *sg*

arricchi'mento [arrikki'mento] *sm* enrichment

arric'chire [arrik'kire] *vt* to enrich; **arricchirsi** *vr* to become rich

arric'chito, -a [arrik'kito] *sm/f* nouveau riche

arricci'are [arrit'tʃare] *vt* to curl; **~ il naso** to turn up one's nose

ar'ridere *vi*: **~ a qn** (*fortuna, successo*) to smile on sb

ar'ringa, -ghe *sf* harangue; (*Dir*) address by counsel

arrischi'are [arris'kjare] *vt* to risk; **arrischiarsi** *vr* to venture, dare

arrischi'ato, -a [arris'kjato] *ag* risky; (*temerario*) reckless, rash

ar'riso, -a *pp di* **arridere**

arri'vare *vi* to arrive; (*avvicinarsi*) to come; (*accadere*) to happen, occur; **~ a** (*livello, grado etc*) to reach; **lui arriva a Roma alle 7** he gets to *o* arrives at Rome at 7; **~ a fare qc** to manage to do sth, succeed in doing sth; **non ci arrivo** I can't reach it; (*fig: non capisco*) I can't understand it

arri'vato, -a *ag* (*persona: di successo*) successful ▪ *sm/f*: **essere un ~** to have made it; **nuovo ~** newcomer; **ben ~!** welcome!; **non sono l'ultimo ~!** (*fig*) I'm no fool!

arrive'derci [arrive'dertʃi] *escl* goodbye!

arrive'derla *escl* (*forma di cortesia*) goodbye!

arri'vismo *sm* (*ambizione*) ambitiousness; (*sociale*) social climbing

arri'vista, -i, e *sm/f* go-getter

ar'rivo *sm* arrival; (*Sport*) finish, finishing line

arro'gante *ag* arrogant

arro'ganza [arro'gantsa] *sf* arrogance

arro'gare *vt*: **arrogarsi il diritto di fare qc** to assume the right to do sth; **arrogarsi il merito di qc** to claim credit for sth

arrossa'mento *sm* reddening

arros'sare *vt* (*occhi, pelle*) to redden, make red; **arrossarsi** *vr* to go *o* become red

arros'sire *vi* (*per vergogna, timidezza*) to blush; (*per gioia*) to flush, blush

arros'tire *vt* to roast; (*pane*) to toast; (*ai ferri*) to grill

ar'rosto *sm, ag inv* roast; **~ di manzo** roast beef

arro'tare *vt* to sharpen; (*investire con un veicolo*) to run over

arro'tino *sm* knife-grinder

arroto'lare *vt* to roll up

arroton'dare *vt* (*forma, oggetto*) to round; (*stipendio*) to add to; (*somma*) to round off

arrovel'larsi *vr* (*anche:* **arrovellarsi il cervello**) to rack one's brains

arroven'tato, -a *ag* red-hot

arruffare *vt* to ruffle; (*fili*) to tangle; (*fig: questione*) to confuse

arruggi'nire [arruddʒi'nire] *vt* to rust; **arrugginirsi** *vr* (*fig*) to become rusty

arruola'mento *sm* (*Mil*) enlistment

arruo'lare *vt* (*Mil*) to enlist; **arruolarsi** *vr* to enlist, join up

arse'nale *sm* (*Mil*) arsenal; (*cantiere navale*) dockyard

ar'senico *sm* arsenic

'arsi *vb vedi* **ardere**

'arso, -a *pp di* **ardere** ▪ *ag* (*bruciato*) burnt; (*arido*) dry

ar'sura *sf* (*calore opprimente*) burning heat; (*siccità*) drought

art. *abbr* (= *articolo*) art.

'arte *sf* art; (*abilità*) skill; **a regola d'~** (*fig*) perfectly; **senz'~ né parte** penniless and out of a job; **arti figurative** visual arts

arte'fatto, -a *ag* (*stile, modi*) affected; (*cibo*) adulterated

ar'tefice [ar'tefitʃe] *sm/f* craftsman(-woman); (*autore*) author

ar'teria *sf* artery

arterios<le'rosi *sf* arteriosclerosis, hardening of the arteries

arteri'oso, -a *ag* arterial

'artico, -a, ci, che *ag* Arctic ▪ *sm*: **l'A~** the Arctic; **il Circolo polare ~** the Arctic Circle; **l'Oceano ~** the Arctic Ocean

artico'lare *ag* (*Anat*) of the joints, articular ▪ *vt* to articulate; (*suddividere*) to divide, split up; **articolarsi** *vr*: **articolarsi in** (*discorso, progetto*) to be divided into

artico'lato, -a *ag* (*linguaggio*) articulate; (*Aut*) articulated

articolazi·one [artikolat'tsjone] *sf* (*Anat, Tecn*) joint; (*di voce, concetto*) articulation

ar·ticolo *sm* article; **~ di fondo** (*Stampa*) leader, leading article; **articoli di marca** branded goods; **un bell'~** (*fig*) a real character

·Artide *sm*: **l'~** the Arctic

artifici·ale [artifi'tʃale] *ag* artificial

artifici·ere [artifi'tʃere] *sm* (*Mil*) artificer; (: *per disinnescare bombe*) bomb-disposal expert

arti·ficio [arti'fitʃo] *sm* (*espediente*) trick, artifice; (*ricerca di effetto*) artificiality

artifici·oso, -a [artifi'tʃoso] *ag* cunning; (*non spontaneo*) affected

artigia·nale [artidʒa'nale] *ag* craft *cpd*

artigia·nato [artidʒa'nato] *sm* craftsmanship; craftsmen *pl*

artigi·ano, -a [arti'dʒano] *sm/f* craftsman(-woman)

artigli·ere [artiʎ'ʎere] *sm* artilleryman

artiglie·ria [artiʎʎe'ria] *sf* artillery

ar·tiglio [ar'tiʎʎo] *sm* claw; (*di rapaci*) talon; **sfoderare gli artigli** (*fig*) to show one's claws

ar·tista, -i, e *sm/f* artist; **un lavoro da ~** (*fig*) a professional piece of work

ar·tistico, -a, ci, che *ag* artistic

·arto *sm* (*Anat*) limb

ar·trite *sf* (*Med*) arthritis

ar·trosi *sf* osteoarthritis

arzigogo·lato, -a [ardzigogo'lato] *ag* tortuous

ar·zillo, -a [ar'dzillo] *ag* lively, sprightly

a·scella [aʃ'ʃɛlla] *sf* (*Anat*) armpit

ascen·dente [aʃʃen'dente] *sm* ancestor; (*fig*) ascendancy; (*Astr*) ascendant

a·scendere [aʃʃendere] *vi*: **~ al trono** to ascend the throne

ascensi·one [aʃʃen'sjone] *sf* (*Alpinismo*) ascent; (*Rel*): **l'A~** the Ascension; **isola dell'A~** Ascension Island

ascen·sore [aʃʃen'sore] *sm* lift

a·scesa [aʃ'ʃesa] *sf* ascent; (*al trono*) accession; (*al potere*) rise

a·scesi [aʃʃezi] *sf* asceticism

a·sceso, -a [aʃʃeso] *pp di* **ascendere**

a·scesso [aʃʃesso] *sm* (*Med*) abscess

a·sceta, -i [aʃʃeta] *sm* ascetic

·ascia ['aʃʃa] (*pl* **asce**) *sf* axe

asciugaca·pelli [aʃʃugaka'pelli] *sm* hair dryer

asciuga·mano [aʃʃuga'mano] *sm* towel

asciu·gare [aʃʃu'gare] *vt* to dry; **asciugarsi** *vr* to dry o.s.; (*diventare asciutto*) to dry

asciuga·trice [aʃʃuga'tritʃe] *sf* spin-dryer

asciut·tezza [aʃʃut'tettsa] *sf* dryness; leanness; curtness

asci·utto, -a [aʃʃutto] *ag* dry; (*fig: magro*) lean; (: *burbero*) curt ■ *sm*: **restare all'~** (*fig*) to be left penniless; **restare a bocca asciutta** (*fig*) to be disappointed

asco·lano, -a *ag* of (*o* from) Ascoli

ascol·tare *vt* to listen to; **~ il consiglio di qn** to listen to *o* heed sb's advice

ascolta·tore, -·trice *sm/f* listener

as·colto *sm*: **essere *o* stare in ~** to be listening; **dare *o* prestare ~ (a)** to pay attention (to); **indice di ~** (*TV, Radio*) audience rating

AS. COM. *sigla f* = **Associazione Commercianti**

as·critto, -a *pp di* **ascrivere**

as·crivere *vt* (*attribuire*): **~ qc a qn** to attribute sth to sb; **~ qc a merito di qn** to give sb credit for sth

a·settico, -a, ci, che *ag* aseptic

asfal·tare *vt* to asphalt

as·falto *sm* asphalt

asfis·sia *sf* asphyxia, asphyxiation

asfissi·ante *ag* (*gas*) asphyxiating; (*fig: calore, ambiente*) stifling, suffocating; (: *persona*) tiresome

asfissi·are *vt* to asphyxiate, suffocate; (*fig: opprimere*) to stifle; (: *infastidire*) to get on sb's nerves ■ *vi* to suffocate, asphyxiate

·Asia *sf*: **l'~** Asia

asi·atico, -a, ci, che *ag, sm/f* Asiatic, Asian

a·silo *sm* refuge, sanctuary; **~ (d'infanzia)** nursery(-school); **~ nido** day nursery, crèche (*for children aged o to 3*); **~ politico** political asylum

asim·metrico, -a, ci, che *ag* asymmetric(al)

·asino *sm* donkey, ass; **la bellezza dell'~** (*fig: di ragazza*) the beauty of youth; **qui casca l'~!** there's the rub!

ASL [azl] *sigla f* (= *Azienda Sanitaria Locale*) local health centre

·asma *sf* asthma

as·matico, -a, ci, che *ag, sm/f* asthmatic

asoci·ale [aso'tʃale] *ag* antisocial

·asola *sf* buttonhole

as·parago, -gi *sm* asparagus *no pl*

as·pergere [as'pɛrdʒere] *vt*: **~ (di *o* con)** to sprinkle (with)

asperità *sf inv* roughness *no pl*; (*fig*) harshness *no pl*

as·persi *etc vb vedi* **aspergere**

as·perso, -a *pp di* **aspergere**

aspet·tare *vt* to wait for; (*anche Comm*) to await; (*aspettarsi*) to expect; (*essere in serbo: notizia, evento etc*) to be in store for, lie ahead of ■ *vi* to wait; **aspettarsi qc** to expect sth; **~ un bambino** to be expecting (a baby); **questo non me l'aspettavo** I wasn't expecting this; **me l'aspettavo!** I thought as much!

aspetta'tiva *sf* expectation; **inferiore all'~** worse than expected; **essere/mettersi in ~** (*Amm*) to be on/take leave of absence

as'petto *sm* (*apparenza*) aspect, appearance, look; (*punto di vista*) point of view; **di bell'~** good-looking

aspi'rante *ag* (*attore etc*) aspiring ■ *sm/f* candidate, applicant

aspira'polvere *sm inv* vacuum cleaner

aspi'rare *vt* (*respirare*) to breathe in, inhale; (*apparecchi*) to suck (up) ■ *vi*: **~ a** to aspire to

aspira'tore *sm* extractor fan

aspirazi'one [aspirat'tsjone] *sf* (*Tecn*) suction; (*anelito*) aspiration

aspi'rina *sf* aspirin

aspor'tare *vt* (*anche Med*) to remove, take away

as'prezza [as'prettsa] *sf* sourness, tartness; pungency; harshness; roughness; rugged nature

'aspro, -a *ag* (*sapore*) sour, tart; (*odore*) acrid, pungent; (*voce, clima, fig*) harsh; (*superficie*) rough; (*paesaggio*) rugged

Ass. *abbr* = **assicurazione**; **assicurata**; **assegno**

assaggi'are [assad'dʒare] *vt* to taste

assag'gini [assad'dʒini] *smpl* (*Cuc*) *selection of first courses*

as'saggio [as'saddʒo] *sm* tasting; (*piccola quantità*) taste; (*campione*) sample

as'sai *av* (*molto*) a lot, much; (: *con ag*) very; (*a sufficienza*) enough ■ *ag inv* (*quantità*) a lot of, much; (*numero*) a lot of, many; **~ contento** very pleased

as'salgo *etc vb vedi* **assalire**

assa'lire *vt* to attack, assail

assali'tore, -trice *sm/f* attacker, assailant

assal'tare *vt* (*Mil*) to storm; (*banca*) to raid; (*treno, diligenza*) to hold up

as'salto *sm* attack, assault; **prendere d'~** (*fig: negozio, treno*) to storm; (: *personalità*) to besiege; **d'~** (*editoria, giornalista etc*) aggressive

assapo'rare *vt* to savour (*Brit*), savor (*US*)

assassi'nare *vt* to murder; (*Pol*) to assassinate; (*fig*) to ruin

assas'sinio *sm* murder; assassination

assas'sino, -a *ag* murderous ■ *sm/f* murderer; assassin

'asse *sm* (*Tecn*) axle; (*Mat*) axis ■ *sf* board; **~ da stiro** ironing board

asse'con'dare *vt*: **~ qn (in qc)** to go along with sb (in sth); **~ i desideri di qn** to go along with sb's wishes; **~ i capricci di qn** to give in to sb's whims

assedi'are *vt* to besiege

as'sedio *sm* siege

asse'gnare [assep'ɲare] *vt* to assign, allot; (*premio*) to award

assegna'tario [assenɲa'tarjo] *sm* (*Dir*) assignee; (*Comm*) recipient; **l'~ del premio** the person awarded the prize

assegnazi'one [assenɲat'tsjone] *sf* (*di casa, somma*) allocation; (*di carica*) assignment; (*di premio, borsa di studio*) awarding

as'segno [as'seɲɲo] *sm* allowance; (*anche*: **assegno bancario**) cheque (*Brit*), check (*US*); **contro ~** cash on delivery; **~ circolare** bank draft; **~ di invalidità** *o* **di malattia** injury *o* sickness benefit; **~ post-datato** post-dated cheque; **~ sbarrato** crossed cheque; **~ non sbarrato** uncrossed cheque; **~ di studio** study grant; **"~ non trasferibile"** "account payee only"; **~ di viaggio** travel(l)er's cheque; **~ a vuoto** dud cheque; **assegni alimentari** alimony *sg*; **assegni familiari** ≈ child benefit *sg*

assem'blaggio [assem'bladdʒo] *sm* (*Industria*) assembly

assem'blare *vt* to assemble

assem'blea *sf* assembly; (*raduno, adunanza*) meeting

assembra'mento *sm* public gathering; **divieto di ~** ban on public meetings

assen'nato, -a *ag* sensible

as'senso *sm* assent, consent

assen'tarsi *vr* to go out

as'sente *ag* absent; (*fig*) faraway, vacant ■ *sm/f* absentee

assente'ismo *sm* absenteeism

assente'ista, -i, e *sm/f* (*dal lavoro*) absentee

assen'tire *vi*: **~ (a)** to agree (to), assent (to)

as'senza [as'sɛntsa] *sf* absence

asse'rire *vt* to maintain, assert

asserragli'arsi [asserraʎ'ʎarsi] *vr*: **~ (in)** to barricade o.s. (in)

asser'vire *vt* to enslave; (*fig: animo, passioni*) to subdue; **asservirsi** *vr*: **asservirsi (a)** to submit (to)

asserzi'one [asser'tsjone] *sf* assertion

assesso'rato *sm* councillorship

asses'sore *sm* councillor

assesta'mento *sm* (*sistemazione*) arrangement; (*Edil, Geo*) settlement

asses'tare *vt* (*mettere in ordine*) to put in order, arrange; **assestarsi** *vr* to settle in; (*Geo*) to settle; **~ un colpo a qn** to deal sb a blow

asse'tato, -a *ag* thirsty, parched

as'setto *sm* order, arrangement; (*Naut, Aer*) trim; **in ~ di guerra** on a war footing; **~ territoriale** country planning

assicu'rare *vt* (*accertare*) to ensure; (*infondere certezza*) to assure; (*fermare, legare*) to make fast, secure; *(fare un contratto di assicurazione)* to insure; **assicurarsi** *vr (accertarsi)*: **assicurarsi (di)** to make sure (of); *(contro il furto etc)*: **assicurarsi (contro)** to insure o.s. (against)

assicu'rato, -a *ag* insured ■ *sf (anche:* **lettera assicurata)** registered letter

assicura'tore, -'trice *ag* insurance *cpd* ■ *sm/f* insurance agent; **società assicuratrice** insurance company

assicurazi'one [assikurat'tsjone] *sf* assurance; insurance; **~ multi-rischio** comprehensive insurance

assidera'mento *sm* exposure

asside'rare *vt* to freeze; **assiderarsi** *vr* to freeze; **morire assiderato** to die of exposure

as'siduo, -a *ag (costante)* assiduous; *(regolare)* regular

assi'eme *av (insieme)* together ■ *prep*: **~ a** (together) with

assil'lante *ag (dubbio, pensiero)* nagging; *(creditore)* pestering

assil'lare *vt* to pester, torment

as'sillo *sm (fig)* worrying thought

assimi'lare *vt* to assimilate

assimilazi'one [assimilat'tsjone] *sf* assimilation

assi'oma, -i *sm* axiom

assio'matico, -a, ci, che *ag* axiomatic

as'sise *sfpl (Dir)* assizes (Brit); **corte d'~** court of assizes, ≈ crown court (Brit); *vedi anche* **Corte d'Assise**

assis'tente *sm/f* assistant; **~ sociale** social worker; **~ universitario** (assistant) lecturer; **~ di volo** *(Aer)* steward/stewardess

assis'tenza [assis'tɛntsa] *sf* assistance; **~ legale** legal aid; **~ ospedaliera** free hospital treatment; **~ sanitaria** health service; **~ sociale** welfare services *pl*

assistenzi'ale [assisten'tsjale] *ag (ente, organizzazione)* welfare *cpd*; *(opera)* charitable

assistenzia'lismo [assistensja'lizmo] *sm (peg)* excessive state aid

as'sistere *vt (aiutare)* to assist, help; *(curare)* to treat ■ *vi*: **~ (a qc)** *(essere presente)* to be present (at sth), attend (sth)

assis'tito, -a *pp di* **assistere**

'asso *sm* ace; **piantare qn in ~** to leave sb in the lurch

associ'are [assoˈtʃare] *vt* to associate; *(rendere partecipe)*: **~ qn a** *(affari)* to take sb into partnership in; *(partito)* to make sb a member of; **associarsi** *vr* to enter into partnership; **associarsi a** to become a member of, join; *(dolori, gioie)* to share in; **~ qn alle carceri** to take sb to prison

associazi'one [assotʃat'tsjone] *sf* association; **~ di categoria** trade association; **~ a o per delinquere** *(Dir)* criminal association; **A~ Europea di Libero Scambio** European Free Trade Association, EFTA; **~ in partecipazione** *(Comm)* joint venture

asso'dare *vt (muro, posizione)* to strengthen; *(fatti, verità)* to ascertain

asso'dato, -a *ag* well-founded

assogget'tare [assoddʒet'tare] *vt* to subject, subjugate; **assoggettarsi** *vr*: **assoggettarsi a** to submit to

asso'lato, -a *ag* sunny

assol'dare *vt* to recruit

as'solsi *etc vb vedi* **assolvere**

as'solto, -a *pp di* **assolvere**

assoluta'mente *av* absolutely

asso'luto, -a *ag* absolute

assoluzi'one [assolut'tsjone] *sf (Dir)* acquittal; *(Rel)* absolution

as'solvere *vt (Dir)* to acquit; *(Rel)* to absolve; *(adempiere)* to carry out, perform

assomigli'are [assomiʎ'ʎare] *vi*: **~ a** to resemble, look like

asson'nato, -a *ag* sleepy

asso'pirsi *vr* to doze off

assor'bente *ag* absorbent ■ *sm*: **~ igienico** sanitary towel; **~ interno** tampon

assor'bire *vt* to absorb; *(fig: far proprio)* to assimilate

assor'dante *ag (rumore, musica)* deafening

assor'dare *vt* to deafen

assorti'mento *sm* assortment

assor'tire *vt (disporre)* to arrange

assor'tito, -a *ag* assorted; *(colori)* matched, matching

as'sorto, -a *ag* absorbed, engrossed

assottigli'are [assottiʎ'ʎare] *vt* to make thin, thin; *(aguzzare)* to sharpen; *(ridurre)* to reduce; **assottigliarsi** *vr* to grow thin; *(fig: ridursi)* to be reduced

assue'fare *vt* to accustom; **assuefarsi** *vr*: **assuefarsi a** to get used to, accustom o.s. to

assue'fatto, -a *pp di* **assuefare**

assuefazi'one [assuefat'tsjone] *sf (Med)* addiction

as'sumere *vt (impiegato)* to take on, engage; *(responsabilità)* to assume, take upon o.s.; *(contegno, espressione)* to assume, put on; *(droga)* to consume

as'sunsi *etc vb vedi* **assumere**

as'sunto, -a *pp di* **assumere** ■ *sm (tesi)* proposition

assunzi'one [assun'tsjone] *sf (di impiegati)* employment, engagement; *(Rel)*: **l'A~** the Assumption

assurdità *sf inv* absurdity; **dire delle ~** to talk nonsense

as'surdo, -a *ag* absurd

'**asta** *sf* pole; (*modo di vendita*) auction

as'tante *sm* bystander

astante'ria *sf* casualty department

as'temio, -a *ag* teetotal ■ *sm/f* teetotaller

aste'nersi *vr*: **~ (da)** to abstain (from), refrain (from); (*Pol*) to abstain (from)

astensi'one *sf* abstention

astensio'nista, -i, e *sm/f* (*Pol*) abstentionist

aste'risco, -schi *sm* asterisk

aste'roide *sm* asteroid

'**astice** ['astitʃe] *sm* lobster

astigi'ano, -a [asti'dʒano] *ag* of (*o* from) Asti

astig'matico, -a, ci, che *ag* astigmatic

asti'nenza [asti'nɛntsa] *sf* abstinence; **essere in crisi di ~** to suffer from withdrawal symptoms

'**astio** *sm* rancour, resentment

asti'oso, -a *ag* resentful

astrat'tismo *sm* (*Arte*) abstract art

as'tratto, -a *ag* abstract

astrin'gente [astrin'dʒente] *ag, sm* astringent

'**astro** *sm* star

astrolo'gia [astrolo'dʒia] *sf* astrology

astro'logico, -a, ci, che [astro'lɔdʒiko] *ag* astrological

as'trologo, -a, ghi, ghe *sm/f* astrologer

astro'nauta, -i, e *sm/f* astronaut

astro'nautica *sf* astronautics *sg*

astro'nave *sf* space ship

astrono'mia *sf* astronomy

astro'nomico, -a, ci, che *ag* astronomic(al)

as'tronomo *sm* astronomer

as'truso, -a *ag* (*discorso, ragionamento*) abstruse

as'tuccio [as'tuttʃo] *sm* case, box, holder

as'tuto, -a *ag* astute, cunning, shrewd

as'tuzia [as'tuttsja] *sf* astuteness, shrewdness; (*azione*) trick

AT *sigla* = **Asti**

ATA *sigla f* = **Associazione Turistica Albergatori**

a'tavico, -a, ci, che *ag* atavistic

ate'ismo *sm* atheism

atelier [atə'lje] *sm inv* (*laboratorio*) workshop; (*studio*) studio; (*sartoria*) fashion house

A'tene *sf* Athens

ate'neo *sm* university

ateni'ese *ag, sm/f* Athenian

'**ateo, -a** *ag, sm/f* atheist

a'tipico, -a, ci, che *ag* atypical

at'lante *sm* atlas; **i Monti dell'A~** the Atlas Mountains

at'lantico, -a, ci, che *ag* Atlantic ■ *sm*: **l'A~**, **l'Oceano A~** the Atlantic, the Atlantic Ocean

at'leta, -i, e *sm/f* athlete

at'letica *sf* athletics *sg*; **~ leggera** track and field events *pl*; **~ pesante** weightlifting and wrestling

atmos'fera *sf* atmosphere

atmos'ferico, -a, ci, che *ag* atmospheric

a'tollo *sm* atoll

a'tomico, -a, ci, che *ag* atomic; (*nucleare*) atomic, atom *cpd*, nuclear

atomizza'tore [atomiddza'tore] *sm* (*di acqua, lacca*) spray; (*di profumo*) atomizer

'**atomo** *sm* atom

'**atono, -a** *ag* (*Fonetica*) unstressed

'**atrio** *sm* entrance hall, lobby

a'troce [a'trotʃe] *ag* (*che provoca orrore*) dreadful; (*terribile*) atrocious

atrocità [atrotʃi'ta] *sf inv* atrocity

atro'fia *sf* atrophy

attacca'brighe [attakka'brige] *sm/f inv* quarrelsome person

attacca'mento *sm* (*fig*) attachment, affection

attacca'panni *sm* hook, peg; (*mobile*) hall stand

attac'care *vt* (*unire*) to attach; (*cucire*) to sew on; (*far aderire*) to stick (on); (*appendere*) to hang (up); (*assalire: anche fig*) to attack; (*iniziare*) to begin, start; (*fig: contagiare*) to pass on ■ *vi* to stick, adhere; **attaccarsi** *vr* to stick, adhere; (*trasmettersi per contagio*) to be contagious; (*afferrarsi*): **attaccarsi (a)** to cling (to); (*fig: affezionarsi*): **attaccarsi (a)** to become attached (to); **~ discorso** to start a conversation; **con me non attacca!** that won't work with me!

attacca'ticcio, -a, ci, ce [attakka'tittʃo] *ag* sticky

attacca'tura *sf* (*di manica*) join; **~ (dei capelli)** hairline

at'tacco, -chi *sm* (*azione offensiva: anche fig*) attack; (*Med*) attack, fit; (*Sci*) binding; (*Elettr*) socket

attanagli'are [attanaʎ'ʎare] *vt* (*anche fig*) to grip

attar'darsi *vr*: **~ a fare qc** (*fermarsi*) to stop to do sth; (*stare più a lungo*) to stay behind to do sth

attec'chire [attek'kire] *vi* (*pianta*) to take root; (*fig*) to catch on

atteggia'mento [atteddʒa'mento] *sm* attitude

atteggi'arsi [atted'dʒarsi] *vr*: **~ a** to pose as

attem'pato, -a *ag* elderly

atten'dente *sm* (*Mil*) orderly, batman

at'tendere *vt* to wait for, await ■ *vi*: **~ a** to attend to

atten'dibile *ag* (*scusa, storia*) credible; (*fonte, testimone, notizia*) reliable; (*persona*) trustworthy

atte'nersi vr: ~ **a** to keep o stick to

atten'tare vi: ~ **a** to make an attempt on

atten'tato sm attack; ~ **alla vita di qn** attempt on sb's life

attenta'tore, -'trice sm/f bomber; ~ **suicida** suicide bomber

at'tento, -a ag attentive; (accurato) careful, thorough ■ escl be careful!; **stare ~ a qc** to pay attention to sth; **attenti!** (Mil) attention!; **attenti al cane** beware of the dog

attenu'ante sf (Dir) extenuating circumstance

attenu'are vt to alleviate, ease; (diminuire) to reduce; **attenuarsi** vr to ease, abate

attenuazi'one [attenuat'tsjone] sf alleviation; easing; reduction

attenzi'one [atten'tsjone] sf attention ■ escl watch out!, be careful!; **coprire qn di attenzioni** to lavish attention on sb

atter'raggio [atter'raddʒo] sm landing; ~ **di fortuna** emergency landing

atter'rare vt to bring down ■ vi to land

atter'rire vt to terrify

at'tesa sf vedi **atteso**

at'tesi etc vb vedi **attendere**

at'teso, -a pp di **attendere** ■ sf waiting; (tempo trascorso aspettando) wait; **essere in attesa di qc** to be waiting for sth; **in attesa di una vostra risposta** (Comm) awaiting your reply; **restiamo in attesa di Vostre ulteriori notizie** (Comm) we look forward to hearing (further) from you

attes'tare vt: ~ **qc/che** to testify to sth//(to the fact) that

attes'tato sm certificate

attestazi'one [attestat'tsjone] sf (certificato) certificate; (dichiarazione) statement

'attico, -ci sm attic

at'tiguo, -a ag adjacent, adjoining

attil'lato, -a ag (vestito) close-fitting, tight; (persona) dressed up

'attimo sm moment; **in un ~** in a moment

atti'nente ag: ~ **a** relating to, concerning

atti'nenza [atti'nentsa] sf connection

at'tingere [at'tindʒere] vt: ~ **a** o **da** (acqua) to draw from; (denaro, notizie) to obtain from

at'tinto, -a pp di **attingere**

atti'rare vt to attract; **attirarsi delle critiche** to incur criticism

atti'tudine sf (disposizione) aptitude; (atteggiamento) attitude

atti'vare vt to activate; (far funzionare) to set going, start

atti'vista, -i, e sm/f activist

attività sf inv activity; (Comm) assets pl; ~ **liquide** (Comm) liquid assets

at'tivo, -a ag active; (Comm) profit-making ■ sm (Comm) assets pl; **in ~** in credit; **chiudere in ~** to show a profit; **avere qc al proprio ~** (fig) to have sth to one's credit

attiz'zare [attit'tsare] vt (fuoco) to poke; (fig) to stir up

attizza'toio [attittsa'tojo] sm poker

'atto, -a ag: ~ **a** fit for, capable of ■ sm act; (azione, gesto) action, act, deed; (Dir: documento) deed, document; **atti** smpl (di congressi etc) proceedings; **essere in ~** to be under way; **mettere in ~** to put into action; **fare ~ di fare qc** to make as if to do sth; **all'~ pratico** in practice; **dare ~ a qn di qc** to give sb credit for sth; ~ **di nascita/morte** birth/death certificate; ~ **di proprietà** title deed; ~ **pubblico** official document; ~ **di vendita** bill of sale; **atti osceni (in luogo pubblico)** (Dir) indecent exposure; **atti verbali** transactions

at'tonito, -a ag dumbfounded, astonished

attorcigli'are [attortʃiʎ'ʎare] vt, **attorcigli'arsi** vr to twist

at'tore, -'trice sm/f actor/actress

attorni'are vt (circondare) to surround; **attorniarsi** vr: **attorniarsi di** to surround o.s. with

at'torno av round, around, about ■ prep: ~ **a** round, around, about

attrac'care vt, vi (Naut) to dock, berth

at'tracco, -chi sm (Naut: manovra) docking, berthing; (luogo) berth

at'trae etc vb vedi **attrarre**

attra'ente ag attractive

at'traggo etc vb vedi **attrarre**

at'trarre vt to attract

at'trassi etc vb vedi **attrarre**

attrat'tiva sf attraction, charm

at'tratto, -a pp di **attrarre**

attraversa'mento sm crossing; ~ **pedonale** pedestrian crossing

attraver'sare vt to cross; (città, bosco, fig: periodo) to go through; (fiume) to run through

attra'verso prep through; (da una parte all'altra) across

attrazi'one [attrat'tsjone] sf attraction

attrez'zare [attret'tsare] vt to equip; (Naut) to rig

attrezza'tura [attrettsa'tura] sf equipment no pl; rigging; **attrezzature per uffici** office equipment

at'trezzo [at'trettso] sm tool, instrument; (Sport) piece of equipment

attribu'ire vt: ~ **qc a qn** (assegnare) to give o award sth to sb; (quadro etc) to attribute sth to sb

attri'buto sm attribute

at'trice [at'tritʃe] *sf vedi* **attore**

at'trito *sm* (*anche fig*) friction

attu'abile *ag* feasible

attuabilità *sf* feasibility

attu'ale *ag* (*presente*) present; (*di attualità*) topical; (*che è in atto*) actual

attualità *sf inv* topicality; (*avvenimento*) current event; **notizie d'~** (*TV*) the news *sg*

attualiz'zare [attualid'dzare] *vt* to update, bring up to date

attual'mente *av* at the moment, at present

attu'are *vt* to carry out; **attuarsi** *vr* to be realized

attuazi'one [attuat'tsjone] *sf* carrying out

attu'tire *vt* to deaden, reduce; **attutirsi** *vr* to die down

A.U. *abbr* = **allievo ufficiale**

au'dace [au'datʃe] *ag* audacious, daring, bold; (*provocante*) provocative; (*sfacciato*) impudent, bold

au'dacia [au'datʃa] *sf* audacity, daring; boldness; provocativeness; impudence

'audio *sm* (*TV, Radio, Cine*) sound

audiocas'setta *sf* (*audio*) cassette

audio'leso, -a *sm/f* person who is hard of hearing

audiovi'sivo, -a *ag* audiovisual

audi'torio *sm*, **audi'torium** *sm inv* auditorium

audizi'one [audit'tsjone] *sf* hearing; (*Mus*) audition

'auge ['audʒe] *sf* (*della gloria, carriera*) height, peak; **essere in ~** to be at the top

augu'rale *ag*: **messaggio ~** greeting; **biglietto ~** greetings card

augu'rare *vt* to wish; **augurarsi qc** to hope for sth

au'gurio *sm* (*presagio*) omen; (*voto di benessere etc*) (good) wish; **essere di buon/cattivo ~** to be of good omen/be ominous; **fare gli auguri a qn** to give sb one's best wishes; **tanti auguri!** all the best!

'aula *sf* (*scolastica*) classroom; (*universitaria*) lecture theatre; (*di edificio pubblico*) hall; **~ magna** main hall; **~ del tribunale** courtroom

aumen'tare *vt, vi* to increase; **~ di peso** (*persona*) to put on weight; **la produzione è aumentata del 50%** production has increased by 50%

au'mento *sm* increase

'aureo, -a *ag* (*di oro*) gold *cpd*; (*fig: colore, periodo*) golden

au'reola *sf* halo

au'rora *sf* dawn

ausili'are *ag, sm, sm/f* auxiliary

au'silio *sm* aid

auspi'cabile *ag* desirable

auspi'care *vt* to call for, express a desire for

aus'picio [aus'pitʃo] *sm* omen; (*protezione*) patronage; **sotto gli auspici di** under the auspices of; **è di buon ~** it augurs well

austerità *sf inv* austerity

aus'tero, -a *ag* austere

aus'trale *ag* southern

Aus'tralia *sf*: **l'~** Australia

australi'ano, -a *ag, sm/f* Australian

'Austria *sf*: **l'~** Austria

aus'triaco, -a, ci, che *ag, sm/f* Austrian

au'tarchico, -a, ci, che [au'tarkiko] *ag* (*sistema*) self-sufficient, autarkic; (*prodotto*) home *cpd*, home-produced

'aut 'aut *sm inv* ultimatum

autenti'care *vt* to authenticate

autenticità [autentitʃi'ta] *sf* authenticity

au'tentico, -a, ci, che *ag* (*quadro, firma*) authentic, genuine; (*fatto*) true, genuine

au'tista, -i *sm* driver; (*personale*) chauffeur

'auto *sf inv* car; **~ blu** official car

autoabbron'zante *ag* self-tanning

autoade'sivo, -a *ag* self-adhesive ▪ *sm* sticker

autoartico'lato *sm* articulated lorry (*Brit*), semi (trailer) (*US*)

autobiogra'fia *sf* autobiography

autobio'grafico, -a, ci, che *ag* autobiographic(al)

auto'blinda *sf* armoured (*Brit*) *o* armored (*US*) car

auto'bomba *sf inv* car carrying a bomb; **l'~ si trovava a pochi metri** the car bomb was a few metres away

auto'botte *sf* tanker

'autobus *sm inv* bus

autocari'cabile *ag*: **scheda ~** top-up card

auto'carro *sm* lorry (*Brit*), truck

autocertificazi'one [autotʃertifikat'tsjone] *sf* self-declaration

autocis'terna [autotʃis'terna] *sf* tanker

autoco'lonna *sf* convoy

autocon'trollo *sm* self-control

autocopia'tivo, -a *ag*: **carta autocopiativa** carbonless paper

autocorri'era *sf* coach, bus

auto'cratico, -a, ci, che *ag* autocratic

auto'critica, -che *sf* self-criticism

au'toctono, -a *ag, sm/f* native

autodemolizi'one [autodemolit'tsjone] *sf* breaker's yard (*Brit*)

autodi'datta, -i, e *sm/f* autodidact, self-taught person

autodi'fesa *sf* self-defence

autoferrotranvi'ario, -a *ag* public transport *cpd*

autogesti'one [autodʒes'tjone] *sf* worker management

autoges'tito, -a [autodʒes'tito] *ag* under worker management

au'tografo, -a *ag, sm* autograph

auto'grill *sm inv* motorway café (*Brit*), roadside restaurant (*US*)

autoim'mune *ag* autoimmune

autolesio'nismo *sm* (*fig*) self-destruction

auto'linea *sf* bus route

au'toma, -i *sm* automaton

auto'matico, -a, ci, che *ag* automatic ■ *sm* (*bottone*) snap fastener; (*fucile*) automatic; **selezione automatica** (*Tel*) direct dialling

automazi'one [automat'tsjone] *sf*: ~ **delle procedure d'ufficio** office automation

automedicazi'one [automedikat'tsjone] *sf* (*medicine, farmaci*): **medicinale di ~** self-medication

auto'mezzo [auto'mɛddzo] *sm* motor vehicle

auto'mobile *sf* (motor) car; ~ **da corsa** racing car (*Brit*), race car (*US*)

automobi'lismo *sm* (*gen*) motoring; (*Sport*) motor racing

automobi'lista, -i, e *sm/f* motorist

automobi'listico, -a, ci, che *ag* car *cpd* (*Brit*), automobile *cpd* (*US*); (*sport*) motor *cpd*

autono'leggio [autono'leddʒo] *sm* car hire (*Brit*), car rental

autono'mia *sf* autonomy; (*di volo*) range

au'tonomo, -a *ag* autonomous; (*sindacato, pensiero*) independent

auto'parco, -chi *sm* (*parcheggio*) car park (*Brit*), parking lot (*US*); (*insieme di automezzi*) transport fleet

auto'pompa *sf* fire engine

autop'sia *sf* post-mortem (examination), autopsy

auto'radio *sf inv* (*apparecchio*) car radio; (*autoveicolo*) radio car

au'tore, -'trice *sm/f* author; **l'~ del furto** the person who committed the robbery; **diritti d'~** copyright *sg*; (*compenso*) royalties

autoregolamentazi'one [autoregolamentat 'tsjone] *sf* self-regulation

auto'revole *ag* authoritative; (*persona*) influential

autori'messa *sf* garage

autorità *sf inv* authority

autori'tratto *sm* self-portrait

autoriz'zare [autorid'dzare] *vt* to authorize, give permission for

autorizzazi'one [autoriddzat'tsjone] *sf* authorization; ~ **a procedere** (*Dir*) authorization to proceed

autos'catto *sm* (*Fot*) timer

autos'contro *sm* dodgem car (*Brit*), bumper car (*US*)

autoscu'ola *sf* driving school

autosno'dato *sm* articulated vehicle

autos'top *sm* hitchhiking

autostop'pista, -i, e *sm/f* hitchhiker

autos'trada *sf* motorway (*Brit*), highway (*US*); ~ **informatica** information superhighway

autosuffici'ente [autosuffi'tʃɛnte] *ag* self-sufficient

autosuffici'enza [autosuffi'tʃɛntsa] *sf* self-sufficiency

auto'treno *sm* articulated lorry (*Brit*), semi (trailer) (*US*)

autove'icolo *sm* motor vehicle

auto'velox® *sm inv* (police) speed camera

autovet'tura *sf* (motor) car

autun'nale *ag* (*di autunno*) autumn *cpd*; (*da autunno*) autumnal

au'tunno *sm* autumn

AV *sigla* = **Avellino**

aval'lare *vt* (*Finanza*) to guarantee; (*fig: sostenere*) to back; (: *confermare*) to confirm

a'vallo *sm* (*Finanza*) guarantee

avam'braccio [avam'brattʃo] (*pl(f)* **avambraccia**) *sm* forearm

avam'posto *sm* (*Mil*) outpost

A'vana *sf*: **l'~** Havana

a'vana *sm inv* (*sigaro*) Havana (cigar); (*colore*) Havana brown

avangu'ardia *sf* vanguard; (*Arte*) avant-garde

avansco'perta *sf* (*Mil*) reconnaissance; **andare in ~** to reconnoitre

a'vanti *av* (*stato in luogo*) in front; (*moto: andare, venire*) forward; (*tempo: prima*) before ■ *prep* (*luogo*): ~ **a** before, in front of; (*tempo*): ~ **Cristo** before Christ ■ *escl* (*entrate*) come (*o go*) in!; (*Mil*) forward!; (*coraggio*) come on! ■ *sm inv* (*Sport*) forward; **il giorno ~** the day before; ~ **e indietro** backwards and forwards; **andare ~** to go forward; (*continuare*) to go on; (*precedere*) to go ahead; (*orologio*) to be fast; **essere ~ negli studi** to be well advanced with one's studies; **mandare ~ la famiglia** to provide for one's family; **mandare ~ un'azienda** to run a business; ~ **il prossimo!** next please!

avan'treno *sm* (*Aut*) front chassis

avanza'mento [avantsa'mento] *sm* (*gen*) advance; (*fig*) progress; promotion

avan'zare [avan'tsare] *vt* (*spostare in avanti*) to move forward, advance; (*domanda*) to put forward; (*promuovere*) to promote; (*essere creditore*): ~ **qc da qn** to be owed sth by sb ■ *vi* (*andare avanti*) to move forward, advance; (*fig: progredire*) to make progress; (*essere d'avanzo*) to be left, remain; **basta e avanza** that's more than enough

avanzato, -a [avan'tsato] *ag* (*teoria, tecnica*) advanced ■ *sf* (*Mil*) advance; **in età avanzata** advanced in years, up in years

avanzo [a'vantso] *sm* (*residuo*) remains *pl*, left-overs *pl*; (*Mat*) remainder; (*Comm*) surplus; (*eccedenza di bilancio*) profit carried forward; **averne d'~ di qc** to have more than enough of sth; **~ di cassa** cash in hand; **~ di galera** (*fig*) jailbird

avaria *sf* (*guasto*) damage; (: *meccanico*) breakdown

avariato, -a *ag* (*merce*) damaged; (*cibo*) off

avarizia [ava'rittsja] *sf* avarice; **crepi l'~!** to hang with the expense!

avaro, -a *ag* avaricious, miserly ■ *sm* miser

avena *sf* oats *pl*

 PAROLA CHIAVE

avere *sm* (*Comm*) credit; **gli averi** (*ricchezze*) wealth *sg*, possessions

■ *vt* **1** (*possedere*) to have; **ha due bambini/una bella casa** she has (got) two children/a lovely house; **ha i capelli lunghi** he has (got) long hair; **non ho da mangiare/bere** I've (got) nothing to eat/drink, I don't have anything to eat/drink

2 (*indossare*) to wear, have on; **aveva una maglietta rossa** he was wearing *o* he had on a red T-shirt; **ha gli occhiali** he wears *o* has glasses

3 (*ricevere*) to get; **hai avuto l'assegno?** did you get *o* have you had the cheque?

4 (*età, dimensione*) to be; **ha 9 anni** he is 9 (years old); **la stanza ha 3 metri di lunghezza** the room is 3 metres in length; *vedi* **fame; paura; sonno** *etc*

5 (*tempo*): **quanti ne abbiamo oggi?** what's the date today?; **ne hai per molto?** will you be long?

6 (*fraseologia*): **avercela con qn** to be angry with sb; **cos'hai?** what's wrong *o* what's the matter (with you)?; **non ha niente a che vedere** *o* **fare con me** it's got nothing to do with me

■ *vb aus* **1** to have; **aver bevuto/mangiato** to have drunk/eaten; **l'ho già visto** I have seen it already; **l'ho visto ieri** I saw it yesterday; **ci ha creduto?** did he believe it?

2 (+ *da* + *infinito*): **avere da fare qc** to have to do sth; **non ho niente da dire** I have nothing to say; **non hai che da chiederlo** you only have to ask him

aviatore, -trice *sm/f* aviator, pilot

aviario, -a *ag* bird *cpd*; **influenza aviaria** bird flu

aviazione [avjat'tsjone] *sf* aviation; (*Mil*) air force; **~ civile** civil aviation

avicoltura *sf* bird breeding; (*di pollame*) poultry farming

avidità *sf* eagerness; greed

avido, -a *ag* eager; (*peg*) greedy

aviere *sm* (*Mil*) airman

avitaminosi *sf* vitamin deficiency

avo *sm* (*antenato*) ancestor; **i nostri avi** our ancestors

avocado *sm* avocado

avorio *sm* ivory

avulso, -a *ag*: **parole avulse dal contesto** words out of context; **~ dalla società** (*fig*) cut off from society

Avv. *abbr* = **avvocato**

avvalersi *vr*: **~ di** to avail o.s. of

avvallamento *sm* sinking *no pl*; (*effetto*) depression

avvalorare *vt* to confirm

avvantaggiare [avvantad'dʒare] *vt* to favour (*Brit*), favor (*US*); **avvantaggiarsi** *vr* (*trarre vantaggio*): **avvantaggiarsi di** to take advantage of; (*prevalere*): **avvantaggiarsi negli affari/sui concorrenti** to get ahead in business/of one's competitors

avvedersi *vr*: **~ di qn/qc** to notice sb/sth

avveduto, -a *ag* (*accorto*) prudent; (*scaltro*) astute

avvelenamento *sm* poisoning

avvelenare *vt* to poison

avvenente *ag* attractive, charming

avvenenza [avve'nɛntsa] *sf* good looks *pl*

avvengo *etc vb vedi* **avvenire**

avvenimento *sm* event

avvenire *vi, vb impers* to happen, occur ■ *sm* future

avvenni *etc vb vedi* **avvenire**

avventarsi *vr*: **~ su** *o* **contro qn/qc** to hurl o.s. *o* rush at sb/sth

avventato, -a *ag* rash, reckless

avventizio, -a [avven'tittsjo] *ag* (*impiegato*) temporary; (*guadagno*) casual

avvento *sm* advent, coming; (*Rel*): **l'A~** Advent

avventore *sm* customer

avventura *sf* adventure; (*amorosa*) affair; **avere spirito d'~** to be adventurous

avventurarsi *vr* to venture

avventuriero, -a *sm/f* adventurer/adventuress

avventuroso, -a *ag* adventurous

avvenuto, -a *pp di* **avvenire**

avverarsi *vr* to come true

avverbio *sm* adverb

avverrò *etc vb vedi* **avvenire**

avver'sare *vt* to oppose

avver'sario, -a *ag* opposing ■ *sm* opponent, adversary

avversi'one *sf* aversion

aversità *sf inv* adversity, misfortune

av'verso, -a *ag* (*contrario*) contrary; (*sfavorevole*) unfavourable (*Brit*), unfavorable (*US*)

avver'tenza [avver'tɛntsa] *sf* (*ammonimento*) warning; (*cautela*) care; (*premessa*) foreword; **avvertenze** *sfpl* (*istruzioni per l'uso*) instructions

avverti'mento *sm* warning

avver'tire *vt* (*avvisare*) to warn; (*rendere consapevole*) to inform, notify; (*percepire*) to feel

av'vezzo, -a [av'vettso] *ag*: ~ **a** used to

avvia'mento *sm* (*atto*) starting; (*effetto*) start; (*Aut*) starting; (: *dispositivo*) starter; (*Comm*) goodwill

avvi'are *vt* (*mettere sul cammino*) to direct; (*impresa, trattative*) to begin, start; (*motore*) to start; **avviarsi** *vr* to set off, set out

avvicenda'mento [avvitʃenda'mento] *sm* alternation; (*Agr*) rotation; **c'è molto ~ di personale** there is a high turnover of staff

avvicen'dare [avvitʃen'dare] *vt*, **avvicen'darsi** *vr* to alternate

avvicina'mento [avvitʃina'mento] *sm* approach

avvici'nare [avvitʃi'nare] *vt* to bring near; (*trattare con: persona*) to approach; **avvicinarsi** *vr*: **avvicinarsi (a qn/qc)** to approach (sb/ sth), draw near (to sb/sth); (*somigliare*) to be similar (to sb/sth), be close (to sb/sth)

avvi'lente *ag* (*umiliante*) humiliating; (*scoraggiante*) discouraging, disheartening

avvili'mento *sm* humiliation; disgrace; discouragement

avvi'lire *vt* (*umiliare*) to humiliate; (*degradare*) to disgrace; (*scoraggiare*) to dishearten, discourage; **avvilirsi** *vr* (*abbattersi*) to lose heart

avvilup'pare *vt* (*avvolgere*) to wrap up; (*ingarbugliare*) to entangle

avvinaz'zato, -a [avvinat'tsato] *ag* drunk

avvin'cente [avvin'tʃɛnte] *ag* (*film, racconto*) enthralling

av'vincere [av'vintʃere] *vt* to charm, enthral

avvinghi'are [avvin'gjare] *vt* to clasp; **avvinghiarsi** *vr*: **avvinghiarsi a** to cling to

av'vinsi *etc vb vedi* **avvincere**

av'vinto, -a *pp di* **avvincere**

av'vio *sm* start, beginning; **dare l'~ a qc** to start sth off; **prendere l'~** to get going, get under way

avvi'saglia [avvi'zaʎʎa] *sf* (*sintomo: di temporale etc*) sign; (*di malattia*) manifestation, sign, symptom; (*scaramuccia*) skirmish

avvi'sare *vt* (*far sapere*) to inform; (*mettere in guardia*) to warn

avvisa'tore *sm* (*apparecchio d'allarme*) alarm; **~ acustico** horn; **~ d'incendio** fire alarm

av'viso *sm* warning; (*annuncio*) announcement; (*affisso*) notice; (*inserzione pubblicitaria*) advertisement; **a mio ~** in my opinion; **mettere qn sull'~** to put sb on their guard; **fino a nuovo ~** until further notice; **~ di chiamata** (*servizio*) call waiting; (*segnale*) call waiting signal; **~ di consegna/ spedizione** (*Comm*) delivery/consignment note; **~ di garanzia** (*Dir*) notification (*of impending investigation and of the right to name a defence laywer*); **~ di pagamento** (*Comm*) payment advice

avvista'mento *sm* sighting

avvi'stare *vt* to sight

avvi'tare *vt* to screw down (*o* in)

avviz'zire [avvit'tsire] *vi* to wither

avvo'cato, -'essa *sm/f* (*Dir*) barrister (*Brit*), lawyer; (*fig*) defender, advocate; **~ del diavolo: fare l'~ del diavolo** to play devil's advocate; **~ difensore** counsel for the defence; **~ di parte civile** counsel for the plaintiff

av'volgere [av'vɔldʒere] *vt* to roll up; (*bobina*) to wind up; (*avviluppare*) to wrap up; **avvolgersi** *vr* (*avvilupparsi*) to wrap o.s. up

avvol'gibile [avvol'dʒibile] *sm* roller blind (*Brit*), blind

avvolgi'mento [avvoldʒi'mento] *sm* winding

av'volsi *etc vb vedi* **avvolgere**

av'volto, -a *pp di* **avvolgere**

avvol'toio *sm* vulture

aza'lea [addza'lɛa] *sf* azalea

Azerbaigi'an [addzɛrbai'dʒan] *sm* Azerbaijan

azerbaig'iano, -a [addzɛrbai'dʒano] *ag* Azerbaijani ■ *sm/f* (*abitante*) Azerbaijani ■ *sm* (*Ling*) Azerbaijani

a'zero, -a [ad'dzero] *sm/f* Azeri

azi'enda [ad'dzjɛnda] *sf* business, firm, concern; **~ agricola** farm; **~ (autonoma) di soggiorno** tourist board; **~ a partecipazione statale** *business in which the State has a financial interest*; **aziende pubbliche** public corporations

azien'dale [addzjen'dale] *ag* company *cpd*; **organizzazione ~** business administration

azio'nare [attsjo'nare] *vt* to activate

azio'nario, -a [attsjo'narjo] *ag* share *cpd*; **capitale ~** share capital; **mercato ~** stock market

azi'one [at'tsjone] *sf* action; (*Comm*) share; **~ sindacale** industrial action; **azioni preferenziali** preference shares (*Brit*), preferred stock *sg* (*US*)

azio'nista, -i, e [attsjo'nista] *sm/f* (*Comm*) shareholder

a'zoto [ad'dzɔto] *sm* nitrogen

az'teco, -a, ci, che [as'tɛko] *ag, sm/f* Aztec

azzan'nare [attsan'nare] *vt* to sink one's teeth into

azzar'dare [addzar'dare] *vt* (*soldi, vita*) to risk, hazard; (*domanda, ipotesi*) to hazard, venture; **azzardarsi** *vr*: **azzardarsi a fare** to dare (to) do

azzar'dato, -a [addzar'dato] *ag* (*impresa*) risky; (*risposta*) rash

az'zardo [ad'dzardo] *sm* risk; **gioco d'~** game of chance

azzec'care [attsek'kare] *vt* (*bersaglio*) to hit, strike; (*risposta, pronostico*) to get right; (*fig: indovinare*) to guess

azzera'mento [addzera'mento] *sm* (*Inform*) reset

azze'rare [addze'rare] *vt* (*Mat, Fisica*) to make equal to zero, reduce to zero; (*Tecn: strumento*) to (re)set to zero

'azzimo, -a ['addzimo] *ag* unleavened ■ *sm* unleavened bread

azzop'pare [attsop'pare] *vt* to lame, make lame

Az'zorre [ad'dzorre] *sfpl*: **le ~** the Azores

azzuffarsi [attsuf'farsi] *vr* to come to blows

az'zurro, -a [ad'dzurro] *ag* blue ■ *sm* (*colore*) blue; **gli azzurri** (*Sport*) the Italian national team

azzur'rognolo, -a [addzur'roɲɲolo] *ag* bluish

Bb

B, b [bi] *sf o m inv (lettera)* B, b; **B come Bologna** ≈ B for Benjamin (*Brit*), ≈ B for Baker (*US*)

BA *sigla* = **Bari**

ba'bau *sm inv* ogre, bogey man

bab'beo *sm* simpleton

'babbo *sm (fam)* dad, daddy; **B~ Natale** Father Christmas

bab'buccia, -ce [bab'buttʃa] *sf* slipper; *(per neonati)* bootee

babbu'ino *sm* baboon

babilo'nese *ag, sm/f* Babylonian

Babi'lonia *sf* Babylonia

ba'bordo *sm (Naut)* port side

baby'sitter ['beɪbɪsɪtəʳ] *sm/f inv* baby-sitter

ba'cato, -a *ag* worm-eaten, rotten; *(fig: mente)* diseased; *(: persona)* corrupt

'bacca, -che *sf* berry

baccalà *sm* dried salted cod; *(fig: peg)* dummy

bac'cano *sm* din, clamour (*Brit*), clamor (*US*)

bac'cello [bat'tʃɛllo] *sm* pod

bac'chetta [bak'ketta] *sf (verga)* stick, rod; *(di direttore d'orchestra)* baton; *(di tamburo)* drumstick; **comandare a ~** to rule with a rod of iron; **~ magica** magic wand

ba'checa, -che [ba'kɛka] *sf (mobile)* showcase, display case; *(Università, in ufficio)* notice board (*Brit*), bulletin board (*US*)

bacia'mano [batʃa'mano] *sm:* **fare il ~ a qn** to kiss sb's hand

baci'are [ba'tʃare] *vt* to kiss; **baciarsi** *vr* to kiss (one another)

ba'cillo [ba'tʃillo] *sm* bacillus, germ

baci'nella [batʃi'nɛlla] *sf* basin

ba'cino [ba'tʃino] *sm* basin; *(Mineralogia)* field, bed; *(Anat)* pelvis; *(Naut)* dock; **~ carbonifero** coalfield; **~ di carenaggio** dry dock; **~ petrolifero** oilfield; **~ d'utenza** catchment area

'bacio ['batʃo] *sm* kiss

'baco, -chi *sm* worm; **~ da seta** silkworm

'bada *sf:* **tenere qn a ~** *(tener d'occhio)* to keep an eye on sb; *(tenere a distanza)* to hold sb at bay

ba'dante *sm/f* care worker

ba'dare *vi (fare attenzione)* to take care, be careful; **~ a** *(occuparsi di)* to look after, take care of; *(dar ascolto)* to pay attention to; **è un tipo che non bada a spese** money is no object to him; **bada ai fatti tuoi!** mind your own business!

ba'dia *sf* abbey

ba'dile *sm* shovel

'baffi *smpl* moustache *sg*, mustache *sg* (*US*); *(di animale)* whiskers; **leccarsi i ~** to lick one's lips; **ridere sotto i ~** to laugh up one's sleeve

bagagli'aio [bagaʎ'ʎajo] *sm* luggage van (*Brit*) *o* car (*US*); *(Aut)* boot (*Brit*), trunk (*US*)

ba'gaglio [ba'gaʎʎo] *sm* luggage *no pl*, baggage *no pl*; **fare/disfare i bagagli** to pack/unpack; **~ a mano** hand luggage

bagat'tella *sf* trifle, trifling matter

Bag'dad *sf* Baghdad

baggia'nata [baddʒa'nata] *sf* foolish action; **dire baggianate** to talk nonsense

bagli'ore [baʎ'ʎore] *sm* flash, dazzling light; **un ~ di speranza** a sudden ray of hope

ba'gnante [baɲ'ɲante] *sm/f* bather

ba'gnare [baɲ'ɲare] *vt* to wet; *(inzuppare)* to soak; *(innaffiare)* to water; *(fiume)* to flow through; *(: mare)* to wash, bathe; *(brindare)* to drink to, toast; **bagnarsi** *vr (al mare)* to go swimming *o* bathing; *(in vasca)* to have a bath

ba'gnato, -a [baɲ'ɲato] *ag* wet; **era come un pulcino ~** he looked like a drowned rat

ba'gnino [baɲ'ɲino] *sm* lifeguard

'bagno ['baɲɲo] *sm* bath; *(locale)* bathroom; **bagni** *smpl (stabilimento)* baths; **fare il ~** to have a bath; *(nel mare)* to go swimming *o* bathing; **fare il ~ a qn** to give sb a bath; **mettere a ~** to soak

bagno'ria [baɲɲoma'ria] *sm:* **cuocere a ~** to cook in a double saucepan (*Brit*) *o* double boiler (*US*)

bagnoschi'uma [baɲɲoskj'uma] *sm inv* bubble bath

Ba'hama [ba'ama] *sfpl:* **le ~** the Bahamas

Bah'rein [ba'rein] *sm*: **il** ~ Bahrain *o* Bahrein

'baia *sf* bay

baio'netta *sf* bayonet

'baita *sf* mountain hut

balaus'trata *sf* balustrade

balbet'tare *vi* to stutter, stammer; (*bimbo*) to babble ■ *vt* to stammer out

bal'buzie [bal'buttsje] *sf* stammer

balbuzi'ente [balbut'tsjɛnte] *ag* stuttering, stammering

Bal'cani *smpl*: **i** ~ the Balkans

bal'canico, -a, ci, che *ag* Balkan

bal'cone *sm* balcony

baldac'chino [baldak'kino] *sm* canopy; **letto a** ~ four-poster (bed)

bal'danza [bal'dantsa] *sf* self-confidence; boldness

'baldo, -a *ag* bold, daring

bal'doria *sf*: **fare** ~ to have a riotous time

Bale'ari *sfpl*: **le isole** ~ the Balearic Islands

ba'lena *sf* whale

bale'nare *vb impers*: **balena** there's lightning ■ *vi* to flash; **mi balenò un'idea** an idea flashed through my mind

baleni'era *sf* (*per la caccia*) whaler, whaling ship

ba'leno *sm* flash of lightning; **in un** ~ in a flash

ba'lera *sf* (*locale*) dance hall; (*pista*) dance floor

ba'lestra *sf* crossbow

'balia *sf* wet-nurse; ~ **asciutta** nanny

ba'lìa *sf*: **in** ~ **di** at the mercy of; **essere lasciato in** ~ **di se stesso** to be left to one's own devices

ba'lilla *sm inv* (*Storia*) member of Fascist youth group

ba'listico, -a, ci, che *ag* ballistic ■ *sf* ballistics *sg*; **perito** ~ ballistics expert

'balla *sf* (*di merci*) bale; (*fandonia*) (tall) story

bal'labile *sm* dance number, dance tune

bal'lare *vt, vi* to dance

bal'lata *sf* ballad

balla'toio *sm* (*terrazzina*) gallery

balle'rina *sf* dancer; ballet dancer; (*scarpa*) pump; ~ **di rivista** chorus girl

balle'rino *sm* dancer; ballet dancer

bal'letto *sm* ballet

'ballo *sm* dance; (*azione*) dancing *no pl*; ~ **in maschera** *o* **mascherato** fancy-dress ball; **essere in** ~ (*fig: persona*) to be involved; (: *cosa*) to be at stake; **tirare in** ~ **qc** to bring sth up, raise sth

ballot'taggio [ballot'taddʒo] *sm* (*Pol*) second ballot

balne'are *ag* seaside *cpd*; (*stagione*) bathing

ba'locco, -chi *sm* toy

ba'lordo, -a *ag* stupid, senseless

bal'samico, -a, ci, che *ag* (*aria, brezza*) balmy; **pomata balsamica** balsam

'balsamo *sm* (*aroma*) balsam; (*lenimento, fig*) balm; (*per capelli*) (hair) conditioner

'baltico, -a, ci, che *ag* Baltic; **il (mar) B**~ the Baltic (Sea)

balu'ardo *sm* bulwark

'balza ['baltsa] *sf* (*dirupo*) crag; (*di stoffa*) frill

bal'zano, -a [bal'tsano] *ag* (*persona, idea*) queer, odd

bal'zare [bal'tsare] *vi* to bounce; (*lanciarsi*) to jump, leap; **la verità balza agli occhi** the truth of the matter is obvious

'balzo ['baltso] *sm* bounce; jump, leap; (*del terreno*) crag; **prendere la palla al** ~ (*fig*) to seize one's opportunity

bam'bagia [bam'badʒa] *sf* (*ovatta*) cotton wool (Brit), absorbent cotton (US); (*cascame*) cotton waste; **tenere qn nella** ~ (*fig*) to mollycoddle sb

bam'bina *sf vedi* **bambino**

bambi'naia *sf* nanny, nurse(maid)

bam'bino, -a *sm/f* child; **fare** ~ to behave childishly

bam'boccio [bam'bɔttʃo] *sm* plump child; (*pupazzo*) rag doll

'bambola *sf* doll

bambo'lotto *sm* male doll

bambù *sm* bamboo

ba'nale *ag* banal, commonplace

banalità *sf inv* banality

ba'nana *sf* banana

ba'nano *sm* banana tree

'banca, -che *sf* bank; ~ **d'affari** merchant bank; ~ **(di) dati** data bank

banca'rella *sf* stall

ban'cario, -a *ag* banking, bank *cpd* ■ *sm* bank clerk

banca'rotta *sf* bankruptcy; **fare** ~ to go bankrupt

bancarotti'ere *sm* bankrupt

ban'chetto [ban'ketto] *sm* banquet

banchi'ere [ban'kjɛre] *sm* banker

ban'china [ban'kina] *sf* (*di porto*) quay; (*per pedoni, ciclisti*) path; (*di stazione*) platform; ~ **cedevole** (*Aut*) soft verge (Brit) *o* shoulder (US); ~ **spartitraffico** (*Aut*) central reservation (Brit), median (strip) (US)

ban'chisa [ban'kiza] *sf* pack ice

'banco, -chi *sm* bench; (*di negozio*) counter; (*di mercato*) stall; (*di officina*) (work)bench; (*Geo, banca*) bank; **sotto** ~ (*fig*) under the counter; **tenere il** ~ (*nei giochi*) to be (the) banker; **tener** ~ (*fig*) to monopolize the conversation; **medicinali da** ~ over-the-counter medicines; ~ **di chiesa** pew; ~ **di corallo** coral reef; ~ **degli imputati** dock; ~ **del Lotto** lottery-ticket office; ~ **di prova** (*fig*) testing ground; ~ **dei testimoni** witness box (Brit) *o* stand (US)

banco'giro [banko'dʒiro] *sm* credit transfer

'Bancomat® *sm inv* (*tessera*) cash card; (*sportello*) cashpoint (Brit), ATM (US)

banco'nota *sf* banknote

'banda *sf* band; (*di stoffa*) band, stripe; (*lato, parte*) side; (*di calcolatore*) tape; **~ larga** broadband; **~ perforata** punch tape

banderu'ola *sf* (*Meteor*) weathercock, weathervane; **essere una ~** (*fig*) to be fickle

bandi'era *sf* flag, banner; **battere ~ italiana** (*nave etc*) to fly the Italian flag; **cambiare ~** (*fig*) to change sides; **~ di comodo** flag of convenience

ban'dire *vt* to proclaim; (*esiliare*) to exile; (*fig*) to dispense with

ban'dito *sm* outlaw, bandit

bandi'tore *sm* (*di aste*) auctioneer

'bando *sm* proclamation; (*esilio*) exile, banishment; **mettere al ~ qn** to exile sb; (*fig*) to freeze sb out; **~ alle ciance!** that's enough talk!

'bandolo *sm* (*di matassa*) end; **trovare il ~ della matassa** (*fig*) to find the key to the problem

Bang'kok [ban'kɔk] *sf* Bangkok

Bangla'desh [bangla'dɛʃ] *sm*: **il ~** Bangladesh

bar *sm inv* bar

'bara *sf* coffin

ba'racca, -che *sf* shed, hut; (*peg*) hovel; **mandare avanti la ~** to keep things going; **piantare ~ e burattini** to throw everything up

barac'cato, -a *sm/f* *person living in temporary camp*

barac'chino [barak'kino] *sm* (*chiosco*) stall; (*apparecchio*) CB radio

barac'cone *sm* booth, stall; **baracconi** *smpl* (*luna park*) funfair *sg* (Brit), amusement park; **fenomeno da ~** circus freak

barac'copoli *sf inv* shanty town

bara'onda *sf* hubbub, bustle

ba'rare *vi* to cheat

'baratro *sm* abyss

barat'tare *vt*: **~ qc con** to barter sth for, swap sth for

ba'ratto *sm* barter

ba'rattolo *sm* (*di latta*) tin; (*di vetro*) jar; (*di coccio*) pot

'barba *sf* beard; **farsi la ~** to shave; **farla in ~ a qn** (*fig*) to fool sb; **servire qn di ~ e capelli** (*fig*) to teach sb a lesson; **che ~!** what a bore!

barbabi'etola *sf* beetroot (Brit), beet (US); **~ da zucchero** sugar beet

Bar'bados *sf* Barbados

bar'barico, -a, ci, che *ag* (*invasione*) barbarian; (*usanze, metodi*) barbaric

bar'barie *sf* barbarity

'barbaro, -a *ag* barbarous ■ *sm* barbarian; **i Barbari** the Barbarians

'barbecue ['ba:bikju:] *sm inv* barbecue

barbi'ere *sm* barber

barbi'turico, -a, ci, che *ag* barbituric ■ *sm* barbiturate

bar'bone *sm* (*cane*) poodle; (*vagabondo*) tramp

bar'buto, -a *ag* bearded

'barca, -che *sf* boat; **una ~ di** (*fig*) heaps of, tons of; **mandare avanti la ~** (*fig*) to keep things going; **~ a remi** rowing boat (Brit), rowboat (US); **~ a vela** sailing boat (Brit), sailboat (US)

barcai'olo *sm* boatman

barcame'narsi *vr* (*nel lavoro*) to get by; (*a parole*) to beat about the bush

Barcel'lona [bartʃel'lona] *sf* Barcelona

barcol'lare *vi* to stagger

bar'cone *sm* (*per ponti di barche*) pontoon

ba'rella *sf* (*lettiga*) stretcher

'Barents: **il mar di ~** the Barents Sea

ba'rese *ag* of (*o from*) Bari

bari'centro [bari'tʃentro] *sm* centre (Brit) *o* center (US) of gravity

ba'rile *sm* barrel, cask

ba'rista, -i, e *sm/f* barman/barmaid; bar owner

ba'ritono *sm* baritone

bar'lume *sm* glimmer, gleam

'baro *sm* (*Carte*) cardsharp

ba'rocco, -a, chi, che *ag, sm* baroque

ba'rometro *sm* barometer

ba'rone *sm* baron; **i baroni della medicina** (*fig peg*) the top brass in the medical faculty

baro'nessa *sf* baroness

'barra *sf* bar; (*Naut*) helm; (*segno grafico*) stroke

bar'rare *vt* to bar

barri'care *vt* to barricade

barri'cata *sf* barricade; **essere dall'altra parte della ~** (*fig*) to be on the other side of the fence

barri'era *sf* barrier; (*Geo*) reef; **la Grande B~ Corallina** the Great Barrier Reef

bar'roccio [bar'rɔttʃo] *sm* cart

ba'ruffa *sf* scuffle; **fare ~** to squabble

barzel'letta [bardzel'letta] *sf* joke, funny story

basa'mento *sm* (*parte inferiore, piedestallo*) base; (*Tecn*) bed, base plate

ba'sare *vt* to base, found; **basarsi** *vr*: **basarsi su** (*fatti, prove*) to be based *o* founded on; (: *persona*) to base one's arguments on

'basco, -a, schi, sche *ag* Basque ■ *sm/f* Basque ■ *sm* (*lingua*) Basque; (*copricapo*) beret

bas'culla *sf* weighing machine, weighbridge

'base *sf* base; (*fig: fondamento*) basis; (*Pol*) rank and file; **di ~** basic; **in ~ a** on the basis of, according to; **in ~ a ciò ...** on that basis ...; **a ~ di caffè** coffee-based; **essere alla ~ di qc** to be at the root of sth; **gettare le basi per qc** to lay the basis o foundations for sth; **avere buone basi** (*Ins*) to have a sound educational background

baseball ['beisbɔːl] *sm* baseball

ba'setta *sf* sideburn

basi'lare *ag* basic, fundamental

Basi'lea *sf* Basle

ba'silica, -che *sf* basilica

ba'silico *sm* basil

bas'sezza [bas'settsa] *sf* (*d'animo, di sentimenti*) baseness; (*azione*) base action

bas'sista, -i, e *sm/f* bass player

'basso, -a *ag* low; (*di statura*) short; (*meridionale*) southern ■ *sm* bottom, lower part; (*Mus*) bass; **a occhi bassi** with eyes lowered; **a ~ prezzo** cheap; **scendere da ~ to** go downstairs; **cadere in ~** (*fig*) to come down in the world; **la bassa Italia** southern Italy; **il ~ Medioevo** the late Middle Ages

basso'fondo (*pl* **bassifondi**) *sm* (*Geo*) shallows *pl*; **i bassifondi (della città)** the seediest parts of the town

bassorili'evo *sm* bas-relief

bas'sotto, -a *ag* squat ■ *sm* (*cane*) dachshund

bas'tardo, -a *ag* (*animale, pianta*) hybrid, crossbreed; (*persona*) illegitimate, bastard (*peg*) ■ *sm/f* illegitimate child, bastard (*peg*); (*cane*) mongrel

bas'tare *vi, vb impers* to be enough, be sufficient; **~ a qn** to be enough for sb; **~ a se stesso** to be self-sufficient; **basta chiedere** o **che chieda a un vigile** you have only to o need only ask a policeman; **basti dire che ...** suffice it to say that ...; **basta!** that's enough!, that will do!; **basta così?** (*al bar etc*) will that be all?; **punto e basta!** and that's that!

basti'an *sm*: **~ contrario** awkward customer

basti'mento *sm* ship, vessel

basti'one *sm* bastion

basto'nare *vt* to beat, thrash; **avere l'aria di un cane bastonato** to look crestfallen

basto'nata *sf* blow (with a stick); **prendere qn a bastonate** to give sb a good beating

baston'cino [baston'tʃino] *sm* (*piccolo bastone*) small stick; (*Tecn*) rod; (*Sci*) ski pole; **bastoncini di pesce** (*Cuc*) fish fingers (*Brit*), fish sticks (*US*)

bas'tone *sm* stick; **bastoni** *smpl* (*Carte*) suit in Neapolitan pack of cards; **~ da passeggio** walking stick; **mettere i bastoni fra le ruote a qn** to put a spoke in sb's wheel

bat'tage [ba'taʒ] *sm inv*: **~ promozionale** o **pubblicitario** publicity campaign

bat'taglia [bat'taʎʎa] *sf* battle

bat'taglio [bat'taʎʎo] *sm* (*di campana*) clapper; (*di porta*) knocker

battagli'one [battaʎ'ʎone] *sm* battalion

bat'tello *sm* boat

bat'tente *sm* (*imposta: di porta*) wing, flap; (*: di finestra*) shutter; (*per bussare*) knocker; (*di orologio*) hammer; **chiudere i battenti** (*fig*) to shut up shop

'battere *vt* to beat; (*grano*) to thresh; (*percorrere*) to scour; (*rintoccare: le ore*) to strike ■ *vi* (*bussare*) to knock; (*urtare*): **~ contro** to hit o strike against; (*pioggia, sole*) to beat down; (*cuore*) to beat; (*Tennis*) to serve; **battersi** *vr* to fight; **~ le mani** to clap; **~ i piedi** to stamp one's feet; **~ su un argomento** to hammer home an argument; **~ a macchina** to type; **~ il marciapiede** (*peg*) to walk the streets, be on the game; **~ un rigore** (*Calcio*) to take a penalty; **~ in testa** (*Aut*) to knock; **in un batter d'occhio** in the twinkling of an eye; **senza ~ ciglio** without batting an eyelid; **battersela** to run off

batte'ria *sf* battery; (*Mus*) drums *pl*; **~ da cucina** pots and pans *pl*

bat'terio *sm* bacterium; **batteri** *smpl* bacteria

batteriolo'gia [batterjolo'dʒia] *sf* bacteriology

bat'tesimo *sm* (*sacramento*) baptism; (*rito*) baptism, christening; **tenere qn a ~** to be godfather (o godmother) to sb

battez'zare [batted'dzare] *vt* to baptize; to christen

battiba'leno *sm*: **in un ~** in a flash

batti'becco, -chi *sm* squabble

batticu'ore *sm* palpitations *pl*; **avere il ~ to** be frightened to death

bat'tigia [bat'tidʒa] *sf* water's edge

batti'mano *sm* applause

batti'panni *sm inv* carpet-beater

battis'tero *sm* baptistry

battis'trada *sm inv* (*di pneumatico*) tread; (*di gara*) pacemaker

battitap'peto *sm inv* upright vacuum cleaner

'battito *sm* beat, throb; **~ cardiaco** heartbeat; **~ della pioggia/dell'orologio** beating of the rain/ticking of the clock

batti'tore *sm* (*Cricket*) batsman; (*Baseball*) batter; (*Caccia*) beater

batti'tura *sf* (*anche*: **battitura a macchina**) typing; (*del grano*) threshing

bat'tuta *sf* blow; (*di macchina da scrivere*) stroke; (*Mus*) bar; beat; (*Teat*) cue; (*di caccia*) beating; (*Polizia*) combing, scouring; (*Tennis*) service; **fare una ~** to crack a joke, make a witty remark; **aver la ~ pronta** (*fig*) to have a ready answer; **è ancora alle prime battute** it's just started

ba'tuffolo *sm* wad

ba'ule *sm* trunk; (*Aut*) boot (*Brit*), trunk (*US*)

bau'xite [bauk'site] *sf* bauxite

'bava *sf* (*di animale*) slaver, slobber; (*di lumaca*) slime; (*di vento*) breath

bava'glino [bavaʎ'ʎino] *sm* bib

ba'vaglio [ba'vaʎʎo] *sm* gag

bava'rese *ag, sm/f* Bavarian

'bavero *sm* collar

Bavi'era *sf* Bavaria

ba'zar [bad'dzar] *sm inv* bazaar

baz'zecola [bad'dzekola] *sf* trifle

bazzi'care [battsi'kare] *vt* (*persona*) to hang about with; (*posto*) to hang about ■ *vi*: ~ **in/con** to hang about/hang about with

BCE *sigla f* (= *Banca centrale europea*) ECB

be'arsi *vr*: ~ **di qc/a fare qc** to delight in sth/in doing sth; ~ **alla vista di** to enjoy looking at

beati'tudine *sf* bliss

be'ato, -a *ag* blessed; (*fig*) happy; ~ **te!** lucky you!

bebè *sm inv* baby

bec'caccia, -ce [bek'kattʃa] *sf* woodcock

bec'care *vt* to peck; (*fig: raffreddore*) to pick up, catch; **beccarsi** *vr* (*fig*) to squabble

bec'cata *sf* peck

beccheggi'are [bekked'dʒare] *vi* to pitch

beccherò *etc* [bekke'rɔ] *vb vedi* **beccare**

bec'chime [bek'kime] *sm* birdseed

bec'chino [bek'kino] *sm* gravedigger

'becco, -chi *sm* beak, bill; (*di caffettiera etc*) spout; lip; (*fig fam*) cuckold; **mettere ~** (*fam*) to butt in; **chiudi il ~!** (*fam*) shut your mouth!, shut your trap!; **non ho il ~ di un quattrino** (*fam*) I'm broke

Be'fana *sf* old woman who, according to legend, brings children their presents at the Epiphany; (*Epifania*) Epiphany; (*donna brutta*): **befana** hag, witch; *see note*

'beffa *sf* practical joke; **farsi ~ o beffe di qn** to make a fool of sb

bef'fardo, -a *ag* scornful, mocking

bef'fare *vt* (*anche*: **beffarsi di**) to make a fool of, mock

'bega, -ghe *sf* quarrel

'begli ['beʎʎi], 'bei *ag vedi* **bello**

beige [beʒ] *ag inv* beige

Bei'rut *sf* Beirut

bel *ag vedi* **bello**

be'lare *vi* to bleat

be'lato *sm* bleating

'belga, -gi, ghe *ag, sm/f* Belgian

'Belgio ['bɛldʒo] *sm*: **il ~** Belgium

Bel'grado *sf* Belgrade

'bella *sf vedi* **bello**

bel'lezza [bel'lettsa] *sf* beauty; **chiudere o finire qc in ~** to finish sth with a flourish; **che ~!** fantastic!; **ho pagato la ~ di 300 euro** I paid 300 euro, no less

belli'coso, -a *ag* warlike

bellige'rante [bellidʒe'rante] *ag* belligerent

bellim'busto *sm* dandy

🔑 PAROLA CHIAVE

'bello, -a (*ag: dav sm* **bel** + C, **bell'** + V, **bello** + s impura, gn, pn, ps, x, z, pl **bei** + C, **begli** + s impura etc o V) *ag* **1** (*oggetto, donna, paesaggio*) beautiful; (*uomo*) handsome; (*tempo*) beautiful, fine, lovely; **farsi bello di qc** to show off about sth; **fare la bella vita** to have an easy life; **le belle arti** fine arts

2 (*quantità*): **una bella cifra** a considerable sum of money; **un bel niente** absolutely nothing

3 (*rafforzativo*): **è una truffa bella e buona!** it's a real fraud!; **oh bella!, anche questa è bella!** (*ironico*) that's nice!; **è bell'e finito** it's already finished

■ *sm/f* (*innamorato*) sweetheart

■ *sm* **1** (*bellezza*) beauty; (*tempo*) fine weather

2: **adesso viene il bello** now comes the best bit; **sul più bello** at the crucial point; **cosa fai di bello?** are you doing anything interesting?

■ *sf* (*anche*: **bella copia**) fair copy; (*Sport, Carte*) decider

■ *av*: **fa bello** the weather is fine, it's fine; **alla bell'e meglio** somehow or other

bellu'nese *ag* of (*o* from) Belluno

'belva *sf* wild animal

belve'dere *sm inv* panoramic viewpoint

benché [ben'ke] *cong* although

'benda *sf* bandage; (*per gli occhi*) blindfold

ben'dare *vt* to bandage; to blindfold

bendis'posto, -a *ag*: ~ **qn/qc** well disposed towards sb/sth

43

bene *av* well; (*completamente, affatto*): **è ben difficile** it's very difficult ■ *ag inv:* **gente ~** well-to-do people ■ *sm* good; (*Comm*) asset; **beni** *smpl* (*averi*) property *sg*, estate *sg*; **io sto ~/poco ~** I'm well/not very well; **va ~** all right; **ben più lungo/caro** much longer/ more expensive; **lo spero ~** I certainly hope so; **volere un ~ dell'anima a qn** to love sb very much; **un uomo per ~** a respectable man; **fare ~** to do the right thing; **fare ~ a** (*salute*) to be good for; **fare del ~ a qn** to do sb a good turn; **di ~ in meglio** better and better; **beni ambientali** environmental assets; **beni di consumo** consumer goods; **beni di consumo durevole** consumer durables; **beni culturali** cultural heritage; **beni immateriali** immaterial *o* intangible assets; **beni patrimoniali** fixed assets; **beni privati** private property *sg*; **beni pubblici** public property *sg*; **beni reali** tangible assets

bene detto, -a *pp di* **benedire** ■ *ag* blessed, holy

bene dire *vt* to bless; to consecrate; **l'ho mandato a farsi ~** (*fig*) I told him to go to hell

benedizi one [benedit'tsjone] *sf* blessing

benedu cato, -a *ag* well-mannered

benefat tore, - trice *sm/f* benefactor/ benefactress

benefi cenza [benefi'tʃɛntsa] *sf* charity

benefici are [benefi'tʃare] *vi:* **~ di** to benefit by, benefit from

benefici ario, -a [benefi'tʃarjo] *ag, sm/f* beneficiary

bene ficio [bene'fitʃo] *sm* benefit; **con ~ d'inventario** (*fig*) with reservations

be nefico, -a, ci, che *ag* beneficial; charitable

Benelux *sm:* **il ~** Benelux, the Benelux countries

beneme renza [beneme'rentsa] *sf* merit

bene merito, -a *ag* meritorious

bene placito [bene'platʃito] *sm* (*approvazione*) approval; (*permesso*) permission

be nessere *sm* well-being

benes tante *ag* well-to-do

benes tare *sm* consent, approval

benevo lenza [benevo'lɛntsa] *sf* benevolence

be nevolo, -a *ag* benevolent

ben godi *sm* land of plenty

benia mino, -a *sm/f* favourite (*Brit*), favorite (*US*)

be nigno, -a [be'niɲɲo] *ag* kind, kindly; (*critica etc*) favourable (*Brit*), favorable (*US*); (*Med*) benign

benintenzio nato, -a [benintentsjo'nato] *ag* well-meaning

benin teso *av* of course; **~ che** *cong* provided that

benpen sante *sm/f* conformist

benser vito *sm:* **dare il ~ a qn** (*sul lavoro*) to give sb the sack, fire sb; (*fig*) to send sb packing

bensì *cong* but (rather)

benve nuto, -a *ag, sm* welcome; **dare il ~ a qn** to welcome sb

ben visto, -a *ag:* **essere ~ (da)** to be well thought of (by)

benvo lere *vt:* **farsi ~ da tutti** to win everybody's affection; **prendere a ~ qn/qc** to take a liking to sb/sth

ben zina [ben'dzina] *sf* petrol (*Brit*), gas (*US*); **fare ~** to get petrol *o* gas; **rimanere senza ~** to run out of petrol *o* gas; **~ verde** unleaded petrol, lead-free petrol

benzi naio [bendzi'najo] *sm* petrol (*Brit*) *o* gas (*US*) pump attendant

be one *sm* heavy drinker

bere *vt* to drink; (*assorbire*) to soak up; **questa volta non me la dai a ~!** I won't be taken in this time!

berga masco, -a, schi, sche *ag* of (*o* from) Bergamo

Bering ['beriŋ]: **il mar di ~** *sm* the Bering Sea

ber lina *sf* (*Aut*) saloon (car) (*Brit*), sedan (*US*); **mettere alla ~** (*fig*) to hold up to ridicule

Ber lino *sf* Berlin; **~ est/ovest** East/West Berlin

Ber muda *sfpl:* **le ~** Bermuda *sg*

ber muda *smpl* (*calzoncini*) Bermuda shorts

Berna *sf* Bern

ber noccolo *sm* bump; (*inclinazione*) flair

ber retto *sm* cap

berrò *etc vb vedi* **bere**

bersagli are [bersaʎ'ʎare] *vt* to shoot at; (*colpire ripetutamente, fig*) to bombard; **bersagliato dalla sfortuna** dogged by ill fortune

bersagli ere [bersaʎ'ʎɛre] *sm* member of rifle regiment in Italian army

ber saglio [ber'saʎʎo] *sm* target

bes temmia *sf* curse; (*Rel*) blasphemy

bestemmi are *vi* to curse, swear; to blaspheme ■ *vt* to curse, swear at; to blaspheme; **~ come un turco** to swear like a trooper

bestia *sf* animal; **lavorare come una ~** to work like a dog; **andare in ~** (*fig*) to fly into a rage; **una ~ rara** (*fig: persona*) an oddball; **~ da soma** beast of burden

besti ale *ag* bestial, brutish; (*fam*): **fa un caldo ~** it's terribly hot; **fa un freddo ~** it's bitterly cold

bestialità *sf inv* (*qualità*) bestiality; **dire/fare una ~ dopo l'altra** to say/do one idiotic thing after another

besti'ame *sm* livestock; (*bovino*) cattle *pl*

Bet'lemme *sf* Bethlehem

betoni'era *sf* cement mixer

'bettola *sf* (*peg*) dive

be'tulla *sf* birch

be'vanda *sf* drink, beverage

bevi'tore, -'trice *sm/f* drinker

'bevo *etc vb vedi* **bere**

be'vuto, -a *pp di* **bere** ∎ *sf* drink

'bevvi *etc vb vedi* **bere**

BG *sigla* = **Bergamo**

BI *sigla f* = **Banca d'Italia** ∎ *sigla* = **Biella**

bi'ada *sf* fodder

bianche'ria [bjanke'ria] *sf* linen; **~ intima** underwear; **~ da donna** ladies' underwear, lingerie

bi'anco, -a, chi, che *ag* white; (*non scritto*) blank ∎ *sm* white; (*intonaco*) whitewash ∎ *sm/f* white, white man/woman; **in ~** (*foglio, assegno*) blank; **in ~ e nero** (*TV, Fot*) black and white; **mangiare in ~** to follow a bland diet; **pesce in ~** boiled fish; **andare in ~** (*non riuscire*) to fail; (*in amore*) to be rejected; **notte bianca** *o* **in ~** sleepless night; **voce bianca** (*Mus*) treble (voice); **votare scheda bianca** to return a blank voting slip; **~ dell'uovo** egg-white

bianco'segno [bjanko'seɲɲo] *sm* signature to a blank document

biancos'pino *sm* hawthorn

biasci'care [bjaʃʃi'kare] *vt* to mumble

biasi'mare *vt* to disapprove of, censure

bi'asimo *sm* disapproval, censure

'bibbia *sf* bible

bibe'ron *sm inv* feeding bottle

'bibita *sf* (soft) drink

bibliogra'fia *sf* bibliography

biblio'teca, -che *sf* library; (*mobile*) bookcase

bibliote'cario, -a *sm/f* librarian

bicame'rale *ag* (*Pol*) two-chamber *cpd*

bicarbo'nato *sm*: **~ (di sodio)** bicarbonate (of soda)

bicchi'ere [bik'kjɛre] *sm* glass; **è (facile) come bere un bicchier d'acqua** it's as easy as pie

bici'cletta [bitʃi'kletta] *sf* bicycle; **andare in ~** to cycle

bi'cipite [bi'tʃipite] *sm* bicep

bidè *sm inv* bidet

bi'dello, -a *sm/f* (*Ins*) janitor

bi'det *sm inv* = **bidè**

bidirezio'nale [bidirettsjo'nale] *ag* bidirectional

bido'nare *vt* (*fam: piantare in asso*) to let down; (: *imbrogliare*) to cheat, swindle

bido'nata *sf* (*fam*) swindle

bi'done *sm* drum, can; (*anche*: **bidone dell'immondizia**) (dust)bin; (*fam: truffa*) swindle; **fare un ~ a qn** (*fam*) to let sb down; to cheat sb

bidon'ville [bidɔ̃'vil] *sf inv* shanty town

bi'eco, -a, chi, che *ag* sinister

bi'ella *sf* (*Tecn*) connecting rod

Bielo'russia *sf* Belarus, Belorussia

bielo'russo, -a *ag, sm/f* Belarussian, Belorussian

bien'nale *ag* biennial ∎ *sf*: **la B~ di Venezia** the Venice Arts Festival; *see note*

bi'ennio *sm* period of two years

bi'erre *sm/f* *member of the Red Brigades*

bi'etola *sf* beet

bifami'liare *ag* (*villa, casetta*) semi-detached

bifo'cale *ag* bifocal

bi'folco, -a, chi, che *sm/f* (*peg*) bumpkin

'bifora *sf* (*Archit*) mullioned window

bifor'carsi *vr* to fork

biforcazi'one [biforkat'tsjone] *sf* fork

bifor'cuto, -a *ag* (*anche fig*) forked

biga'mia *sf* bigamy

'bigamo, -a *ag* bigamous ∎ *sm/f* bigamist

bighello'nare [bigello'nare] *vi* to loaf (about)

bighel'lone, -a [bigel'lone] *sm/f* loafer

bigiotte'ria [bidʒotte'ria] *sf* costume jewellery (*Brit*) *o* jewelry (*US*); (*negozio*) jeweller's (shop) (*Brit*) *o* jewelry store (*US*) (*selling only costume jewellery*)

bigli'ardo [biʎ'ʎardo] *sm* = **biliardo**

bigliet'taio, -a [biʎʎet'tajo] *sm/f* (*nei treni*) ticket inspector; (*in autobus etc*) conductor/ conductress; (*Cine, Teat*) box-office attendant

bigliette'ria [biʎʎette'ria] *sf* (*di stazione*) ticket office; booking office; (*di teatro*) box office

bigli'etto [biʎ'ʎetto] *sm* (*per viaggi, spettacoli etc*) ticket; (*cartoncino*) card; **~ di banca** (bank)note; (*anche*: **biglietto d'auguri/da visita**) greetings/visiting card; **~ d'andata e**

ritorno return (*Brit*) *o* round-trip (*US*) ticket; ~ **elettronico** e-ticket; ~ **omaggio** complimentary ticket

bignè [biɲ'ɲɛ] *sm inv* cream puff

bigo'dino *sm* roller, curler

bi'gotto, -a *ag* over-pious ∎ *sm/f* church fiend

bi'kini *sm inv* bikini

bi'lancia, -ce [bi'lantʃa] *sf* (*pesa*) scales *pl*; (: *di precisione*) balance; (*dello zodiaco*): **B~** Libra; **essere della B~** to be Libra; ~ **commerciale/dei pagamenti** balance of trade/payments

bilanci'are [bilan'tʃare] *vt* (*pesare*) to weigh; (: *fig*) to weigh up; ~ **le uscite e le entrate** (*Comm*) to balance expenditure and revenue

bi'lancio [bi'lantʃo] *sm* (*Comm*) balance (sheet); (*statale*) budget; **far quadrare il** ~ to balance the books; **chiudere il** ~ **in attivo/passivo** to make a profit/loss; **fare il** ~ **di** (*fig*) to assess; ~ **consolidato** consolidated balance; ~ **consuntivo** (final) balance; ~ **preventivo** budget; ~ **pubblico** national budget; ~ **di verifica** trial balance

bilate'rale *ag* bilateral

'**bile** *sf* bile; (*fig*) rage, anger

bili'ardo *sm* billiards *sg*; (*tavolo*) billiard table

'**bilico, -chi** *sm*: **essere in** ~ to be balanced; (*fig*) to be undecided; **tenere qn in** ~ to keep sb in suspense

bi'lingue *ag* bilingual

bili'one *sm* (*mille milioni*) thousand million, billion (*US*); (*milione di milioni*) billion (*Brit*), trillion (*US*)

bilo'cale *sm* two-room flat (*Brit*) *o* apartment (*US*)

'**bimbo, -a** *sm/f* little boy/girl

bimen'sile *ag* fortnightly

bimes'trale *ag* two-monthly, bimonthly

bi'mestre *sm* two-month period; **ogni** ~ every two months

bi'nario, -a *ag* binary ∎ *sm* (railway) track *o* line; (*piattaforma*) platform; ~ **morto** dead-end track

bi'nocolo *sm* binoculars *pl*

bio'chimica [bio'kimika] *sf* biochemistry

biodegra'dabile *ag* biodegradable

biodiversità *sf* biodiversity

bio'etica *sf* bioethics *sg*

bio'etico, -a, ci, che *ag* bioethical

bio'fabbrica *sf factory producing biological control agents*

bio'fisica *sf* biophysics *sg*

biogra'fia *sf* biography

bio'grafico, -a, ci, che *ag* biographical

bi'ografo, -a *sm/f* biographer

biolo'gia [biolo'dʒia] *sf* biology

bio'logico, -a, ci, che [bio'lɔdʒiko] *ag* (*scienze, fenomeni etc*) biological; (*agricoltura, prodotti*) organic

bi'ologo, -a, ghi, ghe *sm/f* biologist

bi'ondo, -a *ag* blond, fair

bi'onico, -a, ci, che *ag* bionic

biop'sia *sf* biopsy

bio'ritmo *sm* biorhythm

bios'fera *sf* biosphere

biotecnolo'gia [bioteknolo'dʒia] *sf* biotechnology

bipar'tito, -a *ag* (*Pol*) two-party *cpd* ∎ *sm* (*Pol*) two-party alliance

'**birba** *sf* rascal, rogue

bir'bante *sm* rascal, rogue

birbo'nata *sf* naughty trick

bir'bone, -a *ag* (*bambino*) naughty ∎ *sm/f* little rascal

biri'chino, -a [biri'kino] *ag* mischievous ∎ *sm/f* scamp, little rascal

bi'rillo *sm* skittle (*Brit*), pin (*US*); **birilli** *smpl* (*gioco*) skittles *sg* (*Brit*), bowling *no pl* (*US*)

Bir'mania *sf*: **la** ~ Burma

bir'mano, -a *ag, sm/f* Burmese (*inv*)

'**biro**® *sf inv* biro®

'**birra** *sf* beer; ~ **scura** stout; **a tutta** ~ (*fig*) at top speed

birre'ria *sf* (*locale*) ≈ bierkeller; (*fabbrica*) brewery

bis *escl, sm inv* encore ∎ *ag inv* (*treno, autobus*) relief *cpd* (*Brit*), additional; (*numero*): **12** ~ 12a

bi'saccia, -ce [bi'zattʃa] *sf* knapsack

Bi'sanzio [bi'zantsjo] *sf* Byzantium

bis'betico, -a, ci, che *ag* ill-tempered, crabby

bisbigli'are [bizbiʎ'ʎare] *vt, vi* to whisper

bis'biglio [biz'biʎʎo] *sm* whisper; (*notizia*) rumour (*Brit*), rumor (*US*)

bisbi'glio [bizbiʎ'ʎio] *sm* whispering

bis'boccia, -ce [biz'bɔttʃa] *sf* binge, spree; **fare** ~ to have a binge

'**bisca, -sche** *sf* gambling house

Bis'caglia [bis'kaʎʎa] *sf*: **il golfo di** ~ the Bay of Biscay

'**bischero** ['biskero] *sm* (*Mus*) peg; (*fam: toscano*) fool, idiot

'**biscia, -sce** ['biʃʃa] *sf* snake; ~ **d'acqua** water snake

biscot'tato, -a *ag* crisp; **fette biscottate** rusks

bis'cotto *sm* biscuit

bisessu'ale *ag, sm/f* bisexual

bises'tile *ag*: **anno** ~ leap year

bisezi'one [biset'tsjone] *sf* dichotomy

bis'lacco, -a, chi, che *ag* odd, weird

bis'lungo, -a, ghi, ghe *ag* oblong

biso'gnare [bizoɲ'ɲare] *vb impers*: **bisogna che tu parta/lo faccia** you'll have to go/do it; **bisogna parlargli** we'll (*o* I'll) have to talk to him ■ *vi* (*esser utile*) to be necessary

bi'sogno [bi'zoɲɲo] *sm* need; **bisogni** *smpl* (*necessità corporali*): **fare i propri bisogni** to relieve o.s.; **avere ~ di qc/di fare qc** to need sth/to do sth; **al ~, in caso di ~** if need be

biso'gnoso, -a [bizoɲ'ɲoso] *ag* needy, poor; **~ di** in need of, needing

bi'sonte *sm* (*Zool*) bison

bis'tecca, -che *sf* steak, beefsteak; **~ al sangue/ai ferri** rare/grilled steak

bisticci'are [bistit'tʃare] *vi*, **bisticci'arsi** *vr* to quarrel, bicker

bis'ticcio [bis'tittʃo] *sm* quarrel, squabble; (*gioco di parole*) pun

bistrat'tare *vt* to maltreat

'bisturi *sm inv* scalpel

bi'sunto, -a *ag* very greasy

bi'torzolo [bi'tortsolo] *sm* (*sulla testa*) bump; (*sul corpo*) lump

'bitter *sm inv* bitters *pl*

bi'tume *sm* bitumen

bivac'care *vi* (*Mil*) to bivouac; (*fig*) to bed down

bi'vacco, -chi *sm* bivouac

'bivio *sm* fork; (*fig*) dilemma

bizan'tino, -a [biddzan'tino] *ag* Byzantine

'bizza ['biddza] *sf* tantrum; **fare le bizze** to throw a tantrum

biz'zarro, -a [bid'dzarro] *ag* bizarre, strange

biz'zeffe [bid'dzeffe]: **a ~** *av* in plenty, galore

BL *sigla* = **Belluno**

blan'dire *vt* to soothe; to flatter

'blando, -a *ag* mild, gentle

blas'femo, -a *ag* blasphemous ■ *sm/f* blasphemer

bla'sone *sm* coat of arms

blate'rare *vi* to chatter

'blatta *sf* cockroach

blin'dare *vt* to armour (*Brit*), armor (*US*)

blin'data *sf* (*macchina*) armoured car *o* limousine

blin'dato, -a *ag* armoured (*Brit*), armored (*US*); **camera blindata** strongroom; **mezzo ~** armoured vehicle; **porta blindata** reinforced door; **vita blindata** life amid maximum security; **vetro ~** bulletproof glass

bloc'care *vt* to block; (*isolare*) to isolate, cut off; (*porto*) to blockade; (*prezzi, beni*) to freeze; (*meccanismo*) to jam; **bloccarsi** *vr* (*motore*) to stall; (*freni, porta*) to jam, stick; (*ascensore*) to get stuck, stop; **ha bloccato la macchina** (*Aut*) he jammed on the brakes

bloccas'terzo [blokkas'tɛrtso] *sm* (*Aut*) steering lock

blocche'rò *etc* [blokke'rɔ] *vb vedi* **bloccare**

bloc'chetto [blok'ketto] *sm* notebook;

(*di biglietti*) book

'blocco, -chi *sm* block; (*Mil*) blockade; (*dei fitti*) restriction; (*quadernetto*) pad; (*fig: unione*) coalition; (*il bloccare*) blocking; isolating; cutting-off; blockading; freezing; jamming; **in ~** (*nell'insieme*) as a whole; (*Comm*) in bulk; **~ cardiaco** cardiac arrest

bloc-'notes [blɔk'nɔt] *sm inv* notebook, notepad

blog [blog] *sm inv* blog

'bloggare *vi* to blog

blu *ag inv, sm inv* dark blue

bluff [blɛf] *sm inv* bluff

bluf'fare *vi* (*anche fig*) to bluff

'blusa *sf* (*camiciotto*) smock; (*camicetta*) blouse

BN *sigla* = **Benevento**

BO *sigla* = **Bologna**

'boa *sm inv* (*Zool*) boa constrictor; (*sciarpa*) feather boa ■ *sf* buoy

bo'ato *sm* rumble, roar

bob [bɔb] *sm inv* bobsleigh

bo'bina *sf* reel, spool; (*di pellicola*) spool; (*di film*) reel; (*Elettr*) coil

'bocca, -che *sf* mouth; **essere di buona ~** to be a hearty eater; (*fig*) to be easily satisfied; **essere sulla ~ di tutti** (*persona, notizia*) to be the talk of the town; **rimanere a ~ asciutta** to have nothing to eat; (*fig*) to be disappointed; **in ~ al lupo!** good luck!; **~ di leone** (*Bot*) snapdragon

boc'caccia, -ce [bok'kattʃa] *sf* (*malalingua*) gossip; (*smorfia*): **fare le boccacce** to pull faces

boc'caglio [bok'kaʎʎo] *sm* (*Tecn*) nozzle; (*di respiratore*) mouthpiece

boc'cale *sm* jug; **~ da birra** tankard

bocca'scena [bokkaʃ'ʃena] *sm inv* proscenium

boc'cata *sf* mouthful; (*di fumo*) puff; **prendere una ~ d'aria** to go out for a breath of (fresh) air

boc'cetta [bot'tʃetta] *sf* small bottle

boccheggi'are [bokked'dʒare] *vi* to gasp

boc'chino [bok'kino] *sm* (*di sigaretta, sigaro: cannella*) cigarette-holder; cigar-holder; (*di pipa, strumenti musicali*) mouthpiece

'boccia, -ce ['bottʃa] *sf* bottle; (*da vino*) decanter, carafe; (*palla di legno, metallo*) bowl; **gioco delle bocce** bowls *sg*

bocci'are [bot'tʃare] *vt* (*proposta, progetto*) to reject; (*Ins*) to fail; (*Bocce*) to hit

boccia'tura [bottʃa'tura] *sf* failure

bocci'olo [bot'tʃolo] *sm* bud

'boccolo *sm* curl

boccon'cino [bokkon'tʃino] *sm* (*pietanza deliziosa*) delicacy

boc'cone *sm* mouthful, morsel; **mangiare un ~** to have a bite to eat

boc'coni *av* face downwards

Bo'emia sf Bohemia

bo'emo, -a ag, sm/f Bohemian

bofonchi'are [bofon'kjare] vi to grumble

Bogotá sf Bogotá

'**boia** sm inv executioner; hangman; **fa un freddo ~** (fam) it's cold as hell; **mondo ~!**, **~ d'un mondo ladro!** (fam) damn!, blast!

boi'ata sf botch

boicot'taggio [boikot'taddʒo] sm boycott

boicot'tare vt to boycott

'**bolgia, -ge** ['bɔldʒa] sf (fig): **c'era una tale ~ al cinema** the cinema was absolutely mobbed

'**bolide** sm (Astr) meteor; (macchina: da corsa) racing car (Brit), race car (US); (: elaborata) performance car; **come un ~** like a flash, at top speed; **entrare/uscire come un ~** to charge in/out

Bo'livia sf: **la ~** Bolivia

bolivi'ano, -a ag, sm/f Bolivian

'**bolla** sf bubble; (Med) blister; (Comm) bill, receipt; **finire in una ~ di sapone** (fig) to come to nothing; **~ di accompagnamento** waybill; **~ di consegna** delivery note; **~ papale** papal bull

bol'lare vt to stamp; (fig) to brand

bol'lente ag boiling; boiling hot; **calmare i bollentei spiriti** to sober up, calm down

bol'letta sf bill; (ricevuta) receipt; **essere in ~** to be hard up; **~ di consegna** delivery note; **~ doganale** clearance certificate; **~ di trasporto aereo** air waybill

bollet'tino sm bulletin; (Comm) note; **~ meteorologico** weather forecast; **~ di ordinazione** order form; **~ di spedizione** consignment note

bolli'cina [bolli'tʃina] sf bubble; **acqua con le ~** fizzy water

bol'lire vt, vi to boil; **qualcosa bolle in pentola** (fig) there's something brewing

bol'lito sm (Cuc) boiled meat

bolli'tore sm (Tecn) boiler; (Cuc: per acqua) kettle; (: per latte) milk pan

bolli'tura sf boiling

'**bollo** sm stamp; **imposta di ~** stamp duty; **~ auto** road tax; **~ per patente** driving licence tax; **~ postale** postmark

bol'lore sm: **dare un ~ a qc** to bring sth to the boil (Brit) o a boil (US); **i bollori della gioventù** youthful enthusiasm sg

Bo'logna [bo'lɔɲɲa] sf Bologna

bolo'gnese [boloɲ'ɲese] ag Bolognese; **spaghetti alla ~** spaghetti bolognese

'**bomba** sf bomb; **tornare a ~** (fig) to get back to the point; **sei stato una ~!** you were tremendous!; **~ atomica** atom bomb; **~ a mano** hand grenade; **~ ad orologeria** time bomb

bombarda'mento sm bombardment; bombing

bombar'dare vt to bombard; (da aereo) to bomb

bombardi'ere sm bomber

bom'betta sf bowler (hat) (Brit), derby (US)

'**bombola** sf cylinder; **~ del gas** gas cylinder

bombo'letta sf spray can

bomboni'era sf box of sweets (as souvenir at weddings, first communions etc)

bo'naccia, -ce [bo'nattʃa] sf dead calm

bonacci'one, -a [bonat'tʃone] ag good-natured ▪ sm/f good-natured sort

bo'nario, -a ag good-natured, kind

bo'nifica, -che sf reclamation; reclaimed land

bo'nifico, -ci sm (riduzione, abbuono) discount; (versamento a terzi) credit transfer

Bonn sf Bonn

bontà sf goodness; (cortesia) kindness; **aver la ~ di fare qc** to be good o kind enough to do sth

'**bonus-malus** sm inv ≈ no-claims bonus

bor'bonico, -a, ci, che ag Bourbon; (fig) backward, out of date

borbot'tare vi to mumble; (stomaco) to rumble

borbot'tio, -ii sm mumbling; rumbling

'**borchia** ['borkja] sf stud

borda'tura sf (Sartoria) border, trim

bor'deaux [bor'dɔ] sm (colore) burgundy, maroon; (vino) Bordeaux

bor'dello sm brothel

'**bordo** sm (Naut) ship's side; (orlo) edge; (striscia di guarnizione) border, trim; **a ~ di** (nave, aereo) aboard, on board; (macchina) in; **sul ~ della strada** at the roadside; **persona d'alto ~** VIP

bor'dura sf border

bor'gata sf hamlet; (a Roma) working-class suburb

bor'ghese [bor'geze] ag (spesso peg) middle-class; bourgeois; **abito ~** civilian dress; **poliziotto in ~** plainclothes policeman

borghe'sia [borge'zia] sf middle classes pl; bourgeoisie

'**borgo, -ghi** sm (paesino) village; (quartiere) district; (sobborgo) suburb

'**boria** sf self-conceit, arrogance

bori'oso, -a ag arrogant

bor'lotto sm kidney bean

'**Borneo** sm: **il ~** Borneo

boro'talco sm talcum powder

bor'raccia, -ce [bor'rattʃa] sf canteen, water-bottle

'**borsa** sf bag; (anche: **borsa da signora**) handbag; (Econ): **la B~ (valori)** the Stock

Exchange; **~ dell'acqua calda** hot-water bottle; **B~ merci** commodity exchange; **~ nera** black market; **~ della spesa** shopping bag; **~ di studio** grant

borsai olo *sm* pickpocket

bor seggio [bor'seddʒo] *sm* pickpocketing

borsel lino *sm* purse

bor sello *sm* gent's handbag

bor setta *sf* handbag

bor sista, -i, e *sm/f* (*Econ*) speculator; (*Ins*) grant-holder

bos caglia [bos'kaʎʎa] *sf* woodlands *pl*

boscai olo, boscaiu olo *sm* woodcutter; forester

bos chetto [bos'ketto] *sm* copse, grove

bosco, -schi *sm* wood

bos coso, -a *ag* wooded

bos niaco, -a, ci, che *ag, sm/f* Bosnian

Bosnia-Erze govina ['bɔsnja erdze'govina] *sf*: **la ~** Bosnia-Herzegovina

bossolo *sm* cartridge case

Bot, bot *sigla m inv vedi* **buono ordinario del Tesoro**

bo tanico, -a, ci, che *ag* botanical ▪ *sm* botanist ▪ *sf* botany

botola *sf* trap door

Bots wana [bots'vana] *sm*: **il ~** Botswana

botta *sf* blow; (*rumore*) bang; **dare (un sacco di) botte a qn** to give sb a good thrashing; **~ e risposta** (*fig*) cut and thrust

botte *sf* barrel, cask; **essere in una ~ di ferro** (*fig*) to be as safe as houses; **volere la ~ piena e la moglie ubriaca** to want to have one's cake and eat it

bot tega, -ghe *sf* shop; (*officina*) workshop; **stare a ~ da qn** to serve one's apprenticeship (with sb); **le Botteghe Oscure** headquarters of the DS, Italian left-wing party

botte gaio, -a *sm/f* shopkeeper

botte ghino [botte'gino] *sm* ticket office; (*del lotto*) public lottery office

bot tiglia [bot'tiʎʎa] *sf* bottle

bottiglie ria [bottiʎʎe'ria] *sf* wine shop

bot tino *sm* (*di guerra*) booty; (*di rapina, furto*) loot; **fare ~ di qc** (*anche fig*) to make off with sth

botto *sm* bang; crash; **di ~** suddenly; **d'un ~** (*fam*) in a flash

bot tone *sm* button; (*Bot*) bud; **stanza dei bottoni** control room; (*fig*) nerve centre; **attaccare (un) ~ a qn** to buttonhole sb

bo vino, -a *ag* bovine; **bovini** *smpl* cattle

box [bɔks] *sm inv* (*per cavalli*) horsebox; (*per macchina*) lock-up; (*per macchina da corsa*) pit; (*per bambini*) playpen

boxe [bɔks] *sf* boxing

boxer ['bɔkser] *sm inv* (*cane*) boxer ▪ *smpl* (*mutande*): **un paio di ~** a pair of boxer shorts

bozza ['bɔttsa] *sf* draft; (*Tip*) proof; **~ di stampa/impaginata** galley/page proof

boz zetto [bot'tsetto] *sm* sketch

bozzolo ['bɔttsolo] *sm* cocoon

BR *sigla fpl* = **Brigate Rosse** ▪ *sigla* = **Brindisi**

braca, -che *sf* (*gamba di pantalone*) trouser leg; **brache** *sfpl* (*fam*) trousers, pants (US); (*mutandoni*) drawers; **calare le brache** (*fig fam*) to chicken out

brac care *vt* to hunt

brac cetto [brat'tʃetto] *sm*: **a ~** arm in arm

braccherò etc [brakke'rɔ] *vb vedi* **braccare**

bracci ale [brat'tʃale] *sm* bracelet; (*per nuotare, anche distintivo*) armband

braccia letto [brattʃa'letto] *sm* bracelet, bangle

bracci ante [brat'tʃante] *sm* (*Agr*) day labourer

bracci ata [brat'tʃata] *sf* armful; (*nel nuoto*) stroke

braccio ['brattʃo] *sm* (*Anat*) (*pl(f)* **braccia**) arm; (*di gru, fiume*) (*pl* **bracci**) arm; (: *di edificio*) wing; **camminare sotto ~** to walk arm in arm; **è il suo ~ destro** he's his right-hand man; **~ di ferro** (*anche fig*) trial of strength; **~ di mare** sound

bracci olo [brat'tʃolo] *sm* (*appoggio*) arm

bracco, -chi *sm* hound

bracconi ere *sm* poacher

brace ['bratʃe] *sf* embers *pl*

braci ere [bra'tʃere] *sm* brazier

braci ola [bra'tʃola] *sf* (*Cuc*) chop

bradipo *sm* (*Zool*) sloth

brado, -a *ag*: **allo stato ~** in the wild o natural state

brama *sf*: **~ (di/di fare)** longing (for/to do), yearning (for/to do)

bra mare *vt*: **~ (qc/di fare qc)** to long (for sth/ to do sth), yearn (for sth/to do sth)

bramo sia *sf*: **~ (di)** longing (for), yearning (for)

branca, -che *sf* branch

branchia ['brankja] *sf* (*Zool*) gill

branco, -chi *sm* (*di cani, lupi*) pack; (*di uccelli, pecore*) flock; (*peg: di persone*) gang, pack

branco lare *vi* to grope, feel one's way

branda *sf* camp bed

bran dello *sm* scrap, shred; **a brandelli** in tatters, in rags; **fare a brandelli** to tear to shreds

bran dina *sf* camp bed (*Brit*), cot (*US*)

bran dire *vt* to brandish

brano *sm* piece; (*di libro*) passage

bra sare *vt* to braise

bra sato *sm* braised beef

Bra sile *sm*: **il ~** Brazil

Bra silia *sf* Brasilia

brasili'ano, -a *ag, sm/f* Brazilian

bra'vata *sf* (*azione spavalda*) act of bravado

'bravo, -a *ag* (*abile*) clever, capable, skilful; (*buono*) good, honest; (: *bambino*) good; (*coraggioso*) brave; ~! well done!; (*al teatro*) bravo!; **su da ~!** (*fam*) there's a good boy!; **mi sono fatto le mie brave 8 ore di lavoro** I put in a full 8 hours' work

bra'vura *sf* cleverness, skill

'breccia, -ce ['brettʃa] *sf* breach; **essere sulla ~** (*fig*) to be going strong; **fare ~ nell'animo** *o* **nel cuore di qn** to find the way to sb's heart

'Brema *sf* Bremen

bre'saola *sf* kind of dried salted beef

bresci'ano, -a [breʃʃano] *ag* of (*o* from) Brescia

Bre'tagna [bre'taɲɲa] *sf*: **la ~** Brittany

bre'tella *sf* (*Aut*) link; **bretelle** *sfpl* braces

brettone, 'bret(t)one *ag, sm/f* Breton

'breve *ag* brief, short; **in ~** in short; **per farla ~** to cut a long story short; **a ~** (*Comm*) short-term

brevet'tare *vt* to patent

bre'vetto *sm* patent; **~ di pilotaggio** pilot's licence (*Brit*) *o* license (*US*)

brevità *sf* brevity

'brezza ['breddza] *sf* breeze

'bricco, -chi *sm* jug; **~ del caffè** coffeepot

bricco'nata *sf* mischievous trick

bric'cone, -a *sm* rogue, rascal

briciola ['britʃola] *sf* crumb

'briciolo ['britʃolo] *sm* (*specie fig*) bit

bridge [bridʒ] *sm* bridge

'briga, -ghe *sf* (*fastidio*) trouble, bother; **attaccar ~** to start a quarrel; **pigliarsi la ~ di fare qc** to take the trouble to do sth

brigadi'ere *sm* (*dei carabinieri etc*) ≈ sergeant

bri'gante *sm* bandit

bri'gata *sf* (*Mil*) brigade; (*gruppo*) group, party; **le Brigate Rosse** (*Pol*) the Red Brigades

briga'tismo *sm* phenomenon of the Red Brigades

briga'tista, -i, e *sm/f* (*Pol*) member of the Red Brigades

'briglia ['briʎʎa] *sf* rein; **a ~ sciolta** at full gallop; (*fig*) at full speed

bril'lante *ag* bright; (*anche fig*) brilliant; (*che luccica*) shining ■ *sm* diamond

brillan'tina *sf* brilliantine

bril'lare *vi* to shine; (*mina*) to blow up ■ *vt* (*mina*) to set off

'brillo, -a *ag* merry, tipsy

'brina *sf* hoarfrost

brin'dare *vi*: **~ a qn/qc** to drink to *o* toast sb/sth

'brindisi *sm inv* toast

'brio *sm* liveliness, go

bri'oche [bri'ɔʃ] *sf inv* brioche (bun)

bri'oso, -a *ag* lively

'briscola *sf* type of card game; (*seme vincente*) trump(s); (*carta*) trump card

bri'tannico, -a, ci, che *ag* British ■ *sm/f* Briton; **i Britannici** the British *pl*

'brivido *sm* shiver; (*di ribrezzo*) shudder; (*fig*) thrill; **racconti del ~** suspense stories

brizzo'lato, -a [brittso'lato] *ag* (*persona*) going grey; (*barba, capelli*) greying

'brocca, -che *sf* jug

broc'cato *sm* brocade

'broccolo *sm* broccoli *no pl*

bro'daglia [bro'daʎʎa] *sf* (*peg*) dishwater

'brodo *sm* broth; (*per cucinare*) stock; **~ ristretto** consommé; **lasciare (cuocere) qn nel suo ~** to let sb stew (in his own juice); **tutto fa ~** every little bit helps

'broglio ['brɔʎʎo] *sm*: **~ elettorale** gerrymandering; **brogli** *smpl* (*Dir*) malpractices

'bromo *sm* (*Chim*) bromine

bron'chite [bron'kite] *sf* (*Med*) bronchitis

'broncio ['brontʃo] *sm* sulky expression; **tenere il ~** to sulk

'bronco, -chi *sm* bronchial tube

bronto'lare *vi* to grumble; (*tuono, stomaco*) to rumble

bronto'lio *sm* grumbling, mumbling

bronto'lone, -a *ag* grumbling ■ *sm/f* grumbler

bron'zina [bron'dzina] *sf* (*Tecn*) bush

'bronzo ['brondzo] *sm* bronze; **che faccia di ~!** what a brass neck!

bross. *abbr* = **in brossura**

bros'sura *sf*: **in ~** (*libro*) limpback

'browser ['brauzer] *sm inv* (*Inform*) browser

bru'care *vt* to browse on, nibble at

brucherà *etc* [bruke'ra] *vb vedi* **brucare**

bruciacchi'are [brutʃak'kjare] *vt* to singe, scorch; **bruciacchiarsi** *vr* to become singed *o* scorched

brucia'pelo [brutʃa'pelo] : **a ~** *av* point-blank

bruci'are [bru'tʃare] *vt* to burn; (*scottare*) to scald ■ *vi* to burn; **~ gli avversari** (*Sport, fig*) to leave the rest of the field behind; **~ le tappe** *o* **i tempi** (*Sport, fig*) to shoot ahead; **bruciarsi la carriera** to put an end to one's career

brucia'tore [brutʃa'tore] *sm* burner

brucia'tura [brutʃa'tura] *sf* (*atto*) burning *no pl*; (*segno*) burn; (*scottatura*) scald

bruci'ore [bru'tʃore] *sm* burning *o* smarting sensation

'bruco, -chi *sm* grub; (*di farfalla*) caterpillar

'brufolo *sm* pimple, spot

brughi'era [bru'gjera] *sf* heath, moor

bruli'care *vi* to swarm

bruli'chio, -ii [bruli'kio] *sm* swarming

'brullo, -a *ag* bare, bleak

'bruma *sf* mist

'bruno, -a *ag* brown, dark; (*persona*) dark(-haired)

brusca'mente *av* (*frenare, fermarsi*) suddenly; (*rispondere, reagire*) sharply

'brusco, -a, schi, sche *ag* (*sapore*) sharp; (*modi, persona*) brusque, abrupt; (*movimento*) abrupt, sudden

bru'sio *sm* buzz, buzzing

bru'tale *ag* brutal

brutalità *sf inv* brutality

'bruto, -a *ag* (*forza*) brute *cpd* ■ *sm* brute

'brutta *sf vedi* **brutto**

brut'tezza [brut'tettsa] *sf* ugliness

'brutto, -a *ag* ugly; (*cattivo*) bad; (*malattia, strada, affare*) nasty, bad ■ *sm*: **guardare qn di ~** to give sb a nasty look ■ *sf* rough copy, first draft; **~ tempo** bad weather; **passare un ~ quarto d'ora** to have a nasty time of it; **vedersela brutta** (*per un attimo*) to have a nasty moment; (*per un periodo*) to have a bad time of it

brut'tura *sf* (*cosa brutta*) ugly thing; (*sudiciume*) filth; (*azione meschina*) mean action

Bru'xelles [bry'sɛl] *sf* Brussels

BS *sigla* = **Brescia**

BSE *sigla f* BSE (= *bovine spongiform encephalopathy*)

B.T. *abbr* (= *bassa tensione*) LT ■ *sigla m inv* = **buono del Tesoro**

btg *abbr* = **battaglione**

Btp *sigla m* = **buono del Tesoro poliennale**; *vedi* **buono**

bub'bone *sm* swelling

'buca, -che *sf* hole; (*avvallamento*) hollow; **~ delle lettere** letterbox

buca'neve *sm inv* snowdrop

bu'care *vt* (*forare*) to make a hole (*o* holes) in; (*pungere*) to pierce; (*biglietto*) to punch; **bucarsi** *vr* (*con eroina*) to mainline; **~ una gomma** to have a puncture; **avere le mani bucate** (*fig*) to be a spendthrift

'Bucarest *sf* Bucharest

bu'cato *sm* (*operazione*) washing; (*panni*) wash, washing

'buccia, -ce ['buttʃa] *sf* skin, peel; (*corteccia*) bark

bucherel'lare [bukerel'lare] *vt* to riddle with holes

bucherò *etc* [buke'rɔ] *vb vedi* **bucare**

'buco, -chi *sm* hole; **fare un ~ nell'acqua** to fail, draw a blank; **farsi un ~** (*fam: drogarsi*) to have a fix; **~ nero** (*anche fig*) black hole

'Budapest *sf* Budapest

'Budda *sm inv* Buddha

bud'dismo *sm* Buddhism

bu'dello *sm* intestine; (*fig: tubo*) tube; (*vicolo*) alley; **budella** *sfpl* bowels, guts

bu'dino *sm* pudding

'bue (*pl* **buoi**) *sm* ox; (*anche*: **carne di bue**) beef; **uovo all'occhio di ~** fried egg

Bu'enos 'Aires *sf* Buenos Aires

'bufalo *sm* buffalo

bu'fera *sf* storm

buf'fetto *sm* flick

'buffo, -a *ag* funny; (*Teat*) comic

buffo'nata *sf* (*azione*) prank, jest; (*parola*) jest

buf'fone *sm* buffoon

bugge'rare [buddʒe'rare] *vt* to swindle, cheat

bu'gia, -gie [bu'dʒia] *sf* lie; (*candeliere*) candleholder

bugi'ardo, -a [bu'dʒardo] *ag* lying, deceitful ■ *sm/f* liar

bugi'gattolo [budʒi'gattolo] *sm* poky little room

'buio, -a *ag* dark ■ *sm* dark, darkness; **fa ~ pesto** it's pitch-dark

'bulbo *sm* (*Bot*) bulb; **~ oculare** eyeball

Bulga'ria *sf*: **la ~** Bulgaria

'bulgaro, -a *ag, sm/f, sm* Bulgarian

buli'mia *sf* bulimia

bul'lismo [bul'lizmo] *sm* bullying

'bullo *sm* (*persona*) tough

bul'lone *sm* bolt

bu'oi *smpl di* **bue**

buona'fede *sf* good faith

buon'anima *sf* = **buon'anima**; *vedi* **anima**

buona'notte *escl* good night! ■ *sf*: **dare la ~ a** to say good night to

buona'sera *escl* good evening!

buoncos'tume *sm* public morality; **la (squadra del) ~** (*Polizia*) the vice squad

buondì *escl* hello!

buongi'orno [bwon'dʒorno] *escl* good morning (*o* afternoon)!

buon'grado *av*: **di ~** willingly

buongus'taio, -a *sm/f* gourmet

buon'gusto *sm* good taste

 PAROLA CHIAVE

bu'ono, -a (*ag: dav sm* **buon** + C *o* V, **buono** + *s impura, gn, pn, ps, z; dav sf* **buon'** + V) *ag* **1** (*gen*) good; **un buon pranzo/ristorante** a good lunch/restaurant; **(stai) buono!** behave!; **che buono!** (*cibo*) this is nice!

2 (*benevolo*): **buono (con)** good (to), kind (to)

3 (*giusto, valido*) right; **al momento buono** at the right moment

4 (*adatto*): **buono a/da** fit for/to; **essere buono a nulla** to be no good *o* use at anything

51

5 (*auguri*): **buon compleanno!** happy birthday!; **buon divertimento!** have a nice time!; **buona fortuna!** good luck!; **buon riposo!** sleep well!; **buon viaggio!** have a good trip!

6: ad ogni buon conto in any case; **tante buone cose!** all the best!; **di buon cuore** (*persona*) goodhearted; **di buon grado** willingly; **le buone maniere** good manners; **di buon mattino** early in the morning; **a buon mercato** cheap; **di buon'ora** early; **mettere una buona parola** to put in a good word; **di buon passo** at a good pace; **buon pro ti faccia!** much good may it do you!; **buon senso** common sense; **la buona società** the upper classes; **una buona volta** once and for all; **alla buona** simple

■ *av* in a simple way, without any fuss; **un tipo alla buona** an easy-going sort
■ *sm/f*: **essere un buono/una buona** to be a good person; **buono a nulla** good for nothing; **i buoni e i cattivi** (*in storia, film*) the goodies and the baddies; **accetterà con le buone o con le cattive** one way or another he's going to agree to it
■ *sm* **1** (*bontà*) goodness, good
2 (*Comm*) voucher, coupon; **buono d'acquisto** credit note; **buono di cassa** cash voucher; **buono di consegna** delivery note; **buono fruttifero** interest-bearing bond; **buono ordinario del Tesoro** short-term Treasury bond; **buono postale fruttifero** interest-bearing bond (*issued by Italian Post Office*); **buono del Tesoro** Treasury bill

buon'senso *sm* = **buon senso**
buontem'pone, -a *sm/f* jovial person
buonu'scita [bwonuʃˈʃita] *sf* (*Industria*) golden handshake; (*di affitti*) *sum paid for the relinquishing of tenancy rights*

buratti'naio *sm* puppeteer, puppet master
burat'tino *sm* puppet
burbero, -a *ag* surly, gruff
burla *sf* prank, trick
bur'lare *vt*: ~ **qc/qn**, **burlarsi di qc/qn** to make fun of sth/sb
bu'rocrate *sm* bureaucrat
buro'cratico, -a, ci, che *ag* bureaucratic
burocra'zia [burokratˈtsia] *sf* bureaucracy
bur'rasca, -sche *sf* storm
burras'coso, -a *ag* stormy
burro *sm* butter
bur'rone *sm* ravine
bus'care *vt* (*anche*: **buscarsi**: *raffreddore*) to get, catch; **buscarle** (*fam*) to get a hiding
buscherò *etc* [buskeˈrɔ] *vb vedi* **buscare**
bus'sare *vi* to knock; ~ **a quattrini** (*fig*) to ask for money
bussola *sf* compass; **perdere la** ~ (*fig*) to lose one's bearings
busta *sf* (*da lettera*) envelope; (*astuccio*) case; **in** ~ **aperta/chiusa** in an unsealed/sealed envelope; ~ **paga** pay packet
busta'rella *sf* bribe, backhander
bus'tina *sf* (*piccola busta*) envelope; (*di cibi, farmaci*) sachet; (*Mil*) forage cap; ~ **di tè** tea bag
busto *sm* bust; (*indumento*) corset, girdle; **a mezzo** ~ (*fotografia, ritratto*) half-length
bu'tano *sm* butane
but'tare *vt* to throw; (*anche*: **buttare via**) to throw away; **buttarsi** *vr* (*saltare*) to jump; ~ **giù** (*scritto*) to scribble down, dash off; (*cibo*) to gulp down; (*edificio*) to pull down, demolish; (*pasta, verdura*) to put into boiling water; **ho buttato là una frase** I mentioned it in passing; **buttiamoci!** (*saltiamo*) let's jump!; (*rischiamo*) let's have a go!; **buttarsi dalla finestra** to jump out of the window
buzzo [ˈbuddzo] *sm* (*fam: pancia*) belly, paunch; **di** ~ **buono** (*con impegno*) with a will

Cc

C, c [tʃi] *sf o m inv* (*lettera*) C, c ■ *abbr* (*Geo*)
= **capo**; (= *Celsius, centigrado*) C; (= *conto*) a/c;
C come Como ≈ C for Charlie

CA *sigla* = **Cagliari**

c.a. *abbr* (*Elettr*) *vedi* **corrente alternata**;
(*Comm*) = **corrente anno**

caba'ret [kaba'rɛ] *sm inv* cabaret

ca'bina *sf* (*di nave*) cabin; (*da spiaggia*) beach
hut; (*di autocarro, treno*) cab; (*di aereo*) cockpit;
(*di ascensore*) cage; **~ di proiezione** (*Cine*)
projection booth; **~ di registrazione**
recording booth; **~ telefonica** callbox,
(tele)phone box *o* booth

cabi'nato *sm* cabin cruiser

ca'blaggio [ka'bladdʒo] *sm* wiring

cablo'gramma *sm* cable(gram)

ca'cao *sm* cocoa

'cacca *sf* (*fam: anche fig*) shit (!)

'caccia ['kattʃa] *sf* hunting; (*con fucile*)
shooting; (*inseguimento*) chase; (*cacciagione*)
game ■ *sm inv* (*aereo*) fighter; (*nave*)
destroyer; **andare a ~** to go hunting; **andare
a ~ di guai** to be asking for trouble; **~ grossa**
big-game hunting; **~ all'uomo** manhunt

cacciabombardi'ere [kattʃabombar'djɛre] *sm*
fighter-bomber

cacciagi'one [kattʃa'dʒone] *sf* game

cacci'are [kat'tʃare] *vt* to hunt; (*mandar via*) to
chase away; (*ficcare*) to shove, stick ■ *vi* to
hunt; **cacciarsi** *vr* (*fam: mettersi*): **cacciarsi
tra la folla** to plunge into the crowd; **dove
s'è cacciata la mia borsa?** where has my
bag got to?; **cacciarsi nei guai** to get into
trouble; **~ fuori qc** to whip *o* pull sth out;
~ un urlo to let out a yell

caccia'tora [kattʃa'tora] *sf* (*giacca*) hunting
jacket; (*Cuc*): **pollo** *etc* **alla ~** chicken *etc*
chasseur

caccia'tore [kattʃa'tore] *sm* hunter; **~ di
frodo** poacher; **~ di dote** fortune-hunter

cacciatorpedini'ere [kattʃatorpedi'njɛre]
sm destroyer

caccia'vite [kattʃa'vite] *sm inv* screwdriver

cache'mire [kaʃ'mir] *sm inv* cashmere

ca'chet [ka'ʃɛ] *sm* (*Med*) capsule; (: *compressa*)
tablet; (*compenso*) fee; (*colorante per capelli*)
rinse

'cachi ['kaki] *sm inv* (*albero, frutto*) persimmon;
(*colore*) khaki ■ *ag inv* khaki

'cacio ['katʃo] *sm* cheese; **essere come il ~ sui
maccheroni** (*fig*) to turn up at the right
moment

'cactus *sm inv* cactus

ca'davere *sm* (*dead*) body, corpse

cada'verico, -a, ci, che *ag* (*fig*) deathly pale

'caddi *etc vb vedi* **cadere**

ca'dente *ag* falling; (*casa*) tumbledown;
(*persona*) decrepit

ca'denza [ka'dɛntsa] *sf* cadence; (*andamento
ritmico*) rhythm; (*Mus*) cadenza

ca'dere *vi* to fall; (*denti, capelli*) to fall out;
(*tetto*) to fall in; **questa gonna cade bene**
this skirt hangs well; **lasciar ~** (*anche fig*) to
drop; **~ dal sonno** to be falling asleep on
one's feet; **~ ammalato** to fall ill; **~ dalle
nuvole** (*fig*) to be taken aback

ca'detto *sm* cadet

cadrò *etc vb vedi* **cadere**

ca'duto, -a *ag* (*morto*) dead ■ *sm* dead soldier
■ *sf* fall; **monumento ai caduti** war
memorial; **caduta di temperatura** drop in
temperature; **la caduta dei capelli** hair
loss; **caduta del sistema** (*Inform*) system
failure

caffè *sm inv* coffee; (*locale*) café; **~ corretto**
coffee with liqueur; **~ in grani** coffee beans;
~ macchiato coffee with a dash of milk;
~ macinato ground coffee

caffe'ina *sf* caffeine

caffel'latte *sm inv* white coffee

caffette'ria *sf* coffee shop

caffetti'era *sf* coffeepot

ca'fone *sm* (*contadino*) peasant; (*peg*) boor

cagio'nare [kadʒo'nare] *vt* to cause, be the
cause of

cagio'nevole [kadʒo'nevole] *ag* delicate, weak

cagli'are [kaʎ'ʎare] *vi* to curdle

cagliari'tano, -a [kaʎʎari'tano] *ag* of (*o* from) Cagliari

'cagna ['kaɲɲa] *sf* (*Zool, peg*) bitch

ca'gnara [kaɲ'ɲara] *sf* (*fig*) uproar

ca'gnesco, -a, schi, sche [kaɲ'ɲesko] *ag* (*fig*): **guardare qn in ~** to scowl at sb

CAI *sigla m* = **Club Alpino Italiano**

'Cairo *sm*: **il ~** Cairo

cala'brese *ag, sm/f* Calabrian

cala'brone *sm* hornet

Cala'hari [kala'ari]: **il Deserto di ~** *sm* the Kalahari Desert

cala'maio *sm* inkpot; inkwell

cala'maro *sm* squid

cala'mita *sf* magnet

calamità *sf inv* calamity, disaster; **~ naturale** natural disaster

ca'lare *vt* (*far discendere*) to lower; (*Maglia*) to decrease ■ *vi* (*discendere*) to go (*o* come) down; (*tramontare*) to set, go down; **~ di peso** to lose weight

ca'lata *sf* (*invasione*) invasion

'calca *sf* throng, press

cal'cagno [kal'kaɲɲo] *sm* heel

cal'care *sm* limestone; (*incrostazione*) (lime)scale ■ *vt* (*premere coi piedi*) to tread, press down; (*premere con forza*) to press down; (*mettere in rilievo*) to stress; **~ le scene** (*fig*) to be on the stage; **~ le orme di qn** (*fig*) to follow in sb's footsteps

'calce ['kaltʃe] *sm*: **in ~** at the foot of the page ■ *sf* lime; **~ viva** quicklime

calces'truzzo [kaltʃes'truttso] *sm* concrete

cal'cetto [kal'tʃetto] *sm* (*calcio-balilla*) table football; (*calcio a cinque*) five-a-side (football)

calcherò *etc* [kalke'rɔ] *vb vedi* **calcare**

calci'are [kal'tʃare] *vt, vi* to kick

calcia'tore [kaltʃa'tore] *sm* footballer (*Brit*), (football) player

cal'cina [kal'tʃina] *sf* (*lime*) mortar

'calcio ['kaltʃo] *sm* (*pedata*) kick; (*sport*) football, soccer; (*di pistola, fucile*) butt; (*Chim*) calcium; **~ d'angolo** (*Sport*) corner (kick); **~ di punizione** (*Sport*) free kick

'calco, -chi *sm* (*Arte*) casting, moulding (*Brit*), molding (*US*); cast, mo(u)ld

calco'lare *vt* to calculate, work out, reckon; (*ponderare*) to weigh (up)

calcola'tore, -'trice *ag* calculating ■ *sm* calculator; (*fig*) calculating person ■ *sf* (*anche*: **macchina calcolatrice**) calculator; **~ digitale** digital computer; **~ elettronico** computer; **~ da tavolo** desktop computer

'calcolo *sm* (*anche Mat*) calculation; (*infinitesimale etc*) calculus; (*Med*) stone; **fare il ~ di qc** to work sth out; **fare i propri calcoli** (*fig*) to weigh the pros and cons; **per ~** out of self-interest

cal'daia *sf* boiler

caldar'rosta *sf* roast chestnut

caldeggi'are [kalded'dʒare] *vt* to support

'caldo, -a *ag* warm; (*molto caldo*) hot; (*fig: appassionato*) keen ■ *sm* heat; **ho ~** I'm warm; I'm hot; **fa ~** it's warm; it's hot; **non mi fa né ~ né freddo** I couldn't care less; **a ~** (*fig*) in the heat of the moment

caleidos'copio *sm* kaleidoscope

calen'dario *sm* calendar

ca'lende *sfpl* calends; **rimandare qc alle ~ greche** to put sth off indefinitely

ca'lesse *sm* gig

'calibro *sm* (*di arma*) calibre, bore; (*Tecn*) callipers *pl*; (*fig*) calibre; **di grosso ~** (*fig*) prominent

'calice ['kalitʃe] *sm* goblet; (*Rel*) chalice

Cali'fornia *sf* California

californi'ano, -a *ag* Californian

ca'ligine [ka'lidʒine] *sf* fog; (*mista con fumo*) smog

calligra'fia *sf* (*scrittura*) handwriting; (*arte*) calligraphy

'callo *sm* callus; (*ai piedi*) corn; **fare il ~ a qc** to get used to sth

'calma *sf* calm; **faccia con ~** take your time

cal'mante *sm* sedative, tranquillizer

cal'mare *vt* to calm; (*lenire*) to soothe; **calmarsi** *vr* to grow calm, calm down; (*vento*) to abate; (*dolori*) to ease

calmi'ere *sm* controlled price

'calmo, -a *ag* calm, quiet

'calo *sm* (*Comm: di prezzi*) fall; (: *di volume*) shrinkage; (: *di peso*) loss

ca'lore *sm* warmth; (*intenso, Fisica*) heat; **essere in ~** (*Zool*) to be on heat

calo'ria *sf* calorie

calo'rifero *sm* radiator

calo'roso, -a *ag* warm; **essere ~** not to feel the cold

calpes'tare *vt* to tread on, trample on; **"è vietato ~ l'erba"** "keep off the grass"

ca'lunnia *sf* slander; (*scritta*) libel

calunni'are *vt* to slander

cal'vario *sm* (*fig*) affliction, cross

cal'vizie [kal'vittsje] *sf* baldness

'calvo, -a *ag* bald

'calza ['kaltsa] *sf* (*da donna*) stocking; (*da uomo*) sock; **fare la ~** to knit

calza'maglia [kaltsa'maʎʎa] *sf* tights *pl*; (*per danza, ginnastica*) leotard

cal'zare [kal'tsare] *vt* (*scarpe, guanti: mettersi*) to put on; (: *portare*) to wear ■ *vi* to fit; **~ a pennello** to fit like a glove

calza'tura [kaltsa'tura] *sf* footwear
calzatu'ri'ficio [kaltsaturi'fitʃo] *sm* shoe *o* footwear factory
cal'zetta [kal'tsetta] *sf* ankle sock; **una mezza ~** (*fig*) a nobody
calzet'tone [kaltset'tone] *sm* heavy knee-length sock
cal'zino [kal'tsino] *sm* sock
calzo'laio [kaltso'lajo] *sm* shoemaker; (*che ripara scarpe*) cobbler
calzole'ria [kaltsole'ria] *sf* (*negozio*) shoe shop; (*arte*) shoemaking
calzon'cini [kaltson'tʃini] *smpl* shorts; **~ da bagno** (swimming) trunks
cal'zone [kal'tsone] *sm* trouser leg; (*Cuc*) savoury turnover made with pizza dough; **calzoni** *smpl* trousers (*Brit*), pants (*US*)
camale'onte *sm* chameleon
cambi'ale *sf* bill (of exchange); (*pagherò cambiario*) promissory note; **~ di comodo** *o* **di favore** accommodation bill
cambia'mento *sm* change; **cambiamenti climatici** climate change *sg*
cambi'are *vt* to change; (*modificare*) to alter, change; (*barattare*): **~ (qc con qn/qc)** to exchange (sth with sb/for sth) ■ *vi* to change, alter; **cambiarsi** *vr* (*variare abito*) to change; **~ casa** to move (house); **~ idea** to change one's mind; **~ treno** to change trains; **~ le carte in tavola** (*fig*) to change one's tune; **~ (l')aria in una stanza** to air a room; **è ora di ~ aria** (*andarsene*) it's time to move on
cambiava'lute *sm inv* exchange office
cambio *sm* change; (*modifica*) alteration, change; (*scambio, Comm*) exchange; (*corso dei cambi*) rate (of exchange); (*Tecn, Aut*) gears *pl*; **in ~ di** in exchange for; **dare il ~ a qn** to take over from sb; **fare il** *o* **un ~** to change (over); **~ a termine** (*Comm*) forward exchange
Cambital *sigla m* = **Ufficio Italiano dei Cambi**
Cam'bogia [kam'bodʒa] *sf*: **la ~** Cambodia
cambogi'ano, -a [kambo'dʒano] *ag, sm/f* Cambodian
cam'busa *sf* storeroom
camera *sf* room; (*anche*: **camera da letto**) bedroom; (*Pol*) chamber, house; **~ ardente** mortuary chapel; **~ d'aria** inner tube; (*di pallone*) bladder; **~ blindata** strongroom; **C~ di Commercio** Chamber of Commerce; **C~ dei Deputati** Chamber of Deputies, ≈ House of Commons (*Brit*), ≈ House of Representatives (*US*); *see note;* **~ a gas** gas chamber; **~ del lavoro** trades union centre (*Brit*), labor union center (*US*); **~ a un letto/a due letti/matrimoniale** single/twin-

bedded/double room; **~ oscura** (*Fot*) dark room; **~ da pranzo** dining room

● **CAMERA DEI DEPUTATI**
●
● The *Camera dei deputati* is the lower house
● of the Italian Parliament and is presided
● over by the "Presidente della Camera"
● who is chosen by the "deputati". Elections
● to the Chamber are normally held every
● 5 years. Since the electoral reform of 1993
● members have been voted in via a system
● which combines a first-past-the-post
● element with proportional representation;
● *see also* "Parlamento".

came'rata, -i, e *sm/f* companion, mate ■ *sf* dormitory
camera'tismo *sm* comradeship
cameri'era *sf* (*domestica*) maid; (*che serve a tavola*) waitress; (*che fa le camere*) chambermaid
cameri'ere *sm* (man)servant; (*di ristorante*) waiter
came'rino *sm* (*Teat*) dressing room
Camerun *sm*: **il ~** Cameroon
camice ['kamitʃe] *sm* (*Rel*) alb; (*per medici etc*) white coat
cami'cetta [kami'tʃetta] *sf* blouse
ca'micia, -cie [ka'mitʃa] *sf* (*da uomo*) shirt; (*da donna*) blouse; **nascere con la ~** (*fig*) to be born lucky; **sudare sette camicie** (*fig*) to have a hell of a time; **~ di forza** straitjacket; **~ da notte** (*da donna*) nightdress; (*da uomo*) nightshirt; **C~ nera** (*fascista*) Blackshirt
camici'aio, -a [kami'tʃajo] *sm/f* (*sarto*) shirtmaker; (*che vende camicie*) shirtseller
camici'ola [kami'tʃola] *sf* vest
camici'otto [kami'tʃotto] *sm* casual shirt; (*per operai*) smock
cami'netto *sm* hearth, fireplace
ca'mino *sm* chimney; (*focolare*) fireplace, hearth
camion *sm inv* lorry (*Brit*), truck (*US*)
camion'cino [kamjon'tʃino] *sm* van
camio'netta *sf* jeep
camio'nista, -i *sm* lorry driver (*Brit*), truck driver (*US*)
camma *sf* cam; **albero a camme** camshaft
cam'mello *sm* (*Zool*) camel; (*tessuto*) camel hair
cam'meo *sm* cameo
cammi'nare *vi* to walk; (*funzionare*) to work, go; **~ a carponi** *o* **a quattro zampe** to go on all fours
cammi'nata *sf* walk; **fare una ~** to go for a walk

cam'mino sm walk; (sentiero) path; (itinerario, direzione, tragitto) way; **mettersi in ~** to set o start off; way; **cammin facendo** on the way; **riprendere il ~** to continue on one's way

camo'milla sf camomile; (infuso) camomile tea

ca'morra sf Camorra; (fig) racket

camor'rista, -i, e sm/f member of the Camorra; (fig) racketeer

ca'moscio [ka'moʃʃo] sm chamois

cam'pagna [kam'paɲɲa] sf country, countryside; (Pol, Comm, Mil) campaign; **in ~** in the country; **andare in ~** to go to the country; **fare una ~** to campaign; **~ promozionale vendite** sales campaign

campa'gnolo, -a [kampaɲ'ɲɔlo] ag country cpd ■ sf (Aut) cross-country vehicle

cam'pale ag field cpd; (fig): **una giornata ~** a hard day

cam'pana sf bell; (anche: **campana di vetro**) bell jar; **sordo come una ~** as deaf as a doorpost; **sentire l'altra ~** (fig) to hear the other side of the story; **~ (per la raccolta del vetro)** bottle bank

campa'nella sf small bell; (di tenda) curtain ring

campa'nello sm (all'uscio, da tavola) bell

campa'nile sm bell tower, belfry

campani'lismo sm parochialism

cam'pano, -a ag of (o from) Campania

cam'pare vi to live; (tirare avanti) to get by, manage; **~ alla giornata** to live from day to day

cam'pato, -a ag: **~ in aria** unsound, unfounded

campeggi'are [kamped'dʒare] vi to camp; (risaltare) to stand out

campeggia'tore, -'trice [kampedd͡ʒa'tore] sm/f camper

cam'peggio [kam'peddʒo] sm camping; (terreno) camp site; **fare (del) ~** to go camping

cam'pestre ag country cpd, rural; **corsa ~** cross-country race

Campi'doglio [kampi'dɔʎʎo] sm: **il ~** the Capitol; see note

⊙ **CAMPIDOGLIO**

⊙ The Campidoglio, one of the Seven Hills
⊙ of Rome, is the home of the "Comune
⊙ di Roma".

'camping ['kæmpiŋ] sm inv camp site

campiona'mento sm sampling

campio'nario, -a ag: **fiera campionaria** trade fair ■ sm collection of samples

campio'nato sm championship

campiona'tura sf (Comm) production of samples; (Statistica) sampling

campi'one, -'essa sm/f (Sport) champion ■ sm (Comm) sample; **~ gratuito** free sample; **prelievi di ~** product samples

'campo sm (gen) field; (Mil) field; (: accampamento) camp; (spazio delimitato: sportivo etc) ground; field; (di quadro) background; **i campi** (campagna) the countryside; **padrone del ~** (fig) victor; **~ da aviazione** airfield; **~ di concentramento** concentration camp; **~ di golf** golf course; **~ lungo** (Cine, TV, Fot) long shot; **~ nomadi** travellers' camp; **~ da tennis** tennis court; **~ visivo** field of vision

campobas'sano, -a ag of (o from) Campobasso

campo'santo (pl **campisanti**) sm cemetery

camuffare vt to disguise; **camuffarsi** vr: **camuffarsi (da)** to disguise o.s. (as); (per ballo in maschera) to dress up (as)

CAN abbr (= Costo, Assicurazione e Nolo) CIF

Can. abbr (Geo) = **canale**

'Canada sm: **il ~** Canada

cana'dese ag, sm/f Canadian ■ sf (anche: **tenda canadese**) ridge tent

ca'naglia [ka'naʎʎa] sf rabble, mob; (persona) scoundrel, rogue

ca'nale sm (anche fig) channel; (artificiale) canal

'canapa sf hemp; **~ indiana** cannabis

Ca'narie sfpl: **le (isole) ~** the Canary Islands, the Canaries

cana'rino sm canary

Can'berra sf Canberra

cancel'lare [kantʃel'lare] vt (con la gomma) to rub out, erase; (con la penna) to strike out; (annullare) to annul, cancel; (disdire) to cancel

cancel'lata [kantʃel'lata] sf railing(s) pl

cancelle'ria [kantʃelle'ria] sf chancery; (quanto necessario per scrivere) stationery

cancelli'ere [kantʃel'ljere] sm chancellor; (di tribunale) clerk of the court

can'cello [kan'tʃello] sm gate

cance'rogeno, -a [kantʃe'rɔdʒeno] ag carcinogenic ■ sm carcinogen

cance'rologo, -a, gi, ghe [kantʃe'rɔlogo] sm/f cancer specialist

cance'roso, -a [kantʃe'roso] ag cancerous ■ sm/f cancer patient

can'crena sf gangrene

'cancro sm (Med) cancer; (dello zodiaco): **C~** Cancer; **essere del C~** to be Cancer

candeggi'are [kanded'dʒare] vt to bleach

candeg'gina [kanded'dʒina] sf bleach

can'deggio [kan'deddʒo] sm bleaching

can'dela sf candle; **~ (di accensione)** (Aut) spark(ing) plug; **una lampadina da 100**

candele (*Elettr*) a 100 watt bulb; **a lume di ~** by candlelight; **tenere la ~** (*fig*) to play gooseberry (*Brit*), act as chaperone

cande'labro *sm* candelabra

candeli'ere *sm* candlestick

cande'lotto *sm* candle; ~ **di dinamite** stick of dynamite; ~ **lacrimogeno** tear gas grenade

candi'dare *vt* to present as candidate; **candidarsi** *vr* to present o.s. as candidate

candi'dato, -a *sm/f* candidate; (*aspirante a una carica*) applicant

candida'tura *sf* candidature; application

'candido, -a *ag* white as snow; (*puro*) pure; (*sincero*) sincere, candid

can'dito, -a *ag* candied

can'dore *sm* brilliant white; purity; sincerity, candour (*Brit*), candor (*US*)

'cane *sm* dog; (*di pistola, fucile*) cock; **fa un freddo ~** it's bitterly cold; **non c'era un ~** there wasn't a soul; **quell'attore è un ~** he's a rotten actor; ~ **da caccia** hunting dog; ~ **da guardia** guard dog; ~ **lupo** alsatian; ~ **da salotto** lap dog; ~ **da slitta** husky

ca'nestro *sm* basket; **fare un ~** (*Sport*) to shoot a basket

'canfora *sf* camphor

cangi'ante [kan'dʒante] *ag* iridescent; **seta ~** shot silk

can'guro *sm* kangaroo

ca'nicola *sf* scorching heat

ca'nile *sm* kennel; (*di allevamento*) kennels *pl*; ~ **municipale** dog pound

ca'nino, -a *ag, sm* canine

'canna *sf* (*pianta*) reed; (: *da zucchero*) cane; (*bastone*) stick, cane; (*di fucile*) barrel; (*di organo*) pipe; (*Droga*) joint; ~ **fumaria** chimney flue; ~ **da pesca** (fishing) rod; ~ **da zucchero** sugar cane

can'nella *sf* (*Cuc*) cinnamon; (*di conduttura, botte*) tap

cannel'loni *smpl* pasta tubes stuffed with sauce and baked

can'neto *sm* bed of reeds

can'nibale *sm* cannibal

cannocchi'ale [kannok'kjale] *sm* telescope

canno'nata *sf*: **è una vera ~!** (*fig*) it's (*o* he's *etc*) fantastic!

can'none *sm* (*Mil*) gun; (: *Storia*) cannon; (*tubo*) pipe, tube; (*piega*) box pleat; (*fig*) ace; **donna ~** fat woman

cannoni'ere *sm* (*Naut*) gunner; (*Calcio*) goal scorer

can'nuccia, -ce [kan'nuttʃa] *sf* (drinking) straw

'canone *sm* canon, criterion; (*mensile, annuo*) rent; fee; **legge dell'equo ~** fair rent act

ca'nonica, -che *sf* presbytery

ca'nonico, -ci *sm* (*Rel*) canon

canoniz'zare [kanonid'dzare] *vt* to canonize

ca'noro, -a *ag* (*uccello*) singing, song *cpd*

ca'notta *sf* vest

canot'taggio [kanot'taddʒo] *sm* rowing

canotti'era *sf* vest (*Brit*), undershirt (*US*)

ca'notto *sm* small boat, dinghy; canoe

cano'vaccio [kano'vattʃo] *sm* (*tela*) canvas; (*strofinaccio*) duster; (*trama*) plot

can'tante *sm/f* singer

can'tare *vt, vi* to sing; ~ **vittoria** to crow; **fare ~ qn** (*fig*) to make sb talk

cantas'torie *sm/f inv* storyteller

cantau'tore, -'trice *sm/f* singer-composer

canterel'lare *vt, vi* to hum, sing to o.s.

canticchi'are [kantik'kjare] *vt, vi* to hum, sing to o.s.

canti'ere *sm* (*Edil*) (building) site; (*anche*: **cantiere navale**) shipyard

canti'lena *sf* (*filastrocca*) lullaby; (*fig*) singsong voice

can'tina *sf* (*locale*) cellar; (*bottega*) wine shop

'canto *sm* song; (*arte*) singing; (*Rel*) chant; chanting; (*Poesia*) poem, lyric; (*parte di una poesia*) canto; (*parte, lato*): **da un ~** on the one hand; **d'altro ~** on the other hand

canto'nata *sf* (*di edificio*) corner; **prendere una ~** (*fig*) to blunder

can'tone *sm* (*in Svizzera*) canton

cantoni'era *ag*: (**casa**) ~ road inspector's house

can'tuccio [kan'tuttʃo] *sm* corner, nook

ca'nuto, -a *ag* white, whitehaired

canzo'nare [kantso'nare] *vt* to tease

canzona'tura [kantsona'tura] *sf* teasing; (*beffa*) joke

can'zone [kan'tsone] *sf* song; (*Poesia*) canzone

canzoni'ere [kantso'njere] *sm* (*Mus*) songbook; (*Letteratura*) collection of poems

'caos *sm inv* chaos

ca'otico, -a, ci, che *ag* chaotic

CAP *sigla m* = **codice di avviamento postale**

cap. *abbr* (= *capitolo*) ch.

ca'pace [ka'patʃe] *ag* able, capable; (*ampio, vasto*) large, capacious; **sei ~ di farlo?** can you *o* are you able to do it?; ~ **d'intendere e di volere** (*Dir*) in full possession of one's faculties

capacità [kapatʃi'ta] *sf inv* ability; (*Dir, di recipiente*) capacity; ~ **produttiva** production capacity

capaci'tarsi [kapatʃi'tarsi] *vr*: ~ **di** to make out, understand

ca'panna *sf* hut

capan'nello *sm* knot (of people)

57

ca'panno *sm* (*di cacciatori*) hide; (*da spiaggia*) bathing hut

capan'none *sm* (*Agr*) barn; (*fabbricato industriale*) (factory) shed

caparbietà *sf* stubbornness

ca'parbio, -a *ag* stubborn

ca'parra *sf* deposit, down payment

capa'tina *sf*: **fare una ~ da qn/in centro** to pop in on sb/into town

capeggi'are [kaped'dʒare] *vt* (*rivolta etc*) to head, lead

ca'pello *sm* hair; **capelli** *smpl* (*capigliatura*) hair *sg*; **averne fin sopra i capelli di qc/qn** to be fed up to the (back) teeth with sth/sb; **mi ci hanno tirato per i capelli** (*fig*) they dragged me into it; **tirato per i capelli** (*spiegazione*) far-fetched

capel'lone, -a *sm/f* hippie

capel'luto, -a *ag*: **cuoio ~ scalp**

capez'zale [kapet'tsale] *sm* bolster; (*fig*) bedside

ca'pezzolo [ka'pettsolo] *sm* nipple

capi'ente *ag* capacious

capi'enza [ka'pjɛntsa] *sf* capacity

capiglia'tura [kapiʎʎa'tura] *sf* hair

capil'lare *ag* (*fig*) detailed ■ *sm* (*Anat: anche:* **vaso capillare**) capillary

ca'pire *vt* to understand; **~ al volo** to catch on straight away; **si capisce!** (*certamente!*) of course!, certainly!

capi'tale *ag* (*mortale*) capital; (*fondamentale*) main *cpd*, chief *cpd* ■ *sf* (*città*) capital ■ *sm* (*Econ*) capital; **~ azionario** equity capital, share capital; **~ d'esercizio** working capital; **~ fisso** capital assets, fixed capital; **~ immobile** real estate; **~ liquido** cash assets *pl*; **~ mobile** movables *pl*; **~ di rischio** risk capital; **~ sociale** (*di società*) authorized capital; (*di club*) funds *pl*; **~ di ventura** venture capital, risk capital

capita'lismo *sm* capitalism

capita'lista, -i, e *ag, sm/f* capitalist

capitaliz'zare [kapitalid'dzare] *vt* to capitalize

capitalizzazi'one [kapitaliddzat'tsjone] *sf* capitalization

capita'nare *vt* to lead; (*Calcio*) to captain

capitane'ria *sf*: **~ (di porto)** port authorities *pl*

capi'tano *sm* captain; **~ di lungo corso** master mariner; **~ di ventura** (*Storia*) mercenary leader

capi'tare *vi* (*giungere casualmente*) to happen to go, find o.s.; (*accadere*) to happen; (*presentarsi: cosa*) to turn up, present itself ■ *vb impers* to happen; **~ a proposito/bene/male** to turn up at the right moment/at a good time/at a bad time; **mi è capitato un guaio** I've had a spot of trouble

capi'tello *sm* (*Archit*) capital

capito'lare *vi* to capitulate

capitolazi'one [kapitolat'tsjone] *sf* capitulation

ca'pitolo *sm* chapter; **capitoli** *smpl* (*Comm*) items; **non ho voce in ~** (*fig*) I have no say in the matter

capi'tombolo *sm* headlong fall, tumble

'capo *sm* (*Anat*) head; (*persona*) head, leader; (*: in ufficio*) head, boss; (*: in tribù*) chief; (*estremità: di tavolo, scale*) head, top; (*: di filo*) end; (*Geo*) cape; **andare a ~** to start a new paragraph; **"punto a ~"** "full stop — new paragraph"; **da ~** over again; **in ~ a** (*tempo*) within; **da un ~ all'altro** from one end to the other; **fra ~ e collo** (*all'improvviso*) out of the blue; **un discorso senza né ~ né coda** a senseless *o* meaningless speech; **~ d'accusa** (*Dir*) charge; **~ di bestiame** head *inv* of cattle; **C~ di Buona Speranza** Cape of Good Hope; **~ di vestiario** item of clothing

capo'banda (*pl* **capibanda**) *sm* (*Mus*) bandmaster; (*di malviventi, fig*) gang leader

ca'poccia [ka'pɔttʃa] *sm inv* (*di lavoranti*) overseer; (*peg: capobanda*) boss

capo'classe (*mpl* **capiclasse**, *fpl* **~**) *sm/f* (*Ins*) ≈ form captain (*Brit*), class president (*US*)

capocu'oco, -chi *sm* head cook

Capo'danno *sm* New Year

capofa'miglia [kapofa'miʎʎa] (*mpl* **capifamiglia**, *fpl* **~**) *sm/f* head of the family

capo'fitto; a ~ *av* headfirst, headlong

capo'giro [kapo'dʒiro] *sm* dizziness *no pl*; **da ~** (*fig*) astonishing, staggering

capo'gruppo (*mpl* **capigruppo**, *fpl* **~**) *sm/f* group leader

capola'voro, -i *sm* masterpiece

capo'linea (*pl* **capilinea**) *sm* terminus; (*fig*) end of the line

capo'lino *sm*: **far ~** to peep out (*o in etc*)

capo'lista (*mpl* **capilista**, *fpl* **~**) *sm/f* (*Pol*) top candidate on electoral list

capolu'ogo (*pl* **capoluoghi** *o* **capiluoghi**) *sm* chief town, administrative centre (*Brit*) *o* center (*US*)

capo'mastro (*pl* **capomastri** *o* **capimastri**) *sm* master builder

capo'rale *sm* (*Mil*) lance corporal (*Brit*), private first class (*US*)

capore'parto (*mpl* **capireparto**, *fpl* **~**) *sm/f* (*di operai*) foreman; (*di ufficio, negozio*) head of department

capo'sala *sf inv* (*Med*) ward sister

capo'saldo (*pl* **capisaldi**) *sm* stronghold; (*fig: fondamento*) basis, cornerstone

capo'squadra (*pl* **capisquadra**) *sm* (*di operai*) foreman, ganger; (*Mil*) squad leader; (*Sport*) team captain

capostazi'one (*pl* **capistazione**)
[kapostat'tsjone] *sm* station master
capos'tipite *sm* progenitor; (*fig*) earliest
example
capo'tavola (*mpl* **capitavola**, *fpl* **~**) *sm/f*
(*persona*) head of the table; **sedere a ~** to sit at
the head of the table
ca'pote [ka'pɔt] *sf inv* (*Aut*) hood (*Brit*), soft top
capo'treno (*pl* **capitreno** *o* **capotreni**) *sm* guard
capouf'ficio [kapouf'fitʃo] *sm/f inv* head clerk
Capo 'Verde *sm*: **il ~** Cape Verde
capo'verso *sm* (*di verso, periodo*) first line; (*Tip*)
indent; (*paragrafo*) paragraph; (*Dir: comma*)
section
capo'volgere [kapo'vɔldʒere] *vt* to overturn;
(*fig*) to reverse; **capovolgersi** *vr* to overturn;
(*barca*) to capsize; (*fig*) to be reversed
capovolgi'mento [kapovɔldʒi'mento] *sm*
(*fig*) reversal, complete change
capo'volto, -a *pp di* **capovolgere** ■ *ag* upside
down; (*barca*) capsized
'cappa *sf* (*mantello*) cape, cloak; (*del camino*)
hood
cap'pella *sf* (*Rel*) chapel
cappel'lano *sm* chaplain
cap'pello *sm* hat; **Tanto di ~!** (*fig*) I take my
hat off to you!; **~ a bombetta** bowler (hat),
derby (*US*); **~ a cilindro** top hat; **~ di paglia**
straw hat
'cappero *sm* caper
cap'pone *sm* capon
cappot'tare *vi* (*Aut*) to overturn
cap'potto *sm* (over)coat
cappuc'cino [kapput'tʃino] *sm* (*frate*)
Capuchin monk; (*bevanda*) cappuccino
cap'puccio [kap'puttʃo] *sm* (*copricapo*) hood;
(*della biro*) cap
'capra *sf* (she-)goat
ca'prese *ag* from (*o* of) Capri
ca'pretto *sm* kid
ca'priccio [ka'prittʃo] *sm* caprice, whim;
(*bizza*) tantrum; **fare i capricci** to be very
naughty; **~ della sorte** quirk of fate
capricci'oso, -a [kaprit'tʃoso] *ag* capricious,
whimsical; naughty
Capri'corno *sm* Capricorn; **essere del ~** (*dello
zodiaco*) to be Capricorn
capri'foglio [kapri'fɔʎʎo] *sm* honeysuckle
capri'ola *sf* somersault
capri'olo *sm* roe deer
'capro *sm* billy-goat; **~ espiatorio** (*fig*)
scapegoat
ca'prone *sm* billy-goat
'capsula *sf* capsule; (*di arma, per bottiglie*) cap
cap'tare *vt* (*Radio, TV*) to pick up; (*cattivarsi*) to
gain, win
CAR *sigla m* = **Centro Addestramento Reclute**

cara'bina *sf* rifle
carabini'ere *sm member of Italian military police
force; see note*

● **CARABINIERI**
●
● Originally part of the armed forces, the
● *Carabinieri* are police who now have civil
● as well as military duties, such as
● maintaining public order. They include
● paratroop units and mounted divisions
● and report to either the Minister of the
● Interior or the Minister of Defence,
● depending on the function they are
● performing.

Ca'racas *sf* Caracas
ca'raffa *sf* carafe
Ca'raibi *smpl*: **il mar dei ~** the Caribbean (Sea)
cara'ibico, -a, ci, che *ag* Caribbean
cara'mella *sf* sweet
cara'mello *sm* caramel
ca'rato *sm* (*di oro, diamante etc*) carat
ca'rattere *sm* character; (*caratteristica*)
characteristic, trait; **avere un buon ~** to be
good-natured; **informazione di ~ tecnico/
confidenziale** information of a technical/
confidential nature; **essere in ~ con qc**
(*intonarsi*) to be in harmony with sth; **~ jolly**
wild card
caratte'rino *sm* difficult nature *o* character
caratte'ristico, -a, ci, che *ag* characteristic
■ *sf* characteristic, feature; **segni
caratteristici** (*su passaporto etc*)
distinguishing marks
caratteriz'zare [karatterid'dzare] *vt* to
characterize, distinguish
carboi'drato *sm* carbohydrate
carbo'naio *sm* (*chi fa carbone*) charcoal-burner;
(*commerciante*) coalman, coal merchant
car'bone *sm* coal; **~ fossile** (pit) coal; **essere
o stare sui carboni ardenti** to be like a cat
on hot bricks
car'bonio *sm* (*Chim*) carbon
carboniz'zare [karbonid'dzare] *vt* (*legna*) to
carbonize; (*: parzialmente*) to char; **morire
carbonizzato** to be burned to death
carbu'rante *sm* (motor) fuel
carbura'tore *sm* carburettor
car'cassa *sf* carcass; (*fig: peg: macchina etc*) (old)
wreck
carce'rato, -a [kartʃe'rato] *sm/f* prisoner
'carcere ['kartʃere] *sm* prison; (*pena*)
imprisonment; **~ di massima sicurezza**
top-security prison
carceri'ere, -a [kartʃe'rjɛre] *sm/f* (*anche fig*)
jailer

carci'ofo [kar'tʃɔfo] *sm* artichoke
cardel'lino *sm* goldfinch
car'diaco, -a, ci, che *ag* cardiac, heart *cpd*
cardi'nale *ag, sm* cardinal
'cardine *sm* hinge
cardiolo'gia [kardjolo'dʒia] *sf* cardiology
cardi'ologo, -gi *sm* heart specialist, cardiologist
'cardo *sm* thistle
ca'rente *ag*: ~ **di** lacking in
ca'renza [ka'rentsa] *sf* lack, scarcity; (*vitaminica*) deficiency
cares'tia *sf* famine; (*penuria*) scarcity, dearth
ca'rezza [ka'rettsa] *sf* caress; **dare** *o* **fare una ~ a** (*persona*) to caress; (*animale*) to stroke, pat
carez'zare [karet'tsare] *vt* to caress, stroke, fondle
carez'zevole [karet'tsevole] *ag* sweet, endearing
'cargo, -ghi *sm* (*nave*) cargo boat, freighter; (*aereo*) freighter
cari'are *vt*, **cari'arsi** *vr* (*denti*) to decay
'carica *sf vedi* **carico**
caricabatte'rie *sm inv* (*Elettr*) battery charger
cari'care *vt* to load; (*aggravare: anche fig*) to weigh down; (*orologio*) to wind up; (*batteria, Mil*) to charge; (*Inform*) to load; **caricarsi** *vr*: **caricarsi di** to burden *o* load o.s. with; (*fig: di responsabilità, impegni*) to burden o.s. with
carica'tura *sf* caricature
'carico, -a, chi, che *ag* (*che porta un peso*): ~ **di** loaded *o* laden with; (*fucile*) loaded; (*orologio*) wound up; (*batteria*) charged; (*colore*) deep; (*caffè, tè*) strong ◼ *sm* (*il caricare*) loading; (*ciò che si carica*) load; (*Comm*) shipment; (*fig: peso*) burden, weight ◼ *sf* (*mansione ufficiale*) office, position; (*Mil, Tecn, Elettr*) charge; ~ **di debiti** up to one's ears in debt; **persona a ~** dependent; **essere a ~ di qn** (*spese etc*) to be charged to sb; (*accusa, prova*) to be against sb; **testimone a ~** witness for the prosecution; **farsi ~ di** (*problema, responsabilità*) to take on; **a ~ del cliente** at the customer's expense; **~ di lavoro** (*di ditta, reparto*) workload; **~ utile** payload; **capacità di ~** cargo capacity; **entrare/essere in carica** to come into/be in office; **ricoprire** *o* **rivestire una carica** to hold a position; **uscire di carica** to leave office; **dare la carica a** (*orologio*) to wind up; (*fig: persona*) to back up; **tornare alla carica** (*fig*) to insist, persist; **ha una forte carica di simpatia** he's very likeable
'carie *sf* (*dentaria*) decay
ca'rino, -a *ag* lovely, pretty, nice; (*simpatico*) nice
ca'risma [ka'rizma] *sm* charisma
caris'matico, -a, ci, che *ag* charismatic

carità *sf* charity; **per ~!** (*escl di rifiuto*) good heavens, no!
carita'tevole *ag* charitable
carnagi'one [karna'dʒone] *sf* complexion
car'nale *ag* (*amore*) carnal; (*fratello*) blood *cpd*
'carne *sf* flesh; (*bovina, ovina etc*) meat; **in ~ e ossa** in the flesh, in person; **essere (bene) in ~** to be well padded, be plump; **non essere né ~ né pesce** (*fig*) to be neither fish nor fowl; **~ di manzo/maiale/pecora** beef/pork/mutton; **~ in scatola** tinned *o* canned meat; **~ tritata** mince (*Brit*), hamburger meat (*US*), minced (*Brit*) *o* ground (*US*) meat
car'nefice [kar'nefitʃe] *sm* executioner; hangman
carnefi'cina [karnefi'tʃina] *sf* carnage; (*fig*) disaster
carne'vale *sm* carnival; **C~** *see note*

◉ **CARNEVALE**
◉
◉ *Carnevale* is the name given to the period
◉ between Epiphany (6 January) and the
◉ beginning of Lent, when people throw
◉ parties, put on processions with
◉ spectacular floats, build bonfires in the
◉ "piazze" and dress up in fabulous
◉ costumes and masks. Building to a peak
◉ just before Lent, *Carnevale* culminates in
◉ the festivities of Martedì grasso (Shrove
◉ Tuesday).

car'nivoro, -a *ag* carnivorous
car'noso, -a *ag* fleshy; (*pianta, frutto, radice*) pulpy; (*labbra*) full
'caro, -a *ag* (*amato*) dear; (*costoso*) dear, expensive; **se ti è cara la vita** if you value your life
ca'rogna [ka'roɲɲa] *sf* carrion; (*fig fam*) swine
caro'sello *sm* merry-go-round
ca'rota *sf* carrot
caro'vana *sf* caravan
caro'vita *sm* high cost of living
'carpa *sf* carp
Car'pazi [kar'patsi] *smpl*: **i ~** the Carpathian Mountains
carpente'ria *sf* carpentry
carpenti'ere *sm* carpenter
car'pire *vt*: **~ qc a qn** (*segreto etc*) to get sth out of sb
car'poni *av* on all fours
car'rabile *ag* suitable for vehicles; **"passo ~"** "keep clear"
car'raio, -a *ag*: **passo ~** vehicle entrance
carré *sm* (*acconciatura*) bob
carreggi'ata [karred'dʒata] *sf* carriageway (*Brit*), roadway; **rimettersi in ~** (*fig*:

recuperare) to catch up; **tenersi in** ~ (*fig*) to keep up to the right path

carrel'lata *sf* (*Cine, TV: tecnica*) tracking; (: *scena*) running shot; ~ **di successi** medley of hit tunes

car'rello *sm* trolley; (*Aer*) undercarriage; (*Cine*) dolly; (*di macchina da scrivere*) carriage

car'retta *sf*: **tirare la** ~ (*fig*) to plod along

car'retto *sm* handcart

carri'era *sf* career; **fare** ~ to get on; **ufficiale di** ~ (*Mil*) regular officer; **a gran** ~ at full speed

carri'ola *sf* wheelbarrow

'carro *sm* cart, wagon; **il Gran/Piccolo C~** (*Astr*) the Great/Little Bear; **mettere il** ~ **avanti ai buoi** (*fig*) to put the cart before the horse; ~ **armato** tank; (*: attrezzi* (*Aut*) breakdown van (*Brit*), tow truck (*US*); ~ **funebre** hearse; ~ **merci/bestiame** (*Ferr*) goods/animal wagon

car'roccio [kar'rɔtʃo] *sm* (*Pol*): **il C~** *symbol of Lega Nord*

car'rozza [kar'rɔttsa] *sf* carriage, coach; ~ **letto** (*Ferr*) sleeper; ~ **ristorante** (*Ferr*) dining car

carroz'zella [karrot'tsɛlla] *sf* (*per bambini*) pram (*Brit*), baby carriage (*US*); (*per invalidi*) wheelchair

carrozze'ria [karrottse'ria] *sf* body, coachwork (*Brit*); (*officina*) coachbuilder's workshop (*Brit*), body shop

carrozzi'ere [karrot'tsjere] *sm* (*Aut: progettista*) car designer; (*: meccanico*) coachbuilder

carroz'zina [karrot'tsina] *sf* pram (*Brit*), baby carriage (*US*)

carroz'zone [karrot'tsone] *sm* (*da circo, di zingari*) caravan

car'rucola *sf* pulley

'carta *sf* paper; (*al ristorante*) menu; (*Geo*) map; plan; (*documento, da gioco*) card; (*costituzione*) charter; **carte** *sfpl* (*documenti*) papers, documents; **alla** ~ (*al ristorante*) à la carte; **cambiare le carte in tavola** (*fig*) to shift one's ground; **fare carte false** (*fig*) to go to great lengths; ~ **assegni** bank card; ~ **assorbente** blotting paper; ~ **bollata** *o* **da bollo** (*Amm*) official stamped paper; ~ **di credito** credit card; ~ **di debito** cash card; ~ **fedeltà** loyalty card; ~ (**geografica**) map; ~ **d'identità** identity card; ~ **igienica** toilet paper; ~ **d'imbarco** (*Aer, Naut*) boarding card, boarding pass; ~ **da lettere** writing paper; ~ **libera** (*Amm*) unstamped paper; ~ **millimetrata** graph paper; ~ **oleata** waxed paper; ~ **da pacchi, ~ da imballo** wrapping paper, brown paper; ~ **da parati** wallpaper; ~ **verde** (*Aut*) green card; ~ **vetrata** sandpaper; ~ **da visita** visiting card

cartacar'bone (*pl* **cartecarbone**) *sf* carbon paper

car'taccia, -ce [kar'tattʃa] *sf* waste paper

cartamo'dello *sm* (*Cucito*) paper pattern

cartamo'neta *sf* paper money

carta'pecora *sf* parchment

carta'pesta *sf* papier-mâché

cartas'traccia [kartas'trattʃa] *sf* waste paper

car'teggio [kar'teddʒo] *sm* correspondence

car'tella *sf* (*scheda*) card; (*custodia: di cartone, Inform*) folder; (: *di uomo d'affari etc*) briefcase; (: *di scolaro*) schoolbag, satchel; ~ **clinica** (*Med*) case sheet

cartel'lino *sm* (*etichetta*) label; (*su porta*) notice; (*scheda*) card; **timbrare il** ~ (*all'entrata*) to clock in; (*all'uscita*) to clock out; ~ **di presenza** clock card, timecard

car'tello *sm* sign; (*pubblicitario*) poster; (*stradale*) sign, signpost; (*in dimostrazioni*) placard; (*Econ*) cartel

cartel'lone *sm* (*pubblicitario*) advertising poster; (*della tombola*) scoring frame; (*Teat*) playbill; **tenere il** ~ (*spettacolo*) to have a long run

carti'era *sf* paper mill

carti'lagine [karti'ladʒine] *sf* cartilage

car'tina *sf* (*Aut, Geo*) map

car'toccio [kar'tɔttʃo] *sm* paper bag; **cuocere al** ~ (*Cuc*) to bake in tinfoil

carto'grafia *sf* cartography

carto'laio, -a *sm/f* stationer

cartolarizzazi'one [kartolariddza'tsjone] *sf* securitization

cartole'ria *sf* stationer's (shop (*Brit*))

carto'lina *sf* postcard; ~ **di auguri** greetings card; ~ **precetto** *o* **rosa** (*Mil*) call-up card

carto'mante *sm/f* fortune-teller (*using cards*)

carton'cino [karton'tʃino] *sm* (*materiale*) thin cardboard; (*biglietto*) card; ~ **della società** compliments slip

car'tone *sm* cardboard; (*del latte, dell'aranciata*) carton; (*Arte*) cartoon; **cartoni animati** (*Cine*) cartoons

car'tuccia, -ce [kar'tuttʃa] *sf* cartridge; ~ **a salve** blank cartridge; **mezza** ~ (*fig: persona*) good-for-nothing

'casa *sf* house; (*specialmente la propria casa*) home; (*Comm*) firm, house; **essere a** ~ to be at home; **vado a** ~ **mia/tua** I'm going home/to your house; ~ **di correzione** ≈ community home (*Brit*), reformatory (*US*); ~ **di cura** nursing home; ~ **editrice** publishing house; **C~ delle Libertà** House of Liberties, *centre-right coalition*; ~ **di riposo** (old people's) home, care home; ~ **dello studente** student hostel; ~ **di tolleranza, ~ d'appuntamenti** brothel; **case popolari** ≈ council houses (*o* flats) (*Brit*), ≈ public housing units (*US*)

ca'sacca, -che *sf* military coat; (*di fantino*) blouse ca'sale *sm* (*gruppo di case*) hamlet; (*casa di campagna*) farmhouse

casa'lingo, -a, ghi, ghe *ag* household, domestic; (*fatto a casa*) home-made; (*semplice*) homely; (*amante della casa*) home-loving ■ *sf* housewife; casalinghi *smpl* (*oggetti*) household articles; cucina casalinga plain home cooking

ca'sata *sf* family lineage

ca'sato *sm* family name

casca'morto *sm* woman-chaser; fare il ~ to chase women

cas'care *vi* to fall; ~ bene/male (*fig*) to land lucky/unlucky; ~ dalle nuvole (*fig*) to be taken aback; ~ dal sonno to be falling asleep on one's feet; caschi il mondo no matter what; non cascherà il mondo se ... it won't be the end of the world if ...

cas'cata *sf* fall; (*d'acqua*) cascade, waterfall

cascherò *etc* [kaske'rɔ] *vb vedi* cascare

ca'scina [kaʃʃina] *sf* farmstead

casci'nale [kaʃʃi'nale] *sm* (*casolare*) farmhouse; (*cascina*) farmstead

'casco (*pl* caschi) *sm* helmet; (*del parrucchiere*) hair-dryer; (*di banane*) bunch; ~ blu (*Mil*) blue helmet (UN *soldier*)

caseggi'ato [kased'dʒato] *sm* (*edificio*) large block of flats (*Brit*) *o* apartment building (US); (*gruppo di case*) group of houses

casei'ficio [kazei'fitʃo] *sm* creamery

ca'sella *sf* pigeonhole; ~ email mailbox; ~ postale post office box

casel'lario *sm* (*mobile*) filing cabinet; (*raccolta di pratiche*) files *pl*; ~ giudiziale court records *pl*; ~ penale police files *pl*

ca'sello *sm* (*di autostrada*) tollgate

case'reccio, -a, ci, ce [kase'rettʃo] *ag* home-made

ca'serma *sf* barracks

caser'tano, -a *ag* of (*o* from) Caserta

ca'sino *sm* (*confusione*) row, racket; (*casa di prostituzione*) brothel

casinò *sm inv* casino

ca'sistica *sf* (*Med*) record of cases; secondo la ~ degli incidenti stradali according to road accident data

'caso *sm* chance; (*fatto, vicenda*) event, incident; (*possibilità*) possibility; (*Med, Ling*) case; a ~ at random; per ~ by chance, by accident; in ogni ~, in tutti i casi in any case, at any rate; in ~ contrario otherwise; al ~ should the opportunity arise; nel ~ che in case; ~ mai if by chance; far ~ a qc/qn to pay attention to sth/sb; fare *o* porre *o* mettere il ~ che to suppose that; fa proprio al ~ nostro it's just what we need; guarda ~ ... strangely enough ...; è il ~ che ce ne

andiamo we'd better go; ~ limite borderline case

caso'lare *sm* cottage

'Caspio *sm*: il mar ~ the Caspian Sea

'caspita *escl* (*di sorpresa*) good heavens!; (*di impazienza*) for goodness' sake!

'cassa *sf* case, crate, box; (*bara*) coffin; (*mobile*) chest; (*involucro: di orologio etc*) case; (*macchina*) cash register; (*luogo di pagamento*) cash desk, checkout (counter); (*fondo*) fund; (*istituto bancario*) bank; battere ~ (*fig*) to come looking for money; ~ automatica prelievi automatic telling machine, cash dispenser; ~ continua night safe; mettere in ~ integrazione = to lay off; C~ del Mezzogiorno *development fund for the South of Italy*; ~ mutua *o* malattia health insurance scheme; ~ di risonanza (*Mus*) soundbox; (*fig*) platform; ~ di risparmio savings bank; ~ rurale e artigiana credit institution (*serving farmers and craftsmen*); ~ toracica (*Anat*) chest

cassa'forte (*pl* casseforti) *sf* safe

cassa'panca (*pl* cassapanche *o* cassepanche) *sf* settle

casseru'ola, casse'rola *sf* saucepan

cas'setta *sf* box; (*per registratore*) cassette; (*Cine, Teat*) box-office takings *pl*; pane a *o* in ~ toasting loaf; film di ~ (*commerciale*) box-office draw; far ~ to be a box-office success; ~ delle lettere letterbox; ~ di sicurezza strongbox

cas'setto *sm* drawer

casset'tone *sm* chest of drawers

cassi'ere, -a *sm/f* cashier; (*di banca*) teller

cassinte'grato, -a *sm/f person who has been laid off*

cas'sone *sm* (*cassa*) large case, large chest

'casta *sf* caste

cas'tagna [kas'taɲɲa] *sf* chestnut; prendere qn in ~ (*fig*) to catch sb in the act

cas'tagno [kas'taɲɲo] *sm* chestnut (tree)

cas'tano, -a *ag* chestnut (brown)

cas'tello *sm* castle; (*Tecn*) scaffolding

casti'gare *vt* to punish

casti'gato, -a *ag* (*casto, modesto*) pure, chaste; (*emendato: prosa, versione*) expurgated, amended

cas'tigo, -ghi *sm* punishment; mettere/ essere in ~ to punish/be punished

castità *sf* chastity

'casto, -a *ag* chaste, pure

cas'toro *sm* beaver

cas'trante *ag* frustrating

cas'trare *vt* to castrate; to geld; to doctor (*Brit*), fix (US); (*fig: iniziativa*) to frustrate

castrone'ria *sf* (*fam*): dire castronerie to talk rubbish

casu'ale *ag* chance *cpd*

ca'supola *sf* simple little cottage

catac'lisma, -i *sm* (*fig*) catastrophe

cata'comba *sf* catacomb

cata'fascio [kata'faʃʃo] *sm*: **andare a ~** to collapse; **mandare a ~** to wreck

cata'litico, -a, ci, che *ag*: **marmitta catalitica** (*Aut*) catalytic converter

cataliz'zare [katalid'dzare] *vt* (*fig*) to act as a catalyst (up)on

cataliz'zato, -a [katalid'dzato] *ag* (*Aut*) with catalytic converter

catalizza'tore [kataliddza'tore] *sm* (*anche fig*) catalyst; (*Aut*) catalytic converter

Cata'logna [kata'loɲɲa] *sf*: **la ~** Catalonia

ca'talogo, -ghi *sm* catalogue; **~ dei prezzi** price list

cata'nese *ag* of (*o* from) Catania

catanza'rese [katandza'rese] *ag* of (*o* from) Catanzaro

cata'pecchia [kata'pekkja] *sf* hovel

cata'pulta *sf* catapult

catarifran'gente [katarifran'dʒɛnte] *sm* (*Aut*) reflector

ca'tarro *sm* catarrh

ca'tarsi *sf inv* catharsis

ca'tasta *sf* stack, pile

ca'tasto *sm* land register; land registry office

ca'tastrofe *sf* catastrophe, disaster

catas'trofico, -a, ci, che *ag* (*evento*) catastrophic; (*persona, previsione*) pessimistic

catastro'fista, -i, e *ag, sm/f* doom-monger; **non fare il ~** don't be so pessimistic

cate'chismo [kate'kizmo] *sm* catechism

catego'ria *sf* category; (*di albergo*) class

cate'gorico, -a, ci, che *ag* categorical

ca'tena *sf* chain; **reazione a ~** chain reaction; **susseguirsi a ~** to happen in quick succession; **~ alimentare** food chain; **~ di montaggio** assembly line; **~ montuosa** mountain range; **catene da neve** (*Aut*) snow chains

cate'naccio [kate'nattʃo] *sm* bolt

cate'nella *sf* (*ornamento*) chain; (*di orologio*) watch chain; (*di porta*) door chain

cate'ratta *sf* cataract; (*chiusa*) sluice gate

ca'terva *sf* (*di cose*) loads *pl*, heaps *pl*; (*di persone*) horde

cate'tere *sm* (*Med*) catheter

cati'nella *sf*: **piovere a catinelle** to pour, rain cats and dogs

ca'tino *sm* basin

ca'todico, -a, ci, che *ag*: **tubo a raggi catodici** cathode-ray tube

ca'torcio [ka'tɔrtʃo] *sm* (*peg*) old wreck

ca'trame *sm* tar

'cattedra *sf* teacher's desk; (*di università*) chair; **salire** *o* **montare in ~** (*fig*) to pontificate

catte'drale *sf* cathedral

catte'dratico, -a, ci, che *ag* (*insegnamento*) university *cpd*; (*ironico*) pedantic ■ *sm/f* professor

catti'veria *sf* (*qualità*) wickedness; (*di bambino*) naughtiness; (*azione*) wicked action; **fare una ~** to do something wicked; to be naughty

cattività *sf* captivity

cat'tivo, -a *ag* bad; (*malvagio*) bad, wicked; (*turbolento: bambino*) bad, naughty; (*: mare*) rough; (*odore, sapore*) nasty, bad ■ *sm/f* bad *o* wicked person; **farsi ~ sangue** to worry, get in a state; **farsi un ~ nome** to earn o.s. a bad reputation; **i cattivi** (*nei film*) the baddies (*Brit*), the bad guys (*US*)

cattocomu'nista, -i, e *ag combining Catholic and communist ideas*

cattoli'cesimo [kattoli'tʃezimo] *sm* Catholicism

cat'tolico, -a, ci, che *ag, sm/f* (Roman) Catholic

cat'tura *sf* capture

cattu'rare *vt* to capture

cau'casico, -a, ci, che *ag, sm/f* Caucasian

'Caucaso *sm*: **il ~** the Caucasus

cauc'ciù [kaut'tʃu] *sm* rubber

'causa *sf* cause; (*Dir*) lawsuit, case, action; **a ~ di** because of; **per ~ sua** because of him; **fare** *o* **muovere ~ a qn** to take legal action against sb; **parte in ~** litigant

cau'sale *ag* (*Ling*) causal ■ *sf* cause, reason

cau'sare *vt* to cause

'caustico, -a, ci, che *ag* caustic

cau'tela *sf* caution, prudence

caute'lare *vt* to protect; **cautelarsi** *vr*: **cautelarsi (da** *o* **contro)** to take precautions (against)

'cauto, -a *ag* cautious, prudent

cauzio'nare [kauttsjo'nare] *vt* to guarantee

cauzi'one [kaut'tsjone] *sf* security; (*Dir*) bail; **rilasciare dietro ~** to release on bail

cav. *abbr* = **cavaliere**

'cava *sf* quarry

caval'care *vt* (*cavallo*) to ride; (*muro*) to sit astride; (*ponte*) to span

caval'cata *sf* ride; (*gruppo di persone*) riding party

cavalca'via *sm inv* flyover

cavalci'oni [kaval'tʃoni]: **a ~ di** *prep* astride

cavali'ere *sm* rider; (*feudale, titolo*) knight; (*soldato*) cavalryman; (*al ballo*) partner

cavalleg'gero [kavalled'dʒero] *sm* (*Mil*) light cavalryman

cavalle'resco, -a, schi, sche *ag* chivalrous
cavalle'ria *sf* chivalry; (*milizia a cavallo*) cavalry
cavalle'rizzo, -a [kavalle'rittso] *sm/f* riding instructor; circus rider
caval'letta *sf* grasshopper; (*dannosa*) locust
caval'letto *sm* (Fot) tripod; (*da pittore*) easel
caval'lina *sf* (*Ginnastica*) horse; (*gioco*) leap-frog; **correre la ~** (*fig*) to sow one's wild oats
ca'vallo *sm* horse; (*Scacchi*) knight; (*Aut: anche:* **cavallo vapore**) horsepower; (*dei pantaloni*) crotch; **a ~** on horseback; **a ~ di** astride, straddling; **siamo a ~** (*fig*) we've made it; **da ~** (*fig: dose*) drastic; (*: febbre*) raging; **vivere a ~ tra due periodi** to straddle two periods; **~ di battaglia** (*Teat*) tour de force; (*fig*) hobbyhorse; **~ da corsa** racehorse; **~ a dondolo** rocking horse; **~ da sella** saddle horse; **~ da soma** packhorse
ca'vare *vt* (*togliere*) to draw out, extract, take out; (*: giacca, scarpe*) to take off; (*: fame, sete, voglia*) to satisfy; **cavarsi** *vr*: **cavarsi da** (*guai, problemi*) to get out of; **cavarsela** to get away with it; to manage, get on all right; **non ci caverà un bel nulla** you'll get nothing out of it (*o him etc*)
cava'tappi *sm inv* corkscrew
ca'verna *sf* cave
caver'noso, -a *ag* (*luogo*) cavernous; (*fig: voce*) deep; (*: tosse*) raucous
ca'vezza [ka'vettsa] *sf* halter
'cavia *sf* guinea pig
cavi'ale *sm* caviar
ca'viglia [ka'viʎʎa] *sf* ankle
cavil'lare *vi* to quibble
ca'villo *sm* quibble
cavil'loso, -a *ag* quibbling, hair-splitting
cavità *sf inv* cavity
'cavo, -a *ag* hollow ■ *sm* (*Anat*) cavity; (*grossa corda*) rope, cable; (*Elettr, Tel*) cable
cavo'lata *sf* (*fam*) stupid thing
cavolfi'ore *sm* cauliflower
'cavolo *sm* cabbage; **non m'importa un ~** (*fam*) I don't give a hoot; **che ~ vuoi?** (*fam*) what the heck do you want?; **~ di Bruxelles** Brussels sprout
caz'zata [kat'tsata] *sf* (*fam!: stupidaggine*) stupid thing, something stupid
'cazzo ['kattso] *sm* (*fam!: pene*) prick (!); **non gliene importa un ~** (*fig fam!*) he doesn't give a damn about it; **fatti i cazzi tuoi** (*fig fam!*) mind your own damn business
caz'zotto [kat'tsɔtto] *sm* punch; **fare a cazzotti** to have a punch-up
cazzu'ola [kat'tswɔla] *sf* trowel
CB *sigla* = **Campobasso**
CC *abbr* = **Carabinieri**

cc *abbr* (= *centimetro cubico*) cc
C.C. *abbr* = **codice civile**
c.c. *abbr* (= *conto corrente*) c/a, a/c; (*Elettr*) *vedi* **corrente continua**
c/c *abbr* (= *conto corrente*) c/a, a/c
C.C.D. *sigla m* (*Pol*: = *Centro Cristiano Democratico*) party originating from Democrazia Cristiana
CCI *sigla f* (= *Camera di Commercio Internazionale*) ICC (= *International Chamber of Commerce*)
CCIAA *abbr* = **Camera di Commercio Industria, Agricoltura e Artigianato**
CCT *sigla m* = **certificato di credito del Tesoro**
C.D. *abbr* (= *Corpo Diplomatico*) CD ■ *sm inv* (= *compact disc*) CD
c.d. *abbr* = **cosiddetto**
C.d.A. *abbr* = **Consiglio di Amministrazione**
c.d.d. *abbr* (= *come dovevasi dimostrare*) QED (= *quod erat demonstrandum*)
C.d.M. *abbr* = **Cassa del Mezzogiorno**
CD-Rom [tʃidi'rɔm] *sigla m inv* (= *Compact Disc Read Only Memory*) CD-Rom
C.d.U. [tʃidi'u] *sigla m* (= *Cristiano Democratici Uniti*) United Christian Democrats (*Italian centre-right political party*)
CE *sigla* = **Caserta**
ce [tʃe] *pron, av vedi* **ci**
C.E. *sigla* = **Consiglio d'Europa**
cec'chino [tʃek'kino] *sm* sniper; (*Pol*) member of parliament who votes against his own party
'cece ['tʃetʃe] *sm* chickpea, garbanzo (US)
Ce'cenia [tʃe'tʃenja] *sf* Chechnya
ce'ceno, -a [tʃe'tʃeno] *ag, sm/f* Chechen
cecità [tʃetʃi'ta] *sf* blindness
'ceco, -a, chi, che ['tʃɛko] *ag, sm/f, sm* Czech; **la Repubblica Ceca** the Czech Republic
Cecoslo'vacchia [tʃekozlo'vakkja] *sf*: **la ~** Czechoslovakia
cecoslo'vacco, -a, chi, che [tʃekozlo'vakko] *ag, sm/f* Czechoslovakian
CED [tʃɛd] *sigla m* = **centro elaborazione dati**
'cedere ['tʃedere] *vt* (*concedere: posto*) to give up; (*Dir*) to transfer, make over ■ *vi* (*cadere*) to give way, subside; **~ (a)** to surrender (to), yield (to), give in (to); **~ il passo (a qn)** to let (sb) pass in front; **~ il passo a qc** (*fig*) to give way to sth; **~ la parola (a qn)** to hand over (to sb)
ce'devole [tʃe'devole] *ag* (*terreno*) soft; (*fig*) yielding
'cedola ['tʃedola] *sf* (*Comm*) coupon; voucher
ce'drata [tʃe'drata] *sf* citron juice
'cedro ['tʃedro] *sm* cedar; (*albero da frutto, frutto*) citron
'CEE ['tʃɛe] *sigla f* = **Comunità Economica Europea**
'ceffo ['tʃeffo] *sm* (*peg*) ugly mug
cef'fone [tʃef'fone] *sm* slap, smack
'ceko, -a ['tʃɛko] *ag, sm/f, sm* = **ceko**

ce'lare [tʃe'lare] vt to conceal; **celarsi** vr to hide

cele'brare [tʃele'brare] vt to celebrate; (*cerimonia*) to hold; **~ le lodi di qc/qn** to sing the praises of sth/sb

celebrazi'one [tʃelebrat'tsjone] sf celebration

'celebre ['tʃɛlebre] ag famous, celebrated

celebrità [tʃelebri'ta] sf inv fame; (*persona*) celebrity

'celere ['tʃɛlere] ag fast, swift; (*corso*) crash cpd ■ sf (*Polizia*) riot police

ce'leste [tʃe'lɛste] ag celestial; heavenly; (*colore*) sky-blue

'celia ['tʃɛlja] sf joke; **per ~** for a joke

celi'bato [tʃeli'bato] sm celibacy

'celibe ['tʃɛlibe] ag single, unmarried ■ sm bachelor

'cella ['tʃɛlla] sf cell; **~ di rigore** punishment cell

cello'phane® [sɛlo'fan] sm cellophane®

'cellula ['tʃɛllula] sf (*Biol, Elettr, Pol*) cell

cellu'lare [tʃellu'lare] ag cellular ■ sm (*furgone*) police van; (*telefono*) cellphone; **segregazione ~** (*Dir*) solitary confinement

cellu'lite [tʃellu'lite] sf cellulitis

'celta ['tʃɛlta] sm/f Celt

'celtico, -a, ci, che ['tʃɛltiko] ag, sm Celtic

'cembalo ['tʃembalo] sm (*Mus*) harpsichord

cemen'tare [tʃemen'tare] vt (*anche fig*) to cement

ce'mento [tʃe'mento] sm cement; **~ armato** reinforced concrete

'cena ['tʃena] sf dinner; (*leggera*) supper

ce'nacolo [tʃe'nakolo] sm (*circolo*) coterie, circle; (*Rel, dipinto*) Last Supper

ce'nare [tʃe'nare] vi to dine, have dinner

'cencio ['tʃentʃo] sm piece of cloth, rag; (*per spolverare*) duster; **essere bianco come un ~** to be as white as a sheet

'cenere ['tʃenere] sf ash

Cene'rentola [tʃene'rentola] sf (*anche fig*) Cinderella

'cenno ['tʃenno] sm (*segno*) sign, signal; (*gesto*) gesture; (*col capo*) nod; (*con la mano*) wave; (*allusione*) hint, mention; (*breve esposizione*) short account; **far ~ di sì/no** to nod (one's head)/shake one's head; **~ d'intesa** sign of agreement; **cenni di storia dell'arte** an outline of the history of art

censi'mento [tʃensi'mento] sm census

cen'sire [tʃen'sire] vt to take a census of

'CENSIS ['tʃensis] sigla m (= Centro Studi Investimenti Sociali) independent institute carrying out research on Italy's social and cultural welfare

cen'sore [tʃen'sore] sm censor

cen'sura [tʃen'sura] sf censorship; censor's office; (*fig*) censure

censu'rare [tʃensu'rare] vt to censor; to censure

cent. abbr = centesimo

centelli'nare [tʃentelli'nare] vt to sip; (*fig*) to savour (*Brit*), savor (*US*)

cente'nario, -a [tʃente'narjo] ag (*che ha cento anni*) hundred-year-old; (*che ricorre ogni cento anni*) centennial, centenary cpd ■ sm/f centenarian ■ sm centenary

cen'tesimo, -a [tʃen'tɛzimo] ag, sm hundredth; (*di euro, dollaro*) cent; **essere senza un ~** to be penniless

cen'tigrado, -a [tʃen'tigrado] ag centigrade; **20 gradi centigradi** 20 degrees centigrade

cen'tilitro [tʃen'tilitro] sm centilitre

cen'timetro [tʃen'timetro] sm centimetre (*Brit*), centimeter (*US*); (*nastro*) measuring tape (*in centimetres*)

centi'naio [tʃenti'najo] (*pl(f)* **centinaia**) sm: **un ~ (di)** a hundred; about a hundred

'cento ['tʃɛnto] num a hundred, one hundred; **per ~** per cent; **al ~ per ~** a hundred per cent; **~ di questi giorni!** many happy returns (of the day)!

cento'dieci [tʃento'djɛtʃi] num one hundred and ten; **~ e lode** (*Università*) ≈ first-class honours

cento'mila [tʃento'mila] num a o one hundred thousand; **te l'ho detto ~ volte** (*fig*) I've told you a thousand times

Cen'trafrica [tʃen'trafrika] sm: **il ~** the Central African Republic

cen'trale [tʃen'trale] ag central ■ sf: **~ elettrica** electric power station; **~ eolica** wind farm; **~ del latte** dairy; **~ di polizia** police headquarters pl; **~ telefonica** (telephone) exchange; **sede ~** head office

centrali'nista [tʃentrali'nista] sm/f operator

centra'lino [tʃentra'lino] sm (telephone) exchange; (*di albergo etc*) switchboard

centraliz'zare [tʃentralid'dzare] vt to centralize

cen'trare [tʃen'trare] vt to hit the centre (*Brit*) o center (*US*) of; (*Tecn*) to centre; **~ una risposta** to get the right answer; **ha centrato il problema** you've hit the nail on the head

centra'vanti [tʃentra'vanti] sm inv centre forward

cen'trifuga [tʃen'trifuga] sf spin-dryer

centrifu'gare [tʃentrifu'gare] vt (*Tecn*) to centrifuge; (*biancheria*) to spin-dry

'centro ['tʃentro] sm centre (*Brit*), center (*US*); **fare ~** to hit the bull's eye; (*Calcio*) to score; (*fig*) to hit the nail on the head; **~ balneare** seaside resort; **~ commerciale** shopping centre; (*città*) commercial centre; **~ di costo** cost centre; **~ elaborazione dati** data-processing unit; **~ ospedaliero** hospital complex; **~ di permanenza temporanea** reception centre; **~ sociale** community centre; **centri vitali** (anche fig) vital organs

centro'destra [tʃentro'dɛstra] sm (Pol) centre right

centromedi'ano [tʃentrome'djano] sm (Calcio) centre half

centrosi'nistra [tʃentrosi'nistra] sm (Pol) centre left

'**ceppo** ['tʃeppo] sm (di albero) stump; (pezzo di legno) log

'**cera** ['tʃera] sf wax; (aspetto) appearance, look; **~ per pavimenti** floor polish

cera'lacca [tʃera'lakka] sf sealing wax

ce'ramica [tʃe'ramika] (pl **ceramiche**) sf ceramic; (Arte) ceramics sg

cerbi'atto [tʃer'bjatto] sm fawn

'**cerca** ['tʃerka] sf: **in** o **alla ~ di** in search of

cercaper'sone [tʃerkaper'sone] sm inv bleeper

cer'care [tʃer'kare] vt to look for, search for
■ vi: **~ di fare qc** to try to do sth

cercherò etc [tʃerke'rɔ] vb vedi **cercare**

'**cerchia** ['tʃerkja] sf circle

cerchi'ato, -a [tʃer'kjato] ag: **occhiali cerchiati d'osso** horn-rimmed spectacles; **avere gli occhi cerchiati** to have dark rings under one's eyes

'**cerchio** ['tʃerkjo] sm circle; (giocattolo, di botte) hoop; **dare un colpo al ~ e uno alla botte** (fig) to keep two things going at the same time

cerchi'one [tʃer'kjone] sm (wheel) rim

cere'ale [tʃere'ale] sm cereal

cere'brale [tʃere'brale] ag cerebral

ceri'monia [tʃeri'mɔnja] sf ceremony; **senza tante cerimonie** (senza formalità) informally; (bruscamente) unceremoniously, without so much as a by-your-leave

cerimoni'ale [tʃerimo'njale] sm etiquette; ceremonial

cerimoni'ere [tʃerimo'njere] sm master of ceremonies

cerimoni'oso, -a [tʃerimo'njoso] ag formal, ceremonious

ce'rino [tʃe'rino] sm wax match

CERN [tʃern] sigla m (= Comitato Europeo di Ricerche Nucleari) CERN

'**cernia** ['tʃernja] sf (Zool) stone bass

cerni'era [tʃer'njera] sf hinge; **~ lampo** zip (fastener) (Brit), zipper (US)

cer'nita ['tʃernita] sf selection; **fare una ~ di** to select

'**cero** ['tʃero] sm (church) candle

ce'rone [tʃe'rone] sm (trucco) greasepaint

ce'rotto [tʃe'rɔtto] sm sticking plaster

certa'mente [tʃerta'mente] av certainly, surely

cer'tezza [tʃer'tettsa] sf certainty

certifi'care [tʃertifi'kare] vt to certify

certifi'cato [tʃertifi'kato] sm certificate; **~ medico/di nascita** medical/birth certificate; **~ di credito del Tesoro** treasury bill

certificazi'one [tʃertifikat'tsjone] sf certification; **~ di bilancio** (Comm) external audit

 PAROLA CHIAVE

'**certo, -a** ['tʃɛrto] ag (sicuro): **certo (di/che)** certain o sure (of/that)
■ det 1 (tale) certain; **un certo signor Smith** a (certain) Mr Smith
2 (qualche; con valore intensivo) some; **dopo un certo tempo** after some time; **un fatto di una certa importanza** a matter of some importance; **di una certa età** past one's prime, not so young
■ pron: **certi, e** (pl) some
■ av (certamente) certainly; (senz'altro) of course; **di certo** certainly; **no (di) certo!**, **certo che no!** certainly not!; **sì certo** yes indeed, certainly

certo'sino [tʃerto'zino] sm Carthusian monk; (liquore) chartreuse; **è un lavoro da ~** it's a pernickety job

cer'tuni [tʃer'tuni] pron pl some (people)

ce'rume [tʃe'rume] sm (ear) wax

'**cerva** ['tʃerva] sf (female) deer, doe

cer'vello [tʃer'vello] (pl **cervelli**, pl(f) **cervella** o **cervelle**) sm brain; **~ elettronico** computer; **avere il** o **essere un ~ fino** to be sharp-witted; **è uscito di ~, gli è dato di volta il ~** he's gone off his head

cervi'cale [tʃervi'kale] ag cervical

'**cervo, -a** ['tʃervo] sm/f stag/hind ■ sm deer; **~ volante** stag beetle

cesel'lare [tʃezel'lare] vt to chisel; (incidere) to engrave

ce'sello [tʃe'zɛllo] sm chisel

ce'soie [tʃe'zoje] sfpl shears

ces'puglio [tʃes'puʎʎo] sm bush

ces'sare [tʃes'sare] vi, vt to stop, cease; **~ di fare qc** to stop doing sth; **"cessato allarme"** "all clear"

ces'sate il fu'oco [tʃes'sate-] sm ceasefire

cessazi'one [tʃessat'tsjone] sf cessation; (interruzione) suspension

cessi'one [tʃes'sjone] sf transfer

'**cesso** ['tʃɛsso] sm (fam: gabinetto) bog

'**cesta** ['tʃesta] sf (large) basket

ces'tello [tʃes'tɛllo] *sm* (*per bottiglie*) crate; (*di lavatrice*) drum

cesti'nare [tʃesti'nare] *vt* to throw away; (*fig: proposta*) to turn down; (: *romanzo*) to reject

ces'tino [tʃes'tino] *sm* basket; (*per la carta straccia*) wastepaper basket; **~ da viaggio** (*Ferr*) packed lunch (*o* dinner)

'cesto ['tʃesto] *sm* basket

ce'sura [tʃe'zura] *sf* caesura

ce'taceo [tʃe'tatʃeo] *sm* sea mammal

'ceto ['tʃɛto] *sm* (*social*) class

'cetra ['tʃetra] *sf* zither; (*fig: di poeta*) lyre

cetrio'lino [tʃetrio'lino] *sm* gherkin

cetri'olo [tʃetri'ɔlo] *sm* cucumber

Cf., Cfr. *abbr* (= *confronta*) cf.

CFC [tʃieffe'tʃi] *abbr mpl* (= *clorofluorocarburi*) CFC

CFS *sigla m* (= *Corpo Forestale dello Stato*) body responsible for the planting and management of forests

cg *abbr* (= *centigrammo*) cg

C.G.I.L. [tʃidʒi'ɛlle] *sigla f* (= *Confederazione Generale Italiana del Lavoro*) trades union organization

CH *sigla* = **Chieti**

cha'let [ʃa'le] *sm inv* chalet

cham'pagne [ʃã'paɲ] *sm inv* champagne

chance [ʃãs] *sf inv* chance

charme [ʃarm] *sm* charm

'charter ['tʃa:tər] *ag inv* (*volo*) charter *cpd*; (*aereo*) chartered ■ *sm inv* chartered plane

chat'tare [tʃat'tare] *vi* to chat; (*online*) to chat

centrosi'nistra [tʃentrosi'nistra] *sm* (*Pol*) centre left

 PAROLA CHIAVE

che [ke] *pron* **1** (*relativo: persona: soggetto*) who; (: *oggetto*) whom, that; (: *cosa, animale*) which, that; **il ragazzo che è venuto** the boy who came; **l'uomo che io vedo** the man (whom) I see; **il libro che è sul tavolo** the book which *o* that is on the table; **il libro che vedi** the book (which *o* that) you see; **la sera che ti ho visto** the evening I saw you

2 (*interrogativo, esclamativo*) what; **che (cosa) fai?** what are you doing?; **a che (cosa) pensi?** what are you thinking about?; **non sa che (cosa) fare** he doesn't know what to do; **sai di che si tratta?** do you know what it's about?; **che (cosa) succede?** what's happening?; **ma che dici!** what are you saying!

3 (*indefinito*): **quell'uomo ha un che di losco** there's something suspicious about that man; **un certo non so che** an indefinable something; **non è un gran che** it's nothing much

■ *det* **1** (*interrogativo: tra tanti*) what; (: *tra pochi*) which; **che tipo di film preferisci?** what sort of film do you prefer?; **che vestito ti vuoi mettere?** what (*o* which) dress do you want to put on?

2 (*esclamativo: seguito da aggettivo*) how; (: *seguito da sostantivo*) what; **che buono!** how delicious!; **che bel vestito!** what a lovely dress!; **che macchina!** what a car!

■ *cong* **1** (*con proposizioni subordinate*) that; **credo che verrà** I think he'll come; **voglio che tu studi** I want you to study; **so che tu c'eri** I know (that) you were there; **non che sia sbagliato, ma ...** not that it's wrong, but ...

2 (*finale*) so that; **vieni qua, che ti veda** come here, so (that) I can see you; **stai attento che non cada** mind it doesn't fall

3 (*temporale*): **arrivai che eri già partito** you had already left when I arrived; **sono anni che non lo vedo** I haven't seen him for years

4 (*in frasi imperative, concessive*): **che venga pure!** let him come by all means!; **che tu sia benedetto!** may God bless you!; **che tu venga o no partiamo lo stesso** we're going whether you come or not

5 (*comparativo: con più, meno*) than; **è più lungo che largo** it's longer than it's wide; **più bella che mai** more beautiful than ever; *vedi anche* **più; meno; così** *etc*

'checca, -che ['kekka] *sf* (*fam: omosessuale*) fairy

chef [ʃɛf] *sm inv* chef

chemiotera'pia [kemjotera'pia] *sf* chemotherapy

chero'sene [kero'zɛne] *sm* kerosene

cheru'bino [keru'bino] *sm* cherub

che'tare [ke'tare] *vt* to hush, silence; **chetarsi** *vr* to quieten down, fall silent

cheti'chella [keti'kɛlla]: **alla ~** *av* stealthily, unobtrusively; **andarsene alla ~** to slip away

'cheto, -a ['keto] *ag* quiet, silent

 PAROLA CHIAVE

chi [ki] *pron* **1** (*interrogativo: soggetto*) who; (: *oggetto*) who, whom; **chi è?** who is it?; **di chi è questo libro?** whose book is this?, whose is this book?; **con chi parli?** who are you talking to?; **a chi pensi?** who are you thinking about?; **chi di voi?** which of you?; **non so a chi rivolgermi** I don't know who to ask

67

2 (relativo) whoever, anyone who; **dillo a chi vuoi** tell whoever you like; **portate chi volete** bring anyone you like; **so io di chi parlo** I know who I'm talking about; **lo riferirò a chi di dovere** I'll pass it on to the relevant person
3 (indefinito): **chi ... chi ...** some ... others ...; **chi dice una cosa, chi dice un'altra** some say one thing, others say another

chiacchie'rare [kjakkje'rare] vi to chat; (discorrere futilmente) to chatter; (far pettegolezzi) to gossip
chiacchie'rata [kjakkje'rata] sf chat; **farsi una ~** to have a chat
chi'acchiere ['kjakkjere] sfpl chatter no pl; gossip no pl; **fare due** o **quattro ~** to have a chat; **perdersi in ~** to waste time talking
chiacchie'rone, -a [kjakkje'rone] ag talkative, chatty gossipy ■ sm/f chatterbox; gossip
chia'mare [kja'mare] vt to call; (rivolgersi a qn) to call (in), send for; **chiamarsi** vr (aver nome) to be called; **mi chiamo Paolo** my name is Paolo, I'm called Paolo; **mandare a ~ qn** to send for sb, call sb in; **~ alle armi** to call up; **~ in giudizio** to summon; **~ qn da parte** to take sb aside
chia'mata [kja'mata] sf (Tel) call; (Mil) call-up; **~ interurbana** long-distance call; **~ con preavviso** person-to-person call; **~ alle urne** (Pol) election
chi'appa ['kjappa] sf (fam: natica) cheek; **chiappe** sfpl bottom sg
chi'ara ['kjara] sf egg white
chia'rezza [kja'rettsa] sf clearness; clarity
chiarifi'care [kjarifi'kare] vt (anche fig) to clarify
chiarificazi'one [kjarifikat'tsjone] sf clarification
chiari'mento [kjari'mento] sm clarification no pl, explanation
chia'rire [kja'rire] vt to make clear; (fig: spiegare) to clear up, explain; **chiarirsi** vr to become clear; **si sono chiariti** they've sorted things out
chi'aro, -a ['kjaro] ag clear; (luminoso) clear, bright; (colore) pale, light ■ av (parlare, vedere) clearly; **si sta facendo ~** the day is dawning; **sia chiara una cosa** let's get one thing straight; **mettere in ~ qc** (fig) to clear sth up; **parliamoci ~** let's be frank; **trasmissione in ~** (TV) uncoded broadcast
chia'rore [kja'rore] sm (diffuse) light
chiaroveg'gente [kjaroveddʒɛnte] sm/f clairvoyant

chi'asso ['kjasso] sm uproar, row; **far ~** to make a din; (fig) to make a fuss; (: notizia) to cause a stir
chias'soso, -a [kjas'soso] ag noisy, rowdy; (vistoso) showy, gaudy
'chiatta ['kjatta] sf barge
chi'ave ['kjave] sf key ■ ag inv key cpd; **chiudere a ~** to lock; **~ d'accensione** (Aut) ignition key; **~ a forcella** fork spanner; **~ inglese** monkey wrench; **in ~ politica** in political terms; **~ di volta** (anche fig) keystone; **chiavi in mano** (contratto) turn-key cpd; **prezzo chiavi in mano** (di macchina) on-the-road price; **~ USB** (Inform) USB key
chiavis'tello [kjavis'tɛllo] sm bolt
chi'azza ['kjattsa] sf stain, splash
chiaz'zare [kjat'tsare] vt to stain, splash
chic [ʃik] ag inv chic, elegant
chicches'sia [kikkes'sia] pron anyone, anybody
'chicco, -chi ['kikko] sm (di cereale, riso) grain; (di caffè) bean; **~ di grandine** hailstone; **~ d'uva** grape
chi'edere ['kjɛdere] vt (per sapere) to ask; (per avere) to ask for ■ vi: **~ di qn** to ask after sb; (al telefono) to ask for o want sb; **chiedersi** vr: **chiedersi (se)** to wonder (whether); **~ qc a qn** to ask sb sth; to ask sb for sth; **~ scusa a qn** to apologize to sb; **~ l'elemosina** to beg; **non chiedo altro** that's all I want
chieri'chetto [kjeri'ketto] sm altar boy
chi'erico, -ci ['kjɛriko] sm cleric; altar boy
chi'esa ['kjeza] sf church
chi'esi etc ['kjɛzi] vb vedi **chiedere**
chi'esto, -a ['kjɛsto] pp di **chiedere**
'Chigi ['kidʒi]: **palazzo ~** sm (Pol) offices of the Italian Prime Minister
'chiglia ['kiʎʎa] sf keel
'chilo ['kilo] sm kilo
chilo'grammo [kilo'grammo] sm kilogram(me)
chilome'traggio [kilome'traddʒo] sm (Aut) ≈ mileage
chilo'metrico, -a, -ci, -che [kilo'mɛtriko] ag kilometric; (fig) endless
chi'lometro [ki'lɔmetro] sm kilometre (Brit), kilometer (US)
'chimico, -a, -ci, -che ['kimiko] ag chemical ■ sm/f chemist ■ sf chemistry
chi'mono [ki'mɔno] sm inv kimono
'china ['kina] sf (pendio) slope, descent; (Bot) cinchona; **(inchiostro di) ~** Indian ink; **risalire la ~** (fig) to be on the road to recovery
chi'nare [ki'nare] vt to lower, bend; **chinarsi** vr to stoop, bend

chincaglie'ria [kinkaʎʎe'ria] sf fancy-goods shop; **chincaglierie** sfpl fancy goods, knick-knacks

chi'nino [ki'nino] sm quinine

chino, -a ['kino] ag: **a capo ~, a testa china** head bent o bowed

chi'occia, -ce ['kjɔttʃa] sf brooding hen

chi'occio, -a, ci, ce ['kjɔttʃo] ag (voce) clucking

chi'occiola ['kjɔttʃola] sf snail; (di indirizzo e-mail) at; **scala a ~** spiral staircase

chi'odo ['kjɔdo] sm nail; (fig) obsession; **~ scaccia ~** (proverbio) one problem drives away another; **roba da chiodi!** it's unbelievable!; **~ di garofano** (Cuc) clove

chi'oma ['kjɔma] sf (capelli) head of hair; (di albero) foliage

chi'osco, -schi ['kjɔsko] sm kiosk, stall

chi'ostro ['kjɔstro] sm cloister

chiro'mante [kiro'mante] sm/f palmist; (indovino) fortune-teller

chirur'gia [kirur'dʒia] sf surgery

chi'rurgico, -a, ci, che [ki'rurdʒiko] ag (anche fig) surgical

chi'rurgo, -ghi o **gi** [ki'rurgo] sm surgeon

chissà [kis'sa] av who knows, I wonder

chi'tarra [ki'tarra] sf guitar

chitar'rista, -i, e [kitar'rista] sm/f guitarist, guitar player

chi'udere ['kjudere] vt to close, shut; (luce, acqua) to put off, turn off; (definitivamente: fabbrica) to close down, shut down; (strada) to close; (recingere) to enclose; (porre termine) to end ■ vi to close, shut; to close down, shut down; to end; **chiudersi** vr to shut, close; (ritirarsi: anche fig) to shut o.s. away; (ferita) to close up; **~ un occhio su** (fig) to turn a blind eye to; **chiudi la bocca!** o **il becco!** (fam) shut up!

chi'unque [ki'unkwe] pron (relativo) whoever; (indefinito) anyone, anybody; **~ sia** whoever it is

chiusi etc ['kjusi] vb vedi **chiudere**

chi'uso, -a ['kjuso] pp di **chiudere** ■ ag (porta) shut, closed; (: a chiave) locked; (senza uscita: strada etc) blocked off; (rubinetto) off; (persona) uncommunicative; (ambiente, club) exclusive ■ sm: **stare al ~** (fig) to be shut up ■ sf (di corso d'acqua) sluice, lock; (recinto) enclosure; (di discorso etc) conclusion, ending; **"~"** (negozio etc) "closed"; **"~ al pubblico"** "no admittance to the public"

chiu'sura [kju'sura] sf closing; shutting; closing o shutting down; enclosing; putting o turning off; ending; (dispositivo) catch; fastening; fastener; **orario di ~** closing time; **~ lampo®** zip (fastener) (Brit), zipper (US)

PAROLA CHIAVE

ci [tʃi] (dav lo, la, li, le, ne diventa **ce**) pron

1 (personale: complemento oggetto) us; (: a noi: complemento di termine) (to) us; (: riflessivo) ourselves; (: reciproco) each other, one another; (impersonale): **ci si veste** we get dressed; **ci ha visti** he's seen us; **non ci ha dato niente** he gave us nothing; **ci vestiamo** we get dressed; **ci amiamo** we love one another o each other; **ci siamo divertiti** we had a good time

2 (dimostrativo: di ciò, su ciò, in ciò etc) about (o on o of) it; **non ci capisco nulla** I can't make head nor tail of it; **non so cosa farci** I don't know what to do about it; **che ci posso fare?** what can I do about it?; **che c'entro io?** what have I got to do with it?; **ci puoi giurare** you can bet on it; **ci puoi contare** you can depend on it; **ci sei?** (sei pronto?) are you ready?; (hai capito?) are you with me?

■ av (qui) here; (lì) there; (moto attraverso luogo): **ci passa sopra un ponte** a bridge passes over it; **non ci passa più nessuno** nobody comes this way any more; **qui ci abito da un anno** I've been living here for a year; **esserci** vedi **essere**

C.I. abbr = **carta d'identità**

CIA ['tʃia] sigla f (= Central Intelligence Agency) CIA

C.ia abbr (= compagnia) Co

cia'batta [tʃa'batta] sf mule, slipper

ciabat'tino [tʃabat'tino] sm cobbler

ciac [tʃak] sm (Cine) clapper board; **~, si gira!** action!

Ci'ad [tʃad] sm: **il ~** Chad

ci'alda ['tʃalda] sf (Cuc) wafer

cial'trone [tʃal'trone] sm good-for-nothing

ciam'bella [tʃam'bɛlla] sf (Cuc) ring-shaped cake; (salvagente) rubber ring

ci'ancia, -ce ['tʃantʃa] sf gossip no pl, tittle-tattle no pl

cianfru'saglie [tʃanfru'zaʎʎe] sfpl bits and pieces

cia'nuro [tʃa'nuro] sm cyanide

ci'ao ['tʃao] escl (all'arrivo) hello!; (alla partenza) cheerio! (Brit), bye!

ciar'lare [tʃar'lare] vi to chatter; (peg) to gossip

ciarla'tano [tʃarla'tano] sm charlatan

cias'cuno, -a [tʃas'kuno] (dav sm: **ciascun** + C, V, **ciascuno** + s impura, gn, pn, ps, x, z; dav sf: **ciascuna** + C, **ciascun'** + V) det, pron each

ci'bare [tʃi'bare] vt to feed; **cibarsi** vr: **cibarsi di** to eat

ci'barie [tʃi'barje] sfpl foodstuffs

ciber'netica [tʃiber'nɛtika] sf cybernetics sg

'cibo ['tʃibo] sm food

ci'cala [tʃi'kala] sf cicada

cica'trice [tʃika'tritʃe] sf scar

cicatriz'zarsi [tʃikatrid'dzarsi] vr to form a
scar, heal (up)

'cicca, -che ['tʃikka] sf cigarette end; (fam:
sigaretta) fag; non vale una ~ (fig) it's
worthless

'ciccia ['tʃittʃa] sf (fam: carne) meat; (: grasso
umano) fat, flesh

cicci'one, -a [tʃit'tʃone] sm/f (fam) fatty

cice'rone [tʃitʃe'rone] sm guide

cicla'mino [tʃikla'mino] sm cyclamen

ci'clismo [tʃi'klizmo] sm cycling

ci'clista, -i, e [tʃi'klista] sm/f cyclist

'ciclo ['tʃiklo] sm cycle; (di malattia) course

ciclomo'tore [tʃiklomo'tore] sm moped

ci'clone [tʃi'klone] sm cyclone

ciclos'tile [tʃiklos'tile] sm cyclostyle (Brit)

ci'cogna [tʃi'koɲɲa] sf stork

ci'coria [tʃi'kɔrja] sf chicory

ci'eco, -a, chi, che ['tʃɛko] ag blind ■ sm/f
blind man(-woman); alla cieca (anche fig)
blindly

ciel'lino, -a [tʃiel'lino] sm/f (Pol) member of CL
movement

ci'elo ['tʃɛlo] sm sky; (Rel) heaven; toccare il ~
con un dito (fig) to walk on air; per amor
del ~! for heavens' sake!

'cifra ['tʃifra] sf (numero) figure, numeral;
(somma di denaro) sum, figure; (monogramma)
monogram, initials pl; (codice) code, cipher

ci'frare [tʃi'frare] vt (messaggio) to code;
(lenzuola etc) to embroider with a monogram

'ciglio ['tʃiʎʎo] sm (margine) edge, verge; (pl(f)
ciglia: delle palpebre) (eye)lash; (sopracciglio)
eyebrow; non ha battuto ~ (fig) he didn't
bat an eyelid

'cigno ['tʃiɲɲo] sm swan

cigo'lante [tʃigo'lante] ag squeaking,
creaking

cigo'lare [tʃigo'lare] vi to squeak, creak

'Cile ['tʃile] sm: il ~ Chile

ci'lecca [tʃi'lekka] sf: far ~ to fail

ci'leno, -a [tʃi'lɛno] ag, sm/f Chilean

cili'egia, -gie o ge [tʃi'ljɛdʒa] sf cherry

cilie'gina [tʃilje'dʒina] sf glacé cherry; la ~
sulla torta (fig) the icing o cherry on the
cake

cili'egio [tʃi'ljɛdʒo] sm cherry tree

cilin'drata [tʃilin'drata] sf (Aut) (cubic)
capacity; una macchina di grossa ~ a big-
engined car

ci'lindro [tʃi'lindro] sm cylinder; (cappello) top
hat

CIM [tʃim] sigla m = centro d'igiene mentale

'cima ['tʃima] sf (sommità) top; (di monte)
top, summit; (estremità) end; (fig: persona)
genius; in ~ a at the top of; da ~ a fondo
from top to bottom; (fig) from beginning
to end

ci'melio [tʃi'mɛljo] sm relic

cimen'tarsi [tʃimen'tarsi] vr: ~ in (atleta,
concorrente) to try one's hand at

'cimice ['tʃimitʃe] sf (Zool) bug; (puntina)
drawing pin (Brit), thumbtack (US)

cimini'era [tʃimi'njɛra] sf chimney; (di nave)
funnel

cimi'tero [tʃimi'tɛro] sm cemetery

ci'murro [tʃi'murro] sm (di cani) distemper

'Cina ['tʃina] sf: la ~ China

cin'cin, cin cin [tʃin'tʃin] escl cheers!

cincischi'are [tʃintʃis'kjare] vi to mess about

'cine ['tʃine] sm inv (fam) cinema

cine'asta, -i, e [tʃine'asta] sm/f person in the
film industry; film-maker

cinegior'nale [tʃinedʒor'nale] sm newsreel

'cinema ['tʃinema] sm inv cinema; ~ muto
silent films; ~ d'essai (locale) avant-garde
cinema, experimental cinema

cinemato'grafico, -a, ci, che
[tʃinemato'grafiko] ag (attore, critica) movie
cpd, film cpd; (festival) film cpd; sala
cinematografica cinema; successo ~ box-
office success

cinema'tografo [tʃinema'tɔgrafo] sm
cinema

cine'presa [tʃine'presa] sf cine-camera

ci'nese [tʃi'nese] ag, sm/f, sm Chinese inv

cine'teca, -che [tʃine'tɛka] sf (collezione) film
collection; (locale) film library

ci'netico, -a, ci, che [tʃi'nɛtiko] ag kinetic

'cingere ['tʃindʒere] vt (attorniare) to surround,
encircle; ~ la vita con una cintura to put a
belt round one's waist; ~ d'assedio to
besiege, lay siege to

'cinghia ['tʃingja] sf strap; (cintura, Tecn) belt;
tirare la ~ (fig) to tighten one's belt

cinghi'ale [tʃin'gjale] sm wild boar

cinguet'tare [tʃingwet'tare] vi to twitter

'cinico, -a, ci, che ['tʃiniko] ag cynical ■ sm/f
cynic

ci'nismo [tʃi'nizmo] sm cynicism

cin'quanta [tʃin'kwanta] num fifty

cinquante'nario [tʃinkwante'narjo] sm
fiftieth anniversary

cinquan'tenne [tʃinkwan'tɛnne] sm/f fifty-
year-old man/woman

cinquan'tesimo, -a [tʃinkwan'tɛzimo] num
fiftieth

cinquan'tina [tʃinkwan'tina] sf (serie): una ~
(di) about fifty; (età): essere sulla ~ to be
about fifty

'**cinque** ['tʃinkwe] *num* five; **avere ~ anni** to be five (years old); **il ~ dicembre 1988** the fifth of December 1988; **alle ~** (*ora*) at five (o'clock); **siamo in ~** there are five of us

cinquecen'tesco, -a, schi, sche [tʃinkwetʃen'tesko] *ag* sixteenth-century

cinque'cento [tʃinkwe'tʃento] *num* five hundred ■ *sm:* **il C~** the sixteenth century

cinque'mila [tʃinkwe'mila] *num* five thousand

'**cinsi** *etc* ['tʃinsi] *vb vedi* **cingere**

'**cinta** ['tʃinta] *sf* (*anche:* **cinta muraria**) city walls *pl;* **muro di ~** (*di giardino etc*) surrounding wall

cin'tare [tʃin'tare] *vt* to enclose

'**cinto, -a** ['tʃinto] *pp di* **cingere**

'**cintola** ['tʃintola] *sf* (*cintura*) belt; (*vita*) waist

cin'tura [tʃin'tura] *sf* belt; **~ di salvataggio** lifebelt (*Brit*), life preserver (*US*); **~ di sicurezza** (*Aut, Aer*) safety o seat belt

cintu'rino [tʃintu'rino] *sm* strap; **~ dell'orologio** watch strap

CIO *sigla m* (= *Comitato Internazionale Olimpico*) IOC (= *International Olympic Committee*)

ciò [tʃɔ] *pron* this; that; **ciò che** what; **ciò nonostante** o **nondimeno** nevertheless, in spite of that; **con tutto ciò** for all that, in spite of everything

ci'occa, -che ['tʃɔkka] *sf* (*di capelli*) lock

ciocco'lata [tʃokko'lata] *sf* chocolate; (*bevanda*) (hot) chocolate; **~ al latte/ fondente** milk/plain chocolate

cioccola'tino [tʃokkola'tino] *sm* chocolate

ciocco'lato [tʃokko'lato] *sm* chocolate

cio'è [tʃo'ɛ] *av* that is (to say)

ciondo'lare [tʃondo'lare] *vt* (*far dondolare*) to dangle, swing ■ *vi* to dangle; (*fig*) to loaf (about)

ci'ondolo ['tʃondolo] *sm* pendant; **~ portafortuna** charm

ciondo'loni [tʃondo'loni] *av*: **con le braccia/ gambe ~** with arms/legs dangling

cionono'stante [tʃononos'tante] *av* nonetheless, nevertheless

ci'otola ['tʃɔtola] *sf* bowl

ci'ottolo ['tʃɔttolo] *sm* pebble; (*di strada*) cobble(stone)

C.I.P. [tʃip] *sigla m* = **comitato interministeriale prezzi**; *vedi* **comitato**

Cipe ['tʃipe] *sigla m* = **comitato interministeriale per la programmazione economica**; *vedi* **comitato**

'**Cipi** ['tʃipi] *sigla m* = **comitato interministeriale per lo sviluppo industriale**; *vedi* **comitato**

ci'piglio [tʃi'piʎʎo] *sm* frown

ci'polla [tʃi'polla] *sf* onion; (*di tulipano etc*) bulb

cipol'lina [tʃipol'lina] *sf* onion; **cipolline sottaceto** pickled onions; **cipolline sottolio** baby onions in oil

ci'presso [tʃi'presso] *sm* cypress (tree)

'**cipria** ['tʃiprja] *sf* (face) powder

cipri'ota, -i, e [tʃipri'ɔta] *ag, sm/f* Cypriot

'**Cipro** ['tʃipro] *sm* Cyprus

'**circa** ['tʃirka] *av* about, roughly ■ *prep* about, concerning; **a mezzogiorno ~** about midday

'**circo, -chi** ['tʃirko] *sm* circus

circo'lare [tʃirko'lare] *vi* to circulate; (*Aut*) to drive (along), move (along) ■ *ag* circular ■ *sf* (*Amm*) circular; (*di autobus*) circle (line); **circola voce che ...** there is a rumour going about that ...; **assegno ~** banker's draft

circolazi'one [tʃirkolat'tsjone] *sf* circulation; (*Aut*): **la ~** (the) traffic; **libretto di ~** log book, registration book; **tassa di ~** road tax; **~ a targhe alterne** *see note*

● CIRCOLAZIONE A TARGHE ALTERNE

● *Circolazione a targhe alterne* was introduced
● by some town councils to combat the
● increase in traffic and pollution in town
● centres. It stipulates that on days with an
● even date, only cars whose number plate
● ends in an even number or a zero may be
● on the road; on days with an odd date,
● only cars with odd registration numbers
● may be used. Public holidays are
● generally, but not always, exempt.

'**circolo** ['tʃirkolo] *sm* circle; **entrare in ~** (*Anat*) to enter the bloodstream

circoncisi'one [tʃirkontʃi'zjone] *sf* circumcision

circon'dare [tʃirkon'dare] *vt* to surround

circondari'ale [tʃirkonda'rjale] *ag*: **casa di pena ~** district prison

circon'dario [tʃirkon'darjo] *sm* (*Dir*) administrative district; (*zona circostante*) neighbourhood (*Brit*), neighborhood (*US*)

circonfe'renza [tʃirkonfe'rɛntsa] *sf* circumference

circonvallazi'one [tʃirkonvallat'tsjone] *sf* ring road (*Brit*), beltway (*US*); (*per evitare una città*) by-pass

circos'critto, -a [tʃirkos'kritto] *pp di* **circoscrivere**

circos'crivere [tʃirkos'krivere] *vt* to circumscribe; (*fig*) to limit, restrict

circoscrizi'one [tʃirkoskrit'tsjone] *sf* (*Amm*) district, area; **~ elettorale** constituency

circos'petto, -a [tʃirkos'pɛtto] *ag* circumspect, cautious

circos'tante [tʃirkos'tante] *ag* surrounding, neighbouring (*Brit*), neighboring (*US*)

circos'tanza [tʃirkos'tantsa] *sf* circumstance; (*occasione*) occasion; **parole di ~** words suited to the occasion

circu'ire [tʃirku'ire] *vt* (*fig*) to fool, take in

cir'cuito [tʃir'kuito] *sm* circuit; **andare in** *o* **fare corto ~** to short-circuit; **~ integrato** integrated circuit

ci'rillico, -a, ci, che [tʃi'rilliko] *ag* Cyrillic

cir'rosi [tʃir'rɔzi] *sf*: **~ epatica** cirrhosis (of the liver)

'C.I.S.A.L. ['tʃizal] *sigla f* (= *Confederazione Italiana Sindacati Autonomi dei Lavoratori*) *trades union organization*

C.I.S.L. [tʃizl] *sigla f* (= *Confederazione Italiana Sindacati Lavoratori*) *trades union organization*

'C.I.S.N.A.L. ['tʃiznal] *sigla f* (= *Confederazione Italiana Sindacati Nazionali dei Lavoratori*) *trades union organization*

'ciste ['tʃiste] *sf* = **cisti**

cis'terna [tʃis'tɛrna] *sf* tank, cistern

'cisti ['tʃisti] *sf inv* cyst

cis'tite [tʃis'tite] *sf* cystitis

C.I.T. [tʃit] *sigla f* = **Compagnia Italiana Turismo**

cit. *abbr* (= *citato, citata*) cit.

ci'tare [tʃi'tare] *vt* (*Dir*) to summon; (*autore*) to quote; (*a esempio, modello*) to cite; **~ qn per danni** to sue sb

citazi'one [tʃitat'tsjone] *sf* summons *sg*; quotation; (*di persona*) mention

ci'tofono [tʃi'tɔfono] *sm* entry phone; (*in uffici*) intercom

cito'logico, -a, ci, che [tʃito'lɔdʒiko] *ag*: **esame ~** *test for detection of cancerous cells*

'citrico, -a, ci, che ['tʃitriko] *ag* citric

città [tʃit'ta] *sf inv* town; (*importante*) city; **~ giardino** garden city; **~ mercato** shopping centre, mall; **~ universitaria** university campus; **C~ del Capo** Cape Town

citta'della [tʃitta'dɛlla] *sf* citadel, stronghold

cittadi'nanza [tʃittadi'nantsa] *sf* citizens *pl*, inhabitants *pl* of a town (*o* city); (*Dir*) citizenship

citta'dino, -a [tʃitta'dino] *ag* town *cpd*; city *cpd* ■ *sm/f* (*di uno Stato*) citizen; (*abitante di città*) town dweller, city dweller

ci'uccio ['tʃuttʃo] *sm* (*fam*) comforter, dummy (*Brit*), pacifier (*US*)

ci'uco, -a, chi, che ['tʃuko] *sm/f* ass

ci'uffo ['tʃuffo] *sm* tuft

ci'urma ['tʃurma] *sf* (*di nave*) crew

ci'vetta [tʃi'vetta] *sf* (*Zool*) owl; (*fig: donna*) coquette, flirt ■ *ag inv*: **auto/nave ~** decoy car/ship; **fare la ~ con qn** to flirt with sb

civet'tare [tʃivet'tare] *vt* to flirt

civette'ria [tʃivette'ria] *sf* coquetry, coquettishness

civettu'olo, -a [tʃivet'twɔlo] *ag* flirtatious

'civico, -a, ci, che ['tʃiviko] *ag* civic; (*museo*) municipal, town *cpd*; **guardia civica** town policeman; **senso ~** public spirit

ci'vile [tʃi'vile] *ag* civil; (*non militare*) civilian; (*nazione*) civilized ■ *sm* civilian; **stato ~** marital status; **abiti civili** civvies

civi'lista, -i, e [tʃivi'lista] *sm/f* (*avvocato*) civil lawyer; (*studioso*) expert in civil law

civiliz'zare [tʃivilid'dzare] *vt* to civilize

civilizzazi'one [tʃiviliddzat'tsjone] *sf* civilization

civiltà [tʃivil'ta] *sf* civilization; (*cortesia*) civility

ci'vismo [tʃi'vizmo] *sm* public spirit

CL [tʃi'elle] *sigla f* (*Pol*: = *Comunione e Liberazione*) *Catholic youth movement* ■ *sigla* = **Caltanissetta**

cl *abbr* (= *centilitro*) cl

'clacson *sm inv* (*Aut*) horn

cla'more *sm* (*frastuono*) din, uproar, clamour (*Brit*), clamor (*US*); (*fig*) outcry

clamo'roso, -a *ag* noisy; (*fig*) sensational

clan *sm inv* clan

clandestinità *sf* (*di attività*) secret nature; **vivere nella ~** to live in hiding; (*ricercato politico*) to live underground

clandes'tino, -a *ag* clandestine; (*Pol*) underground, clandestine ■ *sm/f* stowaway; (*anche*: **immigrato clandestino**) illegal immigrant

clari'netto *sm* clarinet

'classe *sf* class; **di ~** (*fig*) with class; of excellent quality; **~ turistica** (*Aer*) economy class

classi'cismo [klassi'tʃizmo] *sm* classicism

'classico, -a, ci, che *ag* classical; (*tradizionale*: *moda*) classic(al) ■ *sm* classic; classical author; (*anche*: **liceo classico**) *secondary school with emphasis on the humanities*

clas'sifica, -che *sf* classification; (*Sport*) placings *pl*; (*di dischi*) charts *pl*, hit parade

classifi'care *vt* to classify; (*candidato, compito*) to grade; **classificarsi** *vr* to be placed

classifica'tore *sm* filing cabinet

classificazi'one [klassifikat'tsjone] *sf* classification; grading

clas'sista, -i, e *ag* class-conscious ■ *sm/f* class-conscious person

claudi'cante *ag* (*zoppo*) lame; (*fig: prosa*) halting

'clausola *sf* (*Dir*) clause

claustro'fobico, -a, ci, che *ag* claustrophobic

clau'sura *sf* (*Rel*): **monaca di ~** nun belonging to an enclosed order; **fare una vita di ~** (*fig*) to lead a cloistered life

'clava *sf* club

clavi'cembalo [klavi'tʃembalo] *sm* harpsichord

cla'vicola *sf* (*Anat*) collarbone

cle'mente *ag* merciful; (*clima*) mild

cle'menza [kle'mɛntsa] *sf* mercy, clemency; mildness

clep'tomane *sm/f* kleptomaniac

cleri'cale *ag* clerical

'clero *sm* clergy

cles'sidra *sf* (*a sabbia*) hourglass; (*ad acqua*) water clock

clic'care *vi* (*Inform*): ~ **su** to click on

cliché [kli'ʃe] *sm inv* (*Tip*) plate; (*fig*) cliché

cli'ente *sm/f* customer, client

clien'tela *sf* customers *pl*, clientèle

cliente'lismo *sm*: ~ **politico** political nepotism

'clima, -i *sm* climate

cli'matico, -a, ci, che *ag* climatic; **stazione climatica** health resort

climatizza'tore [klimatiddza'tore] *sm* air conditioner

climatizzazi'one [klimatiddzat'tsjone] *sf* air conditioning

'clinico, -a, ci, che *ag* clinical ■ *sm* (*medico*) clinician ■ *sf* (*scienza*) clinical medicine; (*casa di cura*) clinic, nursing home; (*settore d'ospedale*) clinic; **quadro** ~ anamnesis; **avere l'occhio** ~ (*fig*) to have an expert eye

clis'tere *sm* (*Med*) enema; (: *apparecchio*) *device used to give an enema*

clo'aca, -che *sf* sewer

cloche [klɔʃ] *sf inv* control stick, joystick; **cambio a** ~ (*Aut*) floor-mounted gear lever

clo'nare *vt* to clone

clona'zione [klonat'tsjone] *sf* (*Biol, fig*) cloning

'cloro *sm* chlorine

cloro'filla *sf* chlorophyll

cloro'formio *sm* chloroform

club *sm inv* club

cm *abbr* (= *centimetro*) cm

c.m. *abbr* (= *corrente mese*) inst.

CN *sigla* = **Cuneo**

c/n *abbr* = **conto nuovo**

CNEN *sigla m* (= *Comitato Nazionale per l'Energia Nucleare*) ≈ AEA (*Brit*), AEC (*US*)

CNIOP *sigla m* = **Centro Nazionale per l'Istruzione e l'Orientamento Professionale**

CNR *sigla m* (= *Consiglio Nazionale delle Ricerche*) science research council

CNRN *sigla m* = **Comitato Nazionale Ricerche Nucleari**

CO *sigla* = **Como**

Co. *abbr* (= *compagnia*) Co.

c/o *abbr* (= *care of*) c/o

coabi'tare *vi* to live together, live under the same roof

coagu'lare *vt* to coagulate ■ *vi*, **coagularsi** *vr* to coagulate; (*latte*) to curdle

coalizi'one [koalit'tsjone] *sf* coalition

co'atto, -a *ag* (*Dir*) compulsory, forced; **condannare al domicilio** ~ to place under house arrest

'COBAS *sigla mpl* (= *Comitati di base*) *independent trades unions*

'cobra *sm inv* cobra

'coca 'cola® *sf* coca cola®

coca'ina *sf* cocaine

coc'carda *sf* cockade

cocchi'ere [kok'kjɛre] *sm* coachman

'cocchio ['kɔkkjo] *sm* (*carrozza*) coach; (*biga*) chariot

cocci'nella [kottʃi'nɛlla] *sf* ladybird (*Brit*), ladybug (*US*)

'coccio ['kɔttʃo] *sm* earthenware; (*vaso*) earthenware pot; **cocci** *smpl* fragments (of pottery)

cocciu'taggine [kottʃu'taddʒine] *sf* stubbornness, pig-headedness

cocci'uto, -a [kot'tʃuto] *ag* stubborn, pigheaded

'cocco, -chi *sm* (*pianta*) coconut palm; (*frutto*): **noce di** ~ coconut ■ *sm/f* (*fam*) darling; **è il** ~ **della mamma** he's mummy's darling

cocco'drillo *sm* crocodile

cocco'lare *vt* to cuddle, fondle

co'cente [ko'tʃɛnte] *ag* (*anche fig*) burning

cocerò *etc* [kotʃe'rɔ] *vb vedi* **cuocere**

co'comero *sm* watermelon

co'cuzzolo [ko'kuttsolo] *sm* top; (*di capo, cappello*) crown

cod. *abbr* = **codice**

'coda *sf* tail; (*fila di persone, auto*) queue (*Brit*), line (*US*); (*di abiti*) train; **con la** ~ **dell'occhio** out of the corner of one's eye; **mettersi in** ~ to queue (up) (*Brit*), line up (*US*); to join the queue *o* line; ~ **di cavallo** (*acconciatura*) ponytail; **avere la** ~ **di paglia** (*fig*) to have a guilty conscience; ~ **di rospo** (*Cuc*) frogfish tail

codar'dia *sf* cowardice

co'dardo, -a *ag* cowardly ■ *sm/f* coward

co'desto, -a *ag, pron* (*poetico*) this; that

'codice ['kɔditʃe] *sm* code; (*manoscritto antico*) codex; ~ **di avviamento postale** postcode (*Brit*), zip code (*US*); ~ **a barre** bar code; ~ **civile** civil code; ~ **fiscale** tax code; ~ **penale** penal code; ~ **segreto** (*di tessera magnetica*) PIN (number); ~ **della strada** highway code

co'difica *sf* codification; (*Inform*: *di programma*) coding

codifi'care *vt* (*Dir*) to codify; (*cifrare*) to code

codificazi'one [kodifikat'tsjone] sf coding

coercizi'one [koert∫it'tsjone] sf coercion

coe'rente ag coherent

coe'renza [koe'rɛntsa] sf coherence

coesi'one sf cohesion

coe'sistere vi to coexist

coe'taneo, -a ag, sm/f contemporary; **essere ~ di qn** to be the same age as sb

cofa'netto sm casket; **~ dei gioielli** jewel case

'**cofano** sm (Aut) bonnet (Brit), hood (US); (forziere) chest

'**coffa** sf (Naut) top

'**cogli** ['koλλi] prep + det vedi **con**

'**cogliere** ['kɔλλere] vt (fiore, frutto) to pick, gather; (sorprendere) to catch, surprise; (bersaglio) to hit; (fig: momento opportuno etc) to grasp, seize, take; (: capire) to grasp; **~ l'occasione (per fare)** to take the opportunity (to do); **~ sul fatto** o **in flagrante/alla sprovvista** to catch red-handed/unprepared; **~ nel segno** (fig) to hit the nail on the head

cogli'one [koλ'λone] sm (fam!: testicolo): **coglioni** balls (!); (: fig: persona sciocca) jerk; **rompere i coglioni a qn** to get on sb's tits (!)

co'gnac [kɔ'ɲak] sm inv cognac

co'gnato, -a [koɲ'ɲato] sm/f brother-(-sister)-in-law

cognizi'one [koɲɲit'tsjone] sf knowledge; **con ~ di causa** with full knowledge of the facts

co'gnome [koɲ'ɲome] sm surname

'**coi** prep + det vedi **con**

coi'bente ag insulating

coinci'denza [kointʃi'dɛntsa] sf coincidence; (Ferr, Aer, di autobus) connection

coin'cidere [koin'tʃidere] vi to coincide

coin'ciso, -a [koin'tʃizo] pp di **coincidere**

coinqui'lino sm fellow tenant

cointeres'senza [kointeres'sɛntsa] sf (Comm): **avere una ~ in qc** to own shares in sth; **~ dei lavoratori** profit-sharing

coin'volgere [koin'vɔldʒere] vt: **~ in** to involve in

coinvolgi'mento [koinvoldʒi'mento] sm involvement

coin'volto, -a pp di **coinvolgere**

col prep + det vedi **con**

Col. abbr (= colonnello) Col.

colà av there

cola'brodo sm inv strainer

cola'pasta sm inv colander

co'lare vt (liquido) to strain; (pasta) to drain; (oro fuso) to pour ■ vi (sudore) to drip; (botte) to leak; (cera) to melt; **~ a picco** (nave) to sink

co'lata sf (di lava) flow; (Fonderia) casting

colazi'one [kolat'tsjone] sf (anche: **prima colazione**) breakfast; (anche: **seconda colazione**) lunch; **fare ~** to have breakfast (o lunch); **~ di lavoro** working lunch

Coldi'retti abbr f (= Confederazione nazionale coltivatori diretti) federation of Italian farmers

co'lei pron vedi **colui**

co'lera sm (Med) cholera

coleste'rolo sm cholesterol

colf abbr f = **collaboratrice familiare**

'**colgo** etc vb vedi **cogliere**

colibrì sm hummingbird

'**colica** sf (Med) colic

co'lino sm strainer

'**colla** prep + det vedi **con** ■ sf glue; (di farina) paste

collabo'rare vi to collaborate; (con la polizia) to co-operate; **~ a** to collaborate on; (giornale) to contribute to

collabora'tore, -trice sm/f collaborator; (di giornale, rivista) contributor; **~ esterno** freelance; **collaboratrice familiare** home help; **~ di giustizia** = **pentito, a**

collaborazi'one [kollaborat'tsjone] sf collaboration; contribution

col'lana sf necklace; (collezione) collection, series

col'lant [kɔ'lɑ̃] sm inv tights pl

col'lare sm collar

col'lasso sm (Med) collapse

collate'rale ag collateral; **effetti collaterali** side effects

col'laudo sm testing no pl; test

'**colle** prep + det vedi **con** ■ sm hill

col'lega, -ghi, ghe sm/f colleague

collega'mento sm connection; (Mil) liaison; (Radio) link(-up); (Inform) link; **ufficiale di ~** liaison officer; **~ ipertestuale** hyperlink

colle'gare vt to connect, join, link; **collegarsi** vr (Radio, TV) to link up; **collegarsi con** (Tel) to get through to

collegi'ale [kolle'dʒale] ag (riunione, decisione) collective; (Ins) boarding school cpd ■ sm/f boarder; (fig: persona timida e inesperta) schoolboy(-girl)

col'legio [kol'ledʒo] sm college; (convitto) boarding school; **~ elettorale** (Pol) constituency

'**collera** sf anger; **andare in ~** to get angry

col'lerico, -a, ci, che ag quick-tempered, irascible

col'letta sf collection

collettività sf community

collet'tivo, -a ag collective; (interesse) general, everybody's; (biglietto, visita etc) group cpd ■ sm (Pol) (political) group; **società in nome ~** (Comm) partnership

col'letto sm collar; **colletti bianchi** (fig) white-collar workers

collezio'nare [kollettsjo'nare] vt to collect

collezi'one [kollet'tsjone] sf collection

collezio'nista [kollettsjo'nista] sm/f collector

colli'mare vi to correspond, coincide

col'lina sf hill

colli'nare ag hill cpd

col'lirio sm eyewash

collisi'one sf collision

'collo prep + det vedi **con** ■ sm neck; (di abito) neck, collar; (pacco) parcel; **~ del piede** instep

colloca'mento sm (impiego) employment; (disposizione) placing, arrangement; **ufficio di ~ =** Jobcentre (Brit), state (o federal) employment agency (US); **~ a riposo** retirement

collo'care vt (libri, mobili) to place; (persona: trovare un lavoro per) to find a job for, place; (Comm: merce) to find a market for; **~ qn a riposo** to retire sb

collocazi'one [kollokat'tsjone] sf placing; (di libro) classification

colloqui'ale ag (termine etc) colloquial; (tono) informal

col'loquio sm conversation, talk; (ufficiale, per un lavoro) interview; (Ins) preliminary oral exam; **avviare un ~ con qn** (Pol etc) to start talks with sb

col'loso, -a ag sticky

col'lottola sf nape o scruff of the neck; **afferrare qn per la ~** to grab sb by the scruff of the neck

collusi'one sf (Dir) collusion

colluttazi'one [kolluttat'tsjone] sf scuffle

col'mare vt: **~ di** (anche fig) to fill with; (dare in abbondanza) to load o overwhelm with; **~ un divario** (fig) to bridge a gap

'colmo, -a ag: **~ (di)** full (of) ■ sm summit, top; (fig) height; **al ~ della disperazione** in the depths of despair; **è il ~!** it's the last straw!; **e per ~ di sfortuna ...** and to cap it all ...

co'lomba sf vedi **colombo**

Co'lombia sf: **la ~** Colombia

colombi'ano, -a ag, sm/f Colombian

co'lombo, -a sm/f dove; pigeon; **colombi** (fig fam) lovebirds

Co'lonia sf Cologne

co'lonia sf colony; (per bambini) holiday camp; **(acqua di) ~** (eau de) cologne

coloni'ale ag colonial ■ sm/f colonist, settler

co'lonico, -a, ci, che ag: **casa colonica** farmhouse

coloniz'zare [kolonid'dzare] vt to colonize

co'lonna sf column; **~ sonora** (Cine) sound track; **~ vertebrale** spine, spinal column

colon'nello sm colonel

co'lono sm (coltivatore) tenant farmer

colo'rante sm colouring (Brit), coloring (US)

colo'rare vt to colour (Brit), color (US); (disegno) to colo(u)r in

co'lore sm colour (Brit), color (US); (Carte) suit; **a colori** in colo(u)r, colo(u)r cpd; **la gente di ~** colo(u)red people; **diventare di tutti i colori** to turn scarlet; **farne di tutti i colori** to get up to all sorts of mischief; **passarne di tutti i colori** to go through all sorts of problems

colo'rito, -a ag coloured (Brit), colored (US); (viso) rosy, pink; (linguaggio) colourful (Brit), colorful (US) ■ sm (tinta) colour (Brit), color (US); (carnagione) complexion

co'loro pron pl vedi **colui**

colos'sale ag colossal, enormous

co'losso sm colossus

'colpa sf fault; (biasimo) blame; (colpevolezza) guilt; (azione colpevole) offence; (peccato) sin; **di chi è la ~?** whose fault is it?; **è ~ sua** it's his fault; **per ~ di** through, owing to; **senso di ~** sense of guilt; **dare la ~ a qn di qc** to blame sb for sth

col'pevole ag guilty

colpevoliz'zare [kolpevolid'dzare] vt: **~ qn** to make sb feel guilty

col'pire vt to hit, strike; (fig) to strike; **rimanere colpito da qc** to be amazed o struck by sth; **è stato colpito da ordine di cattura** there is a warrant out for his arrest; **~ nel segno** (fig) to hit the nail on the head, be spot on (Brit)

'colpo sm (urto) knock; (fig: affettivo) blow, shock; (: aggressivo) blow; (di pistola) shot; (Med) stroke; (furto) raid; **di ~, tutto d'un ~** suddenly; **fare ~** to make a strong impression; **il motore perde colpi** (Aut) the engine is misfiring; **è morto sul ~** he died instantly; **mi hai fatto venire un ~!** what a fright you gave me!; **ti venisse un ~!** (fam) drop dead!; **~ d'aria** chill; **~ in banca** bank job o raid; **~ basso** (Pugilato, fig) punch below the belt; **~ di fulmine** love at first sight; **~ di grazia** coup de grâce; (fig) finishing blow; **a ~ d'occhio** at a glance; **~ di scena** (Teat) coup de théâtre; (fig) dramatic turn of events; **~ di sole** sunstroke; **colpi di sole** (nei capelli) highlights; **~ di Stato** coup d'état; **~ di telefono** phone call; **~ di testa** (sudden) impulse o whim; **~ di vento** gust (of wind)

col'poso, -a ag: **omicidio ~** manslaughter

'colsi etc vb vedi **cogliere**

coltel'lata sf stab

col'tello *sm* knife; **avere il ~ dalla parte del manico** (*fig*) to have the whip hand; **~ a serramanico** clasp knife

colti'vare *vt* to cultivate; (*verdura*) to grow, cultivate

coltiva'tore *sm* farmer; **~ diretto** small independent farmer

coltivazi'one [koltivat'tsjone] *sf* cultivation; growing; **~ intensiva** intensive farming

'colto, -a *pp di* cogliere ■ *ag* (*istruito*) cultured, educated

'coltre *sf* blanket

col'tura *sf* cultivation; **~ alternata** crop rotation

co'lui, co'lei (*pl* co'loro) *pron* the one; **~ che parla** the one *o* the man *o* the person who is speaking; **colei che amo** the one *o* the woman *o* the person (whom) I love

com. *abbr* = comunale; commissione

'coma *sm inv* coma

comanda'mento *sm* (*Rel*) commandment

coman'dante *sm* (*Mil*) commander, commandant; (*di reggimento*) commanding officer; (*Naut, Aer*) captain

coman'dare *vi* to be in command ■ *vt* to command; (*imporre*) to order, command; **~ a qn di fare** to order sb to do

co'mando *sm* (*ingiunzione*) order, command; (*autorità*) command; (*Tecn*) control; **~ generale** general headquarters *pl*; **~ a distanza** remote control

co'mare *sf* (*madrina*) godmother; (*donna pettegola*) gossip

co'masco, -a, schi, sche *ag* of (*o* from) Como

combaci'are [komba'tʃare] *vi* to meet; (*fig: coincidere*) to coincide, correspond

combat'tente *ag* fighting ■ *sm* combatant; **ex-~** ex-serviceman

combat'tere *vt* to fight; (*fig*) to combat, fight against ■ *vi* to fight

combatti'mento *sm* fight; fighting *no pl*; (*di pugilato*) match; **mettere fuori ~** to knock out

combat'tivo, -a *ag* pugnacious

combat'tuto, -a *ag* (*incerto: persona*) uncertain, undecided; (*gara, partita*) hard fought

combi'nare *vt* to combine; (*organizzare*) to arrange; (*fam: fare*) to make, cause ■ *vi* (*corrispondere*): **~ (con)** to correspond (with)

combinazi'one [kombinat'tsjone] *sf* combination; (*caso fortuito*) coincidence; **per ~** by chance

com'briccola *sf* (*gruppo*) party; (*banda*) gang

combus'tibile *ag* combustible ■ *sm* fuel

combusti'one *sf* combustion

com'butta *sf* (*peg*) gang; **in ~** in league

PAROLA CHIAVE

'come *av* **1** (*alla maniera di*) like; **ti comporti come lui** you behave like him *o* like he does; **bianco come la neve** (as) white as snow; **come se** as if, as though; **com'è vero Dio!** as God is my witness!

2 (*in qualità di*) as a; **lavora come autista** he works as a driver

3 (*interrogativo*) how; **come ti chiami?** what's your name?; **come sta?** how are you?; **com'è il tuo amico?** what is your friend like?; **come?** (*prego?*) pardon?, sorry?; **come mai?** how come?; **come mai non ci hai avvertiti?** how come you didn't warn us?

4 (*esclamativo*): **come sei bravo!** how clever you are!; **come mi dispiace!** I'm terribly sorry!

■ *cong* **1** (*in che modo*) how; **mi ha spiegato come l'ha conosciuto** he told me how he met him; **non so come sia successo** I don't know how it happened; **attento a come parli!** watch your mouth!

2 (*correlativo*) as; (*con comparativi di maggioranza*) than; **non è bravo come pensavo** he isn't as clever as I thought; **è meglio di come pensassi** it's better than I thought

3 (*quasi se*) as; **è come se fosse ancora qui** it's as if he was still here; **come se niente fosse** as if nothing had happened; **come non detto!** let's forget it!

4 (*appena che, quando*) as soon as; **come arrivò, iniziò a lavorare** as soon as he arrived, he set to work; *vedi anche* **così**; **oggi**; **ora**

COMECON *abbr m* (= *Consiglio di Mutua Assistenza Economica*) COMECON

come'done *sm* blackhead

co'meta *sf* comet

'comico, -a, ci, che *ag* (*Teat*) comic; (*buffo*) comical ■ *sm* (*attore*) comedian, comic actor; (*comicità*) comic spirit, comedy

co'mignolo [ko'miɲɲolo] *sm* chimney top

cominci'are [komin'tʃare] *vt, vi* to begin, start; **~ a fare/col fare** to begin to do/by doing; **cominciamo bene!** (*ironico*) we're off to a fine start!

comi'tato *sm* committee; **~ direttivo** steering committee; **~ di gestione** works council; **~ interministeriale prezzi** interdepartmental committee on prices; **~ interministeriale per la programmazione economica** interdepartmental committee for economic planning; **~ interministeriale per lo sviluppo industriale** interdepartmental committee for industrial development

comi'tiva *sf* party, group
co'mizio [ko'mittsjo] *sm* (*Pol*) meeting, assembly; **~ elettorale** election rally
'**comma, -i** *sm* (*Dir*) subsection
com'mando *sm inv* commando (squad)
com'media *sf* comedy; (*opera teatrale*) play; (: *che fa ridere*) comedy; (*fig*) playacting *no pl*
commedi'ante *sm/f* (*peg*) third-rate actor(-actress); (: *fig*) sham
commedi'ografo, -a *sm/f* (*autore*) comedy writer
commemo'rare *vt* to commemorate
commemorazi'one [kommemorat'tsjone] *sf* commemoration
commenda'tore *sm official title awarded for services to one's country*
commen'sale *sm/f* table companion
commen'tare *vt* to comment on; (*testo*) to annotate; (*Radio, TV*) to give a commentary on
commenta'tore, -'trice *sm/f* commentator
com'mento *sm* comment; (*a un testo, Radio, TV*) commentary; **~ musicale** (*Cine*) background music
commerci'ale *ag* commercial, trading; (*peg*) commercial
commercia'lista, -i, e [kommertʃa'lista] *sm/f* (*laureato*) graduate in economics and commerce; (*consulente*) business consultant
commercializ'zare [kommertʃalid'dzare] *vt* to market
commercializzazi'one [kommertʃaliddzat-tsjone] *sf* marketing
commerci'ante [kommer'tʃante] *sm/f* trader, dealer; (*negoziante*) shopkeeper; **~ all'ingrosso** wholesaler; **~ in proprio** sole trader
commerci'are [kommer'tʃare] *vi*: **~ in** to deal *o* trade in **▪** *vt* to deal *o* trade in
com'mercio [kom'mertʃo] *sm* trade, commerce; **essere in ~** (*prodotto*) to be on the market *o* on sale; **essere nel ~** (*persona*) to be in business; **~ all'ingrosso/al minuto** wholesale/retail trade
com'messo, -a *pp di* **commettere ▪** *sm/f* shop assistant (*Brit*), sales clerk (*US*) **▪** *sm* (*impiegato*) clerk **▪** *sf* (*Comm*) order; **~ viaggiatore** commercial traveller
commes'tibile *ag* edible; **commestibili** *smpl* foodstuffs
com'mettere *vt* to commit; (*ordinare*) to commission, order
commi'ato *sm* leave-taking; **prendere ~ da qn** to take one's leave of sb
commi'nare *vt* (*Dir*) to make provision for
commise'rare *vt* to sympathize with, commiserate with

commiserazi'one [kommizerat'tsjone] *sf* commiseration
com'misi *etc vb vedi* **commettere**
commissaria'mento *sm* temporary receivership
commissari'are *vt* to put under temporary receivership
commissari'ato *sm* (*Amm*) commissionership; (: *sede*) commissioner's office; (: *di polizia*) police station
commis'sario *sm* commissioner; (*di pubblica sicurezza*) ≈ (police) superintendent (*Brit*), ≈ (police) captain (*US*); (*Sport*) steward; (*membro di commissione*) member of a committee *o* board; **alto ~** high commissioner; **~ di bordo** (*Naut*) purser; **~ d'esame** member of an examining board; **~ di gara** race official; **~ tecnico** (*Sport*) national coach
commissio'nare *vt* to order, place an order for
commissio'nario *sm* (*Comm*) agent, broker
commissi'one *sf* (*incarico*) errand; (*comitato, percentuale*) commission; (*Comm: ordinazione*) order; **commissioni** *sfpl* (*acquisti*) shopping *sg*; **~ d'esame** examining board; **~ d'inchiesta** committee of enquiry; **~ permanente** standing committee; **commissioni bancarie** bank charges
commit'tente *sm/f* (*Comm*) purchaser, customer
com'mosso, -a *pp di* **commuovere**
commo'vente *ag* moving
commozi'one [kommot'tsjone] *sf* emotion, deep feeling; **~ cerebrale** (*Med*) concussion
commu'overe *vt* to move, affect; **commuoversi** *vr* to be moved
commu'tare *vt* (*pena*) to commute; (*Elettr*) to change *o* switch over
commutazi'one [kommutat'tsjone] *sf* (*Dir, Elettr*) commutation
como *sm inv* chest of drawers
como'dino *sm* bedside table
comodità *sf inv* comfort; convenience
'**comodo, -a** *ag* comfortable; (*facile*) easy; (*conveniente*) convenient; (*utile*) useful, handy **▪** *sm* comfort; convenience; **con ~** at one's convenience *o* leisure; **fare il proprio ~** to do as one pleases; **far ~** to be useful *o* handy; **stia ~!** don't bother to get up!
'**compact disc** *sm inv* compact disc
compae'sano, -a *sm/f* fellow-countryman(-woman); person from the same town
com'pagine [kom'padʒine] *sf* (*squadra*) team
compa'gnia [kompaɲ'ɲia] *sf* company; (*gruppo*) gathering; **fare ~ a qn** to keep sb company; **essere di ~** to be sociable

com'pagno, -a [kom'paɲɲo] sm/f (di classe, gioco) companion; (Pol) comrade; ~ **di lavoro** workmate; ~ **di scuola** schoolfriend; ~ **di viaggio** fellow traveller

com'paio etc vb vedi **comparire**

compa'rare vt to compare

compara'tivo, -a ag, sm comparative

comparazi'one [komparat'tsjone] sf comparison

com'pare sm (padrino) godfather; (complice) accomplice; (fam: amico) old pal, old mate

compa'rire vi to appear; ~ **in giudizio** (Dir) to appear before the court

comparizi'one [komparit'tsjone] sf (Dir) appearance; **mandato di** ~ summons sg

com'parso, -a pp di **comparire** ■ sf appearance; (Teat) walk-on; (Cine) extra

compartecipare [kompartetʃi'pare] vi (Comm): ~ **a** to have a share in

compartecipazi'one [kompartetʃipat'tsjone] sf sharing; (quota) share; ~ **agli utili** profit-sharing; **in** ~ jointly

comparti'mento sm compartment; (Amm) district

com'parvi etc vb vedi **comparire**

compas'sato, -a ag (persona) composed; **freddo e** ~ cool and collected

compassi'one sf compassion, pity; **avere** ~ **di qn** to feel sorry for sb, pity sb; **fare** ~ to arouse pity

compassio'nevole ag compassionate

com'passo sm (pair of) compasses pl; callipers pl

compa'tibile ag (scusabile) excusable; (conciliabile, Inform) compatible

compati'mento sm compassion; indulgence; **con aria di** ~ with a condescending air

compa'tire vt (aver compassione di) to sympathize with, feel sorry for; (scusare) to make allowances for

compatri'ota, -i, e sm/f compatriot

compat'tezza [kompat'tettsa] sf (solidità) compactness; (fig: unità) solidarity

com'patto, -a ag compact; (roccia) solid; (folla) dense; (fig: gruppo, partito) united, close-knit

com'pendio sm summary; (libro) compendium

compen'sare vt (equilibrare) to compensate for, make up for; **compensarsi** vr (reciproco) to balance each other out; ~ **qn di** (rimunerare) to pay o remunerate sb for; (risarcire) to pay compensation to sb for; (fig fatiche, dolori) to reward sb for

compen'sato sm (anche: **legno compensato**) plywood

com'penso sm compensation; payment, remuneration; reward; **in** ~ (d'altra parte) on the other hand

'compera sf purchase; **fare le compere** to do the shopping

compe'rare vt = **comprare**

compe'tente ag competent; (mancia) apt, suitable; (capace) qualified; **rivolgersi all'ufficio** ~ to apply to the office concerned

compe'tenza [kompe'tɛntsa] sf competence; (Dir: autorità) jurisdiction; (Tecn, Comm) expertise; **competenze** sfpl (onorari) fees; **definire le competenze** to establish responsibilities

com'petere vi to compete, vie; (Dir: spettare): ~ **a** to lie within the competence of

competitività sf inv competitiveness

competi'tivo, -a ag competitive

competi'tore, -'trice sm/f competitor

competizi'one [kompetit'tsjone] sf competition; **spirito di** ~ competitive spirit

compia'cente [kompja'tʃɛnte] ag courteous, obliging

compia'cenza [kompja'tʃɛntsa] sf courtesy

compia'cere [kompja'tʃere] vi: ~ **a** to gratify, please ■ vt to please; **compiacersi** vr (provare soddisfazione): **compiacersi di** o **per qc** to be delighted at sth; (rallegrarsi): **compiacersi con qn** to congratulate sb; (degnarsi): **compiacersi di fare** to be so good as to do

compiaci'mento [kompjatʃi'mento] sm satisfaction

compiaci'uto, -a [kompja'tʃuto] pp di **compiacere**

compi'angere [kom'pjandʒere] vt to sympathize with, feel sorry for

compi'anto, -a pp di **compiangere** ■ ag: **il** ~ **presidente** the late lamented president ■ sm mourning, grief

'compiere vt (concludere) to finish, complete; (adempiere) to carry out, fulfil; **compiersi** vr (avverarsi) to be fulfilled, come true; ~ **gli anni** to have one's birthday

compi'lare vt to compile; (modulo) to complete, fill in (Brit), fill out (US)

compila'tore, -'trice sm/f compiler

compilazi'one [kompilat'tsjone] sf compilation; completion

compi'mento sm (termine, conclusione) completion, fulfilment; **portare a** ~ **qc** to conclude sth, bring sth to a conclusion

com'pire vb = **compiere**

'compito sm (incarico) task, duty; (dovere) duty; (Ins) exercise; (: a casa) piece of homework; **fare i compiti** to do one's homework

com'pito, -a ag well-mannered, polite

compiu'tezza [kompju'tettsa] *sf* (*completezza*) completeness; (*perfezione*) perfection

compi'uto, -a *pp di* **compiere** ■ *ag*: **a 20 anni compiuti** at 20 years of age, at age 20; **un fatto ~** a fait accompli

comple'anno *sm* birthday

complemen'tare *ag* complementary; (*Ins: materia*) subsidiary

comple'mento *sm* complement; (*Mil*) reserve (troops); ~ **oggetto** (*Ling*) direct object

comples'sato, -a *ag*, *sm/f*: **essere (un) ~** to be full of complexes *o* hang-ups (*fam*)

complessità *sf* complexity

complessiva'mente *av* (*nell'insieme*) on the whole; (*in tutto*) altogether

comples'sivo, -a *ag* (*globale*) comprehensive, overall; (*totale: cifra*) total; **visione complessiva** overview

com'plesso, -a *ag* complex ■ *sm* (*Psic, Edil*) complex; (*Mus: corale*) ensemble; (: *orchestrina*) band; (: *di musica pop*) group; **in** *o* **nel ~** on the whole

completa'mento *sm* completion

comple'tare *vt* to complete

com'pleto, -a *ag* complete; (*teatro, autobus*) full ■ *sm* suit; **al ~** full; (*tutti presenti*) all present; **essere al ~** (*teatro*) to be sold out; **~ da sci** ski suit

compli'care *vt* to complicate; **complicarsi** *vr* to become complicated

complicazi'one [komplikat'tsjone] *sf* complication; **salvo complicazioni** unless any difficulties arise

'complice ['kɔmplitʃe] *sm/f* accomplice

complicità [komplitʃi'ta] *sf inv* complicity; **un sorriso/uno sguardo di ~** a knowing smile/look

complimen'tarsi *vr*: ~ **con** to congratulate

compli'mento *sm* compliment; **complimenti** *smpl* (*cortesia eccessiva*) ceremony *sg*; **complimenti!** congratulations!; **senza complimenti!** don't stand on ceremony!; make yourself at home!; help yourself!

complot'tare *vi* to plot, conspire

com'plotto *sm* plot, conspiracy

com'pone *etc vb vedi* **comporre**

compo'nente *sm/f* member ■ *sm* component

com'pongo *etc vb vedi* **comporre**

compo'nibile *ag* (*mobili, cucina*) fitted

componi'mento *sm* (*Dir*) settlement; (*Ins*) composition; (*poetico, teatrale*) work

com'porre *vt* (*musica, testo*) to compose; (*mettere in ordine*) to arrange; (*Dir: lite*) to settle; (*Tip*) to set; (*Tel*) to dial; **comporsi** *vr*: **comporsi di** to consist of, be composed of

comportamen'tale *ag* behavioural (*Brit*), behavioral (*US*)

comporta'mento *sm* behaviour (*Brit*), behavior (*US*); (*di prodotto*) performance

compor'tare *vt* (*implicare*) to involve, entail; (*consentire*) to permit, allow (of); **comportarsi** *vr* (*condursi*) to behave

com'posi *etc vb vedi* **comporre**

composi'tore, -'trice *sm/f* composer; (*Tip*) compositor, typesetter

composizi'one [kompozit'tsjone] *sf* composition; (*Dir*) settlement

com'posta *sf vedi* **composto**

compos'tezza [kompos'tettsa] *sf* composure; decorum

com'posto, -a *pp di* **comporre** ■ *ag* (*persona*) composed, self-possessed; (: *decoroso*) dignified; (*formato da più elementi*) compound *cpd* ■ *sm* compound; (*Cuc etc*) mixture ■ *sf* (*Cuc*) stewed fruit *no pl*; (*Agr*) compost

com'prare *vt* to buy; (*corrompere*) to bribe

compra'tore, -'trice *sm/f* buyer, purchaser

compra'vendita *sf* (*Comm*) (contract of) sale; **un atto di ~** a deed of sale

com'prendere *vt* (*contenere*) to comprise, consist of; (*capire*) to understand

compren'donio *sm*: **essere duro di ~** to be slow on the uptake

compren'sibile *ag* understandable

comprensi'one *sf* understanding

compren'sivo, -a *ag* (*prezzo*): ~ **di** inclusive of; (*indulgente*) understanding

compren'sorio *sm* area, territory; (*Amm*) district

com'preso, -a *pp di* **comprendere** ■ *ag* (*incluso*) included; **tutto ~** all included, all-in (*Brit*)

com'pressa *sf vedi* **compresso**

compressi'one *sf* compression

com'presso, -a *pp di* **comprimere** ■ *ag* (*vedi comprimere*) pressed; compressed; repressed ■ *sf* (*Med: garza*) compress; (: *pastiglia*) tablet

compres'sore *sm* compressor; (*anche*: **rullo compressore**) steamroller

compri'mario, -a *sm/f* (*Teat*) supporting actor(-actress)

com'primere *vt* (*premere*) to press; (*Fisica*) to compress; (*fig*) to repress

compro'messo, -a *pp di* **compromettere** ■ *sm* compromise

compro'mettere *vt* to compromise; **compromettersi** *vr* to compromise o.s.

comproprietà *sf* (*Dir*) joint ownership

compro'vare *vt* to confirm

com'punto, -a *ag* contrite; **con fare ~** with a solemn air

compunzi'one [kompun'tsjone] *sf* contrition; solemnity

compu'tare *vt* to calculate; (*addebitare*): ~ **qc a qn** to debit sb with sth

com'puter [kəm'pju:tər] *sm inv* computer

computeriz'zato, -a [komputerid'dzato] *ag* computerized

computerizzazi'one [komputeriddzat'tsjone] *sf* computerization

computiste'ria *sf* accounting, book-keeping

'computo *sm* calculation; **fare il ~ di** to count

comu'nale *ag* municipal, town *cpd*; **consiglio/palazzo** ~ town council/hall; **è un impiegato** ~ he works for the local council

Co'mune *sm* (*Amm*) town council; (*sede*) town hall; *see note*

⊙ **COMUNE**

The *Comune* is the smallest autonomous political and administrative unit. It keeps records of births, marriages and deaths and has the power to levy taxes and vet proposals for public works and town planning. It is run by a "Giunta comunale", which is elected by the "Consiglio Comunale". The *Comune* is headed by the "sindaco" (mayor) who since 1993 has been elected directly by the citizens.

co'mune *ag* common; (*consueto*) common, everyday; (*di livello medio*) average; (*ordinario*) ordinary ■ *sf* (*di persone*) commune; **fuori del** ~ out of the ordinary; **avere in** ~ to have in common, share; **mettere in** ~ to share; **un nostro** ~ **amico** a mutual friend of ours; **fare cassa** ~ to pool one's money

comuni'care *vt* (*notizia*) to pass on, convey; (*malattia*) to pass on; (*ansia etc*) to communicate; (*trasmettere: calore etc*) to transmit, communicate; (*Rel*) to administer communion to ■ *vi* to communicate; **comunicarsi** *vr* (*propagarsi*): **comunicarsi a** to spread to; (*Rel*) to receive communion

comunica'tivo, -a *ag* (*sentimento*) infectious; (*persona*) communicative ■ *sf* communicativeness

comuni'cato *sm* communiqué; ~ **stampa** press release

comunicazi'one [komunikat'tsjone] *sf* communication; (*annuncio*) announcement; (*Tel*): ~ **(telefonica)** (telephone) call; **dare la** ~ **a qn** to put sb through; **ottenere la** ~ to get through; **salvo comunicazioni contrarie da parte Vostra** unless we hear from you to the contrary

comuni'one *sf* communion; ~ **dei beni** (*Dir*: *tra coniugi*) joint ownership of property

comu'nismo *sm* communism

comu'nista, -i, e *ag, sm/f* communist

comunità *sf inv* community; **C~ Economica Europea** European Economic Community; ~ **terapeutica** *rehabilitation centre run by voluntary organizations for people with drug, alcohol etc dependency*

comuni'tario, -a *ag* community *cpd*

co'munque *cong* however, no matter how ■ *av* (*in ogni modo*) in any case; (*tuttavia*) however, nevertheless

con *prep* (*nei seguenti casi* **con** *può fondersi con l'articolo definito:* con + il = **col**, con + la = **colla**, con + gli = **cogli**, con + I = **coi**, con + le = **colle**) with; **partire col treno** to leave by train; ~ **mio grande stupore** to my great astonishment; ~ **la forza** by force; ~ **questo freddo** in this cold weather; ~ **il 1° di ottobre** as of October 1st; ~ **tutto ciò** in spite of that, for all that; ~ **tutto che era arrabbiato** even though he was angry, in spite of the fact that he was angry; **e** ~ **questo?** so what?

co'nato *sm*: ~ **di vomito** retching

'conca, -che *sf* (*Geo*) valley

concate'nare *vt* to link up, connect; **concatenarsi** *vr* to be connected

con'cavo, -a *ag* concave

con'cedere [kon'tʃedere] *vt* (*accordare*) to grant; (*ammettere*) to admit, concede; **concedersi qc** to treat o.s. to sth, allow o.s. sth

concentra'mento [kontʃentra'mento] *sm* concentration

concen'trare [kontʃen'trare] *vt*, **concen'trarsi** *vr* to concentrate

concen'trato [kontʃen'trato] *sm* concentrate; ~ **di pomodoro** tomato purée

concentrazi'one [kontʃentrat'tsjone] *sf* concentration; ~ **orizzontale/verticale** (*Econ*) horizontal/vertical integration

con'centrico, -a, ci, che [kon'tʃentriko] *ag* concentric

conce'pibile [kontʃe'pibile] *ag* conceivable

concepi'mento [kontʃepi'mento] *sm* conception

conce'pire [kontʃe'pire] *vt* (*bambino*) to conceive; (*progetto, idea*) to conceive (of); (*metodo, piano*) to devise; (*situazione*) to imagine, understand

con'cernere [kon'tʃernere] *vt* to concern; **per quanto mi concerne** as far as I'm concerned

concer'tare [kontʃer'tare] *vt* (*Mus*) to harmonize; (*ordire*) to devise, plan; **concertarsi** *vr* to agree

concer'tista, -i, e [kontʃer'tista] *sm/f* (*Mus*) concert performer

con'certo [kon'tʃerto] *sm* (*Mus*) concert; (: *componimento*) concerto

con'cessi *etc* [kon'tʃessi] *vb vedi* **concedere**

concessio'nario [kontʃessjo'narjo] *sm*
(*Comm*) agent, dealer; ~ **esclusivo (di)** sole
agent (for)

concessi'one [kontʃes'sjone] *sf* concession

con'cesso, -a [kon'tʃɛsso] *pp di* **concedere**

con'cetto [kon'tʃɛtto] *sm* (*pensiero, idea*)
concept; (*opinione*) opinion; **è un impiegato
di ~** ≈ he's a white-collar worker

concezi'one [kontʃet'tsjone] *sf* conception;
(*idea*) view, idea

con'chiglia [kon'kiʎʎa] *sf* shell

'concia ['kontʃa] *sf* (*di pelli*) tanning; (*di
tabacco*) curing; (*sostanza*) tannin

conci'are [kon'tʃare] *vt* (*pelli*) to tan; (*tabacco*)
to cure; (*fig: ridurre in cattivo stato*) to beat up;
conciarsi *vr* (*sporcarsi*) to get in a mess;
(*vestirsi male*) to dress badly; **ti hanno
conciato male** *o* **per le feste!** they've really
beaten you up!

concili'abile [kontʃi'ljabile] *ag* compatible

concili'abolo [kontʃi'ljabolo] *sm* secret
meeting

concili'ante [kontʃi'ljante] *ag* conciliatory

concili'are [kontʃi'ljare] *vt* to reconcile;
(*contravvenzione*) to pay on the spot; (*favorire:
sonno*) to be conducive to, induce; (*procurare:
simpatia*) to gain; **conciliarsi qc** to gain *o* win
sth (for o.s.); **conciliarsi qn** to win sb over;
conciliarsi con to be reconciled with

conciliazi'one [kontʃiljat'tsjone] *sf*
reconciliation; (*Dir*) settlement; **la C~** (*Storia*)
the Lateran Pact

con'cilio [kon'tʃiljo] *sm* (*Rel*) council

conci'mare [kontʃi'mare] *vt* to fertilize; (*con
letame*) to manure

con'cime [kon'tʃime] *sm* manure; (*chimico*)
fertilizer

concisi'one [kontʃi'zjone] *sf* concision,
conciseness

con'ciso, -a [kon'tʃizo] *ag* concise, succinct

conci'tato, -a [kontʃi'tato] *ag* excited,
emotional

concitta'dino, -a [kontʃitta'dino] *sm/f* fellow
citizen

con'clave *sm* conclave

con'cludere *vt* to conclude; (*portare a
compimento*) to conclude, finish, bring to an
end; (*operare positivamente*) to achieve ▪ *vi*
(*essere convincente*) to be conclusive;
concludersi *vr* to come to an end, close

conclusi'one *sf* conclusion; (*risultato*) result

conclu'sivo, -a *ag* conclusive; (*finale*) final

con'cluso, -a *pp di* **concludere**

concomi'tanza [konkomi'tantsa] *sf* (*di
circostanze, fatti*) combination

concor'danza [konkor'dantsa] *sf* (*anche Ling*)
agreement

concor'dare *vt* (*prezzo*) to agree on; (*Ling*) to
make agree ▪ *vi* to agree; ~ **una tregua** to
agree to a truce

concor'dato *sm* agreement; (*Rel*) concordat

con'corde *ag* (*d'accordo*) in agreement;
(*simultaneo*) simultaneous

con'cordia *sf* harmony, concord

concor'rente *ag* competing; (*Mat*)
concurrent ▪ *sm/f* (*Sport, Comm*) competitor;
(*a un concorso di bellezza*) contestant

concor'renza [konkor'rentsa] *sf*
competition; ~ **sleale** unfair competition;
a prezzi di ~ at competitive prices

concorrenzi'ale [konkorren'tsjale] *ag*
competitive

con'correre *vi*: ~ **(in)** (*Mat*) to converge *o* meet
(in); ~ **(a)** (*competere*) to compete (for); (: *Ins: a
una cattedra*) to apply (for); (*partecipare: a
un'impresa*) to take part (in), contribute (to)

con'corso, -a *pp di* **concorrere** ▪ *sm*
competition; (*esame*) examination; ~ **di bellezza** beauty contest; ~
di circostanze combination of circumstances;
~ **di colpa** (*Dir*) contributory negligence; **un**
~ **ippico** a showjumping event; ~ **in reato** (*Dir*)
complicity in a crime; ~ **per titoli** competitive
examination for qualified candidates

con'creto, -a *ag* concrete ▪ *sm*: **in** ~ in reality

concu'bina *sf* concubine ▪ *sm*: **sono
concubini** they are living together

concussi'one *sf* (*Dir*) extortion

con'danna *sf* condemnation; sentence;
conviction; ~ **a morte** death sentence

condan'nare *vt* (*disapprovare*) to condemn;
(*Dir*): ~ **a** to sentence to; ~ **per** to convict of

condan'nato, -a *sm/f* convict

con'densa *sf* condensation

conden'sare *vt*, **conden'sarsi** *vr* to condense

condensa'tore *sm* capacitor

condensazi'one [kondensat'tsjone] *sf*
condensation

condi'mento *sm* seasoning; dressing

con'dire *vt* to season; (*insalata*) to dress

condiscen'dente [kondiʃʃen'dɛnte] *ag*
obliging; compliant

condiscen'denza [kondiʃʃen'dɛntsa] *sf*
(*disponibilità*) obligingness; (*arrendevolezza*)
compliance

condi'scendere [kondiʃʃendere] *vi*: ~ **a** to
agree to

condi'sceso, -a [kondiʃʃeso] *pp di*
condiscendere

condi'videre *vt* to share

condi'viso, -a *pp di* **condividere**

condizio'nale [kondittsjo'nale] *ag*
conditional ▪ *sm* (*Ling*) conditional ▪ *sf*
(*Dir*) suspended sentence

condiziona'mento [kondittsjona'mento] *sm* conditioning; ~ **d'aria** air conditioning

condizio'nare [kondittsjo'nare] *vt* to condition; **ad aria condizionata** air-conditioned

condiziona'tore [kondittsjona'tore] *sm* air conditioner

condizi'one [kondit'tsjone] *sf* condition; **condizioni** *sfpl* (*di pagamento etc*) terms, conditions; **a ~ che** on condition that, provided that; **a nessuna ~** on no account; **condizioni a convenirsi** terms to be arranged; **condizioni di lavoro** working conditions; **condizioni di vendita** sales terms

condogli'anze [kondoʎ'ʎantse] *sfpl* condolences

condomini'ale *ag*: **riunione ~** residents' meeting; **spese condominiali** common charges

condo'minio *sm* joint ownership; (*edificio*) jointly-owned building

con'domino *sm* joint owner

condo'nare *vt* (*Dir*) to remit

con'dono *sm* remission; ~ **fiscale** *conditional amnesty for people evading tax*

con'dotta *sf vedi* **condotto**

con'dotto, -a *pp di* **condurre** ◼ *ag*: **medico ~** local authority doctor (*in country district*) ◼ *sm* (*canale, tubo*) pipe, conduit; (*Anat*) duct ◼ *sf* (*modo di comportarsi*) conduct, behaviour (*Brit*), behavior (*US*); (*di un affare etc*) handling; (*di acqua*) piping; (*incarico sanitario*) *country medical practice controlled by a local authority*

condu'cente [kondu'tʃɛnte] *sm* driver

con'duco *etc vb vedi* **condurre**

con'durre *vt* to conduct; (*azienda*) to manage; (*accompagnare: bambino*) to take; (*automobile*) to drive; (*trasportare: acqua, gas*) to convey, conduct; (*fig*) to lead ◼ *vi* to lead; **condursi** *vr* to behave, conduct o.s.; ~ **a termine** to conclude

con'dussi *etc vb vedi* **condurre**

condut'tore, -'trice *ag*: **filo ~** (*fig*) thread; **motivo ~** leitmotiv ◼ *sm* (*di mezzi pubblici*) driver; (*Fisica*) conductor

condut'tura *sf* (*gen*) pipe; (*di acqua, gas*) main

conduzi'one [kondut'tsjone] *sf* (*di affari, ditta*) management; (*Dir: locazione*) lease; (*Fisica*) conduction

confabu'lare *vi* to confab

confa'cente [konfa'tʃɛnte] *ag*: ~ **a qn/qc** suitable for sb/sth; **clima ~ alla salute** healthy climate

CONFAGRICOL'TURA *abbr f* (= *Confederazione generale dell'Agricoltura Italiana*) *confederation of Italian farmers*

CON'FAPI *sigla f* = **Confederazione Nazionale della Piccola Industria**

con'farsi *vr*: ~ **a** to suit, agree with

CONFARTIGIA'NATO [konfartidʒa'nato] *abbr f* = **Confederazione Generale dell'Artigianato Italiano**

con'fatto, -a *pp di* **confarsi**

CONFCOM'MERCIO [konfkom'mɛrtʃo] *abbr f* = **Confederazione Generale del Commercio**

confederazi'one [konfederat'tsjone] *sf* confederation; ~ **imprenditoriale** employers' association

confe'renza [konfe'rɛntsa] *sf* (*discorso*) lecture; (*riunione*) conference; ~ **stampa** press conference

conferenzi'ere, -a [konferen'tsjɛre] *sm/f* lecturer

conferi'mento *sm* conferring, awarding

confe'rire *vt*: ~ **qc a qn** to give sth to sb, confer sth on sb ◼ *vi* to confer

con'ferma *sf* confirmation

confer'mare *vt* to confirm

confes'sare *vt*, **confes'sarsi** *vr* to confess; **andare a confessarsi** (*Rel*) to go to confession

confessio'nale *ag, sm* confessional

confessi'one *sf* confession; (*setta religiosa*) denomination

con'fesso, -a *ag*: **essere reo ~** to have pleaded guilty

confes'sore *sm* confessor

con'fetto *sm* sugared almond; (*Med*) pill

confet'tura *sf* (*gen*) jam; (*di arance*) marmalade

confezio'nare [konfettsjo'nare] *vt* (*vestito*) to make (up); (*merci, pacchi*) to package

confezi'one [konfet'tsjone] *sf* (*di abiti: da uomo*) tailoring; (: *da donna*) dressmaking; (*imballaggio*) packaging; ~ **regalo** gift pack; ~ **risparmio** economy size; ~ **da viaggio** travel pack; **confezioni per signora** ladies' wear *no pl*; **confezioni da uomo** menswear *no pl*

confic'care *vt*: ~ **qc in** to hammer o drive sth into; **conficcarsi** *vr* to stick

confi'dare *vi*: ~ **in** to confide in, rely on ◼ *vt* to confide; **confidarsi con qn** to confide in sb

confi'dente *sm/f* (*persona amica*) confidant/confidante; (*informatore*) informer

confi'denza [konfi'dɛntsa] *sf* (*familiarità*) intimacy, familiarity; (*fiducia*) trust, confidence; (*rivelazione*) confidence; **prendersi (troppe) confidenze** to take liberties; **fare una ~ a qn** to confide something to sb

confidenzi'ale [konfiden'tsjale] *ag* familiar, friendly; (*segreto*) confidential; **in via ~** confidentially

configu'rare vt (Inform) to set; **configurarsi** vr: **configurarsi a** to assume the shape o form of

configurazi'one [konfigurat'tsjone] sf configuration; (Inform) setting

confi'nante ag neighbouring (Brit), neighboring (US)

confi'nare vi: ~ **con** to border on ■ vt (Pol) to intern; (fig) to confine; **confinarsi** vr (isolarsi): **confinarsi in** to shut o.s. up in

confi'nato, -a ag interned ■ sm/f internee

CONFIN'DUSTRIA sigla f (= Confederazione Generale dell'Industria Italiana) employers' association, ≈ CBI (Brit)

con'fine sm boundary; (di paese) border, frontier; **territorio di** ~ border zone

con'fino sm internment

con'fisca sf confiscation

confis'care vt to confiscate

conflagrazi'one [konflagrat'tsjone] sf conflagration

con'flitto sm conflict; **essere in** ~ **con qc** to clash with sth; **essere in** ~ **con qn** to be at loggerheads with sb; ~ **d'interessi** conflict of interests

conflittu'ale ag: **rapporto** ~ relationship based on conflict

conflittualità sf conflicts pl

conflu'enza [konflu'entsa] sf (di fiumi) confluence; (di strade) junction

conflu'ire vi (fiumi) to flow into each other, meet; (strade) to meet

con'fondere vt to mix up, confuse; (imbarazzare) to embarrass; **confondersi** vr (mescolarsi) to mingle; (turbarsi) to be confused; (sbagliare) to get mixed up; ~ **le idee a qn** to mix sb up, confuse sb

confor'mare vt (adeguare): ~ **a** to adapt o conform to; **conformarsi** vr: **conformarsi (a)** to conform (to)

con'forme ag: ~ **a** (simile) similar to; (corrispondente) in keeping with

conforme'mente av accordingly; ~ **a** in accordance with

confor'mismo sm conformity

confor'mista, -i, e sm/f conformist

conformità sf conformity; **in** ~ **a** in conformity with

confor'tare vt to comfort, console

confor'tevole ag (consolante) comforting; (comodo) comfortable

con'forto sm (consolazione, sollievo) comfort, consolation; (conferma) support; **a** ~ **di qc** in support of sth; **i conforti (religiosi)** the last sacraments

confra'ternita sf brotherhood

confron'tare vt to compare; **confrontarsi** vr

(scontrarsi) to have a confrontation

con'fronto sm comparison; (Dir, Mil, Pol) confrontation; **in** o **a** ~ **di** in comparison with, compared to; **nei miei** (o **tuoi** etc) **confronti** towards me (o you etc)

con'fusi etc vb vedi **confondere**

confusi'one sf confusion; (imbarazzo) embarrassment; **far** ~ (disordine) to make a mess; (chiasso) to make a racket; (confondere) to confuse things

con'fuso, -a pp di **confondere** ■ ag (vedi confondere) confused; embarrassed

confu'tare vt to refute

conge'dare [kondʒe'dare] vt to dismiss; (Mil) to demobilize; **congedarsi** vr to take one's leave

con'gedo [kon'dʒedo] sm (anche Mil) leave; **prendere** ~ **da qn** to take one's leave of sb; ~ **assoluto** (Mil) discharge

conge'gnare [kondʒeɲ'ɲare] vt to construct, put together

con'gegno [kon'dʒeɲɲo] sm device, mechanism

congela'mento [kondʒela'mento] sm (gen) freezing; (Med) frostbite; ~ **salariale** wage freeze

conge'lare [kondʒe'lare] vt, **congelarsi** vr to freeze

congela'tore [kondʒela'tore] sm freezer

con'genito, -a [kon'dʒɛnito] ag congenital

con'gerie [kon'dʒɛrje] sf inv (di oggetti) heap; (di idee) muddle, jumble

congestio'nare [kondʒestjo'nare] vt to congest; **essere congestionato** (persona, viso) to be flushed; (zona: per traffico) to be congested

congesti'one [kondʒes'tjone] sf congestion

conget'tura [kondʒet'tura] sf conjecture, supposition

con'giungere [kon'dʒundʒere] vt, **con'giungersi** vr to join (together)

congiunti'vite [kondʒunti'vite] sf conjunctivitis

congiun'tivo [kondʒun'tivo] sm (Ling) subjunctive

congi'unto, -a [kon'dʒunto] pp di **congiungere** ■ ag (unito) joined ■ sm/f (parente) relative

congiun'tura [kondʒun'tura] sf (giuntura) junction, join; (Anat) joint; (circostanza) juncture; (Econ) economic situation

congiuntu'rale [kondʒuntu'rale] ag of the economic situation; **crisi** ~ economic crisis

congiunzi'one [kondʒun'tsjone] sf (Ling) conjunction

congi'ura [kon'dʒura] sf conspiracy

congiu'rare [kondʒu'rare] vi to conspire

conglome'rato sm (Geo) conglomerate; (fig) conglomeration; (Edil) concrete

'Congo sm: **il ~** the Congo

congo'lese ag, sm/f Congolese inv

congratu'larsi vr: **~ con qn per qc** to congratulate sb on sth

congratulazi'oni [kongratulat'tsjoni] sfpl congratulations

con'grega, -ghe sf band, bunch

congregazi'one [kongregat'tsjone] sf congregation

congres'sista, -i, e sm/f participant at a congress

con'gresso sm congress

'congruo, -a ag (prezzo, compenso) adequate, fair; (ragionamento) coherent, consistent

conguagli'are [kongwaʎ'ʎare] vt to balance; (stipendio) to adjust

congu'aglio [kon'gwaʎʎo] sm balancing; adjusting; (somma di denaro) balance; **fare il ~ di** to balance; to adjust

coni'are vt to mint, coin; (fig) to coin

coniazi'one [konjat'tsjone] sf mintage

'conico, -a, ci, che ag conical

co'nifere sfpl conifers

conigli'era [koniʎ'ʎɛra] sf (gabbia) rabbit hutch; (più grande) rabbit run

conigli'etta [koniʎ'ʎetta] sf bunny girl

conigli'etto [koniʎ'ʎetto] sm bunny

co'niglio [ko'niʎʎo] sm rabbit; **sei un ~!** (fig) you're chicken!

coniu'gale ag (amore, diritti) conjugal; (vita) married, conjugal

coniu'gare vt to combine; (Ling) to conjugate; **coniugarsi** vr to get married

coniu'gato, -a ag (Amm) married

coniugazi'one [konjugat'tsjone] sf (Ling) conjugation

'coniuge ['kɔnjudʒe] sm/f spouse

connatu'rato, -a ag inborn

connazio'nale [konnattsjo'nale] sm/f fellow-countryman(-woman)

connessi'one sf connection

con'nesso, -a pp di **connettere**

con'nettere vt to connect, join ■ vi (fig) to think straight

connet'tore sm (Elettr) connector

conni'vente ag conniving

conno'tati smpl distinguishing marks; **rispondere ai ~** to fit the description; **cambiare i ~ a qn** (fam) to beat sb up

con'nubio sm (matrimonio) marriage; (fig) union

'cono sm cone; **~ gelato** ice-cream cone

co'nobbi etc vb vedi **conoscere**

cono'scente [konoʃ'ʃente] sm/f acquaintance

cono'scenza [konoʃ'ʃentsa] sf (il sapere) knowledge no pl; (persona) acquaintance;

(facoltà sensoriale) consciousness no pl; **essere a ~ di qc** to know sth; **portare qn a ~ di qc** to inform sb of sth; **per vostra ~** for your information; **fare la ~ di qn** to make sb's acquaintance; **perdere ~** to lose consciousness; **~ tecnica** know-how

co'noscere [ko'noʃʃere] vt to know; **ci siamo conosciuti a Firenze** we (first) met in Florence; **~ qn di vista** to know sb by sight; **farsi ~** (fig) to make a name for o.s.

conosci'tore, -'trice [konoʃʃi'tore] sm/f connoisseur

conosci'uto, -a [konoʃ'ʃuto] pp di **conoscere** ■ ag well-known

con'quista sf conquest

conquis'tare vt to conquer; (fig) to gain, win

conquista'tore, -'trice sm/f (in guerra) conqueror ■ sm (seduttore) lady-killer

cons. abbr = **consiglio**

consa'crare vt (Rel) to consecrate; (: sacerdote) to ordain; (dedicare) to dedicate; (fig: uso etc) to sanction; **consacrarsi a** to dedicate o.s. to

consangu'ineo, a sm/f blood relation

consa'pevole ag: **~ di** aware of

consapevo'lezza [konsapevo'lettsa] sf awareness, consciousness

conscia'mente [konʃa'mente] av consciously

'conscio, -a, sci, sce ['kɔnʃo] ag: **~ di** aware o conscious of

consecu'tivo, -a ag consecutive; (successivo: giorno) following, next

con'segna [kon'seɲɲa] sf delivery; (merce consegnata) consignment; (custodia) care, custody; (Mil: ordine) orders pl; (: punizione) confinement to barracks; **alla ~** on delivery; **dare qc in ~ a qn** to entrust sth to sb; **passare le consegne a qn** to hand over to sb; **~ a domicilio** home delivery; **~ in contrassegno, pagamento alla ~** cash on delivery; **~ sollecita** prompt delivery

conse'gnare [konseɲ'ɲare] vt to deliver; (affidare) to entrust, hand over; (Mil) to confine to barracks

consegna'tario [konseɲɲa'tarjo] sm consignee

consegu'ente ag consequent

conseguente'mente av consequently

consegu'enza [konse'gwentsa] sf consequence; **per o di ~** consequently

consegui'mento sm (di scopo, risultato etc) achievement, attainment; **al ~ della laurea** on graduation

consegu'ire vt to achieve ■ vi to follow, result; **~ la laurea** to graduate, obtain one's degree

con'senso sm approval, consent

consensu'ale ag (Dir) by mutual consent

consen'tire *vi:* ~ **a** to consent *o* agree to ■ *vt* to allow, permit; **mi si consenta di ringraziare ...** I would like to thank ...
consenzi'ente [konsen'tsjɛnte] *ag (gen, Dir)* consenting
con'serto, -a *ag:* **a braccia conserte** with one's arms folded
con'serva *sf (Cuc)* preserve; ~ **di frutta** jam; ~ **di pomodoro** tomato purée; **conserve alimentari** tinned (*o* canned *o* bottled) foods
conser'vante *sm (per alimenti)* preservative
conser'vare *vt (Cuc)* to preserve; *(custodire)* to keep; *(: dalla distruzione etc)* to preserve, conserve; **conservarsi** *vr* to keep
conserva'tore, -'trice *ag, sm/f (Pol)* conservative
conserva'torio *sm (di musica)* conservatory
conservato'rismo *sm (Pol)* conservatism
conservazi'one [konservat'tsjone] *sf* preservation; conservation; **istinto di** ~ instinct for self-preservation; **a lunga** ~ *(latte, panna)* long-life *cpd*
con'sesso *sm (assemblea)* assembly; *(riunione)* meeting
conside'rabile *ag* worthy of consideration
conside'rare *vt* to consider; *(reputare)* to consider, regard; ~ **molto qn** to think highly of sb
conside'rato, -a *ag (prudente)* cautious, careful; *(stimato)* highly thought of, esteemed
considerazi'one [konsiderat'tsjone] *sf (esame, riflessione)* consideration; *(stima)* regard, esteem; *(pensiero, osservazione)* observation; **prendere in** ~ to take into consideration
conside'revole *ag* considerable
consigli'abile [konsiʎ'ʎabile] *ag* advisable
consigli'are [konsiʎ'ʎare] *vt (persona)* to advise; *(metodo, azione)* to recommend, advise, suggest; **consigliarsi** *vr:* **consigliarsi con qn** to ask sb for advice
consigli'ere, -a [konsiʎ'ʎɛre] *sm/f* adviser ■ *sm:* ~ **d'amministrazione** board member; ~ **comunale** town councillor; ~ **delegato** *(Comm)* managing director
con'siglio [kon'siʎʎo] *sm (suggerimento)* advice *no pl*, piece of advice; *(assemblea)* council; ~ **d'amministrazione** board; **C~ d'Europa** Council of Europe; ~ **di fabbrica** works council; **il C~ dei Ministri** *(Pol)* ≈ the Cabinet; **C~ di stato** *advisory body to the Italian government on administrative matters and their legal implications;* **C~ superiore della magistratura** *state body responsible for judicial appointments and regulations; see note*

CONSIGLI

The *Consiglio dei Ministri*, the Italian Cabinet, is headed by the "Presidente del Consiglio", the Prime Minister, who is the leader of the Government. The *Consiglio superiore della Magistratura*, the magistrates' governing body, ensures their autonomy and independence as enshrined in the Constitution. Chaired by the "Presidente della Repubblica", it mainly deals with appointments and transfers, and can take disciplinary action as required. Of the 30 magistrates elected to the *Consiglio* for a period of four years, 20 are chosen by their fellow magistrates and 10 by Parliament. The "Presidente della Repubblica" and the "Vicepresidente" are ex-officio members.

con'simile *ag* similar
consis'tente *ag* solid; *(fig)* sound, valid
consis'tenza [konsis'tentsa] *sf (di impasto)* consistency; *(di stoffa)* texture; **senza** ~ *(sospetti, voci)* ill-founded, groundless; ~ **di cassa/di magazzino** cash/stock in hand; ~ **patrimoniale** financial solidity
con'sistere *vi:* ~ **in** to consist of
consis'tito, -a *pp di* **consistere**
CONSOB *sigla f (= Commissione nazionale per le società e la borsa) regulatory body for the Italian Stock Exchange*
consoci'arsi [konso'tʃarsi] *vr* to go into partnership
consociati'vismo [konsotʃati'vizmo] *sm (Pol)* pact-building
consocia'tivo, -a [konsotʃa'tivo] *ag (Pol: democrazia)* based on pacts
consoci'ato, -a [konso'tʃato] *ag* associated ■ *sm/f* associate
conso'lante *ag* consoling, comforting
conso'lare *ag* consular ■ *vt (confortare)* to console, comfort; *(rallegrare)* to cheer up; **consolarsi** *vr* to be comforted; to cheer up
conso'lato *sm* consulate
consolazi'one [konsolat'tsjone] *sf* consolation, comfort
console¹ *sm* consul
console² [kɔ̃'sɔl] *sf (quadro di comando)* console
consolida'mento *sm* strengthening; consolidation
consoli'dare *vt* to strengthen, reinforce; *(Mil, terreno)* to consolidate; **consolidarsi** *vr* to consolidate
consolidazi'one [konsolidat'tsjone] *sf* strengthening; consolidation
consommé [kɔ̃sɔ'me] *sm inv* consommé

conso'nante *sf* consonant

conso'nanza [konso'nantsa] *sf* consonance

'consono, -a *ag*: ~ **a** consistent with, consonant with

con'sorte *sm/f* consort

con'sorzio [kon'sɔrtsjo] *sm* consortium; ~ **agrario** farmers' cooperative; ~ **di garanzia** (*Comm*) underwriting syndicate

con'stare *vi*: ~ **di** to consist of ▪ *vb impers*: **mi consta che** it has come to my knowledge that, it appears that; **a quanto mi consta** as far as I know

consta'tare *vt* to establish, verify; (*notare*) to notice, observe

constatazi'one [konstatat'tsjone] *sf* observation; ~ **amichevole** (*in incidenti*) *jointly-agreed statement for insurance purposes*

consu'eto, -a *ag* habitual, usual ▪ *sm*: **come di** ~ as usual

consuetudi'nario, -a *ag*: **diritto** ~ (*Dir*) common law

consue'tudine *sf* habit; (*usanza*) custom

consu'lente *sm/f* consultant; ~ **aziendale/ tecnico** management/technical consultant

consu'lenza [konsu'lentsa] *sf* consultancy; ~ **medica/legale** medical/legal advice; **ufficio di** ~ **fiscale** tax consultancy office; ~ **tecnica** technical consultancy o advice

consul'tare *vt* to consult; **consultarsi** *vr*: **consultarsi con qn** to seek the advice of sb

consultazi'one [konsultat'tsjone] *sf* consultation; **consultazioni** *sfpl* (*Pol*) talks, consultations; **libro di** ~ reference book

consul'tivo, -a *ag* consultative

consul'torio *sm*: ~ **familiare** o **matrimoniale** marriage guidance centre; ~ **pediatrico** children's clinic

consu'mare *vt* (*logorare: abiti, scarpe*) to wear out; (*usare*) to consume, use up; (*mangiare, bere*) to consume; (*Dir*) to consummate; **consumarsi** *vr* to wear out; to be used up; (*anche fig*) to be consumed; (*combustibile*) to burn out

consu'mato, -a *ag* (*vestiti, scarpe, tappeto*) worn; (*persona: esperto*) accomplished

consuma'tore *sm* consumer

consumazi'one [konsumat'tsjone] *sf* (*bibita*) drink; (*spuntino*) snack; (*Dir*) consummation

consu'mismo *sm* consumerism

con'sumo *sm* consumption; wear; use; **generi** o **beni di** ~ consumer goods; **beni di largo** ~ basic commodities; **imposta sui consumi** tax on consumer goods

consun'tivo *sm* (*Econ*) final balance

con'sunto, -a *ag* worn-out; (*viso*) wasted

'conta *sf* (*nei giochi*): **fare la** ~ to see who is going to be "it"

con'tabile *ag* accounts *cpd*, accounting ▪ *sm/f* accountant

contabilità *sf* (*attività, tecnica*) accounting, accountancy; (*insieme dei libri etc*) books *pl*, accounts *pl*; (*ufficio*) ~ accounts department; ~ **finanziaria** financial accounting; ~ **di gestione** management accounting

contachi'lometri [kontaki'lɔmetri] *sm inv* ≈ mileometer

conta'dino, -a *sm/f* countryman(-woman); farm worker; (*peg*) peasant

contagi'are [konta'dʒare] *vt* to infect

con'tagio [kon'tadʒo] *sm* infection; (*per contatto diretto*) contagion; (*epidemia*) epidemic

contagi'oso, -a [konta'dʒoso] *ag* infectious; contagious

conta'giri [konta'dʒiri] *sm inv* (*Aut*) rev counter

conta'gocce [konta'gottʃe] *sm inv* dropper

contami'nare *vt* to contaminate

contaminazi'one [kontaminat'tsjone] *sf* contamination

con'tante *sm* cash; **pagare in contanti** to pay cash

con'tare *vt* to count; (*considerare*) to consider ▪ *vi* to count, be of importance; ~ **su qn** to count o rely on sb; ~ **di fare qc** to intend to do sth; **ha i giorni contati, ha le ore contate** his days are numbered; **la gente che conta** people who matter

contas'catti *sm inv* telephone meter

conta'tore *sm* meter

contat'tare *vt* to contact

con'tatto *sm* contact; **essere in** ~ **con qn** to be in touch with sb; **fare** ~ (*Elettr: fili*) to touch

'conte *sm* count

con'tea *sf* (*Storia*) earldom; (*Amm*) county

conteggi'are [konted'dʒare] *vt* to charge, put on the bill

con'teggio [kon'teddʒo] *sm* calculation

con'tegno [kon'teɲɲo] *sm* (*comportamento*) behaviour (*Brit*), behavior (*US*); (*atteggiamento*) attitude; **darsi un** ~ (*ostentare disinvoltura*) to act nonchalant; (*ricomporsi*) to pull o.s. together

conte'gnoso, -a [konteɲ'ɲoso] *ag* reserved, dignified

contem'plare *vt* to contemplate, gaze at; (*Dir*) to make provision for

contempla'tivo, -a *ag* contemplative

contemplazi'one [kontemplat'tsjone] *sf* contemplation

con'tempo *sm*: **nel** ~ meanwhile, in the meantime

contemporanea'mente *av* simultaneously; at the same time

contempo'raneo, -a *ag, sm/f* contemporary
conten'dente *sm/f* opponent, adversary
con'tendere *vi* (*competere*) to compete; (*litigare*) to quarrel ■ *vt:* ~ **qc a qn** to contend with o be in competition with sb for sth
conte'nere *vt* to contain; **contenersi** *vr* to contain o.s.
conteni'tore *sm* container
conten'tabile *ag:* **difficilmente** ~ difficult to please
conten'tare *vt* to please, satisfy; **contentarsi** *vr:* **contentarsi di** to be satisfied with, content o.s. with; **si contenta di poco** he is easily satisfied
conten'tezza [konten'tettsa] *sf* contentment
conten'tino *sm* sop
con'tento, -a *ag* pleased, glad; ~ **di** pleased with
conte'nuto *ag* (*ira, entusiasmo*) restrained, suppressed; (*forza*) contained ■ *sm* contents *pl*; (*argomento*) content
contenzi'oso, -a [konten'tsjɔso] *ag* (*Dir*) contentious ■ *sm* (*Amm: ufficio*) legal department
con'teso, -a *pp di* **contendere** ■ *sf* dispute, argument
con'tessa *sf* countess
contes'tare *vt* (*Dir*) to notify; (*fig*) to dispute; ~ **il sistema** to protest against the system
contesta'tore, -trice *ag* anti-establishment ■ *sm/f* protester
contestazi'one [kontestat'tsjone] *sf* (*Dir: disputa*) dispute; (*: notifica*) notification; (*Pol*) anti-establishment activity; **in caso di** ~ if there are any objections
con'testo *sm* context
con'tiguo, -a *ag:* ~ (**a**) adjacent (to)
continen'tale *ag* continental
conti'nente *ag* continent ■ *sm* (*Geo*) continent; (*: terra ferma*) mainland
conti'nenza [konti'nentsa] *sf* continence
contin'gente [kontin'dʒɛnte] *ag* contingent ■ *sm* (*Comm*) quota; (*Mil*) contingent
contin'genza [kontin'dʒɛntsa] *sf* circumstance; (**indennità di**) ~ cost-of-living allowance
continua'mente *av* (*senza interruzione*) continuously, nonstop; (*ripetutamente*) continually
continu'are *vt* to continue (with), go on with ■ *vi* to continue, go on; ~ **a fare qc** to go on o continue doing sth; **continua a nevicare/a fare freddo** it's still snowing/cold
continua'tivo, -a *ag* (*occupazione*) permanent; (*periodo*) consecutive
continuazi'one [kontinuat'tsjone] *sf* continuation

continuità *sf* continuity
con'tinuo, -a *ag* (*numerazione*) continuous; (*pioggia*) continual, constant; (*Elettr: corrente*) direct; **di** ~ continually
'conto *sm* (*calcolo*) calculation; (*Comm, Econ*) account; (*di ristorante, albergo*) bill; (*fig: stima*) consideration, esteem; **in** ~ **sospeso (con qn)** to have an outstanding account (with sb); (*fig*) to have a score to settle (with sb); **fare i conti con qn** to settle one's account with sb; **fare** ~ **su qn** to count o rely on sb; **fare** ~ **che** (*supporre*) to suppose that; **rendere** ~ **qn di qc** to be accountable to sb for sth; **rendersi** ~ **di qc/che** to realize sth/that; **tener** ~ **di qn/qc** to take sb/sth into account; **tenere qc da** ~ to take great care of sth; **ad ogni buon** ~ in any case; **di poco/nessun** ~ of little/no importance; **per** ~ **di** on behalf of; **per** ~ **mio** as far as I'm concerned; (*da solo*) on my own; **a conti fatti, in fin dei conti** all things considered; **mi hanno detto strane cose sul suo** ~ I've heard some strange things about him; ~ **capitale** capital account; ~ **cifrato** numbered account; ~ **corrente** current account (*Brit*), checking account (*US*); ~ **corrente postale** Post Office account; ~ **economico** profit and loss account; ~ **in partecipazione** joint account; ~ **passivo** account payable; ~ **profitti e perdite** profit and loss account; ~ **alla rovescia** countdown; ~ **valutario** foreign currency account
con'torcere [kon'tɔrtʃere] *vt* to twist; (*panni*) to wring (out); **contorcersi** *vr* to twist, writhe
contor'nare *vt* to surround; **contornarsi** *vr:* **contornarsi di** to surround o.s. with
con'torno *sm* (*linea*) outline, contour; (*ornamento*) border; (*Cuc*) vegetables *pl*; **fare da** ~ **a** to surround
contorsi'one *sf* contortion
con'torto, -a *pp di* **contorcere**
contrabban'dare *vt* to smuggle
contrabbandi'ere, -a *sm/f* smuggler
contrab'bando *sm* smuggling, contraband; **merce di** ~ contraband, smuggled goods *pl*
contrab'basso *sm* (*Mus*) (double) bass
contraccambi'are *vt* (*favore etc*) to return; **vorrei** ~ I'd like to show my appreciation
contraccet'tivo, -a [kontratt'fet'tivo] *ag, sm* contraceptive
contrac'colpo *sm* rebound; (*di arma da fuoco*) recoil; (*fig*) repercussion
con'trada *sf* street; district; *vedi anche* **Palio**
contrad'detto, -a *pp di* **contraddire**
contrad'dire *vt* to contradict; **contraddirsi** *vr* to contradict o.s.; (*uso reciproco: persone*) to

contradict each other *o* one another; (: *testimonianze etc*) to be contradictory

contraddis'tinguere *vt* (*merce*) to mark; (*fig: atteggiamento, persona*) to distinguish

contraddis'tinto, -a *pp di* **contraddistinguere**

contradditˈtorio, -a *ag* contradictory; (*sentimenti*) conflicting ◼ *sm* (*Dir*) cross-examination

contraddizi'one [kontraddit'tsjone] *sf* contradiction; **cadere in ~** to contradict o.s.; **essere in ~** (*tesi, affermazioni*) to contradict one another; **spirito di ~** argumentativeness

con'trae *etc vb vedi* **contrarre**

contra'ente *sm* contractor

contra'erea *sf* (*Mil*) anti-aircraft artillery

contra'ereo, -a *ag* anti-aircraft

contraf'fare *vt* (*persona*) to mimic; (*voce*) to disguise; (*firma*) to forge, counterfeit

contraf'fatto, -a *pp di* **contraffare** ◼ *ag* counterfeit

contraffazi'one [kontraffat'tsjone] *sf* mimicking *no pl*; disguising *no pl*; forging *no pl*; (*cosa contraffatta*) forgery

contraf'forte *sm* (*Archit*) buttress; (*Geo*) spur

con'traggo *etc vb vedi* **contrarre**

con'tralto *sm* (*Mus*) contralto

contrap'pello *sm* (*Mil*) second roll call

contrappe'sare *vt* to counterbalance; (*fig: decisione*) to weigh up

contrap'peso *sm* counterbalance, counterweight

contrap'porre *vt*: **~ qc a qc** to counter sth with sth; (*paragonare*) to compare sth with sth; **contrapporsi** *vr*: **contrapporsi a qc** to contrast with sth, be opposed to sth

contrap'posto, -a *pp di* **contrapporre**

contraria'mente *av*: **~ a** contrary to

contrari'are *vt* (*contrastare*) to thwart, oppose; (*irritare*) to annoy, bother; **contrariarsi** *vr* to get annoyed

contrari'ato, -a *ag* annoyed

contrarietà *sf* adversity; (*fig*) aversion

con'trario, -a *ag* opposite; (*sfavorevole*) unfavourable (*Brit*), unfavorable (*US*) ◼ *sm* opposite; **essere ~ a qc** (*persona*) to be against sth; **al ~** on the contrary; **in caso ~** otherwise; **avere qualcosa in ~** to have some objection; **non ho niente in ~** I have no objection

con'trarre *vt* (*malattia, debito*) to contract; (*muscoli*) to tense; (*abitudine, vizio*) to pick up; (*accordo, patto*) to enter into; **contrarsi** *vr* to contract; **~ matrimonio** to marry

contrasse'gnare [kontrassen'ɲare] *vt* to mark

contras'segno [kontras'seɲɲo] *sm* (*distintivo*) distinguishing mark; **spedire in ~** (*Comm*) to send COD

con'trassi *etc vb vedi* **contrarre**

contras'tante *ag* contrasting

contras'tare *vt* (*avversare*) to oppose; (*impedire*) to bar; (*negare: diritto*) to contest, dispute ◼ *vi*: **~ (con)** (*essere in disaccordo*) to contrast (with); (*lottare*) to struggle (with)

con'trasto *sm* contrast; (*conflitto*) conflict; (*litigio*) dispute

contrat'tacco *sm* counterattack; **passare al ~** (*fig*) to fight back

contrat'tare *vt, vi* to negotiate

contrat'tempo *sm* hitch

con'tratto, -a *pp di* **contrarre** ◼ *sm* contract; **~ di acquisto** purchase agreement; **~ di affitto, ~ di locazione** lease; **~ collettivo di lavoro** collective agreement; **~ di lavoro** contract of employment; **~ a termine** forward contract

contrattu'ale *ag* contractual; **forza ~** (*di sindacato*) bargaining power

contravve'nire *vi*: **~ a** (*legge*) to contravene; (*obbligo*) to fail to meet

contravven'tore, -'trice *sm/f* offender

contravve'nuto, -a *pp di* **contravvenire**

contravvenzi'one [kontravven'tsjone] *sf* contravention; (*ammenda*) fine

contrazi'one [kontrat'tsjone] *sf* contraction; (*di prezzi etc*) reduction

contribu'ente *sm/f* taxpayer; ratepayer (*Brit*), property tax payer (*US*)

contribu'ire *vi* to contribute

contribu'tivo, -a *ag* contributory

contri'buto *sm* contribution; (*sovvenzione*) subsidy, contribution; (*tassa*) tax; **contributi previdenziali** = national insurance (*Brit*) *o* welfare (*US*) contributions; **contributi sindacali** trade union dues

con'trito, -a *ag* contrite, penitent

'contro *prep* against; **~ di me/lui** against me/him; **pastiglie ~ la tosse** throat lozenges; **~ pagamento** (*Comm*) on payment; **~ ogni mia aspettativa** contrary to my expectations; **per ~** on the other hand

contro'battere *vt* (*fig: a parole*) to answer back; (: *confutare*) to refute

controbilanci'are [kontrobilan'tʃare] *vt* to counterbalance

controcor'rente *av*: **andare ~** (*anche fig*) to swim against the tide

controcul'tura *sf* counterculture

contro'esodo *sm* return from holiday

contro'fax *sm inv* reply to a fax

controffen'siva *sf* counteroffensive

controfi'gura *sf* (*Cine*) double

controfir mare vt to countersign

control lare vt (accertare) to check; (sorvegliare) to watch, control; (tenere nel proprio potere, fig: dominare) to control; **controllarsi** vr to control o.s.

control lato, -a ag (persona) self-possessed; (reazioni) controlled ■ sf (Comm: società) associated company

con trollo sm check; watch; control; **base di ~** (Aer) ground control; **telefono sotto ~** tapped telephone; **visita di ~** (Med) checkup; **~ doganale** customs inspection; **~ di gestione** management control; **~ delle nascite** birth control; **~ di qualità** quality control

control lore sm (Ferr, Autobus) (ticket) inspector; **~ di volo** o **del traffico aereo** air traffic controller

contro luce [kontro'lutʃe] sf inv (Fot) backlit shot ■ av: **(in) ~** against the light; (fotografare) into the light

contro mano av: **guidare ~** to drive on the wrong side of the road; (in un senso unico) to drive the wrong way up a one-way street

contropar tita sf (fig: compenso): **come ~** in return

contropi ede sm (Sport): **azione di ~** sudden counter-attack; **prendere qn in ~** (fig) to catch sb off his (o her) guard

controprodu cente [kontroprodu'tʃɛnte] ag counterproductive

con trordine sm counter-order; **salvo ~** unless I (o you etc) hear to the contrary

contro senso sm (contraddizione) contradiction in terms; (assurdità) nonsense

controspio naggio [kontrospio'naddʒo] sm counterespionage

controva lore sm equivalent (value)

contro vento av against the wind; **navigare ~** (Naut) to sail to windward

contro versia sf controversy; (Dir) dispute; **~ sindacale** industrial dispute

contro verso, -a ag controversial

contro voglia [kontro'vɔʎʎa] av unwillingly

contu mace [kontu'matʃe] ag (Dir): **rendersi ~** to default, fail to appear in court ■ sm/f (Dir) defaulter

contu macia [kontu'matʃa] sf (Dir) default

contun dente ag: **corpo ~** blunt instrument

contur bante ag (sguardo, bellezza) disturbing

contur bare vt to disturb, upset

contusi one sf (Med) bruise

convale scente [konvaleʃ'ʃɛnte] ag, sm/f convalescent

convale scenza [konvaleʃ'ʃɛntsa] sf convalescence

con valida sf (Dir) confirmation; (di biglietto) stamping

convali dare vt (Amm) to validate; (fig: sospetto, dubbio) to confirm

con vegno [kon'veɲɲo] sm (incontro) meeting; (congresso) convention, congress; (luogo) meeting place

conve nevoli smpl civilities

conveni ente ag suitable; (vantaggioso) profitable; (: prezzo) cheap

conveni enza [konve'njɛntsa] sf suitability; advantage; cheapness; **convenienze** sfpl social conventions

conve nire vt to agree upon ■ vi (riunirsi) to gather, assemble; (concordare) to agree; (tornare utile) to be worthwhile ■ vb impers: **conviene fare questo** it is advisable to do this; **conviene andarsene** we should go; **ne convengo** I agree; **come convenuto** as agreed; **in data da ~** on a date to be agreed; **come (si) conviene ad una signorina** as befits a young lady

conven ticola sf (cricca) clique; (riunione) secret meeting

con vento sm (di frati) monastery; (di suore) convent

conve nuto, -a pp di **convenire** ■ sm (cosa pattuita) agreement ■ sm/f (Dir) defendant; **i convenuti** (i presenti) those present

convenzio nale [konventsjo'nale] ag conventional

convenzio nato, -a [konventsjo'nato] ag (ospedale, clinica) providing free health care, ≈ National Health Service cpd (Brit)

convenzi one [konven'tsjone] sf (Dir) agreement; (nella società) convention; **le convenzioni (sociali)** social conventions

conver gente [konver'dʒɛnte] ag convergent

conver genza [konver'dʒɛntsa] sf convergence

con vergere [kon'vɛrdʒere] vi to converge

con versa sf (Rel) lay sister

conver sare vi to have a conversation, converse

conversazi one [konversat'tsjone] sf conversation; **fare ~** (chiacchierare) to chat, have a chat

conversi one sf conversion; **~ ad U** (Aut) U-turn

con verso, -a pp di **convergere**; **per ~** av conversely

conver tire vt (trasformare) to change; (Inform, Pol, Rel) to convert; **convertirsi** vr: **convertirsi (a)** to be converted (to)

conver tito, -a sm/f convert

converti tore sm (Elettr) converter

con vesso, -a ag convex

convin cente [konvin'tʃɛnte] ag convincing

C

con'vincere [kon'vintʃere] vt to convince;
~ **qn di qc** to convince sb of sth; (Dir) to prove
sb guilty of sth; ~ **qn a fare qc** to persuade
sb to do sth

con'vinto, -a pp di **convincere** ■ ag: **reo ~**
(Dir) convicted criminal

convinzi'one [konvin'tsjone] sf conviction,
firm belief

convis'suto, -a pp di **convivere**

convi'tato, -a sm/f guest

con'vitto sm (Ins) boarding school

convi'venza [konvi'vɛntsa] sf living
together; (Dir) cohabitation

con'vivere vi to live together

convivi'ale ag convivial

convo'care vt to call, convene; (Dir)
to summon

convocazi'one [konvokat'tsjone] sf meeting;
summons sg; **lettera di ~** (letter of)
notification to appear o attend

convogli'are [konvoʎ'ʎare] vt to convey;
(dirigere) to direct, send

con'voglio [kon'vɔʎʎo] sm (di veicoli) convoy;
(Ferr) train; ~ **funebre** funeral procession

convo'lare vi: ~ **a (giuste) nozze** (scherzoso)
to tie the knot

convulsi'one sf convulsion

con'vulso, -a ag (pianto) violent, convulsive;
(attività) feverish

COOP abbr f = **cooperativa**

coope'rare vi: ~ **(a)** to cooperate (in)

coopera'tiva sf cooperative

cooperazi'one [kooperat'tsjone] sf
cooperation

coordina'mento sm coordination

coordi'nare vt to coordinate

coordi'nato, -a ag (movimenti) coordinated
■ sf (Ling, Geo, Mat) coordinate ■ smpl:
coordinati (Moda) coordinates

coordinazi'one [koordinat'tsjone] sf
coordination

co'perchio [ko'pɛrkjo] sm cover; (di pentola) lid

co'perta sf cover; (di lana) blanket; (da viaggio)
rug; (Naut) deck

coper'tina sf (Stampa) cover, jacket

co'perto, -a pp di **coprire** ■ ag covered; (cielo)
overcast ■ sm place setting; (posto a tavola)
place; (al ristorante) cover charge; ~ **di** covered
in o with

coper'tone sm (telo impermeabile) tarpaulin;
(Aut) rubber tyre

coper'tura sf (anche Econ, Mil) cover; (di edificio)
roofing; **fare un gioco di ~** (Sport) to play a
defensive game; ~ **assicurativa** insurance
cover

'copia sf copy; (Fot) print; **brutta/bella ~**
rough/final copy; ~ **conforme** (Dir) certified
copy; ~ **omaggio** presentation copy

copi'are vt to copy

copia'trice [kopja'tritʃe] sf copier, copying
machine

copincol'lare vt to copy and paste

copi'one sm (Cine, Teat) script

'coppa sf (bicchiere) goblet; (per frutta, gelato)
dish; (trofeo) cup, trophy; **coppe** sfpl (Carte)
suit in Neapolitan pack of cards

'coppia sf (di persone) couple; (di animali, Sport)
pair

cop'rente ag (colore, cosmetico) covering; (calze)
opaque

copri'capo sm headgear; (cappello) hat

coprifu'oco, -chi sm curfew

copri'letto sm bedspread

copripiu'mino sm inv duvet cover

co'prire vt to cover; (occupare: carica, posto) to
hold; **coprirsi** vr (cielo) to cloud over; (vestirsi)
to wrap up, cover up; (Econ) to cover o.s.;
coprirsi di (macchie, muffa) to become
covered in; ~ **qn di baci** to smother sb with
kisses; ~ **le spese** to break even; **coprirsi le
spalle** (fig) to cover o.s.

coque [kɔk] sf: **uovo alla ~** boiled egg

co'raggio [ko'raddʒo] sm courage, bravery;
~! (forza!) come on!; (animo!) cheer up!; **farsi ~**
to pluck up courage; **hai un bel ~!**
(sfacciataggine) you've got a nerve o cheek!

coraggi'oso, -a [korad'dʒoso] ag courageous,
brave

co'rale ag choral; (approvazione) unanimous

co'rallo sm coral; **il mar dei Coralli** the
Coral Sea

co'rano sm (Rel) Koran

co'razza [ko'rattsa] sf armour (Brit), armor
(US); (di animali) carapace, shell; (Mil)
armo(u)r(-plating)

coraz'zato, -a [korat'tsato] ag (Mil) armoured
(Brit), armored (US) ■ sf battleship

corazzi'ere [korat'tsjere] sm (Storia)
cuirassier; (guardia presidenziale) carabiniere of
the President's guard

corbelle'ria sf stupid remark; **corbellerie** sfpl
(sciocchezze) nonsense no pl

'corda sf cord; (fune) rope; (spago, Mus) string;
dare ~ a qn (fig) to let sb have his (o her) way;
tenere sulla ~ qn (fig) to keep sb on
tenterhooks; **tagliare la ~** (fig) to slip away,
sneak off; **essere giù di ~** to feel down;
corde vocali vocal cords

cor'data sf (Alpinismo) roped party; (fig) alliance
system in financial and business world

cordi'ale ag cordial, warm ■ sm (bevanda)
cordial

cordialità sf inv warmth, cordiality ■ sfpl
(saluti) best wishes

cor'doglio [kor'dɔʎʎo] *sm* grief; *(lutto)* mourning

cor'done *sm* cord, string; *(linea: di polizia)* cordon; ~ **ombelicale** umbilical cord; ~ **sanitario** quarantine line

Co'rea *sf*: **la** ~ Korea; **la ~ del Nord/Sud** North/South Korea

core'ano, -a *ag*, *sm/f* Korean

coreogra'fia *sf* choreography

core'ografo, -a *sm/f* choreographer

cori'aceo, -a [ko'rjatʃeo] *ag* *(Bot, Zool)* coriaceous; *(fig)* tough

cori'andolo *sm* *(Bot)* coriander; **coriandoli** *smpl* *(per carnevale etc)* confetti *no pl*

cori'care *vt* to put to bed; **coricarsi** *vr* to go to bed

coricherò *etc* [korike'rɔ] *vb vedi* **coricare**

Co'rinto *sf* Corinth

co'rista, -i, e *sm/f* *(Rel)* choir member, chorister; *(Teat)* member of the chorus

'corna *sfpl vedi* **corno**

cor'nacchia [kor'nakkja] *sf* crow

corna'musa *sf* bagpipes *pl*

'cornea *sf* *(Anat)* cornea

'corner *sm inv* *(Calcio)* corner (kick); **salvarsi in ~** *(fig: in gara, esame etc)* to get through by the skin of one's teeth

cor'netta *sf* *(Mus)* cornet; *(Tel)* receiver

cor'netto *sm* *(Cuc)* croissant; ~ **acustico** ear trumpet

cor'nice [kor'nitʃe] *sf* frame; *(fig)* background, setting

cornici'one [korni'tʃone] *sm* *(di edificio)* ledge; *(Archit)* cornice

'corno *sm* *(Zool: pl(f)* corna, *Mus)* horn; *(fam)*: **fare le corna a qn** to be unfaithful to sb; **dire peste e corna di qn** to call sb every name under the sun; **un ~!** not on your life!

Corno'vaglia [korno'vaʎʎa] *sf*: **la ~** Cornwall

cor'nuto, -a *ag* *(con corna)* horned; *(fam!: marito)* cuckolded ■ *sm* *(fam!)* cuckold; (: *insulto*) bastard *(!)*

'coro *sm* chorus; *(Rel)* choir

corol'lario *sm* corollary

co'rona *sf* crown; *(di fiori)* wreath

corona'mento *sm* *(di impresa)* completion; *(di carriera)* crowning achievement; **il ~ dei propri sogni** the fulfilment of one's dreams

coro'nare *vt* to crown

coro'naria *sf* coronary artery

'corpo *sm* body; *(cadavere)* (dead) body; *(militare, diplomatico)* corps *inv*; *(di opere)* corpus; **prendere ~** to take shape; **darsi anima e ~ a** to give o.s. heart and soul to; **a ~ a ~** hand-to-hand; ~ **d'armata** army corps; ~ **di ballo** corps de ballet; ~ **dei carabinieri** ≈ police force; ~ **celeste** heavenly body; ~ **di guardia**

(soldati) guard; *(locale)* guardroom; ~ **insegnante** teaching staff; ~ **del reato** material evidence

corpo'rale *ag* bodily; *(punizione)* corporal

corpora'tura *sf* build, physique

corporazi'one [korporat'tsjone] *sf* corporation

cor'poreo, -a *ag* bodily, physical

cor'poso, -a *ag* *(vino)* full-bodied

corpu'lento, -a *ag* stout, corpulent

corpu'lenza [korpu'lɛntsa] *sf* stoutness, corpulence

cor'puscolo *sm* corpuscle

corre'dare *vt*: ~ **di** to provide o furnish with; **domanda corredata dai seguenti documenti** application accompanied by the following documents

cor'redo *sm* equipment; *(di sposa)* trousseau

cor'reggere [kor'rɛddʒere] *vt* to correct; *(compiti)* to correct, mark

cor'rente *ag* *(fiume)* flowing; *(acqua del rubinetto)* running; *(moneta, prezzo)* current; *(comune)* everyday ■ *sm*: **essere al ~ (di)** to be well-informed (about) ■ *sf* *(movimento di liquido)* current, stream; *(spiffero)* draught; *(Elettr, Meteor)* current; *(fig)* trend, tendency; **mettere al ~ (di)** to inform (of); **la vostra lettera del 5 ~ mese** *(in lettere commerciali)* in your letter of the 5th inst.; **articoli di qualità** ~ average-quality products; ~ **alternata (c.a.)** alternating current (AC); ~ **continua (c.c.)** direct current (DC)

corrente'mente *av* *(comunemente)* commonly; **parlare una lingua ~** to speak a language fluently

corren'tista, -i, e *sm/f* (current *(Brit)* o checking *(US)*) account holder

cor'reo, -a *sm/f* *(Dir)* accomplice

'correre *vi* to run; *(precipitarsi)* to rush; *(partecipare a una gara)* to race, run; *(fig: diffondersi)* to go round ■ *vt* *(Sport: gara)* to compete in; *(rischio)* to run; *(pericolo)* to face; ~ **dietro a qn** to run after sb; **corre voce che ...** it is rumoured that ...

corresponsabilità *sf* joint responsibility; *(Dir)* joint liability

corresponsi'one *sf* payment

cor'ressi *etc vb vedi* **correggere**

corret'tezza [korret'tettsa] *sf* *(di comportamento)* correctness; *(Sport)* fair play

cor'retto, -a *pp di* **correggere** ■ *ag* *(comportamento)* correct, proper; **caffè ~ al cognac** coffee laced with brandy

corret'tore, -'trice *sm/f*: ~ **di bozze** proofreader ■ *sm*: **(liquido)** ~ correction fluid

correzi'one [korret'tsjone] *sf* correction; marking; ~ **di bozze** proofreading

cor'rida *sf* bullfight
corri'doio *sm* corridor; **manovre di ~** (*Pol*) lobbying *sg*
corri'dore *sm* (*Sport*) runner; (*: su veicolo*) racer
corri'era *sf* coach (*Brit*), bus
corri'ere *sm* (*diplomatico, di guerra*) courier; (*posta*) mail, post; (*spedizioniere*) carrier
corri'mano *sm* handrail
corrispet'tivo *sm* amount due; **versare a qn il ~ di una prestazione** to pay sb the amount due for his (*o* her) services
corrispon'dente *ag* corresponding ■ *sm/f* correspondent
corrispon'denza [korrispon'dɛntsa] *sf* correspondence; **~ in arrivo/partenza** incoming/outgoing mail
corris'pondere *vi* (*equivalere*): **~ (a)** to correspond (to); (*per lettera*): **~ con** to correspond with ■ *vt* (*stipendio*) to pay; (*fig: amore*) to return
corris'posto, -a *pp di* **corrispondere**
corrobo'rare *vt* to strengthen, fortify; (*fig*) to corroborate, bear out
cor'rodere *vt*, **cor'rodersi** *vr* to corrode
cor'rompere *vt* to corrupt; (*comprare*) to bribe
corrosi'one *sf* corrosion
corro'sivo, -a *ag* corrosive
cor'roso, -a *pp di* **corrodere**
corrotta'mente *av* corruptly
cor'rotto, -a *pp di* **corrompere** ■ *ag* corrupt
corrucci'arsi [korrut'tʃarsi] *vr* to grow angry *o* vexed
corru'gare *vt* to wrinkle; **~ la fronte** to knit one's brows
cor'ruppi *etc vb vedi* **corrompere**
corrut'tela *sf* corruption, depravity
corruzi'one [korrut'tsjone] *sf* corruption; bribery; **~ di minorenne** (*Dir*) corruption of a minor
'corsa *sf* running *no pl*; (*gara*) race; (*di autobus, taxi*) journey, trip; **fare una ~** to run, dash; (*Sport*) to run a race; **andare** *o* **essere di ~** to be in a hurry; **~ automobilistica/ciclistica** motor/cycle racing; **~ campestre** cross-country racing; **~ ad ostacoli** (*Ippica*) steeplechase; (*Atletica*) hurdles race
cor'saro, -a *ag*: **nave corsara** privateer ■ *sm* privateer
'corsi *etc vb vedi* **correre**
cor'sia *sf* (*Aut, Sport*) lane; (*di ospedale*) ward; **~ di emergenza** (*Aut*) hard shoulder; **~ preferenziale** ≈ bus lane; (*fig*) fast track; **~ di sorpasso** (*Aut*) overtaking lane
'Corsica *sf*: **la ~** Corsica
cor'sivo *sm* cursive (writing); (*Tip*) italics *pl*
'corso, -a *pp di* **correre** ■ *ag, sm/f* Corsican ■ *sm* course; (*strada cittadina*) main street;

(*di unità monetaria*) circulation; (*di titoli, valori*) rate, price; **dar libero ~ a** to give free expression to; **in ~** in progress, under way; (*annata*) current; **~ d'acqua** river; stream; (*artificiale*) waterway; **~ serale** evening class; **aver ~ legale** to be legal tender
'corte *sf* (court)yard; (*Dir, regale*) court; **fare la ~ a qn** to court sb; **~ d'appello** court of appeal; **~ di cassazione** final court of appeal; **C~ dei Conti** State audit court; **C~ Costituzionale** special court dealing with constitutional and ministerial matters; **~ marziale** court-martial; *see note*

◉ **CORTE**

◉ The *Corte d'Appello* hears appeals against
◉ sentences passed by courts in both civil
◉ and criminal cases and can modify
◉ sentences where necessary. The *Corte*
◉ *d'Assise* tries serious crimes such as
◉ manslaughter and murder; its judges
◉ include both legal professionals and
◉ members of the public. Similar in
◉ structure, the *Corte d'Assise d'Appello* hears
◉ appeals imposed by these two courts. The
◉ *Corte di Cassazione* is the highest judicial
◉ authority and ensures that the law is
◉ correctly applied by the other courts; it
◉ may call for a re-trial if required. The
◉ politically independent *Corte Costituzionale*
◉ decides whether laws comply with the
◉ principles of the Constitution, and has
◉ the power to impeach the "Presidente
◉ della Repubblica". The *Corte dei Conti*
◉ ensures the Government's compliance
◉ with the law and the Constitution.
◉ Reporting directly to Parliament, it
◉ oversees the financial aspects of the state
◉ budget.

cor'teccia, -ce [kor'tettʃa] *sf* bark
corteggia'mento [korteddʒa'mento] *sm* courtship
corteggi'are [korted'dʒare] *vt* to court
corteggia'tore [korteddʒa'tore] *sm* suitor
cor'teo *sm* procession; **~ funebre** funeral cortège
cor'tese *ag* courteous
corte'sia *sf* courtesy; **fare una ~ a qn** to do sb a favour; **per ~, dov'è ...?** excuse me, please, where is ...?
cortigi'ano, -a [korti'dʒano] *sm/f* courtier ■ *sf* courtesan
cor'tile *sm* (court)yard
cor'tina *sf* curtain; (*anche fig*) screen
corti'sone *sm* cortisone

'**corto, -a** *ag* short ■ *av:* **tagliare** ~ to come straight to the point; **essere a** ~ **di qc** to be short of sth; **essere a** ~ **di parole** to be at a loss for words; **la settimana corta** the 5-day week; ~ **circuito** short-circuit

cortocir'cuito [kortotʃir'kuito] *sm* = **corto circuito**

cortome'traggio [kortome'traddʒo] *sm* short (feature film)

cor'vino, -a *ag* (*capelli*) jet-black

'**corvo** *sm* raven

'**cosa** *sf* thing; (*faccenda*) affair, matter, business *no pl*; (**che**) ~? what?; (**che**) **cos'è?** what is it?; **a** ~ **pensi?** what are you thinking about?; **tante belle cose!** all the best!; **ormai è** ~ **fatta!** (*positivo*) it's in the bag!; (*negativo*) it's done now!; **a cose fatte** when it's all over

'**Cosa 'Nostra** *sf* Cosa Nostra

'**cosca, -sche** *sf* (*di mafiosi*) clan

'**coscia, -sce** ['kɔʃʃa] *sf* thigh; ~ **di pollo** (*Cuc*) chicken leg

cosci'ente [koʃʃɛnte] *ag* conscious; ~ **di** conscious *o* aware of

cosci'enza [koʃʃɛntsa] *sf* conscience; (*consapevolezza*) consciousness; ~ **politica** political awareness

coscienzi'oso, -a [koʃʃen'tsjoso] *ag* conscientious

cosci'otto [koʃʃɔtto] *sm* (*Cuc*) leg

cos'critto *sm* (*Mil*) conscript

coscrizi'one [koskrit'tsjone] *sf* conscription

PAROLA CHIAVE

cosi *av* **1** (*in questo modo*) like this, (in) this way; (*in tal modo*) so; **le cose stanno così** this is the way things stand; **non ho detto così!** I didn't say that!; **come stai?** — (**e**) **così** how are you? — so-so; **e così via** and so on; **per così dire** so to speak; **così sia** amen
2 (*tanto*) so; **così lontano** so far away; **un ragazzo così intelligente** such an intelligent boy
■ *ag inv* (*tale*): **non ho mai visto un film così** I've never seen such a film
■ *cong* **1** (*perciò*) so, therefore; **e così ho deciso di lasciarlo** so I decided to leave him
2: **così ... come** as ... as; **non è così bravo come te** he's not as good as you; **così ... che** so ... that

cosicché [kosik'ke] *cong* so (that)

cosid'detto, -a *ag* so-called

cos'mesi *sf* (*scienza*) cosmetics *sg*; (*prodotti*) cosmetics *pl*; (*trattamento*) beauty treatment

cos'metico, -a, ci, che *ag, sm* cosmetic

'**cosmico, -a, ci, che** *ag* cosmic

'**cosmo** *sm* cosmos

cosmo'nauta, -i, e *sm/f* cosmonaut

cosmopo'lita, -i, e *ag* cosmopolitan

'**coso** *sm* (*fam: oggetto*) thing, thingumajig; (*: aggeggio*) contraption; (*: persona*) what's his name, thingumajig

cos'pargere [kos'pardʒere] *vt:* ~ **di** to sprinkle with

cos'parso, -a *pp di* **cospargere**

cos'petto *sm:* **al** ~ **di** in front of; in the presence of

cospicuità *sf* vast quantity

cos'picuo, -a *ag* considerable, large

cospi'rare *vi* to conspire

cospira'tore, -'trice *sm/f* conspirator

cospirazi'one [kospirat'tsjone] *sf* conspiracy

'**cossi** *etc vb vedi* **cuocere**

Cost. *abbr* = **costituzione**

'**costa** *sf* (*tra terra e mare*) coast(line); (*litorale*) shore; (*pendio*) slope; (*Anat*) rib; **navigare sotto** ~ to hug the coast; **la C~ Azzurra** the French Riviera; **la C~ d'Avorio** the Ivory Coast; **velluto a coste** corduroy

costà *av* there

cos'tante *ag* constant; (*persona*) steadfast ■ *sf* constant

cos'tanza [kos'tantsa] *sf* (*gen*) constancy; (*fermezza*) constancy, steadfastness; **il Lago di C~** Lake Constance

cos'tare *vi, vt* to cost; ~ **caro** to be expensive, cost a lot; ~ **un occhio della testa** to cost a fortune; **costi quel che costi** no matter what

'**Costa 'Rica** *sf:* **la** ~ Costa Rica

cos'tata *sf* (*Cuc: di manzo*) large chop

cos'tato *sm* (*Anat*) ribs *pl*

costeggi'are [kosted'dʒare] *vt* to be close to; to run alongside

cos'tei *pron vedi* **costui**

costellazi'one [kostellat'tsjone] *sf* constellation

coster'nare *vt* to dismay

coster'nato, -a *ag* dismayed

costernazi'one [kosternat'tsjone] *sf* dismay, consternation

costi'ero, -a *ag* coastal, coast *cpd* ■ *sf* stretch of coast

costi'pato, -a *ag* (*stitico*) constipated

costitu'ire *vt* (*comitato, gruppo*) to set up, form; (*collezione*) to put together, build up; (*elementi, parti: comporre*) to make up, constitute; (*rappresentare*) to constitute; (*Dir*) to appoint; **costituirsi** *vr:* **costituirsi (alla polizia)** to give o.s. up (to the police); **costituirsi parte civile** (*Dir*) *to associate in an action with the public prosecutor for damages*; **il fatto non costituisce reato** this is not a crime costitu'tivo, -a *ag* constituent, component; **atto ~** (*Dir: di società*) memorandum of association

costituzio'nale [kostituttsjo'nale] *ag* constitutional

costituzi'one [kostitut'tsjone] *sf* setting up; building up; constitution

'costo *sm* cost; **sotto ~** for less than cost price; **a ogni** *o* **qualunque ~, a tutti i costi** at all costs; **costi di esercizio** running costs; **costi fissi** fixed costs; **costi di gestione** operating costs; **costi di produzione** production costs

'costola *sf* (*Anat*) rib; **ha la polizia alle costole** the police are hard on his heels

costo'letta *sf* (*Cuc*) cutlet

cos'toro *pron pl vedi* **costui**

cos'toso, -a *ag* expensive, costly

cos'tretto, -a *pp di* **costringere**

cos'tringere [kos'trindʒere] *vt*: **~ qn a fare qc** to force sb to do sth

costrit'tivo, -a *ag* coercive

costrizi'one [kostrit'tsjone] *sf* coercion

costru'ire *vt* to construct, build

costrut'tivo, -a *ag* (*Edil*) building *cpd*; (*fig*) constructive

costruzi'one [kostrut'tsjone] *sf* construction, building; **di ~ inglese** British-made

cos'tui, cos'tei (*pl* **cos'toro**) *pron* (*soggetto*) he/she; (*pl*) they; (*complemento*) him/her; (*pl*) them; **si può sapere chi è ~?** (*peg*) just who is that fellow?

cos'tume *sm* (*uso*) custom; (*foggia di vestire, indumento*) costume; **il buon ~** public morality; **donna di facili costumi** woman of easy morals; **~ da bagno** bathing *o* swimming costume (*Brit*), swimsuit; (*da uomo*) bathing *o* swimming trunks *pl*

costu'mista, -i, e *sm/f* costume maker, costume designer

co'tenna *sf* bacon rind

co'togna [ko'toɲɲa] *sf* quince

coto'letta *sf* (*di maiale, montone*) chop; (*di vitello, agnello*) cutlet

coto'nare *vt* (*capelli*) to backcomb

co'tone *sm* cotton; **~ idrofilo** cotton wool (*Brit*), absorbent cotton (*US*)

cotoni'ficio [kotoni'fitʃo] *sm* cotton mill

'cotta *sf* (*Rel*) surplice; (*fam: innamoramento*) crush

'cottimo *sm*: **lavorare a ~** to do piecework

'cotto, -a *pp di* **cuocere** ■ *ag* cooked; (*fam: innamorato*) head-over-heels in love ■ *sm* brickwork; **~ a puntino** cooked to perfection; **dirne di cotte e di crude a qn** to call sb every name under the sun; **farne di cotte e di crude** to get up to all kinds of mischief; **mattone di ~** fired brick; **pavimento in ~** tile floor

cot'tura *sf* cooking; (*in forno*) baking; (*in umido*) stewing; **~ a fuoco lento** simmering; **angolo (di) ~** cooking area

co'vare *vt* to hatch; (*fig: malattia*) to be sickening for; (: *odio, rancore*) to nurse ■ *vi* (*fuoco, fig*) to smoulder (*Brit*), smolder (*US*)

co'vata *sf* (*anche fig*) brood

'covo *sm* den; **~ di terroristi** terrorist base

co'vone *sm* sheaf

'cozza ['kɔttsa] *sf* mussel

coz'zare [kot'tsare] *vi*: **~ contro** to bang into, collide with

'cozzo ['kɔttso] *sm* collision

C.P. *abbr* (= *cartolina postale*) pc; (*Posta*) *vedi* **casella postale**; (*Naut*) **= capitaneria (di porto)**; (*Dir*) **= codice penale**

CPT *sigla m inv* **= Centro di Permanenza Temporanea**

crac'care *vt* (*Inform*) to crack

crack *sm inv* (*droga*) crack

Cra'covia *sf* Cracow

'crampo *sm* cramp

'cranio *sm* skull

cra'tere *sm* crater

cra'vatta *sf* tie; **~ a farfalla** bow tie

cravat'tino *sm* bow tie

cre'anza [kre'antsa] *sf* manners *pl*; **per buona ~** out of politeness

cre'are *vt* to create

creatività *sf* creativity

cre'ato *sm* creation

crea'tore, -'trice *ag* creative ■ *sm/f* creator; **un ~ di alta moda** fashion designer; **andare al C~** to go to meet one's maker

crea'tura *sf* creature; (*bimbo*) baby, infant

creazi'one [kreat'tsjone] *sf* creation; (*fondazione*) foundation, establishment

'crebbi *etc vb vedi* **crescere**

cre'dente *sm/f* (*Rel*) believer

cre'denza [kre'dentsa] *sf* belief; (*armadio*) sideboard

credenzi'ali [kreden'tsjali] *sfpl* credentials

'credere *vt* to believe ■ *vi*: **~ in, ~ a** to believe in; **~ qn onesto** to believe sb (to be) honest; **~ che** to believe *o* think that; **credersi furbo** to think one is clever; **lo credo bene!** I can well believe it!; **fai quello che credi** *o* **come credi** do as you please

cre'dibile *ag* credible, believable

credibilità *sf* credibility

credi'tizio, -a [kredi'tittsjo] *ag* credit

'credito *sm* (*anche Comm*) credit; (*reputazione*) esteem, repute; **comprare a ~** to buy on credit; **~ agevolato** easy credit terms; **~ d'imposta** tax credit

credi'tore, -'trice *sm/f* creditor
'credo *sm inv* creed
'credulo, -a *ag* credulous
credu'lone, -a *sm/f* simpleton, sucker (*fam*)
'crema *sf* cream; (*con uova, zucchero etc*) custard; **~ idratante** moisturizing cream; **~ pasticciera** confectioner's custard; **~ solare** sun cream
cre'mare *vt* to cremate
crema'torio *sm* crematorium
cremazi'one [kremat'tsjone] *sf* cremation
'cremisi *ag inv, sm inv* crimson
Crem'lino *sm:* **il ~** the Kremlin
cremo'nese *ag* of (*o* from) Cremona
cre'moso, -a *ag* creamy
'crepa *sf* crack
cre'paccio [kre'pattʃo] *sm* large crack, fissure; (*di ghiacciaio*) crevasse
crepacu'ore *sm* broken heart
crepa'pelle *av:* **ridere a ~** to split one's sides laughing
cre'pare *vi* (*fam: morire*) to snuff it (*Brit*), kick the bucket; **~ dalle risa** to split one's sides laughing; **~ dall'invidia** to be green with envy
crepi'tare *vi* (*fuoco*) to crackle; (*pioggia*) to patter
crepi'tio, -ii *sm* crackling; pattering
cre'puscolo *sm* twilight, dusk
cre'scendo [kreʃ'ʃendo] *sm* (*Mus*) crescendo
cre'scente [kreʃ'ʃente] *ag* (*gen*) growing, increasing; (*luna*) waxing
'crescere ['kreʃʃere] *vi* to grow ■ *vt* (*figli*) to raise
cre'scione [kreʃ'ʃone] *sm* watercress
'crescita ['kreʃʃita] *sf* growth
cresci'uto, -a [kreʃ'ʃuto] *pp di* **crescere**
'cresima *sf* (*Rel*) confirmation
cresi'mare *vt* to confirm
'crespo, -a *ag* (*capelli*) frizzy; (*tessuto*) puckered ■ *sm* crêpe
'cresta *sf* crest; (*di polli, uccelli*) crest, comb; **alzare la ~** (*fig*) to become cocky; **abbassare la ~** (*fig*) to climb down; **essere sulla ~ dell'onda** (*fig*) to be riding high
'Creta *sf* Crete
'creta *sf* (*gesso*) chalk; (*argilla*) clay
cre'tese *ag, sm/f* Cretan
creti'nata *sf* (*fam*): **dire/fare una ~** to say/do a stupid thing
cre'tino, -a *ag* stupid ■ *sm/f* idiot, fool
CRI *sigla f* = **Croce Rossa Italiana**
cric *sm inv* (*Tecn*) jack
'cricca, -che *sf* clique
'cricco, -chi *sm* = **cric**
cri'ceto [kri'tʃeto] *sm* hamster
crimi'nale *ag, sm/f* criminal

criminalità *sf* crime; **~ organizzata** organized crime
'Criminalpol *abbr* = **polizia criminale**
'crimine *sm* (*Dir*) crime
criminolo'gia [kriminolo'dʒia] *sf* criminology
crimi'noso, -a *ag* criminal
cri'nale *sm* ridge
'crine *sm* horsehair
crini'era *sf* mane
'cripta *sf* crypt
crip'tare *vt* (*TV: programma*) to encrypt
crip'tato, -a *ag* (*programma, messaggio*) encrypted
crisan'temo *sm* chrysanthemum; *vedi anche* **Giorno dei Morti**
'crisi *sf inv* crisis; (*Med*) attack, fit; **essere in ~** (*partito, impresa etc*) to be in a state of crisis; **~ energetica** energy crisis; **~ di nervi** attack *o* fit of nerves
cristalle'ria *sf* (*fabbrica*) crystal glassworks *sg*; (*oggetti*) crystalware
cristal'lino, -a *ag* (*Mineralogia*) crystalline; (*fig: suono, acque*) crystal clear ■ *sm* (*Anat*) crystalline lens
cristalliz'zare [kristallid'dzare] *vi*, **cristalliz'zarsi** *vr* to crystallize; (*fig*) to become fossilized
cris'tallo *sm* crystal
cristia'nesimo *sm* Christianity
cristianità *sf* Christianity; (*i cristiani*) Christendom
cristi'ano, -a *ag, sm/f* Christian; **un povero ~** (*fig*) a poor soul *o* beggar; **comportarsi da ~** (*fig*) to behave in a civilized manner
'cristo *sm:* **C~** Christ; **(un) povero ~** (a) poor beggar
cri'terio *sm* criterion; (*buon senso*) (common) sense
'critica, -che *sf vedi* **critico**
criti'care *vt* to criticize
'critico, -a, ci, che *ag* critical ■ *sm* critic ■ *sf* criticism; **la critica** (*attività*) criticism; (*persone*) the critics *pl*
criti'cone, -a *sm/f* faultfinder
crivel'lare *vt:* **~ (di)** to riddle (with)
cri'vello *sm* riddle
cro'ato, -a *ag, sm/f* Croatian, Croat
Cro'azia [kro'attsja] *sf:* **la ~** Croatia
croc'cante *ag* crisp, crunchy ■ *sm* (*Cuc*) almond crunch
'crocchia ['krɔkkja] *sf* chignon, bun
'crocchio ['krɔkkjo] *sm* (*di persone*) small group, cluster
'croce ['krotʃe] *sf* cross; **in ~** (*di traverso*) crosswise; (*fig*) on tenterhooks; **mettere in ~** (*anche fig: criticare*) to crucify; (*: tormentare*) to nag to death; **la C~ Rossa** the Red Cross; **~ uncinata** swastika

95

croce'figgere etc [krotʃe'fiddʒere]
= **crocifiggere** etc
croceros'sina [krotʃeros'sina] sf Red Cross
nurse
croce'via [krotʃe'via] sm inv crossroads sg
croci'ato, -a [kro'tʃato] ag cross-shaped ■ sm
(anche fig) crusader ■ sf crusade
cro'cicchio [kro'tʃikkjo] sm crossroads sg
croci'era [kro'tʃera] sf (viaggio) cruise; (Archit)
transept; **altezza di ~** (Aer) cruising height;
velocità di ~ (Aer, Naut) cruising speed
croci'figgere [krotʃi'fiddʒere] vt to crucify
crocifissi'one [krotʃifis'sjone] sf crucifixion
croci'fisso, -a [krotʃi'fisso] pp di **crocifiggere**
■ sm crucifix
crogio'larsi [krodʒo'larsi] vr: ~ **al sole** to bask
in the sun
crogi'olo [kro'dʒolo], **crogiu'olo** [kro'dʒwɔlo]
sm crucible; (fig) melting pot
crol'lare vi to collapse
'crollo sm collapse; (di prezzi) slump, sudden
fall
'croma sf (Mus) quaver (Brit), eighth note (US)
cro'mato, -a ag chromium-plated
'cromo sm chrome, chromium
cromo'soma, -i sm chromosome
cronaca, -che sf chronicle; (Stampa) news sg;
(: rubrica) column; (TV, Radio) commentary;
fatto o **episodio di ~** news item; **~ nera**
crime news sg; crime column
'cronico, -a, ci, che ag chronic
cro'nista, -i sm (Stampa) reporter, columnist
cronis'toria sf chronicle; (fig: ironico) blow-by-
blow account
cro'nografo sm (strumento) chronograph
cronolo'gia [kronolo'dʒia] sf chronology
cronome'trare vt to time
cro'nometro sm chronometer; (a scatto)
stopwatch
'crosta sf crust; (Med) scab; (Zool) shell; (di
ghiaccio) layer; (fig peg: quadro) daub
cros'tacei [kros'tatʃei] smpl shellfish
cros'tata sf (Cuc) tart
cros'tino sm (Cuc) crouton; (: da antipasto)
canapé
crucci'are [krut'tʃare] vt to torment, worry;
crucciarsi vr: **crucciarsi per** to torment o.s.
over
'cruccio ['kruttʃo] sm worry, torment
cruci'ale [kru'tʃale] ag crucial
cruci'verba [krutʃi'vɛrba] sm inv crossword
(puzzle)
cru'dele ag cruel
crudeltà sf cruelty
'crudo, -a ag (non cotto) raw; (aspro) harsh,
severe
cru'ento, -a ag bloody

cru'miro sm (peg) blackleg (Brit), scab
'cruna sf eye (of a needle)
'crusca sf bran
crus'cotto sm (Aut) dashboard
CS sigla = **Cosenza**
c.s. abbr = **come sopra**
CSI [tʃi'esse'i] sigla f (= Comunità di Stati
Indipendenti) CIS
CSM [tʃiesse'emme] sigla m (= consiglio superiore
della magistratura) Magistrates' Board of
Supervisors
CT sigla = **Catania**
c.t. abbr = **commissario tecnico**
'Cuba sf Cuba
cu'bano, -a ag, sm/f Cuban
cu'betto sm (small) cube; **~ di ghiaccio** ice
cube
'cubico, -a, ci, che ag cubic
cu'bista sf podium dancer, dancer who performs
on stage in a club
'cubo, -a ag cubic ■ sm cube; **elevare al ~**
(Mat) to cube
cuc'cagna [kuk'kaɲɲa] sf: **paese della ~** land
of plenty; **albero della ~** greasy pole (fig)
cuc'cetta [kut'tʃetta] sf (Ferr) couchette;
(Naut) berth
cucchiai'ata [kukkja'jata] sf spoonful;
tablespoonful
cucchia'ino [kukkja'ino] sm teaspoon; coffee
spoon
cucchi'aio [kuk'kjajo] sm spoon; (da tavola)
tablespoon; (cucchiaiata) spoonful;
tablespoonful
'cuccia, -ce ['kuttʃa] sf dog's bed; **a ~!** down!
cuccio'lata [kuttʃo'lata] sf litter
'cucciolo ['kuttʃolo] sm cub; (di cane) puppy
cu'cina [ku'tʃina] sf (locale) kitchen;
(arte culinaria) cooking, cookery; (le vivande)
food, cooking; (apparecchio) cooker; **di ~**
(libro, lezione) cookery cpd; **~ componibile**
fitted kitchen; **~ economica** kitchen
range
cuci'nare [kutʃi'nare] vt to cook
cuci'nino [kutʃi'nino] sm kitchenette
cu'cire [ku'tʃire] vt to sew, stitch; **~ la bocca
a qn** (fig) to shut sb up
cu'cito, -a [ku'tʃito] sm sewing; (Ins) sewing,
needlework
cuci'trice [kutʃi'tritʃe] sf (Tip: per libri)
stitching machine; (per fogli) stapler
cuci'tura [kutʃi'tura] sf sewing, stitching;
(costura) seam
cucù sm inv, **cu'culo** sm cuckoo
'cuffia sf bonnet, cap; (da infermiera) cap;
(da bagno) (bathing) cap; (per ascoltare)
headphones pl, headset
cu'gino, -a [ku'dʒino] sm/f cousin

○ PAROLA CHIAVE

cui *pron* **1** *(nei complementi indiretti: persona)* whom; *(: oggetto, animale)* which; **la persona/ le persone a cui accennavi** the person/ people you were referring to *o* to whom you were referring; **la penna con cui scrivo** the pen I'm writing with; **il paese da cui viene** the country he comes from; **i libri di cui parlavo** the books I was talking about *o* about which I was talking; **parla varie lingue, fra cui l'inglese** he speaks several languages, including English; **il quartiere in cui abito** the district where I live; **visto il modo in cui ti ha trattato ...** considering how he treated you ...; **la ragione per cui** the reason why; **per cui non so più che fare** that's why I don't know what to do **2** *(inserito tra articolo e sostantivo)* whose; **la donna i cui figli sono scomparsi** the woman whose children have disappeared; **il signore, dal cui figlio ho avuto il libro** the man from whose son I got the book

culi'naria *sf* cookery
culi'nario, -a *ag* culinary
'culla *sf* cradle
cul'lare *vt* to rock; *(fig: idea, speranza)* to cherish; **cullarsi** *vr (gen)* to sway; **cullarsi in vane speranze** *(fig)* to cherish fond hopes; **cullarsi nel dolce far niente** *(fig)* to sit back and relax
culmi'nante *ag*: **posizione ~** *(Astr)* highest point; **punto** *o* **momento ~** *(fig)* climax
culmi'nare *vi*: **~ in** *o* **con** to culminate in
'culmine *sm* top, summit
'culo *sm (fam!)* arse *(Brit!)*, ass *(US!)*; *(: fig: fortuna)*: **aver ~** to have the luck of the devil; **prendere qn per il ~** to take the piss out of sb *(!)*
'culto *sm (religione)* religion; *(adorazione)* worship, adoration; *(venerazione: anche fig)* cult
cul'tura *sf (gen)* culture; *(conoscenza)* education, learning; **di ~** *(persona)* cultured; *(istituto)* cultural, of culture; **~ generale** general knowledge; **~ di massa** mass culture
cultu'rale *ag* cultural
cultu'rismo *sm* body-building
cumu'lare *vt* to accumulate, amass
cumula'tivo, -a *ag* cumulative; *(prezzo)* inclusive; *(biglietto)* group *cpd*
'cumulo *sm (mucchio)* pile, heap; *(Meteor)* cumulus; **~ dei redditi** *(Fisco)* combined incomes; **~ delle pene** *(Dir)* consecutive sentences

'cuneo *sm* wedge
cu'netta *sf (di strada etc)* bump; *(scolo: nelle strade di città)* gutter; *(: di campagna)* ditch
cu'nicolo *sm (galleria)* tunnel; *(di miniera)* pit, shaft; *(di talpa)* hole
cu'oca *sf vedi* **cuoco**
cu'ocere ['kwɔtʃere] *vt (alimenti)* to cook; *(mattoni etc)* to fire ■ *vi* to cook; **~ in umido/a vapore/in padella** to stew/steam/fry; **~ al forno** *(pane)* to bake; *(arrosto)* to roast
cu'oco, -a, chi, che *sm/f* cook; *(di ristorante)* chef
cuoi'ame *sm* leather goods *pl*
cu'oio *sm* leather; **~ capelluto** scalp; **tirare le cuoia** *(fam)* to kick the bucket
cu'ore *sm* heart; **cuori** *smpl (Carte)* hearts; **avere buon ~** to be kind-hearted; **stare a ~ a qn** to be important to sb; **un grazie di ~** heartfelt thanks; **ringraziare di ~** to thank sincerely; **nel profondo del ~** in one's heart of hearts; **avere la morte nel ~** to be sick at heart; **club dei cuori solitari** lonely hearts club
cupi'digia [kupi'didʒa] *sf* greed, covetousness
'cupo, -a *ag* dark; *(suono)* dull; *(fig)* gloomy, dismal
'cupola *sf* dome; *(più piccola)* cupola; *(fig)* Mafia high command
'cura *sf* care; *(Med: trattamento)* (course of) treatment; **aver ~ di** *(occuparsi di)* to look after; **a ~ di** *(libro)* edited by; **fare una ~** to follow a course of treatment; **~ dimagrante** diet
cu'rabile *ag* curable
cu'rante *ag*: **medico ~** doctor (in charge of a patient)
cu'rare *vt (malato, malattia)* to treat; *(: guarire)* to cure; *(aver cura di)* to take care of; *(testo)* to edit; **curarsi** *vr* to take care of o.s.; *(Med)* to follow a course of treatment; **curarsi di** to pay attention to; *(occuparsi di)* to look after
cu'rato *sm* parish priest; *(protestante)* vicar, minister
cura'tore, -'trice *sm/f (Dir)* trustee; *(di antologia etc)* editor; **~ fallimentare** (official) receiver
'curdo, -a *ag* Kurdish ■ *sm/f* Kurd
'curia *sf (Rel)*: **la ~ romana** the Roman curia; **~ notarile** notaries' association *o* guild
curio'saggine [kurjo'saddʒine] *sf* nosiness
curio'sare *vi* to look round, wander round; *(tra libri)* to browse; **~ nei negozi** *o* wander round the shops; **~ nelle faccende altrui** to poke one's nose into other people's affairs
curiosità *sf inv* curiosity; *(cosa rara)* curio, curiosity

curi'oso, -a *ag* (*che vuol sapere*) curious, inquiring; (*ficcanaso*) curious, inquisitive; (*bizzarro*) strange, curious ▪ *sm/f* busybody, nosy parker; **essere ~ di** to be curious about; **una folla di curiosi** a crowd of onlookers

cur'riculum *sm inv*: **~ (vitae)** curriculum vitae

cur'sore *sm* (*Inform*) cursor

'**curva** *sf* curve; (*stradale*) bend, curve

cur'vare *vt* to bend ▪ *vi* (*veicolo*) to take a bend; (*strada*) to bend, curve; **curvarsi** *vr* to bend; (*legno*) to warp

'**curvo, -a** *ag* curved; (*piegato*) bent

CUS *sigla m* = **Centro Universitario Sportivo**

cusci'netto [kuʃʃi'netto] *sm* pad; (*Tecn*) bearing ▪ *ag inv*: **stato ~** buffer state; **~ a sfere** ball bearing

cu'scino [kuʃʃino] *sm* cushion; (*guanciale*) pillow

'**cuspide** *sf* (*Archit*) spire

cus'tode *sm/f* (*di museo*) keeper, custodian; (*di parco*) warden; (*di casa*) concierge; (*di fabbrica, carcere*) guard

cus'todia *sf* care; (*Dir*) custody; (*astuccio*) case, holder; **avere qc in ~** to look after sth; **dare qc in ~ a qn** to entrust sth to sb's care; **agente di ~** prison warder; **~ delle carceri** prison security; **~ cautelare** (*Dir*) remand

custo'dire *vt* (*conservare*) to keep; (*assistere*) to look after, take care of; (*fare la guardia*) to guard

customiz'zare [kustomid'dzare] *vt* (*Inform*) to customize

'**cute** *sf* (*Anat*) skin

cu'ticola *sf* cuticle

C.V. *abbr* = **cavallo vapore**

c.v.d. *abbr* (= *come volevasi dimostrare*) QED (= *quod erat demonstrandum*)

c.vo *abbr* = **corsivo**

cy'clette® [si'klet] *sf inv* exercise bike

CZ *sigla* = **Catanzaro**

Dd

D, d [di] *sf o m inv* (*lettera*) D, d; **D come Domodossola** ≈ D for David (Brit), D for Dog (US)

D *abbr* (= *destra*) R; (*Ferr*) = **diretto**

○ **PAROLA CHIAVE**

da (*da + il* = **dal**, *da + lo* = **dallo**, *da + l'* = **dall'**, *da + la* = **dalla**, *da + i* = **dai**, *da + gli* = **dagli**, *da + le* = **dalle**) *prep* **1** (*agente*) by; **dipinto da un grande artista** painted by a great artist
2 (*causa*) with; **tremare dalla paura** to tremble with fear
3 (*stato in luogo*) at; **abito da lui** I'm living at his house *o* with him; **sono dal giornalaio** I'm at the newsagent's; **era da Francesco** she was at Francesco's (house)
4 (*moto a luogo*) to; (*moto per luogo*) through; **vado da Pietro/dal giornalaio** I'm going to Pietro's (house)/to the newsagent's; **sono passati dalla finestra** they came in through the window
5 (*provenienza, allontanamento*) from; **da ... a** from ... to; **arrivare/partire da Milano** to arrive/depart from Milan; **scendere dal treno/dalla macchina** to get off the train/out of the car; **viene da una famiglia povera** he comes from a poor background; **viene dalla Scozia** he comes from Scotland; **ti chiamo da una cabina** I'm phoning from a call box; **si trova a 5 km da qui** it's 5 km from here
6 (*tempo: durata*) for; (: *a partire da: nel passato*) since; (: *nel futuro*) from; **vivo qui da un anno** I've been living here for a year; **è dalle 3 che ti aspetto** I've been waiting for you since 3 (o'clock); **da mattina a sera** from morning till night; **da oggi in poi** from today onwards; **da bambino** as a child, when I (*o he etc*) was a child
7 (*modo, maniera*) like; **comportarsi da uomo** to behave like a man; **l'ho fatto da me** I did it (by) myself; **non è da lui** it's not like him
8 (*descrittivo*): **una macchina da corsa** a racing car; **è una cosa da poco** it's nothing special; **una ragazza dai capelli biondi** a girl with blonde hair; **sordo da un orecchio** deaf in one ear; **abbigliamento da uomo** menswear; **un vestito da 100 euro** a 100 euro dress; **qualcosa da bere/mangiare** something to drink/eat

dà *vb vedi* **dare**

dab'bene *ag inv* honest, decent

'Dacca *sf* Dacca

dac'capo, da'capo *av* (*di nuovo*) (once) again; (*dal principio*) all over again, from the beginning

dacché [dak'ke] *cong* since

'dado *sm* (*da gioco*) dice *o* die; (*Cuc*) stock cube (Brit), bouillon cube (US); (*Tecn*) (screw) nut; nut; **dadi** *smpl* (game of) dice

daf'fare, da'fare *sm* work, toil; **avere un gran ~** to be very busy

'dagli ['daʎʎi], **'dai** *prep + det vedi* **da**

'daino *sm* (fallow) deer *inv*; (*pelle*) buckskin

Da'kar *sf* Dakar

dal *prep + det vedi* **da**

dal *abbr* (= *decalitro*) dal

dall', 'dalla, 'dalle, 'dallo *prep + det vedi* **da**

dal'tonico, -a, ci, che *ag* colour-blind (Brit), colorblind (US)

dam *abbr* (= *decametro*) dam

'dama *sf* lady; (*nei balli*) partner; (*gioco*) draughts *sg* (Brit), checkers *sg* (US); **far ~** (*nel gioco*) to make a crown; **~ di compagnia** lady's companion; **~ di corte** lady-in-waiting

Da'masco *sf* Damascus

dami'gella [dami'dʒella] *sf* (*Storia*) damsel; (: *titolo*) mistress; **~ d'onore** (*di sposa*) bridesmaid

damigi'ana [dami'dʒana] *sf* demijohn

dam'meno *ag inv*: **per non essere ~ di qn** so as not to be outdone by sb

DAMS *sigla m*: **Disciplina delle Arti, della musica, dello spettacolo** *study of the performing arts*

da'naro *sm* = **denaro**

dana'roso, -a *ag* wealthy

da'nese *ag* Danish ▪ *sm/f* Dane ▪ *sm* (*Ling*) Danish

Dani'marca *sf*: **la ~** Denmark

dan'nare *vt* (*Rel*) to damn; **dannarsi** *vr*: **dannarsi per** (*fig: tormentarsi*) to be worried to death (by); **far ~ qn** to drive sb mad; **dannarsi l'anima per qc** (*affannarsi*) to work o.s. to death for sth; (*tormentarsi*) to worry o.s. to death over sth

dan'nato, -a *ag* damned

dannazi'one [dannat'tsjone] *sf* damnation

danneggi'are [danned'dʒare] *vt* to damage; (*rovinare*) to spoil; (*nuocere*) to harm; **la parte danneggiata** (*Dir*) the injured party

'danno *vb vedi* **dare** ▪ *sm* damage; (*a persona*) harm, injury; **danni** *smpl* (*Dir*) damages; **a ~ di qn** to sb's detriment; **chiedere/risarcire i danni** to sue for/pay damages

dan'noso, -a *ag*: **~ (a o per)** harmful (to), bad (for)

dan'tesco, -a, schi, sche *ag* Dantesque; **l'opera dantesca** Dante's work

Da'nubio *sm*: **il ~** the Danube

'danza ['dantsa] *sf*: **la ~** dancing; **una ~** a dance

dan'zante [dan'tsante] *ag* dancing; **serata ~** dance

dan'zare [dan'tsare] *vt, vi* to dance

danza'tore, -'trice [dantsa'tore] *sm/f* dancer

dapper'tutto *av* everywhere

dap'poco *ag inv* inept; worthless

dap'prima *av* at first

Darda'nelli *smpl*: **i ~** the Dardanelles

'dardo *sm* dart

'dare *sm* (*Comm*) debit ▪ *vt* to give; (*produrre: frutti, suono*) to produce ▪ *vi* (*guardare*): **~ su** to look (out) onto; **darsi** *vr*: **darsi a** to dedicate o.s. to; **quanti anni mi dai?** how old do you think I am?; **danno ancora quel film?** is that film still showing?; **~ da mangiare a qn** to give sb something to eat; **~ per certo qc** to consider sth certain; **~ ad intendere a qn che ...** to lead sb to believe that ...; **~ per morto qn** to give sb up for dead; **~ qc per scontato** to take sth for granted; **darsi ammalato** to report sick; **darsi alla bella vita** to have a good time; **darsi al bere** to take to drink; **darsi al commercio** to go into business; **darsi da fare per fare qc** to go to a lot of bother to do sth; **darsi per vinto** to give in; **può darsi** maybe, perhaps; **si dà il caso che ...** it so happens that ...; **darsela a**

gambe to take to one's heels; **il ~ e l'avere** (*Econ*) debits and credits *pl*

Dar-es-Sa'laam *sf* Dar-es-Salaam

'darsena *sf* dock

'data *sf* date; **in ~ da destinarsi** on a date still to be announced; **in ~ odierna** as of today; **amicizia di lunga o vecchia ~** long-standing friendship; **~ di emissione** date of issue; **~ di nascita** date of birth; **~ di scadenza** expiry date; **~ limite d'utilizzo o di consumo** (*Comm*) best-before date

da'tare *vt* to date ▪ *vi*: **~ da** to date from

da'tato, -a *ag* dated

da'tivo *sm* dative

'dato, -a *ag* (*stabilito*) given ▪ *sm* datum; **dati** *smpl* data *pl*; **~ che** given that; **in dati casi** in certain cases; **è un ~ di fatto** it's a fact; **dati sensibili** sense data

da'tore, -'trice *sm/f*: **~ di lavoro** employer

'dattero *sm* date (*Bot*)

dattilogra'fare *vt* to type

dattilogra'fia *sf* typing

datti'lografo, -a *sm/f* typist

dattilos'critto *sm* typescript

da'vanti *av* in front; (*dirimpetto*) opposite ▪ *ag inv* front ▪ *sm* front; **~ a** *prep* in front of; (*dirimpetto a*) facing, opposite; (*in presenza di*) before, in front of

davan'zale [davan'tsale] *sm* windowsill

da'vanzo, d'a'vanzo [da'vantso] *av* more than enough

dav'vero *av* really, indeed; **dico ~** I mean it

dazi'ario, -a [dat'tsjarjo] *ag* excise *cpd*

'dazio ['dattsjo] *sm* (*somma*) duty; (*luogo*) customs *pl*; **~ d'importazione** import duty

db *abbr* (= *decibel*) dB

DC *sigla f* = **Democrazia Cristiana** (*former political party*)

d.C. *abbr* (= *dopo Cristo*) A.D.

D.D.T. *abbr m* (= *dicloro-difenil-tricloroetano*) D.D.T.

'dea *sf* goddess

'debbo *etc vb vedi* **dovere**

debel'lare *vt* to overcome, conquer

debili'tare *vt* to debilitate

debita'mente *av* duly, properly

'debito, -a *ag* due, proper ▪ *sm* debt; (*Comm: dare*) debit; **a tempo ~** at the right time; **portare a ~ di qn** to debit sb with; **~ consolidato** consolidated debt; **~ d'imposta** tax liability; **~ pubblico** national debt

debi'tore, -'trice *sm/f* debtor

'debole *ag* weak, feeble; (*suono*) faint; (*luce*) dim ▪ *sm* weakness

debo'lezza [debo'lettsa] *sf* weakness

debut'tante *sm/f* (*gen*) beginner, novice; (*Teat*) actor/actress at the beginning of his (*o* her) career

debut'tare vi to make one's début

de'butto sm début

'decade sf period of ten days

deca'dente ag decadent

deca'denza [deka'dɛntsa] sf decline; (Dir) loss, forfeiture

deca'dere vi to decline

deca'duto, -a ag (persona) impoverished; (norma) lapsed

decaffei'nato, -a ag decaffeinated

de'calogo sm (fig) rulebook

de'cano sm (Rel) dean

decan'tare vt (virtù, bravura etc) to praise; (persona) to sing the praises of

decapi'tare vt to decapitate, behead

decappot'tabile ag, sf convertible

dece'duto, -a [detʃe'duto] ag deceased

dece'rare [detʃele'rare] vt, vi to decelerate, slow down

decen'nale [detʃen'nale] ag (che dura 10 anni) ten-year cpd; (che ricorre ogni 10 anni) ten-yearly, every ten years ■ sm (ricorrenza) tenth anniversary

de'cenne [de'tʃɛnne] ag: **un bambino ~** a ten-year-old child, a child of ten

de'cennio [de'tʃɛnnjo] sm decade

de'cente [de'tʃɛnte] ag decent, respectable, proper; (accettabile) satisfactory, decent

decentraliz'zare [detʃentralid'dzare] vt (Amm) to decentralize

decentra'mento [detʃentra'mento] sm decentralization

decen'trare [detʃen'trare] vt to decentralize, move out of o away from the centre

de'cenza [de'tʃɛntsa] sf decency, propriety

de'cesso [de'tʃɛsso] sm death; **atto di ~** death certificate

de'cidere [de'tʃidere] vi to decide, make up one's mind ■ vt: **~ qc** to decide on sth; (questione, lite) to settle sth; **decidersi** vr: **decidersi (a fare)** to decide (to do), make up one's mind (to do); **~ di fare/che** to decide to do/that; **~ di qc** (cosa) to determine sth

deci'frare [detʃi'frare] vt to decode; (fig) to decipher, make out

de'cilitro [de'tʃilitro] sm decilitre (Brit), deciliter (US)

deci'male [detʃi'male] ag decimal

deci'mare [detʃi'mare] vt to decimate

de'cimetro [de'tʃimetro] sm decimetre

'decimo, -a ['dɛtʃimo] num tenth

de'cina [de'tʃina] sf ten; (circa dieci): **una ~ (di)** about ten

de'cisi etc [de'tʃizi] vb vedi **decidere**

decisio'nale [detʃizjo'nale] ag decision-making cpd

decisi'one [detʃi'zjone] sf decision; **prendere una ~** to make a decision; **con ~** decisively, resolutely

deci'sivo, -a [detʃi'zivo] ag (gen) decisive; (fattore) deciding

de'ciso, -a [de'tʃizo] pp di **decidere** ■ ag (persona, carattere) determined; (tono) firm, resolute

declas'sare vt to downgrade; to lower in status; **la declassata** (Ferr) first-class carriage which may be used by second-class passengers

decli'nare vi (pendio) to slope down; (fig: diminuire) to decline; (tramontare) to set, go down ■ vt to decline; **~ le proprie generalità** (fig) to give one's particulars; **~ ogni responsabilità** to disclaim all responsibility

declinazi'one [deklinat'tsjone] sf (Ling) declension

de'clino sm decline

de'clivio sm (downward) slope

decodifi'care vt to decode

decodifica'tore sm decoder

decol'lare vi (Aer) to take off

décolleté [dekol'te] ag inv (abito) low-necked, low-cut ■ sm (di abito) low neckline; (di donna) cleavage

de'collo sm take-off

decolo'rare vt to bleach

decom'porre vt, **decomporsi** vr to decompose

decomposizi'one [dekompozit'tsjone] sf decomposition

decom'posto, -a pp di **decomporre**

decompressi'one sf decompression

deconge'lare [dekondʒe'lare] vt to defrost

decongestio'nare [dekondʒestjo'nare] vt (Med, traffico) to relieve congestion in

deco'rare vt to decorate

decora'tivo, -a ag decorative

decora'tore, -'trice sm (interior) decorator

decorazi'one [dekorat'tsjone] sf decoration

de'coro sm decorum

deco'roso, -a ag decorous, dignified

decor'renza [dekor'rɛntsa] sf: **con ~ da** (as) from

de'correre vi to pass, elapse; (avere effetto) to run, have effect

de'corso, -a pp di **decorrere** ■ sm (evoluzione: anche Med) course

de'crebbi etc vb vedi **decrescere**

de'crepito, -a ag decrepit

de'crescere [de'kreʃere] vi (diminuire) to decrease, diminish; (acque) to subside, go down; (prezzi) to go down

decresci'uto, -a [dekreʃ'ʃuto] pp di **decrescere**

decre'tare vt (norma) to decree; (mobilitazione) to order; **~ lo stato d'emergenza** to declare a state of emergency; ~ **la nomina di qn** to decide on the appointment of sb

de'creto *sm* decree; ~ **legge** *decree with the force of law*; ~ **di sfratto** eviction order

decur'tare *vt* (*debito, somma*) to reduce

decurtazi'one [dekurtat'tsjone] *sf* reduction

'dedalo *sm* maze, labyrinth

'dedica, -che *sf* dedication

dedi'care *vt* to dedicate; **dedicarsi** *vr*: **dedicarsi a** (*votarsi*) to devote o.s. to

dedi'cherò *etc* [dedike'rɔ] *vb vedi* **dedicare**

'dedito, -a *ag*: ~ **a** (*studio etc*) dedicated *o* devoted to; (*vizio*) addicted to

de'dotto, -a *pp di* **dedurre**

de'duco *etc vb vedi* **dedurre**

de'durre *vt* (*concludere*) to deduce; (*defalcare*) to deduct

de'dussi *etc vb vedi* **dedurre**

deduzi'one [dedut'tsjone] *sf* deduction

defal'care *vt* to deduct

defenes'trare *vt* to throw out of the window; (*fig*) to remove from office

defe'rente *ag* respectful, deferential

defe'rire *vt* (*Dir*): ~ **a** to refer to

defezi'one [defet'tsjone] *sf* defection, desertion

defici'ente [defi'tʃɛnte] *ag* (*mancante*): ~ **di** deficient in; (*insufficiente*) insufficient ■ *sm/f* mental defective; (*peg: cretino*) idiot

defici'enza [defi'tʃɛntsa] *sf* deficiency; (*carenza*) shortage; (*fig: lacuna*) weakness

'deficit ['dɛfitʃit] *sm inv* (*Econ*) deficit

defi'nire *vt* to define; (*risolvere*) to settle; (*questione*) to finalize

defini'tivo, -a *ag* definitive, final ■ *sf*: **in definitiva** (*dopotutto*) when all is said and done; (*dunque*) well then

defi'nito, -a *ag* definite; **ben** ~ clear, clear cut

definizi'one [definit'tsjone] *sf* (*gen*) definition; (*di disputa, vertenza*) settlement; (*di tempi, obiettivi*) establishment

deflagrazi'one [deflagrat'tsjone] *sf* explosion

deflazi'one [deflat'tsjone] *sf* (*Econ*) deflation

deflet'tore *sm* (*Aut*) quarterlight (*Brit*), deflector (*US*)

deflu'ire *vi*: ~ **da** (*liquido*) to flow away from; (*fig: capitali*) to flow out of

de'flusso *sm* (*della marea*) ebb

defor'mare *vt* (*alterare*) to put out of shape; (*corpo*) to deform; (*pensiero, fatto*) to distort; **deformarsi** *vr* to lose its shape

deformazi'one [deformat'tsjone] *sf* (*Med*) deformation; **questa è ~ professionale!** that's force of habit because of your (*o his etc*) job!

de'forme *ag* deformed; disfigured

deformità *sf inv* deformity

defrau'dare *vt*: ~ **qn di qc** to defraud sb of sth, cheat sb out of sth

de'funto, -a *ag* late *cpd* ■ *sm/f* deceased

degene'rare [dedʒene'rare] *vi* to degenerate

degenerazi'one [dedʒenerat'tsjone] *sf* degeneration

de'genere [de'dʒenere] *ag* degenerate

de'gente [de'dʒɛnte] *sm/f* bedridden person; (*ricoverato in ospedale*) in-patient

de'genza [de'dʒɛntsa] *sf* confinement to bed; ~ **ospedaliera** period in hospital

'degli ['deʎʎi] *prep + det vedi* **di**

deglu'tire *vt* to swallow

de'gnare [deɲ'ɲare] *vt*: ~ **qn della propria presenza** to honour sb with one's presence; **degnarsi** *vr*: **degnarsi di fare qc** to deign *o* condescend to do sth; **non mi ha degnato di uno sguardo** he wouldn't even look at me

'degno, -a ['deɲɲo] *ag* dignified; ~ **di** worthy of; ~ **di lode** praiseworthy

degra'dare *vt* (*Mil*) to demote; (*privare della dignità*) to degrade; **degradarsi** *vr* to demean o.s.

de'grado *sm*: ~ **urbano** urban decline

degus'tare *vt* to sample, taste

degustazi'one [degustat'tsjone] *sf* sampling, tasting; ~ **di vini** (*locale*) specialist wine bar; ~ **di caffè** (*locale*) specialist coffee shop

'dei *smpl di* **dio** ■ *prep + det vedi* **di**

del *prep + det vedi* **di**

dela'tore, -'trice *sm/f* police informer

delazi'one [delat'tsjone] *sf* informing

'delega, -ghe *sf* (*procura*) proxy; **per ~ notarile** ≈ through a solicitor (*Brit*) *o* lawyer

dele'gare *vt* to delegate

dele'gato *sm* delegate

delegazi'one [delegat'tsjone] *sf* delegation

delegh'erò *etc* [delege'rɔ] *vb vedi* **delegare**

dele'terio, -a *ag* deleterious, noxious

del'fino *sm* (*Zool*) dolphin; (*Storia*) dauphin; (*fig*) probable successor

'Delhi ['dɛli] *sf* Delhi

de'libera *sf* decision

delibe'rare *vt* to come to a decision on ■ *vi* (*Dir*): ~ **(su qc)** to rule (on sth)

delica'tezza [delika'tettsa] *sf* delicacy; frailty; thoughtfulness; tactfulness

deli'cato, -a *ag* delicate; (*salute*) delicate, frail; (*fig: gentile*) thoughtful, considerate; (*: che dimostra tatto*) tactful

delimi'tare *vt* (*anche fig*) to delimit

deline'are *vt* to outline; **delinearsi** *vr* to be outlined; (*fig*) to emerge

delin'quente *sm/f* criminal, delinquent

delin'quenza [delin'kwɛntsa] *sf* criminality, delinquency; **~ minorile** juvenile delinquency

de'liquio *sm* (*Med*) swoon; **cadere in ~** to swoon

deli'rante *ag* (*Med*) delirious; (*fig: folla*) frenzied; (*: discorso, mente*) insane

deli'rare *vi* to be delirious, rave; (*fig*) to rave

de'lirio *sm* delirium; (*ragionamento insensato*) raving; (*fig*): **andare/mandare in ~** to go/send into a frenzy

de'litto *sm* crime; **~ d'onore** *crime committed to avenge one's honour*

delittu'oso, -a *ag* criminal

de'lizia [de'littsja] *sf* delight

delizi'are [delit'tsjare] *vt* to delight; **deliziarsi** *vr*: **deliziarsi di qc/a fare qc** to take delight in sth/in doing sth

delizi'oso, -a [delit'tsjoso] *ag* delightful; (*cibi*) delicious

dell', **'della**, **'delle**, **'dello** *prep + det vedi* **di**

'delta *sm inv* delta

delta'plano *sm* hang-glider; **volo col ~** hang-gliding

delucidazi'one [delutʃidat'tsjone] *sf* clarification *no pl*

delu'dente *ag* disappointing

de'ludere *vt* to disappoint

delusi'one *sf* disappointment

de'luso, -a *pp di* **deludere** ■ *ag* disappointed

dema'gogico, -a, ci, che [dema'gɔdʒiko] *ag* popularity-seeking, demagogic

dema'gogo, -ghi *sm* demagogue

de'manio *sm* state property

de'mente *ag* (*Med*) demented, mentally deranged; (*fig*) crazy, mad

de'menza [de'mɛntsa] *sf* dementia; madness; **~ senile** senile dementia

demenzi'ale [demen'tsjale] *ag* (*fig*) off-the-wall

'demmo *vb vedi* **dare**

demo'cratico, -a, ci, che *ag* democratic

democra'zia [demokrat'tsia] *sf* democracy; **la D~ Cristiana** the Christian Democrat Party

democristi'ano, -a *ag, sm/f* Christian Democrat

demogra'fia *sf* demography

demo'grafico, -a, ci, che *ag* demographic; **incremento ~** increase in population

demo'lire *vt* to demolish

demolizi'one [demolit'tsjone] *sf* demolition

'demone *sm* demon

de'monio *sm* demon, devil; **il D~** the Devil

demoniz'zare [demonid'dzare] *vt* to make a monster of

demonizzazi'one [demoniddzat'tsjone] *sf* demonizing, demonization

demoraliz'zare [demoralid'dzare] *vt* to demoralize; **demoralizzarsi** *vr* to become demoralized

de'mordere *vi*: **non ~ (da)** to refuse to give up

demoti'vare *vt*: **~ qn** to take away sb's motivation

demoti'vato, -a *ag* unmotivated, lacking motivation

de'naro *sm* money; **denari** *smpl* (*Carte*) suit in Neapolitan pack of cards

denatu'rato, -a *ag vedi* **alcool**

deni'grare *vt* to denigrate, run down

denomi'nare *vt* to name; **denominarsi** *vr* to be named o called

denomina'tore *sm* (*Mat*) denominator

denominazi'one [denominat'tsjone] *sf* name; denomination; **~ di origine controllata** *label guaranteeing the quality and origin of a wine*

deno'tare *vt* to denote, indicate

densità *sf inv* density; (*di nebbia*) thickness, denseness; **ad alta/bassa ~ di popolazione** densely/sparsely populated

'denso, -a *ag* thick, dense

den'tale *ag* dental

den'tario, -a *ag* dental

denta'tura *sf* set of teeth, teeth *pl*; (*Tecn: di ruota*) serration

'dente *sm* tooth; (*di forchetta*) prong; (*Geo: cima*) jagged peak; **al ~** (*Cuc: pasta*) cooked so as to be firm when eaten; **mettere i denti** to teethe; **mettere qc sotto i denti** to have a bite to eat; **avere il ~ avvelenato contro** o **con qn** to bear sb a grudge; **~ di leone** (*Bot*) dandelion; **denti del giudizio** wisdom teeth

'dentice ['dɛntitʃe] *sm* (*Zool*) sea bream

denti'era *sf* (set of) false teeth *pl*

denti'fricio [denti'fritʃo] *sm* toothpaste

den'tista, -i, e *sm/f* dentist

'dentro *av* inside; (*in casa*) indoors; (*fig: nell'intimo*) inwardly ■ *prep*: **~ (a)** in; **piegato in ~** folded over; **qui/là ~** in here/there; **~ di sé** (*pensare, brontolare*) to oneself; **tenere tutto ~** to keep everything bottled up (inside o.s.); **darci ~** (*fig fam*) to slog away, work hard

denuclear'izzato, -a [denuklearid'dzato] *ag* denuclearized, nuclear-free

denu'dare *vt* (*persona*) to strip; (*parte del corpo*) to bare; **denudarsi** *vr* to strip

de'nuncia [de'nuntʃa] (*pl* **denunce** o **denuncie**), **de'nunzia** [de'nuntsja] *sf* denunciation; declaration; **fare una ~** o **sporgere ~ contro qn** (*Dir*) to report sb to the police; **~ del reddito** (income) tax return

denunci'are [denun'tʃare], **denunzi'are** [denun'tsjare] *vt* to denounce; (*dichiarare*) to declare; ~ **qn/qc (alla polizia)** to report sb/ sth to the police

denu'trito, -a *ag* undernourished

denutrizi'one [denutrit'tsjone] *sf* malnutrition

deodo'rante *sm* deodorant

deontolo'gia [deontolo'dʒia] *sf (professionale)* professional code of conduct

depenalizzazi'one [depenaliddzat'tsjone] *sf* decriminalization

dépen'dance [depā'dãs] *sf inv* outbuilding

depe'ribile *ag* perishable; **merce ~** perishables *pl*, perishable goods *pl*

deperi'mento *sm (di persona)* wasting away; *(di merci)* deterioration

depe'rire *vi* to waste away

depi'lare *vt* to depilate

depila'torio, -a *ag* hair-removing, depilatory ■ *sm* hair remover, depilatory

depilazi'one [depilat'tsjone] *sf* hair removal, depilation

depis'taggio [depis'taddʒo] *sm* diversion

depis'tare *vt* to set on the wrong track

dépli'ant [depli'ā] *sm inv* leaflet; *(opuscolo)* brochure

deplo'rare *vt* to deplore; to lament

deplo'revole *ag* deplorable

de'pone, de'pongo *etc vb vedi* **deporre**

de'porre *vt (depositare)* to put down; *(rimuovere: da una carica)* to remove; *(: re)* to depose; *(Dir)* to testify; ~ **le armi** *(Mil)* to lay down arms; ~ **le uova** to lay eggs

depor'tare *vt* to deport

depor'tato, -a *sm/f* deportee

deportazi'one [deportat'tsjone] *sf* deportation

de'posi *etc vb vedi* **deporre**

deposi'tante *sm (Comm)* depositor

deposi'tare *vt (gen, Geo, Econ)* to deposit; *(lasciare)* to leave; *(merci)* to store; **depositarsi** *vr (sabbia, polvere)* to settle

deposi'tario *sm (Comm)* depository

de'posito *sm* deposit; *(luogo)* warehouse; depot; *(: Mil)* depot; ~ **bagagli** left-luggage office; ~ **di munizioni** ammunition dump

deposizi'one [depozit'tsjone] *sf* deposition; *(da una carica)* removal; **rendere una falsa ~** to perjure o.s.

de'posto, -a *pp di* **deporre**

depra'vare *vt* to corrupt, pervert

depra'vato, -a *ag* depraved ■ *sm/f* degenerate

depre'care *vt* to deprecate, deplore

depre'dare *vt* to rob, plunder

depressi'one *sf* depression; **area** *o* **zona di ~** *(Meteor)* area of low pressure; *(Econ)* depressed area

de'presso, -a *pp di* **deprimere** ■ *ag* depressed

deprezza'mento [deprettsa'mento] *sm* depreciation

deprez'zare [depret'tsare] *vt (Econ)* to depreciate

depri'mente *ag* depressing

de'primere *vt* to depress

depu'rare *vt* to purify

depura'tore *sm*: ~ **d'acqua** water purifier; ~ **di gas** scrubber

depu'tato, -a *sm/f (Pol)* deputy, ≈ Member of Parliament *(Brit)*, ≈ Congressman(-woman *(US)*); *vedi anche* **Camera dei Deputati**

deputazi'one [deputat'tsjone] *sf* deputation; *(Pol)* position of deputy, ≈ parliamentary seat *(Brit)*, ≈ seat in Congress *(US)*

deraglia'mento [deraʎʎa'mento] *sm* derailment

deragli'are [deraʎ'ʎare] *vi* to be derailed; **far ~** to derail

dera'pare *vi (veicolo)* to skid; *(Sci)* to sideslip

derattizzazi'one [derattiddzat'tsjone] *sf* rodent control

deregolamen'tare *vt* to deregulate

deregolamentazi'one [deregolamentat'tsjone] *sf* deregulation

dere'litto, -a *ag* derelict

dere'tano *sm (fam)* bottom, buttocks *pl*

de'ridere *vt* to mock, deride

de'risi *etc vb vedi* **deridere**

derisi'one *sf* derision, mockery

de'riso, -a *pp di* **deridere**

deri'sorio, -a *ag (gesto, tono)* mocking

de'riva *sf (Naut, Aer)* drift; *(dispositivo: Aer)* fin; *(: Naut)* centre-board *(Brit)*, centerboard *(US)*; **andare alla ~** *(anche fig)* to drift

deri'vare *vi*: ~ **da** to derive from ■ *vt* to derive; *(corso d'acqua)* to divert

deri'vato, -a *ag* derived ■ *sm (Chim, Ling)* derivative; *(prodotto)* by-product

derivazi'one [derivat'tsjone] *sf* derivation; diversion

derma'tite *sf* dermatitis

dermatolo'gia [dermatolo'dʒia] *sf* dermatology

derma'tologo, -a, gi, ghe *sm/f* dermatologist

dermoprotet'tivo, -a *ag (crema, azione)* protecting the skin

'deroga, -ghe *sf* (special) dispensation; **in ~ a** as a (special) dispensation to

dero'gare *vi*: ~ **a** *(Dir)* to repeal in part

der'rate *sfpl* commodities; ~ **alimentari** foodstuffs

deru'bare *vt* to rob

des'critto, -a *pp di* **descrivere**

des'crivere *vt* to describe

descrizi'one [deskrit'tsjone] *sf* description

de'serto, -a *ag* deserted ■ *sm* (*Geo*) desert; **isola deserta** desert island

deside'rabile *ag* desirable

deside'rare *vt* to want, wish for; (*sessualmente*) to desire; ~ **fare/che qn faccia** to want *o* wish to do/sb to do; **desidera fare una passeggiata?** would you like to go for a walk?; **farsi** ~ (*fare il prezioso*) to play hard to get; (*farsi aspettare*) to take one's time; **lascia molto a** ~ it leaves a lot to be desired

desi'derio *sm* wish; (*più intenso, carnale*) desire

deside'roso, -a *ag*: ~ **di** longing *o* eager for

desi'gnare [desiɲ'ɲare] *vt* to designate, appoint; (*data*) to fix; **la vittima designata** the intended victim

designazi'one [desiɲɲat'tsjone] *sf* designation, appointment

desi'nare *vi* to dine, have dinner ■ *sm* dinner

desi'nenza [dezi'nɛntsa] *sf* (*Ling*) ending, inflexion

de'sistere *vi*: ~ **da** to give up, desist from

desis'tito, -a *pp di* **desistere**

deso'lante *ag* distressing

deso'lato, -a *ag* (*paesaggio*) desolate; (*persona: spiacente*) sorry

desolazi'one [dezolat'tsjone] *sf* desolation

'despota, -i *sm* despot

'dessi *etc vb vedi* **dare**

destabiliz'zare [destabilid'dzare] *vt* to destabilize

des'tare *vt* to wake (up); (*fig*) to awaken, arouse; **destarsi** *vr* to wake (up)

'deste *etc vb vedi* **dare**

desti'nare *vt* to destine; (*assegnare*) to appoint, assign; (*indirizzare*) to address; ~ **qc a qn** to intend to give sth to sb, intend sb to have sth

destina'tario, -a *sm/f* (*di lettera*) addressee; (*di merce*) consignee; (*di mandato*) payee

destinazi'one [destinat'tsjone] *sf* destination; (*uso*) purpose

des'tino *sm* destiny, fate

destitu'ire *vt* to dismiss, remove

destituzi'one [destitut'tsjone] *sf* dismissal, removal

'desto, -a *ag* (wide) awake

'destra *sf vedi* **destro**

destreggi'arsi [destred'dʒarsi] *vr* to manoeuvre (*Brit*), maneuver (*US*)

des'trezza [des'trettsa] *sf* skill, dexterity

'destro, -a *ag* right, right-hand; (*abile*) skilful (*Brit*), skillful (*US*), adroit ■ *sf* (*mano*) right hand; (*parte*) right (side); (*Pol*): **la destra** the right ■ *sm* (*Boxe*) right; **a destra** (*essere*) on the right; (*andare*) to the right; **tenere la destra** to keep to the right

de'sumere *vt* (*dedurre*) to infer, deduce; (*trarre: informazioni*) to obtain

de'sunto, -a *pp di* **desumere**

detas'sare *vt* to remove the duty (*o* tax) from

dete'nere *vt* (*incarico, primato*) to hold; (*proprietà*) to have, possess; (*in prigione*) to detain, hold

de'tengo, de'tenni *etc vb vedi* **detenere**

deten'tivo, -a *ag*: **mandato** ~ imprisonment order; **pena detentiva** prison sentence

deten'tore, -'trice *sm/f* (*di titolo, primato etc*) holder

dete'nuto, -a *sm/f* prisoner

detenzi'one [deten'tsjone] *sf* holding; possession; detention

deter'gente [deter'dʒɛnte] *ag* detergent; (*crema, latte*) cleansing ■ *sm* detergent

de'tergere [de'tɛrdʒere] *vt* (*gen*) to clean; (*pelle, viso*) to cleanse; (*sudore*) to wipe (away)

deteriora'mento *sm*: ~ (**di**) deterioration (in)

deterio'rare *vt* to damage; **deteriorarsi** *vr* to deteriorate

deteri'ore *ag* (*merce*) second-rate; (*significato*) pejorative; (*tradizione letteraria*) lesser, minor

determi'nante *ag* decisive, determining

determi'nare *vt* to determine

determina'tivo, -a *ag* determining; **articolo** ~ (*Ling*) definite article

determi'nato, -a *ag* (*gen*) certain; (*particolare*) specific; (*risoluto*) determined, resolute

determinazi'one [determinat'tsjone] *sf* determination; (*decisione*) decision

deter'rente *ag, sm* deterrent

deter'rò *etc vb vedi* **detenere**

deter'sivo *sm* detergent; (*per bucato: in polvere*) washing powder; (*Brit*), soap powder

de'terso, -a *pp di* **detergere**

detes'tare *vt* to detest, hate

deti'ene *etc vb vedi* **detenere**

deto'nare *vi* to detonate

detona'tore *sm* detonator

detonazi'one [detonat'tsjone] *sf* (*di esplosivo*) detonation, explosion; (*di arma*) bang; (*di motore*) pinking (*Brit*), knocking

de'trae, de'traggo *etc vb vedi* **detrarre**

de'trarre *vt*: ~ (**da**) to deduct (from), take away (from)

de'trassi *etc vb vedi* **detrarre**

de'tratto, -a *pp di* **detrarre**

detrazi'one [detrat'tsjone] *sf* deduction; ~ **d'imposta** tax allowance

detri'mento *sm* detriment, harm; **a ~ di** to the detriment of

de'trito *sm* (*Geo*) detritus

detroniz'zare [detronid'dzare] *vt* to dethrone

'detta *sf*: **a ~ di** according to

dettagli'ante [dettaʎ'ʎante] *sm/f* (*Comm*) retailer

d

dettagli'are [dettaʎ'ʎare] *vt* to detail, give full details of

dettagliata'mente [dettaʎʎata'mente] *av* in detail

det'taglio [det'taʎʎo] *sm* detail; (*Comm*): **il ~** retail; **al ~** (*Comm*) retail; separately

det'tame *sm* dictate, precept

det'tare *vt* to dictate; **~ legge** (*fig*) to lay down the law

det'tato *sm* dictation

detta'tura *sf* dictation

'detto, -a *pp di* **dire ■** *ag* (*soprannominato*) called, known as; (*già nominato*) above-mentioned **■** *sm* saying; **~ fatto** no sooner said than done; **presto ~!** it's easier said than done!

detur'pare *vt* to disfigure; (*moralmente*) to sully

devas'tante *ag* (*anche fig*) devastating

devas'tare *vt* to devastate; (*fig*) to ravage

devastazi'one [devastat'tsjone] *sf* devastation, destruction

devi'are *vi*: **~ (da)** to turn off (from) **■** *vt* to divert

devi'ato, -a *ag* (*fig: persona, organizzazione*) corrupt, bent (*col*)

deviazi'one [devjat'tsjone] *sf* (*anche Aut*) diversion; **fare una ~** to make a detour

'devo *etc vb vedi* **dovere**

devo'luto, -a *pp di* **devolvere**

devoluzi'one [devolut'tsjone] *sf* (*Dir*) devolution, transfer

de'volvere *vt* (*Dir*) to transfer, devolve; **~ qc in beneficenza** to give sth to charity

de'voto, -a *ag* (*Rel*) devout, pious; (*affezionato*) devoted

devozi'one [devot'tsjone] *sf* devoutness; (*anche Rel*) devotion

dezip'pare [dedzip'pare] *vt* (*Comput*) to unzip

dg *abbr* (= *decigrammo*) dg

○ **PAROLA CHIAVE**

di (*di + il* = **del**, *di + lo* = **dello**, *di + l'* = **dell'**, *di + la* = **della**, *di + i* = **dei**, *di + gli* = **degli**, *di + le* = **delle**) *prep* **1** (*possesso, specificazione*) of; (*composto da, scritto da*) by; **la macchina di Paolo/di mio fratello** Paolo's/my brother's car; **un amico di mio fratello** a friend of my brother's, one of my brother's friends; **la grandezza della casa** the size of the house; **le foto delle vacanze** the holiday photos; **la città di Firenze** the city of Florence; **il nome di Maria** the name Mary; **un quadro di Botticelli** a painting by Botticelli

2 (*caratterizzazione, misura*) of; **una casa di mattoni** a brick house, a house made of bricks; **un orologio d'oro** a gold watch; **un bimbo di 3 anni** a child of 3, a 3-year-old

child; **una trota di un chilo** a trout weighing a kilo; **una strada di 10 km** a road 10 km long; **un quadro di valore** a valuable picture

3 (*causa, mezzo, modo*) with; **tremare di paura** to tremble with fear; **morire di cancro** to die of cancer; **spalmare di burro** to spread with butter

4 (*argomento*) about, of; **discutere di sport** to talk about sport; **parlare di politica/lavoro** to talk about politics/work

5 (*luogo: provenienza*) from; out of; **essere di Roma** to be from Rome; **uscire di casa** to come out of *o* leave the house

6 (*tempo*) in; **d'estate/d'inverno** in (the) summer/winter; **di notte** by night, at night; **di mattina/sera** in the morning/evening; **di lunedì** on Mondays; **di ora in ora** by the hour

7 (*partitivo*) of; **alcuni di voi/noi** some of you/us; **il più bravo di tutti** the best of all; **il migliore del mondo** the best in the world; **non c'è niente di peggio** there's nothing worse

8 (*paragone*) than; **più veloce di me** faster than me; **guadagna meno di me** he earns less than me

■ *det* (*una certa quantità di*) some; (: *negativo*) any; (: *interrogativo*) any, some; **del pane** (some) bread; **delle caramelle** (some) sweets; **degli amici miei** some friends of mine; **vuoi del vino?** do you want some *o* any wine?

dì *sm* day; **buon dì!** hallo!; **a dì** = **addì**

DIA *sigla f* = **Direzione investigativa antimafia**

dia'bete *sm* diabetes *sg*

dia'betico, -a, ci, che *ag, sm/f* diabetic

dia'bolico, -a, ci, che *ag* diabolical

di'acono *sm* (*Rel*) deacon

dia'dema, -i *sm* diadem; (*di donna*) tiara

di'afano, -a *ag* (*trasparente*) diaphanous; (*pelle*) transparent

dia'framma, -i *sm* (*divisione*) screen; (*Anat, Fot, contraccettivo*) diaphragm

di'agnosi [di'aɲɲozi] *sf* diagnosis *sg*

diagnosti'care [diaɲɲosti'kare] *vt* to diagnose

dia'gnostico, -a, ci, che [diaɲ'ɲɔstiko] *ag* diagnostic; **aiuti diagnostici** (*Inform*) debugging aids

diago'nale *ag, sf* diagonal

dia'gramma, -i *sm* diagram; **~ a barre** bar chart; **~ di flusso** flow chart

dialet'tale *ag* dialectal; **poesia ~** poetry in dialect

dia'letto *sm* dialect

di'alisi *sf* dialysis

dialo'gante *ag*: **unità ~** (*Inform*) interactive terminal

dialo'gare *vi*: **~ (con)** to have a dialogue (with); (*conversare*) to converse (with) ■ *vt* (*scena*) to write the dialogue for

di'alogo, -ghi *sm* dialogue

dia'mante *sm* diamond

di'ametro *sm* diameter

di'amine *escl*: **che ~ ...?** what on earth ...?

diaposi'tiva *sf* transparency, slide

di'aria *sf* daily (expense) allowance

di'ario *sm* diary; **~ di bordo** (*Naut*) log(book); **~ di classe** (*Ins*) class register; **~ degli esami** (*Ins*) exam timetable

diar'rea *sf* diarrhoea

dia'triba *sf* diatribe

diavole'ria *sf* (*azione*) act of mischief; (*aggeggio*) weird contraption

di'avolo *sm* devil; **è un buon ~** he's a good sort; **avere un ~ per capello** to be in a foul temper; **avere una fame/un freddo del ~** to be ravenously hungry/frozen stiff; **mandare qn al ~** (*fam*) to tell sb to go to hell; **fare il ~ a quattro** to kick up a fuss

di'battere *vt* to debate, discuss; **dibattersi** *vr* to struggle

dibatti'mento *sm* (*dibattito*) debate, discussion; (*Dir*) hearing

di'battito *sm* debate, discussion

dic. *abbr* (= *dicembre*) Dec

dicas'tero *sm* ministry

'dice ['ditʃe] *vb vedi* **dire**

di'cembre [di'tʃembre] *sm* December; *vedi anche* **luglio**

dice'ria [ditʃe'ria] *sf* rumour (*Brit*), rumor (*US*), piece of gossip

dichia'rare [dikja'rare] *vt* to declare; **dichiararsi** *vr* to declare o.s.; (*innamorato*) to declare one's love; **si dichiara che ...** it is hereby declared that ...; **dichiararsi vinto** to admit defeat

dichia'rato, -a [dikja'rato] *ag* (*nemico, ateo*) avowed

dichiarazi'one [dikjarat'tsjone] *sf* declaration; **~ dei redditi** statement of income; (*modulo*) tax return

dician'nove [ditʃan'nɔve] *num* nineteen

dicianno'venne [ditʃanno'venne] *ag, sm/f* nineteen-year-old

dicias'sette [ditʃas'sette] *num* seventeen

diciasset'tenne [ditʃasset'tenne] *ag, sm/f* seventeen-year-old

diciot'tenne [ditʃot'tenne] *ag, sm/f* eighteen-year-old

dici'otto [di'tʃotto] *num* eighteen ■ *sm inv* (*Ins*) minimum satisfactory mark awarded in Italian universities

dici'tura [ditʃi'tura] *sf* words *pl*, wording

'dico *etc vb vedi* **dire**

didasca'lia *sf* (*di illustrazione*) caption; (*Cine*) subtitle; (*Teat*) stage directions *pl*

di'dattico, -a, ci, che *ag* didactic; (*metodo, programma*) teaching; (*libro*) educational ■ *sf* didactics *sg*; teaching methodology

di'dentro *av* inside, indoors

didi'etro *av* behind ■ *ag inv* (*ruota, giardino*) back, rear *cpd* ■ *sm* (*di casa*) rear; (*fam: sedere*) backside

di'eci ['djetʃi] *num* ten

dieci'mila [djetʃi'mila] *num* ten thousand

die'cina [dje'tʃina] *sf* = **decina**

di'edi *etc vb vedi* **dare**

di'eresi *sf* dieresis *sg*

'diesel ['diːzəl] *sm inv* diesel engine

dies'sino, -a *ag* (*Pol*) of o belonging to the Democrats of the Left (*Italian left-wing party*)

di'eta *sf* diet; **essere a ~** to be on a diet

die'tetica *sf* dietetics *sg*

die'tologo, -a, gi, ghe *sm/f* dietician

di'etro *av* behind; (*in fondo*) at the back ■ *prep* behind; (*tempo: dopo*) after ■ *sm* (*di foglio, giacca*) back; (*di casa*) back, rear ■ *ag inv* back *cpd*; **le zampe di ~** the hind legs; **~ ricevuta** against receipt; **~ richiesta** on demand; (*scritta*) on application; **andare ~ a** (*anche fig*) to follow; **stare ~ a qn** (*sorvegliare*) to keep an eye on sb; (*corteggiare*) to hang around sb; **portarsi ~ qn/qc** to bring sb/sth with one, bring sb/sth along; **gli hanno riso/parlato ~** they laughed at/talked about him behind his back

di'etro front *escl* about turn! (*Brit*), about face! (*US*) ■ *sm* (*Mil*) about-turn, about-face; (*fig*) volte-face, about-turn, about-face; **fare ~** (*Mil, fig*) to about-turn, about-face; (*tornare indietro*) to turn round

di'fatti *cong* in fact, as a matter of fact

di'fendere *vt* to defend; **difendersi** *vr* (*cavarsela*) to get by; **difendersi da/contro** to defend o.s. from/against; **difendersi dal freddo** to protect o.s. from the cold; **sapersi ~** to know how to look after o.s.

difen'sivo, -a *ag* defensive ■ *sf*: **stare sulla difensiva** (*anche fig*) to be on the defensive

difen'sore, -a *sm/f* defender; **avvocato ~** counsel for the defence (*Brit*) o defense (*US*)

di'fesa *sf vedi* **difeso**

di'fesi *etc vb vedi* **difendere**

di'feso, -a *pp di* **difendere** ■ *sf* defence (*Brit*), defense (*US*); **prendere le difese di qn** to defend sb, take sb's part

difet'tare vi to be defective; **~ di** to be lacking in, lack

difet'tivo, -a ag defective

di'fetto sm (mancanza): **~ di** lack of; (di fabbricazione) fault, flaw, defect; (morale) fault, failing, defect; (fisico) defect; **far ~** to be lacking; **in ~** at fault; in the wrong

difet'toso, -a ag defective, faulty

diffa'mare vt (a parole) to slander; (per iscritto) to libel

diffama'torio, -a ag slanderous; libellous

diffamazi'one [diffamat'tsjone] sf slander; libel

diffe'rente ag different

diffe'renza [diffe'rɛntsa] sf difference; **a ~ di** unlike; **non fare ~ (tra)** to make no distinction (between)

differenzi'ale [differen'tsjale] ag, sm differential; **classi differenziali** (Ins) special classes (for backward children)

differenzi'are [differen'tsjare] vt to differentiate; **differenziarsi da** to differentiate o.s. from; to differ from

diffe'rire vt to postpone, defer ■ vi to be different

diffe'rita sf: **in ~** (trasmettere) prerecorded

difficile [dif'fitʃile] ag difficult; (persona) hard to please, difficult (to please); (poco probabile): **è ~ che sia libero** it is unlikely that he'll be free ■ sm/f: **fare il(la) ~** to be difficult, be awkward ■ sm difficult part; difficulty; **essere ~ nel mangiare** to be fussy about one's food

diffici'mente [diffitʃil'mente] av (con difficoltà) with difficulty; **~ verrà** he's unlikely to come

difficoltà sf inv difficulty

difficol'toso, -a ag (compito) difficult, hard; (persona) difficult, hard to please; **digestione difficoltosa** poor digestion

dif'fida sf (Dir) warning, notice

diffi'dare vi: **~ di** to be suspicious o distrustful of ■ vt (Dir) to warn; **~ qn dal fare qc** to warn sb not to do sth, caution sb against doing sth

diffi'dente ag suspicious, distrustful

diffi'denza [diffi'dɛntsa] sf suspicion, distrust

dif'fondere vt (luce, calore) to diffuse; (notizie) to spread, circulate; **diffondersi** vr to spread

diffusi etc vb vedi **diffondere**

diffusi'one sf diffusion; spread; (anche di giornale) circulation; (Fisica) scattering

dif'fuso, -a pp di **diffondere** ■ ag (Fisica) diffuse; (notizia, malattia etc) widespread; **è opinione diffusa che ...** it's widely held that ....

difi'lato av (direttamente) straight, directly; (subito) straight away

difte'rite sf diphtheria

'diga, -ghe sf dam; (portuale) breakwater

dige'rente [didʒe'rente] ag (apparato) digestive

dige'rire [didʒe'rire] vt to digest

digesti'one [didʒes'tjone] sf digestion

diges'tivo, -a [didʒes'tivo] ag digestive ■ sm (after-dinner) liqueur

Digi'one [di'dʒone] sf Dijon

digi'tale [didʒi'tale] ag digital; (delle dita) finger cpd, digital ■ sf (Bot) foxglove

digi'tare [didʒi'tare] vt (dati) to key (in); (tasto) to press

digiu'nare [didʒu'nare] vi to starve o.s.; (Rel) to fast

digi'uno, -a [di'dʒuno] ag: **essere ~** not to have eaten ■ sm fast; **a ~** on an empty stomach

dignità [diɲɲi'ta] sf inv dignity

digni'tario [diɲɲi'tarjo] sm dignitary

digni'toso, -a [diɲɲi'toso] ag dignified

'DIGOS sigla f (= Divisione Investigazioni Generali e Operazioni Speciali) police department dealing with political security

digressi'one sf digression

digri'gnare [digriɲ'ɲare] vt: **~ i denti** to grind one's teeth

dila'gare vi to flood; (fig) to spread

dilani'are vt to tear to pieces

dilapi'dare vt to squander, waste

dila'tare vt to dilate; (gas) to cause to expand; (passaggio, cavità) to open (up); **dilatarsi** vr to dilate; (Fisica) to expand

dilatazi'one [dilatat'tsjone] sf (Anat) dilation; (di gas, metallo) expansion

dilazio'nare [dilattsjo'nare] vt to delay, defer

dilazi'one [dilat'tsjone] sf deferment

dileggi'are [diled'dʒare] vt to mock, deride

dilegu'are vi, **dilegu'arsi** vr to vanish, disappear

di'lemma, -i sm dilemma

dilet'tante sm/f dilettante; (anche Sport) amateur

dilet'tare vt to give pleasure to, delight; **dilettarsi** vr: **dilettarsi di** to take pleasure in, enjoy

dilet'tevole ag delightful

di'letto, -a ag dear, beloved ■ sm pleasure, delight

dili'gente [dili'dʒente] ag (scrupoloso) diligent; (accurato) careful, accurate

dili'genza [dili'dʒɛntsa] sf diligence; care; (carrozza) stagecoach

dilu'ire vt to dilute

dilun'garsi vr (fig): **~ su** to talk at length on o about

diluvi'are vb impers to pour (down)
di'luvio sm downpour; (inondazione, fig) flood;
il ~ universale the Flood
dima'grante ag slimming cpd
dima'grire vi to get thinner, lose weight
dime'nare vt to wave, shake; **dimenarsi** vr
to toss and turn; (fig) to struggle; **~ la coda**
(cane) to wag its tail
dimensi'one sf dimension; (grandezza) size;
**considerare un discorso nella sua ~
politica** to look at a speech in terms of its
political significance
dimenti'canza [dimenti'kantsa] sf
forgetfulness; (errore) oversight, slip; **per ~**
inadvertently
dimenti'care vt to forget; **dimenticarsi** vr:
dimenticarsi di qc to forget sth
dimentica'toio sm (scherzoso): **cadere/
mettere nel ~** to sink into/consign to
oblivion
di'mentico, -a, chi, che ag: **~ di** (che non
ricorda) forgetful of; (incurante) oblivious of,
unmindful of
di'messo, -a pp di **dimettere** ▪ ag (voce)
subdued; (uomo, abito) modest, humble
dimesti'chezza [dimesti'kettsa] sf
familiarity
di'mettere vt: **~ qn da** to dismiss sb from;
(dall'ospedale) to discharge sb from;
dimettersi vr: **dimettersi (da)** to resign
(from)
dimez'zare [dimed'dzare] vt to halve
diminu'ire vt to reduce, diminish; (prezzi) to
bring down, reduce ▪ vi to decrease,
diminish; (rumore) to die down, die away;
(prezzi) to fall, go down
diminu'tivo, -a ag, sm diminutive
diminuzi'one [diminut'tsjone] sf decreasing,
diminishing; **in ~** on the decrease; **~ della
produttività** fall in productivity
di'misi etc vb vedi **dimettere**
dimissio'nario, -a ag outgoing, resigning
dimissi'oni sfpl resignation sg; **dare** o
presentare le ~ to resign, hand in one's
resignation
di'mora sf residence; **senza fissa ~** of no
fixed address o abode
dimo'rare vi to reside
dimos'trante sm/f (Pol) demonstrator
dimos'trare vt to demonstrate, show;
(provare) to prove, demonstrate; **dimostrarsi**
vr: **dimostrarsi molto abile** to show o.s. o
prove to be very clever; **non dimostra la sua
età** he doesn't look his age; **dimostra
30 anni** he looks about 30 (years old)
dimostra'tivo, -a ag (anche Ling)
demonstrative

dimostrazi'one [dimostrat'tsjone] sf
demonstration; proof
di'namico, -a, ci, che ag dynamic ▪ sf
dynamics sg
dina'mismo sm dynamism
dinami'tardo, -a ag: **attentato ~** dynamite
attack ▪ sm/f dynamiter
dina'mite sf dynamite
'dinamo sf inv dynamo
di'nanzi [di'nantsi]: **~ a** prep in front of
dinas'tia sf dynasty
di'niego, -ghi sm (rifiuto) refusal; (negazione)
denial
dinocco'lato, -a ag lanky; **camminare ~** to
walk with a slouch
dino'sauro sm dinosaur
din'torno av round, (round) about; **dintorni**
smpl outskirts; **nei dintorni di** in the
vicinity o neighbourhood of
'dio (pl **dei**) sm god; **D~** God; **gli dei** the gods;
si crede un ~ he thinks he's wonderful; **D~
mio!** my God!; **D~ ce la mandi buona** let's
hope for the best; **D~ ce ne scampi e liberi!**
God forbid!
di'ocesi [di'ɔtʃezi] sf inv diocese
dios'sina sf dioxin
dipa'nare vt (lana) to wind into a ball; (fig) to
disentangle, sort out
diparti'mento sm department
dipen'dente ag dependent ▪ sm/f employee
dipen'denza [dipen'dɛntsa] sf dependence;
essere alle dipendenze di qn to be
employed by sb o in sb's employ
di'pendere vi: **~ da** to depend on;
(finanziariamente) to be dependent on;
(derivare) to come from, be due to
di'pesi etc vb vedi **dipendere**
di'peso, -a pp di **dipendere**
di'pingere [di'pindʒere] vt to paint
di'pinsi etc vb vedi **dipingere**
di'pinto, -a pp di **dipingere** ▪ sm painting
di'ploma, -i sm diploma
diplo'mare vt to award a diploma to,
graduate (US) ▪ vi to obtain a diploma,
graduate (US)
diplo'matico, -a, ci, che ag diplomatic
▪ sm diplomat
diplo'mato, -a ag qualified ▪ sm/f qualified
person, holder of a diploma
diploma'zia [diplomat'tsia] sf diplomacy
di'porto sm: **imbarcazione da ~** pleasure
craft
dira'dare vt to thin (out); (visite) to reduce,
make less frequent; **diradarsi** vr to disperse;
(nebbia) to clear (up)
dira'mare vt to issue; ▪ vi, **diramarsi** ▪ vr
(strade) to branch

'dire vt to say; (segreto, fatto) to tell; ~ qc a qn to tell sb sth; ~ a qn di fare qc to tell sb to do sth; ~ di sì/no to say yes/no; si dice che ... they say that ...; mi si dice che ... I am told that ...; si direbbe che ... it looks (o sounds) as though ...; dica, signora? (in un negozio) yes, Madam, can I help you?; sa quello che dice he knows what he's talking about; lascialo ~ (esprimersi) let him have his say; (ignoralo) just ignore him; come sarebbe a ~? what do you mean?; che ne diresti di andarcene? how about leaving?; chi l'avrebbe mai detto! who would have thought it!; si dicono esperti they say they are experts; per così ~ so to speak; a dir poco to say the least; non c'è che ~ there's no doubt about it; non dico di no I can't deny it; il che è tutto ~ need I say more?

di'ressi etc vb vedi dirigere

di'retta sf vedi diretto

diretta'mente av (immediatamente) directly, straight; (personalmente) directly; (senza intermediari) direct, straight

diret'tissima sf (tragitto) most direct route; (Dir): processo per ~ summary trial

diret'tissimo sm (Ferr) fast (through) train

diret'tivo, -a ag (Pol, Amm) executive; (Comm) managerial, executive ■ sm leadership, leaders pl ■ sf directive, instruction

di'retto, -a pp di dirigere ■ ag direct ■ sm (Ferr) through train ■ sf: in (linea) diretta (Radio, TV) live; il mio ~ superiore my immediate superior

diret'tore, -'trice sm/f (di azienda) director, manager(-manageress); (di scuola elementare) head (teacher) (Brit), principal (US); ~ amministrativo company secretary (Brit), corporate executive secretary (US); ~ del carcere prison governor (Brit) o warden (US); ~ di filiale branch manager; ~ d'orchestra conductor; ~ di produzione (Cine) producer; ~ sportivo team manager; ~ tecnico (Sport) trainer, coach

direzi'one [diret'tsjone] sf (senso: anche fig) direction; (conduzione: gen) running; (: di partito) leadership; (: di società) management; (: di giornale) editorship; (direttori) management; in ~ di in the direction of, towards

diri'gente [diri'dʒɛnte] ag managerial ■ sm/f executive; (Pol) leader; classe ~ ruling class

diri'genza [diri'dʒɛntsa] sf management; (Pol) leadership

dirigenzi'ale [diridʒen'tsjale] ag managerial

di'rigere [di'ridʒere] vt to direct; (impresa) to run, manage; (Mus) to conduct; dirigersi vr: dirigersi verso o a to make o head for; ~ i

propri passi verso to make one's way towards; il treno era diretto a Pavia the train was heading for Pavia

diri'gibile [diri'dʒibile] sm airship

dirim'petto av opposite; ~ a prep opposite, facing

di'ritto, -a ag straight; (onesto) straight, upright ■ av straight, directly ■ sm right side; (Tennis) forehand; (Maglia) plain stitch, knit stitch; (prerogativa) right; (leggi, scienza): il ~ law; stare ~ to stand up straight; aver ~ a qc to be entitled to sth; punto ~ plain (stitch); andare ~ to go straight on; a buon ~ quite rightly; diritti (d'autore) royalties; ~ di successione right of succession

dirit'tura sf (Sport) straight; (fig) rectitude

diroc'cato, -a ag tumbledown, in ruins

dirom'pente ag (anche fig) explosive

dirotta'mento sm: ~ (aereo) hijack

dirot'tare vt (nave, aereo) to change the course of; (aereo: sotto minaccia) to hijack; (traffico) to divert ■ vi (nave, aereo) to change course

dirotta'tore, -'trice sm/f hijacker

di'rotto, -a ag (pioggia) torrential; (pianto) unrestrained; piovere a ~ to pour, rain cats and dogs; piangere a ~ to cry one's heart out

di'rupo sm crag, precipice

di'sabile sm/f disabled person

disabi'tato, -a ag uninhabited

disabitu'arsi vr: ~ a to get out of the habit of

disac'cordo sm disagreement

disadat'tato, -a ag (Psic) maladjusted

disa'dorno, -a ag plain, unadorned

disaffezi'one [dizaffet'tsjone] sf disaffection

disa'gevole [disa'dʒevole] ag (scomodo) uncomfortable; (difficile) difficult

disagi'ato, -a [diza'dʒato] ag poor, needy; (vita) hard

di'sagio [di'zadʒo] sm discomfort; (disturbo) inconvenience; (fig: imbarazzo) embarrassment; disagi smpl hardship sg, poverty sg; essere a ~ to be ill at ease

di'samina sf close examination

disappro'vare vt to disapprove of

disapprovazi'one [dizapprovat'tsjone] sf disapproval

disap'punto sm disappointment

disarcio'nare [dizartʃo'nare] vt to unhorse

disar'mante ag (fig) disarming

disar'mare vt, vi to disarm

di'sarmo sm (Mil) disarmament

di'sastro sm disaster

disas'troso, -a ag disastrous

disat'tento, -a ag inattentive

disattenzi'one [dizatten'tsjone] sf carelessness, lack of attention

disatti'vare vt (bomba) to de-activate, defuse

disa'vanzo [diza'vantso] *sm* (*Econ*) deficit

disavven'tura *sf* misadventure, mishap

dis'brigo, -ghi *sm* (*prompt*) clearing up *o* settlement

dis'capito *sm*: **a ~ di** to the detriment of

dis'carica, -che *sf* (*di rifiuti*) rubbish tip *o* dump

discen'dente [diʃʃen'dɛnte] *ag* descending ■ *sm/f* descendant

di'scendere [diʃʃɛndere] *vt* to go (*o* come) down ■ *vi* to go (*o* come) down; (*smontare*) to get off; **~ da** (*famiglia*) to be descended from; **~ dalla macchina/dal treno** to get out of the car/out of *o* off the train; **~ da cavallo** to dismount, get off one's horse

di'scepolo, -a [diʃʃepolo] *sm/f* disciple

di'scernere [diʃʃernere] *vt* to discern

discerni'mento [diʃʃerni'mento] *sm* discernment

disce'sista [diʃʃe'sista] *sm/f* downhill skier

di'sceso, -a [diʃʃeso] *pp di* **discendere** ■ *sf* descent; (*pendio*) slope; **in discesa** (*strada*) downhill *cpd*, sloping; **discesa libera** (*Sci*) downhill race

dischi'udere [dis'kjudere] *vt* (*aprire*) to open; (*fig: rivelare*) to disclose, reveal

dischi'usi *etc* [dis'kjusi] *vb vedi* **dischiudere**

dischi'uso, -a [dis'kjuso] *pp di* **dischiudere**

di'scinto, -a [diʃʃinto] *ag* (*anche:* **in abiti discinti**) half-undressed

disci'ogliere [diʃʃɔʎʎere] *vt*, **disci'ogliersi** *vr* to dissolve; (*fondere*) to melt

disci'plina [diʃʃi'plina] *sf* discipline

discipli'nare [diʃʃipli'nare] *ag* disciplinary ■ *vt* to discipline

'disco, -schi *sm* disc, disk; (*Sport*) discus; (*fonografico*) record; (*Inform*) disk; **~ magnetico** (*Inform*) magnetic disk; **~ orario** (*Aut*) parking disc; **~ rigido** (*Inform*) hard disk; **~ volante** flying saucer

discogra'fia *sf* (*tecnica*) recording, record-making; (*industria*) record industry

disco'grafico, -a, ci, che *ag* record *cpd*, recording *cpd* ■ *sm* record producer; **casa discografica** record(ing) company

'discolo, -a *ag* (*bambino*) undisciplined, unruly ■ *sm/f* rascal

discol'pare *vt* to clear of blame; **discolparsi** *vr* to clear o.s., prove one's innocence; (*giustificarsi*) to excuse o.s.

disco'noscere [disko'noʃʃere] *vt* (*figlio*) to disown; (*meriti*) to ignore, disregard

disconosci'uto, -a [diskonoʃʃuto] *pp di* **disconoscere**

discon'tinuo, -a *ag* (*linea*) broken; (*rendimento, stile*) irregular; (*interesse*) sporadic

dis'corde *ag* conflicting, clashing

dis'cordia *sf* discord; (*dissidio*) disagreement, clash

dis'correre *vi*: **~ (di)** to talk (about)

dis'corso, -a *pp di* **discorrere** ■ *sm* speech; (*conversazione*) conversation, talk

dis'costo, -a *ag* faraway, distant ■ *av* far away; **~ da** *prep* far from

disco'teca, -che *sf* (*raccolta*) record library; (*luogo di ballo*) disco(theque)

discre'panza [diskre'pantsa] *sf* discrepancy

dis'creto, -a *ag* discreet; (*abbastanza buono*) reasonable, fair

discrezi'one [diskret'tsjone] *sf* discretion; (*giudizio*) judgment, discernment; **a ~ di** at the discretion of

discrimi'nante *ag* (*fattore, elemento*) decisive ■ *sf* (*Dir*) extenuating circumstance

discrimi'nare *vt* to discrimate

discriminazi'one [diskriminat'tsjone] *sf* discrimination

dis'cussi *etc vb vedi* **discutere**

discussi'one *sf* discussion; (*litigio*) argument; **mettere in ~** to bring into question; **fuori ~** out of the question

dis'cusso, -a *pp di* **discutere**

dis'cutere *vt* to discuss, debate; (*contestare*) to question, dispute ■ *vi* (*conversare*): **~ (di)** to discuss; (*litigare*) to argue

discu'tibile *ag* questionable

disde'gnare [dizdeɲ'ɲare] *vt* to scorn

dis'degno [diz'deɲɲo] *sm* scorn, disdain

disde'gnoso, -a [dizdeɲ'ɲoso] *ag* disdainful, scornful

dis'detto, -a *pp di* **disdire** ■ *sf* cancellation; (*sfortuna*) bad luck

disdi'cevole [dizdi't ʃevole] *ag* improper, unseemly

dis'dire *vt* (*prenotazione*) to cancel; **~ un contratto d'affitto** (*Dir*) to give notice (to quit)

dise'gnare [diseɲ'ɲare] *vt* to draw; (*progettare*) to design; (*fig*) to outline

disegna'tore, -'trice [diseɲɲa'tore] *sm/f* designer

di'segno [di'zeɲɲo] *sm* drawing; (*su stoffa etc*) design; (*fig: schema*) outline; **~ industriale** industrial design; **~ di legge** (*Dir*) bill

diser'bante *sm* weedkiller

disere'dare *vt* to disinherit

diser'tare *vt, vi* to desert

diser'tore *sm* (*Mil*) deserter

diserzi'one [dizer'tsjone] *sf* (*Mil*) desertion

disfaci'mento [disfat ʃi'mento] *sm* (*di cadavere*) decay; (*fig: di istituzione, impero, società*) decline, decay; **in ~** in decay

dis'fare *vt* to undo; (*valigie*) to unpack; (*meccanismo*) to take to pieces; (*lavoro, paese*)

d

to destroy; (*neve*) to melt; **disfarsi** *vr* to come undone; (*neve*) to melt; ~ **il letto** to strip the bed; **disfarsi di qn** (*liberarsi*) to get rid of sb
dis'fatta *sf vedi* **disfatto**
disfat'tista, -i, e *sm/f* defeatist
dis'fatto, -a *pp di* **disfare** ■ *ag* (*gen*) undone, untied; (*letto*) unmade; (*persona: sfinito*) exhausted, worn-out; (: *addolorato*) grief-stricken ■ *sf* (*sconfitta*) rout
disfunzi'one [disfun'tsjone] *sf* (*Med*) dysfunction; ~ **cardiaca** heart trouble
disge'lare [dizdʒe'lare] *vt, vi,* **disge'larsi** *vr* to thaw
dis'gelo [diz'dʒɛlo] *sm* thaw
dis'grazia [diz'grattsja] *sf* (*sventura*) misfortune; (*incidente*) accident, mishap
disgrazi'ato, -a [dizgrat'tsjato] *ag* unfortunate ■ *sm/f* wretch
disgre'gare *vt,* **disgre'garsi** *vr* to break up
disgu'ido *sm* hitch; ~ **postale** error in postal delivery
disgus'tare *vt* to disgust; **disgustarsi** *vr:* **disgustarsi di** to be disgusted by
dis'gusto *sm* disgust
disgus'toso, -a *ag* disgusting
disidra'tare *vt* to dehydrate
disidra'tato, -a *ag* dehydrated
disil'ludere *vt* to disillusion, disenchant
disillusi'one *sf* disillusion, disenchantment
disimpa'rare *vt* to forget
disimpe'gnare [dizimpeɲ'ɲare] *vt* (*persona: da obblighi*): ~ **da** to release from; (*oggetto dato in pegno*) to redeem, get out of pawn; **disimpegnarsi** *vr:* **disimpegnarsi da** (*obblighi*) to release o.s. from, free o.s. from
disincagli'are [dizinkaʎ'ʎare] *vt* (*barca*) to refloat; **disincagliarsi** *vr* to get afloat again
disincan'tato, -a *ag* disenchanted, disillusioned
disincenti'vare [dizintʃenti'vare] *vt* to discourage
disinfes'tare *vt* to disinfest
disinfestazi'one [dizinfestat'tsjone] *sf* disinfestation
disinfet'tante *ag, sm* disinfectant
disinfet'tare *vt* to disinfect
disinfezi'one [dizinfet'tsjone] *sf* disinfection
disingan'nare *vt* to disillusion
disin'ganno *sm* disillusion
disini'bito, -a *ag* uninhibited
disinnes'care *vt* to defuse
disinnes'tare *vt* (*marcia*) to disengage
disinqui'nare *vt* to free from pollution
disinte'grare *vt, vi* to disintegrate
disinteres'sarsi *vr:* ~ **di** to take no interest in
disinte'resse *sm* indifference; (*generosità*) unselfishness

disintossi'care *vt* (*alcolizzato, drogato*) to treat for alcoholism (*o* drug addiction); **disintossicarsi** *vr* to clear out one's system; (*alcolizzato, drogato*) to be treated for alcoholism (*o* drug addiction)
disintossicazi'one [dizintossikat'tsjone] *sf* treatment for alcoholism (*o* drug addiction)
disin'volto, -a *ag* casual, free and easy
disinvol'tura *sf* casualness, ease
disles'sia *sf* dyslexia
disli'vello *sm* difference in height; (*fig*) gap
dislo'care *vt* to station, position
dismi'sura *sf* excess; **a** ~ to excess, excessively
disobbe'dire *etc* = **disubbidire** *etc*
disoccu'pato, -a *ag* unemployed ■ *sm/f* unemployed person
disoccupazi'one [dizokkupat'tsjone] *sf* unemployment
disonestà *sf* dishonesty
diso'nesto, -a *ag* dishonest
disono'rare *vt* to dishonour (*Brit*), dishonor (*US*), bring disgrace upon
diso'nore *sm* dishonour (*Brit*), dishonor (*US*), disgrace
di'sopra *av* (*con contatto*) on top; (*senza contatto*) above; (*al piano superiore*) upstairs ■ *ag inv* (*superiore*) upper ■ *sm inv* top, upper part; **la gente** ~ the people upstairs; **il piano** ~ the floor above
disordi'nare *vt* to mess up, disarrange; (*Mil*) to throw into disorder
disordi'nato, -a *ag* untidy; (*privo di misura*) irregular, wild
di'sordine *sm* (*confusione*) disorder, confusion; (*sregolatezza*) debauchery; **disordini** *smpl* (*Pol etc*) disorder *sg*; (*tumulti*) riots
disor'ganico, -a, ci, che *ag* incoherent, disorganized
disorganiz'zato, -a [dizorganid'dzato] *ag* disorganized
disorienta'mento *sm* (*fig*) confusion, bewilderment
disorien'tare *vt* to disorientate; **disorientarsi** *vr* (*fig*) to get confused, lose one's bearings
disorien'tato, -a *ag* disorientated
disos'sare *vt* (*Cuc*) to bone
di'sotto *av* below, underneath; (*in fondo*) at the bottom; (*al piano inferiore*) downstairs ■ *ag inv* (*inferiore*) lower; bottom *cpd* ■ *sm inv* (*parte inferiore*) lower part; bottom; **la gente** ~ the people downstairs; **il piano** ~ the floor below
dis'paccio [dis'pattʃo] *sm* dispatch
dispa'rato, -a *ag* disparate
'dispari *ag inv* odd, uneven
disparità *sf inv* disparity

dis'parte: **in ~** av (da lato) aside, apart; **tenersi** o **starsene in ~** to keep to o.s., hold aloof

dis'pendio sm (di denaro, energie) expenditure; (: spreco) waste

dispendi'oso, -a ag expensive

dis'pensa sf pantry, larder; (mobile) sideboard; (Dir) exemption; (Rel) dispensation; (fascicolo) number, issue

dispen'sare vt (elemosine, favori) to distribute; (esonerare) to exempt

dispe'rare vi: **~ (di)** to despair (of); **disperarsi** vr to despair

dispe'rato, -a ag (persona) in despair; (caso, tentativo) desperate

disperazi'one [disperat'tsjone] sf despair

dis'perdere vt (disseminare) to disperse; (Mil) to scatter, rout; (fig: consumare) to waste, squander; **disperdersi** vr to disperse; to scatter

dispersi'one sf dispersion, dispersal; (Fisica, Chim) dispersion

disper'sivo, -a ag (lavoro etc) disorganized

dis'perso, -a pp di **disperdere** ■ sm/f missing person; (Mil) missing soldier

dis'petto sm spite no pl, spitefulness no pl; **fare un ~ a qn** to play a (nasty) trick on sb; **a ~ di** in spite of; **con suo grande ~** much to his annoyance

dispet'toso, -a ag spiteful

dispia'cere [dispja'tʃere] sm (rammarico) regret, sorrow; (dolore) grief ■ vi: **~ a** to displease ■ vb impers: **mi dispiace (che)** I am sorry (that); **dispiaceri** smpl (preoccupazioni) troubles, worries; **se non le dispiace, me ne vado adesso** if you don't mind, I'll go now

dispiaci'uto, -a [dispja'tʃuto] pp di **dispiacere** ■ ag sorry

dis'pone, dis'pongo etc vb vedi **disporre**

dispo'nibile ag available; (persona: solerte, gentile) helpful

disponibilità sf inv availability; (solerzia, gentilezza) helpfulness; **disponibilità** sfpl (economiche) resources

dis'porre vt (sistemare) to arrange; (preparare) to prepare; (Dir) to order; (persuadere): **~ qn a** to incline o dispose sb towards ■ vi (decidere) to decide; (usufruire): **~ di** to use, have at one's disposal; (essere dotato): **~ di** to have; **disporsi** vr (ordinarsi) to place o.s., arrange o.s.; **disporsi a fare** to get ready to do; **disporsi all'attacco** to prepare for an attack; **disporsi in cerchio** to form a circle

dis'posi etc vb vedi **disporre**

disposi'tivo sm (meccanismo) device; (Dir) pronouncement; **~ di controllo** o **di**
comando control device; **~ di sicurezza** (gen) safety device; (di arma da fuoco) safety catch

disposizi'one [dispozit'tsjone] sf arrangement, layout; (stato d'animo) mood; (tendenza) bent, inclination; (comando) order; (Dir) provision, regulation; **a ~ di qn** at sb's disposal; **per ~ di legge** by law; **~ testamentaria** provisions of a will

dis'posto, -a pp di **disporre** ■ ag (incline): **~ a fare** disposed o prepared to do

dis'potico, -a, ci, che ag despotic

dispo'tismo sm despotism

disprez'zare [dispret'tsare] vt to despise

dis'prezzo [dis'prettso] sm contempt; **con ~ del pericolo** with a total disregard for the danger involved

disputa sf dispute, quarrel

dispu'tare vt (contendere) to dispute, contest; (Sport: partita) to play; (: gara) to take part in ■ vi to quarrel; **~ di** to discuss; **disputarsi qc** to fight for sth

disqui'sire vi to discourse on

disquisizi'one [diskwizit'tsjone] sf detailed analysis

dissa'crare vt to desecrate

dissangua'mento sm loss of blood

dissangu'are vt (fig: persona) to bleed white; (: patrimonio) to suck dry; **dissanguarsi** vr (Med) to lose blood; (fig) to ruin o.s.; **morire dissanguato** to bleed to death

dissa'pore sm slight disagreement

disse vb vedi **dire**

disse'care vt to dissect

dissec'care vt, **dissec'carsi** vr to dry up

dissemi'nare vt to scatter; (fig: notizie) to spread

dissenna'tezza [dissenna'tettsa] sf foolishness

dis'senso sm dissent; (disapprovazione) disapproval

dissente'ria sf dysentery

dissen'tire vi: **~ (da)** to disagree (with)

disseppel'lire vt (esumare: cadavere) to disinter, exhume; (dissotterrare: anche fig) to dig up, unearth; (: rancori) to resurrect

dissertazi'one [dissertat'tsjone] sf dissertation

disser'vizio [disser'vittsjo] sm inefficiency

disses'tare vt (Econ) to ruin

disses'tato, -a ag (fondo stradale) uneven; (economia, finanze) shaky; **"strada dissestata"** (per lavori in corso) "road up" (Brit), "road out" (US)

dis'sesto sm (financial) ruin

disse'tante ag refreshing

disse'tare vt to quench the thirst of; **dissetarsi** vr to quench one's thirst

dissezi'one [disset'tsjone] *sf* dissection

'**dissi** *vb vedi* **dire**

dissi'dente *ag, sm/f* dissident

dis'sidio *sm* disagreement

dis'simile *ag* different, dissimilar

dissimu'lare *vt* (*fingere*) to dissemble; (*nascondere*) to conceal

dissimula'tore, -'trice *sm/f* dissembler

dissimulazi'one [dissimulat'tsjone] *sf* dissembling; concealment

dissi'pare *vt* to dissipate; (*scialacquare*) to squander, waste

dissipa'tezza [dissipa'tettsa] *sf* dissipation

dissi'pato, -a *ag* dissolute, dissipated

dissipazi'one [dissipat'tsjone] *sf* squandering

dissoci'are [disso'tʃare] *vt* to dissociate

dis'solto, -a *pp di* **dissolvere**

disso'lubile *ag* soluble

dissolu'tezza [dissolu'tettsa] *sf* dissoluteness

dissolu'tivo, -a *ag* (*forza*) divisive; **processo ~** (*anche fig*) process of dissolution

disso'luto, -a *pp di* **dissolvere** ■ *ag* dissolute, licentious

dissol'venza [dissol'vɛntsa] *sf* (*Cine*) fading

dis'solvere *vt* to dissolve; (*neve*) to melt; (*fumo*) to disperse; **dissolversi** *vr* to dissolve; to melt; to disperse

disso'nante *ag* discordant

disso'nanza [disso'nantsa] *sf* (*fig: di opinioni*) clash

dissotter'rare *vt* (*cadavere*) to disinter, exhume; (*tesori, rovine*) to dig up, unearth; (*fig: sentimenti, odio*) to bring up again, resurrect

dissu'adere *vt*: **~ qn da** to dissuade sb from

dissuasi'one *sf* dissuasion

dissu'aso, -a *pp di* **dissuadere**

dissua'sore *sm*: **~ di velocità** (*Aut*) speed bump

distacca'mento *sm* (*Mil*) detachment

distac'care *vt* to detach, separate; (*Sport*) to leave behind; **distaccarsi** *vr* to be detached; (*fig*) to stand out; **distaccarsi da** (*fig: allontanarsi*) to grow away from

dis'tacco, -chi *sm* (*separazione*) separation; (*fig: indifferenza*) detachment; (*Sport*): **vincere con un ~ di ...** to win by a distance of ...

dis'tante *av* far away ■ *ag* distant, far away; **essere ~ (da)** to be a long way (from); **è ~ da qui?** is it far from here?; **essere ~ nel tempo** to be in the distant past

dis'tanza [dis'tantsa] *sf* distance; **comando a ~** remote control; **a ~ di 2 giorni** 2 days later; **tener qn a ~** to keep sb at arm's length; **prendere le distanze da qc/qn** to

dissociate o.s. from sth/sb; **tenere** *o* **mantenere le distanze** to keep one's distance; **~ focale** focal length; **~ di sicurezza** safe distance; (*Aut*) braking distance; **~ di tiro** range; **~ di visibilità** visibility

distanzi'are [distan'tsjare] *vt* to space out, place at intervals; (*Sport*) to outdistance; (*fig: superare*) to outstrip, surpass

dis'tare *vi*: **distiamo pochi chilometri da Roma** we are only a few kilometres (away) from Rome; **dista molto da qui?** is it far (away) from here?; **non dista molto** it's not far (away)

dis'tendere *vt* (*coperta*) to spread out; (*gambe*) to stretch (out); (*mettere a giacere*) to lay; (*rilassare: muscoli, nervi*) to relax; **distendersi** *vr* (*rilassarsi*) to relax; (*sdraiarsi*) to lie down

distensi'one *sf* stretching; relaxation; (*Pol*) détente

disten'sivo, -a *ag* (*gen*) relaxing, restful; (*farmaco*) tranquillizing; (*Pol*) conciliatory

dis'teso, -a *pp di* **distendere** ■ *ag* (*allungato: persona, gamba*) stretched out; (*rilassato: persona, atmosfera*) relaxed ■ *sf* expanse, stretch; **avere un volto ~** to look relaxed

distil'lare *vt* to distil

distil'lato *sm* distillate

distillazi'one [distillat'tsjone] *sf* distillation

distille'ria *sf* distillery

dis'tinguere *vt* to distinguish; **distinguersi** *vr* (*essere riconoscibile*) to be distinguished; (*emergere*) to stand out, be conspicuous, distinguish o.s.; **un vino che si distingue per il suo aroma** a wine with a distinctive bouquet

dis'tinguo *sm inv* distinction

dis'tinta *sf* (*nota*) note; (*elenco*) list; **~ di pagamento** receipt; **~ di versamento** pay-in slip

distin'tivo, -a *ag* distinctive; distinguishing ■ *sm* badge

dis'tinto, -a *pp di* **distinguere** ■ *ag* (*dignitoso ed elegante*) distinguished; **distinti saluti** (*in lettera*) yours faithfully

distinzi'one [distin'tsjone] *sf* distinction; **non faccio distinzioni** (*tra persone*) I don't discriminate; (*tra cose*) it's all one to me; **senza ~ di razza/religione ...** no matter what one's race/creed ...

dis'togliere [dis'tɔʎʎere] *vt*: **~ da** to take away from; (*fig*) to dissuade from

dis'tolto, -a *pp di* **distogliere**

dis'torcere [dis'tɔrtʃere] *vt* to twist; (*fig*) to twist, distort; **distorcersi** *vr* (*contorcersi*) to twist

distorsi'one *sf* (*Med*) sprain; (*Fisica, Ottica*) distortion

dis'torto, -a *pp di* **distorcere**

dis'trarre *vt* to distract; (*divertire*) to entertain, amuse; **distrarsi** *vr* (*non fare attenzione*) to be distracted, let one's mind wander; (*svagarsi*) to amuse *o* enjoy o.s.; **~ lo sguardo** to look away; **non distrarti!** pay attention!

distratta'mente *av* absent-mindedly, without thinking

dis'tratto, -a *pp di* **distrarre** ■ *ag* absent-minded; (*disattento*) inattentive

distrazi'one [distrat'tsjone] *sf* absent-mindedness; inattention; (*svago*) distraction, entertainment; **errori di ~** careless mistakes

dis'tretto *sm* district

distribu'ire *vt* to distribute; (*Carte*) to deal (out); (*consegnare: posta*) to deliver; (*lavoro*) to allocate, assign; (*ripartire*) to share out

distribu'tore *sm* (*di benzina*) petrol (*Brit*) *o* gas (*US*) pump; (*Aut, Elettr*) distributor; (*automatico*) vending machine

distribuzi'one [distribut'tsjone] *sf* distribution; delivery; allocation, assignment; sharing out

distri'care *vt* to disentangle, unravel; **districarsi** *vr* (*tirarsi fuori*): **districarsi da** to get out of, disentangle o.s. from; (*fig: cavarsela*) to manage, get by

dis'truggere [dis'truddʒere] *vt* to destroy

distrut'tivo, -a *ag* destructive

dis'trutto, -a *pp di* **distruggere**

distruzi'one [distrut'tsjone] *sf* destruction

distur'bare *vt* to disturb, trouble; (*sonno, lezioni*) to disturb, interrupt; **disturbarsi** *vr* to put o.s. out; **non si disturbi** please don't bother

dis'turbo *sm* trouble, bother, inconvenience; (*indisposizione*) (slight) disorder, ailment; **disturbi** *smpl* (*Radio, TV*) static *sg*; **~ della quiete pubblica** (*Dir*) disturbance of the peace; **disturbi di stomaco** stomach trouble *sg*

disubbidi'ente *ag* disobedient

disubbidi'enza [dizubbi'djɛntsa] *sf* disobedience; **~ civile** civil disobedience

disubbi'dire *vi*: **~ (a qn)** to disobey (sb)

disuguagli'anza [dizugwaʎ'ʎantsa] *sf* inequality

disugu'ale *ag* unequal; (*diverso*) different; (*irregolare*) uneven

disumanità *sf* inhumanity

disu'mano, -a *ag* inhuman; **un grido ~** a terrible cry

disuni'one *sf* disunity

disu'nire *vt* to divide, disunite

di'suso *sm*: **andare** *o* **cadere in ~** to fall into disuse

'dita *sfpl di* **dito**

di'tale *sm* thimble

di'tata *sf* (*colpo*) jab (with one's finger); (*segno*) fingermark

'dito (*pl(f)* **dita**) *sm* finger; (*misura*) finger, finger's breadth; **~ (del piede)** toe; **mettersi le dita nel naso** to pick one's nose; **mettere il ~ sulla piaga** (*fig*) to touch a sore spot; **non ha mosso un ~ (per aiutarmi)** he didn't lift a finger (to help me); **ormai è segnato a ~** everyone knows about him now

'ditta *sf* firm, business; **macchina della ~** company car

dit'tafono *sm* Dictaphone®

ditta'tore *sm* dictator

ditta'tura *sf* dictatorship

dit'tongo, -ghi *sm* diphthong

di'urno, -a *ag* day *cpd*, daytime *cpd*; **ore diurne** daytime *sg*; **spettacolo ~** matinee; **turno ~** day shift; *vedi anche* **albergo**

'diva *sf vedi* **divo**

diva'gare *vi* to digress

divagazi'one [divagat'tsjone] *sf* digression; **divagazioni sul tema** variations on a theme

divam'pare *vi* to flare up, blaze up

di'vano *sm* sofa; (*senza schienale*) divan; **~ letto** bed settee, sofa bed

divari'care *vt* to open wide

di'vario *sm* difference

di'vengo *etc vb vedi* **divenire**

dive'nire *vi* = **diventare**

di'venni *etc vb vedi* **divenire**

diven'tare *vi* to become; **~ famoso/professore** to become famous/a teacher; **~ vecchio** to grow old; **c'è da ~ matti** it's enough to drive you mad

dive'nuto, -a *pp di* **divenire**

di'verbio *sm* altercation

diver'gente [diver'dʒɛnte] *ag* divergent

diver'genza [diver'dʒɛntsa] *sf* divergence; **~ d'opinioni** difference of opinion

di'vergere [di'vɛrdʒere] *vi* to diverge

diverrò *etc vb vedi* **divenire**

diversa'mente *av* (*in modo differente*) differently; (*altrimenti*) otherwise; **~ da quanto stabilito** contrary to what had been decided

diversifi'care *vt* to diversify, vary; **diversificarsi** *vr*: **diversificarsi (per)** to differ (in)

diversificazi'one [diversifikat'tsjone] *sf* diversification; difference

diversi'one *sf* diversion

diversità *sf inv* difference, diversity; (*varietà*) variety

diver'sivo, -a *ag* diversionary ▪ *sm* diversion, distraction; **fare un'azione diversiva** to create a diversion

di'verso, -a *ag* (*differente*): ~ **(da)** different (from) ▪ *sm* (*omosessuale*) homosexual; **diversi, e** *det pl* several, various; (*Comm*) sundry ▪ *pron pl* several people, many (people)

diver'tente *ag* amusing

diverti'mento *sm* amusement, pleasure; (*passatempo*) pastime, recreation; **buon ~!** enjoy yourself!, have a nice time!

diver'tire *vt* to amuse, entertain; **divertirsi** *vr* to amuse o enjoy o.s.; **divertiti!** enjoy yourself!, have a good time!; **divertirsi alle spalle di qn** to have a laugh at sb's expense

diver'tito, -a *ag* amused

divi'dendo *sm* dividend

di'videre *vt* (*anche Mat*) to divide; (*distribuire, ripartire*) to divide (up), split (up); **dividersi** *vr* (*persone*) to separate, part; (*coppia*) to separate; **dividersi (in)** (*scindersi*) to divide (into), split up (into); (*ramificarsi*) to fork; **è diviso dalla moglie** he's separated from his wife; **si divide tra casa e lavoro** he divides his time between home and work

divi'eto *sm* prohibition; **"~ di accesso"** "no entry"; **"~ di caccia"** "no hunting"; **"~ di parcheggio"** "no parking"; **"~ di sosta"** (*Aut*) "no waiting"

divinco'larsi *vr* to wriggle, writhe

divinità *sf inv* divinity

di'vino, -a *ag* divine

di'visa *sf* (*Mil etc*) uniform; (*Comm*) foreign currency

di'visi *etc vb vedi* **dividere**

divisi'one *sf* division; ~ **in sillabe** syllable division; (*a fine riga*) hyphenation

di'vismo *sm* (*esibizionismo*) playing to the crowd

di'viso, -a *pp di* **dividere**

divi'sorio, -a *ag* (*siepe, muro esterno*) dividing; (*muro interno*) dividing, partition *cpd* ▪ *sm* (*in una stanza*) partition

'divo, -a *sm/f* star; **come una diva** like a prima donna

divo'rare *vt* to devour; ~ **qc con gli occhi** to eye sth greedily

divorzi'are [divor'tsjare] *vi*: ~ **(da qn)** to divorce (sb)

divorzi'ato, -a [divor'tsjato] *ag* divorced ▪ *sm/f* divorcee

di'vorzio [di'vɔrtsjo] *sm* divorce

divul'gare *vt* to divulge, disclose; (*rendere comprensibile*) to popularize; **divulgarsi** *vr* to spread

divulgazi'one [divulgat'tsjone] *sf* (*vedi vb*) disclosure; popularization; spread

dizio'nario [dittsjo'narjo] *sm* dictionary

dizi'one [dit'tsjone] *sf* diction; pronunciation

Dja'karta [dʒa'karta] *sf* Djakarta

dl *abbr* (*= decilitro*) dl

dm *abbr* (*= decimetro*) dm

DNA [di'ennɛa] *sigla m* (*Biol: = acido deossiribonucleico*) DNA ▪ *sigla f* = **direzione nazionale antimafia**

do *sm* (*Mus*) C; (*: solfeggiando la scala*) do(h)

dobbi'amo *vb vedi* **dovere**

D.O.C. [dɔk] *sigla* = **denominazione di origine controllata**

doc. *abbr* = **documento**

'doccia, -ce ['dottʃa] *sf* (*bagno*) shower; (*condotto*) pipe; **fare la ~** to have a shower; **~ fredda** (*fig*) slap in the face

docciaschi'uma [dottʃas'kjuma] *sm inv* shower gel

do'cente [do'tʃɛnte] *ag* teaching ▪ *sm/f* teacher; (*di università*) lecturer; **personale non ~** non-teaching staff

do'cenza [do'tʃɛntsa] *sf* university teaching o lecturing; **ottenere la libera ~** to become a lecturer

D.O.C.G. *sigla* (*= denominazione di origine controllata e garantita*) label guaranteeing the quality and origin of a wine

'docile ['dɔtʃile] *ag* docile

docilità [dotʃili'ta] *sf* docility

documen'tare *vt* to document; **documentarsi** *vr*: **documentarsi (su)** to gather information o material (about)

documen'tario, -a *ag, sm* documentary

documentazi'one [dokumentat'tsjone] *sf* documentation

docu'mento *sm* document; **documenti** *smpl* (*d'identità etc*) papers

Dodecan'neso *sm*: **le Isole del ~** the Dodecanese Islands

dodi'cenne [dodi'tʃenne] *ag, sm/f* twelve-year-old

dodi'cesimo, -a [dodi'tʃɛzimo] *num* twelfth

'dodici ['doditʃi] *num* twelve

do'gana *sf* (*ufficio*) customs *pl*; (*tassa*) (customs) duty; **passare la ~** to go through customs

doga'nale *ag* customs *cpd*

dogani'ere *sm* customs officer

'doglie ['dɔʎʎe] *sfpl* (*Med*) labour *sg* (*Brit*), labor *sg* (*US*), labo(u)r pains

'dogma, -i *sm* dogma

dog'matico, -a, ci, che *ag* dogmatic

'dolce ['doltʃe] *ag* sweet; (*colore*) soft; (*carattere, persona*) gentle, mild; (*fig: mite: clima*) mild; (*non ripido: pendio*) gentle ▪ *sm* (*sapore dolce*) sweetness, sweet taste; (*Cuc: portata*) sweet, dessert; (: *torta*) cake; **il ~ far niente** sweet idleness

dolcemente *av* (*baciare, trattare*) gently; (*sorridere, cantare*) sweetly; (*parlare*) softly

dol'cezza [dol'tʃettsa] *sf* sweetness; softness; mildness; gentleness

dolci'ario, -a [dol'tʃarjo] *ag* confectionery *cpd*

dolci'astro, -a [dol'tʃastro] *ag* (*sapore*) sweetish

dolcifi'cante [doltʃifi'kante] *ag* sweetening ■ *sm* sweetener

dolci'umi [dol'tʃumi] *smpl* sweets

do'lente *ag* sorrowful, sad

do'lere *vi* to be sore, hurt, ache; **dolersi** *vr* to complain; (*essere spiacente*): **dolersi di** to be sorry for; **mi duole la testa** my head aches, I've got a headache

'dolgo *etc vb vedi* **dolere**

'dollaro *sm* dollar

'dolo *sm* (*Dir*) malice; (*frode*) fraud, deceit

Dolo'miti *sfpl:* **le ~** the Dolomites

dolo'rante *ag* aching, sore

do'lore *sm* (*fisico*) pain; (*morale*) sorrow, grief; **se lo scoprono sono dolori!** if they find out there'll be trouble!

dolo'roso, -a *ag* painful; sorrowful, sad

do'loso, -a *ag* (*Dir*) malicious; **incendio ~** arson

'dolsi *etc vb vedi* **dolere**

dom. *abbr* (= *domenica*) Sun

do'manda *sf* (*interrogazione*) question; (*richiesta*) demand; (: *cortese*) request; (*Dir: richiesta scritta*) application; (*Econ*): **la ~** demand; **fare una ~ a qn** to ask sb a question; **fare ~ (per un lavoro)** to apply (for a job); **far regolare ~ (di qc)** to apply through the proper channels (for sth); **fare ~ all'autorità giudiziaria** to apply to the courts; **~ di divorzio** divorce petition; **~ di matrimonio** proposal

doman'dare *vt* (*per avere*) to ask for; (*per sapere*) to ask; (*esigere*) to demand; **domandarsi** *vr* to wonder, ask o.s.; **~ qc a qn** to ask sb for sth; to ask sb sth

do'mani *av* tomorrow ■ *sm* (*l'indomani*) next day, following day; **il ~** (*il futuro*) the future; (*il giorno successivo*) the next day; **un ~** some day; **~ l'altro** the day after tomorrow; **~ (a) otto** tomorrow week, a week tomorrow; **a ~!** see you tomorrow!

do'mare *vt* to tame

doma'tore, -'trice *sm/f* (*gen*) tamer; **~ di cavalli** horsebreaker; **~ di leoni** lion tamer

domat'tina *av* tomorrow morning

do'menica, -che *sf* Sunday; *vedi anche* **martedì**

domeni'cale *ag* Sunday *cpd*

domeni'cano, -a *ag, sm/f* Dominican

do'mestica, -che *sf vedi* **domestico**

do'mestico, -a, ci, che *ag* domestic ■ *sm/f* servant, domestic; **le pareti domestiche** one's own four walls; **animale ~** pet; **una domestica a ore** a daily (woman)

domicili'are [domitʃi'ljare] *ag vedi* **arresto**

domicili'arsi [domitʃi'ljarsi] *vr* to take up residence

domi'cilio [domi'tʃiljo] *sm* (*Dir*) domicile, place of residence; **visita a ~** (*Med*) house call; **"recapito a ~"** "deliveries"; **violazione di ~** (*Dir*) breaking and entering

domi'nante *ag* (*colore, nota*) dominant; (*opinione*) prevailing; (*idea*) main *cpd*, chief *cpd*; (*posizione*) dominating *cpd*; (*classe, partito*) ruling *cpd*

domi'nare *vt* to dominate; (*fig: sentimenti*) to control, master ■ *vi* to be in the dominant position; **dominarsi** *vr* (*controllarsi*) to control o.s.; **~ su** (*fig*) to surpass, outclass

domina'tore, -'trice *ag* ruling *cpd* ■ *sm/f* ruler

dominazi'one [dominat'tsjone] *sf* domination

domini'cano, -a *ag:* **la Repubblica Dominicana** the Dominican Republic

do'minio *sm* dominion; (*fig: campo*) field, domain; **domini coloniali** colonies; **essere di ~ pubblico** (*notizia etc*) to be common knowledge

don *sm* (*Rel*) Father

do'nare *vt* to give, present; (*per beneficenza etc*) to donate ■ *vi* (*fig*): **~ a** to suit, become; **~ sangue** to give blood

dona'tore, -'trice *sm/f* donor; **~ di sangue/di organi** blood/organ donor

donazi'one [donat'tsjone] *sf* donation; **atto di ~** (*Dir*) deed of gift

'donde *av* (*poetico*) whence

dondo'lare *vt* (*cullare*) to rock; **dondolarsi** *vr* to swing, sway

'dondolo *sm:* **sedia/cavallo a ~** rocking chair/ horse

dongio'vanni [dondʒo'vanni] *sm* Don Juan, ladies' man

'donna *sf* woman; (*titolo*) Donna; (*Carte*) queen; **figlio di buona ~!** (*fam*) son of a bitch!; **~ di casa** housewife; **~ a ore** daily (help o woman); **~ delle pulizie** cleaning lady, cleaner; **~ di servizio** maid; **~ di vita** o **di strada** prostitute, streetwalker

donnai'olo *sm* ladykiller

'donnola *sf* weasel

'dono *sm* gift

'doping *sm* doping

dopo *av* (*tempo*) afterwards; (: *più tardi*) later; (*luogo*) after, next ■ *prep* after ■ *cong* (*temporale*): ~ **aver studiato** after having studied ■ *ag inv*: **il giorno** ~ the following day; ~ **mangiato va a dormire** after having eaten *o* after a meal he goes for a sleep; **un anno** ~ a year later; ~ **di me/lui** after me/him; ~ **che** = **dopoché**

dopo'barba *sm inv* after-shave

dopoché [dopo'ke] *cong* after, when

dopodiché [dopodi'ke] *av* after which

dopodo'mani *av* the day after tomorrow

dopogu'erra *sm* postwar years *pl*

dopola'voro *sm* recreational club

dopo'pranzo [dopo'prandzo] *av* after lunch (*o* dinner)

doposcì [dopoʃ'ʃi] *sm inv* après-ski outfit

doposcu'ola *sm inv* school club offering extra tuition and recreational facilities

dopo'sole *sm inv, ag inv*: (**lozione/crema**) ~ aftersun (lotion/cream)

dopo'tutto *av* after all

doppi'aggio [dop'pjaddʒo] *sm* (*Cine*) dubbing

doppi'are *vt* (*Naut*) to round; (*Sport*) to lap; (*Cine*) to dub

doppia'tore, -'trice *sm/f* dubber

doppi'etta *sf* (*fucile*) double-barrelled (*Brit*) *o* double-barreled (*US*) shotgun; (*sparo*) shot from both barrels; (*Calcio*) double; (*Pugilato*) one-two; (*Aut*) double-declutch (*Brit*), double-clutch (*US*)

doppi'ezza [dop'pjettsa] *sf* (*fig: di persona*) duplicity, double-dealing

doppio, -a *ag* double; (*fig: falso*) double-dealing, deceitful ■ *sm* (*quantità*): **il ~ (di)** twice as much (*o* many), double the amount (*o* number) of; (*Sport*) doubles *pl* ■ *av* double; **battere una lettera in doppia copia** to type a letter with a carbon copy; **fare il ~ gioco** (*fig*) to play a double game; **chiudere a doppia mandata** to double-lock; ~ **senso** double entendre; **frase a ~ senso** sentence with a dual meaning; **un utensile a ~ uso** a dual-purpose utensil

doppio'fondo *sm* (*di valigia*) false bottom; (*Naut*) double hull

doppi'one *sm* duplicate (copy)

doppio'petto *sm* double-breasted jacket

dop'pista *sm/f* (*Tennis*) doubles player

do'rare *vt* to gild; (*Cuc*) to brown; ~ **la pillola** (*fig*) to sugar the pill

do'rato, -a *ag* golden; (*ricoperto d'oro*) gilt, gilded

dora'tura *sf* gilding

dormicchi'are [dormik'kjare] *vi* to doze

dormi'ente *ag* sleeping ■ *sm/f* sleeper

dormigli'one, -a [dormiʎ'ʎone] *sm/f* sleepyhead

dor'mire *vi* to sleep; (*essere addormentato*) to be asleep, be sleeping; **il caffè non mi fa** ~ coffee keeps me awake; ~ **come un ghiro** to sleep like a log; ~ **della grossa** to sleep soundly, be dead to the world; ~ **in piedi** (*essere stanco*) to be asleep on one's feet

dor'mita *sf*: **farsi una** ~ to have a good sleep

dormi'torio *sm* dormitory; ~ **pubblico** doss house (*Brit*) *o* flophouse (*US*) (*run by local authority*)

dormi'veglia [dormi'veʎʎa] *sm* drowsiness

dorrò *etc vb vedi* **dolere**

dor'sale *ag*: **spina** ~ backbone, spine

dorso *sm* back; (*di montagna*) ridge, crest; (*di libro*) spine; (*Nuoto*) backstroke; **a** ~ **di cavallo** on horseback

do'saggio [do'zaddʒo] *sm* (*atto*) measuring out; **sbagliare il** ~ to get the proportions wrong

do'sare *vt* to measure out; (*Med*) to dose

'dose *sf* quantity, amount; (*Med*) dose

dossi'er [do'sje] *sm inv* dossier, file

'dosso *sm* (*rilievo*) rise; (: *di strada*) bump; (*dorso*): **levarsi di** ~ **i vestiti** to take one's clothes off; **levarsi un peso di** ~ (*fig*) to take a weight off one's mind

do'tare *vt*: ~ **di** to provide *o* supply with; (*fig*) to endow with

do'tato, -a *ag*: ~ **di** (*attrezzature*) equipped with; (*bellezza, intelligenza*) endowed with; **un uomo** ~ a gifted man

dotazi'one [dotat'tsjone] *sf* (*insieme di beni*) endowment; (*di macchine etc*) equipment; **dare qc in** ~ **a qn** to issue sb with sth, issue sth to sb; **i macchinari in** ~ **alla fabbrica** the machinery in use in the factory

'dote *sf* (*di sposa*) dowry; (*assegnata a un ente*) endowment; (*fig*) gift, talent

Dott. *abbr* (= *dottore*) Dr

'dotto, -a *ag* (*colto*) learned ■ *sm* (*sapiente*) scholar; (*Anat*) duct

dotto'rato *sm* degree; ~ **di ricerca** doctorate, doctor's degree

dot'tore, -'essa *sm/f* doctor

dot'trina *sf* doctrine

Dott.ssa *abbr* (= *dottoressa*) Dr

double-face [dubl'fas] *ag inv* reversible

'dove *av* where; (*in cui*) where, in which; (*dovunque*) wherever ■ *sm*: **per ogni** ~ everywhere; **di dov'è?** where are you from?; **da** ~ **abito vedo tutta la città** I can see the whole city from where I live; **per** ~ **si passa?** which way should we go?; **le dò una mano fin** ~ **posso** I'll help you as much as I can

do'vere *sm* (*obbligo*) duty ■ *vt* (*essere debitore*): ~ **qc (a qn)** to owe (sb) sth ■ *vi* (*obbligo*) to have to; **devo partire domani** (*intenzione*) I'm (due) to leave tomorrow; **dev'essere tardi** (*probabilità*) it must be late; **lui deve farlo** he has to do it, he must do it; **è dovuto partire** he had to leave; **ha dovuto pagare** he had to pay; **doveva accadere** it was bound to happen; **avere il senso del ~** to have a sense of duty; **rivolgersi a chi di ~** to apply to the appropriate authority *o* person; **a ~** (*bene*) properly; (*debitamente*) as he (*o* she *etc*) deserves; **come si deve** (*bene*) properly; (*meritatamente*) properly, as he (*o* she *etc*) deserves; **una persona come si deve** a respectable person

dove'roso, -a *ag* (right and) proper

do'vizia [do'vittsja] *sf* abundance

dovrò *etc vb vedi* **dovere**

do'vunque *av* (*in qualunque luogo*) wherever; (*dappertutto*) everywhere; **~ io vada** wherever I go

dovuta'mente *av* (*debitamente: redigere, compilare*) correctly; (: *rimproverare*) as he (*o* she *etc*) deserves

do'vuto, -a *ag* (*causato*): **~ a** due to ■ *sm* due; **nel modo ~** in the proper way; **ho lavorato più del ~** I worked more than was necessary

doz'zina [dod'dzina] *sf* dozen; **una ~ di uova** a dozen eggs; **di** *o* **da ~** (*scrittore, spettacolo*) second-rate

dozzi'nale [doddzi'nale] *ag* cheap, second-rate

DP *sigla f* (= *Democrazia Proletaria*) political party

'draga, -ghe *sf* dredger

dra'gare *vt* to dredge

dragherò *etc* [drage'rɔ] *vb vedi* **dragare**

'drago, -ghi *sm* dragon; (*fig fam*) genius

'dramma, -i *sm* drama; **fare un ~ di qc** to make a drama out of sth

dram'matico, -a, ci, che *ag* dramatic

drammatiz'zare [drammatid'dzare] *vt* to dramatize

dramma'turgo, -ghi *sm* playwright

drappeggi'are [drapped'dʒare] *vt* to drape

drap'peggio [drap'peddʒo] *sm* (*tessuto*) drapery; (*di abito*) folds

drap'pello *sm* (*Mil*) squad; (*gruppo*) band, group

'drappo *sm* cloth

'drastico, -a, ci, che *ag* drastic

dre'naggio [dre'naddʒo] *sm* drainage

dre'nare *vt* to drain

'Dresda *sf* Dresden

drib'lare *vi* (*Calcio*) to dribble ■ *vt* (*avversario*) to dodge, avoid

'dritto, -a *ag, av* = **diritto** ■ *sm/f* (*fam: furbo*): **è un ~** he's a crafty *o* sly one ■ *sf* (*destra*) right, right hand; (*Naut*) starboard; **a dritta e a manca** (*fig*) on all sides, right, left and centre

driz'zare [drit'tsare] *vt* (*far tornare diritto*) to straighten; (*volgere: sguardo, occhi*) to turn, direct; (*innalzare: antenna, muro*) to erect; **drizzarsi** *vr* to stand up; **~ le orecchie** to prick up one's ears; **drizzarsi in piedi** to rise to one's feet; **drizzarsi a sedere** to sit up

'droga, -ghe *sf* (*sostanza aromatica*) spice; (*stupefacente*) drug; **droghe pesanti/leggere** hard/soft drugs

dro'gare *vt* to drug, dope; **drogarsi** *vr* to take drugs

dro'gato, -a *sm/f* drug addict

droghe'ria [droge'ria] *sf* grocer's (shop) (*Brit*), grocery (store) (*US*)

drogherò *etc* [droge'rɔ] *vb vedi* **drogare**

droghi'ere, -a [dro'gjɛre] *sm/f* grocer

drome'dario *sm* dromedary

DS [di'ɛsse] *smpl* (= *Democratici di Sinistra*) Democrats of the Left (*Italian left-wing party*)

'dubbio, -a *ag* (*incerto*) doubtful, dubious; (*ambiguo*) dubious ■ *sm* (*incertezza*) doubt; **avere il ~ che** to be afraid that, suspect that; **essere in ~ fra** to hesitate between; **mettere in ~ qc** to question sth; **nutrire seri dubbi su qc** to have grave doubts about sth; **senza ~** doubtless, no doubt

dubbi'oso, -a *ag* doubtful, dubious

dubi'tare *vi*: **~ di** (*onestà*) to doubt; (*risultato*) to be doubtful of; **~ di qn** to mistrust sb; **~ di sé** to be unsure of o.s.

Du'blino *sf* Dublin

'duca, -chi *sm* duke

'duce ['dutʃe] *sm* (*Storia*) captain; (: *del fascismo*) duce

du'chessa [du'kessa] *sf* duchess

'due *num* two; **a ~ a ~** two at a time, two by two; **dire ~ parole** to say a few words; **ci metto ~ minuti** I'll have it done in a jiffy

duecen'tesco, -a, schi, sche [duetʃen'tesko] *ag* thirteenth-century

due'cento [due'tʃento] *num* two hundred ■ *sm*: **il D~** the thirteenth century

duel'lare *vi* to fight a duel

du'ello *sm* duel

due'mila *num* two thousand ■ *sm inv*: **il ~** the year two thousand

due'pezzi [due'pɛttsi] *sm* (*costume da bagno*) two-piece swimsuit; (*abito femminile*) two-piece suit

du'etto *sm* duet

'dulcis in 'fundo ['dultʃisin'fundo] *av* to cap it all

'duna *sf* dune

'dunque *cong* (*perciò*) so, therefore; (*riprendendo il discorso*) well (then) ■ *sm inv*: **venire al ~** to come to the point

'duo *sm inv* (*Mus*) duet; (*Teat, Cine, fig*) duo

du'ole *etc vb vedi* **dolere**
du'omo *sm* cathedral
'duplex *sm inv* (*Tel*) party line
dupli'cato *sm* duplicate
'duplice ['duplitʃe] *ag* double, twofold; **in ~ copia** in duplicate
duplicità [duplitʃi'ta] *sf* (*fig*) duplicity
du'rante *prep* during; **vita natural ~ for life**
du'rare *vi* to last; **non può ~!** this can't go on any longer!; **~ fatica a** to have difficulty in; **~ in carica** to remain in office
du'rata *sf* length (of time); duration; **per tutta la ~ di** throughout; **~ media della vita** life expectancy
dura'turo, -a *ag*, **du'revole** *ag* (*ricordo*)

lasting; (*materiale*) durable
du'rezza [du'rettsa] *sf* hardness; stubbornness; harshness; toughness
'duro, -a *ag* (*pietra, lavoro, materasso, problema*) hard; (*persona: ostinato*) stubborn, obstinate; (*: severo*) harsh, hard; (*voce*) harsh; (*carne*) tough ∎ *sm/f* (*persona*) tough one ∎ *av*: **tener ~** (*resistere*) to stand firm, hold out; **avere la pelle dura** (*fig: persona*) to be tough; **fare il ~** to act tough; **~ di comprendonio** slow-witted; **~ d'orecchi** hard of hearing
du'rone *sm* hard skin
'duttile *ag* (*sostanza*) malleable; (*fig: carattere*) docile, biddable; (*: stile*) adaptable
DVD [divu'di] *sm inv* DVD; (*lettore*) DVD player

Ee

E, e [e] *sf o m inv* (*lettera*) E, e; **E come Empoli** ≈ E for Edward (*Brit*), E for Easy (*US*)

E *abbr* (= *est*) E; (*Aut*) = **itinerario europeo**

e (*dav V spesso* **ed**) *cong* and; (*avversativo*) but; (*eppure*) and yet; **e lui?** what about him?; **e compralo!** well buy it then!

è *vb vedi* **essere**

E.A.D. *sigla f* = **elaborazione automatica dei dati**

ebaniste'ria *sf* cabinet-making; (*negozio*) cabinet-maker's shop

'ebano *sm* ebony

eb'bene *cong* well (then)

'ebbi *etc vb vedi* **avere**

eb'brezza [eb'brettsa] *sf* intoxication

'ebbro, -a *ag* drunk; **~ di** (*gioia etc*) beside o.s. *o* wild with

'ebete *ag* stupid, idiotic

ebe'tismo *sm* stupidity

ebollizi'one [ebollit'tsjone] *sf* boiling; **punto di ~** boiling point

e'braico, -a, ci, che *ag* Hebrew, Hebraic ■ *sm* (*Ling*) Hebrew

e'breo, -a *ag* Jewish ■ *sm/f* Jew/Jewess

'Ebridi *sfpl:* **le (isole) ~** the Hebrides

e'burneo, -a *ag* ivory *cpd*

E/C *abbr* = **estratto conto**

eca'tombe *sf* (*strage*) slaughter, massacre

ecc. *abbr* (= *eccetera*) etc

ecce'dente [ettʃe'dɛnte] *sm* surplus

ecce'denza [ettʃe'dɛntsa] *sf* excess, surplus; (*Inform*) overflow

ec'cedere [et'tʃɛdere] *vt* to exceed ■ *vi* to go too far; **~ nel bere/mangiare** to indulge in drink/food to excess

eccel'lente [ettʃel'lɛnte] *ag* excellent; (*cadavere, arresto*) of a prominent person

eccel'lenza [ettʃe'lɛntsa] *sf* excellence; (*titolo*): **Sua E~** His Excellency

ec'cellere [et'tʃɛllere] *vi:* **~ (in)** to excel (at); **~ su tutti** to surpass everyone

ec'celso, -a [et'tʃɛlso] *pp di* **eccellere** ■ *ag* (*cima, montagna*) high; (*fig: ingegno*) great, exceptional

ec'centrico, -a, ci, che [et'tʃɛntriko] *ag* eccentric

ecces'sivo, -a [ettʃes'sivo] *ag* excessive

ec'cesso [et'tʃɛsso] *sm* excess; **all'~** (*gentile, generoso*) to excess, excessively; **dare in eccessi** to fly into a rage; **~ di velocità** (*Aut*) speeding; **~ di zelo** overzealousness

ec'cetera [et'tʃetera] *av* et cetera, and so on

ec'cetto [et'tʃɛtto] *prep* except, with the exception of; **~ che** *cong* except, other than; **~ che (non)** unless

eccettu'are [ettʃettu'are] *vt* to except; **eccettuati i presenti** present company excepted

eccezio'nale [ettʃettsjo'nale] *ag* exceptional; **in via del tutto ~** in this instance, exceptionally

eccezi'one [ettʃet'tsjone] *sf* exception; (*Dir*) objection; **a ~ di** with the exception of, except for; **d'~** exceptional; **fare un'~ alla regola** to make an exception to the rule

ec'chimosi [ek'kimozi] *sf inv* bruise

ec'cidio [et'tʃidjo] *sm* massacre

ecci'tante [ettʃi'tante] *ag* (*gen*) exciting; (*sostanza*) stimulating ■ *sm* stimulant

ecci'tare [ettʃi'tare] *vt* (*curiosità, interesse*) to excite, arouse; (*folla*) to incite; **eccitarsi** *vr* to get excited; (*sessualmente*) to become aroused

eccitazi'one [ettʃitat'tsjone] *sf* excitement

ecclesi'astico, -a, ci, che *ag* ecclesiastical, church *cpd*; clerical ■ *sm* ecclesiastic

'ecco *av* (*per dimostrare*): **~ il treno!** here's *o* here comes the train!; (*dav pronome*): **eccomi!** here I am!; **eccone uno!** here's one (of them)!; (*dav pp*): **~ fatto!** there, that's it done!

ec'come *av* rather; **ti piace? — ~!** do you like it? — I'll say! *o* and how! *o* rather! (*Brit*)

ECG *sigla m* = **elettrocardiogramma**

echeggi'are [eked'dʒare] *vi* to echo

e'clettico, -a, ci, che *ag, sm/f* eclectic

eclet'tismo *sm* eclecticism

eclis'sare *vt* to eclipse; (*fig*) to eclipse, overshadow; **eclissarsi** *vr* (*persona: scherzoso*) to slip away

e'clissi *sf* eclipse

'eco (*pl(m)* **echi**) *sm o f* echo; **suscitò** *o* **ebbe una profonda ~** it caused quite a stir

ecogra'fia *sf* (*Med*) ultrasound

ecolo'gia [ekolo'dʒia] *sf* ecology

eco'logico, -a, ci, che [eko'lɔdʒiko] *ag* ecological

ecolo'gista, -i, e [ekolo'dʒista] *ag* ecological ■ *sm/f* ecologist, environmentalist

e'cologo, -a, gi, ghe *sm/f* ecologist

eco'mafia *sf* mafia involved in crimes related to the environment, in particular the illegal disposal of waste

econo'mato *sm* (*Ins*) bursar's office

econo'mia *sf* economy; (*scienza*) economics *sg*; (*risparmio: azione*) saving; **fare ~** to economize, make economies; **l'~ sommersa** the black (*Brit*) *o* underground (*US*) economy; **~ di mercato** market economy; **~ pianificata** planned economy

eco'nomico, -a, ci, che *ag* economic; (*poco costoso*) economical; **edizione economica** economy edition

econo'mista, -i *sm* economist

economiz'zare [ekonomid'dzare] *vt, vi* to save

e'conomo, -a *ag* thrifty ■ *sm/f* (*Ins*) bursar

ecosis'tema, -i *sm* ecosystem

'ecstasy ['ɛkstasi] *sf inv* ecstasy

'Ecuador *sm*: **l'~** Ecuador

ec'zema [ek'dzɛma] *sm* eczema

ed *cong vedi* **e**

Ed. *abbr* = **editore**

ed. *abbr* = **edizione**

'edera *sf* ivy

e'dicola *sf* newspaper kiosk *o* stand (*US*)

edico'lante *sm/f* news vendor (*in kiosk*)

edifi'cante *ag* edifying

edifi'care *vt* to build; (*fig: teoria, azienda*) to establish; (*indurre al bene*) to edify

edi'ficio [edi'fitʃo] *sm* building; (*fig*) structure

e'dile *ag* building *cpd*

edi'lizio, -a [edi'littsjo] *ag* building *cpd* ■ *sf* building, building trade

Edim'burgo *sf* Edinburgh

'edito, -a *ag* published

edi'tore, -'trice *ag* publishing *cpd* ■ *sm/f* publisher; (*curatore*) editor

edito'ria *sf* publishing

editori'ale *ag* publishing *cpd* ■ *sm* (*articolo di fondo*) editorial, leader

e'ditto *sm* edict

edizi'one [edit'tsjone] *sf* edition; (*tiratura*) printing; **~ a tiratura limitata** limited edition

edo'nismo *sm* hedonism

e'dotto, -a *ag* informed; **rendere qn ~ su qc** to inform sb about sth

edu'canda *sf* boarder

edu'care *vt* to educate; (*gusto, mente*) to train; **~ qn a fare** to train sb to do

educa'tivo, -a *ag* educational

edu'cato, -a *ag* polite, well-mannered

educazi'one [edukat'tsjone] *sf* education; (*familiare*) upbringing; (*comportamento*) (good) manners *pl*; **per ~** out of politeness; **questa è pura mancanza d'~!** this is sheer bad manners!; **~ fisica** (*Ins*) physical training *o* education

educherò *etc* [eduke'rɔ] *vb vedi* **educare**

E.E.D. *sigla f* = **elaborazione elettronica dei dati**

EEG *sigla m* = **elettroencefalogramma**

e'felide *sf* freckle

effemi'nato, -a *ag* effeminate

effe'rato, -a *ag* brutal, savage

efferve'scente [efferveʃ'ʃente] *ag* effervescent

effettiva'mente *av* (*in effetti*) in fact; (*a dire il vero*) really, actually

effet'tivo, -a *ag* (*reale*) real, actual; (*impiegato, professore*) permanent; (*Mil*) regular ■ *sm* (*Mil*) strength; (*di patrimonio etc*) sum total

ef'fetto *sm* effect; (*Comm: cambiale*) bill; (*fig: impressione*) impression; **far ~** (*medicina*) to take effect, (start to) work; **cercare l'~** to seek attention; **in effetti** in fact; **effetti attivi** (*Comm*) bills receivable; **effetti passivi** (*Comm*) bills payable; **effetti personali** personal effects, personal belongings; **~ serra** greenhouse effect; **effetti speciali** (*Cine*) special effects

effettu'are *vt* to effect, carry out

effi'cace [effi'katʃe] *ag* effective

effi'cacia [effi'katʃa] *sf* effectiveness

effici'ente [effi'tʃente] *ag* efficient

efficien'tismo [effitʃen'tizmo] *sm* maximum efficiency

effici'enza [effi'tʃentsa] *sf* efficiency

effigi'are [effi'dʒare] *vt* to represent, portray

ef'figie [ef'fidʒe] *sf inv* effigy

ef'fimero, -a *ag* ephemeral

ef'fluvio *sm* (*anche peg, ironico*) scent, perfume

effusi'one *sf* effusion

e.g. *abbr* (= *exempli gratia*) e.g.

egemo'nia [edʒemo'nia] *sf* hegemony

E'geo [e'dʒɛo] *sm*: **l'~, il mare ~** the Aegean (Sea)

'egida ['ɛdʒida] *sf*: **sotto l'~ di** under the aegis of

E'gitto [e'dʒitto] *sm*: **l'~** Egypt

egizi'ano, -a [edʒit'tsjano] *ag, sm/f* Egyptian

e'gizio, -a [e'dʒittsjo] *ag, sm/f* (ancient) Egyptian

'egli ['eʎʎi] *pron* he; ~ **stesso** he himself

'ego *sm inv* (*Psic*) ego

ego'centrico, -a, ci, che [ego'tʃɛntriko] *ag* egocentric(al) ■ *sm/f* self-centred (*Brit*) o self-centered (*US*) person

egocen'trismo [egotʃen'trizmo] *sm* egocentricity

ego'ismo *sm* selfishness, egoism

ego'ista, -i, e *ag* selfish, egoistic ■ *sm/f* egoist

ego'istico, -a, ci, che *ag* egoistic, selfish

ego'tismo *sm* egotism

ego'tista, -i, e *ag* egotistic ■ *sm/f* egotist

Egr. *abbr* = **Egregio**

e'gregio, -a, gi, gie [e'grɛdʒo] *ag* distinguished; (*nelle lettere*): **E~ Signore** Dear Sir

eguagli'anza *etc* [egwaʎ'ʎantsa] *vedi* **uguaglianza** *etc*

eguali'tario, -a *ag, sm/f* egalitarian

E.I. *abbr* = **Esercito Italiano**

eiaculazi'one [ejakulat'tsjone] *sf* ejaculation; ~ **precoce** premature ejaculation

elabo'rare *vt* (*progetto*) to work out, elaborate; (*dati*) to process; (*digerire*) to digest

elabora'tore *sm* (*Inform*): ~ **elettronico** computer

elaborazi'one [elaborat'tsjone] *sf* elaboration; processing; digestion; ~ **automatica dei dati** (*Inform*) automatic data processing; ~ **elettronica dei dati** (*Inform*) electronic data processing; ~ **testi** (*Inform*) text processing

elar'gire [elar'dʒire] *vt* to hand out

elargizi'one [elardʒit'tsjone] *sf* donation

elasticiz'zato, -a [elastitʃid'dzato] *ag* (*tessuto*) stretch *cpd*

e'lastico, -a, ci, che *ag* elastic; (*fig: andatura*) springy; (: *decisione, vedute*) flexible ■ *sm* (*gommino*) rubber band; (*per il cucito*) elastic *no pl*

ele'fante *sm* elephant

ele'gante *ag* elegant

ele'ganza [ele'gantsa] *sf* elegance

e'leggere [e'lɛddʒere] *vt* to elect

elemen'tare *ag* elementary; **le (scuole) elementari** *vedi* **scuola elementare**; **prima** ~ first year of primary school, ≈ infants' class (*Brit*), ≈ 1st grade (*US*)

ele'mento *sm* element; (*parte componente*) element, component, part; **elementi** *smpl* (*della scienza etc*) elements, rudiments

ele'mosina *sf* charity, alms *pl*; **chiedere l'~** to beg

elemosi'nare *vt* to beg for, ask for ■ *vi* to beg

elen'care *vt* to list

elencherò *etc* [elenke'rɔ] *vb vedi* **elencare**

e'lenco, -chi *sm* list; ~ **nominativo** list of names; ~ **telefonico** telephone directory

e'lessi *etc vb vedi* **eleggere**

elet'tivo, -a *ag* (*carica etc*) elected

e'letto, -a *pp di* **eleggere** ■ *sm/f* (*nominato*) elected member

eletto'rale *ag* electoral, election *cpd*

eletto'rato *sm* electorate

elet'tore, -'trice *sm/f* voter, elector

elet'trauto *sm inv* workshop for car electrical repairs; (*tecnico*) car electrician

elettri'cista, -i [elettri'tʃista] *sm* electrician

elettricità [elettritʃi'ta] *sf* electricity

e'lettrico, -a, ci, che *ag* electric(al)

elettrifi'care *vt* to electrify

elettriz'zante [elettrid'dzante] *ag* (*fig*) electrifying, thrilling

elettriz'zare [elettrid'dzare] *vt* to electrify; **elettrizzarsi** *vr* to become charged with electricity; (*fig: persona*) to be thrilled

e'lettro... *prefisso* electro...

elettrocardio'gramma, -i *sm* electrocardiogram

e'lettrodo *sm* electrode

elettrodo'mestico, -a, ci, che *ag*: **apparecchi elettrodomestici** domestic (electrical) appliances

elettroencefalo'gramma, -i [elettroen-tʃefalo'gramma] *sm* electroencephalogram

elet'trogeno, -a [elet'trɔdʒeno] *ag*: **gruppo ~** generator

elet'trolisi *sf* electrolysis

elettroma'gnetico, -a, ci, che [elettroman'ɲetiko] *ag* electromagnetic

elettromo'trice [elettromo'tritʃe] *sf* electric train

elet'trone *sm* electron

elet'tronico, -a, ci, che *ag* electronic ■ *sf* electronics *sg*

elettro'shock [elettroʃ'ʃɔk] *sm inv* (electro)shock treatment

elettro'tecnico, -a, ci, che *ag* electrotechnical ■ *sm* electrical engineer

ele'vare *vt* to raise; (*edificio*) to erect; (*multa*) to impose; ~ **un numero al quadrato** to square a number

eleva'tezza [eleva'tettsa] *sf* (*altezza*) elevation; (*di animo, pensiero*) loftiness

ele'vato, -a *ag* (*gen*) high; (*cime*) high, lofty; (*fig: stile, sentimenti*) lofty

elevazi'one [elevat'tsjone] *sf* elevation; (*l'elevare*) raising

elezi'one [elet'tsjone] *sf* election; **elezioni** *sfpl* (*Pol*) election(s); **patria d'~** chosen country

'elica, -che *sf* propeller

eli'cottero *sm* helicopter

e'lidere *vt* (*Fonetica*) to elide; elidersi *vr* (*forze*) to cancel each other out, neutralize each other

elimi'nare *vt* to eliminate

elimina'toria *sf* eliminating round

eliminazi'one [eliminat'tsjone] *sf* elimination

'elio *sm* helium

eli'porto *sm* heliport

elisabetti'ano, -a *ag* Elizabethan

eli'sir *sm inv* elixir

e'liso, -a *pp di* elidere

elisoc'corso *sm* helicoper ambulance

eli'tario, -a *ag* elitist

é'lite [e'lit] *sf inv* élite

'ella *pron* she; (*forma di cortesia*) you; ~ stessa she herself; you yourself

el'lisse *sf* ellipse

el'littico, -a, ci, che *ag* elliptic(al)

el'metto *sm* helmet

'elmo *sm* helmet

elogi'are [elo'dʒare] *vt* to praise

elogia'tivo, -a [elodʒa'tivo] *ag* laudatory

e'logio [e'lɔdʒo] *sm* (*discorso, scritto*) eulogy; (*lode*) praise; ~ funebre funeral oration

elo'quente *ag* eloquent; questi dati sono eloquentei these facts speak for themselves

elo'quenza [elo'kwɛntsa] *sf* eloquence

e'loquio *sm* speech, language

elucu'brare *vt* to ponder about *o* over

elucubrazi'oni [elukubrat'tsjoni] *sfpl* (*anche ironico*) cogitations, ponderings

e'ludere *vt* to evade

e'lusi *etc vb vedi* eludere

elusi'one *sf*: ~ d'imposta tax evasion

elu'sivo, -a *ag* evasive

e'luso, -a *pp di* eludere

el'vetico, -a, ci, che *ag* Swiss

emaci'ato, -a [ema'tʃato] *ag* emaciated

e-'mail, e'mail [e'mail] *sf inv, ag inv* email; indirizzo ~ email address

ema'nare *vt* to send out, give off; (*fig: leggi*) to promulgate; (*: decreti*) to issue ■ *vi*: ~ da to come from

emanazi'one [emanat'tsjone] *sf* (*di raggi, calore*) emanation; (*di odori*) exhalation; (*di legge*) promulgation; (*di ordine, circolare*) issuing

emanci'pare [emantʃi'pare] *vt* to emancipate; emanciparsi *vr* (*fig*) to become liberated *o* emancipated

emancipazi'one [emantʃipat'tsjone] *sf* emancipation

emargi'nare [emardʒi'nare] *vt* (*fig: socialmente*) to cast out

emargi'nato, -a [emardʒi'nato] *sm/f* outcast

ematolo'gia [ematolo'dʒia] *sf* haematology (*Brit*), hematology (*US*)

ema'toma, -i *sm* haematoma (*Brit*), hematoma (*US*)

em'blema, -i *sm* emblem

emble'matico, -a, ci, che *ag* emblematic; (*fig: atteggiamento, parole*) symbolic

embo'lia *sf* embolism

embrio'nale, -i, e *ag* embryonic, embryo *cpd*; allo stadio ~ at the embryo stage

embri'one *sm* embryo

emenda'mento *sm* amendment

emen'dare *vt* to amend

emer'gente [emer'dʒɛnte] *ag* emerging

emer'genza [emer'dʒɛntsa] *sf* emergency; in caso di ~ in an emergency

e'mergere [e'mɛrdʒere] *vi* to emerge; (*sommergibile*) to surface; (*fig: distinguersi*) to stand out

e'merito, -a *ag* (*insigne*) distinguished; è un ~ cretino! he's a complete idiot!

e'mersi *etc vb vedi* emergere

e'merso, -a *pp di* emergere ■ *ag* (*Geo*): terre emerse lands above sea level

e'messo, -a *pp di* emettere

e'mettere *vt* (*suono, luce*) to give out, emit; (*onde radio*) to send out; (*assegno, francobollo, ordine*) to issue; (*fig: giudizio*) to express, voice; ~ la sentenza (*Dir*) to pass sentence

emi'crania *sf* migraine

emi'grante *ag, sm/f* emigrant

emi'grare *vi* to emigrate

emi'grato, -a *ag* emigrant ■ *sm/f* emigrant; (*Storia*) émigré

emigrazi'one [emigrat'tsjone] *sf* emigration

emili'ano, -a *ag* of (*o* from) Emilia

emi'nente *ag* eminent, distinguished

emi'nenza [emi'nentsa] *sf* eminence; ~ grigia (*fig*) éminence grise

emi'rato *sm* emirate; gli Emirati Arabi Uniti the United Arab Emirates

e'miro *sm* emir

emis'fero *sm* hemisphere; ~ boreale/ australe northern/southern hemisphere

e'misi *etc vb vedi* emettere

emis'sario *sm* (*Geo*) outlet, effluent; (*inviato*) emissary

emissi'one *sf* (*vedi emettere*) emission; sending out; issue; (*Radio*) broadcast

emit'tente *ag* (*banca*) issuing; (*Radio*) broadcasting, transmitting ■ *sf* (*Radio*) transmitter

emofi'lia *sf* haemophilia (*Brit*), hemophilia (*US*)

emofi'liaco, -a, ci, che *ag, sm/f* haemophiliac (*Brit*), hemophiliac (*US*)

emoglo'bina *sf* haemoglobin (*Brit*), hemoglobin (*US*)

emolli'ente *ag* soothing

emorra'gia, -'gie [emorra'dʒia] *sf* haemorrhage (*Brit*), hemorrhage (*US*)

emor'roidi *sfpl* haemorrhoids (*Brit*), hemorrhoids (*US*)

emos'tatico, -a, ci, che *ag* haemostatic (*Brit*), hemostatic (*US*); **laccio ~** tourniquet; **matita emostatica** styptic pencil

emotività *sf* emotionalism

emo'tivo, -a *ag* emotional

emozio'nante [emottsjo'nante] *ag* exciting, thrilling

emozio'nare [emottsjo'nare] *vt* (*appassionare*) to thrill, excite; (*commuovere*) to move; (*innervosire*) to upset; **emozionarsi** *vr* to be excited; to be moved; to be upset

emozi'one [emot'tsjone] *sf* emotion; (*agitazione*) excitement

'empio, -a *ag* (*sacrilego*) impious; (*spietato*) cruel, pitiless; (*malvagio*) wicked, evil

em'pirico, -a, ci, che *ag* empirical

em'porio *sm* general store

emu'lare *vt* to emulate

'emulo, -a *sm/f* imitator

emulsi'one *sf* emulsion

EN *sigla* = **Enna**

en'ciclica, -che [en'tʃiklika] *sf* (*Rel*) encyclical

enciclope'dia [entʃiklope'dia] *sf* encyclop(a)edia

encomi'abile *ag* commendable, praiseworthy

encomi'are *vt* to commend, praise

en'comio *sm* commendation; **~ solenne** (*Mil*) mention in dispatches

endove'noso, -a *ag* (*Med*) intravenous ■ *sf* intravenous injection

E'NEA *sigla f* = **Comitato nazionale per la ricerca e lo sviluppo dell'Energia Nucleare e delle Energie Alternative**

'E.N.E.L. *sigla m* (= *Ente Nazionale per l'Energia Elettrica*) national electricity company

ener'getico, -a, ci, che [ener'dʒetiko] *ag* (*risorse, crisi*) energy *cpd*; (*sostanza, alimento*) energy-giving

ener'gia, -'gie [ener'dʒia] *sf* (*Fisica*) energy; (*fig*) energy, strength, vigour (*Brit*), vigor (*US*)

e'nergico, -a, ci, che [e'nɛrdʒiko] *ag* energetic, vigorous

'enfasi *sf* emphasis; (*peg*) bombast, pomposity

en'fatico, -a, ci, che *ag* emphatic; pompous

enfatiz'zare [enfatid'dzare] *vt* to emphasize, stress

enfi'sema *sm* emphysema

'ENI *sigla m* = **Ente Nazionale Idrocarburi**

e'nigma, -i *sm* enigma

enig'matico, -a, ci, che *ag* enigmatic

'ENIT *sigla m* (= *Ente Nazionale Italiano per il Turismo*) Italian tourist authority

en'nesimo, -a *ag* (*Mat, fig*) nth; **per l'ennesima volta** for the umpteenth time

enolo'gia [enolo'dʒia] *sf* oenology (*Brit*), enology (*US*)

e'nologo, -gi *sm* wine expert

e'norme *ag* enormous, huge

enormità *sf inv* enormity, huge size; (*assurdità*) absurdity; **non dire enormità!** don't talk nonsense!

eno'teca, -che *sf* (*negozio*) wine bar

'E.N.P.A. *sigla m* (= *Ente Nazionale Protezione Animali*) ≈ RSPCA (*Brit*), ≈ SPCA (*US*)

'E.N.P.A.S. *sigla m* (= *Ente Nazionale di Previdenza e Assistenza per i Dipendenti Statali*) welfare organization for State employees

'ente *sm* (*istituzione*) body, board, corporation; (*Filosofia*) being; **~ locale** local authority (*Brit*), local government (*US*); **~ pubblico** public body; **~ di ricerca** research organization

ente'rite *sf* enteritis

entità *sf* (*Filosofia*) entity; (*di perdita, danni, investimenti*) extent; (*di popolazione*) size; **di molta/poca ~** (*avvenimento, incidente*) of great/little importance

en'trambi, -e *pron pl* both (of them) ■ *ag pl*: **~ i ragazzi** both boys, both of the boys

en'trante *ag* (*prossimo: mese, anno*) next, coming

en'trare *vi* to enter, go (*o* come) in; **~ in** (*luogo*) to enter, go (*o* come) into; (*trovar posto, poter stare*) to fit into; (*essere ammesso a: club etc*) to join, become a member of; **~ in automobile** to get into the car; **far ~ qn** (*visitatore etc*) to show sb in; **~ in società/in commercio con qn** to go into partnership/business with sb; **questo non c'entra** (*fig*) that's got nothing to do with it

en'trata *sf* entrance, entry; **entrate** *sfpl* (*Comm*) receipts, takings; (*Econ*) income *sg*; **"~ libera"** "admission free"; **con l'~ in vigore dei nuovi provvedimenti ...** once the new measures come into effect ...; **entrate tributarie** tax revenue *sg*

'entro *prep* (*temporale*) within; **~ domani** by tomorrow; **~ e non oltre il 25 aprile** no later than 25th April

entro'terra *sm inv* hinterland

entusias'mante *ag* exciting

entusias'mare *vt* to excite, fill with enthusiasm; **entusiasmarsi** *vr*: **entusiasmarsi (per qc/qn)** to become enthusiastic (about sth/sb)

entusi'asmo sm enthusiasm
entusi'asta, -i, e ag enthusiastic ▪ sm/f enthusiast
entusi'astico, -a, ci, che ag enthusiastic
enucle'are vt (formale: chiarire) to explain
enume'rare vt to enumerate, list
enunci'are [enun'tʃare] vt (teoria) to enunciate, set out
en'zima, -i sm enzyme
e'patico, -a, ci, che ag hepatic; **cirrosi epatica** cirrhosis of the liver
epa'tite sf hepatitis
'epico, -a, ci, che ag epic
epide'mia sf epidemic
epi'dermico, -a, ci, che ag (Anat) skin cpd; (fig: interesse, impressioni) superficial
epi'dermide sf skin, epidermis
Epifa'nia sf Epiphany
e'pigono sm imitator
e'pigrafe sf epigraph; (su libro) dedication
epiles'sia sf epilepsy
epi'lettico, -a, ci, che ag, sm/f epileptic
e'pilogo, -ghi sm conclusion
epi'sodico, -a, ci, che ag (romanzo, narrazione) episodic; (fig: occasionale) occasional
epi'sodio sm episode; **sceneggiato a episodi** serial
e'pistola sf epistle
episto'lare ag epistolary; **essere in rapporto o relazione ~ con qn** to correspond o be in correspondence with sb
e'piteto sm epithet
'epoca, -che sf (periodo storico) age, era; (tempo) time; (Geo) age; **mobili d'~** period furniture; **fare ~** (scandalo) to cause a stir; (cantante, moda) to mark a new era
epo'pea sf (anche fig) epic
ep'pure cong and yet, nevertheless
EPT sigla m (= Ente Provinciale per il Turismo) district tourist bureau
epu'rare vt (Pol) to purge
equ'anime ag (imparziale) fair, impartial
equa'tore sm equator
equazi'one [ekwat'tsjone] sf (Mat) equation
e'questre ag equestrian
equi'latero, -a ag equilateral
equili'brare vt to balance
equili'brato, -a ag (carico, fig: giudizio) balanced; (vita) well-regulated; (persona) stable, well-balanced
equi'librio sm balance, equilibrium; **perdere l'~** to lose one's balance; **stare in ~ su** (persona) to balance on; (oggetto) to be balanced on
equili'brismo sm tightrope walking; (fig) juggling
e'quino, -a ag horse cpd, equine

equi'nozio [ekwi'nɔttsjo] sm equinox
equipaggia'mento [ekwipaddʒa'mento] sm (operazione: di nave) equipping, fitting out; (: di spedizione, esercito) equipping, kitting out; (attrezzatura) equipment
equipaggi'are [ekwipad'dʒare] vt to equip; **equipaggiarsi** vr to equip o.s.
equi'paggio [ekwi'paddʒo] sm crew
equipa'rare vt to make equal
é'quipe [e'kip] sf (Sport, gen) team
equità sf equity, fairness
equitazi'one [ekwitat'tsjone] sf (horse-) riding
equiva'lente ag, sm equivalent
equiva'lenza [ekwiva'lɛntsa] sf equivalence
equiva'lere vi: **~ a** to be equivalent to; **equivalersi** vr (forze etc) to counterbalance each other; (soluzioni) to amount to the same thing; **equivale a dire che ...** that is the same as saying that ...
equi'valso, -a pp di **equivalere**
equivo'care vi to misunderstand
e'quivoco, -a, ci, che ag equivocal, ambiguous; (sospetto) dubious ▪ sm misunderstanding; **a scanso di equivoci** to avoid any misunderstanding; **giocare sull'~** to equivocate
'equo, -a ag fair, just
'era sf era
'era etc vb vedi **essere**
erari'ale ag: **ufficio ~** = tax office; **imposte erariali** revenue taxes; **spese erariali** public expenditure sg
e'rario sm: **l'~** = the Treasury
'erba sf grass; (aromatica, medicinale) herb; **in ~** (fig) budding; **fare di ogni ~ un fascio** (fig) to lump everything (o everybody) together
er'baccia, -ce [er'battʃa] sf weed
er'bivoro, -a ag herbivorous ▪ sm/f herbivore
erbo'rista, -i, e sm/f herbalist
erboriste'ria sf (scienza) study of medicinal herbs; (negozio) herbalist's (shop)
er'boso, -a ag grassy
e'rede sm/f heir; **~ legittimo** heir-at-law
eredità sf (Dir) inheritance; (Biol) heredity; **lasciare qc in ~ a qn** to leave o bequeath sth to sb
eredi'tare vt to inherit
eredi'tario, -a ag hereditary
erediti'era sf heiress
ere'mita, -i sm hermit
eremi'taggio [eremi'taddʒo] sm hermitage
'eremo sm hermitage; (fig) retreat
ere'sia sf heresy
e'ressi etc vb vedi **erigere**

e'retico, -a, ci, che *ag* heretical ■ *sm/f* heretic

e'retto, -a *pp di* erigere ■ *ag* erect, upright

erezi'one [eret'tsjone] *sf* (*Fisiol*) erection

ergasto'lano, -a *sm/f* prisoner serving a life sentence, lifer (*fam*)

er'gastolo *sm* (*Dir: pena*) life imprisonment; (: *luogo di pena*) prison (*for those serving life sentences*)

ergono'mia *sf* ergonomics *sg*

ergo'nomico, -a, ci, che *ag* ergonomic(al)

'erica *sf* heather

e'rigere [e'ridʒere] *vt* to erect, raise; (*fig: fondare*) to found

eri'tema *sm* (*Med*) inflammation, erythema; ~ solare sunburn

Eri'trea *sf* Eritrea

ermel'lino *sm* ermine

er'metico, -a, ci, che *ag* hermetic

'ernia *sf* (*Med*) hernia; ~ del disco slipped disc

'ero *vb vedi* essere

e'rodere *vt* to erode

e'roe *sm* hero

ero'gare *vt* (*somme*) to distribute; (*gas, servizi*) to supply

erogazi'one [erogat'tsjone] *sf* distribution; supply

e'roico, -a, ci, che *ag* heroic

ero'ina *sf* heroine; (*droga*) heroin

ero'ismo *sm* heroism

'eros *sm* Eros

erosi'one *sf* erosion

e'roso, -a *pp di* erodere

e'rotico, -a, ci, che *ag* erotic

ero'tismo *sm* eroticism

'erpete *sm* herpes *sg*

'erpice ['erpitʃe] *sm* (*Agr*) harrow

er'rare *vi* (*vagare*) to wander, roam; (*sbagliare*) to be mistaken

er'roneo, -a *ag* erroneous, wrong

er'rore *sm* error, mistake; (*morale*) error; per ~ by mistake; ~ giudiziario miscarriage of justice

'erto, -a *ag* (very) steep ■ *sf* steep slope; stare all'erta to be on the alert

eru'dire *vt* to teach, educate

eru'dito, -a *ag* learned, erudite

erut'tare *vt* (*vulcano*) to throw out, belch

eruzi'one [erut'tsjone] *sf* eruption; (*Med*) rash

es. *abbr* (= *esempio*) e.g.

E.S. *sigla m* (= *elettroshock*) ECT

E.S.A. ['eza] *sigla m* (= *European Space Agency*) ESA

esacer'bare [ezatʃer'bare] *vt* to exacerbate

esage'rare [ezadʒe'rare] *vt* to exaggerate ■ *vi* to exaggerate; (*eccedere*) to go too far; senza ~ without exaggeration

esage'rato, -a [ezadʒe'rato] *ag* (*notizia, proporzioni*) exaggerated; (*curiosità, pignoleria*) excessive; (*prezzo*) exorbitant ■ *sm/f*: sei il solito ~ you are exaggerating as usual

esagerazi'one [esadʒerat'tsjone] *sf* exaggeration

esago'nale *ag* hexagonal

e'sagono *sm* hexagon

esa'lare *vt* (*odori*) to give off ■ *vi*: ~ (da) to emanate (from); ~ l'ultimo respiro (*fig*) to breathe one's last

esalazi'one [ezalat'tsjone] *sf* (*emissione*) exhalation; (*odore*) fumes *pl*

esal'tante *ag* exciting

esal'tare *vt* to exalt; (*entusiasmare*) to excite, stir; esaltarsi *vr*: esaltarsi (per qc) to grow excited (about sth)

esal'tato, -a *sm/f* fanatic

esaltazi'one [ezaltat'tsjone] *sf* (*elogio*) extolling, exalting; (*nervosa*) intense excitement; (*mistica*) exaltation

e'same *sm* examination; (*Ins*) exam, examination; fare o dare un ~ to sit o take an exam; fare un ~ di coscienza to search one's conscience; ~ di guida driving test; ~ del sangue blood test

esami'nare *vt* to examine

e'sangue *ag* bloodless; (*fig: pallido*) pale, wan; (: *privo di vigore*) lifeless

e'sanime *ag* lifeless

esaspe'rare *vt* to exasperate; (*situazione*) to exacerbate; esasperarsi *vr* to become annoyed o exasperated

esasperazi'one [ezasperat'tsjone] *sf* exasperation

esatta'mente *av* exactly; accurately, precisely

esat'tezza [ezat'tettsa] *sf* exactitude, accuracy, precision; per l'~ to be precise

e'satto, -a *pp di* esigere ■ *ag* (*calcolo, ora*) correct, right, exact; (*preciso*) accurate, precise; (*puntuale*) punctual

esat'tore *sm* (*di imposte etc*) collector

esat'toria *sf*: ~ comunale district rates office (*Brit*) o assessor's office (*US*)

esau'dire *vt* to grant, fulfil (*Brit*), fulfill (*US*)

esauri'ente *ag* exhaustive

esauri'mento *sm* exhaustion; ~ nervoso nervous breakdown; svendita (fino) ad ~ della merce clearance sale

esau'rire *vt* (*stancare*) to exhaust, wear out; (*provviste, miniera*) to exhaust; esaurirsi *vr* to exhaust o.s., wear o.s. out; (*provviste*) to run out

esau'rito, -a *ag* exhausted; (*merci*) sold out; (*libri*) out of print; essere ~ (*persona*) to be run down; registrare il tutto ~ (*Teat*) to have a full house e'sausto, -a *ag* exhausted

esauto'rare *vt* (*dirigente, funzionario*) to deprive of authority

esazi'one [ezat'tsjone] *sf* collection (of taxes)

'esca (*pl* **esche**) *sf* bait

escamo'tage [ɛskamɔ'taʒ] *sm* subterfuge

escande'scenza [eskandeʃʃɛntsa] *sf*: **dare in escandescenze** to lose one's temper, fly into a rage

'esce ['eʃʃe] *vb vedi* **uscire**

eschi'mese [eski'mese] *ag, sm/f, sm* Eskimo

'esci ['ɛʃʃi] *vb vedi* **uscire**

escl. *abbr* (= *escluso*) excl

escla'mare *vi* to exclaim, cry out

esclama'tivo, -a *ag*: **punto ~** exclamation mark

esclamazi'one [esklamat'tsjone] *sf* exclamation

es'cludere *vt* to exclude

es'clusi *etc vb vedi* **escludere**

esclusi'one *sf* exclusion; **a ~ di, fatta ~ per** except (for), apart from; **senza ~ (alcuna)** without exception; **procedere per ~** to follow a process of elimination; **senza ~ di colpi** (*fig*) with no holds barred

esclu'siva *sf vedi* **esclusivo**

esclusiva'mente *av* exclusively, solely

esclu'sivo, -a *ag* exclusive ■ *sf* (*Dir, Comm*) exclusive *o* sole rights *pl*

es'cluso, -a *pp di* **escludere** ■ *ag*: **nessuno ~** without exception; **IVA esclusa** excluding VAT, exclusive of VAT

'esco *vb vedi* **uscire**

escogi'tare [eskodʒi'tare] *vt* to devise, think up

'escono *vb vedi* **uscire**

escoriazi'one [eskorjat'tsjone] *sf* abrasion, graze

escre'menti *smpl* excrement *sg*, faeces

escursi'one *sf* (*gita*) excursion, trip; (*a piedi*) hike, walk; (*Meteor*): **~ termica** temperature range

escursio'nista, -i, e *sm/f* (*gitante*) (day) tripper; (*a piedi*) hiker, walker

ese'crare *vt* to loathe, abhor

esecu'tivo, -a *ag, sm* executive

esecu'tore, -'trice *sm/f* (*Mus*) performer; (*Dir*) executor

esecuzi'one [ezekut'tsjone] *sf* execution, carrying out; (*Mus*) performance; **~ capitale** execution

ese'geta, -i [eze'dʒɛta] *sm* commentator

esegu'ire *vt* to carry out, execute; (*Mus*) to perform, execute

e'sempio *sm* example; **per ~** for example, for instance; **fare un ~** to give an example

esem'plare *ag* exemplary ■ *sm* example; (*copia*) copy; (*Bot, Zool, Geo*) specimen

esemplifi'care *vt* to exemplify

esen'tare *vt*: **~ qn/qc da** to exempt sb/sth from

esen'tasse *ag inv* tax-free

e'sente *ag*: **~ da** (*dispensato da*) exempt from; (*privo di*) free from

esenzi'one [ezen'tsjone] *sf* exemption

e'sequie *sfpl* funeral rites; funeral service *sg*

eser'cente [ezer'tʃɛnte] *sm/f* trader, dealer; shopkeeper

eserci'tare [ezertʃi'tare] *vt* (*professione*) to practise (*Brit*), practice (*US*); (*allenare: corpo, mente*) to exercise, train; (*diritto*) to exercise; (*influenza, pressione*) to exert; **esercitarsi** *vr* to practise; **esercitarsi nella guida** to practise one's driving

esercitazi'one [ezertʃitat'tsjone] *sf* (*scolastica, militare*) exercise; **esercitazioni di tiro** target practice *sg*

e'sercito [e'zɛrtʃito] *sm* army

eser'cizio [ezer'tʃittsjo] *sm* practice; (*compito, movimento*) exercise; (*azienda*) business, concern; (*Econ*): **~ finanziario** financial year; **in ~** (*medico etc*) practising (*Brit*), practicing (*US*); **nell'~ delle proprie funzioni** in the execution of one's duties

esfoli'ante *sm* exfoliator

esi'bire *vt* to exhibit, display; (*documenti*) to produce, present; **esibirsi** *vr* (*attore*) to perform; (*fig*) to show off

esibizi'one [ezibit'tsjone] *sf* exhibition; (*di documento*) presentation; (*spettacolo*) show, performance

esibizio'nista, -i, e [ezibittsjo'nista] *sm/f* exhibitionist

esi'gente [ezi'dʒɛnte] *ag* demanding

esi'genza [ezi'dʒɛntsa] *sf* demand, requirement

e'sigere [e'zidʒere] *vt* (*pretendere*) to demand; (*richiedere*) to demand, require; (*imposte*) to collect

esi'gibile [ezi'dʒibile] *ag* payable

e'siguo, -a *ag* small, slight

esila'rante *ag* hilarious; **gas ~** laughing gas

'esile *ag* (*persona*) slender, slim; (*stelo*) thin; (*voce*) faint

esili'are *vt* to exile

esili'ato, -a *ag* exiled ■ *sm/f* exile

e'silio *sm* exile

e'simere *vt*: **~ qn/qc da** to exempt sb/sth from; **esimersi** *vr*: **esimersi da** to get out of

esis'tente *ag* existing; (*attuale*) present, current

esis'tenza [ezis'tɛntsa] *sf* existence

esistenzia'lismo [ezistentsja'lizmo] *sm* existentialism

e'sistere *vi* to exist; **esiste più di una versione dell'opera** there is more than one version of the work; **non esiste!** (*fam*) no way!

esis'tito, -a *pp di* **esistere**

esi'tante *ag* hesitant; (*voce*) faltering

esi'tare *vi* to hesitate

esitazi'one [ezitat'tsjone] *sf* hesitation

'esito *sm* result, outcome

'eskimo *sm* (*giaccone*) parka

'esodo *sm* exodus

e'sofago, -gi *sm* oesophagus (*Brit*), esophagus (*US*)

esone'rare *vt*: ~ **qn da** to exempt sb from

esorbi'tante *ag* exorbitant, excessive

esor'cismo [ezor'tʃizmo] *sm* exorcism

esor'cista, -i [ezor'tʃista] *sm* exorcist

esorciz'zare [ezortʃid'dzare] *vt* to exorcize

esordi'ente *sm/f* beginner

e'sordio *sm* debut

esor'dire *vi* (*nel teatro*) to make one's debut; (*fig*) to start out, begin (one's career); **esordì dicendo che ...** he began by saying (that) ...

esor'tare *vt*: ~ **qn a fare** to urge sb to do

esortazi'one [ezortat'tsjone] *sf* exhortation

e'soso, -a *ag* (*prezzo*) exorbitant; (*persona: avido*) grasping

eso'terico, -a, ci, che *ag* esoteric

e'sotico, -a, ci, che *ag* exotic

es'pandere *vt* to expand; (*confini*) to extend; (*influenza*) to extend, spread; **espandersi** *vr* to expand

espansi'one *sf* expansion

espansività *sf* expansiveness

espan'sivo, -a *ag* expansive, communicative

es'panso, -a *pp di* **espandere**

espatri'are *vi* to leave one's country

es'patrio *sm* expatriation; **permesso di ~** authorization to leave the country

espedi'ente *sm* expedient; **vivere di espedienti** to live by one's wits

es'pellere *vt* to expel

esperi'enza [espe'rjɛntsa] *sf* experience; (*Sci: prova*) experiment; **parlare per ~** to speak from experience

esperi'mento *sm* experiment; **fare un ~** to carry out *o* do an experiment

es'perto, -a *ag, sm/f* expert

espi'anto *sm* (*Med*) removal

espi'are *vt* to atone for

espiazi'one [espiat'tsjone] *sf*: ~ **(di)** expiation (of), atonement (for)

espi'rare *vt, vi* to breathe out

espleta'mento *sm* (*Amm*) carrying out

esple'tare *vt* (*Amm*) to carry out

espli'care *vt* (*attività*) to carry out, perform

esplica'tivo, -a *ag* explanatory

es'plicito, -a [es'plitʃito] *ag* explicit

es'plodere *vi* (*anche fig*) to explode ■ *vt* to fire

esplo'rare *vt* to explore

esplora'tore, -'trice *sm/f* explorer; (*anche:* **giovane esploratore**) (boy) scout/(girl) guide (*Brit*) *o* scout (*US*) ■ *sm* (*Naut*) scout (ship)

esplorazi'one [esplorat'tsjone] *sf* exploration; **mandare qn in ~** (*Mil*) to send sb to scout ahead

esplosi'one *sf* (*anche fig*) explosion

explo'sivo, -a *ag, sm* explosive

es'ploso, -a *pp di* **esplodere**

es'pone *etc vb vedi* **esporre**

espo'nente *sm/f* (*rappresentante*) representative

esponenzi'ale [esponen'tsjale] *ag* (*Mat*) exponential

es'pongo, es'poni *vb vedi* **esporre**

es'porre *vt* (*merci*) to display; (*quadro*) to exhibit, show; (*fatti, idee*) to explain, set out; (*porre in pericolo, Fot*) to expose; **esporsi** *vr*: **esporsi a** (*sole, pericolo*) to expose o.s. to; (*critiche*) to lay o.s. open to

espor'tare *vt* to export

esporta'tore, -'trice *ag* exporting ■ *sm* exporter

esportazi'one [esportat'tsjone] *sf* (*azione*) exportation, export; (*insieme di prodotti*) exports *pl*

es'pose *etc vb vedi* **esporre**

espo'simetro *sm* exposure meter

esposizi'one [espozit'tsjone] *sf* displaying; exhibiting; setting out; (*anche Fot*) exposure; (*mostra*) exhibition; (*narrazione*) explanation, exposition

es'posto, -a *pp di* **esporre** ■ *ag*: ~ **a nord** facing north, north-facing ■ *sm* (*Amm*) statement, account; (: *petizione*) petition

espressi'one *sf* expression

espres'sivo, -a *ag* expressive

es'presso, -a *pp di* **esprimere** ■ *ag* express ■ *sm* (*lettera*) express letter; (*anche:* **treno espresso**) express train; (*anche:* **caffè espresso**) espresso

es'primere *vt* to express; **esprimersi** *vr* to express o.s.

espropri'are *vt* (*terreni, edifici*) to place a compulsory purchase order on; (*persona*) to dispossess

espropriazi'one [esproprjat'tsjone] *sf*, es'proprio *sm* expropriation; ~ **per pubblica utilità** compulsory purchase

espu'gnare [espun'ɲare] *vt* to take by force, storm

es'pulsi *etc vb vedi* **espellere**

espulsi'one *sf* expulsion

es'pulso, -a *pp di* **espellere**

'**essa** *pron f*, '**esse** *pron fpl vedi* **esso**
es'senza [es'sɛntsa] *sf* essence
essenzi'ale [essen'tsjale] *ag* essential; *(stile, linea)* simple ■ *sm*: l'~ the main o most important thing

PAROLA CHIAVE

'**essere** *sm* being; **essere umano** human being

■ *vb copulativo* **1** *(con attributo, sostantivo)* to be; **sei giovane/simpatico** you are o you're young/nice; **è medico** he is o he's a doctor

2 *(+ di: appartenere)* to be; **di chi è la penna?** whose pen is it?; **è di Carla** it is o it's Carla's, it belongs to Carla

3 *(+ di: provenire)* to be; **è di Venezia** he is o he's from Venice

4 *(data, ora)*: **è il 15 agosto** it is o it's the 15th of August; **è lunedì** it is o it's Monday; **che ora è?, che ore sono?** what time is it?; **è l'una** it is o it's one o'clock; **sono le due** it is o it's two o'clock

5 *(costare)*: **quant'è?** how much is it?; **sono 20 euro** it's 20 euros

■ *vb aus* **1** *(attivo)*: **essere arrivato/venuto** to have arrived/come; **è già partita** she has already left

2 *(passivo)* to be; **essere fatto da** to be made by; **è stata uccisa** she has been killed

3 *(riflessivo)*: **si sono lavati** they washed, they got washed

4 *(+ da + infinito)*: **è da farsi subito** it must be done o is to be done immediately

■ *vi* **1** *(esistere, trovarsi)* to be; **sono a casa** I'm at home; **essere in piedi/seduto** to be standing/sitting

2 *(succedere)*: **sarà quel che sarà** what will be will be; **sia quel che sia, io me ne vado** come what may, I'm going now

3: **esserci**: **c'è** there is; **ci sono** there are; **che c'è?** what's the matter?, what is it?; **non c'è niente da fare** there's nothing we can do; **c'è da sperare che ...** one can only hope that ...; **ci sono!** *(sono pronto)* I'm ready; *(ho capito)* I get it!; *vedi* **ci**

■ *vb impers*: **è tardi/Pasqua** it's late/Easter; **è mezzanotte** it's midnight; **è bello/caldo/freddo** it's nice/hot/cold; **è possibile che venga** he may come; **è così** that's the way it is

'**essi** *pron mpl vedi* **esso**
essic'care *vt (gen)* to dry; *(legname)* to season; *(cibi)* to desiccate; *(bacino, palude)* to drain; **essiccarsi** *vr (fiume, pozzo)* to dry up; *(vernice)* to dry (out)

'**esso, -a** *pron* it; *(riferito a persona: soggetto)* he/she; *(: complemento)* him/her; **essi, e** *pron pl (complemento)* them

est *sm* east; **i paesi dell'E~** the Eastern bloc *sg*
'**estasi** *sf* ecstasy
estasi'are *vt* to send into raptures; **estasiarsi** *vr*: **estasiarsi (davanti a)** to go into ecstasies (over), go into raptures (over)
es'tate *sf* summer
es'tatico, -a, ci, che *ag* ecstatic
estempo'raneo, -a *ag (discorso)* extempore, impromptu; *(brano musicale)* impromptu
es'tendere *vt* to extend; **estendersi** *vr (diffondersi)* to spread; *(territorio, confini)* to extend
estensi'one *sf* extension; *(di superficie)* expanse; *(di voce)* range
estenu'ante *ag* wearing, tiring
estenu'are *vt (stancare)* to wear out, tire out
esteri'ore *ag* outward, external
esteriorità *sf inv* outward appearance
esterioriz'zare [esterjorid'dzare] *vt (gioia etc)* to show
ester'nare *vt* to express; **~ un sospetto** to voice a suspicion
es'terno, -a *ag (porta, muro)* outer, outside; *(scala)* outside; *(alunno, impressione)* external ■ *sm* outside, exterior ■ *sm/f (allievo)* day pupil; "**per uso ~**" "for external use only"; **gli esterni sono stati girati a Glasgow** *(Cine)* the location shots were taken in Glasgow
'**estero, -a** *ag* foreign ■ *sm*: **all'~** abroad; **Ministero degli Esteri, gli Esteri** Ministry for Foreign Affairs, ≈ Foreign Office *(Brit)*, ≈ State Department *(US)*
esterofi'lia *sf* excessive love of foreign things
esterre'fatto, -a *ag (costernato)* horrified; *(sbalordito)* astounded
es'tesi *etc vb vedi* **estendere**
es'teso, -a *pp di* **estendere** ■ *ag* extensive, large; **scrivere per ~** to write in full
estetica'mente *av* aesthetically
es'tetico, -a, ci, che *ag* aesthetic ■ *sf (disciplina)* aesthetics *sg*; *(bellezza)* attractiveness; **chirurgia estetica** cosmetic surgery; **cura estetica** beauty treatment
este'tista, -i, e *sm/f* beautician
'**estimo** *sm* valuation; *(disciplina)* surveying
es'tinguere *vt* to extinguish, put out; *(debito)* to pay off; *(conto)* to close; **estinguersi** *vr* to go out; *(specie)* to become extinct
es'tinsi *etc vb vedi* **estinguere**
es'tinto, -a *pp di* **estinguere**
estin'tore *sm* (fire) extinguisher
estinzi'one [estin'tsjone] *sf* putting out; *(di specie)* extinction; *(di debito)* payment; *(di conto)* closing

estir'pare *vt* (*pianta*) to uproot, pull up; (*dente*) to extract; (*tumore*) to remove; (*fig: vizio*) to eradicate

es'tivo, -a *ag* summer *cpd*

'estone *ag, sm/f, sm* Estonian

Es'tonia *sf:* l'~ Estonia

es'torcere [es'tɔrtʃere] *vt:* ~ **qc (a qn)** to extort sth (from sb)

estorsi'one *sf* extortion

es'torto, -a *pp di* **estorcere**

estra'dare *vt* to extradite

estradizi'one [estradit'tsjone] *sf* extradition

es'trae, es'traggo *vb vedi* **estrarre**

es'traneo, -a *ag* foreign; (*discorso*) extraneous, unrelated ■ *sm/f* stranger; **rimanere ~ a qc** to take no part in sth; **sentirsi ~ a** (*famiglia, società*) to feel alienated from; **"ingresso vietato agli estranei"** "no admittance to unauthorized personnel"

estrani'arsi *vr:* ~ **(da)** to cut o.s. off (from)

es'trarre *vt* to extract; (*minerali*) to mine; (*sorteggiare*) to draw; ~ **a sorte** to draw lots

es'trassi *etc vb vedi* **estrarre**

es'tratto, -a *pp di* **estrarre** ■ *sm* extract; (*di documento*) abstract; ~ **conto** (bank) statement; ~ **di nascita** birth certificate

estrazi'one [estrat'tsjone] *sf* extraction; mining; drawing *no pl*; draw

estrema'mente *av* extremely

estre'mismo *sm* extremism

estre'mista, -i, e *sm/f* extremist

estremità *sf inv* extremity, end ■ *sfpl* (*Anat*) extremities

es'tremo, -a *ag* extreme; (*ultimo: ora, tentativo*) final, last ■ *sm* extreme; (*di pazienza, forza*) limit, end; **estremi** *smpl* (*Dir*) essential elements; (*Amm: dati essenziali*) details, particulars; **l'E~ Oriente** the Far East

estrinse'care *vt* to express, show

'estro *sm* (*capriccio*) whim, fancy; (*ispirazione creativa*) inspiration

estro'messo, -a *pp di* **estromettere**

estro'mettere *vt:* ~ **(da)** (*partito, club etc*) to expel (from); (*discussione*) to exclude (from)

estromissi'one *sf* expulsion

es'troso, -a *ag* whimsical, capricious; inspired

estro'verso, -a *ag, sm* extrovert

estu'ario *sm* estuary

esube'rante *ag* exuberant; (*Comm*) redundant (*Brit*)

esube'ranza [ezube'rantsa] *sf* (*di persona*) exuberance; ~ **di personale** (*Comm*) overmanning (*Brit*), over-staffing (*US*)

e'subero *sm:* ~ **di personale** surplus staff; **in** ~ redundant, due to be laid off

esu'lare *vi:* ~ **da** (*competenza*) to be beyond; (*compiti*) not to be part of

'esule *sm/f* exile

esul'tanza [ezul'tantsa] *sf* exultation

esul'tare *vi* to exult

esu'mare *vt* (*salma*) to exhume, disinter; (*fig*) to unearth

età *sf inv* age; **all'età di 8 anni** at the age of 8, at 8 years of age; **ha la mia età** he (*o* she) is the same age as me *o* as I am; **di mezza età** middle-aged; **raggiungere la maggiore età** to come of age; **essere in età minore** to be under age; **in età avanzata** advanced in years

eta'nolo *sm* ethanol

etc. *abbr* etc.

'etere *sm* ether; **via ~** on the airwaves

e'tereo, -a *ag* ethereal

eternità *sf* eternity

e'terno, -a *ag* eternal; (*interminabile: lamenti, attesa*) never-ending; **in ~** for ever, eternally

etero'geneo, -a [etero'dʒɛneo] *ag* heterogeneous

eterosessu'ale *ag, sm/f* heterosexual

'etica *sf vedi* **etico**

eti'chetta [eti'ketta] *sf* label; (*cerimoniale*): l'~ etiquette

'etico, -a, ci, che *ag* ethical ■ *sf* ethics *sg*

eti'lometro *sm* Breathalyzer®

etimolo'gia, -'gie [etimolo'dʒia] *sf* etymology

etimo'logico, -a, ci, che [etimo'lɔdʒiko] *ag* etymological

e'tiope *ag, sm/f* Ethiopian

Eti'opia *sf:* l'~ Ethiopia

eti'opico, -a, ci, che *ag, sm* (*Ling*) Ethiopian

'Etna *sm:* l'~ Etna

'etnico, -a, ci, che *ag* ethnic

e'trusco, -a, schi, sche *ag, sm/f* Etruscan

'ettaro *sm* hectare (= 10,000 m²)

'etto *abbr m* = **ettogrammo**

etto'grammo *sm* hectogram(me) (= 100 grams)

et'tolitro *sm* hectolitre (*Brit*), hectoliter (*US*)

et'tometro *sm* hectometre

EU *abbr* = **Europa**

euca'lipto *sm* eucalyptus

Eucaris'tia *sf:* l'~ the Eucharist

eufe'mismo *sm* euphemism

eufe'mistico, -a, ci, che *ag* euphemistic

eufo'ria *sf* euphoria

eu'forico, -a, ci, che *ag* euphoric

Eu'rasia *sf* Eurasia

eurasi'atico, -a, ci, che *ag, sm/f* Eurasian

Eura'tom *sigla f* (= Comunità Europea dell'Energia Atomica) Euratom

eu'ristico, -a, ci, che *ag* heuristic

'euro *sm inv* (*divisa*) euro

e

euro'corpo *sm* European force
eurodepu'tato *sm* Euro MP
eurodi'visa *sf* Eurocurrency
euro'dollaro *sm* Eurodollar
Euro'landia *sf* Euroland
euromer'cato *sm* Euromarket
euro'missile *sm* Euro-missile
Eu'ropa *sf*: **l'~** Europe
europarlamen'tare *sm/f* Member of the European Parliament, MEP
euro'peo, -a *ag, sm/f* European
euro'scettico, -a, ci, che [euroʃʃettiko] *sm/f* Euro-sceptic
eutana'sia *sf* euthanasia
E.V. *abbr* = **Eccellenza Vostra**
evacu'are *vt* to evacuate
evacuazi'one [evakuat'tsjone] *sf* evacuation
e'vadere *vi (fuggire)*: **~ da** to escape from ■ *vt (sbrigare)* to deal with, dispatch; *(tasse)* to evade
evan'gelico, -a, ci, che [evan'dʒeliko] *ag* evangelical
evange'lista, -i [evandʒe'lista] *sm* evangelist
evapo'rare *vi* to evaporate
evaporazi'one [evaporat'tsjone] *sf* evaporation
e'vasi *etc vb vedi* **evadere**
evasi'one *sf (vedi evadere)* escape; dispatch; **dare ~ ad un ordine** to carry out *o* execute an order; **letteratura d'~** escapist literature; **~ fiscale** tax evasion
eva'sivo, -a *ag* evasive
e'vaso, -a *pp di* **evadere** ■ *sm* escapee
eva'sore *sm*: **~ (fiscale)** tax evader
eveni'enza [eve'njɛntsa] *sf*: **nell'~ che ciò succeda** should that happen; **essere pronto ad ogni ~** to be ready for anything *o* any eventuality
e'vento *sm* event
eventu'ale *ag* possible
eventualità *sf inv* eventuality, possibility; **nell'~ di** in the event of
eventual'mente *av* if need be, if necessary
'Everest *sm*: **l'~, il Monte ~** (Mount) Everest
eversi'one *sf* subversion

ever'sivo, -a *ag* subversive
evi'dente *ag* evident, obvious
evidente'mente *av* evidently; *(palesemente)* obviously, evidently
evi'denza [evi'dɛntsa] *sf* obviousness; **mettere in ~** to point out, highlight; **tenere in ~** qc to bear sth in mind
evidenzi'are [eviden'tsjare] *vt (sottolineare)* to emphasize, highlight; *(con evidenziatore)* to highlight
evidenzia'tore [evidentsja'tore] *sm (penna)* highlighter
evi'rare *vt* to castrate
evi'tabile *ag* avoidable
evi'tare *vt* to avoid; **~ di fare** to avoid doing; **~ qc a qn** to spare sb sth
'evo *sm* age, epoch
evo'care *vt* to evoke
evoca'tivo, -a *ag* evocative
evocherò *etc* [evoke'rɔ] *vb vedi* **evocare**
evolu'tivo, -a *ag (gen, Biol)* evolutionary; *(Med)* progressive
evo'luto, -a *pp di* **evolversi** ■ *ag (popolo, civiltà)* (highly) developed, advanced; *(persona: emancipato)* independent; *(: senza pregiudizi)* broad-minded
evoluzi'one [evolut'tsjone] *sf* evolution
e'volversi *vr* to evolve; **con l'~ della situazione** as the situation develops
ev'viva *escl* hurrah!; **~ il re!** long live the king!, hurrah for the king!
ex *prefisso* ex-, former ■ *sm/f inv* ex-boyfriend/girlfriend
ex 'aequo [ɛg'zɛkwo] *av*: **classificarsi primo ~** to come joint first, come equal first
'extra *ag inv, sm inv* extra
extracomuni'tario, -a *ag* non-EEC ■ *sm/f* non-EEC national *(often referring to non-European immigrant)*
extraconiu'gale *ag* extramarital
extraparlamen'tare *ag* extraparliamentary
extrasensori'ale *ag*: **percezione ~** extrasensory perception
extrater'restre *ag, sm/f* extraterrestrial
extraur'bano, -a *ag* suburban

F, f ['ɛffe] *sf o m inv (lettera)* F, f; **F come Firenze** ≈ F for Frederick (*Brit*), F for Fox (*US*)

F *abbr* (= *Fahrenheit*) F

F. *abbr* (= *fiume*) R

fa *vb vedi* **fare** ■ *sm inv* (*Mus*) F; (: *solfeggiando la scala*) fa ■ *av*: **10 anni fa** 10 years ago

fabbi'sogno [fabbi'zoɲɲo] *sm* needs *pl*, requirements *pl*; **il ~ nazionale di petrolio** the country's oil requirements; **~ del settore pubblico** public sector borrowing requirement (*Brit*), government debt borrowing (*US*)

'fabbrica *sf* factory

fabbri'cante *sm* manufacturer, maker

fabbri'care *vt* to build; (*produrre*) to manufacture, make; (*fig*) to fabricate, invent

fabbri'cato *sm* building

fabbricazi'one [fabbrikat'tsjone] *sf* building, fabrication; making, manufacture, manufacturing

'fabbro *sm* (black)smith

fac'cenda [fat'tʃɛnda] *sf* matter, affair; (*cosa da fare*) task, chore; **le faccende domestiche** the housework *sg*

faccendi'ere [fattʃen'djɛre] *sm* wheeler-dealer, (shady) operator

fac'cetta [fat'tʃetta] *sf* (*di pietra preziosa*) facet

fac'chino [fak'kino] *sm* porter

'faccia, -ce ['fattʃa] *sf* face; (*di moneta, medaglia*) side; **~ a ~** face to face; **di ~ a** opposite, facing; **avere la ~ (tosta) di dire/ fare qc** to have the cheek o nerve to say/do sth; **fare qc alla ~ di qn** to do sth to spite sb; **leggere qc in ~ a qn** to see sth written all over sb's face

facci'ata [fat'tʃata] *sf* façade; (*di pagina*) side

'faccio *etc* ['fattʃo] *vb vedi* **fare**

fac'cina [fat'tʃina] *sf* (*Comput*) emoticon

fa'cente [fa'tʃente]: **~ funzione** *sm* (*Amm*) deputy

fa'cessi *etc* [fa'tʃessi] *vb vedi* **fare**

fa'ceto, -a [fa'tʃeto] *ag* witty, humorous

fa'cevo *etc* [fa'tʃevo] *vb vedi* **fare**

fa'cezia [fa'tʃɛttsja] *sf* witticism, witty remark

fa'chiro [fa'kiro] *sm* fakir

'facile ['fatʃile] *ag* easy; (*affabile*) easy-going; (*disposto*): **~ a** inclined to, prone to; (*probabile*): **è ~ che piova** it's likely to rain; **donna di facili costumi** woman of easy virtue, loose woman

facilità [fatʃili'ta] *sf* easiness; (*disposizione, dono*) aptitude

facili'tare [fatʃili'tare] *vt* to make easier

facilitazi'one [fatʃilitat'tsjone] *sf* (*gen*) facilities *pl*; **facilitazioni di pagamento** easy terms, credit facilities

facil'mente [fatʃil'mente] *av* (*gen*) easily; (*probabilmente*) probably

faci'lone, -a [fatʃi'lone] *sm/f* (*peg*) happy-go-lucky person

facino'roso, -a [fatʃino'roso] *ag* violent

facoltà *sf inv* faculty; (*Chim*) property; (*autorità*) power

facolta'tivo, -a *ag* optional; (*fermata d'autobus*) request *cpd*

facol'toso, -a *ag* wealthy, rich

fac'simile *sm* facsimile

'faggio ['faddʒo] *sm* beech

fagi'ano [fa'dʒano] *sm* pheasant

fagio'lino [fadʒo'lino] *sm* French (*Brit*) o string bean

fagi'olo [fa'dʒɔlo] *sm* bean; **capitare a ~** to come at the right time

fagoci'tare [fagotʃi'tare] *vt* (*fig: industria etc*) to absorb, swallow up; (*scherzoso: cibo*) to devour

fa'gotto *sm* bundle; (*Mus*) bassoon; **far ~** (*fig*) to pack up and go

'fai *vb vedi* **fare**

'faida *sf* feud

'fai-da-'te *sm inv* DIY, do-it-yourself

fa'ina *sf* (*Zool*) stone marten

'Fahrenheit ['faːrənheit] *sm* Fahrenheit

fa'lange [fa'landʒe] *sf* (*Anat, Mil*) phalanx

fal'cata *sf* stride

falce ['faltʃe] sf scythe; ~ **e martello** (Pol) hammer and sickle

fal'cetto [fal'tʃetto] sm sickle

falci'are [fal'tʃare] vt to cut; (fig) to mow down

falcia'trice [faltʃa'tritʃe] sf (per fieno) reaping machine; (per erba) mowing machine

'falco, -chi sm (anche fig) hawk

fal'cone sm falcon

'falda sf (Geo) layer, stratum; (di cappello) brim; (di cappotto) tails pl; (di monte) lower slope; (di tetto) pitch; (di neve) flake; **abito a falde** tails pl

fale'gname [faleɲ'ɲame] sm joiner

fa'lena sf (Zool) moth

'Falkland ['fɔːlklənd] sfpl: **le isole ~** the Falkland Islands

fal'lace [fal'latʃe] ag misleading, deceptive

'fallico, -a, ci, che ag phallic

fallimen'tare ag (Comm) bankruptcy cpd; **bilancio ~** negative balance, deficit; **diritto ~** bankruptcy law

falli'mento sm failure; bankruptcy

fal'lire vi (non riuscire): ~ **(in)** to fail (in); (Dir) to go bankrupt ■ vt (colpo, bersaglio) to miss

fal'lito, -a ag unsuccessful; bankrupt ■ sm/f bankrupt

'fallo sm error, mistake; (imperfezione) defect, flaw; (Sport) foul; fault; (Anat) phallus; **senza ~** without fail; **cogliere qn in ~** to catch sb out; **mettere il piede in ~** to slip

fal'locrate sm male chauvinist

falò sm inv bonfire

fal'sare vt to distort, misrepresent

falsa'riga, -ghe sf lined page, ruled page; **sulla ~ di ...** (fig) along the lines of ...

fal'sario sm forger; counterfeiter

falsifi'care vt to forge; (monete) to forge, counterfeit

falsità sf inv (di persona, notizia) falseness; (bugia) falsehood, lie

'falso, -a ag false; (errato) wrong; (falsificato) forged; fake; (: oro, gioielli) imitation cpd ■ sm forgery; **essere un ~ magro** to be heavier than one looks; **giurare il ~** to commit perjury; **~ in atto pubblico** forgery (of a legal document)

'fama sf fame; (reputazione) reputation, name

'fame sf hunger; **aver ~** to be hungry; **fare la ~** (fig) to starve, exist at subsistence level

fa'melico, -a, ci, che ag ravenous

famige'rato, -a [famidʒe'rato] ag notorious, ill-famed

fa'miglia [fa'miʎʎa] sf family

famili'are ag (della famiglia) family cpd; (ben noto) familiar; (rapporti, atmosfera) friendly; (Ling) informal, colloquial ■ sm/f relative, relation; **una vettura ~** a family car

familiarità sf familiarity; friendliness; informality

familiariz'zare [familjarid'dzare] vi: ~ **con qn** to get to know sb; **abbiamo familiarizzato subito** we got on well together from the start

fa'moso, -a ag famous, well-known

fa'nale sm (Aut) light, lamp (Brit); (luce stradale, Naut) light; (di faro) beacon

fa'natico, -a, ci, che ag fanatical; (del teatro, calcio etc): ~ **di** o **per** mad o crazy about ■ sm/f fanatic; (tifoso) fan

fana'tismo sm fanaticism

fanciul'lezza [fantʃul'lettsa] sf childhood

fanci'ullo, -a [fan'tʃullo] sm/f child

fan'donia sf tall story; **fandonie** sfpl nonsense sg

fan'fara sf brass band; (musica) fanfare

fanfa'rone sm braggart

fan'ghiglia [fan'giʎʎa] sf mire, mud

'fango, -ghi sm mud; **fare i fanghi** (Med) to take a course of mud baths

fan'goso, -a ag muddy

'fanno vb vedi **fare**

fannul'lone, -a sm/f idler, loafer

fantasci'enza [fantaʃ'ʃentsa] sf science fiction

fanta'sia sf fantasy, imagination; (capriccio) whim, caprice ■ ag inv: **vestito ~** patterned dress

fantasi'oso, -a ag (dotato di fantasia) imaginative; (bizzarro) fanciful, strange

fan'tasma, -i sm ghost, phantom

fantasti'care vi to daydream

fantastiche'ria [fantastike'ria] sf daydream

fan'tastico, -a, ci, che ag fantastic; (potenza, ingegno) imaginative

'fante sm infantryman; (Carte) jack, knave (Brit)

fante'ria sf infantry

fan'tino sm jockey

fan'toccio [fan'tɔttʃo] sm puppet

fanto'matico, -a, ci, che ag (nave, esercito) phantom cpd; (personaggio) mysterious

FAO sigla f FAO (= Food and Agriculture Organization)

fara'butto sm crook

fara'ona sf guinea fowl

fara'one sm (Storia) Pharaoh

fara'onico, -a, ci, che ag of the Pharaohs; (fig) enormous, huge

far'cire [far'tʃire] vt (carni, peperoni etc) to stuff; (torte) to fill

fard [far] sm inv blusher

far'dello sm bundle; (fig) burden

PAROLA CHIAVE

fare *sm* 1 (*modo di fare*): **con fare distratto** absent-mindedly; **ha un fare simpatico** he has a pleasant manner
2: **sul far del giorno/della notte** at daybreak/nightfall

■ *vt* 1 (*fabbricare, creare*) to make; (: *casa*) to build; (: *assegno*) to make out; **fare una promessa/un film** to make a promise/a film; **fare rumore** to make a noise
2 (*effettuare: lavoro, attività, studi*) to do; (: *sport*) to play; **cosa fa?** (*adesso*) what are you doing?; (*di professione*) what do you do?; **fare psicologia/italiano** to do psychology/Italian; **fare tennis** to play tennis; **fare un viaggio** to go on a trip *o* journey; **fare una passeggiata** to go for a walk; **fare la spesa** to do the shopping
3 (*funzione*) to be; (*Teat*) to play; **fare il medico** to be a doctor; **fare il malato** (*fingere*) to act the invalid
4 (*suscitare: sentimenti*): **fare paura a qn** to frighten sb; **mi fa rabbia** it makes me angry; **(non) fa niente** (*non importa*) it doesn't matter
5 (*ammontare*): **3 più 3 fa 6** 3 and 3 are *o* make 6; **fanno 6 euro** that's 6 euros; **Roma fa oltre 2.000.000 di abitanti** Rome has over 2,000,000 inhabitants; **che ora fai?** what time do you make it?
6 (+ *infinito*): **far fare qc a qn** (*obbligare*) to make sb do sth; (*permettere*) to let sb do sth; **fare piangere/ridere qn** to make sb cry/laugh; **fare venire qn** to send for sb; **fammi vedere** let me see; **far partire il motore** to start (up) the engine; **far riparare la macchina/costruire una casa** to get *o* have the car repaired/a house built
7: **farsi: farsi una gonna** to make o.s. a skirt; **farsi un nome** to make a name for o. s.; **farsi la permanente** to get a perm; **farsi notare** to get o.s. noticed; **farsi tagliare i capelli** to get one's hair cut; **farsi operare** to have an operation
8 (*fraseologia*): **farcela** to succeed, manage; **non ce la faccio più** I can't go on; **ce la faremo** we'll make it; **me l'hanno fatta!** I've been done!; **lo facevo più giovane** I thought he was younger; **fare sì/no con la testa** to nod/shake one's head

■ *vi* 1 (*agire*) to act, do; **fate come volete** do as you like; **fare presto** to be quick; **fare da** to act as; **non c'è niente da fare** it's no use; **saperci fare con qn/qc** to know how to deal with sb/sth; **ci sa fare** she's very good at it; **faccia pure!** go ahead!

2 (*dire*) to say; **"davvero?" fece** "really?" he said
3: **fare per** (*essere adatto*) to be suitable for; **fare per fare qc** to be about to do sth; **fece per andarsene** he made as if to leave
4: **farsi: si fa così** you do it like this, this is the way it's done; **non si fa così!** (*rimprovero*) that's no way to behave!; **la festa non si fa** the party is off
5: **fare a gara con qn** to compete with sb; **fare a pugni** to come to blows; **fare in tempo a fare** to be in time to do

■ *vb impers*: **fa bel tempo** the weather is fine; **fa caldo/freddo** it's hot/cold; **fa notte** it's getting dark

■ **farsi** *vr* 1 (*diventare*) to become; **farsi prete** to become a priest; **farsi grande/vecchio** to grow tall/old
2 (*spostarsi*): **farsi avanti/indietro** to move forward/back; **fatti più in là** move along a bit
3 (*fam: drogarsi*) to be a junkie

fa'retra *sf* quiver
far'falla *sf* butterfly
farfugli'are [farfuʎ'ʎare] *vt, vi* to mumble, mutter
fa'rina *sf* flour; ~ **gialla** maize (*Brit*) *o* corn (*US*) flour; ~ **integrale** wholemeal (*Brit*) *o* whole-wheat (*US*) flour; **questa non è ~ del tuo sacco** (*fig*) this isn't your own idea (*o* work)
fari'nacei [fari'natʃei] *smpl* starches
fa'ringe [fa'rindʒe] *sf* (*Anat*) pharynx
farin'gite [farin'dʒite] *sf* pharyngitis
fari'noso, -a *ag* (*patate*) floury; (*neve, mela*) powdery
farma'ceutico, -a, ci, che [farma'tʃeutiko] *ag* pharmaceutical
farma'cia, -cie [farma'tʃia] *sf* pharmacy; (*negozio*) chemist's (shop) (*Brit*), pharmacy
farma'cista, -i, e [farma'tʃista] *sm/f* chemist (*Brit*), pharmacist
farmaco (*pl* **farmaci** *o* **farmachi**) *sm* drug, medicine
farneti'care *vi* to rave, be delirious
faro *sm* (*Naut*) lighthouse; (*Aer*) beacon; (*Aut*) headlight, headlamp (*Brit*)
farragi'noso, -a [farradʒi'noso] *ag* (*stile*) muddled, confused
farsa *sf* farce
far'sesco, -a, schi, sche *ag* farcical
fasc. *abbr* = **fascicolo**
fascia, -sce ['faʃʃa] *sf* band, strip; (*Med*) bandage; (*di sindaco, ufficiale*) sash; (*parte di territorio*) strip, belt; (*di contribuenti etc*) group, band; **essere in fasce** (*anche fig*) to be in one's infancy; ~ **oraria** time band

f

135

fasci'are [faʃʃare] vt to bind; (Med) to bandage; (bambino) to put a nappy (Brit) o diaper (US) on

fascia'tura [faʃʃa'tura] sf (azione) bandaging; (fascia) bandage

fa'scicolo [faʃʃikolo] sm (di documenti) file, dossier; (di rivista) issue, number; (opuscolo) booklet, pamphlet

'fascino ['faʃʃino] sm charm, fascination

'fascio ['faʃʃo] sm bundle, sheaf; (di fiori) bunch; (di luce) beam; (Pol): **il F~** the Fascist Party

fa'scismo [faʃʃizmo] sm fascism

fa'scista, -i, e [faʃʃista] ag, sm/f fascist

'fase sf phase; (Tecn) stroke; **in ~ di espansione** in a period of expansion; **essere fuori ~** (motore) to be rough (Brit), run roughly; (fig) to feel rough (Brit) o rotten

fas'tidio sm bother, trouble; **dare ~ a qn** to bother o annoy sb; **sento ~ allo stomaco** my stomach's upset; **avere fastidi con la polizia** to have trouble o bother with the police

fastidi'oso, -a ag annoying, tiresome; (schifiltoso) fastidious

'fasto sm pomp, splendour (Brit), splendor (US)

fas'toso, -a ag sumptuous, lavish

fa'sullo, -a ag (gen) fake; (dichiarazione, persona) false; (pretesto) bogus

'fata sf fairy

fa'tale ag fatal; (inevitabile) inevitable; (fig) irresistible

fata'lismo sm fatalism

fatalità sf inv inevitability; (avversità) misfortune; (fato) fate, destiny

fa'tato, -a ag (spada, chiave) magic; (castello) enchanted

fa'tica, -che sf hard work, toil; (sforzo) effort; (di metalli) fatigue; **a ~** with difficulty; **respirare a ~** to have difficulty (in) breathing; **fare ~ a fare qc** to find it difficult to do sth; **animale da ~** beast of burden

fati'caccia, -ce [fati'kattʃa] sf: **fu una ~** it was hard work, it was a hell of a job (fam)

fati'care vi to toil; **~ a fare qc** to have difficulty doing sth

fati'cata sf hard work

fa'tichi etc [fa'tiki] vb vedi **faticare**

fati'coso, -a ag (viaggio, camminata) tiring, exhausting; (lavoro) laborious

fa'tidico, -a, ci, che ag fateful

'fato sm fate, destiny

Fatt. abbr (= fattura) inv

fat'taccio [fat'tattʃo] sm foul deed

fat'tezze [fat'tettse] sfpl features

fat'tibile ag feasible, possible

fattis'pecie [fattis'petʃe] sf: **nella o in ~ in** this case o instance

'fatto, -a pp di **fare** ■ ag: **un uomo ~** a grown man ■ sm fact; (azione) deed; (avvenimento) event, occurrence; (di romanzo, film) action, story; **~ a mano/in casa** hand-/home-made; **è ben fatta** she has a nice figure; **cogliere qn sul ~** to catch sb red-handed; **il ~ sta o è che** the fact remains o is that; **in ~ di** as for, as far as ... is concerned; **fare i fatti propri** to mind one's own business; **è uno che sa il ~ suo** he knows what he's about; **gli ho detto il ~ suo** I told him what I thought of him; **porre qn di fronte al ~ compiuto** to present sb with a fait accompli; **coppia/ unione di ~** long-standing relationship

fat'tore sm (Agr) farm manager; (Mat: elemento costitutivo) factor

fatto'ria sf farm; (casa) farmhouse

fatto'rino sm errand boy; (di ufficio) office boy; (d'albergo) porter

fattucchi'era [fattuk'kjera] sf witch

fat'tura sf (Comm) invoice; (di abito) tailoring; (malia) spell; **pagamento contro presentazione ~** payment on invoice

fattu'rare vt (Comm) to invoice; (prodotto) to produce; (vino) to adulterate

fattu'rato sm (Comm) turnover

fatturazi'one [fatturat'tsjone] sf billing, invoicing

'fatuo, -a ag vain, fatuous; **fuoco ~** (anche fig) will-o'-the-wisp

'fauci ['fautʃi] sfpl (di leone etc) jaws; (di vulcano) mouth sg

'fauna sf fauna

'fausto, -a ag (formale) happy; **un ~ presagio** a good omen

fau'tore, -'trice sm/f advocate, supporter

'fava sf broad bean

fa'vella sf speech

fa'villa sf spark

'favo sm (di api) honeycomb

'favola sf (fiaba) fairy tale; (d'intento morale) fable; (fandonia) yarn; **essere la ~ del paese** (oggetto di critica) to be the talk of the town; (zimbello) to be a laughing stock

favo'loso, -a ag fabulous; (incredibile) incredible

fa'vore sm favour (Brit), favor (US); **per ~** please; **prezzo/trattamento di ~** preferential price/treatment; **condizioni di ~** (Comm) favo(u)rable terms; **fare un ~ a qn** to do sb a favo(u)r; **col ~ delle tenebre** under cover of darkness

favoreggia'mento [favoreddʒa'mento] sm (Dir) aiding and abetting

favo'revole *ag* favourable (*Brit*), favorable (*US*)

favo'rire *vt* to favour (*Brit*), favor (*US*); (*il commercio, l'industria, le arti*) to promote, encourage; **vuole ~?** won't you help yourself?; **favorisca in salotto** please come into the sitting room; **mi favorisca i documenti** please may I see your papers?

favori'tismo *sm* favouritism (*Brit*), favoritism (*US*)

favo'rito, -a *ag, sm/f* favourite (*Brit*), favorite (*US*)

fax *sm inv* fax; **mandare qc via ~** to fax sth

fa'xare *vt* to fax

fazi'one [fat'tsjone] *sf* faction

faziosità [fattsjosi'ta] *sf* sectarianism

fazzo'letto [fattso'letto] *sm* handkerchief; (*per la testa*) (*head*)scarf

F.B.I. *sigla f* (= *Federal Bureau of Investigation*) FBI

F.C. *abbr* = **fuoricorso**

f.co *abbr* = **franco**

FE *sigla* = **Ferrara**

febb. *abbr* (= *febbraio*) Feb

feb'braio *sm* February; *vedi anche* **luglio**

'febbre *sf* fever; **aver la ~** to have a high temperature; **~ da fieno** hay fever

feb'brile *ag* (*anche fig*) feverish

feccia, -ce ['fettʃa] *sf* dregs *pl*

feci ['fɛtʃi] *sfpl* faeces, excrement *sg*

feci *etc* ['fɛtʃi] *vb vedi* **fare**

'fecola *sf* potato flour

fecon'dare *vt* to fertilize

fecondazi'one [fekondat'tsjone] *sf* fertilization; **~ artificiale** artificial insemination

fecondità *sf* fertility

fe'condo, -a *ag* fertile

'Fedcom *sigla m* = **Fondo Europeo di Cooperazione Monetaria**

'fede *sf* (*credenza*) belief, faith; (*Rel*) faith; (*fiducia*) faith, trust; (*fedeltà*) loyalty; (*anello*) wedding ring; (*attestato*) certificate; **aver ~ in qn** to have faith in sb; **tener ~ a** (*ideale*) to remain loyal to; (*giuramento, promessa*) to keep; **in buona/cattiva ~** in good/bad faith; **"in ~"** (*Dir*) "in witness whereof"

fe'dele *ag* (*leale*): **~ (a)** faithful (to); (*veritiero*) true, accurate ■ *sm/f* follower; **i fedeli** (*Rel*) the faithful

fedeltà *sf* faithfulness; (*coniugale*) fidelity; (*esattezza: di copia, traduzione*) accuracy; **alta ~** (*Radio*) high fidelity

'federa *sf* pillowslip, pillowcase

fede'rale *ag* federal

federa'lismo *sm* (*Pol*) federalism

federa'lista, -i, e *ag, sm/f* (*Pol*) federalist

federazi'one [federat'tsjone] *sf* federation

Feder'caccia [feder'kattʃa] *abbr f* (= *Federazione Italiana della Caccia*) hunting federation

Feder'calcio [feder'kaltʃo] *abbr m* (= *Federazione Italiana Gioco Calcio*) Italian football association

Federcon'sorzi [federkon'sɔrtsi] *abbr f* (= *Federazione Italiana dei Consorzi Agrari*) federation of farmers' cooperatives

fe'difrago, -a, ghi, ghe *ag* faithless, perfidious

fe'dina *sf* (*Dir*): **~ (penale)** record; **avere la ~ penale sporca** to have a police record

'fegato *sm* liver; (*fig*) guts *pl*, nerve; **mangiarsi** *o* **rodersi il ~** to be consumed with rage

'felce ['feltʃe] *sf* fern

fe'lice [fe'litʃe] *ag* happy; (*fortunato*) lucky

felicità [felitʃi'ta] *sf* happiness

felici'tarsi [felitʃi'tarsi] *vr* (*congratularsi*): **~ con qn per qc** to congratulate sb on sth

felicitazi'oni [felitʃitat'tsjoni] *sfpl* congratulations

fe'lino, -a *ag, sm* feline

'felpa *sf* sweatshirt

fel'pato, -a *ag* (*tessuto*) brushed; (*passo*) stealthy; **con passo ~** stealthily

'feltro *sm* felt

'femmina *sf* (*Zool, Tecn*) female; (*figlia*) girl, daughter; (*spesso peg*) woman

femmi'nile *ag* feminine; (*sesso*) female; (*lavoro, giornale*) woman's, women's; (*moda*) women's ■ *sm* (*Ling*) feminine

femminilità *sf* femininity

femmi'nismo *sm* feminism

femmi'nista, -i, e *ag, sm/f* feminist

'femore *sm* thighbone, femur

'fendere *vt* to cut through

fendi'nebbia *sm* (*Aut*) fog lamp

fendi'tura *sf* (*gen*) crack; (*di roccia*) cleft, crack

fe'nomeno *sm* phenomenon

'feretro *sm* coffin

feri'ale *ag*: **giorno ~** weekday, working day

'ferie *sfpl* holidays (*Brit*), vacation *sg* (*US*); **andare in ~** to go on holiday *o* vacation; **25 giorni di ~ pagate** 25 days' holiday *o* vacation with pay

feri'mento *sm* wounding

fe'rire *vt* to injure; (*deliberatamente: Mil etc*) to wound; (*colpire*) to hurt; **ferirsi** *vr* to hurt o.s., injure o.s.

fe'rito, -a *sm/f* wounded *o* injured man/ woman ■ *sf* injury; wound

feri'toia *sf* slit

'ferma *sf* (*Mil*) (period of) service; (*Caccia*): **cane da ~** pointer

ferma'carte *sm inv* paperweight

fermacra'vatta *sm inv* tiepin (*Brit*), tie tack (*US*)

f

137

fer'maglio [fer'maʎʎo] *sm* clasp; (*gioiello*) brooch; (*per documenti*) clip

ferma'mente *av* firmly

fer'mare *vt* to stop, halt; (*Polizia*) to detain, hold; (*bottone etc*) to fasten, fix ■ *vi* to stop; **fermarsi** *vr* to stop, halt; **fermarsi a fare qc** to stop to do sth

fer'mata *sf* stop; ~ **dell'autobus** bus stop

fermen'tare *vi* to ferment; (*fig*) to be in a ferment

fermentazi'one [fermentat'tsjone] *sf* fermentation

fer'mento *sm* (*anche fig*) ferment; (*lievito*) yeast; **fermenti lattici** probiotics, probiotic bacteria

fer'mezza [fer'mettsa] *sf* (*fig*) firmness, steadfastness

'fermo, -a *ag* still, motionless; (*veicolo*) stationary; (*orologio*) not working; (*saldo: anche fig*) firm; (*voce, mano*) steady ■ *escl* stop!; keep still! ■ *sm* (*chiusura*) catch, lock; (*Dir*): ~ **di polizia** police detention; ~ **restando che ...** it being understood that ...

'fermo 'posta *av, sm inv* poste restante (Brit), general delivery (US)

fe'roce [fe'rɔtʃe] *ag* (*animale*) wild, fierce, ferocious; (*persona*) cruel, fierce; (*fame, dolore*) raging

fe'rocia, -cie [fe'rɔtʃa] *sf* ferocity

Ferr. *abbr* = **ferrovia**

fer'raglia [fer'raʎʎa] *sf* scrap iron

ferra'gosto *sm* (*festa*) feast of the Assumption; (*periodo*) August holidays *pl* (Brit) *o* vacation (US); *see note*

● **FERRAGOSTO**

Ferragosto, 15 August, is a national holiday. Marking the feast of the Assumption, its origins are religious but in recent years it has simply become the most important public holiday of the summer season. Most people take some extra time off work and head out of town to the holiday resorts. Consequently, most of industry and commerce grinds to a standstill.

ferra'menta *sfpl* ironmongery *sg* (Brit), hardware *sg*; **negozio di** ~ ironmonger's (Brit), hardware shop *o* store (US)

fer'rare *vt* (*cavallo*) to shoe

fer'rato, -a *ag* (Ferr): **strada ferrata** railway line (Brit), railroad line (US); (*fig*): **essere ~ in** (*materia*) to be well up in

ferra'vecchio [ferra'vɛkkjo] *sm* scrap merchant

'ferreo, -a *ag* iron *cpd*

ferri'era *sf* ironworks *inv*

'ferro *sm* iron; **una bistecca ai ferri** a grilled steak; **mettere a ~ e fuoco** to put to the sword; **essere ai ferri corti** (*fig*) to be at daggers drawn; **tocca ~!** touch wood!; ~ **battuto** wrought iron; ~ **di cavallo** horseshoe; ~ **da stiro** iron; **ferri da calza** knitting needles; **i ferri del mestiere** the tools of the trade

ferrotranvi'ario, -a *ag* public transport *cpd*

Ferrotranvi'eri *abbr f* (= *Federazione Nazionale Lavoratori Autoferrotranvieri e Internavigatori*) transport workers' union

ferro'vecchio [ferro'vɛkkjo] *sm* = **ferravecchio**

ferro'via *sf* railway (Brit), railroad (US)

ferrovi'ario, -a *ag* railway *cpd* (Brit), railroad *cpd* (US)

ferrovi'ere *sm* railwayman (Brit), railroad man (US)

'fertile *ag* fertile

fertilità *sf* fertility

fertiliz'zante [fertilid'dzante] *sm* fertilizer

fertiliz'zare [fertilid'dzare] *vt* to fertilize

fer'vente *ag* fervent, ardent

'fervere *vi*: **fervono i preparativi per ...** they are making feverish preparations for ...

'fervido, -a *ag* fervent, ardent

fer'vore *sm* fervour (Brit), fervor (US), ardour (Brit), ardor (US); (*punto culminante*) height

'fesa *sf* (*Cuc*) rump of veal

fesse'ria *sf* stupidity; **dire fesserie** to talk nonsense

'fesso, -a *pp di* **fendere** ■ *ag* (*fam: sciocco*) crazy, cracked

fes'sura *sf* crack, split; (*per gettone, moneta*) slot

'festa *sf* (*religiosa*) feast; (*pubblica*) holiday; (*compleanno*) birthday; (*onomastico*) name day; (*ricevimento*) celebration, party; **far ~** to have a holiday; (*far baldoria*) to live it up; **far ~ a qn** to give sb a warm welcome; **essere vestito a ~** to be dressed up to the nines; ~ **comandata** (*Rel*) holiday of obligation; **la ~ della mamma/del papà** Mother's/Father's Day; **la F~ della Repubblica** *see note*

● **FESTA DELLA REPUBBLICA**

The *Festa della Repubblica*, 2 June, celebrates the founding of the Italian Republic after the fall of the monarchy and the subsequent referendum in 1946. It is marked by military parades and political speeches.

festeggia'menti [festeddʒa'menti] *smpl* celebrations

festeggi·are [fested'dʒare] vt to celebrate; (persona) to have a celebration for

fes·tino sm party; (con balli) ball

fes·tivo, -a ag (atmosfera) festive; **giorno ~** holiday

fes·toso, -a ag merry, joyful

fe·tente ag (puzzolente) fetid; (comportamento) disgusting ■ sm/f (fam) stinker, rotter (Brit)

fe·ticcio [fe'tittʃo] sm fetish

'feto sm foetus (Brit), fetus (US)

fe·tore sm stench, stink

'fetta sf slice

fet·tuccia, -ce [fet'tuttʃa] sf tape, ribbon

fettuc·cine [fettut'tʃine] sfpl (Cuc) ribbon-shaped pasta

feu·dale ag feudal

'feudo sm (Storia) fief; (fig) stronghold

ff abbr (Amm) = **facente funzione**; (= fogli) pp

FF.AA abbr = **forze armate**

FG sigla = **Foggia**

FI sigla = **Firenze** ■ abbr = **Forza Italia**

fi·aba sf fairy tale

fia·besco, -a, schi, sche ag fairy-tale cpd

fi·acca sf weariness; (svogliatezza) listlessness; **battere la ~** to shirk

fiac·care vt to weaken

fiacche·rò etc [fjakke'rɔ] vb vedi **fiaccare**

fi·acco, -a, chi, che ag (stanco) tired, weary; (svogliato) listless; (debole) weak; (mercato) slack

fi·accola sf torch

fiacco·lata sf torchlight procession

fi·ala sf phial

fi·amma sf flame; (Naut) pennant

fiam·mante ag (colore) flaming; **nuovo ~** brand new

fiam·mata sf blaze

fiammeggi·are [fjammed'dʒare] vi to blaze

fiam·mifero sm match

fiam·mingo, -a, ghi, ghe ag Flemish ■ sm/f Fleming ■ sm (Ling) Flemish; (Zool) flamingo; **i Fiamminghi** the Flemish

fian·cata sf (di nave etc) side; (Naut) broadside

fiancheggi·are [fjanked'dʒare] vt to border; (fig) to support, back (up); (Mil) to flank

fi·anco, -chi sm side; (di persona) hip; (Mil) flank; **di ~** sideways, from the side; **a ~ a ~** side by side; **prestare il proprio ~ alle critiche** to leave o.s. open to criticism; **~ destr/sinistr!** (Mil) right/left turn!

Fi·andre sfpl: **le ~** Flanders sg

fiaschette·ria [fjaskette'ria] sf wine shop

fi·asco, -schi sm flask; (fig) fiasco; **fare ~** to be a fiasco

fia·tare vi (fig: parlare): **senza ~** without saying a word

fi·ato sm breath; (resistenza) stamina; **fiati** smpl (Mus) wind instruments; **avere il ~**

grosso to be out of breath; **prendere ~** to catch one's breath; **bere qc tutto d'un ~** to drink sth in one go o gulp

'fibbia sf buckle

'fibra sf fibre, fiber (US); (fig) constitution; **~ ottica** optical fibre; **~ di vetro** fibreglass (Brit), fiberglass (US)

ficca·naso (mpl **ficcanasi**, fpl **~**) sm/f busybody, nos(e)y parker

fic·care vt to push, thrust, drive; **ficcarsi** vr (andare a finire) to get to; **~ il naso negli affari altrui** (fig) to poke o stick one's nose into other people's business; **ficcarsi nei pasticci o nei guai** to get into hot water o a fix

ficche·rò etc [fikke'rɔ] vb vedi **ficcare**

fiche [fiʃ] sf inv (nei giochi d'azzardo) chip

'fico, -chi sm (pianta) fig tree; (frutto) fig; **~ d'India** prickly pear; **~ secco** dried fig

fiction ['fikʃon] sf inv TV drama

fidanza·mento [fidantsa'mento] sm engagement

fidan·zarsi [fidan'tsarsi] vr to get engaged

fidan·zato, -a [fidan'tsato] sm/f fiancé/fiancée

fi·darsi vr: **~ di** to trust; **~ è bene non ~ è meglio** (proverbio) better safe than sorry

fi·dato, -a ag reliable, trustworthy

fide·ismo sm unquestioning belief

fide·istico, -a, ci, che ag (atteggiamento, posizione) totally uncritical

fideius·sore sm (Dir) guarantor

fideliz·zare [fidelid'dzare] vt: **~ la clientela** to build customer loyalty; **fidelizzarsi** vr to stay loyal

'fido, -a ag faithful, loyal ■ sm (Comm) credit

fi·ducia [fi'dutʃa] sf confidence, trust; **incarico di ~** position of trust, responsible position; **persona di ~** reliable person; **è il mio uomo di ~** he is my right-hand man; **porre la questione di ~** (Pol) to ask for a vote of confidence

fiduci·oso, -a [fidu'tʃoso] ag trusting

fi·ele sm (Med) bile; (fig) bitterness

fie·nile sm hayloft

fi·eno sm hay

fi·era sf fair; (animale) wild beast; **~ di beneficenza** charity bazaar; **~ campionaria** trade fair

fie·rezza [fje'rettsa] sf pride

fi·ero, -a ag proud; (crudele) fierce, cruel; (audace) bold

fi·evole ag (luce) dim; (suono) weak

F.I.F.A. sigla f (= Fédération Internationale de Football Association) FIFA

'fifa sf (fam): **aver ~** to have the jitters

fi·fone, -a sm/f (fam, scherzoso) coward

fig. *abbr* (= *figura*) fig

FIGC *sigla f* (= *Federazione Italiana Gioco Calcio*) Italian football association

Figi ['fidʒi] *sfpl*: **le isole ~** Fiji, the Fiji Islands

figlia ['fiʎʎa] *sf* daughter; (*Comm*) counterfoil (*Brit*), stub

figliare [fiʎ'ʎare] *vi* to give birth

figliastro, -a [fiʎ'ʎastro] *sm/f* stepson(-daughter)

figlio ['fiʎʎo] *sm* son; (*senza distinzione di sesso*) child; **~ d'arte: essere ~ d'arte** to come from a theatrical (*o* musical *etc*) family; **~ di puttana** (*fam!*) son of a bitch (!); **~ unico** only child

figlioccio, -a, ci, ce [fiʎ'ʎɔttʃo] *sm/f* godchild, godson(-daughter)

figliola [fiʎ'ʎɔla] *sf* daughter; (*fig: ragazza*) girl

figliolo [fiʎ'ʎɔlo] *sm* (*anche fig: ragazzo*) son

figura *sf* figure; (*forma, aspetto esterno*) form, shape; (*illustrazione*) picture, illustration; **far ~** to look smart; **fare una brutta ~** to make a bad impression; **che ~!** how embarrassing!

figuraccia, -ce [figu'rattʃa] *sf*: **fare una ~** to create a bad impression

figurare *vi* to appear ■ *vt*: **figurarsi qc** to imagine sth; **figurarsi** *vr*: **figurati!** imagine that!; **ti do noia? — ma figurati!** am I disturbing you? — not at all!

figurativo, -a *ag* figurative

figurina *sf* (*statuetta*) figurine; (*cartoncino*) picture card

figurinista, -i, e *sm/f* dress designer

figurino *sm* fashion sketch

figuro *sm*: **un losco ~** a suspicious character

figurone *sm*: **fare un ~** (*persona, oggetto*) to look terrific; (*persona: con un discorso etc*) to make an excellent impression

fila *sf* row, line; (*coda*) queue; (*serie*) series, string; **di ~** in succession; **fare la ~** to queue; **in ~ indiana** in single file

filamento *sm* filament

filanca® *sf* stretch material

filanda *sf* spinning mill

filante *ag*: **stella ~** (*stella cadente*) shooting star; (*striscia di carta*) streamer

filantropia *sf* philanthropy

filantropico, -a, ci, che *ag* philanthropic(al)

filantropo *sm* philanthropist

filare *vt* to spin; (*Naut*) to pay out ■ *vi* (*baco, ragno*) to spin; (*formaggio fuso*) to go stringy; (*liquido*) to trickle; (*discorso*) to hang together; (*fam: amoreggiare*) to go steady; (*muoversi a forte velocità*) to go at full speed; (*andarsene lestamente*) to make o.s. scarce ■ *sm* (*di alberi etc*) row, line; **~ diritto** (*fig*) to toe the line

filarmonico, -a, ci, che *ag* philharmonic

filastrocca, -che *sf* nursery rhyme

filatelia *sf* philately, stamp collecting

filato, -a *ag* spun ■ *sm* yarn ■ *av*: **vai dritto ~ a casa** go straight home; **3 giorni filati** 3 days running *o* on end

filatura *sf* spinning; (*luogo*) spinning mill

filetto *sm* (*ornamento*) braid, trimming; (*di vite*) thread; (*di carne*) fillet

filiale *ag* filial ■ *sf* (*di impresa*) branch

filibustiere *sm* pirate; (*fig*) adventurer

filigrana *sf* (*in oreficeria*) filigree; (*su carta*) watermark

filippica *sf* invective

Filippine *sfpl*: **le ~** the Philippines

filippino, -a *ag, sm/f* Filipino

film *sm inv* film

filmare *vt* to film

filmato *sm* short film

filmina *sf* film strip

filo *sm* (*anche fig*) thread; (*filato*) yarn; (*metallico*) wire; (*di lama, rasoio*) edge; **con un ~ di voce** in a whisper; **un ~ d'aria** (*fig*) a breath of air; **dare del ~ da torcere a qn** to create difficulties for sb, make life difficult for sb; **fare il ~ a qn** (*corteggiare*) to be after sb, chase sb; **per ~ e per segno** in detail; **~ d'erba** blade of grass; **~ interdentale** dental floss; **~ di perle** string of pearls; **~ di Scozia** fine cotton yarn; **~ spinato** barbed wire

filoamericano, -a *ag* pro-American

filobus *sm inv* trolley bus

filodiffusione *sf* rediffusion

filodrammatico, -a, ci, che *ag*: **(compagnia) filodrammatica** amateur dramatic society ■ *sm/f* amateur actor/actress

filoncino [filon'tʃino] *sm* ≈ French stick

filone *sm* (*di minerali*) seam, vein; (*pane*) ≈ Vienna loaf; (*fig*) trend

filosofia *sf* philosophy

filosofico, -a, ci, che *ag* philosophical

filosofo, -a *sm/f* philosopher

filosovietico, -a, ci, che *ag* pro-Soviet

filovia *sf* (*linea*) trolley line; (*bus*) trolley bus

filtrare *vt, vi* to filter

filtro *sm* filter; (*pozione*) potion; **~ dell'olio** (*Aut*) oil filter

filza ['filtsa] *sf* (*anche fig*) string

FIN *sigla f* = Federazione Italiana Nuoto

fin *av, prep* = **fino**

finale *ag* final ■ *sm* (*di libro, film*) end, ending; (*Mus*) finale ■ *sf* (*Sport*) final

finalista, -i, e *sm/f* finalist

finalità *sf* (*scopo*) aim, purpose

finalizzare [finalid'dzare] *vt*: **~ a** to direct towards

finalmente *av* finally, at last

fi'nanza [fi'nantsa] *sf* finance; **finanze** *sfpl* (*di individuo, Stato*) finances; (**Guardia di**) ~ (*di frontiera*) ≈ Customs and Excise (*Brit*), ≈ Customs Service (*US*); (**Intendenza di**) ~ ≈ Inland Revenue (*Brit*), ≈ Internal Revenue Service (*US*); **Ministro delle finanze** Minister of Finance, ≈ Chancellor of the Exchequer (*Brit*), ≈ Secretary of the Treasury (*US*)

finanzia'mento [finantsja'mento] *sm* (*azione*) financing; (*denaro fornito*) funds *pl*

finanzi'are [finan'tsjare] *vt* to finance, fund

finanzi'ario, -a [finan'tsjarjo] *ag* financial ■ *sf* (*anche:* **società finanziaria**) investment company; (*anche:* **legge finanziaria**) finance act, ≈ budget (*Brit*)

finanzia'tore, -'trice *ag:* **ente ~, società finanziatrice** backer ■ *sm/f* backer

finanzi'ere [finan'tsjere] *sm* financier; (*guardia di finanza: doganale*) customs officer; (: *tributaria*) Inland Revenue official (*Brit*), Internal Revenue official (*US*)

finché [fin'ke] *cong* (*per tutto il tempo che*) as long as; (*fino al momento in cui*) until; ~ **vorrai** as long as you like; **aspetta ~ non esca** wait until he goes (*o* comes) out

'fine *ag* (*lamina, carta*) thin; (*capelli, polvere*) fine; (*vista, udito*) keen, sharp; (*persona: raffinata*) refined, distinguished; (*osservazione*) subtle ■ *sf* end ■ *sm* aim, purpose; (*esito*) result, outcome; **in** *o* **alla ~** in the end, finally; **alla fin ~** at the end of the day, in the end; **che ~ ha fatto?** what became of him?; **buona ~ e buon principio!** (*augurio*) happy New Year!; **a fin di bene** with the best of intentions; **al ~ di fare qc** (in order) to do sth; **condurre qc a buon ~** to bring sth to a successful conclusion; **secondo ~** ulterior motive

fine setti'mana *sm o f inv* weekend

fi'nestra *sf* window

fines'trino *sm* (*di treno, auto*) window

fi'nezza [fi'nettsa] *sf* thinness; fineness; keenness; sharpness; refinement; subtlety

'fingere ['findʒere] *vt* to feign; (*supporre*) to imagine, suppose; **fingersi** *vr:* **fingersi ubriaco/pazzo** to pretend to be drunk/crazy; ~ **di fare** to pretend to do

fini'menti *smpl* (*di cavallo etc*) harness *sg*

fini'mondo *sm* pandemonium

fi'nire *vt* to finish ■ *vi* to finish, end ■ *sm:* **sul ~ della festa** towards the end of the party; ~ **di fare** (*compiere*) to finish doing; (*smettere*) to stop doing; ~ **in galera** to end up *o* finish up in prison; **farla finita** (*con la vita*) to put an end to one's life; **farla finita con qc** to have done with sth; **com'è andata a ~?** what happened in the end?; **finiscila!** stop it!

fini'tura *sf* finish

finlan'dese *ag* Finnish ■ *sm/f* Finn ■ *sm* (*Ling*) Finnish

Fin'landia *sf:* **la ~** Finland

'fino, -a *ag* (*capelli, seta*) fine; (*oro*) pure; (*fig: acuto*) shrewd ■ *av* (*spesso troncato in fin:* pure, anche) even ■ *prep* (*spesso troncato in fin: tempo*): **fin quando?** till when?; (: *luogo*) **fin qui** as far as here; ~ **a** (*tempo*) until, till; (*luogo*) as far as, (up) to; **fin da domani** from tomorrow onwards; **fin da ieri** since yesterday; **fin dalla nascita** from *o* since birth

fi'nocchio [fi'nɔkkjo] *sm* fennel; (*fam peg: pederasta*) queer

fi'nora *av* up till now

'finsi *etc vb vedi* **fingere**

'finto, -a *pp di* **fingere** ■ *ag* (*capelli, dente*) false; (*fiori*) artificial; (*cuoio, pelle*) imitation *cpd*; (*fig: simulato: pazzia etc*) feigned, sham ■ *sf* pretence (*Brit*), pretense (*US*), sham; (*Sport*) feint; **far finta (di fare)** to pretend (to do); **l'ho detto per finta** I was only pretending; (*per scherzo*) I was only kidding

finzi'one [fin'tsjone] *sf* pretence (*Brit*), pretense (*US*), sham

fioc'care *vi* (*neve*) to fall; (*fig: insulti etc*) to fall thick and fast

fi'occo, -chi *sm* (*di nastro*) bow; (*di stoffa, lana*) flock; (*di neve*) flake; (*Naut*) jib; **coi fiocchi** (*fig*) first-rate; **fiocchi di granoturco** cornflakes

fi'ocina ['fjɔtʃina] *sf* harpoon

fi'oco, -a, chi, che *ag* faint, dim

fi'onda *sf* catapult

fio'raio, -a *sm/f* florist

fiorda'liso *sm* (*Bot*) cornflower

fi'ordo *sm* fjord

fi'ore *sm* flower; **fiori** *smpl* (*Carte*) clubs; **nel ~ degli anni** in one's prime; **a fior d'acqua** on the surface of the water; **a fior di labbra** in a whisper; **aver i nervi a fior di pelle** to be on edge; **fior di latte** cream; **è costato fior di soldi** it cost a pretty penny; **il fior ~ della società** the cream of society; ~ **all'occhiello** feather in the cap; **fiori di campo** wild flowers

fio'rente *ag* (*industria, paese*) flourishing; (*salute*) blooming; (*petto*) ample

fioren'tino, -a *ag, sm/f* Florentine ■ *sf* (*Cuc*) T-bone steak

fio'retto *sm* (*Scherma*) foil

fio'rino *sm* florin

fio'rire *vi* (*rosa*) to flower; (*albero*) to blossom; (*fig*) to flourish

fio'rista, -i, e *sm/f* florist

fiori'tura *sf* (*di pianta*) flowering, blooming; (*di albero*) blossoming; (*fig: di commercio, arte*) flourishing; (*insieme dei fiori*) flowers *pl*; (*Mus*) fioritura

fi'otto *sm* (*di lacrime*) flow, flood; (*di sangue*) gush, spurt

FIPE *sigla f* = **Federazione Italiana Pubblici Esercizi**

Fi'renze [fi'rɛntse] *sf* Florence

firma *sf* signature; (*reputazione*) name

firma'mento *sm* firmament

fir'mare *vt* to sign

firma'tario, -a *sm/f* signatory

fisar'monica, -che *sf* accordion

fis'cale *ag* fiscal, tax *cpd*; (*meticoloso*) punctilious; **medico ~** *doctor employed by Social Security to verify cases of sick leave*

fisca'lista, -i, e *sm/f* tax consultant

fiscaliz'zare [fiskalid'dzare] *vt* to exempt from taxes

fischi'are [fis'kjare] *vi* to whistle ▪ *vt* to whistle; (*attore*) to boo, hiss; **mi fischian le orecchie** my ears are singing; (*fig*) my ears are burning

fischiet'tare [fiskjet'tare] *vi, vt* to whistle

fischi'etto [fis'kjetto] *sm* (*strumento*) whistle

fischio ['fiskjo] *sm* whistle; **prendere fischi per fiaschi** to get hold of the wrong end of the stick

fisco *sm* tax authorities *pl*, ≈ Inland Revenue (*Brit*), ≈ Internal Revenue Service (*US*)

fisica *sf vedi* **fisico**

fisica'mente *av* physically

fisico, -a, ci, che *ag* physical ▪ *sm/f* physicist ▪ *sm* physique ▪ *sf* physics *sg*

fisima *sf* fixation

fisiolo'gia [fizjolo'dʒia] *sf* physiology

fisiono'mia *sf* face, physiognomy

fisiotera'pia *sf* physiotherapy

fisiotera'pista *sm/f* physiotherapist

fis'saggio [fis'saddʒo] *sm* (*Fot*) fixing

fis'sante *ag* (spray, lozione) holding

fis'sare *vt* to fix, fasten; (*guardare intensamente*) to stare at; (*data, condizioni*) to fix, establish, set; (*prenotare*) to book; **fissarsi** *vr*: **fissarsi su** (*sguardo, attenzione*) to focus on; (*fig: idea*) to become obsessed with

fissazi'one [fissat'tsjone] *sf* (*Psic*) fixation

fissi'one *sf* fission

fisso, -a *ag* fixed; (*stipendio, impiego*) regular ▪ *av*: **guardar ~ qn/qc** to stare at sb/sth; **avere un ragazzo ~** to have a steady boyfriend; **senza fissa dimora** of no fixed abode; **telefono ~** landline

fitoterma'lismo *sm* herbal hydrotherapy

fitta *sf vedi* **fitto**

fit'tavolo *sm* tenant

fit'tizio, -a [fit'tittsjo] *ag* fictitious, imaginary

fitto, -a *ag* thick, dense; (*pioggia*) heavy ▪ *sm* (*affitto, pigione*) rent ▪ *sf* sharp pain; **una fitta al cuore** (*fig*) a pang of grief; **nel ~ del bosco** in the heart o depths of the wood

fiu'mana *sf* torrent; (*fig*) stream, flood

fi'ume *sm* river ▪ *ag inv*: **processo ~** long-running trial; **scorrere a fiumi** (*acqua, sangue*) to flow in torrents

fiu'tare *vt* to smell, sniff; (*animale*) to scent; (*fig: inganno*) to get wind of, smell; **~ tabacco** to take snuff; **~ cocaina** to snort cocaine

fi'uto *sm* (sense of) smell; (*fig*) nose

'flaccido, -a ['flattʃido] *ag* flabby

fla'cone *sm* bottle

flagel'lare [fladʒel'lare] *vt* to flog, scourge; (*onde*) to beat against

fla'gello [fla'dʒello] *sm* scourge

fla'grante *ag* flagrant; **cogliere qn in ~** to catch sb red-handed

fla'nella *sf* flannel

flash [flaʃ] *sm inv* (*Fot*) flash; (*giornalistico*) newsflash

flau'tista, -i *sm/f* flautist

'flauto *sm* flute

'flebile *ag* faint, feeble

fle'bite *sf* phlebitis

'flemma *sf* (*calma*) coolness, phlegm; (*Med*) phlegm

flem'matico, -a, ci, che *ag* phlegmatic, cool

fles'sibile *ag* pliable; (*fig: che si adatta*) flexible

flessi'one *sf* (*gen*) bending; (*Ginnastica: a terra*) sit-up; (*: in piedi*) forward bend; (*: sulle gambe*) knee-bend; (*diminuzione*) slight drop, slight fall; (*Ling*) inflection; **fare una ~** to bend; **una ~ economica** a downward trend in the economy

'flesso, -a *pp di* **flettere**

flessu'oso, -a *ag* supple, lithe; (*andatura*) flowing, graceful

'flettere *vt* to bend

'flipper ['flipper] *sm inv* pinball machine

flirt [flə:t] *sm inv* brief romance, flirtation

flir'tare *vi* to flirt

F.lli *abbr* (= *fratelli*) Bros

'flora *sf* flora

'florido, -a *ag* flourishing; (*fig*) glowing with health

'floscio, -a, sci, sce ['floʃʃo] *ag* (*cappello*) floppy, soft; (*muscoli*) flabby

'flotta *sf* fleet

flot'tante *sm* (*Econ*): **titoli a largo ~** blue chips, stocks on the market

'fluido, -a *ag, sm* fluid

flu'ire *vi* to flow

fluore'scente [fluoreʃʃɛnte] *ag* fluorescent

flu'oro *sm* fluorine

fluo'ruro *sm* fluoride

'**flusso** sm flow; (Fisica, Med) flux; ~ **e riflusso** ebb and flow; ~ **di cassa** (Comm) cash flow

'**flutti** smpl waves

fluttu'are vi to rise and fall; (Econ) to fluctuate

fluvi'ale ag river cpd, fluvial

FM abbr vedi **modulazione di frequenza**

FMI sigla m = **Fondo Monetario Internazionale**

FO sigla = **Forlì**

fo'bia sf phobia

'**foca, -che** sf (Zool) seal

fo'caccia, -ce [fo'kattʃa] sf kind of pizza; (dolce) bun; **rendere pan per** ~ to get one's own back, give tit for tat

fo'cale ag focal

focaliz'zare [fokalid'dzare] vt (Fot: immagine) to get into focus; (fig: situazione) to get into perspective; ~ **l'attenzione su** to focus one's attention on

foce ['fotʃe] sf (Geo) mouth

fo'chista, -i [fo'kista] sm (Ferr) stoker, fireman

foco'laio sm (Med) centre (Brit) o center (US) of infection; (fig) hotbed

foco'lare sm hearth, fireside; (Tecn) furnace

fo'coso, -a ag fiery; (cavallo) mettlesome, fiery

'**fodera** sf (di vestito) lining; (di libro, poltrona) cover

fode'rare vt to line; to cover

'**fodero** sm (di spada) scabbard; (di pugnale) sheath; (di pistola) holster

'**foga** sf enthusiasm, ardour (Brit), ardor (US)

'**foggia, -ge** ['fɔddʒa] sf (maniera) style; (aspetto) form, shape; (moda) fashion, style

foggi'are [fod'dʒare] vt to shape; to style

'**foglia** ['fɔʎʎa] sf leaf; **ha mangiato la** ~ (fig) he's caught on; ~ **d'argento/d'oro** silver/gold leaf

fogli'ame [foʎ'ʎame] sm foliage, leaves pl

fogli'etto [foʎ'ʎetto] sm (piccolo foglio) slip of paper, piece of paper; (manifestino) leaflet, handout

'**foglio** ['fɔʎʎo] sm (di carta) sheet (of paper); (di metallo) sheet; (documento) document; (banconota) (bank)note; ~ **di calcolo** spreadsheet; ~ **rosa** (Aut) provisional licence; ~ **di via** (Dir) expulsion order; ~ **volante** pamphlet

'**fogna** ['foɲɲa] sf drain, sewer

fogna'tura [foɲɲa'tura] sf drainage, sewerage

föhn [fø:n] sm inv hair-dryer

fo'lata sf gust

fol'clore sm folklore

folclo'ristico, -a, ci, che ag folk cpd

folgo'rare vt (fulmine) to strike down; (: alta tensione) to electrocute

folgorazi'one [folgorat'tsjone] sf electrocution; **ebbe una** ~ (fig: idea) he had a brainwave

'**folgore** sf thunderbolt

folksono'mia sf (Inform) folksonomy

'**folla** sf crowd, throng

'**folle** ag mad, insane; (Tecn) idle; **in** ~ (Aut) in neutral

fol'letto sm elf

fol'lia sf folly, foolishness; foolish act; (pazzia) madness, lunacy; **amare qn alla** ~ to love sb to distraction; **costare una** ~ to cost the earth

'**folto, -a** ag thick

fomen'tare vt to stir up, foment

fon sm inv = **föhn**

fon'dale sm (del mare) bottom; (Teat) backdrop; **il** ~ **marino** the sea bed

fondamen'tale ag fundamental, basic

fondamenta'lista, -i, e ag, sm/f (Rel) fundamentalist

fonda'mento sm foundation; **fondamenta** sfpl (Edil) foundations

fon'dare vt to found; (fig: dar base): ~ **qc su** to base sth on; **fondarsi** vr (teorie): **fondarsi (su)** to be based (on)

fonda'tezza [fonda'tettsa] sf (di ragioni) soundness; (di dubbio, sospetto) basis in fact

fon'dato, -a ag (ragioni) sound; (dubbio, sospetto) well-founded

fondazi'one [fondat'tsjone] sf foundation

fon'dente ag: **cioccolato** ~ plain o dark chocolate

'**fondere** vt (neve) to melt; (metallo) to fuse, melt; (fig: colori) to merge, blend; (: imprese, gruppi) to merge ■ vi to melt; **fondersi** vr to melt; (fig: partiti, correnti) to unite, merge

fonde'ria sf foundry

fondi'ario, -a ag land cpd

fon'dina sf (piatto fondo) soup plate; (portapistola) holster

'**fondo, -a** ag deep ■ sm (di recipiente, pozzo) bottom; (di stanza) back; (quantità di liquido che resta, deposito) dregs pl; (sfondo) background; (unità immobiliare) property, estate; (somma di denaro) fund; (Sport) long-distance race; **fondi** smpl (denaro) funds; **a notte fonda** at dead of night; **in** ~ **a** at the bottom of; at the back of; (strada) at the end of; **laggiù in** ~ (lontano) over there; (in profondità) down there; **in** ~ (fig) after all, all things considered; **andare fino in** ~ **a** (fig) to examine thoroughly; **andare a** ~ (nave) to sink; **conoscere a** ~ to know inside out; **dar** ~ **a** (fig: provvisti, soldi) to use up; **toccare il ~** (fig) to plumb the depths; **a ~ perduto** (Comm) without security; **~ comune di investimento** investment trust; **F~ Monetario Internazionale** International Monetary Fund; **~ di previdenza** social insurance fund; **~ di riserva** reserve fund; **~ urbano** town property; **fondi di caffè** coffee grounds; **fondi d'esercizio** working capital sg; **fondi liquidi** ready money sg, liquid assets; **fondi di magazzino** old o unsold stock sg; **fondi neri** slush fund sg

fondo'tinta sm inv (cosmetico) foundation

fo'nema sm phoneme

fo'netica sf phonetics sg

fo'netico, -a, ci, che ag phonetic

fon'tana sf fountain

fonta'nella sf drinking fountain

'fonte sf spring, source; (fig) source ■ sm: **~ battesimale** (Rel) font

fon'tina sm full fat hard, sweet cheese

'footing ['futiŋ] sm jogging

forag'giare [forad'dʒare] vt (cavalli) to fodder; (fig: partito etc) to bankroll

fo'raggio [fo'raddʒo] sm fodder, forage

fo'rare vt to pierce, make a hole in; (pallone) to burst; (pneumatico) to puncture; (biglietto) to punch; **forarsi** vr (gen) to develop a hole; (Aut, pallone, timpano) to burst; **~ una gomma** to burst a tyre (Brit) o tire (US)

fora'tura sf piercing; bursting; puncturing; punching

'forbici ['fɔrbitʃi] sfpl scissors

forbi'cina [forbi'tʃina] sf earwig

for'bito, -a ag (stile, modi) polished

'forca, -che sf (Agr) fork, pitchfork; (patibolo) gallows sg

for'cella [for'tʃɛlla] sf (Tecn) fork; (di monte) pass

for'chetta [for'ketta] sf fork; **essere una buona ~** to enjoy one's food

for'cina [for'tʃina] sf hairpin

'forcipe ['fɔrtʃipe] sm forceps pl

for'cone sm pitchfork

fo'rense ag (linguaggio) legal; **avvocato ~** barrister (Brit), lawyer

fo'resta sf forest; **la F~ Nera** the Black Forest

fores'tale ag forest cpd; **guardia ~** forester

foreste'ria sf (di convento, palazzo etc) guest rooms pl, guest quarters pl

foresti'ero, -a ag foreign ■ sm/f foreigner

for'fait [fɔr'fɛ] sm inv: **(prezzo a) ~** fixed price, set price; **dichiarare ~** (Sport) to withdraw; (fig) to give up

forfe'tario, -a ag: **prezzo ~** (da pagare) fixed o set price; (da ricevere) lump sum

'forfora sf dandruff

'forgia, -ge ['fɔrdʒa] sf forge

forgi'are [for'dʒare] vt to forge

'forma sf form; (aspetto esteriore) form, shape; (Dir: procedura) procedure; (per calzature) last; (stampo da cucina) mould (Brit), mold (US); **forme** sfpl (del corpo) figure, shape; **le forme** (convenzioni) appearances; **errori di ~** stylistic errors; **essere in ~** to be in good shape; **mantenersi in ~** to keep fit; **in ~ ufficiale/ privata** officially/privately; **una ~ di formaggio** a (whole) cheese

formag'gino [formad'dʒino] sm processed cheese

for'maggio [for'maddʒo] sm cheese

for'male ag formal

formalità sf inv formality

formaliz'zare [formalid'dzare] vt to formalize

for'mare vt to form, shape, make; (numero di telefono) to dial; (fig: carattere) to form, mould (Brit), mold (US); **formarsi** vr to form, take shape; **il treno si forma a Milano** the train starts from Milan

for'mato sm format, size

format'tare vt (Inform) to format

formattazi'one [formattat'tsjone] sf (Inform) formatting

formazi'one [format'tsjone] sf formation; (fig: educazione) training; **~ continua** continuing education; **~ permanente** lifelong learning; **~ professionale** vocational training

for'mica, -che sf ant

formi'caio sm anthill

formico'lare vi (gamba, braccio) to tingle; (brulicare: anche fig): **~ di** to be swarming with; **mi formicola la gamba** I've got pins and needles in my leg, my leg's tingling

formico'lio sm pins and needles pl; swarming

formi'dabile ag powerful, formidable; (straordinario) remarkable

for'moso, -a ag shapely

'formula sf formula; **~ di cortesia** (nelle lettere) letter ending

formu'lare vt to formulate

for'nace [for'natʃe] sf (per laterizi etc) kiln; (per metalli) furnace

for'naio sm baker

for'nello sm (elettrico, a gas) ring; (di pipa) bowl

for'nire vt: **~ qn di qc, fornire qc a qn** to provide o supply sb with sth, supply sth to sb; **fornirsi** vr: **fornirsi di** (procurarsi) to provide o.s. with

for'nito, -a ag: **ben ~** (negozio) well-stocked

forni'tore, -'trice ag: **ditta fornitrice di ...** company supplying ... ■ sm/f supplier

forni'tura sf supply

'forno sm (di cucina) oven; (panetteria) bakery; (Tecn: per calce etc) kiln; (: per metalli) furnace; **fare i forni** (Med) to undergo heat treatment

'foro sm (buco) hole; (Storia) forum; (tribunale) (law) court

'forse av perhaps, maybe; (circa) about; **essere in ~** to be in doubt

forsen'nato, -a ag mad, crazy, insane

'forte ag strong; (suono) loud; (spesa) considerable, great ■ av strongly; (velocemente) fast; (a voce alta) loud(ly); (violentemente) hard ■ sm (edificio) fort; (specialità) forte, strong point; **piatto ~** (Cuc) main dish; **avere un ~ mal di testa/raffreddore** to have a bad headache/cold; **essere ~ in qc** to be good at sth; **farsi ~ di qc** to make use of sth; **dare man ~ a qn** to back sb up, support sb; **usare le maniere forti** to use strong-arm tactics

for'tezza [for'tettsa] sf (morale) strength; (luogo fortificato) fortress

fortifi'care vt to fortify, strengthen

for'tuito, -a ag fortuitous, chance cpd

for'tuna sf (destino) fortune, luck; (buona sorte) success, fortune; (eredità, averi) fortune; **per ~** luckily, fortunately; **di ~** makeshift, improvised; **atterraggio di ~** emergency landing

fortu'nale sm storm

fortunata'mente av luckily, fortunately

fortu'nato, -a ag lucky, fortunate; (coronato da successo) successful

fortu'noso, -a ag (vita) eventful; (avvenimento) unlucky

fo'runcolo sm (Med) boil

forvi'are vt, vi = **fuorviare**

'forza ['fɔrtsa] sf strength; (potere) power; (Fisica) force ■ escl come on!; **forze** sfpl (fisiche) strength sg; (Mil) forces; **per ~** against one's will; (naturalmente) of course; **per ~ di cose** by force of circumstances; **a viva ~** by force; **a ~ di** by dint of; **farsi ~** (coraggio) to pluck up one's courage; **bella ~!** (ironico) how clever of you (o him etc)!; **~ lavoro** work force, manpower; **per causa di ~ maggiore** (Dir) by reason of an act of God; (per estensione) due to circumstances beyond one's control; **la ~ pubblica** the police pl; **~ di pace** peacekeeping force; **~ di vendita** (Comm) sales force; **~ di volontà** willpower; **le forze armate** the armed forces; **F~ Italia** (Pol) moderate right-wing party

for'zare [for'tsare] vt to force; (cassaforte, porta) to force (open); (voce) to strain; **~ qn a fare** to force sb to do

for'zato, -a [for'tsato] ag forced ■ sm (Dir) prisoner sentenced to hard labour (Brit) o labor (US)

forzi'ere [for'tsjɛre] sm strongbox; (di pirati) treasure chest

for'zista, -i, e [for'tsista] ag of Forza Italia ■ sm/f member (o supporter) of Forza Italia

for'zuto, -a [for'tsuto] ag big and strong

fos'chia [fos'kia] sf mist, haze

'fosco, -a, schi, sche ag dark, gloomy; **dipingere qc a tinte fosche** (fig) to paint a gloomy picture of sth

fos'fato sm phosphate

fosfore'scente [fosforeʃ'ʃɛnte] ag phosphorescent; (lancetta dell'orologio etc) luminous

'fosforo sm phosphorous

'fossa sf pit; (di cimitero) grave; **~ comune** mass grave

fos'sato sm ditch; (di fortezza) moat

fos'setta sf dimple

'fossi etc vb vedi **essere**

'fossile ag, sm fossil (cpd)

'fosso sm ditch; (Mil) trench

'foste etc vb vedi **essere**

'foto sf inv photo; **~ ricordo** souvenir photo; **~ tessera** passport(-type) photo

foto... prefisso photo...

foto'camera sf: **~ digitale** digital camera

fotocomposi'tore sm filmsetter

foto'copia sf photocopy

fotocopi'are vt to photocopy

fotocopiste'ria sf photocopy shop

fotofo'nino sm camera phone

foto'genico, -a, ci, che [foto'dʒɛniko] ag photogenic

fotogra'fare vt to photograph

fotogra'fia sf (procedimento) photography; (immagine) photograph; **fare una ~** to take a photograph; **una ~ a colori/in bianco e nero** a colour/black and white photograph

foto'grafico, -a, ci, che ag photographic; **macchina fotografica** camera

fo'tografo, -a sm/f photographer

foto'gramma, -i sm (Cine) frame

fotomo'dello, -a sm/f fashion model

fotomon'taggio [fotomon'taddʒo] sm photomontage

fotore'porter sm/f inv newspaper (o magazine) photographer

fotoro'manzo [fotoro'mandzo] sm romantic picture story

foto'sintesi sf photosynthesis

fotovol'taico, -a, ci, che ag (sistema, pannello) photovoltaic

'fottere vt (fam!: avere rapporti sessuali) to fuck (!), screw (!); (: rubare) to pinch, swipe; (: fregare): **mi hanno fottuto** they played a dirty trick on me; **vai a farti ~!** fuck off! (!)

fot'tuto, -a ag (fam!) bloody, fucking (!)

fou'lard [fu'lar] sm inv scarf

FR *sigla* = **Frosinone**

fra *prep* = **tra**

fracas'sare *vt* to shatter, smash;
fracassarsi *vr* to shatter, smash; (*veicolo*)
to crash

fra'casso *sm* smash; crash; (*baccano*) din,
racket

'fradicio, -a, ci, ce ['fraditʃo] *ag* (*guasto*)
rotten; (*molto bagnato*) soaking (wet);
ubriaco ~ blind drunk

'fragile ['fradʒile] *ag* fragile; (*salute*) delicate;
(*nervi, vetro*) brittle

fragilità [fradʒili'ta] *sf* (*vedi ag*) fragility;
delicacy; brittleness

'fragola *sf* strawberry

fra'gore *sm* (*di cascate, carro armato*) roar; (*di
tuono*) rumble

frago'roso, -a *ag* deafening; **ridere in modo
~** to roar with laughter

fra'grante *ag* fragrant

fraintendi'mento *sm* misunderstanding

frain'tendere *vt* to misunderstand

frain'teso, -a *pp di* **fraintendere**

fram'mento *sm* fragment

fram'misto, -a *ag*: **~ a** interspersed with

'frana *sf* landslide; (*fig: persona*): **essere una ~**
to be useless, be a walking disaster area

fra'nare *vi* to slip, slide down

franca'mente *av* frankly

fran'cese [fran'tʃeze] *ag* French ▪ *sm/f*
Frenchman(-woman) ▪ *sm* (*Ling*) French;
i Francesi the French

fran'chezza [fran'kettsa] *sf* frankness,
openness

fran'chigia, -gie [fran'kidʒa] *sf* (*Amm*)
exemption; (*Dir*) franchise; (*Naut*) shore
leave; **~ doganale** exemption from customs
duty

'Francia ['frantʃa] *sf*: **la ~** France

'franco, -a, chi, che *ag* (*Comm*) free; (*sincero*)
frank, open, sincere ▪ *sm* (*moneta*) franc;
farla franca (*fig*) to get off scot-free; **~ a
bordo** free on board; **~ di dogana** duty-free;
~ a domicilio delivered free of charge; **~
fabbrica** ex factory, ex works; **prezzo ~
fabbrica** ex-works price; **~ magazzino** ex
warehouse; **~ di porto** carriage free; **~
vagone** free on rail; **~ tiratore** sniper; (*Pol*)
*member of parliament who votes against his own
party*

franco'bollo *sm* (postage) stamp

franco-cana'dese *ag, sm/f* French Canadian

Franco'forte *sf* Frankfurt

fran'gente [fran'dʒente] *sm* (*onda*) breaker;
(*scoglio emergente*) reef; (*circostanza*) situation,
circumstance

'frangia, -ge ['frandʒa] *sf* fringe

frangi'flutti [frandʒi'flutti] *sm inv*
breakwater

frangi'vento [frandʒi'vento] *sm* windbreak

fran'toio *sm* (*Agr*) olive press; (*Tecn*) crusher

frantu'mare *vt*, **frantu'marsi** *vr* to break
into pieces, shatter

fran'tumi *smpl* pieces, bits; (*schegge*) splinters;
andare in ~, mandare in ~ to shatter, smash
to pieces *o* smithereens

frappé *sm* (*Cuc*) milk shake

fra'sario *sm* (*gergo*) vocabulary, language

'frasca, -sche *sf* (leafy) branch; **saltare di
palo in ~** to jump from one subject to
another

'frase *sf* (*Ling*) sentence; (*locuzione, espressione,
Mus*) phrase; **~ fatta** set phrase

fraseolo'gia [frazeolo'dʒia] *sf* phraseology

'frassino *sm* ash (tree)

frastagli'ato, -a [frasta'ʎʎato] *ag* (*costa*)
indented, jagged

frastor'nare *vt* (*intontire*) to daze; (*confondere*)
to bewilder, befuddle

frastor'nato, -a *ag* dazed; bewildered

frastu'ono *sm* hubbub, din

'frate *sm* friar, monk

fratel'lanza [fratel'lantsa] *sf* brotherhood;
(*associazione*) fraternity

fratel'lastro *sm* stepbrother; (*con genitore in
comune*) half brother

fra'tello *sm* brother; **fratelli** *smpl* brothers;
(*nel senso di fratelli e sorelle*) brothers and sisters

fra'terno, -a *ag* fraternal, brotherly

fratri'cida, -i, e [fratri'tʃida] *ag* fratricidal
▪ *sm/f* fratricide; **guerra ~** civil war

frat'taglie [frat'taʎʎe] *sfpl* (*Cuc: gen*) offal *sg*;
(: *di pollo*) giblets

frat'tanto *av* in the meantime, meanwhile

frat'tempo *sm*: **nel ~** in the meantime,
meanwhile

frat'tura *sf* fracture; (*fig*) split, break

frattu'rare *vt* to fracture

fraudo'lento, -a *ag* fraudulent

fraziona'mento [frattsjona'mento] *sm*
division, splitting up

frazio'nare [frattsjo'nare] *vt* to divide, split
up

frazi'one [frat'tsjone] *sf* fraction; (*borgata*): **~
di comune** hamlet

'freccia, -ce ['frettʃa] *sf* arrow; **~ di direzione**
(*Aut*) indicator

frec'ciata [fret'tʃata] *sf*: **lanciare una ~** to
make a cutting remark

fred'dare *vt* to shoot dead

fred'dezza [fred'dettsa] *sf* coldness

'freddo, -a *ag, sm* cold; **fa ~** it's cold; **aver ~** to
be cold; **soffrire il ~** to feel the cold; **a ~** (*fig*)
deliberately

freddo'loso, -a *ag* sensitive to the cold

fred'dura *sf* pun

'freezer ['frizer] *sm inv* fridge-freezer

fre'gare *vt* to rub; (*fam: truffare*) to take in, cheat; (*: rubare*) to swipe, pinch; **fregarsene** (*fam!*): **chi se ne frega?** who gives a damn (about it)?

fre'gata *sf* rub; (*fam*) swindle; (*Naut*) frigate

frega'tura *sf* (*fam: imbroglio*) rip-off; (*: delusione*) let-down

fregherò *etc* [frege'rɔ] *vb vedi* **fregare**

'fregio ['fredʒo] *sm* (*Archit*) frieze; (*ornamento*) decoration

'fremere *vi*: ~ **di** to tremble *o* quiver with; ~ **d'impazienza** to be champing at the bit

'fremito *sm* tremor, quiver

fre'nare *vt* (*veicolo*) to slow down; (*cavallo*) to rein in; (*lacrime*) to restrain, hold back ■ *vi* to brake; **frenarsi** *vr* (*fig*) to restrain o.s., control o.s.

fre'nata *sf*: **fare una** ~ to brake

frene'sia *sf* frenzy

fre'netico, -a, ci, che *ag* frenetic

'freno *sm* brake; (*morso*) bit; **tenere a** ~ (*passioni etc*) to restrain; **tenere a ~ la lingua** to hold one's tongue; **~ a disco** disc brake; **~ a mano** handbrake

'freon® *sm inv* (*Chim*) Freon®

frequen'tare *vt* (*scuola, corso*) to attend; (*locale, bar*) to go to, frequent; (*persone*) to see (often)

frequen'tato, -a *ag* (*locale*) busy

fre'quente *ag* frequent; **di ~** frequently

fre'quenza [fre'kwɛntsa] *sf* frequency; (*Ins*) attendance

fre'sare *vt* (*Tecn*) to mill

fres'chezza [fres'kettsa] *sf* freshness

'fresco, -a, schi, sche *ag* fresh; (*temperatura*) cool; (*notizia*) recent, fresh ■ *sm*: **godere il ~** to enjoy the cool air; **~ di bucato** newly washed; **stare ~** (*fig*) to be in for it; **mettere al ~** to put in a cool place; (*fig: in prigione*) to put inside *o* in the cooler

fres'cura *sf* cool

'fresia *sf* freesia

'fretta *sf* hurry, haste; **in ~** in a hurry; **in ~ e furia** in a mad rush; **aver ~** to be in a hurry; **far ~ a qn** to hurry sb

frettolosa'mente *av* hurriedly, in a rush

fretto'loso, -a *ag* (*persona*) in a hurry; (*lavoro etc*) hurried, rushed

fri'abile *ag* (*terreno*) friable; (*pasta*) crumbly

'friggere ['friddʒere] *vt* to fry ■ *vi* (*olio etc*) to sizzle; **vai a farti ~!** (*fam*) get lost!

frigidità [fridʒidi'ta] *sf* frigidity

'frigido, -a ['fridʒido] *ag* (*Med*) frigid

fri'gnare [frin'nare] *vi* to whine, snivel

fri'gnone, -a [frin'none] *sm/f* whiner, sniveller

'frigo, -ghi *sm* fridge

frigo'bar *sm inv* minibar

frigo'rifero, -a *ag* refrigerating ■ *sm* refrigerator; **cella frigorifera** cold store

fringu'ello *sm* chaffinch

'frissi *etc vb vedi* **friggere**

frit'tata *sf* omelet(te); **fare una ~** (*fig*) to make a mess of things

frit'tella *sf* (*Cuc*) pancake; (*: ripiena*) fritter

'fritto, -a *pp di* **friggere** ■ *ag* fried ■ *sm* fried food; **ormai siamo fritti!** (*fig fam*) now we've had it!; **è un argomento ~ e rifritto** that's old hat; **~ misto** mixed fry

frit'tura *sf* (*cibo*) fried food; **~ di pesce** mixed fried fish

friu'lano, -a *ag* of (*o* from) Friuli

frivo'lezza [frivo'lettsa] *sf* frivolity

'frivolo, -a *ag* frivolous

frizi'one [frit'tsjone] *sf* friction; (*di pelle*) rub, rub-down; (*Aut*) clutch

friz'zante [frid'dzante] *ag* (*anche fig*) sparkling

'frizzo ['friddzo] *sm* witticism

fro'dare *vt* to defraud, cheat

'frode *sf* fraud; **~ fiscale** tax evasion

'frodo *sm*: **di ~** illegal, contraband; **pescatore di ~, cacciatore di ~** poacher

'frogia, -gie ['frɔdʒa] *sf* (*di cavallo etc*) nostril

'frollo, -a *ag* (*carne*) tender; (*: selvaggina*) high; (*fig: persona*) soft; **pasta frolla** short(crust) pastry

'fronda *sf* (*leafy*) branch; (*di partito politico*) internal opposition; **fronde** *sfpl* (*di albero*) foliage *sg*

fron'tale *ag* frontal; (*scontro*) head-on

'fronte *sf* (*Anat*) forehead; (*di edificio*) front, façade ■ *sm* (*Mil, Pol, Meteor*) front; **a ~, di ~** facing, opposite; **di ~ a** (*posizione*) opposite, facing, in front of; (*a paragone di*) compared with; **far ~ a** (*nemico, problema*) to confront; (*responsabilità*) to face up to; (*spese*) to cope with

fronteggi'are [fronted'dʒare] *vt* (*avversari, difficoltà*) to face, stand up to; (*spese*) to cope with

frontes'pizio [frontes'pittsjo] *sm* (*Archit*) frontispiece; (*di libro*) title page

fronti'era *sf* border, frontier

fron'tone *sm* pediment

'fronzolo ['frondzolo] *sm* frill

'frotta *sf* crowd; **in ~, a frotte** in their hundreds, in droves

'frottola *sf* fib; **raccontare un sacco di frottole** to tell a pack of lies

fru'gale *ag* frugal

fru'gare *vi* to rummage ■ *vt* to search

frugherò *etc* [fruge'rɔ] *vb vedi* **frugare**

frui'tore *sm* user

fruizi'one [fruit'tsjone] *sf* use

frul'lare *vt* (*Cuc*) to whisk ◼ *vi* (*uccelli*) to flutter; **cosa ti frulla in mente?** what is going on in that mind of yours?

frul'lato *sm* (*Cuc*) milk shake; (: *con solo frutta*) fruit drink

frulla'tore *sm* electric mixer

frul'lino *sm* whisk

fru'mento *sm* wheat

frusci'are [fruʃ'ʃare] *vi* to rustle

fru'scio [fruʃ'ʃio] *sm* rustle; rustling

'frusta *sf* whip; (*Cuc*) whisk

frus'tare *vt* to whip

frus'tata *sf* lash

frus'tino *sm* riding crop

frus'trare *vt* to frustrate

frus'trato, -a *ag* frustrated

frustrazi'one [frustrat'tsjone] *sf* frustration

'frutta *sf* fruit; (*portata*) dessert; ~ **candita/ secca** candied/dried fruit

frut'tare *vi* (*investimenti, deposito*) to bear dividends, give a return; **il mio deposito in banca (mi) frutta il 10%** my bank deposits bring (me) in 10%; **quella gara gli fruttò la medaglia d'oro** he won the gold medal in that competition

frut'teto *sm* orchard

frutticol'tura *sf* fruit growing

frut'tifero, -a *ag* (*albero etc*) fruit-bearing; (*fig: che frutta*) fruitful, profitable; **deposito ~** interest-bearing deposit

frutti'vendolo, -a *sm/f* greengrocer (*Brit*), produce dealer (*US*)

'frutto *sm* fruit; (*fig: risultato*) result(s); (*Econ: interesse*) interest; (: *reddito*) income; **è ~ della tua immaginazione** it's a figment of your imagination; **frutti di mare** seafood *sg*

fruttu'oso, -a *ag* fruitful, profitable

FS *abbr* (= *Ferrovie dello Stato*) *Italian railways*

f.t. *abbr* = **fuori testo**

f.to *abbr* (= *firmato*) signed

fu *vb vedi* **essere** ◼ *ag inv:* **il fu Paolo Bianchi** the late Paolo Bianchi

fuci'lare [futʃi'lare] *vt* to shoot

fuci'lata [futʃi'lata] *sf* rifle shot

fucilazi'one [futʃilat'tsjone] *sf* execution (by firing squad)

fu'cile [fu'tʃile] *sm* rifle, gun; (*da caccia*) shotgun, gun; **~ a canne mozze** sawn-off shotgun

fu'cina [fu'tʃina] *sf* forge

'fuco, -chi *sm* drone

'fucsia *sf* fuchsia

'fuga, -ghe *sf* escape, flight; (*di gas, liquidi*) leak; (*Mus*) fugue; **mettere qn in ~** to put sb to flight; **~ di cervelli** brain drain

fu'gace [fu'gatʃe] *ag* fleeting, transient

fu'gare *vt* (*dubbi, incertezze*) to dispel, drive out

fug'gevole [fud'dʒevole] *ag* fleeting

fuggi'asco, -a, schi, sche [fud'dʒasko] *ag, sm/f* fugitive

fuggi'fuggi [fuddʒi'fuddʒi] *sm* scramble, stampede

fug'gire [fud'dʒire] *vi* to flee, run away; (*fig: passar veloce*) to fly ◼ *vt* to avoid

fuggi'tivo, -a [fuddʒi'tivo] *sm/f* fugitive, runaway

'fui *vb vedi* **essere**

'fulcro *sm* (*Fisica*) fulcrum; (*fig: di teoria, questione*) central o key point

ful'gore *sm* brilliance, splendour (*Brit*), splendor (*US*)

fu'liggine [fu'liddʒine] *sf* soot

fulmi'nare *vt* (*elettricità*) to electrocute; (*con arma da fuoco*) to shoot dead; **fulminarsi** *vr* (*lampadina*) to go, blow; (*fig: con lo sguardo*): **mi fulminò (con uno sguardo)** he looked daggers at me

'fulmine *sm* bolt of lightning; **fulmini** *smpl* lightning *sg*; **~ a ciel sereno** bolt from the blue

ful'mineo, -a *ag* (*fig: scatto*) rapid; (: *minaccioso*) threatening

'fulvo, -a *ag* tawny

fuma'iolo *sm* (*di nave*) funnel; (*di fabbrica*) chimney

fu'mante *ag* (*piatto etc*) steaming

fu'mare *vi* to smoke; (*emettere vapore*) to steam ◼ *vt* to smoke

fu'mario, -a *ag*: **canna fumaria** flue

fu'mata *sf* (*segnale*) smoke signal; **farsi una ~** to have a smoke; **~ bianca/nera** (*in Vaticano*) signal that a new pope has/has not been elected

fuma'tore, -trice *sm/f* smoker

fu'metto *sm* comic strip; **giornale a fumetti** comic

'fummo *vb vedi* **essere**

'fumo *sm* smoke; (*vapore*) steam; (*il fumare tabacco*) smoking; **fumi** *smpl* (*industriali etc*) fumes; **vendere ~** to deceive, cheat; **è tutto ~ e niente arrosto** it has no substance to it; **i fumi dell'alcool** (*fig*) the after-effects of drink; **~ passivo** passive smoking

fu'mogeno, -a [fu'mɔdʒeno] *ag* (*candelotto*) smoke *cpd* ◼ *sm* smoke bomb; **cortina fumogena** smoke screen

fu'moso, -a *ag* smoky; (*fig*) muddled

fu'nambolo, -a *sm/f* tightrope walker

'fune *sf* rope, cord; (*più grossa*) cable

'funebre *ag* (*rito*) funeral; (*aspetto*) gloomy, funereal

fune'rale *sm* funeral

fu'nesto, -a *ag (incidente)* fatal; *(errore, decisione)* fatal, disastrous; *(atmosfera)* gloomy, dismal
'fungere ['fundʒere] *vi:* ~ **da** to act as
'fungo, -ghi *sm* fungus; *(commestibile)* mushroom; ~ **velenoso** toadstool; **crescere come i funghi** *(fig)* to spring up overnight
funico'lare *sf* funicular railway
funi'via *sf* cable railway
'funsi *etc vb vedi* **fungere**
'funto, -a *pp di* **fungere**
funzio'nare [funtsjo'nare] *vi* to work, function; *(fungere):* ~ **da** to act as
funzio'nario [funtsjo'narjo] *sm* official; ~ **statale** civil servant
funzi'one [fun'tsjone] *sf* function; *(carica)* post, position; *(Rel)* service; **in** ~ *(meccanismo)* in operation; **in** ~ **di** *(come)* as; **vive in** ~ **dei figli** he lives for his children; **far** ~ **di** to act as; **fare la** ~ **di qn** *(farne le veci)* to take sb's place
fu'oco, -chi *sm* fire; *(fornello)* ring; *(Fot, Fisica)* focus; **dare** ~ **a qc** to set fire to sth; **far** ~ *(sparare)* to fire; **prendere** ~ to catch fire; ~ **d'artificio** firework; ~ **di paglia** flash in the pan; ~ **sacro** *o* **di Sant'Antonio** *(Med: fam)* shingles *sg*
fuorché [fwor'ke] *cong, prep* except
FU'ORI *sigla m (= Fronte Unitario Omosessuale Rivoluzionario Italiano)* gay liberation movement
fu'ori *av* outside; *(all'aperto)* outdoors, outside; *(fuori di casa, Sport)* out; *(esclamativo)* get out! ■ *prep:* ~ **(di)** out of, outside ■ *sm* outside; **essere in** ~ *(sporgere)* to stick out; **lasciar** ~ **qc/qn** to leave sth/sb out; **far** ~ *(fam: soldi)* to spend; *(: cioccolatini)* to eat up; *(: rubare)* to nick; **far** ~ **qn** *(fam)* to kill sb, do sb in; **essere tagliato** ~ *(da un gruppo, ambiente)* to be excluded; **essere** ~ **di sé** to be beside oneself; ~ **luogo** *(inopportuno)* out of place, uncalled for; ~ **mano** out of the way, remote; ~ **pasto** between meals; ~ **pericolo** out of danger; ~ **dai piedi!** get out of the way!; ~ **servizio** out of order; ~ **stagione** out of season; **illustrazione** ~ **testo** *(Stampa)* plate; ~ **uso** out of use
fuori'bordo *sm inv* speedboat (with outboard motor); outboard motor
fuori'busta *sm inv* unofficial payment
fuori'classe *sm/f inv* (undisputed) champion
fuori'corso *ag inv (moneta)* no longer in circulation; *(Ins):* **(studente)** ~ *undergraduate who has not completed a course in due time*
fuorigi'oco [fwori'dʒɔko] *sm* offside
fuori'legge [fwori'leddʒe] *sm/f inv* outlaw
fuoriprog'ramma *sm inv (TV, Radio)* unscheduled programme; *(fig)* change of plan *o* programme

fuori'serie *ag inv (auto etc)* custom-built ■ *sf* custom-built car
fuoris'trada *sm (Aut)* cross-country vehicle
fuoru'scito, -a [fworuʃˈʃito], **fuoriu'scito, -a** [fworiuʃˈʃito] *sm/f* exile ■ *sf (di gas)* leakage, escape; *(di sangue, linfa)* seepage
fuorvi'are *vt* to mislead; *(fig)* to lead astray ■ *vi* to go astray
furbacchi'one, -a [furbakˈkjone] *sm/f* cunning old devil
fur'bizia [furˈbittsja] *sf (vedi ag)* cleverness; cunning; **una** ~ a cunning trick
'furbo, -a *ag* clever, smart; *(peg)* cunning ■ *sm/f:* **fare il** ~ to (try to) be clever *o* smart; **fatti** ~! show a bit of sense!
fu'rente *ag:* ~ **(contro)** furious (with)
fure'ria *sf (Mil)* orderly room
fu'retto *sm* ferret
fur'fante *sm* rascal, scoundrel
furgon'cino [furgon'tʃino] *sm* small van
fur'gone *sm* van
'furia *sf (ira)* fury, rage; *(fig: impeto)* fury, violence; *(fretta)* rush; **a** ~ **di** by dint of; **andare su tutte le furie** to fly into a rage
furi'bondo, -a *ag* furious
furi'ere *sm* quartermaster
furi'oso, -a *ag* furious; *(mare, vento)* raging
'furono *vb vedi* **essere**
fu'rore *sm* fury; *(esaltazione)* frenzy; **far** ~ to be all the rage
furtiva'mente *av* furtively
fur'tivo, -a *ag* furtive
'furto *sm* theft; ~ **con scasso** burglary
'fusa *sfpl:* **fare le** ~ to purr
fu'scello [fuʃˈʃello] *sm* twig
fu'seaux *smpl inv* leggings
'fusi *etc vb vedi* **fondere**
fu'sibile *sm (Elettr)* fuse
fusi'one *sf (di metalli)* fusion, melting; *(colata)* casting; *(Comm)* merger; *(fig)* merging
'fuso, -a *pp di* **fondere** ■ *sm (Filatura)* spindle; **diritto come un** ~ as stiff as a ramrod; ~ **orario** time zone
fusoli'era *sf (Aer)* fusillage
fus'tagno [fusˈtaɲɲo] *sm* corduroy
fus'tella *sf (su scatola di medicinali)* tear-off tab
fusti'gare *vt (frustare)* to flog; *(fig: costumi)* to censure, denounce
fus'tino *sm (di detersivo)* tub
'fusto *sm* stem; *(Anat, di albero)* trunk; *(recipiente)* drum, can; *(fam)* he-man
'futile *ag* vain, futile
futilità *sf inv* futility
futu'rismo *sm* futurism

Gg

G, g [dʒi] sf o m inv (lettera) G, g; **G come Genova** ≈ G for George

g abbr (= grammo) g

G8 [dʒi'otto] smpl G8 (= Group of Eight)

G20 [dʒi'venti] smpl G20 (= Group of Twenty)

gabar'dine [gabar'din] sm (tessuto) gabardine; (soprabito) gabardine raincoat

gab'bare vt to take in, dupe; **gabbarsi** vr: **gabbarsi di qn** to make fun of sb

'gabbia sf cage; (Dir) dock; (da imballaggio) crate; **la ~ degli accusati** (Dir) the dock; **~ dell'ascensore** lift (Brit) o elevator (US) shaft; **~ toracica** (Anat) rib cage

gabbi'ano sm (sea)gull

gabi'netto sm (Med etc) consulting room; (Pol) ministry; (di decenza) toilet, lavatory; (Ins: di fisica etc) laboratory

Ga'bon sm: **il ~** Gabon

ga'elico, -a, ci, che ag, sm Gaelic

gaffe [gaf] sf inv blunder, boob (fam)

gagli'ardo, -a [gaʎ'ʎardo] ag strong, vigorous

gai'ezza [ga'jettsa] sf gaiety, cheerfulness

'gaio, -a ag cheerful

'gala sf (sfarzo) pomp; (festa) gala

ga'lante ag gallant, courteous; (avventura, poesia) amorous

galante'ria sf gallantry

galantu'omo (pl **galantuomini**) sm gentleman

Ga'lapagos sfpl: **le (isole) ~** the Galapagos Islands

ga'lassia sf galaxy

gala'teo sm (good) manners pl, etiquette

gale'otto sm (rematore) galley slave; (carcerato) convict

ga'lera sf (Naut) galley; (prigione) prison

'galla sf: **a ~** afloat; **venire a ~** to surface, come to the surface; (fig: verità) to come out

galleggia'mento [galleddʒa'mento] sm floating; **linea di ~** (di nave) waterline

galleggi'ante [galled'dʒante] ag floating ■ sm (natante) barge; (di pescatore, lenza, Tecn) float

galleggi'are [galled'dʒare] vi to float

galle'ria sf (traforo) tunnel; (Archit, d'arte) gallery; (Teat) circle; (strada coperta con negozi) arcade; **~ del vento o aerodinamica** (Aer) wind tunnel

'Galles sm: **il ~** Wales

gal'lese ag Welsh ■ sm/f Welshman(-woman) ■ sm (Ling) Welsh; **i Gallesi** the Welsh

gal'letta sf cracker; (Naut) ship's biscuit

gal'letto sm young cock, cockerel; (fig) cocky young man; **fare il ~** to play the gallant

'Gallia sf: **la ~** Gaul

gal'lina sf hen; **andare a letto con le galline** to go to bed early

gal'lismo sm machismo

'gallo sm cock; **al canto del ~** at daybreak, at cockcrow; **fare il ~** to play the gallant

gal'lone sm piece of braid; (Mil) stripe; (unità di misura) gallon

galop'pare vi to gallop

galop'pino sm errand boy; (Pol) canvasser

ga'loppo sm gallop; **al o di ~** at a gallop

galvaniz'zare [galvanid'dzare] vt to galvanize

'gamba sf leg; (asta: di lettera) stem; **in ~** (in buona salute) well; (bravo, sveglio) bright, smart; **prendere qc sotto ~** (fig) to treat sth too lightly; **scappare a gambe levate** to take to one's heels; **gambe!** scatter!

gam'bale sm legging

gambe'retto sm shrimp

'gambero sm (di acqua dolce) crayfish; (di mare) prawn

'Gambia sf: **la ~** the Gambia

gambiz'zare [gambid'dzare] vt to kneecap

'gambo sm stem; (di frutta) stalk

ga'mella sf mess tin

'gamma sf (Mus) scale; (di colori, fig) range; **~ di prodotti** product range

ga'nascia, -sce [ga'naʃʃa] sf jaw; **ganasce del freno** (Aut) brake shoes

'gancio ['gantʃo] sm hook

'Gange ['gandʒe] sm: **il ~** the Ganges

'**gangheri** ['gangeri] *smpl*: **uscire dai** ~ (*fig*) to fly into a temper

gan'grena *sf* = **cancrena**

'**gara** *sf* competition; (*Sport*) competition; contest; match; (: *corsa*) race; **fare a** ~ to compete, vie; ~ **d'appalto** (*Comm*) tender

ga'rage [ga'raʒ] *sm inv* garage

ga'rante *sm/f* guarantor

garan'tire *vt* to guarantee; (*debito*) to stand surety for; (*dare per certo*) to assure

garan'tismo *sm* protection of civil liberties

garan'tista, -i, e *ag* concerned with civil liberties

garan'zia [garan'tsia] *sf* guarantee; (*pegno*) security; **in** ~ under guarantee

gar'bare *vi*: **non mi garba** I don't like it (*o* him *etc*)

garba'tezza [garba'tettsa] *sf* courtesy, politeness

gar'bato, -a *ag* courteous, polite

'**garbo** *sm* (*buone maniere*) politeness, courtesy; (*di vestito etc*) grace, style

gar'buglio [gar'buʎʎo] *sm* tangle; (*fig*) muddle, mess

gareggi'are [gared'dʒare] *vi* to compete

garga'nella *sf*: **a** ~ from the bottle

garga'rismo *sm* gargle; **fare i gargarismi** to gargle

ga'ritta *sf* (*di caserma*) sentry box

ga'rofano *sm* carnation; **chiodo di** ~ clove

gar'retto *sm* hock

gar'rire *vi* to chirp

'**garrulo, -a** *ag* (*uccello*) chirping; (*persona*: *loquace*) garrulous, talkative

'**garza** ['gardza] *sf* (*per bende*) gauze

gar'zone [gar'dzone] *sm* (*di negozio*) boy

gas *sm inv* gas; **a tutto** ~ at full speed; **dare** ~ (*Aut*) to accelerate; ~ **lacrimogeno** tear gas; ~ **naturale** natural gas

ga'sare *etc* = **gassare** *etc*

ga'sato, -a *sm/f* (*fam*: *persona*) freak

gas'dotto *sm* gas pipeline

ga'solio *sm* diesel (oil)

ga's(s)are *vt* to aerate, carbonate; (*asfissiare*) to gas; **gas(s)arsi** *vr* (*fam*) to get excited

ga's(s)ato, -a *ag* (*bibita*) aerated, fizzy

gas'soso, -a *ag* gaseous; gassy ■ *sf* fizzy drink

'**gastrico, -a, ci, che** *ag* gastric

gast'rite *sf* gastritis

gastroente'rite *sf* gastroenteritis

gastrono'mia *sf* gastronomy

gas'tronomo, -a *sm/f* gourmet, gastronome

G.A.T.T. *sigla m* (= *General Agreement on Tariffs and Trade*) GATT

'**gatta** *sf* cat, she-cat; **una** ~ **da pelare** (*fam*) a thankless task; **qui** ~ **ci cova!** I smell a rat!, there's something fishy going on here!

gatta'buia *sf* (*fam scherzoso*: *prigione*) clink

gat'tino *sm* kitten

'**gatto** *sm* cat, tomcat; ~ **delle nevi** (*Aut, Sci*) snowcat; ~ **a nove code** cat-o'-nine-tails; ~ **selvatico** wildcat

gatto'pardo *sm*: ~ **africano** serval; ~ **americano** ocelot

gat'tuccio [gat'tuttʃo] *sm* dogfish

gau'dente *sm/f* pleasure-seeker

'**gaudio** *sm* joy, happiness

ga'vetta *sf* (*Mil*) mess tin; **venire dalla** ~ (*Mil, fig*) to rise from the ranks

'**gazza** ['gaddza] *sf* magpie

gaz'zarra [gad'dzarra] *sf* racket, din

gaz'zella [gad'dzɛlla] *sf* gazelle; (*dei carabinieri*) (high-speed) police car

gaz'zetta [gad'dzetta] *sf* news sheet; **G~ Ufficiale** *official publication containing details of new laws*

gaz'zoso, -a [gad'dzoso] *ag* = **gassoso**

Gazz. Uff. *abbr* = **Gazzetta Ufficiale**

GB *sigla* (= *Gran Bretagna*) GB

G.C. *abbr* = **genio civile**

G.d.F. *abbr* = **guardia di finanza**

GE *sigla* = **Genova**

gel [dʒɛl] *sm inv* gel

ge'lare [dʒe'lare] *vt, vi, vb impers* to freeze; **mi ha gelato il sangue** (*fig*) it made my blood run cold

ge'lata [dʒe'lata] *sf* frost

gela'taio, -a [dʒela'tajo] *sm/f* ice-cream vendor

gelate'ria [dʒelate'ria] *sf* ice-cream shop

gela'tina [dʒela'tina] *sf* gelatine; ~ **esplosiva** gelignite; ~ **di frutta** fruit jelly

gelati'noso, -a [dʒelati'noso] *ag* gelatinous, jelly-like

ge'lato, -a [dʒe'lato] *ag* frozen ■ *sm* ice cream

'**gelido, -a** ['dʒɛlido] *ag* icy, ice-cold

'**gelo** ['dʒɛlo] *sm* (*temperatura*) intense cold; (*brina*) frost; (*fig*) chill

ge'lone [dʒe'lone] *sm* chilblain

gelo'sia [dʒelo'sia] *sf* jealousy

ge'loso, -a [dʒe'loso] *ag* jealous

'**gelso** ['dʒɛlso] *sm* mulberry (tree)

gelso'mino [dʒelso'mino] *sm* jasmine

gemel'laggio [dʒemel'laddʒo] *sm* twinning

gemel'lare [dʒemel'lare] *ag* twin *cpd* ■ *vt* (*città*) to twin

ge'mello, -a [dʒe'mɛllo] *ag, sm/f* twin; **gemelli** *smpl* (*di camicia*) cufflinks; (*dello zodiaco*): **Gemelli** Gemini *sg*; **essere dei Gemelli** to be Gemini

'**gemere** ['dʒɛmere] *vi* to moan, groan; (*cigolare*) to creak; (*gocciolare*) to drip, ooze

'**gemito** ['dʒɛmito] *sm* moan, groan

151

'gemma ['dʒɛmma] *sf* (*Bot*) bud; (*pietra preziosa*) gem

Gen. *abbr* (*Mil*: = *generale*) Gen

gen. *abbr* (= *generale, generalmente*) gen

gen'darme [dʒen'darme] *sm* policeman; (*fig*) martinet

'gene ['dʒɛne] *sm* gene

genealo'gia, -'gie [dʒenealo'dʒia] *sf* genealogy

genea'logico, -a, ci, che [dʒenea'lɔdʒiko] *ag* genealogical; **albero** ~ family tree

gene'rale [dʒene'rale] *ag, sm* general; **in** ~ (*per sommi capi*) in general terms; (*di solito*) usually, in general; **a** ~ **richiesta** by popular request

generalità [dʒenerali'ta] *sfpl* (*dati d'identità*) particulars

generaliz'zare [dʒeneralid'dzare] *vt, vi* to generalize

generalizzazi'one [dʒeneraliddzat'tsjone] *sf* generalization

general'mente [dʒeneral'mente] *av* generally

gene'rare [dʒene'rare] *vt* (*dar vita*) to give birth to; (*produrre*) to produce; (*causare*) to arouse; (*Tecn*) to produce, generate

genera'tore [dʒenera'tore] *sm* (*Tecn*) generator

generazi'one [dʒenerat'tsjone] *sf* generation

'genere ['dʒenere] *sm* kind, type, sort; (*Biol*) genus; (*merce*) article, product; (*Ling*) gender; (*Arte, Letteratura*) genre; **in** ~ generally, as a rule; **cose del** *o* **di questo** ~ such things; **il** ~ **umano** mankind; **generi alimentari** foodstuffs; **generi di consumo** consumer goods; **generi di prima necessità** basic essentials

ge'nerico, -a, ci, che [dʒe'nɛriko] *ag* generic; (*vago*) vague, imprecise; **medico** ~ general practitioner

'genero ['dʒɛnero] *sm* son-in-law

generosità [dʒenerosi'ta] *sf* generosity

gene'roso, -a [dʒene'roso] *ag* generous

'genesi ['dʒɛnezi] *sf* genesis

ge'netico, -a, ci, che [dʒe'nɛtiko] *ag* genetic; ▪ *sf* genetics *sg*

gen'giva [dʒen'dʒiva] *sf* (*Anat*) gum

ge'nia [dʒe'nia] *sf* (*peg*) mob, gang

geni'ale [dʒe'njale] *ag* (*persona*) of genius; (*idea*) ingenious, brilliant

'genio ['dʒɛnjo] *sm* genius; (*attitudine, talento*) talent, flair, genius; **andare a** ~ **a qn** to be to sb's liking, appeal to sb; ~ **civile** civil engineers *pl*; **il** ~ (**militare**) the Engineers

geni'tale [dʒeni'tale] *ag* genital; **genitali** *smpl* genitals

geni'tore [dʒeni'tore] *sm* parent, father *o* mother; **genitori** *smpl* parents

genn. *abbr* (= *gennaio*) Jan

gen'naio [dʒen'najo] *sm* January; *vedi anche* **luglio**

geno'cidio [dʒeno'tʃidjo] *sm* genocide

'Genova ['dʒɛnova] *sf* Genoa

geno'vese [dʒeno'vese] *ag, sm/f* Genoese (*pl inv*)

gen'taglia [dʒen'taʎʎa] *sf* (*peg*) rabble

'gente ['dʒɛnte] *sf* people *pl*

gentil'donna [dʒentil'dɔnna] *sf* lady

gen'tile [dʒen'tile] *ag* (*persona, atto*) kind; (: *garbato*) courteous, polite; (*nelle lettere*): **G~ Signore** Dear Sir; (: *sulla busta*): **G~ Signor Fernando Villa** Mr Fernando Villa

genti'lezza [dʒenti'lettsa] *sf* kindness; courtesy, politeness; **per** ~ (*per favore*) please

gentilu'omo [dʒenti'lwɔmo] (*pl* **gentiluomini**) *sm* gentleman

genuflessi'one [dʒenufles'sjone] *sf* genuflection

genu'ino, -a [dʒenu'ino] *ag* (*prodotto*) natural; (*persona, sentimento*) genuine, sincere

geogra'fia [dʒeogra'fia] *sf* geography

geo'grafico, -a, ci, che [dʒeo'grafiko] *ag* geographical

ge'ografo, -a [dʒe'ɔgrafo] *sm/f* geographer

geolo'gia [dʒeolo'dʒia] *sf* geology

geo'logico, -a, ci, che [dʒeo'lɔdʒiko] *ag* geological

ge'ometra, -i, e [dʒe'ɔmetra] *sm/f* (*professionista*) surveyor

geome'tria [dʒeome'tria] *sf* geometry

geo'metrico, -a, ci, che [dʒeo'mɛtriko] *ag* geometric(al)

geopo'litico, -a, ci, che [dʒeopo'litiko] *ag* geopolitical

Ge'orgia [dʒe'ɔrdʒa] *sf* Georgia

geor'giano, -a [dʒeor'dʒano] *ag, sm/f* Georgian

ge'ranio [dʒe'ranjo] *sm* geranium

ge'rarca, -chi [dʒe'rarka] *sm* (*Storia*: *nel fascismo*) party official

gerar'chia [dʒerar'kia] *sf* hierarchy

ge'rarchico, -a, ci, che [dʒe'rarkiko] *ag* hierarchical

ge'rente [dʒe'rɛnte] *sm/f* manager/manageress

ge'renza [dʒe'rɛntsa] *sf* management

ger'gale [dʒer'gale] *ag* slang *cpd*

'gergo, -ghi ['dʒergo] *sm* jargon; slang

geria'tria [dʒerja'tria] *sf* geriatrics *sg*

geri'atrico, -a, ci, che [dʒe'rjatriko] *ag* geriatric

'gerla ['dʒɛrla] *sf* conical wicker basket

Ger'mania [dʒer'manja] *sf*: **la** ~ Germany; **la** ~ **occidentale/orientale** West/East Germany

germe ['dʒɛrme] *sm* germ; (*fig*) seed

germinazi'one [dʒɛrminat'tsjone] *sf* germination

germogli'are [dʒɛrmoʎ'ʎare] *vi* (*emettere germogli*) to sprout; (*germinare*) to germinate

ger'moglio [dʒer'moʎʎo] *sm* shoot; (*gemma*) bud

gero'glifico, -ci [dʒero'glifiko] *sm* hieroglyphic

geron'tologo, -a, gi, ghe [dʒeron'tɔlogo] *sm/f* specialist in geriatrics

ge'rundio [dʒe'rundjo] *sm* gerund

Gerusa'lemme [dʒeruza'lɛmme] *sf* Jerusalem

gesso ['dʒɛsso] *sm* chalk; (*Scultura, Med, Edil*) plaster; (*statua*) plaster figure; (*minerale*) gypsum

gesta ['dʒɛsta] *sfpl* (*letterario*) deeds, feats

ges'tante [dʒes'tante] *sf* expectant mother

gestazi'one [dʒestat'tsjone] *sf* gestation

gestico'lare [dʒestiko'lare] *vi* to gesticulate

gestio'nale [dʒestjo'nale] *ag* administrative, management *cpd*

gesti'one [dʒes'tjone] *sf* management; **~ di magazzino** stock control; **~ patrimoniale** investment management

ges'tire [dʒes'tire] *vt* to run, manage

gesto ['dʒɛsto] *sm* gesture

ges'tore [dʒes'tore] *sm* manager

Gesù [dʒe'zu] *sm* Jesus; **~ bambino** the Christ Child

gesu'ita, -i [dʒezu'ita] *sm* Jesuit

get'tare [dʒet'tare] *vt* to throw; (*anche:* **gettare via**) to throw away o out; (*Scultura*) to cast; (*Edil*) to lay; (*acqua*) to spout; (*grido*) to utter; **gettarsi** *vr:* **gettarsi in** (*impresa*) to throw o.s. into; (*mischia*) to hurl o.s. into; (*fiume*) to flow into; **~ uno sguardo su** to take a quick look at

get'tata [dʒet'tata] *sf* (*di cemento, gesso, metalli*) cast; (*diga*) jetty

gettito ['dʒettito] *sm* revenue

getto ['dʒetto] *sm* (*di gas, liquido, Aer*) jet; (*Bot*) shoot; **a ~ continuo** uninterruptedly; **di ~** (*fig*) straight off, in one go

get'tone [dʒet'tone] *sm* token; (*per giochi*) counter; (*: roulette etc*) chip; **~ di presenza** attendance fee; **~ telefonico** telephone token

gettoni'era [dʒetto'njera] *sf* telephone-token dispenser

geyser ['gaizə] *sm inv* geyser

Ghana ['gana] *sm:* **il ~** Ghana

ghenga, -ghe ['gɛnga] *sf* (*fam*) gang, crowd

ghe'pardo [ge'pardo] *sm* cheetah

gher'mire [ger'mire] *vt* to grasp, clasp, clutch

ghetta ['getta] *sf* (*gambale*) gaiter

ghettiz'zare [gettid'dzare] *vt* to segregate

ghetto ['getto] *sm* ghetto

ghiacci'aia [gjat'tʃaja] *sf* (*anche fig*) icebox

ghiacci'aio [gjat'tʃajo] *sm* glacier

ghiacci'are [gjat'tʃare] *vt* to freeze; (*fig*): **~ qn** to make sb's blood run cold ■ *vi* to freeze, ice over

ghiacci'ato, -a [gjat'tʃato] *ag* frozen; (*bevanda*) ice-cold

ghi'accio ['gjattʃo] *sm* ice

ghiacci'olo [gjat'tʃɔlo] *sm* icicle; (*tipo di gelato*) ice lolly (*Brit*), popsicle (*US*)

ghi'aia ['gjaja] *sf* gravel

ghi'anda ['gjanda] *sf* (*Bot*) acorn

ghi'andola ['gjandola] *sf* gland

ghiando'lare [gjando'lare] *ag* glandular

ghigliot'tina [giʎʎot'tina] *sf* guillotine

ghi'gnare [giɲ'ɲare] *vi* to sneer

ghigno ['giɲɲo] *sm* (*espressione*) sneer; (*risata*) mocking laugh

ghingheri ['gingeri] *smpl:* **in ~** all dolled up; **mettersi in ~** to put on one's Sunday best

ghi'otto, -a ['gjotto] *ag* greedy; (*cibo*) delicious, appetizing

ghiot'tone, -a [gjot'tone] *sm/f* glutton

ghiottone'ria [gjottone'ria] *sf* greed, gluttony; (*cibo*) delicacy, titbit (*Brit*), tidbit (*US*)

ghiri'goro [giri'goro] *sm* scribble, squiggle

ghir'landa [gir'landa] *sf* garland, wreath

ghiro ['giro] *sm* dormouse

ghisa ['giza] *sf* cast iron

G.I. *abbr* = **giudice istruttore**

già [dʒa] *av* already; (*ex, in precedenza*) formerly ■ *escl* of course!, yes indeed!; **già che ci sei ...** while you are at it ...

gi'acca, -che ['dʒakka] *sf* jacket; **~ a vento** windcheater (*Brit*), windbreaker (*US*)

giacché [dʒak'ke] *cong* since, as

giac'chetta [dʒak'ketta] *sf* (*light*) jacket

giaccio *etc* ['dʒattʃo] *vb vedi* **giacere**

giac'cone [dʒak'kone] *sm* heavy jacket

gia'cenza [dʒa'tʃɛntsa] *sf:* **merce in ~** goods in stock; **capitale in ~** uninvested capital; **giacenze di magazzino** unsold stock

gia'cere [dʒa'tʃere] *vi* to lie

giaci'mento [dʒatʃi'mento] *sm* deposit

gia'cinto [dʒa'tʃinto] *sm* hyacinth

giaci'uto, -a [dʒa'tʃuto] *pp di* **giacere**

gi'acqui *etc* ['dʒakkwi] *vb vedi* **giacere**

gi'ada ['dʒada] *sf* jade

giaggi'olo [dʒad'dʒɔlo] *sm* iris

giagu'aro [dʒa'gwaro] *sm* jaguar

gial'lastro, -a [dʒal'lastro] *ag* yellowish; (*carnagione*) sallow

gi'allo ['dʒallo] *ag* yellow; (*carnagione*) sallow ■ *sm* yellow; (*anche:* **romanzo giallo**) detective novel; (*anche:* **film giallo**) detective film; ~ **dell'uovo** yolk; **il mar G~** the Yellow Sea

gial'lognolo, -a [dʒal'loɲɲolo] *ag* yellowish, dirty yellow

Gia'maica [dʒa'maika] *sf*: **la ~** Jamaica

giamai'cano, -a [dʒamai'kano] *ag, sm/f* Jamaican

giam'mai [dʒam'mai] *av* never

Giap'pone [dʒap'pone] *sm*: **il ~** Japan

giappo'nese [dʒappo'nese] *ag, sm/f, sm* Japanese *inv*

gi'ara ['dʒara] *sf* jar

giardi'naggio [dʒardi'naddʒo] *sm* gardening

giardi'netta [dʒardi'netta] *sf* estate car (*Brit*), station wagon (*US*)

giardini'ere, -a [dʒardi'njɛre] *sm/f* gardener ■ *sf* (*misto di sottaceti*) mixed pickles *pl*; (*automobile*) = **giardinetta**

giar'dino [dʒar'dino] *sm* garden; ~ **d'infanzia** nursery school; ~ **pubblico** public gardens *pl*, (public) park; ~ **zoologico** zoo

giarretti'era [dʒarret'tjɛra] *sf* garter

Gi'ava ['dʒava] *sf* Java

giavel'lotto [dʒavel'lɔtto] *sm* javelin

gib'boso, -a [dʒib'boso] *ag* (*superficie*) bumpy; (*naso*) crooked

Gibil'terra [dʒibil'tɛrra] *sf* Gibraltar

gi'gante, -'essa [dʒi'gante] *sm/f* giant ■ *ag* giant, gigantic; (*Comm*) giant-size

gigan'tesco, -a, schi, sche [dʒigan'tesko] *ag* gigantic

gigantogra'fia [dʒigantogra'fia] *sf* (*Fot*) blow-up

'giglio ['dʒiʎʎo] *sm* lily

gilè [dʒi'lɛ] *sm inv* waistcoat

gin [dʒin] *sm inv* gin

gin'cana [dʒin'kana] *sf* gymkhana

ginecolo'gia [dʒinekolo'dʒia] *sf* gynaecology (*Brit*), gynecology (*US*)

gine'cologo, -a, gi, ghe [dʒine'kɔlogo] *sm/f* gynaecologist (*Brit*), gynecologist (*US*)

gi'nepro [dʒi'nepro] *sm* juniper

gi'nestra [dʒi'nɛstra] *sf* (*Bot*) broom

Gi'nevra [dʒi'nevra] *sf* Geneva; **il Lago di ~** Lake Geneva

gingil'larsi [dʒindʒil'larsi] *vr* to fritter away one's time; (*giocare*): ~ **con** to fiddle with

gin'gillo [dʒin'dʒillo] *sm* plaything

gin'nasio [dʒin'nazjo] *sm the 4th and 5th year of secondary school in Italy*

gin'nasta, -i, e [dʒin'nasta] *sm/f* gymnast

gin'nastica [dʒin'nastika] *sf* gymnastics *sg*; (*esercizio fisico*) keep-fit exercises *pl*; (*Ins*) physical education

'ginnico, -a, ci, che ['dʒinniko] *ag* gymnastic

gi'nocchio [dʒi'nɔkkjo] (*pl(f)* **ginocchi**, *pl(m)* **ginocchia**) *sm* knee; **stare in ~** to kneel,

be on one's knees; **mettersi in ~** to kneel (down)

ginocchi'oni [dʒinok'kjoni] *av* on one's knees

gio'care [dʒo'kare] *vt* to play; (*scommettere*) to stake, wager, bet; (*ingannare*) to take in ■ *vi* to play; (*a roulette etc*) to gamble; (*fig*) to play a part, be important; (*Tecn: meccanismo*) to be loose; ~ **a** (*gioco, sport*) to play; (*cavalli*) to bet on; ~ **d'astuzia** to be crafty; **giocarsi la carriera** to put one's career at risk; **giocarsi tutto** to risk everything; **a che gioco giochiamo?** what are you playing at?

gioca'tore, -'trice [dʒoka'tore] *sm/f* player; gambler

gio'cattolo [dʒo'kattolo] *sm* toy

giocherel'lare [dʒokerel'lare] *vi*: ~ **con** (*giocattolo*) to play with; (*distrattamente*) to fiddle with

giocherò *etc* [dʒoke'rɔ] *vb vedi* **giocare**

gio'chetto [dʒo'ketto] *sm* (*gioco*) game; (*tranello*) trick; (*fig*): **è un ~** it's child's play

gi'oco, -chi ['dʒɔko] *sm* game; (*divertimento, Tecn*) play; (*al casinò*) gambling; (*Carte*) hand; (*insieme di pezzi etc necessari per un gioco*) set; **per** ~ for fun; **fare il doppio ~ con qn** to double-cross sb; **prendersi ~ di qn** to pull sb's leg; **stare al ~ di qn** to play along with sb; **è in ~ la mia reputazione** my reputation is at stake; ~ **d'azzardo** game of chance; ~ **della palla** ball game; ~ **degli scacchi** chess set; **i Giochi Olimpici** the Olympic Games

gioco'forza [dʒoko'fɔrtsa] *sm*: **essere ~** to be inevitable

giocoli'ere [dʒoko'ljɛre] *sm* juggler

gio'coso, -a [dʒo'koso] *ag* playful, jesting

gio'gaia [dʒo'gaja] *sf* (*Geo*) range of mountains

gi'ogo, -ghi ['dʒogo] *sm* yoke

gi'oia ['dʒɔja] *sf* joy, delight; (*pietra preziosa*) jewel, precious stone

gioielle'ria [dʒojelle'ria] *sf* jeweller's (*Brit*) *o* jeweler's (*US*) craft; (*negozio*) jewel(l)er's (shop)

gioielli'ere, -a [dʒojel'ljɛre] *sm/f* jeweller (*Brit*), jeweler (*US*)

gioi'ello [dʒo'jɛllo] *sm* jewel, piece of jewellery (*Brit*) *o* jewelry (*US*); **gioielli** *smpl* (*gioie*) jewel(l)ery *sg*

gioi'oso, -a [dʒo'joso] *ag* joyful

Gior'dania [dʒor'danja] *sf*: **la ~** Jordan

Gior'dano [dʒor'dano] *sm*: **il ~** the Jordan

gior'dano, -a [dʒor'dano] *ag, sm/f* Jordanian

giorna'laio, -a [dʒorna'lajo] *sm/f* newsagent (*Brit*), newsdealer (*US*)

gior'nale [dʒor'nale] *sm* (news)paper; (*diario*) journal, diary; (*Comm*) journal; ~ **di bordo** (*Naut*) ship's log; ~ **radio** radio news *sg*

giorna'letto [dʒorna'letto] *sm* (children's) comic

giornali'ero, -a [dʒorna'ljɛro] *ag* daily; (*che varia: umore*) changeable ■ *sm* day labourer (*Brit*) *o* laborer (*US*)

giorna'lino [dʒorna'lino] *sm* children's comic

giorna'lismo [dʒorna'lizmo] *sm* journalism

giorna'lista, -i, e [dʒorna'lista] *sm/f* journalist

giorna'listico, -a, ci, che [dʒorna'listiko] *ag* journalistic; **stile ~** journalese

giornal'mente [dʒornal'mente] *av* daily

gior'nata [dʒor'nata] *sf* day; (*paga*) day's wages, day's pay; **durante la ~ di ieri** yesterday; **fresco di ~** (*uovo*) freshly laid; **vivere alla ~** to live from day to day; **~ lavorativa** working day

gi'orno ['dʒorno] *sm* day; (*opposto alla notte*) day, daytime; (*luce del giorno*) daylight; **al ~** per day; **di ~** by day; **~ per ~** day by day; **al ~ d'oggi** nowadays; **tutto il santo ~** all day long; **il G~ dei Morti** *see note*

◉ **IL GIORNO DEI MORTI**

◉ Il *Giorno dei Morti*, All Souls' Day, falls on
◉ 2 November. At this time of year people
◉ visit cemeteries to lay flowers on the
◉ graves of their loved ones.

gi'ostra ['dʒɔstra] *sf* (*per bimbi*) merry-go-round; (*torneo storico*) joust

gios'trare [dʒos'trare] *vi* (*Storia*) to joust, tilt; **giostrarsi** *vr* to manage

giov. *abbr* (= *giovedì*) Thur(s)

giova'mento [dʒova'mento] *sm* benefit, help

gi'ovane ['dʒovane] *ag* young; (*aspetto*) youthful ■ *sm/f* youth/girl, young man(-woman); **i giovani** young people; **è ~ del mestiere** he's new to the job

giova'netto, -a [dʒova'netto] *sm/f* young man(-woman)

giova'nile [dʒova'nile] *ag* youthful; (*scritti*) early; (*errore*) of youth

giova'notto [dʒova'nɔtto] *sm* young man

gio'vare [dʒo'vare] *vi:* **~ a** (*essere utile*) to be useful to; (*far bene*) to be good for ■ *vb impers* (*essere bene, utile*) to be useful; **giovarsi** *vr:* **giovarsi di qc** to make use of sth; **a che giova prendersela?** what's the point of getting upset?

Gi'ove ['dʒɔve] *sm* (*Mitologia*) Jove; (*Astr*) Jupiter

giovedì [dʒove'di] *sm inv* Thursday; *vedi anche* **martedì**

gio'venca, -che [dʒo'vɛnka] *sf* heifer

gioventù [dʒoven'tu] *sf* (*periodo*) youth; (*i giovani*) young people *pl*, youth

giovi'ale [dʒo'vjale] *ag* jovial, jolly

giovi'nastro [dʒovi'nastro] *sm* young thug

giovin'cello [dʒovin'tʃɛllo] *sm* young lad

giovi'nezza [dʒovi'nettsa] *sf* youth

gip [dʒip] *sigla m inv* (= *giudice per le indagini preliminari*) judge for preliminary enquiries

gira'dischi [dʒira'diski] *sm inv* record player

gi'raffa [dʒi'raffa] *sf* giraffe; (*TV, Cine, Radio*) boom

gira'mento [dʒira'mento] *sm:* **~ di testa** fit of dizziness

gira'mondo [dʒira'mondo] *sm/f inv* globetrotter

gi'randola [dʒi'randola] *sf* (*fuoco d'artificio*) Catherine wheel; (*giocattolo*) toy windmill; (*banderuola*) weather vane, weathercock

gi'rante [dʒi'rante] *sm/f* (*di assegno*) endorser

gi'rare [dʒi'rare] *vt* (*far ruotare*) to turn; (*percorrere, visitare*) to go round; (*Cine*) to shoot; (*: film: come regista*) to make; (*Comm*) to endorse ■ *vi* to turn; (*più veloce*) to spin; (*andare in giro*) to wander, go around; **girarsi** *vr* to turn; **~ attorno a** to go round; to revolve round; **si girava e rigirava nel letto** he tossed and turned in bed; **far ~ la testa a qn** to make sb dizzy; (*fig*) to turn sb's head; **gira al largo** keep your distance; **girala come ti pare** (*fig*) look at it whichever way you like; **gira e rigira ...** after a lot of driving (*o* walking) about ...; (*fig*) whichever way you look at it; **cosa ti gira?** (*fam*) what's got into you?; **mi ha fatto ~ le scatole** (*fam*) he drove me crazy

girar'rosto [dʒirar'rɔsto] *sm* (*Cuc*) spit

gira'sole [dʒira'sole] *sm* sunflower

gi'rata [dʒi'rata] *sf* (*passeggiata*) stroll; (*con veicolo*) drive; (*Comm*) endorsement

gira'tario, -a [dʒira'tarjo] *sm/f* endorsee

gira'volta [dʒira'vɔlta] *sf* twirl, turn; (*curva*) sharp bend; (*fig*) about-turn

gi'rello [dʒi'rɛllo] *sm* (*di bambino*) Babywalker® (*Brit*), go-cart (*US*); (*taglio di carne*) topside (*Brit*), top round (*US*)

gi'retto [dʒi'retto] *sm* (*passeggiata*) walk, stroll; (*: in macchina*) drive, spin; (*: in bicicletta*) ride

gi'revole [dʒi'revole] *ag* revolving, turning

gi'rino [dʒi'rino] *sm* tadpole

'giro ['dʒiro] *sm* (*circuito, cerchio*) circle; (*di chiave, manovella*) turn; (*viaggio*) tour, excursion; (*passeggiata*) stroll, walk; (*in macchina*) drive; (*in bicicletta*) ride; (*Sport: della pista*) lap; (*di denaro*) circulation; (*Carte*) hand; (*Tecn*) revolution; **fare un ~** to go for a walk (*o* a drive *o* a ride); **fare il ~ di** (*parco, città*) to go round; **andare in ~** (*a piedi*) to go about, walk around; **guardarsi in ~** to look around; **prendere in ~ qn** (fig) to take sb for a ride; **a stretto ~ di posta** by return of post; **nel ~ di un mese** in a month's time; **essere nel ~** (fig) to belong to a circle (of friends); **~ d'affari** (viaggio) business tour; (Comm) turnover; **~ di parole** circumlocution; **~ di prova** (Aut) test drive; **~ turistico** sightseeing tour; **~ vita** waist measurement

giro collo [dʒiro'kɔllo] sm: **a ~** crewneck cpd

giro conto [dʒiro'konto] sm (Econ) credit transfer

gi rone [dʒi'rone] sm (Sport) series of games; **~ di andata/ritorno** (Calcio) first/second half of the season

gironzo lare [dʒirondzo'lare] vi to stroll about

giro tondo [dʒiro'tondo] sm ring-a-ring-o'-roses (Brit), ring-around-the-rosey (US); **in ~** in a circle

girova gare [dʒirova'gare] vi to wander about

gi rovago, -a, ghi, ghe [dʒi'rɔvago] sm/f (vagabondo) tramp; (venditore) peddler; **una compagnia di girovaghi** (attori) a company of strolling actors

gita ['dʒita] sf excursion, trip; **fare una ~** to go for a trip, go on an outing

gi tano, -a [dʒi'tano] sm/f gipsy

gi tante [dʒi'tante] sm/f member of a tour

giù [dʒu] av down; (dabbasso) downstairs; **in giù** downwards, down; **la mia casa è un po' più in giù** my house is a bit further on; **giù di lì** (pressappoco) thereabouts; **bambini dai 6 anni in giù** children aged 6 and under; **cadere giù per le scale** to fall down the stairs; **giù le mani!** hands off!; **essere giù** (fig: di salute) to be run down; (: di spirito) to be depressed; **quel tipo non mi va giù** I can't stand that guy

gi ubba ['dʒubba] sf jacket

giub botto [dʒub'bɔtto] sm jerkin; **~ antiproiettile** bulletproof vest

giubi lare [dʒubi'lare] vi to rejoice

gi ubilo ['dʒubilo] sm rejoicing

giudi care [dʒudi'kare] vt to judge; (accusato) to try; (lite) to arbitrate in; **~ qn/qc bello** to consider sb/sth (to be) beautiful

giudi cato [dʒudi'kato] sm (Dir): **passare in ~** to pass final judgment

gi udice ['dʒuditʃe] sm judge; **~ collegiale** member of the court; **~ conciliatore** justice of the peace; **~ istruttore** examining (Brit) o committing (US) magistrate; **~ popolare** member of a jury

giudizi ale [dʒudit'tsjale] ag judicial

giudizi ario, -a [dʒudit'tsjarjo] ag legal, judicial

giu dizio [dʒu'dittsjo] sm judgment; (opinione) opinion; (Dir) judgment, sentence; (: processo) trial; (: verdetto) verdict; (: processo) trial; (: verdetto) verdict; **aver ~** to be wise o prudent; **essere in attesa di ~** to be awaiting trial; **citare in ~** to summons; **l'imputato è stato rinviato a ~** the accused has been committed for trial

giudizi oso, -a [dʒudit'tsjoso] ag prudent, judicious

gi uggiola ['dʒuddʒola] sf: **andare in brodo di giuggiole** (fam) to be over the moon

gi ugno ['dʒuɲɲo] sm June; vedi anche **luglio**

giu livo, -a [dʒu'livo] ag merry

giul lare [dʒul'lare] sm jester

giu menta [dʒu'menta] sf mare

gi unco, -chi ['dʒunko] sm (Bot) rush

gi ungere ['dʒundʒere] vi to arrive ■ vt (mani etc) to join; **~ a** to arrive at, reach; **~ nuovo a qn** to come as news to sb; **~ in porto** to reach harbour; (fig) to be brought to a successful outcome

gi ungla ['dʒungla] sf jungle

gi unsi etc ['dʒunsi] vb vedi **giungere**

gi unto, -a ['dʒunto] pp di **giungere** ■ sm (Tecn) coupling, joint ■ sf addition; (organo esecutivo, amministrativo) council, board; **per giunta** into the bargain, in addition; **giunta militare** military junta; vedi anche **Comune**; **Provincia**; **Regione**

giun tura [dʒun'tura] sf joint

giuo care [dʒwo'kare] vt, vi = **giocare**

giu oco ['dʒwɔko] sm = **gioco**

giura mento [dʒura'mento] sm oath; **~ falso** perjury

giu rare [dʒu'rare] vt to swear ■ vi to swear, take an oath; **gliel'ho giurata** I swore I would get even with him

giu rato, -a [dʒu'rato] ag: **nemico ~** sworn enemy ■ sm/f juror, juryman(-woman)

giu ria [dʒu'ria] sf jury

giu ridico, -a, ci, che [dʒu'ridiko] ag legal

giurisdizi one [dʒurizdit'tsjone] sf jurisdiction

giurispru denza [dʒurispru'dɛntsa] sf jurisprudence

giu rista, -i, e [dʒu'rista] sm/f jurist

giustap porre [dʒustap'porre] vt to juxtapose

giustapposizi one [dʒustappozit'tsjone] sf juxtaposition

giustap posto, -a [dʒustap'posto] pp di **giustapporre**

giustifi care [dʒustifi'kare] vt to justify; **giustificarsi** vr: **giustificarsi di** o **per qc** to justify o excuse o.s. for sth

giustifica tivo, -a [dʒustifika'tivo] ag (Amm): **nota** o **pezza giustificativa** receipt

giustificazi'one [dʒustifikat'tsjone] sf justification; (Ins) (note of) excuse

gius'tizia [dʒus'tittsja] sf justice; **farsi ~ (da sé)** (vendicarsi) to take the law into one's own hands

giustizi'are [dʒustit'tsjare] vt to execute, put to death

giustizi'ere [dʒustit'tsjɛre] sm executioner

gi'usto, -a ['dʒusto] ag (equo) fair, just; (vero) true, correct; (adatto) right, suitable; (preciso) exact, correct ■ av (esattamente) exactly, precisely; (per l'appunto, appena) just; **arrivare ~** to arrive just in time; **ho ~ bisogno di te** you're just the person I need

'glabro, -a ag hairless

glaci'ale [gla'tʃale] ag glacial

gla'diolo sm gladiolus

'glandola sf = **ghiandola**

'glassa sf (Cuc) icing

glau'coma sm glaucoma

gli [ʎi] det mpl (dav V, s impura, gn, pn, ps, x, z) the ■ pron (a lui) to him; (a esso) to it; (in coppia con lo, la, li, le, ne: a lui, a lei, a loro etc): **gliele do** I'm giving them to him (o her o them); **gliene ho parlato** I spoke to him (o her o them) about it; vedi anche **il**

glice'mia [glitʃe'mia] sf glycaemia

glice'rina [glitʃe'rina] sf glycerine

'glicine ['glitʃine] sm wistaria

gli'ela etc ['ʎela] vedi **gli**

glo'bale ag overall; (vista) global

'globo sm globe

'globulo sm (Anat): **~ rosso/bianco** red/white corpuscle

glocalizzazi'one [glokaliddza'tsjone] sf glocalization

'gloria sf glory; **farsi ~ di qc** to pride o.s. on sth, take pride in sth

glori'arsi vr: **~ di qc** to pride o.s. on sth, glory o take pride in sth

glorifi'care vt to glorify

glori'oso, -a ag glorious

glos'sario sm glossary

glu'cosio sm glucose

'gluteo sm gluteus; **glutei** smpl buttocks

GM abbr = **genio militare**

'gnocchi ['ɲɔkki] smpl (Cuc) small dumplings made of semolina pasta o potato

'gnomo ['ɲɔmo] sm gnome

'gnorri ['ɲɔrri] sm/f inv: **non fare lo ~!** stop acting as if you didn't know anything about it!

GO sigla = **Gorizia**

'goal ['goul] sm inv (Sport) goal

'gobba sf (Anat) hump; (protuberanza) bump

'gobbo, -a ag hunchbacked; (ricurvo) round-shouldered ■ sm/f hunchback

'Gobi smpl: **il Deserto dei ~** the Gobi Desert

'goccia, -ce ['gottʃa] sf drop; **~ di rugiada** dewdrop; **somigliarsi come due gocce d'acqua** to be as like as two peas in a pod; **è la ~ che fa traboccare il vaso!** it's the last straw!

'goccio ['gottʃo] sm drop, spot

goccio'lare [gottʃo'lare] vi, vt to drip

goccio'lio [gottʃo'lio] sm dripping

go'dere vi (compiacersi): **~ (di)** to be delighted (at), rejoice (at); (trarre vantaggio): **~ di** to enjoy, benefit from ■ vt to enjoy; **godersi la vita** to enjoy life; **godersela** to have a good time, enjoy o.s.

godi'mento sm enjoyment

godrò etc vb vedi **godere**

gof'faggine [gof'faddʒine] sf clumsiness

'goffo, -a ag clumsy, awkward

'gogna ['goɲɲa] sf pillory

gol sm inv = **goal**

'gola sf (Anat) throat; (golosità) gluttony, greed; (di camino) flue; (di monte) gorge; **fare ~** (anche fig) to tempt; **ricacciare il pianto o le lacrime in ~** to swallow one's tears

go'letta sf (Naut) schooner

golf sm inv (Sport) golf; (maglia) cardigan

'golfo sm gulf

goli'ardico, -a, ci, che ag (canto, vita) student cpd

go'loso, -a ag greedy

'golpe sm inv (Pol) coup

gomi'tata sf: **dare una ~ a qn** to elbow sb; **farsi avanti a (forza o furia di) gomitate** to elbow one's way through; **fare a gomitate per qc** to fight to get sth

'gomito sm elbow; (di strada etc) sharp bend

go'mitolo sm ball

'gomma sf rubber; (colla) gum; (per cancellare) rubber, eraser; (di veicolo) tyre (Brit), tire (US); **~ da masticare** chewing gum; **~ a terra** flat tyre

gommapi'uma® sf foam rubber

gom'mino sm rubber tip; (rondella) rubber washer

gom'mista, -i, e sm/f tyre (Brit) o tire (US) specialist; (rivenditore) tyre o tire merchant

gom'mone sm rubber dinghy

gom'moso, -a ag rubbery

'gondola sf gondola

gondoli'ere sm gondolier

gonfa'lone sm banner

gonfi'are vt (pallone) to blow up, inflate; (dilatare, ingrossare) to swell; (fig: notizia) to exaggerate; **gonfiarsi** vr to swell; (fiume) to rise

'gonfio, -a ag swollen; (stomaco) bloated; (palloncino, gomme) inflated, blown up; (con pompa) pumped up; (vela) full; **occhi gonfi di**

pianto eyes swollen with tears; **~ di orgoglio** (*persona*) puffed up (with pride); **avere il portafoglio ~** to have a bulging wallet

gonfi ore *sm* swelling

gongo'lare *vi* to look pleased with o.s.; **~ di gioia** to be overjoyed

'**gonna** *sf* skirt; **~ pantalone** culottes *pl*

'**gonzo** ['gondzo] *sm* simpleton, fool

googlare [gu'glare] *vt* (*Inform*) to google

gorgheggi'are [gorged'dʒare] *vi* to warble; to trill

gor'gheggio [gor'geddʒo] *sm* (*Mus, di uccello*) trill

'**gorgo, -ghi** *sm* whirlpool

gorgogli'are [gorgoʎ'ʎare] *vi* to gurgle

gorgo'glio [gorgoʎ'ʎio] *sm* gurgling

go'rilla *sm inv* gorilla; (*guardia del corpo*) bodyguard

'**Gotha** *sm inv* (*del cinema, letteratura, industria*) leading lights *pl*

'**gotico, -a, ci, che** *ag, sm* Gothic

'**gotta** *sf* gout

gover'nante *sm/f* ruler ■ *sf* (*di bambini*) governess; (*donna di servizio*) housekeeper

gover'nare *vt* (*stato*) to govern, rule; (*pilotare, guidare*) to steer; (*bestiame*) to tend, look after

governa'tivo, -a *ag* (*politica, decreto*) government *cpd*, governmental; (*stampa*) pro-government

governa'tore *sm* governor

go'verno *sm* government; **~ ombra** shadow cabinet

'**gozzo** ['gottso] *sm* (*Zool*) crop; (*Med*) goitre; (*fig fam*) throat

gozzovigli'are [gottsoviʎ'ʎare] *vi* to make merry, carouse

GPL [dʒipi'ɛlle] *sigla m* (= *Gas di Petrolio Liquefatto*) LPG (= *Liquefied Petroleum Gas*)

gpm *abbr* (= *giri per minuto*) rpm

GPS [dʒipi'esse] *sigla m* GPS (= *Global Positioning System*)

GR [dʒi'erre] *sigla* = **Grosseto** ■ *sigla m* (= *giornale radio*) radio news

gracchi'are [grak'kjare] *vi* to caw

graci'dare [gratʃi'dare] *vi* to croak

graci'dio, -ii [gratʃi'dio] *sm* croaking

'**gracile** ['gratʃile] *ag* frail, delicate

gra'dasso *sm* boaster

gradata'mente *av* gradually, by degrees

gradazi'one [gradat'tsjone] *sf* (*sfumatura*) gradation; **~ alcolica** alcoholic content

gra'devole *ag* pleasant, agreeable

gradi'mento *sm* pleasure, satisfaction; **essere di mio** (*o* **tuo** *etc*) **~** to be to my (*o* your *etc*) liking

gradi'nata *sf* flight of steps; (*in teatro, stadio*) tiers *pl*

gra'dino *sm* step; (*Alpinismo*) foothold

gra'dire *vt* (*accettare con piacere*) to accept; (*desiderare*) to wish, like; **gradisce una tazza di tè?** would you like a cup of tea?

gra'dito, -a *ag* welcome

'**grado** *sm* (*Mat, Fisica etc*) degree; (*stadio*) degree, level; (*Mil, sociale*) rank; **essere in ~ di fare** to be in a position to do; **di buon ~** willingly; **per gradi** by degrees; **un cugino di primo/ secondo ~** a first/second cousin; **subire il terzo ~** (*anche fig*) to be given the third degree

gradu'ale *ag* gradual

gradu'are *vt* to grade

gradu'ato, -a *ag* (*esercizi*) graded; (*scala, termometro*) graduated ■ *sm* (*Mil*) non-commissioned officer

gradua'toria *sf* (*di concorso*) list; (*per la promozione*) order of seniority

'**graffa** *sf* (*gancio*) clip; (*segno grafico*) brace

graf'fetta *sf* paper clip

graffi'are *vt* to scratch

graffia'tura *sf* scratch

'**graffio** *sm* scratch

graf'fiti *smpl* graffiti

gra'fia *sf* spelling; (*scrittura*) handwriting

'**grafico, -a, ci, che** *ag* graphic ■ *sm* graph; (*persona*) graphic designer ■ *sf* graphic arts *pl*; **~ a torta** pie chart

gra'migna [gra'miɲɲa] *sf* weed; couch grass

gram'matica, -che *sf* grammar

grammati'cale *ag* grammatical

'**grammo** *sm* gram(me)

gram'mofono *sm* gramophone

'**gramo, -a** *ag* (*vita*) wretched

gran *ag vedi* **grande**

'**grana** *sf* (*granello, di minerali, corpi spezzati*) grain; (*fam: seccatura*) trouble; (*: soldi*) cash ■ *sm inv* cheese similar to Parmesan

gra'naglie [gra'naʎʎe] *sfpl* corn *sg*, seed *sg*

gra'naio *sm* granary, barn

gra'nata *sf* (*frutto*) pomegranate; (*pietra preziosa*) garnet; (*proiettile*) grenade

granati'ere *sm* (*Mil*) grenadier; (*fig*) fine figure of a man

Gran Bre'tagna [granbre'taɲɲa] *sf*: **la ~** Great Britain

gran'cassa *sf* (*Mus*) bass drum

'**granchio** ['grankjo] *sm* crab; (*fig*) blunder; **prendere un ~** (*fig*) to blunder

grandango'lare *sm* wide-angle lens *sg*

gran'dangolo *sm* (*Fot*) wide-angle lens *sg*

'**grande** *ag* (*qualche volta* **gran** + C, **grand'** + V) (*grosso, largo, vasto*) big, large; (*alto*) tall; (*lungo*) long; (*in sensi astratti*) great ■ *sm/f* (*persona adulta*) adult, grown-up; (*chi ha ingegno e potenza*) great man(-woman); **mio fratello più ~** my big *o* older brother; **il gran**

pubblico the general public; **di gran classe** (*prodotto*) high-class; **cosa farai da ~?** what will you be o do when you grow up?; **fare le cose in ~** to do things in style; **fare il ~** (*strafare*) to act big; **una gran bella donna** a very beautiful woman; **non è una gran cosa** o **un gran che** it's nothing special; **non ne so gran che** I don't know very much about it

grandeggi'are [granded'dʒare] vi (*emergere per grandezza*): **~ su** to tower over; (*darsi arie*) to put on airs

gran'dezza [gran'dettsa] sf (*dimensione*) size; (*fig*) greatness; **in ~ naturale** lifesize; **manie di ~** delusions of grandeur

grandi'nare vb impers to hail

'grandine sf hail

grandi'oso, -a ag grand, grandiose

gran'duca, -chi sm grand duke

grandu'cato sm grand duchy

grandu'chessa [grandu'kessa] sf grand duchess

gra'nello sm (*di cereali, uva*) seed; (*di frutta*) pip; (*di sabbia, sale etc*) grain

gra'nita sf kind of water ice

gra'nito sm granite

'grano sm (*in quasi tutti i sensi*) grain; (*frumento*) wheat; (*di rosario, collana*) bead; **~ di pepe** peppercorn

gran'turco sm maize

'granulo sm granule; (*Med*) pellet

'grappa sf rough, strong brandy

'grappolo sm bunch, cluster

'graspo sm bunch (of grapes)

gras'setto sm (*Tip*) bold (type) (*Brit*), bold face

'grasso, -a ag fat; (*cibo*) fatty; (*pelle*) greasy; (*terreno*) rich; (*fig: guadagno, annata*) plentiful; (: *volgare*) coarse, lewd ▪ sm (*di persona, animale*) fat; (*sostanza che unge*) grease

gras'soccio, -a, ci, ce [gras'sɔttʃo] ag plump

gras'sone, -a sm/f (*fam: persona*) dumpling

'grata sf grating

gra'ticcio [gra'tittʃo] sm trellis; (*stuoia*) mat

gra'ticola sf grill

gra'tifica, -che sf bonus; **~ natalizia** Christmas bonus

gratificazi'one [gratifikat'tsjone] sf (*soddisfazione*) satisfaction, reward

grati'nare vt (*Cuc*) to cook au gratin

'gratis av free, for nothing

grati'tudine sf gratitude

'grato, -a ag grateful

gratta'capo sm worry, headache

grattaci'elo [gratta'tʃɛlo] sm skyscraper

gratta e 'sosta sm inv scratch card used to pay for parking

gratta e 'vinci [grattae'vintʃi] sm (*lotteria*) lottery; (*biglietto*) scratchcard

grat'tare vt (*pelle*) to scratch; (*raschiare*) to scrape; (*pane, formaggio, carote*) to grate; (*fam: rubare*) to pinch ▪ vi (*stridere*) to grate; (*Aut*) to grind; **grattarsi** vr to scratch o.s.; **grattarsi la pancia** (*fig*) to twiddle one's thumbs

grat'tata sf scratch; **fare una ~** (*Aut: fam*) to grind the gears

grat'tugia, -gie [grat'tudʒa] sf grater

grattugi'are [grattu'dʒare] vt to grate; **pane grattugiato** breadcrumbs pl

gratuità sf (*fig*) gratuitousness

gra'tuito, -a ag free; (*fig*) gratuitous

gra'vame sm tax; (*fig*) burden, weight

gra'vare vt to burden ▪ vi: **~ su** to weigh on

'grave ag (*danno, pericolo, peccato etc*) grave, serious; (*responsabilità*) heavy, grave; (*contegno*) grave, solemn; (*voce, suono*) deep, low-pitched; (*Ling*): **accento ~** grave accent ▪ sm (*Fisica*) (heavy) body; **un malato ~** a person who is seriously ill

grave'mente av (*ammalato, ferito*) seriously

gravi'danza [gravi'dantsa] sf pregnancy

'gravido, -a ag pregnant

gravità sf seriousness; (*anche Fisica*) gravity

gravi'tare vi (*Fisica*): **~ intorno a** to gravitate round

gra'voso, -a ag heavy, onerous

'grazia ['grattsja] sf grace; (*favore*) favour (*Brit*), favor (*US*); (*Dir*) pardon; **di ~** (*ironico*) if you please; **troppa ~!** (*ironico*) you're too generous!; **quanta ~ di Dio!** what abundance!; **entrare nelle grazie di qn** to win sb's favour; **Ministero di G~ e Giustizia** Ministry of Justice, ≈ Lord Chancellor's Office (*Brit*), ≈ Department of Justice (*US*)

grazi'are [grat'tsjare] vt (*Dir*) to pardon

'grazie ['grattsje] escl thank you!; **~ mille!** o **tante!** o **infinite!** thank you very much!; **~ a** thanks to

grazi'oso, -a [grat'tsjoso] ag charming, delightful; (*gentile*) gracious

'Grecia ['grɛtʃa] sf: **la ~** Greece

'greco, -a, ci, che ag, sm/f, sm Greek

gre'gario sm (*Ciclismo*) supporting rider

'gregge ['greddʒe] (*pl(f)* **greggi**) sm flock

'greggio, -a, gi, ge ['greddʒo] ag raw, unrefined; (*diamante*) rough, uncut; (*tessuto*) unbleached ▪ sm (*anche:* **petrolio greggio**) crude (oil)

grembi'ule sm apron; (*sopravveste*) overall

'grembo sm lap; (*ventre della madre*) womb

gre'mito, -a ag: **~ (di)** packed o crowded (with)

'greto sm (*esposto*) gravel bed of a river

'gretto, -a ag mean, stingy; (*fig*) narrow-minded

g

greve *ag* heavy

grezzo, -a ['greddzo] *ag* = **greggio**

gridare *vi* (*per chiamare*) to shout, cry (out); (*strillare*) to scream, yell ■ *vt* to shout (out), yell (out); ~ **aiuto** to cry *o* shout for help

grido (*pl*(*m*) **gridi**, *pl*(*f*) **grida**) *sm* shout, cry; scream, yell; (*di animale*) cry; **di** ~ famous; **all'ultimo** ~ in the latest style

grigio, -a, gi, gie ['gridʒo] *ag*, *sm* grey (*Brit*), gray (*US*)

griglia ['griʎʎa] *sf* (*per arrostire*) grill; (*Elettr*) grid; (*inferriata*) grating; **alla** ~ (*Cuc*) grilled

grigliata [griʎ'ʎata] *sf* (*Cuc*) grill

grilletto *sm* trigger

grillo *sm* (*Zool*) cricket; (*fig*) whim; **ha dei grilli per la testa** his head is full of nonsense

grimaldello *sm* picklock

grinfia *sf*: **cadere nelle grinfie di qn** (*fig*) to fall into sb's clutches

grinta *sf* grim expression; (*Sport*) fighting spirit; **avere molta** ~ to be very determined

grintoso, -a *ag* forceful

grinza ['grintsa] *sf* crease, wrinkle; (*ruga*) wrinkle; **il tuo ragionamento non fa una** ~ your argument is faultless

grinzoso, -a [grin'tsoso] *ag* wrinkled; creased

grippare *vi* (*Tecn*) to seize

grissino *sm* bread-stick

groenlandese *ag* Greenland *cpd* ■ *sm/f* Greenlander

Groenlandia *sf*: **la** ~ Greenland

gronda *sf* eaves *pl*

grondaia *sf* gutter

grondante *ag* dripping

grondare *vi* to pour; (*essere bagnato*): ~ **di** to be dripping with ■ *vt* to drip with

groppa *sf* (*di animale*) back, rump; (*fam*: *dell'uomo*) back, shoulders *pl*

groppo *sm* tangle; **avere un** ~ **alla gola** (*fig*) to have a lump in one's throat

grossa *sf* (*unità di misura*) gross

grossezza [gros'settsa] *sf* size; thickness

grossista, -i, e *sm/f* (*Comm*) wholesaler

grosso, -a *ag* big, large; (*di spessore*) thick; (*grossolano*: *anche fig*) coarse; (*grave*, *insopportabile*) serious, great; (*tempo, mare*) rough ■ *sm*: **il** ~ **di** the bulk of; **un pezzo** ~ (*fig*) a VIP, a bigwig; **farla grossa** to do something very stupid; **dirle grosse** to tell tall stories (*Brit*) *o* tales (*US*); **questa è grossa!** that's a good one!; **sbagliarsi di** ~ to be completely wrong; **dormire della grossa** to sleep like a log

grossolanità *sf* coarseness

grossolano, -a *ag* rough, coarse; (*fig*) coarse, crude; (: *errore*) stupid

grosso modo *av* roughly

grotta *sf* cave; grotto

grottesco, -a, schi, sche *ag* grotesque

groviera *sm o f* gruyère (cheese)

groviglio [gro'viʎʎo] *sm* tangle; (*fig*) muddle

gru *sf inv* crane

gruccia, -ce ['gruttʃa] *sf* (*per camminare*) crutch; (*per abiti*) coat-hanger

grugnire [gruɲ'ɲire] *vi* to grunt

grugnito [gruɲ'ɲito] *sm* grunt

grugno ['gruɲɲo] *sm* snout; (*fam*: *faccia*) mug

grullo, -a *ag* silly, stupid

grumo *sm* (*di sangue*) clot; (*di farina etc*) lump

grumoso, -a *ag* lumpy

gruppo *sm* group; ~ **sanguigno** blood group

gruviera *sm o f* = **groviera**

gruzzolo ['gruttsolo] *sm* (*di denaro*) hoard

GT *abbr* (*Aut*: = *gran turismo*) GT

G.U. *abbr* = **Gazzetta Ufficiale**

guadagnare [gwadaɲ'ɲare] *vt* (*ottenere*) to gain; (*soldi, stipendio*) to earn; (*vincere*) to win; (*raggiungere*) to reach; **tanto di guadagnato!** so much the better!

guadagno [gwa'daɲɲo] *sm* earnings *pl*; (*Comm*) profit; (*vantaggio, utile*) advantage, gain; ~ **di capitale** capital gains *pl*; ~ **lordo/netto** gross/net earnings *pl*

guado *sm* ford; **passare a** ~ to ford

guai *escl*: ~ **a te** (*o* **lui** *etc*)! woe betide you (*o* him *etc*)!

guaina *sf* (*fodero*) sheath; (*indumento per donna*) girdle

guaio *sm* trouble, mishap; (*inconveniente*) trouble, snag

guaire *vi* to whine, yelp

guaito *sm* (*di cane*) yelp, whine; (*il guaire*) yelping, whining

guancia, -ce ['gwantʃa] *sf* cheek

guanciale [gwan'tʃale] *sm* pillow; **dormire fra due guanciali** (*fig*) to sleep easy, have no worries

guanto *sm* glove; **trattare qn con i guanti** (*fig*) to handle sb with kid gloves; **gettare/raccogliere il** ~ (*fig*) to throw down/take up the gauntlet

guantone *sm* boxing glove

guardaboschi [gwarda'bɔski] *sm inv* forester

guardacaccia [gwarda'kattʃa] *sm inv* gamekeeper

guardacoste *sm inv* coastguard; (*nave*) coastguard patrol vessel

guardalinee *sm inv* (*Sport*) linesman

guardamacchine [gwarda'makkine] *sm/f inv* car-park (*Brit*) *o* parking lot (*US*) attendant

guardare *vt* (*con lo sguardo*: *osservare*) to look at; (*film, televisione*) to watch; (*custodire*) to look after, take care of ■ *vi* to look; (*badare*): ~ **a** to pay attention to; (*luoghi: esser orientato*): ~ **a** to face; **guardarsi** *vr* to look at o.s.; ~ **di** to try to; **guardarsi da** (*astenersi*) to refrain from; (*stare in guardia*) to beware of; **guardarsi dal fare** to take care not to do; **ma guarda un po'!** good heavens!; **e guarda caso ...** as if by coincidence ...; ~ **dall'alto in basso** to look down on sb; **non ~ in faccia a nessuno** (*fig*) to have no regard for anybody; ~ **di traverso** to scowl o frown at; ~ **a vista qn** to keep a close watch on sb

guarda'roba *sm inv* wardrobe; (*locale*) cloakroom

guardarobi'ere, -a *sm/f* cloakroom attendant

guardasi'gilli [gwardasi'dʒilli] *sm inv* ≈ Lord Chancellor (*Brit*), ≈ Attorney General (*US*)

gu'ardia *sf* (*individuo, corpo*) guard; (*sorveglianza*) watch; **fare la ~ a qc/qn** to guard sth/sb; **stare in ~** (*fig*) to be on one's guard; **il medico di ~** the doctor on call; **il fiume ha raggiunto il livello di ~** the river has reached the high-water mark; ~ **carceraria** (*prison*) warder (*Brit*) o guard (*US*); ~ **del corpo** bodyguard; ~ **di finanza** (*corpo*) customs *pl*; (*persona*) customs officer; *see note*; ~ **forestale** forest ranger; ~ **giurata** security guard; ~ **medica** emergency doctor service; ~ **municipale** town policeman; ~ **notturna** night security guard; ~ **di pubblica sicurezza** policeman

- **GUARDIA DI FINANZA**

  The *Guardia di Finanza* is a military body which deals with infringements of the laws governing income tax and monopolies. It reports to the Ministers of Finance, Justice or Agriculture, depending on the function it is performing.

guardia'caccia [gwardja'kattʃa] *sm inv* = **guardacaccia**

guardi'ano, -a *sm/f* (*di carcere*) warder (*Brit*), guard (*US*); (*di villa etc*) caretaker; (*di museo*) custodian; (*di zoo*) keeper; ~ **notturno** night watchman

guar'dina *sf* cell

guar'dingo, -a, ghi, ghe *ag* wary, cautious

guardi'ola *sf* porter's lodge; (*Mil*) look-out tower

guarigi'one [gwari'dʒone] *sf* recovery

gua'rire *vt* (*persona, malattia*) to cure; (*ferita*) to heal ■ *vi* to recover, be cured; to heal (up)

guarnigi'one [gwarni'dʒone] *sf* garrison

guar'nire *vt* (*ornare: abiti*) to trim; (*Cuc*) to garnish

guarnizi'one [gwarnit'tsjone] *sf* trimming; garnish; (*Tecn*) gasket

guasta'feste *sm/f inv* spoilsport

guas'tare *vt* to spoil, ruin; (*meccanismo*) to break; **guastarsi** *vr* (*cibo*) to go bad; (*meccanismo*) to break down; (*tempo*) to change for the worse; (*amici*) to quarrel, fall out

gu'asto, -a *ag* (*non funzionante*) broken; (: *telefono etc*) out of order; (*andato a male*) bad, rotten; (: *dente*) decayed, bad; (*fig: corrotto*) depraved ■ *sm* breakdown; (*avaria*) failure; ~ **al motore** engine failure

Guate'mala *sm*: **il ~** Guatemala

guatemal'teco, -a, ci, che *ag, sm/f* Guatemalan

gu'ercio, -a, ci, ce ['gwertʃo] *ag* cross-eyed

gu'erra *sf* war; (*tecnica: atomica, chimica etc*) warfare; **fare la ~ (a)** to wage war (against); **la ~ fredda** the Cold War; ~ **mondiale** world war; ~ **preventiva** preventive war; **la prima/seconda ~ mondiale** the First/ Second World War

guerrafon'daio *sm* warmonger

guerreggi'are [gwerred'dʒare] *vi* to wage war

guer'resco, -a, schi, sche *ag* (*di guerra*) war *cpd*; (*incline alla guerra*) warlike

guerri'ero, -a *ag* warlike ■ *sm* warrior

guer'riglia [gwer'riʎʎa] *sf* guerrilla warfare

guerrigli'ero [gwerriʎ'ʎɛro] *sm* guerrilla

'gufo *sm* owl

'guglia ['guʎʎa] *sf* (*Archit*) spire; (*di roccia*) needle

Gui'ana *sf*: **la ~ francese** French Guiana

gu'ida *sf* (*persona*) guide; (*libro*) guide(book); (*comando, direzione*) guidance, direction; (*Aut*) driving; (: *sterzo*) steering; (*tappeto*) runner; ~ **a destra/sinistra** (*Aut*) right-/left-hand drive; **essere alla ~ di** (*governo*) to head; (*spedizione, paese*) to lead; **far da ~ a qn** (*mostrare la strada*) to show sb the way; (*in una città*) to show sb (a)round; ~ **telefonica** telephone directory

gui'dare *vt* to guide; (*condurre a capo*) to lead; (*auto*) to drive; (*aereo, nave*) to pilot; **sa ~?** can you drive?

guida'tore, -'trice *sm/f* (*conducente*) driver

Gui'nea *sf*: **la Repubblica di ~** the Republic of Guinea; **la ~ Equatoriale** Equatorial Guinea

guin'zaglio [gwin'tsaʎʎo] *sm* leash, lead

gu'isa *sf*: **a ~ di** like, in the manner of

guiz'zare [gwit'tsare] *vi* to dart; to flicker; to leap; ~ **via** (*fuggire*) to slip away

gu'izzo ['gwittso] *sm* (*di animali*) dart; (*di fulmine*) flash

'guru *sm inv* (*Rel, anche fig*) guru

'guscio ['guʃʃo] *sm* shell

g

gus'tare vt (cibi) to taste; (: assaporare con piacere) to enjoy, savour (Brit), savor (US); (fig) to enjoy, appreciate ■ vi: ~ **a** to please; **non mi gusta affatto** I don't like it at all
gusta'tivo, -a ag: **papille gustative** taste buds
'gusto sm (senso) taste; (sapore) taste, flavour (Brit), flavor (US); (godimento) enjoyment; **al ~**

di fragola strawberry-flavo(u)red; **di ~ barocco** in the baroque style; **mangiare di ~** to eat heartily; **prenderci ~: ci ha preso ~** he's acquired a taste for it, he's got to like it
gus'toso, -a ag tasty; (fig) agreeable
guttu'rale ag guttural
Gu'yana [gu'jana] sf: **la ~** Guyana

Hh

H, h ['akka] *sf o m inv* (*lettera*) H, h ■ *abbr*
(= *ora*) hr; (= *etto, altezza*) h; **H come hotel** ≈
H for Harry (*Brit*), H for How (*US*)
ha¹, 'hai [a, ai] *vb vedi* **avere**
ha² *abbr* (= *ettaro*) ha
Ha'iti [a'iti] *sf* Haiti
haiti'ano, -a [ai'tjano] *ag, sm/f* Haitian
hall [hɔːl] *sf inv* hall, foyer
'handicap ['handikap] *sm inv* handicap
handicap'pato, -a [andikap'pato] *ag*
handicapped ■ *sm/f* handicapped person,
disabled person
'hanno ['anno] *vb vedi* **avere**
ha'scisc [aʃʃiʃ] *sm* hashish
hawai'ano, -a [ava'jano] *ag, sm/f*
Hawaiian
Ha'waii [a'vai] *sfpl*: **le ~** Hawaii *sg*
'Helsinki ['ɛlsinki] *sf* Helsinki

'herpes ['ɛrpes] *sm* (*Med*) herpes *sg*;
~ zoster shingles *sg*
hg *abbr* (= *ettogrammo*) hg
'hi-fi ['haifai] *sm inv, ag inv* hi-fi
Hima'laia [ima'laja] *sm*: **l'~** the Himalayas *pl*
hl *abbr* (= *ettolitro*) hl
ho [ɔ] *vb vedi* **avere**
'hobby ['hɔbi] *sm inv* hobby
'hockey ['hɔki] *sm* hockey; **~ su ghiaccio**
ice hockey
'holding ['houldiŋ] *sf inv* holding company
Hon'duras [on'duras] *sm* Honduras
'Hong Kong ['ɔkɔg] *sf* Hong Kong
Hono'lulu [ono'lulu] *sf* Honolulu
'hostess ['houstis] *sf inv* air hostess (*Brit*) o
stewardess
ho'tel [o'tɛl] *sm inv* hotel
Hz *abbr* (= *hertz*) Hz

h

I i

I, i [i] *sf o m inv* (*lettera*) I, i; **I come Imola** ≈ I for Isaac (*Brit*), I for Item (*US*)

i *det mpl* the; *vedi anche* **il**

IACP *sigla m* (= *Istituto Autonomo per le Case Popolari*) public housing association

i'ato *sm* hiatus

i'berico, -a, ci, che *ag* Iberian; **la Penisola Iberica** the Iberian Peninsula

iber'nare *vi* to hibernate ■ *vt* (*Med*) to induce hypothermia in

ibernazi'one [ibernat'tsjone] *sf* hibernation

ibid. *abbr* (= *ibidem*) ib(id)

'ibrido, -a *ag, sm* hybrid

IC *abbr* = **intercity**

'ICE ['itʃe] *sigla m* (= *Istituto nazionale per il Commercio Estero*) overseas trade board

i'cona *sf* icon

id *abbr* (= *idem*) do.

Id'dio *sm* God

i'dea *sf* idea; (*opinione*) opinion, view; (*ideale*) ideal; **avere le idee chiare** to know one's mind; **cambiare ~** to change one's mind; **dare l'~ di** to seem, look like; **neanche** *o* **neppure per ~!** certainly not!, no way!; **~ fissa** obsession

ide'ale *ag, sm* ideal

idea'lismo *sm* idealism

idea'lista, -i, e *sm/f* idealist

idea'listico, -a, ci, che *ag* idealistic

idealiz'zare [idealid'dzare] *vt* to idealize

ide'are *vt* (*immaginare*) to think up, conceive; (*progettare*) to plan

idea'tore, -'trice *sm/f* author

i'dentico, -a, ci, che *ag* identical

identifi'care *vt* to identify

identificazi'one [identifikat'tsjone] *sf* identification

identità *sf inv* identity

ideolo'gia, -'gie [ideolo'dʒia] *sf* ideology

ideo'logico, -a, ci, che [ideo'lɔdʒiko] *ag* ideological

idil'liaco, -a, ci, che *ag* = **idillico**

i'dillico, -a, ci, che *ag* idyllic

i'dillio *sm* idyll; **tra di loro è nato un ~** they have fallen in love

idi'oma, -i *sm* idiom, language

idio'matico, -a, ci, che *ag* idiomatic; **frase idiomatica** idiom

idiosincra'sia *sf* idiosyncrasy

idi'ota, -i, e *ag* idiotic ■ *sm/f* idiot

idio'zia [idjot'tsia] *sf* idiocy; (*atto, discorso*) idiotic thing to do (*o* say)

ido'latra, -i, e *ag* idolatrous ■ *sm/f* idolater

idola'trare *vt* to worship; (*fig*) to idolize

idola'tria *sf* idolatry

'idolo *sm* idol

idoneità *sf* suitability; **esame** *m* **di ~** qualifying examination

i'doneo, -a *ag*: **~ a** suitable for, fit for; (*Mil*) fit for; (*qualificato*) qualified for

i'drante *sm* hydrant

idra'tante *ag* (*crema*) moisturizing ■ *sm* moisturizer

idra'tare *vt* (*pelle*) to moisturize

idratazi'one [idratat'tsjone] *sf* moisturizing

i'draulico, -a, ci, che *ag* hydraulic ■ *sm* plumber ■ *sf* hydraulics *sg*

'idrico, -a, ci, che *ag* water *cpd*

idrocar'buro *sm* hydrocarbon

idroe'lettrico, -a, ci, che *ag* hydroelectric

i'drofilo, -a *ag*: **cotone ~** cotton wool (*Brit*), absorbent cotton (*US*)

idrofo'bia *sf* rabies *sg*

i'drofobo, -a *ag* rabid; (*fig*) furious

i'drogeno [i'drɔdʒeno] *sm* hydrogen

idroli'pidico, -a, ci, che *ag* hydrolipid

idro'porto *sm* (*Aer*) seaplane base

idrorepel'lente *ag* water-repellent

idros'calo *sm* = **idroporto**

idrovo'lante *sm* seaplane

i'ella *sf* bad luck

iel'lato, -a *ag* plagued by bad luck

i'ena *sf* hyena

ie'ratico, -a, ci, che *ag* (*Rel: scrittura*) hieratic; (*fig: atteggiamento*) solemn i'eri *av, sm* yesterday; **il giornale di ~** yesterday's paper; **~ l'altro** the day before yesterday; **~ sera** yesterday evening

ietta'tore, -'trice *sm/f* jinx

igi'ene [i'dʒɛne] *sf* hygiene; **norme d'~** sanitary regulations; **ufficio d'~** public health office; **~ mentale** mental health; **~ pubblica** public health

igi'enico, -a, ci, che [i'dʒɛniko] *ag* hygienic; (*salubre*) healthy

igloo [i'glu] *sm inv* igloo; (*tenda*) dome tent

IGM *sigla m* (= *Ispettorato Generale della Motorizzazione*) road traffic inspectorate

i'gnaro, -a [iɲ'ɲaro] *ag*: **~ di** unaware of, ignorant of

i'gnifugo, -a, ghi, ghe [iɲ'ɲifugo] *ag* flame-resistant, fireproof

i'gnobile [iɲ'ɲɔbile] *ag* despicable, vile

igno'minia [iɲɲo'minja] *sf* ignominy

igno'rante [iɲɲo'rante] *ag* ignorant

igno'ranza [iɲɲo'rantsa] *sf* ignorance

igno'rare [iɲɲo'rare] *vt* (*non sapere, conoscere*) to be ignorant o unaware of, not to know; (*fingere di non vedere, sentire*) to ignore

i'gnoto, -a [iɲ'ɲɔto] *ag* unknown ■ *sm/f*: **figlio di ignoti** child of unknown parentage; **il Milite I~** the Unknown Soldier

⭕ **PAROLA CHIAVE**

il (*pl(m)* **i**; *diventa* **lo** (*pl* **gli**) *davanti a s impura, gn, pn, ps, x, z; f* **la** (*pl* **le**)) *det m* **1** the; **il libro/lo studente/l'acqua** the book/the student/the water; **gli scolari** the pupils

2 (*astrazione*): **il coraggio/l'amore/la giovinezza** courage/love/youth

3 (*tempo*): **il mattino/la sera** in the morning/evening; **il venerdì** (*abitualmente*) on Fridays; (*quel giorno*) on (the) Friday; **la settimana prossima** next week

4 (*distributivo*) a, an; **2 euro il chilo/paio** 2 euros a o per kilo/pair

5 (*partitivo*) some, any; **hai messo lo zucchero?** have you added sugar?; **hai comprato il latte?** did you buy (some o any) milk?

6 (*possesso*): **aprire gli occhi** to open one's eyes; **rompersi la gamba** to break one's leg; **avere i capelli neri/il naso rosso** to have dark hair/a red nose; **mettiti le scarpe** put your shoes on

7 (*con nomi propri*): **il Petrarca** Petrarch; **il Presidente Bush** President Bush; **dov'è la Francesca?** where's Francesca?

8 (*con nomi geografici*): **il Tevere** the Tiber; **l'Italia** Italy; **il Regno Unito** the United Kingdom; **l'Everest** Everest

'ilare *ag* cheerful

ilarità *sf* hilarity, mirth

ill. *abbr* (= *illustrazione, illustrato*) ill.

illangui'dire *vi* to grow weak o feeble

illazi'one [illat'tsjone] *sf* inference, deduction

il'lecito, -a [il'letʃito] *ag* illicit

ille'gale *ag* illegal

illegalità *sf* illegality

illeg'gibile [illed'dʒibile] *ag* illegible

illegittimità [illedʒittimi'ta] *sf* illegitimacy

ille'gittimo, -a [ille'dʒittimo] *ag* illegitimate

il'leso, -a *ag* unhurt, unharmed

illette'rato, -a *ag* illiterate

illiba'tezza [illiba'tettsa] *sf* (*di donna*) virginity

illi'bato, -a *ag*: **donna illibata** virgin

illimi'tato, -a *ag* boundless; unlimited

illivi'dire *vi* (*volto, mani*) to turn livid; (*cielo*) to grow leaden

ill.mo *abbr* = **illustrissimo**

il'logico, -a, ci, che [il'lɔdʒiko] *ag* illogical

il'ludere *vt* to deceive, delude; **illudersi** *vr* to deceive o.s., delude o.s.

illumi'nare *vt* to light up, illuminate; (*fig*) to enlighten; **illuminarsi** *vr* to light up; **~ a giorno** (*con riflettori*) to floodlight

illumi'nato, -a *ag* (*fig: sovrano, spirito*) enlightened

illuminazi'one [illuminat'tsjone] *sf* lighting; illumination; floodlighting; (*fig*) flash of inspiration

illumi'nismo *sm* (*Storia*): **l'I~** the Enlightenment

il'lusi *etc vb vedi* **illudere**

illusi'one *sf* illusion; **farsi delle illusioni** to delude o.s.

illusio'nismo *sm* conjuring

illusio'nista, -i, e *sm/f* conjurer

il'luso, -a *pp di* **illudere**

illu'sorio, -a *ag* illusory

illus'trare *vt* to illustrate

illustra'tivo, -a *ag* illustrative

illustrazi'one [illustrat'tsjone] *sf* illustration

il'lustre *ag* eminent, renowned

illus'trissimo, -a *ag* (*negli indirizzi*) very revered

'ILOR *sigla f* = **imposta locale sui redditi**

IM *sigla* = **Imperia**

imbacuc'care *vt*, **imbacuc'carsi** *vr* to wrap up

imbaldan'zire [imbaldan'tsire] *vt* to give confidence to; **imbaldanzirsi** *vr* to grow bold

imbal'laggio [imbal'laddʒo] *sm* packing *no pl*

imbal'lare *vt* to pack; (*Aut*) to race; **imballarsi** *vr* (*Aut*) to race

imbalsa'mare *vt* to embalm

imbalsa'mato, -a *ag* embalmed

imbambo'lato, -a *ag* (*sguardo, espressione*) vacant, blank

imban'dire *vt*: ~ **un banchetto** to prepare a lavish feast

imban'dito, -a *ag*: **tavola imbandita** lavishly *o* sumptuously decked table

imbaraz'zante [imbarat'tsante] *ag* embarrassing, awkward

imbaraz'zare [imbarat'tsare] *vt* (*mettere a disagio*) to embarrass; (*ostacolare: movimenti*) to hamper; (: *stomaco*) to lie heavily on; **imbarazzarsi** *vr* to become embarrassed

imbaraz'zato, -a [imbarat'tsato] *ag* embarrassed; **avere lo stomaco ~** to have an upset stomach

imba'razzo [imba'rattso] *sm* (*disagio*) embarrassment; (*perplessità*) puzzlement, bewilderment; **essere** *o* **trovarsi in ~** to be in an awkward situation *o* predicament; **mettere in ~** to embarrass; **~ di stomaco** indigestion

imbarbari'mento *sm* (*di civiltà, costumi*) barbarization

imbarca'dero *sm* landing stage

imbar'care *vt* (*passeggeri*) to embark; (*merci*) to load; **imbarcarsi** *vr*: **imbarcarsi su** to board; **imbarcarsi per l'America** to sail for America; **imbarcarsi in** (*fig: affare*) to embark on

imbarcazi'one [imbarkat'tsjone] *sf* (small) boat, (small) craft *inv*; **~ di salvataggio** lifeboat

im'barco, -chi *sm* embarkation; loading; boarding; (*banchina*) landing stage; **carta d'~** boarding pass (Brit), boarding card

imbastar'dire *vt* to bastardize, debase; **imbastardirsi** *vr* to degenerate, become debased

imbas'tire *vt* (*cucire*) to tack; (*fig: abbozzare*) to sketch, outline

im'battersi *vr*: **~ in** (*incontrare*) to bump *o* run into

imbat'tibile *ag* unbeatable, invincible

imbavagli'are [imbavaʎ'ʎare] *vt* to gag

imbec'care *vt* (*uccelli*) to feed; (*fig*) to prompt, put words into sb's mouth

imbec'cata *sf* (*Teat*) prompt; **dare l'~ a qn** to prompt sb; (*fig*) to give sb their cue

imbe'cille [imbe'tʃille] *ag* idiotic ■ *sm/f* idiot; (*Med*) imbecile

imbecillità [imbetʃilli'ta] *sf inv* (*Med, fig*) imbecility, idiocy; **dire ~** to talk nonsense

imbellet'tare *vt* (*viso*) to make up, put make-up on; **imbellettarsi** *vr* to make o.s. up, put on one's make-up

imbel'lire *vt* to adorn, embellish ■ *vi* to grow more beautiful

im'berbe *ag* beardless; **un giovanotto ~** a callow youth

imbestia'lire *vt* to infuriate; **imbestialirsi** *vr* to become infuriated, fly into a rage

im'bevere *vt* to soak; **imbeversi** *vr*: **imbeversi di** to soak up, absorb

imbe'vuto, -a *ag*: **~ (di)** soaked (in)

imbian'care *vt* to whiten; (*muro*) to whitewash ■ *vi* to become *o* turn white

imbianca'tura *sf* (*di muro: con bianco di calce*) whitewashing; (: *con altre pitture*) painting

imbian'chino [imbjan'kino] *sm* (house) painter, painter and decorator

imbion'dire *vt* (*capelli*) to lighten; (*Cuc: cipolla*) to brown; **imbiondirsi** *vr* (*capelli*) to lighten, go blonde, go fair; (*messi*) to turn golden, ripen

imbizzar'rirsi [imbiddzar'rirsi] *vr* (*cavallo*) to become frisky

imboc'care *vt* (*bambino*) to feed; (*entrare: strada*) to enter, turn into ■ *vi*: **~ in** (*strada*) to lead into; (: *fiume*) to flow into

imbocca'tura *sf* mouth; (*di strada, porto*) entrance; (*Mus, del morso*) mouthpiece

im'bocco, -chi *sm* entrance

imboni'tore *sm* (*di spettacolo, circo*) barker

imborghe'sire [imborge'zire] *vi*, **imborghe'sirsi** *vr* to become bourgeois

imbos'care *vt* to hide; **imboscarsi** *vr* (*Mil*) to evade military service

imbos'cata *sf* ambush

imbos'cato *sm* draft dodger (US)

imboschi'mento [imboski'mento] *sm* afforestation

imbottigli'are [imbottiʎ'ʎare] *vt* to bottle; (*Naut*) to blockade; (*Mil*) to hem in; **imbottigliarsi** *vr* to be stuck in a traffic jam

imbot'tire *vt* to stuff; (*giacca*) to pad; **imbottirsi** *vr*: **imbottirsi di** (*rimpinzarsi*) to stuff o.s. with

imbot'tito, -a *ag* (*sedia*) upholstered; (*giacca*) padded ■ *sf* quilt

imbotti'tura *sf* stuffing; padding

imbracci'are [imbrat'tʃare] *vt* (*fucile*) to shoulder; (*scudo*) to grasp

imbra'nato, -a *ag* clumsy, awkward ■ *sm/f* clumsy person

imbratta'carte *sm/f* (*peg*) scribbler

imbrat'tare *vt* to dirty, smear, daub; **imbrattarsi** *vr*: **imbrattarsi (di)** to dirty o.s. (with)

imbratta'tele *sm/f* (*peg*) dauber

imbrigli'are [imbriʎ'ʎare] *vt* to bridle

imbroc'care *vt* (*fig*) to guess correctly

imbrogli'are [imbroʎ'ʎare] *vt* to mix up; (*fig: raggirare*) to deceive, cheat; (: *confondere*) to confuse, mix up; **imbrogliarsi** *vr* to get tangled; (*fig*) to become confused

im'broglio [im'brɔʎʎo] sm (groviglio) tangle; (situazione confusa) mess; (truffa) swindle, trick

imbrogli'one, -a [imbroʎ'ʎone] sm/f cheat, swindler

imbronci'ato, -a [imbron'tʃato] ag (persona) sulky; (cielo) cloudy, threatening

imbru'nire vi, vb impers to grow dark; **all'~** at dusk

imbrut'tire vt to make ugly ■ vi to become ugly

imbu'care vt to post

imbur'rare vt to butter

imbuti'forme ag funnel-shaped

im'buto sm funnel

I.M.C.T.C. sigla (= Ispettorato Generale della Motorizzazione Civile e dei Trasporti in Concessione) ≈ DVLA

i'mene sm hymen

imi'tare vt to imitate; (riprodurre) to copy; (assomigliare) to look like

imita'tore, -'trice sm/f (gen) imitator; (Teat) impersonator, impressionist

imitazi'one [imitat'tsjone] sf imitation

immaco'lato, -a ag spotless; immaculate

immagazzi'nare [immagaddzi'nare] vt to store

immagi'nabile [immadʒi'nabile] ag imaginable

immagi'nare [immadʒi'nare] vt to imagine; (supporre) to suppose; (inventare) to invent; **s'immagini!** don't mention it!, not at all!

immagi'nario, -a [immadʒi'narjo] ag imaginary

immagina'tiva [immadʒina'tiva] sf imagination

immaginazi'one [immadʒinat'tsjone] sf imagination; (cosa immaginata) fancy

im'magine [im'madʒine] sf image; (rappresentazione grafica, mentale) picture

immagi'noso, -a [immadʒi'noso] ag (linguaggio, stile) fantastic

immalinco'nire vt to sadden, depress; **immalinconirsi** vr to become depressed, become melancholy

imman'cabile ag unfailing

immancabil'mente av without fail, unfailingly

im'mane ag (smisurato) huge; (spaventoso, inumano) terrible

imma'nente ag (Filosofia) inherent, immanent

immangi'abile [imman'dʒabile] ag inedible

immatrico'lare vt to register; **immatricolarsi** vr (Ins) to matriculate, enrol

immatricolazi'one [immatrikolat'tsjone] sf registration; matriculation; enrolment

immaturità sf immaturity

imma'turo, -a ag (frutto) unripe; (persona) immature; (prematuro) premature

immedesi'marsi vr: **~ in** to identify with

immediata'mente av immediately, at once

immedia'tezza [immedja'tettsa] sf immediacy

immedi'ato, -a ag immediate

immemo'rabile ag immemorial; **da tempo ~** from time immemorial

im'memore ag: **~ di** forgetful of

immensità sf immensity

im'menso, -a ag immense

im'mergere [im'mɛrdʒere] vt to immerse, plunge; **immergersi** vr to plunge; (sommergibile) to dive, submerge; (dedicarsi a): **immergersi in** to immerse o.s. in

immeri'tato, -a ag undeserved

immeri'tevole ag undeserving, unworthy

immersi'one sf immersion; (di sommergibile) submersion, dive; (di palombaro) dive; **linea di ~** (Naut) water line

im'merso, -a pp di **immergere**

im'messo, -a pp di **immettere**

im'mettere vt: **~ (in)** to introduce (into); **~ dati in un computer** to enter data on a computer

immi'grante ag, sm/f immigrant

immi'grare vi to immigrate

immi'grato, -a sm/f immigrant

immigrazi'one [immigrat'tsjone] sf immigration

immi'nente ag imminent

immi'nenza [immi'nɛntsa] sf imminence

immischi'are [immis'kjare] vt: **~ qn in** to involve sb in; **immischiarsi** vr: **immischiarsi in** to interfere o meddle in

immiseri'mento sm impoverishment

immise'rire vt to impoverish

immis'sario sm (Geo) affluent, tributary

immissi'one sf (gen) introduction; (di aria, gas) intake; **~ di dati** (Inform) data entry

im'mobile ag motionless, still; **(beni) immobili** real estate sg

immobili'are ag (Dir) property cpd; **patrimonio ~** real estate; **società ~** property company

immobi'lismo sm inertia

immobilità sf immobility

immobiliz'zare [immobilid'dzare] vt to immobilize; (Econ) to lock up

immobi'lizzo [immobi'liddzo] sm: **spese d'~** capital expenditure

immo'destia sf immodesty

immo'desto, -a ag immodest

immo'lare vt to sacrifice

immondez'zaio [immondet'tsajo] sm rubbish dump

167

immon'dizia [immon'dittsja] *sf* dirt, filth; (*spesso al pl: spazzatura, rifiuti*) rubbish *no pl*, refuse *no pl*
immo'rale *ag* immoral
immoralità *sf* immorality
immorta'lare *vt* to immortalize
immor'tale *ag* immortal
immortalità *sf* immortality
im'mune (*esente*) exempt; (*Med, Dir*) immune
immunità *sf* immunity; ~ **diplomatica** diplomatic immunity; ~ **parlamentare** parliamentary privilege
immuniz'zare [immunid'dzare] *vt* (*Med*) to immunize
immunizzazi'one [immuniddzat'tsjone] *sf* immunization
immunodefi'cienza [immunodefi'tʃɛntsa] *sf*: ~ **acquisita** acquired immunodeficiency
immuno'logico, -a, ci, che [immuno'lɔdʒiko] *ag* immunological
immu'tabile *ag* immutable; unchanging
impac'care *vt* to pack
impacchet'tare [impakket'tare] *vt* to pack up
impacci'are [impat'tʃare] *vt* to hinder, hamper
impacci'ato, -a [impat'tʃato] *ag* awkward, clumsy; (*imbarazzato*) embarrassed
im'paccio [im'pattʃo] *sm* obstacle; (*imbarazzo*) embarrassment; (*situazione imbarazzante*) awkward situation
im'pacco, -chi *sm* (*Med*) compress
impadro'nirsi *vr*: ~ **di** to seize, take possession of; (*fig: apprendere a fondo*) to master
impa'gabile *ag* priceless
impagi'nare [impadʒi'nare] *vt* (*Tip*) to paginate, page (up)
impaginazi'one [impadʒinat'tsjone] *sf* pagination
impagli'are [impaʎ'ʎare] *vt* to stuff (with straw)
impa'lato, -a *ag* (*fig*) stiff as a board
impalca'tura *sf* scaffolding; (*anche fig*) framework
impalli'dire *vi* to turn pale; (*fig*) to fade
impalli'nare *vt* to riddle with shot
impal'pabile *ag* impalpable
impa'nare *vt* (*Cuc*) to dip (*o* roll) in breadcrumbs, bread (*US*)
impanta'narsi *vr* to sink (in the mud); (*fig*) to get bogged down
impape'rarsi *vr* to stumble over a word
impappi'narsi *vr* to stammer, falter
impa'rare *vt* to learn; **così impari!** that'll teach you!

impara'ticcio [impara'tittʃo] *sm* half-baked notions *pl*
impareggi'abile [impared'dʒabile] *ag* incomparable
imparen'tarsi *vr*: ~ **con** (*famiglia*) to marry into
'impari *ag inv* (*disuguale*) unequal; (*dispari*) odd
impar'tire *vt* to bestow, give
imparzi'ale [impar'tsjale] *ag* impartial, unbiased
imparzialità [impartsjali'ta] *sf* impartiality
impas'sibile *ag* impassive
impas'tare *vt* (*pasta*) to knead; (*colori*) to mix
impastic'carsi *vr* to pop pills
im'pasto *sm* (*l'impastare: di pane*) kneading; (: *di cemento*) mixing; (*pasta*) dough; (*anche fig*) mixture
im'patto *sm* impact; ~ **ambientale** impact on the environment
impau'rire *vt* to scare, frighten ■ *vi* (*anche*: **impaurirsi**) to become scared *o* frightened
im'pavido, -a *ag* intrepid, fearless
impazi'ente [impat'tsjɛnte] *ag* impatient
impazi'enza [impat'tsjɛntsa] *sf* impatience
impaz'zata [impat'tsata] *sf*: **all'~** (*precipitosamente*) at breakneck speed; (*colpire*) wildly
impaz'zire [impat'tsire] *vi* to go mad; ~ **per qn/qc** to be crazy about sb/sth
impec'cabile *ag* impeccable
impedi'mento *sm* obstacle, hindrance
impe'dire *vt* (*vietare*): ~ **a qn di fare** to prevent sb from doing; (*ostruire*) to obstruct; (*impacciare*) to hamper, hinder
impe'gnare [impeɲ'ɲare] *vt* (*dare in pegno*) to pawn; (*onore etc*) to pledge; (*prenotare*) to book, reserve; (*obbligare*) to oblige; (*occupare*) to keep busy; (*Mil: nemico*) to engage; **impegnarsi** *vr* (*vincolarsi*): **impegnarsi a fare** to undertake to do; (*mettersi risolutamente*): **impegnarsi in qc** to devote o.s. to sth; **impegnarsi con qn** (*accordarsi*) to come to an agreement with sb
impegna'tivo, -a [impeɲɲa'tivo] *ag* binding; (*lavoro*) demanding, exacting
impe'gnato, -a [impeɲ'ɲato] *ag* (*occupato*) busy; (*fig: romanzo, autore*) committed, engagé
im'pegno [im'peɲɲo] *sm* (*obbligo*) obligation; (*promessa*) promise, pledge; (*zelo*) diligence, zeal; (*compito: d'autore*) commitment; **impegni di lavoro** business commitments
impego'larsi *vr* (*fig*): ~ **in** to get heavily involved in
impela'garsi *vr* = **impegolarsi**
impel'lente *ag* pressing, urgent
impene'trabile *ag* impenetrable
impen'narsi *vr* (*cavallo*) to rear up; (*Aer*) to go into a climb; (*fig*) to bridle

impen'nata sf (di cavallo) rearing up; (di aereo) climb, nose-up; (fig: scatto d'ira) burst of anger; (: di prezzi etc) sudden increase

impen'sabile ag (inaccettabile) unthinkable; (difficile da concepire) inconceivable

impen'sato, -a ag unforeseen, unexpected

impensie'rire vt, **impensie'rirsi** vr to worry

impe'rante ag prevailing

impe'rare vi (anche fig) to reign, rule

impera'tivo, -a ag, sm imperative

impera'tore, - trice sm/f emperor/empress

impercet'tibile [impertʃet'tibile] ag imperceptible

imperdo'nabile ag unforgivable, unpardonable

imper'fetto, -a ag imperfect ■ sm (Ling) imperfect (tense)

imperfezi'one [imperfet'tsjone] sf imperfection

imperi'ale ag imperial

imperia'lismo sm imperialism

imperia'lista, -i, e ag imperialist

imperi'oso, -a ag (persona) imperious; (motivo, esigenza) urgent, pressing

imperi'turo, -a ag everlasting

impe'rizia [impe'rittsja] sf lack of experience

imperma'lirsi vr to take offence

imperme'abile ag waterproof ■ sm raincoat

imperni'are vt: ~ **qc su** to hinge sth on; (fig: discorso, relazione etc) to base sth on; **imperniarsi** vr (fig): **imperniarsi su** to be based on

im'pero sm empire; (forza, autorità) rule, control

imperscru'tabile ag inscrutable

imperso'nale ag impersonal

imperso'nare vt to personify; (Teat) to play, act (the part of); **impersonarsi** vr: **impersonarsi in un ruolo** to get into a part, live a part

imper'territo, -a ag unperturbed

imperti'nente ag impertinent

imperti'nenza [imperti'nɛntsa] sf impertinence

impertur'babile ag imperturbable

imperver'sare vi to rage

im'pervio, -a ag (luogo) inaccessible; (strada) impassable

impeto sm (moto, forza) force, impetus; (assalto) onslaught; (fig: impulso) impulse; (: slancio) transport; **con ~** (parlare) forcefully, energetically

impet'tito, -a ag stiff, erect; **camminare ~** to strut

impetu'oso, -a ag (vento) strong, raging; (persona) impetuous

impian'tare vt (motore) to install; (azienda, discussione) to establish, start

impian'tistica sf plant design and installation

impi'anto sm (installazione) installation; (apparecchiature) plant; (sistema) system; ~ **elettrico** wiring; ~ **sportivo** sports complex; **impianti di risalita** (Sci) ski lifts

impias'trare, impiastricci'are [impjastrit'tʃare] vt to smear, dirty

impi'astro sm poultice; (fig fam: persona) nuisance

impiccagi'one [impikka'dʒone] sf hanging

impic'care vt to hang; **impiccarsi** vr to hang o.s.

impicci'are [impit'tʃare] vt to hinder, hamper; **impicciarsi** vr to meddle, interfere; **impicciati degli affari tuoi!** mind your own business!

im'piccio [im'pittʃo] sm (ostacolo) hindrance; (seccatura) trouble, bother; (affare imbrogliato) mess; **essere d'~** to be in the way; **cavare o togliere qn dagli impicci** to get sb out of trouble

impicci'one, -a [impit'tʃone] sm/f busybody

impie'gare vt (usare) to use, employ; (assumere) to employ, take on; (spendere: denaro, tempo) to spend; (investire) to invest; **impiegarsi** vr to get a job, obtain employment; **impiego un quarto d'ora per andare a casa** it takes me o I take a quarter of an hour to get home

impiega'tizio, -a [impjega'tittsjo] ag clerical, white-collar cpd; **lavoro/ceto ~** clerical o white-collar work/workers pl

impie'gato, -a sm/f employee; ~ **statale** state employee

impi'ego, -ghi sm (uso) use; (occupazione) employment; (posto di lavoro) (regular) job, post; (Econ) investment; ~ **pubblico** job in the public sector

impieto'sire vt to move to pity; **impietosirsi** vr to be moved to pity

impie'toso, -a ag pitiless, cruel

impie'trire vt (anche fig) to petrify

impigli'are [impiʎ'ʎare] vt to catch, entangle; **impigliarsi** vr to get caught up o entangled

impi'grire vt to make lazy ■ vi (anche: **impigrirsi**) to grow lazy

impingu'are vt (maiale etc) to fatten; (fig: tasche, casse dello Stato) to stuff with money

impiom'bare vt (pacco) to seal (with lead); (dente) to fill

impla'cabile ag implacable

implemen'tare vt to implement

impli'care vt to imply; (coinvolgere) to involve; **implicarsi** vr: **implicarsi (in)** to become involved (in)

implicazi'one [implikat'tsjone] *sf* implication

im'plicito, -a [im'plitʃito] *ag* implicit

implo'rare *vt* to implore

implorazi'one [implorat'tsjone] *sf* plea, entreaty

impolli'nare *vt* to pollinate

impollinazi'one [impollinat'tsjone] *sf* pollination

impolve'rare *vt* to cover with dust; **impolverarsi** *vr* to get dusty

impoma'tare *vt* (*pelle*) to put ointment on; (*capelli*) to pomade; (*baffi*) to wax; **impomatarsi** *vr* (*fam*) to get spruced up

imponde'rabile *ag* imponderable

im'pone *etc vb vedi* **imporre**

impo'nente *ag* imposing, impressive

im'pongo *etc vb vedi* **imporre**

impo'nibile *ag* taxable ■ *sm* taxable income

impopo'lare *ag* unpopular

impopolarità *sf* unpopularity

im'porre *vt* to impose; (*costringere*) to force, make; (*far valere*) to impose, enforce; **imporsi** *vr* (*persona*) to assert o.s.; (*cosa: rendersi necessario*) to become necessary; (*aver successo: moda, attore*) to become popular; ~ **a qn di fare** to force sb to do, make sb do

impor'tante *ag* important

impor'tanza [impor'tantsa] *sf* importance; **dare** ~ **a qc** to attach importance to sth; **darsi** ~ to give o.s. airs

impor'tare *vt* (*introdurre dall'estero*) to import ■ *vi* to matter, be important ■ *vb impers* (*essere necessario*) to be necessary; (*interessare*) to matter; **non importa!** it doesn't matter!; **non me ne importa!** I don't care!

importa'tore, -'trice *ag* importing ■ *sm/f* importer

importazi'one [importat'tsjone] *sf* importation; (*merci importate*) imports *pl*

im'porto *sm* (*total*) amount

importu'nare *vt* to bother

impor'tuno, -a *ag* irksome, annoying

im'posi *etc vb vedi* **imporre**

imposizi'one [impozit'tsjone] *sf* imposition; (*ordine*) order, command; (*onere, imposta*) tax

imposses'sarsi *vr*: ~ **di** to seize, take possession of

impos'sibile *ag* impossible; **fare l'**~ to do one's utmost, do all one can

impossibilità *sf* impossibility; **essere nell'**~ **di fare qc** to be unable to do sth

impossibili'tato, -a *ag*: **essere** ~ **a fare qc** to be unable to do sth

im'posta *sf* (*di finestra*) shutter; (*tassa*) tax; ~ **indiretta sui consumi** excise duty *o* tax; ~ **locale sui redditi (ILOR)** tax on unearned

income; ~ **patrimoniale** property tax; ~ **sul reddito** income tax; ~ **sul reddito delle persone fisiche** personal income tax; ~ **di successione** capital transfer tax (*Brit*), inheritance tax (*US*); ~ **sugli utili** tax on profits; ~ **sul valore aggiunto** value added tax (*Brit*), sales tax (*US*)

impos'tare *vt* (*imbucare*) to post; (*servizio, organizzazione*) to set up; (*lavoro*) to organize, plan; (*resoconto, rapporto*) to plan; (*problema*) to set out, formulate; (*Tip: pagina*) to lay out; ~ **la voce** (*Mus*) to pitch one's voice

impostazi'one [impostat'tsjone] *sf* (*di lettera*) posting (*Brit*), mailing (*US*); (*di problema, questione*) formulation, statement; (*di lavoro*) organization, planning; (*di attività*) setting up; (*Mus: di voce*) pitch

im'posto, -a *pp di* **imporre**

impos'tore, -a *sm/f* impostor

impo'tente *ag* weak, powerless; (*anche Med*) impotent

impo'tenza [impo'tɛntsa] *sf* weakness, powerlessness; impotence

impove'rire *vt* to impoverish ■ *vi* (*anche*: **impoverirsi**) to become poor

imprati'cabile *ag* (*strada*) impassable; (*campo da gioco*) unplayable

imprati'chire [imprati'kire] *vt* to train; **impratichirsi** *vr*: **impratichirsi in qc** to practise (*Brit*) *o* practice (*US*) sth

impre'care *vi* to curse, swear; ~ **contro** to hurl abuse at

imprecazi'one [imprekat'tsjone] *sf* abuse, curse

impreci'sato, -a [impretʃi'zato] *ag* (*non preciso: quantità, numero*) indeterminate

imprecisi'one [impretʃi'zjone] *sf* imprecision; inaccuracy

impre'ciso, -a [impre'tʃizo] *ag* imprecise, vague; (*calcolo*) inaccurate

impre'gnare [impreɲ'ɲare] *vt*: ~ **(di)** (*imbevere*) to soak *o* impregnate (with); (*riempire: anche fig*) to fill (with)

imprendi'tore *sm* (*industriale*) entrepreneur; (*appaltatore*) contractor; **piccolo** ~ small businessman

imprendito'ria *sf* enterprise; (*imprenditori*) entrepreneurs *pl*

imprenditori'ale *ag* (*ceto, classe*) entrepreneurial

imprepa'rato, -a *ag*: ~ **(a)** (*gen*) unprepared (for); (*lavoratore*) untrained (for); **cogliere qn** ~ to catch sb unawares

impreparazi'one [impreparat'tsjone] *sf* lack of preparation

im'presa *sf* (*iniziativa*) enterprise; (*azione*) exploit; (*azienda*) firm, concern; ~ **familiare**

family firm; **~ pubblica** state-owned enterprise

impre'sario sm (Teat) manager, impresario; **~ di pompe funebri** funeral director

imprescin'dibile [impreʃʃin'dibile] ag not to be ignored

im'pressi etc vb vedi **imprimere**

impressio'nante ag impressive; upsetting

impressio'nare vt to impress; (turbare) to upset; (Fot) to expose; **impressionarsi** vr to be easily upset

impressi'one sf impression; (fig: sensazione) sensation, feeling; (stampa) printing; **fare ~** (colpire) to impress; (turbare) to frighten, upset; **fare buona/cattiva ~ a** to make a good/bad impression on

im'presso, -a pp di **imprimere**

impres'tare vt: **~ qc a qn** to lend sth to sb

impreve'dibile ag unforeseeable; (persona) unpredictable

imprevi'dente ag lacking in foresight

imprevi'denza [imprevi'dɛntsa] sf lack of foresight

impre'visto, -a ag unexpected, unforeseen ◾ sm unforeseen event; **salvo imprevisti** unless anything unexpected happens

imprezio'sire [imprettsjo'sire] vt: **~ di** to embellish with

imprigiona'mento [impridʒona'mento] sm imprisonment

imprigio'nare [impridʒo'nare] vt to imprison

im'primere vt (anche fig) to impress, stamp; (comunicare: movimento) to transmit, give

impro'babile ag improbable, unlikely

'improbo, -a ag (fatica, lavoro) hard, laborious

improdut'tivo, -a ag (investimento) unprofitable; (terreno) unfruitful; (fig: sforzo) fruitless

im'pronta sf imprint, impression, sign; (di piede, mano) print; (fig) mark, stamp; **~ digitale** fingerprint; **~ di carbonio** carbon footprint; **rilevamento delle impronte genetiche** genetic fingerprinting

impro'perio sm insult

impropo'nibile ag which cannot be proposed o suggested

im'proprio, -a ag improper; **arma impropria** offensive weapon

improro'gabile ag (termine) that cannot be extended

improvvisa'mente av suddenly; unexpectedly

improvvi'sare vt to improvise; **improvvisarsi** vr: **improvvisarsi cuoco** to (decide to) act as cook

improvvi'sata sf (pleasant) surprise

improvvisazi'one [improvvizat'tsjone] sf improvisation; **spirito d'~** spirit of invention

improv'viso, -a ag (imprevisto) unexpected; (subitaneo) sudden; **all'~** unexpectedly; suddenly

impru'dente ag foolish, imprudent; (osservazione) unwise

impru'denza [impru'dɛntsa] sf foolishness, imprudence; **è stata un'~** that was a foolish o an imprudent thing to do

impu'dente ag impudent

impu'denza [impu'dɛntsa] sf impudence

impudi'cizia [impudi'tʃittsja] sf immodesty

impu'dico, -a, chi, che ag immodest

impu'gnare [impuɲ'ɲare] vt to grasp, grip; (Dir) to contest

impugna'tura [impuɲɲa'tura] sf grip, grasp; (manico) handle; (: di spada) hilt

impulsività sf impulsiveness

impul'sivo, -a ag impulsive

im'pulso sm impulse; **dare un ~ alle vendite** to boost sales

impune'mente av with impunity

impunità sf impunity

impun'tarsi vr to stop dead, refuse to budge; (fig) to be obstinate

impun'tura sf stitching

impurità sf inv impurity

im'puro, -a ag impure

impu'tare vt (ascrivere): **~ qc a** to attribute sth to; (Dir: accusare): **~ qn di** to charge sb with, accuse sb of

impu'tato, -a sm/f (Dir) accused, defendant

imputazi'one [imputat'tsjone] sf (Dir) charge; (di spese) allocation

imputri'dire vi to rot

◯ **PAROLA CHIAVE**

in (in+il = **nel**, in+lo = **nello**, in+l' = **nell'**, in+la = **nella**, in+i = **nei**, in+gli = **negli**, in+le = **nelle**)
prep **1** (stato in luogo) in; **vivere in Italia/città** to live in Italy/town; **essere in casa/ufficio** to be at home/the office; **è nel cassetto/in salotto** it's in the drawer/in the sitting room; **se fossi in te** if I were you
2 (moto a luogo) to; (: dentro) into; **andare in Germania/città** to go to Germany/town; **andare in ufficio** to go to the office; **entrare in macchina/casa** to get into the car/go into the house
3 (tempo) in; **nel 1989** in 1989; **in giugno/estate** in June/summer; **l'ha fatto in sei mesi** he did it in six months; **in gioventù, io ...** when I was young, I ...
4 (modo, maniera) in; **in silenzio** in silence; **parlare in tedesco** to speak (in) German; **in abito da sera** in evening dress; **in guerra** at war; **in vacanza** on holiday; **Maria Bianchi**

in Rossi Maria Rossi née Bianchi
5 (*mezzo*) by; **viaggiare in autobus/treno** to travel by bus/train
6 (*materia*) made of; **in marmo** made of marble, marble *cpd*; **una collana in oro** a gold necklace
7 (*misura*) in; **siamo in quattro** there are four of us; **in tutto** in all
8 (*fine*): **dare in dono** to give as a gift; **spende tutto in alcool** he spends all his money on drink; **in onore di** in honour of

i'**nabile** *ag*: ~ **a** incapable of; (*fisicamente, Mil*) unfit for
inabilità *sf*: ~ (**a**) unfitness (for)
inabis'sare *vt* (*nave*) to sink; **inabissarsi** *vr* to go down
inabi'tabile *ag* uninhabitable
inabi'tato, -a *ag* uninhabited
inacces'sibile [inattʃes'sibile] *ag* (*luogo*) inaccessible; (*persona*) unapproachable; (*mistero*) unfathomable
inaccet'tabile [inattʃet'tabile] *ag* unacceptable
inacer'bire [inatʃer'bire] *vt* to exacerbate; **inacerbirsi** *vr* (*persona*) to become embittered
inaci'dire [inatʃi'dire] *vt* (*persona, carattere*) to embitter; **inacidirsi** *vr* (*latte*) to go sour; (*fig: persona, carattere*) to become sour, become embittered
ina'datto, -a *ag*: ~ (**a**) unsuitable *o* unfit (for)
inadegu'ato, -a *ag* inadequate
inadempi'ente *ag* defaulting ■ *sm/f* defaulter
inadempi'enza [inadem'pjɛntsa] *sf*: ~ **a un contratto** non-fulfilment of a contract; **dovuto alle inadempienze dei funzionari** due to negligence on the part of the officials
inadempi'mento *sm* non-fulfilment
inaffer'rabile *ag* elusive; (*concetto, senso*) difficult to grasp
'INAIL *sigla m* (= *Istituto Nazionale per l'Assicurazione contro gli Infortuni sul Lavoro*) *state body providing sickness benefit in the event of accidents at work*
ina'lare *vt* to inhale
inala'tore *sm* inhaler
inalazi'one [inalat'tsjone] *sf* inhalation
inalbe'rare *vt* (*Naut*) to hoist, raise; **inalberarsi** *vr* (*fig*) to flare up, fly off the handle
inalte'rabile *ag* unchangeable; (*colore*) fast, permanent; (*affetto*) constant
inalte'rato, -a *ag* unchanged
inami'dare *vt* to starch
inami'dato, -a *ag* starched
inammis'sibile *ag* inadmissible

inani'mato, -a *ag* inanimate; (*senza vita: corpo*) lifeless
inappa'gabile *ag* insatiable
inappel'labile *ag* (*decisione*) final, irrevocable; (*Dir*) final, not open to appeal
inappe'tenza [inappe'tɛntsa] *sf* (*Med*) lack of appetite
inappun'tabile *ag* irreproachable, flawless
inar'care *vt* (*schiena*) to arch; (*sopracciglia*) to raise; **inarcarsi** *vr* to arch
inaridi'mento *sm* (*anche fig*) drying up
inari'dire *vt* to make arid, dry up ■ *vi* (*anche*: **inaridirsi**) to dry up, become arid
inarres'tabile *ag* (*processo*) irreversible; (*emorragia*) that cannot be stemmed; (*corsa del tempo*) relentless
inascol'tato, -a *ag* unheeded, unheard
inaspettata'mente *av* unexpectedly
inaspet'tato, -a *ag* unexpected
inas'prire *vt* (*disciplina*) to tighten up, make harsher; (*carattere*) to embitter; (*rapporti*) to make worse; **inasprirsi** *vr* to become harsher; to become bitter; to become worse
inattac'cabile *ag* (*anche fig*) unassailable; (*alibi*) cast-iron
inatten'dibile *ag* unreliable
inat'teso, -a *ag* unexpected
inat'tivo, -a *ag* inactive, idle; (*Chim*) inactive
inattu'abile *ag* impracticable
inau'dito, -a *ag* unheard of
inaugu'rale *ag* inaugural
inaugu'rare *vt* to inaugurate, open; (*monumento*) to unveil
inaugurazi'one [inaugurat'tsjone] *sf* inauguration; unveiling
inavve'duto, -a *ag* careless, inadvertent
inavver'tenza [inavver'tɛntsa] *sf* carelessness, inadvertence
inavvertita'mente *av* inadvertently, unintentionally
inavvici'nabile [inavvitʃi'nabile] *ag* unapproachable
'Inca *ag inv, sm/f inv* Inca
incagli'are [inkaʎ'ʎare] *vi* (*Naut: anche*: **incagliarsi**) to run aground
incalco'labile *ag* incalculable
incal'lito, -a *ag* calloused; (*fig*) hardened, inveterate; (: *insensibile*) hard
incal'zante [inkal'tsante] *ag* urgent, insistent; (*crisi*) imminent
incal'zare [inkal'tsare] *vt* to follow *o* pursue closely; (*fig*) to press ■ *vi* (*urgere*) to be pressing; (*essere imminente*) to be imminent
incame'rare *vt* (*Dir*) to expropriate
incammi'nare *vt* (*fig: avviare*) to start up; **incamminarsi** *vr* to set off

incana'lare vt (anche fig) to channel; **incanalarsi** vr (folla): **incanalarsi verso** to converge on

incancre'nire vi, **incancre'nirsi** vi to become gangrenous

incande'scente [inkandeʃʃente] ag incandescent, white-hot

incan'tare vt to enchant, bewitch; **incantarsi** vr (rimanere intontito) to be spellbound; to be in a daze; (meccanismo: bloccarsi) to jam

incanta'tore, -'trice ag enchanting, bewitching ■ sm/f enchanter/enchantress

incan'tesimo sm spell, charm

incan'tevole ag charming, enchanting

in'canto sm spell, charm, enchantment; (asta) auction; **come per ~** as if by magic; **ti sta d'~!** (vestito etc) it really suits you!; **mettere all'~** to put up for auction

incanu'tire vi to go white

inca'pace [inka'patʃe] ag incapable

incapacità [inkapatʃi'ta] sf inability; (Dir) incapacity; **~ d'intendere e di volere** diminished responsibility

incapo'nirsi vr to be stubborn, be determined

incap'pare vi: **~ in qc/qn** (anche fig) to run into sth/sb

incappucci'are [inkapput'tʃare] vt to put a hood on; **incappucciarsi** vr (persona) to put on a hood

incapricci'arsi [inkaprit'tʃarsi] vr: **~ di** to take a fancy to o for

incapsu'lare vt (dente) to crown

incarce'rare [inkartʃe'rare] vt to imprison

incari'care vt: **~ qn di fare** to give sb the responsibility of doing; **incaricarsi** vr: **incaricarsi di** to take care o charge of

incari'cato, -a ag: **~ (di)** in charge (of), responsible (for) ■ sm/f delegate, representative; **docente ~** (di università) lecturer without tenure; **~ d'affari** (Pol) chargé d'affaires

in'carico, -chi sm task, job; (Ins) temporary post

incar'nare vt to embody; **incarnarsi** vr to be embodied; (Rel) to become incarnate

incarnazi'one [inkarnat'tsjone] sf incarnation; (fig) embodiment

incarta'mento sm dossier, file

incartapeco'rito, -a ag (pelle) wizened, shrivelled (Brit), shriveled (US)

incar'tare vt to wrap (in paper)

incasel'lare vt (posta) to sort; (fig: nozioni) to pigeonhole

incas'sare vt (merce) to pack (in cases); (gemma: incastonare) to set; (Econ: riscuotere) to collect; (Pugilato: colpi) to take, stand up to

in'casso sm cashing, encashment; (introito) takings pl

incasto'nare vt to set

incastona'tura sf setting

incas'trare vt to fit in, insert; (fig: intrappolare) to catch; **incastrarsi** vr (combaciare) to fit together; (restare bloccato) to become stuck

in'castro sm slot, groove; (punto di unione) joint; **gioco a ~** interlocking puzzle

incate'nare vt to chain up

incatra'mare vt to tar

incatti'vire vt to make wicked; **incattivirsi** vr to turn nasty

in'cauto, -a ag imprudent, rash

inca'vare vt to hollow out

inca'vato, -a ag hollow; (occhi) sunken

in'cavo sm hollow; (solco) groove

incavo'larsi vr (fam) to lose one's temper, get annoyed

incaz'zarsi [inkat'tsarsi] vr (fam!) to get steamed up

in'cedere [in'tʃedere] vi (poetico) to advance solemnly ■ sm solemn gait

incendi'are [intʃen'djare] vt to set fire to; **incendiarsi** vr to catch fire, burst into flames

incendi'ario, -a [intʃen'djarjo] ag incendiary ■ sm/f arsonist

in'cendio [in'tʃendjo] sm fire

incene'rire [intʃene'rire] vt to burn to ashes, incinerate; (cadavere) to cremate; **incenerirsi** vr to be burnt to ashes

inceneri'tore [intʃeneri'tore] sm incinerator

in'censo [in'tʃenso] sm incense

incensu'rato, -a [intʃensu'rato] ag (Dir): **essere ~** to have a clean record

incenti'vare [intʃenti'vare] vt (produzione, vendite) to boost; (persona) to motivate

incen'tivo [intʃen'tivo] sm incentive

incen'trarsi [intʃen'trarsi] vr: **~ su** (fig) to centre (Brit) o center (US) on

incep'pare [intʃep'pare] vt to obstruct, hamper; **incepparsi** vr to jam

ince'rata [intʃe'rata] sf (tela) tarpaulin; (impermeabile) oilskins pl

incer'tezza [intʃer'tettsa] sf uncertainty

in'certo, -a [in'tʃerto] ag uncertain; (irresoluto) undecided, hesitating ■ sm uncertainty; **gli incerti del mestiere** the risks of the job

incespi'care [intʃespi'kare] vi: **~ (in qc)** to trip (over sth)

inces'sante [intʃes'sante] ag incessant

in'cesto [in'tʃesto] sm incest

incestu'oso, -a [intʃestu'oso] ag incestuous

in'cetta [in'tʃetta] sf buying up; **fare ~ di qc** to buy up sth

inchi'esta [in'kjɛsta] sf investigation, inquiry

inchi'nare [inki'nare] *vt* to bow; **inchinarsi**
vr to bend down; (*per riverenza*) to bow;
(: *donna*) to curtsy

in'chino [in'kino] *sm* bow; curtsy

inchio'dare [inkjo'dare] *vt* to nail (down); ~
la macchina (*Aut*) to jam on the brakes

inchi'ostro [in'kjɔstro] *sm* ink; ~ **simpatico**
invisible ink

inciam'pare [intʃam'pare] *vi* to trip, stumble

inci'ampo [in'tʃampo] *sm* obstacle; **essere
d'~ a qn** (*fig*) to be in sb's way

inciden'tale [intʃiden'tale] *ag* incidental

incidental'mente [intʃidental'mente] *av* (*per
caso*) by chance; (*per inciso*) incidentally, by
the way

inci'dente [intʃi'dɛnte] *sm* accident; (*episodio*)
incident; **e con questo l'~ è chiuso** and that
is the end of the matter; ~ **d'auto** car
accident; ~ **diplomatico** diplomatic incident

inci'denza [intʃi'dɛntsa] *sf* incidence; **avere
una forte ~ su qc** to affect sth greatly

in'cidere [in'tʃidere] *vi*: ~ **su** to bear upon,
affect ■ *vt* (*tagliare incavando*) to cut into;
(*Arte*) to engrave; to etch; (*canzone*) to record

in'cinta [in'tʃinta] *ag f* pregnant

incipi'ente [intʃi'pjɛnte] *ag* incipient

incipri'are [intʃi'prjare] *vt* to powder

in'circa [in'tʃirka] *av*: **all'~** more or less, very
nearly

in'cisi *etc* [in'tʃizi] *vb vedi* **incidere**

incisi'one [intʃi'zjone] *sf* cut; (*disegno*)
engraving; etching; (*registrazione*) recording;
(*Med*) incision

inci'sivo, -a [intʃi'zivo] *ag* incisive; (*Anat*):
(**dente**) ~ incisor

in'ciso, -a [in'tʃizo] *pp di* **incidere** ■ *sm*: **per ~**
incidentally, by the way

inci'sore [intʃi'zore] *sm* (*Arte*) engraver

incita'mento [intʃita'mento] *sm* incitement

inci'tare [intʃi'tare] *vt* to incite

inci'vile [intʃi'vile] *ag* uncivilized; (*villano*)
impolite

incivi'lire [intʃivi'lire] *vt* to civilize

inciviltà [intʃivil'ta] *sf* (*di popolazione*)
barbarism; (*fig: di trattamento*) barbarity;
(: *maleducazione*) incivility, rudeness

incl. *abbr* (= *incluso*) encl.

incle'mente *ag* (*giudice, sentenza*) severe,
harsh; (*fig: clima*) harsh; (: *tempo*) inclement

incle'menza [inkle'mentsa] *sf* severity;
harshness; inclemency

incli'nabile *ag* (*schienale*) reclinable

incli'nare *vt* to tilt ■ *vi* (*fig*): ~ **a qc/a fare** to
incline towards sth/doing; to tend towards
sth/to do; **inclinarsi** *vr* (*barca*) to list; (*aereo*)
to bank

incli'nato, -a *ag* sloping

inclinazi'one [inklinat'tsjone] *sf* slope; (*fig*)
inclination, tendency

in'cline *ag*: ~ **a** inclined to

in'cludere *vt* to include; (*accludere*) to enclose

inclusi'one *sf* inclusion

inclu'sivo, -a *ag*: ~ **di** inclusive of

in'cluso, -a *pp di* **includere** ■ *ag* included;
enclosed

incoe'rente *ag* incoherent; (*contraddittorio*)
inconsistent

incoe'renza [inkoe'rɛntsa] *sf* incoherence;
inconsistency

in'cognito, -a [in'kɔɲɲito] *ag* unknown
■ *sm*: **in ~** incognito ■ *sf* (*Mat, fig*) unknown
quantity

incol'lare *vt* to glue, gum; (*unire con colla*) to
stick together; ~ **gli occhi addosso a qn** (*fig*)
to fix one's eyes on sb

incolla'tura *sf* (*Ippica*): **vincere/perdere di
un'~** to win/lose by a head

incolon'nare *vt* to draw up in columns

inco'lore *ag* colourless (*Brit*), colorless (*US*)

incol'pare *vt*: ~ **qn di** to charge sb with

in'colto, -a *ag* (*terreno*) uncultivated;
(*trascurato: capelli*) neglected; (*persona*)
uneducated

in'colume *ag* safe and sound, unhurt

incolumità *sf* safety

incom'bente *ag* (*pericolo*) imminent,
impending

incom'benza [inkom'bɛntsa] *sf* duty, task

in'combere *vi* (*sovrastare minacciando*): ~ **su** to
threaten, hang over

incominci'are [inkomin'tʃare] *vi, vt* to begin,
start

incomo'dare *vt* to trouble, inconvenience;
incomodarsi *vr* to put o.s. out

in'comodo, -a *ag* uncomfortable;
(*inopportuno*) inconvenient ■ *sm*
inconvenience, bother

incompa'rabile *ag* incomparable

incompa'tibile *ag* incompatible

incompatibilità *sf* incompatibility; ~ **di
carattere** (mutual) incompatibility

incompe'tente *ag* incompetent

incompe'tenza [inkompe'tɛntsa] *sf*
incompetence

incompi'uto, -a *ag* unfinished, incomplete

incom'pleto, -a *ag* incomplete

incompren'sibile *ag* incomprehensible

incomprensi'one *sf* incomprehension

incom'preso, -a *ag* not understood;
misunderstood

inconce'pibile [inkontʃe'pibile] *ag*
inconceivable

inconcili'abile [inkontʃi'ljabile] *ag*
irreconcilable

inconclu'dente *ag* inconclusive; (*persona*) ineffectual

incondizio'nato, -a [inkondittsjo'nato] *ag* unconditional

inconfes'sabile *ag* (*pensiero, peccato*) unmentionable

inconfon'dibile *ag* unmistakable

inconfu'tabile *ag* irrefutable

incongru'ente *ag* inconsistent

incongru'enza [inkongru'ɛntsa] *sf* inconsistency

in'congruo, -a *ag* incongruous

inconsa'pevole *ag*: ~ **di** unaware of, ignorant of

inconsapevo'lezza [inkonsapevo'lettsa] *sf* ignorance, lack of awareness

in'conscio, -a, sci, sce [in'kɔnʃo] *ag* unconscious ■ *sm* (*Psic*): **l'~** the unconscious

inconsis'tente *ag* (*patrimonio*) insubstantial; (*dubbio*) unfounded; (*ragionamento, prove*) tenuous, flimsy

inconsis'tenza [inkonsis'tɛntsa] *sf* insubstantial nature; lack of foundation; flimsiness

inconso'labile *ag* inconsolable

inconsu'eto, -a *ag* unusual

incon'sulto, -a *ag* rash

inconte'nibile *ag* (*rabbia*) uncontrollable; (*entusiasmo*) irrepressible

inconten'tabile *ag* (*desiderio, avidità*) insatiable; (*persona: capriccioso*) hard to please, very demanding

incontes'tabile *ag* incontrovertible, indisputable

incontes'tato, -a *ag* undisputed

inconti'nenza [inkonti'nɛntsa] *sf* incontinence

incon'trare *vt* to meet; (*difficoltà*) to meet with; **incontrarsi** *vr* to meet

incon'trario *av*: **all'~** (*sottosopra*) upside down; (*alla rovescia*) back to front; (*all'indietro*) backwards; (*nel senso contrario*) the other way round

incontras'tabile *ag* incontrovertible, indisputable

incontras'tato, -a *ag* (*successo, vittoria, verità*) uncontested, undisputed

in'contro *av*: ~ **a** (*verso*) towards ■ *sm* meeting; (*Sport*) match; meeting; (*fortuito*) encounter; **venire ~ a** (*richieste, esigenze*) to comply with; ~ **di calcio** football match (*Brit*), soccer game (*US*)

incontrol'labile *ag* uncontrollable

inconveni'ente *sm* drawback, snag

incoraggia'mento [inkoraddʒa'mento] *sm* encouragement; **premio d'~** consolation prize

incoraggi'are [inkorad'dʒare] *vt* to encourage

incor'nare *vt* to gore

incornici'are [inkorni'tʃare] *vt* to frame

incoro'nare *vt* to crown

incoronazi'one [inkoronat'tsjone] *sf* coronation

incorpo'rare *vt* to incorporate; (*fig: annettere*) to annex

incorreg'gibile [inkorred'dʒibile] *ag* incorrigible

in'correre *vi*: ~ **in** to meet with, run into

incorrut'tibile *ag* incorruptible

in'corso, -a *pp di* **incorrere**

incosci'ente [inkoʃ'ʃɛnte] *ag* (*inconscio*) unconscious; (*irresponsabile*) reckless, thoughtless

incosci'enza [inkoʃ'ʃɛntsa] *sf* unconsciousness; recklessness, thoughtlessness

incos'tante *ag* (*studente, impiegato*) inconsistent; (*carattere*) fickle, inconstant; (*rendimento*) sporadic

incos'tanza [inkos'tantsa] *sf* inconstancy, fickleness

incostituzio'nale [inkostituttsjo'nale] *ag* unconstitutional

incre'dibile *ag* incredible, unbelievable

incredulità *sf* incredulity

in'credulo, -a *ag* incredulous, disbelieving

incremen'tare *vt* to increase; (*dar sviluppo a*) to promote

incre'mento *sm* (*sviluppo*) development; (*aumento numerico*) increase, growth

incresci'oso, -a [inkreʃ'ʃoso] *ag* (*spiacevole*) unpleasant; regrettable

incres'pare *vt* (*capelli*) to curl; (*acque*) to ripple; **incresparsi** *vr* (*vedi vt*) to curl; to ripple

incrimi'nare *vt* (*Dir*) to charge

incriminazi'one [inkriminat'tsjone] *sf* (*atto d'accusa*) indictment, charge

incri'nare *vt* to crack; (*fig: rapporti, amicizia*) to cause to deteriorate; **incrinarsi** *vr* to crack; to deteriorate

incrina'tura *sf* crack; (*fig*) rift

incroci'are [inkro'tʃare] *vt* to cross; (*incontrare*) to meet ■ *vi* (*Naut, Aer*) to cruise; **incrociarsi** *vr* (*strade*) to cross, intersect; (*persone, veicoli*) to pass each other; ~ **le braccia/le gambe** to fold one's arms/cross one's legs

incrocia'tore [inkrotʃa'tore] *sm* cruiser

in'crocio [in'krotʃo] *sm* (*anche Ferr*) crossing; (*di strade*) crossroads

incrol'labile *ag* (*fede*) unshakeable, firm

incros'tare *vt* to encrust; **incrostarsi** *vr*: **incrostarsi di** to become encrusted with

incrostazi'one [inkrostat'tsjone] *sf* encrustation; (*di calcare*) scale; (*nelle tubature*) fur (*Brit*), scale

incru'ento, -a *ag* (*battaglia*) without bloodshed, bloodless

incuba'trice [inkuba'tritʃe] *sf* incubator

incubazi'one [inkubat'tsjone] *sf* incubation

'incubo *sm* nightmare

in'cudine *sf* anvil; **trovarsi** *o* **essere tra l'~ e il martello** (*fig*) to be between the devil and the deep blue sea

incul'care *vt*: ~ **qc in** to inculcate sth into, instill sth into

incune'are *vt* to wedge

incu'pire *vt* (*rendere scuro*) to darken; (*fig: intristire*) to fill with gloom ◼ *vi* (*vedi vt*) to darken; to become gloomy

incu'rabile *ag* incurable

incu'rante *ag*: ~ **(di)** heedless (of), careless (of)

in'curia *sf* negligence

incurio'sire *vt* to make curious; **incuriosirsi** *vr* to become curious

incursi'one *sf* raid

incur'vare *vt*, **incur'varsi** *vr* to bend, curve

in'cusso, -a *pp di* **incutere**

incusto'dito, -a *ag* unguarded, unattended; **passaggio a livello** ~ unmanned level crossing

in'cutere *vt* to arouse; ~ **timore/rispetto a qn** to strike fear into sb/command sb's respect

'indaco *sm* indigo

indaffa'rato, -a *ag* busy

inda'gare *vt* to investigate

indaga'tore, -'trice *ag* (*sguardo, domanda*) searching; (*mente*) inquiring

in'dagine [in'dadʒine] *sf* investigation, inquiry; (*ricerca*) research, study; ~ **di mercato** market survey

indebita'mente *av* (*immeritatamente*) undeservedly; (*erroneamente*) wrongfully

indebi'tare *vt*: ~ **qn** to get sb into debt; **indebitarsi** *vr* to run *o* get into debt

in'debito, -a *ag* undeserved; wrongful

indeboli'mento *sm* weakening; (*debolezza*) weakness

indebo'lire *vt, vi* (*anche*: **indebolirsi**) to weaken

inde'cente [inde'tʃɛnte] *ag* indecent

inde'cenza [inde'tʃɛntsa] *sf* indecency; **è un'~!** (*vergogna*) it's scandalous!, it's a disgrace!

indeci'frabile [indetʃi'frabile] *ag* indecipherable

indecisi'one [indetʃi'zjone] *sf* indecisiveness; indecision

inde'ciso, -a [inde'tʃizo] *ag* indecisive; (*irresoluto*) undecided

indeco'roso, -a *ag* (*comportamento*) indecorous, unseemly

inde'fesso, -a *ag* untiring, indefatigable

indefi'nibile *ag* indefinable

indefi'nito, -a *ag* (*anche Ling*) indefinite; (*impreciso, non determinato*) undefined

indefor'mabile *ag* crushproof

in'degno, -a [in'deɲɲo] *ag* (*atto*) shameful; (*persona*) unworthy

inde'lebile *ag* indelible

indelica'tezza [indelika'tettsa] *sf* tactlessness

indeli'cato, -a *ag* (*domanda*) indiscreet, tactless

indemoni'ato, -a *ag* possessed (by the devil)

in'denne *ag* unhurt, uninjured

indennità *sf inv* (*rimborso: di spese*) allowance; (: *di perdita*) compensation, indemnity; ~ **di contingenza** cost-of-living allowance; ~ **di fine rapporto** severance payment (*on retirement, redundancy or when taking up other employment*); ~ **di trasferta** travel expenses *pl*

indenniz'zare [indennid'dzare] *vt* to compensate

inden'nizzo [inden'niddzo] *sm* (*somma*) compensation, indemnity

indero'gabile *ag* binding

indescri'vibile *ag* indescribable

indeside'rabile *ag* undesirable

indeside'rato, -a *ag* unwanted

indetermina'tezza [indetermina'tettsa] *sf* vagueness

indetermina'tivo, -a *ag* (*Ling*) indefinite

indetermi'nato, -a *ag* indefinite, indeterminate

in'detto, -a *pp di* **indire**

'India *sf*: **l'~** India; **le Indie occidentali** the West Indies

indi'ano, -a *ag* Indian ◼ *sm/f* (*d'India*) Indian; (*d'America*) Red Indian; **l'Oceano I~** the Indian Ocean

indiavo'lato, -a *ag* possessed (by the devil); (*vivace, violento*) wild

indi'care *vt* (*mostrare*) to show, indicate; (: *col dito*) to point to, point out; (*consigliare*) to suggest, recommend

indica'tivo, -a *ag* indicative ◼ *sm* (*Ling*) indicative (mood)

indi'cato, -a *ag* (*consigliato*) advisable; (*adatto*): ~ **per** suitable for, appropriate for

indica'tore, -'trice *ag* indicating ◼ *sm* (*elenco*) guide; directory; (*Tecn*) gauge; indicator; **cartello** ~ sign; ~ **della benzina** petrol (*Brit*) *o* gas (*US*) gauge, fuel gauge; ~ **di velocità** (*Aut*) speedometer; (*Aer*) airspeed indicator

indicazi'one [indikat'tsjone] *sf* indication; (*informazione*) piece of information; **indicazioni per l'uso** instructions for use

indice ['inditʃe] *sm* (*Anat: dito*) index finger, forefinger; (*lancetta*) needle, pointer; (*fig: indizio*) sign; (*Tecn, Mat, nei libri*) index; ~ **azionario** share index; ~ **di gradimento** (*Radio, TV*) popularity rating; ~ **dei prezzi al consumo** ~ retail price index

indicherò *etc* [indike'rɔ] *vb vedi* **indicare**

indi'cibile [indi'tʃibile] *ag* inexpressible

indiciz'zare [inditʃid'dzare] *vt*: ~ **al costo della vita** to index-link (*Brit*), index (*US*)

indiciz'zato, -a [inditʃid'dzato] *ag* (*polizza, salario etc*) index-linked (*Brit*), indexed (*US*)

indicizzazi'one [inditʃiddzat'tsjone] *sf* indexing

indietreggi'are [indjetred'dʒare] *vi* to draw back, retreat

indi'etro *av* back; (*guardare*) behind, back; (*andare, cadere: anche*: **all'indietro**) backwards; **rimanere** ~ to be left behind; **essere** ~ (*col lavoro*) to be behind; (*orologio*) to be slow; **rimandare qc** ~ to send sth back; **non vado né avanti né** ~ (*fig*) I'm not getting anywhere, I'm getting nowhere

indi'feso, -a *ag* (*città, confine*) undefended; (*persona*) defenceless (*Brit*), defenseless (*US*), helpless

indiffe'rente *ag* indifferent ■ *sm*: **fare l'**~ to pretend to be indifferent, be *o* act casual; (*fingere di non vedere o sentire*) to pretend not to notice

indiffe'renza [indiffe'rentsa] *sf* indifference

in'digeno, -a [in'didʒeno] *ag* indigenous, native ■ *sm/f* native

indi'gente [indi'dʒɛnte] *ag* poverty-stricken, destitute

indi'genza [indi'dʒɛntsa] *sf* extreme poverty

indigesti'one [indidʒes'tjone] *sf* indigestion

indi'gesto, -a [indi'dʒɛsto] *ag* indigestible

indi'gnare [indiɲ'ɲare] *vt* to fill with indignation; **indignarsi** *vr* to be (*o* get) indignant

indignazi'one [indiɲɲat'tsjone] *sf* indignation

indimenti'cabile *ag* unforgettable

'indio, -a *ag, sm/f* (*South American*) Indian

indipen'dente *ag* independent

indipendente'mente *av* independently; ~ **dal fatto che gli piaccia o meno, verrà!** he's coming, whether he likes it or not!

indipen'denza [indipen'dɛntsa] *sf* independence

in'dire *vt* (*concorso*) to announce; (*elezioni*) to call

indi'retto, -a *ag* indirect

indiriz'zare [indirit'tsare] *vt* (*dirigere*) to direct; (*mandare*) to send; (*lettera*) to address; ~ **la parola a qn** to address sb

indiriz'zario [indirit'tsarjo] *sm* mailing list

indi'rizzo [indi'rittso] *sm* address; (*direzione*) direction; (*avvio*) trend, course; ~ **Internet** web address

indisci'plina [indiʃʃi'plina] *sf* indiscipline

indiscipli'nato, -a [indiʃʃipli'nato] *ag* undisciplined, unruly

indis'creto, -a *ag* indiscreet

indiscrezi'one [indiskret'tsjone] *sf* indiscretion

indiscrimi'nato, -a *ag* indiscriminate

indis'cusso, -a *ag* unquestioned

indiscu'tibile *ag* indisputable, unquestionable

indispen'sabile *ag* indispensable, essential

indispet'tire *vt* to irritate, annoy ■ *vi* (*anche*: **indispettirsi**) to get irritated *o* annoyed

indispo'nente *ag* irritating, annoying

indis'porre *vt* to antagonize

indisposizi'one [indispozit'tsjone] *sf* (*slight*) indisposition

indis'posto, -a *pp di* **indisporre** ■ *ag* indisposed, unwell

indisso'lubile *ag* indissoluble

indissolubil'mente *av* indissolubly

indistinta'mente *av* (*senza distinzioni*) indiscriminately, without exception; (*in modo indefinito: vedere, sentire*) vaguely, faintly

indis'tinto, -a *ag* indistinct

indistrut'tibile *ag* indestructible

in'divia *sf* endive

individu'ale *ag* individual

individua'lismo *sm* individualism

individua'lista, -i, e *sm/f* individualist

individualità *sf* individuality

individual'mente *av* individually

individu'are *vt* (*dar forma distinta a*) to characterize; (*determinare*) to locate; (*riconoscere*) to single out

indi'viduo *sm* individual

indivi'sibile *ag* indivisible; **quei due sono indivisibili** (*fig*) those two are inseparable

indizi'are [indit'tsjare] *vt*: ~ **qn di qc** to cast suspicion on sb for sth

indizi'ato, -a [indit'tsjato] *ag* suspected ■ *sm/f* suspect

in'dizio [in'dittsjo] *sm* (*segno*) sign, indication; (*Polizia*) clue; (*Dir*) piece of evidence

Indo'cina [indo'tʃina] *sf*: **l'**~ Indochina

'indole *sf* nature, character

indo'lente *ag* indolent

indo'lenza [indo'lɛntsa] *sf* indolence

indolen'zire [indolen'tsire] *vt* (*gambe, braccia etc*) to make stiff, cause to ache; (: *intorpidire*) to numb; **indolenzirsi** *vr* to become stiff; to go numb

indolen'zito, -a [indolen'tsito] *ag* stiff, aching; (*intorpidito*) numb

indo'lore *ag* (*anche fig*) painless

indo'mani *sm*: **l'~** the next day, the following day

Indo'nesia *sf*: **l'~** Indonesia

indonesi'ano, -a *ag, sm/f, sm* Indonesian

indo'rare *vt* (*rivestire in oro*) to gild; (*Cuc*) to dip in egg yolk; **~ la pillola** (*fig*) to sugar the pill

indos'sare *vt* (*mettere indosso*) to put on; (*avere indosso*) to have on

indossa'tore, -'trice *sm/f* model

in'dotto, -a *pp di* **indurre**

indottri'nare *vt* to indoctrinate

indovi'nare *vt* (*scoprire*) to guess; (*immaginare*) to imagine, guess; (*il futuro*) to foretell; **tirare a ~** to make a shot in the dark

indovi'nato, -a *ag* successful; (*scelta*) inspired

indovi'nello *sm* riddle

indo'vino, -a *sm/f* fortuneteller

indù *ag, sm/f* Hindu

indubbia'mente *av* undoubtedly

in'dubbio, -a *ag* certain, undoubted

in'duco *etc vb vedi* **indurre**

indugi'are [indu'dʒare] *vi* to take one's time, delay

in'dugio [in'dudʒo] *sm* (*ritardo*) delay; **senza ~** without delay

indul'gente [indul'dʒɛnte] *ag* indulgent; (*giudice*) lenient

indul'genza [indul'dʒɛntsa] *sf* indulgence; leniency

in'dulgere [in'duldʒere] *vi*: **~ a** (*accondiscendere*) to comply with; (*abbandonarsi*) to indulge in

in'dulto, -a *pp di* **indulgere** ◼ *sm* (*Dir*) pardon

indu'mento *sm* article of clothing, garment; **indumenti** *smpl* (*vestiti*) clothes; **indumenti intimi** underwear *sg*

induri'mento *sm* hardening

indu'rire *vt* to harden ◼ *vi* (*anche*: **indurirsi**) to harden, become hard

in'durre *vt*: **~ qn a fare qc** to induce *o* persuade sb to do sth; **~ qn in errore** to mislead sb; **~ in tentazione** to lead into temptation

in'dussi *etc vb vedi* **indurre**

in'dustria *sf* industry; **la piccola/grande ~** small/big business

industri'ale *ag* industrial ◼ *sm* industrialist

industrializ'zare [industrjalid'dzare] *vt* to industrialize

industrializzazi'one [industrjaliddzat'tsjone] *sf* industrialization

industri'arsi *vr* to do one's best, try hard

industri'oso, -a *ag* industrious, hard-working

induzi'one [indut'tsjone] *sf* induction

inebe'tito, -a *ag* dazed, stunned

inebri'are *vt* (*anche fig*) to intoxicate; **inebriarsi** *vr* to become intoxicated

inecce'pibile [inettʃe'pibile] *ag* unexceptionable

i'nedia *sf* starvation

i'nedito, -a *ag* unpublished

inef'fabile *ag* ineffable

ineffi'cace [ineffi'katʃe] *ag* ineffective

ineffi'cacia [ineffi'katʃa] *sf* inefficacy, ineffectiveness

ineffi'ente [ineffi'tʃɛnte] *ag* inefficient

ineffici'enza [ineffi'tʃɛntsa] *sf* inefficiency

ineguagli'abile [inegwaʎ'ʎabile] *ag* incomparable, matchless

ineguagli'anza [inegwaʎ'ʎantsa] *sf* (*sociale*) inequality; (*di superficie, livello*) unevenness

inegu'ale *ag* unequal; (*irregolare*) uneven

inelut'tabile *ag* inescapable

ineluttabilità *sf* inescapability

inenar'rabile *ag* unutterable

inequivo'cabile *ag* unequivocal

ine'rente *ag*: **~ a** concerning, regarding

i'nerme *ag* unarmed, defenceless (*Brit*), defenseless (*US*)

inerpi'carsi *vr*: **~ (su)** to clamber (up)

i'nerte *ag* inert; (*inattivo*) indolent, sluggish

i'nerzia [i'nɛrtsja] *sf* inertia; indolence, sluggishness

inesat'tezza [inezat'tettsa] *sf* inaccuracy

ine'satto, -a *ag* (*impreciso*) inaccurate, inexact; (*erroneo*) incorrect; (*Amm: non riscosso*) uncollected

inesau'ribile *ag* inexhaustible

inesis'tente *ag* non-existent

ineso'rabile *ag* inexorable, relentless

inesorabil'mente *av* inexorably

inesperi'enza [inespe'rjɛntsa] *sf* inexperience

ines'perto, -a *ag* inexperienced

inespli'cabile *ag* inexplicable

inesplo'rato, -a *ag* unexplored

ines'ploso, -a *ag* unexploded

inespres'sivo, -a *ag* (*viso*) expressionless, inexpressive

ines'presso, -a *ag* unexpressed

inespri'mibile *ag* inexpressible

inespu'gnabile [inespuɲ'ɲabile] *ag* (*fortezza, torre etc*) impregnable

ineste'tismo *sm* beauty problem

inesti'mabile *ag* inestimable; (*valore*) incalculable

inestir'pabile *ag* ineradicable
inestri'cabile *ag* (*anche fig*) impenetrable
inetti'tudine *sf* ineptitude
i'netto, -a *ag* (*incapace*) inept; (*che non ha attitudine*): ~ **(a)** unsuited (to)
ine'vaso, -a *ag* (*ordine, corrispondenza*) outstanding
inevi'tabile *ag* inevitable
inevitabil'mente *av* inevitably
i'nezia [i'nɛttsja] *sf* trifle, thing of no importance
infagot'tare *vt* to bundle up, wrap up; **infagottarsi** *vr* to wrap up
infal'libile *ag* infallible
infallibilità *sf* infallibility
infa'mante *ag* (*accusa*) defamatory, slanderous
infa'mare *vt* to defame
in'fame *ag* infamous; (*fig: cosa, compito*) awful, dreadful
in'famia *sf* infamy
infan'gare *vt* (*sporcare*) to cover with mud; (*nome, reputazione*) to sully; **infangarsi** *vr* to get covered in mud; to be sullied
infan'tile *ag* child *cpd*; childlike; (*adulto, azione*) childish; **letteratura** ~ children's books *pl*
in'fanzia [in'fantsja] *sf* childhood; (*bambini*) children *pl*; **prima** ~ babyhood, infancy
infari'nare *vt* to cover with (*o* sprinkle with *o* dip in) flour; ~ **di zucchero** to sprinkle with sugar
infarina'tura *sf* (*fig*) smattering
in'farto *sm* (*Med*): ~ **(cardiaco)** coronary
infasti'dire *vt* to annoy, irritate; **infastidirsi** *vr* to get annoyed *o* irritated
infati'cabile *ag* tireless, untiring
in'fatti *cong* as a matter of fact, in fact, actually
infatu'arsi *vr*: ~ **di** *o* **per** to become infatuated with, fall for
infatuazi'one [infatuat'tsjone] *sf* infatuation
in'fausto, -a *ag* unpropitious, unfavourable (*Brit*), unfavorable (*US*)
infecondità *sf* infertility
infe'condo, -a *ag* infertile
infe'dele *ag* unfaithful
infedeltà *sf* infidelity
infe'lice [infe'litʃe] *ag* unhappy; (*sfortunato*) unlucky, unfortunate; (*inopportuno*) inopportune, ill-timed; (*mal riuscito: lavoro*) bad, poor
infelicità [infelitʃi'ta] *sf* unhappiness
infel'trire *vi*, **infeltrirsi** *vr* (*lana*) to become matted
infe'renza [infe'rɛntsa] *sf* inference

inferi'ore *ag* lower; (*per intelligenza, qualità*) inferior ■ *sm/f* inferior; ~ **a** (*numero, quantità*) less *o* smaller than; (*meno buono*) inferior to; ~ **alla media** below average
inferiorità *sf* inferiority
infe'rire *vt* (*dedurre*) to infer, deduce
inferme'ria *sf* infirmary; (*di scuola, nave*) sick bay
infermi'ere, -a *sm/f* nurse
infermità *sf inv* illness; infirmity; ~ **di mente** mental illness
in'fermo, -a *ag* (*ammalato*) ill; (*debole*) infirm; ~ **di mente** mentally ill
infer'nale *ag* infernal; (*proposito, complotto*) diabolical; **un tempo** ~ (*fam*) hellish weather
in'ferno *sm* hell; **soffrire le pene dell'~** (*fig*) to go through hell
infero'cire [infero'tʃire] *vt* to make fierce ■ *vi*, **inferocirsi** *vr* to become fierce
inferri'ata *sf* grating
infervo'rare *vt* to arouse enthusiasm in; **infervorarsi** *vr* to get excited, get carried away
infes'tare *vt* to infest
infet'tare *vt* to infect; **infettarsi** *vr* to become infected
infet'tivo, -a *ag* infectious
in'fetto, -a *ag* infected; (*acque*) polluted, contaminated
infezi'one [infet'tsjone] *sf* infection
infiac'chire [infjak'kire] *vt* to weaken ■ *vi* (*anche*: **infiacchirsi**) to grow weak
infiam'mabile *ag* inflammable
infiam'mare *vt* to set alight; (*fig, Med*) to inflame; **infiammarsi** *vr* to catch fire; (*Med*) to become inflamed; (*fig*): **infiammarsi di** to be fired with
infiammazi'one [infjammat'tsjone] *sf* (*Med*) inflammation
infias'care *vt* to bottle
infici'are [infi'tʃare] *vt* (*Dir: atto, dichiarazione*) to challenge
in'fido, -a *ag* unreliable, treacherous
infie'rire *vi*: ~ **su** (*fisicamente*) to attack furiously; (*verbalmente*) to rage at; (*epidemia*) to rage over
in'figgere [in'fiddʒere] *vt*: ~ **qc in** to thrust *o* drive sth into
infi'lare *vt* (*ago*) to thread; (*mettere: chiave*) to insert; (: *vestito*) to slip *o* put on; (*strada*) to turn into, take; **infilarsi** *vr*: **infilarsi in** to slip into; (*indossare*) to slip on; ~ **un anello al dito** to slip a ring on one's finger; ~ **l'uscio** to slip in; to slip out; **infilarsi la giacca** to put on one's jacket
infil'trarsi *vr* to penetrate, seep through; (*Mil*)

179

to infiltrate

infil'trato, -a *sm/f* infiltrator

infiltrazi'one [infiltrat'tsjone] *sf* infiltration

infil'zare [infil'tsare] *vt* (*infilare*) to string together; (*trafiggere*) to pierce

infimo, -a *ag* lowest; **un albergo di ~ ordine** a third-rate hotel

in'fine *av* finally; (*insomma*) in short

infin'gardo, -a *ag* lazy ▪ *sm/f* slacker

infinità *sf* infinity; (*in quantità*): **un'~ di** an infinite number of

infinitesi'male *ag* infinitesimal

infi'nito, -a *ag* infinite; (*Ling*) infinitive ▪ *sm* infinity; (*Ling*) infinitive; **all'~** (*senza fine*) endlessly; (*Ling*) in the infinitive

infinocchi'are [infinok'kjare] *vt* (*fam*) to hoodwink

infiore'scenza [infjoreʃ'ʃentsa] *sf* inflorescence

infir'mare *vt* (*Dir*) to invalidate

infischi'arsi [infis'kjarsi] *vr*: **~ di** not to care about

in'fisso, -a *pp di* **infiggere** ▪ *sm* fixture; (*di porta, finestra*) frame

infit'tire *vt, vi* (*anche*: **infittirsi**) to thicken

inflazio'nare [inflattsjo'nare] *vt* to inflate

inflazi'one [inflat'tsjone] *sf* inflation

inflazio'nistico, -a, ci, che [inflattsjo'nistiko] *ag* inflationary

infles'sibile *ag* inflexible; (*ferreo*) unyielding

inflessi'one *sf* inflexion

in'fliggere [in'fliddʒere] *vt* to inflict

in'flissi *etc vb vedi* **infliggere**

in'flitto, -a *pp di* **infliggere**

influ'ente *ag* influential

influ'enza [influ'entsa] *sf* influence; (*Med*) influenza, flu; **~ aviaria** bird flu; **~ suina** swine flu

influen'zare [influen'tsare] *vt* to influence, have an influence on

influ'ire *vi*: **~ su** to influence

in'flusso *sm* influence

INFN *sigla m* = **Istituto Nazionale di Fisica Nucleare**

info'cato, -a *ag* = **infuocato**

info'gnarsi [infoɲ'ɲarsi] *vr* (*fam*) to get into a mess; **~ in un mare di debiti** to be up to one's o the eyes in debt

infol'tire *vt, vi* to thicken

infon'dato, -a *ag* unfounded, groundless

in'fondere *vt*: **~ qc in qn** to instill sth in sb; **~ fiducia in qn** to inspire sb with confidence

infor'care *vt* to fork (up); (*bicicletta, cavallo*) to get on; (*occhiali*) to put on

infor'male *ag* informal

infor'mare *vt* to inform, tell; **informarsi** *vr*: **informarsi (di** o **su)** to inquire (about);

tenere informato qn to keep sb informed

infor'matico, -a, ci, che *ag* (*settore*) computer *cpd* ▪ *sf* computer science

informa'tivo, -a *ag* informative; **a titolo ~** for information only

informatiz'zare [informatid'dzare] *vt* to computerize

infor'mato, -a *ag* informed; **tenersi ~** to keep o.s. (well-)informed

informa'tore *sm* informer

informazi'one [informat'tsjone] *sf* piece of information; **informazioni** *sfpl* information *sg*; **chiedere un'~** to ask for (some) information; **~ di garanzia** (*Dir*) = **avviso di garanzia**

in'forme *ag* shapeless

informico'larsi, informico'lirsi *vr*: **mi si è informicolata una gamba** I've got pins and needles in my leg

infor'nare *vt* to put in the oven

infor'nata *sf* (*anche fig*) batch

infortu'narsi *vr* to injure o.s., have an accident

infortu'nato, -a *ag* injured, hurt ▪ *sm/f* injured person

infor'tunio *sm* accident; **~ sul lavoro** industrial accident, accident at work

infortu'nistica *sf* study of (industrial) accidents

infos'sarsi *vr* (*terreno*) to sink; (*guance*) to become hollow

infos'sato, -a *ag* hollow; (*occhi*) deep-set; (: *per malattia*) sunken

infradici'are [infradi'tʃare] *vt* (*inzuppare*) to soak, drench; (*marcire*) to rot; **infradiciarsi** *vr* to get soaked, get drenched; to rot

infra'dito *sm inv* (*calzatura*) flip flop (*Brit*), thong (*US*)

in'frangere [in'frandʒere] *vt* to smash; (*fig: legge, patti*) to break; **infrangersi** *vr* to smash, break

infran'gibile [infran'dʒibile] *ag* unbreakable

in'franto, -a *pp di* **infrangere** ▪ *ag* broken

infra'rosso, -a *ag, sm* infrared

infrasettima'nale *ag* midweek *cpd*

infrastrut'tura *sf* infrastructure

infrazi'one [infrat'tsjone] *sf*: **~ a** breaking of, violation of

infredda'tura *sf* slight cold

infreddo'lito, -a *ag* cold, chilled

infre'quente *ag* infrequent, rare

infrol'lire *vi*, **infrol'lirsi** *vr* (*selvaggina*) to become high

infruttu'oso, -a *ag* fruitless

infuo'cato, -a *ag* (*metallo*) red-hot; (*sabbia*) burning; (*fig: discorso*) heated, passionate

infu'ori *av* out; **all'~** outwards; **all'~ di** (*eccetto*) except, with the exception of

infuri'are vi to rage; **infuriarsi** vr to fly into a rage

infusi'one sf infusion

in'fuso, -a pp di **infondere** ▪ ag: **scienza infusa** (anche ironico) innate knowledge ▪ sm infusion; ~ **di camomilla** camomile tea

Ing. abbr = **ingegnere**

ingabbi'are vt to (put in a) cage

ingaggi'are [ingad'dʒare] vt (assumere con compenso) to take on, hire; (Sport) to sign on; (Mil) to engage

in'gaggio [in'gaddʒo] sm hiring; signing on

ingagliar'dire [ingaʎʎar'dire] vt to strengthen, invigorate ▪ vi (anche: **ingagliardirsi**) to grow stronger

ingan'nare vt to deceive; (coniuge) to be unfaithful to; (fisco) to cheat; (eludere) to dodge, elude; (fig: tempo) to while away ▪ vi (apparenza) to be deceptive; **ingannarsi** vr to be mistaken, be wrong

inganna'tore, -'trice ag deceptive; (persona) deceitful

ingan'nevole ag deceptive

in'ganno sm deceit, deception; (azione) trick; (menzogna, frode) cheat, swindle; (illusione) illusion

ingarbugli'are [ingarbuʎ'ʎare] vt to tangle; (fig) to confuse, muddle; **ingarbugliarsi** vr to become confused o muddled

ingarbu'gliato, -a [ingarbuʎ'ʎato] ag tangled; confused, muddled

inge'gnarsi [indʒeɲ'ɲarsi] vr to do one's best, try hard; ~ **per vivere** to live by one's wits; **basta ~ un po'** you just need a bit of ingenuity

inge'gnere [indʒeɲ'ɲɛre] sm engineer; ~ **civile/navale** civil/naval engineer

ingegne'ria [indʒeɲɲe'ria] sf engineering

in'gegno [in'dʒeɲɲo] sm (intelligenza) intelligence, brains pl; (capacità creativa) ingenuity; (disposizione) talent

ingegnosità [indʒeɲɲosi'ta] sf ingenuity

inge'gnoso, -a [indʒeɲ'ɲoso] ag ingenious, clever

ingelo'sire [indʒelo'sire] vt to make jealous ▪ vi (anche: **ingelosirsi**) to become jealous

in'gente [in'dʒɛnte] ag huge, enormous

ingenti'lire [indʒenti'lire] vt to refine, civilize; **ingentilirsi** vr to become more refined, become more civilized

ingenuità [indʒenui'ta] sf ingenuousness

in'genuo, -a [in'dʒɛnuo] ag ingenuous, naïve

inge'renza [indʒe'rɛntsa] sf interference

inge'rire [indʒe'rire] vt to ingest

inges'sare [indʒes'sare] vt (Med) to put in plaster

ingessa'tura [indʒessa'tura] sf plaster

Inghil'terra [ingil'tɛrra] sf: **l'~** England

inghiot'tire [ingjot'tire] vt to swallow

in'ghippo [in'gippo] sm trick

ingial'lire [indʒal'lire] vi to go yellow

ingigan'tire [indʒigan'tire] vt to enlarge, magnify ▪ vi to become gigantic o enormous

inginocchi'arsi [indʒinok'kjarsi] vr to kneel (down)

inginocchia'toio [indʒinokkja'tojo] sm prie-dieu

ingioiel'lare [indʒojel'lare] vt to bejewel, adorn with jewels

ingiù [in'dʒu] av down, downwards

ingi'ungere [in'dʒundʒere] vt: ~ **a qn di fare qc** to enjoin o order sb to do sth

ingi'unto, -a [in'dʒunto] pp di **ingiungere**

ingiunzi'one [indʒun'tsjone] sf injunction, command; ~ **di pagamento** final demand

ingi'uria [in'dʒurja] sf insult; (fig: danno) damage

ingiuri'are [indʒu'rjare] vt to insult, abuse

ingiuri'oso, -a [indʒu'rjoso] ag insulting, abusive

ingiusta'mente [indʒusta'mente] av unjustly

ingiustifi'cabile [indʒustifi'kabile] ag unjustifiable

ingiustifi'cato, -a [indʒustifi'kato] ag unjustified

ingius'tizia [indʒus'tittsja] sf injustice

ingi'usto, -a [in'dʒusto] ag unjust, unfair

in'glese ag English ▪ sm/f Englishman(-woman) ▪ sm (Ling) English; **gli Inglesi** the English; **andarsene** o **filare all'~** to take French leave

inglori'oso, -a ag inglorious

ingob'bire vi, **ingob'birsi** vr to become stooped

ingoi'are vt to gulp (down); (fig) to swallow (up); **ha dovuto ~ il rospo** (fig) he had to accept the situation

ingol'fare vt, **ingol'farsi** vr (motore) to flood

ingolo'sire vt: ~ **qn** to make sb's mouth water; (fig) to attract sb ▪ vi (anche: **ingolosirsi**): ~ **(di)** (anche fig) to become greedy (for)

ingom'brante ag cumbersome

ingom'brare vt (strada) to block; (stanza) to clutter up

in'gombro, -a ag: ~ **di** (strada) blocked by; (stanza) cluttered up with ▪ sm obstacle; **essere d'~** to be in the way; **per ragioni di ~** for reasons of space

ingor'digia [ingor'didʒa] sf: ~ **(di)** greed (for); avidity (for)

in'gordo, -a ag: ~ **di** greedy for; (fig) greedy o avid for ▪ sm/f glutton

ingor'gare vt to block; **ingorgarsi** vr to be blocked up, be choked up

in'gorgo, -ghi sm blockage, obstruction; (anche: **ingorgo stradale**) traffic jam

ingoz'zare [ingot'tsare] vt (animali) to fatten; (fig: persona) to stuff; **ingozzarsi** vr: **ingozzarsi (di)** to stuff o.s. (with)

ingra'naggio [ingra'naddʒo] sm (Tecn) gear; (di orologio) mechanism; **gli ingranaggi della burocrazia** the bureaucratic machinery

ingra'nare vi to mesh, engage ■ vt to engage; **~ la marcia** to get into gear

ingrandi'mento sm enlargement; extension; magnification; growth; expansion

ingran'dire vt (anche Fot) to enlarge; (estendere) to extend; (Ottica, fig) to magnify ■ vi (anche: **ingrandirsi**) to become larger o bigger; (aumentare) to grow, increase; (espandersi) to expand

ingrandi'tore sm (Fot) enlarger

ingras'saggio [ingras'saddʒo] sm greasing

ingras'sare vt to make fat; (animali) to fatten; (Agr: terreno) to manure; (lubrificare) to grease ■ vi (anche: **ingrassarsi**) to get fat, put on weight

ingrati'tudine sf ingratitude

in'grato, -a ag ungrateful; (lavoro) thankless, unrewarding

ingrazi'are [ingrat'tsjare] vt: **ingraziarsi qn** to ingratiate o.s. with sb

ingredi'ente sm ingredient

in'gresso sm (porta) entrance; (atrio) hall; (l'entrare) entrance, entry; (facoltà di entrare) admission; **"~ libero"** "admission free"; **~ principale** main entrance; **~ di servizio** tradesmen's entrance

ingros'sare vt to increase; (folla, livello) to swell ■ vi (anche: **ingrossarsi**) to increase; to swell

in'grosso av: **all'~** (Comm) wholesale; (all'incirca) roughly, about

ingru'gnato, -a [ingruɲ'ɲato] ag grumpy

inguai'arsi vr to get into trouble

inguai'nare vt to sheathe

ingual'cibile [ingwal'tʃibile] ag crease-resistant

ingua'ribile ag incurable

'inguine sm (Anat) groin

ingurgi'tare [ingurdʒi'tare] vt to gulp down

ini'bire vt to forbid, prohibit; (Psic) to inhibit

ini'bito, -a ag inhibited ■ sm/f inhibited person

inibi'torio, -a ag (Psic) inhibitory, inhibitive; (provvedimento, misure) restrictive

inibizi'one [inibit'tsjone] sf prohibition; inhibition

iniet'tare vt to inject; **iniettarsi** vr: **iniettarsi di sangue** (occhi) to become bloodshot

iniet'tore sm injector

iniezi'one [injet'tsjone] sf injection

inimi'care vt to alienate, make hostile; **inimicarsi** vr: **inimicarsi con qn** to fall out with sb; **si è inimicato gli amici di un tempo** he has alienated his old friends

inimi'cizia [inimi'tʃittsja] sf animosity

inimi'tabile ag inimitable

inimmagi'nabile [inimmadʒi'nabile] ag unimaginable

ininfiam'mabile ag non-flammable

inintelli'gibile [inintelli'dʒibile] ag unintelligible

ininterrotta'mente av non-stop, continuously

ininter'rotto, -a ag (fila) unbroken; (rumore) uninterrupted

iniquità sf inv iniquity; (atto) wicked action

i'niquo, -a ag iniquitous

inizi'ale [init'tsjale] ag, sf initial

inizializ'zare [inittsjalid'dzare] vt (Inform) to boot

inizial'mente [inittsjal'mente] av initially, at first

inizi'are [init'tsjare] vi, vt to begin, start; **~ qn a** to initiate sb into; (pittura etc) to introduce sb to; **~ a fare qc** to start doing sth

inizia'tiva [inittsja'tiva] sf initiative; **~ privata** private enterprise

inizia'tore, -'trice [inittsja'tore] sm/f initiator

i'nizio [i'nittsjo] sm beginning; **all'~** at the beginning, at the start; **dare ~ a qc** to start sth, get sth going; **essere agli inizi** (progetto, lavoro etc) to be in the initial stages

innaffi'are etc = **annaffiare** etc

innal'zare [innal'tsare] vt (sollevare, alzare) to raise; (rizzare) to erect; **innalzarsi** vr to rise

innamora'mento sm falling in love

innamo'rare vt to enchant, charm; **innamorarsi** vr: **innamorarsi (di qn)** to fall in love (with sb)

innamo'rato, -a ag (che nutre amore): **~ (di)** in love (with); (appassionato): **~ di** very fond of ■ sm/f lover; (anche scherzoso) sweetheart

in'nanzi [in'nantsi] av (stato in luogo) in front, ahead; (moto a luogo) forward, on; (tempo: prima) before ■ prep (prima) before; **~ a** in front of; **d'ora ~** from now on; **farsi ~** to step forward; **~ tempo** ahead of time

innanzi'tutto [innantsi'tutto] av above all; (per prima cosa) first of all

in'nato, -a ag innate

innatu'rale ag unnatural

inne'gabile *ag* undeniable

inneggi'are [inned'dʒare] *vi*: ~ **a** to sing hymns to; *(fig)* to sing the praises of

innervo'sire *vt*: ~ **qn** to get on sb's nerves; **innervosirsi** *vr* to get irritated o upset

innes'care *vt* to prime

in'nesco, -schi *sm* primer

innes'tare *vt* (*Bot, Med*) to graft; (*Tecn*) to engage; (*inserire: presa*) to insert

in'nesto *sm* graft; grafting *no pl*; (*Tecn*) clutch; (*Elettr*) connection

'inno *sm* hymn; ~ **nazionale** national anthem

inno'cente [inno'tʃɛnte] *ag* innocent

inno'cenza [inno'tʃɛntsa] *sf* innocence

in'nocuo, -a *ag* innocuous, harmless

innomi'nato, -a *ag* unnamed

inno'vare *vt* to change, make innovations in

innova'tivo, -a *ag* innovative

innovazi'one [innovat'tsjone] *sf* innovation

innume'revole *ag* innumerable

inocu'lare *vt* (*Med*) to inoculate

ino'doro, -a *ag* odourless (*Brit*), odorless (*US*)

inoffen'sivo, -a *ag* harmless

inol'trare *vt* (*Amm*) to pass on, forward; **inoltrarsi** *vr* (*addentrarsi*) to advance, go forward

inol'trato, -a *ag*: **a notte inoltrata** late at night; **a primavera inoltrata** late in the spring

i'noltre *av* besides, moreover

i'noltro *sm* (*Amm*) forwarding

inon'dare *vt* to flood

inondazi'one [inondat'tsjone] *sf* flooding *no pl*; flood

inope'roso, -a *ag* inactive, idle

inopi'nato, -a *ag* unexpected

inoppor'tuno, -a *ag* untimely, ill-timed; (*poco adatto*) inappropriate; (*momento*) inopportune

inoppu'gnabile [inoppuɲ'ɲabile] *ag* incontrovertible

inor'ganico, -a, ci, che *ag* inorganic

inorgo'glire [inorgoʎ'ʎire] *vt* to make proud ■ *vi* (*anche*: **inorgoglirsi**) to become proud; **inorgoglirsi di qc** to pride o.s. on sth

inorri'dire *vt* to horrify ■ *vi* to be horrified

inospi'tale *ag* inhospitable

inosser'vante *ag*: **essere ~ di** to fail to comply with

inosser'vato, -a *ag* (*non notato*) unobserved; (*non rispettato*) not observed, not kept; **passare ~** to go unobserved, escape notice

inossi'dabile *ag* stainless

INPS *sigla m* (= *Istituto Nazionale Previdenza Sociale*) social security service

inqua'drare *vt* (*foto, immagine*) to frame; (*fig*) to situate, set

inquadra'tura *sf* (*Cine, Fot: atto*) framing; (: *immagine*) shot; (: *sequenza*) sequence

inqualifi'cabile *ag* unspeakable

inquie'tante *ag* disturbing, worrying

inquie'tare *vt* (*turbare*) to disturb, worry; **inquietarsi** *vr* to worry, become anxious; (*impazientirsi*) to get upset

inqui'eto, -a *ag* restless; (*preoccupato*) worried, anxious

inquie'tudine *sf* anxiety, worry

inqui'lino, -a *sm/f* tenant

inquina'mento *sm* pollution

inqui'nare *vt* to pollute

inqui'rente *ag* (*Dir*): **magistrato ~** examining (*Brit*) o committing (*US*) magistrate; **commissione ~** commission of inquiry

inqui'sire *vt, vi* to investigate

inqui'sito, -a *ag* (*persona*) under investigation

inquisi'tore, -'trice *ag* (*sguardo*) inquiring

inquisizi'one [inkwizit'tsjone] *sf* inquisition

insabbia'mento *sm* (*fig*) shelving

insabbi'are *vt* (*fig: pratica*) to shelve; **insabbiarsi** *vr* (*barca*) to run aground; (*fig: pratica*) to be shelved

insac'care *vt* (*grano, farina etc*) to bag, put into sacks; (*carne*) to put into sausage skins

insac'cati *smpl* (*Cuc*) sausages

insa'lata *sf* salad; (*pianta*) lettuce; ~ **mista** mixed salad

insalati'era *sf* salad bowl

insa'lubre *ag* unhealthy

insa'nabile *ag* (*piaga*) which cannot be healed; (*situazione*) irremediable; (*odio*) implacable

insangui'nare *vt* to stain with blood

in'sania *sf* insanity

in'sano, -a *ag* (*pazzo, folle*) insane

insapo'nare *vt* to soap; **insaponarsi le mani** to soap one's hands

insapo'nata *sf*: **dare un' ~ a qc** to give sth a (quick) soaping

insapo'rire *vt* to flavour (*Brit*), flavor (*US*); (*con spezie*) to season; **insaporirsi** *vr* to acquire flavo(u)r

insa'poro, -a *ag* tasteless, insipid

insa'puta *sf*: **all' ~ di qn** without sb knowing

insazi'abile [insat'tsjabile] *ag* insatiable

inscato'lare *vt* (*frutta, carne*) to can

insce'nare [inʃe'nare] *vt* (*Teat*) to stage, put on; (*fig*) to stage

inscin'dibile [inʃin'dibile] *ag* (*fattori*) inseparable; (*legame*) indissoluble

insec'chire [insek'kire] *vt* (*seccare*) to dry up; (: *piante*) to wither ■ *vi* to dry up, become dry; to wither

insedia'mento *sm* (*Amm: in carica, ufficio*) installation; (*villaggio, colonia*) settlement

183

insedi'are vt (Amm) to install; **insediarsi** vr (Amm) to take up office; (colonia, profughi etc) to settle; (Mil) to take up positions

in'segna [in'seɲɲa] sf sign; (emblema) sign, emblem; (bandiera) flag, banner; **insegne** sfpl (decorazioni) insignia pl

insegna'mento [inseɲɲa'mento] sm teaching; **trarre ~ da un'esperienza** to learn from an experience, draw a lesson from an experience; **che ti serva da ~** let this be a lesson to you

inse'gnante [inseɲ'ɲante] ag teaching; ■ sm/f teacher

inse'gnare [inseɲ'ɲare] vt, vi to teach; **~ a qn qc** to teach sb sth; **~ a qn a fare qc** to teach sb (how) to do sth; **come lei ben m'insegna ...** (ironico) as you will doubtless be aware ...

insegui'mento sm pursuit, chase; **darsi all'~ di qn** to give chase to sb

insegu'ire vt to pursue, chase

insegui'tore, -trice sm/f pursuer

insel'lare vt to saddle

inselvati'chire [inselvati'kire] vt (persona) to make unsociable ■ vi (anche: **inselvatichirsi**) to grow wild; (persona) to become unsociable

inseminazi'one [inseminat'tsjone] sf insemination

insena'tura sf inlet, creek

insen'sato, -a ag senseless, stupid

insen'sibile ag (anche fig) insensitive

insensibilità sf insensitivity, insensibility

insepa'rabile ag inseparable

inse'polto, -a ag unburied

inseri'mento sm (gen) insertion; **problemi di ~** (di persona) adjustment problems

inse'rire vt to insert; (Elettr) to connect; (allegare) to enclose; **inserirsi** vr (fig): **inserirsi in** to become part of; **~ un annuncio sul giornale** to put o place an advertisement in the newspaper

in'serto sm (pubblicazione) insert; **~ filmato** (film) clip

inser'vibile ag useless

inservi'ente sm/f attendant

inserzi'one [inser'tsjone] sf insertion; (avviso) advertisement; **fare un'~ sul giornale** to put an advertisement in the newspaper

inserzio'nista, -i, e [insertsjo'nista] sm/f advertiser

insetti'cida, -i [insetti'tʃida] sm insecticide

in'setto sm insect

insicu'rezza [insiku'rettsa] sf insecurity

insi'curo, -a ag insecure

in'sidia sf snare, trap; (pericolo) hidden danger; **tendere un'~ a qn** to lay o set a trap for sb

insidi'are vt (Mil) to harass; **~ la vita di qn** to make an attempt on sb's life

insidi'oso, -a ag insidious

insi'eme av together; (contemporaneamente) at the same time ■ prep: **~ o con** together with ■ sm whole; (Mat, servizio, assortimento) set; (Moda) ensemble, outfit; **tutti ~** all together; **tutto ~** all together; (in una volta) at one go; **nell'~** on the whole; **d'~** (veduta etc) overall

in'signe [in'siɲɲe] ag (persona) famous, distinguished, eminent; (città, monumento) notable

insignifi'cante [insiɲɲifi'kante] ag insignificant

insi'gnire [insiɲ'ɲire] vt: **~ qn di** to honour (Brit) o honor (US) sb with, decorate sb with

insin'cero, -a [insin'tʃero] ag insincere

insinda'cabile ag unquestionable

insinu'ante ag (osservazione, sguardo) insinuating; (maniere) ingratiating

insinu'are vt (introdurre): **~ qc in** to slip o slide sth into; (fig) to insinuate, imply; **insinuarsi** vr: **insinuarsi in** to seep into; (fig) to creep into; to worm one's way into

insinuazi'one [insinuat'tsjone] sf (fig) insinuation

in'sipido, -a ag insipid

insis'tente ag insistent; (pioggia, dolore) persistent

insistente'mente av repeatedly

insis'tenza [insis'tentsa] sf insistence; persistence

in'sistere vi: **~ su qc** to insist on sth; **~ in qc/a fare** (perseverare) to persist in sth/in doing

insis'tito, -a pp di **insistere**

'insito, -a ag: **~ (in)** inherent (in)

insoddis'fatto, -a ag dissatisfied

insoddisfazi'one [insoddisfat'tsjone] sf dissatisfaction

insoffe'rente ag intolerant

insoffe'renza [insoffe'rentsa] sf impatience

insolazi'one [insolat'tsjone] sf (Med) sunstroke

inso'lente ag insolent

insolen'tire vi to grow insolent ■ vt to insult, be rude to

inso'lenza [inso'lentsa] sf insolence

in'solito, -a ag unusual, out of the ordinary

inso'lubile ag insoluble

inso'luto, -a ag (non risolto) unsolved; (non pagato) unpaid, outstanding

insol'vente ag (Dir) insolvent

insol'venza [insol'ventsa] sf (Dir) insolvency

insol'vibile ag insolvent

in'somma av (in breve, in conclusione) in short; (dunque) well ■ escl for heaven's sake!

inson'dabile *ag* unfathomable

in'sonne *ag* sleepless

in'sonnia *sf* insomnia, sleeplessness

insonno'lito, -a *ag* sleepy, drowsy

insonorizzazi'one [insonoriddzat'tsjone] *sf* soundproofing

insoppor'tabile *ag* unbearable

insoppri'mibile *ag* insuppressible

insor'genza [insor'dʒɛntsa] *sf* (*di malattia*) onset

in'sorgere [in'sordʒere] *vi* (*ribellarsi*) to rise up, rebel; (*apparire*) to come up, arise

insormon'tabile *ag* (*ostacolo*) insurmountable, insuperable

in'sorsi *etc vb vedi* **insorgere**

in'sorto, -a *pp di* **insorgere** ■ *sm/f* rebel, insurgent

insospet'tabile *ag* (*al di sopra di ogni sospetto*) above suspicion; (*inatteso*) unsuspected

insospet'tire *vt* to make suspicious ■ *vi* (*anche:* **insospettirsi**) to become suspicious

insoste'nibile *ag* (*posizione, teoria*) untenable; (*dolore, situazione*) intolerable, unbearable; **le spese di manutenzione sono insostenibili** the maintenance costs are excessive

insostitu'ibile *ag* (*persona*) irreplaceable; (*aiuto, presenza*) invaluable

insoz'zare [insot'tsare] *vt* (*pavimento*) to make dirty; (*fig: reputazione, memoria*) to tarnish, sully; **insozzarsi** *vr* to get dirty

inspe'rabile *ag*: **la guarigione/salvezza era ~** there was no hope of a cure/of rescue; **abbiamo ottenuto risultati insperabili** the results we achieved were far better than we had hoped

inspe'rato, -a *ag* unhoped-for

inspie'gabile *ag* inexplicable

inspi'rare *vt* to breathe in, inhale

in'stabile *ag* (*carico, indole*) unstable; (*tempo*) unsettled; (*equilibrio*) unsteady

instabilità *sf* instability; (*di tempo*) changeability

instal'lare *vt* to install; **installarsi** *vr* (*sistemarsi*): **installarsi in** to settle in

installazi'one [installat'tsjone] *sf* installation

instan'cabile *ag* untiring, indefatigable

instau'rare *vt* to establish

instaurazi'one [instaurat'tsjone] *sf* establishment

instil'lare *vt* to instil

instra'dare *vt* = **istradare**

insù *av* up, upwards; **guardare all'~** to look up *o* upwards; **naso all'~** turned-up nose

insubordinazi'one [insubordinat'tsjone] *sf* insubordination

insuc'cesso [insut'tʃɛsso] *sm* failure, flop

insudici'are [insudi'tʃare] *vt* to dirty; **insudiciarsi** *vr* to get dirty

insuffici'ente [insuffi'tʃɛnte] *ag* insufficient; (*compito, allievo*) inadequate

insuffici'enza [insuffi'tʃɛntsa] *sf* insufficiency; inadequacy; (*Ins*) fail; **~ di prove** lack of evidence

insu'lare *ag* insular

insu'lina *sf* insulin

in'sulso, -a *ag* (*sciocco*) inane, silly; (*persona*) dull, insipid

insul'tare *vt* to insult, affront

in'sulto *sm* insult, affront

insupe'rabile *ag* (*ostacolo, difficoltà*) insuperable, insurmountable; (*eccellente: qualità, prodotto*) unbeatable; (*: persona, interpretazione*) unequalled

insuper'bire *vt* to make proud, make arrogant; **insuperbirsi** *vr* to become arrogant

insurrezi'one [insurret'tsjone] *sf* revolt, insurrection

insussis'tente *ag* non-existent

intac'care *vt* (*fare tacche*) to cut into; (*corrodere*) to corrode; (*fig: cominciare ad usare: risparmi*) to break into; (*: ledere*) to damage

intagli'are [intaʎ'ʎare] *vt* to carve

intaglia'tore, -'trice [intaʎʎa'tore] *sm/f* engraver

in'taglio [in'taʎʎo] *sm* carving

intan'gibile [intan'dʒibile] *ag* (*bene, patrimonio*) untouchable; (*fig: diritto*) inviolable

in'tanto *av* (*nel frattempo*) meanwhile, in the meantime; (*per cominciare*) just to begin with; **~ che** *cong* while

intarsi'are *vt* to inlay

in'tarsio *sm* inlaying *no pl*, marquetry *no pl*; inlay

intasa'mento *sm* (*ostruzione*) blockage, obstruction; (*Aut: ingorgo*) traffic jam

inta'sare *vt* to choke (up), block (up); (*Aut*) to obstruct, block; **intasarsi** *vr* to become choked *o* blocked

intas'care *vt* to pocket

in'tatto, -a *ag* intact; (*puro*) unsullied

intavo'lare *vt* to start, enter into

inte'gerrimo, -a [inte'dʒɛrrimo] *ag* honest, upright

inte'grale *ag* complete; (*pane, farina*) wholemeal (*Brit*), wholewheat (*US*); **film in versione ~** uncut version of a film; **calcolo ~** (*Mat*) integral calculus; **edizione ~** unabridged edition

inte'grante *ag*: **parte ~** integral part

inte'grare *vt* to complete; (*Mat*) to integrate; **integrarsi** *vr* (*persona*) to become integrated

integra'tivo, -a *ag* (*assegno*) supplementary; (Ins): **esame** ~ *assessment test sat when changing schools*

integra'tore *sm*: **integratori alimentari** nutritional supplements

integrazi'one [integrat'tsjone] *sf* integration

integrità *sf* integrity

'integro, -a *ag* (*intatto, intero*) complete, whole; (*retto*) upright

intelaia'tura *sf* frame; (*fig*) structure, framework

intel'letto *sm* intellect

intellettu'ale *ag, sm/f* intellectual

intellettua'loide (*peg*) *ag* pseudo-intellectual ■ *sm/f* pseudo-intellectual, would-be intellectual

intelli'gente [intelli'dʒɛnte] *ag* intelligent

intelli'genza [intelli'dʒɛntsa] *sf* intelligence

intelli'ghenzia [intelli'gɛntsja] *sf* intelligentsia

intelli'gibile [intelli'dʒibile] *ag* intelligible

inteme'rato, -a *ag* (*persona, vita*) blameless, irreproachable; (*coscienza*) clear; (*fama*) unblemished

intempe'rante *ag* intemperate, immoderate

intempe'ranza [intempe'rantsa] *sf* intemperance; **intemperanze** *sfpl* (*eccessi*) excesses

intem'perie *sfpl* bad weather *sg*

intempes'tivo, -a *ag* untimely

inten'dente *sm*: ~ **di Finanza** inland (*Brit*) *o* internal (*US*) revenue officer

inten'denza [inten'dɛntsa] *sf*: ~ **di Finanza** inland (*Brit*) *o* internal (*US*) revenue office

in'tendere *vt* (*avere intenzione*): ~ **fare qc** to intend *o* mean to do sth; (*comprendere*) to understand; (*udire*) to hear; (*significare*) to mean; **intendersi** *vr* (*conoscere*): **intendersi di** to know a lot about, be a connoisseur of; (*accordarsi*) to get on (well); **intendersi con qn su qc** to come to an agreement with sb about sth; **intendersela con qn** (*avere una relazione amorosa*) to have an affair with sb; **mi ha dato a ~ che ...** he led me to believe that ...; **non vuole ~ ragione** he won't listen to reason; **s'intende!** naturally!, of course!; **intendiamoci** let's get it quite clear; **ci siamo intesi?** is that clear?, is that understood?

intendi'mento *sm* (*intelligenza*) understanding; (*proposito*) intention

intendi'tore, -'trice *sm/f* connoisseur, expert; **a buon intenditor poche parole** (*proverbio*) a word is enough to the wise

intene'rire *vt* (*fig*) to move (to pity); **intenerirsi** *vr* (*fig*) to be moved

intensifi'care *vt*, **intensifi'carsi** *vr* to intensify

intensità *sf* intensity; (*del vento*) force, strength

inten'sivo, -a *ag* intensive

in'tenso, -a *ag* (*luce, profumo*) strong; (*colore*) intense, deep

inten'tare *vt* (Dir): ~ **causa contro qn** to start *o* institute proceedings against sb

inten'tato, -a *ag*: **non lasciare nulla d'**~ to leave no stone unturned, try everything

in'tento, -a *ag* (*teso, assorto*): ~ **(a)** intent (on), absorbed (in) ■ *sm* aim, purpose; **fare qc con l'**~ **di** to do sth with the intention of; **riuscire nell'**~ to achieve one's aim

intenzio'nale [intentsjo'nale] *ag* intentional; (Dir: *omicidio*) premeditated; **fallo** ~ (*Sport*) deliberate foul

intenzio'nato, -a [intentsjo'nato] *ag*: **essere** ~ **a fare qc** to intend to do sth, have the intention of doing sth; **ben** ~ well-meaning, well-intentioned; **mal** ~ ill-intentioned

intenzi'one [inten'tsjone] *sf* intention; (Dir) intent; **avere** ~ **di fare qc** to intend to do sth, have the intention of doing sth

intera'gire [intera'dʒire] *vi* to interact

intera'mente *av* entirely, completely

interat'tivo, -a *ag* interactive

interazi'one [interat'tsjone] *sf* interaction

interca'lare *sm* pet phrase, stock phrase ■ *vt* to insert

interca'pedine *sf* gap, cavity

inter'cedere [inter'tʃedere] *vi* to intercede

intercessi'one [intertʃes'sjone] *sf* intercession

intercetta'mento [intertʃetta'mento] *sm* = **intercettazione**

intercet'tare [intertʃet'tare] *vt* to intercept

intercettazi'one [intertʃettat'tsjone] *sf*: ~ **telefonica** telephone tapping

intercity [inter'siti] *sm inv* (Ferr) ≈ intercity (train)

intercon'nettere *vt* to interconnect

inter'correre *vi* (*esserci*) to exist; (*passare*: *tempo*) to elapse

inter'corso, -a *pp di* **intercorrere**

inter'detto, -a *pp di* **interdire** ■ *ag* forbidden, prohibited; (*sconcertato*) dumbfounded ■ *sm* (Rel) interdict; **rimanere** ~ to be taken aback

inter'dire *vt* to forbid, prohibit, ban; (Rel) to interdict; (Dir) to deprive of civil rights

interdizi'one [interdit'tsjone] *sf* prohibition, ban

interessa'mento *sm* interest; (*intervento*) intervention, good offices *pl*

interes'sante *ag* interesting; **essere in stato** ~ to be expecting (a baby)

interes'sare *vt* to interest; (*concernere*) to concern, be of interest to; (*far intervenire*): ~ **qn**

a to draw sb's attention to ■ *vi*: **~ a** to interest, matter to; **interessarsi** *vr (mostrare interesse)*: **interessarsi a** to take an interest in, be interested in; *(occuparsi)*: **interessarsi di** to take care of; **precipitazioni che interessano le regioni settentrionali** rainfall affecting the north; **si è interessato di farmi avere quei biglietti** he took the trouble to get me those tickets

interes'sato, -a *ag (coinvolto)* interested, involved; *(peg)*: **essere ~** to act out of pure self-interest ■ *sm/f (coinvolto)* person concerned; **a tutti gli interessati** to all those concerned, to all interested parties

inte'resse *sm (anche Comm)* interest; *(tornaconto)*: **fare qc per ~** to do sth out of self-interest; **~ maturato** *(Econ)* accrued interest; **~ privato in atti di ufficio** *(Amm)* abuse of public office

interes'senza [interes'sɛntsa] *sf (Econ)* profit-sharing

inter'faccia, -ce [inter'fattʃa] *sf (Inform)* interface; **~ utente** user interface

interfacci'are [interfat'tʃare] *vt (Inform)* to interface

interfe'renza [interfe'rɛntsa] *sf* interference

interfe'rire *vi* to interfere

inter'fono *sm* intercom; *(apparecchio)* internal phone

interiezi'one [interjet'tsjone] *sf* exclamation, interjection

'interim *sm inv (periodo)* interim, interval; **ministro ad ~** acting o interim minister; *(incarico)* temporary appointment

interi'nale *ag*: **lavoro ~** temporary work *(through an agency)*; **lavoratore ~** temporary worker

interi'ora *sfpl* entrails

interi'ore *ag* inner *cpd*; **parte ~** inside

interiorità *sf* inner being

interioriz'zare [interjorid'dzare] *vt* to internalize

inter'linea *sf (Dattilografia)* spacing; *(Tip)* leading; **doppia ~** double spacing

interlocu'tore, -'trice *sm/f* speaker

interlocu'torio, -a *ag* interlocutory

inter'ludio *sm (Mus)* interlude

intermedi'ario, -a *ag, sm/f* intermediary

intermediazi'one [intermedjat'tsjone] *sf* mediation

inter'medio, -a *ag* intermediate

inter'mezzo [inter'mɛddzo] *sm (intervallo)* interval; *(breve spettacolo)* intermezzo

intermi'nabile *ag* interminable, endless

intermit'tente *ag* intermittent

intermit'tenza [intermit'tɛntsa] *sf*: **ad ~** intermittent

interna'mento *sm* internment; confinement (to a mental hospital)

inter'nare *vt (arrestare)* to intern; *(Med)* to confine to a mental hospital

inter'nato, -a *ag* interned; confined (to a mental hospital) ■ *sm/f* internee; inmate (of a mental hospital) ■ *sm (collegio)* boarding school; *(Med)* period as a houseman *(Brit)* o an intern *(US)*

internazio'nale [internattsjo'nale] *ag* international

'Internet ['internet] *sf* internet; **in ~** on the internet

inter'nista, -i, e *sm/f* specialist in internal medicine

in'terno, -a *ag (di dentro)* internal, interior, inner; *(: mare)* inland; *(nazionale)* domestic; *(allievo)* boarding ■ *sm* inside, interior; *(di paese)* interior; *(fodera)* lining; *(di appartamento)* flat *(Brit)* o apartment *(US)* (number); *(Tel)* extension ■ *sm/f (Ins)* boarder; **interni** *smpl (Cine)* interior shots; **commissione interna** *(Ins)* internal examination board; **"per uso ~"** *(Med)* "to be taken internally"; **all'~** inside; **Ministero degli Interni** Ministry of the Interior, ≈ Home Office *(Brit)*, ≈ Department of the Interior *(US)*; **notizie dall'~** *(Stampa)* home news

in'tero, -a *ag (integro, intatto)* whole, entire; *(completo, totale)* complete; *(numero)* whole; *(non ridotto: biglietto)* full

interpel'lanza [interpel'lantsa] *sf*: **presentare un'~** *(Pol)* to ask a (parliamentary) question; **~ parlamentare** interpellation

interpel'lare *vt* to consult; *(Pol)* to question

INTER'POL *sigla f* (= International Criminal Police Organization) INTERPOL

inter'porre *vt (ostacolo)*: **~ qc a qc** to put sth in the way of sth; *(influenza)* to use; **interporsi** *vr* to intervene; **~ appello** *(Dir)* to appeal; **interporsi fra** *(mettersi in mezzo)* to come between

inter'posto, -a *pp di* **interporre**

interpre'tare *vt (spiegare, tradurre)* to interpret; *(Mus, Teat)* to perform; *(personaggio, sonata)* to play; *(canzone)* to sing

interpretari'ato *sm* interpreting

interpretazi'one [interpretat'tsjone] *sf* interpretation

in'terprete *sm/f* interpreter; *(Teat)* actor/actress, performer; *(Mus)* performer; **farsi ~ di** to act as a spokesman for

interpunzi'one [interpun'tsjone] *sf* punctuation; **segni di ~** punctuation marks

inter'rare vt (seme, pianta) to plant; (tubature etc) to lay underground; (Mil: pezzo d'artiglieria) to dig in; (riempire di terra: canale) to fill in

interregio'nale [interredʒo'nale] sm train that travels between two or more regions of Italy

interro'gare vt to question; (Ins) to test

interroga'tivo, -a ag (occhi, sguardo) questioning, inquiring; (Ling) interrogative ■ sm question; (fig) mystery

interroga'torio, -a ag interrogatory, questioning ■ sm (Dir) questioning no pl

interrogazi'one [interrogat'tsjone] sf questioning no pl; (Ins) oral test; (Pol): ~ (parlamentare) question

inter'rompere vt to interrupt; (studi, trattative) to break off, interrupt; **interrompersi** vr to break off, stop

inter'rotto, -a pp di **interrompere**

interrut'tore sm switch

interruzi'one [interrut'tsjone] sf (vedi interrompere) interruption; break; ~ **di gravidanza** termination of pregnancy

interse'care vt, **interse'carsi** vr to intersect

inter'stizio [inter'stittsjo] sm interstice, crack

interur'bano, -a ag inter-city; (Tel: chiamata) trunk cpd (Brit), long-distance; (: telefono) long-distance ■ sf trunk call (Brit), long-distance call

inter'vallo sm interval; (spazio) space, gap; ~ **pubblicitario** (TV) commercial break

interve'nire vi (partecipare): ~ **a** to take part in; (intromettersi: anche Pol) to intervene; (Med: operare) to operate

interven'tista, -i, e ag, sm/f interventionist

inter'vento sm participation; (intromissione) intervention; (Med) operation; (breve discorso) speech; **fare un ~ nel corso di** (dibattito, programma) to take part in

interve'nuto, -a pp di **intervenire** ■ sm: **gli intervenuti** those present

inter'vista sf interview

intervis'tare vt to interview

intervista'tore, -'trice sm/f interviewer

in'teso, -a pp di **intendere** ■ ag agreed ■ sf understanding; (accordo) agreement, understanding; **resta ~ che ...** it is understood that ...; **non darsi per ~ di qc** to take no notice of sth; **uno sguardo d'intesa** a knowing look

in'tessere vt to weave together; (fig: trama, storia) to weave

intes'tare vt (lettera) to address; (proprietà): ~ **a** to register in the name of; ~ **un assegno a qn** to make out a cheque to sb

intesta'tario, -a sm/f holder

intes'tato, -a ag (proprietà, casa, conto) in the name of; (assegno) made out to; **carta intestata** headed paper

intestazi'one [intestat'tsjone] sf heading; (su carta da lettere) letterhead; (registrazione) registration

intesti'nale ag intestinal

intes'tino, -a ag (lotte) internal, civil ■ sm (Anat) intestine

intiepi'dire vt (riscaldare) to warm (up); (raffreddare) to cool (down); (fig: amicizia etc) to cool; **intiepidirsi** vr to warm (up); to cool (down); to cool

Inti'fada sf Intifada

intima'mente av intimately; **sono ~ convinto che ...** I'm firmly o deeply convinced that ...; **i due fatti sono ~ connessi** the two events are closely connected

inti'mare vt to order, command; ~ **la resa a qn** (Mil) to call upon sb to surrender

intimazi'one [intimat'tsjone] sf order, command

intimida'torio, -a ag threatening

intimidazi'one [intimidat'tsjone] sf intimidation

intimi'dire vt to intimidate ■ vi (anche: **intimidirsi**) to grow shy

intimità sf intimacy; privacy; (familiarità) familiarity

'intimo, -a ag intimate; (affetti, vita) private; (fig: profondo) inmost ■ sm (persona) intimate o close friend; (dell'animo) bottom, depths pl; **parti intime** (Anat) private parts; **rapporti intimi** (sessuali) intimate relations

intimo'rire vt to frighten; **intimorirsi** vr to become frightened

in'tingere [in'tindʒere] vt to dip

in'tingolo sm sauce; (pietanza) stew

in'tinto, -a pp di **intingere**

intiriz'zire [intirid'dzire] vt to numb ■ vi, **intirizzirsi** vr to go numb

intiriz'zito, -a [intirid'dzito] ag numb (with cold)

intito'lare vt to give a title to; (dedicare) to dedicate; **intitolarsi** vr (libro, film) to be called

intolle'rabile ag intolerable

intolle'rante ag intolerant

intolle'ranza [intolle'rantsa] sf intolerance

intona'care vt to plaster

in'tonaco (mpl **intonaci** o **intonachi**) sm plaster

into'nare vt (canto) to start to sing; (armonizzare) to match; **intonarsi** vr (colori) to go together; **intonarsi a** (carnagione) to suit; (abito) to go with, match

intonazi'one [intonat'tsjone] sf intonation

inton'tire *vt* to stun, daze ■ *vi*, **intontirsi** *vr* to be stunned *o* dazed

inton'tito, -a *ag* stunned, dazed; ~ **dal sonno** stupid with sleep

in'toppo *sm* stumbling block, obstacle

intorbi'dire *vt* (*liquido*) to make turbid; (*mente*) to cloud; ~ **le acque** (*fig*) to muddy the waters

in'torno *av* around; ~ **a** *prep* (*attorno a*) around; (*riguardo, circa*) about

intorpi'dire *vt* to numb; (*fig*) to make sluggish ■ *vi* (*anche*: **intorpidirsi**) to grow numb; (*fig*) to become sluggish

intossi'care *vt* to poison

intossicazi'one [intossikat'tsjone] *sf* poisoning

intradu'cibile [intradu'tʃibile] *ag* untranslatable

intralci'are [intral'tʃare] *vt* to hamper, hold up

in'tralcio [in'traltʃo] *sm* hitch

intrallaz'zare [intrallat'tsare] *vi* to intrigue, scheme

intral'lazzo [intral'lattso] *sm* (*Pol*) intrigue, manoeuvre (*Brit*), maneuver (*US*); (*traffico losco*) racket

intramon'tabile *ag* timeless

intramusco'lare *ag* intramuscular

Intranet ['intranet] *sf* Intranet

intransi'gente [intransi'dʒente] *ag* intransigent, uncompromising

intransi'genza [intransi'dʒentsa] *sf* intransigence

intransi'tivo, -a *ag, sm* intransitive

intrappo'lare *vt* to trap; **rimanere intrappolato** to be trapped; **farsi ~** to get caught

intrapren'dente *ag* enterprising, go-ahead; (*con le donne*) forward, bold

intrapren'denza [intrapren'dentsa] *sf* audacity, initiative; (*con le donne*) boldness

intra'prendere *vt* to undertake; (*carriera*) to embark (up)on

intra'preso, -a *pp di* **intraprendere**

intrat'tabile *ag* intractable

intratte'nere *vt* (*divertire*) to entertain; (*chiacchierando*) to engage in conversation; (*rapporti*) to have, maintain; **intrattenersi** *vr* to linger; **intrattenersi su qc** to dwell on sth

intratteni'mento *sm* entertainment

intrave'dere *vt* to catch a glimpse of; (*fig*) to foresee

intrecci'are [intret'tʃare] *vt* (*capelli*) to plait, braid; (*intessere: anche fig*) to weave, interweave, intertwine; **intrecciarsi** *vr* to intertwine, become interwoven; ~ **le mani** to clasp one's hands; ~ **una relazione amorosa** (*fig*) to begin an affair

in'treccio [in'trettʃo] *sm* (*fig: trama*) plot, story

in'trepido, -a *ag* fearless, intrepid

intri'care *vt* (*fili*) to tangle; (*fig: faccenda*) to complicate; **intricarsi** *vr* to become tangled; to become complicated

in'trico, -chi *sm* (*anche fig*) tangle

intri'gante *ag* scheming ■ *sm/f* schemer, intriguer

intri'gare *vi* to manoeuvre (*Brit*), maneuver (*US*), scheme

in'trigo, -ghi *sm* plot, intrigue

in'trinseco, -a, ci, che *ag* intrinsic

in'triso, -a *ag*: ~ (**di**) soaked (in)

intris'tire *vi* (*persona: diventare triste*) to grow sad; (*pianta*) to wilt

intro'dotto, -a *pp di* **introdurre**

intro'durre *vt* to introduce; (*chiave etc*): ~ **qc in** to insert sth into; (*persona: far entrare*) to show in; **introdursi** *vr* (*moda, tecniche*) to be introduced; **introdursi in** (*persona: penetrare*) to enter; (: *entrare furtivamente*) to steal *o* slip into

in'troito *sm* income, revenue

intro'messo, -a *pp di* **intromettersi**

intro'mettersi *vr* to interfere, meddle; (*interporsi*) to intervene

intromissi'one *sf* interference, meddling; intervention

introspezi'one [introspet'tsjone] *sf* introspection

intro'vabile *ag* (*persona, oggetto*) who (*o* which) cannot be found; (*libro etc*) unobtainable

intro'verso, -a *ag* introverted ■ *sm/f* introvert

intrufo'larsi *vr*: ~ (**in**) (*stanza*) to sneak (into), slip (into); (*conversazione*) to butt in (on)

in'truglio [in'truʎʎo] *sm* concoction

intrusi'one *sf* intrusion; interference

in'truso, -a *sm/f* intruder

intu'ire *vt* to perceive by intuition; (*rendersi conto*) to realize

in'tuito *sm* intuition; (*perspicacia*) perspicacity

intuizi'one [intuit'tsjone] *sf* intuition

inturgi'dire [inturdʒi'dire] *vi*, **inturgi'dirsi** *vr* to swell

inumanità *sf inv* inhumanity

inu'mano, -a *ag* inhuman

inu'mare *vt* (*seppellire*) to bury, inter

inumazi'one [inumat'tsjone] *sf* burial, interment

inumi'dire *vt* to dampen, moisten; **inumidirsi** *vr* to become damp *o* wet

inurba'mento *sm* urbanization

inusi'tato, -a *ag* unusual

i'nutile *ag* useless; (*superfluo*) pointless, unnecessary; **è stato tutto ~!** it was all in vain!

inutilità *sf* uselessness; pointlessness

inutiliz'zabile [inutilid'dzabile] *ag* unusable

inutil'mente *av* (*senza risultato*) fruitlessly; (*senza utilità, scopo*) unnecessarily, needlessly; **l'ho cercato ~** I looked for him in vain; **ti preoccupi ~** there's nothing for you to worry about, there's no need for you to worry

inva'dente *ag* (*fig*) intrusive

inva'denza [inva'dɛntsa] *sf* intrusiveness

in'vadere *vt* to invade; (*affollare*) to swarm into, overrun; (*acque*) to flood

invadi'trice [invadi'tritʃe] *ag f vedi* **invasore**

inva'ghirsi [inva'girsi] *vr:* **~ di** to take a fancy to

invali'cabile *ag* (*montagna*) impassable

invali'dare *vt* to invalidate

invalidità *sf* infirmity; disability; (*Dir*) invalidity

in'valido, -a *ag* (*infermo*) infirm; (*al lavoro*) disabled; (*Dir: nullo*) invalid ▪ *sm/f* invalid; disabled person; **~ di guerra** disabled ex-serviceman; **~ del lavoro** industrially disabled person

in'valso, -a *ag* (*diffuso*) established

in'vano *av* in vain

invari'abile *ag* invariable

invari'ato, -a *ag* unchanged

inva'sare *vt* (*pianta*) to pot

inva'sato, -a *ag* possessed (by the devil) ▪ *sm/f* person possessed by the devil; **urlare come un ~** to shout like a madman

invasi'one *sf* invasion

in'vaso, -a *pp di* **invadere**

inva'sore, invadi'trice [invadi'tritʃe] *ag* invading ▪ *sm/f* invader

invecchia'mento [invekkja'mento] *sm* growing old; ageing; **questo whisky ha un ~ di 12 anni** this whisky has been matured for 12 years

invecchi'are [invek'kjare] *vi* (*persona*) to grow old; (*vino, popolazione*) to age; (*moda*) to become dated ▪ *vt* to age; (*far apparire più vecchio*) to make look older; **lo trovo invecchiato** I find he has aged

in'vece [in'vetʃe] *av* instead; (*al contrario*) on the contrary; **~ di** *prep* instead of

inve'ire *vi:* **~ contro** to rail against

invele'nire *vt* to embitter; **invelenirsi** *vr* to become bitter

inven'duto, -a *ag* unsold

inven'tare *vt* to invent; (*pericoli, pettegolezzi*) to make up, invent

inventari'are *vt* to make an inventory of, inventory

inven'tario *sm* inventory; (*Comm*) stocktaking *no pl*

inven'tivo, -a *ag* inventive ▪ *sf* inventiveness

inven'tore, -'trice *sm/f* inventor

invenzi'one [inven'tsjone] *sf* invention; (*bugia*) lie, story

invere'condia *sf* shamelessness, immodesty

inver'nale *ag* winter *cpd*; (*simile all'inverno*) wintry

in'verno *sm* winter; **d'~** in (the) winter

invero'simile *ag* unlikely ▪ *sm:* **ha dell'~** it's hard to believe, it's incredible

inversi'one *sf* inversion; **"divieto d'~"** (*Aut*) "no U-turns"

in'verso, -a *ag* opposite; (*Mat*) inverse ▪ *sm* contrary, opposite; **in senso ~** in the opposite direction; **in ordine ~** in reverse order

inverte'brato, -a *ag, sm* invertebrate

inver'tire *vt* to invert; (*disposizione, posti*) to change; (*ruoli*) to exchange; **~ la marcia** (*Aut*) to do a U-turn; **~ la rotta** (*Naut*) to go about; (*fig*) to do a U-turn

inver'tito, -a *sm/f* homosexual

investi'gare *vt, vi* to investigate

investiga'tivo, -a *ag:* **squadra investigativa** detective squad

investiga'tore, -'trice *sm/f* investigator, detective

investigazi'one [investigat'tsjone] *sf* investigation, inquiry

investi'mento *sm* (*Econ*) investment; (*di veicolo*) crash, collision; (*di pedone*) knocking down

inves'tire *vt* (*denaro*) to invest; (*veicolo: pedone*) to knock down; (*: altro veicolo*) to crash into; (*apostrofare*) to assail; (*incaricare*): **~ qn di** to invest sb with; **investirsi** *vr* (*fig*): **investirsi di una parte** to enter thoroughly into a role

investi'tore, -'trice *sm/f* driver responsible for an accident

investi'tura *sf* investiture

invete'rato, -a *ag* inveterate

invet'tiva *sf* invective

invi'are *vt* to send

invi'ato, -a *sm/f* envoy; (*Stampa*) correspondent

in'vidia *sf* envy; **fare ~ a qn** to make sb envious

invidi'abile *ag* enviable

invidi'are *vt:* **~ qn (per qc)** to envy sb (for sth); **~ qc a qn** to envy sb sth; **non aver nulla da ~ a nessuno** to be as good as the next one

invidi'oso, -a *ag* envious

invin'cibile [invin'tʃibile] *ag* invincible

in'vio, -'vii *sm* sending; (*insieme di merci*) consignment; (*tasto*) Return (key), Enter (key)

invio'labile *ag* inviolable

invio'lato, -a *ag* (*diritto, segreto*) inviolate; (*foresta*) virgin *cpd*; (*montagna, vetta*) unscaled

invipe'rire *vi*, **invipe'rirsi** *vr* to become furious, fly into a temper

invipe'rito, -a *ag* furious

invis'chiare [invis'kjare] *vt* (*fig*): ~ **qn in qc** to involve sb in sth, mix sb up in sth; **invischiarsi** *vr*: **invischiarsi (con qn/in qc)** to get mixed up *o* involved (with sb/in sth)

invi'sibile *ag* invisible

in'viso, -a *ag*: ~ **a** unpopular with

invi'tante *ag* (*proposta, odorino*) inviting; (*sorriso*) appealing, attractive

invi'tare *vt* to invite; ~ **qn a fare** to invite sb to do

invi'tato, -a *sm/f* guest

in'vito *sm* invitation; **dietro ~ del sig. Rossi** at Mr Rossi's invitation

invo'care *vt* (*chiedere: aiuto, pace*) to cry out for; (*appellarsi: la legge, Dio*) to appeal to, invoke

invogli'are [invoʎ'ʎare] *vt*: ~ **qn a fare** to tempt sb to do, induce sb to do

involon'tario, -a *ag* (*errore*) unintentional; (*gesto*) involuntary

invol'tino *sm* (*Cuc*) roulade

in'volto *sm* (*pacco*) parcel; (*fagotto*) bundle

in'volucro *sm* cover, wrapping

involu'tivo, -a *ag*: **subire un processo ~** to regress

invo'luto, -a *ag* involved, intricate

involuzi'one [involut'tsjone] *sf* (*di stile*) convolutedness; (*regresso*): **subire un'~** to regress

invulne'rabile *ag* invulnerable

inzacche'rare [intsakke'rare] *vt* to spatter with mud; **inzaccherarsi** *vr* to get muddy

inzup'pare [intsup'pare] *vt* to soak; **inzupparsi** *vr* to get soaked; **inzuppò i biscotti nel latte** he dipped the biscuits in the milk

'io *pron* I ■ *sm inv*: **l'io** the ego, the self; **io stesso(a)** I myself; **sono io** it's me

i'odio *sm* iodine

i'ogurt *sm inv* = **yoghurt**

i'one *sm* ion

I'onio *sm*: **lo ~, il mar ~** the Ionian (Sea)

ionizza'tore [joniddza'tore] *sm* ioniser

'iosa; a ~ *av* in abundance, in great quantity

IPAB *sigla fpl* (= *Istituzioni pubbliche di Assistenza e Beneficenza*) charitable institutions

i'perbole *sf* (*Letteratura*) hyperbole; (*Mat*) hyperbola

iper'bolico, -a, ci, che *ag* (*Letteratura, Mat*) hyperbolic(al); (*fig: esagerato*) exaggerated

ipermer'cato *sm* hypermarket

ipersen'sibile *ag* (*persona*) hypersensitive; (*Fot: lastra, pellicola*) hypersensitized

ipertecno'logico, -a, ci, che [ipertekno'lɔdʒiko] *ag* hi-tech

ipertensi'one *sf* high blood pressure, hypertension

iper'testo *sm* hypertext

ipertestu'ale *ag* (*Comput*): **collegamento~**, **link ~** hyperlink

ip'nosi *sf* hypnosis

ip'notico, -a, ci, che *ag* hypnotic

ipno'tismo *sm* hypnotism

ipnotiz'zare [ipnotid'dzare] *vt* to hypnotize

ipoaller'genico, -a, ci, che [ipoaller'dʒeniko] *ag* hypoallergenic

ipocon'dria *sf* hypochondria

ipocon'driaco, -a, ci, che *ag, sm/f* hypochondriac

ipocri'sia *sf* hypocrisy

i'pocrita, -i, e *ag* hypocritical ■ *sm/f* hypocrite

ipo'sodico, -a, ci, che *ag* low sodium *cpd*

ipo'teca, -che *sf* mortgage

ipote'care *vt* to mortgage

ipote'nusa *sf* hypotenuse

i'potesi *sf inv* hypothesis; **facciamo l'~ che ..., ammettiamo per ~ che ...** let's suppose *o* assume that ...; **nella peggiore/migliore delle ~** at worst/best; **nell'~ che venga** should he come, if he comes; **se per ~ io partissi ...** just supposing I were to leave ....

ipo'tetico, -a, ci, che *ag* hypothetical

ipotiz'zare [ipotid'dzare] *vt*: ~ **che** to form the hypothesis that

'ippico, -a, ci, che *ag* horse *cpd* ■ *sf* horseracing

ippocas'tano *sm* horse chestnut

ip'podromo *sm* racecourse

ippo'potamo *sm* hippopotamus

'ipsilon *sf o m inv* (*lettera*) Y, y; (: *dell'alfabeto greco*) epsilon

IP'SOA *sigla m* (= *Istituto Post-Universitario per lo Studio dell'Organizzazione Aziendale*) postgraduate institute of business administration

IR *abbr* (*Ferr*) = **interregionale**

IRA *sigla f* (= *Irish Republican Army*) IRA

'ira *sf* anger, wrath

ira'cheno, -a [ira'kɛno] *ag, sm/f* Iraqi

I'ran *sm*: **l'~** Iran

irani'ano, -a *ag, sm/f* Iranian

I'raq *sm*: **l'~** Iraq

iras'cibile [iraʃ'ʃibile] *ag* quick-tempered

IRCE ['irtʃe] *sigla m* = **Istituto per le relazioni culturali con l'Estero**

'IRI *sigla m* (= *Istituto per la Ricostruzione Industriale*) state-controlled industrial investment office

'iride *sf* (*arcobaleno*) rainbow; (*Anat, Bot*) iris

'iris *sm inv* iris

Ir'landa *sf*: **l'~** Ireland; **l'~ del Nord** Northern Ireland, Ulster; **la Repubblica d'~** Eire, the Republic of Ireland; **il mar d'~** the Irish Sea

irlan'dese *ag* Irish ■ *sm/f* Irishman(-woman); **gli Irlandesi** the Irish

iro'nia *sf* irony

i'ronico, -a, ci, che *ag* ironic(al)

ironiz'zare [ironid'dzare] *vt, vi*: **~ su** to be ironical about

i'roso, -a *ag* (*sguardo, tono*) angry, wrathful; (*persona*) irascible

'IRPEF *sigla f* = **imposta sul reddito delle persone fisiche**

ir'pino, -a *ag* of (*o* from) Irpinia

irradi'are *vt* to radiate; (*raggi di luce: illuminare*) to shine on ■ *vi* (*diffondersi: anche*: **irradiarsi**) to radiate

irradiazi'one [irradjat'tsjone] *sf* radiation

irraggiun'gibile [irraddʒun'dʒibile] *ag* unreachable; (*fig: meta*) unattainable

irragio'nevole [irradʒo'nevole] *ag* (*privo di ragione*) irrational; (*fig: persona, pretese, prezzo*) unreasonable

irrazio'nale [irrattsjo'nale] *ag* irrational

irre'ale *ag* unreal

irrealiz'zabile [irrealid'dzabile] *ag* (*sogno, desiderio*) unattainable, unrealizable; (*progetto*) unworkable, impracticable

irrealtà *sf* unreality

irrecupe'rabile *ag* (*gen*) irretrievable; (*fig: persona*) irredeemable

irrecu'sabile *ag* (*offerta*) not to be refused; (*prova*) irrefutable

irreden'tista, -i, e *ag, sm/f* (*Storia*) Irredentist

irrefre'nabile *ag* uncontrollable

irrefu'tabile *ag* irrefutable

irrego'lare *ag* irregular; (*terreno*) uneven

irregolarità *sf inv* irregularity; unevenness *no pl*

irremo'vibile *ag* (*fig*) unshakeable, unyielding

irrepa'rabile *ag* irreparable; (*fig*) inevitable

irrepe'ribile *ag* nowhere to be found

irrepren'sibile *ag* irreproachable

irrequi'eto, -a *ag* restless

irresis'tibile *ag* irresistible

irreso'luto, -a *ag* irresolute

irrespi'rabile *ag* (*aria*) unbreathable; (*fig: opprimere*) stifling, oppressive; (*: malsano*) unhealthy

irrespon'sabile *ag* irresponsible

irrestrin'gibile [irrestrin'dʒibile] *ag* unshrinkable, non-shrink (*Brit*)

irre'tire *vt* to seduce

irrever'sibile *ag* irreversible

irrevo'cabile *ag* irrevocable

irricono'scibile [irrikonoʃʃibile] *ag* unrecognizable

irridu'cibile [irridu'tʃibile] *ag* irreducible; (*fig*) unshakeable

irrifles'sivo, -a *ag* thoughtless

irri'gare *vt* (*annaffiare*) to irrigate; (*fiume etc*) to flow through

irrigazi'one [irrigat'tsjone] *sf* irrigation

irrigidi'mento [irridʒidi'mento] *sm* stiffening; hardening; tightening

irrigi'dire [irridʒi'dire] *vt* to stiffen; (*disciplina*) to tighten; **irrigidirsi** *vr* to stiffen; (*posizione, atteggiamento*) to harden

irriguar'doso, -a *ag* disrespectful

irrile'vante *ag* (*trascurabile*) insignificant

irrimedi'abile *ag*: **un errore ~** a mistake which cannot be rectified; **non è ~!** we can do something about it!

irrinunci'abile [irrinun'tʃabile] *ag* vital; which cannot be abandoned

irripe'tibile *ag* unrepeatable

irri'solto, -a *ag* (*problema*) unresolved

irri'sorio, -a *ag* derisory

irrispet'toso, -a *ag* disrespectful

irri'tabile *ag* irritable

irri'tante *ag* (*atteggiamento*) irritating, annoying; (*Med*) irritant

irri'tare *vt* (*mettere di malumore*) to irritate, annoy; (*Med*) to irritate; **irritarsi** *vr* (*stizzirsi*) to become irritated *o* annoyed; (*Med*) to become irritated

irritazi'one [irritat'tsjone] *sf* irritation; annoyance

irrive'rente *ag* irreverent

irrobus'tire *vt* (*persona*) to make stronger, make more robust; (*muscoli*) to strengthen; **irrobustirsi** *vr* to become stronger

ir'rompere *vi*: **~ in** to burst into

irro'rare *vt* to sprinkle; (*Agr*) to spray

ir'rotto, -a *pp di* **irrompere**

irru'ente *ag* (*fig*) impetuous, violent

irru'enza [irru'entsa] *sf* impetuousness; **con ~** impetuously

ir'ruppi *etc vb vedi* **irrompere**

irruvi'dire *vt* to roughen ■ *vi* (*anche*: **irruvidirsi**) to become rough

irruzi'one [irrut'tsjone] *sf*: **fare ~ in** to burst into; (*polizia*) to raid

ir'suto, -a *ag* (*petto*) hairy; (*barba*) bristly

'irto, -a *ag* bristly; **~ di** bristling with

Is. *abbr* (= *isola*) I

ISBN *abbr* (= *International Standard Book Number*) ISBN

is'crissi *etc vb vedi* **iscrivere**

is'critto, -a *pp di* **iscrivere** ■ *sm/f* member; **gli iscritti alla gara** the competitors; **per** *o* **in ~** in writing

is'crivere *vt* to register, enter; (*persona*): **~ (a)** to register (in), enrol (in); **iscriversi** *vr*:

iscriversi (a) (club, partito) to join; (università) to register o enrol (at); (esame, concorso) to register o enter (for)

iscrizi'one [iskrit'tsjone] sf (epigrafe etc) inscription; (a scuola, società etc) enrolment; registration

'ISEF sigla m = **Istituto Superiore di Educazione Fisica**

Is'lam sm: **l'~** Islam

is'lamico, -a, ci, che ag Islamic

Is'landa sf: **l'~** Iceland

islan'dese ag Icelandic ■ sm/f Icelander ■ sm (Ling) Icelandic

'isola sf island; **~ pedonale** (Aut) pedestrian precinct

isola'mento sm isolation; (Tecn) insulation; **essere in cella di ~** to be in solitary confinement; **~ acustico** soundproofing; **~ termico** thermal insulation

iso'lano, -a ag island cpd ■ sm/f islander

iso'lante ag insulating ■ sm insulator

iso'lare vt to isolate; (Tecn) to insulate; (: acusticamente) to soundproof

iso'lato, -a ag isolated; insulated ■ sm (edificio) block

isolazio'nismo [isolattsjo'nismo] sm isolationism

i'sotopo sm isotope

ispessi'mento sm thickening

ispes'sire vt to thicken; **ispessirsi** vr to get thicker, thicken

ispetto'rato sm inspectorate

ispet'tore, -'trice sm/f inspector; (Comm) supervisor; **~ di zona** (Comm) area supervisor o manager; **~ di reparto** shop walker (Brit), floor walker (US)

ispezio'nare [ispettsjo'nare] vt to inspect

ispezi'one [ispet'tsjone] sf inspection

'ispido, -a ag bristly, shaggy

ispi'rare vt to inspire; **ispirarsi** vr: **ispirarsi a** to draw one's inspiration from; (conformarsi) to be based on; **l'idea m'ispira** the idea appeals to me

ispira'tore, -'trice ag inspiring ■ sm/f inspirer; (di ribellione) instigator

ispirazi'one [ispirat'tsjone] sf inspiration; **secondo l'~ del momento** according to the mood of the moment

israeli'ano, -a ag, sm/f Israeli

israe'lita, -i, e sm/f Jew/Jewess; (Storia) Israelite

israe'litico, -a, ci, che ag Jewish

is'sare vt to hoist; **~ l'ancora** to weigh anchor

Istanbul sf Istanbul

istan'taneo, -a ag instantaneous ■ sf (Fot) snapshot

is'tante sm instant, moment; **all'~, sull'~** instantly, immediately

is'tanza [is'tantsa] sf petition, request; **giudice di prima ~** (Dir) judge of the court of first instance; **giudizio di seconda ~** judgment on appeal; **in ultima ~** (fig) finally; **~ di divorzio** petition for divorce

'ISTAT sigla m = **Istituto Centrale di Statistica**

'ISTEL sigla f = **Indagine sull'ascolto delle televisioni in Italia**

is'terico, -a, ci, che ag hysterical

isteri'lire vt (terreno) to render infertile; (fig: fantasia) to dry up; **isterilirsi** vr to become infertile; to dry up

iste'rismo sm hysteria

isti'gare vt to incite

istigazi'one [istigat'tsjone] sf instigation; **~ a delinquere** (Dir) incitement to crime

istin'tivo, -a ag instinctive

is'tinto sm instinct

istitu'ire vt (fondare) to institute, found; (porre: confronto) to establish; (intraprendere: inchiesta) to set up

isti'tuto sm institute; (di università) department; (ente, Dir) institution; **~ di bellezza** beauty salon; **~ di credito** bank, banking institution; **~ tecnico commerciale** ≈ commercial college; **~ tecnico industriale statale** ≈ technical college

istitu'tore, -'trice sm/f (fondatore) founder; (precettore) tutor, governess

istituzi'one [istitut'tsjone] sf institution; **istituzioni** sfpl (Dir) institutes; **lotta alle istituzioni** struggle against the Establishment

'istmo sm (Geo) isthmus

isto'gramma, -i sm histogram

istra'dare vt (fig: persona): **~ (a/verso)** to direct (to/towards)

istri'ano, -a ag, sm/f Istrian

'istrice ['istritʃe] sm porcupine

istri'one sm (peg) ham (actor)

istru'ire vt (insegnare) to teach; (ammaestrare) to train; (informare) to instruct, inform; (Dir) to prepare

istru'ito, -a ag educated

istrut'tivo, -a ag instructive

istrut'tore, -'trice sm/f instructor ■ ag: **giudice ~** examining (Brit) o committing (US) magistrate

istrut'toria sf (Dir) (preliminary) investigation and hearing; **formalizzare un'~** to proceed to a formal hearing

istruzi'one [istrut'tsjone] sf (gen) training; (Ins, cultura) education; (direttiva) instruction; (Dir) = **istruttoria**; **Ministero della Pubblica I~** Ministry of Education; **istruzioni di spedizione** forwarding

193

instructions; **istruzioni per l'uso**
instructions (for use)

istupi'dire vt (colpo) to stun, daze; (: droga, stanchezza) to stupefy; **istupidirsi** vr to become stupid

'ISVE sigla m (= Istituto di Studi per lo Sviluppo Economico) institute for research into economic development

I'talia sf: **l'~** Italy

itali'ano, -a ag Italian ■ sm/f Italian ■ sm (Ling) Italian; **gli Italiani** the Italians

ITC sigla m = **istituto tecnico commerciale**

'iter sm passage, course; **l'~ burocratico** the bureaucratic process

itine'rante ag wandering, itinerant; **mostra ~** touring exhibition; **spettacolo ~** travelling (Brit) o traveling (US) show, touring show

itine'rario sm itinerary

'ITIS sigla m = **istituto tecnico industriale statale**

itte'rizia [itte'rittsja] sf (Med) jaundice

'ittico, -a, ci, che ag fish cpd; fishing cpd

IUD sigla m inv (= intra-uterine device) IUD

Iugos'lavia sf = **Jugoslavia**

iugos'lavo, -a ag, sm/f = **jugoslavo, a**

i'uta sf jute

'I.V.A. sigla f = **imposta sul valore aggiunto**

'ivi av (formale, poetico) therein; (nelle citazioni) ibid

Jj

J, j [i'lunga] *sm o f inv* (*lettera*) J, j; **J come Jersey** ≈ J for Jack (Brit), J for Jig (US)

jazz [dʒaz] *sm* jazz

jaz'zista, -i [dʒad'dzista] *sm* jazz player

jeans [dʒinz] *smpl* jeans

jeep [dʒip] *sm inv* jeep

'jersey ['dʒɛrzi] *sm inv* jersey (cloth)

'jockey ['dʒɔki] *sm inv* (*Carte*) jack; (*fantino*) jockey

'jogging ['dʒɔgiŋ] *sm* jogging; **fare ~** to go jogging

'jolly ['dʒɔli] *sm inv* joker

jr. *abbr* (= *junior*) Jr., jr.

ju'do [dʒu'dɔ] *sm* judo

Jugos'lavia [jugoz'lavja] *sf*: **la ~** Yugoslavia

jugos'lavo, -a *ag, sm/f* Yugoslav(ian)

juke 'box ['dʒuk'bɔks] *sm inv* jukebox

j

Kk

K, k ['kappa] *sf o m inv (lettera)* K, k ■ *abbr*
(= *kilo-, chilo-*) k; (*Inform*) K; **K come Kursaal**
≈ K for King
Kam'pala *sf* Kampala
kara'oke [kara'oke] *sm inv* karaoke
karatè [kara'tɛ] *sm* karate
Kashmir ['kaʃmir] *sm*: **il** ~ Kashmir
ka'yak [ka'jak] *sm inv* kayak
Ka'zakistan [ɪa'dzakistan] *sm* Kazakhstan
ka'zako, -a [ka'dzako] *ag, sm/f* Kazakh
'Kenia ['kenja] *sm*: **il** ~ Kenya
keni'ano, -a *ag, sm/f* Kenyan
keni'ota, -i, e *ag, sm/f* Kenyan
'Kenya ['kenja] *sm*: **il** ~ Kenya
kero'sene [kero'zɛne] *sm* = **cherosene**
kg *abbr* (= *chilogrammo*) kg
kib'butz [kib'buts] *sm inv* kibbutz
Kilimangi'aro [kiliman'dʒaro] *sm*: **il** ~
Kilimanjaro

killer ['killer] *sm inv* gunman, hired gun
kilo *etc* = **chilo** *etc*
kilt [kilt] *sm inv* kilt
ki'mono [ki'mɔno] *sm* = **chimono**
Kir'ghizistan [kir'gidzistan] *sm* Kyrgyzstan
kir'ghiso, -a [kir'gizo] *ag, sm/f* Kyrgyz
kitsch [kitʃ] *sm* kitsch
'kiwi ['kiwi] *sm inv* kiwi (fruit)
km *abbr* (= *chilometro*) km
kmq *abbr* (= *chilometro quadrato*) km^2
ko'ala [ko'ala] *sm inv* koala (bear)
koso'varo, -a *ag, sm/f* Kosovan
'Kosovo *sm* Kosovo
KR *sigla* = **Crotone**
'krapfen ['krapfən] *sm inv* doughnut
Ku'ala Lum'par *sf* Kuala Lumpur
Ku'wait [ku'vait] *sm*: **il** ~ Kuwait
kW *abbr* (= *kilowatt, chilowatt*) kW
kWh *abbr* (= *kilowattora*) kW/h

Ll

L, l ['ɛlle] *sf o m inv* (*lettera*) L, l ▪ *abbr* (= *lira*) L; (= *L come Livorno*) ≈ L for Lucy (Brit), L for Love (US)

l *abbr* (= *litro*) l

l' *det vedi* **la**; **lo**

la *det f* (*dav V l'*) the ▪ *pron* (*dav V l'*) (*oggetto: persona*) her; (: *cosa*) it; (: *forma di cortesia*) you ▪ *sm inv* (*Mus*) A; (: *solfeggiando la scala*) la; *vedi anche* **il**

là *av* there; **di là** (*da quel luogo*) from there; (*in quel luogo*) in there; (*dall'altra parte*) over there; **di là di** beyond; **per di là** that way; **più in là** further on; (*tempo*) later on; **là dentro/sopra/sotto** in/up (*o* on) /under there; **là per là** (*sul momento*) there and then; **essere in là con gli anni** to be getting on (in years); **essere più di là che di qua** to be more dead than alive; **va' là!** come off it!; **stavolta è andato troppo in là** this time he's gone too far; *vedi anche* **quello**

labbro *sm* (*Anat*: *pl*(*f*) **labbra**) lip

labile *ag* fleeting, ephemeral

labirinto *sm* labyrinth, maze

laboratorio *sm* (*di ricerca*) laboratory; (*di arti, mestieri*) workshop; **~ linguistico** language laboratory

laborioso, -a *ag* (*faticoso*) laborious; (*attivo*) hard-working

laburista, -i, e *ag* Labour *cpd* (Brit) ▪ *sm/f* Labour Party member (Brit)

lacca, -che *sf* lacquer; (*per unghie*) nail varnish (Brit), nail polish

laccare *vt* (*mobili*) to varnish, lacquer

laccio ['lattʃo] *sm* noose; (*legaccio, tirante*) lasso; (*di scarpa*) lace; **~ emostatico** (*Med*) tourniquet

lacerante [latʃe'rante] *ag* (*suono*) piercing, shrill

lacerare [latʃe'rare] *vt* to tear to shreds, lacerate; **lacerarsi** *vr* to tear

lacerazione [latʃerat'tsjone] *sf* (*anche Med*) tear

lacero, -a ['latʃero] *ag* (*logoro*) torn, tattered; (*Med*) lacerated; **ferita ~-contusa** injury with lacerations and bruising

laconico, -a, ci, che *ag* laconic, brief

lacrima *sf* tear; (*goccia*) drop; **in lacrime** in tears

lacrimare *vi* to water

lacrimevole *ag* heartrending, pitiful

lacrimogeno, -a [lakri'mɔdʒeno] *ag*: **gas ~** tear gas

lacrimoso, -a *ag* tearful

lacuna *sf* (*fig*) gap

lacustre *ag* lake *cpd*

laddove *cong* whereas

ladro *sm* thief; **al ~!** stop thief!

ladrocinio [ladro'tʃinjo] *sm* theft, robbery

ladruncolo, -a *sm/f* petty thief

laggiù [lad'dʒu] *av* down there; (*di là*) over there

lagna ['laɲɲa] *sf* (*fam*: *persona, cosa*) drag, bore; **fare la ~** to whine, moan

lagnanza [laɲ'ɲantsa] *sf* complaint

lagnarsi [laɲ'ɲarsi] *vr*: **~ (di)** to complain (about)

lago, -ghi *sm* lake

Lagos ['lagos] *sf* Lagos

lagrima *etc* = **lacrima** *etc*

laguna *sf* lagoon

lagunare *ag* lagoon *cpd*

laico, -a, ci, che *ag* (*apostolato*) lay; (*vita*) secular; (*scuola*) non-denominational ▪ *sm/f* layman(-woman) ▪ *sm* lay brother

laido, -a *ag* filthy, foul; (*fig*: *osceno*) obscene, filthy

lama *sf* blade ▪ *sm inv* (*Zool*) llama; (*Rel*) lama

lambiccare *vt* to distil; **lambiccarsi il cervello** to rack one's brains

lambire *vt* (*fig*: *fiamme*) to lick; (*acqua*) to lap

lambretta® *sf* scooter

lamella *sf* (*di metallo etc*) thin sheet, thin strip; (*di fungo*) gill

lamentare *vt* to lament; **lamentarsi** *vr* (*emettere lamenti*) to moan, groan;

(*rammaricarsi*): **lamentarsi (di)** to complain (about)

lamen'tela *sf* complaining *no pl*

lamen'tevole *ag* (*voce*) complaining, plaintive; (*stato*) lamentable, pitiful

la'mento *sm* moan, groan; (*per la morte di qn*) lament

lamen'toso, -a *ag* plaintive

la'metta *sf* razor blade

lami'era *sf* sheet metal

'lamina *sf* (*lastra sottile*) thin sheet (*o layer o plate*); ~ **d'oro** gold leaf; gold foil

lami'nare *vt* to laminate

lami'nato, -a *ag* laminated; (*tessuto*) lamé ■ *sm* laminate

'lampada *sf* lamp; ~ **a petrolio/a gas** oil/gas lamp; ~ **a spirito** blowlamp (*Brit*), blowtorch; ~ **a stelo** standard lamp (*Brit*), floor lamp; ~ **da tavolo** table lamp

lampa'dario *sm* chandelier

lampa'dina *sf* light bulb; ~ **tascabile** pocket torch (*Brit*), flashlight (*US*)

lam'pante *ag* (*fig: evidente*) crystal clear, evident

lam'para *sf* fishing lamp; (*barca*) boat for fishing by lamplight (*in Mediterranean*)

lampeggi'are [lamped'dʒare] *vi* (*luce, fari*) to flash ■ *vb impers*: **lampeggia** there's lightning

lampeggia'tore [lampeddʒa'tore] *sm* (*Aut*) indicator

lampi'one *sm* street light *o* lamp (*Brit*)

'lampo *sm* (*Meteor*) flash of lightning; (*di luce, fig*) flash ■ *ag inv*: **cerniera** ~ zip (fastener) (*Brit*), zipper (*US*); **guerra** ~ blitzkrieg; **lampi** *smpl* (*Meteor*) lightning *no pl*; **passare come un** ~ to flash past *o* by

lam'pone *sm* raspberry

'lana *sf* wool; ~ **d'acciaio** steel wool; **pura** ~ **vergine** pure new wool; ~ **di vetro** glass wool

lan'cetta [lan'tʃetta] *sf* (*indice*) pointer, needle; (*di orologio*) hand

'lancia, -ce ['lantʃa] *sf* (*arma*) lance; (: *picca*) spear; (*di pompa antincendio*) nozzle; (*imbarcazione*) launch; **partire** ~ **in resta** (*fig*) to set off ready for battle; **spezzare una** ~ **in favore di qn** (*fig*) to come to sb's defence; ~ **di salvataggio** lifeboat

lancia'bombe [lantʃa'bombe] *sm inv* (*Mil*) mortar

lanciafi'amme [lantʃa'fjamme] *sm inv* flamethrower

lancia'missili [lantʃa'missili] *ag inv* missile-launching ■ *sm inv* missile launcher

lancia'razzi [lantʃa'raddzi] *ag inv* rocket-launching ■ *sm inv* rocket launcher

lanci'are [lan'tʃare] *vt* to throw, hurl, fling; (*Sport*) to throw; (*far partire: automobile*) to get up to full speed; (*bombe*) to drop; (*razzo, prodotto, moda*) to launch; (*emettere: grido*) to give out; **lanciarsi** *vr*: **lanciarsi contro/su** to throw *o* hurl *o* fling o.s. against/on; **lanciarsi in** (*fig*) to embark on; ~ **un cavallo** to give a horse his head; ~ **il disco** (*Sport*) to throw the discus; ~ **il peso** (*Sport*) to put the shot; **lanciarsi all'inseguimento di qn** to set off in pursuit of sb; **lanciarsi col paracadute** to parachute

lanci'ato, -a [lan'tʃato] *ag* (*affermato: attore, prodotto*) well-known, famous; (*veicolo*) speeding along, racing along

lanci'nante [lantʃi'nante] *ag* (*dolore*) shooting, throbbing; (*grido*) piercing

'lancio ['lantʃo] *sm* throwing *no pl*; throw; dropping *no pl*; drop; launching *no pl*; launch; ~ **del disco** (*Sport*) throwing the discus; ~ **del peso** (*Sport*) putting the shot

'landa *sf* (*Geo*) moor

'languido, -a *ag* (*fiacco*) languid, weak; (*tenero, malinconico*) languishing

langu'ire *vi* to languish; (*conversazione*) to flag

langu'ore *sm* weakness, languor

lani'ero, -a *ag* wool *cpd*, woollen (*Brit*), woolen (*US*)

lani'ficio [lani'fitʃo] *sm* woollen (*Brit*) *o* woolen (*US*) mill

lano'lina *sf* lanolin(e)

la'noso, -a *ag* woolly

lan'terna *sf* lantern; (*faro*) lighthouse

lanter'nino *sm*: **cercarsele col** ~ to be asking for trouble

la'nugine [la'nudʒine] *sf* down

'Laos *sm* Laos

lapalissi'ano, -a *ag* self-evident

La 'Paz [la'pas] *sf* La Paz

lapi'dare *vt* to stone

lapi'dario, -a *ag* (*fig*) terse

'lapide *sf* (*di sepolcro*) tombstone; (*commemorativa*) plaque

la'pin [la'pɛ̃] *sm inv* coney

'lapis *sm inv* pencil

lap'pone *ag, sm/f, sm* Lapp

Lap'ponia *sf*: **la** ~ Lapland

'lapsus *sm inv* slip

laptop ['læp tɔp] *sm inv* laptop (computer)

'lardo *sm* bacon fat, lard

lar'ghezza [lar'gettsa] *sf* width; breadth; looseness; generosity; ~ **di vedute** broad-mindedness

lar'gire [lar'dʒire] *vt* to give generously

'largo, -a, ghi, ghe *ag* wide, broad; (*maniche*) wide; (*abito: troppo ampio*) loose; (*fig*) generous ■ *sm* width; breadth; (*mare aperto*): **il** ~ the open sea ■ *sf*: **stare** *o* **tenersi alla larga (da qn/qc)** to keep one's distance (from sb/sth), keep away (from sb/sth); **~ due metri** two metres wide; **~ di spalle** broad-shouldered; **di larghe vedute** broad-minded; **in larga misura** to a great *o* large extent; **su larga scala** on a large scale; **di manica larga** generous, open-handed; **al ~ di Genova** off (the coast of) Genoa; **farsi ~ tra la folla** to push one's way through the crowd

larice ['laritʃe] *sm* (Bot) larch

laringe [la'rindʒe] *sf* larynx

laringite [larin'dʒite] *sf* laryngitis

laringoiatra, -i, e *sm/f* (medico) throat specialist

larva *sf* larva; (fig) shadow

lasagne [la'zaɲɲe] *sfpl* lasagna *sg*

lasciapassare [laʃʃapas'sare] *sm inv* pass, permit

lasciare [laʃʃare] *vt* to leave; (abbandonare) to leave, abandon, give up; (cessare di tenere) to let go of ■ *vb aus*: **~ qn fare qc** to let sb do sth ■ *vi*: **~ di fare** (smettere) to stop doing; **lasciarsi andare/truffare** to let o.s. go/be cheated; **~ andare** *o* **correre** *o* **perdere** to let things go their own way; **~ stare qc/qn** to leave sth/sb alone; **~ qn erede** to make sb one's heir; **~ la presa** to lose one's grip; **~ il segno (su qc)** to leave a mark (on sth); (fig) to leave one's mark (on sth); **~ (molto) a desiderare** to leave much to be desired; **ci ha lasciato la vita** it cost him his life

lascito ['laʃʃito] *sm* (Dir) legacy

lascivia [laʃʃivja] *sf* lust, lasciviousness

lascivo, -a [laʃʃivo] *ag* lascivious

laser ['lazer] *ag, sm inv*: **(raggio) ~** laser (beam)

lassativo, a *ag, sm* laxative

lassismo *sm* laxity

lasso *sm*: **~ di tempo** interval

lassù *av* up there

lastra *sf* (di pietra) slab; (di metallo, Fot) plate; (di ghiaccio, vetro) sheet; (radiografica) X-ray (plate)

lastricare *vt* to pave

lastricato *sm* paving

lastrico (mpl **lastrici** *o* **lastrichi**) *sm* paving; **essere sul ~** (fig) to be penniless; **gettare qn sul ~** (fig) to leave sb destitute

lastrone *sm* (Alpinismo) sheer rock face

latente *ag* latent

laterale *ag* lateral, side *cpd*; (uscita, ingresso etc) side *cpd* ■ *sm* (Calcio) half-back

lateralmente *av* sideways

laterizio [late'rittsjo] *sm* (perforated) brick

latifondista, -i, e *sm/f* large agricultural landowner

latifondo *sm* large estate

latino, -a *ag, sm* Latin

latinoamericano, -a *ag, sm/f* Latin-American

latitante *ag*: **essere ~** to be on the run ■ *sm/f* fugitive (from justice)

latitanza [lati'tantsa] *sf*: **darsi alla ~** to go into hiding

latitudine *sf* latitude

lato, -a *ag*: **in senso ~** broadly speaking ■ *sm* side; (fig) aspect, point of view; **d'altro ~** (d'altra parte) on the other hand

latrare *vi* to bark

latrato *sm* howling

latrina *sf* public lavatory

latrocinio [latro'tʃinjo] *sm* = **ladrocinio**

latta *sf* tin (plate); (recipiente) tin, can

lattaio, -a *sm/f* (distributore) milkman(-woman); (commerciante) dairyman(-woman)

lattante *ag* unweaned ■ *sm/f* breast-fed baby

latte *sm* milk; **fratello di ~** foster brother; **avere ancora il ~ alla bocca** (fig) to be still wet behind the ears; **tutto ~ e miele** (fig) all smiles; **~ detergente** cleansing milk *o* lotion; **~ intero** full-cream milk; **~ a lunga conservazione** UHT milk; **~ magro** *o* **scremato** skimmed milk; **~ secco** *o* **in polvere** dried *o* powdered milk

latteo, -a *ag* milky; (dieta, prodotto) milk *cpd*

latteria *sf* dairy

latticini [latti'tʃini] *smpl* dairy *o* milk products

lattina *sf* (di birra etc) can

lattuga, -ghe *sf* lettuce

laurea *sf* ≈ degree; **~ breve** university degree awarded at the end of a three-year course; **avere una ~ in chimica** to have a degree in chemistry *o* a chemistry degree; see note

○ **LAUREA**

○ The Laurea is awarded to students who
○ successfully complete their degree
○ courses. Traditionally, this takes between
○ four and six years; a major element of the
○ final examinations is the presentation
○ and discussion of a dissertation. A
○ shorter, more vocational course of study,
○ taking from two to three years, is also
○ available; at the end of this time students
○ receive a diploma called the Laurea breve.

laureando, -a *sm/f* final-year student

laureare *vt* to confer a degree on; **laurearsi** *vr* to graduate

laure'ato, -a *ag, sm/f* graduate

'lauro *sm* laurel

'lauto, -a *ag (pranzo, mancia)* lavish; **lauti guadagni** handsome profits

'lava *sf* lava

lavabianche'ria [lavabjanke'ria] *sf inv* washing machine

la'vabo *sm* washbasin

la'vaggio [la'vaddʒo] *sm* washing *no pl*; **~ del cervello** brainwashing *no pl*

la'vagna [la'vaɲɲa] *sf (Geo)* slate; *(di scuola)* blackboard; **~ luminosa** overhead projector

la'vanda *sf (anche Med)* wash; *(Bot)* lavender; **fare una ~ gastrica a qn** to pump sb's stomach

lavan'daia *sf* washerwoman

lavande'ria *sf (di ospedale, caserma etc)* laundry; **~ automatica** launderette; **~ a secco** dry-cleaner's

lavan'dino *sm* sink; *(del bagno)* washbasin

lavapi'atti *sm/f* dishwasher

la'vare *vt* to wash; **lavarsi** *vr* to wash, have a wash; **~ a secco** to dry-clean; **~ i panni sporchi in pubblico** *(fig)* to wash one's dirty linen in public; **lavarsi le mani/i denti** to wash one's hands/clean one's teeth

lava'secco *sm o f inv* dry-cleaner's

lavasto'viglie [lavasto'viʎʎe] *sm o f inv (macchina)* dishwasher

la'vata *sf* wash; *(fig)*: **dare una ~ di capo a qn** to give sb a good telling-off

lava'tivo *sm (clistere)* enema; *(buono a nulla)* good-for-nothing, idler

lava'toio *sm (public)* washhouse

lava'trice [lava'tritʃe] *sf* washing machine

lava'tura *sf* washing *no pl*; **~ di piatti** dishwater

la'vello *sm (kitchen)* sink

la'vina *sf* snowslide

lavo'rante *sm/f* worker

lavo'rare *vi* to work; *(fig: bar, studio etc)* to do good business ■ *vt* to work; **~ a** to work on; **~ a maglia** to knit; **~ di fantasia** *(suggestionarsi)* to imagine things; *(fantasticare)* to let one's imagination run free; **lavorarsi qn** *(fig: convincere)* to work on sb

lavora'tivo, -a *ag* working

lavora'tore, -'trice *sm/f* worker ■ *ag* working

lavorazi'one [lavorat'tsjone] *sf (gen)* working; *(di legno, pietra)* carving; *(di film)* making; *(di prodotto)* manufacture; *(modo di esecuzione)* workmanship

lavo'rio *sm* intense activity

la'voro *sm* work; *(occupazione)* job, work *no pl*; *(opera)* piece of work, job; *(Econ)* labour *(Brit)*,

labor *(US)*; **Ministero del L~** Department of Employment *(Brit)*, Department of Labor *(US)*; **(fare) i lavori di casa** (to do) the housework *sg*; **lavori forzati** hard labour *sg*; **i lavori del parlamento** the parliamentary session *sg*; **lavori pubblici** public works

lazi'ale [lat'tsjale] *ag* of *(o* from) Lazio

lazza'retto [laddza'retto] *sm* leper hospital

lazza'rone [laddza'rone] *sm* scoundrel

'lazzo ['laddzo] *sm* jest

LC *sigla* = **Lecco**

LE *sigla* = **Lecce**

le *det fpl* the ■ *pron (oggetto)* them; *(: a lei, a essa)* (to) her; *(: forma di cortesia)* (to) you; *vedi anche* **il**

le'ale *ag* loyal; *(sincero)* sincere; *(onesto)* fair

lea'lista, -i, e *sm/f* loyalist

lealtà *sf* loyalty; sincerity; fairness

'leasing ['liːziŋ] *sm* leasing; lease

'lebbra *sf* leprosy

'lecca 'lecca *sm inv* lollipop

leccapi'edi *sm/f inv (peg)* toady, bootlicker

lec'care *vt* to lick; *(gatto: latte etc)* to lick *o* lap up; *(fig)* to flatter; **leccarsi** *vr (fig)* to preen o.s.; **leccarsi i baffi** to lick one's lips

lec'cato, -a *ag* affected ■ *sf* lick

leccherò *etc* [lekke'rɔ] *vb vedi* **leccare**

'leccio ['lettʃo] *sm* holm oak, ilex

leccor'nia *sf* titbit, delicacy

'lecito, -a ['letʃito] *ag* permitted, allowed; **se mi è ~** if I may; **mi sia ~ far presente che …** may I point out that …

'ledere *vt* to damage, injure; **~ gli interessi di qn** to be prejudicial to sb's interests

'lega, -ghe *sf (anche Pol)* league; *(di metalli)* alloy; **metallo di bassa ~** base metal; **gente di bassa ~** common *o* vulgar people; **L lega Nord** *(Pol)* federalist party

le'gaccio [le'gattʃo] *sm* string, lace

le'gale *ag* legal ■ *sm* lawyer; **corso ~ delle monete** official exchange rate; **medicina ~** forensic medicine; **studio ~** lawyer's office

legalità *sf* legality, lawfulness

legaliz'zare [legalid'dzare] *vt* to legalize; *(documento)* to authenticate

legalizzazi'one [legaliddzat'tsjone] *sf (vedi vt)* legalization; authentication

le'game *sm (corda, fig: affettivo)* tie, bond; *(nesso logico)* link, connection; **~ di sangue *o* di parentela** family tie

lega'mento *sm (Anat)* ligament

le'gare *vt (prigioniero, capelli, cane)* to tie (up); *(libro)* to bind; *(Chim)* to alloy; *(fig: collegare)* to bind, join ■ *vi (far lega)* to unite; *(fig)* to get on well; **è pazzo da ~** *(fam)* he should be locked up

lega'tario, -a *sm/f (Dir)* legatee

le'gato sm (Rel) legate; (Dir) legacy, bequest

legato'ria sf (attività) bookbinding; (negozio) bookbinder's

lega'tura sf (di libro) binding; (Mus) ligature

legazi'one [legat'tsjone] sf legation

le'genda [le'dʒɛnda] sf (di carta geografica etc) = leggenda

'legge ['leddʒe] sf law; ~ procedurale procedural law

leg'genda [led'dʒɛnda] sf (narrazione) legend; (di carta geografica etc) key, legend

leggen'dario, -a [leddʒen'darjo] ag legendary

'leggere ['lɛddʒere] vt, vi to read; ~ il pensiero di qn to read sb's mind o thoughts

legge'rezza [leddʒe'rettsa] sf lightness; thoughtlessness; fickleness

leg'gero, -a [led'dʒɛro] ag light; (agile, snello) nimble, agile, light; (tè, caffè) weak; (fig: non grave, piccolo) slight; (: spensierato) thoughtless; (: incostante) fickle; free and easy; una ragazza leggera (fig) a flighty girl; alla leggera thoughtlessly

leggi'adro, -a [led'dʒadro] ag pretty, lovely; (movimenti) graceful

leg'gibile [led'dʒibile] ag legible; (libro) readable, worth reading

leg'gio, -'gii [led'dʒio] sm lectern; (Mus) music stand

leghe'rò etc [lege'rɔ] vb vedi legare

le'ghismo [le'gismo] sm political movement with federalist tendencies

le'ghista, -i, e [le'gista] ag (Pol) of a "lega" (especially Lega Nord) ■ sm/f member (o supporter) of a "lega" (especially Lega Nord)

legife'rare [ledʒife'rare] vi to legislate

legio'nario [ledʒo'narjo] sm (romano) legionary; (volontario) legionnaire

legi'one [le'dʒone] sf legion; ~ straniera foreign legion

legisla'tivo, -a [ledʒizla'tivo] ag legislative

legisla'tore [ledʒizla'tore] sm legislator

legisla'tura [ledʒizla'tura] sf legislature

legislazi'one [ledʒizlat'tsjone] sf legislation

legitti'mare [ledʒitti'mare] vt (figlio) to legitimize; (comportamento etc) to justify

legittimità [ledʒittimi'ta] sf legitimacy

le'gittimo, -a [le'dʒittimo] ag legitimate; (fig: giustificato, lecito) justified, legitimate; legittima difesa (Dir) self-defence (Brit), self-defense (US)

'legna ['leɲɲa] sf firewood

le'gnaia [leɲ'ɲaja] sf woodshed

legnai'olo [leɲɲa'jɔlo] sm woodcutter

le'gname [leɲ'ɲame] sm wood, timber

le'gnata [leɲ'ɲata] sf blow with a stick; dare a qn un sacco di legnate to give sb a good hiding

'legno ['leɲɲo] sm wood; (pezzo di legno) piece of wood; di ~ wooden; ~ compensato plywood

le'gnoso, -a [leɲ'ɲoso] ag (di legno) wooden; (come il legno) woody; (carne) tough

le'gume sm (Bot) pulse; legumi smpl (fagioli, piselli etc) pulses

'lei pron (soggetto) she; (oggetto: per dare rilievo, con preposizione) her; (forma di cortesia: anche: Lei) you ■ sf inv: la mia ~ my beloved ■ sm: dare del ~ a qn to address sb as "lei"; ~ stessa she herself; you yourself; è ~ it's her

'lembo sm (di abito, strada) edge; (striscia sottile: di terra) strip

'lemma, -i sm headword

'lemme 'lemme av (very) very slowly

'lena sf (fig) energy, stamina; di buona ~ (lavorare, camminare) at a good pace

Lenin'grado sf Leningrad

le'nire vt to soothe

lenta'mente av slowly

'lente sf (Ottica) lens sg; ~ d'ingrandimento magnifying glass; lenti a contatto, lenti corneali contact lenses; lenti (a contatto) morbide soft lenses; lenti (a contatto) rigide hard lenses

len'tezza [len'tettsa] sf slowness

len'ticchia [len'tikkja] sf (Bot) lentil

len'tiggine [len'tiddʒine] sf freckle

'lento, -a ag slow; (molle: fune) slack; (non stretto: vite, abito) loose ■ sm (ballo) slow dance

'lenza ['lentsa] sf fishing line

lenzu'olo [len'tswɔlo] sm sheet; lenzuola sfpl pair of sheets; ~ funebre shroud

leon'cino [leon'tʃino] sm lion cub

le'one sm lion; (dello zodiaco): L~ Leo; essere del L~ to be Leo

leo'pardo sm leopard

lepo'rino, -a ag: labbro ~ harelip

'lepre sf hare

'lercio, -a, ci, ce ['lɛrtʃo] ag filthy

lerci'ume [ler'tʃume] sm filth

'lesbico, -a, ci, che ag, sf lesbian

'lesi etc vb vedi ledere

lesi'nare vt to be stingy with ■ vi: ~ (su) to skimp (on), be stingy (with)

lesi'one sf (Med) lesion; (Dir) injury, damage; (Edil) crack

le'sivo, -a ag: ~ (di) damaging (to), detrimental (to)

'leso, -a pp di ledere ■ ag (offeso) injured; parte lesa (Dir) injured party; lesa maestà lese-majesty

Le'sotho [le'soto] sm Lesotho

les'sare vt (Cuc) to boil

'lessi etc vb vedi leggere

lessi'cale ag lexical

'lessico, -ci *sm* vocabulary; (*dizionario*) lexicon

lessicogra'fia *sf* lexicography

lessi'cografo, -a *sm/f* lexicographer

'lesso, -a *ag* boiled ■ *sm* boiled meat

'lesto, -a *ag* quick; (*agile*) nimble; **~ di mano** (*per rubare*) light-fingered; (*per picchiare*) free with one's fists

lesto'fante *sm* swindler, con man

le'tale *ag* lethal, deadly

leta'maio *sm* dunghill

le'tame *sm* manure, dung

le'targo, -ghi *sm* lethargy; (*Zool*) hibernation

le'tizia [le'tittsja] *sf* joy, happiness

'letta *sf*: **dare una ~ a** qc to glance o look through sth

'lettera *sf* letter; **lettere** *sfpl* (*letteratura*) literature *sg*; (*studi umanistici*) arts (subjects); **alla ~** literally; **in lettere** in words, in full; **diventar ~ morta** (*legge*) to become a dead letter; **restar ~ morta** (*consiglio, invito*) to go unheeded; **~ di accompagnamento** accompanying letter; **~ assicurata** registered letter; **~ di cambio** (*Comm*) bill of exchange; **~ di credito** (*Comm*) letter of credit; **~ di intenti** letter of intent; **~ di presentazione** o **raccomandazione** letter of introduction; **~ raccomandata** recorded delivery (*Brit*) o certified (*US*) letter; **~ di trasporto aereo** (*Comm*) air waybill

lette'rale *ag* literal

letteral'mente *av* literally

lette'rario, -a *ag* literary

lette'rato, -a *ag* well-read, scholarly

lettera'tura *sf* literature

let'tiga, -ghe *sf* (*portantina*) litter; (*barella*) stretcher

let'tino *sm* cot (*Brit*), crib (*US*); (*per il sole*) sun lounger

'letto, -a *pp di* **leggere** ■ *sm* bed; **andare a ~** to go to bed; **~ a castello** bunk beds *pl*; **~ a una piazza/a due piazze** o **matrimoniale** single/double bed

'lettone *ag, sm/f* Latvian ■ *sm* (*Ling*) Latvian

Let'tonia *sf*: **la ~** Latvia

letto'rato *sm* (*Ins*) lectorship, assistantship; (*Rel*) lectorate

let'tore, -'trice *sm/f* reader; (*Ins*) (foreign language) assistant (*Brit*), (foreign) teaching assistant (*US*) ■ *sm*: **~ ottico (di caratteri)** optical character reader; **~ CD/DVD** CD/DVD player; **~ MP3/MP4** MP3/MP4 player

let'tura *sf* reading

leuce'mia [leutʃe'mia] *sf* leukaemia

'leva *sf* lever; (*Mil*) conscription; **far ~ su** qn to work on sb; **essere di ~** to be due for call-up; **~ del cambio** (*Aut*) gear lever

le'vante *sm* east; (*vento*) East wind; **il L~** the Levant

le'vare *vt* (*occhi, braccio*) to raise; (*sollevare, togliere: tassa, divieto*) to lift; (: *indumenti*) to take off, remove; (*rimuovere*) to take away; (: *dal di sopra*) to take off; (: *dal di dentro*) to take out; **levarsi** *vr* to get up; (*sole*) to rise; **~ le tende** (*fig*) to pack up and leave; **levarsi il pensiero** to put one's mind at rest; **levati di mezzo** o **di lì** o **di torno!** get out of my way!

le'vata *sf* (*di posta*) collection

leva'taccia, -ce [leva'tattʃa] *sf* early rise

leva'toio, -a *ag*: **ponte ~** drawbridge

leva'trice [leva'tritʃe] *sf* midwife

leva'tura *sf* intelligence, mental capacity

levi'gare *vt* to smooth; (*con carta vetrata*) to sand

levi'gato, -a *ag* (*superficie*) smooth; (*fig: stile*) polished; (: *viso*) flawless

levità *sf* lightness

levri'ere *sm* greyhound

lezi'one [let'tsjone] *sf* lesson; (*all'università, sgridata*) lecture; **fare ~** to teach; to lecture

lezi'oso, -a [let'tsjoso] *ag* affected; simpering

'lezzo ['leddzo] *sm* stench, stink

LI *sigla* = **Livorno**

li *pron pl* (*oggetto*) them

lì *av* there; **di** o **da lì** from there; **per di lì** that way; **di lì a pochi giorni** a few days later; **lì per lì** there and then; at first; **essere lì (lì) per fare** to be on the point of doing, be about to do; **lì dentro** in there; **lì sotto** under there; **lì sopra** on there; up there; **tutto lì** that's all; *vedi anche* **quello**

libagi'one [liba'dʒone] *sf* libation

liba'nese *ag, sm/f* Lebanese *inv*

Li'bano *sm*: **il ~** the Lebanon

'libbra *sf* (*peso*) pound

li'beccio [li'bettʃo] *sm* south-west wind

li'bello *sm* libel

li'bellula *sf* dragonfly

libe'rale *ag, sm/f* liberal

liberaliz'zare [liberalid'dzare] *vt* to liberalize

libe'rare *vt* (*rendere libero: prigioniero*) to release; (: *popolo*) to free, liberate; (*sgombrare: passaggio*) to clear; (: *stanza*) to vacate; (*produrre: energia*) to release; **liberarsi** *vr*: **liberarsi di** qc/qn to get rid of sth/sb

libera'tore, -'trice *ag* liberating ■ *sm/f* liberator

liberazi'one [liberat'tsjone] *sf* (*di prigioniero*) release; (*di popolo*) liberation; **che ~!** what a relief!; **la L~** *see note*

● **LIBERAZIONE**
●
● The *Liberazione* is a national holiday which falls on 25 April. It commemorates the

● liberation of Italy in 1945 from German
● forces and Mussolini's government and
● marks the end of the war on Italian soil.

li'bercolo *sm* (*peg*) worthless book
Li'beria *sf*: **la** ~ Liberia
liberi'ano, -a *ag, sm/f* Liberian
libe'rismo *sm* (*Econ*) laissez-faire
'libero, -a *ag* free; (*strada*) clear; (*non occupato: posto etc*) vacant, free; (*Tel*) not engaged; ~ **di fare qc** free to do sth; ~ **da** free from; **una donna di liberi costumi** a woman of loose morals; **avere via libera** to have a free hand; **dare via libera a qn** to give sb the go-ahead; **via libera!** all clear!; ~ **arbitrio** free will; ~ **professionista** self-employed professional person; ~ **scambio** free trade; **libera uscita** (*Mil*) leave
liberoscam'bismo *sm* (*Econ*) free trade
liber'tà *sf inv* freedom; (*tempo disponibile*) free time ■ *sfpl* (*licenza*) liberties; **essere in** ~ **provvisoria/vigilata** to be released without bail/be on probation; ~ **di riunione** right to hold meetings
liber'tario, -a *ag* libertarian
liber'tino, -a *ag, sm/f* libertine
'liberty ['liberti] *ag inv, sm* art nouveau
'Libia *sf*: **la** ~ Libya
'libico, -a, ci, che *ag, sm/f* Libyan
li'bidine *sf* lust
libidi'noso, -a *ag* lustful, libidinous
li'bido *sf* libido
li'braio *sm* bookseller
li'brario, -a *ag* book *cpd*
li'brarsi *vr* to hover
libre'ria *sf* (*bottega*) bookshop; (*stanza*) library; (*mobile*) bookcase
li'bretto *sm* booklet; (*taccuino*) notebook; (*Mus*) libretto; ~ **degli assegni** chequebook (*Brit*), checkbook (*US*); ~ **di circolazione** (*Aut*) logbook; ~ **di deposito** (bank) deposit book; ~ **di risparmio** (savings) bankbook, passbook; ~ **universitario** student's report book
'libro *sm* book; ~ **bianco** (*Pol*) white paper; ~ **di cassa** cash book; ~ **di consultazione** reference book; ~ **mastro** ledger; ~ **paga** payroll; ~ **tascabile** paperback; ~ **di testo** textbook; **libri contabili** (account) books; **libri sociali** company records
li'cantropo *sm* werewolf
lice'ale [litʃe'ale] *ag* secondary school *cpd* (*Brit*), high school *cpd* (*US*) ■ *sm/f* secondary school *o* high school pupil
li'cenza [li'tʃɛntsa] *sf* (*permesso*) permission, leave; (*di pesca, caccia, circolazione*) permit, licence (*Brit*), license (*US*); (*Mil*) leave; (*Ins*)

school-leaving certificate; (*libertà*) liberty; (*sfrenatezza*) licentiousness; **andare in** ~ (*Mil*) to go on leave; **su** ~ **di ...** (*Comm*) under licence from ...; ~ **di esportazione** export licence; ~ **di fabbricazione** manufacturer's licence; ~ **poetica** poetic licence
licenzia'mento [litʃentsja'mento] *sm* dismissal
licenzi'are [litʃen'tsjare] *vt* (*impiegato*) to dismiss; (*Ins*) to award a certificate to; **licenziarsi** *vr* (*impiegato*) to resign, hand in one's notice; (*Ins*) to obtain one's school-leaving certificate
licenziosità [litʃentsjosi'ta] *sf* licentiousness
licenzi'oso, -a [litʃen'tsjoso] *ag* licentious
li'ceo [li'tʃɛo] *sm* (*Ins*) secondary (*Brit*) *o* high (*US*) school (*for 14- to 19-year-olds*); ~ **classico/scientifico** secondary or high school specializing in classics/scientific subjects
li'chene [li'kɛne] *sm* (*Bot*) lichen
'lido *sm* beach, shore
'Liechtenstein ['liktənstain] *sm*: **il** ~ Liechtenstein
li'eto, -a *ag* happy, glad; **"molto** ~ **"** (*nelle presentazioni*) "pleased to meet you"; **a** ~ **fine** with a happy ending
li'eve *ag* light; (*di poco conto*) slight; (*sommesso: voce*) faint, soft
lievi'tare *vi* (*anche fig*) to rise ■ *vt* to leaven
li'evito *sm* yeast; ~ **di birra** brewer's yeast
'ligio, -a, gi, gie ['lidʒo] *ag* faithful, loyal
li'gnaggio [liɲ'naddʒo] *sm* descent, lineage
'ligure *ag* Ligurian; **la Riviera L**~ the Italian Riviera
Li'kud [li'kud] *sm* Likud
'lilla, lillà *sm inv* lilac
'Lima *sf* Lima
'lima *sf* file; ~ **da unghie** nail file
limacci'oso, -a [limat'tʃoso] *ag* muddy
li'mare *vt* to file (down); (*fig*) to polish
'limbo *sm* (*Rel*) limbo
li'metta *sf* nail file
limi'tare *vt* to limit, restrict; (*circoscrivere*) to bound, surround
limitata'mente *av* to a limited extent; ~ **alle mie possibilità** in so far as I am able
limi'tato, -a *ag* limited, restricted
limitazi'one [limitat'tsjone] *sf* limitation, restriction
'limite *sm* limit; (*confine*) border, boundary ■ *ag inv*: **caso** ~ extreme case; **al** ~ if the worst comes to the worst (*Brit*), if worst comes to worst (*US*); ~ **di velocità** speed limit
li'mitrofo, -a *ag* neighbouring (*Brit*), neighboring (*US*)
'limo *sm* mud, slime; (*Geo*) silt

limo'nata *sf* lemonade (*Brit*), (lemon) soda (*US*); (*spremuta*) lemon squash (*Brit*), lemonade (*US*)

li'mone *sm* (*pianta*) lemon tree; (*frutto*) lemon

limpi'dezza [limpi'dettsa]· *sf* clearness; (*di discorso*) clarity

'limpido, -a *ag* (*acqua*) limpid, clear; (*cielo*) clear; (*fig: discorso*) clear, lucid

'lince ['lintʃe] *sf* lynx

linci'aggio [lin'tʃaddʒo] *sm* lynching

linci'are [lin'tʃare] *vt* to lynch

'lindo, -a *ag* tidy, spick and span; (*biancheria*) clean

'linea *sf* (*gen*) line; (*di mezzi pubblici di trasporto: itinerario*) route; (: *servizio*) service; (*di prodotto: collezione*) collection; (: *stile*) style; **a grandi linee** in outline; **mantenere la ~** to look after one's figure; **è caduta la ~** (*Tel*) I (*o you etc*) have been cut off; **di ~: aereo di ~** airliner; **nave di ~** liner; **volo di ~** scheduled flight; **in ~ diretta da** (*TV, Radio*) coming to you direct from; **~ aerea** airline; **~ continua** solid line; **~ di partenza/d'arrivo** (*Sport*) starting/finishing line; **~ punteggiata** dotted line; **~ di tiro** line of fire

linea'menti *smpl* features; (*fig*) outlines

line'are *ag* linear; (*fig*) coherent, logical

line'etta *sf* (*trattino*) dash; (*d'unione*) hyphen

'linfa *sf* (*Bot*) sap; (*Anat*) lymph; **~ vitale** (*fig*) lifeblood

lin'gotto *sm* ingot, bar

'lingua *sf* (*Anat, Cuc*) tongue; (*idioma*) language; **mostrare la ~** to stick out one's tongue; **di ~ italiana** Italian-speaking; **~ madre** mother tongue; **una ~ di terra** a spit of land

lingu'accia [lin'gwattʃa] *sf* (*fig*) spiteful gossip

linguacci'uto, -a [lingwat'tʃuto] *ag* gossipy

lingu'aggio [lin'gwaddʒo] *sm* language; **~ giuridico** legal language; **~ macchina** (*Inform*) machine language; **~ di programmazione** (*Inform*) programming language

lingu'etta *sf* (*di strumento*) reed; (*di scarpa, Tecn*) tongue; (*di busta*) flap

lingu'ista, -i, e *sm/f* linguist

lingu'istico, -a, ci, che *ag* linguistic ■ *sf* linguistics *sg*

lini'mento *sm* liniment

'lino *sm* (*pianta*) flax; (*tessuto*) linen

li'noleum *sm inv* linoleum, lino

liofiliz'zare [liofilid'dzare] *vt* to freeze-dry

liofiliz'zati [liofilid'dzati] *smpl* freeze-dried foods

Li'one *sf* Lyons

liposuzi'one [liposut'tsjone] *sf* liposuction

'LIPU *sigla f* (= *Lega Italiana Protezione Uccelli*) society for the protection of birds

liqu'ame *sm* liquid sewage

lique'fare *vt* (*render liquido*) to liquefy; (*fondere*) to melt; **liquefarsi** *vr* to liquefy; to melt

lique'fatto, -a *pp di* **liquefare**

liqui'dare *vt* (*società, beni, persona: uccidere*) to liquidate; (*persona: sbarazzarsene*) to get rid of; (*conto, problema*) to settle; (*Comm: merce*) to sell off, clear

liquidazi'one [likwidat'tsjone] *sf* (*di società, persona*) liquidation; (*di conto*) settlement; (*di problema*) settling; (*Comm: di merce*) clearance sale; (*Amm*) severance pay (*on retirement, redundancy, or when taking up other employment*)

liquidità *sf* liquidity

'liquido, -a *ag, sm* liquid; **denaro ~** cash, ready money; **~ per freni** brake fluid

liqui'gas® *sm inv* Calor gas® (*Brit*), butane

liqui'rizia [likwi'rittsja] *sf* liquorice

li'quore *sm* liqueur

liquo'roso, -a *ag*: **vino ~** dessert wine

'lira *sf* (*unità monetaria*) lira; (*Mus*) lyre; **~ sterlina** pound sterling

'lirico, -a, ci, che *ag* lyric(al); (*Mus*) lyric ■ *sf* (*poesia*) lyric poetry; (*componimento poetico*) lyric; (*Mus*) opera; **cantante/teatro ~** opera singer/house

li'rismo *sm* lyricism

Lis'bona *sf* Lisbon

'lisca, -sche *sf* (*di pesce*) fishbone

lisci'are [liʃʃare] *vt* to smooth; (*fig*) to flatter; **lisciarsi i capelli** to straighten one's hair

'liscio, -a, sci, sce ['liʃʃo] *ag* smooth; (*capelli*) straight; (*mobile*) plain; (*bevanda alcolica*) neat; (*fig*) straightforward, simple ■ *av*: **andare ~** to go smoothly; **passarla liscia** to get away with it

'liso, -a *ag* worn out, threadbare

'lista *sf* (*striscia*) strip; (*elenco*) list; **~ elettorale** electoral roll; **~ delle vivande** menu

lis'tare *vt*: **~ (di)** to edge (with), border (with)

lis'tato *sm* (*Inform*) list, listing

lis'tino *sm* list; **~ di borsa** the Stock Exchange list; **~ dei cambi** (foreign) exchange rate; **~ dei prezzi** price list

lita'nia *sf* litany

'lite *sf* quarrel, argument; (*Dir*) lawsuit

liti'gare *vi* to quarrel; (*Dir*) to litigate

li'tigio [li'tidʒo] *sm* quarrel

litigi'oso, -a [liti'dʒoso] *ag* quarrelsome; (*Dir*) litigious

litogra'fia *sf* (*sistema*) lithography; (*stampa*) lithograph

lito'grafico, -a, ci, che *ag* lithographic

lito'rale *ag* coastal, coast *cpd* ■ *sm* coast

lito'raneo, -a *ag* coastal

'litro *sm* litre (*Brit*), liter (*US*)

lit'torio, -a *ag* (*Storia*) lictorial; **fascio ~** fasces *pl*

Litu'ania *sf*: **la ~** Lithuania

litu'ano, -a *ag, sm/f, sm* Lithuanian

litur'gia, -'gie [litur'dʒia] *sf* liturgy

li'uto *sm* lute

li'vella *sf* level; **~ a bolla d'aria** spirit level

livel'lare *vt* to level, make level; **livellarsi** *vr* to become level; (*fig*) to level out, balance out

livella'trice [livella'tritʃe] *sf* steamroller

li'vello *sm* level; (*fig*) level, standard; **ad alto ~** (*fig*) high-level; **a ~ mondiale** world-wide; **a ~ di confidenza** confidentially; **~ di magazzino** stock level; **~ del mare** sea level; **sul ~ del mare** above sea level; **~ occupazionale** level of employment; **~ retributivo** salary level

'livido, -a *ag* livid; (*per percosse*) bruised, black and blue; (*cielo*) leaden ■ *sm* bruise

li'vore *sm* malice, spite

Li'vorno *sf* Livorno, Leghorn

li'vrea *sf* livery

'lizza ['littsa] *sf* lists *pl*; **essere in ~ per** (*fig*) to compete for; **scendere in ~** (*anche fig*) to enter the lists

LO *sigla* = **Lodi**

lo *det m* (*dav s impura, gn, pn, ps, x, z; dav V* **l'**) the ■ *pron* (*dav V* **l'**: *oggetto: persona*) him; (: *cosa*) it; **lo sapevo** I knew it; **lo so** I know; **sii buono, anche se lui non lo è** be good, even if he isn't; *vedi anche* **il**

lob'bista, -i, e *sm/f* lobbyist

'lobby *sf inv* lobby

'lobo *sm* lobe; **~ dell'orecchio** ear lobe

lo'cale *ag* local ■ *sm* room; (*luogo pubblico*) premises *pl*; **~ notturno** nightclub

locali'tà *sf inv* locality

localiz'zare [lokalid'dzare] *vt* (*circoscrivere*) to confine, localize; (*accertare*) to locate, place

lo'canda *sf* inn

locandi'ere, -a *sm/f* innkeeper

locan'dina *sf* (*Teat*) poster

lo'care *vt* (*casa*) to rent out, let; (*macchina*) to hire out (*Brit*), rent (out)

loca'tario, -a *sm/f* tenant

loca'tivo, -a *ag* (*Dir*) rentable

loca'tore, -'trice *sm/f* landlord/lady

locazi'one [lokat'tsjone] *sf* (*da parte del locatario*) renting *no pl*; (*da parte del locatore*) renting out *no pl*, letting *no pl*; (**contratto di**) **~** lease; (**canone di**) **~** rent; **dare in ~** to rent out, let

locomo'tiva *sf* locomotive

locomo'tore *sm* electric locomotive

locomo'trice [lokomo'tritʃe] *sf* = **locomotore**

locomozi'one [lokomot'tsjone] *sf* locomotion; **mezzi di ~** vehicles, means of transport

'loculo *sm* burial recess

lo'custa *sf* locust

locuzi'one [lokut'tsjone] *sf* phrase, expression

lo'dare *vt* to praise

'lode *sf* praise; (*Ins*): **laurearsi con 110 e ~** ≈ to graduate with first-class honours (*Brit*), ≈ to graduate summa cum laude (*US*)

'loden *sm inv* (*stoffa*) loden; (*cappotto*) loden overcoat

lo'devole *ag* praiseworthy

loga'ritmo *sm* logarithm

log'garsi *vr* (*Inform*) to log in

'loggia, -ge ['lɔddʒa] *sf* (*Archit*) loggia; (*circolo massonico*) lodge

loggi'one [lod'dʒone] *sm* (*di teatro*): **il ~** the Gods *sg*

logica'mente [lodʒika'mente] *av* naturally, obviously

logici'tà [lodʒitʃi'ta] *sf* logicality

'logico, -a, ci, che ['lɔdʒiko] *ag* logical ■ *sf* logic

lo'gistica [lo'dʒistika] *sf* logistics *sg*

'logo *sm inv* logo

logora'mento *sm* (*di vestiti etc*) wear

logo'rante *ag* exhausting

logo'rare *vt* to wear out; (*sciupare*) to waste; **logorarsi** *vr* to wear out; (*fig*) to wear o.s. out

logo'rio *sm* wear and tear; (*fig*) strain

'logoro, -a *ag* (*stoffa*) worn out, threadbare; (*persona*) worn out

'Loira *sf*: **la ~** the Loire

lom'baggine [lom'baddʒine] *sf* lumbago

Lombar'dia *sf*: **la ~** Lombardy

lom'bardo, -a *ag, sm/f* Lombard

lom'bare *ag* (*Anat, Med*) lumbar

lom'bata *sf* (*taglio di carne*) loin

'lombo *sm* (*Anat*) loin

lom'brico, -chi *sm* earthworm

londi'nese *ag* London *cpd* ■ *sm/f* Londoner

'Londra *sf* London

lon'ganime *ag* forbearing

longevi'tà [londʒevi'ta] *sf* longevity

lon'gevo, -a [lon'dʒevo] *ag* long-lived

longi'lineo, -a [londʒi'lineo] *ag* long-limbed

longi'tudine [londʒi'tudine] *sf* longitude

lontana'mente *av* remotely; **non ci pensavo neppure ~** it didn't even occur to me

lonta'nanza [lonta'nantsa] *sf* distance; absence

lon'tano, -a *ag* (*distante*) distant, faraway; (*assente*) absent; (*vago: sospetto*) slight, remote; (*tempo: remoto*) far-off, distant; (*parente*) distant, remote ■ *av* far; **è lontana la casa?** is it far to the house?, is the house far from here?; **è ~ un chilometro** it's a kilometre away *o* a kilometre from here; **più** ~ farther; **da** *o* **di** ~ from a distance; ~ **da** a long way from; **alla lontana** slightly, vaguely

lontra *sf* otter

lo'quace [lo'kwatʃe] *ag* talkative, loquacious; *(fig: gesto etc)* eloquent

loquacità [lokwatʃi'ta] *sf* talkativeness, loquacity

lordo, -a *ag* dirty, filthy; *(peso, stipendio)* gross; ~ **d'imposta** pre-tax

Lo'rena *sf (Geo)* Lorraine

loro *pron pl (oggetto, con preposizione)* them; *(complemento di termine)* to them; *(soggetto)* they; *(forma di cortesia: anche:* **Loro**) you; to you; **il(la)** ~, **i(le)** ~ their; *(forma di cortesia: anche:* **Loro**) your ■ *pron* theirs; *(forma di cortesia: anche:* **Loro**) yours ■ *sm inv:* **il** ~ their *(o* your) money ■ *sf inv:* **la** ~ *(opinione)* their *(o* your) view; **i** ~ *(famiglia)* their *(o* your) family; *(amici etc)* their *(o* your own people; **un** ~ **amico** a friend of theirs; **è dalla** ~ he's on their *(o* your) side; **ne hanno fatto un'altra** they've *(o* you've) done it again; ~ **stessi(e)** they themselves; you yourselves

lo'sanga, -ghe *sf* diamond, lozenge

Lo'sanna *sf* Lausanne

losco, -a, schi, sche *ag (fig)* shady, suspicious

lotta *sf* struggle, fight; *(Sport)* wrestling; **essere in** ~ **(con)** to be in conflict (with); **fare la** ~ **(con)** to wrestle (with); ~ **armata** armed struggle; ~ **di classe** *(Pol)* class struggle; ~ **libera** *(Sport)* all-in wrestling *(Brit)*, freestyle

lot'tare *vi* to fight, struggle; to wrestle

lotta'tore, -'trice *sm/f* wrestler

lotte'ria *sf* lottery; *(di gara ippica)* sweepstake

lottiz'zare [lottid'dzare] *vt* to divide into plots; *(fig)* to share out

lottizzazi'one [lottiddzat'tsjone] *sf* division into plots; *(fig)* share-out

lotto *sm (gioco)* (state) lottery; *(parte)* lot; *(Edil)* site; **vincere un terno al** ~ *(anche fig)* to hit the jackpot

lozi'one [lot'tsjone] *sf* lotion

LT *sigla* = **Latina**

LU *sigla* = **Lucca**

lubrifi'cante *sm* lubricant

lubrifi'care *vt* to lubricate

lu'cano, -a *ag* of *(o* from) Lucania

luc'chetto [luk'ketto] *sm* padlock

lucci'care [luttʃi'kare] *vi* to sparkle; *(oro)* to glitter; *(stella)* to twinkle; *(occhi)* to glisten

lucci'chio [luttʃi'kio] *sm* sparkling; glittering; twinkling; glistening

lucci'cone [luttʃi'kone] *sm:* **avere i luccicони agli occhi** to have tears in one's eyes

luccio ['luttʃo] *sm (Zool)* pike

lucciola ['luttʃola] *sf (Zool)* firefly; glowworm; *(fam, fig: prostituta)* girl *(o* woman) on the game

luce ['lutʃe] *sf* light; *(finestra)* window; **alla** ~ **di** by the light of; **fare qc alla** ~ **del sole** *(fig)* to do sth in the open; **dare alla** ~ *(bambino)* to give birth to; **fare** ~ **su qc** *(fig)* to shed *o* throw light on sth; ~ **del sole/della luna** sun/moonlight

lu'cente [lu'tʃente] *ag* shining

lucen'tezza [lutʃen'tettsa] *sf* shine

lu'cerna [lu'tʃerna] *sf* oil lamp

lucer'nario [lutʃer'narjo] *sm* skylight

lu'certola [lu'tʃertola] *sf* lizard

luci'dare [lutʃi'dare] *vt* to polish; *(ricalcare)* to trace

lucida'trice [lutʃida'tritʃe] *sf* floor polisher

lucidità [lutʃidi'ta] *sf* lucidity

lucido, -a ['lutʃido] *ag* shining, bright; *(lucidato)* polished; *(fig)* lucid ■ *sm* shine, lustre *(Brit)*, luster *(US)*; *(per scarpe etc)* polish; *(disegno)* tracing

lu'cignolo [lu'tʃiɲɲolo] *sm* wick

luc'rare *vt* to make money out of

lucra'tivo, -a *ag* lucrative; **a scopo** ~ for gain

lucro *sm* profit, gain; **a scopo di** ~ for gain; **organizzazione senza scopo di** ~ non-profit-making *(Brit) o* non-profit *(US)* organization

lu'croso, -a *ag* lucrative, profitable

luculli'ano, -a *ag (pasto)* sumptuous

lu'dibrio *sm* mockery *no pl;* *(oggetto di scherno)* laughing stock

lue *sf* syphilis

luglio ['luʎʎo] *sm* July; **nel mese di** ~ in July, in the month of July; **il primo** ~ the first of July; **arrivare il 2** ~ to arrive on the 2nd of July; **all'inizio/alla fine di** ~ at the beginning/at the end of July; **durante il mese di** ~ during July; **a** ~ **del prossimo anno** in July of next year; **ogni anno a** ~ every July; **che fai a** ~? what are you doing in July?; **ha piovuto molto a** ~ **quest'anno** July was very wet this year

lugubre *ag* gloomy

lui *pron (soggetto)* he; *(oggetto: per dare rilievo, con preposizione)* him ■ *sm inv:* **il mio** ~ my beloved; ~ **stesso** he himself; **è** ~ it's him

lu'maca, -che *sf* slug; *(chiocciola)* snail

luma'cone *sm* (large) slug; *(fig)* slowcoach *(Brit)*, slowpoke *(US)*

lume *sm* light; *(lampada)* lamp; ~ **a olio** oil lamp; **chiedere lumi a qn** *(fig)* to ask sb for advice; **a** ~ **di naso** *(fig)* by rule of thumb

lumi'cino [lumi'tʃino] *sm* small *o* faint light; **essere (ridotto) al** ~ *(fig)* to be at death's door

lumi'era *sf* chandelier

lumi'nare sm luminary
lumi'naria sf (per feste) illuminations pl
lumine'scente [lumineʃʃɛnte] ag luminescent
lu'mino sm small light; ~ **da notte** night-light; ~ **per i morti** candle for the dead
luminosità sf brightness; (fig: di sorriso, volto) radiance
lumi'noso, -a ag (che emette luce) luminous; (cielo, colore, stanza) bright; (sorgente) of light, light cpd; (fig: sorriso) bright, radiant; **insegna luminosa** neon sign
lun. abbr (= lunedì) Mon.
'**luna** sf moon; ~ **nuova/piena** new/full moon; **avere la** ~ to be in a bad mood; ~ **di miele** honeymoon
'**luna park** sm inv amusement park, funfair
lu'nare ag lunar, moon cpd
lu'nario sm almanac; **sbarcare il** ~ to make ends meet
lu'natico, -a, ci, che ag whimsical, temperamental
lunedì sm inv Monday; vedi anche **martedì**
lun'gaggine [lun'gaddʒine] sf slowness; **lungaggini della burocrazia** red tape
lunga'mente av (a lungo) for a long time; (estesamente) at length
lun'garno sm embankment along the Arno
lun'ghezza [lun'gettsa] sf length; ~ **d'onda** (Fisica) wavelength
'**lungi** ['lundʒi]: ~ **da** prep far from
lungimi'rante [lundʒimi'rante] ag far-sighted
'**lungo, -a, ghi, ghe** ag long; (lento: persona) slow; (diluito: caffè, brodo) weak, watery, thin ■ sm length ■ prep along; ~ **3 metri** 3 metres long; **avere la barba lunga** to be unshaven; **a** ~ for a long time; **a** ~ **andare** in the long run; **di gran lunga** (molto) by far; **andare in** ~ o **per le lunghe** to drag on; **saperla lunga** to know what's what; **in** ~ **e in largo** far and wide, all over; ~ **il corso dei secoli** throughout the centuries; **navigazione di** ~ **corso** ocean-going navigation
lungofi'ume sm embankment
lungo'lago sm road round a lake
lungo'mare sm promenade
lungome'traggio [lungome'traddʒo] sm (Cine) feature film
lungo'tevere sm embankment along the Tiber

lu'notto sm (Aut) rear o back window; ~ **termico** heated rear window
lu'ogo, -ghi sm place; (posto: di incidente etc) scene, site; (punto, passo di libro) passage; **in** ~ **di** instead of; **in primo** ~ in the first place; **aver** ~ to take place; **dar** ~ **a** to give rise to; ~ **comune** commonplace; ~ **del delitto** scene of the crime; ~ **geometrico** locus; ~ **di nascita** birthplace; (Amm) place of birth; ~ **di pena** prison, penitentiary; ~ **di provenienza** place of origin
luogote'nente sm (Mil) lieutenant
lupacchi'otto [lupak'kjɔtto] sm (Zool) (wolf) cub
lu'para sf sawn-off shotgun
lu'petto sm (Zool) (wolf) cub; (negli scouts) cub scout
'**lupo, -a** sm/f wolf/she-wolf; **cane** ~ alsatian (dog) (Brit), German shepherd (dog); **tempo da lupi** filthy weather
'**luppolo** sm (Bot) hop
'**lurido, -a** ag filthy
luri'dume sm filth
lu'singa, -ghe sf (spesso al pl) flattery no pl
lusin'gare vt to flatter
lusinghi'ero, -a [luzin'gjɛro] ag flattering, gratifying
lus'sare vt (Med) to dislocate
lussazi'one [lussat'tsjone] sf (Med) dislocation
lussembur'ghese [lussembur'gese] ag of (o from) Luxembourg ■ sm/f native (o inhabitant) of Luxembourg
Lussem'burgo sm (stato): **il** ~ Luxembourg ■ sf (città) Luxembourg
'**lusso** sm luxury; **di** ~ luxury cpd
lussu'oso, -a ag luxurious
lussureggi'are [lussured'dʒare] vi to be luxuriant
lus'suria sf lust
lussuri'oso, -a ag lascivious, lustful
lus'trare vt to polish, shine
lustras'carpe sm/f inv shoeshine
lus'trino sm sequin
'**lustro, -a** ag shiny; (pelliccia) glossy ■ sm shine, gloss; (fig) prestige, glory; (quinquennio) five-year period
lute'rano, -a ag, sm/f Lutheran
'**lutto** sm mourning; **essere in/portare il** ~ to be in/wear mourning

Mm

M, m ['ɛmme] *sf o m inv* (*lettera*) M, m;
M come Milano M for Mary (*Brit*), M for
Mike (*US*)

m. *abbr* = **mese; metro; miglia; monte**

ma *cong* but; **ma insomma!** for goodness
sake!; **ma no!** of course not!

'macabro, -a *ag* gruesome, macabre

ma'caco, -chi *sm* (*Zool*) macaque

macché [mak'ke] *escl* not at all!, certainly not!

macche'roni [makke'roni] *smpl* macaroni *sg*

'macchia ['makkja] *sf* stain, spot; (*chiazza di
diverso colore*) spot splash, patch; (*tipo di
boscaglia*) scrub; **~ d'inchiostro** ink stain;
estendersi a ~ d'olio (*fig*) to spread rapidly;
darsi/vivere alla ~ (*fig*) to go into/live in
hiding

macchi'are [mak'kjare] *vt* (*sporcare*) to stain,
mark; **macchiarsi** *vr* (*persona*) to get o.s.
dirty; (*stoffa*) to stain; to get stained *o*
marked; **macchiarsi di un delitto** to be
guilty of a crime

macchi'ato, -a [mak'kjato] *ag* (*pelle, pelo*)
spotted; **~ di** stained with; **caffè ~** coffee
with a dash of milk

macchi'etta [mak'kjetta] *sf* (*disegno*) sketch,
caricature; (*Teat*) caricature; (*fig: persona*)
character

'macchina ['makkina] *sf* machine; (*motore,
locomotiva*) engine; (*automobile*) car; (*fig:
meccanismo*) machinery; **andare in ~** (*Aut*) to
go by car; (*Stampa*) to go to press; **salire in ~**
to get into the car; **venire in ~** to come by
car; **sala macchine** (*Naut*) engine room; **~
da cucire** sewing machine; **~ fotografica**
camera; **~ da presa** cine *o* movie camera; **~
da scrivere** typewriter; **~ utensile** machine
tool; **~ a vapore** steam engine

macchinal'mente [makkinal'mente] *av*
mechanically

macchi'nare [makki'nare] *vt* to plot

macchi'nario [makki'narjo] *sm* machinery

macchinazi'one [makkinat'tsjone] *sf* plot,
machination

macchi'netta [makki'netta] *sf* (*fam:
caffettiera*) percolator; (: *accendino*) lighter

macchi'nista, -i [makki'nista] *sm* (*di treno*)
engine-driver; (*di nave*) engineer; (*Teat, TV*)
stagehand

macchi'noso, -a [makki'noso] *ag* complex,
complicated

ma'cedone [ma'tʃɛdone] *ag, sm/f* Macedonian

Mace'donia [matʃe'dɔnja] *sm* Macedonia

mace'donia [matʃe'dɔnja] *sf* fruit salad

macel'laio [matʃel'lajo] *sm* butcher

macel'lare [matʃel'lare] *vt* to slaughter,
butcher

macellazi'one [matʃellat'tsjone] *sf*
slaughtering, butchering

macelle'ria [matʃelle'ria] *sf* butcher's (shop)

ma'cello [ma'tʃɛllo] *sm* (*mattatoio*)
slaughterhouse, abattoir (*Brit*); (*fig*)
slaughter, massacre; (: *disastro*) shambles *sg*

mace'rare [matʃe'rare] *vt* to macerate; (*Cuc*)
to marinate; **macerarsi** *vr* to waste away;
(*fig*): **macerarsi in** to be consumed with

macerazi'one [matʃerat'tsjone] *sf*
maceration

ma'cerie [ma'tʃɛrje] *sfpl* rubble *sg*, debris *sg*

'macero ['matʃero] *sm* (*operazione*) pulping;
(*stabilimento*) pulping mill; **carta da ~** paper
for pulping

machia'vellico, -a, ci, che [makja'vɛlliko] *ag*
(*anche fig*) Machiavellian

ma'cigno [ma'tʃiɲɲo] *sm* (*masso*) rock,
boulder

maci'lento, -a [matʃi'lɛnto] *ag* emaciated

'macina ['matʃina] *sf* (*pietra*) millstone;
(*macchina*) grinder

macinacaffè [matʃinakaf'fɛ] *sm inv* coffee
grinder

macina'pepe [matʃina'pepe] *sm inv*
peppermill

maci'nare [matʃi'nare] *vt* to grind; (*carne*) to
mince (*Brit*), grind (*US*)

maci'nato [matʃi'nato] *sm* meal, flour; (*carne*)
minced (*Brit*) *o* ground (*US*) meat

maci'nino [matʃi'nino] *sm* (*per caffè*) coffee grinder; (*per pepe*) peppermill; (*scherzoso: macchina*) old banger (Brit), clunker (US)

maciul'lare [matʃul'lare] *vt* (*canapa, lino*) to brake; (*fig: braccio etc*) to crush

'**macro** ... *prefisso* macro...

macrobi'otico, -a *ag* macrobiotic ■ *sf* macrobiotics *sg*

macu'lato, -a *ag* (*pelo*) spotted

Ma'dama: palazzo ~ *sm* (*Pol*) seat of the Italian Chamber of Senators

made in Italy [meɪdɪ'nɪtəlɪ] *sm*: **il ~** Italian exports *pl* (*especially fashion goods*)

Ma'dera *sf* (*Geo*) Madeira ■ *sm inv* (*vino*) Madeira

'**madido, -a** *ag*: **~ (di)** wet o moist (with)

Ma'donna *sf* (*Rel*) Our Lady

mador'nale *ag* enormous, huge

'**madre** *sf* mother; (*matrice di bolletta*) counterfoil ■ *ag inv* mother *cpd*; **ragazza ~** unmarried mother; **scena ~** (*Teat*) principal scene; (*fig*) terrible scene

madre'lingua *sf* mother tongue, native language

madre'patria *sf* mother country, native land

madre'perla *sf* mother-of-pearl

Ma'drid *sf* Madrid

madri'gale *sm* madrigal

madri'leno, -a *ag* of (o from) Madrid ■ *sm/f* person from Madrid

ma'drina *sf* godmother

maestà *sf inv* majesty; **Sua M~ la Regina** Her Majesty the Queen

maestosità *sf* majesty

maes'toso, -a *ag* majestic

ma'estra *sf vedi* **maestro**

maes'trale *sm* north-west wind

maes'tranze [maes'trantse] *sfpl* workforce *sg*

maes'tria *sf* mastery, skill

ma'estro, -a *sm/f* (*Ins: anche*: **maestro di scuola** o **elementare**) primary (Brit) o grade school (US) teacher; (*esperto*) expert ■ *sm* (*artigiano, fig: guida*) master; (*Mus*) maestro ■ *ag* (*principale*) main; (*di grande abilità*) masterly, skilful (Brit), skillful (US); **un colpo da ~** (*fig*) a masterly move; **muro ~** main wall; **strada maestra** main road; **maestra d'asilo** nursery teacher; **~ di ballo** dancing master; **~ di cerimonie** master of ceremonies; **~ d'orchestra** conductor, director (US); **~ di scherma** fencing master; **~ di sci** ski instructor

'**mafia** *sf* Mafia

mafi'oso *sm* member of the Mafia

'**maga, -ghe** *sf* sorceress

ma'gagna [ma'gaɲɲa] *sf* defect, flaw, blemish; (*noia, guaio*) problem

ma'gari *escl* (*esprime desiderio*): **~ fosse vero!** if only it were true!; **ti piacerebbe andare in Scozia? — ~!** would you like to go to Scotland? — I certainly would! ■ *av* (*anche*) even; (*forse*) perhaps

magazzi'naggio [magaddzi'naddʒo] *sm*: **(spese di) ~** storage charges *pl*, warehousing charges *pl*

magazzini'ere [magaddzi'njɛre] *sm* warehouseman

magaz'zino [magad'dzino] *sm* warehouse; **grande ~** department store; **~ doganale** bonded warehouse

'**maggio** ['maddʒo] *sm* May; *vedi anche* **luglio**

maggio'rana [maddʒo'rana] *sf* (*Bot*) (sweet) marjoram

maggio'ranza [maddʒo'rantsa] *sf* majority; **nella ~ dei casi** in most cases

maggio'rare [maddʒo'rare] *vt* to increase, raise

maggiorazi'one [maddʒorat'tsjone] *sf* (*Comm*) rise, increase

maggior'domo [maddʒor'dɔmo] *sm* butler

maggi'ore [mad'dʒore] *ag* (*comparativo: più grande*) bigger, larger; taller; greater; (: *più vecchio: sorella, fratello*) older, elder; (: *di grado superiore*) senior; (: *più importante, Mil, Mus*) major; (*superlativo*) biggest, largest; tallest; greatest; oldest, eldest ■ *sm/f* (*di grado*) superior; (*di età*) elder; (*Mil*) major; (: *Aer*) squadron leader; **la maggior parte** the majority; **andare per la ~** (*cantante, attore etc*) to be very popular, be "in"

maggio'renne [maddʒo'rɛnne] *ag* of age ■ *sm/f* person who has come of age

maggiori'tario, -a [maddʒori'tarjo] *ag* majority *cpd*; (*Pol: anche*: **sistema maggioritario**) first-past-the-post system

maggior'mente [maddʒor'mente] *av* much more; (*con senso superlativo*) most

ma'gia [ma'dʒia] *sf* magic

'**magico, -a, ci, che** ['madʒiko] *ag* magic; (*fig*) fascinating, charming, magical

'**magio** ['madʒo] *sm* (*Rel*): **i re Magi** the Magi, the Three Wise Men

magis'tero [madʒis'tero] *sm* teaching; (*fig: maestria*) skill; (*Ins*): **Facoltà di M~** ≈ teachers' training college

magis'trale [madʒis'trale] *ag* primary (Brit) o grade school (US) teachers', primary (Brit) o grade school (US) teaching; (*abile*) skilful (Brit), skillful (US); **istituto ~** secondary school *for the training of primary teachers*

magis'trato [madʒis'trato] *sm* magistrate

magistra'tura [madʒistra'tura] *sf* magistrature; (*magistrati*): **la ~** the Bench

m

maglia ['maʎʎa] *sf* stitch; (*lavoro ai ferri*) knitting *no pl*; (*tessuto, Sport*) jersey; (*maglione*) jersey, sweater; (*di catena*) link; (*di rete*) mesh; **avviare/diminuire le maglie** to cast on/cast off; **lavorare a ~, fare la ~** to knit; **~ diritta/rovescia** plain/purl

maglie'ria [maʎʎe'ria] *sf* knitwear; (*negozio*) knitwear shop; **macchina per ~** knitting machine

magli'etta [maʎ'ʎetta] *sf* (*canottiera*) vest; (*tipo camicia*) T-shirt

magli'ficio [maʎʎi'fitʃo] *sm* knitwear factory

ma'glina [maʎ'ʎina] *sf* (*tessuto*) jersey

maglio ['maʎʎo] *sm* mallet; (*macchina*) power hammer

magli'one [maʎ'ʎone] *sm* jersey, sweater

magma *sm* magma; (*fig*) mass

ma'gnaccia [maɲ'ɲattʃa] *sm inv* (*peg*) pimp

magnanimità [maɲɲanimi'ta] *sf* magnanimity

ma'gnanimo, -a [maɲ'ɲanimo] *ag* magnanimous

ma'gnate [maɲ'ɲate] *sm* tycoon, magnate

ma'gnesia [maɲ'ɲɛzja] *sf* (*Chim*) magnesia

ma'gnesio [maɲ'ɲɛzjo] *sm* (*Chim*) magnesium; **al ~** (*lampada, flash*) magnesium *cpd*

ma'gnete [maɲ'ɲɛte] *sm* magnet

ma'gnetico, -a, ci, che [maɲ'ɲɛtiko] *ag* magnetic

magne'tismo [maɲɲe'tizmo] *sm* magnetism

magnetiz'zare [maɲɲetid'dzare] *vt* (*Fisica*) to magnetize; (*fig*) to mesmerize

magne'tofono [maɲɲe'tɔfono] *sm* tape recorder

magnifica'mente [maɲɲifika'mente] *av* magnificently, extremely well

magnifi'cenza [maɲɲifi'tʃentsa] *sf* magnificence, splendour (*Brit*), splendor (*US*)

ma'gnifico, -a, ci, che [maɲ'ɲifiko] *ag* magnificent, splendid; (*ospite*) generous

magno, -a ['maɲɲo] *ag*: **aula magnoa** main hall

ma'gnolia [maɲ'ɲɔlja] *sf* magnolia

mago, -ghi *sm* (*stregone*) magician, wizard; (*illusionista*) magician

ma'grezza [ma'grettsa] *sf* thinness

magro, -a *ag* (*very*) thin, skinny; (*carne*) lean; (*formaggio*) low-fat; (*fig: scarso,*) meagre (*Brit*), meager (*US*), poor; (: *meschino: scusa*) poor, lame; **mangiare di ~** not to eat meat

mai *av* (*nessuna volta*) never; (*talvolta*) ever; **non ... ~** never; **~ più** never again; **come ~?** why (*o* how) on earth?; **chi/dove/quando ~?** whoever/wherever/whenever?

mai'ale *sm* (*Zool*) pig; (*carne*) pork

mail ['meil] *sf inv* = **e-mail**

mai'olica *sf* majolica

maio'nese *sf* mayonnaise

Mai'orca *sf* Majorca

mais *sm* maize (*Brit*), corn (*US*)

mai'uscolo, -a *ag* (*lettera*) capital ■ *sf* capital letter ■ *sm* capital letters *pl*; (*Tip*) upper case; **scrivere tutto (in) ~** to write everything in capitals *o* in capital letters

mal *av, sm vedi* **male**

mala *sf* (*gergo*) underworld

malac'corto, -a *ag* rash, careless

mala'fede *sf* bad faith

malaf'fare; **di ~** *ag* (*gente*) shady, dishonest; **donna di ~** prostitute

mala'gevole [mala'dʒevole] *ag* difficult, hard

mala'grazia [mala'grattsja] *sf*: **con ~** with bad grace, impolitely

mala'lingua (*pl* **malelingue**) *sf* gossip (*person*)

mala'mente *av* badly; (*sgarbatamente*) rudely

malan'dato, -a *ag* (*persona: di salute*) in poor health; (: *di condizioni finanziarie*) badly off; (*trascurato*) shabby

ma'lanimo *sm* ill will, malevolence; **di ~** unwillingly

ma'lanno *sm* (*disgrazia*) misfortune; (*malattia*) ailment

mala'pena *sf*: **a ~** hardly, scarcely

ma'laria *sf* malaria

ma'larico, -a, ci, che *ag* malarial

mala'sorte *sf* bad luck

mala'ticcio, -a [mala'tittʃo] *ag* sickly

ma'lato, -a *ag* ill, sick; (*gamba*) bad; (*pianta*) diseased ■ *sm/f* sick person; (*in ospedale*) patient; **darsi ~** (*sul lavoro etc*) to go sick

malat'tia *sf* (*infettiva etc*) illness, disease; (*cattiva salute*) illness, sickness; (*di pianta*) disease; **mettersi in ~** to go on sick leave; **fare una ~ di qc** (*fig: disperarsi*) to get in a state about sth

malaugu'rato, -a *ag* ill-fated, unlucky

malau'gurio *sm* bad *o* ill omen; **uccello del ~** bird of ill omen

mala'vita *sf* underworld

malavi'toso, -a *sm/f* gangster

mala'voglia [mala'vɔʎʎa]: **di ~** *av* unwillingly, reluctantly

Ma'lawi [ma'lavi] *sm*: **il ~** Malawi

Mala'ysia *sf* Malaysia

malaysi'ano, -a *ag, sm/f* Malaysian

malcapi'tato, -a *ag* unlucky, unfortunate ■ *sm/f* unfortunate person

mal'concio, -a, ci, ce [mal'kontʃo] *ag* in a sorry state

malcon'tento *sm* discontent

malcos'tume *sm* immorality

mal'destro, -a *ag* (*inabile*) inexpert, inexperienced; (*goffo*) awkward

maldicente [maldi'tʃɛnte] *ag* slanderous

maldicenza [maldi'tʃɛntsa] *sf* malicious gossip

maldisposto, -a *ag*: ~ **(verso)** ill-disposed (towards)

Maldive *sfpl*: **le** ~ the Maldives

'male *av* badly ▪ *sm* (*ciò che è ingiusto,*) evil; (*danno, svantaggio*) harm; (*sventura*) misfortune; (*dolore fisico,*) pain, ache; **sentirsi** ~ to feel ill; **aver mal di cuore/ fegato** to have a heart/liver complaint; **aver mal di denti/d'orecchi/di testa** to have toothache/earache/a headache; **aver mal di gola** to have a sore throat; **aver ~ ai piedi** to have sore feet; **far** ~ (*dolere*) to hurt; **far ~ alla salute** to be bad for one's health; **far del ~ a qn** to hurt *o* harm sb; **parlar ~ di qn** to speak ill of sb; **restare** *o* **rimanere** ~ to be sorry; to be disappointed to be hurt; **trattar ~ qn** to ill-treat sb; **andare a ~** to go off *o* bad; **come va?** — **non c'è** ~ how are you? — not bad; **di ~ in peggio** from bad to worse; **per ~ che vada** however badly things go; **non avertene a ~, non prendertela a ~** don't take it to heart; **mal comune mezzo gaudio** (*proverbio*) a trouble shared is a trouble halved; **mal d'auto** carsickness; **mal di mare** seasickness

maledetto, -a *pp di* **maledire** ▪ *ag* cursed, damned; (*fig fam*) damned, blasted

maledire *vt* to curse

maledizione [maledit'tsjone] *sf* curse; **~!** damn it!

maleducato, -a *ag* rude, ill-mannered

maleducazione [maledukat'tsjone] *sf* rudeness

malefatta *sf* misdeed

maleficio [male'fitʃo] *sm* witchcraft

malefico, -a, ci, che *ag* (*aria, cibo*) harmful, bad; (*influsso, azione*) evil

malese *ag, sm/f* Malay(an) ▪ *sm* (*Ling*) Malay

Malesia *sf* Malaya

malessere *sm* indisposition, slight illness; (*fig*) uneasiness

malevolenza [malevo'lɛntsa] *sf* malevolence

malevolo, -a *ag* malevolent

malfamato, -a *ag* notorious

malfatto, -a *ag* (*persona*) deformed; (*oggetto*) badly made; (*lavoro*) badly done

malfattore, -trice *sm/f* wrongdoer

malfermo, -a *ag* unsteady, shaky; (*salute*) poor, delicate

malformazione [malformat'tsjone] *sf* malformation

'malga, -ghe *sf* Alpine hut

malgoverno *sm* maladministration

malgrado *prep* in spite of, despite ▪ *cong* although; **mio** *o* **tuo** *etc* ~ against my (*o* your *etc*) will

ma'lia *sf* spell; (*fig: fascino*) charm

maliardo, -a *ag* (*occhi, sorriso*) bewitching ▪ *sf* enchantress

malignamente [malippa'mente] *av* maliciously

malignare [malip'pare] *vi*: ~ **su** to malign, speak ill of

malignità [malippi'ta] *sf inv* (*qualità*) malice, spite; (*osservazione*) spiteful remark; **con** ~ spitefully, maliciously

maligno, -a [ma'lippo] *ag* (*malvagio*) malicious, malignant; (*Med*) malignant

malinconia *sf* melancholy, gloom

malinconico, -a, ci, che *ag* melancholy

malincuore: a ~ *av* reluctantly, unwillingly

malinformato, -a *ag* misinformed

malintenzionato, -a [malintentsjo'nato] *ag* ill-intentioned

malinteso, -a *ag* misunderstood; (*riguardo, senso del dovere*) mistaken, wrong ▪ *sm* misunderstanding

malizia [ma'littsja] *sf* (*malignità*) malice; (*furbizia*) cunning; (*espediente*) trick

malizioso, -a [malit'tsjoso] *ag* malicious; cunning; (*vivace, birichino*) mischievous

malleabile *ag* malleable

malloppo *sm* (*fam: refurtiva*) loot

malmenare *vt* to beat up; (*fig*) to ill-treat

malmesso, -a *ag* shabby

malnutrito, -a *ag* undernourished

malnutrizione [malnutrit'tsjone] *sf* malnutrition

'malo, -a *ag*: **in** ~ **modo** badly

malocchio [ma'lɔkkjo] *sm* evil eye

ma'lora *sf* (*fam*): **andare in** ~ to go to the dogs; **va in ~!** go to hell!

ma'lore *sm* (sudden) illness

malridotto, -a *ag* (*abiti, scarpe, persona*) in a sorry state; (*casa, macchina*) dilapidated, in a poor state of repair

malsano, -a *ag* unhealthy

malsicuro, -a *ag* unsafe

Malta *sf* Malta

'malta *sf* (*Edil*) mortar

maltempo *sm* bad weather

'malto *sm* malt

maltolto *sm* ill-gotten gains *pl*

maltrattamento *sm* ill treatment

maltrattare *vt* to ill-treat

malumore *sm* bad mood; (*irritabilità*) bad temper; (*discordia*) ill feeling; **di** ~ in a bad mood

'malva *sf* (*Bot*) mallow ▪ *ag, sm inv* mauve

m

211

mal'vagio, -a, gi, gie [mal'vadʒo] *ag* wicked, evil

malvagità [malvadʒi'ta] *sf inv* (*qualità*) wickedness; (*azione*) wicked deed

malva'sia *sf Italian dessert wine*

malversazi'one [malversat'tsjone] *sf* (*Dir*) embezzlement

malves'tito, -a *ag* badly dressed, ill-clad

mal'visto, -a *ag*: ~ **(da)** disliked (by), unpopular (with)

malvi'vente *sm* criminal

malvolenti'eri *av* unwillingly, reluctantly

malvo'lere *vt*: **farsi ~ da qn** to make o.s. unpopular with sb ■ *sm*: **prendere qn a ~** to take a dislike to sb

'mamma *sf* mum(my) (*Brit*), mom (*US*); ~ **mia!** my goodness!

mam'mario, -a *ag* (*Anat*) mammary

mam'mella *sf* (*Anat*) breast; (*di vacca, capra etc*) udder

mam'mifero *sm* mammal

mam'mismo *sm* *excessive attachment to one's mother*

'mammola *sf* (*Bot*) violet

'manager ['mænidʒə] *sm inv* manager

manageri'ale [manadʒe'rjale] *ag* managerial

ma'nata *sf* (*colpo*) slap; (*quantità*) handful

'manca *sf* left (hand); **a destra e a ~** left, right and centre, on all sides

manca'mento *sm* (*di forze*) (feeling of) faintness, weakness

man'canza [man'kantsa] *sf* lack; (*carenza*) shortage, scarcity; (*fallo*) fault; (*imperfezione*) failing, shortcoming; **per ~ di tempo** through lack of time; **in ~ di meglio** for lack of anything better; **sentire la ~ di qc/qn** to miss sth/sb

man'care *vi* (*essere insufficiente*) to be lacking; (*venir meno*) to fail; (*sbagliare*) to be wrong, make a mistake; (*non esserci*) to be missing, not to be there; (*essere lontano*): ~ **(da)** to be away (from) ■ *vt* to miss; ~ **di** to lack; ~ **a** (*promessa*) to fail to keep; **tu mi manchi** I miss you; **mancò poco che morisse** he very nearly died; **mancano ancora 10 sterline** we're still £10 short; **manca un quarto alle 6** it's a quarter to 6; **non mancherò** I won't forget, I'll make sure I do; **ci mancherebbe altro!** of course I (*o you etc*) will!; ~ **da casa** to be away from home; ~ **di rispetto a** *o* **verso qn** to be lacking in respect towards sb, be disrespectful towards sb; ~ **di parola** not to keep one's word, go back on one's word; **sentirsi ~** to feel faint

man'cato, -a *ag* (*tentativo*) unsuccessful; (*artista*) failed

manche [mɑ̃ʃ] *sf inv* (*Sport*) heat

mancherò *etc* [manke'rɔ] *vb vedi* **mancare**

man'chevole [man'kevole] *ag* (*insufficiente*) inadequate, insufficient

manchevo'lezza [mankevo'lettsa] *sf* (*scorrettezza*) fault, shortcoming

'mancia, -ce ['mantʃa] *sf* tip; ~ **competente** reward

manci'ata [man'tʃata] *sf* handful

man'cino, -a [man'tʃino] *ag* (*braccio*) left; (*persona*) left-handed; (*fig*) underhand

'manco *av* (*nemmeno*): ~ **per sogno** *o* **per idea!** not on your life!

man'dante *sm/f* (*Dir*) principal; (*istigatore*) instigator

manda'rancio [manda'rantʃo] *sm* clementine

man'dare *vt* to send; (*far funzionare: macchina*) to drive; (*emettere*) to send out; (*: grido*) to give, utter, let out; ~ **avanti** (*persona*) to send ahead; (*fig: famiglia*) to provide for; (*ditta*) to look after, run; (*: pratica*) to attend to; ~ **a chiamare qn** to send for sb; ~ **giù** to send down; (*anche fig*) to swallow; ~ **in onda** (*Radio, TV*) to broadcast; ~ **in rovina** to ruin; ~ **via** to send away; (*licenziare*) to fire

manda'rino *sm* mandarin (orange); (*cinese*) mandarin

man'data *sf* (*quantità*) lot, batch; (*di chiave*) turn; **chiudere a doppia ~** to double-lock

manda'tario *sm* (*Dir*) representative, agent

man'dato *sm* (*incarico*) commission; (*Dir: provvedimento*) warrant; (*di deputato etc*) mandate; (*ordine di pagamento*) postal *o* money order; ~ **d'arresto**, ~ **di cattura** warrant for arrest; ~ **di comparizione** summons *sg*; ~ **di perquisizione** search warrant

man'dibola *sf* mandible, jaw

mando'lino *sm* mandolin(e)

'mandorla *sf* almond

mandor'lato *sm* nut brittle

'mandorlo *sm* almond tree

'mandria *sf* herd

mandri'ano *sm* cowherd, herdsman

man'drino *sm* (*Tecn*) mandrel

maneg'gevole [maned'dʒevole] *ag* easy to handle

maneggi'are [maned'dʒare] *vt* (*creta, cera*) to mould (*Brit*), mold (*US*), work, fashion; (*arnesi, utensili*) to handle; (*: adoperare*) to use; (*fig: persone, denaro*) to handle, deal with

ma'neggio [ma'neddʒo] *sm* moulding (*Brit*), molding (*US*); handling use; (*intrigo*) plot, scheme; (*per cavalli*) riding school

ma'nesco, -a, schi, sche *ag* free with one's fists

ma'nette *sfpl* handcuffs

manga'nello *sm* club

manga'nese *sm* manganese

mange'reccio, -a, ci, ce [mandʒe'rettʃo] *ag* edible

mangi'abile [man'dʒabile] *ag* edible, eatable

mangia'dischi [mandʒa'diski] *sm inv* record player

mangia'nastri [mandʒa'nastri] *sm inv* cassette-recorder

mangi'are [man'dʒare] *vt* to eat; (*intaccare*) to eat into *o* away; (*Carte, Scacchi etc*) to take ■ *vi* to eat ■ *sm* eating; (*cibo*) food; (*cucina*) cooking; **fare da ~** to do the cooking; **mangiarsi le parole** to mumble; **mangiarsi le unghie** to bite one's nails

mangia'soldi [mandʒa'sɔldi] *ag inv* (*fam*): **macchinetta ~** one-armed bandit

mangia'toia [mandʒa'toja] *sf* feeding-trough

man'gime [man'dʒime] *sm* fodder

mangiucchi'are [mandʒuk'kjare] *vt* to nibble

'mango, -ghi *sm* mango

ma'nia *sf* (*Psic*) mania; (*fig*) obsession, craze; **avere la ~ di fare qc** to have a habit of doing sth; **~ di persecuzione** persecution complex *o* mania

mania'cale *ag* (*Psic*) maniacal; (*fanatico*) fanatical

ma'niaco, -a, ci, che *ag* suffering from a mania; **~ (di)** obsessed (by), crazy (about)

'manica, -che *sf* sleeve; (*fig: gruppo*) gang, bunch; (*Geo*): **la M~, il Canale della M~** the (English) Channel; **senza maniche** sleeveless; **essere in maniche di camicia** to be in one's shirt sleeves; **essere di ~ larga/stretta** to be easy-going/strict; **~ a vento** (*Aer*) wind sock

manica'retto *sm* titbit (*Brit*), tidbit (*US*)

mani'chetta [mani'ketta] *sf* (*Tecn*) hose

mani'chino [mani'kino] *sm* (*di sarto, vetrina*) dummy

'manico, -ci *sm* handle; (*Mus*) neck; **~ di scopa** broomstick

mani'comio *sm* mental hospital; (*fig*) madhouse

mani'cotto *sm* muff; (*Tecn*) coupling; sleeve

mani'cure *sm o f inv* manicure ■ *sf inv* manicurist

mani'era *sf* way, manner; (*stile*) style, manner; **maniere** *sfpl* manners; **in ~ che** so that; **in ~ da** so as to; **alla ~ di** in *o* after the style of; **in una ~ o nell'altra** one way or another; **in tutte le maniere** at all costs; **usare buone maniere con qn** to be polite to sb; **usare le maniere forti** to use strong-arm tactics

manie'rato, -a *ag* affected

mani'ero *sm* manor

manifat'tura *sf* (*lavorazione*) manufacture; (*stabilimento*) factory

manifatturi'ero, -a *ag* manufacturing

manifes'tante *sm/f* demonstrator

manifes'tare *vt* to show, display; (*esprimere*) to express; (*rivelare*) to reveal, disclose ■ *vi* to demonstrate; **manifestarsi** *vr* to show o.s.; **manifestarsi amico** to prove o.s. (to be) a friend

manifestazi'one [manifestat'tsjone] *sf* show, display expression; (*sintomo*) sign, symptom; (*dimostrazione pubblica*) demonstration; (*cerimonia*) event

manifes'tino *sm* leaflet

mani'festo, -a *ag* obvious, evident ■ *sm* poster, bill; (*scritto ideologico*) manifesto

ma'niglia [ma'niʎʎa] *sf* handle; (*sostegno: negli autobus etc*) strap

Ma'nila *sf* Manila

manipo'lare *vt* to manipulate; (*alterare: vino*) to adulterate

manipolazi'one [manipolat'tsjone] *sf* manipulation; adulteration

ma'nipolo *sm* (*drappello*) handful

manis'calco, -chi *sm* blacksmith, farrier (*Brit*)

'manna *sf* (*Rel*) manna

man'naia *sf* (*del boia*) (executioner's) axe *o* ax (*US*); (*per carni*) cleaver

man'naro, -a *ag*: **lupo ~** werewolf

'mano, -i *sf* hand; (*strato: di vernice etc*) coat; **a ~** by hand; **cucito a ~** hand-sewn; **fatto a ~** handmade; **alla ~** (*persona*) easy-going; **fuori ~** out of the way; **di prima ~** (*notizia*) first-hand; **di seconda ~** second-hand; **man ~** little by little, gradually; **man ~ che** as; **a piene mani** (*fig*) generously; **avere le mani bucate** to spend money like water; **aver le mani in pasta** to be in the know; **avere qc per le mani** (*progetto, lavoro*) to have sth in hand; **dare una ~ a qn** to lend sb a hand; **dare una ~ di vernice a qc** to give sth a coat of paint; **darsi *o* stringersi la ~** to shake hands; **forzare la ~** to go too far; **mettere ~ a qc** to have a hand in sth; **mettere le mani avanti** (*fig*) to safeguard o.s.; **restare a mani vuote** to be left empty-handed; **venire alle mani** to come to blows; **mani in alto!** hands up!; **mani pulite** *see note*

● **MANI PULITE**
●
● *Mani pulite* ("clean hands") is a term used
● to describe the judicial operation of the
● early 1990s to gather evidence against
● politicians and industrialists who were
● implicated in bribery and corruption
● scandals.

m

mano'dopera *sf* labour (Brit), labor (US)
mano'messo, -a *pp di* **manomettere**
ma'nometro *sm* gauge, manometer
mano'mettere *vt* (*alterare*) to tamper with;
(*aprire indebitamente*) to break open illegally
manomissi'one *sf* (*di prove etc*) tampering;
(*di lettera*) opening
ma'nopola *sf* (*dell'armatura*) gauntlet; (*guanto*)
mitt; (*di impugnatura*) hand-grip; (*pomello*)
knob
manos'critto, -a *ag* handwritten ■ *sm*
manuscript
manova'lanza [manova'lantsa] *sf* unskilled
workers *pl*
mano'vale *sm* labourer (Brit), laborer (US)
mano'vella *sf* handle; (*Tecn*) crank
ma'novra *sf* manoeuvre (Brit), maneuver
(US); (*Ferr*) shunting; **manovre di corridoio**
palace intrigues
mano'vrare *vt* (*veicolo*) to manoeuvre (Brit),
maneuver (US); (*macchina, congegno*) to operate;
(*fig: persona*) to manipulate ■ *vi* to manoeuvre
manro'vescio [manro'veʃʃo] *sm* slap (*with
back of hand*)
man'sarda *sf* attic
mansi'one *sf* task, duty, job
mansu'eto, -a *ag* (*animale*) tame; (*persona*)
gentle, docile
mansue'tudine *sf* tameness gentleness,
docility
man'tello *sm* cloak; (*fig: di neve etc*) blanket,
mantle; (*Tecn: involucro*) casing, shell; (*Zool*)
coat
mante'nere *vt* to maintain; (*adempiere:
promesse*) to keep, abide by; (*provvedere a*) to
support, maintain; **mantenersi** *vr*:
mantenersi calmo/giovane to stay calm/
young; **~ i contatti con qn** to keep in touch
with sb
manteni'mento *sm* maintenance
mante'nuto, -a *sm/f* gigolo/kept woman
'mantice ['mantitʃe] *sm* bellows *pl*; (*di carrozza,
automobile*) hood
'manto *sm* cloak; **~ stradale** road surface
'Mantova *sf* Mantua
manto'vano, -a *ag* of (*o from*) Mantua
manu'ale *ag* manual ■ *sm* (*testo*) manual,
handbook
manua'listico, -a, ci, che *ag* textbook *cpd*
manual'mente *av* manually, by hand
ma'nubrio *sm* handle; (*di bicicletta etc*)
handlebars *pl*; (*Sport*) dumbbell
manu'fatto *sm* manufactured article;
manufatti *smpl* manufactured goods
manutenzi'one [manuten'tsjone] *sf*
maintenance, upkeep; (*d'impianti*)
maintenance, servicing

'manzo ['mandzo] *sm* (*Zool*) steer; (*carne*) beef
Mao'metto *sm* Mohammed
'mappa *sf* (*Geo*) map
mappa'mondo *sm* map of the world; (*globo
girevole*) globe
ma'rasma, -i *sm* (*fig*) decay, decline
mara'tona *sf* marathon
'marca, -che *sf* mark; (*bollo*) stamp; (*Comm:
di prodotti*) brand; (*contrassegno, scontrino*)
ticket, check; **prodotti di (gran) ~** high-
class products; **~ da bollo** official stamp
mar'care *vt* (*munire di contrassegno*) to mark;
(*a fuoco*) to brand; (*Sport: gol*) to score;
(*: avversario*) to mark; (*accentuare*) to stress;
~ visita (*Mil*) to report sick
mar'cato, -a *ag* (*lineamenti, accento etc*)
pronounced
'Marche ['marke] *sfpl*: **le ~** the Marches
(*region of central Italy*)
marche'rò etc [marke'rɔ] *vb vedi* **marcare**
mar'chese, -a [mar'keze] *sm/f* marquis o
marquess/marchioness
marchi'ano, -a [mar'kjano] *ag* (*errore*)
glaring, gross
marchi'are [mar'kjare] *vt* to brand
marchigi'ano, -a [marki'dʒano] *ag* of (*o
from*) the Marches
'marchio ['markjo] *sm* (*di bestiame, Comm: fig*)
brand; **~ depositato** registered trademark;
~ di fabbrica trademark
'marcia, -ce ['martʃa] *sf* (*anche Mus, Mil*)
march; (*funzionamento*) running; (*il
camminare*) walking; (*Aut*) gear; **mettere in ~**
to start; **mettersi in ~** to get moving; **far ~
indietro** (*Aut*) to reverse; (*fig*) to back-pedal;
~ forzata forced march; **~ funebre** funeral
march
marciapi'ede [martʃa'pjɛde] *sm* (*di strada*)
pavement (Brit), sidewalk (US); (*Ferr*)
platform
marci'are [mar'tʃare] *vi* to march;
(*andare: treno, macchina*) to go; (*funzionare*)
to run, work
'marcio, -a, ci, ce ['martʃo] *ag* (*frutta, legno*)
rotten, bad; (*Med*) festering; (*fig*) corrupt,
rotten ■ *sm*: **c'è del ~ in questa storia** (*fig*)
there's something fishy about this business;
avere torto ~ to be utterly wrong
mar'cire [mar'tʃire] *vi* (*andare a male*) to go bad,
rot; (*suppurare*) to fester; (*fig*) to rot
marci'ume [mar'tʃume] *sm* (*parte guasta: di cibi
etc*) rotten part, bad part; (*di radice, pianta*) rot;
(*fig: corruzione*) rottenness, corruption
'marco, -chi *sm* (*unità monetaria*) mark
'mare *sm* sea; **di ~** (*brezza, acqua, uccelli, pesce*)
sea *cpd*; **in ~** at sea; **per ~** by sea; **sul ~** (*barca*)
on the sea; (*villaggio, località*) by o beside the

sea; **andare al ~** (in vacanza etc) to go to the seaside; **il mar Caspio** the Caspian Sea; **il mar Morto** the Dead Sea; **il mar Nero** the Black Sea; **il ~ del Nord** the North Sea; **il mar Rosso** the Red Sea; **il mar dei Sargassi** the Sargasso Sea; **i mari del Sud** the South Seas

ma'rea sf tide; **alta/bassa ~** high/low tide

mareggi'ata [mared'dʒata] sf heavy sea

ma'remma sf (Geo) maremma, swampy coastal area

marem'mano, -a ag (zona, macchia) swampy; (della Maremma) of o from the Maremma

mare'moto sm seaquake

maresci'allo [mareʃʃallo] sm (Mil) marshal; (sottufficiale) warrant officer

marez'zato, -a [mared'dzato] ag (seta etc) watered, moiré; (legno) veined; (carta) marbled

marga'rina sf margarine

marghe'rita [marge'rita] sf (ox-eye) daisy, marguerite; (di stampante) daisy wheel

margheri'tina [margeri'tina] sf daisy

margi'nale [mardʒi'nale] ag marginal

'margine ['mardʒine] sm margin; (di bosco, via) edge, border; **avere un buon ~ di tempo/denaro** to have plenty of time/money; **~ di guadagno** o **di utile** profit margin; **~ di sicurezza** safety margin

mariju'ana [mæri'waːnə] sf marijuana

ma'rina sf navy; (costa) coast; (quadro) seascape; **~ mercantile** merchant navy (Brit) o marine (US); **~ militare** ≈ Royal Navy (Brit), ≈ Navy (US)

mari'naio sm sailor

mari'nare vt (Cuc) to marinate; **~ la scuola** to play truant

mari'naro, -a ag (tradizione, popolo) seafaring; (Cuc) with seafood; **alla marinara** (vestito, cappello) sailor cpd; **borgo ~** district where fishing folk live

mari'nata sf marinade

ma'rino, -a ag sea cpd, marine

mario'netta sf puppet

mari'tare vt to marry; **maritarsi** vr: **maritarsi** o **con qn** to marry sb, get married to sb

mari'tato, -a ag married

ma'rito sm husband; **prendere ~** to get married; **ragazza (in età) da ~** girl of marriageable age

ma'rittimo, -a ag maritime, sea cpd

mar'maglia [mar'maʎʎa] sf mob, riff-raff

marmel'lata sf jam; (di agrumi) marmalade

mar'mitta sf (recipiente) pot; (Aut) silencer; **~ catalitica** catalytic converter

'marmo sm marble

mar'mocchio [mar'mɔkkjo] sm (fam) (little) kid

mar'motta sf (Zool) marmot

maroc'chino, -a [marok'kino] ag, sm/f Moroccan

Ma'rocco sm: **il ~** Morocco

ma'roso sm breaker

'marra sf hoe

Marra'kesh [marra'keʃ] sf Marrakesh

mar'rone ag inv brown ■ sm (Bot) chestnut

mar'sala sm inv (vino) Marsala (wine)

Mar'siglia [mar'siʎʎa] sf Marseilles

mar'sina sf tails pl, tail coat

mar'supio sm (Zool) pouch, marsupium

mart. abbr (= martedì) Tue(s)

'Marte sm (Astr, Mitologia) Mars

martedì sm inv Tuesday; **il** o **il ~** on Tuesdays; **oggi è ~ 3 aprile** (the date) today is Tuesday 3rd April; **~ stavo male** I wasn't well on Tuesday; **il giornale di ~** Tuesday's newspaper; **~ grasso** Shrove Tuesday

martel'lante ag (fig: dolore) throbbing

martel'lare vt to hammer ■ vi (pulsare) to throb; (cuore) to thump

martel'letto sm (di pianoforte) hammer; (di macchina da scrivere) typebar; (di giudice, nelle vendite all'asta) gavel; (Med) percussion hammer

mar'tello sm hammer; (di uscio) knocker; **suonare a ~** (fig: campane) to sound the tocsin; **~ pneumatico** pneumatic drill

marti'netto sm (Tecn) jack

martin'gala sf (di giacca) half-belt; (di cavallo) martingale

'martire sm/f martyr

mar'tirio sm martyrdom; (fig) agony, torture

martori'are vt to torment, torture

mar'xismo sm Marxism

mar'xista, -i, e ag, sm/f Marxist

marza'pane [martsa'pane] sm marzipan

marzi'ale [mar'tsjale] ag martial

'marzo ['martso] sm March; vedi **luglio**

marzo'lino, -a [martso'lino] ag March cpd

mascalzo'nata [maskaltso'nata] sf dirty trick

mascal'zone [maskal'tsone] sm rascal, scoundrel

mas'cara sm inv mascara

mascar'pone sm soft cream cheese often used in desserts

ma'scella [maʃʃella] sf (Anat) jaw

'maschera ['maskera] sf mask; (travestimento) disguise; (per un ballo etc) fancy dress; (Teat, Cine) usher/usherette; (personaggio del teatro) stock character; **in ~** (mascherato) masked; **ballo in ~** fancy-dress ball; **gettare la ~** (fig) to reveal o.s.;

m

~ antigas/subacquea gas/diving mask; **~ di bellezza** face pack

masche'rare [maske'rare] *vt* to mask; (*travestire*) to disguise; to dress up; (*fig: celare*) to hide, conceal; (*Mil*) to camouflage; **mascherarsi** *vr*: **mascherarsi da** to disguise o.s. as; to dress up as; (*fig*) to masquerade as

masche'rina [maske'rina] *sf* (*piccola maschera*) mask; (*di animale*) patch; (*di scarpe*) toe-cap; (*Aut*) radiator grill

mas'chile [mas'kile] *ag* masculine; (*sesso, popolazione*) male; (*abiti*) men's; (*per ragazzi: scuola*) boys'

maschio, -a ['maskjo] *ag* (*Biol*) male; (*virile*) manly ■ *sm* (*anche Zool, Tecn*) male; (*uomo*) man; (*ragazzo*) boy; (*figlio*) son

masco'lino, -a *ag* masculine

mas'cotte [mas'kɔt] *sf inv* mascot

maso'chismo [mazo'kizmo] *sm* masochism

maso'chista, -i, e [mazo'kista] *ag* masochistic ■ *sm/f* masochist

'massa *sf* mass; (*di errori etc*): **una ~ di** heaps of, masses of; (*di gente*) mass, multitude; (*Elettr*) earth; **in ~** (*Comm*) in bulk; (*tutti insieme*) en masse; **adunata in ~** mass meeting; **manifestazione/cultura di ~** mass demonstration/culture; **produrre in ~** to mass-produce; **la ~ (del popolo)** the masses *pl*

massa'crante *ag* exhausting, gruelling

massa'crare *vt* to massacre, slaughter

mas'sacro *sm* massacre, slaughter; (*fig*) mess, disaster

massaggi'are [massad'dʒare] *vt* to massage

massaggia'tore, -'trice [massaddʒa'tore] *sm/f* masseur/masseuse

mas'saggio [mas'saddʒo] *sm* massage

mas'saia *sf* housewife

masse'ria *sf* large farm

masse'rizie [masse'rittsje] *sf pl* (household) furnishings

massicci'ata [massit'tʃata] *sf* (*di strada, ferrovia*) ballast

mas'siccio, -a, ci, ce [mas'sittʃo] *ag* (*oro, legno*) solid; (*palazzo*) massive; (*corporatura*) stout ■ *sm* (*Geo*) massif

'massima *sf vedi* **massimo**

massi'male *sm* maximum; (*Comm*) ceiling, limit

'massimo, -a *ag, sm* maximum ■ *sf* (*sentenza, regola*) maxim; (*Meteor*) maximum temperature; **in linea di massima** generally speaking; **arrivare entro il tempo ~** to arrive within the time limit; **al ~** at (the) most; **sfruttare qc al ~** to make full use of sth; **arriverò al ~ alle 5** I'll arrive at 5 at the latest; **erano presenti le**

massimoe autorità all the most important dignitaries were there; **il ~ della pena** (*Dir*) the maximum penalty

mas'sivo, -a *ag* (*intervento*) en masse; (*emigrazione*) mass; (*emorragia*) massive

'masso *sm* rock, boulder

mas'sone *sm* freemason

massone'ria *sf* freemasonry

mas'sonico, -a, ci, che *ag* masonic

mas'tello *sm* tub

masteriz'zare [masterid'dzare] *vt* to burn

masterizza'tore [masteriddza'tore] *sm* CD burner o writer

masti'care *vt* to chew

'mastice ['mastitʃe] *sm* mastic; (*per vetri*) putty

mas'tino *sm* mastiff

masto'dontico, -a, ci, che *ag* gigantic

mastur'barsi *vr* to masturbate

masturbazi'one [masturbat'tsjone] *sf* masturbation

ma'tassa *sf* skein

mate'matico, -a, ci, che *ag* mathematical ■ *sm/f* mathematician ■ *sf* mathematics *sg*

materas'sino *sm* mat; **~ gonfiabile** air bed

mate'rasso *sm* mattress; **~ a molle** spring o interior-sprung mattress

ma'teria *sf* (*Fisica*) matter; (*Tecn, Comm*) material, matter *no pl*; (*disciplina*) subject; (*argomento*) subject matter, material; **prima di entrare in ~ ...** before discussing the matter in hand ...; **un esperto in ~ (di musica etc)** an expert on the subject (of music etc); **sono ignorante in ~** I know nothing about it; **~ cerebrale** cerebral matter; **~ grassa** fat; **~ grigia** (*anche fig*) grey matter; **materie plastiche** plastics; **materie prime** raw materials

materi'ale *ag* material; (*fig: grossolano*) rough, rude ■ *sm* material; (*insieme di strumenti etc*) equipment *no pl*, materials *pl*; **~ da costruzione** building materials *pl*

materia'lista, -i, e *ag* materialistic ■ *sm/f* materialist

materializ'zarsi [materjalid'dzarsi] *vr* to materialize

material'mente *av* (*fisicamente*) materially; (*economicamente*) financially

mater'nità *sf* motherhood, maternity; (*clinica*) maternity hospital; **in (congedo di) ~** on maternity leave

ma'terno, -a *ag* (*amore, cura etc*) maternal, motherly; (*nonno*) maternal; (*lingua, terra*) mother *cpd*; *vedi anche* **scuola**

ma'tita *sf* pencil; **matite colorate** crayons; **~ per gli occhi** eyeliner (pencil)

ma'trice [ma'tritʃe] *sf* matrix; (*Comm*) counterfoil; (*fig: origine*) background

ma'tricola *sf* (*registro*) register; (*numero*) registration number; (*nell'università*) freshman, fresher (*Brit fam*)

ma'trigna [ma'triɲɲa] *sf* stepmother

matrimoni'ale *ag* matrimonial, marriage *cpd*; **camera/letto** ~ double room/bed

matri'monio *sm* marriage, matrimony; (*durata*) marriage, married life; (*cerimonia*) wedding

ma'trona *sf* (*fig*) matronly woman

matta'toio *sm* abattoir (*Brit*), slaughterhouse

mat'tina *sf* morning; **la** o **alla** o **di** ~ in the morning; **di prima** ~, **la** ~ **presto** early in the morning; **dalla** ~ **alla sera** (*continuamente*) from morning to night; (*improvvisamente: cambiare*) overnight

matti'nata *sf* morning; (*spettacolo*) matinée, afternoon performance; **in** ~ in the course of the morning; **nella** ~ in the morning; **nella tarda** ~ at the end of the morning; **nella tarda** ~ **di sabato** late on Saturday morning

mattini'ero, -a *ag*: **essere** ~ to be an early riser

mat'tino *sm* morning; **di buon** ~ early in the morning

'matto, -a *ag* mad, crazy; (*fig: falso*) false, imitation; (*opaco*) matt, dull ■ *sm/f* madman/woman; **avere una voglia matta di qc** to be dying for sth; **far diventare** ~ **qn** to drive sb mad o crazy; **una gabbia di matti** (*fig*) a madhouse

mat'tone *sm* brick; (*fig*): **questo libro/film è un** ~ this book/film is heavy going

matto'nella *sf* tile

mattu'tino, -a *ag* morning *cpd*

matu'rare *vi* (*anche: maturarsi: frutta, grano*) to ripen; (*ascesso*) to come to a head; (*fig: persona, idea, Econ*) to mature ■ *vt* to ripen, to (make) mature; ~ **una decisione** to come to a decision

maturità *sf* maturity; (*di frutta*) ripeness, maturity; (*Ins*) school-leaving examination, ≈ GCE A-levels (*Brit*)

ma'turo, -a *ag* mature; (*frutto*) ripe, mature

ma'tusa *sm/f inv* (*scherzoso*) old fogey

Mauri'tania *sf*: **la** ~ Mauritania

Mau'rizio [mau'rittsjo] *sf*: (**l'isola di**) ~ Mauritius

mauso'leo *sm* mausoleum

max. *abbr* (= *massimo*) max

'maxi... *prefisso* maxi...

maxipro'cesso [maksipro'tʃesso] *sm see note*

● **MAXIPROCESSO**

A *maxiprocesso* is a criminal trial which is characterized by the large number of co-defendants. These people are usually members of terrorist or criminal organizations. The trials are often lengthy and many witnesses may be called to give evidence.

maxis'chermo [maksis'kermo] *sm* giant screen

'mazza ['mattsa] *sf* (*bastone*) club; (*martello*) sledge-hammer; (*Sport: da golf*) club; (: *da baseball, cricket*) bat

maz'zata [mat'tsata] *sf* (*anche fig*) heavy blow

maz'zetta [mat'tsetta] *sf* (*di banconote etc*) bundle; (*fig*) rake-off

'mazzo ['mattso] *sm* (*di fiori, chiavi etc*) bunch; (*di carte da gioco*) pack

MC *sigla* = **Macerata**

m.c.d. *abbr* (= *minimo comune denominatore*) lcd

m.c.m. *abbr* (= *minimo comune multiplo*) lcm

ME *sigla* = **Messina**

me *pron* me; **sei bravo quanto me** you are as clever as I (am) o as me

me'andro *sm* meander

M.E.C. [mɛk] *abbr m* = **Mercato Comune Europeo**

'Mecca *sf* (*anche fig*): **La** ~ Mecca

meccanica'mente *av* mechanically

mec'canico, -a, ci, che *ag* mechanical ■ *sm* mechanic ■ *sf* mechanics *sg*; (*attività tecnologica*) mechanical engineering; (*meccanismo*) mechanism; **officina meccanica** garage

mecca'nismo *sm* mechanism

meccaniz'zare [mekkanid'dzare] *vt* to mechanize

meccanizzazi'one [mekkaniddzat'tsjone] *sf* mechanization

meccanogra'fia *sf* (mechanical) data processing

meccano'grafico, -a, ci, che *ag*: **centro** ~ data processing department

mece'nate [metʃe'nate] *sm* patron

mèche [mɛʃ] *sf inv* streak; **farsi le** ~ to have one's hair streaked

me'daglia [me'daʎʎa] *sf* medal; ~ **d'oro** (*oggetto*) gold medal; (*persona*) gold medallist (*Brit*) o medalist (*US*)

medagli'one [medaʎ'ʎone] *sm* (*Archit*) medallion; (*gioiello*) locket

me'desimo, -a *ag* same; (*in persona*): **io** ~ I myself

'media *sf vedi* **medio**

media'mente *av* on average

medi'ano, -a *ag* median; (*valore*) mean ■ *sm* (*Calcio*) half-back

medi'ante *prep* by means of

medi'are *vt* (*fare da mediatore*) to act as mediator in; (*Mat*) to average

medi'ato, -a ag indirect
media'tore, -'trice sm/f mediator; (Comm) middle man, agent; **fare da ~ fra** to mediate between
mediazi'one [medjat'tsjone] sf mediation; (Comm: azione, compenso) brokerage
medica'mento sm medicine, drug
medi'care vt to treat; (ferita) to dress
medi'cato, -a ag (garza, shampoo) medicated
medicazi'one [medikat'tsjone] sf treatment, medication dressing; **fare una ~ a qn** to dress sb's wounds
medi'cina [medi'tʃina] sf medicine; **~ legale** forensic medicine
medici'nale [meditʃi'nale] ag medicinal
■ sm drug, medicine
'medico, -a, ci, che ag medical ■ sm doctor; **~ di bordo** ship's doctor; **~ di famiglia** family doctor; **~ fiscale** doctor who examines patients signed off sick for a lengthy period by their private doctor; **~ generico** general practitioner, GP
medie'vale ag medieval
'medio, -a ag average; (punto, ceto) middle; (altezza, statura) medium ■ sm (dito) middle finger ■ sf average; (Mat) mean; (Ins: voto) end-of-term average; **medie** sfpl vedi **scuola media inferiore**; **licenza media** leaving certificate awarded at the end of 3 years of secondary education; **in media** on average; **al di sopra/ sotto della media** above/below average; **viaggiare ad una media di ...** to travel at an average speed of ...; **il M~ Oriente** the Middle East
medi'ocre ag (gen) mediocre; (qualità, stipendio) poor
mediocrità sf mediocrity; poorness
medioe'vale ag = **medievale**
Medio'evo sm Middle Ages pl
medita'bondo, -a ag thoughtful
medi'tare vt to ponder over, meditate on; (progettare) to plan, think out ■ vi to meditate
medi'tato, -a ag (gen) meditated; (parole) carefully-weighed; (vendetta) premeditated; **ben ~** (piano) well worked-out, neat
meditazi'one [meditat'tsjone] sf meditation
mediter'raneo, -a ag Mediterranean; **il (mare) M~** the Mediterranean (Sea)
'medium sm/f inv medium
me'dusa sf (Zool) jellyfish
me'gafono sm megaphone
mega'lomane ag, sm/f megalomaniac
me'gera [me'dʒɛra] sf (peg: donna) shrew
'meglio ['mɛʎʎo] av, ag inv better; (con senso superlativo) best ■ sm (la cosa migliore): **il ~** the best (thing); **faresti ~ ad andartene** you

had better leave; **alla ~** as best one can; **andar di bene in ~** to get better and better; **fare del proprio ~** to do one's best; **per il ~** for the best; **aver la ~ su qn** to get the better of sb
'mela sf apple; **~ cotogna** quince
mela'grana sf pomegranate
melan'zana [melan'dzana] sf aubergine (Brit), eggplant (US)
me'lassa sf molasses sg, treacle
me'lenso, -a ag dull, stupid
me'lissa sf (Bot) balm
mel'lifluo, -a ag (peg) sugary, honeyed
'melma sf mud, mire
'melo sm apple tree
melo'dia sf melody
me'lodico, -a, ci, che ag melodic
melodi'oso, -a ag melodious
melo'dramma, -i sm melodrama
me'lone sm (musk) melon
'membra sfpl vedi **membro**
mem'brana sf membrane
'membro sm (person) (pl(m) **membri**) member; (arto) (pl(f) **membra**) limb
memo'rabile ag memorable
memo'randum sm inv memorandum
'memore ag: **~ di** (ricordando) mindful of; (riconoscente) grateful for
me'moria sf (anche Inform) memory; **memorie** sfpl (opera autobiografica) memoirs; **a ~** (imparare, sapere) by heart; **a ~ d'uomo** within living memory; **~ di sola lettura** (Inform) read-only memory; **~ tampone** (Inform) buffer
memori'ale sm (raccolta di memorie) memoirs pl; (Dir) memorial
memoriz'zare [memorid'dzare] vt (gen) to memorize; (Inform) to store
memorizzazi'one [memoriddzat'tsjone] sf memorization; storage
'mena sf scheme
mena'dito; a ~ av perfectly, thoroughly; **sapere qc a ~** to have sth at one's fingertips
mena'gramo sm/f inv jinx, Jonah
me'nare vt to lead; (picchiare) to hit, beat; (dare: colpi) to deal; **~ la coda** (cane) to wag its tail; **~ qc per le lunghe** to drag sth out; **~ il can per l'aia** (fig) to beat about (Brit) o around (US) the bush
mendi'cante sm/f beggar
mendi'care vt to beg for ■ vi to beg
menefre'ghismo [menefre'gizmo] sm (fam) couldn't-care-less attitude
me'ninge [me'nindʒe] sf (Med) meninx; **spremersi le meningi** to rack one's brains
menin'gite [menin'dʒite] sf meningitis
me'nisco sm (Anat, Mat, Fisica) meniscus

○ **PAROLA CHIAVE**

'**meno** av **1** (in minore misura) less; **dovresti mangiare meno** you should eat less, you shouldn't eat so much; **è sempre meno facile** it's getting less and less easy; **ne voglio di meno** I don't want so much
2 (comparativo): **meno … di** not as … as, less … than; **sono meno alto di te** I'm not as tall as you (are), I'm less tall than you (are); **meno … che** not as … as, less … than; **meno che mai** less than ever; **è meno intelligente che ricco** he's more rich than intelligent; **meno fumo più mangio** the less I smoke the more I eat; **meno di quanto pensassi** less than I thought
3 (superlativo) least; **il meno dotato degli studenti** the least gifted of the students; **è quello che compro meno spesso** it's the one I buy least often
4 (Mat) minus; **8 meno 5** 8 minus 5, 8 take away 5; **sono le 8 meno un quarto** it's a quarter to 8; **meno 5 gradi** 5 degrees below zero, minus 5 degrees; **mille euro in meno** a thousand euros less; **ha preso 6 meno** (a scuola) he scraped a pass; **cento euro meno le spese** a hundred euros minus o less expenses
5 (fraseologia): **quanto meno poteva telefonare** he could at least have phoned; **non so se accettare o meno** I don't know whether to accept or not; **non essere da meno di** not to be outdone by; **fare a meno di qc/qn** to do without sth/sb; **non potevo fare a meno di ridere** I couldn't help laughing; **meno male!** thank goodness!; **meno male che sei arrivato** it's a good job that you've come
■ ag inv (tempo, denaro) less; (errori, persone) fewer; **ha fatto meno errori di tutti** he made fewer mistakes than anyone, he made the fewest mistakes of all
■ sm inv **1: il meno** (il minimo) the least; **parlare del più e del meno** to talk about this and that; **era il meno che ti potesse succedere** it was the least you could have expected
2 (Mat) minus
■ prep (eccetto) except (for), apart from; **tutti meno lui** everybody apart from o except him; **a meno che, a meno di** unless; **a meno che non piova** unless it rains; **non posso, a meno di prendere ferie** I can't, unless I take some leave; vedi anche **più**

meno'mare vt (danneggiare) to maim, disable

meno'mato, -a ag (persona) disabled ■ sm/f disabled person
menomazi'one [menomat'tsjone] sf disablement
meno'pausa sf menopause
'**mensa** sf (locale) canteen; (Mil) mess; (: nelle università) refectory
men'sile ag monthly ■ sm (periodico) monthly (magazine); (stipendio) monthly salary
mensil'mente av (ogni mese) every month; (una volta al mese) monthly
'**mensola** sf bracket; (ripiano) shelf; (Archit) corbel
'**menta** sf mint; (anche: **menta piperita**) peppermint; (bibita) peppermint cordial; (caramella) mint, peppermint
men'tale ag mental
mentalità sf inv mentality
mental'mente av mentally
'**mente** sf mind; **imparare/sapere qc a ~** to learn/know sth by heart; **avere in ~ qc** to have sth in mind; **avere in ~ di fare qc** to intend to do sth; **fare venire in ~ qc a qn** to remind sb of sth; **mettersi in ~ di fare qc** to make up one's mind to do sth; **passare di ~ a qn** to slip sb's mind; **tenere a ~ qc** to bear sth in mind; **a ~ fredda** objectively; **lasciami fare ~ locale** let me think
mente'catto, -a ag half-witted ■ sm/f halfwit, imbecile
men'tire vi to lie
men'tito, -a ag: **sotto mentite spoglie** under false pretences (Brit) o pretenses (US)
'**mento** sm chin; **doppio ~** double chin
men'tolo sm menthol
'**mentre** cong (temporale) while; (avversativo) whereas ■ sm: **in quel ~** at that very moment
menù sm inv (set) menu; **~ turistico** standard o tourists' menu
menzio'nare [mentsjo'nare] vt to mention
menzi'one [men'tsjone] sf mention; **fare ~ di** to mention
men'zogna [men'tsɔɲɲa] sf lie
menzo'gnero, -a [mentsoɲ'ɲɛro] ag false, untrue
mera'viglia [mera'viʎʎa] sf amazement, wonder; (persona, cosa) marvel, wonder; **a ~** perfectly, wonderfully
meravigli'are [meraviʎ'ʎare] vt to amaze, astonish; **meravigliarsi** vr: **meravigliarsi (di)** to marvel (at); (stupirsi) to be amazed (at), be astonished (at); **mi meraviglio di te!** I'm surprised at you!; **non c'è da meravigliarsi** it's not surprising
meravigli'oso, -a [meraviʎ'ʎoso] ag wonderful, marvellous (Brit), marvelous (US)

m

merc. *abbr* (= *mercoledì*) Wed
mer'cante *sm* merchant; ~ **d'arte** art dealer; ~ **di cavalli** horse dealer
mercanteggi'are [merkanted'dʒare] *vt* (*onore, voto*) to sell ■ *vi* to bargain, haggle
mercan'tile *ag* commercial, mercantile; (*nave, marina*) merchant *cpd* ■ *sm* (*nave*) merchantman
mercan'zia [merkan'tsia] *sf* merchandise, goods *pl*
merca'tino *sm* (*rionale*) local street market; (*Econ*) unofficial stock market
mer'cato *sm* market; **di ~** (*economia, prezzo, ricerche*) market *cpd*; **mettere** o **lanciare qc sul ~** to launch sth on the market; **a buon ~** cheap; ~ **dei cambi** exchange market; **M~ Comune (Europeo)** (European) Common Market; ~ **del lavoro** labour market, job market; ~ **nero** black market; ~ **al rialzo/al ribasso** (*Borsa*) sellers'/buyers' market
merce ['mɛrtʃe] *sf* goods *pl*, merchandise; ~ **deperibile** perishable goods *pl*
mercé [mer'tʃe] *sf* mercy; **essere alla ~ di qn** to be at sb's mercy
merce'nario, -a [mertʃe'narjo] *ag, sm* mercenary
merce'ria [mertʃe'ria] *sf* (*articoli*) haberdashery (*Brit*), notions *pl* (*US*); (*bottega*) haberdasher's shop (*Brit*), notions store (*US*)
mercoledì *sm inv* Wednesday; ~ **delle Ceneri** Ash Wednesday; *see note*; *vedi anche* **martedì**

● **MERCOLEDÌ DELLE CENERI**
●
● In the Catholic church, *Mercoledì delle Ceneri*
● signals the beginning of Lent.
● Churchgoers are marked on the forehead
● with ash from the burning of the olive
● branch. Ash Wednesday is traditionally
● a day of fasting, abstinence and
● repentance.

mer'curio *sm* mercury
'merda *sf* (*fam!*) shit (!)
me'renda *sf* afternoon snack
meren'dina *sf* snack
meridi'ano, -a *ag* (*di mezzogiorno*) midday *cpd*, noonday ■ *sm* meridian ■ *sf* (*orologio*) sundial
meridio'nale *ag* southern ■ *sm/f* southerner
meridi'one *sm* south
me'ringa, -ghe *sf* (*Cuc*) meringue
meri'tare *vt* to deserve, merit ■ *vb impers* (*valere la pena*): **merita andare** it is worth going; **non merita neanche parlarne** it's not worth talking about; **per quel che merita** for what it's worth

meri'tevole *ag* worthy
'merito *sm* merit; (*valore*) worth; **dare ~ a qn di** to give sb credit for; **finire a pari ~** to finish joint first (*o second etc*); to tie; **in ~ a** as regards, with regard to; **entrare nel ~ di una questione** to go into a matter; **non so niente in ~** I don't know anything about it
meritocra'zia [meritokrat'tsia] *sf* meritocracy
meri'torio, -a *ag* praiseworthy
mer'letto *sm* lace
'merlo *sm* (*Zool*) blackbird; (*Archit*) battlement
mer'luzzo [mer'luttso] *sm* (*Zool*) cod
'mescere ['meʃʃere] *vt* to pour (out)
meschinità [meskini'ta] *sf* wretchedness; meagreness; meanness; narrow-mindedness
mes'chino, -a [mes'kino] *ag* wretched; (*scarso*) meagre (*Brit*), meager (*US*); (*persona: gretta*) mean; (*limitata*) narrow-minded, petty; **fare una figura meschina** to cut a poor figure
'mescita ['meʃʃita] *sf* wine shop
mesci'uto, -a [meʃʃuto] *pp di* **mescere**
mesco'lanza [mesko'lantsa] *sf* mixture
mesco'lare *vt* to mix; (*vini, colori*) to blend; (*mettere in disordine*) to mix up, muddle up; (*carte*) to shuffle; **mescolarsi** *vr* to mix; to blend; to get mixed up; (*fig*): **mescolarsi in** to get mixed up in, meddle in
'mese *sm* month; **il ~ scorso** last month; **il corrente ~** this month
'messa *sf* (*Rel*) mass; (*il mettere*): ~ **a fuoco** focusing; ~ **in moto** starting; ~ **in piega** (*acconciatura*) set; ~ **a punto** (*Tecn*) adjustment; (*Aut*) tuning; (*fig*) clarification; ~ **in scena** = **messinscena**
messagge'rie [messaddʒe'rie] *sfpl* (*ditta: di distribuzione*) distributors; (*di trasporto*) freight company
messag'gero [messad'dʒɛro] *sm* messenger
messaggi'arsi [messad'dʒarsi] *vr*: **messaggiamoci** we'll text each other
messag'gino [messad'dʒino] *sm* (*di telefonino*) text (message)
mes'saggio [mes'saddʒo] *sm* message
messag'gistica [messad'dʒistica] *sf*: ~ **immediata** (*Inform*) instant messaging; **programma di ~ immediata** instant messenger
mes'sale *sm* (*Rel*) missal
'messe *sf* harvest
Mes'sia *sm inv* (*Rel*): **il ~** the Messiah
messi'cano, -a *ag, sm/f* Mexican
'Messico *sm*: **il ~** Mexico; **Città del ~** Mexico City
messin'scena [messin'ʃena] *sf* (*Teat*) production

'messo, -a *pp di* mettere ■ *sm* messenger
mestie'rante *sm/f* (*peg*) money-grubber;
   (*: scrittore*) hack
mesti'ere *sm* (*professione*) job; (*manuale*) trade;
   (*artigianale*) craft; (*fig: abilità nel lavoro*) skill,
   technique; **di ~** by *o* to trade; **essere del ~** to
   know the tricks of the trade
mes'tizia [mes'tittsja] *sf* sadness,
   melancholy
'mesto, -a *ag* sad, melancholy
'mestolo *sm* (*Cuc*) ladle
mestru'ale *ag* menstrual
mestruazi'one [mestruat'tsjone] *sf*
   menstruation; **avere le mestruazioni** to
   have one's period
'meta *sf* destination; (*fig*) aim, goal
metà *sf inv* half; (*punto di mezzo*) middle;
   dividere qc a *o* **per ~** to divide sth in half,
   halve sth; **fare a ~ (di qc con qn)** to go
   halves (with sb in sth); **a ~ prezzo** at half
   price; **a ~ settimana** midweek; **a ~ strada**
   halfway; **verso la ~ del mese** halfway
   through the month, towards the middle of
   the month; **dire le cose a ~** to leave some
   things unsaid; **fare le cose a ~** to leave
   things half-done; **la mia dolce ~** (*fam
   scherzoso*) my better half
metabo'lismo *sm* metabolism
meta'done *sm* methadone
meta'fisica *sf* metaphysics *sg*
me'tafora *sf* metaphor
meta'forico, -a, ci, che *ag* metaphorical
me'tallico, -a, ci, che *ag* (*di metallo*) metal *cpd*;
   (*splendore, rumore etc*) metallic
metalliz'zato, -a [metallid'dzato] *ag*
   (*verniciatura*) metallic
me'tallo *sm* metal; **di ~** metal *cpd*
metallur'gia [metallur'dʒia] *sf* metallurgy
metalmec'canico, -a, ci, che *ag* engineering
   cpd ■ *sm* engineering worker
meta'morfosi *sf* metamorphosis
me'tano *sm* methane
me'teora *sf* meteor
meteo'rite *sm* meteorite
meteorolo'gia [meteorolo'dʒia] *sf*
   meteorology
meteoro'logico, -a, ci, che [meteoro'lɔdʒiko]
   ag meteorological, weather *cpd*
meteo'rologo, -a, ghi, ghe *sm/f* meteorologist
me'ticcio, -a, ci, ce [me'tittʃo] *sm/f* half-
   caste, half-breed
meticolosità *sf* meticulousness
metico'loso, -a *ag* meticulous
me'todico, -a, ci, che *ag* methodical
'metodo *sm* method; (*manuale*) tutor (*Brit*),
   manual; **far qc con/senza ~** to do sth
   methodically/unmethodically

me'traggio [me'traddʒo] *sm* (*Sartoria*) length;
   (*Cine*) footage; **film a lungo ~** feature film;
   film a corto ~ short film
metra'tura *sf* length
'metrico, -a, ci, che *ag* metric; (*Poesia*)
   metrical ■ *sf* metrics *sg*
'metro *sm* metre (*Brit*), meter (*US*); (*nastro*)
   tape measure; (*asta*) (metre) rule
metrò *sm inv* underground (*Brit*), subway (*US*)
metro'notte *sm inv* night security guard
me'tropoli *sf* metropolis
metropoli'tano, -a *ag* metropolitan ■ *sf*
   underground (*Brit*), subway (*US*);
   metropolitana leggera metro (*mainly on the
   surface*)
metroses'suale *ag* metrosexual
'mettere *vt* to put; (*abito*) to put on; (*: portare*)
   to wear; (*installare: telefono*) to put in; (*fig:
   provocare*): **~ fame/allegria a qn** to make sb
   hungry/happy; (*supporre*): **mettiamo che ...**
   let's suppose *o* say that ...; **mettersi** *vr*
   (*persona*) to put o.s.; (*oggetto*) to go; (*disporsi:
   faccenda*) to turn out; **mettersi a piangere/
   ridere** to start crying/laughing, start *o*
   begin to cry/laugh; **mettersi a sedere**
   to sit down; **mettersi al lavoro** to set to
   work; **mettersi a letto** to get into bed;
   (*per malattia*) to take to one's bed; **mettersi
   il cappello** to put on one's hat; **mettersi
   sotto** to get down to things; **mettersi in
   società** to set up in business; **si sono messi
   insieme** (*coppia*) they've started going out
   together (*Brit*) *o* dating (*US*); **metterci**:
   metterci molta cura/molto tempo
   to take a lot of care/a lot of time; **mettercela
   tutta** to do one's best; **ci ho messo 3 ore
   per venire** it's taken me 3 hours to get here;
   ~ un annuncio sul giornale to place an
   advertisement in the paper; **~ a confronto**
   to compare; **~ in conto** (*somma etc*) to put
   on account; **~ in luce** (*problemi, errori*) to
   stress, highlight; **~ a tacere qn/qc** to keep
   sb/sth quiet; **~ su casa** to set up house;
   ~ su un negozio to start a shop; **~ su peso**
   to put on weight; **~ via** to put away
mez'zadro [med'dzadro] *sm* (*Agr*)
   sharecropper
mezza'luna [meddza'luna] (*pl* mezzelune)
   sf half-moon; (*dell'islamismo*) crescent;
   (*coltello*) (semicircular) chopping knife
mezza'nino [meddza'nino] *sm* mezzanine
   (floor)
mez'zano, -a [med'dzano] *ag* (*medio*)
   average, medium; (*figlio*) middle *cpd*
   ■ *sm/f* (*intermediario*) go-between; (*ruffiano*)
   pimp
mezza'notte [meddza'nɔtte] *sf* midnight

m

mezzo, -a ['mɛddzo] *ag* half; **un ~ litro/
panino** half a litre/roll ■ *av* half-; **~ morto**
half-dead ■ *sm* (*metà*) half; (*parte centrale: di
strada etc*) middle; (*per raggiungere un fine*)
means *sg*; (*veicolo*) vehicle; (*nell'indicare l'ora*):
le nove e ~ half past nine; **mezzogiorno e ~**
half past twelve ■ *sf*: **la mezza** half-past
twelve (in the afternoon); **mezzi** *smpl*
(*possibilità economiche*) means; **di mezza età**
middle-aged; **aver una mezza idea di fare
qc** to have half a mind to do sth; **è stato un ~
scandalo** it almost caused a scandal; **un
soprabito di mezza stagione** a spring (*o*
autumn) coat; **a mezza voce** in an
undertone; **una volta e ~ più grande** one
and a half times bigger; **di ~** middle, in the
middle; **andarci di ~** (*patir danno*) to suffer;
esserci di ~ (*ostacolo*) to be in the way;
levarsi *o* **togliersi di ~** to get out of the way;
mettersi di ~ to interfere; **togliere di ~**
(*persona, cosa*) to get rid of; (*fam: uccidere*) to
bump off; **non c'è una via di ~** there's no
middle course; **in ~ a** in the middle of; **nel
bel ~ (di)** right in the middle (of); **per** *o* **a ~ di**
by means of; **a ~ corriere** by carrier; **mezzi
di comunicazione di massa** mass media *pl*;
mezzi pubblici public transport *sg*; **mezzi
di trasporto** means of transport
mezzogi'orno [meddzo'dʒorno] *sm* midday,
noon; (*Geo*) south; **a ~** at 12 (o'clock) *o* midday
o noon; **il ~ d'Italia** southern Italy
mezz'ora [med'dzora] *sf* half-hour, half an
hour
MI *sigla* = **Milano**
mi *pron* (*dav lo, la, li, le, ne diventa* **me**) (*oggetto*)
me; (*complemento di termine*) (to) me; (*riflessivo*)
myself ■ *sm* (*Mus*) E; (*: solfeggiando la scala*)
mi; **mi aiuti?** will you help me?; **me ne ha
parlato** he spoke to me about it, he told me
about it; **mi servo da solo** I'll help myself
mia *vedi* **mio**
miago'lare *vi* to miaow, mew
Mib *sigla m, ag* (= *indice borsa Milano*) Milan
Stock Exchange Index
mica *sf* (*Chim*) mica ■ *av* (*fam*): **non ... ~** not ...
at all; **non sono ~ stanco** I'm not a bit tired;
non sarà ~ partito? he wouldn't have left,
would he?; **~ male** not bad
miccia, -ce ['mittʃa] *sf* fuse
micidi'ale [mitʃi'djale] *ag* fatal; (*dannosissimo*)
deadly
micio, -a, ci, cie ['mitʃo] *sm/f* pussy (cat)
microbiolo'gia [mikrobiolo'dʒia] *sf*
microbiology
microbo *sm* microbe
microcir'cuito [mikrotʃir'kuito] *sm*
microcircuit

micro'fibra *sf* microfibre
micro'film *sm inv* microfilm
mi'crofono *sm* microphone
microinfor'matica *sf* microcomputing
micro'onda *sf* microwave
microproces'sore [mikroprotʃes'sore] *sm*
microprocessor
micros'copico, -a, ci, che *ag* microscopic
micros'copio *sm* microscope
micro'solco, -chi *sm* (*solco*) microgroove;
(*disco: a 33 giri*) long-playing record, LP; (*: a 45
giri*) extended-play record, EP
micros'pia *sf* hidden microphone, bug (*fam*)
mi'dollo (*pl(f)* **midolla**) *sm* (*Anat*) marrow;
~ spinale spinal cord
mie (*pl* **miei**) *vedi* **mio**
mi'ele *sm* honey
mi'etere *vt* (*Agr*) to reap, harvest; (*fig: vite*) to
take, claim
mietitrebbia'trice [mjetitrebbja'tritʃe] *sf*
combine harvester
mieti'trice [mjeti'tritʃe] *sf* (*macchina*)
harvester
mieti'tura *sf* (*raccolto*) harvest; (*lavoro*)
harvesting; (*tempo*) harvest-time
miglia ['miʎʎa] *sfpl di* **miglio**
migli'aio [miʎ'ʎajo] (*pl(f)* **migliaia**) *sm*
thousand; **un ~ (di)** about a thousand; **a
migliaia** by the thousand, in thousands
miglio¹ ['miʎʎo] (*pl(f)* **miglia**) *sm* (*unità di
misura*) mile; **~ marino** *o* **nautico** nautical
mile
miglio² ['miʎʎo] *sm* (*Bot*) millet
migliora'mento [miʎʎora'mento] *sm*
improvement
miglio'rare [miʎʎo'rare] *vt, vi* to improve
migli'ore [miʎ'ʎore] *ag* (*comparativo*) better;
(*superlativo*) best ■ *sm*: **il ~** the best (thing)
■ *sm/f*: **il(la) ~** the best (person); **il miglior
vino di questa regione** the best wine in this
area; **i migliori auguri** best wishes
miglio'ria [miʎʎo'ria] *sf* improvement
mignolo ['miɲɲolo] *sm* (*Anat*) little finger,
pinkie; (*: dito del piede*) little toe
mi'grare *vi* to migrate
migrazi'one [migrat'tsjone] *sf* migration
mila *pl di* **mille**
mila'nese *ag* Milanese ■ *sm/f* person from
Milan; **i milanesi** the Milanese; **cotoletta
alla ~** (*Cuc*) Wiener schnitzel; **risotto alla ~**
(*Cuc*) *risotto with saffron*
Mi'lano *sf* Milan
miliar'dario, -a *ag, sm/f* millionaire
mili'ardo *sm* thousand million (*Brit*), billion
(*US*)
mili'are *ag*: **pietra ~** milestone
milio'nario, -a *ag, sm/f* millionaire

mili'one sm million; **un ~ di euro** a million euros

mili'tante ag, sm/f militant

mili'tanza [mili'tantsa] sf militancy

mili'tare vi (Mil) to be a soldier, serve; (fig: in un partito) to be a militant ■ ag military ■ sm serviceman; **fare il ~** to do one's military service; **~ di carriera** regular (soldier)

milita'resco, -a, schi, sche ag (portamento) military cpd

'milite sm soldier

mi'lizia [mi'littsja] sf (corpo armato) militia

milizi'ano [milit'tsjano] sm militiaman

millanta'tore, -'trice sm/f boaster

millante'ria sf (qualità) boastfulness

'mille (pl **mila**) num a o one thousand; **diecimila** ten thousand

mille'foglie [mille'fɔʎʎe] sm inv (Cuc) cream o vanilla slice

mil'lennio sm millennium

millepi'edi sm inv centipede

mil'lesimo, -a ag, sm thousandth

milli'grammo sm milligram(me)

mil'lilitro sm millilitre (Brit), milliliter (US)

mil'limetro sm millimetre (Brit), millimeter (US)

'milza ['miltsa] sf (Anat) spleen

mi'metico, -a, ci, che ag (arte) mimetic; **tuta mimetica** (Mil) camouflage

mime'tismo sm camouflage

mimetiz'zare [mimetid'dzare] vt to camouflage; **mimetizzarsi** vr to camouflage o.s.

'mimica sf (arte) mime

'mimo sm (attore, componimento) mime

mi'mosa sf mimosa

min. abbr (= minuto, minimo) min

'mina sf (esplosiva) mine; (di matita) lead

mi'naccia, -ce [mi'nattʃa] sf threat; **sotto la ~ di** under threat of

minacci'are [minat'tʃare] vt to threaten; **~ qn di morte** to threaten to kill sb; **~ di fare qc** to threaten to do sth; **minaccia di piovere** it looks like rain

minacci'oso, -a [minat'tʃoso] ag threatening

mi'nare vt (Mil) to mine; (fig) to undermine

mina'tore sm miner

mina'torio, -a ag threatening

minchi'one, -a [min'kjone] ag (fam) idiotic ■ sm/f idiot

mine'rale ag, sm mineral

mineralo'gia [mineralo'dʒia] sf mineralogy

mine'rario, -a ag (delle miniere) mining; (dei minerali) ore cpd

mi'nestra sf soup; **~ in brodo** noodle soup; **~ di verdura** vegetable soup

mines'trone sm thick vegetable and pasta soup

mingher'lino, -a [minger'lino] ag thin, slender

'mini ag inv mini ■ sf inv miniskirt

minia'tura sf miniature

mini'bar sm inv minibar

minielabora'tore sm minicomputer

mini'era sf mine; **~ di carbone** coalmine; (impresa) colliery (Brit), coalmine

mini'gonna sf miniskirt

minima'lista, -i, e ag, sm/f minimalist

minimiz'zare [minimid'dzare] vt to minimize

'minimo, -a ag minimum, least, slightest; (piccolissimo) very small, slight; (il più basso) lowest, minimum ■ sm minimum; **al ~** at least; **girare al ~** (Aut) to idle; **il ~ indispensabile** the bare minimum; **il ~ della pena** the minimum sentence

minis'tero sm (Pol, Rel) ministry; (governo) government; (Dir): **Pubblico M~** State Prosecutor; **M~ delle Finanze** Ministry of Finance, ≈ Treasury

mi'nistro sm (Pol, Rel) minister; **M~ delle Finanze** Minister of Finance, ≈ Chancellor of the Exchequer (Brit)

mino'ranza [mino'rantsa] sf minority; **essere in ~** to be in the minority

mino'rato, -a ag handicapped ■ sm/f physically o mentally) handicapped person

minorazi'one [minorat'tsjone] sf handicap

Mi'norca sf Minorca

mi'nore ag (comparativo) less; (più piccolo) smaller; (numero) lower; (inferiore) lower, inferior; (meno importante) minor; (più giovane) younger; (superlativo) least; smallest; lowest; least important; youngest ■ sm/f (minorenne) minor, person under age; **in misura ~** to a lesser extent; **questo è il male ~** this is the lesser evil

mino'renne ag under age ■ sm/f minor, person under age

mino'rile ag juvenile; **carcere ~** young offenders' institution; **delinquenza ~** juvenile delinquency

minori'tario, -a ag minority cpd

mi'nuscolo, -a ag (scrittura, carattere) small; (piccolissimo) tiny ■ sf small letter ■ sm small letters pl; (Tip) lower case; **scrivere tutto (in) ~** to write everything in small letters

mi'nuta sf rough copy, draft

mi'nuto, -a ag tiny, minute; (pioggia) fine; (corporatura) delicate, fine; (lavoro) detailed ■ sm (unità di misura) minute; **al ~** (Comm) retail; **avere i minuti contati** to have very little time

m

mi'nuzia [mi'nuttsja] *sf* (*cura*) meticulousness; (*particolare*) detail

minuziosa'mente [minuttsjosa'mente] *av* meticulously; in minute detail

minuzi'oso, -a [minut'tsjoso] *ag* (*persona, descrizione*) meticulous; (*esame*) minute

'mio, 'mia, mi'ei, 'mie *det*: **il ~, la mia** *etc* my *pron*: **il ~, la mia** *etc* mine ■ *sm*: **ho speso del ~** I spent my own money ■ *sf*: **la mia** (*opinione*) my view; **i miei** my family; **un ~ amico** a friend of mine; **per amor ~** for my sake; **è dalla mia** he is on my side; **anch'io ho avuto le mie** (*disavventure*) I've had my problems too; **ne ho fatta una delle mie!** (*sciocchezze*) I've done it again!; **cerco di stare sulle mie** I try to keep myself to myself

'miope *ag* short-sighted

mio'pia *sf* short-sightedness, myopia; (*fig*) short-sightedness

'mira *sf* (*anche fig*) aim; **avere una buona/ cattiva ~** to be a good/bad shot; **prendere la ~** to take aim; **prendere di ~ qn** (*fig*) to pick on sb

mi'rabile *ag* admirable, wonderful

mi'racolo *sm* miracle

miraco'loso, -a *ag* miraculous

mi'raggio [mi'raddʒo] *sm* mirage

mi'rare *vi*: **~ a** to aim at

mi'rato, -a *ag* targetted

mi'riade *sf* myriad

mi'rino *sm* (*Tecn*) sight; (*Fot*) viewer, viewfinder

mir'tillo *sm* bilberry (*Brit*), blueberry (*US*), whortleberry

'mirto *sm* myrtle

mi'santropo, -a *sm/f* misanthropist

mi'scela [miʃ'ʃela] *sf* mixture; (*di caffè*) blend

miscel'lanea [miʃʃel'lanea] *sf* miscellany

'mischia ['miskja] *sf* scuffle; (*Rugby*) scrum, scrummage

mischi'are [mis'kjare] *vt*, **mischi'arsi** *vr* to mix, blend

misco'noscere [misko'noʃʃere] *vt* (*qualità, coraggio etc*) to fail to appreciate

miscre'dente *ag* (*Rel*) misbelieving; (*: incredulo*) unbelieving ■ *sm/f* misbeliever; unbeliever

mis'cuglio [mis'kuʎʎo] *sm* mixture, hotchpotch, jumble

'mise *vb vedi* **mettere**

mise'rabile *ag* (*infelice*) miserable, wretched; (*povero*) poverty-stricken; (*di scarso valore*) miserable

mi'seria *sf* extreme poverty; (*infelicità*) misery; **miserie** *sfpl* (*del mondo etc*) misfortunes, troubles; **costare una ~** to cost next to nothing; **piangere ~** to plead poverty;

ridursi in ~ to be reduced to poverty; **porca ~!** (*fam*) (bloody) hell!

miseri'cordia *sf* mercy, pity

misericordi'oso, -a *ag* merciful

'misero, -a *ag* miserable, wretched; (*povero*) poverty-stricken; (*insufficiente*) miserable

mis'fatto *sm* misdeed, crime

'misi *vb vedi* **mettere**

mi'sogino [mi'zɔdʒino] *sm* misogynist

'missile *sm* missile; **~ cruise** *o* **di crociera** cruise missile; **~ terra-aria** surface-to-air missile

missio'nario, -a *ag, sm/f* missionary

missi'one *sf* mission

misteri'oso, -a *ag* mysterious

mis'tero *sm* mystery; **fare ~ di qc** to make a mystery out of sth; **quanti misteri!** why all the mystery?

'mistico, -a, ci, che *ag* mystic(al) ■ *sm* mystic

mistifi'care *vt* to fool, bamboozle

'misto, -a *ag* mixed; (*scuola*) mixed, coeducational ■ *sm* mixture; **un tessuto in ~ lino** a linen mix

mis'tura *sf* mixture

mi'sura *sf* measure; (*misurazione, dimensione*) measurement; (*taglia*) size; (*provvedimento*) measure, step; (*moderazione*) moderation; (*Mus*) time; (*: divisione*) bar; (*fig: limite*) bounds *pl*, limit; **in ~ di** in accordance with, according to; **nella ~ in cui** inasmuch as, insofar as; **in giusta ~** moderately; **oltre ~** beyond measure; **su ~** made to measure; **in ugual ~** equally, in the same way; **a ~ d'uomo** on a human scale; **passare la ~** to overstep the mark, go too far; **prendere le misure a qn** to take sb's measurements, measure sb; **prendere le misure di qc** to measure sth; **ho preso le mie misure** I've taken the necessary steps; **non ha il senso della ~** he doesn't know when to stop; **~ di lunghezza/capacità** measure of length/ capacity; **misure di sicurezza/ prevenzione** safety/precautionary measures

misu'rare *vt* (*ambiente, stoffa*) to measure; (*terreno*) to survey; (*abito*) to try on; (*pesare*) to weigh; (*fig: parole etc*) to weigh up; (*: spese, cibo*) to limit ■ *vi* to measure; **misurarsi** *vr*: **misurarsi con qn** to have a confrontation with sb; (*competere*) to compete with sb

misu'rato, -a *ag* (*ponderato*) measured; (*prudente*) cautious; (*moderato*) moderate

misurazi'one [mizurat'tsjone] *sf* measuring; (*di terreni*) surveying

'mite *ag* mild; (*prezzo*) moderate, reasonable

'mitico, -a, ci, che *ag* mythical

miti'gare *vt* to mitigate, lessen; *(lenire)* to soothe, relieve; **mitigarsi** *vr (odio)* to subside; *(tempo)* to become milder

'mitilo *sm* mussel

'mito *sm* myth

mitolo'gia, -'gie [mitolo'dʒia] *sf* mythology

mito'logico, -a, ci, che [mito'lɔdʒiko] *ag* mythological

'mitra *sf (Rel)* mitre *(Brit)*, miter *(US)* ■ *sm inv (arma)* sub-machine gun

mitragli'are [mitraʎ'ʎare] *vt* to machine-gun

mitraglia'tore, -'trice [mitraʎʎa'tore] *ag*: **fucile ~** sub-machine gun ■ *sf* machine gun

mitteleuro'peo, -a *ag* Central European

mit'tente *sm/f* sender

ml *abbr (= millilitro)* ml

MLD *sigla m* = **Movimento per la Liberazione della Donna**

MM *abbr* = **Metropolitana Milanese**

mm *abbr (= millimetro)* mm

M.M. *abbr* = **marina militare**

mms *sigla m inv (= multimedia messaging service)* *(servizio)* MMS *(= multimedia messaging service)*; *(messaggio)* MMS message

MN *sigla* = **Mantova**

M/N, m/n *abbr (= motonave)* MV

MO *sigla* = **Modena**

M.O. *abbr* = **Medio Oriente**

mo' *sm*: **a ~di** *prep* like; **a ~di esempio** by way of example

'mobile *ag* mobile; *(parte di macchina)* moving; *(Dir: bene)* movable, personal ■ *sm (arredamento)* piece of furniture; **mobili** *smpl* furniture *sg*

mo'bilia *sf* furniture

mobili'are *ag (Dir)* personal, movable

mo'bilio *sm* = **mobilia**

mobilità *sf* mobility

mobili'tare *vt* to mobilize; **~ l'opinione pubblica** to rouse public opinion

mobilitazi'one [mobilitat'tsjone] *sf* mobilization

mocas'sino *sm* moccasin

mocci'oso, -a [mot'tʃoso] *sm/f (bambino piccolo)* little kid; *(peg)* snotty-nosed kid

'moccolo *sm (di candela)* candle end; *(fam: bestemmia)* oath; *(moccio)* snot; **reggere il ~** to play gooseberry *(Brit)* act as chaperon(e)

'moda *sf* fashion; **alla ~, di ~** fashionable, in fashion

modalità *sf inv* formality; **seguire attentamente le ~ d'uso** to follow the instructions carefully; **~ giuridiche** legal procedures; **~ di pagamento** method of payment

mo'della *sf* model

model'lare *vt (creta)* to model, shape; **modellarsi** *vr*: **modellarsi su** to model o.s. on

mo'dello *sm* model; *(stampo)* mould *(Brit)*, mold *(US)* ■ *ag inv* model *cpd*

'modem *sm inv* modem

mode'nese *ag* of *(o* from) Modena

mode'rare *vt* to moderate; **moderarsi** *vr* to restrain o.s.; **~ la velocità** to reduce speed; **~ i termini** to weigh one's words

mode'rato, -a *ag* moderate

modera'tore, -'trice *sm/f* moderator

moderazi'one [moderat'tsjone] *sf* moderation

moderniz'zare [modernid'dzare] *vt* to bring up to date, modernize; **modernizzarsi** *vr* to get up to date

mo'derno, -a *ag* modern

mo'destia *sf* modesty; **~ a parte ...** in all modesty ..., though I say it myself ...

mo'desto, -a *ag* modest

'modico, -a, ci, che *ag* reasonable, moderate

mo'difica, -che *sf* modification; **subire delle modifiche** to undergo some modifications

modifi'cabile *ag* modifiable

modifi'care *vt* to modify, alter; **modificarsi** *vr* to alter, change

mo'dista *sf* milliner

'modo *sm* way, manner; *(mezzo)* means, way; *(occasione)* opportunity; *(Ling)* mood; *(Mus)* mode; **modi** *smpl (maniere)* manners; **a suo ~, a ~ suo** in his own way; **ad o in ogni ~** anyway; **di o in ~ che** so that; **in ~ da** so as to; **in tutti i modi** at all costs; *(comunque sia)* anyway; *(in ogni caso)* in any case; **in un certo qual ~** in a way, in some ways; **in qualche ~** somehow or other; **oltre ~** extremely; **~ di dire** turn of phrase; **per ~ di dire** so to speak; **fare a ~ proprio** to do as one likes; **fare le cose a ~** to do things properly; **una persona a ~** a well-mannered person; **c'è ~ e ~ di farlo** there's a right way and a wrong way of doing it

modu'lare *vt* to modulate ■ *ag* modular

modulazi'one [modulat'tsjone] *sf* modulation; **~ di frequenza FM** frequency modulation (FM)

'modulo *sm (modello)* form; *(Archit: lunare, di comando)* module; **~ di domanda** application form; **~ d'iscrizione** enrolment form; **~ di versamento** deposit slip

Moga'discio [moga'diʃʃo] *sm* Mogadishu

'mogano *sm* mahogany

'mogio, -a, gi, gie ['mɔdʒo] *ag* down in the dumps, dejected

'moglie ['moʎʎe] *sf* wife

225

mo'hair [mɔ'ɛr] *sm* mohair
mo'ine *sfpl* cajolery *sg*; (*leziosità*) affectation *sg*;
fare le ~ a qn to cajole sb
'**mola** *sf* millstone; (*utensile abrasivo*)
grindstone
mo'lare *vt* to grind ■ *ag* (*pietra*) mill *cpd* ■ *sm*
(*dente*) molar
'**mole** *sf* mass; (*dimensioni*) size; (*edificio
grandioso*) massive structure; **una ~ di lavoro**
masses (*Brit*) *o* loads of work
mo'lecola *sf* molecule
moles'tare *vt* to bother, annoy
mo'lestia *sf* annoyance, bother; **recar ~ a qn**
to bother sb; **molestie sessuali** sexual
harassment *sg*
mo'lesto, -a *ag* annoying
moli'sano, -a *ag* of (*o* from) Molise
'**molla** *sf* spring; **molle** *sfpl* (*per camino*) tongs;
prendere qn con le molle to treat sb with
kid gloves
mol'lare *vt* to release, let go; (*Naut*) to ease;
(*fig: ceffone*) to give ■ *vi* (*cedere*) to give in; **~
gli ormeggi** (*Naut*) to cast off; **~ la presa** to
let go
'**molle** *ag* soft; (*muscoli*) flabby; (*fig: debole*)
weak, feeble
molleggi'ato, -a [molled'dʒato] *ag* (*letto*)
sprung; (*auto*) with good suspension
mol'leggio [mol'leddʒo] *sm* (*per veicoli*)
suspension; (*elasticità*) springiness;
(*Ginnastica*) knee-bends *pl*
mol'letta *sf* (*per capelli*) hairgrip; (*per panni
stesi*) clothes peg (*Brit*) *o* pin (*US*); **mollette**
sfpl (*per zucchero*) tongs
mol'lezza [mol'lettsa] *sf* softness flabbiness
weakness, feebleness; **mollezze** *sfpl*: **vivere
nelle mollezze** to live in the lap of luxury
mol'lica, -che *sf* crumb, soft part
mol'liccio, -a, ci, ce [mol'littʃo] *ag* (*terreno,
impasto*) soggy; (*frutta*) soft; (*floscio: mano*)
limp; (*muscolo*) flabby
mol'lusco, -schi *sm* mollusc
'**molo** *sm* jetty, pier
mol'teplice [mol'teplitʃe] *ag* (*formato di più
elementi*) complex; **molteplici** *pl* (*svariati:
interessi, attività*) numerous, various
molteplicità [molteplitʃi'ta] *sf* multiplicity
moltipli'care *vt* to multiply; **moltiplicarsi** *vr*
to multiply; (*richieste*) to increase in number
moltiplicazi'one [moltiplikat'tsjone] *sf*
multiplication
molti'tudine *sf* multitude; **una ~ di** a vast
number *o* a multitude of
'**molto, -a** *det* (*quantità*) a lot of, much;
(*numero*) a lot of, many; **~ pane/carbone** a lot
of bread/coal; **molta gente** a lot of people,
many people; **molti libri** a lot of books,

many books; **non ho ~ tempo** I haven't got
much time; **per ~ (tempo)** for a long time;
ci vuole ~ (tempo)? will it take long?;
arriverà fra non ~ he'll arrive soon; **ne hai
per ~?** will you be long? ■ *av* a lot, (very)
much; **viaggia ~** he travels a lot; **non
viaggia ~** he doesn't travel much *o* a lot
(*intensivo con aggettivi, avverbi*), very; (*: con
participio passato*) (very) much; **~ buono** very
good; **~ migliore, ~ meglio** much *o* a lot
better ■ *pron* much, a lot; **molti, e** (*pl*)
many, a lot; **molti pensano che ...** many
(people) think that ...; **molte sono rimaste
a casa** a lot of them stayed at home; **c'era
gente, ma non molta** there were people
there, but not many
momentanea'mente *av* at the moment, at
present
momen'taneo, -a *ag* momentary, fleeting
mo'mento *sm* moment; **da un ~ all'altro**
at any moment; (*all'improvviso*) suddenly;
al ~ di fare just as I was (*o* you were *o* he
was *etc*) doing; **a momenti** (*da un mo'mento
all'altro*) any time *o* moment now; (*quasi*)
nearly; **per il ~** for the time being; **dal ~ che**
ever since; (*dato che*) since; **~ culminante**
climax
'**monaca, -che** *sf* nun
'**Monaco** *sf* Monaco; **~ (di Baviera)** Munich
'**monaco, -ci** *sm* monk
mo'narca, -chi *sm* monarch
monar'chia [monar'kia] *sf* monarchy
mo'narchico, -a, ci, che [mo'narkiko] *ag*
(*stato, autorità*) monarchic; (*partito, fede*)
monarchist ■ *sm/f* monarchist
monas'tero *sm* (*di monaci*) monastery; (*di
monache*) convent
mo'nastico, -a, ci, che *ag* monastic
'**monco, -a, chi, che** *ag* maimed; (*fig*)
incomplete; **~ d'un braccio** one-armed
mon'cone *sm* stump
mon'dana *sf* prostitute
mondanità *sf* (*frivolezza*) worldliness; **le ~**
(*piaceri*) the pleasures of the world
mon'dano, -a *ag* (*anche fig*) worldly; (*dell'alta
società*) society *cpd*; fashionable
mon'dare *vt* (*frutta, patate*) to peel; (*piselli*) to
shell; (*pulire*) to clean
mondez'zaio [mondet'tsajo] *sm* rubbish
(*Brit*) *o* garbage (*US*) dump
mondi'ale *ag* (*campionato, popolazione*) world
cpd; (*influenza*) world-wide; **di fama ~** world
famous
'**mondo** *sm* world; (*grande quantità*): **un ~ di**
lots of, a host of; **il gran** *o* **bel ~** high society;
per niente al ~, per nessuna cosa al ~ not
for all the world; **da che ~ è ~** since time *o*

the world began; **mandare qn all'altro** ~ to kill sb; **mettere/venire al** ~ to bring/come into the world; **vivere fuori dal** ~ to be out of touch with the real world; **(sono) cose dell'altro** ~! it's incredible!; **com'è piccolo il** ~! it's a small world!

mone'gasco, -a, schi, sche *ag, sm/f* Monegasque

monelle'ria *sf* prank, naughty trick

mo'nello, -a *sm/f* street urchin; (*ragazzo vivace*) scamp, imp

mo'neta *sf* coin; (*Econ: valuta*) currency; (*denaro spicciolo*) (small) change; ~ **estera** foreign currency; ~ **legale** legal tender

mone'tario, -a *ag* monetary

Mon'golia *sf*: **la** ~ Mongolia

mon'golico, -a, ci, che *ag* Mongolian

mongo'lismo *sm* Down's syndrome

'mongolo, -a *ag* Mongolian ■ *sm/f, sm* Mongol, Mongolian

mongo'loide *ag, sm/f* (*Med*) mongol

'monito *sm* warning

'monitor *sm inv* (*Tecn, TV*) monitor

monito'raggio [monito'raddʒo] *sm* monitoring

monito'rare *vt* to monitor

mo'nocolo *sm* (*lente*) monocle, eyeglass

monoco'lore *ag* (*Pol*): **governo** ~ one-party government

monoga'mia *sf* monogamy

mo'nogamo, -a *ag* monogamous ■ *sm* monogamist

monogra'fia *sf* monograph

mono'gramma, -i *sm* monogram

mono'lingue *ag* monolingual

monolo'cale *sm* ≈ studio flat

mo'nologo, -ghi *sm* monologue

mono'pattino *sm* scooter

mono'polio *sm* monopoly; ~ **di stato** government monopoly

monopoliz'zare [monopolid'dzare] *vt* to monopolize

mono'sillabo, -a *ag* monosyllabic ■ *sm* monosyllable

monoto'nia *sf* monotony

mo'notono, -a *ag* monotonous

mono'uso *ag inv* disposable

monovo'lume *sf inv* people carrier, people mover

Mons. *abbr* (= *Monsignore*) Mgr

monsi'gnore [monsiɲ'ɲore] *sm* (*Rel: titolo*) Your (*o* His) Grace

mon'sone *sm* monsoon

monta'carichi [monta'kariki] *sm inv* hoist, goods lift

mon'taggio [mon'taddʒo] *sm* (*Tecn*) assembly; (*Cine*) editing

mon'tagna [mon'taɲɲa] *sf* mountain; (*zona montuosa*): **la** ~ the mountains *pl*; **andare in** ~ to go to the mountains; **aria/strada di** ~ mountain air/road; **casa di** ~ house in the mountains; **montagne russe** roller coaster *sg*

monta'gnoso, -a [montaɲ'ɲoso] *ag* mountainous

monta'naro, -a *ag* mountain *cpd* ■ *sm/f* mountain dweller

mon'tano, -a *ag* mountain *cpd*

mon'tante *sm* (*di porta*) jamb; (*di finestra*) upright; (*Calcio: palo*) post; (*Pugilato*) upper cut; (*Comm*) total amount

mon'tare *vt* to go (*o* come) up; (*cavallo*) to ride; (*apparecchiatura*) to set up, assemble; (*Cuc*) to whip; (*Zool*) to cover; (*incastonare*) to mount, set; (*Cine*) to edit; (*Fot*) to mount ■ *vi* to go (*o* come) up; (*a cavallo*): ~ **bene/male** to ride well/badly; (*aumentare di livello, volume*) to rise; **montarsi** *vr* to become big-headed; ~ **qc** to exaggerate sth; ~ **qn** *o* **la testa a qn** to turn sb's head; **montarsi la testa** to become big-headed; ~ **in bicicletta/macchina/treno** to get on a bicycle/ into a car/on a train; ~ **a cavallo** to get on *o* mount a horse; ~ **la guardia** (*Mil*) to mount guard

monta'tura *sf* assembling *no pl*; (*di occhiali*) frames *pl*; (*di gioiello*) mounting, setting; (*fig*): ~ **pubblicitaria** publicity stunt

montavi'vande *sm inv* dumbwaiter

'monte *sm* mountain; **a** ~ upstream; **andare a** ~ (*fig*) to come to nothing; **mandare a** ~ **qc** (*fig*) to upset sth, cause sth to fail; **il M~ Bianco** Mont Blanc; **il M~ Everest** Mount Everest; ~ **di pietà** pawnshop; ~ **premi** prize

Monteci'torio [montetʃi'torjo] *sm*: **palazzo** ~ (*Pol*) seat of the Italian Chamber of Deputies

montene'grino, -a *ag, sm/f* Montenegrin

monte'negro *sm* Montenegro

mont'gomery [mənt'ɡʌməri] *sm inv* duffel coat

mon'tone *sm* (*Zool*) ram; (*anche*: **giacca di montone**) sheepskin (jacket); **carne di** ~ mutton

montuosità *sf* mountainous nature

montu'oso, -a *ag* mountainous

monu'mento *sm* monument

mo'quette [mɔ'kɛt] *sf* fitted carpet

'mora *sf* (*del rovo*) blackberry; (*del gelso*) mulberry; (*Dir*) delay; (*somma*) arrears *pl*

mo'rale *ag* moral ■ *sf* (*scienza*) ethics *sg*, moral philosophy; (*complesso di norme*) moral standards *pl*, morality; (*condotta*) morals *pl*; (*insegnamento morale*) moral ■ *sm* morale; **la** ~ **della favola** the moral of the tale; **essere giù di** ~ to be feeling down; **aver il** ~ **alto/a terra** to be in good/low spirits

m

mora'lista, -i, e *ag* moralistic ■ *sm/f* moralist

morali'tà *sf* morality; *(condotta)* morals *pl*

moraliz'zare [moralid'dzare] *vt (costumi, vita pubblica)* to set moral standards for

moralizzazi'one [moraliddzat'tsjone] *sf* setting of moral standards

mora'toria *sf (Dir)* moratorium

morbi'dezza [morbi'dettsa] *sf* softness; smoothness; tenderness

'morbido, -a *ag* soft; *(pelle)* soft, smooth; *(carne)* tender

mor'billo *sm (Med)* measles *sg*

'morbo *sm* disease

mor'boso, -a *ag (fig)* morbid

'morchia ['morkja] *sf (residuo grasso)* dregs *pl*; oily deposit

mor'dente *sm (fig: di satira, critica)* bite; *(di persona)* drive

'mordere *vt* to bite; *(addentare)* to bite into; *(corrodere)* to eat into

mordicchi'are [mordik'kjare] *vt (gen)* to chew at

mo'rente *ag* dying ■ *sm/f* dying man/woman

mor'fina *sf* morphine

mo'ria *sf* high mortality

mori'bondo, -a *ag* dying, moribund

morige'rato, -a [moridʒe'rato] *ag* of good morals

mo'rire *vi* to die; *(abitudine, civiltà)* to die out; **~ di dolore** to die of a broken heart; **~ di fame** to die of hunger; *(fig)* to be starving; **~ di freddo** to freeze to death; *(fig)* to be frozen; **~ d'invidia** to be green with envy; **~ di noia/paura** to be bored/scared to death; **~ dalla voglia di fare qc** to be dying to do sth; **fa un caldo da ~** it's terribly hot

mormo'rare *vi* to murmur; *(brontolare)* to grumble; **si mormora che ...** it's rumoured *(Brit)* o rumored *(US)* that ...; **la gente mormora** people are talking

mormo'rio *sm* murmuring; grumbling

'moro, -a *ag* dark(-haired), dark(-complexioned); **i Mori** *smpl (Storia)* the Moors

mo'roso, -a *ag* in arrears ■ *sm/f (fam: innamorato)* sweetheart

'morsa *sf (Tecn)* vice *(Brit)*, vise *(US)*; *(fig: stretta)* grip

mor'setto *sm (Tecn)* clamp; *(Elettr)* terminal

morsi'care *vt* to nibble (at), gnaw (at); *(insetto)* to bite

'morso, -a *pp di* **mordere** ■ *sm* bite; *(di insetto)* sting; *(parte della briglia)* bit; **dare un ~ a qc/qn** to bite sth/sb; **i morsi della fame** pangs of hunger

morta'della *sf (Cuc)* mortadella *(type of salted pork meat)*

mor'taio *sm* mortar

mor'tale *ag, sm* mortal

mortali'tà *sf* mortality; *(Statistica)* mortality, death rate

'morte *sf* death; **in punto di ~** at death's door; **ferito a ~** *(soldato)* mortally wounded; *(in incidente)* fatally injured; **essere annoiato a ~** to be bored to death o to tears; **avercela a ~ con qn** to be bitterly resentful of sb; **avere la ~ nel cuore** to have a heavy heart

mortifi'care *vt* to mortify

'morto, -a *pp di* **morire** ■ *ag* dead ■ *sm/f* dead man/woman; **i morti** the dead; **fare il ~** *(nell'acqua)* to float on one's back; **un ~ di fame** *(fig peg)* a down-and-out; **le campane suonavano a ~** the funeral bells were tolling; *vedi anche* **Giorno dei Morti**

mor'torio *sm (anche fig)* funeral

mo'saico, -ci *sm* mosaic; **l'ultimo tassello del ~** *(fig)* the last piece of the puzzle

'Mosca *sf* Moscow

'mosca, -sche *sf* fly; **rimanere** o **restare con un pugno di mosche** *(fig)* to be left empty-handed; **non si sentiva volare una ~** *(fig)* you could have heard a pin drop; **~ cieca** blind-man's buff

mos'cato *sm* muscatel (wine)

mosce'rino [moʃʃe'rino] *sm* midge, gnat

mos'chea [mos'kεa] *sf* mosque

mos'chetto [mos'ketto] *sm* musket

moschet'tone [mosket'tone] *sm (gancio)* spring clip; *(Alpinismo)* karabiner, snaplink

moschi'cida, -i, e [moski'tʃida] *ag* fly *cpd*; **carta ~** flypaper

'moscio, -a, sci, sce ['moʃʃo] *ag (fig)* lifeless; **ha la "r" moscia** he can't roll his "r"s

mos'cone *sm (Zool)* bluebottle; *(barca)* pedalo; *(: a remi)* kind of pedalo with oars

mosco'vita, -i, e *ag, sm/f* Muscovite

'mossa *sf* movement; *(nel gioco)* move; **darsi una ~** *(fig)* to give o.s. a shake; **prendere le mosse da qc** to come about as the result of sth

'mossi *etc vb vedi* **muovere**

'mosso, -a *pp di* **muovere** ■ *ag (mare)* rough; *(capelli)* wavy; *(Fot)* blurred; *(ritmo, prosa)* animated

mos'tarda *sf* mustard

'mosto *sm* must

'mostra *sf* exhibition, show; *(ostentazione)* show; **in ~** on show; **far ~ di** *(fingere)* to pretend; **far ~ di sé** to show off; **mettersi in ~** to draw attention to o.s.

mos'trare *vt* to show ■ *vi*: **~ di fare** to pretend to do; **mostrarsi** *vr* to appear; **~ la lingua** to stick out one's tongue

'mostro sm monster

mostru'oso, -a ag monstrous

mo'tel sm inv motel

moti'vare vt (causare) to cause; (giustificare) to justify, account for

motivazi'one [motivat'tsjone] sf justification; (Psic) motivation

mo'tivo sm (causa) reason, cause; (movente) motive; (letterario) (central) theme; (disegno) motif, design, pattern; (Mus) motif; **per quale ~?** why?, for what reason?; **per motivi di salute** for health reasons, on health grounds; **motivi personali** personal reasons

'moto sm (anche Fisica) motion; (movimento, gesto) movement; (esercizio fisico) exercise; (sommossa) rising, revolt; (commozione) feeling, impulse ■ sf inv (motocicletta) motorbike; **fare del ~** to take some exercise; **un ~ d'impazienza** an impatient gesture; **mettere in ~** to set in motion; (Aut) to start up; **~ d'acqua** Jet Ski®

moto'carro sm three-wheeler van

motoci'cletta [mototʃi'kletta] sf motorcycle

motoci'clismo [mototʃi'klizmo] sm motorcycling, motorcycle racing

motoci'clista, -i, e [mototʃi'klista] sm/f motorcyclist

moto'nave sf motor vessel

motopesche'reccio [motopeske'rettʃo] sm motor fishing vessel

mo'tore, -'trice ag motor; (Tecn) driving ■ sm engine, motor ■ sf (Tecn) engine, motor; **albero ~** drive shaft; **forza motrice** driving force; **a ~** cpd, power-driven; **~ a combustione interna/a reazione** internal combustion/jet engine; **~ di ricerca** (Inform) search engine

moto'rino sm moped; **~ di avviamento** (Aut) starter

motoriz'zato, -a [motorid'dzato] ag (truppe) motorized; (persona) having a car o transport

motorizzazi'one [motoriddzat'tsjone] sf (ufficio tecnico e organizzativo): **(ufficio della) ~** road traffic office

motos'cafo sm motorboat

motove'detta sf motor patrol vessel

mo'trice [mo'tritʃe] sf vedi **motore**

mot'teggio [mot'teddʒo] sm banter

'motto sm (battuta scherzosa) witty remark; (frase emblematica) motto, maxim

mountain bike sf inv mountain bike

'mouse ['maus] sm inv (Inform) mouse

mo'vente sm motive

mo'venza [mo'vɛntsa] sf movement

movimen'tare vt to liven up

movimen'tato, -a ag (festa, partita) lively; (riunione) animated; (strada, vita) busy; (soggiorno) eventful

movi'mento sm movement; (fig) activity, hustle and bustle; (Mus) tempo, movement; **essere sempre in ~** to be always on the go; **fare un po' di ~** (esercizio fisico) to take some exercise; **c'è molto ~ in città** the town is very busy; **~ di capitali** movement of capital; **M~ per la Liberazione della Donna** Women's Movement

movi'ola sf moviola; **rivedere qc alla ~** to see an action (Brit) o instant (US) replay of sth

Mozam'bico [moddzam'biko] sm: **il ~** Mozambique

mozi'one [mot'tsjone] sf (Pol) motion; **~ d'ordine** (Pol) point of order

mozzafi'ato [mottsa'fjato] ag inv breathtaking

moz'zare [mot'tsare] vt to cut off; (coda) to dock; **~ il fiato o il respiro a qn** (fig) to take sb's breath away

mozza'rella [mottsa'rella] sf mozzarella

mozzi'cone [mottsi'kone] sm stub, butt, end; (anche: **mozzicone di sigaretta**) cigarette end

'mozzo¹ ['mɔddzo] sm (Meccanica) hub

'mozzo² ['mottso] sm (Naut) ship's boy; **~ di stalla** stable boy

mq abbr (= metro quadro) sq.m

MS sigla = **Massa Carrara**

M.S.I. sigla m (= Movimento Sociale Italiano) former right-wing political party

Mti abbr = **monti**

'mucca, -che sf cow; **~ pazza** BSE; **(morbo della) ~ pazza** mad cow disease, BSE; **l'emergenza ~ pazza** the mad cow crisis

'mucchio ['mukkjo] sm pile, heap; (fig): **un ~ di** lots of, heaps of

mucil'lagine [mutʃil'ladʒine] sf (Bot) mucilage (green slime produced by plants growing in water)

'muco, -chi sm mucus

mu'cosa sf mucous membrane

'muesli ['mjusli] sm muesli

'muffa sf mould (Brit), mold (US), mildew; **fare la ~** to go mouldy (Brit) o moldy (US)

mugghi'are [mug'gjare] vi (fig: mare, tuono) to roar; (vento) to howl

mug'gire [mud'dʒire] vi (vacca) to low, moo; (toro) to bellow; (fig) to roar

mug'gito [mud'dʒito] sm moo; bellow; roar

mu'ghetto [mu'getto] sm lily of the valley

mu'gnaio, -a [muɲ'ɲajo] sm/f miller

mugo'lare vi (cane) to whimper, whine; (fig: persona) to moan

mugu'gnare [muguɲ'ɲare] vi (fam) to mutter, mumble

mulatti'era *sf* mule track

mu'latto, -a *ag, sm/f* mulatto

muli'nare *vi* to whirl, spin round (and round)

muli'nello *sm* (*moto vorticoso*) eddy, whirl; (*di canna da pesca*) reel; (*Naut*) windlass

mu'lino *sm* mill; **~ a vento** windmill

'mulo *sm* mule

'multa *sf* fine

mul'tare *vt* to fine

multico'lore *ag* multicoloured (*Brit*), multicolored (*US*)

multi'etnico, -a, ci, che *ag* multiethnic

multi'forme *ag* (*paesaggio, attività, interessi*) varied; (*ingegno*) versatile

multimedi'ale *ag* multimedia *cpd*

multinazio'nale [multinattsjo'nale] *ag, sf* multinational; **forza ~ di pace** multinational peace-keeping force

'multiplo, -a *ag, sm* multiple

multiu'tenza [multiu'tɛntsa] *sf* (*Inform*) time sharing

'mummia *sf* mummy

'mungere ['mundʒere] *vt* (*anche fig*) to milk

mungi'tura [mundʒi'tura] *sf* milking

munici'pale [munitʃi'pale] *ag* (*gen*) municipal; **palazzo ~** town hall; **autorità municipali** local authorities (*Brit*), local government *sg*

muni'cipio [muni'tʃipjo] *sm* town council; (*edificio*) town hall; **sposarsi in ~ ≈** to get married in a registry office (*Brit*), have a civil marriage

munifi'cenza [munifi'tʃɛntsa] *sf* munificence

mu'nifico, -a, ci, che *ag* munificent, generous

mu'nire *vt*: **~ qc/qn di** to equip sth/sb with; **~ di firma** (*documento*) to sign

munizi'oni [munit'tsjoni] *sfpl* (*Mil*) ammunition *sg*

'munsi *etc vb vedi* **mungere**

'munto, -a *pp di* **mungere**

mu'oio *etc vb vedi* **morire**

mu'overe *vt* to move; (*ruota, macchina*) to drive; (*sollevare: questione, obiezione*) to raise, bring up; (*accusa*) to make, bring forward; **muoversi** *vr* to move; **~ causa a qn** (*Dir*) to take legal action against sb; **~ a compassione** to move to pity; **~ guerra a** *o* **contro qn** to wage war against sb; **~ mari e monti** to move heaven and earth; **~ al pianto** to move to tears; **~ i primi passi** to take one's first steps; (*fig*) to be starting out; **muoviti!** hurry up!, get a move on!

'mura *sfpl vedi* **muro**

mu'raglia [mu'raʎʎa] *sf* (high) wall

mu'rale *ag* wall *cpd*; mural

mu'rare *vt* (*persona, porta*) to wall up

mu'rario, -a *ag* building *cpd*; **arte muraria** masonry

mura'tore *sm* (*con pietre*) mason; (*con mattoni*) bricklayer

mura'tura *sf* (*lavoro murario*) masonry; **casa in ~** (*di pietra*) stonebuilt house; (*di mattoni*) brick house

'muro *sm* wall; **mura** *sfpl* (*cinta cittadina*) walls; **a ~** wall *cpd*; (*armadio etc*) built-in; **mettere al ~** (*fucilare*) to shoot *o* execute (by firing squad); **~ di cinta** surrounding wall; **~ divisorio** dividing wall; **~ del suono** sound barrier

'musa *sf* muse

'muschio ['muskjo] *sm* (*Zool*) musk; (*Bot*) moss

musco'lare *ag* muscular, muscle *cpd*

muscola'tura *sf* muscle structure

'muscolo *sm* (*Anat*) muscle

musco'loso, -a *ag* muscular

mu'seo *sm* museum

museru'ola *sf* muzzle

'musica *sf* music; **~ da ballo/camera** dance/chamber music

musi'cale *ag* musical

musicas'setta *sf* (pre-recorded) cassette

musi'cista, -i, e [muzi'tʃista] *sm/f* musician

musi'comane *sm/f* music lover

'muso *sm* muzzle; (*di auto, aereo*) nose; **tenere il ~** to sulk

mu'sone, -a *sm/f* sulky person

'mussola *sf* muslin

mus(s)ul'mano, -a *ag, sm/f* Muslim, Moslem

'muta *sf* (*di animali*) moulting (*Brit*), molting (*US*); (*di serpenti*) sloughing; (*per immersioni subacquee*) diving suit; (*gruppo di cani*) pack

mu'tabile *ag* changeable

muta'mento *sm* change

mu'tande *sfpl* (*da uomo*) (under)pants

mutan'dine *sfpl* (*da donna, bambino*) pants (*Brit*), briefs; **~ di plastica** plastic pants

mu'tare *vt, vi* to change, alter

mutazi'one [mutat'tsjone] *sf* change, alteration; (*Biol*) mutation

mu'tevole *ag* changeable

muti'lare *vt* to mutilate, maim; (*fig*) to mutilate, deface

muti'lato, -a *sm/f* disabled person; (*through loss of limbs*): **~ di guerra** disabled ex-serviceman (*Brit*) *o* war veteran (*US*)

mutilazi'one [mutilat'tsjone] *sf* mutilation

mu'tismo *sm* (*Med*) mutism; (*atteggiamento*) (stubborn) silence

'muto, -a *ag* (*Med*) dumb; (*emozione, dolore, Cine*) silent; (*Ling*) silent, mute; (*carta geografica*) blank; **~ per lo stupore** *etc* speechless with amazement *etc*; **ha fatto scena muta** he didn't utter a word '**mutua** *sf* (*anche*: **cassa mutua**) health insurance scheme; **medico della ~** ≈ National Health Service doctor (*Brit*)

mutu'are *vt* (*fig*) to borrow

mutu'ato, -a *sm/f* member of a health insurance scheme

'**mutuo, -a** *ag* (*reciproco*) mutual ■ *sm* (*Econ*) (long-term) loan; **~ ipotecario** mortgage

Nn

N, n ['εnne] *sf o m (lettera)* N, n; **N come Napoli** ≈ N for Nellie (*Brit*), N for Nan (*US*)
N *abbr* (= *nord*) N
n *abbr* (= *numero*) no
NA *sigla* = **Napoli**
na'babbo *sm* (*anche fig*) nabob
'nacchere ['nakkere] *sfpl* castanets
NAD *sigla m* = **nucleo anti-droga**
na'dir *sm* (*Astr*) nadir
'nafta *sf* naphtha; (*per motori diesel*) diesel oil
nafta'lina *sf* (*Chim*) naphthalene; (*tarmicida*) mothballs *pl*
'naia *sf* (*Zool*) cobra; (*Mil*) *slang term for national service*
na'if [na'if] *ag inv* naïve
'nailon *sm* = **nylon**
Nai'robi *sf* Nairobi
'nanna *sf* (*linguaggio infantile*): **andare a ~** to go to beddy-byes
'nano, -a *ag, sm/f* dwarf
napole'tano, -a *ag, sm/f* Neapolitan ■ *sf* (*macchinetta da caffè*) Neapolitan coffee pot
'Napoli *sf* Naples
'nappa *sf* tassel
nar'ciso [nar'tʃizo] *sm* narcissus
'narcos *sm inv* (*colombiano*) Colombian drug trafficker
narco'dollari *smpl* drug money *sg*
nar'cosi *sf* general anaesthesia, narcosis
nar'cotico, -ci *ag* narcotic
narcotraffi'cante *sm/f* drug trafficker
narco'traffico *sm* drug trade
na'rice [na'ritʃe] *sf* nostril
nar'rare *vt* to tell the story of, recount
narra'tivo, -a *ag* narrative ■ *sf* (*branca*) fiction
narra'tore, -'trice *sm/f* narrator
narrazi'one [narrat'tsjone] *sf* narration; (*racconto*) story, tale
N.A.S.A. ['naza] *sigla f* (= *National Aeronautics and Space Administration*) NASA
na'sale *ag* nasal
na'scente [naʃʃɛnte] *ag* (*sole, luna*) rising

'nascere ['naʃʃere] *vi* (*bambino*) to be born; (*pianta*) to come o spring up; (*fiume*) to rise, have its source; (*sole*) to rise; (*dente*) to come through; (*fig: derivare, conseguire*): **~ da** to arise from, be born out of; **è nata nel 1952** she was born in 1952; **da cosa nasce cosa** one thing leads to another
'nascita ['naʃʃita] *sf* birth
nasci'turo, -a [naʃʃi'turo] *sm/f* future child; **come si chiamerà il ~?** what's the baby going to be called?
nas'condere *vt* to hide, conceal; **nascondersi** *vr* to hide
nascon'diglio [naskon'diʎʎo] *sm* hiding place
nascon'dino *sm* (*gioco*) hide-and-seek
nas'cosi *etc vb vedi* **nascondere**
nas'costo, -a *pp di* **nascondere** ■ *ag* hidden; **di ~** secretly
na'sello *sm* (*Zool*) hake
'naso *sm* nose
Nas'sau *sf* Nassau
'nastro *sm* ribbon; (*magnetico, isolante, Sport*) tape; **~ adesivo** adhesive tape; **~ trasportatore** conveyor belt
nas'turzio [nas'turtsjo] *sm* nasturtium
na'tale *ag* of one's birth ■ *sm* (*Rel*): **N~** Christmas; (*giorno della nascita*) birthday; **natali** *smpl*: **di illustri/umili natali** of noble/humble birth
nata'lità *sf* birth rate
nata'lizio, -a [nata'littsjo] *ag* (*del Natale*) Christmas *cpd*
na'tante *sm* craft *inv*, boat
'natica, -che *sf* (*Anat*) buttock
na'tio, -a, tii, tie *ag* native
Nativi'tà *sf* (*Rel*) Nativity
na'tivo, -a *ag, sm/f* native
'nato, -a *pp di* **nascere** ■ *ag*: **un attore ~ a** born actor; **nata Pieri** née Pieri
'N.A.T.O. *sigla f* NATO (= *North Atlantic Treaty Organization*)
na'tura *sf* nature; **pagare in ~** to pay in kind; **~ morta** still life

natu'rale *ag* natural ◼ *sm*: **al ~** (*alimenti*) served plain; (*ritratto*) life-size; (**ma**) **è ~!** (*in risposte*) of course!; **a grandezza ~** life-size; **acqua ~** spring water

natura'lezza [natura'lettsa] *sf* naturalness

natura'lista, -i, e *sm/f* naturalist

naturaliz'zare [naturalid'dzare] *vt* to naturalize

natural'mente *av* naturally; (*certamente, sì*) of course

natu'rismo *sm* naturism, nudism

natu'rista, -i, e *ag, sm/f* naturist, nudist

naufra'gare *vi* (*nave*) to be wrecked; (*persona*) to be shipwrecked; (*fig*) to fall through

nau'fragio [nau'fradʒo] *sm* shipwreck; (*fig*) ruin, failure

'naufrago, -ghi *sm* castaway, shipwreck victim

'nausea *sf* nausea; **avere la ~** to feel sick (*Brit*) *o* ill (*US*); **fino alla ~** ad nauseam

nausea'bondo, -a *ag*; **nause'ante** *ag* nauseating, sickening

nause'are *vt* to nauseate, make (feel) sick (*Brit*) *o* ill (*US*)

'nautico, -a, ci, che *ag* nautical ◼ *sf* (art of) navigation; **salone ~** (*mostra*) boat show

na'vale *ag* naval; **battaglia ~** naval battle; (*gioco*) battleships *pl*

na'vata *sf* (*anche*: **navata centrale**) nave; (*anche*: **navata laterale**) aisle

'nave *sf* ship, vessel; **~ da carico** cargo ship, freighter; **~ cisterna** tanker; **~ da guerra** warship; **~ di linea** liner; **~ passeggeri** passenger ship; **~ portaerei** aircraft carrier; **~ spaziale** spaceship

na'vetta *sf* shuttle; (*servizio di collegamento*) shuttle (service)

navi'cella [navi'tʃella] *sf* (*di aerostato*) gondola; **~ spaziale** spaceship

navi'gabile *ag* navigable

navi'gante *sm* sailor, seaman

navi'gare *vi* to sail; **~ in cattive acque** (*fig*) to be in deep water; **~ in Internet** to surf the Net

navi'gato, -a *ag* (*fig: esperto*) experienced

naviga'tore, -'trice *sm/f* (*gen*) navigator; **~ solitario** single-handed sailor; **~ satellite** satellite navigator

navigazi'one [navigat'tsjone] *sf* navigation; **dopo una settimana di ~** after a week at sea

na'viglio [na'viʎʎo] *sm* fleet, ships *pl*; (*canale artificiale*) canal; **~ da pesca** fishing fleet

nazio'nale [nattsjo'nale] *ag* national ◼ *sf* (*Sport*) national team

naziona'lismo [nattsjona'lizmo] *sm* nationalism

naziona'lista, -i, e [nattsjona'lista] *ag, sm/f* nationalist

nazionalità [nattsjonali'ta] *sf inv* nationality

nazionaliz'zare [nattsjonalid'dzare] *vt* to nationalize

nazionalizzazi'one [nattsjonaliddzat'tsjone] *sf* nationalization

nazi'one [nat'tsjone] *sf* nation

naziskin ['nɑːtsiskin] *sm inv* Nazi skinhead

na'zismo [nat'tsizmo] *sm* Nazism

na'zista, -i, e [nat'tsista] *ag, sm/f* Nazi

NB *abbr* (= *nota bene*) NB

N.d.A. *abbr* (= *nota dell'autore*) author's note

N.d.D. *abbr* = **nota della direzione**

N.d.E. *abbr* (= *nota dell'editore*) publisher's note

N.d.R. *abbr* (= *nota della redazione*) editor's note

'nd'rangheta [nd'rangeta] *sf* Calabrian Mafia

N.d.T. *abbr* (= *nota del traduttore*) translator's note

 PAROLA CHIAVE

ne *pron* **1** (*di lui, lei, loro*) of him/her/them; about him/her/them; **ne riconosco la voce** I recognize his (*o* her) voice

2 (*di questa, quella cosa*) of it; about it; **ne voglio ancora** I want some more (of it *o* them); **non parliamone più!** let's not talk about it any more!

3 (*da ciò*) from this; **ne deduco che l'avete trovato** I gather you've found it; **ne consegue che ...** it follows therefore, that ...

4 (*con valore partitivo*): **hai dei libri? — sì, ne ho** have you any books? — yes, I have (some); **hai del pane? — no, non ne ho** have you any bread? — no, I haven't any; **quanti anni hai? — ne ho 17** how old are you? — I'm 17

◼ *av* (*moto da luogo: da lì*) from there; **ne vengo ora** I've just come from there

né *cong*: **né ... né** neither ... nor; **né l'uno né l'altro lo vuole** neither of them wants it; **né più né meno** no more no less; **non parla né l'italiano né il tedesco** he speaks neither Italian nor German, he doesn't speak either Italian or German; **non piove né nevica** it isn't raining or snowing

N.E. *abbr* (= *nordest*) NE

ne'anche [ne'anke] *av, cong* not even; **non ... ~** not even; **~ se volesse potrebbe venire** he couldn't come even if he wanted to; **non l'ho visto — neanch'io** I didn't see him — neither did I *o* I didn't either; **~ per idea** *o* **sogno!** not on your life!; **non ci penso ~!** I wouldn't dream of it!; **~ a pagarlo lo farebbe** he wouldn't do it even if you paid him

'**nebbia** *sf* fog; (*foschia*) mist
nebbi'oso, -a *ag* foggy; misty
nebulizza'tore [nebuliddza'tore] *sm* atomizer
nebu'losa *sf* nebula
nebulosità *sf* haziness
nebu'loso, -a *ag* (*atmosfera, cielo*) hazy; (*fig*) hazy, vague
néces'saire [nese'sɛr] *sm inv*: ~ **da viaggio** overnight case *o* bag
necessaria'mente [netʃessarja'mente] *av* necessarily
neces'sario, -a [netʃes'sarjo] *ag* necessary ■ *sm*: **fare il** ~ to do what is necessary; **lo stretto** ~ the bare essentials *pl*
necessità [netʃessi'ta] *sf inv* necessity; (*povertà*) need, poverty; **trovarsi nella** ~ **di fare qc** to be forced *o* obliged to do sth, have to do sth
necessi'tare [netʃessi'tare] *vt* to require ■ *vi* (*aver bisogno*): ~ **di** to need
necro'logio [nekro'lɔdʒo] *sm* obituary notice; (*registro*) register of deaths
ne'fando, -a *ag* infamous, wicked
ne'fasto, -a *ag* inauspicious, ill-omened
ne'gare *vt* to deny; (*rifiutare*) to deny, refuse; ~ **di aver fatto/che** to deny having done/ that
negativa'mente *av* negatively; **rispondere** ~ to give a negative response
nega'tivo, -a *ag, sf, sm* negative
negazi'one [negat'tsjone] *sf* negation
negherò *etc* [nege'rɔ] *vb vedi* **negare**
ne'gletto, -a [ne'gletto] *ag* (*trascurato*) neglected
'**negli** ['neʎʎi] *prep+det vedi* **in**
négli'gé [negli'ʒe] *sm inv* negligee
negli'gente [negli'dʒɛnte] *ag* negligent, careless
negli'genza [negli'dʒɛntsa] *sf* negligence, carelessness
negozi'abile [negot'tsjabile] *ag* negotiable
negozi'ante [negot'tsjante] *sm/f* trader, dealer; (*bottegaio*) shopkeeper (*Brit*), storekeeper (*US*)
negozi'are [negot'tsjare] *vt* to negotiate ■ *vi*: ~ **in** to trade *o* deal in
negozi'ato [negot'tsjato] *sm* negotiation
negozia'tore, -trice [negottsja'tore] *sm/f* negotiator
ne'gozio [ne'gɔttsjo] *sm* (*locale*) shop (*Brit*), store (*US*); (*affare*) (piece of) business *no pl*; (*Dir*): ~ **giuridico** legal transaction
negri'ere, -a, negri'ero, -a *sm/f* slave trader; (*fig*) slave driver
'**negro, -a** *ag, sm/f* Negro
negro'mante *sm/f* necromancer

negroman'zia [negroman'tsia] *sf* necromancy
'**nei,** '**nel,** '**nell',** '**nella,** '**nelle,** '**nello** *prep+det vedi* **in**
'**nembo** *sm* (*Meteor*) nimbus
ne'mico, -a, ci, che *ag* hostile; (*Mil*) enemy *cpd* ■ *sm/f* enemy; **essere ~ di** to be strongly averse *o* opposed to
nem'meno *av, cong* = **neanche**
'**nenia** *sf* dirge; (*motivo monotono*) monotonous tune
'**neo** *sm* mole; (*fig*) (slight) flaw
'**neo...** *prefisso* neo...
neofa'scista, -i, e [neofaʃ'ʃista] *sm/f* neofascist
neolo'gismo [neolo'dʒizmo] *sm* neologism
'**neon** *sm* (*Chim*) neon
neo'nato, -a *ag* newborn ■ *sm/f* newborn baby
neozelan'dese [neoddzelan'dese] *ag* New Zealand *cpd* ■ *sm/f* New Zealander
Ne'pal *sm*: **il ~** Nepal
nepo'tismo *sm* nepotism
nep'pure *av, cong* = **neanche**
ner'bata *sf* (*colpo*) blow; (*sferzata*) whiplash
'**nerbo** *sm* lash; (*fig*) strength, backbone
nerbo'ruto, -a *ag* muscular; robust
ne'retto *sm* (*Tip*) bold type
'**nero, -a** *ag* black; (*scuro*) dark ■ *sm* black; **nella miseria più nera** in utter *o* abject poverty; **essere di umore ~, essere ~** to be in a filthy mood; **mettere qc ~ su bianco** to put sth down in black and white; **vedere tutto ~** to look on the black side (of things)
nero'fumo *sm* lampblack
nerva'tura *sf* (*Anat*) nervous system; (*Bot*) veining; (*Archit, Tecn*) rib
'**nervo** *sm* (*Anat*) nerve; (*Bot*) vein; **avere i nervi** to be on edge; **dare sui nervi a qn** to get on sb's nerves; **tenere/avere i nervi saldi** to keep/be calm; **che nervi!** damn (it)!
nervo'sismo *sm* (*Psic*) nervousness; (*irritazione*) irritability
ner'voso, -a *ag* nervous; (*irritabile*) irritable ■ *sm* (*fam*): **far venire il ~ a qn** to get on sb's nerves; **farsi prendere dal ~** to let o.s. get irritated
'**nespola** *sf* (*Bot*) medlar; (*fig*) blow, punch
'**nespolo** *sm* medlar tree
'**nesso** *sm* connection, link

 PAROLA CHIAVE

nes'suno, -a (*det: dav sm* **nessun** + C, V, **nessuno** + *s impura, gn, pn, ps, x, z; dav sf* **nessuna** + C, **nessun'** + V) *det* **1** (*non uno*) no; (*espressione negativa*) + any; **non c'è nessun libro** there isn't any book, there is no book; **nessun altro** no one else, nobody else; **nessun'altra cosa** nothing else; **in nessun luogo** nowhere

2 (*qualche*) any; **hai nessuna obiezione?** do you have any objections?

■ *pron* **1** (*non uno*) no one, nobody; (*espressione negativa +*) any(one); (*: cosa*) (*espressione negativa*) + any; **nessuno è venuto, non è venuto nessuno** nobody came

2 (*qualcuno*) anyone, anybody; **ha telefonato nessuno?** did anyone phone?

netta'mente *av* clearly
net'tare¹ *vt* to clean
'nettare² ['nɛttare] *sm* nectar
net'tezza [net'tettsa] *sf* cleanness, cleanliness; **~ urbana** cleansing department (*Brit*), department of sanitation (*US*)
'netto, -a *ag* (*pulito*) clean; (*chiaro*) clear, clear-cut; (*deciso*) definite; (*Econ*) net; **tagliare qc di ~** to cut sth clean off; **taglio ~ col passato** (*fig*) clean break with the past
nettur'bino *sm* dustman (*Brit*), garbage collector (*US*)
'neuro... *prefisso* neuro...
neurochirur'gia [neurokirur'dʒia] *sf* neurosurgery
neurolo'gia [neurolo'dʒia] *sf* neurology
neuro'logico, -a, ci, che [neuro'lɔdʒiko] *ag* neurological
neu'rologo, -a, gi, ghe *sm/f* neurologist
neu'rosi *sf inv* = **nevrosi**
neu'trale *ag* neutral
neutralità *sf* neutrality
neutraliz'zare [neutralid'dzare] *vt* to neutralize
'neutro, -a *ag* neutral; (*Ling*) neuter ■ *sm* (*Ling*) neuter
neu'trone *sm* neutron
ne'vaio *sm* snowfield
'neve *sf* snow; **montare a ~** (*Cuc*) to whip up; **~ carbonica** dry ice
nevi'care *vb impers* to snow
nevi'cata *sf* snowfall
ne'vischio [ne'viskjo] *sm* sleet
ne'voso, -a *ag* snowy; snow-covered
nevral'gia [nevral'dʒia] *sf* neuralgia
ne'vralgico, -a, ci, che [ne'vraldʒiko] *ag*: **punto ~** (*Med*) nerve centre; (*fig*) crucial point
nevras'tenico, -a, ci, che *ag* (*Med*) neurasthenic; (*fig*) hot-tempered ■ *sm/f* neurasthenic; hot-tempered person
ne'vrosi *sf inv* neurosis
ne'vrotico, -a, ci, che *ag, sm/f* (*anche fig*) neurotic

Nia'gara *sm*: **le cascate del ~** the Niagara Falls
'nibbio *sm* (*Zool*) kite
Nica'ragua *sm*: **il ~** Nicaragua
nicaragu'ense *ag, sm/f* Nicaraguan
'nicchia ['nikkja] *sf* niche; (*naturale*) cavity, hollow; **~ di mercato** (*Comm*) niche market
nicchi'are [nik'kjare] *vi* to shilly-shally, hesitate
'nichel ['nikel] *sm* nickel
nichi'lismo [niki'lizmo] *sm* nihilism
Nico'sia *sf* Nicosia
nico'tina *sf* nicotine
nidi'ata *sf* (*di uccelli, fig: di bambini*) brood; (*di altri animali*) litter
nidifi'care *vi* to nest
'nido *sm* nest ■ *ag inv*: **asilo ~** day nursery, crèche (*for children aged 0 to 3*); **a ~ d'ape** (*tessuto etc*) honeycomb *cpd*

 PAROLA CHIAVE

ni'ente *pron* **1** (*nessuna cosa*) nothing; **niente può fermarlo** nothing can stop him; **niente di niente** absolutely nothing; **grazie! — di niente!** thank you! — not at all!; **nient'altro** nothing else; **nient'altro che** nothing but; **niente affatto** not at all, not in the least; **come se niente fosse** as if nothing had happened; **cose da niente** trivial matters; **per niente** (*gratis, invano*) for nothing; **non per niente, ma ...** not for any particular reason, but ...; **poco o niente** next to nothing; **un uomo da niente** a man of no consequence

2 (*qualcosa*): **hai bisogno di niente?** do you need anything?

3: **non ... niente** nothing; (*espressione negativa*) anything; **non ho visto niente** I saw nothing, I didn't see anything; **non può farci niente** he can't do anything about it; **(non) fa niente** (*non importa*) it doesn't matter; **non ho niente da dire** I have nothing o haven't anything to say

■ *ag inv*: **niente paura!** never fear!; **e niente scuse!** and I don't want to hear excuses!

■ *sm* nothing; **un bel niente** absolutely nothing; **basta un niente per farla piangere** the slightest thing is enough to make her cry; **finire in niente** to come to nothing

■ *av* (*in nessuna misura*): **non ... niente** not ... at all; **non è (per) niente buono** it isn't good at all; **non ci penso per niente** (*non ne ho nessuna intenzione*) I wouldn't think of it; **niente male!** not bad at all!

nientedi'meno, niente'meno *av* actually, even ■ *escl* really!, I say!

'Niger ['nidʒer] *sm*: **il** ~ Niger; *(fiume)* the Niger

Ni'geria [ni'dʒɛrja] *sf* Nigeria

nigeri'ano, -a [nidʒe'rjano] *ag, sm/f* Nigerian

'Nilo *sm*: **il** ~ the Nile

'nimbo *sm* halo

'ninfa *sf* nymph

nin'fea *sf* water lily

nin'fomane *sf* nymphomaniac

ninna'nanna *sf* lullaby

'ninnolo *sm* (*balocco*) plaything; (*gingillo*) knick-knack

ni'pote *sm/f* (*di zii*) nephew/niece; (*di nonni*) grandson/daughter, grandchild

nip'ponico, -a, ci, che *ag* Japanese

niti'dezza [niti'dettsa] *sf* (*gen*) clearness; (*di stile*) clarity; (*Fot, TV*) sharpness

'nitido, -a *ag* clear; (*immagine*) sharp

ni'trato *sm* nitrate

'nitrico, -a, ci, che *ag* nitric

ni'trire *vi* to neigh

ni'trito *sm* (*di cavallo*) neighing *no pl*; neigh; (*Chim*) nitrite

nitroglice'rina [nitroglitʃe'rina] *sf* nitroglycerine

'niveo, -a *ag* snow-white

'Nizza ['nittsa] *sf* Nice

nn *abbr* (= *numeri*) nos

NO *sigla* = **Novara**

no *av* (*risposta*) no; **vieni o no?** are you coming or not?; **come no!** of course!, certainly!; **perché no?** why not?

N.O. *abbr* (= *nordovest*) NW

nobil'donna *sf* noblewoman

'nobile *ag* noble ■ *sm/f* noble, nobleman/woman

nobili'are *ag* noble

nobili'tare *vt* (*anche fig*) to ennoble; **nobilitarsi** *vr* (*rendersi insigne*) to distinguish o.s.

nobiltà *sf* nobility; (*di azione etc*) nobleness

nobilu'omo (*pl* **nobiluomini**) *sm* nobleman

'nocca, -che *sf* (*Anat*) knuckle

'noccio *etc* ['nɔttʃo] *vb vedi* **nuocere**

nocci'ola [not'tʃɔla] *sf* hazelnut ■ *ag inv* (*anche*: **color nocciola**) hazel, light brown

noccio'lina [nottʃo'lina] *sf* (*anche*: **nocciolina**) peanut

'nocciolo¹ ['nɔttʃolo] *sm* (*di frutto*) stone; (*fig*) heart, core

'nocciolo² [not'tʃolo] *sm* (*albero*) hazel

'noce ['notʃe] *sm* (*albero*) walnut tree ■ *sf* (*frutto*) walnut; **una** ~ **di burro** (*Cuc*) a knob of butter (*Brit*), a dab of butter (*US*); ~ **di cocco** coconut; ~ **moscata** nutmeg

noce'pesca, -sche [notʃe'pɛska] *sf* nectarine

no'cevo *etc* [no'tʃevo] *vb vedi* **nuocere**

noci'uto [no'tʃuto] *pp di* **nuocere**

no'civo, -a [no'tʃivo] *ag* harmful, noxious

'nocqui *etc vb vedi* **nuocere**

'nodo *sm* (*di cravatta, legname, Naut*) knot; (*Aut, Ferr*) junction; (*Med, Astr, Bot*) node; (*fig*: *legame*) bond, tie; (: *punto centrale*) heart, crux; **avere un** ~ **alla gola** to have a lump in one's throat; **tutti i nodi vengono al pettine** (*proverbio*) your sins will find you out

no'doso, -a *ag* (*tronco*) gnarled

'nodulo *sm* (*Anat, Bot*) nodule

no-'global [no-'global] *ag inv* anti-globalization *cpd*

'noi *pron* (*soggetto*) we; (*oggetto*: *per dare rilievo, con preposizione*) us; ~ **stessi(e)** we ourselves; (*oggetto*) ourselves; **da** ~ (*nel nostro paese*) in our country, where we come from; (*a casa nostra*) at our house

'noia *sf* boredom; (*disturbo, impaccio*) bother *no pl*, trouble *no pl*; **avere qn/qc a** ~ not to like sb/sth; **mi è venuto a** ~ I'm tired of it; **dare** ~ **a** to annoy; **avere delle noie con qn** to have trouble with sb

noi'altri *pron* we

noi'oso, -a *ag* boring; (*fastidioso*) annoying, troublesome

noleggi'are [noled'dʒare] *vt* (*prendere a noleggio*) to hire (*Brit*), rent; (*dare a noleggio*) to hire out (*Brit*), rent out; (*aereo, nave*) to charter

noleggia'tore, -'trice [noledzza'tore] *sm/f* hirer (*Brit*), renter; charterer

no'leggio [no'leddʒo] *sm* hire (*Brit*), rental charter

no'lente *ag*: **volente o** ~ whether one likes it or not, willy-nilly

'nolo *sm* hire (*Brit*), rental charter; (*per trasporto merci*) freight; **prendere/dare a** ~ **qc** to hire/hire out sth (*Brit*), rent/rent out sth

'nomade *ag* nomadic ■ *sm/f* nomad

noma'dismo *sm* nomadism

'nome *sm* name; (*Ling*) noun; **in o a** ~ **di** in the name of; **di** *o* **per** ~ (*chiamato*) called, named; **conoscere qn di** ~ to know sb by name; **fare il** ~ **di qn** to name sb; **faccia pure il mio** ~ feel free to mention my name; ~ **d'arte** stage name; ~ **di battesimo** Christian name; ~ **depositato** trade name; ~ **di famiglia** surname; ~ **da ragazza** maiden name; ~ **da sposata** married name; ~ **utente** login

no'mea *sf* notoriety

nomencla'tura *sf* nomenclature

nomenkla'tura *sf* (*di partito, stato*) nomenklatura

no'mignolo [no'miɲɲolo] *sm* nickname

'nomina *sf* appointment

nomi'nale *ag* nominal; (*Ling*) noun *cpd*

nomi'nare *vt* to name; (*eleggere*) to appoint; (*citare*) to mention; **non l'ho mai sentito ~** I've never heard of it (*o him*)

nomination [nomi'neʃʃon] *sf inv* (*in reality show*) nomination

nomina'tivo, -a *ag* (*intestato: titolo*) registered; (*libretto*) personal; (*Ling*) nominative ■ *sm* (*nome*) name; (*Ling*) nominative; **elenco ~** list of names

non *av* not ■ *prefisso* non-; **grazie — ~ c'è di che** thank you — don't mention it; **i ~ credenti** the unbelievers; **~ autosufficiente** (*persona anziana*) needing care; *vedi anche* **affatto; appena** *etc*

nonché [non'ke] *cong* (*tanto più, tanto meno*) let alone; (*e inoltre*) as well as

nonconfor'mista, -i, e *ag, sm/f* nonconformist

noncu'rante *ag*: **~ (di)** careless (of), indifferent (to); **con fare ~** with a nonchalant air

noncu'ranza [nonku'rantsa] *sf* carelessness, indifference; **un'aria di ~** a nonchalant air

nondi'meno *cong* (*tuttavia*) however; (*nonostante*) nevertheless

'**nonno, -a** *sm/f* grandfather/mother; (*in senso più familiare*) grandma/grandpa; **nonni** *smpl* grandparents

non'nulla *sm inv*: **un ~** nothing, a trifle

'**nono, -a** *num* ninth

nonos'tante *prep* in spite of, notwithstanding ■ *cong* although, even though

non plus 'ultra *sm inv*: **il ~ (di)** the last word (in)

nontiscordardimé *sm inv* (*Bot*) forget-me-not

nord *sm* north ■ *ag inv* north; (*regione*) northern; **verso ~** north, northwards; **l'America del N~** North America

nor'dest *sm* north-east

'**nordico, -a, ci, che** *ag* nordic, northern European

nor'dista, -i, e *ag, sm/f* Yankee

nor'dovest *sm* north-west

Norim'berga *sf* Nuremberg

'**norma** *sf* (*principio*) norm; (*regola*) regulation, rule; (*consuetudine*) custom, rule; **di ~** normally; **a ~ di legge** according to law, as laid down by law; **al di sopra della ~** above average, above the norm; **per sua ~ e regola** for your information; **proporsi una ~ di vita** to set o.s. rules to live by; **norme di sicurezza** safety regulations; **norme per l'uso** instructions for use

nor'male *ag* normal

normalità *sf* normality

normaliz'zare [normalid'dzare] *vt* to normalize, bring back to normal

normal'mente *av* normally

Norman'dia *sf*: **la ~** Normandy

nor'manno, -a *ag, sm/f* Norman

norma'tivo, -a *ag* normative ■ *sf* regulations *pl*

norve'gese [norve'dʒese] *ag, sm/f, sm* Norwegian

Nor'vegia [nor'vɛdʒa] *sf*: **la ~** Norway

noso'comio *sm* hospital

nostal'gia [nostal'dʒia] *sf* (*di casa, paese*) homesickness; (*del passato*) nostalgia

nos'talgico, -a, ci, che [nos'taldʒiko] *ag* homesick; nostalgic ■ *sm/f* (*Pol*) *person who hopes for the return of Fascism*

nos'trano, -a *ag* local; (*pianta, frutta*) home-produced

'**nostro, -a** *det*: **il(la) ~(a)** *etc* our ■ *pron*: **il(la) ~(a)** *etc* ours ■ *sm*: **abbiamo speso del ~** we spent our own money ■ *sf*: **la nostra** (*opinione*) our view; **i nostri** our family; our own people; **è dei nostri** he's one of us; **è dalla nostra** (*parte*) he's on our side; **anche noi abbiamo avuto le nostre** (*disavventure*) we've had our problems too; **alla nostra!** (*brindisi*) to us!

nos'tromo *sm* boatswain

'**nota** *sf* (*segno*) mark; (*comunicazione scritta, Mus*) note; (*fattura*) bill; (*elenco*) list; **prendere ~ di qc** to note sth, make a note of sth, write sth down; (*fig: fare attenzione*) to note sth, take note of sth; **degno di ~** noteworthy, worthy of note; **note caratteristiche** distinguishing marks *o* features; **note a piè di pagina** footnotes

no'tabile *ag* notable; (*persona*) important ■ *sm* prominent citizen

no'taio *sm* notary

no'tare *vt* (*segnare: errori*) to mark; (*registrare*) to note (down), write down; (*rilevare, osservare*) to note, notice; **farsi ~** to get o.s. noticed

nota'rile *ag*: **atto ~** legal document (*authorized by a notary*); **studio ~** notary's office

notazi'one [notat'tsjone] *sf* (*Mus*) notation

no'tevole *ag* (*talento*) notable, remarkable; (*peso*) considerable

no'tifica, -che *sf* notification

notifi'care *vt* (*Dir*): **~ qc a qn** to notify sb of sth, give sb notice of sth

notificazi'one [notifikat'tsjone] *sf* notification

no'tizia [no'tittsja] *sf* (piece of) news *sg*; (*informazione*) piece of information; **notizie** *sfpl* news *sg*; information *sg*

notizi'ario [notit'tsjarjo] *sm* (*Radio, TV, Stampa*) news *sg*

n

'noto, -a *ag* (well-)known

notorietà *sf* fame; notoriety

no'torio, -a *ag* well-known; *(peg)* notorious

not'tambulo, -a *sm/f* night-bird *(fig)*

not'tata *sf* night

'notte *sf* night; **di** ~ at night; *(durante la notte)* in the night, during the night; **questa** ~ *(passata)* last night; *(che viene)* tonight; **nella** ~ **dei tempi** in the mists of time; **come va?** — **peggio che andar di** ~ how are things? — worse than ever; ~ **bianca** sleepless night

notte'tempo *av* at night; during the night

'nottola *sf* (Zool) noctule

not'turno, -a *ag* nocturnal; *(servizio, guardiano)* night *cpd* ■ *sf* (Sport) evening fixture (Brit) o match

nov. *abbr* (= *novembre*) Nov

no'vanta *num* ninety

novan'tenne *ag, sm/f* ninety-year-old

novan'tesimo, -a *num* ninetieth

novan'tina *sf*: **una** ~ **(di)** about ninety

'nove *num* nine

novecen'tesco, -a, schi, sche [novetʃen'tesko] *ag* twentieth-century

nove'cento [nove'tʃɛnto] *num* nine hundred ■ *sm*: **il N**~ the twentieth century

no'vella *sf* (Letteratura) short story

novel'lino, -a *ag* (pivello) green, inexperienced

novel'lista, -i, e *sm/f* short-story writer

novel'listica *sf* (arte) short-story writing; *(insieme di racconti)* short stories *pl*

no'vello, -a *ag* (piante, patate) new; *(insalata, verdura)* early; *(sposo)* newly-married

no'vembre *sm* November; *vedi anche* **luglio**

novem'brino, -a *ag* November *cpd*

nove'mila *num* nine thousand

noven'nale *ag* (che dura 9 anni) nine-year *cpd*; *(ogni 9 anni)* nine-yearly

novi'lunio *sm* (Astr) new moon

novità *sf inv* novelty; *(innovazione)* innovation; *(cosa originale, insolita)* something new; *(notizia)* (piece of) news *sg*; **le** ~ **della moda** the latest fashions

novizi'ato [novit'tsjato] *sm* (Rel) novitiate; *(tirocinio)* apprenticeship

no'vizio, -a [no'vittsjo] *sm/f* (Rel) novice; *(tirocinante)* beginner, apprentice

nozi'one [not'tsjone] *sf* notion, idea; **nozioni** *sfpl* (rudimenti) basic knowledge *sg*, rudiments

nozio'nismo [nottsjo'nizmo] *sm* superficial knowledge

nozio'nistico, -a, ci, che [nottsjo'nistiko] *ag* superficial

'nozze ['nɔttse] *sfpl* wedding *sg*, marriage *sg*; ~ **d'argento/d'oro** silver/golden wedding *sg*

ns. *abbr* (Comm) = **nostro**

NU *sigla* = **Nuoro**

N.U. *sigla* (= *Nazioni Unite*) UN

'nube *sf* cloud

nubi'fragio [nubi'fradʒo] *sm* cloudburst

'nubile *ag* (donna) unmarried, single

'nuca, -che *sf* nape of the neck

nucle'are *ag* nuclear ■ *sm*: **il** ~ nuclear energy

'nucleo *sm* nucleus; *(gruppo)* team, unit, group; *(Mil, Polizia)* squad; ~ **antidroga** anti-drugs squad; **il** ~ **familiare** the family unit

nu'dismo *sm* nudism

nu'dista, -i, -e *sm/f* nudist

nudità *sf inv* nudity, nakedness; *(di paesaggio)* bareness ■ *sfpl* (parti nude del corpo) nakedness *sg*

'nudo, -a *ag* (persona) bare, naked, nude; *(membra)* bare, naked; *(montagna)* bare ■ *sm* (Arte) nude; **a occhio** ~ to the naked eye; **a piedi nudi** barefoot; **mettere a** ~ *(cuore, verità)* to lay bare; **gli ha detto** ~ **e crudo che** ... he told him bluntly that ...

'nugolo *sm*: **un** ~ **di** a whole host of

'nulla *pron, av* = **niente** ■ *sm*: **il** ~ nothing; **svanire nel** ~ to vanish into thin air; **basta un** ~ **per farlo arrabbiare** he gets annoyed over the slightest thing

nulla'osta *sm inv* authorization

nullate'nente *ag*: **essere** ~ to own nothing ■ *sm/f* person with no property

nullità *sf inv* nullity; *(persona)* nonentity

'nullo, -a *ag* useless, worthless; *(Dir)* null (and void); *(Sport)*: **incontro** ~ draw

nume'rale *ag, sm* numeral

nume'rare *vt* to number

numera'tore *sm* (Mat) numerator; *(macchina)* numbering device

numerazi'one [numerat'tsjone] *sf* numbering; *(araba, decimale)* notation

nu'merico, -a, ci, che *ag* numerical

'numero *sm* number; *(romano, arabo)* numeral; *(di spettacolo)* act, turn; **dare i numeri** *(farneticare)* not to be all there; **tanto per fare** ~ **invitiamo anche lui** why don't we invite him to make up the numbers?; **ha tutti i numeri per riuscire** he's got what it takes to succeed; **che** ~ **tuo fratello!** your brother is a real character!; ~ **civico** house number; ~ **chiuso** (Università) selective entry system; ~ **doppio** (di rivista) issue with supplement; ~ **di scarpe** size of shoe; ~ **verde** (Tel) ≈ Freephone®

nume'roso, -a *ag* numerous, many; *(folla, famiglia)* large

numis'matica *sf* numismatics *sg*, coin collecting

'nunzio ['nuntsjo] *sm* (Rel) nuncio

nu'occio *etc* ['nwɔttʃo] *vb vedi* **nuocere**

nu'ocere ['nwɔtʃere] vi: ~ **a** to harm, damage; **il tentar non nuoce** (proverbio) there's no harm in trying

nuoci'uto, -a [nwo'tʃuto] pp di **nuocere**

nu'ora sf daughter-in-law

nuo'tare vi to swim; (galleggiare: oggetti) to float; ~ **a rana/sul dorso** to do the breast stroke/backstroke

nuo'tata sf swim

nuota'tore, -'trice sm/f swimmer

nu'oto sm swimming

nu'ova sf vedi **nuovo**

nuova'mente av again

Nu'ova York sf New York

Nu'ova Ze'landa [-dze'landa] sf: **la ~** New Zealand

nu'ovo, -a ag new ■ sf (notizia) (piece of) news sg; **come ~** as good as new; **di ~** again; **fino a ~ ordine** until further notice; **il suo volto non mi è ~** I know his face; **rimettere a ~** (cosa, macchina) to do up like new; **anno ~,**

vita nuova! it's time to turn over a new leaf!; **~ fiammante** o **di zecca** brand-new; **la Nuova Guinea** New Guinea; **la Nuova Inghilterra** New England; **la Nuova Scozia** Nova Scotia

nu'trice [nu'tritʃe] sf wet nurse

nutri'ente ag nutritious, nourishing; (crema, balsamo) nourishing

nutri'mento sm food, nourishment

nu'trire vt to feed; (fig: sentimenti) to harbour (Brit), harbor (US), nurse

nutri'tivo, -a ag nutritional; (alimento) nutritious

nu'trito, -a ag (numeroso) large; (fitto) heavy; **ben/mal ~** well/poorly fed

nutrizi'one [nutrit'tsjone] sf nutrition

'nuvolo, -a ag cloudy ■ sf cloud

nuvolosità sf cloudiness

nuvo'loso, -a ag cloudy

nuzi'ale [nut'tsjale] ag nuptial; wedding cpd

'nylon ['nailən] sm nylon

Oo

O, o [ɔ] *sf o m inv* (*lettera*) O, o; **O come Otranto** ≈ O for Oliver (*Brit*), O for Oboe (*US*)

o *cong* (*dav V spesso*): **od** or; **o ... o** either ... or; **o l'uno o l'altro** either (of them); **o meglio** or rather

O. *abbr* (= *ovest*) W

'oasi *sf inv* oasis

obbedi'ente *etc vedi* **ubbidiente** *etc*

obbiet'tare *etc vedi* **obiettare** *etc*

obbli'gare *vt* (*costringere*): **~ qn a fare** to force *o* oblige sb to do; (*Dir*) to bind; **obbligarsi** *vr*: **obbligarsi a fare** to undertake to do; **obbligarsi per qn** (*Dir*) to stand surety for sb, act as guarantor for sb

obbliga'tissimo, -a *ag* (*ringraziamento*): ~! much obliged!

obbli'gato, -a *ag* (*costretto, grato*) obliged; (*percorso, tappa*) set, fixed; **passaggio ~** (*fig*) essential requirement

obbliga'torio, -a *ag* compulsory, obligatory

obbligazi'one [obbligat'tsjone] *sf* obligation; (*Comm*) bond, debenture; **~ dello Stato** government bond; **obbligazioni convertibili** convertible loan stock, convertible debentures

obbligazio'nista, -i, e [obbligattsjo'nista] *sm/f* bond-holder

'obbligo, -ghi *sm* obligation; (*dovere*) duty; **avere l'~ di fare, essere nell'~ di fare** to be obliged to do; **essere d'~** (*discorso, applauso*) to be called for; **avere degli obblighi con** *o* **verso qn** to be under an obligation to sb, be indebted to sb; **le formalità d'~** the necessary formalities

obb.mo *abbr* = **obbligatissimo**

ob'brobrio *sm* disgrace; (*fig*) mess, eyesore

obe'lisco, -schi *sm* obelisk

obe'rato, -a *ag*: **~ di** (*lavoro*) overloaded *o* overburdened with; (*debiti*) crippled with

obesità *sf* obesity

o'beso, -a *ag* obese

obiet'tare *vt*: **~ che** to object that; **~ su** to object to sth, raise objections concerning sth

obiettiva'mente *av* objectively

obiettività *sf* objectivity

obiet'tivo, -a *ag* objective ■ *sm* (*Ottica, Fot*) lens *sg*, objective; (*Mil*) *fig*, objective

obiet'tore *sm* objector; **~ di coscienza** conscientious objector

obiezi'one [objet'tsjone] *sf* objection

obi'torio *sm* morgue

o'bliquo, -a *ag* oblique; (*inclinato*) slanting; (*fig*) devious, underhand; **sguardo ~** sidelong glance

oblite'rare *vt* (*francobollo*) to cancel; (*biglietto*) to stamp

oblitera'trice [oblitera'tritʃe] *sf* (*anche*: **macchina obliteratrice**) cancelling machine; stamping machine

oblò *sm inv* porthole

o'blungo, -a, ghi, ghe *ag* oblong

'oboe *sm* oboe

'obolo *sm* (*elemosina*) (small) offering, mite

obsole'scenza [obsoleʃʃɛntsa] *sf* (*Econ*) obsolescence

obso'leto, -a *ag* obsolete

OC *abbr* (= *onde corte*) SW

'oca (*pl* **oche**) *sf* goose

o'caggine [o'kaddʒine] *sf* silliness, stupidity

occasio'nale *ag* (*incontro*) chance; (*cliente, guadagni*) casual, occasional

occasi'one *sf* (*caso favorevole*) opportunity; (*causa, motivo, circostanza*) occasion; (*Comm*) bargain; **all'~** should the need arise; **alla prima ~** at the first, opportunity; **d'~** (*a buon prezzo*) bargain *cpd*; (*usato*) secondhand

occhi'aia [ok'kjaja] *sf* eye socket; **occhiaie** *sfpl* (*sotto gli occhi*) shadows (under the eyes)

occhi'ali [ok'kjali] *smpl* glasses, spectacles; **~ da sole** sunglasses

occhi'ata [ok'kjata] *sf* look, glance; **dare un'~ a** to have a look at

occhieggi'are [okkjed'dʒare] *vi* (*apparire qua e là*) to peep (out)

occhi'ello [ok'kjɛllo] *sm* buttonhole; (*asola*) eyelet

occhio [ˈɔkkjo] *sm* eye; ~! careful!, watch out!; **a ~ nudo** with the naked eye; **a quattr'occhii** privately, in private; **avere ~** to have a good eye; **chiudere un ~ (su)** (*fig*) to turn a blind eye (to), shut one's eyes (to); **costare un ~ della testa** to cost a fortune; **dare all'~** *o* **nell'~ a qn** to catch sb's eye; **fare l'~ a qc** to get used to sth; **tenere d'~ qn** to keep an eye on sb; **vedere di buon/mal ~ qc** to look favourably/unfavourably on sth

occhiolino [okkjoˈlino] *sm*: **fare l'~ a qn** to wink at sb

occidentale [ottʃidenˈtale] *ag* western ■ *sm/f* Westerner

occidente [ottʃiˈdɛnte] *sm* west; (*Pol*): **l'O~** the West; **a ~** in the west

occipite [otˈtʃipite] *sm* back of the head, occiput (*Anat*)

occludere *vt* to block

occlusione *sf* blockage, obstruction

occluso, -a *pp di* **occludere**

occorrente *ag* necessary ■ *sm* all that is necessary

occorrenza [okkorˈrɛntsa] *sf* necessity, need; **all'~** in case of need

occorrere *vi* to be needed, be required ■ *vb impers*: **occorre farlo** it must be done; **occorre che tu parta** you must leave, you'll have to leave; **mi occorrono i soldi** I need the money

occorso, -a *pp di* **occorrere**

occultamento *sm* concealment

occultare *vt* to hide, conceal

occulto, -a *ag* hidden, concealed; (*scienze, forze*) occult

occupante *sm/f* (*di casa*) occupier, occupant; **~ abusivo** squatter

occupare *vt* to occupy; (*manodopera*) to employ; (*ingombrare*) to occupy, take up; **occuparsi** *vr* to occupy o.s., keep o.s. busy; (*impiegarsi*) to get a job; **occuparsi di** (*interessarsi*) to take an interest in; (*prendersi cura di*) to look after, take care of

occupato, -a *ag* (*Mil, Pol*) occupied; (*persona: affaccendato*) busy; (*posto, sedia*) taken; (*toilette, Tel*) engaged

occupazionale [okkupattsjoˈnale] *ag* employment *cpd*, of employment

occupazione [okkupatˈtsjone] *sf* occupation; (*impiego, lavoro*) job; (*Econ*) employment

Oceania [otʃeˈanja] *sf*: **l'~** Oceania

oceano [oˈtʃɛano] *sm* ocean

ocra *sf* ochre

OCSE *sigla f* (= *Organizzazione per la Cooperazione e lo Sviluppo Economico*) OECD (= *Organization for Economic Cooperation and Development*)

oculare *ag* ocular, eye *cpd*; **testimone ~** eye witness

oculatezza [okulaˈtettsa] *sf* caution; shrewdness

oculato, -a *ag* (*attento*) cautious, prudent; (*accorto*) shrewd

oculista, -i, e *sm/f* eye specialist, oculist

od *cong vedi* **o**

ode *sf* ode

ode *etc vb vedi* **udire**

odiare *vt* to hate, detest

odierno, -a *ag* today's, of today; (*attuale*) present; **in data odierna** (*formale*) today

odio *sm* hatred; **avere in ~ qc/qn** to hate *o* detest sth/sb

odioso, -a *ag* hateful, odious; **rendersi ~ (a)** to make o.s. unpopular (with)

odo *etc vb vedi* **udire**

odontoiatra, -i, e *sm/f* dentist, dental surgeon

odontoiatria *sf* dentistry

odontotecnico, -ci *sm* dental technician

odorare *vt* (*annusare*) to smell; (*profumare*) to perfume, scent ■ *vi*: **~ (di)** to smell (of)

odorato *sm* sense of smell

odore *sm* smell; **gli odori** (*Cuc*) (aromatic) herbs; **sentire ~ di qc** to smell sth; **morire in ~ di santità** (*Rel*) to die in the odour (*Brit*) *o* odor (*US*) of sanctity

odoroso, -a *ag* sweet-smelling

offendere *vt* to offend; (*violare*) to break, violate; (*insultare*) to insult; (*ferire*) to hurt; **offendersi** *vr* (*con senso reciproco*) to insult one another; (*risentirsi*): **offendersi (di)** to take offence (at), be offended (by)

offensivo, -a *ag, sf* offensive

offensore *sm* offender; (*Mil*) aggressor

offerente *sm* (*in aste*): **al migliore ~** to the highest bidder

offerto, -a *pp di* **offrire** ■ *sf* offer; (*donazione, anche: Rel*) offering; (*in gara d'appalto*) tender; (*in aste*) bid; (*Econ*) supply; **fare un'offerta** to make an offer; (*per appalto*) to tender; (*ad un'asta*) to bid; **offerta pubblica d'acquisto** takeover bid; **offerta pubblica di vendita** public offer for sale; **offerta reale** tender; **"offerte d'impiego"** (*Stampa*) "situations vacant" (*Brit*), "help wanted" (*US*)

offeso, -a *pp di* **offendere** ■ *ag* offended; (*fisicamente*) hurt, injured ■ *sm/f* offended party ■ *sf* insult, affront; (*Mil*) attack; (*Dir*) offence (*Brit*), offense (*US*); **essere ~ con qn** to be annoyed with sb; **parte offesa** (*Dir*) plaintiff

officiare [offiˈtʃare] *vi* (*Rel*) to officiate

officina [offiˈtʃina] *sf* workshop

offrire *vt* to offer; **offrirsi** *vr* (*proporsi*) to offer (o.s.), volunteer; (*occasione*) to present itself;

(*esporsi*): **offrirsi a** to expose o.s. to; **ti offro da bere** I'll buy you a drink; **"offresi posto di segretaria"** "secretarial vacancy", "vacancy for secretary"; **"segretaria offresi"** "secretary seeks post"

offus'care *vt* to obscure, darken; (*fig*: *intelletto*) to dim, cloud; (*fama*) to obscure, overshadow; **offuscarsi** *vr* to grow dark to cloud, grow dim to be obscured

of'talmico, -a, ci, che *ag* ophthalmic

oggettività [oddʒettivi'ta] *sf* objectivity

ogget'tivo, -a [oddʒet'tivo] *ag* objective

og'getto [od'dʒɛtto] *sm* object; (*materia, argomento*) subject (matter); (*in lettere commerciali*): ~ ... re ...; **essere ~ di** (*critiche, controversia*) to be the subject of; (*odio, pietà etc*) to be the object of; **essere ~ di scherno** to be a laughing stock; **in ~ a quanto detto** (*in lettere*) as regards the matter mentioned above; **oggetti preziosi** valuables, articles of value; **oggetti smarriti** lost property *sg* (*Brit*), lost and found *sg* (*US*)

'**oggi** ['ɔddʒi] *av, sm* today; ~ **stesso** today, this very day; ~ **come** ~ at present, as things stand; **dall' ~ al domani** from one day to the next; **a tutt'** ~ up till now, till today; **le spese a tutt'~ sono** ... expenses to date are ...; ~ **a otto** a week today

oggigi'orno [oddʒi'dʒorno] *av* nowadays

o'giva [o'dʒiva] *sf* ogive, pointed arch

OGM [ɔdʒi'ɛmme] *sigla mpl* (= *organismi geneticamente modificati*) GMO (= *genetically modified organisms*)

'**ogni** ['oɲɲi] *det* every, each; (*tutti*) all; (*con valore distributivo*) every; ~ **uomo è mortale** all men are mortal; **viene ~ due giorni** he comes every two days; ~ **cosa** everything; **ad ~ costo** at all costs, at any price; **in ~ luogo** everywhere; ~ **tanto** every so often; ~ **volta che** every time that

Ognis'santi [oɲɲis'santi] *sm* All Saints' Day

o'gnuno [oɲ'ɲuno] *pron* everyone, everybody

'**ohi** *escl* oh!; (*esprimente dolore*) ow!

ohimè *escl* oh dear!

'**OIL** *sigla f* (= *Organizzazione Internazionale del Lavoro*) ILO

OL *abbr* (= *onde lunghe*) LW

O'landa *sf*: **l'**~ Holland

olan'dese *ag* Dutch ▪ *sm* (*Ling*) Dutch ▪ *sm/f* Dutchman/woman; **gli Olandesi** the Dutch

ole'andro *sm* oleander

ole'ato, -a *ag*: **carta oleata** greaseproof paper (*Brit*), wax paper (*US*)

oleo'dotto *sm* oil pipeline

ole'oso, -a *ag* oily; (*che contiene olio*) oil *cpd*

o'lezzo [o'leddzo] *sm* fragrance

ol'fatto *sm* sense of smell

oli'are *vt* to oil

olia'tore *sm* oil can, oiler

oli'era *sf* oil cruet

oligar'chia [oligar'kia] *sf* oligarchy

olim'piadi *sfpl* Olympic Games

o'limpico, -a, ci, che *ag* Olympic

'**olio** *sm* oil; (*Pittura*): **un (quadro a)** ~ an oil painting; **sott'~** (*Cuc*) in oil; **oli essenziali** essential oils; ~ **di fegato di merluzzo** cod liver oil; ~ **d'oliva** olive oil; ~ **santo** holy oil; ~ **di semi** vegetable oil; ~ **solare** suntan oil

o'liva *sf* olive

oli'vastro, -a *ag* olive(-coloured) (*Brit*), olive(-colored) (*US*); (*carnagione*) sallow

oli'veto *sm* olive grove

o'livo *sm* olive tree

'**olmo** *sm* elm

olo'causto *sm* holocaust

OLP *sigla f* (= *Organizzazione per la Liberazione della Palestina*) PLO

oltraggi'are [oltrad'dʒare] *vt* to offend, insult

ol'traggio [ol'traddʒo] *sm* offence (*Brit*), offense (*US*), insult; (*Dir*): ~ **al pudore** indecent behaviour (*Brit*) o behavior (*US*); ~ **alla corte** contempt of court

oltraggi'oso, -a [oltrad'dʒoso] *ag* offensive

ol'tralpe *av* beyond the Alps

ol'tranza [ol'trantsa] *sf*: **a** ~ to the last, to the bitter end; **sciopero ad** ~ all-out strike

oltran'zismo [oltran'tsizmo] *sm* (*Pol*) extremism

oltran'zista, -i, e [oltran'tsista] *sm/f* (*Pol*) extremist

'**oltre** *av* (*più in là*) further; (*di più*: *aspettare*) longer, more ▪ *prep* (*di là da*) beyond, over, on the other side of; (*più di*) more than, over; (*in aggiunta a*) besides; (*eccetto*): ~ **a** except, apart from; ~ **a tutto** on top of all that

oltrecor'tina *av* behind the Iron Curtain; **paesi d'**~ Iron Curtain countries

oltre'manica *av* across the Channel

oltre'mare *av* overseas

oltre'modo *av* extremely, greatly

oltreo'ceano [oltreo'tʃeano] *av* overseas ▪ *sm*: **paesi d'**~ overseas countries

oltrepas'sare *vt* to go beyond, exceed

oltre'tomba *sm inv*: **l'**~ the hereafter

OM *abbr* (= *onde medie*) MW; (*Mil*) = **ospedale militare**

o'maggio [o'maddʒo] *sm* (*dono*) gift; (*segno di rispetto*) homage, tribute; **omaggi** *smpl* (*complimenti*) respects; **in** ~ (*copia, biglietto*) complimentary; **rendere ~ a** to pay homage o tribute to; **presentare i propri omaggi a qn** (*formale*) to pay one's respects to sb

'**Oman** *sm*: **l'**~ Oman

ombeli'cale *ag* umbilical

ombe'lico, -chi *sm* navel

'ombra *sf (zona non assolata, fantasma)* shade; *(sagoma scura)* shadow ■ *ag inv*: **bandiera ~** flag of convenience; **governo ~** *(Pol)* shadow cabinet; **sedere all'~** to sit in the shade; **nell'~** *(tramare, agire)* secretly; **restare nell'~** *(fig: persona)* to remain in obscurity; **senza ~ di dubbio** without the shadow of a doubt

ombreggi'are [ombred'dʒare] *vt* to shade

om'brello *sm* umbrella; **~ da sole** parasol, sunshade

ombrel'lone *sm* beach umbrella

om'bretto *sm* eyeshadow

om'broso, -a *ag* shady, shaded; *(cavallo)* nervous, skittish; *(persona)* touchy, easily offended

ome'lette [ɔmə'lɛt] *sf inv* omelet(te)

ome'lia *sf (Rel)* homily, sermon

ome'opata *sm/f* hom(o)eopath

omeopa'tia *sf* hom(o)eopathy

omeo'patico, -a, ci, che *ag* hom(o)eopathic ■ *sm* hom(o)eopath

omertà *sf* conspiracy of silence

o'messo, -a *pp di* **omettere**

o'mettere *vt* to omit, leave out; **~ di fare** to omit *o* fail to do

omi'cida, -i, e [omi'tʃida] *ag* homicidal, murderous ■ *sm/f* murderer/murderess

omi'cidio [omi'tʃidjo] *sm* murder; **~ colposo** *(Dir)* culpable homicide; **~ premeditato** *(Dir)* murder

o'misi *etc vb vedi* **omettere**

omissi'one *sf* omission; **reato d'~** criminal negligence; **~ di atti d'ufficio** negligence; *(by a public employee):* **~ di denuncia** failure to report a crime; **~ di soccorso** *(Dir)* failure to stop and give assistance

omogeneiz'zato [omodʒeneid'dzato] *sm* baby food

omo'geneo, -a [omo'dʒɛneo] *ag* homogeneous

omolo'gare *vt (Dir)* to approve, recognize; *(ratificare)* to ratify

omologazi'one [omologat'tsjone] *sf* approval; ratification

o'mologo, -a, ghi, ghe *ag* homologous, corresponding ■ *sm/f* opposite number

o'monimo, a *sm/f* namesake *sm (Ling)* homonym

omosessu'ale *ag, sm/f* homosexual

O.M.S. *sigla f =* **Organizzazione Mondiale della Sanità**

On. *abbr (Pol) =* **onorevole**

'oncia, -ce ['ontʃa] *sf* ounce

'onda *sf* wave; **mettere** *o* **mandare in ~** *(Radio, TV)* to broadcast; **andare in ~** *(Radio,*

TV) to go on the air; **onde corte/medie/lunghe** short/medium/long wave *sg*; **l'~ verde** *(Aut)* synchronized traffic lights *pl*

on'data *sf* wave, billow; *(fig)* wave, surge; **a ondate** in waves; **~ di caldo** heatwave; **~ di freddo** cold spell *o* snap

'onde *cong (affinché: con il congiuntivo)* so that, in order that; *(: con l'infinito)* so as to, in order to

ondeggi'are [onded'dʒare] *vi (acqua)* to ripple; *(muoversi sulle onde: barca)* to rock, roll; *(fig: muoversi come le onde, barcollare)* to sway; *(essere incerto)* to waver

on'doso, -a *ag (moto)* of the waves

ondu'lato, -a *ag (capelli)* wavy; *(terreno)* undulating; **cartone ~** corrugated paper; **lamiera ondulata** sheet of corrugated iron

ondula'torio, -a *ag* undulating; *(Fisica)* undulatory, wave *cpd*

ondulazi'one [ondulat'tsjone] *sf* undulation; *(acconciatura)* wave

one'rato, -a *ag*: **~ di** burdened with, loaded with

'onere *sm* burden; **~ finanziario** financial charge; **oneri fiscali** taxes

one'roso, -a *ag (fig)* heavy, onerous

onestà *sf* honesty

onesta'mente *av* honestly; fairly, virtuously; *(in verità)* honestly, frankly

o'nesto, -a *ag (probo, retto)* honest; *(giusto)* fair; *(casto)* chaste, virtuous

'onice ['onitʃe] *sf* onyx

o'nirico, -a, ci, che *ag* dreamlike, dream *cpd*

onnipo'tente *ag* omnipotent

onnipre'sente *ag* omnipresent; *(scherzoso)* ubiquitous

onnisci'ente [onniʃʃente] *ag* omniscient

onniveg'gente [onnived'dʒente] *ag* all-seeing

ono'mastico, -ci *sm* name day

onomato'pea *sf* onomatopoeia

onomato'peico, -a, ci, che *ag* onomatopoeic

ono'ranze [ono'rantse] *sfpl* honours (Brit), honors (US)

ono'rare *vt* to honour (Brit), honor (US); *(far onore a)* to do credit to; **onorarsi** *vr*: **onorarsi di qc/di fare** to feel hono(u)red by sth/to do

ono'rario, -a *ag* honorary ■ *sm* fee

onora'tissimo, -a *ag (in presentazioni):* **~!** delighted to meet you!

ono'rato, -a *ag (reputazione, famiglia, carriera)* distinguished; **essere ~ di fare qc** to have the honour to do sth *o* of doing sth; **~ di conoscerla!** (it is) a pleasure to meet you!

o'nore *sm* honour (Brit), honor (US); **in ~ di** in hono(u)r of; **fare gli onori di casa** to play host (*o* hostess); **fare ~ a** to hono(u)r; *(pranzo)* to do justice to; *(famiglia)* to be a credit to;

farsi ~ to distinguish o.s.; **posto d'**~ place of hono(u)r; **a onor del vero ...** to tell the truth ...

ono'revole *ag* honourable (*Brit*), honorable (*US*) ▪ *sm/f* (*Pol*) ≈ Member of Parliament (*Brit*), ≈ Congressman/woman (*US*)

onorifi'cenza [onorifi'tʃɛntsa] *sf* honour (*Brit*), honor (*US*); decoration

ono'rifico, -a, ci, che *ag* honorary

'**onta** *sf* shame, disgrace; **ad** ~ **di** despite, notwithstanding

on'tano *sm* alder

'**O.N.U.** *sigla f* (= *Organizzazione delle Nazioni Unite*) UN, UNO

'**OPA** *sigla f* = **offerta pubblica d'acquisto**

o'paco, -a, chi, che *ag* (*vetro*) opaque; (*metallo*) dull, matt

o'pale *sm o f* opal

'**O.P.E.C.** *sigla f* (= *Organization of Petroleum Exporting Countries*) OPEC

'**opera** *sf* (*gen*) work; (*azione rilevante*) action, deed, work; (*Mus*) work; opus; (*melodramma*) opera; (*teatro*) opera house; (*ente*) institution, organization; **per** ~ **sua** thanks to him; **fare** ~ **di persuasione presso qn** to try to convince sb; **mettersi/essere all'** to get down to/be at work; ~ **d'arte** work of art; ~ **buffa** comic opera; ~ **lirica** (grand) opera; ~ **pia** religious charity; **opere pubbliche** (**OO. PP.**) public works; **opere di restauro/di scavo** restoration/excavation work *sg*

ope'raio, -a *ag* working-class; workers'; (*Zool: ape, formica*) worker *cpd* ▪ *sm/f* worker; **classe operaia** working class; ~ **di fabbrica** factory worker; ~ **a giornata** day labourer (*Brit*) o laborer (*US*); ~ **specializzato** o **qualificato** skilled worker; ~ **non specializzato** semi-skilled worker

ope'rare *vt* to carry out, make; (*Med*) to operate on ▪ *vi* to operate, work; (*rimedio*) to act, work; (*Med*) to operate; **operarsi** *vr* to occur, take place; (*Med*) to have an operation; **operarsi d'appendicite** to have one's appendix out; ~ **qn d'urgenza** to perform an emergency operation on sb

opera'tivo, -a *ag* operative, operating; **piano** ~ (*Mil*) plan of operations

ope'rato *sm* (*comportamento*) actions *pl*

opera'tore, -'trice *sm/f* operator; (*TV, Cine*) cameraman; **aperto solo agli operatori** (*Comm*) open to the trade only; ~ **di borsa** dealer on the stock exchange; ~ **ecologico** refuse collector; ~ **economico** agent, broker; ~ **del suono** sound recordist; ~ **turistico** tour operator

opera'torio, -a *ag* (*Med*) operating

operazi'one [operat'tsjone] *sf* operation

ope'retta *sf* (*Mus*) operetta, light opera

operosità *sf* industry

ope'roso, -a *ag* industrious, hard-working

opi'ficio [opi'fitʃo] *sm* factory, works *pl*

opi'nabile *ag* (*discutibile*) debatable, questionable; **è** ~ it is a matter of opinion

opini'one *sf* opinion; **avere il coraggio delle proprie opinioni** to have the courage of one's convictions; **l'** ~ **pubblica** public opinion

opinio'nista, -i, e *sm/f* (political) columnist

op là *escl* (*per far saltare*) hup!; (*a bimbo che è caduto*) upsy-daisy!

'**oppio** *sm* opium

oppi'omane *sm/f* opium addict

oppo'nente *ag* opposing ▪ *sm/f* opponent

op'pongo *etc vb vedi* **opporre**

op'porre *vt* to oppose; **opporsi** *vr*: **opporsi (a qc)** to oppose (sth); to object (to sth); ~ **resistenza/un rifiuto** to offer resistance/to refuse

opportu'nista, -i, e *sm/f* opportunist

opportunità *sf inv* opportunity; (*convenienza*) opportuneness, timeliness

oppor'tuno, -a *ag* timely, opportune; (*giusto*) right, appropriate; **a tempo** ~ at the right o the appropriate time

op'posi *etc vb vedi* **opporre**

opposi'tore, -'trice *sm/f* opposer, opponent

opposizi'one [oppozit'tsjone] *sf* opposition; (*Dir*) objection; **essere in netta** ~ (*idee, opinioni*) to clash, be in complete opposition; **fare** ~ **a qn/qc** to oppose sb/sth

op'posto, -a *pp di* **opporre** ▪ *ag* opposite; (*opinioni*) conflicting ▪ *sm* opposite, contrary; **all'** ~ on the contrary

oppressi'one *sf* oppression

oppres'sivo, -a *ag* oppressive

op'presso, -a *pp di* **opprimere**

oppres'sore *sm* oppressor

oppri'mente *ag* (*caldo, noia*) oppressive; (*persona*) tiresome; (*deprimente*) depressing

op'primere *vt* (*premere, gravare*) to weigh down; (*estenuare: caldo*) to suffocate, oppress; (*tiranneggiare: popolo*) to oppress

oppu'gnare [oppuɲ'ɲare] *vt* (*fig*) to refute

op'pure *cong* or (else)

op'tare *vi*: ~ **per** (*scegliere*) to opt for, decide upon; (*Borsa*) to take (out) an option on

'**optimum** *sm inv* optimum

opu'lento, -a *ag* (*ricco*) rich, wealthy, affluent; (*arredamento etc*) opulent

opu'lenza [opu'lɛntsa] *sf* (*vedi ag*) richness, wealth, affluence; opulence

o'puscolo *sm* booklet, pamphlet

OPV *sigla f* = **offerta pubblica di vendita**

opzio'nale [optsjo'nale] *ag* optional

opzi'one [op'tsjone] *sf* option
OR *sigla* = **Oristano**
'ora *sf* (*60 minuti*) hour; (*momento*) time
  ■ *av* (*adesso*) now; (*poco fa*): **è uscito proprio**
  ~ he's just gone out; (*tra poco*) presently, in a
  minute; (*correlativo*): **~ ..., ~ now ... now;**
  che ~ è?, che ore sono? what time is it?;
  domani a quest'~ this time tomorrow;
  non veder l'~ di fare to long to do, look
  forward to doing; **fare le ore piccole** to stay
  up till the early hours (of the morning) *o* the
  small hours; **è ~ di partire** it's time to go;
  di buon' ~ early; **alla buon'~!** at last!; **~**
  legale *o* **estiva** summer time (*Brit*), daylight
  saving time (*US*); **~ locale** local time; **~ di**
  pranzo lunchtime; **~ di punta** (*Aut*) rush
  hour; **d'~ in avanti** *o* **poi** from now on; **or ~**
  just now, a moment ago; **~ come ~** right
  now, at present; **10 anni or sono** 10 years
  ago
o'racolo *sm* oracle
'orafo *sm* goldsmith
o'rale *ag, sm* oral
oral'mente *av* orally
ora'mai *av* = **ormai**
o'rario, -a *ag* hourly; (*fuso, segnale*) time *cpd*;
  (*velocità*) per hour ■ *sm* timetable, schedule;
  (*di visite etc*) hours *pl*; time(s) (*pl*); **~ di**
  apertura/chiusura opening/closing time;
  ~ di apertura degli sportelli bank opening
  hours; **~ elastico** *o* **flessibile** (*Industria*)
  flexitime; **~ ferroviario** railway timetable;
  ~ di lavoro/d'ufficio working/office hours
o'rata *sf* sea bream
ora'tore, -'trice *sm/f* speaker; orator
ora'torio, -a *ag* oratorical ■ *sm* (*Rel*) oratory;
  (*Mus*) oratorio ■ *sf* (*arte*) oratory
orazi'one [orat'tsjone] *sf* (*Rel*) prayer;
  (*discorso*) speech, oration
or'bene *cong* so, well (then)
'orbita *sf* (*Astr, Fisica*) orbit; (*Anat*) (eye-)socket
orbi'tare *vi* to orbit
'orbo, -a *ag* blind
'Orcadi *sfpl*: **le (isole) ~** the Orkney Islands,
  the Orkneys
or'chestra [or'kɛstra] *sf* orchestra
orches'trale [orkes'trale] *ag* orchestral
  ■ *sm/f* orchestra player
orches'trare [orkes'trare] *vt* to orchestrate;
  (*fig*) to stage-manage
orchi'dea [orki'dɛa] *sf* orchid
'orcio ['ortʃo] *sm* jar
'orco, -chi *sm* ogre
'orda *sf* horde
or'digno [or'diɲɲo] *sm*: **~ esplosivo** explosive
  device
ordi'nale *ag, sm* ordinal

ordina'mento *sm* order, arrangement;
  (*regolamento*) regulations *pl*, rules *pl*; **~**
  scolastico/giuridico education/legal
  system
ordi'nanza [ordi'nantsa] *sf* (*Dir, Mil*) order;
  (*Amm: decreto*) decree; (*persona: Mil*) orderly,
  batman; **d'~** (*Mil*) regulation *cpd*; **ufficiale**
  d'~ orderly; **~ municipale** by(e)-law
ordi'nare *vt* (*mettere in ordine*) to arrange,
  organize; (*Comm*) to order; (*prescrivere:*
  medicina) to prescribe; (*comandare*): **~ a qn di**
  fare qc to order *o* command sb to do sth; (*Rel*)
  to ordain
ordi'nario, -a *ag* (*comune*) ordinary;
  (*grossolano*) coarse, common ■ *sm* ordinary;
  (*di università*) full professor
ordina'tivo, -a *ag* regulating, governing
  ■ *sm* (*Comm*) order
ordi'nato, -a *ag* tidy, orderly
ordinazi'one [ordinat'tsjone] *sf* (*Comm*)
  order; (*Rel*) ordination; **fare un'~ di qc** to
  put in an order for sth, order sth; **eseguire**
  qc su ~ to make sth to order
'ordine *sm* order; (*carattere*): **d'~ pratico** of a
  practical nature; **all'~** (*Comm: assegno*) to
  order; **di prim'~** first-class; **fino a nuovo ~**
  until further notice; **essere in ~** (*documenti*)
  to be in order; (*persona, stanza*) to be tidy;
  mettere in ~ to put in order, tidy (up);
  richiamare all'~ to call to order; **le forze**
  dell'~ the forces of law and order; **~**
  d'acquisto purchase order; **l'~ degli**
  avvocati ≈ the Bar; **~ del giorno** (*di seduta*)
  agenda; (*Mil*) order of the day; **l'~ dei medici**
  ≈ the Medical Association; **~ di pagamento**
  standing order (*Brit*), automatic payment
  (*US*); **l'~ pubblico** law and order; **ordini**
  (sacri) (*Rel*) holy orders
or'dire *vt* (*fig*) to plot, scheme
or'dito *sm* (*di tessuto*) warp
orecchi'abile [orek'kjabile] *ag* (*canzone*)
  catchy
orec'chino [orek'kino] *sm* earring
o'recchio [o'rekkjo] (*pl(f)* **orecchie**) *sm* (*Anat*)
  ear; **avere ~** to have a good ear (for music);
  venire all'~ di qn to come to sb's attention;
  fare orecchie da mercante (a) to turn a
  deaf ear (to)
orecchi'oni [orek'kjoni] *smpl* (*Med*) mumps *sg*
o'refice [o'refitʃe] *sm* goldsmith; jeweller
  (*Brit*), jeweler (*US*)
orefice'ria [orefitʃe'ria] *sf* (*arte*) goldsmith's
  art; (*negozio*) jeweller's (shop) (*Brit*), jewelry
  store (*US*)
'orfano, -a *ag* orphan(ed) ■ *sm/f* orphan; **~ di**
  padre/madre fatherless/motherless
orfano'trofio *sm* orphanage

o

245

orga'netto *sm* barrel organ; (*fam: armonica a bocca*) mouth organ; (*fisarmonica*) accordion

or'ganico, -a, ci, che *ag* organic ■ *sm* personnel, staff

organi'gramma, -i *sm* organization chart; (*Inform*) computer flow chart

orga'nismo *sm* (*Biol*) organism; (*Anat, Amm*) body, organism

orga'nista, -i, e *sm/f* organist

organiz'zare [organid'dzare] *vt* to organize; **organizzarsi** *vr* to get organized

organizza'tivo, -a [organiddza'tivo] *ag* organizational

organizza'tore, -'trice [organiddza'tore] *ag* organizing ■ *sm/f* organizer

organizzazi'one [organiddzat'tsjone] *sf* (*azione*) organizing, arranging; (*risultato*) organization; **O~ Mondiale della Sanità** World Health Organization

'**organo** *sm* organ; (*di congegno*) part; (*portavoce*) spokesman/woman, mouthpiece; **organi di trasmissione** (*Tecn*) transmission (unit) *sg*

or'gasmo *sm* (*Fisiol*) orgasm; (*fig*) agitation, anxiety

'**orgia, -ge** ['ɔrdʒa] *sf* orgy

or'goglio [or'gɔʎʎo] *sm* pride

orgogli'oso, -a [orgoʎ'ʎoso] *ag* proud

orien'tabile *ag* adjustable

orien'tale *ag* (*paese, regione*) eastern; (*tappeti, lingua, civiltà*) oriental

orienta'mento *sm* positioning; orientation; direction; **senso di ~** sense of direction; **perdere l'~** to lose one's bearings; **~ professionale** careers guidance

orien'tare *vt* (*situare*) to position; (*carta, bussola*) to orientate; (*fig*) to direct; **orientarsi** *vr* to find one's bearings; (*fig: tendere*) to tend, lean; (*indirizzarsi*): **orientarsi verso** to take up, go in for

orienta'tivo, -a *ag* indicative, for guidance; **a scopo ~** for guidance

ori'ente *sm* east; **l'O~** the East, the Orient; **il Medio/l'Estremo O~** the Middle/Far East; **a ~** in the east

ori'ficio [ori'fitʃo], **ori'fizio** [ori'fittsjo] *sm* (*apertura*) opening; (*di tubo*) mouth; (*Anat*) orifice

o'rigano *sm* oregano

origi'nale [oridʒi'nale] *ag* original; (*bizzarro*) eccentric ■ *sm* original

originalità [oridʒinali'ta] *sf* originality; eccentricity

origi'nare [oridʒi'nare] *vt* to bring about, produce ■ *vi*: **~ da** to arise *o* spring from

origi'nario, -a [oridʒi'narjo] *ag* original; **essere ~ di** to be a native of; (*animale, pianta*) to be indigenous to, be native to

o'rigine [o'ridʒine] *sf* origin; **all'~** originally; **d'~ inglese** of English origin; **avere ~ da** to originate from; **dare ~ a** to give rise to

origli'are [oriʎ'ʎare] *vi*: **~ (a)** to eavesdrop (on)

o'rina *sf* urine

ori'nale *sm* chamberpot

ori'nare *vi* to urinate ■ *vt* to pass

orina'toio *sm* (*public*) urinal

ori'undo, -a *ag*: **essere ~ di Milano** *etc* to be of Milanese *etc* extraction *o* origin ■ *sm/f* person of foreign extraction *o* origin

orizzon'tale [oriddzon'tale] *ag* horizontal

oriz'zonte [orid'dzonte] *sm* horizon

ORL *sigla f* (*Med*: = *otorinolaringoiatria*) ENT

or'lare *vt* to hem

orla'tura *sf* (*azione*) hemming *no pl*; (*orlo*) hem

'**orlo** *sm* edge, border; (*di recipiente*) rim, brim; (*di vestito etc*) hem; **pieno fino all'~** full to the brim, brimful; **sull'~ della pazzia/della rovina** on the brink *o* verge of madness/ruin; **~ a giorno** hemstitch

'**orma** *sf* (*di persona*) footprint; (*di animale*) track; (*impronta, traccia*) mark, trace; **seguire** *o* **calcare le orme di qn** to follow in sb's footsteps

or'mai *av* by now, by this time; (*adesso*) now; (*quasi*) almost, nearly

ormeggi'are [ormed'dʒare] *vt*, **ormeggi'arsi** *vr* (*Naut*) to moor

or'meggio [or'meddʒo] *sm* (*atto*) mooring *no pl*; (*luogo*) moorings *pl*; **posto d'~** berth

ormo'nale *ag* hormonal; (*disfunzione, cura*) hormone *cpd*; **terapia ~** hormone therapy

or'mone *sm* hormone

ornamen'tale *ag* ornamental, decorative

orna'mento *sm* ornament, decoration

or'nare *vt* to adorn, decorate; **ornarsi** *vr*: **ornarsi (di)** to deck o.s. (out) (with)

or'nato, -a *ag* ornate

ornitolo'gia [ornitolo'dʒia] *sf* ornithology

orni'tologo, -a, gi, ghe *sm/f* ornithologist

'**oro** *sm* gold; **d'~, in ~** gold *cpd*; **d'~** (*colore, occasione*) golden; (*persona*) marvellous (*Brit*), marvelous (*US*); **un affare d'~** a real bargain; **prendere qc per ~ colato** to take sth as gospel (truth); **~ nero** black gold; **~ zecchino** pure gold

orologe'ria [orolodʒe'ria] *sf* watchmaking *no pl*; watchmaker's (shop), clockmaker's (shop); **bomba a ~** time bomb

orologi'aio [orolo'dʒajo] *sm* watchmaker; clockmaker

oro'logio [oro'lɔdʒo] *sm* clock; (*da tasca, da polso*) watch; **~ biologico** biological clock; **~ da polso** wristwatch; **~ al quarzo** quartz watch; **~ a sveglia** alarm clock o'roscopo *sm* horoscope

or'rendo, -a *ag* (*spaventoso*) horrible, awful; (*bruttissimo*) hideous

or'ribile *ag* horrible

'orrido, -a *ag* fearful, horrid

orripi'lante *ag* hair-raising, horrifying

or'rore *sm* horror; avere in ~ qn/qc to loathe o detest sb/sth; **mi fanno ~** I loathe o detest them

orsacchi'otto [orsak'kjɔtto] *sm* teddy bear

'orso *sm* bear; **~ bruno/bianco** brown/polar bear

orsù *escl* come now!

or'taggio [or'taddʒo] *sm* vegetable

or'tensia *sf* hydrangea

or'tica, -che *sf* (stinging) nettle

orti'caria *sf* nettle rash

orticol'tura *sf* horticulture

'orto *sm* vegetable garden, kitchen garden; (*Agr*) market garden (*Brit*), truck farm (*US*); **~ botanico** botanical garden(s) (*pl*)

orto'dosso, -a *ag* orthodox

ortofrut'ticolo, -a *ag* fruit and vegetable *cpd*

ortogo'nale *ag* perpendicular

ortogra'fia *sf* spelling

orto'lano, -a *sm/f* (*venditore*) greengrocer (*Brit*), produce dealer (*US*)

ortope'dia *sf* orthopaedics *sg* (*Brit*), orthopedics *sg* (*US*)

orto'pedico, -a, ci, che *ag* orthopaedic (*Brit*), orthopedic (*US*) ■ *sm* orthopaedic specialist (*Brit*), orthopedist (*US*)

orzai'olo [ordza'jɔlo], orziaiu'olo [ordza'jwɔlo] *sm* (*Med*) stye

or'zata [or'dzata] *sf* barley water

'orzo ['ɔrdzo] *sm* barley

'OSA *sigla f* (= *Organizzazione degli Stati Americani*) OAS (= *Organization of American States*)

o'sare *vt, vi* to dare; **~ fare** to dare (to) do; **come osi?** how dare you?

oscenità [oʃʃeni'ta] *sf inv* obscenity

o'sceno, -a [oʃ'ʃɛno] *ag* obscene; (*ripugnante*) ghastly

oscil'lare [oʃʃil'lare] *vi* (*pendolo*) to swing; (*dondolare: al vento etc*) to rock; (*variare*) to fluctuate; (*Tecn*) to oscillate; (*fig*): **~ fra** to waver between

oscillazi'one [oʃʃillat'tsjone] *sf* oscillation; (*di prezzi, temperatura*) fluctuation

oscura'mento *sm* darkening; obscuring; (*in tempo di guerra*) blackout

oscu'rare *vt* to darken, obscure; (*fig*) to obscure; **oscurarsi** *vr* (*cielo*) to darken, cloud over; (*persona*): **si oscurò in volto** his face clouded over

oscurità *sf* (*vedi ag*) darkness; obscurity; gloominess

os'curo, -a *ag* dark; (*fig: incomprensibile*) obscure; (*umile: vita, natali*) humble, obscure; (*triste: pensiero*) gloomy, sombre ■ *sm*: **all'~** in the dark; **tenere qn all'~ di qc** to keep sb in the dark about sth

'Oslo *sf* Oslo

ospe'dale *sm* hospital

ospedali'ero, -a *ag* hospital *cpd*

ospi'tale *ag* hospitable

ospitalità *sf* hospitality

ospi'tare *vt* to give hospitality to; (*albergo*) to accommodate

'ospite *sm/f* (*persona che ospita*) host/hostess; (*persona ospitata*) guest

os'pizio [os'pittsjo] *sm* (*per vecchi etc*) home

'ossa *sfpl vedi* osso

os'sario *sm* (*Mil*) war memorial (*with burial place*)

ossa'tura *sf* (*Anat*) skeletal structure, frame; (*Tecn, fig*) framework

'osseo, -a *ag* bony; (*tessuto etc*) bone *cpd*

osse'quente *ag*: **~ alla legge** law-abiding

os'sequio *sm* deference, respect; **ossequi** *smpl* (*saluto*) respects, regards; **porgere i propri ossequi a qn** (*formale*) to pay one's respects to sb; **ossequi alla signora!** (give my) regards to your wife!

ossequi'oso, -a *ag* obsequious

osser'vanza [osser'vantsa] *sf* observance

osser'vare *vt* to observe, watch; (*esaminare*) to examine; (*notare, rilevare*) to notice, observe; (*Dir: la legge*) to observe, respect; (*mantenere: silenzio*) to keep, observe; **far ~ qc a qn** to point sth out to sb

osserva'tore, -'trice *ag* observant, perceptive ■ *sm/f* observer

osserva'torio *sm* (*Astr*) observatory; (*Mil*) observation post

osservazi'one [osservat'tsjone] *sf* observation; (*di legge etc*) observance; (*considerazione critica*) observation, remark; (*rimprovero*) reproof; **in ~** under observation; **fare un'~** to make a remark; to raise an objection; **fare un'~ a qn** to criticize sb

ossessio'nare *vt* to obsess, haunt; (*tormentare*) to torment, harass

ossessi'one *sf* obsession; (*seccatura*) nuisance

osses'sivo, -a *ag* obsessive, haunting troublesome

os'sesso, -a *ag* (*spiritato*) possessed

os'sia *cong* that is, to be precise

ossi'buchi [ossi'buki] *smpl di* ossobuco

ossi'dare *vt*, ossi'darsi *vr* to oxidize

ossidazi'one [ossidat'tsjone] *sf* oxidization, oxidation

'ossido *sm* oxide; **~ di carbonio** carbon monoxide

ossige'nare [ossidʒe'nare] vt to oxygenate; (decolorare) to bleach; **acqua ossigenata** hydrogen peroxide

os'sigeno [os'sidʒeno] sm oxygen

'osso sm (Anat: pl(f) **ossa**) bone; **d'~** (bottone etc) of bone, bone cpd; **avere le ossa rotte** to be dead o dog tired; **bagnato fino all'~** soaked to the skin; **essere ridotto all'~** (fig: magro) to be just skin and bone; (senza soldi) to be in dire straits; **rompersi l'~ del collo** to break one's neck; **rimetterci l'~ del collo** (fig) to ruin o.s., lose everything; **un ~ duro** (persona, impresa) a tough number; **~ di seppia** cuttlebone

osso'buco (pl **ossibuchi**) sm (Cuc) marrowbone; (piatto) stew made with knuckle of veal in tomato sauce

os'suto, -a ag bony

ostaco'lare vt to block, obstruct

os'tacolo sm obstacle; (Equitazione) hurdle, jump; **essere di ~ a qn/qc** (fig) to stand in the way of sb/sth

os'taggio [os'taddʒo] sm hostage

'oste, ostessa sm/f innkeeper

osteggi'are [osted'dʒare] vt to oppose, be opposed to

os'tello sm hostel; **~ della gioventù** youth hostel

osten'sorio sm (Rel) monstrance

osten'tare vt to make a show of, flaunt

ostentazi'one [ostentat'tsjone] sf ostentation, show

oste'ria sf inn

os'tessa sf vedi **oste**

os'tetrico, -a, ci, che ag obstetric ■ sm obstetrician ■ sf midwife

'ostia sf (Rel) host; (per medicinali) wafer

'ostico, -a, ci, che ag difficult, tough

os'tile ag hostile

ostilità sf hostility ■ sfpl (Mil) hostilities

osti'narsi vr to insist, dig one's heels in; **~ a fare** to persist (obstinately) in doing

osti'nato, -a ag (caparbio) obstinate; (tenace) persistent, determined

ostinazi'one [ostinat'tsjone] sf obstinacy; persistence

ostra'cismo [ostra'tʃizmo] sm ostracism

'ostrica, -che sf oyster

ostru'ire vt to obstruct, block

ostruzi'one [ostrut'tsjone] sf obstruction, blockage

ostruzio'nismo [ostruttsjo'nizmo] sm (Pol) obstructionism; (Sport) obstruction; **fare dell'~ a** (progetto, legge) to obstruct; **~ sindacale** work-to-rule (Brit), slowdown (US)

o'tite sf ear infection

otorinolaringoiatra, oto'rino(laringoi'atra), -i, e sm/f ear, nose and throat specialist

'otre sm (recipiente) goatskin

ott. abbr (= ottobre) Oct

ottago'nale ag octagonal

ot'tagono sm octagon

ot'tano sm octane; **numero di ottani** octane rating

ot'tanta num eighty

ottan'tenne ag eighty-year-old ■ sm/f octogenarian

ottan'tesimo, -a num eightieth

ottan'tina sf: **una ~ (di)** about eighty

ot'tavo, -a num eighth ■ sf octave

ottempe'ranza [ottempe'rantsa] sf: **in ~ a** (Amm) in accordance with, in compliance with

ottempe'rare vi: **~ a** to comply with, obey

ottene'brare vt to darken; (fig) to cloud

otte'nere vt to obtain, get; (risultato) to achieve, obtain

'ottico, -a, ci, che ag (della vista: nervo) optic; (dell'ottica) optical ■ sm optician ■ sf (scienza) optics sg; (Fot: lenti, prismi etc) optics pl

otti'male ag optimal, optimum

ottima'mente av excellently, very well

otti'mismo sm optimism

otti'mista, -i, e sm/f optimist

ottimiz'zare [ottimid'dzare] vt to optimize

ottimizzazi'one [ottimiddzat'tsjone] sf optimization

'ottimo, -a ag excellent, very good

'otto num eight

ot'tobre sm October; vedi anche **luglio**

otto'brino, -a ag October cpd

ottocen'tesco, -a, schi, sche [ottotʃen'tesko] ag nineteenth-century

otto'cento [otto'tʃento] num eight hundred ■ sm: **l'O~** the nineteenth century

otto'mila num eight thousand

ot'tone sm brass; **gli ottoni** (Mus) the brass

ottuage'nario, -a [ottuadʒe'narjo] ag, sm/f octogenarian

ot'tundere vt (fig) to dull

ottu'rare vt to close (up); (dente) to fill

ottura'tore sm (Fot) shutter; (nelle armi) breechblock

otturazi'one [otturat'tsjone] sf closing (up); (dentaria) filling

ottusità sf (vedi ag) obtuseness; dullness

ot'tuso, -a pp di **ottundere** ■ ag (Mat, fig) obtuse; (suono) dull

o'vaia sf, **o'vaio** sm (Anat) ovary

o'vale ag, sm oval

o'varico, -a ag ovarian

o'vatta sf cotton wool; (per imbottire) padding, wadding

ovat'tare vt (imbottire) to pad; (fig: smorzare) to muffle

ovazi'one [ovat'tsjone] sf ovation

'**ovest** sm west; **a ~ (di)** west (of); **verso ~** westward(s)

o'vile sm pen, enclosure; **tornare all'~** (fig) to return to the fold

o'vino, -a ag sheep cpd, ovine

'**O.V.N.I.** sigla m (= oggetto volante non identificato) UFO

ovulazi'one [ovulat'tsjone] sf ovulation

'**ovulo** sm (Fisiol) ovum

o'vunque av = **dovunque**

ov'vero cong (ossia) that is, to be precise; (oppure) or (else)

ovvi'are vi: **~ a** to obviate

'**ovvio, -a** ag obvious

ozi'are [ot'tsjare] vi to laze around

'**ozio** ['ɔttsjo] sm idleness; (tempo libero) leisure; **ore d'~** leisure time; **stare in ~** to be idle

ozi'oso, -a [ot'tsjoso] ag idle

o'zono [od'dzono] sm ozone; **lo strato d'~** the ozone layer

ozonos'fera [oddzonos'fɛra] sf ozone layer

Pp

P, p [pi] *sf o m inv* (*lettera*) P, p; **P come Padova** ≈ P for Peter

P *abbr* (= *peso*) wt (= *parcheggio*); P

p. *abbr* (= *pagina*) p

P2 *abbr f* (= *la* (*loggia*) P2) the P2 masonic lodge

PA *sigla* = Palermo

P.A. *abbr* = pubblica amministrazione

pa'care *vt* to calm; **pacarsi** *vr* (*tempesta, disordini*) to subside

paca'tezza [paka'tettsa] *sf* quietness, calmness

pa'cato, -a *ag* quiet, calm

'pacca, -che *sf* slap

pac'chetto [pak'ketto] *sm* packet;
~ **applicativo** (*Inform*) applications package;
~ **azionario** (*Finanza*) shareholding;
~ **software** (*Inform*) software package;
~ **turistico** package holiday (*Brit*) *o* tour

pacchi'ano, -a [pak'kjano] *ag* (*colori*) garish; (*abiti, arredamento*) vulgar, garish

'pacco, -chi *sm* parcel; (*involto*) bundle;
~ **postale** parcel

paccot'tiglia [pakkot'tiʎʎa] *sf* trash, junk

'pace ['patʃe] *sf* peace; **darsi** ~ to resign o.s.;
fare (la) ~ **con qn** to make it up with sb

pachis'tano, -a [pakis'tano] *ag, sm/f* Pakistani

pacifi'care [patʃifi'kare] *vt* (*riconciliare*) to reconcile, make peace between; (*mettere in pace*) to pacify

pacificazi'one [patʃifikat'tsjone] *sf* (*vedi vt*) reconciliation; pacification

pa'cifico, -a, ci, che [pa'tʃifiko] *ag* (*persona*) peaceable; (*vita*) peaceful; (*fig: indiscusso*) indisputable; (*ovvio*) obvious, clear ▪ *sm*: **i l P~, l'Oceano P~** the Pacific (Ocean)

paci'fismo [patʃi'fizmo] *sm* pacifism

paci'fista, -i, e [patʃi'fista] *sm/f* pacifist

PACS [paks] *sigla mpl* civil partnerships

pa'dano, -a *ag* of the Po; **la pianura padana** the Lombardy plain

pa'della *sf* frying pan; (*per infermi*) bedpan

padigli'one [padiʎ'ʎone] *sm* pavilion

'Padova *sf* Padua

pado'vano, -a *ag* of (*o* from) Padua

'padre *sm* father; **padri** *smpl* (*antenati*) forefathers

Padre'terno *sm*: **il** ~ God the Father

pa'drino *sm* godfather

padro'nale *ag* (*scala, entrata*) main, principal;
casa ~ country house

padro'nanza [padro'nantsa] *sf* command, mastery

padro'nato *sm*: **il** ~ the ruling class

pa'drone, -a *sm/f* master/mistress;
(*proprietario*) owner; (*datore di lavoro*) employer;
essere ~ **di sé** to be in control of o.s.; **~/a di casa** master/mistress of the house; (*per gli inquilini*) landlord/lady

padroneggi'are [padroned'dʒare] *vt* (*fig: sentimenti*) to master, control; (*materia*) to master, know thoroughly; **padroneggiarsi** *vr* to control o.s.

pae'saggio [pae'zaddʒo] *sm* landscape

paesag'gista, -i, e [paezad'dʒista] *sm/f* (*pittore*) landscape painter

pae'sano, -a *ag* country *cpd* ▪ *sm/f* villager, countryman/woman

pa'ese *sm* (*nazione*) country, nation; (*terra*) country, land; (*villaggio*) village; ~ **di provenienza** country of origin; **i Paesi Bassi** the Netherlands

paf'futo, -a *ag* chubby, plump

'paga, -ghe *sf* pay, wages *pl*; **giorno di** ~ pay day

pa'gabile *ag* payable; ~ **alla consegna/a vista** payable on delivery/on demand

pa'gaia *sf* paddle

paga'mento *sm* payment; ~ **anticipato** payment in advance; ~ **alla consegna** payment on delivery; ~ **all'ordine** cash with order; **la TV a** ~ payTV

pa'gano, -a *ag, sm/f* pagan

pa'gare *vt* to pay; (*acquisto, fig: colpa*) to pay for; (*contraccambiare*) to repay, pay back ▪ *vi* to pay; **quanto l'ha pagato?** how much did you pay for it?; **~ con carta di credito** to pay by credit card; **~ in contanti** to pay cash; **~ di persona** (fig) to suffer the consequences; **l'ho pagata cara** (fig) I paid dearly for it

pa'gella [pa'dʒɛlla] sf (Ins) school report (Brit), report card (US)

'paggio ['paddʒo] sm page(boy)

pagherò [page'rɔ] vb vedi **pagare** ■ sm inv IOU; **~ cambiario** promissory note

'pagina ['padʒina] sf page; **Pagine bianche** phone book, telephone directory; **Pagine Gialle**® Yellow Pages®

'paglia ['paʎʎa] sf straw; **avere la coda di ~** (fig) to have a guilty conscience; **fuoco di ~** (fig) flash in the pan

pagliac'cetto [paʎʎat'tʃetto] sm (per bambini) rompers pl

pagliac'ciata [paʎʎat'tʃata] sf farce

pagli'accio [paʎ'ʎattʃo] sm clown

pagli'aio [paʎ'ʎajo] sm haystack

paglie'riccio [paʎʎe'rittʃo] sm straw mattress

paglie'rino, -a [paʎʎe'rino] ag: **giallo ~** pale yellow

pagli'etta [paʎ'ʎetta] sf (cappello per uomo) (straw) boater; (per tegami etc) steel wool

pagli'uzza [paʎ'ʎuttsa] sf (blade of) straw; (d'oro etc) tiny particle, speck

pa'gnotta [paɲ'ɲɔtta] sf round loaf

'pago, -a, ghi, ghe ag: **~ (di)** satisfied (with)

pa'goda sf pagoda

pail'lette [pa'jɛt] sf inv sequin

'paio (pl(f) paia) sm pair; **un ~ di occhiali** a pair of glasses; **un ~ di** (alcuni) a couple of; **è un altro ~ di maniche** (fig) that's another kettle of fish

'paio etc vb vedi **parere**

pai'olo, paiu'olo sm (copper) pot

'Pakistan sm: **il ~** Pakistan

pakis'tano, -a ag, sm/f = **pachistano**

pal. abbr = **palude**

'pala sf shovel; (di remo, ventilatore, elica) blade; (di ruota) paddle

palan'drana sf (scherzoso: abito lungo e largo) tent

pa'lata sf shovelful; **fare soldi a palate** to make a mint

pala'tale ag (Anat, Ling) palatal

pa'lato sm palate

pa'lazzo [pa'lattso] sm (reggia) palace; (edificio) building; **~ di giustizia** courthouse; **~ dello sport** sports stadium; see note

was acquired by the state in 1919 and became the seat of the Ministry of Foreign Affairs; since 1961 it has housed the Prime Minister's office and hosted Cabinet meetings. Palazzo Madama, another sixteenth-century building which was originally built for the Medici family, has been the home of the Senate since 1871. Palazzo di Montecitorio, completed in 1694, has housed the "Camera dei deputati" since 1870.

pal'chetto [pal'ketto] sm shelf

'palco, -chi sm (Teat) box; (tavolato) platform, stand; (ripiano) layer

palco'scenico, -ci [palkoʃ'ʃɛniko] sm (Teat) stage

palermi'tano, -a ag of (o from) Palermo ■ sm/f person from Palermo

Pa'lermo sf Palermo

pale'sare vt to reveal, disclose; **palesarsi** vr to reveal o show o.s.

pa'lese ag clear, evident

Pales'tina sf: **la ~** Palestine

palesti'nese ag, sm/f Palestinian

pa'lestra sf gymnasium; (esercizio atletico) exercise, training; (fig) training ground, school

paletot [pal'to] sm inv overcoat

pa'letta sf spade; (per il focolare) shovel; (del capostazione) signalling disc

pa'letto sm stake, peg; (spranga) bolt

palin'sesto sm (Storia) palimpsest; (TV, Radio) programme (Brit) o program (US) schedule

'palio sm (gara): **il P~** horse race run at Siena; **mettere qc in ~** to offer sth as a prize; see note

palis'sandro sm rosewood

paliz'zata [palit'tsata] sf palisade

'palla sf ball; (pallottola) bullet; **prendere** (fig) to seize one's opportunity

pallaca'nestro *sf* basketball
pallanu'oto *sf* water polo
palla'volo *sf* volleyball
palleggi'are [palled'dʒare] *vi* (*Calcio*) to practise (*Brit*) o practice (*US*) with the ball; (*Tennis*) to knock up
pallia'tivo *sm* palliative; (*fig*) stopgap measure
'pallido, -a *ag* pale
pal'lina *sf* (*bilia*) marble
pal'lino *sm* (*Biliardo*) cue ball; (*Bocce*) jack; (*proiettile*) pellet; (*pois*) dot; **bianco a pallini blu** white with blue dots; **avere il ~ di** (*fig*) to be crazy about
pallon'cino [pallon'tʃino] *sm* balloon; (*lampioncino*) Chinese lantern
pal'lone *sm* (*palla*) ball; (*Calcio*) football; (*aerostato*) balloon; **gioco del ~** ball game
pal'lore *sm* pallor, paleness
pal'lottola *sf* pellet; (*proiettile*) bullet
'palma *sf* (*Anat*) = **palmo**; (*Bot*) palm; **~ da datteri** date palm
pal'mato, -a *ag* (*Zool: piede*) webbed; (*Bot*) palmate
pal'mipede *ag* web-footed
pal'mizio [pal'mittsjo] *sm* (*palma*) palm tree; (*ramo*) palm
'palmo *sm* (*Anat*) palm; **essere alto un ~** (*fig*) to be tiny; **restare con un ~ di naso** (*fig*) to be badly disappointed
'palo *sm* (*legno appuntito*) stake; (*sostegno*) pole; **fare da** o **il ~** (*fig*) to act as look-out; **saltare di ~ in frasca** (*fig*) to jump from one topic to another
palom'baro *sm* diver
pa'lombo *sm* (*pesce*) dogfish
pal'pare *vt* to feel, finger
'palpebra *sf* eyelid
palpi'tare *vi* (*cuore, polso*) to beat; (*più forte*) to pound, throb; (*fremere*) to quiver
palpitazi'one [palpitat'tsjone] *sf* palpitation
'palpito *sm* (*del cuore*) beat; (*fig: d'amore etc*) throb
paltò *sm inv* overcoat
pa'lude *sf* marsh, swamp
palu'doso, -a *ag* marshy, swampy
pa'lustre *ag* marsh *cpd*, swamp *cpd*
'pampino *sm* vine leaf
pana'cea [pana'tʃea] *sf* panacea
'Panama *sf* Panama; **il canale di ~** the Panama Canal
pana'mense *ag, sm/f* Panamanian
'panca, -che *sf* bench
pancarrè *sm* sliced bread
pan'cetta [pan'tʃetta] *sf* (*Cuc*) bacon
pan'chetto [pan'ketto] *sm* stool; footstool
pan'china [pan'kina] *sf* garden seat; (*di giardino pubblico*) (park) bench

'pancia, -ce ['pantʃa] *sf* belly, stomach; **mettere** o **fare ~** to be getting a paunch; **avere mal di ~** to have stomach ache o a sore stomach
panci'era [pan'tʃera] *sf* corset
panci'olle [pan'tʃolle] *av*: **stare in ~** to lounge about (*Brit*) o around
panci'otto [pan'tʃotto] *sm* waistcoat
pan'ciuto, -a [pan'tʃuto] *ag* (*persona*) potbellied; (*vaso, bottiglia*) rounded
'pancreas *sm inv* pancreas
'panda *sm inv* panda
pande'mia *sf* pandemic
pande'monio *sm* pandemonium
pan'doro *sm* *type of sponge cake eaten at Christmas*
'pane *sm* bread; (*pagnotta*) loaf (of bread); (*forma*): **un ~ di burro/cera** *etc* a pat of butter/bar of wax *etc*; **guadagnarsi il ~** to earn one's living; **dire ~ al ~, vino al vino** (*fig*) to call a spade a spade; **rendere pan per focaccia** (*fig*) to give tit for tat; **~ casereccio** homemade bread; **~ a cassetta** sliced bread; **~ integrale** wholemeal bread; **~ di segale** rye bread; **pan di Spagna** sponge cake; **~ tostato** toast
pane'girico [pane'dʒiriko] *sm* (*fig*) panegyric
panette'ria *sf* (*forno*) bakery; (*negozio*) baker's (shop), bakery
panetti'ere, -a *sm/f* baker
panet'tone *sm* *a kind of spiced brioche with sultanas (eaten at Christmas)*
'panfilo *sm* yacht
pan'forte *sm* *Sienese nougat-type delicacy*
pangrat'tato *sm* breadcrumbs *pl*
'panico, -a, ci, che *ag, sm* panic; **essere in preda al ~** to be panic-stricken; **lasciarsi prendere dal ~** to panic
pani'ere *sm* basket
panifica'tore, -'trice *sm/f* bread-maker, baker
pani'ficio [pani'fitʃo] *sm* (*forno*) bakery; (*negozio*) baker's (shop), bakery
pa'nino *sm* roll; **~ imbottito** filled roll; sandwich
panino'teca, -che *sf* sandwich bar
'panna *sf* (*Cuc*) cream; (*Aut*) = **panne**; **~ di cucina** cooking cream; **~ montata** whipped cream
'panne *sf inv* (*Aut*) breakdown; **essere in ~** to have broken down
pan'nello *sm* panel; **~ di controllo** control panel; **~ solare** solar panel
'panno *sm* cloth; **panni** *smpl* (*abiti*) clothes; **mettiti nei miei panni** (*fig*) put yourself in my shoes
pan'nocchia [pan'nɔkkja] *sf* (*di mais etc*) ear
panno'lino *sm* (*per bambini*) nappy (*Brit*), diaper (*US*)

panno'lone *sm* incontinence pad

pano'rama, -i *sm* panorama

pano'ramico, -a, ci, che *ag* panoramic; **strada panoramica** scenic route

pantacol'lant *smpl* leggings

panta'loni *smpl* trousers (Brit), pants (US), pair *sg* of trousers *o* pants

pan'tano *sm* bog

pan'tera *sf* panther

'pantheon ['panteon] *sm inv* pantheon

pan'tofola *sf* slipper

panto'mima *sf* pantomime

pan'zana [pan'tsana] *sf* fib, tall story

pao'nazzo, -a [pao'nattso] *ag* purple

'papa, -i *sm* pope

papà *sm inv* dad(dy); **figlio di ~** spoilt young man

pa'pale *ag* papal

pa'pato *sm* papacy

pa'pavero *sm* poppy

'papero, -a *sm/f* (Zool) gosling ▪ *sf* (fig) slip of the tongue, blunder

papi'llon [papi'jɔ̃] *sm inv* bow tie

pa'piro *sm* papyrus

'pappa *sf* baby cereal

pappa'gallo *sm* parrot; (fig: uomo) Romeo

pappa'gorgia, -ge [pappa'gɔrdʒa] *sf* double chin

pappar'della *sf* (fig) rigmarole

pap'pare *vt* (fam: anche: **papparsi**) to gobble up

par. *abbr* (= paragrafo) par

'para *sf*: **suole di ~** crepe soles

parà *abbr m inv* (= paracadutista) para

pa'rabola *sf* (Mat) parabola; (Rel) parable

para'bolico, -a, ci, che *ag* (Mat) parabolic; *vedi anche* **antenna**

para'brezza [para'breddza] *sm inv* (Aut) windscreen (Brit), windshield (US)

paracadu'tare *vt*, **paracadu'tarsi** *vr* to parachute

paraca'dute *sm inv* parachute

paracadu'tismo *sm* parachuting

paracadu'tista, -i, e *sm/f* parachutist; (Mil) paratrooper

para'carro *sm* kerbstone (Brit), curbstone (US)

paradi'siaco, -a, ci, che *ag* heavenly

para'diso *sm* paradise; **~ fiscale** tax haven

parados'sale *ag* paradoxical

para'dosso *sm* paradox

para'fango, -ghi *sm* mudguard

paraf'fina *sf* paraffin, paraffin wax

parafra'sare *vt* to paraphrase

pa'rafrasi *sf inv* paraphrase

para'fulmine *sm* lightning conductor

pa'raggi [pa'raddʒi] *smpl*: **nei ~** in the vicinity, in the neighbourhood (Brit) *o* neighborhood (US)

parago'nare *vt*: **~ con/a** to compare with/to

para'gone *sm* comparison; (esempio analogo) analogy, parallel; **reggere al ~** to stand comparison

pa'ragrafo *sm* paragraph

paraguai'ano, -a *ag*, *sm/f* Paraguayan

Paragu'ay [para'gwai] *sm*: **il ~** Paraguay

pa'ralisi *sf inv* paralysis

para'litico, -a, ci, che *ag*, *sm/f* paralytic

paraliz'zare [paralid'dzare] *vt* to paralyze

parallela'mente *av* in parallel

paralle'lismo *sm* (Mat) parallelism; (fig: corrispondenza) similarities pl

paral'lelo, -a *ag* parallel ▪ *sm* (Geo) parallel; (comparazione): **fare un ~ tra** to draw a parallel between ▪ *sf* parallel (line); **parallele** *sfpl* (attrezzo ginnico) parallel bars

para'lume *sm* lampshade

para'medico, -a, ci, che *ag* paramedical

para'menti *smpl* (Rel) vestments

pa'rametro *sm* parameter

paramili'tare *ag* paramilitary

pa'ranco, -chi *sm* hoist

para'noia *sf* paranoia; **andare/mandare in ~** (fam) to freak/be freaked out

para'noico, -a, ci, che *ag*, *sm/f* paranoid; (fam: angosciato) freaked (out)

paranor'male *ag* paranormal

para'occhi [para'ɔkki] *smpl* blinkers (Brit), blinders (US)

paraolim'piadi *sfpl* paralympics

para'petto *sm* parapet

para'piglia [para'piʎʎa] *sm* commotion

parapsicolo'gia [parapsikolo'dʒia] *sf* parapsychology

pa'rare *vt* (addobbare) to adorn, deck; (proteggere) to shield, protect; (scansare: colpo) to parry; (Calcio) to save ▪ *vi*: **dove vuole andare a ~?** what are you driving at?; **pararsi** *vr* (presentarsi) to appear, present o.s.

parasco'lastico, -a, ci, che *ag* (attività) extracurricular

para'sole *sm inv* parasol, sunshade

paras'sita, -i *sm* parasite

parassi'tario, -a *ag* parasitic

parasta'tale *ag* state-controlled

paras'tato *sm* employees in the state-controlled sector

pa'rata *sf* (Sport) save; (Mil) review, parade

pa'rati *smpl* hangings pl; **carta da ~** wallpaper

para'tia *sf* (di nave) bulkhead

para'urti *sm inv* (Aut) bumper

para'vento *sm* folding screen; **fare da ~ a qn** (fig) to shield sb

par'cella [par'tʃella] *sf* fee

parcheggi'are [parked'dʒare] *vt* to park

p

253

parcheggia'tore, -'trice [parkeddʒa'tore] *sm/f* parking attendant

par'cheggio [par'keddʒo] *sm* parking *no pl*; (*luogo*) car park (*Brit*), parking lot (*US*); (*singolo posto*) parking space

par'chimetro [par'kimetro] *sm* parking meter

'**parco, -chi** *sm* park; (*spazio per deposito*) depot; (*complesso di veicoli*) fleet

'**parco, -a, chi, che** *ag*: **~ (in)** (*sobrio*) moderate (in); (*avaro*) sparing (with)

par'cometro *sm* (*Aut*) (Pay and Display) ticket machine

pa'recchio, -a [pa'rekkjo] *det* quite a lot of; (*tempo*) quite a lot of, a long ■ *pron* quite a lot, quite a bit; (*tempo*) quite a while, a long time ■ *av* (*con ag*) quite, rather; (*con vb*) quite a lot, quite a bit; **parecchi, e** *det pl* quite a lot of, several ■ *pron pl* quite a lot, several

pareggi'are [pared'dʒare] *vt* to make equal; (*terreno*) to level, make level; (*bilancio, conti*) to balance ■ *vi* (*Sport*) to draw

pa'reggio [pa'reddʒo] *sm* (*Econ*) balance; (*Sport*) draw

paren'tado *sm* relatives *pl*, relations *pl*

pa'rente *sm/f* relative, relation

paren'tela *sf* (*vincolo di sangue: fig*) relationship; (*insieme dei parenti*) relations *pl*, relatives *pl*

pa'rentesi *sf* (*segno grafico*) bracket, parenthesis; (*frase incisa*) parenthesis; (*digressione*) parenthesis, digression; **tra ~** in brackets; (*fig*) incidentally

pa'rere *sm* (*opinione*) opinion; (*consiglio*) advice, opinion; **a mio ~** in my opinion ■ *vi* to seem, appear ■ *vb impers*: **pare che** it seems it appears that, they say that; **mi pare che** it seems to me that; **mi pare di sì/no** I think so/don't think so; **fai come ti pare** do as you like; **che ti pare del mio libro?** what do you think of my book?

pa'rete *sf* wall

'**pargolo, -a** *sm/f* child

'**pari** *ag inv* (*uguale*) equal, same; (*in giochi*) equal drawn, tied; (*Mat*) even ■ *sm inv* (*Pol: di Gran Bretagna*) peer ■ *sm/f inv* peer, equal; **copiato ~ ~** copied word for word; **siamo ~** (*fig*) we are quits *o* even; **alla ~** on the same level; (*Borsa*) at par; **ragazza alla ~** au pair (girl); **mettersi alla ~ con** to place o.s. on the same level as; **mettersi in ~ con** to catch up with; **andare di ~ passo con qn** to keep pace with sb

parifi'care *vt* (*scuola*) to recognize officially

parifi'cato, -a *ag*: **scuola parificata** *officially recognized private school*

Pa'rigi [pa'ridʒi] *sf* Paris

pari'gino, -a [pari'dʒino] *ag, sm/f* Parisian

pa'riglia [pa'riʎʎa] *sf* pair; **rendere la ~** to give tit for tat

parità *sf* parity, equality; (*Sport*) draw, tie

pari'tetico, -a, ci, che *ag*: **commissione paritetica** joint committee; **rapporto ~** equal relationship

parlamen'tare *ag* parliamentary ■ *sm/f* ≈ Member of Parliament (*Brit*), ≈ Congressman/woman (*US*) ■ *vi* to negotiate, parley

parla'mento *sm* parliament; *see note*

parlan'tina *sf* (*fam*) talkativeness; **avere una buona ~** to have the gift of the gab

par'lare *vi* to speak, talk; (*confidare cose segrete*) to talk ■ *vt* to speak; **~ (a qn) di** to speak *o* talk (to sb) about; **~ chiaro** to speak one's mind; **~ male di qn/qc** to speak ill of sb/sth; **~ del più e del meno** to talk of this and that; **ne ho sentito ~** I have heard it mentioned; **non parliamone più** let's just forget about it; **i dati parlano** (*fig*) the facts speak for themselves

par'lata *sf* (*dialetto*) dialect

parla'tore, -'trice *sm/f* speaker

parla'torio *sm* (*di carcere etc*) visiting room; (*Rel*) parlour (*Brit*), parlor (*US*)

parlot'tare *vi* to mutter

parmigi'ano, -a [parmi'dʒano] *ag* Parma *cpd* of (*o* from) Parma ■ *sm* (*grana*) Parmesan (cheese); **alla parmigiana** (*Cuc*) with Parmesan cheese

paro'dia *sf* parody

parodi'are *vt* to parody

pa'rola *sf* word; (*facoltà*) speech; **parole** *sfpl* (*chiacchiere*) talk *sg*; **chiedere la ~** to ask permission to speak; **dare la ~ a qn** to call on sb to speak; **dare la propria ~ a qn** to give sb one's word; **mantenere la ~** to keep one's word; **mettere una buona ~ per qn** to put in a good word for sb; **passare dalle parole ai fatti** to get down to business; **prendere la ~** to take the floor; **rimanere senza parole** to be speechless; **rimangiarsi la ~** to go back on one's word; **non ho parole per ringraziarla** I don't know how to thank you; **rivolgere la ~ a qn** to speak to sb; **non è**

detta l'ultima ~ that's not the end of the matter; **è una persona di ~** he is a man of his word; **in parole povere** in plain English; **~ d'onore** word of honour; **~ d'ordine** (*Mil*) password; **parole incrociate** crossword (puzzle) *sg*

paro'laccia, -ce [paro'lattʃa] *sf* bad word, swearword

paros'sismo *sm* paroxysm

par'quet [par'kɛ] *sm* parquet (flooring)

parrò *etc vb vedi* **parere**

par'rocchia [par'rɔkkja] *sf* parish; (*chiesa*) parish church

parrocchi'ano, -a [parrok'kjano] *sm/f* parishioner

'parroco, -ci *sm* parish priest

par'rucca, -che *sf* wig

parrucchi'ere, -a [parruk'kjɛre] *sm/f* hairdresser ■ *sm* barber

parruc'cone *sm* (*peg*) old fogey

parsi'monia *sf* frugality, thrift

parsimoni'oso, -a *ag* frugal, thrifty

'parso, -a *pp di* **parere**

'parte *sf* part; (*lato*) side; (*quota spettante a ciascuno*) share; (*direzione*) direction; (*Pol*) party; faction; (*Dir*) party; **a ~** *ag* separate ■ *av* separately; **scherzi a ~** joking aside; **a ~ ciò** apart from that; **inviare a ~** (*campioni etc*) to send under separate cover; **da ~** (*in disparte*) to one side, aside; **mettere/prendere da ~** to put/take aside; **d'altra ~** on the other hand; **da ~ di** (*per conto di*) on behalf of; **da ~ mia** as far as I'm concerned, as for me; **da ~ di madre** on his (*o* her *etc*) mother's side; **essere dalla ~ della ragione** to be in the right; **da ~ a ~** right through; **da qualche ~** somewhere; **da nessuna ~** nowhere; **da questa ~** (*in questa direzione*) this way; **da ogni ~** on all sides, everywhere; (*moto da luogo*) from all sides; **fare ~ di qc** to belong to sth; **prendere ~ a qc** to take part in sth; **prendere le parti di qn** to take sb's side; **mettere qn a ~ di qc** to inform sb of sth; **costituirsi ~ civile contro qn** (*Dir*) to associate in an action with the public prosecutor against sb; **la ~ lesa** (*Dir*) the injured party; **le parti in causa** the parties concerned; **parti sociali** representatives of workers and employers

parteci'pante [partetʃi'pante] *sm/f*: **~ (a)** (*a riunione, dibattito*) participant (in); (*a gara sportiva*) competitor (in); (*a concorso*) entrant (to)

parteci'pare [partetʃi'pare] *vi*: **~ a** to take part in, participate in; (*utili etc*) to share in; (*spese etc*) to contribute to; (*dolore, successo di qn*) to share (in) ■ *vt*: **~ le nozze (a)** to announce one's wedding (to)

partecipazi'one [partetʃipat'tsjone] *sf* participation; sharing; (*Econ*) interest; **~ a banda armata** (*Dir*) belonging to an armed gang; **~ di maggioranza/minoranza** controlling/minority interest; **~ agli utili** profit-sharing; **partecipazioni di nozze** *wedding announcement card*; **ministro delle Partecipazioni statali** *minister responsible for companies in which the state has a financial interest*

par'tecipe [par'tetʃipe] *ag* participating; **essere ~ di** to take part in, participate in; (*gioia, dolore*) to share (in); (*consapevole*) to be aware of

parteggi'are [parted'dʒare] *vi*: **~ per** to side with, be on the side of

par'tenza [par'tentsa] *sf* departure; (*Sport*) start; **essere in ~** to be about to leave, be leaving; **passeggeri in ~ per** passengers travelling (*Brit*) *o* traveling (*US*) to; **siamo tornati al punto di ~** (*fig*) we are back where we started; **falsa ~** (*anche fig*) false start

parti'cella [parti'tʃɛlla] *sf* particle

parti'cipio [parti'tʃipjo] *sm* participle

partico'lare *ag* (*specifico*) particular; (*proprio*) personal, private; (*speciale*) special, particular; (*caratteristico*) distinctive; (*fuori dal comune*) peculiar ■ *sm* detail, particular; **in ~** in particular, particularly; **entrare nei particolari** to go into details

particolareggi'ato, -a [partikolared'dʒato] *ag* (extremely) detailed

particolarità *sf inv* (*carattere eccezionale*) peculiarity; (*dettaglio*) particularity, detail; (*caratteristica*) characteristic, feature

partigi'ano, -a [parti'dʒano] *ag* partisan ■ *sm* (*fautore*) supporter, champion; (*Mil*) partisan

par'tire *vi* to go, leave; (*allontanarsi*) to go (*o* drive *etc*) away *o* off; (*petardo, colpo*) to go off; (*fig: avere inizio, Sport*) to start; **sono partita da Roma alle 7** I left Rome at 7; **il volo parte da Ciampino** the flight leaves from Ciampino; **a ~ da** from; **la seconda a ~ da destra** the second from the right; **~ in quarta** to drive off at top speed; (*fig*) to be very enthusiastic

par'tita *sf* (*Comm*) lot, consignment; (*Econ: registrazione*) entry, item; (*Carte, Sport: gioco*) game; (*competizione*) match, game; **~ di caccia** hunting party; **~ IVA** VAT account; **~ semplice/doppia** (*Comm*) single-/double-entry book-keeping

par'tito *sm* (*Pol*) party; (*decisione*) decision, resolution; (*persona da maritare*) match; **per ~ preso** on principle; **mettere la testa a ~** to settle down

partitocra'zia [partitokrat'tsia] *sf hijacking of institutions by the party system*

parti'tura *sf* (*Mus*) score

'parto *sm* (*Med*) labour (*Brit*), labor (*US*); **sala ~ labo(u)r room; morire di ~** to die in childbirth

partori'ente *sf* woman in labour (*Brit*) o labor (*US*)

parto'rire *vt* to give birth to; (*fig*) to produce

par'venza [par'vɛntsa] *sf* semblance

'parvi *etc vb vedi* **parere**

parzi'ale [par'tsjale] *ag* (*limitato*) partial; (*non obiettivo*) biased, partial

parzialità [partsjali'ta] *sf*: **~ a favore di** partiality (for), bias (towards); **~ contro** bias (against)

'pascere ['paʃʃere] *vi* to graze ■ *vt* (*brucare*) to graze on; (*far pascolare*) to graze, pasture

pasci'uto, -a [paʃ'ʃuto] *pp di* **pascere** ■ *ag*: **ben ~** plump

pasco'lare *vt, vi* to graze

'pascolo *sm* pasture

'Pasqua *sf* Easter; **isola di ~** Easter Island

pas'quale *ag* Easter *cpd*

pasqu'etta *sf* Easter Monday

pas'sabile *ag* fairly good, passable

pas'saggio [pas'saddʒo] *sm* passing *no pl*, passage; (*traversata*) crossing *no pl*, passage; (*luogo, prezzo della traversata, brano di libro etc*) passage; (*su veicolo altrui*) lift (*Brit*), ride; (*Sport*) pass; **di ~** (*persona*) passing through; **~ pedonale/a livello** pedestrian/level (*Brit*) o grade (*US*) crossing; **~ di proprietà** transfer of ownership

passamane'ria *sf* braid, trimming

passamon'tagna [passamon'taɲɲa] *sm inv* balaclava

pas'sante *sm/f* passer-by ■ *sm* loop

passa'porto *sm* passport

pas'sare *vi* (*andare*) to go; (*veicolo, pedone*) to pass (by), go by; (*fare una breve sosta: postino etc*) to come, call; (*amico: per fare una visita*) to call o drop in; (*sole, aria, luce*) to get through; (*trascorrere: giorni, tempo*) to pass, go by; (*fig: proposta di legge*) to be passed; (*dolore*) to pass, go away; (*Carte*) to pass ■ *vt* (*attraversare*) to cross; (*trasmettere: messaggio*): **~ qc a qn** to pass sth on to sb; (*dare*): **~ qc a qn** to pass sth to sb, give sb sth; (*trascorrere: tempo*) to spend; (*superare: esame*) to pass; (*triturare: verdura*) to strain; (*approvare*) to pass, approve; (*oltrepassare, sorpassare: anche fig*) to go beyond, pass; (*fig: subire*) to go through; **~ da ... a** to pass from ... to; **~ di padre in figlio** to be handed down o to pass from father to son; **~ per** (*anche fig*) to go through; **~ per stupido/un genio** to be taken for a fool/a genius; **~ sopra** (*anche fig*) to pass over; **~ attraverso** (*anche fig*) to go through; **~ ad altro** to change

the subject; (*in una riunione*) to discuss the next item; **~ in banca/ufficio** to call (in) at the bank/office; **~ alla storia** to pass into history; **~ a un esame** to go up (to the next class) after an exam; **~ di moda** to go out of fashion; **~ a prendere qc/qn** to call and pick sth/sb up; **le passo il Signor X** (*al telefono*) here is Mr X, I'm putting you through to Mr X; **farsi ~ per** to pass o.s. off as, pretend to be; **lasciar ~ qn/qc** to let sb/sth through; **col ~ degli anni** (*riferito al presente*) as time goes by; (*riferito al passato*) as time passed o went by; **il peggio è passato** the worst is over; **30 anni e passa** well over 30 years ago; **~ una mano di vernice su qc** to give sth a coat of paint; **passarsela: come te la passi?** how are you getting on o along?

pas'sata *sf*: **dare una ~ di vernice a qc** to give sth a coat of paint; **dare una ~ al giornale** to have a look at the paper, skim through the paper

passa'tempo *sm* pastime, hobby

pas'sato, -a *ag* (*scorso*) last; (*finito: gloria, generazioni*) past; (*usanze*) out of date; (*sfiorito*) faded ■ *sm* (*Ling*) past (tense); **l'anno ~** last year; **nel corso degli anni passati** over the past years; **nei tempi passati** in the past; **sono le 8 passate** it's past o after 8 o'clock; **è acqua passata** (*fig*) it's over and done with; **~ prossimo** (*Ling*) present perfect; **~ remoto** (*Ling*) past historic; **~ di verdura** (*Cuc*) vegetable purée

passa'tutto *sm inv*, **passaver'dura** *sm inv* vegetable mill

passeg'gero, -a [passed'dʒero] *ag* passing ■ *sm/f* passenger

passeggi'are [passed'dʒare] *vi* to go for a walk; (*in veicolo*) to go for a drive

passeggi'ata [passed'dʒata] *sf* walk; drive; (*luogo*) promenade; **fare una ~** to go for a walk (o drive)

passeg'gino [passed'dʒino] *sm* pushchair (*Brit*), stroller (*US*)

pas'seggio [pas'seddʒo] *sm* walk, stroll; (*luogo*) promenade; **andare a ~** to go for a walk o a stroll

passe'rella *sf* footbridge; (*di nave, aereo*) gangway; (*pedana*) catwalk

'passero *sm* sparrow

pas'sibile *ag*: **~ di** liable to

passio'nale *ag* (*temperamento*) passionate; **delitto ~** crime of passion

passi'one *sf* passion

passività *sf* (*qualità*) passivity, passiveness; (*Comm*) liability

pas'sivo, -a *ag* passive ■ *sm* (*Ling*) passive; (*Econ*) debit; (*complesso dei debiti*) liabilities *pl*

passo *sm* step; (*andatura*) pace; (*rumore*) (foot)step; (*orma*) footprint; (*passaggio: fig: brano*) passage; (*valico*) pass; **a ~ d'uomo** at walking pace; (*Aut*) dead slow; **~ (a) ~** step by step; **fare due** *o* **quattro passi** to go for a walk *o* a stroll; **andare al ~ coi tempi** to keep up with the times; **di questo ~** (*fig*) at this rate; **fare i primi passi** (*anche fig*) to take one's first steps; **fare il gran ~** (*fig*) to take the plunge; **fare un ~ falso** (*fig*) to make the wrong move; **tornare sui propri passi** to retrace one's steps; **"~ carraio"** "vehicle entrance — keep clear"

pasta *sf* (*Cuc*) dough; (*impasto per dolce*) pastry; (*anche*: **pasta alimentare**) pasta; (*massa molle di materia*) paste; (*fig: indole*) nature; **paste** *sfpl* (*pasticcini*) pastries; **~ in brodo** noodle soup; **~ sfoglia** puff pastry *o* paste (US)

pastasciutta [pastaʃʃutta] *sf* pasta

pasteggiare [pasted'dʒare] *vi*: **~ a vino/champagne** to have wine/champagne with one's meal

pastella *sf* batter

pastello *sm* pastel

pastetta *sf* (*Cuc*) = **pastella**

pasticca, -che *sf* = **pastiglia**

pasticceria [pastittʃe'ria] *sf* (*pasticcini*) pastries *pl*, cakes *pl*; (*negozio*) cake shop; (*arte*) confectionery

pasticciare [pastit'tʃare] *vt* to mess up, make a mess of ■ *vi* to make a mess

pasticciere, -a [pastit'tʃere] *sm/f* pastrycook confectioner

pasticcino [pastit'tʃino] *sm* petit four

pasticcio [pas'tittʃo] *sm* (*Cuc*) pie; (*lavoro disordinato, imbroglio*) mess; **trovarsi nei pasticci** to get into trouble

pastificio [pasti'fitʃo] *sm* pasta factory

pastiglia [pas'tiʎʎa] *sf* pastille, lozenge

pastina *sf* small pasta shapes used in soup

pastinaca, -che *sf* parsnip

pasto *sm* meal; **vino da ~** table wine

pastoia *sf* (*fig*): **~ burocratica** red tape

pastone *sm* (*per animali*) mash; (*peg*) overcooked stodge

pastorale *ag* pastoral

pastore *sm* shepherd; (*Rel*) pastor, minister; (*anche*: **cane pastore**) sheepdog; **~ scozzese** (*Zool*) collie; **~ tedesco** (*Zool*) Alsatian (dog) (*Brit*) German shepherd (dog)

pastorizia [pasto'rittsja] *sf* sheep-rearing, sheep farming

pastorizzare [pastorid'dzare] *vt* to pasteurize

pastoso, -a *ag* doughy; pasty; (*fig: voce, colore*) mellow, soft

pastrano *sm* greatcoat

patacca, -che *sf* (*distintivo*) medal, decoration; (*fig: macchia*) grease spot, grease mark; (*articolo scadente*) bit of rubbish

patata *sf* potato; **patate fritte** chips (*Brit*), French fries

patatine *sfpl* (*potato*) crisps (*Brit*) *o* chips (*US*)

patatrac *sm* (*crollo: anche fig*) crash

pâté [pa'te] *sm inv* pâté; **~ di fegato d'oca** pâté de foie gras

patella *sf* (*Zool*) limpet

patema, -i *sm* anxiety, worry

patentato, -a *ag* (*munito di patente*) licensed, certified; (*fig scherzoso: qualificato*) utter, thorough

patente *sf* licence (*Brit*), license (*US*); (*anche*: **patente di guida**) driving licence (*Brit*), driver's license (*US*); **~ a punti** *driving licence with penalty points*

patentino *sm* temporary licence (*Brit*) *o* license (*US*)

paternalismo *sm* paternalism

paternalista *sm* paternalist

paternalistico, -a, ci, che *ag* paternalistic

paternità *sf* paternity, fatherhood

paterno, -a *ag* (*affetto, consigli*) fatherly; (*casa, autorità*) paternal

patetico, -a, ci, che *ag* pathetic; (*commovente*) moving, touching

pathos ['patos] *sm* pathos

patibolo *sm* gallows *sg*, scaffold

patimento *sm* suffering

patina *sf* (*su rame etc*) patina; (*sulla lingua*) fur, coating

patire *vt, vi* to suffer

patito, -a *sm/f* enthusiast, fan, lover

patologia [patolo'dʒia] *sf* pathology

patologico, -a, ci, che [pato'lɔdʒiko] *ag* pathological

patologo, -a, gi, ghe *sm/f* pathologist

patria *sf* homeland; **amor di ~** patriotism

patriarca, -chi *sm* patriarch

patrigno [pa'trinno] *sm* stepfather

patrimoniale *ag* (*rendita*) from property ■ *sf* (*anche*: **imposta patrimoniale**) property tax

patrimonio *sm* estate, property; (*fig*) heritage; **mi è costato un ~** (*fig*) it cost me a fortune, I paid a fortune for it; **~ spirituale/culturale** spiritual/cultural heritage; **~ ereditario** (*fig*) hereditary characteristics *pl*; **~ pubblico** public property

patrio, -a, ii, ie *ag* (*di patria*) native *cpd*, of one's country; (*Dir*): **patria potestà** parental authority; **amor ~** love of one's country

patriota, -i, e *sm/f* patriot

patriottico, -a, ci, che *ag* patriotic

patriottismo *sm* patriotism

p

patroci'nare [patrotʃi'nare] vt (Dir: difendere) to defend; (sostenere) to sponsor, support

patro'cinio [patro'tʃinjo] sm defence (Brit), defense (US); support, sponsorship

patro'nato sm patronage; (istituzione benefica) charitable institution o society

pa'trono sm (Rel) patron saint; (socio di patronato) patron; (Dir) counsel

'**patta** sf flap; (dei pantaloni) fly

patteggia'mento [patteddʒa'mento] sm (Dir) plea bargaining

patteggi'are [patted'dʒare] vt, vi to negotiate

patti'naggio [patti'naddʒo] sm skating

patti'nare vi to skate; ~ **sul ghiaccio** to ice-skate

pattina'tore, -'trice sm/f skater

'**pattino** sm skate; (di slitta) runner; (Aer) skid; (Tecn) sliding block; **pattini (da ghiaccio)** (ice) skates; **pattini in linea** rollerblades; **pattini a rotelle** roller skates

pat'tino sm (barca) kind of pedalo with oars

pat'tista, -i, e ag (Pol) of Patto per l'Italia ▪ sm/f (Pol) member (o supporter) of Patto per l'Italia

'**patto** sm (accordo) pact, agreement; (condizione) term, condition; **a ~ che** on condition that; **a nessun ~** under no circumstances; **venire o scendere a patti (con)** to come to an agreement (with); **P~ per l'Italia** (Pol) centrist party

pat'tuglia [pat'tuʎʎa] sf (Mil) patrol

pattugli'are [pattuʎ'ʎare] vt to patrol

pattu'ire vt to reach an agreement on

pattumi'era sf (dust)bin (Brit), ashcan (US)

pa'ura sf fear; **aver ~ di/di fare/che** to be frightened o afraid of/of doing/that; **far ~ a** to frighten; **per ~ di/che** for fear of/that; **ho ~ di sì/no** I am afraid so/not

pau'roso, -a ag (che fa paura) frightening; (che ha paura) fearful, timorous

'**pausa** sf (sosta) break; (nel parlare, Mus) pause

paven'tato, -a ag much-feared

pa'vese ag of (o from) Pavia

'**pavido, -a** ag (letterario) fearful

pavimen'tare vt (stanza) to floor; (strada) to pave

pavimentazi'one [pavimentat'tsjone] sf flooring; paving

pavi'mento sm floor

pa'vone sm peacock

pavoneggi'arsi [pavoned'dʒarsi] vr to strut about, show off

pazien'tare [pattsjen'tare] vi to be patient

pazi'ente [pat'tsjɛnte] ag, sm/f patient

pazi'enza [pat'tsjɛntsa] sf patience; **perdere la ~** to lose (one's) patience

pazza'mente [pattsa'mente] av madly; **essere ~ innamorato** to be madly in love

paz'zesco, -a, schi, sche [pat'tsesko] ag mad, crazy

paz'zia [pat'tsia] sf (Med) madness, insanity; (di azione, decisione) madness, folly; **è stata una ~!** it was sheer madness!

'**pazzo, -a** ['pattso] ag (Med) mad, insane; (strano) wild, mad ▪ sm/f madman/woman; **~ di** (gioia, amore etc) mad o crazy with; **~ per qc/qn** mad o crazy about sth/sb; **essere ~ da legare** to be raving mad o a raving lunatic

PC sigla = **Piacenza** ▪ sigla m inv [pi'tʃi] (= personal computer) PC

p.c. abbr = **per condoglianze; per conoscenza**

p.c.c. abbr (= per copia conforme) cc

P.C.I. sigla m (= Partito Comunista Italiano) former political party

PCUS sigla m = **Partito Comunista dell'Unione Sovietica**

PD sigla = **Padova**

P.D. abbr = **partita doppia**

PE sigla = **Pescara**

'**pecca, -che** sf defect, flaw, fault

peccami'noso, -a ag sinful

pec'care vi to sin; (fig) to err

pec'cato sm sin; **è un ~ che** it's a pity that; **che ~!** what a shame o pity!; **un ~ di gioventù** (fig) a youthful error o indiscretion

pecca'tore, -'trice sm/f sinner

peccherò etc [pekke'rɔ] vb vedi **peccare**

'**pece** ['petʃe] sf pitch

pechi'nese [peki'nese] ag, sm/f Pekin(g)ese inv ▪ sm (anche: **cane pechinese**) Pekin(g)ese inv, Peke

Pe'chino [pe'kino] sf Beijing, Peking

'**pecora** sf sheep; **~ nera** (fig) black sheep

peco'raio sm shepherd

peco'rella sf lamb; **la ~ smarrita** the lost sheep; **cielo a pecorelle** (fig: nuvole) mackerel sky

peco'rino sm sheep's milk cheese

pecu'lato sm (Dir) embezzlement

peculi'are ag: **~ di** peculiar to

peculiarità sf peculiarity

pecuni'ario, -a ag financial, money cpd

pe'daggio [pe'daddʒo] sm toll

pedago'gia [pedago'dʒia] sf pedagogy, educational methods pl

peda'gogico, -a, ci, che [peda'gɔdʒiko] ag pedagogic(al)

peda'gogo, -a, ghi, ghe sm/f pedagogue

peda'lare vi to pedal; (andare in bicicletta) to cycle

pe'dale sm pedal

pe'dana sf footboard; (Sport: nel salto) springboard; (: nella scherma) piste

pe'dante ag pedantic ▪ sm/f pedant

pedante'ria sf pedantry

pe'data *sf (impronta)* footprint; *(colpo)* kick; **prendere a pedate qn/qc** to kick sb/sth

pede'rasta, -i *sm* pederast

pe'destre *ag* prosaic, pedestrian

pedi'atra, -i, e *sm/f* paediatrician *(Brit)* pediatrician *(US)*

pedia'tria *sf* paediatrics *sg (Brit)*, pediatrics *sg (US)*

pedi'atrico, -a, ci, che *ag* pediatric

pedi'cure *sm/f inv* chiropodist *(Brit)*, podiatrist *(US)*

pedigree *sm inv* pedigree

pedi'luvio *sm* footbath

pe'dina *sf (della dama)* draughtsman *(Brit)*, draftsman *(US)*; *(fig)* pawn

pedi'nare *vt* to shadow, tail

pe'dofilo, -a *ag, sm/f* paedophile

pedo'nale *ag* pedestrian

pe'done, -a *sm/f* pedestrian ▪ *sm (Scacchi)* pawn

peeling ['piling] *sm inv (Cosmesi)* facial scrub

'peggio ['peddʒo] *av, ag inv* worse ▪ *sm o f:* **il o la ~** the worst; **cambiare in ~** to get o become worse; **alla ~** at worst, if the worst comes to the worst; **tirare avanti alla meno ~** to get along as best one can; **avere la ~** to come off worse, get the worst of it

peggiora'mento [peddʒora'mento] *sm* worsening

peggio'rare [peddʒo'rare] *vt* to make worse, worsen ▪ *vi* to grow worse, worsen

peggiora'tivo, -a [peddʒora'tivo] *ag* pejorative

peggi'ore [ped'dʒore] *ag (comparativo)* worse; *(superlativo)* worst ▪ *sm/f:* **il(la) ~** the worst (person); **nel ~ dei casi** if the worst comes to the worst

'pegno ['peɲɲo] *sm (Dir)* security, pledge; *(nei giochi di società)* forfeit; *(fig)* pledge, token; **dare in ~ qc** to pawn sth; **in ~ d'amicizia** as a token of friendship; **banco dei pegni** pawnshop

pelapa'tate *sm inv* potato peeler

pe'lare *vt (spennare)* to pluck; *(spellare)* to skin; *(sbucciare)* to peel; *(fig)* to make pay through the nose; **pelarsi** *vr* to go bald

pe'lato, -a *ag (sbucciato)* peeled; *(calvo)* bald; **(pomodori) pelati** peeled tomatoes

pel'lame *sm* skins *pl*, hides *pl*

'pelle *sf* skin; *(di animale)* skin, hide; *(cuoio)* leather; **essere ~ ed ossa** to be skin and bone; **avere la ~ d'oca** to have goose pimples o goose flesh; **avere i nervi a fior di ~** to be edgy; **non stare più nella ~ dalla gioia** to be beside o.s. with delight; **lasciarci la ~** to lose one's life; **amici per la ~** firm o close friends

pellegri'naggio [pellegri'naddʒo] *sm* pilgrimage

pelle'grino, -a *sm/f* pilgrim

pelle'rossa *(pl* **pellirosse)** *sm/f* Red Indian

pellette'ria *sf (articoli)* leather goods *pl*; *(negozio)* leather goods shop

pelli'cano *sm* pelican

pellicce'ria [pellittʃe'ria] *sf (negozio)* furrier's (shop); *(quantità di pellicce)* furs *pl*

pel'liccia, -ce [pel'littʃa] *sf (mantello di animale)* coat, fur; *(indumento)* fur coat; **~ ecologica** fake fur

pellicci'aio [pellit'tʃajo] *sm* furrier

pel'licola *sf (membrana sottile)* film, layer; *(Fot, Cine)* film

pelli'rossa *sm/f* = **pellerossa**

'pelo *sm* hair; *(pelame)* coat, hair; *(pelliccia)* fur; *(di tappeto)* pile; *(di liquido)* surface; **per un ~: per un ~ non ho perduto il treno** I very nearly missed the train; **c'è mancato un ~ che affogasse** he narrowly escaped drowning; **cercare il ~ nell'uovo** *(fig)* to pick holes, split hairs; **non aver peli sulla lingua** *(fig)* to speak one's mind

pe'loso, -a *ag* hairy

'peltro *sm* pewter

pe'luche [pə'lyʃ] *sm* plush; **giocattoli di ~** soft toys

pe'luria *sf* down

'pelvi *sf inv* pelvis

'pelvico, -a, ci, che *ag* pelvic

'pena *sf (Dir)* sentence; *(punizione)* punishment; *(sofferenza)* sadness *no pl*, sorrow; *(fatica)* trouble *no pl*, effort; *(difficoltà)* difficulty; **far ~** to be pitiful; **mi fai ~** I feel sorry for you; **essere o stare in ~ (per qc/qn)** to worry o be anxious (about sth/sb); **prendersi o darsi la ~ di fare** to go to the trouble of doing; **vale la ~ farlo** it's worth doing, it's worth it; **non ne vale la ~** it's not worth the effort, it's not worth it; **~ di morte** death sentence; **~ pecuniaria** fine

pe'nale *ag* penal ▪ *sf (anche:* **clausola penale)** penalty clause; **causa ~** criminal trial; **diritto ~** criminal law; **pagare la ~** to pay the penalty

pena'lista, -i, e *sm/f (avvocato)* criminal lawyer

penalità *sf inv* penalty

penaliz'zare [penalid'dzare] *vt (Sport)* to penalize

penalizzazi'one [penaliddzat'tsjone] *sf (Sport)* penalty

pe'nare *vi (patire)* to suffer; *(faticare)* to struggle

pen'dente *ag* hanging; leaning ▪ *sm (ciondolo)* pendant; *(orecchino)* drop earring

p

pen'denza [pen'dɛntsa] *sf* slope, slant; (*grado d'inclinazione*) gradient; (*Econ*) outstanding account

'**pendere** *vi* (*essere appeso*): ~ **da** to hang from; (*essere inclinato*) to lean; (*fig: incombere*): ~ **su** to hang over

pen'dice [pen'ditʃe] *sf* (*di monte*) slope

pen'dio, -ii *sm* slope, slant; (*luogo in pendenza*) slope

'**pendola** *sf* pendulum clock

pendo'lare *ag* pendulum *cpd*, pendular ■ *sm/f* commuter

pendola'rismo *sm* commuting

'**pendolo** *sm* (*peso*) pendulum; (*anche:* **orologio a pendolo**) pendulum clock

'**pene** *sm* penis

pene'trante *ag* piercing, penetrating

pene'trare *vi* to come *o* get in ■ *vt* to penetrate; ~ **in** to enter; (*proiettile*) to penetrate; (*acqua, aria*) to go *o* come into

penetrazi'one [penetrat'tsjone] *sf* penetration

penicil'lina [penitʃil'lina] *sf* penicillin

peninsu'lare *ag* peninsular; **l'Italia** ~ mainland Italy

pe'nisola *sf* peninsula

peni'tente *sm/f* penitent

peni'tenza [peni'tɛntsa] *sf* penitence; (*punizione*) penance

penitenzi'ario [peniten'tsjarjo] *sm* prison

'**penna** *sf* (*di uccello*) feather; (*per scrivere*) pen; **penne** *sfpl* (*Cuc*) quills (*type of pasta*); ~ **a feltro/stilografica/a sfera** felt-tip/fountain/ballpoint pen

pen'nacchio [pen'nakkjo] *sm* (*ornamento*) plume; **un ~ di fumo** (*fig*) a plume *o* spiral of smoke

penna'rello *sm* felt(-tip) pen

pennel'lare *vi* to paint

pennel'lata *sf* brushstroke

pen'nello *sm* brush; (*per dipingere*) (paint)brush; **a ~** (*perfettamente*) to perfection, perfectly; ~ **per la barba** shaving brush

Pen'nini *smpl*: **i ~** the Pennines

pen'nino *sm* nib

pen'none *sm* (*Naut*) yard; (*stendardo*) banner, standard

pen'nuto *sm* bird

pe'nombra *sf* half-light, dim light

pe'noso, -a *ag* painful, distressing; (*faticoso*) tiring, laborious

pen'sare *vi* to think ■ *vt* to think; (*inventare, escogitare*) to think out; ~ **a** to think of; (*amico, vacanze*) to think of *o* about; (*problema*) to think about; ~ **di fare qc** to think of doing sth; ~ **bene/male di qn** to think well/badly of sb, have a good/bad opinion of sb; **penso di sì** I think so; **penso di no** I don't think so; **a pensarci bene ...** on second thoughts (*Brit*) *o* thought (*US*) ...; **non voglio nemmeno pensarci** I don't even want to think about it; **ci penso io** I'll see to *o* take care of it

pen'sata *sf* (*trovata*) idea, thought

pensa'tore, -'trice *sm/f* thinker

pensie'rino *sm* (*dono*) little gift; (*pensiero*): **ci farò un ~** I'll think about it

pensi'ero *sm* thought; (*modo di pensare, dottrina*) thinking *no pl*; (*preoccupazione*) worry, care, trouble; **darsi ~ per qc** to worry about sth; **stare in ~ per qn** to be worried about sb; **un ~ gentile** (*anche fig: dono etc*) a kind thought

pensie'roso, -a *ag* thoughtful

'**pensile** *ag* hanging ■ *sm* (*in cucina*) wall cupboard

pensi'lina *sf* (*in stazione*) platform roof

pensiona'mento *sm* retirement; ~ **anticipato** early retirement

pensio'nante *sm/f* (*presso una famiglia*) lodger; (*di albergo*) guest

pensio'nato, -a *sm/f* pensioner ■ *sm* (*istituto*) hostel

pensi'one *sf* (*al prestatore di lavoro*) pension; (*vitto e alloggio*) board and lodging; (*albergo*) boarding house; **andare in ~** to retire; **mezza ~** half board; ~ **completa** full board; ~ **d'invalidità** disablement pension; ~ **per la vecchiaia** old-age pension

pensio'nistico, -a, ci, che *ag* pension *cpd*

pen'soso, -a *ag* thoughtful, pensive, lost in thought

pen'tagono *sm* pentagon; **il P~** the Pentagon

pentag'ramma, -i *sm* (*Mus*) staff, stave

pentapar'tito *sm* (*Pol*) five-party coalition government

pen'tathlon ['pɛntatlon] *sm* (*Sport*) pentathlon

Pente'coste *sf* Pentecost, Whit Sunday (*Brit*)

penti'mento *sm* repentance, contrition

pen'tirsi *vr*: ~ **di** to repent of; (*rammaricarsi*) to regret, be sorry for

penti'tismo *sm confessions from terrorists and members of organized crime rackets; see note*

○ **PENTITISMO**
○
○ The practice of *pentitismo* first emerged in
○ Italy during the 1970s, a period marked by
● major terrorist activity. Once arrested,
● some members of terrorist groups would
● collaborate with the authorities by
● providing information in return for a
● reduced sentence, or indeed for their own
● reasons. In recent years it has become

- common practice for members of Mafia
- organizations to become "pentiti",
- and special legislation has had to be
- introduced to provide for the sentencing
- and personal protection of these
- informants.

pen'tito, -a *sm/f* ≈ supergrass (*Brit*), *terrorist/ criminal who turns police informer*

'pentola *sf* pot; **~ a pressione** pressure cooker

pe'nultimo, -a *ag* last but one (*Brit*), next to last, penultimate

pe'nuria *sf* shortage

penzo'lare [pendzo'lare] *vi* to dangle, hang loosely

penzo'loni [pendzo'loni] *av* dangling, hanging down; **stare ~** to dangle, hang down

pe'pato, -a *ag* (*condito con pepe*) peppery, hot; (*fig: pungente*) sharp

'pepe *sm* pepper; **~ macinato/in grani/nero** ground/whole/black pepper

pepero'nata *sf* stewed peppers, tomatoes and onions

peperon'cino [peperon'tʃino] *sm* chilli pepper

pepe'rone *sm:* **~ (rosso)** red pepper, capsicum; **~ (verde)** green pepper, capsicum; **rosso come un ~** as red as a beetroot (*Brit*), fire-engine red (*US*); **peperoni ripieni** stuffed peppers

pe'pita *sf* nugget

 PAROLA CHIAVE

per *prep* **1** (*moto attraverso luogo*) through; **i ladri sono passati per la finestra** the thieves got in (*o* out) through the window; **l'ho cercato per tutta la casa** I've searched the whole house *o* all over the house for it
2 (*moto a luogo*) for, to; **partire per la Germania/il mare** to leave for Germany/the sea; **il treno per Roma** the Rome train, the train for *o* to Rome; **proseguire per Londra** to go on to London
3 (*stato in luogo*): **seduto/sdraiato per terra** sitting/lying on the ground
4 (*tempo*) for; **per anni/tanto tempo** for years/a long time; **per tutta l'estate** throughout the summer, all summer long; **lo rividi per Natale** I saw him again at Christmas; **lo faccio per lunedì** I'll do it for Monday
5 (*mezzo, maniera*) by; **per lettera/ferrovia/ via aerea** by letter/rail/airmail; **prendere qn per un braccio** to take sb by the arm

6 (*causa, scopo*) for; **assente per malattia** absent because of *o* through *o* owing to illness; **ottimo per il mal di gola** excellent for sore throats; **per abitudine** out of habit, from habit
7 (*limitazione*) for; **è troppo difficile per lui** it's too difficult for him; **per quel che mi riguarda** as far as I'm concerned; **per poco che sia** however little it may be; **per questa volta ti perdono** I'll forgive you this time
8 (*prezzo, misura*) for; (*distributivo*) a, per; **venduto per 3 milioni** sold for 3 million; **la strada continua per 3 km** the street goes on for 3 km; **15 euro per persona** 15 euros a *o* per person; **uno per volta** one at a time; **uno per uno** one by one; **giorno per giorno** day by day; **due per parte** two either side; **5 per cento** 5 per cent; **3 per 4 fa 12** 3 times 4 equals 12; **dividere/moltiplicare 12 per 4** to divide/multiply 12 by 4
9 (*in qualità di*) as; (*al posto di*) for; **avere qn per professore** to have sb as a teacher; **ti ho preso per Mario** I mistook you for Mario, I thought you were Mario; **dare per morto qn** to give sb up for dead; **lo prenderanno per pazzo** they'll think he's crazy
10 (*seguito da vb: finale*): **per fare qc** (so as) to do sth, in order to do sth; (*causale*): **per aver fatto qc** for having done sth; **studia per passare l'esame** he's studying in order to *o* (so as) to pass his exam; **l'hanno punito per aver rubato i soldi** he was punished for having stolen the money; **è abbastanza grande per andarci da solo** he's big enough to go on his own

'pera *sf* pear

pe'raltro *av* moreover, what's more

per'bacco *escl* by Jove!

per'bene *ag inv* respectable, decent ■ *av* (*con cura*) properly, well

perbe'nismo *sm* (so-called) respectability

percentu'ale [pertʃentu'ale] *sf* percentage; (*commissione*) commission

perce'pire [pertʃe'pire] *vt* (*sentire*) to perceive; (*ricevere*) to receive

percet'tibile [pertʃet'tibile] *ag* perceptible

percezi'one [pertʃet'tsjone] *sf* perception

 PAROLA CHIAVE

perché [per'ke] *av* why; **perché no?** why not?; **perché non vuoi andarci?** why don't you want to go?; **spiegami perché l'hai fatto** tell me why you did it
■ *cong* (*causale*) **1** because; **non posso uscire**

perché ho da fare I can't go out because
o as I've a lot to do
2 (*finale*) in order that, so that; **te lo do
perché tu lo legga** I'm giving it to you so
(that) you can read it
3 (*consecutivo*): **è troppo forte perché si
possa batterlo** he's too strong to be beaten
■ *sm inv* reason; **il perché di** the reason for;
non c'è un vero perché there's no real
reason for it

perciò [per't∫ɔ] *cong* so, for this (*o* that) reason
per'correre *vt* (*luogo*) to go all over; (*paese*) to
travel up and down, go all over; (*distanza*) to
cover
percor'ribile *ag* (*strada*) which can be
followed
per'corso, -a *pp di* **percorrere** ■ *sm* (*tragitto*)
journey; (*tratto*) route
per'cosso, -a *pp di* **percuotere** ■ *sf* blow
percu'otere *vt* to hit, strike
percussi'one *sf* percussion; **strumenti a ~**
(*Mus*) percussion instruments
per'dente *ag* losing ■ *sm/f* loser
'perdere *vt* to lose; (*lasciarsi sfuggire*) to miss;
(*sprecare: tempo, denaro*) to waste; (*mandare in
rovina: persona*) to ruin ■ *vi* to lose; (*serbatoio
etc*) to leak; **perdersi** *vr* (*smarrirsi*) to get lost;
(*svanire*) to disappear, vanish; **saper ~** to be a
good loser; **lascia ~!** forget it!, never mind!;
non ho niente da ~ (*fig*) I've got nothing to
lose; **è un'occasione da non ~** it's a
marvellous opportunity; (*affare*) it's a great
bargain; **è fatica persa** it's a waste of effort;
~ al gioco to lose money gambling; **~ di
vista qn** (*anche fig*) to lose sight of sb;
perdersi di vista to lose sight of each other;
(*fig*) to lose touch; **perdersi alla vista** to
disappear from sight; **perdersi in
chiacchiere** to waste time talking
perdifi'ato: **a ~** *av* (*correre*) at breathtaking
speed; (*gridare*) at the top of one's voice
perdigi'orno [perdi'dʒorno] *sm/f inv* idler,
waster
'perdita *sf* loss; (*spreco*) waste; (*fuoriuscita*)
leak; **siamo in ~** (*Comm*) we are running at a
loss; **a ~ d'occhio** as far as the eye can see
perdi'tempo *sm/f inv* waster, idler
perdizi'one [perdit'tsjone] *sf* (*Rel*) perdition,
damnation; **luogo di ~** place of ill repute
perdo'nare *vt* to pardon, forgive; (*scusare*) to
excuse, pardon; **per farsi ~** in order to be
forgiven; **perdona la domanda ...** if you
don't mind my asking ...; **vogliate ~ il (mio)
ritardo** my apologies for being late; **un
male che non perdona** an incurable
disease

per'dono *sm* forgiveness; (*Dir*) pardon;
chiedere ~ a qn (per) to ask for sb's
forgiveness (for); (*scusarsi*) to apologize to sb
(for)
perdu'rare *vi* to go on, last; (*perseverare*) to
persist
perduta'mente *av* desperately, passionately
per'duto, -a *pp di* **perdere** ■ *ag* (*gen*) lost;
sentirsi *o* **vedersi ~** (*fig*) to realize the
hopelessness of one's position; **una donna
perduta** (*fig*) a fallen woman
peregri'nare *vi* to wander, roam
pe'renne *ag* eternal, perpetual, perennial;
(*Bot*) perennial
peren'torio, -a *ag* peremptory; (*definitivo*)
final
perfetta'mente *av* perfectly; **sai ~ che ...** you
know perfectly well that ...
per'fetto, -a *ag* perfect ■ *sm* (*Ling*) perfect
(tense)
perfeziona'mento [perfettsjona'mento] *sm*:
~ (di) improvement (in), perfection (of);
corso di ~ proficiency course
perfezio'nare [perfettsjo'nare] *vt* to improve,
perfect; **perfezionarsi** *vr* to improve
perfezi'one [perfet'tsjone] *sf* perfection
perfezio'nismo [perfettsjo'nizmo] *sm*
perfectionism
perfezio'nista, -i, e [perfettsjo'nista] *sm/f*
perfectionist
per'fidia *sf* perfidy
'perfido, -a *ag* perfidious, treacherous
per'fino *av* even
perfo'rare *vt* to pierce; (*Med*) to perforate;
(*banda, schede*) to punch; (*trivellare*) to drill
perfora'tore, -'trice *sm/f* punch-card
operator ■ *sm* (*utensile*) punch; (*Inform*): **~ di
schede** card punch ■ *sf* (*Tecn*) boring *o*
drilling machine; (*Inform*) card punch
perforazi'one [perforat'tsjone] *sf* piercing;
perforation; punching drilling
perga'mena *sf* parchment
'pergola *sf* pergola
pergo'lato *sm* pergola
perico'lante *ag* precarious
pe'ricolo *sm* danger; **essere fuori ~** to be out
of danger; (*Med*) to be off the danger list;
mettere in ~ to endanger, put in danger
perico'loso, -a *ag* dangerous
perife'ria *sf* (*anche fig*) periphery; (*di città*)
outskirts *pl*
peri'ferico, -a, ci, che *ag* (*Anat, Inform*)
peripheral; (*zona*) outlying
pe'rifrasi *sf inv* circumlocution
pe'rimetro *sm* perimeter
peri'odico, -a, ci, che *ag* periodic(al); (*Mat*)
recurring ■ *sm* periodical

pe'riodo *sm* period; ~ **contabile** accounting period; ~ **di prova** trial period

peripe'zie [peripet'tsie] *sfpl* ups and downs, vicissitudes

'**periplo** *sm* circumnavigation

pe'rire *vi* to perish, die

peris'copio *sm* periscope

pe'rito, -a *ag* expert, skilled ■ *sm/f* expert; (*agronomo, navale*) surveyor; **un ~ chimico** a qualified chemist

perito'nite *sf* peritonitis

pe'rizia [pe'rittsja] *sf* (*abilità*) ability; (*giudizio tecnico*) expert opinion; expert's report; ~ **psichiatrica** psychiatrist's report

peri'zoma, -i [peri'dzoma] *sm* G-string

'**perla** *sf* pearl

per'lina *sf* bead

perli'nato *sm* matchboarding

perlo'meno *av* (*almeno*) at least

perlopiù *av* (*quasi sempre*) in most cases, usually

perlus'trare *vt* to patrol

perlustrazi'one [perlustrat'tsjone] *sf* patrol, reconnaissance; **andare in ~** to go on patrol

perma'loso, -a *ag* touchy

perma'nente *ag* permanent ■ *sf* permanent wave, perm

perma'nenza [perma'nɛntsa] *sf* permanence; (*soggiorno*) stay; **buona ~!** enjoy your stay!

perma'nere *vi* to remain

per'mango *vb vedi* **permanere**

per'masi *vb vedi* **permanere**

perme'abile *ag* permeable

perme'are *vt* to permeate

per'messo, -a *pp di* **permettere** ■ *sm* (*autorizzazione*) permission, leave; (*dato a militare, impiegato*) leave; (*licenza*) licence (*Brit*), license (*US*), permit; (*Mil: foglio*) pass; ~?, **è ~?** (*posso entrare?*) may I come in?; (*posso passare?*) excuse me; ~ **di lavoro/pesca** work/fishing permit

per'mettere *vt* to allow, permit; ~ **a qn qc/di fare qc** to allow sb sth/to do sth; **permettersi** *vr:* **permettersi qc/di fare qc** (*concedersi*) to allow o.s. sth/to do sth; (*avere la possibilità*) to afford sth/to do sth; **permettete che mi presenti** let me introduce myself, may I introduce myself?; **mi sia permesso di sottolineare che ...** may I take the liberty of pointing out that ...

per'misi *etc vb vedi* **permettere**

permis'sivo, -a *ag* permissive

'**permuta** *sf* (*Dir*) transfer; (*Comm*) trade-in; **accettare qc in ~** to take sth as a trade-in; **valore di ~** (*di macchina etc*) trade-in value

permu'tare *vt* to exchange; (*Mat*) to permute

per'nacchia [per'nakkja] *sf* (*fam*): **fare una ~** to blow a raspberry

per'nice [per'nitʃe] *sf* partridge

'**perno** *sm* pivot

pernotta'mento *sm* overnight stay

pernot'tare *vi* to spend the night, stay overnight

'**pero** *sm* pear tree

però *cong* (*ma*) but; (*tuttavia*) however, nevertheless

pero'rare *vt* (*Dir: fig*): ~ **la causa di qn** to plead sb's case

perpendico'lare *ag, sf* perpendicular

perpen'dicolo *sm:* **a ~** perpendicularly

perpe'trare *vt* to perpetrate

perpetu'are *vt* to perpetuate

per'petuo, -a *ag* perpetual

perplessità *sf inv* perplexity

per'plesso, -a *ag* perplexed, puzzled

perqui'sire *vt* to search

perquisizi'one [perkwizit'tsjone] *sf* (police) search; **mandato di ~** search warrant

'**perse** *etc vb vedi* **perdere**

persecu'tore *sm* persecutor

persecuzi'one [persekut'tsjone] *sf* persecution

persegu'ibile *ag* (*Dir*): **essere ~ per legge** to be liable to prosecution

persegu'ire *vt* to pursue; (*Dir*) to prosecute

persegui'tare *vt* to persecute

perseve'rante *ag* persevering

perseve'ranza [perseve'rantsa] *sf* perseverance

perseve'rare *vi* to persevere

'**persi** *etc vb vedi* **perdere**

'**Persia** *sf:* **la ~** Persia

persi'ano, -a *ag, sm/f* Persian ■ *sf* shutter; **persiana avvolgibile** roller blind

'**persico, -a, ci, che** *ag:* **il golfo P~** the Persian Gulf; **pesce ~** perch

per'sino *av* = **perfino**

persis'tente *ag* persistent

persis'tenza [persis'tɛntsa] *sf* persistence

per'sistere *vi* to persist; ~ **a fare** to persist in doing

persis'tito, -a *pp di* **persistere**

'**perso, -a** *pp di* **perdere** ■ *ag* (*smarrito: anche fig*) lost; (*sprecato*) wasted; **fare qc a tempo ~** to do sth in one's spare time; ~ **per ~** I've (*o* we've *etc*) got nothing further to lose

per'sona *sf* person; (*qualcuno*): **una ~** someone, somebody; (*espressione*) anyone *o* anybody; **persone** *sfpl* people *pl*; **non c'è ~ che ...** there's nobody who ..., there isn't anybody who ...; **in ~, di ~** in person; **per interposta ~** through an intermediary *o* a third party; ~ **giuridica** (*Dir*) legal person

perso'naggio [perso'naddʒo] *sm* (*persona ragguardevole*) personality, figure; (*tipo*) character, individual; (*Letteratura*) character

perso'nale *ag* personal ■ *sm* staff, personnel; (*figura fisica*) build ■ *sf* (*mostra*) one-man *o* one-woman exhibition

personalità *sf inv* personality

personaliz'zare [personalid'dzare] *vt* (*arredamento, stile*) to personalize; (*adattare*) to customize

personaliz'zato, -a [personalid'dzato] *ag* personalized

personal'mente *av* personally

personifi'care *vt* to personify; (*simboleggiare*) to embody

personificazi'one [personifikat'tsjone] *sf* (*vedi vb*) personification; embodiment

perspi'cace [perspi'katʃe] *ag* shrewd, discerning

perspi'cacia [perspi'katʃa] *sf* perspicacity, shrewdness

persu'adere *vt*: ~ **qn (di qc/a fare)** to persuade sb (of sth/to do)

persuasi'one *sf* persuasion

persua'sivo, -a *ag* persuasive

persu'aso, -a *pp di* **persuadere**

per'tanto *cong* (*quindi*) so, therefore

'pertica, -che *sf* pole

perti'nace [perti'natʃe] *ag* determined; persistent

perti'nente *ag*: ~ **(a)** relevant (to), pertinent (to)

perti'nenza [perti'nɛntsa] *sf* (*attinenza*) pertinence, relevance; (*competenza*): **essere di ~ di qn** to be sb's business

per'tosse *sf* whooping cough

per'tugio [per'tudʒo] *sm* hole, opening

pertur'bare *vt* to disrupt; (*persona*) to disturb, perturb

perturbazi'one [perturbat'tsjone] *sf* disruption; disturbance

Perù *sm*: **il ~** Peru

peru'gino, -a [peru'dʒino] *ag* (*o from*), Perugia

peruvi'ano, -a *ag, sm/f* Peruvian

per'vadere *vt* to pervade

per'vaso, -a *pp di* **pervadere**

perve'nire *vi*: ~ **a** to reach, arrive at, come to; (*venire in possesso*) **gli pervenne una fortuna** he inherited a fortune; **far ~ qc a** to have sth sent to

perve'nuto, -a *pp di* **pervenire**

perversi'one *sf* perversion

perversità *sf* perversity

per'verso, -a *ag* perverted

perver'tire *vt* to pervert

perver'tito, -a *sm/f* pervert

pervi'cace [pervi'katʃe] *ag* stubborn, obstinate

pervi'cacia [pervi'katʃa] *sf* stubbornness, obstinacy

per'vinca, -che *sf* periwinkle ■ *sm inv* (*colore*) periwinkle (blue)

p.es. *abbr* (= *per esempio*) e.g.

'pesa *sf* weighing *no pl* weighbridge

pe'sante *ag* heavy; (*fig: noioso*) dull, boring

pesan'tezza [pesan'tettsa] *sf* (*anche fig*) heaviness; **avere ~ di stomaco** to feel bloated

pesaper'sone *ag inv*: **(bilancia)** ~ (weighing) scales *pl*; (*automatica*) weighing machine

pe'sare *vt* to weigh ■ *vi* (*avere un peso*) to weigh; (*essere pesante*) to be heavy; (*fig*) to carry weight; ~ **su** (*fig*) to lie heavy on; to influence to hang over; **mi pesa sgridarlo** I find it hard to scold him; **tutta la responsabilità pesa su di lui** all the responsibility rests on his shoulders; **è una situazione che mi pesa** it's a difficult situation for me; **il suo parere pesa molto** his opinion counts for a lot; ~ **le parole** to weigh one's words

'pesca (*pl* **pesche**) *sf* (*frutto*) peach; (*il pescare*) fishing; **andare a** ~ to go fishing; ~ **di beneficenza** (*lotteria*) lucky dip; ~ **con la lenza** angling; ~ **subacquea** underwater fishing

pes'caggio [pes'kaddʒo] *sm* (*Naut*) draught (*Brit*), draft (*US*)

pes'care *vt* (*pesce*) to fish for; to catch; (*qc nell'acqua*) to fish out; (*fig: trovare*) to get hold of, find

pesca'tore *sm* fisherman; (*con lenza*) angler

'pesce ['peʃʃe] *sm* fish *gen inv*; **Pesci** (*dello zodiaco*) Pisces; **essere dei Pesci** to be Pisces; **non saper che pesci prendere** (*fig*) not to know which way to turn; ~ **d'aprile!** April Fool!; *see note*; ~ **martello** hammerhead; ~ **rosso** goldfish; ~ **spada** swordfish

● **IL PESCE D'APRILE**

● *Il pesce d'aprile* is a sort of April Fool's joke, played on 1 April. Originally it took its name from a paper fish which was secretly attached to a person's back but nowadays all sorts of practical jokes are popular.

pesce'cane [peʃʃe'kane] *sm* shark

pesche'reccio [peske'rettʃo] *sm* fishing boat

pesche'ria [peske'ria] *sf* fishmonger's (shop) (*Brit*), fish store (*US*)

pescherò *etc* [peske'rɔ] *vb vedi* **pescare**

peschi·era [pes'kjɛra] *sf* fishpond
pesci·vendolo, -a [peʃʃi'vendolo] *sm/f* fishmonger (*Brit*), fish merchant (*US*)
pesco, -schi *sm* peach tree
pes·coso, -a *ag* teeming with fish
pe·seta *sf* peseta
peso *sm* weight; (*Sport*) shot; **dar ~ a qc** to attach importance to sth; **essere di ~ a qn** (*fig*) to be a burden to sb; **rubare sul ~** to give short weight; **lo portarono via di ~** they carried him away bodily; **avere due pesi e due misure** (*fig*) to have double standards; **~ lordo/netto** gross/net weight; **~ piuma/mosca/gallo/medio/massimo** (*Pugilato*) feather/fly/bantam/middle/heavyweight
pessi·mismo *sm* pessimism
pessi·mista, -i, e *ag* pessimistic ■ *sm/f* pessimist
pessimo, -a *ag* very bad, awful; **di pessima qualità** of very poor quality
pes·tare *vt* to tread on, trample on; (*sale, pepe*) to grind; (*uva, aglio*) to crush; (*fig: picchiare*): **~ qn** to beat sb up; **~ i piedi** to stamp one's feet; **~ i piedi a qn** (*anche fig*) to tread on sb's toes
peste *sf* plague; (*persona*) nuisance, pest
pes·tello *sm* pestle
pesti·cida, -i [pesti'tʃida] *sm* pesticide
pes·tifero, -a *ag* (*anche fig*) pestilential, pestiferous; (*odore*) noxious
pesti·lenza [pesti'lentsa] *sf* pestilence; (*fetore*) stench
pesto, -a *ag*: **c'è buio ~** it's pitch dark ■ *sm* (*Cuc*) *sauce made with basil, garlic, cheese and oil*; **occhio ~** black eye
petalo *sm* (*Bot*) petal
pe·tardo *sm* firecracker, banger (*Brit*)
petizi·one [petit'tsjone] *sf* petition; **fare una ~ a** to petition
peto *sm* (*fam!*) fart (!)
petro·dollaro *sm* petrodollar
petrol·chimica [petrol'kimika] *sf* petrochemical industry
petroli·era *sf* (*nave*) oil tanker
petroli·ere *sm* (*industriale*) oilman; (*tecnico*) worker in the oil industry
petroli·ero, -a *ag* oil *cpd*
petro·lifero, -a *ag* oil *cpd*
pe·trolio *sm* oil, petroleum; (*per lampada, fornello*) paraffin (*Brit*), kerosene (*US*); **lume a ~** oil o paraffin o kerosene lamp; **~ grezzo** crude oil
pettego·lare *vi* to gossip
pettego·lezzo [pettego'leddzo] *sm* gossip *no pl*; **fare pettegolezzi** to gossip
pet·tegolo, -a *ag* gossipy ■ *sm/f* gossip
petti·nare *vt* to comb (the hair of); **pettinarsi** *vr* to comb one's hair

pettina·tura *sf* (*acconciatura*) hairstyle
pettine *sm* comb; (*Zool*) scallop
petti·rosso *sm* robin
petto *sm* chest; (*seno*) breast, bust; (*Cuc: di carne bovina*) brisket; (*di pollo etc*) breast; **prendere qn/qc di ~** to face up to sb/sth; **a doppio ~** (*abito*) double-breasted
petto·rale *ag* pectoral
petto·rina *sf* (*di grembiule*) bib
petto·ruto, -a *ag* broad-chested; full-breasted
petu·lante *ag* insolent
pe·tunia *sf* petunia
pezza ['pettsa] *sf* piece of cloth; (*toppa*) patch; (*cencio*) rag, cloth; (*Amm*): **~ d'appoggio** o **giustificativa** voucher; **trattare qn come una ~ da piedi** to treat sb like a doormat
pez·zato, -a [pet'tsato] *ag* piebald
pez·zente [pet'tsɛnte] *sm/f* beggar
pezzo ['pettso] *sm* (*gen*) piece; (*brandello, frammento*) piece, bit; (*di macchina, arnese etc*) part; (*Stampa*) article; (*di tempo*): **aspettare un ~** to wait quite a while o some time; **andare a pezzi** to break into pieces; **essere a pezzi** (*oggetto*) to be in pieces o bits; (*fig: persona*) to be shattered; **un bel ~ d'uomo** a fine figure of a man; **abito a due pezzi** two-piece suit; **essere tutto d'un ~** (*fig*) to be a man (o woman) of integrity; **~ di cronaca** (*Stampa*) report; **~ grosso** (*fig*) bigwig; **~ di ricambio** spare part
PG *sigla* = **Perugia**
P.G. *abbr* = **procuratore generale**
pH [pi'akka] *sm inv* (*Chim*) pH
PI *sigla* = **Pisa**
P.I. *abbr* = **Pubblica Istruzione**
pi·accio *etc* ['pjattʃo] *vb vedi* **piacere**
pia·cente [pja'tʃɛnte] *ag* attractive, pleasant
pia·cere [pja'tʃere] *vi* to please ■ *sm* pleasure; (*favore*) favour (*Brit*), favor (*US*); **una ragazza che piace** (*piacevole*) a likeable girl; (*attraente*) an attractive girl; **~ a: mi piace** I like it; **quei ragazzi non mi piacciono** I don't like those boys; **gli piacerebbe andare al cinema** he would like to go to the cinema; **il suo discorso è piaciuto molto** his speech was well received; **"~!"** (*nelle presentazioni*) "pleased to meet you!"; **con ~** certainly, with pleasure; **per ~** please; **fare un ~ a qn** to do sb a favour; **mi fa ~ per lui** I am pleased for him; **mi farebbe ~ rivederlo** I would like to see him again
pia·cevole [pja'tʃevole] *ag* pleasant, agreeable
piaci·mento [pjatʃi'mento] *sm*: **a ~** (*a volontà*) as much as one likes, at will; **lo farà a suo ~** he'll do it when it suits him

p

265

piaci'uto, -a [pja'tʃuto] *pp di* **piacere**

pi'acqui *etc vb vedi* **piacere**

pi'aga, -ghe *sf* (*lesione*) sore; (*ferita: anche fig*) wound; (*fig: flagello*) scourge, curse; (*persona*) pest, nuisance

piagnis'teo [pjaɲɲis'tɛo] *sm* whining, whimpering

piagnuco'lare [pjaɲɲuko'lare] *vi* to whimper

piagnuco'lio, -ii [pjaɲɲuko'lio] *sm* whimpering

piagnuco'loso, -a [pjaɲɲuko'loso] *ag* whiny, whimpering, moaning

pi'alla *sf* (*arnese*) plane

pial'lare *vt* to plane

pialla'trice [pjalla'tritʃe] *sf* planing machine

pi'ana *sf* stretch of level ground; (*più esteso*) plain

pianeggi'ante [pjaned'dʒante] *ag* flat, level

piane'rottolo *sm* landing

pia'neta *sm* (*Astr*) planet

pi'angere ['pjandʒere] *vi* to cry, weep; (*occhi*) to water ■ *vt* to cry, weep; (*lamentare*) to bewail, lament; **~ la morte di qn** to mourn sb's death

pianifi'care *vt* to plan

pianificazi'one [pjanifikat'tsjone] *sf* (*Econ*) planning; **~ aziendale** corporate planning

pia'nista, -i, e *sm/f* pianist

pi'ano, -a *ag* (*piatto*) flat, level; (*Mat*) plane; (*facile*) straightforward, simple; (*chiaro*) clear, plain ■ *av* (*adagio*) slowly; (*a bassa voce*) softly; (*con cautela*) slowly, carefully ■ *sm* (*Mat*) plane; (*Geo*) plain; (*livello*) level, plane; (*di edificio*) floor; (*programma*) plan; (*Mus*) piano; **pian ~** very slowly; (*poco a poco*) little by little; **una casa di 3 piani** a 3-storey (*Brit*) *o* 3-storied (*US*) house; **al ~ di sopra/di sotto** on the floor above/below; **all'ultimo ~** on the top floor; **al ~ terra** on the ground floor; **in primo/secondo ~** (*Fot, Cine etc*) in the foreground/background; **fare un primo ~** (*Fot, Cine*) to take a close-up; **di primo ~** (*fig*) prominent, high-ranking; **un fattore di secondo ~** a secondary *o* minor factor; **passare in secondo ~** to become less important; **mettere tutto sullo stesso ~** to lump everything together, give equal importance to everything; **tutto secondo i piani** all according to plan; **~ di lavoro** (*superficie*) worktop; (*programma*) work plan; **~ regolatore** (*Urbanistica*) town-planning scheme; **~ stradale** road surface

piano'forte *sm* piano, pianoforte

piano'terra *sm inv* = **piano terra**

pi'ansi *etc vb vedi* **piangere**

pi'anta *sf* (*Bot*) plant; (*Anat: anche*: **pianta del piede**) sole (of the foot); (*grafico*) plan; (*cartina* *topografica*) map; **ufficio a ~ aperta** open-plan office; **in ~ stabile** on the permanent staff; **~ stradale** street map, street plan

piantagi'one [pjanta'dʒone] *sf* plantation

pianta'grane *sm/f inv* troublemaker

pian'tare *vt* to plant; (*conficcare*) to drive *o* hammer in; (*tenda*) to put up, pitch; (*fig: lasciare*) to leave, desert; **piantarsi** *vr*: **piantarsi davanti a qn** to plant o.s. in front of sb; **~ qn in asso** to leave sb in the lurch; **~ grane** (*fig*) to cause trouble; **piantala!** (*fam*) cut it out!

pian'tato, -a *ag*: **ben ~** (*persona*) well-built

pianta'tore *sm* planter

pianter'reno *sm* ground floor

pian'tina *sf* (*di edificio, città*) (small) map; (*Bot*) (small) plant

pi'anto, -a *pp di* **piangere** ■ *sm* tears *pl*, crying

pianto'nare *vt* to guard, watch over

pian'tone *sm* (*vigilante*) sentry, guard; (*soldato*) orderly; (*Aut*) steering column

pia'nura *sf* plain

pi'astra *sf* plate; (*di pietra*) slab; (*di fornello*) hotplate; **panino alla ~** ≈ toasted sandwich; **~ di registrazione** tape deck

pias'trella *sf* tile

piastrel'lare *vt* to tile

pias'trina *sf* (*Anat*) platelet; (*Mil*) identity disc (*Brit*) *o* tag (*US*)

piatta'forma *sf* (*anche fig*) platform; **~ continentale** (*Geo*) continental shelf; **~ girevole** (*Tecn*) turntable; **~ di lancio** (*Mil*) launching pad *o* platform; **~ rivendicativa** *document prepared by the unions in an industry, setting out their claims*

piat'tello *sm* clay pigeon; **tiro al ~** clay-pigeon shooting (*Brit*), trapshooting

piat'tino *sm* (*di tazza*) saucer

pi'atto, -a *ag* flat; (*fig: scialbo*) dull ■ *sm* (*recipiente, vivanda*) dish; (*portata*) course; (*parte piana*) flat (part); **piatti** *smpl* (*Mus*) cymbals; **un ~ di minestra** a plate of soup; **~ fondo** soup dish; **~ forte** main course; **~ del giorno** dish of the day, plat du jour; **~ del giradischi** turntable; **piatti già pronti** (*Cuc*) ready-cooked dishes

pi'azza ['pjattsa] *sf* square; (*Comm*) market; (*letto, lenzuolo*): **a una ~** single; **a due piazze** double; **far ~ pulita** to make a clean sweep; **mettere in ~** (*fig: rendere pubblico*) to make public; **scendere in ~** (*fig*) to take to the streets, demonstrate; **~ d'armi** (*Mil*) parade ground

piazza'forte [pjattsa'forte] *pl*, **piazze'forti** *sf* (*Mil*) stronghold

piaz'zale [pjat'tsale] *sm* (large) square

piazza'mento [pjattsa'mento] *sm* (*Sport*) place, placing

piaz'zare [pjat'tsare] vt to place; (Comm) to market, sell; **piazzarsi** vr (Sport) to be placed; **piazzarsi bene** to finish with the leaders o in a good position

piaz'zista, -i [pjat'tsista] sm (Comm) commercial traveller

piaz'zola [pjat'tsɔla] sf (Aut) lay-by (Brit), (roadside) stopping place; (di tenda) pitch

'picca, -che sf pike; **picche** sfpl (Carte) spades; **rispondere picche a qn** (fig) to give sb a flat refusal

pic'cante ag hot, pungent; (fig) racy

pic'carsi vr: ~ **di fare** to pride o.s. on one's ability to do; ~ **per qc** to take offence (Brit) o offense (US) at sth

picchet'taggio [pikket'taddʒo] sm picketing

picchet'tare [pikket'tare] vt to picket

pic'chetto [pik'ketto] sm (Mil, di scioperanti) picket

picchi'are [pik'kjare] vt (persona: colpire) to hit, strike; (prendere a botte) to beat (up); (battere) to beat; (sbattere) to bang ■ vi (bussare) to knock; (: con forza) to bang; (colpire) to hit, strike; (sole) to beat down

picchi'ata [pik'kjata] sf knock; bang; blow; (percosse) beating, thrashing; (Aer) dive; **scendere in ~** to (nose-)dive

picchiet'tare [pikkjet'tare] vt (punteggiare) to spot, dot; (colpire) to tap

'picchio ['pikkjo] sm woodpecker

pic'cino, -a [pit'tʃino] ag tiny, very small

picci'olo [pit'tʃɔlo] sm (Bot) stalk

piccio'naia [pittʃo'naja] sf pigeon-loft; (Teat): **la ~** the gods sg (Brit), the gallery

picci'one [pit'tʃone] sm pigeon; **pigliare due piccioni con una fava** (fig) to kill two birds with one stone

'picco, -chi sm peak; **a ~** vertically; **colare a ~** (Naut, fig) to sink

picco'lezza [pikko'lettsa] sf (dimensione) smallness; (fig: grettezza) meanness, pettiness; (inezia) trifle

'piccolo, -a ag small; (oggetto, mano, di età: bambino) small, little; (dav sostantivo: di breve durata: viaggio) short; (fig) mean, petty ■ sm/f child, little one ■ sm: **nel mio ~** in my own small way; **piccoli** smpl (di animale) young pl; **in ~** in miniature; **la piccola borghesia** the lower middle classes; (peg) the petty bourgeoisie

pic'cone sm pick(-axe)

pic'cozza [pik'kɔttsa] sf ice-axe

pic'nic sm inv picnic; **fare un ~** to have a picnic

pidies'sino, -a ag (Pol) of P.D.S. ■ sm/f member (o supporter) of P.D.S.

pi'docchio [pi'dɔkkjo] sm louse

pidocchi'oso, -a [pidok'kjoso] ag (infestato) lousy; (fig: taccagno) mean, stingy, tight

pidu'ista, -i, e ag P2 cpd (masonic lodge) ■ sm member of the P2 masonic lodge

piè sm inv: **a ogni piè sospinto** (fig) at every step; **saltare a piè pari** (omettere) to skip; **a piè di pagina** at the foot of the page; **note a piè di pagina** footnotes

pi'ede sm foot; (di mobile) leg; **in piedi** standing; **a piedi** on foot; **a piedi nudi** barefoot; **su due piedi** (fig) at once; **mettere qc in piedi** (azienda etc) to set sth up; **prendere ~** (fig) to gain ground, catch on; **puntare i piedi** (fig) to dig one's heels in; **sentirsi mancare la terra sotto i piedi** to feel lost; **non sta in piedi** (persona) he can't stand; (fig: scusa etc) it doesn't hold water; **tenere in piedi** (persona) to keep on his (o her) feet; (fig: ditta etc) to keep going; **a ~ libero** (Dir) on bail; **sul ~ di guerra** (Mil) ready for action; **~ di porco** crowbar

piedipi'atti sm inv (peg: poliziotto) cop

piedis'tallo, piedes'tallo sm pedestal

pi'ega, -ghe sf (piegatura, Geo) fold; (di gonna) pleat; (di pantaloni) crease; (grinza) wrinkle, crease; **prendere una brutta** o **cattiva ~** (fig: persona) to get into bad ways; (situazione) to take a turn for the worse; **non fa una ~** (fig: ragionamento) it's faultless; **non ha fatto una ~** (fig: persona) he didn't bat an eye(lid) (Brit) o an eye(lash) (US)

piega'mento sm folding; bending; ~ **sulle gambe** (Ginnastica) kneebend

pie'gare vt to fold; (braccia, gambe, testa) to bend ■ vi to bend; **piegarsi** vr to bend; (fig): **piegarsi (a)** to yield (to), submit (to)

piega'tura sf folding no pl; bending no pl; fold bend

piegherò etc [pjege'rɔ] vb vedi **piegare**

pieghet'tare [pjeget'tare] vt to pleat

pie'ghevole [pje'gevole] ag pliable, flexible; (porta) folding; (fig) yielding, docile

Pie'monte sm: **il ~** Piedmont

piemon'tese ag, sm/f Piedmontese

pi'ena sf vedi **pieno**

pie'nezza [pje'nettsa] sf fullness

pi'eno, -a ag full; (muro, mattone) solid ■ sm (colmo) height, peak; (carico) full load ■ sf (di fiume) flood, spate; (gran folla) crowd, throng; ~ **di** full of; **a piene mani** abundantly; **a tempo ~** full-time; **a pieni voti** (eleggere) unanimously; **laurearsi a pieni voti** to graduate with full marks; **in ~ giorno** in broad daylight; **in ~ inverno** in the depths of winter; **in piena notte** in the middle of the night; **in piena stagione** at the height of the season; **in ~** (completamente: sbagliare)

p

completely; (colpire, centrare) bang o right in the middle; **avere pieni poteri** to have full powers; **nel ~ possesso delle sue facoltà** in full possession of his faculties; **fare il ~ (di benzina)** to fill up (with petrol)

pie'none sm: **c'era il ~ al cinema/al teatro** the cinema/the theatre was packed

'piercing ['pirsing] sm: **farsi il ~ all'ombelico** to have one's navel pierced

pietà sf pity; (Rel) piety; **senza ~** (agire) ruthlessly; (persona) pitiless, ruthless; **avere ~ di** (compassione) to pity, feel sorry for; (misericordia) to have pity o mercy on; **far ~** to arouse pity; (peg) to be terrible

pie'tanza [pje'tantsa] sf dish, course

pie'toso, -a ag (compassionevole) pitying, compassionate; (che desta pietà) pitiful

pi'etra sf stone; **mettiamoci una ~ sopra** (fig) let bygones be bygones; **~ preziosa** precious stone, gem; **~ dello scandalo** (fig) cause of scandal

pie'traia sf (terreno) stony ground

pietrifi'care vt to petrify; (fig) to transfix, paralyze

piet'rina sf (per accendino) flint

pie'trisco, -schi sm crushed stone, road metal

pi'eve sf parish church

'piffero sm (Mus) pipe

pigi'ama [pi'dʒama] sm pyjamas pl

'pigia 'pigia ['pidʒa'pidʒa] sm crowd, press

pigi'are [pi'dʒare] vt to press

pigia'trice [pidʒa'tritʃe] sf (macchina) wine press

pigi'one [pi'dʒone] sf rent

pigli'are [piʎ'ʎare] vt to take, grab; (afferrare) to catch

'piglio ['piʎʎo] sm look, expression

pig'mento sm pigment

pig'meo, -a sm/f pygmy

'pigna ['pinɲa] sf pine cone

pignole'ria [pinɲole'ria] sf fastidiousness, fussiness

pi'gnolo, -a [pin'ɲɔlo] ag pernickety

pigno'rare [pinɲo'rare] vt (Dir) to distrain

pigo'lare vi to cheep, chirp

pigo'lio sm cheeping, chirping

pigra'mente av lazily

pi'grizia [pi'grittsja] sf laziness

'pigro, -a ag lazy; (fig: ottuso) slow, dull

PIL sigla m = **prodotto interno lordo**

'pila sf (catasta, di ponte) pile; (Elettr) battery; (fam: torcia) torch (Brit), flashlight; **a ~, a pile** battery-operated

pi'lastro sm pillar

'pile ['pail] sm inv fleece

'pillola sf pill; **prendere la ~** (contraccettivo) to be on the pill; **~ del giorno dopo** morning-after pill

pi'lone sm (di ponte) pier; (di linea elettrica) pylon

pi'lota, -i, e sm/f pilot; (Aut) driver ■ ag inv pilot cpd; **~ automatico** automatic pilot

pilo'taggio [pilo'taddʒo] sm: **cabina di ~** flight deck

pilo'tare vt to pilot; to drive

piluc'care vt to nibble at

pi'mento sm pimento, allspice

pim'pante ag lively, full of beans

pinaco'teca, -che sf art gallery

pi'neta sf pinewood

ping-'pong [piŋ'pɔŋ] sm table tennis

'pingue ag fat, corpulent

pingu'edine sf corpulence

pingu'ino sm (Zool) penguin

'pinna sf fin; (di pinguino, spatola di gomma) flipper

pin'nacolo sm pinnacle

'pino sm pine (tree)

pi'nolo sm pine kernel

'pinta sf pint

'pinza ['pintsa] sf pliers pl; (Med) forceps pl; (Zool) pincer

pin'zette [pin'tsette] sfpl tweezers

'pio, -a, 'pii, 'pie ag pious; (opere, istituzione) charitable, charity cpd

piogge'rella [pjoddʒe'rella] sf drizzle

pi'oggia, -ge ['pjɔddʒa] sf rain; (fig: di regali, fiori) shower; (di insulti) hail; **sotto la ~** in the rain; **~ acida** acid rain

pi'olo sm peg; (di scala) rung

piom'bare vi to fall heavily; (gettarsi con impeto): **~ su** to fall upon, assail ■ vt (dente) to fill

piomba'tura sf (di dente) filling

piom'bino sm (sigillo) (lead) seal; (del filo a piombo) plummet; (Pesca) sinker

pi'ombo sm (Chim) lead; (sigillo) (lead) seal; (proiettile) (lead) shot; **a ~** (cadere) straight down; (muro etc) plumb; **andare con i piedi di ~** (fig) to tread carefully; **senza ~** (benzina) unleaded, lead-free; **anni di ~** (fig) era of terrorist outrages

pioni'ere, -a sm/f pioneer

pi'oppo sm poplar

pio'vano, -a ag: **acqua piovana** rainwater

pi'overe vb impers to rain ■ vi (fig: scendere dall'alto) to rain down; (affluire in gran numero): **~ in** to pour into; **non ci piove sopra** (fig) there's no doubt about it

pioviggi'nare [pjoviddʒi'nare] vb impers to drizzle

piovosità sf rainfall

pio'voso, -a ag rainy

pi'ovra sf octopus

pi'ovve etc vb vedi **piovere**

'pipa sf pipe

pipì *sf (fam)*: **fare ~** to have a wee (wee)
pipi'strello *sm (Zool)* bat
pi'ramide *sf* pyramid
pi'ranha *sm inv* piranha
pi'rata, -i *sm* pirate; **~ informatico** hacker; **~ della strada** hit-and-run driver
Pire'nei *smpl*: **i ~** the Pyrenees
pi'retro *sm* pyrethrum
'pirico, -a, ci, che *ag*: **polvere pirica** gunpowder
pi'rite *sf* pyrite
piro'etta *sf* pirouette
pi'rofilo, -a *ag* heat-resistant ■ *sf* heat-resistant glass; *(tegame)* heat-resistant dish
pi'roga, -ghe *sf* dug-out canoe
pi'romane *sm/f* arsonist
pi'roscafo *sm* steamer, steamship
'Pisa *sf* Pisa
pi'sano, -a *ag* Pisan
pisci'are [piʃʃare] *vi (fam!)* to piss (!), pee (!)
pi'scina [piʃʃina] *sf* (swimming) pool
pi'sello *sm* pea
piso'lino *sm* nap; **fare un ~** to have a nap
'pista *sf (traccia)* track, trail; *(di stadio)* track; *(di pattinaggio)* rink; *(da sci)* run; *(Aer)* runway; *(di circo)* ring; **~ da ballo** dance floor; **~ ciclabile** cycle lane; **~ di lancio** launch(ing) pad; **~ di rullaggio** *(Aer)* taxiway; **~ di volo** *(Aer)* runway
pis'tacchio [pis'takkjo] *sm* pistachio (tree), pistachio (nut)
pis'tillo *sm (Bot)* pistil
pis'tola *sf* pistol, gun; **~ a spruzzo** spray gun; **~ a tamburo** revolver
pis'tone *sm* piston
pi'tocco, -chi *sm* skinflint, miser
pi'tone *sm* python
'pittima *sf (fig)* bore
pit'tore, -'trice *sm/f* painter
pitto'resco, -a, schi, sche *ag* picturesque
pit'torico, -a, ci, che *ag* of painting, pictorial
pit'tura *sf* painting; **~ fresca** wet paint
pittu'rare *vt* to paint

○ **PAROLA CHIAVE**

più *av* **1** *(in maggiore quantità)* more; **più del solito** more than usual; **in più, di più** more; **ne voglio di più** I want some more; **ci sono 3 persone in** *o* **di più** there are 3 more *o* extra people; **costa di più** it's more expensive; **una volta di più** once more; **più o meno** more or less; **né più né meno** no more, no less; **per di più** *(inoltre)* what's more, moreover; **è sempre più difficile** it is getting more and more difficult; **chi più chi meno hanno tutti contribuito** everybody

made a contribution of some sort; **più dormo e più dormirei** the more I sleep the more I want to sleep

2 *(comparativo)* more; *(se monosillabo, spesso)* : **+ ...er; più ... di/che** more ... than; **più intelligente di lui** more intelligent than him; **più furbo di te** smarter than you; **più tardi di ...** later than ...; **lavoro più di te/di Paola** I work harder than you/than Paola; **è più fortunato che bravo** he is lucky rather than skilled; **più di quanto pensassi** more than I thought; **più che altro** mainly; **più che mai** more than ever

3 *(superlativo)* most; *(se monosillabo, spesso)*: **+ ...est; il più grande/intelligente** the biggest/most intelligent; **è quello che compro più spesso** that's the one I buy most often; **al più presto** as soon as possible; **al più tardi** at the latest

4 *(negazione)*: **non ... più** no more, no longer; **non ho più soldi** I've got no more money, I don't have any more money; **non lavoro più** I'm no longer working, I don't work any more; **non ce n'è più** there isn't any left; **non c'è più nessuno** there's no one left; **non c'è più niente da fare** there's nothing more to be done; **a più non posso** *(gridare)* at the top of one's voice; *(correre)* as fast as one can

5 *(Mat)* plus; **4 più 5 fa 9** 4 plus 5 equals 9; **più 5 gradi** 5 degrees above freezing, plus 5; **6 più** *(a scuola)* just above a pass

■ *prep* plus; **500.000 più le spese** 500,000 plus expenses; **siamo in quattro più il nonno** there are four of us, plus grandpa

■ *ag inv* **1**: **più ... (di)** more ... (than); **più denaro/tempo** more money/time; **più persone di quante ci aspettassimo** more people than we expected

2 *(numerosi, diversi)* several; **l'aspettai per più giorni** I waited for it for several days

■ *sm* **1** *(la maggior parte)*: **il più è fatto** most of it is done; **il più delle volte** more often than not, generally; **parlare del più e del meno** to talk about this and that

2 *(Mat)* plus (sign)

3: **i più** the majority

piuccheper'fetto [pjukkeper'fɛtto] *sm (Ling)* pluperfect, past perfect
pi'uma *sf* feather; **piume** *sfpl* down *sg*; *(piumaggio)* plumage *sg*, feathers
piu'maggio [pju'maddʒo] *sm* plumage, feathers *pl*
piu'mino *sm* (eider)down; *(per letto)* eiderdown; *(tipo danese)* duvet, continental quilt; *(giacca)* quilted jacket; *(with goose-*

P

feather padding: per cipria) powder puff; (*per spolverare*) feather duster

piut'tosto *av* rather; **~ che** (*anziché*) rather than

'**piva** *sf*: **con le pive nel sacco** (*fig*) empty-handed

pi'**vello, -a** *sm/f* greenhorn

'**pizza** ['pittsa] *sf* (*Cuc*) pizza; (*Cine*) reel

pizze'**ria** [pittse'ria] *sf place where pizzas are made, sold or eaten*

pizzi'**cagnolo, -a** [pittsi'kaɲɲolo] *sm/f* specialist grocer

pizzi'**care** [pittsi'kare] *vt* (*stringere*) to nip, pinch; (*pungere*) to sting; to bite; (*Mus*) to pluck ■ *vi* (*prudere*) to itch, be itchy; (*cibo*) to be hot *o* spicy

pizziche'**ria** [pittsike'ria] *sf* delicatessen (shop)

'**pizzico, chi** ['pittsiko] *sm* (*pizzicotto*) pinch, nip; (*piccola quantità*) pinch, dash; (*d'insetto*) sting; bite

pizzi'**cotto** [pittsi'kɔtto] *sm* pinch, nip

'**pizzo** ['pittso] *sm* (*merletto*) lace; (*barbetta*) goatee beard; (*tangente*) protection money

pla'**care** *vt* to placate, soothe; **placarsi** *vr* to calm down

'**placca, -che** *sf* plate; (*con iscrizione*) plaque; (*anche*: **placca dentaria**) (dental) plaque

plac'**care** *vt* to plate; **placcato in oro/argento** gold-/silver-plated

pla'**centa** [pla'tʃɛnta] *sf* placenta

placidità [platʃidi'ta] *sf* calm, peacefulness

'**placido, -a** ['platʃido] *ag* placid, calm

plafoni'**era** *sf* ceiling light

plagi'**are** [pla'dʒare] *vt* (*copiare*) to plagiarize; (*Dir: influenzare*) to coerce

'**plagio** ['pladʒo] *sm* plagiarism; (*Dir*) duress

'**plaid** [plɛd] *sm inv* (travelling) rug (*Brit*), lap robe (*US*)

pla'**nare** *vi* (*Aer*) to glide

'**plancia, -ce** ['plantʃa] *sf* (*Naut*) bridge; (*Aut: cruscotto*) dashboard

'**plancton** *sm inv* plankton

plane'**tario, -a** *ag* planetary ■ *sm* (*locale*) planetarium

planis'**fero** *sm* planisphere

plan'**tare** *sm* arch support

'**plasma** *sm* plasma

plas'**mare** *vt* to mould (*Brit*), mold (*US*), shape

'**plastico, -a, ci, che** *ag* plastic ■ *sm* (*rappresentazione*) relief model; (*esplosivo*): **bomba al ~** plastic bomb ■ *sf* (*arte*) plastic arts *pl*; (*Med*) plastic surgery; (*sostanza*) plastic; **in materiale ~** plastic

plasti'**lina**® *sf* plasticine®

'**platano** *sm* plane tree

pla'**tea** *sf* (*Teat*) stalls *pl* (*Brit*), orchestra (*US*)

'**plate'ale** *ag* (*gesto, atteggiamento*) theatrical

plateal'**mente** *av* theatrically

'**platino** *sm* platinum

pla'**tonico, -a, ci, che** *ag* platonic

plau'**dire** *vi*: **~ a** to applaud

plau'**sibile** *ag* plausible

'**plauso** *sm* (*fig*) approval

'**playback** ['plei bæk] *sm*: **cantare in ~** to mime

'**playboy** ['pleibɔi] *sm inv* playboy

'**playmaker** ['pleimeikəʳ] *sm/f inv* (*Sport*) playmaker

'**play-off** ['plɛɪɔf] *sm inv* (*Sport*) play-off

ple'**baglia** [ple'baʎʎa] *sf* (*peg*) rabble, mob

'**plebe** *sf* common people

ple'**beo, -a** *ag* plebeian; (*volgare*) coarse, common

plebi'**scito** [plebiʃ'ʃito] *sm* plebiscite

ple'**nario, -a** *ag* plenary

pleni'**lunio** *sm* full moon

plenipotenzi'**ario, -a** [plenipoten'tsjarjo] *ag* plenipotentiary

'**plenum** *sm inv* plenum

'**plettro** *sm* plectrum

'**pleura** *sf* (*Anat*) pleura

pleu'**rite** *sf* pleurisy

P.L.I. *sigla m* (= *Partito Liberale Italiano*) *former political party*

'**plico, -chi** *sm* (*pacco*) parcel; **in ~ a parte** (*Comm*) under separate cover

plissé [pli'se] *ag inv* plissé *cpd* ■ *sm inv* (*anche*: **tessuto plissé**) plissé

plisset'**tato, -a** *ag* plissé *cpd*

plo'**tone** *sm* (*Mil*) platoon; **~ d'esecuzione** firing squad

'**plumbeo, -a** *ag* leaden

plu'**rale** *ag, sm* plural

plura'**lismo** *sm* pluralism

pluralità *sf* plurality; (*maggioranza*) majority

plusva'**lenza** [pluzva'lɛntsa] *sf* capital gain

plusva'**lore** *sm* (*Econ*) surplus

plu'**tonio** *sm* plutonium

pluvi'**ale** *ag* rain *cpd*

pluvi'**ometro** *sm* rain gauge

P.M. *abbr* (*Pol*) = **Pubblico Ministero**; (= *Polizia Militare*) MP (= *Military Police*)

pm *abbr* = **peso molecolare**

PMI *sigla fpl* (= *Piccole e Medie Imprese*) SME (= *Small and Medium-sized Enterprises*)

PN *sigla* = **Pordenone**

pneu'**matico, -a, ci, che** *ag* inflatable; (*Tecn*) pneumatic ■ *sm* (*Aut*) tyre (*Brit*), tire (*US*)

PNL *sigla m* = **prodotto nazionale lordo**

PO *sigla* = **Prato**

Po *sm*: **il Po** the Po

po' *av, sm vedi* **poco**

P.O. *abbr* = **posta ordinaria**

po'chezza [po'kettsa] *sf* insufficiency, shortage; *(fig: meschinità)* meanness, smallness

 PAROLA CHIAVE

'**poco, -a, chi, che** *ag (quantità)* little, not much; *(numero)* few, not many; **poco pane/denaro/spazio** little *o* not much bread/money/space; **con poca spesa** without spending much; **a poco prezzo** at a low price, cheap; **poco (tempo) fa** a short time ago; **poche persone/idee** few *o* not many people/ideas; **è un tipo di poche parole** he's a man of few words

 ■ *av* **1** *(in piccola quantità)* little, not much; *(numero limitato)* few, not many; **guadagna poco** he doesn't earn much, he earns little **2** *(con ag, av)* (a) little, not very; **è poco più vecchia di lui** she's a little *o* slightly older than him; **è poco socievole** he's not very sociable; **sta poco bene** he isn't very well **3** *(tempo)*: **poco dopo/prima** shortly afterwards/before; **il film dura poco** the film doesn't last very long; **ci vediamo molto poco** we don't see each other very often, we hardly ever see each other **4**: **un po'** a little, a bit; **è un po' corto** it's a little *o* a bit short; **arriverà fra un po'** he'll arrive shortly *o* in a little while **5**: **a dir poco** to say the least; **a poco a poco** little by little; **per poco non cadevo** I nearly fell; **è una cosa da poco** it's nothing, it's of no importance; **una persona da poco** a worthless person

 ■ *pron* (a) little; **pochi, poche** *(pl: persone)* few (people); *(cose)* few; **ci vediamo tra poco** see you soon; **pochi lo sanno** not many people know it; **ci vuole tempo ed io ne ho poco** it takes time, and I haven't got much to spare

 ■ *sm* **1** little; **vive del poco che ha** he lives on the little he has **2**: **un po'** a little; **un po' di zucchero** a little sugar; **un bel po' di denaro** quite a lot of money; **un po' per ciascuno** a bit each

podcast [podkast] *sm* podcast
po'dere *sm (Agr)* farm
pode'roso, -a *ag* powerful
podestà *sm inv (nel fascismo)* podestà, mayor
'**podio** *sm* dais, platform; *(Mus)* podium
po'dismo *sm (Sport: marcia)* walking; *(corsa)* running
po'dista, -i, e *sm/f* walker; runner
po'ema, -i *sm* poem
poe'sia *sf (arte)* poetry; *(componimento)* poem
po'eta, -'essa *sm/f* poet/poetess

poe'tare *vi* to write poetry
po'etico, -a, ci, che *ag* poetic(al)
poggi'are [pod'dʒare] *vt* to lean, rest; *(posare)* to lay, place
poggia'testa [poddʒa'tɛsta] *sm inv (Aut)* headrest
'**poggio** ['pɔddʒo] *sm* hillock, knoll
poggi'olo [pod'dʒɔlo] *sm* balcony
'**poi** *av* then; *(alla fine)* finally, at last ■ *sm*: **pensare al ~** to think of the future; **e ~** *(inoltre)* and besides; **questa ~ (è bella)** *(ironico)* that's a good one!; **d'ora in ~** from now on; **da domani in ~** from tomorrow onwards
poi'ana *sf* buzzard
poiché [poi'ke] *cong* since, as
pois [pwa] *sm inv* spot, *(polka)* dot; **a ~** spotted, polka-dot *cpd*
'**poker** *sm* poker
po'lacco, -a, chi, che *ag* Polish ■ *sm/f* Pole
po'lare *ag* polar
polariz'zare [polarid'dzare] *vt (anche fig)* to polarize
'**polca, -che** *sf* polka
po'lemico, -a, ci, che *ag* polemical, controversial ■ *sf* controversy; **fare polemiche** to be contentious
polemiz'zare [polemid'dzare] *vi*: **~ (su qc)** to argue (about sth)
po'lenta *sf (Cuc)* sort of thick porridge made with maize flour
polen'tone, -a *sm/f* slowcoach *(Brit)*, slowpoke *(US)*
pole'sano, -a *ag* of *(o* from) Polesine *(area between the Po and the Adige)*
POL'FER *abbr f* = **Polizia Ferroviaria**
'**poli...** *prefisso* poly...
poliambula'torio *sm (Med)* health clinic
poli'clinico, -ci *sm* general hospital, polyclinic
poli'edro *sm* polyhedron
poli'estere *sm* polyester
poliga'mia *sf* polygamy
polig'lotta, -i, e *ag, sm/f* polyglot
po'ligono *sm* polygon; **~ di tiro** rifle range
Poli'nesia *sf*: **la ~** Polynesia
polinesi'ano, -a *ag, sm/f* Polynesian
poliomielite, 'polio(mie'lite) *sf* polio(myelitis)
'**polipo** *sm* polyp
polisti'rolo *sm* polystyrene
poli'tecnico, -ci *sm* postgraduate technical college
po'litica, -che *sf vedi* **politico**
politi'cante *sm/f (peg)* petty politician
politiciz'zare [polititʃid'dzare] *vt* to politicize
po'litico, -a, ci, che *ag* political ■ *sm/f* politician ■ *sf* politics *sg*; *(linea di condotta)*

policy; **elezioni politiche** parliamentary (*Brit*) *o* congressional (*US*) election(s); **uomo ~** politician; **darsi alla politica** to go into politics; **fare politica** (*militante*) to be a political activist; (*come professione*) to be in politics; **la politica del governo** the government's policies; **politica aziendale** company policy; **politica estera** foreign policy; **politica dei prezzi** prices policy; **politica dei redditi** incomes policy

poliva'lente *ag* multi-purpose

poli'zia [polit'tsia] *sf* police; **~ giudiziaria** ≈ Criminal Investigation Department (CID) (*Brit*), Federal Bureau of Investigation (FBI) (*US*); **~ sanitaria/tributaria** health/tax inspectorate; **~ stradale** traffic police; **~ di stato** *see note*

○ **POLIZIA DI STATO**
○
○ The remit of the *polizia di stato* is to
○ maintain public order, to uphold the law,
○ and to prevent and investigate crime.
○ This is a civilian branch of the police
○ force; male and female officers perform
○ similar duties. The *polizia di stato* reports to
○ the Minister of the Interior.

polizi'esco, -a, schi, sche [polit'tsjesko] *ag* police *cpd*; (*film, romanzo*) detective *cpd*

polizi'otto [polit'tsjɔtto] *sm* policeman; **cane ~** police dog; **donna ~** policewoman; **~ di quartiere** local police officer

'polizza ['pɔlittsa] *sf* (*Comm*) bill; **~ di assicurazione** insurance policy; **~ di carico** bill of lading

pol'laio *sm* henhouse

pollai'olo, -a *sm/f* poulterer (*Brit*), poultryman

pol'lame *sm* poultry

pol'lastra *sf* pullet; (*fig: ragazza*) chick, wench

pol'lastro *sm* (*Zool*) cockerel

'pollice ['pɔllitʃe] *sm* thumb; (*unità di*) inch

'polline *sm* pollen

'pollo *sm* chicken; **far ridere i polli** (*situazione, persona*) to be utterly ridiculous

polmo'nare *ag* lung *cpd*, pulmonary

pol'mone *sm* lung

polmo'nite *sf* pneumonia; **~ atipica** SARS

'Polo *sm* (*Pol*) centre-right coalition

'polo *sm* (*Geo, Fisica*) pole; (*gioco*) polo ▪ *sf inv* (*maglia*) polo shirt; **il P~ sud/nord** the South/North Pole

Po'lonia *sf*: **la ~** Poland

'polpa *sf* flesh, pulp; (*carne*) lean meat

pol'paccio [pol'pattʃo] *sm* (*Anat*) calf

polpas'trello *sm* fingertip

pol'petta *sf* (*Cuc*) meatball

polpet'tone *sm* (*Cuc*) meatloaf

'polpo *sm* octopus

pol'poso, -a *ag* fleshy

pol'sino *sm* cuff

'polso *sm* (*Anat*) wrist; (*pulsazione*) pulse; (*fig: forza*) drive, vigour (*Brit*), vigor (*US*); **avere ~** (*fig*) to be strong; **un uomo di ~** a man of nerve

pol'tiglia [pol'tiʎʎa] *sf* (*composto*) mash, mush; (*di fango e neve*) slush

pol'trire *vi* to laze about

pol'trona *sf* armchair; (*Teat: posto*) seat in the front stalls (*Brit*) *o* the orchestra (*US*)

poltron'cina [poltron'tʃina] *sf* (*Teat*) seat in the back stalls (*Brit*) *o* the orchestra (*US*)

pol'trone *ag* lazy, slothful

'polvere *sf* dust; (*anche*: **polvere da sparo**) (gun)powder; (*sostanza ridotta minutissima*) powder, dust; **caffè in ~** instant coffee; **latte in ~** dried *o* powdered milk; **sapone in ~** soap powder; **~ d'oro** gold dust; **~ pirica** *o* **da sparo** gunpowder; **polveri sottili** particulates

polveri'era *sf* powder magazine

polve'rina *sf* (*gen, Med*) powder; (*gergo: cocaina*) snow

polveriz'zare [polverid'dzare] *vt* to pulverize; (*nebulizzare*) to atomize; (*fig*) to crush, pulverize; (*record*) to smash

polve'rone *sm* thick cloud of dust

polve'roso, -a *ag* dusty

po'mata *sf* ointment, cream

po'mello *sm* knob

pomeridi'ano, -a *ag* afternoon *cpd*; **nelle ore pomeridiane** in the afternoon

pome'riggio [pome'riddʒo] *sm* afternoon; **nel primo/tardo ~** in the early/late afternoon

'pomice ['pomitʃe] *sf* pumice

pomici'are [pomi'tʃare] *vi* (*fam*) to neck

'pomo *sm* (*mela*) apple; (*ornamentale*) knob; (*di sella*) pommel; **~ d'Adamo** (*Anat*) Adam's apple

pomo'doro *sm* tomato

'pompa *sf* pump; (*sfarzo*) pomp (and ceremony); **~ antincendio** fire hose; **~ di benzina** petrol (*Brit*) *o* gas (*US*) pump; (*distributore*) filling *o* gas (*US*) station; **impresa di pompe funebri** funeral parlour *sg* (*Brit*), undertaker's *sg*, mortician's (*US*)

pom'pare *vt* to pump; (*trarre*) to pump out; (*gonfiare d'aria*) to pump up

pompei'ano, -a *ag* of (*o* from) Pompei

pom'pelmo *sm* grapefruit

pompi'ere *sm* fireman

pom'pon [pom'pɔn] *sm inv* pompom, pompon

pom'poso, -a *ag* pompous

ponde'rare *vt* to ponder over, consider carefully

ponde'roso, -a *ag* (*anche fig*) weighty

po'nente *sm* west

'pongo *vb vedi* **porre**

'poni *vb vedi* **porre**

'ponte *sm* bridge; (*di nave*) deck; (: *anche*: **ponte di comando**) bridge; (*impalcatura*) scaffold; **vivere sotto i ponti** to be a tramp; **fare il ~** (*fig*) to take the extra day off; (*between 2 public holidays*): **governo ~** interim government; **~ aereo** airlift; **~ di barche** (*Mil*) pontoon bridge; **~ di coperta** (*Naut*) upper deck; **~ levatoio** drawbridge; **~ radio** radio link; **~ sospeso** suspension bridge

pon'tefice [pon'tefitʃe] *sm* (*Rel*) pontiff

ponti'cello [ponti'tʃɛllo] *sm* (*di occhiali, Mus*) bridge

pontifi'care *vi* (*anche fig*) to pontificate

pontifi'cato *sm* pontificate

ponti'ficio, -a, ci, cie [ponti'fitʃo] *ag* papal; **Stato P~** Papal State

pon'tile *sm* jetty

'pony ['pɔni] *sm inv* pony

pool [pu:l] *sm inv* (*consorzio*) consortium; (*organismo internazionale*) pool; (*di esperti, ricercatori*) team; (*antimafia, antidroga*) working party

pop [pɔp] *ag inv* pop *cpd*

'popcorn ['pɔpkɔːn] *sm inv* popcorn

'popeline ['pɔpelin] *sm* poplin

popò *sm inv* (*sedere*) botty

popo'lano, -a *ag* popular, of the people ■ *sm/f* man/woman of the people

popo'lare *ag* popular; (*quartiere, clientela*) working-class; (*Pol*) of P.P.I. ■ *sm/f* (*Pol*) member (*o* supporter) of P.P.I. ■ *vt* (*rendere abitato*) to populate; **popolarsi** *vr* to fill with people, get crowded; **manifestazione ~** mass demonstration; **repubblica ~** people's republic

popolarità *sf* popularity

popolazi'one [popolat'tsjone] *sf* population

'popolo *sm* people

popo'loso, -a *ag* densely populated

po'pone *sm* melon

'poppa *sf* (*di nave*) stern; (*fam: mammella*) breast; **a ~** aft, astern

pop'pante *sm/f* unweaned infant; (*fig*) whippersnapper

pop'pare *vt* to suck

pop'pata *sf* (*allattamento*) feed

poppa'toio *sm* (*feeding*) bottle

popu'lista, -i, e *ag* populist

por'caio *sm* (*anche fig*) pigsty

por'cata *sf* (*libro, film etc*) load of rubbish; **fare una ~ a qn** to play a dirty trick on sb

porcel'lana [portʃel'lana] *sf* porcelain, china; (*oggetto*) piece of porcelain

porcel'lino, -a [portʃel'lino] *sm/f* piglet; **~ d'India** guinea pig

porche'ria [porke'ria] *sf* filth, muck; (*fig: oscenità*) obscenity; (*azione disonesta*) dirty trick; (*cosa mal fatta*) rubbish

por'chetta [por'ketta] *sf* roast sucking pig

por'cile [por'tʃile] *sm* pigsty

por'cino, -a [por'tʃino] *ag* of pigs, pork *cpd* ■ *sm* (*fungo*) type of edible mushroom

'porco, -ci *sm* pig; (*carne*) pork

porcos'pino *sm* porcupine

'porfido *sm* porphyry

'porgere ['pɔrdʒere] *vt* to hand, give; (*tendere*) to hold out

'porno *ag inv* porn, porno

pornogra'fia *sf* pornography

porno'grafico, -a, ci, che *ag* pornographic

'poro *sm* pore

po'roso, -a *ag* porous

'porpora *sf* purple

'porre *vt* (*mettere*) to put; (*collocare*) to place; (*posare*) to lay (down), put (down); (*fig: supporre*): **poniamo (il caso) che ...** let's suppose that ...; **porsi** *vr* (*mettersi*): **porsi a sedere/in cammino** to sit down/, set off; **~ le basi di** (*fig*) to lay the foundations of, establish; **~ una domanda a qn** to ask sb a question, put a question to sb; **~ la propria fiducia in** to place one's trust in sb; **~ fine** *o* **termine a qc** to put an end *o* a stop to sth; **posto che ...** supposing that ..., on the assumption that ...; **porsi in salvo** to save o.s.

'porro *sm* (*Bot*) leek; (*Med*) wart

'porsi *etc vb vedi* **porgere**

'porta *sf* door; (*Sport*) goal; (*Inform*) port; **porte** *sfpl* (*di città*) gates; **mettere qn alla ~** to throw sb out; **sbattere** *o* **chiudere la ~ in faccia a qn** (*anche fig*) to slam the door in sb's face; **trovare tutte le porte chiuse** (*fig*) to find the way barred; **a porte chiuse** (*Dir*) in camera; **l'inverno è alle porte** (*fig*) winter is upon us; **vendita ~ a ~** door-to-door selling; **~ di servizio** tradesmen's entrance; **~ di sicurezza** emergency exit; **~ stagna** watertight door

portaba'gagli [portaba'gaʎʎi] *sm inv* (*facchino*) porter; (*Aut, Ferr*) luggage rack

portabandi'era *sm inv* standard bearer

porta'borse *sm inv* (*peg*) lackey

portabot'tiglie [portabot'tiʎʎe] *sm inv* bottle rack

porta-CD [portatʃi'di] *sm inv* CD rack; (*astuccio*) CD holder

porta'cenere [porta'tʃenere] *sm inv* ashtray

P

portachi'avi [porta'kjavi] *sm inv* keyring

porta'cipria [porta'tʃiprja] *sm inv* powder compact

porta'erei *sf inv* (*nave*) aircraft carrier ■ *sm inv* (*aereo*) aircraft transporter

portafi'nestra (*pl* **portefinestre**) *sf* French window

porta'foglio [porta'fɔʎʎo] *sm* (*busta*) wallet; (*cartella*) briefcase; (*Pol, Borsa*) portfolio; **~ titoli** investment portfolio

portagi'oie [porta'dʒɔje], **portagioi'elli** [portadʒo'jɛlli] *sm inv* jewellery (*Brit*) *o* jewelry (*US*) box

por'tale *sm* portal

porta'lettere *sm/f inv* postman/woman (*Brit*), mailman/woman (*US*)

porta'mento *sm* carriage, bearing

portamo'nete *sm inv* purse

por'tante *ag* (*muro etc*) supporting, load-bearing

portan'tina *sf* sedan chair; (*per ammalati*) stretcher

portaog'getti [portaod'dʒetti] *ag inv*: **vano ~** (*in macchina*) glove compartment

portaom'brelli *sm inv* umbrella stand

porta'pacchi [porta'pakki] *sm inv* (*di moto, bicicletta*) luggage rack

porta'penne [porta'penne] *sm inv* pen holder; (*astuccio*) pencil case

por'tare *vt* (*sostenere, sorreggere: peso, bambino, pacco*) to carry; (*indossare: abito, occhiali*) to wear; (*capelli lunghi*) to have; (*avere: nome, titolo*) to have, bear; (*recare*): **~ qc a qn** to take (*o* bring) sth to sb; (*fig: sentimenti*) to bear; **portarsi** *vr* (*recarsi*) to go; **~ avanti** (*discorso, idea*) to pursue; **~ via** to take away; (*rubare*) to take; **~ i bambini a spasso** to take the children for a walk; **~ fortuna** to bring good luck; **~ qc alla bocca** to lift *o* put sth to one's lips; **porta bene i suoi anni** he's wearing well; **dove porta questa strada?** where does this road lead?, where does this road take you?; **il documento porta la tua firma** the document has *o* bears your signature; **non gli porto rancore** I don't bear him a grudge; **la polizia si è portata sul luogo del disastro** the police went to the scene of the disaster

portarit'ratti *sm inv* photo(graph) frame

portari'viste *sm inv* magazine rack

portasa'pone *sm inv* soap dish

portasiga'rette *sm inv* cigarette case

portas'pilli *sm inv* pincushion

por'tata *sf* (*vivanda*) course; (*Aut*) carrying (*o* loading) capacity; (*di arma*) range; (*volume d'acqua*) (rate of) flow; (*fig: limite*) scope, capability; (*: importanza*) impact, import; **alla ~ di tutti** (*conoscenza*) within everybody's

capabilities; (*prezzo*) within everybody's means; **a/fuori ~ (di)** within/out of reach (of); **a ~ di mano** within (arm's) reach; **di grande ~** of great importance

por'tatile *ag* portable

por'tato, -a *ag* (*incline*): **~ a** inclined *o* apt to

porta'tore, -'trice *sm/f* (*anche Comm*) bearer; (*Med*) carrier; **pagabile al ~** payable to the bearer; **~ di handicap** disabled person

portatovagli'olo [portatovaʎ'ʎɔlo] *sm* napkin ring

portau'ovo *sm inv* eggcup

porta'voce [porta'votʃe] *sm/f inv* spokesman/woman

por'tello *sm* (*di portone*) door; (*Naut*) hatch

portel'lone *sm* (*Naut, Aer*) hold door

por'tento *sm* wonder, marvel

porten'toso, -a *ag* wonderful, marvellous (*Brit*), marvelous (*US*)

porti'cato *sm* portico

'portico, -ci *sm* portico; (*riparo*) lean-to

porti'era *sf* (*Aut*) door

porti'ere *sm* (*portinaio*) concierge, caretaker; (*di hotel*) porter; (*nel calcio*) goalkeeper

porti'naio, -a *sm/f* concierge, caretaker

portine'ria *sf* caretaker's lodge

'porto, -a *pp di* **porgere** ■ *sm* (*Naut*) harbour (*Brit*), harbor (*US*), port; (*spesa di trasporto*) carriage ■ *sm inv* port (wine); **andare** *o* **giungere in ~** (*fig*) to come to a successful conclusion; **condurre qc in ~** to bring sth to a successful conclusion; **~ d'armi** gun licence (*Brit*) *o* license (*US*); **~ fluviale** river port; **~ franco** free port; **~ marittimo** seaport; **~ militare** naval base; **~ pagato** carriage paid, post free *o* paid; **~ di scalo** port of call

Porto'gallo *sm*: **il ~** Portugal

porto'ghese [porto'gese] *ag, sm/f, sm* Portuguese *inv*

por'tone *sm* main entrance, main door

portori'cano, -a *ag, sm/f* Puerto Rican

Porto'rico *sf* Puerto Rico

portu'ale *ag* harbour *cpd* (*Brit*), harbor *cpd* (*US*), port *cpd* ■ *sm* dock worker

porzi'one [por'tsjone] *sf* portion, share; (*di cibo*) portion, helping

'posa *sf* (*Fot*) exposure; (*atteggiamento, di modello*) pose; (*riposo*): **lavorare senza ~** to work without a break; **mettersi in ~** to pose; **teatro di ~** photographic studio

posa'cenere [posa'tʃenere] *sm inv* ashtray

po'sare *vt* to put (down), lay (down) ■ *vi* (*ponte, edificio, teoria*): **~ su** to rest on; (*Fot: atteggiarsi*) to pose; **posarsi** *vr* (*ape, aereo*) to land; (*uccello*) to alight; (*sguardo*) to settle

po'sata *sf* piece of cutlery; **posate** *sfpl* cutlery *sg*

posa'tezza [posa'tettsa] sf (di persona) composure; (di discorso) balanced nature

po'sato, -a ag steady; (discorso) balanced

pos'critto sm postscript

'posi etc vb vedi **porre**

positiva'mente av positively; (rispondere) in the affirmative, affirmatively

posi'tivo, -a ag positive

posizi'one [pozit'tsjone] sf position; **farsi una ~** to make one's way in the world; **prendere ~** (fig) to take a stand; **luci di ~** (Aut) sidelights

posolo'gia, - 'gie [pozolo'dʒia] sf dosage, directions pl for use

pos'porre vt to place after; (differire) to postpone, defer

pos'posto, -a pp di **posporre**

posse'dere vt to own, possess; (qualità, virtù) to have, possess; (conoscere a fondo: lingua etc) to have a thorough knowledge of; (ira etc) to possess

possedi'mento sm possession

pos'sente ag strong, powerful

posses'sivo, -a ag possessive

pos'sesso sm possession; **essere in ~ di** to be in possession of sth; **prendere ~** to take possession of sth; **entrare in ~** to come into one's inheritance

posses'sore sm owner

pos'sibile ag possible ■ sm: **fare tutto il ~** to do everything possible; **nei limiti del ~** as far as possible; **al più tardi ~** as late as possible; **vieni prima ~** come as soon as possible

possibi'lista, -i, e ag: **essere ~** to keep an open mind

possibilità sf inv possibility ■ sfpl (mezzi) means; **aver la ~ di fare** to be in a position to do; to have the opportunity to do; **nei limiti delle nostre ~** in so far as we can

possibil'mente av if possible

possi'dente sm/f landowner

possi'edo etc vb vedi **possedere**

'posso etc vb vedi **potere**

post ... prefisso post...

'posta sf (servizio) post, postal service; (corrispondenza) post, mail; (ufficio postale) post office; (nei giochi d'azzardo) stake; (Caccia) hide (Brit), blind (US); **poste** sfpl (amministrazione) post office; **fare la ~ a qn** (fig) to lie in wait for sb; **la ~ in gioco è troppo alta** (fig) there's too much at stake; **a bella ~** (apposta) on purpose; **piccola ~** (su giornale) letters to the editor, letters page; **~ aerea** airmail; **~ elettronica** electronic mail; **~ ordinaria** = second-class mail; **~ prioritaria** first class (post); **Poste e Telecomunicazioni** postal

and telecommunications service; **ministro delle Poste e Telecomunicazioni** Postmaster General

posta'giro [posta'dʒiro] sm post office cheque (Brit) o check (US), postal giro (Brit)

pos'tale ag postal, post office cpd ■ sm (treno) mail train; (nave) mail boat; (furgone) mail van; **timbro ~** postmark

postazi'one [postat'tsjone] sf (Mil) emplacement

post'bellico, -a, ci, che ag postwar

postda'tare vt to postdate

posteggi'are [posted'dʒare] vt, vi to park

posteggia'tore, - 'trice [postedd ʒa'tore] sm/f car-park attendant (Brit), parking-lot attendant (US)

pos'teggio [pos'teddʒo] sm car park (Brit), parking lot (US); (di taxi) rank (Brit), stand (US)

postelegra'fonico, -a, ci, che ag postal and telecommunications cpd

'poster sm inv poster

'posteri smpl posterity sg; **i nostri ~** our descendants

posteri'ore ag (dietro) back; (dopo) later ■ sm (fam: sedere) behind

posteri'ori: a ~ ag inv after the event; (dopo sostantivo) av ~ looking back

pos'ticcio, -a, ci, ce [pos'tittʃo] ag false ■ sm hairpiece

postici'pare [postitʃi'pare] vt to defer, postpone

pos'tilla sf marginal note

pos'tino sm postman (Brit), mailman (US)

'posto, -a pp di **porre** ■ sm (sito, posizione) place; (impiego) job; (spazio libero) room, space; (di parcheggio) space; (sedile: al teatro, in treno etc) seat; (Mil) post; **a ~** (in ordine) in place, tidy; (fig) settled; (: persona) reliable; **mettere a ~** (riordinare) to tidy (up), put in order; (faccende: sistemare) to straighten out; **prender ~** to take a seat; **al ~ di** in place of; **sul ~** on the spot; **~ di blocco** roadblock; **~ di lavoro** job; **~ di polizia** police station; **~ telefonico pubblico** public telephone; **~ di villeggiatura** holiday (Brit) o tourist spot; **posti in piedi** (Teat: in autobus) standing room

postopera'torio, -a ag (Med) postoperative

pos'tribolo sm brothel

post'scriptum sm inv postscript

'postumo, -a ag posthumous; (tardivo) belated; **postumi** smpl (conseguenze) after-effects, consequences

po'tabile ag drinkable; **acqua ~** drinking water

po'tare vt to prune

po'tassio *sm* potassium

pota'tura *sf* pruning

po'tente *ag (nazione)* strong, powerful; *(veleno, farmaco)* potent, strong

poten'tino, -a *ag* of (*o* from) Potenza

Po'tenza [po'tɛntsa] *sf* Potenza

po'tenza [po'tɛntsa] *sf* power; *(forza)* strength; **all'ennesima ~** to the nth degree; **le Grandi Potenze** the Great Powers; **~ militare** military might *o* strength

potenzi'ale [poten'tsjale] *ag, sm* potential

potenzia'mento [potentsja'mento] *sm* development

potenzi'are [poten'tsjare] *vt* to develop

 PAROLA CHIAVE

po'tere *sm* power; **al potere** *(partito etc)* in power; **potere d'acquisto** purchasing power; **potere esecutivo** executive power; **potere giudiziario** legal power; **potere legislativo** legislative power

■ *vb aus* **1** *(essere in grado di)* can, be able to; **non ha potuto ripararlo** he couldn't *o* he wasn't able to repair it; **non è potuto venire** he couldn't *o* he wasn't able to come; **spiacente di non poter aiutare** sorry not to be able to help

2 *(avere il permesso)* can, may, be allowed to; **posso entrare?** can *o* may I come in?; **posso chiederti, dove sei stato?** where, may I ask, have you been?

3 *(eventualità)* may, might, could; **potrebbe essere vero** it might *o* could be true; **può aver avuto un incidente** he may *o* might *o* could have had an accident; **può darsi** perhaps; **può darsi** *o* **può essere che non venga** he may *o* might not come

4 *(augurio)*: **potessi almeno parlargli!** if only I could speak to him!

5 *(suggerimento)*: **potresti almeno scusarti!** you could at least apologize!

■ *vt* can, be able to; **può molto per noi** he can do a lot for us; **non ne posso più** *(per stanchezza)* I'm exhausted; *(per rabbia)* I can't take any more

potestà *sf (potere)* power; *(Dir)* authority

potrò *etc vb vedi* **potere**

pove'raccio, -a, ci, ce [pove'rattʃo] *sm/f* poor devil

'povero, -a *ag* poor; *(disadorno)* plain, bare

■ *sm/f* poor man/woman; **i poveri** the poor; **~ di** lacking in, having little; **minerale ~ di ferro** ore with a low iron content; **paese ~ di risorse** country short of *o* lacking in resources

povertà *sf* poverty; **~ energetica** fuel poverty

pozi'one [pot'tsjone] *sf* potion

'pozza ['pottsa] *sf* pool

poz'zanghera [pot'tsangera] *sf* puddle

'pozzo ['pottso] *sm* well; *(cava: di carbone)* pit; *(di miniera)* shaft; **~ nero** cesspit; **~ petrolifero** oil well

pp. *abbr* (= *pagine*) pp

p.p. *abbr* (= *per procura*) pp

P.P.I. *sigla m* (Pol: *Partito Popolare Italiano*) party originating from D.C.

PP.TT. *abbr* = **Poste e Telecomunicazioni**

PR *sigla* = **Parma** ■ *sigla m* (Pol) = **Partito Radicale**

P.R. *abbr* = **piano regolatore**; **procuratore della Repubblica**

'Praga *sf* Prague

prag'matico, -a, ci, che *ag* pragmatic

pram'matica *sf* custom; **essere di ~** to be customary

pranotera'pia *sf* pranotherapy

pran'zare [pran'dzare] *vi* to dine, have dinner; to lunch, have lunch

'pranzo ['prandzo] *sm* dinner; *(a mezzogiorno)* lunch

'prassi *sf* usual procedure

'pratica, -che *sf* practice; *(esperienza)* experience; *(conoscenza)* knowledge, familiarity; *(tirocinio)* training, practice; *(Amm: affare)* matter, case; *(:incartamento)* file, dossier; **in ~** *(praticamente)* in practice; **mettere in ~** to put into practice; **fare le pratiche per** *(Amm)* to do the paperwork for; **~ restrittiva** restrictive practice; **pratiche illecite** dishonest practices

prati'cabile *ag (progetto)* practicable, feasible; *(luogo)* passable, practicable

pratica'mente *av (in modo pratico)* in a practical way, practically; *(quasi)* practically, almost

prati'cante *sm/f* apprentice, trainee; *(Rel)* (regular) churchgoer

prati'care *vt* to practise *(Brit)*, practice *(US)*; *(Sport: tennis etc)* to play; *(nuoto, scherma etc)* to go in for; *(eseguire: apertura, buco)* to make; **~ uno sconto** to give a discount

praticità [pratitʃi'ta] *sf* practicality, practicalness; **per ~** for practicality's sake

'pratico, -a, ci, che *ag* practical; **~ di** *(esperto)* experienced *o* skilled in; *(familiare)* familiar with; **all'atto ~** in practice; **è ~ del mestiere** he knows his trade; **mi è più ~ venire di pomeriggio** it's more convenient for me to come in the afternoon

'prato *sm* meadow; *(di giardino)* lawn

preal'larme *sm* warning (signal)

Pre'alpi *sfpl*: **le ~** (the) Pre-Alps

preal'pino, -a *ag* of the Pre-Alps

pre'ambolo *sm* preamble; **senza tanti preamboli** without beating about (*Brit*) *o* around (*US*) the bush

preannunci'are [preannun'tʃare], **preannunzi'are** [preannun'tsjare] *vt* to give advance notice of

preavvi'sare *vt* to give advance notice of

preav'viso *sm* notice; **telefonata con ~** personal *o* person to person call

pre'bellico, -a, ci, che *ag* prewar *cpd*

precari'ato *sm* temporary employment

precarietà *sf* precariousness

pre'cario, -a *ag* precarious; (*Ins*) temporary, without tenure

precauzio'nale [prekauttsjo'nale] *ag* precautionary

precauzi'one [prekaut'tsjone] *sf* caution, care; (*misura*) precaution; **prendere precauzioni** to take precautions

prece'dente [pretʃe'dɛnte] *ag* previous ▪ *sm* precedent; **il discorso/film ~** the previous *o* preceding speech/film; **senza precedenti** unprecedented; **precedenti penali** (*Dir*) criminal record *sg*

precedente'mente [pretʃedente'mente] *av* previously

prece'denza [pretʃe'dɛntsa] *sf* priority, precedence; (*Aut*) right of way; **dare ~ assoluta a qc** to give sth top priority

pre'cedere [pre'tʃɛdere] *vt* to precede, go *o* (come) before

precet'tare [pretʃet'tare] *vt* (*lavoratori*) to order back to work (*via an injunction*)

precettazi'one [pretʃettat'tsjone] *sf* (*di lavoratori*) order to resume work

pre'cetto [pre'tʃɛtto] *sm* precept; (*Mil*) call-up notice

precet'tore [pretʃet'tore] *sm* (*private*) tutor

precipi'tare [pretʃipi'tare] *vi* (*cadere*) to fall headlong; (*fig: situazione*) to get out of control ▪ *vt* (*gettare dall'alto in basso*) to hurl, fling; (*fig: affrettare*) to rush; **precipitarsi** *vr* (*gettarsi*) to hurl *o* fling o.s.; (*affrettarsi*) to rush

precipi'tato, -a [pretʃipi'tato] *ag* hasty ▪ *sm* (*Chim*) precipitate

precipitazi'one [pretʃipitat'tsjone] *sf* (*Meteor*) precipitation; (*fig*) haste

precipi'toso, -a [pretʃipi'toso] *ag* (*caduta, fuga*) headlong; (*fig: avventato*) rash, reckless; (*affrettato*) hasty, rushed

preci'pizio [pretʃi'pittsjo] *sm* precipice; **a ~** (*fig: correre*) headlong

pre'cipuo, -a [pre'tʃipuo] *ag* principal, main

precisa'mente [pretʃiza'mente] *av* (*gen*) precisely; (*con esattezza*) exactly

preci'sare [pretʃi'zare] *vt* to state, specify; (*spiegare*) to explain (in detail); **vi preciseremo la data in seguito** we'll let you know the exact date later; **tengo a ~ che ...** I must point out that ...

precisazi'one [pretʃizat'tsjone] *sf* clarification

precisi'one [pretʃi'zjone] *sf* precision; accuracy; **strumenti di ~** precision instruments

pre'ciso, -a [pre'tʃizo] *ag* (*esatto*) precise; (*accurato*) accurate, precise; (*deciso: idea*) precise, definite; (*uguale*): **2 vestiti precisi** 2 dresses exactly the same; **sono le 9 precise** it's exactly 9 o'clock

pre'cludere *vt* to block, obstruct

pre'cluso, -a *pp di* **precludere**

pre'coce [pre'kɔtʃe] *ag* early; (*bambino*) precocious; (*vecchiaia*) premature

precocità [prekotʃi'ta] *sf* (*di morte*) untimeliness; (*di bambino*) precociousness

precon'cetto, -a [prekon'tʃetto] *ag* preconceived ▪ *sm* preconceived idea, prejudice

pre'correre *vt* to anticipate; **~ i tempi** to be ahead of one's time

precorri'tore, -'trice *sm/f* precursor, forerunner

pre'corso, -a *pp di* **precorrere**

precur'sore *sm* forerunner, precursor

'preda *sf* (*bottino*) booty; (*animale: fig*) prey; **essere ~ di** to fall prey to; **essere in ~ a** to be prey to

pre'dare *vt* to plunder

preda'tore *sm* predator

predeces'sore, -a [predetʃes'sore] *sm/f* predecessor

pre'della *sf* platform, dais; altar-step

predesti'nare *vt* to predestine

predestinazi'one [predestinat'tsjone] *sf* predestination

pre'detto, -a *pp di* **predire** ▪ *ag* aforesaid, aforementioned

'predica, -che *sf* sermon; (*fig*) lecture, talking-to

predi'care *vt, vi* to preach

predica'tivo, -a *ag* predicative

predi'cato *sm* (*Ling*) predicate

predi'letto, -a *pp di* **prediligere** ▪ *ag, sm/f* favourite (*Brit*), favorite (*US*)

predilezi'one [predilet'tsjone] *sf* fondness, partiality; **avere una ~ per qc/qn** to be partial to sth/fond of sb

predi'ligere [predi'lidʒere] *vt* to prefer, have a preference for

pre'dire *vt* to foretell, predict

predis'porre *vt* to get ready, prepare; **~ qn a qc** to predispose sb to sth

predisposizi'one [predispozit'tsjone] *sf* (*Med*) predisposition; (*attitudine*) bent, aptitude; **avere ~ alla musica** to have a bent for music

predis'posto, -a *pp di* **predisporre**

predizi'one [predit'tsjone] *sf* prediction

predomi'nante *ag* predominant

predomi'nare *vi* (*prevalere*) to predominate; (*eccellere*) to excel

predo'minio *sm* predominance; supremacy

preesis'tente *ag* pre-existent

pree'sistere *vi* to pre-exist

preesis'tito, -a *pp di* **preesistere**

prefabbri'cato, -a *ag* (*Edil*) prefabricated

prefazi'one [prefat'tsjone] *sf* preface, foreword

prefe'renza [prefe'rɛntsa] *sf* preference; **a ~ di** rather than; **di ~** preferably, by preference; **non ho preferenze** I have no preferences either way, I don't mind

preferenzi'ale [preferen'tsjale] *ag* preferential; **corsia ~** (*Aut*) bus and taxi lane

prefe'ribile *ag:* **~ (a)** preferable (to), better (than); **sarebbe ~ andarsene** it would be better to go

preferibil'mente *av* preferably

prefe'rire *vt* to prefer, like better; **~ il caffè al tè** to prefer coffee to tea, like coffee better than tea

pre'fetto *sm* prefect

prefet'tura *sf* prefecture

pre'figgersi [pre'fiddʒersi] *vr:* **~ uno scopo** to set o.s. a goal

prefigu'rare *vt* (*simboleggiare*) to foreshadow; (*prevedere*) to foresee

pre'fisso, -a *pp di* **prefiggersi** ■ *sm* (*Ling*) prefix; (*Tel*) dialling (*Brit*) *o* dial (*US*) code

Preg. *abbr* = **pregiatissimo**

pre'gare *vi* to pray ■ *vt* (*Rel*) to pray to; (*implorare*) to beg; (*chiedere*): **~ qn di fare** to ask sb to do; **farsi ~** to need coaxing *o* persuading

pre'gevole [pre'dʒevole] *ag* valuable

pregherò *etc* [prege'rɔ] *vb vedi* **pregare**

preghi'era [pre'gjɛra] *sf* (*Rel*) prayer; (*domanda*) request

pregi'arsi [pre'dʒarsi] *vr:* **mi pregio di farle sapere che ...** I am pleased to inform you that ...

pregia'tissimo, -a [predʒa'tissimo] *ag* (*in lettere*): **~ Signor G. Agnelli** G. Agnelli Esquire

pregi'ato, -a [pre'dʒato] *ag* (*opera*) valuable; (*tessuto*) fine; (*valuta*) strong; **vino ~** vintage wine

'pregio ['prɛdʒo] *sm* (*stima*) esteem, regard; (*qualità*) (good) quality, merit; (*valore*) value,

worth; **il ~ di questo sistema è ...** the merit of this system is ...; **oggetto di ~** valuable object

pregiudi'care [predʒudi'kare] *vt* to prejudice, harm, be detrimental to

pregiudi'cato, -a [predʒudi'kato] *sm/f* (*Dir*) previous offender

pregiu'dizio [predʒu'dittsjo] *sm* (*idea errata*) prejudice; (*danno*) harm *no pl*

preg'nante [preɲ'ɲante] *ag* (*fig*) pregnant, meaningful

'pregno, -a ['preɲɲo] *ag* (*saturo*): **~ di** full of, saturated with

'prego *escl* (*a chi ringrazia*) don't mention it!; (*invitando qn ad accomodarsi*) please sit down!; (*invitando qn ad andare prima*) after you!

pregus'tare *vt* to look forward to

preis'toria *sf* prehistory

preis'torico, -a, ci, che *ag* prehistoric

pre'lato *sm* prelate

prela'vaggio [prela'vaddʒo] *sm* pre-wash

prelazi'one [prelat'tsjone] *sf* (*Dir*) pre-emption; **avere il diritto di ~ su qc** to have the first option on sth

preleva'mento *sm* (*Banca*) withdrawal; (*di merce*) picking up, collection

prele'vare *vt* (*denaro*) to withdraw; (*campione*) to take; (*merce*) to pick up, collect; (*polizia*) to take, capture

preli'evo *sm* (*Banca*) withdrawal; (*Med*): **fare un ~ (di)** to take a sample (of)

prelimi'nare *ag* preliminary; **preliminari** *smpl* preliminary talks; preliminaries

pre'ludere *vi:* **~ a** (*preannunciare: crisi, guerra, temporale*) to herald, be a sign of; (*introdurre: dibattito etc*) to introduce, be a prelude to

pre'ludio *sm* prelude

pre'luso, -a *pp di* **preludere**

pre-ma'man [prema'mã] *sm inv* maternity dress

prematrimoni'ale *ag* premarital

prema'turo, -a *ag* premature

premedi'tare *vt* to premeditate, plan

premeditazi'one [premeditat'tsjone] *sf* (*Dir*) premeditation; **con ~** *ag* premeditated ■ *av* with intent

pre'mere *vt* to press ■ *vi:* **~ su** to press down on; (*fig*) to put pressure on; **~ a** (*fig: importare*) to matter to; **~ il grilletto** to pull the trigger

pre'messo, -a *pp di* **premettere** ■ *sf* introductory statement, introduction; **mancano le premesse per una buona riuscita** we lack the basis for a successful outcome

pre'mettere *vt* to put before; (*dire prima*) to start by saying, state first; **premetto che ...** I must say first of all that ...; **premesso**

che ... given that ...; **ciò premesso** ... that having been said ...

premi'are vt to give a prize to; (fig: merito, onestà) to reward

premiazi'one [premjat'tsjone] sf prize giving

'premier ['prɛmjer] sm inv premier

premi'nente ag pre-eminent

'premio sm prize; (ricompensa) reward; (Comm) premium; (Amm: indennità) bonus; **in ~ per** as a prize (o reward) for; **~ d'ingaggio** (Sport) signing-on fee; **~ di produzione** productivity bonus

pre'misi etc vb vedi **premettere**

premoni'tore, -'trice ag premonitory

premonizi'one [premonit'tsjone] sf premonition

premu'nirsi vr: **~ di** to provide o.s. with; **~ contro** to protect o.s. from, guard o.s. against

pre'mura sf (fretta) haste, hurry; (riguardo) attention, care; **aver ~** to be in a hurry; **far ~ a qn** to hurry sb; **usare ogni ~ nei riguardi di qn, circondare qn di premure** to be very attentive to sb

premu'roso, -a ag thoughtful, considerate

prena'tale ag antenatal

'prendere vt to take; (andare a prendere) to get, fetch; (ottenere) to get; (guadagnare) to get, earn; (catturare: ladro, pesce) to catch; (collaboratore, dipendente) to take on; (passeggero) to pick up; (chiedere: somma, prezzo) to charge, ask; (trattare: persona) to handle ■ vi (colla, cemento) to set; (pianta) to take; (fuoco: nel camino) to catch; (voltare): **~ a destra** to turn (to the) right; **prendersi** vr (azzuffarsi): **prendersi a pugni** to come to blows; **prende qualcosa?** (da bere, da mangiare) would you like something to eat (o drink)?; **prendo un caffè** I'll have a coffee; **~ a fare qc** to start doing sth; **~ qn/qc per** (scambiare) to take sb/ sth for; **~ l'abitudine di** to get into the habit of; **~ fuoco** to catch fire; **~ le generalità di qn** to take down sb's particulars; **~ nota di** to take note of; **~ parte a** to take part in; **prendersi cura di qn/qc** to look after sb/sth; **prendersi un impegno** to take on a commitment; **prendersela** (adirarsi) to get annoyed; (preoccuparsi) to get upset, worry

prendi'sole sm inv sundress

preno'tare vt to book, reserve

prenotazi'one [prenotat'tsjone] sf booking, reservation

'prensile ag prehensile

preoccu'pante ag worrying

preoccu'pare vt to worry; **preoccuparsi** vr: **preoccuparsi di qn/qc** to worry about sb/sth; **preoccuparsi per qn** to be anxious for sb

preoccupazi'one [preokkupat'tsjone] sf worry, anxiety

preordi'nato, -a ag preordained

prepa'rare vt to prepare; (esame, concorso) to prepare for; **prepararsi** vr (vestirsi) to get ready; **prepararsi a qc/a fare** to get ready o prepare (o.s.) for sth/to do; **~ da mangiare** to prepare a meal

prepara'tivi smpl preparations

prepa'rato, -a ag (gen) prepared; (pronto) ready ■ sm (prodotto) preparation

prepara'torio, -a ag preparatory

preparazi'one [preparat'tsjone] sf preparation; **non ha la necessaria ~ per svolgere questo lavoro** he lacks the qualifications necessary for the job

prepensiona'mento sm early retirement

preponde'rante ag predominant

pre'porre vt to place before; (fig) to prefer

preposizi'one [prepozit'tsjone] sf (Ling) preposition

pre'posto, -a pp di **preporre**

prepo'tente ag (persona) domineering, arrogant; (bisogno, desiderio) overwhelming, pressing ■ sm/f bully

prepo'tenza [prepo'tɛntsa] sf arrogance; (comportamento) arrogant behaviour (Brit) o behavior (US)

pre'puzio [pre'puttsjo] sm (Anat) foreskin

preroga'tiva sf prerogative

'presa sf taking no pl; catching no pl; (di città) capture; (indurimento: di cemento) setting; (appiglio, Sport) hold; (di acqua, gas) (supply) point; (Elettr): **~ (di corrente)** socket; (al muro) point; (piccola quantità: di sale etc) pinch; (Carte) trick; **far ~** (colla) to set; **ha fatto ~ sul pubblico** (fig) it caught the public's imagination; **a ~ rapida** (cemento) quick-setting; **di forte ~** (fig) with wide appeal; **essere alle prese con qc** (fig) to be struggling with sth; **macchina da ~** (Cine) cine camera (Brit), movie camera (US); **~ d'aria** air inlet; **~ diretta** (Aut) direct drive; **~ in giro** leg-pull (Brit), joke; **~ di posizione** stand

pre'sagio [pre'zadʒo] sm omen

presa'gire [preza'dʒire] vt to foresee

presa'lario sm (Ins) grant

'presbite ag long-sighted

presbiteri'ano, -a ag, sm/f Presbyterian

presbi'terio sm presbytery

pre'scindere [preʃʃindere] vi: **~ da** to leave out of consideration; **a ~ da** apart from

pre'scisso, -a [preʃʃisso] pp di **prescindere**

presco'lastico, -a, ci, che ag pre-school cpd

pres'critto, -a pp di **prescrivere**

pres'crivere vt to prescribe

p

prescrizi'one [preskrit'tsjone] *sf* (*Med, Dir*) prescription; (*norma*) rule, regulation; **cadere in ~** (*Dir*) to become statute-barred

'prese *etc vb vedi* **prendere**

presen'tare *vt* to present; (*far conoscere*): **~ qn (a)** to introduce sb (to); (*Amm: inoltrare*) to submit; **presentarsi** *vr* (*recarsi, farsi vedere*) to present o.s., appear; (*farsi*) to introduce o.s.; (*occasione*) to arise; **~ qc in un'esposizione** to show *o* display sth at an exhibition; **~ qn in società** to introduce sb into society; **presentarsi come candidato** (*Pol*) to stand (*Brit*) *o* run (*US*) as a candidate; **presentarsi bene/male** to have a good/poor appearance; **la situazione si presenta difficile** things aren't looking too good, things look a bit tricky

presentazi'one [prezentat'tsjone] *sf* presentation; introduction

pre'sente *ag* present; (*questo*) this ■ *sm* present ■ *sf* (*lettera*): **con la ~ vi comunico ...** this is to inform you that ... ■ *sm/f* person present; **i presenti** those present; **aver ~ qc/qn** to remember sth/sb; **essere ~ a una riunione** to be present at *o* attend a meeting; **tener ~ qn/qc** to keep sb/sth in mind; **esclusi i presenti** present company excepted

presenti'mento *sm* premonition

pre'senza [pre'zɛntsa] *sf* presence; (*aspetto esteriore*) appearance; **in ~ di** in (the) presence of; **di bella ~** of good appearance; **~ di spirito** presence of mind

presenzi'are [prezen'tsjare] *vi*: **~ a** to be present at, attend

pre'sepe, pre'sepio *sm* crib

preser'vare *vt* to protect

preserva'tivo *sm* sheath, condom

'presi *etc vb vedi* **prendere**

'preside *sm/f* (*Ins*) head (teacher) (*Brit*), principal (*US*); (*di facoltà universitaria*) dean

presi'dente *sm* (*Pol*) president; (*di assemblea, Comm*) chairman; **il P~ della Camera** (*Pol*) ≈ the Speaker; **P~ del Consiglio (dei Ministri)** ≈ Prime Minister; **P~ della Repubblica** President of the Republic; *see note*

presiden'tessa *sf* president; (*moglie*) president's wife; (*di assemblea, Comm*) chairwoman

presi'denza [presi'dɛntsa] *sf* presidency; office of president; chairmanship; **assumere la ~** to become president; to take the chair; **essere alla ~** to be president (*o* chairman); **candidato alla ~** presidential candidate; candidate for the chairmanship

presidenzi'ale [presidɛn'tsjale] *ag* presidential

presidi'are *vt* to garrison

pre'sidio *sm* garrison

presi'edere *vt* to preside over ■ *vi*: **~ a** to direct, be in charge of

'preso, -a *pp di* **prendere**

'pressa *sf* (*Tecn*) press

pres'sante *ag* (*bisogno, richiesta*) urgent, pressing

pressap'poco *av* about, roughly, approximately

pres'sare *vt* (*anche fig*) to press; **~ qn con richieste** to pursue sb with demands

pressi'one *sf* pressure; **far ~ su qn** to put pressure on sb; **subire forti pressioni** to be under strong pressure; **~ sanguigna** blood pressure

'presso *av* (*vicino*) nearby, close at hand ■ *prep* (*vicino a*) near; (*accanto a*) beside, next to; (*in casa di*): **~ qn** at sb's home; (*nelle lettere*) care of; (*alle dipendenza di*): **lavora ~ di noi** he works for *o* with us ■ *smpl*: **nei pressi di** near, in the vicinity of; **ha avuto grande successo ~ i giovani** it has been a hit with young people

pressoché [presso'ke] *av* nearly, almost

pressuriz'zare [pressurid'dzare] *vt* to pressurize

prestabi'lire *vt* to arrange beforehand, arrange in advance

presta'nome *sm/f inv* (*peg*) figurehead

pres'tante *ag* good-looking

pres'tanza [pres'tantsa] *sf* (*robust*) good looks *pl*

pres'tare *vt*: ~ (**qc a qn**) to lend (sb sth *o* sth to sb); **prestarsi** *vr* (*offrirsi*): **prestarsi a fare** to offer to do; (*essere adatto*): **prestarsi a** to lend itself to, be suitable for; ~ **aiuto** to lend a hand; ~ **ascolto** *o* **orecchio** to listen; ~ **attenzione** to pay attention; ~ **fede a qc/qn** to give credence to sth/sb; ~ **giuramento** to take an oath; **la frase si presta a molteplici interpretazioni** the phrase lends itself to numerous interpretations

prestazi'one [prestat'tsjone] *sf* (*Tecn, Sport*) performance; **prestazioni** *sfpl* (*di persona: servizi*) services

prestigia'tore, -'trice [prestidʒa'tore] *sm/f* conjurer

pres'tigio [pres'tidʒo] *sm* (*potere*) prestige; (*illusione*): **gioco di** ~ conjuring trick

prestigi'oso, -a [presti'dʒoso] *ag* prestigious

prestito *sm* lending *no pl*; loan; **dar in** ~ to lend; **prendere in** ~ to borrow; ~ **bancario** bank loan; ~ **pubblico** public borrowing

presto *av* (*tra poco*) soon; (*in fretta*) quickly; (*di buon'ora*) early; **a** ~ see you soon; ~ **o tardi** sooner or later; **fare** ~ **a fare qc** to hurry up and do sth; (*non costare fatica*) to have no trouble doing sth; **si fa** ~ **a criticare** it's easy to criticize; **è ancora** ~ **per decidere** it's still too early *o* too soon to decide

pre'sumere *vt* to presume, assume

presu'mibile *ag* (*dati, risultati*) likely

pre'sunsi *etc vb vedi* **presumere**

pre'sunto, -a *pp di* **presumere** ■ *ag*: **il** ~ **colpevole** the alleged culprit

presuntu'oso, -a *ag* presumptuous

presunzi'one [prezun'tsjone] *sf* presumption

presup'porre *vt* to suppose; to presuppose

presup'posto, -a *pp di* **presupporre** ■ *sm* (*premessa*) supposition, premise; **partendo dal** ~ **che** ... assuming that ...; **mancano i presupposti necessari** the necessary conditions are lacking

prete *sm* priest

preten'dente *sm/f* pretender ■ *sm* (*corteggiatore*) suitor

pre'tendere *vt* (*esigere*) to demand, require; (*sostenere*): ~ **che** to claim that; **pretende di aver sempre ragione** he thinks he's always right

pretenzi'oso, -a [preten'tsjoso] *ag* pretentious

preterintenzio'nale [preterintentsjo'nale] *ag* (*Dir*): **omicidio** ~ manslaughter

pre'teso, -a *pp di* **pretendere** ■ *sf* (*esigenza*) claim, demand; (*presunzione, sfarzo*) pretentiousness; **avanzare una pretesa** to put forward a claim *o* demand; **senza pretese** *ag* unpretentious ■ *av* unpretentiously

pre'testo *sm* pretext, excuse; **con il** ~ **di** on the pretext of

pretestu'oso, -a *ag* (*data, motivo*) used as an excuse

pre'tore *sm* magistrate

pre'tura *sf* (*Dir: sede*) magistrate's court (*Brit*), circuit *o* superior court (*US*); (: *magistratura*) magistracy

preva'lente *ag* prevailing

prevalente'mente *av* mainly, for the most part

preva'lenza [preva'lentsa] *sf* predominance

preva'lere *vi* to prevail

pre'valso, -a *pp di* **prevalere**

prevari'care *vi* (*abusare del potere*) to abuse one's power

prevaricazi'one [prevarikat'tsjone] *sf* (*abuso di potere*) abuse of power

preve'dere *vt* (*indovinare*) to foresee; (*presagire*) to foretell; (*considerare*) to make provision for; **nulla lasciava** ~ **che** ... there was nothing to suggest *o* to make one think that ...; **come previsto** as expected; **spese previste** anticipated expenditure; **previsto per martedì** scheduled for Tuesday

prev'edibile *ag* predictable; **non era assolutamente** ~ **che** ... no one could have foreseen that ...

prevedibil'mente *av* as one would expect

preve'nire *vt* (*anticipare: obiezione*) to forestall; (*domanda*) to anticipate; (*evitare*) to avoid, prevent; (*avvertire*): ~ **qn** (**di**) to warn sb (of); to inform sb (of)

preventi'vare *vt* (*Comm*) to estimate

preven'tivo, -a *ag* preventive ■ *sm* (*Comm*) estimate; **fare un** ~ to give an estimate; **bilancio** ~ budget; **carcere** ~ custody; (*pending trial*)

preve'nuto, -a *ag* (*mal disposto*): ~ (**contro qc/ qn**) prejudiced (against sth/sb)

prevenzi'one [preven'tsjone] *sf* prevention; (*preconcetto*) prejudice

previ'dente *ag* showing foresight; prudent

previ'denza [previ'dentsa] *sf* foresight; **istituto di** ~ provident institution; ~ **sociale** social security (*Brit*), welfare (*US*)

pre'vidi *etc vb vedi* **prevedere**

previo, -a *ag* (*Comm*): ~ **avviso** upon notice; ~ **pagamento** upon payment

previsi'one *sf* forecast, prediction; **previsioni meteorologiche** *o* **del tempo** weather forecast *sg*

pre'visto, -a *pp di* **prevedere** ■ *sm*: **piú/ meno del** ~ more/less than expected; **prima del** ~ earlier than expected

p

281

prezi'oso, -a [pret'tsjoso] *ag* precious; (*aiuto, consiglio*) invaluable ■ *sm* jewel; valuable

prez'zemolo [pret'tsemolo] *sm* parsley

'prezzo ['prɛttso] *sm* price; **a ~ di costo** at cost, at cost price (*Brit*); **tirare sul ~** to bargain, haggle; **il ~ pattuito è 1000 di euro** the agreed price is 1000 euros; **~ d'acquisto/di vendita** buying/selling price; **~ di fabbrica** factory price; **~ di mercato** market price; **~ scontato** reduced price; **~ unitario** unit price

P.R.I. *sigla m* (= *Partito Repubblicano Italiano*) *former political party*

prigi'one [pri'dʒone] *sf* prison

prigio'nia [pridʒo'nia] *sf* imprisonment

prigioni'ero, -a [pridʒo'njɛro] *ag* captive ■ *sm/f* prisoner

'prima *sf vedi* **primo** ■ *av* before; (*in anticipo*) in advance, beforehand; (*per l'addietro*) at one time, formerly; (*più presto*) sooner, earlier; (*in primo luogo*) first ■ *cong*: **~ di fare/che parta** before doing/he leaves; **~ di** *prep* before; **~ o poi** sooner or later; **due giorni ~** two days before *o* earlier; **~ d'ora** before now

pri'mario, -a *ag* primary; (*principale*) chief, leading, primary ■ *sm/f* (*medico*) head physician, chief physician

pri'mate *sm* (*Rel, Zool*) primate

prima'tista, -i, e *sm/f* (*Sport*) record holder

pri'mato *sm* supremacy; (*Sport*) record

prima'vera *sf* spring

primave'rile *ag* spring *cpd*

primeggi'are [primed'dʒare] *vi* to excel, be one of the best

primi'tivo, -a *ag* (*gen*) primitive; (*significato*) original

pri'mizie [pri'mittsje] *sfpl* early produce *sg*

'primo, -a *ag* first; (*fig*) initial; basic; prime ■ *sm/f* first (one) ■ *sm* (*Cuc*) first course; (*in date*): **il ~ luglio** the first of July ■ *sf* (*Teat*) first night; (*Cine*) première; (*Aut*) first (gear); **le prime ore del mattino** the early hours of the morning; **di prima mattina** early in the morning; **in prima pagina** (*Stampa*) on the front page; **ai primi freddi** at the first sign of cold weather; **ai primi di maggio** at the beginning of May; **i primi del Novecento** the early twentieth century; **viaggiare in prima** to travel first-class; **per prima cosa** firstly; **in ~ luogo** first of all, in the first place; **di prim'ordine** *o* **prima qualità** first-class, first-rate; **in un ~ tempo** *o* **momento** at first; **prima donna** leading lady; (*di opera lirica*) prima donna

primo'genito, -a [primo'dʒenito] *ag, sm/f* firstborn

pri'mordi *smpl* beginnings

primordi'ale *ag* primordial

'primula *sf* primrose

princi'pale [printʃi'pale] *ag* main, principal ■ *sm* manager, boss; **sede ~** head office

principal'mente [printʃipal'mente] *av* mainly, principally

princi'pato [printʃi'pato] *sm* principality

'principe ['printʃipe] *sm* prince; **~ ereditario** crown prince

princi'pesco, -a, schi, sche [printʃi'pesko] *ag* (*anche fig*) princely

princi'pessa [printʃi'pessa] *sf* princess

principi'ante [printʃi'pjante] *sm/f* beginner

principi'are [printʃi'pjare] *vt, vi* to start, begin

prin'cipio [prin'tʃipjo] *sm* (*inizio*) beginning, start; (*origine*) origin, cause; (*concetto, norma*) principle; **al** *o* **in ~** at first; **fin dal ~** right from the start; **per ~** on principle; **una questione di ~** a matter of principle; **una persona di sani principi morali** a person of sound moral principles; **~ attivo** active ingredient

pri'ore *sm* (*Rel*) prior

pri'ori: a ~ *ag inv* prior; **a priori** *av* at first glance; initially; **a priori**

priorità *sf* priority; **avere la ~ (su)** to have priority (over)

priori'tario, -a *ag* (*scelta*) first; (*interesse*) overriding; **posta prioritaria** first class (post)

'prisma, -i *sm* prism

pri'vare *vt*: **~ qn di** to deprive sb of; **privarsi** *vr*: **privarsi di** to go *o* do without

priva'tiva *sf* (*Econ*) monopoly

privatiz'zare [privatid'dzare] *vt* to privatize

privatizzazi'one [privatiddzat'tsjone] *sf* privatization

pri'vato, -a *ag* private ■ *sm/f* (*anche: privato cittadino*) private citizen; **in ~** in private; **diritto ~** (*Dir*) civil law; **ritirarsi a vita privata** to withdraw from public life; **"non vendiamo a privati"** "wholesale only"

privazi'one [privat'tsjone] *sf* privation, hardship

privilegi'are [privile'dʒare] *vt* to favour (*Brit*), favor (*US*)

privilegi'ato, -a [privile'dʒato] *ag* (*individuo, classe*) privileged; (*trattamento, Comm: credito*) preferential; **azioni privilegiate** preference shares (*Brit*), preferred stock (*US*)

privi'legio [privi'lɛdʒo] *sm* privilege; **avere il ~ di fare** to have the privilege of doing, be privileged to do

'privo, -a *ag*: **~ di** without, lacking

pro *prep* for, on behalf of ■ *sm inv* (*utilità*) advantage, benefit; **a che ~?** what's the use?; **il ~ e il contro** the pros and cons

pro'babile *ag* probable, likely

probabilità *sf inv* probability; **con molta ~**
very probably, in all probability

probabil'mente *av* probably

pro'bante *ag* convincing

pro'blema, -i *sm* problem

proble'matico, -a, ci, che *ag* problematic;
(*incerto*) doubtful ■ *sf* problems *pl*

pro'boscide [pro'bɔʃʃide] *sf* (*di elefante*) trunk

procacci'are [prokat'tʃare] *vt* to get, obtain

procaccia'tore [prokattʃa'tore] *sm*: **~ d'affari**
sales executive

pro'cace [pro'katʃe] *ag* (*donna, aspetto*)
provocative

pro'cedere [pro'tʃɛdere] *vi* to proceed;
(*comportarsi*) to behave; (*iniziare*): **~ a** to start; **~**
contro (*Dir*) to start legal proceedings
against; **~ oltre** to go on ahead; **prima di ~**
oltre before going any further; **gli affari**
procedono bene business is going well;
bisogna ~ con cautela we have to proceed
cautiously; **non luogo a ~** (*Dir*) nonsuit

procedi'mento [protʃedi'mento] *sm* (*modo di*
condurre) procedure; (*di avvenimenti*) course;
(*Tecn*) process; **~ penale** (*Dir*) criminal
proceedings *pl*

proce'dura [protʃe'dura] *sf* (*Dir*) procedure

proces'sare [protʃes'sare] *vt* (*Dir*) to try

processi'one [protʃes'sjone] *sf* procession

pro'cesso [pro'tʃɛsso] *sm* (*Dir*) trial;
proceedings *pl*; (*metodo*) process; **essere**
sotto ~ to be on trial; **mettere sotto ~** (*anche*
fig) to put on trial; **~ di fabbricazione**
manufacturing process; **~ di pace** peace
process

processu'ale [protʃessu'ale] *ag* (*Dir*): **atti**
processuali records of a trial; **spese**
processuali legal costs

Proc. Gen. *abbr* = **procuratore generale**

pro'cinto [pro'tʃinto] *sm*: **in ~ di fare** about to
do, on the point of doing

pro'clama, -i *sm* proclamation

procla'mare *vt* to proclaim

proclamazi'one [proklamat'tsjone] *sf*
proclamation, declaration

procrasti'nare *vt* (*data*) to postpone;
(*pagamento*) to defer

procre'are *vt* to procreate

pro'cura *sf* (*Dir*) proxy, power of attorney;
(*ufficio*) attorney's office; **per ~** by proxy; **la**
P~ della Repubblica the Public Prosecutor's
Office

procu'rare *vt*: **~ qc a qn** (*fornire*) to get *o* obtain
sth for sb; (*causare: noie etc*) to bring *o* give sb
sth

procura'tore, -'trice *sm/f* (*Dir*) ≈ solicitor;
(: *chi ha la procura*) holder of power of attorney;

~ generale (*in corte d'appello*) public
prosecutor; (*in corte di cassazione*) Attorney
General; **~ legale** = solicitor (*Brit*), lawyer; **~**
della Repubblica (*in corte d'assise, tribunale*)
public prosecutor

prodi'gare *vt* to be lavish with; **prodigarsi**
vr: **prodigarsi per qn** to do all one can for sb

pro'digio [pro'didʒo] *sm* marvel, wonder;
(*persona*) prodigy

prodigi'oso, -a [prodi'dʒoso] *ag* prodigious;
phenomenal

'prodigo, -a, ghi, ghe *ag* lavish, extravagant

pro'dotto, -a [pro'dɔtto] *pp di* **produrre** ■ *sm* product; **~**
di base primary product; **~ finale** end
product; **~ interno lordo** gross domestic
product; **~ nazionale lordo** gross national
product; **prodotti agricoli** farm produce *sg*;
prodotti di bellezza cosmetics; **prodotti**
chimici chemicals

pro'duco *etc vb vedi* **produrre**

pro'durre *vt* to produce

pro'dussi *etc vb vedi* **produrre**

produttività *sf* productivity

produt'tivo, -a *ag* productive

produt'tore, -'trice *ag* producing *cpd* ■ *sm/f*
producer; **paese ~ di petrolio** oil-producing
country

produzi'one [produt'tsjone] *sf* production;
(*rendimento*) output; **~ in serie** mass
production

pro'emio *sm* introduction, preface

Prof . *abbr* (= *professore*) Prof

profa'nare *vt* to desecrate

pro'fano, -a *ag* (*mondano*) secular, profane;
(*sacrilego*) profane

profe'rire *vt* to utter

profes'sare *vt* to profess; (*medicina etc*) to
practise (*Brit*), practice (*US*)

professio'nale *ag* professional; **scuola ~**
training college

professi'one *sf* profession; **di ~** professional,
by profession; **libera ~** profession

professio'nista, -i, e *sm/f* professional

profes'sore, -'essa *sm/f* (*Ins*) teacher; (: *di*
università) lecturer; (*titolare di cattedra*)
professor; **~ d'orchestra** member of an
orchestra

pro'feta, -i *sm* prophet

pro'fetico, -a, ci, che *ag* prophetic

profetiz'zare [profetid'dzare] *vt* to prophesy

profe'zia [profet'tsia] *sf* prophecy

pro'ficuo, -a *ag* useful, profitable

profi'lare *vt* to outline; (*ornare: vestito*) to edge;
profilarsi *vr* to stand out, be silhouetted; to
loom up

profi'lassi *sf* (*Med*) preventive treatment,
prophylaxis

profi'lattico, -a, ci, che *ag* prophylactic ◾ *sm* (*anticoncezionale*) sheath, condom

pro'filo *sm* profile; (*breve descrizione*) sketch, outline; **di ~** in profile

profit'tare *vi*: **~ di** (*trarre profitto*) to profit by; (*approfittare*) to take advantage of

pro'fitto *sm* advantage, profit, benefit; (*fig*: *progresso*) progress; (*Comm*) profit; **ricavare un ~ da** to make a profit from *o* out of; **vendere con ~** to sell at a profit; **conto profitti e perdite** profit and loss account

pro'fondere *vt* (*lodi*) to lavish; (*denaro*) to squander; **profondersi** *vr*: **profondersi in** to be profuse in

profondità *sf inv* depth

pro'fondo, -a *ag* deep; (*rancore, meditazione*) profound ◾ *sm* depth(s) (*pl*), bottom; **~ 8 metri** 8 metres deep

pro'forma *ag* routine *cpd* ◾ *sm inv* formality ◾ *av*: **fare qc ~** to do sth as a formality

profugo, -a, ghi, ghe *sm/f* refugee

profu'mare *vt* to perfume ◾ *vi* to be fragrant; **profumarsi** *vr* to put on perfume *o* scent

profumata'mente *av*: **pagare qc ~** to pay through the nose for sth

profu'mato, -a *ag* (*fiore, aria*) fragrant; (*fazzoletto, saponetta*) scented; (*pelle*) sweet-smelling; (*persona*) with perfume on

profume'ria *sf* perfumery; (*negozio*) perfume shop

pro'fumo *sm* (*prodotto*) perfume, scent; (*fragranza*) scent, fragrance

profusi'one *sf* profusion; **a ~** in plenty

pro'fuso, -a *pp di* **profondere**

progeni'tore, -'trice [prodʒeni'tore] *sm/f* ancestor

proget'tare [prodʒet'tare] *vt* to plan; (*Tecn*: *edificio*) to plan, design; **~ di fare qc** to plan to do sth

progettazi'one [prodʒettat'tsjone] *sf* planning; **in corso di ~** at the planning stage

proget'tista, -i, e [prodʒet'tista] *sm/f* designer

pro'getto [pro'dʒetto] *sm* plan; (*idea*) plan, project; **avere in ~ di fare qc** to be planning to do sth; **~ di legge** (*Pol*) bill

prognosi ['proɲɲozi] *sf* (*Med*) prognosis; **essere in ~ riservata** to be on the danger list

pro'gramma, -i *sm* programme (*Brit*), program (*US*); (*TV, Radio*) program(me)s *pl*; (*Ins*) syllabus, curriculum; (*Inform*) program; **avere in ~ di fare qc** to be planning to do sth; **~ applicativo** (*Inform*) application program

program'mare *vt* (*TV, Radio*) to put on; (*Inform*) to program; (*Econ*) to plan

programma'tore, -'trice *sm/f* (*Inform*) computer programmer (*Brit*) *o* programer (*US*)

programmazi'one [programmat'tsjone] *sf* programming (*Brit*), programing (*US*); planning

progre'dire *vi* to progress, make progress

progressi'one *sf* progression

progres'sista, -i, e *ag, sm/f* progressive

progressiva'mente *av* progressively

progres'sivo, -a *ag* progressive

pro'gresso *sm* progress *no pl*; **fare progressi** to make progress

proi'bire *vt* to forbid, prohibit; **~ a qn di fare qc** (*vietare*) to forbid sb to do sth; (*impedire*) to prevent sb from doing sth

proibi'tivo, -a *ag* prohibitive

proi'bito, -a *ag* forbidden; **"è ~ l'accesso"** "no admittance"; **"è ~ fumare"** "no smoking"

proibizi'one [proibit'tsjone] *sf* prohibition

proibizio'nismo [proibittsjo'nizmo] *sm* prohibition

proiet'tare *vt* (*gen, Geom, Cine*) to project; (*presentare*) to show, screen; (*luce, ombra*) to throw, cast, project

proi'ettile *sm* projectile, bullet *o* shell *etc*

proiet'tore *sm* (*Cine*) projector; (*Aut*) headlamp; (*Mil*) searchlight

proiezi'one [projet'tsjone] *sf* (*Cine*) projection; showing

'prole *sf* children *pl*, offspring

proletari'ato *sm* proletariat

prole'tario, -a *ag, sm/f* proletarian

prolife'rare *vi* (*fig*) to proliferate

pro'lifico, -a, ci, che *ag* prolific

pro'lisso, -a *ag* verbose

'prologo, -ghi *sm* prologue

pro'lunga, -ghe *sf* (*di cavo elettrico etc*) extension

prolunga'mento *sm* (*gen*) extension; (*di strada*) continuation

prolun'gare *vt* (*discorso, attesa*) to prolong; (*linea, termine*) to extend

prome'moria *sm inv* memorandum

pro'messa *sf* promise; **fare/mantenere una ~** to make/keep a promise

pro'messo, -a *pp di* **promettere**

promet'tente *ag* promising

pro'mettere *vt* to promise ◾ *vi* to be *o* look promising; **~ a qn di fare** to promise sb that one will do

promi'nente *ag* prominent

promi'nenza [promi'nɛntsa] *sf* prominence

promiscuità *sf* promiscuousness

pro'miscuo, -a *ag*: **matrimonio ~** mixed marriage; **nome ~** (*Ling*) common-gender noun

pro'misi *etc vb vedi* **promettere**

promon'torio sm promontory, headland

pro'mosso, -a pp di **promuovere**

promo'tore, -'trice sm/f promoter, organizer

promozio'nale [promottsjo'nale] ag promotional; **"vendita ~"** "special offer"

promozi'one [promot'tsjone] sf promotion; **~ delle vendite** sales promotion

promul'gare vt to promulgate

promulgazi'one [promulgat'tsjone] sf promulgation

promu'overe vt to promote

proni'pote sm/f (di nonni) great-grandchild, great-grandson/granddaughter; (di zii) great-nephew/niece; **pronipoti** smpl (discendenti) descendants

pro'nome sm (Ling) pronoun

pronomi'nale ag pronominal

pronosti'care vt to foretell, predict

pro'nostico, -ci sm forecast

pron'tezza [pron'tettsa] sf readiness; quickness, promptness; **~ di riflessi** quick reflexes; **~ di spirito/mente** readiness of wit/mind

'pronto, -a ag ready; (rapido) fast, quick, prompt; **~!** (Tel) hello!; **essere ~ a fare qc** to be ready to do sth; **~ all'ira** quick-tempered; **a pronta cassa** (Comm) cash (Brit) o collect (US) on delivery; **pronta consegna** (Comm) prompt delivery; **~ soccorso** (trattamento) first aid; (reparto) A&E (Brit), ER (US)

prontu'ario sm manual, handbook

pro'nuncia [pro'nuntʃa] sf pronunciation

pronunci'are [pronun'tʃare] vt (parola, sentenza) to pronounce; (dire) to utter; (discorso) to deliver; **pronunciarsi** vr to declare one's opinion; **pronunciarsi a favore di/contro** to pronounce o.s. in favour of/against; **non mi pronuncio** I'm not prepared to comment

pronunci'ato, -a [pronun'tʃato] ag (spiccato) pronounced, marked; (sporgente) prominent

pro'nunzia etc [pro'nuntsja] = **pronuncia** etc

propa'ganda sf propaganda

propagan'dare vt (idea) to propagandize; (prodotto, invenzione) to push, plug (fam)

propa'gare vt (Fisica, Biol) to propagate; (notizia, idea, malattia) to spread; **propagarsi** vr to propagate; to spread

propagazi'one [propagat'tsjone] sf (vedi vb) propagation; spreading

prope'deutico, -a, ci, che ag (corso, trattato) introductory

pro'pendere vi: **~ per** to favour (Brit), favor (US), lean towards

propensi'one sf inclination, propensity; **avere ~ a credere che ...** to be inclined to think that ...

pro'penso, -a pp di **propendere** ◾ ag: **essere ~ a qc** to be in favour (Brit) o favor (US) of sth; **essere ~ a fare qc** to be inclined to do sth

propi'nare vt to administer

pro'pizio, a [pro'pittsjo] ag favourable (Brit), favorable (US)

pro'porre vt (suggerire): **~ qc (a qn)** to suggest sth (to sb); (candidato) to put forward; (legge, brindisi) to propose; **~ di fare** to suggest o propose doing; **proporsi di fare** to propose o intend to do; **proporsi una meta** to set o.s. a goal

proporzio'nale [proportsjo'nale] ag proportional; **(sistema) ~** (Pol) proportional representation system

proporzio'nato, -a [proportsjo'nato] ag: **~ a** proportionate to, proportional to; **ben ~** well-proportioned

proporzi'one [propor'tsjone] sf proportion; **in ~ a** in proportion to

pro'posito sm (intenzione) intention, aim; (argomento) subject, matter; **a ~ di** regarding, with regard to; **a questo ~** on this subject; **di ~** (apposta) deliberately, on purpose; **a ~** by the way; **capitare a ~** (cosa, persona) to turn up at the right time

proposizi'one [propozit'tsjone] sf (Ling) clause; (periodo) sentence

pro'posto, -a pp di **proporre** ◾ sf proposal; (suggerimento) suggestion; **fare una proposta** to put forward a proposal; to make a suggestion; **proposta di legge** (Pol) bill

propria'mente av (correttamente) properly, correctly; (in modo specifico) specifically; **~ detto** in the strict sense of the word

proprietà sf inv (ciò che si possiede) property gen no pl, estate; (caratteristica) property; (correttezza) correctness; **essere di ~ di qn** to belong to sb; **~ edilizia** (developed) property; **~ privata** private property

proprie'tario, -a sm/f owner; (di albergo etc) proprietor, owner; (per l'inquilino) landlord/lady; **~ terriero** landowner

'proprio, -a ag (possessivo) own's; (: impersonale) one's; (esatto) exact, correct, proper; (senso, significato) literal; (Ling: nome) proper; (particolare): **~ di** characteristic of, peculiar to ◾ av (precisamente) just, exactly; (davvero) really; (affatto): **non ... ~** not ... at all ◾ sm (Comm): **mettersi in ~** to set up on one's own; **l'ha visto con i (suoi) propri occhi** he saw it with his own eyes

propu'gnare [propuɲ'ɲare] vt to support

propulsi'one sf propulsion; **a ~ atomica** atomic-powered

propul'sore sm (Tecn) propeller

'prora sf (Naut) bow(s) (pl), prow

proroga, -ghe *sf* extension; postponement
proro'gare *vt* to extend; (*differire*) to postpone, defer
pro'rompere *vi* to burst out
pro'rotto, -a *pp di* **prorompere**
pro'ruppi *etc vb vedi* **prorompere**
'prosa *sf* prose; (*Teat*): **la stagione della ~** the theatre season; **attore di ~** theatre actor; **compagnia di ~** theatrical company
pro'saico, -a, ci, che *ag* (*fig*) prosaic, mundane
pro'sciogliere [proʃʃoʎʎere] *vt* to release; (*Dir*) to acquit
prosciogli'mento [proʃʃoʎʎi'mento] *sm* acquittal
prosci'olto, -a [proʃʃɔlto] *pp di* **prosciogliere**
prosciu'gare [proʃʃu'gare] *vt* (*terreni*) to drain, reclaim; **prosciugarsi** *vr* to dry up
prosci'utto [proʃʃutto] *sm* ham
pros'critto, -a *pp di* **proscrivere** ◾ *sm/f* exile; outlaw
pros'crivere *vt* to exile, banish
proscrizi'one [proskrit'tsjone] *sf* (*esilio*) banishment, exile
prosecuzi'one [prosekut'tsjone] *sf* continuation
prosegui'mento *sm* continuation; **buon ~!** all the best!; (*a chi viaggia*) enjoy the rest of your journey!
prosegu'ire *vt* to carry on with, continue ◾ *vi* to carry on, go on
pro'selito *sm* (*Rel, Pol*) convert
prospe'rare *vi* to thrive
prosperità *sf* prosperity
'prospero, -a *ag* (*fiorente*) flourishing, thriving, prosperous
prospe'roso, -a *ag* (*robusto*) hale and hearty; (*ragazza*) buxom
prospet'tare *vt* (*esporre*) to point out, show; (*ipotesi*) to advance; (*affare*) to outline; **prospettarsi** *vr* to look, appear
prospet'tiva *sf* (*Arte*) perspective; (*veduta*) view; (*fig: previsione, possibilità*) prospect
pros'petto *sm* (*Disegno*) elevation; (*veduta*) view, prospect; (*facciata*) façade, front; (*tabella*) table; (*sommario*) summary
prospici'ente [prospi'tʃente] *ag*: **~ qc** facing o overlooking sth
prossima'mente *av* soon
prossimità *sf* nearness, proximity; **in ~ di** near (to), close to; **in ~ delle feste natalizie** as Christmas approaches
'prossimo, -a *ag* (*vicino*): **~ a** near (to), close to; (*che viene subito dopo*) next; (*parente*) close ◾ *sm* neighbour (*Brit*), neighbor (*US*), fellow man; **nei prossimi giorni** in the next few days; **in un ~ futuro** in the near future; **~**

venturo (pv) (*Amm*): **venerdì ~ venturo** next Friday
'prostata *sf* prostate (gland)
prostitu'irsi *vr* to prostitute o.s.
prosti'tuta *sf* prostitute
prostituzi'one [prostitut'tsjone] *sf* prostitution
pros'trare *vt* (*fig*) to exhaust, wear out; **prostrarsi** *vr* (*fig*) to humble o.s.; **prostrato dal dolore** overcome o prostrate with grief
prostrazi'one [prostrat'tsjone] *sf* prostration
protago'nista, -i, e *sm/f* protagonist
pro'teggere [pro'tɛddʒere] *vt* to protect
proteggi'slip [protɛddʒi'slip] *sm inv* panty liner
pro'teico, -a, ci, che *ag* protein *cpd*; **altamente ~** high in protein
prote'ina *sf* protein
pro'tendere *vt* to stretch out
'protesi *sf inv* (*Med*) prosthesis
pro'teso, -a *pp di* **protendere**
pro'testa *sf* protest
protes'tante *ag, sm/f* Protestant
protes'tare *vt, vi* to protest; **protestarsi** *vr*: **protestarsi innocente** *etc* to protest one's innocence o that one is innocent *etc*
pro'testo *sm* (*Dir*) protest; **mandare una cambiale in ~** to dishonour (*Brit*) o dishonor (*US*) a bill
protet'tivo, -a *ag* protective
pro'tetto, -a *pp di* **proteggere**
protetto'rato *sm* protectorate
protet'tore, -'trice *sm/f* protector; (*sostenitore*) patron ◾ *ag* (*Rel*): **santo ~** patron saint; **società protettrice dei consumatori** consumer protection society
protezi'one [protet'tsjone] *sf* protection; (*patrocinio*) patronage; **misure di ~** protective measures; **~ civile** civil defence (*Brit*) o defense (*US*)
protezio'nismo [protettsjo'nizmo] *sm* protectionism
protocol'lare *vt* to register ◾ *ag* formal; of protocol
proto'collo *sm* protocol; (*registro*) register of documents ◾ *ag inv*: **foglio ~** foolscap; **numero di ~** reference number
pro'tone *sm* proton
proto'tipo *sm* prototype
pro'trarre *vt* (*prolungare*) to prolong; **protrarsi** *vr* to go on, continue
pro'tratto, -a *pp di* **protrarre**
protube'ranza [protube'rantsa] *sf* protuberance, bulge
Prov. *abbr* (= *provincia*) Prov
'prova *sf* (*esperimento, cimento*) test, trial; (*tentativo*) attempt, try; (*Mat*) proof *no pl*; (*Dir*)

evidence *no pl*, proof *no pl*; (*Ins*) exam, test; (*Teat*) rehearsal; (*di abito*) fitting; **a ~ di** (*in testimonianza di*) as proof of; **a ~ di fuoco** fireproof; **assumere in ~** (*per lavoro*) to employ on a trial basis; **essere in ~** (*persona: per lavoro*) to be on trial; **mettere alla ~** to put to the test; **giro di ~** test *o* trial run; **fino a ~ contraria** until (it's) proved otherwise; **~ a carico/a discarico** (*Dir*) evidence for the prosecution/for the defence; **~ documentale** (*Dir*) documentary evidence; **~ generale** (*Teat*) dress rehearsal; **~ testimoniale** (*Dir*) testimonial evidence

pro'vare *vt* (*sperimentare*) to test; (*tentare*) to try, attempt; (*assaggiare*) to try, taste; (*sperimentare in sé*) to experience; (*sentire*) to feel; (*cimentare*) to put to the test; (*dimostrare*) to prove; (*abito*) to try on; **provarsi** *vr*: **provarsi (a fare)** to try *o* attempt (to do); **~ a fare** to try *o* attempt to do

proveni'enza [prove'njɛntsa] *sf* origin, source

prove'nire *vi*: **~ da** to come from

pro'venti *smpl* revenue *sg*

prove'nuto, -a *pp di* provenire

Pro'venza [pro'vɛntsa] *sf*: **la ~** Provence

proven'zale [proven'tsale] *ag* Provençal

pro'verbio *sm* proverb

pro'vetta *sf* test tube; **bambino in ~** test-tube baby

pro'vetto, -a *ag* skilled, experienced

pro'vider [pro'vaider] *sm inv* (*Inform*) service provider

pro'vincia [pro'vintʃa] (*fpl* **province** *o* **provincie**) *sf* province; *see note*

provinci'ale [provin'tʃale] *ag* provincial; (**strada**) **~** main road (*Brit*), highway (*US*)

pro'vino *sm* (*Cine*) screen test; (*campione*) specimen

provo'cante *ag* (*attraente*) provocative

provo'care *vt* (*causare*) to cause, bring about; (*eccitare: riso, pietà*) to arouse; (*irritare, sfidare*) to provoke

provoca'tore, -'trice *sm/f* agitator ■ *ag*: **agente ~** agent provocateur

provoca'torio, -a *ag* provocative

provocazi'one [provokat'tsjone] *sf* provocation

provve'dere *vi* (*disporre*): **~ (a)** to provide (for); (*prendere un provvedimento*) to take steps, act ■ *vt*: **~ qc a qn** to supply sth to sb; **provvedersi** *vr*: **provvedersi di** to provide o.s. with

provvedi'mento *sm* measure; (*di previdenza*) precaution; **~ disciplinare** disciplinary measure

provvedito'rato *sm* (*Amm*): **~ agli studi** divisional education offices *pl*

provvedi'tore *sm* (*Amm*): **~ agli studi** divisional director of education

provvi'denza [provvi'dɛntsa] *sf*: **la ~** providence

provvidenzi'ale [provviden'tsjale] *ag* providential

provvigi'one [provvi'dʒone] *sf* (*Comm*) commission; **lavoro/stipendio a ~** job/salary on a commission basis

provvi'sorio, -a *ag* temporary; (*governo*) temporary, provisional

prov'vista *sf* (*riserva*) supply, stock; **fare ~ di** to stock up with

prov'visto, -a *pp di* provvedere ■ *sf* provision, supply

pro'zia [prot'tsia] *sf* great-aunt

pro'zio, -'zii [prot'tsio] *sm* great-uncle

'prua *sf* (*Naut*) = **prora**

pru'dente *ag* cautious, prudent; (*assennato*) sensible, wise

pru'denza [pru'dɛntsa] *sf* prudence, caution; wisdom; **per ~** as a precaution, to be on the safe side

'prudere *vi* to itch, be itchy

'prugna ['pruɲɲa] *sf* plum; **~ secca** prune

prurigi'noso, -a [pruridʒi'noso] *ag* itchy

pru'rito *sm* itchiness *no pl*; itch

PS *sigla* = **Pesaro**

P.S. *abbr* (= *postscriptum*) PS; (*Comm*) = **partita semplice** ■ *sigla f* = **Pubblica Sicurezza**

P.S.D.I. *sigla m* (= *Partito Socialista Democratico Italiano*) *former political party*

pseu'donimo *sm* pseudonym

PSI *sigla m* (*Pol*) = **Partito Socialista Italiano**

psica'nalisi *sf* psychoanalysis

psicana'lista, -i, e *sm/f* psychoanalyst

psicanaliz'zare [psikanalid'dzare] *vt* to psychoanalyse

'psiche ['psike] sf psyche
psiche'delico, -a, ci, che [psike'dɛliko] ag
psychedelic
psichi'atra, -i, e [psi'kjatra] sm/f psychiatrist
psichia'tria [psikja'tria] sf psychiatry
psichi'atrico, -a, ci, che [psi'kjatriko] ag
(caso) psychiatric; (reparto, ospedale)
psychiatric, mental
'psichico, -a, ci, che ['psikiko] ag
psychological
psico'farmaco, -ci sm (Med) drug used in
treatment of mental conditions
psicolo'gia [psikolo'dʒia] sf psychology
psico'logico, -a, ci, che [psiko'lɔdʒiko] ag
psychological
psi'cologo, -a, gi, ghe sm/f psychologist
psico'patico, -a, ci, che ag psychopathic
■ sm/f psychopath
psi'cosi sf inv (Med) psychosis; (fig) obsessive
fear
psicoso'matico, -a, ci, che ag
psychosomatic
PT sigla = Pistoia
Pt. abbr (Geo: = punta) Pt
P.T. abbr (= Posta e Telegrafi) ≈ PO (= Post Office);
(Fisco) = polizia tributaria
P.ta abbr = porta
pubbli'care vt to publish
pubblicazi'one [pubblikat'tsjone] sf
publication; ~ periodica periodical;
pubblicazioni (matrimoniali) (pl)
(marriage) banns
pubbli'cista, -i, e [pubbli'tʃista] sm/f (Stampa)
freelance journalist
pubblicità [pubblitʃi'ta] sf (diffusione)
publicity; (attività) advertising; (annunci nei
giornali) advertisements pl; fare ~ a qc to
advertise sth
pubblici'tario, -a [pubblitʃi'tarjo] ag
advertising cpd; (trovata, film) publicity cpd
■ sm advertising agent; annuncio o avviso ~
advertisement
'pubblico, -a, ci, che ag public; (statale: scuola
etc) state cpd ■ sm public; (spettatori)
audience; in ~ in public; la pubblica
amministrazione public administration;
un ~ esercizio a catering (o hotel o
entertainment) business; ~ funzionario
civil servant; Ministero della Pubblica
Istruzione ≈ Department of Education and
Science (Brit), ≈ Department of Health,
Education and Welfare (US); P~ Ministero
Public Prosecutor's Office; la Pubblica
Sicurezza the police
'pube sm (Anat) pubis
pubertà sf puberty
'pudico, -a, ci, che ag modest

pu'dore sm modesty
puericul'tura sf infant care
pue'rile ag childish
pu'erpera sf woman who has just given birth
pugi'lato [pudʒi'lato] sm boxing
'pugile ['pudʒile] sm boxer
pugli'ese [puʎ'ʎese] ag of (o from) Puglia
pugna'lare [pupɲa'lare] vt to stab
pu'gnale [puɲ'ɲale] sm dagger
'pugno ['puɲɲo] sm fist; (colpo) punch;
(quantità) fistful; avere qn in ~ to have sb in
the palm of one's hand; tenere la
situazione in ~ to have control of the
situation; scrivere qc di proprio ~ to write
sth in one's own hand
'pulce ['pultʃe] sf flea
pul'cino [pul'tʃino] sm chick
pu'ledro, -a sm/f colt/filly
pu'leggia, -ge [pu'leddʒa] sf pulley
pu'lire vt to clean; (lucidare) to polish; far ~ qc
to have sth cleaned; ~ a secco to dry-clean
pu'lito, -a ag (anche fig) clean; (ordinato) neat,
tidy ■ sf quick clean; avere la coscienza
pulita to have a clear conscience
puli'tura sf cleaning; ~ a secco dry-cleaning
puli'zia [pulit'tsia] sf (atto) cleaning;
(condizione) cleanness; fare le pulizie to do
the cleaning, do the housework; ~ etnica
ethnic cleansing
'pullman sm inv coach (Brit), bus
pull'over sm inv pullover, jumper
pullu'lare vi to swarm, teem
pul'mino sm minibus
'pulpito sm pulpit
pul'sante sm (push-)button
pul'sare vi to pulsate, beat
pulsazi'one [pulsat'tsjone] sf beat
pul'viscolo sm fine dust
'puma sm inv puma
pun'gente [pun'dʒente] ag prickly; stinging;
(anche fig) biting
'pungere ['pundʒere] vt to prick; (insetto,
ortica) to sting; (freddo) to bite; ~ qn sul vivo
(fig) to cut sb to the quick
pungigli'one [pundʒiʎ'ʎone] sm sting
pungo'lare vt to goad
pu'nire vt to punish
puni'tivo, -a ag punitive
punizi'one [punit'tsjone] sf punishment;
(Sport) penalty
'punsi etc vb vedi pungere
'punta sf point; (parte terminale) tip, end; (di
monte) peak; (di costa) promontory; (minima
parte) touch, trace; in ~ di piedi on tiptoe;
ore di ~ peak hours; uomo di ~ (Sport, Pol)
front-rank o leading man; doppie punte
split ends

pun'tare vt (piedi a terra, gomiti sul tavolo) to plant; (dirigere: pistola) to point; (scommettere): ~ **su** to bet on ■ vi (mirare): ~ **a** to aim at; (avviarsi): ~ **su** to head o make for; (fig: contare): ~ **su** to count o rely on

puntas'pilli sm inv = **portaspilli**

pun'tata sf (gita) short trip; (scommessa) bet; (parte di opera) instalment (Brit), installment (US); **farò una ~ a Parigi** I'll pay a flying visit to Paris; **romanzo a puntate** serial

punteggi'are [punted'dʒare] vt to punctuate

punteggia'tura [punteddʒa'tura] sf punctuation

pun'teggio [pun'teddʒo] sm score

puntel'lare vt to support

pun'tello sm prop, support

punteru'olo sm (Tecn) punch; (per stoffa) bodkin

pun'tiglio [pun'tiʎʎo] sm obstinacy, stubbornness

puntigli'oso, -a [puntiʎ'ʎoso] ag punctilious

pun'tina sf: ~ **da disegno** drawing pin (Brit), thumb tack (US); **puntine** sfpl (Aut) points

pun'tino sm dot; **fare qc a ~** to do sth properly; **arrivare a ~** to arrive just at the right moment; **cotto a ~** cooked to perfection; **mettere i puntini sulle "i"** (fig) to dot the i's and cross the t's

'punto, -a pp di **pungere** ■ sm (segno, macchiolina) dot; (Ling) full stop; (Mat, momento, di punteggio: fig: argomento) point; (di indirizzo e-mail) dot; (posto) spot; (a scuola) mark; (nel cucire, nella maglia, Med) stitch ■ av: **non ... ~** not ... at all; **due punti** (inv: Ling) colon; **ad un certo ~** at a certain point; **fino ad un certo ~** (fig) to a certain extent; **sul ~ di fare** (just) about to do; **fare il ~** (Naut) to take a bearing; **fare il ~ della situazione** (analisi) to take stock of the situation; (riassunto) to sum up the situation; **alle 6 in ~** at 6 o'clock sharp o on the dot; **essere a buon ~** to have reached a satisfactory stage; **mettere a ~** to adjust; (motore) to tune; (cannocchiale) to focus; (fig) to settle; **venire al ~** to come to the point; **vestito di tutto ~** all dressed up; **di ~ in bianco** point-blank; **~ d'arrivo** arrival point; **~ cardinale** point of the compass, cardinal point; **~ debole** weak point; **~ esclamativo/interrogativo** exclamation/question mark; **~ d'incontro** meeting place, meeting point; **~ morto** standstill; **~ nero** (comedone) blackhead; **~ nevralgico** (anche fig) nerve centre (Brit) o center (US); **~ di partenza** (anche fig) starting point; **~ di riferimento** landmark; (fig) point of reference; **~ di vendita** retail outlet; **~ e virgola** semicolon; **~ di vista** (fig) point

of view; **punti di sospensione** suspension points

puntu'ale ag punctual

puntualità sf punctuality

puntualiz'zare [puntualid'dzare] vt to make clear

puntual'mente av (gen) on time; (ironico: al solito) as usual

pun'tura sf (di ago) prick; (di insetto) sting, bite; (Med) puncture; (iniezione) injection; (dolore) sharp pain

punzecchi'are [puntsek'kjare] vt to prick; (fig) to tease

punzo'nare [puntso'nare] vt (Tecn) to stamp

pun'zone [pun'tsone] sm (per metalli) stamp, die

può vb vedi **potere**

puoi vb vedi **potere**

'pupa sf doll

pu'pazzo [pu'pattso] sm puppet

pu'pillo, -a sm/f (Dir) ward; (prediletto) favourite (Brit), favorite (US), pet ■ sf (Anat) pupil

purché [pur'ke] cong provided that, on condition that

'pure cong (tuttavia) and yet, nevertheless; (anche se) even if ■ av (anche) too, also; **pur di** (al fine di) just to; **faccia ~!** go ahead!, please do!

purè sm, **pu'rea** sf (Cuc) purée; (di patate) mashed potatoes

pu'rezza [pu'rettsa] sf purity

'purga, -ghe sf purging no pl; purge

pur'gante sm (Med) purgative, purge

pur'gare vt (Med, Pol) to purge; (pulire) to clean

purga'torio sm purgatory

purifi'care vt to purify; (metallo) to refine

purificazi'one [purifikat'tsjone] sf purification; refinement

puri'tano, -a ag, sm/f puritan

'puro, -a ag pure; (acqua) clear, limpid; (vino) undiluted; **di razza pura** thoroughbred; **per ~ caso** by sheer chance, purely by chance

puro'sangue sm/f inv thoroughbred

pur'troppo av unfortunately

pus sm pus

pusil'lanime ag cowardly

'pustola sf pimple

puta'caso av just supposing, suppose

puti'ferio sm rumpus, row

putre'fare vi to putrefy, rot

putre'fatto, -a pp di **putrefare**

putrefazi'one [putrefat'tsjone] sf putrefaction

'putrido, -a ag putrid, rotten

put'tana sf (fam!) whore (!)

'putto sm cupid

'**puzza** ['puttsa] *sf* = **puzzo**

puz'zare [put'tsare] *vi* to stink; **la faccenda puzza (d'imbroglio)** the whole business stinks

'**puzzo** ['puttso] *sm* stink, foul smell

'**puzzola** ['puttsola] *sf* polecat

puzzo'lente [puttso'lɛnte] *ag* stinking

PV *sigla* = **Pavia**

pv *abbr* = **prossimo venturo**

P.V.C. [pivi'tʃi] *sigla m* (= *polyvinyl chloride*) PVC

PZ *sigla* = **Potenza**

p. za *abbr* = **piazza**

Qq

Q, q [ku] *sf o m inv* (*lettera*) Q, q; **Q come Quarto** ≈ Q for Queen

q *abbr* (= *quintale*) q

Qa'tar [ka'tar] *sm*: **il ~** Qatar

q.b. *abbr* (= *quanto basta*) as needed; (= *zucchero q.b.*) sugar to taste

Q.G. *abbr* = **quartier generale**

Q.I. *abbr* = **quoziente d'intelligenza**

qua *av* here; **in ~** (*verso questa parte*) this way; **~ dentro/sotto** *etc* in/under here *etc*; **da un anno in ~** for a year now; **da quando in ~?** since when?; **per di ~** (*passare*) this way; **al di ~ di** (*fiume, strada*) on this side of; *vedi* **questo**

'quacchero, -a ['kwakkero] *sm/f* Quaker

qua'derno *sm* notebook; (*per scuola*) exercise book

qua'drangolo *sm* quadrangle

qua'drante *sm* quadrant; (*di orologio*) face

qua'drare *vi* (*bilancio*) to balance, tally; (*fig: corrispondere*): **~ (con)** to correspond (with) ■ *vt* (*Mat*) to square; **far ~ il bilancio** to balance the books; **non mi quadra** I don't like it

qua'drato, -a *ag* square; (*fig: equilibrato*) level-headed, sensible; (*peg*) square ■ *sm* (*Mat*) square; (*Pugilato*) ring; **5 al ~** 5 squared

quadret'tato, -a *ag* (*foglio*) squared; (*tessuto*) checked

qua'dretto *sm*: **a quadretti** (*tessuto*) checked; (*foglio*) squared

quadrien'nale *ag* (*che dura 4 anni*) four-year *cpd*; (*che avviene ogni 4 anni*) four-yearly

quadri'foglio [kwadri'fɔʎʎo] *sm* four-leaf clover

quadri'mestre *sm* (*periodo*) four-month period; (*Ins*) term

'quadro *sm* (*pittura*) painting, picture; (*quadrato*) square; (*tabella*) table, chart; (*Tecn*) board, panel; (*Teat*) scene; (*fig: scena, spettacolo*) sight; (*descrizione*) outline, description; **quadri** *smpl* (*Pol*) party organizers; (*Comm*) managerial staff; (*Mil*) cadres; (*Carte*) diamonds; **a quadri** (*disegno*) checked; **fare un ~ della situazione** to outline the situation; **~ clinico** (*Med*) case history; **~ di comando** control panel; **quadri intermedi** middle management *sg*

qua'drupede *sm* quadruped

quadrupli'care *vt* to quadruple

qua'druplo, -a *ag, sm* quadruple

quaggiù [kwad'dʒu] *av* down here

'quaglia ['kwaʎʎa] *sf* quail

 PAROLA CHIAVE

'qualche ['kwalke] *det* **1** some, a few; (*in interrogative*) any; **ho comprato qualche libro** I've bought some *o* a few books; **~ volta** sometimes; **hai qualche sigaretta?** have you any cigarettes?
2 (*uno*): **c'è qualche medico?** is there a doctor?; **in qualche modo** somehow
3 (*un certo, parecchio*) some; **un personaggio di qualche rilievo** a figure of some importance
4: **qualche cosa** = **qualcosa**

qualche'duno [kwalke'duno] *pron* = **qualcuno**

qual'cosa *pron* something; (*in espressioni interrogative*) anything; **qualcos'altro** something else; anything else; **~ di nuovo** something new; anything new; **~ da mangiare** something to eat; anything to eat; **c'è ~ che non va?** is there something *o* anything wrong?

qual'cuno *pron* (*persona*) someone, somebody; (*in espressioni interrogative*) anyone, anybody; (*alcuni*) some; **~ è favorevole a noi** some are on our side; **qualcun altro** someone *o* somebody else; anyone *o* anybody else

 PAROLA CHIAVE

'quale (*spesso troncato in* **qual**) *det* **1** (*interrogativo*) what; (*scegliendo tra due o più cose o persone*) which; **quale uomo/denaro?** what man/

q

money?; which man/money?; **quali sono i tuoi programmi?** what are your plans?; **quale stanza preferisci?** which room do you prefer?

2 (*relativo: come*): **il risultato fu quale ci si aspettava** the result was as expected
3 (*in elenchi*) such as, like; **piante quali l'edera** plants such as o like ivy
4 (*esclamativo*) what; **quale disgrazia!** what bad luck!
5: **in un certo qual modo** in a way, in some ways; **per la qual cosa** for which reason ■ *pron* **1** (*interrogativo*) which; **quale dei due scegli?** which of the two do you want?
2 (*relativo*): **il(la) quale** (*persona: soggetto*) who; (*oggetto, con preposizione*) whom; (*cosa*) which; (*possessivo*) whose; **suo padre, il quale è avvocato, ...** his father, who is a lawyer, ...; **a tutti coloro i quali fossero interessati ...** to whom it may concern ...; **il signore con il quale parlavo** the gentleman to whom I was speaking; **l'albergo al quale ci siamo fermati** the hotel where we stayed o which we stayed at; **la signora della quale ammiriamo la bellezza** the lady whose beauty we admire
■ *av* (*in qualità di, come*) as; **quale sindaco di questa città** as mayor of this town

qua'lifica, -che *sf* qualification; (*titolo*) title
qualifi'care *vt* to qualify; (*definire*): **~ qn/qc come** to describe sb/sth as; **qualificarsi** *vr* (*Sport*) to qualify; **qualificarsi a un concorso** to pass a competitive exam
qualifica'tivo, -a *ag* qualifying
qualifi'cato, -a *ag* (*dotato di qualifica*) qualified; (*esperto, abile*) skilled; **non mi ritengo ~ per questo lavoro** I don't think I'm qualified for this job; **è un medico molto ~** he is a very distinguished doctor
qualificazi'one [kwalifikat'tsjone] *sf* qualification; **gara di ~** (*Sport*) qualifying event
qualità *sf inv* quality; **di ottima** o **prima ~** top quality; **in ~ di** in one's capacity as; **in ~ di amica** as a friend; **articoli di ogni ~** all sorts of goods; **controllo (di) ~** quality control; **prodotto di ~** quality product
qualita'tivo, -a *ag* qualitative
qua'lora *cong* in case, if
qual'siasi, qua'lunque *det inv* any; (*quale che sia*) whatever; (*discriminativo*) whichever; (*posposto: mediocre*) poor, indifferent; ordinary; **mettiti un vestito ~** put on any old dress; **~ cosa** anything; **~ cosa accada** whatever happens; **a ~ costo** at any cost, whatever the cost; **l'uomo ~** the man in the street; **~ persona** anyone, anybody

qualunqu'ista, -i, e *sm/f* person indifferent to politics
'quando *cong, av* when; **~ sarò ricco** when I'm rich; **da ~** (*dacché*) since; (*interrogativo*): **da ~ sei qui?** how long have you been here?; **di ~ in ~** from time to time; **quand'anche** even if
quantifi'care *vt* to quantify
quantità *sf inv* quantity; (*gran numero*): **una ~ di** a great deal of; a lot of; **in grande ~** in large quantities
quantita'tivo, -a *ag* quantitative ■ *sm* (*Comm: di merce*) amount, quantity

 PAROLA CHIAVE

'quanto, -a *det* **1** (*interrogativo: quantità*) how much; (*numero*) how many; **quanto pane/denaro?** how much bread/money?; **quanti libri/ragazzi?** how many books/boys?; **quanto tempo?** how long?; **quanti anni hai?** how old are you?
2 (*esclamativo*): **quante storie!** what a lot of nonsense!; **quanto tempo sprecato!** what a waste of time!
3 (*relativo: quantità*) as much ... as; (*: numero*) as many ... as; **ho quanto denaro mi occorre** I have as much money as I need; **prendi quanti libri vuoi** take as many books as you like
■ *pron* **1** (*interrogativo: quantità*) how much; (*: numero*) how many; (*tempo*) how long; **quanto mi dai?** how much will you give me?; **quanti me ne hai portati?** how many did you bring me?; **quanto starai via?** how long will you be away (for)?; **da quanto sei qui?** how long have you been here?; **quanti ne abbiamo oggi?** what's the date today?
2 (*relativo: quantità*) as much as; (*: numero*) as many as; **farò quanto posso** I'll do as much as I can; **a quanto dice lui** according to him; **in risposta a quanto esposto nella sua lettera ...** in answer to the points raised in your letter; **possono venire quanti sono stati invitati** all those who have been invited can come
■ *av* **1** (*interrogativo: con ag, av*) how; (*con vb*) how much; **quanto stanco ti sembrava?** how tired did he seem to you?; **quanto corre la tua moto?** how fast can your motorbike go?; **quanto costa?** how much does it cost?; **quant'è?** how much is it?
2 (*esclamativo: con ag, av*) how; (*con vb*) how much; **quanto sono felice!** how happy I am!; **sapessi quanto abbiamo camminato!** if you knew how far we've walked!; **studierò quanto posso** I'll study as much as

o all I can; **quanto prima** as soon as possible; **quanto più ... tanto meno** the more ... the less; **quanto più ... tanto più** the more ... the more

3: **in quanto** (in qualità di) as; (perché, per il fatto che) as, since; **in quanto legale della signora** as the lady's lawyer; **non è possibile in quanto non possiamo permettercelo** it isn't possible, since we can't afford it; **(in) quanto a** (per ciò che riguarda) as for, as regards; **(in) quanto a lui** as far as he's concerned

4: **per quanto** (nonostante, anche se) however; **per quanto si sforzi, non ce la farà** try as he may, he won't manage it; **per quanto sia brava, fa degli errori** however good she may be, she makes mistakes; **per quanto io sappia** as far as I know

quan'tunque cong although, though
qua'ranta num forty
quaran'tena sf quarantine
quaran'tenne ag, sm/f forty-year-old
quaran'tennio sm (period of) forty years
quaran'tesimo, -a num fortieth
quaran'tina sf: **una ~ (di)** about forty
quaran'totto sm inv forty-eight; **fare un ~** (fam) to raise hell
Qua'resima sf: **la ~** Lent
'quarta sf vedi **quarto**
quar'tetto sm quartet(te)
quarti'ere sm district, area; (Mil) quarters pl; **~ generale** headquarters pl; **~ residenziale** residential area o district; **i quartieri alti** the smart districts
'quarto, -a ag fourth ■ sm fourth; (quarta parte) quarter ■ sf (Aut) fourth (gear); (Ins: elementare) fourth year of primary school; (:superiore) seventh year of secondary school; **un ~ di vino** a quarter-litre (Brit) o quarter-liter (US) bottle of wine; **le 6 e un ~** a quarter past (Brit) o after (US) 6; **~ d'ora** quarter of an hour; **tre quarti d'ora** three quarters of an hour; **le otto e tre quarti, le nove meno un ~** (a) quarter to (Brit) o of (US) nine; **passare un brutto ~ d'ora** (fig) to have a bad o nasty time of it; **quarti di finale** (Sport) quarter finals
'quarzo ['kwartso] sm quartz
'quasi av almost, nearly ■ cong (anche: **quasi che**) as if; **(non) ... ~ mai** hardly ever; **~ ~ me ne andrei** I've half a mind to leave
quas'sù av up here
'quatto, -a ag crouched, squatting; (silenzioso) silent; **~ ~** very quietly; stealthily
quattordi'cenne [kwattordi'tʃenne] ag, sm/f fourteen-year-old
quat'tordici [kwat'torditʃi] num fourteen

quat'trini smpl money sg, cash sg
'quattro num four; **in ~ e quattr'otto** in less than no time; **dirne ~ a qn** to give sb a piece of one's mind; **fare il diavolo a ~** to kick up a rumpus; **fare ~ chiacchiere** to have a chat; **farsi in ~ per qn** to go out of one's way for sb, put o.s. out for sb
quat'trocchi [kwat'trɔkki] sm inv (fig fam: persona con occhiali) four-eyes; **a ~** av (tra 2 persone) face to face; (privatamente) in private
quattrocen'tesco, -a, schi, sche [kwattrotʃen'tesko] ag fifteenth-century
quattro'cento [kwattro'tʃento] num four hundred ■ sm: **il Q~** the fifteenth century
quattro'mila num four thousand

⊙ **PAROLA CHIAVE**

'quello, -a (dav sm **quel** + C, **quell'** + V, **quello** + s impura, gn, pn, ps, x, z; pl **quei** + C, **quegli** + V o s impura, gn, pn, ps, x, z; dav sf **quella** + C, **quell'** + V; pl **quelle**) det that; those pl; **quella casa** that house; **quegli uomini** those men; **voglio quella camicia (lì o là)** I want that shirt; **quello è mio fratello** that's my brother ■ pron **1** (dimostrativo) that one; those ones pl; (ciò) that; **conosci quella?** do you know her?; **prendo quello bianco** I'll take the white one; **chi è quello?** who's that?; **prendiamo quello (lì o là)** let's take that one (there); **in quel di Milano** in the Milan area o region **2** (relativo): **quello(a) che** (persona) the one (who); (cosa) the one (which), the one (that); **quelli(e) che** (persone) those who; (cose) those which; **è lui quello che non voleva venire** he's the one who didn't want to come; **ho fatto quello che potevo** I did what I could; **è quella che ti ho prestato** that's the one I lent you; **è proprio quello che gli ho detto** that's exactly what I told him; **da quello che ho sentito** from what I've heard

'quercia, -ce ['kwɛrtʃa] sf oak (tree); (legno) oak; **la Q~** (Pol) symbol of P.D.S.
que'rela sf (Dir) (legal) action
quere'lare vt to bring an action against
que'sito sm question, query; problem
'questi pron (poetico) this person
questio'nario sm questionnaire
questi'one sf problem, question; (controversia) issue; (litigio) quarrel; **in ~** in question; **il caso in ~** the matter at hand; **la persona in ~** the person involved; **non voglio essere chiamato in ~** I don't want to be dragged into the argument; **fuor di ~** out of the question; **è ~ di tempo** it's a matter o question of time

q

PAROLA CHIAVE

'questo, -a 1 det (dimostrativo) this; these pl;
~ **libro (qui** o **qua)** this book; **io prendo
questo cappotto, tu quello** I'll take this
coat, you take that one; **quest'oggi** today;
questa sera this evening
2 (enfatico): **non fatemi più prendere di
queste paure** don't frighten me like that
again ■ pron (dimostrativo) this (one), these
(ones) pl; (ciò) this; **prendo questo (qui** o
qua) I'll take this one; **preferisci questi o
quelli?** do you prefer these (ones) or those
(ones)?; **questo intendevo io** this is what
I meant; **questo non dovevi dirlo** you
shouldn't have said that; **e con questo?** so
what?; **e con questo se n'è andato** and
with that he left; **con tutto questo** in spite
of this, despite all this; **questo è quanto**
that's all

ques'tore sm public official in charge of the police in
the provincial capital, reporting to the prefetto,
≈ chief constable (Brit), ≈ police
commissioner (US)
'questua sf collection (of alms)
ques'tura sf police headquarters pl
questu'rino sm (fam: poliziotto) cop
qui av here; **da** o **di** ~ from here; **di** ~ **in avanti**
from now on; **di** ~ **a poco/una settimana** in
a little while/a week's time; ~ **dentro/
sopra/vicino** in/up/near here; vedi **questo**
quie'scenza [kwjeʃʃɛntsa] sf (Amm): **porre
qn in** ~ to retire sb
quie'tanza [kwje'tantsa] sf receipt
quie'tare vt to calm, soothe
qui'ete sf quiet, quietness; calmness;
stillness; peace; **turbare la** ~ **pubblica** (Dir)
to disturb the peace
qui'eto, -a ag quiet; (notte) calm, still; (mare)
calm; **l'ho fatto per il** ~ **vivere** I did it for a
quiet life
'quindi av then ■ cong therefore, so
quindi'cenne [kwindi'tʃɛnne] ag, sm/f
fifteen-year-old
'quindici ['kwinditʃi] num fifteen; ~ **giorni** a
fortnight (Brit), two weeks
quindi'cina [kwindi'tʃina] sf (serie): **una** ~ **(di)**
about fifteen; **fra una** ~ **di giorni** in a

fortnight (Brit) o two weeks
quindici'nale [kwinditʃi'nale] ag fortnightly
(Brit), semimonthly (US) ■ sm (rivista)
fortnightly magazine (Brit), semimonthly (US)
quinquen'nale ag (che dura 5 anni) five-year
cpd; (che avviene ogni 5 anni) five-yearly
quin'quennio sm period of five years
'quinta sf vedi **quinto**
quin'tale sm quintal (100 kg)
quin'tetto sm quintet(te)
'quinto, -a num fifth ■ sf (Aut) fifth (gear);
(Ins: elementare) fifth year of primary school;
(:superiore) final year of secondary school; (Teat)
wing; **un** ~ **della popolazione** a fifth of the
population; **tre quinti** three fifths; **in
quinta pagina** on the fifth page, on page
five
qui pro quo sm inv misunderstanding
Quiri'nale sm see note

'Quito sf Quito
quiz [kwidz] sm inv (domanda) question;
(anche: **gioco a quiz**) quiz game
'quorum sm quorum
'quota sf (parte) quota, share; (Aer) height,
altitude; (Ippica) odds pl; **prendere/perdere**
~ (Aer) to gain/lose height o altitude; ~
imponibile taxable income; ~ **d'iscrizione**
(Ins) enrolment fee; (ad una gara) entry fee;
(ad un club) membership fee; ~ **di mercato**
market share; **quote rosa** (Pol) quota for
women
quo'tare vt (Borsa) to quote; (valutare: anche fig)
to value; **è un pittore molto quotato** he is
rated highly as a painter
quotazi'one [kwotat'tsjone] sf quotation
quotidiana'mente av daily, every day
quotidi'ano, -a ag daily; (banale) everyday
■ sm (giornale) daily (paper)
quozi'ente [kwot'tsjɛnte] sm (Mat) quotient;
~ **di crescita zero** zero growth rate;
~ **d'intelligenza** intelligence quotient

Rr

R, r ['erre] *sf o m* (*lettera*) R, r; **R come Roma**
≈ R for Robert (*Brit*), R for Roger (*US*)
R *abbr* (*Posta*) = **raccomandata**; (*Ferr*) = **rapido**
RA *sigla* = **Ravenna**
ra'barbaro *sm* rhubarb
Ra'bat *sf* Rabat
rabberci'are [rabber'tʃare] *vt* (*anche fig*) to
patch up
'rabbia *sf* (*ira*) anger, rage; (*accanimento, furia*)
fury; (*Med: idrofobia*) rabies *sg*
rab'bino *sm* rabbi
rabbi'oso, -a *ag* angry, furious; (*facile all'ira*)
quick-tempered; (*forze, acqua etc*) furious,
raging; (*Med*) rabid, mad
rabbo'nire *vt*, **rabbo'nirsi** *vr* to calm down
rabbrivi'dire *vi* to shudder, shiver
rabbui'arsi *vr* to grow dark
rabdo'mante *sm* water diviner
racc. *abbr* (*Posta*) = **raccomandata**
raccapez'zarsi [rakkapet'tsarsi] *vr*: **non ~** to
be at a loss
raccapricci'ante [rakkaprit'tʃante] *ag*
horrifying
racca'priccio [rakka'prittʃo] *sm* horror
raccatta'palle *sm inv* (*Sport*) ballboy
raccat'tare *vt* to pick up
rac'chetta [rak'ketta] *sf* (*per tennis*) racket; (*per
ping-pong*) bat; **~ da neve** snowshoe; **~ da sci**
ski stick
'racchio, -a ['rakkjo] *ag* (*fam*) ugly
racchi'udere [rak'kjudere] *vt* to contain
racchi'uso, -a [rak'kjuso] *pp di* **racchiudere**
rac'cogliere [rak'kɔʎʎere] *vt* to collect;
(*raccattare*) to pick up; (*frutti, fiori*) to pick,
pluck; (*Agr*) to harvest; (*approvazione: voti*) to
win; (*profughi*) to take in; (*vele*) to furl; (*capelli*)
to put up; **raccogliersi** *vr* to gather; (*fig*) to
gather one's thoughts; to meditate; **non ha
raccolto** (*allusione*) he didn't take the hint;
(*frecciata*) he took no notice of it; **~ i frutti
del proprio lavoro** (*fig*) to reap the benefits
of one's work; **~ le idee** (*fig*) to gather one's
thoughts

raccogli'mento [rakkoʎʎi'mento] *sm*
meditation
raccogli'tore [rakkoʎʎi'tore] *sm* (*cartella*)
folder, binder; **~ a fogli mobili** loose-leaf
binder
rac'colto, -a *pp di* **raccogliere** ■ *ag* (*persona:
pensoso*) thoughtful; (*luogo: appartato*)
secluded, quiet ■ *sm* (*Agr*) crop, harvest ■ *sf*
collecting *no pl*; collection; (*Agr*) harvesting
no pl, gathering *no pl*; harvest, crop; **fare la
raccolta di qc** to collect sth; **chiamare a
raccolta** to gather together; **raccolta
differenziata** (*dei rifiuti*) *separate collection of
different kinds of household waste*
raccoman'dabile *ag* (highly) commendable;
è un tipo poco ~ he is not to be trusted
raccoman'dare *vt* to recommend; (*affidare*) to
entrust; **raccomandarsi** *vr*: **raccomandarsi
a qn** to commend o.s. to sb; **~ a qn di fare qc**
to recommend that sb does sth; **~ a qn di
non fare qc** to tell *o* warn sb not to do sth;
~ qn a qn/alle cure di qn to entrust sb to
sb/to sb's care; **mi raccomando!** don't forget!
raccoman'dato, -a *ag* (*lettera, pacco*) recorded-
delivery (*Brit*), certified (*US*); (*candidato*)
recommended ■ *sm/f*: **essere un(a) ~(a) di
ferro** to have friends in high places ■ *sf*
(*anche: **lettera raccomandata***) recorded-
delivery letter; **raccomandata con ricevuta
di ritorno (Rr)** recorded-delivery letter with
advice of receipt
raccomandazi'one [rakkomandat'tsjone] *sf*
recommendation; **lettera di ~** letter of
introduction
raccomo'dare *vt* (*riparare*) to repair, mend
raccon'tare *vt*: **~ (a qn)** (*dire*) to tell (sb);
(*narrare*) to relate (to sb), tell (sb) about; **a me
non la racconti** don't try and kid me; **cosa
mi racconti di nuovo?** what's new?
rac'conto *sm* telling *no pl*, relating *no pl*; (*fatto
raccontato*) story, tale; (*genere letterario*) short
story; **racconti per bambini** children's
stories

r

raccorci'are [rakkor'tʃare] *vt* to shorten
raccor'dare *vt* to link up, join
rac'cordo *sm* (*Tecn: giunzione*) connection, joint; (: *di autostrada*) slip road (*Brit*) entrance (*o exit*) ramp (*US*); ~ **anulare** (*Aut*) ring road (*Brit*), beltway (*US*)
ra'chitico, -a, ci, che [ra'kitiko] *ag* suffering from rickets; (*fig*) scraggy, scrawny
rachi'tismo [raki'tizmo] *sm* (*Med*) rickets *sg*
racimo'lare [ratʃimo'lare] *vt* (*fig*) to scrape together, glean
'rada *sf* (*natural*) harbour (*Brit*) *o* harbor (*US*)
'radar *sm inv* radar
raddol'cire [raddol'tʃire] *vt* (*persona: carattere*) to soften; **raddolcirsi** *vr* (*tempo*) to grow milder; (*persona*) to soften, mellow
raddoppia'mento *sm* doubling
raddoppi'are *vt, vi* to double
rad'doppio *sm* (*gen*) doubling; (*Biliardo*) double; (*Equitazione*) gallop
raddriz'zare [raddrit'tsare] *vt* to straighten; (*fig: correggere*) to put straight, correct
'radere *vt* (*barba*) to shave off; (*mento*) to shave; (*fig: rasentare*) to graze; to skim; **radersi** *vr* to shave (o.s.); ~ **al suolo** to raze to the ground
radi'ale *ag* radial
radi'ante *ag* (*calore, energia*) radiant
radi'are *vt* to strike off
radia'tore *sm* radiator
radiazi'one [radjat'tsjone] *sf* (*Fisica*) radiation; (*cancellazione*) striking off
'radica *sf* (*Bot*): ~ **di noce** walnut (wood)
radi'cale *ag* radical ■ *sm* (*Ling*) root; (*Mat, Pol*) radical; **radicali liberi** free radicals
radi'cato, -a *ag* (*pregiudizio, credenza*) deep-seated, deeply-rooted
ra'dicchio [ra'dikkjo] *sm* variety of chicory
ra'dice [ra'ditʃe] *sf* root; **segno di** ~ (*Mat*) radical sign; **colpire alla** ~ (*fig*) to strike at the root; **mettere radici** (*idee, odio etc*) to take root; (*persona*) to put down roots; ~ **quadrata** (*Mat*) square root
'radio *sf inv* ■ *sm* (*Chim*) radium; **trasmettere per** ~ to broadcast; **stazione/ponte** ~ radio station/link; ~ **ricevente/trasmittente** receiver/transmitter
radioabbo'nato, -a *sm/f* radio subscriber
radioama'tore, -'trice *sm/f* amateur radio operator, ham (*fam*)
radioascolta'tore, -'trice *sm/f* (*radio*) listener
radioattività *sf* radioactivity
radioat'tivo, -a *ag* radioactive
radiocoman'dare *vt* to operate by remote control
radiocoman'dato, -a *ag* remote-controlled

radioco'mando *sm* remote control
radiocomunicazi'one [radjokomunikat'tsjone] *sf* radio message
radio'cronaca, -che *sf* radio commentary
radiocro'nista, -i, e *sm/f* radio commentator
radiodiffusi'one *sf* (*radio*) broadcasting
radio'fonico, -a, ci, che *ag* radio *cpd*
radiogra'fare *vt* to X-ray
radiogra'fia *sf* radiography; (*foto*) X-ray photograph
radio'lina *sf* portable radio, transistor (radio)
radiolo'gia [radjolo'dʒia] *sf* radiology
radi'ologo, -a, gi, ghe *sm/f* radiologist
radiorice'vente [radjoritʃe'vɛnte] *sf* (*anche:* **apparecchio radioricevente**) receiver
radi'oso, -a *ag* radiant
radiostazi'one [radjostat'tsjone] *sf* radio station
radios'veglia [radjoz'veʎʎa] *sf* radio alarm
radio'taxi *sm inv* radio taxi
radio'tecnico, -a, ci, che *ag* radio engineering *cpd* ■ *sm* radio engineer
radiotelegra'fista, -i, e *sm/f* radiotelegrapher
radiotera'pia *sf* radiotherapy
radiotrasmit'tente *ag* (*radio*) broadcasting *cpd* ■ *sf* (*radio*) broadcasting station
'rado, -a *ag* (*capelli*) sparse, thin; (*visite*) infrequent; **di** ~ rarely; **non di** ~ not uncommonly
radu'nare *vt*, **radu'narsi** *vr* to gather, assemble
radu'nata *sf* (*Mil*) muster
ra'duno *sm* gathering, meeting
ra'dura *sf* clearing
'rafano *sm* horseradish
raffazzo'nare [raffattso'nare] *vt* to patch up
raf'fermo, -a *ag* stale
'raffica, -che *sf* (*Meteor*) gust (of wind); ~ **di colpi** (*di fucile*) burst of gunfire
raffigu'rare *vt* to represent
raffigurazi'one [raffigurat'tsjone] *sf* representation, depiction
raffi'nare *vt* to refine
raffina'tezza [raffina'tettsa] *sf* refinement
raffi'nato, -a *ag* refined
raffinazi'one [raffinat'tsjone] *sf* (*di sostanza*) refining; ~ **del petrolio** oil refining
raffine'ria *sf* refinery
raffor'zare [raffor'tsare] *vt* to reinforce
rafforza'tivo, -a [raffortsa'tivo] *ag* (*Ling*) intensifying ■ *sm* (*Ling*) intensifier
raffredda'mento *sm* cooling
raffred'dare *vt* to cool; (*fig*) to dampen, have a cooling effect on; **raffreddarsi** *vr* to grow cool *o* cold; (*prendere un raffreddore*) to catch a cold; (*fig*) to cool (off)

raffred'dato, -a *ag* (*Med*): **essere ~** to have a cold

raffred'dore *sm* (*Med*) cold

raffron'tare *vt* to compare

raf'fronto *sm* comparison

'**rafia** *sf* (*fibra*) raffia

raga'nella *sf* (*Zool*) tree frog

ra'gazzo, -a [ra'gattso] *sm/f* boy/girl; (*fam: fidanzato*) boyfriend/girlfriend; **nome da ragazza** maiden name; **ragazza madre** unmarried mother; **ragazza squillo** call girl

ragge'lare [raddʒe'lare] *vt, vi*, **ragge'larsi** *vr* to freeze

raggi'ante [rad'dʒante] *ag* radiant, shining; **~ di gioia** beaming *o* radiant with joy

raggi'era [rad'dʒera] *sf* (*di ruota*) spokes *pl*; **a ~** with a sunburst pattern

'**raggio** ['raddʒo] *sm* (*di sole etc*) ray; (*Mat: distanza*) radius; (*di ruota etc*) spoke; **nel ~ di 20 km** within a radius of 20 km *o* a 20-km radius; **a largo ~** (*esplorazione, incursione*) wide-ranging; **~ d'azione** range; **~ laser** laser beam; **raggi X** X-rays

raggi'rare [raddʒi'rare] *vt* to take in, trick

rag'giro [rad'dʒiro] *sm* trick

raggi'ungere [rad'dʒundʒere] *vt* to reach; (*persona: riprendere*) to catch up (with); (*bersaglio*) to hit; (*fig: meta*) to achieve; **~ il proprio scopo** to reach one's goal, achieve one's aim; **~ un accordo** to come to *o* reach an agreement

raggi'unto, -a [rad'dʒunto] *pp di* **raggiungere**

raggomito'larsi *vr* to curl up

raggranel'lare *vt* to scrape together

raggrin'zare [raggrin'tsare] *vt, vi* (*anche:* **raggrinzarsi**) to wrinkle

raggrin'zire [raggrin'tsire] *vt* = **raggrinzare**

raggru'mare *vt*, **raggru'marsi** *vr* (*sangue, latte*) to clot

raggruppa'mento *sm* (*azione*) grouping; (*gruppo*) group; (*Mil*) unit

raggrup'pare *vt* to group (together)

ragguagli'are [raggwaʎ'ʎare] *vt* (*paragonare*) to compare; (*informare*) to inform

raggu'aglio [rag'gwaʎʎo] *sm* comparison; (*informazione, relazione*) piece of information

ragguar'devole *ag* (*degno di riguardo*) distinguished, notable; (*notevole: somma*) considerable

'**ragia** ['radʒa] *sf*: **acqua ~** turpentine

ragiona'mento [radʒona'mento] *sm* reasoning *no pl*; argument

ragio'nare [radʒo'nare] *vi* (*usare la ragione*) to reason; (*discorrere*) **~ (di)** to argue (about); **cerca di ~** try and be reasonable

ragi'one [ra'dʒone] *sf* reason; (*dimostrazione, prova*) argument, reason; (*diritto*) right; **aver**

~ to be right; aver ~ di qn to get the better of sb; **dare ~ a qn** (*persona*) to side with sb; (*fatto*) to prove sb right; **farsi una ~ di qc** to accept sth, come to terms with sth; **in ~ di** at the rate of; **a** *o* **con ~** rightly, justly; **perdere la ~** to become insane; (*fig*) to take leave of one's senses; **a ragion veduta** after due consideration; **per ragioni di famiglia** for family reasons; **~ di scambio** terms of trade; **~ sociale** (*Comm*) corporate name; **ragion di stato** reason of State

ragione'ria [radʒone'ria] *sf* accountancy; (*ufficio*) accounts department

ragio'nevole [radʒo'nevole] *ag* reasonable

ragioni'ere, -a [radʒo'njere] *sm/f* accountant

ragli'are [raʎ'ʎare] *vi* to bray

ragna'tela [raɲɲa'tela] *sf* cobweb, spider's web

'**ragno** ['raɲɲo] *sm* spider; **non cavare un ~ dal buco** (*fig*) to draw a blank

ragù *sm inv* (*Cuc*) meat sauce (*for pasta*)

RAI-TV [raiti'vu] *sigla f* (= *Radio televisione italiana*) *Italian Broadcasting Company*

rallegra'menti *smpl* congratulations

ralle'grare *vt* to cheer up; **rallegrarsi** *vr* to cheer up; (*provare allegrezza*) to rejoice; **rallegrarsi con qn** to congratulate sb

rallenta'mento *sm* slowing down; slackening

rallen'tare *vt, vi* to slow down; **~ il passo** to slacken one's pace

rallenta'tore *sm* (*Cine*) slow-motion camera; **al ~** (*anche fig*) in slow motion

raman'zina [raman'dzina] *sf* lecture, telling-off

ra'mare *vt* (*superficie*) to copper, coat with copper; (*Agr: vite*) to spray with copper sulphate

ra'marro *sm* green lizard

ra'mato, -a *ag* (*oggetto: rivestito di rame*) copper-coated, coppered; (*capelli, barba*) coppery, copper-coloured (*Brit*), copper-colored (*US*)

'**rame** *sm* (*Chim*) copper; **di ~** copper *cpd*; **incisione su ~** copperplate

ramifi'care *vi* (*Bot*) to put out branches; **ramificarsi** *vr* (*diramarsi*) to branch out; (*Med: tumore, vene*) to ramify; **ramificarsi in** (*biforcarsi*) to branch into

ramificazi'one [ramifikat'tsjone] *sf* ramification

ra'mingo, -a, ghi, ghe *ag* (*poetico*): **andare ~** to go wandering, wander

ra'mino *sm* (*Carte*) rummy

rammari'carsi *vr*: **~ (di)** (*rincrescersi*) to be sorry (about), regret; (*lamentarsi*) to complain (about)

ram'marico, -chi *sm* regret

r

rammen'dare vt to mend; (calza) to darn
ram'mendo sm mending no pl; darning no pl;
mend darn
rammen'tare vt to remember, recall;
rammentarsi vr: **rammentarsi (di qc)** to
remember (sth); ~ **qc a qn** to remind sb of sth
rammol'lire vt to soften ■ vi (anche:
rammollirsi) to go soft
rammol'lito, -a ag weak ■ sm/f weakling
'**ramo** sm branch; (di commercio) field; **non è il
mio** ~ it's not my field o line
ramo'scello [ramoʃʃello] sm twig
'**rampa** sf flight (of stairs); ~ **di lancio**
launching pad
rampi'cante ag (Bot) climbing
ram'pino sm (gancio) hook; (Naut) grapnel
ram'pollo sm (di acqua) spring; (Bot: germoglio)
shoot; (fig: discendente) descendant
ram'pone sm harpoon; (Alpinismo) crampon
'**rana** sf frog; ~ **pescatrice** angler fish
'**rancido, -a** ['rantʃido] ag rancid
'**rancio** ['rantʃo] sm (Mil) mess; **ora del** ~ mess
time
ran'core sm rancour (Brit), rancor (US),
resentment; **portare** ~ **a qn, provare** ~ **per** o
verso qn to bear sb a grudge
ran'dagio, -a, gi, gie o **ge** [ran'dadʒo] ag
(gatto, cane) stray
ran'dello sm club, cudgel
'**rango, -ghi** sm (grado) rank; (condizione sociale)
station, social standing; **persone di** ~
inferiore people of lower standing; **uscire
dai ranghi** to fall out; (fig) to step out of line
Ran'gun sf Rangoon
rannicchi'arsi [rannik'kjarsi] vr to crouch,
huddle
rannuvo'larsi vr to cloud over, become
overcast
ra'nocchio [ra'nɔkkjo] sm (edible) frog
ranto'lare vi to wheeze
ranto'lio sm (il respirare affannoso) wheezing;
(di agonizzante) death rattle
'**rantolo** sm wheeze; death rattle
ra'nuncolo sm (Bot) buttercup
'**rapa** sf (Bot) turnip
ra'pace [ra'patʃe] ag (animale) predatory; (fig)
rapacious, grasping ■ sm bird of prey
ra'pare vt (capelli) to crop, cut very short
'**rapida** sf vedi **rapido**
rapida'mente av quickly, rapidly
rapidità sf speed
'**rapido, -a** ag fast; (esame, occhiata) quick,
rapid ■ sm (Ferr) express (train) ■ sf (di
fiume) rapid
rapi'mento sm kidnapping; (fig) rapture
ra'pina sf robbery; ~ **in banca** bank robbery;
~ **a mano armata** armed robbery

rapi'nare vt to rob
rapina'tore, -trice sm/f robber
ra'pire vt (cose) to steal; (persone) to kidnap;
(fig) to enrapture, delight
ra'pito, -a ag (persona) kidnapped; (fig: in
estasi): **ascoltare** ~ **qn** to be captivated by sb's
words ■ sm/f kidnapped person
rapi'tore, -trice sm/f kidnapper
rappacifi'care [rappatʃifi'kare] vt (riconciliare)
to reconcile; **rappacificarsi** vr (uso) to be
reconciled, make it up (fam)
rappacificazi'one [rappatʃifikat'tsjone] sf
reconciliation
rappez'zare [rappet'tsare] vt to patch
rappor'tare vt (confrontare) to compare;
(riprodurre) to reproduce
rap'porto sm (resoconto) report; (legame)
relationship; (Mat, Tecn) ratio; **rapporti** smpl
(fra persone, paesi) relations; **in** ~ **a quanto è
successo** with regard to o in relation to what
happened; **fare** ~ **a qn su qc** to report sth to
sb; **andare a** ~ **da qn** to report to sb;
chiamare qn a ~ (Mil) to summon sb;
essere in buoni/cattivi rapporti con qn to
be on good/bad terms with sb; ~ **d'affari,** ~
di lavoro business relations; ~ **di
compressione** (Tecn) pressure ratio; ~
coniugale marital relationship; ~ **di
trasmissione** (Tecn) gear; **rapporti
sessuali** sexual intercourse sg
rap'prendersi vr to coagulate, clot; (latte) to
curdle
rappre'saglia [rappre'saʎʎa] sf reprisal,
retaliation
rappresen'tante sm/f representative; ~ **di
commercio** sales representative, sales rep;
(fam): ~ **sindacale** union delegate o
representative
rappresen'tanza [rapprezen'tantsa] sf
delegation, deputation; (Comm: ufficio, sede)
agency; **in** ~ **di qn** on behalf of sb; **spese di** ~
entertainment expenses; **macchina di** ~
official car; **avere la** ~ **di** to be the agent for;
~ **esclusiva** sole agency; **avere la** ~ **esclusiva**
to be sole agent
rappresen'tare vt to represent; (Teat) to
perform; **farsi** ~ **dal proprio legale** to be
represented by one's lawyer
rappresenta'tivo, -a ag representative
■ sf (di partito, sindacale) representative group;
(Sport: squadra) representative (team)
rappresentazi'one [rapprezentat'tsjone] sf
representation; performing no pl; (spettacolo)
performance; **prima** ~ **assoluta** world
première
rap'preso, -a pp di **rapprendere**
rapso'dia sf rhapsody

'**raptus** *sm inv*: ~ **di follia** fit of madness
rara'mente *av* seldom, rarely
rare'fare *vt*, **rare'farsi** *vr* to rarefy
rare'fatto, -a *pp di* **rarefare** ■ *ag* rarefied
rarefazi'one [rarefat'tsjone] *sf* rarefaction
rarità *sf inv* rarity
'**raro, -a** *ag* rare
ra'sare *vt* (*barba etc*) to shave off; (*siepi, erba*) to trim, cut; **rasarsi** *vr* to shave (o.s.)
ra'sato, -a *ag* (*erba*) trimmed, cut; (*tessuto*) smooth; **avere la barba rasata** to be clean-shaven
rasa'tura *sf* shave
raschia'mento [raskja'mento] *sm* (*Med*) curettage; ~ **uterino** D and C
raschi'are [ras'kjare] *vt* to scrape; (*macchia, fango*) to scrape off ■ *vi* to clear one's throat
rasen'tare *vt* (*andar rasente*) to keep close to; (*sfiorare*) to skim along (*o over*); (*fig*) to border on
ra'sente *prep*: ~ (**a**) close to, very near
'**raso, -a** *pp di* **radere** ■ *ag* (*barba*) shaved; (*capelli*) cropped; (*con misure di capacità*) level; (*pieno: bicchiere*) full to the brim ■ *sm* (*tessuto*) satin; ~ **terra** close to the ground; **volare ~ terra** to hedgehop; **un cucchiaio ~ a** level spoonful
ra'soio *sm* razor; ~ **elettrico** electric shaver *o* razor
ras'pare *vt* (*levigare*) to rasp; (*grattare*) to scratch
'**raspo** *sm* (*di uva*) grape stalk
ras'segna [ras'seɲɲa] *sf* (*Mil*) inspection, review; (*esame*) inspection; (*resoconto*) review, survey; (*pubblicazione letteraria etc*) review; (*mostra*) exhibition, show; **passare in ~** (*Mil: fig*) to review
rasse'gnare [rasseɲ'ɲare] *vt*: ~ **le dimissioni** to resign, hand in one's resignation; **rassegnarsi** *vr* (*accettare*): **rassegnarsi (a qc/a fare)** to resign o.s. (to sth/to doing)
rassegnazi'one [rasseɲɲat'tsjone] *sf* resignation
rassere'nare *vt* (*persona*) to cheer up; **rasserenarsi** *vr* (*tempo*) to clear up
rasset'tare *vt* to tidy, put in order; (*aggiustare*) to repair, mend
rassicu'rante *ag* reassuring
rassicu'rare *vt* to reassure; **rassicurarsi** *vr* to take heart, recover one's confidence
rassicurazi'one [rassikurat'tsjone] *sf* reassurance
rasso'dare *vt* to harden, stiffen; (*fig*) to strengthen, consolidate
rassomigli'anza [rassomiʎ'ʎantsa] *sf* resemblance
rassomigli'are [rassomiʎ'ʎare] *vi*: ~ **a** to resemble, look like

rastrella'mento *sm* (*Mil: di polizia*) (thorough) search
rastrel'lare *vt* to rake; (*fig: perlustrare*) to comb
rastrelli'era *sf* rack; (*per piatti*) dish rack
ras'trello *sm* rake
'**rata** *sf* (*quota*) instalment, installment (*US*); **pagare a rate** to pay by instal(l)ments *o* on hire purchase (*Brit*); **comprare/vendere a rate** to buy/sell on hire purchase (*Brit*) *o* on the installment plan (*US*)
rate'ale *ag*: **pagamento ~** payment by instal(l)ments; **vendita ~** hire purchase (*Brit*), installment plan (*US*)
rate'are *vt* to divide into instal(l)ments
rateazi'one [rateat'tsjone] *sf* division into instal(l)ments
rateiz'zare [rateid'dzare] *vt* = **rateare**
'**rateo** *sm* (*Comm*) accrual
ra'tifica, -che *sf* ratification
ratifi'care *vt* (*Dir*) to ratify
'**ratto** *sm* (*Dir*) abduction; (*Zool*) rat
rattop'pare *vt* to patch
rat'toppo *sm* patching *no pl*; patch
rattrap'pire *vt* to make stiff; **rattrappirsi** *vr* to be stiff
rattris'tare *vt* to sadden; **rattristarsi** *vr* to become sad
rau'cedine [rau'tʃedine] *sf* hoarseness
'**rauco, -a, chi, che** *ag* hoarse
rava'nello *sm* radish
raven'nate *ag* of (*o from*) Ravenna
ravi'oli *smpl* ravioli *sg*
ravve'dersi *vr* to mend one's ways
ravvi'are *vt* (*capelli*) to tidy; **ravviarsi i capelli** to tidy one's hair
ravvicina'mento [ravvitʃina'mento] *sm* (*tra persone*) reconciliation; (*Pol: tra paesi etc*) rapprochement
ravvici'nare [ravvitʃi'nare] *vt* (*avvicinare*): ~ **qc a** to bring sth nearer to; (*oggetti*) to bring closer together; (*fig: persone*) to reconcile, bring together; **ravvicinarsi** *vr* to be reconciled
ravvi'sare *vt* to recognize
ravvi'vare *vt* to revive; (*fig*) to brighten up, enliven; **ravvivarsi** *vr* to revive; to brighten up
Rawal'pindi [raval'pindi] *sf* Rawalpindi
razio'cinio [rattsjo'tʃinjo] *sm* reasoning *no pl*; reason; (*buon senso*) common sense
razio'nale [rattsjo'nale] *ag* rational
razionalità [rattsjonali'ta] *sf* rationality; (*buon senso*) common sense
razionaliz'zare [rattsjonalid'dzare] *vt* (*metodo, lavoro, programma*) to rationalize; (*problema, situazione*) to approach rationally

r

raziona'mento [rattsjona'mento] *sm* rationing

razio'nare [rattsjo'nare] *vt* to ration

razi'one [rat'tsjone] *sf* ration; (*porzione*) portion, share

'razza ['rattsa] *sf* race; (*Zool*) breed; (*discendenza, stirpe*) stock, race; (*sorta*) sort, kind

raz'zia [rat'tsia] *sf* raid, foray

razzi'ale [rat'tsjale] *ag* racial

raz'zismo [rat'tsizmo] *sm* racism, racialism

raz'zista, -i, e [rat'tsista] *ag, sm/f* racist, racialist

'razzo ['raddzo] *sm* rocket; **~ di segnalazione** flare; **~ vettore** vector rocket

razzo'lare [rattso'lare] *vi* (*galline*) to scratch about

RC *sigla* = **Reggio Calabria**

RDT *sigla f vedi* **Repubblica Democratica Tedesca**

RE *sigla* = **Reggio Emilia**

re *sm inv* (*sovrano*) king; (*Mus*) D; (: *solfeggiando la scala*) re; **i Re Magi** the Three Wise Men, the Magi

rea'gente [rea'dʒɛnte] *sm* reagent

rea'gire [rea'dʒire] *vi* to react

re'ale *ag* real; (*di, da re*) royal ■ *sm*: **il ~** reality; **i Reali** the Royal family

rea'lismo *sm* realism

rea'lista, -i, e *sm/f* realist; (*Pol*) royalist

rea'listico, -a, ci, che *ag* realistic

reality [ri'aliti] *sm inv* reality show

realiz'zare [realid'dzare] *vt* (*progetto etc*) to realize, carry out; (*sogno, desiderio*) to realize, fulfil; (*scopo*) to achieve; (*Comm: titoli etc*) to realize; (*Calcio etc*) to score; **realizzarsi** *vr* to be realized

realizzazi'one [realiddzat'tsjone] *sf* realization; fulfilment; achievement; **~ scenica** stage production

rea'lizzo [rea'liddzo] *sm* (*conversione in denaro*) conversion into cash; (*vendita forzata*) clearance sale

real'mente *av* really, actually

realtà *sf inv* reality; **in ~** (*in effetti*) in fact; (*a dire il vero*) really

re'ame *sm* kingdom, realm; (*fig*) realm

re'ato *sm* offence (*Brit*), offense (*US*)

reat'tore *sm* (*Fisica*) reactor; (*Aer: aereo*) jet; (*motore*) jet engine

reazio'nario, -a [reattsjo'narjo] *ag, sm/f* (*Pol*) reactionary

reazi'one [reat'tsjone] *sf* reaction; **motore/ aereo a ~** jet engine/plane; **forze della ~** reactionary forces; **~ a catena** (*anche fig*) chain reaction

'rebbio *sm* prong

'rebus *sm inv* rebus; (*fig*) puzzle; enigma

recapi'tare *vt* to deliver

re'capito *sm* (*indirizzo*) address; (*consegna*) delivery; **ha un ~ telefonico?** do you have a telephone number where you can be reached?; **~ a domicilio** home delivery (service)

re'care *vt* (*portare*) to bring; (*avere su di sé*) to carry, bear; (*cagionare*) to cause, bring; **recarsi** *vr* to go; **recarsi in città/a scuola** to go into town/to school; **~ danno a qn** to harm sb, cause harm to sb

re'cedere [re'tʃedere] *vi* to withdraw

recensi'one [retʃen'sjone] *sf* review

recen'sire [retʃen'sire] *vt* to review

recen'sore, -a [retʃen'sore] *sm/f* reviewer

re'cente [re'tʃente] *ag* recent; **di ~** recently; **più ~** latest, most recent

recente'mente [retʃente'mente] *av* recently

rece'pire [retʃe'pire] *vt* to understand, take in

recessi'one [retʃes'sjone] *sf* (*Econ*) recession

re'cesso [re'tʃesso] *sm* (*azione*) recession, receding; (*Dir*) withdrawal; (*luogo*) recess

recherò *etc* [reke'rɔ] *vb vedi* **recare**

re'cidere [re'tʃidere] *vt* to cut off, chop off

reci'divo, -a [retʃi'divo] *sm/f* (*Dir*) second (*o habitual*) offender, recidivist ■ *sf* recidivism

recin'tare [retʃin'tare] *vt* to enclose, fence off

re'cinto [re'tʃinto] *sm* enclosure; (*ciò che recinge*) fence; surrounding wall

recinzi'one [retʃin'tsjone] *sf* (*azione*) enclosure, fencing-off; (*recinto: di legno*) fence; (: *di mattoni*) wall; (*reticolato*) wire fencing; (*a sbarre*) railings *pl*

recipi'ente [retʃi'pjɛnte] *sm* container

re'ciproco, -a, ci, che [re'tʃiproko] *ag* reciprocal

re'ciso, -a [re'tʃizo] *pp di* **recidere**

'recita ['rɛtʃita] *sf* performance

'recital ['rɛtʃital] *sm inv* recital

reci'tare [retʃi'tare] *vt* (*poesia, lezione*) to recite; (*dramma*) to perform; (*ruolo*) to play *o* act (the part of)

recitazi'one [retʃitat'tsjone] *sf* recitation; (*di attore*) acting; **scuola di ~** drama school

recla'mare *vi* to complain ■ *vt* (*richiedere*) to demand

ré'clame [re'klam] *sf inv* advertising *no pl*; advertisement, advert (*Brit*), ad (*fam*)

reclamiz'zare [reklamid'dzare] *vt* to advertise

re'clamo *sm* complaint; **sporgere ~ a** to complain to, make a complaint to

recli'nabile *ag* (*sedile*) reclining

recli'nare *vt* (*capo*) to bow, lower; (*sedile*) to tilt

reclusi'one *sf* (*Dir*) imprisonment

re'cluso, -a *sm/f* prisoner

'recluta *sf* recruit

recluta'mento *sm* recruitment

reclu'tare *vt* to recruit

re'condito, -a *ag* secluded; *(fig)* secret, hidden

'record *ag inv* record *cpd* ■ *sm inv* record; **in tempo ~, a tempo di ~** in record time; **detenere il ~ di** to hold the record for; **~ mondiale** world record

recrimi'nare *vi:* **~ (su qc)** to complain (about sth)

recriminazi'one [rekriminat'tsjone] *sf* recrimination

recrude'scenza [rekrudeʃʃɛntsa] *sf* fresh outbreak

recupe'rare *etc* = **ricuperare** *etc*

redargu'ire *vt* to rebuke

re'dassi *etc vb vedi* **redigere**

re'datto, -a *pp di* **redigere**

redat'tore, -trice *sm/f (Stampa)* editor; *(: di articolo)* writer; *(di dizionario etc)* compiler; **~ capo** chief editor

redazi'one [redat'tsjone] *sf* editing; writing; *(sede)* editorial office(s); *(personale)* editorial staff; *(versione)* version

reddi'tizio, a [reddi'tittsjo] *ag* profitable

'reddito *sm* income; *(dello Stato)* revenue; *(di un capitale)* yield; **~ complessivo** gross income; **~ disponibile** disposable income; **~ fisso** fixed income; **~ imponibile/non imponibile** taxable/non-taxable income; **~ da lavoro** earned income; **~ nazionale** national income; **~ pubblico** public revenue

re'densi *etc vb vedi* **redimere**

re'dento, -a *pp di* **redimere**

reden'tore *sm:* **il R~** the Redeemer

redenzi'one [reden'tsjone] *sf* redemption

re'digere [re'didʒere] *vt* to write; *(contratto)* to draw up

re'dimere *vt* to deliver; *(Rel)* to redeem

'redini *sfpl* reins

redi'vivo, -a *ag* returned to life, reborn

'reduce ['redutʃe] *ag (gen):* **~ da** returning from, back from ■ *sm/f* survivor; *(veterano)* veteran; **essere ~ da** *(esame, colloquio)* to have been through; *(malattia)* to be just over

'refe *sm* thread

refe'rendum *sm inv* referendum

refe'renza [refe'rɛntsa] *sf* reference

re'ferto *sm* medical report

refet'torio *sm* refectory

refezi'one [refet'tsjone] *sf (Ins)* school meal

refrat'tario, -a *ag* refractory; *(fig):* **essere ~ alla matematica** to have no aptitude for mathematics

refrige'rante [refridʒe'rante] *ag (Tecn)* cooling, refrigerating; *(bevanda)* refreshing ■ *sm (Chim: fluido)* coolant; *(Tecn: apparecchio)* refrigerator

refrige'rare [refridʒe'rare] *vt* to refrigerate; *(rinfrescare)* to cool, refresh

refrigerazi'one [refridʒerat'tsjone] *sf* refrigeration; *(Tecn)* cooling; **~ ad acqua** *(Aut)* water-cooling

refri'gerio [refri'dʒɛrjo] *sm:* **trovare ~** to find somewhere cool

refur'tiva *sf* stolen goods *pl*

Reg. *abbr* (= *reggimento*) Regt; *(Amm)* = **regolamento**

rega'lare *vt* to give (as a present), make a present of

re'gale *ag* regal

re'galo *sm* gift, present ■ *ag inv:* **confezione ~** gift pack; **fare un ~ a qn** to give sb a present; **"articoli da ~"** "gifts"

re'gata *sf* regatta

reg'gente [red'dʒɛnte] *ag (proposizione)* main; *(sovrano)* reigning ■ *sm/f* regent; **principe ~** prince regent

reg'genza [red'dʒɛntsa] *sf* regency

'reggere ['rɛddʒere] *vt (tenere)* to hold; *(sostenere)* to support, bear, hold up; *(portare)* to carry, bear; *(resistere)* to withstand; *(dirigere: impresa)* to manage, run; *(governare)* to rule, govern; *(Ling)* to take, be followed by ■ *vi (resistere):* **~ a** to stand up to, hold out against; *(sopportare):* **~ a** to stand; *(durare)* to last; *(fig: teoria etc)* to hold water; **reggersi** *vr (stare ritto)* to stand; *(fig: dominarsi)* to control o.s.; **reggersi sulle gambe** *o* **in piedi** to stand up

'reggia, -ge ['rɛddʒa] *sf* royal palace

reggi'calze [reddʒi'kaltse] *sm inv* suspender belt

reggi'mento [reddʒi'mento] *sm (Mil)* regiment

reggi'petto [reddʒi'pɛtto], **reggi'seno** [reddʒi'seno] *sm* bra

re'gia, -gie [re'dʒia] *sf (TV, Cine etc)* direction

re'gime [re'dʒime] *sm (Pol)* regime; *(Dir: aureo, patrimoniale etc)* system; *(Med)* diet; *(Tecn)* (engine) speed; **~ di giri** *(di motore)* revs *pl* per minute; **~ vegetariano** vegetarian diet

re'gina [re'dʒina] *sf* queen

'regio, -a, gi, gie ['rɛdʒo] *ag* royal

regio'nale [redʒo'nale] *ag* regional

regi'one [re'dʒone] *sf (gen)* region; *(territorio)* region, area; *see note*

○ **REGIONE**

The *Regione* is the biggest administrative unit in Italy. Each of the 20 *Regioni* consists of a variable number of "Province", which in turn are subdivided into "Comuni". Each of the regions has a "capoluogo", its chief province (for example, Florence is the chief province of

r

the region of Tuscany). Five regions have
special status and wider powers: Val
d'Aosta, Friuli-Venezia Giulia, Trentino-
Alto Adige, Sicily and Sardinia. A *Regione*
is run by the "Giunta regionale", which is
elected by the "Consiglio regionale"; both
are presided over by a "Presidente". The
"Giunta" has legislative powers within
the region over the police, public health,
schools, town planning and agriculture.

re'gista, -i, e [re'dʒista] *sm/f* (*TV, Cine etc*)
director

regis'trare [redʒis'trare] *vt* (*Amm*) to register;
(*Comm*) to enter; (*notare*) to report, note;
(*canzone, conversazione: strumento di misura*) to
record; (*mettere a punto*) to adjust, regulate;
~ **i bagagli** (*Aer*) to check in one's luggage;
~ **i freni** (*Tecn*) to adjust the brakes

registra'tore [redʒistra'tore] *sm* (*strumento*)
recorder, register; (*magnetofono*) tape
recorder; ~ **di cassa** cash register; ~ **a
cassette** cassette recorder; ~ **di volo** (*Aer*)
flight recorder, black box (*fam*)

registrazi'one [redʒistrat'tsjone] *sf*
registration; entry; reporting recording
adjustment; ~ **bagagli** (*Aer*) check-in

re'gistro [re'dʒistro] *sm* (*libro: Mus, Tecn, Ling*)
register; (*Dir*) registry; (*Comm*): ~ (**di cassa**)
ledger; **ufficio del** ~ registrar's office; ~ **di
bordo** logbook; **registri contabili** (account)
books

re'gnante [reɲ'ɲante] *ag* reigning, ruling
■ *sm/f* ruler

re'gnare [reɲ'ɲare] *vi* to reign, rule; (*fig*) to
reign

'regno ['reɲɲo] *sm* kingdom; (*periodo*) reign;
(*fig*) realm; **il** ~ **animale/vegetale** the
animal/vegetable kingdom; **il R~ Unito** the
United Kingdom

'regola *sf* rule; **a** ~ **d'arte** duly; perfectly;
essere in ~ (*dipendente*) to be a registered
employee; (*fig: essere pulito*) to be clean; **fare
le cose in** ~ to do things properly; **avere le
carte in** ~ (*gen*) to have one's papers in order;
(*fig: essere adatto*) to be the right person; **per
tua (norma e)** ~ for your information;
un'eccezione alla ~ an exception to the rule

rego'labile *ag* adjustable

regolamen'tare *ag* (*distanza, velocità*)
regulation *cpd*, proper; (*disposizione*) statutory
■ *vt* (*gen*) to control; **entro il tempo** ~
within the time allowed, within the
prescribed time

regola'mento *sm* (*complesso di norme*)
regulations *pl*; (*di debito*) settlement; ~ **di
conti** (*fig*) settling of scores

rego'lare *ag* regular; (*velocità*) steady;
(*superficie*) even; (*passo*) steady, even;
(*in regola: documento*) in order ■ *vt* to regulate,
control; (*apparecchio*) to adjust, regulate;
(*questione, conto, debito*) to settle; **regolarsi** *vr*
(*moderarsi*): **regolarsi nel bere/nello
spendere** to control one's drinking/
spending; (*comportarsi*) to behave, act;
presentare ~ **domanda** to apply through
the proper channels; ~ **i conti** (*fig*) to settle
old scores

regolarità *sf inv* regularity; steadiness;
evenness; (*nel pagare*) punctuality

regolariz'zare [regolarid'dzare] *vt* (*posizione*)
to regularize; (*debito*) to settle

rego'lata *sf*: **darsi una** ~ to pull o.s. together

regola'tezza [regola'tettsa] *sf* (*ordine*)
orderliness; (*moderazione*) moderation

rego'lato, -a *ag* (*ordinato*) orderly; (*moderato*)
moderate

regola'tore *sm* (*Tecn*) regulator; ~ **di
frequenza/di volume** frequency/volume
control

'regolo *sm* ruler; ~ **calcolatore** slide rule

regre'dire *vi* to regress

regressi'one *sf* regression

re'gresso *sm* (*fig: declino*) decline

rei'etto, -a *sm/f* outcast

reincarnazi'one [reinkarnat'tsjone] *sf*
reincarnation

reinte'grare *vt* (*produzione*) to restore; (*energie*)
to recover; (*dipendente*) to reinstate

reintegrazi'one [reintegrat'tsjone] *sf* (*di
produzione*) restoration; (*di dipendente*)
reinstatement

relativa'mente *av* relatively

relatività *sf* relativity

rela'tivo, -a *ag* relative; (*attinente*) relevant;
(*rispettivo*) respective; ~ **a** (*che concerne*)
relating to, concerning; (*proporzionato*) in
proportion to

rela'tore, -'trice *sm/f* (*gen*) spokesman/
woman; (*Ins: di tesi*) supervisor

re'lax [re'laks] *sm* relaxation

relazi'one [relat'tsjone] *sf* (*fra cose, persone*)
relation(ship); (*resoconto*) report, account;
relazioni *sfpl* (*conoscenze*) connections;
essere in ~ to be connected; **mettere in** ~
(*fatti, elementi*) to make the connection
between; **in** ~ **a quanto detto prima** with
regard to what has already been said; **essere
in buone relazioni con qn** to be on good
terms with sb; **fare una** ~ to make a report,
give an account; **relazioni pubbliche (RP)**
public relations (PR)

rele'gare *vt* to banish; (*fig*) to relegate

religi'one [reli'dʒone] *sf* religion

religi'oso, -a [reli'dʒoso] *ag* religious ▪ *sm/f* monk/nun

re'liquia *sf* relic

re'litto *sm* wreck; *(fig)* down-and-out

re'mainder [ri'meindər] *sm inv (libro)* remainder

'**re'make** ['ri:'meik] *sm inv (Cine)* remake

re'mare *vi* to row

remini'scenze [reminiʃʃentse] *sfpl* reminiscences

remissi'one *sf* remission; *(deferenza)* submissiveness, compliance; **~ del debito** remission of debt; **~ di querela** *(Dir)* withdrawal of an action

remissività *sf* submissiveness

remis'sivo, -a *ag* submissive, compliant

'**remo** *sm* oar

'**remora** *sf (poetico: indugio)* hesitation

re'moto, -a *ag* remote

remune'rare *etc* = **rimunerare** *etc*

'**rena** *sf* sand

re'nale *ag* kidney *cpd*

'**rendere** *vt (ridare)* to return, give back; *(: saluto etc)* to return; *(produrre)* to yield, bring in; *(esprimere, tradurre)* to render; *(far diventare):* **~ qc possibile** to make sth possible ▪ *vi (fruttare: ditta)* to be profitable; *(: investimento, campo)* to yield, be productive; **~ grazie a qn** to thank sb; **~ omaggio a qn** to honour sb; **~ un servizio a qn** to do sb a service; **~ una testimonianza** to give evidence; **~ la visita** to pay a return visit; **non so se rendo l'idea** I don't know whether I'm making myself clear; **rendersi utile** to make o.s. useful; **rendersi conto di qc** to realize sth

rendi'conto *sm (rapporto)* report, account; *(Amm, Comm)* statement of account

rendi'mento *sm (reddito)* yield; *(di manodopera, Tecn)* efficiency; *(capacità)* output; *(di studenti)* performance

'**rendita** *sf (di individuo)* private o unearned income; *(Comm)* revenue; **~ annua** annuity; **~ vitalizia** life annuity

'**rene** *sm* kidney

'**reni** *sfpl* back *sg*

reni'tente *ag* reluctant, unwilling; **~ ai consigli di qn** unwilling to follow sb's advice; **essere ~ alla leva** *(Mil)* to fail to report for military service

'**renna** *sf* reindeer *inv*

'**Reno** *sm:* **il ~** the Rhine

'**reo, -a** *sm/f (Dir)* offender

re'parto *sm* department, section; *(Mil)* detachment; **~ acquisti** purchasing office

repel'lente *ag* repulsive; *(Chim: insettifugo):* **liquido ~** (liquid) repellent

repen'taglio [repen'taʎʎo] *sm:* **mettere a ~** to jeopardize, risk

repen'tino, -a *ag* sudden, unexpected

repe'ribile *ag* available

repe'rire *vt* to find, trace

re'perto *sm (Archeologia)* find; *(Med)* report; *(anche:* **reperto giudiziario**) exhibit

reper'torio *sm (Teat)* repertory; *(elenco)* index, (alphabetical) list

'**replica, -che** *sf* repetition reply, answer; *(obiezione)* objection; *(Teat, Cine)* repeat performance; *(copia)* replica

repli'care *vt (ripetere)* to repeat; *(rispondere)* to answer, reply

repor'tage [rəpɔr'taʒ] *sm inv (Stampa)* report

repressi'one *sf* repression

repres'sivo, -a *ag* repressive

re'presso, -a *pp di* **reprimere**

re'primere *vt* to suppress, repress

re'pubblica, -che *sf* republic; **la R~ Democratica Tedesca (RDT)** the German Democratic Republic (GDR); **la R~ Federale Tedesca (RFT)** the Federal Republic of Germany (FRG); **la Prima/la Seconda R~** *terms used to refer to Italy before and after the political changes resulting from the 1994 elections; vedi anche* **Festa della Repubblica; Seconda Repubblica**

repubbli'cano, -a *ag, sm/f* republican

repu'tare *vt* to consider, judge

reputazi'one [reputat'tsjone] *sf* reputation; **farsi una cattiva ~** to get o.s. a bad name

'**requie** *sf* rest; **dare ~ a qn** to give sb some peace; **senza ~** unceasingly

'**requiem** *sm inv (preghiera)* requiem, prayer for the dead; *(fig: ufficio funebre)* requiem

requi'sire *vt* to requisition

requi'sito *sm* requirement; **avere i requisiti necessari per un lavoro** to have the necessary qualifications for a job

requisi'toria *sf (Dir)* closing speech (for the prosecution)

requisizi'one [rekwizit'tsjone] *sf* requisition

'**resa** *sf (l'arrendersi)* surrender; *(restituzione, rendimento)* return; **~ dei conti** rendering of accounts; *(fig)* day of reckoning

re'scindere [reʃ'ʃindere] *vt (Dir)* to rescind, annul

re'scisso, -a [reʃ'ʃisso] *pp di* **rescindere**

reset'tare *vt (Inform)* to reset

'**resi** *etc vb vedi* **rendere**

resi'dente *ag* resident

resi'denza [resi'dentsa] *sf* residence

residenzi'ale [residen'tsjale] *ag* residential

residu'ale *ag* residual

re'siduo, -a *ag* residual, remaining ▪ *sm* remainder; *(Chim)* residue; **residui industriali** industrial waste *sg*

'resina *sf* resin

resis'tente *ag* (*che resiste*): ~ **a** resistant to; (*forte*) strong; (*duraturo*) long-lasting, durable; ~ **all'acqua** waterproof; ~ **al caldo** heat-resistant; ~ **al fuoco** fireproof; ~ **al gelo** frost-resistant

resis'tenza [resis'tɛntsa] *sf* (*gen, Elettr*) resistance; (*di persona: fisica*) stamina, endurance; (: *mentale*) endurance, resistance; **opporre** ~ (**a**) to offer *o* put up resistance (to); (*decisione, scelta*) to show opposition (to); **la R~** *see note*

re'sistere *vi* to resist; ~ **a** (*assalto, tentazioni*) to resist; (*dolore: pianta*) to withstand; (*non patir danno*) to be resistant to

resis'tito, -a *pp di* **resistere**

'reso, -a *pp di* **rendere**

reso'conto *sm* report, account

respin'gente [respin'dʒɛnte] *sm* (*Ferr*) buffer

res'pingere [res'pindʒere] *vt* to drive back, repel; (*rifiutare: pacco, lettera*) to return; (: *invito*) to refuse; (: *proposta*) to reject, turn down; (*Ins: bocciare*) to fail

res'pinto, -a *pp di* **respingere**

respi'rare *vi* to breathe; (*fig*) to get one's breath; to breathe again ▪ *vt* to breathe (in), inhale

respira'tore *sm* respirator

respira'torio, -a *ag* respiratory

respirazi'one [respirat'tsjone] *sf* breathing; ~ **artificiale** artificial respiration; ~ **bocca a bocca** mouth-to-mouth resuscitation, kiss of life; (*fam*)

res'piro *sm* breathing *no pl*; (*singolo atto*) breath; (*fig*) respite, rest; **mandare un ~ di sollievo** to give a sigh of relief; **trattenere il ~** to hold one's breath; **lavorare senza ~** to work non-stop; **di ampio ~** (*opera, lavoro*) far-reaching

respon'sabile *ag* responsible ▪ *sm/f* person responsible; (*capo*) person in charge; ~ **di** responsible for; (*Dir*) liable for

responsabilità *sf inv* responsibility; (*legale*) liability; **assumere la ~ di** to take on the responsibility for; **affidare a qn la ~ di qc** to make sb responsible for sth; ~ **patrimoniale** debt liability; ~ **penale** criminal liability

responsabiliz'zare [responsabilid'dzare] *vt*: ~ **qn** to make sb feel responsible

res'ponso *sm* answer; (*Dir*) verdict

'ressa *sf* crowd, throng

'ressi *etc vb vedi* **reggere**

res'tare *vi* (*rimanere*) to remain, stay; (*diventare*): ~ **orfano/cieco** to become *o* be left an orphan/become blind; (*trovarsi*): ~ **sorpreso** to be surprised; (*avanzare*) to be left, remain; ~ **d'accordo** to agree; **non resta più niente** there's nothing left; **restano pochi giorni** there are only a few days left; **che resti tra di noi** this is just between ourselves; ~ **in buoni rapporti** to remain on good terms; ~ **senza parole** to be left speechless

restau'rare *vt* to restore

restaura'tore, -'trice *sm/f* restorer

restaurazi'one [restaurat'tsjone] *sf* (*Pol*) restoration

res'tauro *sm* (*di edifici etc*) restoration; **in ~** under repair; **sotto ~** (*dipinto*) being restored; **chiuso per restauri** closed for repairs

res'tio, -a, 'tii, 'tie *ag* restive; (*persona*): ~ **a** reluctant to

restitu'ire *vt* to return, give back; (*energie, forze*) to restore

restituzi'one [restitut'tsjone] *sf* return; (*di soldi*) repayment

'resto *sm* remainder, rest; (*denaro*) change; (*Mat*) remainder; **resti** *smpl* leftovers; (*di città*) remains; **del ~** moreover, besides; **resti mortali** (mortal) remains

res'tringere [res'trindʒere] *vt* to reduce; (*vestito*) to take in; (*stoffa*) to shrink; (*fig*) to restrict, limit; **restringersi** *vr* (*strada*) to narrow; (*stoffa*) to shrink

restrit'tivo, -a *ag* restrictive

restrizi'one [restrit'tsjone] *sf* restriction

resurrezi'one [resurret'tsjone] *sf* = **risurrezione**

resusci'tare [resuʃʃi'tare] *vt, vi* = **risuscitare**

re'tata *sf* (*Pesca*) haul, catch; **fare una ~ di** (*fig: persone*) to round up

'rete *sf* net; (*di recinzione*) wire netting; (*Aut, Ferr, di spionaggio etc*) network; (*fig*) trap, snare; **segnare una ~** (*Calcio*) to score a goal; ~ **ferroviaria/stradale/di distribuzione** railway/road/distribution network; ~ **del letto** (sprung) bed base; ~ **da pesca** fishing net; ~ **sociale** social network; ~ **(televisiva)** (*sistema*) network; (*canale*) channel; **la R~** the web; **calze a ~** fishnet tights *o* stockings

reti'cente [reti'tʃɛnte] *ag* reticent

reti'cenza [reti'tʃɛntsa] *sf* reticence

retico'lato *sm* grid; (*rete metallica*) wire netting; (*di filo spinato*) barbed wire fence

'**retina** *sf* (*Anat*) retina

re'torico, -a, ci, che *ag* rhetorical ■ *sf* rhetoric

retribu'ire *vt* to pay; (*premiare*) to reward; **un lavoro mal retribuito** a poorly-paid job

retribu'tivo, -a *ag* pay *cpd*

retribuzi'one [retribut'tsjone] *sf* payment; reward

re'trivo, -a *ag* (*fig*) reactionary

'**retro** *sm inv* back ■ *av* (*dietro*): **vedi ~** see over(leaf)

retroattività *sf* retroactivity

retroat'tivo, -a *ag* (*Dir: legge*) retroactive; (*Amm: salario*) backdated

retrobot'tega, -ghe *sf* back shop

retro'cedere [retro'tʃɛdere] *vi* to withdraw ■ *vt* (*Calcio*) to relegate; (*Mil*) to degrade; (*Amm*) to demote

retrocessi'one [retrotʃes'sjone] *sf* (*di impiegato*) demotion

retro'cesso, -a [retro'tʃɛsso] *pp di* **retrocedere**

retroda'tare *vt* (*Amm*) to backdate

re'trogrado, -a *ag* (*fig*) reactionary, backward-looking

retrogu'ardia *sf* (*anche fig*) rearguard

retro'marcia [retro'martʃa] *sf* (*Aut*) reverse; (*dispositivo*) reverse gear

retro'scena [retroʃ'ʃɛna] *sf inv* (*Teat*) backstage ■ *sm inv* (*fig*) behind-the-scenes activity

retrospet'tivo, -a *ag* retrospective ■ *sf* (*Arte*) retrospective (exhibition)

retros'tante *ag*: **~ (a)** at the back (of)

retro'terra *sm* hinterland

retro'via *sf* (*Mil*) zone behind the front; **mandare nelle retrovie** to send to the rear

retrovi'sore *sm* (*Aut*) (rear-view) mirror

'**retta** *sf* (*Mat*) straight line; (*di convitto*) charge for bed and board; (*fig: ascolto*): **dar ~ a** to listen to, pay attention to

rettango'lare *ag* rectangular

ret'tangolo, -a *ag* right-angled ■ *sm* rectangle

ret'tifica, -che *sf* rectification, correction

rettifi'care *vt* (*curva*) to straighten; (*fig*) to rectify, correct

'**rettile** *sm* reptile

retti'lineo, -a *ag* rectilinear

retti'tudine *sf* rectitude, uprightness

'**retto, -a** *pp di* **reggere** ■ *ag* straight; (*Mat*): **angolo ~** right angle; (*onesto*) honest, upright; (*giusto, esatto*) correct, proper, right

ret'tore *sm* (*Rel*) rector; (*di università*) ≈ chancellor

reuma'tismo *sm* rheumatism

Rev. *abbr* (= *Reverendo*) Rev(d)

reve'rendo, -a *ag*: **il ~ padre Belli** the Reverend Father Belli

reve'rente *ag* = **riverente**

reve'renza [reve'rɛntsa] *sf* = **riverenza**

rever'sibile *ag* reversible

revisio'nare *vt* (*conti*) to audit; (*Tecn*) to overhaul, service; (*Dir: processo*) to review; (*componimento*) to revise

revisi'one *sf* auditing *no pl*; audit servicing *no pl*; overhaul review revision; **~ di bilancio** audit; **~ di bozze** proofreading; **~ contabile interna** internal audit

revi'sore *sm*: **~ di conti/bozze** auditor/proofreader

'**revoca** *sf* revocation

revo'care *vt* to revoke

re'volver *sm inv* revolver

revolve'rata *sf* revolver shot

'**Reykjavik** ['reikjavik] *sf* Reykjavik

RFT *sigla f vedi* **Repubblica Federale Tedesca**

ri'abbia *etc vb vedi* **riavere**

riabili'tare *vt* to rehabilitate; (*fig*) to restore to favour (*Brit*) *o* favor (*US*)

riabilitazi'one [riabilitat'tsjone] *sf* rehabilitation

riac'cendere [riat'tʃɛndere] *vt* (*sigaretta, fuoco, gas*) to light again; (*luce, radio, TV*) to switch on again; (*fig: sentimenti: interesse*) to rekindle, revive; **riaccendersi** *vr* (*fuoco*) to catch again; (*luce, radio, TV*) to come back on again; (*fig: sentimenti*) to revive, be rekindled

riac'ceso, -a [riat'tʃeso] *pp di* **riaccendere**

riacqui'stare *vt* (*gen*) to buy again; (*ciò che si era venduto*) to buy back; (*fig: buonumore, sangue freddo, libertà*) to regain; **~ la salute** to recover (one's health); **~ le forze** to regain one's strength

Ri'ad *sf* Riyadh

riaddormen'tare *vt* to put to sleep again; **riaddormentarsi** *vr* to fall asleep again

riallac'ciare [riallat'tʃare] *vt* (*cintura, cavo etc*) to refasten, tie up *o* fasten again; (*fig: rapporti, amicizia*) to resume, renew; **riallacciarsi** *vr*: **riallacciarsi a** (*fig: a discorso, tema*) to resume, take up again

rial'zare [rial'tsare] *vt* to raise, lift; (*alzare di più*) to heighten, raise; (*aumentare: prezzi*) to increase, raise ■ *vi* (*prezzi*) to rise, increase

rial'zato, -a [rial'tsato] *ag*: **piano ~** mezzanine, entresol

rial'zista, -i [rial'tsista] *sm* (*Borsa*) bull

ri'alzo [ri'altso] *sm* (*di prezzi*) increase, rise; (*sporgenza*) rise; **giocare al ~** (*Borsa*) to bull

r

rian'dare vi: ~ **(in)**, ~ **(a)** to go back (to), return (to)

riani'mare vt (Med) to resuscitate; (fig: rallegrare) to cheer up; (dar coraggio) to give heart to; **rianimarsi** vr to recover consciousness; to cheer up; to take heart

rianimazi'one [rianimat'tsjone] sf (Med) resuscitation; **centro di ~** intensive care unit

ria'perto, -a pp di **riaprire**

riaper'tura sf reopening

riappa'rire vi to reappear

riap'parso, -a pp di **riapparire**

riap'pendere vt to rehang; (Tel) to hang up

ria'prire vt, **ria'prirsi** vr to reopen, open again

ri'armo sm (Mil) rearmament

ri'arso, -a ag (terreno) arid; (gola) parched; (labbra) dry

riasset'tare vt (vedi sm) to rearrange; to reorganize

rias'setto sm (di stanza etc) rearrangement; (ordinamento) reorganization

rias'sumere vt (riprendere) to resume; (impiegare di nuovo) to re-employ; (sintetizzare) to summarize

rias'sunto, -a pp di **riassumere** ■ sm summary

riattac'care vt (attaccare di nuovo): ~ **(a)** (manifesto, francobollo) to stick back (on); (bottone) to sew back (on); (quadro, chiavi) to hang back up (on); ~ **(il telefono** o **il ricevitore)** to hang up (the receiver)

riatti'vare vt to reactivate

ria'vere vt to have again; (avere indietro) to get back; (riacquistare) to recover; **riaversi** vr to recover; (da svenimento, stordimento) to come round

riba'dire vt (fig) to confirm

ri'balta sf (sportello) flap; (Teat: proscenio) front of the stage; (apparecchio d'illuminazione) footlights pl; (fig) limelight; **tornare alla ~** (personaggio) to make a comeback; (problema) to come up again

ribal'tabile ag (sedile) tip-up

ribal'tare vt, vi (anche: **ribaltarsi**) to turn over, tip over

ribas'sare vt to lower, bring down ■ vi to come down, fall

ribas'sista, -i sm (Borsa) bear

ri'basso sm reduction, fall; **essere in ~** (azioni, prezzi) to be down; (fig: popolarità) to be on the decline; **giocare al ~** (Borsa) to bear

ri'battere vt (battere di nuovo) to beat again; (con macchina da scrivere) to type again; (palla) to return; (confutare) to refute; ~ **che** to retort that

ribattez'zare [ribatted'dzare] vt to rename

ribel'larsi vr: ~ **(a)** to rebel (against)

ri'belle ag (soldati) rebel; (ragazzo) rebellious ■ sm/f rebel

ribelli'one sf rebellion

'ribes sm inv currant; ~ **nero** blackcurrant; ~ **rosso** redcurrant

ribol'lire vi (fermentare) to ferment; (fare bolle) to bubble, boil; (fig) to seethe

ri'brezzo [ri'breddzo] sm disgust, loathing; **far ~ a** to disgust

ributtante ag disgusting, revolting

ricacci'are [rikat'tʃare] vt (respingere) to drive back; ~ **qn fuori** to throw sb out

rica'dere vi to fall again; (scendere a terra: fig: nel peccato etc) to fall back; (vestiti, capelli etc) to hang (down); (riversarsi: fatiche, colpe): ~ **su** to fall on

rica'duta sf (Med) relapse

rical'care vt (disegni) to trace; (fig) to follow faithfully

ricalci'trare [rikaltʃi'trare] vi (cavalli, asini, muli) to kick

rica'mare vt to embroider

ricambi'are vt to change again; (contraccambiare) to return

ri'cambio sm exchange, return; (Fisiol) metabolism; **ricambi** smpl: **pezzi di ~** spare parts; ~ **della manodopera** labour turnover

ri'camo sm embroidery; **senza ricami** (fig) without frills

ricapito'lare vt to recapitulate, sum up

ricapitolazi'one [rikapitolat'tsjone] sf recapitulation, summary

ricari'care vt (arma, macchina fotografica) to reload; (penna) to refill; (orologio, giocattolo) to rewind; (Elettr) to recharge

ricat'tare vt to blackmail

ricatta'tore, -'trice sm/f blackmailer

ri'catto sm blackmail; **fare un ~ a qn** to blackmail sb; **subire un ~** to be blackmailed

rica'vare vt (estrarre) to draw out, extract; (ottenere) to obtain, gain

rica'vato sm (di vendite) proceeds pl

ri'cavo sm proceeds pl; (Contabilità) revenue

ric'chezza [rik'kettsa] sf wealth; (fig) richness; **ricchezze** sfpl (beni) wealth sg, riches; **ricchezze naturali** natural resources

'riccio, -a, ci, ce ['rittʃo] ag curly ■ sm (Zool) hedgehog; (anche: **riccio di mare**) sea urchin

'ricciolo ['rittʃolo] sm curl

ricci'uto, -a [rit'tʃuto] ag curly

'ricco, -a, chi, che ag rich; (persona, paese) rich, wealthy ■ sm/f rich man/woman; **i ricchi** the rich; ~ **di** (idee, illustrazioni etc) full of; (risorse, fauna etc) rich in

ri'cerca, -che [ri'tʃerka] sf search; (indagine) investigation, inquiry; (studio): **la ~** research; **una ~** piece of research; **mettersi alla ~ di** to go in search of, look o search o hunt for; **essere alla ~ di** to be searching for, be looking for; **~ di mercato** market research; **~ operativa** operational research

ricer'care [ritʃer'kare] vt (motivi, cause) to look for, try to determine; (successo, piacere) to pursue; (onore, gloria) to seek

ricerca'tezza [ritʃerka'tettsa] sf (raffinatezza) refinement; (peg) affectation

ricer'cato, -a [ritʃer'kato] ag (apprezzato) much sought-after; (affettato) studied, affected ■ sm/f (Polizia) wanted man/woman

ricerca'tore, -'trice [ritʃerka'tore] sm/f (Ins) researcher

ricetrasmit'tente [ritʃetrazmit'tɛnte] sf two-way radio, transceiver

ri'cetta [ri'tʃetta] sf (Med) prescription; (Cuc) recipe; (fig: antidoto): **~ contro** remedy for

ricet'tacolo [ritʃet'takolo] sm (peg: luogo malfamato) den

ricet'tario [ritʃet'tarjo] sm (Med) prescription pad; (Cuc) recipe book

ricetta'tore, -'trice [ritʃetta'tore] sm/f (Dir) receiver (of stolen goods)

ricettazi'one [ritʃettat'tsjone] sf (Dir) receiving (stolen goods)

ricet'tivo, -a [ritʃet'tivo] ag receptive

rice'vente [ritʃe'vɛnte] ag (Radio, TV) receiving ■ sm/f (Comm) receiver

ri'cevere [ri'tʃevere] vt to receive; (stipendio, lettera) to get, receive; (accogliere: ospite) to welcome; (vedere: cliente, rappresentante etc) to see; **"confermiamo di aver ricevuto tale merce"** (Comm) "we acknowledge receipt of these goods"

ricevi'mento [ritʃevi'mento] sm receiving no pl; (trattenimento) reception; **al ~ della merce** on receipt of the goods

ricevi'tore [ritʃevi'tore] sm (Tecn) receiver; **~ delle imposte** tax collector

ricevito'ria [ritʃevito'ria] sf (Fisco): **~ (delle imposte)** Inland Revenue (Brit) o Internal Revenue (US) Office; **~ del lotto** lottery office

rice'vuta [ritʃe'vuta] sf receipt; **accusare ~ di qc** (Comm) to acknowledge receipt of sth; **~ fiscale** official receipt (for tax purposes); **~ di ritorno** (Posta) advice of receipt; **~ di versamento** receipt of payment

ricezi'one [ritʃet'tsjone] sf (Radio, TV) reception

richia'mare [rikja'mare] vt (chiamare indietro, ritelefonare) to call back; (ambasciatore, truppe) to recall; (rimproverare) to reprimand; (attrare)

to attract, draw; **richiamarsi** vr: **richiamarsi a** (riferirsi a) to refer to; **~ qn all'ordine** to call sb to order; **desidero ~ la vostra attenzione su ...** I would like to draw your attention to ...

richi'amo [ri'kjamo] sm call; recall; reprimand; attraction

richie'dente [rikje'dente] sm/f applicant

richi'edere [ri'kjɛdere] vt to ask again for; (chiedere indietro): **~ qc** to ask for sth back; (chiedere: per sapere) to ask; (: per avere) to ask for; (Amm: documenti) to apply for; (esigere) to need, require; **essere molto richiesto** to be in great demand

richi'esto, -a [ri'kjɛsto] pp di **richiedere** ■ sf (domanda) request; (Amm) application, request; (esigenza) demand, request; **a richiesta** on request

rici'claggio [ritʃi'kladdʒo] sm (fig) laundering; **~ di materiale** recycling; **~ di denaro sporco** money laundering

rici'clare [ritʃi'klare] vt (vetro, carta, bottiglie) to recycle; (fig: personale) to retrain

'ricino ['ritʃino] sm: **olio di ~** castor oil

ricogni'tore [rikoɲɲi'tore] sm (Aer) reconnaissance aircraft

ricognizi'one [rikoɲɲit'tsjone] sf (Mil) reconnaissance; (Dir) recognition, acknowledgement

ricolle'gare vt (collegare nuovamente: gen) to join again, link again; (connettere: fatti): **~ (a, con)** to connect (with); **ricollegarsi** vr: **ricollegarsi a** (fatti connettersi) to be connected to; (persona: riferirsi) to refer to

ri'colmo, -a ag: **~ (di)** (bicchiere) full to the brim (with); (stanza) full (of)

ricominci'are [rikomin'tʃare] vt, vi to start again, begin again; **~ a fare qc** to begin doing o to do sth again, start doing o to do sth again

ricom'pensa sf reward

ricompen'sare vt to reward

ricom'porsi vr to compose o.s., regain one's composure

ricom'posto, -a pp di **ricomporsi**

riconcili'are [rikontʃi'ljare] vt to reconcile; **riconciliarsi** vr to be reconciled

riconciliazi'one [rikontʃiliat'tsjone] sf reconciliation

ricon'dotto, -a pp di **ricondurre**

ricon'durre vt to bring (o take) back

ricon'ferma sf reconfirmation

riconfer'mare vt to reconfirm

ricongiungi'mento [rikondʒundʒi'mento] sm (di famiglia, coniugi) reconciliation; **~ familiare** (Dir: di immigrati) family reunification

r

307

ricono'scente [rikonoʃʃɛnte] *ag* grateful

ricono'scenza [rikonoʃʃɛntsa] *sf* gratitude

rico'noscere [riko'noʃʃere] *vt* to recognize; (*Dir: figlio, debito*) to acknowledge; (*ammettere: errore*) to admit, acknowledge; **~ qn colpevole** to find sb guilty

riconosci'mento [rikonoʃʃi'mento] *sm* recognition; acknowledgement; (*identificazione*) identification; **come ~ dei servizi resi** in recognition of services rendered; **documento di ~** means of identification; **segno di ~** distinguishing mark; **programma per il ~ vocale** (*Inform*) voice recognition program

riconosci'uto, -a [rikonoʃʃuto] *pp di* **riconoscere**

riconquis'tare *vt* (*Mil*) to reconquer; (*libertà, stima*) to win back

rico'perto, -a *pp di* **ricoprire**

ricopi'are *vt* to copy

rico'prire *vt* to re-cover; (*coprire*) to cover; (*occupare: carica*) to hold

ricor'dare *vt* to remember, recall; (*richiamare alla memoria*): **~ qc a qn** to remind sb of sth; **ricordarsi** *vr*: **ricordarsi (di)** to remember; **ricordarsi di qc/di aver fatto** to remember sth/having done

ri'cordo *sm* memory; (*regalo*) keepsake, souvenir; (*di viaggio*) souvenir; **ricordi** *smpl* (*memorie*) memoirs

ricor'rente *ag* recurrent, recurring

ricor'renza [rikor'rɛntsa] *sf* recurrence; (*festività*) anniversary

ri'correre *vi* (*ripetersi*) to recur; **~ a** (*rivolgersi*) to turn to; (*Dir*) to appeal to; (*servirsi di*) to have recourse to; **~ in appello** to lodge an appeal

ri'corso, -a *pp di* **ricorrere** ■ *sm* recurrence; (*Dir*) appeal; **far ~ a** = **ricorrere a**

ricostitu'ente *ag* (*Med*): **cura ~** tonic treatment ■ *sm* (*Med*) tonic

ricostitu'ire *vt* (*società*) to build up again; (*governo, partito*) to re-form; **ricostituirsi** *vr* (*gruppo etc*) to re-form

ricostru'ire *vt* (*casa*) to rebuild; (*fatti*) to reconstruct

ricostruzi'one [rikostrut'tsjone] *sf* rebuilding *no pl*; reconstruction

ri'cotta *sf* soft white unsalted cheese made from sheep's milk

ricove'rare *vt* to give shelter to; **~ qn in ospedale** to admit sb to hospital

ricove'rato, -a *sm/f* patient

ri'covero *sm* shelter, refuge; (*Mil*) shelter; (*Med*) admission (to hospital); **~ antiaereo** air-raid shelter

ricre'are *vt* to recreate; (*rinvigorire*) to restore; (*fig: distrarre*) to amuse

ricrea'tivo, -a *ag* recreational

ricreazi'one [rikreat'tsjone] *sf* recreation, entertainment; (*Ins*) break

ri'credersi *vr* to change one's mind

ricupe'rare *vt* (*rientrare in possesso di*) to recover, get back; (*tempo perduto*) to make up for; (*Naut*) to salvage; (*: naufraghi*) to rescue; (*delinquente*) to rehabilitate; **~ lo svantaggio** (*Sport*) to close the gap

ri'cupero *sm* (*gen*) recovery; (*di relitto etc*) salvaging; **capacità di ~** resilience

ricu'sare *vt* to refuse

ridacchi'are [ridak'kjare] *vi* to snigger

ri'dare *vt* to return, give back

'ridda *sf* (*di ammiratori etc*) swarm; (*di pensieri*) jumble

ri'dente *ag* (*occhi, volto*) smiling; (*paesaggio*) delightful

'ridere *vi* to laugh; (*deridere, beffare*): **~ di** to laugh at, make fun of; **non c'è niente da ~**, **c'è poco da ~** it's not a laughing matter

rides'tare *vt* (*fig: ricordi, passioni*) to reawaken

ri'detto, -a *pp di* **ridire**

ridico'laggine [ridiko'laddʒine] *sf* (*di situazione*) absurdity; (*cosa detta o fatta*) nonsense *no pl*

ridicoliz'zare [ridikolid'dzare] *vt* to ridicule

ri'dicolo, -a *ag* ridiculous, absurd ■ *sm*: **cadere nel ~** to become ridiculous; **rendersi ~** to make a fool of o.s.

ridimensiona'mento *sm* reorganization; (*di fatto storico*) reappraisal

ridimensio'nare *vt* to reorganize; (*fig*) to see in the right perspective

ri'dire *vt* to repeat; (*criticare*) to find fault with; to object to; **trova sempre qualcosa da ~** he always manages to find fault

ridon'dante *ag* redundant

ri'dosso *sm*: **a ~ di** (*dietro*) behind; (*contro*) against

ri'dotto, -a *pp di* **ridurre**

ri'duco *etc vb vedi* **ridurre**

ri'durre *vt* (*anche Chim, Mat*) to reduce; (*prezzo, spese*) to cut, reduce; (*accorciare: opera letteraria*) to abridge; (*Radio, TV*) to adapt; **ridursi** *vr* (*diminuirsi*) to be reduced, shrink; **ridursi a** to be reduced to; **ridursi a pelle e ossa** to be reduced to skin and bone

ri'dussi *etc vb vedi* **ridurre**

ridut'tore *sm* (*Tecn, Chim, Elettr*) reducer

riduzi'one [ridut'tsjone] *sf* reduction; abridgement; adaptation

ri'ebbi *etc vb vedi* **riavere**

riecheg'giare [rieked'dʒare] *vi* to re-echo

riedu'care *vt* (*persona, arto*) to re-educate; (*malato*) to rehabilitate

rieducazi'one [riedukat'tsjone] *sf* re-education; rehabilitation; **centro di ~** rehabilitation centre

rie'leggere [rie'lɛddʒere] *vt* to re-elect

rie'letto, -a *pp di* **rieleggere**

riempi'mento *sm* filling (up)

riem'pire *vt* to fill (up); *(modulo)* to fill in *o* out; **riempirsi** *vr* to fill (up); *(mangiare troppo)* to stuff o.s.; **~ qc di** to fill sth (up) with

riempi'tivo, -a *ag* filling ▪ *sm (anche fig)* filler

rien'tranza [rien'trantsa] *sf* recess; indentation

rien'trare *vi (entrare di nuovo)* to go (*o* come) back in; *(tornare)* to return; *(fare una rientranza)* to go in, curve inwards; to be indented; *(riguardare)*: **~ in** to be included among, form part of; **~ (a casa)** to get back home; **non rientriamo nelle spese** we are not within our budget

ri'entro *sm (ritorno)* return; *(di astronave)* re-entry; **è iniziato il grande ~** *(estivo)* people are coming back from their (summer) holidays

riepilo'gare *vt* to summarize ▪ *vi* to recapitulate

rie'pilogo, -ghi *sm* recapitulation; **fare un ~ di qc** to summarize sth

rie'same *sm* re-examination

riesami'nare *vt* to re-examine

ri'esco *etc vb vedi* **riuscire**

ri'essere *vi:* **ci risiamo!** *(fam)* we're back to this again!

rievo'care *vt (passato)* to recall; *(commemorare: figura, meriti)* to commemorate

rievocazi'one [rievokat'tsjone] *sf (vedi vt)* recalling; commemoration

rifaci'mento [rifatʃi'mento] *sm (di film)* remake; *(di opera letteraria)* rehashing

ri'fare *vt* to do again; *(ricostruire)* to make again; *(nodo)* to tie again, do up again; *(imitare)* to imitate, copy; **rifarsi** *vr (risarcirsi)*: **rifarsi di** to make up for; *(vendicarsi)*: **rifarsi di qc su qn** to get one's own back on sb for sth; *(riferirsi)*: **rifarsi a** *(periodo, fenomeno storico)* to go back to; **~ il letto** to make the bed; **rifarsi una vita** to make a new life for o.s.

ri'fatto, -a *pp di* **rifare**

riferi'mento *sm* reference; **in** *o* **con ~ a** with reference to; **far ~ a** to refer to

rife'rire *vt (riportare)* to report; *(ascrivere)*: **~ qc a** to attribute sth to ▪ *vi* to do a report; **riferirsi** *vr:* **riferirsi a** to refer to; **riferirò** I'll pass on the message

rifi'lare *vt (tagliare a filo)* to trim; *(fam: affibbiare)*: **~ qc a qn** to palm sth off on sb

rifi'nire *vt* to finish off, put the finishing touches to

rifini'tura *sf* finishing touch; **rifiniture** *sfpl (di mobile, auto)* finish *sg*

rifiu'tare *vt* to refuse; **~ di fare** to refuse to do

rifi'uto *sm* refusal; **rifiuti** *smpl (spazzatura)* rubbish *sg*, refuse *sg*; **rifiuti solidi urbani** solid urban waste *sg*

riflessi'one *sf (Fisica)* reflection; *(il pensare)* thought, reflection; *(osservazione)* remark

rifles'sivo, -a *ag (persona)* thoughtful, reflective; *(Ling)* reflexive

ri'flesso, -a *pp di* **riflettere** ▪ *sm (di luce, su specchio)* reflection; *(Fisiol)* reflex; *(su capelli)* light; *(fig)* effect; **di** *o* **per ~** indirectly; **avere i riflessi pronti** to have quick reflexes

riflessolo'gia [riflessolo'dʒia] *sf:* **~ (plantare)** reflexology

ri'flettere *vt* to reflect ▪ *vi* to think; **riflettersi** *vr* to be reflected; *(ripercuotersi)*: **riflettersi su** to have repercussions on; **~ su** to think over

riflet'tore *sm* reflector; *(proiettore)* floodlight; *(Mil)* searchlight

ri'flusso *sm* flowing back; *(della marea)* ebb; **un'epoca di ~** an era of nostalgia

rifocil'larsi [rifotʃil'larsi] *vr (poetico)* to take refreshment

rifondazi'one [rifondat'tsjone] *sf (Pol):* **R~ Comunista** *hard left party, originating from former P.C.I.*

ri'fondere *vt (rimborsare)* to refund, repay; **~ le spese a qn** to refund sb's expenses; **~ i danni a qn** to compensate sb for damages

ri'forma *sf* reform; *(Mil)* declaration of unfitness for service; discharge; *(on health grounds)*: **la R~** *(Rel)* the Reformation

rifor'mare *vt* to re-form; *(cambiare, innovare)* to reform; *(Mil: recluta)* to declare unfit for service; *(soldato)* to invalid out, discharge

riforma'tore, -'trice *ag* reforming ▪ *sm/f* reformer

riforma'torio *sm (Dir)* community home (Brit), reformatory (US)

rifor'mista, -i, -e *ag, sm/f* reformist

riforni'mento *sm* supplying, providing; restocking; *(di carburante)* refuelling; **rifornimenti** *smpl* supplies, provisions; **fare ~ di** *(viveri)* to stock up with; *(benzina)* to fill up with; **posto di ~** filling *o* gas (US) station

rifor'nire *vt (provvedere)*: **~ di** to supply *o* provide with; *(fornire di nuovo: casa etc)* to restock

ri'frangere [ri'frandʒere] *vt* to refract

ri'fratto, -a *pp di* **rifrangere**

rifrazi'one [rifrat'tsjone] *sf* refraction

rifug'gire [rifud'dʒire] *vi* to escape again; *(fig):* **~ da** to shun

rifugi'arsi [rifu'dʒarsi] *vr* to take refuge

rifugi'ato, -a [rifu'dʒato] *sm/f* refugee

ri'fugio [ri'fudʒo] *sm* refuge, shelter; (*in montagna*) shelter; ~ **antiaereo** air-raid shelter

ri'fuso, -a *pp di* **rifondere**

'riga, -ghe *sf* line; (*striscia*) stripe; (*di persone, cose*) line, row; (*regolo*) ruler; (*scriminatura*) parting; **mettersi in ~** to line up; **a righe** (*foglio*) lined; (*vestito*) striped; **buttare giù due righe** (*note*) to jot down a few notes; **mandami due righe appena arrivi** drop me a line as soon as you arrive

ri'gagnolo [ri'gaɲɲolo] *sm* rivulet

ri'gare *vt* (*foglio*) to rule ▪ *vi*: ~ **diritto** (*fig*) to toe the line

rigassifica'tore *sm* regasification terminal

riga'toni *smpl* (*Cuc*) short, ridged pasta shapes

rigatti'ere *sm* junk dealer

riga'tura *sf* (*di pagina, quaderno*) lining, ruling; (*di fucile*) rifling

rigene'rare [ridʒene'rare] *vt* (*gen, Tecn*) to regenerate; (*forze*) to restore; (*gomma*) to retread; **rigenerarsi** *vr* (*gen*) to regenerate; (*ramo, tumore*) to regenerate, grow again; **gomma rigenerata** retread

rigenerazi'one [ridʒenerat'tsjone] *sf* regeneration

riget'tare [ridʒet'tare] *vt* (*gettare indietro*) to throw back; (*fig: respingere*) to reject; (*vomitare*) to bring o throw up

ri'getto [ri'dʒetto] *sm* (*anche Med*) rejection

ri'ghello [ri'gello] *sm* ruler

righerò *etc* [rige'rɔ] *vb vedi* **rigare**

rigi'dezza [ridʒi'dettsa], **rigidità** [ridʒidi'ta] *sf* rigidity; stiffness; severity, rigours *pl* (*Brit*), rigors *pl* (*US*); strictness

'rigido, a ['ridʒido] *ag* rigid, stiff; (*membra etc: indurite*) stiff; (*Meteor*) harsh, severe; (*fig*) strict

rigi'rare [ridʒi'rare] *vt* to turn; **rigirarsi** *vr* to turn round; (*nel letto*) to turn over; ~ **qc tra le mani** to turn sth over in one's hands; ~ **il discorso** to change the subject

'rigo, -ghi *sm* line; (*Mus*) staff, stave

rigogli'oso, -a [rigoʎ'ʎoso] *ag* (*pianta*) luxuriant; (*fig: commercio, sviluppo*) thriving

rigonfia'mento *sm* (*Anat*) swelling; (*su legno, intonaco etc*) bulge

ri'gonfio, -a *ag* swollen; (*grembiule, sporta*): ~ **di** bulging with

ri'gore *sm* (*Meteor*) harshness, rigours *pl* (*Brit*), rigors *pl* (*US*); (*fig*) severity, strictness; (*anche:* **calcio di rigore**) penalty; **di ~** compulsory; **"è di ~ l'abito da sera"** "evening dress"; **area di ~** (*Calcio*) penalty box (*Brit*); **a rigor di termini** strictly speaking

rigorosità *sf* strictness; rigour (*Brit*), rigor (*US*)

rigo'roso, -a *ag* (*severo: persona, ordine*) strict; (*preciso*) rigorous

rigover'nare *vt* to wash (up)

riguar'dare *vt* to look at again; (*considerare*) to regard, consider; (*concernere*) to regard, concern; **riguardarsi** *vr* (*aver cura di sé*) to look after o.s.; **per quel che mi riguarda** as far as I'm concerned; **sono affari che non ti riguardano** it's none of your business

rigu'ardo *sm* (*attenzione*) care; (*considerazione*) regard, respect; ~ **a** concerning, with regard to; **per ~ a** out of respect for; **ospite/ persona di ~** very important guest/person; **non aver riguardi nell'agire/nel parlare** to act/speak freely

riguar'doso, -a *ag* (*rispettoso*) respectful; (*premuroso*) considerate, thoughtful

rigurgi'tare [rigurdʒi'tare] *vi* (*liquido*): ~ **da** to gush out from; (*recipiente: traboccare*): ~ **di** to overflow with

ri'gurgito [ri'gurdʒito] *sm* (*Med*) regurgitation; (*fig: ritorno, risveglio*) revival

rilanci'are [rilan'tʃare] *vt* (*lanciare di nuovo: gen*) to throw again; (*moda*) to bring back; (*prodotto*) to re-launch; ~ **un'offerta** (*asta*) to make a higher bid

ri'lancio [ri'lantʃo] *sm* (*Carte: di offerta*) raising

rilasci'are [rilaʃ'ʃare] *vt* (*rimettere in libertà*) to release; (*Amm: documenti*) to issue; (*intervista*) to give; ~ **delle dichiarazioni** to make a statement

ri'lascio [ri'laʃʃo] *sm* release; issue

rilassa'mento *sm* (*gen, Med*) relaxation

rilas'sare *vt* to relax; **rilassarsi** *vr* to relax; (*fig: disciplina*) to become slack

rilassa'tezza [rilassa'tettsa] *sf* (*fig: di costumi, disciplina*) laxity

rilas'sato, -a *ag* (*persona, muscoli*) relaxed; (*disciplina, costumi*) lax

rile'gare *vt* (*libro*) to bind

rilega'tura *sf* binding

ri'leggere [ri'lɛddʒere] *vt* to reread, read again; (*rivedere*) to read over

ri'lento: a ~ *av* slowly

ri'letto, -a *pp di* **rileggere**

rilet'tura *sf* (*vedi vt*) rereading; reading over

rileva'mento *sm* (*topografico, statistico*) survey; (*Naut*) bearing

rile'vante *ag* considerable; important

rile'vanza [rile'vantsa] *sf* importance

rile'vare *vt* (*ricavare*) to find; (*notare*) to notice; (*mettere in evidenza*) to point out; (*venire a conoscere: notizia*) to learn; (*raccogliere: dati*) to gather, collect; (*Topografia*) to survey; (*Mil*) to relieve; (*Comm*) to take over

rilevazi'one [rilevat'tsjone] *sf* survey

rili'evo *sm* (*Arte, Geo*) relief; (*fig: rilevanza*) importance; (*osservazione*) point, remark; (*Topografia*) survey; **dar ~ a** *o* **mettere in ~ qc** (*fig*) to bring sth out, highlight sth; **di poco/ nessun ~** (*fig*) of little/no importance; **un personaggio di ~** an important person

rilut'tante *ag* reluctant

rilut'tanza [rilut'tantsa] *sf* reluctance

'**rima** *sf* rhyme; (*verso*) verse; **far ~ con** to rhyme with; **rispondere a qn per le rime** to give sb tit for tat

riman'dare *vt* to send again; (*restituire, rinviare*) to send back, return; (*differire*): **~ qc (a)** to postpone sth *o* put sth off (till); (*fare riferimento*): **~ qn a** to refer sb to; **essere rimandato** (*Ins*) to have to resit one's exams

ri'mando *sm* (*rinvio*) return; (*dilazione*) postponement; (*riferimento*) cross-reference

rimaneggi'are [rimaned'dʒare] *vt* (*testo*) to reshape, recast; (*Pol*) to reshuffle

rima'nente *ag* remaining ■ *sm* rest, remainder; **i rimanenti** (*persone*) the rest of them, the others

rima'nenza [rima'nɛntsa] *sf* rest, remainder; **rimanenze** *sfpl* (*Comm*) unsold stock *sg*

rima'nere *vi* (*restare*) to remain, stay; (*avanzare*) to be left, remain; (*restare stupito*) to be amazed; (*restare, mancare*): **rimangono poche settimane a Pasqua** there are only a few weeks left till Easter; (*diventare*): **~ vedovo** to be left a widower; (*trovarsi*): **~ confuso/ sorpreso** to be confused/surprised; **rimane da vedere se** it remains to be seen whether

rimangi'are [riman'dʒare] *vt* to eat again; **rimangiarsi la parola/una promessa** (*fig*) to go back on one's word/one's promise

ri'mango *etc vb vedi* **rimanere**

ri'mare *vt, vi* to rhyme

rimargi'nare [rimardʒi'nare] *vt, vi*, **rimargi'narsi** to heal

ri'masto, -a *pp di* **rimanere**

rima'sugli [rima'suʎʎi] *smpl* leftovers

rimbal'zare [rimbal'tsare] *vi* to bounce back, rebound; (*proiettile*) to ricochet

rim'balzo [rim'baltso] *sm* rebound; ricochet

rimbam'bire *vi* to be in one's dotage; (*rincretinire*) to grow foolish

rimbam'bito, -a *ag* senile, gaga; (*fam*): **un vecchio ~** a doddering old man

rimbec'care *vt* (*persona*) to answer back; (*offesa*) to return

rimbecil'lire [rimbetʃil'lire] *vi*, **rimbecil'lirsi** *vr* to become stupid

rimboc'care *vt* (*orlo*) to turn up; (*coperta*) to tuck in; (*maniche, pantaloni*) to turn *o* roll up

rimbom'bare *vi* to resound; (*artiglieria*) to boom; (*tuono*) to rumble

rim'bombo *sm* (*vedi vi*) boom; rumble

rimbor'sare *vt* to pay back, repay; **~ qc a qn** to reimburse sb for sth

rim'borso *sm* repayment; (*di spese, biglietto*) refund; **~ d'imposta** tax rebate

rimboschi'mento [rimboski'mento] *sm* reafforestation

rimbos'chire [rimbos'kire] *vt* to reafforest

rimbrot'tare *vt* to reproach

rim'brotto *sm* reproach

rimedi'are *vi*: **~ a** to remedy ■ *vt* (*fam: procurarsi*) to scrape *o* get together; **~ da vivere** to scrape a living

ri'medio *sm* (*medicina*) medicine; (*cura: fig*) remedy, cure; **porre ~ a qc** to remedy sth; **non c'è ~** there's no way out, there's nothing to be done about it

rimesco'lare *vt* to mix well, stir well; (*carte*) to shuffle; **sentirsi ~ il sangue** (*per rabbia*) to feel one's blood boil

ri'messa *sf* (*locale: per veicoli*) garage; (*per aerei*) hangar; (*Comm: di merce*) consignment; (*di denaro*) remittance; (*Tennis*) return; (*Calcio: anche:* **rimessa in gioco**) throw-in

ri'messo, -a *pp di* **rimettere**

rimes'tare *vt* (*mescolare*) to mix well, stir well; (*fig: passato*) to drag up again

ri'mettere *vt* (*mettere di nuovo*) to put back; (*indossare di nuovo*): **~ qc** to put sth back on, put sth on again; (*restituire*) to return, give back; (*affidare*) to entrust; (: *decisione*) to refer; (*condonare*) to remit; (*Comm: merci*) to deliver; (: *denaro*) to remit; (*vomitare*) to bring up; (*perdere: anche:* **rimetterci**) to lose; **rimettersi** *vr*: **rimettersi a** (*affidarsi*) to trust; **~ a nuovo** (*casa etc*) to do up (Brit) *o* over (US); **rimetterci di tasca propria** to be out of pocket; **rimettersi al bello** (*tempo*) to clear up; **rimettersi in cammino** to set off again; **rimettersi al lavoro** to start working again; **rimettersi in salute** to get better, recover one's health

rimi'nese *ag* of (*o* from) Rimini

ri'misi *etc vb vedi* **rimettere**

'**rimmel**® *sm inv* mascara

rimoderna'mento *sm* modernization

rimoder'nare *vt* to modernize

ri'monta *sf* (*Sport: gen*) recovery

rimon'tare *vt* (*meccanismo*) to reassemble; (*tenda*) to put up again ■ *vi* (*salire di nuovo*): **~ in** (*macchina, treno*) to get back into; (*Sport*) to close the gap

rimorchi'are [rimor'kjare] *vt* to tow; (*fig: ragazza*) to pick up

rimorchia'tore [rimorkja'tore] *sm* (*Naut*) tug(boat)

r

ri'morchio [ri'mɔrkjo] *sm* tow; (*veicolo*) trailer; **andare a ~** to be towed; **prendere a ~ to tow; cavo da ~** towrope; **autocarro con ~** articulated lorry (Brit) semi(trailer) (US)

ri'morso *sm* remorse; **avere il ~ di aver fatto qc** to deeply regret having done sth

ri'mosso, -a *pp di* **rimuovere**

rimos'tranza [rimos'trantsa] *sf* protest, complaint; **fare le proprie rimostranze a qn** to remonstrate with sb

rimozi'one [rimot'tsjone] *sf* removal; (*da un impiego*) dismissal; (*Psic*) repression; **"~ forzata"** "illegally parked vehicles will be removed at owner's expense"

rimpas'tare *vt* (*Pol: ministero*) to reshuffle

rim'pasto *sm* (*Pol*) reshuffle; **~ ministeriale** cabinet reshuffle

rimpatri'are *vi* to return home ■ *vt* to repatriate

rim'patrio *sm* repatriation

rimpi'angere [rim'pjandʒere] *vt* to regret; (*persona*) to miss; **~ di (non) aver fatto qc** to regret (not) having done sth

rimpi'anto, -a *pp di* **rimpiangere** ■ *sm* regret

rimpiat'tino *sm* hide-and-seek

rimpiaz'zare [rimpjat'tsare] *vt* to replace

rimpiccio'lire [rimpittʃo'lire] *vt* to make smaller ■ *vi* (*anche*: **rimpicciolirsi**) to become smaller

rimpin'zare [rimpin'tsare] *vt*: **~ di** to cram o stuff with

rimprove'rare *vt* to rebuke, reprimand

rim'provero *sm* rebuke, reprimand; **di ~** (*tono, occhiata*) reproachful; (*parole*) of reproach

rimugi'nare [rimudʒi'nare] *vt* (*fig*) to turn over in one's mind

rimune'rare *vt* (*retribuire*) to remunerate; (*ricompensare: sacrificio etc*) to reward; **un lavoro ben rimunerato** a well-paid job

rimunera'tivo, -a *ag* (*lavoro, attività*) remunerative, profitable

rimunerazi'one [rimunerat'tsjone] *sf* remuneration; (*premio*) reward

rimu'overe *vt* to remove; (*destituire*) to dismiss; (*fig: distogliere*) to dissuade

rinascimen'tale [rinaʃʃimen'tale] *ag* Renaissance *cpd*, of the Renaissance

Rinasci'mento [rinaʃʃi'mento] *sm*: **il ~** the Renaissance

ri'nascita [ri'naʃʃita] *sf* rebirth, revival

rincal'zare [rinkal'tsare] *vt* (*palo, albero*) to support, prop up; (*lenzuola*) to tuck in

rin'calzo [rin'kaltso] *sm* support, prop; (*rinforzo*) reinforcement; (*Sport*) reserve (player); **rincalzi** *smpl* (*Mil*) reserves

rinca'rare *vt* to increase the price of ■ *vi* to go up, become more expensive; **~ la dose** (*fig*) to pile it on

rin'caro *sm*: **~ (di)** (*prezzi, costo della vita*) increase (in); (*prodotto*) increase in the price (of)

rinca'sare *vi* to go home

rinchi'udere [rin'kjudere] *vt* to shut (o lock) up; **rinchiudersi** *vr*: **rinchiudersi in** to shut o.s. up in; **rinchiudersi in se stesso** to withdraw into o.s.

rinchi'uso, -a [rin'kjuso] *pp di* **rinchiudere**

rincitrul'lirsi [rintʃitrul'lirsi] *vr* to grow foolish

rin'correre *vt* to chase, run after

rin'corso, -a *pp di* **rincorrere** ■ *sf* short run

rin'crescere [rin'kreʃʃere] *vb impers*: **mi rincresce che/di non poter fare** I'm sorry that/I can't do, I regret that/being unable to do

rincresci'mento [rinkreʃʃi'mento] *sm* regret

rincresci'uto, -a [rinkreʃ'ʃuto] *pp di* **rincrescere**

rincu'lare *vi* to draw back; (*arma*) to recoil

rinfacci'are [rinfat'tʃare] *vt* (*fig*): **~ qc a qn** to throw sth in sb's face

rinfoco'lare *vt* (*fig: odio, passioni*) to rekindle; (*risentimento, rabbia*) to stir up

rinfor'zare [rinfor'tsare] *vt* to reinforce, strengthen ■ *vi* (*anche*: **rinforzarsi**) to grow stronger

rin'forzo [rin'fortso] *sm*: **mettere un ~ a** to strengthen; **rinforzi** *smpl* (*Mil*) reinforcements; **di ~** (*asse, sbarra*) strengthening; (*esercito*) supporting; (*personale*) extra, additional

rinfran'care *vt* to encourage, reassure

rinfres'cante *ag* (*bibita*) refreshing

rinfres'care *vt* (*atmosfera, temperatura*) to cool (down); (*abito, pareti*) to freshen up ■ *vi* (*tempo*) to grow cooler; **rinfrescarsi** *vr* (*ristorarsi*) to refresh o.s.; (*lavarsi*) to freshen up; **~ la memoria a qn** to refresh sb's memory

rin'fresco, -schi *sm* (*festa*) party; **rinfreschi** *smpl* (*cibi e bevande*) refreshments

rin'fusa *sf*: **alla ~** in confusion, higgledy-piggledy

ringhi'are [rin'gjare] *vi* to growl, snarl

ringhi'era [rin'gjɛra] *sf* railing; (*delle scale*) banister(s) (*pl*)

'ringhio ['ringjo] *sm* growl, snarl

ringhi'oso, -a [rin'gjoso] *ag* growling, snarling

ringiova'nire [rindʒova'nire] *vt* (*vestito, acconciatura etc*): **~ qn** to make sb look younger; (*vacanze etc*) to rejuvenate ■ *vi* (*anche*: **ringiovanirsi**) to become (*o* look) younger

ringrazia'mento [ringrattsja'mento] *sm* thanks *pl*; **lettera/biglietto di** ~ thank you letter/card

ringrazi'are [ringrat'tsjare] *vt* to thank; ~ **qn di qc** to thank sb for sth; ~ **qn per aver fatto qc** to thank sb for doing sth

rinne'gare *vt* (*fede*) to renounce; (*figlio*) to disown, repudiate

rinne'gato, -a *sm/f* renegade

rinno'vabile *ag* (*contratto, energia*) renewable

rinnova'mento *sm* renewal; (*economico*) revival

rinno'vare *vt* to renew; (*ripetere*) to repeat, renew; **rinnovarsi** *vr* (*fenomeno*) to be repeated, recur

rin'novo *sm* (*di contratto*) renewal; **"chiuso per ~ (dei) locali"** (*negozio*) "closed for alterations"

rinoce'ronte [rinotʃe'ronte] *sm* rhinoceros

rino'mato, -a *ag* renowned, celebrated

rinsal'dare *vt* to strengthen

rinsa'vire *vi* to come to one's senses

rinsec'chito, -a [rinsek'kito] *ag* (*vecchio, albero*) thin, gaunt

rinta'narsi *vr* (*animale*) to go into its den; (*persona: nascondersi*) to hide

rintoc'care *vi* (*campana*) to toll; (*orologio*) to strike

rin'tocco, -chi *sm* toll

rintracci'are [rintrat'tʃare] *vt* to track down; (*persona scomparsa, documento*) to trace

rintro'nare *vi* to boom, roar ■ *vt* (*assordare*) to deafen; (*stordire*) to stun

rintuz'zare [rintut'tsare] *vt* (*fig: sentimento*) to check, repress; (*accusa*) to refute

ri'nuncia [ri'nuntʃa] *sf* renunciation; ~ **a** (*carica*) resignation from; (*eredità*) relinquishment of; ~ **agli atti del giudizio** (*Dir*) abandonment of a claim

rinunci'are [rinun'tʃare] *vi*: ~ **a** to give up, renounce; ~ **a fare qc** to give up doing sth

rinuncia'tario, -a [rinuntʃa'tarjo] *ag* defeatist

ri'nunzia *etc* [ri'nuntsja] = **rinuncia** *etc*

rinveni'mento *sm* (*ritrovamento*) recovery; (*scoperta*) discovery; (*Metallurgia*) tempering

rinve'nire *vt* to find, recover; (*scoprire*) to discover, find out ■ *vi* (*riprendere i sensi*) to come round; (*riprendere l'aspetto naturale*) to revive

rinve'nuto, -a *pp di* **rinvenire**

rinver'dire *vi* (*bosco, ramo*) to become green again

rinvi'are *vt* (*rimandare indietro*) to send back, return; (*differire*): ~ **qc (a)** to postpone sth *o* put sth off (till); (*: seduta*) to adjourn sth (till);

(*fare un rimando*): ~ **qn a** to refer sb to; ~ **a giudizio** (*Dir*) to commit for trial

rinvigo'rire *vt* to strengthen

rin'vio, -'vii *sm* (*rimando*) return; (*differimento*) postponement; (*di seduta*) adjournment; (*in un testo*) cross-reference; ~ **a giudizio** (*Dir*) indictment

riò *etc vb vedi* **riavere**

Rio de Ja'neiro ['riodedʒa'neiro] *sf* Rio de Janeiro

rio'nale *ag* (*mercato, cinema*) local, district *cpd*

ri'one *sm* district, quarter

riordina'mento *sm* (*di ente, azienda*) reorganization

riordi'nare *vt* (*rimettere in ordine*) to tidy; (*riorganizzare*) to reorganize

riorganiz'zare [riorganid'dzare] *vt* to reorganize

riorganizzazi'one [riorganiddzat'tsjone] *sf* reorganization

ripa'gare *vt* to repay

ripa'rare *vt* (*proteggere*) to protect, defend; (*correggere: male, torto*) to make up for; (*: errore*) to put right; (*aggiustare*) to repair ■ *vi* (*mettere rimedio*): ~ **a** to make up for; **ripararsi** *vr* (*rifugiarsi*) to take refuge *o* shelter

ripa'rato, -a *ag* (*posto*) sheltered

riparazi'one [riparat'tsjone] *sf* (*di un torto*) reparation; (*di guasto, scarpe*) repairing *no pl*; repair; (*risarcimento*) compensation; (*Ins*): **esame di** ~ resit (*Brit*), test retake (*US*)

ri'paro *sm* (*protezione*) shelter, protection; (*rimedio*) remedy; **al ~ da** (*sole, vento*) sheltered from; **mettersi al ~** to take shelter; **correre ai ripari** (*fig*) to take remedial action

ripar'tire *vt* (*dividere*) to divide up; (*distribuire*) to share out, distribute ■ *vi* to leave again; (*motore*) to start again

ripartizi'one [ripartit'tsjone] *sf* division sharing out, distribution; (*Amm: dipartimento*) department

ripas'sare *vi* to come (*o* go) back ■ *vt* (*scritto, lezione*) to go over (again)

ri'passo *sm* (*di lezione*) revision (*Brit*), review (*US*)

ripensa'mento *sm* second thoughts *pl* (*Brit*), change of mind; **avere un ~** to have second thoughts, change one's mind

ripen'sare *vi* to think; (*cambiare idea*) to change one's mind; (*tornare col pensiero*): ~ **a** to recall; **a ripensarci ...** on thinking it over ...

riper'correre *vt* (*itinerario*) to travel over again; (*strada*) to go along again; (*fig: ricordi, passato*) to go back over

riper'corso, -a *pp di* **ripercorrere**

riper'cosso, -a *pp di* **ripercuotersi**

ripercu'otersi *vr*: ~ **su** (*fig*) to have repercussions on

r

313

ripercussi'one sf (fig): **avere una ~** o **delle ripercussioni su** to have repercussions on

ripes'care vt (pesce) to catch again; (persona, cosa) to fish out; (fig: ritrovare) to dig out

ripe'tente sm/f student repeating the year, repeater (US)

ri'petere vt to repeat; (ripassare) to go over

ripeti'tore sm (Radio, TV) relay

ripetizi'one [ripetit'tsjone] sf repetition; (di lezione) revision; **ripetizioni** sfpl (Ins) private tutoring o coaching sg; **fucile a ~** repeating rifle

ripetuta'mente av repeatedly, again and again

ripi'ano sm (Geo) terrace; (di mobile) shelf

ri'picca sf: **per ~** out of spite

'ripido, -a ag steep

ripiega'mento sm (Mil) retreat

ripie'gare vt to refold; (piegare più volte) to fold (up) ■ vi (Mil) to retreat, fall back; (fig: accontentarsi): **~ su** to make do with; **ripiegarsi** vr to bend

ripi'ego, -ghi sm expedient; **una soluzione di ~** a makeshift solution

ripi'eno, -a ag full; (Cuc) stuffed; (panino) filled ■ sm (Cuc) stuffing

ri'pone vb vedi **riporre**

ri'pongo vb vedi **riporre**

ri'porre vt (porre al suo posto) to put back, replace; (mettere via) to put away; (fiducia, speranza): **~ qc in qn** to place o put sth in sb

ripor'tare vt (portare indietro) to bring (o take) back; (riferire) to report; (citare) to quote; (ricevere) to receive, get; (vittoria) to gain; (successo) to have; (Mat) to carry; (Comm) to carry forward; **riportarsi** vr: **riportarsi a** (anche fig) to go back to; (riferirsi a) to refer to; **~ danni** to suffer damage; **ha riportato gravi ferite** he was seriously injured

ri'porto sm amount carried over; amount carried forward

ripo'sante ag (gen) restful; (musica, colore) soothing

ripo'sare vt (bicchiere, valigia) to put down; (dare sollievo) to rest ■ vi to rest; **riposarsi** vr to rest; **qui riposa …** (su tomba) here lies …

ripo'sato, -a ag (viso, aspetto) rested; (mente) fresh

ri'posi etc vb vedi **riporre**

ri'poso sm rest; (Mil): **~!** at ease!; **a ~** (in pensione) retired; **giorno di ~** day off; **"oggi ~"** (Cine, Teat) "no performance today"; (ristorante) "closed today"

ripos'tiglio [ripos'tiʎʎo] sm lumber room (Brit), storage room (US)

ri'posto, -a pp di **riporre** ■ ag (fig: senso, significato) hidden

ri'prendere vt (prigioniero, fortezza) to recapture; (prendere indietro) to take back; (ricominciare: lavoro) to resume; (andare a prendere) to fetch, come back for; (assumere di nuovo: impiegati) to take on again, re-employ; (rimproverare) to tell off; (restringere: abito) to take in; (Cine) to shoot; **riprendersi** vr to recover; (correggersi) to correct o.s.; **~ a fare qc** to start doing sth again; **~ il cammino** to set off again; **~ i sensi** to recover consciousness; **~ sonno** to go back to sleep

ripresen'tare vt (certificato) to submit again; (domanda) to put forward again; (persona) to introduce again; **ripresentarsi** vr (ritornare: persona) to come back; (: occasione) to arise again; **ripresentarsi a** (esame) to sit (Brit) o take (US) again; (concorso) to enter again; **ripresentarsi come candidato** (Pol) to stand (Brit) o run (US) again (as a candidate)

ri'preso, -a pp di **riprendere** ■ sf recapture; resumption; (economica, da malattia, emozione) recovery; (Aut) acceleration no pl; (Teat, Cine) rerun; (Cine: presa) shooting no pl; shot; (Sport) second half; (Pugilato) round; **a più riprese** on several occasions, several times

ripristi'nare vt to restore

ri'pristino sm (gen) restoration; (di tradizioni) revival

ripro'dotto, -a pp di **riprodurre**

ripro'durre vt to reproduce; **riprodursi** vr (Biol) to reproduce; (riformarsi) to form again

riprodut'tivo, -a ag reproductive

riprodut'tore, -'trice ag (organo) reproductive ■ sm: **~ acustico** pick-up; **~ a cassetta** cassette player

riproduzi'one [riprodut'tsjone] sf reproduction; **~ vietata** all rights reserved

ripro'messo, -a pp di **ripromettersi**

ripro'mettersi vt (aspettarsi): **~ qc da** to expect sth from; (intendere): **~ di fare qc** to intend to do sth

ripro'porre vt: **riproporsi di fare qc** to intend to do sth

ripro'posto, -a pp di **riproporre**

ri'prova sf confirmation; **a ~ di** as confirmation of

ripro'vare vt (provare di nuovo: gen) to try again; (: vestito) to try on again; (: sensazione) to experience again ■ vi (tentare): **~ (a fare qc)** to try (to do sth) again; **riproverò più tardi** I'll try again later

ripro'vevole ag reprehensible

ripudi'are vt to repudiate, disown

ri'pudio sm repudiation, disowning

ripu'gnante [ripuɲ'ɲante] ag disgusting, repulsive

ripu'gnanza [ripuɲ'ɲantsa] *sf* repugnance, disgust

ripu'gnare [ripuɲ'ɲare] *vi*: **~ a qn** to repel *o* disgust sb

ripu'lire *vt* to clean up; (*ladri*) to clean out; (*perfezionare*) to polish, refine

ripulsi'one *sf* (*Fisica, fig*) repulsion

ri'quadro *sm* square; (*Archit*) panel

RIS [ris] *sigla m* (= *Reparto Investigazioni Scientifiche*) ≈ CID, branch of the Carabinieri

ri'sacca, -che *sf* backwash

ri'saia *sf* paddy field

risa'lire *vi* (*ritornare in su*) to go back up; **~ a** (*ritornare con la mente*) to go back to; (*datare da*) to date back to, go back to

risa'lita *sf*: **mezzi di ~** (*Sci*) ski lifts

risal'tare *vi* (*fig: distinguersi*) to stand out; (*Archit*) to project, jut out

ri'salto *sm* prominence; (*sporgenza*) projection; **mettere** *o* **porre in ~ qc** to make sth stand out

risana'mento *sm* (*economico*) improvement; (*bonifica*) reclamation; **~ del bilancio** reorganization of the budget; **~ edilizio** building improvement

risa'nare *vt* (*guarire*) to heal, cure; (*palude*) to reclaim; (*economia*) to improve; (*bilancio*) to reorganize

risa'pere *vt*: **~ qc** to come to know of sth

risa'puto, -a *ag*: **è ~ che ...** everyone knows that ..., it's common knowledge that ...

risarci'mento [risartʃi'mento] *sm*: **~ (di)** compensation (for); **aver diritto al ~ dei danni** to be entitled to damages

risar'cire [risar'tʃire] *vt* (*cose*) to pay compensation for; (*persona*): **~ qn di qc** to compensate sb for sth; **~ i danni a qn** to pay sb damages

ri'sata *sf* laugh

riscalda'mento *sm* heating; **~ centrale** central heating

riscal'dare *vt* (*scaldare*) to heat; (*mani, persona*) to warm; (*minestra*) to reheat; **riscaldarsi** *vr* to warm up

ris'caldo *sm* (*fam*) (slight) inflammation

riscat'tare *vt* (*prigioniero*) to ransom, pay a ransom for; (*Dir*) to redeem; **riscattarsi** *vr* (*da disonore*) to redeem o.s.

ris'catto *sm* ransom; redemption

rischia'rare [riskja'rare] *vt* (*illuminare*) to light up; (*colore*) to make lighter; **rischiararsi** *vr* (*tempo*) to clear up; (*cielo*) to clear; (*fig: volto*) to brighten up; **rischiararsi la voce** to clear one's throat

rischi'are [ris'kjare] *vt* to risk ■ *vi*: **~ di fare qc** to risk *o* run the risk of doing sth

'rischio ['riskjo] *sm* risk; **a ~** (*zona, situazione*) at risk, vulnerable; **a proprio ~ e pericolo** at

one's own risk; **correre il ~ di fare qc** to run the risk of doing sth; **~ del mestiere** occupational hazard

rischi'oso, -a [ris'kjoso] *ag* risky, dangerous

risciac'quare [riʃʃak'kware] *vt* to rinse

risci'acquo [riʃʃakkwo] *sm* rinse

riscon'trare *vt* (*confrontare: due cose*) to compare; (*esaminare*) to check, verify; (*rilevare*) to find

ris'contro *sm* comparison check, verification; (*Amm: lettera di risposta*) reply; **mettere a ~** to compare; **in attesa di un vostro cortese ~** we look forward to your reply

risco'perto, -a *pp di* **riscoprire**

risco'prire *vt* to rediscover

riscossi'one *sf* collection

ris'cosso, -a *pp di* **riscuotere** ■ *sf* (*riconquista*) recovery, reconquest

riscri'vibile *ag* (*CD, DVD*) rewritable

riscu'otere *vt* (*ritirare una somma dovuta*) to collect; (*stipendio*) to draw, collect; (*fig: successo etc*) to win, earn; **riscuotersi** *vr*: **riscuotersi (da)** to shake o.s. (out of), rouse o.s. (from); **~ un assegno** to cash a cheque

'rise *etc vb vedi* **ridere**

risenti'mento *sm* resentment

risen'tire *vt* to hear again; (*provare*) to feel ■ *vi*: **~ di** to feel (*o* show) the effects of; **risentirsi** *vr*: **risentirsi di** *o* **per** to take offence (*Brit*) *o* offense (*US*) at, resent

risen'tito, -a *ag* resentful

ri'serbo *sm* reserve

ri'serva *sf* reserve; (*di caccia, pesca*) preserve; (*restrizione, di indigeni*) reservation; (*Calcio*) substitute; **fare ~ di** (*cibo*) to get in a supply of; **tenere di ~** to keep in reserve; **con le dovute riserve** with certain reservations; **ha accettato con la ~ di potersi ritirare** he accepted with the proviso that he could pull out

riser'vare *vt* (*tenere in serbo*) to keep, put aside; (*prenotare*) to book, reserve; **riservarsi** *vr*: **riservarsi di fare qc** to intend to do sth; **riservarsi il diritto di fare qc** to reserve the right to do sth

riserva'tezza [riserva'tettsa] *sf* reserve

riser'vato, -a *ag* (*prenotato: fig: persona*) reserved; (*confidenziale*) confidential; (*lettera, informazione*) confidential

'risi *etc vb vedi* **ridere**

ri'sibile *ag* laughable

risi'cato, -a *ag* (*vittoria etc*) very narrow

risi'edere *vi*: **~ a** *o* **in** to reside in

'risma *sf* (*di carta*) ream; (*fig*) kind, sort

'riso¹, -a *pp di* **ridere** ■ *sm* (*pl(f)* **risa**) (*il ridere*): **un ~** a laugh; **il ~** laughter; **uno scoppio di risa** a burst of laughter

'riso² *sm* (*pianta*) rice

riso'lino *sm* snigger

risolle'vare *vt* (*sollevare di nuovo: testa*) to raise again, lift up again; (*fig: questione*) to raise again, bring up again; (*morale*) to raise; **risollevarsi** *vr* (*da terra*) to rise again; (*fig: da malattia*) to recover; ~ **le sorti di qc** to improve the chances of sth

ri'solsi *etc vb vedi* **risolvere**

ri'solto, -a *pp di* **risolvere**

risolu'tezza [risolu'tettsa] *sf* determination

risolu'tivo, -a *ag* (*determinante*) decisive; (*che risolve*): **arrivare ad una formula risolutiva** to come up with a formula to resolve a situation

riso'luto, -a *ag* determined, resolute

risoluzi'one [risolut'tsjone] *sf* solving *no pl*; (*Mat*) solution; (*decisione, di immagine*) resolution; (*Dir: di contratto*) annulment, cancellation

ri'solvere *vt* (*difficoltà, controversia*) to resolve; (*problema*) to solve; (*decidere*): ~ **di fare** to resolve to do; **risolversi** *vr* (*decidersi*): **risolversi a fare** to make up one's mind to do; (*andare a finire*): **risolversi in** to end up, turn out; **risolversi in nulla** to come to nothing

risol'vibile *ag* solvable

riso'nanza [riso'nantsa] *sf* resonance; **aver vasta** ~ (*fig: fatto etc*) to be known far and wide; ~ **magnetica** magnetic resonance

riso'nare *vt, vi* = **risuonare**

ri'sorgere [ri'sordʒere] *vi* to rise again

risorgimen'tale [risordʒimen'tale] *ag* of the Risorgimento

risorgi'mento [risordʒi'mento] *sm* revival; **il R~** (*Storia*) the Risorgimento; *see note*

● **RISORGIMENTO**
●
● The *Risorgimento*, the period stretching
● from the early nineteenth century to 1861
● and the proclamation of the Kingdom of
● Italy, saw considerable upheaval and
● change. Political and personal freedom
● took on new importance as the events of
● the French Revolution unfolded. The
● *Risorgimento* paved the way for the
● unification of Italy in 1871.

ri'sorsa *sf* expedient, resort; **risorse** *sfpl* (*naturali, finanziarie etc*) resources; **persona piena di risorse** resourceful person

ri'sorsi *etc vb vedi* **risorgere**

ri'sorto, -a *pp di* **risorgere**

ri'sotto *sm* (*Cuc*) risotto

risparmi'are *vt* to save; (*non uccidere*) to spare ■ *vi* to save; ~ **qc a qn** to spare sb sth; ~

fatica/fiato to save one's energy/breath; **risparmiati il disturbo** *o* **la fatica** (*anche ironico*) save yourself the trouble

risparmia'tore, -'trice *sm/f* saver

ris'parmio *sm* saving *no pl*; (*denaro*) savings *pl*

rispecchi'are [rispek'kjare] *vt* to reflect; **rispecchiarsi** *vr* to be reflected

rispe'dire *vt* to send back; ~ **qc a qn** to send sth back to sb

rispet'tabile *ag* respectable; (*considerevole: somma*) sizeable, considerable

rispet'tare *vt* to respect; (*legge*) to obey, comply with, abide by; (*promessa*) to keep; **farsi** ~ to command respect; ~ **le distanze** to keep one's distance; ~ **i tempi** to keep to schedule; **ogni medico che si rispetti** every self-respecting doctor

rispettiva'mente *av* respectively

rispet'tivo, -a *ag* respective

ris'petto *sm* respect; **rispetti** *smpl* (*saluti*) respects, regards; ~ **a** (*in paragone a*) compared to; (*in relazione a*) as regards, as for; ~ **(di** *o* **per)** (*norme, leggi*) observance (of), compliance (with); **portare** ~ **a qn/qc** to have *o* feel respect for sb/sth; **mancare di** ~ **a qn** to be disrespectful to sb; **con** ~ **parlando** with respect, if you will excuse my saying so; **(porga) i miei rispetti alla signora** (give) my regards to your wife

rispet'toso, -a *ag* respectful

risplen'dente *ag* (*giornata, sole*) bright, shining; (*occhi*) sparkling

ris'plendere *vi* to shine

rispon'dente *ag*: ~ **a** in keeping *o* conformity with

rispon'denza [rispon'dɛntsa] *sf* correspondence

ris'pondere *vi* to answer, reply; (*freni*) to respond; ~ **a** (*domanda*) to answer, reply to; (*persona*) to answer; (*invito*) to reply to; (*provocazione: veicolo, apparecchio*) to respond to; (*corrispondere a*) to correspond to; (*speranze, bisogno*) to answer; ~ **a qn di qc** (*essere responsabile*) to be answerable to sb for sth

rispo'sarsi *vr* to get married again, remarry

ris'posto, -a *pp di* **rispondere** ■ *sf* answer, reply; **in risposta a** in reply to; **dare una risposta** to give an answer; **diamo risposta alla vostra lettera del ...** in reply to your letter of ...

'rissa *sf* brawl

ris'soso, -a *ag* quarrelsome

rist. *abbr* = **ristampa**

ristabi'lire *vt* to re-establish, restore; (*persona: riposo etc*) to restore to health; **ristabilirsi** *vr* to recover

rista'gnare [ristaɲ'ɲare] *vi* (*acqua*) to become stagnant; (*sangue*) to cease flowing; (*fig: industria*) to stagnate

ris'tagno [ris'taɲɲo] *sm* stagnation; **c'è un ~ delle vendite** business is slack

ris'tampa *sf* reprinting *no pl*; reprint

ristam'pare *vt* to reprint

risto'rante *sm* restaurant

risto'rare *vt* (*persona, forze*) to revive, refresh; **ristorarsi** *vr* (*rifocillarsi*) to have something to eat and drink; (*riposarsi*) to rest, have a rest

ristora'tore, -'trice *ag* refreshing, reviving ■ *sm* (*gestore di ristorante*) restaurateur

ris'toro *sm* (*bevanda, cibo*) refreshment; **posto di ~** (*Ferr*) buffet, snack bar; **servizio di ~** (*Ferr*) refreshments *pl*

ristret'tezza [ristret'tettsa] *sf* (*strettezza*) narrowness; (*fig: scarsezza*) scarcity, lack; (: *meschinità*) meanness; **ristrettezze** *sfpl* (*povertà*) poverty *sg*

ris'tretto, -a *pp di* **restringere** ■ *ag* (*racchiuso*) enclosed, hemmed in; (*angusto*) narrow; (*limitato*): **~ (a)** restricted *o* limited (to); (*Cuc: brodo*) thick; (*caffè*) extra strong

ristruttu'rare *vt* (*azienda*) to reorganize; (*edificio*) to restore; (*appartamento*) to alter; (*crema, balsamo*) to repair

ristrutturazi'one [ristrutturat'tsjone] *sf* reorganization; restoration; alteration

risucchi'are [risuk'kjare] *vt* to suck in

ri'succhio [ri'sukkjo] *sm* (*di acqua*) undertow, pull; (*di aria*) suction

risul'tare *vi* (*dimostrarsi*) to prove (to be), turn out (to be); (*riuscire*): **~ vincitore** to emerge as the winner; **~ da** (*provenire*) to result from, be the result of; **mi risulta che …** I understand that …, as far as I know …; **(ne) risulta che …** it follows that …; **non mi risulta** not as far as I know

risul'tato *sm* result

risuo'nare *vi* (*rimbombare*) to resound

risurrezi'one [risurret'tsjone] *sf* (*Rel*) resurrection

risusci'tare [risuʃʃi'tare] *vt* to resuscitate, restore to life; (*fig*) to revive, bring back ■ *vi* to rise (from the dead)

risvegli'are [rizveʎ'ʎare] *vt* (*gen*) to wake up, waken; (*fig: interesse*) to stir up, arouse; (*curiosità*) to arouse; (*fig: dall'inerzia etc*): **~ qn (da)** to rouse sb (from); **risvegliarsi** *vr* to wake up, awaken; (*fig: interesse, curiosità*) to be aroused

ris'veglio [riz'veʎʎo] *sm* waking up; (*fig*) revival

ris'volto *sm* (*di giacca*) lapel; (*di pantaloni*) turn-up (Brit), cuff (US); (*di manica*) cuff; (*di tasca*) flap; (*di libro*) inside flap; (*fig*) implication

ritagli'are [ritaʎ'ʎare] *vt* (*tagliar via*) to cut out

ri'taglio [ri'taʎʎo] *sm* (*di giornale*) cutting, clipping; (*di stoffa etc*) scrap; **nei ritagli di tempo** in one's spare time

ritar'dare *vi* (*persona, treno*) to be late; (*orologio*) to be slow ■ *vt* (*rallentare*) to slow down; (*impedire*) to delay, hold up; (*differire*) to postpone, delay; **~ il pagamento** to defer payment

ritarda'tario, -a *sm/f* latecomer

ritar'dato, -a *ag* (*Psic*) retarded

ri'tardo *sm* delay; (*di persona aspettata*) lateness *no pl*; (*fig: mentale*) backwardness; **in ~** late

ri'tegno [ri'teɲɲo] *sm* restraint

ritem'prare *vt* (*forze, spirito*) to restore

rite'nere *vt* (*trattenere*) to hold back; (: *somma*) to deduct; (*giudicare*) to consider, believe

ri'tengo *vb vedi* **ritenere**

ri'tenni *vb vedi* **ritenere**

riten'tare *vt* to try again, make another attempt at

rite'nuta *sf* (*sul salario*) deduction; **~ d'acconto** advance deduction of tax; **~ alla fonte** (*Fisco*) taxation at source

riterrò *etc vb vedi* **ritenere**

ritiene *etc vb vedi* **ritenere**

riti'rare *vt* to withdraw; (*Pol: richiamare*) to recall; (*andare a prendere: pacco etc*) to collect, pick up; **ritirarsi** *vr* to withdraw; (*da un'attività*) to retire; (*stoffa*) to shrink; (*marea*) to recede; **gli hanno ritirato la patente** they disqualified him from driving (Brit), they took away his licence (Brit) *o* license (US); **ritirarsi a vita privata** to withdraw from public life

riti'rata *sf* (*Mil*) retreat; (*latrina*) lavatory

riti'rato, -a *ag* secluded; **fare vita ritirata** to live in seclusion

ri'tiro *sm* (*di truppe, candidati, soldi*) withdrawal; (*di pacchi*) collection; (*di passaporto*) confiscation; (*da attività*) retirement; (*luogo appartato*) retreat

rit'mato, -a *ag* rhythmic(al)

'ritmico, -a, ci, che *ag* rhythmic(al)

'ritmo *sm* rhythm; (*fig*) rate; (*della vita*) pace, tempo; **al ~ di** at a speed *o* rate of; **ballare al ~ di valzer** to waltz

'rito *sm* rite; **di ~** usual, customary

ritoc'care *vt* (*disegno, fotografia*) to touch up; (*testo*) to alter

ri'tocco, -chi *sm* touching up *no pl*; alteration

ri'torcere [ri'tɔrtʃere] *vt* (*filato*) to twist; (*fig: accusa, insulto*) to throw back; **ritorcersi** *vr* (*tornare a danno di*): **ritorcersi contro** to turn against

ritor'nare *vi* to return, go *o* come back; (*ripresentarsi*) to recur; (*ridiventare*): **~ ricco** to

r

become rich again ■ vt (*restituire*) to return, give back

ritor'nello sm refrain

ri'torno sm return; **durante il (viaggio di)** ~ on the return trip, on the way back; **al** ~ (*tornando*) on the way back; **essere di** ~ to be back; **far** ~ to return; **avere un** ~ **di fiamma** (*Aut*) to backfire; (*fig: persona*) to be back in love again

ritorsi'one sf (*rappresaglia*) retaliation

ri'torto, -a pp di **ritorcere** ■ ag (*cotone, corda*) twisted

ri'trarre vt (*trarre indietro, via*) to withdraw; (*distogliere: sguardo*) to turn away; (*rappresentare*) to portray, depict; (*ricavare*) to get, obtain; **ritrarsi** vr to move back

ritrat'tare vt (*disdire*) to retract, take back; (*trattare nuovamente*) to deal with again

ritrattazi'one [ritrattat'tsjone] sf withdrawal

ritrat'tista, -i, e sm/f portrait painter

ri'tratto, -a pp di **ritrarre** ■ sm portrait

ritro'sia sf (*riluttanza*) reluctance, unwillingness; (*timidezza*) shyness

ri'troso, -a ag (*restio*): ~ **(a)** reluctant (to); (*schivo*) shy; **andare a** ~ to go backwards

ritrova'mento sm (*di cadavere, oggetto smarrito etc*) finding; (*oggetto ritrovato*) find

ritro'vare vt to find; (*salute*) to regain; (*persona*) to find; to meet again; **ritrovarsi** vr (*essere, capitare*) to find o.s.; (*raccapezzarsi*) to find one's way; (*con senso reciproco*) to meet (again)

ritro'vato sm discovery

ri'trovo sm meeting place; ~ **notturno** night club

'ritto, -a ag (*in piedi*) standing, on one's feet; (*levato in alto*) erect, raised; (*capelli*) standing on end; (*posto verticalmente*) upright

ritu'ale ag, sm ritual

riuni'one sf (*adunanza*) meeting; (*riconciliazione*) reunion; **essere in** ~ to be at a meeting

riu'nire vt (*ricongiungere*) to join (together); (*riconciliare*) to reunite, bring together (again); **riunirsi** vr (*adunarsi*) to meet; (*tornare a stare insieme*) to be reunited; **siamo qui riuniti per festeggiare il vostro anniversario** we are gathered here to celebrate your anniversary

riu'scire [riuʃ'ʃire] vi (*uscire di nuovo*) to go out again, go back out; (*aver esito: fatti, azioni*) to go, turn out; (*aver successo*) to succeed, be successful; (*essere, apparire*) to be, prove; (*raggiungere il fine*) to manage, succeed; ~ **a fare qc** to manage o be able to do sth; **questo mi riesce nuovo** this is new to me

riu'scita [riuʃ'ʃita] sf (*esito*) result, outcome; (*buon esito*) success

riutiliz'zare [riutilid'dzare] vt to use again, re-use

'riva sf (*di fiume*) bank; (*di lago, mare*) shore; **in** ~ **al mare** on the (sea) shore

ri'vale ag rival cpd ■ sm/f rival; **non avere rivali** (*anche fig*) to be unrivalled

rivaleggi'are [rivaled'dʒare] vi to compete, vie

rivalità sf rivalry

ri'valsa sf (*rivincita*) revenge; (*risarcimento*) compensation; **prendersi una** ~ **su qn** to take revenge on sb

rivalu'tare vt (*Econ*) to revalue

rivalutazi'one [rivalutat'tsjone] sf (*Econ*) revaluation; (*fig*) re-evaluation

rivan'gare vt (*ricordi etc*) to dig up (again)

rive'dere vt to see again; (*ripassare*) to revise; (*verificare*) to check

rivedrò etc vb vedi **rivedere**

rive'lare vt to reveal; (*divulgare*) to reveal, disclose; (*dare indizio*) to reveal, show; **rivelarsi** vr (*manifestarsi*) to be revealed; **rivelarsi onesto** etc to prove to be honest etc

rivela'tore, -'trice ag revealing ■ sm (*Tecn*) detector; (*Fot*) developer

rivelazi'one [rivelat'tsjone] sf revelation

ri'vendere vt (*vendere: di nuovo*) to resell, sell again; (*al dettaglio*) to retail, sell retail

rivendi'care vt to claim, demand

rivendicazi'one [rivendikat'tsjone] sf claim; **rivendicazioni salariali** wage claims

ri'vendita sf (*bottega*) retailer's (shop); ~ **di tabacchi** tobacconist's (shop)

rivendi'tore, -'trice sm/f retailer; ~ **autorizzato** authorized dealer

riverbe'rare vt to reflect

ri'verbero sm (*di luce, calore*) reflection; (*di suono*) reverberation

rive'rente ag reverent, respectful

rive'renza [rive'rentsa] sf reverence; (*inchino*) bow; curtsey

rive'rire vt (*rispettare*) to revere; (*salutare*) to pay one's respects to

river'sare vt (*anche fig*) to pour; **riversarsi** vr (*fig: persone*) to pour out

rivesti'mento sm covering; coating

rives'tire vt to dress again; (*ricoprire*) to cover; (*con vernice*) to coat; (*fig: carica*) to hold; **rivestirsi** vr to get dressed again, to change (one's clothes); ~ **di piastrelle** to tile

ri'vidi etc vb vedi **rivedere**

rivi'era sf coast; **la** ~ **italiana** the Italian Riviera

ri'vincita [ri'vintʃita] sf (*Sport*) return match; (*fig*) revenge; **prendersi la** ~ **(su qn)** to take o get one's revenge (on sb)

rivis'suto, -a *pp di* **rivivere**

ri'vista *sf* review; (*periodico*) magazine, review; (*Teat*) revue; variety show

ri'visto, -a *pp di* **rivedere**

rivitaliz'zante [rivitalid'dzante] *ag* revitalizing

rivitaliz'zare [rivitalid'dzare] *vt* to revitalize

ri'vivere *vi* (*riacquistare forza*) to come alive again; (*tornare in uso*) to be revived ■ *vt* to relive

'rivo *sm* stream

ri'volgere [ri'vɔldʒere] *vt* (*attenzione, sguardo*) to turn, direct; (*parole*) to address; **rivolgersi** *vr* to turn round; (*fig: dirigersi per informazioni*): **rivolgersi a** to go and see, go and speak to; **~ un'accusa/una critica a qn** to accuse/ criticize sb; **rivolgersi all'ufficio competente** to apply to the office concerned

rivolgi'mento [rivoldʒi'mento] *sm* upheaval

ri'volsi *etc vb vedi* **rivolgere**

ri'volta *sf* revolt, rebellion

rivol'tante *ag* revolting, disgusting

rivol'tare *vt* to turn over; (*con l'interno all'esterno*) to turn inside out; (*disgustare: stomaco*) to upset, turn; (*fig*) to revolt, disgust; **rivoltarsi** *vr* (*ribellarsi*): **rivoltarsi (a)** to rebel (against)

rivol'tella *sf* revolver

ri'volto, -a *pp di* **rivolgere**

rivol'toso, -a *ag* rebellious ■ *sm/f* rebel

rivoluzio'nare [rivoluttsjo'nare] *vt* to revolutionize

rivoluzio'nario, a [rivoluttsjo'narjo] *ag, sm/f* revolutionary

rivoluzi'one [rivolut'tsjone] *sf* revolution

riz'zare [rit'tsare] *vt* to raise, erect; **rizzarsi** *vr* to stand up; (*capelli*) to stand on end; **rizzarsi in piedi** to stand up, get to one's feet

RN *sigla* = **Rimini**

RNA *sigla m* RNA (= *ribonucleic acid*)

RO *sigla* = **Rovigo**

'roba *sf* stuff, things *pl*; (*possessi, beni*) belongings *pl*, things *pl*, possessions *pl*; **~ da mangiare** things to eat, food; **~ da matti!** it's sheer madness *o* lunacy!

robi'vecchi [robi'vɛkki] *sm/f inv* junk dealer

'robot *sm inv* robot

ro'botica *sf* robotics *sg*

robus'tezza [robus'tettsa] *sf* (*di persona, pianta*) robustness, sturdiness; (*di edificio, ponte*) soundness

ro'busto, -a *ag* robust, sturdy; (*solido: catena*) strong; (*edificio, ponte*) sound, solid; (*vino*) full-bodied

'rocca, -che *sf* fortress

rocca'forte *sf* stronghold

roc'chetto [rok'ketto] *sm* reel, spool

'roccia, -ce ['rɔttʃa] *sf* rock; **fare ~** (*Sport*) to go rock climbing

roccia'tore, -'trice [rottʃa'tore] *sm/f* rock climber

rocci'oso, -a [rot'tʃoso] *ag* rocky; **le Montagne Rocciose** the Rocky Mountains

'roco, -a, chi, che *ag* hoarse

ro'daggio [ro'daddʒo] *sm* running (*Brit*) *o* breaking (*US*) in; **in ~** running *o* breaking in; **periodo di ~** (*fig*) period of adjustment

'Rodano *sm*: **il ~** the Rhone

ro'dare *vt* (*Aut, Tecn*) to run (*Brit*) *o* break (*US*) in

ro'deo *sm* rodeo

'rodere *vt* to gnaw (at); (*distruggere poco a poco*) to eat into

'Rodi *sf* Rhodes

rodi'tore *sm* (*Zool*) rodent

rodo'dendro *sm* rhododendron

'rogito ['rɔdʒito] *sm* (*Dir*) (notary's) deed

'rogna ['rɔɲɲa] *sf* (*Med*) scabies *sg*; (*di animale*) mange; (*fig*) bother, nuisance

ro'gnone [roɲ'ɲone] *sm* (*Cuc*) kidney

ro'gnoso, -a [roɲ'ɲoso] *ag* (*persona*) scabby; (*animale*) mangy; (*fig*) troublesome

'rogo, -ghi *sm* (*per cadaveri*) (funeral) pyre; (*supplizio*): **il ~** the stake

rol'lare *vi* (*Naut, Aer*) to roll

rol'lino *sm* = **rullino**

rol'lio *sm* roll(ing)

'Roma *sf* Rome

roma'gnolo, -a [romaɲ'ɲɔlo] *ag* of (*o* from) Romagna

roma'nesco, -a, schi, sche *ag* Roman ■ *sm* Roman dialect

Roma'nia *sf*: **la ~** Romania

ro'manico, -a, ci, che *ag* Romanesque

ro'mano, -a *ag, sm/f* Roman; **fare alla romana** to go Dutch

romantiche'ria [romantike'ria] *sf* sentimentality

romanti'cismo [romanti'tʃizmo] *sm* romanticism

ro'mantico, -a, ci, che *ag* romantic

ro'manza [ro'mandza] *sf* (*Mus, Letteratura*) romance

roman'zare [roman'dzare] *vt* to romanticize

roman'zesco, -a, schi, sche [roman'dzesko] *ag* (*stile, personaggi*) fictional; (*fig*) storybook *cpd*

romanzi'ere [roman'dzjɛre] *sm* novelist

ro'manzo, -a [ro'mandzo] *ag* (*Ling*) romance *cpd* ■ *sm* (*medievale*) romance; (*moderno*) novel; **~ d'amore** love story; **~ d'appendice** serial (story); **~ cavalleresco** tale of chivalry; **~ poliziesco, ~ giallo** detective story; **~ rosa** romantic novel

r

rom'bare vi to rumble, thunder, roar

'rombo sm rumble, thunder, roar; (Mat) rhombus; (Zool) turbot

ro'meno, -a ag, sm/f, sm = **rumeno**

'rompere vt to break; (conversazione, fidanzamento) to break off ∎ vi to break; **rompersi** vr to break; **mi rompe le scatole** (fam) he (o she) is a pain in the neck; **rompersi un braccio** to break an arm

rompi'capo sm worry, headache; (indovinello) puzzle; (in enigmistica) brain-teaser

rompi'collo sm daredevil

rompighi'accio [rompi'gjattʃo] sm (Naut) icebreaker

rompis'catole sm/f inv (fam) pest, pain in the neck

'ronda sf (Mil) rounds pl, patrol

ron'della sf (Tecn) washer

'rondine sf (Zool) swallow

ron'done sm (Zool) swift

ron'fare vi (russare) to snore

ron'zare [ron'dzare] vi to buzz, hum

ron'zino [ron'dzino] sm (peg: cavallo) nag

ron'zio, -ii [ron'dzio] sm buzzing, humming; **~ auricolare** (Med) tinnitus sg

'rosa sf rose; (fig: gruppo): **~ dei candidati** list of candidates ∎ ag inv, sm pink

ro'saio sm (pianta) rosebush, rose tree; (giardino) rose garden

ro'sario sm (Rel) rosary

ro'sato, -a ag pink, rosy ∎ sm (vino) rosé (wine)

ro'seo, -a ag (anche fig) rosy

ro'seto sm rose garden

ro'setta sf (diamante) rose-cut diamond; (rondella) washer

'rosi vb vedi **rodere**

rosicchi'are [rosik'kjare] vt to gnaw (at); (mangiucchiare) to nibble (at)

rosma'rino sm rosemary

'roso, -a pp di **rodere**

roso'lare vt (Cuc) to brown

roso'lia sf (Med) German measles sg, rubella

'rospo sm (Zool) toad; **mandar giù** o **ingoiare un** o **il ~** (fig) to swallow a bitter pill; **sputa il ~!** out with it!

ros'setto sm (per labbra) lipstick; (per guance) rouge

ros'siccio, -a, ci, ce [ros'sittʃo] ag reddish

'rosso, -a ag, sm, sm/f red; **diventare ~ (per la vergogna)** to blush o go red (with o for shame); **il mar R~** the Red Sea; **~ d'uovo** egg yolk

ros'sore sm flush, blush

rosticce'ria [rostittʃe'ria] sf shop selling roast meat and other cooked food

'rostro sm rostrum; (becco) beak

ro'tabile ag (percorribile): **strada ~** roadway; (Ferr): **materiale ~** rolling stock

ro'taia sf rut, track; (Ferr) rail

ro'tare vt, vi to rotate

rota'tivo, -a ag rotating, rotation cpd

rotazi'one [rotat'tsjone] sf rotation

rote'are vt, vi to whirl; **~ gli occhi** to roll one's eyes

ro'tella sf small wheel; (di mobile) castor

roto'calco, -chi sm (Tip) rotogravure; (rivista) illustrated magazine

roto'lare vt, vi to roll; **rotolarsi** vr to roll (about)

roto'lio sm rolling

'rotolo sm (di carta, stoffa) roll; (di corda) coil; **andare a rotoli** (fig) to go to rack and ruin; **mandare a rotoli** (fig) to ruin

ro'tondo, -a ag round ∎ sf rotunda

ro'tore sm rotor

'rotta sf (Aer, Naut) course, route; (Mil) rout; **a ~ di collo** at breakneck speed; **essere in ~ con qn** to be on bad terms with sb; **fare ~ su** o **per** o **verso** to head for o towards; **cambiare ~** (anche fig) to change course; **in ~ di collisione** on a collision course; **ufficiale di ~** navigator, navigating officer

rotta'mare vt to scrap old vehicles in return for incentives

rotta'zione [rottamat'tsjone] sf the scrapping of old vehicles in return for incentives

rot'tame sm fragment, scrap, broken bit; **rottami** smpl (di nave aereo etc) wreckage sg; **rottami di ferro** scrap iron sg

'rotto, -a pp di **rompere** ∎ ag broken; (calzoni) torn, split; (persona: pratico, resistente): **~ a** accustomed o inured to ∎ sm: **per il ~ della cuffia** by the skin of one's teeth; **rotti** smpl: **20 euro e rotti** 20-odd euros

rot'tura sf (azione) breaking no pl; (di rapporti) breaking off; (Med) fracture, break

rou'lotte [ru'lɔt] sf inv caravan

ro'vente ag red-hot

'rovere sm oak

ro'vescia [ro'veʃʃa] sf: **alla ~** upside-down, inside-out; **oggi mi va tutto alla ~** everything is going wrong (for me) today

rovesci'are [roveʃ'ʃare] vt (versare in giù) to pour; (accidentalmente) to spill; (capovolgere) to turn upside down; (gettare a terra) to knock down; (fig: governo) to overthrow; (piegare all'indietro: testa) to throw back; **rovesciarsi** vr (sedia, macchina) to overturn; (barca) to capsize; (liquido) to spill; (fig: situazione) to be reversed

ro'vescio, sci [ro'veʃʃo] sm other side, wrong side; (della mano) back; (di moneta) reverse; (pioggia) sudden downpour; (fig) setback; (Maglia: anche: **punto rovescio**) purl (stitch);

(Tennis) backhand (stroke); **a ~** (sottosopra) upside-down; (con l'esterno all'interno) inside-out; **capire qc a ~** to misunderstand sth; **~ di fortuna** setback

ro'vina sf ruin; **rovine** sfpl ruins; **andare in ~** (andare a pezzi) to collapse; (fig) to go to rack and ruin; **mandare qc/qn in ~** to ruin sth/sb

rovi'nare vi to collapse, fall down ■ vt (far cadere giù: casa) to demolish; (danneggiare: fig) to ruin

rovi'nato, -a ag ruined, damaged; (fig: persona) ruined

rovi'noso, -a ag ruinous

rovis'tare vt (casa) to ransack; (tasche) to rummage in (o through)

'rovo sm (Bot) blackberry o bramble bush

roz'zezza [rod'dzettsa] sf roughness, coarseness

'rozzo, -a ['roddzo] ag rough, coarse

RP sigla fpl vedi **relazioni pubbliche**

R.R. abbr (Posta) = **ricevuta di ritorno**

Rr abbr (Posta) = **raccomandata con ricevuta di ritorno**

RSVP abbr (= répondez s'il vous plaît) RSVP

'ruba sf: **andare a ~** to sell like hot cakes

rubacu'ori sm inv ladykiller

ru'bare vt to steal; **~ qc a qn** to steal sth from sb

rubi'condo, -a ag ruddy

rubi'netto sm tap, faucet (US)

ru'bino sm ruby

ru'bizzo, -a [ru'bittso] ag lively, sprightly

'rublo sm rouble

ru'brica, -che sf (di giornale: colonna) column; (: pagina) page; (quadernetto) index book; (per indirizzi) address book

'rude ag tough, rough

'rudere sm (rovina) ruins pl

rudimen'tale ag rudimentary, basic

rudi'menti smpl rudiments; basic principles

ruffi'ano sm pimp

'ruga, -ghe sf wrinkle

'ruggine ['ruddʒine] sf rust

rug'gire [rud'dʒire] vi to roar

rug'gito [rud'dʒito] sm roar

rugi'ada [ru'dʒada] sf dew

ru'goso, -a ag wrinkled; (scabro: superficie etc) rough

rul'lare vi (tamburo, nave) to roll; (aereo) to taxi

rul'lino sm (Fot) roll of film, spool

rul'lio, -ii sm (di tamburi) roll

'rullo sm (di tamburi) roll; (arnese cilindrico, Tip) roller; **~ compressore** steam roller; **~ di pellicola** roll of film

rum sm rum

ru'meno, -a ag, sm/f, sm Romanian

rumi'nante sm (Zool) ruminant

rumi'nare vt (Zool) to ruminate; (fig) to ruminate on o over, chew over

ru'more sm: **un ~** a noise, a sound; **il ~** noise; **fare ~** to make a noise; **un ~ di passi** the sound of footsteps; **la notizia ha fatto molto ~** (fig) the news aroused great interest

rumoreggi'are [rumored'dʒare] vi (tuono etc) to rumble; (fig: folla) to clamour (Brit), clamor (US)

rumo'roso, -a ag noisy

ru'olo sm (Teat, fig) role, part; (elenco) roll, register, list; **di ~** permanent, on the permanent staff; **professore di ~** (Ins) ≈ lecturer with tenure; **fuori ~** (personale, insegnante) temporary

ru'ota sf wheel; **a ~** (forma) circular; **~ anteriore/posteriore** front/back wheel; **andare a ~ libera** to freewheel; **parlare a ~ libera** (fig) to speak freely; **~ di scorta** spare wheel

ruo'tare vt, vi = **rotare**

'rupe sf cliff, rock

ru'pestre ag rocky

ru'pia sf rupee

'ruppi etc vb vedi **rompere**

ru'rale ag rural, country cpd

ru'scello [ruʃʃello] sm stream

'ruspa sf excavator

rus'pante ag (pollo) free-range

rus'sare vi to snore

'Russia sf: **la ~** Russia

'russo, -a ag, sm/f, sm Russian

'rustico, -a, ci, che ag country cpd, rural; (arredamento) rustic; (fig) rough, unrefined ■ sm (fabbricato: per attrezzi) shed; (: per abitazione) farm labourer's (Brit) o farmhand's cottage

'ruta sf (Bot) rue

rut'tare vi to belch

'rutto sm belch

'ruvido, -a ag rough, coarse

ruzzo'lare [ruttso'lare] vi to tumble down

ruzzo'lone [ruttso'lone] sm tumble, fall

ruzzo'loni [ruttso'loni] av: **cadere ~** to tumble down; **fare le scale ~** to tumble down the stairs

r

Ss

S, s ['esse] *sf o m* (*lettera*) S, s; **S come Savona** ≈ S for Sugar

s *abbr* (= *secondo*) sec.

S. *abbr* (= *sud*) S; (= *santo*) St

SA *sigla* = **Salerno** ■ *abbr* = **società anonima**

sa *vb vedi* **sapere**

sab. *abbr* (= *sabato*) Sat.

'**sabato** *sm* Saturday; *vedi anche* **martedì**

'**sabbia** *sf* sand; **sabbie mobili** quicksand(s *pl*)

sabbia'tura *sf* (*Med*) sand bath; (*Tecn*) sand-blasting; **fare le sabbiature** to take sand baths

sabbi'oso, -a *ag* sandy

sabo'taggio [sabo'taddʒo] *sm* sabotage

sabo'tare *vt* to sabotage

sabota'tore, -'trice *sm/f* saboteur

'**sacca, -che** *sf* bag; (*bisaccia*) haversack; (*insenatura*) inlet; **~ d'aria** air pocket; **~ da viaggio** travelling bag

sacca'rina *sf* saccharin(e)

sac'cente [sat'tʃɛnte] *sm/f* know-all (*Brit*), know-it-all (*US*)

saccheggi'are [sakked'dʒare] *vt* to sack, plunder

sac'cheggio [sak'keddʒo] *sm* sack(ing)

sac'chetto [sak'ketto] *sm* (small) bag; (small) sack; **~ di carta/di plastica** paper/plastic bag

'**sacco, -chi** *sm* bag; (*per carbone etc*) sack; (*Anat, Biol*) sac; (*tela*) sacking; (*saccheggio*) sack(ing); (*fig: grande quantità*): **un ~ di** lots of, heaps of; **cogliere o prendere qn con le mani nel ~** to catch sb red-handed; **vuotare il ~** to confess, spill the beans; **mettere qn nel ~** to cheat sb; **colazione al ~** packed lunch; **~ a pelo** sleeping bag; **~ per i rifiuti** bin bag (*Brit*), garbage bag (*US*)

sacer'dote [satʃer'dote] *sm* priest

sacer'dozio [satʃer'dɔttsjo] *sm* priesthood

'**Sacra Co'rona U'nita** *sf the mafia in Puglia*

sacra'mento *sm* sacrament

sa'crario *sm* memorial chapel

sacres'tano *sm* = **sagrestano**

sacres'tia *sf* = **sagrestia**

sacrifi'care *vt* to sacrifice; **sacrificarsi** *vr* to sacrifice o.s.; (*privarsi di qc*) to make sacrifices

sacrifi'cato, -a *ag* sacrificed; (*non valorizzato*) wasted; **una vita sacrificata** a life of sacrifice

sacri'ficio [sakri'fitʃo] *sm* sacrifice

sacri'legio [sakri'lɛdʒo] *sm* sacrilege

sa'crilego, -a, ghi, ghe *ag* (*Rel*) sacrilegious

'**sacro, -a** *ag* sacred

sacro'santo, -a *ag* sacrosanct

'**sadico, -a, ci, che** *ag* sadistic ■ *sm/f* sadist

sa'dismo *sm* sadism

sadomaso'chismo [sadomazo'kismo] *sm* sadomasochism

sa'etta *sf* arrow; (*fulmine: anche fig*) thunderbolt

sa'fari *sm inv* safari

sa'gace [sa'gatʃe] *ag* shrewd, sagacious

sa'gacia [sa'gatʃa] *sf* sagacity, shrewdness

sag'gezza [sad'dʒettsa] *sf* wisdom

saggi'are [sad'dʒare] *vt* (*metalli*) to assay; (*fig*) to test

'**saggio, -a, gi, ge** ['saddʒo] *ag* wise ■ *sm* (*persona*) sage; (*operazione sperimentale*) test; (: *dell'oro*) assay; (*fig: prova*) proof; (*campione indicativo*) sample; (*scritto: letterario*) essay; (: *Ins*) written test; **dare ~ di** to give proof of; **in ~** as a sample

sag'gistica [sad'dʒistika] *sf* ≈ non-fiction

Sagit'tario [sadʒit'tarjo] *sm* Sagittarius; **essere del ~** to be Sagittarius

'**sagoma** *sf* (*profilo*) outline, profile; (*forma*) form, shape; (*Tecn*) template; (*bersaglio*) target; (*fig: persona*) character

'**sagra** *sf* festival

sa'grato *sm* churchyard

sagres'tano *sm* sacristan; sexton

sagres'tia *sf* sacristy; (*culto protestante*) vestry

Sa'hara [sa'ara] *sm*: **il (Deserto del) ~** the Sahara (Desert)

sahari'ana [saa'rjana] *sf* bush jacket

'**sai** *vb vedi* **sapere**

'saio sm (Rel) habit

'sala sf hall; (stanza) room; (Cine: di proiezione) screen; ~ **d'aspetto** waiting room; ~ **da ballo** ballroom; ~ **(dei) comandi** control room; ~ **per concerti** concert hall; ~ **per conferenze** (Ins) lecture hall; (in aziende) conference room; ~ **corse** betting shop; ~ **giochi** amusement arcade; ~ **da gioco** gaming room; ~ **macchine** (Naut) engine room; ~ **operatoria** (Med) operating theatre (Brit) o room (US); ~ **da pranzo** dining room; ~ **per ricevimenti** banqueting hall; ~ **delle udienze** (Dir) courtroom

sa'lace [sa'latʃe] ag (spinto, piccante) salacious, saucy; (mordace) cutting, biting

sala'mandra sf salamander

sa'lame sm salami no pl, salami sausage

sala'moia sf (Cuc) brine

sa'lare vt to salt

salari'ale ag wage cpd, pay cpd; **aumento ~** wage o pay increase (Brit) o raise (US)

salari'ato, -a sm/f wage-earner

sa'lario sm pay, wages pl; ~ **base** basic wage; ~ **minimo garantito** guaranteed minimum wage

sa'las'sare vt (Med) to bleed

sa'lasso sm (Med) bleeding, bloodletting; (fig: forte spesa) drain

sala'tino sm cracker, salted biscuit

sa'lato, -a ag (sapore) salty; (Cuc) salted, salt cpd; (fig: discorso etc) biting, sharp; (: prezzi) steep, stiff

sal'dare vt (congiungere) to join, bind; (parti metalliche) to solder; (: con saldatura autogena) to weld; (conto) to settle, pay

salda'tore sm (operaio) solderer; welder; (utensile) soldering iron

salda'trice [salda'tritʃe] sf (macchina) welder, welding machine; ~ **ad arco** arc welder

salda'tura sf soldering; welding; (punto saldato) soldered joint; weld; ~ **autogena** welding; ~ **dolce** soft soldering

sal'dezza [sal'dettsa] sf firmness, strength

'saldo, -a ag (resistente, forte) strong, firm; (fermo) firm, steady, stable; (fig) firm, steadfast ■ sm (svendita) sale; (di conto) settlement; (Econ) balance; **pagare a ~** to pay in full; ~ **attivo** credit; ~ **passivo** deficit; ~ **da riportare** balance carried forward

'sale sm salt; (fig) wit; **sali** smpl (Med: da annusare) smelling salts; **sotto ~** salted; **restare di ~** (fig) to be dumbfounded; **ha poco ~ in zucca** he doesn't have much sense; ~ **da cucina**, ~ **grosso** cooking salt; ~ **da tavola**, ~ **fino** table salt; **sali da bagno** bath salts; **sali minerali** mineral salts; **sali e tabacchi** tobacconist's (shop)

sal'gemma [sal'dʒemma] sm rock salt

'salgo etc vb vedi **salire**

'salice ['salitʃe] sm willow; ~ **piangente** weeping willow

sali'ente ag (fig) salient, main

sali'era sf salt cellar

sa'lino, -a ag saline ■ sf saltworks sg

sa'lire vi to go (o come) up; (aereo etc) to climb, go up; (passeggero) to get on; (sentiero, prezzi, livello) to go up, rise ■ vt (scale, gradini) to go (o come) up; ~ **su** to climb (up); ~ **sul treno/ sull'autobus** to board the train/the bus; ~ **in macchina** to get into the car; ~ **a cavallo** to mount; ~ **al potere** to rise to power; ~ **al trono** to ascend the throne; ~ **alle stelle** (prezzi) to rocket

sali'scendi [saliʃ'ʃendi] sm inv latch

sa'lita sf climb, ascent; (erta) hill, slope; **in ~** uphill

sa'liva sf saliva

'salma sf corpse

sal'mastro, -a ag (acqua) salt cpd; (sapore) salty ■ sm (sapore) salty taste; (odore) salty smell

salmì sm (Cuc) salmi; **lepre in ~** salmi of hare

'salmo sm psalm

sal'mone sm salmon

salmo'nella sf salmonella

Salo'mone: le isole ~ sfpl the Solomon Islands

sa'lone sm (stanza) sitting room, lounge; (in albergo) lounge; (di ricevimento) reception room; (su nave) lounge, saloon; (mostra) show, exhibition; (negozio: di parrucchiere) hairdresser's (salon); ~ **dell'automobile** motor show; ~ **di bellezza** beauty salon

salo'pette [salɔ'pɛt] sf inv dungarees pl

salotti'ero, -a ag mundane

sa'lotto sm lounge, sitting room; (mobilio) lounge suite

sal'pare vi (Naut) to set sail; (anche: **salpare l'ancora**) to weigh anchor

'salsa sf (Cuc) sauce; **in tutte le salse** (fig) in all kinds of ways; ~ **di pomodoro** tomato sauce

sal'sedine sf (del mare, vento) saltiness; (incrostazione) (dried) salt

sal'siccia, -ce [sal'sittʃa] sf pork sausage

salsi'era sf sauceboat (Brit), gravy boat

'salso sm saltiness

sal'tare vi to jump, leap; (esplodere) to blow up, explode; (: valvola) to blow; (venir via) to pop off; (non aver luogo: corso etc) to be cancelled ■ vt to jump (over), leap (over); (fig: pranzo, capitolo) to skip, miss (out); (Cuc) to sauté; **far ~** to blow up; (serratura: forzare) to break; **far ~ il banco** (Gioco) to break the bank; **farsi ~ le cervella** to blow one's brains out; **ma che ti**

salta in mente? what are you thinking of?;
~ **da un argomento all'altro** to jump from
one subject to another; ~ **addosso a qn**
(*aggredire*) to attack sb; ~ **fuori** to jump out,
leap out; (*venire trovato*) to turn up; ~ **fuori
con** (*frase, commento*) to come out with; ~ **giù
da qc** to jump off sth, jump down from sth
saltel'lare *vi* to skip; to hop
sal'tello *sm* hop, little jump
saltim'banco, -chi *sm* acrobat
'**salto** *sm* jump; (*Sport*) jumping; (*dislivello*)
drop; **fare un** ~ to jump, leap; **fare un** ~ **da
qn** to pop over to sb's (place); ~ **in alto/lungo**
high/long jump; ~ **con l'asta** pole vaulting;
~ **mortale** somersault; **un** ~ **di qualità**
(*miglioramento*) significant improvement
saltu'ario, -a *ag* occasional, irregular
sa'lubre *ag* healthy, salubrious
sa'lume *sm* (*Cuc*) cured pork; **salumi** *smpl*
(*insaccati*) cured pork meats
salume'ria *sf* delicatessen
salumi'ere, -a *sm/f* = delicatessen owner
salumi'ficio [salumi'fitʃo] *sm* cured pork
meat factory
salu'tare *ag* healthy; (*fig*) salutary, beneficial
■ *vt* (*per dire buon giorno, fig*) to greet; (*per dire
addio*) to say goodbye to; (*Mil*) to salute; **mi
saluti sua moglie** my regards to your wife
sa'lute *sf* health; ~! (*a chi starnutisce*) bless
you!; (*nei brindisi*) cheers!; **bere alla** ~ **di qn** to
drink (to) sb's health; **la** ~ **pubblica** public
welfare; **godere di buona** ~ to be healthy,
enjoy good health
sa'luto *sm* (*gesto*) wave; (*parola*) greeting; (*Mil*)
salute; **gli ha tolto il** ~ he no longer says
hello to him; **cari saluti, tanti saluti** best
regards; **vogliate gradire i nostri più
distinti saluti** yours faithfully; **i miei
saluti alla sua signora** my regards to your
wife
'**salva** *sf* salvo
salvacon'dotto *sm* (*Mil*) safe-conduct
salvada'naio *sm* moneybox, piggy bank
salvado'regno, -a [salvado'reɲɲo] *ag, sm/f*
Salvadorean
salva'gente [salva'dʒɛnte] *sm* (*Naut*)
lifebuoy; (*pl inv: stradale*) traffic island; ~ **a
ciambella** lifebelt; ~ **a giubbotto** lifejacket
(*Brit*), life preserver (*US*)
salvaguar'dare *vt* to safeguard
salvagu'ardia *sf* safeguard; **a** ~ **di** for the
safeguard of
sal'vare *vt* to save; (*trarre da un pericolo*) to
rescue; (*proteggere*) to protect; **salvarsi** *vr* to
save o.s.; to escape; ~ **la vita a qn** to save sb's
life; ~ **le apparenze** to keep up appearances;
si salvi chi può! every man for himself!

salvas'chermo [salvas'kermo] *sm* (*Inform*)
screen saver
salva'slip® *sm inv* panty liner
salva'taggio [salva'taddʒo] *sm* rescue
salva'tore, -'trice *sm/f* saviour (*Brit*), savior
(*US*)
salvazi'one [salvat'tsjone] *sf* (*Rel*) salvation
'**salve** *escl* (*fam*) hi!
sal'vezza [sal'vettsa] *sf* salvation; (*sicurezza*)
safety
'**salvia** *sf* (*Bot*) sage
salvi'etta *sf* napkin, serviette
'**salvo, -a** *ag* safe, unhurt, unharmed; (*fuori
pericolo*) safe, out of danger ■ *sm:* **in** ~ safe
■ *prep* (*eccetto*) except; ~ **che** *cong* (*a meno che*)
unless; (*eccetto che*) except (that); **mettere qc
in** ~ to put sth in a safe place; **mettersi in** ~
to reach safety; **portare qn in** ~ to lead sb to
safety; ~ **contrordini** barring instructions
to the contrary; ~ **errori e omissioni** errors
and omissions excepted; ~ **imprevisti**
barring accidents
sam'buca *sf* (*liquore*) sambuca (*type of anisette*)
sam'buco *sm* elder (tree)
sa'nare *vt* to heal, cure; (*economia*) to put right
sana'toria *sf* (*Dir*) act of indemnity
sana'torio *sm* sanatorium (*Brit*), sanitarium
(*US*)
san'cire [san'tʃire] *vt* to sanction
'**sandalo** *sm* (*Bot*) sandalwood; (*calzatura*)
sandal
san'gria [san'gria] *sf* (*bibita*) sangria
'**sangue** *sm* blood; **farsi cattivo** ~ to fret, get
worked up; **all'ultimo** ~ (*duello, lotta*) to the
death; **non corre buon** ~ **tra di loro** there's
bad blood between them; **buon** ~ **non
mente!** blood will out!; ~ **freddo** (*fig*) sang-
froid, calm; **a** ~ **freddo** in cold blood
sangu'igno, -a [san'gwiɲɲo] *ag* blood *cpd*;
(*colore*) blood-red
sangui'nante *ag* bleeding
sangui'nare *vi* to bleed
sangui'nario, -a *ag* bloodthirsty
sangui'noso, -a *ag* bloody
sangui'suga, -ghe *sf* leech
sanità *sf* health; (*salubrità*) healthiness;
Ministero della S~ Department of Health;
~ **mentale** sanity; ~ **pubblica** public health
sani'tario, -a *ag* health *cpd*; (*condizioni*)
sanitary ■ *sm* (*Amm*) doctor; **Ufficiale S~**
Health Officer; (**impianti**) **sanitari**
bathroom *o* sanitary fittings
San Ma'rino *sf*: **la Repubblica di** ~ the
Republic of San Marino
'**sanno** *vb vedi* **sapere**
'**sano, -a** *ag* healthy; (*denti, costituzione*)
healthy, sound; (*integro*) whole, unbroken;

(fig: politica, consigli) sound; **~ di mente** sane; **di sana pianta** completely, entirely; **~ e salvo** safe and sound

San Silvestro [san sil'vestro] *sm (giorno)* New Year's Eve

Santi'ago *sf:* **~ (del Cile)** Santiago (de Chile)

santifi'care *vt* to sanctify; *(feste)* to observe

san'tino *sm* holy picture

san'tissimo, -a *ag:* **il S~ Sacramento** the Holy Sacrament; **il Padre S~** *(papa)* the Holy Father

santità *sf* sanctity; holiness; **Sua/Vostra ~** *(titolo di papa)* His/Your Holiness

'santo, -a *ag* holy; *(fig)* saintly; *(seguito da nome proprio: dav sm* **san** + C, **sant'** + V, **santo** + s impura, gn, pn, ps, x, z; dav sf **santa** + C, **sant'** + V) saint ■ *sm/f* saint; **parole sante!** very true!; **tutto il ~ giorno** the whole blessed day, all day long; **non c'è ~ che tenga!** that's no excuse!; **la Santa Sede** the Holy See

san'tone *sm* holy man

santu'ario *sm* sanctuary

sanzio'nare [santsjo'nare] *vt* to sanction

sanzi'one [san'tsjone] *sf* sanction; *(penale, civile)* sanction, penalty; **sanzioni economiche** economic sanctions

sa'pere *vt* to know; *(essere capace di):* **so nuotare** I know how to swim, I can swim ■ *vi:* **~ di** *(aver sapore)* to taste of; *(aver odore)* to smell of ■ *sm* knowledge; **far ~ qc a qn** to inform sb about sth, let sb know sth; **venire a ~ qc (da qn)** to find out o hear about sth (from sb); **non ne vuole più ~ di lei** he doesn't want to have anything more to do with her; **mi sa che non sia vero** I don't think that's true

sapi'ente *ag (dotto)* learned; *(che rivela abilità)* masterly ■ *sm/f* scholar

sapien'tone, -a *sm/f (peg)* know-all (Brit), know-it-all (US)

sapi'enza [sa'pjɛntsa] *sf* wisdom

sa'pone *sm* soap; **~ da barba** shaving soap; **~ da bucato** washing soap; **~ liquido** liquid soap; **~ in scaglie** soapflakes *pl*

sapo'netta *sf* cake o bar o tablet of soap

sa'pore *sm* taste, flavour (Brit), flavor (US)

sapo'rito, -a *ag* tasty; *(fig: arguto)* witty; *(: piccante)* racy

sappi'amo *vb vedi* **sapere**

saprò *etc vb vedi* **sapere**

sapu'tello, -a *sm/f* know-all (Brit), know-it-all (US)

sarà *etc vb vedi* **essere**

sara'banda *sf (fig)* uproar

saraci'nesca, -sche [saratʃi'neska] *sf (serranda)* rolling shutter

sar'casmo *sm* sarcasm *no pl;* sarcastic remark

sar'castico, -a, ci, che *ag* sarcastic

sarchi'are [sar'kjare] *vt (Agr)* to hoe

sar'cofago *(mpl* **sarcofagi** o **sarcofaghi**) *sm* sarcophagus

Sar'degna [sar'deɲɲa] *sf:* **la ~** Sardinia

sar'dina *sf* sardine

'sardo, -a *ag, sm/f* Sardinian

sar'donico, -a, ci, che *ag* sardonic

sa'rei *etc vb vedi* **essere**

SARS *sf (= severe acute respiratory syndrome)* SARS

'sarta *sf vedi* **sarto**

'sartia *sf (Naut)* stay

'sarto, -a *sm/f* tailor/dressmaker; **~ d'alta moda** couturier

sarto'ria *sf* tailor's (shop); dressmaker's (shop); *(casa di moda)* fashion house; *(arte)* couture

sassai'ola *sf* hail of stones

sas'sata *sf* blow with a stone; **tirare una ~ contro** o **a qc/qn** to throw a stone at sth/sb

'sasso *sm* stone; *(ciottolo)* pebble; *(masso)* rock; **restare** o **rimanere di ~** to be dumbfounded

sassofo'nista, -i, e *sm/f* saxophonist

sas'sofono *sm* saxophone

sas'sone *ag, sm/f, sm* Saxon

sas'soso, -a *ag* stony; pebbly

'Satana *sm* Satan

sa'tanico, -a, ci, che *ag* satanic, fiendish

sa'tellite *sm, ag* satellite

'satira *sf* satire

satireggi'are [satired'dʒare] *vt* to satirize ■ *vi (fare della satira)* to be satirical; *(scrivere satire)* to write satires

sa'tirico, -a, ci, che *ag* satiric(al)

sa'tollo, -a *ag* full, replete

satu'rare *vt* to saturate

saturazi'one [saturat'tsjone] *sf* saturation

'saturo, -a *ag* saturated; *(fig):* **~ di** full of; **~ d'acqua** *(terreno)* waterlogged

'SAUB *sigla f (= Struttura Amministrativa Unificata di Base)* state welfare system

'sauna *sf* sauna; **fare la ~** to have o take a sauna

sa'vana *sf* savannah

'savio, -a *ag* wise, sensible ■ *sm* wise man

Sa'voia *sf:* **la ~** Savoy

savoi'ardo, -a *ag* of Savoy, Savoyard ■ *sm (biscotto)* sponge finger

sazi'are [sat'tsjare] *vt* to satisfy, satiate; **saziarsi** *vr (riempirsi di cibo):* **saziarsi (di)** to eat one's fill (of); *(fig):* **saziarsi di** to grow tired o weary of

sazietà [sattsje'ta] *sf* satiety, satiation

'sazio, -a ['sattsjo] *ag:* **~ (di)** sated (with), full (of); *(fig: stufo)* fed up (with), sick (of)

sbada'taggine [zbada'taddʒine] *sf (sventatezza)* carelessness; *(azione)* oversight

sba'dato, -a *ag* careless, inattentive

sbadigli'are [zbadiʎ'ʎare] *vi* to yawn

S

sba'diglio [zba'diλλo] *sm* yawn; **fare uno** ~ to yawn

'sbafo *sm*: **a** ~ at somebody else's expense

sbagli'are [zbaλ'λare] *vt* to make a mistake in, get wrong ■ *vi* (*fare errori*) to make a mistake (*o mistakes*), be mistaken; (*ingannarsi*) to be wrong; (*operare in modo non giusto*) to err; **sbagliarsi** *vr* to make a mistake, be mistaken, be wrong; ~ **la mira/ strada** to miss one's aim/take the wrong road; **scusi, ho sbagliato numero** (*Tel*) sorry, I've got the wrong number; **non c'è da sbagliarsi** there can be no mistake

sbagli'ato, -a [zbaλ'λato] *ag* (*gen*) wrong; (*compito*) full of mistakes; (*conclusione*) erroneous

'sbaglio ['zbaλλo] *sm* mistake, error; (*morale*) error; **fare uno** ~ to make a mistake

sbales'trato, -a *ag* (*persona: scombussolato*) unsettled

sbal'lare *vt* (*merce*) to unpack ■ *vi* (*nel fare un conto*) to overestimate; (*Droga: gergo*) to get high

sbal'lato, -a *ag* (*calcolo*) wrong; (*fam: ragionamento, persona*) screwy

'sballo *sm* (*Droga: gergo*) trip

sballot'tare *vt* to toss (about)

sbalor'dire *vt* to stun, amaze ■ *vi* to be stunned, be amazed

sbalordi'tivo, -a *ag* amazing; (*prezzo*) incredible, absurd

sbal'zare [zbal'tsare] *vt* to throw, hurl; (*fig: da una carica*) to remove, dismiss ■ *vi* (*balzare*) to bounce; (*saltare*) to leap, bound

'sbalzo ['zbaltso] *sm* (*spostamento improvviso*) jolt, jerk; **a sbalzi** jerkily; (*fig*) in fits and starts; **uno** ~ **di temperatura** a sudden change in temperature

sban'care *vt* (*nei giochi*) to break the bank at (*o of*); (*fig*) to ruin, bankrupt

sbanda'mento *sm* (*Naut*) list; (*Aut*) skid; (*fig: di persona*) confusion; **ha avuto un periodo di** ~ he went off the rails for a bit

sban'dare *vi* (*Naut*) to list; (*Aut*) to skid; **sbandarsi** *vr* (*folla*) to disperse; (*truppe*) to scatter; (*fig: famiglia*) to break up

sban'data *sf* (*Aut*) skid; (*Naut*) list; **prendere una** ~ **per qn** (*fig*) to fall for sb

sban'dato, -a *sm/f* mixed-up person

sbandie'rare *vt* (*bandiera*) to wave; (*fig*) to parade, show off

'sbando *sm*: **essere allo** ~ to drift

sbarac'care *vt* (*libri, piatti etc*) to clear (up)

sbaragli'are [zbaraλ'λare] *vt* (*Mil*) to rout; (*in gare sportive etc*) to beat, defeat

sba'raglio [zba'raλλo] *sm*: **gettarsi allo** ~ (*soldato*) to throw o.s. into the fray; (*fig*) to risk everything

sbaraz'zarsi [zbarat'tsarsi] *vr*: ~ **di** to get rid of, rid o.s. of

sbaraz'zino, -a [zbarat'tsino] *ag* impish, cheeky

sbar'bare *vt*, **sbar'barsi** *vr* to shave

sbarba'tello *sm* novice, greenhorn

sbar'care *vt* (*passeggeri*) to disembark; (*merci*) to unload ■ *vi* to disembark

'sbarco *sm* disembarkation; unloading; (*Mil*) landing

'sbarra *sf* bar; (*di passaggio a livello*) barrier; (*Dir*): **mettere/presentarsi alla** ~ to bring/ appear before the court

sbarra'mento *sm* (*stradale*) barrier; (*diga*) dam, barrage; (*Mil*) barrage; (*Pol*) cut-off point (*level of support below which a political party is excluded from representation in Parliament*)

sbar'rare *vt* (*bloccare*) to block, bar; (*cancellare: assegno*) to cross (*Brit*); ~ **il passo** to bar the way; ~ **gli occhi** to open one's eyes wide

sbar'rato, -a *ag* (*porta*) barred; (*passaggio*) blocked, barred; (*strada*) blocked, obstructed; (*occhi*) staring; (*assegno*) crossed (*Brit*)

'sbattere *vt* (*porta*) to bang; (*tappeti, ali, Cuc*) to beat; (*urtare*) to knock, hit ■ *vi* (*porta, finestra*) to bang; (*agitarsi: ali, vele etc*) to flap; ~ **qn fuori/in galera** to throw sb out/into prison; **me ne sbatto!** (*fam*) I don't give a damn!

sbat'tuto, -a *ag* (*viso, aria*) dejected, worn out; (*uovo*) beaten

sba'vare *vi* to dribble; (*colore*) to smear, smudge

sbava'tura *sf* (*di persone*) dribbling; (*di lumache*) slime; (*di rossetto, vernice*) smear

sbelli'carsi *vr*: ~ **dalle risa** to split one's sides laughing

'sberla *sf* slap

sber'leffo *sm*: **fare uno** ~ **a qn** to make a face at sb

sbia'dire *vi* (*anche*: **sbiadirsi**) ■ *vt* to fade

sbia'dito, -a *ag* faded; (*fig*) colourless (*Brit*), colorless (*US*), dull

sbian'care *vt* to whiten; (*tessuto*) to bleach ■ *vi* (*impallidire*) to grow pale *o* white

sbi'eco, -a, chi, che *ag* (*storto*) squint, askew; **di** ~: **guardare qn di** ~ (*fig*) to look askance at sb; **tagliare una stoffa di** ~ to cut material on the bias

sbigot'tire *vt* to dismay, stun ■ *vi* (*anche*: **sbigottirsi**) to be dismayed

sbilanci'are [zbilan'tʃare] *vt* to throw off balance; **sbilanciarsi** *vr* (*perdere l'equilibrio*) to overbalance, lose one's balance; (*fig: compromettersi*) to compromise o.s.

sbi'lenco, -a, chi, che *ag* (*persona*) crooked, misshapen; (*fig: idea, ragionamento*) twisted

sbirci'are [zbir'tʃare] *vt* to cast sidelong glances at, eye

sbirci'ata [zbir'tʃata] *sf*: **dare una ~ a qc** to glance at sth, have a look at sth

'**sbirro** *sm* (*peg*) cop

sbizzar'rirsi [zbiddzar'rirsi] *vr* to indulge one's whims

sbloc'care *vt* to unblock, free; (*freno*) to release; (*prezzi, affitti*) to free from controls; **sbloccarsi** *vr* (*gen*) to become unblocked; (*passaggio, strada*) to clear, become unblocked; **la situazione si è sbloccata** things are moving again

'**sblocco, -chi** *sm* (*vedi vt*) unblocking, freeing; release

sboc'care *vi*: **~ in** (*fiume*) to flow into; (*strada*) to lead into; (*persona*) to come (out) into; (*fig*: *concludersi*) to end (up) in

sboc'cato, -a *ag* (*persona*) foul-mouthed; (*linguaggio*) foul

sbocci'are [zbot'tʃare] *vi* (*fiore*) to bloom, open (out)

'**sbocco, -chi** *sm* (*di fiume*) mouth; (*di strada*) end; (*di tubazione, Comm*) outlet; (*uscita: anche fig*) way out; **una strada senza ~** a dead end; **siamo in una situazione senza sbocchi** there's no way out of this for us

sbocconcel'lare [zbokkontʃel'lare] *vt*: **~ (qc)** to nibble (at sth)

sbollen'tare *vt* (*Cuc*) to parboil

sbol'lire *vi* (*fig*) to cool down, calm down

'**sbornia** *sf* (*fam*): **prendersi una ~** to get plastered

sbor'sare *vt* (*denaro*) to pay out

sbot'tare *vi*: **~ in una risata/per la collera** to burst out laughing/explode with anger

sbotto'nare *vt* to unbutton, undo

sbra'cato, -a *ag* slovenly

sbracci'arsi [zbrat'tʃarsi] *vr* to wave (one's arms about)

sbracci'ato, -a [zbrat'tʃato] *ag* (*camicia*) sleeveless; (*persona*) bare-armed

sbrai'tare *vi* to yell, bawl

sbra'nare *vt* to tear to pieces

sbricio'lare [zbritʃo'lare] *vt*, **sbricio'larsi** *vr* to crumble

sbri'gare *vt* to deal with, get through; (*cliente*) to attend to, deal with; **sbrigarsi** *vr* to hurry (up)

sbriga'tivo, -a *ag* (*persona, modo*) quick, expeditious; (*giudizio*) hasty

sbrina'mento *sm* defrosting

sbri'nare *vt* to defrost

sbrindel'lato, -a *ag* tattered, in tatters

sbrodo'lare *vt* to stain, dirty

sbron'zarsi [zbron'tsarsi] *vr* (*fam*) to get sozzled

'**sbronzo, -a** ['zbrontso] *ag* (*fam*) sozzled ▪ *sf*: **prendersi una sbronza** to get sozzled

sbruf'fone, -a *sm/f* boaster, braggart

sbu'care *vi* (*apparire*) to pop out (*o* up)

sbucci'are [zbut'tʃare] *vt* (*arancia, patata*) to peel; (*piselli*) to shell; **sbucciarsi un ginocchio** to graze one's knee

sbucherò *etc* [zbuke'rɔ] *vb vedi* **sbucare**

sbudel'larsi *vr*: **~ dalle risa** to split one's sides laughing

sbuf'fare *vi* (*persona, cavallo*) to snort; (: *ansimare*) to puff, pant; (*treno*) to puff

'**sbuffo** *sm* (*di aria, fumo, vapore*) puff; **maniche a ~** puff(ed) sleeves

sc. *abbr* (*Teat*: = *scena*) sc.

'**scabbia** *sf* (*Med*) scabies *sg*

'**scabro, -a** *ag* rough, harsh; (*fig*) concise, terse

sca'broso, -a *ag* (*fig*: *difficile*) difficult, thorny; (: *imbarazzante*) embarrassing; (: *sconcio*) indecent

scacchi'era [skak'kjera] *sf* chessboard

scacchiere [skak'kjere] *sm* (*Mil*) sector; **S~** (*in Gran Bretagna*) Exchequer

scaccia'cani [skattʃa'kani] *sm o f inv* pistol with blanks

scacciapensi'eri [skattʃapen'sjɛri] *sm inv* (*Mus*) jew's-harp

scacci'are [skat'tʃare] *vt* to chase away *o* out, drive away *o* out; **~ qn di casa** to turn sb out of the house

'**scacco, -chi** *sm* (*pezzo del gioco*) chessman; (*quadretto di scacchiera*) square; (*fig*) setback, reverse; **scacchi** *smpl* (*gioco*) chess *sg*; **a scacchi** (*tessuto*) check(ed); **subire uno ~** (*fig*: *sconfitta*) to suffer a setback

scacco'matto *sm* checkmate; **dare ~ a qn** (*anche fig*) to checkmate sb

'**scaddi** *etc vb vedi* **scadere**

sca'dente *ag* shoddy, of poor quality

sca'denza [ska'dentsa] *sf* (*di cambiale, contratto*) maturity; (*di passaporto*) expiry date; **a breve/lunga ~** short-/long-term; **data di ~** expiry date; **~ a termine** fixed deadline

sca'dere *vi* (*contratto etc*) to expire; (*debito*) to fall due; (*valore, forze, peso*) to decline, go down

sca'fandro *sm* (*di palombaro*) diving suit; (*di astronauta*) spacesuit

scaffala'tura *sf* shelving, shelves *pl*

scaf'fale *sm* shelf; (*mobile*) set of shelves

sca'fista *sm* (*di immigrati*) people smuggler (*by boat*)

'**scafo** *sm* (*Naut, Aer*) hull

scagio'nare [skadʒo'nare] *vt* to exonerate, free from blame

'**scaglia** ['skaʎʎa] *sf* (*Zool*) scale; (*scheggia*) chip, flake

scagli'are [skaʎ'ʎare] vt (lanciare: anche fig) to hurl, fling; **scagliarsi** vr: **scagliarsi su** o **contro** to hurl o fling o.s. at; (fig) to rail at

scagliona'mento [skaʎʎona'mento] sm (Mil) arrangement in echelons

scaglio'nare [skaʎʎo'nare] vt (pagamenti) to space out, spread out; (Mil) to echelon

scagli'one [skaʎ'ʎone] sm (Mil) echelon; (Geo) terrace; **a scaglioni** in groups

sca'gnozzo [skaɲ'ɲɔttso] sm (peg) lackey

'Scala: **la** ~ see note

○ **LA SCALA**
○
○
○ Milan's la Scala first opened its doors in
○ 1778 with a performance of Salieri's
○ opera, "L'Europa riconosciuta". Built on
○ the site of the church of Santa Maria della
○ Scala, the theatre suffered serious
○ damage in the bombing campaigns of
○ 1943 but reopened in 1946 with a concert
○ conducted by Toscanini. Enjoying world-
○ wide renown for its opera, la Scala also has
○ a famous school of classical dance.

'scala sf (a gradini etc) staircase, stairs pl; (a pioli, di corda) ladder; (Mus, Geo, di colori, valori, fig) scale; **scale** sfpl (scalinata) stairs; **su larga** o **vasta ~** on a large scale; **su piccola ~**, **su ~ ridotta** on a small scale; **su ~ nazionale/mondiale** on a national/worldwide scale; **in ~ di 1 a 100.000** on a scale of 1 cm to 1 km; **riproduzione in ~** reproduction to scale; **~ a chiocciola** spiral staircase; **~ a libretto** stepladder; **~ di misure** system of weights and measures; **~ mobile** escalator; (Econ) sliding scale; **~ mobile (dei salari)** index-linked pay scale; **~ di sicurezza** (antincendio) fire escape

sca'lare vt (Alpinismo, muro) to climb, scale; (debito) to scale down, reduce; **questa somma vi viene scalata dal prezzo originale** this sum is deducted from the original price

sca'lata sf scaling no pl, climbing no pl; (arrampicata, fig) climb; **dare la ~ a** (fig) to make a bid for

scala'tore, -'trice sm/f climber

scalca'gnato, -a [skalkaɲ'ɲato] ag (logoro) worn; (persona) shabby

scalci'are [skal'tʃare] vi to kick

scalci'nato, -a [skaltʃi'nato] ag (fig peg) shabby

scalda'bagno [skalda'baɲɲo] sm water heater

scal'dare vt to heat; **scaldarsi** vr to warm up, heat up; (al fuoco, al sole) to warm o.s.; (fig) to get excited; **~ la sedia** (fig) to twiddle one's thumbs

scaldavi'vande sm inv dish warmer

scal'dino sm (per mani) hand-warmer; (per piedi) foot-warmer; (per letto) bedwarmer

scal'fire vt to scratch

scalfit'tura sf scratch

scali'nata sf staircase

sca'lino sm (anche fig) step; (di scala a pioli) rung

scal'mana sf (hot) flush

scalma'narsi vr (affaticarsi) to rush about, rush around; (agitarsi, darsi da fare) to get all hot and bothered; (arrabbiarsi) to get excited, get steamed up

scalma'nato, -a sm/f hothead

'scalo sm (Naut) slipway; (: porto d'approdo) port of call; (Aer) stopover; **fare ~ (a)** (Naut) to call (at), put in (at); (Aer) to land (at), make a stop (at); **volo senza ~** non-stop flight; **~ merci** (Ferr) goods (Brit) o freight yard

sca'logna [ska'loɲɲa] sf (fam) bad luck

scalo'gnato, -a [skaloɲ'ɲato] ag (fam) unlucky

scalop'pina sf (Cuc) escalope

scal'pello sm chisel

scalpi'tare vi (cavallo) to paw the ground; (persona) to stamp one's feet

scal'pore sm noise, row; **far ~** (notizia) to cause a sensation o a stir

'scaltro, -a ag cunning, shrewd

scal'zare [skal'tsare] vt (albero) to bare the roots of; (muro: fig: autorità) to undermine

'scalzo, -a ['skaltso] ag barefoot

scambi'are vt to exchange; (confondere): **~ qn/qc per** to take o mistake sb/sth for; **mi hanno scambiato il cappello** they've given me the wrong hat

scambi'evole ag mutual, reciprocal

'scambio sm exchange; (Comm) trade; (Ferr) points pl; **fare (uno) ~** to make a swap; **libero ~** free trade; **scambi con l'estero** foreign trade

scamosci'ato, -a [skamoʃ'ʃato] ag suede

scampa'gnata [skampaɲ'ɲata] sf trip to the country

scampa'nare vi to peal

scam'pare vt (salvare) to rescue, save; (evitare: morte, prigione) to escape ■ vi: **~ (a qc)** to survive (sth), escape (sth); **scamparla bella** to have a narrow escape

'scampo sm (salvezza) escape; (Zool) prawn; **cercare ~ nella fuga** to seek safety in flight; **non c'è (via di) ~** there's no way out

'scampolo sm remnant

scanala'tura sf (incavo) channel, groove

scandagli'are [skandaʎ'ʎare] vt (Naut) to sound; (fig) to sound out; to probe

scanda'listico, -a, ci, che *ag* (*settimanale etc*) sensational

scandaliz'zare [skandalid'dzare] *vt* to shock, scandalize; **scandalizzarsi** *vr* to be shocked

'**scandalo** *sm* scandal; **dare ~** to cause a scandal

scanda'loso, -a *ag* scandalous, shocking

Scandi'navia *sf*: **la ~** Scandinavia

scandi'navo, -a *ag, sm/f* Scandinavian

scan'dire *vt* (*versi*) to scan; (*parole*) to articulate, pronounce distinctly; **~ il tempo** (*Mus*) to beat time

scan'nare *vt* (*animale*) to butcher, slaughter; (*persona*) to cut o slit the throat of

'**scanner** ['skanner] *sm inv* scanner

scanneriz'zare [skannerid'dzare] *vt* to scan

'**scanno** *sm* seat, bench

scansafa'tiche [skansafa'tike] *sm/f inv* idler, loafer

scan'sare *vt* (*rimuovere*) to move (aside), shift; (*schivare: schiaffo*) to dodge; (*sfuggire*) to avoid; **scansarsi** *vr* to move aside

scan'sia *sf* shelves *pl*; (*per libri*) bookcase

'**scanso** *sm*: **a ~ di** in order to avoid, as a precaution against; **a ~ di equivoci** to avoid (any) misunderstanding

scanti'nato *sm* basement

scanto'nare *vi* to turn the corner; (*svignarsela*) to sneak off

scanzo'nato, -a [skantso'nato] *ag* easy-going

scapacci'one [skapat'tʃone] *sm* clout, slap

scapes'trato, -a *ag* dissolute

'**scapito** *sm* (*perdita*) loss; (*danno*) damage, detriment; **a ~ di** to the detriment of

'**scapola** *sf* shoulder blade

'**scapolo** *sm* bachelor

scappa'mento *sm* (*Aut*) exhaust

scap'pare *vi* (*fuggire*) to escape; (*andare via in fretta*) to rush off; **~ di prigione** to escape from prison; **~ di mano** (*oggetto*) to slip out of one's hands; **~ di mente a qn** to slip sb's mind; **lasciarsi ~** (*occasione, affare*) to miss, let go by; (*dettaglio*) to overlook; (*parola*) to let slip; (*prigioniero*) to let escape; **mi scappò detto** I let it slip

scap'pata *sf* quick visit o call

scappa'tella *sf* escapade

scappa'toia *sf* way out

scara'beo *sm* beetle

scarabocchi'are [skarabok'kjare] *vt* to scribble, scrawl

scara'bocchio [skara'bokkjo] *sm* scribble, scrawl

scara'faggio [skara'faddʒo] *sm* cockroach

scaraman'zia [skaraman'tsia] *sf*: **per ~** for luck

scara'muccia, -ce [skara'muttʃa] *sf* skirmish

scaraven'tare *vt* to fling, hurl

scarce'rare [skartʃe'rare] *vt* to release (from prison)

scarcerazi'one [skartʃerat'tsjone] *sf* release (from prison)

scardi'nare *vt* to take off its hinges

'**scarica, -che** *sf* (*di più armi*) volley of shots; (*di sassi, pugni*) hail, shower; (*Elettr*) discharge; **~ di mitra** burst of machine-gun fire

scari'care *vt* (*merci, camion etc*) to unload; (*passeggeri*) to set down; (*da Internet*) to download; (*arma*) to unload; (: *sparare, Elettr*) to discharge; (*corso d'acqua*) to empty, pour; (*fig: liberare da un peso*) to unburden, relieve; **scaricarsi** *vr* (*orologio*) to run o wind down; (*batteria, accumulatore*) to go flat (*Brit*) o dead; (*fig: rilassarsi*) to unwind; (: *sfogarsi*) to let off steam; **~ le proprie responsabilità su qn** to off-load one's responsibilities onto sb; **~ la colpa addosso a qn** to blame sb; **il fulmine si scaricò su un albero** the lightning struck a tree

scarica'tore *sm* loader; (*di porto*) docker

'**scarico, -a, chi, che** *ag* unloaded; (*orologio*) run down; (*batteria, accumulatore*) dead, flat (*Brit*) ■ *sm* (*di merci, materiali*) unloading; (*di immondizie*) dumping, tipping (*Brit*); (: *luogo*) rubbish dump; (*Tecn: deflusso*) draining; (: *dispositivo*) drain; (*Aut*) exhaust; **~ del lavandino** waste outlet

scarlat'tina *sf* scarlet fever

scar'latto, -a *ag* scarlet

'**scarno, -a** *ag* thin, bony

'**scarpa** *sf* shoe; **fare le scarpe a qn** (*fig*) to double-cross sb; **scarpe da ginnastica** gym shoes; **scarpe coi tacchi (alti)** high-heeled shoes; **scarpe col tacco basso** low-heeled shoes; **scarpe senza tacco** flat shoes; **scarpe da tennis** tennis shoes

scar'pata *sf* escarpment

scarpi'era *sf* shoe rack

scar'pone *sm* boot; **scarponi da montagna** climbing boots; **scarponi da sci** ski-boots

scarroz'zare [skarrot'tsare] *vt* to drive around

scarseggi'are [skarsed'dʒare] *vi* to be scarce; **~ di** to be short of, lack

scar'sezza [skar'settsa] *sf* scarcity, lack

'**scarso, -a** *ag* (*insufficiente*) insufficient, meagre (*Brit*), meager (*US*); (*povero: annata*) poor, lean; (*Ins: voto*) poor; **~ di** lacking in; **3 chili scarsi** just under 3 kilos

scartabel'lare *vt* to skim through, glance through

scarta'faccio [skarta'fattʃo] *sm* notebook

scarta'mento *sm* (*Ferr*) gauge; **~ normale/ ridotto** standard/narrow gauge

S

scar'tare vt (pacco) to unwrap; (idea) to reject; (Mil) to declare unfit for military service; (carte da gioco) to discard; (Calcio) to dodge (past) ◼ vi to swerve

'**scarto** sm (cosa scartata, anche Comm) reject; (di veicolo) swerve; (differenza) gap, difference; ~ **salariale** wage differential

scar'toffie sfpl (peg) papers pl

scas'sare vt (fam: rompere) to wreck

scassi'nare vt to break, force

'**scasso** sm vedi **furto**

scate'nare vt (fig) to incite, stir up; **scatenarsi** vr (temporale) to break; (rivolta) to break out; (persona: infuriarsi) to rage

scate'nato, -a ag wild

'**scatola** sf box; (di latta) tin (Brit), can; **cibi in ~** tinned (Brit) o canned foods; **una ~ di cioccolatini** a box of chocolates; **comprare qc a ~ chiusa** to buy sth sight unseen; ~ **cranica** cranium

scato'lone sm box

scat'tante ag quick off the mark; (agile) agile

scat'tare vt (fotografia) to take ◼ vi (congegno, molla etc) to be released; (balzare) to spring up; (Sport) to put on a spurt; (fig: per l'ira) to fly into a rage; (legge, provvedimento) to come into effect; ~ **in piedi** to spring to one's feet; **far ~** to release

'**scatto** sm (dispositivo) release; (: di arma da fuoco) trigger mechanism; (rumore) click; (balzo) jump, start; (Sport) spurt; (fig: di ira etc) fit; (: di stipendio) increment; **di ~** suddenly; **serratura a ~** spring lock

scatu'rire vi to gush, spring

scaval'care vt (ostacolo) to pass (o climb) over; (fig) to get ahead of, overtake

sca'vare vt (terreno) to dig; (legno) to hollow out; (pozzo, galleria) to bore; (città sepolta etc) to excavate

scava'trice [skava'tritʃe] sf (macchina) excavator

scavezza'collo [skavettsa'kɔllo] sm daredevil

'**scavo** sm excavating no pl; excavation

scazzot'tare [skattsot'tare] vt (fam) to beat up, give a thrashing to

sce'gliere ['ʃeʎʎere] vt (gen) to choose; (candidato, prodotto) to choose, select; ~ **di fare** to choose to do

sce'icco, -chi [ʃe'ikko] sm sheik

'**scelgo** etc ['ʃelgo] vb vedi **scegliere**

scelle'rato, -a [ʃelle'rato] ag wicked, evil

scel'lino [ʃel'lino] sm shilling

'**scelto, -a** ['ʃelto] pp di **scegliere** ◼ ag (gruppo) carefully selected; (frutta, verdura) choice, top quality; (Mil: specializzato) crack cpd, highly skilled ◼ sf choice; (selezione) selection, choice; **frutta o formaggi a scelta** choice of fruit or cheese; **fare una scelta** to make a choice, choose; **non avere scelta** to have no choice o option; **di prima scelta** top grade o quality

sce'mare [ʃe'mare] vt, vi to diminish

sce'menza [ʃe'mentsa] sf stupidity no pl; stupid thing (to do o say)

'**scemo, -a** ['ʃemo] ag stupid, silly

'**scempio** ['ʃempjo] sm slaughter, massacre; (fig) ruin; **far ~ di** (fig) to play havoc with, ruin

'**scena** ['ʃena] sf (gen) scene; (palcoscenico) stage; **le scene** (fig: teatro) the stage; **andare in ~** to be staged o put on o performed; **mettere in ~** to stage; **uscire di ~** to leave the stage; (fig) to leave the scene; **fare una ~** (fig) to make a scene; **ha fatto ~ muta** (fig) he didn't open his mouth

sce'nario [ʃe'narjo] sm scenery; (di film) scenario

sce'nata [ʃe'nata] sf row, scene

'**scendere** ['ʃendere] vi to go (o come) down; (strada, sole) to go down; (notte) to fall; (passeggero: fermarsi) to get out, alight; (fig: temperatura, prezzi) to fall, drop ◼ vt (scale, pendio) to go (o come) down; ~ **dalle scale** to go (o come) down the stairs; ~ **dal treno** to get off o out of the train; ~ **dalla macchina** to get out of the car; ~ **da cavallo** to dismount, get off one's horse; ~ **ad un albergo** to put up o stay at a hotel

scenegg'iato [ʃened'dʒato] sm television drama

sceneggia'tore, -'trice [ʃenedʒa'tore] sm/f script-writer

sceneggia'tura [ʃenedʒa'tura] sf (Teat) scenario; (Cine) screenplay, scenario

'**scenico, -a, ci, che** ['ʃeniko] ag stage cpd

sceno'grafia [ʃenogra'fia] sf (Teat) stage design; (Cine) set design; (elementi scenici) scenery

sce'nografo, -a [ʃe'nografo] sm/f set designer

sce'riffo [ʃe'riffo] sm sheriff

scervel'larsi [ʃervel'larsi] vr: ~ **(su qc)** to rack one's brains (over sth)

scervel'lato, -a [ʃervel'lato] ag featherbrained

'**sceso, -a** ['ʃeso] pp di **scendere**

scetti'cismo [ʃetti'tʃizmo] sm scepticism (Brit), skepticism (US)

'**scettico, -a, ci, che** ['ʃettiko] ag sceptical (Brit), skeptical (US)

'**scettro** ['ʃettro] sm sceptre (Brit), scepter (US)

'**scheda** ['skɛda] sf (index) card; (TV, Radio) (brief) report; ~ **audio** (Inform) sound card; ~ **bianca/nulla** (Pol) unmarked/spoiled ballot paper; ~ **a circuito stampato** printed-circuit board; **~ elettorale** ballot paper; **~ madre** (*Inform*) motherboard; **~ perforata** punch card; **~ ricaricabile** (*Tel*) top-up card; **~ telefonica** phone card; **~ video** (*Inform*) video card

sche'dare [ske'dare] *vt* (*dati*) to file; (*libri*) to catalogue; (*registrare: anche Polizia*) to put on one's files

sche'dario [ske'darjo] *sm* file; (*mobile*) filing cabinet

sche'dato, -a [ske'dato] *ag* with a (police) record ■ *sm/f* person with a (police) record

sche'dina [ske'dina] *sf* ≈ pools coupon (*Brit*)

'scheggia, -ge ['skeddʒa] *sf* splinter, sliver; **~ impazzita** (*fig*) maverick

sche'letrico, -a, ci, che [ske'lɛtriko] *ag* (*anche Anat*) skeletal; (*fig: essenziale*) skeleton *cpd*

'scheletro ['skɛletro] *sm* skeleton; **avere uno ~ nell'armadio** (*fig*) to have a skeleton in the cupboard

'schema, -i ['skema] *sm* (*diagramma*) diagram, sketch; (*progetto, abbozzo*) outline, plan; **ribellarsi agli schemi** to rebel against traditional values; **secondo gli schemi tradizionali** in accordance with traditional values

sche'matico, -a, ci, che [ske'matiko] *ag* schematic

schematiz'zare [skematid'dzare] *vt* to schematize

'scherma ['skerma] *sf* fencing

scher'maglia [sker'maʎʎa] *sf* (*fig*) skirmish

scher'mirsi [sker'mirsi] *vr* to defend o.s.

'schermo ['skermo] *sm* shield, screen; (*Cine, TV*) screen

schermogra'fia [skermogra'fia] *sf* X-rays *pl*

scher'nire [sker'nire] *vt* to mock, sneer at

'scherno ['skerno] *sm* mockery, derision; **farsi ~ di** to sneer at; **essere oggetto di ~** to be a laughing stock

scher'zare [sker'tsare] *vi* to joke

'scherzo ['skertso] *sm* joke; (*tiro*) trick; (*Mus*) scherzo; **è uno ~!** (*una cosa facile*) it's child's play!, it's easy!; **per ~** for a joke *o* a laugh; **fare un brutto ~ a qn** to play a nasty trick on sb; **scherzi a parte** seriously, joking apart

scher'zoso, -a [sker'tsoso] *ag* (*tono, gesto*) playful; (*osservazione*) facetious; **è un tipo ~** he likes a joke

schiaccia'noci [skjattʃa'notʃi] *sm inv* nutcracker

schiacci'ante [skjat'tʃante] *ag* overwhelming

schiacci'are [skjat'tʃare] *vt* (*dito*) to crush; (*noci*) to crack; **~ un pisolino** to have a nap

schiaffeggi'are [skjaffed'dʒare] *vt* to slap

schi'affo ['skjaffo] *sm* slap; **prendere qn a schiaffi** to slap sb's face; **uno ~ morale** a slap in the face, a rebuff

schiamaz'zare [skjamat'tsare] *vi* to squawk, cackle

schia'mazzo [skja'mattso] *sm* (*fig: chiasso*) din, racket

schian'tare [skjan'tare] *vt* to break, tear apart; **schiantarsi** *vr* to break (up), shatter; **schiantarsi al suolo** (*aereo*) to crash (to the ground)

schi'anto ['skjanto] *sm* (*rumore*) crash; tearing sound; **è uno ~!** (*fam*) it's (*o* he's *o* she's) terrific!; **di ~** all of a sudden

schia'rire [skja'rire] *vt* to lighten, make lighter ■ *vi* (*anche*: **schiarirsi**) to grow lighter; (*tornar sereno*) to clear, brighten up; **schiarirsi la voce** to clear one's throat

schia'rita [skja'rita] *sf* (*Meteor*) bright spell; (*fig*) improvement, turn for the better

schiat'tare [skjat'tare] *vi* to burst; **~ d'invidia** to be green with envy; **~ di rabbia** to be beside o.s. with rage

schiavitù [skjavi'tu] *sf* slavery

schiaviz'zare [skjavid'dzare] *vt* to enslave

schi'avo, -a ['skjavo] *sm/f* slave

schi'ena ['skjɛna] *sf* (*Anat*) back

schie'nale [skje'nale] *sm* (*di sedia*) back

schi'era ['skjɛra] *sf* (*Mil*) rank; (*gruppo*) group, band; **villette a ~** ≈ terraced houses

schiera'mento [skjera'mento] *sm* (*Mil, Sport*) formation; (*fig*) alliance

schie'rare [skje'rare] *vt* (*esercito*) to line up, draw up, marshal; **schierarsi** *vr* to line up; (*fig*): **schierarsi con** *o* **dalla parte di/contro qn** to side with/oppose sb

schi'etto, -a ['skjɛtto] *ag* (*puro*) pure; (*fig*) frank, straightforward

schi'fare [ski'fare] *vt* to disgust

schi'fezza [ski'fettsa] *sf*: **essere una ~** (*cibo, bibita etc*) to be disgusting; (*film, libro*) to be dreadful

schifil'toso, -a [skifil'toso] *ag* fussy, difficult

'schifo ['skifo] *sm* disgust; **fare ~** (*essere fatto male, dare pessimi risultati*) to be awful; **mi fa ~** it makes me sick, it's disgusting; **quel libro è uno ~** that book's rotten

schi'foso, -a [ski'foso] *ag* disgusting, revolting; (*molto scadente*) rotten, lousy

schioc'care [skjok'kare] *vt* (*frusta*) to crack; (*dita*) to snap; (*lingua*) to click; **~ le labbra** to smack one's lips

schioppet'tata [skjoppet'tata] *sf* gunshot

schi'oppo ['skjɔppo] *sm* rifle, gun

schi'udere ['skjudere] *vt*, **schi'udersi** *vr* to open

S

331

schi'uma ['skjuma] *sf* foam; (*di sapone*) lather; (*di latte*) froth

schiu'mare [skju'mare] *vt* to skim ▪ *vi* to foam

schi'uso, -a ['skjuso] *pp di* **schiudere**

schi'vare [ski'vare] *vt* to dodge, avoid

'schivo, -a ['skivo] *ag* (*ritroso*) stand-offish, reserved; (*timido*) shy

schizofre'nia [skiddzofre'nia] *sf* schizophrenia

schizo'frenico, -a, ci, che [skiddzo'freniko] *ag* schizophrenic

schiz'zare [skit'tsare] *vt* (*spruzzare*) to spurt, squirt; (*sporcare*) to splash, spatter; (*fig: abbozzare*) to sketch ▪ *vi* to spurt, squirt; (*saltar fuori*) to dart up (*o off etc*); ~ **via** (*animale, persona*) to dart away; (*macchina, moto*) to accelerate away

schizzi'noso, -a [skittsi'noso] *ag* fussy, finicky

'schizzo ['skittso] *sm* (*di liquido*) spurt; splash, spatter; (*abbozzo*) sketch

sci [ʃi] *sm inv* (*attrezzo*) ski; (*attività*) skiing; ~ **di fondo** cross-country skiing, ski touring (*US*); ~ **nautico** water-skiing

'scia ['ʃia] (*pl* **scie**) *sf* (*di imbarcazione*) wake; (*di profumo*) trail

scià [ʃa] *sm inv* shah

sci'abola ['ʃabola] *sf* sabre (*Brit*), saber (*US*)

scia'callo [ʃa'kallo] *sm* jackal; (*fig peg: profittatore*) shark, profiteer; (: *ladro*) looter

sciac'quare [ʃak'kware] *vt* to rinse

scia'gura [ʃa'gura] *sf* disaster, calamity

sciagu'rato, -a [ʃagu'rato] *ag* unfortunate; (*malvagio*) wicked

scialac'quare [ʃalak'kware] *vt* to squander

scia'lare [ʃa'lare] *vi* to throw one's money around

sci'albo, -a ['ʃalbo] *ag* pale, dull; (*fig*) dull, colourless (*Brit*), colorless (*US*)

sci'alle ['ʃalle] *sm* shawl

sci'alo ['ʃalo] *sm* squandering, waste

scia'luppa [ʃa'luppa] *sf* (*Naut*) sloop; (*anche*: **scialuppa di salvataggio**) lifeboat

scia'mare [ʃa'mare] *vi* to swarm

sci'ame ['ʃame] *sm* swarm

scian'cato, -a [ʃan'kato] *ag* lame; (*mobile*) rickety

sci'are [ʃi'are] *vi* to ski; **andare a** ~ to go skiing

sci'arpa ['ʃarpa] *sf* scarf; (*fascia*) sash

scia'tore, -trice [ʃia'tore] *sm/f* skier

sciat'tezza [ʃat'tettsa] *sf* slovenliness

sci'atto, -a ['ʃatto] *ag* (*persona: nell'aspetto*) slovenly, unkempt; (: *nel lavoro*) sloppy, careless

'scibile ['ʃibile] *sm* knowledge

scien'tifico, -a, ci, che [ʃen'tifiko] *ag* scientific; **la (polizia) scientifica** the forensic department

sci'enza ['ʃentsa] *sf* science; (*sapere*) knowledge; **scienze** *sfpl* (*Ins*) science *sg*; **scienze naturali** natural sciences; **scienze politiche** political science *sg*

scienzi'ato, -a [ʃen'tsjato] *sm/f* scientist

'Scilly ['ʃilli]: **le isole** ~ *sfpl* the Scilly Isles

'scimmia ['ʃimmja] *sf* monkey

scimmiot'tare [ʃimmjot'tare] *vt* to ape, mimic

scimpanzé [ʃimpan'tse] *sm inv* chimpanzee

scimu'nito, -a [ʃimu'nito] *ag* silly, idiotic

'scindere ['ʃindere] *vt*, **'scindersi** *vr* to split (up)

scin'tilla [ʃin'tilla] *sf* spark

scintil'lare [ʃintil'lare] *vi* to spark; (*acqua, occhi*) to sparkle

scintil'lio [ʃintil'lio] *sm* sparkling

scioc'care [ʃok'kare] *vt* to shock

scioc'chezza [ʃok'kettsa] *sf* stupidity *no pl*; stupid *o* foolish thing; **dire sciocchezze** to talk nonsense

sci'occo, -a, chi, che ['ʃɔkko] *ag* stupid, foolish

sci'ogliere ['ʃɔʎʎere] *vt* (*nodo*) to untie; (*capelli*) to loosen; (*persona, animale*) to untie, release; (*fig: persona*): ~ **da** to release from; (*neve*) to melt; (*nell'acqua: zucchero etc*) to dissolve; (*fig: mistero*) to solve; (*porre fine a: contratto*) to cancel; (: *società, matrimonio*) to dissolve; (: *riunione*) to bring to an end; **sciogliersi** *vr* to loosen, come untied; to melt; to dissolve; (*assemblea, corteo, duo*) to break up; ~ **i muscoli** to limber up; ~ **il ghiaccio** (*fig*) to break the ice; ~ **le vele** (*Naut*) to set sail; **sciogliersi dai legami** (*fig*) to free o.s. from all ties

sci'olgo etc ['ʃɔlgo] *vb vedi* **sciogliere**

sciol'tezza [ʃol'tettsa] *sf* agility; suppleness; ease

sci'olto, -a ['ʃɔlto] *pp di* **sciogliere** ▪ *ag* loose; (*agile*) agile, nimble; (*disinvolto*) free and easy; **essere** ~ **nei movimenti** to be supple; **versi sciolti** (*Poesia*) blank verse

sciope'rante [ʃope'rante] *sm/f* striker

sciope'rare [ʃope'rare] *vi* to strike, go on strike

sci'opero ['ʃɔpero] *sm* strike; **fare** ~ to strike; **entrare in** ~ to go on *o* come out on strike; ~ **bianco** work-to-rule (*Brit*), slowdown (*US*); ~ **della fame** hunger strike; ~ **selvaggio** wildcat strike; ~ **a singhiozzo** on-off strike; ~ **di solidarietà** sympathy strike

sciori'nare [ʃori'nare] *vt* (*ostentare*) to show off, display

scio'via [ʃio'via] *sf* ski lift

sciovi'nismo [ʃovi'nizmo] *sm* chauvinism
sciovi'nista, -i, e [ʃovi'nista] *sm/f* chauvinist
sci'pito, -a [ʃi'pito] *ag* insipid
scip'pare [ʃip'pare] *vt*: ~ **qn** to snatch sb's bag
scippa'tore [ʃippa'tore] *sm* bag-snatcher
'scippo ['ʃippo] *sm* bag-snatching
sci'rocco [ʃi'rɔkko] *sm* sirocco
sci'roppo [ʃi'rɔppo] *sm* syrup; ~ **per la tosse** cough syrup, cough mixture
'scisma, -i ['ʃizma] *sm* (Rel) schism
scissi'one [ʃis'sjone] *sf* (anche fig) split, division; (Fisica) fission
'scisso, -a ['ʃisso] *pp di* **scindere**
sciu'pare [ʃu'pare] *vt* (abito, libro, appetito) to spoil, ruin; (tempo, denaro) to waste; **sciuparsi** *vr* to get spoilt o ruined; (rovinarsi la salute) to ruin one's health
scivo'lare [ʃivo'lare] *vi* to slide o glide along; (involontariamente) to slip, slide
'scivolo ['ʃivolo] *sm* slide; (Tecn) chute
scivo'loso, -a [ʃivo'loso] *ag* slippery
scle'rosi *sf* sclerosis
scoc'care *vt* (freccia) to shoot ■ *vi* (guizzare) to shoot up; (battere: ora) to strike
scoccherò etc [skokke'rɔ] *vb vedi* **scoccare**
scocci'are [skot'tʃare] *vt* to bother, annoy; **scocciarsi** *vr* to be bothered o annoyed
scoccia'tore, -'trice [skottʃa'tore] *sm/f* nuisance, pest (fam)
scoccia'tura [skottʃa'tura] *sf* nuisance, bore
sco'della *sf* bowl
scodinzo'lare [skodintso'lare] *vi* to wag its tail
scogli'era [skoʎ'ʎɛra] *sf* reef; (rupe) cliff
'scoglio ['skɔʎʎo] *sm* (al mare) rock; (fig: ostacolo) difficulty, stumbling block
scogli'oso, -a [skoʎ'ʎoso] *ag* rocky
scoi'attolo *sm* squirrel
scola'pasta *sm inv* colander
sco'lare *ag*: **età** ~ school age ■ *vt* to drain ■ *vi* to drip
scola'resca *sf* schoolchildren *pl*, pupils *pl*
sco'laro, -a *sm/f* pupil, schoolboy(-girl)
sco'lastico, -a, ci, che *ag* (gen) scholastic; (libro, anno, divisa) school *cpd*
scol'lare *vt* (staccare) to unstick; **scollarsi** *vr* to come unstuck
scol'lato, -a *ag* (vestito) low-cut, low-necked; (donna) wearing a low-cut dress (o blouse etc)
scolla'tura *sf* neckline
'scolo *sm* drainage; (sbocco) drain; (acqua) waste water; **canale di** ~ drain; **tubo di** ~ drainpipe
scolo'rire *vt* to fade; to discolour (Brit), discolor (US) ■ *vi* (anche: **scolorirsi**) to fade, to become discolo(u)red; (impallidire) to turn pale

scol'pire *vt* to carve, sculpt
scombi'nare *vt* to mess up, upset
scombi'nato, -a *ag* confused, muddled
scombusso'lare *vt* to upset
scom'messo, -a *pp di* **scommettere** ■ *sf* bet, wager; **fare una scommessa** to bet
scom'mettere *vt, vi* to bet
scomo'dare *vt* to trouble, bother, disturb; (fig: nome famoso) to involve, drag in; **scomodarsi** *vr* to put o.s. out; **scomodarsi a fare** to go to the bother o trouble of doing
scomodità *sf inv* (di sedia, letto etc) discomfort; (di orario, sistemazione etc) inconvenience
'scomodo, -a *ag* uncomfortable; (sistemazione, posto) awkward, inconvenient
scompagi'nare [skompadʒi'nare] *vt* to upset, throw into disorder
scompag'nato, -a [skompaɲ'ɲato] *ag* (calzini, guanti) odd
scompa'rire *vi* (sparire) to disappear, vanish; (fig) to be insignificant
scom'parso, -a *pp di* **scomparire** ■ *sf* disappearance; (fig: morte) passing away, death
scomparti'mento *sm* (Ferr) compartment; (sezione) division
scom'parto *sm* compartment, division
scom'penso *sm* imbalance, lack of balance
scompigli'are [skompiʎ'ʎare] *vt* (cassetto, capelli) to mess up, disarrange; (fig: piani) to upset
scom'piglio [skom'piʎʎo] *sm* mess, confusion
scom'porre *vt* (parola, numero) to break up; (Chim) to decompose; **scomporsi** *vr* (Chim) to decompose; (fig) to get upset, lose one's composure; **senza scomporsi** unperturbed
scom'posto, -a *pp di* **scomporre** ■ *ag* (gesto) unseemly; (capelli) ruffled, dishevelled
sco'munica, -che *sf* excommunication
scomuni'care *vt* to excommunicate
sconcer'tante [skontʃer'tante] *ag* disconcerting
sconcer'tare [skontʃer'tare] *vt* to disconcert, bewilder
'sconcio, -a, ci, ce ['skontʃo] *ag* (osceno) indecent, obscene ■ *sm* (cosa riprovevole, mal fatta) disgrace
sconclusio'nato, -a *ag* incoherent, illogical
sconfes'sare *vt* to renounce, disavow; to repudiate
scon'figgere [skon'fiddʒere] *vt* to defeat, overcome
sconfi'nare *vi* to cross the border; (in proprietà privata) to trespass; (fig): ~ **da** to stray o digress from

sconfi'nato, -a *ag* boundless, unlimited

scon'fitto, -a *pp di* **sconfiggere** ■ *sf* defeat

sconfor'tante, -a *ag* discouraging, disheartening

sconfor'tare *vt* to discourage, dishearten; **sconfortarsi** *vr* to become discouraged, become disheartened, lose heart

scon'forto *sm* despondency

sconge'lare [skondʒe'lare] *vt* to defrost

scongiu'rare [skondʒu'rare] *vt* (*implorare*) to beseech, implore; (*eludere: pericolo*) to ward off, avert

scongi'uro [skon'dʒuro] *sm* (*esorcismo*) exorcism; **fare gli scongiuri** to touch wood (*Brit*), knock on wood (*US*)

scon'nesso, -a *ag* (*fig: discorso*) incoherent, rambling

sconosci'uto, -a [skonoʃʃuto] *ag* unknown; new, strange ■ *sm/f* stranger, unknown person

sconquas'sare *vt* to shatter, smash

scon'quasso *sm* (*danno*) damage; (*fig*) confusion

sconside'rato, -a *ag* thoughtless, rash

sconsigli'are [skonsiʎ'ʎare] *vt*: **~ qc a qn** to advise sb against sth; **~ qn dal fare qc** to advise sb not to do *o* against doing sth

sconso'lato, -a *ag* disconsolate

scon'tare *vt* (*Comm: detrarre*) to deduct; (*: debito*) to pay off; (*: cambiale*) to discount; (*pena*) to serve; (*colpa, errori*) to pay for, suffer for

scon'tato, -a *ag* (*previsto*) foreseen, taken for granted; (*prezzo, merce*) discounted, at a discount; **dare per ~ che** to take it for granted that

sconten'tare *vt* to displease, dissatisfy

sconten'tezza [skonten'tettsa] *sf* displeasure, dissatisfaction

scon'tento, -a *ag*: **~ (di)** discontented *o* dissatisfied (with) ■ *sm* discontent, dissatisfaction

'sconto *sm* discount; **fare** *o* **concedere uno ~** to give a discount; **uno ~ del 10%** a 10% discount

scon'trarsi *vr* (*treni etc*) to crash, collide; (*venire ad uno scontro, fig*) to clash; **~ con** to crash into, collide with

scon'trino *sm* ticket

'scontro *sm* (*Mil, fig*) clash; (*di veicoli*) crash, collision; **~ a fuoco** shoot-out

scon'troso, -a *ag* sullen, surly; (*permaloso*) touchy

sconveni'ente *ag* unseemly, improper

sconvol'gente [skonvol'dʒɛnte] *ag* (*notizia, brutta esperienza*) upsetting, disturbing; (*bellezza*) amazing; (*passione*) overwhelming

scon'volgere [skon'vɔldʒere] *vt* to throw into confusion, upset; (*turbare*) to shake, disturb, upset

scon'volto, -a *pp di* **sconvolgere** ■ *ag* (*persona*) distraught, very upset

'scopa *sf* broom; (*Carte*) Italian card game

sco'pare *vt* to sweep; (*fam!*) to bonk (!)

sco'pata *sf* (*fam!*) bonk (!)

scoperchi'are [skoper'kjare] *vt* (*pentola, vaso*) to take the lid off, uncover; (*casa*) to take the roof off

sco'perto, -a *pp di* **scoprire** ■ *ag* uncovered; (*capo*) uncovered, bare; (*macchina*) open; (*Mil*) exposed, without cover; (*conto*) overdrawn ■ *sf* discovery ■ *sm*: **allo ~** (*dormire etc*) out in the open; **assegno ~** uncovered cheque; **avere un conto ~** to be overdrawn

'scopo *sm* aim, purpose; **a che ~?** what for?; **adatto allo ~** fit for its purpose; **allo ~ di fare qc** in order to do sth; **a ~ di lucro** for gain *o* money; **senza ~** (*fare, cercare*) pointlessly

scoppi'are *vi* (*spaccarsi*) to burst; (*esplodere*) to explode; (*fig*) to break out; **~ in pianto** *o* **a piangere** to burst out crying; **~ dalle risa** *o* **dal ridere** to split one's sides laughing; **~ dal caldo** to be boiling; **~ di salute** to be the picture of health

scoppiet'tare *vi* to crackle

'scoppio *sm* explosion; (*di tuono, arma etc*) crash, bang; (*di pneumatico*) bang; (*fig: di guerra*) outbreak; **a ~ ritardato** delayed-action; **reazione a ~ ritardato** delayed *o* slow reaction; **uno ~ di risa** a burst of laughter; **uno ~ di collera** an explosion of anger

sco'prire *vt* to discover; (*liberare da ciò che copre*) to uncover; (*: monumento*) to unveil; **scoprirsi** *vr* to put on lighter clothes; (*fig*) to give o.s. away

scopri'tore, -'trice *sm/f* discoverer

scoraggi'are [skorad'dʒare] *vt* to discourage; **scoraggiarsi** *vr* to become discouraged, lose heart

scor'butico, -a, ci, che *ag* (*fig*) cantankerous

scorcia'toia [skortʃa'toja] *sf* short cut

'scorcio ['skortʃo] *sm* (*Arte*) foreshortening; (*di secolo, periodo*) end, close; **~ panoramico** vista

scor'dare *vt* to forget; **scordarsi** *vr*: **scordarsi di qc/di fare** to forget sth/to do

sco'reggia [sko'reddʒa] (*fam!*) *sf* fart (!)

scoreggi'are [skored'dʒare] (*fam!*) *vi* to fart (!)

'scorgere ['skɔrdʒere] *vt* to make out, distinguish, see

sco'ria *sf* (*di metalli*) slag; (*vulcanica*) scoria; **scorie radioattive** (*Fisica*) radioactive waste *sg*

'scorno sm ignominy, disgrace

scorpacci'ata [skorpat'tʃata] sf: **fare una ~ (di)** to stuff o.s. (with), eat one's fill (of)

scorpi'one sm scorpion; (*dello zodiaco*): **S~** Scorpio; **essere dello S~** to be Scorpio

'scorporo sm (*Pol*) *transfer of votes aimed at increasing the chances of representation for minority parties*

scorraz'zare [skorrat'tsare] vi to run about

'scorrere vt (*giornale, lettera*) to run o skim through ■ vi (*liquido, fiume*) to run, flow; (*fune*) to run; (*cassetto, porta*) to slide easily; (*tempo*) to pass (by)

scorre'ria sf raid, incursion

scorret'tezza [skorret'tettsa] sf incorrectness; lack of politeness, rudeness; unfairness; **commettere una ~** (*essere sleale*) to be unfair

scor'retto, -a ag (*sbagliato*) incorrect; (*sgarbato*) impolite; (*sconveniente*) improper; (*sleale*) unfair; (*gioco*) foul

scor'revole ag (*porta*) sliding; (*fig: stile*) fluent, flowing

scorri'banda sf (*Mil*) raid; (*escursione*) trip, excursion

'scorsi etc vb vedi **scorgere**

'scorso, -a pp di **scorrere** ■ ag last ■ sf quick look, glance; **lo ~ mese** last month

scor'soio, -a ag: **nodo ~** noose

'scorta sf (*di personalità, convoglio*) escort; (*provvista*) supply, stock; **sotto la ~ di due agenti** escorted by two policemen; **fare ~ di** to stock up with, get in a supply of; **di ~** (*materiali*) spare; **ruota di ~** spare wheel

scor'tare vt to escort

scor'tese ag discourteous, rude

scorte'sia sf discourtesy, rudeness; (*azione*) discourtesy

scorti'care vt to skin

'scorto, -a pp di **scorgere**

'scorza ['skɔrdza] sf (*di albero*) bark; (*di agrumi*) peel, skin

sco'sceso, -a [skoʃ'ʃeso] ag steep

'scosso, -a pp di **scuotere** ■ ag (*turbato*) shaken, upset ■ sf jerk, jolt, shake; (*Elettr, fig*) shock; **prendere la scossa** to get an electric shock; **scossa di terremoto** earth tremor

scos'sone sm: **dare uno ~ a qn** to give sb a shake; **procedere a scossoni** to jolt o jerk along

scos'tante ag (*fig*) off-putting (*Brit*), unpleasant

scos'tare vt to move (away), shift; **scostarsi** vr to move away

scostu'mato, -a ag immoral, dissolute

scotch [skɔtʃ] sm inv (*whisky*) Scotch® (*nastro adesivo*) Scotch tape®, Sellotape®

scot'tante ag (*fig: urgente*) pressing; (: *delicato*) delicate

scot'tare vt (*ustionare*) to burn; (: *con liquido bollente*) to scald ■ vi to burn; (*caffè*) to be too hot

scotta'tura sf burn; scald

'scotto, -a ag overcooked ■ sm (*fig*): **pagare lo ~ (di)** to pay the penalty (for)

sco'vare vt to drive out, flush out; (*fig*) to discover

'Scozia ['skɔttsja] sf: **la ~** Scotland

scoz'zese [skot'tsese] ag Scottish ■ sm/f Scot

screan'zato, -a [skrean'tsato] ag ill-mannered ■ sm/f boor

scredi'tare vt to discredit

scre'mare vt to skim

scre'mato, -a ag skimmed; **parzialmente ~** semi-skimmed

screpo'lare vt, **screpo'larsi** vr to crack

screpola'tura sf cracking no pl; crack

screzi'ato, -a [skret'tsjato] ag streaked

'screzio ['skrettsjo] sm disagreement

scribac'chino [skribak'kino] sm (*peg: impiegato*) penpusher; (: *scrittore*) hack

scricchio'lare [skrikkjo'lare] vi to creak, squeak

scricchio'lio [skrikkjo'lio] sm creaking

'scricciolo ['skrittʃolo] sm wren

'scrigno ['skriɲɲo] sm casket

scrimina'tura sf parting

'scrissi etc vb vedi **scrivere**

'scritto, -a pp di **scrivere** ■ ag written ■ sm writing; (*lettera*) letter, note ■ sf inscription; **scritti** smpl (*letterari etc*) work(s), writings; **per** o **in ~** in writing

scrit'toio sm writing desk

scrit'tore, -'trice sm/f writer

scrit'tura sf writing; (*Comm*) entry; (*contratto*) contract; (*Rel*): **la Sacra S~** the Scriptures pl; **scritture** sfpl (*Comm*) accounts, books

scrittu'rare vt (*Teat, Cine*) to sign up, engage; (*Comm*) to enter

scriva'nia sf desk

scri'vano sm (*amanuense*) scribe; (*impiegato*) clerk

scri'vente sm/f writer

'scrivere vt to write; **come si scrive?** how is it spelt?, how do you write it?; **~ qc a qn** to write sth to sb; **~ qc a macchina** to type sth; **~ a penna/matita** to write in pen/pencil; **~ qc maiuscolo/minuscolo** to write sth in capital/small letters

scroc'care vt (*fam*) to scrounge, cadge

scroc'cone, -a sm/f scrounger

'**scrofa** *sf* (*Zool*) sow
scrol'lare *vt* to shake; **scrollarsi** *vr* (*anche fig*)
to give o.s. a shake; ~ **le spalle/il capo** to
shrug one's shoulders/shake one's head;
scrollarsi qc di dosso (*anche fig*) to shake
sth off
scrol'lata *sf* shake; ~ **di spalle** shrug (of one's
shoulders)
scrosci'ante [skroʃʃante] *ag* (*pioggia*) pouring;
(*fig: applausi*) thunderous
scrosci'are [skroʃʃare] *vi* (*pioggia*) to pour
down, pelt down; (*torrente, fig: applausi*) to
thunder, roar
'**scroscio** ['skrɔʃʃo] *sm* pelting; thunder, roar;
(*di applausi*) burst
scros'tare *vt* (*intonaco*) to scrape off, strip;
scrostarsi *vr* to peel off, flake off
'**scrupolo** *sm* scruple; (*meticolosità*) care,
conscientiousness; **essere senza scrupoli**
to be unscrupulous
scrupo'loso, -a *ag* scrupulous;
conscientious
scru'tare *vt* to scrutinize; (*intenzioni, causa*)
to examine, scrutinize
scruta'tore, -trice *sm/f* (*Pol*) scrutineer
scruti'nare *vt* (*voti*) to count
scru'tinio *sm* (*votazione*) ballot; (*insieme delle
operazioni*) poll; (*Ins*) meeting for assignment of
marks at end of a term or year
scu'cire [sku'tʃire] *vt* (*orlo etc*) to unpick, undo;
scucirsi *vr* to come unstitched
scude'ria *sf* stable
scu'detto *sm* (*Sport*) (championship) shield;
(*distintivo*) badge
scu'discio [sku'diʃʃo] *sm* (riding) crop,
(riding) whip
'**scudo** *sm* shield; **farsi ~ di** *o* **con qc** to shield
o.s. with sth; ~ **aereo/missilistico** air/
missile defence (*Brit*) *o* defense (*US*); ~
termico heat shield
sculacci'are [skulat'tʃare] *vt* to spank
sculacci'one [skulat'tʃone] *sm* spanking
scul'tore, -trice *sm/f* sculptor
scul'tura *sf* sculpture
scu'ola *sf* school; ~ **elementare** *o* **primaria**
primary (*Brit*) *o* grade (*US*) school (*for children
from 6 to 11 years of age*); ~ **guida** driving school;
~ **materna** *o* **dell'infanzia** nursery school
(*for children aged 3 to 6*); ~ **secondaria di primo
grado** first 3 years of secondary school, for children
from 11 to 14 years of age; ~ **secondaria di
secondo grado** secondary school (*for children
aged 14 to 18*); ~ **dell'obbligo** compulsory
education; ~ **privata/pubblica** private/state
school; **scuole serali** evening classes,
night school *sg*; ~ **tecnica** technical college;
see note

SCUOLA

Italian children first go to school at the
age of three. They remain at the "scuola
materna" until they are six, when they
move on to the "scuola primaria" for
another five years. After this come three
years of "scuola secondaria di primo
grado". Students who wish to continue
their schooling attend "scuola secondaria
di secondo grado", choosing between
several types of institution which
specialize in different subject areas.

scu'otere *vt* to shake; **scuotersi** *vr* to jump,
be startled; (*fig: muoversi*) to rouse o.s., stir
o.s.; (: *turbarsi*) to be shaken
'**scure** *sf* axe, ax (*US*)
scu'rire *vt* to darken, make darker
'**scuro, -a** *ag* dark; (*fig: espressione*) grim ■ *sm*
darkness; dark colour (*Brit*) *o* color (*US*);
(*imposta*) (window) shutter; **verde/rosso** *etc*
~ dark green/red *etc*
scur'rile *ag* scurrilous
'**scusa** *sf* excuse; **scuse** *sfpl* apology *sg*,
apologies; **chiedere ~ a qn (per)** to
apologize to sb (for); **chiedo ~** I'm sorry;
(*disturbando etc*) excuse me; **vi prego di
accettare le mie scuse** please accept my
apologies
scu'sare *vt* to excuse; **scusarsi** *vr*: **scusarsi
(di)** to apologize (for); **(mi) scusi** I'm sorry;
(*per richiamare l'attenzione*) excuse me
S.C.V. *sigla* = **Stato della Città del Vaticano**
sdebi'tarsi *vt*: ~ **(con qn di** *o* **per qc)** (*anche fig*)
to repay (sb for sth)
sde'gnare [zdeɲ'ɲare] *vt* to scorn, despise;
sdegnarsi *vr* (*adirarsi*) to get angry
sde'gnato, -a [zdeɲ'ɲato] *ag* indignant,
angry
'**sdegno** ['zdeɲɲo] *sm* scorn, disdain
sdegnosa'mente [zdeɲɲosa'mente] *av*
scornfully, disdainfully
sde'gnoso, -a [zdeɲ'ɲoso] *ag* scornful,
disdainful
sdilin'quirsi *vr* (*illanguidirsi*) to become
sentimental
sdoga'nare *vt* (*Comm*) to clear through
customs
sdolci'nato, -a [zdoltʃi'nato] *ag* mawkish,
oversentimental
sdoppia'mento *sm* (*Chim: di composto*)
splitting; (*Psic*): ~ **della personalità** split
personality
sdoppi'are *vt* (*dividere*) to divide *o* split in two
sdrai'arsi *vr* to stretch out, lie down
'**sdraio** *sm*: **sedia a ~** deck chair

sdrammatiz'zare [zdrammatid'dzare] *vt* to play down, minimize

sdruccio'lare [zdruttʃo'lare] *vi* to slip, slide

sdruccio'levole [zdruttʃo'levole] *ag* slippery

sdru'cito, -a [zdru'tʃito] *ag* (*strappato*) torn; (*logoro*) threadbare

🔵 **PAROLA CHIAVE**

se *pron vedi* **si**

■ *cong* **1** (*condizionale, ipotetica*) if; **se nevica non vengo** I won't come if it snows; **se fossi in te** if I were you; **sarei rimasto se me l'avessero chiesto** I would have stayed if they'd asked me; **non puoi fare altro se non telefonare** all you can do is phone; **se mai** if, if ever; **siamo noi se mai che le siamo grati** it is we who should be grateful to you; **se no** (*altrimenti*) or (else), otherwise; **se non** (*anzi*) if not; (*tranne*) except; **se non altro** if nothing else, at least; **se solo** *o* **solamente** if only

2 (*in frasi dubitative, interrogative indirette*) if, whether; **non so se scrivere o telefonare** I don't know whether *o* if I should write or phone

S.E. *abbr* (= *sud-est*) SE; (= *Sua Eccellenza*) HE

sé *pron* (*gen*) oneself; (*esso, essa, lui, lei, loro*) itself; himself; herself; themselves; **sé stesso(a)** oneself; itself; himself; herself; **sé stessi(e)** (*pl*) themselves; **di per sé non è un problema** it's no problem in itself; **parlare tra sé e sé** to talk to oneself; **va da sé che ...** it goes without saying that ..., it's obvious that ..., it stands to reason that ...; **è un caso a sé** *o* **a sé stante** it's a special case; **un uomo che s'è fatto da sé** a self-made man

S.E.A.T.O. *sigla f* (= *Southeast Asia Treaty Organization*) SEATO

seb'bene *cong* although, though

'sebo *sm* sebum

sec. *abbr* (= *secolo*) c

'SECAM *sigla m* (= *séquentiel couleur à mémoire*) SECAM

'secca *sf vedi* **secco**

secca'mente *av* (*rispondere, rifiutare*) sharply, curtly

sec'care *vt* to dry; (*prosciugare*) to dry up; (*fig: importunare*) to annoy, bother ■ *vi* to dry; to dry up; **seccarsi** *vr* to dry; to dry up; (*fig*) to grow annoyed; **si è seccato molto** he was very annoyed

sec'cato, -a *ag* (*fig: infastidito*) bothered, annoyed; (: *stufo*) fed up

secca'tore, -'trice *sm/f* nuisance, bother

secca'tura *sf* (*fig*) bother *no pl*, trouble *no pl*

seccherò *etc* [sekke'rɔ] *vb vedi* **seccare**

'secchia ['sekkja] *sf* bucket, pail

secchi'ello [sek'kjɛllo] *sm* (*per bambini*) bucket, pail

'secchio ['sekkjo] *sm* bucket, pail; ~ **della spazzatura** *o* **delle immondizie** dustbin (*Brit*), garbage can (*US*)

'secco, -a, chi, che *ag* dry; (*fichi, pesce*) dried; (*foglie, ramo*) withered; (*magro: persona*) thin, skinny; (*fig: risposta, modo di fare*) curt, abrupt; (: *colpo*) clean, sharp ■ *sm* (*siccità*) drought ■ *sf* (*del mare*) shallows *pl*; **restarci** ~ (*fig: morire sul colpo*) to drop dead; **avere la gola secca** to feel dry, be parched; **lavare a** ~ to dry-clean; **tirare a** ~ (*barca*) to beach

secen'tesco, -a, schi, sche [setʃen'tesko] *ag* = **seicentesco**

se'cernere [se'tʃɛrnere] *vt* to secrete

seco'lare *ag* age-old, centuries-old; (*laico, mondano*) secular

'secolo *sm* century; (*epoca*) age

se'conda *sf vedi* **secondo**; **la S~ Repubblica** *see note*

secondaria'mente *av* secondly

secon'dario, -a *ag* secondary; **scuola/ istruzione secondaria** secondary school/ education

secon'dino *sm* prison officer, warder (*Brit*)

se'condo, -a *ag* second ■ *sm* second; (*di pranzo*) main course ■ *sf* (*Aut*) second (gear); (*Ferr*) second class ■ *prep* according to; (*nel modo prescritto*) in accordance with; ~ **me** in my opinion, to my mind; ~ **la legge/quanto si era deciso** in accordance with the law/the decision taken; **di seconda classe** second-class; **di seconda mano** second-hand; **viaggiare in seconda** to travel second-class; **comandante in seconda** second-in-command; **a seconda di** *prep* according to; in accordance with

secondo'genito, -a [sekondo'dʒɛnito] *sm/f* second-born

S

secrezi'one [sekret'tsjone] *sf* secretion

'**sedano** *sm* celery

se'dare *vt* (*dolore*) to soothe; (*rivolta*) to put down, suppress

seda'tivo, -a *ag, sm* sedative

'**sede** *sf* (*luogo di residenza*) (place of) residence; (*di ditta: principale*) head office; (*: secondaria*) branch (office); (*di organizzazione*) headquarters *pl*; (*di governo, parlamento*) seat; (*Rel*) see; **in ~ di** (*in occasione di*) during; **in altra ~** on another occasion; **in ~ legislativa** in legislative sitting; **prendere ~** to take up residence; **un'azienda con diverse sedi in città** a firm with several branches in the city; **~ centrale** head office; **~ sociale** registered office

seden'tario, -a *ag* sedentary

se'dere *vi* to sit, be seated; **sedersi** *vr* to sit down ■ *sm* (*deretano*) bottom; **posto a ~** seat

'**sedia** *sf* chair; **~ elettrica** electric chair; **~ a rotelle** wheelchair

sedi'cenne [sedi'tʃɛnne] *ag, sm/f* sixteen-year-old

sedi'cente [sedi'tʃɛnte] *ag* self-styled

sedi'cesimo, -a [sedi'tʃɛzimo] *num* sixteenth

'**sedici** ['seditʃi] *num* sixteen

se'dile *sm* seat; (*panchina*) bench

sedimen'tare *vi* to leave a sediment

sedi'mento *sm* sediment

sedizi'one [sedit'tsjone] *sf* revolt, rebellion

sedizi'oso, -a [sedit'tsjoso] *ag* seditious

se'dotto, -a *pp di* **sedurre**

sedu'cente [sedu'tʃɛnte] *ag* seductive; (*proposta*) very attractive

se'durre *vt* to seduce

se'duta *sf* session, sitting; (*riunione*) meeting; **essere in ~** to be in session, be sitting; **~ stante** (*fig*) immediately; **~ spiritica** seance

sedut'tore, -'trice *sm/f* seducer/seductress

seduzi'one [sedut'tsjone] *sf* seduction; (*fascino*) charm, appeal

SEeO *abbr* (= *salvo errori e omissioni*) E & OE

'**sega, -ghe** *sf* saw; **~ circolare** circular saw; **~ a mano** handsaw

'**segale** *sf* rye

se'gare *vt* to saw; (*recidere*) to saw off

sega'tura *sf* (*residuo*) sawdust

'**seggio** ['seddʒo] *sm* seat; **~ elettorale** polling station

'**seggiola** ['seddʒola] *sf* chair

seggio'lino [seddʒo'lino] *sm* seat; (*per bambini*) child's chair; **~ di sicurezza** (*Aut*) child safety seat

seggio'lone [seddʒo'lone] *sm* (*per bambini*) highchair

seggio'via [seddʒo'via] *sf* chairlift

seghe'ria [sege'ria] *sf* sawmill

segherò *etc* [sege'rɔ] *vb vedi* **segare**

seghet'tato, -a [seget'tato] *ag* serrated

se'ghetto [se'getto] *sm* hacksaw

seg'mento *sm* segment

segna'lare [seɲɲa'lare] *vt* (*essere segno di*) to indicate, be a sign of; (*avvertire*) to signal; (*menzionare*) to indicate; (*: fatto, risultato, aumento*) to report; (*: errore, dettaglio*) to point out; (*Aut*) to signal, indicate; **segnalarsi** *vr* (*distinguersi*) to distinguish o.s.; **~ qn a qn** (*per lavoro etc*) to bring sb to sb's attention

segnalazi'one [seɲɲalat'tsjone] *sf* (*azione*) signalling; (*segnale*) signal; (*annuncio*) report; (*raccomandazione*) recommendation

se'gnale [seɲ'ɲale] *sm* signal; (*cartello*): **~ stradale** road sign; **~ acustico** acoustic *o* sound signal; (*di segreteria telefonica*) tone; **~ d'allarme** alarm; (*Ferr*) communication cord; **~ di linea libera** (*Tel*) dialling (*Brit*) *o* dial (*US*) tone; **~ luminoso** light signal; **~ di occupato** (*Tel*) engaged tone (*Brit*), busy signal (*US*); **~ orario** (*Radio*) time signal

segna'letica [seɲɲa'lɛtika] *sf* signalling, signposting; **~ stradale** road signs *pl*

segna'libro [seɲɲa'libro] *sm* (*anche Inform*) bookmark

segna'punti [seɲɲa'punti] *sm/f inv* scorer, scorekeeper

se'gnare [seɲ'ɲare] *vt* to mark; (*prendere nota*) to note; (*indicare*) to indicate, mark; (*Sport: goal*) to score; **segnarsi** *vr* (*Rel*) to make the sign of the cross, cross o.s.

'**segno** ['seɲɲo] *sm* sign; (*impronta, contrassegno*) mark; (*bersaglio*) target; **fare ~ di sì/no** to nod (one's head)/shake one's head; **fare ~ a qn di fermarsi** to motion (to) sb to stop; **cogliere** *o* **colpire nel ~** (*fig*) to hit the mark; **in** *o* **come ~ d'amicizia** as a mark *o* token of friendship; **"segni particolari"** (*su documento etc*) "distinguishing marks"

segre'gare *vt* to segregate, isolate

segregazi'one [segregat'tsjone] *sf* segregation

se'greta *sf vedi* **segreto**

segre'tario, -a *sm/f* secretary; **~ comunale** town clerk; **~ del partito** party leader; **S~ di Stato** Secretary of State

segrete'ria *sf* (*di ditta, scuola*) (secretary's) office; (*d'organizzazione internazionale*) secretariat; (*Pol etc: carica*) office of Secretary; **~ telefonica** answering service

segre'tezza [segre'tettsa] *sf* secrecy; **notizie della massima ~** confidential information; **in tutta ~** in secret; (*confidenzialmente*) in confidence

se'greto, -a *ag* secret ■ *sm* secret ■ *sf* dungeon; **in ~** in secret, secretly; **il ~**

professionale professional secrecy; **un ~ professionale** a professional secret

segu'ace [se'gwatʃe] *sm/f* follower, disciple

segu'ente *ag* following, next; **nel modo ~** as follows, in the following way

se'gugio [se'gudʒo] *sm* hound, hunting dog; *(fig)* private eye, sleuth

segu'ire *vt* to follow; *(frequentare: corso)* to attend ■ *vi* to follow; *(continuare: testo)* to continue; **~ i consigli di qn** to follow *o* to take sb's advice; **~ gli avvenimenti di attualità** to follow *o* keep up with current events; **come segue** as follows; **"segue"** "to be continued"

segui'tare *vt* to continue, carry on with ■ *vi* to continue, carry on

'seguito *sm* (*scorta*) suite, retinue; *(discepoli)* followers *pl*; *(serie)* sequence, series *sg*; *(continuazione)* continuation; *(conseguenza)* result; **di ~** at a stretch, on end; **in ~** later on; **in ~ a, a ~ di** following; *(a causa di)* as a result of, owing to; **essere al ~ di qn** to be among sb's suite, be one of sb's retinue; **non aver ~** *(conseguenze)* to have no repercussions; **facciamo ~ alla lettera del ...** further to *o* in answer to your letter of ...

'sei *vb vedi* **essere** ■ *num* six

Sei'celle [sei'tʃelle] *sfpl:* **le ~ the** Seychelles

seicen'tesco, -a, schi, sche [seitʃen'tesko] *ag* seventeenth-century

sei'cento [sei'tʃento] *num* six hundred ■ *sm:* **il S~** the seventeenth century

sei'mila *num* six thousand

'selce ['seltʃe] *sf* flint, flintstone

selci'ato [sel'tʃato] *sm* cobbled surface

selet'tivo, -a *ag* selective

selet'tore *sm* (*Tecn*) selector

selezio'nare [selettsjo'nare] *vt* to select

selezi'one [selet'tsjone] *sf* selection; **fare una ~** to make a selection *o* choice

'sella *sf* saddle

sel'lare *vt* to saddle

sel'lino *sm* saddle

seltz *sm inv* soda (water)

'selva *sf* (*bosco*) wood; *(foresta)* forest

selvag'gina [selvad'dʒina] *sf* (*animali*) game

sel'vaggio, -a, gi, ge [sel'vaddʒo] *ag* wild; *(tribù)* savage, uncivilized; *(fig: brutale)* savage, brutal; *(: incontrollato: fenomeno, aumento etc)* uncontrolled ■ *sm/f* savage; **inflazione selvaggia** runaway inflation

sel'vatico, -a, ci, che *ag* wild

S.Em. *abbr* (= *Sua Eminenza*) HE

se'maforo *sm* (*Aut*) traffic lights *pl*

se'mantico, -a *ag* semantic ■ *sf* semantics *sg*

sembi'anza [sem'bjantsa] *sf* (*poetico: aspetto*) appearance; **sembianze** *sfpl* (*lineamenti*)

features; *(fig: falsa apparenza)* semblance *sg*

sem'brare *vi* to seem ■ *vb impers:* **sembra che** it seems that; **mi sembra che** it seems to me that; *(penso che)* I think (that); **~ di essere** to seem to be; **non mi sembra vero!** I can't believe it!

'seme *sm* seed; *(sperma)* semen; *(Carte)* suit

se'mente *sf* seed

semes'trale *ag* (*che dura 6 mesi*) six-month *cpd*; *(che avviene ogni 6 mesi)* six-monthly

se'mestre *sm* half-year, six-month period

'semi ... *prefisso* semi ...

semi'cerchio [semi'tʃerkjo] *sm* semicircle

semicondut'tore *sm* semiconductor

semidetenzi'one [semideten'tsjone] *sf* custodial sentence whereby individual must spend a minimum of 10 hours per day in prison

semifi'nale *sf* semifinal

semi'freddo, -a *ag* (*Cuc*) chilled ■ *sm* ice-cream cake

semiliber'tà *sf* custodial sentence which allows prisoner to study or work outside prison for part of the day

'semina *sf* (*Agr*) sowing

semi'nare *vt* to sow

semi'nario *sm* seminar; *(Rel)* seminary

semi'nato *sm:* **uscire dal ~** *(fig)* to wander off the point

seminter'rato *sm* basement; *(appartamento)* basement flat *(Brit)* *o* apartment *(US)*

semi'ologo, -a, gi, ghe *sm/f* semiologist

semi'otica *sf* semiotics *sg*

se'mitico, -a, ci, che *ag* semitic

semivu'oto, -a *ag* half-empty

sem'mai = se mai

'semola *sf* bran; **~ di grano duro** durum wheat

semo'lato *ag:* **zucchero ~** caster sugar

semo'lino *sm* semolina

'semplice ['semplitʃe] *ag* simple; *(di un solo elemento)* single; **è una ~ formalità** it's a mere formality

semplice'mente [semplitʃe'mente] *av* simply

sempli'cistico, -a, ci, che [sempli'tʃistiko] *ag* simplistic

semplicità [semplitʃi'ta] *sf* simplicity

semplifi'care *vt* to simplify

semplificazi'one [semplifikat'tsjone] *sf* simplification; **fare una ~ di** to simplify

'sempre *av* always; *(ancora)* still; **posso ~ tentare** I can always *o* still try; **da ~** always; **per ~** forever; **una volta per ~** once and for all; **~ che** *cong* as long as, provided (that); **~ più** more and more; **~ meno** less and less; **va ~ meglio** things are getting better and better; **è ~ più giovane** she gets younger and

339

younger; **è ~ meglio che niente** it's better than nothing; **è (pur) ~ tuo fratello** he is still your brother (however); **c'è ~ la possibilità che ...** there's still a chance that ..., there's always the possibility that ...
sempre'verde *ag, sm o f (Bot)* evergreen
Sen. *abbr* (= *senatore*) Sen.
senape *sf (Cuc)* mustard
se'nato *sm* senate; **il S~** *see note*

sena'tore, -trice *sm/f* senator
Senegal *sm*: **il ~** Senegal
senega'lese *ag, sm/f* Senegalese *inv*
se'nese *ag* of (o from) Siena
se'nile *ag* senile
Senna *sf*: **la ~** the Seine
senno *sm* judgment, (common) sense; **col ~ di poi** with hindsight
sennò *av* = **se no**
seno *sm (Anat: petto, mammella)* breast; (: *grembo, fig*) womb; (: *cavità*) sinus; *(Geo)* inlet, creek; *(Mat)* sine; **in ~ al partito/all'organizzazione** within the party/the organization
sen'sale *sm (Comm)* agent
sensa'tezza [sensa'tettsa] *sf* good sense, good judgment
sen'sato, -a *ag* sensible
sensazio'nale [sensattsjo'nale] *ag* sensational
sensazi'one [sensat'tsjone] *sf* feeling, sensation; **fare ~** to cause a sensation, create a stir; **avere la ~ che** to have a feeling that
sen'sibile *ag* sensitive; (*ai sensi*) perceptible; (*rilevante, notevole*) appreciable, noticeable; **~ a** sensitive to
sensibilità *sf* sensitivity
sensibiliz'zare [sensibilid'dzare] *vt (fig)* to make aware, awaken
senso *sm (Fisiol, istinto)* sense; (*impressione, sensazione*) feeling, sensation; (*significato*)

meaning, sense; (*direzione*) direction; **sensi** *smpl (coscienza)* consciousness *sg*; (*sensualità*) senses; **perdere/riprendere i sensi** to lose/regain consciousness; **avere ~ pratico** to be practical; **avere un sesto ~** to have a sixth sense; **fare ~ a** (*ripugnare*) to disgust, repel; **ciò non ha ~** that doesn't make sense; **senza** *o* **privo di ~** meaningless; **nel ~ che** in the sense that; **nel vero ~ della parola** in the true sense of the word; **nel ~ della lunghezza** lengthwise, lengthways; **nel ~ della larghezza** widthwise; **ho dato disposizioni in quel ~** I've given instructions to that end *o* effect; **~ comune** common sense; **~ del dovere** sense of duty; **in ~ opposto** in the opposite direction; **in ~ orario/antiorario** clockwise/anticlockwise; **~ dell'umorismo** sense of humour; **a ~ unico** one-way; **"~ vietato"** *(Aut)* "no entry"
sensu'ale *ag* sensual; sensuous
sensualità *sf* sensuality; sensuousness
sen'tenza [sen'tentsa] *sf (Dir)* sentence; (*massima*) maxim
sentenzi'are [senten'tsjare] *vi (Dir)* to pass judgment
senti'ero *sm* path
sentimen'tale *ag* sentimental; (*vita, avventura*) love *cpd*
senti'mento *sm* feeling
senti'nella *sf* sentry
sen'tire *vt (percepire al tatto, fig)* to feel; (*udire*) to hear; (*ascoltare*) to listen to; (*odore*) to smell; (*avvertire con il gusto, assaggiare*) to taste ■ *vi*: **~ di** (*avere sapore*) to taste of; (*avere odore*) to smell of; **sentirsi** *vr (uso reciproco)* to be in touch; **sentirsi bene/male** to feel well/unwell *o* ill; **sentirsi di fare qc** (*essere disposto*) to feel like doing sth; **~ la mancanza di qn** to miss sb; **ho sentito dire che ...** I have heard that ...; **a ~ lui ...** to hear him talk ...; **fatti ~** keep in touch; **intendo ~ il mio legale/il parere di un medico** I'm going to consult my lawyer/a doctor
sentita'mente *av* sincerely; **ringraziare ~** to thank sincerely
sen'tito, -a *ag (sincero)* sincere, warm; **per ~ dire** by hearsay
sen'tore *sm* rumour (Brit), rumor (US), talk; **aver ~ di qc** to hear about sth
senza ['sentsa] *prep, cong* without; **~ dir nulla** without saying a word; **~ dire che ...** not to mention the fact that ...; **~ contare che ...** without considering that ...; **fare ~ qc** to do without sth; **~ di me** without me; **~ che io lo sapessi** without me *o* my knowing; **~ amici** friendless; **senz'altro** of course, certainly; **~ dubbio** no doubt; **~ scrupoli**

unscrupulous; **i ~ lavoro** the jobless, the unemployed; **i ~ tetto** the homeless

senza'tetto [sentsa'tetto] *sm/f inv* homeless person; **i ~** the homeless

sepa'rare *vt* to separate; (*dividere*) to divide; (*tenere distinto*) to distinguish; **separarsi** *vr* (*coniugi*) to separate, part; (*amici*) to part; **· separarsi da** (*coniuge*) to separate o part from; (*amico, socio*) to part company with; (*oggetto*) to part with

separata'mente *av* separately

sepa'rato, -a *ag* (*letti, conto etc*) separate; (*coniugi*) separated

separazi'one [separat'tsjone] *sf* separation; **~ dei beni** division of property

séparé [sepa're] *sm inv* screen

se'polcro *sm* sepulchre (*Brit*), sepulcher (*US*)

se'polto, -a *pp di* **seppellire**

sepol'tura *sf* burial; **dare ~ a qn** to bury sb

seppel'lire *vt* to bury

'seppi *etc vb vedi* **sapere**

'seppia *sf* cuttlefish ■ *ag inv* sepia

sep'pure *cong* even if

se'quela *sf* (*di avvenimenti*) series, sequence; (*di offese, ingiurie*) string

se'quenza [se'kwentsa] *sf* sequence

sequenzi'ale [sekwen'tsjale] *ag* sequential

seques'trare *vt* (*Dir*) to impound; (*rapire*) to kidnap; (*costringere in un luogo*) to keep, confine

se'questro *sm* (*Dir*) impoundment; **~ di persona** kidnapping

se'quoia *sf* sequoia

'sera *sf* evening; **di ~** in the evening; **domani ~** tomorrow evening, tomorrow night; **questa ~** this evening, tonight

se'rale *ag* evening *cpd*; **scuola ~** evening classes *pl*, night school

se'rata *sf* evening; (*ricevimento*) party

ser'bare *vt* to keep; (*mettere da parte*) to put aside; **~ rancore/odio verso qn** to bear sb a grudge/hate sb

serba'toio *sm* tank; (*cisterna*) cistern

'serbo *ag* Serbian ■ *sm/f* Serbian, Serb ■ *sm* (*Ling*) Serbian; (*il serbare*): **mettere/tenere** o **avere in ~ qc** to put/keep sth aside

serbocro'ato, -a *ag, sm* Serbo-Croat

serena'mente *av* serenely, calmly

sere'nata *sf* (*Mus*) serenade

serenità *sf* serenity

se'reno, -a *ag* (*tempo, cielo*) clear; (*fig*) serene, calm ■ *sm* (*tempo*) good weather; **un fulmine a ciel ~** (*fig*) a bolt from the blue

serg. *abbr* (= *sergente*) Sgt.

ser'gente [ser'dʒente] *sm* (*Mil*) sergeant

seri'ale *ag* (*Inform*) serial

seria'mente *av* (*con serietà, in modo grave*) seriously; **lavorare ~** to take one's job seriously

'serie *sf inv* (*successione*) series *inv*; (*gruppo, collezione di chiavi etc*) set; (*Sport*) division; league; (*Comm*): **modello di ~/fuori ~** standard/custom-built model; **in ~** in quick succession; (*Comm*) mass *cpd*; **tutta una ~ di problemi** a whole string o series of problems

serietà *sf* seriousness; reliability

'serio, -a *ag* serious; (*impiegato*) responsible, reliable; (*ditta, cliente*) reliable, dependable; **sul ~** (*davvero*) really, truly; (*seriamente*) seriously, in earnest; **dico sul ~** I'm serious; **faccio sul ~** I mean it; **prendere qc/qn sul ~** to take sth/sb, seriously

seri'oso, -a *ag* (*persona, modi*): **un po' ~** a bit too serious

ser'mone *sm* sermon

'serpe *sf* snake; (*fig peg*) viper

serpeggi'are [serped'dʒare] *vi* to wind; (*fig*) to spread

ser'pente *sm* snake; **~ a sonagli** rattlesnake

'serra *sf* greenhouse; hothouse; (*Geo*) sierra

serra'manico *sm*: **coltello a ~** jack-knife

serranda *sf* roller shutter

ser'rare *vt* to close, shut; (*a chiave*) to lock; (*stringere*) to tighten; (*serrare: nemico*) to close in on; **~ i pugni/i denti** to clench one's fists/ teeth; **~ le file** to close ranks

ser'rata *sf* (*Industria*) lockout

ser'rato, -a *ag* (*veloce*): **a ritmo ~** quickly, fast

serra'tura *sf* lock

'serva *sf vedi* **servo**

'server ['server] *sm inv* (*Inform*) server

ser'vigio [ser'vidʒo] *sm* favour (*Brit*), favor (*US*), service

ser'vire *vt* to serve; (*clienti: al ristorante*) to wait on; (*: al negozio*) to serve, attend to; (*fig: giovare*) to aid, help; (*Carte*) to deal ■ *vi* (*Tennis*) to serve; (*essere utile*): **~ a qn** to be of use to sb; **~ a qc/a fare** (*utensile etc*) to be used for sth/for doing; **~ (a qn) da** to serve as (for sb); **servirsi** *vr* (*usare*): **servirsi di** to use; (*prendere: cibo*): **servirsi (di)** to help o.s. (to); (*essere cliente abituale*): **servirsi da** to be a regular customer at, go to; **non mi serve più** I don't need it any more; **non serve che lei vada** you don't need to go

servitù *sf* servitude; slavery; (*personale di servizio*) servants *pl* domestic staff, domestic staff

servizi'evole [servit'tsjevole] *ag* obliging, willing to help

ser'vizio [ser'vittsjo] *sm* service; (*al ristorante: sul conto*) service (charge); (*Stampa, TV, Radio*) report; (*da tè, caffè etc*) set, service; **servizi** *smpl* (*di casa*) kitchen and bathroom; (*Econ*) services; **essere di ~** to be on duty; **fuori ~** (*telefono etc*) out of order; **~ compreso/**

escluso service included/not included; **entrata di** ~ service o tradesman's (Brit) entrance; **casa con doppi servizi** house with two bathrooms; **~ assistenza clienti** after-sales service; **~ civile** ≈ community service; **~ in diretta** (TV, Radio) live coverage; **~ fotografico** (Stampa) photo feature; **~ militare** military service; **~ d'ordine** (Polizia) police patrol; (di manifestanti) team of stewards (responsible for crowd control); **servizi segreti** secret service sg; **servizi di sicurezza** security forces

'**servo, a** sm/f servant

servo'freno sm (Aut) servo brake

servos'terzo [servos'tɛrtso] sm (Aut) power steering

'**sesamo** sm (Bot) sesame

ses'santa num sixty

sessan'tenne ag, sm/f sixty-year-old

sessan'tesimo, -a num sixtieth

sessan'tina sf: **una ~ (di)** about sixty

sessantot'tino, -a sm/f a person who took part in the events of 1968

sessan'totto sm see note

sessi'one sf session

'**sesso** sm sex; **il ~ debole/forte** the weaker/stronger sex

sessu'ale ag sexual, sex cpd

sessualità sf sexuality

sessu'ologo, -a, gi, ghe sm/f sexologist, sex specialist

ses'tante sm sextant

'**sesto, -a** num sixth ■ sm: **rimettere in ~** (aggiustare) to put back in order; (fig: persona) to put back on his (o her) feet; **rimettersi in ~** (riprendersi) to recover, get well; (riassettarsi) to tidy o.s. up

'**seta** sf silk

setacci'are [setat'tʃare] vt (farina etc) to sift, sieve; (fig: zona) to search, comb

se'taccio [se'tattʃo] sm sieve; **passare al ~** (fig) to search, comb

'**sete** sf thirst; **avere ~** to be thirsty; **~ di potere** thirst for power

seti'ficio [seti'fitʃo] sm silk factory

'**setola** sf bristle

sett. abbr (= settembre) Sept.

'**setta** sf sect

set'tanta num seventy

settan'tenne ag, sm/f seventy-year-old

settan'tesimo, -a num seventieth

settan'tina sf: **una ~ (di)** about seventy

'**sette** num seven

settecen'tesco, -a, schi, sche [settetʃen'tesko] ag eighteenth-century

sette'cento [sette'tʃɛnto] num seven hundred ■ sm: **il S~** the eighteenth century

set'tembre sm September; vedi anche **luglio**

sette'mila num seven thousand

settentrio'nale ag northern ■ sm/f northerner

settentri'one sm north

'**settico, -a, ci, che** ag (Med) septic

setti'mana sf week; **la ~ scorsa/prossima** last/next week; **a metà ~** in the middle of the week; **~ bianca** winter-sport holiday

settima'nale ag, sm weekly

'**settimo, -a** num seventh

set'tore sm sector; **~ privato/pubblico** private/public sector; **~ terziario** service industries pl

Se'ul sf Seoul

severità sf severity

se'vero, -a ag severe

sevizi'are [sevit'tsjare] vt to torture

se'vizie [se'vittsje] sfpl torture sg

'**sexy** ['seksi] ag inv sexy

sez. abbr = **sezione**

sezio'nare [settsjo'nare] vt to divide into sections; (Med) to dissect

sezi'one [set'tsjone] sf section; (Med) dissection

sfaccen'dato, -a [sfattʃen'dato] ag idle

sfaccetta'tura [sfattʃetta'tura] sf (azione) faceting; (parte sfaccettata, fig) facet

sfacchi'nare [sfakki'nare] vi (fam) to toil, drudge

sfacchi'nata [sfakki'nata] sf (fam) chore, drudgery no pl

sfaccia'taggine [sfattʃa'taddʒine] sf insolence, cheek

sfacci'ato, -a [sfat'tʃato] ag (maleducato) cheeky, impudent; (vistoso) gaudy

sfa'celo [sfa'tʃɛlo] sm (fig) ruin, collapse

sfal'darsi vr to flake (off)

sfal'sare vt to offset

sfa'mare vt (nutrire) to feed; (soddisfare la fame): **~ qn** to satisfy sb's hunger; **sfamarsi** vr to satisfy one's hunger, fill o.s. up

sfarfal'lio sm (Cine, TV) flickering

'**sfarzo** ['sfartso] sm pomp, splendour (Brit), splendor (US)

sfar'zoso, -a [sfar'tsoso] ag splendid, magnificent

sfasa'mento sm (Elettr) phase displacement; (fig) confusion, bewilderment

sfa'sato, -a ag (Elettr, motore) out of phase; (fig: persona) confused, bewildered

sfasci'are [sfaʃ'ʃare] vt (ferita) to unbandage; (distruggere: porta) to smash, shatter; **sfasciarsi** vr (rompersi) to smash, shatter

sfa'tare vt (leggenda) to explode

sfati'cato, -a sm/f idler, loafer

'**sfatto, -a** ag (letto) unmade; (orlo etc) undone; (gelato, neve) melted; (frutta) overripe; (riso, pasta etc) overdone, overcooked; (fam: persona, corpo) flabby

sfavil'lare vi to spark, send out sparks; (risplendere) to sparkle

sfa'vore sm disfavour (Brit), disfavor (US), disapproval

sfavo'revole ag unfavourable (Brit), unfavorable (US)

sfega'tato, -a ag fanatical

'**sfera** sf sphere

'**sferico, -a, ci, che** ag spherical

sfer'rare vt (fig: colpo) to land, deal; (: attacco) to launch

sfer'zante [sfer'tsante] ag (critiche, parole) stinging

sfer'zare [sfer'tsare] vt to whip; (fig) to lash out at

sfian'care vt to wear out, exhaust; **sfiancarsi** vr to exhaust o.s., wear o.s. out

sfia'tare vi to allow air (o gas etc) to escape

sfiata'toio sm blowhole; (Tecn) vent

sfi'brante ag exhausting, energy-sapping

sfi'brare vt (indebolire) to exhaust, enervate

sfi'brato, -a ag exhausted, worn out

'**sfida** sf challenge

sfi'dante ag challenging ■ sm/f challenger

sfi'dare vt to challenge; (fig) to defy, brave; ~ **qn a fare qc** to challenge sb to do sth; ~ **un pericolo** to brave a danger; **sfido che ...** I dare say (that) ...

sfi'ducia [sfi'dutʃa] sf distrust, mistrust; **avere ~ in qn/qc** to distrust sb/sth

sfiduci'ato, -a [sfidu'tʃato] ag lacking confidence

sfigato, -a (fam) ag: **essere ~** (sfortunato) to be unlucky ■ sm/f (fallito, sfortunato) loser; (fuori moda) dork

sfigu'rare vt (persona) to disfigure; (quadro, statua) to deface ■ vi (far cattiva figura) to make a bad impression

sfilacci'are [sfilat'tʃare] vt, vi, **sfilacci'arsi** vr to fray

sfi'lare vt (ago) to unthread; (abito, scarpe) to slip off ■ vi (truppe) to march past, parade; (manifestanti) to march; **sfilarsi** vr (perle etc) to come unstrung; (orlo, tessuto) to fray; (calza) to run, ladder

sfi'lata sf (Mil) parade; (di manifestanti) march; ~ **di moda** fashion show

'**sfilza** ['sfiltsa] sf (di case) row; (di errori) series inv

'**sfinge** ['sfindʒe] sf sphinx

sfini'mento sm exhaustion

sfi'nito, -a ag exhausted

sfio'rare vt to brush (against); (argomento) to touch upon; ~ **la velocità di 150 km/h** to touch 150 km/h

sfio'rire vi to wither, fade

'**sfitto, -a** ag vacant, empty

sfo'cato, -a ag (Fot) out of focus

sfoci'are [sfo'tʃare] vi: ~ **in** to flow into; (fig: malcontento) to develop into

sfode'rato, -a ag (vestito) unlined

sfo'gare vt to vent, pour out; **sfogarsi** vr (sfogare la propria rabbia) to give vent to one's anger; (confidarsi): **sfogarsi (con)** to pour out one's feelings (to); **non sfogarti su di me!** don't take your bad temper out on me!

sfoggi'are [sfod'dʒare] vt, vi to show off

'**sfoggio** ['sfɔddʒo] sm show, display; **fare ~ di** to show off, display

sfogherò etc [sfoge'rɔ] vb vedi **sfogare**

'**sfoglia** ['sfɔʎʎa] sf sheet of pasta dough; **pasta ~** (Cuc) puff pastry

sfogli'are [sfoʎ'ʎare] vt (libro) to leaf through

'**sfogo, -ghi** sm outlet; (eruzione cutanea) rash; (fig) outburst; **dare ~ a** (fig) to give vent to

sfolgo'rante ag (luce) blazing; (fig: vittoria) brilliant

sfolgo'rare vi to blaze

sfolla'gente [sfolla'dʒɛnte] sm inv truncheon (Brit), billy (US)

sfol'lare vt to empty, clear ■ vi to disperse; ~ **da** (città) to evacuate

sfol'lato, -a ag evacuated ■ sm/f evacuee

sfol'tire vt, **sfol'tirsi** vr to thin (out)

sfon'dare vt (porta) to break down; (scarpe) to wear a hole in; (cesto, scatola) to burst, knock the bottom out of; (Mil) to break through ■ vi (riuscire) to make a name for o.s.

sfon'dato, -a ag (scarpe) worn out; (scatola) burst; (sedia) broken, damaged; **essere ricco ~** to be rolling in it

'**sfondo** sm background

sfo'rare vi to overrun

sfor'mare vt to put out of shape, knock out of shape; **sformarsi** vr to lose shape, get out of shape

S

343

sfor'mato, -a ag (che ha perso forma) shapeless ■ sm (Cuc) type of soufflé

sfor'nare vt (pane) to take out of the oven; (fig) to churn out

sfor'nito, -a ag: ~ **di** lacking in, without; (negozio) out of

sfor'tuna sf misfortune, ill luck no pl; **avere ~** to be unlucky; **che ~!** how unfortunate!

sfortu'nato, -a ag unlucky; (impresa, film) unsuccessful

sfor'zare [sfor'tsare] vt to force; (voce, occhi) to strain; **sforzarsi** vr: **sforzarsi di** o **a** o **per fare** to try hard to do

'sforzo ['sfɔrtso] sm effort; (tensione eccessiva, Tecn) strain; **fare uno ~** to make an effort; **essere sotto ~** (motore, macchina, fig: persona) to be under stress

'sfottere vt (fam) to tease

sfracel'lare [sfratʃel'lare] vt, **sfracel'larsi** vr to smash

sfrat'tare vt to evict

'sfratto sm eviction; **dare lo ~ a qn** to give sb notice to quit

sfrecci'are [sfret'tʃare] vi to shoot o flash past

sfre'gare vt (strofinare) to rub; (graffiare) to scratch; **sfregarsi le mani** to rub one's hands; **~ un fiammifero** to strike a match

sfregi'are [sfre'dʒare] vt to slash, gash; (persona) to disfigure; (quadro) to deface

'sfregio ['sfredʒo] sm gash; scar; (fig) insult

sfre'nato, -a ag (fig) unrestrained, unbridled

sfron'dare vt (albero) to prune, thin out; (fig: discorso, scritto) to prune (down)

sfronta'tezza [sfronta'tettsa] sf impudence, cheek

sfron'tato, -a ag impudent, cheeky

sfrutta'mento sm exploitation

sfrut'tare vt (terreno) to overwork, exhaust; (miniera) to exploit, work; (fig: operai, occasione, potere) to exploit

sfrutta'tore, -'trice sm/f exploiter

sfug'gente [sfud'dʒente] ag (fig: sguardo) elusive; (mento) receding

sfug'gire [sfud'dʒire] vi to escape; **~ a** (custode) to escape (from); (morte) to escape; **~ a qn** (dettaglio, nome) to escape sb; **~ di mano a qn** to slip out of sb's hand (o hands); **lasciarsi ~ un'occasione** to let an opportunity go by; **~ al controllo** (macchina) to go out of control; (situazione) to be no longer under control

sfug'gita [sfud'dʒita] sf: **di ~** (rapidamente, in fretta) in passing

sfu'mare vt (colori, contorni) to soften, shade off ■ vi to shade (off), fade; (fig: svanire) to vanish, disappear; (: speranze) to come to nothing

sfuma'tura sf shading off no pl; (tonalità) shade, tone; (fig) touch, hint

sfuo'cato, -a ag = **sfocato**

sfuri'ata sf (scatto di collera) fit of anger; (rimprovero) sharp rebuke

'sfuso, -a ag (caramelle etc) loose, unpacked; (vino) unbottled; (birra) draught (Brit), draft (US)

sg. abbr = **seguente**

sga'bello sm stool

sgabuz'zino [zgabud'dzino] sm lumber room

sgambet'tare vi to kick one's legs about

sgam'betto sm: **far lo ~ a qn** to trip sb up; (fig) to oust sb

sganasci'arsi [zganaʃ'ʃarsi] vr: **~ dalle risa** to roar with laughter

sganci'are [zgan'tʃare] vt to unhook; (chiusura) to unfasten, undo; (Ferr) to uncouple; (bombe: da aereo) to release, drop; (fig: fam: soldi) to fork out; **sganciarsi** vr to come unhooked; to come unfastened, come undone; to uncouple; (fig): **sganciarsi (da)** to get away (from)

sganghe'rato, -a [zgange'rato] ag (porta) off its hinges; (auto) ramshackle; (riso) wild, boisterous

sgar'bato, -a ag rude, impolite

'sgarbo sm: **fare uno ~ a qn** to be rude to sb

sgargi'ante [zgar'dʒante] ag gaudy, showy

sgar'rare vi (persona) to step out of line; (orologio: essere avanti) to gain; (: essere indietro) to lose

'sgarro sm inaccuracy

sgattaio'lare vi to sneak away o off

sge'lare [zdʒe'lare] vi, vt to thaw

'sghembo, -a ['zgembo] ag (obliquo) slanting; (storto) crooked

sghignaz'zare [zgiɲɲat'tsare] vi to laugh scornfully

sghignaz'zata [zgiɲɲat'tsata] sf scornful laugh

sgob'bare vi (fam: scolaro) to swot; (: operaio) to slog

sgoccio'lare [zgottʃo'lare] vt (vuotare) to drain (to the last drop) ■ vi (acqua) to drip; (recipiente) to drain

'sgoccioli ['zgottʃoli] smpl: **essere agli ~** (lavoro, provviste etc) to be nearly finished; (periodo) to be nearly over; **siamo agli ~** we've nearly finished, the end is in sight

sgo'larsi vr to talk (o shout o sing) o.s. hoarse

sgomberare, sgomb(e)'rare vt to clear; (andarsene da: stanza) to vacate; (evacuare) to evacuate

'sgombero sm vedi **sgombro**

'sgombro, -a ag: **~ (di)** clear (of), free (from) ■ sm (Zool) mackerel; (anche: **sgombero**)

clearing; vacating; evacuation; (: *trasloco*)
removal

sgomen'tare *vt* to dismay; **sgomentarsi** *vr*
to be dismayed

sgo'mento, -a *ag* dismayed ■ *sm* dismay,
consternation

sgomi'nare *vt* (*nemico*) to rout; (*avversario*) to
defeat; (*fig*: *epidemia*) to overcome

sgonfi'are *vt* to let down, deflate; **sgonfiarsi**
vr to go down

'sgonfio, -a *ag* (*pneumatico, pallone*) flat

'sgorbio *sm* blot; scribble

sgor'gare *vi* to gush (out)

sgoz'zare [zgot'tsare] *vt* to cut the throat of

sgra'devole *ag* unpleasant, disagreeable

sgra'dito, -a *ag* unpleasant, unwelcome

sgraffi'gnare [zgraffiɲ'ɲare] *vt* (*fam*) to
pinch, swipe

sgrammati'cato, -a *ag* ungrammatical

sgra'nare *vt* (*piselli*) to shell; ~ **gli occhi** to
open one's eyes wide

sgran'chirsi [zgran'kirsi] *vr* to stretch; ~ **le
gambe** to stretch one's legs

sgranocchi'are [zgranok'kjare] *vt* to munch

sgras'sare *vt* to remove the grease from

'sgravio *sm*: ~ **fiscale** *o* **contributivo** tax
relief

sgrazi'ato, -a [zgrat'tsjato] *ag* clumsy,
ungainly

sgreto'lare *vt* to cause to crumble;
sgretolarsi *vr* to crumble

sgri'dare *vt* to scold

sgri'data *sf* scolding

sguai'ato, -a *ag* coarse, vulgar

sguai'nare *vt* to draw, unsheathe

sgual'cire [zgwal'tʃire] *vt* to crumple (up),
crease

sgual'drina *sf* (*peg*) slut

sgu'ardo *sm* (*occhiata*) look, glance;
(*espressione*) look (in one's eye); **dare uno ~ a
qc** to glance at sth, cast a glance *o* an eye over
sth; **alzare** *o* **sollevare lo ~** to raise one's
eyes, look up; **cercare qc/qn con lo ~** to look
around for sth/sb

'sguattero, -a *sm/f* scullery boy(-maid)

sguaz'zare [zgwat'tsare] *vi* (*nell'acqua*) to
splash about; (*nella melma*) to wallow; ~
nell'oro to be rolling in money

sguinzagli'are [zgwintsaʎ'ʎare] *vt* to let off
the leash; (*fig*: *persona*): ~ **qn dietro a qn** to
set sb on sb

sgusci'are [zguʃ'ʃare] *vt* to shell ■ *vi* (*sfuggire
di mano*) to slip; ~ **via** to slip *o* slink away

'shaker ['ʃeikaʳ] *sm inv* (cocktail) shaker

'shampoo ['ʃampo] *sm inv* shampoo

'shiatzu ['tʃiatsu] *sm, ag inv* shiatsu

shoc'care [ʃok'kare] *vt* = **shockare**

shock [ʃok] *sm inv* shock

shoc'kare [ʃok'kare] *vt* to shock

SI *sigla* = **Siena**

 PAROLA CHIAVE

si (*dav lo, la, li, le, ne diventa* **se**) *pron* **1** (*riflessivo*:
maschile) himself; (: *femminile*) herself;
(: *neutro*) itself; (: *impersonale*) oneself; (: *pl*)
themselves; **lavarsi** to wash (oneself); **si è
tagliato** he has cut himself; **si credono
importanti** they think a lot of themselves
2 (*con complemento oggetto*): **lavarsi le mani** to
wash one's hands; **sporcarsi i pantaloni** to
get one's trousers dirty; **si sta lavando i
capelli** he (*o* she) is washing his (*o* her) hair
3 (*reciproco*) one another, each other; **si
amano** they love one another *o* each other
4 (*passivo*): **si ripara facilmente** it is easily
repaired; **affittasi camera** room to let
5 (*impersonale*): **si dice che ...** they *o* people
say that ...; **si vede che è vecchio** one *o* you
can see that it's old; **non si fa credito** we do
not give credit; **ci si sbaglia facilmente** it's
easy to make a mistake
6 (*noi*) we; **tra poco si parte** we're leaving
soon

sì *av* yes ■ *sm*: **non mi aspettavo un sì** I
didn't expect him (*o* her *etc*) to say yes; **per
me è sì** I should think so, I expect so;
saranno stati sì e no in 20 there must have
been about 20 of them; **uno sì e uno no**
every other one; **un giorno sì e uno no**
every other day; **dire di sì** to say yes; **spero/
penso di sì** I hope/think so; **fece di sì col
capo** he nodded (his head); **e sì che ...** and to
think that ...

'sia *cong*: ~ ... ~ (*o* ... *o*): ~ **che lavori, ~ che non
lavori** whether he works or not; (*tanto ...
quanto*): **verranno ~ Luigi ~ suo fratello**
both Luigi and his brother will be coming

'sia *etc vb vedi* **essere**

SIAE *sigla f* = **Società Italiana Autori ed
Editori**

Si'am *sm*: **il ~** Siam

sia'mese *ag, sm/f* siamese *inv*

si'amo *vb vedi* **essere**

Si'beria *sf*: **la ~** Siberia

siberi'ano, -a *ag, sm/f* Siberian

sibi'lare *vi* to hiss; (*fischiare*) to whistle

'sibilo *sm* hiss; whistle

si'cario *sm* hired killer

sicché [sik'ke] *cong* (*perciò*) so (that), therefore;
(*e quindi*) (and) so

siccità [sittʃi'ta] *sf* drought

sic'come *cong* since, as

Si'cilia [si'tʃilja] *sf*: **la ~** Sicily
sicili'ano, -a [sitʃi'ljano] *ag, sm/f* Sicilian
sico'moro *sm* sycamore
'siculo, -a *ag, sm/f* Sicilian
si'cura *sf* (*di arma, spilla*) safety catch; (*di portiera*) safety lock
sicura'mente *av* certainly
sicu'rezza [siku'rettsa] *sf* safety; security; confidence; certainty; **di ~** safety *cpd*; **la ~ stradale** road safety; **avere la ~ di qc** to be sure *o* certain of sth; **lo so con ~** I am quite certain; **ha risposto con molta ~** he answered very confidently
si'curo, -a *ag* safe; (*ben difeso*) secure; (*fiducioso*) confident; (*certo*) sure, certain; (*notizia, amico*) reliable; (*esperto*) skilled ■ *av* (*anche:* **di sicuro**) certainly ■ *sm*: **andare sul ~** to play safe; **essere/mettere al ~** to be safe/put in a safe place; **~ di sé** self-confident, sure of o.s.; **sentirsi ~** to feel safe *o* secure; **essere ~ di/ che** to be sure of/that; **da fonte sicura** from reliable sources
siderur'gia [siderur'dʒia] *sf* iron and steel industry
side'rurgico, -a, ci, che [side'rurdʒiko] *ag* iron and steel *cpd*
'sidro *sm* cider
si'edo *etc vb vedi* **sedere**
si'epe *sf* hedge
si'ero *sm* (*Med*) serum; **~ antivipera** snake bite serum; **~ del latte** whey
sieronegatività *sf inv* HIV-negative status
sieronega'tivo, -a *ag* HIV-negative ■ *sm/f* HIV-negative person
sieropositività *sf inv* HIV-positive status
sieroposi'tivo, -a *ag* HIV-positive ■ *sm/f* HIV-positive person
si'erra *sf* (*Geo*) sierra
Si'erra Le'one *sf*: **la ~** Sierra Leone
si'esta *sf* siesta, (afternoon) nap
si'ete *vb vedi* **essere**
si'filide *sf* syphilis
si'fone *sm* siphon
Sig. *abbr* (= *signore*) Mr
siga'retta *sf* cigarette
'sigaro *sm* cigar
Sigg. *abbr* (= *signori*) Messrs
sigil'lare [sidʒil'lare] *vt* to seal
si'gillo [si'dʒillo] *sm* seal
'sigla *sf* (*iniziali*) initials *pl*; (*abbreviazione*) acronym, abbreviation; **~ automobilistica** *abbreviation of province on vehicle number plate*; **~ musicale** signature tune
si'glare *vt* to initial
Sig.na *abbr* (= *signorina*) Miss
signifi'care [siɲɲifi'kare] *vt* to mean; **cosa significa?** what does this mean?

significa'tivo, -a [siɲɲifika'tivo] *ag* significant
signifi'cato [siɲɲifi'kato] *sm* meaning
si'gnora [si'ɲora] *sf* lady; **la ~ X** Mrs X; **buon giorno S~/Signore/Signorina** good morning; (*deferente*) good morning Madam/ Sir/Madam; (*quando si conosce il nome*) good morning Mrs/Mr/Miss X; **Gentile S~/ Signore/Signorina** (*in una lettera*) Dear Madam/Sir/Madam; **Gentile** (*o Cara*) **S~ Rossi** Dear Mrs Rossi; **Gentile S~ Anna Rossi** (*sulle buste*) Mrs Anna Rossi; **il signor Rossi e ~** Mr Rossi and his wife; **signore e signori** ladies and gentlemen; **le presento la mia ~** may I introduce my wife?
si'gnore [si'ɲore] *sm* gentleman; (*padrone*) lord, master; (*Rel*): **il S~** the Lord; **il signor X** Mr X; **signor Presidente** Mr Chairman; **Gentile** (*o Caro*) **Signor Rossi** (*in lettere*) Dear Mr Rossi; **Gentile Signor Paolo Rossi** (*sulle buste*) Mr Paolo Rossi; **i signori Bianchi** (*coniugi*) Mr and Mrs Bianchi; *vedi anche* **signora**
signo'ria [siɲɲo'ria] *sf* (*Storia*) seignory, signoria; **S~ Vostra** (*Amm*) you
signo'rile [siɲɲo'rile] *ag* refined
signorilità [siɲɲorili'ta] *sf* (*raffinatezza*) refinement; (*eleganza*) elegance
signo'rina [siɲɲo'rina] *sf* young lady; **la ~ X** Miss X; **Gentile** (*o Cara*) **S~ Rossi** (*in lettere*) Dear Miss Rossi; **Gentile S~ Anna Rossi** (*sulle buste*) Miss Anna Rossi; *vedi anche* **signora**
signo'rino [siɲɲo'rino] *sm* young master
Sig.ra *abbr* (= *signora*) Mrs
silenzia'tore [silentsja'tore] *sm* silencer
si'lenzio [si'lɛntsjo] *sm* silence; **fare ~** to be quiet, stop talking; **far passare qc sotto ~** to keep quiet about sth, hush sth up
silenzi'oso, -a [silen'tsjoso] *ag* silent, quiet
'silice ['silitʃe] *sf* silica
si'licio [si'litʃo] *sm* silicon; **piastrina di ~** silicon chip
sili'cone *sm* silicone
'sillaba *sf* syllable
silu'rare *vt* to torpedo; (*fig: privare del comando*) to oust
si'luro *sm* torpedo
SIM [sim] *sigla f inv* (*Tel*): **~ card** SIM card
simbi'osi *sf* (*Biol, fig*) symbiosis
simboleggi'are [simboled'dʒare] *vt* to symbolize
sim'bolico, -a, ci, che *ag* symbolic(al)
simbo'lismo *sm* symbolism
'simbolo *sm* symbol
simi'lare *ag* similar
'simile *ag* (*analogo*) similar; (*di questo tipo*): **un uomo ~** such a man, a man like this ■ *sm*

(*persona*) fellow man; **libri simili** such books; **~ a** similar to; **non ho mai visto niente di ~** I've never seen anything like that; **è insegnante o qualcosa di ~** he's a teacher or something like that; **vendono vasi e simili** they sell vases and things like that; **i suoi simili** one's fellow men; one's peers

simili'tudine *sf* (*Ling*) simile

simme'tria *sf* symmetry

sim'metrico, -a, ci, che *ag* symmetric(al)

simpa'tia *sf* (*qualità*) pleasantness; (*inclinazione*) liking; **avere ~ per qn** to like sb, have a liking for sb; **con ~** (*su lettera etc*) with much affection

sim'patico, -a, ci, che *ag* (*persona*) nice, pleasant, likeable; (*casa, albergo etc*) nice, pleasant

simpatiz'zante [simpatid'dzante] *sm/f* sympathizer

simpatiz'zare [simpatid'dzare] *vi:* **~ con** to take a liking to

sim'posio *sm* symposium

simu'lacro *sm* (*monumento, statua*) image; (*fig*) semblance

simu'lare *vt* to sham, simulate; (*Tecn*) to simulate

simulazi'one [simulat'tsjone] *sf* shamming; simulation

simul'taneo, -a *ag* simultaneous

sin. *abbr* (= *sinistra*) L

sina'goga, -ghe *sf* synagogue

sincera'mente [sintʃera'mente] *av* (*gen*) sincerely; (*francamente*) honestly, sincerely

since'rarsi [sintʃe'rarsi] *vr:* **~ (di qc)** to make sure (of sth)

sincerità [sintʃeri'ta] *sf* sincerity

sin'cero, -a [sin'tʃero] *ag* (*genuino*) sincere; (*onesto*) genuine

'sincope *sf* syncopation; (*Med*) blackout

sincro'nia *sf* (*di movimento*) synchronism

sin'cronico, -a, ci, che *ag* synchronic

sincroniz'zare [sinkronid'dzare] *vt* to synchronize

sinda'cale *ag* (trade-)union *cpd*

sindaca'lista, -i, e *sm/f* trade unionist

sinda'care *vt* (*controllare*) to inspect; (*fig: criticare*) to criticize

sinda'cato *sm* (*di lavoratori*) (trade) union; **~ dei datori di lavoro** employers' association

'sindaco, -ci *sm* mayor

'sindrome *sf* (*Med*) syndrome

siner'gia, -gie [siner'dʒia] *sf* (*anche fig*) synergy

sinfo'nia *sf* (*Mus*) symphony

sin'fonico, -a, ci, che *ag* symphonic; (*orchestra*) symphony *cpd*

singa'lese *ag, sm/f* Sin(g)halese *inv*

Singa'pore *sf* Singapore

singhioz'zare [singjot'tsare] *vi* to sob; to hiccup

singhi'ozzo [sin'gjottso] *sm* (*di pianto*) sob; (*Med*) hiccup; **avere il ~** to have the hiccups; **a ~** (*fig*) by fits and starts

singo'lare *ag* (*insolito*) remarkable, singular; (*Ling*) singular ▪ *sm* (*Ling*) singular; (*Tennis*): **~ maschile/femminile** men's(-women's) singles

singolar'mente *av* (*separatamente*) individually, one at a time; (*in modo strano*) strangely, peculiarly, oddly

'singolo, -a *ag* single, individual ▪ *sm* (*persona*) individual; (*Tennis*) = **singolare**; **ogni ~ individuo** each individual; **camera singola** single room

sinis'trato, -a *ag* damaged ▪ *sm/f* disaster victim; **zona sinistrata** disaster area

si'nistro, -a *ag* left, left-hand; (*fig*) sinister ▪ *sm* (*incidente*) accident ▪ *sf* (*Pol*) left (wing); **a sinistra** on the left; (*direzione*) to the left; **a sinistra di** to the left of; **di sinistra** left-wing; **tenere la sinistra** to keep to the left; **guida a sinistra** left-hand drive

'sino *prep* = **fino**

si'nonimo, -a *ag* synonymous ▪ *sm* synonym; **~ di** synonymous with

sin'tassi *sf* syntax

sin'tattico, -a, ci, che *ag* syntactic

'sintesi *sf* synthesis; (*riassunto*) summary, résumé; **in ~** in brief, in short

sin'tetico, -a, ci, che *ag* synthetic; (*conciso*) brief, concise

sintetiz'zare [sintetid'dzare] *vt* to synthesize; (*riassumere*) to summarize

sintetizza'tore [sintetiddza'tore] *sm* (*Mus*) synthesizer; **~ di voce** voice synthesizer

sinto'matico, -a, ci, che *ag* symptomatic

'sintomo *sm* symptom

sinto'nia *sf* (*Radio*) tuning; **essere in ~ con qn** (*fig*) to be on the same wavelength as sb

sintoniz'zare [sintonid'dzare] *vt* to tune (in); **sintonizzarsi** *vr:* **sintonizzarsi su** to tune in to

sintonizza'tore [sintoniddza'tore] *sm* tuner

sinu'oso, -a *ag* (*strada*) winding

sinu'site *sf* sinusitis

SIP *sigla f* (= *Società Italiana per l'esercizio telefonico*) *former name of Italian telephone company*

si'pario *sm* (*Teat*) curtain

si'rena *sf* (*apparecchio*) siren; (*nella mitologia, fig*) siren, mermaid; **~ d'allarme** (*per incendio*) fire alarm; (*per furto*) burglar alarm

'Siria *sf:* **la ~** Syria

siri'ano, -a *ag, sm/f* Syrian

347

si'ringa, -ghe *sf* syringe

'sisma, -i *sm* earthquake

'SISMI *sigla m* (= *Servizio per l'Informazione e la Sicurezza Militari*) military security service

'sismico, -a, ci, che *ag* seismic; (*zona*) earthquake *cpd*

sis'mografo *sm* seismograph

sissi'gnore [sissin'nore] *av* (*a un superiore*) yes, sir; (*enfatico*) yes indeed, of course

sis'tema, -i *sm* system; (*metodo*) method, way; **trovare il ~ per fare qc** to find a way to do sth; **~ decimale/metrico** decimal/metric system; **~ operativo** (*Inform*) operating system; **~ solare** solar system; **~ di vita** way of life

siste'mare *vt* (*mettere a posto*) to tidy, put in order; (*risolvere: questione*) to sort out, settle; (*procurare un lavoro a*) to find a job for; (*dare un alloggio a*) to settle, find accommodation (*Brit*) *o* accommodations (*US*) for; **sistemarsi** *vr* (*problema*) to be settled; (*persona: trovare alloggio*) to find accommodation(s); (: *trovarsi un lavoro*) to get fixed up with a job; **ti sistemo io!** I'll soon sort you out!; **~ qn in un albergo** to fix sb up with a hotel

sistematica'mente *av* systematically

siste'matico, -a, ci, che *ag* systematic

sistemazi'one [sistemat'tsjone] *sf* arrangement, order; settlement; employment; accommodation (*Brit*), accommodations (*US*)

'sito, -a *ag* (*Amm*) situated ▪ *sm* (*letterario*) place; **~ Internet** website

situ'are *vt* to site, situate

situ'ato, -a *ag*: **~ a/su** situated at/on

situazi'one [situat'tsjone] *sf* situation; **vista la sua ~ familiare** given your family situation *o* circumstances; **nella sua ~** in your position *o* situation; **mi trovo in una ~ critica** I'm in a very difficult situation *o* position

'skai® *sm* Leatherette®

ski-lift [ski'lift] *sm inv* ski lift

ski pass [ski'pɑːs] *sm inv* ski pass

slacci'are [zlat'tʃare] *vt* to undo, unfasten

slanci'arsi [zlan'tʃarsi] *vr* to dash, fling o.s.

slanci'ato, -a [zlan'tʃato] *ag* slender

'slancio ['zlantʃo] *sm* dash, leap; (*fig*) surge; **in uno ~ d'affetto** in a burst *o* rush of affection; **di ~** impetuously

sla'vato, -a *ag* faded, washed out; (*fig: viso, occhi*) pale, colourless (*Brit*), colorless (*US*)

sla'vina *sf* snowslide

'slavo, -a *ag* Slav(onic), Slavic

sle'ale *ag* disloyal; (*concorrenza etc*) unfair

slealtà *sf* disloyalty; unfairness

sle'gare *vt* to untie

slip *sm inv* (*mutandine*) briefs *pl*; (*da bagno: per uomo*) (swimming) trunks *pl*; (: *per donna*) bikini bottoms *pl*

'slitta *sf* sledge; (*trainata*) sleigh

slitta'mento *sm* slipping; skidding; postponement; **~ salariale** wage drift

slit'tare *vi* to slip, slide; (*Aut*) to skid; (*incontro, conferenza*) to be put off, be postponed

s.l.m. *abbr* (= *sul livello del mare*) a.s.l.

slo'gare *vt* (*Med*) to dislocate; (: *caviglia, polso*) to sprain

sloga'tura *sf* dislocation; sprain

sloggi'are [zlod'dʒare] *vt* (*inquilino*) to turn out; (*nemico*) to drive out, dislodge ▪ *vi* to move out

Slo'vacchia [zlo'vakkja] *sf* Slovakia

slo'vacco, -a, ci, che *ag*, *sm/f* Slovak, Slovakian; **la Repubblica Slovacca** the Slovak Republic

Slo'venia *sf* Slovenia

slo'veno, -a *ag*, *sm/f* Slovene, Slovenian ▪ *sm* (*Ling*) Slovene

S.M. *abbr* (*Mil*) = **Stato Maggiore**; (= *Sua Maestà*) HM

smac'cato, -a *ag* (*fig*) excessive

smacchi'are [zmak'kjare] *vt* to remove stains from

smacchia'tore [zmakkja'tore] *sm* stain remover

'smacco, -chi *sm* humiliating defeat

smagli'ante [zmaʎ'ʎante] *ag* brilliant, dazzling

smagli'are [zmaʎ'ʎare] *vt*, **smagli'arsi** *vr* (*calza*) to ladder

smaglia'tura [zmaʎʎa'tura] *sf* (*su maglia, calza*) ladder (*Brit*), run; (*Med: sulla pelle*) stretch mark

sma'grire *vt* to make thin ▪ *vi* to get *o* grow thin, lose weight

sma'grito, -a *ag*: **essere ~** to have lost a lot of weight

smalizi'ato, -a [zmalit'tsjato] *ag* shrewd, cunning

smal'tare *vt* to enamel; (*ceramica*) to glaze; (*unghie*) to varnish

smalti'mento *sm* (*di rifiuti*) disposal

smal'tire *vt* (*merce*) to sell off; (*rifiuti*) to dispose of; (*cibo*) to digest; (*peso*) to lose; (*rabbia*) to get over; **~ la sbornia** to sober up

'smalto *sm* (*anche di denti*) enamel; (*per ceramica*) glaze; **~ per unghie** nail varnish

smance'rie [zmantʃe'rie] *sfpl* mawkishness *sg*

'smania *sf* agitation, restlessness; (*fig*): **~ di** thirst for, craving for; **avere la ~ addosso** to have the fidgets; **avere la ~ di fare** to long *o* yearn to do

smani'are vi (agitarsi) to be restless o agitated; (fig): ~ **di fare** to long o yearn to do

smantella'mento sm dismantling

smantel'lare vt to dismantle

smar'carsi vr (Sport) to get free of marking

smargi'asso [zmar'dʒasso] sm show-off

smarri'mento sm loss; (fig) bewilderment; dismay

smar'rire vt to lose; (non riuscire a trovare) to mislay; **smarrirsi** vr (perdersi) to lose one's way, get lost; (: oggetto) to go astray

smar'rito, -a ag (oggetto) lost; (fig: confuso: persona) bewildered, nonplussed; (: sguardo) bewildered; **ufficio oggetti smarriti** lost property office (Brit), lost and found (US)

smasche'rare [zmaske'rare] vt to unmask

SME abbr = **Stato Maggiore Esercito** ■ sigla m (= Sistema Monetario Europeo) EMS (= European Monetary System)

smem'brare vt (gruppo, partito etc) to split; **smembrarsi** vr to split up

smemo'rato, -a ag forgetful

smen'tire vt (negare) to deny; (testimonianza) to refute; (reputazione) to give the lie to; **smentirsi** vr to be inconsistent

smen'tita sf denial; refutation

sme'raldo sm, ag inv emerald

smerci'are [zmer'tʃare] vt (Comm) to sell; (: svendere) to sell off

'smercio ['zmɛrtʃo] sm sale; **avere poco/molto ~** to have poor/good sales

smerigli'ato, -a [zmeriʎ'ʎato] ag: **carta smerigliata** emery paper; **vetro ~** frosted glass

sme'riglio [zme'riʎʎo] sm emery

'smesso, -a pp di **smettere** ■ ag: **abiti smessi** cast-offs

'smettere vt to stop; (vestiti) to stop wearing ■ vi to stop, cease; ~ **di fare** to stop doing

smidol'lato, -a ag spineless ■ sm/f spineless person

smilitarizzazi'one [zmilitariddzat'tsjone] sf demilitarization

'smilzo, -a ['zmiltso] ag thin, lean

sminu'ire vt to diminish, lessen; (fig) to belittle; ~ **l'importanza di qc** to play sth down

sminuz'zare [zminut'tsare] vt to break into small pieces; to crumble

'smisi etc vb vedi **smettere**

smista'mento sm (di posta) sorting; (Ferr) shunting

smis'tare vt (pacchi etc) to sort; (Ferr) to shunt

smisu'rato, -a ag boundless, immeasurable; (grandissimo) immense, enormous

smitiz'zare [zmitid'dzare] vt to debunk

smobili'tare vt to demobilize

smobilitazi'one [zmobilitat'tsjone] sf demobilization

smobi'lizzo [zmobi'liddzo] sm (Comm) disinvestment

smo'dato, -a ag excessive, unrestrained

smode'rato, -a ag immoderate

smog [zmɔg] sm inv smog

'smoking ['smoukiŋ] sm inv dinner jacket (Brit), tuxedo (US)

smon'tare vt (mobile, macchina etc) to take to pieces, dismantle; (fig: scoraggiare) to dishearten ■ vi (scendere: da cavallo) to dismount; (: da treno) to get off; (terminare il lavoro) to stop (work); **smontarsi** vr to lose heart; to lose one's enthusiasm

smorfia sf grimace; (atteggiamento lezioso) simpering; **fare smorfie** to make faces; to simper

smorfi'oso, -a ag simpering

'smorto, -a ag (viso) pale, wan; (colore) dull

smor'zare [zmor'tsare] vt (suoni) to deaden; (colori) to tone down; (luce) to dim; (sete) to quench; (entusiasmo) to dampen; **smorzarsi** vr (suono, luce) to fade; (entusiasmo) to dampen

'smosso, -a pp di **smuovere**

smotta'mento sm landslide

sms ['ɛsse'emme'esse] sm inv text (message)

'smunto, -a ag haggard, pinched

smu'overe vt to move, shift; (fig: commuovere) to move; (: dall'inerzia) to rouse, stir; **smuoversi** vr to move, shift

smus'sare vt (angolo) to round off, smooth; (lama etc) to blunt; **smussarsi** vr to become blunt

s.n. abbr = **senza numero**

snatu'rato, -a ag inhuman, heartless

snazionaliz'zare [znattsjonalid'dzare] vt to denationalize

snelli'mento sm (di traffico) speeding up; (di procedura) streamlining

snel'lire vt (persona) to make slim; (traffico) to speed up; (procedura) to streamline; **snellirsi** vr (persona) to (get) slim; (traffico) to speed up

'snello, -a ag (agile) agile; (svelto) slender, slim

sner'vante ag (attesa, lavoro) exasperating

sner'vare vt to enervate, wear out; **snervarsi** vr to become enervated

sni'dare vt to drive out, flush out

sniffare [znif'fare] vt (fam: cocaina) to snort

snob'bare vt to snub

sno'bismo sm snobbery

snoccio'lare [znottʃo'lare] vt (frutta) to stone; (fig: orazioni) to rattle off; (: verità) to blab; (: fam: soldi) to shell out

sno'dabile ag (lampada) adjustable; (tubo, braccio) hinged

S

sno'dare vt to untie, undo; (rendere agile, mobile) to loosen; **snodarsi** vr to come loose; (articolarsi) to bend; (strada, fiume) to wind

SO sigla = **Sondrio**

so vb vedi **sapere**

S.O. abbr (= sudovest) SW

so'ave ag (voce, maniera) gentle; (volto) delicate, sweet; (musica) soft, sweet; (profumo) delicate

soavità sf gentleness; delicacy; sweetness; softness

sobbal'zare [sobbal'tsare] vi to jolt, jerk; (trasalire) to jump, start

sob'balzo [sob'baltso] sm jerk, jolt; jump, start

sobbar'carsi vr: ~ **a** to take on, undertake

sob'borgo, -ghi sm suburb

sobil'lare vt to stir up, incite

sobrio, -a ag sober

Soc. abbr (= società) Soc.

socchi'udere [sok'kjudere] vt (porta) to leave ajar; (occhi) to half-close

socchi'uso, -a [sok'kjuso] pp di **socchiudere** ■ ag (porta, finestra) ajar; (occhi) half-closed

soc'combere vi to succumb, give way

soc'correre vt to help, assist

soccorri'tore, -'trice sm/f rescuer

soc'corso, -a pp di **soccorrere** ■ sm help, aid, assistance; **soccorsi** smpl relief sg, aid sg; **prestare ~ a qn** to help o assist sb; **venire in ~ di qn** to help sb, come to sb's aid; **operazioni di ~** rescue operations; **~ stradale** breakdown service

socialdemo'cratico, -a, ci, che [sotʃaldemo'kratiko] sm/f Social Democrat

soci'ale [so'tʃale] ag social; (di associazione) club cpd, association cpd

socia'lismo [sotʃa'lizmo] sm socialism

socia'lista, -i, e [sotʃa'lista] ag, sm/f socialist

socializ'zare [sotʃalid'dzare] vi to socialize

società [sotʃe'ta] sf inv society; (sportiva) club; (Comm) company; **in ~ con qn** in partnership with sb; **mettersi in ~ con qn** to go into business with sb; **l'alta ~** high society; **~ anonima** ≈ limited (Brit) o incorporated (US) company; **~ per azioni** joint-stock company; **~ di comodo** shell company; **~ fiduciaria** trust company; **~ di mutuo soccorso** friendly society (Brit), benefit society (US); **~ a responsabilità limitata** type of limited liability company

soci'evole [so'tʃevole] ag sociable

socievo'lezza [sotʃevo'lettsa] sf sociableness

socio ['sɔtʃo] sm (Dir, Comm) partner; (membro di associazione) member

sociolo'gia [sotʃolo'dʒia] sf sociology

soci'ologo, -a, gi, ghe [so'tʃɔlogo] sm/f sociologist

soda sf (Chim) soda; (acqua gassata) soda (water)

soda'lizio [soda'littsjo] sm association, society

soddisfa'cente [soddisfa'tʃɛnte] ag satisfactory

soddis'fare vt, vi: ~ **a** to satisfy; (impegno) to fulfil; (debito) to pay off; (richiesta) to meet, comply with; (offesa) to make amends for

soddis'fatto, -a pp di **soddisfare** ■ ag satisfied, pleased; **essere ~ di** to be satisfied o pleased with

soddisfazi'one [soddisfat'tsjone] sf satisfaction

sodio sm (Chim) sodium

sodo, -a ag firm, hard ■ sm: **venire al ~** to come to the point ■ av (picchiare, lavorare) hard; **dormire ~** to sleep soundly

sofà sm inv sofa

soffe'renza [soffe'rɛntsa] sf suffering; (Comm): **in ~** unpaid

sof'ferto, -a pp di **soffrire** ■ ag (vittoria) hard-fought; (distacco, decisione) painful

soffi'are vt to blow; (notizia, segreto) to whisper ■ vi to blow; (sbuffare) to puff (and blow); **soffiarsi il naso** to blow one's nose; **~ qc/qn a qn** (fig) to pinch o steal sth/sb from sb; **~ via qc** to blow sth away

soffi'ata sf (fam) tip-off; **fare una ~ alla polizia** to tip off the police

soffice ['sɔffitʃe] ag soft

soffi'etto sm (Mus, per fuoco) bellows pl; **porta a ~** folding door

soffio sm (di vento) breath; (di fumo) puff; (Med) murmur

soffi'one sm (Bot) dandelion

sof'fitta sf attic

sof'fitto sm ceiling

soffo'cante ag suffocating, stifling

soffo'care vi (anche: **soffocarsi**) to suffocate, choke ■ vt to suffocate, choke; (fig) to stifle, suppress

soffocazi'one [soffokat'tsjone] sf suffocation

soffrig'gere [soffrid'dʒere] vt to fry lightly

sof'frire vt to suffer, endure; (sopportare) to bear, stand ■ vi to suffer; to be in pain; **~ (di) qc** (Med) to suffer from sth

soffritto, -a pp di **soffriggere** ■ sm (Cuc) fried mixture of herbs, bacon and onions

sof'fuso, -a ag (di luce) suffused

So'fia sf (Geo) Sofia

sofisti'care vt (vino, cibo) to adulterate

sofisti'cato, -a ag sophisticated; (vino) adulterated

sofisticazi'one [sofistikat'tsjone] sf adulteration

software ['sɔftwɛə] sm: **~ applicativo** applications package

sogget'tivo, -a [soddʒet'tivo] *ag* subjective
sog'getto, -a [sod'dʒetto] *ag*: ~ **a** (*sottomesso*) subject to; (*esposto: a variazioni, danni etc*) subject *o* liable to ◼ *sm* subject; ~ **a tassa** taxable; **recitare a ~** (*Teat*) to improvise
soggezi'one [soddʒet'tsjone] *sf* subjection; (*timidezza*) awe; **avere ~ di qn** to be ill at ease in sb's presence
sogghi'gnare [soggin'ɲare] *vi* to sneer
sog'ghigno [sog'giɲɲo] *sm* sneer
soggia'cere [soddʒa'tʃere] *vi*: ~ **a** to be subjected to
soggio'gare [soddʒo'gare] *vt* to subdue, subjugate
soggior'nare [soddʒor'nare] *vi* to stay
soggi'orno [sod'dʒorno] *sm* (*invernale, marino*) stay; (*stanza*) living room
soggi'ungere [sod'dʒundʒere] *vt* to add
soggi'unto, -a [sod'dʒunto] *pp di* **soggiungere**
'soglia ['sɔʎʎa] *sf* doorstep; (*anche fig*) threshold
'sogliola ['sɔʎʎola] *sf* (*Zool*) sole
so'gnante [soɲ'ɲante] *ag* dreamy
so'gnare [soɲ'ɲare] *vt, vi* to dream; ~ **a occhi aperti** to daydream
sogna'tore, -'trice [soɲɲa'tore] *sm/f* dreamer
'sogno ['soɲɲo] *sm* dream
'soia *sf* (*Bot*) soya
sol *sm* (*Mus*) G; (: *solfeggiando la scala*) so(h)
so'laio *sm* (*soffitta*) attic
sola'mente *av* only, just
so'lare *ag* solar, sun *cpd*
sol'care *vt* (*terreno, fig: mari*) to plough (*Brit*), plow (*US*)
'solco, -chi *sm* (*scavo, fig: ruga*) furrow; (*incavo*) rut, track; (*di disco*) groove; (*scia*) wake
sol'dato *sm* soldier; ~ **di leva** conscript; ~ **semplice** private
'soldo *sm* (*fig*): **non avere un ~** to be penniless; **non vale un ~** it's not worth a penny; **soldi** *smpl* (*denaro*) money *sg*
'sole *sm* sun; (*luce*) sun(light); (*tempo assolato*) sun(shine); **prendere il ~** to sunbathe; **il S~ che ride** (*Pol*) symbol of the Italian Green party
soleggi'ato, -a [soled'dʒato] *ag* sunny
so'lenne *ag* solemn
solennità *sf* solemnity; (*festività*) holiday, feast day
so'lere *vt*: ~ **fare qc** to be in the habit of doing sth ◼ *vb impers*: **come suole accadere** as is usually the case, as usually happens; **come si suol dire** as they say
so'lerte *ag* diligent
so'lerzia [so'lertsja] *sf* diligence
so'letta *sf* (*per scarpe*) insole
sol'fato *sm* sulphate (*Brit*), sulfate (*US*)

sol'forico, -a, ci, che *ag* sulphuric (*Brit*), sulfuric (*US*); **acido ~** sulphuric *o* sulfuric acid
sol'furo *sm* sulphur (*Brit*), sulfur (*US*)
soli'dale *ag* in agreement; **essere ~ con qn** (*essere d'accordo*) to be in agreement with sb; (*appoggiare*) to be behind sb
solidarietà *sf* solidarity
solidifi'care *vt, vi* (*anche*: **solidificarsi**) to solidify
solidità *sf* solidity
'solido, -a *ag* solid; (*forte, robusto*) sturdy, solid; (*fig: ditta*) sound, solid ◼ *sm* (*Mat*) solid
soli'loquio *sm* soliloquy
so'lista, -i, e *ag* solo ◼ *sm/f* soloist
solita'mente *av* usually, as a rule
soli'tario, -a *ag* (*senza compagnia*) solitary, lonely; (*solo, isolato*) solitary, lone; (*deserto*) lonely ◼ *sm* (*gioiello, gioco*) solitaire
'solito, -a *ag* usual; **essere ~ fare** to be in the habit of doing; **di ~** usually; **più tardi del ~** later than usual; **come al ~** as usual; **siamo alle solite!** (*fam*) here we go again!
soli'tudine *sf* solitude
sollaz'zare [sollat'tsare] *vt* to entertain; **sollazzarsi** *vr* to amuse o.s.
sol'lazzo [sol'lattso] *sm* amusement
solleci'tare [solletʃi'tare] *vt* (*lavoro*) to speed up; (*persona*) to urge on; (*chiedere con insistenza*) to press for, request urgently; (*stimolare*): ~ **qn a fare** to urge sb to do; (*Tecn*) to stress
sollecitazi'one [solletʃitat'tsjone] *sf* entreaty, request; (*fig*) incentive; (*Tecn*) stress; **lettera di ~** (*Comm*) reminder
sol'lecito, -a [sol'letʃito] *ag* prompt, quick ◼ *sm* (*Comm*) reminder; ~ **di pagamento** payment reminder
solleci'tudine [solletʃi'tudine] *sf* promptness, speed
solleti'care *vt* to tickle
sol'letico *sm* tickling; **soffrire il ~** to be ticklish
solleva'mento *sm* raising; lifting; (*ribellione*) revolt; ~ **pesi** (*sport*) weight-lifting
solle'vare *vt* to lift, raise; (*fig: persona: alleggerire*): ~ **(da)** to relieve (of); (: *dar conforto*) to comfort, relieve; (: *questione*) to raise; (: *far insorgere*) to stir (to revolt); **sollevarsi** *vr* to rise; (*fig: riprendersi*) to recover; (: *ribellarsi*) to rise up; **sollevarsi da terra** (*persona*) to get up from the ground; (*aereo*) to take off; **sentirsi sollevato** to feel relieved
solli'evo *sm* relief; (*conforto*) comfort; **con mio grande ~** to my great relief
'solo, -a *ag* alone; (*in senso spirituale: isolato*) lonely; (*unico*): **un ~ libro** only one book, a single book; (*con ag numerale*): **veniamo noi**

tre soli just *o* only the three of us are coming ■ *av* (*soltanto*) only, just; **~ che** *cong* but; **è il ~ proprietario** he's the sole proprietor; **l'incontrò due sole volte** he only met him twice; **non ~ ... ma anche** not only ... but also; **fare qc da ~** to do sth (all) by oneself; **vive (da) ~** he lives on his own; **possiamo vederci da soli?** can I see you in private?

sol'stizio [sol'stittsjo] *sm* solstice

sol'tanto *av* only

so'lubile *ag* (*sostanza*) soluble; **caffè ~** instant coffee

soluzi'one [solut'tsjone] *sf* solution; **senza ~ di continuità** uninterruptedly

sol'vente *ag, sm* solvent; **~ per unghie** nail polish remover; **~ per vernici** paint remover

sol'venza [sol'vɛntsa] *sf* (*Comm*) solvency

'soma *sf* load, burden; **bestia da ~** beast of burden

So'malia *sf*: **la ~** Somalia

'somalo, -a *ag, sm/f, sm* Somali

so'maro *sm* ass, donkey

so'matico, -a, ci, che *ag* somatic

somigli'anza [somiʎ'ʎantsa] *sf* resemblance

somigli'are [somiʎ'ʎare] *vi*: **~ a** to be like, resemble; (*nell'aspetto fisico*) to look like; **somigliarsi** *vr* to be (*o* look) alike

'somma *sf* (*Mat*) sum; (*di denaro*) sum (of money); (*complesso di varie cose*) whole amount, sum total; **tirare le somme** (*fig*) to sum up; **tirate le somme** (*fig*) all things considered

som'mare *vt* to add up; (*aggiungere*) to add; **tutto sommato** all things considered

som'mario, -a *ag* (*racconto, indagine*) brief; (*giustizia*) summary ■ *sm* summary

som'mergere [som'mɛrdʒere] *vt* to submerge

sommer'gibile [sommer'dʒibile] *sm* submarine

som'merso, -a *pp di* **sommergere**

som'messo, -a *ag* (*voce*) soft, subdued

somminis'trare *vt* to give, administer

sommità *sf inv* summit, top; (*fig*) height

'sommo, -a *ag* highest; (*rispetto*) highest, greatest; (*poeta, artista*) great, outstanding ■ *sm* (*fig*) height; **per sommi capi** in short, in brief

som'mossa *sf* uprising

sommozza'tore [sommottsa'tore] *sm* (deep-sea) diver; (*Mil*) frogman

so'naglio [so'naʎʎo] *sm* (*di mucche etc*) bell; (*per bambini*) rattle

so'nante *ag*: **denaro** *o* **moneta ~** (ready) cash

so'nare *etc* = **suonare** *etc*

'sonda *sf* (*Med, Meteor, Aer*) probe; (*Mineralogia*) drill ■ *ag inv*: **pallone ~** weather balloon

son'daggio [son'daddʒo] *sm* sounding; probe; boring, drilling; (*indagine*) survey; **~ d'opinioni** opinion poll

son'dare *vt* (*Naut*) to sound; (*atmosfera, piaga*) to probe; (*Mineralogia*) to bore, drill; (*fig: opinione etc*) to survey, poll

so'netto *sm* sonnet

son'nambulo, -a *sm/f* sleepwalker

sonnecchi'are [sonnek'kjare] *vi* to doze, nod

sonnel'lino *sm* nap

son'nifero *sm* sleeping drug (*o* pill)

'sonno *sm* sleep; **aver ~** to be sleepy; **prendere ~** to fall asleep

sonno'lento, -a *ag* sleepy, drowsy; (*movimenti*) sluggish

sonno'lenza [sonno'lɛntsa] *sf* sleepiness, drowsiness

'sono *vb vedi* **essere**

sonoriz'zare [sonorid'dzare] *vt* (*Ling*) to voice; (*Cine*) to add a sound-track to

so'noro, -a *ag* (*ambiente*) resonant; (*voce*) sonorous, ringing; (*onde, film*) sound *cpd* ■ *sm*: **il ~** (*Cine*) the talkies *pl*

sontu'oso, -a *ag* sumptuous

so'pire *vt* (*fig: dolore, tensione*) to soothe

so'pore *sm* drowsiness

sopo'rifero, -a *ag* soporific

soppe'rire *vi*: **~ a** to provide for; **~ alla mancanza di qc** to make up for the lack of sth

soppe'sare *vt* to weigh in one's hand(s), feel the weight of; (*fig*) to weigh up

soppian'tare *vt* to supplant

soppi'atto *av*: **di ~** secretly; furtively

soppor'tabile *ag* tolerable, bearable

soppor'tare *vt* (*reggere*) to support; (*subire: perdita, spese*) to bear, sustain; (*soffrire: dolore*) to bear, endure; (*cosa: freddo*) to withstand; (*persona: freddo, vino*) to take; (*tollerare*) to put up with, tolerate

sopportazi'one [sopportat'tsjone] *sf* patience; **avere spirito di ~**, **avere capacità di ~** to be long-suffering

soppressi'one *sf* abolition; withdrawal; suppression; deletion; elimination, liquidation

sop'presso, -a *pp di* **sopprimere**

sop'primere *vt* (*carica, privilegi etc*) to abolish, do away with; (*servizio*) to withdraw; (*pubblicazione*) to suppress; (*parola, frase*) to delete; (*uccidere*) to eliminate, liquidate

'sopra *prep* (*gen*) on; (*al di sopra di, più in alto di*) above; over; (*riguardo a*) on, about ■ *av* on top; (*attaccato, scritto*) on it; (*al di sopra*) above; (*al piano superiore*) upstairs; **donne ~ i 30 anni** women over 30 (years of age); **100 metri ~ il livello del mare** 100 metres above sea level;

5 gradi ~ lo zero 5 degrees above zero; **abito di ~** I live upstairs; **essere al di ~ di ogni sospetto** to be above suspicion; **per i motivi ~ illustrati** for the above-mentioned reasons, for the reasons shown above; **dormirci ~** (fig) to sleep on it; **passar ~ a qc** (anche fig) to pass over sth

so'prabito sm overcoat

sopraccen'nato, -a [soprattʃen'nato] ag above-mentioned

soprac'ciglio [soprat'tʃiʎʎo] (pl(f) **sopracciglia**) sm eyebrow

sopracco'perta sf (di letto) bedspread; (di libro) jacket

soprad'detto, -a ag aforesaid

sopraf'fare vt to overcome, overwhelm

sopraf'fatto, -a pp di **sopraffare**

sopraffazi'one [sopraffat'tsjone] sf overwhelming, overpowering

sopraf'fino, -a ag (pranzo, vino) excellent; (fig) masterly

sopraggi'ungere [soprad'dʒundʒere] vi (giungere all'improvviso) to arrive (unexpectedly); (accadere) to occur (unexpectedly)

sopraggi'unto, -a [soprad'dʒunto] pp di **sopraggiungere**

soprallu'ogo, -ghi sm (di esperti) inspection; (di polizia) on-the-spot investigation

sopram'mobile sm ornament

soprannatu'rale ag supernatural

sopran'nome sm nickname

soprannomi'nare vt to nickname

sopran'numero av: **in ~** in excess

so'prano, -a sm/f (persona) soprano ■ sm (voce) soprano

soprappensi'ero av lost in thought

soprappiù sm surplus, extra; **in ~** extra, surplus; (per giunta) besides, in addition

sopras'salto sm: **di ~** with a start, with a jump

soprasse'dere vi: **~ a** to delay, put off

soprat'tassa sf surtax

soprat'tutto av (anzitutto) above all; (specialmente) especially

sopravvalu'tare vt (persona, capacità) to overestimate

sopravve'nire vi to arrive, appear; (fatto) to occur

soprav'vento sm: **avere/prendere il ~ su qn** to have/get the upper hand over sb

sopravvis'suto, -a pp di **sopravvivere** ■ sm/f survivor

sopravvi'venza [sopravvi'vɛntsa] sf survival

soprav'vivere vi to survive; (continuare a vivere): **~ (in)** to live on (in); **~ a** (incidente etc) to survive; (persona) to outlive

sopre'levata sf (di strada, ferrovia) elevated section

soprinten'dente sm/f supervisor; (statale: di belle arti etc) keeper

soprinten'denza [soprinten'dɛntsa] sf supervision; (ente): **~ alle Belle Arti** government department responsible for monuments and artistic treasures

soprin'tendere vi: **~ a** to superintend, supervise

soprin'teso, -a pp di **soprintendere**

so'pruso sm abuse of power; **subire un ~** to be abused

soq'quadro sm: **mettere a ~** to turn upside-down

sor'betto sm sorbet, water ice (Brit)

sor'bire vt to sip; (fig) to put up with

'sorcio ['sortʃo] sm mouse

'sordido, -a ag sordid; (fig: gretto) stingy

sor'dina sf: **in ~** softly; (fig) on the sly

sordità sf deafness

'sordo, -a ag deaf; (rumore) muffled; (dolore) dull; (lotta) silent, hidden; (odio, rancore) veiled ■ sm/f deaf person

sordo'muto, -a ag deaf-and-dumb ■ sm/f deaf-mute

so'rella sf sister

sorel'lastra sf stepsister; (con genitore in comune) half sister

sor'gente [sor'dʒɛnte] sf (acqua che sgorga) spring; (di fiume, Fisica, fig) source; **acqua di ~** spring water; **~ di calore** source of heat; **~ termale** thermal spring

'sorgere ['sordʒere] vi to rise; (scaturire) to spring, rise; (fig: difficoltà) to arise ■ sm: **al ~ del sole** at sunrise

sori'ano, -a ag, sm/f tabby

sormon'tare vt (fig) to overcome, surmount

sorni'one, -a ag sly

sorpas'sare vt (Aut) to overtake; (fig) to surpass; (: eccedere) to exceed, go beyond; **~ in altezza** to be higher than; (persona) to be taller than

sorpas'sato, -a ag (metodo, moda) outmoded, old-fashioned; (macchina) obsolete

sor'passo sm (Aut) overtaking

sorpren'dente ag surprising; (eccezionale, inaspettato) astonishing, amazing

sor'prendere vt (cogliere: in flagrante etc) to catch; (stupire) to surprise; **sorprendersi** vr: **sorprendersi (di)** to be surprised (at)

sor'preso, -a pp di **sorprendere** ■ sf surprise; **fare una sorpresa a qn** to give sb a surprise; **prendere qn di sorpresa** to take sb by surprise o unawares

sor'reggere [sor'rɛddʒere] vt to support, hold up; (fig) to sustain

353

sor'retto, -a pp di **sorreggere**

sor'ridere vi to smile

sor'riso, -a pp di **sorridere** ■ sm smile

sor'sata sf gulp; **bere a sorsate** to gulp

sorseggi'are [sorsed'dʒare] vt to sip

'sorsi etc vb vedi **sorgere**

'sorso sm sip; **d'un ~, in un ~ solo** at one gulp

'sorta sf sort, kind; **di ~** whatever, of any kind at all; **ogni ~ di** all sorts of; **di ogni ~** of every kind

'sorte sf (fato) fate, destiny; (evento fortuito) chance; **tirare a ~** to draw lots; **tentare la ~** to try one's luck

sorteggi'are [sorted'dʒare] vt to draw for

sor'teggio [sor'teddʒo] sm draw

sorti'legio [sorti'lɛdʒo] sm witchcraft no pl; (incantesimo) spell; **fare un ~ a qn** to cast a spell on sb

sor'tire vt (ottenere) to produce

sor'tita sf (Mil) sortie

'sorto, -a pp di **sorgere**

sorvegli'ante [sorveʎ'ʎante] sm/f (di carcere) guard, warder (Brit); (di fabbrica etc) supervisor

sorvegli'anza [sorveʎ'ʎantsa] sf watch; supervision; (Polizia, Mil) surveillance

sorvegli'are [sorveʎ'ʎare] vt (bambino, bagagli, prigioniero) to watch, keep an eye on; (malato) to watch over; (territorio, casa) to watch o keep watch over; (lavori) to supervise

sorvo'lare vt (territorio) to fly over ■ vi: **~ su** (fig) to skim over

S.O.S. sigla m mayday, SOS

'sosia sm inv double

sos'pendere vt (appendere) to hang (up); (interrompere, privare di una carica) to suspend; (rimandare) to defer; **~ un quadro al muro/ un lampadario al soffitto** to hang a picture on the wall/a chandelier from the ceiling; **~ qn dal suo incarico** to suspend sb from office

sospensi'one sf (anche Chim, Aut) suspension; deferment; **~ condizionale della pena** (Dir) suspended sentence

sos'peso, -a pp di **sospendere** ■ ag (appeso): **~ a** hanging on (o from); (treno, autobus) cancelled; **in ~** in abeyance; (conto) outstanding; **tenere in ~** (fig) to keep in suspense; **col fiato ~** with bated breath

sospet'tare vt to suspect ■ vi: **~ di** to suspect; (diffidare) to be suspicious of

sos'petto, -a ag suspicious ■ sm suspicion; **destare sospetti** to arouse suspicion

sospet'toso, -a ag suspicious

sos'pingere [sos'pindʒere] vt to drive, push

sos'pinto, -a pp di **sospingere**

sospi'rare vi to sigh ■ vt to long for, yearn for

sos'piro sm sigh; **~ di sollievo** sigh of relief

'sosta sf (fermata) stop, halt; (pausa) pause, break; **senza ~** non-stop, without a break

sostanti'vato, -a ag (Ling): **aggettivo ~** adjective used as a noun

sostan'tivo sm noun, substantive

sos'tanza [sos'tantsa] sf substance; **sostanze** sfpl (ricchezze) wealth sg, possessions; **in ~** in short, to sum up; **la ~ del discorso** the essence of the speech

sostanzi'ale [sostan'tsjale] ag substantial

sostanzi'oso, -a [sostan'tsjoso] ag (cibo) nourishing, substantial

sos'tare vi (fermarsi) to stop (for a while), stay; (fare una pausa) to take a break

sos'tegno [sos'teɲɲo] sm support; **a ~ di** in support of; **muro di ~** supporting wall

soste'nere vt to support; (prendere su di sé) to take on, bear; (resistere) to withstand, stand up to; (affermare): **~ che** to maintain that; **sostenersi** vr to hold o.s. up, support o.s.; (fig) to keep up one's strength; **~ qn** (moralmente) to be a support to sb; (difendere) to stand up for sb, take sb's part; **~ gli esami** to sit exams; **~ il confronto** to bear o stand comparison

soste'nibile ag (tesi) tenable; (spese) bearable; (sviluppo) sustainable

sosteni'tore, -trice sm/f supporter

sostenta'mento sm maintenance, support; **mezzi di ~** means of support

soste'nuto, -a ag (stile) elevated; (velocità, ritmo) sustained; (prezzo) high ■ sm/f: **fare il(la) ~(a)** to be standoffish, keep one's distance

sostitu'ire vt (mettere al posto di): **~ qn/qc a** to substitute sb/sth for; (prendere il posto di) to replace, take the place of

sostitu'tivo, -a ag (Amm: documento, certificato) equivalent

sosti'tuto, -a sm/f substitute; **~ procuratore della Repubblica** (Dir) deputy public prosecutor

sostituzi'one [sostitut'tsjone] sf substitution; **in ~ di** as a substitute for, in place of

sotta'ceti [sotta'tʃeti] smpl pickles

sot'tana sf (sottoveste) underskirt; (gonna) skirt; (Rel) soutane, cassock

sot'tecchi [sot'tekki] av: **guardare di ~** to steal a glance at

sotter'fugio [sotter'fudʒo] sm subterfuge

sotter'raneo, -a ag underground ■ sm cellar

sotter'rare vt to bury

sottigli'ezza [sottiʎ'ʎettsa] sf thinness; slimness; (fig: acutezza) subtlety; shrewdness; **sottigliezze** sfpl (pedanteria) quibbles

sot'tile *ag* thin; (*figura, caviglia*) thin, slim, slender; (*fine: polvere, capelli*) fine; (*fig: leggero*) light; (: *vista*) sharp, keen; (: *olfatto*) fine, discriminating; (: *mente*) subtle; shrewd ■ *sm*: **non andare per il ~** not to mince matters

sottiliz'zare [sottilid'dzare] *vi* to split hairs

sottin'tendere *vt* (*intendere qc non espresso*) to understand; (*implicare*) to imply; **lasciare ~ che** to let it be understood that

sottin'teso, -a *pp di* **sottintendere** ■ *sm* allusion; **parlare senza sottintesi** to speak plainly

'**sotto** *prep* (*gen*) under; (*più in basso di*) below ■ *av* underneath, beneath; below; (*al piano inferiore*) di **~** downstairs; (**al piano) di ~** downstairs; **~ il monte** at the foot of the mountain; **~ la pioggia/il sole** in the rain/sun(shine); **tutti quelli ~ i 18 anni** all those under 18 (years of age) (*Brit*) *o* under age 18 (*US*); **~ il livello del mare** below sea level; **~ il chilo** under *o* less than a kilo; **ha 5 impiegati ~ di sé** he has 5 clerks under him; **siamo ~ Natale/Pasqua** it's nearly Christmas/Easter; **~ un certo punto di vista** in a sense; **~ forma di** in the form of; **~ falso nome** under a false name; **~ terra** underground; **~ voce** in a low voice; **chiuso ~ vuoto** vacuum packed

sotto'banco *av* (*di nascosto: vendere, comprare*) under the counter; (*agire*) in an underhand way

sottobicchi'ere [sottobik'kjere] *sm* mat, coaster

sotto'bosco, -schi *sm* undergrowth *no pl*

sotto'braccio [sotto'brattʃo] *av* by the arm; **prendere qn ~** to take sb by the arm; **camminare ~ a qn** to walk arm in arm with sb

sottochi'ave [sotto'kjave] *av* under lock and key

sottoco'perta *av* (*Naut*) below deck

sotto'costo *av* below cost (price)

sottocu'taneo, -a *ag* subcutaneous

sottoes'posto, -a *ag* (*fotografia, pellicola*) underexposed

sotto'fondo *sm* background; **~ musicale** background music

sotto'gamba *av*: **prendere qc ~** not to take sth seriously

sotto'gonna *sf* underskirt

sottogo'verno *sm* political patronage

sotto'gruppo *sm* subgroup; (*di partito*) faction

sottoline'are *vt* to underline; (*fig*) to emphasize, stress

sott'olio *av, ag inv* in oil

sotto'mano *av* (*a portata di mano*) within reach, to hand; (*di nascosto*) secretly

sottoma'rino, -a *ag* (*flora*) submarine; (*cavo, navigazione*) underwater ■ *sm* (*Naut*) submarine

sotto'messo, -a *pp di* **sottomettere** ■ *ag* submissive

sotto'mettere *vt* to subdue, subjugate; **sottomettersi** *vr* to submit

sottomissi'one *sf* submission

sottopas'saggio [sottopas'saddʒo] *sm* (*Aut*) underpass; (*pedonale*) subway, underpass

sotto'porre *vt* (*costringere*) to subject; (*fig: presentare*) to submit; **sottoporsi** *vr* to submit; **sottoporsi a** (*subire*) to undergo

sotto'posto, -a *pp di* **sottoporre**

sottopro'dotto *sm* by-product

sottoproduzi'one [sottoprodut'tsjone] *sf* underproduction

sottoproletari'ato *sm*: **il ~** the underprivileged class

sot'tordine *av*: **passare in ~** to become of minor importance

sottos'cala *sm inv* (*ripostiglio*) cupboard (*Brit*) *o* closet (*US*) under the stairs; (*stanza*) room under the stairs

sottos'critto, -a *pp di* **sottoscrivere** ■ *sm/f*: **io ~, il ~** the undersigned

sottos'crivere *vt* to sign ■ *vi*: **~ a** to subscribe to

sottoscrizi'one [sottoskrit'tsjone] *sf* signing; subscription

sottosegre'tario *sm*: **S~ di Stato** undersecretary of state (*Brit*), assistant secretary of state (*US*)

sotto'sopra *av* upside-down

sottos'tante *ag* (*piani*) lower; **nella valle ~** in the valley below

sottos'tare *vi*: **~ a** (*assoggettarsi a*) to submit to; (: *richieste*) to give in to; (*subire: prova*) to undergo

sottosu'olo *sm* subsoil

sottosvilup'pato, -a *ag* underdeveloped

sottosvi'luppo *sm* underdevelopment

sottote'nente *sm* (*Mil*) second lieutenant

sotto'terra *av* underground

sotto'tetto *sm* attic

sotto'titolo *sm* subtitle

sottovalu'tare *vt* (*persona, prova*) to underestimate, underrate

sotto'vento *av* (*Naut*) leeward(s) ■ *ag inv* (*lato*) leeward, lee

sotto'veste *sf* underskirt

sotto'voce [sotto'votʃe] *av* in a low voice

sottovu'oto *av*: **confezionare ~** to vacuum-pack ■ *ag*: **confezione ~** vacuum pack

sot'trarre *vt* (*Mat*) to subtract, take away; **sottrarsi** *vr*: **sottrarsi a** (*sfuggire*) to escape; (*evitare*) to avoid; **~ qn/qc a** (*togliere*) to

S

355

remove sb/sth from; (*salvare*) to save *o* rescue sb/sth from; ~ **qc a qn** (*rubare*) to steal sth from sb; **sottratte le spese** once expenses have been deducted

sot'tratto, -a *pp di* **sottrarre**

sottrazi'one [sottrat'tsjone] *sf* (*Mat*) subtraction; (*furto*) removal

sottuffici'ale [sottuffi'tʃale] *sm* (*Mil*) non-commissioned officer; (*Naut*) petty officer

soufflé [su'fle] *sm inv* (*Cuc*) soufflé

souve'nir [suv(ə)'nir] *sm inv* souvenir

so'vente *av* often

soverchi'are [sover'kjare] *vt* to overpower, overwhelm

soverchie'ria [soverkje'ria] *sf* (*prepotenza*) abuse (of power)

sovi'etico, -a, ci, che *ag* Soviet ■ *sm/f* Soviet citizen

sovrabbon'dante *ag* overabundant

sovrabbon'danza [sovrabbon'dantsa] *sf* overabundance; **in ~** in excess

sovraccari'care *vt* to overload

sovrac'carico, -a, chi, che *ag*: ~ **(di)** overloaded (with) ■ *sm* excess load; ~ **di lavoro** extra work

sovraesposizi'one [sovraespozit'tsjone] *sf* (*Fot*) overexposure

sovraffol'lato, -a *ag* overcrowded

sovraimmagazzi'nare [sovraimmagaddzi'nare] *vt* to overstock

sovranità *sf* sovereignty; (*fig: superiorità*) supremacy

sovrannatu'rale *ag* = **soprannaturale**

so'vrano, -a *ag* sovereign; (*fig: sommo*) supreme ■ *sm/f* sovereign, monarch

sovrappopolazi'one [sovrappopolat'tsjone] *sf* overpopulation

sovrap'porre *vt* to place on top of, put on top of; (*Fot, Geom*) to superimpose; **sovrapporsi** *vr* (*fig: aggiungersi*) to be added; (*Fot*) to be superimposed

sovrapposizi'one [sovrapposit'tsjone] *sf* superimposition

sovrap'posto, -a *pp di* **sovrapporre**

sovrapproduzi'one [sovrapprodut'tsjone] *sf* overproduction

sovras'tante *ag* overhanging; (*fig*) imminent

sovras'tare *vt* (*vallata, fiume*) to overhang; (*fig*) to hang over, threaten

sovrastrut'tura *sf* superstructure

sovrecci'tare [sovrettʃi'tare] *vt* to overexcite

sovrimpressi'one *sf* (*Fot, Cine*) double exposure; **immagini in ~** superimposed images

sovrinten'dente *etc* = **soprintendente** *etc*

sovru'mano, -a *ag* superhuman

sovve'nire *vi* (*venire in mente*): ~ **a** to occur to

sovvenzio'nare [sovventsjo'nare] *vt* to subsidize

sovvenzi'one [sovven'tsjone] *sf* subsidy, grant

sovver'sivo, -a *ag* subversive

sovverti'mento *sm* subversion, undermining

sovver'tire *vt* (*Pol: ordine, stato*) to subvert, undermine

'sozzo, -a ['sottso] *ag* filthy, dirty

SP *sigla* = **La Spezia**

S.P. *abbr* = **strada provinciale**; *vedi* **provinciale**

S.p.A. *abbr vedi* **società per azioni**

spac'care *vt* to split, break; (*legna*) to chop; (*fig*) to divide; **spaccarsi** *vr* to split, break

spacca'tura *sf* split

spaccherò *etc* [spakke'rɔ] *vb vedi* **spaccare**

spacci'are [spat'tʃare] *vt* (*vendere*) to sell (off); (*mettere in circolazione*) to circulate; (*droga*) to peddle, push; **spacciarsi** *vr*: **spacciarsi per** (*farsi credere*) to pass o.s. off as, pretend to be

spacci'ato, -a [spat'tʃato] *ag* (*fam: malato, fuggiasco*): **essere ~** to be done for

spaccia'tore, -'trice [spattʃa'tore] *sm/f* (*di droga*) pusher; (*di denaro falso*) dealer

'spaccio ['spattʃo] *sm* (*di merce rubata, droga*): ~ **(di)** trafficking (in); (*di denaro falso*): ~ **(di)** passing (of); (*vendita*) sale; (*bottega*) shop

'spacco, -chi *sm* (*fenditura*) split, crack; (*strappo*) tear; (*di gonna*) slit

spac'cone *sm/f* boaster, braggart

'spada *sf* sword

spadroneggi'are [spadroned'dʒare] *vi* to swagger

spae'sato, -a *ag* disorientated, lost

spaghet'tata [spaget'tata] *sf* spaghetti meal

spa'ghetti [spa'getti] *smpl* (*Cuc*) spaghetti *sg*

'Spagna ['spaɲɲa] *sf*: **la ~** Spain

spa'gnolo, -a [spaɲ'ɲɔlo] *ag* Spanish ■ *sm/f* Spaniard ■ *sm* (*Ling*) Spanish; **gli Spagnoli** the Spanish

'spago, -ghi *sm* string, twine; **dare ~ a qn** (*fig*) to let sb have his (*o* her) way

spai'ato, -a *ag* (*calza, guanto*) odd

spalan'care *vt*, **spalan'carsi** *vr* to open wide

spa'lare *vt* to shovel

'spalla *sf* shoulder; (*fig: Teat*) stooge; **spalle** *sfpl* (*dorso*) back; **di spalle** from behind; **seduto alle mie spalle** sitting behind me; **prendere/colpire qn alle spalle** to take/hit sb from behind; **mettere qn con le spalle al muro** (*fig*) to put sb with his (*o* her) back to the wall; **vivere alle spalle di qn** (*fig*) to live off sb

spal'lata *sf* (*urto*) shove *o* push with the shoulder; **dare una ~ a qc** to give sth a push *o* shove with one's shoulder

spalleggi'are [spalled'dʒare] vt to back up, support

spal'letta sf (parapetto) parapet

spalli'era sf (di sedia etc) back; (di letto: da capo) head(board); (: da piedi) foot(board); (Ginnastica) wall bars pl

spal'lina sf (Mil) epaulette; (di sottoveste, maglietta) strap; **senza spalline** strapless

spal'mare vt to spread

'spalti smpl (di stadio) terraces (Brit), ≈ bleachers (US)

spamming ['spammin] sm (Internet) spamming

'spandere vt to spread; (versare) to pour (out); **spandersi** vr to spread; ~ **lacrime** to shed tears

'spanto, -a pp di **spandere**

spa'rare vt to fire ▪ vi (far fuoco) to fire; (tirare) to shoot; ~ **a qn/qc** to shoot sb/sth, fire at sb/sth

spa'rato sm (di camicia) dicky

spara'tore sm gunman

spara'toria sf exchange of shots

sparecchi'are [sparek'kjare] vt: ~ **(la tavola)** to clear the table

spa'reggio [spa'reddʒo] sm (Sport) play-off

'spargere ['spardʒere] vt (sparpagliare) to scatter; (versare: vino) to spill; (: lacrime, sangue) to shed; (diffondere) to spread; (emanare) to give off (o out); **spargersi** vr (voce, notizia) to spread; (persone) to scatter; **si è sparsa una voce sul suo conto** there is a rumour going round about him

spargi'mento [spardʒi'mento] sm scattering; spilling; shedding; ~ **di sangue** bloodshed

spa'rire vi to disappear, vanish; ~ **dalla circolazione** (fig fam) to lie low, keep a low profile

sparizi'one [sparit'tsjone] sf disappearance

spar'lare vi: ~ **di** to run down, speak ill of

'sparo sm shot

sparpagli'are [sparpaʎ'ʎare] vt, **sparpagli'arsi** vr to scatter

'sparso, -a pp di **spargere** ▪ ag scattered; (sciolto) loose; **in ordine** ~ (Mil) in open order

sparti'acque sm (Geo) watershed

sparti'neve sm inv snowplough (Brit), snowplow (US)

spar'tire vt (eredità, bottino) to share out; (avversari) to separate

spar'tito sm (Mus) score

sparti'traffico sm inv (Aut) central reservation (Brit), median (strip) (US)

spartizi'one [spartit'tsjone] sf division

spa'ruto, -a ag (viso etc) haggard

sparvi'ero sm (Zool) sparrowhawk

spasi'mante sm suitor

spasi'mare vi to be in agony; ~ **di fare** (fig) to yearn to do; ~ **per qn** to be madly in love

with sb

'spasimo sm pang

'spasmo sm (Med) spasm

spas'modico, -a, -ci, -che ag (angoscioso) agonizing; (Med) spasmodic

spas'sarsela vi to enjoy o.s., have a good time

spassio'nato, -a ag dispassionate, impartial

'spasso sm (divertimento) amusement, enjoyment; **andare a** ~ to go out for a walk; **essere a** ~ (fig) to be out of work; **mandare qn a** ~ (fig) to give sb the sack

spas'soso, -a ag amusing, entertaining

'spastico, -a, -ci, -che ag, sm/f spastic

'spatola sf spatula

spau'racchio [spau'rakkjo] sm scarecrow

spau'rire vt to frighten, terrify

spavalde'ria sf boldness, arrogance

spa'valdo, -a ag arrogant, bold

spaventa'passeri sm inv scarecrow

spaven'tare vt to frighten, scare; **spaventarsi** vr to become frightened, become scared

spa'vento sm fear, fright; **far ~ a qn** to give sb a fright

spaven'toso, -a ag frightening, terrible; (fig fam) tremendous, fantastic

spazi'ale [spat'tsjale] ag (volo, nave, tuta) space cpd; (Archit, Geom) spatial

spazia'tura [spattsja'tura] sf (Tip) spacing

spazien'tire [spattsjen'tire] vi (anche: **spazientirsi**) to lose one's patience

'spazio ['spattsjo] sm space; (posto) room, space; **fare ~ per qc/qn** to make room for sth/sb; **nello ~ di un'ora** within an hour, in the space of an hour; **dare ~ a** (fig) to make room for; ~ **aereo** airspace

spazi'oso, -a [spat'tsjoso] ag spacious

spazzaca'mino [spattsaka'mino] sm chimney sweep

spazza'neve [spattsa'neve] sm inv (spartineve, Sci) snowplough (Brit), snowplow (US)

spaz'zare [spat'tsare] vt to sweep; (foglie etc) to sweep up; (cacciare) to sweep away

spazza'tura [spattsa'tura] sf sweepings pl; (immondizia) rubbish

spaz'zino [spat'tsino] sm street sweeper

'spazzola ['spattsola] sf brush; ~ **per abiti** clothesbrush; ~ **da capelli** hairbrush

spazzo'lare [spattso'lare] vt to brush

spazzo'lino [spattso'lino] sm (small) brush; ~ **da denti** toothbrush

specchi'arsi [spek'kjarsi] vr to look at o.s. in a mirror; (riflettersi) to be mirrored, be reflected

specchi'era [spek'kjera] sf large mirror; (mobile) dressing table

specchi'etto [spek'kjetto] sm (tabella) table, chart; ~ **da borsetta** pocket mirror; ~ **retrovisore** (Aut) rear-view mirror

specchio ['spɛkkjo] *sm* mirror; (*tabella*) table, chart; **uno ~ d'acqua** a sheet of water

speci'ale [spe'tʃale] *ag* special; **in special modo** especially; **inviato ~** (*Radio, TV, Stampa*) special correspondent; **offerta ~** special offer; **poteri/leggi speciali** (*Pol*) emergency powers/legislation

specia'lista, -i, e [spetʃa'lista] *sm/f* specialist

specia'listico, -a, ci, che [spetʃa'listiko] *ag* (*conoscenza, preparazione*) specialized

specialità [spetʃali'ta] *sf inv* speciality; (*branca di studio*) special field, speciality

specializ'zare [spetʃalid'dzare] *vt* (*industria*) to make more specialized; **specializzarsi** *vr*: **specializzarsi (in)** to specialize (in)

specializ'zato, -a [spetʃalid'dzato] *ag* (*manodopera*) skilled; **operaio non ~** semiskilled worker; **essere ~ in** to be a specialist in

specializzazi'one [spetʃaliddzat'tsjone] *sf* specialization; **prendere la ~ in** to specialize in

special'mente [spetʃal'mente] *av* especially, particularly

specie ['spɛtʃe] *sf inv* (*Biol, Bot, Zool*) species *inv*; (*tipo*) kind, sort ■ *av* especially, particularly; **una ~ di** a kind of; **fare ~ a qn** to surprise sb; **la ~ umana** mankind

spe'cifica, -che [spe'tʃifika] *sf* specification

specifi'care [spetʃifi'kare] *vt* to specify, state

specificata'mente [spetʃifikata'mente] *av* in detail

spe'cifico, -a, ci, che [spe'tʃifiko] *ag* specific

speck [ʃpɛk] *sm inv kind of smoked ham*

specu'lare *vi*: **~ su** (*Comm*) to speculate in; (*sfruttare*) to exploit; (*meditare*) to speculate on

specula'tore, -trice *sm/f* (*Comm*) speculator

speculazi'one [spekulat'tsjone] *sf* speculation

spe'dire *vt* to send; (*Comm*) to dispatch, forward; **~ per posta** to post (*Brit*), mail (*US*); **~ per mare** to ship

spedita'mente *av* quickly; **camminare ~** to walk at a brisk pace

spe'dito, -a *ag* (*gen*) quick; **con passo ~** at a brisk pace

spedizi'one [spedit'tsjone] *sf* sending; (*collo*) consignment; (*scientifica etc*) expedition; (*Comm*) forwarding; shipping; **fare una ~** to send a consignment; **agenzia di ~** forwarding agency; **spese di ~** postal charges; (*Comm*) forwarding charges

spedizioni'ere [spedittsjo'njere] *sm* forwarding agent, shipping agent

spegnere ['speɲɲere] *vt* (*fuoco, sigaretta*) to put out, extinguish; (*apparecchio elettrico*) to turn *o* switch off; (*gas*) to turn off; (*fig: suoni, passioni*) to stifle; (*debito*) to extinguish; **spegnersi** *vr* to go out; to go off; (*morire*) to pass away

speleolo'gia [speleolo'dʒia] *sf* (*studio*) speleology; (*pratica*) potholing (*Brit*), speleology

spele'ologo, -a, gi, ghe *sm/f* speleologist; potholer

spel'lare *vt* (*scuoiare*) to skin; (*scorticare*) to graze; **spellarsi** *vr* to peel

spendacci'one, -a [spendat'tʃone] *sm/f* spendthrift

spendere *vt* to spend; **~ una buona parola per qn** (*fig*) to put in a good word for sb

spengo *etc vb vedi* **spegnere**

spen'nare *vt* to pluck

spensi *etc vb vedi* **spegnere**

spensiera'tezza [spensjera'tettsa] *sf* carefreeness, lightheartedness

spensie'rato, -a *ag* carefree

spento, -a *pp di* **spegnere** ■ *ag* (*suono*) muffled; (*colore*) dull; (*sigaretta*) out; (*civiltà, vulcano*) extinct

spe'ranza [spe'rantsa] *sf* hope; **nella ~ di rivederti** hoping to see *o* in the hope of seeing you again; **pieno di speranze** hopeful; **senza ~** (*situazione*) hopeless; (*amare*) without hope

speran'zoso, -a [speran'tsoso] *ag* hopeful

spe'rare *vt* to hope for ■ *vi*: **~ in** to trust in; **~ che/di fare** to hope that/to do; **lo spero, spero di sì** I hope so; **tutto fa ~ per il meglio** everything leads one to hope for the best

sper'duto, -a *ag* (*isolato*) out-of-the-way; (*persona: smarrita, a disagio*) lost

spergi'uro, -a [sper'dʒuro] *sm/f* perjurer ■ *sm* perjury

speric'olato, -a *ag* fearless, daring; (*guidatore*) reckless

sperimen'tale *ag* experimental; **fare qc in via ~** to try sth out

sperimen'tare *vt* to experiment with, test; (*fig*) to test, put to the test

sperimentazi'one [sperimentat'tsjone] *sf* experimentation

sperma, -i *sm* (*Biol*) sperm

spermato'zoo, -i [spermatod'dzɔo] *sm* spermatozoon

spe'rone *sm* spur

sperpe'rare *vt* to squander

sperpero *sm* (*di denaro*) squandering, waste; (*di cibo, materiali*) waste

spesa *sf* (*soldi spesi*) expense; (*costo*) cost; (*acquisto*) purchase; (*fam: acquisto del cibo quotidiano*) shopping; **spese** *sfpl* expenses; (*Comm*) costs; charges; **ridurre le spese** (*gen*) to cut down; (*Comm*) to reduce expenditure; **fare la ~** to do the shopping; **fare le spese di qc** (*fig*) to pay the price for sth; **a spese di** (*a carico di*) at the expense of; **con la modica ~ di 200 euro** for the modest sum o outlay of 200 euros; **~ pubblica** public expenditure; **spese accessorie** incidental expenses; **spese generali** overheads; **spese di gestione** operating expenses; **spese d'impianto** initial outlay; **spese legali** legal costs; **spese di manutenzione, spese di mantenimento** maintenance costs; **spese postali** postage *sg*; **spese di sbarco e sdoganamento** landing charges; **spese di trasporto** handling charge; **spese di viaggio** travelling (*Brit*) o traveling (*US*) expenses

spe'sare *vt*: **viaggio tutto spesato** all-expenses-paid trip

'speso, -a *pp di* **spendere**

'spesso, -a *ag* (*fitto*) thick; (*frequente*) frequent ■ *av* often; **spesse volte** frequently, often

spes'sore *sm* thickness; **ha uno ~ di 20 cm** it is 20 cm thick

Spett. *abbr vedi* **spettabile**

spet'tabile *ag* (*abbr*): **Spett.** (*in lettere*): **~ ditta X** Messrs X and Co; **avvertiamo la ~ clientela ...** we inform our customers ...

spettaco'lare *ag* spectacular

spet'tacolo *sm* (*rappresentazione*) performance, show; (*vista, scena*) sight; **dare ~ di sé** to make an exhibition o a spectacle of o.s.

spettaco'loso, -a *ag* spectacular

spet'tanza [spet'tantsa] *sf* (*competenza*) concern; **non è di mia ~** it's no concern of mine

spet'tare *vi*: **~ a** (*decisione*) to be up to; (*stipendio*) to be due to; **spetta a lei decidere** it's up to you to decide

spetta'tore, -'trice *sm/f* (*Cine, Teat*) member of the audience; (*di avvenimento*) onlooker, witness

spette'go'lare *vi* to gossip

spetti'nare *vt*: **~ qn** to ruffle sb's hair; **spettinarsi** *vr* to get one's hair in a mess

spet'trale *ag* spectral, ghostly

'spettro *sm* (*fantasma*) spectre (*Brit*), specter (*US*); (*Fisica*) spectrum

'spezie ['spɛttsje] *sfpl* (*Cuc*) spices

spez'zare [spet'tsare] *vt* (*rompere*) to break; (*fig: interrompere*) to break up; **spezzarsi** *vr* to break

spezza'tino [spettsa'tino] *sm* (*Cuc*) stew

spez'zato, -a [spet'tsato] *ag* (*unghia, ramo, braccio*) broken ■ *sm* (*abito maschile*) coordinated jacket and trousers (*Brit*) o pants (*US*); **fare orario ~** to work a split shift

spezzet'tare [spettset'tare] *vt* to break up (*o chop*) into small pieces

spez'zino, -a [spet'tsino] *ag* of (*o* from) La Spezia

spez'zone [spet'tsone] *sm* (*Cine*) clip

'spia *sf* spy; (*confidente della polizia*) informer; (*Elettr*) indicating light; warning light; (*fessura*) peephole; (*fig: sintomo*) sign, indication; **~ dell'olio** (*Aut*) oil warning light

spiacci'care [spjattʃi'kare] *vt* to squash, crush

spia'cente [spja'tʃente] *ag* sorry; **essere ~ di qc/di fare qc** to be sorry about sth/for doing sth; **siamo spiacenti di dovervi annunciare che ...** we regret to announce that ...

spia'cevole [spja'tʃevole] *ag* unpleasant, disagreeable

spi'aggia, -ge ['spjaddʒa] *sf* beach

spia'nare *vt* (*terreno*) to level, make level; (*edificio*) to raze to the ground; (*pasta*) to roll out; (*rendere liscio*) to smooth (out)

spi'ano *sm*: **a tutto ~** (*lavorare*) non-stop, without a break; (*spendere*) lavishly

spian'tato, -a *ag* penniless, ruined

spi'are *vt* to spy on; (*occasione etc*) to watch o wait for

spi'ata *sf* tip-off

spiattel'lare *vt* (*fam: verità, segreto*) to blurt out

spi'azzo ['spjattso] *sm* open space; (*radura*) clearing

spic'care *vt* (*assegno, mandato di cattura*) to issue ■ *vi* (*risaltare*) to stand out; **~ il volo** to fly off; (*fig*) to spread one's wings; **~ un balzo** to jump, leap

spic'cato, -a *ag* (*marcato*) marked, strong; (*notevole*) remarkable

spiccherò *etc* [spikke'rɔ] *vb vedi* **spiccare**

'spicchio ['spikkjo] *sm* (*di agrumi*) segment; (*di aglio*) clove; (*parte*) piece, slice

spicci'are [spit'tʃare] *vt* (*faccenda, impegno*) to finish off; **spicciarsi** *vr* (*fare in fretta*) to hurry up, get a move on

'spiccio, -a, ci, ce ['spittʃo] *ag* (*modi, mezzi*) quick; **andare per le spicce** to be quick off the mark, waste no time

spicci'olata [spittʃo'lata] *av*: **alla ~** in dribs and drabs, a few at a time

'spicciolo, -a ['spittʃolo] *ag*: **moneta spicciola** small change; **spiccioli** *smpl* (small) change

'spicco, -chi *sm*: **fare ~** to stand out; **di ~** outstanding, prominent; (*tema*) main, principal

spie'dino *sm* (*utensile*) skewer; (*cibo*) kebab

spi'edo *sm* (*Cuc*) spit; **pollo allo ~** spit-roasted chicken

spiega'mento sm (Mil): ~ **di forze** deployment of forces

spie'gare vt (far capire) to explain; (tovaglia) to unfold; (vele) to unfurl; **spiegarsi** vr to explain o.s., make o.s. clear; ~ **qc a qn** to explain sth to sb; **il problema si spiega** one can understand the problem; **non mi spiego come ...** I can't understand how ...

spiegazi'one [spjegat'tsjone] sf explanation; **avere una ~ con qn** to have it out with sb

spiegaz'zare [spjegat'tsare] vt to crease, crumple

spiegherò etc [spjege'rɔ] vb vedi **spiegare**

spie'tato, -a ag ruthless, pitiless

spiffe'rare vt (fam) to blurt out, blab

'spiffero sm draught (Brit), draft (US)

'spiga, -ghe sf (Bot) ear

spigli'ato, -a [spiʎ'ʎato] ag self-possessed, self-confident

spigo'lare vt (anche fig) to glean

'spigolo sm corner; (Geom) edge

spigo'loso, -a ag (mobile) angular; (persona, carattere) difficult

'spilla sf brooch; (da cravatta, cappello) pin

spil'lare vt (vino, fig) to tap; ~ **denaro/notizie a qn** to tap sb for money/information

'spillo sm pin; (spilla) brooch; **tacco a ~** stiletto heel (Brit), spike heel (US); ~ **di sicurezza** o **da balia** safety pin; ~ **di sicurezza** (Mil) (safety) pin

spilorce'ria [spilortʃe'ria] sf meanness, stinginess

spi'lorcio, -a, ci, ce [spi'lortʃo] ag mean, stingy

spilun'gone sm/f beanpole

'spina sf (Bot) thorn; (Zool) spine, prickle; (di pesce) bone; (Elettr) plug; (di botte) bunghole; **birra alla ~** draught beer; **stare sulle spine** (fig) to be on tenterhooks; ~ **dorsale** (Anat) backbone

spi'nacio [spi'natʃo] sm spinach no pl; (Cuc): **spinaci** spinach sg

spi'nale ag (Anat) spinal

spi'nato, -a ag (fornito di spine): **filo ~** barbed wire; (tessuto) herringbone cpd

spi'nello sm (Droga: gergo) joint

'spingere ['spindʒere] vt to push; (condurre: anche fig) to drive; (stimolare): ~ **qn a fare** to urge o press sb to do; **spingersi** vr (inoltrarsi) to push on, carry on; **spingersi troppo lontano** (anche fig) to go too far

'spino sm (Bot) thorn bush

spi'noso, -a ag thorny, prickly

'spinsi etc vb vedi **spingere**

spinte'rogeno [spinte'rɔdʒeno] sm (Aut) coil ignition

'spinto, -a pp di **spingere** ■ sf (urto) push; (Fisica) thrust; (fig: stimolo) incentive, spur; (: appoggio) string-pulling no pl; **dare una spinta a qn** (fig) to pull strings for sb

spinto'nare vt to shove, push

spin'tone sm push, shove

spio'naggio [spio'naddʒo] sm espionage, spying

spion'cino [spion'tʃino] sm peephole

spi'one, -a sm/f (spia) informer; (ragazzino, collega) telltale, sneak

spio'nistico, -a, ci, che ag (organizzazione) spy cpd; **rete spionistica** spy ring

spi'overe vi (scorrere) to flow down; (ricadere) to hang down, fall

'spira sf coil

spi'raglio [spi'raʎʎo] sm (fessura) chink, narrow opening; (raggio di luce, fig) glimmer, gleam

spi'rale sf spiral; (contraccettivo) coil; **a ~** spiral(-shaped); ~ **inflazionistica** inflationary spiral

spi'rare vi (vento) to blow; (morire) to expire, pass away

spiri'tato, -a ag possessed; (fig: persona, espressione) wild

spiri'tismo sm spiritualism

'spirito sm (Rel, Chim, disposizione d'animo, di legge etc, fantasma) spirit; (pensieri, intelletto) mind; (arguzia) wit; (umorismo) humour, wit; **in buone condizioni di ~** in the right frame of mind; **è una persona di ~** he has a sense of humour (Brit) o humor (US); **battuta di ~** joke; ~ **di classe** class consciousness; **non ha ~ di parte** he never takes sides; **lo S~ Santo** the Holy Spirit o Ghost

spirito'saggine [spirito'saddʒine] sf witticism; (peg) wisecrack

spiri'toso, -a ag witty

spiritu'ale ag spiritual

splen'dente ag (giornata) bright, sunny; (occhi) shining; (pavimento) shining, gleaming

'splendere vi to shine

'splendido, -a ag splendid; (splendente) shining; (sfarzoso) magnificent, splendid

splen'dore sm splendour (Brit), splendor (US); (luce intensa) brilliance, brightness

spodes'tare vt to deprive of power; (sovrano) to depose

'spoglia ['spɔʎʎa] sf vedi **spoglio**

spogli'are [spoʎ'ʎare] vt (svestire) to undress; (privare, fig: depredare): ~ **qn di qc** to deprive sb of sth; (togliere ornamenti: anche fig): ~ **qn/qc di** to strip sb/sth of; **spogliarsi** vr to undress, strip; **spogliarsi di** (ricchezze etc) to deprive o.s. of, give up; (pregiudizi) to rid o.s. of

spoglia'rello [spoʎʎa'rɛllo] *sm* striptease
spoglia'toio [spoʎʎa'tojo] *sm* dressing room; (*di scuola etc*) cloakroom; (*Sport*) changing room
'**spoglio, -a** ['spɔʎʎo] *ag* (*pianta, terreno*) bare; (*privo*): ~ **di** stripped of; lacking in, without ■ *sm* (*di voti*) counting ■ *sf* (*Zool*) skin, hide; (: *di rettile*) slough; **spoglie** *sfpl* (*salma*) remains; (*preda*) spoils, booty *sg*
'**spola** *sf* shuttle; (*bobina*) spool; **fare la ~ (fra)** to go to and fro *o* shuttle (between)
spo'letta *sf* (*Cucito: bobina*) spool; (*di bomba*) fuse
spol'pare *vt* to strip the flesh off
spolve'rare *vt* (*anche Cuc*) to dust; (*con spazzola*) to brush; (*con battipanni*) to beat; (*fig: mangiare*) to polish off ■ *vi* to dust
spolve'rino *sm* (*soprabito*) dust coat
'**sponda** *sf* (*di fiume*) bank; (*di mare, lago*) shore; (*bordo*) edge
sponsoriz'zare [sponsorid'dzare] *vt* to sponsor
sponsorizzazi'one [sponsoriddzat'tsjone] *sf* sponsorship
spontanea'mente *av* (*comportarsi*) naturally; (*agire*) spontaneously; (*reagire*) instinctively, spontaneously
spon'taneo, -a *ag* spontaneous; (*persona*) unaffected, natural; **di sua spontanea volontà** of his own free will
spopo'lare *vt* to depopulate ■ *vi* (*attirare folla*) to draw the crowds; **spopolarsi** *vr* to become depopulated
spo'radico, -a, ci, che *ag* sporadic
sporcacci'one, -a [sporkat'tʃone] *sm/f* (*peg*) pig, filthy person
spor'care *vt* to dirty, make dirty; (*fig*) to sully, soil; **sporcarsi** *vr* to get dirty
spor'cizia [spor'tʃittsja] *sf* (*stato*) dirtiness; (*sudiciume*) dirt, filth; (*fig: cosa oscena*) obscenity
'**sporco, -a, chi, che** *ag* dirty, filthy; **avere la coscienza sporca** to have a guilty conscience
spor'genza [spor'dʒɛntsa] *sf* projection
spor'gere ['spɔrdʒere] *vt* to put out, stretch out ■ *vi* (*venire in fuori*) to stick out; **sporgersi** *vr* to lean out; **~ querela contro qn** (*Dir*) to take legal action against sb
'**sporsi** *etc vb vedi* **sporgere**
sport *sm inv* sport
'**sporta** *sf* shopping bag
spor'tello *sm* (*di treno, auto etc*) door; (*di banca, ufficio*) window, counter; **~ automatico** (*Banca*) cash dispenser, automated telling machine
spor'tivo, -a *ag* (*gara, giornale*) sports *cpd*; (*persona*) sporty; (*abito*) casual; (*spirito,*

atteggiamento) sporting ■ *sm/f* sportsman(-woman); **campo** ~ playing field; **giacca sportiva** sports (*Brit*) *o* sport (*US*) jacket
'**sporto, -a** *pp di* **sporgere**
'**sposa** *sf* bride; (*moglie*) wife; **abito** *o* **vestito da** ~ wedding dress
sposa'lizio [spoza'littsjo] *sm* wedding
spo'sare *vt* to marry; (*fig: idea, fede*) to espouse; **sposarsi** *vr* to get married, marry; **sposarsi con qn** to marry sb, get married to sb
spo'sato, -a *ag* married
'**sposo** *sm* (*bride*)groom; (*marito*) husband; **gli sposi** the newlyweds
spos'sante *ag* exhausting
spossa'tezza [spossa'tettsa] *sf* exhaustion
spos'sato, -a *ag* exhausted, weary
sposta'mento *sm* movement, change of position
spos'tare *vt* to move, shift; (*cambiare: orario*) to change; **spostarsi** *vr* to move; **hanno spostato la partenza di qualche giorno** they postponed *o* put off their departure by a few days
spot [spɔt] *sm inv* (*faretto*) spotlight, spot; (*TV*) advert, commercial, ad
'**spranga, -ghe** *sf* (*sbarra*) bar; (*catenaccio*) bolt
spran'gare *vt* to bar; to bolt
spray ['sprai] *sm inv* (*dispositivo, sostanza*) spray ■ *ag inv* (*bombola, confezione*) spray *cpd*
'**sprazzo** ['sprattso] *sm* (*di sole etc*) flash; (*fig: di gioia etc*) burst
spre'care *vt* to waste; **sprecarsi** *vr* (*persona*) to waste one's energy
'**spreco, -chi** *sm* waste
spre'gevole [spre'dʒevole] *ag* contemptible, despicable
'**spregio** ['spredʒo] *sm* scorn, disdain
spregiudi'cato, -a [spredʒudi'kato] *ag* unprejudiced, unbiased; (*peg*) unscrupulous
spre'mere *vt* to squeeze; **spremersi le meningi** (*fig*) to rack one's brains
spre'muta *sf* fresh fruit juice; **~ d'arancia** fresh orange juice
sprez'zante [spret'tsante] *ag* scornful, contemptuous
'**sprezzo** ['sprettso] *sm* contempt, scorn, disdain
sprigio'nare [spridʒo'nare] *vt* to give off, emit; **sprigionarsi** *vr* to emanate; (*uscire con impeto*) to burst out
spriz'zare [sprit'tsare] *vt, vi* to spurt; **~ gioia/ salute** to be bursting with joy/health
sprofon'dare *vi* to sink; (*casa*) to collapse; (*suolo*) to give way, subside; **sprofondarsi** *vr*: **sprofondarsi in** (*poltrona*) to sink into; (*fig*) to become immersed *o* absorbed in

S

sproloqui'are vi to ramble on

spro'loquio sm rambling speech

spro'nare vt to spur (on)

'sprone sm (sperone, fig) spur

sproporzio'nato, -a [sproportsjo'nato] ag disproportionate, out of all proportion

sproporzi'one [spropor'tsjone] sf disproportion

sproposi'tato, -a ag (lettera, discorso) full of mistakes; (fig: costo) excessive, enormous

spro'posito sm blunder; **a ~** at the wrong time; (rispondere, parlare) irrelevantly

sprovve'duto, -a ag inexperienced, naïve

sprov'visto, -a ag (mancante): **~ di** lacking in, without; **ne siamo sprovvisti** (negozio) we are out of it (o them); **alla sprovvista** unawares

spruz'zare [sprut'tsare] vt (a nebulizzazione) to spray; (aspergere) to sprinkle; (inzaccherare) to splash

spruzza'tore [spruttsa'tore] sm (per profumi) spray, atomizer; (per biancheria) sprinkler, spray

'spruzzo ['spruttso] sm spray; splash; **verniciatura a ~** spray painting

spudora'tezza [spudora'tettsa] sf shamelessness

spudo'rato, -a ag shameless

'spugna ['spuɲɲa] sf (Zool) sponge; (tessuto) towelling

spu'gnoso, -a [spuɲ'ɲoso] ag spongy

spulci'are [spul'tʃare] vt (animali) to rid of fleas; (fig: testo, compito) to examine thoroughly

'spuma sf (schiuma) foam; (bibita) fizzy drink

spu'mante sm sparkling wine

spumeggi'ante [spumed'dʒante] ag (vino, fig) sparkling; (birra, mare) foaming

spu'mone sm (Cuc) mousse

spun'tare sm: **allo ~ del sole** at sunrise; **allo ~ del giorno** at daybreak ■ vt (coltello) to break the point of; (capelli) to trim; (elenco) to tick off (Brit), check off (US) ■ vi (uscire: germogli) to sprout; (: capelli) to begin to grow; (: denti) to come through; (apparire) to appear (suddenly); **spuntarsi** vr to become blunt, lose its point; **spuntarla** (fig) to make it, win through

spun'tino sm snack

'spunto sm (Teat, Mus) cue; (fig) starting point; **dare lo ~ a** to give rise to; **prendere ~ da qc** to take sth as one's starting point

spur'gare vt (fogna) to clean, clear; **spurgarsi** vr (Med) to expectorate

spu'tare vt to spit out; (fig) to belch (out) ■ vi to spit

'sputo sm spittle no pl, spit no pl

sputta'nare vt (fam) to bad-mouth

'squadra sf (strumento) (set) square; (gruppo) team, squad; (di operai) gang, squad; (Mil) squad; (: Aer, Naut) squadron; (Sport) team; **lavoro a squadre** teamwork; **~ mobile/del buon costume** (Polizia) flying/vice squad

squa'drare vt to square, make square; (osservare) to look at closely

squa'driglia [skwa'driʎʎa] sf (Aer) flight; (Naut) squadron

squa'drone sm squadron

squagli'arsi [skwaʎ'ʎarsi] vr to melt; (fig) to sneak off

squa'lifica, -che sf disqualification

squalifi'care vt to disqualify

'squallido, -a ag wretched, bleak

squal'lore sm wretchedness, bleakness

'squalo sm shark

'squama sf scale

squa'mare vt to scale; **squamarsi** vr to flake o peel (off)

squarcia'gola [skwartʃa'gola]: **a ~** av at the top of one's voice

squarci'are [skwar'tʃare] vt (muro, corpo) to rip open; (tessuto) to rip; (fig: tenebre, silenzio) to split; (: nuvole) to pierce

'squarcio ['skwartʃo] sm (ferita) gash; (in lenzuolo, abito) rip; (in un muro) breach; (in una nave) hole; (brano) passage, excerpt; **uno ~ di sole** a burst of sunlight

squar'tare vt to quarter, cut up; (cadavere) to dismember

squattri'nato, -a ag penniless ■ sm/f pauper

squili'brare vt to unbalance

squili'brato, -a ag (Psic) unbalanced ■ sm/f deranged person

squi'librio sm (differenza, sbilancio) imbalance; (Psic) derangement

squil'lante ag (suono) shrill, sharp; (voce) shrill

squil'lare vi (campanello, telefono) to ring (out); (tromba) to blare

'squillo sm ring, ringing no pl; blare ■ sf inv (anche: **ragazza squillo**) call girl

squi'sito, -a ag exquisite; (cibo) delicious; (persona) delightful

squit'tire vi (uccello) to squawk; (topo) to squeak

SR sigla = **Siracusa**

sradi'care vt to uproot; (fig) to eradicate

sragio'nare [zradʒo'nare] vi to talk nonsense, rave

sregola'tezza [zregola'tettsa] sf (nel mangiare, bere) lack of moderation; (di vita) dissoluteness, dissipation

srego'lato, -a ag (senza ordine: vita) disorderly; (smodato) immoderate; (dissoluto) dissolute

Sri 'Lanka [sri'lanka] *sm*: **lo** ~ Sri Lanka

S.r.l. *abbr vedi* **società a responsabilità limitata**

sroto'lare *vt*, **sroto'larsi** *vr* to unroll

SS *sigla* = **Sassari**

S.S. *abbr* (*Rel*) = **Sua Santità**; **Santa Sede**; **santi, santissimo**; (*Aut*) = **strada statale**; *vedi* **statale**

S.S.N. *abbr* (= *Servizio Sanitario Nazionale*) ≈ NHS

sta *etc vb vedi* **stare**

'**stabbio** *sm* (*recinto*) pen, fold; (*di maiali*) pigsty; (*letame*) manure

'**stabile** *ag* stable, steady; (*tempo: non variabile*) settled; (*Teat: compagnia*) resident ■ *sm* (*edificio*) building; **teatro** ~ civic theatre

stabili'mento *sm* (*edificio*) establishment; (*fabbrica*) plant, factory; ~ **balneare** bathing establishment; ~ **tessile** textile mill

stabi'lire *vt* to establish; (*fissare: prezzi, data*) to fix; (*decidere*) to decide; **stabilirsi** *vr* (*prendere dimora*) to settle; **resta stabilito che ...** it is agreed that ...

stabilità *sf* stability

stabiliz'zare [stabilid'dzare] *vt* to stabilize

stabilizza'tore [stabiliddza'tore] *sm* stabilizer; (*fig*) stabilizing force

stabilizzazi'one [stabiliddzat'tsjone] *sf* stabilization

stacano'vista, -i, e *sm/f* (*ironico*) eager beaver

stac'care *vt* (*levare*) to detach, remove; (*separare: anche fig*) to separate, divide; (*strappare*) to tear off (*o* out); (*scandire: parole*) to pronounce clearly; (*Sport*) to leave behind; **staccarsi** *vr* (*bottone etc*) to come off; (*scostarsi*): **staccarsi (da)** to move away (from); (*fig: separarsi*): **staccarsi da** to leave; **non** ~ **gli occhi da qn** not to take one's eyes off sb; ~ **la televisione/il telefono** to disconnect the television/the phone; ~ **un assegno** to write a cheque

staccio'nata [stattʃo'nata] *sf* (*gen*) fence; (*Ippica*) hurdle

'**stacco, -chi** *sm* (*intervallo*) gap; (: *tra due scene*) break; (*differenza*) difference; (*Sport: nel salto*) takeoff

sta'dera *sf* lever scales *pl*

'**stadio** *sm* (*Sport*) stadium; (*periodo, fase*) phase, stage

'**staffa** *sf* (*di sella, Tecn*) stirrup; **perdere le staffe** (*fig*) to fly off the handle

staf'fetta *sf* (*messo*) dispatch rider; (*Sport*) relay race

stagflazi'one [stagflat'tsjone] *sf* (*Econ*) stagflation

stagio'nale [stadʒo'nale] *ag* seasonal ■ *sm/f* seasonal worker

stagio'nare [stadʒo'nare] *vt* (*legno*) to season; (*formaggi, vino*) to mature

stagio'nato, -a [stadʒo'nato] *ag* (*vedi vb*) seasoned; matured; (*scherzoso: attempato*) getting on in years

stagi'one [sta'dʒone] *sf* season; **alta/bassa** ~ high/low season

stagli'arsi [staʎ'ʎarsi] *vr* to stand out, be silhouetted

sta'gnante [staɲ'ɲante] *ag* stagnant

sta'gnare [staɲ'ɲare] *vt* (*vaso, tegame*) to tin-plate; (*barca, botte*) to make watertight; (*sangue*) to stop ■ *vi* to stagnate

sta'gnino [staɲ'ɲino] *sm* tinsmith

'**stagno, -a** ['staɲɲo] *ag* (*a tenuta d'acqua*) watertight; (*a tenuta d'aria*) airtight ■ *sm* (*acquitrino*) pond; (*Chim*) tin

sta'gnola [staɲ'ɲɔla] *sf* tinfoil

stalag'mite *sf* stalagmite

stalat'tite *sf* stalactite

stali'nismo *sm* (*Pol*) Stalinism

'**stalla** *sf* (*per bovini*) cowshed; (*per cavalli*) stable

stalli'ere *sm* groom, stableboy

'**stallo** *sm* stall, seat; (*Scacchi*) stalemate; (*Aer*) stall; **situazione di** ~ (*fig*) stalemate

stal'lone *sm* stallion

sta'mani, stamat'tina *av* this morning

stam'becco, -chi *sm* ibex

stam'berga, -ghe *sf* hovel

stami'nale *ag*: **cellula** ~ stem cell; **ricerca sulle cellule staminali** stem-cell research

'**stampa** *sf* (*Tip, Fot: tecnica*) printing; (*impressione, copia fotografica*) print; (*insieme di quotidiani, giornalisti etc*): **la** ~ the press; **andare in** ~ to go to press; **mandare in** ~ to pass for press; **errore di** ~ printing error; **prova di** ~ print sample; **libertà di** ~ freedom of the press; **"stampe"** "printed matter"

stam'pante *sf* (*Inform*) printer; ~ **seriale/termica** serial/thermal printer

stam'pare *vt* to print; (*pubblicare*) to publish; (*coniare*) to strike, coin; (*imprimere: anche fig*) to impress

stampa'tello *sm* block letters *pl*

stam'pato, -a *ag* printed ■ *sm* (*opuscolo*) leaflet; (*modulo*) form; **stampati** *smpl* printed matter *sg*

stam'pella *sf* crutch

stampigli'are [stampiʎ'ʎare] *vt* to stamp

stampiglia'tura [stampiʎʎa'tura] *sf* (*atto*) stamping; (*marchio*) stamp

'**stampo** *sm* mould; (*fig: indole*) type, kind, sort

sta'nare *vt* to drive out

stan'care *vt* to tire, make tired; (*annoiare*) to bore; (*infastidire*) to annoy; **stancarsi** *vr* to get tired, tire o.s. out; **stancarsi (di)** (*stufarsi*) to grow weary (of), grow tired (of)

S

stan'chezza [stan'kettsa] *sf* tiredness, fatigue

'**stanco, -a, chi, che** *ag* tired; ~ **di** tired of, fed up with

stand [stand] *sm inv* (*in fiera*) stand

'**standard** ['standǝrd] *sm inv* (*livello*) standard

standardiz'zare [standardid'dzare] *vt* to standardize

stan'dista, -i, e *sm/f* (*in una fiera etc*) person responsible for a stand

'**stanga, -ghe** *sm* bar; (*di carro*) shaft

stan'gare *vt* (*fig: cliente*) to overcharge; (: *studente*) to fail

stan'gata *sf* (*colpo: anche fig*) blow; (*cattivo risultato*) poor result; (*Calcio*) shot

stan'ghetta [stan'getta] *sf* (*di occhiali*) leg; (*Mus, di scrittura*) bar

'**stanno** *vb vedi* **stare**

sta'notte *av* tonight; (*notte passata*) last night

'**stante** *prep* owing to, because of; **a sé ~** (*appartamento, casa*) independent, separate

stan'tio, -a, 'tii, 'tie *ag* stale; (*burro*) rancid; (*fig*) old

stan'tuffo *sm* piston

'**stanza** ['stantsa] *sf* room; (*Poesia*) stanza; **essere di ~ a** (*Mil*) to be stationed in; **~ da bagno** bathroom; **~ da letto** bedroom

stanzia'mento [stantsja'mento] *sm* allocation

stanzi'are [stan'tsjare] *vt* to allocate

stan'zino [stan'tsino] *sm* (*ripostiglio*) storeroom; (*spogliatoio*) changing room (*Brit*), locker room (*US*)

stap'pare *vt* to uncork; (*tappo a corona*) to uncap

star [star] *sf* (*attore, attrice etc*) star

'**stare** *vi* (*restare in un luogo*) to stay, remain; (*abitare*) to stay, live; (*essere situato*) to be, be situated; (*anche*: **stare in piedi**) to stand; (*essere, trovarsi*) to be; (*dipendere*): **se stesse in me** if it were up to me, if it depended on me; (*seguito da gerundio*): **sta studiando** he's studying; **~ per fare qc** to be about to do sth; **starci** (*esserci spazio*): **nel baule non ci sta più niente** there's no more room in the boot; (*accettare*): **ci stai?** is that okay with you?; **~ a** (*attenersi a*) to follow, stick to; (*seguito dall'infinito*): **~ a sentire** to listen; **staremo a vedere** let's wait and see; **stiamo a discutere** we're talking; (*toccare a*): **sta a te giocare** it's your turn to play; **sta a te decidere** it's up to you to decide; **~ a qn** (*abiti etc*) to fit sb; **queste scarpe mi stanno strette** these shoes are tight for me; **il rosso ti sta bene** red suits you; **come sta?** how are you?; **io sto bene/male** I'm very well/not very well; **~ fermo** to keep *o* stay still; **~ seduto** to sit, be sitting; **~ zitto** to keep quiet; **stando così le cose** given the situation; **stando a ciò che dice lui** according to him *o* to his version

starnaz'zare [starnat'tsare] *vi* to squawk

starnu'tire *vi* to sneeze

star'nuto *sm* sneeze

sta'sera *av* this evening, tonight

'**stasi** *sf* (*Med, fig*) stasis

sta'tale *ag* state *cpd*, government *cpd* ∎ *sm/f* state employee; (*nell'amministrazione*) ≈ civil servant; **bilancio ~** national budget; **strada ~** ≈ trunk (*Brit*) *o* main road

stataliz'zare [statalid'dzare] *vt* to nationalize, put under state control

'**statico, -a, ci, che** *ag* (*Elettr, fig*) static

sta'tista, -i *sm* statesman

sta'tistico, -a, ci, che *ag* statistical ∎ *sf* statistic; (*scienza*) statistics *sg*; **fare una statistica** to carry out a statistical examination

'**stato, -a** *pp di* **essere**; **stare** ∎ *sm* (*condizione*) state, condition; (*Pol*) state; (*Dir*) status; **essere in ~ d'accusa** (*Dir*) to be committed for trial; **essere in ~ d'arresto** (*Dir*) to be under arrest; **essere in ~ interessante** to be pregnant; **~ d'assedio/d'emergenza** state of siege/emergency; **~ civile** (*Amm*) marital status; **~ di famiglia** (*Amm*) *certificate giving details of a household and its dependents*; **~ maggiore** (*Mil*) general staff; **~ patrimoniale** (*Comm*) statement of assets and liabilities; **gli Stati Uniti (d'America)** the United States (of America)

'**statua** *sf* statue

statuni'tense *ag* United States *cpd*, of the United States

sta'tura *sf* (*Anat*) height; (*fig*) stature; **essere alto/basso di ~** to be tall/short *o* small

sta'tuto *sm* (*Dir*) statute; **regione a ~ speciale** *Italian region with political autonomy in certain matters*; **~ della società** (*Comm*) articles *pl* of association

sta'volta *av* this time

staziona'mento [stattsjona'mento] *sm* (*Aut*) parking; (: *sosta*) waiting; **freno di ~** handbrake

stazio'nare [stattsjo'nare] *vi* (*veicoli*) to be parked

stazio'nario, a [stattsjo'narjo] *ag* stationary; (*fig*) unchanged

stazi'one [stat'tsjone] *sf* station; (*balneare, invernale etc*) resort; **~ degli autobus** bus station; **~ balneare** seaside resort; **~ climatica** health resort; **~ ferroviaria** railway (*Brit*) *o* railroad (*US*) station; **~ invernale** winter sports resort; **~ di lavoro** work station; **~ di polizia** police station (*in* *small town);* ~ **di servizio** service *o* petrol *(Brit) o* filling station; ~ **termale** spa

stazza ['stattsa] *sf* tonnage

st. civ. *abbr* = **stato civile**

stecca, -che *sf* stick; *(di ombrello)* rib; *(di sigarette)* carton; *(Med)* splint; *(stonatura):* **fare una** ~ to sing *(o* play) a wrong note

stec'cato *sm* fence

stec'chito, -a [stek'kito] *ag* dried up; *(persona)* skinny; **lasciar** ~ **qn** *(fig)* to leave sb flabbergasted; **morto** ~ stone dead

stella *sf* star; ~ **alpina** *(Bot)* edelweiss; ~ **cadente** *o* **filante** shooting star; ~ **di mare** *(Zool)* starfish; ~ **di Natale** *(Bot)* poinsettia

stel'lato, -a *ag (cielo, notte)* starry

stelo *sm* stem; *(asta)* rod; **lampada a** ~ standard lamp *(Brit),* floor lamp

stemma, -i *sm* coat of arms

stemmo *vb vedi* **stare**

stempe'rare *vt (calce, colore)* to dissolve

stempi'ato, -a *ag* with a receding hairline

stempia'tura *sf* receding hairline

sten'dardo *sm* standard

stendere *vt (braccia, gambe)* to stretch (out); *(tovaglia)* to spread (out); *(bucato)* to hang out; *(mettere a giacere)* to lay (down); *(spalmare: colore)* to spread; *(mettere per iscritto)* to draw up; **stendersi** *vr (coricarsi)* to stretch out, lie down; *(estendersi)* to extend, stretch

stendibianche'ria [stendibjanke'ria] *sm inv* clotheshorse

stendi'toio *sm (locale)* drying room; *(stendibiancheria)* clotheshorse

stenodattilogra'fia *sf* shorthand typing *(Brit),* stenography *(US)*

stenodatti'lografo, -a *sm/f* shorthand typist *(Brit),* stenographer *(US)*

stenogra'fare *vt* to take down in shorthand

stenogra'fia *sf* shorthand

ste'nografo, -a *sm/f* stenographer

sten'tare *vi:* ~ **a fare** to find it hard to do, have difficulty doing

sten'tato, -a *ag (compito, stile)* laboured *(Brit),* labored *(US); (sorriso)* forced

stento *sm (fatica)* difficulty; **stenti** *smpl (privazioni)* hardship *sg,* privation *sg;* **a** ~ *av* with difficulty, barely

steppa *sf* steppe

sterco *sm* dung

stereo *ag* stereo

stereofo'nia *sf* stereophony

stereo'fonico, -a, ci, che *ag* stereophonic

stereoti'pato, -a *ag* stereotyped

stere'otipo *sm* stereotype; **pensare per stereotipi** to think in clichés

sterile *ag* sterile; *(terra)* barren; *(fig)* futile, fruitless

sterilità *sf* sterility

steriliz'zare [sterilid'dzare] *vt* to sterilize

sterilizzazi'one [steriliddzat'tsjone] *sf* sterilization

ster'lina *sf* pound (sterling)

stermi'nare *vt* to exterminate, wipe out

stermi'nato, -a *ag* immense, endless

ster'minio *sm* extermination, destruction; **campo di** ~ death camp

sterno *sm (Anat)* breastbone

ster'paglia [ster'paʎʎa] *sf* brushwood

sterpo *sm* dry twig

ster'rare *vt* to excavate

ster'zare [ster'tsare] *vt, vi (Aut)* to steer

sterzo ['stertso] *sm* steering; *(volante)* steering wheel

steso, -a *pp di* **stendere**

stessi *etc vb vedi* **stare**

stesso, -a *ag* same; *(rafforzativo: in persona, proprio):* **il re** ~ the king himself *o* in person ▪ *pron:* **lo(la)** ~**(a)** the same (one); **quello** ~ **giorno** that very day; **i suoi stessi avversari lo ammirano** even his enemies admire him; **fa lo** ~ it doesn't matter; **parto lo** ~ I'm going all the same; **per me è lo** ~ it's all the same to me, it doesn't matter to me; *vedi* **io; tu** *etc*

ste'sura *sf (azione)* drafting *no pl,* drawing up *no pl; (documento)* draft

stetos'copio *sm* stethoscope

stetti *etc vb vedi* **stare**

stia *sf* hutch

stia *etc vb vedi* **stare**

stigma, -i *sm* stigma

stigmate *sfpl (Rel)* stigmata

sti'lare *vt* to draw up, draft

stile *sm* style; *(classe)* style, class; *(Sport):* ~ **libero** freestyle; **mobili in** ~ period furniture; **in grande** ~ in great style; **è proprio nel suo** ~ *(fig)* it's just like him

sti'lismo *sm* concern for style

sti'lista, -i, e *sm/f* designer

sti'listico, -a, ci, che *ag* stylistic

stiliz'zato, -a [stilid'dzato] *ag* stylized

stil'lare *vi (trasudare)* to ooze; *(gocciolare)* to drip

stilli'cidio [stilli'tʃidjo] *sm (fig)* continual pestering *(o* moaning *etc)*

stilo'grafica, -che *sf (anche:* **penna stilografica)** fountain pen

Stim. *abbr* = **stimata**

stima *sf* esteem; valuation; assessment, estimate; **avere** ~ **di qn** to have respect for sb; **godere della** ~ **di qn** to enjoy sb's respect; **fare la** ~ **di qc** to estimate the value of sth

sti'mare *vt (persona)* to esteem, hold in high regard; *(terreno, casa etc)* to value; *(stabilire in* *misura approssimativa*) to estimate, assess; (*ritenere*): ~ **che** to consider that; **stimarsi fortunato** to consider o.s. (to be) lucky

Stim.ma *abbr* = **stimatissima**

stimo'lante *ag* stimulating ■ *sm* (*Med*) stimulant

stimo'lare *vt* to stimulate; (*incitare*): ~ **qn (a fare)** to spur sb on (to do)

stimolazi'one [stimolat'tsjone] *sf* stimulation

'stimolo *sm* (*anche fig*) stimulus

'stinco, -chi *sm* shin; shinbone

'stingere ['stindʒere] *vt, vi* (*anche:* **stingersi**) to fade

'stinto, -a *pp di* **stingere**

sti'pare *vt* to cram, pack; **stiparsi** *vr* (*accalcarsi*) to crowd, throng

stipendi'are *vt* (*pagare*) to pay (a salary to)

stipendi'ato, -a *ag* salaried ■ *sm/f* salaried worker

sti'pendio *sm* salary

'stipite *sm* (*di porta, finestra*) jamb

stipu'lare *vt* (*redigere*) to draw up

stipulazi'one [stipulat'tsjone] *sf* (*di contratto: stesura*) drafting; (: *firma*) signing

stiracchi'are [stirak'kjare] *vt* (*fig: significato di una parola*) to stretch, force; **stiracchiarsi** *vr* (*persona*) to stretch

stira'mento *sm* (*Med*) sprain

sti'rare *vt* (*abito*) to iron; (*distendere*) to stretch; (*strappare: muscolo*) to strain; **stirarsi** *vr* (*fam*) to stretch (o.s.)

stira'tura *sf* ironing

'stirpe *sf* birth, stock; descendants *pl*

stiti'chezza [stiti'kettsa] *sf* constipation

'stitico, -a, ci, che *ag* constipated

'stiva *sf* (*di nave*) hold

sti'vale *sm* boot

stiva'letto *sm* ankle boot

sti'vare *vt* to stow, load

'stizza ['stittsa] *sf* anger, vexation

stiz'zire [stit'tsire] *vt* to irritate ■ *vi*, **stizzirsi** *vr* to become irritated, become vexed

stiz'zoso, -a [stit'tsoso] *ag* (*persona*) quick-tempered, irascible; (*risposta*) angry

stocca'fisso *sm* stockfish, dried cod

Stoc'carda *sf* Stuttgart

stoc'cata *sf* (*colpo*) stab, thrust; (*fig*) gibe, cutting remark

Stoc'colma *sf* Stockholm

stock [stɔk] *sm inv* (*Comm*) stock

'stoffa *sf* material, fabric; (*fig*): **aver la ~ di** to have the makings of; **avere della ~** to have what it takes

stoi'cismo [stoi'tʃizmo] *sm* stoicism

'stoico, -a, ci, che *ag* stoic(al)

sto'ino *sm* doormat

'stola *sf* stole

stol'tezza [stol'tettsa] *sf* stupidity; (*azione*) foolish action

'stolto, -a *ag* stupid, foolish

'stomaco, -chi *sm* stomach; **dare di ~** to vomit, be sick

sto'nare *vt* to sing (*o* play) out of tune ■ *vi* to be out of tune, sing (*o* play) out of tune; (*fig*) to be out of place, jar; (: *colori*) to clash

sto'nato, -a *ag* (*persona*) off-key; (*strumento*) off-key, out of tune

stona'tura *sf* (*suono*) false note

stop *sm inv* (*Telegrafia*) stop; (*Aut: cartello*) stop sign; (: *fanalino d'arresto*) brake-light (*Brit*), stoplight

'stoppa *sf* tow

'stoppia *sf* (*Agr*) stubble

stop'pino *sm* (*di candela*) wick; (*miccia*) fuse

'storcere ['stɔrtʃere] *vt* to twist; **storcersi** *vr* to writhe, twist; ~ **il naso** (*fig*) to turn up one's nose; **storcersi la caviglia** to twist one's ankle

stordi'mento *sm* (*gen*) dizziness; (*da droga*) stupefaction

stor'dire *vt* (*intontire*) to stun, daze; **stordirsi** *vr*: **stordirsi col bere** to dull one's senses with drink

stor'dito, -a *ag* stunned; (*sventato*) scatterbrained, heedless

'storia *sf* (*scienza, avvenimenti*) history; (*racconto, bugia*) story; (*faccenda, questione*) business *no pl*; (*pretesto*) excuse, pretext; **storie** *sfpl* (*smancerie*) fuss *sg*; **passare alla ~** to go down in history; **non ha fatto storie** he didn't make a fuss

storicità [storitʃi'ta] *sf* historical authenticity

'storico, -a, ci, che *ag* historic(al) ■ *sm/f* historian

storiogra'fia *sf* historiography

stori'one *sm* (*Zool*) sturgeon

stor'mire *vi* to rustle

'stormo *sm* (*di uccelli*) flock

stor'nare *vt* (*Comm*) to transfer

stor'nello *sm* kind of folk song

'storno *sm* starling

storpi'are *vt* to cripple, maim; (*fig: parole*) to mangle; (: *significato*) to twist

storpia'tura *sf* (*fig: di parola*) twisting, distortion

'storpio, -a *ag* crippled, maimed

'storsi *etc vb vedi* **storcere**

'storto, -a *pp di* **storcere** ■ *ag* (*chiodo*) twisted, bent; (*gamba, quadro*) crooked; (*fig: ragionamento*) false, wrong ■ *sf* (*distorsione*) sprain, twist; (*recipiente*) retort ■ *av*: **guardare ~ qn** (*fig*) to look askance at sb; **andar ~** to go wrong

sto'viglie [sto'viʎʎe] *sfpl* dishes *pl*, crockery

str. *abbr (Geo)* = **stretto**

'strabico, -a, ci, che *ag* squint-eyed; *(occhi)* squint

strabili'ante *ag* astonishing, amazing

strabili'are *vi* to astonish, amaze

stra'bismo *sm* squinting

strabuz'zare [strabud'dzare] *vt:* ~ **gli occhi** to open one's eyes wide

stra'carico, -a, chi, che *ag* overloaded

strac'chino [strak'kino] *sm type of soft cheese*

stracci'are [strat'tʃare] *vt* to tear

'straccio, -a, ci, ce ['strattʃo] *ag:* **carta straccia** waste paper ■ *sm* rag; *(per pulire)* cloth, duster

stracci'one, -a [strat'tʃone] *sm/f* ragamuffin

stracci'vendolo [strattʃi'vendolo] *sm* ragman

'stracco, -a, chi, che *ag:* ~ **(morto)** exhausted, dead tired

stra'cotto, -a *ag* overcooked ■ *sm (Cuc)* beef stew

'strada *sf* road; *(di città)* street; *(cammino, via, fig)* way; ~ **facendo** on the way; **tre ore di** ~ **(a piedi)/(in macchina)** three hours' walk/ drive; **essere sulla buona** ~ *(nella vita)* to be on the right road *o* path; *(con indagine etc)* to be on the right track; **essere fuori** ~ *(fig)* to be on the wrong track; **fare** ~ **a qn** to show sb the way; **fare** *o* **farsi** ~ *(fig: persona)* to get on in life; **portare qn sulla cattiva** ~ to lead sb astray; **donna di** ~ *(fig peg)* streetwalker; **ragazzo di** ~ *(fig peg)* street urchin; ~ **ferrata** railway *(Brit)*, railroad *(US)*; ~ **principale** main road; ~ **senza uscita** dead end, cul-de-sac

stra'dale *ag* road *cpd*; *(polizia, regolamento)* traffic *cpd*

stra'dario *sm* street guide

stra'dino *sm* road worker

strafalci'one [strafal'tʃone] *sm* blunder, howler

stra'fare *vi* to overdo it

stra'fatto, -a *pp di* **strafare**

stra'foro; di ~ *av (di nascosto)* on the sly

strafot'tente *ag:* **è** ~ he doesn't give a damn, he couldn't care less

strafot'tenza [strafot'tɛntsa] *sf* arrogance

'strage ['stradʒe] *sf* massacre, slaughter

stra'grande *ag:* **la** ~ **maggioranza** the overwhelming majority

stralci'are [stral'tʃare] *vt* to remove

'stralcio ['straltʃo] *sm (Comm):* **vendere in** ~ to sell off (at bargain prices) ■ *ag inv:* **legge** ~ abridged version of an act

stralu'nato, -a *ag (occhi)* rolling; *(persona)* beside o.s., very upset

stramaz'zare [stramat'tsare] *vi* to fall heavily

strambe'ria *sf* eccentricity

'strambo, -a *ag* strange, queer

strampa'lato, -a *ag* odd, eccentric

strana'mente *av* oddly, strangely; **e lui,** ~, **ha accettato** and surprisingly, he agreed

stra'nezza [stra'nettsa] *sf* strangeness

strango'lare *vt* to strangle; **strangolarsi** *vr* to choke

strani'ero, -a *ag* foreign ■ *sm/f* foreigner

stra'nito, -a *ag* dazed

'strano, -a *ag* strange, odd

straordi'nario, -a *ag* extraordinary; *(treno etc)* special ■ *sm (lavoro)* overtime

strapaz'zare [strapat'tsare] *vt* to ill-treat; **strapazzarsi** *vr* to tire o.s. out, overdo things

strapaz'zato, -a [strapat'tsato] *ag:* **uova strapazzate** scrambled eggs

stra'pazzo [stra'pattso] *sm* strain, fatigue; **da** ~ *(fig)* third-rate

strapi'eno, -a *ag* full to overflowing

strapi'ombo *sm* overhanging rock; **a** ~ overhanging

strapo'tere *sm* excessive power

strappa'lacrime *ag inv (fam):* **romanzo** *(o* **film** *etc)* ~ tear-jerker

strap'pare *vt (gen)* to tear, rip; *(pagina etc)* to tear off, tear out; *(sradicare)* to pull up; *(togliere):* ~ **qc a qn** to snatch sth from sb; *(fig)* to wrest sth from sb; **strapparsi** *vr (lacerarsi)* to rip, tear; *(rompersi)* to break; **strapparsi un muscolo** to tear a muscle

strap'pato, -a *ag* torn, ripped

'strappo *sm (strattone)* pull, tug; *(lacerazione)* tear, rip; *(fig fam: passaggio)* lift *(Brit)*, ride *(US)*; **fare uno** ~ **alla regola** to make an exception to the rule; ~ **muscolare** torn muscle

strapun'tino *sm* jump *o* foldaway seat

strari'pare *vi* to overflow

Stras'burgo *sf* Strasbourg

strasci'care [straʃʃi'kare] *vt* to trail; *(piedi)* to drag; ~ **le parole** to drawl

'strascico, -chi ['straʃʃiko] *sm (di abito)* train; *(conseguenza)* after-effect

strata'gemma, -i [strata'dʒɛmma] *sm* stratagem

stra'tega, -ghi *sm* strategist

strate'gia, -'gie [strate'dʒia] *sf* strategy

stra'tegico, -a, ci, che [stra'tɛdʒiko] *ag* strategic

'strato *sm* layer; *(rivestimento)* coat, coating; *(Geo, fig)* stratum; *(Meteor)* stratus

stratos'fera *sf* stratosphere

strat'tone *sm* tug, jerk; **dare uno** ~ **a qc** to tug *o* jerk sth, give sth a tug *o* jerk

stravac'cato, -a *ag* sprawling

strava'gante *ag* odd, eccentric

strava'ganza [strava'gantsa] *sf* eccentricity

stra'vecchio, -a [stra'vɛkkjo] *ag* very old

strave'dere *vi*: ~ **per qn** to dote on sb

stra'visto, -a *pp di* **stravedere**

stra'vizio [stra'vittsjo] *sm* excess

stra'volgere [stra'vɔldʒere] *vt* (*volto*) to contort; (*fig: animo*) to trouble deeply; (: *verità*) to twist, distort

stra'volto, -a *pp di* **stravolgere** ■ *ag* (*persona: per stanchezza etc*) in a terrible state; (: *per sofferenza*) distraught

strazi'ante [strat'tsjante] *ag* (*scena*) harrowing; (*urlo*) bloodcurdling; (*dolore*) excruciating

strazi'are [strat'tsjare] *vt* to torture, torment

'strazio ['strattsjo] *sm* torture; (*fig: cosa fatta male*): **essere uno ~** to be appalling; **fare ~ di** (*corpo, vittima*) to mutilate

'strega, -ghe *sf* witch

stre'gare *vt* to bewitch

stre'gone *sm* (*mago*) wizard; (*di tribù*) witch doctor

stregone'ria *sf* (*pratica*) witchcraft; **fare una ~** to cast a spell

'stregua *sf*: **alla ~ di** by the same standard as

stre'mare *vt* to exhaust

'stremo *sm*: **essere allo ~** to be at the end of one's tether

'strenna *sf*: **~ natalizia** (*regalo*) Christmas present; (*libro*) book published for the Christmas market

'strenuo, -a *ag* brave, courageous

strepi'tare *vi* to yell and shout

'strepito *sm* (*di voci, folla*) clamour (*Brit*), clamor (*US*); (*di catene*) clanking, rattling

strepi'toso, -a *ag* clamorous, deafening; (*fig: successo*) resounding

stres'sante *ag* stressful

stres'sare *vt* to put under stress

stres'sato, -a *ag* under stress

'stretta *sf vedi* **stretto**

stretta'mente *av* tightly; (*rigorosamente*) strictly

stret'tezza [stret'tettsa] *sf* narrowness; **strettezze** *sfpl* (*povertà*) poverty *sg*, straitened circumstances

'stretto, -a *pp di* **stringere** ■ *ag* (*corridoio, limiti*) narrow; (*gonna, scarpe, nodo, curva*) tight; (*intimo: parente, amico*) close; (*rigoroso: osservanza*) strict; (*preciso: significato*) precise, exact ■ *sm* (*braccio di mare*) strait ■ *sf* (*di mano*) grasp; (*finanziaria*) squeeze; (*fig: dolore, turbamento*) pang; **a denti stretti** with clenched teeth; **lo ~ necessario** the bare minimum; **una stretta di mano** a handshake; **una stretta al cuore** a sudden

sadness; **essere alle strette** to have one's back to the wall

stret'toia *sf* bottleneck; (*fig*) tricky situation

stri'ato, -a *ag* streaked

stria'tura *sf* (*atto*) streaking; (*effetto*) streaks *pl*

stric'nina *sf* strychnine

'strida *sfpl* screaming *sg*

stri'dente *ag* strident

'stridere *vi* (*porta*) to squeak; (*animale*) to screech, shriek; (*colori*) to clash

'strido (*pl(f)* **strida**) *sm* screech, shriek

stri'dore *sm* screeching, shrieking

'stridulo, -a *ag* shrill

'striglia ['strɪʎʎa] *sf* currycomb

strigli'are [strɪʎ'ʎare] *vt* (*cavallo*) to curry

strigli'ata [strɪʎ'ʎata] *sf* (*di cavallo*) currying; (*fig*): **dare una ~ a qn** to give sb a scolding

stril'lare *vt, vi* to scream, shriek

'strillo *sm* scream, shriek

stril'lone *sm* newspaper seller

strimin'zito, -a [strimin'tsito] *ag* (*misero*) shabby; (*molto magro*) skinny

strimpel'lare *vt* (*Mus*) to strum

'stringa, -ghe *sf* lace; (*Inform*) string

strin'gare *vt* (*fig: discorso*) to condense

strin'gato, -a *ag* (*fig*) concise

'stringere ['strindʒere] *vt* (*avvicinare due cose*) to press (together), squeeze (together); (*tenere stretto*) to hold tight, clasp, clutch; (*pugno, mascella, denti*) to clench; (*labbra*) to compress; (*avvitare*) to tighten; (*abito*) to take in; (*scarpe*) to pinch, be tight for; (*fig: concludere: patto*) to make; (: *accelerare: passo*) to quicken ■ *vi* (*incalzare*) to be pressing; **stringersi** *vr* (*accostarsi*): **stringersi a** to press o.s. up against; **~ la mano a qn** to shake sb's hand; **~ gli occhi** to screw up one's eyes; **~ amicizia con qn** to make friends with sb; **stringi stringi** in conclusion; **il tempo stringe** time is short

'strinsi *etc vb vedi* **stringere**

'striscia, -sce ['strɪʃʃa] *sf* (*di carta, tessuto etc*) strip; (*riga*) stripe; **strisce (pedonali)** zebra crossing *sg*; **a strisce** striped

strisci'ante [strɪʃ'ʃante] *ag* (*fig peg*) unctuous; (*Econ: inflazione*) creeping

strisci'are [strɪʃ'ʃare] *vt* (*piedi*) to drag; (*muro, macchina*) to graze ■ *vi* to crawl, creep

'striscio ['strɪʃʃo] *sm* graze; (*Med*) smear; **colpire di ~** to graze

strisci'one [strɪʃ'ʃone] *sm* banner

strito'lare *vt* to grind

striz'zare [strit'tsare] *vt* (*arancia*) to squeeze; (*panni*) to wring (out); **~ l'occhio** to wink

striz'zata [strit'tsata] *sf*: **dare una ~ a qc** to give sth a wring; **una ~ d'occhio** a wink

'strofa *sf*, **'strofe** *sf inv* strophe

strofi'naccio [strofi'nattʃo] *sm* duster, cloth; (*per piatti*) dishcloth; (*per pavimenti*) floorcloth

strofi'nare *vt* to rub

stron'care *vt* to break off; (*fig: ribellione*) to suppress, put down; (*: film, libro*) to tear to pieces

'stronzo ['strontso] *sm* (*sterco*) turd; (*fig fam!: persona*) shit (!)

stropicci'are [stropit'tʃare] *vt* to rub

stroz'zare [strot'tsare] *vt* (*soffocare*) to choke, strangle; **strozzarsi** *vr* to choke

strozza'tura [strottsa'tura] *sf* (*restringimento*) narrowing; (*di strada etc*) bottleneck

stroz'zino, -a [strot'tsino] *sm/f* (*usuraio*) usurer; (*fig*) shark

struc'care *vt* to remove make-up from; **struccarsi** *vr* to remove one's make-up

'struggere ['struddʒere] *vt* (*fig*) to consume; **struggersi** *vr* (*fig*): **struggersi di** to be consumed with

struggi'mento [struddʒi'mento] *sm* (*desiderio*) yearning

strumen'tale *ag* (*Mus*) instrumental

strumentaliz'zare [strumentalid'dzare] *vt* to exploit, use to one's own ends

strumentalizzazi'one [strumentaliddzat-tsjone] *sf* exploitation

strumentazi'one [strumentat'tsjone] *sf* (*Mus*) orchestration; (*Tecn*) instrumentation

stru'mento *sm* (*arnese, fig*) instrument, tool; (*Mus*) instrument; **~ a corda** *o* **ad arco/a fiato** string(ed)/wind instrument

'strussi *etc vb vedi* **struggere**

'strutto *sm* lard

strut'tura *sf* structure

struttu'rare *vt* to structure

'struzzo ['struttso] *sm* ostrich; **fare lo ~, fare la politica dello ~** to bury one's head in the sand

stuc'care *vt* (*muro*) to plaster; (*vetro*) to putty; (*decorare con stucchi*) to stucco

stucca'tore, -'trice *sm/f* plasterer; (*artista*) stucco worker

stuc'chevole [stuk'kevole] *ag* nauseating; (*fig*) tedious, boring

'stucco, -chi *sm* plaster; (*da vetri*) putty; (*ornamentale*) stucco; **rimanere di ~** (*fig*) to be dumbfounded

stu'dente, -'essa *sm/f* student; (*scolaro*) pupil, schoolboy(-girl)

studen'tesco, -a, schi, sche *ag* student *cpd*

studi'are *vt* to study; **studiarsi** *vr* (*sforzarsi*): **studiarsi di fare** to try *o* endeavour (*Brit*) *o* endeavor (*US*) to do

studi'ato, -a *ag* (*modi, sorriso*) affected

'studio *sm* studying; (*ricerca, saggio, stanza*)

study; (*di professionista*) office; (*di artista, Cine, TV, Radio*) studio; (*di medico*) surgery (*Brit*), office (*US*); **studi** *smpl* (*Ins*) studies; **alla fine degli studi** at the end of one's course (of studies); **secondo recenti studi, appare che ...** recent research indicates that ...; **la proposta è allo ~** the proposal is under consideration; **~ legale** lawyer's office

studi'oso, -a *ag* studious, hardworking ■ *sm/f* scholar

'stufa *sf* stove; **~ elettrica** electric fire *o* heater; **~ a legna/carbone** wood-burning/coal stove

stu'fare *vt* (*Cuc*) to stew; (*fig fam*) to bore

stu'fato *sm* (*Cuc*) stew

'stufo, -a *ag* (*fam*): **essere ~ di** to be fed up with, be sick and tired of

stu'oia *sf* mat

stu'olo *sm* crowd, host

stupefa'cente [stupefa'tʃɛnte] *ag* stunning, astounding ■ *sm* drug, narcotic

stupe'fare *vt* to stun, astound

stupe'fatto, -a *pp di* **stupefare**

stupefazi'one [stupefat'tsjone] *sf* astonishment

stu'pendo, -a *ag* marvellous, wonderful

stupi'daggine [stupi'daddʒine] *sf* stupid thing (to do *o* say)

stupidità *sf* stupidity

'stupido, -a *ag* stupid

stu'pire *vt* to amaze, stun ■ *vi* (*anche:* **stupirsi**): **~ (di)** to be amazed (at), be stunned (by); **non c'è da stupirsi** that's not surprising

stu'pore *sm* amazement, astonishment

stu'prare *vt* to rape

stupra'tore *sm* rapist

'stupro *sm* rape

stu'rare *vt* (*lavandino*) to clear

stuzzica'denti [stuttsika'dɛnti] *sm* toothpick

stuzzi'cante [stuttsi'kante] *ag* (*gen*) stimulating; (*appetitoso*) appetizing

stuzzi'care [stuttsi'kare] *vt* (*ferita etc*) to poke (at), prod (at); (*fig*) to tease; (*: appetito*) to whet; (*: curiosità*) to stimulate; **~ i denti** to pick one's teeth

 PAROLA CHIAVE

su (*su + il* = **sul**, *su + lo* = **sullo**, *su + l'* = **sull'**, *su + la* = **sulla**, *su + i* = **sui**, *su + gli* = **sugli**, *su + le* = **sulle**) *prep* **1** (*gen*) on; (*moto*) on(to); (*in cima a*) on (top of); **mettilo sul tavolo** put it on the table; **salire sul treno** to get on the train; **un paesino sul mare** a village by the sea; **è sulla destra** it's on the right; **cento metri sul livello del mare** a hundred metres above sea level; **fecero rotta su Palermo** they set out for Palermo; **sul vestito portava un golf rosso** she was wearing a red sweater over her dress

2 (*argomento*) about, on; **un libro su Cesare** a book on *o* about Caesar

3 (*circa*) about; **costerà sui 3 milioni** it will cost about 3 million; **una ragazza sui 17 anni** a girl of about 17 (years of age)

4: **su misura** made to measure; **su ordinazione** to order; **su richiesta** on request; **3 casi su dieci** 3 cases out of 10

■ *av* **1** (*in alto, verso l'alto*) up; **vieni su** come on up; **guarda su** look up; **andare su e giù** to go up and down; **su le mani!** hands up!; **in su** (*verso l'alto*) up(wards); (*in poi*) onwards; **vieni su da me?** are you going to come up?; **dai 20 anni in su** from the age of 20 onwards

2 (*addosso*) on; **cos'hai su?** what have you got on?

■ *escl* come on!; **su avanti, muoviti!** come on, hurry up!; **su coraggio!** come on, cheer up!

'**sua** *vedi* **suo**
sua'dente *ag* persuasive
sub *sm/f inv* skin-diver
su'bacqueo, -a *ag* underwater ■ *sm* skin-diver
subaffit'tare *vt* to sublet
subaf'fitto *sm* (*contratto*) sublet
subal'terno, -a *ag, sm* subordinate; (*Mil*) subaltern
subappal'tare *vt* to subcontract
subap'palto *sm* subcontract
sub'buglio [sub'buʎʎo] *sm* confusion, turmoil; **essere/mettere in ~** to be in/throw into a turmoil
sub'conscio, -a [sub'kɔnʃo] *ag, sm* subconscious
subcosci'ente [subkoʃʃɛnte] *sm* subconscious
'**subdolo, -a** *ag* underhand, sneaky
suben'trare *vi*: **~ a qn in qc** to take over sth from sb; **sono subentrati altri problemi** other problems arose
su'bire *vt* to suffer, endure
subis'sare *vt* (*fig*): **~ di** to overwhelm with, load with
subi'taneo, -a *ag* sudden
'**subito** *av* immediately, at once, straight away
subli'mare *vt* (*Psic*) to sublimate; (*Chim*) to sublime
su'blime *ag* sublime
sublo'care *vt* to sublease
sublocazi'one [sublokat'tsjone] *sf* sublease

subnor'male *ag* subnormal ■ *sm/f* mentally handicapped person
subodo'rare *vt* (*insidia etc*) to smell, suspect
subordi'nare *vt* to subordinate
subordi'nato, -a *ag* subordinate; (*dipendente*): **~ a** dependent on, subject to
subordinazi'one [subordinat'tsjone] *sf* subordination
su'bordine *sm*: **in ~** secondarily
subur'bano, -a *ag* suburban
succe'daneo [sutt'ʃe'daneo] *sm* substitute
suc'cedere [sut'tʃedere] *vi* (*prendere il posto di qn*): **~ a** to succeed; (*venire dopo*): **~ a** to follow; (*accadere*) to happen; **succedersi** *vr* to follow each other; **~ al trono** to succeed to the throne; **sono cose che succedono** these things happen
successi'one [suttʃes'sjone] *sf* succession; **tassa di ~** death duty (*Brit*), inheritance tax (*US*)
successiva'mente [suttʃessiva'mente] *av* subsequently
succes'sivo, -a [suttʃes'sivo] *ag* successive; **il giorno ~** the following day; **in un momento ~** subsequently
suc'cesso, -a [sut'tʃɛsso] *pp di* **succedere** ■ *sm* (*esito*) outcome; (*buona riuscita*) success; **di ~** (*libro, personaggio*) successful; **avere ~** (*persona*) to be successful; (*idea*) to be well received
succes'sore [suttʃes'sore] *sm* successor
succhi'are [suk'kjare] *vt* to suck (up)
succhi'otto [suk'kjɔtto] *sm* dummy (*Brit*), pacifier (*US*), comforter (*US*)
suc'cinto, -a [sut'tʃinto] *ag* (*discorso*) succinct; (*abito*) brief
'**succo, -chi** *sm* juice; (*fig*) essence, gist; **~ di frutta/pomodoro** fruit/tomato juice
suc'coso, -a *ag* juicy; (*fig*) pithy
'**succube** *sm/f* victim; **essere ~ di qn** to be dominated by sb
succur'sale *sf* branch (office)
sud *sm* south ■ *ag inv* south; (*regione*) southern; **verso ~** south, southwards; **l'Italia del S~** Southern Italy; **l'America del S~** South America
Su'dafrica *sm*: **il ~** South Africa
sudafri'cano, -a *ag, sm/f* South African
Suda'merica *sm*: **il ~** South America
sudameri'cano, -a *ag, sm/f* South American
Su'dan *sm*: **il ~** (the) Sudan
suda'nese *ag, sm/f* Sudanese *inv*
su'dare *vi* to perspire, sweat; **~ freddo** to come out in a cold sweat
su'dato, -a *ag* (*persona, mani*) sweaty; (*fig: denaro*) hard-earned ■ *sf* (*anche fig*) sweat; **una vittoria sudata** a hard-won victory;

ho fatto una bella sudata per finirlo in tempo it was a real sweat to get it finished in time

sud'detto, -a *ag* above-mentioned

suddi'tanza [suddi'tantsa] *sf* subjection; *(cittadinanza)* citizenship

sud'dito, -a *sm/f* subject

suddi'videre *vt* to subdivide

suddivisi'one *sf* subdivision

suddi'viso, -a *pp di* **suddividere**

su'dest *sm* south-east; **vento di** ~ south-easterly wind; **il ~ asiatico** South-East Asia

sudice'ria [suditʃe'ria] *sf (qualità)* filthiness, dirtiness; *(cosa sporca)* dirty thing

'sudicio, -a, ci, ce ['suditʃo] *ag* dirty, filthy

sudici'ume [sudi'tʃume] *sm* dirt, filth

su'doku *sm inv* sudoku

su'dore *sm* perspiration, sweat

su'dovest *sm* south-west; **vento di** ~ south-westerly wind

'sue *vedi* **suo**

'Suez ['suez] *sm*: **il Canale di** ~ the Suez Canal

suffici'ente [suffi'tʃɛnte] *ag* enough, sufficient; *(borioso)* self-important; *(Ins)* satisfactory

sufficiente'mente [suffitʃɛnte'mente] *av* sufficiently, enough; *(guadagnare, darsi da fare)* enough

suffici'enza [suffi'tʃɛntsa] *sf (Ins)* pass mark; **con un'aria di** ~ *(fig)* with a condescending air; **a** ~ enough; **ne ho avuto a** ~! I've had enough of this!

suf'fisso *sm (Ling)* suffix

suffra'gare *vt* to support

suf'fragio [suf'fradʒo] *sm (voto)* vote; ~ **universale** universal suffrage

suggel'lare [suddʒel'lare] *vt (fig)* to seal

suggeri'mento [suddʒeri'mento] *sm* suggestion; *(consiglio)* piece of advice, advice *no pl*; **dietro suo** ~ on his advice

sugge'rire [suddʒe'rire] *vt (risposta)* to tell; *(consigliare)* to advise; *(proporre)* to suggest; *(Teat)* to prompt; ~ **a qn di fare qc** to suggest to sb that he *(o* she) do sth

suggeri'tore, -'trice [suddʒeri'tore] *sm/f (Teat)* prompter

suggestio'nare [suddʒestjo'nare] *vt* to influence

suggesti'one [suddʒes'tjone] *sf (Psic)* suggestion; *(istigazione)* instigation

sugges'tivo, -a [suddʒes'tivo] *ag (paesaggio)* evocative; *(teoria)* interesting, attractive

'sughero ['sugero] *sm* cork

'sugli ['suʎʎi] *prep+det vedi* **su**

'sugo, -ghi *sm (succo)* juice; *(di carne)* gravy; *(condimento)* sauce; *(fig)* gist, essence

su'goso, -a *ag (frutto)* juicy; *(fig: articolo etc)* pithy

'sui *prep+det vedi* **su**

sui'cida, -i, e [sui'tʃida] *ag* suicidal ◾ *sm/f* suicide

suici'darsi [suitʃi'darsi] *vr* to commit suicide

sui'cidio [sui'tʃidjo] *sm* suicide

su'ino, -a *ag*: **carne suina** pork ◾ *sm* pig; **suini** *smpl* swine *pl*

sul, sull', 'sulla, 'sulle, 'sullo *prep+det vedi* **su**

sulfa'midico, -a, ci, che *ag, sm (Med)* sulphonamide

sulta'nina *sf*: **(uva)** ~ sultana

sul'tano, -a *sm/f* sultan/sultana

Su'matra *sf* Sumatra

'summit ['summit] *sm inv* summit

S.U.N.I.A. *sigla m (= sindacato unitario nazionale inquilini e assegnatari) national association of tenants*

sunnomi'nato, -a *ag* aforesaid *cpd*

'sunto *sm* summary

'suo, 'sua, 'sue, su'oi *det*: **il ~, la sua** *etc (di lui)* his; *(di lei)* her; *(di esso)* its; *(con valore indefinito)* one's, his/her; *(forma di cortesia: anche:* **Suo**) your *pron*: **il ~, la sua** *etc* his; hers; yours ◾ *sm*: **ha speso del** ~ he *(o* she *etc)* spent his *(o* her *etc)* own money ◾ *sf*: **la sua** *(opinione)* his *(o* her *etc)* view; **i suoi** *(parenti)* his *(o* her *etc)* family; **un ~ amico** a friend of his *(o* hers *etc)*; **è dalla sua** he's on his *(o* her *etc)* side; **anche lui ha avuto le sue** *(disavventure)* he's had his problems too; **sta sulle sue** he keeps himself to himself

su'ocero, -a ['swɔtʃero] *sm/f* father(-mother)-in-law; **i suoceri** *(pl)* father- and mother-in-law

su'oi *vedi* **suo**

su'ola *sf (di scarpa)* sole

su'olo *sm (terreno)* ground; *(terra)* soil

suo'nare *vt (Mus)* to play; *(campana)* to ring; *(ore)* to strike; *(clacson, allarme)* to sound ◾ *vi* to play; *(telefono, campana)* to ring; *(ore)* to strike; *(clacson, fig: parole)* to sound

suo'nato, -a *ag (compiuto)*: **ha cinquant'anni suonati** he is well over fifty

suona'tore, -'trice *sm/f* player; ~ **ambulante** street musician

suone'ria *sf (di sveglia)* alarm; *(di telefono)* ringtone

su'ono *sm* sound

su'ora *sf (Rel)* nun; **Suor Maria** Sister Maria

'super *ag inv*: **(benzina)** ~ ≈ four-star (petrol) (Brit), ≈ premium (US)

supera'mento *sm (di ostacolo)* overcoming; *(di montagna)* crossing

supe'rare *vt (oltrepassare: limite)* to exceed, surpass; *(attraversare: fiume)* to cross; *(sorpassare: veicolo)* to overtake; *(fig: essere più bravo di)* to surpass, outdo; *(: difficoltà)* to

S

overcome; (: *esame*) to get through; ~ **qn in altezza/peso** to be taller/heavier than sb; **ha superato la cinquantina** he's over fifty (years of age); ~ **i limiti di velocità** to exceed the speed limit; **stavolta ha superato se stesso** this time he has surpassed himself

supe'rato, -a *ag* outmoded

supe'rattico, -ci *sm* penthouse

su'perbia *sf* pride

su'perbo, -a *ag* proud; (*fig*) magnificent, superb

supercondut'tore *sm* superconductor

superena'lotto *sm* Italian national lottery

superfici'ale [superfi'tʃale] *ag* superficial

superficialità [superfitʃali'ta] *sf* superficiality

super'ficie, -ci [super'fitʃe] *sf* surface; **tornare in ~** (*a galla*) to return to the surface; (*fig: problemi etc*) to resurface; ~ **alare** (*Aer*) wing area; ~ **velica** (*Naut*) sail area

su'perfluo, -a *ag* superfluous

superi'ora *sf* (*Rel: anche:* **madre superiora**) mother superior

superi'ore *ag* (*piano, arto, classi*) upper; (*più elevato: temperatura, livello*): ~ **(a)** higher (than); (*migliore*): ~ **(a)** superior (to) ■ *sfpl*: **le superiori** (*Ins*) *vedi* **scuola media superiore**; **il corso ~ di un fiume** the upper reaches of a river; **scuola media ~** ≈ senior comprehensive school (*Brit*), ≈ senior high (school) (*US*)

superiorità *sf* superiority

superla'tivo, -a *ag, sm* superlative

superla'voro *sm* overwork

super'market [super'market] *sm inv* = **supermercato**

supermer'cato *sm* supermarket

super'nova *sf* supernova

superpo'tenza [superpo'tentsa] *sf* (*Pol*) superpower

super'sonico, -a, ci, che *ag* supersonic

su'perstite *ag* surviving ■ *sm/f* survivor

superstizi'one [superstit'tsjone] *sf* superstition

superstizi'oso, -a [superstit'tsjoso] *ag* superstitious

super'strada *sf* ≈ expressway

supervisi'one *sf* supervision

supervi'sore *sm* supervisor

su'pino, -a *ag* supine; **accettazione supina** (*fig*) blind acceptance

suppel'lettile *sf* furnishings *pl*

suppergiù [supper'dʒu] *av* more or less, roughly

suppl. *abbr* (= *supplemento*) supp(l)

supplemen'tare *ag* extra; (*treno*) relief *cpd*; (*entrate*) additional

supple'mento *sm* supplement

sup'plente *ag* temporary; (*insegnante*) supply *cpd* (*Brit*), substitute *cpd* (*US*) ■ *sm/f* temporary member of staff; supply (*o* substitute) teacher

sup'lenza [sup'plɛntsa] *sf*: **fare ~** to do supply (*Brit*) *o* substitute (*US*) teaching

supple'tivo, -a *ag* (*gen*) supplementary; (*sessione d'esami*) extra

'supplica, -che *sf* (*preghiera*) plea; (*domanda scritta*) petition, request

suppli'care *vt* to implore, beseech

suppli'chevole [suppli'kevole] *ag* imploring

sup'plire *vi*: ~ **a** to make up for, compensate for

sup'plizio [sup'plittsjo] *sm* torture

sup'pongo, sup'poni *etc vb vedi* **supporre**

sup'porre *vt* to suppose; **supponiamo che ...** let's *o* just suppose that ...

sup'porto *sm* (*sostegno*) support

supposizi'one [suppozit'tsjone] *sf* supposition

sup'posta *sf* (*Med*) suppository

sup'posto, -a *pp di* **supporre**

suppu'rare *vi* to suppurate

suprema'zia [supremat'tsia] *sf* supremacy

su'premo, -a *ag* supreme; **Suprema Corte (di Cassazione)** Supreme Court

surclas'sare *vt* to outclass

surge'lare [surdʒe'lare] *vt* to (deep-)freeze

surge'lato, -a [surdʒe'lato] *ag* (deep-)frozen ■ *smpl*: **i surgelati** frozen food *sg*

surme'nage [syrmə'naʒ] *sm* (*fisico*) overwork; (*mentale*) mental strain; (*Sport*) overtraining

sur'plus *sm inv* (*Econ*) surplus; ~ **di manodopera** overmanning

surre'ale *ag* surrealistic

surriscalda'mento *sm* (*gen, Tecn*) overheating

surriscal'dare *vt* to overheat

surro'gato *sm* substitute

suscet'tibile [suʃʃet'tibile] *ag* (*sensibile*) touchy, sensitive; (*soggetto*): ~ **di miglioramento** that can be improved, open to improvement

suscettibilità [suʃʃettibili'ta] *sf* touchiness; **urtare la ~ di qn** to hurt sb's feelings

susci'tare [suʃʃi'tare] *vt* to provoke, arouse

su'sina *sf* plum

su'sino *sm* plum (tree)

sussegu'ire *vt* to follow; **susseguirsi** *vr* to follow one another

sussidi'ario, -a *ag* subsidiary; (*treno*) relief *cpd*; (*fermata*) extra

sus'sidio *sm* subsidy; (*aiuto*) aid; **sussidi didattici/audiovisivi** teaching/audiovisual aids; ~ **di disoccupazione** unemployment benefit (*Brit*) *o* benefits (*US*); ~ **per malattia** sickness benefit

sussi'ego *sm* haughtiness; **con aria di ~** haughtily

sussis'tenza [sussis'tɛntsa] *sf* subsistence

sus'sistere *vi* to exist; (*essere fondato*) to be valid *o* sound

sussul'tare *vi* to shudder

sus'sulto *sm* start

sussur'rare *vt, vi* to whisper, murmur; **si sussurra che ...** it's rumoured (*Brit*) *o* rumored (*US*) that ...

sus'surro *sm* whisper, murmur

su'tura *sf* (*Med*) suture

sutu'rare *vt* to stitch up, suture

suv'via *escl* come on!

SV *sigla* = **Savona**

S.V. *abbr* = **Signoria Vostra**

sva'gare *vt* (*divertire*) to amuse; (*distrarre*): **~ qn** to take sb's mind off things; **svagarsi** *vr* to amuse o.s.; to take one's mind off things

sva'gato, -a *ag* (*persona*) absent-minded; (*scolaro*) inattentive

'svago, -ghi *sm* (*riposo*) relaxation; (*ricreazione*) amusement; (*passatempo*) pastime

svaligi'are [zvali'dʒare] *vt* to rob, burgle (*Brit*), burglarize (*US*)

svaligia'tore, -'trice [zvalidʒa'tore] *sm/f* (*di banca*) robber; (*di casa*) burglar

svalu'tare *vt* (*Econ*) to devalue; (*fig*) to belittle; **svalutarsi** *vr* (*Econ*) to be devalued

svalutazi'one [zvalutat'tsjone] *sf* devaluation

svam'pito, -a *ag* absent-minded ■ *sm/f* absent-minded person

sva'nire *vi* to disappear, vanish

sva'nito, -a *ag* (*fig: persona*) absent-minded

svantaggi'ato, -a [zvantad'dʒato] *ag* at a disadvantage

svan'taggio [zvan'taddʒo] *sm* disadvantage; (*inconveniente*) drawback, disadvantage; **tornerà a suo ~** it will work against you

svantaggi'oso [zvantad'dʒoso] *ag* disadvantageous; **è un'offerta svantaggiosa per me** it's not in my interest to accept this offer; **è un prezzo ~** it is not an attractive price

svapo'rare *vi* to evaporate

svapo'rato, -a *ag* (*bibita*) flat

svari'ato, -a *ag* (*vario, diverso*) varied; (*numeroso*) various

svastica, -che *sf* swastika

sve'dese *ag* Swedish ■ *sm/f* Swede ■ *sm* (*Ling*) Swedish

'sveglia ['zveʎʎa] *sf* waking up; (*orologio*) alarm (clock); **suonare la ~** (*Mil*) to sound the reveille; **~ telefonica** alarm call

svegli'are [zveʎ'ʎare] *vt* to wake up; (*fig*) to awaken, arouse; **svegliarsi** *vr* to wake up; (*fig*) to be revived, reawaken

'sveglio, a ['zveʎʎo] *ag* awake; (*fig*) alert, quick-witted

sve'lare *vt* to reveal

svel'tezza [zvel'tettsa] *sf* (*gen*) speed; (*mentale*) quick-wittedness

svel'tire *vt* (*gen*) to speed up; (*procedura*) to streamline

'svelto, -a *ag* (*passo*) quick; (*mente*) quick, alert; (*linea*) slim, slender; **alla svelta** quickly

'svendere *vt* to sell off, clear

'svendita *sf* (*Comm*) (clearance) sale

sve'nevole *ag* mawkish

'svengo *etc vb vedi* **svenire**

sveni'mento *sm* fainting fit, faint

sve'nire *vi* to faint

sven'tare *vt* to foil, thwart

sventa'tezza [zventa'tettsa] *sf* (*distrazione*) absent-mindedness; (*mancanza di prudenza*) rashness

sven'tato, -a *ag* (*distratto*) scatterbrained; (*imprudente*) rash

'sventola *sf* (*colpo*) slap; **orecchie a ~** sticking-out ears

svento'lare *vt, vi* to wave, flutter

sven'trare *vt* to disembowel

sven'tura *sf* misfortune

sventu'rato, -a *ag* unlucky, unfortunate

sve'nuto, -a *pp di* **svenire**

svergo'gnare [zvergoɲ'ɲare] *vt* to shame

svergo'gnato, -a [zvergoɲ'ɲato] *ag* shameless ■ *sm/f* shameless person

sver'nare *vi* to spend the winter

sverrò *etc vb vedi* **svenire**

sves'tire *vt* to undress; **svestirsi** *vr* to get undressed

'Svezia ['zvɛttsja] *sf*: **la ~** Sweden

svez'zare [zvet'tsare] *vt* to wean

svi'are *vt* to divert; (*fig*) to lead astray; **sviarsi** *vr* to go astray

svico'lare *vi* to slip down an alley; (*fig*) to sneak off

svi'gnarsela [zviɲ'ɲarsela] *vr* to slip away, sneak off

svili'mento *sm* debasement

svi'lire *vt* to debase

svilup'pare *vt*, **svilup'parsi** *vr* to develop

sviluppa'tore, -'trice (*Inform*) *sm/f* developer

svi'luppo *sm* development; (*di industria*) expansion; **in via di ~** in the process of development; **paesi in via di ~** developing countries

svinco'lare *vt* to free, release; (*merce*) to clear

'svincolo *sm* (*Comm*) clearance; (*stradale*) motorway (*Brit*) *o* expressway (*US*) intersection

svisce'rare [zviʃʃe'rare] *vt* (*fig: argomento*) to examine in depth

S

svisce'rato, -a [zviʃʃe'rato] *ag (amore, odio)* passionate

'svista *sf* oversight

svi'tare *vt* to unscrew

'Svizzera ['zvittsera] *sf*: **la ~** Switzerland

'svizzero, -a ['zvittsero] *ag, sm/f* Swiss

svoglia'tezza [zvoʎʎa'tettsa] *sf* listlessness; indolence

svogli'ato, -a [zvoʎ'ʎato] *ag* listless; *(pigro)* lazy, indolent

svolaz'zare [zvolat'tsare] *vi* to flutter

'svolgere ['zvoldʒere] *vt* to unwind; *(srotolare)* to unroll; *(fig: argomento)* to develop; *(: piano, programma)* to carry out; **svolgersi** *vr* to unwind; to unroll; *(fig: aver luogo)* to take place; *(: procedere)* to go on; **tutto si è svolto secondo i piani** everything went according to plan

svolgi'mento [zvoldʒi'mento] *sm* development; carrying out; *(andamento)* course

'svolsi *etc vb vedi* **svolgere**

'svolta *sf (atto)* turning *no pl*; *(curva)* turn, bend; *(fig)* turning-point; **essere ad una ~ nella propria vita** to be at a crossroads in one's life

svol'tare *vi* to turn

'svolto, -a *pp di* **svolgere**

svuo'tare *vt* to empty (out)

'Swaziland ['swadziland] *sm*: **lo ~** Swaziland

Tt

T, t [ti] *sf o m inv* (*lettera*) T, t; **T come Taranto** ≈ T for Tommy

T *abbr* = **tabaccheria**

t *abbr* = **tara; tonnellata**

TA *sigla* = **Taranto**

tabac'caio, -a *sm/f* tobacconist

tabacche'ria [tabakke'ria] *sf* tobacconist's (shop)

tabacchi'era [tabak'kjɛra] *sf* snuffbox

ta'bacco, -chi *sm* tobacco

ta'bella *sf* (*tavola*) table; (*elenco*) list; ~ **di marcia** schedule; ~ **dei prezzi** price list

tabel'lone *sm* (*per pubblicità*) billboard; (*per informazioni*) notice board (*Brit*), bulletin board (*US*); (: *in stazione*) timetable board

taber'nacolo *sm* tabernacle

tabù *ag, sm inv* taboo

'tabula 'rasa *sf* tabula rasa; **fare** ~ (*fig*) to make a clean sweep

tabu'lare *vt* to tabulate

tabu'lato *sm* (*Inform*) printout

tabula'tore *sm* tabulator

TAC *sigla f* (*Med*: = *Tomografia Assiale Computerizzata*) CAT

'tacca, -che *sf* notch, nick; **di mezza** ~ (*fig*) mediocre

taccagne'ria [takkaɲɲe'ria] *sf* meanness, stinginess

tac'cagno, -a [tak'kaɲɲo] *ag* mean, stingy

tac'cheggio [tak'keddʒo] *sm* shoplifting

tac'chino [tak'kino] *sm* turkey

'taccia, -ce ['tattʃa] *sf* bad reputation

tacci'are [tat'tʃare] *vt*: ~ **qn di** (*vigliaccheria etc*) to accuse sb of

'taccio *etc* ['tattʃo] *vb vedi* **tacere**

'tacco, -chi *sm* heel

taccu'ino *sm* notebook

ta'cere [ta'tʃere] *vi* to be silent o quiet; (*smettere di parlare*) to fall silent ■ *vt* to keep to oneself, say nothing about; **far** ~ **qn** to make sb be quiet; (*fig*) to silence sb; **mettere a** ~ **qc** to hush sth up

tachicar'dia [takikar'dia] *sf* (*Med*) tachycardia

ta'chimetro [ta'kimetro] *sm* speedometer

'tacito, -a ['tatʃito] *ag* silent; (*sottinteso*) tacit, unspoken

taci'turno, -a [tatʃi'turno] *ag* taciturn

taci'uto, -a [ta'tʃuto] *pp di* **tacere**

'tacqui *etc vb vedi* **tacere**

ta'fano *sm* horsefly

taffe'ruglio [taffe'ruʎʎo] *sm* brawl, scuffle

taffettà *sm* taffeta

'taglia ['taʎʎa] *sf* (*statura*) height; (*misura*) size; (*riscatto*) ransom; (*ricompensa*) reward; **taglie forti** (*Abbigliamento*) outsize

taglia'boschi [taʎʎa'bɔski] *sm inv* woodcutter

taglia'carte [taʎʎa'karte] *sm inv* paperknife

taglia'legna [taʎʎa'leɲɲa] *sm inv* woodcutter

tagli'ando [taʎ'ʎando] *sm* coupon

tagli'are [taʎ'ʎare] *vt* to cut; (*recidere, interrompere*) to cut off; (*intersecare*) to cut across, intersect; (*carne*) to carve; (*vini*) to blend ■ *vi* to cut; (*prendere una scorciatoia*) to take a short-cut; ~ **la strada a qn** to cut across in front of sb; ~ **corto** (*fig*) to cut short

taglia'telle [taʎʎa'telle] *sfpl* tagliatelle *pl*

tagli'ato, -a [taʎ'ʎato] *ag*: **essere** ~ **per qc** (*fig*) to be cut out for sth

taglia'trice [taʎʎa'tritʃe] *sf* (*Tecn*) cutter

taglia'unghie [taʎʎa'ungje] *sm inv* nail clippers *pl*

taglieggi'are [taʎʎed'dʒare] *vt* to exact a tribute from

tagli'ente [taʎ'ʎɛnte] *ag* sharp

tagli'ere [taʎ'ʎɛre] *sm* chopping board; (*per il pane*) bread board

'taglio ['taʎʎo] *sm* (*anche fig*) cut; (*azione*) cutting *no pl*; (*di carne*) piece; (*di stoffa*) length; (*di vini*) blending; **di** ~ on edge, edgeways; **banconote di piccolo/grosso** ~ notes of small/large denomination; **un bel** ~ **di capelli** a nice haircut o hairstyle; **pizza al** ~ pizza by the slice

tagli'ola [taʎ'ʎɔla] *sf* trap, snare

t

tagli'one [taʎ'ʎone] *sm*: **la legge del ~** the concept of an eye for an eye and a tooth for a tooth

tagliuz'zare [taʎʎut'tsare] *vt* to cut into small pieces

Ta'hiti [ta'iti] *sf* Tahiti

tailan'dese *ag, sm/f, sm* Thai

Tai'landia *sf*: **la ~** Thailand

tai'lleur [ta'jœr] *sm inv* lady's suit

'talamo *sm* (*poetico*) marriage bed

'talco *sm* talcum powder

 PAROLA CHIAVE

'tale *det* **1** (*simile, così grande*) such; **un(a) tale ...** such a ...; **non accetto tali discorsi** I won't allow such talk; **è di una tale arroganza** he is so arrogant; **fa una tale confusione!** he makes such a mess! **2** (*persona o cosa indeterminata*) such-and-such; **il giorno tale all'ora tale** on such-and-such a day at such-and-such a time; **la tal persona** that person; **ha telefonato una tale Giovanna** somebody called Giovanna phoned **3** (*nelle similitudini*): **tale ... tale** like ... like; **tale padre tale figlio** like father, like son; **hai il vestito tale quale il mio** your dress is just *o* exactly like mine
■ *pron* (*indefinito: persona*): **un(a) tale** someone; **quel** (*o* **quella**) **tale** that person, that man (*o* woman); **il tal dei tali** what's-his-name

tale'bano *sm* Taliban

ta'lento *sm* talent

talis'mano *sm* talisman

talk-'show [tɔlk'ʃo] *sm inv* talk *o* chat show

tallo'nare *vt* to pursue; **~ il pallone** (*Calcio, Rugby*) to heel the ball

tallon'cino [tallon'tʃino] *sm* counterfoil (*Brit*), stub; **~ del prezzo** (*di medicinali*) tear-off tag

tal'lone *sm* heel

tal'mente *av* so

ta'lora *av* = **talvolta**

'talpa *sf* (*anche fig*) mole

tal'volta *av* sometimes, at times

tambu'rello *sm* tambourine

tambu'rino *sm* drummer boy

tam'buro *sm* drum; **freni a ~** drum brakes; **pistola a ~** revolver; **a ~ battente** (*fig*) immediately, at once

Ta'migi [ta'midʒi] *sm*: **il ~** the Thames

tampona'mento *sm* (*Aut*) collision; **~ a catena** pile-up

tampo'nare *vt* (*otturare*) to plug; (*urtare: macchina*) to crash *o* ram into

tam'pone *sm* (*Med*) wad, pad; (*per timbri*) ink-pad; (*respingente*) buffer; **~ assorbente** tampon

'tamtam *sm inv* (*fig*) grapevine

'tana *sf* lair, den; (*fig*) den, hideout

'tanfo *sm* (*di muffa*) musty smell; (*puzza*) stench

tan'gente [tan'dʒente] *ag* (*Mat*): **~ a** tangential to ■ *sf* tangent; (*quota*) share; (*denaro estorto*) rake-off (*fam*), cut

tangen'topoli [tandʒen'topoli] *sf* (*Pol, Media*) Bribesville; *see note*

tangenzi'ale [tandʒen'tsjale] *sf* (*strada*) bypass

Tangeri ['tandʒeri] *sf* Tangiers

tan'gibile [tan'dʒibile] *ag* tangible

tangibil'mente [tandʒibil'mente] *av* tangibly

tango, -ghi *sm* tango

'tanica, -che *sf* jerry can

tan'nino *sm* tannin

tan'tino: **un tan'tino** *av* (*un po'*) a little, a bit; (*alquanto*) rather

 PAROLA CHIAVE

'tanto, -a *det* **1** (*molto: quantità*) a lot of, much; (*: numero*) a lot of, many; **tanto pane/latte** a lot of bread/milk; **tanto tempo** a lot of time, a long time; **tanti auguri!** all the best!; **tante grazie** many thanks; **tante persone** a lot of people, many people; **tante volte** many times, often; **ogni tanti chilometri** every so many kilometres **2** (*così tanto: quantità*) so much, such a lot of; (*: numero*) so many, such a lot of; **tanta fatica per niente!** a lot of trouble for nothing!; **ha tanto coraggio che ...** he's got so much courage that ..., he's so brave that ...; **ho aspettato per tanto tempo** I waited so long *o* for such a long time **3**: **tanto ... quanto** (*quantità*) as much ... as; (*numero*) as many ... as; **ho tanta pazienza**

quanta ne hai tu I have as much patience as you have o as you; **ha tanti amici quanti nemici** he has as many friends as he has enemies

■ *pron* **1** (*molto*) much, a lot; (*così tanto*) so much, such a lot; **tanti, e** many, a lot; so many; such a lot; **credevo ce ne fosse tanto** I thought there was (such) a lot, I thought there was plenty; **una persona come tante** a person just like any other; **è passato tanto** (*tempo*) it's been so long; **è tanto che aspetto** I've been waiting for a long time; **tanto di guadagnato!** so much the better! **2: tanto quanto** (*denaro*) as much as; (*cioccolatini*) as many as; **ne ho tanto quanto basta** I have as much as I need; **due volte tanto** twice as much

3 (*indeterminato*) so much; **tanto per l'affitto, tanto per il gas** so much for the rent, so much for the gas; **costa un tanto al metro** it costs so much per metre; **di tanto in tanto, ogni tanto** every so often; **tanto vale che ...** I (*o* we *etc*) may as well ...; **tanto meglio!** so much the better!; **tanto peggio per lui!** so much the worse for him!; **se tanto mi dà tanto** if that's how things are; **guardare qc con tanto d'occhi** to gaze wide-eyed at sth

■ *av* **1** (*molto*) very; **vengo tanto volentieri** I'd be very glad to come; **non ci vuole tanto a capirlo** it doesn't take much to understand it

2 (*così tanto: con ag, av*) so; (*: con vb*) so much, such a lot; **è tanto bella!** she's so beautiful!; **non urlare tanto (forte)** don't shout so much; **sto tanto meglio adesso** I'm so much better now; **era tanto bella da non credere** she was incredibly beautiful; **tanto ... che** so ... (that); **tanto ... da** so ... as

3: tanto ... quanto as ... as; **conosco tanto Carlo quanto suo padre** I know both Carlo and his father; **non è poi tanto complicato quanto sembra** it's not as difficult as it seems; **è tanto bella quanto buona** she is as good as she is beautiful; **tanto più insisti, tanto più non mollerà** the more you insist, the more stubborn he'll be; **quanto più ... tanto meno** the more ... the less; **quanto più lo conosco tanto meno mi piace** the better I know him the less I like him

4 (*solamente*) just; **tanto per cambiare/scherzare** just for a change/a joke; **una volta tanto** for once

5 (*a lungo*) (for) long

■ *cong* after all; **non insistere, tanto è inutile** don't keep on, it's no use; **lascia**

stare, tanto è troppo tardi forget it, it's too late

Tanza'nia [tandza'nia] *sf*: **la ~** Tanzania
tapi'oca *sf* tapioca
ta'piro *sm* (*Zool*) tapir
'tappa *sf* (*luogo di sosta, fermata*) stop, halt; (*parte di un percorso*) stage, leg; (*Sport*) lap; **a tappe** in stages; **bruciare le tappe** (*fig*) to be a whizz kid
tappa'buchi [tappa'buki] *sm inv* stopgap; **fare da ~** to act as a stopgap
tap'pare *vt* to plug, stop up; (*bottiglia*) to cork; **tapparsi il naso** to hold one's nose; **tapparsi le orecchie** to turn a deaf ear; **tapparsi gli occhi** to turn a blind eye
tappa'rella *sf* rolling shutter
tappe'tino *sm* (*per auto*) car mat; **~ antiscivolo** (*da bagno*) non-slip mat
tap'peto *sm* carpet; (*anche*: **tappetino**) rug; (*di tavolo*) cloth; (*Sport*): **andare al ~** to go down for the count; **mettere sul ~** (*fig*) to bring up for discussion
tappez'zare [tappet'tsare] *vt* (*con carta*) to paper; (*rivestire*): **~ qc (di)** to cover sth (with)
tappezze'ria [tappettse'ria] *sf* (*arredamento*) soft furnishings *pl*; (*carta da parati*) wall covering; (*di automobile*) upholstery; **far da ~** (*fig*) to be a wallflower
tappezzi'ere [tappet'tsjere] *sm* upholsterer
'tappo *sm* stopper; (*in sughero*) cork; **~ a corona** bottle top; **~ a vite** screw top
TAR *sigla m* = **Tribunale Amministrativo Regionale**
'tara *sf* (*peso*) tare; (*Med*) hereditary defect; (*difetto*) flaw
taran'tella *sf* tarantella
ta'rantola *sf* tarantula
ta'rare *vt* (*Comm*) to tare; (*Tecn*) to calibrate
ta'rato, -a *ag* (*Comm*) tared; (*Med*) with a hereditary defect
tara'tura *sf* (*Comm*) taring; (*Tecn*) calibration
tarchi'ato, -a [tar'kjato] *ag* stocky, thickset
tar'dare *vi* to be late ■ *vt* to delay; **~ a fare** to delay doing
'tardi *av* late; **più ~** later (on); **al più ~** at the latest; **sul ~** (*verso sera*) late in the day; **far ~** to be late; (*restare alzato*) to stay up late
tar'divo, -a *ag* (*primavera*) late; (*rimedio*) belated, tardy; (*fig: bambino*) retarded
'tardo, -a *ag* (*lento, fig: ottuso*) slow; (*tempo: avanzato*) late
tar'dona *sf* (*peg*): **essere una ~** to be mutton dressed as lamb
'targa, -ghe *sf* plate; (*Aut*) number (*Brit*) *o* license (*US*) plate; *vedi anche* **circolazione**
tar'gare *vt* (*Aut*) to register

t

377

targ'hetta [tar'getta] *sf (con nome: su porta)* nameplate; (: *su bagaglio*) name tag

ta'riffa *sf (gen)* rate, tariff; *(di trasporti)* fare; *(elenco)* price list; tariff; **la ~ in vigore** the going rate; **~ normale/ridotta** standard/reduced rate; *(su mezzi di trasporto)* full/concessionary fare; **~ salariale** wage rate; **~ unica** flat rate; **tariffe doganali** customs rates *o* tariff; **tariffe postali/telefoniche** postal/telephone charges

tariffario, -ii *ag*: **aumento ~** increase in charges *o* rates ■ *sm* tariff, table of charges

'tarlo *sm* woodworm

'tarma *sf* moth

tarmi'cida, -i [tarmi'tʃida] *ag, sm* moth-killer

ta'rocco, -chi *sm* tarot card; **tarocchi** *smpl (gioco)* tarot *sg*

tar'pare *vt (fig)*: **~ le ali a qn** to clip sb's wings

tartagli'are [tartaʎ'ʎare] *vi* to stutter, stammer

'tartaro, -a *ag, sm (in tutti i sensi)* tartar

tarta'ruga, -ghe *sf* tortoise; *(di mare)* turtle; *(materiale)* tortoiseshell

tartas'sare *vt (fam)*: **~ qn** to give sb the works; **~ qn a un esame** to give sb a grilling at an exam

tar'tina *sf* canapé

tar'tufo *sm (Bot)* truffle

'tasca, -sche *sf* pocket; **da ~** pocket *cpd*; **fare i conti in ~ a qn** *(fig)* to meddle in sb's affairs

tas'cabile *ag (libro)* pocket *cpd*

tasca'pane *sm* haversack

tas'chino [tas'kino] *sm* breast pocket

Tas'mania *sf*: **la ~** Tasmania

'tassa *sf (imposta)* tax; *(doganale)* duty; *(per iscrizione: a scuola etc)* fee; **~ di circolazione/di soggiorno** road/tourist tax

tas'sametro *sm* taximeter

tas'sare *vt* to tax; to levy a duty on

tassa'tivo, -a *ag* peremptory

tassazi'one [tassat'tsjone] *sf* taxation; **soggetto a ~** taxable

tas'sello *sm (di legno, pietra)* plug; *(assaggio)* wedge

tas'sì *sm inv* = **taxi**

tas'sista, -i, e *sm/f* taxi driver

'tasso *sm (di natalità, d'interesse etc)* rate; *(Bot)* yew; *(Zool)* badger; **~ di cambio/d'interesse** rate of exchange/interest; **~ di crescita** growth rate

tas'tare *vt* to feel; **~ il terreno** *(fig)* to see how the land lies

tasti'era *sf* keyboard

tastie'rino *sm*: **~ numerico** numeric keypad

'tasto *sm* key; *(tatto)* touch, feel; **toccare un ~ delicato** *(fig)* to touch on a delicate subject; **toccare il ~ giusto** *(fig)* to strike the right

note; **~ funzione** *(Inform)* function key; **~ delle maiuscole** *(su macchina da scrivere etc)* shift key

tas'toni *av*: **procedere (a) ~** to grope one's way forward

'tata *sf (linguaggio infantile)* nanny

'tattico, -a, ci, che *ag* tactical ■ *sf* tactics *pl*

'tatto *sm (senso)* touch; *(fig)* tact; **duro al ~** hard to the touch; **aver ~** to be tactful, have tact

tatu'aggio [tatu'addʒo] *sm* tattooing; *(disegno)* tattoo

tatu'are *vt* to tattoo

tauma'turgico, -a, ci, che [tauma'turdʒiko] *ag (fig)* miraculous

TAV [tav] *sigla m o f inv* (= *treno alta velocità*) high-speed train; *(sistema)* high-speed rail system

ta'verna *sf (osteria)* tavern

'tavola *sf* table; *(asse)* plank, board; *(lastra)* tablet; *(quadro)* panel (painting); *(illustrazione)* plate; **~ calda** snack bar; **~ pieghevole** folding table

tavo'lata *sf* company at table

tavo'lato *sm* boarding; *(pavimento)* wooden floor

tavo'letta *sf* tablet, bar; **a ~** *(Aut)* flat out

tavo'lino *sm* small table; *(scrivania)* desk; **~ da tè/gioco** coffee/card table; **mettersi a ~** to get down to work; **decidere qc a ~** *(fig)* to decide sth on a theoretical level

'tavolo *sm* table; **~ da disegno** drawing board; **~ da lavoro** desk; *(Tecn)* workbench; **~ operatorio** *(Med)* operating table

tavo'lozza [tavo'lɔttsa] *sf (Arte)* palette

'taxi *sm inv* taxi

'tazza ['tattsa] *sf* cup; **~ da caffè/tè** coffee/tea cup; **una ~ di caffè/tè** a cup of coffee/tea

taz'zina [tat'tsina] *sf* coffee cup

TBC *abbr f* (= *tubercolosi*) TB

TCI *sigla m* = **Touring Club Italiano**

TE *sigla* = **Teramo**

te *pron (soggetto: in forme comparative, oggetto)* you

tè *sm inv* tea; *(trattenimento)* tea party

tea'trale *ag* theatrical

te'atro *sm* theatre; **~ comico** comedy; **~ di posa** film studio

'tecnico, -a, ci, che *ag* technical ■ *sm/f* technician ■ *sf* technique; *(tecnologia)* technology

tecnolo'gia [teknolo'dʒia] *sf* technology; **alta ~** high technology, hi-tech

tecno'logico, -a, ci, che [tekno'lɔdʒiko] *ag* technological

te'desco, -a, schi, sche *ag, sm/f, sm* German; **~ orientale/occidentale** East/West German

tedi'are *vt (infastidire)* to bother, annoy; *(annoiare)* to bore 'tedio *sm* tedium, boredom

tedi'oso, -a *ag* tedious, boring

te'game *sm* (*Cuc*) pan; **al ~** fried

'teglia ['teʎʎa] *sf* (*Cuc: per dolci*) (baking) tin (*Brit*), cake pan (*US*); (*: per arrosti*) (roasting) tin

'tegola *sf* tile

Teh'ran *sf* Tehran

tei'era *sf* teapot

te'ina *sf* (*Chim*) theine

tel. *abbr* (= *telefono*) tel

'tela *sf* (*tessuto*) cloth; (*per vele, quadri*) canvas; (*dipinto*) canvas, painting; **di ~** (*calzoni*) (heavy) cotton *cpd*; (*scarpe, borsa*) canvas *cpd*; **~ cerata** oilcloth; **~ di ragno** spider's web

te'laio *sm* (*apparecchio*) loom; (*struttura*) frame

Tel A'viv *sf* Tel Aviv

tele... *prefisso* tele...

teleabbo'nato *sm* television licence holder

tele'camera *sf* television camera

telecoman'dare *vt* to operate by remote control

teleco'mando *sm* remote control; (*dispositivo*) remote-control device

telecomunicazi'oni [telekomunikat'tsjoni] *sfpl* telecommunications

teleconfe'renza *sf* teleconferencing

tele'cronaca, -che *sf* television report

telecro'nista, -i, e *sm/f* (television) commentator

tele'ferica, -che *sf* cableway

tele'film *sm inv* television film

telefo'nare *vi* to telephone, ring; (*fare una chiamata*) to make a phone call ■ *vt* to telephone; **~ a qn** to telephone sb, phone *o* ring *o* call sb (up)

telefo'nata *sf* (telephone) call; **~ urbana/interurbana** local/long-distance call; **~ a carico del destinatario** reverse charge (*Brit*) *o* collect (*US*) call; **~ con preavviso** person-to-person call

telefonica'mente *av* by (tele)phone

tele'fonico, -a, ci, che *ag* (tele)phone *cpd*

telefo'nino *sm* (*cellulare*) mobile phone

telefo'nista, -i, e *sm/f* telephonist; (*d'impresa*) switchboard operator

te'lefono *sm* telephone; **essere al ~** to be on the (tele)phone; **~ a gettoni** ≈ pay phone; **~ azzurro** ≈ Childline; **~ interno** internal phone; **~ pubblico** public phone, call box (*Brit*); **~ rosa** ≈ rape crisis

telegior'nale [teledʒor'nale] *sm* television news (programme)

telegra'fare *vt, vi* to telegraph, cable

telegra'fia *sf* telegraphy

tele'grafico, -a, ci, che *ag* telegraph *cpd*, telegraphic

telegra'fista, -i, e *sm/f* telegraphist, telegraph operator

te'legrafo *sm* telegraph; (*ufficio*) telegraph office

tele'gramma, -i *sm* telegram

telela'voro *sm* teleworking

tele'matica *sf* data transmission; telematics *sg*

teleno'vela *sf* soap opera

teleobiet'tivo *sm* telephoto lens *sg*

telepa'tia *sf* telepathy

tele'quiz [tele'kwits] *sm inv* (*TV*) game show

teles'chermo [teles'kɛrmo] *sm* television screen

teles'copio *sm* telescope

telescri'vente *sf* teleprinter (*Brit*), teletypewriter (*US*)

teleselet'tivo, -a *ag*: **prefisso ~** dialling code (*Brit*), dial code (*US*)

teleselezi'one [teleselet'tsjone] *sf* direct dialling

telespetta'tore, -'trice *sm/f* (television) viewer

tele'text *sm inv* teletext

tele'vendita [tele'vendita] *sf* teleshopping

tele'video *sm* videotext service

televisi'one *sf* television; see note

● **TELEVISIONE**

● Three state-owned channels, RAI 1, 2 and
● 3, and a large number of private
● companies broadcast television
● programmes in Italy. Some of the latter
● function at purely local level, while
● others are regional; some form part of a
● network, while others remain
● independent. As a public corporation, RAI
● reports to the Post and
● Telecommunications Ministry. Both RAI
● and the private-sector channels compete
● for advertising revenues.

televi'sore *sm* television set

'telex *sm inv* telex

'telo *sm* length of cloth

te'lone *sm* (*per merci etc*) tarpaulin; (*sipario*) drop curtain

'tema, -i *sm* theme; (*Ins*) essay, composition

te'matica *sf* basic themes *pl*

teme'rario, -a *ag* rash, reckless

te'mere *vt* to fear, be afraid of; (*essere sensibile a: freddo, calore*) to be sensitive to ■ *vi* to be afraid; (*essere preoccupato*): **~ per** to worry about, fear for; **~ di/che** to be afraid of/that

'tempera *sf* (*pittura*) tempera; (*dipinto*) painting in tempera

temperama'tite *sm inv* pencil sharpener
tempera'mento *sm* temperament
tempe'rante *ag* moderate
tempe'rare *vt* (*aguzzare*) to sharpen; (*fig*) to moderate, control, temper
tempe'rato, -a *ag* moderate, temperate; (*clima*) temperate
tempera'tura *sf* temperature; ~ **ambiente** room temperature
tempe'rino *sm* penknife
tem'pesta *sf* storm; ~ **di sabbia/neve** sand/snowstorm
tempes'tare *vt* (*percuotere*): ~ **qn di colpi** to rain blows on sb; (*bombardare*): ~ **qn di domande** to bombard sb with questions; (*ornare*) to stud
tempestività *sf* timeliness
tempes'tivo, -a *ag* timely
tempes'toso, -a *ag* stormy
'tempia *sf* (*Anat*) temple
'tempio *sm* (*edificio*) temple
tem'pismo *sm* sense of timing
tem'pistiche [tem'pistike] *sfpl* (*Comm*) time and motion
'tempo *sm* (*Meteor*) weather; (*cronologico*) time; (*epoca*) time, times *pl*; (*di film, gioco: parte*) part; (*Mus*) time; (: *battuta*) beat; (*Ling*) tense; **un ~** once; **da ~** for a long time now; ~ **fa** some time ago; **poco ~ dopo** not long after; **a ~ e luogo** at the right time and place; **ogni cosa a suo ~** we'll (*o* you'll *etc*) deal with it in due course; **al ~ stesso** *o* **a un ~** at the same time; **per ~** early; **per qualche ~** for a while; **trovare il ~ di fare qc** to find the time to do sth; **aver fatto il proprio ~** to have had its (*o* his *etc*) day; **primo/secondo ~** (*Teat*) first/second part; (*Sport*) first/second half; **rispettare i tempi** to keep to the timetable; **stringere i tempi** to speed things up; **con i tempi che corrono** these days; **in questi ultimi tempi** of late; **ai miei tempi** in my day; ~ **di cottura** cooking time; **in ~ utile** in due time *o* course; **tempi di esecuzione** (*Comm*) time scale *sg*; **tempi di lavorazione** (*Comm*) throughput time *sg*; **tempi morti** (*Comm*) downtime *sg*, idle time *sg*
tempo'rale *ag* temporal ■ *sm* (*Meteor*) (thunder)storm
tempora'lesco, -a, schi, sche *ag* stormy
tempo'raneo, -a *ag* temporary
temporeggi'are [tempored'dʒare] *vi* to play for time, temporize
'tempra *sf* (*Tecn: atto*) tempering, hardening; (: *effetto*) temper; (*fig: costituzione fisica*) constitution; (: *intellettuale*) temperament
tem'prare *vt* to temper

te'nace [te'natʃe] *ag* strong, tough; (*fig*) tenacious
te'nacia [te'natʃa] *sf* tenacity
te'naglie [te'naʎʎe] *sfpl* pincers *pl*
'tenda *sf* (*riparo*) awning; (*di finestra*) curtain; (*per campeggio etc*) tent
ten'daggio [ten'daddʒo] *sm* curtaining, curtains *pl*, drapes *pl* (US)
ten'denza [ten'dentsa] *sf* tendency; (*orientamento*) trend; **avere ~** *o* **per qc** to have a bent for sth; ~ **al rialzo/ribasso** (*Borsa*) upward/downward trend
tendenziosità [tendentsjosi'ta] *sf* tendentiousness
tendenzi'oso, -a [tenden'tsjoso] *ag* tendentious, bias(s)ed
'tendere *vt* (*allungare al massimo*) to stretch, draw tight; (*porgere: mano*) to hold out; (*fig: trappola*) to lay, set ■ *vi*: ~ **a qc/a fare** to tend towards sth/to do; **tutti i nostri sforzi sono tesi a ...** all our efforts are geared towards ...; ~ **l'orecchio** to prick up one's ears; **il tempo tende al caldo** the weather is getting hot; **un blu che tende al verde** a greenish blue
ten'dina *sf* curtain
'tendine *sm* tendon, sinew
ten'done *sm* (*da circo*) big top
ten'dopoli *sf inv* (large) camp
'tenebre *sfpl* darkness *sg*
tene'broso, -a *ag* dark, gloomy
te'nente *sm* lieutenant
te'nere *vt* to hold; (*conservare, mantenere*) to keep; (*ritenere, considerare*) to consider; (*spazio: occupare*) to take up, occupy; (*seguire: strada*) to keep to; (*dare: lezione, conferenza*) to give ■ *vi* to hold; (*colori*) to be fast; (*dare importanza*): ~ **a** to care about; ~ **a fare** to want to do, be keen to do; **tenersi** *vr* (*stare in una determinata posizione*) to stand; (*stimarsi*) to consider o.s.; (*aggrapparsi*): **tenersi a** to hold on to; (*attenersi*): **tenersi a** to stick to; ~ **in gran conto** *o* **considerazione qn** to have a high regard for sb, think highly of sb; ~ **conto di qc** to take sth into consideration; ~ **presente qc** to bear sth in mind; **non ci sono scuse che tengano** I'll take no excuses; **tenersi per la mano** (*uso reciproco*) to hold hands; **tenersi in piedi** to stay on one's feet
tene'rezza [tene'rettsa] *sf* tenderness
'tenero, -a *ag* tender; (*pietra, cera, colore*) soft; (*fig*) tender, loving ■ *sm*: **tra quei due c'è del ~** there's a romance budding between those two
'tengo *etc vb vedi* **tenere**
'tenia *sf* tapeworm
'tenni *etc vb vedi* **tenere**
'tennis *sm* tennis; ~ **da tavolo** table tennis

ten'nista, -i, e *sm/f* tennis player

te'nore *sm* (*tono*) tone; (*Mus*) tenor; **~ di vita** way of life; (*livello*) standard of living

tensi'one *sf* tension; **ad alta ~** (*Elettr*) high-voltage *cpd*, high-tension *cpd*

tentaco'lare *ag* tentacular; (*fig: città*) magnet-like

ten'tacolo *sm* tentacle

ten'tare *vt* (*indurre*) to tempt; (*provare*): **~ qc/di fare** to attempt o try sth/to do; **~ la sorte** to try one's luck

tenta'tivo *sm* attempt

tentazi'one [tentat'tsjone] *sf* temptation; **aver la ~ di fare** to be tempted to do

tentenna'mento *sm* (*fig*) hesitation, wavering; **dopo molti tentennamenti** after much hesitation

tenten'nare *vi* to shake, be unsteady; (*fig*) to hesitate, waver ■ *vt*: **~ il capo** to shake one's head

ten'toni *av*: **andare a ~** (*anche fig*) to grope one's way

'tenue *ag* (*sottile*) fine; (*colore*) soft; (*fig*) slender, slight

te'nuta *sf* (*capacità*) capacity; (*divisa*) uniform; (*abito*) dress; (*Agr*) estate; **a ~ d'aria** airtight; **~ di strada** roadholding power; **in ~ da lavoro** in one's working clothes; **in ~ da sci** in a skiing outfit

teolo'gia [teolo'dʒia] *sf* theology

teo'logico, -a, ci, che [teo'lɔdʒiko] *ag* theological

te'ologo, -gi *sm* theologian

teo'rema, -i *sm* theorem

teo'ria *sf* theory; **in ~** in theory, theoretically

te'orico, -a, ci, che *ag* theoretic(al) ■ *sm* theorist, theoretician; **a livello ~**, **in linea teorica** theoretically

teoriz'zare [teorid'dzare] *vt* to theorize

'tepido, -a *ag* = **tiepido**

te'pore *sm* warmth

'teppa *sf* mob, hooligans *pl*

tep'paglia [tep'paʎʎa] *sf* hooligans *pl*

tep'pismo *sm* hooliganism

tep'pista, -i *sm* hooligan

tera'peutico, -a, ci, che *ag* therapeutic

tera'pia *sf* therapy; **~ di gruppo** group therapy

tera'pista, -i, e *sm/f* therapist

tergicris'tallo [terdʒikris'tallo] *sm* windscreen (*Brit*) o windshield (*US*) wiper

tergiver'sare [terdʒiver'sare] *vi* to shilly-shally

'tergo *sm*: **a ~** behind; **vedi a ~** please turn over

'terital® *sm inv* Terylene®

ter'male *ag* thermal

'terme *sfpl* thermal baths

'termico, -a, ci, che *ag* thermal; **centrale termica** thermal power station

termi'nale *ag* (*fase, parte*) final; (*Med*) terminal ■ *sm* terminal; **tratto ~** (*di fiume*) lower reaches *pl*

termi'nare *vt* to end; (*lavoro*) to finish ■ *vi* to end

terminazi'one [terminat'tsjone] *sf* (*fine*) end; (*Ling*) ending; **terminazioni nervose** (*Anat*) nerve endings

'termine *sm* term; (*fine, estremità*) end; (*di territorio*) boundary, limit; **fissare un ~** to set a deadline; **portare a ~ qc** to bring sth to a conclusion; **contratto a ~** (*Comm*) forward contract; **a breve/lungo ~** short-/long-term; **ai termini di legge** by law; **in altri termini** in other words; **parlare senza mezzi termini** to talk frankly, not to mince one's words

terminolo'gia [terminolo'dʒia] *sf* terminology

'termite *sf* termite

termoco'perta *sf* electric blanket

ter'mometro *sm* thermometer

termonucle'are *ag* thermonuclear

'termos *sm inv* = **thermos**

termosi'fone *sm* radiator; (**riscaldamento a**) **~** central heating

ter'mostato *sm* thermostat

'terna *sf* set of three; (*lista di tre nomi*) list of three candidates

'terno *sm* (*al lotto etc*) (set of) three winning numbers; **vincere un ~ al lotto** (*fig*) to hit the jackpot

'terra *sf* (*gen, Elettr*) earth; (*sostanza*) soil, earth; (*opposto al mare*) land *no pl*; (*regione, paese*) land; (*argilla*) clay; **terre** *sfpl* (*possedimento*) lands, land *sg*; **a o per ~** (*stato*) on the ground (*o floor*); (*moto*) to the ground, down; **mettere a ~** (*Elettr*) to earth; **essere a ~** (*fig: depresso*) to be at rock bottom; **via ~** (*viaggiare*) by land, overland; **strada in ~ battuta** dirt track; **~ di nessuno** no man's land; **la T~ Santa** the Holy Land; **~ di Siena** sienna; **~ ~** (*fig: persona, argomento*) prosaic, pedestrian

terra-'aria *ag inv* (*Mil*) ground-to-air

terra'cotta *sf* terracotta; **vasellame di ~** earthenware

terra'ferma *sf* dry land, terra firma; (*continente*) mainland

ter'raglia [ter'raʎʎa] *sf* pottery; **terraglie** *sfpl* (*oggetti*) crockery *sg*, earthenware *sg*

Terra'nova *sf*: **la ~** Newfoundland

terrapi'eno *sm* embankment, bank

terra-'terra *ag inv* (*Mil*) surface-to-surface

ter'razza [ter'rattsa] *sf*, **ter'razzo** [ter'rattso] *sm* terrace

terremo'tato, -a *ag* (*zona*) devastated by an earthquake ■ *sm/f* earthquake victim

terre'moto *sm* earthquake

ter'reno, -a *ag* (*vita, beni*) earthly ■ *sm* (*suolo, fig*) ground; (*Comm*) land *no pl*, plot (of land); site; (*Sport, Mil*) field; **perdere ~** (*anche fig*) to lose ground; **un ~ montuoso** a mountainous terrain; **~ alluvionale** (*Geo*) alluvial soil

'terreo, -a *ag* (*viso, colorito*) wan

ter'restre *ag* (*superficie*) of the earth, earth's; (*di terra: battaglia, animale*) land *cpd*; (*Rel*) earthly, worldly

ter'ribile *ag* terrible, dreadful

ter'riccio [ter'rittʃo] *sm* soil

terri'ero, -a *ag*: **proprietà terriera** landed property; **proprietario ~** landowner

terrifi'cante *ag* terrifying

ter'rina *sf* (*zuppiera*) tureen

territori'ale *ag* territorial

terri'torio *sm* territory

ter'rone, -a *sm/f derogatory term used by Northern Italians to describe Southern Italians*

ter'rore *sm* terror; **avere il ~ di qc** to be terrified of sth

terro'rismo *sm* terrorism

terro'rista, -i, e *sm/f* terrorist

terroriz'zare [terrorid'dzare] *vt* to terrorize

'terso, -a *ag* clear

ter'zetto [ter'tsetto] *sm* (*Mus*) trio, terzetto; (*di persone*) trio

terzi'ario, -a [ter'tsjarjo] *ag* (*Geo, Econ*) tertiary

ter'zino [ter'tsino] *sm* (*Calcio*) fullback, back

'terzo, -a ['tertso] *ag* third ■ *sm* (*frazione*) third; (*Dir*) third party ■ *sf* (*gen*) third; (*Aut*) third (gear); (*di trasporti*) third class; (*Scol: elementare*) third year at primary school; (*: media*) third year at secondary school; (*: superiore*) sixth year at secondary school; **terzi** *smpl* (*altri*) others, other people; **agire per conto di terzi** to act on behalf of a third party; **assicurazione contro terzi** third-party insurance (*Brit*), liability insurance (*US*); **la terza età** old age; **il ~ mondo** the Third World; **di terz'ordine** third rate; **la terza pagina** (*Stampa*) the Arts page

'tesa *sf* brim; **a larghe tese** wide-brimmed

'teschio ['teskjo] *sm* skull

'tesi *sf inv* thesis; **~ di laurea** degree thesis

'tesi *etc vb vedi* **tendere**

'teso, -a *pp di* **tendere** ■ *ag* (*tirato*) taut, tight; (*fig*) tense

tesore'ria *sf* treasury

tesori'ere *sm* treasurer

te'soro *sm* treasure; **il Ministero del T~** the Treasury; **far ~ dei consigli di qn** to take sb's advice to heart

'tessera *sf* (*documento*) card; (*di abbonato*) season ticket; (*di giornalista*) pass; **ha la ~ del partito** he's a party member; **~ elettorale** ballot paper

tesse'rare *vt* (*iscrivere*) to give a membership card to

tesse'rato, -a *sm/f* (*di società sportiva etc*) (fully paid-up) member; (*Pol*) (card-carrying) member

'tessere *vt* to weave; **~ le lodi di qn** (*fig*) to sing sb's praises

'tessile *ag, sm* textile

tessi'tore, -'trice *sm/f* weaver

tessi'tura *sf* weaving

tes'suto *sm* fabric, material; (*Biol*) tissue; (*fig*) web

'testa *sf* head; (*di cose: estremità, parte anteriore*) head, front; **50 euro a ~** 50 euros apiece *o* a head *o* per person; **a ~ alta** with one's head held high; **a ~ bassa** (*correre*) headlong; (*con aria dimessa*) with head bowed; **di ~** *ag* (*vettura etc*) front; **dare alla ~** to go to one's head; **fare di ~ propria** to go one's own way; **in ~** (*Sport*) in the lead; **essere in ~ alla classifica** (*corridore*) to be number one; (*squadra*) to be at the top of the league table; (*disco*) to be top of the charts, be number one; **essere alla ~ di qc** (*società*) to be the head of; (*esercito*) to be at the head of; **tenere ~ a qn** (*nemico etc*) to stand up to sb; **una ~ d'aglio** a bulb of garlic; **~ o croce?** heads or tails?; **avere la ~ dura** to be stubborn; **~ di serie** (*Tennis*) seed, seeded player

testa-'coda *sm inv* (*Aut*) spin

testamen'tario, -a *ag* (*Dir*) testamentary; **le sue disposizioni testamentarie** the provisions of his will

testa'mento *sm* (*atto*) will, testament; **l'Antico/il Nuovo T~** (*Rel*) the Old/New Testament

testar'daggine [testar'daddʒine] *sf* stubbornness, obstinacy

tes'tardo, -a *ag* stubborn, pig-headed

tes'tare *vt* to test

tes'tata *sf* (*parte anteriore*) head; (*intestazione*) heading; **missile a ~ nucleare** missile with a nuclear warhead

'teste *sm/f* witness

tes'ticolo *sm* testicle

testi'era *sf* (*del letto*) headboard; (*di cavallo*) headpiece

testi'mone *sm/f* (*Dir*) witness; **fare da ~ alle nozze di qn** to be a witness at sb's wedding; **~ oculare** eye witness

testimoni'anza [testimo'njantsa] *sf (atto)* deposition; *(effetto)* evidence; *(fig: prova)* proof; **accusare qn di falsa ~** to accuse sb of perjury; **rilasciare una ~** to give evidence

testimoni'are *vt* to testify; *(fig)* to bear witness to, testify to ■ *vi* to give evidence, testify; **~ il vero** to tell the truth; **~ il falso** to perjure o.s.

tes'tina *sf (di giradischi, registratore)* head

'**testo** *sm* text; **fare ~** *(opera, autore)* to be authoritative; *(fig: dichiarazione)* to carry weight

testoste'rone *sm* testosterone

testu'ale *ag* textual; **le sue parole testuali** his *(o* her) actual words

tes'tuggine [tes'tuddʒine] *sf* tortoise; *(di mare)* turtle

'**tetano** *sm (Med)* tetanus

'**tetro, -a** *ag* gloomy

'**tetta** *sf (fam)* boob, tit

tetta'rella *sf* teat

'**tetto** *sm* roof; **abbandonare il ~ coniugale** to desert one's family; **~ a cupola** dome

tet'toia *sf* roofing; canopy

'**Tevere** *sm*: **il ~** the Tiber

TG [tid'dʒi] *abbr m* (= *telegiornale*) TV news *sg*

'**thermos**® ['termos] *sm inv* vacuum *o* Thermos® flask

'**thriller** ['θrilə], '**thrilling** ['θriliŋ] *sm inv* thriller

ti *pron (dav lo, la, li, le, ne diventa* **te**) *(oggetto)* you; *(complemento di termine)* (to) you; *(riflessivo)* yourself; **ti aiuto?** can I give you a hand?; **te lo ha dato?** did he give it to you?; **ti sei lavato?** have you washed?

ti'ara *sf (Rel)* tiara

'**Tibet** *sm*: **il ~** Tibet

tibe'tano, -a *ag, sm/f* Tibetan

'**tibia** *sf* tibia, shinbone

tic *sm inv* tic, (nervous) twitch; *(fig)* mannerism

ticchet'tio [tikket'tio] *sm (di macchina da scrivere)* clatter; *(di orologio)* ticking; *(della pioggia)* patter

'**ticchio** ['tikkjo] *sm (ghiribizzo)* whim; *(tic)* tic, (nervous) twitch

'**ticket** *sm inv (Med)* prescription charge (Brit)

ti'ene *etc vb vedi* **tenere**

ti'epido, -a *ag* lukewarm, tepid

ti'fare *vi*: **~ per** to be a fan of; *(parteggiare)* to side with

'**tifo** *sm (Med)* typhus; *(fig)*: **fare il ~ per** to be a fan of

tifoi'dea *sf* typhoid

ti'fone *sm* typhoon

ti'foso, -a *sm/f (Sport etc)* fan

tight ['tait] *sm inv* morning suit

tigì [tid'dʒi] *sm inv* TV news

'**tiglio** ['tiλλo] *sm* lime (tree), linden (tree)

'**tigna** ['tiɲɲa] *sf (Med)* ringworm

ti'grato, -a *ag* striped

'**tigre** *sf* tiger

tilt *sm*: **andare in ~** *(fig)* to go haywire

tim'ballo *sm (strumento)* kettledrum; *(Cuc)* timbale

tim'brare *vt* to stamp; *(annullare: francobolli)* to postmark; **~ il cartellino** to clock in

'**timbro** *sm* stamp; *(Mus)* timbre, tone

timi'dezza [timi'dettsa] *sf* shyness, timidity

'**timido, -a** *ag* shy, timid

'**timo** *sm* thyme

ti'mone *sm (Naut)* rudder

timoni'ere *sm* helmsman

timo'rato, -a *ag* conscientious; **~ di Dio** God-fearing

ti'more *sm (paura)* fear; *(rispetto)* awe; **avere ~ di qc/qn** *(paura)* to be afraid of sth/sb

timo'roso, -a *ag* timid, timorous

'**timpano** *sm (Anat)* eardrum; *(Mus)*: **timpani** kettledrums, timpani

'**tinca, -che** *sf (Zool)* tench

ti'nello *sm* small dining room

'**tingere** ['tindʒere] *vt* to dye

'**tino** *sm* vat

ti'nozza [ti'nɔttsa] *sf* tub

'**tinsi** *etc vb vedi* **tingere**

'**tinta** *sf (materia colorante)* dye; *(colore)* colour (Brit), color (US), shade

tinta'rella *sf (fam)* (sun)tan

tintin'nare *vi* to tinkle

tintin'nio *sm* tinkling

'**tinto, -a** *pp di* **tingere**

tinto'ria *sf (officina)* dyeworks *sg*; *(lavasecco)* dry cleaner's (shop)

tin'tura *sf (operazione)* dyeing; *(colorante)* dye; **~ di iodio** tincture of iodine

'**tipico, -a, ci, che** *ag* typical

'**tipo** *sm* type; *(genere)* kind, type; *(fam)* chap, fellow; **vestiti di tutti i tipi** all kinds of clothes; **sul ~ di questo** of this sort; **sei un bel ~!** you're a fine one!

tipogra'fia *sf* typography

tipo'grafico, -a, ci, che *ag* typographic(al)

ti'pografo *sm* typographer

tip 'tap [tip'tap] *sm (ballo)* tap dancing

T.I.R. *sigla m* (= *Transports Internationaux Routiers*) *International Heavy Goods Vehicle*

'**tira e 'molla** *sm inv* tug-of-war

ti'raggio [ti'raddʒo] *sm (di camino etc)* draught (Brit), draft (US)

Ti'rana *sf* Tirana

tiranneggi'are [tiranned'dʒare] *vt* to tyrannize

tiran'nia *sf* tyranny

ti'ranno, -a *ag* tyrannical ▪ *sm* tyrant
ti'rante *sm* (*Naut, di tenda etc*) guy; (*Edil*) brace
tirapi'edi *sm/f inv* hanger-on
tira'pugni [tira'puɲɲi] *sm inv* knuckle-duster
ti'rare *vt* (*gen*) to pull; (*estrarre*): ~ **qc da** to take
o pull sth out of; to get sth out of; to extract
sth from; (*chiudere: tenda etc*) to draw, pull;
(*tracciare, disegnare*) to draw, trace; (*lanciare:
sasso, palla*) to throw; (*stampare*) to print;
(*pistola, freccia*) to fire ▪ *vi* (*pipa, camino*) to
draw; (*vento*) to blow; (*abito*) to be tight; (*fare
fuoco*) to fire; (*fare del tiro, Calcio*) to shoot; ~ **qn
da parte** to take *o* draw sb aside; ~ **un
sospiro (di sollievo)** to heave a sigh (of
relief); ~ **a indovinare** to take a guess; ~ **sul
prezzo** to bargain; ~ **avanti** *vi* to struggle on
▪ *vt* (*famiglia*) to provide for; (*ditta*) to look
after; ~ **fuori** to take out, pull out; ~ **giù** to
pull down; ~ **su** to pull up; (*capelli*) to put up;
(*fig: bambino*) to bring up; **tirarsi indietro** to
move back; (*fig*) to back out; **tirarsi su** to
pull o.s. up; (*fig*) to cheer o.s. up
ti'rato, -a *ag* (*teso*) taut; (*fig: teso, stanco*) drawn
tira'tore *sm* gunman; **un buon** ~ a good shot;
~ **scelto** marksman
tira'tura *sf* (*azione*) printing; (*di libro*) (print)
run; (*di giornale*) circulation
tirchie'ria [tirkje'ria] *sf* meanness,
stinginess
'tirchio, -a ['tirkjo] *ag* mean, stingy
tiri'tera *sf* drivel, hot air
'tiro *sm* shooting *no pl*, firing *no pl*; (*colpo, sparo*)
shot; (*di palla: lancio*) throwing *no pl*; throw;
(*fig*) trick; **essere a** ~ to be in range; **giocare
un brutto** ~ *o* un ~ **mancino a qn** to play a
dirty trick on s.b.; **cavallo da** ~ draught (*Brit*)
o draft (*US*) horse; ~ **a segno** target shooting;
(*luogo*) shooting range
tiroci'nante [tirotʃi'nante] *ag, sm/f*
apprentice *cpd*; trainee *cpd*
tiro'cinio [tiro'tʃinjo] *sm* apprenticeship;
(*professionale*) training
ti'roide *sf* thyroid (gland)
tiro'lese *ag, sm/f* Tyrolean, Tyrolese *inv*
Ti'rolo *sm*: **il** ~ the Tyrol
tir'rennico, -a, ci, che *ag* Tyrrhenian
Tir'reno *sm*: **il (mar)** ~ the Tyrrhenian Sea
ti'sana *sf* herb tea
'tisi *sf* (*Med*) consumption
'tisico, -a, ci, che *ag* (*Med*) consumptive; (*fig:
gracile*) frail ▪ *sm/f* consumptive (person)
ti'tanico, -a, ci, che *ag* gigantic, enormous
ti'tano *sm* (*Mitologia, fig*) titan
tito'lare *ag* appointed; (*sovrano*) titular ▪ *sm/f*
incumbent; (*proprietario*) owner; (*Calcio*)
regular player
tito'lato, -a *ag* (*persona*) titled

'titolo *sm* title; (*di giornale*) headline; (*diploma*)
qualification; (*Comm*) security; (: *azione*)
share; **a che** ~? for what reason?; **a** ~ **di
amicizia** out of friendship; **a** ~ **di cronaca**
for your information; **a** ~ **di premio** as a
prize; ~ **di credito** share; ~ **obbligazionario**
bond; ~ **al portatore** bearer bond; ~ **di
proprietà** title deed; **titoli di stato**
government securities; **titoli di testa** (*Cine*)
credits
titu'bante *ag* hesitant, irresolute
tivù *sf inv* (*fam*) telly (*Brit*), TV
'tizio, a ['tittsjo] *sm/f* fellow, chap
tiz'zone [tit'tsone] *sm* brand
T.M.G. *abbr* (= *tempo medio di Greenwich*) GMT
TN *sigla* = **Trento**
TNT *sigla m* (= *trinitrotoluolo*) TNT
TO *sigla* = **Torino**
toast [toust] *sm inv* toasted sandwich
toc'cante *ag* touching
toc'care *vt* to touch; (*tastare*) to feel; (*fig:
riguardare*) to concern; (: *commuovere*) to touch,
move; (: *pungere*) to hurt, wound; (: *far cenno a:
argomento*) to touch on, mention ▪ *vi*: ~ **a**
(*accadere*) to happen to; (*spettare*) to be up to;
tocca a te difenderci it's up to you to defend
us; **a chi tocca?** whose turn is it?; **mi toccò
pagare** I had to pay; ~ **il fondo** (*in acqua*) to
touch the bottom; (*fig*) to touch rock bottom;
~ **con mano** (*fig*) to find out for o.s.; ~ **qn sul
vivo** to cut sb to the quick
tocca'sana *sm inv* cure-all, panacea
toccherò *etc* [tokke'rɔ] *vb vedi* **toccare**
'tocco, -chi *sm* touch; (*Arte*) stroke, touch
toe'letta *sf* = **toilette**
'toga, -ghe *sf* toga; (*di magistrato, professore*)
gown
'togliere ['tɔʎʎere] *vt* (*rimuovere*) to take away
(*o* off), remove; (*riprendere, non concedere più*) to
take away, remove; (*Mat*) to take away,
subtract; (*liberare*) to free; ~ **qc a qn** to take
sth (away) from sb; **ciò non toglie che** ...
nevertheless ..., be that as it may ...;
togliersi il cappello to take off one's hat
'Togo *sm*: **il** ~ Togo
toilette [twa'let] *sf inv* (*gabinetto*) toilet;
(*cosmesi*) make-up; (*abbigliamento*) gown,
dress; (*mobile*) dressing table; **fare** ~ to get
made up, make o.s. beautiful
'Tokyo *sf* Tokyo
to'letta *sf* = **toilette**
'tolgo *etc vb vedi* **togliere**
tolle'rante *ag* tolerant
tolle'ranza [tolle'rantsa] *sf* tolerance; **casa
di** ~ brothel
tolle'rare *vt* to tolerate; **non tollero
repliche** I won't stand for objections; **non**

sono tollerati i ritardi lateness will not be tolerated

To'losa *sf* Toulouse

'tolsi *etc vb vedi* **togliere**

'tolto, -a *pp di* **togliere**

to'maia *sf (di scarpa)* upper

'tomba *sf* tomb

tom'bale *ag:* **pietra ~** tombstone, gravestone

tom'bino *sm* manhole cover

'tombola *sf (gioco)* tombola; *(ruzzolone)* tumble

'tomo *sm* volume

tomogra'fia *sf (Med)* tomography; **~ assiale computerizzata** computerized axial tomography

'tonaca, -che *sf (Rel)* habit

to'nare *vi =* **tuonare**

'tondo, -a *ag* round

'tonfo *sm* splash; *(rumore sordo)* thud; *(caduta):* **fare un ~** to take a tumble

'tonico, -a, ci, che *ag* tonic ∎ *sm* tonic; *(cosmetico)* toner

tonifi'cante *ag* invigorating, bracing

tonifi'care *vt (muscoli, pelle)* to tone up; *(irrobustire)* to invigorate, brace

ton'nara *sf* tuna-fishing nets *pl*

ton'nato, -a *ag (Cuc):* **salsa tonnata** tuna fish sauce; **vitello ~** veal with tuna fish sauce

tonnel'laggio [tonnel'laddʒo] *sm (Naut)* tonnage

tonnel'lata *sf* ton

'tonno *sm* tuna (fish)

'tono *sm (gen, Mus)* tone; *(di colore)* shade, tone; **rispondere a ~** *(a proposito)* to answer to the point; *(nello stesso modo)* to answer in kind; *(per le rime)* to answer back

ton'silla *sf* tonsil

tonsil'lite *sf* tonsillitis

ton'sura *sf* tonsure

'tonto, -a *ag* dull, stupid ∎ *sm/f* blockhead, dunce; **fare il finto ~** to play dumb

top [tɔp] *sm inv (vertice, camicetta)* top

to'paia *sf (di topo)* mousehole; *(di ratto)* rat's nest; *(fig: casa etc)* hovel, dump

to'pazio [to'pattsjo] *sm* topaz

topi'cida, -i [topi'tʃida] *sm* rat poison

'topless ['tɔplis] *sm inv* topless bathing costume

'topo *sm* mouse; **~ d'albergo** *(fig)* hotel thief; **~ di biblioteca** *(fig)* bookworm

topogra'fia *sf* topography

topog'rafico, -a, ci, che *ag* topographic, topographical

to'ponimo *sm* place name

'toppa *sf (serratura)* keyhole; *(pezza)* patch

to'race [to'ratʃe] *sm* chest

'torba *sf* peat

'torbido, -a *ag (liquido)* cloudy; *(: fiume)* muddy; *(fig)* dark; troubled ∎ *sm:* **pescare nel ~** *(fig)* to fish in troubled waters

'torcere ['tɔrtʃere] *vt* to twist; *(biancheria)* to wring (out); **torcersi** *vr* to twist, writhe; **dare del filo da ~ a qn** to make life *o* things difficult for sb

torchi'are [tor'kjare] *vt* to press

'torchio ['tɔrkjo] *sm* press; **mettere qn sotto il ~** *(fig fam: interrogare)* to grill sb; **~ tipografico** printing press

'torcia, -ce ['tɔrtʃa] *sf* torch; **~ elettrica** torch *(Brit)*, flashlight *(US)*

torci'collo [tortʃi'kɔllo] *sm* stiff neck

'tordo *sm* thrush

to'rero *sm* bullfighter, toreador

tori'nese *ag* of *(o* from*)* Turin ∎ *sm/f* person from Turin

To'rino *sf* Turin

tor'menta *sf* snowstorm

tormen'tare *vt* to torment; **tormentarsi** *vr* to fret, worry o.s.

tor'mento *sm* torment

torna'conto *sm* advantage, benefit

tor'nado *sm* tornado

tor'nante *sm* hairpin bend *(Brit) o* curve *(US)*

tor'nare *vi* to return, go *(o* come*)* back; *(ridiventare: anche fig)* to become (again); *(riuscire giusto, esatto: conto)* to work out; *(risultare)* to turn out (to be), prove (to be); **~ al punto di partenza** to start again; **~ a casa** to go *(o* come*)* home; **i conti tornano** the accounts balance; **~ utile** to prove *o* turn out (to be) useful

torna'sole *sm inv* litmus

tor'neo *sm* tournament

'tornio *sm* lathe

tor'nire *vt (Tecn)* to turn (on a lathe); *(fig)* to shape, polish

tor'nito, -a *ag (gambe, caviglie)* well-shaped

'toro *sm* bull; *(dello zodiaco):* **T~** Taurus; **essere del T~** to be Taurus

tor'pedine *sf* torpedo

torpedini'era *sf* torpedo boat

tor'pore *sm* torpor

'torre *sf* tower; *(Scacchi)* rook, castle; **~ di controllo** *(Aer)* control tower

torrefazi'one [torrefat'tsjone] *sf* roasting

torreggi'are [torred'dʒare] *vi:* **~ (su)** to tower (over)

tor'rente *sm* torrent

torren'tizio, -a [torren'tittsjo] *ag* torrential

torrenzi'ale [torren'tsjale] *ag* torrential

tor'retta *sf* turret

'torrido, -a *ag* torrid

torri'one *sm* keep

tor'rone *sm* nougat

'torsi *etc vb vedi* **torcere**

torsi'one *sf* twisting; (*Tecn*) torsion

'torso *sm* torso, trunk; (*Arte*) torso; **a ~ nudo** bare-chested

'torsolo *sm* (*di cavolo etc*) stump; (*di frutta*) core

'torta *sf* cake

tortel'lini *smpl* (*Cuc*) tortellini

torti'era *sf* cake tin (*Brit*), cake pan (*US*)

'torto, -a *pp di* **torcere** ■ *ag* (*ritorto*) twisted; (*storto*) twisted, crooked ■ *sm* (*ingiustizia*) wrong; (*colpa*) fault; **a ~** wrongly; **a ~ o a ragione** rightly or wrongly; **aver ~** to be wrong; **fare un ~ a qn** to wrong sb; **essere/passare dalla parte del ~** to be/put o.s. in the wrong; **lui non ha tutti i torti** there's something in what he says

'tortora *sf* turtle dove

tortu'oso, -a *ag* (*strada*) twisting; (*fig*) tortuous

tor'tura *sf* torture

tortu'rare *vt* to torture

'torvo, -a *ag* menacing, grim

tosa'erba *sm o f inv* (lawn)mower

to'sare *vt* (*pecora*) to shear; (*cane*) to clip; (*siepe*) to clip, trim

tosa'tura *sf* (*di pecore*) shearing; (*di cani*) clipping; (*di siepi*) trimming, clipping

Tos'cana *sf*: **la ~** Tuscany

tos'cano, -a *ag, sm/f* Tuscan ■ *sm* (*anche*: **sigaro toscano**) strong Italian cigar

'tosse *sf* cough

tossicità [tossitʃi'ta] *sf* toxicity

'tossico, -a, ci, che *ag* toxic; (*Econ*): **titolo ~** toxic asset

tossicodipen'dente *sm/f* drug addict

tossicodipen'denza [tossikodipen'dɛntsa] *sf* drug addiction

tossi'comane *sm/f* drug addict

tossicoma'nia *sf* drug addiction

tos'sina *sf* toxin

tos'sire *vi* to cough

tosta'pane *sm inv* toaster

tos'tare *vt* to toast; (*caffè*) to roast

tosta'tura *sf* (*di pane*) toasting; (*di caffè*) roasting

'tosto, -a *ag*: **faccia tosta** cheek ■ *av* at once, immediately; **~ che** as soon as

to'tale *ag, sm* total

totalità *sf*: **la ~ di** all of, the total amount (*o number*) of; the whole + *sg*

totali'tario, -a *ag* totalitarian; (*totale*) complete, total; **adesione totalitaria** complete support

totalita'rismo *sm* (*Pol*) totalitarianism

totaliz'zare [totalid'dzare] *vt* to total; (*Sport*: *punti*) to score

totalizza'tore [totaliddza'tore] *sm* (*Tecn*)

totalizator; (*Ippica*) totalizator, tote (*fam*)

to'tip *sm* gambling pool betting on horse racing

toto'calcio [toto'kaltʃo] *sm* gambling pool betting on football results, ≈ (football) pools *pl* (*Brit*)

tou'pet [tu'pɛ] *sm inv* toupee

tour [tur] *sm inv* (*giro*) tour; (*Ciclismo*) tour de France

tour de 'force ['tur də 'fɔrs] *sm inv* (*Sport: anche fig*) tour de force

tour'née [tur'ne] *sf* tour; **essere in ~** to be on tour

to'vaglia [to'vaʎʎa] *sf* tablecloth

tovagli'olo [tovaʎ'ʎɔlo] *sm* napkin

'tozzo, -a ['tɔttso] *ag* squat ■ *sm*: **~ di pane** crust of bread

TP *sigla* = **Trapani**

TR *sigla* = **Terni**

Tr *abbr* (*Comm*) = **tratta**

tra *prep* (*di due persone, cose*) between; (*di più persone, cose*) among(st); (*tempo: entro*) within, in; **prendere qn ~ le braccia** to take sb in one's arms; **litigano ~ (di) loro** they're fighting amongst themselves; **~ 5 giorni** in 5 days' time; **~ breve** o **poco** soon; **sé e sé** (*parlare etc*) to oneself; **sia detto ~ noi ...** between you and me ...; **~ una cosa e l'altra** what with one thing and another

trabal'lante *ag* shaky

trabal'lare *vi* to stagger, totter

tra'biccolo *sm* (*peg: auto*) old banger (*Brit*), jalopy

traboc'care *vi* to overflow

traboc'chetto [trabok'ketto] *sm* (*fig*) trap ■ *ag inv* trap *cpd*; **domanda ~** trick question

traca'gnotto, -a [trakaɲ'ɲɔtto] *ag* dumpy ■ *sm/f* dumpy person

tracan'nare *vt* to gulp down

'traccia, -ce ['trattʃa] *sf* (*segno, striscia*) trail, track; (*orma*) tracks *pl*; (*residuo, testimonianza*) trace, sign; (*abbozzo*) outline; **essere sulle tracce di qn** to be on sb's trail

tracci'are [trat'tʃare] *vt* to trace, mark (out); (*disegnare*) to draw; (*fig: abbozzare*) to outline; **~ un quadro della situazione** to outline the situation

tracci'ato [trat'tʃato] *sm* (*grafico*) layout, plan; **~ di gara** (*Sport*) race route

tra'chea [tra'kɛa] *sf* windpipe, trachea

tra'colla *sf* shoulder strap; **portare qc a ~** to carry sth over one's shoulder; **borsa a ~** shoulder bag

tra'collo *sm* (*fig*) collapse, ruin; **~ finanziario** crash; **avere un ~** (*Med*) to have a setback; (*Comm*) to collapse

traco'tante *ag* overbearing, arrogant

traco'tanza [trako'tantsa] *sf* arrogance

trad. *abbr* = **traduzione**

tradi'mento *sm* betrayal; *(Dir, Mil)* treason;
a ~ by surprise; **alto ~** high treason

tra'dire *vt* to betray; *(coniuge)* to be unfaithful
to; *(doveri: mancare)* to fail in; *(rivelare)* to give
away, reveal; **ha tradito le attese di tutti**
he let everyone down

tradi'tore, -'trice *sm/f* traitor

tradizio'nale [traditts̩jo'nale] *ag* traditional

tradizi'one [tradit'tsjone] *sf* tradition

tra'dotto, -a *pp di* **tradurre** ■ *sf (Mil)* troop train

tra'durre *vt* to translate; *(spiegare)* to render,
convey; *(Dir):* **~ qn in carcere/tribunale** to
take sb to prison/court; **~ in cifre** to put into
figures; **~ in atto** *(fig)* to put into effect

tradut'tore, -'trice *sm/f* translator

traduzi'one [tradut'tsjone] *sf* translation;
(Dir) transfer

'trae *vb vedi* **trarre**

tra'ente *sm/f (Econ)* drawer

trafe'lato, -a *ag* out of breath

traffi'cante *sm/f* dealer; *(peg)* trafficker

traffi'care *vi (commerciare):* **~ (in)** to trade (in),
deal (in); *(affaccendarsi)* to busy o.s. ■ *vt (peg)*
to traffic in

traffi'cato, -a *ag (strada, zona)* busy

'traffico, -ci *sm* traffic; *(commercio)* trade,
traffic; **~ aereo/ferroviario** air/rail traffic; **~
di droga** drug trafficking; **~ stradale** traffic

tra'figgere [tra'fiddʒere] *vt* to run through,
stab; *(fig)* to pierce

tra'fila *sf* procedure

trafi'letto *sm (di giornale)* short article

tra'fitto, -a *pp di* **trafiggere**

trafo'rare *vt* to bore, drill

tra'foro *sm (azione)* boring, drilling; *(galleria)*
tunnel

trafu'gare *vt* to purloin

tra'gedia [tra'dʒɛdja] *sf* tragedy

'traggo *etc vb vedi* **trarre**

traghet'tare [traget'tare] *vt* to ferry

tra'ghetto [tra'getto] *sm* crossing; *(barca)*
ferry(boat)

tragicità [tradʒitʃi'ta] *sf* tragedy

'tragico, -a, ci, che ['tradʒiko] *ag* tragic ■ *sm*
(autore) tragedian; **prendere tutto sul ~** *(fig)*
to take everything far too seriously

tragi'comico, -a, ci, che [tradʒi'kɔmiko] *ag*
tragicomic

tra'gitto [tra'dʒitto] *sm (passaggio)* crossing;
(viaggio) journey

tragu'ardo *sm (Sport)* finishing line; *(fig)* goal,
aim

'trai *etc vb vedi* **trarre**

traiet'toria *sf* trajectory

trai'nante *ag (cavo, fune)* towing; *(fig: persona,
settore)* driving

trai'nare *vt* to drag, haul; *(rimorchiare)* to tow

'training ['treinin(g)] *sm inv* training

'traino *sm (carro)* wagon; *(slitta)* sledge; *(carico)*
load

tralasci'are [tralaʃ'ʃare] *vt (studi)* to neglect;
(dettagli) to leave out, omit

'tralcio ['traltʃo] *sm (Bot)* shoot

tra'liccio [tra'littʃo] *sm (tela)* ticking;
(struttura) trellis; *(Elettr)* pylon

tram *sm inv* tram (Brit), streetcar (US)

'trama *sf (filo)* weft, woof; *(fig: argomento,
maneggio)* plot

traman'dare *vt* to pass on, hand down

tra'mare *vt (fig)* to scheme, plot

tram'busto *sm* turmoil

trames'tio *sm* bustle

tramez'zino [tramed'dzino] *sm* sandwich

tra'mezzo [tra'mɛddzo] *sm* partition

'tramite *prep* through ■ *sm* means *pl;* **agire/
fare da ~** to act as/be a go-between

tramon'tana *sf (Meteor)* north wind

tramon'tare *vi* to set, go down

tra'monto *sm* setting; *(del sole)* sunset

tramor'tire *vi* to faint ■ *vt* to stun

trampo'lino *sm (per tuffi)* springboard, diving
board; *(per lo sci)* ski-jump

'trampolo *sm* stilt

tramu'tare *vt:* **~ in** to change into

trance [traːns] *sf inv (di medium)* trance;
cadere in ~ to fall into a trance

'trancia, -ce ['trantʃa] *sf* slice; *(cesoia)*
shearing machine

tranci'are [tran'tʃare] *vt (Tecn)* to shear

'trancio ['trantʃo] *sm* slice

tra'nello *sm* trap; **tendere un ~ a qn** to set a
trap for sb; **cadere in un ~** to fall into a trap

trangugi'are [trangu'dʒare] *vt* to gulp down

'tranne *prep* except (for), but (for); **~ che** *cong*
unless; **tutti i giorni ~ il venerdì** every day
except o with the exception of Friday

tranquil'lante *sm (Med)* tranquillizer

tranquillità *sf* calm, stillness; quietness;
peace of mind

tranquilliz'zare [trankwillid'dzare] *vt* to
reassure

tran'quillo, -a *ag* calm, quiet; *(bambino,
scolaro)* quiet; *(sereno)* with one's mind at rest;
sta' ~ don't worry

transat'lantico, -a, ci, che *ag* transatlantic
■ *sm* transatlantic liner; *(Pol) corridor used as a
meeting place by members of the lower chamber of the
Italian Parliament; see note*

> ● **TRANSATLANTICO**
> ●
> ● The *transatlantico* is a room in the Palazzo
> ● di Montecitorio which is used by
> ● "deputati" between parliamentary

sessions for relaxation and conversation.
It is also used for media interviews and
press conferences.

tran'satto, -a *pp di* **transigere**
transazi'one [transat'tsjone] *sf* (*Dir*)
settlement; (*Comm*) transaction, deal
tran'senna *sf* barrier
tran'setto *sm* transept
trans'genico, -a, ci, che [trans'dʒɛniko] *ag*
genetically modified
transiberi'ano, -a *ag* trans-Siberian
tran'sigere [tran'sidʒere] *vi* (*Dir*) to reach a
settlement; (*venire a patti*) to compromise,
come to an agreement
tran'sistor *sm inv*, **transis'tore** *sm* transistor
transi'tabile *ag* passable
transi'tare *vi* to pass
transi'tivo, -a *ag* transitive
'transito *sm* transit; **di ~** (*merci*) in transit;
(*stazione*) transit *cpd*; **"divieto di ~"** "no
entry"; **"~ interrotto"** "road closed"
transi'torio, -a *ag* transitory, transient;
(*provvisorio*) provisional
transizi'one [transit'tsjone] *sf* transition
tran'tran *sm* routine; **il solito ~** the same old
routine
tran'via *sf* tramway (*Brit*), streetcar line (*US*)
tranvi'ario, -a *ag* tram *cpd* (*Brit*), streetcar *cpd*
(*US*); **linea tranviaria** tramline, streetcar
line
tranvi'ere *sm* (*conducente*) tram driver (*Brit*),
streetcar driver (*US*); (*bigliettaio*) tram *o*
streetcar conductor
trapa'nare *vt* (*Tecn*) to drill
'trapano *sm* (*utensile*) drill; (: *Med*) trepan
trapas'sare *vt* to pierce
trapas'sato *sm* (*Ling*) past perfect
tra'passo *sm* passage; **~ di proprietà** (*di case*)
conveyancing; (*di auto etc*) legal transfer
trape'lare *vi* to leak, drip; (*fig*) to leak out
tra'pezio [tra'pɛttsjo] *sm* (*Mat*) trapezium;
(*attrezzo ginnico*) trapeze
trape'zista, -i, e [trapet'tsista] *sm/f* trapeze
artist
trapian'tare *vt* to transplant
trapi'anto *sm* transplanting; (*Med*)
transplant
'trappola *sf* trap
tra'punta *sf* quilt
'trarre *vt* to draw, pull; (*prendere, tirare fuori*)
to take (out), draw; (*derivare*) to obtain;
~ beneficio *o* **profitto da qc** to benefit
from sth; **~ le conclusioni** to draw one's
own conclusions; **~ esempio da qn** to follow
sb's example; **~ guadagno** to make a profit;
~ qn d'impaccio to get sb out of an awkward

situation; **~ origine da qc** to have its
origins *o* originate in sth; **~ in salvo** to
rescue
trasa'lire *vi* to start, jump
trasan'dato, -a *ag* shabby
trasbor'dare *vt* to transfer; (*Naut*) to
tran(s)ship ■ *vi* (*Naut*) to change ship; (*Aer*)
to change plane; (*Ferr*) to change (trains)
trascenden'tale [traʃʃenden'tale] *ag*
transcendental
tra'scendere [traʃ'ʃendere] *vt* (*Filosofia, Rel*) to
transcend; (*fig: superare*) to surpass, go
beyond
tra'sceso, -a [traʃ'ʃeso] *pp di* **trascendere**
trasci'nare [traʃʃi'nare] *vt* to drag;
trascinarsi *vr* to drag o.s. along; (*fig*) to drag
on
tras'correre *vt* (*tempo*) to spend, pass ■ *vi*
to pass
tras'corso, -a *pp di* **trascorrere** ■ *ag* past
■ *sm* mistake
tras'critto, -a *pp di* **trascrivere**
tras'crivere *vt* to transcribe
trascrizi'one [traskrit'tsjone] *sf*
transcription
trascu'rare *vt* to neglect; (*non considerare*) to
disregard
trascura'tezza [traskura'tettsa] *sf*
carelessness, negligence
trascu'rato, -a *ag* (*casa*) neglected; (*persona*)
careless, negligent
traseco'lato, -a *ag* astounded, amazed
trasferi'mento *sm* transfer; (*trasloco*)
removal, move
trasfe'rire *vt* to transfer; **trasferirsi** *vr* to
move
tras'ferta *sf* transfer; (*indennità*) travelling
expenses *pl*; (*Sport*) away game
trasfigu'rare *vt* to transfigure
trasfor'mare *vt* to transform, change
trasforma'tore *sm* transformer
trasformazi'one [trasformat'tsjone] *sf*
transformation
trasfusi'one *sf* (*Med*) transfusion
trasgre'dire *vt* to break, infringe; (*ordini*) to
disobey
trasgressi'one *sf* breaking, infringement;
disobeying
trasgres'sivo, -a *ag* (*personaggio, atteggiamento*)
rule-breaking
trasgres'sore, trasgredi'trice
[trazgredi'tritʃe] *sm/f* (*Dir*) transgressor
tras'lato, -a *ag* metaphorical, figurative
traslo'care *vt* to move, transfer; **traslocarsi**
vr to move
tras'loco, -chi *sm* removal
tras'messo, -a *pp di* **trasmettere**

tras'mettere vt (passare): ~ qc a qn to pass sth on to sb; (mandare) to send; (Tecn, Tel, Med) to transmit; (TV, Radio) to broadcast

trasmetti'tore sm transmitter

trasmissi'one sf (gen, Fisica, Tecn) transmission; (passaggio) transmission, passing on; (TV, Radio) broadcast

trasmit'tente sf transmitting o broadcasting station

traso'gnato, -a [trasoɲ'ɲato] ag dreamy

traspa'rente ag transparent

traspa'renza [traspa'rentsa] sf transparency; **guardare qc in** ~ to look at sth against the light

traspa'rire vi to show (through)

tras'parso, -a pp di **trasparire**

traspi'rare vi to perspire; (fig) to come to light, leak out

traspirazi'one [traspirat'tsjone] sf perspiration

tras'porre vt to transpose

traspor'tare vt to carry, move; (merce) to transport, convey; **lasciarsi** ~ (da qc) (fig) to let o.s. be carried away (by sth)

tras'porto sm transport; (fig) rapture, passion; **con** ~ passionately; **compagnia di** ~ carriers pl; (per strada) hauliers pl (Brit), haulers pl (US); **mezzi di** ~ means of transport; **nave/aereo da** ~ transport ship/aircraft inv; ~ **(funebre)** funeral procession; ~ **marittimo/aereo** sea/air transport; ~ **stradale** (road) haulage; **i trasporti pubblici** public transport

tras'posto, -a pp di **trasporre**

'**trassi** etc vb vedi **trarre**

trastul'lare vt to amuse; **trastullarsi** vr to amuse o.s.

tras'tullo sm game

trasu'dare vi (filtrare) to ooze; (sudare) to sweat ■ vt to ooze with

trasver'sale ag (taglio, sbarra) cross(-); (retta) transverse; **via** ~ side street

trasvo'lare vt to fly over

'**tratta** sf (Econ) draft; (di persone): **la ~ delle bianche** the white slave trade; ~ **documentaria** documentary bill of exchange

tratta'mento sm treatment; (servizio) service; **ricevere un buon** ~ (cliente) to get good service; ~ **di bellezza** beauty treatment; ~ **di fine rapporto** (Comm) severance pay

trat'tare vt (gen) to treat; (commerciare) to deal in; (svolgere: argomento) to discuss, deal with; (negoziare) to negotiate ■ vi: ~ **di** to deal with; ~ **con** (persona) to deal with; **si tratta di** ... it's about...; **si tratterebbe solo di poche ore** it would just be a matter of a few hours

tratta'tiva sf negotiation; **trattative** sfpl (tra governi, stati) talks; **essere in** ~ **con** to be in negotiation with

trat'tato sm (testo) treatise; (accordo) treaty; ~ **commerciale** trade agreement; ~ **di pace** peace treaty

trattazi'one [trattat'tsjone] sf treatment

tratteggi'are [tratted'dʒare] vt (disegnare: a tratti) to sketch, outline; (: col tratteggio) to hatch

trat'teggio [trat'teddʒo] sm hatching

tratte'nere vt (far rimanere: persona) to detain; (tenere, frenare, reprimere) to hold back, keep back; (astenersi dal consegnare) to hold, keep; (detrarre: somma) to deduct; **trattenersi** vr (astenersi) to restrain o.s., stop o.s.; (soffermarsi) to stay, remain; **sono stato trattenuto in ufficio** I was delayed at the office

tratteni'mento sm entertainment; (festa) party

tratte'nuta sf deduction

trat'tino sm dash; (in parole composte) hyphen

'**tratto, -a** pp di **trarre** ■ sm (di penna, matita) stroke; (parte) part, piece; (di strada) stretch; (di mare, cielo) expanse; (di tempo) period (of time); **tratti** smpl (caratteristiche) features; (modo di) ways, manners; **a un** ~, **d'un** ~ suddenly

trat'tore sm tractor

tratto'ria sf (small) restaurant

'**trauma, -i** sm trauma; ~ **cranico** concussion

trau'matico, -a, ci, che ag traumatic

traumatiz'zare [traumatid'dzare] vt (Med) to traumatize; (fig: impressionare) to shock

tra'vaglio [tra'vaʎʎo] sm (angoscia) pain, suffering; (Med) pains pl; ~ **di parto** labour pains

trava'sare vt to pour; (vino) to decant

tra'vaso sm pouring; decanting

trava'tura sf beams pl

'**trave** sf beam

tra'veggole sfpl: **avere le** ~ to be seeing things

tra'versa sf (trave) crosspiece; (via) sidestreet; (Ferr) sleeper (Brit), (railroad) tie (US); (Calcio) crossbar

traver'sare vt to cross

traver'sata sf crossing; (Aer) flight, trip

traver'sie sfpl mishaps, misfortunes

traver'sina sf (Ferr) sleeper (Brit), (railroad) tie (US)

tra'verso, -a ag oblique; **di** ~ ag askew ■ av sideways; **andare di** ~ (cibo) to go down the wrong way; **messo di** ~ sideways on; **guardare di** ~ to look askance at; **via traversa** side road; **ottenere qc per vie traverse** (fig) to obtain sth in an underhand way

389

travesti'mento *sm* disguise
traves'tire *vt* to disguise; **travestirsi** *vr* to disguise o.s.
traves'tito *sm* transvestite
travi'are *vt* (*fig*) to lead astray
travi'sare *vt* (*fig*) to distort, misrepresent
travol'gente [travol'dʒɛnte] *ag* overwhelming
tra'volgere [tra'vɔldʒere] *vt* to sweep away, carry away; (*fig*) to overwhelm
tra'volto, -a *pp di* **travolgere**
trazi'one [trat'tsjone] *sf* traction; ~ **anteriore/posteriore** (*Aut*) front-wheel/rear-wheel drive
tre *num* three
tre'alberi *sm inv* (*Naut*) three-master
'trebbia *sf* (*Agr: operazione*) threshing; (: *stagione*) threshing season
trebbi'are *vt* to thresh
trebbia'trice [trebbja'tritʃe] *sf* threshing machine
trebbia'tura *sf* threshing
'treccia, -ce ['trettʃa] *sf* plait, braid; **lavorato a trecce** (*pullover etc*) cable-knit
trecen'tesco, -a, schi, sche [tretʃen'tesko] *ag* fourteenth-century
tre'cento [tre'tʃɛnto] *num* three hundred ■ *sm*: **il T~** the fourteenth century
tredi'cenne [tredi'tʃɛnne] *ag, sm/f* thirteen-year-old
tredi'cesimo, -a [tredi'tʃɛzimo] *num* thirteenth ■ *sf* Christmas bonus of a month's pay
'tredici ['treditʃi] *num* thirteen ■ *sm inv*: **fare ~** (*Totocalcio*) to win the pools (*Brit*)
'tregua *sf* truce; (*fig*) respite; **senza ~** non-stop, without stopping, uninterruptedly
tre'mante *ag* trembling, shaking
tre'mare *vi* to tremble, shake; ~ **di** (*freddo etc*) to shiver o tremble with; (*paura, rabbia*) to shake o tremble with
trema'rella *sf* shivers *pl*
tremen'tina *sf* turpentine
tre'mila *num* three thousand
'tremito *sm* trembling *no pl*; shaking *no pl*; shivering *no pl*
tremo'lare *vi* to tremble; (*luce*) to flicker; (*foglie*) to quiver
tremo'lio *sm* (*vedi vi*) tremble; flicker; quiver
tre'more *sm* tremor
'treno *sm* train; (*Aut*): ~ **di gomme** set of tyres; ~ **locale/diretto/espresso** local/fast/express train; ~ **merci** goods (*Brit*) o freight train; ~ **rapido** express (train) (*for which supplement must be paid*); ~ **straordinario** special train; ~ **viaggiatori** passenger train; *see note*

'trenta *num* thirty ■ *sm inv* (*Ins*): ~ **e lode** full marks plus distinction o cum laude
tren'tenne *ag, sm/f* thirty-year-old
tren'tennio *sm* period of thirty years
tren'tesimo, -a *num* thirtieth
tren'tina *sf*: **una ~ (di)** thirty or so, about thirty
tren'tino, -a *ag* of (o from) Trento
trepi'dante *ag* anxious
trepi'dare *vi* to be anxious; ~ **per qn** to be anxious about sb
'trepido, -a *ag* anxious
treppi'ede *sm* tripod; (*Cuc*) trivet
tre'quarti *sm inv* three-quarter-length coat
'tresca, -sche *sf* (*fig*) intrigue; (: *relazione amorosa*) affair
'trespolo *sm* trestle
trevigi'ano, -a [trevi'dʒano] *ag* of (o from) Treviso
triango'lare *ag* triangular
tri'angolo *sm* triangle
tribo'lare *vi* (*patire*) to suffer; (*fare fatica*) to have a lot of trouble
tribolazi'one [tribolat'tsjone] *sf* suffering, tribulation
tri'bordo *sm* (*Naut*) starboard
tribù *sf inv* tribe
tri'buna *sf* (*podio*) platform; (*in aule etc*) gallery; (*di stadio*) stand; ~ **della stampa/riservata al pubblico** press/public gallery
tribu'nale *sm* court; **presentarsi o comparire in** ~ to appear in court; ~ **militare** military tribunal; ~ **supremo** supreme court
tribu'tare *vt* to bestow; ~ **gli onori dovuti a qn** to pay tribute to sb
tribu'tario, -a *ag* (*imposta*) fiscal, tax *cpd*; (*Geo*): **essere ~ di** to be a tributary of

tri'buto sm tax; (fig) tribute

tri'checo, -chi [tri'kɛko] sm (Zool) walrus

tri'ciclo [tri'tʃiklo] sm tricycle

trico'lore ag three-coloured (Brit), three-colored (US) ■ sm tricolo(u)r; (bandiera italiana) Italian flag

tri'dente sm trident

trien'nale ag (che dura 3 anni) three-year cpd; (che avviene ogni 3 anni) three-yearly

tri'ennio sm period of three years

tries'tino, -a ag of (o from) Trieste

tri'fase ag (Elettr) three-phase

tri'foglio [tri'fɔʎʎo] sm clover

trifo'lato, -a ag (Cuc) cooked in oil, garlic and parsley

'triglia ['triʎʎa] sf red mullet

trigonome'tria sf trigonometry

tril'lare vi (Mus) to trill

'trillo sm trill

tri'mestre sm period of three months; (Ins) term, quarter (US); (Comm) quarter

trimo'tore sm (Aer) three-engined plane

'trina sf lace

trin'cea [trin'tʃea] sf trench

trince'rare [trintʃe'rare] vt to entrench

trinci'are [trin'tʃare] vt to cut up

Trinidad sm: ~ **e Tobago** Trinidad and Tobago

Trinità sf (Rel) Trinity

'trio (pl **trii**) sm trio

trion'fale ag triumphal, triumphant

trion'fante ag triumphant

trion'fare vi to triumph, win; ~ **su** to triumph over, overcome

tri'onfo sm triumph

tripli'care vt to triple

'triplice ['triplitʃe] ag triple; **in ~ copia** in triplicate

'triplo, -a ag triple, treble ■ sm: **il ~ (di)** three times as much (as); **la spesa è tripla** it costs three times as much

'tripode sm tripod

'Tripoli sf Tripoli

'trippa sf (Cuc) tripe

tri'pudio sm triumph, jubilation; (fig: di colori) galaxy

tris sm inv (Carte): ~ **d'assi/di re** etc three aces/kings etc

'triste ag sad; (luogo) dreary, gloomy

tris'tezza [tris'tettsa] sf sadness; gloominess

'tristo, -a ag (cattivo) wicked, evil; (meschino) sorry, poor

trita'carne sm inv mincer, grinder (US)

trita'ghiaccio [trita'gjattʃo] sm inv ice crusher

tri'tare vt to mince, grind (US)

trita'tutto sm inv mincer, grinder (US)

'trito, -a ag (tritato) minced, ground (US); ~ **e ritrito** (idee, argomenti, frasi) trite, hackneyed

tri'tolo sm trinitrotoluene

tri'tone sm (Zool) newt

'trittico, -ci sm (Arte) triptych

tritu'rare vt to grind

tri'vella sf drill

trivel'lare vt to drill

trivellazi'one [trivellat'tsjone] sf drilling; **torre di ~** derrick

trivi'ale ag vulgar, low

trivialità sf inv (volgarità) coarseness, crudeness; (: osservazione) coarse o crude remark

tro'feo sm trophy

'trogolo sm (per maiali) trough

'troia sf (Zool) sow; (fig peg) whore

'tromba sf (Mus) trumpet; (Aut) horn; ~ **d'aria** whirlwind; ~ **delle scale** stairwell

trombet'tista, -i, e sm/f trumpeter, trumpet (player)

trom'bone sm trombone

trom'bosi sf thrombosis

tron'care vt to cut off; (spezzare) to break off

'tronco, -a, chi, che ag cut off; broken off; (Ling) truncated ■ sm (Bot, Anat) trunk; (fig: tratto) section; (: pezzo: di lancia) stump; **licenziare qn in ~** (fig) to fire sb on the spot

troneggi'are [troned'dʒare] vi: ~ **(su)** to tower (over)

'tronfio, -a ag conceited

'trono sm throne

tropi'cale ag tropical

'tropico, -ci sm tropic; ~ **del Cancro/Capricorno** Tropic of Cancer/Capricorn; **i tropici** the tropics

 PAROLA CHIAVE

'troppo, -a det (in eccesso: quantità) too much; (: numero) too many; **ho messo troppo zucchero** I put too much sugar in; **c'era troppa gente** there were too many people
■ pron (in eccesso: quantità) too much; (: numero) too many; **ne hai messo troppo** you've put in too much; **meglio troppi che pochi** better too many than too few
■ av (eccessivamente: con ag, av) too; (: con vb) too much; **troppo amaro/tardi** too bitter/late; **lavora troppo** he works too much; **troppo buono da parte tua!** (anche ironico) you're too kind!; **di troppo** too much; too many; **qualche tazza di troppo** a few cups too many; **5 euro di troppo** 5 euros too much; **essere di troppo** to be in the way

'trota sf trout

trot'tare vi to trot

trotterel'lare vi to trot along; (bambino) to toddle

'trotto sm trot

'trottola sf spinning top

tro'vare vt to find; (giudicare): **trovo che** I find o think that; **trovarsi** vr (reciproco: incontrarsi) to meet; (essere, stare) to be; (arrivare, capitare) to find o.s.; **andare a ~ qn** to go and see sb; **~ qn colpevole** to find sb guilty; **trovo giusto/sbagliato che ...** I think/don't think it's right that ...; **trovarsi bene/male** (in un luogo, con qn) to get on well/badly; **trovarsi d'accordo con qn** to be in agreement with sb

tro'vata sf good idea; **~ pubblicitaria** advertising gimmick

trova'tello, -a sm/f foundling

truc'care vt (falsare) to fake; (attore etc) to make up; (travestire) to disguise; (Sport) to fix; (Aut) to soup up; **truccarsi** vr to make up (one's face)

trucca'tore, -'trice sm/f (Cine, Teat) make-up artist

'trucco, -chi sm trick; (cosmesi) make-up; **i trucchi del mestiere** the tricks of the trade

'truce ['trutʃe] ag fierce

truci'dare [trutʃi'dare] vt to slaughter

'truciolo ['trutʃolo] sm shaving

'truffa sf fraud, swindle

truf'fare vt to swindle, cheat

truffa'tore, -'trice sm/f swindler, cheat

'truppa sf troop

TS sigla = **Trieste**

tu pron you; **tu stesso(a)** you yourself; **dare del tu a qn** to address sb as "tu"; **trovarsi a tu per tu con qn** to find o.s. face to face with sb

'tua vedi **tuo**

'tuba sf (Mus) tuba; (cappello) top hat

tu'bare vi to coo

tuba'tura sf, **tubazi'one** [tubat'tsjone] ■ sf piping no pl, pipes pl

tuberco'losi sf tuberculosis

'tubero sm (Bot) tuber

tu'betto sm tube

tu'bino sm (cappello) bowler (Brit), derby (US); (abito da donna) sheath dress

'tubo sm tube; (per conduttore) pipe; **~ digerente** (Anat) digestive tract; **~ di scappamento** (Aut) exhaust pipe

tubo'lare ag tubular ■ sm tubeless tyre (Brit) o tire (US)

'tue vedi **tuo**

tuf'fare vt to plunge; (intingere) to dip; **tuffarsi** vr to plunge, dive

tuffa'tore, -'trice sm/f (Sport) diver

'tuffo sm dive; (breve bagno) dip

tu'gurio sm hovel

tuli'pano sm tulip

'tulle sm (tessuto) tulle

tume'fare vt to cause to swell; **tumefarsi** vr to swell

'tumido, -a ag swollen

tu'more sm (Med) tumour (Brit), tumor (US)

tumulazi'one [tumulat'tsjone] sf burial

tu'multo sm uproar, commotion; (sommossa) riot; (fig) turmoil

tumultu'oso, -a ag rowdy, unruly; (fig) turbulent, stormy

tungs'teno sm tungsten

'tunica, -che sf tunic

'Tunisi sf Tunis

Tuni'sia sf: **la ~** Tunisia

tuni'sino, -a ag, sm/f Tunisian

'tunnel sm inv tunnel

'tuo, 'tua, tu'oi, 'tue det: **il ~, la tua** etc your pron: **il ~, la tua** etc yours ■ sm: **hai speso del ~?** did you spend your own money? ■ sf: **la tua** (opinione) your view; **i tuoi** (genitori, famiglia) your family; **una tua amica** a friend of yours; **è dalla tua** he is on your side; **alla tua!** (brindisi) your health!; **ne hai fatta una delle tue!** (sciocchezze) you've done it again!

tuo'nare vi to thunder; **tuona** it is thundering, there's some thunder

tu'ono sm thunder

tu'orlo sm yolk

tu'racciolo [tu'rattʃolo] sm cap, top; (di sughero) cork

tu'rare vt to stop, plug; (con sughero) to cork; **turarsi il naso** to hold one's nose

'turba sf (folla) crowd, throng; (: peg) mob; **turbe** sfpl disorder(s); **soffrire di turbe psichiche** to suffer from a mental disorder

turba'mento sm disturbance; (di animo) anxiety, agitation

tur'bante sm turban

tur'bare vt to disturb, trouble; **~ la quiete pubblica** (Dir) to disturb the peace

tur'bato, -a ag upset; (preoccupato, ansioso) anxious

tur'bina sf turbine

turbi'nare vi to whirl

'turbine sm whirlwind; **~ di neve** swirl of snow; **~ di polvere/sabbia** dust/sandstorm

turbi'noso, -a ag (vento, danza etc) whirling

turbo'lento, -a ag turbulent; (ragazzo) boisterous, unruly

turbo'lenza [turbo'lɛntsa] sf turbulence

turboreat'tore sm turbojet engine

tur'chese [tur'kese] ag, sm, sf turquoise

Tur'chia [tur'kia] sf: **la ~** Turkey

tur'chino, -a [tur'kino] ag deep blue

'turco, -a, chi, che ag Turkish ■ sm/f Turk/ Turkish woman ■ sm (Ling) Turkish; **parlare ~** (fig) to talk double Dutch

'turgido, -a ['turdʒido] ag swollen

tu'rismo sm tourism

tu'rista, -i, e sm/f tourist

tu'ristico, -a, ci, che ag tourist cpd

tur'nista, -i, e sm/f shift worker

'turno sm turn; (di lavoro) shift; **di ~** (soldato, medico, custode) on duty; **a ~** (rispondere) in turn; (lavorare) in shifts; **fare a ~ a fare qc** to take turns to do sth; **è il suo ~** it's your (o his etc) turn

'turpe ag filthy, vile

turpi'loquio sm obscene language

'tuta sf overalls pl; (Sport) tracksuit; **~ mimetica** (Mil) camouflage clothing; **~ spaziale** spacesuit; **~ subacquea** wetsuit

tu'tela sf (Dir: di minore) guardianship; (: protezione) protection; (difesa) defence (Brit), defense (US); **~ dell'ambiente** environmental protection; **~ del consumatore** consumer protection

tute'lare vt to protect, defend ■ ag (Dir): **giudice ~** judge with responsibility for guardianship cases

tutor ['tiutor] sm inv (Auto) electronic camera system for measuring average speed on motorways

tu'tore, -'trice sm/f (Dir) guardian

tutta'via cong nevertheless, yet

 PAROLA CHIAVE

'tutto, -a det **1** (intero) all; **tutto il latte** all the milk; **tutta la notte** all night, the whole night; **tutto il libro** the whole book; **tutta una bottiglia** a whole bottle; **in tutto il mondo** all over the world

2 (pl, collettivo) all; every; **tutti i libri** all the books; **tutte le notti** every night; **tutti i venerdì** every Friday; **tutti gli uomini** all the men; (collettivo) all men; **tutte le volte che** every time (that); **tutti e due** both o each of us (o them o you); **tutti e cinque** all

five of us (o them o you)

3 (completamente): **era tutta sporca** she was all dirty; **tremava tutto** he was trembling all over; **è tutta sua madre** she's just o exactly like her mother

4: **a tutt'oggi** so far, up till now; **a tutta velocità** at full o top speed

■ pron **1** (ogni cosa) everything, all; (qualsiasi cosa) anything; **ha mangiato tutto** he's eaten everything; **dimmi tutto** tell me all about it; **tutto compreso** all included, all-in (Brit); **tutto considerato** all things considered; **con tutto che** (malgrado) although; **del tutto** completely; **100 euro in tutto** 100 euros in all; **in tutto eravamo 50** there were 50 of us in all; **in tutto e per tutto** completely; **il che è tutto dire** and that's saying a lot

2: **tutti, e** (ognuno) all, everybody; **vengono tutti** they are all coming, everybody's coming; **tutti sanno che** everybody knows that; **tutti quanti** all and sundry

■ av (completamente) entirely, quite; **è tutto il contrario** it's quite o exactly the opposite; **tutt'al più: saranno stati tutt'al più una cinquantina** there were about fifty of them at (the very) most; **tutt'al più possiamo prendere un treno** if the worst comes to the worst we can take a train; **tutt'altro** on the contrary; **è tutt'altro che felice** he's anything but happy; **tutt'intorno** all around; **tutt'a un tratto** suddenly ■ sm: **il tutto** the whole lot, all of it; **il tutto si è svolto senza incidenti** it all went off without incident; **il tutto le costerà due milioni** the whole thing will cost you two million

tutto'fare ag inv: **domestica ~** general maid; **ragazzo ~** office boy ■ sm/f inv handyman(-woman)

tut'tora av still

tutù sm inv tutu, ballet skirt

TV [ti'vu] sf inv (= televisione) TV ■ sigla = **Treviso**

t

Uu

U, u [u] *sf o m inv* (*lettera*) U, u; **U come Udine**
≈ U for Uncle; **inversione ad U** U-turn
ub'bia *sf* (*letterario*) irrational fear
ubbidi'ente *ag* obedient
ubbidi'enza [ubbi'djɛntsa] *sf* obedience
ubbi'dire *vi* to obey; **~ a** to obey; (*veicolo,
macchina*) to respond to
ubicazi'one [ubikat'tsjone] *sf* site, location
ubiquità *sf*: **non ho il dono dell'~** I can't be
everywhere at once
ubria'care *vt*: **~ qn** to get sb drunk; (*alcool*) to
make sb drunk; (*fig*) to make sb's head spin *o*
reel; **ubriacarsi** *vr* to get drunk; **ubriacarsi
di** (*fig*) to become intoxicated with
ubria'chezza [ubria'kettsa] *sf* drunkenness
ubri'aco, -a, chi, che *ag, sm/f* drunk
ubria'cone *sm* drunkard
uccellagi'one [uttʃella'dʒone] *sf* bird
catching
uccelli'era [uttʃel'ljɛra] *sf* aviary
uccel'lino [uttʃel'lino] *sm* baby bird, chick
uc'cello [ut'tʃello] *sm* bird
uc'cidere [ut'tʃidere] *vt* to kill; **uccidersi** *vr*
(*suicidarsi*) to kill o.s.; (*perdere la vita*) to be
killed
uccisi'one [uttʃi'zjone] *sf* killing
uc'ciso, -a [ut'tʃizo] *pp di* **uccidere**
ucci'sore [uttʃi'zore] *sm* killer
U'craina *sf* Ukraine
u'craino, -a *ag, sm/f* Ukrainian
UD *sigla* = **Udine**
U.D.C. *sigla f* (*Pol*: = *Unione di Centro*) centre party
u'dente *sm/f*: **i non udenti** the hard of
hearing
u'dibile *ag* audible
udi'enza [u'djɛntsa] *sf* audience; (*Dir*)
hearing; **dare ~ (a)** to grant an audience (to);
~ a porte chiuse hearing in camera
u'dire *vt* to hear
udi'tivo, -a *ag* auditory
u'dito *sm* (sense of) hearing
udi'tore, -trice *sm/f* listener; (*Ins*)
unregistered student (*attending lectures*)

udi'torio *sm* (*persone*) audience
U.E. *abbr* = **uso esterno**
UE *sigla f* (= *Unione Europea*) EU
UEFA *sigla f* UEFA (= *Union of European Football
Associations*)
UEM *sigla f* (= *Unione economica e monetaria*) EMU
'uffa *escl* tut!
uffici'ale [uffi'tʃale] *ag* official ■ *sm* (*Amm*)
official, officer; (*Mil*) officer; **pubblico ~**
public official; **~ giudiziario** clerk of the
court; **~ di marina** naval officer; **~ sanitario**
health inspector; **~ di stato civile** registrar
ufficializ'zare [uffitʃalid'dzare] *vt* to make
official
uf'ficio [uf'fitʃo] *sm* (*gen*) office; (*dovere*) duty;
(*mansione*) task, function, job; (*agenzia*)
agency, bureau; (*Rel*) service; **d'~** *ag* office
cpd; official ■ *av* officially; **provvedere d'~**
to act officially; **convocare d'~** (*Dir*) to
summons; **difensore** *o* **avvocato d'~** (*Dir*)
court-appointed counsel for the defence; **~
brevetti** patent office; **~ di collocamento**
employment office; **~ informazioni**
information bureau; **~ oggetti smarriti**
lost property office (*Brit*), lost and found (*US*);
~ postale post office; **~ vendite/del
personale** sales/personnel department
uffici'oso, -a [uffi'tʃoso] *ag* unofficial
'UFO *sm inv* (= *unidentified flying object*) UFO
'ufo: a ~ *av* free, for nothing
U'ganda *sf*: **l'~** Uganda
'uggia ['uddʒa] *sf* (*noia*) boredom; (*fastidio*)
bore; **avere/prendere qn in ~** to dislike/take
a dislike to sb
uggi'oso, -a [ud'dʒoso] *ag* tiresome; (*tempo*)
dull
'ugola *sf* uvula
uguagli'anza [ugwaʎ'ʎantsa] *sf* equality
uguagli'are [ugwaʎ'ʎare] *vt* to make equal;
(*essere uguale*) to equal, be equal to; (*livellare*)
to level; **uguagliarsi** *vr*: **uguagliarsi a**
o **con qn** (*paragonarsi*) to compare o.s.
to sb

ugu'ale *ag* equal; (*identico*) identical, the same; (*uniforme*) level, even ■ *av*: **costano ~** they cost the same; **sono bravi ~** they're equally good

ugual'mente *av* equally; (*lo stesso*) all the same

U.I. *abbr* = **uso interno**

UIL *sigla f* (= *Unione Italiana del Lavoro*) trade union federation

'**ulcera** ['ultʃera] *sf* ulcer

ulcerazi'one [ultʃerat'tsjone] *sf* ulceration

u'liva *etc* = **oliva** *etc*

U'livo *sm* (*Pol*) centre-left coalition

ulteri'ore *ag* further

ultima'mente *av* lately, of late

ulti'mare *vt* to finish, complete

ulti'matum *sm inv* ultimatum

ulti'missime *sfpl* latest news *sg*

'**ultimo, -a** *ag* (*finale*) last; (*estremo*) farthest, utmost; (*recente: notizia, moda*) latest; (*fig: sommo, fondamentale*) ultimate ■ *sm/f* last (one); **fino all' ~** to the last, until the end; **da ~, in ~** in the end; **per ~** (*entrare, arrivare*) last; **abitare all' ~ piano** to live on the top floor; **in ultima pagina** (*di giornale*) on the back page; **negli ultimi tempi** recently; **all' ~ momento** at the last minute; **... la vostra lettera del 7 aprile ~ scorso ...** your letter of April 7th last; **in ultima analisi** in the final *o* last analysis; **in ~ luogo** finally

ultrà *sm/f* ultra

ultrasi'nistra *sf* (*Pol*) extreme left

ultrasu'ono *sm* ultrasound

ultravio'letto, -a *ag* ultraviolet

ulu'lare *vi* to howl

ulu'lato *sm* howling *no pl*; howl

umana'mente *av* (*con umanità*) humanely; (*nei limiti delle capacità umane*) humanly

uma'nesimo *sm* humanism

umanità *sf* humanity

umani'tario, -a *ag* humanitarian

umaniz'zare [umanid'dzare] *vt* to humanize

u'mano, -a *ag* human; (*comprensivo*) humane

umbi'lico *sm* = **ombelico**

'**umbro, -a** *ag* of (*o* from) Umbria

umet'tare *vt* to dampen, moisten

umi'diccio, -a, ci, ce [umi'dittʃo] *ag* (*terreno*) damp; (*mano*) moist, clammy

umidifi'care *vt* to humidify

umidifica'tore *sm* humidifier

umidità *sf* dampness; moistness; humidity

'**umido, -a** *ag* damp; (*mano, occhi*) moist; (*clima*) humid ■ *sm* dampness, damp; **carne in ~** stew

'**umile** *ag* humble

umili'ante *ag* humiliating

umili'are *vt* to humiliate; **umiliarsi** *vr* to humble o.s.

umiliazi'one [umiljat'tsjone] *sf* humiliation

umiltà *sf* humility, humbleness

u'more *sm* (*disposizione d'animo*) mood; (*carattere*) temper; **di buon/cattivo ~** in a good/bad mood

umo'rismo *sm* humour (*Brit*), humor (*US*); **avere il senso dell' ~** to have a sense of humo(u)r

umo'rista, -i, e *sm/f* humorist

umo'ristico, -a, ci, che *ag* humorous, funny

un, un', una *vedi* **uno**

u'nanime *ag* unanimous

unanimità *sf* unanimity; **all' ~** unanimously

'**una 'tantum** *ag* one-off *cpd* ■ *sf* (*imposta*) one-off tax

unci'nato, -a [untʃi'nato] *ag* (*amo*) barbed; (*ferro*) hooked; **croce uncinata** swastika

unci'netto [untʃi'netto] *sm* crochet hook

un'cino [un'tʃino] *sm* hook

undi'cenne [undi'tʃɛnne] *ag, sm/f* eleven-year-old

undi'cesimo, -a [undi'tʃɛzimo] *ag* eleventh

'**undici** ['unditʃi] *num* eleven

U'NESCO *sigla f* (= *United Nations Educational, Scientific and Cultural Organization*) UNESCO

'**ungere** ['undʒere] *vt* to grease, oil; (*Rel*) to anoint; (*fig*) to flatter, butter up; **ungersi** *vr* (*sporcarsi*) to get covered in grease; **ungersi con la crema** to put on cream

unghe'rese [unge'rese] *ag, sm/f, sm* Hungarian

Unghe'ria [unge'ria] *sf*: **l' ~** Hungary

'**unghia** ['ungja] *sf* (*Anat*) nail; (*di animale*) claw; (*di rapace*) talon; (*di cavallo*) hoof; **pagare sull' ~** (*fig*) to pay on the nail

unghi'ata [un'gjata] *sf* (*graffio*) scratch

ungu'ento *sm* ointment

unica'mente *av* only

'**UNICEF** ['unitʃef] *sigla m* (= *United Nations International Children's Emergency Fund*) UNICEF

'**unico, -a, ci, che** *ag* (*solo*) only; (*ineguagliabile*) unique; (*singolo: binario*) single; **è figlio ~** he's an only child; **atto ~** (*Teat*) one-act play; **agente ~** (*Comm*) sole agent

uni'corno *sm* unicorn

unifi'care *vt* to unite, unify; (*sistemi*) to standardize

unificazi'one [unifikat'tsjone] *sf* unification; standardization

unifor'mare *vt* (*terreno, superficie*) to level; **uniformarsi** *vr*: **uniformarsi a** to conform to; **~ qc a** to adjust *o* relate sth to

uni'forme *ag* uniform; (*superficie*) even ■ *sf* (*divisa*) uniform; **alta ~** dress uniform

uniformità *sf* uniformity; evenness

unilate'rale *ag* one-sided; (*Dir, Pol*) unilateral

u

uninomi'nale *ag* (*Pol: collegio, sistema*) single-candidate *cpd*

uni'one *sf* union; (*fig: concordia*) unity, harmony; **l'U~** (*Pol*) coalition of centre-left parties; **U~ economica e monetaria** economic and monetary union; **U~ Europea** European Union; **l'U~ Sovietica** the Soviet Union

u'nire *vt* to unite; (*congiungere*) to join, connect; (*: ingredienti, colori*) to combine; (*in matrimonio*) to unite, join together; **unirsi** *vr* to unite; (*in matrimonio*) to be joined together; **~ qc a** to unite sth with; to join *o* connect sth with; to combine sth with; **unirsi a** (*gruppo, società*) to join

u'nisono *sm*: **all'~** in unison

unità *sf inv* (*unione, concordia*) unity; (*Mat, Mil, Comm, di misura*) unit; **~ centrale (di elaborazione)** (*Inform*) central processing unit; **~ disco** (*Inform*) disk drive; **~ monetaria** monetary unit

uni'tario, -a *ag* unitary; **prezzo ~** price per unit

u'nito, -a *ag* (*paese*) united; (*amici, famiglia*) close; **in tinta unita** plain, self-coloured (*Brit*), self-colored (*US*)

univer'sale *ag* universal; general

universalità *sf* universality

universal'mente *av* universally

università *sf inv* university

universi'tario, -a *ag* university *cpd* ■ *sm/f* (*studente*) university student; (*insegnante*) academic, university lecturer

uni'verso *sm* universe

u'nivoco, -a, ci, che *ag* unambiguous

⬤ PAROLA CHIAVE

'uno, -a (*dav sm* **un** + C, V, **uno** + *s impura, gn, pn, ps, x, z; dav sf* **un'** + V, **una** + C) *det* **1** a; (*dav vocale*) an; **un bambino** a child; **una strada** a street; **uno zingaro** a gypsy

2 (*intensivo*): **ho avuto una paura!** I got such a fright!

■ *pron* **1** one; **ce n'è uno qui** there's one here; **prendine uno** take one (of them); **l'uno o l'altro** either (of them); **l'uno e l'altro** both (of them); **aiutarsi l'un l'altro** to help one another *o* each other; **sono entrati l'uno dopo l'altro** they came in one after the other; **a uno a uno** one by one; **metà per uno** half each

2 (*un tale*) someone, somebody; **ho incontrato uno che ti conosce** I met somebody who knows you

3 (*con valore impersonale*) one, you; **se uno vuole** if one wants, if you want; **cosa fa uno in quella situazione?** what does one do in that situation?

■ *num* one; **una mela e due pere** one apple and two pears; **uno più uno fa due** one plus one equals two, one and one are two

■ *sf*: **è l'una** it's one (o'clock)

'unsi *etc vb vedi* **ungere**

'unto, -a *pp di* **ungere** ■ *ag* greasy, oily ■ *sm* grease

untu'oso, -a *ag* greasy, oily

unzi'one [un'tsjone] *sf*: **l'Estrema U~** (*Rel*) Extreme Unction

u'omo (*pl* **uomini**) *sm* man; **da ~** (*abito, scarpe*) men's, for men; **a memoria d'~** since the world began; **a passo d'~** at walking pace; **~ d'affari** businessman; **~ d'azione** man of action; **~ di fiducia** right-hand man; **~ di mondo** man of the world; **~ di paglia** stooge; **~ rana** frogman; **l'~ della strada** the man in the street

u'opo *sm*: **all'~** if necessary

u'ovo (*pl(f)* **uova**) *sm* egg; **cercare il pelo nell'~** (*fig*) to split hairs; **~ affogato** *o* **in camicia** poached egg; **~ bazzotto/sodo** soft-/hard-boiled egg; **~ alla coque** boiled egg; **~ di Pasqua** Easter egg; **~ al tegame** *o* **all'occhio di bue** fried egg; **uova strapazzate** scrambled eggs

ura'gano *sm* hurricane

U'rali *smpl*: **gli ~**: **i Monti ~** the Urals, the Ural Mountains

u'ranio *sm* uranium; **~ impoverito** depleted uranium

urba'nista, -i, e *sm/f* town planner

urba'nistica *sf* town planning

urbanità *sf* urbanity

ur'bano, -a *ag* urban, city *cpd*, town *cpd*; (*Tel: chiamata*) local; (*fig*) urbane

ur'gente [ur'dʒente] *ag* urgent

ur'genza [ur'dʒentsa] *sf* urgency; **in caso d'~** in (case of) an emergency; **d'~** *ag* emergency ■ *av* urgently, as a matter of urgency; **non c'è ~** there's no hurry; **questo lavoro va fatto con ~** this work is urgent

'urgere ['urdʒere] *vi* to be needed urgently

u'rina *etc* = **orina** *etc*

ur'lare *vi* (*persona*) to scream, yell; (*animale, vento*) to howl ■ *vt* to scream, yell

'urlo (*pl(m)* **urli**, *pl(f)* **urla**) *sm* scream, yell; howl

'urna *sf* urn; (*elettorale*) ballot box; **andare alle urne** to go to the polls

URP [urp] *sigla m* (= *Ufficio Relazioni con il Pubblico*) PR Office

urrà *escl* hurrah!

U.R.S.S. *sigla f* = **Unione delle Repubbliche Socialiste Sovietiche**; **l'~** the USSR ur'tare *vt* to bump into, knock against; (*fig*: *irritare*) to annoy ■ *vi*: ~ **contro** *o* **in** to bump into, knock against; (*fig*: *imbattersi*) to come up against; **urtarsi** *vr* (*reciproco*: *scontrarsi*) to collide; (:*fig*) to clash; (*irritarsi*) to get annoyed

'urto *sm* (*colpo*) knock, bump; (*scontro*) crash, collision; (*fig*) clash; **terapia d'**~ (*Med*) shock treatment

uruguai'ano, -a *ag, sm/f* Uruguayan

Urugu'ay *sm*: **l'**~ Uruguay

u.s. *abbr* = **ultimo scorso**

'USA *smpl*: **gli** ~ the USA

u'sanza [u'zantsa] *sf* custom; (*moda*) fashion

u'sare *vt* to use, employ ■ *vi* (*essere di moda*) to be fashionable; (*servirsi*): ~ **di** to use; (: *diritto*) to exercise; (*essere solito*): ~ **fare** to be in the habit of doing, be accustomed to doing ■ *vb impers*: **qui usa così** it's the custom round here; ~ **la massima cura nel fare qc** to exercise great care when doing sth

u'sato, -a *ag* used; (*consumato*) worn; (*di seconda mano*) used, second-hand ■ *sm* second-hand goods *pl*

u'scente [uʃʃɛnte] *ag* (*Amm*) outgoing

usci'ere [uʃʃɛre] *sm* usher

'uscio ['uʃʃo] *sm* door

u'scire [uʃʃire] *vi* (*gen*) to come out; (*partire, andare a passeggio, a uno spettacolo etc*) to go out; (*essere sorteggiato: numero*) to come up; ~ **da** (*gen*) to leave; (*posto*) to go (*o* come) out of, leave; (*solco, vasca etc*) to come out of; (*muro*) to stick out of; (*competenza etc*) to be outside; (*infanzia, adolescenza*) to leave behind; (*famiglia nobile etc*) to come from; ~ **da** *o* **di casa** to go out; (*fig*) to leave home; ~ **in automobile** to go out in the car, go for a drive; ~ **di strada** (*Aut*) to go off *o* leave the road

u'scita [uʃʃita] *sf* (*passaggio, varco*) exit, way out; (*per divertimento*) outing; (*Econ: somma*) expenditure; (*fig: battuta*) witty remark; **"vietata l'**~" "no exit"; ~ **di sicurezza** emergency exit

usi'gnolo [uziɲ'ɲɔlo] *sm* nightingale

'uso *sm* (*utilizzazione*) use; (*esercizio*) practice (*Brit*), practise (*US*); (*abitudine*) custom; **fare** ~ **di qc** to use sth; **con l'**~ with practice; **a** ~ **di**

for (the use of); **d'**~ (*corrente*) in use; **fuori** ~ out of use; **essere in** ~ to be in common *o* current use

ustio'nare *vt* to burn; **ustionarsi** *vr* to burn o.s.

usti'one *sf* burn

usu'ale *ag* common, everyday

usufru'ire *vi*: ~ **di** (*giovarsi di*) to take advantage of, make use of

usu'frutto *sm* (*Dir*) usufruct

u'sura *sf* usury; (*logoramento*) wear (and tear)

usu'raio *sm* usurer

usur'pare *vt* to usurp

usurpa'tore, -'trice *sm/f* usurper

uten'sile *sm* tool, implement ■ *ag*: **macchina** ~ machine tool; **utensili da cucina** kitchen utensils

utensile'ria *sf* (*utensili*) tools *pl*; (*reparto*) tool room

u'tente *sm/f* user; (*di gas etc*) consumer; (*del telefono*) subscriber; ~ **finale** end user

'utero *sm* uterus, womb; ~ **in affitto** host womb

'utile *ag* useful ■ *sm* (*vantaggio*) advantage, benefit; (*Econ*) profit; **rendersi** ~ to be helpful; **in tempo** ~ **per** in time for; **unire l'**~ **al dilettevole** to combine business with pleasure; **partecipare agli utili** (*Econ*) to share in the profits

utilità *sf* usefulness *no pl*; use; (*vantaggio*) benefit; **essere di grande** ~ to be very useful

utili'tario, -a *ag* utilitarian ■ *sf* (*Aut*) economy car

utiliz'zare [utilid'dzare] *vt* to use, make use of, utilize

utilizzazi'one [utiliddzat'tsjone] *sf* utilization, use

uti'lizzo [uti'liddzo] *sm* (*Amm*) utilization; (*Banca: di credito*) availment

util'mente *av* usefully, profitably

uto'pia *sf* utopia; **è pura** ~ that's sheer utopianism

uto'pistico, -a, ci, che *ag* utopian

UVA *abbr* (= *ultravioletto prossimo*) UVA

'uva *sf* grapes *pl*; ~ **passa** raisins *pl*; ~ **spina** gooseberry

UVB *abbr* (= *ultravioletto lontano*) UVB

Vv

V, v [vi, vu] *sf o m inv (lettera)* V, v; **V come Venezia** ≈ V for Victor

V *abbr* (= *volt*) V

v. *abbr* (= *vedi, verso, versetto*) v.

VA *sigla* = **Varese**

va, va' *vb vedi* **andare**

va'cante *ag* vacant

va'canza [va'kantsa] *sf* (*l'essere vacante*) vacancy; (*riposo, ferie*) holiday(s pl) (*Brit*), vacation (*US*); (*giorno di permesso*) day off, holiday; **vacanze** *sfpl* (*periodo di ferie*) holidays, vacation *sg*; **essere/andare in** ~ to be/go on holiday *o* vacation; **far** ~ to have a holiday; **vacanze estive** summer holiday(s) *o* vacation

'vacca, -che *sf* cow

vacci'nare [vattʃi'nare] *vt* to vaccinate; **farsi** ~ to have a vaccination, get vaccinated

vaccinazi'one [vattʃinat'tsjone] *sf* vaccination

vac'cino [vat'tʃino] *sm* (*Med*) vaccine

vacil'lante [vatʃil'lante] *ag* (*edificio, vecchio*) shaky, unsteady; (*fiamma*) flickering; (*salute, memoria*) shaky, failing

vacil'lare [vatʃil'lare] *vi* to sway; (*fiamma*) to flicker; (*fig: memoria, coraggio*) to be failing, falter

'vacuo, -a *ag* (*fig*) empty, vacuous ■ *sm* vacuum

'vado *etc vb vedi* **andare**

vagabon'daggio [vagabon'daddʒo] *sm* wandering, roaming; (*Dir*) vagrancy

vagabon'dare *vi* to roam, wander

vaga'bondo, -a *sm/f* tramp, vagrant; (*fannullone*) idler, loafer

va'gare *vi* to wander

vagheggi'are [vaged'dʒare] *vt* to long for, dream of

vaghe'rò *etc* [vage'rɔ] *vb vedi* **vagare**

va'ghezza [va'gettsa] *sf* vagueness

va'gina [va'dʒina] *sf* vagina

va'gire [va'dʒire] *vi* to whimper

va'gito [va'dʒito] *sm* cry, wailing

'vaglia ['vaʎʎa] *sm inv* money order; ~ **cambiario** promissory note; ~ **postale** postal order

vagli'are [vaʎ'ʎare] *vt* to sift; (*fig*) to weigh up

'vaglio ['vaʎʎo] *sm* sieve; **passare al** ~ (*fig*) to examine closely

'vago, -a, ghi, ghe *ag* vague

va'gone *sm* (*Ferr: per passeggeri*) carriage (*Brit*), car (*US*); (*: per merci*) truck, wagon; ~ **letto** sleeper, sleeping car; ~ **ristorante** dining *o* restaurant car

'vai *vb vedi* **andare**

vai'olo *sm* smallpox

val. *abbr* = **valuta**

va'langa, -ghe *sf* avalanche

va'lente *ag* able, talented

va'lenza [va'lɛntsa] *sf* (*fig: significato*) content; (*Chim*) valency

va'lere *vi* (*avere forza, potenza*) to have influence; (*essere valido*) to be valid; (*avere vigore, autorità*) to hold, apply; (*essere capace: poeta, studente*) to be good, be able ■ *vt* (*prezzo, sforzo*) to be worth; (*corrispondere*) to correspond to; (*procurare*): ~ **qc a qn** to earn sb sth; **valersi** *vr*: **valersi di** to make use of, take advantage of; **far** ~ (*autorità etc*) to assert; **far** ~ **le proprie ragioni** to make o.s. heard; **farsi** ~ to make o.s. appreciated *o* respected; **vale a dire** that is to say; ~ **la pena** to be worth the effort *o* worth it; **l'uno vale l'altro** the one is as good as the other, they amount to the same thing; **non vale niente** it's worthless; **valersi dei consigli di qn** to take *o* act upon sb's advice

valeri'ana *sf* (*Bot, Med*) valerian

va'levole *ag* valid

'valgo *etc vb vedi* **valere**

vali'care *vt* to cross

'valico, -chi *sm* (*passo*) pass

validità *sf* validity

'valido, -a *ag* valid; (*rimedio*) effective; (*persona*) worthwhile; **essere di** ~ **aiuto a qn** to be a great help to sb

valige'ria [validʒe'ria] sf (assortimento) leather goods pl; (fabbrica) leather goods factory; (negozio) leather goods shop

vali'getta [vali'dʒetta] sf: **~ ventiquattrore** overnight bag o case

va'ligia, -gie o **ge** [va'lidʒa] sf (suit)case; **fare le valigie** to pack (up); **~ diplomatica** diplomatic bag

val'lata sf valley

'valle sf valley; **a ~** (di fiume) downstream; **scendere a ~** to go downhill

val'letto sm valet

valligi'ano, -a [valli'dʒano] sm/f inhabitant of a valley

va'lore sm (gen, Comm) value; (merito) merit, worth; (coraggio) valour (Brit), valor (US), courage; (Finanza: titolo) security; **valori** smpl (oggetti preziosi) valuables; **crescere/diminuire di ~** to go up/down in value, gain/lose in value; **è di gran ~** it's worth a lot, it's very valuable; **privo di ~** worthless; **~ contabile** book value; **~ effettivo** real value; **~ nominale** o **facciale** nominal value; **~ di realizzo** break-up value; **~ di riscatto** surrender value; **valori bollati** (revenue) stamps

valoriz'zare [valorid'dzare] vt (terreno) to develop; (fig) to make the most of

valo'roso, -a ag courageous

'valso, -a pp di **valere**

va'luta sf currency, money; (Banca): **~ 15 gennaio** interest to run from January 15th; **~ estera** foreign currency

valu'tare vt (casa, gioiello, fig) to value; (stabilire: peso, entrate, fig) to estimate

valu'tario, -a ag (Finanza: norme) currency cpd

valutazi'one [valutat'tsjone] sf valuation; estimate

'valva sf (Zool, Bot) valve

'valvola sf (Tecn, Anat) valve; (Elettr) fuse; **~ a farfalla del carburatore** (Aut) throttle; **~ di sicurezza** safety valve

'valzer ['valtser] sm inv waltz

vam'pata sf (di fiamma) blaze; (di calore) blast; (: al viso) flush

vam'piro sm vampire

vana'gloria sf boastfulness

van'dalico, -a, ci, che ag vandal cpd; **atto ~** act of vandalism

vanda'lismo sm vandalism

'vandalo sm vandal

vaneggia'mento [vanedd ʒa'mento] sm raving, delirium

vaneggi'are [vaned'dʒare] vi to rave

va'nesio, -a ag vain, conceited

'vanga, -ghe sf spade

van'gare vt to dig

van'gelo [van'dʒɛlo] sm gospel

vanifi'care vt to nullify

va'niglia [va'niʎʎa] sf vanilla

vanigli'ato, -a [vaniʎ'ʎato] ag: **zucchero ~** (Cuc) vanilla sugar

vanità sf vanity; (di promessa) emptiness; (di sforzo) futility

vani'toso, -a ag vain, conceited

'vanno vb vedi **andare**

'vano, -a ag vain ■ sm (spazio) space; (apertura) opening; (stanza) room; **il ~ della porta** the doorway; **il ~ portabagagli** (Aut) the boot (Brit), the trunk (US)

van'taggio [van'taddʒo] sm advantage; **trarre ~ da qc** to benefit from sth; **essere/portarsi in ~** (Sport) to be in/take the lead

vantaggi'oso, -a [vantad'dʒoso] ag advantageous, favourable (Brit), favorable (US)

van'tare vt to praise, speak highly of; **vantarsi** vr: **vantarsi (di/di aver fatto)** to boast o brag (about/about having done)

vante'ria sf boasting

'vanto sm boasting; (merito) virtue, merit; (gloria) pride

'vanvera sf: **a ~** haphazardly; **parlare a ~** to talk nonsense

va'pore sm vapour (Brit), vapor (US); (anche: **vapore acqueo**) steam; (nave) steamer; **a ~** (turbina etc) steam cpd; **al ~** (Cuc) steamed

vapo'retto sm steamer

vapori'era sf (Ferr) steam engine

vaporiz'zare [vaporid'dzare] vt to vaporize

vaporizza'tore [vaporiddza'tore] sm spray

vaporizzazi'one [vaporiddzat'tsjone] sf vaporization

vapo'roso, -a ag (tessuto) filmy; (capelli) soft and full

va'rare vt (Naut, fig) to launch; (Dir) to pass

var'care vt to cross

'varco, -chi sm passage; **aprirsi un ~ tra la folla** to push one's way through the crowd

vare'china [vare'kina] sf bleach

vari'abile ag variable; (tempo, umore) changeable, variable ■ sf (Mat) variable

vari'ante sf (gen) variation, change; (di piano) modification; (Ling) variant; (Sport) alternative route

vari'are vt, vi to vary; **~ di opinione** to change one's mind

variazi'one [varjat'tsjone] sf variation, change; (Mus) variation; **una ~ di programma** a change of plan

va'rice [va'ritʃe] sf varicose vein

vari'cella [vari'tʃella] sf chickenpox

vari'coso, -a ag varicose

varie'gato, -a ag variegated

399

varietà *sf inv* variety ◼ *sm inv* variety show
vario, -a *ag* varied; *(parecchi: col sostantivo al pl)*
various; *(mutevole: umore)* changeable; **varie**
sfpl: **varie ed eventuali** *(nell'ordine del giorno)*
any other business
vario'pinto, -a *ag* multicoloured (Brit),
multicolored (US)
'varo *sm* (Naut, *fig)* launch; *(di leggi)* passing
varrò *etc vb vedi* **valere**
Var'savia *sf* Warsaw
va'saio *sm* potter
'vasca, -sche *sf* basin; *(anche:* **vasca da**
bagno*)* bathtub, bath
va'scello [vaʃʃello] *sm* (Naut) vessel, ship
vas'chetta [vas'ketta] *sf (per gelato)* tub; *(per*
sviluppare fotografie) dish
vase'lina *sf* vaseline
vasel'lame *sm (stoviglie)* crockery; (: *di*
porcellana) china; **~ d'oro/d'argento** gold/
silver plate
'vaso *sm (recipiente)* pot; (: *barattolo)* jar;
(: *decorativo)* vase; (Anat) vessel; **~ da fiori**
vase; *(per piante)* flowerpot
vas'sallo *sm* vassal
vas'soio *sm* tray
vas'tità *sf* vastness
'vasto, -a *ag* vast, immense; **di vaste**
proporzioni *(incendio)* huge; *(fenomeno,*
rivolta) widespread; **su vasta scala** on a vast *o*
huge scale
Vati'cano *sm*: **il ~** the Vatican; **la Città del ~**
the Vatican City
VB *sigla* = **Vibo Valenza**
VC *sigla* = **Vercelli**
VE *sigla* = **Venezia** ◼ *abbr* = **Vostra Eccellenza**
ve *pron, av vedi* **vi**
vecchi'aia [vek'kjaja] *sf* old age
'vecchio, -a ['vɛkkjo] *ag* old ◼ *sm/f* old
man(-woman); **i vecchi** the old; **è un mio ~**
amico he's an old friend of mine; **è un**
uomo ~ stile *o* **stampo** he's an old-
fashioned man; **è ~ del mestiere** he's an old
hand at the job
'vece ['vetʃe] *sf*: **in ~ di** in the place of, for;
fare le veci di qn to take sb's place; **firma**
del padre o di chi ne fa le veci signature of
the father or guardian
ve'dere *vt, vi* to see; **vedersi** *vr* to meet, see
one another; **~ di fare qc** to see (to it) that
sth is done, make sure that sth is done;
avere a che ~ con to have to do with; **far ~ qc**
a qn to show sb sth; **farsi ~** to show o.s.;
(farsi vivo) to show one's face; **farsi ~ da un**
medico to go and see a doctor; **modo di ~**
outlook, view of things; **vedi pagina 8**
(rimando) see page 8; **è da ~ se ...** it remains to
be seen whether ...; **non vedo la ragione di**

farlo I can't see any reason to do it; **si era**
visto costretto a ... he found himself forced
to ...; **non (ci) si vede** *(è buio etc)* you can't see
a thing; **ci vediamo domani!** see you
tomorrow!; **non lo posso ~** *(fig)* I can't stand
him
ve'detta *sf (sentinella, posto)* look-out; *(Naut)*
patrol boat
ve'dette [və'dɛt] *sf inv (attrice)* star
'vedovo, -a *sm/f* widower/widow; **rimaner ~**
to be widowed
vedrò *etc vb vedi* **vedere**
ve'duta *sf* view; **di larghe** *o* **ampie vedute**
broad-minded; **di vedute limitate** narrow-
minded
vee'mente *ag (discorso, azione)* vehement;
(assalto) vigorous; *(passione)* overwhelming
vee'menza [vee'mɛntsa] *sf* vehemence; **con**
~ vehemently
vege'tale [vedʒe'tale] *ag, sm* vegetable
vege'tare [vedʒe'tare] *vi (fig)* to vegetate
vegetari'ano, -a [vedʒeta'rjano] *ag, sm/f*
vegetarian
vegeta'tivo, -a *ag* vegetative
vegetazi'one [vedʒetat'tsjone] *sf* vegetation
'vegeto, -a ['vɛdʒeto] *ag (pianta)* thriving;
(persona) strong, vigorous
veg'gente [ved'dʒɛnte] *sm/f (indovino)*
clairvoyant
'veglia ['veʎʎa] *sf (sorveglianza)* watch;
(trattenimento) evening gathering; **tra la ~ e il**
sonno half awake; **fare la ~ a un malato** to
watch over a sick person; **~ funebre** wake
vegli'ardo, -a [veʎ'ʎardo] *sm/f* venerable old
man/woman
vegli'are [veʎ'ʎare] *vi* to stay *o* sit up; *(stare*
vigile) to watch; to keep watch ◼ *vt (malato,*
morto) to watch over, sit up with
vegli'one [veʎ'ʎone] *sm* ball, dance
ve'icolo *sm* vehicle; **~ spaziale** spacecraft *inv*
'vela *sf (Naut: tela)* sail; *(sport)* sailing; **tutto**
va a gonfie vele *(fig)* everything is going
perfectly
ve'lare *vt* to veil; **velarsi** *vr (occhi, luna)* to
mist over; *(voce)* to become husky; **velarsi il**
viso to cover one's face (with a veil)
ve'lato, -a *ag* veiled
vela'tura *sf (Naut)* sails *pl*
veleggi'are [veled'dʒare] *vi* to sail; *(Aer)* to
glide
ve'leno *sm* poison
vele'noso, -a *ag* poisonous
ve'letta *sf (di cappello)* veil
veli'ero *sm* sailing ship
ve'lina *sf*: **carta ~** *(per imballare)* tissue paper;
(: *per copie)* flimsy paper; *(copia)* carbon copy
ve'lista, -i, e *sm/f* yachtsman(-woman)

ve'livolo *sm* aircraft

velleità *sf inv* vain ambition, vain desire

vellei'tario, -a *ag* unrealistic

'vello *sm* fleece

vellu'tato, -a *ag* (*stoffa, pesca, colore*) velvety; (*voce*) mellow

vel'luto *sm* velvet; ~ **a coste** cord

'velo *sm* veil; (*tessuto*) voile

ve'loce [ve'lotʃe] *ag* fast, quick ■ *av* fast, quickly

velo'cista, -i, e [velo'tʃista] *sm/f* (*Sport*) sprinter

velocità [velotʃi'ta] *sf* speed; **a forte ~** at high speed; **~ di crociera** cruising speed

ve'lodromo *sm* velodrome

ven. *abbr* (= *venerdì*) Fri.

'vena *sf* (*gen*) vein; (*filone*) vein, seam; (*fig: ispirazione*) inspiration; (*: umore*) mood; **essere in ~ di qc** to be in the mood for sth

ve'nale *ag* (*prezzo, valore*) market *cpd*; (*fig*) venal; mercenary

venalità *sf* venality

ve'nato, -a *ag* (*marmo*) veined, streaked; (*legno*) grained

vena'torio, -a *ag* hunting; **la stagione venatoria** the hunting season

vena'tura *sf* (*di marmo*) vein, streak; (*di legno*) grain

ven'demmia *sf* (*raccolta*) grape harvest; (*quantità d'uva*) grape crop, grapes *pl*; (*vino ottenuto*) vintage

vendemmi'are *vt* to harvest ■ *vi* to harvest the grapes

'vendere *vt* to sell; ~ **all'ingrosso/al dettaglio** *o* **minuto** to sell wholesale/retail; ~ **all'asta** to auction, sell by auction; **"vendesi"** "for sale"

ven'detta *sf* revenge

vendi'care *vt* to avenge; **vendicarsi** *vr*: **vendicarsi (di)** to avenge o.s. (for); (*per rancore*) to take one's revenge (for); **vendicarsi su qn** to revenge o.s. on sb

vendica'tivo, -a *ag* vindictive

'vendita *sf* sale; **la ~** (*attività*) selling; (*smercio*) sales *pl*; **in ~** on sale; **mettere in ~** to put on sale; **in ~ presso** on sale at; **contratto di ~** sales agreement; **reparto vendite** sales department; ~ **all'asta** sale by auction; ~ **al dettaglio** *o* **minuto** retail; ~ **all'ingrosso** wholesale

vendi'tore, -'trice *sm/f* seller, vendor; (*gestore di negozio*) trader, dealer

ven'duto, -a *ag* (*merce*) sold; (*fig: corrotto*) corrupt

ve'nefico, -a, ci, che *ag* poisonous

vene'rabile *ag*, vene'rando, -a ■ *ag* venerable

vene'rare *vt* to venerate

venerazi'one [venerat'tsjone] *sf* veneration

venerdì *sm inv* Friday; **V~ Santo** Good Friday; *vedi anche* **martedì**

'Venere *sm, sf* Venus

ve'nereo, -a *ag* venereal

'veneto, -a *ag* of (*o* from) the Veneto

'veneto-giuli'ano, -a ['vɛnetodʒu'ljano] *ag* of (*o* from) Venezia-Giulia

Ve'nezia [ve'nettsja] *sf* Venice

venezi'ano, -a [venet'tsjano] *ag, sm/f* Venetian

Venezu'ela [venettsu'ela] *sm*: **il ~** Venezuela

venezue'lano, -a [venettsue'lano] *ag, sm/f* Venezuelan

'vengo *etc vb vedi* **venire**

veni'ale *ag* venial

ve'nire *vi* to come; (*riuscire: dolce, fotografia*) to turn out; (*come ausiliare: essere*): **viene ammirato da tutti** he is admired by everyone; ~ **da** to come from; **quanto viene?** how much does it cost?; **far ~** (*mandare a chiamare*) to send for; (*medico*) to call, send for; ~ **a capo di qc** to unravel sth, sort sth out; ~ **al dunque** *o* **nocciolo** *o* **fatto** to come to the point; ~ **fuori** to come out; ~ **giù** to come down; ~ **meno** (*svenire*) to faint; ~ **meno a qc** not to fulfil sth; ~ **su** to come up; ~ **via** to come away; ~ **a sapere qc** to learn sth; ~ **a trovare qn** to come and see sb; **negli anni a** ~ in the years to come, in future; **è venuto il momento di ...** the time has come to ...

'venni *etc vb vedi* **venire**

ven'taglio [ven'taʎʎo] *sm* fan

ven'tata *sf* gust (of wind)

venten'nale *ag* (*che dura 20 anni*) twenty-year *cpd*; (*che ricorre ogni 20 anni*) which takes place every twenty years

ven'tenne *ag, sm/f* twenty-year-old

ven'tennio *sm* period of twenty years; **il ~ fascista** the Fascist period

ven'tesimo, -a *num* twentieth

'venti *num* twenty

venti'lare *vt* (*stanza*) to air, ventilate; (*fig: idea, proposta*) to air

venti'lato, -a *ag* (*camera, zona*) airy; **poco ~** airless

ventila'tore *sm* fan; (*su parete, finestra*) ventilator, fan

ventilazi'one [ventilat'tsjone] *sf* ventilation

ven'tina *sf*: **una ~ (di)** around twenty, twenty or so

ventiquat'tr'ore *sfpl* (*periodo*) twenty-four hours ■ *sf inv* (*Sport*) twenty-four-hour race; (*valigetta*) overnight case

venti'sette *num* twenty-seven; **il ~** (*giorno di paga*) (monthly) pay day

ventitré *num* twenty-three ■ *sfpl*: **portava il cappello sulle ~** he wore his hat at a jaunty angle

'**vento** *sm* wind; **c'è ~** it's windy; **un colpo di ~** a gust of wind; **contro ~** against the wind; **~ contrario** (*Naut*) headwind

'**ventola** *sf* (*Aut, Tecn*) fan

ven'**tosa** *sf* (*Zool*) sucker; (*di gomma*) suction pad

ven'**toso, -a** *ag* windy

ven'**totto** *num* twenty-eight

'**ventre** *sm* stomach

ven'**triloquo** *sm* ventriloquist

ven'**tuno** *num* twenty-one

ven'**tura** *sf*: **andare alla ~** to trust to luck; **soldato di ~** mercenary

ven'**turo, -a** *ag* next, coming

ve'**nuto, -a** *pp di* **venire** ■ *sm/f*: **il(la) primo(a) ~(a)** the first person who comes along ■ *sf* coming, arrival

ver. *abbr* = **versamento**

'**vera** *sf* wedding ring

ve'**race** [ve'ratʃe] *ag* (*testimone*) truthful; (*testimonianza*) accurate; (*cibi*) real, genuine

vera'**mente** *av* really

ve'**randa** *sf* veranda(h)

ver'**bale** *ag* verbal ■ *sm* (*di riunione*) minutes *pl*; **accordo ~** verbal agreement; **mettere a ~** to place in the minutes *o* on record

'**verbo** *sm* (*Ling*) verb; (*parola*) word; (*Rel*): **il V~** the Word

ver'**boso, -a** *ag* verbose, wordy

ver'**dastro, -a** *ag* greenish

'**verde** *ag, sm* green; **~ bottiglia/oliva** (*inv*) bottle/olive green; **benzina ~** lead-free *o* unleaded petrol; **i Verdi** (*Pol*) the Greens; **essere al ~** (*fig*) to be broke

verdeggi'**ante** [verded'dʒante] *ag* green, verdant

verde'**rame** *sm* verdigris

ver'**detto** *sm* verdict

ver'**dura** *sf* vegetables *pl*

vere'**condia** *sf* modesty

vere'**condo, -a** *ag* modest

'**verga, -ghe** *sf* rod

ver'**gato, -a** *ag* (*foglio*) ruled

vergi'**nale** [verdʒi'nale] *ag* virginal

'**vergine** ['verdʒine] *sf* virgin; (*dello zodiaco*): **V~** Virgo ■ *ag* virgin; (*ragazza*): **essere ~** to be a virgin; **essere della V~** (*dello zodiaco*) to be Virgo; **pura lana ~** pure new wool; **olio ~ d'oliva** unrefined olive oil

vergi'**nità** [verdʒini'ta] *sf* virginity

ver'**gogna** [ver'goɲɲa] *sf* shame; (*timidezza*) shyness, embarrassment

vergo'**gnarsi** [vergoɲ'ɲarsi] *vr*: **~ (di)** to be *o* feel ashamed (of); to be shy (about), be embarrassed (about)

vergo'**gnoso, -a** [vergoɲ'ɲoso] *ag* ashamed; (*timido*) shy, embarrassed; (*causa di vergogna: azione*) shameful

veridi'**cità** [veriditʃi'ta] *sf* truthfulness

ve'**ridico, -a, ci, che** *ag* truthful

ve'**rifica, -che** *sf* checking *no pl*; check; **fare una ~ di** (*freni, testimonianza, firma*) to check; **~ contabile** (*Finanza*) audit

verifi'**care** *vt* (*controllare*) to check; (*confermare*) to confirm, bear out; (*Finanza*) to audit

ve'**rità** *sf inv* truth; **a dire la ~, per la ~** truth to tell, actually

veriti'**ero, -a** *ag* (*che dice la verità*) truthful; (*conforme a verità*) true

'**verme** *sm* worm

vermi'**celli** [vermi'tʃelli] *smpl* vermicelli *sg*

ver'**miglio** [ver'miʎʎo] *sm* vermilion, scarlet

'**vermut** *sm inv* vermouth

ver'**nacolo** *sm* vernacular

ver'**nice** [ver'nitʃe] *sf* (*colorazione*) paint; (*trasparente*) varnish; (*pelle*) patent leather; **"~ fresca"** "wet paint"

vernici'**are** [verni'tʃare] *vt* to paint; to varnish

vernicia'**tura** [vernitʃa'tura] *sf* painting; varnishing

'**vero, -a** *ag* (*veridico: fatti, testimonianza*) true; (*autentico*) real ■ *sm* (*verità*) truth; (*realtà*) (real) life; **un ~ e proprio delinquente** a real criminal, an out and out criminal; **tant'è ~ che ...** so much so that ...; **a onor del ~, a dire il ~** to tell the truth

Ve'**rona** *sf* Verona

vero'**nese** *ag* of (*o* from) Verona

vero'**simile** *ag* likely, probable

ver'**rò** *etc vb vedi* **venire**

ver'**ruca, -che** *sf* wart

versa'**mento** *sm* (*pagamento*) payment; (*deposito di denaro*) deposit

ver'**sante** *sm* slopes *pl*, side

ver'**sare** *vt* (*fare uscire: vino, farina*) to pour (out); (*spargere: lacrime, sangue*) to shed; (*rovesciare*) to spill; (*Econ*) to pay; (*: depositare*) to deposit, pay in ■ *vi*: **~ in gravi difficoltà** to find o.s. with serious problems; **versarsi** *vr* (*rovesciarsi*) to spill; (*fiume, folla*): **versarsi (in)** to pour (into)

versa'**tile** *ag* versatile

versati'**lità** *sf* versatility

ver'**sato, -a** *ag*: **~ in** to be (well-)versed in

ver'**setto** *sm* (*Rel*) verse

versi'**one** *sf* version; (*traduzione*) translation

'**verso** *sm* (*di poesia*) verse, line; (*di animale, uccello, venditore ambulante*) cry; (*direzione*) direction; (*modo*) way; (*di foglio di carta*) verso; (*di moneta*) reverse; **versi** *smpl* (*poesia*) verse *sg*; **per un ~ o per l'altro** one way or another;

prendere qn/qc per il ~ giusto to approach sb/sth the right way; **rifare il ~ a qn** (*imitare*) to mimic sb; **non c'è ~ di persuaderlo** there's no way of persuading him, he can't be persuaded ■ *prep* (*in direzione di*) toward(s); (*nei pressi di*) near, around (about); (*in senso temporale*) about, around; (*nei confronti di*) for; **~ di me** towards me; **~ l'alto** upwards; **~ il basso** downwards; **~ sera** towards evening

'**vertebra** *sf* vertebra

verte'brale *ag* vertebral; **colonna ~** spinal column, spine

verte'brato, -a *ag, sm* vertebrate

ver'tenza [ver'tɛntsa] *sf* (*lite*) lawsuit, case; (*sindacale*) dispute

'**vertere** *vi*: **~ su** to deal with, be about

verti'cale *ag, sf* vertical

'**vertice** ['vertitʃe] *sm* summit, top; (*Mat*) vertex; **conferenza al ~** (*Pol*) summit conference

ver'tigine [ver'tidʒine] *sf* dizziness *no pl*; dizzy spell; (*Med*) vertigo; **avere le vertigini** to feel dizzy

vertigi'noso, -a [vertidʒi'noso] *ag* (*altezza*) dizzy; (*fig*) breathtakingly high (*o deep etc*)

'**verza** ['verdza] *sf* Savoy cabbage

ve'scica, -che [veʃ'ʃika] *sf* (*Anat*) bladder; (*Med*) blister

vesco'vile *ag* episcopal

'**vescovo** *sm* bishop

'**vespa** *sf* wasp; (®: *veicolo*) (motor) scooter

ves'paio *sm* wasps' nest; **suscitare un ~** (*fig*) to stir up a hornets' nest

vespasi'ano *sm* urinal

'**vespro** *sm* (*Rel*) vespers *pl*

ves'sare *vt* to oppress

vessazi'one [vessat'tsjone] *sf* oppression

ves'sillo *sm* standard; (*bandiera*) flag

ves'taglia [ves'taʎʎa] *sf* dressing gown, robe (*US*)

'**veste** *sf* garment; (*rivestimento*) covering; (*qualità, facoltà*) capacity; **vesti** *sfpl* clothes, clothing *sg*; **in ~ ufficiale** (*fig*) in an official capacity; **in ~ di** in the guise of, as; **~ da camera** dressing gown, robe (*US*); **~ editoriale** layout

vesti'ario *sm* wardrobe, clothes *pl*; **capo di ~** article of clothing, garment

ves'tibolo *sm* (*entrance*) hall

ves'tigia [ves'tidʒa] *sfpl* (*tracce*) vestiges, traces; (*rovine*) ruins, remains

ves'tire *vt* (*bambino, malato*) to dress; (*avere indosso*) to have on, wear; **vestirsi** *vr* to dress, get dressed; **vestirsi da** (*negozio, sarto*) to buy *o* get one's clothes at

ves'tito, -a *ag* dressed ■ *sm* garment; (*da donna*) dress; (*da uomo*) suit; **vestiti** *smpl*

(*indumenti*) clothes; **~ di bianco** dressed in white

Ve'suvio *sm*: **il ~** Vesuvius

vete'rano, -a *ag, sm/f* veteran

veteri'nario, -a *ag* veterinary ■ *sm* veterinary surgeon (*Brit*), veterinarian (*US*), vet ■ *sf* veterinary medicine

'**veto** *sm inv* veto; **porre il ~ a qc** to veto sth

ve'traio *sm* glassmaker; (*per finestre*) glazier

ve'trato, -a *ag* (*porta, finestra*) glazed; (*che contiene vetro*) glass *cpd* ■ *sf* glass door (*o* window); (*di chiesa*) stained glass window; **carta vetrata** sandpaper

vetre'ria *sf* (*stabilimento*) glassworks *sg*; (*oggetti di vetro*) glassware

ve'trina *sf* (*di negozio*) (shop) window; (*armadio*) display cabinet

vetri'nista, -i, e *sm/f* window dresser

ve'trino *sm* slide

vetri'olo *sm* vitriol

'**vetro** *sm* glass; (*per finestra, porta*) pane (of glass); **~ blindato** bulletproof glass; **~ infrangibile** shatterproof glass; **~ di sicurezza** safety glass; **i vetri di Murano** Murano glassware *sg*

ve'troso, -a *ag* vitreous

'**vetta** *sf* peak, summit, top

vet'tore *sm* (*Mat, Fisica*) vector; (*chi trasporta*) carrier

vetto'vaglie [vetto'vaʎʎe] *sfpl* supplies

vet'tura *sf* (*carrozza*) carriage; (*Ferr*) carriage (*Brit*), car (*US*); (*auto*) car (*Brit*), automobile (*US*); **~ di piazza** hackney carriage

vettu'rino *sm* coach driver, coachman

vezzeggi'are [vettsed'dʒare] *vt* to fondle, caress

vezzeggia'tivo [vettsedd'ʒa'tivo] *sm* (*Ling*) term of endearment

'**vezzo** ['vettso] *sm* habit; **vezzi** *smpl* (*smancerie*) affected ways; (*leggiadria*) charms

vez'zoso, -a [vet'tsoso] *ag* (*grazioso*) charming, pretty; (*lezioso*) affected

V.F. *abbr* = **vigili del fuoco**

V.G. *abbr* = **Vostra Grazia**

VI *sigla* = **Vicenza**

vi (*dav lo, la, li, le, ne diventa* **ve**) *pron* (*oggetto*) you; (*complemento di termine*) (to) you; (*riflessivo*) yourselves; (*reciproco*) each other ■ *av* (*lì*) there; (*qui*) here; (*per questo/quel luogo*) through here/there; **vi è/sono** there is/are

'**via** *sf* (*gen*) way; (*strada*) street; (*sentiero, pista*) path, track; (*Amm: procedimento*) channels *pl* ■ *prep* (*passando per*) via, by way of ■ *av* away ■ *escl* go away!; (*suvvia*) come on!; (*Sport*) go! ■ *sm* (*Sport*) starting signal; **per ~ di** (*a causa di*) because of, on account of; **in** *o* **per ~** on the way; **in ~ di guarigione** (*fig*) on the road

v

to recovery; **per ~ aerea** by air; (*lettere*) by airmail; **~ satellite** by satellite; **andare/ essere ~** to go/be away; **~ ~** (*pian piano*) gradually; **~ ~ che** (*a mano a mano*) as; **e ~ dicendo, e ~ di questo passo** and so on (and so forth); **dare il ~** (*Sport*) to give the starting signal; **dare il ~ a un progetto** to give the green light to a project; **hanno dato il ~ ai lavori** they've begun o started work; **in ~ amichevole** in a friendly manner; **comporre una disputa in ~ amichevole** (*Dir*) to settle a dispute out of court; **in ~ eccezionale** as an exception; **in ~ privata** o **confidenziale** (*dire etc*) in confidence; **in ~ provvisoria** provisionally; **V~ lattea** (*Astr*) Milky Way; **~ di mezzo** middle course; **non c'è ~ di scampo** o **d'uscita** there's no way out; **vie di comunicazione** communication routes

viabilità *sf* (*di strada*) practicability; (*rete stradale*) roads *pl*, road network

via'dotto *sm* viaduct

viaggi'are [viad'dʒare] *vi* to travel; **le merci viaggiano via mare** the goods go by sea

viaggia'tore, -'trice [viadd'ʒatore] *ag* travelling (*Brit*), traveling (*US*) ■ *sm* traveller (*Brit*), traveler (*US*), passenger

vi'aggio [vi'addʒo] *sm* travel(ling); (*tragitto*) journey, trip; **buon ~!** have a good trip!; **~ d'affari** business trip; **~ di nozze** honeymoon; **~ organizzato** package tour o holiday

vi'ale *sm* avenue

vian'dante *sm/f* vagrant

vi'atico, -ci *sm* (*Rel*) viaticum; (*fig*) encouragement

via'vai *sm* coming and going, bustle

vi'brare *vi* to vibrate; (*agitarsi*): **~ (di)** to quiver (with)

vibra'tore *sm* vibrator

vibrazi'one [vibrat'tsjone] *sf* vibration

vi'cario *sm* (*apostolico etc*) vicar

'vice ['vitʃe] *sm/f* deputy ■ *prefisso* vice

vice'console [vitʃe'kɔnsole] *sm* vice-consul

vicediret'tore, -'trice [vitʃediret'tore] *sm/f* assistant manager(-manageress); (*di giornale etc*) deputy editor

vi'cenda [vi'tʃɛnda] *sf* event; **vicende** *sfpl* (*sorte*) fortunes; **a ~** in turn; **con alterne vicende** with mixed fortunes

vicen'devole [vitʃen'devole] *ag* mutual, reciprocal

vicen'tino, -a [vitʃen'tino] *ag* of (o from) Vicenza

vicepresi'dente [vitʃepresi'dɛnte] *sm* vice-president, vice-chairman

vice'versa [vitʃe'vɛrsa] *av* vice versa; **da Roma a Pisa e ~** from Rome to Pisa and back

vi'chingo, -a, ghi, ghe [vi'kingo] *ag, sm/f* Viking

vici'nanza [vitʃi'nantsa] *sf* nearness, closeness; **vicinanze** *sfpl* (*paraggi*) neighbourhood (*Brit*), neighborhood (*US*), vicinity

vici'nato [vitʃi'nato] *sm* neighbourhood (*Brit*), neighborhood (*US*); (*vicini*) neighbo(u)rs *pl*

vi'cino, -a [vi'tʃino] *ag* (*gen*) near; (*nello spazio*) near, nearby; (*accanto*) next; (*nel tempo*) near, close at hand ■ *sm/f* neighbour (*Brit*), neighbor (*US*) ■ *av* near, close; **da ~** (*guardare*) close up; (*esaminare, seguire*) closely; (*conoscere*) well, intimately; **~ a** *prep* near (to), close to; (*accanto a*) beside; **mi sono stati molto vicini** (*fig*) they were very supportive towards me; **~ di casa** neighbo(u)r

vicissi'tudini [vitʃissi'tudini] *sfpl* trials and tribulations

'vicolo *sm* alley; **~ cieco** blind alley

'video *sm inv* (*TV: schermo*) screen

video'camera *sf* camcorder

videocas'setta *sf* videocassette

videochia'mare [videokja'mare] *vt* to video call

videodipen'dente *sm/f* telly addict ■ *ag*: **un pigrone ~** a couch potato

videofo'nino *sm* video mobile

videogi'oco, -chi [video'dʒɔko] *sm* video game

videono'leggio [videono'leddʒo] *sm* video rental

videoregistra'tore [videoredʒistra'tore] *sm* (*apparecchio*) video (recorder)

video'teca, -che *sf* video shop

videote'lefono *sm* videophone

videotermi'nale *sm* visual display unit

'vidi *etc vb vedi* **vedere**

vidi'mare *vt* (*Amm*) to authenticate

vidimazi'one [vidimat'tsjone] *sf* (*Amm*) authentication

Vi'enna *sf* Vienna

vien'nese *ag, sm/f* Viennese *inv*

vie'tare *vt* to forbid; (*Amm*) to prohibit; (*libro*) to ban; **~ a qn di fare** to forbid sb to do; to prohibit sb from doing

vie'tato, -a *ag* (*vedi vb*) forbidden; prohibited; banned; **"~ fumare/l'ingresso"** "no smoking/admittance"; **~ ai minori di 14/18 anni** prohibited to children under 14/18; **"senso ~"** (*Aut*) "no entry"; **"sosta vietata"** (*Aut*) "no parking"

Viet'nam *sm*: **il ~** Vietnam

vietna'mita, -i, e *ag, sm/f, sm* Vietnamese *inv*

vi'eto, -a *ag* worthless

vi'gente [vi'dʒɛnte] *ag* in force

vigere ['vidʒere] vi (difettivo: si usa solo alla terza persona) to be in force; **in casa mia vige l'abitudine di ...** at home we are in the habit of ...

vigilante [vidʒi'lante] ag vigilant, watchful

vigilanza [vidʒi'lantsa] sf vigilance; (sorveglianza: di operai, alunni) supervision; (: di sospetti, criminali) surveillance; **~ notturna** night-watchman service

vigilare [vidʒi'lare] vt to watch over, keep an eye on; **~ che** to make sure that, see to it that

vigilato, -a [vidʒi'lato] sm/f (Dir) person under police surveillance

vigilatrice [vidʒila'tritʃe] sf: **~ d'infanzia** nursery-school teacher; **~ scolastica** school health officer

vigile ['vidʒile] ag watchful ■ sm (anche: **vigile urbano**) policeman (in towns); **~ del fuoco** fireman; see note

vigilessa [vidʒi'lessa] sf (traffic) policewoman

vigilia [vi'dʒilja] sf (giorno antecedente) eve; **la ~ di Natale** Christmas Eve

vigliaccheria [viʎʎakke'ria] sf cowardice

vigliacco, -a, chi, che [viʎ'ʎakko] ag cowardly ■ sm/f coward

vigna ['viɲɲa] sf, **vigneto** [viɲ'ɲeto] sm vineyard

vignetta [viɲ'ɲetta] sf cartoon; (Auto; vignetta autostradale : tassa) car tax (for motorways); (: adesivo) sticker showing that this tax has been paid

vigogna [vi'goɲɲa] sf vicuña

vigore sm vigour (Brit), vigor (US); (Dir): **essere/entrare in ~** to be in/come into force; **non è più in ~** it is no longer in force, it no longer applies

vigoroso, -a ag vigorous

vile ag (spregevole) low, mean, base; (codardo) cowardly

vilipendere vt to despise, scorn

vilipendio sm contempt, scorn

vilipeso, -a pp di **vilipendere**

villa sf villa

villaggio [vil'laddʒo] sm village; **~ turistico** holiday village

villania sf rudeness, lack of manners; **fare (o dire) una ~ a qn** to be rude to sb

villano, -a ag rude, ill-mannered ■ sm/f boor

villeggiante [villed'dʒante] sm/f holiday-maker (Brit), vacationer (US)

villeggiare [villed'dʒare] vi to holiday, spend one's holidays, vacation (US)

villeggiatura [villeddʒa'tura] sf holiday(s pl) (Brit), vacation (US); **luogo di ~** (holiday) resort

villetta sf, **villino** sm small house (with a garden), cottage

villoso, -a ag hairy

viltà sf cowardice no pl; (gesto) cowardly act

Viminale sm see note

vimine sm wicker; **mobili di vimini** wicker furniture sg

vinaio sm wine merchant

vincere ['vintʃere] vt (in guerra, al gioco, a una gara) to defeat, beat; (premio, guerra, partita) to win; (fig) to overcome, conquer ■ vi to win; **~ qn in** (abilità, bellezza) to surpass sb in

vincita ['vintʃita] sf win; (denaro vinto) winnings pl

vincitore, -trice [vintʃi'tore] sm/f winner; (Mil) victor

vincolante ag binding

vincolare vt to bind; (Comm: denaro) to tie up

vincolato, -a ag: **deposito ~** (Comm) fixed deposit

vincolo sm (fig) bond, tie; (Dir) obligation

vinicolo, -a ag wine cpd; **regione vinicola** wine-producing area

vinificazione [vinifikat'tsjone] sf wine-making

vino sm wine; **~ bianco/rosso** white/red wine

vinsi etc vb vedi **vincere**

vinto, -a pp di **vincere** ■ ag: **darla vinta a qn** to let sb have his (o her) way; **darsi per ~** to give up, give in

viola sf (Bot) violet; (Mus) viola ■ ag, sm inv (colore) purple

violare vt (chiesa) to desecrate, violate; (giuramento, legge) to violate

violazione [violat'tsjone] sf desecration; violation; **~ di domicilio** (Dir) breaking and entering

violentare vt to use violence on; (donna) to rape

violento, -a ag violent

violenza [vio'lɛntsa] sf violence; **~ carnale** rape

violetto, -a ag, sm (colore) violet ■ sf (Bot) violet

V

violi'nista, -i, e *sm/f* violinist
vio'lino *sm* violin
violoncel'lista, -i, e [violontʃel'lista] *sm/f* cellist, cello player
violon'cello [violon'tʃɛllo] *sm* cello
vi'ottolo *sm* path, track
VIP *sm/f inv* (= *Very Important Person*) VIP
'vipera *sf* viper, adder
vi'raggio [vi'raddʒo] *sm* (*Naut, Aer*) turn; (*Fot*) toning
vi'rale *ag* viral
vi'rare *vi* (*Naut*) to come about; (*Aer*) to turn; (*Fot*) to tone; **~ di bordo** to change course
vi'rata *sf* coming about; turning; change of course
'virgola *sf* (*Ling*) comma; (*Mat*) point
virgo'lette *sfpl* inverted commas, quotation marks
vi'rile *ag* (*proprio dell'uomo*) masculine; (*non puerile, da uomo*) manly, virile
virili'tà *sf* masculinity; manliness; (*sessuale*) virility
virtù *sf inv* virtue; **in** *o* **per ~ di** by virtue of, by
virtu'ale *ag* virtual
virtu'oso, -a *ag* virtuous ■ *sm/f* (*Mus etc*) virtuoso
viru'lento, -a *ag* virulent
'virus *sm inv* virus
visa'gista, -i, e [viza'dʒista] *sm/f* beautician
visce'rale [viʃʃe'rale] *ag* (*Med*) visceral; (*fig*) profound, deep-rooted
'viscere ['viʃʃere] *sm* (*Anat*) internal organ ■ *sfpl* (*di animale*) entrails *pl*; (*fig*) depths *pl*, bowels *pl*
'vischio ['viskjo] *sm* (*Bot*) mistletoe; (*pania*) birdlime
vischi'oso, -a [vis'kjoso] *ag* sticky
viscidità [viʃʃidi'ta] *sf* sliminess
'viscido, -a ['viʃʃido] *ag* slimy
vis'conte, -'essa *sm/f* viscount/viscountess
viscosità *sf* viscosity
vis'coso, -a *ag* viscous
vi'sibile *ag* visible
visi'bilio *sm*: **andare in ~** to go into raptures
visibilità *sf* visibility
visi'era *sf* (*di elmo*) visor; (*di berretto*) peak
visio'nare *vt* (*gen*) to look at, examine; (*Cine*) to screen
visio'nario, -a *ag, sm/f* visionary
visi'one *sf* vision; **prendere ~ di qc** to examine sth, look sth over; **prima/seconda ~** (*Cine*) first/second showing
'visita *sf* visit; (*Med*) visit, call; (: *esame*) examination; **far ~ a qn, andare in ~ da qn** to visit sb, pay sb a visit; **in ~ ufficiale in Italia** on an official visit to Italy; **orario di visite** (*ospedale*) visiting hours; **~ di controllo** (*Med*) checkup; **~ a domicilio** house call; **~ guidata** guided tour; **~ sanitaria** sanitary inspection
visi'tare *vt* to visit; (*Med*) to visit, call on; (: *esaminare*) to examine
visita'tore, -'trice *sm/f* visitor
vi'sivo, -a *ag* visual
'viso *sm* face; **fare buon ~ a cattivo gioco** to make the best of things
vi'sone *sm* mink
vi'sore *sm* (*Fot*) viewer
'vispo, -a *ag* quick, lively
'vissi *etc vb vedi* **vivere**
vis'suto, -a *pp di* **vivere** ■ *ag* (*aria, modo di fare*) experienced
'vista *sf* (*facoltà*) (eye)sight; (*fatto di vedere*): **la ~ di** the sight of; (*veduta*) view; **con ~ sul lago** with a view over the lake; **sparare a ~** to shoot on sight; **pagabile a ~** payable on demand; **in ~** in sight; **avere in ~ qc** to have sth in view; **mettersi in ~** to draw attention to o.s.; (*peg*) to show off; **perdere qn di ~** to lose sight of sb; (*fig*) to lose touch with sb; **far ~ di fare** to pretend to do; **a ~ d'occhio** as far as the eye can see; (*fig*) before one's very eyes
vis'tare *vt* to approve; (*Amm: passaporto*) to visa
'visto, -a *pp di* **vedere** ■ *sm* visa; **~ che** *cong* seeing (that); **~ d'ingresso/di transito** entry/transit visa; **~ permanente/di soggiorno** permanent/tourist visa
vis'toso, -a *ag* gaudy, garish; (*ingente*) considerable
visu'ale *ag* visual
visualiz'zare [vizualid'dzare] *vt* to visualize
visualizza'tore [vizualiddza'tore] *sm* (*Inform*) visual display unit, VDU
visualizzazi'one [vizualiddzat'tsjone] *sf* (*Inform*) display
'vita *sf* life; (*Anat*) waist; **essere in ~** to be alive; **pieno di ~** full of life; **a ~** for life; **membro a ~** life member
vi'tale *ag* vital
vitalità *sf* vitality
vita'lizio, -a [vita'littsjo] *ag* life *cpd* ■ *sm* life annuity
vita'mina *sf* vitamin
'vite *sf* (*Bot*) vine; (*Tecn*) screw; **giro di ~** (*anche fig*) turn of the screw
vi'tello *sm* (*Zool*) calf; (*carne*) veal; (*pelle*) calfskin
vi'ticcio [vi'tittʃo] *sm* (*Bot*) tendril
viticol'tore *sm* wine grower
viticol'tura *sf* wine growing
'vitreo, -a *ag* vitreous; (*occhio, sguardo*) glassy
'vittima *sf* victim

vitti'mismo *sm* self-pity
'vitto *sm* food; (*in un albergo etc*) board; **~ e alloggio** board and lodging
vit'toria *sf* victory
vittori'ano, -a *ag* Victorian
vittori'oso, -a *ag* victorious
vitupe'rare *vt* to rail at *o* against
vi'uzza [vi'uttsa] *sf* (*in città*) alley
'viva *escl*: **~ il re!** long live the king!
vivacchi'are [vivak'kjare] *vi* to scrape a living
vi'vace [vi'vatʃe] *ag* (*vivo, animato*) lively; (*: mente*) lively, sharp; (*colore*) bright
vivacità [vivatʃi'ta] *sf* liveliness; brightness
vivaciz'zare [vivatʃid'dzare] *vt* to liven up
vi'vaio *sm* (*di pesci*) hatchery; (*Agr*) nursery
viva'mente *av* (*commuoversi*) deeply, profoundly; (*ringraziare etc*) sincerely, warmly
vi'vanda *sf* food; (*piatto*) dish
viva'voce [viva'votʃe] *sm inv* (*dispositivo*) loudspeaker ■ *ag inv*: **telefono ~** speakerphone; **mettere in ~** to switch on the loudspeaker
vi'vente *ag* living, alive; **i viventi** the living
'vivere *vi* to live ■ *vt* to live; (*passare: brutto momento*) to live through, go through; (*sentire: gioie, pene di qn*) to share ■ *sm* life; (*anche:* **modo di vivere**) way of life; **viveri** *smpl* food *sg*, provisions; **~ di** to live on
vi'veur [vi'vœr] *sm inv* pleasure-seeker
'vivido, -a *ag* (*colore*) vivid, bright
vivifi'care *vt* to enliven, give life to; (*piante etc*) to revive
vivisezi'one [viviset'tsjone] *sf* vivisection
'vivo, -a *ag* (*vivente*) alive, living; (*fig*) lively; (*: colore*) bright, brilliant ■ *sm*: **entrare nel ~ di una questione** to get to the heart of a matter; **i vivi** the living; **esperimenti su animali vivi** experiments on live *o* living animals; **~ e vegeto** hale and hearty; **farsi ~** (*fig*) to show one's face; to keep in touch; **con ~ rammarico** with deep regret; **congratulazioni vivissime** heartiest congratulations; **con i più vivi ringraziamenti** with deepest *o* warmest thanks; **ritrarre dal ~** to paint from life; **pungere qn nel ~** (*fig*) to cut sb to the quick
vivrò *etc vb vedi* **vivere**
vizi'are [vit'tsjare] *vt* (*bambino*) to spoil; (*corrompere moralmente*) to corrupt; (*Dir*) to invalidate
vizi'ato, -a [vit'tsjato] *ag* spoilt; (*aria, acqua*) polluted; (*Dir*) invalid, invalidated
'vizio ['vittsjo] *sm* (*morale*) vice; (*cattiva abitudine*) bad habit; (*imperfezione*) flaw, defect; (*errore*) fault, mistake; **~ di forma** legal flaw *o* irregularity; **~ procedurale** procedural error

vizi'oso, -a [vit'tsjoso] *ag* depraved; (*inesatto*) incorrect; **circolo ~** vicious circle
V.le *abbr* = **viale**
vocabo'lario *sm* (*dizionario*) dictionary; (*lessico*) vocabulary
vo'cabolo *sm* word
vo'cale *ag* vocal ■ *sf* vowel
vocazi'one [vokat'tsjone] *sf* vocation; (*fig*) natural bent
'voce ['votʃe] *sf* voice; (*diceria*) rumour (*Brit*), rumor (*US*); (*di un elenco: in bilancio*) item; (*di dizionario*) entry; **parlare a alta/bassa ~** to speak in a loud/low *o* soft voice; **fare la ~ grossa** to raise one's voice; **dar ~ a qc** to voice sth, give voice to sth; **a gran ~** in a loud voice, loudly; **te lo dico a ~** I'll tell you when I see you; **a una ~** unanimously; **aver ~ in capitolo** (*fig*) to have a say in the matter; **voci di corridoio** rumours
voci'are [vo'tʃare] *vi* to shout, yell
vocife'rante [votʃife'rante] *ag* noisy
vo'cio [vo'tʃio] *sm* shouting
'vodka *sf inv* vodka
'voga *sf* (*Naut*) rowing; (*usanza*): **essere in ~** to be in fashion *o* in vogue
vo'gare *vi* to row
voga'tore, -trice *sm/f* oarsman(-woman) ■ *sm* rowing machine
vogherò *etc vb vedi* **vogare**
'voglia ['vɔʎʎa] *sf* desire, wish; (*macchia*) birthmark; **aver ~ di qc/di fare** to feel like sth/like doing; (*più forte*) to want sth/to do; **di buona ~** willingly
'voglio *etc* ['vɔʎʎo] *vb vedi* **volere**
vogli'oso, -a [voʎ'ʎoso] *ag* (*sguardo etc*) longing; (*più forte*) full of desire
'voi *pron* you; **~ stessi(e)** you yourselves
voi'altri *pron* you
vol. *abbr* (= *volume*) vol.
vo'lano *sm* (*Sport*) shuttlecock; (*Tecn*) flywheel
vo'lant [vɔ'l] *sm inv* frill
vo'lante *ag* flying ■ *sm* (steering) wheel ■ *sf* (*Polizia: anche:* **squadra volante**) flying squad
volanti'naggio [volanti'naddʒo] *sm* leafleting
volanti'nare *vt* (*distribuire volantini*) to leaflet, hand out leaflets
volan'tino *sm* leaflet
vo'lare *vi* (*uccello, aereo, fig*) to fly; (*cappello*) to blow away *o* off, fly away *o* off; **~ via** to fly away *o* off
vo'lata *sf* flight; (*d'uccelli*) flock, flight; (*corsa*) rush; (*Sport*) final sprint; **passare di ~ da qn** to drop in on sb briefly
vo'latile *ag* (*Chim*) volatile ■ *sm* (*Zool*) bird
volatiliz'zarsi [volatilid'dzarsi] *vr* (*Chim*) to volatilize; (*fig*) to vanish, disappear

vo'lente *ag*: **verrai ~ o nolente** you'll come whether you like it or not
volente'roso, -a *ag* willing, keen
volenti'eri *av* willingly; **"~"** "with pleasure", "I'd be glad to"

⬤ PAROLA CHIAVE

vo'lere *sm* will, wish(es); **contro il volere di** against the wishes of; **per volere di qn** in obedience to sb's will *o* wishes
■ *vt* **1** (*esigere, desiderare*) to want; **volere fare qc** to want to do sth; **volere che qn faccia qc** to want sb to do sth; **vorrei andarmene** I'd like to go; **vorrei che se ne andasse** I'd like him to go; **vorrei quello lì!** I'd like that one; **volevo parlartene** I meant to talk to you about it; **come vuoi** as you like; **la vogliono al telefono** there's a call for you; **che tu lo voglia o no** whether you like it or not; **vuoi un caffè?** would you like a coffee?; **senza volere** (*inavvertitamente*) without meaning to, unintentionally; **te la sei voluta** you asked for it; **la tradizione vuole che ...** custom requires that ...; **la leggenda vuole che ...** legend has it that ...
2 (*consentire*): **vogliate attendere, per piacere** please wait; **vogliamo andare?** shall we go?; **vuole essere così gentile da ...?** would you be so kind as to ...?; **non ha voluto ricevermi** he wouldn't see me
3: **volerci** (*essere necessario: materiale, attenzione*) to be needed; (: *tempo*) to take; **quanta farina ci vuole per questa torta?** how much flour do you need for this cake?; **ci vuole un'ora per arrivare a Venezia** it takes an hour to get to Venice; **è quel che ci vuole** it's just what is needed
4: **voler bene a qn** (*amore*) to love sb; (*affetto*) to be fond of sb, like sb very much; **voler male a qn** to dislike sb; **volerne a qn** to bear sb a grudge; **voler dire** to mean; **voglio dire ...** I mean ...; **volevo ben dire!** I thought as much!

vol'gare *ag* vulgar
volgarità *sf* vulgarity
volgariz'zare [volgarid'dzare] *vt* to popularize
volgar'mente *av* (*in modo volgare*) vulgarly, coarsely; (*del popolo*) commonly, popularly
'volgere ['vɔldʒere] *vt* to turn ■ *vi* to turn; (*tendere*): **~ a**: **il tempo volge al brutto/al bello** the weather is breaking/is setting fair; **un rosso che volge al viola** a red verging on purple; **volgersi** *vr* to turn; **~ al peggio** to take a turn for the worse; **~ al termine** to draw to an end

'volgo *sm* common people
voli'era *sf* aviary
voli'tivo, -a *ag* strong-willed
'volli *etc vb vedi* **volere**
'volo *sm* flight; **ci sono due ore di ~ da Londra a Milano** it's a two-hour flight between London and Milan; **al ~**: **colpire qc al ~** to hit sth as it flies past; **prendere al ~** (*autobus, treno*) to catch at the last possible moment; (*palla*) to catch as it flies past; (*occasione*) to seize; **capire al ~** to understand straight away; **veduta a ~ d'uccello** bird's-eye view; **~ di linea** scheduled flight
volontà *sf inv* will; **a ~** (*mangiare, bere*) as much as one likes; **buona/cattiva ~** goodwill/lack of goodwill; **le sue ultime ~** (*testamento*) his last will and testament *sg*
volontaria'mente *av* voluntarily
volontari'ato *sm* (*Mil*) voluntary service; (*lavoro*) voluntary work
volon'tario, -a *ag* voluntary ■ *sm* (*Mil*) volunteer
'volpe *sf* fox
vol'pino, -a *ag* (*pelo, coda*) fox's; (*aspetto, astuzia*) fox-like ■ *sm* (*cane*) Pomeranian
vol'pone, -a *sm/f* (*fig*) old fox
'volsi *etc vb vedi* **volgere**
volt *sm inv* (*Elettr*) volt
'volta *sf* (*momento, circostanza*) time; (*turno, giro*) turn; (*curva*) turn, bend; (*Archit*) vault; (*direzione*): **partire alla ~ di** to set off for; **a mia** (*o* **tua** *etc*) **~** in turn; **una ~** once; **una ~ sola** only once; **c'era una ~** once upon a time there was; **le cose di una ~** the things of the past; **due volte** twice; **tre volte** three times; **una cosa per ~** one thing at a time; **una ~ o l'altra** one of these days; **una ~ per tutte** once and for all; **una ~ tanto** just for once; **lo facciamo un'altra ~** we'll do it another time *o* some other time; **a volte** at times, sometimes; **di ~ in ~** from time to time; **una ~ che** (*temporale*) once; (*causale*) since; **3 volte 4** 3 times 4; **ti ha dato di ~ il cervello?** have you gone out of your mind?
volta'faccia [volta'fattʃa] *sm inv* (*fig*) volte-face
vol'taggio [vol'taddʒo] *sm* (*Elettr*) voltage
vol'tare *vt* to turn; (*girare: moneta*) to turn over; (*rigirare*) to turn round ■ *vi* to turn; **voltarsi** *vr* to turn; to turn over; to turn round
voltas'tomaco *sm* nausea; (*fig*) disgust
volteggi'are [volted'dʒare] *vi* (*volare*) to circle; (*in equitazione*) to do trick riding; (*in ginnastica*) to vault
'volto, -a *pp di* **volgere** ■ *ag* (*inteso a*): **il mio discorso è ~ a spiegare ...** in my speech I intend to explain ... ■ *sm* face

vo'lubile *ag* changeable, fickle
vo'lume *sm* volume
volumi'noso, -a *ag* voluminous, bulky
vo'luta *sf* (*gen*) spiral; (*Archit*) volute
voluttà *sf* sensual pleasure *o* delight
voluttu'oso, -a *ag* voluptuous
vomi'tare *vt, vi* to vomit
'vomito *sm* vomit; **ho il ~** I feel sick
'vongola *sf* clam
vo'race [vo'ratʃe] *ag* voracious, greedy
voracità [voratʃi'ta] *sf* voracity, voraciousness
vo'ragine [vo'radʒine] *sf* abyss, chasm
vorrò *etc vb vedi* **volere**
'vortice ['vɔrtitʃe] *sm* whirl, vortex; (*fig*) whirl
vorti'coso, -a *ag* whirling
'vostro, -a *det*: **il(la) ~(a)** *etc* your ■ *pron*: **il(la) ~(a)** *etc* yours ■ *sm*: **avete speso del ~?** did you spend your own money? ■ *sf*: **la vostra** (*opinione*) your view; **i vostri** (*famiglia*) your family; **un ~ amico** a friend of yours; **è dei vostri, è dalla vostra** he's on your side; **l'ultima vostra** (*Comm: lettera*) your most recent letter; **alla vostra!** (*brindisi*) here's to you!, your health!
vo'tante *sm/f* voter
vo'tare *vi* to vote ■ *vt* (*sottoporre a votazione*) to take a vote on; (*approvare*) to vote for; (*Rel*): **~ qc a** to dedicate sth to; **votarsi** *vr* to devote o.s. to

votazi'one [votat'tsjone] *sf* vote, voting; **votazioni** *sfpl* (*Pol*) votes; (*Ins*) marks
'voto *sm* (*Pol*) vote; (*Ins*) mark (*Brit*), grade (*US*); (*Rel*) vow; (*: offerta*) votive offering; **aver voti belli/brutti** (*Ins*) to get good/bad marks *o* grades; **prendere i voti** to take one's vows; **~ di fiducia** vote of confidence
V.P. *abbr* (= *vicepresidente*) VP
VR *sigla* = **Verona**
v.r. *abbr* (= *vedi retro*) PTO
vs. *abbr* (= *vostro*) yr
v.s. *abbr* = **vedi sopra**
VT *sigla* = **Viterbo**
V.U. *abbr* = **vigile urbano**
vul'canico, -a, ci, che *ag* volcanic
vulcanizzazi'one [vulkaniddzat'tsjone] *sf* vulcanization
vul'cano *sm* volcano
vulne'rabile *ag* vulnerable
vulnerabilità *sf* vulnerability
vu'oi, vu'ole *vb vedi* **volere**
vuo'tare *vt,* **vuo'tarsi** *vr* to empty
vu'oto, -a *ag* empty; (*fig: privo*): **~ di** (*senso etc*) devoid of ■ *sm* empty space, gap; (*spazio in bianco*) blank; (*Fisica*) vacuum; (*fig: mancanza*) gap, void; **a mani vuote** empty-handed; **assegno a ~** dud cheque (*Brit*), bad check (*US*); **~ d'aria** air pocket; **"~ a perdere"** "no deposit"; **"~ a rendere"** "returnable bottle"

V

Ww

W, w ['dɔppjovu] *sf o m inv* (*lettera*) W, w;
 W come Washington ≈ W for William
W *abbr* = **viva, evviva**
wafer ['vafer] *sm inv* (*Cuc, Elettr*) wafer
wagon-lit [vagɔ'li] *sm inv* (*Ferr*) sleeping car
walkman® ['wɔːkmən] *sm inv* Walkman®
water closet ['wɔːtə'klɔzɪt] *sm inv* toilet,
 lavatory
watt [vat] *sm inv* (*Elettr*) watt
wattora [vat'tora] *sm inv* (*Elettr*) watt-hour
WC *sm inv* WC
web [web] *sm:* **il ~** the web; **cercare nel ~**

to search the web ■ *ag inv:* **pagina ~** webpage
webcam [web'kam] *sf inv* (*Comput*) webcam
weekend ['wiːkend] *sm inv* weekend
western ['wɛstern] *ag* (*Cine*) cowboy *cpd*
 ■ *sm inv* western, cowboy film; **~ all'italiana**
 spaghetti western
whisky ['wiski] *sm inv* whisky
Wi-Fi [uai'fai] (*Comput*) *nm* Wi-Fi ■ *ag inv*
 Wi-Fi
windsurf ['windsəːf] *sm inv* (*tavola*)
 windsurfer, sailboard; (*sport*) windsurfing
würstel ['vyrstəl] *sm inv* frankfurter

X, x [iks] *sf o m inv* (*lettera*) X, x; **X come Xeres** ≈ X for Xmas
xenofo'bia [ksenofo'bia] *sf* xenophobia
xe'nofobo, -a [kse'nɔfobo] *ag* xenophobic ■ *sm/f* xenophobe

'xeres ['ksɛres] *sm inv* sherry
xero'copia [ksero'kɔpja] *sf* xerox®, photocopy
xerocopi'are [kseroko'pjare] *vt* to photocopy
xi'lofono [ksi'lɔfono] *sm* xylophone

Y, y ['ipsilon] *sf o m inv (lettera)* Y, y; **Y come Yacht** ≈ Y for Yellow *(Brit)*, ≈ Y for Yoke *(US)*
yacht [jɔt] *sm inv* yacht
ˈ**yankee** ['jæŋki] *sm/f inv* Yank, Yankee
Y.C.I. *abbr* = **Yacht Club d'Italia**

ˈ**Yemen** ['jemen] *sm*: **lo ~** Yemen
yen [jen] *sm inv (moneta)* yen
ˈ**yiddish** ['jidiʃ] *ag inv, sm inv* Yiddish
ˈ**yoga** ['jɔga] *ag inv, sm* yoga *(cpd)*
yogurt ['jɔgurt] *sm inv* yog(h)urt

Zz

Z, z ['dzɛta] *sf o m inv (lettera)* Z, z; **Z come Zara** ≈ Z for Zebra

zabai'one [dzaba'jone] *sm dessert made of egg yolks, sugar and marsala*

zaf'fata [tsaf'fata] *sf (tanfo)* stench

zaffe'rano [dzaffe'rano] *sm* saffron

zaf'firo [dzaf'firo] *sm* sapphire

'zagara ['dzagara] *sf* orange blossom

zai'netto [dzai'netto] *sm* (small) rucksack

'zaino ['dzaino] *sm* rucksack

Za'ire [dza'ire] *sm:* **lo ~** Zaire

'Zambia ['dzambja] *sm:* **lo ~** Zambia

'zampa ['tsampa] *sf (di animale: gamba)* leg; (*: piede*) paw; **a quattro zampe** on all fours; **zampe di gallina** *(calligrafia)* scrawl; *(rughe)* crow's feet

zam'pata [tsam'pata] *sf (di cane, gatto)* blow with a paw

zampet'tare [tsampet'tare] *vi* to scamper

zampil'lare [tsampil'lare] *vi* to gush, spurt

zam'pillo [tsam'pillo] *sm* gush, spurt

zam'pino [tsam'pino] *sm* paw; **qui c'è sotto il suo ~** *(fig)* he's had a hand in this

zam'pogna [tsam'poɲɲa] *sf instrument similar to bagpipes*

'zanna ['tsanna] *sf (di elefante)* tusk; *(di carnivori)* fang

zan'zara [dzan'dzara] *sf* mosquito

zanzari'era [dzandza'rjera] *sf* mosquito net

'zappa ['tsappa] *sf* hoe

zap'pare [tsap'pare] *vt* to hoe

zappa'tura [tsappa'tura] *sf (Agr)* hoeing

'zapping ['tsapɪŋ] *sm (TV)* channel-hopping

zar, za'rina [tsar, tsa'rina] *sm/f* tsar/tsarina

zat'tera ['dzattera] *sf* raft

za'vorra [dza'vɔrra] *sf* ballast

'zazzera ['tsattsera] *sf* shock of hair

'zebra ['dzɛbra] *sf* zebra; **zebre** *sfpl (Aut)* zebra crossing *sg (Brit)*, crosswalk *sg (US)*

ze'brato, -a [dze'brato] *ag* with black and white stripes; **strisce zebrate, attraversamento ~** *(Aut)* zebra crossing *(Brit)*, crosswalk *(US)*

zecca, -che ['tsekka] *sf (Zool)* tick; *(officina di monete)* mint

zec'chino [tsek'kino] *sm* gold coin; **oro ~** pure gold

ze'lante [dze'lante] *ag* zealous

'zelo ['dzɛlo] *sm* zeal

'zenit ['dzɛnit] *sm* zenith

'zenzero ['dzendzero] *sm* ginger

'zeppa ['tseppa] *sf* wedge

'zeppo, -a ['tseppo] *ag:* **~ di** crammed *o* packed with

zer'bino [dzer'bino] *sm* doormat

'zero ['dzɛro] *sm* zero, nought; **vincere per tre a ~** *(Sport)* to win three-nil

'zeta ['dzɛta] *sm o f* zed, (the letter) z

'zia ['tsia] *sf* aunt

zibel'lino [dzibel'lino] *sm* sable

zi'gano, -a [tsi'gano] *ag, sm/f* gypsy

'zigomo ['dzigomo] *sm* cheekbone

zigri'nare [dzigri'nare] *vt (gen)* to knurl; *(pellame)* to grain; *(monete)* to mill

zig'zag [dzig'dzag] *sm inv* zigzag; **andare a ~** to zigzag

Zim'babwe [tsim'babwe] *sm:* **lo ~** Zimbabwe

zim'bello [dzim'bɛllo] *sm (oggetto di burle)* laughing-stock

'zinco ['dzinko] *sm* zinc

zinga'resco, -a, schi, sche [dzinga'resko] *ag* gypsy *cpd*

'zingaro, -a ['dzingaro] *sm/f* gypsy

'zio ['tsio] *(pl* **zii***) sm* uncle; **zii** *smpl (zio e zia)* uncle and aunt

zip'pare [dzip'pare] *vt (Inform)* to zip

zi'tella [dzi'tɛlla] *sf* spinster; *(peg)* old maid

zit'tire [tsit'tire] *vt* to silence, hush *o* shut up ■ *vi* to hiss

'zitto, -a ['tsitto] *ag* quiet, silent; **sta' ~!** be quiet!

ziz'zania [dzid'dzanja] *sf (Bot)* darnel; *(fig)* discord; **gettare** *o* **seminare ~** to sow discord

'zoccolo ['tsɔkkolo] *sm (calzatura)* clog; *(di cavallo etc)* hoof; *(Archit)* plinth; *(di parete)* skirting (board); *(di armadio)* base

z

zodia'cale [dzodia'kale] *ag* zodiac *cpd*; **segno** ~ sign of the zodiac

zo'diaco [dzo'diako] *sm* zodiac

zolfa'nello [tsolfa'nɛllo] *sm* (sulphur) match

'zolfo ['tsolfo] *sm* sulphur (*Brit*), sulfur (*US*)

'zolla ['dzolla] *sf* clod (of earth)

zol'letta [dzol'letta] *sf* sugar lump

'zona ['dzɔna] *sf* zone, area; **~ di depressione** (*Meteor*) trough of low pressure; **~ erogena** erogenous zone; **~ pedonale** pedestrian precinct; **~ verde** (*di abitato*) green area

'zonzo ['dzondzo]: **a ~** *av*: **andare a ~** to wander about, stroll about

'zoo ['dzɔo] *sm inv* zoo

zoolo'gia [dzoolo'dʒia] *sf* zoology

zoo'logico, -a, ci, che [dzoo'lɔdʒiko] *ag* zoological

zo'ologo, -a, gi, ghe [dzo'ɔlogo] *sm/f* zoologist

zoosa'fari [dzoosa'fari] *sm inv* safari park

zoo'tecnico, -a, ci, che [dzoo'tekniko] *ag* zootechnical; **il patrimonio ~ di un paese** a country's livestock resources

zoppi'care [tsoppi'kare] *vi* to limp; (*fig: mobile*) to be shaky, rickety

'zoppo, -a ['tsɔppo] *ag* lame; (*fig: mobile*) shaky, rickety

zoti'cone [dzoti'kone] *sm* lout

ZTL [dzetati'ɛlle] *sigla f* (= *Zona a Traffico Limitato*) *controlled traffic zone*

zu'ava [dzu'ava] *sf*: **pantaloni alla ~** knickerbockers

'zucca, -che ['tsukka] *sf* (*Bot*) marrow (*Brit*), vegetable marrow (*US*); pumpkin; (*scherzoso*) head

zucche'rare [tsukke'rare] *vt* to put sugar in

zucche'rato, -a [tsukke'rato] *ag* sweet, sweetened

zuccheri'era [tsukke'rjɛra] *sf* sugar bowl

zuccheri'ficio [tsukkeri'fitʃo] *sm* sugar refinery

zucche'rino, -a [tsukke'rino] *ag* sugary, sweet

'zucchero ['tsukkero] *sm* sugar; **~ di canna** cane sugar; **~ caramellato** caramel; **~ filato** candy floss, cotton candy (*US*); **~ a velo** icing sugar (*Brit*), confectioner's sugar (*US*)

zucche'roso, -a [tsukke'roso] *ag* sugary

zuc'china [tsuk'kina] *sf*, **zuc'chino** [tsuk'kino] *sm* courgette (*Brit*), zucchini (*US*)

zuc'cotto [tsuk'kɔtto] *sm* ice-cream sponge

'zuffa ['tsuffa] *sf* brawl

zufo'lare [tsufo'lare] *vt, vi* to whistle

'zufolo ['tsufolo] *sm* (*Mus*) flageolet

'zuppa ['tsuppa] *sf* soup; (*fig*) mixture, muddle; **~ inglese** (*Cuc*) *dessert made with sponge cake, custard and chocolate*, ≈ trifle (*Brit*)

zuppi'era [tsup'pjɛra] *sf* soup tureen

'zuppo, -a ['tsuppo] *ag*: **~ (di)** drenched (with), soaked (with)

Zu'rigo [dzu'rigo] *sf* Zurich

Aa

A, a [eɪ] *n* (*letter*) A, a *for m inv* (*Scol: mark*)
≈ 10 (*ottimo*); (*Mus*): **A** la *m*; **A for Andrew**,
(*US*) **A for Able** ≈ A come Ancona; **from A to
Z** dall'A alla Z; **A road** *n* (*Brit Aut*) ≈ strada
statale; **A shares** *npl* (*Brit Stock Exchange*)
azioni *fpl* senza diritto di voto; **A to Z**® *n*
stradario

O **KEYWORD**

a [ə] (*before vowel or silent h: an*) *indef art* **1** un,
uno (+ *s impure, gn, pn, ps, x, z*), una *f*, un' + *vowel*;
a book un libro; **a mirror** uno specchio; **an
apple** una mela; **she's a doctor** è medico
2 (*instead of the number "one"*) un, una *f*; **a year
ago** un anno fa; **a hundred/thousand
pounds** cento/mille sterline
3 (*in expressing ratios, prices etc*) a, per; **3 a day/
week** 3 al giorno/alla settimana; **10 km an
hour** 10 km all'ora; **£5 a person** 5 sterline a
persona *or* per persona

a. *abbr* = **acre**
A2 *n abbr* (*Brit: Scol*) *seconda parte del diploma di
studi superiori chiamato "A level"*
AA *n abbr* (*Brit*: = *Automobile Association*) ≈ A.C.I.
m (= *Automobile Club d'Italia*); (*US*: = *Associate in/
of Arts*) *titolo di studio*; (= *Alcoholics Anonymous*)
A.A. *f* (= *Anonima Alcolisti*); (*Mil*) = **anti-aircraft**
AAA *n abbr* (= *American Automobile Association*)
≈ A.C.I. *m* (= *Automobile Club d'Italia*); (*Brit*)
= **Amateur Athletics Association**
A & R *n abbr* (*Mus*) = **artists and repertoire**;
~ man talent scout *m inv*
AAUP *n abbr* (= *American Association of University
Professors*) *associazione dei professori universitari*
AB *abbr* (*Brit*) = **able-bodied seaman**; (*Canada*)
= **Alberta**
aback [ə'bæk] *adv*: **to be taken ~** essere
sbalordito(-a)
abacus (*pl* **abaci**) ['æbəkəs, -saɪ] *n*
pallottoliere *m*, abaco
abandon [ə'bændən] *vt* abbandonare ■ *n*

abbandono; **to ~ ship** abbandonare la nave
abandoned [ə'bændənd] *adj* (*child, house etc*)
abbandonato(-a); (*unrestrained: manner*)
disinvolto(-a)
abase [ə'beɪs] *vt*: **to ~ o.s. (so far as to do)**
umiliarsi *or* abbassarsi (al punto di fare)
abashed [ə'bæʃt] *adj* imbarazzato(-a)
abate [ə'beɪt] *vi* calmarsi
abatement [ə'beɪtmənt] *n* (*of pollution, noise*)
soppressione *f*, eliminazione *f*; **noise ~
society** associazione *f* per la lotta contro
i rumori
abattoir ['æbətwɑːʳ] *n* (*Brit*) mattatoio
abbey ['æbɪ] *n* abbazia, badia
abbot ['æbət] *n* abate *m*
abbreviate [ə'briːvɪeɪt] *vt* abbreviare
abbreviation [əbriːvɪ'eɪʃən] *n* abbreviazione *f*
ABC *n abbr* (= *American Broadcasting Company*) *rete
televisiva americana*
abdicate ['æbdɪkeɪt] *vt* abdicare a ■ *vi* abdicare
abdication [æbdɪ'keɪʃən] *n* abdicazione *f*
abdomen ['æbdəmən] *n* addome *m*
abdominal [æb'dɔmɪnl] *adj* addominale
abduct [æb'dʌkt] *vt* rapire
abduction [æb'dʌkʃən] *n* rapimento
Aberdonian [æbə'dəunɪən] *adj* di Aberdeen
■ *n* abitante *m/f* di Aberdeen, originario(-a)
di Aberdeen
aberration [æbə'reɪʃən] *n* aberrazione *f*
abet [ə'bɛt] *vt see* **aid**
abeyance [ə'beɪəns] *n*: **in ~** in sospeso
abhor [əb'hɔːʳ] *vt* aborrire
abhorrent [əb'hɔrənt] *adj* odioso(-a)
abide [ə'baɪd] *vt* sopportare
▶ **abide by** *vt fus* conformarsi a
abiding [ə'baɪdɪŋ] *adj* (*memory etc*) persistente,
duraturo(-a)
ability [ə'bɪlɪtɪ] *n* abilità *f inv*; **to the best of
my ~** con il massimo impegno
abject ['æbdʒɛkt] *adj* (*poverty*) abietto(-a);
(*apology*) umiliante; (*coward*) indegno(-a), vile
ablaze [ə'bleɪz] *adj* in fiamme; **~ with light**
risplendente di luce

able ['eɪbl] *adj* capace; **to be ~ to do sth**
essere capace di fare qc, poter fare qc
able-bodied ['eɪbl'bɔdɪd] *adj* robusto(-a)
able-bodied seaman *n* (*Brit*) marinaio scelto
ably ['eɪblɪ] *adv* abilmente
ABM *n abbr* (= *anti-ballistic missile*) ABM *m*
abnormal [æb'nɔːməl] *adj* anormale
abnormality [æbnɔː'mælɪtɪ] *n* (*condition*)
anormalità; (*instance*) anomalia
aboard [ə'bɔːd] *adv* a bordo ■ *prep* a bordo di;
~ the train in *or* sul treno
abode [ə'bəud] *n* (*old*) dimora; (*Law*)
domicilio, dimora; **of no fixed ~** senza fissa
dimora
abolish [ə'bɔlɪʃ] *vt* abolire
abolition [æbəu'lɪʃən] *n* abolizione *f*
abominable [ə'bɔmɪnəbl] *adj* abominevole
aborigine [æbə'rɪdʒɪnɪ] *n* aborigeno(-a)
abort [ə'bɔːt] *vt* (*Med, fig*) abortire; (*Comput*)
interrompere l'esecuzione di
abortion [ɔ'bɔːʃən] *n* aborto; **to have an ~**
avere un aborto, abortire
abortionist [ə'bɔːʃənɪst] *n* abortista *m/f*
abortive [ə'bɔːtɪv] *adj* abortivo(-a)
abound [ə'baund] *vi* abbondare; **to ~ in**
abbondare di

KEYWORD

about [ə'baut] *adv* **1** (*approximately*) circa,
quasi; **about a hundred/thousand** un
centinaio/migliaio, circa cento/mille; **it
takes about 10 hours** ci vogliono circa 10
ore; **at about 2 o'clock** verso le 2; **I've just
about finished** ho quasi finito; **it's about
here** è qui intorno, è qui vicino
2 (*referring to place*) qua e là, in giro; **to leave
things lying about** lasciare delle cose in
giro; **to run about** correre qua e là; **to walk
about** camminare; **is Paul about?** (*Brit*) hai
visto Paul in giro?; **it's the other way about**
(*Brit*) è il contrario
3: to be about to do sth stare per fare qc;
I'm not about to do all that for nothing
non ho intenzione di fare tutto questo per
niente
■ *prep* **1** (*relating to*) su, di; **a book about
London** un libro su Londra; **what is it
about?** di che si tratta?; (*book, film etc*) di cosa
tratta?; **we talked about it** ne abbiamo
parlato; **do something about it!** fai
qualcosa!; **what** *or* **how about doing this?**
che ne dici di fare questo?
2 (*referring to place*): **to walk about the town**
camminare per la città; **her clothes were
scattered about the room** i suoi vestiti
erano sparsi *or* in giro per tutta la stanza

about-face [ə'baut'feɪs] *n*, **about-turn**
[ə'baut'təːn] *n* (*Mil*) dietro front *m inv*
above [ə'bʌv] *adv, prep* sopra; **mentioned ~**
suddetto; **costing ~ £10** più caro di 10
sterline; **he's not ~ a bit of blackmail** non
rifuggirebbe dal ricatto; **~ all** soprattutto
aboveboard [ə'bʌv'bɔːd] *adj* aperto(-a);
onesto(-a)
abrasion [ə'breɪʒən] *n* abrasione *f*
abrasive [ə'breɪzɪv] *adj* abrasivo(-a)
abreast [ə'brest] *adv* di fianco; **3 ~** per 3 di
fronte; **to keep ~ of** tenersi aggiornato su
abridge [ə'brɪdʒ] *vt* ridurre
abroad [ə'brɔːd] *adv* all'estero; **there is a
rumour ~ that ...** (*fig*) si sente dire in giro
che ..., circola la voce che ...
abrupt [ə'brʌpt] *adj* (*steep*) erto(-a); (*sudden*)
improvviso(-a); (*gruff, blunt*) brusco(-a)
abscess ['æbsɪs] *n* ascesso
abscond [əb'skɔnd] *vi* scappare
absence ['æbsəns] *n* assenza; **in the ~ of**
(*person*) in assenza di; (*thing*) in mancanza di
absent ['æbsənt] *adj* assente; **to be ~
without leave** (*Mil etc*) essere assente
ingiustificato
absentee [æbsən'tiː] *n* assente *m/f*
absenteeism [æbsən'tiːɪzəm] *n* assenteismo
absent-minded ['æbsənt'maɪndɪd] *adj*
distratto(-a)
absent-mindedness ['æbsənt'maɪndɪdnɪs]
n distrazione *f*
absolute ['æbsəluːt] *adj* assoluto(-a)
absolutely [æbsə'luːtlɪ] *adv* assolutamente
absolve [əb'zɔlv] *vt*: **to ~ sb (from)** (*sin etc*)
assolvere qn (da); **to ~ sb from** (*oath*)
sciogliere qn da
absorb [əb'sɔːb] *vt* assorbire; **to be absorbed
in a book** essere immerso(-a) in un libro
absorbent [əb'sɔːbənt] *adj* assorbente
absorbent cotton *n* (*US*) cotone *m* idrofilo
absorbing [əb'sɔːbɪŋ] *adj* avvincente, molto
interessante
absorption [əb'sɔːpʃən] *n* assorbimento
abstain [əb'steɪn] *vi*: **to ~ (from)** astenersi
(da)
abstemious [əb'stiːmɪəs] *adj* astemio(-a)
abstention [əb'stɛnʃən] *n* astensione *f*
abstinence ['æbstɪnəns] *n* astinenza
abstract ['æbstrækt] *adj* astratto(-a) ■ *n*
(*summary*) riassunto ■ *vt* [æb'strækt] estrarre
absurd [əb'səːd] *adj* assurdo(-a)
absurdity [əb'səːdɪtɪ] *n* assurdità *f inv*
ABTA ['æbtə] *n abbr* = **Association of British
Travel Agents**
Abu Dhabi ['æbuː'dɑːbɪ] *n* Abu Dhabi *f*
abundance [ə'bʌndəns] *n* abbondanza
abundant [ə'bʌndənt] *adj* abbondante

abuse n [əˈbjuːs] abuso; (insults) ingiurie fpl
■ vt [əˈbjuːz] abusare di; **open to ~** che si
presta ad abusi
abusive [əˈbjuːsɪv] adj ingiurioso(-a)
abysmal [əˈbɪzməl] adj spaventoso(-a)
abyss [əˈbɪs] n abisso
AC n abbr (US) = **athletic club**
a/c abbr (Banking etc: = account, account current) c
academic [ækəˈdɛmɪk] adj accademico(-a);
(pej: issue) puramente formale ■ n
universitario(-a)
academic year n anno accademico
academy [əˈkædəmɪ] n (learned body)
accademia; (school) scuola privata; **military/
naval ~** scuola militare/navale; **~ of music**
conservatorio
ACAS [ˈeɪkæs] n abbr (Brit: = Advisory, Conciliation
and Arbitration Service) comitato governativo per il
miglioramento della contrattazione collettiva
accede [ækˈsiːd] vi: **to ~ to** (request) accedere
a; (throne) ascendere a
accelerate [ækˈsɛləreɪt] vt, vi accelerare
acceleration [æksɛləˈreɪʃən] n accelerazione f
accelerator [ækˈsɛləreɪtər] n acceleratore m
accent [ˈæksɛnt] n accento
accentuate [ækˈsɛntjueɪt] vt (syllable)
accentuare; (need, difference etc) accentuare,
mettere in risalto or in evidenza
accept [əkˈsɛpt] vt accettare
acceptable [əkˈsɛptəbl] adj accettabile
acceptance [əkˈsɛptəns] n accettazione f;
to meet with general ~ incontrare il favore
or il consenso generale
access [ˈæksɛs] n accesso ■ vt (Comput)
accedere a; **to have ~ to** avere accesso a;
the burglars gained ~ through a window
i ladri sono riusciti a penetrare da or
attraverso una finestra
accessible [ækˈsɛsəbl] adj accessibile
accession [ækˈsɛʃən] n (addition) aggiunta;
(to library) accessione f, acquisto; (of king)
ascesa or salita al trono
accessory [ækˈsɛsərɪ] n accessorio; **toilet
accessories** npl (Brit) articoli mpl da toilette
access road n strada d'accesso; (to motorway)
raccordo di entrata
access time n (Comput) tempo di accesso
accident [ˈæksɪdənt] n incidente m; (chance)
caso; **to meet with** or **to have an ~** avere un
incidente; **accidents at work** infortuni mpl
sul lavoro; **by ~** per caso
accidental [æksɪˈdɛntl] adj accidentale
accidentally [æksɪˈdɛntəlɪ] adv per caso
accident insurance n assicurazione f contro
gli infortuni
accident-prone [ˈæksɪdəntˈprəun] adj: **he's
very ~** è un vero passaguai

acclaim [əˈkleɪm] vt acclamare
■ n acclamazione f
acclamation [ækləˈmeɪʃən] n (approval)
acclamazione f; (applause) applauso
acclimatize [əˈklaɪmətaɪz], (US) **acclimate**
[əˈklaɪmeɪt] vt: **to become acclimatized**
acclimatarsi
accolade [ˈækəleɪd] n encomio
accommodate [əˈkɔmədeɪt] vt alloggiare;
(oblige, help) favorire; **this car
accommodates 4 people comfortably**
quest'auto può trasportare comodamente
4 persone
accommodating [əˈkɔmədeɪtɪŋ] adj
compiacente
accommodation [əkɔməˈdeɪʃən] n, (US)
accommodations [əkɔməˈdeɪʃənz] npl
alloggio; **seating ~** (Brit) posti a sedere; **"~ to
let"** (Brit) "camere in affitto"; **have you
any ~?** avete posto?
accompaniment [əˈkʌmpənɪmənt] n
accompagnamento
accompanist [əˈkʌmpənɪst] n (Mus)
accompagnatore(-trice)
accompany [əˈkʌmpənɪ] vt accompagnare
accomplice [əˈkʌmplɪs] n complice m/f
accomplish [əˈkʌmplɪʃ] vt compiere; (achieve)
ottenere
accomplished [əˈkʌmplɪʃt] adj (person)
esperto(-a)
accomplishment [əˈkʌmplɪʃmənt] n
compimento; (thing achieved) risultato;
accomplishments npl (skills) doti fpl
accord [əˈkɔːd] n accordo ■ vt accordare;
of his own ~ di propria iniziativa; **with
one ~** all'unanimità, di comune accordo
accordance [əˈkɔːdəns] n: **in ~ with** in
conformità
according [əˈkɔːdɪŋ]: **~ to** prep secondo; **it
went ~ to plan** è andata secondo il previsto
accordingly [əˈkɔːdɪŋlɪ] adv in conformità
accordion [əˈkɔːdɪən] n fisarmonica
accost [əˈkɔst] vt avvicinare
account [əˈkaunt] n (Comm) conto; (report)
descrizione f; **accounts** npl (Comm) conti;
"~ payee only" (Brit) "assegno non
trasferibile"; **to keep an ~ of** tenere nota di;
**to bring sb to ~ for sth/for having done
sth** chiedere a qn di render conto di qc/per
aver fatto qc; **by all accounts** a quanto si
dice; **of little ~** di poca importanza; **on ~**
in acconto; **to buy sth on ~** comprare qc a
credito; **on no ~** per nessun motivo; **on ~ of**
a causa di; **to take into ~, take ~ of** tener
conto di
▶ **account for** vt fus (explain) spiegare;
giustificare; **all the children were**

accounted for nessun bambino mancava all'appello

accountability [ə'kauntə'bɪlɪtɪ] *n* responsabilità

accountable [ə'kauntəbl] *adj* responsabile; **to be held ~ for sth** dover rispondere di qc

accountancy [ə'kauntənsɪ] *n* ragioneria

accountant [ə'kauntənt] *n* ragioniere(-a)

accounting [ə'kauntɪŋ] *n* contabilità

accounting period *n* esercizio finanziario, periodo contabile

account number *n* numero di conto

account payable *n* conto passivo

account receivable *n* conto da esigere

accredited [ə'krɛdɪtɪd] *adj* accreditato(-a)

accretion [ə'kri:ʃən] *n* accrescimento

accrue [ə'kru:] *vi* (*mount up*) aumentare; **to ~ to** derivare a; **accrued charges** ratei *mpl* passivi; **accrued interest** interesse *m* maturato

accumulate [ə'kju:mjuleɪt] *vt* accumulare ■ *vi* accumularsi

accumulation [əkju:mju'leɪʃən] *n* accumulazione *f*

accuracy ['ækjurəsɪ] *n* precisione *f*

accurate ['ækjurɪt] *adj* preciso(-a)

accurately ['ækjurɪtlɪ] *adv* precisamente

accusation [ækju'zeɪʃən] *n* accusa

accusative [ə'kju:zətɪv] *n* (*Ling*) accusativo

accuse [ə'kju:z] *vt* accusare

accused [ə'kju:zd] *n* accusato(-a)

accuser [ə'kju:zə'] *n* accusatore(-trice)

accustom [ə'kʌstəm] *vt* abituare; **to ~ o.s. to sth** abituarsi a qc

accustomed [ə'kʌstəmd] *adj* (*usual*) abituale; **~ to** abituato(-a) a

AC/DC *abbr* (= *alternating current/direct current*) c.a./c.c.

ACE [eɪs] *n abbr* = **American Council on Education**

ace [eɪs] *n* asso; **within an ~ of** (*Brit*) a un pelo da

acerbic [ə'sə:bɪk] *adj* (*also fig*) acido(-a)

acetate ['æsɪteɪt] *n* acetato

ache [eɪk] *n* male *m*, dolore *m* ■ *vi* (*be sore*) far male, dolere; (*yearn*): **to ~ to do sth** morire dalla voglia di fare qc; **I've got stomach ~** *or* (*US*) **a stomach ~** ho mal di stomaco; **my head aches** mi fa male la testa; **I'm aching all over** mi duole dappertutto

achieve [ə'tʃi:v] *vt* (*aim*) raggiungere; (*victory, success*) ottenere; (*task*) compiere

achievement [ə'tʃi:vmənt] *n* compimento; successo

Achilles heel [ə'kɪli:z-] *n* tallone *m* d'Achille

acid ['æsɪd] *adj* acido(-a) ■ *n* acido

acidity [ə'sɪdɪtɪ] *n* acidità

acid rain *n* pioggia acida

acid test *n* (*fig*) prova del fuoco

acknowledge [ək'nɔlɪdʒ] *vt* riconoscere; (*letter: also:* **acknowledge receipt of**) accusare ricevuta di

acknowledgement [ək'nɔlɪdʒmənt] *n* riconoscimento; (*of letter*) conferma; **acknowledgements** *npl* (*in book*) ringraziamenti *mpl*

ACLU *n abbr* (= *American Civil Liberties Union*) unione americana per le libertà civili

acme ['ækmɪ] *n* culmine *m*, acme *m*

acne ['æknɪ] *n* acne *f*

acorn ['eɪkɔ:n] *n* ghianda

acoustic [ə'ku:stɪk] *adj* acustico(-a); *see also* **acoustics**

acoustic coupler [-'kʌplə'] *n* (*Comput*) accoppiatore *m* acustico

acoustics [ə'ku:stɪks] *n, npl* acustica

acquaint [ə'kweɪnt] *vt*: **to ~ sb with sth** far sapere qc a qn; **to be acquainted with** (*person*) conoscere

acquaintance [ə'kweɪntəns] *n* conoscenza; (*person*) conoscente *m/f*; **to make sb's ~** fare la conoscenza di qn

acquiesce [ækwɪ'ɛs] *vi* (*agree*): **to ~ (in)** acconsentire (a)

acquire [ə'kwaɪə'] *vt* acquistare

acquired [ə'kwaɪəd] *adj* acquisito(-a); **it's an ~ taste** è una cosa che si impara ad apprezzare

acquisition [ækwɪ'zɪʃən] *n* acquisto

acquisitive [ə'kwɪzɪtɪv] *adj* a cui piace accumulare le cose

acquit [ə'kwɪt] *vt* assolvere; **to ~ o.s. well** comportarsi bene

acquittal [ə'kwɪtl] *n* assoluzione *f*

acre ['eɪkə'] *n* acro (= 4047 *m²*)

acreage ['eɪkərɪdʒ] *n* superficie *f* in acri

acrid ['ækrɪd] *adj* (*smell*) acre, pungente; (*fig*) pungente

acrimonious [ækrɪ'məunɪəs] *adj* astioso(-a)

acrobat ['ækrəbæt] *n* acrobata *m/f*

acrobatic [ækrə'bætɪk] *adj* acrobatico(-a)

acrobatics [ækrə'bætɪks] *n* acrobatica ■ *npl* acrobazie *fpl*

Acropolis [ə'krɔpəlɪs] *n*: **the ~** l'Acropoli *f*

across [ə'krɔs] *prep* (*on the other side*) dall'altra parte di; (*crosswise*) attraverso ■ *adv* dall'altra parte; in larghezza; **to walk ~ (the road)** attraversare (la strada); **to take sb ~ the road** far attraversare la strada a qn; **~ from** di fronte a; **the lake is 12 km ~** il lago ha una larghezza di 12 km *or* è largo 12 km; **to get sth ~ to sb** (*fig*) far capire qc a qn

acrylic [ə'krɪlɪk] *adj* acrilico(-a) ■ *n* acrilico

ACT *n abbr* (= *American College Test*) esame di ammissione a college

act [ækt] *n* atto; (*in music-hall etc*) numero; (*Law*) decreto ■ *vi* agire; (*Theat*) recitare; (*pretend*) fingere ■ *vt* (*part*) recitare; **to catch sb in the ~** cogliere qn in flagrante *or* sul fatto; **it's only an ~** è tutta scena, è solo una messinscena; **~ of God** (*Law*) calamità *f inv* naturale; **to ~ Hamlet** (*Brit*) recitare la parte di Amleto; **to ~ the fool** (*Brit*) fare lo stupido; **to ~ as** agire da; **it acts as a deterrent** serve da deterrente; **acting in my capacity as chairman, I ...** in qualità di presidente, io ...
  ▶ **act on** *vt*: **to ~ on sth** agire in base a qc
  ▶ **act out** *vt* (*event*) ricostruire; (*fantasies*) dare forma concreta a

acting ['æktɪŋ] *adj* che fa le funzioni di ■ *n* (*of actor*) recitazione *f*; (*activity*): **to do some ~** fare del teatro (*or* del cinema); **he is the ~ manager** fa le veci del direttore

action ['ækʃən] *n* azione *f*; (*Mil*) combattimento; (*Law*) processo ■ *vt* (*Comm: request*) evadere; (*tasks*) portare a termine; **to take ~** agire; **to put a plan into ~** realizzare un piano; **out of ~** fuori combattimento; (*machine etc*) fuori servizio; **killed in ~** (*Mil*) ucciso in combattimento; **to bring an ~ against sb** (*Law*) intentare causa contro qn

action replay *n* (*Brit TV*) replay *m inv*

activate ['æktɪveɪt] *vt* (*mechanism*) fare funzionare; (*Chem, Physics*) rendere attivo(-a)

active ['æktɪv] *adj* attivo(-a); **to play an ~ part in** partecipare attivamente a

active duty *n* (*US Mil*) = **active service**

actively ['æktɪvlɪ] *adv* attivamente

active partner *n* (*Comm*) socio effettivo

active service *n* (*Brit Mil*): **to be on ~** prestar servizio in zona di operazioni

activist ['æktɪvɪst] *n* attivista *m/f*

activity [æk'tɪvɪtɪ] *n* attività *f inv*

activity holiday *n* vacanza attiva (*in bici, a cavallo, in barca, a vela ecc.*)

actor ['æktər] *n* attore *m*

actress ['æktrɪs] *n* attrice *f*

actual ['æktjuəl] *adj* reale, vero(-a)

actually ['æktjuəlɪ] *adv* veramente; (*even*) addirittura

actuary ['æktjuərɪ] *n* attuario(-a)

actuate ['æktjueɪt] *vt* attivare

acuity [ə'kjuːɪtɪ] *n* acutezza

acumen ['ækjumən] *n* acume *m*; **business ~** fiuto negli affari

acupuncture ['ækjupʌŋktʃər] *n* agopuntura

AD *adv abbr* (= *Anno Domini*) d. C. ■ *n abbr* (*US Mil*) = **active duty**

ad [æd] *n abbr* = **advertisement**

adamant ['ædəmənt] *adj* irremovibile

Adam's apple ['ædəmz-] *n* pomo di Adamo

adapt [ə'dæpt] *vt* adattare ■ *vi*: **to ~ (to)** adattarsi (a)

adaptability [ədæptə'bɪlɪtɪ] *n* adattabilità

adaptable [ə'dæptəbl] *adj* (*device*) adattabile; (*person*) che sa adattarsi

adaptation [ædæp'teɪʃən] *n* adattamento

adapter, adaptor [ə'dæptər] *n* (*Elec*) adattatore *m*

add [æd] *vt* aggiungere; (*figures*) addizionare ■ *vi*: **to ~ to** (*increase*) aumentare ■ *n* (*Internet*): **thanks for the ~** grazie per avermi aggiunto (come amico)
  ▶ **add on** *vt* aggiungere
  ▶ **add up** *vt* (*figures*) addizionare ■ *vi* (*fig*): **it doesn't ~ up** non ha senso; **it doesn't ~ up to much** non è un granché

adder ['ædər] *n* vipera

addict ['ædɪkt] *n* tossicomane *m/f*; (*fig*) fanatico(-a); **heroin ~** eroinomane *m/f*; **drug ~** tossicodipendente *m/f*, tossicomane *m/f*

addicted [ə'dɪktɪd] *adj*: **to be ~ to** (*drink etc*) essere dedito(-a) a; (*fig: football etc*) essere tifoso(-a) di

addiction [ə'dɪkʃən] *n* (*Med*) tossicomania

Addis Ababa ['ædɪs'æbəbə] *n* Addis Abeba *f*

addition [ə'dɪʃən] *n* addizione *f*; **in ~** inoltre; **in ~ to** oltre

additional [ə'dɪʃənl] *adj* supplementare

additive ['ædɪtɪv] *n* additivo

address [ə'drɛs] *n* (*gen, Comput*) indirizzo; (*talk*) discorso ■ *vt* indirizzare; (*speak to*) fare un discorso a; **form of ~** (*gen*) formula di cortesia; (*in letters*) formula d'indirizzo *or* di intestazione; **to ~ o.s. to sth** indirizzare le proprie energie verso qc

address book *n* rubrica

addressee [ædrɛ'siː] *n* destinatario(-a)

Aden ['eɪdən] *n*: **the Gulf of ~** il golfo di Aden

adenoids ['ædɪnɔɪdz] *npl* adenoidi *fpl*

adept ['ædɛpt] *adj*: **~ at** esperto(-a) in

adequate ['ædɪkwɪt] *adj* (*description, reward*) adeguato(-a); (*amount*) sufficiente; **to feel ~ to a task** sentirsi all'altezza di un compito

adequately ['ædɪkwɪtlɪ] *adv* adeguatamente; sufficientemente

adhere [əd'hɪər] *vi*: **to ~ to** aderire a; (*fig: rule, decision*) seguire

adhesion [əd'hiːʒən] *n* adesione *f*

adhesive [əd'hiːzɪv] *adj* adesivo(-a) ■ *n* adesivo; **~ tape** (*Brit: for parcels etc*) nastro adesivo; (*US: Med*) cerotto adesivo

ad hoc [æd'hɔk] *adj* (*decision*) ad hoc *inv*; (*committee*) apposito(-a)

ad infinitum ['ædɪnfɪ'naɪtəm] *adv* all'infinito

adjacent [ə'dʒeɪsənt] *adj* adiacente; **~ to** accanto a

419

adjective ['ædʒɛktɪv] n aggettivo
adjoin [ə'dʒɔɪn] vt essere contiguo(-a) or attiguo(-a) a
adjoining [ə'dʒɔɪnɪŋ] adj accanto inv, adiacente ■ prep accanto a
adjourn [ə'dʒəːn] vt rimandare, aggiornare; (US: end) sospendere ■ vi sospendere la seduta; (Parliament) sospendere i lavori; (go) spostarsi; **to ~ a meeting till the following week** aggiornare or rinviare un incontro alla settimana seguente; **they adjourned to the pub** (col) si sono trasferiti al pub
adjournment [ə'dʒəːnmənt] n rinvio, aggiornamento; sospensione f
Adjt abbr (Mil) = **adjutant**
adjudicate [ə'dʒuːdɪkeɪt] vt (contest) giudicare; (claim) decidere su
adjudication [ədʒuːdɪ'keɪʃən] n decisione f
adjust [ə'dʒʌst] vt aggiustare; (Comm) rettificare ■ vi: **to ~ (to)** adattarsi (a)
adjustable [ə'dʒʌstəbl] adj regolabile
adjuster [ə'dʒʌstəʳ] n see **loss adjuster**
adjustment [ə'dʒʌstmənt] n adattamento; (of prices, wages) aggiustamento
adjutant ['ædʒətənt] n aiutante m
ad-lib [æd'lɪb] vt, vi improvvisare ■ n improvvisazione f ■ adv: **ad lib** a piacere, a volontà
adman ['ædmæn] n (col) pubblicitario
admin [æd'mɪn] n abbr (col) = **administration**
administer [əd'mɪnɪstəʳ] vt amministrare; (justice) somministrare
administration [ədmɪnɪs'treɪʃən] n amministrazione f; **the A~** (US) il Governo
administrative [əd'mɪnɪstrətɪv] adj amministrativo(-a)
administrator [əd'mɪnɪstreɪtəʳ] n amministratore(-trice)
admirable ['ædmərəbl] adj ammirevole
admiral ['ædmərəl] n ammiraglio
Admiralty ['ædmərəltɪ] n (Brit: also: **Admiralty Board**) Ministero della Marina
admiration [ædmə'reɪʃən] n ammirazione f
admirer [əd'maɪərəʳ] n ammiratore(-trice)
admiring [əd'maɪərɪŋ] adj (glance etc) di ammirazione
admissible [əd'mɪsəbl] adj ammissibile
admission [əd'mɪʃən] n ammissione f; (to exhibition, night club etc) ingresso; (confession) confessione f; **by his own ~** per sua ammissione; **"~ free", "free ~"** "ingresso gratuito"
admit [əd'mɪt] vt ammettere; far entrare; (agree) riconoscere; **"children not admitted"** "vietato l'ingresso ai bambini"; **this ticket admits two** questo biglietto è valido per due persone; **I must ~ that …**

devo ammettere or confessare che …
▶ **admit of** vt fus lasciare adito a
▶ **admit to** vt fus riconoscere
admittance [əd'mɪtəns] n ingresso; **"no ~"** "vietato l'ingresso"
admittedly [əd'mɪtɪdlɪ] adv bisogna pur riconoscere (che)
admonish [əd'mɔnɪʃ] vt ammonire
ad nauseam [æd'nɔːzɪæm] adv fino alla nausea, a non finire
ado [ə'duː] n: **without (any) more ~** senza più indugi
adolescence [ædəu'lɛsns] n adolescenza
adolescent [ædəu'lɛsnt] adj, n adolescente m/f
adopt [ə'dɔpt] vt adottare
adopted [ə'dɔptɪd] adj adottivo(-a)
adoption [ə'dɔpʃən] n adozione f
adore [ə'dɔːʳ] vt adorare
adoring [ə'dɔːrɪŋ] adj adorante; **his ~ wife** sua moglie che lo adora
adoringly [ə'dɔːrɪŋlɪ] adv con adorazione
adorn [ə'dɔːn] vt ornare
adornment [ə'dɔːnmənt] n ornamento
ADP n abbr = **automatic data processing**
adrenalin [ə'drɛnəlɪn] n adrenalina; **it gets the ~ going** ti dà una carica
Adriatic [eɪdrɪ'ætɪk], **Adriatic Sea** [eɪdrɪ'ætɪk-] n Adriatico
adrift [ə'drɪft] adv alla deriva; **to come ~** (boat) andare alla deriva
adroit [ə'drɔɪt] adj abile, destro(-a)
ADSL n abbr (= asymmetric digital subscriber line) ADSL m
ADT abbr (US: = Atlantic Daylight Time) ora legale di New York
adult ['ædʌlt] n adulto(-a)
adult education n scuola per adulti
adulterate [ə'dʌltəreɪt] vt adulterare
adulterer [ə'dʌltərəʳ] n adultero
adulteress [ə'dʌltərɪs] n adultera
adultery [ə'dʌltərɪ] n adulterio
adulthood ['ædʌlthud] n età adulta
advance [əd'vɑːns] n avanzamento; (money) anticipo ■ vt avanzare; (date, money) anticipare ■ vi avanzare; **in ~** in anticipo; **to make advances to sb** (gen) fare degli approcci a qn; (amorously) fare delle avances a qn
advanced [əd'vɑːnst] adj avanzato(-a); (Scol: studies) superiore; **~ in years** avanti negli anni
advancement [əd'vɑːnsmənt] n avanzamento
advance notice n preavviso
advantage [əd'vɑːntɪdʒ] n (also Tennis) vantaggio; **to take ~ of** approfittarsi di; **it's to our ~** è nel nostro interesse, torna a nostro vantaggio

advantageous [ædvən'teɪdʒəs] *adj*
vantaggioso(-a)

advent ['ædvənt] *n* avvento; **A~** (*Rel*) Avvento

Advent calendar *n* calendario dell'Avvento

adventure [əd'vɛntʃəʳ] *n* avventura

adventure playground *n* area attrezzata di
giochi per bambini con funi, strutture in legno etc

adventurous [əd'vɛntʃərəs] *adj*
avventuroso(-a)

adverb ['ædvəːb] *n* avverbio

adversary ['ædvəsərɪ] *n* avversario(-a)

adverse ['ædvəːs] *adj* avverso(-a); **in ~
circumstances** nelle avversità; **~ to**
contrario(-a) a

adversity [əd'vəːsɪtɪ] *n* avversità

advert ['ædvəːt] *n abbr* (*Brit*) = **advertisement**

advertise ['ædvətaɪz] *vi, vt* fare pubblicità *or*
réclame (a), fare un'inserzione (per vendere);
to ~ for (*staff*) cercare tramite annuncio

advertisement [əd'vəːtɪsmənt] *n* (*Comm*)
réclame *f inv*, pubblicità *f inv*; (*in classified ads*)
inserzione *f*

advertiser ['ædvətaɪzəʳ] *n* azienda che
reclamizza un prodotto; (*in newspaper*)
inserzionista *m/f*

advertising ['ædvətaɪzɪŋ] *n* pubblicità

advertising agency *n* agenzia pubblicitaria
or di pubblicità

advertising campaign *n* campagna
pubblicitaria

advice [əd'vaɪs] *n* consigli *mpl*; (*notification*)
avviso; **piece of ~** consiglio; **to ask (sb) for ~**
chiedere il consiglio (di qn), chiedere un
consiglio (a qn); **legal ~** consulenza legale

advice note *n* (*Brit*) avviso di spedizione

advisable [əd'vaɪzəbl] *adj* consigliabile

advise [əd'vaɪz] *vt* consigliare; **to ~ sb of sth**
informare qn di qc; **to ~ sb against sth/
against doing sth** sconsigliare qc a qn/a qn
di fare qc; **you will be well/ill advised to go**
fareste bene/male ad andare

advisedly [əd'vaɪzɪdlɪ] *adv* (*deliberately*)
deliberatamente

adviser [əd'vaɪzəʳ] *n* consigliere(-a);
(*in business*) consulente *m/f*, consigliere(-a)

advisory [əd'vaɪzərɪ] *adj* consultivo(-a);
in an ~ capacity in veste di consulente

advocate [*n* ['ædvəkɪt] (*upholder*)
sostenitore(-trice) ◆ *vt* ['ædvəkeɪt]
propugnare; **to be an ~ of** essere a favore di

advt. *abbr* = **advertisement**

AEA *n abbr* (*Brit*: = *Atomic Energy Authority*) *ente
di controllo sulla ricerca e lo sviluppo dell'energia
atomica*

AEC *n abbr* (*US*: = *Atomic Energy Commission*) *ente
di controllo sulla ricerca e lo sviluppo dell'energia
atomica*

Aegean [iː'dʒiːən], **Aegean Sea** [iː'dʒiːən-] *n*
(mare *m*) Egeo

aegis ['iːdʒɪs] *n*: **under the ~ of** sotto gli
auspici di

aeon ['iːən] *n* eternità *f inv*

aerial ['ɛərɪəl] *n* antenna ◼ *adj* aereo(-a)

aerobatics ['ɛərəu'bætɪks] *npl* acrobazia *sg*
aerea; (*stunts*) acrobazie *fpl* aeree

aerobics [ɛə'rəubɪks] *n* aerobica

aerodrome ['ɛərədrəum] *n* (*Brit*) aerodromo

aerodynamic ['ɛərəudaɪ'næmɪk] *adj*
aerodinamico(-a)

aeronautics [ɛərə'nɔːtɪks] *n* aeronautica

aeroplane ['ɛərəpleɪn] *n* aeroplano

aerosol ['ɛərəsɔl] *n* aerosol *m inv*

aerospace industry ['ɛərəuspeɪs-] *n*
industria aerospaziale

aesthetic [ɪs'θɛtɪk] *adj* estetico(-a)

afar [ə'fɑːʳ] *adv* lontano; **from ~** da lontano

AFB *n abbr* (*US*) = **Air Force Base**

AFDC *n abbr* (*US*: = *Aid to Families with Dependent
Children*) ≈ A.F. (= *assegni familiari*)

affable ['æfəbl] *adj* affabile

affair [ə'fɛəʳ] *n* affare *m*; (*also*: **love affair**)
relazione *f* amorosa; **affairs** *npl* (*business*)
affari; **the Watergate ~** il caso Watergate

affect [ə'fɛkt] *vt* toccare; (*feign*) fingere

affectation [æfɛk'teɪʃən] *n* affettazione *f*

affected [ə'fɛktɪd] *adj* affettato(-a)

affection [ə'fɛkʃən] *n* affetto

affectionate [ə'fɛkʃənɪt] *adj* affettuoso(-a)

affectionately [ə'fɛkʃənɪtlɪ] *adv*
affettuosamente

affidavit [æfɪ'deɪvɪt] *n* (*Law*) affidavit *m inv*

affiliated [ə'fɪlieɪtɪd] *adj* affiliato(-a); **~
company** filiale *f*

affinity [ə'fɪnɪtɪ] *n* affinità *f inv*

affirm [ə'fəːm] *vt* affermare, asserire

affirmation [æfə'meɪʃən] *n* affermazione *f*

affirmative [ə'fəːmətɪv] *adj* affermativo(-a)
◼ *n*: **in the ~** affermativamente

affix [ə'fɪks] *vt* apporre; attaccare

afflict [ə'flɪkt] *vt* affliggere

affliction [ə'flɪkʃən] *n* afflizione *f*

affluence ['æfluəns] *n* ricchezza

affluent ['æfluənt] *adj* ricco(-a); **the ~
society** la società del benessere

afford [ə'fɔːd] *vt* permettersi; (*provide*)
fornire; **I can't ~ the time** non ho
veramente il tempo; **can we ~ a car?**
possiamo permetterci un'automobile?

affordable [ə'fɔːdəbl] *adj* (che ha un prezzo)
abbordabile

affray [ə'freɪ] *n* (*Brit Law*) rissa

affront [ə'frʌnt] *n* affronto

affronted [ə'frʌntɪd] *adj* insultato(-a)

Afghan ['æfgæn] *adj, n* afgano(-a)

421

Afghanistan [æf'gænɪstɑːn] n Afganistan m

afield [ə'fiːld] adv: **far ~** lontano

AFL-CIO n abbr (= American Federation of Labor and Congress of Industrial Organizations) confederazione sindacale

afloat [ə'fləut] adj, adv a galla

afoot [ə'fut] adv: **there is something ~** si sta preparando qualcosa

aforementioned [ə'fɔːmɛnʃənd] adj suddetto(-a)

aforesaid [ə'fɔːsɛd] adj suddetto(-a), predetto(-a)

afraid [ə'freɪd] adj impaurito(-a); **to be ~ of** aver paura di; **to be ~ of doing** or **to do** aver paura di fare; **I am ~ that I'll be late** mi dispiace, ma farò tardi; **I'm ~ so!** ho paura di sì!, temo proprio di sì!; **I'm ~ not** no, mi dispiace, purtroppo no

afresh [ə'frɛʃ] adv di nuovo

Africa ['æfrɪkə] n Africa

African ['æfrɪkən] adj, n africano(a)

Afrikaans [æfrɪ'kɑːns] n afrikaans m

Afrikaner [æfrɪ'kɑːnəʳ] n africander m inv

Afro-American ['æfrəuə'mɛrɪkən] adj afroamericano(-a)

Afro-Caribbean ['æfrəukærɪ'bɪən] adj afrocaraibico(-a)

AFT n abbr (= American Federation of Teachers) sindacato degli insegnanti

aft [ɑːft] adv a poppa, verso poppa

after ['ɑːftəʳ] prep, adv dopo; **~ dinner** dopo cena; **the day ~ tomorrow** dopodomani; **what/who are you ~?** che/chi cerca?; **the police are ~ him** è ricercato dalla polizia; **~ you!** prima lei!, dopo di lei!; **~ all** dopo tutto

afterbirth ['ɑːftəbːθ] n placenta

aftercare ['ɑːftəkɛəʳ] n (Brit Med) assistenza medica post-degenza

after-effects ['ɑːftərɪfɛkts] npl conseguenze fpl; (of illness) postumi mpl

afterlife ['ɑːftəlaɪf] n vita dell'al di là

aftermath ['ɑːftəmæθ] n conseguenze fpl; **in the ~ of** nel periodo dopo

afternoon ['ɑːftə'nuːn] n pomeriggio; **good ~!** buon giorno!

afters ['ɑːftəz] n (Brit col: dessert) dessert m inv

after-sales service [ɑːftə'seɪlz-] n servizio assistenza clienti

after-shave ['ɑːftəʃeɪv], **after-shave lotion** ['ɑːftəʃeɪv-] n dopobarba m inv

aftershock ['ɑːftəʃɔk] n scossa di assestamento

aftersun ['ɑːftəsʌn] adj: **~ (lotion/cream)** (lozione f /crema) doposole m inv

aftertaste ['ɑːftəteɪst] n retrogusto

afterthought ['ɑːftəθɔːt] n: **as an ~** come aggiunta

afterwards ['ɑːftəwədz] adv dopo

again [ə'gɛn] adv di nuovo; **to begin/see ~** ricominciare/rivedere; **he opened it ~** l'ha aperto di nuovo, l'ha riaperto; **not ... ~** non ... più; **~ and ~** ripetutamente; **now and ~** di tanto in tanto, a volte

against [ə'gɛnst] prep contro; **~ a blue background** su uno sfondo azzurro; **leaning ~ the desk** appoggiato alla scrivania; **(as) ~** (Brit) in confronto a, contro

age [eɪdʒ] n età f inv ▪ vt, vi invecchiare; **what ~ is he?** quanti anni ha?; **he is 20 years of ~** ha 20 anni; **under ~** minorenne; **to come of ~** diventare maggiorenne; **it's been ages since ...** sono secoli che ...

aged ['eɪdʒd] adj: **~ 10** di 10 anni; ▪ npl ['eɪdʒɪd]: **the ~** gli anziani

age group n generazione f; **the 40 to 50 ~** le persone fra i 40 e i 50 anni

ageing ['eɪdʒɪŋ] adj che diventa vecchio(-a); **an ~ film star** una diva stagionata

ageless ['eɪdʒlɪs] adj senza età

age limit n limite m d'età

agency ['eɪdʒənsɪ] n agenzia; **through** or **by the ~ of** grazie a

agenda [ə'dʒɛndə] n ordine m del giorno; **on the ~** all'ordine del giorno

agent ['eɪdʒənt] n agente m

aggravate ['ægrəveɪt] vt aggravare, peggiorare; (annoy) esasperare

aggravation [ægrə'veɪʃən] n peggioramento; esasperazione f

aggregate ['ægrɪgeɪt] n aggregato; **on ~** (Sport) con punteggio complessivo

aggression [ə'grɛʃən] n aggressione f

aggressive [ə'grɛsɪv] adj aggressivo(-a)

aggressiveness [ə'grɛsɪvnɪs] n aggressività

aggressor [ə'grɛsəʳ] n aggressore m

aggrieved [ə'griːvd] adj addolorato(-a)

aggro ['ægrəu] n (col: behaviour) aggressività f inv; (: hassle) rottura

aghast [ə'gɑːst] adj sbigottito(-a)

agile ['ædʒaɪl] adj agile

agility [ə'dʒɪlɪtɪ] n agilità f inv

agitate ['ædʒɪteɪt] vt turbare; agitare ▪ vi: **to ~ for** agitarsi per

agitator ['ædʒɪteɪtəʳ] n agitatore(-trice)

AGM n abbr = **annual general meeting**

agnostic [æg'nɔstɪk] adj, n agnostico(-a)

ago [ə'gəu] adv: **2 days ~** 2 giorni fa; **not long ~** poco tempo fa; **as long ~ as 1960** già nel 1960; **how long ~?** quanto tempo fa?

agog [ə'gɔg] adj: **~ (all) ~ (for)** ansioso(-a) (di), impaziente (di)

agonize ['ægənaɪz] vi: **to ~ (over)** angosciarsi (per)

agonizing ['ægənaɪzɪŋ] adj straziante

agony ['ægənɪ] n agonia; **I was in ~** avevo dei dolori atroci

agony aunt n (Brit col) chi tiene la rubrica della posta del cuore

agony column n posta del cuore

agree [ə'gri:] vt (price) pattuire ■ vi: **to ~ (with)** essere d'accordo (con); (Ling) concordare (con); **to ~ to sth/to do sth** accettare qc/di fare qc; **to ~ that** (admit) ammettere che; **to ~ on sth** accordarsi su qc; **it was agreed that ...** è stato deciso (di comune accordo) che ...; **garlic doesn't ~ with me** l'aglio non mi va

agreeable [ə'gri:əbl] adj gradevole; (willing) disposto(-a); **are you ~ to this?** è d'accordo con questo?

agreed [ə'gri:d] adj (time, place) stabilito(-a); **to be ~** essere d'accordo

agreement [ə'gri:mənt] n accordo; **in ~** d'accordo; **by mutual ~** di comune accordo

agricultural [ægrɪ'kʌltʃərəl] adj agricolo(-a)

agriculture ['ægrɪkʌltʃəʳ] n agricoltura

aground [ə'graund] adv: **to run ~** arenarsi

ahead [ə'hɛd] adv avanti; davanti; **~ of** davanti a; (fig: schedule etc) in anticipo su; **~ of time** in anticipo; **go ~!** avanti!; **go right** or **straight ~** tiri diritto; **they were (right) ~ of us** erano (proprio) davanti a noi

AI n abbr = **Amnesty International**; (Comput) = **artificial intelligence**

AIB n abbr (Brit: = Accident Investigation Bureau) ufficio d'inchiesta per incidenti aerei e simili

AID n abbr = **artificial insemination by donor**; (US: = Agency for International Development) A.I.D. f

aid [eɪd] n aiuto ■ vt aiutare; **with the ~ of** con l'aiuto di; **in ~ of** a favore di; **to ~ and abet** (Law) essere complice di

aide [eɪd] n (person) aiutante m

aide-de-camp ['eɪddə'kɔŋ] n (Mil) aiutante m di campo

AIDS [eɪdz] n abbr (= acquired immune (or immuno-) deficiency syndrome) A.I.D.S. f

AIH n abbr = **artificial insemination by husband**

ailing ['eɪlɪŋ] adj sofferente; (fig: economy, industry etc) in difficoltà

ailment ['eɪlmənt] n indisposizione f

aim [eɪm] vt: **to ~ sth at** (gun) mirare qc a, puntare qc a; (camera, remark) rivolgere qc a; (missile) lanciare qc contro; (blow etc) tirare qc a ■ vi (also: **to take aim**) prendere la mira ■ n mira; **to ~ at** mirare; **to ~ to do** aver l'intenzione di fare

aimless ['eɪmlɪs] adj, **aimlessly** ['eɪmlɪslɪ] adv senza scopo

ain't [eɪnt] (col) = **am not; aren't; isn't**

air [ɛəʳ] n aria ■ vt (room, bed) arieggiare; (clothes) far prendere aria a; (idea, grievance) esprimere pubblicamente, manifestare; (views) far conoscere ■ cpd (currents) d'aria; (attack) aereo(-a); **by ~** (travel) in aereo; **to be on the ~** (Radio, TV: station) trasmettere; (: programme) essere in onda

air bag n airbag m inv

air base n base f aerea

airbed ['ɛəbɛd] n (Brit) materassino

airborne ['ɛəbɔ:n] adj (plane) in volo; (troops) aerotrasportato(-a); **as soon as the plane was ~** appena l'aereo ebbe decollato

air cargo n carico trasportato per via aerea

air-conditioned ['ɛəkən'dɪʃənd] adj con or ad aria condizionata

air conditioning n condizionamento d'aria

air-cooled ['ɛəku:ld] adj raffreddato(-a) ad aria

aircraft ['ɛəkrɑ:ft] n pl inv apparecchio

aircraft carrier n portaerei f inv

air cushion n cuscino gonfiabile; (Tech) cuscino d'aria

airfield ['ɛəfi:ld] n campo d'aviazione

Air Force n aviazione f militare

air freight n spedizione f di merci per via aerea; (goods) carico spedito per via aerea

airgun ['ɛəgʌn] n fucile m ad aria compressa

air hostess n hostess f inv

airily ['ɛərɪlɪ] adv con disinvoltura

airing ['ɛərɪŋ] n: **to give an ~ to** (linen) far prendere aria a; (room) arieggiare; (fig: ideas etc) ventilare

air letter n (Brit) aerogramma m

airlift ['ɛəlɪft] n ponte m aereo

airline ['ɛəlaɪn] n linea aerea

airliner ['ɛəlaɪnəʳ] n aereo di linea

airlock ['ɛəlɔk] n cassa d'aria

air mail n posta aerea; **by ~** per via or posta aerea

air mattress n materassino gonfiabile

airplane ['ɛəpleɪn] n (US) aeroplano

air pocket n vuoto d'aria

airport ['ɛəpɔ:t] n aeroporto

air rage n comportamento aggressivo dei passeggeri di un aereo

air raid n incursione f aerea

air rifle n fucile m ad aria compressa

airsick ['ɛəsɪk] adj: **to be ~** soffrire di mal d'aereo

airspace ['ɛəspeɪs] n spazio aereo

airspeed ['ɛəspi:d] n velocità f inv di crociera (Aer)

airstrip ['ɛəstrɪp] n pista d'atterraggio

air terminal n air-terminal m inv

airtight ['ɛətaɪt] adj ermetico(-a)

air time n (Radio) spazio radiofonico; (TV) spazio televisivo

air traffic control n controllo del traffico aereo
air traffic controller n controllore m del traffico aereo
airway ['ɛəweɪ] n (Aviat) rotte fpl aeree; (Anat) vie fpl respiratorie
airy ['ɛərɪ] adj arioso(-a); (manners) noncurante
aisle [aɪl] n (of church) navata laterale; navata centrale; (of plane) corridoio
aisle seat n (on plane) posto sul corridoio
ajar [ə'dʒɑːʳ] adj socchiuso(-a)
AK abbr (US) = **Alaska**
aka abbr (= also known as) alias
akin [ə'kɪn] prep: ~ **to** simile a
AL abbr (US) = **Alabama**
ALA n abbr = **American Library Association**
Ala. abbr (US) = **Alabama**
à la carte [ɑːlɑː'kɑːt] adv alla carta
alacrity [ə'lækrɪtɪ] n: **with ~** con prontezza
alarm [ə'lɑːm] n allarme m ▪ vt allarmare
alarm clock n sveglia
alarmed [ə'lɑːmd] adj (person) allarmato(-a); (house, car etc) dotato(-a) di allarme
alarming [ə'lɑːmɪŋ] adj allarmante, preoccupante
alarmingly [ə'lɑːmɪŋlɪ] adv in modo allarmante; **~ close** pericolosamente vicino
alarmist [ə'lɑːmɪst] n allarmista m/f
alas [ə'læs] excl ohimè!, ahimè!
Alas. abbr (US) = **Alaska**
Alaska [ə'læskə] n Alasca
Albania [æl'beɪnɪə] n Albania
Albanian [æl'beɪnɪən] adj albanese
▪ n albanese m/f; (Ling) albanese m
albatross ['ælbətrɔs] n albatro, albatros m inv
albeit [ɔːl'biːɪt] conj sebbene + sub, benché + sub
album ['ælbəm] n album m inv; (L.P.) 33 giri m inv, L.P. m inv
albumen ['ælbjumɪn] n albume m
alchemy ['ælkɪmɪ] n alchimia
alcohol ['ælkəhɔl] n alcool m
alcohol-free ['ælkəhɔl'friː] adj analcolico(-a)
alcoholic [ælkə'hɔlɪk] adj alcolico(-a)
▪ n alcolizzato(-a)
alcoholism ['ælkəhɔlɪzəm] n alcolismo
alcove ['ælkəuv] n alcova
Ald. abbr = **alderman**
alderman ['ɔːldəmən] n consigliere m comunale
ale [eɪl] n birra
alert [ə'ləːt] adj vivo(-a); (watchful) vigile
▪ n allarme m ▪ vt: **to ~ sb (to sth)** avvisare qn (di qc), avvertire qn (di qc); **to ~ sb to the dangers of sth** mettere qn in guardia contro qc; **on the ~** all'erta
Aleutian Islands [ə'luːʃən-] npl isole fpl Aleutine

A level n (Brit) diploma di studi superiori
Alexandria [ælɪg'zændrɪə] n Alessandria (d'Egitto)
alfresco [æl'freskəu] adj, adv all'aperto
algebra ['ældʒɪbrə] n algebra
Algeria [æl'dʒɪərɪə] n Algeria
Algerian [æl'dʒɪərɪən] adj, n algerino(-a)
Algiers [æl'dʒɪəz] n Algeri f
algorithm ['ælgərɪðəm] n algoritmo
alias ['eɪlɪəs] adv alias ▪ n pseudonimo, falso nome m
alibi ['ælɪbaɪ] n alibi m inv
alien ['eɪlɪən] n straniero(-a) ▪ adj: ~ **(to)** estraneo(-a) (a)
alienate ['eɪlɪəneɪt] vt alienare
alienation [eɪlɪə'neɪʃən] n alienazione f
alight [ə'laɪt] adj acceso(-a) ▪ vi scendere; (bird) posarsi
align [ə'laɪn] vt allineare
alignment [ə'laɪnmənt] n allineamento; **out of ~ (with)** non allineato (con)
alike [ə'laɪk] adj simile ▪ adv allo stesso modo; **to look ~** assomigliarsi; **winter and summer ~** sia d'estate che d'inverno
alimony ['ælɪmənɪ] n (payment) alimenti mpl
alive [ə'laɪv] adj vivo(-a); (active) attivo(-a); ~ **with** pieno(-a) di; ~ **to** conscio(-a) di
alkali ['ælkəlaɪ] n alcali m inv

 KEYWORD

all [ɔːl] adj tutto(-a); **all day** tutto il giorno; **all night** tutta la notte; **all men** tutti gli uomini; **all five girls** tutt'e cinque le ragazze; **all five came** sono venuti tutti e cinque; **all the books** tutti i libri; **all the food** tutto il cibo; **all the time** tutto il tempo; (always) sempre; **all his life** tutta la vita; **for all their efforts** nonostante tutti i loro sforzi
▪ pron **1** tutto(-a); **is that all?** non c'è altro?; (in shop) basta così?; **all of them** tutti(-e); **all of it** tutto(-a); **I ate it all, I ate all of it** l'ho mangiato tutto; **all of us went** tutti noi siamo andati; **all of the boys went** tutti i ragazzi sono andati
2 (in phrases): **above all** soprattutto; **after all** dopotutto; **at all: not at all** (in answer to question) niente affatto; (in answer to thanks) prego!, di niente!, s'immagini!; **I'm not at all tired** non sono affatto stanco; **anything at all will do** andrà bene qualsiasi cosa; **all in all** tutto sommato
▪ adv: **all alone** tutto(-a) solo(-a); **to be/feel all in** (Brit col) essere/sentirsi sfinito(-a) or distrutto(-a); **all out** adv: **to go all out** mettercela tutta; **it's not as hard as all**

that non è poi così difficile; **all the more/
the better** tanto più/meglio; **all but** quasi;
the score is two all il punteggio è di due a
due *or* è due pari

allay [ə'leɪ] *vt (fears)* dissipare
all clear *n (Mil)* cessato allarme *m inv*; *(fig)*
okay *m*
allegation [ælɪ'geɪʃən] *n* asserzione *f*
allege [ə'lɛdʒ] *vt* asserire; **he is alleged to
have said ...** avrebbe detto che ...
alleged [ə'lɛdʒd] *adj* presunto(-a)
allegedly [ə'lɛdʒɪdlɪ] *adv* secondo quanto si
asserisce
allegiance [ə'liːdʒəns] *n* fedeltà
allegory ['ælɪgərɪ] *n* allegoria
all-embracing ['ɔːlɪm'breɪsɪŋ] *adj* universale
allergic [ə'lɜːdʒɪk] *adj*: **~ to** allergico(-a) a
allergy ['ælədʒɪ] *n* allergia
alleviate [ə'liːvɪeɪt] *vt* alleviare
alley ['ælɪ] *n* vicolo; *(in garden)* vialetto
alleyway ['ælɪweɪ] *n* vicolo
alliance [ə'laɪəns] *n* alleanza
allied ['ælaɪd] *adj* alleato(-a)
alligator ['ælɪgeɪtə'] *n* alligatore *m*
all-important ['ɔːlɪm'pɔːtənt] *adj*
importantissimo(-a)
all-in ['ɔːlɪn] *adj, adv (Brit: charge)* tutto
compreso
all-in wrestling *n (Brit)* lotta americana
alliteration [əlɪtə'reɪʃən] *n* allitterazione *f*
all-night ['ɔːl'naɪt] *adj* aperto(-a) *(or* che dura)
tutta la notte
allocate ['æləkeɪt] *vt (share out)* distribuire;
(duties, sum, time): **to ~ sth to** assegnare qc a;
to ~ sth for stanziare qc per
allocation [æləu'keɪʃən] *n*: **~ (of money)**
stanziamento
allot [ə'lɒt] *vt (share out)* spartire; **to ~ sth to**
(time) dare qc a; *(duties)* assegnare qc a; **in the
allotted time** nel tempo fissato *or*
prestabilito
allotment [ə'lɒtmənt] *n (share)* spartizione *f*;
(garden) lotto di terra
all-out ['ɔːlaut] *adj (effort etc)* totale ◾ *adv*:
to go all out for mettercela tutta per
allow [ə'lau] *vt (practice, behaviour)* permettere;
(sum to spend etc) accordare; *(sum, time
estimated)* dare; *(concede)*: **to ~ that**
ammettere che; **to ~ sb to do** permettere a
qn di fare; **he is allowed to (do it)** lo può
fare; **smoking is not allowed** è vietato
fumare, non è permesso fumare; **we must ~
3 days for the journey** dobbiamo calcolare
3 giorni per il viaggio
▶ **allow for** *vt fus* tener conto di
allowance [ə'lauəns] *n (money received)*

assegno; *(for travelling, accommodation)*
indennità *f inv*; *(Tax)* detrazione *f* di imposta;
to make ~(s) for tener conto di; *(person)*
scusare
alloy ['ælɔɪ] *n* lega
all right *adv (feel, work)* bene; *(as answer)* va
bene
all-round ['ɔːl'raund] *adj* completo(-a)
all-rounder [ɔːl'raundə'] *n (Brit)*: **to be a good
~** essere bravo(-a) in tutto
allspice ['ɔːlspaɪs] *n* pepe *m* della Giamaica
all-time ['ɔːl'taɪm] *adj (record)* assoluto(-a)
allude [ə'luːd] *vi*: **to ~ to** alludere a
alluring [ə'ljuərɪŋ] *adj* seducente
allusion [ə'luːʒən] *n* allusione *f*
alluvium [ə'luːvɪəm] *n* materiale *m*
alluvionale
ally *n* ['ælaɪ] alleato ◾ *vt* [ə'laɪ]: **to ~ o.s. with**
allearsi con
almighty [ɔːl'maɪtɪ] *adj* onnipotente
almond ['aːmənd] *n* mandorla
almost ['ɔːlməust] *adv* quasi; **he ~ fell** per
poco non è caduto
alms [aːmz] *n* elemosina
aloft [ə'lɒft] *adv* in alto; *(Naut)* sull'alberatura
alone [ə'ləun] *adj, adv* solo(-a); **to leave sb ~**
lasciare qn in pace; **to leave sth ~** lasciare
stare qc; **let ~ ...** figuriamoci poi ..., tanto
meno ...
along [ə'lɒŋ] *prep* lungo ◾ *adv*: **is he
coming ~?** viene con noi?; **he was hopping/
limping ~** veniva saltellando/zoppicando;
~ with insieme con
alongside [ə'lɒŋ'saɪd] *prep* accanto a; lungo
◾ *adv* accanto; *(Naut)* sottobordo; **we brought
our boat ~** *(of a pier/shore etc)* abbiamo
accostato la barca (al molo/alla riva *etc*)
aloof [ə'luːf] *adj* distaccato(-a) ◾ *adv* a
distanza, in disparte; **to stand ~** tenersi a
distanza *or* in disparte
aloofness [ə'luːfnɪs] *n* distacco, riserbo
aloud [ə'laud] *adv* ad alta voce
alphabet ['ælfəbet] *n* alfabeto
alphabetical [ælfə'betɪkəl] *adj* alfabetico(-a);
in ~ order in ordine alfabetico
alphanumeric [ælfənjuː'merɪk] *adj*
alfanumerico(-a)
alpine ['ælpaɪn] *adj* alpino(-a); **~ hut** rifugio
alpino; **~ pasture** pascolo alpestre; **~ skiing**
sci alpino
Alps [ælps] *npl*: **the ~** le Alpi
already [ɔːl'redɪ] *adv* già
alright ['ɔːl'raɪt] *adv (Brit)* = **all right**
Alsatian [æl'seɪʃən] *n (Brit: dog)* pastore *m*
tedesco, (cane *m*) lupo
also ['ɔːlsəu] *adv* anche
Alta. *abbr (Canada)* = **Alberta**

altar ['ɔltər] n altare m

alter ['ɔltər] vt, vi alterare

alteration [ɔltə'reɪʃən] n modificazione f, alterazione f; **alterations** (Sewing, Archit) modifiche fpl; **timetable subject to** ~ orario soggetto a variazioni

altercation [ɔːtə'keɪʃən] n alterco, litigio

alternate adj [ɔl'tə:nɪt] alterno(-a) ■ vi ['ɔltə:neɪt] alternare; **on** ~ **days** ogni due giorni

alternately [ɔl'tə:nɪtlɪ] adv alternatamente

alternating current ['ɔltəneɪtɪŋ-] n corrente f alternata

alternative [ɔl'tə:nətɪv] adj (solutions) alternativo(-a); (solution) altro(-a) ■ n (choice) alternativa; (other possibility) altra possibilità

alternatively [ɔl'tə:nətɪvlɪ] adv altrimenti, come alternativa

alternative medicine n medicina alternativa

alternator ['ɔltə:neɪtər] n (Aut) alternatore m

although [ɔːl'ðəu] conj benché + sub, sebbene + sub

altitude ['æltɪtjuːd] n altitudine f

alto ['æltəu] n contralto

altogether [ɔːltə'gɛðər] adv del tutto, completamente; (on the whole) tutto considerato; (in all) in tutto; **how much is that** ~? quant'è in tutto?

altruism ['æltruːɪzəm] n altruismo

altruistic [æltru'ɪstɪk] adj altruistico(-a)

aluminium [ælju'mɪnɪəm], (US) **aluminum** [ə'luːmɪnəm] n alluminio

always ['ɔːlweɪz] adv sempre

Alzheimer's ['æltshaɪməz] n (also: **Alzheimer's disease**) morbo di Alzheimer

AM abbr (= amplitude modulation) AM ■ n abbr (= Assembly Member) deputato gallese

am [æm] vb see **be**

a.m. adv abbr (= ante meridiem) della mattina

AMA n abbr = **American Medical Association**

amalgam [ə'mælgəm] n amalgama m

amalgamate [ə'mælgəmeɪt] vt amalgamare ■ vi amalgamarsi

amalgamation [əmælgə'meɪʃən] n amalgamazione f; (Comm) fusione f

amass [ə'mæs] vt ammassare

amateur ['æmətər] n dilettante m/f ■ adj (Sport) dilettante; ~ **dramatics** n filodrammatica

amateurish ['æmətərɪʃ] adj (pej) da dilettante

amaze [ə'meɪz] vt stupire; **to be amazed (at)** essere sbalordito(-a) (da)

amazement [ə'meɪzmənt] n stupore m

amazing [ə'meɪzɪŋ] adj sorprendente, sbalorditivo(-a); (bargain, offer) sensazionale

amazingly [ə'meɪzɪŋlɪ] adv incredibilmente, sbalorditivamente

Amazon ['æməzən] n (Mythology) Amazzone f; (river): **the** ~ il Rio delle Amazzoni ■ cpd (basin, jungle) amazzonico(-a)

Amazonian [æmə'zəunɪən] adj amazzonico(-a)

ambassador [æm'bæsədər] n ambasciatore(-trice)

amber ['æmbər] n ambra; **at** ~ (Brit Aut) giallo

ambidextrous [æmbɪ'dɛkstrəs] adj ambidestro(-a)

ambience ['æmbɪəns] n ambiente m

ambiguity [æmbɪ'gjuɪtɪ] n ambiguità f inv

ambiguous [æm'bɪgjuəs] adj ambiguo(-a)

ambition [æm'bɪʃən] n ambizione f; **to achieve one's** ~ realizzare le proprie aspirazioni or ambizioni

ambitious [æm'bɪʃəs] adj ambizioso(-a)

ambivalent [æm'bɪvələnt] adj ambivalente

amble ['æmbl] vi (also: **to amble along**) camminare tranquillamente

ambulance ['æmbjuləns] n ambulanza

ambush ['æmbuʃ] n imboscata ■ vt fare un'imboscata a

ameba [ə'miːbə] n (US) = **amoeba**

ameliorate [ə'miːlɪəreɪt] vt migliorare

amen ['ɑː'mɛn] excl così sia, amen

amenable [ə'miːnəbl] adj: ~ **to** (advice etc) ben disposto(-a) a

amend [ə'mɛnd] vt (law) emendare; (text) correggere ■ vi emendarsi; **to make amends** fare ammenda

amendment [ə'mɛndmənt] n emendamento; correzione f

amenities [ə'miːnɪtɪz] npl attrezzature fpl ricreative e culturali

amenity [ə'miːnɪtɪ] n amenità f inv

America [ə'mɛrɪkə] n America

American [ə'mɛrɪkən] adj, n americano(-a)

americanize [ə'mɛrɪkənaɪz] vt americanizzare

amethyst ['æmɪθɪst] n ametista

Amex ['æmɛks] n abbr = **American Stock Exchange**

amiable ['eɪmɪəbl] adj amabile, gentile

amicable ['æmɪkəbl] adj amichevole

amicably ['æmɪkəblɪ] adv: **to part** ~ lasciarsi senza rancori

amid [ə'mɪd], **amidst** [ə'mɪdst] prep fra, tra, in mezzo a

amiss [ə'mɪs] adj, adv: **there's something** ~ c'è qualcosa che non va bene; **don't take it** ~ non avertene a male

ammo ['æməu] n abbr (col) = **ammunition**

ammonia [ə'məunɪə] n ammoniaca

ammunition [æmju'nɪʃən] n munizioni fpl; (fig) arma

ammunition dump n deposito di munizioni

amnesia [æm'niːzɪə] *n* amnesia
amnesty ['æmnɪstɪ] *n* amnistia; **to grant an ~ to** concedere l'amnistia a, amnistiare
Amnesty International *n* Amnesty International *f*
amoeba, *(US)* **ameba** [ə'miːbə] *n* ameba
amok [ə'mɔk] *adv*: **to run ~** diventare pazzo(-a) furioso(-a)
among [ə'mʌŋ], **amongst** [ə'mʌŋst] *prep* fra, tra, in mezzo a
amoral [eɪ'mɔrəl] *adj* amorale
amorous ['æmərəs] *adj* amoroso(-a)
amorphous [ə'mɔːfəs] *adj* amorfo(-a)
amortization [əmɔːtaɪ'zeɪʃən] *n* *(Comm)* ammortamento
amount [ə'maunt] *n* *(sum of money)* somma; *(of bill etc)* importo; *(quantity)* quantità *f inv* ▪ *vi*: **to ~ to** *(total)* ammontare a; *(be same as)* essere come; **this amounts to a refusal** questo equivale a un rifiuto
amp ['æmp], **ampère** ['æmpɛəʳ] *n* ampere *m inv*; **a 13 ~ plug** una spina con fusibile da 13 ampere
ampersand ['æmpəsænd] *n* e *f* commerciale
amphetamine [æm'fɛtəmiːn] *n* anfetamina
amphibian [æm'fɪbɪən] *n* anfibio
amphibious [æm'fɪbɪəs] *adj* anfibio(-a)
amphitheatre, *(US)* **amphitheater** ['æmfɪθɪətəʳ] *n* anfiteatro
ample ['æmpl] *adj* ampio(-a); spazioso(-a); *(enough)*: **this is ~** questo è più che sufficiente; **to have ~ time/room** avere assai tempo/posto
amplifier ['æmplɪfaɪəʳ] *n* amplificatore *m*
amplify ['æmplɪfaɪ] *vt* amplificare
amply ['æmplɪ] *adv* ampiamente
ampoule, *(US)* **ampule** ['æmpuːl] *n* *(Med)* fiala
amputate ['æmpjuteɪt] *vt* amputare
amputee [æmpju'tiː] *n* mutilato(-a), chi ha subito un'amputazione
Amsterdam [æmstə'dæm] *n* Amsterdam *f*
amt *abbr* = **amount**
amuck [ə'mʌk] *adv* = **amok**
amuse [ə'mjuːz] *vt* divertire; **to ~ o.s. with sth/by doing sth** divertirsi con qc/a fare qc; **to be amused at** essere divertito da; **he was not amused** non l'ha trovato divertente
amusement [ə'mjuːzmənt] *n* divertimento; **much to my ~** con mio grande spasso
amusement arcade *n* sala giochi *(solo con macchinette a gettoni)*
amusement park *n* luna park *m inv*
amusing [ə'mjuːzɪŋ] *adj* divertente
an [æn, ən, n] *indef art see* **a**
ANA *n abbr* = **American Newspaper Association; American Nurses Association**
anachronism [ə'nækrənɪzəm] *n* anacronismo

anaemia [ə'niːmɪə] *n* anemia
anaemic [ə'niːmɪk] *adj* anemico(-a)
anaesthetic [ænɪs'θɛtɪk] *adj* anestetico(-a) ▪ *n* anestetico; **local/general ~** anestesia locale/totale; **under the ~** sotto anestesia
anaesthetist [æ'niːsθɪtɪst] *n* anestesista *m/f*
anagram ['ænəgræm] *n* anagramma *m*
anal ['eɪnl] *adj* anale
analgesic [ænæl'dʒiːsɪk] *adj* analgesico(-a) ▪ *n* analgesico
analog, analogue ['ænəlɔg] *adj* *(watch, computer)* analogico(-a)
analogous [ə'næləgəs] *adj*: **~ to** *or* **with** analogo(-a) a
analogy [ə'nælədʒɪ] *n* analogia; **to draw an ~ between** fare un'analogia tra
analyse ['ænəlaɪz] *vt* *(Brit)* analizzare
analysis *(pl* **analyses)** [ə'næləsɪs, -siːz] *n* analisi *f inv*; **in the last ~** in ultima analisi
analyst ['ænəlɪst] *n* *(political analyst etc)* analista *m/f*; *(US)* *(psic)* analista *m/f*
analytic [ænə'lɪtɪk], **analytical** [ænə'lɪtɪkl] *adj* analitico(-a)
analyze ['ænəlaɪz] *vt* *(US)* = **analyse**
anarchic [æ'nɑːkɪk] *adj* anarchico(-a)
anarchist ['ænəkɪst] *adj, n* anarchico(-a)
anarchy ['ænəkɪ] *n* anarchia
anathema [ə'næθɪmə] *n*: **it is ~ to him** non ne vuol neanche sentir parlare
anatomical [ænə'tɔmɪkl] *adj* anatomico(-a)
anatomy [ə'nætəmɪ] *n* anatomia
ANC *n abbr* = **African National Congress**
ancestor ['ænsɪstəʳ] *n* antenato(-a)
ancestral [æn'sɛstrəl] *adj* avito(-a)
ancestry ['ænsɪstrɪ] *n* antenati *mpl*; ascendenza
anchor ['æŋkəʳ] *n* ancora ▪ *vi* *(also:* **to drop anchor)** gettare l'ancora ▪ *vt* ancorare; **to weigh ~** salpare *or* levare l'ancora
anchorage ['æŋkərɪdʒ] *n* ancoraggio
anchor man *n* *(TV, Radio)* anchorman *m inv*
anchor woman *n* *(TV, Radio)* anchorwoman *f inv*
anchovy ['æntʃəvɪ] *n* acciuga
ancient ['eɪnʃənt] *adj* antico(-a); *(fig)* anziano(-a); **~ monument** monumento storico
ancillary [æn'sɪlərɪ] *adj* ausiliario(-a)
and [ænd] *conj* e *(often 'ed' before vowel)*; **~ so on** e così via; **try ~ do it** prova a farlo; **come ~ sit here** vieni a sedere qui; **better ~ better** sempre meglio; **more ~ more** sempre di più
Andes ['ændiːz] *npl*: **the ~** le Ande
Andorra [æn'dɔːrə] *n* Andorra
anecdote ['ænɪkdəut] *n* aneddoto
anemia *etc* [ə'niːmɪə] = **anaemia** *etc*
anemone [ə'nɛmənɪ] *n* *(Bot)* anemone *m*; *(sea anemone)* anemone *m* di mare, attinia

anesthetic etc [ænɪs'θεtɪk] = **anaesthetic** etc
anew [ə'njuː] adv di nuovo
angel ['eɪndʒəl] n angelo
angel dust n sedativo usato a scopo allucinogeno
anger ['æŋgəʳ] n rabbia ∎ vt arrabbiare
angina [æn'dʒaɪnə] n angina pectoris
angle ['æŋgl] n angolo ∎ vi: **to ~ for** (fig) cercare di avere; **from their ~** dal loro punto di vista
angler ['æŋgləʳ] n pescatore m con la lenza
Anglican ['æŋglɪkən] adj, n anglicano(-a)
anglicize ['æŋglɪsaɪz] vt anglicizzare
angling ['æŋglɪŋ] n pesca con la lenza
Anglo- ['æŋgləu] prefix anglo...; **~Italian** adj, n italobritannico(-a)
Anglo-Saxon ['æŋgləu'sæksən] adj, n anglosassone m/f
Angola [æŋ'gəulə] n Angola
Angolan [æŋ'gəulən] adj, n angolano(-a)
angrily ['æŋgrɪlɪ] adv con rabbia
angry ['æŋgrɪ] adj arrabbiato(-a), furioso(-a); **to be ~ with sb/at sth** essere in collera con qn/per qc; **to get ~** arrabbiarsi; **to make sb ~** fare arrabbiare qn
anguish ['æŋgwɪʃ] n angoscia
anguished ['æŋgwɪʃt] adj angosciato(-a), pieno(-a) d'angoscia
angular ['æŋgjuləʳ] adj angolare
animal ['ænɪməl] adj, n animale m
animal rights npl diritti mpl degli animali
animate vt ['ænɪmeɪt] animare ∎ adj ['ænɪmɪt] animato(-a)
animated ['ænɪmeɪtɪd] adj animato(-a)
animation [ænɪ'meɪʃən] n animazione f
animosity [ænɪ'mɔsɪtɪ] n animosità
aniseed ['ænɪsiːd] n semi mpl di anice
Ankara ['æŋkərə] n Ankara
ankle ['æŋkl] n caviglia
ankle socks npl calzini mpl
annex n ['ænεks] (Brit: also: **annexe**) edificio annesso ∎ vt [ə'nεks] annettere
annexation [ænεk'seɪʃən] n annessione f
annihilate [ə'naɪəleɪt] vt annientare
annihilation [ənaɪə'leɪʃən] n annientamento
anniversary [ænɪ'vəːsərɪ] n anniversario
anniversary dinner n cena commemorativa
annotate ['ænəuteɪt] vt annotare
announce [ə'nauns] vt annunciare;
he announced that he wasn't going ha dichiarato che non (ci) sarebbe andato
announcement [ə'naunsmənt] n annuncio; (letter, card) partecipazione f; **I'd like to make an ~** ho una comunicazione da fare
announcer [ə'naunsəʳ] n (Radio, TV: between programmes) annunciatore(-trice); (: in a programme) presentatore(-trice)
annoy [ə'nɔɪ] vt dare fastidio a; **to be**

annoyed (at sth/with sb) essere seccato or irritato (per qc/con qn); **don't get annoyed!** non irritarti!
annoyance [ə'nɔɪəns] n fastidio; (cause of annoyance) noia
annoying [ə'nɔɪɪŋ] adj irritante, seccante
annual ['ænjuəl] adj annuale ∎ n (Bot) pianta annua; (book) annuario
annual general meeting n (Brit) assemblea generale
annually ['ænjuəlɪ] adv annualmente
annual report n relazione f annuale
annuity [ə'njuːɪtɪ] n annualità f inv; **life ~** vitalizio
annul [ə'nʌl] vt annullare; (law) rescindere
annulment [ə'nʌlmənt] n annullamento; rescissione f
annum ['ænəm] n see **per annum**
Annunciation [ənʌnsɪ'eɪʃən] n Annunciazione f
anode ['ænəud] n anodo
anoint [ə'nɔɪnt] vt ungere
anomalous [ə'nɔmələs] adj anomalo(-a)
anomaly [ə'nɔməlɪ] n anomalia
anon. [ə'nɔn] abbr = **anonymous**
anonymity [ænə'nɪmɪtɪ] n anonimato
anonymous [ə'nɔnɪməs] adj anonimo(-a); **to remain ~** mantenere l'anonimato
anorak ['ænəræk] n giacca a vento
anorexia [ænə'rεksɪə] n (also: **anorexia nervosa**) anoressia
anorexic [ænə'rεksɪk] adj, n anoressico(-a)
another [ə'nʌðəʳ] adj: **~ book** (one more) un altro libro, ancora un libro; (a different one) un altro libro ∎ pron un altro/un'altra, ancora uno(-a); **~ drink?** ancora qualcosa da bere?; **in ~ 5 years** fra altri 5 anni; see also **one**
ANSI n abbr (= American National Standards Institution) Istituto americano di standardizzazione
answer ['ɑːnsəʳ] n risposta; soluzione f ∎ vi rispondere ∎ vt (reply to) rispondere a; (problem) risolvere; (prayer) esaudire; **in ~ to your letter** in risposta alla sua lettera; **to ~ the phone** rispondere (al telefono); **to ~ the bell** rispondere al campanello; **to ~ the door** aprire la porta
▶ **answer back** vi ribattere
▶ **answer for** vt fus essere responsabile di
▶ **answer to** vt fus (description) corrispondere a
answerable ['ɑːnsərəbl] adj: **~ (to sb/for sth)** responsabile (verso qn/di qc); **I am ~ to no-one** non devo rispondere a nessuno
answering machine ['ɑːnsərɪŋ-] n segreteria (telefonica) automatica
ant [ænt] n formica
ANTA n abbr = **American National Theater and Academy**

antagonism [æn'tægənızəm] *n*
antagonismo
antagonist [æn'tægənıst] *n* antagonista *m/f*
antagonistic [æntægə'nıstık] *adj*
antagonistico(-a)
antagonize [æn'tægənaız] *vt* provocare
l'ostilità di
Antarctic [ænt'ɑːktık] *n*: **the ~** l'Antartide *f*
■ *adj* antartico(-a)
Antarctica [ænt'ɑːktıkə] *n* Antartide *f*
Antarctic Circle *n* Circolo polare antartico
Antarctic Ocean *n* Oceano antartico
ante ['æntı] *n* (*Cards, fig*): **to up the ~** alzare la
posta in palio
ante... ['æntı] *prefix* anti..., ante..., pre...
anteater ['æntiːtəʳ] *n* formichiere *m*
antecedent [æntı'siːdənt] *n* antecedente *m*,
precedente *m*
antechamber ['æntıtʃeımbəʳ] *n* anticamera
antelope ['æntıləup] *n* antilope *f*
antenatal ['æntı'neıtl] *adj* prenatale
antenatal clinic *n* assistenza medica preparto
antenna (*pl* **antennae**) [æn'tɛnə, -niː] *n*
antenna
anthem ['ænθəm] *n* antifona; **national ~**
inno nazionale
ant-hill ['ænthıl] *n* formicaio
anthology [æn'θɔlədʒı] *n* antologia
anthropologist [ænθrə'pɔlədʒıst] *n*
antropologo(-a)
anthropology [ænθrə'pɔlədʒı] *n*
antropologia
anti- ['æntı] *prefix* anti...
anti-aircraft ['æntı'ɛəkrɑːft] *adj* antiaereo(-a)
antiballistic ['æntıbə'lıstık] *adj*
antibalistico(-a)
antibiotic ['æntıbaı'ɔtık] *adj* antibiotico(-a)
■ *n* antibiotico
antibody ['æntıbɔdı] *n* anticorpo
anticipate [æn'tısıpeıt] *vt* prevedere;
pregustare; (*wishes, request*) prevenire;
as anticipated come previsto; **this is worse
than I anticipated** è peggio di quel che
immaginavo *or* pensavo
anticipation [æntısı'peıʃən] *n* anticipazione
f; (*expectation*) aspettative *fpl*; **thanking you
in ~** vi ringrazio in anticipo
anticlimax ['æntı'klaımæks] *n*: **it was an ~**
fu una completa delusione
anticlockwise ['æntı'klɔkwaız] *adj* in senso
antiorario
antics ['æntıks] *npl* buffonerie *fpl*
anticyclone ['æntı'saıkləun] *n* anticiclone *m*
antidote ['æntıdəut] *n* antidoto
antifreeze ['æntıfriːz] *n* anticongelante *m*
anti-globalization [æntıgləubəlaı'zeıʃən] *adj*
antiglobalizzazione *inv*

antihistamine [æntı'hıstəmın] *n*
antistaminico
Antilles [æn'tıliːz] *npl*: **the ~** le Antille
antipathy [æn'tıpəθı] *n* antipatia
antiperspirant ['æntı'pəːspərənt] *adj*
antitraspirante
Antipodean [æntıpə'diːən] *adj* degli Antipodi
Antipodes [æn'tıpədiːz] *npl*: **the ~** gli Antipodi
antiquarian [æntı'kwɛərıən] *adj*:
~ bookshop libreria antiquaria ■ *n*
antiquario(-a)
antiquated ['æntıkweıtıd] *adj* antiquato(-a)
antique [æn'tiːk] *n* antichità *f inv* ■ *adj*
antico(-a)
antique dealer *n* antiquario(-a)
antique shop *n* negozio d'antichità
antiquity [æn'tıkwıtı] *n* antichità *f inv*
anti-semitic ['æntısı'mıtık] *adj*
antisemitico(-a), antisemita
anti-semitism ['æntı'sɛmıtızəm] *n*
antisemitismo
antiseptic [æntı'sɛptık] *adj* antisettico(-a)
■ *n* antisettico
antisocial ['æntı'səuʃəl] *adj* asociale; (*against
society*) antisociale
antitank [æntı'tæŋk] *adj* anticarro *inv*
antithesis (*pl* **antitheses**) [æn'tıθısıs, -sıːz] *n*
antitesi *f inv*; (*contrast*) carattere *m* antitetico
anti-trust [æntı'trʌst] *adj* (*Comm*):
~ legislation legislazione *f* antitrust *inv*
antiviral [æntı'vaıərəl] *adj* (*Med*) antivirale
antivirus [æntı'vaıərəs] *adj* (*Comput*)
antivirus *inv*; **~ software** antivirus *m inv*
antlers ['æntləz] *npl* palchi *mpl*
Antwerp ['æntwəːp] *n* Anversa
anus ['eınəs] *n* ano
anvil ['ænvıl] *n* incudine *f*
anxiety [æŋ'zaıətı] *n* ansia; (*keenness*): **~ to do**
smania di fare
anxious ['æŋkʃəs] *adj* ansioso(-a),
inquieto(-a); (*keen*): **~ to do/that** impaziente
di fare/che + *sub*; **I'm very ~ about you** sono
molto preoccupato *or* in pensiero per te
anxiously ['æŋkʃəslı] *adv* ansiosamente, con
ansia

○ KEYWORD

any ['ɛnı] *adj* **1** (*in questions etc*): **have you any
butter?** hai del burro?, hai un po' di burro?;
have you any children? hai bambini?; **if
there are any tickets left** se ci sono ancora
(dei) biglietti, se c'è ancora qualche biglietto
2 (*with negative*): **I haven't any money/books**
non ho soldi/libri; **without any difficulty**
senza nessuna *or* alcuna difficoltà
3 (*no matter which*) qualsiasi, qualunque;

choose any book you like scegli un libro qualsiasi
4 (*in phrases*): **in any case** in ogni caso; **any day now** da un giorno all'altro; **at any moment** in qualsiasi momento, da un momento all'altro; **at any rate** ad ogni modo ▪ *pron* **1** (*in questions, with negative*): **have you got any?** ne hai?; **can any of you sing?** qualcuno di voi sa cantare?; **I haven't any (of them)** non ne ho
2 (*no matter which one(s)*): **take any of those books (you like)** prendi uno qualsiasi di quei libri
▪ *adv* **1** (*in questions etc*): **do you want any more soup/sandwiches?** vuoi ancora un po' di minestra/degli altri panini?; **are you feeling any better?** ti senti meglio?
2 (*with negative*): **I can't hear him any more** non lo sento più; **don't wait any longer** non aspettare più

anybody ['ɛnɪbɒdɪ] *pron* qualsiasi persona; (*in interrogative sentences*) qualcuno; (*in negative sentences*): **I don't see ~** non vedo nessuno
anyhow ['ɛnɪhaʊ] *adv* in qualsiasi modo; (*haphazardly*) come capita; **I shall go ~** ci andrò lo stesso *or* comunque
anyone ['ɛnɪwʌn] *pron* = **anybody**
anyplace ['ɛnɪpleɪs] *adv* (*US col*) = **anywhere**
anything ['ɛnɪθɪŋ] *pron* qualsiasi cosa; (*in interrogative sentences*) qualcosa; (*in negative sentences*) non ... niente, non ... nulla; **~ else?** (*in shop*) basta (così)?; **it can cost ~ between £15 and £20** può costare qualcosa come 15 o 20 sterline
anytime ['ɛnɪtaɪm] *adv* in qualunque momento; quando vuole
anyway ['ɛnɪweɪ] *adv* in *or* ad ogni modo
anywhere ['ɛnɪwɛəʳ] *adv* da qualsiasi parte; (*in interrogative sentences*) da qualche parte; **I don't see him ~** non lo vedo da nessuna parte; **~ in the world** dovunque nel mondo
Anzac ['ænzæk] *n abbr* (= *Australia-New Zealand Army Corps*) A.N.Z.A.C. *m*; (*soldier*) soldato dell'A.N.Z.A.C.; *vedi nota*

⬤ **ANZAC DAY**

L' *Anzac Day* è una festa nazionale australiana e neozelandese che cade il 25 aprile e commemora il famoso sbarco delle forze armate congiunte dei due paesi a Gallipoli nel 1915, durante la prima guerra mondiale.

apart [ə'pɑːt] *adv* (*to one side*) a parte;

(*separately*) separatamente; **with one's legs ~** con le gambe divaricate; **10 miles/a long way ~** a 10 miglia di distanza/molto lontani l'uno dall'altro; **they are living ~** sono separati; **~ from** *prep* a parte, eccetto
apartheid [ə'pɑːteɪt] *n* apartheid *f*
apartment [ə'pɑːtmənt] *n* (*US*) appartamento; **apartments** *npl* appartamento ammobiliato
apartment building *n* (*US*) stabile *m*, caseggiato
apathetic [æpə'θɛtɪk] *adj* apatico(-a)
apathy ['æpəθɪ] *n* apatia
APB *n abbr* (*US*: = *all points bulletin: police expression*) *espressione della polizia che significa* "*trovate e arrestate il sospetto*"
ape [eɪp] *n* scimmia ▪ *vt* scimmiottare
Apennines ['æpənaɪnz] *npl*: **the ~** gli Apennini
aperitif [ə'pɛrɪtiːf] *n* aperitivo
aperture ['æpəɪʃjʊəʳ] *n* apertura
APEX ['eɪpɛks] *n abbr* (*Aviat*: = *advance purchase excursion*) APEX *m inv*
apex ['eɪpɛks] *n* apice *m*
aphid ['æfɪd] *n* afide *f*
aphrodisiac [æfrəʊ'dɪzɪæk] *adj* afrodisiaco(-a) ▪ *n* afrodisiaco
API *n abbr* = **American Press Institute**
apiece [ə'piːs] *adv* ciascuno(-a)
aplomb [ə'plɔm] *n* disinvoltura
APO *n abbr* (*US*: = *Army Post Office*) ufficio postale dell'esercito
apocalypse [ə'pɔkəlɪps] *n* apocalisse *f*
apolitical [eɪpə'lɪtɪkl] *adj* apolitico(-a)
apologetic [əpɔlə'dʒɛtɪk] *adj* (*tone, letter*) di scusa; **to be very ~ about** scusarsi moltissimo di
apologetically [əpɔlə'dʒɛtɪkəlɪ] *adv* per scusarsi
apologize [ə'pɔlədʒaɪz] *vi*: **to ~ (for sth to sb)** scusarsi (di qc a qn), chiedere scusa (a qn per qc)
apology [ə'pɔlədʒɪ] *n* scuse *fpl*; **please accept my apologies** la prego di accettare le mie scuse
apoplectic [æpə'plɛktɪk] *adj* (*Med*) apoplettico(-a); **~ with rage** (*col*) livido(-a) per la rabbia
apoplexy ['æpəplɛksɪ] *n* apoplessia
apostle [ə'pɔsl] *n* apostolo
apostrophe [ə'pɔstrəfɪ] *n* (*sign*) apostrofo
app *n abbr* (*Comput*) = **application**
appal [ə'pɔːl] *vt* atterrire; sgomentare
Appalachian Mountains [æpə'leɪʃən-] *npl*: **the ~** i Monti Appalachi
appalling [ə'pɔːlɪŋ] *adj* spaventoso(-a); **she's an ~ cook** è un disastro come cuoca
apparatus [æpə'reɪtəs] *n* apparato
apparel [ə'pærl] *n* (*US*) abbigliamento, confezioni *fpl*

apparent [ə'pærənt] *adj* evidente
apparently [ə'pærəntlı] *adv* evidentemente, a quanto pare
apparition [æpə'rɪʃən] *n* apparizione *f*
appeal [ə'piːl] *vi* (*Law*) appellarsi alla legge
■ *n* (*Law*) appello; (*request*) richiesta; (*charm*) attrattiva; **to ~ for** chiedere (con insistenza); **to ~ to** (*person*) appellarsi a; (*thing*) piacere a; **to ~ to sb for mercy** chiedere pietà a qn; **it doesn't ~ to me** mi dice poco; **right of ~** diritto d'appello
appealing [ə'piːlɪŋ] *adj* (*moving*) commovente; (*attractive*) attraente
appear [ə'pɪər] *vi* apparire; (*Law*) comparire; (*publication*) essere pubblicato(-a); (*seem*) sembrare; **it would ~ that** sembra che; **to ~ in Hamlet** recitare nell'Amleto; **to ~ on TV** presentarsi in televisione
appearance [ə'pɪərəns] *n* apparizione *f*; (*look, aspect*) aspetto; **to put in** or **make an ~** fare atto di presenza; **by order of ~** in ordine di apparizione; **to keep up appearances** salvare le apparenze; **to all appearances** a giudicar dalle apparenze
appease [ə'piːz] *vt* calmare, appagare
appeasement [ə'piːzmənt] *n* (*Pol*) appeasement *m inv*
append [ə'pend] *vt* (*Comput*) aggiungere in coda
appendage [ə'pendɪdʒ] *n* aggiunta
appendicitis [əpɛndɪ'saɪtɪs] *n* appendicite *f*
appendix (*pl* **appendices**) [ə'pendɪks, -siːz] *n* appendice *f*; **to have one's ~ out** operarsi or farsi operare di appendicite
appetite ['æpɪtaɪt] *n* appetito; **that walk has given me an ~** la passeggiata mi ha messo appetito
appetizer ['æpɪtaɪzər] *n* (*food*) stuzzichino; (*drink*) aperitivo
appetizing ['æpɪtaɪzɪŋ] *adj* appetitoso(-a)
applaud [ə'plɔːd] *vt*, *vi* applaudire
applause [ə'plɔːz] *n* applauso
apple ['æpl] *n* mela; (*also*: **apple tree**) melo; **the ~ of one's eye** la pupilla dei propri occhi
apple turnover *n* sfogliatella alle mele
appliance [ə'plaɪəns] *n* apparecchio; **electrical appliances** elettrodomestici *mpl*
applicable [ə'plɪkəbl] *adj* applicabile; **to be ~ to** essere valido per; **the law is ~ from January** la legge entrerà in vigore in gennaio
applicant ['æplɪkənt] *n* candidato(-a); (*Admin: for benefit etc*) chi ha fatto domanda or richiesta
application [æplɪ'keɪʃən] *n* applicazione *f*; (*for a job, a grant etc*) domanda; (*Comput*) applicazione *f*; **on ~** su richiesta

application form *n* modulo di domanda
application program *n* (*Comput*) programma applicativo
applications package *n* (*Comput*) software *m inv* applicativo
applied [ə'plaɪd] *adj* applicato(-a); **~ arts** arti *fpl* applicate
apply [ə'plaɪ] *vt*: **to ~ (to)** (*paint, ointment*) dare (a); (*theory, technique*) applicare (a) ■ *vi*: **to ~ to** (*ask*) rivolgersi a; (*be suitable for, relevant to*) riguardare, riferirsi a; **to ~ (for)** (*permit, grant, job*) fare domanda (per); **to ~ the brakes** frenare; **to ~ o.s. to** dedicarsi a
appoint [ə'pɔɪnt] *vt* nominare
appointee [əpɔɪn'tiː] *n* incaricato(-a)
appointment [ə'pɔɪntmənt] *n* nomina; (*arrangement to meet*) appuntamento; **by ~** su or per appuntamento; **to make an ~ with sb** prendere un appuntamento con qn; (*Press*): **"appointments (vacant)"** "offerte *fpl* di impiego"
apportion [ə'pɔːʃən] *vt* attribuire
appraisal [ə'preɪzl] *n* valutazione *f*
appraise [ə'preɪz] *vt* (*value*) valutare, fare una stima di; (*situation etc*) fare il bilancio di
appreciable [ə'priːʃəbl] *adj* apprezzabile
appreciably [ə'priːʃəblɪ] *adv* notevolmente, sensibilmente
appreciate [ə'priːʃɪeɪt] *vt* (*like*) apprezzare; (*be grateful for*) essere riconoscente di; (*be aware of*) rendersi conto di ■ *vi* (*Comm*) aumentare; **I appreciated your help** ti sono grato per l'aiuto
appreciation [əpriːʃɪ'eɪʃən] *n* apprezzamento; (*Finance*) aumento del valore
appreciative [ə'priːʃɪətɪv] *adj* (*person*) sensibile; (*comment*) elogiativo(-a)
apprehend [æprɪ'hend] *vt* (*arrest*) arrestare; (*understand*) comprendere
apprehension [æprɪ'henʃən] *n* (*fear*) inquietudine *f*
apprehensive [æprɪ'hensɪv] *adj* apprensivo(-a)
apprentice [ə'prentɪs] *n* apprendista *m/f* ■ *vt*: **to be apprenticed to** lavorare come apprendista presso
apprenticeship [ə'prentɪsʃɪp] *n* apprendistato; **to serve one's ~** fare il proprio apprendistato or tirocinio
appro. ['æprəu] *abbr* (*Brit Comm: col*) = **approval**
approach [ə'prəutʃ] *vi* avvicinarsi ■ *vt* (*come near*) avvicinarsi a; (*ask, apply to*) rivolgersi a; (*subject, passer-by*) avvicinare ■ *n* approccio; accesso; (*to problem*) modo di affrontare; **to ~ sb about sth** rivolgersi a qn per qc

approachable [ə'prəutʃəbl] *adj* accessibile
approach road *n* strada d'accesso
approbation [æprə'beɪʃən] *n* approvazione *f*, benestare *m*
appropriate *vt* [ə'prəuprɪeɪt] *(take)* appropriarsi di ■ *adj* [ə'prəuprɪɪt] appropriato(-a), adatto(-a); **it would not be ~ for me to comment** non sta a me fare dei commenti
appropriately [ə'prəuprɪɪtlɪ] *adv* in modo appropriato
appropriation [əprəuprɪ'eɪʃən] *n* stanziamento
approval [ə'pru:vəl] *n* approvazione *f*; **on ~** *(Comm)* in prova, in esame; **to meet with sb's ~** soddisfare qn, essere di gradimento di qn
approve [ə'pru:v] *vt, vi* approvare
  ▶ **approve of** *vt fus* approvare
approved school *n* *(Brit: old)* riformatorio
approvingly [ə'pɾu:vɪŋlɪ] *adv* in approvazione
approx. *abbr* = **approximately**
approximate *adj* [ə'prɔksɪmɪt] approssimativo(-a) ■ *vt* [ə'prɔksɪmeɪt] essere un'approssimazione di, avvicinarsi a
approximately [ə'prɔksɪmətlɪ] *adv* circa
approximation [ə'prɔksɪ'meɪʃən] *n* approssimazione *f*
apr *n abbr* (= *annual percentage rate*) tasso di percentuale annuo
Apr. *abbr* (= *April*) apr.
apricot ['eɪprɪkɔt] *n* albicocca
April ['eɪprəl] *n* aprile *m*; **~ fool!** pesce d'aprile!; *see also* **July**
April Fools' Day *n* vedi nota

● **APRIL FOOLS' DAY**

April Fools' Day è il primo aprile, il giorno degli scherzi e delle burle. Il nome deriva dal fatto che, se una persona cade nella trappola che gli è stata tesa, fa la figura del fool, cioè dello sciocco. Di recente gli scherzi stanno diventando sempre più elaborati, e persino i giornalisti a volte inventano vicende incredibili per burlarsi dei lettori.

apron ['eɪprən] *n* grembiule *m*; *(Aviat)* area di stazionamento
apse [æps] *n* *(Archit)* abside *f*
APT *n abbr* (Brit: = *advanced passenger train*) treno ad altissima velocità
apt [æpt] *adj* *(suitable)* adatto(-a); *(able)* capace; *(likely)*: **to be ~ to do** avere tendenza a fare
Apt. *abbr* = **apartment**

aptitude ['æptɪtju:d] *n* abilità *f inv*
aptitude test *n* test *m inv* attitudinale
aptly ['æptlɪ] *adv* appropriatamente, in modo adatto
aqualung ['ækwəlʌŋ] *n* autorespiratore *m*
aquarium [ə'kwɛərɪəm] *n* acquario
Aquarius [ə'kwɛərɪəs] *n* Acquario; **to be ~** essere dell'Acquario
aquatic [ə'kwætɪk] *adj* acquatico(-a)
aqueduct ['ækwɪdʌkt] *n* acquedotto
AR *abbr* (US) = **Arkansas**
ARA *n abbr* (Brit) = **Associate of the Royal Academy**
Arab ['ærəb] *adj, n* arabo(-a)
Arabia [ə'reɪbɪə] *n* Arabia
Arabian [ə'reɪbɪən] *adj* arabo(-a)
Arabian Desert *n* Deserto arabico
Arabian Sea *n* mare *m* Arabico
Arabic ['ærəbɪk] *adj* arabico(-a) ■ *n* arabo
Arabic numerals *npl* numeri *mpl* arabi, numerazione *f* araba
arable ['ærəbl] *adj* arabile
ARAM *n abbr* (Brit) = **Associate of the Royal Academy of Music**
arbiter ['ɑ:bɪtər] *n* arbitro
arbitrary ['ɑ:bɪtrərɪ] *adj* arbitrario(-a)
arbitrate ['ɑ:bɪtreɪt] *vi* arbitrare
arbitration [ɑ:bɪ'treɪʃən] *n* *(Law)* arbitrato; *(Industry)* arbitraggio
arbitrator ['ɑ:bɪtreɪtər] *n* arbitro
ARC *n abbr* (= *American Red Cross*) C.R.I. *f* (= *Croce Rossa Italiana*)
arc [ɑ:k] *n* arco
arcade [ɑ:'keɪd] *n* portico; *(passage with shops)* galleria
arch [ɑ:tʃ] *n* arco; *(of foot)* arco plantare ■ *vt* inarcare ■ *prefix*: **~(-)** grande *(before n)*; per eccellenza
archaeological [ɑ:kɪə'lɔdʒɪkəl] *adj* archeologico(-a)
archaeologist [ɑ:kɪ'ɔlədʒɪst] *n* archeologo(-a)
archaeology [ɑ:kɪ'ɔlədʒɪ] *n* archeologia
archaic [ɑ:'keɪɪk] *adj* arcaico(-a)
archangel ['ɑ:keɪndʒəl] *n* arcangelo
archbishop [ɑ:tʃ'bɪʃəp] *n* arcivescovo
arched [ɑ:tʃt] *adj* arcuato(-a), ad arco
arch-enemy ['ɑ:tʃ'ɛnɪmɪ] *n* arcinemico(-a)
archeology *etc* [ɑ:kɪ'ɔlədʒɪ] = **archaeology** *etc*
archer ['ɑ:tʃər] *n* arciere *m*
archery ['ɑ:tʃərɪ] *n* tiro all'arco
archetypal ['ɑ:kɪtaɪpəl] *adj* tipico(-a)
archetype ['ɑ:kɪtaɪp] *n* archetipo
archipelago [ɑ:kɪ'pɛlɪgəu] *n* arcipelago
architect ['ɑ:kɪtɛkt] *n* architetto
architectural [ɑ:kɪ'tɛktʃərəl] *adj* architettonico(-a)
architecture ['ɑ:kɪtɛktʃər] *n* architettura

archive file n (Comput) file m inv di archivio
archives ['ɑːkaɪvz] npl archivi mpl
archivist ['ɑːkɪvɪst] n archivista m/f
archway ['ɑːtʃweɪ] n arco
ARCM n abbr (Brit) = **Associate of the Royal College of Music**
Arctic ['ɑːktɪk] adj artico(-a) ■ n: **the ~** l'Artico
Arctic Circle n Circolo polare artico
Arctic Ocean n Oceano artico
ARD n abbr (US Med) = **acute respiratory disease**
ardent ['ɑːdənt] adj ardente
ardour, (US) **ardor** ['ɑːdər] n ardore m
arduous ['ɑːdjuəs] adj arduo(-a)
are [ɑːr] vb see **be**
area ['ɛərɪə] n (Geom) area; (zone) zona; (: smaller) settore m; **dining ~** zona pranzo; **the London ~** la zona di Londra
area code n (US Tel) prefisso
arena [əˈriːnə] n arena
aren't [ɑːnt] = **are not**
Argentina [ɑːdʒənˈtiːnə] n Argentina
Argentinian [ɑːdʒənˈtɪnɪən] adj, n argentino(-a)
arguable ['ɑːgjuəbl] adj discutibile; **it is ~ whether ...** è una cosa discutibile se ... + sub
arguably ['ɑːgjuəblɪ] adv: **it is ~ ...** si può sostenere che sia ...
argue ['ɑːgjuː] vi (quarrel) litigare; (reason) ragionare ■ vt (debate: case, matter) dibattere; **to ~ that** sostenere che; **to ~ about sth (with sb)** litigare per or a proposito di qc (con qn)
argument ['ɑːgjumənt] n (reasons) argomento; (quarrel) lite f; (debate) discussione f; **~ for/against** argomento a or in favore di/contro
argumentative [ɑːgjuˈmɛntətɪv] adj litigioso(-a)
aria ['ɑːrɪə] n aria
ARIBA n abbr (Brit) = **Associate of the Royal Institute of British Architects**
arid ['ærɪd] adj arido(-a)
aridity [əˈrɪdɪtɪ] n aridità
Aries ['ɛərɪz] n Ariete m; **to be ~** essere dell'Ariete
arise (pt **arose**, pp **arisen**) [əˈraɪz, əˈrəuz, əˈrɪzn] vi alzarsi; (opportunity, problem) presentarsi; **to ~ from** risultare da; **should the need ~** dovesse presentarsi la necessità, in caso di necessità
aristocracy [ærɪsˈtɔkrəsɪ] n aristocrazia
aristocrat ['ærɪstəkræt] n aristocratico(-a)
aristocratic [ærɪstəˈkrætɪk] adj aristocratico(-a)
arithmetic [əˈrɪθmətɪk] n aritmetica
arithmetical [ærɪθˈmɛtɪkəl] adj aritmetico(-a)
Ariz. abbr (US) = **Arizona**

ark [ɑːk] n: **Noah's A~** l'arca di Noè
Ark. abbr (US) = **Arkansas**
arm [ɑːm] n braccio; (Mil: branch) arma ■ vt armare; **~ in ~** a braccetto; see also **arms**
armaments ['ɑːməmənts] npl (weapons) armamenti mpl
armband ['ɑːmbænd] n bracciale m
armchair ['ɑːmtʃɛər] n poltrona
armed [ɑːmd] adj armato(-a)
armed forces npl forze fpl armate
armed robbery n rapina a mano armata
Armenia [ɑːˈmiːnɪə] n Armenia
Armenian [ɑːˈmiːnɪən] adj armeno(-a) ■ n armeno(-a); (Ling) armeno
armful ['ɑːmful] n bracciata
armistice ['ɑːmɪstɪs] n armistizio
armour, (US) **armor** ['ɑːmər] n armatura; (also: **armour-plating**) corazza, blindatura; (Mil: tanks) mezzi mpl blindati
armoured car, (US) **armored car** n autoblinda f inv
armoury, (US) **armory** ['ɑːmərɪ] n arsenale m
armpit ['ɑːmpɪt] n ascella
armrest ['ɑːmrɛst] n bracciolo
arms [ɑːmz] npl (weapons) armi fpl; (Heraldry) stemma m
arms control n controllo degli armamenti
arms race n corsa agli armamenti
army ['ɑːmɪ] n esercito
aroma [əˈrəumə] n aroma
aromatherapy [ərəuməˈθɛrəpɪ] n aromaterapia
aromatic [ærəˈmætɪk] adj aromatico(-a)
arose [əˈrəuz] pt of **arise**
around [əˈraund] adv attorno, intorno ■ prep intorno a; (fig: about): **~ £5/3 o'clock** circa 5 sterline/le 3; **is he ~?** è in giro?
arousal [əˈrauzəl] n (sexual etc) eccitazione f; (awakening) risveglio
arouse [əˈrauz] vt (sleeper) svegliare; (curiosity, passions) suscitare
arrange [əˈreɪndʒ] vt sistemare; (programme) preparare ■ vi: **we have arranged for a taxi to pick you up** la faremo venire a prendere da un taxi; **it was arranged that ...** è stato deciso or stabilito che ...; **to ~ to do sth** mettersi d'accordo per fare qc
arrangement [əˈreɪndʒmənt] n sistemazione f; (plans etc); **arrangements** npl progetti mpl, piani mpl; **by ~** su richiesta; **to come to an ~ (with sb)** venire ad un accordo (con qn), mettersi d'accordo or accordarsi (con qn); **I'll make arrangements for you to be met** darò disposizioni or istruzioni perché ci sia qualcuno ad incontrarla
arrant ['ærənt] adj: **~ nonsense** colossali sciocchezze fpl

433

array [ə'reɪ] *n* fila; (*Comput*) array *m inv*, insiemi *mpl*

arrears [ə'rɪəz] *npl* arretrati *mpl*; **to be in ~ with one's rent** essere in arretrato con l'affitto

arrest [ə'rɛst] *vt* arrestare; (*sb's attention*) attirare ◼ *n* arresto; **under ~** in arresto

arresting [ə'rɛstɪŋ] *adj* (*fig*) che colpisce

arrival [ə'raɪvəl] *n* arrivo; (*person*) arrivato(-a); **new ~** nuovo venuto

arrive [ə'raɪv] *vi* arrivare
  ▸ **arrive at** *vt fus* arrivare a

arrogance ['ærəgəns] *n* arroganza

arrogant ['ærəgənt] *adj* arrogante

arrow ['ærəu] *n* freccia

arse [ɑ:s] *n* (*Brit col!*) culo (*!*)

arsenal ['ɑ:sɪnl] *n* arsenale *m*

arsenic ['ɑ:snɪk] *n* arsenico

arson ['ɑ:sn] *n* incendio doloso

art [ɑ:t] *n* arte *f*; (*craft*) mestiere *m*; **work of ~** opera d'arte; *see also* **arts**

artefact, (*US*) **artifact** ['ɑ:tɪfækt] *n* manufatto

arterial [ɑ:'tɪərɪəl] *adj* (*Anat*) arterioso(-a); (*road etc*) di grande comunicazione; **~ roads** le (grandi *or* principali) arterie

artery ['ɑ:tərɪ] *n* arteria

artful ['ɑ:tful] *adj* furbo(-a)

art gallery *n* galleria d'arte

arthritis [ɑ:'θraɪtɪs] *n* artrite *f*

artichoke ['ɑ:tɪtʃəuk] *n* carciofo; **Jerusalem ~** topinambur *m inv*

article ['ɑ:tɪkl] *n* articolo; **articles** *npl* (*Brit Law: training*) contratto di tirocinio; **articles of clothing** indumenti *mpl*

articles of association *npl* (*Comm*) statuto sociale

articulate *adj* [ɑ:'tɪkjulɪt] (*person*) che si esprime forbitamente; (*speech*) articolato(-a) ◼ *vi* [ɑ:'tɪkjuleɪt] articolare

articulated lorry *n* (*Brit*) autotreno

artifact ['ɑ:tɪfækt] *n* (*US*) = **artefact**

artifice ['ɑ:tɪfɪs] *n* (*cunning*) abilità, destrezza; (*trick*) artificio

artificial [ɑ:tɪ'fɪʃəl] *adj* artificiale

artificial insemination [-ɪnsɛmɪ'neɪʃən] *n* fecondazione *f* artificiale

artificial intelligence *n* intelligenza artificiale

artificial respiration *n* respirazione *f* artificiale

artillery [ɑ:'tɪlərɪ] *n* artiglieria

artisan ['ɑ:tɪzæn] *n* artigiano(-a)

artist ['ɑ:tɪst] *n* artista *m/f*

artistic [ɑ:'tɪstɪk] *adj* artistico(-a)

artistry ['ɑ:tɪstrɪ] *n* arte *f*

artless ['ɑ:tlɪs] *adj* semplice, ingenuo(-a)

arts [ɑ:ts] *npl* (*Scol*) lettere *fpl*

art school *n* scuola d'arte

artwork ['ɑ:twə:k] *n* materiale *m* illustrativo

ARV *n abbr* (= *American Revised Version*) traduzione della Bibbia

AS *n abbr* (*US Scol*: = *Associate in Science*) titolo di studio

 KEYWORD

as [æz] *conj* **1** (*referring to time*) mentre; **as the years went by** col passare degli anni; **he came in as I was leaving** arrivò mentre stavo uscendo; **as from tomorrow** da domani

2 (*in comparisons*): **as big as** grande come; **twice as big as** due volte più grande di; **as much/many as** tanto quanto/tanti quanti; **as soon as possible** prima possibile

3 (*since, because*) dal momento che, siccome

4 (*referring to manner, way*) come; **big as it is** grande com'è; **much as I like them, ...** per quanto mi siano simpatici, ...; **do as you wish** fa' come vuoi; **as she said** come ha detto lei

5 (*concerning*): **as for** *or* **to that** per quanto riguarda *or* quanto a quello

6: **as if** *or* **though** come se; **he looked as if he was ill** sembrava stare male; *see also* **long; such; well**

  ◼ *prep*: **he works as a driver** fa l'autista; **as chairman of the company, he ...** come presidente della compagnia, lui ...; **he gave me it as a present** me lo ha regalato

ASA *n abbr* (= *American Standards Association*) associazione per la normalizzazione; (*Brit*: = *Advertising Standards Association*) ≈ Istituto di Autodisciplina Pubblicitaria

a.s.a.p. *abbr* (= *as soon as possible*) prima possibile

asbestos [æz'bɛstəs] *n* asbesto, amianto

ASBO ['æzbəu] *n abbr* (*Brit*: = *antisocial behaviour order*) provvedimento restrittivo per comportamento antisociale

ascend [ə'sɛnd] *vt* salire

ascendancy [ə'sɛndənsɪ] *n* ascendente *m*

ascendant [ə'sɛndənt] *n*: **to be in the ~** essere in auge

ascension [ə'sɛnʃən] *n*: **the A~** (*Rel*) l'Ascensione *f*

Ascension Island *n* isola dell'Ascensione

ascent [ə'sɛnt] *n* salita

ascertain [æsə'teɪn] *vt* accertare

ascetic [ə'sɛtɪk] *adj* ascetico(-a)

asceticism [ə'sɛtɪsɪzəm] *n* ascetismo

ASCII ['æski:] *n abbr* (= *American Standard Code*

for Information Interchange) ASCII *m*

ascribe [ə'skraɪb] *vt*: **to ~ sth to** attribuire qc a

ASCU *n abbr* (US) = **Association of State Colleges and Universities**

ASE *n abbr* = **American Stock Exchange**

ASH [æʃ] *n abbr* (Brit: = *Action on Smoking and Health*) iniziativa contro il fumo

ash [æʃ] *n* (*dust*) cenere *f*; ~ **(tree)** frassino

ashamed [ə'ʃeɪmd] *adj* vergognoso(-a); **to be ~ of** vergognarsi di; **to be ~ (of o.s.) for having done** vergognarsi di aver fatto

ashen ['æʃən] *adj* (*pale*) livido(-a)

ashore [ə'ʃɔːʳ] *adv* a terra; **to go ~** sbarcare

ashtray ['æʃtreɪ] *n* portacenere *m*

Ash Wednesday *n* Mercoledì *m inv* delle Ceneri

Asia Minor *n* Asia minore

Asian ['eɪʃən] *adj, n* asiatico(-a)

Asiatic [eɪsɪ'ætɪk] *adj* asiatico(-a)

aside [ə'saɪd] *adv* da parte ■ *n* a parte *m*; **to take sb ~** prendere qn da parte; ~ **from** (*as well as*) oltre a; (*except for*) a parte

ask [ɑːsk] *vt* (*request*) chiedere; (*question*) domandare; (*invite*) invitare; **to ~ about sth** informarsi su *or* di qc; **to ~ sb sth/sb to do sth** chiedere qc a qn/a qn di fare qc; **to ~ sb about sth** chiedere a qn di qc; **to ~ (sb) a question** fare una domanda (a qn); **to ~ sb the time** chiedere l'ora a qn; **to ~ sb out to dinner** invitare qn a mangiare fuori; **you should ~ at the information desk** dovreste rivolgersi all'ufficio informazioni

▸ **ask after** *vt fus* chiedere di

▸ **ask for** *vt fus* chiedere; **it's just asking for trouble** *or* **for it** è proprio (come) andarsele a cercare

askance [ə'skɑːns] *adv*: **to look ~ at sb** guardare qn di traverso

askew [ə'skjuː] *adv* di traverso, storto

asking price ['ɑːskɪŋ-] *n* prezzo di partenza

asleep [ə'sliːp] *adj* addormentato(-a); **to be ~** dormire; **to fall ~** addormentarsi

ASLEF ['æzlɛf] *n abbr* (Brit: = *Associated Society of Locomotive Engineers and Firemen*) sindacato dei conducenti dei treni e dei macchinisti

AS level *n abbr* (= *Advanced Subsidiary level*) prima parte del diploma di studi superiori chiamato "A level"

asp [æsp] *n* cobra *m inv* egiziano

asparagus [əs'pærəgəs] *n* asparagi *mpl*

asparagus tips *npl* punte *fpl* d'asparagi

ASPCA *n abbr* (= *American Society for the Prevention of Cruelty to Animals*) ≈ E.N.P.A. *m* (= *Ente Nazionale per la Protezione degli Animali*)

aspect ['æspɛkt] *n* aspetto

aspersions [əs'pə:ʃənz] *npl*: **to cast ~ on** diffamare

asphalt ['æsfælt] *n* asfalto

asphyxiate [æs'fɪksɪeɪt] *vt* asfissiare

asphyxiation [æsfɪksɪ'eɪʃən] *n* asfissia

aspiration [æspə'reɪʃən] *n* aspirazione *f*

aspire [əs'paɪəʳ] *vi*: **to ~ to** aspirare a

aspirin ['æsprɪn] *n* aspirina

aspiring [əs'paɪərɪŋ] *adj* aspirante

ass [æs] *n* asino; (*US col!*) culo (!)

assail [ə'seɪl] *vt* assalire

assailant [ə'seɪlənt] *n* assalitore *m*

assassin [ə'sæsɪn] *n* assassino

assassinate [ə'sæsɪneɪt] *vt* assassinare

assassination [əsæsɪ'neɪʃən] *n* assassinio

assault [ə'sɔːlt] *n* (Mil) assalto; (*gen: attack*) aggressione *f*; (*Law*): ~ **(and battery)** minacce e vie di fatto *fpl* ■ *vt* assaltare; aggredire; (*sexually*) violentare

assemble [ə'sɛmbl] *vt* riunire; (Tech) montare ■ *vi* riunirsi

assembly [ə'sɛmblɪ] *n* (*meeting*) assemblea; (*construction*) montaggio

assembly language *n* (Comput) linguaggio assemblativo

assembly line *n* catena di montaggio

assent [ə'sɛnt] *n* assenso, consenso ■ *vi* assentire; **to ~ (to sth)** approvare (qc)

assert [ə'sə:t] *vt* asserire; (*insist on*) far valere; **to ~ o.s.** farsi valere

assertion [ə'sə:ʃən] *n* asserzione *f*

assertive [ə'sə:tɪv] *adj* che sa imporsi

assess [ə'sɛs] *vt* valutare

assessment [ə'sɛsmənt] *n* valutazione *f*; (*judgment*): ~ **(of)** giudizio (su)

assessor [ə'sɛsəʳ] *n* perito; funzionario del fisco

asset ['æsɛt] *n* vantaggio; (*person*) elemento prezioso; **assets** *npl* (Comm) beni *mpl*; disponibilità *fpl*; attivo

asset-stripping ['æsɛt'strɪpɪŋ] *n* (Comm) acquisto di una società in fallimento con lo scopo di rivenderne le attività

assiduous [ə'sɪdjuəs] *adj* assiduo(-a)

assign [ə'saɪn] *vt*: **to ~ (to)** (*task*) assegnare (a); (*resources*) riservare (a); (*cause, meaning*) attribuire (a); **to ~ a date to sth** fissare la data di qc

assignment [ə'saɪnmənt] *n* compito

assimilate [ə'sɪmɪleɪt] *vt* assimilare

assimilation [əsɪmɪ'leɪʃən] *n* assimilazione *f*

assist [ə'sɪst] *vt* assistere, aiutare

assistance [ə'sɪstəns] *n* assistenza, aiuto

assistant [ə'sɪstənt] *n* assistente *m/f*; (Brit: *also*: **shop assistant**) commesso(-a)

assistant manager *n* vicedirettore *m*

assizes [ə'saɪzɪz] *npl* assise *fpl*

associate [ə'səuʃɪt] *adj* associato(-a); (*member*) aggiunto(-a) ■ *n* collega *m/f*;

435

(*in business*) socio(-a) ■ *vb* [əˈsəuʃɪeɪt] *vt*
associare ■ *vi*: **to ~ with sb** frequentare qn
associated company [əˈsəusɪˈeɪtɪd-] *n*
società collegata
associate director *n* amministratore *m*
aggiunto
association [əsəusɪˈeɪʃən] *n* associazione *f*;
in ~ with in collaborazione con
association football *n* (*Brit*) (gioco del) calcio
assorted [əˈsɔːtɪd] *adj* assortito(-a); **in ~
sizes** in diverse taglie
assortment [əˈsɔːtmənt] *n* assortimento
Asst. *abbr* = **assistant**
assuage [əˈsweɪdʒ] *vt* alleviare
assume [əˈsjuːm] *vt* supporre; (*responsibilities
etc*) assumere; (*attitude, name*) prendere
assumed name *n* nome *m* falso
assumption [əˈsʌmpʃən] *n* supposizione *f*,
ipotesi *f inv*; **on the ~ that ...** partendo dal
presupposto che ...
assurance [əˈʃuərəns] *n* assicurazione *f*;
(*self-confidence*) fiducia in se stesso; **I can give
you no assurances** non posso assicurarle *or*
garantirle niente
assure [əˈʃuəʳ] *vt* assicurare
assured [əˈʃuəd] *adj* (*confident*) sicuro(-a);
(*certain: promotion etc*) assicurato(-a)
AST *abbr* (*US: = Atlantic Standard Time*) ora
invernale di New York
asterisk [ˈæstərɪsk] *n* asterisco
astern [əˈstəːn] *adv* a poppa
asteroid [ˈæstərɔɪd] *n* asteroide *m*
asthma [ˈæsmə] *n* asma
asthmatic [æsˈmætɪk] *adj, n* asmatico(-a)
astigmatism [əˈstɪgmətɪzəm] *n*
astigmatismo
astir [əˈstəːʳ] *adv* in piedi; (*excited*) in
fermento
astonish [əˈstɒnɪʃ] *vt* stupire
astonishing [əˈstɒnɪʃɪŋ] *adj* sorprendente,
stupefacente; **I find it ~ that ...** mi stupisce
che ...
astonishingly [əˈstɒnɪʃɪŋlɪ] *adv*
straordinariamente, incredibilmente
astonishment [əˈstɒnɪʃmənt] *n* stupore *m*;
to my ~ con mia gran meraviglia, con mio
grande stupore
astound [əˈstaund] *vt* sbalordire
astray [əˈstreɪ] *adv*: **to go ~** smarrirsi; (*fig*)
traviarsi; **to go ~ in one's calculations**
sbagliare i calcoli
astride [əˈstraɪd] *adv* a cavalcioni ■ *prep*
a cavalcioni di
astringent [əsˈtrɪndʒənt] *adj, n* astringente *m*
astrologer [əsˈtrɒlədʒəʳ] *n* astrologo(-a)
astrology [əsˈtrɒlədʒɪ] *n* astrologia
astronaut [ˈæstrənɔːt] *n* astronauta *m/f*

astronomer [əsˈtrɒnəməʳ] *n* astronomo(-a)
astronomical [æstrəˈnɒmɪkl] *adj*
astronomico(-a)
astronomy [əsˈtrɒnəmɪ] *n* astronomia
astrophysics [ˈæstrəuˈfɪzɪks] *n* astrofisica
astute [əsˈtjuːt] *adj* astuto(-a)
asunder [əˈsʌndəʳ] *adv*: **to tear ~** strappare
ASV *n abbr* (*= American Standard Version*)
traduzione della Bibbia
asylum [əˈsaɪləm] *n* asilo; (*lunatic asylum*)
manicomio; **to seek political ~** chiedere
asilo politico
asymmetric [eɪsɪˈmɛtrɪk], **asymmetrical**
[eɪsɪˈmɛtrɪkəl] *adj* asimmetrico(-a)

 KEYWORD

at [æt] *prep* **1** (*referring to position, direction*) a;
at the top in cima; **at the desk** al banco,
alla scrivania; **at home/school** a casa/
scuola; **at Paolo's** da Paolo; **at the baker's**
dal panettiere; **to look at sth** guardare qc;
to throw sth at sb lanciare qc a qn
2 (*referring to time*) a; **at 4 o'clock** alle 4;
at night di notte; **at Christmas** a Natale;
at times a volte
3 (*referring to rates, speed etc*) a; **at £1 a kilo**
a 1 sterlina al chilo; **two at a time** due alla
volta, due per volta; **at 50 km/h** a 50 km/h;
at full speed a tutta velocità
4 (*referring to manner*): **at a stroke** d'un solo
colpo; **at peace** in pace
5 (*referring to activity*): **to be at work** essere al
lavoro; **to play at cowboys** giocare ai
cowboy; **to be good at sth/doing sth** essere
bravo in qc/a fare qc
6 (*referring to cause*): **shocked/surprised/
annoyed at sth** colpito da/sorpreso da/
arrabbiato per qc; **I went at his suggestion**
ci sono andato dietro suo consiglio
7 (*Comput: symbol*) chiocciola

ate [eɪt] *pt of* **eat**
atheism [ˈeɪθɪɪzəm] *n* ateismo
atheist [ˈeɪθɪɪst] *n* ateo(-a)
Athenian [əˈθiːnɪən] *adj, n* ateniese *m/f*
Athens [ˈæθɪnz] *n* Atene *f*
athlete [ˈæθliːt] *n* atleta *m/f*
athletic [æθˈlɛtɪk] *adj* atletico(-a)
athletics [æθˈlɛtɪks] *n* atletica
Atlantic [ətˈlæntɪk] *adj* atlantico(-a) ■ *n*:
the ~ (Ocean) l'Atlantico, l'Oceano Atlantico
atlas [ˈætləs] *n* atlante *m*
Atlas Mountains *npl*: **the ~** i Monti
dell'Atlante
ATM *abbr* (*= automated telling machine*) cassa
automatica prelievi, sportello automatico

atmosphere ['ætməsfɪəʳ] n atmosfera; (air) aria

atmospheric [ætməs'fɛrɪk] adj atmosferico(-a)

atmospherics [ætməs'fɛrɪks] npl (Radio) scariche fpl

atoll ['ætɔl] n atollo

atom ['ætəm] n atomo

atom bomb n bomba atomica

atomic [ə'tɔmɪk] adj atomico(-a)

atomic bomb n bomba atomica

atomizer ['ætəmaɪzəʳ] n atomizzatore m

atone [ə'təun] vi: **to ~ for** espiare

atonement [ə'təunmənt] n espiazione f

ATP n abbr = **Association of Tennis Professionals**

atrocious [ə'trəuʃəs] adj atroce, pessimo(-a)

atrocity [ə'trɔsɪtɪ] n atrocità f inv

atrophy ['ætrəfɪ] n atrofia ■ vi atrofizzarsi

attach [ə'tætʃ] vt attaccare; (document, letter) allegare; (Mil: troops) assegnare; **to be attached to sb/sth** (to like) essere affezionato(-a) a qn/qc; **the attached letter** la lettera acclusa or allegata

attaché [ə'tæʃeɪ] n addetto

attaché case n valigetta per documenti

attachment [ə'tætʃmənt] n (tool) accessorio; (love): **~ (to)** affetto (per); (Comput) allegato

attack [ə'tæk] vt attaccare; (task etc) iniziare; (problem) affrontare ■ n attacco; (also: **heart attack**) infarto

attacker [ə'tækəʳ] n aggressore m, assalitore(-trice)

attain [ə'teɪn] vt (also: **to attain to**) arrivare a, raggiungere

attainments [ə'teɪnmənts] npl cognizioni fpl

attempt [ə'tɛmpt] n tentativo ■ vt tentare; **attempted murder** (Law) tentato omicidio; **to make an ~ on sb's life** attentare alla vita di qn; **he made no ~ to help** non ha (neanche) tentato or cercato di aiutare

attend [ə'tɛnd] vt frequentare; (meeting, talk) andare a; (patient) assistere
  ▶ **attend to** vt fus (needs, affairs etc) prendersi cura di; (customer) occuparsi di

attendance [ə'tɛndəns] n (being present) presenza; (people present) gente f presente

attendant [ə'tɛndənt] n custode m/f; persona di servizio ■ adj concomitante

attention [ə'tɛnʃən] n attenzione f; **attentions** premure fpl, attenzioni fpl; **~!** (Mil) attenti!; **at ~** (Mil) sull'attenti; **for the ~ of** (Admin) per l'attenzione di; **it has come to my ~ that ...** sono venuto a conoscenza (del fatto) che ...

attentive [ə'tɛntɪv] adj attento(-a); (kind) premuroso(-a)

attentively [ə'tɛntɪvlɪ] adv attentamente

attenuate [ə'tɛnjueɪt] vt attenuare ■ vi attenuarsi

attest [ə'tɛst] vi: **to ~ to** attestare

attic ['ætɪk] n soffitta

attire [ə'taɪəʳ] n abbigliamento

attitude ['ætɪtjuːd] n (behaviour) atteggiamento; (posture) posa; (view): **~ (to)** punto di vista (nei confronti di)

attorney [ə'təːnɪ] n (US: lawyer) avvocato; (having proxy) mandatario; **power of ~** procura

Attorney General n (Brit) Procuratore m Generale; (US) Ministro della Giustizia

attract [ə'trækt] vt attirare

attraction [ə'trækʃən] n (gen pl: pleasant things) attrattiva; (Physics, fig: towards sth) attrazione f

attractive [ə'træktɪv] adj attraente; (idea, offer, price) allettante, interessante

attribute n ['ætrɪbjuːt] attributo ■ vt [ə'trɪbjuːt]: **to ~ sth to** attribuire qc a

attrition [ə'trɪʃən] n: **war of ~** guerra di logoramento

Atty. Gen. abbr = **Attorney General**

atypical [eɪ'tɪpɪkl] adj atipico(-a)

AU n abbr (= African Union) Unione Africana

aubergine ['əubəʒiːn] n melanzana

auburn ['ɔːbən] adj tizianesco(-a)

auction ['ɔːkʃən] n (also: **sale by auction**) asta ■ vt (also: **to sell by auction**) vendere all'asta; (also: **to put up for auction**) mettere all'asta

auctioneer [ɔːkʃə'nɪəʳ] n banditore m

auction room n sala dell'asta

audacious [ɔː'deɪʃəs] adj (bold) audace; (impudent) sfrontato(-a)

audacity [ɔː'dæsɪtɪ] n audacia

audible ['ɔːdɪbl] adj udibile

audience ['ɔːdɪəns] n (people) pubblico; spettatori mpl; ascoltatori mpl; (interview) udienza

audio-typist ['ɔːdɪəu'taɪpɪst] n dattilografo(-a) che trascrive da nastro

audiovisual [ɔːdɪəu'vɪzjuəl] adj audiovisivo(-a); **~ aids** sussidi mpl audiovisivi

audit ['ɔːdɪt] n revisione f, verifica ■ vt rivedere, verificare

audition [ɔː'dɪʃən] n (Theat) audizione f; (Cine) provino ■ vi fare un'audizione (or un provino)

auditor ['ɔːdɪtəʳ] n revisore m

auditorium [ɔːdɪ'tɔːrɪəm] n sala, auditorio

Aug. abbr (= August) ago., ag.

augment [ɔːg'mɛnt] vt, vi aumentare

augur ['ɔːgəʳ] vt (be a sign of) predire ■ vi: **it augurs well** promette bene

August ['ɔːgəst] n agosto; see also **July**

437

august [ɔː'gʌst] *adj* augusto(-a)

aunt [ɑːnt] *n* zia

auntie, aunty ['ɑːntɪ] *n* zietta

au pair ['əu'pɛəʳ] *n* (*also*: **au pair girl**) (ragazza *f*) alla pari *inv*

aura ['ɔːrə] *n* aura

auspices ['ɔːspɪsɪz] *npl*: **under the ~ of** sotto gli auspici di

auspicious [ɔːs'pɪʃəs] *adj* propizio(-a)

austere [ɔs'tɪəʳ] *adj* austero(-a)

austerity [ɔs'tɛrɪtɪ] *n* austerità *f inv*

Australasia [ɔstrə'leɪzɪə] *n* Australasia

Australia [ɔs'treɪlɪə] *n* Australia

Australian [ɔs'treɪlɪən] *adj, n* australiano(-a)

Austria ['ɔstrɪə] *n* Austria

Austrian ['ɔstrɪən] *adj, n* austriaco(-a)

AUT *n abbr* (*Brit*: = *Association of University Teachers*) associazione dei docenti universitari

authentic [ɔː'θɛntɪk] *adj* autentico(-a)

authenticate [ɔː'θɛntɪkeɪt] *vt* autenticare

authenticity [ɔːθɛn'tɪsɪtɪ] *n* autenticità

author ['ɔːθəʳ] *n* autore(-trice)

authoritarian [ɔːθɔrɪ'tɛərɪən] *adj* autoritario(-a)

authoritative [ɔː'θɔrɪtətɪv] *adj* (*account etc*) autorevole; (*manner*) autoritario(-a)

authority [ɔː'θɔrɪtɪ] *n* autorità *f inv*; (*permission*) autorizzazione *f*; **the authorities** *npl* le autorità; **to have ~ to do sth** avere l'autorizzazione a fare *or* il diritto di fare qc

authorization [ɔːθəraɪ'zeɪʃən] *n* autorizzazione *f*

authorize ['ɔːθəraɪz] *vt* autorizzare

authorized capital *n* capitale *m* nominale

authorship ['ɔːθəʃɪp] *n* paternità (*letteraria etc*)

autistic [ɔː'tɪstɪk] *adj* autistico(-a)

auto ['ɔːtəu] *n* (*US*) auto *f inv*

autobiography [ɔːtəbaɪ'ɔgrəfɪ] *n* autobiografia

autocratic [ɔːtə'krætɪk] *adj* autocratico(-a)

Autocue® ['ɔːtəukjuː] *n* (*Brit*) gobbo (TV)

autograph ['ɔːtəgrɑːf] *n* autografo ■ *vt* firmare

autoimmune [ɔːtəʊɪ'mjuːn] *adj* autoimmune

automat ['ɔːtəmæt] *n* (*US*) tavola calda fornita esclusivamente di distributori automatici

automated ['ɔːtəmeɪtɪd] *adj* automatizzato(-a)

automatic [ɔːtə'mætɪk] *adj* automatico(-a) ■ *n* (*gun*) arma automatica; (*car*) automobile *f* con cambio automatico; (*washing machine*) lavatrice *f* automatica

automatically [ɔːtə'mætɪklɪ] *adv* automaticamente

automatic data processing *n* elaborazione *f* automatica dei dati

automation [ɔːtə'meɪʃən] *n* automazione *f*

automaton (*pl* **automata**) [ɔː'tɔmətən, -tə] *n* automa *m*

automobile ['ɔːtəməbiːl] *n* (*US*) automobile *f*

autonomous [ɔː'tɔnəməs] *adj* autonomo(-a)

autopsy ['ɔːtɔpsɪ] *n* autopsia

autumn ['ɔːtəm] *n* autunno

auxiliary [ɔːg'zɪlɪərɪ] *adj* ausiliario(-a) ■ *n* ausiliare *m/f*

AV *n abbr* (= *Authorized Version*) traduzione inglese della Bibbia ■ *abbr* = **audiovisual**

Av. *abbr* = **avenue**

avail [ə'veɪl] *vt*: **to ~ o.s. of** servirsi di; approfittarsi di ■ *n*: **to no ~** inutilmente

availability [əveɪlə'bɪlɪtɪ] *n* disponibilità

available [ə'veɪləbl] *adj* disponibile; **every ~ means** tutti i mezzi disponibili; **to make sth ~ to sb** mettere qc a disposizione di qn; **is the manager ~?** è libero il direttore?

avalanche ['ævəlɑːnʃ] *n* valanga

avant-garde ['ævɑ̃'gɑːd] *adj* d'avanguardia

avarice ['ævərɪs] *n* avarizia

avaricious [ævə'rɪʃəs] *adj* avaro(-a)

avdp. *abbr* (= *avoirdupois*) sistema ponderale anglosassone basato su libbra, oncia e multipli

Ave. *abbr* = **avenue**

avenge [ə'vɛndʒ] *vt* vendicare

avenue ['ævənjuː] *n* viale *m*

average ['ævərɪdʒ] *n* media ■ *adj* medio(-a) ■ *vt* (*also*: **average out at**) aggirarsi in media su, essere in media di; **on ~** in media; **above/ below (the) ~** sopra/sotto la media

averse [ə'vəːs] *adj*: **to be ~ to sth/doing** essere contrario(-a) a qc/a fare; **I wouldn't be ~ to a drink** non avrei nulla in contrario a bere qualcosa

aversion [ə'vəːʃən] *n* avversione *f*

avert [ə'vəːt] *vt* evitare, prevenire; (*one's eyes*) distogliere

avian flu ['eɪvɪən-] *n* influenza aviaria

aviary ['eɪvɪərɪ] *n* voliera, uccelliera

aviation [eɪvɪ'eɪʃən] *n* aviazione *f*

avid ['ævɪd] *adj* avido(-a)

avidly ['ævɪdlɪ] *adv* avidamente

avocado [ævə'kɑːdəu] *n* (*Brit*: *also*: **avocado pear**) avocado *m inv*

avoid [ə'vɔɪd] *vt* evitare

avoidable [ə'vɔɪdəbl] *adj* evitabile

avoidance [ə'vɔɪdəns] *n* l'evitare *m*

avowed [ə'vaud] *adj* dichiarato(-a)

AVP *n abbr* (*US*) = **assistant vice-president**

AWACS ['eɪwæks] *n abbr* (= *airborne warning and control system*) sistema di allarme e controllo in volo

await [ə'weɪt] *vt* aspettare; **awaiting attention** (*Comm*: *letter*) in attesa di risposta; (: *order*) in attesa di essere evaso; **long awaited** tanto atteso(-a)

a

awake [ə'weɪk] *adj* sveglio(-a) ■ *vb* (*pt* **awoke**, *pp* **awoken** *or* **awaked**) *vt* svegliare ■ *vi* svegliarsi; ~ **to** consapevole di

awakening [ə'weɪknɪŋ] *n* risveglio

award [ə'wɔːd] *n* premio; (*Law*) decreto ■ *vt* assegnare; (*Law: damages*) decretare

aware [ə'wɛə^r] *adj*: ~ **of** (*conscious*) conscio(-a) di; (*informed*) informato(-a) di; **to become ~ of** accorgersi di; **politically/socially ~** politicamente/socialmente preparato; **I am fully ~ that ...** mi rendo perfettamente conto che ...

awareness [ə'wɛənɪs] *n* consapevolezza; coscienza; **to develop people's ~ (of)** sensibilizzare la gente (a)

awash [ə'wɔʃ] *adj*: ~ (**with**) inondato(-a) (da)

away [ə'weɪ] *adj, adv* via; lontano(-a); **two kilometres ~** a due chilometri di distanza; **two hours ~ by car** a due ore di distanza in macchina; **the holiday was two weeks ~** mancavano due settimane alle vacanze; **~ from** lontano da; **he's ~ for a week** è andato via per una settimana; **he's ~ in Milan** è (andato) a Milano; **to take ~** *vt* portare via; **he was working/pedalling** *etc* ~ *la particella indica la continuità e l'energia dell'azione*, lavorava/pedalava *etc* più che poteva; **to fade/wither** *etc* ~ *la particella rinforza l'idea della diminuzione*

away game *n* (*Sport*) partita fuori casa

awe [ɔː] *n* timore *m*

awe-inspiring ['ɔːɪnspaɪərɪŋ], **awesome** ['ɔːsəm] *adj* imponente

awestruck ['ɔːstrʌk] *adj* sgomento(-a)

awful ['ɔːfəl] *adj* terribile; **an ~ lot of** (*people, cars, dogs*) un numero incredibile di; (*jam, flowers*) una quantità incredibile di

awfully ['ɔːflɪ] *adv* (*very*) terribilmente

awhile [ə'waɪl] *adv* (per) un po'

awkward ['ɔːkwəd] *adj* (*clumsy*) goffo(-a); (*inconvenient*) scomodo(-a); (*embarrassing*) imbarazzante; (*difficult*) delicato(-a), difficile

awkwardness ['ɔːkwədnɪs] *n* goffaggine *f*; scomodità; imbarazzo; delicatezza, difficoltà

awl ['ɔːl] *n* punteruolo

awning ['ɔːnɪŋ] *n* (*of tent*) veranda; (*of shop, hotel etc*) tenda

awoke [ə'wəuk] *pt of* **awake**

awoken [ə'wəukən] *pp of* **awake**

AWOL ['eɪwɔl] *abbr* (*Mil etc*) = **absent without leave**

awry [ə'raɪ] *adv* di traverso ■ *adj* storto(-a); **to go ~** andare a monte

axe, (US) **ax** [æks] *n* scure *f* ■ *vt* (*project etc*) abolire; (*jobs*) sopprimere; **to have an ~ to grind** (*fig*) fare i propri interessi *or* il proprio tornaconto

axiom ['æksɪəm] *n* assioma *m*

axiomatic [æksɪəu'mætɪk] *adj* assiomatico(-a)

axis (*pl* **axes**) ['æksɪs, -siːz] *n* asse *m*

axle ['æksl] *n* (*also*: **axle-tree**) asse *m*

ay, aye [aɪ] *excl* (*yes*) sì

AYH *n abbr* = **American Youth Hostels**

AZ *abbr* (US) = **Arizona**

azalea [ə'zeɪlɪə] *n* azalea

Azerbaijan [æzəbaɪ'dʒɑːn] *n* Azerbaigian *m*

Azerbaijani [æzəbaɪ'dʒɑːnɪ], **Azeri** [ə'zɛərɪ] *adj, n* azerbaigiano(-a), azero(-a)

Azores [ə'zɔːz] *npl*: **the ~** le Azzorre

AZT *n abbr* (= *azidothymidine*) AZT *m*

Aztec ['æztɛk] *adj, n* azteco(-a)

azure ['eɪʒə^r] *adj* azzurro(-a)

Bb

B, b [biː] *n* (*letter*) B, b *f or m inv*; (*Scol: mark*) ≈
8 (buono); (*Mus*): **B** si *m*; **B for Benjamin**, (US)
B for Baker ≈ B come Bologna; **B road** *n*
(*Brit Aut*) ≈ strada secondaria

b. *abbr* = **born**

BA *n abbr* = **British Academy**; (*Scol*)
= **Bachelor of Arts**

babble ['bæbl] *vi* cianciare; mormorare
■ *n* ciance *fpl* mormorio

babe [beɪb] *n* (*col*): **she's a real** ~ è uno
schianto di ragazza

baboon [bə'buːn] *n* babbuino

baby ['beɪbɪ] *n* bambino(-a)

baby carriage *n* (US) carrozzina

baby grand *n* (*also*: **baby grand piano**)
pianoforte *m* a mezza coda

babyhood ['beɪbɪhud] *n* prima infanzia

babyish ['beɪbɪɪʃ] *adj* infantile

baby-minder ['beɪbɪ'maɪndə'] *n* (*Brit*)
bambinaia (*che tiene i bambini mentre la madre
lavora*)

baby-sit ['beɪbɪsɪt] *vi* fare la (*or* la) babysitter

baby-sitter ['beɪbɪsɪtə'] *n* baby-sitter *m/f inv*

bachelor ['bætʃələ'] *n* scapolo; **B~ of Arts/
Science (BA/BSc)** ≈ laureato(-a) in lettere/
scienze; **B~ of Arts/Science degree (BA/
BSc)** *n* ≈ laurea in lettere/scienze; *vedi nota*

bachelorhood ['bætʃələhud] *n* celibato

bachelor party *n* (US) festa di addio al
celibato

back [bæk] *n* (*of person, horse*) dorso, schiena;
(*of hand*) dorso; (*of house, car*) didietro; (*of train*)
coda; (*of chair*) schienale *m*; (*of page*) rovescio;
(*Football*) difensore *m*; ~ **to front**
all'incontrario; **to break the** ~ **of a job** (*Brit*)
fare il grosso *or* il peggio di un lavoro; **to
have one's** ~ **to the wall** (*fig*) essere *or*
trovarsi con le spalle al muro ■ *vt* (*financially*)
finanziare; (*candidate: also*: **back up**)
appoggiare; (*horse: at races*) puntare su; (*car*)
guidare a marcia indietro ■ *vi* indietreggiare;
(*car etc*) fare marcia indietro ■ *adj* (*in compounds*)
posteriore, di dietro; arretrato(-a); ~ **seats/
wheels** (*Aut*) sedili *mpl*/ruote *fpl* posteriori;
~ **payments/rent** arretrati *mpl*; ~ **garden/
room** giardino/stanza sul retro (della casa);
to take a ~ **seat** (*fig*) restare in secondo piano
■ *adv* (*not forward*) indietro; (*returned*): **he's** ~
è tornato; **when will you be** ~? quando
torni?; **he ran** ~ tornò indietro di corsa;
throw the ball ~ (*restitution*) ritira la palla;
can I have it ~? posso riaverlo?; **he called** ~
(*again*) ha richiamato

▶ **back down** *vi* (*fig*) fare marcia indietro

▶ **back on to** *vt fus*: **the house backs on to
the golf course** il retro della casa dà sul
campo da golf

▶ **back out** *vi* (*of promise*) tirarsi indietro

▶ **back up** *vt* (*support*) appoggiare, sostenere;
(*Comput*) fare una copia di riserva di

backache ['bækeɪk] *n* mal *m* di schiena

backbencher ['bæk'bentʃə'] *n* (*Brit*) parlamentare
che non ha incarichi né al governo né all'opposizione

back benches *npl posti in Parlamento occupati dai
backbencher; vedi nota*

all'opposizione. Nelle file davanti ad essi
siedono i "frontbencher"; *vedi anche* "front
bench".

backbiting ['bækbaɪtɪŋ] *n* maldicenza
backbone ['bækbəun] *n* spina dorsale; **the ~
of the organization** l'anima
dell'organizzazione
backchat ['bæktʃæt] *n* (*Brit col*) impertinenza
backcloth ['bækklɔθ] *n* (*Brit*) scena di sfondo
backcomb ['bækkəum] *vt* (*Brit*) cotonare
backdate [bæk'deɪt] *vt* (*letter*) retrodatare;
backdated pay rise aumento retroattivo
backdrop ['bækdrɔp] *n* = **backcloth**
backer ['bækə'] *n* sostenitore(-trice); (*Comm*)
fautore *m*
backfire ['bæk'faɪə'] *vi* (*Aut*) dar ritorni di
fiamma; (*plans*) fallire
backgammon ['bækgæmən] *n* tavola reale
background ['bækgraund] *n* sfondo; (*of
events, Comput*) background *m inv*; (*basic
knowledge*) base *f*; (*experience*) esperienza ■ *cpd*
(*noise, music*) di fondo; ~ **reading** letture *fpl*
sull'argomento; **family** ~ ambiente *m*
familiare
backhand ['bækhænd] *n* (*Tennis: also:*
backhand stroke) rovescio
backhanded [bæk'hændɪd] *adj* (*fig*)
ambiguo(-a)
backhander ['bækhændə'] *n* (*Brit: bribe*)
bustarella
backing ['bækɪŋ] *n* (*Comm*) finanziamento;
(*Mus*) accompagnamento; (*fig*) appoggio
backlash ['bæklæʃ] *n* contraccolpo,
ripercussione *f*
backlog ['bæklɔg] *n*: ~ **of work** lavoro
arretrato
back number *n* (*of magazine etc*) numero
arretrato
backpack ['bækpæk] *n* zaino
backpacker ['bækpækə'] *n* chi viaggia con zaino
e sacco a pelo
back pay *n* arretrato di paga
backpedal ['bækpɛdl] *vi* pedalare
all'indietro; (*fig*) far marcia indietro
backseat driver ['bæksi:t-] *n* passeggero che dà
consigli non richiesti al guidatore
backside [bæk'saɪd] *n* (*col*) sedere *m*
backslash ['bækslæʃ] *n* backslash *m inv*, barra
obliqua inversa
backslide ['bækslaɪd] *vi* ricadere
backspace ['bækspeɪs] *vi* (*in typing*) battere il
tasto di ritorno
backstage [bæk'steɪdʒ] *adv* nel retroscena
back street *n* vicolo
back-street ['bækstri:t] *adj*: ~ **abortionist**
praticante *m/f* di aborti clandestini

backstroke ['bækstrəuk] *n* nuoto sul dorso
backtrack ['bæktræk] *vi* = **backpedal**
backup ['bækʌp] *adj* (*train, plane*)
supplementare; (*Comput*) di riserva ■ *n*
(*support*) appoggio, sostegno; (*Comput: also:*
backup file) file *m inv* di riserva
backward ['bækwəd] *adj* (*movement*) indietro
inv; (*person*) tardivo(-a); (*country*) arretrato(-a);
~ **and forward movement** movimento
avanti e indietro
backwards ['bækwədz] *adv* indietro; (*fall,
walk*) all'indietro; **to know sth** ~ *or* (*US*)
~ **and forwards** (*col*) sapere qc a menadito
backwater ['bækwɔ:tə'] *n* (*fig*) posto morto
back yard *n* cortile *m* sul retro
bacon ['beɪkən] *n* pancetta
bacteria [bæk'tɪərɪə] *npl* batteri *mpl*
bacteriology [bæktɪərɪ'ɔlədʒɪ] *n*
batteriologia
bad [bæd] *adj* cattivo(-a); (*child*) cattivello(-a);
(*meat, food*) andato(-a) a male; **his ~ leg** la sua
gamba malata; **to go ~** (*meat, food*) andare a
male; **to have a ~ time of it** passarsela
male; **I feel ~ about it** (*guilty*) mi sento un
po' in colpa; ~ **debt** credito difficile da
recuperare; ~ **faith** malafede *f*
baddie, baddy ['bædɪ] *n* (*col: Cine etc*) cattivo(-a)
bade [bæd] *pt of* **bid**
badge [bædʒ] *n* insegna; (*of policeman*)
stemma *m*; (*stick-on*) adesivo
badger ['bædʒə'] *n* tasso ■ *vt* tormentare
badly ['bædlɪ] *adv* (*work, dress etc*) male;
things are going ~ le cose vanno male; ~
wounded gravemente ferito; **he needs it** ~
ne ha gran bisogno; ~ **off** *adj* povero(-a)
bad-mannered [bæd'mænəd] *adj*
maleducato(-a), sgarbato(-a)
badminton ['bædmɪntən] *n* badminton *m*
bad-tempered [bæd'tɛmpəd] *adj* irritabile;
(*in bad mood*) di malumore
baffle ['bæfl] *vt* (*puzzle*) confondere
baffling ['bæflɪŋ] *adj* sconcertante
bag [bæg] *n* sacco; (*handbag etc*) borsa;
(*of hunter*) carniere *m*; bottino ■ *vt* (*col: take*)
mettersi in tasca; prendersi; **bags of** (*col: lots
of*) un sacco di; **to pack one's bags** fare le
valigie; **bags under the eyes** borse sotto gli
occhi
bagful ['bægful] *n* sacco (pieno)
baggage ['bægɪdʒ] *n* bagagli *mpl*
baggage allowance *n* peso bagaglio
consentito
baggage car *n* (*US*) bagagliaio
baggage claim *n* ritiro bagagli
baggy ['bægɪ] *adj* largo(-a), sformato(-a)
Baghdad [bæg'dæd] *n* Bagdad *f*
bag lady *n* (*col*) stracciona, barbona

bagpipes ['bægpaɪps] npl cornamusa
bag-snatcher ['bægsnætʃəʳ] n (Brit) scippatore(-trice)
bag-snatching ['bægsnætʃɪŋ] n (Brit) scippo
Bahamas [bə'hɑːməz] npl: **the** ~ le isole Bahama
Bahrain [bɑː'reɪn] n Bahrein m
bail [beɪl] n cauzione f ■ vt (prisoner: also: **to grant bail to**) concedere la libertà provvisoria su cauzione a; (Naut: also: **bail out**) see **bale out**; **to be released on** ~ essere rilasciato(-a) su cauzione
  ▸ **bail out** vt (prisoner) ottenere la libertà provvisoria su cauzione di; (fig) tirare fuori dai guai ■ vi see **bale out**
bailiff ['beɪlɪf] n usciere m; fattore m
bait [beɪt] n esca ■ vt (hook) innescare; (trap) munire di esca; (fig) tormentare
bake [beɪk] vt cuocere al forno ■ vi cuocersi al forno
baked beans npl fagioli mpl all'uccelletto
baked potato n patata (con la buccia) cotta al forno
baker ['beɪkəʳ] n fornaio(-a), panettiere(-a)
bakery ['beɪkərɪ] n panetteria
baking ['beɪkɪŋ] n cottura (al forno)
baking powder n lievito in polvere
baking tin n stampo, tortiera
baking tray n teglia
balaclava [bælə'klɑːvə] n (also: **balaclava helmet**) passamontagna m inv
balance ['bæləns] n equilibrio; (Comm: sum) bilancio; (scales) bilancia ■ vt tenere in equilibrio; (pros and cons) soppesare; (budget) far quadrare; (account) pareggiare; (compensate) contrappesare; ~ **of trade/payments** bilancia commerciale/dei pagamenti; ~ **brought forward** saldo riportato; ~ **carried forward** saldo da riportare; **to** ~ **the books** fare il bilancio
balanced ['bælənst] adj (personality, diet) equilibrato(-a)
balance sheet n bilancio
balcony ['bælkənɪ] n balcone m
bald [bɔːld] adj calvo(-a)
baldness ['bɔːldnɪs] n calvizie f
bale [beɪl] n balla
  ▸ **bale out** vt (Naut: water) vuotare; (: boat) aggottare ■ vi (of a plane) gettarsi col paracadute
Balearic Islands [bælɪ'ærɪk] npl: **the** ~ le (isole) Baleari
baleful ['beɪlful] adj funesto(-a)
balk [bɔːlk] vi: **to** ~ **(at)** tirarsi indietro (davanti a); (horse) recalcitrare (davanti a)
Balkan ['bɔːlkən] adj balcanico(-a) ■ n: **the Balkans** i Balcani

ball [bɔːl] n palla; (football) pallone m; (for golf) pallina; (dance) ballo; **to play** ~ giocare a palla (con qn); (fig) stare al gioco (di qn); **to be on the** ~ (fig: competent) essere in gamba; (: alert) stare all'erta; **to start the** ~ **rolling** (fig) fare la prima mossa; **the** ~ **is in your court** (fig) a lei la prossima mossa; see also **balls**
ballad ['bæləd] n ballata
ballast ['bæləst] n zavorra
ball bearing n cuscinetto a sfere
ball cock n galleggiante m
ballerina [bælə'riːnə] n ballerina
ballet ['bæleɪ] n balletto
ballet dancer n ballerino(-a)
ballistic [bə'lɪstɪk] adj balistico(-a)
ballistics [bə'lɪstɪks] n balistica
balloon [bə'luːn] n pallone m; (in comic strip) fumetto ■ vi gonfiarsi
balloonist [bə'luːnɪst] n aeronauta m/f
ballot ['bælət] n scrutinio
ballot box n urna (per le schede)
ballot paper n scheda
ballpark ['bɔːlpɑːk] n (US) stadio di baseball
ballpark figure n (col) cifra approssimativa
ball-point pen ['bɔːlpɔɪnt-] n penna a sfera
ballroom ['bɔːlrum] n sala da ballo
balls [bɔːlz] npl (col!) coglioni mpl (!)
balm [bɑːm] n balsamo
balmy ['bɑːmɪ] adj (breeze, air) balsamico(-a); (Brit col) = **barmy**
BALPA ['bælpə] n abbr (= British Airline Pilots' Association) sindacato dei piloti
balsa ['bɔːlsə], **balsa wood** n (legno di) balsa
balsam ['bɔːlsəm] n balsamo
Baltic ['bɔːltɪk] adj, n: **the** ~ **Sea** il (mar) Baltico
balustrade [bæləs'treɪd] n balaustrata
bamboo [bæm'buː] n bambù m
bamboozle [bæm'buːzl] vt (col) infinocchiare
ban [bæn] n interdizione f ■ vt interdire; **he was banned from driving** (Brit) gli hanno ritirato la patente
banal [bə'nɑːl] adj banale
banana [bə'nɑːnə] n banana
band [bænd] n banda; (at a dance) orchestra; (Mil) fanfara
  ▸ **band together** vi collegarsi
bandage ['bændɪdʒ] n benda
Band-Aid® ['bændeɪd] n (US) cerotto
B & B n abbr = **bed and breakfast**
bandit ['bændɪt] n bandito
bandstand ['bændstænd] n palco dell'orchestra
bandwagon ['bændwægən] n: **to jump on the** ~ (fig) seguire la corrente
bandy ['bændɪ] vt (jokes, insults) scambiare

▶ **bandy about** *vt* far circolare

bandy-legged ['bændɪ'lɛgɪd] *adj* dalle gambe storte

bane [beɪn] *n*: **it** (*or* **he** *etc*) **is the ~ of my life** è la mia rovina

bang [bæŋ] *n* botta; (*of door*) lo sbattere; (*blow*) colpo ◼ *vt* battere (violentemente); (*door*) sbattere ◼ *vi* scoppiare; sbattere; **to ~ at the door** picchiare alla porta; **to ~ into sth** sbattere contro qc ◼ *adv*: **to be ~ on time** (*Brit col*) spaccare il secondo; *see also* **bangs**

banger ['bæŋəʳ] *n* (*Brit: car: also*: **old banger**) macinino; (*Brit col: sausage*) salsiccia; (*firework*) mortaretto

Bangkok ['bæŋkɔk] *n* Bangkok *f*

Bangladesh [baːŋglə'dɛʃ] *n* Bangladesh *m*

bangle ['bæŋgl] *n* braccialetto

bangs [bæŋz] *npl* (*US: fringe*) frangia, frangetta

banish ['bænɪʃ] *vt* bandire

banister ['bænɪstə] *n*, **banisters** ['bænɪstəz] *npl* ringhiera

banjo (*pl* **banjoes** *or* **banjos**) ['bændʒəu] *n* banjo *m inv*

bank [bæŋk] *n* (*for money*) banca, banco; (*of river, lake*) riva, sponda; (*of earth*) banco ◼ *vi* (*Aviat*) inclinarsi in virata; (*Comm*): **they ~ with Pitt's** sono clienti di Pitt's

▶ **bank on** *vt fus* contare su

bank account *n* conto in banca

bank balance *n* saldo; **a healthy ~** un solido conto in banca

bank card *n* = **banker's card**

bank charges *npl* (*Brit*) spese *fpl* bancarie

bank draft *n* assegno circolare *or* bancario

banker ['bæŋkəʳ] *n* banchiere *m*; **~'s card** (*Brit*) carta *f* assegni *inv*; **~'s order** (*Brit*) ordine *m* di banca

bank giro *n* bancogiro

bank holiday *n* (*Brit*) giorno di festa; *vedi nota*

⬤ **BANK HOLIDAY**

Una *bank holiday*, in Gran Bretagna, è una giornata in cui le banche e molti negozi sono chiusi. Generalmente le *bank holiday* cadono di lunedì e molti ne approfittano per fare una breve vacanza fuori città. Di conseguenza, durante questi fine settimana lunghi ("*bank holiday weekend*") si verifica un notevole aumento del traffico sulle strade, negli aeroporti e nelle stazioni e molte località turistiche registrano il tutto esaurito.

banking ['bæŋkɪŋ] *n* attività bancaria; professione *f* di banchiere

banking hours *npl* orario di sportello

bank loan *n* prestito bancario

bank manager *n* direttore *m* di banca

banknote ['bæŋknəut] *n* banconota

bank rate *n* tasso bancario

bankrupt ['bæŋkrʌpt] *adj, n* fallito(-a); **to go ~** fallire

bankruptcy ['bæŋkrʌptsɪ] *n* fallimento

bank statement *n* estratto conto

banned substance *n* sostanza al bando (*nello sport*)

banner ['bænəʳ] *n* striscione *m*

bannister ['bænɪstə] *n*, **bannisters** ['bænɪstəz] *npl see* **banister**

banns [bænz] *npl* pubblicazioni *fpl* di matrimonio

banquet ['bæŋkwɪt] *n* banchetto

bantam-weight ['bæntəmweɪt] *n* peso gallo

banter ['bæntəʳ] *n* scherzi *mpl* bonari

baptism ['bæptɪzəm] *n* battesimo

Baptist ['bæptɪst] *adj, n* battista (*m/f*)

baptize [bæp'taɪz] *vt* battezzare

bar [baːʳ] *n* barra; (*of window etc*) sbarra; (*of chocolate*) tavoletta; (*fig*) ostacolo; restrizione *f*; (*pub*) bar *m inv*; (*counter: in pub*) banco; (*Mus*) battuta ◼ *vt* (*road, window*) sbarrare; (*person*) escludere; (*activity*) interdire; **~ of soap** saponetta; **the B~** (*Law*) l'Ordine *m* degli avvocati; **behind bars** (*prisoner*) dietro le sbarre; **~ none** senza eccezione

Barbados [baː'beɪdɔs] *n* Barbados *fsg*

barbaric [baː'bærɪk], **barbarous** ['baːbərəs] *adj* barbaro(-a), barbarico(-a)

barbecue ['baːbɪkjuː] *n* barbecue *m inv*

barbed wire ['baːbd-] *n* filo spinato

barber ['baːbəʳ] *n* barbiere *m*

barbiturate [baː'bɪtjurɪt] *n* barbiturico

Barcelona [baːsɪ'ləunə] *n* Barcellona

bar chart *n* diagramma *m* di frequenza

bar code *n* codice *m* a barre

bare [bɛəʳ] *adj* nudo(-a) ◼ *vt* scoprire, denudare; (*teeth*) mostrare; **the ~ essentials** lo stretto necessario

bareback ['bɛəbæk] *adv* senza sella

barefaced ['bɛəfeɪst] *adj* sfacciato(-a)

barefoot ['bɛəfut] *adj, adv* scalzo(-a)

bareheaded [bɛə'hɛdɪd] *adj, adv* a capo scoperto

barely ['bɛəlɪ] *adv* appena

Barents Sea ['bærənts-] *n*: **the ~** il mar di Barents

bargain ['baːgɪn] *n* (*transaction*) contratto; (*good buy*) affare *m* ◼ *vi* (*haggle*) tirare sul prezzo; (*trade*) contrattare; **into the ~** per giunta

▶ **bargain for** *vt fus* (*col*): **to ~ for sth** aspettarsi qc; **he got more than he bargained for** gli è andata peggio di quel che si aspettasse

443

bargaining ['bɑːgənɪŋ] n contrattazione f
bargaining position n: **to be in a weak/ strong ~** non avere/avere potere contrattuale
barge [bɑːdʒ] n chiatta
 ▶ **barge in** vi (walk in) piombare dentro; (interrupt talk) intromettersi a sproposito
 ▶ **barge into** vt fus urtare contro
baritone ['bærɪtəʊn] n baritono
barium meal ['bɛərɪəm-] n (pasto di) bario
bark [bɑːk] n (of tree) corteccia; (of dog) abbaio ■ vi abbaiare
barley ['bɑːlɪ] n orzo
barley sugar n zucchero d'orzo
barmaid ['bɑːmeɪd] n cameriera al banco
barman ['bɑːmən] n barista m
barmy ['bɑːmɪ] adj (Brit col) tocco(-a)
barn [bɑːn] n granaio; (for animals) stalla
barnacle ['bɑːnəkl] n cirripede m
barn owl n barbagianni m inv
barometer [bə'rɒmɪtər] n barometro
baron ['bærən] n barone m; (fig) magnate m; **the oil barons** i magnati del petrolio; **the press barons** i baroni della stampa
baroness ['bærənɪs] n baronessa
baronet ['bærənɪt] n baronetto
barrack ['bærək] vt (Brit): **to ~ sb** subissare qn di grida e fischi
barracking ['bærəkɪŋ] n (Brit): **to give sb a ~** subissare qn di grida e fischi
barracks ['bærəks] npl caserma
barrage ['bærɑːʒ] n (Mil) sbarramento; **a ~ of questions** una raffica di or un fuoco di fila di domande
barrel ['bærəl] n barile m; (of gun) canna
barrel organ n organetto a cilindro
barren ['bærən] adj sterile; (soil) arido(-a)
barricade [bærɪ'keɪd] n barricata ■ vt barricare
barrier ['bærɪər] n barriera; (Brit: also: **crash barrier**) guardrail m inv
barrier cream n (Brit) crema protettiva
barring ['bɑːrɪŋ] prep salvo
barrister ['bærɪstər] n (Brit) avvocato; vedi nota

 ● **BARRISTER**
 ●
 ● Il barrister è un membro della più
 ● prestigiosa delle due branche della
 ● professione legale (l'altra è quella dei
 ● "solicitor"); la sua funzione è quella di
 ● rappresentare i propri clienti in tutte le
 ● corti ("magistrates' court", "crown court" e
 ● "Court of Appeal"), generalmente seguendo
 ● le istruzioni del caso preparate dai
 ● "solicitor".

barrow ['bærəʊ] n (cart) carriola

barstool ['bɑːstuːl] n sgabello
Bart. abbr (Brit) = **baronet**
bartender ['bɑːtɛndər] n (US) barista m
barter ['bɑːtər] n baratto ■ vt: **to ~ sth for** barattare qc con
base [beɪs] n base f ■ adj vile ■ vt: **to ~ sth on** basare qc su; **to ~ at** (troops) mettere di stanza a; **coffee-based** a base di caffè; **a Paris-based firm** una ditta con sede centrale a Parigi; **I'm based in London** sono di base or ho base a Londra
baseball ['beɪsbɔːl] n baseball m
baseboard ['beɪsbɔːd] n (US) zoccolo, battiscopa m inv
base camp n campo m base inv
Basel [bɑːl] n = **Basle**
baseline ['beɪslaɪn] n (Tennis) linea di fondo
basement ['beɪsmənt] n seminterrato; (of shop) sotterraneo
base rate n tasso di base
bases ['beɪsiːz] npl of **basis**; ['beɪsɪz] npl of **base**
bash [bæʃ] vt (col) picchiare ■ n: **I'll have a ~ (at it)** (Brit col) ci proverò; **bashed in** adj sfondato(-a)
 ▶ **bash up** vt (col: car) sfasciare; (: Brit: person) riempire di or prendere a botte
bashful ['bæʃful] adj timido(-a)
bashing ['bæʃɪŋ] n: **Paki-/queer-~** atti mpl di violenza contro i pachistani/gli omosessuali
BASIC ['beɪsɪk] n (Comput) BASIC m
basic ['beɪsɪk] adj (principles, precautions, rules) elementare; (salary) base inv (after n)
basically ['beɪsɪklɪ] adv fondamentalmente, sostanzialmente
basic rate n (of tax) aliquota minima
basil ['bæzl] n basilico
basin ['beɪsn] n (vessel, also Geo) bacino; (also: **washbasin**) lavabo; (Brit: for food) terrina
basis (pl **bases**) ['beɪsɪs, -siːz] n base f; **on the ~ of what you've said** in base alle sue asserzioni
bask [bɑːsk] vi: **to ~ in the sun** crogiolarsi al sole
basket ['bɑːskɪt] n cesta; (smaller) cestino; (with handle) paniere m
basketball ['bɑːskɪtbɔːl] n pallacanestro f
basketball player n cestista m/f
Basle [bɑːl] n Basilea
basmati rice [bəz'mætɪ-] n riso basmati
Basque [bæsk] adj, n basco(-a)
bass [beɪs] n (Mus) basso
bass clef n chiave f di basso
bassoon [bə'suːn] n fagotto
bastard ['bɑːstəd] n bastardo(-a); (col!) stronzo (!)

baste [beɪst] vt (Culin) ungere con grasso; (Sewing) imbastire

bastion ['bæstɪən] n bastione m; (fig) baluardo

bat [bæt] n pipistrello; (for baseball etc) mazza; (Brit: for table tennis) racchetta; **off one's own ~** di propria iniziativa ■ vt: **he didn't ~ an eyelid** non battè ciglio

batch [bætʃ] n (of bread) infornata; (of papers) cumulo; (of applicants, letters) gruppo; (of work) sezione f; (of goods) partita, lotto

batch processing n (Comput) elaborazione f a blocchi

bated ['beɪtɪd] adj: **with ~ breath** col fiato sospeso

bath (pl **baths**) [bɑːθ, bɑːðz] n bagno; (bathtub) vasca da bagno ■ vt far fare il bagno a; **to have a ~** fare un bagno; see also **baths**

bathchair ['bɑːθtʃɛəʳ] n (Brit) poltrona a rotelle

bathe [beɪð] vi fare il bagno ■ vt bagnare; (wound etc) lavare

bather ['beɪðəʳ] n bagnante m/f

bathing ['beɪðɪŋ] n bagni mpl

bathing cap n cuffia da bagno

bathing costume, (US) **bathing suit** n costume m da bagno

bathmat ['bɑːθmæt] n tappetino da bagno

bathrobe ['bɑːθrəub] n accappatoio

bathroom ['bɑːθrum] n stanza da bagno

baths [bɑːðz] npl bagni mpl pubblici

bath towel n asciugamano da bagno

bathtub ['bɑːθtʌb] n (vasca da) bagno

batman ['bætmən] n (Brit Mil) attendente m

baton ['bætən] n bastone m; (Mus) bacchetta

battalion [bə'tælɪən] n battaglione m

batten ['bætən] n (Carpentry) assicella, correntino; (for flooring) tavola per pavimenti; (Naut) serretta; (: on sail) stecca

▶ **batten down** vt (Naut): **to ~ down the hatches** chiudere i boccaporti

batter ['bætəʳ] vt battere ■ n pastetta

battered ['bætəd] adj (hat) sformato(-a); (pan) ammaccato(-a); **~ wife/baby** consorte f/bambino(-a) maltrattato(-a)

battering ram ['bætərɪŋ-] n ariete m

battery ['bætərɪ] n batteria; (of torch) pila

battery charger n caricabatterie m inv

battle ['bætl] n battaglia ■ vi battagliare, lottare; **to fight a losing ~** (fig) battersi per una causa persa; **that's half the ~** (col) è già una mezza vittoria

battle dress n uniforme f da combattimento

battlefield ['bætlfiːld] n campo di battaglia

battlements ['bætlmənts] npl bastioni mpl

battleship ['bætlʃɪp] n nave f da guerra

batty ['bætɪ] adj (col: person) svitato(-a), strambo(-a); (behaviour, idea) strampalato(-a)

bauble ['bɔːbl] n ninnolo

baud [bɔːd] n (Comput) baud m inv

baulk [bɔːlk] vi = **balk**

bauxite ['bɔːksaɪt] n bauxite f

Bavaria [bə'vɛərɪə] n Bavaria

Bavarian [bə'vɛərɪən] adj, n bavarese (m/f)

bawdy ['bɔːdɪ] adj piccante

bawl [bɔːl] vi urlare

bay [beɪ] n (of sea) baia; (Brit: for parking) piazzola di sosta; (: for loading) piazzale m di (sosta e) carico; **to hold sb at ~** tenere qn a bada

bay leaf n foglia d'alloro

bayonet ['beɪənɪt] n baionetta

bay tree n alloro

bay window n bovindo

bazaar [bə'zɑːʳ] n bazar m inv; vendita di beneficenza

bazooka [bə'zuːkə] n bazooka m inv

BB n abbr (Brit: = Boys' Brigade) organizzazione giovanile a fine educativo

BBB n abbr (US: = Better Business Bureau) organismo per la difesa dei consumatori

BBC n abbr (= British Broadcasting Corporation) vedi nota

> **BBC**
>
> La BBC è l'azienda statale che fornisce il servizio radiofonico e televisivo in Gran Bretagna. Pur dovendo rispondere al Parlamento del proprio operato, la BBC non è soggetta al controllo dello stato per scelte e programmi, anche perché si autofinanzia con il ricavato dei canoni d'abbonamento. La BBC ha canali televisivi digitali e terrestri, oltre a diverse emittenti radiofoniche nazionali e locali. Fornisce un servizio di informazione internazionale, il "BBC World Service", trasmesso in tutto il mondo.

BBE n abbr (US: = Benevolent and Protective Order of Elks) organizzazione filantropica

BC adv abbr (= before Christ) a.C. ■ abbr (Canada) = **British Columbia**

BCG n abbr (= Bacillus Calmette-Guérin) vaccino antitubercolare

BD n abbr (= Bachelor of Divinity) titolo di studio

B/D abbr = **bank draft**

BDS n abbr (= Bachelor of Dental Surgery) titolo di studio

⊙ KEYWORD

be [biː] (*pt* **was, were,** *pp* **been**) *aux vb* **1** (*with present participle: forming continuous tenses*): **what are you doing?** che fai?, che stai facendo?; **they're coming tomorrow** vengono domani; **I've been waiting for her for hours** sono ore che l'aspetto

2 (*with pp: forming passives*) essere; **to be killed** essere *or* venire ucciso(-a); **the box had been opened** la scatola era stata aperta; **the thief was nowhere to be seen** il ladro non si trovava da nessuna parte

3 (*in tag questions*): **it was fun, wasn't it?** è stato divertente, no?; **he's good-looking, isn't he?** è un bell'uomo, vero?; **she's back, is she?** così è tornata, eh?

4 (+ *to* + *infinitive*): **the house is to be sold** abbiamo (*or* hanno *etc*) intenzione di vendere casa; **you're to be congratulated for all your work** dovremo farvi i complimenti per tutto il vostro lavoro; **am I to understand that ...?** devo dedurre che ...?; **he's not to open it** non deve aprirlo; **he was to have come yesterday** sarebbe dovuto venire ieri

◼ *vb* + *complement* **1** (*gen*) essere; **I'm English** sono inglese; **I'm tired** sono stanco(-a); **I'm hot/cold** ho caldo/freddo; **he's a doctor** è medico; **2 and 2 are 4** 2 più 2 fa 4; **be careful!** sta attento!; **be good** sii buono; **if I were you ...** se fossi in te ...

2 (*of health*) stare; **how are you?** come sta?; **he's very ill** sta molto male

3 (*of age*): **how old are you?** quanti anni hai?; **I'm sixteen (years old)** ho sedici anni

4 (*cost*) costare; **how much was the meal?** quant'era *or* quanto costava il pranzo?; **that'll be £5, please** (sono) 5 sterline, per favore

◼ *vi* **1** (*exist, occur etc*) essere, esistere; **the best singer that ever was** il migliore cantante mai esistito *or* di tutti tempi; **be that as it may** comunque sia, sia come sia; **so be it** sia pure, e sia

2 (*referring to place*) essere, trovarsi; **I won't be here tomorrow** non ci sarò domani; **Edinburgh is in Scotland** Edimburgo si trova in Scozia

3 (*referring to movement*): **where have you been?** dove sei stato?; **I've been to China** sono stato in Cina

◼ *impers vb* **1** (*referring to time, distance*) essere; **it's 5 o'clock** sono le 5; **it's the 28th of April** è il 28 aprile; **it's 10 km to the village** di qui al paese sono 10 km

2 (*referring to the weather*) fare; **it's too hot/cold** fa troppo caldo/freddo; **it's windy** c'è vento

3 (*emphatic*): **it's me** sono io; **it's only me** sono solo io; **it was Maria who paid the bill** è stata Maria che ha pagato il conto

B/E *abbr* = **bill of exchange**
beach [biːtʃ] *n* spiaggia ◼ *vt* tirare in secco
beach buggy *n* dune buggy *f inv*
beachcomber [ˈbiːtʃkəʊməʳ] *n* vagabondo (*che s'aggira sulla spiaggia*)
beachwear [ˈbiːtʃwɛəʳ] *n* articoli *mpl* da spiaggia
beacon [ˈbiːkən] *n* (*lighthouse*) faro; (*marker*) segnale *m*; (*also*: **radio beacon**) radiofaro
bead [biːd] *n* perlina; (*of dew, sweat*) goccia; **beads** *npl* (*necklace*) collana
beady [ˈbiːdɪ] *adj*: **~ eyes** occhi *mpl* piccoli e penetranti
beagle [ˈbiːgl] *n* cane *m* da lepre
beak [biːk] *n* becco
beaker [ˈbiːkəʳ] *n* coppa
beam [biːm] *n* trave *f*; (*of light*) raggio; (*Radio*) fascio (d'onde) ◼ *vi* brillare; (*smile*): **to ~ at sb** rivolgere un radioso sorriso a qn; **to drive on full** *or* **main ~** *or* (*US*) **high ~** guidare con gli abbaglianti accesi
beaming [ˈbiːmɪŋ] *adj* (*sun, smile*) raggiante
bean [biːn] *n* fagiolo; (*coffee bean*) chicco
beanpole [ˈbiːnpəʊl] *n* (*col*) spilungone(-a)
beansprouts [ˈbiːnsprauts] *npl* germogli *mpl* di soia
bear [bɛəʳ] *n* orso; (*Stock Exchange*) ribassista *m/f* ◼ *vb* (*pt* **bore,** *pp* **borne**) [bɔːʳ, bɔːn] *vt* (*gen*) portare; (*produce: fruit*) produrre, dare; (: *traces, signs*) mostrare; (*Comm: interest*) fruttare; (*endure*) sopportare ◼ *vi*: **to ~ right/left** piegare a destra/sinistra; **to ~ the responsibility of** assumersi la responsabilità di; **to ~ comparison with** reggere al paragone con; **I can't ~ him** non lo posso soffrire *or* sopportare; **to bring pressure to ~ on sb** fare pressione su qn
▸ **bear out** *vt* (*theory, suspicion*) confermare, convalidare
▸ **bear up** *vi* farsi coraggio; **he bore up well under the strain** ha sopportato bene lo stress
▸ **bear with** *vt fus* (*sb's moods, temper*) sopportare (con pazienza); **~ with me a minute** solo un attimo, prego
bearable [ˈbɛərəbl] *adj* sopportabile
beard [bɪəd] *n* barba
bearded [ˈbɪədɪd] *adj* barbuto(-a)
bearer [ˈbɛərəʳ] *n* portatore *m*; (*of passport*) titolare *m/f*
bearing [ˈbɛərɪŋ] *n* portamento; (*connection*) rapporto; **bearings** *npl* (*also*: **ball bearings**) cuscinetti *mpl* a sfere; **to take a ~** fare un

rilevamento; **to find one's bearings** orientarsi

beast [biːst] *n* bestia

beastly ['biːstlɪ] *adj* meschino(-a); (*weather*) da cani

beat [biːt] *n* colpo; (*of heart*) battito; (*Mus*) tempo; battuta; (*of policeman*) giro ■ *vt* (*pt ~, pp* **beaten**) battere; **off the beaten track** fuori mano; **to ~ about the bush** menare il cane per l'aia; **to ~ time** battere il tempo; **that beats everything!** (*col*) questo è il colmo!

▶ **beat down** *vt* (*door*) abbattere, buttare giù; (*price*) far abbassare; (*seller*) far scendere ■ *vi* (*rain*) scrosciare; (*sun*) picchiare

▶ **beat off** *vt* respingere

▶ **beat up** *vt* (*col: person*) picchiare; (*eggs*) sbattere

beater ['biːtə^r] *n* (*for eggs, cream*) frullino

beating ['biːtɪŋ] *n* botte *fpl*; (*defeat*) batosta; **to take a ~** prendere una (bella) batosta

beat-up [biːt'ʌp] *adj* (*col*) scassato(-a)

beautician [bjuː'tɪʃən] *n* estetista *m/f*

beautiful ['bjuːtɪful] *adj* bello(-a)

beautify ['bjuːtɪfaɪ] *vt* abbellire

beauty ['bjuːtɪ] *n* bellezza; (*concept*) bello; **the ~ of it is that …** il bello è che …

beauty contest *n* concorso di bellezza

beauty queen *n* miss *f inv*, reginetta di bellezza

beauty salon *n* istituto di bellezza

beauty sleep *n*: **to get one's ~** farsi un sonno ristoratore

beauty spot *n* neo; (*Brit Tourism*) luogo pittoresco

beaver ['biːvə^r] *n* castoro

becalmed [bɪ'kɑːmd] *adj* in bonaccia

became [bɪ'keɪm] *pt of* **become**

because [bɪ'kɔz] *conj* perché; **~ of** *prep* a causa di

beck [bɛk] *n*: **to be at sb's ~ and call** essere a completa disposizione di qn

beckon ['bɛkən] *vt* (*also*: **beckon to**) chiamare con un cenno

become [bɪ'kʌm] *vt* (*irreg: like* **come**) diventare; **to ~ fat/thin** ingrassarsi/dimagrire; **to ~ angry** arrabbiarsi; **it became known that …** si è venuto a sapere che …; **what has ~ of him?** che gli è successo?

becoming [bɪ'kʌmɪŋ] *adj* (*behaviour*) che si conviene; (*clothes*) grazioso(-a)

BECTU ['bɛktuː] *n abbr* (*Brit*) = **Broadcasting Entertainment Cinematographic and Theatre Union**

BEd *n abbr* (= *Bachelor of Education*) laurea con abilitazione all'insegnamento

bed [bɛd] *n* letto; (*of flowers*) aiuola; (*of coal, clay*) strato; (*of sea, lake*) fondo; **to go to ~** andare a letto

▶ **bed down** *vi* sistemarsi (per dormire)

bed and breakfast *n* (*terms*) camera con colazione; (*place*) ≈ pensione *f* familiare; *vedi nota*

⬤ **BED AND BREAKFAST (B & B)**
◌
◌ I *bed and breakfasts*, anche *B & Bs*, sono
◌ piccole pensioni a conduzione familiare,
◌ in case private o fattorie, dove si affittano
◌ camere e viene servita al mattino la
◌ tradizionale colazione all'inglese. Queste
◌ pensioni offrono un servizio di camera
◌ con prima colazione, appunto *bed and*
◌ *breakfast*, a prezzi più contenuti rispetto
◌ agli alberghi.

bedbug ['bɛdbʌg] *n* cimice *f*

bedclothes ['bɛdkləuðz] *npl* coperte e lenzuola *fpl*

bedcover ['bɛdkʌvə^r] *n* copriletto

bedding ['bɛdɪŋ] *n* coperte e lenzuola *fpl*

bedevil [bɪ'dɛvl] *vt* (*person*) tormentare; (*plans*) ostacolare continuamente

bedfellow ['bɛdfɛləu] *n*: **they are strange bedfellows** (*fig*) fanno una coppia ben strana

bedlam ['bɛdləm] *n* baraonda

bedpan ['bɛdpæn] *n* padella

bedpost ['bɛdpəust] *n* colonnina del letto

bedraggled [bɪ'drægld] *adj* sbrindellato(-a); (*wet*) fradicio(-a)

bedridden ['bɛdrɪdən] *adj* costretto(-a) a letto

bedrock ['bɛdrɔk] *n* (*Geo*) basamento; (*fig*) fatti *mpl* di base

bedroom ['bɛdrum] *n* camera da letto

Beds *abbr* (*Brit*) = **Bedfordshire**

bed settee *n* divano *m* letto *inv*

bedside ['bɛdsaɪd] *n*: **at sb's ~** al capezzale di qn

bedside lamp *n* lampada da comodino

bedsit ['bɛdsɪt], **bedsitter** ['bɛdsɪtə^r] *n* (*Brit*) monolocale *m*

bedspread ['bɛdsprɛd] *n* copriletto

bedtime ['bɛdtaɪm] *n*: **it's ~** è ora di andare a letto

bee [biː] *n* ape *f*; **to have a ~ in one's bonnet (about sth)** avere la fissazione (di qc)

beech [biːtʃ] *n* faggio

beef [biːf] *n* manzo

▶ **beef up** *vt* (*col*) rinforzare

beefburger ['biːfbəːgə^r] *n* hamburger *m inv*

beefeater ['biːfiːtə^r] *n* guardia della Torre di Londra

beehive ['biːhaɪv] n alveare m
bee-keeping ['biːkiːpɪŋ] n apicoltura
beeline ['biːlaɪn] n: **to make a ~ for** buttarsi a capo fitto verso
been [biːn] pp of **be**
beep [biːp] n (of horn) colpo di clacson; (of phone etc) segnale m (acustico), bip m inv ■ vi suonare
beeper ['biːpər] n (of doctor etc) cercapersone m inv
beer [bɪər] n birra
beer belly n (col) stomaco da bevitore
beer can n lattina di birra
beetle ['biːtl] n scarafaggio; coleottero
beetroot ['biːtruːt] n (Brit) barbabietola
befall [bɪ'fɔːl] vi, vt (irreg: like **fall**) accadere (a)
befit [bɪ'fɪt] vt addirsi a
before [bɪ'fɔːr] prep (in time) prima di; (in space) davanti a ■ conj prima che + sub; prima di ■ adv prima; **~ going** prima di andare; **~ she goes** prima che vada; **the week ~** la settimana prima; **I've seen it ~** l'ho già visto; **I've never seen it ~** è la prima volta che lo vedo
beforehand [bɪ'fɔːhænd] adv in anticipo
befriend [bɪ'frɛnd] vt assistere; mostrarsi amico a
befuddled [bɪ'fʌdld] adj confuso(-a)
beg [bɛg] vi chiedere l'elemosina ■ vt chiedere in elemosina; (favour) chiedere; (entreat) pregare; **I ~ your pardon** (apologising) mi scusi; (not hearing) scusi?; **this begs the question of …** questo presuppone che sia già risolto il problema di …
began [bɪ'gæn] pt of **begin**
beggar ['bɛgər] n (also: **beggarman, beggarwoman**) mendicante m/f
begin (pt **began**, pp **begun**) [bɪ'gɪn, bɪ'gæn, bɪ'gʌn] vt, vi cominciare; **to ~ doing** or **to do sth** incominciare or iniziare a fare qc; **I can't ~ to thank you** non so proprio come ringraziarla; **to ~ with, I'd like to know …** tanto per cominciare vorrei sapere …; **beginning from Monday** a partire da lunedì
beginner [bɪ'gɪnər] n principiante m/f
beginning [bɪ'gɪnɪŋ] n inizio, principio; **right from the ~** fin dall'inizio
begrudge [bɪ'grʌdʒ] vt: **to ~ sb sth** dare qc a qn a malincuore; invidiare qn per qc
beguile [bɪ'gaɪl] vt incantare
beguiling [bɪ'gaɪlɪŋ] adj (charming) allettante; (deluding) ingannevole
begun [bɪ'gʌn] pp of **begin**
behalf [bɪ'hɑːf] n: **on ~ of**, (US) **in ~ of** per conto di; a nome di

behave [bɪ'heɪv] vi comportarsi; (well: also: **behave o.s.**) comportarsi bene
behaviour, (US) **behavior** [bɪ'heɪvjər] n comportamento, condotta
behead [bɪ'hɛd] vt decapitare
beheld [bɪ'hɛld] pt, pp of **behold**
behind [bɪ'haɪnd] prep dietro; (followed by pronoun) dietro di; (time) in ritardo con ■ adv dietro; in ritardo ■ n didietro; **we're ~ them in technology** siamo più indietro or più arretrati di loro nella tecnica; **~ the scenes** dietro le quinte; **to be ~ (schedule) with sth** essere indietro con qc; (payments) essere in arretrato con qc; **to leave sth ~** dimenticare di prendere qc
behold [bɪ'həuld] vt (irreg: like **hold**) vedere, scorgere
beige [beɪʒ] adj beige inv
Beijing [beɪ'dʒɪŋ] n Pechino f
being ['biːɪŋ] n essere m; **to come into ~** cominciare ad esistere
Beirut [beɪ'ruːt] n Beirut f
Belarus ['bɛlærus] n Bielorussia
Belarussian [bɛlə'rʌʃən] adj bielorusso(-a) ■ n bielorusso(-a); (Ling) bielorusso
belated [bɪ'leɪtɪd] adj tardo(-a)
belch [bɛltʃ] vi ruttare ■ vt (gen: also: **belch out**: smoke etc) eruttare
beleaguered [bɪ'liːgəd] adj (city) assediato(-a); (army) accerchiato(-a); (fig) assillato(-a)
Belfast ['bɛlfɑːst] n Belfast f
belfry ['bɛlfrɪ] n campanile m
Belgian ['bɛldʒən] adj, n belga (m/f)
Belgium ['bɛldʒəm] n Belgio
Belgrade [bɛl'greɪd] n Belgrado f
belie [bɪ'laɪ] vt smentire; (give false impression of) nascondere
belief [bɪ'liːf] n (opinion) opinione f, convinzione f; (trust, faith) fede f; (acceptance as true) credenza; **in the ~ that** nella convinzione che; **it's beyond ~** è incredibile
believe [bɪ'liːv] vt, vi credere; **to ~ in** (God) credere in; (ghosts) credere a; (method) avere fiducia in; **I don't ~ in corporal punishment** sono contrario alle punizioni corporali; **he is believed to be abroad** si pensa (che) sia all'estero
believer [bɪ'liːvər] n (Rel) credente m/f; (in idea, activity): **to be a ~ in** credere in
belittle [bɪ'lɪtl] vt sminuire
Belize [bɛ'liːz] n Belize m
bell [bɛl] n campana; (small, on door, electric) campanello; **that rings a ~** (fig) mi ricorda qualcosa
bell-bottoms ['bɛlbɔtəmz] npl calzoni mpl a zampa d'elefante

bellboy ['bɛlbɔɪ], (US) **bellhop** ['bɛlhɔp] n ragazzo d'albergo, fattorino d'albergo

belligerent [bɪ'lɪdʒərənt] adj (at war) belligerante; (fig) bellicoso(-a)

bellow ['bɛləʊ] vi muggire; (cry) urlare (a squarciagola) ■ vt (orders) urlare (a squarciagola)

bellows ['bɛləʊz] npl soffietto

bell push n (Brit) pulsante m del campanello

belly ['bɛlɪ] n pancia

bellyache ['bɛlɪeɪk] n mal m di pancia ■ vi (col) mugugnare

bellybutton ['bɛlɪbʌtn] n ombelico

bellyful ['bɛlɪful] n (col): **to have had a ~ of** (fig) averne piene le tasche (di)

belong [bɪ'lɔŋ] vi: **to ~ to** appartenere a; (club etc) essere socio di; **this book belongs here** questo libro va qui

belongings [bɪ'lɔŋɪŋz] npl cose fpl, roba; **personal ~** effetti mpl personali

Belorussia [bɛləʊ'rʌʃə] n Bielorussia

Belorussian [bɛləʊ'rʌʃən] adj, n = **Belarussian**

beloved [bɪ'lʌvɪd] adj adorato(-a)

below [bɪ'ləʊ] prep sotto, al di sotto di ■ adv sotto, di sotto; giù; **see ~** vedi sotto or oltre; **temperatures ~ normal** temperature al di sotto del normale

belt [bɛlt] n cintura; (Tech) cinghia ■ vt (thrash) picchiare ■ vi (Brit col) filarsela; **industrial ~** zona industriale
▶ **belt out** vt (song) cantare a squarciagola
▶ **belt up** vi (Brit col) chiudere la boccaccia

beltway ['bɛltweɪ] n (US Aut) circonvallazione f; (: motorway) autostrada

bemoan [bɪ'məʊn] vt lamentare

bemused [bɪ'mju:zd] adj perplesso(-a), stupito(-a)

bench [bɛntʃ] n panca; (in workshop) banco; **the B~** (Law) la Corte

bench mark n banco di prova

bend [bɛnd] vb (pt, pp **bent**) [bɛnt] vt curvare; (leg, arm) piegare ■ vi curvarsi; piegarsi ■ n (Brit: in road) curva; (in pipe, river) gomito
▶ **bend down** vi chinarsi
▶ **bend over** vi piegarsi

bends [bɛndz] npl (Med) embolia

beneath [bɪ'ni:θ] prep sotto, al di sotto di; (unworthy of) indegno(-a) di ■ adv sotto, di sotto

benefactor ['bɛnɪfæktə'] n benefattore m

benefactress ['bɛnɪfæktrɪs] n benefattrice f

beneficial [bɛnɪ'fɪʃəl] adj che fa bene; vantaggioso(-a); **~ to** che giova a

beneficiary [bɛnɪ'fɪʃərɪ] n (Law) beneficiario(-a)

benefit ['bɛnɪfɪt] n beneficio, vantaggio; (allowance of money) indennità f inv ■ vt far

bene a ■ vi: **he'll ~ from it** ne trarrà beneficio or profitto

benefit performance n spettacolo di beneficenza

Benelux ['bɛnɪlʌks] n Benelux m

benevolent [bɪ'nɛvələnt] adj benevolo(-a)

BEng n abbr (= Bachelor of Engineering) laurea in ingegneria

benign [bɪ'naɪn] adj benevolo(-a); (Med) benigno(-a)

bent [bɛnt] pt, pp of **bend** ■ n inclinazione f ■ adj (wire, pipe) piegato(-a), storto(-a); (col: dishonest) losco(-a); **to be ~ on** essere deciso(-a) a

bequeath [bɪ'kwi:ð] vt lasciare in eredità

bequest [bɪ'kwɛst] n lascito

bereaved [bɪ'ri:vd] adj in lutto ■ npl: **the ~** i familiari in lutto

bereavement [bɪ'ri:vmənt] n lutto

beret ['bɛreɪ] n berretto

Bering Sea ['bɛrɪŋ-] n: **the ~** il mar di Bering

berk [bə:k] n (Brit col!) coglione(-a) (!)

Berks abbr (Brit) = **Berkshire**

Berlin [bə:'lɪn] n Berlino f; **East/West ~** Berlino est/ovest

berm [bə:m] n (US Aut) corsia d'emergenza

Bermuda [bə:'mju:də] n le Bermude

Bermuda shorts npl bermuda mpl

Bern [bə:n] n Berna f

berry ['bɛrɪ] n bacca

berserk [bə'sə:k] adj: **to go ~** montare su tutte le furie

berth [bə:θ] n (bed) cuccetta; (for ship) ormeggio ■ vi (in harbour) entrare in porto; (at anchor) gettare l'ancora; **to give sb a wide ~** (fig) tenersi alla larga da qn

beseech (pt, pp **besought**) [bɪ'si:tʃ, bɪ'sɔ:t] vt implorare

beset (pt, pp **~**) [bɪ'sɛt] vt assalire ■ adj: **a policy ~ with dangers** una politica irta or piena di pericoli

besetting [bɪ'sɛtɪŋ] adj: **his ~ sin** il suo più grande difetto

beside [bɪ'saɪd] prep accanto a; (compared with) rispetto a, in confronto a; **to be ~ o.s. (with anger)** essere fuori di sé; **that's ~ the point** non c'entra

besides [bɪ'saɪdz] adv inoltre, per di più ■ prep oltre a; (except) a parte

besiege [bɪ'si:dʒ] vt (town) assediare; (fig) tempestare

besotted [bɪ'sɔtɪd] adj (Brit): **~ with** infatuato(-a) di

besought [bɪ'sɔ:t] pt, pp of **beseech**

bespectacled [bɪ'spɛktɪkld] adj occhialuto(-a)

bespoke [bɪ'spəʊk] adj (Brit: garment) su misura; **~ tailor** sarto

b

best [bɛst] *adj* migliore ■ *adv* meglio; **the ~ thing to do is ...** la cosa migliore da fare *or* farsi è ...; **the ~ part of** (*quantity*) la maggior parte di; **at ~** tutt'al più; **to make the ~ of sth** cavare il meglio possibile da qc; **to do one's ~** fare del proprio meglio; **to the ~ of my knowledge** per quel che ne so; **to the ~ of my ability** al massimo delle mie capacità; **he's not exactly patient at the ~ of times** non è mai molto paziente

best-before date *n* (*Comm*) data limite d'utilizzo *or* di consumo

best man *n* testimone *m* dello sposo

bestow [bɪ'stəu] *vt*: **to ~ sth on sb** conferire qc a qn

bestseller ['bɛst'sɛlə^r] *n* bestseller *m inv*

bet [bɛt] *n* scommessa ■ *vt, vi* (*pt, pp ~ or* **betted**) scommettere; **it's a safe ~** (*fig*) è molto probabile

Bethlehem ['bɛθlɪhɛm] *n* Betlemme *f*

betray [bɪ'treɪ] *vt* tradire

betrayal [bɪ'treɪəl] *n* tradimento

better ['bɛtə^r] *adj* migliore ■ *adv* meglio ■ *vt* migliorare ■ *n*: **to get the ~ of** avere la meglio su; **you had ~ do it** è meglio che lo faccia; **he thought ~ of it** cambiò idea; **to get ~** migliorare; **a change for the ~** un cambiamento in meglio; **that's ~!** così va meglio!; **I had ~ go** dovrei andare; **~ off** *adj* più ricco(-a); (*fig*): **you'd be ~ off this way** starebbe meglio così

betting ['bɛtɪŋ] *n* scommesse *fpl*

betting shop *n* (*Brit*) ufficio dell'allibratore

between [bɪ'twiːn] *prep* tra ■ *adv* in mezzo, nel mezzo; **the road ~ here and London** la strada da qui a Londra; **we only had £5 ~ us** fra tutti e due avevamo solo 5 sterline

bevel ['bɛvl] *n* (*also*: **bevel(led) edge**) profilo smussato

beverage ['bɛvərɪdʒ] *n* bevanda

bevy ['bɛvɪ] *n*: **a ~ of** una banda di

bewail [bɪ'weɪl] *vt* lamentare

beware [bɪ'wɛə^r] *vt, vi*: **to ~ (of)** stare attento(-a) (a)

bewildered [bɪ'wɪldəd] *adj* sconcertato(-a), confuso(-a)

bewildering [bɪ'wɪldərɪŋ] *adj* sconcertante, sbalorditivo(-a)

bewitching [bɪ'wɪtʃɪŋ] *adj* affascinante

beyond [bɪ'jɔnd] *prep* (*in space*) oltre; (*exceeding*) al di sopra di ■ *adv* di là; **~ doubt** senza dubbio; **~ repair** irreparabile

b/f *abbr* = **brought forward**

BFPO *n abbr* (= *British Forces Post Office*) recapito delle truppe britanniche all'estero

bhp *n abbr* (*Aut*: = *brake horsepower*) c.v. (= *cavallo vapore*)

bi... [baɪ] *prefix* bi...

biannual [baɪ'ænjuəl] *adj* semestrale

bias ['baɪəs] *n* (*prejudice*) pregiudizio; (*preference*) preferenza

biased, biassed ['baɪəst] *adj* parziale; **to be bias(s)ed against** essere prevenuto(-a) contro

biathlon [baɪ'æθlən] *n* biathlon *m*

bib [bɪb] *n* bavaglino

Bible ['baɪbl] *n* Bibbia

bibliography [bɪblɪ'ɔgrəfɪ] *n* bibliografia

bicarbonate of soda [baɪ'kɑːbənɪt-] *n* bicarbonato (di sodio)

bicentenary [baɪsɛn'tiːnərɪ], **bicentennial** [baɪsɛn'tɛnɪəl] *n* bicentenario

biceps ['baɪsɛps] *n* bicipite *m*

bicker ['bɪkə^r] *vi* bisticciare

bicycle ['baɪsɪkl] *n* bicicletta

bicycle path *n*, **bicycle track** *n* sentiero ciclabile

bicycle pump *n* pompa della bicicletta

bid [bɪd] *n* offerta; (*attempt*) tentativo ■ *vb* (*pt* **bade** *or* **~**, *pp* **bidden** *or* **~**) *vi* fare un'offerta ■ *vt* fare un'offerta di; **to ~ sb good day** dire buon giorno a qn

bidder ['bɪdə^r] *n*: **the highest ~** il maggior offerente

bidding ['bɪdɪŋ] *n* offerte *fpl*

bide [baɪd] *vt*: **to ~ one's time** aspettare il momento giusto

bidet ['biːdeɪ] *n* bidè *m inv*

bidirectional ['baɪdɪ'rɛkʃənl] *adj* bidirezionale

biennial [baɪ'ɛnɪəl] *adj* biennale ■ *n* (*pianta*) biennale *f*

bier [bɪə^r] *n* bara

bifocals [baɪ'fəuklz] *npl* occhiali *mpl* bifocali

big [bɪg] *adj* grande; grosso(-a); **my ~ brother** mio fratello maggiore; **to do things in a ~ way** fare le cose in grande

bigamy ['bɪgəmɪ] *n* bigamia

big dipper [-'dɪpə^r] *n* montagne *fpl* russe, otto *m inv* volante

big end *n* (*Aut*) testa di biella

biggish ['bɪgɪʃ] *adj see* **big** piuttosto grande, piuttosto grosso(-a); **a ~ rent** un affitto piuttosto alto

bigheaded ['bɪg'hɛdɪd] *adj* presuntuoso(-a)

big-hearted ['bɪg'hɑːtɪd] *adj* generoso(-a)

bigot ['bɪgət] *n* persona gretta

bigoted ['bɪgətɪd] *adj* gretto(-a)

bigotry ['bɪgətrɪ] *n* grettezza

big toe *n* alluce *m*

big top *n* tendone *m* del circo

big wheel *n* (*at fair*) ruota (panoramica)

bigwig ['bɪgwɪg] *n* (*col*) pezzo grosso

bike [baɪk] *n* bici *f inv*

bike lane n pista ciclabile
bikini [bɪˈkiːnɪ] n bikini m inv
bilateral [baɪˈlætərl] adj bilaterale
bile [baɪl] n bile f
bilingual [baɪˈlɪŋgwəl] adj bilingue
bilious [ˈbɪlɪəs] adj biliare; (fig) bilioso(-a)
bill [bɪl] n (in hotel, restaurant) conto; (Comm) fattura; (for gas, electricity) bolletta, conto; (Pol) atto; (US: banknote) banconota; (notice) avviso; (Theat): **on the ~** in cartellone; (of bird) becco ■ vt mandare il conto a; **may I have the ~ please?** posso avere il conto per piacere?; **"stick** or **post no bills"** "divieto di affissione"; **to fit** or **fill the ~** (fig) fare al caso; **~ of exchange** cambiale f, tratta; **~ of lading** polizza di carico; **~ of sale** atto di vendita
billboard [ˈbɪlbɔːd] n tabellone m
billet [ˈbɪlɪt] n alloggio ■ vt (troops etc) alloggiare
billfold [ˈbɪlfəʊld] n (US) portafoglio
billiards [ˈbɪljədz] n biliardo
billion [ˈbɪljən] n (Brit) bilione m; (US) miliardo
billow [ˈbɪləʊ] n (of smoke) nuvola; (of sail) rigonfiamento ■ vi (smoke) alzarsi in volute; (sail) gonfiarsi
bills payable npl effetti mpl passivi
bills receivable npl effetti mpl attivi
billy goat [ˈbɪlɪgəʊt] n caprone m, becco
bimbo [ˈbɪmbəʊ] n (col) pollastrella, svampitella
bin [bɪn] n bidone m; (Brit: also: **dustbin**) pattumiera; (: also: **litter bin**) cestino
binary [ˈbaɪnərɪ] adj binario(-a)
bind (pt, pp **bound**) [baɪnd, baʊnd] vt legare; (oblige) obbligare
▶ **bind over** vt (Law) dare la condizionale a
▶ **bind up** vt (wound) fasciare, bendare; **to be bound up in** (work, research etc) essere completamente assorbito da; **to be bound up with** (person) dedicarsi completamente a
binder [ˈbaɪndəʳ] n (file) classificatore m
binding [ˈbaɪndɪŋ] n (of book) legatura ■ adj (contract) vincolante
binge [bɪndʒ] n (col): **to go on a ~** fare baldoria
binge drinker n persona che di norma beve troppo
bingo [ˈbɪŋgəʊ] n gioco simile alla tombola
bin liner n sacchetto per l'immondizia
binoculars [bɪˈnɔkjuləz] npl binocolo
biochemistry [baɪəʊˈkɛmɪstrɪ] n biochimica
biodegradable [ˈbaɪəʊdɪˈgreɪdəbl] adj biodegradabile
biodiversity [ˈbaɪəʊdaɪˈvəːsɪtɪ] n biodiversità f inv
biofuel [ˈbaɪəʊfjuəl] n carburante m biologico

biographer [baɪˈɔgrəfəʳ] n biografo(-a)
biographic [baɪəˈgræfɪk], **biographical** [baɪəˈgræfɪkl] adj biografico(-a)
biography [baɪˈɔgrəfɪ] n biografia
biological [baɪəˈlɔdʒɪkl] adj biologico(-a)
biological clock n orologio biologico
biologist [baɪˈɔlədʒɪst] n biologo(-a)
biology [baɪˈɔlədʒɪ] n biologia
biometric [baɪəʊˈmɛtrɪk] adj biometrico(-a)
biophysics [baɪəʊˈfɪzɪks] n biofisica
biopic [ˈbaɪəʊpɪk] n film m inv biografia inv
biopsy [ˈbaɪɔpsɪ] n biopsia
biosphere [ˈbaɪəʊsfɪəʳ] n biosfera
biotechnology [baɪəʊtɛkˈnɔlədʒɪ] n biotecnologia
bioterrorism [baɪəʊˈtɛrərɪzəm] n bioterrorismo
birch [bəːtʃ] n betulla
bird [bəːd] n uccello; (Brit col: girl) bambola
bird flu n influenza aviaria
bird of prey n (uccello) rapace m
bird's-eye view [ˈbəːdzaɪ-] n vista panoramica
bird watcher n ornitologo(-a) dilettante
Biro® [ˈbaɪrəʊ] n biro® f inv
birth [bəːθ] n nascita; **to give ~ to** dare alla luce; (fig) dare inizio a
birth certificate n certificato di nascita
birth control n controllo delle nascite; contraccezione f
birthday [ˈbəːθdeɪ] n compleanno
birthmark [ˈbəːθmɑːk] n voglia
birthplace [ˈbəːθpleɪs] n luogo di nascita
birth rate n indice m di natalità
Biscay [ˈbɪskeɪ] n: **the Bay of ~** il golfo di Biscaglia
biscuit [ˈbɪskɪt] n (Brit) biscotto; (US) panino al latte
bisect [baɪˈsɛkt] vt tagliare in due (parti); (Math) bisecare
bisexual [ˈbaɪˈsɛksjuəl] adj, n bisessuale (m/f)
bishop [ˈbɪʃəp] n vescovo; (Chess) alfiere m
bistro [ˈbiːstrəʊ] n bistrò m inv
bit [bɪt] pt of **bite** ■ n pezzo; (of tool) punta; (of horse) morso; (Comput) bit m inv; (US: coin) ottavo di dollaro; **a ~ of** un po' di; **a ~ mad/dangerous** un po' matto/pericoloso; **~ by ~** a poco a poco; **to do one's ~** fare la propria parte; **to come to bits** (break) andare a pezzi; **bring all your bits and pieces** porta tutte le tue cose
bitch [bɪtʃ] n (dog) cagna; (col!) puttana (!)
bite [baɪt] vt, vi (pt **bit**, pp **bitten**) mordere ■ n morso; (insect bite) puntura; (mouthful) boccone m; **let's have a ~ (to eat)** mangiamo un boccone; **to ~ one's nails** mangiarsi le unghie

biting ['baɪtɪŋ] *adj* pungente
bit part *n* (*Theat*) particina
bitten ['bɪtn] *pp of* **bite**
bitter ['bɪtəʳ] *adj* amaro(-a); (*wind, criticism*) pungente; (*icy: weather*) gelido(-a) ■ *n* (*Brit: beer*) birra amara; **to the ~ end** a oltranza
bitterly ['bɪtəlɪ] *adv* (*disappoint, complain, weep*) amaramente; (*oppose, criticise*) aspramente; (*jealous*) profondamente; **it's ~ cold** fa un freddo gelido
bitterness ['bɪtənɪs] *n* amarezza; gusto amaro
bittersweet ['bɪtəswiːt] *adj* agrodolce
bitty ['bɪtɪ] *adj* (*Brit col*) frammentario(-a)
bitumen ['bɪtjumɪn] *n* bitume *m*
bivouac ['bɪvuæk] *n* bivacco
bizarre [bɪ'zɑːʳ] *adj* bizzarro(-a)
bk *abbr* = **bank**; **book**
BL *n abbr* (= *Bachelor of Law(s), Bachelor of Letters*) titolo di studio; (*US*: = *Bachelor of Literature*) titolo di studio
B/L *abbr* = **bill of lading**
blab [blæb] *vi* parlare troppo ■ *vt* (*also*: **blab out**) spifferare
black [blæk] *adj* nero(-a) ■ *n* nero; (*person*): **B~** negro(-a) ■ *vt* (*Brit Industry*) boicottare; **~ coffee** caffè *m inv* nero; **to give sb a ~ eye** fare un occhio nero a qn; **in the ~** (*in credit*) in attivo; **there it is in ~ and white** (*fig*) eccolo nero su bianco; **~ and blue** *adj* tutto(-a) pesto(-a)
 ▶ **black out** *vi* (*faint*) svenire
black belt *n* (*Sport*) cintura nera; (*US: area*): **the ~** zona abitata principalmente da negri
blackberry ['blækbərɪ] *n* mora
blackbird ['blækbəːd] *n* merlo
blackboard ['blækbɔːd] *n* lavagna
black box *n* (*Aviat*) scatola nera
Black Country *n* (*Brit*): **the ~** zona carbonifera del centro dell'Inghilterra
blackcurrant [blæk'kʌrənt] *n* ribes *m inv*
black economy *n* (*Brit*) economia sommersa
blacken ['blækn] *vt* annerire
Black Forest *n*: **the ~** la Foresta Nera
blackhead ['blækhɛd] *n* punto nero, comedone *m*
black hole *n* (*Astron*) buco nero
black ice *n* strato trasparente di ghiaccio
blackjack ['blækdʒæk] *n* (*Cards*) ventuno; (*US: truncheon*) manganello
blackleg ['blæklɛg] *n* (*Brit*) crumiro
blacklist ['blæklɪst] *n* lista nera ■ *vt* mettere sulla lista nera
blackmail ['blækmeɪl] *n* ricatto ■ *vt* ricattare
blackmailer ['blækmeɪləʳ] *n* ricattatore(-trice)
black market *n* mercato nero

blackout ['blækaut] *n* oscuramento; (*fainting*) svenimento; (*TV*) interruzione *f* delle trasmissioni
black pepper *n* pepe *m* nero
Black Sea *n*: **the ~** il mar Nero
black sheep *n* pecora nera
blacksmith ['blæksmɪθ] *n* fabbro ferraio
black spot *n* (*Aut*) luogo famigerato per gli incidenti
bladder ['blædəʳ] *n* vescica
blade [bleɪd] *n* lama; (*of oar*) pala; **~ of grass** filo d'erba
blame [bleɪm] *n* colpa ■ *vt*: **to ~ sb/sth for sth** dare la colpa di qc a qn/qc; **who's to ~?** chi è colpevole?; **I'm not to ~** non è colpa mia
blameless ['bleɪmlɪs] *adj* irreprensibile
blanch [blɑːntʃ] *vi* (*person*) sbiancare in viso ■ *vt* (*Culin*) scottare
bland [blænd] *adj* mite; (*taste*) blando(-a)
blank [blæŋk] *adj* bianco(-a); (*look*) distratto(-a) ■ *n* spazio vuoto; (*cartridge*) cartuccia a salve; **to draw a ~** (*fig*) non aver nessun risultato
blank cheque, (*US*) **blank check** *n* assegno in bianco; **to give sb a ~ to do** (*fig*) dare carta bianca a qn per fare
blanket ['blæŋkɪt] *n* coperta ■ *adj* (*statement, agreement*) globale
blanket cover *n*: **to give ~** (*insurance policy*) coprire tutti i rischi
blare [blɛəʳ] *vi* strombettare; (*radio*) suonare a tutto volume
blasé ['blɑːzeɪ] *adj* blasé *inv*
blasphemous ['blæsfɪməs] *adj* blasfemo(-a)
blasphemy ['blæsfɪmɪ] *n* bestemmia
blast [blɑːst] *n* (*of wind*) raffica; (*of air, steam*) getto; (*bomb blast*) esplosione *f* ■ *vt* far saltare ■ *excl* (*Brit col*) mannaggia!; **(at) full ~** a tutta forza
 ▶ **blast off** *vi* (*Space*) essere lanciato(-a)
blast-off ['blɑːstɔf] *n* (*Space*) lancio
blatant ['bleɪtənt] *adj* flagrante
blatantly ['bleɪtəntlɪ] *adv*: **it's ~ obvious** è lampante
blaze [bleɪz] *n* (*fire*) incendio; (*glow: of fire, sun etc*) bagliore *m*; (*fig*) vampata ■ *vi* (*fire*) ardere, fiammeggiare; (*fig*) infiammarsi ■ *vt*: **to ~ a trail** (*fig*) tracciare una via nuova; **in a ~ of publicity** circondato da grande pubblicità
blazer ['bleɪzəʳ] *n* blazer *m inv*
bleach [bliːtʃ] *n* (*also*: **household bleach**) varechina ■ *vt* (*material*) candeggiare
bleached ['bliːtʃt] *adj* (*hair*) decolorato(-a)
bleachers ['bliːtʃəz] *npl* (*US*) posti *mpl* di gradinata

bleak [bli:k] *adj (prospect, future)* tetro(-a); *(landscape)* desolato(-a); *(weather)* gelido(-a)

bleary-eyed ['blɪərɪ'aɪd] *adj* dagli occhi offuscati

bleat [bli:t] *vi* belare

bleed *(pt, pp* **bled)** [bli:d, blɛd] *vt* dissanguare; *(brakes, radiator)* spurgare ▪ *vi* sanguinare; **my nose is bleeding** mi viene fuori sangue dal naso

bleep [bli:p] *n* breve segnale *m* acustico, bip *m inv* ▪ *vi* suonare ▪ *vt (doctor)* chiamare con il cercapersone

bleeper ['bli:pəʳ] *n (of doctor etc)* cercapersone *m inv*

blemish ['blɛmɪʃ] *n* macchia

blend [blɛnd] *n* miscela ▪ *vt* mescolare ▪ *vi (colours etc)* armonizzare

blender ['blɛndəʳ] *n (Culin)* frullatore *m*

bless *(pt, pp* **blessed** *or* **blest)** [blɛs, blɛst] *vt* benedire; **~ you!** *(sneezing)* salute!; **to be blessed with** godere di

blessed ['blɛsɪd] *adj (Rel: holy)* benedetto(-a); *(happy)* beato(-a); **every ~ day** tutti i santi giorni

blessing ['blɛsɪŋ] *n* benedizione *f*; fortuna; **to count one's blessings** ringraziare Iddio, ritenersi fortunato; **it was a ~ in disguise** in fondo è stato un bene

blest [blɛst] *pt, pp of* **bless**

blew [blu:] *pt of* **blow**

blight [blaɪt] *n (of plants)* golpe *f* ▪ *vt (hopes etc)* deludere; *(life)* rovinare

blimey ['blaɪmɪ] *excl (Brit col)* accidenti!

blind [blaɪnd] *adj* cieco(-a) ▪ *n (for window)* avvolgibile *m; (Venetian blind)* veneziana ▪ *vt* accecare; **to turn a ~ eye (on** *or* **to)** chiudere un occhio (su)

blind alley *n* vicolo cieco

blind corner *n (Brit)* svolta cieca

blind date *n* appuntamento combinato *(tra due persone che non si conoscono)*

blinders ['blaɪndəz] *npl (US)* = **blinkers**

blindfold ['blaɪndfəuld] *n* benda ▪ *adj, adv* bendato(-a) ▪ *vt* bendare gli occhi a

blinding ['blaɪndɪŋ] *adj (flash, light)* accecante; *(pain)* atroce

blindly ['blaɪndlɪ] *adv* ciecamente

blindness ['blaɪndnɪs] *n* cecità

blind spot *n (Aut etc)* punto cieco; *(fig)* punto debole

bling [blɪŋ] *n* gioielli vistosi

blink [blɪŋk] *vi* battere gli occhi; *(light)* lampeggiare ▪ *n:* **to be on the ~** *(col)* essere scassato(-a)

blinkers ['blɪŋkəz] *npl (Brit)* paraocchi *mpl*

blinking ['blɪŋkɪŋ] *adj (Brit col):* **this ~ ...** questo(-a) maledetto(-a) ...

blip [blɪp] *n (on radar etc)* segnale *m* intermittente; *(on graph)* piccola variazione *f; (fig)* momentanea battuta d'arresto

bliss [blɪs] *n* estasi *f*

blissful ['blɪsfəl] *adj (event, day)* stupendo(-a), meraviglioso(-a); *(smile)* beato(-a); **in ~ ignorance** nella (più) beata ignoranza

blissfully ['blɪsfəlɪ] *adv (sigh, smile)* beatamente; **~ happy** magnificamente felice

blister ['blɪstəʳ] *n (on skin)* vescica; *(on paintwork)* bolla ▪ *vi (paint)* coprirsi di bolle

BLit, BLitt *n abbr (= Bachelor of Literature)* titolo di studio

blithe [blaɪð] *adj* gioioso(-a), allegro(-a)

blithely ['blaɪðlɪ] *adv* allegramente

blithering ['blɪðərɪŋ] *adj (col):* **this ~ idiot** questa razza d'idiota

blitz [blɪts] *n* blitz *m;* **to have a ~ on sth** *(fig)* prendere d'assalto qc

blizzard ['blɪzəd] *n* bufera di neve

bloated ['bləutɪd] *adj* gonfio(-a)

blob [blɔb] *n (drop)* goccia; *(stain, spot)* macchia

bloc [blɔk] *n (Pol)* blocco

block [blɔk] *n (gen, Comput)* blocco; *(in pipes)* ingombro; *(toy)* cubo; *(of buildings)* isolato ▪ *vt (gen, Comput)* bloccare; **~ of flats** caseggiato; **3 blocks from here** a 3 isolati di distanza da qui; **mental ~** blocco mentale
  ▸ **block up** *vt* bloccare; *(pipe)* ingorgare, intasare

blockade [blɔ'keɪd] *n* blocco ▪ *vt* assediare

blockage ['blɔkɪdʒ] *n* ostacolo

block and tackle *n (Tech)* paranco

block booking *n* prenotazione *f* in blocco

blockbuster ['blɔkbʌstəʳ] *n* libro *or* film *etc* sensazionale

block capitals *npl* stampatello

blockhead ['blɔkhɛd] *n* testa di legno

block letters *npl* stampatello

block vote *n (Brit)* voto per delega

blog [blɔg] *n* blog *m inv* ▪ *vi* scrivere blog, bloggare

blogger [blɔgəʳ] *n (Comput)* blogger *m/f inv*

blogging [blɔgɪŋ] *n* blogging *m* ▪ *adj:* **~ website** sito di blogging

bloke [bləuk] *n (Brit col)* tizio

blond, blonde [blɔnd] *n (man)* biondo; *(woman)* bionda ▪ *adj* biondo(-a)

blood [blʌd] *n* sangue *m;* **new ~** *(fig)* nuova linfa

blood bank *n* banca del sangue

blood count *n* conteggio di globuli rossi e bianchi

bloodcurdling ['blʌdkə:dlɪŋ] *adj* raccapricciante, da far gelare il sangue

blood donor *n* donatore(-trice) di sangue

453

blood group n gruppo sanguigno

bloodhound ['blʌdhaund] n segugio

bloodless ['blʌdlɪs] adj (pale) smorto(-a), esangue; (coup) senza spargimento di sangue

bloodletting ['blʌdlɛtɪŋ] n (Med) salasso; (fig) spargimento di sangue

blood poisoning n setticemia

blood pressure n pressione f sanguigna; **to have high/low ~** avere la pressione alta/ bassa

bloodshed ['blʌdʃɛd] n spargimento di sangue

bloodshot ['blʌdʃɔt] adj: **~ eyes** occhi iniettati di sangue

bloodstained ['blʌdsteɪnd] adj macchiato(-a) di sangue

bloodstream ['blʌdstriːm] n flusso del sangue

blood test n analisi f inv del sangue

bloodthirsty ['blʌdθəːstɪ] adj assetato(-a) di sangue

blood transfusion n trasfusione f di sangue

blood type n gruppo sanguigno

blood vessel n vaso sanguigno

bloody ['blʌdɪ] adj sanguinoso(-a); (Brit col!): **this ~ ...** questo maledetto ...; **a ~ awful day** (col!) una giornata di merda (!); **~ good** (col!) maledettamente buono

bloody-minded ['blʌdɪ'maɪndɪd] adj (Brit col) indisponente

bloom [bluːm] n fiore m ■ vi essere in fiore

blooming ['bluːmɪŋ] adj (col): **this ~ ...** questo(-a) dannato(-a) ...

blossom ['blɔsəm] n fiore m; (with pl sense) fiori mpl ■ vi essere in fiore; **to ~ into** (fig) diventare

blot [blɔt] n macchia ■ vt macchiare; **to be a ~ on the landscape** rovinare il paesaggio; **to ~ one's copy book** (fig) farla grossa

  ▶ **blot out** vt (memories) cancellare; (view) nascondere; (nation, city) annientare

blotchy ['blɔtʃɪ] adj (complexion) coperto(-a) di macchie

blotter ['blɔtə'] n tampone m (di carta assorbente)

blotting paper ['blɔtɪŋ-] n carta assorbente

blotto ['blɔtəu] adj (col) sbronzo(-a)

blouse [blauz] n camicetta

blow [bləu] n colpo ■ vb (pt **blew**, pp **blown**) vi soffiare ■ vt (fuse) far saltare; **to come to blows** venire alle mani; **to ~ one's nose** soffiarsi il naso; **to ~ a whistle** fischiare

  ▶ **blow away** vi volare via ■ vt portare via

  ▶ **blow down** vt abbattere

  ▶ **blow off** vt far volare via; **to ~ off course** far uscire di rotta

  ▶ **blow out** vi scoppiare

  ▶ **blow over** vi calmarsi

  ▶ **blow up** vi saltare in aria ■ vt far saltare in aria; (tyre) gonfiare; (Phot) ingrandire

blow-dry ['bləudraɪ] n (hairstyle) messa in piega a föhn ■ vt asciugare con il föhn

blowlamp ['bləulæmp] n (Brit) lampada a benzina per saldare

blown [bləun] pp of **blow**

blowout ['bləuaut] n (of tyre) scoppio; (col: big meal) abbuffata

blowtorch ['bləutɔːtʃ] n lampada a benzina per saldare

blowzy ['blauzɪ] adj trasandato(-a)

BLS n abbr (US) = **Bureau of Labor Statistics**

blubber ['blʌbə'] n grasso di balena ■ vi (pej) piangere forte

bludgeon ['blʌdʒən] vt prendere a randellate

blue [bluː] adj azzurro(-a), celeste; (darker) blu inv; **~ film/joke** film/barzelletta pornografico(a); **(only) once in a ~ moon** a ogni morte di papa; **out of the ~** (fig) all'improvviso; see also **blues**

blue baby n neonato cianotico

bluebell ['bluːbɛl] n giacinto di bosco

bluebottle ['bluːbɔtl] n moscone m

blue cheese n formaggio tipo gorgonzola

blue-chip ['bluːtʃɪp] adj: **~ investment** investimento sicuro

blue-collar worker ['bluːkɔlə'-] n operaio(-a)

blue jeans npl blue-jeans mpl

blueprint ['bluːprɪnt] n cianografia; (fig): **~ (for)** formula (di)

blues [bluːz] npl: **the ~** (Mus) il blues; **to have the ~** (col: feeling) essere a terra

bluff [blʌf] vi bluffare ■ n bluff m inv; (promontory) promontorio scosceso ■ adj (person) brusco(-a); **to call sb's ~** mettere alla prova il bluff di qn

blunder ['blʌndə'] n abbaglio ■ vi prendere un abbaglio; **to ~ into sb/sth** andare a sbattere contro qn/qc

blunt [blʌnt] adj (edge) smussato(-a); (point) spuntato(-a); (knife) che non taglia; (person) brusco(-a) ■ vt smussare; spuntare; **this pencil is ~** questa matita non ha più la punta; **~ instrument** (Law) corpo contundente

bluntly ['blʌntlɪ] adv (speak) senza mezzi termini

bluntness ['blʌntnɪs] n (of person) brutale franchezza

blur [bləː'] n cosa offuscata ■ vt offuscare

blurb [bləːb] n trafiletto pubblicitario

blurred [bləːd] adj (photo) mosso(-a); (TV) sfuocato(-a)

blurt out [bləːt-] vt lasciarsi sfuggire

blush [blʌʃ] vi arrossire ■ n rossore m

blusher ['blʌʃəʳ] n fard m inv
bluster ['blʌstəʳ] n spacconate fpl; (threats) vuote minacce fpl ■ vi fare lo spaccone; minacciare a vuoto
blustering ['blʌstərɪŋ] adj (tone etc) da spaccone
blustery ['blʌstərɪ] adj (weather) burrascoso(-a)
Blvd abbr = **boulevard**
BM n abbr = **British Museum**; (Scol: = Bachelor of Medicine) titolo di studio
BMA n abbr = **British Medical Association**
BMJ n abbr = **British Medical Journal**
BMus n abbr (= Bachelor of Music) titolo di studio
BMX n abbr (= bicycle motocross) BMX f inv; ~ **bike** mountain bike f inv per cross
bn abbr = **billion**
BO n abbr (col: = body odour) odori mpl sgradevoli (del corpo); = **box office**
boar [bɔːʳ] n cinghiale m
board [bɔːd] n tavola; (on wall) tabellone m; (for chess etc) scacchiera; (committee) consiglio, comitato; (in firm) consiglio d'amministrazione; (Naut, Aviat): **on** ~ a bordo ■ vt (ship) salire a bordo di; (train) salire su; **full** ~ (Brit) pensione f completa; **half** ~ (Brit) mezza pensione; ~ **and lodging** vitto e alloggio; **above** ~ (fig) regolare; **across the** ~ (fig) adv per tutte le categorie; adj generale; **to go by the** ~ venir messo(-a) da parte
▶ **board up** vt (door) chiudere con assi
boarder ['bɔːdəʳ] n pensionante m/f; (Scol) convittore(-trice)
board game n gioco da tavolo
boarding card ['bɔːdɪŋ-] n (Aviat, Naut) carta d'imbarco
boarding house n pensione f
boarding party n squadra di ispezione (del carico di una nave)
boarding pass n (Brit) = **boarding card**
boarding school n collegio
board meeting n riunione f di consiglio
board room n sala del consiglio
boardwalk ['bɔːdwɔːk] n (US) passeggiata a mare
boast [bəust] vi: **to** ~ (**about** or **of**) vantarsi (di) ■ vt vantare ■ n vanteria; vanto
boastful ['bəustful] adj vanaglorioso(-a)
boastfulness ['bəustfulnɪs] n vanagloria
boat [bəut] n nave f; (small) barca; **to go by** ~ andare in barca or in nave; **we're all in the same** ~ (fig) siamo tutti nella stessa barca
boater ['bəutəʳ] n (hat) paglietta
boating ['bəutɪŋ] n canottaggio
boat people n boat people mpl
boatswain ['bəusn] n nostromo

bob [bɔb] vi (boat, cork on water: also: **bob up and down**) andare su e giù ■ n (Brit col) = **shilling**
▶ **bob up** vi saltare fuori
bobbin ['bɔbɪn] n bobina; (of sewing machine) rocchetto
bobby ['bɔbɪ] n (Brit col) ≈ poliziotto
bobsleigh ['bɔbsleɪ] n bob m inv
bode [bəud] vi: **to** ~ **well/ill (for)** essere di buon/cattivo auspicio (per)
bodice ['bɔdɪs] n corsetto
bodily ['bɔdɪlɪ] adj (comfort, needs) materiale; (pain) fisico(-a) ■ adv (carry) in braccio; (lift) di peso
body ['bɔdɪ] n corpo; (of car) carrozzeria; (of plane) fusoliera; (organization) associazione f, organizzazione f; (quantity) quantità f inv; (of speech, document) parte f principale; (also: **body stocking**) body m inv; **in a** ~ in massa; **ruling** ~ direttivo; **a wine with** ~ un vino corposo
body blow n (fig) duro colpo
body-building ['bɔdɪ'bɪldɪŋ] n culturismo
bodyguard ['bɔdɪɡɑːd] n guardia del corpo
body language n linguaggio del corpo
body repairs npl (Aut) lavori mpl di carrozzeria
body search n perquisizione f personale; **to submit to** or **undergo a** ~ essere sottoposto(-a) a perquisizione personale
bodywork ['bɔdɪwɜːk] n carrozzeria
boffin ['bɔfɪn] n scienziato
bog [bɔɡ] n palude f ■ vt: **to get bogged down** (fig) impantanarsi
bogey ['bəuɡɪ] n (worry) spauracchio; (also: **bogey man**) babau m inv
boggle ['bɔɡl] vi: **the mind boggles** è incredibile
Bogotá [bəuɡə'tɑː] n Bogotà f
bogus ['bəuɡəs] adj falso(-a); finto(-a)
Bohemia [bəu'hiːmɪə] n Boemia
Bohemian [bəu'hiːmɪən] adj, n boemo(-a)
boil [bɔɪl] vt, vi bollire ■ n (Med) foruncolo; **to come to the** or (US) **a** ~ raggiungere l'ebollizione; **to bring to the** or (US) **a** ~ portare a ebollizione; **boiled egg** uovo alla coque; **boiled potatoes** patate fpl bollite or lesse
▶ **boil down** vi (fig): **to** ~ **down to** ridursi a
▶ **boil over** vi traboccare (bollendo)
boiler ['bɔɪləʳ] n caldaia
boiler suit n (Brit) tuta
boiling ['bɔɪlɪŋ] adj bollente; **I'm** ~ (**hot**) (col) sto morendo di caldo
boiling point n punto di ebollizione
boil-in-the-bag [bɔɪlɪnðə'bæɡ] adj (rice etc) da bollire nel sacchetto
boisterous ['bɔɪstərəs] adj chiassoso(-a)
bold [bəuld] adj audace; (child) impudente; (outline) chiaro(-a); (colour) deciso(-a)

455

boldness ['bəʊldnɪs] n audacia; impudenza
bold type n (Typ) neretto, grassetto
Bolivia [bə'lɪvɪə] n Bolivia
Bolivian [bə'lɪvɪən] adj, n boliviano(-a)
bollard ['bɒləd] n (Naut) bitta; (Brit Aut)
colonnina luminosa
Bollywood ['bɒlɪwud] n Bollywood f
bolshy ['bɒlʃɪ] adj (Brit col) piantagrane,
ribelle; **to be in a ~ mood** essere in vena di
piantar grane
bolster ['bəʊlstə'] n capezzale m
▶ **bolster up** vt sostenere
bolt [bəʊlt] n chiavistello; (with nut) bullone
m ■ adv: ~ **upright** diritto(-a) come un fuso
■ vt serrare; (food) mangiare in fretta ■ vi
scappare via; **a ~ from the blue** (fig) un
fulmine a ciel sereno
bomb [bɒm] n bomba ■ vt bombardare
bombard [bɒm'bɑːd] vt bombardare
bombardment [bɒm'bɑːdmənt] n
bombardamento
bombastic [bɒm'bæstɪk] adj ampolloso(-a)
bomb disposal n: ~ **expert** artificiere m;
~ **unit** corpo degli artificieri
bomber ['bɒmə'] n bombardiere m; (terrorist)
dinamitardo(-a)
bombing ['bɒmɪŋ] n bombardamento
bomb scare n stato di allarme (per sospetta
presenza di una bomba)
bombshell ['bɒmʃɛl] n (fig) notizia bomba
bomb site n luogo bombardato
bona fide ['bəʊnə'faɪdɪ] adj sincero(-a);
(offer) onesto(-a)
bonanza [bə'nænzə] n cuccagna
bond [bɒnd] n legame m; (binding promise,
Finance) obbligazione f; **in ~** (of goods) in
attesa di sdoganamento
bondage ['bɒndɪdʒ] n schiavitù f
bonded warehouse ['bɒndɪd-] n magazzino
doganale
bone [bəʊn] n osso; (of fish) spina, lisca
■ vt disossare; togliere le spine a
bone china n porcellana fine
bone-dry ['bəʊn'draɪ] adj asciuttissimo(-a)
bone idle adj: **to be ~** essere un(a)
fannullone(-a)
bone marrow n midollo osseo
boner ['bəʊnə'] n (US) gaffe f inv
bonfire ['bɒnfaɪə'] n falò m inv
bonk [bɒŋk] vt, vi (hum, col) scopare (!)
bonkers ['bɒŋkəz] adj (Brit col) suonato(-a)
Bonn [bɒn] n Bonn f
bonnet ['bɒnɪt] n cuffia; (Brit: of car) cofano
bonny ['bɒnɪ] adj (esp Scottish) bello(-a), carino(-a)
bonus ['bəʊnəs] n premio; (on wages) gratifica
bony ['bəʊnɪ] adj (thin: person) ossuto(-a),
angoloso(-a); (arm, face, Med: tissue) osseo(-a);

(meat) pieno(-a) di ossi; (fish) pieno(-a) di
spine
boo [buː] excl ba! ■ vt fischiare ■ n fischio
boob [buːb] n (col: breast) tetta; (: Brit: mistake)
gaffe f inv
booby prize ['buːbɪ-] n premio per il peggior
contendente
booby trap ['buːbɪ-] n trabocchetto; (bomb)
congegno che esplode al contatto
booby-trapped ['buːbɪtræpt] adj: **a ~ car**
una macchina con dell'esplosivo a bordo
book [buk] n libro; (of stamps etc) blocchetto
■ vt (ticket, seat, room) prenotare; (driver)
multare; (football player) ammonire; **books**
npl (Comm) conti mpl; **to keep the books**
(Comm) tenere la contabilità; **by the ~**
secondo le regole; **to throw the ~ at sb**
incriminare qn seriamente or con tutte le
aggravanti
▶ **book in** vi (Brit: at hotel) prendere una
camera
▶ **book up** vt riservare, prenotare; **the hotel
is booked up** l'albergo è al completo; **all seats
are booked up** è tutto esaurito
bookable ['bukəbl] adj: **seats are ~** si possono
prenotare i posti
bookcase ['bukkeɪs] n scaffale m
book ends npl reggilibri mpl
booking ['bukɪŋ] n (Brit) prenotazione f
booking office n (Brit) biglietteria
book-keeping ['buk'kiːpɪŋ] n contabilità
booklet ['buklɪt] n opuscolo, libretto
bookmaker ['bukmeɪkə'] n allibratore m
bookmark ['bukmɑːk] n (also Comput) n
segnalibro ■ vt (Comput) mettere un
segnalibro a; (internet) aggiungere a
"Preferiti"
bookseller ['bukssɛlə'] n libraio
bookshelf ['bukʃɛlf] n mensola (per libri);
bookshelves npl (bookcase) libreria
bookshop ['bukʃɒp] n libreria
bookstall ['bukstɔːl] n bancarella di libri
bookstore ['bukstɔː'] n = **bookshop**
book token n buono m libri inv
book value n valore m contabile
bookworm ['bukwəːm] n (fig) topo di
biblioteca
boom [buːm] n (noise) rimbombo; (busy period)
boom m inv ■ vi rimbombare; andare a
gonfie vele
boomerang ['buːməræŋ] n boomerang m inv
■ vi (fig) avere effetto contrario; **to ~ on sb**
(fig) ritorcersi contro qn
boom town n città f inv in rapidissima
espansione
boon [buːn] n vantaggio
boorish ['buərɪʃ] adj maleducato(-a)

boost [buːst] n spinta ■ vt spingere; (increase: sales, production) incentivare; **to give a ~ to** (morale) tirar su; **it gave a ~ to his confidence** è stata per lui un'iniezione di fiducia

booster ['buːstə^r] n (Elec) amplificatore m; (TV) amplificatore m di segnale; (also: **booster rocket**) razzo vettore; (Med) richiamo

booster seat n (Aut: for children) seggiolino di sicurezza

boot [buːt] n stivale m; (ankle boot) stivaletto; (for hiking) scarpone m da montagna; (for football etc) scarpa; (Brit: of car) portabagagli m inv ■ vt (Comput) inizializzare; **to ~** (in addition) per giunta, in più; **to give sb the ~** (col) mettere qn alla porta

booth [buːð] n (at fair) baraccone m; (of cinema, telephone etc) cabina; (also: **voting booth**) cabina (elettorale)

bootleg ['buːtlɛg] adj di contrabbando; **~ record** registrazione f pirata inv

booty ['buːtɪ] n bottino

booze [buːz] (col) n alcool m ■ vi trincare

boozer ['buːzə^r] n (col: person) beone m; (Brit col: pub) osteria

border ['bɔːdə^r] n orlo; margine m; (of a country) frontiera; **the B~** la frontiera tra l'Inghilterra e la Scozia; **the Borders** la zona di confine tra l'Inghilterra e la Scozia

▶ **border on** vt fus confinare con

borderline ['bɔːdəlaɪn] n (fig) linea di demarcazione ■ adj: **~ case** caso limite

bore [bɔː^r] pt of **bear** ■ vt (hole) perforare; (person) annoiare ■ n (person) seccatore(-trice); (of gun) calibro; **he's bored to tears** or **bored to death** or **bored stiff** è annoiato a morte, si annoia da morire

boredom ['bɔːdəm] n noia

boring ['bɔːrɪŋ] adj noioso(-a)

born [bɔːn] adj: **to be ~** nascere; **I was ~ in 1960** sono nato nel 1960; **~ blind** cieco dalla nascita; **a ~ comedian** un comico nato

born-again [bɔːnə'gɛn] adj: **~ Christian** convertito(-a) alla chiesa evangelica

borne [bɔːn] pp of **bear**

Borneo ['bɔːnɪəu] n Borneo

borough ['bʌrə] n comune m

borrow ['bɔrəu] vt: **to ~ sth (from sb)** prendere in prestito qc (da qn); **may I ~ your car?** può prestarmi la macchina?

borrower ['bɔrəuə^r] n (gen) chi prende a prestito; (Econ) mutuatario(-a)

borrowing ['bɔrəuɪŋ] n prestito

borstal ['bɔːstl] n (Brit) riformatorio

Bosnia ['bɔznɪə] n Bosnia

Bosnia-Herzegovina ['bɔznɪəhɛrzə'gəuviːnə]

n (also: **Bosnia-Hercegovina**) Bosnia-Erzegovina

Bosnian ['bɔznɪən] adj, n bosniaco(-a)

bosom ['buzəm] n petto; (fig) seno

bosom friend n amico(-a) del cuore

boss [bɔs] n capo ■ vt (also: **boss about** or **around**) comandare a bacchetta; **stop bossing everyone about!** smettila di dare ordini a tutti!

bossy ['bɔsɪ] adj prepotente

bosun ['bəusn] n nostromo

botanical [bə'tænɪkl] adj botanico(-a)

botanist ['bɔtənɪst] n botanico(-a)

botany ['bɔtənɪ] n botanica

botch [bɔtʃ] vt fare un pasticcio di

both [bəuθ] adj entrambi(-e), tutt'e due ■ pron: **~ of them** entrambi(-e) ■ adv: **they sell ~ meat and poultry** vendono insieme la carne ed il pollame; **~ of us went, we ~ went** ci siamo andati tutt'e due

bother ['bɔðə^r] vt (worry) preoccupare; (annoy) infastidire ■ vi (gen: also: **bother o.s.**) preoccuparsi ■ n: **it is a ~ to have to do** è una seccatura dover fare ■ excl uffa!, accidenti!; **to ~ doing sth** darsi la pena di fare qc; **I'm sorry to ~ you** mi dispiace disturbarla; **please don't ~** non si scomodi; **it's no ~** non c'è problema

Botswana [bɔt'swɑːnə] n Botswana m

bottle ['bɔtl] n bottiglia; (of perfume, shampoo etc) flacone m; (baby's) biberon m inv ■ vt imbottigliare; **~ of wine/milk** bottiglia di vino/latte; **wine/milk ~** bottiglia da vino/del latte

▶ **bottle up** vt contenere

bottle bank n contenitore m per la raccolta del vetro

bottle-fed ['bɔtlfɛd] adj allattato(-a) artificialmente

bottleneck ['bɔtlnɛk] n ingorgo

bottle-opener ['bɔtləupnə^r] n apribottiglie m inv

bottom ['bɔtəm] n fondo; (of mountain, tree, hill) piedi mpl; (buttocks) sedere m ■ adj più basso(-a), ultimo(-a); **at the ~ of** in fondo a; **to get to the ~ of sth** (fig) andare al fondo di or in fondo a qc

bottomless ['bɔtəmlɪs] adj senza fondo

bottom line n: **the ~ is ...** in ultima analisi ...

botulism ['bɔtjulɪzəm] n botulismo

bough [bau] n ramo

bought [bɔːt] pt, pp of **buy**

boulder ['bəuldə^r] n masso (tondeggiante)

boulevard ['buːlvɑːd] n viale m

bounce [bauns] vi (ball) rimbalzare; (cheque) essere restituito(-a) ■ vt far rimbalzare ■ n (rebound) rimbalzo; **to ~ in** entrare di slancio or con foga; **he's got plenty of ~** *(fig)* è molto esuberante

bouncer ['baunsə^r] *n* buttafuori *m inv*

bouncy castle® ['baunsı-] *n grande castello gonfiabile per giocare*

bound [baund] *pt, pp of* **bind** ■ *n* *(gen pl)* limite *m*; *(leap)* salto ■ *vt* *(leap)* saltare; *(limit)* delimitare ■ *adj*: **to be ~ to do sth** *(obliged)* essere costretto(-a) a fare qc; **he's ~ to fail** *(likely)* è certo di fallire; **~ for** diretto(-a) a; **out of bounds** il cui accesso è vietato

boundary ['baundrı] *n* confine *m*

boundless ['baundlıs] *adj* illimitato(-a)

bountiful ['bauntıful] *adj* *(person)* munifico(-a); *(God)* misericordioso(-a); *(supply)* abbondante

bounty ['bauntı] *n* *(generosity)* liberalità, munificenza; *(reward)* taglia

bounty hunter *n* cacciatore *m* di taglie

bouquet ['bukeı] *n* bouquet *m inv*

bourbon ['buəbən] *n* *(US: also:* **bourbon whiskey)** bourbon *m inv*

bourgeois ['buəʒwɑ:] *adj, n* borghese *(m/f)*

bout [baut] *n* periodo *m*; *(of malaria etc)* attacco; *(Boxing etc)* incontro

boutique [bu:'ti:k] *n* boutique *f inv*

bow[1] [bəu] *n* nodo; *(weapon)* arco; *(Mus)* archetto

bow[2] [bau] *n* *(with body)* inchino; *(Naut: also:* **bows)** prua ■ *vi* inchinarsi; *(yield):* **to ~ to** *or* **before** sottomettersi a; **to ~ to the inevitable** rassegnarsi all'inevitabile

bowels [bauəlz] *npl* intestini *mpl*; *(fig)* viscere *fpl*

bowl [bəul] *n* *(for eating)* scodella; *(for washing)* bacino; *(ball)* boccia; *(of pipe)* fornello; *(US: stadium)* stadio ■ *vi* *(Cricket)* servire (la palla); *see also* **bowls**

▶ **bowl over** *vt* *(fig)* sconcertare

bow-legged ['bəu'legıd] *adj* dalle gambe storte

bowler ['bəulə^r] *n* giocatore *m* di bocce; *(Cricket)* giocatore che serve la palla; *(Brit: also:* **bowler hat)** bombetta

bowling ['bəulıŋ] *n* *(game)* gioco delle bocce; bowling *m*

bowling alley *n* pista da bowling

bowling green *n* campo di bocce

bowls [bəulz] *n* gioco delle bocce

bow tie *n* cravatta a farfalla

box [bɔks] *n* scatola; *(also:* **cardboard box)** (scatola di) cartone *m*; *(crate; also for money)* cassetta; *(Theat)* palco; *(Brit Aut)* area d'incrocio ■ *vi* fare pugilato ■ *vt* mettere in (una) scatola; *(Sport)* combattere contro

boxer ['bɔksə^r] *n* *(person)* pugile *m*; *(dog)* boxer *m inv*

boxing ['bɔksıŋ] *n* *(Sport)* pugilato

Boxing Day *n* *(Brit)* = Santo Stefano; *vedi nota*

boxing gloves *npl* guantoni *mpl* da pugile

boxing ring *n* ring *m inv*

box number *n* *(for advertisements)* casella

box office *n* biglietteria

box room *n* ripostiglio

boy [bɔı] *n* ragazzo; *(small)* bambino; *(son)* figlio; *(servant)* servo

boy band *n* *gruppo pop di soli ragazzi maschi creato per far presa su un pubblico giovane*

boycott ['bɔıkɔt] *n* boicottaggio ■ *vt* boicottare

boyfriend ['bɔıfrɛnd] *n* ragazzo

boyish ['bɔııʃ] *adj* di or da ragazzo

bp *abbr* = **bishop**

bra [brɑ:] *n* reggipetto, reggiseno

brace [breıs] *n* sostegno; *(on teeth)* apparecchio correttore; *(tool)* trapano; *(Typ: also:* **brace bracket)** graffa ■ *vt* rinforzare, sostenere; **to ~ o.s.** *(fig)* farsi coraggio; *see also* **braces**

bracelet ['breıslıt] *n* braccialetto

braces ['breısız] *npl* *(Brit)* bretelle *fpl*

bracing ['breısıŋ] *adj* invigorante

bracken ['brækən] *n* felce *f*

bracket ['brækıt] *n* *(Tech)* mensola; *(group)* gruppo; *(Typ)* parentesi *f inv* ■ *vt* mettere fra parentesi; *(fig: also:* **bracket together)** mettere insieme; **in brackets** tra parentesi; **round/square brackets** parentesi tonde/ quadre; **income ~** fascia di reddito

brackish ['brækıʃ] *adj* *(water)* salmastro(-a)

brag [bræg] *vi* vantarsi

braid [breıd] *n* *(trimming)* passamano; *(of hair)* treccia

Braille [breıl] *n* braille *m*

brain [breın] *n* cervello; **brains** *npl* cervella *fpl*; **he's got brains** è intelligente

brainchild ['breıntʃaıld] *n* creatura, creazione *f*

braindead ['breındɛd] *adj* *(Med)* che ha subito morte cerebrale; *(col)* cerebroleso(-a), deficiente

brainless ['breınlıs] *adj* deficiente, stupido(-a)

brainstorm ['breınstɔ:m] *n* *(fig)* attacco di pazzia; *(US)* = **brainwave**

brainwash ['breɪnwɔʃ] *vt* fare un lavaggio di cervello a

brainwave ['breɪnweɪv] *n* lampo di genio

brainy ['breɪnɪ] *adj* intelligente

braise [breɪz] *vt* brasare

brake [breɪk] *n* (*on vehicle*) freno ■ *vt, vi* frenare

brake light *n* (fanalino dello) stop *m inv*

brake pedal *n* pedale *m* del freno

bramble ['bræmbl] *n* rovo; (*fruit*) mora

bran [bræn] *n* crusca

branch [brɑːntʃ] *n* ramo; (*Comm*) succursale *f*, filiale *f* ■ *vi* diramarsi
  ▶ **branch out** *vi*: **to ~ out into** intraprendere una nuova attività nel ramo di

branch line *n* (*Rail*) linea secondaria

branch manager *n* direttore *m* di filiale

brand [brænd] *n* marca ■ *vt* (*cattle*) marcare (a ferro rovente); (*fig: pej*): **to ~ sb a communist** *etc* definire qn come comunista *etc*

brandish ['brændɪʃ] *vt* brandire

brand name *n* marca

brand-new ['brænd'njuː] *adj* nuovo(-a) di zecca

brandy ['brændɪ] *n* brandy *m inv*

brash [bræʃ] *adj* sfacciato(-a)

Brasilia [brə'zɪljə] *n* Brasilia

brass [brɑːs] *n* ottone *m*; **the ~** (*Mus*) gli ottoni

brass band *n* fanfara

brassière ['bræsɪəʳ] *n* reggipetto, reggiseno

brass tacks *npl*: **to get down to ~** (*col*) venire al sodo

brat [bræt] *n* (*pej*) marmocchio, monello(-a)

bravado [brə'vɑːdəu] *n* spavalderia

brave [breɪv] *adj* coraggioso(-a) ■ *n* guerriero *m* pellerossa *inv* ■ *vt* affrontare

bravery ['breɪvərɪ] *n* coraggio

bravo [brɑː'vəu] *excl* bravo!, bene!

brawl [brɔːl] *n* rissa ■ *vi* azzuffarsi

brawn [brɔːn] *n* muscolo; (*meat*) carne *f* di testa di maiale

brawny ['brɔːnɪ] *adj* muscoloso(-a)

bray [breɪ] *n* raglio ■ *vi* ragliare

brazen ['breɪzn] *adj* svergognato(-a) ■ *vt*: **to ~ it out** fare lo sfacciato

brazier ['breɪzɪəʳ] *n* braciere *m*

Brazil [brə'zɪl] *n* Brasile *m*

Brazilian [brə'zɪljən] *adj, n* brasiliano(-a)

Brazil nut *n* noce *f* del Brasile

breach [briːtʃ] *vt* aprire una breccia in ■ *n* (*gap*) breccia, varco; (*estrangement*) rottura; (*of duty*) abuso; (*breaking*): **~ of contract** rottura di contratto; **~ of the peace** violazione *f* dell'ordine pubblico; **~ of trust** abuso di fiducia

bread [bred] *n* pane *m*; (*col: money*) grana; **to earn one's daily ~** guadagnarsi il pane;

to know which side one's ~ is buttered on saper fare i propri interessi; **~ and butter** *n* pane e burro; (*fig*) mezzi *mpl* di sussistenza

breadbin ['bredbɪn] *n* (*Brit*) cassetta *f* portapane *inv*

breadboard ['bredbɔːd] *n* tagliere *m* (*per il pane*); (*Comput*) pannello per esperimenti

breadbox ['bredbɔks] *n* (*US*) cassetta *f* portapane *inv*

breadcrumbs ['bredkrʌmz] *npl* briciole *fpl*; (*Culin*) pangrattato

breadline ['bredlaɪn] *n*: **to be on the ~** avere appena denaro per vivere

breadth [bretθ] *n* larghezza

breadwinner ['bredwɪnəʳ] *n* chi guadagna il pane per tutta la famiglia

break [breɪk] *vb* (*pt* **broke**, *pp* **broken**) *vt* rompere; (*law*) violare; (*promise*) mancare a ■ *vi* rompersi; (*weather*) cambiare ■ *n* (*gap*) breccia; (*fracture*) rottura; (*rest, also Scol*) intervallo; (: *short*) pausa; (*chance*) possibilità *f inv*; (*holiday*) vacanza; **to ~ one's leg** *etc* rompersi la gamba *etc*; **to ~ a record** battere un primato; **to ~ the news to sb** comunicare per primo la notizia a qn; **to ~ with sb** (*fig*) rompere con qn; **to ~ even** *vi* coprire le spese; **to ~ free** *or* **loose** liberarsi; **without a ~** senza una pausa; **to have** *or* **take a ~** (*few minutes*) fare una pausa; (*holiday*) prendere un po' di riposo; **a lucky ~** un colpo di fortuna
  ▶ **break down** *vt* (*figures, data*) analizzare; (*door etc*) buttare giù, abbattere; (*resistance*) stroncare ■ *vi* crollare; (*Med*) avere un esaurimento (nervoso); (*Aut*) guastarsi
  ▶ **break in** *vt* (*horse etc*) domare ■ *vi* (*burglar*) fare irruzione
  ▶ **break into** *vt fus* (*house*) fare irruzione in
  ▶ **break off** *vi* (*speaker*) interrompersi; (*branch*) troncarsi ■ *vt* (*talks, engagement*) rompere
  ▶ **break open** *vt* (*door etc*) sfondare
  ▶ **break out** *vi* evadere; **to ~ out in spots** coprirsi di macchie
  ▶ **break through** *vi*: **the sun broke through** il sole ha fatto capolino tra le nuvole ■ *vt* (*defences, barrier*) sfondare, penetrare in; (*crowd*) aprirsi un varco in *or* tra, aprirsi un passaggio in *or* tra
  ▶ **break up** *vi* (*partnership*) sciogliersi; (*friends*) separarsi; **the line's** *or* **you're breaking up** la linea è disturbata ■ *vt* fare in pezzi, spaccare; (*fight etc*) interrompere, far cessare; (*marriage*) finire

breakable ['breɪkəbl] *adj* fragile; **breakables** *npl* oggetti *mpl* fragili

breakage ['breɪkɪdʒ] *n* rottura; **to pay for breakages** pagare i danni

breakaway ['breɪkəweɪ] *adj* (*group etc*) scissionista, dissidente

break-dancing ['breɪkdɑːnsɪŋ] *n* breakdance *f*

breakdown ['breɪkdaun] *n* (*Aut*) guasto; (*in communications*) interruzione *f*; (*Med: also:* **nervous breakdown**) esaurimento nervoso; (*of payments etc*) resoconto

breakdown service *n* (*Brit*) servizio riparazioni

breakdown van *n* carro *m* attrezzi *inv*

breaker ['breɪkə'] *n* frangente *m*

breakeven ['breɪk'iːvn] *cpd:* ~ **chart** diagramma *m* del punto di rottura *or* pareggio; ~ **point** punto di rottura *or* pareggio

breakfast ['brɛkfəst] *n* colazione *f*

breakfast cereal *n* fiocchi *mpl* d'avena *or* di mais *etc*

break-in ['breɪkɪn] *n* irruzione *f*

breaking point ['breɪkɪŋ-] *n* punto di rottura

breakthrough ['breɪkθruː] *n* (*Mil*) breccia; (*fig*) passo avanti

break-up ['breɪkʌp] *n* (*of partnership, marriage*) rottura

break-up value *n* (*Comm*) valore *m* di realizzo

breakwater ['breɪkwɔːtə'] *n* frangiflutti *m inv*

breast [brɛst] *n* (*of woman*) seno; (*chest*) petto

breast-feed ['brɛstfiːd] *vt* (*irreg: like* **feed**) allattare (al seno)

breast pocket *n* taschino

breast-stroke ['brɛststrəuk] *n* nuoto a rana

breath [brɛθ] *n* fiato; **out of** ~ senza fiato; **to go out for a** ~ **of air** andare a prendere una boccata d'aria

Breathalyser® ['brɛθəlaɪzə'] *n* alcoltest *m inv*

breathe [briːð] *vt, vi* respirare; **I won't** ~ **a word about it** non fiaterò
  ▶ **breathe in** *vi* inspirare ■ *vt* respirare
  ▶ **breathe out** *vt, vi* espirare

breather ['briːðə'] *n* attimo di respiro

breathing ['briːðɪŋ] *n* respiro, respirazione *f*

breathing space *n* (*fig*) attimo di respiro

breathless ['brɛθlɪs] *adj* senza fiato; (*with excitement*) con il fiato sospeso

breath-taking ['brɛθteɪkɪŋ] *adj* sbalorditivo(-a)

breath test *n* ~ prova del palloncino

-bred [brɛd] *suffix:* **to be well/ill**~ essere ben educato(-a)/maleducato(-a)

breed [briːd] *vb* (*pt, pp* **bred**) *vt* allevare; (*fig: hate, suspicion*) generare, provocare ■ *vi* riprodursi ■ *n* razza, varietà *f inv*

breeder ['briːdə'] *n* (*Physics: also:* **breeder reactor**) reattore *m* autofertilizzante

breeding ['briːdɪŋ] *n* riproduzione *f*; allevamento

breeze [briːz] *n* brezza

breeze block *n* (*Brit*) mattone composto di scorie di coke

breezy ['briːzɪ] *adj* arioso(-a); allegro(-a)

Breton ['brɛtən] *adj, n* brettone (*m/f*)

brevity ['brɛvɪtɪ] *n* brevità

brew [bruː] *vt* (*tea*) fare un infuso di; (*beer*) fare; (*plot*) tramare ■ *vi* (*tea*) essere in infusione; (*beer*) essere in fermentazione; (*fig*) bollire in pentola

brewer ['bruːə'] *n* birraio

brewery ['bruːərɪ] *n* fabbrica di birra

briar ['braɪə'] *n* (*thorny bush*) rovo; (*wild rose*) rosa selvatica

bribe [braɪb] *n* bustarella ■ *vt* comprare; **to** ~ **sb to do sth** pagare qn sottobanco perché faccia qc

bribery ['braɪbərɪ] *n* corruzione *f*

bric-a-brac ['brɪkəbræk] *n* bric-a-brac *m*

brick [brɪk] *n* mattone *m*

bricklayer ['brɪkleɪə'] *n* muratore *m*

brickwork ['brɪkwəːk] *n* muratura in mattoni

brickworks ['brɪkwəːks] *n* fabbrica di mattoni

bridal ['braɪdl] *adj* nuziale; ~ **party** corteo nuziale

bride [braɪd] *n* sposa

bridegroom ['braɪdgruːm] *n* sposo

bridesmaid ['braɪdzmeɪd] *n* damigella d'onore

bridge [brɪdʒ] *n* ponte *m*; (*Naut*) ponte di comando; (*of nose*) dorso; (*Cards, Dentistry*) bridge *m inv* ■ *vt* (*river*) fare un ponte sopra; (*gap*) colmare

bridging loan ['brɪdʒɪŋ-] *n* (*Brit*) anticipazione *f* sul mutuo

bridle ['braɪdl] *n* briglia ■ *vt* tenere a freno; (*horse*) mettere la briglia a ■ *vi* (*in anger etc*) adombrarsi, adontarsi

bridle path *n* sentiero (per cavalli)

brief [briːf] *adj* breve ■ *n* (*Law*) comparsa ■ *vt* (*Mil etc*) dare istruzioni a; **in** ~ ... in breve ..., a farla breve ...; **to** ~ **sb (about sth)** mettere qn al corrente (di qc); *see also* **briefs**

briefcase ['briːfkeɪs] *n* cartella

briefing ['briːfɪŋ] *n* istruzioni *fpl*

briefly ['briːflɪ] *adv* (*speak, visit*) brevemente; (*glimpse*) di sfuggita

briefness ['briːfnɪs] *n* brevità

briefs [briːfs] *npl* mutande *fpl*

Brig. *abbr* = **brigadier**

brigade [brɪ'geɪd] *n* (*Mil*) brigata

brigadier [brɪgə'dɪə'] *n* generale *m* di brigata

bright [braɪt] *adj* luminoso(-a); (*person*) sveglio(-a); (*colour*) vivace; **to look on the** ~ **side** vedere il lato positivo delle cose

brighten ['braɪtn] (*also:* **brighten up**) *vt* (*room*) rendere luminoso(-a); rallegrare ■ vi schiarirsi; (person) rallegrarsi

brightly ['braɪtlɪ] adv (shine) vivamente, intensamente; (smile) radiosamente; (talk) con animazione

brill [brɪl] excl (Brit col) stupendo!, fantastico!

brilliance ['brɪljəns] n splendore m; (fig: of person) genialità, talento

brilliant ['brɪljənt] adj brillante; (sunshine) sfolgorante

brim [brɪm] n orlo

brimful ['brɪm'ful] adj pieno(-a) or colmo(-a) fino all'orlo; (fig) pieno(-a)

brine [braɪn] n acqua salmastra; (Culin) salamoia

bring (pt, pp **brought**) [brɪŋ, brɔːt] vt portare; **to ~ sth to an end** mettere fine a qc; **I can't ~ myself to sack him** non so risolvermi a licenziarlo

▶ **bring about** vt causare

▶ **bring back** vt riportare

▶ **bring down** vt (lower) far scendere; (shoot down) abbattere; (government) far cadere

▶ **bring forward** vt portare avanti; (in time) anticipare; (Book-keeping) riportare

▶ **bring in** vt (person) fare entrare; (object) portare; (Pol: bill) presentare; (: legislation) introdurre; (Law: verdict) emettere; (produce: income) rendere

▶ **bring off** vt (task, plan) portare a compimento; (deal) concludere

▶ **bring out** vt (meaning) mettere in evidenza; (new product) lanciare; (book) pubblicare, fare uscire

▶ **bring round** or **to** vt (unconscious person) far rinvenire

▶ **bring up** vt allevare; (question) introdurre

brink [brɪŋk] n orlo; **on the ~ of doing sth** sul punto di fare qc; **she was on the ~ of tears** era lì lì per piangere

brisk [brɪsk] adj (person, tone) spiccio(-a), sbrigativo(-a); (: abrupt) brusco(-a); (wind) fresco(-a); (trade etc) vivace, attivo(-a); **to go for a ~ walk** fare una camminata di buon passo; **business is ~** gli affari vanno bene

bristle ['brɪsl] n setola ■ vi rizzarsi; **bristling with** irto(-a) di

bristly ['brɪslɪ] adj (chin) ispido(-a); (beard, hair) irsuto(-a), setoloso(-a)

Brit [brɪt] n abbr (col: = British person) britannico(-a)

Britain ['brɪtən] n Gran Bretagna

British ['brɪtɪʃ] adj britannico(-a); **the British** npl i Britannici; **the ~ Isles** npl le Isole Britanniche

British Summer Time n ora legale (in Gran Bretagna)

Briton ['brɪtən] n britannico(-a)

Brittany ['brɪtənɪ] n Bretagna

brittle ['brɪtl] adj fragile

Br(o) abbr (Rel) = **brother**

broach [brəʊtʃ] vt (subject) affrontare

broad [brɔːd] adj largo(-a); (distinction) generale; (accent) spiccato(-a) ■ n (US col) bellona; **~ hint** allusione f esplicita; **in ~ daylight** in pieno giorno; **the ~ outlines** le grandi linee

broadband ['brɔːdbænd] adj (Comput) a banda larga ■ n banda larga

broad bean n fava

broadcast ['brɔːdkɑːst] n trasmissione f ■ vb (pt, pp **~**) vt trasmettere per radio (or per televisione) ■ vi fare una trasmissione

broadcaster ['brɔːdkɑːstə'] n annunciatore(-trice) radiotelevisivo(-a) (or radiofonico(-a))

broadcasting ['brɔːdkɑːstɪŋ] n radiodiffusione f; televisione f

broadcasting station n stazione f trasmittente

broaden ['brɔːdn] vt allargare ■ vi allargarsi

broadly ['brɔːdlɪ] adv (fig) in generale

broad-minded ['brɔːd'maɪndɪd] adj di mente aperta

broadsheet ['brɔːdʃiːt] n (Brit) giornale m (si contrappone al tabloid che è di formato più piccolo)

broccoli ['brɔkəlɪ] n (Bot) broccolo; (Culin) broccoli mpl

brochure ['brəʊʃjʊə'] n dépliant m inv

brogue [brəʊg] n (shoe) scarpa rozza in cuoio; (accent) accento irlandese

broil [brɔɪl] vt cuocere a fuoco vivo

broke [brəʊk] pt of **break** ■ adj (col) squattrinato(-a); **to go ~** fare fallimento

broken ['brəʊkən] pp of **break** ■ adj (gen) rotto(-a); (stick, promise, vow) spezzato(-a); (marriage) fallito(-a); **he comes from a ~ home** i suoi sono divisi; **in ~ French/ English** in un francese/inglese stentato

broken-down ['brəʊkən'daun] adj (car) in panne, rotto(-a); (machine) guasto(-a), fuori uso; (house) abbandonato(-a), in rovina

broken-hearted ['brəʊkən'hɑːtɪd] adj: **to be ~** avere il cuore spezzato

broker ['brəʊkə'] n agente m

brokerage ['brəʊkərɪdʒ] n (Comm) commissione f di intermediazione

brolly ['brɔlɪ] n (Brit col) ombrello

bronchitis [brɔŋ'kaɪtɪs] n bronchite f

bronze [brɔnz] n bronzo

bronzed [brɔnzd] adj abbronzato(-a)

brooch [brəʊtʃ] n spilla

brood [bruːd] n covata ■ vi (hen) covare; (person) rimuginare

broody ['bruːdɪ] *adj (fig)* cupo(-a) e taciturno(-a)
brook [bruk] *n* ruscello
broom [bruːm] *n* scopa
broomstick ['bruːmstɪk] *n* manico di scopa
Bros. *abbr (Comm: = brothers)* F.lli (= *Fratelli*)
broth [brɔθ] *n* brodo
brothel ['brɔθl] *n* bordello
brother ['brʌðəʳ] *n* fratello
brotherhood ['brʌðəhud] *n* fratellanza; confraternità *f inv*
brother-in-law ['brʌðərɪnlɔː] *n* cognato
brotherly ['brʌðəlɪ] *adj* fraterno(-a)
brought [brɔːt] *pt, pp of* **bring**
brought forward *adj (Comm)* riportato(-a)
brow [brau] *n* fronte *f; (rare, gen: also:* **eyebrow**) sopracciglio; *(of hill)* cima
browbeat ['braubiːt] *vt* intimidire
brown [braun] *adj* bruno(-a), marrone; *(hair)* castano(-a) ■ *n (colour)* color *m* bruno *or* marrone ■ *vt (Culin)* rosolare; **to go ~** *(person)* abbronzarsi; *(leaves)* ingiallire
brown bread *n* pane *m* integrale, pane nero
brownie ['braunɪ] *n* giovane esploratrice *f*
brown paper *n* carta da pacchi *or* da imballaggio
brown rice *n* riso greggio
brown sugar *n* zucchero greggio
browse [brauz] *vi (animal)* brucare; *(in bookshop etc)* curiosare; *(Comput)* navigare (in Internet) ■ *vt:* **to ~ the web** navigare in Internet ■ *n:* **to have a ~ (around)** dare un'occhiata (in giro); **to ~ through a book** sfogliare un libro
browser ['brauzəʳ] *n (Comput)* browser *m inv*
bruise [bruːz] *n* ammaccatura; *(on person)* livido ■ *vt* ammaccare; *(leg etc)* farsi un livido a; *(fig: feelings)* urtare ■ *vi (fruit)* ammaccarsi
Brum [brʌm] *n abbr,* **Brummagem** ['brʌmədʒəm] *n (col)* = **Birmingham**
Brummie ['brʌmɪ] *n (col)* abitante *m/f* di Birmingham, originario(-a) di Birmingham
brunch [brʌntʃ] *n ricca colazione consumata in tarda mattinata*
brunette [bruː'net] *n* bruna
brunt [brʌnt] *n:* **the ~ of** *(attack, criticism etc)* il peso maggiore di
brush [brʌʃ] *n* spazzola; *(quarrel)* schermaglia ■ *vt* spazzolare; *(gen: also:* **brush past, brush against**) sfiorare; **to have a ~ with sb** *(verbally)* avere uno scontro con qn; *(physically)* venire a diverbio *or* alle mani con qn; **to have a ~ with the police** avere delle noie con la polizia
▶ **brush aside** *vt* scostare
▶ **brush up** *vt (knowledge)* rinfrescare

brushed [brʌʃt] *adj (Tech: steel, chrome etc)* sabbiato(-a); *(nylon, denim etc)* pettinato(-a)
brush-off ['brʌʃɔf] *n:* **to give sb the ~** dare il ben servito a qn
brushwood ['brʌʃwud] *n* macchia
brusque [bruːsk] *adj (person, manner)* brusco(-a); *(tone)* secco(-a)
Brussels ['brʌslz] *n* Bruxelles *f*
Brussels sprout *n* cavolo di Bruxelles
brutal ['bruːtl] *adj* brutale
brutality [bruː'tælɪtɪ] *n* brutalità
brutalize ['bruːtəlaɪz] *vt (harden)* abbrutire; *(ill-treat)* brutalizzare
brute [bruːt] *n* bestia; **by ~ force** con la forza, a viva forza
brutish ['bruːtɪʃ] *adj* da bruto
BS *n abbr (US: = Bachelor of Science)* titolo di studio
bs *abbr =* **bill of sale**
BSA *n abbr (US) =* **Boy Scouts of America**
BSc *n abbr =* **Bachelor of Science**
BSE *n abbr (= bovine spongiform encephalopathy)* encefalite *f* bovina spongiforme
BSI *n abbr (= British Standards Institution)* associazione per la normalizzazione
BST *abbr (= British Summer Time)* ora legale
Bt. *abbr (Brit) =* **baronet**
btu *n abbr (= British thermal unit)* Btu *m* (= 1054.2 joules)
bubble ['bʌbl] *n* bolla ■ *vi* ribollire; *(sparkle, fig)* essere effervescente
bubble bath *n* bagno *m* schiuma *inv*
bubblejet printer ['bʌbldʒet-] *n* stampante *f* a getto d'inchiostro
bubbly ['bʌblɪ] *adj (also fig)* frizzante ■ *n (col: champagne)* spumante *m*
Bucharest [buː'kə'rest] *n* Bucarest *f*
buck [bʌk] *n* maschio *(di camoscio, caprone, coniglio etc); (US col)* dollaro ■ *vi* sgroppare; **to pass the ~ (to sb)** scaricare (su di qn) la propria responsabilità
▶ **buck up** *vi (cheer up)* rianimarsi ■ *vt:* **to ~ one's ideas up** mettere la testa a partito
bucket ['bʌkɪt] *n* secchio ■ *vi (Brit col):* **the rain is bucketing (down)** piove a catinelle
Buckingham Palace ['bʌkɪŋəm-] *n vedi nota*

● **BUCKINGHAM PALACE**

○ *Buckingham Palace* è la residenza ufficiale a Londra del sovrano britannico. Costruita nel 1703 per il duca di Buckingham, fu acquistata nel 1762 dal re Giorgio III e ricostruita tra il 1821 e il 1838 sotto la guida dell'architetto John Nash. All'inizio del Novecento alcune sue parti sono state ulteriormente modificate.

buckle ['bʌkl] n fibbia ■ vt affibbiare; (warp) deformare
▶ **buckle down** vi mettersi sotto
Bucks [bʌks] abbr (Brit) = **Buckinghamshire**
bud [bʌd] n gemma; (of flower) boccio ■ vi germogliare; (flower) sbocciare
Budapest [bju:də'pɛst] n Budapest f
Buddha ['budə] n Budda m
Buddhism ['budɪzəm] n buddismo
Buddhist ['budɪst] adj, n buddista (m/f)
budding ['bʌdɪŋ] adj (flower) in boccio; (poet etc) in erba
buddy ['bʌdɪ] n (US) compagno
budge [bʌdʒ] vt scostare ■ vi spostarsi
budgerigar ['bʌdʒərɪgɑːʳ] n pappagallino
budget ['bʌdʒɪt] n bilancio preventivo ■ vi: **to ~ for sth** fare il bilancio per qc; **I'm on a tight ~** devo contare la lira; **she works out her ~ every month** fa il preventivo delle spese ogni mese
budgie ['bʌdʒɪ] n = **budgerigar**
Buenos Aires ['bweɪnɔs'aɪrɪz] n Buenos Aires f
buff [bʌf] adj color camoscio inv ■ n (enthusiast) appassionato(-a)
buffalo (pl ~ or **buffaloes**) ['bʌfələu] n bufalo; (US) bisonte m
buffer ['bʌfəʳ] n respingente m; (Comput) memoria tampone, buffer m inv ■ vi (Comput) fare il buffering, trasferire nella memoria tampone
buffering ['bʌfərɪŋ] n (Comput) buffering m inv, trasferimento nella memoria tampone
buffer state n stato cuscinetto
buffer zone n zona f cuscinetto inv
buffet n ['bufeɪ] (food, Brit: bar) buffet m inv ■ vt ['bʌfɪt] schiaffeggiare scuotere; urtare
buffet car n (Brit Rail) ≈ servizio ristoro
buffet lunch n pranzo in piedi
buffoon [bə'fu:n] n buffone m
bug [bʌg] n (insect) cimice f; (: gen) insetto; (fig: germ) virus m inv; (spy device) microfono spia; (Comput) bug m inv, errore m nel programma ■ vt mettere sotto controllo; (room) installare microfoni spia in; (annoy) scocciare; **I've got the travel ~** (fig) mi è presa la mania dei viaggi
bugbear ['bʌgbɛəʳ] n spauracchio
bugger ['bʌgəʳ] (col!) n bastardo (!) ■ vb: **~ off!** vaffanculo! (!); **~ (it)!** merda! (!)
bugle ['bju:gl] n tromba
build [bɪld] n (of person) corporatura ■ vt (pt, pp **built**) [bɪlt] costruire
▶ **build on** vt fus (fig) prendere il via da
▶ **build up** vt (establish: business) costruire; (: reputation) fare, consolidare; (increase: production) allargare, incrementare; **don't ~**

your hopes up too soon non sperarci troppo
builder ['bɪldəʳ] n costruttore m
building ['bɪldɪŋ] n costruzione f; edificio; (also: **building trade**) edilizia
building contractor n costruttore m, imprenditore m (edile)
building industry n industria edilizia
building site n cantiere m di costruzione
building society n; vedi nota

● **BUILDING SOCIETY**
●
● Le building societies sono società
● immobiliari e finanziarie che forniscono
● numerosi servizi bancari ai clienti che vi
● investono i risparmi, e in particolare
● concedono mutui per l'acquisto della
● casa.

building trade n = **building industry**
build-up ['bɪldʌp] n (of gas etc) accumulo; (publicity): **to give sb/sth a good ~** fare buona pubblicità a qn/qc
built [bɪlt] pt, pp of **build**; **well-~** robusto(-a)
built-in ['bɪlt'ɪn] adj (cupboard) a muro; (device) incorporato(-a)
built-up area ['bɪltʌp-] n abitato
bulb [bʌlb] n (Bot) bulbo; (Elec) lampadina
bulbous ['bʌlbəs] adj bulboso(-a)
Bulgaria [bʌl'gɛərɪə] n Bulgaria
Bulgarian [bʌl'gɛərɪən] adj bulgaro(-a) ■ n bulgaro(-a); (Ling) bulgaro
bulge [bʌldʒ] n rigonfiamento; (in birth rate, sales) punta ■ vi essere protuberante or rigonfio(-a); **to be bulging with** essere pieno(-a) or zeppo(-a) di
bulimia [bə'lɪmɪə] n bulimia
bulk [bʌlk] n massa, volume m; **the ~ of** il grosso di; **(to buy) in ~** (comprare) in grande quantità
bulk buying n acquisto di merce in grande quantità
bulk carrier n grossa nave f da carico
bulkhead ['bʌlkhɛd] n paratia
bulky ['bʌlkɪ] adj grosso(-a); voluminoso(-a)
bull [bul] n toro; (Stock Exchange) rialzista m/f; (Rel) bolla (papale)
bulldog ['buldɔg] n bulldog m inv
bulldoze ['buldəuz] vt aprire or spianare col bulldozer; **I was bulldozed into doing it** (fig, col) mi ci hanno costretto con la prepotenza
bulldozer ['buldəuzəʳ] n bulldozer m inv
bullet ['bulɪt] n pallottola
bulletin ['bulɪtɪn] n bollettino
bulletin board n (Comput) bulletin board m inv

bullet point n punto; **bullet points** elenco sg puntato

bullet-proof ['bulɪtpruːf] adj a prova di proiettile; ~ **vest** giubbotto antiproiettile

bullfight ['bulfaɪt] n corrida

bullfighter ['bulfaɪtəʳ] n torero

bullfighting ['bulfaɪtɪŋ] n tauromachia

bullion ['buljən] n oro or argento in lingotti

bullock ['bulək] n giovenco

bullring ['bulrɪŋ] n arena (per corride)

bull's-eye ['bulzaɪ] n centro del bersaglio

bullshit ['bulʃɪt] (col!) excl, n stronzate fpl (!)
■ vi raccontare stronzate (!) ■ vt raccontare stronzate a (!)

bully ['bulɪ] n prepotente m ■ vt angariare; (frighten) intimidire

bullying ['bulɪɪŋ] n prepotenze fpl

bum [bʌm] n (col: backside) culo; (tramp) vagabondo(-a); (US: idler) fannullone(-a)
▶ **bum around** vi (col) fare il vagabondo

bumblebee ['bʌmblbiː] n (Zool) bombo

bumf [bʌmf] n (col: forms etc) scartoffie fpl

bump [bʌmp] n (blow) colpo; (jolt) scossa; (noise) botto; (on road etc) protuberanza; (on head) bernoccolo ■ vt battere; (car) urtare, sbattere
▶ **bump along** vi procedere sobbalzando
▶ **bump into** vt fus scontrarsi con; (col: meet) imbattersi in, incontrare per caso

bumper ['bʌmpəʳ] n (Brit) paraurti m inv
■ adj: ~ **harvest** raccolto eccezionale

bumper cars npl (US) autoscontri mpl

bumph [bʌmf] n = **bumf**

bumptious ['bʌmpʃəs] adj presuntuoso(-a)

bumpy ['bʌmpɪ] adj (road) dissestato(-a); (journey, flight) movimentato(-a)

bun [bʌn] n focaccia; (of hair) crocchia

bunch [bʌntʃ] n (of flowers, keys) mazzo; (of bananas) ciuffo; (of people) gruppo; ~ **of grapes** grappolo d'uva

bundle ['bʌndl] n fascio ■ vt (also: **bundle up**) legare in un fascio; (put): **to ~ sth/sb into** spingere qc/qn in
▶ **bundle off** vt (person) mandare via in gran fretta
▶ **bundle out** vt far uscire (senza tante cerimonie)

bun fight n (Brit: col) tè m inv (ricevimento)

bung [bʌŋ] n tappo ■ vt (Brit: throw: also: **bung into**) buttare; (also: **bung up**: pipe, hole) tappare, otturare; **my nose is bunged up** (col) ho il naso otturato

bungalow ['bʌŋgələu] n bungalow m inv

bungee jumping ['bʌndʒiː'dʒʌmpɪŋ] n salto nel vuoto da ponti, grattacieli etc con un cavo fissato alla caviglia

bungle ['bʌŋgl] vt abborracciare

bunion ['bʌnjən] n callo (al piede)

bunk [bʌŋk] n cuccetta
▶ **bunk off** vi (Brit col): **to ~ off school** marinare la scuola; **I'll ~ off at 3 this afternoon** oggi me la filo dal lavoro alle 3

bunk beds npl letti mpl a castello

bunker ['bʌŋkəʳ] n (coal store) ripostiglio per il carbone; (Mil, Golf) bunker m inv

bunny ['bʌnɪ] n (also: **bunny rabbit**) coniglietto

bunny girl n coniglietta

bunny hill n (US Ski) pista per principianti

bunting ['bʌntɪŋ] n pavesi mpl, bandierine fpl

buoy [bɔɪ] n boa
▶ **buoy up** vt tenere a galla; (fig) sostenere

buoyancy ['bɔɪənsɪ] n (of ship) galleggiabilità

buoyant ['bɔɪənt] adj galleggiante; (fig) vivace; (Comm: market) sostenuto(-a); (: prices, currency) stabile

burden ['bəːdn] n carico, fardello ■ vt caricare; (oppress) opprimere; **to be a ~ to sb** essere di peso a qn

bureau (pl **bureaux**) ['bjuərəu, -z] n (Brit: writing desk) scrivania; (US: chest of drawers) cassettone m; (office) ufficio, agenzia

bureaucracy [bjuə'rɔkrəsɪ] n burocrazia

bureaucrat ['bjuərəkræt] n burocrate m/f

bureaucratic [bjuərə'krætɪk] adj burocratico(-a)

burgeon ['bəːdʒən] vi svilupparsi rapidamente

burger ['bəːgəʳ] n hamburger m inv

burglar ['bəːgləʳ] n scassinatore m

burglar alarm n antifurto m inv

burglarize ['bəːgləraɪz] vt (US) svaligiare

burglary ['bəːglərɪ] n furto con scasso

burgle ['bəːgl] vt svaligiare

Burgundy ['bəːgəndɪ] n Borgogna

burial ['berɪəl] n sepoltura

burial ground n cimitero

burly ['bəːlɪ] adj robusto(-a)

Burma ['bəːmə] n Birmania; see **Myanmar**

Burmese [bəː'miːz] adj birmano(-a) ■ n (pl inv) birmano(-a); (Ling) birmano

burn [bəːn] vt, vi (pt, pp **burned** or **burnt**) bruciare
■ n bruciatura, scottatura; (Med) ustione f; **I've burnt myself!** mi sono bruciato!; **the cigarette burnt a hole in her dress** si è fatta un buco nel vestito con la sigaretta
▶ **burn down** vt distruggere col fuoco
▶ **burn out** vt (writer etc): **to ~ o.s. out** esaurirsi

burner ['bəːnəʳ] n fornello

burning ['bəːnɪŋ] adj (building, forest) in fiamme; (issue, question) scottante

burnish ['bəːnɪʃ] vt brunire

Burns Night n vedi nota

BURNS NIGHT

Burns Night è la festa celebrata il 25 gennaio per commemorare il poeta scozzese Robert Burns (1759–1796). Gli scozzesi festeggiano questa data con una cena a base de "haggis" e whisky, spesso al suono di una cornamusa durante la cena vengono recitate le poesie di Robert Burns e vengono letti discorsi alla sua memoria.

burnt [bə:nt] *pt, pp of* **burn**
burnt sugar *n* (*Brit*) caramello
burp [bə:p] (*col*) *n* rutto ▪ *vi* ruttare
burrow ['bʌrəu] *n* tana ▪ *vt* scavare
bursar ['bə:sə'] *n* economo(-a); (*Brit: student*) borsista *m/f*
bursary ['bə:sərɪ] *n* (*Brit*) borsa di studio
burst [bə:st] *vb* (*pt, pp* ~) *vt* far scoppiare *or* esplodere ▪ *vi* esplodere; (*tyre*) scoppiare ▪ *n* scoppio; (*also*: **burst pipe**) rottura nel tubo, perdita; ~ **of energy/laughter** scoppio d'energia/di risa; **a ~ of applause** uno scroscio d'applausi; **a ~ of speed** uno scatto (di velocità); ~ **blood vessel** rottura di un vaso sanguigno; **the river has ~ its banks** il fiume ha rotto gli argini *or* ha straripato; **to ~ into flames/tears** scoppiare in fiamme/lacrime; **to be bursting with** essere pronto a scoppiare di; **to ~ out laughing** scoppiare a ridere; **to ~ open** *vi* aprirsi improvvisamente; (*door*) spalancarsi
▸ **burst into** *vt fus* (*room etc*) irrompere in
▸ **burst out of** *vt fus* precipitarsi fuori da
bury ['bɛrɪ] *vt* seppellire; **to ~ one's face in one's hands** nascondere la faccia tra le mani; **to ~ one's head in the sand** (*fig*) fare (la politica del)lo struzzo; **to ~ the hatchet** (*fig*) seppellire l'ascia di guerra
bus (*pl* **buses**) [bʌs,'bʌsɪz] *n* autobus *m inv*
bus boy *n* (*US*) aiuto *inv* cameriere(-a)
bush [buʃ] *n* cespuglio; (*scrub land*) macchia
bushed [buʃt] *adj* (*col*) distrutto(-a)
bushel ['buʃl] *n* staio
bushfire ['buʃfaɪə'] *n* grande incendio in aperta campagna
bushy ['buʃɪ] *adj* (*plant, tail, beard*) folto(-a); (*eyebrows*) irsuto(-a)
busily ['bɪzɪlɪ] *adv* con impegno, alacremente
business ['bɪznɪs] *n* (*matter*) affare *m*; (*trading*) affari *mpl*; (*firm*) azienda; (*job, duty*) lavoro; **to be away on ~** essere andato via per affari; **I'm here on ~** sono qui per affari; **to do ~ with sb** fare affari con qn; **he's in the insurance ~** lavora nel campo delle assicurazioni; **it's none of my ~** questo non mi riguarda; **he means ~** non scherza

business address *n* indirizzo di lavoro *or* d'ufficio
business card *n* biglietto da visita della ditta
businesslike ['bɪznɪslaɪk] *adj* serio(-a); efficiente
businessman ['bɪznɪsmən] *n* uomo d'affari
business trip *n* viaggio d'affari
businesswoman ['bɪznɪswumən] *n* donna d'affari
busker ['bʌskə'] *n* (*Brit*) suonatore(-trice) ambulante
bus lane *n* (*Brit*) corsia riservata agli autobus
bus shelter *n* pensilina (*alla fermata dell'autobus*)
bus station *n* stazione *f* delle autolinee, autostazione *f*
bus stop *n* fermata d'autobus
bust [bʌst] *n* (*Art*) busto; (*bosom*) seno ▪ *adj* (*broken*) rotto(-a) ▪ *vt* (*col: Police: arrest*) pizzicare, beccare; **to go ~** fallire
bustle ['bʌsl] *n* movimento, attività ▪ *vi* darsi da fare
bustling ['bʌslɪŋ] *adj* (*person*) indaffarato(-a); (*town*) animato(-a)
bust-up ['bʌstʌp] *n* (*Brit col*) lite *f*
busty ['bʌstɪ] *adj* (*col*) tettone(-a)
busy ['bɪzɪ] *adj* occupato(-a); (*shop, street*) molto frequentato(-a) ▪ *vt*: **to ~ o.s.** darsi da fare; **he's a ~ man** (*normally*) è un uomo molto occupato; (*temporarily*) ha molto da fare, è molto occupato
busybody ['bɪzɪbɔdɪ] *n* ficcanaso *m/f inv*
busy signal *n* (*US*) segnale *m* di occupato

KEYWORD

but [bʌt] *conj* ma; **I'd love to come, but I'm busy** vorrei tanto venire, ma ho da fare
▪ *prep* (*apart from, except*) eccetto, tranne, meno; **nothing but** nient'altro che; **he was nothing but trouble** non dava altro che guai; **no-one but him** solo lui; **no-one but him can do it** nessuno può farlo tranne lui; **the last but one** (*Brit*) il/la penultimo(-a); **but for you/your help** se non fosse per te/per il tuo aiuto; **anything but that** tutto ma non questo; **anything but finished** tutt'altro che finito
▪ *adv* (*just, only*) solo, soltanto; **she's but a child** è solo una bambina; **had I but known** se solo avessi saputo; **I can but try** tentar non nuoce; **all but finished** quasi finito

butane ['bju:teɪn] *n* (*also*: **butane gas**) butano
butch [butʃ] *adj* (*woman: pej*) mascolino(-a); (*man*) macho *inv*
butcher ['butʃə'] *n* macellaio ▪ *vt* macellare; ~**'s (shop)** macelleria

butler [ˈbʌtləʳ] *n* maggiordomo

butt [bʌt] *n* (*cask*) grossa botte *f*; (*thick end*) estremità *f inv* più grossa; (*of gun*) calcio; (*of cigarette*) mozzicone *m*; (*Brit fig: target*) oggetto ■ *vt* cozzare
▶ **butt in** *vi* (*interrupt*) interrompere

butter [ˈbʌtəʳ] *n* burro ■ *vt* imburrare

buttercup [ˈbʌtəkʌp] *n* ranuncolo

butter dish *n* burriera

butterfingers [ˈbʌtəfɪŋgəz] *n* (*col*) mani *fpl* di ricotta

butterfly [ˈbʌtəflaɪ] *n* farfalla; (*Swimming: also*: **butterfly stroke**) (nuoto a) farfalla

buttocks [ˈbʌtəks] *npl* natiche *fpl*

button [ˈbʌtn] *n* bottone *m* ■ *vt* (*also*: **button up**) abbottonare ■ *vi* abbottonarsi

buttonhole [ˈbʌtnhəul] *n* asola, occhiello ■ *vt* (*person*) attaccar bottone a

buttress [ˈbʌtrɪs] *n* contrafforte *m*

buxom [ˈbʌksəm] *adj* formoso(-a)

buy [baɪ] *vt* (*pt, pp* **bought**) [lɔːt] comprare, acquistare ■ *n*: **a good/bad ~** un buon/cattivo acquisto *or* affare; **to ~ sb sth/sth from sb** comprare qc per qn/qc da qn; **to ~ sb a drink** offrire da bere a qn
▶ **buy back** *vt* riprendersi, prendersi indietro
▶ **buy in** *vt* (*Brit: goods*) far provvista di
▶ **buy into** *vt fus* (*Brit Comm*) acquistare delle azioni di
▶ **buy off** *vt* (*col: bribe*) comprare
▶ **buy out** *vt* (*business*) rilevare
▶ **buy up** *vt* accaparrare

buyer [ˈbaɪəʳ] *n* compratore(-trice); **~'s market** mercato favorevole ai compratori

buy-out [ˈbaɪaut] *n* (*Comm*) *acquisto di una società da parte dei suoi dipendenti*

buzz [bʌz] *n* ronzio; (*col: phone call*) colpo di telefono ■ *vi* ronzare ■ *vt* (*call on intercom*) chiamare al citofono; (*: with buzzer*) chiamare col cicalino; (*Aviat: plane, building*) passare rasente; **my head is buzzing** mi gira la testa
▶ **buzz off** *vi* (*Brit col*) filare, levarsi di torno

buzzard [ˈbʌzəd] *n* poiana

buzzer [ˈbʌzəʳ] *n* cicalino

buzz word *n* (*col*) termine *m* in voga

 KEYWORD

by [baɪ] *prep* **1** (*referring to cause, agent*) da; **killed by lightning** ucciso da un fulmine; **surrounded by a fence** circondato da uno steccato; **a painting by Picasso** un quadro di Picasso

2 (*referring to method, manner, means*): **by bus/car/train** in autobus/macchina/treno, con l'autobus/la macchina/il treno; **to pay by cheque** pagare con (un) assegno; **by moonlight** al chiaro di luna; **by saving hard, he ...** risparmiando molto, lui ...

3 (*via, through*) per; **we came by Dover** siamo venuti via Dover

4 (*close to, past*) accanto a; **the house by the river** la casa sul fiume; **a holiday by the sea** una vacanza al mare; **she sat by his bed** si sedette accanto al suo letto; **she rushed by me** mi è passata accanto correndo; **I go by the post office every day** passo davanti all'ufficio postale ogni giorno

5 (*not later than*) per, entro; **by 4 o'clock** per *or* entro le 4; **by this time tomorrow** domani a quest'ora; **by the time I got here it was too late** quando sono arrivato era ormai troppo tardi

6 (*during*): **by day/night** di giorno/notte

7 (*amount*) a; **by the kilo** a chili; **paid by the hour** pagato all'ora; **to increase by the hour** aumentare di ora in ora; **one by one** uno per uno; **little by little** a poco a poco

8 (*Math, measure*): **to divide/multiply by 3** dividere/moltiplicare per 3; **a room 3 metres by 4** una stanza di 3 metri per 4; **it's broader by a metre** è un metro più largo, è più largo di un metro

9 (*according to*) per; **to play by the rules** attenersi alle regole; **it's all right by me** per me va bene

10: **(all) by oneself** (tutto(-a)) solo(-a); **he did it (all) by himself** lo ha fatto (tutto) da solo

11: **by the way** a proposito; **this wasn't my idea by the way** tra l'altro l'idea non è stata mia

■ *adv* **1** *see* **go**; **pass** *etc*

2: **by and by** (*in past*) poco dopo; (*in future*) fra breve; **by and large** nel complesso

bye [ˈbaɪ], **bye-bye** [ˈbaɪˈbaɪ] *excl* ciao!, arrivederci!

bye-law [ˈbaɪlɔː] *n* legge *f* locale

by-election [ˈbaɪɪlɛkʃən] *n* (*Brit*) elezione *f* straordinaria; *vedi nota*

BY-ELECTION

Una *by-election* in Gran Bretagna e in alcuni paesi del Commonwealth è un'elezione che si tiene per coprire un posto in Parlamento resosi vacante, a governo ancora in carica. é importante in quanto serve a misurare il consenso degli elettori in vista delle successive elezioni politiche.

Byelorussia [bjɛləu'rʌʃə] *n* Bielorussia, Belorussia

Byelorussian [bjɛləu'rʌʃən] *adj, n* = **Belarussian**

bygone ['baɪɡɔn] *adj* passato(-a) ■ *n*: **let bygones be bygones** mettiamoci una pietra sopra

by-law ['baɪlɔ:] *n* legge *f* locale

bypass ['baɪpɑ:s] *n* circonvallazione *f*; (*Med*) by-pass *m inv* ■ *vt* fare una deviazione intorno a

by-product ['baɪprɔdʌkt] *n* sottoprodotto; (*fig*) conseguenza secondaria

byre ['baɪəʳ] *n* (*Brit*) stalla

bystander ['baɪstændəʳ] *n* spettatore(-trice)

byte [baɪt] *n* (*Comput*) byte *m inv*

byway ['baɪweɪ] *n* strada secondaria

byword ['baɪwə:d] *n*: **to be a ~ for** essere sinonimo di

by-your-leave ['baɪjɔ:'li:v] *n*: **without so much as a ~** senza nemmeno chiedere il permesso

b

467

Cc

C, c [siː] *n* (*letter*) C, c *f* or *m* inv; (*Scol: mark*) ≈ 6 (*sufficiente*); (*Mus*): **C** do; **C for Charlie** ≈ C come Como

C *abbr* (= *Celsius, centigrade*) C

c. *abbr* (= *century*) sec.; (= *circa*) c; (*US etc*) = **cent(s)**

CA *abbr* – **Central America**; (*US*) – **California** ■ *n abbr* (*Brit*) = **chartered accountant**

ca. *abbr* (= *circa*) ca

c/a *abbr* = **capital account; credit account; current account**

CAA *n abbr* (*Brit*: = *Civil Aviation Authority*, US: = *Civil Aeronautics Authority*) *organismo di controllo e di sviluppo dell'aviazione civile*

CAB *n abbr* (*Brit*: = *Citizens' Advice Bureau*) *organizzazione per la tutela del consumatore*

cab [kæb] *n* taxi *m* inv; (*of train, truck*) cabina; (*horsedrawn*) carrozza

cabaret ['kæbəreɪ] *n* cabaret *m* inv

cabbage ['kæbɪdʒ] *n* cavolo

cabbie, cabby ['kæbɪ] *n* (*col*) tassista *m/f*

cab driver *n* tassista *m/f*

cabin ['kæbɪn] *n* capanna; (*on ship*) cabina

cabin cruiser *n* cabinato

cabinet ['kæbɪnɪt] *n* (*Pol*) consiglio dei ministri; (*furniture*) armadietto; (*also*: **display cabinet**) vetrinetta; **cocktail ~** mobile *m* bar inv

cabinet-maker ['kæbɪnɪt'meɪkər] *n* stipettaio

cabinet minister *n* ministro (*membro del Consiglio*)

cable ['keɪbl] *n* cavo; fune *f*; (*Tel*) cablogramma *m* ■ *vt* telegrafare

cable-car ['keɪblkɑːr] *n* funivia

cablegram ['keɪblɡræm] *n* cablogramma *m*

cable railway *n* funicolare *f*

cable television *n* televisione *f* via cavo

cache [kæʃ] *n* nascondiglio; **a ~ of food** *etc* un deposito segreto di viveri *etc*

cackle ['kækl] *vi* schiamazzare

cactus (*pl* **cacti**) ['kæktəs, -taɪ] *n* cactus *m* inv

CAD *n abbr* (= *computer-aided design*)

progettazione *f* con l'ausilio dell'elaboratore

caddie ['kædɪ] *n* caddie *m* inv

cadet [kə'dɛt] *n* (*Mil*) cadetto; **police ~** allievo poliziotto

cadge [kædʒ] *vt* (*col*) scroccare; **to ~ a meal (off sb)** scroccare un pranzo (a qn)

cadre ['kædrɪ] *n* quadro

Caesarean, (*US*) **Cesarean** [siː'zɛərɪən] *adj*: **~ (section)** (*taglio*) cesareo

CAF *abbr* (*Brit*: = *cost and freight*) Caf *m*

café ['kæfeɪ] *n* caffè *m* inv

cafeteria [kæfɪ'tɪərɪə] *n* self-service *m* inv

caffein, caffeine ['kæfiːn] *n* caffeina

cage [keɪdʒ] *n* gabbia ■ *vt* mettere in gabbia

cagey ['keɪdʒɪ] *adj* (*col*) chiuso(-a); guardingo(-a)

cagoule [kə'ɡuːl] *n* K-way® *m* inv

cahoots [kə'huːts] *n*: **to be in ~ (with sb)** essere in combutta (con qn)

CAI *n abbr* (= *computer-aided instruction*) istruzione *f* assistita dall'elaboratore

Cairo ['kaɪərəu] *n* il Cairo

cajole [kə'dʒəul] *vt* allettare

cake [keɪk] *n* torta; **~ of soap** saponetta; **it's a piece of ~** (*col*) è una cosa da nulla; **he wants to have his ~ and eat it (too)** (*fig*) vuole la botte piena e la moglie ubriaca

caked [keɪkt] *adj*: **~ with** incrostato(-a) di

cake shop *n* pasticceria

Cal. *abbr* (*US*) = **California**

calamitous [kə'læmɪtəs] *adj* disastroso(-a)

calamity [kə'læmɪtɪ] *n* calamità *f* inv

calcium ['kælsɪəm] *n* calcio

calculate ['kælkjuleɪt] *vt* calcolare; (*estimate: chances, effect*) valutare

▶ **calculate on** *vt fus*: **to ~ on sth/on doing sth** contare su qc/di fare qc

calculated ['kælkjuleɪtɪd] *adj* calcolato(-a), intenzionale; **a ~ risk** un rischio calcolato

calculating ['kælkjuleɪtɪŋ] *adj* calcolatore(-trice)

calculation [kælkju'leɪʃən] *n* calcolo

calculator ['kælkjuleɪtər] *n* calcolatrice *f*

calculus ['kælkjuləs] n calcolo; **integral/
differential** ~ calcolo integrale/
differenziale
calendar ['kæləndə^r] n calendario
calendar year n anno civile
calf (pl **calves**) [kɑːf, kɑːvz] n (of cow) vitello;
(of other animals) piccolo; (also: **calfskin**) (pelle f
di) vitello; (Anat) polpaccio
caliber ['kælɪbə^r] n (US) = **calibre**
calibrate ['kælɪbreɪt] vt (gun etc) calibrare;
(scale of measuring instrument) tarare
calibre, (US) **caliber** ['kælɪbə^r] n calibro
calico ['kælɪkəu] n tela grezza, cotone m
grezzo; (US) cotonina stampata
Calif. abbr (US) = **California**
California [kælɪ'fɔːnɪə] n California
calipers ['kælɪpəz] npl (US) = **callipers**
call [kɔːl] vt (gen, also Tel) chiamare; (announce:
flight) annunciare; (meeting, strike) indire,
proclamare ∎ vi chiamare; (visit: also: **call in**,
call round) passare ∎ n (shout) grido, urlo;
(visit) visita; (summons: for flight etc) chiamata;
(fig: lure) richiamo; (also: **telephone call**)
telefonata; **to be on** ~ essere a disposizione;
to make a ~ telefonare, fare una telefonata;
please give me a ~ **at 7** per piacere mi
chiami alle 7; **to pay a** ~ **on sb** fare (una)
visita a qn; **there's not much** ~ **for these
items** non c'è molta richiesta di questi
articoli; **she's called Jane** si chiama Jane;
who is calling? (Tel) chi parla?; **London
calling** (Radio) qui Londra
  ▶ **call at** vt fus (ship) fare scalo a; (train)
fermarsi a
  ▶ **call back** vi (return) ritornare; (Tel)
ritelefonare, richiamare ∎ vt (Tel)
ritelefonare a, richiamare
  ▶ **call for** vt fus (demand: action etc) richiedere;
(collect: person) passare a prendere; (: goods)
ritirare
  ▶ **call in** vt (doctor, expert, police) chiamare, far
venire
  ▶ **call off** vt (meeting, race) disdire; (deal)
cancellare; (dog) richiamare; **the strike was
called off** lo sciopero è stato revocato
  ▶ **call on** vt fus (visit) passare da; (request): **to** ~
on sb to do chiedere a qn di fare
  ▶ **call out** vi urlare ∎ vt (doctor, police, troops)
chiamare
  ▶ **call up** vt (Mil) richiamare
Callanetics® [kælə'nɛtɪks] nsg tipo di
ginnastica basata sulla ripetizione di piccoli
movimenti
callbox ['kɔːlbɔks] n (Brit) cabina telefonica
call centre n centro informazioni
telefoniche
caller ['kɔːlə^r] n persona che chiama;

visitatore(-trice); **hold the line,** ~! (Tel)
rimanga in linea, signore (or signora)!
call girl n ragazza f squillo inv
call-in ['kɔːlɪn] n (US) = **phone-in**
calling ['kɔːlɪŋ] n vocazione f
calling card n (US) biglietto da visita
callipers, (US) **calipers** ['kælɪpəz] npl (Med)
gambale m; (Math) calibro
callous ['kæləs] adj indurito(-a), insensibile
callousness ['kæləsnɪs] n insensibilità
callow ['kæləu] adj immaturo(-a)
calm [kɑːm] adj calmo(-a) ∎ n calma ∎ vt
calmare
  ▶ **calm down** vi calmarsi ∎ vt calmare
calmly ['kɑːmlɪ] adv con calma
calmness ['kɑːmnɪs] n calma
Calor gas® ['kælə^r-] n (Brit) butano
calorie ['kælərɪ] n caloria; **low-~ product**
prodotto a basso contenuto di calorie
calve [kɑːv] vi figliare
calves [kɑːvz] npl of **calf**
CAM n abbr (= computer-aided manufacturing)
fabbricazione f con l'ausilio dell'elaboratore
camber ['kæmbə^r] n (of road) bombatura
Cambodia [kæm'bəudjə] n Cambogia
Cambodian [kæm'bəudɪən] adj, n
cambogiano(-a)
Cambs abbr (Brit) = **Cambridgeshire**
camcorder ['kæmkɔːdə^r] n videocamera
came [keɪm] pt of **come**
camel ['kæməl] n cammello
cameo ['kæmɪəu] n cammeo
camera ['kæmərə] n macchina fotografica;
(Cine, TV) telecamera; (also: **cinecamera,
movie camera**) cinepresa; **in** ~ a porte
chiuse
cameraman ['kæmərəmæn] n cameraman
m inv
camera phone n telefonino con fotocamera
integrata
Cameroon, Cameroun ['kæməruːn] n
Camerun m
camouflage ['kæməflɑːʒ] n camuffamento;
(Mil) mimetizzazione f ∎ vt camuffare;
mimetizzare
camp [kæmp] n campeggio; (Mil) campo ∎ vi
campeggiare; accamparsi; **to go camping**
andare in campeggio
campaign [kæm'peɪn] n (Mil, Pol etc)
campagna ∎ vi: **to** ~ **(for/against)** (also fig)
fare una campagna (per/contro)
campaigner [kæm'peɪnə^r] n: ~ **for**
fautore(-trice) di; ~ **against**
oppositore(-trice) di
campbed ['kæmp'bɛd] n (Brit) brandina
camper ['kæmpə^r] n campeggiatore(-trice)
camping ['kæmpɪŋ] n campeggio

C

camp site, camping site n campeggio
campus ['kæmpəs] n campus m inv
camshaft ['kæmʃɑːft] n albero a camme
can¹ [kæn] n (of milk) scatola; (of oil) bidone m; (of water) tanica; (tin) scatola ■ vt mettere in scatola; **a ~ of beer** una lattina di birra; **to carry the ~** (Brit col) prendere la colpa

 KEYWORD

can² [kæn] (negative **cannot, can't**, conditional and pt **could**) aux vb **1** (be able to) potere;
I can't go any further non posso andare oltre; **you can do it if you try** sei in grado di farlo – basta provarci; **I'll help you all I can** ti aiuterò come potrò; **I can't see you** non ti vedo; **can you hear me?** mi senti?, riesci a sentirmi?
2 (know how to) sapere, essere capace di; **I can swim** so nuotare; **can you speak French?** parla francese?
3 (may) potere; **could I have a word with you?** posso parlarle un momento?
4 (expressing disbelief, puzzlement etc): **it can't be true!** non può essere vero!; **what CAN he want?** cosa può mai volere?
5 (expressing possibility, suggestion etc): **he could be in the library** può darsi che sia in biblioteca; **they could have forgotten** potrebbero essersene dimenticati; **she could have been delayed** può aver avuto un contrattempo

Canada ['kænədə] n Canada m
Canadian [kə'neɪdɪən] adj, n canadese (m/f)
canal [kə'næl] n canale m
canary [kə'nɛərɪ] n canarino
Canary Islands, Canaries [kə'nɛərɪz] npl: **the ~** le (isole) Canarie
Canberra ['kænbərə] n Camberra
cancel ['kænsəl] vt annullare; (train) sopprimere; (cross out) cancellare
 ▶ **cancel out** vt (Math) semplificare; (fig) annullare; **they ~ each other out** (also fig) si annullano a vicenda
cancellation [kænsə'leɪʃən] n annullamento; soppressione f; cancellazione f; (Tourism) prenotazione f annullata
cancer ['kænsə'] n cancro; **C~** (sign) Cancro; **to be C~** essere del Cancro
cancerous ['kænsərəs] adj canceroso(-a)
cancer patient n malato(-a) di cancro
cancer research n ricerca sul cancro
C and F abbr (Brit: = cost and freight) Caf m
candid ['kændɪd] adj onesto(-a)
candidacy ['kændɪdəsɪ] n candidatura
candidate ['kændɪdeɪt] n candidato(-a)

candidature ['kændɪdətʃə'] n (Brit)
 = **candidacy**
candied ['kændɪd] adj candito(-a); **~ apple** (US) mela caramellata
candle ['kændl] n candela
candlelight ['kændl'laɪt] n: **by ~** a lume di candela
candlestick ['kændlstɪk] n (also: **candle holder**) bugia; (bigger, ornate) candeliere m
candour, (US) **candor** ['kændə'] n sincerità
C & W n abbr = **country and western (music)**
candy ['kændɪ] n zucchero candito; (US) caramella; caramelle fpl
candy-floss ['kændɪflɔs] n (Brit) zucchero filato
candy store n (US) = pasticceria
cane [keɪn] n canna; (for baskets, chairs etc) bambù m; (Scol) verga; (for walking) bastone m (da passeggio) ■ vt (Brit Scol) punire a colpi di verga
canine ['kænaɪn] adj canino(-a)
canister ['kænɪstə'] n scatola metallica
cannabis ['kænəbɪs] n canapa indiana
canned ['kænd] adj (food) in scatola; (col: recorded: music) registrato(-a); (Brit col: drunk) sbronzo(-a); (US col: worker) licenziato(-a)
cannibal ['kænɪbəl] n cannibale m/f
cannibalism ['kænɪbəlɪzəm] n cannibalismo
cannon (pl **~** or **cannons**) ['kænən] n (gun) cannone m
cannonball ['kænənbɔːl] n palla di cannone
cannon fodder n carne f da macello
cannot ['kænɔt] = **can not**
canny ['kænɪ] adj furbo(-a)
canoe [kə'nuː] n canoa; (Sport) canotto
canoeing [kə'nuːɪŋ] n (sport) canottaggio
canoeist [kə'nuːɪst] n canottiere m
canon ['kænən] n (clergyman) canonico; (standard) canone m
canonize ['kænənaɪz] vt canonizzare
can opener [-əupnə'] n apriscatole m inv
canopy ['kænəpɪ] n baldacchino
cant [kænt] n gergo ■ vt inclinare
 ■ vi inclinarsi
can't [kænt] = **can not**
Cantab. abbr (Brit: = cantabrigiensis) of Cambridge
cantankerous [kæn'tæŋkərəs] adj stizzoso(-a)
canteen [kæn'tiːn] n mensa; (Brit: of cutlery) portaposate m inv
canter ['kæntə'] n piccolo galoppo
 ■ vi andare al piccolo galoppo
cantilever ['kæntɪliːvə'] n trave f a sbalzo
canvas ['kænvəs] n tela; **under ~** (camping) sotto la tenda; (Naut) sotto la vela
canvass ['kænvəs] vt (Comm: district) fare un'indagine di mercato in; (: citizens, opinions)

fare un sondaggio di; (*Pol: district*) fare un giro elettorale di; (: *person*) fare propaganda elettorale a

canvasser ['kænvəsəʳ] *n* (*Comm*) agente *m* viaggiatore, piazzista *m*; (*Pol*) propagandista *m/f* (elettorale)

canvassing ['kænvəsɪŋ] *n* sollecitazione *f*

canyon ['kænjən] *n* canyon *m inv*

CAP *n abbr* (= *Common Agricultural Policy*) PAC *f*

cap [kæp] *n* (*also Brit Football*) berretto; (*of pen*) coperchio; (*of bottle*) tappo; (*for swimming*) cuffia; (*Brit: contraceptive: also:* **Dutch cap**) diaframma *m* ▪ *vt* tappare; (*outdo*) superare; **capped with** ricoperto(-a) di; **and to ~ it all, he ...** (*Brit*) e per completare l'opera, lui ...

capability [keɪpə'bɪlɪtɪ] *n* capacità *f inv*, abilità *f inv*

capable ['keɪpəbl] *adj* capace; **~ of** capace di; suscettibile di

capacious [kə'peɪʃəs] *adj* capace

capacity [kə'pæsɪtɪ] *n* capacità *f inv*; (*of lift etc*) capienza; **in his ~ as** nella sua qualità di; **to work at full ~** lavorare al massimo delle proprie capacità; **this work is beyond my ~** questo lavoro supera le mie possibilità; **filled to ~** pieno zeppo; **in an advisory ~** a titolo consultativo

cape [keɪp] *n* (*garment*) cappa; (*Geo*) capo

Cape of Good Hope *n* Capo di Buona Speranza

caper ['keɪpəʳ] *n* (*Culin: also:* **capers**) cappero; (*leap*) saltello; (*escapade*) birichinata

Cape Town *n* Città del Capo

capita ['kæpɪtə] *see* **per capita**

capital ['kæpɪtl] *n* (*also:* **capital city**) capitale *f*; (*money*) capitale *m*; (*also:* **capital letter**) (lettera) maiuscola

capital account *n* conto capitale

capital allowance *n* ammortamento fiscale

capital assets *npl* capitale *m* fisso

capital expenditure *n* spese *fpl* in capitale

capital gains tax *n* imposta sulla plusvalenza

capital goods *n* beni *mpl* d'investimento, beni *mpl* capitali

capital-intensive ['kæpɪtlɪn'tɛnsɪv] *adj* ad alta intensità di capitale

capitalism ['kæpɪtəlɪzəm] *n* capitalismo

capitalist ['kæpɪtəlɪst] *adj, n* capitalista (*m/f*)

capitalize ['kæpɪtəlaɪz] *vt* (*provide with capital*) capitalizzare

▶ **capitalize on** *vt fus* (*fig*) trarre vantaggio da

capital punishment *n* pena capitale

capital transfer tax *n* (*Brit*) imposta sui trasferimenti di capitali

Capitol ['kæpɪtl] *n*: **the ~** il Campidoglio; *vedi nota*

⬤ Capitol

⬤ Il *Capitol* è l'edificio che ospita le riunioni del Congresso degli Stati Uniti. é situato sull'omonimo colle, "Capitol Hill", a Washington DC. In molti stati americani il termine Capitol viene usato per indicare l'edificio dove si riuniscono i rappresentanti dello stato.

capitulate [kə'pɪtjuleɪt] *vi* capitolare

capitulation [kəpɪtju'leɪʃən] *n* capitolazione *f*

capricious [kə'prɪʃəs] *adj* capriccioso(-a)

Capricorn ['kæprɪkɔ:n] *n* Capricorno; **to be ~** essere del Capricorno

caps [kæps] *abbr* = **capital letters**

capsize [kæp'saɪz] *vt* capovolgere ▪ *vi* capovolgersi

capstan ['kæpstən] *n* argano

capsule ['kæpsju:l] *n* capsula

Capt. *abbr* (= *captain*) Cap.

captain ['kæptɪn] *n* capitano ▪ *vt* capitanare

caption ['kæpʃən] *n* leggenda

captivate ['kæptɪveɪt] *vt* avvincere

captive ['kæptɪv] *adj, n* prigioniero(-a)

captivity [kæp'tɪvɪtɪ] *n* prigionia; **in ~** (*animal*) in cattività

captor ['kæptəʳ] *n* (*lawful*) chi ha catturato; (*unlawful*) rapitore *m*

capture ['kæptʃəʳ] *vt* catturare, prendere; (*attention*) attirare ▪ *n* cattura; (*data capture*) registrazione *f* o rilevazione *f* di dati

car [kɑ:ʳ] *n* macchina, automobile *f*; (*US Rail*) carrozza; **by ~** in macchina

Caracas [kə'rækəs] *n* Caracas *f*

carafe [kə'ræf] *n* caraffa

carafe wine *n* (*in restaurant*) ≈ vino sfuso

caramel ['kærəməl] *n* caramello

carat ['kærət] *n* carato; **18 ~ gold** oro a 18 carati

caravan ['kærəvæn] *n* roulotte *f inv*

caravan site *n* (*Brit*) campeggio per roulotte

caraway ['kærəweɪ] *n*: **~ seed** seme *m* di cumino

carbohydrates [kɑ:bəu'haɪdreɪts] *npl* (*foods*) carboidrati *mpl*

carbolic acid [kɑ:'bɔlɪk-] *n* acido fenico, fenolo

car bomb *n* ordigno esplosivo collocato in una macchina; **a ~ went off yesterday** ieri è esplosa un'autobomba

carbon ['kɑ:bən] *n* carbonio

carbonated ['kɑ:bəneɪtəd] *adj* (*drink*) gassato(-a)

carbon copy *n* copia *f* carbone *inv*

carbon dioxide [-daɪˈɒksaɪd] n diossido di carbonio

carbon footprint n impronta di carbonio

carbon paper n carta carbone

carbon ribbon n nastro carbonato

car boot sale n mercatino dell'usato dove la merce viene esposta nel bagagliaio delle macchine

carburettor, (US) **carburetor** [kɑːbjuˈretəʳ] n carburatore m

carcass [ˈkɑːkəs] n carcassa

carcinogenic [kɑːsɪnəˈdʒɛnɪk] adj cancerogeno(-a)

card [kɑːd] n carta; (thin cardboard) cartoncino; (visiting card etc) biglietto; (membership card) tessera; (Christmas card etc) cartolina; **to play cards** giocare a carte

cardamom [ˈkɑːdəməm] n cardamomo

cardboard [ˈkɑːdbɔːd] n cartone m

cardboard box n (scatola di) cartone m

cardboard city n luogo dove dormono in scatole di cartone emarginati senzatetto

card-carrying member [ˈkɑːdˈkærɪŋ-] n tesserato(-a)

card game n gioco di carte

cardiac [ˈkɑːdɪæk] adj cardiaco(-a)

cardigan [ˈkɑːdɪgən] n cardigan m inv

cardinal [ˈkɑːdɪnl] adj, n cardinale (m)

card index n schedario

cardphone [ˈkɑːdfəun] n telefono a scheda (magnetica)

cardsharp [ˈkɑːdʃɑːp] n baro

card vote n (Brit) voto (palese) per delega

CARE [kɛəʳ] n abbr = **Cooperative for American Relief Everywhere**

care [kɛəʳ] n cura, attenzione f; (worry) preoccupazione f ■ vi: **to ~ about** interessarsi di; **would you ~ to/for ...?** le piacerebbe ...?; **I wouldn't ~ to do it** non lo vorrei fare; **in sb's ~** alle cure di qn; **to take ~ fare attenzione**; **to take ~ of** curarsi di; (details, arrangements) occuparsi di; **I don't ~** non me ne importa; **I couldn't ~ less** non me ne importa un bel niente; **~ of** (c/o) (on letter) presso; **"with ~" "fragile"**; **the child has been taken into ~** il bambino è stato preso in custodia

▶ **care for** vt fus aver cura di; (like) voler bene a

careen [kəˈriːn] vi (ship) sbandare ■ vt carenare

career [kəˈrɪəʳ] n carriera; (occupation) professione f ■ vi (also: **career along**) andare di (gran) carriera

career girl n donna dedita alla carriera

careers officer n consulente m/f d'orientamento professionale

carefree [ˈkɛəfriː] adj sgombro(-a) di preoccupazioni

careful [ˈkɛəful] adj attento(-a); (cautious) cauto(-a); **(be) ~!** attenzione!; **he's very ~ with his money** bada molto alle spese

carefully [ˈkɛəfəlɪ] adv con cura; cautamente

careless [ˈkɛəlɪs] adj negligente; (remark) privo(-a) di tatto

carelessly [ˈkɛəlɪslɪ] adv negligentemente; senza tatto; (without thinking) distrattamente

carelessness [ˈkɛəlɪsnɪs] n negligenza; mancanza di tatto

carer [ˈkɛərəʳ] n chi si occupa di un familiare anziano o invalido

caress [kəˈrɛs] n carezza ■ vt accarezzare

caretaker [ˈkɛəteɪkəʳ] n custode m

caretaker government n (Brit) governo m ponte inv

car-ferry [ˈkɑːfɛrɪ] n traghetto

cargo (pl **cargoes**) [ˈkɑːgəu] n carico

cargo boat n cargo

cargo plane n aereo di linea da carico

car hire n (Brit) autonoleggio

Caribbean [kærɪˈbiːən] adj caraibico(-a); **the ~ (Sea)** il Mar dei Caraibi

caricature [ˈkærɪkətjuəʳ] n caricatura

caring [ˈkɛərɪŋ] adj (person) premuroso(-a); (society, organization) umanitario(-a)

carnage [ˈkɑːnɪdʒ] n carneficina

carnal [ˈkɑːnl] adj carnale

carnation [kɑːˈneɪʃən] n garofano

carnival [ˈkɑːnɪvəl] n (public celebration) carnevale m; (US: funfair) luna park m inv

carnivorous [kɑːˈnɪvərəs] adj carnivoro(-a)

carol [ˈkærəl] n: **(Christmas) ~** canto di Natale

carouse [kəˈrauz] vi far baldoria

carousel [kærəˈsɛl] n (US) giostra

carp [kɑːp] n (fish) carpa

▶ **carp at** vt fus trovare a ridire su

car park n parcheggio

carpenter [ˈkɑːpɪntəʳ] n carpentiere m

carpentry [ˈkɑːpɪntrɪ] n carpenteria

carpet [ˈkɑːpɪt] n tappeto; (Brit: fitted carpet) moquette f inv ■ vt coprire con tappeto

carpet bombing n bombardamento a tappeto

carpet slippers npl pantofole fpl

carpet sweeper n scopatappeti m inv

car phone n telefonino per auto

car rental n (US) autonoleggio

carriage [ˈkærɪdʒ] n vettura; (of goods) trasporto; (of typewriter) carrello; (bearing) portamento; **~ forward** porto assegnato; **~ free** franco di porto; **~ paid** porto pagato

carriage return n (on typewriter etc) leva (or tasto) del ritorno a capo

carriageway [ˈkærɪdʒweɪ] n (Brit: part of road) carreggiata

carrier ['kærɪəʳ] *n* (*of disease*) portatore(-trice); (*Comm*) impresa di trasporti; (*Naut*) portaerei *f inv*
carrier bag *n* (*Brit*) sacchetto
carrier pigeon *n* colombo viaggiatore
carrion ['kærɪən] *n* carogna
carrot ['kærət] *n* carota
carry ['kærɪ] *vt* (*person*) portare; (*vehicle*) trasportare; (*a motion, bill*) far passare; (*involve: responsibilities etc*) comportare; (*Comm: goods*) tenere; (: *interest*) avere; (*Math: figure*) riportare ■ *vi* (*sound*) farsi sentire; **this loan carries 10% interest** questo prestito è sulla base di un interesse del 10%; **to be carried away** (*fig*) farsi trascinare
▶ **carry forward** *vt* (*Math, Comm*) riportare
▶ **carry on** *vi*: **to ~ on with sth/doing** continuare qc/a fare ■ *vt* mandare avanti
▶ **carry out** *vt* (*orders*) eseguire; (*investigation*) svolgere; (*accomplish etc: plan*) realizzare; (*perform, implement: idea, threat*) mettere in pratica
carrycot ['kærɪkɔt] *n* (*Brit*) culla portabile
carry-on [kærɪ'ɔn] *n* (*col: fuss*) casino, confusione *f*; (: *annoying behaviour*): **I've had enough of your ~!** mi hai proprio scocciato!
cart [kɑːt] *n* carro ■ *vt* (*col*) trascinare, scarrozzare
carte blanche ['kɑːt'blɒnʃ] *n*: **to give sb ~** dare carta bianca a qn
cartel [kɑː'tɛl] *n* (*Comm*) cartello
cartilage ['kɑːtɪlɪdʒ] *n* cartilagine *f*
cartographer [kɑː'tɔgrəfəʳ] *n* cartografo(-a)
cartography [kɑː'tɔgrəfɪ] *n* cartografia
carton ['kɑːtən] *n* (*box*) scatola di cartone; (*of yogurt*) cartone *m*; (*of cigarettes*) stecca
cartoon [kɑː'tuːn] *n* (*in newspaper etc*) vignetta; (*Cine, TV*) cartone *m* animato; (*Art*) cartone
cartoonist [kɑː'tuːnɪst] *n* vignettista *m/f*; cartonista *m/f*
cartridge ['kɑːtrɪdʒ] *n* (*for gun, pen*) cartuccia; (*for camera*) caricatore *m*; (*music tape*) cassetta; (*of record player*) testina
cartwheel ['kɑːtwiːl] *n*: **to turn a ~** (*Sport etc*) fare la ruota
carve [kɑːv] *vt* (*meat*) trinciare; (*wood, stone*) intagliare
▶ **carve up** *vt* (*meat*) tagliare; (*fig: country*) suddividere
carving ['kɑːvɪŋ] *n* (*in wood etc*) scultura
carving knife *n* trinciante *m*
car wash *n* lavaggio auto
Casablanca [kæsə'blæŋkə] *n* Casablanca
cascade [kæs'keɪd] *n* cascata ■ *vi* scendere a cascata
case [keɪs] *n* caso; (*Law*) causa, processo; (*box*) scatola, (*also*: **suitcase**) valigia; (*Typ*): **lower/upper ~** (carattere *m*) minuscolo/maiuscolo; **to have a good ~** avere pretese legittime; **there's a strong ~ for reform** ci sono validi argomenti a favore della riforma; **in ~ of** in caso di; **in ~ he** caso mai lui; **just in ~** in caso di bisogno
case history *n* (*Med*) cartella clinica
case-sensitive ['keɪs'sɛnsɪtɪv] *adj* (*Comput*) sensibile alle maiuscole o minuscole
case study *n* studio di un caso
cash [kæʃ] *n* (*coins, notes*) soldi *mpl*, denaro; (*col: money*) quattrini *mpl* ■ *vt* incassare; **to pay (in) ~** pagare in contanti; **to be short of ~** essere a corto di soldi; **~ with order/on delivery (COD)** (*Comm*) pagamento all'ordinazione/alla consegna
▶ **cash in** *vt* (*insurance policy etc*) riscuotere, riconvertire
▶ **cash in on** *vt fus*: **to ~ in on sth** sfruttare qc
cash account *n* conto *m* cassa *inv*
cash-and-carry ['kæʃənd'kærɪ] *n* cash and carry *m inv*
cashbook ['kæʃbuk] *n* giornale *m* di cassa
cash box *n* cassetta per il denaro spicciolo
cash card *n* carta per prelievi automatici
cash desk *n* (*Brit*) cassa
cash discount *n* sconto per contanti
cash dispenser *n* sportello automatico
cashew [kæ'ʃuː] *n* (*also*: **cashew nut**) anacardio
cash flow *n* cash-flow *m inv*, liquidità *f inv*
cashier [kæ'ʃɪəʳ] *n* cassiere(-a) ■ *vt* (*esp Mil*) destituire
cashmere ['kæʃmɪəʳ] *n* cachemire *m*
cash payment *n* pagamento in contanti
cash price *n* prezzo per contanti
cash register *n* registratore *m* di cassa
cash sale *n* vendita per contanti
casing ['keɪsɪŋ] *n* rivestimento
casino [kə'siːnəu] *n* casinò *m inv*
cask [kɑːsk] *n* botte *f*
casket ['kɑːskɪt] *n* cofanetto; (*US: coffin*) bara
Caspian Sea ['kæspɪən-] *n*: **the ~** il mar Caspio
casserole ['kæsərəul] *n* casseruola; (*food*): **chicken ~** pollo in casseruola
cassette [kæ'sɛt] *n* cassetta
cassette deck *n* piastra di registrazione
cassette player *n* riproduttore *m* a cassette
cassette recorder *n* registratore *m* a cassette
cast [kɑːst] *vt* (*pt, pp* **~**) (*throw*) gettare; (*shed*) perdere; spogliarsi di; (*metal*) gettare, fondere; (*Theat*): **to ~ sb as Hamlet** scegliere qn per la parte di Amleto ■ *n* (*Theat*) complesso di attori; (*mould*) forma; (*also*: **plaster cast**) ingessatura; **to ~ one's vote** votare, dare il voto

▶ **cast aside** vt (reject) mettere da parte
▶ **cast off** vi (Naut) salpare; (Knitting) diminuire, calare ■ vt (Naut) disormeggiare; (Knitting) diminuire, calare
▶ **cast on** (Knitting) vt avviare ■ vi avviare (le maglie)
castanets [kæstə'nɛts] npl castagnette fpl
castaway ['kɑːstəwəɪ] n naufrago(-a)
caste [kɑːst] n casta
caster sugar ['kɑːstə-] n zucchero semolato
casting vote ['kɑːstɪŋ-] n (Brit) voto decisivo
cast iron n ghisa ■ adj: **cast-iron** (fig: will, alibi) di ferro, d'acciaio
castle ['kɑːsl] n castello; (fortified) rocca
castor ['kɑːstəʳ] n (wheel) rotella
castor oil n olio di ricino
castrate [kæs'treɪt] vt castrare
casual ['kæʒjul] adj (by chance) casuale, fortuito(-a); (irregular: work etc) avventizio(-a); (unconcerned) noncurante, indifferente; **~ wear** casual m
casual labour n manodopera avventizia
casually ['kæʒjulɪ] adv con disinvoltura; (by chance) casualmente
casualty ['kæʒjultɪ] n ferito(-a); (dead) morto(-a), vittima; **heavy casualties** grosse perdite fpl
casualty ward n (Brit) pronto soccorso
cat [kæt] n gatto
catacombs ['kætəkuːmz] npl catacombe fpl
catalogue, (US) **catalog** ['kætələɡ] n catalogo ■ vt catalogare
catalyst ['kætəlɪst] n catalizzatore m
catalytic converter [kætə'lɪtɪkkən'vəːtəʳ] n marmitta catalitica, catalizzatore m
catapult ['kætəpʌlt] n catapulta; fionda
cataract ['kætərækt] n (also Med) cateratta
catarrh [kə'tɑːʳ] n catarro
catastrophe [kə'tæstrəfɪ] n catastrofe f
catastrophic [kætə'strɔfɪk] adj catastrofico(-a)
catcall ['kætkɔːl] n (at meeting etc) fischio
catch [kætʃ] vb (pt, pp **caught**) [kɔːt] vt (train, thief, cold) acchiappare; (ball) afferrare; (person: by surprise) sorprendere; (understand) comprendere; (get entangled) impigliare ■ vi (fire) prendere ■ n (fish etc caught) retata, presa; (trick) inganno; (Tech) gancio (pt, pp **to ~ sb's attention** or **eye**) attirare l'attenzione di qn; **to ~ fire** prendere fuoco; **to ~ sight of** scorgere
▶ **catch on** vi (become popular) affermarsi, far presa; (understand): **to ~ on (to sth)** capire (qc)
▶ **catch out** vt (Brit fig: with trick question) cogliere in fallo
▶ **catch up** vi mettersi in pari ■ vt (also: **catch up with**) raggiungere

catching ['kætʃɪŋ] adj (Med) contagioso(-a)
catchment area ['kætʃmənt-] n (Brit Scol) circoscrizione f scolare; (Geo) bacino pluviale
catch phrase n slogan m inv; frase f fatta
catch-22 ['kætʃtwɛntɪ'tuː] n: **it's a ~ situation** non c'è via d'uscita
catchy ['kætʃɪ] adj orecchiabile
catechism ['kætɪkɪzəm] n catechismo
categoric [kætɪ'ɡɔrɪk], **categorical** [kætɪ'ɡɔrɪkl] adj categorico(-a)
categorize ['kætɪɡəraɪz] vt categorizzare
category ['kætɪɡərɪ] n categoria
cater ['keɪtəʳ] vi: **to ~ (for)** provvedere da mangiare (per)
▶ **cater for** vt fus (Brit: needs) provvedere a; (: readers, consumers) incontrare i gusti di
caterer ['keɪtərəʳ] n fornitore m
catering ['keɪtərɪŋ] n approvvigionamento
catering trade n settore m ristoranti
caterpillar ['kætəpɪləʳ] n (Zool) bruco ■ cpd (vehicle) cingolato(-a); **~ track** cingolo
cat flap n gattaiola
cathedral [kə'θiːdrəl] n cattedrale f, duomo
cathode ['kæθəud] n catodo
cathode ray tube n tubo a raggi catodici
catholic ['kæθəlɪk] adj universale; aperto(-a); eclettico(-a); **C~** adj, n (Rel) cattolico(-a)
CAT scanner [kæt-] n (Med: = computerized axial tomography scanner) (rilevatore m per la) TAC f inv
cat's-eye ['kæts'aɪ] n (Brit Aut) catarifrangente m
catsup ['kætsəp] n (US) ketchup m inv
cattle ['kætl] npl bestiame m, bestie fpl
catty ['kætɪ] adj maligno(-a), dispettoso(-a)
catwalk ['kætwɔːk] n passerella
Caucasian [kɔː'keɪzɪən] adj, n caucasico(-a)
Caucasus ['kɔːkəsəs] n Caucaso
caucus ['kɔːkəs] n (US Pol) (riunione f del) comitato elettorale; (Brit Pol: group) comitato di dirigenti; vedi nota

⦿ **CAUCUS**
⦿
⦿ Caucus è il termine usato, specialmente
⦿ negli Stati Uniti, per indicare una
⦿ riunione informale dei rappresentanti di
⦿ spicco di un partito politico che precede
⦿ una riunione ufficiale. Con uso estensivo,
⦿ la parola indica il nucleo direttivo di un
⦿ partito politico.

caught [kɔːt] pt, pp of **catch**
cauliflower ['kɔlɪflauəʳ] n cavolfiore m
cause [kɔːz] n causa ■ vt causare; **there is no ~ for concern** non c'è ragione di preoccuparsi; **to ~ sb to do sth** far fare qc a qn; **to ~ sth to be done** far fare qc

causeway ['kɔːzweɪ] *n* strada rialzata
caustic ['kɔːstɪk] *adj* caustico(-a)
caution ['kɔːʃən] *n* prudenza; (*warning*) avvertimento ◼ *vt* ammonire
cautious ['kɔːʃəs] *adj* cauto(-a), prudente
cautiously ['kɔːʃəslɪ] *adv* prudentemente
cautiousness ['kɔːʃəsnɪs] *n* cautela
cavalier [kævə'lɪəʳ] *n* (*knight*) cavaliere *m* ◼ *adj* (*pej: offhand*) brusco(-a)
cavalry ['kævəlrɪ] *n* cavalleria
cave [keɪv] *n* caverna, grotta ◼ *vi*: **to go caving** fare speleologia
▶ **cave in** *vi* (*roof etc*) crollare
caveman ['keɪvmæn] *n* uomo delle caverne
cavern ['kævən] *n* caverna
caviar, caviare ['kævɪɑːʳ] *n* caviale *m*
cavity ['kævɪtɪ] *n* cavità *f inv*
cavity wall insulation *n* isolamento per pareti a intercapedine
cavort [kə'vɔːt] *vi* far capriole
cayenne [keɪ'ɛn], **cayenne pepper** [keɪ'ɛn-] *n* pepe *m* di Caienna
CB *n abbr* (Brit: = *Companion (of the Order) of the Bath*) titolo; (= *Citizens' Band (Radio)*) C.B *m*; **CB radio (set)** baracchino
CBC *n abbr* = **Canadian Broadcasting Corporation**
CBE *n abbr* (Brit: = *Companion (of the Order) of the British Empire*) titolo
CBI *n abbr* (= *Confederation of British Industry*) ≈ CONFINDUSTRIA (= *Confederazione Generale dell'Industria Italiana*)
CBS *n abbr* (US) = **Columbia Broadcasting System**
CC *abbr* (Brit) = **county council**
cc *abbr* (= *cubic centimetre*) cc; (*on letter etc*) = **carbon copy**
CCA *n abbr* (US: = *Circuit Court of Appeals*) corte *f* d'appello itinerante
CCTV *n abbr* = **closed-circuit television**
CCU *n abbr* (US: = *coronary care unit*) unità coronarica
CD *n abbr* (= *compact disk*) compact disc *m inv*; **CD player** lettore *m* CD; (*Mil*) = **Civil Defence (Corps)** (Brit), **Civil Defense** (US) ◼ *abbr* (Brit: = *Corps Diplomatique*) C.D.
CD burner *n* masterizzatore *m*
CDC *n abbr* (US) = **center for disease control**
CD-I® *n* CD-I *m inv*, compact disc *m inv* interattivo
Cdr. *abbr* (= *commander*) Com
CD-ROM ['siː'diː'rɔm] *n abbr* (= *compact disc read-only memory*) CD-ROM *m inv*
CDT *abbr* (US: = *Central Daylight Time*) ora legale del centro; (Brit: Scol: = *Craft, Design and Technology*) educazione tecnica
CDW *n abbr* = **collision damage waiver**

CD writer *n* masterizzatore *m*
cease [siːs] *vt*, *vi* cessare
ceasefire ['siːsfaɪəʳ] *n* cessate il fuoco *m inv*
ceaseless ['siːslɪs] *adj* incessante, continuo(-a)
CED *n abbr* (US) = **Committee for Economic Development**
cedar ['siːdəʳ] *n* cedro
cede [siːd] *vt* cedere
CEEB *n abbr* (US: = *College Entrance Examination Board*) commissione per l'esame di ammissione al college
ceilidh ['keɪlɪ] *n* festa con musiche e danze popolari scozzesi o irlandesi
ceiling ['siːlɪŋ] *n* soffitto; (*fig: upper limit*) tetto, limite *m* massimo
celebrate ['sɛlɪbreɪt] *vt*, *vi* celebrare
celebrated ['sɛlɪbreɪtɪd] *adj* celebre
celebration [sɛlɪ'breɪʃən] *n* celebrazione *f*
celebrity [sɪ'lɛbrɪtɪ] *n* celebrità *f inv*
celeriac [sə'lɛrɪæk] *n* sedano *m* rapa *inv*
celery ['sɛlərɪ] *n* sedano
celestial [sɪ'lɛstɪəl] *adj* celeste
celibacy ['sɛlɪbəsɪ] *n* celibato
cell [sɛl] *n* cella; (*Biol*) cellula; (*Elec*) elemento (di batteria)
cellar ['sɛləʳ] *n* sottosuolo, cantina
cellist ['tʃɛlɪst] *n* violoncellista *m/f*
cello ['tʃɛləu] *n* violoncello
cellophane® ['sɛləfeɪn] *n* cellophane® *m*
cellphone ['sɛlfəun] *n* cellulare *m*
cellular ['sɛljuləʳ] *adj* cellulare
celluloid ['sɛljulɔɪd] *n* celluloide *f*
cellulose ['sɛljuləus] *n* cellulosa
Celsius ['sɛlsɪəs] *adj* Celsius *inv*
Celt [kɛlt, sɛlt] *n* celta *m/f*
Celtic ['kɛltɪk, 'sɛltɪk] *adj* celtico(-a) ◼ *n* (*Ling*) celtico
cement [sə'mɛnt] *n* cemento ◼ *vt* cementare
cement mixer *n* betoniera
cemetery ['sɛmɪtrɪ] *n* cimitero
cenotaph ['sɛnətɑːf] *n* cenotafio
censor ['sɛnsəʳ] *n* censore *m* ◼ *vt* censurare
censorship ['sɛnsəʃɪp] *n* censura
censure ['sɛnʃəʳ] *vt* censurare
census ['sɛnsəs] *n* censimento
cent [sɛnt] *n* (*of dollar, euro*) centesimo; *see also* **per cent**
centenary [sɛn'tiːnərɪ], **centennial** [sɛn'tɛnɪəl] *n* centenario
center ['sɛntəʳ] *n*, *vt* (US) = **centre**
centigrade ['sɛntɪgreɪd] *adj* centigrado(-a)
centilitre, (US) **centiliter** ['sɛntɪliːtəʳ] *n* centilitro
centimetre, (US) **centimeter** ['sɛntɪmiːtəʳ] *n* centimetro

centipede ['sɛntɪpiːd] *n* centopiedi *m inv*
central ['sɛntrəl] *adj* centrale
Central African Republic *n* Repubblica centrafricana
Central America *n* America centrale
central heating *n* riscaldamento centrale
centralize ['sɛntrəlaɪz] *vt* accentrare
central processing unit *n* (*Comput*) unità *f inv* centrale di elaborazione
central reservation *n* (*Brit Aut*) banchina *f* spartitraffico *inv*
centre, (*US*) **center** ['sɛntəʳ] *n* centro ◾ *vt* (*concentrate*): **to ~ (on)** concentrare (su)
centrefold, (*US*) **centerfold** ['sɛntəfəuld] *n* (*Press*) poster *m* (all'interno di rivista)
centre-forward ['sɛntə'fɔːwəd] *n* (*Sport*) centroavanti *m inv*
centre-half ['sɛntə'hɑːf] *n* (*Sport*) centromediano
centrepiece, (*US*) **centerpiece** ['sɛntəpiːs] *n* centrotavola *m*; (*fig*) punto centrale
centre spread *n* (*Brit*) pubblicità a doppia pagina
centre-stage [sɛntə'steɪdʒ] *n*: **to take ~** porsi al centro dell'attenzione
centrifugal [sɛn'trɪfjugəl] *adj* centrifugo(-a)
centrifuge ['sɛntrɪfjuːʒ] *n* centrifuga
century ['sɛntjurɪ] *n* secolo; **in the twentieth ~** nel ventesimo secolo
CEO *n abbr* = **chief executive officer**
ceramic [sɪ'ræmɪk] *adj* ceramico(-a)
cereal ['siːrɪəl] *n* cereale *m*
cerebral ['sɛrɪbrəl] *adj* cerebrale
ceremonial [sɛrɪ'məunɪəl] *n* cerimoniale *m*; (*rite*) rito
ceremony ['sɛrɪmənɪ] *n* cerimonia; **to stand on ~** fare complimenti
cert [səːt] *n* (*Brit col*): **it's a dead ~** non c'è alcun dubbio
certain ['səːtən] *adj* certo(-a); **to make ~ of** assicurarsi di; **for ~** per certo, di sicuro
certainly ['səːtənlɪ] *adv* certamente, certo
certainty ['səːtəntɪ] *n* certezza
certificate [sə'tɪfɪkɪt] *n* certificato; diploma *m*
certified letter ['səːtɪfaɪd-] *n* (*US*) lettera raccomandata
certified public accountant ['səːtɪfaɪd-] *n* (*US*) ≈ commercialista *m/f*
certify ['səːtɪfaɪ] *vt* certificare ◾ *vi*: **to ~ to** attestare a
cervical ['səːvɪkl] *adj*: **~ cancer** cancro della cervice, tumore *m* al collo dell'utero; **~ smear** Pap-test *m inv*
cervix ['səːvɪks] *n* cervice *f*
Cesarean [siː'zɛərɪən] *adj, n* (*US*) = **Caesarean**
cessation [sə'seɪʃən] *n* cessazione *f*; arresto

cesspit ['sɛspɪt] *n* pozzo nero
CET *abbr* (= *Central European Time*) *fuso orario*
Ceylon [sɪ'lɔn] *n* Ceylon *f*
cf. *abbr* (= *compare*) cfr
c/f *abbr* (*Comm*) = **carried forward**
CFC *n abbr* (= *chlorofluorocarbon*) CFC *m inv*
CG *n abbr* (*US*) = **coastguard**
cg *abbr* (= *centigram*) cg
CH *n abbr* (*Brit*: = *Companion of Honour*) titolo
ch. *abbr* (= *chapter*) cap
Chad [tʃæd] *n* Chad *m*
chafe [tʃeɪf] *vt* fregare, irritare ◾ *vi* (*fig*): **to ~ against** scontrarsi con
chaffinch ['tʃæfɪntʃ] *n* fringuello
chagrin ['ʃægrɪn] *n* disappunto, dispiacere *m*
chain [tʃeɪn] *n* catena ◾ *vt* (*also*: **chain up**) incatenare
chain reaction *n* reazione *f* a catena
chain-smoke ['tʃeɪnsməuk] *vi* fumare una sigaretta dopo l'altra
chain store *n* negozio a catena
chair [tʃɛəʳ] *n* sedia; (*armchair*) poltrona; (*of university*) cattedra ◾ *vt* (*meeting*) presiedere; **the ~** (*US*: *electric chair*) la sedia elettrica
chairlift ['tʃɛəlɪft] *n* seggiovia
chairman ['tʃɛəmən] *n* presidente *m*
chairperson ['tʃɛəpəːsn] *n* presidente(-essa)
chairwoman ['tʃɛəwumən] *n* presidentessa
chalet ['ʃæleɪ] *n* chalet *m inv*
chalice ['tʃælɪs] *n* calice *m*
chalk [tʃɔːk] *n* gesso
> **chalk up** *vt* scrivere col gesso; (*fig*: *success*) ottenere; (: *victory*) riportare
challenge ['tʃælɪndʒ] *n* sfida ◾ *vt* sfidare; (*statement, right*) mettere in dubbio; **to ~ sb to a fight/game** sfidare qn a battersi/ad una partita; **to ~ sb to do** sfidare qn a fare
challenger ['tʃælɪndʒəʳ] *n* (*Sport*) sfidante *m/f*
challenging ['tʃælɪndʒɪŋ] *adj* sfidante; (*remark, look*) provocatorio(-a)
chamber ['tʃeɪmbəʳ] *n* camera; **~ of commerce** camera di commercio
chambermaid ['tʃeɪmbəmeɪd] *n* cameriera
chamber music *n* musica da camera
chamberpot ['tʃeɪmbəpɔt] *n* vaso da notte
chameleon [kə'miːlɪən] *n* camaleonte *m*
chamois ['ʃæmwɑː] *n* camoscio
chamois leather ['ʃæmɪ-] *n* pelle *f* di camoscio
champagne [ʃæm'peɪn] *n* champagne *m inv*
champers ['ʃæmpəz] *nsg* (*col*) sciampagna
champion ['tʃæmpɪən] *n* campione(-essa); (*of cause*) difensore *m* ◾ *vt* difendere, lottare per
championship ['tʃæmpɪənʃɪp] *n* campionato
chance [tʃɑːns] *n* caso; (*opportunity*) occasione *f*; (*likelihood*) possibilità *f inv* ◾ *vt*: **to ~ it**

rischiare, provarci ■ *adj* fortuito(-a); **there
is little ~ of his coming** è molto
improbabile che venga; **to take a ~**
rischiare; **by ~** per caso; **it's the ~ of a
lifetime** è un'occasione unica; **the chances
are that ...** probabilmente ..., è probabile
che ... + *sub*; **to ~ to do sth** (*formal: happen*) fare
per caso qc
▶ **chance (up)on** *vt fus* (*person*) incontrare per
caso, imbattersi in; (*thing*) trovare per caso

chancel ['tʃɑːnsəl] *n* coro

chancellor ['tʃɑːnsələ^r] *n* cancelliere *m*; (*of
university*) rettore *m* (onorario); **C~ of the
Exchequer** (*Brit*) Cancelliere *m* dello
Scacchiere

chandelier [ʃændə'lɪə^r] *n* lampadario

change [tʃeɪndʒ] *vt* cambiare; (*transform*):
to ~ sb into trasformare qn in ■ *vi*
cambiarsi; (*be transformed*): **to ~ into**
trasformarsi in ■ *n* cambiamento; (*money*)
resto; **to ~ one's mind** cambiare idea; **to ~
gear** (*Aut*) cambiare (marcia); **she changed
into an old skirt** si è cambiata e ha messo
una vecchia gonna; **a ~ of clothes** un
cambio (di vestiti); **for a ~** tanto per
cambiare; **small ~** spiccioli *mpl*, moneta;
keep the ~ tenga il resto; **can you give me ~
for £1?** mi può cambiare una sterlina?

changeable ['tʃeɪndʒəbl] *adj* (*weather*)
variabile; (*person*) mutevole

change machine *n* distributore *m*
automatico di monete

changeover ['tʃeɪndʒəuvə^r] *n* cambiamento,
passaggio

changing ['tʃeɪndʒɪŋ] *adj* che cambia;
(*colours*) cangiante

changing room *n* (*Brit: in shop*) camerino;
(: *Sport*) spogliatoio

channel ['tʃænl] *n* canale *m*; (*of river, sea*) alveo
■ *vt* canalizzare; (*fig: interest, energies*): **to ~
into** concentrare su, indirizzare verso;
through the usual channels per le solite
vie; **the (English) C~** la Manica; **green/red
~** (*Customs*) uscita "niente da dichiarare"/
"merci da dichiarare"

channel-hopping ['tʃænlhɔpɪŋ] *n* (*TV*)
zapping *m*

Channel Islands *npl*: **the ~** le Isole Normanne

Channel Tunnel *n*: **the ~** il tunnel della
Manica

chant [tʃɑːnt] *n* canto; salmodia; (*of crowd*)
slogan *m inv* ■ *vt* cantare; salmodiare; **the
demonstrators chanted their disapproval**
i dimostranti lanciavano slogan di protesta

chaos ['keɪɔs] *n* caos *m*

chaos theory *n* teoria del caos

chaotic [keɪ'ɔtɪk] *adj* caotico(-a)

chap [tʃæp] *n* (*Brit col: man*) tipo ■ *vt* (*skin*)
screpolare; **old ~** vecchio mio

chapel ['tʃæpl] *n* cappella

chaperone ['ʃæpərəun] *n*
accompagnatore(-trice) ■ *vt* accompagnare

chaplain ['tʃæplɪn] *n* cappellano

chapped [tʃæpt] *adj* (*skin, lips*) screpolato(-a)

chapter ['tʃæptə^r] *n* capitolo

char [tʃɑː^r] *vt* (*burn*) carbonizzare ■ *vi* (*Brit:
cleaner*) lavorare come domestica (a ore) ■ *n*
(*Brit*) = **charlady**

character ['kærɪktə^r] *n* (*gen, Comput*) carattere
m; (*in novel, film*) personaggio; (*eccentric*)
originale *m*; **a person of good ~** una persona
a modo

character code *n* (*Comput*) codice *m* di
carattere

characteristic ['kærɪktə'rɪstɪk] *adj*
caratteristico(-a) ■ *n* caratteristica; **~ of**
tipico(-a) di

characterize ['kærɪktəraɪz] *vt* caratterizzare;
(*describe*): **to ~ (as)** descrivere (come)

charade [ʃə'rɑːd] *n* sciarada

charcoal ['tʃɑːkəul] *n* carbone *m* di legna

charge [tʃɑːdʒ] *n* accusa; (*cost*) prezzo; (*of gun,
battery, Mil: attack*) carica ■ *vt* (*gun, battery,
Mil: enemy*) caricare; (*customer*) fare pagare a;
(*sum*) fare pagare; (*Law*): **to ~ sb (with)**
accusare qn (di) ■ *vi* (*gen with: up, along etc*)
lanciarsi; **charges** *npl*: **bank charges**
commissioni *fpl* bancarie; **labour charges**
costi *mpl* del lavoro; **to ~ in/out** precipitarsi
dentro/fuori; **to ~ up/down** lanciarsi su/giù
per; **is there a ~?** c'è da pagare?; **there's no
~ non** c'è niente da pagare; **extra ~**
supplemento; **to take ~ of** incaricarsi di;
to be in ~ of essere responsabile per; **to have
~ of sb** aver cura di qn; **how much do you ~
for this repair?** quanto chiede per la
riparazione?; **to ~ an expense (up) to sb**
addebitare una spesa a qn; **~ it to my
account** lo metta *or* addebiti sul mio conto

charge account *n* conto

charge card *n* carta di credito commerciale

chargé d'affaires ['ʃɑːʒeɪdæ'feə^r] *n* incaricato
d'affari

chargehand ['tʃɑːdʒhænd] *n* (*Brit*)
caposquadra *m/f*

charger ['tʃɑːdʒə^r] *n* (*also*: **battery charger**)
caricabatterie *m inv*; (*old: warhorse*) destriero

chariot ['tʃærɪət] *n* carro

charitable ['tʃærɪtəbl] *adj* caritatevole

charity ['tʃærɪtɪ] *n* carità; (*organization*) opera pia

charlady ['tʃɑːleɪdɪ] *n* (*Brit*) domestica a ore

charlatan ['ʃɑːlətən] *n* ciarlatano

charm [tʃɑːm] *n* fascino; (*on bracelet*) ciondolo
■ *vt* affascinare, incantare

charm bracelet n braccialetto con ciondoli

charming ['tʃɑ:mɪŋ] adj affascinante

chart [tʃɑ:t] n tabella; grafico; (map) carta nautica; (weather chart) carta del tempo ■ vt fare una carta nautica di; (sales, progress) tracciare il grafico di; **to be in the charts** (record, pop group) essere in classifica

charter ['tʃɑ:təʳ] vt (plane) noleggiare ■ n (document) carta; **on** ~ a nolo

chartered accountant ['tʃɑ:təd-] n (Brit) ragioniere(-a) professionista

charter flight n volo m charter inv

charwoman ['tʃɑ:wumən] n = **charlady**

chase [tʃeɪs] vt inseguire; (also: **chase away**) cacciare ■ n caccia

▸ **chase down** vt (US) = **chase up**

▸ **chase up** vt (Brit: person) scovare; (: information) scoprire, raccogliere

chasm ['kæzəm] n abisso

chassis ['ʃæsɪ] n telaio

chastened ['tʃeɪsnd] adj abbattuto(-a), provato(-a)

chastening ['tʃeɪsnɪŋ] adj che fa riflettere

chastise [tʃæs'taɪz] vt punire, castigare

chastity ['tʃæstɪtɪ] n castità

chat [tʃæt] vi (also: **have a chat**) chiacchierare; (on the internet) chattare ■ n chiacchierata

▸ **chat up** vt (Brit col: girl) abbordare

chatline ['tʃætlaɪn] n servicio telefonico che permette a più utenti di conversare insieme

chat room n chat line f inv

chat show n (Brit) talk show m inv, conversazione f televisiva

chattel ['tʃætl] n see **goods**

chatter ['tʃætəʳ] vi (person) ciarlare ■ n ciarle fpl; **her teeth were chattering** batteva i denti

chatterbox ['tʃætəbɔks] n chiacchierone(-a)

chattering classes ['tʃætərɪŋ-] npl: **the** ~ (col, pej) ≈ gli intellettuali da salotto

chatty ['tʃætɪ] adj (style) familiare; (person) chiacchierino(-a)

chauffeur ['ʃəufəʳ] n autista m

chauvinism ['ʃəuvɪnɪzəm] n (also: **male chauvinism**) maschilismo; (nationalism) sciovinismo

chauvinist ['ʃəuvɪnɪst] n (also: **male chauvinist**) maschilista m; (nationalist) sciovinista m/f

chauvinistic [ʃəuvɪ'nɪstɪk] adj sciovinistico(-a)

chav [tʃæv] n (Brit: pej) giovane della periferia urbana poco colto che indossa abiti sportivi di particolari marche

ChE abbr = **chemical engineer**

cheap [tʃi:p] adj a buon mercato; (reduced: fare, ticket) ridotto(-a); (joke) grossolano(-a); (poor quality) di cattiva qualità ■ a buon mercato; **cheaper** meno caro; ~ **day return** biglietto giornaliero ridotto di andata e ritorno; ~ **money** denaro a basso tasso di interesse

cheapen ['tʃi:pn] vt ribassare; (fig) avvilire

cheaply ['tʃi:plɪ] adv a buon prezzo, a buon mercato

cheat [tʃi:t] vi imbrogliare; (at school) copiare ■ vt ingannare; (rob) defraudare ■ n imbroglione m; copione m; (trick) inganno; **he's been cheating on his wife** ha tradito sua moglie

cheating ['tʃi:tɪŋ] n imbrogliare m; copiare m

check [tʃɛk] vt verificare; (passport, ticket) controllare; (halt) fermare; (restrain) contenere ■ vi (official etc) informarsi ■ n verifica; controllo; (curb) freno; (bill) conto; (pattern: gen pl) quadretti mpl; (US) = **cheque** ■ adj (also: **checked**: pattern, cloth) a scacchi, a quadretti; **to** ~ **with sb** chiedere a qn; **to keep a** ~ **on sb/sth** controllare qn/qc, fare attenzione a qn/qc

▸ **check in** vi (in hotel) registrare; (at airport) presentarsi all'accettazione ■ vt (luggage) depositare

▸ **check off** vt segnare

▸ **check out** vi (from hotel) saldare il conto ■ vt (luggage) ritirare; (investigate: story) controllare, verificare; (: person) prendere informazioni su

▸ **check up** vi: **to** ~ **up (on sth)** investigare (qc); **to** ~ **up on sb** informarsi sul conto di qn

checkbook ['tʃɛkbuk] n (US) = **chequebook**

checkered ['tʃɛkəd] adj (US) = **chequered**

checkers ['tʃɛkəz] n (US) dama

check guarantee card n (US) carta f assegni inv

check-in ['tʃɛkɪn] n (also: **check-in desk**: at airport) check-in m inv, accettazione f (bagagli inv)

checking account ['tʃɛkɪŋ-] n (US) conto corrente

checklist ['tʃɛklɪst] n lista di controllo

checkmate ['tʃɛkmeɪt] n scaccomatto

checkout ['tʃɛkaut] n (in supermarket) cassa

checkpoint ['tʃɛkpɔɪnt] n posto di blocco

checkroom ['tʃɛkrum] n (US) deposito m bagagli inv

checkup ['tʃɛkʌp] n (Med) controllo medico

cheek [tʃi:k] n guancia; (impudence) faccia tosta

cheekbone ['tʃi:kbəun] n zigomo

cheeky ['tʃi:kɪ] adj sfacciato(-a)

cheep [tʃi:p] n (of bird) pigolio ■ vi pigolare

cheer [tʃɪəʳ] vt applaudire; (gladden)

rallegrare ■ vi applaudire ■ n (gen pl)
applausi mpl; evviva mpl; **cheers!** salute!
▶ **cheer on** vt (person etc) incitare
▶ **cheer up** vi rallegrarsi, farsi animo
■ vt rallegrare
cheerful ['tʃɪəful] adj allegro(-a)
cheerfulness ['tʃɪəfulnɪs] n allegria
cheerio ['tʃɪərɪ'əu] excl (Brit) ciao!
cheerleader ['tʃɪəli:dəʳ] n cheerleader f inv
cheerless ['tʃɪəlɪs] adj triste
cheese [tʃi:z] n formaggio
cheeseboard ['tʃi:zbɔ:d] n piatto del (or per il)
formaggio
cheeseburger ['tʃi:zbə:gəʳ] n cheeseburger m inv
cheesecake ['tʃi:zkeɪk] n specie di torta di ricotta,
a volte con frutta
cheetah ['tʃi:tə] n ghepardo
chef [ʃɛf] n capocuoco
chemical ['kɛmɪkl] adj chimico(-a) ■ n
prodotto chimico
chemical engineering n ingegneria chimica
chemist ['kɛmɪst] n (Brit: pharmacist)
farmacista m/f; (scientist) chimico(-a); **~'s
shop** n (Brit) farmacia
chemistry ['kɛmɪstrɪ] n chimica
chemo ['ki:məu] n chemio f inv
chemotherapy [ki:məu'θɛrəpɪ] n
chemioterapia
cheque, (US) **check** [tʃɛk] n assegno; **to pay
by** ~ pagare per assegno or con un assegno
chequebook, (US) **checkbook** ['tʃɛkbuk] n
libretto degli assegni
cheque card n (Brit) carta f assegni inv
chequered, (US) **checkered** ['tʃɛkəd] adj (fig)
movimentato(-a)
cherish ['tʃɛrɪʃ] vt aver caro; (hope etc) nutrire
cheroot [ʃə'ru:t] n sigaro spuntato
cherry ['tʃɛrɪ] n ciliegia
Ches abbr (Brit) = **Cheshire**
chess [tʃɛs] n scacchi mpl
chessboard ['tʃɛsbɔ:d] n scacchiera
chessman ['tʃɛsmæn] n pezzo degli scacchi
chessplayer ['tʃɛspleɪəʳ] n scacchista m/f
chest [tʃɛst] n petto; (box) cassa; **to get sth
off one's ~** (col) sputare il rospo; **~ of
drawers** cassettone m
chest measurement n giro m torace inv
chestnut ['tʃɛsnʌt] n castagna; (also:
chestnut tree) castagno ■ adj castano(-a)
chesty ['tʃɛstɪ] adj: **~ cough** tosse f bronchiale
chew [tʃu:] vt masticare
chewing gum ['tʃu:ɪŋ-] n chewing gum m
chic [ʃi:k] adj elegante
chick [tʃɪk] n pulcino; (US col) pollastrella
chicken ['tʃɪkɪn] n pollo; (col: coward) coniglio
▶ **chicken out** vi (col) avere fifa; **to ~ out of
sth** tirarsi indietro da qc per fifa or paura

chicken feed n (fig) miseria
chickenpox ['tʃɪkɪnpɔks] n varicella
chick flick n (col) filmetto rosa
chickpea ['tʃɪkpi:] n cece m
chicory ['tʃɪkərɪ] n cicoria
chide [tʃaɪd] vt rimproverare
chief [tʃi:f] n capo ■ adj principale; **C~ of
Staff** (Mil) Capo di Stato Maggiore
chief constable n (Brit) ≈ questore m
chief executive, (US) **chief executive
officer** n direttore m generale
chiefly ['tʃi:flɪ] adv per lo più, soprattutto
chief operating officer n direttore(-trice)
operativo(-a)
chiffon ['ʃɪfɔn] n chiffon m inv
chilblain ['tʃɪlbleɪn] n gelone m
child (pl **children**) [tʃaɪld, 'tʃɪldrən] n
bambino(-a)
child abuse n molestie fpl a minori
child abuser [-ə'bju:zəʳ] n molestatore(-trice)
di bambini
child benefit n (Brit) ≈ assegni mpl familiari
childbirth ['tʃaɪldbə:θ] n parto
childhood ['tʃaɪldhud] n infanzia
childish ['tʃaɪldɪʃ] adj puerile
childless ['tʃaɪldlɪs] adj senza figli
childlike ['tʃaɪldlaɪk] adj fanciullesco(-a)
child minder n (Brit) bambinaia
child prodigy n bambino m prodigio inv
children ['tʃɪldrən] npl of **child**
children's home n istituto per l'infanzia
Chile ['tʃɪlɪ] n Cile m
Chilean ['tʃɪlɪən] adj, n cileno(-a)
chill [tʃɪl] n freddo; (Med) infreddatura ■ adj
freddo(-a), gelido(-a) ■ vt raffreddare;
(Culin) mettere in fresco; **"serve chilled"**
"servire fresco"
▶ **chill out** vi (esp US: col) darsi una calmata
chilli, (US) **chili** ['tʃɪlɪ] n peperoncino
chilling ['tʃɪlɪŋ] adj agghiacciante; (wind)
gelido(-a)
chilly ['tʃɪlɪ] adj freddo(-a), fresco(-a); (sensitive
to cold) freddoloso(-a); **to feel ~** sentirsi
infreddolito(-a)
chime [tʃaɪm] n carillon m inv ■ vi suonare,
scampanare
chimney ['tʃɪmnɪ] n camino
chimney sweep n spazzacamino
chimpanzee [tʃɪmpæn'zi:] n scimpanzé m inv
chin [tʃɪn] n mento
China ['tʃaɪnə] n Cina
china ['tʃaɪnə] n porcellana
Chinese [tʃaɪ'ni:z] adj cinese ■ n (pl inv)
cinese m/f; (Ling) cinese m
chink [tʃɪŋk] n (opening) fessura; (noise) tintinnio
chinwag ['tʃɪnwæg] n (col): **to have a ~** fare
una chiacchierata

chip [tʃɪp] n (gen pl: Culin) patatina fritta; (: US: also: **potato chip**) patatina; (of wood, glass, stone) scheggia; (in gambling) fiche f inv (Comput: microchip) chip m inv ■ vt (cup, plate) scheggiare; **when the chips are down** (fig) al momento critico
  ▶ **chip in** vi (col: contribute) contribuire; (: interrupt) intromettersi
chip and PIN n sistema m chip e PIN;
  ~ **machine** lettore m di carte chip e PIN;
  ~ **card** carta chip e PIN
chipboard ['tʃɪpbɔːd] n agglomerato
chipmunk ['tʃɪpmʌŋk] n tamia m striato
chippings ['tʃɪpɪŋz] npl: **loose** ~ brecciame m
chip shop n (Brit) vedi nota

chiropodist [kɪ'rɔpədɪst] n (Brit) pedicure m/f inv
chiropody [kɪ'rɔpədɪ] n (Brit) mestiere m di callista
chirp [tʃəːp] n cinguettio; (of crickets) cri cri m ■ vi cinguettare
chirpy ['tʃəːpɪ] adj (col) frizzante
chisel ['tʃɪzl] n cesello
chitchat ['tʃɪttʃæt] n (col) chiacchiere fpl
chivalrous ['ʃɪvəlrəs] adj cavalleresco(-a)
chivalry ['ʃɪvlrɪ] n cavalleria; cortesia
chives [tʃaɪvz] npl erba cipollina
chloride ['klɔːraɪd] n cloruro
chlorinate ['klɔrɪneɪt] vt clorare
chlorine ['klɔːriːn] n cloro
chock [tʃɔk] n zeppa
chock-a-block ['tʃɔkə'blɔk], **chockfull** ['tʃɔk'ful] adj pieno(-a) zeppo(-a)
chocolate ['tʃɔklɪt] n (substance) cioccolato, cioccolata; (drink) cioccolata; (a sweet) cioccolatino
choice [tʃɔɪs] n scelta ■ adj scelto(-a); **a wide** ~ un'ampia scelta; **I did it by** or **from** ~ l'ho fatto di mia volontà or per mia scelta
choir ['kwaɪə'] n coro
choirboy ['kwaɪəbɔɪ] n corista m fanciullo
choke [tʃəuk] vi soffocare ■ vt soffocare; (block) ingombrare ■ n (Aut) valvola dell'aria
cholera ['kɔlərə] n colera m
cholesterol [kə'lɛstərɔl] n colesterolo
choose (pt **chose**, pp **chosen**) [tʃuːz, tʃəuz, 'tʃəuzn] vt scegliere; **to** ~ **to do** decidere di

fare; preferire fare; **to** ~ **between** scegliere tra; **to** ~ **from** scegliere da or tra
choosy ['tʃuːzɪ] adj: **(to be)** ~ (fare lo/la) schizzinoso(-a)
chop [tʃɔp] vt (wood) spaccare; (Culin: also: **chop up**) tritare ■ n colpo netto; (Culin) costoletta; **to get the** ~ (Brit col: project) essere bocciato(-a); (: person: be sacked) essere licenziato(-a); see also **chops**
  ▶ **chop down** vt (tree) abbattere
choppy ['tʃɔpɪ] adj (sea) mosso(-a)
chops [tʃɔps] npl (jaws) mascelle fpl
chopsticks ['tʃɔpstɪks] npl bastoncini mpl cinesi
choral ['kɔːrəl] adj corale
chord [kɔːd] n (Mus) accordo
chore [tʃɔː'] n faccenda; **household chores** faccende fpl domestiche
choreographer [kɔrɪ'ɔgrəfə'] n coreografo(-a)
choreography [kɔrɪ'ɔgrəfɪ] n coreografia
chorister ['kɔrɪstə'] n corista m/f
chortle ['tʃɔːtl] vi ridacchiare
chorus ['kɔːrəs] n coro; (repeated part of song, also fig) ritornello
chose [tʃəuz] pt of **choose**
chosen ['tʃəuzn] pp of **choose**
chowder ['tʃaudə'] n zuppa di pesce
Christ [kraɪst] n Cristo
christen ['krɪsn] vt battezzare
christening ['krɪsnɪŋ] n battesimo
Christian ['krɪstɪən] adj, n cristiano(-a)
Christianity [krɪstɪ'ænɪtɪ] n cristianesimo
Christian name n nome m di battesimo
Christmas ['krɪsməs] n Natale m; **happy** or **merry** ~! Buon Natale!
Christmas card n cartolina di Natale
Christmas Day n il giorno di Natale
Christmas Eve n la vigilia di Natale
Christmas Island n isola di Christmas
Christmas tree n albero di Natale
chrome [krəum] n = **chromium**
chromium ['krəumɪəm] n cromo; (also: **chromium plating**) cromatura
chromosome ['krəuməsəum] n cromosoma m
chronic ['krɔnɪk] adj cronico(-a); (fig: liar, smoker) incallito(-a)
chronicle ['krɔnɪkl] n cronaca
chronological [krɔnə'lɔdʒɪkl] adj cronologico(-a)
chrysanthemum [krɪ'sænθəməm] n crisantemo
chubby ['tʃʌbɪ] adj paffuto(-a)
chuck [tʃʌk] vt buttare, gettare; **to** ~ **(up** or **in)** (Brit: job, person) piantare
  ▶ **chuck out** vt buttar fuori
chuckle ['tʃʌkl] vi ridere sommessamente

chuffed [tʃʌft] *adj* (*col*): **to be ~ about sth** essere arcicontento(-a) di qc

chug [tʃʌg] *vi* (*also:* **chug along**: *train*) muoversi sbuffando

chum [tʃʌm] *n* compagno(-a)

chump [tʃʌmp] *n* (*col*) idiota *m/f*

chunk [tʃʌŋk] *n* pezzo; (*of bread*) tocco

chunky [tʃʌŋkɪ] *adj* (*furniture etc*) basso(-a) e largo(-a); (*person*) ben piantato(-a); (*knitwear*) di lana grossa

Chunnel [tʃʌnəl] *n* = **Channel Tunnel**

church [tʃəːtʃ] *n* chiesa; **the C~ of England** la Chiesa anglicana

churchyard [tʃəːtʃjɑːd] *n* sagrato

churlish [tʃəːlɪʃ] *adj* rozzo(-a), sgarbato(-a)

churn [tʃəːn] *n* (*for butter*) zangola; (*also:* **milk churn**) bidone *m*
▶ **churn out** *vt* sfornare

chute [ʃuːt] *n* cascata; (*also:* **rubbish chute**) canale *m* di scarico; (*Brit*: *children's slide*) scivolo

chutney [tʃʌtnɪ] *n* salsa piccante (di frutta, zucchero e spezie)

CIA *n abbr* (*US:* = *Central Intelligence Agency*) C.I.A. *f*

CID *n abbr* (*Brit*) = **Criminal Investigation Department**

cider [saɪdəʳ] *n* sidro

CIF *abbr* (= *cost, insurance, and freight*) C.I.F. *m*

cigar [sɪgɑːʳ] *n* sigaro

cigarette [sɪgəret] *n* sigaretta

cigarette case *n* portasigarette *m inv*

cigarette end *n* mozzicone *m*

cigarette holder *n* bocchino

C-in-C *abbr* = **commander-in-chief**

cinch [sɪntʃ] *n* (*col*): **it's a ~** è presto fatto; (*sure thing*) è una cosa sicura

cinder [sɪndəʳ] *n* cenere *f*

Cinderella [sɪndərelə] *n* Cenerentola

cine-camera [sɪnɪkæmərə] *n* (*Brit*) cinepresa

cine-film [sɪnɪfɪlm] *n* (*Brit*) pellicola

cinema [sɪnəmə] *n* cinema *m inv*

cine-projector [sɪnɪprədʒektəʳ] *n* (*Brit*) proiettore *m*

cinnamon [sɪnəmən] *n* cannella

cipher [saɪfəʳ] *n* cifra; (*fig*: *faceless employee etc*) persona di nessun conto; **in ~** in codice

circa [səːkə] *prep* circa

circle [səːkl] *n* cerchio; (*of friends etc*) circolo; (*in cinema*) galleria ■ *vi* girare in circolo
■ *vt* (*surround*) circondare; (*move round*) girare intorno a

circuit [səːkɪt] *n* circuito

circuit board *n* (*Comput*) tavola dei circuiti

circuitous [səːkjuɪtəs] *adj* indiretto(-a)

circular [səːkjuləʳ] *adj* circolare ■ *n* (*letter*) circolare *f*; (*as advertisement*) volantino pubblicitario

circulate [səːkjuleɪt] *vi* circolare; (*person: socially*) girare e andare un po' da tutti
■ *vt* far circolare

circulating capital [səːkjuleɪtɪŋ-] *n* (*Comm*) capitale *m* d'esercizio

circulation [səːkjuleɪʃən] *n* circolazione *f*; (*of newspaper*) tiratura

circumcise [səːkəmsaɪz] *vt* circoncidere

circumference [səkʌmfərəns] *n* circonferenza

circumflex [səːkəmfleks] *n* (*also:* **circumflex accent**) accento circonflesso

circumscribe [səːkəmskraɪb] *vt* circoscrivere; (*fig*: *limit*) limitare

circumspect [səːkəmspekt] *adj* circospetto(-a)

circumstances [səːkəmstənsɪz] *npl* circostanze *fpl*; (*financial condition*) condizioni *fpl* finanziarie; **in the ~** date le circostanze; **under no ~** per nessun motivo

circumstantial [səːkəmstænʃəl] *adj* (*report, statement*) circostanziato(-a), dettagliato(-a); **~ evidence** prova indiretta

circumvent [səːkəmvent] *vt* (*rule etc*) aggirare

circus [səːkəs] *n* circo; (*also:* **Circus**: *in place names*) piazza (di forma circolare)

cirrhosis [sɪrəusɪs] *n* (*also:* **cirrhosis of the liver**) cirrosi *f inv* (epatica)

CIS *n abbr* (= *Commonwealth of Independent States*) CSI *f*

cissy [sɪsɪ] *n* = **sissy**

cistern [sɪstən] *n* cisterna; (*in toilet*) serbatoio d'acqua

citation [saɪteɪʃən] *n* citazione *f*

cite [saɪt] *vt* citare

citizen [sɪtɪzn] *n* (*Pol*) cittadino(-a); (*resident*): **the citizens of this town** gli abitanti di questa città

Citizens' Advice Bureau *n* (*Brit*) *organizzazione di volontari che offre gratuitamente assistenza legale e finanziaria*

citizenship [sɪtɪznʃɪp] *n* cittadinanza

citric acid [sɪtrɪk] *n* acido citrico

citrus fruit [sɪtrəs-] *n* agrume *m*

city [sɪtɪ] *n* città *f inv*; **the C~** la Città di Londra (*centro commerciale*)

city centre *n* centro della città

City Hall *n* (*US*) ≈ Comune *m*

City Technology College *n* (*Brit*) istituto tecnico superiore (*finanziato dall'industria*)

civic [sɪvɪk] *adj* civico(-a)

civic centre *n* (*Brit*) centro civico

civil [sɪvɪl] *adj* civile; (*polite*) educato(-a), gentile

civil disobedience n disubbidienza civile
civil engineer n ingegnere m civile
civil engineering n ingegneria civile
civilian [sɪ'vɪliən] adj, n borghese (m/f)
civilization [sɪvɪlaɪ'zeɪʃən] n civiltà f inv
civilized ['sɪvɪlaɪzd] adj civilizzato(-a); (fig) cortese
civil law n codice m civile; (study) diritto civile
civil liberties npl libertà fpl civili
civil rights npl diritti mpl civili
civil servant n impiegato(-a) statale
Civil Service n amministrazione f statale
civil war n guerra civile
civvies ['sɪvɪz] npl (col): **in ~** in borghese
CJD n abbr (= Creutzfeld-Jakob disease) malattia di Creutzfeldt-Jakob
cl abbr (= centilitre) cl
clad [klæd] adj: **~ (in)** vestito(-a) (di)
claim [kleɪm] vt (rights etc) rivendicare; (damages) richiedere; (assert) sostenere, pretendere ■ vi (for insurance) fare una domanda d'indennizzo ■ n rivendicazione f; pretesa; (right) diritto; **to ~ that/to be** sostenere che/di essere; **(insurance) ~** domanda d'indennizzo; **to put in a ~ for sth** fare una richiesta di qc
claimant ['kleɪmənt] n (Admin, Law) richiedente m/f
claim form n (gen) modulo di richiesta; (for expenses) modulo di rimborso spese
clairvoyant [kleə'vɔɪənt] n chiaroveggente m/f
clam [klæm] n vongola
  ▶ **clam up** vi (col) azzittirsi
clamber ['klæmbəʳ] vi arrampicarsi
clammy ['klæmɪ] adj (weather) caldo(-a) umido(-a); (hands) viscido(-a)
clamour, (US) **clamor** ['klæməʳ] n (noise) clamore m; (protest) protesta ■ vi: **to ~ for sth** chiedere a gran voce qc
clamp [klæmp] n pinza; morsa ■ vt ammorsare
  ▶ **clamp down** vt fus (fig): **to ~ down (on)** dare un giro di vite (a)
clampdown ['klæmpdaun] n stretta, giro di vite; **a ~ on sth/sb** un giro di vite a qc/qn
clan [klæn] n clan m inv
clandestine [klæn'dɛstɪn] adj clandestino(-a)
clang [klæŋ] n fragore m, suono metallico
clanger ['klæŋəʳ] n: **to drop a ~** (Brit col) fare una gaffe
clansman ['klænzmən] n membro di un clan
clap [klæp] vi applaudire ■ vt: **to ~ one's hands** battere le mani ■ n: **a ~ of thunder** un tuono

clapping ['klæpɪŋ] n applausi mpl
claptrap ['klæptræp] n (col) stupidaggini fpl
claret ['klærət] n vino di Bordeaux
clarification [klærɪfɪ'keɪʃən] n (fig) chiarificazione f, chiarimento
clarify ['klærɪfaɪ] vt chiarificare, chiarire
clarinet [klærɪ'nɛt] n clarinetto
clarity ['klærɪtɪ] n chiarezza
clash [klæʃ] n frastuono; (fig) scontro ■ vi (Mil, fig: have an argument) scontrarsi; (colours) stridere; (dates, events) coincidere
clasp [klɑːsp] n fermaglio, fibbia ■ vt stringere
class [klɑːs] n classe f; (group, category) tipo, categoria ■ vt classificare
class-conscious ['klɑːskɔnʃəs] adj che ha coscienza di classe
class consciousness n coscienza di classe
classic ['klæsɪk] adj classico(-a) ■ n classico
classical ['klæsɪkəl] adj classico(-a)
classics ['klæsɪks] npl (Scol) studi mpl umanistici
classification [klæsɪfɪ'keɪʃən] n classificazione f
classified ['klæsɪfaɪd] adj (information) segreto(-a), riservato(-a); **~ ads** annunci economici
classify ['klæsɪfaɪ] vt classificare
classless society ['klɑːslɪs-] n società f inv senza distinzioni di classe
classmate ['klɑːsmeɪt] n compagno(-a) di classe
classroom ['klɑːsrum] n aula
classroom assistant n assistente m/f in classe dell'insegnante
clatter ['klætəʳ] n acciottolio; scalpitio ■ vi acciottolare; scalpitare
clause [klɔːz] n clausola; (Ling) proposizione f
claustrophobia [klɔːstrə'fəubɪə] n claustrofobia
claustrophobic [klɔːstrə'fəubɪk] adj claustrofobico(-a)
claw [klɔː] n tenaglia; (of bird of prey) artiglio; (of lobster) pinza ■ vt graffiare; afferrare
clay [kleɪ] n argilla
clean [kliːn] adj pulito(-a); (clear, smooth) netto(-a) ■ vt pulire ■ adv: **he ~ forgot** si è completamente dimenticato; **to come ~** (col: admit guilt) confessare; **to have a ~ driving licence** or (US) **record** non aver mai preso contravvenzioni; **to ~ one's teeth** (Brit) lavarsi i denti
  ▶ **clean off** vt togliere
  ▶ **clean out** vt ripulire
  ▶ **clean up** vi far pulizia ■ vt (also fig) ripulire; (fig: make profit): **to ~ up on** fare una barca di soldi con

clean-cut ['kli:n'kʌt] *adj* (*man*) curato(-a); (*situation etc*) ben definito(-a)

cleaner ['kli:nə^r] *n* (*person*) uomo/donna delle pulizie; (*also*: **dry cleaner**) tintore(-a); (*product*) smacchiatore *m*

cleaning ['kli:nɪŋ] *n* pulizia

cleaning lady *n* donna delle pulizie

cleanliness ['klɛnlɪnɪs] *n* pulizia

cleanly ['kli:nlɪ] *adv* in modo netto

cleanse [klɛnz] *vt* pulire; purificare

cleanser ['klɛnzə^r] *n* detergente *m*; (*cosmetic*) latte *m* detergente

clean-shaven ['kli:n'ʃeɪvn] *adj* sbarbato(-a)

cleansing department ['klɛnzɪŋ-] *n* (*Brit*) nettezza urbana

clean sweep *n*: **to make a ~ (of)** fare piazza pulita (di)

clean-up ['kli:nʌp] *n* pulizia

clear [klɪə^r] *adj* chiaro(-a); (*road, way*) libero(-a); (*profit, majority*) netto(-a) ▪ *vt* sgombrare; liberare; (*site, woodland*) spianare; (*Comm: goods*) liquidare; (*Law: suspect*) discolpare; (*obstacle*) superare; (*cheque*) fare la compensazione di ▪ *vi* (*weather*) rasserenarsi; (*fog*) andarsene ▪ *adv*: **~ of** distante da ▪ *n*: **to be in the ~** (*out of debt*) essere in attivo; (*out of suspicion*) essere a posto; (*out of danger*) essere fuori pericolo; **to ~ the table** sparecchiare (la tavola); **to ~ one's throat** schiarirsi la gola; **to ~ a profit** avere un profitto netto; **to make o.s. ~** spiegarsi bene; **to make it ~ to sb that ...** far capire a qn che ...; **I have a ~ day tomorrow** (*Brit*) non ho impegni domani; **to keep ~ of sb/sth** tenersi lontano da qn/qc, stare alla larga da qn/qc

▸ **clear off** *vi* (*col: leave*) svignarsela

▸ **clear up** *vi* schiarirsi ▪ *vt* mettere in ordine; (*mystery*) risolvere

clearance ['klɪərəns] *n* (*removal*) sgombro; (*free space*) spazio; (*permission*) autorizzazione *f*, permesso

clearance sale *n* vendita di liquidazione

clear-cut ['klɪə'kʌt] *adj* ben delineato(-a), distinto(-a)

clearing ['klɪərɪŋ] *n* radura; (*Brit Banking*) clearing *m*

clearing bank *n* (*Brit*) banca che fa uso della camera di compensazione

clearing house *n* (*Comm*) camera di compensazione

clearly ['klɪəlɪ] *adv* chiaramente

clearway ['klɪəweɪ] *n* (*Brit*) strada con divieto di sosta

cleavage ['kli:vɪdʒ] *n* (*of woman*) scollatura

cleaver ['kli:və^r] *n* mannaia

clef [klɛf] *n* (*Mus*) chiave *f*

cleft [klɛft] *n* (*in rock*) crepa, fenditura

clemency ['klɛmənsɪ] *n* clemenza

clement ['klɛmənt] *adj* (*weather*) mite, clemente

clench [klɛntʃ] *vt* stringere

clergy ['klə:dʒɪ] *n* clero

clergyman ['klə:dʒɪmən] *n* ecclesiastico

clerical ['klɛrɪkl] *adj* d'impiegato; (*Rel*) clericale

clerk [klɑ:k, (*US*) klə:rk] *n* impiegato(-a); (*US: salesman/woman*) commesso(-a); **C~ of the Court** (*Law*) cancelliere *m*

clever ['klɛvə^r] *adj* (*mentally*) intelligente; (*deft, skilful*) abile; (*device, arrangement*) ingegnoso(-a)

cleverly ['klɛvəlɪ] *adv* abilmente

clew [klu:] *n* (*US*) = **clue**

cliché ['kli:ʃeɪ] *n* cliché *m inv*

click [klɪk] *vi* scattare ▪ *vt*: **to ~ one's tongue** schioccare la lingua; **to ~ one's heels** battere i tacchi

clickable ['klɪkəbl] *adj* cliccabile

client ['klaɪənt] *n* cliente *m/f*

clientele [kli:ā:n'tɛl] *n* clientela

cliff [klɪf] *n* scogliera scoscesa, rupe *f*

cliffhanger ['klɪfhæŋə^r] *n* (*TV, fig*) episodio (*or situazione etc*) ricco(-a) di suspense

climactic [klaɪ'mæktɪk] *adj* culminante

climate ['klaɪmɪt] *n* clima *m*

climate change *n* cambiamenti *mpl* climatici

climax ['klaɪmæks] *n* culmine *m*; (*of play etc*) momento più emozionante; (*sexual climax*) orgasmo

climb [klaɪm] *vi* salire; (*clamber*) arrampicarsi; (*plane*) prendere quota ▪ *vt* salire; (*Climbing*) scalare ▪ *n* salita; arrampicata; scalata; **to ~ over a wall** scavalcare un muro

▸ **climb down** *vi* scendere; (*Brit fig*) far marcia indietro

climbdown ['klaɪmdaun] *n* (*Brit*) ritirata

climber ['klaɪmə^r] *n* (*also*: **rock climber**) rocciatore(-trice); alpinista *m/f*

climbing ['klaɪmɪŋ] *n* (*also*: **rock climbing**) alpinismo

clinch [klɪntʃ] *vt* (*deal*) concludere

clincher ['klɪntʃə^r] *n* (*col*): **that was the ~** quello è stato il fattore decisivo

cling (*pt, pp* **clung**) [klɪŋ, klʌŋ] *vi*: **to ~ (to)** tenersi stretto(-a) (a); (*clothes*) aderire strettamente (a)

clingfilm ['klɪŋfɪlm] *n* pellicola trasparente (*per alimenti*)

clinic ['klɪnɪk] *n* clinica; (*session*) seduta; serie *f* di sedute

clinical ['klɪnɪkəl] *adj* clinico(-a); (*fig*) freddo(-a), distaccato(-a)

clink [klɪŋk] *vi* tintinnare

clip [klɪp] *n* (*for hair*) forcina; (*also*: **paper clip**) graffetta; (*Brit: also*: **bulldog clip**) fermafogli *m inv*; (*holding hose etc*) anello d'attacco ▪ *vt* (*also*: **clip together**: *papers*) attaccare insieme; (*hair, nails*) tagliare; (*hedge*) tosare

clippers ['klɪpəz] *npl* macchinetta per capelli; (*also*: **nail clippers**) forbicine *fpl* per le unghie

clipping ['klɪpɪŋ] *n* (*from newspaper*) ritaglio

clique [kliːk] *n* cricca

cloak [kləuk] *n* mantello ▪ *vt* avvolgere

cloakroom ['kləukrum] *n* (*for coats etc*) guardaroba *m inv*; (*Brit: W.C.*) gabinetti *mpl*

clock [klɔk] *n* orologio; (*of taxi*) tassametro; **around the ~** ventiquattr'ore su ventiquattro; **to sleep round the ~** *or* **the ~-round** dormire un giorno intero; **to work against the ~** lavorare in gara col tempo; **30,000 on the ~** (*Brit Aut*) 30.000 sul contachilometri
  ▶ **clock in, clock on** *vi* (*Brit*) timbrare il cartellino (all'entrata)
  ▶ **clock off, clock out** *vi* (*Brit*) timbrare il cartellino (all'uscita)
  ▶ **clock up** *vt* (*miles, hours etc*) fare

clockwise ['klɔkwaɪz] *adv* in senso orario

clockwork ['klɔkwəːk] *n* movimento *or* meccanismo a orologeria ▪ *adj* (*toy, train*) a molla

clog [klɔg] *n* zoccolo ▪ *vt* intasare ▪ *vi* intasarsi, bloccarsi

cloister ['klɔɪstəʳ] *n* chiostro

clone [kləun] *n* clone *m* ▪ *vt* clonare

close¹ [kləus] *adj* vicino(-a); (*writing, texture*) fitto(-a); (*watch*) stretto(-a); (*examination*) attento(-a); (*weather*) afoso(-a) ▪ *adv* vicino, dappresso; **~ to** *prep* vicino a; **~ by, ~ at hand** qui (*or* lì) vicino; **how ~ is Edinburgh to Glasgow?** quanto dista Edimburgo da Glasgow? **a ~ friend** un amico intimo; **to have a ~ shave** (*fig*) scamparla bella; **at ~ quarters** da vicino

close² [kləuz] *vt* chiudere; (*bargain, deal*) concludere ▪ *vi* (*shop etc*) chiudere; (*lid, door etc*) chiudersi; (*end*) finire ▪ *n* (*end*) fine *f*; **to bring sth to a ~** terminare qc
  ▶ **close down** *vt* chiudere (definitivamente) ▪ *vi* cessare (definitivamente)
  ▶ **close in** *vi* (*hunters*) stringersi attorno; (*evening, night, fog*) calare; **to ~ in on sb** accerchiare qn; **the days are closing in** le giornate si accorciano
  ▶ **close off** *vt* (*area*) chiudere

closed [kləuzd] *adj* chiuso(-a)

closed-circuit ['kləuzd'səːkɪt] *adj*: **~ television** televisione *f* a circuito chiuso

closed shop *n* azienda *o* fabbrica che impiega solo aderenti ai sindacati

close-knit ['kləus'nɪt] *adj* (*family, community*) molto unito(-a)

closely ['kləuslɪ] *adv* (*examine, watch*) da vicino; **we are ~ related** siamo parenti stretti; **a ~ guarded secret** un assoluto segreto

close season ['kləuz-] *n* (*Football*) periodo di vacanza del campionato; (*Hunting*) stagione *f* di chiusura (*di caccia, pesca etc*)

closet ['klɔzɪt] *n* (*cupboard*) armadio

close-up ['kləusʌp] *n* primo piano

closing ['kləuzɪŋ] *adj* (*stages, remarks*) conclusivo(-a), finale; **~ price** (*Stock Exchange*) prezzo di chiusura

closing time *n* orario di chiusura

closure ['kləuʒəʳ] *n* chiusura

clot [klɔt] *n* (*also*: **blood clot**) coagulo; (*col: idiot*) scemo(-a) ▪ *vi* coagularsi

cloth [klɔθ] *n* (*material*) tessuto, stoffa; (*Brit: also*: **teacloth**) strofinaccio; (*also*: **tablecloth**) tovaglia

clothe [kləuð] *vt* vestire

clothes [kləuðz] *npl* abiti *mpl*, vestiti *mpl*; **to put one's ~ on** vestirsi; **to take one's ~ off** togliersi i vestiti, svestirsi

clothes brush *n* spazzola per abiti

clothes line *n* corda (per stendere il bucato)

clothes peg, (*US*) **clothes pin** *n* molletta

clothing ['kləuðɪŋ] *n* = **clothes**

clotted cream ['klɔtɪd-] *n* (*Brit*) panna rappresa

cloud [klaud] *n* nuvola; (*of dust, smoke, gas*) nube *f* ▪ *vt* (*liquid*) intorbidire; **to ~ the issue** distogliere dal problema; **every ~ has a silver lining** (*proverb*) non tutto il male vien per nuocere
  ▶ **cloud over** *vi* rannuvolarsi; (*fig*) offuscarsi

cloudburst ['klaudbəːst] *n* acquazzone *m*

cloud-cuckoo-land ['klaud'kuku:'lænd] *n* (*Brit*) mondo dei sogni

cloudy ['klaudɪ] *adj* nuvoloso(-a); (*liquid*) torbido(-a)

clout [klaut] *n* (*blow*) colpo; (*fig*) influenza ▪ *vt* dare un colpo a

clove [kləuv] *n* chiodo di garofano; **~ of garlic** spicchio d'aglio

clover ['kləuvəʳ] *n* trifoglio

cloverleaf ['kləuvəli:f] *n* foglia di trifoglio; (*Aut*) raccordo (a quadrifoglio)

clown [klaun] *n* pagliaccio ▪ *vi* (*also*: **clown about, clown around**) fare il pagliaccio

cloying ['klɔɪɪŋ] *adj* (*taste, smell*) nauseabondo(-a)

club [klʌb] *n* (*society*) club *m inv*, circolo; (*weapon, Golf*) mazza ▪ *vt* bastonare ▪ *vi*:

to ~ **together** associarsi; **clubs** npl (Cards) fiori mpl

club car n (US Rail) carrozza or vagone m ristorante

club class n (Aviat) classe f club

clubhouse ['klʌbhaus] n sede f del circolo

club soda n (US) = **soda**

cluck [klʌk] vi chiocciare

clue [kluː] n indizio; (in crosswords) definizione f; **I haven't a ~** non ho la minima idea

clued up, (US) **clued in** [kluːd-] adj (col) (ben) informato(-a)

clump [klʌmp] n: ~ **of trees** folto d'alberi

clumsy ['klʌmzɪ] adj (person) goffo(-a), maldestro(-a); (object) malfatto(-a), mal costruito(-a)

clung [klʌŋ] pt, pp of **cling**

cluster ['klʌstəʳ] n gruppo ▪ vi raggrupparsi

clutch [klʌtʃ] n (grip, grasp) presa, stretta; (Aut) frizione f ▪ vt afferrare, stringere forte; **to ~ at** aggrapparsi a

clutter ['klʌtəʳ] vt (also: **clutter up**) ingombrare ▪ n confusione f, disordine m

cm abbr (= centimetre) cm

CNAA n abbr (Brit: = Council for National Academic Awards) organizzazione che conferisce premi accademici

CND n abbr (Brit) = **Campaign for Nuclear Disarmament**

CO n abbr (= commanding officer) Com.; (Brit) = **Commonwealth Office** ▪ abbr (US) = **Colorado**

Co. abbr = **county**; (= company) C., C.ia

c/o abbr (= care of) c/o

coach [kəutʃ] n (bus) pullman m inv; (horse-drawn, of train) carrozza; (Sport) allenatore(-trice) ▪ vt allenare

coach trip n viaggio in pullman

coagulate [kəu'ægjuleɪt] vt coagulare ▪ vi coagularsi

coal [kəul] n carbone m

coalface ['kəulfeɪs] n fronte f

coalfield ['kəulfiːld] n bacino carbonifero

coalition [kəuə'lɪʃən] n coalizione f

coalman ['kəulmən] n negoziante m di carbone

coalmine ['kəulmaɪn] n miniera di carbone

coalminer ['kəulmaɪnəʳ] n minatore m

coalmining ['kəulmaɪnɪŋ] n estrazione f del carbone

coarse [kɔːs] adj (salt, sand etc) grosso(-a); (cloth, person) rozzo(-a); (vulgar: character, laugh) volgare

coast [kəust] n costa ▪ vi (with cycle etc) scendere a ruota libera

coastal ['kəustəl] adj costiero(-a)

coaster ['kəustəʳ] n (Naut) nave f da cabotaggio; (for glass) sottobicchiere m

coastguard ['kəustgɑːd] n guardia costiera

coastline ['kəustlaɪn] n linea costiera

coat [kəut] n cappotto; (of animal) pelo; (of paint) mano f ▪ vt coprire; ~ **of arms** n stemma m

coat hanger n attaccapanni m inv

coating ['kəutɪŋ] n rivestimento

co-author ['kəu'ɔːθəʳ] n coautore(-trice)

coax [kəuks] vt indurre (con moine)

cob [kɔb] n see **corn**

cobbler ['kɔbləʳ] n calzolaio

cobbles ['kɔblz], **cobblestones** ['kɔblstəunz] npl ciottoli mpl

COBOL ['kəubɔl] n COBOL m

cobra ['kəubrə] n cobra m inv

cobweb ['kɔbwɛb] n ragnatela

cocaine [kə'keɪn] n cocaina

cock [kɔk] n (rooster) gallo; (male bird) maschio ▪ vt (gun) armare; **to ~ one's ears** (fig) drizzare le orecchie

cock-a-hoop [kɔkə'huːp] adj euforico(-a)

cockerel ['kɔkərəl] n galletto

cock-eyed ['kɔkaɪd] adj (fig) storto(-a); strampalato(-a)

cockle ['kɔkl] n cardio

cockney ['kɔknɪ] n cockney m/f inv (abitante dei quartieri popolari dell'East End di Londra)

cockpit ['kɔkpɪt] n abitacolo

cockroach ['kɔkrəutʃ] n blatta

cocktail ['kɔkteɪl] n cocktail m inv; **prawn ~**, (US) **shrimp ~** cocktail m inv di gamberetti

cocktail cabinet n mobile m bar inv

cocktail party n cocktail m inv

cocktail shaker n shaker m inv

cocky ['kɔkɪ] adj spavaldo(-a), arrogante

cocoa ['kəukəu] n cacao

coconut ['kəukənʌt] n noce f di cocco

cocoon [kə'kuːn] n bozzolo

COD abbr = **cash on delivery**; (US) = **collect on delivery**

cod [kɔd] n merluzzo

code [kəud] n codice m; ~ **of behaviour** regole fpl di condotta; ~ **of practice** codice professionale

codeine ['kəudiːn] n codeina

codger ['kɔdʒəʳ] n (Brit col): **an old ~** un simpatico nonnetto

codicil ['kɔdɪsɪl] n codicillo

codify ['kəudɪfaɪ] vt codificare

cod-liver oil ['kɔdlɪvəʳ-] n olio di fegato di merluzzo

co-driver ['kəu'draɪvəʳ] n (in race) copilota m; (of lorry) secondo autista m

co-ed ['kəu'ɛd] adj abbr = **coeducational** ▪ n abbr (US: female student) studentessa presso un'università mista; (Brit: school) scuola mista

coeducational [ˈkəʊɛdjuˈkeɪʃənl] *adj* misto(-a)

coerce [kəʊˈəːs] *vt* costringere

coercion [kəʊˈəːʃən] *n* coercizione *f*

coexistence [ˈkəʊɪgˈzɪstəns] *n* coesistenza

C. of C. *n abbr* = **chamber of commerce**

C of E *abbr* = **Church of England**

coffee [ˈkɔfɪ] *n* caffè *m inv*; **white ~**, (US)
~ with cream caffellatte *m*

coffee bar *n* (Brit) caffè *m inv*

coffee bean *n* grano *or* chicco di caffè

coffee break *n* pausa per il caffè

coffeecake [ˈkɔfɪkeɪk] *n* (US) panino dolce
all'uva

coffee cup *n* tazzina da caffè

coffeepot [ˈkɔfɪpɔt] *n* caffettiera

coffee table *n* tavolino da tè

coffin [ˈkɔfɪn] *n* bara

C of I *abbr* = **Church of Ireland**

C of S *abbr* = **Church of Scotland**

cog [kɔg] *n* dente *m*

cogent [ˈkəʊdʒənt] *adj* convincente

cognac [ˈkɔnjæk] *n* cognac *m inv*

cogwheel [ˈkɔgwiːl] *n* ruota dentata

cohabit [kəʊˈhæbɪt] *vi* (formal): **to ~ (with sb)**
coabitare (con qn)

coherent [kəʊˈhɪərənt] *adj* coerente

cohesion [kəʊˈhiːʒən] *n* coesione *f*

cohesive [kəʊˈhiːsɪv] *adj* (fig) unificante,
coesivo(-a)

COI *n abbr* (Brit) = **Central Office of
Information**

coil [kɔɪl] *n* rotolo; (one loop) anello; (Aut, Elec)
bobina; (contraceptive) spirale *f*; (of smoke) filo
■ *vt* avvolgere

coin [kɔɪn] *n* moneta ■ *vt* (word) coniare

coinage [ˈkɔɪnɪdʒ] *n* sistema *m* monetario

coin-box [ˈkɔɪnbɔks] *n* (Brit) cabina telefonica

coincide [kəʊɪnˈsaɪd] *vi* coincidere

coincidence [kəʊˈɪnsɪdəns] *n*
combinazione *f*

coin-operated [ˈkɔɪnˈɔpəreɪtɪd] *adj* (machine)
(che funziona) a monete

Coke® [kəʊk] *n* (Coca-Cola) coca *f inv*

coke [kəʊk] *n* coke *m*

Col. *abbr* = **colonel**; (US) = **Colorado**

COLA *n abbr* (US: = cost-of-living adjustment)
≈ scala mobile

colander [ˈkɔləndər] *n* colino

cold [kəʊld] *adj* freddo(-a) ■ *n* freddo; (Med)
raffreddore *m*; **it's ~** fa freddo; **to be ~** aver
freddo; **to catch ~** prendere freddo; **to catch
a ~** prendere un raffreddore; **in ~ blood** a
sangue freddo; **to have ~ feet** avere i piedi
freddi; (fig) aver la fifa; **to give sb the ~
shoulder** ignorare qn

cold-blooded [kəʊldˈblʌdɪd] *adj* (Zool) a
sangue freddo

cold call *n* chiamata pubblicitaria non
richiesta

cold cream *n* crema emolliente

coldly [ˈkəʊldlɪ] *adv* freddamente

cold sore *n* erpete *m*

cold sweat *n*: **to be in a ~ (about sth)** sudare
freddo (per qc)

cold turkey *n* (col): **to go ~** avere la scimmia
(drogato)

Cold War *n*: **the ~** la guerra fredda

coleslaw [ˈkəʊlslɔː] *n* insalata di cavolo bianco

colic [ˈkɔlɪk] *n* colica

colicky [ˈkɔlɪkɪ] *adj* che soffre di coliche

collaborate [kəˈlæbəreɪt] *vi* collaborare

collaboration [kəlæbəˈreɪʃən] *n*
collaborazione *f*

collaborator [kəˈlæbəreɪtər] *n*
collaboratore(-trice)

collage [kɔˈlɑːʒ] *n* (Art) collage *m inv*

collagen [ˈkɔlədʒən] *n* collageno

collapse [kəˈlæps] *vi* (gen) crollare;
(government) cadere; (Med) avere un collasso;
(plans) fallire ■ *n* crollo, caduta, collasso;
fallimento

collapsible [kəˈlæpsəbl] *adj* pieghevole

collar [ˈkɔlər] *n* (of coat, shirt) colletto; (for dog)
collare *m*; (Tech) anello, fascetta ■ *vt* (col:
person, object) beccare

collarbone [ˈkɔləbəʊn] *n* clavicola

collate [kɔˈleɪt] *vt* collazionare

collateral [kɔˈlætərəl] *n* garanzia

collation [kɔˈleɪʃən] *n* collazione *f*

colleague [ˈkɔliːg] *n* collega *m/f*

collect [kəˈlɛkt] *vt* (gen) raccogliere; (as a
hobby) fare collezione di; (Brit: call for)
prendere; (money owed, pension) riscuotere;
(donations, subscriptions) fare una colletta di
■ *vi* (people) adunarsi, riunirsi; (rubbish etc)
ammucchiarsi ■ *adv* (US Tel): **to call ~** fare
una chiamata a carico del destinatario; **to ~
one's thoughts** raccogliere le idee; **~ on
delivery** (US Comm) pagamento alla consegna

collected [kəˈlɛktɪd] *adj*: **~ works** opere *fpl*
raccolte

collection [kəˈlɛkʃən] *n* collezione *f*; raccolta;
(for money) colletta; (Post) levata

collective [kəˈlɛktɪv] *adj* collettivo(-a)
■ *n* collettivo

collective bargaining *n* trattative *fpl*
(sindacali) collettive

collector [kəˈlɛktər] *n* collezionista *m/f*; (of
taxes) esattore *m*; **~'s item** *or* **piece** pezzo da
collezionista

college [ˈkɔlɪdʒ] *n* (Scol) college *m inv*; (of
technology, agriculture etc) istituto superiore;
(body) collegio; **~ of education** ≈ facoltà *f inv*
di Magistero

collide [kə'laɪd] *vi*: **to ~ (with)** scontrarsi (con)

collie ['kɔlɪ] *n* (*dog*) collie *m inv*

colliery ['kɔlɪərɪ] *n* (*Brit*) miniera di carbone

collision [kə'lɪʒən] *n* collisione *f*, scontro; **to be on a ~ course** (*also fig*) essere in rotta di collisione

collision damage waiver *n* (*Insurance*) copertura per i danni alla vettura

colloquial [kə'ləukwɪəl] *adj* familiare

collusion [kə'luːʒən] *n* collusione *f*; **in ~ with** in accordo segreto con

Colo. *abbr* (*US*) = **Colorado**

Cologne [kə'ləun] *n* Colonia

cologne [kə'ləun] *n* (*also*: **eau de cologne**) acqua di colonia

Colombia [kə'lɔmbɪə] *n* Colombia

Colombian [kə'lɔmbɪən] *adj, n* colombiano(-a)

colon ['kəulən] *n* (*sign*) due punti *mpl*; (*Med*) colon *m inv*

colonel ['kəːnl] *n* colonnello

colonial [kə'ləunɪəl] *adj* coloniale

colonize ['kɔlənaɪz] *vt* colonizzare

colony ['kɔlənɪ] *n* colonia

color *etc* ['kʌlər] (*US*) = **colour** *etc*

Colorado beetle [kɔlə'rɑːdəu-] *n* dorifora

colossal [kə'lɔsl] *adj* colossale

colour, (*US*) **color** ['kʌlər] *n* colore *m* ∎ *vt* colorare; (*tint, dye*) tingere; (*fig: affect*) influenzare ∎ *vi* arrossire ∎ *cpd* (*film, photograph, television*) a colori; **colours** *npl* (*of party, club*) emblemi *mpl*

colour bar, (*US*) **color bar** *n* discriminazione *f* razziale (*in locali etc*)

colour-blind, (*US*) **color-blind** ['kʌləblaɪnd] *adj* daltonico(-a)

coloured, (*US*) **colored** ['kʌləd] *adj* colorato(-a); (*photo*) a colori ∎ *n*: **colo(u)reds** gente *f* di colore

colour film, (*US*) **color film** *n* (*for camera*) pellicola a colori

colourful, (*US*) **colorful** ['kʌləful] *adj* pieno(-a) di colore, a vivaci colori; (*personality*) colorato(-a)

colouring, (*US*) **coloring** ['kʌlərɪŋ] *n* colorazione *f*; (*complexion*) colorito

colour scheme, (*US*) **color scheme** *n* combinazione *f* di colori

colour supplement *n* (*Brit Press*) supplemento a colori

colour television, (*US*) **color television** *n* televisione *f* a colori

colt [kəult] *n* puledro

column ['kɔləm] *n* colonna; (*fashion column, sports column etc*) rubrica; **the editorial ~** l'articolo di fondo

columnist ['kɔləmnɪst] *n* articolista *m/f*

coma ['kəumə] *n* coma *m inv*

comb [kəum] *n* pettine *m* ∎ *vt* (*hair*) pettinare; (*area*) battere a tappeto

combat ['kɔmbæt] *n* combattimento ∎ *vt* combattere, lottare contro

combination [kɔmbɪ'neɪʃən] *n* combinazione *f*

combination lock *n* serratura a combinazione

combine [kəm'baɪn] *vt* combinare; (*one quality with another*): **to ~ sth with sth** unire qc a qc ∎ *vi* unirsi; (*Chem*) combinarsi ∎ *n* ['kɔmbaɪn] lega; (*Econ*) associazione *f*; **a combined effort** uno sforzo collettivo

combine, combine harvester *n* mietitrebbia

combo ['kɔmbəu] *n* (*Jazz etc*) gruppo

combustible [kəm'bʌstɪbl] *adj* combustibile

combustion [kəm'bʌstʃən] *n* combustione *f*

come (*pt* **came**, *pp* **~**) [kʌm, keɪm] *vi* venire; (*arrive*) venire, arrivare; **~ with me** vieni con me; **we've just ~ from Paris** siamo appena arrivati da Parigi; **nothing came of it** non è saltato fuori niente; **to ~ into sight** *or* **view** apparire; **to ~ to** (*decision etc*) raggiungere; **to ~ undone/loose** slacciarsi/allentarsi; **coming!** vengo!; **if it comes to it** nella peggiore delle ipotesi

▶ **come about** *vi* succedere

▶ **come across** *vt fus* trovare per caso ∎ *vi*: **to ~ across well/badly** fare una buona/cattiva impressione

▶ **come along** *vi* (*pupil, work*) fare progressi; **~ along!** avanti!, andiamo!, forza!

▶ **come apart** *vi* andare in pezzi; (*become detached*) staccarsi

▶ **come away** *vi* venire via; (*become detached*) staccarsi

▶ **come back** *vi* ritornare; (*reply: col*): **can I ~ back to you on that one?** possiamo riparlarne più tardi?

▶ **come by** *vt fus* (*acquire*) ottenere; procurarsi

▶ **come down** *vi* scendere; (*prices*) calare; (*buildings*) essere demolito(-a)

▶ **come forward** *vi* farsi avanti; presentarsi

▶ **come from** *vt fus* venire da; provenire da

▶ **come in** *vi* entrare

▶ **come in for** *vt fus* (*criticism etc*) ricevere

▶ **come into** *vt fus* (*money*) ereditare

▶ **come off** *vi* (*button*) staccarsi; (*stain*) andar via; (*attempt*) riuscire

▶ **come on** *vi* (*lights, electricity*) accendersi; (*pupil, undertaking*) fare progressi; **~ on!** avanti!, andiamo!, forza!

▶ **come out** *vi* uscire; (*strike*) entrare in sciopero

487

▶ **come over** *vt fus:* **I don't know what's ~ over him!** non so cosa gli sia successo!

▶ **come round** *vi (after faint, operation)* riprendere conoscenza, rinvenire

▶ **come through** *vi (survive)* sopravvivere, farcela; **the call came through** ci hanno passato la telefonata

▶ **come to** *vi* rinvenire ■ *vt (add up to: amount):* **how much does it ~ to?** quanto costa?, quanto viene?

▶ **come under** *vt fus (heading)* trovarsi sotto; *(influence)* cadere sotto, subire

▶ **come up** *vi* venire su

▶ **come up against** *vt fus (resistance, difficulties)* urtare contro

▶ **come up to** *vt fus* arrivare (fino) a; **the film didn't ~ up to our expectations** il film ci ha delusi

▶ **come up with** *vt fus:* **he came up with an idea** venne fuori con un'idea

▶ **come upon** *vt fus* trovare per caso

comeback ['kʌmbæk] *n (Theat etc)* ritorno; *(reaction)* reazione *f; (response)* risultato, risposta

comedian [kə'miːdɪən] *n* comico

comedienne [kəmi:dɪ'ɛn] *n* attrice *f* comica

comedown ['kʌmdaun] *n* rovescio

comedy ['kɔmɪdɪ] *n* commedia

comet ['kɔmɪt] *n* cometa

comeuppance [kʌm'ʌpəns] *n:* **to get one's ~** ricevere ciò che si merita

comfort ['kʌmfət] *n* comodità *f inv,* benessere *m; (solace)* consolazione *f,* conforto ■ *vt* consolare, confortare; *see also* **comforts**

comfortable ['kʌmfətəbl] *adj* comodo(-a); *(income, majority)* più che sufficiente; **I don't feel very ~ about it** non mi sento molto tranquillo

comfortably ['kʌmfətəblɪ] *adv (sit)* comodamente; *(live)* bene

comforter ['kʌmfətər] *n (US)* trapunta

comforts ['kʌmfəts] *npl* comforts *mpl,* comodità *fpl*

comfort station *n (US)* gabinetti *mpl*

comic ['kɔmɪk] *adj* comico(-a) ■ *n* comico; *(magazine)* giornaletto

comical ['kɔmɪkl] *adj* divertente, buffo(-a)

comic strip *n* fumetto

coming ['kʌmɪŋ] *n* arrivo ■ *adj (next)* prossimo(-a); *(future)* futuro(-a); **in the ~ weeks** nelle prossime settimane

comings and goings *npl,* **coming and going** *n* andirivieni *m inv*

Comintern ['kɔmɪntəːn] *n* KOMINTERN *m*

comma ['kɔmə] *n* virgola

command [kə'mɑːnd] *n* ordine *m,* comando; *(Mil: authority)* comando; *(mastery)* padronanza; *(Comput)* command *m inv,* comando ■ *vt* comandare; **to ~ sb to do** ordinare a qn di fare; **to have/take ~ of** avere/prendere il comando di; **to have at one's ~** *(money, resources etc)* avere a propria disposizione

command economy *n =* **planned economy**

commandeer [kɔmən'dɪər] *vt* requisire

commander [kə'mɑːndər] *n* capo; *(Mil)* comandante *m*

commander-in-chief [kə'mɑːndərɪn'tʃiːf] *n (Mil)* comandante *m* in capo

commanding [kə'mɑːndɪŋ] *adj (appearance)* imponente; *(voice, tone)* autorevole; *(lead, position)* dominante

commanding officer *n* comandante *m*

commandment [kə'mɑːndmənt] *n (Rel)* comandamento

command module *n (Space)* modulo di comando

commando [kə'mɑːndəu] *n* commando *m inv;* membro di un commando

commemorate [kə'mɛməreɪt] *vt* commemorare

commemoration [kəmɛmə'reɪʃən] *n* commemorazione *f*

commemorative [kə'mɛmərətɪv] *adj* commemorativo(-a)

commence [kə'mɛns] *vt, vi* cominciare

commend [kə'mɛnd] *vt* lodare; raccomandare

commendable [kə'mɛndəbl] *adj* lodevole

commendation [kɔmɛn'deɪʃən] *n* lode *f;* raccomandazione *f; (for bravery etc)* encomio

commensurate [kə'mɛnʃərɪt] *adj:* **~ with** proporzionato(-a) a

comment ['kɔment] *n* commento ■ *vi:* **to ~ (on)** fare commenti (su); **to ~ that** osservare che; **"no ~"** "niente da dire"

commentary ['kɔməntərɪ] *n* commentario; *(Sport)* radiocronaca; telecronaca

commentator ['kɔmənteɪtər] *n* commentatore(-trice); *(Sport)* radiocronista *m/f;* telecronista *m/f*

commerce ['kɔmə:s] *n* commercio

commercial [kə'mə:ʃəl] *adj* commerciale ■ *n (TV: also:* **commercial break)** pubblicità *f inv*

commercial bank *n* banca commerciale

commercial college *n ≈* istituto commerciale

commercialism [kə'mə:ʃəlɪzəm] *n* affarismo

commercial television *n* televisione *f* commerciale

commercial traveller *n* commesso viaggiatore

commercial vehicle *n* veicolo commerciale

commiserate [kə'mɪzəreɪt] *vi:* **to ~ with**

condolersi con

commission [kə'mɪʃən] *n* commissione *f*; (*for salesman*) commissione, provvigione *f* ■ *vt* (*Mil*) nominare (al comando); (*work of art*) commissionare; **I get 10%** ~ ricevo il 10% sulle vendite; **out of** ~ (*Naut*) in disarmo; (*machine*) fuori uso; **to** ~ **sb to do sth** incaricare qn di fare qc; **to** ~ **sth from sb** (*painting etc*) commissionare qc a qn; ~ **of inquiry** (*Brit*) commissione *f* d'inchiesta

commissionaire [kəmɪʃə'nɛəʳ] *n* (*Brit: at shop, cinema etc*) portiere *m* in livrea

commissioner [kə'mɪʃənəʳ] *n* commissionario; (*Police*) questore *m*

commit [kə'mɪt] *vt* (*act*) commettere; (*to sb's care*) affidare; **to** ~ **o.s.** (**to do**) impegnarsi (a fare); **to** ~ **suicide** suicidarsi; **to** ~ **sb for trial** rinviare qn a giudizio

commitment [kə'mɪtmənt] *n* impegno

committed [kə'mɪtɪd] *adj* (*writer*) impegnato(-a); (*Christian*) convinto(-a)

committee [kə'mɪtɪ] *n* comitato; **to be on a** ~ far parte di un comitato *or* di una commissione

committee meeting *n* riunione *f* di comitato *or* di commissione

commodity [kə'mɔdɪtɪ] *n* prodotto, articolo; (*food*) derrata

commodity exchange *n* borsa *f* merci *inv*

common ['kɔmən] *adj* comune; (*pej*) volgare; (*usual*) normale ■ *n* terreno comune; **in** ~ in comune; **in** ~ **use** di uso comune; **it's** ~ **knowledge that** è di dominio pubblico che; **to the** ~ **good** nell'interesse generale, per il bene comune; *see also* **Commons**

common cold *n*: **the** ~ il raffreddore

common denominator *n* denominatore *m* comune

commoner ['kɔmənəʳ] *n* cittadino(-a) (non nobile)

common ground *n* (*fig*) terreno comune

common land *n* terreno di uso pubblico

common law *n* diritto consuetudinario

common-law ['kɔmənlɔ:] *adj*: ~ **wife** convivente *f* more uxorio

commonly ['kɔmənlɪ] *adv* comunemente, usualmente

Common Market *n* Mercato Comune

commonplace ['kɔmənpleɪs] *adj* banale, ordinario(-a)

commonroom ['kɔmənrum] *n* sala di riunione; (*Scol*) sala dei professori

Commons ['kɔmənz] *npl* (*Brit Pol*): **the (House of)** ~ la Camera dei Comuni

common sense *n* buon senso

Commonwealth ['kɔmənwɛlθ] *n*: **the** ~ il Commonwealth; *vedi nota*

commotion [kə'məʊʃən] *n* confusione *f*, tumulto

communal ['kɔmju:nl] *adj* (*life*) comunale; (*for common use*) pubblico(-a)

commune *n* ['kɔmju:n] (*group*) comune *f* ■ *vi* [kə'mju:n]: **to** ~ **with** mettersi in comunione con

communicate [kə'mju:nɪkeɪt] *vt* comunicare, trasmettere ■ *vi*: **to** ~ **(with)** comunicare (con)

communication [kəmju:nɪ'keɪʃən] *n* comunicazione *f*

communication cord *n* (*Brit*) segnale *m* d'allarme

communications network *n* rete *f* delle comunicazioni

communications satellite *n* satellite *m* per telecomunicazioni

communicative [kə'mju:nɪkətɪv] *adj* (*gen*) loquace

communion [kə'mju:nɪən] *n* (*also*: **Holy Communion**) comunione *f*

communiqué [kə'mju:nɪkeɪ] *n* comunicato

communism ['kɔmjunɪzəm] *n* comunismo

communist ['kɔmjunɪst] *adj*, *n* comunista (*m/f*)

community [kə'mju:nɪtɪ] *n* comunità *f inv*

community centre *n* circolo ricreativo

community chest *n* (*US*) fondo di beneficenza

community health centre *n* centro socio-sanitario

community home *n* (*Brit*) riformatorio

community service *n* (*Brit*) ≈ lavoro sostitutivo

community spirit *n* spirito civico

commutation ticket [kɔmju'teɪʃən-] *n* (*US*) biglietto di abbonamento

commute [kə'mju:t] *vi* fare il pendolare ■ *vt* (*Law*) commutare

commuter [kə'mju:təʳ] *n* pendolare *m/f*

compact *adj* [kəm'pækt] compatto(-a) ■ *n* ['kɔmpækt] (*also*: **powder compact**) portacipria *m inv*

compact disc *n* compact disc *m inv*; ~ **player** lettore *m* CD *inv*

companion [kəm'pænjən] *n* compagno(-a)
companionship [kəm'pænjənʃɪp] *n*
compagnia
companionway [kəm'pænjənweɪ] *n* (*Naut*)
scala
company ['kʌmpənɪ] *n* (*also Comm, Mil, Theat*)
compagnia; **he's good ~** è di buona
compagnia; **we have ~** abbiamo ospiti; **to
keep sb ~** tenere compagnia a qn; **to part ~
with** separarsi da; **Smith and C~** Smith e soci
company car *n* macchina (di proprietà) della
ditta
company director *n* amministratore *m*,
consigliere *m* di amministrazione
company secretary *n* (*Brit Comm*)
segretario(-a) generale
comparable ['kɒmpərəbl] *adj* comparabile
comparative [kəm'pærətɪv] *adj* (*freedom, cost*)
relativo(-a); (*adjective, adverb etc*)
comparativo(-a); (*literature*) comparato(-a)
comparatively [kəm'pærətɪvlɪ] *adv*
relativamente
compare [kəm'pɛəʳ] *vt*: **to ~ sth/sb with/to**
confrontare qc/qn con/a ■ *vi*: **to ~ (with)**
reggere il confronto (con); **compared with**
or **to** a paragone di, rispetto a; **how do the
prices ~?** che differenza di prezzo c'è?
comparison [kəm'pærɪsn] *n* confronto;
in ~ (with) a confronto (di)
compartment [kəm'pɑːtmənt] *n*
compartimento; (*Rail*) scompartimento
compass ['kʌmpəs] *n* bussola; (**a pair of)
compasses** (*Math*) compasso; **within the ~
of** entro i limiti di
compassion [kəm'pæʃən] *n* compassione *f*
compassionate [kəm'pæʃənɪt] *adj*
compassionevole; **on ~ grounds** per motivi
personali
compassionate leave *n* congedo
straordinario (*per gravi motivi di famiglia*)
compatibility [kəmpætɪ'bɪlɪtɪ] *n*
compatibilità
compatible [kəm'pætɪbl] *adj* compatibile
compel [kəm'pɛl] *vt* costringere, obbligare
compelling [kəm'pɛlɪŋ] *adj* (*fig: argument*)
irresistibile
compendium [kəm'pɛndɪəm] *n* compendio
compensate ['kɒmpənseɪt] *vt* risarcire
■ *vi*: **to ~ for** compensare
compensation [kɒmpən'seɪʃən] *n*
compensazione *f*; (*money*) risarcimento
compère ['kɒmpɛəʳ] *n* presentatore(-trice)
compete [kəm'piːt] *vi* (*take part*) concorrere;
(*vie*): **to ~ (with)** fare concorrenza (a)
competence ['kɒmpɪtəns] *n* competenza
competent ['kɒmpɪtənt] *adj* competente
competing [kəm'piːtɪŋ] *adj* (*theories, ideas*)

opposto(-a); (*companies*) in concorrenza;
three ~ explanations (of) tre spiegazioni
contrastanti tra di loro (di)
competition [kɒmpɪ'tɪʃən] *n* gara, concorso;
(*Sport*) gara; (*Econ*) concorrenza; **in ~ with** in
concorrenza con
competitive [kəm'pɛtɪtɪv] *adj* (*sports*)
agonistico(-a); (*person*) che ha spirito di
competizione; (*Econ*) concorrenziale
competitive examination *n* concorso
competitor [kəm'pɛtɪtəʳ] *n* concorrente *m/f*
compile [kəm'paɪl] *vt* compilare
complacency [kəm'pleɪsnsɪ] *n* compiacenza
di sé
complacent [kəm'pleɪsnt] *adj*
compiaciuto(-a) di sé
complain [kəm'pleɪn] *vi*: **to ~ (about)**
lagnarsi (di); (*in shop etc*) reclamare (per)
▸ **complain of** *vt fus* (*Med*) accusare
complaint [kəm'pleɪnt] *n* lamento; reclamo;
(*Med*) malattia
complement *n* ['kɒmplɪmənt] complemento;
(*especially of ship's crew etc*) effettivo ■ *vt*
['kɒmplɪmɛnt] (*enhance*) accompagnarsi
bene a
complementary [kɒmplɪ'mɛntərɪ] *adj*
complementare
complete [kəm'pliːt] *adj* completo(-a) ■ *vt*
completare; (*form*) riempire; **it's a ~ disaster**
è un vero disastro
completely [kəm'pliːtlɪ] *adv* completamente
completion [kəm'pliːʃən] *n* completamento;
to be nearing ~ essere in fase di
completamento; **on ~ of contract** alla firma
del contratto
complex ['kɒmplɛks] *adj* complesso(-a)
■ *n* (*Psych, buildings etc*) complesso
complexion [kəm'plɛkʃən] *n* (*of face*)
carnagione *f*; (*of event etc*) aspetto
complexity [kəm'plɛksɪtɪ] *n* complessità *f inv*
compliance [kəm'plaɪəns] *n* acquiescenza;
in ~ with (*orders, wishes etc*) in conformità con
compliant [kəm'plaɪənt] *adj* acquiescente,
arrendevole
complicate ['kɒmplɪkeɪt] *vt* complicare
complicated ['kɒmplɪkeɪtɪd] *adj*
complicato(-a)
complication [kɒmplɪ'keɪʃən] *n*
complicazione *f*
compliment *n* ['kɒmplɪmənt] complimento
■ *vt* ['kɒmplɪmɛnt] fare un complimento a;
compliments *npl* complimenti *mpl*; rispetti
mpl; **to pay sb a ~** fare un complimento a qn;
to ~ sb (on sth/on doing sth) congratularsi
or complimentarsi con qn (per qc/per aver
fatto qc)
complimentary [kɒmplɪ'mɛntərɪ] *adj*

complimentoso(-a), elogiativo(-a); *(free)* in omaggio

complimentary ticket *n* biglietto d'omaggio

compliments slip *n* cartoncino della società

comply [kəm'plaɪ] *vi*: **to ~ with** assentire a; conformarsi a

component [kəm'pəunənt] *adj, n* componente *(m)*

compose [kəm'pəuz] *vt* comporre; **to ~ o.s.** ricomporsi; **composed of** composto(-a) di

composed [kəm'pəuzd] *adj* calmo(-a)

composer [kəm'pəuzər] *n (Mus)* compositore(-trice)

composite ['kɔmpəzɪt] *adj* composito(-a); *(Math)* composto(-a)

composition [kɔmpə'zɪʃən] *n* composizione *f*

compost ['kɔmpɔst] *n* composta, concime *m*

composure [kəm'pəuʒər] *n* calma

compound ['kɔmpaund] *n (Chem, Ling)* composto; *(enclosure)* recinto ■ *adj* composto(-a) ■ *vt* [kəm'paund] *(fig: problem, difficulty)* peggiorare

compound fracture *n* frattura esposta

compound interest *n* interesse *m* composto

comprehend [kɔmprɪ'hɛnd] *vt* comprendere, capire

comprehension [kɔmprɪ'hɛnʃən] *n* comprensione *f*

comprehensive [kɔmprɪ'hɛnsɪv] *adj* comprensivo(-a)

comprehensive insurance policy *n* polizza multi-rischio *inv*

comprehensive (school) *n (Brit) scuola secondaria aperta a tutti*

compress *vt* [kəm'prɛs] comprimere ■ *n* ['kɔmprɛs] *(Med)* compressa

compression [kəm'prɛʃən] *n* compressione *f*

comprise [kəm'praɪz] *vt (also: **be comprised of**)* comprendere

compromise ['kɔmprəmaɪz] *n* compromesso ■ *vt* compromettere ■ *vi* venire a un compromesso ■ *cpd (decision, solution)* di compromesso

compulsion [kəm'pʌlʃən] *n* costrizione *f*; **under ~** sotto pressioni

compulsive [kəm'pʌlsɪv] *adj (Psych)* incontrollabile; **he's a ~ smoker** non riesce a controllarsi nel fumare

compulsory [kəm'pʌlsərɪ] *adj* obbligatorio(-a)

compulsory purchase *n* espropriazione *f*

compunction [kəm'pʌŋkʃən] *n* scrupolo; **to have no ~ about doing sth** non farsi scrupoli a fare qc

computer [kəm'pju:tər] *n* computer *m inv*, elaboratore *m* elettronico

computer game *n* computer game *m inv*

computerization [kəmpju:təraɪ'zeɪʃən] *n* computerizzazione *f*

computerize [kəm'pju:təraɪz] *vt* computerizzare

computer language *n* linguaggio *m* macchina *inv*

computer literate *adj*: **to be ~** essere in grado di usare il computer

computer peripheral *n* unità periferica

computer program *n* programma *m* di computer

computer programmer *n* programmatore(-trice)

computer programming *n* programmazione *f* di computer

computer science *n* informatica

computer scientist *n* informatico(-a)

computing [kəm'pju:tɪŋ] *n* informatica

comrade ['kɔmrɪd] *n* compagno(-a)

comradeship ['kɔmrɪdʃɪp] *n* cameratismo

Comsat® ['kɔmsæt] *n abbr* = **communications satellite**

con [kɔn] *vt (col)* truffare ■ *n* truffa; **to ~ sb into doing sth** indurre qn a fare qc con raggiri

concave ['kɔnkeɪv] *adj* concavo(-a)

conceal [kən'si:l] *vt* nascondere

concede [kən'si:d] *vt* concedere ■ *vi* fare una concessione

conceit [kən'si:t] *n* presunzione *f*, vanità

conceited [kən'si:tɪd] *adj* presuntuoso(-a), vanitoso(-a)

conceivable [kən'si:vəbl] *adj* concepibile; **it is ~ that ...** può anche darsi che ...

conceivably [kən'si:vəblɪ] *adv*: **he may ~ be right** può anche darsi che abbia ragione

conceive [kən'si:v] *vt* concepire ■ *vi* concepire un bambino; **to ~ of sth/of doing sth** immaginare qc/di fare qc

concentrate ['kɔnsəntreɪt] *vi* concentrarsi ■ *vt* concentrare

concentration [kɔnsən'treɪʃən] *n* concentrazione *f*

concentration camp *n* campo di concentramento

concentric [kɔn'sɛntrɪk] *adj* concentrico(-a)

concept ['kɔnsɛpt] *n* concetto

conception [kən'sɛpʃən] *n* concezione *f*; *(idea)* idea, concetto

concern [kən'sə:n] *n* affare *m*; *(Comm)* azienda, ditta; *(anxiety)* preoccupazione *f* ■ *vt* riguardare; **to be concerned (about)** preoccuparsi (di); **to be concerned with** occuparsi di; **as far as I am concerned** per quanto mi riguarda; **"to whom it may ~"** "a tutti gli interessati"; **the department**

concerned (*under discussion*) l'ufficio in questione; (*relevant*) l'ufficio competente
concerning [kən'sɜ:nɪŋ] *prep* riguardo a, circa
concert ['kɔnsət] *n* concerto; **in** ~ di concerto
concerted [kən'sə:tɪd] *adj* concertato(-a)
concert hall *n* sala da concerti
concertina [kɔnsə'ti:nə] *n* piccola fisarmonica ■ *vi* ridursi come una fisarmonica
concerto [kən'tʃə:təu] *n* concerto
concession [kən'sɛʃən] *n* concessione *f*
concessionaire [kənsɛʃə'nɛəʳ] *n* concessionario
concessionary [kən'sɛʃənərɪ] *adj* (*ticket, fare*) a prezzo ridotto
conciliation [kənsɪlɪ'eɪʃən] *n* conciliazione *f*
conciliatory [kən'sɪlɪətrɪ] *adj* conciliativo(-a)
concise [kən'saɪs] *adj* conciso(-a)
conclave ['kɔnkleɪv] *n* riunione *f* segreta; (*Rel*) conclave *m*
conclude [kən'klu:d] *vt* concludere ■ *vi* (*speaker*) concludere; (*events*): **to** ~ (**with**) concludersi (con)
concluding [kən'klu:dɪŋ] *adj* (*remarks etc*) conclusivo(-a), finale
conclusion [kən'klu:ʒən] *n* conclusione *f*; **to come to the** ~ **that** ... concludere che ..., arrivare alla conclusione che ...
conclusive [kən'klu:sɪv] *adj* conclusivo(-a)
concoct [kən'kɔkt] *vt* inventare
concoction [kən'kɔkʃən] *n* (*food, drink*) miscuglio
concord ['kɔŋkɔ:d] *n* (*harmony*) armonia, concordia; (*treaty*) accordo
concourse ['kɔŋkɔ:s] *n* (*hall*) atrio
concrete ['kɔŋkri:t] *n* calcestruzzo ■ *adj* concreto(-a); (*Constr*) di calcestruzzo
concrete mixer *n* betoniera
concur [kən'kə:ʳ] *vi* concordare
concurrently [kən'kʌrntlɪ] *adv* simultaneamente
concussion [kən'kʌʃən] *n* (*Med*) commozione *f* cerebrale
condemn [kən'dɛm] *vt* condannare
condemnation [kɔndɛm'neɪʃən] *n* condanna
condensation [kɔndɛn'seɪʃən] *n* condensazione *f*
condense [kən'dɛns] *vi* condensarsi ■ *vt* condensare
condensed milk *n* latte *m* condensato
condescend [kɔndɪ'sɛnd] *vi* condiscendere; **to** ~ **to do sth** degnarsi di fare qc
condescending [kɔndɪ'sɛndɪŋ] *adj* condiscendente
condition [kən'dɪʃən] *n* condizione *f*; (*disease*) malattia ■ *vt* condizionare, regolare; **in good/poor** ~ in buone/cattive condizioni;

to have a heart ~ soffrire di (mal di) cuore; **weather conditions** condizioni meteorologiche; **on** ~ **that** a condizione che + *sub*, a condizione di
conditional [kən'dɪʃənl] *adj* condizionale; **to be** ~ **upon** dipendere da
conditioner [kən'dɪʃənəʳ] *n* (*for hair*) balsamo
condo ['kɔndəu] *n abbr* (*US col*) = **condominium**
condolences [kən'dəulənsɪz] *npl* condoglianze *fpl*
condom ['kɔndəm] *n* preservativo
condominium [kɔndə'mɪnɪəm] *n* (*US*) condominio
condone [kən'dəun] *vt* condonare
conducive [kən'dju:sɪv] *adj*: ~ **to** favorevole a
conduct *n* ['kɔndʌkt] condotta ■ *vt* [kən'dʌkt] condurre; (*manage*) dirigere; amministrare; (*Mus*) dirigere; **to** ~ **o.s.** comportarsi
conductor [kən'dʌktəʳ] *n* (*of orchestra*) direttore *m* d'orchestra; (*on bus*) bigliettaio; (*US Rail*) controllore *m*; (*Elec*) conduttore *m*
conductress [kən'dʌktrɪs] *n* (*on bus*) bigliettaia
conduit ['kɔndɪt] *n* condotto; tubo
cone [kəun] *n* cono; (*Bot*) pigna
confectioner [kən'fɛkʃənəʳ] *n*: ~'**s (shop)** ≈ pasticceria
confectionery [kən'fɛkʃənərɪ] *n* dolciumi *mpl*
confederate [kən'fɛdərɪt] *adj* confederato(-a) ■ *n* (*pej*) complice *m/f*; (*US Hist*) confederato
confederation [kənfɛdə'reɪʃən] *n* confederazione *f*
confer [kən'fə:ʳ] *vt*: **to** ~ **sth on** conferire qc a ■ *vi* conferire; **to** ~ (**with sb about sth**) consultarsi (con qn su qc)
conference ['kɔnfərns] *n* congresso; **to be in** ~ essere in riunione
conference room *n* sala *f* conferenze *inv*
confess [kən'fɛs] *vt* confessare, ammettere ■ *vi* confessarsi
confession [kən'fɛʃən] *n* confessione *f*
confessional [kən'fɛʃənl] *n* confessionale *m*
confessor [kən'fɛsəʳ] *n* confessore *m*
confetti [kən'fɛtɪ] *n* coriandoli *mpl*
confide [kən'faɪd] *vi*: **to** ~ **in** confidarsi con
confidence ['kɔnfɪdns] *n* confidenza; (*trust*) fiducia; (*also*: **self-confidence**) sicurezza di sé; **to tell sb sth in strict** ~ dire qc a qn in via strettamente confidenziale; **to have (every)** ~ **that** ... essere assolutamente certo(-a) che ...; **motion of no** ~ mozione *f* di sfiducia
confidence trick *n* truffa
confident ['kɔnfɪdənt] *adj* sicuro(-a); (*also*: **self-confident**) sicuro(-a) di sé
confidential [kɔnfɪ'dɛnʃəl] *adj* riservato(-a); (*secretary*) particolare

confidentiality [ˌkɒnfɪdɛnʃɪˈælɪtɪ] n riservatezza, carattere m confidenziale
configuration [kənˌfɪgjuˈreɪʃən] n (Comput) configurazione f
confine [kənˈfaɪn] vt limitare; (shut up) rinchiudere; **to ~ o.s. to doing sth** limitarsi a fare qc; see also **confines**
confined [kənˈfaɪnd] adj (space) ristretto(-a)
confinement [kənˈfaɪnmənt] n prigionia; (Mil) consegna; (Med) parto
confines [ˈkɒnfaɪnz] npl confini mpl
confirm [kənˈfəːm] vt confermare; (Rel) cresimare
confirmation [ˌkɒnfəˈmeɪʃən] n conferma; cresima
confirmed [kənˈfəːmd] adj inveterato(-a)
confiscate [ˈkɒnfɪskeɪt] vt confiscare
confiscation [ˌkɒnfɪsˈkeɪʃən] n confisca
conflagration [ˌkɒnfləˈgreɪʃən] n conflagrazione f
conflict n [ˈkɒnflɪkt] conflitto ■ vi [kənˈflɪkt] essere in conflitto
conflicting [kənˈflɪktɪŋ] adj contrastante; (reports, evidence, opinions) contraddittorio(-a)
conform [kənˈfɔːm] vi: **to ~ (to)** conformarsi (a)
conformist [kənˈfɔːmɪst] n conformista m/f
confound [kənˈfaund] vt confondere; (amaze) sconcertare
confounded [kənˈfaundɪd] adj maledetto(-a)
confront [kənˈfrʌnt] vt confrontare; (enemy, danger) affrontare
confrontation [ˌkɒnfrənˈteɪʃən] n scontro
confrontational [ˌkɒnfrənˈteɪʃənəl] adj polemico(-a), aggressivo(-a)
confuse [kənˈfjuːz] vt imbrogliare; (one thing with another) confondere
confused [kənˈfjuːzd] adj confuso(-a); **to get ~** confondersi
confusing [kənˈfjuːzɪŋ] adj che fa confondere
confusion [kənˈfjuːʒən] n confusione f
congeal [kənˈdʒiːl] vi (blood) congelarsi
congenial [kənˈdʒiːnɪəl] adj (person) simpatico(-a); (place, work, company) piacevole
congenital [kənˈdʒɛnɪtl] adj congenito(-a)
conger eel [ˈkɒŋgər-] n grongo
congested [kənˈdʒɛstɪd] adj congestionato(-a); (telephone lines) sovraccarico(-a)
congestion [kənˈdʒɛstʃən] n congestione f
congestion charge n pedaggio da pagare per poter circolare in automobile nel centro di alcune città, introdotto per la prima volta a Londra nel 2002
conglomerate [kənˈglɒmərɪt] n (Comm) conglomerato
conglomeration [kənˌglɒməˈreɪʃən] n conglomerazione f

Congo [ˈkɒŋgəu] n Congo
congratulate [kənˈgrætjuleɪt] vt: **to ~ sb (on)** congratularsi con qn (per or di)
congratulations [kənˌgrætjuˈleɪʃənz] npl: **~ (on)** congratulazioni fpl (per) ■ excl congratulazioni!, rallegramenti!
congregate [ˈkɒŋgrɪgeɪt] vi congregarsi, riunirsi
congregation [ˌkɒŋgrɪˈgeɪʃən] n congregazione f
congress [ˈkɒŋgrɛs] n congresso; (US Pol): **C~** il Congresso; vedi nota

◉ **CONGRESS**
◉
◉ Il Congress è l'assemblea statunitense che
◉ si riunisce a Washington D.C. nel
◉ "Capitol" per elaborare e discutere le
◉ leggi federali. è costituita dalla "House of
◉ Representatives" (435 membri, eletti nei
◉ vari stati in base al numero degli
◉ abitanti) e dal "Senate" (100 senatori, due
◉ per ogni stato). Sia i membri della "House
◉ of Representatives" che quelli del
◉ "Senate" sono eletti direttamente dal
◉ popolo.

congressman [ˈkɒŋgrɛsmən] n (US) membro del Congresso
congresswoman [ˈkɒŋgrɛswumən] n (US) (donna) membro del Congresso
conical [ˈkɒnɪkl] adj conico(-a)
conifer [ˈkɒnɪfər] n conifero
coniferous [kəˈnɪfərəs] adj (forest) di conifere
conjecture [kənˈdʒɛktʃər] n congettura ■ vt, vi congetturare
conjoined twin [kənˈdʒɔɪnd-] n fratello (or sorella) siamese
conjugal [ˈkɒndʒugl] adj coniugale
conjugate [ˈkɒndʒugeɪt] vt coniugare
conjugation [ˌkɒndʒəˈgeɪʃən] n coniugazione f
conjunction [kənˈdʒʌŋkʃən] n congiunzione f; **in ~ with** in accordo con, insieme con
conjunctivitis [kəndʒʌŋktɪˈvaɪtɪs] n congiuntivite f
conjure [ˈkʌndʒər] vi fare giochi di prestigio
▶ **conjure up** vt (ghost, spirit) evocare; (memories) rievocare
conjurer [ˈkʌndʒərər] n prestigiatore(-trice), prestidigitatore(-trice)
conjuring trick [ˈkʌndʒərɪŋ-] n gioco di prestigio
conker [ˈkɒŋkər] n (Brit col) castagna (d'ippocastano)
conk out [kɒŋk-] vi (col) andare in panne
conman [ˈkɒnmæn] n truffatore m
Conn. abbr (US) = **Connecticut**

connect [kə'nɛkt] *vt* connettere, collegare; (*Elec*) collegare; (*fig*) associare ■ *vi* (*train*): **to ~ with** essere in coincidenza con; **to be connected with** aver rapporti con; essere imparentato(-a) con; **I am trying to ~ you** (*Tel*) sto cercando di darle la linea

connection [kə'nɛkʃən] *n* relazione *f*, rapporto; (*Elec*) connessione *f*; (*Tel*) collegamento; (*train etc*) coincidenza; **in ~ with** con riferimento a, a proposito di; **what is the ~ between them?** in che modo sono legati?; **business connections** rapporti d'affari; **to miss/get one's ~** (*train etc*) perdere/prendere la coincidenza

connexion [kə'nɛkʃən] *n* (*Brit*) = **connection**

conning tower ['kɔnɪŋ-] *n* torretta di comando

connive [kə'naɪv] *vi*: **to ~ at** essere connivente in

connoisseur [kɔnɪ'səːʳ] *n* conoscitore(-trice)

connotation [kɔnə'teɪʃən] *n* connotazione *f*

connubial [kə'njuːbɪəl] *adj* coniugale

conquer ['kɔŋkəʳ] *vt* conquistare; (*feelings*) vincere

conqueror ['kɔŋkərəʳ] *n* conquistatore *m*

conquest ['kɔŋkwɛst] *n* conquista

cons [kɔnz] *npl see* **pro**; **convenience**

conscience ['kɔnʃəns] *n* coscienza; **in all ~** onestamente, in coscienza

conscientious [kɔnʃɪ'ɛnʃəs] *adj* coscienzioso(-a)

conscientious objector *n* obiettore *m* di coscienza

conscious ['kɔnʃəs] *adj* consapevole; (*Med*) conscio(-a); (*deliberate: insult, error*) intenzionale, voluto(-a); **to become ~ of sth/that** rendersi conto di qc/che

consciousness ['kɔnʃəsnɪs] *n* consapevolezza; (*Med*) coscienza; **to lose/ regain ~** perdere/riprendere coscienza

conscript ['kɔnskrɪpt] *n* coscritto

conscription [kən'skrɪpʃən] *n* coscrizione *f*

consecrate ['kɔnsɪkreɪt] *vt* consacrare

consecutive [kən'sɛkjutɪv] *adj* consecutivo(-a); **on 3 ~ occasions** 3 volte di fila

consensus [kən'sɛnsəs] *n* consenso; **the ~ of opinion** l'opinione *f* unanime *or* comune

consent [kən'sɛnt] *n* consenso ■ *vi*: **to ~ (to)** acconsentire (a); **age of ~** età legale (per avere rapporti sessuali); **by common ~** di comune accordo

consenting adults [kən'sɛntɪŋ-] *npl* adulti *mpl* consenzienti

consequence ['kɔnsɪkwəns] *n* conseguenza, risultato; importanza; **in ~** di conseguenza

consequently ['kɔnsɪkwəntlɪ] *adv* di conseguenza, dunque

conservation [kɔnsə'veɪʃən] *n* conservazione *f*; (*also*: **nature conservation**) tutela dell'ambiente; **energy ~** risparmio energetico

conservationist [kɔnsə'veɪʃənɪst] *n* fautore(-trice) della tutela dell'ambiente

conservative [kən'səːvətɪv] *adj* conservatore(-trice); (*cautious*) cauto(-a); **C~** *adj*, *n* (*Brit Pol*) conservatore(-trice); **the C~ Party** il partito conservatore

conservatory [kən'səːvətrɪ] *n* (*greenhouse*) serra

conserve [kən'səːv] *vt* conservare ■ *n* conserva

consider [kən'sɪdəʳ] *vt* considerare; (*take into account*) tener conto di; **to ~ doing sth** considerare la possibilità di fare qc; **all things considered** tutto sommato *or* considerato; **~ yourself lucky** puoi dirti fortunato

considerable [kən'sɪdərəbl] *adj* considerevole, notevole

considerably [kən'sɪdərəblɪ] *adv* notevolmente, decisamente

considerate [kən'sɪdərɪt] *adj* premuroso(-a)

consideration [kənsɪdə'reɪʃən] *n* considerazione *f*; (*reward*) rimunerazione *f*; **out of ~ for** per riguardo a; **under ~** in esame; **my first ~ is my family** il mio primo pensiero è per la mia famiglia

considered [kən'sɪdəd] *adj*: **it is my ~ opinion that** ... dopo lunga riflessione il mio parere è che ...

considering [kən'sɪdərɪŋ] *prep* in considerazione di; **~ (that)** se si considera (che)

consign [kən'saɪn] *vt* consegnare; (*send: goods*) spedire

consignee [kɔnsaɪ'niː] *n* consegnatario(-a), destinatario(-a)

consignment [kən'saɪnmənt] *n* consegna; spedizione *f*

consignment note *n* (*Comm*) nota di spedizione

consignor [kən'saɪnəʳ] *n* mittente *m/f*

consist [kən'sɪst] *vi*: **to ~ of** constare di, essere composto(-a) di

consistency [kən'sɪstənsɪ] *n* consistenza; (*fig*) coerenza

consistent [kən'sɪstənt] *adj* coerente; (*constant*) costante; **~ with** compatibile con

consolation [kɔnsə'leɪʃən] *n* consolazione *f*

console *vt* [kən'səul] consolare ■ *n* ['kɔnsəul] quadro di comando

consolidate [kən'sɔlɪdeɪt] *vt* consolidare

consols ['kɔnsɔlz] *npl* (*Stock Exchange*) titoli *mpl* del debito consolidato

consommé [kən'sɔmeɪ] n consommé m inv, brodo ristretto

consonant ['kɔnsənənt] n consonante f

consort ['kɔnsɔ:t] n consorte m/f; **prince ~** principe m consorte ■ vi [kən'sɔ:t] (often pej): **to ~ with sb** frequentare qn

consortium [kən'sɔ:tɪəm] n consorzio

conspicuous [kən'spɪkjuəs] adj cospicuo(-a); **to make o.s. ~** farsi notare

conspiracy [kən'spɪrəsɪ] n congiura, cospirazione f

conspiratorial [kənspɪrə'tɔ:rɪəl] adj cospiratorio(-a)

conspire [kən'spaɪər] vi congiurare, cospirare

constable ['kʌnstəbl] n (Brit: also: **police constable**) ≈ poliziotto, agente m di polizia

constabulary [kən'stæbjulərɪ] n forze fpl dell'ordine

constant ['kɔnstənt] adj costante; continuo(-a)

constantly ['kɔnstəntlɪ] adv costantemente; continuamente

constellation [kɔnstə'leɪʃən] n costellazione f

consternation [kɔnstə'neɪʃən] n costernazione f

constipated ['kɔnstɪpeɪtɪd] adj stitico(-a)

constipation [kɔnstɪ'peɪʃən] n stitichezza

constituency [kən'stɪtjuənsɪ] n collegio elettorale; (people) elettori mpl (del collegio); vedi nota

⦿ **CONSTITUENCY**

Con il termine constituency viene indicato sia un collegio elettorale che i suoi elettori. In Gran Bretagna ogni collegio elegge un rappresentante che in seguito incontra regolarmente i propri elettori in riunioni chiamate "surgeries" per discutere questioni di interesse locale.

constituency party n sezione f locale (del partito)

constituent [kən'stɪtjuənt] n elettore(-trice); (part) elemento componente

constitute ['kɔnstɪtju:t] vt costituire

constitution [kɔnstɪ'tju:ʃən] n costituzione f

constitutional [kɔnstɪ'tju:ʃənl] adj costituzionale

constitutional monarchy n monarchia costituzionale

constrain [kən'streɪn] vt costringere

constrained [kən'streɪnd] adj costretto(-a)

constraint [kən'streɪnt] n (restraint) limitazione f, costrizione f; (embarrassment) imbarazzo, soggezione f

constrict [kən'strɪkt] vt comprimere; opprimere

construct [kən'strʌkt] vt costruire

construction [kən'strʌkʃən] n costruzione f; (fig: interpretation) interpretazione f; **under ~** in costruzione

construction industry n edilizia, industria edile

constructive [kən'strʌktɪv] adj costruttivo(-a)

construe [kən'stru:] vt interpretare

consul ['kɔnsl] n console m

consulate ['kɔnsjulɪt] n consolato

consult [kən'sʌlt] vt: **to ~ sb (about sth)** consultare qn (su or riguardo a qc)

consultancy [kən'sʌltənsɪ] n consulenza

consultancy fee n onorario di consulenza

consultant [kən'sʌltənt] n (Med) consulente m medico; (other specialist) consulente ■ cpd: **~ engineer** n ingegnere m consulente; **~ paediatrician** n specialista m/f in pediatria; **legal/management ~** consulente legale/gestionale

consultation [kɔnsəl'teɪʃən] n consultazione f; (Med, Law) consulto; **in ~ with** consultandosi con

consultative [kən'sʌltətɪv] adj di consulenza

consulting room [kən'sʌltɪŋ-] n (Brit) ambulatorio

consume [kən'sju:m] vt consumare

consumer [kən'sju:mər] n consumatore(-trice); (of electricity, gas etc) utente m/f

consumer credit n credito al consumatore

consumer durables npl prodotti mpl di consumo durevole

consumer goods npl beni mpl di consumo

consumerism [kən'sju:mərɪzəm] n (consumer protection) tutela del consumatore; (Econ) consumismo

consumer society n società dei consumi

consumer watchdog n comitato di difesa dei consumatori

consummate ['kɔnsʌmeɪt] vt consumare

consumption [kən'sʌmpʃən] n consumo; (Med) consunzione f; **not fit for human ~** non commestibile

cont. abbr (= continued) segue

contact ['kɔntækt] n contatto; (person) conoscenza ■ vt mettersi in contatto con; **to be in ~ with sb/sth** essere in contatto con qn/qc; **business contacts** contatti mpl d'affari

contact lenses npl lenti fpl a contatto

contagious [kən'teɪdʒəs] adj contagioso(-a)

contain [kən'teɪn] vt contenere; **to ~ o.s.** contenersi

container [kən'teɪnər] n recipiente m; (for shipping etc) container m

containerize [kən'teɪnəraɪz] vt mettere in container

container ship n nave f container inv

contaminate [kən'tæmɪneɪt] vt contaminare

contamination [kəntæmɪ'neɪʃən] n contaminazione f

cont'd abbr (= continued) segue

contemplate ['kɔntəmpleɪt] vt contemplare; (consider) pensare a (or di)

contemplation [kɔntəm'pleɪʃən] n contemplazione f

contemporary [kən'tɛmpərərɪ] adj contemporaneo(-a); (design) moderno(-a) ∎ n contemporaneo(-a); (of the same age) coetaneo(-a)

contempt [kən'tɛmpt] n disprezzo; ~ **of court** (Law) oltraggio alla Corte

contemptible [kən'tɛmptəbl] adj spregevole, vergognoso(-a)

contemptuous [kən'tɛmptjuəs] adj sdegnoso(-a)

contend [kən'tɛnd] vt: **to ~ that** sostenere che ∎ vi: **to ~ with** lottare contro; **he has a lot to ~ with** ha un sacco di guai

contender [kən'tɛndər] n contendente m/f; concorrente m/f

content [kən'tɛnt] adj contento(-a), soddisfatto(-a) ∎ vt contentare, soddisfare ∎ n ['kɔntɛnt] contenuto; **contents** npl contenuto; (of barrel etc: capacity) capacità f inv; **(table of) contents** indice m; **to be ~ with** essere contento di; **to ~ o.s. with sth/with doing sth** accontentarsi di qc/di fare qc

contented [kən'tɛntɪd] adj contento(-a), soddisfatto(-a)

contentedly [kən'tɛntɪdlɪ] adv con soddisfazione

contention [kən'tɛnʃən] n contesa; (assertion) tesi f inv; **bone of ~** pomo della discordia

contentious [kən'tɛnʃəs] adj polemico(-a)

contentment [kən'tɛntmənt] n contentezza

contest n ['kɔntɛst] lotta; (competition) gara, concorso ∎ vt [kən'tɛst] contestare; (Law) impugnare; (compete for) contendere

contestant [kən'tɛstənt] n concorrente m/f; (in fight) avversario(-a)

context ['kɔntɛkst] n contesto; **in/out of ~** nel/fuori dal contesto

continent ['kɔntɪnənt] n continente m; **the C~** (Brit) l'Europa continentale; **on the C~** in Europa

continental [kɔntɪ'nɛntl] adj continentale ∎ n (Brit) abitante m/f dell'Europa continentale

continental breakfast n colazione f all'europea

continental quilt n (Brit) piumino

contingency [kən'tɪndʒənsɪ] n eventualità f inv

contingency plan n misura d'emergenza

contingent [kən'tɪndʒənt] n contingenza ∎ adj: **to be ~ upon** dipendere da

continual [kən'tɪnjuəl] adj continuo(-a)

continually [kən'tɪnjuəlɪ] adv di continuo

continuation [kəntɪnju'eɪʃən] n continuazione f; (after interruption) ripresa; (of story) seguito

continue [kən'tɪnjuː] vi continuare ∎ vt continuare; (start again) riprendere; **to be continued** (story) continua; **continued on page 10** segue or continua a pagina 10

continuing education [kən'tɪnjuɪŋ-] n corsi mpl per adulti

continuity [kɔntɪ'njuːɪtɪ] n continuità; (Cine) (ordine m della) sceneggiatura

continuity girl n (Cine) segretaria di edizione

continuous [kən'tɪnjuəs] adj continuo(-a), ininterrotto(-a); ~ **performance** (Cine) spettacolo continuato; ~ **stationery** (Comput) carta a moduli continui

continuously [kən'tɪnjuəslɪ] adv (repeatedly) continuamente; (uninterruptedly) ininterrottamente

contort [kən'tɔːt] vt contorcere

contortion [kən'tɔːʃən] n contorcimento; (of acrobat) contorsione f

contortionist [kən'tɔːʃənɪst] n contorsionista m/f

contour ['kɔntuər] n contorno, profilo; (also: **contour line**) curva di livello

contraband ['kɔntrəbænd] n contrabbando ∎ adj di contrabbando

contraception [kɔntrə'sɛpʃən] n contraccezione f

contraceptive [kɔntrə'sɛptɪv] adj contraccettivo(-a) ∎ n contraccettivo

contract n ['kɔntrækt] contratto ∎ cpd ['kɔntrækt] (price, date) del contratto; (work) a contratto ∎ vi [kən'trækt] (Comm): **to ~ to do sth** fare un contratto per fare qc; (become smaller) contrarre; **to be under ~ to do sth** aver stipulato un contratto per fare qc; ~ **of employment** contratto di lavoro
  ▶ **contract in** vi impegnarsi (con un contratto); (Brit Admin) scegliere di pagare i contributi per una pensione
  ▶ **contract out** vi: **to ~ out (of)** ritirarsi (da); (Brit Admin) (scegliere di) non pagare i contributi per una pensione

contraction [kən'trækʃən] n contrazione f

contractor [kən'træktər] n imprenditore m

contractual [kən'træktjuəl] adj contrattuale

contradict [kɔntrə'dɪkt] vt contraddire

contradiction [kɔntrə'dɪkʃən] n contraddizione f; **to be in ~ with** discordare con

contradictory [kɔntrə'dɪktərɪ] *adj*
contraddittorio(-a)
contralto [kən'træltəu] *n* contralto
contraption [kən'træpʃən] *n (pej)* aggeggio
contrary¹ ['kɔntrərɪ] *adj* contrario(-a);
(unfavourable) avverso(-a), contrario(-a) ■ *n*
contrario; **on the** ~ al contrario; **unless you
hear to the** ~ a meno che non si disdica; ~ **to
what we thought** a differenza di *or*
contrariamente a quanto pensavamo
contrary² [kən'trɛərɪ] *(perverse)* bisbetico(-a)
contrast *n* ['kɔntrɑːst] contrasto ■ *vt*
[kən'trɑːst] mettere in contrasto; **in** ~ **to** *or*
with a differenza di, contrariamente a
contrasting [kən'trɑːstɪŋ] *adj* contrastante,
di contrasto
contravene [kɔntrə'viːn] *vt* contravvenire
contravention [kɔntrə'vɛnʃən] *n*: ~ **(of)**
contravvenzione *f* (a), infrazione *f* (di)
contribute [kən'trɪbjuːt] *vi* contribuire ■ *vt*:
to ~ **£10/an article to** dare 10 sterline/un
articolo a; **to** ~ **to** contribuire a; *(newspaper)*
scrivere per; *(discussion)* partecipare a
contribution [kɔntrɪ'bjuːʃən] *n* contribuzione *f*
contributor [kən'trɪbjutə^r] *n (to newspaper)*
collaboratore(-trice)
contributory [kən'trɪbjutərɪ] *adj (cause)* che
contribuisce; **it was a** ~ **factor in** … quello
ha contribuito a …
contributory pension scheme *n (Brit)*
*sistema di pensionamento finanziato congiuntamente
dai contributi del lavoratore e del datore di lavoro*
contrite ['kɔntraɪt] *adj* contrito(-a)
contrivance [kən'traɪvəns] *n* congegno;
espediente *m*
contrive [kən'traɪv] *vt* inventare; escogitare
■ *vi*: **to** ~ **to do** fare in modo di fare
control [kən'trəul] *vt* dominare; *(firm,
operation etc)* dirigere; *(check)* controllare;
(disease, fire) arginare, limitare ■ *n* controllo;
controls *npl* comandi *mpl*; **to take** ~ **of**
assumere il controllo di; **to be in** ~ **of** aver
autorità su; essere responsabile di;
controllare; **to** ~ **o.s.** controllarsi;
everything is under ~ tutto è sotto
controllo; **the car went out of** ~ la
macchina non rispondeva ai comandi;
circumstances beyond our ~ circostanze *fpl*
che non dipendono da noi
control key *n (Comput)* tasto di controllo
controlled substance [kən'trəuld-] *n*
sostanza stupefacente
controller [kən'trəulə^r] *n* controllore *m*
controlling interest [kən'trəulɪŋ-] *n (Comm)*
maggioranza delle azioni
control panel *n (on aircraft, ship, TV etc)* quadro
dei comandi

control point *n* punto di controllo
control room *n (Naut, Mil)* sala di comando;
(Radio, TV) sala di regia
control tower *n (Aviat)* torre *f* di controllo
control unit *n (Comput)* unità *f inv* di controllo
controversial [kɔntrə'vəːʃl] *adj*
controverso(-a), polemico(-a)
controversy ['kɔntrəvəːsɪ] *n* controversia,
polemica
conurbation [kɔnə:'beɪʃən] *n* conurbazione *f*
convalesce [kɔnvə'lɛs] *vi* rimettersi in salute
convalescence [kɔnvə'lɛsns] *n*
convalescenza
convalescent [kɔnvə'lɛsnt] *adj, n*
convalescente *(m/f)*
convector [kən'vɛktə^r] *n* convettore *m*
convene [kən'viːn] *vt* convocare; *(meeting)*
organizzare ■ *vi* convenire, adunarsi
convenience [kən'viːnɪəns] *n* comodità *f inv*;
at your ~ a suo comodo; **at your earliest** ~
(Comm) appena possibile; **all modern
conveniences**, *(Brit)* **all mod cons** tutte le
comodità moderne
convenience foods *npl* cibi *mpl* precotti
convenient [kən'viːnɪənt] *adj* conveniente,
comodo(-a); **if it is** ~ **to you** se per lei va
bene, se non la incomoda
conveniently [kən'viːnɪəntlɪ] *adv (happen)*
a proposito; *(situated)* in un posto comodo
convent ['kɔnvənt] *n* convento
convention [kən'vɛnʃən] *n* convenzione *f*;
(meeting) convegno
conventional [kən'vɛnʃənl] *adj* convenzionale
convent school *n* scuola retta da suore
converge [kən'vəːdʒ] *vi* convergere
conversant [kən'vəːsnt] *adj*: **to be** ~ **with**
essere al corrente di; essere pratico(-a) di
conversation [kɔnvə'seɪʃən] *n* conversazione *f*
conversational [kɔnvə'seɪʃənl] *adj* non
formale; *(Comput)* conversazionale; ~ **Italian**
l'italiano parlato
conversationalist [kɔnvə'seɪʃnəlɪst] *n*
conversatore(-trice)
converse *n* ['kɔnvəːs] contrario, opposto
■ *vi* [kən'vəːs]: **to** ~ **(with sb about sth)**
conversare (con qn su qc)
conversely [kɔn'vəːslɪ] *adv* al contrario,
per contro
conversion [kən'vəːʃən] *n* conversione *f*;
(Brit: of house) trasformazione *f*,
rimodernamento
conversion table *n* tavola di equivalenze
convert *vt* [kən'vəːt] *(Rel, Comm)* convertire;
(alter) trasformare ■ *n* ['kɔnvəːt]
convertito(-a)
convertible [kən'vəːtəbl] *n* macchina
decappottabile

convex ['kɔnvɛks] *adj* convesso(-a)
convey [kən'veɪ] *vt* trasportare; (*thanks*) comunicare; (*idea*) dare
conveyance [kən'veɪəns] *n* (*of goods*) trasporto; (*vehicle*) mezzo di trasporto
conveyancing [kən'veɪənsɪŋ] *n* (*Law*) redazione *f* di transazioni di proprietà
conveyor belt *n* nastro trasportatore
convict *vt* [kən'vɪkt] dichiarare colpevole ■ *n* ['kɔnvɪkt] carcerato(-a)
conviction [kən'vɪkʃən] *n* condanna; (*belief*) convinzione *f*
convince [kən'vɪns] *vt*: **to ~ sb (of sth/that)** convincere qn (di qc/che), persuadere qn (di qc/che)
convincing [kən'vɪnsɪŋ] *adj* convincente
convincingly [kən'vɪnsɪŋlɪ] *adv* in modo convincente
convivial [kən'vɪvɪəl] *adj* allegro(-a)
convoluted ['kɔnvəluːtɪd] *adj* (*shape*) attorcigliato(-a), avvolto(-a); (*argument*) involuto(-a)
convoy ['kɔnvɔɪ] *n* convoglio
convulse [kən'vʌls] *vt* sconvolgere; **to be convulsed with laughter** contorcersi dalle risa
convulsion [kən'vʌlʃən] *n* convulsione *f*
COO *n abbr* = **chief operating officer**
coo [kuː] *vi* tubare
cook [kuk] *vt* cucinare, cuocere; (*meal*) preparare ■ *vi* cuocere; (*person*) cucinare ■ *n* cuoco(-a)
  ▸ **cook up** *vt* (*col: excuse, story*) improvvisare, inventare
cookbook ['kukbuk] *n* = **cookery book**
cooker ['kukəʳ] *n* fornello, cucina
cookery book *n* (*Brit*) libro di cucina
cookie ['kukɪ] *n* (*US*) biscotto; (*Comput*) cookie *m inv*
cooking ['kukɪŋ] *n* cucina ■ *cpd* (*apples, chocolate*) da cuocere; (*utensils, salt, foil*) da cucina
cookout ['kukaut] *n* (*US*) pranzo (cucinato) all'aperto
cool [kuːl] *adj* fresco(-a); (*not afraid*) calmo(-a); (*unfriendly*) freddo(-a); (*impertinent*) sfacciato(-a) ■ *vt* raffreddare, rinfrescare ■ *vi* raffreddarsi, rinfrescarsi; **it's ~** (*weather*) fa fresco; **to keep sth ~ or in a ~ place** tenere qc in fresco
  ▸ **cool down** *vi* raffreddarsi; (*fig: person, situation*) calmarsi
coolant ['kuːlənt] *n* (liquido) refrigerante *m*
cool box, (*US*) **cooler** ['kuːləʳ] *n* borsa termica
cooling ['kuːlɪŋ] *adj* (*breeze*) fresco(-a)
cooling tower *n* torre *f* di raffreddamento

coolly ['kuːlɪ] *adv* (*calmly*) con calma, tranquillamente; (*audaciously*) come se niente fosse; (*unenthusiastically*) freddamente
coolness ['kuːlnɪs] *n* freschezza; sangue *m* freddo, calma
coop [kuːp] *n* stia ■ *vt*: **to ~ up** (*fig*) rinchiudere
co-op ['kəuɔp] *n abbr* (= *cooperative (society*)) coop *f*
cooperate [kəu'ɔpəreɪt] *vi* cooperare, collaborare
cooperation [kəuɔpə'reɪʃən] *n* cooperazione *f*, collaborazione *f*
cooperative [kəu'ɔpərətɪv] *adj* cooperativo(-a) ■ *n* cooperativa
coopt [kəu'ɔpt] *vt*: **to ~ sb into sth** cooptare qn per qc
coordinate *vt* [kəu'ɔːdɪneɪt] coordinare ■ *n* [kəu'ɔːdɪnət] (*Math*) coordinata; **coordinates** *npl* (*clothes*) coordinati *mpl*
coordination [kəuɔːdɪ'neɪʃən] *n* coordinazione *f*
coot [kuːt] *n* folaga
co-ownership [kəu'əunəʃɪp] *n* comproprietà
cop [kɔp] *n* (*col*) sbirro
cope [kəup] *vi* farcela; **to ~ with** (*problems*) far fronte a
Copenhagen [kəupən'heɪgən] *n* Copenhagen *f*
copier ['kɔpɪəʳ] *n* (*also*: **photocopier**) (foto)copiatrice *f*
co-pilot ['kəupaɪlət] *n* secondo pilota *m*
copious ['kəupɪəs] *adj* copioso(-a), abbondante
copper ['kɔpəʳ] *n* rame *m*; (*col: policeman*) sbirro; **coppers** *npl* spiccioli *mpl*
coppice ['kɔpɪs], **copse** [kɔps] *n* bosco ceduo
copulate ['kɔpjuleɪt] *vi* accoppiarsi
copy ['kɔpɪ] *n* copia; (*book etc*) esemplare *m*; (*material: for printing*) materiale *m*, testo ■ *vt* (*gen, Comput*) copiare; (*imitate*) imitare; **rough/fair ~** brutta/bella (copia); **to make good ~** (*fig*) fare notizia
  ▸ **copy out** *vt* ricopiare, trascrivere
copycat ['kɔpɪkæt] *n* (*pej*) copione *m*
copyright ['kɔpɪraɪt] *n* diritto d'autore; **~ reserved** tutti i diritti riservati
copy typist *n* dattilografo(-a)
copywriter ['kɔpɪraɪtəʳ] *n* redattore *m* pubblicitario
coral ['kɔrəl] *n* corallo
coral reef *n* barriera corallina
Coral Sea *n*: **the ~** il mar dei Coralli
cord [kɔːd] *n* corda; (*Elec*) filo; (*fabric*) velluto a coste; **cords** *npl* (*trousers*) calzoni *mpl* (di velluto) a coste
cordial ['kɔːdɪəl] *adj, n* cordiale (*m*)
cordless ['kɔːdlɪs] *adj* senza cavo

cordon ['kɔːdn] n cordone m
  ▶ **cordon off** vt fare cordone intorno a
corduroy ['kɔːdərɔɪ] n fustagno
CORE [kɔːʳ] n abbr (US) = **Congress of Racial Equality**
core [kɔːʳ] n (of fruit) torsolo; (Tech) centro; (of earth, nuclear reactor) nucleo; (of problem etc) cuore m, nocciolo ■ vt estrarre il torsolo da; **rotten to the ~** marcio fino al midollo
Corfu [kɔː'fuː] n Corfù f
coriander [kɔrɪ'ændəʳ] n coriandolo
cork [kɔːk] n sughero; (of bottle) tappo
corkage ['kɔːkɪdʒ] n somma da pagare se il cliente porta il proprio vino
corked [kɔːkt], (US) **corky** ['kɔːkɪ] adj (wine) che sa di tappo
corkscrew ['kɔːkskruː] n cavatappi m inv
cormorant ['kɔːmərnt] n cormorano
corn [kɔːn] n (Brit: wheat) grano; (US: maize) granturco; (on foot) callo; **~ on the cob** (Culin) pannocchia cotta
cornea ['kɔːnɪə] n cornea
corned beef ['kɔːnd-] n carne f di manzo in scatola
corner ['kɔːnəʳ] n angolo; (Aut) curva; (Football: also: **corner kick**) corner m inv, calcio d'angolo ■ vt intrappolare; mettere con le spalle al muro; (Comm: market) accaparrare ■ vi prendere una curva; **to cut corners** (fig) prendere una scorciatoia
corner flag n (Football) bandierina d'angolo
corner kick n (Football) calcio d'angolo
cornerstone ['kɔːnəstəun] n pietra angolare
cornet ['kɔːnɪt] n (Mus) cornetta; (Brit: of ice-cream) cono
cornflakes ['kɔːnfleɪks] npl fiocchi mpl di granturco
cornflour ['kɔːnflauəʳ] n (Brit) ≈ fecola di patate
cornice ['kɔːnɪs] n cornicione m; cornice f
Cornish ['kɔːnɪʃ] adj della Cornovaglia
corn oil n olio di mais
cornstarch ['kɔːnstɑːtʃ] n (US) = **cornflour**
cornucopia [kɔːnju'kəupɪə] n grande abbondanza
Cornwall ['kɔːnwəl] n Cornovaglia
corny ['kɔːnɪ] adj (col) trito(-a)
corollary [kə'rɔlərɪ] n corollario
coronary ['kɔrənərɪ] n: **~ (thrombosis)** trombosi f coronaria
coronation [kɔrə'neɪʃən] n incoronazione f
coroner ['kɔrənəʳ] n magistrato incaricato di indagare la causa di morte in circostanze sospette
coronet ['kɔrənɪt] n diadema m
Corp. abbr = **corporation**
corporal ['kɔːpərl] n caporalmaggiore m
  ■ adj: **~ punishment** pena corporale

corporate ['kɔːpərɪt] adj comune; (Comm) costituito(-a) (in corporazione)
corporate hospitality n omaggi mpl ai clienti (come biglietti per spettacoli, cene etc)
corporate identity, corporate image n (of organization) immagine f di marca
corporation [kɔːpə'reɪʃən] n (of town) consiglio comunale; (Comm) ente m
corporation tax n ≈ imposta societaria
corps [kɔːʳ ʃ] (pl **~**) [kɔːz] n corpo; **press ~** ufficio m stampa inv
corpse [kɔːps] n cadavere m
corpuscle ['kɔːpʌsl] n corpuscolo
corral [kə'rɑːl] n recinto
correct [kə'rɛkt] adj (accurate) corretto(-a), esatto(-a); (proper) corretto(-a) ■ vt correggere; **you are ~** ha ragione
correction [kə'rɛkʃən] n correzione f
correlate ['kɔrɪleɪt] vt mettere in correlazione ■ vi: **to ~ with** essere in rapporto con
correlation [kɔrɪ'leɪʃən] n correlazione f
correspond [kɔrɪs'pɔnd] vi corrispondere
correspondence [kɔrɪs'pɔndəns] n corrispondenza
correspondence course n corso per corrispondenza
correspondent [kɔrɪs'pɔndənt] n corrispondente m/f
corridor ['kɔrɪdɔːʳ] n corridoio
corroborate [kə'rɔbəreɪt] vt corroborare, confermare
corrode [kə'rəud] vt corrodere ■ vi corrodersi
corrosion [kə'rəuʒən] n corrosione f
corrosive [kə'rəuzɪv] adj corrosivo(-a)
corrugated ['kɔrəgeɪtɪd] adj increspato(-a), ondulato(-a)
corrugated iron n lamiera di ferro ondulata
corrupt [kə'rʌpt] adj corrotto(-a) ■ vt corrompere; **~ practices** (dishonesty, bribery) pratiche fpl illecite
corruption [kə'rʌpʃən] n corruzione f
corset ['kɔːsɪt] n busto
Corsica ['kɔːsɪkə] n Corsica
Corsican ['kɔːsɪkən] adj, n corso(-a)
cortège [kɔː'teɪʒ] n corteo
cortisone ['kɔːtɪzəun] n cortisone m
coruscating ['kɔrəskeɪtɪŋ] adj scintillante
cosh [kɔʃ] n (Brit) randello (corto)
cosignatory [kəu'sɪgnətərɪ] n cofirmatario(-a)
cosiness ['kəuzɪnɪs] n intimità
cos lettuce ['kɔs-] n lattuga romana
cosmetic [kɔz'mɛtɪk] n cosmetico ■ adj (preparation) cosmetico(-a); (surgery) estetico(-a); (fig: reforms) ornamentale

C

cosmic ['kɔzmɪk] *adj* cosmico(-a)
cosmonaut ['kɔzmənɔːt] *n* cosmonauta *m/f*
cosmopolitan [kɔzmə'pɔlɪtn] *adj* cosmopolita
cosmos ['kɔzmɔs] *n* cosmo
cosset ['kɔsɪt] *vt* vezzeggiare
cost [kɔst] *n* costo ■ *vb (pt, pp ~) vi* costare
■ *vt* stabilire il prezzo di; **costs** *npl (Law)*
spese *fpl*; **it costs £5/too much** costa
5 sterline/troppo; **it ~ him his life/job**
gli costò la vita/il suo lavoro; **how much
does it ~?** quanto costa?, quanto viene?;
what will it ~ to have it repaired? quanto
costerà farlo riparare?; **~ of living** costo della
vita; **at all costs** a ogni costo
cost accountant *n* analizzatore *m* dei costi
co-star ['kəʊstɑːʳ] *n* attore/trice della stessa
importanza del protagonista
Costa Rica ['kɔstə'riːkə] *n* Costa Rica
cost centre *n* centro di costo
cost control *n* controllo dei costi
cost-effective ['kɔstɪ'fɛktɪv] *adj (gen)*
conveniente, economico(-a); *(Comm)*
redditizio(-a), conveniente
cost-effectiveness ['kɔstɪ'fɛktɪvnɪs] *n*
convenienza
costing ['kɔstɪŋ] *n* (determinazione *f* dei)
costi *mpl*
costly ['kɔstlɪ] *adj* costoso(-a), caro(-a)
cost-of-living ['kɔstəv'lɪvɪŋ] *adj*: **~ allowance**
indennità *f inv* di contingenza; **~ index**
indice *m* della scala mobile
cost price *n (Brit)* prezzo all'ingrosso
costume ['kɔstjuːm] *n* costume *m*; *(lady's suit)*
tailleur *m inv*; *(Brit: also:* **swimming costume***)*
costume da bagno
costume jewellery *n* bigiotteria
cosy, *(US)* **cozy** ['kəʊzɪ] *adj* intimo(-a); *(room,
atmosphere)* accogliente
cot [kɔt] *n (Brit: child's)* lettino; *(US: folding bed)*
brandina
cot death *n* improvvisa e inspiegabile morte nel
sonno di un neonato
Cotswolds ['kɔtswəʊldz] *npl*: **the ~** zona
collinare del Gloucestershire
cottage ['kɔtɪdʒ] *n* cottage *m inv*
cottage cheese *n* fiocchi *mpl* di latte magro
cottage industry *n* industria artigianale basata
sul lavoro a cottimo
cottage pie *n* piatto a base di carne macinata in
sugo e purè di patate
cotton ['kɔtn] *n* cotone *m*; **~ dress** *etc* vestito
etc di cotone
▶ **cotton on** *vi (col)*: **to ~ on (to sth)** afferrare
(qc)
cotton wool *n (Brit)* cotone *m* idrofilo
couch [kautʃ] *n* sofà *m inv*; *(in doctor's surgery)*
lettino ■ *vt* esprimere

couchette [kuːʃɛt] *n* cuccetta
couch potato *n (col)* pigrone(-a)
teledipendente
cough [kɔf] *vi* tossire ■ *n* tosse *f*
cough drop *n* pasticca per la tosse
cough mixture, cough syrup *n* sciroppo
per la tosse
could [kud] *pt of* **can²**
couldn't ['kudnt] = **could not**
council ['kaunsl] *n* consiglio; **city** *or* **town ~**
consiglio comunale; **C~ of Europe** Consiglio
d'Europa
council estate *n (Brit)* quartiere *m* di case
popolari
council house *n (Brit)* casa popolare
council housing *n* alloggi *mpl* popolari
councillor ['kaunsələʳ] *n* consigliere(-a)
council tax *n (Brit)* tassa comunale sulla proprietà
counsel ['kaunsl] *n* avvocato; consultazione *f*
■ *vt*: **to ~ sth/sb to do sth** consigliare qc/a
qn di fare qc; **~ for the defence/the
prosecution** avvocato difensore/di parte
civile
counsellor, *(US)* **counselor** ['kaunsləʳ] *n*
consigliere(-a); *(US: lawyer)* avvocato(-essa)
count [kaunt] *vt*, *vi* contare ■ *n* conto;
(nobleman) conte *m*; **to ~ (up) to 10** contare
fino a 10; **to ~ the cost of** calcolare il costo
di; **not counting the children** senza
contare i bambini; **10 counting him** 10
compreso lui; **~ yourself lucky** considerati
fortunato; **it counts for very little** non
conta molto, non ha molta importanza;
to keep ~ of sth tenere il conto di qc
▶ **count on** *vt fus* contare su; **to ~ on doing
sth** contare di fare qc
▶ **count up** *vt* addizionare
countdown ['kauntdaun] *n* conto alla
rovescia
countenance ['kauntɪnəns] *n* volto, aspetto
■ *vt* approvare
counter ['kauntəʳ] *n* banco; *(position: in post
office, bank)* sportello; *(in game)* gettone *m*;
(Tech) contatore *m* ■ *vt* opporsi a; *(blow)*
parare ■ *adv*: **~ to** contro; in opposizione a;
to buy under the ~ *(fig)* comperare
sottobanco; **to ~ sth with sth/by doing sth**
rispondere a qc con qc/facendo qc
counteract ['kauntər'ækt] *vt* agire in
opposizione a; *(poison etc)* annullare gli
effetti di
counterattack ['kauntərətæk] *n*
contrattacco ■ *vi* contrattaccare
counterbalance ['kauntəbæləns] *vt*
contrappesare
counter-clockwise ['kauntə'klɔkwaɪz] *adv*
in senso antiorario

counter-espionage [kauntər'ɛspɪənɑːʒ] n
controspionaggio

counterfeit ['kauntəfɪt] n contraffazione f,
falso ■ vt contraffare, falsificare ■ adj
falso(-a)

counterfoil ['kauntəfɔɪl] n matrice f

counterintelligence ['kauntərɪn'tɛlɪdʒəns]
n = **counter-espionage**

countermand ['kauntəmɑːnd] vt annullare

countermeasure ['kauntəmɛʒər] n
contromisura

counteroffensive ['kauntərə'fɛnsɪv] n
controffensiva

counterpane ['kauntəpeɪn] n copriletto m inv

counterpart ['kauntəpɑːt] n (of document etc)
copia; (of person) corrispondente m/f

counterproductive ['kauntəprə'dʌktɪv] adj
controproducente

counterproposal ['kauntəprə'pəuzl] n
controproposta

countersign ['kauntəsaɪn] vt controfirmare

countersink ['kauntəsɪŋk] vt (hole) svasare

counterterrorism ['kauntə'terərɪzəm] n
antiterrorismo

countess ['kauntɪs] n contessa

countless ['kauntlɪs] adj innumerevole

countrified ['kʌntrɪfaɪd] adj rustico(-a),
campagnolo(-a)

country ['kʌntrɪ] n paese m; (native land)
patria; (as opposed to town) campagna; (region)
regione f; **in the ~** in campagna;
mountainous ~ territorio montagnoso

**country and western, country and
western music** n musica country e
western, country m

country dancing n (Brit) danza popolare

country house n villa in campagna

countryman ['kʌntrɪmən] n (national)
compatriota m; (rural) contadino

countryside ['kʌntrɪsaɪd] n campagna

country-wide ['kʌntrɪ'waɪd] adj diffuso(-a)
in tutto il paese ■ adv in tutto il paese

county ['kauntɪ] n contea

county council n (Brit) consiglio di contea

county town n (Brit) capoluogo

coup (pl **coups**) [kuː, kuːz] n (also: **coup d'état**)
colpo di Stato; (triumph) bel colpo

coupé [kuː'peɪ] n coupé m inv

couple ['kʌpl] n coppia ■ vt (carriages)
agganciare; (Tech) accoppiare; (ideas, names)
associare; **a ~ of** un paio di

couplet ['kʌplɪt] n distico

coupling ['kʌplɪŋ] n (Rail) agganciamento

coupon ['kuːpɔn] n (voucher) buono; (Comm)
coupon m inv

courage ['kʌrɪdʒ] n coraggio

courageous [kə'reɪdʒəs] adj coraggioso(-a)

courgette [kuə'ʒɛt] n (Brit) zucchina

courier ['kurɪər] n corriere m; (for tourists) guida

course [kɔːs] n corso; (of ship) rotta; (for golf)
campo; (part of meal) piatto; **first ~** primo
piatto; **of ~** adv senz'altro, naturalmente;
(no) of ~ not! certo che no!, no di certo!; **in
the ~ of the next few days** nel corso dei
prossimi giorni; **in due ~** a tempo debito;
~ (of action) modo d'agire; **the best ~
would be to ...** la cosa migliore sarebbe ...;
we have no other ~ but to ... non possiamo
far altro che ...; **~ of lectures** corso di lezioni;
a ~ of treatment (Med) una cura

court [kɔːt] n corte f; (Tennis) campo ■ vt
(woman) fare la corte a; (fig: favour, popularity)
cercare di conquistare; (: death, disaster)
sfiorare, rasentare; **out of ~** (Law: settle) in
via amichevole; **to take to ~** citare in
tribunale; **C~ of Appeal** corte d'appello

courteous ['kəːtɪəs] adj cortese

courtesan [kɔːtɪ'zæn] n cortigiana

courtesy ['kəːtəsɪ] n cortesia; **by ~ of** per
gentile concessione di

courtesy bus n navetta gratuita (di hotel,
aeroporto)

courtesy car n vettura sostitutiva

courtesy light n (Aut) luce f interna

court-house ['kɔːthaus] n (US) palazzo di
giustizia

courtier ['kɔːtɪər] n cortigiano(-a)

court martial (pl **courts martial**) n corte f
marziale

courtroom ['kɔːtrum] n tribunale m

court shoe n scarpa f décolleté inv

courtyard ['kɔːtjɑːd] n cortile m

cousin ['kʌzn] n cugino(-a)

cove [kəuv] n piccola baia

covenant ['kʌvənənt] n accordo ■ vt: **to ~ to
do sth** impegnarsi (per iscritto) a fare qc

Coventry ['kɔvəntrɪ] n: **to send sb to ~** (fig)
dare l'ostracismo a qn

cover ['kʌvər] vt (gen) coprire; (distance)
coprire, percorrere; (Press: report on) fare un
servizio su ■ n (of pan) coperchio; (over
furniture) fodera; (of book) copertina; (shelter)
riparo; (Comm, Insurance) copertura; **to take ~**
mettersi al coperto; **under ~** al riparo;
under ~ of darkness protetto dall'oscurità;
under separate ~ (Comm) a parte, in plico
separato; **£10 will ~ everything** 10 sterline
saranno sufficienti

▸ **cover up** vt (child, object): **to ~ up (with)**
coprire (di); (fig: hide: truth, facts) nascondere
■ vi: **to ~ up for sb** (fig) coprire qn

coverage ['kʌvərɪdʒ] n (Press, TV, Radio): **to
give full ~ to** fare un ampio servizio su

coveralls ['kʌvərɔːlz] npl (US) tuta

501

cover charge n coperto
covering ['kʌvərɪŋ] n copertura
covering letter, (US) **cover letter** n lettera d'accompagnamento
cover note n (Insurance) polizza (di assicurazione) provvisoria
cover price n prezzo di copertina
covert ['kʌvət] adj nascosto(-a); (glance) di sottecchi, furtivo(-a)
cover-up ['kʌvərʌp] n occultamento (di informazioni)
covet ['kʌvɪt] vt bramare
cow [kau] n vacca ■ cpd femmina ■ vt intimidire; ~ **elephant** n elefantessa
cowardice ['kauədɪs] n vigliaccheria
cowardly ['kauədlɪ] adj vigliacco(-a)
cowboy ['kaubɔɪ] n cow-boy m inv
cower ['kauəʳ] vi acquattarsi
cowshed ['kauʃed] n stalla
cowslip ['kauslɪp] n (Bot) primula (odorata)
coxswain ['kɔksn] n (also: **cox**) timoniere m
coy [kɔɪ] adj falsamente timido(-a)
coyote [kɔɪ'əutɪ] n coyote m inv
cozy ['kəuzɪ] adj (US) = **cosy**
CP n abbr (= Communist Party) P.C. m
cp. abbr (= compare) cfr.
CPA n abbr (US) = **certified public accountant**
CPI n abbr (US: = Consumer Price Index) indice dei prezzi al consumo
Cpl. abbr = **corporal**
CP/M n abbr (= Control Program for Microcomputers) CP/M m
c.p.s. abbr (= characters per second) c.p.s.
CPSA n abbr (Brit: = Civil and Public Services Association) sindacato dei servizi pubblici
CPU n abbr = **central processing unit**
cr. abbr = **credit; creditor**
crab [kræb] n granchio
crab apple n mela selvatica
crack [kræk] n (split, slit) fessura, crepa; incrinatura; (noise) schiocco; (: of gun) scoppio; (joke) battuta; (col: attempt): **to have a ~ at sth** tentare qc; (Drugs) crack m inv ■ vt spaccare; incrinare; (whip) schioccare; (nut) schiacciare; (case, mystery: solve) risolvere; (code) decifrare ■ cpd (athlete) di prim'ordine; **to ~ jokes** (col) dire battute, scherzare; **to get cracking** (col) darsi una mossa
  ▶ **crack down on** vt fus prendere serie misure contro, porre freno a
  ▶ **crack up** vi crollare
crackdown ['krækdaun] n repressione f
cracked [krækt] adj (col) matto(-a)
cracker ['krækəʳ] n cracker m inv; (firework) petardo; (Christmas cracker) mortaretto natalizio (con sorpresa); **a ~ of a ...** (Brit col)

un(-a) ... formidabile; **he's crackers** (Brit col) è tocco
crackle ['krækl] vi crepitare
crackling ['kræklɪŋ] n crepitio; (on radio, telephone) disturbo; (of pork) cotenna croccante (del maiale)
crackpot ['krækpɔt] n (col) imbecille m/f con idee assurde, assurdo(-a)
cradle ['kreɪdl] n culla ■ vt (child) tenere fra le braccia; (object) reggere tra le braccia
craft [krɑːft] n mestiere m; (cunning) astuzia; (boat) naviglio
craftsman ['krɑːftsmən] n artigiano
craftsmanship ['krɑːftsmənʃɪp] n abilità
crafty ['krɑːftɪ] adj furbo(-a), astuto(-a)
crag [kræg] n roccia
cram [kræm] vt (fill): **to ~ sth with** riempire qc di; (put): **to ~ sth into** stipare qc in
cramming ['kræmɪŋ] n (fig: pej) sgobbare m
cramp [kræmp] n crampo ■ vt soffocare, impedire
cramped [kræmpt] adj ristretto(-a)
crampon ['kræmpən] n (Climbing) rampone m
cranberry ['krænbərɪ] n mirtillo
crane [kreɪn] n gru f inv ■ vt, vi: **to ~ forward, to ~ one's neck** allungare il collo
cranium (pl **crania**) ['kreɪnɪəm, 'kreɪnɪə] n cranio
crank [kræŋk] n manovella; (person) persona stramba
crankshaft ['kræŋkʃɑːft] n albero a gomiti
cranky ['kræŋkɪ] adj eccentrico(-a); (bad-tempered): **to be ~** avere i nervi
cranny ['krænɪ] n see **nook**
crap [kræp] n (col!) fesserie fpl; **to have a ~** cacare (!)
crappy ['kræpɪ] adj (col) di merda (!)
crash [kræʃ] n fragore m; (of car) incidente m; (of plane) caduta; (of business) fallimento; (Stock Exchange) crollo ■ vt fracassare ■ vi (plane) fracassarsi; (car) avere un incidente; (two cars) scontrarsi; (fig) fallire, andare in rovina; **to ~ into** scontrarsi con; **he crashed the car into a wall** andò a sbattere contro un muro con la macchina
crash barrier n (Brit Aut) guardrail m inv
crash course n corso intensivo
crash helmet n casco
crash landing n atterraggio di fortuna
crass [kræs] adj crasso(-a)
crate [kreɪt] n gabbia
crater ['kreɪtəʳ] n cratere m
cravat, cravate [krə'væt] n fazzoletto da collo
crave [kreɪv] vi: **to ~ for** desiderare ardentemente
craving ['kreɪvɪŋ] n: ~ **(for)** (for food, cigarettes etc) (gran) voglia (di)

crawl [krɔ:l] *vi* strisciare carponi; *(child)*
andare a gattoni; *(vehicle)* avanzare
lentamente ∎ *n (Swimming)* crawl *m*; **to ~ to
sb** *(col: suck up)* arruffianarsi qn
crawler lane ['krɔ:lə⁻-] *n (Brit Aut) corsia
riservata al traffico lento*
crayfish ['kreɪfɪʃ] *n (pl inv)* gambero (d'acqua
dolce)
crayon ['kreɪən] *n* matita colorata
craze [kreɪz] *n* mania
crazed [kreɪzd] *adj (look, person)* folle,
pazzo(-a); *(pottery, glaze)* incrinato(-a)
crazy ['kreɪzɪ] *adj* matto(-a); **to go ~** uscir di
senno, impazzire; **to be ~ about sb** *(col: keen)*
essere pazzo di qn; **to be ~ about sth** andare
matto per qc
crazy paving *n (Brit)* lastricato a mosaico
irregolare
creak [kri:k] *vi* cigolare, scricchiolare
cream [kri:m] *n* crema; *(fresh)* panna ∎ *adj
(colour)* color crema *inv*; **whipped ~** panna
montata
  ▶ **cream off** *vt (best talents, part of profits)*
  portarsi via
cream cake *n* torta alla panna
cream cheese *n* formaggio fresco
creamery ['kri:mərɪ] *n (shop)* latteria; *(factory)*
caseificio
creamy ['kri:mɪ] *adj* cremoso(-a)
crease [kri:s] *n* grinza; *(deliberate)* piega
∎ *vt* sgualcire ∎ *vi* sgualcirsi
crease-resistant ['kri:srɪzɪstənt] *adj*
ingualcibile
create [kri:'eɪt] *vt* creare; *(fuss, noise)* fare
creation [kri:'eɪʃən] *n* creazione *f*
creative [kri:'eɪtɪv] *adj* creativo(-a)
creativity [kri:eɪ'tɪvɪtɪ] *n* creatività
creator [kri:'eɪtə⁻] *n* creatore(-trice)
creature ['kri:tʃə⁻] *n* creatura
crèche, creche [krɛʃ] *n* asilo infantile
credence ['kri:dns] *n* credenza, fede *f*
credentials [krɪ'dɛnʃlz] *npl (papers)*
credenziali *fpl*; *(letters of reference)* referenze *fpl*
credibility [krɛdɪ'bɪlɪtɪ] *n* credibilità
credible ['krɛdɪbl] *adj* credibile; *(witness,
source)* attendibile
credit ['krɛdɪt] *n* credito; onore *m*; *(Scol: esp
US)* certificato del compimento di una parte del corso
universitario ∎ *vt (Comm)* accreditare; *(believe:
also:* **give credit to***)* credere, prestar fede a;
to ~ £5 to sb accreditare 5 sterline a qn;
to ~ sb with sth *(fig)* attribuire qc a qn; **on ~**
a credito; **to one's ~** a proprio onore; **to take
the ~ for** farsi il merito di; **to be in ~** *(person)*
essere creditore(-trice); *(bank account)* essere
coperto(-a); **he's a ~ to his family** fa onore
alla sua famiglia; *see also* **credits**

creditable ['krɛdɪtəbl] *adj* che fa onore,
degno(-a) di lode
credit account *n* conto di credito
credit agency *n (Brit)* agenzia di analisi di
credito
credit balance *n* saldo attivo
credit bureau *n (US)* agenzia di analisi di
credito
credit card *n* carta di credito
credit control *n* controllo dei crediti
credit crunch *n* improvvisa stretta di credito
credit facilities *npl* agevolazioni *fpl* creditizie
credit limit *n* limite *m* di credito
credit note *n (Brit)* nota di credito
creditor ['krɛdɪtə⁻] *n* creditore(-trice)
credits ['krɛdɪts] *npl (Cine)* titoli *mpl*
credit transfer *n* bancogiro, postagiro
creditworthy ['krɛdɪt'wə:ðɪ] *adj*
autorizzabile al credito
credulity [krɪ'dju:lɪtɪ] *n* credulità
creed [kri:d] *n* credo; dottrina
creek [kri:k] *n* insenatura; *(US)* piccolo
fiume *m*
creel [kri:l] *n* cestino per il pesce; *(also:
lobster creel)* nassa
creep [kri:p] *vi (pt, pp* **crept**) [krɛpt] avanzare
furtivamente *(or* pian piano*)*; *(plant)*
arrampicarsi ∎ *n (col)*: **he's a ~** è un tipo
viscido; **it gives me the creeps** *(col)* mi fa
venire la pelle d'oca; **to ~ up on sb**
avvicinarsi quatto quatto a qn; *(fig: old age etc)*
cogliere qn alla sprovvista
creeper ['kri:pə⁻] *n* pianta rampicante
creepy ['kri:pɪ] *adj (frightening)* che fa
accapponare la pelle
creepy-crawly ['kri:pɪ'krɔ:lɪ] *n (col)*
bestiolina, insetto
cremate [krɪ'meɪt] *vt* cremare
cremation [krɪ'meɪʃən] *n* cremazione *f*
crematorium *(pl* **crematoria***)* [krɛmə'tɔ:rɪəm,
-'tɔ:rɪə] *n* forno crematorio
creosote ['krɪəsəut] *n* creosoto
crêpe [kreɪp] *n* crespo
crêpe bandage *n (Brit)* fascia elastica
crêpe paper *n* carta crespa
crêpe sole *n* suola di para
crept [krɛpt] *pt, pp of* **creep**
crescendo [krɪ'ʃɛndəu] *n* crescendo
crescent ['krɛsnt] *n (shape)* mezzaluna;
(street) strada semicircolare
cress [krɛs] *n* crescione *m*
crest [krɛst] *n* cresta; *(of helmet)*
pennacchiera; *(of coat of arms)* cimiero
crestfallen ['krɛstfɔ:lən] *adj* mortificato(-a)
Crete ['kri:t] *n* Creta
crevasse [krɪ'væs] *n* crepaccio
crevice ['krɛvɪs] *n* fessura, crepa

crew [kru:] n equipaggio; (Cine) troupe f inv; (gang) banda, compagnia

crew-cut ['kru:kʌt] n: **to have a ~** avere i capelli a spazzola

crew-neck ['kru:nɛk] n girocollo

crib [krɪb] n culla; (Rel) presepio ■ vt (col) copiare

cribbage ['krɪbɪdʒ] n tipo di gioco di carte

crick [krɪk] n crampo; **~ in the neck** torcicollo

cricket ['krɪkɪt] n (insect) grillo; (game) cricket m

cricketer ['krɪkɪtə'] n giocatore m di cricket

crime [kraɪm] n (in general) criminalità; (instance) crimine m, delitto

crime wave n ondata di criminalità

criminal ['krɪmɪnl] adj, n criminale (m/f); **C~ Investigation Department (CID)** ≈ polizia giudiziaria

crimp [krɪmp] vt arricciare

crimson ['krɪmzn] adj color cremisi inv

cringe [krɪndʒ] vi acquattarsi; (fig) essere servile

crinkle ['krɪŋkl] vt arricciare, increspare

cripple ['krɪpl] n zoppo(-a) ■ vt azzoppare; (ship, plane) avariare; (production, exports) rovinare; **crippled with arthritis** sciancato(-a) per l'artrite

crippling ['krɪplɪŋ] adj (taxes, debts) esorbitante; (disease) molto debilitante

crisis (pl **crises**) ['kraɪsɪs, -si:z] n crisi f inv

crisp [krɪsp] adj croccante; (fig) frizzante, vivace; deciso(-a)

crisps [krɪsps] npl (Brit) patatine fpl fritte

criss-cross ['krɪskrɔs] adj incrociato(-a) ■ vt incrociarsi

criterion (pl **criteria**) [kraɪ'tɪərɪən, -'tɪərɪə] n criterio

critic ['krɪtɪk] n critico(-a)

critical ['krɪtɪkl] adj critico(-a); **to be ~ of sb/ sth** criticare qn/qc, essere critico verso qn/qc

critically ['krɪtɪklɪ] adv criticamente; **~ ill** gravemente malato

criticism ['krɪtɪsɪzəm] n critica

criticize ['krɪtɪsaɪz] vt criticare

critique [krɪ'ti:k] n critica, saggio critico

croak [krəuk] vi gracchiare

Croat ['krəuæt] adj, n = **Croatian**

Croatia [krəu'eɪʃə] n Croazia

Croatian [krəu'eɪʃən] adj croato(-a) ■ n croato(-a); (Ling) croato

crochet ['krəuʃeɪ] n lavoro all'uncinetto

crock [krɔk] n coccio; (col: person: also: **old crock**) rottame m; (: car etc) caffettiera, rottame m

crockery ['krɔkərɪ] n vasellame m; (plates, cups etc) stoviglie fpl

crocodile ['krɔkədaɪl] n coccodrillo

crocus ['krəukəs] n croco

croft [krɔft] n (Brit) piccolo podere m

crofter ['krɔftə'] n (Brit) affittuario di un piccolo podere

crone [krəun] n strega

crony ['krəunɪ] n (col) amicone(-a)

crook [kruk] n truffatore m; (of shepherd) bastone m

crooked ['krukɪd] adj curvo(-a), storto(-a); (person, action) disonesto(-a)

crop [krɔp] n raccolto; (produce) coltivazione f; (of bird) gozzo, ingluvie f ■ vt (cut: hair) tagliare, rapare; (animals: grass) brucare

▶ **crop up** vi presentarsi

cropper ['krɔpə'] n: **to come a ~** (col) fare fiasco

crop spraying n spruzzatura di antiparassitari

croquet ['krəukeɪ] n croquet m

croquette [krə'kɛt] n crocchetta

cross [krɔs] n croce f; (Biol) incrocio ■ vt (street etc) attraversare; (arms, legs, Biol) incrociare; (cheque) sbarrare; (thwart: person, plan) contrastare, ostacolare ■ vi: **the boat crosses from … to …** la barca fa la traversata da … a … ■ adj di cattivo umore; **to ~ o.s.** fare il segno della croce, segnarsi; **we have a crossed line** (Brit: on telephone) c'è un'interferenza; **they've got their lines crossed** (fig) si sono fraintesi; **to be/get ~ with sb (about sth)** essere arrabbiato(-a)/ arrabbiarsi con qn (per qc)

▶ **cross out** vt cancellare

▶ **cross over** vi attraversare

crossbar ['krɔsbɑ:'] n traversa

crossbow ['krɔsbəu] n balestra

crossbreed ['krɔsbri:d] n incrocio

cross-Channel ferry ['krɔs'tʃænl-] n traghetto che attraversa la Manica

cross-check ['krɔstʃɛk] n controprova ■ vi fare una controprova

crosscountry [krɔs'kʌntrɪ], **crosscountry race** [krɔs'kʌntrɪ-] n cross-country m inv

cross-dressing [krɔs'drɛsɪŋ] n travestitismo

cross-examination ['krɔsɪgzæmɪ'neɪʃən] n (Law) controinterrogatorio

cross-examine ['krɔsɪg'zæmɪn] vt (Law) sottoporre a controinterrogatorio

cross-eyed ['krɔsaɪd] adj strabico(-a)

crossfire ['krɔsfaɪə'] n fuoco incrociato

crossing ['krɔsɪŋ] n incrocio; (sea-passage) traversata; (also: **pedestrian crossing**) passaggio pedonale

crossing point n valico di frontiera

cross-purposes ['krɔs'pə:pəsɪz] npl: **to be at ~ with sb** (misunderstand) fraintendere qn; **to talk at ~** fraintendersi

cross-question [krɔs'kwɛstʃən] vt (Law)
= **cross-examine**; (fig) sottoporre ad un
interrogatorio
cross-reference ['krɔs'rɛfərəns] n rinvio,
rimando
crossroads ['krɔsrəudz] n incrocio
cross section n (Biol) sezione f trasversale; (in
population) settore m rappresentativo
crosswalk ['krɔswɔ:k] n (US) strisce fpl
pedonali, passaggio pedonale
crosswind ['krɔswɪnd] n vento di traverso
crosswise ['krɔswaɪz] adv di traverso
crossword ['krɔswə:d] n cruciverba m inv
crotch [krɔtʃ] n (Anat) inforcatura; (of
garment) pattina
crotchet ['krɔtʃɪt] n (Mus) semiminima
crotchety ['krɔtʃɪtɪ] adj (person) burbero(-a)
crouch [krautʃ] vi acquattarsi;
rannicchiarsi
croup [kru:p] n (Med) crup m
crouton ['kru:tɔn] n crostino
crow [krəu] n (bird) cornacchia; (of cock) canto
del gallo ■ vi (cock) cantare; (fig) vantarsi;
cantar vittoria
crowbar ['krəubɑ:ʳ] n piede m di porco
crowd [kraud] n folla ■ vt affollare, stipare
■ vi affollarsi; **crowds of people** un sacco di
gente
crowded ['kraudɪd] adj affollato(-a); ~ **with**
stipato(-a) di
crowd scene n (Cine, Theat) scena di massa
crown [kraun] n corona; (of head) calotta
cranica; (of hat) cocuzzolo; (of hill) cima ■ vt
incoronare; (tooth) incapsulare; **and to ~ it
all ...** (fig) e per giunta ..., e come se non
bastasse ...; vedi nota

● CROWN COURT

Nel sistema legale inglese, la crown court è
un tribunale penale che si sposta da una
città all'altra. È formata da una giuria
locale ed è presieduta da un giudice che si
sposta assieme alla "court". Vi si
discutono i reati più gravi, mentre dei
reati minori si occupano le "magistrates'
courts", presiedute da un giudice di pace,
ma senza giuria. È il giudice di pace che
decide se passare o meno un caso alla
crown court.

crowning ['kraunɪŋ] adj (achievement, glory)
supremo(-a)
crown jewels npl gioielli mpl della Corona
crown prince n principe m ereditario
crow's-feet ['krəuzfi:t] npl zampe fpl di
gallina

crow's-nest ['krəuznɛst] n (on sailing-ship)
coffa
crucial ['kru:ʃl] adj cruciale, decisivo(-a);
~ **to** essenziale per
crucifix ['kru:sɪfɪks] n crocifisso
crucifixion [kru:sɪ'fɪkʃən] n crocifissione f
crucify ['kru:sɪfaɪ] vt crocifiggere, mettere in
croce; (fig) distruggere, fare a pezzi
crude [kru:d] adj (materials) greggio(-a); non
raffinato(-a); (fig: basic) crudo(-a),
primitivo(-a); (: vulgar) rozzo(-a),
grossolano(-a)
crude, crude oil n (petrolio) greggio
cruel ['kruəl] adj crudele
cruelty ['kruəltɪ] n crudeltà f inv
cruet ['kru:ɪt] n ampolla
cruise [kru:z] n crociera ■ vi andare a
velocità di crociera; (taxi) circolare
cruise missile n missile m cruise inv
cruiser ['kru:zəʳ] n incrociatore m
cruising speed ['kru:zɪŋ-] n velocità f inv di
crociera
crumb [krʌm] n briciola
crumble ['krʌmbl] vt sbriciolare ■ vi
sbriciolarsi; (plaster etc) sgretolarsi; (land,
earth) franare; (building, fig) crollare
crumbly ['krʌmblɪ] adj friabile
crummy ['krʌmɪ] adj (col: cheap) di infima
categoria; (: depressed) giù inv
crumpet ['krʌmpɪt] n specie di frittella
crumple ['krʌmpl] vt raggrinzare,
spiegazzare
crunch [krʌntʃ] vt sgranocchiare; (underfoot)
scricchiolare ■ n (fig) punto or momento
cruciale
crunchy ['krʌntʃɪ] adj croccante
crusade [kru:'seɪd] n crociata ■ vi (fig): **to ~
for/against** fare una crociata per/contro
crusader [kru:'seɪdəʳ] n crociato; (fig): ~ **(for)**
sostenitore(-trice) (di)
crush [krʌʃ] n folla; (love): **to have a ~ on sb**
avere una cotta per qn; (drink): **lemon ~**
spremuta di limone ■ vt schiacciare;
(crumple) sgualcire; (grind, break up: garlic, ice)
tritare; (: grapes) pigiare
crush barrier n (Brit) transenna
crushing ['krʌʃɪŋ] adj schiacciante
crust [krʌst] n crosta
crustacean [krʌs'teɪʃən] n crostaceo
crusty ['krʌstɪ] adj (bread) croccante; (person)
brontolone(-a); (remark) brusco(-a)
crutch [krʌtʃ] n (Med) gruccia; (support)
sostegno; (also: **crotch**) pattina
crux [krʌks] n nodo
cry [kraɪ] vi piangere; (shout: also: **cry out**)
urlare ■ n urlo, grido; (of animal) verso; **to ~
for help** gridare aiuto; **what are you crying**

505

about? perché piangi?; **she had a good ~** si è fatta un bel pianto; **it's a far ~ from ...** *(fig)* è tutt'un'altra cosa da ...
▶ **cry off** *vi* ritirarsi
crying ['kraɪɪŋ] *adj (fig)* palese; urgente
crypt [krɪpt] *n* cripta
cryptic ['krɪptɪk] *adj* ermetico(-a)
crystal ['krɪstl] *n* cristallo
crystal-clear ['krɪstl'klɪər] *adj* cristallino(-a); *(fig)* chiaro(-a) (come il sole)
crystallize ['krɪstəlaɪz] *vi* cristallizzarsi ▪ *vt (fig)* concretizzare, concretare; **crystallized fruits** *(Brit)* frutta candita
CSA *n abbr (US)* = **Confederate States of America**; *(Brit: = Child Support Agency)* istituto a difesa dei figli di coppie separate, che si adopera affinché venga rispettato l'obbligo del mantenimento
CSC *n abbr (= Civil Service Commission)* commissione per il reclutamento dei funzionari statali
CS gas *n (Brit)* tipo di gas lacrimogeno
CST *abbr (US: = Central Standard Time)* fuso orario
CT *abbr (US)* = **Connecticut**
ct *abbr* = **cent**; **court**
CTC *n abbr (Brit: = city technology college)* istituto tecnico superiore
cu. *abbr* = **cubic**
cub [kʌb] *n* cucciolo; *(also:* **cub scout)** lupetto
Cuba ['kju:bə] *n* Cuba
Cuban ['kju:bən] *adj, n* cubano(-a)
cubbyhole ['kʌbɪhəʊl] *n* angolino
cube [kju:b] *n* cubo ▪ *vt (Math)* elevare al cubo
cube root *n* radice *f* cubica
cubic ['kju:bɪk] *adj* cubico(-a); **~ metre** *etc* metro *etc* cubo; **~ capacity** *(Aut)* cilindrata
cubicle ['kju:bɪkl] *n* scompartimento separato; cabina
cuckoo ['kʊku:] *n* cucù *m inv*
cuckoo clock *n* orologio a cucù
cucumber ['kju:kʌmbər] *n* cetriolo
cud [kʌd] *n*: **to chew the ~** ruminare
cuddle ['kʌdl] *vt* abbracciare, coccolare ▪ *vi* abbracciarsi
cuddly ['kʌdlɪ] *adj* da coccolare
cudgel ['kʌdʒl] *n* randello ▪ *vt*: **to ~ one's brains** scervellarsi, spremere le meningi
cue [kju:] *n* stecca; *(Theat etc)* segnale *m*
cuff [kʌf] *n (of shirt, coat etc)* polsino; *(US: on trousers)* = **turnup**; *(blow)* schiaffo ▪ *vt* dare uno schiaffo a; **off the ~** *adv* improvvisando
cufflink ['kʌflɪŋk] *n* gemello
cu. ft. *abbr* = **cubic feet**
cu. in. *abbr* = **cubic inches**
cuisine [kwɪ'zi:n] *n* cucina
cul-de-sac ['kʌldəsæk] *n* vicolo cieco
culinary ['kʌlɪnərɪ] *adj* culinario(-a)
cull [kʌl] *vt (kill selectively: animals)* selezionare e abbattere

culminate ['kʌlmɪneɪt] *vi*: **to ~ in** culminare con
culmination [kʌlmɪ'neɪʃən] *n* culmine *m*
culottes [kju:'lɒts] *npl* gonna *f* pantalone *inv*
culpable ['kʌlpəbl] *adj* colpevole
culprit ['kʌlprɪt] *n* colpevole *m/f*
cult [kʌlt] *n* culto
cult figure *n* idolo
cultivate ['kʌltɪveɪt] *vt (also fig)* coltivare
cultivation [kʌltɪ'veɪʃən] *n* coltivazione *f*
cultural ['kʌltʃərəl] *adj* culturale
culture ['kʌltʃər] *n (also fig)* cultura
cultured ['kʌltʃəd] *adj* colto(-a)
cumbersome ['kʌmbəsəm] *adj* ingombrante
cumin ['kʌmɪn] *n (spice)* cumino
cumulative ['kju:mjulətɪv] *adj* cumulativo(-a)
cunning ['kʌnɪŋ] *n* astuzia, furberia ▪ *adj* astuto(-a), furbo(-a); *(clever: device, idea)* ingegnoso(-a)
cunt [kʌnt] *n (col!)* figa (!); *(insult)* stronzo(-a) (!)
cup [kʌp] *n* tazza; *(prize)* coppa; **a ~ of tea** una tazza di tè
cupboard ['kʌbəd] *n* armadio
cup final *n (Brit Football)* finale *f* di coppa
Cupid ['kju:pɪd] *n* Cupido; *(figurine):* **cupid** cupido
cupidity [kju:'pɪdɪtɪ] *n* cupidigia
cupola ['kju:pələ] *n* cupola
cuppa ['kʌpə] *n (Brit col)* tazza di tè
cup-tie ['kʌptaɪ] *n (Brit Football)* partita di coppa
curable ['kjʊərəbl] *adj* curabile
curate ['kjʊərɪt] *n* cappellano
curator [kjʊə'reɪtər] *n* direttore *m (di museo etc)*
curb [kə:b] *vt* tenere a freno; *(expenditure)* limitare ▪ *n* freno; *(US)* = **kerb**
curd cheese [kə:d-] *n* cagliata
curdle ['kə:dl] *vi* cagliare
curds [kə:dz] *npl* latte *m* cagliato
cure [kjʊər] *vt* guarire; *(Culin)* trattare; affumicare; essiccare ▪ *n* rimedio; **to be cured of sth** essere guarito(-a) da qc
cure-all ['kjʊərɔ:l] *n (also fig)* panacea, toccasana *m inv*
curfew ['kə:fju:] *n* coprifuoco
curio ['kjʊərɪəʊ] *n* curiosità *f inv*
curiosity [kjʊərɪ'ɒsɪtɪ] *n* curiosità
curious ['kjʊərɪəs] *adj* curioso(-a); **I'm ~ about him** m'incuriosisce
curiously ['kjʊərɪəslɪ] *adv* con curiosità; *(strangely)* stranamente; **~ enough, ...** per quanto possa sembrare strano, ...
curl [kə:l] *n* riccio; *(of smoke etc)* anello ▪ *vt* ondulare; *(tightly)* arricciare ▪ *vi* arricciarsi
▶ **curl up** *vi* avvolgersi a spirale; rannicchiarsi

curler ['kə:lə^r] n bigodino; (Sport) giocatore(-trice) di curling

curlew ['kə:lu:] n chiurlo

curling ['kə:lɪŋ] n (Sport) curling m

curling tongs, (US) **curling irons** npl (for hair) arricciacapelli m inv

curly ['kə:lɪ] adj ricciuto(-a)

currant ['kʌrnt] n uva passa

currency ['kʌrnsɪ] n moneta; **foreign ~** divisa estera; **to gain ~** (fig) acquistare larga diffusione

current ['kʌrnt] adj corrente; (tendency, price, event) attuale ■ n corrente f; **in ~ use** in uso corrente, d'uso comune; **the ~ issue of a magazine** l'ultimo numero di una rivista; **direct/alternating ~** (Elec) corrente continua/alternata

current account n (Brit) conto corrente

current affairs npl attualità fpl

current assets npl (Comm) attivo realizzabile e disponibile

current liabilities npl (Comm) passività fpl correnti

currently ['kʌrntlɪ] adv attualmente

curriculum (pl **curriculums** or **curricula**) [kə'rɪkjuləm, -lə] n curriculum m inv

curriculum vitae [-'vi:taɪ] n curriculum vitae m inv

curry ['kʌrɪ] n curry m inv ■ vt: **to ~ favour with** cercare di attirarsi i favori di; **chicken ~** pollo al curry

curry powder n curry m

curse [kə:s] vt maledire ■ vi bestemmiare ■ n maledizione f; bestemmia

cursor ['kə:sə^r] n (Comput) cursore m

cursory ['kə:sərɪ] adj superficiale

curt [kə:t] adj secco(-a)

curtail [kə:'teɪl] vt (visit etc) accorciare; (expenses etc) ridurre, decurtare

curtain ['kə:tn] n tenda; (Theat) sipario; **to draw the curtains** (together) chiudere or tirare le tende; (apart) aprire le tende

curtain call n (Theat) chiamata alla ribalta

curtsy, curtsey ['kə:tsɪ] n inchino, riverenza ■ vi fare un inchino or una riverenza

curvature ['kə:vətʃə^r] n curvatura

curve [kə:v] n curva ■ vt curvare ■ vi curvarsi; (road) fare una curva

curved [kə:vd] adj curvo(-a)

cushion ['kuʃən] n cuscino ■ vt (shock) fare da cuscinetto a

cushy ['kuʃɪ] adj (col): **a ~ job** un lavoro di tutto riposo; **to have a ~ time** spassarsela

custard ['kʌstəd] n (for pouring) crema

custard powder n (Brit) crema pasticcera in polvere

custodial sentence [kʌs'təudɪəl-] n condanna a pena detentiva

custodian [kʌs'təudɪən] n custode m/f; (of museum etc) soprintendente m/f

custody ['kʌstədɪ] n (of child) custodia; (for offenders) arresto; **to take sb into ~** mettere qn in detenzione preventiva; **in the ~ of** alla custodia di

custom ['kʌstəm] n costume m, usanza; (Law) consuetudine f; (Comm) clientela; see also **customs**

customary ['kʌstəmərɪ] adj consueto(-a); **it is ~ to do** è consuetudine fare

custom-built ['kʌstəm'bɪlt] adj see **custom-made**

customer ['kʌstəmə^r] n cliente m/f; **he's an awkward ~** (col) è un tipo incontentabile

customer profile n profilo del cliente

customized ['kʌstəmaɪzd] adj personalizzato(-a); (car) fuoriserie inv

custom-made ['kʌstəm'meɪd] adj (clothes) fatto(-a) su misura; (other goods: also: **custom-built**) fatto(-a) su ordinazione

customs ['kʌstəmz] npl dogana; **to go through (the) ~** passare la dogana

Customs and Excise n (Brit) Ufficio Dazi e Dogana

customs officer n doganiere m

cut [kʌt] vb (pt, pp **~**) vt tagliare; (shape, make) intagliare; (reduce) ridurre; (col: avoid: class, lecture, appointment) saltare ■ vi tagliare; (intersect) tagliarsi ■ n taglio; (in salary etc) riduzione f; **cold cuts** npl (US) affettati mpl; **power ~** mancanza di corrente elettrica; **to ~ one's finger** tagliarsi un dito; **to get one's hair ~** farsi tagliare i capelli; **to ~ a tooth** mettere un dente; **to ~ sb/sth short** interrompere qn/qc; **to ~ sb dead** ignorare qn completamente

▶ **cut back** vt (plants) tagliare; (production, expenditure) ridurre

▶ **cut down** vt (tree) abbattere; (consumption, expenses) ridurre; **to ~ sb down to size** (fig) sgonfiare or ridimensionare qn

▶ **cut down on** vt fus ridurre

▶ **cut in** vi: **to ~ in (on)** (interrupt conversation) intromettersi (in); (Aut) tagliare la strada (a)

▶ **cut off** vt tagliare; (fig) isolare; **we've been ~ off** (Tel) è caduta la linea

▶ **cut out** vt tagliare; (picture) ritagliare

▶ **cut up** vt (gen) tagliare; (chop: food) sminuzzare

cut-and-dried ['kʌtən'draɪd] adj (also: **cut-and-dry**) assodato(-a)

cutaway ['kʌtəweɪ] adj, n: **~ (drawing)** spaccato

cutback ['kʌtbæk] n riduzione f

507

cute [kjuːt] *adj* grazioso(-a); (*clever*) astuto(-a)
cut glass *n* cristallo
cuticle ['kjuːtɪkl] *n* (*on nail*) pellicina, cuticola
cutlery ['kʌtlərɪ] *n* posate *fpl*
cutlet ['kʌtlɪt] *n* costoletta
cutoff ['kʌtɔf] *n* (*also*: **cutoff point**) limite *m*
cutoff switch *n* interruttore *m*
cutout ['kʌtaut] *n* (*switch*) interruttore *m*; (*paper, cardboard figure*) ritaglio
cut-price ['kʌt'praɪs], (US) **cut-rate** ['kʌt'reɪt] *adj* a prezzo ridotto
cutthroat ['kʌtθrəut] *n* assassino ■ *adj*: **~ competition** concorrenza spietata
cutting ['kʌtɪŋ] *adj* tagliente; (*fig*) pungente ■ *n* (*Brit*: *Press*) ritaglio (di giornale); (: *Rail*) trincea; (*Cine*) montaggio
cutting edge *n* (*of knife*) taglio, filo; **on** *or* **at the ~ of sth** all'avanguardia di qc
cuttlefish ['kʌtlfɪʃ] *n* seppia
cut-up ['kʌtʌp] *adj* stravolto(-a)
CV *n abbr* = **curriculum vitae**
CWO *abbr* = **cash with order**
cwt. *abbr* = **hundredweight**
cyanide ['saɪənaɪd] *n* cianuro
cybercafé ['saɪbəkæfeɪ] *n* cybercaffè *m inv*
cybercrime ['saɪbəkraɪm] *n* delinquenza informatica
cybernetics [saɪbə'nɛtɪks] *n* cibernetica
cyberterrorism [saɪbə'tɛrərɪzəm] *n* ciberterrorismo
cyclamen ['sɪkləmən] *n* ciclamino
cycle ['saɪkl] *n* ciclo; (*bicycle*) bicicletta ■ *vi* andare in bicicletta
cycle path *n* percorso ciclabile

cycle race *n* gara *or* corsa ciclistica
cycle rack *n* portabiciclette *m inv*
cycle track *n* percorso ciclabile; (*in velodrome*) pista
cycling ['saɪklɪŋ] *n* ciclismo; **to go on a ~ holiday** (*Brit*) fare una vacanza in bicicletta
cyclist ['saɪklɪst] *n* ciclista *m/f*
cyclone ['saɪkləun] *n* ciclone *m*
cygnet ['sɪɡnɪt] *n* cigno giovane
cylinder ['sɪlɪndəʳ] *n* cilindro
cylinder capacity *n* cilindrata
cylinder head *n* testata
cylinder head gasket *n* guarnizione *f* della testata del cilindro
cymbals ['sɪmblz] *npl* cembali *mpl*
cynic ['sɪnɪk] *n* cinico(-a)
cynical ['sɪnɪkl] *adj* cinico(-a)
cynicism ['sɪnɪsɪzəm] *n* cinismo
cypress ['saɪprɪs] *n* cipresso
Cypriot ['sɪprɪət] *adj*, *n* cipriota (*m/f*)
Cyprus ['saɪprəs] *n* Cipro
cyst [sɪst] *n* cisti *f inv*
cystitis [sɪ'staɪtɪs] *n* cistite *f*
CZ *n abbr* (US: = *Canal Zone*) zona del Canale di Panama
czar [zɑːʳ] *n* zar *m inv*
Czech [tʃɛk] *adj* ceco(-a) ■ *n* ceco(-a); (*Ling*) ceco; **the ~ Republic** la Repubblica Ceca
Czechoslovak [tʃɛkə'sləuvæk] *adj*, *n* = **Czechoslovakian**
Czechoslovakia [tʃɛkəslə'vækɪə] *n* Cecoslovacchia
Czechoslovakian [tʃɛkəslə'vækɪən] *adj*, *n* cecoslovacco(-a)

Dd

D, d [di:] *n* (*letter*) D, d *f or m inv*; (*Mus*): **D** re *m*; **D for David**, (*US*) **D for Dog** ≈ D come Domodossola

D *abbr* (*US Pol*) = **democrat(ic)**

d *abbr* (*Brit: old*) = **penny**

d. *abbr* = **died**

DA *n abbr* (*US*) = **district attorney**

dab [dæb] *vt* (*eyes, wound*) tamponare; (*paint, cream*) applicare (con leggeri colpetti); **a ~ of paint** un colpetto di vernice

dabble ['dæbl] *vi*: **to ~ in** occuparsi (da dilettante) di

Dacca ['dækə] *n* Dacca *f*

dachshund ['dækshund] *n* bassotto

dad [dæd], **daddy** ['dædɪ] *n* babbo, papà *m inv*

daddy-long-legs [dædɪ'lɒŋlɛgz] *n* tipula, zanzarone *m*

daffodil ['dæfədɪl] *n* trombone *m*, giunchiglia

daft [dɑːft] *adj* sciocco(-a); **to be ~ about sb** perdere la testa per qn; **to be ~ about sth** andare pazzo per qc

dagger ['dægə'] *n* pugnale *m*

dahlia ['deɪljə] *n* dalia

daily ['deɪlɪ] *adj* quotidiano(-a), giornaliero(-a) ■ *n* quotidiano; (*Brit: servant*) donna di servizio ■ *adv* tutti i giorni; **twice ~** due volte al giorno

dainty ['deɪntɪ] *adj* delicato(-a), grazioso(-a)

dairy ['dɛərɪ] *n* (*shop*) latteria; (*on farm*) caseificio ■ *cpd* caseario(-a)

dairy cow *n* mucca da latte

dairy farm *n* caseificio

dairy produce *n* latticini *mpl*

dais ['deɪɪs] *n* pedana, palco

daisy ['deɪzɪ] *n* margherita

daisy wheel *n* (*on printer*) margherita

daisy-wheel printer ['deɪzɪwiːl-] *n* stampante *f* a margherita

Dakar ['dækə'] *n* Dakar *f*

dale [deɪl] *n* valle *f*

dally ['dælɪ] *vi* trastullarsi

dalmatian [dæl'meɪʃən] *n* (*dog*) dalmata *m*

dam [dæm] *n* diga; (*reservoir*) bacino artificiale ■ *vt* sbarrare; costruire dighe su

damage ['dæmɪdʒ] *n* danno, danni *mpl*; (*fig*) danno ■ *vt* danneggiare; (*fig*) recar danno a; **~ to property** danni materiali

damages ['dæmɪdʒɪz] *npl* (*Law*) danni *mpl*; **to pay £5000 in ~** pagare 5000 sterline di indennizzo

damaging ['dæmɪdʒɪŋ] *adj*: **~ (to)** nocivo(-a) (a)

Damascus [də'mɑːskəs] *n* Damasco *f*

dame [deɪm] *n* (*title, US col*) donna; (*Theat*) vecchia signora (*ruolo comico di donna recitato da un uomo*)

damn [dæm] *vt* condannare; (*curse*) maledire ■ *n* (*col*): **I don't give a ~** non me ne importa un fico ■ *adj* (*col*): **this ~ ...** questo maledetto ...; **~ (it)!** accidenti!

damnable ['dæmnəbl] *adj* (*col: behaviour*) vergognoso(-a); (: *weather*) schifoso(-a)

damnation [dæm'neɪʃən] *n* (*Rel*) dannazione *f* ■ *excl* (*col*) dannazione!, diavolo!

damning ['dæmɪŋ] *adj* (*evidence*) schiacciante

damp [dæmp] *adj* umido(-a) ■ *n* umidità, umido ■ *vt* (*also*: **dampen**: *cloth, rag*) inumidire, bagnare; (*enthusiasm etc*) spegnere

dampcourse ['dæmpkɔːs] *n* strato *m* isolante antiumido *inv*

damper ['dæmpə'] *n* (*Mus*) sordina; (*of fire*) valvola di tiraggio; **to put a ~ on sth** (*fig: atmosphere*) gelare; (: *enthusiasm*) far sbollire

dampness ['dæmpnɪs] *n* umidità, umido

damson ['dæmzən] *n* susina damaschina

dance [dɑːns] *n* danza, ballo; (*ball*) ballo ■ *vi* ballare; **to ~ about** saltellare

dance hall *n* dancing *m inv*, sala da ballo

dancer ['dɑːnsə'] *n* danzatore(-trice); (*professional*) ballerino(-a)

dancing ['dɑːnsɪŋ] *n* danza, ballo

D and C *n abbr* (*Med*: = *dilation and curettage*) raschiamento

dandelion ['dændɪlaɪən] *n* dente *m* di leone

dandruff ['dændrəf] *n* forfora

D & T *n abbr* (*Brit: Scol*) = **design and technology**

dandy ['dændɪ] n dandy m inv, elegantone m
∎ adj (US col) fantastico(-a)

Dane [deɪn] n danese m/f

danger ['deɪndʒəʳ] n pericolo; **there is a ~ of fire** c'è pericolo di incendio; **in ~** in pericolo; **out of ~** fuori pericolo; **he was in ~ of falling** rischiava di cadere

danger list n (Med): **on the ~** in prognosi riservata

dangerous ['deɪndʒrəs] adj pericoloso(-a)

dangerously ['deɪndʒrəslɪ] adv: **~ ill** in pericolo di vita

danger zone n area di pericolo

dangle ['dæŋgl] vt dondolare; (fig) far balenare ∎ vi pendolare

Danish ['deɪnɪʃ] adj danese ∎ n (Ling) danese m

Danish pastry n dolce m di pasta sfoglia

dank [dæŋk] adj freddo(-a) e umido(-a)

Danube ['dænjuːb] n: **the ~** il Danubio

dapper ['dæpəʳ] adj lindo(-a)

Dardanelles [dɑːdəˈnɛlz] npl Dardanelli mpl

dare [dɛəʳ] vt: **to ~ sb to do** sfidare qn a fare ∎ vi: **to ~ (to) do sth** osare fare qc; **I daren't tell him** (Brit) non oso dirglielo; **I ~ say he'll turn up** immagino che spunterà

daredevil ['dɛədɛvl] n scavezzacollo m/f

Dar-es-Salaam ['dɑːrɛssəˈlɑːm] n Dar-es-Salaam f

daring ['dɛərɪŋ] adj audace, ardito(-a)

dark [dɑːk] adj (night, room) buio(-a), scuro(-a); (colour, complexion) scuro(-a); (fig) cupo(-a), tetro(-a), nero(-a) ∎ n: **in the ~** al buio; **it is/ is getting ~** è/si sta facendo buio; **in the ~ about** (fig) all'oscuro di; **after ~** a notte fatta; **~ chocolate** cioccolata amara

darken ['dɑːkən] vt (room) oscurare; (photo, painting) far scuro(-a) ∎ vi oscurarsi; imbrunirsi

dark glasses npl occhiali mpl scuri

dark horse n (fig) incognita

darkly ['dɑːklɪ] adv (gloomily) cupamente, con aria cupa; (in a sinister way) minacciosamente

darkness ['dɑːknɪs] n oscurità, buio

darkroom ['dɑːkruːm] n camera oscura

darling ['dɑːlɪŋ] adj caro(-a) ∎ n tesoro

darn [dɑːn] vt rammendare

dart [dɑːt] n freccetta ∎ vi: **to ~ towards** (also: **make a dart towards**) precipitarsi verso; **to ~ along** passare come un razzo; **to ~ away** guizzare via; see also **darts**

dartboard ['dɑːtbɔːd] n bersaglio (per freccette)

darts [dɑːts] n tiro al bersaglio (con freccette)

dash [dæʃ] n (sign) lineetta; (small quantity: of liquid) goccio, goccino; (: of soda) spruzzo ∎ vt (missile) gettare; (hopes) infrangere ∎ vi: **to ~**

towards (also: **make a dash towards**) precipitarsi verso

▶ **dash away** vi scappare via

dashboard ['dæʃbɔːd] n cruscotto

dashing ['dæʃɪŋ] adj ardito(-a)

dastardly ['dæstədlɪ] adj vile

DAT n abbr (= digital audio tape) cassetta f digitale audio inv

data ['deɪtə] npl dati mpl

database ['deɪtəbeɪs] n database m, base f di dati

data capture n registrazione f or rilevazione f di dati

data processing n elaborazione f (elettronica) dei dati

data transmission n trasmissione f di dati

date [deɪt] n data; (appointment) appuntamento; (fruit) dattero ∎ vt datare; (col: girl etc) uscire con; **what's the ~ today?** quanti ne abbiamo oggi?; **~ of birth** data di nascita; **closing ~** scadenza, termine m; **to ~** adv fino a oggi; **out of ~** scaduto(-a); (old-fashioned) passato(-a) di moda; **up to ~** moderno(-a), aggiornato(-a); **to bring up to ~** (correspondence, information) aggiornare; (method) modernizzare; (person) aggiornare, mettere al corrente; **dated the 13th** datato il 13; **thank you for your letter dated 5th July** or **July 5th** (US) la ringrazio per la sua lettera in data 5 luglio

dated ['deɪtɪd] adj passato(-a) di moda

dateline ['deɪtlaɪn] n linea del cambiamento di data

date rape n stupro perpetrato da persona conosciuta

date stamp n timbro datario

daub [dɔːb] vt imbrattare

daughter ['dɔːtəʳ] n figlia

daughter-in-law ['dɔːtərɪnlɔː] n nuora

daunt [dɔːnt] vt intimidire

daunting ['dɔːntɪŋ] adj non invidiabile

dauntless ['dɔːntlɪs] adj intrepido(-a)

dawdle ['dɔːdl] vi bighellonare; **to ~ over one's work** gingillarsi con il lavoro

dawn [dɔːn] n alba ∎ vi (day) spuntare; (fig) venire in mente; **at ~** all'alba; **from ~ to dusk** dall'alba al tramonto; **it dawned on him that ...** gli è venuto in mente che ...

dawn chorus n (Brit) coro mattutino degli uccelli

day [deɪ] n giorno; (as duration) giornata; (period of time, age) tempo, epoca; **the ~ before** il giorno avanti or prima; **the ~ after, the following ~** il giorno dopo, il giorno seguente; **the ~ before yesterday** l'altroieri; **the ~ after tomorrow** dopodomani; **(on) that ~** quel giorno; **(on) the ~ that ...** il giorno che or in cui ...; **to work an 8-hour ~**

avere una giornata lavorativa di 8 ore; **by ~** di giorno; **~ by ~** giorno per giorno; **paid by the ~** pagato(-a) a giornata; **these days, in the present ~** di questi tempi, oggigiorno
daybook ['deɪbuk] n (Brit) brogliaccio
day boy n (Scol) alunno esterno
daybreak ['deɪbreɪk] n spuntar m del giorno
day care centre n scuola materna
daydream ['deɪdriːm] n sogno a occhi aperti
  ■ vi sognare a occhi aperti
day girl n (Scol) alunna esterna
daylight ['deɪlaɪt] n luce f del giorno
daylight robbery n: **it's ~!** (Brit col) è un vero furto!
Daylight Saving Time n (US) ora legale
day release n: **to be on ~** avere un giorno di congedo alla settimana per formazione professionale
day return, day return ticket n (Brit) biglietto giornaliero di andata e ritorno
day shift n turno di giorno
daytime ['deɪtaɪm] n giorno
day-to-day ['deɪtə'deɪ] adj (routine) quotidiano(-a); (expenses) giornaliero(-a); **on a ~ basis** a giornata
day trader n (Stock Exchange) day dealer m/f inv, operatore che compra e vende titoli nel corso della stessa giornata
day trip n gita (di un giorno)
day tripper n gitante m/f
daze [deɪz] vt (drug) inebetire; (blow) stordire
  ■ n: **in a ~** inebetito(-a), stordito(-a)
dazzle ['dæzl] vt abbagliare
dazzling ['dæzlɪŋ] adj (light) abbagliante; (colour) violento(-a); (smile) smagliante
dB abbr (= decibel) db
DC abbr (Elec: = direct current) c.c.; (US) = **District of Columbia**
DCC® n abbr = **digital compact cassette**
DD n abbr (= Doctor of Divinity) titolo di studio
dd. abbr (Comm) = **delivered**
DD abbr = **direct debit**
D-day ['diːdeɪ] n giorno dello sbarco alleato in Normandia
DDS n abbr (US: = Doctor of Dental Science, Doctor of Dental Surgery) titoli di studio
DDT n abbr (= dichlorodiphenyl trichloroethane) D.D.T. m
DE abbr (US) = **Delaware**
deacon ['diːkən] n diacono
dead [dɛd] adj morto(-a); (numb) intirizzito(-a) ■ adv assolutamente, perfettamente; **the dead** npl i morti; **he was shot ~** fu colpito a morte; **~ on time** in perfetto orario; **~ tired** stanco(-a) morto(-a); **to stop ~** fermarsi in tronco; **the line has gone ~** (Tel) è caduta la linea
dead beat adj (col) stanco(-a) morto(-a)

deaden ['dɛdn] vt (blow, sound) ammortire; (make numb) intirizzire
dead end n vicolo cieco
dead-end ['dɛdɛnd] adj: **a ~ job** un lavoro senza sbocchi
dead heat n (Sport): **to finish in a ~** finire alla pari
dead-letter office [dɛd'lɛtə-] n ufficio della posta in giacenza
deadline ['dɛdlaɪn] n scadenza; **to work to a ~** avere una scadenza
deadlock ['dɛdlɔk] n punto morto
dead loss n (col): **to be a ~** (person, thing) non valere niente
deadly ['dɛdlɪ] adj mortale; (weapon, poison) micidiale ■ adv: **~ dull** di una noia micidiale
deadpan ['dɛdpæn] adj a faccia impassibile
Dead Sea n: **the ~** il mar Morto
deaf [dɛf] adj sordo(-a); **to turn a ~ ear to sth** fare orecchi da mercante a qc
deaf-aid ['dɛfeɪd] n apparecchio per la sordità
deaf-and-dumb ['dɛfən'dʌm] adj (person) sordomuto(-a); (alphabet) dei sordomuti
deafen ['dɛfn] vt assordare
deafening ['dɛfnɪŋ] adj fragoroso(-a), assordante
deaf-mute ['dɛfmjuːt] n sordomuto(-a)
deafness ['dɛfnɪs] n sordità
deal [diːl] n accordo; (business deal) affare m
  ■ vt (pt, pp **dealt**) [dɛlt] (blow, cards) dare; **to strike a ~ with sb** fare un affare con qn; **it's a ~!** (col) affare fatto!; **he got a bad/fair ~ from them** l'hanno trattato male/bene; **a good ~ of, a great ~ of** molto(-a)
  ▶ **deal in** vt fus (Comm) occuparsi di
  ▶ **deal with** vt fus (Comm) fare affari con, trattare con; (handle) occuparsi di; (be about: book etc) trattare di
dealer ['diːlər] n commerciante m/f
dealership ['diːləʃɪp] n rivenditore m
dealings ['diːlɪŋz] npl rapporti mpl; (in goods, shares) transazioni fpl
dealt [dɛlt] pt, pp of **deal**
dean [diːn] n (Rel) decano; (Scol) preside m di facoltà (or di collegio)
dear [dɪər] adj caro(-a) ■ n: **my ~** caro mio/cara mia; **~ me!** Dio mio!; **D~ Sir/Madam** (in letter) Egregio Signore/Egregia Signora; **D~ Mr/Mrs X** Gentile Signor/Signora X
dearly ['dɪəlɪ] adv (love) moltissimo; (pay) a caro prezzo
dear money n (Comm) denaro ad alto interesse
dearth [dəːθ] n scarsità, carestia
death [dɛθ] n morte f; (Admin) decesso

deathbed ['dεθbεd] n letto di morte

death certificate n atto di decesso

death duty n (Brit) imposta or tassa di successione

deathly ['dεθlɪ] adj di morte ◼ adv come un cadavere

death penalty n pena di morte

death rate n indice m di mortalità

death row [-rəʊ] n (US): **to be on ~** essere nel braccio della morte

death sentence n condanna a morte

death squad n squadra della morte

deathtrap ['dεθtræp] n trappola mortale

deb [dεb] n abbr (col) = **debutante**

debacle [deɪ'bɑːkl] n (defeat) disfatta; (collapse) sfacelo

debar [dɪ'bɑːʳ] vt: **to ~ sb from a club** etc escludere qn da un club etc; **to ~ sb from doing** vietare a qn di fare

debase [dɪ'beɪs] vt (currency) adulterare; (person) degradare

debatable [dɪ'beɪtəbl] adj discutibile; **it is ~ whether ...** è in dubbio se ...

debate [dɪ'beɪt] n dibattito ◼ vt dibattere, discutere ◼ vi (consider): **to ~ whether** riflettere se

debauchery [dɪ'bɔːtʃərɪ] n dissolutezza

debenture [dɪ'bεntʃəʳ] n (Comm) obbligazione f

debilitate [dɪ'bɪlɪteɪt] vt debilitare

debit ['dεbɪt] n debito ◼ vt: **to ~ a sum to sb** or **to sb's account** addebitare una somma a qn

debit balance n saldo debitore

debit note n nota di addebito

debonair [dεbə'nεəʳ] adj gioviale e disinvolto(-a)

debrief [diː'briːf] vt chiamare a rapporto (a operazione ultimata)

debriefing [diː'briːfɪŋ] n rapporto

debris ['dεbriː] n detriti mpl

debt [dεt] n debito; **to be in ~** essere indebitato(-a); **debts of £5000** debiti per 5000 sterline; **bad ~** debito insoluto

debt collector n agente m di recupero crediti

debtor ['dεtəʳ] n debitore(-trice)

debug [diː'bʌg] vt (Comput) localizzare e rimuovere errori in

debunk [diː'bʌŋk] vt (col: theory) demistificare; (: claim) smentire; (: person, institution) screditare

debut ['deɪbjuː] n debutto

debutante ['dεbjutɑːnt] n debuttante f

Dec. abbr (= December) dic.

decade ['dεkeɪd] n decennio

decadence ['dεkədəns] n decadenza

decadent ['dεkədənt] adj decadente

de-caff ['diːkæf] n (col) decaffeinato

decaffeinated [dɪ'kæfɪneɪtɪd] adj decaffeinato(-a)

decamp [dɪ'kæmp] vi (col) filarsela, levare le tende

decant [dɪ'kænt] vt (wine) travasare

decanter [dɪ'kæntəʳ] n caraffa

decarbonize [diː'kɑːbənaɪz] vt (Aut) decarburare

decathlon [dɪ'kæθlən] n decathlon m

decay [dɪ'keɪ] n decadimento; imputridimento; (fig) rovina; (also: **tooth decay**) carie f ◼ vi (rot) imputridire; (fig) andare in rovina

decease [dɪ'siːs] n decesso

deceased [dɪ'siːst] n: **the ~** il(la) defunto(a)

deceit [dɪ'siːt] n inganno

deceitful [dɪ'siːtful] adj ingannevole, perfido(-a)

deceive [dɪ'siːv] vt ingannare; **to ~ o.s.** illudersi, ingannarsi

decelerate [diː'sεləreɪt] vt, vi rallentare

December [dɪ'sεmbəʳ] n dicembre m; see also **July**

decency ['diːsənsɪ] n decenza

decent ['diːsənt] adj decente; **they were very ~ about it** si sono comportati da signori riguardo a ciò

decently ['diːsəntlɪ] adv (respectably) decentemente, convenientemente; (kindly) gentilmente

decentralization [diːsεntrəlaɪ'zeɪʃən] n decentramento

decentralize [diː'sεntrəlaɪz] vt decentrare

deception [dɪ'sεpʃən] n inganno

deceptive [dɪ'sεptɪv] adj ingannevole

decibel ['dεsɪbεl] n decibel m inv

decide [dɪ'saɪd] vt (person) far prendere una decisione a; (question, argument) risolvere, decidere ◼ vi decidere, decidersi; **to ~ to do/ that** decidere di fare/che; **to ~ on** decidere per; **to ~ against doing sth** decidere di non fare qc

decided [dɪ'saɪdɪd] adj (resolute) deciso(-a); (clear, definite) netto(-a), chiaro(-a)

decidedly [dɪ'saɪdɪdlɪ] adv indubbiamente; decisamente

deciding [dɪ'saɪdɪŋ] adj decisivo(-a)

deciduous [dɪ'sɪdjuəs] adj deciduo(-a)

decimal ['dεsɪməl] adj, n decimale (m); **to 3 ~ places** al terzo decimale

decimalize ['dεsɪməlaɪz] vt (Brit) convertire al sistema metrico decimale

decimal point n ≈ virgola

decimate ['dεsɪmeɪt] vt decimare

decipher [dɪ'saɪfəʳ] vt decifrare

decision [dɪ'sɪʒən] n decisione f; **to make a ~** prendere una decisione

decisive [dɪ'saɪsɪv] adj (victory, factor) decisivo(-a); (influence) determinante;

(*manner, person*) risoluto(-a), deciso(-a); (*reply*) deciso(-a), categorico(-a)

deck [dɛk] *n* (*Naut*) ponte *m*; (*of cards*) mazzo; (*of bus*): **top** ~ imperiale *m*; **to go up on** ~ salire in coperta; **below** ~ sotto coperta; **cassette** ~ piastra (di registrazione); **record** ~ piatto (giradischi)

deckchair ['dɛktʃɛəʳ] *n* sedia a sdraio

deck hand *n* marinaio

declaration [dɛklə'reɪʃən] *n* dichiarazione *f*

declare [dɪ'klɛəʳ] *vt* dichiarare

declassify [diː'klæsɪfaɪ] *vt* rendere accessibile al pubblico

decline [dɪ'klaɪn] *n* (*decay*) declino; (*lessening*) ribasso ■ *vt* declinare; rifiutare ■ *vi* declinare; diminuire; ~ **in living standards** abbassamento del tenore di vita; **to** ~ **to do sth** rifiutar(si) di fare qc

declutch [diː'klʌtʃ] *vi* (*Brit*) premere la frizione

decode [diː'kəud] *vt* decifrare

decoder [diː'kəudəʳ] *n* (*Comput, TV*) decodificatore *m*

decompose [diːkəm'pəuz] *vi* decomporre

decomposition [diːkɔmpə'zɪʃən] *n* decomposizione *f*

decompression [diːkəm'prɛʃən] *n* decompressione *f*

decompression chamber *n* camera di decompressione

decongestant [diːkən'dʒɛstənt] *n* decongestionante *m*

decontaminate [diːkən'tæmɪneɪt] *vt* decontaminare

decontrol [diːkən'trəul] *vt* (*trade*) liberalizzare; (*prices*) togliere il controllo governativo a

decor ['deɪkɔːʳ] *n* decorazione *f*

decorate ['dɛkəreɪt] *vt* (*adorn, give a medal to*) decorare; (*paint and paper*) pitturare e tappezzare

decoration [dɛkə'reɪʃən] *n* decorazione *f*

decorative ['dɛkərətɪv] *adj* decorativo(-a)

decorator ['dɛkəreɪtəʳ] *n* decoratore(-trice)

decorum [dɪ'kɔːrəm] *n* decoro

decoy ['diːkɔɪ] *n* zimbello; **they used him as a** ~ **for the enemy** l'hanno usato come esca per il nemico

decrease *n* ['diːkriːs] diminuzione *f* ■ *vt, vi* [diː'kriːs] diminuire; **to be on the** ~ essere in diminuzione

decreasing [diː'kriːsɪŋ] *adj* sempre meno *inv*

decree [dɪ'kriː] *n* decreto ■ *vt*: **to** ~ (**that**) decretare (che + *sub*); ~ **absolute** sentenza di divorzio definitiva; ~ **nisi** [-'naɪsaɪ] sentenza provvisoria di divorzio

decrepit [dɪ'krɛpɪt] *adj* decrepito(-a); (*building*) cadente

decry [dɪ'kraɪ] *vt* condannare, deplorare

dedicate ['dɛdɪkeɪt] *vt* consacrare; (*book etc*) dedicare

dedicated ['dɛdɪkeɪtɪd] *adj* coscienzioso(-a); (*Comput*) specializzato(-a), dedicato(-a)

dedication [dɛdɪ'keɪʃən] *n* (*devotion*) dedizione *f*; (*in book*) dedica

deduce [dɪ'djuːs] *vt* dedurre

deduct [dɪ'dʌkt] *vt*: **to** ~ **sth (from)** dedurre qc (da); (*from wage etc*) trattenere qc (da)

deduction [dɪ'dʌkʃən] *n* (*deducting*) deduzione *f*; (*from wage etc*) trattenuta; (*deducing*) deduzione *f*, conclusione *f*

deed [diːd] *n* azione *f*, atto; (*Law*) atto; ~ **of covenant** atto di donazione

deem [diːm] *vt* (*formal*) giudicare, ritenere; **to** ~ **it wise to do** ritenere prudente fare

deep [diːp] *adj* profondo(-a) ■ *adv*: ~ **in snow** affondato(-a) nella neve; **spectators stood 20** ~ c'erano 20 file di spettatori; **knee-~ in water** in acqua fino alle ginocchia; **4 metres** ~ profondo(a) 4 metri; **he took a** ~ **breath** fece un respiro profondo

deepen ['diːpn] *vt* (*hole*) approfondire ■ *vi* approfondirsi; (*darkness*) farsi più intenso(-a)

deep-freeze [diːp'friːz] *n* congelatore *m* ■ *vt* congelare

deep-fry ['diːp'fraɪ] *vt* friggere in olio abbondante

deeply ['diːplɪ] *adv* profondamente; **to regret sth** ~ rammaricarsi sinceramente di qc

deep-rooted ['diːp'ruːtɪd] *adj* (*prejudice*) profondamente radicato(-a); (*affection*) profondo(-a); (*habit*) inveterato(-a)

deep-sea diver ['diːp'siː-] *n* palombaro

deep-sea diving *n* immersione *f* in alto mare

deep-sea fishing *n* pesca d'alto mare

deep-seated ['diːp'siːtɪd] *adj* (*beliefs*) radicato(-a)

deep-set ['diːpset] *adj* (*eyes*) infossato(-a)

deep-vein thrombosis ['diːpveɪn-] *n* trombosi *f inv* venosa profonda

deer [dɪəʳ] *n* (*pl inv*): **the** ~ i cervidi (*Zool*); (**red**) ~ cervo; (**fallow**) ~ daino; (**roe**) ~ capriolo

deerskin ['dɪəskɪn] *n* pelle *f* di daino

deerstalker ['dɪəstɔːkəʳ] *n* berretto da cacciatore

deface [dɪ'feɪs] *vt* imbrattare

defamation [dɛfə'meɪʃən] *n* diffamazione *f*

defamatory [dɪ'fæmətərɪ] *adj* diffamatorio(-a)

default [dɪ'fɔːlt] *vi* (*Law*) essere contumace; (*gen*) essere inadempiente ■ *n* (*Comput: also:* **default value**) default *m inv*; (*Law*) in contumacia; (*Sport*) per abbandono; **to** ~ **on a debt** non onorare un debito

defaulter [dɪ'fɔːltəʳ] *n* (*on debt*) inadempiente *m/f*

default option n (*Comput*) opzione f di default
defeat [dɪ'fiːt] n sconfitta ▪ vt (*team, opponents*) sconfiggere; (*fig: plans, efforts*) frustrare
defeatism [dɪ'fiːtɪzəm] n disfattismo
defeatist [dɪ'fiːtɪst] adj, n disfattista (*m/f*)
defecate ['dɛfəkeɪt] vi defecare
defect n ['diːfɛkt] difetto ▪ vi [dɪ'fɛkt]: **to ~ to the enemy/the West** passare al nemico/all'Ovest; **physical ~** difetto fisico; **mental ~** anomalia mentale
defective [dɪ'fɛktɪv] adj difettoso(-a)
defector [dɪ'fɛktər] n rifugiato(-a) politico(-a)
defence, (*US*) **defense** [dɪ'fɛns] n difesa; **in ~ of** in difesa di; **the Ministry of D~,** (*US*) **the Department of Defense** il Ministero della Difesa; **witness for the ~** teste m/f a difesa
defenceless [dɪ'fɛnslɪs] adj senza difesa
defend [dɪ'fɛnd] vt difendere; (*decision, action*) giustificare; (*opinion*) sostenere
defendant [dɪ'fɛndənt] n imputato(-a)
defender [dɪ'fɛndər] n difensore(-a)
defending champion n (*Sport*) campione(-essa) in carica
defending counsel n (*Law*) avvocato difensore
defense [dɪ'fɛns] n (*US*) = **defence**
defensive [dɪ'fɛnsɪv] adj difensivo(-a) ▪ n difensiva; **on the ~** sulla difensiva
defer [dɪ'fəːr] vt (*postpone*) differire, rinviare ▪ vi (*submit*): **to ~ to sb/sth** rimettersi a qn/qc
deference ['dɛfərəns] n deferenza; riguardo; **out of** or **in ~ to** per riguardo a
defiance [dɪ'faɪəns] n sfida; **in ~ of** a dispetto di
defiant [dɪ'faɪənt] adj (*attitude*) di sfida; (*person*) ribelle
defiantly [dɪ'faɪəntlɪ] adv con aria di sfida
deficiency [dɪ'fɪʃənsɪ] n deficienza; carenza; (*Comm*) ammanco
deficiency disease n malattia da carenza
deficient [dɪ'fɪʃənt] adj deficiente; insufficiente; **to be ~ in** mancare di
deficit ['dɛfɪsɪt] n disavanzo
defile [dɪ'faɪl] vt contaminare ▪ vi sfilare ▪ n ['diːfaɪl] gola, stretta
define [dɪ'faɪn] vt (*gen, Comput*) definire
definite ['dɛfɪnɪt] adj (*fixed*) definito(-a), preciso(-a); (*clear, obvious*) ben definito(-a), esatto(-a); (*Ling*) determinativo(-a); **he was ~ about it** ne era sicuro
definitely ['dɛfɪnɪtlɪ] adv indubbiamente
definition [dɛfɪ'nɪʃən] n definizione f
definitive [dɪ'fɪnɪtɪv] adj definitivo(-a)
deflate [diː'fleɪt] vt sgonfiare; (*Econ*) deflazionare; (*pompous person*) fare abbassare la cresta a

deflation [diː'fleɪʃən] n (*Econ*) deflazione f
deflationary [diː'fleɪʃənrɪ] adj (*Econ*) deflazionistico(-a)
deflect [dɪ'flɛkt] vt deflettere, deviare
defog ['diː'fɒg] vt (*US Aut*) sbrinare
defogger ['diː'fɒgər] n (*US Aut*) sbrinatore m
deform [dɪ'fɔːm] vt deformare
deformed [dɪ'fɔːmd] adj deforme
deformity [dɪ'fɔːmɪtɪ] n deformità f inv
Defra n abbr (*Brit*) = **Department for Environment, Food and Rural Affairs**
defraud [dɪ'frɔːd] vt: **to ~ (of)** defraudare (di)
defray [dɪ'freɪ] vt: **to ~ sb's expenses** sostenere le spese di qn
defrost [diː'frɒst] vt (*fridge*) disgelare; (*frozen food*) scongelare
deft [dɛft] adj svelto(-a), destro(-a)
defunct [dɪ'fʌŋkt] adj defunto(-a)
defuse [diː'fjuːz] vt disinnescare; (*fig*) distendere
defy [dɪ'faɪ] vt sfidare; (*efforts etc*) resistere a; (*refuse to obey: person*) rifiutare di obbedire a
degenerate vi [dɪ'dʒɛnəreɪt] degenerare ▪ adj [dɪ'dʒɛnərɪt] degenere
degradation [dɛgrə'deɪʃən] n degradazione f
degrade [dɪ'greɪd] vt degradare
degrading [dɪ'greɪdɪŋ] adj degradante
degree [dɪ'griː] n grado; (*Scol*) laurea (universitaria); **10 degrees below freezing** 10 gradi sotto zero; **a (first) ~ in maths** una laurea in matematica; **a considerable ~ of risk** una grossa percentuale di rischio; **by degrees** (*gradually*) gradualmente, a poco a poco; **to some ~, to a certain ~** fino a un certo punto, in certa misura
dehydrated [diːhaɪ'dreɪtɪd] adj disidratato(-a); (*milk, eggs*) in polvere
dehydration [diːhaɪ'dreɪʃən] n disidratazione f
de-ice [diː'aɪs] vt (*windscreen*) disgelare
de-icer ['diː'aɪsər] n sbrinatore m
deign [deɪn] vi: **to ~ to do** degnarsi di fare
deity ['diːɪtɪ] n divinità f inv; dio/dea
déjà vu [deɪʒɑ:'vuː] n déjà vu m inv
dejected [dɪ'dʒɛktɪd] adj abbattuto(-a), avvilito(-a)
dejection [dɪ'dʒɛkʃən] n abbattimento, avvilimento
Del. abbr (*US*) = **Delaware**
delay [dɪ'leɪ] vt (*journey, operation*) ritardare, rinviare; (*travellers, trains*) ritardare; (*payment*) differire ▪ n ritardo; **without ~** senza ritardo
delayed-action [dɪ'leɪd'ækʃən] adj a azione ritardata
delectable [dɪ'lɛktəbl] adj delizioso(-a)
delegate n ['dɛlɪgɪt] delegato(-a) ▪ vt

['dɛlɪgeɪt] delegare; **to ~ sth to sb/sb to do sth** delegare qc a qn/qn a fare qc

delegation [dɛlɪ'geɪʃən] *n* delegazione *f*; (*of work etc*) delega

delete [dɪ'liːt] *vt* (*gen, Comput*) cancellare

Delhi ['dɛlɪ] *n* Delhi *f*

deli ['dɛlɪ] *n* = **delicatessen**

deliberate *adj* [dɪ'lɪbərɪt] (*intentional*) intenzionale; (*slow*) misurato(-a) ◼ *vi* [dɪ'lɪbəreɪt] deliberare, riflettere

deliberately [dɪ'lɪbərɪtlɪ] *adv* (*on purpose*) deliberatamente

deliberation [dɪlɪbə'reɪʃən] *n* (*consideration*) riflessione *f*; (*discussion*) discussione *f*, deliberazione *f*

delicacy ['dɛlɪkəsɪ] *n* delicatezza

delicate ['dɛlɪkɪt] *adj* delicato(-a)

delicately ['dɛlɪkɪtlɪ] *adv* (*gen*) delicatamente; (*act, express*) con delicatezza

delicatessen [dɛlɪkə'tɛsn] *n* ≈ salumeria

delicious [dɪ'lɪʃəs] *adj* delizioso(-a), squisito(-a)

delight [dɪ'laɪt] *n* delizia, gran piacere *m* ◼ *vt* dilettare; **it is a ~ to the eyes** è un piacere guardarlo; **to ~ in** divertirsi a; **to be the ~ of** essere la gioia di

delighted [dɪ'laɪtɪd] *adj*: **~ (at** or **with sth)** contentissimo(-a) (di qc), felice (di qc); **to be ~ to do sth/that** essere felice di fare qc/che +*sub*; **I'd be ~** con grande piacere

delightful [dɪ'laɪtful] *adj* (*person, place, meal*) delizioso(-a); (*smile, manner*) incantevole

delimit [di:'lɪmɪt] *vt* delimitare

delineate [dɪ'lɪnɪeɪt] *vt* delineare

delinquency [dɪ'lɪŋkwənsɪ] *n* delinquenza

delinquent [dɪ'lɪŋkwənt] *adj, n* delinquente (*m/f*)

delirious [dɪ'lɪrɪəs] *adj* (*Med, fig*) delirante, in delirio; **to be ~** delirare; (*fig*) farneticare

delirium [dɪ'lɪrɪəm] *n* delirio

deliver [dɪ'lɪvə^r] *vt* (*mail*) distribuire; (*goods*) consegnare; (*speech*) pronunciare; (*free*) liberare; (*Med*) far partorire; **to ~ a message** fare un'ambasciata; **to ~ the goods** (*fig*) partorire

deliverance [dɪ'lɪvrəns] *n* liberazione *f*

delivery [dɪ'lɪvərɪ] *n* distribuzione *f*; consegna; (*of speaker*) dizione *f*; (*Med*) parto; **to take ~ of** prendere in consegna

delivery note *n* bolla di consegna

delivery van, (*US*) **delivery truck** *n* furgoncino (per le consegne)

delta ['dɛltə] *n* delta *m*

delude [dɪ'luːd] *vt* deludere, illudere

deluge ['dɛljuːdʒ] *n* diluvio ◼ *vt* (*fig*): **to ~ (with)** subissare (di), inondare (di)

delusion [dɪ'luːʒən] *n* illusione *f*

de luxe [də'lʌks] *adj* di lusso

delve [dɛlv] *vi*: **to ~ into** frugare in; (*subject*) far ricerche in

Dem. *abbr* (*US Pol*) = **Democrat(ic)**

demagogue ['dɛməgɔg] *n* demagogo

demand [dɪ'mɑːnd] *vt* richiedere ◼ *n* richiesta; (*Econ*) domanda; **to ~ sth (from** or **of sb)** pretendere qc (da qn), esigere qc (da qn); **in ~** ricercato(-a), richiesto(-a); **on ~** a richiesta

demand draft *n* (*Comm*) tratta a vista

demanding [dɪ'mɑːndɪŋ] *adj* (*boss*) esigente; (*work*) impegnativo(-a)

demarcation [di:mɑː'keɪʃən] *n* demarcazione *f*

demarcation dispute *n* (*Industry*) controversia settoriale (*or* di categoria)

demean [dɪ'miːn] *vt*: **to ~ o.s.** umiliarsi

demeanour, (*US*) **demeanor** [dɪ'miːnə^r] *n* comportamento; contegno

demented [dɪ'mɛntɪd] *adj* demente, impazzito(-a)

demilitarized zone [di:'mɪlɪtəraɪzd-] *n* zona smilitarizzata

demise [dɪ'maɪz] *n* decesso

demist [di:'mɪst] *vt* (*Brit Aut*) sbrinare

demister [di:'mɪstə^r] *n* (*Brit Aut*) sbrinatore *m*

demo ['dɛməu] *n abbr* (*col*) = **demonstration**

demobilize [di:'məubɪlaɪz] *vt* smobilitare

democracy [dɪ'mɔkrəsɪ] *n* democrazia

democrat ['dɛməkræt] *n* democratico(-a)

democratic [dɛmə'krætɪk] *adj* democratico(-a); **the D~ Party** (*US*) il partito democratico

demography [dɪ'mɔgrəfɪ] *n* demografia

demolish [dɪ'mɔlɪʃ] *vt* demolire

demolition [dɛmə'lɪʃən] *n* demolizione *f*

demon ['diːmən] *n* (*also fig*) demonio ◼ *cpd*: **a ~ squash player** un mago dello squash; **a ~ driver** un guidatore folle

demonstrate ['dɛmənstreɪt] *vt* dimostrare, provare ◼ *vi*: **to ~ (for/against)** dimostrare (per/contro), manifestare (per/contro)

demonstration [dɛmən'streɪʃən] *n* dimostrazione *f*; (*Pol*) manifestazione *f*, dimostrazione; **to hold a ~** (*Pol*) tenere una manifestazione, fare una dimostrazione

demonstrative [dɪ'mɔnstrətɪv] *adj* dimostrativo(-a)

demonstrator ['dɛmənstreɪtə^r] *n* (*Pol*) dimostrante *m/f*; (*Comm: sales person*) dimostratore(-trice); (*: car, computer etc*) modello per dimostrazione

demoralize [dɪ'mɔrəlaɪz] *vt* demoralizzare

demote [dɪ'məut] *vt* far retrocedere

demotion [dɪ'məuʃən] *n* retrocessione *f*, degradazione *f*

d

demur [dɪˈməːʳ] vi (formal): **to ~ (at)** sollevare obiezioni (a or su) ■ n: **without ~** senza obiezioni

demure [dɪˈmjuəʳ] adj contegnoso(-a)

demurrage [dɪˈmʌrɪdʒ] n diritti mpl di immagazzinaggio; spese fpl di controstallia

den [den] n tana, covo

denationalization [ˈdiːnæʃnəlaɪˈzeɪʃən] n denazionalizzazione f

denationalize [diːˈnæʃnəlaɪz] vt snazionalizzare

denial [dɪˈnaɪəl] n diniego; rifiuto

denier [ˈdɛnɪəʳ] n denaro (di filati, calze)

denigrate [ˈdɛnɪɡreɪt] vt denigrare

denim [ˈdɛnɪm] n tessuto di cotone ritorto; see also **denims**

denim jacket n giubbotto di jeans

denims [ˈdɛnɪmz] npl blue jeans mpl

denizen [ˈdɛnɪzən] n (inhabitant) abitante m/f; (foreigner) straniero(-a) naturalizzato(-a)

Denmark [ˈdɛnmɑːk] n Danimarca

denomination [dɪnɔmɪˈneɪʃən] n (of money) valore m; (Rel) confessione f

denominator [dɪˈnɔmɪneɪtəʳ] n denominatore m

denote [dɪˈnəut] vt denotare

denounce [dɪˈnauns] vt denunciare

dense [dɛns] adj fitto(-a); (stupid) ottuso(-a), duro(-a)

densely [ˈdɛnslɪ] adv: **~ wooded** fittamente boscoso(-a); **~ populated** densamente popolato(-a)

density [ˈdɛnsɪtɪ] n densità f inv; **single/double ~ disk** (Comput) disco a singola/doppia densità di registrazione

dent [dɛnt] n ammaccatura ■ vt (also: **make a dent in**) ammaccare; (fig) intaccare

dental [ˈdɛntl] adj dentale

dental floss [-flɔs] n filo interdentale

dental surgeon n medico(-a) dentista

dentist [ˈdɛntɪst] n dentista m/f; **~'s surgery** (Brit) gabinetto dentistico

dentistry [ˈdɛntɪstrɪ] n odontoiatria

denture [ˈdɛntʃəʳ] n, **dentures** [ˈdɛntʃəz] npl dentiera

denunciation [dɪnʌnsɪˈeɪʃən] n denuncia

deny [dɪˈnaɪ] vt negare; (refuse) rifiutare; **he denies having said it** nega di averlo detto

deodorant [diːˈəudərənt] n deodorante m

depart [dɪˈpɑːt] vi partire; **to ~ from** (leave) allontanarsi da, partire da; (fig) deviare da

departed [dɪˈpɑːtɪd] adj estinto(-a) ■ n: **the ~** il caro estinto/la cara estinta

department [dɪˈpɑːtmənt] n (Comm) reparto; (Scol) sezione f, dipartimento; (Pol) ministero; **that's not my ~** (also fig) questo non è di mia competenza; **D~ of State** (US) Dipartimento di Stato

departmental [dɪpɑːtˈmɛntl] adj (dispute) settoriale; (meeting) di sezione; **~ manager** caporeparto m/f

department store n grande magazzino

departure [dɪˈpɑːtʃəʳ] n partenza; (fig): **~ from** deviazione f da; **a new ~** una novità

departure lounge n sala d'attesa

depend [dɪˈpɛnd] vi: **to ~ (up)on** dipendere da; (rely on) contare su; (be dependent on) dipendere (economicamente) da, essere a carico di; **it depends** dipende; **depending on the result ...** a seconda del risultato ...

dependable [dɪˈpɛndəbl] adj fidato(-a); (car etc) affidabile

dependant [dɪˈpɛndənt] n persona a carico

dependence [dɪˈpɛndəns] n dipendenza

dependent [dɪˈpɛndənt] adj: **to be ~ (on)** (gen) dipendere (da); (child, relative) essere a carico (di) ■ n = **dependant**

depict [dɪˈpɪkt] vt (in picture) dipingere; (in words) descrivere

depilatory [dɪˈpɪlətərɪ] n (also: **depilatory cream**) crema depilatoria

depleted [dɪˈpliːtɪd] adj diminuito(-a)

deplorable [dɪˈplɔːrəbl] adj deplorevole, lamentevole

deplore [dɪˈplɔːʳ] vt deplorare

deploy [dɪˈplɔɪ] vt dispiegare

depopulate [diːˈpɔpjuleɪt] vt spopolare

depopulation [ˈdiːpɔpjuˈleɪʃən] n spopolamento

deport [dɪˈpɔːt] vt deportare; espellere

deportation [diːpɔːˈteɪʃən] n deportazione f

deportation order n foglio di via obbligatorio

deportee [diːpɔːˈtiː] n deportato(-a)

deportment [dɪˈpɔːtmənt] n portamento

depose [dɪˈpəuz] vt deporre

deposit [dɪˈpɔzɪt] n (Comm, Geo) deposito; (of ore, oil) giacimento; (Chem) sedimento; (part payment) acconto; (for hired goods etc) cauzione f ■ vt depositare; dare in acconto; (luggage etc) mettere or lasciare in deposito; **to put down a ~ of £50** versare una caparra di 50 sterline

deposit account n conto vincolato

depositor [dɪˈpɔzɪtəʳ] n depositante m/f

depository [dɪˈpɔzɪtərɪ] n (person) depositario(-a); (place) deposito

depot [ˈdɛpəu] n deposito

depraved [dɪˈpreɪvd] adj depravato(-a)

depravity [dɪˈprævɪtɪ] n depravazione f

deprecate [ˈdɛprɪkeɪt] vt deprecare

deprecating [ˈdɛprɪkeɪtɪŋ] adj (disapproving) di biasimo; (apologetic): **a ~ smile** un sorriso di scusa

depreciate [dɪˈpriːʃieɪt] vt svalutare ■ vi svalutarsi

depreciation [dɪpriːʃɪ'eɪʃən] n svalutazione f
depress [dɪ'prɛs] vt deprimere; (press down) premere
depressant [dɪ'prɛsnt] n (Med) sedativo
depressed [dɪ'prɛst] adj (person) depresso(-a), abbattuto(-a); (area) depresso(-a); (Comm: market, trade) stagnante, in ribasso; **to get ~** deprimersi
depressing [dɪ'prɛsɪŋ] adj deprimente
depression [dɪ'prɛʃən] n depressione f
deprivation [dɛprɪ'veɪʃən] n privazione f; (state) indigenza; (Psych) carenza affettiva
deprive [dɪ'praɪv] vt: **to ~ sb of** privare qn di
deprived [dɪ'praɪvd] adj disgraziato(-a)
dept. abbr = **department**
depth [dɛpθ] n profondità f inv; **at a ~ of 3 metres** a una profondità di 3 metri, a 3 metri di profondità; **in the depths of** nel profondo di; nel cuore di; **in the depths of winter** in pieno inverno; **to study sth in ~** studiare qc in profondità; **to be out of one's ~** (Brit: swimmer) essere dove non si tocca; (fig) non sentirsi all'altezza della situazione
depth charge n carica di profondità
deputation [dɛpju'teɪʃən] n deputazione f, delegazione f
deputize ['dɛpjutaɪz] vi: **to ~ for** svolgere le funzioni di
deputy ['dɛpjutɪ] n (replacement) supplente m/f; (second in command) vice m/f ■ cpd: **~ chairman** vicepresidente m; **~ head** (Scol) vicepreside m/f; **~ leader** (Brit Pol) sottosegretario
derail [dɪ'reɪl] vt far deragliare; **to be derailed** deragliare
derailment [dɪ'reɪlmənt] n deragliamento
deranged [dɪ'reɪndʒd] adj: **to be (mentally) ~** essere pazzo(a)
derby ['dəːbɪ] n (US) bombetta
deregulate [diː'rɛgjuleɪt] vt eliminare la regolamentazione di
deregulation ['diːrɛgju'leɪʃən] n eliminazione f della regolamentazione
derelict ['dɛrɪlɪkt] adj abbandonato(-a)
deride [dɪ'raɪd] vt deridere
derision [dɪ'rɪʒən] n derisione f
derisive [dɪ'raɪsɪv] adj di derisione
derisory [dɪ'raɪsərɪ] adj (sum) irrisorio(-a)
derivation [dɛrɪ'veɪʃən] n derivazione f
derivative [dɪ'rɪvətɪv] n derivato ■ adj derivato(-a)
derive [dɪ'raɪv] vt: **to ~ sth from** derivare qc da; trarre qc da ■ vi: **to ~ from** derivare da
dermatitis [dəːmə'taɪtɪs] n dermatite f
dermatology [dəːmə'tɔlədʒɪ] n dermatologia
derogatory [dɪ'rɔgətərɪ] adj denigratorio(-a)
derrick ['dɛrɪk] n gru f inv; (for oil) derrick m inv
derv [dəːv] n (Brit) gasolio

desalination [diːsælɪ'neɪʃən] n desalinizzazione f, dissalazione f
descend [dɪ'sɛnd] vt, vi discendere, scendere; **to ~ from** discendere da; **in descending order of importance** in ordine decrescente d'importanza
▶ **descend on** vt fus (enemy, angry person) assalire, piombare su; (misfortune) arrivare addosso a; (fig: gloom, silence) scendere su; **visitors descended (up)on us** ci sono arrivate visite tra capo e collo
descendant [dɪ'sɛndənt] n discendente m/f
descent [dɪ'sɛnt] n discesa; (origin) discendenza, famiglia
describe [dɪs'kraɪb] vt descrivere
description [dɪs'krɪpʃən] n descrizione f; (sort) genere m, specie f; **of every ~** di ogni genere e specie
descriptive [dɪs'krɪptɪv] adj descrittivo(-a)
desecrate ['dɛsɪkreɪt] vt profanare
desert n ['dɛzət] deserto vb [dɪ'zəːt] vt lasciare, abbandonare ■ vi (Mil) disertare; see also **deserts**
deserter [dɪ'zəːtə'] n disertore m
desertion [dɪ'zəːʃən] n diserzione f
desert island n isola deserta
deserts [dɪ'zəːts] npl: **to get one's just ~** avere ciò che si merita
deserve [dɪ'zəːv] vt meritare
deservedly [dɪ'zəːvɪdlɪ] adv meritatamente, giustamente
deserving [dɪ'zəːvɪŋ] adj (person) meritevole, degno(-a); (cause) meritorio(-a)
desiccated ['dɛsɪkeɪtɪd] adj essiccato(-a)
design [dɪ'zaɪn] n (sketch) disegno; (: of dress, car) modello; (layout, shape) linea; (pattern) fantasia; (Comm) disegno tecnico; (intention) intenzione f ■ vt disegnare; progettare; **to have designs on** aver mire su; **well-designed** ben concepito; **industrial ~** disegno industriale
design and technology n (Brit: Scol) progettazione f e tecnologie fpl
designate vt ['dɛzɪgneɪt] designare ■ adj ['dɛzɪgnɪt] designato(-a)
designation [dɛzɪg'neɪʃən] n designazione f
designer [dɪ'zaɪnə'] n (Tech) disegnatore(-trice), progettista m/f; (of furniture) designer m/f inv; (fashion designer) disegnatore(-trice) di moda; (of theatre sets) scenografo(-a)
designer baby n bambino progettato geneticamente prima della nascita
desirability [dɪzaɪərə'bɪlɪtɪ] n desiderabilità; vantaggio
desirable [dɪ'zaɪərəbl] adj desiderabile; **it is ~ that** è opportuno che + sub

517

desire [dɪ'zaɪə^r] n desiderio, voglia ■ vt
desiderare, volere; **to ~ sth/to do sth/that**
desiderare qc/di fare qc/che + sub

desirous [dɪ'zaɪərəs] adj: **~ of** desideroso(-a)
di

desk [dɛsk] n (in office) scrivania; (for pupil)
banco; (Brit: in shop, restaurant) cassa; (in hotel)
ricevimento; (at airport) accettazione f

desk job n lavoro d'ufficio

desktop computer ['dɛsktɔp-] n personal m
inv, personal computer m inv

desktop publishing n desktop publishing m

desolate ['dɛsəlɪt] adj desolato(-a)

desolation [dɛsə'leɪʃən] n desolazione f

despair [dɪs'pɛə^r] n disperazione f ■ vi: **to ~
of** disperare di; **in ~** disperato(-a)

despatch [dɪs'pætʃ] n, vt = **dispatch**

desperate ['dɛspərɪt] adj disperato(-a);
(measures) estremo(-a); (fugitive) capace di
tutto; **we are getting ~** siamo sull'orlo della
disperazione

desperately ['dɛspərɪtlɪ] adv
disperatamente; (very) terribilmente,
estremamente; **~ ill** in pericolo di vita

desperation [dɛspə'reɪʃən] n disperazione f;
in ~ per disperazione

despicable [dɪs'pɪkəbl] adj disprezzabile

despise [dɪs'paɪz] vt disprezzare, sdegnare

despite [dɪs'paɪt] prep malgrado, a dispetto
di, nonostante

despondent [dɪs'pɔndənt] adj abbattuto(-a),
scoraggiato(-a)

despot ['dɛspɔt] n despota m

dessert [dɪ'zə:t] n dolce m; frutta

dessertspoon [dɪ'zə:tspu:n] n cucchiaio da
dolci

destabilize [di:'steɪbɪlaɪz] vt privare di
stabilità; (fig) destabilizzare

destination [dɛstɪ'neɪʃən] n destinazione f

destine ['dɛstɪn] vt destinare

destined ['dɛstɪnd] adj: **to be ~ to do sth**
essere destinato(a) a fare qc; **~ for London**
diretto a Londra, con destinazione Londra

destiny ['dɛstɪnɪ] n destino

destitute ['dɛstɪtju:t] adj indigente,
bisognoso(-a); **~ of** privo(a) di

destroy [dɪs'trɔɪ] vt distruggere

destroyer [dɪs'trɔɪə^r] n (Naut)
cacciatorpediniere m

destruction [dɪs'trʌkʃən] n distruzione f

destructive [dɪs'trʌktɪv] adj distruttivo(-a)

desultory ['dɛsəltərɪ] adj (reading)
disordinato(-a); (conversation) sconnesso(-a);
(contact) saltuario(-a), irregolare

detach [dɪ'tætʃ] vt staccare, distaccare

detachable [dɪ'tætʃəbl] adj staccabile

detached [dɪ'tætʃt] adj (attitude) distante

detached house n villa

detachment [dɪ'tætʃmənt] n (Mil)
distaccamento; (fig) distacco

detail ['di:teɪl] n particolare m, dettaglio;
(Mil) piccolo distaccamento ■ vt dettagliare,
particolareggiare; (Mil): **to ~ sb (for)**
assegnare qn (a); **in ~** nei particolari; **to go
into ~(s)** scendere nei particolari

detailed ['di:teɪld] adj particolareggiato(-a)

detain [dɪ'teɪn] vt trattenere; (in captivity)
detenere

detainee [di:teɪ'ni:] n detenuto(-a)

detect [dɪ'tɛkt] vt scoprire, scorgere; (Med,
Police, Radar etc) individuare

detection [dɪ'tɛkʃən] n scoperta;
individuazione f; **crime ~** indagini fpl
criminali; **to escape ~** (criminal) eludere le
ricerche; (mistake) passare inosservato(-a)

detective [dɪ'tɛktɪv] n investigatore(-trice);
private ~ investigatore m privato

detective story n giallo

detector [dɪ'tɛktə^r] n rivelatore m

détente [deɪ'ta:nt] n distensione f

detention [dɪ'tɛnʃən] n detenzione f; (Scol)
permanenza forzata per punizione

deter [dɪ'tə:^r] vt dissuadere

detergent [dɪ'tə:dʒənt] n detersivo

deteriorate [dɪ'tɪərɪəreɪt] vi deteriorarsi

deterioration [dɪtɪərɪə'reɪʃən] n
deterioramento

determination [dɪtə:mɪ'neɪʃən] n
determinazione f

determine [dɪ'tə:mɪn] vt determinare;
to ~ to do sth decidere di fare qc

determined [dɪ'tə:mɪnd] adj (person)
risoluto(-a), deciso(-a); **to be ~ to do sth**
essere determinato or deciso a fare qc; **a ~
effort** uno sforzo di volontà

deterrence [dɪ'tɛrəns] n deterrenza

deterrent [dɪ'tɛrənt] n deterrente m; **to act
as a ~** fungere da deterrente

detest [dɪ'tɛst] vt detestare

detestable [dɪ'tɛstəbl] adj detestabile,
abominevole

detonate ['dɛtəneɪt] vi detonare ■ vt far
detonare

detonator ['dɛtəneɪtə^r] n detonatore m

detour ['di:tuə^r] n deviazione f

detract [dɪ'trækt] vt: **to ~ from** detrarre da

detractor [dɪ'træktə^r] n detrattore(-trice)

detriment ['dɛtrɪmənt] n: **to the ~ of** a
detrimento di; **without ~ to** senza danno a

detrimental [dɛtrɪ'mɛntl] adj: **~ to**
dannoso(-a) a, nocivo(-a) a

deuce [dju:s] n (Tennis) quaranta pari m inv

devaluation [di:vælju'eɪʃən] n svalutazione f

devalue ['di:'vælju:] vt svalutare

devastate ['dɛvəsteɪt] *vt* devastare; **he was devastated by the news** la notizia fu per lui un colpo terribile

devastating ['dɛvəsteɪtɪŋ] *adj* devastatore(-trice)

devastation [dɛvə'steɪʃən] *n* devastazione *f*

develop [dɪ'vɛləp] *vt* sviluppare; (*habit*) prendere (gradualmente) ▪ *vi* svilupparsi; (*facts, symptoms: appear*) manifestarsi, rivelarsi; **to ~ a taste for sth** imparare a gustare qc; **to ~ into** diventare

developer [dɪ'vɛləpə^r] *n* (*Phot*) sviluppatore *m*; **property ~** costruttore *m* (edile)

developing country [dɪ'vɛləpɪŋ-] *n* paese *m* in via di sviluppo

development [dɪ'vɛləpmənt] *n* sviluppo

development area *n* area di sviluppo industriale

deviant ['di:vɪənt] *adj* deviante

deviate ['di:vɪeɪt] *vi*: **to ~ (from)** deviare (da)

deviation [di:vɪ'eɪʃən] *n* deviazione *f*

device [dɪ'vaɪs] *n* (*apparatus*) congegno; (*explosive device*) ordigno esplosivo

devil ['dɛvl] *n* diavolo; demonio

devilish ['dɛvlɪʃ] *adj* diabolico(-a)

devil-may-care ['dɛvlmeɪ'kɛə^r] *adj* impudente

devil's advocate *n*: **to play ~** fare l'avvocato del diavolo

devious ['di:vɪəs] *adj* (*means*) indiretto(-a), tortuoso(-a); (*person*) subdolo(-a)

devise [dɪ'vaɪz] *vt* escogitare, concepire

devoid [dɪ'vɔɪd] *adj*: **~ of** privo(-a) di

devolution [di:və'lu:ʃən] *n* (*Pol*) decentramento

devolve [dɪ'vɔlv] *vi*: **to ~ (up)on** ricadere su

devote [dɪ'vəut] *vt*: **to ~ sth to** dedicare qc a

devoted [dɪ'vəutɪd] *adj* devoto(-a); **to be ~ to** essere molto attaccato(-a) a

devotee [dɛvəu'ti:] *n* (*Rel*) adepto(-a); (*Mus, Sport*) appassionato(-a)

devotion [dɪ'vəuʃən] *n* devozione *f*, attaccamento; (*Rel*) atto di devozione, preghiera

devour [dɪ'vauə^r] *vt* divorare

devout [dɪ'vaut] *adj* pio(-a), devoto(-a)

dew [dju:] *n* rugiada

dexterity [dɛks'tɛrɪtɪ] *n* destrezza

dexterous, dextrous ['dɛkstrəs] *adj* (*skilful*) destro(-a), abile; (*movement*) agile

DfEE *n abbr* (*Brit*: = *Department for Education and Employment*) Ministero della pubblica istruzione e dell'occupazione

dg *abbr* (= *decigram*) dg

diabetes [daɪə'bi:ti:z] *n* diabete *m*

diabetic [daɪə'bɛtɪk] *adj* diabetico(-a); (*chocolate, jam*) per diabetici ▪ *n* diabetico(-a)

diabolical [daɪə'bɔlɪkl] *adj* diabolico(-a); (*col: dreadful*) infernale, atroce

diaeresis [daɪ'ɛrɪsɪs] *n* dieresi *f inv*

diagnose [daɪəg'nəuz] *vt* diagnosticare

diagnosis (*pl* **diagnoses**) [daɪəg'nəusɪs, -si:z] *n* diagnosi *f inv*

diagonal [daɪ'ægənl] *adj, n* diagonale (*f*)

diagram ['daɪəgræm] *n* diagramma *m*

dial ['daɪəl] *n* quadrante *m*; (*on telephone*) disco combinatore ▪ *vt* (*number*) fare; **to ~ a wrong number** sbagliare numero; **can I ~ London direct?** si può chiamare Londra in teleselezione?

dial. *abbr* = **dialect**

dialect ['daɪəlɛkt] *n* dialetto

dialling code ['daɪəlɪŋ-], (*US*) **area code** *n* prefisso

dialling tone ['daɪəlɪŋ-], (*US*) **dial tone** *n* segnale *m* di linea libera

dialogue ['daɪələɡ] *n* dialogo

dialysis [daɪ'ælɪsɪs] *n* dialisi *f*

diameter [daɪ'æmɪtə^r] *n* diametro

diametrically [daɪə'mɛtrɪklɪ] *adv*: **~ opposed (to)** diametralmente opposto(-a) (a)

diamond ['daɪəmənd] *n* diamante *m*; (*shape*) rombo; **diamonds** *npl* (*Cards*) quadri *mpl*

diamond ring *n* anello di brillanti; (*with one diamond*) anello con brillante

diaper ['daɪəpə^r] *n* (*US*) pannolino

diaphragm ['daɪəfræm] *n* diaframma *m*

diarrhoea, (*US*) **diarrhea** [daɪə'ri:ə] *n* diarrea

diary ['daɪərɪ] *n* (*daily account*) diario; (*book*) agenda; **to keep a ~** tenere un diario

diatribe ['daɪətraɪb] *n* diatriba

dice [daɪs] *n* (*pl inv*) dado ▪ *vt* (*Culin*) tagliare a dadini

dicey ['daɪsɪ] *adj* (*col*): **it's a bit ~** è un po' un rischio

dichotomy [daɪ'kɔtəmɪ] *n* dicotomia

dickhead ['dɪkhɛd] *n* (*Brit col!*) testa *m* di cazzo (!)

Dictaphone® ['dɪktəfəun] *n* dittafono

dictate *vt* [dɪk'teɪt] dettare ▪ *vi*: **to ~ to** (*person*) dare ordini a, dettar legge a ▪ *n* ['dɪkteɪt] dettame *m*; **I won't be dictated to** non ricevo ordini

dictation [dɪk'teɪʃən] *n* dettato; (*to secretary etc*) dettatura; **at ~ speed** a velocità di dettatura

dictator [dɪk'teɪtə^r] *n* dittatore *m*

dictatorship [dɪk'teɪtəʃɪp] *n* dittatura

diction ['dɪkʃən] *n* dizione *f*

dictionary ['dɪkʃənrɪ] *n* dizionario

did [dɪd] *pt of* **do**

didactic [daɪ'dæktɪk] *adj* didattico(-a)

didn't = **did not**

d

die [daɪ] n (pl **dies**) conio; matrice f; stampo
■ vi morire; **to be dying** star morendo;
to be dying for sth/to do sth morire dalla
voglia di qc/di fare qc; **to ~ (of** or **from)**
morire (di)
▶ **die away** vi spegnersi a poco a poco
▶ **die down** vi abbassarsi
▶ **die out** vi estinguersi
diehard ['daɪhɑːd] n reazionario(-a)
diesel ['diːzl] n diesel m
diesel engine n motore m diesel inv
diesel fuel, diesel oil n gasolio (per motori
diesel)
diet ['daɪət] n alimentazione f; (restricted food)
dieta ■ vi (also: **be on a diet**) stare a dieta;
to live on a ~ of nutrirsi di
dietician [daɪə'tɪʃən] n dietologo(-a)
differ ['dɪfəʳ] vi: **to ~ from sth** differire da qc;
essere diverso(-a) da qc; **to ~ from sb over**
sth essere in disaccordo con qn su qc
difference ['dɪfrəns] n differenza; (quarrel)
screzio; **it makes no ~ to me** per me è lo
stesso; **to settle one's differences** risolvere
la situazione
different ['dɪfrənt] adj diverso(-a)
differential [dɪfə'renʃəl] n (Aut, in wages)
differenziale m
differentiate [dɪfə'renʃɪeɪt] vi differenziarsi;
to ~ between discriminare fra, fare
differenza fra
differently ['dɪfrəntlɪ] adv diversamente
difficult ['dɪfɪkəlt] adj difficile; **~ to**
understand difficile da capire
difficulty ['dɪfɪkəltɪ] n difficoltà f inv; **to have**
difficulties with (police, landlord etc) avere
noie con; **to be in ~** essere or trovarsi in
difficoltà
diffidence ['dɪfɪdəns] n mancanza di sicurezza
diffident ['dɪfɪdənt] adj sfiduciato(-a)
diffuse adj [dɪ'fjuːs] diffuso(-a) ■ vt [dɪ'fjuːz]
diffondere, emanare
dig [dɪg] vb (pt, pp **dug**) [dʌg] vt (hole) scavare;
(garden) vangare ■ vi scavare ■ n (prod)
gomitata; (fig) frecciata; (Archaeology) scavo,
scavi mpl; **to ~ into** (snow, soil) scavare; **to ~**
into one's pockets for sth frugarsi le
tasche cercando qc; **to ~ one's nails into**
conficcare le unghie in; see also **digs**
▶ **dig in** vi (col: eat) attaccare a mangiare;
(also: **dig o.s. in**: Mil) trincerarsi; (: fig)
insediarsi, installarsi ■ vt (compost)
interrare; (knife, claw) affondare; **to ~ in**
one's heels (fig) impuntarsi
▶ **dig out** vt (survivors, car from snow) tirar fuori
(scavando), estrarre (scavando)
▶ **dig up** vt scavare; (tree etc) sradicare
digest [daɪ'dʒest] vt digerire

digestible [dɪ'dʒestəbl] adj digeribile
digestion [dɪ'dʒestʃən] n digestione f
digestive [dɪ'dʒestɪv] adj digestivo(-a);
~ system apparato digerente
digit ['dɪdʒɪt] n cifra; (finger) dito
digital ['dɪdʒɪtəl] adj digitale
digital camera n fotocamera digitale
digital compact cassette n piastra digitale
per CD
digital radio n radio digitale
digital TV n televisione f digitale
dignified ['dɪgnɪfaɪd] adj dignitoso(-a)
dignitary ['dɪgnɪtərɪ] n dignitario
dignity ['dɪgnɪtɪ] n dignità
digress [daɪ'gres] vi: **to ~ from** divagare da
digression [daɪ'greʃən] n digressione f
digs [dɪgz] npl (Brit col) camera ammobiliata
dilapidated [dɪ'læpɪdeɪtɪd] adj cadente
dilate [daɪ'leɪt] vt dilatare ■ vi dilatarsi
dilatory ['dɪlətərɪ] adj dilatorio(-a)
dilemma [daɪ'lemə] n dilemma m; **to be in a**
~ essere di fronte a un dilemma
diligent ['dɪlɪdʒənt] adj diligente
dill [dɪl] n aneto
dilly-dally ['dɪlɪdælɪ] vi gingillarsi
dilute [daɪ'luːt] vt diluire; (with water)
annacquare ■ adj diluito(-a)
dim [dɪm] adj (light, eyesight) debole; (memory,
outline) vago(-a); (stupid) ottuso(-a) ■ vt (light:
also US Aut) abbassare; **to take a ~ view of**
sth non vedere di buon occhio qc
dime [daɪm] n (US) = **10 cents**
dimension [dɪ'menʃən] n dimensione f
-dimensional [dɪ'menʃənl] adj suffix: **two-**
bi-dimensionale
diminish [dɪ'mɪnɪʃ] vt, vi diminuire
diminished [dɪ'mɪnɪʃt] adj: **~ responsibility**
(Law) incapacità d'intendere e di volere
diminutive [dɪ'mɪnjutɪv] adj minuscolo(-a)
■ n (Ling) diminutivo
dimly ['dɪmlɪ] adv debolmente;
indistintamente
dimmer ['dɪməʳ] n (also: **dimmer switch**)
dimmer m inv, interruttore m a reostato;
dimmers npl (US Aut) anabbaglianti mpl;
(: parking lights) luci fpl di posizione
dimple ['dɪmpl] n fossetta
dim-witted ['dɪm'wɪtɪd] adj (col) sciocco(-a),
stupido(-a)
din [dɪn] n chiasso, fracasso ■ vt: **to ~ sth**
into sb (col) ficcare qc in testa a qn
dine [daɪn] vi pranzare
diner ['daɪnəʳ] n (person: in restaurant) cliente m;
(Rail) carrozza or vagone m ristorante; (US:
eating place) tavola calda
dinghy ['dɪŋgɪ] n battello pneumatico;
(also: **sailing dinghy**) dinghy m inv

dingy ['dɪndʒɪ] *adj* grigio(-a)
dining area ['daɪnɪŋ-] *n* zona pranzo *inv*
dining car *n* vagone *m* ristorante
dining room *n* sala da pranzo
dinner ['dɪnəʳ] *n* pranzo; *(evening meal)* cena; *(public)* banchetto; **~'s ready!** a tavola!
dinner jacket *n* smoking *m inv*
dinner party *n* cena
dinner service *n* servizio da tavola
dinner time *n* ora di pranzo *(or* cena)
dinosaur ['daɪnəsɔːʳ] *n* dinosauro
dint [dɪnt] *n*: **by ~ of (doing) sth** a forza di (fare) qc
diocese ['daɪəsɪs] *n* diocesi *f inv*
dioxide [daɪˈɒksaɪd] *n* biossido
dip [dɪp] *n (slope)* discesa; *(in sea)* bagno ■ *vt* immergere, bagnare; *(Brit Aut: lights)* abbassare ■ *vi (road)* essere in pendenza; *(bird, plane)* abbassarsi
Dip. *abbr (Brit)* = **diploma**
diphtheria [dɪfˈθɪərɪə] *n* difterite *f*
diphthong ['dɪfθɒŋ] *n* dittongo
diploma [dɪˈpləʊmə] *n* diploma *m*
diplomacy [dɪˈpləʊməsɪ] *n* diplomazia
diplomat ['dɪpləmæt] *n* diplomatico
diplomatic [dɪpləˈmætɪk] *adj* diplomatico(-a); **to break off ~ relations** rompere le relazioni diplomatiche
diplomatic corps *n* corpo diplomatico
diplomatic immunity *n* immunità *f inv* diplomatica
dipstick ['dɪpstɪk] *n (Aut)* indicatore *m* di livello dell'olio
dipswitch ['dɪpswɪtʃ] *n (Brit Aut)* levetta dei fari
dire [daɪəʳ] *adj* terribile; estremo(-a)
direct [daɪˈrɛkt] *adj* diretto(-a); *(manner, person)* franco(-a), esplicito(-a) ■ *vt* dirigere; **to ~ sb to do sth** dare direttive a qn di fare qc; **can you ~ me to ...?** mi può indicare la strada per ...?
direct cost *n (Comm)* costo diretto
direct current *n (Elec)* corrente *f* continua
direct debit *n (Banking)* addebito effettuato per ordine di un cliente di banca
direct dialling *n (Tel)* ≈ teleselezione *f*
direct hit *n (Mil)* colpo diretto
direction [dɪˈrɛkʃən] *n* direzione *f*; *(of play, film, programme)* regia; **directions** *npl (advice)* chiarimenti *mpl*; *(instructions: to a place)* indicazioni *fpl*; **directions for use** istruzioni *fpl*; **to ask for directions** chiedere la strada; **sense of ~** senso dell'orientamento; **in the ~ of** in direzione di
directive [dɪˈrɛktɪv] *n* direttiva, ordine *m*; **a government ~** una disposizione governativa

direct labour *n* manodopera diretta
directly [dɪˈrɛktlɪ] *adv (in straight line)* direttamente; *(at once)* subito
direct mail *n* pubblicità diretta
direct mailshot *n (Brit)* materiale *m* pubblicitario ad approccio diretto
directness [daɪˈrɛktnɪs] *n (of person, speech)* franchezza
director [dɪˈrɛktəʳ] *n* direttore(-trice), amministratore(-trice); *(Theat, Cine, TV)* regista *m/f*; **D~ of Public Prosecutions** *(Brit)* ≈ Procuratore *m* della Repubblica
directory [dɪˈrɛktərɪ] *n* elenco; *(street directory)* stradario; *(trade directory)* repertorio del commercio; *(Comput)* directory *m inv*
directory enquiries, *(US)* **directory assistance** *n (Tel)* servizio informazioni, informazioni *fpl* elenco abbonati
dirt [dəːt] *n* sporcizia; immondizia; **to treat sb like ~** trattare qn come uno straccio
dirt-cheap ['dəːt'tʃiːp] *adj* da due soldi
dirt road *n* strada non asfaltata
dirty ['dəːtɪ] *adj* sporco(-a) ■ *vt* sporcare; **~ bomb** bomba convenzionale contenente materiale radioattivo; **~ story** storia oscena; **~ trick** brutto scherzo
disability [dɪsəˈbɪlɪtɪ] *n* invalidità *f inv*; *(Law)* incapacità *f inv*
disability allowance *n* pensione *f* d'invalidità
disable [dɪsˈeɪbl] *vt (illness, accident)* rendere invalido(-a); *(tank, gun)* mettere fuori uso
disabled [dɪsˈeɪbld] *adj* invalido(-a); *(maimed)* mutilato(-a); *(through illness, old age)* inabile
disadvantage [dɪsədˈvɑːntɪdʒ] *n* svantaggio
disadvantaged [dɪsədˈvɑːntɪdʒd] *adj (person)* svantaggiato(-a)
disadvantageous [dɪsædvɑːnˈteɪdʒəs] *adj* svantaggioso(-a)
disaffected [dɪsəˈfɛktɪd] *adj*: **~ (to or towards)** scontento(-a) di, insoddisfatto(-a) di
disaffection [dɪsəˈfɛkʃən] *n* malcontento, insoddisfazione *f*
disagree [dɪsəˈɡriː] *vi (differ)* discordare; *(be against, think otherwise)*: **to ~ (with)** essere in disaccordo (con), dissentire (da); **I ~ with you** non sono d'accordo con lei; **garlic disagrees with me** l'aglio non mi va
disagreeable [dɪsəˈɡriːəbl] *adj* sgradevole; *(person)* antipatico(-a)
disagreement [dɪsəˈɡriːmənt] *n* disaccordo; *(quarrel)* dissapore *m*; **to have a ~ with sb** litigare con qn
disallow ['dɪsəˈlaʊ] *vt* respingere; *(Brit Football: goal)* annullare
disappear [dɪsəˈpɪəʳ] *vi* scomparire
disappearance [dɪsəˈpɪərəns] *n* scomparsa

disappoint [dɪsə'pɔɪnt] vt deludere
disappointed [dɪsə'pɔɪntɪd] adj deluso(-a)
disappointing [dɪsə'pɔɪntɪŋ] adj deludente
disappointment [dɪsə'pɔɪntmənt] n delusione f
disapproval [dɪsə'pruːvəl] n disapprovazione f
disapprove [dɪsə'pruːv] vi: **to ~ of** disapprovare
disapproving [dɪsə'pruːvɪŋ] adj di disapprovazione
disarm [dɪs'ɑːm] vt disarmare
disarmament [dɪs'ɑːməmənt] n disarmo
disarming [dɪs'ɑːmɪŋ] adj (smile) disarmante
disarray [dɪsə'reɪ] n: **in ~** (troops) in rotta; (thoughts) confuso(-a); (clothes) in disordine; **to throw into ~** buttare all'aria
disaster [dɪ'zɑːstər] n disastro
disaster area n zona disastrata
disastrous [dɪ'zɑːstrəs] adj disastroso(-a)
disband [dɪs'bænd] vt sbandare; (Mil) congedare ▪ vi sciogliersi
disbelief [ˈdɪsbə'liːf] n incredulità; **in ~** incredulo(-a)
disbelieve [ˈdɪsbə'liːv] vt (person, story) non credere a, mettere in dubbio; **I don't ~ you** vorrei poterle credere
disc [dɪsk] n disco
disc. abbr (Comm) = **discount**
discard [dɪs'kɑːd] vt (old things) scartare; (fig) abbandonare
disc brake n freno a disco
discern [dɪ'sɜːn] vt discernere, distinguere
discernible [dɪ'sɜːnəbl] adj percepibile
discerning [dɪ'sɜːnɪŋ] adj perspicace
discharge vt [dɪs'tʃɑːdʒ] (duties) compiere; (settle: debt) pagare, estinguere; (Elec, waste etc) scaricare; (Med) emettere; (patient) dimettere; (employee) licenziare; (soldier) congedare; (defendant) liberare ▪ n ['dɪstʃɑːdʒ] (Elec) scarica; (Med, of gas, chemicals) emissione f; (vaginal discharge) perdite fpl (bianche); (dismissal) licenziamento; congedo; liberazione f; **to ~ one's gun** fare fuoco
discharged bankrupt [dɪs'tʃɑːdʒd-] n fallito cui il tribunale ha concesso la riabilitazione
disciple [dɪ'saɪpl] n discepolo
disciplinary ['dɪsɪplɪnərɪ] adj disciplinare; **to take ~ action against sb** prendere un provvedimento disciplinare contro qn
discipline ['dɪsɪplɪn] n disciplina ▪ vt disciplinare; (punish) punire; **to ~ o.s. to do sth** imporsi di fare qc
disc jockey n disc jockey m inv
disclaim [dɪs'kleɪm] vt negare, smentire
disclaimer [dɪs'kleɪmər] n smentita;

to issue a ~ pubblicare una smentita
disclose [dɪs'kləuz] vt rivelare, svelare
disclosure [dɪs'kləuʒər] n rivelazione f
disco ['dɪskəu] n abbr = **discothèque**
discolour, (US) **discolor** [dɪs'kʌlər] vt scolorire; (sth white) ingiallire ▪ vi sbiadire, scolorirsi; (sth white) ingiallire
discolouration, (US) **discoloration** [dɪskʌlə'reɪʃən] n scolorimento
discoloured, (US) **discolored** [dɪs'kʌləd] adj scolorito(-a), ingiallito(-a)
discomfort [dɪs'kʌmfət] n disagio; (lack of comfort) scomodità f inv
disconcert [dɪskən'sɜːt] vt sconcertare
disconnect [dɪskə'nɛkt] vt sconnettere, staccare; (Elec, Radio) staccare; (gas, water) chiudere
disconnected [dɪskə'nɛktɪd] adj (speech, thought) sconnesso(-a)
disconsolate [dɪs'kɔnsəlɪt] adj sconsolato(-a)
discontent [dɪskən'tɛnt] n scontentezza
discontented [dɪskən'tɛntɪd] adj scontento(-a)
discontinue [dɪskən'tɪnjuː] vt smettere, cessare; **"discontinued"** (Comm) "sospeso"
discord ['dɪskɔːd] n disaccordo; (Mus) dissonanza
discordant [dɪs'kɔːdənt] adj discordante; dissonante
discothèque ['dɪskəutɛk] n discoteca
discount n ['dɪskaunt] sconto ▪ vt [dɪs'kaunt] scontare; (report etc) non badare a; **at a ~** con uno sconto; **to give sb a ~ on sth** fare uno sconto a qn su qc; **~ for cash** sconto m cassa inv
discount house n (Finance) casa di sconto, discount house f inv; (Comm: also: **discount store**) discount m inv
discount rate n tasso di sconto
discourage [dɪs'kʌrɪdʒ] vt scoraggiare; (dissuade, deter) tentare di dissuadere
discouragement [dɪs'kʌrɪdʒmənt] n (dissuasion) disapprovazione f; (depression) scoraggiamento; **to act as a ~ to** ostacolare
discouraging [dɪs'kʌrɪdʒɪŋ] adj scoraggiante
discourteous [dɪs'kɜːtɪəs] adj scortese
discover [dɪs'kʌvər] vt scoprire
discovery [dɪs'kʌvərɪ] n scoperta
discredit [dɪs'krɛdɪt] vt screditare; mettere in dubbio ▪ n discredito
discreet [dɪ'skriːt] adj discreto(-a)
discreetly [dɪ'skriːtlɪ] adv con discrezione
discrepancy [dɪ'skrɛpənsɪ] n discrepanza
discretion [dɪ'skrɛʃən] n discrezione f; **use your own ~** giudichi lei
discretionary [dɪs'krɛʃənərɪ] adj (powers) discrezionale

discriminate [dɪˈskrɪmɪneɪt] *vi:* **to ~ between** distinguere tra; **to ~ against** discriminare contro

discriminating [dɪsˈkrɪmɪneɪtɪŋ] *adj (ear, taste)* fine, giudizioso(-a); *(person)* esigente; *(tax, duty)* discriminante

discrimination [dɪskrɪmɪˈneɪʃən] *n* discriminazione *f*; *(judgement)* discernimento; **racial/sexual ~** discriminazione razziale/sessuale

discus [ˈdɪskəs] *n* disco

discuss [dɪˈskʌs] *vt* discutere; *(debate)* dibattere

discussion [dɪˈskʌʃən] *n* discussione *f*; **under ~** in discussione

discussion forum *n (Comput)* forum *m inv* di discussione

disdain [dɪsˈdeɪn] *n* disdegno

disease [dɪˈziːz] *n* malattia

diseased [dɪˈziːzd] *adj* malato(-a)

disembark [dɪsɪmˈbɑːk] *vt, vi* sbarcare

disembarkation [dɪsɛmbɑːˈkeɪʃən] *n* sbarco

disembodied [dɪsɪmˈbɔdɪd] *adj* disincarnato(-a)

disembowel [dɪsɪmˈbauəl] *vt* sbudellare, sventrare

disenchanted [dɪsɪnˈtʃɑːntɪd] *adj* disincantato(-a); **~ (with)** deluso(-a) (da)

disenfranchise [dɪsɪnˈfræntʃaɪz] *vt* privare del diritto di voto; *(Comm)* revocare una condizione di privilegio commerciale a

disengage [dɪsɪnˈgeɪdʒ] *vt* disimpegnare; *(Tech)* distaccare; *(Aut)* disinnestare

disentangle [dɪsɪnˈtæŋgl] *vt* sbrogliare

disfavour, *(US)* **disfavor** [dɪsˈfeɪvə^r] *n* sfavore *m*; disgrazia

disfigure [dɪsˈfɪgə^r] *vt* sfigurare

disgorge [dɪsˈgɔːdʒ] *vt (river)* riversare

disgrace [dɪsˈgreɪs] *n* vergogna; *(disfavour)* disgrazia ■ *vt* disonorare, far cadere in disgrazia

disgraceful [dɪsˈgreɪsful] *adj* scandaloso(-a), vergognoso(-a)

disgruntled [dɪsˈgrʌntld] *adj* scontento(-a), di cattivo umore

disguise [dɪsˈgaɪz] *n* travestimento ■ *vt* travestire; *(voice)* contraffare; *(feelings etc)* mascherare; **to ~ o.s. as** travestirsi da; **in ~** travestito(-a); **there's no disguising the fact that ...** non si può nascondere (il fatto) che ...

disgust [dɪsˈgʌst] *n* disgusto, nausea ■ *vt* disgustare, far schifo a

disgusting [dɪsˈgʌstɪŋ] *adj* disgustoso(-a)

dish [dɪʃ] *n* piatto; **to do** *or* **wash the dishes** fare i piatti

▶ **dish out** *vt (food)* servire; *(advice)* elargire; *(money)* tirare fuori; *(exam papers)* distribuire

▶ **dish up** *vt (food)* servire; *(facts, statistics)* presentare

dishcloth [ˈdɪʃklɔθ] *n* strofinaccio dei piatti

dishearten [dɪsˈhɑːtn] *vt* scoraggiare

dishevelled, *(US)* **disheveled** [dɪˈʃɛvəld] *adj* arruffato(-a), scapigliato(-a)

dishonest [dɪsˈɔnɪst] *adj* disonesto(-a)

dishonesty [dɪsˈɔnɪstɪ] *n* disonestà

dishonour, *(US)* **dishonor** [dɪsˈɔnə^r] *n* disonore *m*

dishonourable, *(US)* **dishonorable** [dɪsˈɔnərəbl] *adj* disonorevole

dish soap *n (US)* detersivo liquido (per stoviglie)

dishtowel [ˈdɪʃtauəl] *n* strofinaccio dei piatti

dishwasher [ˈdɪʃwɔʃə^r] *n* lavastoviglie *f inv*; *(person)* sguattero(-a)

dishy [ˈdɪʃɪ] *adj (Brit col)* figo(-a)

disillusion [dɪsɪˈluːʒən] *vt* disilludere, disingannare ■ *n* disillusione *f*; **to become disillusioned (with)** perdere le illusioni (su)

disillusionment [dɪsɪˈluːʒənmənt] *n* disillusione *f*

disincentive [dɪsɪnˈsɛntɪv] *n:* **to act as a ~ (to)** agire da freno (su); **to be a ~ to** scoraggiare

disinclined [dɪsɪnˈklaɪnd] *adj:* **to be ~ to do sth** essere poco propenso(-a) a fare qc

disinfect [dɪsɪnˈfɛkt] *vt* disinfettare

disinfectant [dɪsɪnˈfɛktənt] *n* disinfettante *m*

disinflation [dɪsɪnˈfleɪʃən] *n* disinflazione *f*

disinformation [dɪsɪnfəˈmeɪʃən] *n* disinformazione *f*

disinherit [dɪsɪnˈhɛrɪt] *vt* diseredare

disintegrate [dɪsˈɪntɪgreɪt] *vi* disintegrarsi

disinterested [dɪsˈɪntrəstɪd] *adj* disinteressato(-a)

disjointed [dɪsˈdʒɔɪntɪd] *adj* sconnesso(-a)

disk [dɪsk] *n (Comput)* disco; **single-/double-sided ~** disco *m* monofaccia *inv* /a doppia faccia

disk drive *n* disk drive *m inv*, unità *f inv* a dischi magnetici

diskette [dɪsˈkɛt] *n (Comput)* dischetto

disk operating system *n* sistema *m* operativo a disco

dislike [dɪsˈlaɪk] *n* antipatia, avversione *f* ■ *vt:* **he dislikes it** non gli piace; **I ~ the idea** l'idea non mi va; **to take a ~ to sb/sth** prendere in antipatia qn/qc

dislocate [ˈdɪsləkeɪt] *vt (Med)* slogare; *(fig)* disorganizzare; **he dislocated his shoulder** si è lussato una spalla

dislodge [dɪsˈlɔdʒ] *vt* rimuovere, staccare; *(enemy)* sloggiare

disloyal [dɪsˈlɔɪəl] *adj* sleale

dismal [ˈdɪzml] *adj* triste, cupo(-a)

dismantle [dɪs'mæntl] vt smantellare, smontare; (fort, warship) disarmare

dismast [dɪs'mɑːst] vt disalberare

dismay [dɪs'meɪ] n costernazione f ■ vt sgomentare; **much to my ~** con mio gran stupore

dismiss [dɪs'mɪs] vt congedare; (employee) licenziare; (idea) scacciare; (Law) respingere ■ vi (Mil) rompere i ranghi

dismissal [dɪs'mɪsəl] n congedo; licenziamento

dismount [dɪs'maunt] vi scendere ■ vt (rider) disarcionare

disobedience [dɪsə'biːdɪəns] n disubbidienza

disobedient [dɪsə'biːdɪənt] adj disubbidiente

disobey [dɪsə'beɪ] vt disubbidire; (rule) trasgredire

disorder [dɪs'ɔːdəʳ] n disordine m; (rioting) tumulto; (Med) disturbo; **civil ~** disordini mpl interni

disorderly [dɪs'ɔːdəlɪ] adj disordinato(-a), tumultuoso(-a)

disorderly conduct n (Law) comportamento atto a turbare l'ordine pubblico

disorganize [dɪs'ɔːgənaɪz] vt disorganizzare

disorganized [dɪs'ɔːgənaɪzd] adj (person, life) disorganizzato(-a); (system, meeting) male organizzato(-a)

disorientated [dɪs'ɔːrɪenteɪtɪd] adj disorientato(-a)

disown [dɪs'əun] vt ripudiare

disparaging [dɪs'pærɪdʒɪŋ] adj spregiativo(-a), sprezzante; **to be ~ about sb/sth** denigrare qn/qc

disparate ['dɪspərɪt] adj disparato(-a)

disparity [dɪs'pærɪtɪ] n disparità f inv

dispassionate [dɪs'pæʃənət] adj calmo(-a), freddo(-a); imparziale

dispatch [dɪs'pætʃ] vt spedire, inviare; (deal with: business) sbrigare ■ n spedizione f, invio; (Mil, Press) dispaccio

dispatch department n reparto spedizioni

dispatch rider n (Mil) corriere m, portaordini m inv

dispel [dɪs'pɛl] vt dissipare, scacciare

dispensary [dɪs'pɛnsərɪ] n farmacia; (in chemist's) dispensario

dispense [dɪs'pɛns] vt distribuire, amministrare; (medicine) preparare e dare; **to ~ sb from** dispensare qn da
▸ **dispense with** vt fus fare a meno di; (make unnecessary) rendere superfluo(-a)

dispenser [dɪs'pɛnsəʳ] n (container) distributore m

dispensing chemist n (Brit) farmacista m/f

dispersal [dɪs'pəːsl] n dispersione f

disperse [dɪs'pəːs] vt disperdere; (knowledge) disseminare ■ vi disperdersi

dispirited [dɪs'pɪrɪtɪd] adj scoraggiato(-a), abbattuto(-a)

displace [dɪs'pleɪs] vt spostare

displaced person n (Pol) profugo(-a)

displacement [dɪs'pleɪsmənt] n spostamento

display [dɪs'pleɪ] n mostra; esposizione f; (of feeling etc) manifestazione f; (military display) parata (militare); (computer display) display m inv; (pej) ostentazione f ■ vt mostrare; (goods) esporre; (results) affiggere; (departure times) indicare; **on ~** (gen) in mostra; (goods) in vetrina

display advertising n pubblicità tabellare

displease [dɪs'pliːz] vt dispiacere a, scontentare; **displeased with** scontento(-a) di

displeasure [dɪs'plɛʒəʳ] n dispiacere m

disposable [dɪs'pəuzəbl] adj (pack etc) a perdere; (income) disponibile; **~ nappy** (Brit) pannolino di carta

disposal [dɪs'pəuzl] n (of rubbish) evacuazione f; distruzione f; (of property etc: by selling) vendita; (: by giving away) cessione f; **at one's ~** alla sua disposizione; **to put sth at sb's ~** mettere qc a disposizione di qn

dispose [dɪs'pəuz] vt disporre
▸ **dispose of** vt fus (time, money) disporre di; (Comm: sell) vendere; (unwanted goods) sbarazzarsi di; (problem) eliminare

disposed [dɪs'pəuzd] adj: **~ to do** disposto(-a) a fare

disposition [dɪspə'zɪʃən] n disposizione f; (temperament) carattere m

dispossess ['dɪspə'zɛs] vt: **to ~ sb (of)** spossessare qn (di)

disproportion [dɪsprə'pɔːʃən] n sproporzione f

disproportionate [dɪsprə'pɔːʃənət] adj sproporzionato(-a)

disprove [dɪs'pruːv] vt confutare

dispute [dɪs'pjuːt] n disputa; (also: **industrial dispute**) controversia (sindacale) ■ vt contestare; (matter) discutere; (victory) disputare; **to be in** or **under ~** (matter) essere in discussione; (territory) essere oggetto di contesa

disqualification [dɪskwɔlɪfɪ'keɪʃən] n squalifica; **~ (from driving)** (Brit) ritiro della patente

disqualify [dɪs'kwɔlɪfaɪ] vt (Sport) squalificare; **to ~ sb from sth/from doing** rendere qn incapace a qc/a fare; squalificare qn da qc/da fare; **to ~ sb from driving** (Brit) ritirare la patente a qn

disquiet [dɪs'kwaɪət] n inquietudine f

disquieting [dɪsˈkwaɪətɪŋ] *adj* inquietante, allarmante

disregard [dɪsrɪˈgɑːd] *vt* non far caso a, non badare a ■ *n* (*indifference*): ~ (**for**) (*feelings*) insensibilità (a), indifferenza (verso); (*danger*) noncuranza (di); (*money*) disprezzo (di)

disrepair [dɪsrɪˈpɛər] *n* cattivo stato; **to fall into** ~ (*building*) andare in rovina; (*street*) deteriorarsi

disreputable [dɪsˈrɛpjutəbl] *adj* (*person*) di cattiva fama; (*area*) malfamato(-a), poco raccomandabile

disrepute [ˈdɪsrɪˈpjuːt] *n* disonore *m*, vergogna; **to bring into** ~ rovinare la reputazione di

disrespectful [dɪsrɪˈspɛktful] *adj* che manca di rispetto

disrupt [dɪsˈrʌpt] *vt* (*meeting, lesson*) disturbare, interrompere; (*public transport*) creare scompiglio in; (*plans*) scombussolare

disruption [dɪsˈrʌpʃən] *n* disordine *m*; interruzione *f*

disruptive [dɪsˈrʌptɪv] *adj* (*influence*) negativo(-a), deleterio(-a); (*strike action*) paralizzante

dissatisfaction [dɪssætɪsˈfækʃən] *n* scontentezza, insoddisfazione *f*

dissatisfied [dɪsˈsætɪsfaɪd] *adj*: ~ (**with**) scontento(a) *or* insoddisfatto(a) (di)

dissect [dɪˈsɛkt] *vt* sezionare; (*fig*) sviscerare

disseminate [dɪˈsɛmɪneɪt] *vt* disseminare

dissent [dɪˈsɛnt] *n* dissenso

dissenter [dɪˈsɛntər] *n* (*Rel, Pol etc*) dissidente *m/f*

dissertation [dɪsəˈteɪʃən] *n* (*Scol*) tesi *f* inv, dissertazione *f*

disservice [dɪsˈsəːvɪs] *n*: **to do sb a** ~ fare un cattivo servizio a qn

dissident [ˈdɪsɪdnt] *adj* dissidente; (*speech, voice*) di dissenso ■ *n* dissidente *m/f*

dissimilar [dɪˈsɪmɪlər] *adj*: ~ (**to**) dissimile *or* diverso(a) (da)

dissipate [ˈdɪsɪpeɪt] *vt* dissipare

dissipated [ˈdɪsɪpeɪtɪd] *adj* dissipato(-a)

dissociate [dɪˈsəuʃɪeɪt] *vt* dissociare; **to ~ o.s. from** dichiarare di non avere niente a che fare con

dissolute [ˈdɪsəluːt] *adj* dissoluto(-a), licenzioso(-a)

dissolve [dɪˈzɔlv] *vt* dissolvere, sciogliere; (*Comm, Pol, marriage*) sciogliere ■ *vi* dissolversi, sciogliersi; (*fig*) svanire

dissuade [dɪˈsweɪd] *vt*: **to ~ sb (from)** dissuadere qn (da)

distaff side [ˈdɪstɑːf-] *n* ramo femminile di una famiglia

distance [ˈdɪstns] *n* distanza; **in the** ~ in lontananza; **what's the ~ to London?**

quanto dista Londra?; **it's within walking** ~ ci si arriva a piedi; **at a ~ of 2 metres** a 2 metri di distanza

distant [ˈdɪstnt] *adj* lontano(-a), distante; (*manner*) riservato(-a), freddo(-a)

distaste [dɪsˈteɪst] *n* ripugnanza

distasteful [dɪsˈteɪstful] *adj* ripugnante, sgradevole

Dist. Atty. *abbr* (*US*) = **district attorney**

distemper [dɪsˈtɛmpər] *n* (*paint*) tempera; (*of dogs*) cimurro

distend [dɪsˈtɛnd] *vt* dilatare ■ *vi* dilatarsi

distended [dɪsˈtɛndɪd] *adj* (*stomach*) dilatato(-a)

distil, (*US*) **distill** [dɪsˈtɪl] *vt* distillare

distillery [dɪsˈtɪlərɪ] *n* distilleria

distinct [dɪsˈtɪŋkt] *adj* distinto(-a); (*preference, progress*) definito(-a); **as ~ from** a differenza di

distinction [dɪsˈtɪŋkʃən] *n* distinzione *f*; (*in exam*) lode *f*; **to draw a ~ between** fare distinzione tra; **a writer of ~** uno scrittore di notevoli qualità

distinctive [dɪsˈtɪŋktɪv] *adj* distintivo(-a)

distinctly [dɪsˈtɪŋktlɪ] *adv* distintamente; (*remember*) chiaramente; (*unhappy, better*) decisamente

distinguish [dɪsˈtɪŋgwɪʃ] *vt* distinguere; discernere ■ *vi*: **to ~ (between)** distinguere (tra); **to ~ o.s.** distinguersi

distinguished [dɪsˈtɪŋgwɪʃt] *adj* (*eminent*) eminente; (*career*) brillante; (*refined*) distinto(-a), signorile

distinguishing [dɪsˈtɪŋgwɪʃɪŋ] *adj* (*feature*) distinto(-a), caratteristico(-a)

distort [dɪsˈtɔːt] *vt* (*also fig*) distorcere; (*account, news*) falsare; (*Tech*) deformare

distortion [dɪsˈtɔːʃən] *n* (*gen*) distorsione *f*; (*of truth etc*) alterazione *f*; (*of facts*) travisamento; (*Tech*) deformazione *f*

distract [dɪsˈtrækt] *vt* distrarre

distracted [dɪsˈtræktɪd] *adj* distratto(-a)

distraction [dɪsˈtrækʃən] *n* distrazione *f*; **to drive sb to** ~ spingere qn alla pazzia

distraught [dɪsˈtrɔːt] *adj* stravolto(-a)

distress [dɪsˈtrɛs] *n* angoscia; (*pain*) dolore *m* ■ *vt* affliggere; **in** ~ (*ship etc*) in pericolo, in difficoltà; **distressed area** (*Brit*) zona sinistrata

distressing [dɪsˈtrɛsɪŋ] *adj* doloroso(-a), penoso(-a)

distress signal *n* segnale *m* di pericolo

distribute [dɪsˈtrɪbjuːt] *vt* distribuire

distribution [dɪstrɪˈbjuːʃən] *n* distribuzione *f*

distribution cost *n* costo di distribuzione

distributor [dɪsˈtrɪbjutər] *n* distributore *m*; (*Comm*) concessionario

district [ˈdɪstrɪkt] *n* (*of country*) regione *f*; (*of town*) quartiere *m*; (*Admin*) distretto

d

district attorney n (US) ≈ sostituto procuratore m della Repubblica

district council n *organo di amministrazione regionale; vedi nota*

⬤ **DISTRICT COUNCIL**
⬤
⬤ In Inghilterra e in Galles, il *district*
⬤ *council* è l'organo responsabile
⬤ dell'amministrazione dei paesi più
⬤ piccoli e dei distretti di campagna. È
⬤ finanziato tramite una tassa locale e
⬤ riceve un contributo da parte del governo.
⬤ I district councils vengono eletti a livello
⬤ locale ogni quattro anni. L'organo
⬤ amministrativo nelle città è invece il
⬤ "city council".

district nurse n (Brit) infermiera di quartiere

distrust [dɪs'trʌst] n diffidenza, sfiducia ■ vi non aver fiducia in

distrustful [dɪs'trʌstful] adj diffidente

disturb [dɪs'təːb] vt disturbare; (*inconvenience*) scomodare; **sorry to ~ you** scusi se la disturbo

disturbance [dɪs'təːbəns] n disturbo; (*political etc*) tumulto; (*by drunks etc*) disordini mpl; **~ of the peace** disturbo della quiete pubblica; **to cause a ~** provocare disordini

disturbed [dɪs'təːbd] adj turbato(-a); **to be emotionally ~** avere problemi emotivi; **to be mentally ~** essere malato(-a) di mente

disturbing [dɪs'təːbɪŋ] adj sconvolgente

disuse [dɪs'juːs] n: **to fall into ~** cadere in disuso

disused [dɪs'juːzd] adj abbandonato(-a)

ditch [dɪtʃ] n fossa ■ vt (col) piantare in asso

dither ['dɪðəʳ] vi vacillare

ditto ['dɪtəu] adv idem

divan [dɪ'væn] n divano

divan bed n divano letto inv

dive [daɪv] n tuffo; (*of submarine*) immersione f; (*Aviat*) picchiata; (*pej*) buco ■ vi tuffarsi

diver ['daɪvəʳ] n tuffatore(-trice); (*deep-sea diver*) palombaro

diverge [daɪ'vəːdʒ] vi divergere

divergent [daɪ'vəːdʒənt] adj divergente

diverse [daɪ'vəːs] adj vario(-a)

diversification [daɪvəːsɪfɪ'keɪʃən] n diversificazione f

diversify [daɪ'vəːsɪfaɪ] vt diversificare

diversion [daɪ'vəːʃən] n (Brit Aut) deviazione f; (*distraction*) divertimento

diversionary tactics [daɪ'vəːʃənrɪ-] npl tattica fsg diversiva

diversity [daɪ'vəːsɪtɪ] n diversità f inv, varietà f inv

divert [daɪ'vəːt] vt (*traffic, river*) deviare; (*train, plane*) dirottare; (*amuse*) divertire

divest [daɪ'vɛst] vt: **to ~ sb of** spogliare qn di

divide [dɪ'vaɪd] vt dividere; (*separate*) separare ■ vi dividersi; **to ~ (between** or **among)** dividere (tra), ripartire (tra); **40 divided by 5** 40 diviso 5

▶ **divide out** vt: **to ~ out (between** or **among)** (*sweets etc*) distribuire (tra); (*tasks*) distribuire or ripartire (tra)

divided [dɪ'vaɪdɪd] adj (*country*) diviso(-a); (*opinions*) discordi

divided highway n (US) strada a doppia carreggiata

divided skirt n gonna f pantalone inv

dividend ['dɪvɪdɛnd] n dividendo

dividend cover n rapporto dividendo profitti

dividers [dɪ'vaɪdəz] npl compasso a punte fisse

divine [dɪ'vaɪn] adj divino(-a) ■ vt (*future*) divinare, predire; (*truth*) indovinare; (*water, metal*) individuare tramite radioestesia

diving ['daɪvɪŋ] n tuffo

diving board n trampolino

diving suit n scafandro

divinity [dɪ'vɪnɪtɪ] n divinità f inv; teologia

division [dɪ'vɪʒən] n divisione f; separazione f; (Brit Football) serie f inv; **~ of labour** divisione f del lavoro

divisive [dɪ'vaɪsɪv] adj che è causa di discordia

divorce [dɪ'vɔːs] n divorzio ■ vt divorziare da

divorced [dɪ'vɔːst] adj divorziato(-a)

divorcee [dɪvɔː'siː] n divorziato(-a)

divot ['dɪvət] n (Golf) zolla di terra (*sollevata accidentalmente*)

divulge [daɪ'vʌldʒ] vt divulgare, rivelare

D.I.Y. adj, n abbr (Brit) = **do-it-yourself**

dizziness ['dɪzɪnɪs] n vertigini fpl

dizzy ['dɪzɪ] adj (*height*) vertiginoso(-a); **to make sb ~** far girare la testa a qn; **to feel ~** avere il capogiro; **I feel ~** mi gira la testa, ho il capogiro

DJ n abbr = **disc jockey**

dj n abbr = **dinner jacket**

Djakarta [dʒə'kɑːtə] n Giakarta

DJIA n abbr (US Stock Exchange: = Dow-Jones Industrial Average) indice m Dow-Jones

dl abbr (= decilitre) dl

DLit, DLitt n abbr = **Doctor of Literature; Doctor of Letters**

dm abbr (= decimetre) dm

DMus n abbr = **Doctor of Music**

DMZ n abbr (= demilitarized zone) zona smilitarizzata

DNA n abbr (= deoxyribonucleic acid) DNA m; **~ test** test m inv del DNA

○ KEYWORD

do [duː] (*pt* **did**, *pp* **done**) *n* (*col: party etc*) festa;
it was rather a grand do è stato un
ricevimento piuttosto importante
■ *vb* **1** (*in negative constructions*) non tradotto;
I don't understand non capisco
2 (*to form questions*) non tradotto; **didn't you
know?** non lo sapevi?; **why didn't you
come?** perché non sei venuto?
3 (*for emphasis, in polite expressions*): **she does
seem rather late** sembra essere piuttosto in
ritardo; **I DO wish I could ...** magari potessi
...; **but I DO like it!** sì che mi piace!; **do sit
down** si accomodi la prego, prego si sieda;
do take care! mi raccomando, stai attento!
4 (*used to avoid repeating vb*): **she swims better
than I do** lei nuota meglio di me; **do you
agree? — yes, I do/no, I don't** sei d'accordo?
— sì/no; **she lives in Glasgow — so do I** lei
vive a Glasgow — anch'io; **he asked me to
help him and I did** mi ha chiesto di aiutarlo
ed io l'ho fatto; **they come here often — do
they?** vengono qui spesso — ah sì?, davvero?
5 (*in question tags*): **you like him, don't you?**
ti piace, vero?; **I don't know him, do I?** non
lo conosco, vero?
■ *vt* (*gen, carry out, perform etc*) fare; **what are
you doing tonight?** che fai stasera?; **what
can I do for you?** (*in shop*) desidera?; **I'll do
all I can** farò tutto il possibile; **to do the
cooking** cucinare; **to do the washing-up**
fare i piatti; **to do one's teeth** lavarsi i
denti; **to do one's hair/nails** farsi i capelli/
le unghie; **the car was doing 100** la
macchina faceva i 100 all'ora; **how do you
like your steak done?** come preferisce la
bistecca?; **well done** ben cotto(a)
■ *vi* **1** (*act, behave*) fare; **do as I do** faccia come
me, faccia come faccio io; **what did he do
with the cat?** che ne ha fatto del gatto?
2 (*get on, fare*) andare; **he's doing well/badly
at school** va bene/male a scuola; **how do
you do?** piacere!
3 (*suit*) andare bene; **this room will do**
questa stanza va bene
4 (*be sufficient*) bastare; **will £10 do?**
basteranno 10 sterline?; **that'll do** basta
così; **that'll do!** (*in annoyance*) ora basta!;
to make do (with) arrangiarsi (con)
▶ **do away with** *vt fus* (*kill*) far fuori; (*abolish*)
abolire
▶ **do for** *vt fus* (*Brit col: clean for*) fare i servizi per
▶ **do out of** *vt fus*: **to do sb out of sth** fregare
qc a qn
▶ **do up** *vt* (*laces*) allacciare; (*dress, buttons*)
abbottonare; (*renovate: room, house*) rimettere

a nuovo, rifare; **to do o.s. up** farsi bello(a)
▶ **do with** *vt fus* (*need*) aver bisogno di;
I could do with some help/a drink un
aiuto/un bicchierino non guasterebbe;
it could do with a wash una lavata non gli
farebbe male; (*be connected*): **what has it got
to do with you?** e tu che c'entri?; **I won't
have anything to do with it** non voglio
avere niente a che farci; **it has to do with
money** si tratta di soldi
▶ **do without** *vi* fare senza
■ *vt fus* fare a meno di

do. *abbr* = **ditto**
DOA *abbr* (= *dead on arrival*) morto(a) durante il
trasporto
d.o.b. *abbr* = **date of birth**
doc [dɔk] *n* (*col*) dottore(-essa)
docile ['dəusaɪl] *adj* docile
dock [dɔk] *n* bacino; (*wharf*) molo; (*Law*)
banco degli imputati ■ *vi* entrare in bacino
■ *vt* (*pay etc*) decurtare
dock dues *npl* diritti *mpl* di banchina
docker ['dɔkər] *n* scaricatore *m*
docket ['dɔkɪt] *n* (*on parcel etc*) etichetta,
cartellino
dockyard ['dɔkjɑːd] *n* cantiere *m* navale
doctor ['dɔktər] *n* medico, dottore(-essa);
(*PhD etc*) dottore(-essa) ■ *vt* (*interfere with:
food, drink*) adulterare; (: *text, document*)
alterare, manipolare; **~'s office** (*US*)
gabinetto medico, ambulatorio; **D~ of
Philosophy (PhD)** dottorato di ricerca;
(*person*) titolare *m/f* di un dottorato di ricerca
doctorate ['dɔktərɪt] *n* dottorato di ricerca;
vedi nota

◉ **DOCTORATE**

Il *doctorate* è il riconoscimento accademico
più prestigioso in tutti i campi del sapere
e viene conferito in seguito alla
presentazione di una tesi originale di
fronte ad una commissione di esperti.
Generalmente tale tesi è un compendio
del lavoro svolto durante più anni di
studi; *vedi anche* "Bachelor's degree",
"Master's degree".

doctrine ['dɔktrɪn] *n* dottrina
docudrama [dɔkju'drɑːmə] *n* (*TV*)
ricostruzione *f* filmata
document *n* ['dɔkjumənt] documento
■ *vt* ['dɔkjument] documentare
documentary [dɔkju'mentərɪ] *adj*
documentario(-a); (*evidence*)
documentato(-a) ■ *n* documentario

527

documentation [dɔkjumən'teɪʃən] *n*
documentazione *f*
DOD *n abbr* (US) = **Department of Defense**
doddering ['dɔdərɪŋ] *adj* traballante
doddery ['dɔdərɪ] *adj* malfermo(-a)
doddle ['dɔdl] *n*: **it's a ~** (*col*) è un gioco da
ragazzi
Dodecanese Islands [dəudɪkə'niːz-] *npl* Isole
fpl del Dodecanneso
dodge [dɔdʒ] *n* trucco; schivata ■ *vt*
schivare, eludere ■ *vi* scansarsi; (*Sport*) fare
una schivata; **to ~ out of the way** scansarsi;
to ~ through the traffic destreggiarsi nel
traffico
dodgems ['dɔdʒəmz] *npl* (*Brit*) autoscontri
mpl
dodgy ['dɔdʒɪ] *adj* (*col: uncertain*) rischioso(-a);
(*untrustworthy*) sospetto(-a)
DOE *n abbr* (US) = **Department of Energy**
doe [dəu] *n* (*deer*) femmina di daino; (*rabbit*)
coniglia
does [dʌz] *see* **do**
doesn't ['dʌznt] = **does not**
dog [dɔg] *n* cane *m* ■ *vt* (*follow closely*)
pedinare; (*fig: memory etc*) perseguitare; **to go
to the dogs** (*person*) ridursi male, lasciarsi
andare; (*nation etc*) andare in malora
dog biscuits *npl* biscotti *mpl* per cani
dog collar *n* collare *m* di cane; (*fig*) collarino
dog-eared ['dɔgɪəd] *adj* (*book*) con orecchie
dog food *n* cibo per cani
dogged ['dɔgɪd] *adj* ostinato(-a), tenace
doggie, doggy ['dɔgɪ] *n* (*col*) cane *m*,
cagnolino
doggy bag *n* sacchetto per gli avanzi (*da
portare a casa*)
dogma ['dɔgmə] *n* dogma *m*
dogmatic [dɔg'mætɪk] *adj* dogmatico(-a)
do-gooder [duː'gudəʳ] *n* (*col, pej*): **to be a ~**
fare il filantropo
dogsbody ['dɔgzbɔdɪ] *n* (*Brit*) factotum *m inv*
doily ['dɔɪlɪ] *n* centrino di carta sottopiatto
doing ['duːɪŋ] *n*: **this is your ~** è opera tua,
sei stato tu
doings ['duːɪŋz] *npl* attività *fpl*
do-it-yourself ['duːɪtjɔː'self] *n* il far da sé
doldrums ['dɔldrəmz] *npl* (*fig*): **to be in the ~**
essere giù; (*business*) attraversare un
momento difficile
dole [dəul] *n* (*Brit*) sussidio di
disoccupazione; **to be on the ~** vivere del
sussidio
▶ **dole out** *vt* distribuire
doleful ['dəulful] *adj* triste, doloroso(-a)
doll [dɔl] *n* bambola
▶ **doll up** *vt*: **to ~ o.s. up** farsi bello(a)
dollar ['dɔləʳ] *n* dollaro

dollop ['dɔləp] *n* (*of food*) cucchiaiata
dolly ['dɔlɪ] *n* bambola
dolphin ['dɔlfɪn] *n* delfino
domain [də'meɪn] *n* dominio; (*fig*) campo,
sfera
dome [dəum] *n* cupola
domestic [də'mɛstɪk] *adj* (*duty, happiness,
animal*) domestico(-a); (*policy, affairs, flights*)
nazionale; (*news*) dall'interno
domesticated [də'mɛstɪkeɪtɪd] *adj*
addomesticato(-a); (*person*) casalingo(-a)
domesticity [dəumɛs'tɪsɪtɪ] *n* vita di
famiglia
domestic servant *n* domestico(-a)
domicile ['dɔmɪsaɪl] *n* domicilio
dominant ['dɔmɪnənt] *adj* dominante
dominate ['dɔmɪneɪt] *vt* dominare
domination [dɔmɪ'neɪʃən] *n* dominazione *f*
domineering [dɔmɪ'nɪərɪŋ] *adj* dispotico(-a),
autoritario(-a)
Dominican Republic [də'mɪnɪkən-] *n*
Repubblica Dominicana
dominion [də'mɪnɪən] *n* dominio, sovranità;
(*Brit Pol*) dominion *m inv*
domino (*pl* **dominoes**) ['dɔmɪnəu] *n* domino;
dominoes *npl* (*game*) gioco del domino
don [dɔn] *n* (*Brit*) docente *m/f*
universitario(-a) ■ *vt* indossare
donate [də'neɪt] *vt* donare
donation [də'neɪʃən] *n* donazione *f*
done [dʌn] *pp of* **do**
donkey ['dɔŋkɪ] *n* asino
donkey-work ['dɔŋkɪwəːk] *n* (*Brit col*) lavoro
ingrato
donor ['dəunəʳ] *n* donatore(-trice)
donor card *n* tessera di donatore di organi
don't [dəunt] *vb* = **do not**
donut ['dəunʌt] *n* (US) = **doughnut**
doodle ['duːdl] *n* scarabocchio ■ *vi*
scarabocchiare
doom [duːm] *n* destino; rovina ■ *vt*: **to be
doomed (to failure)** essere predestinato(-a)
(a fallire)
doomsday ['duːmzdeɪ] *n* il giorno del
Giudizio
door [dɔːʳ] *n* porta; (*of vehicle*) sportello,
portiera; **from ~ to ~** di porta in porta
doorbell ['dɔːbɛl] *n* campanello
door handle *n* maniglia
doorman ['dɔːmæn] *n* (*in hotel*) portiere *m* in
livrea; (*in block of flats*) portinaio
doormat ['dɔːmæt] *n* stuoia della porta
doorstep ['dɔːstɛp] *n* gradino della porta
door-to-door ['dɔːtə'dɔːʳ] *adj*: **~ selling**
vendita porta a porta
doorway ['dɔːweɪ] *n* porta; **in the ~** nel vano
della porta

dope [dəup] *n* (*col: drugs*) roba; (: *information*) dati *mpl* ◼ *vt* (*horse etc*) drogare

dopey ['dəupɪ] *adj* (*col*) inebetito(-a)

dormant ['dɔːmənt] *adj* inattivo(-a); (*fig*) latente

dormer ['dɔːmə'] *n* (*also*: **dormer window**) abbaino

dormice ['dɔːmaɪs] *npl of* **dormouse**

dormitory ['dɔːmɪtrɪ] *n* dormitorio; (*US: hall of residence*) casa dello studente

dormouse (*pl* **dormice**) ['dɔːmaus, -maɪs] *n* ghiro

DOS [dɔs] *n abbr* = **disk operating system**

dosage ['dəusɪdʒ] *n* (*on medicine bottle*) posologia

dose [dəus] *n* dose *f*; (*Brit: bout*) attacco ◼ *vt*: **to ~ sb with sth** somministrare qc a qn; **a ~ of flu** una bella influenza

dosser ['dɔsə'] *n* (*Brit col*) barbone(-a)

doss house ['dɔs-] *n* (*Brit*) asilo notturno

dossier ['dɔsɪeɪ] *n* dossier *m inv*

DOT *n abbr* (*US*) = **Department of Transportation**

dot [dɔt] *n* punto; macchiolina ◼ *vt*: **dotted with** punteggiato(a) di; **on the ~** in punto

dotcom [dɔt'kɔm] *n* azienda che opera in Internet

dot command *n* (*Comput*) dot command *m inv*

dote [dəut]: **to ~ on** *vt fus* essere infatuato(a) di

dot-matrix printer [dɔt'meɪtrɪks-] *n* stampante *f* a matrice a punti

dotted line ['dɔtɪd-] *n* linea punteggiata; **to sign on the ~** firmare (nell'apposito spazio); (*fig*) accettare

dotty ['dɔtɪ] *adj* (*col*) strambo(-a)

double ['dʌbl] *adj* doppio(-a) ◼ *adv* (*fold*) in due, doppio; (*twice*): **to cost ~ sth** costare il doppio (di qc) ◼ *n* sosia *m inv*; (*Cine*) controfigura ◼ *vt* raddoppiare; (*fold*) piegare doppio *or* in due ◼ *vi* raddoppiarsi; **spelt with a ~ "l"** scritto con due elle *or* con doppia elle; **~ five two six (5526)** (*Brit Tel*) cinque cinque due sei; **on the ~**, (*Brit*) **at the ~** a passo di corsa; **to ~ as** (*have two uses etc*) funzionare *or* servire anche da; *see also* **doubles**

▶ **double back** *vi* (*person*) tornare sui propri passi

▶ **double up** *vi* (*bend over*) piegarsi in due; (*share room*) dividere la stanza

double bass *n* contrabbasso

double bed *n* letto matrimoniale

double-breasted ['dʌbl'brɛstɪd] *adj* a doppio petto

double-check ['dʌbl'tʃɛk] *vt, vi* ricontrollare

double-clutch ['dʌbl'klʌtʃ] *vi* (*US*) fare la doppietta

double cream *n* (*Brit*) doppia panna

doublecross ['dʌbl'krɔs] *vt* fare il doppio gioco con

doubledecker ['dʌbl'dɛkə'] *n* autobus *m inv* a due piani

double declutch *vi* (*Brit*) fare la doppietta

double exposure *n* (*Phot*) sovrimpressione *f*

double glazing *n* (*Brit*) doppi vetri *mpl*

double-page ['dʌblpeɪdʒ] *adj*: **~ spread** pubblicità a doppia pagina

double parking *n* parcheggio in doppia fila

double room *n* camera per due

doubles ['dʌblz] *n* (*Tennis*) doppio

double time *n* tariffa doppia per lavoro straordinario

double whammy [-'wæmɪ] *n* doppia mazzata (*fig*)

doubly ['dʌblɪ] *adv* doppiamente

doubt [daut] *n* dubbio ◼ *vt* dubitare di; **to ~ that** dubitare che + *sub*; **without (a) ~** senza dubbio; **beyond ~** fuor di dubbio; **I ~ it very much** ho i miei dubbi, nutro seri dubbi in proposito

doubtful ['dautful] *adj* dubbioso(-a), incerto(-a); (*person*) equivoco(-a); **to be ~ about sth** avere dei dubbi su qc, non essere convinto di qc; **I'm a bit ~** non ne sono sicuro

doubtless ['dautlɪs] *adv* indubbiamente

dough [dəu] *n* pasta, impasto; (*col: money*) grana

doughnut, (*US*) **donut** ['dəunʌt] *n* bombolone *m*

dour [duə'] *adj* arcigno(-a)

douse [daus] *vt* (*with water*) infradiciare; (*flames*) spegnere

dove [dʌv] *n* colombo(-a)

Dover ['dəuvə'] *n* Dover *f*

dovetail ['dʌvteɪl] *n*: **~ joint** incastro a coda di rondine ◼ *vi* (*fig*) combaciare

dowager ['dauədʒə'] *n* vedova titolata

dowdy ['daudɪ] *adj* trasandato(-a), malvestito(-a)

Dow-Jones average ['dau'dʒəunz-] *n* (*US*) indice *m* Dow-Jones

down [daun] *n* (*fluff*) piumino; (*hill*) collina, colle *m* ◼ *adv* giù, di sotto ◼ *prep* giù per ◼ *vt* (*col: drink*) scolarsi; **~ there** laggiù, là in fondo; **~ here** quaggiù; **I'll be ~ in a minute** scendo tra un minuto; **the price of meat is ~** il prezzo della carne è sceso; **I've got it ~ in my diary** ce l'ho sulla mia agenda; **to pay £2 ~** dare 2 sterline in acconto *or* di anticipo; **I've been ~ with flu** sono stato a letto con l'influenza; **England is two goals ~** l'Inghilterra sta perdendo per due goal; **to ~ tools** (*Brit*) incrociare le braccia; **~ with X!** abbasso X!

529

down-and-out ['daunəndaut] *n* (*tramp*) barbone *m*

down-at-heel ['daunət'hi:l] *adj* scalcagnato(-a); (*fig*) trasandato(-a)

downbeat ['daunbi:t] *n* (*Mus*) tempo in battere ■ *adj* (*col*) volutamente distaccato(-a)

downcast ['daunkɑ:st] *adj* abbattuto(-a)

downer ['daunəʳ] *n* (*col*: *drug*) farmaco depressivo; **to be on a ~** (*depressed*) essere giù

downfall ['daunfɔ:l] *n* caduta; rovina

downgrade ['daungreɪd] *vt* (*job, hotel*) declassare; (*employee*) degradare

downhearted [daun'hɑ:tɪd] *adj* scoraggiato(-a)

downhill ['daun'hɪl] *adv* verso il basso ■ *n* (*Ski: also:* **downhill race**) discesa libera; **to go ~** andare in discesa; (*business*) andare a rotoli

Downing Street ['daunɪŋ-] *n*: **10 ~** residenza *del primo ministro inglese; vedi nota*

● **DOWNING STREET**

Downing Street è la via di Westminster che porta da Whitehall al parco di St James dove, al numero 10, si trova la residenza del primo ministro inglese e, al numero 11, quella del Cancelliere dello Scacchiere. Spesso si usa *Downing Street* per indicare il governo britannico.

download ['daunləud] *vt* (*Comput*) scaricare ■ *n* (*Comput*) file *m inv* da scaricare

downloadable *adj* (*Comput*) scaricabile

down-market ['daun'mɑ:kɪt] *adj* rivolto(-a) ad una fascia di mercato inferiore

down payment *n* acconto

downplay ['daunpleɪ] *vt* (*US*) minimizzare

downpour ['daunpɔ:ʳ] *n* scroscio di pioggia

downright ['daunraɪt] *adj* franco(-a); (*refusal*) assoluto(-a)

Downs [daunz] *npl* (*Brit*): **the ~** colline ricche di *gesso nel sud-est dell'Inghilterra*

downsize ['daun'saɪz] *vt* (*workforce*) ridurre

Down's syndrome *n* sindrome *f* di Down

downstairs ['daun'stɛəz] *adv* di sotto; al piano inferiore; **to come ~**, **go ~** scendere giù

downstream ['daun'stri:m] *adv* a valle

downtime ['dauntaɪm] *n* (*Comm*) tempi *mpl* morti

down-to-earth ['dauntu'ə:θ] *adj* pratico(-a)

downtown ['daun'taun] *adv* in città ■ *adj* (*US*): **~ Chicago** il centro di Chicago

downtrodden ['dauntrɒdn] *adj* oppresso(-a)

down under *adv* agli antipodi

downward ['daunwəd] *adj* in giù, in discesa; **a ~ trend** una diminuzione progressiva ■ *adv* in giù, in discesa

downwards ['daunwədz] *adv* in giù, in discesa

dowry ['dauri] *n* dote *f*

doz. *abbr* = **dozen**

doze [dəuz] *vi* sonnecchiare
▶ **doze off** *vi* appisolarsi

dozen ['dʌzn] *n* dozzina; **a ~ books** una dozzina di libri; **80p a ~** 80 pence la dozzina; **dozens of times** centinaia *or* migliaia di volte

DPh, DPhil *n abbr* (= *Doctor of Philosophy*) ≈ dottorato di ricerca

DPP *n abbr* (*Brit*) = **Director of Public Prosecutions**

DPT *n abbr* (*Med:* = *diphtheria, pertussis, tetanus*) vaccino

Dr, Dr. *abbr* (= *doctor*) Dr, Dott./Dott.ssa

dr *abbr* (*Comm*) = **debtor**

Dr. *abbr* (*in street names*) = **drive**

drab [dræb] *adj* tetro(-a), grigio(-a)

draft [drɑ:ft] *n* abbozzo; (*Comm*) tratta; (*US Mil*) contingente *m*; (*: call-up*) leva ■ *vt* abbozzare; (*document, report*) stendere (in versione preliminare); *see also* **draught**

drag [dræg] *vt* trascinare; (*river*) dragare ■ *vi* trascinarsi ■ *n* (*Aviat, Naut*) resistenza (aerodinamica); (*col: person*) noioso(-a); (*: task*) noia; (*women's clothing*): **in ~** travestito (da donna)
▶ **drag away** *vt*: **to ~ away (from)** tirare via (da)
▶ **drag on** *vi* tirar avanti lentamente

dragnet ['drægnet] *n* giacchio; (*fig*) rastrellamento

dragon ['drægən] *n* drago

dragonfly ['drægənflaɪ] *n* libellula

dragoon [drə'gu:n] *n* (*cavalryman*) dragone *m* ■ *vt*: **to ~ sb into doing sth** (*Brit*) costringere qn a fare qc

drain [dreɪn] *n* canale *m* di scolo; (*for sewage*) fogna; (*on resources*) salasso ■ *vt* (*land, marshes*) prosciugare; (*vegetables*) scolare; (*reservoir etc*) vuotare ■ *vi* (*water*) defluire; **to feel drained** sentirsi svuotato(-a), sentirsi sfinito(-a)

drainage ['dreɪnɪdʒ] *n* prosciugamento; fognatura

draining board ['dreɪnɪŋ-], (*US*) **drainboard** ['dreɪnbɔ:d] *n* piano del lavello

drainpipe ['dreɪnpaɪp] *n* tubo di scarico

drake [dreɪk] *n* maschio dell'anatra

dram [dræm] *n* bicchierino (di whisky *etc*)

drama ['drɑ:mə] *n* (*art*) dramma *m*, teatro; (*play*) commedia; (*event*) dramma

dramatic [drə'mætɪk] *adj* drammatico(-a)

dramatically [drə'mætɪklɪ] *adv* in modo spettacolare

dramatist ['dræmətɪst] n drammaturgo(-a)

dramatize ['dræmətaɪz] vt (events etc) drammatizzare; (adapt: novel: for TV) ridurre or adattare per la televisione; (: for cinema) ridurre or adattare per lo schermo

drank [dræŋk] pt of **drink**

drape [dreɪp] vt drappeggiare; see also **drapes**

draper ['dreɪpə^r] n (Brit) negoziante m/f di stoffe

drapes [dreɪps] npl (US) tende fpl

drastic ['dræstɪk] adj drastico(-a)

drastically ['dræstɪklɪ] adv drasticamente

draught, (US) **draft** [drɑːft] n corrente f d'aria; (Naut) pescaggio; **on ~** (beer) alla spina; see also **draughts**

draught beer n birra alla spina

draughtboard ['drɑːftbɔːd] n scacchiera

draughts [drɑːfts] n (Brit) (gioco della) dama

draughtsman, (US) **draftsman** ['drɑːftsmən] n disegnatore m

draughtsmanship, (US) **draftsmanship** ['drɑːftsmənʃɪp] n disegno tecnico; (skill) arte f del disegno

draw [drɔː] vb (pt **drew**, pp **drawn**) [druː, drɔːn] vt tirare; (attract) attirare; (picture) disegnare; (line, circle) tracciare; (money) ritirare; (formulate: conclusion) trarre, ricavare; (: comparison, distinction): **to ~ (between)** fare (tra) ■ vi (Sport) pareggiare ■ n (Sport) pareggio; (in lottery) estrazione f; (attraction) attrazione f; **to ~ to a close** avvicinarsi alla conclusione; **to ~ near** vi avvicinarsi

  ▶ **draw back** vi: **to ~ back (from)** indietreggiare (di fronte a), tirarsi indietro (di fronte a)

  ▶ **draw in** vi (Brit: car) accostarsi; (: train) entrare in stazione

  ▶ **draw on** vt (resources) attingere a; (imagination, person) far ricorso a

  ▶ **draw out** vi (lengthen) allungarsi ■ vt (money) ritirare

  ▶ **draw up** vi (stop) arrestarsi, fermarsi ■ vt (document) compilare; (plans) formulare

drawback ['drɔːbæk] n svantaggio, inconveniente m

drawbridge ['drɔːbrɪdʒ] n ponte m levatoio

drawee [drɔːˈiː] n trattario

drawer [drɔːr] n cassetto; ['drɔːər] (of cheque) riscuotitore(-trice)

drawing ['drɔːɪŋ] n disegno

drawing board n tavola da disegno

drawing pin n (Brit) puntina da disegno

drawing room n salotto

drawl [drɔːl] n pronuncia strascicata

drawn [drɔːn] pp of **draw** ■ adj (haggard: with tiredness) tirato(-a); (: with pain) contratto(-a) (dal dolore)

drawstring ['drɔːstrɪŋ] n laccio (per stringere maglie, sacche etc)

dread [drɛd] n terrore m ■ vt tremare all'idea di

dreadful ['drɛdful] adj terribile; **I feel ~!** (ill) mi sento uno straccio!; (ashamed) vorrei scomparire (dalla vergogna)!

dream [driːm] n sogno ■ vt, vi (pt, pp **dreamed** or **dreamt**) [drɛmt] sognare; **to have a ~ about sb/sth** fare un sogno su qn/qc; **sweet dreams!** sogni d'oro!

  ▶ **dream up** vt (reason, excuse) inventare; (plan, idea) escogitare

dreamer ['driːmər] n sognatore(-trice)

dreamt [drɛmt] pt, pp of **dream**

dreamy ['driːmɪ] adj (look, voice) sognante; (person) distratto(-a), sognatore(-trice)

dreary ['drɪərɪ] adj tetro(-a); monotono(-a)

dredge [drɛdʒ] vt dragare

  ▶ **dredge up** vt tirare alla superficie; (fig: unpleasant facts) rivangare

dredger ['drɛdʒər] n draga; (Brit: also: **sugar dredger**) spargizucchero m inv

dregs [drɛgz] npl feccia

drench [drɛntʃ] vt inzuppare; **drenched to the skin** bagnato(a) fino all'osso, bagnato(a) fradicio(a)

dress [drɛs] n vestito; (clothing) abbigliamento ■ vt vestire; (wound) fasciare; (food) condire; preparare; (shop window) allestire ■ vi vestirsi; **to ~ o.s., to get dressed** vestirsi; **she dresses very well** veste molto bene

  ▶ **dress up** vi vestirsi a festa; (in fancy dress) vestirsi in costume

dress circle n prima galleria

dress designer n disegnatore(-trice) di moda

dresser ['drɛsər] n (Theat) assistente m/f del camerino; (also: **window dresser**) vetrinista m/f; (furniture) credenza

dressing ['drɛsɪŋ] n (Med) benda; (Culin) condimento

dressing gown n (Brit) vestaglia

dressing room n (Theat) camerino; (Sport) spogliatoio

dressing table n toilette f inv

dressmaker ['drɛsmeɪkər] n sarta

dressmaking ['drɛsmeɪkɪŋ] n sartoria; confezioni fpl per donna

dress rehearsal n prova generale

dress shirt n camicia da sera

dressy ['drɛsɪ] adj (col) elegante

drew [druː] pt of **draw**

dribble ['drɪbl] vi gocciolare; (baby) sbavare; (Football) dribblare ■ vt dribblare

dried [draɪd] adj (fruit, beans) secco(-a); (eggs, milk) in polvere

d

drier ['draɪə^r] n = **dryer**

drift [drɪft] n (of current etc) direzione f; forza; (of sand, snow) cumulo; (general meaning) senso ■ vi (boat) essere trasportato(-a) dalla corrente; (sand, snow) ammucchiarsi; **to catch sb's ~** capire dove qn vuole arrivare; **to let things ~** lasciare che le cose vadano come vogliono; **to ~ apart** (friends) perdersi di vista; (lovers) allontanarsi l'uno dall'altro

drifter ['drɪftə^r] n persona che fa una vita da zingaro

driftwood ['drɪftwud] n resti mpl della mareggiata

drill [drɪl] n trapano; (Mil) esercitazione f ■ vt trapanare; (soldiers) esercitare, addestrare; (pupils: in grammar) fare esercitare ■ vi (for oil) fare trivellazioni

drilling ['drɪlɪŋ] n (for oil) trivellazione f

drilling rig n (on land) torre f di perforazione; (at sea) piattaforma (per trivellazioni subacquee)

drily ['draɪlɪ] adv = **dryly**

drink [drɪŋk] n bevanda, bibita ■ vt, vi (pt **drank**, pp **drunk**) [dræŋk, drʌŋk] bere; **to have a ~** bere qualcosa; **a ~ of water** un bicchier d'acqua; **would you like something to ~?** vuole qualcosa da bere?; **we had drinks before lunch** abbiamo preso l'aperitivo

▶ **drink in** vt (person: fresh air) aspirare; (: story) ascoltare avidamente; (: sight) ammirare, bersi con gli occhi

drinkable ['drɪŋkəbl] adj (not poisonous) potabile; (palatable) bevibile

drink-driving ['drɪŋk'draɪvɪŋ] n guida in stato di ebbrezza

drinker ['drɪŋkə^r] n bevitore(-trice)

drinking ['drɪŋkɪŋ] n (drunkenness) il bere, alcoolismo

drinking fountain n fontanella

drinking water n acqua potabile

drip [drɪp] n goccia; (dripping) sgocciolio; (Med) fleboclisi f inv; (col: spineless person) lavativo ■ vi gocciolare; (washing) sgocciolare; (wall) trasudare

drip-dry ['drɪp'draɪ] adj (shirt) che non si stira

drip-feed ['drɪpfi:d] vt alimentare mediante fleboclisi

dripping ['drɪpɪŋ] n (Culin) grasso d'arrosto ■ adj: **~ wet** fradicio(a)

drive [draɪv] n passeggiata or giro in macchina; (also: **driveway**) viale m d'accesso; (energy) energia; (Psych) impulso; bisogno; (push) sforzo eccezionale; campagna; (Sport) drive m inv; (Tech) trasmissione f; (Comput: also: **disk drive**) disk drive m inv, unità f inv a dischi magnetici ■ vb (pt **drove**, pp **driven**)

[drəuv, 'drɪvn] vt (vehicle) guidare; (nail) piantare; (push) cacciare, spingere; (Tech: motor) azionare; far funzionare ■ vi (Aut: at controls) guidare; (: travel) andare in macchina; **to go for a ~** andare a fare un giro in macchina; **it's 3 hours' ~ from London** è a 3 ore di macchina da Londra; **left-/right-hand ~** (Aut) guida a sinistra/destra; **front-/rear-wheel ~** (Aut) trazione f anteriore/posteriore; **to ~ sb to (do) sth** spingere qn a (fare) qc; **he drives a taxi** fa il tassista; **to ~ at 50 km an hour** guidare or andare a 50 km all'ora

▶ **drive at** vt fus (fig: intend, mean) mirare a, voler dire

▶ **drive on** vi proseguire, andare (più) avanti ■ vt (incite, encourage) sospingere, spingere

drive-by ['draɪvbaɪ] n (also: **drive-by shooting**) sparatoria dalla macchina; **he was killed in a ~ shooting** lo hanno ammazzato sparandogli da una macchina in corsa

drive-in ['draɪvɪn] adj, n (esp US) drive-in (m inv)

drive-in window n (US) sportello di drive-in

drivel ['drɪvl] n (col: nonsense) ciance fpl

driven ['drɪvn] pp of **drive**

driver ['draɪvə^r] n conducente m/f; (of taxi) tassista m; (of bus) autista m; (Comput) driver m inv

driver's license n (US) patente f di guida

driveway ['draɪvweɪ] n viale m d'accesso

driving ['draɪvɪŋ] adj: **~ rain** pioggia sferzante ■ n guida

driving force n forza trainante

driving instructor n istruttore(-trice) di scuola guida

driving lesson n lezione f di guida

driving licence n (Brit) patente f di guida

driving school n scuola f guida inv

driving test n esame m di guida

drizzle ['drɪzl] n pioggerella ■ vi piovigginare

droll [drəul] adj buffo(-a)

dromedary ['drɔmədərɪ] n dromedario

drone [drəun] n ronzio; (male bee) fuco ■ vi (bee, aircraft, engine) ronzare; (also: **drone on**: person) continuare a parlare (in modo monotono); (: voice) continuare a ronzare

drool [dru:l] vi sbavare; **to ~ over sb/sth** (fig) andare in estasi per qn/qc

droop [dru:p] vi abbassarsi; languire

drop [drɔp] n goccia; (fall: in price) calo, ribasso; (: in salary) riduzione f, taglio; (also: **parachute drop**) lancio; (steep incline) salto ■ vt lasciar cadere; (voice, eyes, price) abbassare; (set down from car) far scendere ■ vi cascare; (decrease: wind, temperature, price, voice)

calare; (*numbers, attendance*) diminuire;
drops *npl* (*Med*) gocce *fpl*; **cough drops**
pastiglie *fpl* per la tosse; **a ~ of 10%** un calo
del 10%; **to ~ sb a line** mandare due righe a
qn; **to ~ anchor** gettare l'ancora
▶ **drop in** *vi* (*col: visit*): **to ~ in (on)** fare un
salto (da), passare (da)
▶ **drop off** *vi* (*sleep*) addormentarsi ■ *vt*:
to ~ sb off far scendere qn
▶ **drop out** *vi* (*withdraw*) ritirarsi; (*student etc*)
smettere di studiare
droplet ['drɔplɪt] *n* gocciolina
dropout ['drɔpaut] *n* (*from society/university*)
chi ha abbandonato (la società/gli studi)
dropper ['drɔpər] *n* (*Med*) contagocce *m inv*
droppings ['drɔpɪŋz] *npl* sterco
dross [drɔs] *n* scoria; scarto
drought [draut] *n* siccità *f inv*
drove [drəuv] *pt of* **drive** ■ *n*: **droves of
people** una moltitudine di persone
drown [draun] *vt* affogare; (*also: **drown out**:
sound*) coprire ■ *vi* affogare
drowse [drauz] *vi* sonnecchiare
drowsy ['drauzɪ] *adj* sonnolento(-a),
assonnato(-a)
drudge [drʌdʒ] *n* (*person*) uomo/donna di
fatica; (*job*) faticaccia
drudgery ['drʌdʒərɪ] *n* fatica improba;
housework is sheer ~ le faccende
domestiche sono alienanti
drug [drʌg] *n* farmaco; (*narcotic*) droga ■ *vt*
drogare; **he's on drugs** si droga; (*Med*) segue
una cura
drug abuser [-ə'bjuːzər] *n* chi fa uso di droghe
drug addict *n* tossicomane *m/f*
druggist ['drʌgɪst] *n* (*US*) farmacista *m/f*
drug peddler *n* spacciatore(-trice) di droga
drugstore ['drʌgstɔːr] *n* (*US*) negozio di generi
vari e di articoli di farmacia con un bar
drum [drʌm] *n* tamburo; (*for oil, petrol*) fusto
■ *vt*: **to ~ one's fingers on the table**
tamburellare con le dita sulla tavola;
drums *npl* (*Mus*) batteria
▶ **drum up** *vt* (*enthusiasm, support*)
conquistarsi
drummer ['drʌmər] *n* batterista *m/f*
drum roll *n* rullio di tamburi
drumstick ['drʌmstɪk] *n* (*Mus*) bacchetta;
(*chicken leg*) coscia di pollo
drunk [drʌŋk] *pp of* **drink** ■ *adj* ubriaco(-a),
ebbro(-a) ■ *n* ubriacone(-a); **to get ~**
ubriacarsi, prendere una sbornia
drunkard ['drʌŋkəd] *n* ubriacone(-a)
drunken ['drʌŋkən] *adj* ubriaco(-a), da
ubriaco; **~ driving** guida in stato di ebbrezza
drunkenness ['drʌŋkənnɪs] *n* ubriachezza;
ebbrezza

dry [draɪ] *adj* secco(-a); (*day, clothes: fig: humour*)
asciutto(-a); (*uninteresting: lecture, subject*) poco
avvincente ■ *vt* seccare; (*clothes, hair, hands*)
asciugare ■ *vi* asciugarsi; **on ~ land** sulla
terraferma; **to ~ one's hands/hair/eyes**
asciugarsi le mani/i capelli/gli occhi
▶ **dry up** *vi* seccarsi; (*source of supply*)
esaurirsi; (*fig: imagination etc*) inaridirsi;
(*fall silent: speaker*) azzittirsi
dry-clean [draɪ'kliːn] *vt* pulire *or* lavare a
secco
dry-cleaner's [draɪ'kliːnəz] *n* lavasecco *m inv*
dry-cleaning [draɪ'kliːnɪŋ] *n* pulitura a secco
dry dock *n* (*Naut*) bacino di carenaggio
dryer ['draɪər] *n* (*for hair*) föhn *m inv*,
asciugacapelli *m inv*; (*for clothes*)
asciugabiancheria *m inv*
dry goods *npl* (*Comm*) tessuti *mpl* e mercerie *fpl*
dry goods store *n* (*US*) negozio di stoffe
dry ice *n* ghiaccio secco
dryly ['draɪlɪ] *adv* con fare asciutto
dryness ['draɪnɪs] *n* secchezza; (*of ground*)
aridità
dry rot *n* fungo del legno
dry run *n* (*fig*) prova
dry ski slope *n* pista artificiale
DSc *n abbr* (= *Doctor of Science*) titolo di studio
DSS *n abbr* (*Brit*) = **Department of Social
Security**; *see* **social security**
DST *abbr* = **Daylight Saving Time**
DTI *n abbr* (*Brit*) = **Department of Trade and
Industry**; *see* **trade**
DTP *n abbr* = **desktop publishing**; (*Med*:
= *diphtheria, tetanus, pertussis*) vaccino
DT's *n abbr* (*col*) = **delirium tremens**
dual ['djuəl] *adj* doppio(-a)
dual carriageway *n* (*Brit*) strada a doppia
carreggiata
dual-control ['djuəlkən'trəul] *adj* con doppi
comandi
dual nationality *n* doppia nazionalità
dual-purpose ['djuəl'pə:pəs] *adj* a doppio uso
dubbed [dʌbd] *adj* (*Cine*) doppiato(-a);
(*nicknamed*) soprannominato(-a)
dubious ['djuːbɪəs] *adj* dubbio(-a); (*character,
manner*) ambiguo(-a), equivoco(-a); **I'm very
~ about it** ho i miei dubbi in proposito
Dublin ['dʌblɪn] *n* Dublino *f*
Dubliner ['dʌblɪnər] *n* dublinese *m/f*
duchess ['dʌtʃɪs] *n* duchessa
duck [dʌk] *n* anatra ■ *vi* abbassare la testa
■ *vt* spingere sotto (l'acqua)
duckling ['dʌklɪŋ] *n* anatroccolo
duct [dʌkt] *n* condotto; (*Anat*) canale *m*
dud [dʌd] *n* (*shell*) proiettile *m* che fa cilecca;
it's a ~ (*object, tool*) è inutile, non funziona
■ *adj* (*Brit: cheque*) a vuoto; (*note, coin*) falso(-a)

533

due [djuː] *adj* dovuto(-a); (*expected*) atteso(-a); (*fitting*) giusto(-a) ■ *n* dovuto ■ *adv*: ~ **north** diritto verso nord; **dues** *npl* (*for club, union*) quota; (*in harbour*) diritti *mpl* di porto; **in ~ course** a tempo debito; finalmente; ~ **to** dovuto a; a causa di; **the rent's ~ on the 30th** l'affitto scade il 30; **the train is ~ at 8** il treno è atteso per le 8; **she is ~ back tomorrow** dovrebbe essere di ritorno domani; **I am ~ 6 days' leave** mi spettano 6 giorni di ferie

due date *n* data di scadenza

duel ['djuəl] *n* duello

duet [djuːˈɛt] *n* duetto

duff [dʌf] *adj* (*Brit col*) barboso(-a)

duffelbag, duffle bag ['dʌflbæg] *n* sacca da viaggio di tela

duffelcoat, duffle coat ['dʌflkəut] *n* montgomery *m inv*

duffer ['dʌfəʳ] *n* (*col*) schiappa

dug [dʌg] *pt, pp* of **dig**

dugout ['dʌgaut] *n* (*Football*) panchina

duke [djuːk] *n* duca *m*

dull [dʌl] *adj* (*boring*) noioso(-a); (*slow-witted*) ottuso(-a); (*sound, pain*) sordo(-a); (*weather, day*) fosco(-a), scuro(-a); (*blade*) smussato(-a) ■ *vt* (*pain, grief*) attutire; (*mind, senses*) intorpidire

duly ['djuːlɪ] *adv* (*on time*) a tempo debito; (*as expected*) debitamente

dumb [dʌm] *adj* muto(-a); (*stupid*) stupido(-a); **to be struck ~** (*fig*) ammutolire, restare senza parole

dumbbell ['dʌmbɛl] *n* (*Sport*) manubrio, peso

dumbfounded [dʌmˈfaundɪd] *adj* stupito(-a), stordito(-a)

dummy ['dʌmɪ] *n* (*tailor's model*) manichino; (*Sport*) finto; (*Brit: for baby*) tettarella ■ *adj* falso(-a), finto(-a)

dummy run *n* giro di prova

dump [dʌmp] *n* mucchio di rifiuti; (*place*) luogo di scarico; (*Mil*) deposito; (*Comput*) scaricamento, dump *m inv* ■ *vt* (*put down*) scaricare; mettere giù; (*get rid of*) buttar via; (*Comm: goods*) svendere; (*Comput*) scaricare; **to be (down) in the dumps** (*col*) essere giù di corda

dumping ['dʌmpɪŋ] *n* (*Econ*) dumping *m*; (*of rubbish*): **"no ~"** "vietato lo scarico"

dumpling ['dʌmplɪŋ] *n* specie di gnocco

dumpy ['dʌmpɪ] *adj* tracagnotto(-a)

dunce [dʌns] *n* asino

dune [djuːn] *n* duna

dung [dʌŋ] *n* concime *m*

dungarees [dʌŋɡəˈriːz] *npl* tuta

dungeon ['dʌndʒən] *n* prigione *f* sotterranea

dunk [dʌŋk] *vt* inzuppare

duo ['djuːəu] *n* (*gen, Mus*) duo *m inv*

duodenal [djuːəuˈdiːnl] *adj* (*ulcer*) duodenale

duodenum [djuːəuˈdiːnəm] *n* duodeno

dupe [djuːp] *vt* gabbare, ingannare

duplex ['djuːplɛks] *n* (*US: also*: **duplex apartment**) appartamento su due piani

duplicate *n* ['djuːplɪkət] doppio; (*copy of letter etc*) duplicato ■ *vt* ['djuːplɪkeɪt] raddoppiare; (*on machine*) ciclostilare ■ *adj* (*copy*) conforme, esattamente uguale; **in ~** in duplice copia; ~ **key** duplicato (della chiave)

duplicating machine ['djuːplɪkeɪtɪŋ-], **duplicator** ['djuːplɪkeɪtəʳ] *n* duplicatore *m*

duplicity [djuːˈplɪsɪtɪ] *n* doppiezza, duplicità

Dur. *abbr* (*Brit*) = **Durham**

durability [djuərəˈbɪlɪtɪ] *n* durevolezza; resistenza

durable ['djuərəbl] *adj* durevole; (*clothes, metal*) resistente

duration [djuəˈreɪʃən] *n* durata

duress [djuəˈrɛs] *n*: **under ~** sotto costrizione

Durex® ['djuərɛks] *n* (*Brit*) preservativo

during ['djuərɪŋ] *prep* durante, nel corso di

dusk [dʌsk] *n* crepuscolo

dusky ['dʌskɪ] *adj* scuro(-a)

dust [dʌst] *n* polvere *f* ■ *vt* (*furniture*) spolverare; (*cake etc*): **to ~ with** cospargere con
▸ **dust off** *vt* rispolverare

dustbin ['dʌstbɪn] *n* (*Brit*) pattumiera

duster ['dʌstəʳ] *n* straccio per la polvere

dust jacket *n* sopraccoperta

dustman ['dʌstmən] *n* (*Brit*) netturbino

dustpan ['dʌstpæn] *n* pattumiera

dusty ['dʌstɪ] *adj* polveroso(-a)

Dutch [dʌtʃ] *adj* olandese ■ *n* (*Ling*) olandese *m* ■ *adv*: **to go ~** or **dutch** fare alla romana; **the ~** gli Olandesi

Dutch auction *n* asta all'olandese

Dutchman ['dʌtʃmən] *n* olandese *m*

Dutchwoman ['dʌtʃwumən] *n* olandese *f*

dutiable ['djuːtɪəbl] *adj* soggetto(-a) a dazio

dutiful ['djuːtɪful] *adj* (*child*) rispettoso(-a); (*husband*) premuroso(-a); (*employee*) coscienzioso(-a)

duty ['djuːtɪ] *n* dovere *m*; (*tax*) dazio, tassa; **duties** *npl* mansioni *fpl*; **on ~** di servizio; (*Med: in hospital*) di guardia; **off ~** libero(-a), fuori servizio; **to make it one's ~ to do sth** assumersi l'obbligo di fare qc; **to pay ~ on sth** pagare il dazio su qc

duty-free ['djuːtɪˈfriː] *adj* esente da dazio; ~ **shop** duty free *m inv*

duty officer *n* (*Mil etc*) ufficiale *m* di servizio

duvet ['duːveɪ] *n* piumino, piumone *m*

DV *abbr* (= *Deo volente*) D.V.

DVD *n abbr* (= *digital versatile or video disc*) DVD *m inv*

DVD burner *n* masterizzatore *m* (di) DVD

DVD player n lettore m DVD
DVD writer n masterizzatore m (di) DVD
DVLA n abbr (Brit: = Driver and Vehicle Licensing
  Agency) ≈ I.M.C.T.C. m (= Ispettorato Generale della
  Motorizzazione Civile e dei Trasporti in Concessione)
DVM n abbr (US: = Doctor of Veterinary Medicine)
  titolo di studio
DVT n abbr = **deep-vein thrombosis**
dwarf [dwɔːf] n nano(-a) ■ vt far apparire
  piccolo
dwell (pt, pp **dwelt**) [dwel, dwɛlt] vi dimorare
  ▶ **dwell on** vt fus indugiare su
dweller ['dwɛləʳ] n abitante m/f; **city ~**
  cittadino(-a)
dwelling ['dwɛlɪŋ] n dimora
dwelt [dwɛlt] pt, pp of **dwell**
dwindle ['dwɪndl] vi diminuire, decrescere
dwindling ['dwɪndlɪŋ] adj (strength, interest)
  che si affievolisce; (resources, supplies) in

diminuzione
dye [daɪ] n colore m; (chemical) colorante m,
  tintura ■ vt tingere; **hair ~** tinta per capelli
dyestuffs ['daɪstʌfs] npl coloranti mpl
dying ['daɪɪŋ] adj morente, moribondo(-a)
dyke [daɪk] n diga; (channel) canale m di scolo;
  (causeway) sentiero rialzato
dynamic [daɪ'næmɪk] adj dinamico(-a)
dynamics [daɪ'næmɪks] n, npl dinamica
dynamite ['daɪnəmaɪt] n dinamite f ■ vt far
  saltare con la dinamite
dynamo ['daɪnəməu] n dinamo f inv
dynasty ['dɪnəstɪ] n dinastia
dysentery ['dɪsntrɪ] n dissenteria
dyslexia [dɪs'lɛksɪə] n dislessia
dyslexic [dɪs'lɛksɪk] adj, n dislessico(-a)
dyspepsia [dɪs'pɛpsɪə] n dispepsia
dystrophy ['dɪstrəfɪ] n distrofia; **muscular ~**
  distrofia muscolare

d

535

Ee

E, e [i:] *n* (*letter*) E, e *f or m inv*; (*Mus*): **E** mi *m*; **E
for Edward**, (*US*) **E for Easy** ≈ E come Empoli
E *abbr* (= *east*) E ■ *n abbr* (= *Ecstasy*) ecstasy *f inv*
e- [i:] *prefix* e-
E111 *n abbr* (*also*: **form E111**) E111 (*modulo UE per
rimborso spese mediche*)
ea. *abbr* = **each**
each [i:tʃ] *adj* ogni, ciascuno(-a) ■ *pron*
ciascuno(-a), ognuno(-a); **~ one** ognuno(a);
~ other si (*or* ci *etc*); **they hate ~ other** si
odiano (l'un l'altro); **you are jealous of ~
other** siete gelosi l'uno dell'altro; **~ day** ogni
giorno; **they have 2 books ~** hanno 2 libri
ciascuno; **they cost £5 ~** costano 5 sterline
l'uno; **~ of us** ciascuno *or* ognuno di noi
eager ['i:gəʳ] *adj* impaziente; desideroso(-a);
ardente; (*keen: pupil*) appassionato(-a),
attento(-a); **to be ~ to do sth** non veder l'ora
di fare qc; essere desideroso di fare qc; **to be
~ for** essere desideroso di, aver gran voglia di
eagle ['i:gl] *n* aquila
E & OE *abbr* (= *errors and omissions excepted*) S.E.O.
ear [ɪəʳ] *n* orecchio; (*of corn*) pannocchia; **up
to the ears in debt** nei debiti fino al collo
earache ['ɪəreɪk] *n* mal *m* d'orecchi
eardrum ['ɪədrʌm] *n* timpano
earful ['ɪəful] *n*: **to give sb an ~** fare una
ramanzina a qn
earl [ə:l] *n* conte *m*
earlier ['ə:lɪəʳ] *adj* (*date etc*) anteriore; (*edition
etc*) precedente, anteriore ■ *adv* prima;
I can't come any ~ non posso venire prima
early ['ə:lɪ] *adv* presto, di buon'ora; (*ahead of
time*) in anticipo ■ *adj* precoce;
anticipato(-a); che si fa vedere di buon'ora;
(*man*) primitivo(-a); (*Christians, settlers*)
primo(-a); **~ in the morning/afternoon**
nelle prime ore del mattino/del pomeriggio;
you're ~! sei in anticipo!; **have an ~ night/
start** vada a letto/parta presto; **in the ~** *or* **~
in the spring/19th century** all'inizio della
primavera/dell'Ottocento; **she's in her ~
forties** ha appena passato la quarantina;

at your earliest convenience (*Comm*) non
appena possibile
early retirement *n* ritiro anticipato
early warning system *n* sistema *m* del
preallarme
earmark ['ɪəmɑ:k] *vt*: **to ~ sth for** destinare
qc a
earn [ə:n] *vt* guadagnare; (*rest, reward*)
meritare; (*Comm: yield*) maturare; **to ~ one's
living** guadagnarsi da vivere; **this earned
him much praise, he earned much praise
for this** si è attirato grandi lodi per questo
earned income *n* reddito da lavoro
earnest ['ə:nɪst] *adj* serio(-a) ■ *n* (*also*:
earnest money) caparra; **in ~** *adv* sul serio
earnings ['ə:nɪŋz] *npl* guadagni *mpl*; (*of
company etc*) proventi *mpl*; (*salary*) stipendio
ear, nose and throat specialist *n*
otorinolaringoiatra *m/f*
earphones ['ɪəfəunz] *npl* cuffia
earplugs ['ɪəplʌgz] *npl* tappi *mpl* per le
orecchie
earring ['ɪərɪŋ] *n* orecchino
earshot ['ɪəʃɔt] *n*: **out of/within ~** fuori
portata/a portata d'orecchio
earth [ə:θ] *n* (*gen also Brit: Elec*) terra; (*of fox etc*)
tana ■ *vt* (*Brit Elec*) mettere a terra
earthenware ['ə:θənwɛəʳ] *n* terracotta;
stoviglie *fpl* di terracotta ■ *adj* di terracotta
earthly ['ə:θlɪ] *adj* terreno(-a); **~ paradise**
paradiso terrestre; **there is no ~ reason to
think ...** non vi è ragione di pensare ...
earthquake ['ə:θkweɪk] *n* terremoto
earth-shattering ['ə:θʃætərɪŋ] *adj*
stupefacente
earth tremor *n* scossa sismica
earthworks ['ə:θwə:ks] *npl* lavori *mpl* di sterro
earthworm ['ə:θwə:m] *n* lombrico
earthy ['ə:θɪ] *adj* (*fig*) grossolano(-a)
earwax ['ɪəwæks] *n* cerume *m*
earwig ['ɪəwɪg] *n* forbicina
ease [i:z] *n* agio, comodo ■ *vt* (*soothe*)
calmare; (*loosen*) allentare ■ *vi* (*situation*)

allentarsi, distendersi; **life of** ~ vita comoda; **with** ~ senza difficoltà; **at** ~ a proprio agio; (*Mil*) a riposo; **to feel at** ~**/ill at** ~ sentirsi a proprio agio/a disagio; **to** ~ **sth out/in** tirare fuori/infilare qc con delicatezza; facilitare l'uscita/l'entrata di qc
▶ **ease off, ease up** *vi* diminuire; (*slow down*) rallentarsi; (*fig*) rilassarsi
easel ['i:zl] *n* cavalletto
easily ['i:zɪlɪ] *adv* facilmente
easiness ['i:zɪnɪs] *n* facilità, semplicità; (*of manners*) disinvoltura
east [i:st] *n* est *m* ■ *adj* dell'est ■ *adv* a oriente; **the E~** l'Oriente *m*; (*Pol*) i Paesi dell'Est
Easter ['i:stə'] *n* Pasqua ■ *adj* (*holidays*) pasquale, di Pasqua
Easter egg *n* uovo di Pasqua
Easter Island *n* isola di Pasqua
easterly ['i:stəlɪ] *adj* dall'est, d'oriente
Easter Monday *n* Pasquetta
eastern ['i:stən] *adj* orientale, d'oriente; **E~ Europe** l'Europa orientale; **the E~ bloc** (*Pol*) i Paesi dell'Est
Easter Sunday *n* domenica di Pasqua
East Germany *n* (*formerly*) Germania dell'Est
eastward ['i:stwəd], **eastwards** ['i:stwədz] *adv* verso est, verso levante
easy ['i:zɪ] *adj* facile; (*manner*) disinvolto(-a); (*carefree: life*) agiato(-a), tranquillo(-a) ■ *adv*: **to take it** *or* **things** ~ prendersela con calma; **I'm** ~ (*col*) non ho problemi; **easier said than done** tra il dire e il fare c'è di mezzo il mare; **payment on** ~ **terms** (*Comm*) facilitazioni *fpl* di pagamento
easy chair *n* poltrona
easy-going ['i:zɪ'gəuɪŋ] *adj* accomodante
eat (*pt* **ate**, *pp* **eaten**) [i:t, eɪt, 'i:tn] *vt* mangiare
▶ **eat away** *vt* (*sea*) erodere; (*acid*) corrodere
▶ **eat away at, eat into** *vt fus* rodere
▶ **eat out** *vi* mangiare fuori
▶ **eat up** *vt* (*meal etc*) finire di mangiare; **it eats up electricity** consuma un sacco di corrente
eatable ['i:təbl] *adj* mangiabile; (*safe to eat*) commestibile
eaten ['i:tn] *pp of* **eat**
eau de Cologne ['əudəkə'ləun] *n* acqua di colonia
eaves [i:vz] *npl* gronda
eavesdrop ['i:vzdrɔp] *vi*: **to** ~ **(on a conversation)** origliare (una conversazione)
ebb [ɛb] *n* riflusso ■ *vi* rifluire; (*fig: also:* **ebb away**) declinare; ~ **and flow** flusso e riflusso; **to be at a low** ~ (*fig: person, spirits*) avere il morale a terra; (*: business*) andar male

ebb tide *n* marea discendente
ebony ['ɛbənɪ] *n* ebano
ebullient [ɪ'bʌlɪənt] *adj* esuberante
ECB *n abbr* (= *European Central Bank*) BCE *f*
eccentric [ɪk'sɛntrɪk] *adj, n* eccentrico(-a)
ecclesiastic [ɪkliːzɪ'æstɪk] *n* ecclesiastico ■ *adj* ecclesiastico(-a)
ecclesiastical [ɪkliːzɪ'æstɪkəl] *adj* ecclesiastico(-a)
ECG *n abbr* = **electrocardiogram**
echo (*pl* **echoes**) ['ɛkəu] *n* eco *m or f* ■ *vt* ripetere; fare eco a ■ *vi* echeggiare; dare un eco
éclair ['eɪkleə'] *n* ≈ bignè *m inv*
eclipse [ɪ'klɪps] *n* eclissi *f inv* ■ *vt* eclissare
eco... ['i:kəu] *prefix* eco...
eco-friendly [i:kəu'frɛndlɪ] *adj* ecologico(-a)
ecological [i:kə'lɔdʒɪkəl] *adj* ecologico(-a)
ecologist [ɪ'kɔlədʒɪst] *n* ecologo(-a)
ecology [ɪ'kɔlədʒɪ] *n* ecologia
e-commerce [i:'kɔməːs] *n* commercio elettronico, e-commerce *m inv*
economic [i:kə'nɔmɪk] *adj* economico(-a); (*profitable: price*) vantaggioso(-a); (*business*) che rende
economical [i:kə'nɔmɪkəl] *adj* economico(-a); (*person*) economo(-a)
economically [i:kə'nɔmɪklɪ] *adv* con economia; (*regarding economics*) dal punto di vista economico
economics [i:kə'nɔmɪks] *n* economia ■ *npl* aspetto *or* lato economico
economist [ɪ'kɔnəmɪst] *n* economista *m/f*
economize [ɪ'kɔnəmaɪz] *vi* risparmiare, fare economia
economy [ɪ'kɔnəmɪ] *n* economia; **economies of scale** (*Comm*) economie *fpl* di scala
economy class *n* (*Aviat etc*) classe *f* turistica
economy size *n* confezione *f* economica
ecosystem ['i:kəusɪstəm] *n* ecosistema *m*
eco-tourism [i:kəu'tuərɪzəm] *n* ecoturismo
ECSC *n abbr* (= *European Coal & Steel Community*) C.E.C.A. *f* (= *Comunità Europea del Carbone e dell'Acciaio*)
ecstasy ['ɛkstəsɪ] *n* estasi *f inv*; **to go into ecstasies over** andare in estasi davanti a; **E~** (*drug*) ecstasy *f inv*
ecstatic [ɛks'tætɪk] *adj* estatico(-a), in estasi
ECT *n abbr* = **electroconvulsive therapy**
ECU, ecu ['eɪkjuː] *n abbr* (= *European Currency Unit*) ECU *f inv*, ecu *f inv*
Ecuador ['ɛkwədɔː'] *n* Ecuador *m*
ecumenical [i:kju'mɛnɪkl] *adj* ecumenico(-a)
eczema ['ɛksɪmə] *n* eczema *m*
eddy ['ɛdɪ] *n* mulinello
edge [ɛdʒ] *n* margine *m*; (*of table, plate, cup*) orlo; (*of knife etc*) taglio ■ *vt* bordare ■ *vi*:

to ~ **away from** sgattaiolare da; **to ~ past** passar rasente; **to ~ forward** avanzare a poco a poco; **on ~** (fig) = **edgy**; **to have the ~ on** essere in vantaggio su

edgeways ['ɛdʒweɪz] adv di fianco; **he couldn't get a word in ~** non riuscì a dire una parola

edging ['ɛdʒɪŋ] n bordo

edgy ['ɛdʒɪ] adj nervoso(-a)

edible ['ɛdɪbl] adj commestibile; (meal) mangiabile

edict ['i:dɪkt] n editto

edifice ['ɛdɪfɪs] n edificio

edifying ['ɛdɪfaɪɪŋ] adj edificante

Edinburgh ['ɛdɪnbərə] n Edimburgo f

edit ['ɛdɪt] vt curare; (newspaper, magazine) dirigere; (Comput) correggere e modificare, editare

edition [ɪ'dɪʃən] n edizione f

editor ['ɛdɪtər] n (in newspaper) redattore(-trice); redattore(-trice) capo; (of sb's work) curatore(-trice); (film editor) responsabile m/f del montaggio

editorial [ɛdɪ'tɔ:rɪəl] adj redazionale, editoriale ▪ n editoriale m; **the ~ staff** la redazione

EDP n abbr = **electronic data processing**

EDT abbr (US: = Eastern Daylight Time) ora legale di New York

educate ['ɛdjukeɪt] vt istruire; educare

educated guess ['ɛdjukeɪtɪd-] n ipotesi f ben fondata

education [ɛdju'keɪʃən] n (teaching) insegnamento; istruzione f; (knowledge, culture) cultura; (Scol: subject etc) pedagogia; **primary** or (US) **elementary/secondary ~** scuola primaria/secondaria

educational [ɛdju'keɪʃənl] adj pedagogico(-a); scolastico(-a); istruttivo(-a); **~ technology** tecnologie fpl applicate alla didattica

Edwardian [ɛd'wɔ:dɪən] adj edoardiano(-a)

EE abbr = **electrical engineer**

EEG n abbr = **electroencephalogram**

eel [i:l] n anguilla

EENT n abbr (US Med) = **eye, ear, nose and throat**

EEOC n abbr (US) = **Equal Employment Opportunity Commission**

eerie ['ɪərɪ] adj che fa accapponare la pelle

EET abbr (= Eastern European Time) fuso orario

effect [ɪ'fɛkt] n effetto ▪ vt effettuare; **to take ~** (law) entrare in vigore; (drug) fare effetto; **to have an ~ on sb/sth** avere or produrre un effetto su qn/qc; **to put into ~** (plan) attuare; **in ~** effettivamente; **his letter is to the ~ that ...** il contenuto della

sua lettera è che ...; *see also* **effects**

effective [ɪ'fɛktɪv] adj efficace; (striking: display, outfit) che fa colpo; **~ date** data d'entrata in vigore; **to become ~** (law) entrare in vigore

effectively [ɪ'fɛktɪvlɪ] adv (efficiently) efficacemente; (strikingly) ad effetto; (in reality) di fatto; (in effect) in effetti

effectiveness [ɪ'fɛktɪvnɪs] n efficacia

effects [ɪ'fɛkts] npl (Theat) effetti mpl scenici; (property) effetti mpl

effeminate [ɪ'fɛmɪnɪt] adj effeminato(-a)

effervescent [ɛfə'vɛsnt] adj effervescente

efficacy ['ɛfɪkəsɪ] n efficacia

efficiency [ɪ'fɪʃənsɪ] n efficienza; rendimento effettivo

efficiency apartment n (US) miniappartamento

efficient [ɪ'fɪʃənt] adj efficiente; (remedy, product, system) efficace; (machine, car) che ha un buon rendimento

efficiently [ɪ'fɪʃəntlɪ] adv efficientemente; efficacemente

effigy ['ɛfɪdʒɪ] n effigie f

effluent ['ɛfluənt] n effluente m

effort ['ɛfət] n sforzo; **to make an ~ to do sth** sforzarsi di fare qc

effortless ['ɛfətlɪs] adj senza sforzo, facile

effrontery [ɪ'frʌntərɪ] n sfrontatezza

effusive [ɪ'fju:sɪv] adj (person) espansivo(-a); (welcome, letter) caloroso(-a); (thanks, apologies) interminabile

EFL n abbr (Scol) = **English as a foreign language**

EFTA ['ɛftə] n abbr (= European Free Trade Association) E.F.T.A. f

e.g. adv abbr (= exempli gratia: for example) p.es.

egalitarian [ɪgælɪ'tɛərɪən] adj egualitario(-a)

egg [ɛg] n uovo
  ▶ **egg on** vt incitare

eggcup ['ɛgkʌp] n portauovo m inv

eggplant ['ɛgplɑ:nt] n (esp US) melanzana

eggshell ['ɛgʃɛl] n guscio d'uovo ▪ adj (colour) guscio d'uovo inv

egg-timer ['ɛgtaɪmər] n clessidra (per misurare il tempo di cottura delle uova)

egg white n albume m, bianco d'uovo

egg yolk n tuorlo, rosso (d'uovo)

ego ['i:gəu] n ego m inv

egoism ['ɛgəuɪzəm] n egoismo

egoist ['ɛgəuɪst] n egoista m/f

egotism ['ɛgəutɪzəm] n egotismo

egotist ['ɛgəutɪst] n egotista m/f

ego trip n: **to be on an ~** gasarsi

Egypt ['i:dʒɪpt] n Egitto

Egyptian [ɪ'dʒɪpʃən] adj, n egiziano(-a)

eiderdown ['aɪdədaun] n piumino

eight [eɪt] *num* otto
eighteen ['eɪ'ti:n] *num* diciotto
eighth [eɪtθ] *num* ottavo(-a)
eighty [eɪtɪ] *num* ottanta
Eire ['ɛərə] *n* Repubblica d'Irlanda
EIS *n abbr* (= *Educational Institute of Scotland*) *principale sindacato degli insegnanti in Scozia*
either ['aɪðər'] *adj* l'uno(-a) o l'altro(-a); (*both, each*) ciascuno(-a); **on ~ side** su ciascun lato
■ *pron:* **~ (of them)** (o) l'uno(a) o l'altro(a);
I don't like ~ non mi piace né l'uno né l'altro
■ *adv* neanche; **no, I don't ~** no, neanch'io
■ *conj:* **~ good or bad** o buono o cattivo;
I haven't seen ~ one or the other non ho visto né l'uno né l'altro
ejaculation [ɪdʒækju'leɪʃən] *n* (*Physiol*) eiaculazione *f*
eject [ɪ'dʒɛkt] *vt* espellere; lanciare ■ *vi* (*pilot*) catapultarsi
ejector seat [ɪ'dʒɛktə-] *n* sedile *m* eiettabile
eke [i:k]: **to ~ out** *vt* far durare; aumentare
EKG *n abbr* (*US*) = **electrocardiogram**
el [ɛl] *n abbr* (*US col*) = **elevated railroad**
elaborate *adj* [ɪ'læbərɪt] elaborato(-a), minuzioso(-a) ■ *vb* [ɪ'læbəreɪt] *vt* elaborare ■ *vi* entrare in dettagli
elapse [ɪ'læps] *vi* trascorrere, passare
elastic [ɪ'læstɪk] *adj* elastico(-a) ■ *n* elastico
elastic band *n* (*Brit*) elastico
elasticity [ɪlæs'tɪsɪtɪ] *n* elasticità
elated [ɪ'leɪtɪd] *adj* pieno(-a) di gioia
elation [ɪ'leɪʃən] *n* gioia
elbow ['ɛlbəu] *n* gomito ■ *vt:* **to ~ one's way through the crowd** farsi largo tra la folla a gomitate
elbow grease *n:* **to use a bit of ~** usare un po' di olio di gomiti
elbowroom ['ɛlbəurum] *n* spazio
elder ['ɛldər'] *adj* maggiore, più vecchio(-a) ■ *n* (*tree*) sambuco; **one's elders** i più anziani
elderly ['ɛldəlɪ] *adj* anziano(-a) ■ *npl:* **the ~** gli anziani
elder statesman *n anziano uomo politico in pensione, ma ancora influente*; (*of company*) anziano(-a) consigliere(-a)
eldest ['ɛldɪst] *adj, n:* **the ~ (child)** il(la) maggiore (dei bambini)
elect [ɪ'lɛkt] *vt* eleggere; (*choose*): **to ~ to do** decidere di fare ■ *adj:* **the president ~** il presidente designato
election [ɪ'lɛkʃən] *n* elezione *f*; **to hold an ~** indire un'elezione
election campaign *n* campagna elettorale
electioneering [ɪlɛkʃə'nɪərɪŋ] *n* propaganda elettorale
elector [ɪ'lɛktər'] *n* elettore(-trice)

electoral [ɪ'lɛktərəl] *adj* elettorale
electoral college *n* collegio elettorale
electoral roll *n* (*Brit*) registro elettorale
electoral system *n* sistema *m* elettorale
electorate [ɪ'lɛktərɪt] *n* elettorato
electric [ɪ'lɛktrɪk] *adj* elettrico(-a)
electrical [ɪ'lɛktrɪkəl] *adj* elettrico(-a)
electrical engineer *n* ingegnere *m* elettrotecnico
electrical failure *n* guasto all'impianto elettrico
electric blanket *n* coperta elettrica
electric chair *n* sedia elettrica
electric cooker *n* cucina elettrica
electric current *n* corrente *f* elettrica
electric fire *n* (*Brit*) stufa elettrica
electrician [ɪlɛk'trɪʃən] *n* elettricista *m*
electricity [ɪlɛk'trɪsɪtɪ] *n* elettricità;
to switch on/off the ~ attaccare/staccare la corrente
electricity board *n* (*Brit*) ente *m* regionale per l'energia elettrica
electric light *n* luce *f* elettrica
electric shock *n* scossa (elettrica)
electrify [ɪ'lɛktrɪfaɪ] *vt* (*Rail*) elettrificare; (*audience*) elettrizzare
electro... [ɪ'lɛktrəu] *prefix* elettro...
electrocardiogram [ɪ'lɛktrə'ka:dɪəgræm] *n* elettrocardiogramma *m*
electroconvulsive therapy [ɪ'lɛktrə-kən'vʌlsɪv-] *n* elettroshockterapia
electrocute [ɪ'lɛktrəkju:t] *vt* fulminare
electrode [ɪ'lɛktrəud] *n* elettrodo
electroencephalogram [ɪ'lɛktrəuen'sɛfələ-græm] *n* (*Med*) elettroencefalogramma *m*
electrolysis [ɪlɛk'trɔlɪsɪs] *n* elettrolisi *f*
electromagnetic [ɪ'lɛktrəumæg'nɛtɪk] *n* elettromagnetico(-a)
electron [ɪ'lɛktrɔn] *n* elettrone *m*
electronic [ɪlɛk'trɔnɪk] *adj* elettronico(-a); *see also* **electronics**
electronic data processing *n* elaborazione *f* elettronica di dati
electronic mail *n* posta elettronica
electronics [ɪlɛk'trɔnɪks] *n* elettronica
electron microscope *n* microscopio elettronico
electroplated [ɪ'lɛktrəu'pleɪtɪd] *adj* galvanizzato(-a)
electrotherapy [ɪ'lɛktrəu'θɛrəpɪ] *n* elettroterapia
elegance ['ɛlɪgəns] *n* eleganza
elegant ['ɛlɪgənt] *adj* elegante
element ['ɛlɪmənt] *n* elemento; (*of heater, kettle etc*) resistenza
elementary [ɛlɪ'mɛntərɪ] *adj* elementare
elementary school *n* (*US*) *vedi nota*

e

Negli Stati Uniti e in Canada, i bambini frequentano la *elementary school* per almeno sei anni, a volte anche per otto. Negli Stati Uniti si chiama anche "grade school" o "grammar school".

elephant ['ɛlɪfənt] *n* elefante(-essa)
elevate ['ɛlɪveɪt] *vt* elevare
elevated railroad, el *n* (*US*) (ferrovia) sopraelevata
elevation [ɛlɪ'veɪʃən] *n* elevazione *f*; (*height*) altitudine *f*
elevator ['ɛlɪveɪtə'] *n* elevatore *m*; (*US: lift*) ascensore *m*
eleven [ɪ'lɛvn] *num* undici
elevenses [ɪ'lɛvnzɪz] *npl* (*Brit*) caffè *m* a metà mattina
eleventh [ɪ'lɛvnθ] *adj* undicesimo(-a); **at the ~ hour** (*fig*) all'ultimo minuto
elf (*pl* **elves**) [ɛlf, ɛlvz] *n* elfo
elicit [ɪ'lɪsɪt] *vt*: **to ~ (from)** trarre (da), cavare fuori (da); **to ~ sth (from sb)** strappare qc (a qn)
eligible ['ɛlɪdʒəbl] *adj* eleggibile; (*for membership*) che ha i requisiti; **to be ~ for a pension** essere pensionabile
eliminate [ɪ'lɪmɪneɪt] *vt* eliminare
elimination [ɪlɪmɪ'neɪʃən] *n* eliminazione *f*; **by process of ~** per eliminazione
élite [eɪ'liːt] *n* élite *f inv*
elitist [eɪ'liːtɪst] *adj* (*pej*) elitario(-a)
elixir [ɪ'lɪksə'] *n* elisir *m inv*
Elizabethan [ɪlɪzə'biːθən] *n* elisabettiano(-a)
ellipse [ɪ'lɪps] *n* ellisse *f*
elliptical [ɪ'lɪptɪkl] *adj* ellittico(-a)
elm [ɛlm] *n* olmo
elocution [ɛlə'kjuːʃən] *n* elocuzione *f*
elongated ['iːlɔŋgeɪtɪd] *adj* allungato(-a)
elope [ɪ'ləup] *vi* (*lovers*) scappare
elopement [ɪ'ləupmənt] *n* fuga romantica
eloquence ['ɛləkwəns] *n* eloquenza
eloquent ['ɛləkwənt] *adj* eloquente
else [ɛls] *adv* altro; **something ~** qualcos'altro; **somewhere ~** altrove; **everywhere ~** in qualsiasi altro luogo; **where ~?** in quale altro luogo?; **little ~** poco altro; **everyone ~** tutti gli altri; **nothing ~** nient'altro; **or ~** (*otherwise*) altrimenti; **is there anything ~ I can do?** posso fare qualcos'altro?
elsewhere [ɛls'wɛə'] *adv* altrove
ELT *n abbr* (*Scol*) = **English Language Teaching**
elucidate [ɪ'luːsɪdeɪt] *vt* delucidare
elude [ɪ'luːd] *vt* eludere

elusive [ɪ'luːsɪv] *adj* elusivo(-a); (*answer*) evasivo(-a); **he is very ~** è proprio inafferrabile *or* irraggiungibile
elves [ɛlvz] *npl of* **elf**
emaciated [ɪ'meɪsɪeɪtɪd] *adj* emaciato(-a)
email ['iːmeɪl] *n abbr* (= *electronic mail*) posta elettronica ■ *vt*: **to ~ sb** comunicare con qn mediante posta elettronica; **~ address** indirizzo di posta elettronica; **~ account** account *m inv* di posta elettronica
emanate ['ɛməneɪt] *vi*: **to ~ from** emanare da
emancipate [ɪ'mænsɪpeɪt] *vt* emancipare
emancipation [ɪmænsɪ'peɪʃən] *n* emancipazione *f*
emasculate [ɪ'mæskjuleɪt] *vt* (*fig*) rendere impotente
embalm [ɪm'bɑːm] *vt* imbalsamare
embankment [ɪm'bæŋkmənt] *n* (*of road, railway*) massicciata; (*riverside*) argine *m*; (*dyke*) diga
embargo [ɪm'bɑːgəu] *n* (*pl* **embargoes**) (*Comm, Naut*) embargo ■ *vt* mettere l'embargo su; **to put an ~ on sth** mettere l'embargo su qc
embark [ɪm'bɑːk] *vi*: **to ~ (on)** imbarcarsi (su) ■ *vt* imbarcare; **to ~ on** (*fig*) imbarcarsi in; (*journey*) intraprendere
embarkation [ɛmbɑː'keɪʃən] *n* imbarco
embarkation card *n* carta d'imbarco
embarrass [ɪm'bærəs] *vt* imbarazzare; **to be embarrassed** essere imbarazzato(-a)
embarrassing [ɪm'bærəsɪŋ] *adj* imbarazzante
embarrassment [ɪm'bærəsmənt] *n* imbarazzo
embassy ['ɛmbəsɪ] *n* ambasciata; **the Italian E~** l'ambasciata d'Italia
embed [ɪm'bɛd] *vt* conficcare; incastrare
embellish [ɪm'bɛlɪʃ] *vt* abbellire; **to ~ (with)** (*fig: story, truth*) infiorare (con)
embers ['ɛmbəz] *npl* braci *fpl*
embezzle [ɪm'bɛzl] *vt* appropriarsi indebitamente di
embezzlement [ɪm'bɛzlmənt] *n* appropriazione *f* indebita, malversazione *f*
embezzler [ɪm'bɛzlə'] *n* malversatore(-trice)
embitter [ɪm'bɪtə'] *vt* amareggiare; inasprire
emblem ['ɛmbləm] *n* emblema *m*
embodiment [ɪm'bɔdɪmənt] *n* personificazione *f*, incarnazione *f*
embody [ɪm'bɔdɪ] *vt* (*features*) racchiudere, comprendere; (*ideas*) dar forma concreta a, esprimere
embolden [ɪm'bəuldn] *vt* incitare
embolism ['ɛmbəlɪzəm] *n* embolia
embossed [ɪm'bɔst] *adj* in rilievo; goffrato(-a); **~ with ...** con in rilievo ...

embrace [ɪmˈbreɪs] vt abbracciare; (include) comprendere ▪ vi abbracciarsi ▪ n abbraccio

embroider [ɪmˈbrɔɪdəʳ] vt ricamare; (fig: story) abbellire

embroidery [ɪmˈbrɔɪdərɪ] n ricamo

embroil [ɪmˈbrɔɪl] vt: **to become embroiled (in sth)** restare invischiato(a) (in qc)

embryo [ˈembrɪəu] n (also fig) embrione m

emcee [ɛmˈsiː] n abbr = **master of ceremonies**

emend [ɪˈmend] vt (text) correggere, emendare

emerald [ˈemərəld] n smeraldo

emerge [ɪˈmɜːdʒ] vi apparire, sorgere; **it emerges that** (Brit) risulta che

emergence [ɪˈmɜːdʒəns] n apparizione f; (of nation) nascita

emergency [ɪˈmɜːdʒənsɪ] n emergenza; **in an ~** in caso di emergenza; **to declare a state of ~** dichiarare lo stato di emergenza

emergency exit n uscita di sicurezza

emergency landing n atterraggio forzato

emergency lane n (US Aut) corsia d'emergenza

emergency road service n (US) servizio riparazioni

emergency service n servizio di pronto intervento

emergency stop n (Brit Aut) frenata improvvisa

emergent [ɪˈmɜːdʒənt] adj: **~ nation** paese m in via di sviluppo

emery board [ˈemərɪ-] n limetta di carta smerigliata

emery paper n carta smerigliata

emetic [ɪˈmetɪk] n emetico

emigrant [ˈemɪgrənt] n emigrante m/f

emigrate [ˈemɪgreɪt] vi emigrare

emigration [emɪˈgreɪʃən] n emigrazione f

émigré [ˈemɪgreɪ] n emigrato(-a)

eminence [ˈemɪnəns] n eminenza

eminent [ˈemɪnənt] adj eminente

eminently [ˈemɪnəntlɪ] adv assolutamente, perfettamente

emirate [ɛˈmɪərɪt] n emirato

emission [ɪˈmɪʃən] n (of gas, radiation) emissione f

emit [ɪˈmɪt] vt emettere

emolument [ɪˈmɔljumənt] n (often pl: formal) emolumento

emoticon [ɪˈməutɪkən] n (Comput) faccina

emotion [ɪˈməuʃən] n emozione f; (love, jealousy etc) sentimento

emotional [ɪˈməuʃənl] adj (person) emotivo(-a); (scene) commovente; (tone, speech) carico(-a) d'emozione

emotionally [ɪˈməuʃnəlɪ] adv (behave, be involved) sentimentalmente; (speak) con emozione; **~ disturbed** con turbe emotive

emotive [ɪˈməutɪv] adj emotivo(-a); **~ power** capacità di commuovere

empathy [ˈempəθɪ] n immedesimazione f; **to feel ~ with sb** immedesimarsi con i sentimenti di qn

emperor [ˈempərəʳ] n imperatore m

emphasis (pl **emphases**) [ˈemfəsɪs, -siːz] n enfasi f inv; importanza; **to lay** or **place ~ on sth** (fig) mettere in risalto or in evidenza qc; **the ~ is on sport** si dà molta importanza allo sport

emphasize [ˈemfəsaɪz] vt (word, point) sottolineare; (feature) mettere in evidenza

emphatic [ɪmˈfætɪk] adj (strong) vigoroso(-a); (unambiguous, clear) netto(-a), categorico(-a)

emphatically [ɪmˈfætɪkəlɪ] adv vigorosamente; nettamente

emphysema [emfɪˈsiːmə] n (Med) enfisema m

empire [ˈempaɪəʳ] n impero

empirical [emˈpɪrɪkl] adj empirico(-a)

employ [ɪmˈplɔɪ] vt (make use of: thing, method, person) impiegare, servirsi di; (give job to) dare lavoro a, impiegare; **he's employed in a bank** lavora in banca

employee [ɪmplɔɪˈiː] n impiegato(-a)

employer [ɪmˈplɔɪəʳ] n principale m/f, datore m di lavoro

employment [ɪmˈplɔɪmənt] n impiego; **to find ~** trovare impiego or lavoro; **without ~** disoccupato(a); **place of ~** posto di lavoro

employment agency n agenzia di collocamento

employment exchange n (Brit) ufficio m collocamento inv

empower [ɪmˈpauəʳ] vt: **to ~ sb to do** concedere autorità a qn di fare

empress [ˈemprɪs] n imperatrice f

emptiness [ˈemptɪnɪs] n vuoto

empty [ˈemptɪ] adj vuoto(-a); (street, area) deserto(-a); (threat, promise) vano(-a) ▪ n (bottle) vuoto ▪ vt vuotare ▪ vi vuotarsi; (liquid) scaricarsi; **on an ~ stomach** a stomaco vuoto; **to ~ into** (river) gettarsi in

empty-handed [emptɪˈhændɪd] adj a mani vuote

empty-headed [emptɪˈhedɪd] adj sciocco(-a)

EMS n abbr (= European Monetary System) S.M.E. m

EMT n abbr (US) = **emergency medical technician**

EMU n abbr (= European Monetary Union) Unità f monetaria europea; (= economic and monetary union) UEM f

emulate [ˈemjuleɪt] vt emulare

emulsion [ɪˈmʌlʃən] n emulsione f; (also: **emulsion paint**) colore m a tempera

enable [ɪˈneɪbl] vt: **to ~ sb to do** permettere a qn di fare

enact [ɪn'ækt] vt (law) emanare; (play, scene) rappresentare

enamel [ɪ'næməl] n smalto

enamel paint n vernice f a smalto

enamoured [ɪ'næməd] adj: ~ of innamorato(a) di

enc. abbr (on letters etc: = enclosed, enclosure) all., alleg.

encampment [ɪn'kæmpmənt] n accampamento

encased [ɪn'keɪst] adj: ~ in racchiuso(a) in, rivestito(a) di

enchant [ɪn'tʃɑ:nt] vt incantare; (magic spell) catturare

enchanting [ɪn'tʃɑ:ntɪŋ] adj incantevole, affascinante

encircle [ɪn'sə:kl] vt accerchiare

encl. abbr (on letters etc: = enclosed, enclosure) all., alleg.

enclose [ɪn'kləuz] vt (land) circondare, recingere; (letter etc): **to ~ (with)** allegare (con); **please find enclosed** trovi qui accluso

enclosure [ɪn'kləuʒəʳ] n recinto; (Comm) allegato

encoder [ɪn'kəudəʳ] n (Comput) codificatore m

encompass [ɪn'kʌmpəs] vt comprendere

encore [ɔŋ'kɔːʳ] excl, n bis (m inv)

encounter [ɪn'kauntəʳ] n incontro ∎ vt incontrare

encourage [ɪn'kʌrɪdʒ] vt incoraggiare; (industry, growth etc) favorire; **to ~ sb to do sth** incoraggiare qn a fare qc

encouragement [ɪn'kʌrɪdʒmənt] n incoraggiamento

encouraging [ɪn'kʌrɪdʒɪŋ] adj incoraggiante

encroach [ɪn'krəutʃ] vi: **to ~ (up)on** (rights) usurpare; (time) abusare di; (land) oltrepassare i limiti di

encrusted [ɪn'krʌstɪd] adj: ~ **with** incrostato(a) di

encumbered [ɪn'kʌmbəd] adj: **to be ~ (with)** essere carico(a) di

encyclopedia, encyclopaedia [ɛnsaɪklə u'pi:dɪə] n enciclopedia

end [ɛnd] n fine f; (aim) fine m; (of table) bordo estremo; (of line, rope etc) estremità f inv; (of pointed object) punta; (of town) parte f ∎ vt finire; (also: **bring to an end, put an end to**) mettere fine a ∎ vi finire; **from ~ to ~** da un'estremità all'altra; **to come to an ~** arrivare alla fine, finire; **to be at an ~** essere finito; **in the ~** alla fine; **at the ~ of the street** in fondo alla strada; **at the ~ of the day** (Brit fig) in fin dei conti; **on ~** (object) ritto(a); **to stand on ~** (hair) rizzarsi; **for 5 hours on ~** per 5 ore di fila; **for hours on ~** per ore e ore; **to this ~, with this ~ in view**

a questo fine; **to ~ (with)** concludere (con)
 ▶ **end up** vi: **to ~ up** finire in

endanger [ɪn'deɪndʒəʳ] vt mettere in pericolo; **an endangered species** una specie in via di estinzione

endear [ɪn'dɪəʳ] vt: **to ~ o.s. to sb** accattivarsi le simpatie di qn

endearing [ɪn'dɪərɪŋ] adj accattivante

endearment [ɪn'dɪəmənt] n: **to whisper endearments** sussurrare tenerezze; **term of ~** vezzeggiativo, parola affettuosa

endeavour, (US) **endeavor** [ɪn'dɛvəʳ] n sforzo, tentativo ∎ vi: **to ~ to do** cercare or sforzarsi di fare

endemic [ɛn'dɛmɪk] adj endemico(-a)

ending ['ɛndɪŋ] n fine f, conclusione f; (Ling) desinenza

endive ['ɛndaɪv] n (curly) indivia (riccia); (smooth, flat) indivia belga

endless ['ɛndlɪs] adj senza fine; (patience, resources) infinito(-a); (possibilities) illimitato(-a)

endorse [ɪn'dɔːs] vt (cheque) girare; (approve) approvare, appoggiare

endorsee [ɪndɔː'siː] n giratario(-a)

endorsement [ɪn'dɔːsmənt] n (approval) approvazione f; (signature) firma; (Brit: on driving licence) contravvenzione registrata sulla patente

endorser [ɪn'dɔːsəʳ] n girante m/f

endow [ɪn'dau] vt (prize) istituire; (hospital) fondare; (provide with money) devolvere denaro a; (equip): **to ~ with** fornire di, dotare di

endowment [ɪn'daumənt] n istituzione f; fondazione f; (amount) donazione f

endowment mortgage n mutuo che viene ripagato sotto forma di un'assicurazione a vita

endowment policy n polizza-vita mista

end product n (Industry) prodotto finito; (fig) risultato

end result n risultato finale

endurable [ɪn'djuərəbl] adj sopportabile

endurance [ɪn'djuərəns] n resistenza; pazienza

endurance test n prova di resistenza

endure [ɪn'djuəʳ] vt sopportare, resistere a ∎ vi durare

enduring [ɪn'djuərɪŋ] adj duraturo(-a)

end user n (Comput) consumatore(-trice) effettivo(-a)

enema ['ɛnɪmə] n (Med) clistere m

enemy ['ɛnəmɪ] adj, n nemico(-a); **to make an ~ of sb** inimicarsi qn

energetic [ɛnə'dʒɛtɪk] adj energico(-a), attivo(-a)

energy ['ɛnədʒɪ] n energia; **Department of E~** (US) Ministero dell'Energia

energy crisis *n* crisi *f* energetica
energy-saving ['ɛnədʒɪ'seɪvɪŋ] *adj* (*policy*) del risparmio energetico; (*device*) che risparmia energia
enervating ['ɛnə:veɪtɪŋ] *adj* debilitante
enforce [ɪn'fɔːs] *vt* (*Law*) applicare, far osservare
enforced [ɪn'fɔːst] *adj* forzato(-a)
enfranchise [ɪn'fræntʃaɪz] *vt* (*give vote to*) concedere il diritto di voto a; (*set free*) affrancare
engage [ɪn'geɪdʒ] *vt* (*hire*) assumere; (*lawyer*) incaricare; (*attention, interest*) assorbire; (*Mil*) attaccare; (*Tech*): **to ~ gear/the clutch** innestare la marcia/la frizione ■ *vi* (*Tech*) ingranare; **to ~ in** impegnarsi in; **he is engaged in research/a survey** si occupa di ricerca/di un'inchiesta; **to ~ sb in conversation** attaccare conversazione con qn
engaged [ɪn'geɪdʒd] *adj* (*Brit: busy, in use*) occupato(-a); (*betrothed*) fidanzato(-a); **to get ~** fidanzarsi
engaged tone *n* (*Brit Tel*) segnale *m* di occupato
engagement [ɪn'geɪdʒmənt] *n* impegno, obbligo; appuntamento; (*to marry*) fidanzamento; (*Mil*) combattimento; **I have a previous ~** ho già un impegno
engagement ring *n* anello di fidanzamento
engaging [ɪn'geɪdʒɪŋ] *adj* attraente
engender [ɪn'dʒɛndə'] *vt* produrre, causare
engine ['ɛndʒɪn] *n* (*Aut*) motore *m*; (*Rail*) locomotiva
engine driver *n* (*Brit: of train*) macchinista *m*
engineer [ɛndʒɪ'nɪə'] *n* ingegnere *m*; (*Brit: for domestic appliances*) tecnico; (*US Rail*) macchinista *m*; **civil/mechanical ~** ingegnere civile/meccanico
engineering [ɛndʒɪ'nɪərɪŋ] *n* ingegneria ■ *cpd* (*works, factory, worker etc*) metalmeccanico(-a)
engine failure *n* guasto al motore
engine trouble *n* panne *f*
England ['ɪŋglənd] *n* Inghilterra
English ['ɪŋglɪʃ] *adj* inglese ■ *n* (*Ling*) inglese *m*; **the English** *npl* gli Inglesi; **to be an ~ speaker** essere anglofono(a)
English Channel *n*: **the ~** il Canale della Manica
Englishman ['ɪŋglɪʃmən] *n* inglese *m*
English-speaking ['ɪŋglɪʃspiːkɪŋ] *adj* di lingua inglese
Englishwoman ['ɪŋglɪʃwumən] *n* inglese *f*
engrave [ɪn'greɪv] *vt* incidere
engraving [ɪn'greɪvɪŋ] *n* incisione *f*
engrossed [ɪn'grəust] *adj*: **~ in** assorbito(a) da, preso(a) da
engulf [ɪn'gʌlf] *vt* inghiottire

enhance [ɪn'hɑːns] *vt* accrescere; (*position, reputation*) migliorare
enigma [ɪ'nɪgmə] *n* enigma *m*
enigmatic [ɛnɪg'mætɪk] *adj* enigmatico(-a)
enjoy [ɪn'dʒɔɪ] *vt* godere; (*have: success, fortune*) avere; (*have benefit of: health*) godere (di); **I ~ dancing** mi piace ballare; **to ~ o.s.** godersela, divertirsi
enjoyable [ɪn'dʒɔɪəbl] *adj* piacevole
enjoyment [ɪn'dʒɔɪmənt] *n* piacere *m*, godimento
enlarge [ɪn'lɑːdʒ] *vt* ingrandire ■ *vi*: **to ~ on** (*subject*) dilungarsi su
enlarged [ɪn'lɑːdʒd] *adj* (*edition*) ampliato(-a); (*Med: organ, gland*) ingrossato(-a)
enlargement [ɪn'lɑːdʒmənt] *n* (*Phot*) ingrandimento
enlighten [ɪn'laɪtn] *vt* illuminare; dare chiarimenti a
enlightened [ɪn'laɪtnd] *adj* illuminato(-a)
enlightening [ɪn'laɪtnɪŋ] *adj* istruttivo(-a)
enlightenment [ɪn'laɪtnmənt] *n* progresso culturale; chiarimenti *mpl*; (*Hist*): **the E~** l'Illuminismo
enlist [ɪn'lɪst] *vt* arruolare; (*support*) procurare ■ *vi* arruolarsi; **enlisted man** (*US Mil*) soldato semplice
enliven [ɪn'laɪvn] *vt* (*people*) rallegrare; (*events*) ravvivare
enmity ['ɛnmɪtɪ] *n* inimicizia
ennoble [ɪ'nəubl] *vt* nobilitare; (*with title*) conferire un titolo nobiliare a
enormity [ɪ'nɔːmɪtɪ] *n* enormità *f inv*
enormous [ɪ'nɔːməs] *adj* enorme
enormously [ɪ'nɔːməslɪ] *adv* enormemente
enough [ɪ'nʌf] *adj, n*: **~ time/books** assai tempo/libri; **have you got ~?** ne ha abbastanza *or* a sufficienza? ■ *adv*: **big ~** abbastanza grande; **he has not worked ~** non ha lavorato abbastanza; **~!** basta!; **it's hot ~ (as it is)!** fa abbastanza caldo così!; **will £5 be ~?** bastano 5 sterline?; **that's ~** basta; **I've had ~!** non ne posso più!; **he was kind ~ to lend me the money** è stato così gentile da prestarmi i soldi; **... which, funnily ~** ... che, strano a dirsi
enquire [ɪn'kwaɪə'] *vt, vi* = **inquire**
enrage [ɪn'reɪdʒ] *vt* fare arrabbiare
enrich [ɪn'rɪtʃ] *vt* arricchire
enrol, (*US*) **enroll** [ɪn'rəul] *vt* iscrivere; (*at university*) immatricolare ■ *vi* iscriversi
enrolment, (*US*) **enrollment** [ɪn'rəulmənt] *n* iscrizione *f*
en route [ɔn'ruːt] *adv*: **~ for/from/to** in viaggio per/da/a
ensconced [ɪn'skɔnst] *adj*: **~ in** ben sistemato(a) in

ensemble [ãːnˈsãːmbl] *n* (*Mus*) ensemble *m inv*

enshrine [ɪnˈʃraɪn] *vt* conservare come una reliquia

ensign *n* (*Naut*) [ˈɛnsən] bandiera; (*Mil*) [ˈɛnsaɪn] portabandiera *m inv*

enslave [ɪnˈsleɪv] *vt* fare schiavo

ensue [ɪnˈsjuː] *vi* seguire, risultare

ensure [ɪnˈʃuəʳ] *vt* assicurare; garantire;
to ~ that assicurarsi che

ENT *n abbr* (*Med*: = *ear, nose and throat*) O.R.L.

entail [ɪnˈteɪl] *vt* comportare

entangle [ɪnˈtæŋgl] *vt* (*thread etc*) impigliare;
to become entangled in sth (*fig*) rimanere impegolato in qc

enter [ˈɛntəʳ] *vt* (*gen*) entrare in; (*club*) associarsi a; (*profession*) intraprendere; (*army*) arruolarsi in; (*competition*) partecipare a; (*sb for a competition*) iscrivere; (*write down*) registrare; (*Comput*: *data*) introdurre, inserire ▪ *vi* entrare
▸ **enter for** *vt fus* iscriversi a
▸ **enter into** *vt fus* (*explanation*) cominciare a dare; (*debate*) partecipare a; (*agreement*) concludere; (*negotiations*) prendere parte a
▸ **enter (up)on** *vt fus* cominciare

enteritis [ɛntəˈraɪtɪs] *n* enterite *f*

enterprise [ˈɛntəpraɪz] *n* (*undertaking, company*) impresa; (*spirit*) iniziativa

enterprising [ˈɛntəpraɪzɪŋ] *adj* intraprendente

entertain [ɛntəˈteɪn] *vt* divertire; (*invite*) ricevere; (*idea, plan*) nutrire

entertainer [ɛntəˈteɪnəʳ] *n* comico(-a)

entertaining [ɛntəˈteɪnɪŋ] *adj* divertente
▪ *n*: **to do a lot of ~** avere molti ospiti

entertainment [ɛntəˈteɪnmənt] *n* (*amusement*) divertimento; (*show*) spettacolo

entertainment allowance *n* spese *fpl* di rappresentanza

enthral [ɪnˈθrɔːl] *vt* affascinare, avvincere

enthralled [ɪnˈθrɔːld] *adj* affascinato(-a)

enthralling [ɪnˈθrɔːlɪŋ] *adj* avvincente

enthuse [ɪnˈθuːz] *vi*: **to ~ (about** *or* **over)** entusiasmarsi (per)

enthusiasm [ɪnˈθuːzɪæzəm] *n* entusiasmo

enthusiast [ɪnˈθuːzɪæst] *n* entusiasta *m/f*;
a jazz *etc* **~** un appassionato di jazz *etc*

enthusiastic [ɪnθuːzɪˈæstɪk] *adj* entusiasta, entusiastico(-a); **to be ~ about sth/sb** essere appassionato di qc/entusiasta di qn

entice [ɪnˈtaɪs] *vt* allettare, sedurre

enticing [ɪnˈtaɪsɪŋ] *adj* allettante

entire [ɪnˈtaɪəʳ] *adj* intero(-a)

entirely [ɪnˈtaɪəlɪ] *adv* completamente, interamente

entirety [ɪnˈtaɪərətɪ] *n*: **in its ~** nel suo complesso

entitle [ɪnˈtaɪtl] *vt* (*give right*): **to ~ sb to sth/ to do** dare diritto a qn a qc/a fare

entitled [ɪnˈtaɪtld] *adj* (*book*) che si intitola;
to be ~ to sth/to do sth avere diritto a qc/a fare qc

entity [ˈɛntɪtɪ] *n* entità *f inv*

entrails [ˈɛntreɪlz] *npl* interiora *fpl*

entrance *n* [ˈɛntrns] entrata, ingresso; (*of person*) entrata ▪ *vt* [ɪnˈtrɑːns] incantare, rapire; **to gain ~ to** (*university etc*) essere ammesso a

entrance examination *n* (*to school*) esame *m* di ammissione

entrance fee *n* tassa d'iscrizione; (*to museum etc*) prezzo d'ingresso

entrance ramp *n* (*US Aut*) rampa di accesso

entrancing [ɪnˈtrɑːnsɪŋ] *adj* incantevole

entrant [ˈɛntrnt] *n* partecipante *m/f*; concorrente *m/f*; (*Brit*: *in exam*) candidato(-a)

entreat [ɛnˈtriːt] *vt* supplicare

entreaty [ɪnˈtriːtɪ] *n* supplica, preghiera

entrée [ˈɔntreɪ] *n* (*Culin*) prima portata

entrenched [ɛnˈtrɛntʃt] *adj* radicato(-a)

entrepreneur [ˈɔntrəprəˈnəːʳ] *n* imprenditore *m*

entrepreneurial [ˈɔntrəprəˈnəːrɪəl] *adj* imprenditoriale

entrust [ɪnˈtrʌst] *vt*: **to ~ sth to** affidare qc a

entry [ˈɛntrɪ] *n* entrata; (*way in*) entrata, ingresso; (*in dictionary*) voce *f*; (*in diary, ship's log*) annotazione *f*; (*in account book, ledger, list*) registrazione *f*; **"no ~"** "vietato l'ingresso"; (*Aut*) "divieto di accesso"; **single/double ~ book-keeping** partita semplice/doppia

entry form *n* modulo d'iscrizione

entry phone *n* (*Brit*) citofono

entwine [ɪnˈtwaɪn] *vt* intrecciare

E number *n* sigla di additivo alimentare

enumerate [ɪˈnjuːməreɪt] *vt* enumerare

enunciate [ɪˈnʌnsɪeɪt] *vt* enunciare; pronunciare

envelop [ɪnˈvɛləp] *vt* avvolgere, avviluppare

envelope [ˈɛnvələup] *n* busta

enviable [ˈɛnvɪəbl] *adj* invidiabile

envious [ˈɛnvɪəs] *adj* invidioso(-a)

environment [ɪnˈvaɪərənmənt] *n* ambiente *m*; **Department of the E~** (*Brit*) ≈ Ministero dell'Ambiente

environmental [ɪnvaɪərənˈmɛntl] *adj* ecologico(-a); ambientale; **~ studies** (*in school etc*) ecologia

environmentalist [ɪnvaɪərənˈmɛntəlɪst] *n* studioso(-a) della protezione dell'ambiente

environmentally [ɪnvaɪərənˈmɛntəlɪ] *adv*: **~ sound/friendly** che rispetta l'ambiente

Environmental Protection Agency *n* (*US*) ≈ Ministero dell'Ambiente

envisage [ɪn'vɪzɪdʒ] vt immaginare; prevedere

envision [ɪn'vɪʒən] vt concepire, prevedere

envoy ['ɛnvɔɪ] n inviato(-a)

envy ['ɛnvɪ] n invidia ■ vt invidiare; **to ~ sb sth** invidiare qn per qc

enzyme ['ɛnzaɪm] n enzima m

EPA n abbr (US) = **Environmental Protection Agency**

ephemeral [ɪ'fɛmərəl] adj effimero(-a)

epic ['ɛpɪk] n poema m epico ■ adj epico(-a)

epicentre, (US) **epicenter** ['ɛpɪsɛntər] n epicentro

epidemic [ɛpɪ'dɛmɪk] n epidemia

epilepsy ['ɛpɪlɛpsɪ] n epilessia

epileptic [ɛpɪ'lɛptɪk] adj, n epilettico(-a)

epilogue ['ɛpɪlɔg] n epilogo

Epiphany [ɪ'pɪfənɪ] n Epifania

episcopal [ɪ'pɪskəpəl] adj episcopale

episode ['ɛpɪsəud] n episodio

epistle [ɪ'pɪsl] n epistola

epitaph ['ɛpɪtɑːf] n epitaffio

epithet ['ɛpɪθɛt] n epiteto

epitome [ɪ'pɪtəmɪ] n epitome f; quintessenza

epitomize [ɪ'pɪtəmaɪz] vt (fig) incarnare

epoch ['iːpɔk] n epoca

epoch-making ['iːpɔkmeɪkɪŋ] adj che fa epoca

eponymous [ɪ'pɔnɪməs] adj dello stesso nome

equable ['ɛkwəbl] adj uniforme; (climate) costante; (character) equilibrato(-a)

equal ['iːkwl] adj, n uguale (m/f) ■ vt uguagliare; **~ to** (task) all'altezza di

equality [iː'kwɔlɪtɪ] n uguaglianza

equalize ['iːkwəlaɪz] vt, vi pareggiare

equalizer ['iːkwəlaɪzər] n punto del pareggio

equally ['iːkwəlɪ] adv ugualmente; **they are ~ clever** sono intelligenti allo stesso modo

Equal Opportunities Commission, (US) **Equal Employment Opportunity Commission** n commissione contro discriminazioni sessuali o razziali nel mondo del lavoro

equal sign, equals sign n segno d'uguaglianza

equanimity [ɛkwə'nɪmɪtɪ] n serenità

equate [ɪ'kweɪt] vt: **to ~ sth with** considerare qc uguale a; (compare) paragonare qc con; **to ~ A to B** mettere in equazione A e B

equation [ɪ'kweɪʃən] n (Math) equazione f

equator [ɪ'kweɪtər] n equatore m

Equatorial Guinea [ɛkwə'tɔːrɪəl-] n Guinea Equatoriale

equestrian [ɪ'kwɛstrɪən] adj equestre ■ n cavaliere/amazzone

equilibrium [iːkwɪ'lɪbrɪəm] n equilibrio

equinox ['iːkwɪnɔks] n equinozio

equip [ɪ'kwɪp] vt equipaggiare, attrezzare; **to ~ sb/sth with** fornire qn/qc di; **equipped with** (machinery etc) dotato(a) di; **he is well equipped for the job** ha i requisiti necessari per quel lavoro

equipment [ɪ'kwɪpmənt] n attrezzatura; (electrical etc) apparecchiatura

equitable ['ɛkwɪtəbl] adj equo(-a), giusto(-a)

equities ['ɛkwɪtɪz] npl (Brit Comm) azioni fpl ordinarie

equity ['ɛkwɪtɪ] n equità

equity capital n capitale m azionario

equivalent [ɪ'kwɪvələnt] adj, n equivalente (m); **to be ~ to** equivalere a

equivocal [ɪ'kwɪvəkl] adj equivoco(-a); (open to suspicion) dubbio(-a)

equivocate [ɪ'kwɪvəkeɪt] vi esprimersi in modo equivoco

equivocation [ɪkwɪvə'keɪʃən] n parole fpl equivoche

ER abbr (Brit) = **Elizabeth Regina**

ERA n abbr (US Pol) = **Equal Rights Amendment**

era ['ɪərə] n era, età f inv

eradicate [ɪ'rædɪkeɪt] vt sradicare

erase [ɪ'reɪz] vt cancellare

eraser [ɪ'reɪzər] n gomma

erect [ɪ'rɛkt] adj eretto(-a) ■ vt costruire; (monument, tent) alzare

erection [ɪ'rɛkʃən] n (also Physiol) erezione f; (of building) costruzione f; (of machinery) montaggio

ergonomics [əːgə'nɔmɪks] n ergonomia

ERISA n abbr (US: = Employee Retirement Income Security Act) legge relativa al pensionamento statale

Eritrea [ɛrɪ'treɪə] n Eritrea

ERM n abbr (= Exchange Rate Mechanism) meccanismo dei tassi di cambio

ermine ['əːmɪn] n ermellino

ERNIE ['əːnɪ] n abbr (Brit: = Electronic Random Number Indicator Equipment) sistema che seleziona i numeri vincenti di buoni del Tesoro

erode [ɪ'rəud] vt erodere; (metal) corrodere

erogenous zone [ɪ'rɔdʒənəs-] n zona erogena

erosion [ɪ'rəuʒən] n erosione f

erotic [ɪ'rɔtɪk] adj erotico(-a)

eroticism [ɪ'rɔtɪsɪzəm] n erotismo

err [əːr] vi errare; (Rel) peccare

errand ['ɛrənd] n commissione f; (also: **to run errands**) fare commissioni; **~ of mercy** atto di carità

errand boy n fattorino

erratic [ɪ'rætɪk] adj imprevedibile; (person, mood) incostante

erroneous [ɪ'rəunɪəs] adj erroneo(-a)

error ['ɛrər] n errore m; **typing/spelling ~**

errore di battitura/di ortografia; **in ~ per errore; errors and omissions excepted** salvo errori ed omissioni

error message n (Comput) messaggio di errore

erstwhile ['ə:stwaɪl] adv allora, un tempo ▪ adj di allora

erudite ['ɛrjudaɪt] adj erudito(-a)

erupt [ɪ'rʌpt] vi erompere; (volcano) mettersi (or essere) in eruzione

eruption [ɪ'rʌpʃən] n eruzione f; (of anger, violence) esplosione f

ESA n abbr (= European Space Agency) ESA f

escalate ['ɛskəleɪt] vi intensificarsi; (costs) salire

escalation [ɛskə'leɪʃən] n escalation f; (of prices) aumento

escalation clause n clausola di revisione

escalator ['ɛskəleɪtə'] n scala mobile

escapade [ɛskə'peɪd] n scappatella; avventura

escape [ɪ'skeɪp] n evasione f; fuga; (of gas etc) fuga, fuoriuscita ▪ vi fuggire; (from jail) evadere, scappare; (fig) sfuggire; (leak) uscire ▪ vt sfuggire a; **to ~ from sb** sfuggire a qn; **to ~ to** (another place) fuggire in; (freedom, safety) fuggire verso; **to ~ notice** passare inosservato(a)

escape artist n mago della fuga

escape clause n clausola scappatoia

escapee [ɪskeɪ'pi:] n evaso(-a)

escape hatch n (in submarine, space rocket) portello di sicurezza

escape key n (Comput) tasto di escape, tasto per cambio di codice

escape route n percorso della fuga

escapism [ɪs'keɪpɪzəm] n evasione f (dalla realtà)

escapist [ɪs'keɪpɪst] adj d'evasione ▪ n persona che cerca di evadere dalla realtà

escapologist [ɛskə'pɒlədʒɪst] n (Brit) = **escape artist**

escarpment [ɪs'kɑ:pmənt] n scarpata

eschew [ɪs'tʃu:] vt evitare

escort n ['ɛskɔ:t] scorta; (to dance etc): **her ~** il suo cavaliere; **his ~** la sua dama ▪ vt [ɪ'skɔ:t] scortare; accompagnare

escort agency n agenzia di hostess

Eskimo ['ɛskɪməu] adj eschimese ▪ n eschimese m/f; (Ling) eschimese m

ESL n abbr (Scol) = **English as a Second Language**

esophagus [i:'sɒfəgəs] n (US) = **oesophagus**

esoteric [ɛsəu'tɛrɪk] adj esoterico(-a)

ESP n abbr = **extrasensory perception**; (Scol) = **English for Specific (or Special) Purposes**

esp. abbr (= especially) spec.

especially [ɪ'spɛʃlɪ] adv specialmente; (above all) soprattutto; (specifically) espressamente; (particularly) particolarmente

espionage ['ɛspɪəna:ʒ] n spionaggio

esplanade [ɛsplə'neɪd] n lungomare m

espouse [ɪ'spauz] vt abbracciare

Esquire [ɪ'skwaɪə'] n (Brit): **J. Brown, Esquire** Signor J. Brown

essay ['ɛseɪ] n (Scol) composizione f; (Literature) saggio

essence ['ɛsns] n essenza; **in ~** in sostanza; **speed is of the ~** la velocità è di estrema importanza

essential [ɪ'sɛnʃəl] adj essenziale; (basic) fondamentale ▪ n elemento essenziale; **it is ~ that** è essenziale che + sub

essentially [ɪ'sɛnʃəlɪ] adv essenzialmente

EST abbr (US: = Eastern Standard Time) fuso orario

est. abbr = **established; estimate(d)**

establish [ɪ'stæblɪʃ] vt stabilire; (business) mettere su; (one's power etc) confermare; (prove: fact, identity, sb's innocence) dimostrare

establishment [ɪs'tæblɪʃmənt] n stabilimento; (business) azienda; **the E~** la classe dirigente; l'establishment m; **a teaching ~** un istituto d'istruzione

estate [ɪ'steɪt] n proprietà f inv; (Law) beni mpl, patrimonio; (Brit: also: **housing estate**) complesso edilizio

estate agency n (Brit) agenzia immobiliare

estate agent n (Brit) agente m immobiliare

estate car n (Brit) giardiniera

esteem [ɪ'sti:m] n stima ▪ vt considerare; stimare; **I hold him in high ~** gode di tutta la mia stima

esthetic [ɪs'θɛtɪk] adj (US) = **aesthetic**

estimate n ['ɛstɪmət] stima; (Comm) preventivo ▪ vt ['ɛstɪmeɪt] stimare, valutare ▪ vi (Brit Comm): **to ~ for** fare il preventivo per; **to give sb an ~ of** fare a qn una valutazione approssimativa (or un preventivo) di; **at a rough ~** approssimativamente

estimation [ɛstɪ'meɪʃən] n stima; opinione f; **in my ~** a mio giudizio, a mio avviso

Estonia [ɛ'stəunɪə] n Estonia

Estonian [ɛ'stəunɪən] adj estone inv ▪ n estone m/f; (Ling) estone m

estranged [ɪ'streɪndʒd] adj separato(-a)

estrangement [ɪs'treɪndʒmənt] n alienazione f

estrogen ['i:strəudʒən] n (US) = **oestrogen**

estuary ['ɛstjuərɪ] n estuario

ET abbr (= Eastern Time) fuso orario; (Brit: = Employment Training) corso di formazione professionale per disoccupati

ETA n abbr (= estimated time of arrival) ora di arrivo prevista

e-tailer ['i:teɪləʳ] n venditore(-trice) in Internet

e-tailing ['i:teɪlɪŋ] n commercio in Internet

et al. abbr (= et alii: and others) ed altri

etc. abbr (= et cetera) ecc., etc.

etch [ɛtʃ] vt incidere all'acquaforte

etching ['ɛtʃɪŋ] n acquaforte f

ETD n abbr (= estimated time of departure) ora di partenza prevista

eternal [ɪ'tə:nl] adj eterno(-a)

eternity [ɪ'tə:nɪtɪ] n eternità

ether ['i:θəʳ] n etere m

ethereal [ɪ'θɪərɪəl] adj etereo(-a)

ethical ['ɛθɪkl] adj etico(-a), morale

ethics ['ɛθɪks] n etica ■ npl morale f

Ethiopia [i:θɪ'əupɪə] n Etiopia

Ethiopian [i:θɪ'əupɪən] adj, n etiope (m/f)

ethnic ['ɛθnɪk] adj etnico(-a)

ethnic cleansing [-'klɛnzɪŋ] n pulizia etnica

ethnic minority n minoranza etnica

ethnology [ɛθ'nɔlədʒɪ] n etnologia

ethos ['i:θɔs] n (of culture, group) norma di vita

e-ticket ['i:tɪkɪt] n e-ticket m inv, biglietto elettronico

etiquette ['ɛtɪkɛt] n etichetta

ETV n abbr (US) = **Educational Television**

etymology [ɛtɪ'mɔlədʒɪ] n etimologia

EU n abbr (= European Union) UE f

eucalyptus [ju:kə'lɪptəs] n eucalipto

eulogy ['ju:lədʒɪ] n elogio

euphemism ['ju:fəmɪzəm] n eufemismo

euphemistic [ju:fə'mɪstɪk] adj eufemistico(-a)

euphoria [ju:'fɔ:rɪə] n euforia

Eurasia [juə'reɪʃə] n Eurasia

Eurasian [juə'reɪʃən] adj, n eurasiano(-a)

Euratom [juə'rætəm] n abbr (= European Atomic Energy Community) EURATOM f

euro ['juərəu] n (currency) euro m inv

Euro- ['juərəu] prefix euro-

Eurocheque ['juərəutʃɛk] n eurochèque m inv

Eurocrat ['juərəukræt] n eurocrate m/f

Eurodollar ['juərəudɔləʳ] n eurodollaro

Euroland ['juərəulænd] n Eurolandia

Europe ['juərəp] n Europa

European [juərə'pi:ən] adj, n europeo(-a)

European Court of Justice n Corte f di Giustizia della Comunità Europea

Europol ['juərəupɔl] n Europol f

Euro-sceptic ['juərəuskɛptɪk] n euroscettico(-a)

Eurozone ['juərəuzəun] n zona euro

euthanasia [ju:θə'neɪzɪə] n eutanasia

evacuate [ɪ'vækjueɪt] vt evacuare

evacuation [ɪvækju'eɪʃən] n evacuazione f

evacuee [ɪvækju'i:] n sfollato(-a)

evade [ɪ'veɪd] vt eludere; (duties etc) sottrarsi a

evaluate [ɪ'væljueɪt] vt valutare

evangelist [ɪ'vændʒəlɪst] n evangelista m

evangelize [ɪ'vændʒəlaɪz] vt evangelizzare

evaporate [ɪ'væpəreɪt] vi evaporare ■ vt far evaporare

evaporated milk n latte m concentrato

evaporation [ɪvæpə'reɪʃən] n evaporazione f

evasion [ɪ'veɪʒən] n evasione f

evasive [ɪ'veɪsɪv] adj evasivo(-a)

eve [i:v] n: **on the ~ of** alla vigilia di

even ['i:vn] adj regolare; (number) pari inv ■ adv anche, perfino; **~ if, ~ though** anche se; **~ more** ancora di più; **he loves her ~ more** la ama anche di più; **~ faster** ancora più veloce; **~ so** ciò nonostante; **not ~ ...** nemmeno ...; **to break ~** finire in pari or alla pari; **to get ~ with sb** dare la pari a qn ▶ **even out** vi pareggiare

even-handed ['i:vn'hændɪd] adj imparziale, equo(-a)

evening ['i:vnɪŋ] n sera; (as duration, event) serata; **in the ~** la sera; **this ~** stasera, questa sera; **tomorrow/yesterday ~** domani/ieri sera

evening class n corso serale

evening dress n (woman's) abito da sera; **in ~** (man) in abito scuro; (woman) in abito lungo

evenly ['i:vnlɪ] adv (distribute, space, spread) uniformemente; (divide) in parti uguali

evensong ['i:vnsɔŋ] n ≈ vespro

event [ɪ'vent] n avvenimento; (Sport) gara; **in the ~ of** in caso di; **at all events**, (Brit) **in any ~** in ogni caso; **in the ~** in realtà, di fatto; **in the course of events** nel corso degli eventi

eventful [ɪ'ventful] adj denso(-a) di eventi

eventing [ɪ'ventɪŋ] n (Horseriding) concorso ippico

eventual [ɪ'ventʃuəl] adj finale

eventuality [ɪventʃu'ælɪtɪ] n possibilità f inv, eventualità f inv

eventually [ɪ'ventʃuəlɪ] adv finalmente

ever ['ɛvəʳ] adv mai; (at all times) sempre; **for ~** per sempre; **the best ~** il migliore che ci sia mai stato; **hardly ~** non ... quasi mai; **did you ~ meet him?** l'hai mai incontrato?; **have you ~ been there?** c'è mai stato?; **~ so pretty** così bello(a); **thank you ~ so much** grazie mille; **yours ~** (Brit: in letters) sempre tuo; **~ since** adv da allora ■ conj sin da quando

Everest ['ɛvərɪst] n (also: **Mount Everest**) Everest m

evergreen ['ɛvəgri:n] n sempreverde m

everlasting [ɛvə'lɑ:stɪŋ] adj eterno(-a)

every ['ɛvrɪ] adj ogni; **~ day** tutti i giorni, ogni giorno; **~ other/third day** ogni due/tre giorni; **~ other car** una macchina su due; **~ now and then** ogni tanto, di quando in quando; **I have ~ confidence in him** ho piena fiducia in lui

everybody ['ɛvrɪbɒdɪ] *pron* ognuno, tutti *pl*; **~ else** tutti gli altri; **~ knows about it** lo sanno tutti

everyday ['ɛvrɪdeɪ] *adj* quotidiano(-a); di ogni giorno; (*use, occurrence, experience*) comune; (*expression*) di uso corrente

everyone ['ɛvrɪwʌn] = **everybody**

everything ['ɛvrɪθɪŋ] *pron* tutto, ogni cosa; **~ is ready** è tutto pronto; **he did ~ possible** ha fatto tutto il possibile

everywhere ['ɛvrɪwɛər] *adv* in ogni luogo, dappertutto; (*wherever*) ovunque; **~ you go you meet ...** ovunque si vada si trova ...

evict [ɪ'vɪkt] *vt* sfrattare

eviction [ɪ'vɪkʃən] *n* sfratto

eviction notice *n* avviso di sfratto

evidence ['ɛvɪdəns] *n* (*proof*) prova; (*of witness*) testimonianza; (*sign*): **to show ~ of** dare segni di; **to give ~** deporre; **in ~** (*obvious*) in evidenza; in vista

evident ['ɛvɪdənt] *adj* evidente

evidently ['ɛvɪdəntlɪ] *adv* evidentemente

evil ['iːvl] *adj* cattivo(-a), maligno(-a) ◼ *n* male *m*

evince [ɪ'vɪns] *vt* manifestare

evocative [ɪ'vɒkətɪv] *adj* evocativo(-a)

evoke [ɪ'vəuk] *vt* evocare; (*admiration*) suscitare

evolution [iːvə'luːʃən] *n* evoluzione *f*

evolve [ɪ'vɒlv] *vt* elaborare ◼ *vi* svilupparsi, evolversi

ewe [juː] *n* pecora

ex- [ɛks] *prefix* ex; (*out of*): **the price ~works** il prezzo franco fabbrica

exacerbate [ɪk'sæsəbeɪt] *vt* (*pain*) aggravare; (*fig: relations, situation*) esacerbare, esasperare

exact [ɪg'zækt] *adj* esatto(-a) ◼ *vt*: **to ~ sth (from)** estorcere qc (da); esigere qc (da)

exacting [ɪg'zæktɪŋ] *adj* esigente; (*work*) faticoso(-a)

exactitude [ɪg'zæktɪtjuːd] *n* esattezza, precisione *f*

exactly [ɪg'zæktlɪ] *adv* esattamente; **~!** esatto!

exaggerate [ɪg'zædʒəreɪt] *vt, vi* esagerare

exaggeration [ɪgzædʒə'reɪʃən] *n* esagerazione *f*

exalt [ɪg'zɔːlt] *vt* esaltare; elevare

exalted [ɪg'zɔːltɪd] *adj* (*rank, person*) elevato(-a); (*elated*) esaltato(-a)

exam [ɪg'zæm] *n abbr* (*Scol*) = **examination**

examination [ɪgzæmɪ'neɪʃən] *n* (*Scol*) esame *m*; (*Med*) controllo; **to take** *or* **sit an ~** (*Brit*) sostenere *or* dare un esame; **the matter is under ~** la questione è all'esame

examine [ɪg'zæmɪn] *vt* esaminare; (*Scol:*

orally, *Law: person*) interrogare; (*inspect: machine, premises*) ispezionare; (*luggage, passport*) controllare; (*Med*) visitare

examiner [ɪg'zæmɪnər] *n* esaminatore(-trice)

example [ɪg'zɑːmpl] *n* esempio; **for ~** ad *or* per esempio; **to set a good/bad ~** dare il buon/cattivo esempio

exasperate [ɪg'zɑːspəreɪt] *vt* esasperare; **exasperated by** (*or* **at** *or* **with**) esasperato da

exasperating [ɪg'zɑːspəreɪtɪŋ] *adj* esasperante

exasperation [ɪgzɑːspə'reɪʃən] *n* esasperazione *f*

excavate ['ɛkskəveɪt] *vt* scavare

excavation [ɛkskə'veɪʃən] *n* escavazione *f*

excavator ['ɛkskəveɪtər] *n* scavatore *m*, scavatrice *f*

exceed [ɪk'siːd] *vt* superare; (*one's powers, time limit*) oltrepassare

exceedingly [ɪk'siːdɪŋlɪ] *adv* eccessivamente

excel [ɪk'sɛl] *vi* eccellere ◼ *vt* sorpassare; **to ~ o.s.** (*Brit*) superare se stesso

excellence ['ɛksələns] *n* eccellenza

Excellency ['ɛksələnsɪ] *n*: **His ~** Sua Eccellenza

excellent ['ɛksələnt] *adj* eccellente

except [ɪk'sɛpt] *prep* (*also:* **except for**, **excepting**) salvo, all'infuori di, eccetto ◼ *vt* escludere; **~ if/when** salvo se/quando; **~ that** salvo che

exception [ɪk'sɛpʃən] *n* eccezione *f*; **to take ~ to** trovare a ridire su; **with the ~ of** ad eccezione di

exceptional [ɪk'sɛpʃənl] *adj* eccezionale

excerpt ['ɛksəːpt] *n* estratto

excess [ɪk'sɛs] *n* eccesso; **in ~ of** al di sopra di

excess baggage *n* bagaglio in eccedenza

excess fare *n* supplemento

excessive [ɪk'sɛsɪv] *adj* eccessivo(-a)

excess supply *n* eccesso di offerta

exchange [ɪks'tʃeɪndʒ] *n* scambio; (*also:* **telephone exchange**) centralino ◼ *vt*: **to ~ (for)** scambiare (con); **in ~ for** in cambio di; **foreign ~** (*Comm*) cambio

exchange control *n* controllo sui cambi

exchange market *n* mercato dei cambi

exchange rate *n* tasso di cambio

Exchequer [ɪks'tʃekər] *n*: **the ~** (*Brit*) lo Scacchiere, ≈ il ministero delle Finanze

excisable [ɪk'saɪzəbl] *adj* soggetto(-a) a dazio

excise *n* ['ɛksaɪz] imposta, dazio ◼ *vt* [ɛk'saɪz] recidere

excise duties *npl* dazi *mpl*

excitable [ɪk'saɪtəbl] *adj* eccitabile

excite [ɪk'saɪt] *vt* eccitare; **to get excited** eccitarsi

excitement [ɪk'saɪtmənt] *n* eccitazione *f*; agitazione *f*

exciting [ɪk'saɪtɪŋ] *adj* avventuroso(-a); *(film, book)* appassionante

excl. *abbr* (= *excluding, exclusive (of)*) escl.

exclaim [ɪk'skleɪm] *vi* esclamare

exclamation [ɛksklə'meɪʃən] *n* esclamazione *f*

exclamation mark *n* punto esclamativo

exclude [ɪk'sklu:d] *vt* escludere

excluding [ɪk'sklu:dɪŋ] *prep*: ~ **VAT** IVA esclusa

exclusion [ɪk'sklu:ʒən] *n* esclusione *f*; **to the ~ of** escludendo

exclusion clause *n* clausola di esclusione

exclusion zone *n* area interdetta

exclusive [ɪk'sklu:sɪv] *adj* esclusivo(-a); *(club)* selettivo(-a); *(district)* snob *inv* ■ *adv (Comm)* non compreso; ~ **of VAT** IVA esclusa; ~ **of postage** spese postali escluse; ~ **of service** servizio escluso; **from 1st to 15th March** ~ dal 1° al 15 marzo esclusi; ~ **rights** *npl (Comm)* diritti *mpl* esclusivi

exclusively [ɪk'sklu:sɪvlɪ] *adv* esclusivamente

excommunicate [ɛkskə'mju:nɪkeɪt] *vt* scomunicare

excrement ['ɛkskrəmənt] *n* escremento

excruciating [ɪk'skru:ʃɪeɪtɪŋ] *adj* straziante, atroce

excursion [ɪk'skə:ʃən] *n* escursione *f*, gita

excursion ticket *n* biglietto a tariffa escursionistica

excusable [ɪk'skju:zəbl] *adj* scusabile

excuse *n* [ɪk'skju:s] scusa ■ *vt* [ɪk'skju:z] scusare; *(justify)* giustificare; **to make excuses for sb** trovare giustificazioni per qn; **to ~ sb from** *(activity)* dispensare qn da; ~ **me!** mi scusi!; **now if you will ~ me,** ... ora, mi scusi ma ...; **to ~ o.s. (for (doing) sth)** giustificarsi (per (aver fatto) qc)

ex-directory ['ɛksdɪ'rɛktərɪ] *adj (Brit)*: ~ **(phone) number** numero non compreso nell'elenco telefonico

execrable ['ɛksɪkrəbl] *adj (gen)* pessimo(-a); *(manners)* esecrabile

execute ['ɛksɪkju:t] *vt (prisoner)* giustiziare; *(plan etc)* eseguire

execution [ɛksɪ'kju:ʃən] *n* esecuzione *f*

executioner [ɛksɪ'kju:ʃnə'] *n* boia *m inv*

executive [ɪg'zɛkjutɪv] *n (Comm)* dirigente *m*; *(Pol)* esecutivo ■ *adj* esecutivo(-a); *(secretary)* di direzione; *(offices, suite)* della direzione; *(car, plane)* dirigenziale; *(position, job, duties)* direttivo(-a)

executive director *n* amministratore(-trice)

executor [ɪg'zɛkjutə'] *n* esecutore(-trice) testamentario(-a)

exemplary [ɪg'zɛmplərɪ] *adj* esemplare

exemplify [ɪg'zɛmplɪfaɪ] *vt* esemplificare

exempt [ɪg'zɛmpt] *adj*: ~ **(from)** *(person: from tax)* esentato(-a) (da); (: *from military service etc)* esonerato(-a) (da); *(goods)* esente (da) ■ *vt*: **to ~ sb from** esentare qn da

exemption [ɪg'zɛmpʃən] *n* esenzione *f*

exercise ['ɛksəsaɪz] *n* esercizio ■ *vt* esercitare; *(dog)* portar fuori ■ *vi (also:* **take exercise)** fare del movimento *or* moto

exercise bike *n* cyclette® *f inv*

exercise book *n* quaderno

exert [ɪg'zə:t] *vt* esercitare; *(strength, force)* impiegare; **to ~ o.s.** sforzarsi

exertion [ɪg'zə:ʃən] *n* sforzo

ex gratia ['ɛks'greɪʃə] *adj*: ~ **payment** gratifica

exhale [ɛks'heɪl] *vt, vi* espirare

exhaust [ɪg'zɔ:st] *n (also:* **exhaust fumes)** scappamento; *(also:* **exhaust pipe)** tubo di scappamento ■ *vt* esaurire; **to ~ o.s.** sfiancarsi

exhausted [ɪg'zɔ:stɪd] *adj* esaurito(-a)

exhausting [ɪg'zɔ:stɪŋ] *adj* estenuante

exhaustion [ɪg'zɔ:stʃən] *n* esaurimento; **nervous ~** sovraffaticamento mentale

exhaustive [ɪg'zɔ:stɪv] *adj* esauriente

exhibit [ɪg'zɪbɪt] *n (Art)* oggetto esposto; *(Law)* documento *or* oggetto esibito ■ *vt* esporre; *(courage, skill)* dimostrare

exhibition [ɛksɪ'bɪʃən] *n* mostra, esposizione *f*; *(of rudeness etc)* spettacolo; **to make an ~ of o.s.** dare spettacolo di sé

exhibitionist [ɛksɪ'bɪʃənɪst] *n* esibizionista *m/f*

exhibitor [ɪg'zɪbɪtə'] *n* espositore(-trice)

exhilarating [ɪg'zɪləreɪtɪŋ] *adj* esilarante; stimolante

exhilaration [ɪgzɪlə'reɪʃən] *n* esaltazione *f*, ebbrezza

exhort [ɪg'zɔ:t] *vt* esortare

exile ['ɛksaɪl] *n* esilio; *(person)* esiliato(-a) ■ *vt* esiliare; **in ~** in esilio

exist [ɪg'zɪst] *vi* esistere

existence [ɪg'zɪstəns] *n* esistenza; **to be in ~** esistere

existentialism [ɛgzɪs'tɛnʃəlɪzəm] *n* esistenzialismo

existing [ɪg'zɪstɪŋ] *adj (laws, regime)* attuale

exit ['ɛksɪt] *n* uscita ■ *vi (Comput, Theat)* uscire

exit poll *n* exit poll *m inv*, sondaggio all'uscita dei seggi

exit ramp *n (US Aut)* rampa di uscita

exit visa *n* visto d'uscita

exodus ['ɛksədəs] *n* esodo

ex officio ['ɛksə'fɪʃɪəu] *adj, adv* d'ufficio

exonerate [ɪg'zɔnəreɪt] *vt*: **to ~ from** discolpare da

exorbitant [ɪg'zɔːbɪtənt] *adj* (*price*) esorbitante; (*demands*) spropositato(-a)

exorcize ['ɛksɔːsaɪz] *vt* esorcizzare

exotic [ɪg'zɔtɪk] *adj* esotico(-a)

expand [ɪk'spænd] *vt* (*chest, economy etc*) sviluppare; (*market, operations*) espandere; (*influence*) estendere; (*horizons*) allargare ■ *vi* svilupparsi; (*gas*) espandersi; (*metal*) dilatarsi; **to ~ on** (*notes, story etc*) ampliare

expanse [ɪk'spæns] *n* distesa, estensione *f*

expansion [ɪk'spænʃən] *n* (*gen*) espansione *f*; (*of town, economy*) sviluppo; (*of metal*) dilatazione *f*

expansionism [ɪk'spænʃənɪzəm] *n* espansionismo

expansionist [ɪk'spænʃənɪst] *adj* espansionistico(-a)

expatriate *n* [ɛks'pætrɪət] espatriato(-a) ■ *vt* [ɛks'pætrɪeɪt] espatriare

expect [ɪk'spɛkt] *vt* (*anticipate*) prevedere, aspettarsi, prevedere *or* aspettarsi che + *sub*; (*count on*) contare su; (*hope for*) sperare; (*require*) richiedere, esigere; (*suppose*) supporre; (*await, also baby*) aspettare ■ *vi*: **to be expecting** essere in stato interessante; **to ~ sb to do** aspettarsi che qn faccia; **to ~ to do sth** pensare *or* contare di fare qc; **as expected** come previsto; **I ~ so** credo di sì

expectancy [ɪk'spɛktənsɪ] *n* attesa; **life ~** probabilità *fpl* di vita

expectant [ɪk'spɛktənt] *adj* pieno(-a) di aspettative

expectantly [ɪk'spɛktəntlɪ] *adv* (*look, listen*) con un'aria d'attesa

expectant mother *n* gestante *f*

expectation [ɛkspɛk'teɪʃən] *n* aspettativa; speranza; **in ~ of** in previsione di; **against** *or* **contrary to all ~(s)** contro ogni aspettativa; **to come** *or* **live up to sb's expectations** rispondere alle attese di qn

expedience [ɪk'spiːdɪəns], **expediency** [ɪk'spiːdɪənsɪ] *n* convenienza; **for the sake of ~** per una questione di comodità

expedient [ɪk'spiːdɪənt] *adj* conveniente; vantaggioso(-a) ■ *n* espediente *m*

expedite ['ɛkspədaɪt] *vt* sbrigare; facilitare

expedition [ɛkspə'dɪʃən] *n* spedizione *f*

expeditionary force [ɛkspə'dɪʃənərɪ-] *n* corpo di spedizione

expeditious [ɛkspə'dɪʃəs] *adj* sollecito(-a), rapido(-a)

expel [ɪk'spɛl] *vt* espellere

expend [ɪk'spɛnd] *vt* spendere; (*use up*) consumare

expendable [ɪk'spɛndəbl] *adj* sacrificabile

expenditure [ɪk'spɛndɪtʃər] *n* spesa; (*of time, effort*) dispendio

expense [ɪk'spɛns] *n* spesa; (*high cost*) costo; **expenses** *npl* (*Comm*) spese *fpl*, indennità *fpl*; **to go to the ~ of** sobbarcarsi la spesa di; **at great ~** con grande impiego di mezzi; **at the ~ of** a spese di

expense account *n* conto *m* spese *inv*

expensive [ɪk'spɛnsɪv] *adj* caro(-a), costoso(-a); **she has ~ tastes** le piacciono le cose costose

experience [ɪk'spɪərɪəns] *n* esperienza ■ *vt* (*pleasure*) provare; (*hardship*) soffrire; **to learn by ~** imparare per esperienza

experienced [ɪk'spɪərɪənst] *adj* che ha esperienza

experiment *n* [ɪk'spɛrɪmənt] esperimento, esperienza ■ *vi* [ɪk'spɛrɪmɛnt] fare esperimenti; **to perform** *or* **carry out an ~** fare un esperimento; **as an ~** a titolo di esperimento; **to ~ with a new vaccine** sperimentare un nuovo vaccino

experimental [ɪkspɛrɪ'mɛntl] *adj* sperimentale; **at the ~ stage** in via di sperimentazione

expert ['ɛkspəːt] *adj, n* esperto(a); **~ witness** (*Law*) esperto(-a); **~ in** *or* **at doing sth** esperto nel fare qc; **an ~ on sth** un esperto di qc

expertise [ɛkspəː'tiːz] *n* competenza

expire [ɪk'spaɪər] *vi* (*period of time, licence*) scadere

expiry [ɪk'spaɪərɪ] *n* scadenza

explain [ɪk'spleɪn] *vt* spiegare
▶ **explain away** *vt* dar ragione di

explanation [ɛksplə'neɪʃən] *n* spiegazione *f*; **to find an ~ for sth** trovare la spiegazione di qc

explanatory [ɪk'splænətrɪ] *adj* esplicativo(-a)

expletive [ɪk'spliːtɪv] *n* imprecazione *f*

explicit [ɪk'splɪsɪt] *adj* esplicito(-a); (*definite*) netto(-a)

explode [ɪk'spləud] *vi* esplodere ■ *vt* (*fig: theory*) demolire; **to ~ a myth** distruggere un mito

exploit *n* ['ɛksplɔɪt] impresa ■ *vt* [ɪk'splɔɪt] sfruttare

exploitation [ɛksplɔɪ'teɪʃən] *n* sfruttamento

exploration [ɛksplə'reɪʃən] *n* esplorazione *f*

exploratory [ɪk'splɔrətrɪ] *adj* (*fig: talks*) esplorativo(-a); **~ operation** (*Med*) intervento d'esplorazione

explore [ɪk'splɔːr] *vt* esplorare; (*possibilities*) esaminare

explorer [ɪk'splɔːrər] *n* esploratore(-trice)

explosion [ɪk'spləuʒən] *n* esplosione *f*

explosive [ɪk'spləusɪv] *adj* esplosivo(-a) ■ *n* esplosivo

exponent [ɪk'spəunənt] *n* esponente *m/f*

export *vt* [ɛk'spɔːt] esportare ■ *n* ['ɛkspɔːt]

esportazione *f*; articolo di esportazione ■ *cpd* d'esportazione

exportation [ɛkspɔː'teɪʃən] *n* esportazione *f*

exporter [ɪk'spɔːtəʳ] *n* esportatore *m*

export licence *n* licenza d'esportazione

expose [ɪk'spəuz] *vt* esporre; (*unmask*) smascherare; **to ~ o.s.** (*Law*) oltraggiare il pudore

exposed [ɪk'spəuzd] *adj* (*land, house*) esposto(-a); (*Elec: wire*) scoperto(-a); (*pipe, beam*) a vista

exposition [ɛkspə'zɪʃən] *n* esposizione *f*

exposure [ɪk'spəuʒəʳ] *n* esposizione *f*; (*Phot*) posa; (*Med*) assideramento; **to die of ~** morire assiderato(-a)

exposure meter *n* esposimetro

expound [ɪk'spaund] *vt* esporre; (*theory, text*) spiegare

express [ɪk'sprɛs] *adj* (*definite*) chiaro(-a), espresso(-a); (*Brit: letter etc*) espresso *inv* ■ *n* (*train*) espresso ■ *adv*: **to send sth ~** spedire qc per espresso ■ *vt* esprimere; **to ~ o.s.** esprimersi

expression [ɪk'sprɛʃən] *n* espressione *f*

expressionism [ɪk'sprɛʃənɪzəm] *n* espressionismo

expressive [ɪk'sprɛsɪv] *adj* espressivo(-a)

expressly [ɪk'sprɛslɪ] *adv* espressamente

expressway [ɪk'sprɛsweɪ] *n* (*US*) autostrada che attraversa la città

expropriate [ɛks'prəuprɪeɪt] *vt* espropriare

expulsion [ɪk'spʌlʃən] *n* espulsione *f*

exquisite [ɛk'skwɪzɪt] *adj* squisito(-a)

ex-serviceman ['ɛks'səːvɪsmən] *n* ex combattente *m*

ext. *abbr* (*Tel: = extension*) int. (*= interno*)

extemporize [ɪk'stɛmpəraɪz] *vi* improvvisare

extend [ɪk'stɛnd] *vt* (*visit*) protrarre; (*road, deadline*) prolungare; (*building*) ampliare; (*offer*) offrire, porgere; (*Comm: credit*) accordare ■ *vi* (*land*) estendersi

extension [ɪk'stɛnʃən] *n* (*of road, term*) prolungamento; (*of contract, deadline*) proroga; (*building*) annesso; (*to wire, table*) prolunga; (*telephone*) interno; (: *in private house*) apparecchio supplementare; **~ 3718** (*Tel*) interno 3718

extension cable *n* (*Elec*) prolunga

extensive [ɪk'stɛnsɪv] *adj* esteso(-a), ampio(-a); (*damage*) su larga scala; (*alterations*) notevole; (*inquiries*) esauriente; (*use*) grande

extensively [ɪk'stɛnsɪvlɪ] *adv* (*altered, damaged etc*) radicalmente; **he's travelled ~** ha viaggiato molto

extent [ɪk'stɛnt] *n* estensione *f*; (*of knowledge, activities, power*) portata; (*degree: of damage, loss*) proporzioni *fpl*; **to some ~** fino a un certo

punto; **to a certain/large ~** in certa/larga misura; **to what ~?** fino a che punto?; **to such an ~ that ...** a tal punto che ...

extenuating [ɪk'stɛnjueɪtɪŋ] *adj*: **~ circumstances** attenuanti *fpl*

exterior [ɛk'stɪərɪəʳ] *adj* esteriore, esterno(-a) ■ *n* esteriore *m*, esterno; aspetto (esteriore)

exterminate [ɪk'stəːmɪneɪt] *vt* sterminare

extermination [ɪkstəːmɪ'neɪʃən] *n* sterminio

external [ɛk'stəːnl] *adj* esterno(-a), esteriore ■ *n*: **the externals** le apparenze; **for ~ use only** (*Med*) solo per uso esterno; **~ affairs** (*Pol*) affari *mpl* esteri

externally [ɛk'stəːnəlɪ] *adv* esternamente

extinct [ɪk'stɪŋkt] *adj* estinto(-a)

extinction [ɪk'stɪŋkʃən] *n* estinzione *f*

extinguish [ɪk'stɪŋgwɪʃ] *vt* estinguere

extinguisher [ɪk'stɪŋgwɪʃəʳ] *n* estintore *m*

extol, (*US*) **extoll** [ɪk'stəul] *vt* (*merits, virtues*) magnificare; (*person*) celebrare

extort [ɪk'stɔːt] *vt*: **to ~ sth from** estorcere qc (da)

extortion [ɪk'stɔːʃən] *n* estorsione *f*

extortionate [ɪk'stɔːʃənɪt] *adj* esorbitante

extra ['ɛkstrə] *adj* extra *inv*, supplementare ■ *adv* (*in addition*) di più ■ *n* supplemento; (*Theat*) comparso; **wine will cost ~** il vino è extra; **~ large sizes** taglie *fpl* forti

extra... ['ɛkstrə] *prefix* extra...

extract *vt* [ɪk'strækt] estrarre; (*money, promise*) strappare ■ *n* ['ɛkstrækt] estratto; (*passage*) brano

extraction [ɪk'strækʃən] *n* estrazione *f*; (*descent*) origine *f*

extractor fan [ɪk'stræktəʳ-] *n* aspiratore *m*

extracurricular [ɛkstrəkə'rɪkjuləʳ] *adj* (*Scol*) parascolastico(-a)

extradite ['ɛkstrədaɪt] *vt* estradare

extradition [ɛkstrə'dɪʃən] *n* estradizione *f*

extramarital [ɛkstrə'mærɪtl] *adj* extraconiugale

extramural [ɛkstrə'mjuərl] *adj* fuori dell'università

extraneous [ɛk'streɪnɪəs] *adj*: **~ to** estraneo(a) a

extraordinary [ɪk'strɔːdnrɪ] *adj* straordinario(-a); **the ~ thing is that ...** la cosa strana è che ...

extraordinary general meeting *n* assemblea straordinaria

extrapolation [ɪkstræpə'leɪʃən] *n* estrapolazione *f*

extrasensory perception [ɛkstrə'sɛnsərɪ-] *n* percezione *f* extrasensoriale

extra time *n* (*Football*) tempo supplementare

extravagance [ɪk'strævəgəns] *n* (*excessive spending*) sperpero; (*thing bought*) stravaganza

e

extravagant [ɪk'strævəgənt] *adj*
stravagante; (*in spending: person*) prodigo(-a);
(*: tastes*) dispendioso(-a)

extreme [ɪk'striːm] *adj* estremo(-a) ■ *n*
estremo; **extremes of temperature**
eccessivi sbalzi *mpl* di temperatura; **the ~
left/right** (*Pol*) l'estrema sinistra/destra

extremely [ɪk'striːmlɪ] *adv* estremamente

extremist [ɪk'striːmɪst] *adj, n* estremista (*m/f*)

extremity [ɪk'strɛmɪtɪ] *n* estremità *f inv*

extricate ['ɛkstrɪkeɪt] *vt*: **to ~ sth from**
districare qc (da)

extrovert ['ɛkstrəvɜːt] *n* estroverso(-a)

exuberance [ɪg'zuːbərəns] *n* esuberanza

exuberant [ɪg'zjuːbərənt] *adj* esuberante

exude [ɪg'zjuːd] *vt* trasudare; (*fig*) emanare

exult [ɪg'zʌlt] *vi* esultare, gioire

exultant [ɪg'zʌltənt] *adj* (*person, smile*)
esultante; (*shout, expression*) di giubilo

exultation [ɛgzʌl'teɪʃən] *n* giubilo; **in ~**
per la gioia

eye [aɪ] *n* occhio; (*of needle*) cruna ■ *vt*
osservare; **to keep an ~ on** tenere d'occhio;
in the public ~ esposto(a) al pubblico; **as far
as the ~ can see** a perdita d'occhio; **with an
~ to doing sth** (*Brit*) con l'idea di far qc; **to
have an ~ for sth** avere occhio per qc;
there's more to this than meets the ~
non è così semplice come sembra

eyeball ['aɪbɔːl] *n* globo dell'occhio

eyebath ['aɪbɑːθ] *n* occhino

eyebrow ['aɪbrau] *n* sopracciglio

eyebrow pencil *n* matita per le sopracciglia

eye-catching ['aɪkætʃɪŋ] *adj* che colpisce
l'occhio

eye cup *n* (*US*) = **eyebath**

eyedrops ['aɪdrɒps] *npl* gocce *fpl* oculari,
collirio

eyeful ['aɪful] *n*: **to get an ~ (of sth)** (*col*)
avere l'occasione di dare una bella sbirciata
(a qc)

eyeglass ['aɪglɑːs] *n* monocolo

eyelash ['aɪlæʃ] *n* ciglio

eyelet ['aɪlɪt] *n* occhiello

eye-level ['aɪlɛvl] *adj* all'altezza degli occhi

eyelid ['aɪlɪd] *n* palpebra

eyeliner ['aɪlaɪnəʳ] *n* eye-liner *m inv*

eye-opener ['aɪəupnəʳ] *n* rivelazione *f*

eyeshadow ['aɪʃædəu] *n* ombretto

eyesight ['aɪsaɪt] *n* vista

eyesore ['aɪsɔːʳ] *n* pugno nell'occhio

eyestrain ['aɪstreɪn] *n*: **to get ~** stancarsi gli
occhi

eye-tooth (*pl* **eye-teeth**) ['aɪtuːθ, -tiːθ] *n*
canino superiore; **to give one's eye-teeth
for sth/to do sth** (*fig*) dare non so che cosa
per qc/per fare qc

eyewash ['aɪwɒʃ] *n* collirio; (*fig*) sciocchezze *fpl*

eye witness *n* testimone *m/f* oculare

eyrie ['ɪərɪ] *n* nido (d'aquila)

Ff

F, f [ɛf] n (letter) F, f or m inv; (Mus): **F** fa m;
F for Frederick, (US) **F for Fox** ≈ F come
Firenze

F. abbr (= Fahrenheit) F

FA n abbr (Brit) = **Football Association**

FAA n abbr (US) = **Federal Aviation
Administration**

fable ['feɪbl] n favola

fabric ['fæbrɪk] n stoffa, tessuto; (Archit)
struttura

fabricate ['fæbrɪkeɪt] vt fabbricare

fabrication [fæbrɪ'keɪʃən] n fabbricazione f

fabric ribbon n (for typewriter) dattilonastro di
tessuto

fabulous ['fæbjuləs] adj favoloso(-a);
(col: super) favoloso(-a), fantastico(-a)

façade [fə'sɑːd] n facciata; (fig) apparenza

face [feɪs] n faccia, viso, volto; (expression)
faccia; (grimace) smorfia; (of clock) quadrante
m; (of building) facciata; (side, surface) faccia; (of
mountain, cliff) parete f ■ vt fronteggiare; (fig)
affrontare; ~ **down** (person) bocconi; (object) a
faccia in giù; **to lose/save** ~ perdere/salvare
la faccia; **to pull a** ~ fare una smorfia; **in
the** ~ **of** (difficulties etc) di fronte a; **on the** ~
of it a prima vista; **to** ~ **the fact that** ...
riconoscere or ammettere che ...
▶ **face up to** vt fus affrontare, far fronte a

face cloth n (Brit) guanto di spugna

face cream n crema per il viso

faceless ['feɪslɪs] adj anonimo(-a)

face lift n lifting m inv; (of façade etc) ripulita

face powder n cipria

face-saving ['feɪs'seɪvɪŋ] adj che salva la
faccia

facet ['fæsɪt] n faccetta, sfaccettatura; (fig)
sfaccettatura

facetious [fə'siːʃəs] adj faceto(-a)

face-to-face ['feɪstə'feɪs] adv faccia a faccia

face value ['feɪs'vælju:] n (of coin) valore m
facciale or nominale; **to take sth at** ~ (fig)
giudicare qc dalle apparenze

facia ['feɪʃə] n = **fascia**

facial ['feɪʃəl] adj facciale ■ n trattamento
del viso

facile ['fæsaɪl] adj facile; superficiale

facilitate [fə'sɪlɪteɪt] vt facilitare

facility [fə'sɪlɪtɪ] n facilità; **facilities** npl
attrezzature fpl; **credit facilities**
facilitazioni fpl di credito

facing ['feɪsɪŋ] n (of wall etc) rivestimento;
(Sewing) paramontura

facsimile [fæk'sɪmɪlɪ] n facsimile m inv

facsimile machine n telecopiatrice f

fact [fækt] n fatto; **in** ~ infatti; **to know for
a** ~ **that** ... sapere per certo che ...; **the** ~ (**of
the matter**) **is that** ... la verità è che ...; **the
facts of life** (sex) i fatti riguardanti la vita
sessuale; (fig) le realtà della vita

fact-finding ['fækt.faɪndɪŋ] adj: **a** ~ **tour/
mission** un viaggio/una missione
d'inchiesta

faction ['fækʃən] n fazione f

factional ['fækʃənl] adj: ~ **fighting** scontri
mpl tra fazioni

factor ['fæktə'] n fattore m; (Comm: company)
organizzazione specializzata nell'incasso di crediti per
conto terzi; (: agent) agente m depositario ■ vi
incassare crediti per conto terzi; **human** ~
elemento umano; **safety** ~ coefficiente m di
sicurezza

factory ['fæktərɪ] n fabbrica, stabilimento

factory farming n (Brit) allevamento su scala
industriale

factory floor n: **the** ~ (workers) gli operai;
(area) il reparto produzione; **on the** ~ nel
reparto produzione

factory ship n nave f fattoria inv

factual ['fæktjuəl] adj che si attiene ai fatti

faculty ['fækəltɪ] n facoltà f inv; (US: teaching
staff) corpo insegnante

fad [fæd] n mania; capriccio

fade [feɪd] vi sbiadire, sbiadirsi; (light, sound,
hope) attenuarsi, affievolirsi; (flower) appassire
▶ **fade in** vt (picture) aprire in dissolvenza;
(sound) aumentare gradualmente d'intensità

▶ **fade out** vt (picture) chiudere in dissolvenza; (sound) diminuire gradualmente d'intensità

faeces, (US) **feces** ['fiːsiːz] npl feci fpl

fag [fæg] n (Brit col: cigarette) cicca; (: chore) sfacchinata; (US col: homosexual) frocio

fag end n (Brit col) mozzicone m

fagged out ['fægd-] adj (Brit col) stanco(-a) morto(-a)

fail [feɪl] vt (exam) non superare; (candidate) bocciare; (courage, memory) mancare a ■ vi fallire; (student) essere respinto(-a); (supplies) mancare; (eyesight, health, light: also: **be failing**) venire a mancare; (brakes) non funzionare; **to ~ to do sth** (neglect) mancare di fare qc; (be unable) non riuscire a fare qc; **without ~** senza fallo; certamente

failing ['feɪlɪŋ] n difetto ■ prep in mancanza di; ~ **that** se questo non è possibile

failsafe ['feɪlseɪf] adj (device etc) di sicurezza

failure ['feɪljəʳ] n fallimento; (person) fallito(-a); (mechanical etc) guasto; (in exam) insuccesso, bocciatura; (of crops) perdita; **his ~ to come** il fatto che non sia venuto; **it was a complete ~** è stato un vero fiasco

faint [feɪnt] adj debole; (recollection) vago(-a); (mark) indistinto(-a); (smell, breeze, trace) leggero(-a) ■ vi svenire; **to feel ~** sentirsi svenire

faintest ['feɪntɪst] adj: **I haven't the ~ idea** non ho la più pallida idea

faint-hearted [feɪnt'hɑːtɪd] adj pusillanime

faintly ['feɪntlɪ] adv debolmente; vagamente

faintness ['feɪntnɪs] n debolezza

fair [fɛəʳ] adj (person, decision) giusto(-a), equo(-a); (hair etc) biondo(-a); (skin, complexion) bianco(-a); (weather) bello(-a), clemente; (good enough) assai buono(-a); (sizeable) bello(-a) ■ adv: **to play ~** giocare correttamente ■ n fiera; (Brit: funfair) luna park m inv; (also: **trade fair**) fiera campionaria; **it's not ~!** non è giusto!; **a ~ amount of** un bel po' di

fair copy n bella copia

fair game n: **to be ~** (person) essere bersaglio legittimo

fairground ['fɛəgraund] n luna park m inv

fair-haired [fɛə'hɛəd] adj (person) biondo(-a)

fairly ['fɛəlɪ] adv equamente; (quite) abbastanza

fairness ['fɛənɪs] n equità, giustizia; **in all ~** per essere giusti, a dire il vero

fair play n correttezza

fair trade n commercio equo e solidale

fairy ['fɛərɪ] n fata

fairy godmother n fata buona

fairy lights npl (Brit) lanternine fpl colorate

fairy tale n fiaba

faith [feɪθ] n fede f; (trust) fiducia; (sect) religione f, fede f; **to have ~ in sb/sth** avere fiducia in qn/qc

faithful ['feɪθful] adj fedele

faithfully ['feɪθfəlɪ] adv fedelmente; **yours ~** (Brit: in letters) distinti saluti

faith healer n guaritore(-trice)

fake [feɪk] n imitazione f; (picture) falso; (person) impostore(-a) ■ adj falso(-a) ■ vt (accounts) falsificare; (illness) fingere; (painting) contraffare; **his illness is a ~** fa finta di essere malato

falcon ['fɔːlkən] n falco, falcone m

Falkland Islands ['fɔːlklənd-] npl: **the ~** le isole Falkland

fall [fɔːl] n caduta; (decrease) diminuzione f, calo; (in temperature) abbassamento; (in price) ribasso; (US: autumn) autunno ■ vi (pt **fell**, pp **fallen**) [fɛl, 'fɔːlən] cadere; (temperature, price) abbassare; **a ~ of earth** uno smottamento; **a ~ of snow** (Brit) una nevicata; **to ~ in love (with sb/sth)** innamorarsi (di qn/qc); **to ~ short of** (sb's expectations) non corrispondere a; **to ~ flat** vi (on one's face) cadere bocconi; (joke) fare cilecca; (plan) fallire; see also **falls**

▶ **fall apart** vi cadere a pezzi

▶ **fall back** vi indietreggiare; (Mil) ritirarsi

▶ **fall back on** vt fus ripiegare su; **to have sth to ~ back on** avere qc di riserva

▶ **fall behind** vi rimanere indietro; (fig: with payments) essere in arretrato

▶ **fall down** vi (person) cadere; (building, hopes) crollare

▶ **fall for** vt fus (person) prendere una cotta per; **to ~ for a trick** (or **a story** etc) cascarci

▶ **fall in** vi crollare; (Mil) mettersi in riga

▶ **fall in with** vt fus (sb's plans etc) trovarsi d'accordo con

▶ **fall off** vi cadere; (diminish) diminuire, abbassarsi

▶ **fall out** vi (friends etc) litigare

▶ **fall over** vi cadere

▶ **fall through** vi (plan, project) fallire

fallacy ['fæləsɪ] n errore m

fallback ['fɔːlbæk] adj: ~ **position** posizione f di ripiego

fallen ['fɔːlən] pp of **fall**

fallible ['fælɪbl] adj fallibile

falling ['fɔːlɪŋ] adj: ~ **market** (Comm) mercato in ribasso

falling-off ['fɔːlɪŋ'ɔf] n calo

fallopian tube [fə'ləupɪən-] n (Anat) tuba di Falloppio

fallout ['fɔːlaut] n fall-out m

fallout shelter n rifugio antiatomico

fallow ['fæləu] adj incolto(-a); a maggese

falls [fɔ:lz] *npl* (*waterfall*) cascate *fpl*
false [fɔ:ls] *adj* falso(-a); **under ~ pretences**
con l'inganno
false alarm *n* falso allarme *m*
falsehood ['fɔ:lshud] *n* menzogna
falsely ['fɔ:lslɪ] *adv* (*accuse*) a torto
false teeth *npl* (*Brit*) denti *mpl* finti
falsify ['fɔ:lsɪfaɪ] *vt* falsificare; (*figures*)
alterare
falter ['fɔ:ltə'] *vi* esitare, vacillare
fame [feɪm] *n* fama, celebrità
familiar [fə'mɪlɪə'] *adj* familiare; (*common*)
comune; (*close*) intimo(-a); **to be ~ with**
(*subject*) conoscere; **to make o.s. ~ with**
familiarizzarsi con; **to be on ~ terms with**
essere in confidenza con
familiarity [fəmɪlɪ'ærɪtɪ] *n* familiarità;
intimità
familiarize [fə'mɪlɪəraɪz] *vt*: **to ~ sb with sth**
far conoscere qc a qn
family ['fæmɪlɪ] *n* famiglia
family allowance *n* (*Brit*) assegni *mpl*
familiari
family business *n* impresa familiare
family credit *n* (*Brit*) ≈ assegni *mpl* familiari
family doctor *n* medico di famiglia
family life *n* vita familiare
family man *n* padre *m* di famiglia
family planning clinic *n* consultorio
familiare
family tree *n* albergo genealogico
famine ['fæmɪn] *n* carestia
famished ['fæmɪʃt] *adj* affamato(-a); **I'm ~!**
(*col*) ho una fame da lupo!
famous ['feɪməs] *adj* famoso(-a)
famously ['feɪməslɪ] *adv* (*get on*) a meraviglia
fan [fæn] *n* (*folding*) ventaglio; (*machine*)
ventilatore *m*; (*person*) ammiratore(-trice);
(*Sport*) tifoso(-a) ■ *vt* far vento a; (*fire, quarrel*)
alimentare
▶ **fan out** *vi* spargersi (a ventaglio)
fanatic [fə'nætɪk] *n* fanatico(-a)
fanatical [fə'nætɪkl] *adj* fanatico(-a)
fan belt *n* cinghia del ventilatore
fancied ['fænsɪd] *adj* immaginario(-a)
fanciful ['fænsɪful] *adj* fantasioso(-a); (*object*)
di fantasia
fan club *n* fan club *m inv*
fancy ['fænsɪ] *n* immaginazione *f*, fantasia;
(*whim*) capriccio ■ *cpd* (di) fantasia *inv* ■ *vt*
(*feel like, want*) aver voglia di; (*imagine*)
immaginare, credere; **to take a ~ to**
incapricciarsi di; **it took** *or* **caught my ~** mi
è piaciuto; **when the ~ takes him** quando
ne ha voglia; **to ~ that** immaginare che; **he**
fancies her gli piace
fancy dress *n* costume *m* (per maschera)

fancy-dress ball *n* ballo in maschera
fancy goods *npl* articoli *mpl* di ogni genere
fanfare ['fænfɛə'] *n* fanfara
fanfold paper ['fænfəuld-] *n* carta a moduli
continui
fang [fæŋ] *n* zanna; (*of snake*) dente *m*
fan heater *n* (*Brit*) stufa ad aria calda
fanlight ['fænlaɪt] *n* lunetta
fanny ['fænɪ] *n* (*Brit col!*) figa (!); (*US col*) culo (!)
fantasize ['fæntəsaɪz] *vi* fantasticare,
sognare
fantastic [fæn'tæstɪk] *adj* fantastico(-a)
fantasy ['fæntəsɪ] *n* fantasia,
immaginazione *f*; fantasticheria; chimera
fanzine ['fænziːn] *n* rivista specialistica (*per*
appassionati)
FAO *n abbr* (= *Food and Agriculture Organization*)
FAO *f*
FAQ *abbr* (= *free alongside quay*) franco lungo
banchina; (*Comput*: = *frequently asked*
question(s)) FAQ
far [fɑ:'] *adj*: **the ~ side/end** l'altra parte/
l'altro capo; **the ~ left/right** (*Pol*) l'estrema
sinistra/destra ■ *adv* lontano; **is it ~ to**
London? è lontana Londra?; **it's not ~ (from**
here) non è lontano (da qui); **~ away**, **~ off**
lontano, distante; **~ better** assai migliore; **~**
from lontano da; **by ~** di gran lunga; **as ~**
back as the 13th century già nel duecento;
go as ~ as the farm vada fino alla fattoria;
as ~ as I know per quel che so; **as ~ as**
possible nei limiti del possibile; **how ~ have**
you got with your work? dov'è arrivato con
il suo lavoro?
faraway ['fɑ:rəweɪ] *adj* lontano(-a); (*voice,*
look) assente
farce [fɑ:s] *n* farsa
farcical ['fɑ:sɪkəl] *adj* farsesco(-a)
fare [fɛə'] *n* (*on trains, buses*) tariffa; (*in taxi*)
prezzo della corsa; (*food*) vitto, cibo ■ *vi*
passarsela; **full ~** tariffa completa
Far East *n*: **the ~** l'Estremo Oriente *m*
farewell [fɛə'wɛl] *excl, n* addio ■ *cpd* (*party etc*)
d'addio
far-fetched ['fɑ:'fɛtʃt] *adj* (*explanation*)
stiracchiato(-a), forzato(-a); (*idea, scheme,*
story) inverosimile
farm [fɑ:m] *n* fattoria, podere *m* ■ *vt* coltivare
▶ **farm out** *vt* (*work*) dare in consegna
farmer ['fɑ:mə'] *n* coltivatore(-trice),
agricoltore(-trice)
farmhand ['fɑ:mhænd] *n* bracciante *m*
agricolo
farmhouse ['fɑ:mhaus] *n* fattoria
farming ['fɑ:mɪŋ] *n* agricoltura; **intensive ~**
coltura intensiva; **sheep ~** allevamento di
pecore

f

farm labourer n = **farmhand**
farmland ['fɑːmlænd] n terreno da coltivare
farm produce n prodotti mpl agricoli
farm worker n = **farmhand**
farmyard ['fɑːmjɑːd] n aia
Faroe Islands ['fɛərəu-], **Faroes** ['fɛərəuz] npl: **the ~** le isole Faeroer
far-reaching ['fɑːˈriːtʃɪŋ] adj di vasta portata
far-sighted ['fɑːˈsaɪtɪd] adj presbite; (fig) lungimirante
fart [fɑːt] (col!) n scoreggia (!) ▪ vi scoreggiare (!)
farther ['fɑːðəʳ] adv più lontano ▪ adj più lontano(-a)
farthest ['fɑːðɪst] adv superlative of **far**
FAS abbr (Brit: = free alongside ship) franco banchina nave
fascia ['feɪʃɪə] n (Aut) cruscotto; (of mobile phone) mascherina
fascinate ['fæsɪneɪt] vt affascinare
fascinating ['fæsɪneɪtɪŋ] adj affascinante
fascination [fæsɪˈneɪʃən] n fascino
fascism ['fæʃɪzəm] n fascismo
fascist ['fæʃɪst] adj, n fascista m/f
fashion ['fæʃən] n moda; (manner) maniera, modo ▪ vt foggiare, formare; **in ~** alla moda; **out of ~** passato(a) di moda; **after a ~** (finish, manage etc) così così; **in the Greek ~** alla greca
fashionable ['fæʃənəbl] adj alla moda, di moda; (writer) di grido
fashion designer n disegnatore(-trice) di moda
fashionista [fæʃəˈnɪstə] n fashionista m/f, maniaco(-a) della moda
fashion show n sfilata di moda
fast [fɑːst] adj rapido(-a), svelto(-a), veloce; (clock): **to be ~** andare avanti; (dye, colour) solido(-a) ▪ adv rapidamente; (stuck, held) saldamente ▪ n digiuno ▪ vi digiunare; **~ asleep** profondamente addormentato; **as ~ as I can** più in fretta possibile; **my watch is 5 minutes ~** il mio orologio va avanti di 5 minuti
fasten ['fɑːsn] vt chiudere, fissare; (coat) abbottonare, allacciare ▪ vi chiudersi, fissarsi; abbottonarsi, allacciarsi
▸ **fasten (up)on** vt fus (idea) cogliere al volo
fastener ['fɑːsnəʳ], **fastening** ['fɑːsnɪŋ] n fermaglio, chiusura; (Brit: zip fastener) chiusura lampo
fast food n fast food m inv
fastidious [fæsˈtɪdɪəs] adj esigente, difficile
fast lane n (Aut) ≈ corsia di sorpasso
fat [fæt] adj grasso(-a) ▪ n grasso; **to live off the ~ of the land** vivere nel lusso, avere ogni ben di Dio
fatal ['feɪtl] adj fatale; mortale; disastroso(-a)

fatalism ['feɪtəlɪzəm] n fatalismo
fatality [fəˈtælɪtɪ] n morto(-a), vittima
fatally ['feɪtəlɪ] adv a morte
fate [feɪt] n destino; (of person) sorte f; **to meet one's ~** trovare la morte
fated ['feɪtɪd] adj (governed by fate) destinato(-a); (person, project etc) destinato(-a) a finire male
fateful ['feɪtful] adj fatidico(-a)
fat-free ['fætfriː] adj senza grassi
father ['fɑːðəʳ] n padre m
Father Christmas n Babbo Natale
fatherhood ['fɑːðəhuːd] n paternità
father-in-law ['fɑːðərɪnlɔː] n suocero
fatherland ['fɑːðəlænd] n patria
fatherly ['fɑːðəlɪ] adj paterno(-a)
fathom ['fæðəm] n braccio (= 1828 mm) ▪ vt (mystery) penetrare, sondare
fatigue [fəˈtiːg] n stanchezza; (Mil) corvé f; **metal ~** fatica del metallo
fatness ['fætnɪs] n grassezza
fatten ['fætn] vt, vi ingrassare; **chocolate is fattening** la cioccolata fa ingrassare
fatty ['fætɪ] adj (food) grasso(-a) ▪ n (col) ciccione(-a)
fatuous ['fætjuəs] adj fatuo(-a)
faucet ['fɔːsɪt] n (US) rubinetto
fault [fɔːlt] n colpa; (Tennis) fallo; (defect) difetto; (Geo) faglia ▪ vt criticare; **it's my ~** è colpa mia; **to find ~ with** trovare da ridire su; **at ~** in fallo; **generous to a ~** eccessivamente generoso
faultless ['fɔːltlɪs] adj perfetto(-a); senza difetto; impeccabile
faulty ['fɔːltɪ] adj difettoso(-a)
fauna ['fɔːnə] n fauna
faux pas [fəuˈpɑː] n gaffe f inv
favour, (US) **favor** ['feɪvəʳ] n favore m ▪ vt (proposition) favorire, essere favorevole a; (pupil etc) favorire; (team, horse) dare per vincente; **to do sb a ~** fare un favore or una cortesia a qn; **in ~ of** in favore di; **to be in ~ of sth/of doing sth** essere favorevole a qc/a fare qc; **to find ~ with sb** (person) entrare nelle buone grazie di qn; (suggestion) avere l'approvazione di qn
favourable, (US) **favorable** ['feɪvərəbl] adj favorevole
favourably, (US) **favorably** ['feɪvərəblɪ] adv favorevolmente
favourite, (US) **favorite** ['feɪvrɪt] adj, n favorito(-a)
favouritism, (US) **favoritism** ['feɪvrɪtɪzəm] n favoritismo
fawn [fɔːn] n daino ▪ adj (also: **fawn-coloured**) marrone chiaro inv ▪ vi: **to ~ (up)on** adulare servilmente

fax [fæks] n (document, machine) facsimile m inv ▪ vt teletrasmettere, spedire in facsimile

FBI n abbr (US: = Federal Bureau of Investigation) FBI f

FCC n abbr (US) = **Federal Communications Commission**

FCO n abbr (Brit: = Foreign and Commonwealth Office) ≈ Ufficio affari esteri

FD n abbr (US) = **fire department**

FDA n abbr (US) = **Food and Drug Administration**

FE n abbr = **further education**

fear [fɪər] n paura, timore m ▪ vt aver paura di, temere ▪ vi: **to ~ for** temere per, essere in ansia per; **~ of heights** vertigini fpl; **for ~ of** per paura di; **to ~ that** avere paura di (or che +sub), temere di (or che +sub)

fearful ['fɪəful] adj pauroso(-a); (sight, noise) terribile, spaventoso(-a); (frightened): **to be ~ of** temere

fearfully ['fɪəfəlɪ] adv (timidly) timorosamente; (col: very) terribilmente, spaventosamente

fearless ['fɪəlɪs] adj intrepido(-a), senza paura

fearsome ['fɪəsəm] adj (opponent) formidabile, terribile; (sight) terrificante

feasibility [fiːzə'bɪlɪtɪ] n praticabilità

feasibility study n studio delle possibilità di realizzazione

feasible ['fiːzəbl] adj fattibile, realizzabile

feast [fiːst] n festa, banchetto; (Rel: also: **feast day**) festa ▪ vi banchettare; **to ~ on** godersi, gustare

feat [fiːt] n impresa, fatto insigne

feather ['fɛðər] n penna ▪ cpd (mattress, bed, pillow) di piume ▪ vt: **to ~ one's nest** (fig) arricchirsi

feather-weight ['fɛðəweɪt] n peso m piuma inv

feature ['fiːtʃər] n caratteristica; (article) articolo ▪ vt (film) avere come protagonista ▪ vi figurare; **features** npl (of face) fisionomia; **a (special) ~ on sth/sb** un servizio speciale su qc/qn; **it featured prominently in ...** ha avuto un posto di prima importanza in ...

feature film n film m inv principale

featureless ['fiːtʃəlɪs] adj anonimo(-a), senza caratteri distinti

Feb. [fɛb] abbr (= February) febb.

February ['fɛbruərɪ] n febbraio; see also **July**

feces ['fiːsiːz] npl (US) = **faeces**

feckless ['fɛklɪs] adj irresponsabile, incosciente

Fed [fɛd] abbr (US) = **federal; federation**

fed [fɛd] pt, pp of **feed; to be fed up** essere stufo(-a)

Fed. [fɛd] n abbr (US col) = **Federal Reserve Board**

federal ['fɛdərəl] adj federale

Federal Republic of Germany n Repubblica Federale Tedesca

Federal Reserve Board n (US) organo di controllo del sistema bancario statunitense

Federal Trade Commission n (US) organismo di protezione contro le pratiche commerciali abusive

federation [fɛdə'reɪʃən] n federazione f

fee [fiː] n pagamento; (of doctor, lawyer) onorario; (for examination) tassa d'esame; **school fees** tasse fpl scolastiche; **entrance ~, membership ~** quota d'iscrizione; **for a small ~** per una somma modesta

feeble ['fiːbl] adj debole

feeble-minded [fiːbl'maɪndɪd] adj deficiente

feed [fiːd] n (of baby) pappa ▪ vt (pt, pp **fed**) [fɛd] nutrire; (horse etc) dare da mangiare a; (fire, machine) alimentare ▪ vi (baby, animal) mangiare; **to ~ material into sth** introdurre materiale in qc; **to ~ data/ information into sth** inserire dati/ informazioni in qc

▸ **feed back** vt (results) riferire

▸ **feed on** vt fus nutrirsi di

feedback ['fiːdbæk] n feed-back m; (from person) reazioni fpl

feeder ['fiːdər] n (bib) bavaglino

feeding bottle ['fiːdɪŋ-] n (Brit) biberon m inv

feel [fiːl] n sensazione f; (sense of touch) tatto; (of substance) consistenza ▪ vt (pt, pp **felt**) [fɛlt] toccare; palpare; tastare; (cold, pain, anger) sentire; (grief) provare; (think, believe): **to ~ that** pensare che; **I ~ that you ought to do it** penso che dovreste farlo; **to ~ hungry/ cold** aver fame/freddo; **to ~ lonely/better** sentirsi solo/meglio; **I don't ~ well** non mi sento bene; **to ~ sorry for** dispiacersi per; **it feels soft** è morbido al tatto; **it feels colder out here** sembra più freddo qui fuori; **it feels like velvet** sembra velluto (al tatto); **to ~ like** (want) aver voglia di; **to ~ about or around for** cercare a tastoni; **to ~ about or around in one's pocket for** frugarsi in tasca per cercare; **I'm still feeling my way** (fig) sto ancora tastando il terreno; **to get the ~ of sth** (fig) abituarsi a qc

feeler ['fiːlər] n (of insect) antenna; **to put out feelers** (fig) fare un sondaggio

feelgood ['fiːlgud] adj (film, song) allegro(-a) e a lieto fine

feeling ['fiːlɪŋ] n sensazione f; sentimento; (impression) senso, impressione f; **to hurt sb's feelings** offendere qn; **what are your feelings about the matter?** che cosa ne pensa?; **my ~ is that ...** ho l'impressione

f

che ...; **I got the ~ that** ... ho avuto l'impressione che ...; **feelings ran high about it** la cosa aveva provocato grande eccitazione

fee-paying school ['fi:peɪɪŋ-] n scuola privata

feet [fi:t] npl of **foot**

feign [feɪn] vt fingere, simulare

felicitous [fɪ'lɪsɪtəs] adj felice

fell [fɛl] pt of **fall** ■ vt (tree) abbattere; (person) atterrare ■ adj: **with one ~ blow** con un colpo terribile; **at one ~ swoop** in un colpo solo ■ n (Brit: mountain) monte m; (: moorland): **the fells** la brughiera

fellow ['fɛləu] n individuo, tipo; (comrade) compagno; (of learned society) membro; (of university) ≈ docente m/f ■ cpd: **their ~ prisoners/students** i loro compagni di prigione/studio

fellow citizen n concittadino(-a)

fellow countryman n compatriota m

fellow feeling n simpatia

fellow men npl simili mpl

fellowship ['fɛləuʃɪp] n associazione f; compagnia; (Scol) specie di borsa di studio universitaria

fellow traveller n compagno(-a) di viaggio; (Pol) simpatizzante m/f

fell-walking ['fɛlwɔ:kɪŋ] n (Brit) passeggiate fpl in montagna

felon ['fɛlən] n (Law) criminale m/f

felony ['fɛlənɪ] n (Law) reato, crimine m

felt [fɛlt] pt, pp of **feel** ■ n feltro

felt-tip pen ['fɛlttɪp-] n pennarello

female ['fi:meɪl] n (Zool) femmina; (pej: woman) donna, femmina ■ adj femminile; (Biol, Elec) femmina inv; **male and ~ students** studenti e studentesse

female impersonator n (Theat) attore comico che fa parti da donna

feminine ['fɛmɪnɪn] adj, n femminile (m)

femininity [fɛmɪ'nɪnɪtɪ] n femminilità

feminism ['fɛmɪnɪzəm] n femminismo

feminist ['fɛmɪnɪst] n femminista m/f

fen [fɛn] n (Brit): **the Fens** la regione delle Fen

fence [fɛns] n recinto; (Sport) ostacolo; (col: person) ricettatore(-trice) ■ vt (also: **fence in**) recingere ■ vi schermire; **to sit on the ~** (fig) rimanere neutrale

fencing ['fɛnsɪŋ] n (Sport) scherma

fend [fɛnd] vi: **to ~ for o.s.** arrangiarsi

▶ **fend off** vt (attack, attacker) respingere, difendersi da; (blow) parare; (awkward question) eludere

fender ['fɛndə'] n parafuoco; (US) parafango; paraurti m inv

fennel ['fɛnl] n finocchio

ferment vi [fə'mɛnt] fermentare ■ n ['fə:mɛnt] agitazione f, eccitazione f

fermentation [fə:mɛn'teɪʃən] n fermentazione f

fern [fə:n] n felce f

ferocious [fə'rəuʃəs] adj feroce

ferocity [fə'rɔsɪtɪ] n ferocità

ferret ['fɛrɪt] n furetto

▶ **ferret about, ferret around** vi frugare

▶ **ferret out** vt (person) scovare, scoprire; (secret, truth) scoprire

ferry ['fɛrɪ] n (small) traghetto; (large: also: **ferryboat**) nave f traghetto inv ■ vt traghettare; **to ~ sth/sb across** or **over** traghettare qc/qn da una parte all'altra

ferryman ['fɛrɪmən] n traghettatore m

fertile ['fə:taɪl] adj fertile; (Biol) fecondo(-a); **~ period** periodo di fecondità

fertility [fə'tɪlɪtɪ] n fertilità; fecondità

fertility drug n farmaco fecondativo

fertilize ['fə:tɪlaɪz] vt fertilizzare; fecondare

fertilizer ['fə:tɪlaɪzə'] n fertilizzante m

fervent ['fə:vənt] adj ardente, fervente

fervour, (US) **fervor** ['fə:və'] n fervore m, ardore m

fester ['fɛstə'] vi suppurare

festival ['fɛstɪvəl] n (Rel) festa; (Art, Mus) festival m inv

festive ['fɛstɪv] adj di festa; **the ~ season** (Brit: Christmas) il periodo delle feste

festivities [fɛs'tɪvɪtɪz] npl festeggiamenti mpl

festoon [fɛ'stu:n] vt: **to ~ with** ornare di; decorare con

fetch [fɛtʃ] vt andare a prendere; (sell for) essere venduto(-a) per; **how much did it ~?** a or per quanto lo ha venduto?

▶ **fetch up** vi (Brit) andare a finire

fetching ['fɛtʃɪŋ] adj attraente

fête [feɪt] n festa

fetid ['fɛtɪd] adj fetido(-a)

fetish ['fɛtɪʃ] n feticcio

fetter ['fɛtə'] vt (person) incatenare; (horse) legare; (fig) ostacolare

fetters ['fɛtəz] npl catene fpl

fettle ['fɛtl] n (Brit): **in fine ~** in gran forma

fetus ['fi:təs] n (US) = **foetus**

feud [fju:d] n contesa, lotta ■ vi essere in lotta; **a family ~** una lite in famiglia

feudal ['fju:dl] adj feudale

feudalism ['fju:dəlɪzəm] n feudalesimo

fever ['fi:və'] n febbre f; **he has a ~** ha la febbre

feverish ['fi:vərɪʃ] adj (also fig) febbrile; (person) febbricitante

few [fju:] adj pochi(-e) ■ pron alcuni(-e); **~ succeed** pochi ci riescono; **they were ~** erano pochi; **a ~ ...** qualche ...; **I know a ~**

ne conosco alcuni; **a good ~, quite a ~** parecchi; **in the next ~ days** nei prossimi giorni; **in the past ~ days** negli ultimi giorni, in questi ultimi giorni; **every ~ days/ months** ogni due o tre giorni/mesi; **a ~ more days** qualche altro giorno

fewer ['fjuːəʳ] adj meno inv; meno numerosi(-e) ▪ pron meno; **they are ~ now** adesso ce ne sono di meno

fewest ['fjuːɪst] adj il minor numero di

FFA n abbr = **Future Farmers of America**

FH abbr (Brit) = **fire hydrant**

FHA n abbr (US) = **Federal Housing Administration**

fiancé [fɪ'ɑ̃ːŋseɪ] n fidanzato

fiancée [fɪ'ɑ̃ːŋseɪ] n fidanzata

fiasco [fɪ'æskəʊ] n fiasco

fib [fɪb] n piccola bugia

fibre, (US) **fiber** ['faɪbəʳ] n fibra

fibreboard, (US) **fiberboard** ['faɪbəbɔːd] n pannello di fibre

fibre-glass, (US) **fiber-glass** ['faɪbəglɑːs] n fibra di vetro

fibrositis [faɪbrə'saɪtɪs] n cellulite f

FICA n abbr (US) = **Federal Insurance Contributions Act**

fickle ['fɪkl] adj incostante, capriccioso(-a)

fiction ['fɪkʃən] n narrativa; (sth made up) finzione f

fictional ['fɪkʃənl] adj immaginario(-a)

fictionalize ['fɪkʃənəlaɪz] vt romanzare

fictitious [fɪk'tɪʃəs] adj fittizio(-a)

fiddle ['fɪdl] n (Mus) violino; (cheating) imbroglio; truffa ▪ vt (Brit: accounts) falsificare, falsare; **tax ~** frode f fiscale; **to work a ~** fare un imbroglio
  ▶ **fiddle with** vt fus gingillarsi con

fiddler ['fɪdləʳ] n violinista m/f

fiddly ['fɪdlɪ] adj (task) da certosino; (object) complesso(-a)

fidelity [fɪ'dɛlɪtɪ] n fedeltà; (accuracy) esattezza

fidget ['fɪdʒɪt] vi agitarsi

fidgety ['fɪdʒɪtɪ] adj agitato(-a)

fiduciary [fɪ'duːʃɪərɪ] n fiduciario

field [fiːld] n (gen, Comput) campo; **to lead the ~** (Sport, Comm) essere in testa, essere al primo posto; **to have a ~ day** (fig) divertirsi, spassarsela

field glasses npl binocolo (da campagna)

field hospital n ospedale m da campo

field marshal n feldmaresciallo

fieldwork ['fiːldwəːk] n ricerche fpl esterne; (Archeology, Geo) lavoro sul campo

fiend [fiːnd] n demonio

fiendish ['fiːndɪʃ] adj demoniaco(-a)

fierce [fɪəs] adj (look, fighting) fiero(-a); (wind)

furioso(-a); (attack) feroce; (enemy) acerrimo(-a)

fiery ['faɪərɪ] adj ardente; infocato(-a)

FIFA ['fiːfə] n abbr (= Fédération Internationale de Football Association) F.I.F.A. f

fifteen [fɪf'tiːn] num quindici

fifth [fɪfθ] num quinto(-a)

fiftieth ['fɪftɪɪθ] num cinquantesimo(-a)

fifty ['fɪftɪ] num cinquanta

fifty-fifty ['fɪftɪ'fɪftɪ] adj, adv: **to go ~ with sb** fare a metà con qn; **we have a ~ chance of success** abbiamo una probabilità su due di successo

fig [fɪg] n fico

fight [faɪt] n zuffa, rissa; (Mil) battaglia, combattimento; (against cancer etc) lotta ▪ vb (pt, pp **fought**) [fɔːt] vt combattere; (cancer, alcoholism) lottare contro, combattere; (Law: case) difendere ▪ vi battersi, combattere; (quarrel): **to ~ (with sb)** litigare (con qn); (fig): **to ~ (for/against)** lottare (per/contro)
  ▶ **fight back** vi difendersi; (Sport, after illness) riprendersi ▪ vt (tears) ricacciare
  ▶ **fight down** vt (anger, anxiety) vincere; (urge) reprimere
  ▶ **fight off** vt (attack, attacker) respingere; (disease, sleep, urge) lottare contro
  ▶ **fight out** vt: **to ~ it out** risolvere la questione a pugni

fighter ['faɪtəʳ] n combattente m; (plane) aeroplano da caccia

fighter-bomber ['faɪtəbɔməʳ] n cacciabombardiere m

fighter pilot n pilota m di caccia

fighting ['faɪtɪŋ] n combattimento; (in streets) scontri mpl

figment ['fɪgmənt] n: **a ~ of the imagination** un parto della fantasia

figurative ['fɪgjurətɪv] adj figurato(-a)

figure ['fɪgəʳ] n (Drawing, Geom, person) figura; (number, cipher) cifra; (body, outline) forma ▪ vi (appear) figurare; (US: make sense) spiegarsi; essere logico(-a) ▪ vt (US: think, calculate) pensare, immaginare; **public ~** personaggio pubblico; **~ of speech** figura retorica
  ▶ **figure on** vt fus (US) contare su
  ▶ **figure out** vt riuscire a capire; calcolare

figurehead ['fɪgəhɛd] n (Naut) polena; (pej) prestanome m/f inv

figure skating n pattinaggio artistico

Fiji ['fiːdʒiː] n, **Fiji Islands** npl le (isole) Figi

filament ['fɪləmənt] n filamento

filch [fɪltʃ] vt (col: steal) grattare

file [faɪl] n (tool) lima; (for nails) limetta; (dossier) incartamento; (in cabinet) scheda; (folder) cartellina; (for loose leaf) raccoglitore m; (row) fila; (Comput) archivio, file m inv ▪ vt

559

(*nails, wood*) limare; (*papers*) archiviare; (*Law: claim*) presentare ■ *vi:* **to ~ in/out** entrare/uscire in fila; **to ~ past** marciare in fila davanti a; **to ~ a suit against sb** intentare causa contro qn

file name *n* (*Comput*) nome *m* del file

filibuster ['fɪlɪbʌstə'] *n* (*also:* **filibusterer**) ostruzionista *m/f* ■ *vi* fare ostruzionismo

filing ['faɪlɪŋ] *n* archiviare *m*; *see also* **filings**

filing cabinet *n* casellario

filing clerk *n* archivista *m/f*

filings ['faɪlɪŋz] *npl* limatura

Filipino [fɪlɪ'piːnəu] *n* filippino(-a); (*Ling*) tagal *m*

fill [fɪl] *vt* riempire; (*tooth*) otturare; (*job*) coprire; (*supply: order, requirements, need*) soddisfare ■ *n:* **to eat one's ~** mangiare a sazietà; **we've already filled that vacancy** abbiamo già assunto qualcuno per quel posto

▶ **fill in** *vt* (*hole*) riempire; (*form*) compilare; (*details, report*) completare ■ *vi:* **to ~ in for sb** sostituire qn; **to ~ sb in on sth** (*col*) mettere qn al corrente di qc

▶ **fill out** *vt* (*form, receipt*) riempire

▶ **fill up** *vt* riempire ■ *vi* (*Aut*) fare il pieno; **~ it up, please** (*Aut*) mi faccia il pieno, per piacere

fillet ['fɪlɪt] *n* filetto

fillet steak *n* bistecca di filetto

filling ['fɪlɪŋ] *n* (*Culin*) impasto, ripieno; (*for tooth*) otturazione *f*

filling station *n* stazione *f* di rifornimento

fillip ['fɪlɪp] *n* incentivo, stimolo

filly ['fɪlɪ] *n* puledra

film [fɪlm] *n* (*Cine*) film *m inv*; (*Phot*) pellicola; (*thin layer*) velo ■ *vt* (*scene*) filmare

film script *n* copione *m*

film star *n* divo(-a) dello schermo

filmstrip ['fɪlmstrɪp] *n* filmina

film studio *n* studio cinematografico

Filofax® ['faɪləufæks] *n* agenda ad anelli

filter ['fɪltə'] *n* filtro ■ *vt* filtrare

▶ **filter in, filter through** *vi* (*news*) trapelare

filter coffee *n* caffè *m* da passare al filtro

filter lane *n* (*Brit Aut*) corsia di svincolo

filter tip *n* filtro

filth [fɪlθ] *n* sporcizia; (*fig*) oscenità

filthy ['fɪlθɪ] *adj* lordo(-a), sozzo(-a); (*language*) osceno(-a)

fin [fɪn] *n* (*of fish*) pinna

final ['faɪnl] *adj* finale, ultimo(-a); definitivo(-a) ■ *n* (*Sport*) finale *f*; **finals** *npl* (*Scol*) esami *mpl* finali; **~ demand** ingiunzione *f* di pagamento

finale [fɪ'nɑːlɪ] *n* finale *m*

finalist ['faɪnəlɪst] *n* (*Sport*) finalista *m/f*

finality [faɪ'nælɪtɪ] *n* irrevocabilità; **with an air of ~** con risolutezza

finalize ['faɪnəlaɪz] *vt* mettere a punto

finally ['faɪnlɪ] *adv* (*lastly*) alla fine; (*eventually*) finalmente; (*once and for all*) definitivamente

finance [faɪ'næns] *n* finanza; (*funds*) fondi *mpl*, capitale *m* ■ *vt* finanziare; **finances** *npl* finanze *fpl*

financial [faɪ'nænʃəl] *adj* finanziario(-a); **~ statement** estratto conto finanziario

financial adviser *n* consulente *m/f* finanziario(-a)

financially [faɪ'nænʃəlɪ] *adv* finanziariamente

financial year *n* anno finanziario, esercizio finanziario

financier [faɪ'nænsɪə'] *n* finanziatore *m*

find [faɪnd] *vt* (*pt, pp* **found**) [faund] trovare; (*lost object*) ritrovare ■ *n* trovata, scoperta; **to ~ (some) difficulty in doing sth** trovare delle difficoltà nel fare qc; **to ~ sb guilty** (*Law*) giudicare qn colpevole

▶ **find out** *vt* informarsi di; (*truth, secret*) scoprire; (*person*) cogliere in fallo ■ *vi:* **to ~ out about** informarsi su; (*by chance*) venire a sapere

findings ['faɪndɪŋz] *npl* (*Law*) sentenza, conclusioni *fpl*; (*of report*) conclusioni

fine [faɪn] *adj* bello(-a); ottimo(-a); (*thin, subtle*) fine ■ *adv* (*well*) molto bene; (*small*) finemente ■ *n* (*Law*) multa ■ *vt* (*Law*) multare; **he's ~** sta bene; **the weather is ~** il tempo è bello; **you're doing ~** te la cavi benissimo; **to cut it ~** (*with time, money*) farcela per un pelo

fine arts *npl* belle arti *fpl*

finely ['faɪnlɪ] *adv* (*splendidly*) in modo stupendo; (*chop*) finemente; (*adjust*) con precisione

fine print *n:* **the ~** i caratteri minuti

finery ['faɪnərɪ] *n* abiti *mpl* eleganti

finesse [fɪ'nɛs] *n* finezza

fine-tooth comb ['faɪntuː θ-] *n:* **to go through sth with a ~** (*fig*) passare qc al setaccio

finger ['fɪŋgə'] *n* dito ■ *vt* toccare, tastare

fingernail ['fɪŋgəneɪl] *n* unghia

fingerprint ['fɪŋgəprɪnt] *n* impronta digitale ■ *vt* (*person*) prendere le impronte digitali di

fingerstall ['fɪŋgəstɔːl] *n* ditale *m*

fingertip ['fɪŋgətɪp] *n* punta del dito; **to have sth at one's fingertips** (*fig*) avere qc sulla punta delle dita

finicky ['fɪnɪkɪ] *adj* esigente, pignolo(-a); minuzioso(-a)

finish ['fɪnɪʃ] *n* fine *f*; (*Sport: place*) traguardo;

(polish etc) finitura ■ *vt* finire; *(use up)*
esaurire ■ *vi* finire; *(session)* terminare; **to ~
doing sth** finire di fare qc; **to ~ first/second**
(Sport) arrivare primo/secondo; **she's
finished with him** ha chiuso con lui
▶ **finish off** *vt* compiere; *(kill)* uccidere
▶ **finish up** *vi, vt* finire
finished ['fɪnɪʃt] *adj (product)* finito(-a);
(performance) perfetto(-a); *(col: tired)* sfinito(-a)
finishing line ['fɪnɪʃɪŋ-] *n* linea d'arrivo
finishing school *n* scuola privata di
perfezionamento *(per signorine)*
finishing touches *npl* ultimi ritocchi *mpl*
finite ['faɪnaɪt] *adj* limitato(-a); *(verb)* finito(-a)
Finland ['fɪnlənd] *n* Finlandia
Finn [fɪn] *n* finlandese *m/f*
Finnish ['fɪnɪʃ] *adj* finlandese ■ *n (Ling)*
finlandese *m*
fiord [fjɔːd] *n* fiordo
fir [fəːʳ] *n* abete *m*
fire [faɪəʳ] *n* fuoco; incendio ■ *vt (discharge)*:
to ~ a gun scaricare un fucile; *(fig)*
infiammare; *(dismiss)* licenziare ■ *vi*
sparare, far fuoco; **on ~** in fiamme; **insured
against ~** assicurato contro gli incendi;
electric/gas ~ stufa elettrica/a gas; **to set ~
to sth, set sth on ~** dar fuoco a qc,
incendiare qc; **to be/come under ~ (from)**
essere/finire sotto il fuoco *or* il tiro (di)
fire alarm *n* allarme *m* d'incendio
firearm ['faɪərɑːm] *n* arma da fuoco
fire brigade *n (Brit)* (corpo dei) pompieri *mpl*
fire chief *n (US)* = **fire master**
fire department *n (US)* = **fire brigade**
fire door *n* porta *f* rompifuoco *inv*
fire drill *n* esercitazione *f* antincendio
fire engine *n* autopompa
fire escape *n* scala di sicurezza
fire extinguisher *n* estintore *m*
fireguard ['faɪəgɑːd] *n (Brit)* parafuoco
fire hazard *n*: **that's a ~** comporta rischi in
caso d'incendio
fire hydrant *n* idrante *m*
fire insurance *n* assicurazione *f* contro gli
incendi
fireman ['faɪəmən] *n* pompiere *m*
fire master *n (Brit)* comandante *m* dei vigili
del fuoco
fireplace ['faɪəpleɪs] *n* focolare *m*
fireplug ['faɪəplʌg] *n (US)* = **fire hydrant**
fire practice *n* = **fire drill**
fireproof ['faɪəpruːf] *adj* resistente al fuoco
fire regulations *npl* norme *fpl* antincendio
fire screen *n* parafuoco
fireside ['faɪəsaɪd] *n* angolo del focolare
fire station *n* caserma dei pompieri
firewall ['faɪəwɔːl] *n* firewall *m inv*

firewood ['faɪəwud] *n* legna
firework ['faɪəwəːk] *n* fuoco d'artificio
firing ['faɪərɪŋ] *n (Mil)* spari *mpl*, tiro
firing line *n* linea del fuoco; **to be in the ~**
(fig) essere sotto tiro
firing squad *n* plotone *m* d'esecuzione
firm [fəːm] *adj* fermo(-a); *(offer, decision)*
definitivo(-a) ■ *n* ditta, azienda; **to be a ~
believer in sth** credere fermamente in qc
firmly ['fəːmlɪ] *adv* fermamente
firmness ['fəːmnɪs] *n* fermezza
first [fəːst] *adj* primo(-a) ■ *adv (before others)* il
primo, la prima; *(before other things)* per primo;
(for the first time) per la prima volta; *(when
listing reasons etc)* per prima cosa ■ *n (person: in
race)* primo(-a); *(Brit Scol)* laurea con lode;
(Aut) prima; **at ~** dapprima, all'inizio; **~ of
all** prima di tutto; **in the ~ instance** prima
di tutto, in primo luogo; **I'll do it ~ thing
tomorrow** lo farò per prima cosa domani;
from the (very) ~ fin dall'inizio, fin dal
primo momento; **the ~ of January** il primo
(di) gennaio
first aid *n* pronto soccorso
first-aid kit ['fəːst'eɪd-] *n* cassetta pronto
soccorso
first-class ['fəːst'klɑːs] *adj* di prima classe
first-class mail *n* ≈ espresso
first-hand ['fəːst'hænd] *adj* di prima mano;
diretto(-a)
first lady *n (US)* moglie *f* del presidente
firstly ['fəːstlɪ] *adv* in primo luogo
first name *n* nome *m* di battesimo
first night *n (Theat)* prima
first-rate ['fəːst'reɪt] *adj* di prima qualità,
ottimo(-a)
first-time buyer ['fəːsttaɪm-] *n* acquirente
m/f di prima casa
First World War *n*: **the ~** la prima guerra
mondiale
fir tree *n* abete *m*
fiscal ['fɪskəl] *adj* fiscale; **~ year** anno fiscale
fish [fɪʃ] *n (pl inv)* pesce *m* ■ *vt, vi* pescare; **to ~
a river** pescare in un fiume; **to go fishing**
andare a pesca
▶ **fish out** *vt (from water)* ripescare; *(from box
etc)* tirare fuori
fish-and-chip shop [fɪʃən'tʃɪp-] *n*
≈ friggitoria; *see* **chip shop**
fishbone ['fɪʃbəun] *n* lisca, spina
fisherman ['fɪʃəmən] *n* pescatore *m*
fishery ['fɪʃərɪ] *n* zona da pesca
fish factory *n (Brit)* fabbrica per la
lavorazione del pesce
fish farm *n* vivaio
fish fingers *npl (Brit)* bastoncini *mpl* di pesce
(surgelati)

561

fish hook n amo
fishing boat ['fɪʃɪŋ-] n barca da pesca
fishing industry n industria della pesca
fishing line n lenza
fishing net n rete f da pesca
fishing rod n canna da pesca
fishing tackle n attrezzatura da pesca
fish market n mercato del pesce
fishmonger ['fɪʃmʌŋgəʳ] n pescivendolo;
~**'s (shop)** pescheria
fish slice n (Brit) posata per servire il pesce
fish sticks npl (US) = **fish fingers**
fishy ['fɪʃɪ] adj (fig) sospetto(-a)
fission ['fɪʃən] n fissione f; **atomic/nuclear** ~
fissione atomica/nucleare
fissure ['fɪʃəʳ] n fessura
fist [fɪst] n pugno
fistfight ['fɪstfaɪt] n scazzottata
fit [fɪt] adj (Med, Sport) in forma; (proper)
adatto(-a), appropriato(-a); conveniente
■ vt (clothes) stare bene a; (match: facts etc)
concordare con; (: description) corrispondere a;
(adjust) aggiustare; (put in, attach) mettere;
installare; (equip) fornire, equipaggiare
■ vi (clothes) stare bene; (parts) andare bene,
adattarsi; (in space, gap) entrare ■ n (Med)
attacco; ~ **to** in grado di; ~ **for** adatto(a) a;
degno(a) di; **to keep** ~ tenersi in forma; ~
for work (after illness) in grado di riprendere
il lavoro; **do as you think** or **see** ~ faccia
come meglio crede; **this dress is a tight/
good** ~ questo vestito è stretto/sta bene;
~ **of anger/enthusiasm** accesso d'ira/
d'entusiasmo; **to have a** ~ (Med) avere un
attacco di convulsioni; (col) andare su tutte
le furie; **by fits and starts** a sbalzi
▶ **fit in** vi accordarsi; adattarsi ■ vt (object)
far entrare; (fig: appointment, visitor) trovare il
tempo per; **to** ~ **in with sb's plans** adattarsi
ai progetti di qn
▶ **fit out** vt (Brit: also: **fit up**) equipaggiare
fitful ['fɪtful] adj saltuario(-a)
fitment ['fɪtmənt] n componibile m
fitness ['fɪtnɪs] n (Med) forma fisica;
(of remark) appropriatezza
fitted ['fɪtɪd] adj: ~ **carpet** moquette f inv;
~ **cupboards** armadi mpl a muro; ~ **kitchen**
(Brit) cucina componibile
fitter ['fɪtəʳ] n aggiustatore m or montatore m
meccanico; (Dressmaking) sarto(-a)
fitting ['fɪtɪŋ] adj appropriato(-a) ■ n
(of dress) prova; (of piece of equipment)
montaggio, aggiustaggio; see also **fittings**
fitting room n (in shop) camerino
fittings ['fɪtɪŋz] npl impianti mpl
five [faɪv] num cinque
five-day week ['faɪvdeɪ-] n settimana di 5
giorni (lavorativi)

fiver ['faɪvəʳ] n (col: Brit) biglietto da cinque
sterline; (: US) biglietto da cinque dollari
fix [fɪks] vt fissare; (mend) riparare; (make
ready: meal, drink) preparare ■ n: **to be in a** ~
essere nei guai; **the fight was a** ~ (col)
l'incontro è stato truccato
▶ **fix up** vt (arrange: date, meeting) fissare,
stabilire; **to** ~ **sb up with sth** procurare
qc a qn
fixation [fɪk'seɪʃən] n (Psych, fig) fissazione f,
ossessione f
fixed [fɪkst] adj (prices etc) fisso(-a); **there's a**
~ **charge** c'è una quota fissa; **how are you** ~
for money? (col) a soldi come stai?
fixed assets npl beni mpl patrimoniali
fixed penalty, fixed penalty fine n
contravvenzione f a importo fisso
fixture ['fɪkstʃəʳ] n impianto (fisso); (Sport)
incontro (del calendario sportivo)
fizz [fɪz] vi frizzare
fizzle ['fɪzl] vi frizzare; (also: **fizzle out**:
enthusiasm, interest) smorzarsi, svanire; (: plan)
fallire
fizzy ['fɪzɪ] adj frizzante; gassato(-a)
fjord [fjɔːd] n = **fiord**
FL, Fla. abbr (US) = **Florida**
flabbergasted ['flæbəgɑːstɪd] adj
sbalordito(-a)
flabby ['flæbɪ] adj flaccido(-a)
flag [flæg] n bandiera; (also: **flagstone**) pietra
da lastricare ■ vi stancarsi; affievolirsi; ~ **of
convenience** bandiera di convenienza
▶ **flag down** vt fare segno (di fermarsi) a
flagon ['flægən] n bottiglione m
flagpole ['flægpəul] n albero
flagrant ['fleɪgrənt] adj flagrante
flag stop n (US: for bus) fermata facoltativa,
fermata a richiesta
flair [flɛəʳ] n (for business etc) fiuto; (for languages
etc) facilità
flak [flæk] n (Mil) fuoco d'artiglieria;
(col: criticism) critiche fpl
flake [fleɪk] n (of rust, paint) scaglia; (of snow,
soap powder) fiocco ■ vi (also: **flake off**) sfaldarsi
flaky ['fleɪkɪ] adj (paintwork) scrostato(-a);
(skin) squamoso(-a); ~ **pastry** (Culin) pasta
sfoglia
flamboyant [flæm'bɔɪənt] adj sgargiante
flame [fleɪm] n fiamma; **old** ~ (col) vecchia
fiamma
flamingo [flə'mɪŋgəu] n fenicottero,
fiammingo
flammable ['flæməbl] adj infiammabile
flan [flæn] n (Brit) flan m inv
Flanders ['flɑːndəz] n Fiandre fpl
flange [flændʒ] n flangia; (on wheel) suola

flank [flæŋk] *n* fianco

flannel ['flænl] *n* (*Brit: also:* **face flannel**) guanto di spugna; (*fabric*) flanella; **flannels** *npl* pantaloni *mpl* di flanella

flannelette [flænə'lɛt] *n* flanella di cotone

flap [flæp] *n* (*of pocket*) patta; (*of envelope*) lembo; (*Aviat*) flap *m inv* ■ *vt* (*wings*) battere ■ *vi* (*sail, flag*) sbattere; (*col: also:* **be in a flap**) essere in agitazione

flapjack ['flæpdʒæk] *n* (*US: pancake*) frittella; (*Brit: biscuit*) biscotto di avena

flare [flɛəʳ] *n* razzo; (*in skirt etc*) svasatura
▸ **flare up** *vi* andare in fiamme; (*fig: person*) infiammarsi di rabbia; (: *revolt*) scoppiare

flared ['flɛəd] *adj* (*trousers*) svasato(-a)

flash [flæʃ] *n* vampata; (*also:* **news flash**) notizia *f* lampo *inv*; (*Phot*) flash *m inv*; (*US: torch*) torcia elettrica, lampadina tascabile ■ *vt* accendere e spegnere; (*send: message*) trasmettere; (*flaunt*) ostentare ■ *vi* brillare; (*light on ambulance, eyes etc*) lampeggiare; **in a ~** in un lampo; **~ of inspiration** lampo di genio; **to ~ one's headlights** lampeggiare; **he flashed by** *or* **past** ci passò davanti come un lampo

flashback ['flæʃbæk] *n* flashback *m inv*

flashbulb ['flæʃbʌlb] *n* cubo *m* flash *inv*

flash card *n* (*Scol*) scheda didattica

flashcube ['flæʃkju:b] *n* flash *m inv*

flasher ['flæʃəʳ] *n* (*Aut*) lampeggiatore *m*

flashlight ['flæʃlaɪt] *n* (*torch*) lampadina tascabile

flashpoint ['flæʃpɔɪnt] *n* punto di infiammabilità; (*fig*) livello critico

flashy ['flæʃɪ] *adj* (*pej*) vistoso(-a)

flask [flɑːsk] *n* fiasco; (*Chem*) beuta; (*also:* **vacuum flask**) thermos® *m inv*

flat [flæt] *adj* piatto(-a); (*tyre*) sgonfio(-a), a terra; (*battery*) scarico(-a); (*denial*) netto(-a); (*Mus*) bemolle *inv*; (: *voice*) stonato(-a); (: *instrument*) scordato(-a) ■ *n* (*Brit: rooms*) appartamento; (*Mus*) bemolle *m*; (*Aut*) pneumatico sgonfio ■ *adv*: (**to work**) **~ out** (lavorare) a più non posso; **~ rate of pay** tariffa unica di pagamento

flat-footed ['flæt'futɪd] *adj*: **to be ~** avere i piedi piatti

flatly ['flætlɪ] *adv* categoricamente, nettamente

flatmate ['flætmeɪt] *n* (*Brit*): **he's my ~** divide l'appartamento con me

flatness ['flætnɪs] *n* (*of land*) assenza di rilievi

flat-pack ['flætpæk] *adj*: **~ furniture** mobili *mpl* in kit ■ *n*: **flat pack** kit *m inv*

flat-screen ['flætskri:n] *adj* a schermo piatto

flatten ['flætn] *vt* (*also:* **flatten out**) appiattire; (*house, city*) abbattere, radere al suolo

flatter ['flætəʳ] *vt* lusingare; (*show to advantage*) donare a

flatterer ['flætərəʳ] *n* adulatore(-trice)

flattering ['flætərɪŋ] *adj* lusinghiero(-a); (*clothes etc*) che dona, che abbellisce

flattery ['flætərɪ] *n* adulazione *f*

flatulence ['flætjuləns] *n* flatulenza

flaunt [flɔ:nt] *vt* fare mostra di

flavour, (*US*) **flavor** ['fleɪvəʳ] *n* gusto, sapore *m* ■ *vt* insaporire, aggiungere sapore a; **vanilla-flavoured** al gusto di vaniglia

flavouring, (*US*) **flavoring** ['fleɪvərɪŋ] *n* essenza (artificiale)

flaw [flɔ:] *n* difetto

flawless ['flɔ:lɪs] *adj* senza difetti

flax [flæks] *n* lino

flaxen ['flæksən] *adj* biondo(-a)

flea [fli:] *n* pulce *f*

flea market *n* mercato delle pulci

fleck [flɛk] *n* (*of mud, paint, colour*) macchiolina; (*of dust*) granello ■ *vt* (*with blood, mud etc*) macchiettare; **brown flecked with white** marrone screziato di bianco

fled [flɛd] *pt, pp of* **flee**

fledgeling, fledgling ['flɛdʒlɪŋ] *n* uccellino

flee (*pt, pp* **fled**) [fli:, flɛd] *vt* fuggire da ■ *vi* fuggire, scappare

fleece [fli:s] *n* vello; (*garment*) pile *m inv* ■ *vt* (*col*) pelare

fleecy ['fli:sɪ] *adj* (*blanket*) soffice; (*cloud*) come ovatta

fleet [fli:t] *n* flotta; (*of lorries etc*) convoglio; (*of cars*) parco

fleeting ['fli:tɪŋ] *adj* fugace, fuggitivo(-a); (*visit*) volante

Flemish ['flɛmɪʃ] *adj* fiammingo(-a) ■ *n* (*Ling*) fiammingo; **the Flemish** *npl* i Fiamminghi

flesh [flɛʃ] *n* carne *f*; (*of fruit*) polpa

flesh wound *n* ferita superficiale

flew [flu:] *pt of* **fly**

flex [flɛks] *n* filo (flessibile) ■ *vt* flettere; (*muscles*) contrarre

flexibility [flɛksɪ'bɪlɪtɪ] *n* flessibilità

flexible ['flɛksəbl] *adj* flessibile

flexitime ['flɛksɪtaɪm] *n* orario flessibile

flick [flɪk] *n* colpetto; *see also* **flicks**
▸ **flick through** *vt fus* sfogliare

flicker ['flɪkəʳ] *vi* tremolare ■ *n* tremolio; **a ~ of light** un breve bagliore

flick knife *n* (*Brit*) coltello a serramanico

flicks *npl*: **the ~** (*col*) il cine

flier ['flaɪəʳ] *n* aviatore *m*

flight [flaɪt] *n* volo; (*escape*) fuga; (*also:* **flight of steps**) scalinata; **to take ~** darsi alla fuga; **to put to ~** mettere in fuga

flight attendant *n* (*US*) steward *m*, hostess *f inv*

flight crew n equipaggio
flight deck n (Aviat) cabina di controllo; (Naut) ponte m di comando
flight path n (of aircraft) rotta di volo; (of rocket, projectile) traiettoria
flight recorder n registratore m di volo
flimsy ['flɪmzɪ] adj (fabric) inconsistente; (excuse) meschino(-a)
flinch [flɪntʃ] vi ritirarsi; **to ~ from** tirarsi indietro di fronte a
fling (pt, pp **flung**) [flɪŋ, flʌŋ] vt lanciare, gettare ▪ n (love affair) avventura
flint [flɪnt] n selce f; (in lighter) pietrina
flip [flɪp] n colpetto ▪ vt dare un colpetto a; (US: pancake) far saltare (in aria) ▪ vi: **to ~ for sth** (US) fare a testa e croce per qc
▸ **flip through** vt fus (book, records) dare una scorsa a
flippant ['flɪpənt] adj senza rispetto, irriverente
flipper ['flɪpəʳ] n pinna
flip side n (of record) retro
flirt [fləːt] vi flirtare ▪ n civetta
flirtation [fləː'teɪʃən] n flirt m inv
flit [flɪt] vi svolazzare
float [fləʊt] n galleggiante m; (in procession) carro; (sum of money) somma ▪ vi galleggiare; (bather) fare il morto; (Comm: currency) fluttuare ▪ vt far galleggiare; (loan, business) lanciare; **to ~ an idea** ventilare un'idea
floating ['fləʊtɪŋ] adj a galla; **~ vote** voto oscillante; **~ voter** elettore m indeciso
flock [flɒk] n gregge m; (of people) folla; (of birds) stormo
floe [fləʊ] n (also: **ice floe**) banchisa
flog [flɒg] vt flagellare
flood [flʌd] n alluvione f; (of words, tears etc) diluvio ▪ vt inondare, allagare; (Aut: carburettor) ingolfare; **in ~** in pieno; **to ~ the market** (Comm) inondare il mercato
flooding ['flʌdɪŋ] n inondazione f
floodlight ['flʌdlaɪt] n riflettore m ▪ vt illuminare a giorno
floodlit ['flʌdlɪt] pt, pp of **floodlight** ▪ adj illuminato(-a) a giorno
flood tide n alta marea, marea crescente
floodwater ['flʌdwɔːtəʳ] n acque fpl (di inondazione)
floor [flɔːʳ] n pavimento; (storey) piano; (of sea, valley) fondo; (fig: at meeting): **the ~** il pubblico ▪ vt pavimentare; (knock down) atterrare; (baffle) confondere; (silence) far tacere; **on the ~** sul pavimento, per terra; **ground ~**, (US) **first ~** pianterreno; **first ~**, (US) **second ~** primo piano; **top ~** ultimo piano; **to have the ~** (speaker) prendere la parola

floorboard ['flɔːbɔːd] n tavellone m di legno
flooring ['flɔːrɪŋ] n (floor) pavimento; (material) materiale m per pavimentazioni
floor lamp n (US) lampada a stelo
floor show n spettacolo di varietà
floorwalker ['flɔːwɔːkəʳ] n (esp US) ispettore m di reparto
flop [flɒp] n fiasco ▪ vi (fail) far fiasco
floppy ['flɒpɪ] adj floscio(-a), molle ▪ n (Comput) = **floppy disk**; **~ hat** cappello floscio
floppy disk n floppy disk m inv
flora ['flɔːrə] n flora
floral ['flɔːrl] adj floreale
Florence ['flɒrəns] n Firenze f
Florentine ['flɒrəntaɪn] adj fiorentino(-a)
florid ['flɒrɪd] adj (complexion) florido(-a); (style) fiorito(-a)
florist ['flɒrɪst] n fioraio(-a); **at the ~'s (shop)** dal fioraio
flotation [fləʊ'teɪʃən] n (Comm) lancio
flounce [flaʊns] n balzo
▸ **flounce out** vi uscire stizzito(-a)
flounder ['flaʊndəʳ] vi annaspare ▪ n (Zool) passera di mare
flour ['flaʊəʳ] n farina
flourish ['flʌrɪʃ] vi fiorire ▪ vt brandire ▪ n abbellimento; svolazzo; (of trumpets) fanfara
flourishing ['flʌrɪʃɪŋ] adj prosperoso(-a), fiorente
flout [flaʊt] vt (order) contravvenire a; (convention) sfidare
flow [fləʊ] n flusso; circolazione f; (of river, also Elec) corrente f ▪ vi fluire; (traffic, blood in veins) circolare; (hair) scendere
flow chart n schema m di flusso
flow diagram n organigramma m
flower ['flaʊəʳ] n fiore m ▪ vi fiorire; **in ~** in fiore
flower bed n aiuola
flowerpot ['flaʊəpɒt] n vaso da fiori
flowery ['flaʊərɪ] adj fiorito(-a)
flown [fləʊn] pp of **fly**
flu [fluː] n influenza
fluctuate ['flʌktjʊeɪt] vi fluttuare, oscillare
fluctuation [flʌktjʊ'eɪʃən] n fluttuazione f, oscillazione f
flue [fluː] n canna fumaria
fluency ['fluːənsɪ] n facilità, scioltezza; **his ~ in English** la sua scioltezza nel parlare l'inglese
fluent ['fluːənt] adj (speech) facile, sciolto(-a); **he's a ~ speaker/reader** si esprime/legge senza difficoltà; **he speaks ~ Italian, he's ~ in Italian** parla l'italiano correntemente
fluently ['fluːəntlɪ] adv con facilità, correntemente
fluff [flʌf] n lanugine f

fluffy ['flʌfɪ] *adj* lanuginoso(-a); (*toy*) di peluche

fluid ['fluːɪd] *adj* fluido(-a) ■ *n* fluido; (*in diet*) liquido

fluid ounce *n* (*Brit*) = 0.028 l; 0.05 *pints*

fluke [fluːk] *n* (*col*) colpo di fortuna

flummox ['flʌməks] *vt* rendere perplesso(-a)

flung [flʌŋ] *pt, pp of* **fling**

flunky ['flʌŋkɪ] *n* tirapiedi *m/f inv*

fluorescent [fluə'rɛsnt] *adj* fluorescente

fluoride ['fluəraɪd] *n* fluoruro

fluorine ['fluəriːn] *n* fluoro

flurry ['flʌrɪ] *n* (*of snow*) tempesta; **a ~ of activity/excitement** una febbre di attività/un'improvvisa agitazione

flush [flʌʃ] *n* rossore *m*; (*fig*) ebbrezza ■ *vt* ripulire con un getto d'acqua; (*also:* **flush out**: *birds*) far alzare in volo; (: *animals, fig*: *criminal*) stanare ■ *vi* arrossire ■ *adj*: **~ with** a livello di, pari a; **~ against** aderente a; **hot flushes** (*Med*) vampate *fpl* di calore; **to ~ the toilet** tirare l'acqua

flushed [flʌʃt] *adj* tutto(-a) rosso(-a)

fluster ['flʌstər] *n* agitazione *f*

flustered ['flʌstəd] *adj* sconvolto(-a)

flute [fluːt] *n* flauto

flutter ['flʌtər] *n* agitazione *f*; (*of wings*) frullio ■ *vi* (*bird*) battere le ali

flux [flʌks] *n*: **in a state of ~** in continuo mutamento

fly [flaɪ] *n* (*insect*) mosca; (*on trousers: also:* **flies**) bracchetta ■ *vb* (*pt* **flew**, *pp* **flown**) [fluː, fləʊn] *vt* pilotare; (*passengers, cargo*) trasportare (in aereo); (*distances*) percorrere ■ *vi* volare; (*passengers*) andare in aereo; (*escape*) fuggire; (*flag*) sventolare; **to ~ open** spalancarsi all'improvviso; **to ~ off the handle** perdere le staffe, uscire dai gangheri

▶ **fly away** *vi* volar via

▶ **fly in** *vi* (*plane*) arrivare; (*person*) arrivare in aereo

▶ **fly off** *vi* volare via

▶ **fly out** *vi* (*plane*) partire; (*person*) partire in aereo

fly-fishing ['flaɪfɪʃɪŋ] *n* pesca con la mosca

flying ['flaɪɪŋ] *n* (*activity*) aviazione *f*; (*action*) volo ■ *adj*: **~ visit** visita volante; **with ~ colours** con risultati brillanti; **he doesn't like ~** non gli piace viaggiare in aereo

flying buttress *n* arco rampante

flying picket *n* picchetto (*proveniente da fabbriche non direttamente coinvolte nello sciopero*)

flying saucer *n* disco volante

flying squad *n* (*Police*) (squadra) volante *f*

flying start *n*: **to get off to a ~** partire come un razzo

flyleaf ['flaɪliːf] *n* risguardo

flyover ['flaɪəʊvər] *n* (*Brit: bridge*) cavalcavia *m inv*

flypast ['flaɪpɑːst] *n* esibizione *f* della pattuglia aerea

flysheet ['flaɪʃiːt] *n* (*for tent*) sopratetto

flyweight ['flaɪweɪt] *n* (*Sport*) peso *m* mosca *inv*

flywheel ['flaɪwiːl] *n* volano

FM *abbr* = **frequency modulation**; (*Brit Mil*) = **Field Marshal**

FMB *n abbr* (*US*) = **Federal Maritime Board**

FMCS *n abbr* (*US*): = *Federal Mediation and Conciliation Services*) organismo di conciliazione in caso di conflitti sul lavoro

FO *n abbr* (*Brit*) = **Foreign Office**

foal [fəʊl] *n* puledro

foam [fəʊm] *n* schiuma ■ *vi* schiumare

foam rubber *n* gommapiuma®

FOB *abbr* (= *free on board*) franco a bordo

fob [fɔb] *vt*: **to ~ sb off with** appioppare qn con; sbarazzarsi di qn con ■ *n* (*also:* **watch fob**: *chain*) catena per orologio; (: *band of cloth*) nastro per orologio

foc *abbr* (*Brit*) = **free of charge**

focal ['fəʊkəl] *adj* focale

focal point *n* punto focale

focus ['fəʊkəs] *n* (*pl* **focuses**) fuoco; (*of interest*) centro ■ *vt* (*field glasses etc*) mettere a fuoco; (*light rays*) far convergere ■ *vi*: **to ~ on** (*with camera*) mettere a fuoco; (*person*) fissare lo sguardo su; **in ~** a fuoco; **out of ~** sfocato(-a)

focus group *n* (*Pol*) gruppo di discussione, focus group *m inv*

fodder ['fɔdər] *n* foraggio

FOE *n abbr* (= *Friends of the Earth*) Amici *mpl* della Terra; (*US*: = *Fraternal Order of Eagles*) *organizzazione filantropica*

foe [fəʊ] *n* nemico

foetus, (*US*) **fetus** ['fiːtəs] *n* feto

fog [fɔg] *n* nebbia

fogbound ['fɔgbaʊnd] *adj* fermo(-a) a causa della nebbia

foggy ['fɔgɪ] *adj* nebbioso(-a); **it's ~** c'è nebbia

fog lamp, (*US*) **fog light** *n* (*Aut*) faro *m* antinebbia *inv*

foible ['fɔɪbl] *n* debolezza, punto debole

foil [fɔɪl] *vt* confondere, frustrare ■ *n* lamina di metallo; (*also:* **kitchen foil**) foglio di alluminio; (*Fencing*) fioretto; **to act as a ~ to** (*fig*) far risaltare

foist [fɔɪst] *vt*: **to ~ sth on sb** rifilare qc a qn

fold [fəʊld] *n* (*bend, crease*) piega; (*Agr*) ovile *m*; (*fig*) gregge *m* ■ *vt* piegare; **to ~ one's arms** incrociare le braccia

▶ **fold up** *vi* (*map etc*) piegarsi; (*business*) crollare ■ *vt* (*map etc*) piegare, ripiegare

folder ['fəuldə^r] *n* (*for papers*) cartella; cartellina; (*binder*) raccoglitore *m*

folding ['fəuldɪŋ] *adj* (*chair, bed*) pieghevole

foliage ['fəulɪɪdʒ] *n* fogliame *m*

folk [fəuk] *npl* gente *f* ■ *cpd* popolare; **folks** *npl* famiglia

folklore ['fəuklɔ:^{r}] *n* folclore *m*

folk music *n* musica folk *inv*

folk singer *n* cantante *m/f* folk *inv*

folksong ['fəuksɔŋ] *n* canto popolare

follow ['fɔləu] *vt* seguire ■ *vi* seguire; (*result*) conseguire, risultare; **to ~ sb's advice** seguire il consiglio di qn; **I don't quite ~ you** non ti capisco *or* seguo affatto; **to ~ in sb's footsteps** seguire le orme di qn; **it follows that ...** ne consegue che ...; **he followed suit** lui ha fatto lo stesso

▶ **follow on** *vi* (*continue*): **to ~ on from** seguire

▶ **follow out** *vt* (*implement: idea, plan*) eseguire, portare a termine

▶ **follow through** *vt* = **follow out**

▶ **follow up** *vt* (*victory*) sfruttare; (*letter, offer*) fare seguito a; (*case*) seguire

follower ['fɔləuə^r] *n* seguace *m/f*, discepolo(-a)

following ['fɔləuɪŋ] *adj* seguente, successivo(-a) ■ *n* seguito, discepoli *mpl*

follow-up ['fɔləuʌp] *n* seguito

folly ['fɔlɪ] *n* pazzia, follia

fond [fɔnd] *adj* (*memory, look*) tenero(-a), affettuoso(-a); **to be ~ of** volere bene a; **she's ~ of swimming** le piace nuotare

fondle ['fɔndl] *vt* accarezzare

fondly ['fɔndlɪ] *adv* (*lovingly*) affettuosamente; (*naïvely*): **he ~ believed that ...** ha avuto l'ingenuità di credere che ...

fondness ['fɔndnɪs] *n* affetto; **~ (for sth)** predilezione *f* (per qc)

font [fɔnt] *n* (*Rel*) fonte *m* (battesimale); (*Typ*) stile *m* di carattere

food [fu:d] *n* cibo

food chain *n* catena alimentare

food mixer *n* frullatore *m*

food poisoning *n* intossicazione *f* alimentare

food processor *n* tritatutto *m inv* elettrico

food stamp *n* (*US*) buono alimentare dato agli indigenti

foodstuffs ['fu:dstʌfs] *npl* generi *fpl* alimentari

fool [fu:l] *n* sciocco(-a); (*Hist: of king*) buffone *m*; (*Culin*) frullato ■ *vt* ingannare ■ *vi* (*gen*): **~ around** fare lo sciocco; **to make a ~ of sb** prendere in giro qn; **to make a ~ of o.s.** coprirsi di ridicolo; **you can't ~ me** non mi inganna

▶ **fool about, fool around** *vi* (*waste time*) perdere tempo

foolhardy ['fu:lhɑ:dɪ] *adj* avventato(-a)

foolish ['fu:lɪʃ] *adj* scemo(-a), stupido(-a); imprudente

foolishly ['fu:lɪʃlɪ] *adv* stupidamente

foolishness ['fu:lɪʃnɪs] *n* stupidità

foolproof ['fu:lpru:f] *adj* (*plan etc*) sicurissimo(-a)

foolscap ['fu:lskæp] *n* carta protocollo

foot [fut] *n* (*pl* **feet**) [fi:t] piede *m*; (*measure*) piede (= 304 mm; = 12 inches); (*of animal*) zampa; (*of page, stairs etc*) fondo ■ *vt* (*bill*) pagare; **on ~** a piedi; **to put one's ~ down** (*Aut*) schiacciare l'accelleratore; (*say no*) imporsi; **to find one's feet** ambientarsi

footage ['futɪdʒ] *n* (*Cine: length*) ≈ metraggio; (: *material*) sequenza

foot and mouth, foot and mouth disease *n* afta epizootica

football ['fu:tbɔ:l] *n* pallone *m*; (*sport: Brit*) calcio; (: *US*) football *m* americano

footballer ['fu:tbɔ:lə^r] *n* (*Brit*) = **football player**

football ground *n* campo di calcio

football match *n* (*Brit*) partita di calcio

football player *n* (*Brit*) calciatore *m*; (*US*) giocatore *m* di football americano

footbrake ['fu:tbreɪk] *n* freno a pedale

footbridge ['fu:tbrɪdʒ] *n* passerella

foothills ['fu:thɪlz] *npl* contrafforti *fpl*

foothold ['fu:thəuld] *n* punto d'appoggio

footing ['fu:tɪŋ] *n* (*fig*) posizione *f*; **to lose one's ~** mettere un piede in fallo; **on an equal ~** in condizioni di parità

footlights ['fu:tlaɪts] *npl* luci *fpl* della ribalta

footman ['fu:tmən] *n* lacchè *m inv*

footnote ['fu:tnəut] *n* nota (a piè di pagina)

footpath ['fu:tpɑ:θ] *n* sentiero; (*in street*) marciapiede *m*

footprint ['fu:tprɪnt] *n* orma, impronta

footrest ['fu:trest] *n* poggiapiedi *m inv*

footsie ['fu:tsɪ] *n* (*col*): **to play ~ with sb** fare piedino a qn

Footsie ['fu:tsɪ], **Footsie index** ['fu:tsɪ-] *n* (*col*) = **Financial Times Stock Exchange 100 Index**

footsore ['fu:tsɔ:^{r}] *adj*: **to be ~** avere mal di piedi

footstep ['fu:tstep] *n* passo

footwear ['fu:twɛə^r] *n* calzatura

FOR *abbr* (= *free on rail*) franco vagone

 KEYWORD

for [fɔ:^{r}] *prep* **1** (*indicating destination, intention, purpose*) per; **the train for London** il treno per Londra; **he went for the paper** è andato a prendere il giornale; **it's time for lunch** è ora di pranzo; **what's it for?** a che serve?; **what for?** (*why*) perché?

2 (*on behalf of, representing*) per; **to work for sb/ sth** lavorare per qn/qc; **I'll ask him for you** glielo chiederò a nome tuo; **G for George** ≈ G come George

3 (*because of*) per, a causa di; **for this reason** per questo motivo

4 (*with regard to*) per; **it's cold for July** è freddo per luglio; **for everyone who voted yes, 50 voted no** per ogni voto a favore ce n'erano 50 contro

5 (*in exchange for*) per; **I sold it for £5** l'ho venduto per 5 sterline

6 (*in favour of*) per, a favore di; **are you for or against us?** sei con noi o contro di noi?; **I'm all for it** sono completamente a favore

7 (*referring to distance, time*) per; **there are roadworks for 5 km** ci sono lavori in corso per 5 km; **he was away for 2 years** è stato via per 2 anni; **she will be away for a month** starà via un mese; **it hasn't rained for 3 weeks** non piove da 3 settimane; **can you do it for tomorrow?** può farlo per domani?

8 (*with infinitive clauses*): **it is not for me to decide** non sta a me decidere; **it would be best for you to leave** sarebbe meglio che lei se ne andasse; **there is still time for you to do it** ha ancora tempo per farlo; **for this to be possible …** perché ciò sia possibile …

9 (*in spite of*) nonostante; **for all his complaints, he's very fond of her** nonostante tutte le sue lamentele, le vuole molto bene

■ *conj* (*since, as: formal*) dal momento che, poiché

forage ['fɒrɪdʒ] *vi* foraggiare
forage cap *n* bustina
foray ['fɒreɪ] *n* incursione *f*
forbad, forbade [fə'bæd] *pt of* **forbid**
forbearing [fɔː'bɛərɪŋ] *adj* paziente, tollerante
forbid (*pt* **forbad(e)**, *pp* **forbidden**) [fə'bɪd, -'bæd, -'bɪdn] *vt* vietare, interdire; **to ~ sb to do sth** proibire a qn di fare qc
forbidding [fə'bɪdɪŋ] *adj* arcigno(-a), d'aspetto minaccioso
force [fɔːs] *n* forza ■ *vt* forzare; (*obtain by force: smile, confession*) strappare; **the Forces** *npl* (*Brit*) le forze armate; **in ~** (*in large numbers*) in gran numero; (*law*) in vigore; **to come into ~** entrare in vigore; **a ~ 5 wind** un vento forza 5; **to join forces** unire le forze; **the sales ~** (*Comm*) l'effettivo dei rappresentanti;

to ~ sb to do sth costringere qn a fare qc
▶ **force back** *vt* (*crowd, enemy*) respingere; (*tears*) ingoiare
▶ **force down** *vt* (*food*) sforzarsi di mangiare
forced [fɔːst] *adj* forzato(-a)
force-feed ['fɔːsfiːd] *vt* sottoporre ad alimentazione forzata
forceful ['fɔːsful] *adj* forte, vigoroso(-a)
forcemeat ['fɔːsmiːt] *n* (*Brit Culin*) ripieno
forceps ['fɔːsɪps] *npl* forcipe *m*
forcibly ['fɔːsəblɪ] *adv* con la forza; (*vigorously*) vigorosamente
ford [fɔːd] *n* guado ■ *vt* guadare
fore [fɔːʳ] *n*: **to the ~** in prima linea; **to come to the ~** mettersi in evidenza
forearm ['fɔːrɑːm] *n* avambraccio
forebear ['fɔːbɛəʳ] *n* antenato
foreboding [fɔː'bəʊdɪŋ] *n* presagio di male
forecast ['fɔːkɑːst] *n* previsione *f*; (*weather forecast*) previsioni *fpl* del tempo ■ *vt* (*irreg: like* **cast**) prevedere
foreclose [fɔː'kləʊz] *vt* (*Law: also:* **foreclose on**) sequestrare l'immobile ipotecato di
foreclosure [fɔː'kləʊʒəʳ] *n* sequestro di immobile ipotecato
forecourt ['fɔːkɔːt] *n* (*of garage*) corte *f* esterna
forefathers ['fɔːfɑːðəz] *npl* antenati *mpl*, avi *mpl*
forefinger ['fɔːfɪŋgəʳ] *n* (*dito*) indice *m*
forefront ['fɔːfrʌnt] *n*: **in the ~ of** all'avanguardia di
forego [fɔː'gəʊ] *vt* = **forgo**
foregoing ['fɔːgəʊɪŋ] *adj* precedente
foregone ['fɔːgɒn] *pp of* **forego** ■ *adj*: **it's a ~ conclusion** è una conclusione scontata
foreground ['fɔːgraʊnd] *n* primo piano ■ *cpd* (*Comput*) foreground *inv*, di primo piano
forehand ['fɔːhænd] *n* (*Tennis*) diritto
forehead ['fɔːrɪd] *n* fronte *f*
foreign ['fɒrən] *adj* straniero(-a); (*trade*) estero(-a)
foreign body *n* corpo estraneo
foreign currency *n* valuta estera
foreigner ['fɒrənəʳ] *n* straniero(-a)
foreign exchange *n* cambio di valuta; (*currency*) valuta estera
foreign exchange market *n* mercato delle valute
foreign exchange rate *n* cambio
foreign investment *n* investimento all'estero
foreign minister *n* ministro degli Affari esteri
Foreign Office *n* (*Brit*) Ministero degli Esteri
foreign secretary *n* (*Brit*) ministro degli Affari esteri
foreleg ['fɔːlɛg] *n* zampa anteriore

foreman ['fɔːmən] *n* caposquadra *m*; (*Law: of jury*) portavoce *m* della giuria

foremost ['fɔːməust] *adj* principale; più in vista ■ *adv*: **first and ~** innanzitutto

forename ['fɔːneɪm] *n* nome *m* di battesimo

forensic [fə'rɛnsɪk] *adj*: **~ medicine** medicina legale; **~ expert** esperto della (polizia) scientifica

foreplay ['fɔːpleɪ] *n* preliminari *mpl*

forerunner ['fɔːrʌnə'] *n* precursore *m*

foresee (*pt* **foresaw**, *pp* **foreseen**) [fɔː'siː, -'sɔː, -'siːn] *vt* prevedere

foreseeable [fɔː'siːəbl] *adj* prevedibile

foreseen [fɔː'siːn] *pp* of **foresee**

foreshadow [fɔː'ʃædəu] *vt* presagire, far prevedere

foreshorten [fɔː'ʃɔːtn] *vt* (*figure, scene*) rappresentare in scorcio

foresight ['fɔːsaɪt] *n* previdenza

foreskin ['fɔːskɪn] *n* (*Anat*) prepuzio

forest ['fɔrɪst] *n* foresta

forestall [fɔː'stɔːl] *vt* prevenire

forestry ['fɔrɪstrɪ] *n* silvicoltura

foretaste ['fɔːteɪst] *n* pregustazione *f*

foretell (*pt*, *pp* **foretold**) [fɔː'tɛl, -'təuld] *vt* predire

forethought ['fɔːθɔːt] *n* previdenza

foretold [fɔː'təuld] *pt*, *pp* of **foretell**

forever [fə'rɛvə'] *adv* per sempre; (*fig*) sempre, di continuo

forewarn [fɔː'wɔːn] *vt* avvisare in precedenza

forewent [fɔː'wɛnt] *pt* of **forego**

foreword ['fɔːwəːd] *n* prefazione *f*

forfeit ['fɔːfɪt] *n* ammenda, pena ■ *vt* perdere; (*one's happiness, health*) giocarsi

forgave [fə'geɪv] *pt* of **forgive**

forge [fɔːdʒ] *n* fucina ■ *vt* falsificare; (*signature*) contraffare, falsificare; (*wrought iron*) fucinare, foggiare
▶ **forge ahead** *vi* tirare avanti

forger ['fɔːdʒə'] *n* contraffattore *m*

forgery ['fɔːdʒərɪ] *n* falso; (*activity*) contraffazione *f*

forget (*pt* **forgot**, *pp* **forgotten**) [fə'gɛt, -'gɔt, -'gɔtn] *vt*, *vi* dimenticare

forgetful [fə'gɛtful] *adj* di corta memoria; **~ of** dimentico(a) di

forgetfulness [fə'gɛtfulnɪs] *n* smemoratezza; (*oblivion*) oblio

forget-me-not [fə'gɛtmɪnɔt] *n* nontiscordardimé *m inv*

forgive (*pt* **forgave**, *pp* **forgiven**) [fə'gɪv, -'geɪv, -'gɪvn] *vt* perdonare; **to ~ sb for sth/ for doing sth** perdonare qc a qn/a qn di aver fatto qc

forgiveness [fə'gɪvnɪs] *n* perdono

forgiving [fə'gɪvɪŋ] *adj* indulgente

forgo (*pt* **forwent**, *pp* **forgone**) [fɔː'gəu, -'wɛnt, -'gɔn] *vt* rinunciare a

forgot [fə'gɔt] *pt* of **forget**

forgotten [fə'gɔtn] *pp* of **forget**

fork [fɔːk] *n* (*for eating*) forchetta; (*for gardening*) forca; (*of roads*) bivio; (*of railways*) inforcazione *f* ■ *vi* (*road*) biforcarsi
▶ **fork out** (*col: pay*) *vt* sborsare ■ *vi* pagare

forked [fɔːkt] *adj* (*lightning*) a zigzag

fork-lift truck ['fɔːklɪft-] *n* carrello elevatore

forlorn [fə'lɔːn] *adj* (*person*) sconsolato(-a); (*deserted: cottage*) abbandonato(-a); (*desperate: attempt*) disperato(-a)

form [fɔːm] *n* forma; (*Scol*) classe *f*; (*questionnaire*) modulo ■ *vt* formare; (*circle, queue etc*) fare; **in the ~ of** a forma di, sotto forma di; **to be in good ~** (*Sport, fig*) essere in forma; **in top ~** in gran forma; **to ~ part of sth** far parte di qc

formal ['fɔːməl] *adj* (*offer, receipt*) vero(-a) e proprio(-a); (*person*) cerimonioso(-a); (*occasion, dinner*) formale, ufficiale; (*Art, Philosophy*) formale; **~ dress** abito da cerimonia; (*evening dress*) abito da sera

formality [fɔː'mælɪtɪ] *n* formalità *f inv*

formalize ['fɔːməlaɪz] *vt* rendere ufficiale

formally ['fɔːməlɪ] *adv* ufficialmente; formalmente; cerimoniosamente; **to be ~ invited** ricevere un invito ufficiale

format ['fɔːmæt] *n* formato ■ *vt* (*Comput*) formattare

formation [fɔː'meɪʃən] *n* formazione *f*

formative ['fɔːmətɪv] *adj*: **~ years** anni *mpl* formativi

former ['fɔːmə'] *adj* vecchio(-a) (*before n*), ex *inv* (*before n*); **the ~ president** l'ex presidente; **the ~ ... the latter** quello ... questo; **the ~ Yugoslavia/Soviet Union** l'ex Jugoslavia/ Unione Sovietica

formerly ['fɔːməlɪ] *adv* in passato

form feed *n* (*on printer*) alimentazione *f* modulo

formidable ['fɔːmɪdəbl] *adj* formidabile

formula ['fɔːmjulə] *n* formula; **F~ One** (*Aut*) formula uno

formulate ['fɔːmjuleɪt] *vt* formulare

fornicate ['fɔːnɪkeɪt] *vi* fornicare

forsake (*pt* **forsook**, *pp* **forsaken**) [fə'seɪk, -'suk, -'seɪkən] *vt* abbandonare

fort [fɔːt] *n* forte *m*; **to hold the ~** (*fig*) prendere le redini (della situazione)

forte ['fɔːtɪ] *n* forte *m*

forth [fɔːθ] *adv* in avanti; **to go back and ~** andare avanti e indietro; **and so ~** e così via

forthcoming [fɔːθ'kʌmɪŋ] *adj* prossimo(-a); (*character*) aperto(-a), comunicativo(-a)

forthright ['fɔːθraɪt] *adj* franco(-a), schietto(-a)

forthwith [fɔːθ'wɪθ] *adv* immediatamente, subito

fortieth ['fɔːtɪɪθ] *num* quarantesimo(-a)

fortification [fɔːtɪfɪ'keɪʃən] *n* fortificazione *f*

fortified wine *n* vino ad alta gradazione alcolica

fortify ['fɔːtɪfaɪ] *vt* fortificare

fortitude ['fɔːtɪtjuːd] *n* forza d'animo

fortnight ['fɔːtnaɪt] *n* (*Brit*) quindici giorni *mpl*, due settimane *fpl*; **it's a ~ since ...** sono due settimane da quando ...

fortnightly ['fɔːtnaɪtlɪ] *adj* bimensile ▪ *adv* ogni quindici giorni

FORTRAN ['fɔːtræn] *n* FORTRAN *m*

fortress ['fɔːtrɪs] *n* fortezza, rocca

fortuitous [fɔː'tjuːɪtəs] *adj* fortuito(-a)

fortunate ['fɔːtʃənɪt] *adj* fortunato(-a); **he is ~ to have ...** ha la fortuna di avere ...; **it is ~ that** è una fortuna che + *sub*

fortunately ['fɔːtʃənɪtlɪ] *adv* fortunatamente

fortune ['fɔːtʃən] *n* fortuna; **to make a ~** farsi una fortuna

fortuneteller ['fɔːtʃəntɛlər] *n* indovino(-a)

forty ['fɔːtɪ] *num* quaranta

forum ['fɔːrəm] *n* foro; (*fig*) luogo di pubblica discussione

forward ['fɔːwəd] *adj* (*movement, position*) in avanti; (*not shy*) sfacciato(-a); (*Comm: delivery, sales, exchange*) a termine ▪ *adv* avanti ▪ *n* (*Sport*) avanti *m inv* ▪ *vt* (*letter*) inoltrare; (*parcel, goods*) spedire; (*fig*) promuovere, appoggiare; **to move ~** avanzare; **"please ~"** "si prega di inoltrare"; **~ planning** programmazione *f* in anticipo

forwards ['fɔːwədz] *adv* avanti

forwent [fɔː'wɛnt] *pt of* **forgo**

fossil ['fɔsl] *adj, n* fossile (*m*); **~ fuel** combustibile *m* fossile

foster ['fɔstər] *vt* incoraggiare, nutrire; (*child*) avere in affidamento

foster brother *n* fratellastro

foster child *n* bambino(-a) preso(-a) in affidamento

foster mother *n* madre *f* affidataria

fought [fɔːt] *pt, pp of* **fight**

foul [faul] *adj* (*smell, food*) cattivo(-a); (*weather*) brutto(-a), orribile; (*language*) osceno(-a); (*deed*) infame ▪ *n* (*Football*) fallo ▪ *vt* sporcare; (*football player*) commettere un fallo su; (*entangle: anchor, propeller*) impigliarsi in

foul play *n* (*Sport*) gioco scorretto; **~ is not suspected** si è scartata l'ipotesi del delitto (*or* dell'attentato *etc*)

found [faund] *pt, pp of* **find** ▪ *vt* (*establish*) fondare

foundation [faun'deɪʃən] *n* (*act*) fondazione *f*; (*base*) base *f*; (*also:* **foundation cream**)

fondo tinta; **foundations** *npl* (*of building*) fondamenta *fpl*; **to lay the foundations** gettare le fondamenta

foundation stone *n* prima pietra

founder ['faundər] *n* fondatore(-trice) ▪ *vi* affondare

founding ['faundɪŋ] *adj*: **~ fathers** (*US*) padri *mpl* fondatori; **~ member** socio fondatore

foundry ['faundrɪ] *n* fonderia

fount [faunt] *n* fonte *f*; (*Typ*) stile *m* di carattere

fountain ['fauntɪn] *n* fontana

fountain pen *n* penna stilografica

four [fɔːr] *num* quattro; **on all fours** a carponi

four-letter word ['fɔːlɛtə-] *n* parolaccia

four-poster ['fɔː'pəustər] *n* (*also:* **four-poster bed**) letto a quattro colonne

foursome ['fɔːsəm] *n* partita a quattro; uscita in quattro

fourteen ['fɔːtiːn] *num* quattordici

fourth [fɔːθ] *num* quarto(-a) ▪ *n* (*Aut: also:* **fourth gear**) quarta

four-wheel drive ['fɔːwiːl-] *n* (*Aut*): **with ~** con quattro ruote motrici

fowl [faul] *n* pollame *m*; volatile *m*

fox [fɔks] *n* volpe *f* ▪ *vt* confondere

fox fur *n* volpe *f*, pelliccia di volpe

foxglove ['fɔksglʌv] *n* (*Bot*) digitale *f*

fox-hunting ['fɔkshʌntɪŋ] *n* caccia alla volpe

foyer ['fɔɪeɪ] *n* atrio; (*Theat*) ridotto

FPA *n abbr* (*Brit*: = *Family Planning Association*) ≈ A.I.E.D. *f* (= *Associazione Italiana Educazione Demografica*)

Fr. *abbr* (*Rel*) = **father; friar**

fr. *abbr* (= *franc*) fr.

fracas ['frækɑː] *n* rissa, lite *f*

fraction ['frækʃən] *n* frazione *f*

fractionally ['frækʃnəlɪ] *adv* un tantino, minimamente

fractious ['frækʃəs] *adj* irritabile

fracture ['fræktʃər] *n* frattura ▪ *vt* fratturare

fragile ['frædʒaɪl] *adj* fragile

fragment ['frægmənt] *n* frammento

fragmentary ['frægməntərɪ] *adj* frammentario(-a)

fragrance ['freɪgrəns] *n* fragranza, profumo

fragrant ['freɪgrənt] *adj* fragrante, profumato(-a)

frail [freɪl] *adj* debole, delicato(-a)

frame [freɪm] *n* (*of building*) armatura; (*of human, animal*) ossatura, corpo; (*of picture*) cornice *f*; (*of door, window*) telaio; (*of spectacles: also:* **frames**) montatura ▪ *vt* (*picture*) incorniciare; **to ~ sb** (col) incastrare qn; **~ of mind** stato d'animo

framework ['freɪmwə:k] n struttura

France [frɑːns] n Francia

franchise ['fræntʃaɪz] n (Pol) diritto di voto; (Comm) concessione f

franchisee [fræntʃaɪ'zi:] n concessionaria

franchiser ['fræntʃaɪzəʳ] n concedente m

frank [fræŋk] adj franco(-a), aperto(-a) ▪ vt (letter) affrancare

Frankfurt ['fræŋkfəːt] n Francoforte f

frankfurter ['fræŋkfəːtəʳ] n würstel m inv

franking machine ['fræŋkɪŋ-] n macchina affrancatrice

frankly ['fræŋklɪ] adv francamente, sinceramente

frankness ['fræŋknɪs] n franchezza

frantic ['fræntɪk] adj (activity, pace) frenetico(-a); (desperate: need, desire) pazzo(-a), sfrenato(-a); (: search) affannoso(-a); (person) fuori di sé

frantically ['fræntɪklɪ] adv freneticamente; affannosamente

fraternal [frə'təːnl] adj fraterno(-a)

fraternity [frə'təːnɪtɪ] n (club) associazione f; (spirit) fratellanza

fraternize ['frætənaɪz] vi fraternizzare

fraud [frɔːd] n truffa; (Law) frode f; (person) impostore(-a)

fraudulent ['frɔːdjulənt] adj fraudolento(-a)

fraught [frɔːt] adj (tense) teso(-a); **~ with** pieno(a) di, intriso(a) da

fray [freɪ] n baruffa ▪ vt logorare ▪ vi logorarsi; **to return to the ~** tornare nella mischia; **tempers were getting frayed** cominciavano ad innervosirsi; **her nerves were frayed** aveva i nervi a pezzi

FRB n abbr (US) = **Federal Reserve Board**

FRCM n abbr (Brit) = **Fellow of the Royal College of Music**

FRCO n abbr (Brit) = **Fellow of the Royal College of Organists**

FRCP n abbr (Brit) = **Fellow of the Royal College of Physicians**

FRCS n abbr (Brit) = **Fellow of the Royal College of Surgeons**

freak [fri:k] n fenomeno, mostro; (col: enthusiast) fanatico(-a) ▪ adj (storm, conditions) anormale; (victory) inatteso(-a)
  ▸ **freak out** vi (col) andare fuori di testa

freakish ['fri:kɪʃ] adj (result, appearance) strano(-a), bizzarro(-a); (weather) anormale

freckle ['frɛkl] n lentiggine f

free [fri:] adj libero(-a); (gratis) gratuito(-a); (liberal) generoso(-a) ▪ vt (prisoner, jammed person) liberare; (jammed object) districare; **~ (of charge)** gratuitamente; **admission ~**

entrata libera; **to give sb a ~ hand** dare carta bianca a qn; **~ and easy** rilassato

freebie ['fri:bɪ] n (col): **it's a ~** è in omaggio

freedom ['fri:dəm] n libertà

freedom fighter n combattente m/f per la libertà

free enterprise n liberalismo economico

Freefone® ['fri:fəun] n (Brit) = numero verde

free-for-all ['fri:fərɔːl] n parapiglia m generale

free gift n regalo, omaggio

freehold ['fri:həuld] n proprietà assoluta

free kick n (Sport) calcio libero

freelance ['fri:lɑːns] adj indipendente; **~ work** collaborazione f esterna

freeloader ['fri:ləudəʳ] n (pej) scroccone(-a)

freely ['fri:lɪ] adv liberamente; (liberally) liberalmente

free-market economy [fri:'mɑːkɪt-] n economia di libero mercato

freemason ['fri:meɪsn] n massone m

freemasonry ['fri:meɪsnrɪ] n massoneria

freepost ['fri:pəust] n affrancatura a carica del destinatario

free-range ['fri:'reɪndʒ] adj (eggs) di gallina ruspante

free sample n campione m gratuito

free speech n libertà di parola

freestyle ['fri:staɪl] n (in swimming) stile m libero

free trade n libero scambio

freeway ['fri:weɪ] n (US) superstrada

freewheel [fri:'wi:l] vi andare a ruota libera

freewheeling [fri:'wi:lɪŋ] adj a ruota libera

free will n libero arbitrio; **of one's own ~** di spontanea volontà

freeze [fri:z] vb (pt **froze**, pp **frozen**) [frəuz, 'frəuzn] vi gelare ▪ vt gelare; (food) congelare; (prices, salaries) bloccare ▪ n gelo; blocco
  ▸ **freeze over** vi (lake, river) ghiacciarsi; (windows, windscreen) coprirsi di ghiaccio
  ▸ **freeze up** vi gelarsi

freeze-dried ['fri:zdraɪd] adj liofilizzato(-a)

freezer ['fri:zəʳ] n congelatore m

freezing ['fri:zɪŋ] adj: **I'm ~** mi sto congelando ▪ n (also: **freezing point**) punto di congelamento; **3 degrees below ~** 3 gradi sotto zero

freight [freɪt] n (goods) merce f, merci f pl; (money charged) spese f pl di trasporto; **~ forward** spese a carico del destinatario; **~ inward** spese di trasporto sulla merce in entrata

freight car n (US) carro m merci inv

freighter ['freɪtəʳ] n (Naut) nave f da carico

freight forwarder [-'fɔ:wədə^r] *n* spedizioniere *m*

freight train *n* (*US*) treno *m* merci *inv*

French [frɛntʃ] *adj* francese ■ *n* (*Ling*) francese *m*; **the French** *npl* i Francesi

French bean *n* fagiolino

French Canadian *adj*, *n* franco-canadese (*m/f*)

French dressing *n* (*Culin*) condimento per insalata

French fried potatoes, (*US*) **French fries** *npl* patate *fpl* fritte

French Guiana [-gaɪˈænə] *n* Guiana francese

French loaf *n* ≈ filoncino

Frenchman ['frɛntʃmən] *n* francese *m*

French Riviera *n*: **the ~** la Costa Azzurra

French stick *n* baguette *f inv*

French window *n* portafinestra

Frenchwoman ['frɛntʃwumən] *n* francese *f*

frenetic [frəˈnɛtɪk] *adj* frenetico(-a)

frenzy ['frɛnzɪ] *n* frenesia

frequency ['fri:kwənsɪ] *n* frequenza

frequency modulation *n* modulazione *f* di frequenza

frequent *adj* ['fri:kwənt] frequente ■ *vt* [frɪˈkwɛnt] frequentare

frequently ['fri:kwəntlɪ] *adv* frequentemente, spesso

fresco ['frɛskəʊ] *n* affresco

fresh [frɛʃ] *adj* fresco(-a); (*new*) nuovo(-a); (*cheeky*) sfacciato(-a); **to make a ~ start** cominciare da capo

freshen ['frɛʃən] *vi* (*wind, air*) rinfrescare
  ▸ **freshen up** *vi* rinfrescarsi

freshener ['frɛʃnə^r] *n*: **skin ~** tonico rinfrescante; **air ~** deodorante *m* per ambienti

fresher ['frɛʃə^r] *n* (*Brit Scol: col*) = **freshman**

freshly ['frɛʃlɪ] *adv* di recente, di fresco

freshman ['frɛʃmən] *n* (*Scol*) matricola

freshness ['frɛʃnɪs] *n* freschezza

freshwater ['frɛʃwɔːtə^r] *adj* (*fish*) d'acqua dolce

fret [frɛt] *vi* agitarsi, affliggersi

fretful ['frɛtful] *adj* (*child*) irritabile

Freudian ['frɔɪdɪən] *adj* freudiano(-a); **~ slip** lapsus *m inv* freudiano

FRG *n abbr* = **Federal Republic of Germany**

Fri. *abbr* (= *Friday*) ven.

friar ['fraɪə^r] *n* frate *m*

friction ['frɪkʃən] *n* frizione *f*, attrito

friction feed *n* (*on printer*) trascinamento ad attrito

Friday ['fraɪdɪ] *n* venerdì *m inv*; *see also* **Tuesday**

fridge [frɪdʒ] *n* (*Brit*) frigo, frigorifero

fridge-freezer ['frɪdʒ'fri:zə^r] *n* freezer *m inv*

fried [fraɪd] *pt*, *pp* of **fry** ■ *adj* fritto(-a); **~ egg** uovo fritto

friend [frɛnd] *n* amico(-a); **to make friends with** fare amicizia con ■ *vt* (*Internet*) aggiungere come amico

friendliness ['frɛndlɪnɪs] *n* amichevolezza

friendly ['frɛndlɪ] *adj* amichevole ■ *n* (*also*: **friendly match**) partita amichevole; **to be ~ with** essere amico di; **to be ~ to** essere cordiale con

friendly fire *n* fuoco amico

friendly society *n* società *f inv* di mutuo soccorso

friendship ['frɛndʃɪp] *n* amicizia

frieze [fri:z] *n* fregio

frigate ['frɪgɪt] *n* (*Naut: modern*) fregata

fright [fraɪt] *n* paura, spavento; **to take ~** spaventarsi; **she looks a ~!** guarda com'è conciata!

frighten ['fraɪtn] *vt* spaventare, far paura a
  ▸ **frighten away**, **frighten off** *vt* (*birds, children etc*) scacciare (facendogli paura)

frightened ['fraɪtnd] *adj*: **to be ~ (of)** avere paura (di)

frightening ['fraɪtnɪŋ] *adj* spaventoso(-a), pauroso(-a)

frightful ['fraɪtful] *adj* orribile

frightfully ['fraɪtfulɪ] *adv* terribilmente; **I'm ~ sorry** mi dispiace moltissimo

frigid ['frɪdʒɪd] *adj* (*woman*) frigido(-a)

frigidity [frɪˈdʒɪdɪtɪ] *n* frigidità

frill [frɪl] *n* balza; **no frills** (*fig*) senza fronzoli

frilly ['frɪlɪ] *adj* (*clothes, lampshade*) pieno(-a) di fronzoli

fringe [frɪndʒ] *n* frangia; (*edge: of forest etc*) margine *m*; (*fig*): **on the ~** al margine

fringe benefits *npl* vantaggi *mpl*

fringe theatre *n* teatro d'avanguardia

Frisbee® ['frɪzbɪ] *n* frisbee® *m inv*

frisk [frɪsk] *vt* perquisire

frisky ['frɪskɪ] *adj* vivace, vispo(-a)

fritter ['frɪtə^r] *n* frittella
  ▸ **fritter away** *vt* sprecare

frivolity [frɪˈvɔlɪtɪ] *n* frivolezza

frivolous ['frɪvələs] *adj* frivolo(-a)

frizzy ['frɪzɪ] *adj* crespo(-a)

fro [frəʊ] *adv*: **to and ~** avanti e indietro

frock [frɔk] *n* vestito

frog [frɔg] *n* rana; **to have a ~ in one's throat** avere la voce rauca

frogman ['frɔgmən] *n* uomo *m* rana *inv*

frogmarch ['frɔgmɑːtʃ] *vt* (*Brit*): **to ~ sb in/out** portar qn dentro/fuori con la forza

frolic ['frɔlɪk] *vi* sgambettare

 KEYWORD

from [frɔm] *prep* **1** (*indicating starting place, origin etc*) da; **where do you come from?, where**

f

are you from? da dove viene?, di dov'è?; **where has he come from?** da dove arriva?; **from London to Glasgow** da Londra a Glasgow; **a letter from my sister** una lettera da mia sorella; **tell him from me that ...** gli dica da parte mia che ... **2** (*indicating time*) da; **from one o'clock to** or **until** or **till two** dall'una alle due; **(as) from Friday** a partire da venerdì; **from January (on)** da gennaio, a partire da gennaio **3** (*indicating distance*) da; **the hotel is 1 km from the beach** l'albergo è a 1 km dalla spiaggia **4** (*indicating price, number etc*) da; **from a pound** da una sterlina in su; **prices range from £10 to £50** i prezzi vanno dalle 10 alle 50 sterline **5** (*indicating difference*) da; **he can't tell red from green** non sa distinguere il rosso dal verde **6** (*because of, on the basis of*): **from what he says** da quanto dice lui; **weak from hunger** debole per la fame

frond [frɔnd] *n* fronda
front [frʌnt] *n* (*of house, dress*) davanti *m inv*; (*of train*) testa; (*of book*) copertina; (*promenade: also:* **sea front**) lungomare *m*; (*Mil, Pol, Meteor*) fronte *m*; (*fig: appearances*) fronte *f* ▪ *adj* primo(-a); anteriore, davanti *inv* ▪ *vi*: **to ~ onto sth** dare su qc, guardare verso qc; **in ~ (of)** davanti (a)
frontage ['frʌntɪdʒ] *n* facciata
frontal ['frʌntl] *adj* frontale
front bench *n* posti in Parlamento occupati dai frontbencher; vedi nota

⊙ **FRONT BENCH**
⊙
⊙ Nel Parlamento britannico, si chiamano
⊙ *front bench* gli scanni della "House of
⊙ Commons" che si trovano alla sinistra e
⊙ alla destra dello "Speaker" davanti ai
⊙ "backbenches". I *front bench* sono occupati
⊙ dai "frontbenchers", parlamentari che
⊙ ricoprono una carica di governo o che
⊙ fanno parte dello "shadow cabinet"
⊙ dell'opposizione.

frontbencher ['frʌnt'bɛntʃəʳ] *n* (*Brit*) parlamentare con carica al governo o all'opposizione
front desk *n* (*US: in hotel*) reception *f inv*; (*: at doctor's*) accettazione *f*
front door *n* porta d'entrata; (*of car*) sportello anteriore
frontier ['frʌntɪəʳ] *n* frontiera
frontispiece ['frʌntɪspiːs] *n* frontespizio
front page *n* prima pagina

front room *n* (*Brit*) salotto
front runner *n* (*fig*) favorito(-a)
front-wheel drive ['frʌntwiːl-] *n* trasmissione *f* anteriore
frost [frɔst] *n* gelo; (*also:* **hoarfrost**) brina
frostbite ['frɔstbaɪt] *n* congelamento
frosted ['frɔstɪd] *adj* (*glass*) smerigliato(-a); (*US: cake*) glassato(-a)
frosting ['frɔstɪŋ] *n* (*US: on cake*) glassa
frosty ['frɔstɪ] *adj* (*window*) coperto(-a) di ghiaccio; (*welcome*) gelido(-a)
froth [frɔθ] *n* spuma; schiuma
frown [fraun] *n* cipiglio ▪ *vi* acciglarsi
 ▶ **frown on** *vt fus* (*fig*) disapprovare
froze [frəuz] *pt of* **freeze**
frozen ['frəuzn] *pp of* **freeze** ▪ *adj* (*food*) congelato(-a); (*Comm: assets*) bloccato(-a)
FRS *n abbr* (*Brit*) = **Fellow of the Royal Society**; (*US: = Federal Reserve System*) sistema bancario degli Stati Uniti
frugal ['fruːgəl] *adj* frugale; (*person*) economo(a)
fruit [fruːt] *n* (*pl inv*) frutto; (*collectively*) frutta
fruiterer ['fruːtərəʳ] *n* fruttivendolo; **at the ~'s (shop)** dal fruttivendolo
fruit fly *n* mosca della frutta
fruitful ['fruːtful] *adj* fruttuoso(-a); (*plant*) fruttifero(-a); (*soil*) fertile
fruition [fruː'ɪʃən] *n*: **to come to ~** realizzarsi
fruit juice *n* succo di frutta
fruitless ['fruːtlɪs] *adj* (*fig*) vano(-a), inutile
fruit machine *n* (*Brit*) macchina *f* mangiasoldi *inv*
fruit salad *n* macedonia
frump [frʌmp] *n*: **to feel a ~** sentirsi infagottato(-a)
frustrate [frʌs'treɪt] *vt* frustrare
frustrated [frʌs'treɪtɪd] *adj* frustrato(-a)
frustrating [frʌs'treɪtɪŋ] *adj* (*job*) frustrante; (*day*) disastroso(-a)
frustration [frʌs'treɪʃən] *n* frustrazione *f*
fry (*pt, pp* **fried**) [fraɪ, -d] *vt* friggere ▪ *npl*: **the small ~** i pesci piccoli
frying pan ['fraɪɪŋ-] *n* padella
FT *n abbr* (*Brit*: = *Financial Times*) giornale finanziario; **the FT index** l'indice FT
ft. *abbr* = **foot; feet**
FTC *n abbr* (*US*) = **Federal Trade Commission**
FT-SE 100 Index *n abbr* = **Financial Times Stock Exchange 100 Index**
fuchsia ['fjuːʃə] *n* fucsia
fuck [fʌk] *vt, vi* (*col!*) fottere (!); **~ off!** vaffanculo! (!)
fuddled ['fʌdld] *adj* (*muddled*) confuso(-a); (*col: tipsy*) brillo(-a)
fuddy-duddy ['fʌdɪdʌdɪ] *n* (*pej*) parruccone *m*
fudge [fʌdʒ] *n* (*Culin*) specie di caramella a base di latte, burro e zucchero ▪ *vt* (*issue, problem*) evitare

fuel [fjuǝl] *n* (*for heating*) combustibile *m*; (*for propelling*) carburante *m* ▪ *vt* (*furnace etc*) alimentare; (*aircraft, ship etc*) rifornire di carburante
fuel oil *n* nafta
fuel poverty *n* povertà energetica
fuel pump *n* (*Aut*) pompa del carburante
fuel tank *n* deposito *m* nafta *inv*; (*on vehicle*) serbatoio (della benzina)
fug [fʌg] *n* (*Brit*) aria viziata
fugitive ['fju:dʒɪtɪv] *n* fuggitivo(-a), profugo(-a); (*from prison*) evaso(-a)
fulfil, (*US*) **fulfill** [ful'fɪl] *vt* (*function*) compiere; (*order*) eseguire; (*wish, desire*) soddisfare, appagare
fulfilled [ful'fɪld] *adj* (*person*) realizzato(-a), soddisfatto(-a)
fulfilment, (*US*) **fulfillment** [ful'fɪlmǝnt] *n* (*of wishes*) soddisfazione *f*, appagamento
full [ful] *adj* pieno(-a); (*details, skirt*) ampio(-a); (*price*) intero(-a) ▪ *adv*: **to know ~ well that** sapere benissimo che; **~ (up)** (*hotel etc*) al completo; **I'm ~ (up)** sono pieno; **a ~ two hours** due ore intere; **at ~ speed** a tutta velocità; **in ~** per intero; **to pay in ~** pagare tutto; **~ name** nome *m* e cognome *m*; **~ employment** piena occupazione
fullback ['fulbæk] *n* (*Rugby, Football*) terzino
full-blooded ['ful'blʌdɪd] *adj* (*vigorous: attack*) energico(-a); (*virile: male*) virile
full-cream ['ful'kri:m] *adj*: **~ milk** (*Brit*) latte *m* intero
full-grown ['ful'grǝun] *adj* maturo(-a)
full-length ['ful'lɛŋθ] *adj* (*portrait*) in piedi; (*film*) a lungometraggio
full moon *n* luna piena
full-scale ['fulskeɪl] *adj* (*plan, model*) in grandezza naturale; (*search, retreat*) su vasta scala
full-sized ['ful'saɪzd] *adj* (*portrait etc*) a grandezza naturale
full stop *n* punto
full-time ['ful'taɪm] *adj, adv* (*work*) a tempo pieno ▪ *n* (*Sport*) fine *f* partita
fully ['fulɪ] *adv* interamente, pienamente, completamente; (*at least*): **~ as big** almeno così grosso
fully-fledged ['fulɪ'flɛdʒd] *adj* (*bird*) adulto(-a); (*fig: teacher, member etc*) a tutti gli effetti
fulsome ['fulsǝm] *adj* (*pej: praise*) esagerato(-a), eccessivo(-a); (: *manner*) insincero
fumble ['fʌmbl] *vi* brancolare, andare a tentoni ▪ *vt* (*ball*) lasciarsi sfuggire
▸ **fumble with** *vt fus* trafficare
fume [fju:m] *vi* essere furioso(-a); **fumes** *npl* esalazioni *fpl*, vapori *mpl*

fumigate ['fju:mɪgeɪt] *vt* suffumicare
fun [fʌn] *n* divertimento, spasso; **to have ~** divertirsi; **for ~** per scherzo; **it's not much ~** non è molto divertente; **to make ~ of** prendersi gioco di
function ['fʌŋkʃǝn] *n* funzione *f*; cerimonia, ricevimento ▪ *vi* funzionare; **to ~ as** fungere da, funzionare da
functional ['fʌŋkʃǝnl] *adj* funzionale
function key *n* (*Comput*) tasto di funzioni
fund [fʌnd] *n* fondo, cassa; (*source*) fondo; (*store*) riserva; **funds** *npl* (*money*) fondi *mpl*
fundamental [fʌndǝ'mɛntl] *adj* fondamentale; **fundamentals** *npl* basi *fpl*
fundamentalism [fʌndǝ'mɛntǝlɪzǝm] *n* fondamentalismo
fundamentalist [fʌndǝ'mɛntǝlɪst] *n* fondamentalista *m/f*
fundamentally [fʌndǝ'mɛntǝlɪ] *adv* essenzialmente, fondamentalmente
funding ['fʌndɪŋ] *n* finanziamento
fund-raising ['fʌndreɪzɪŋ] *n* raccolta di fondi
funeral ['fju:nǝrǝl] *n* funerale *m*
funeral director *n* impresario di pompe funebri
funeral parlour *n* impresa di pompe funebri
funeral service *n* ufficio funebre
funereal [fju:'nɪǝrɪǝl] *adj* funereo(-a), lugubre
fun fair *n* luna park *m inv*
fungus (*pl* **fungi**) ['fʌŋgǝs, -gaɪ] *n* fungo; (*mould*) muffa
funicular [fju:'nɪkjulǝˈ] *adj* (*also*: **funicular railway**) funicolare *f*
funky ['fʌŋkɪ] *adj* (*music*) funky *inv*; (*col: excellent*) figo(-a)
funnel ['fʌnl] *n* imbuto; (*of ship*) ciminiera
funnily ['fʌnɪlɪ] *adv* in modo divertente; (*oddly*) stranamente
funny ['fʌnɪ] *adj* divertente, buffo(-a); (*strange*) strano(-a), bizzarro(-a)
funny bone *n* osso cubitale
fun run *n* marcia non competitiva
fur [fǝ:ˈ] *n* pelo; pelliccia; pelle *f*; (*Brit: in kettle etc*) deposito calcare
fur coat *n* pelliccia
furious ['fjuǝrǝs] *adj* furioso(-a); (*effort*) accanito(-a); (*argument*) violento(-a)
furiously ['fjuǝrǝslɪ] *adv* furiosamente; accanitamente
furl [fǝ:l] *vt* (*sail*) piegare
furlong ['fǝ:lɔŋ] *n* 201.17 *m* (*termine ippico*)
furlough ['fǝ:lǝu] *n* (*US*) congedo, permesso
furnace ['fǝ:nɪs] *n* fornace *f*
furnish ['fǝ:nɪʃ] *vt* ammobiliare; (*supply*) fornire; **furnished flat** *or* (*US*) **apartment** appartamento ammobiliato

furnishings [ˈfəːnɪʃɪŋz] *npl* mobili *mpl*, mobilia

furniture [ˈfəːnɪtʃəʳ] *n* mobili *mpl*; **piece of ~** mobile *m*

furore [fjuəˈrɔːrɪ] *n* (*protests*) scalpore *m*; (*enthusiasm*) entusiasmo

furrier [ˈfʌrɪəʳ] *n* pellicciaio(-a)

furrow [ˈfʌrəu] *n* solco ■ *vt* (*forehead*) segnare di rughe

furry [ˈfəːrɪ] *adj* (*animal*) peloso(-a); (*toy*) di peluche

further [ˈfəːðəʳ] *adj* supplementare, altro(-a); nuovo(-a); più lontano(-a) ■ *adv* più lontano; (*more*) di più; (*moreover*) inoltre ■ *vt* favorire, promuovere; **until ~ notice** fino a nuovo avviso; **how much ~ is it?** quanto manca *or* dista?; **~ to your letter of ...** (*Comm*) con riferimento alla vostra lettera del ...; **to ~ one's interests** fare i propri interessi

further education *n* = corsi *mpl* di formazione

furthermore [fəːðəˈmɔːʳ] *adv* inoltre, per di più

furthermost [ˈfəːðəməust] *adj* più lontano(-a)

furthest [ˈfəːðɪst] *adv superlative of* **far**

furtive [ˈfəːtɪv] *adj* furtivo(-a)

fury [ˈfjuərɪ] *n* furore *m*

fuse, (*US*) **fuze** [fjuːz] *n* fusibile *m*; (*for bomb etc*) miccia, spoletta ■ *vt* fondere; (*Elec*) **to ~ the lights** far saltare i fusibili ■ *vi* fondersi; **a ~ has blown** è saltato un fusibile

fuse box *n* cassetta dei fusibili

fuselage [ˈfjuːzəlɑːʒ] *n* fusoliera

fuse wire *n* filo (di fusibile)

fusillade [fjuːzɪˈleɪd] *n* scarica di fucileria; (*fig*) fuoco di fila, serie *f inv* incalzante

fusion [ˈfjuːʒən] *n* fusione *f*

fuss [fʌs] *n* chiasso, trambusto, confusione *f*; (*complaining*) storie *fpl* ■ *vt* (*person*) infastidire, scocciare ■ *vi* agitarsi; **to make a ~** fare delle storie; **to make a ~ of sb** coprire qn di attenzioni
▸ **fuss over** *vt fus* (*person*) circondare di premure

fusspot [ˈfʌspɔt] *n* (*col*): **he's such a ~** fa sempre tante storie

fussy [ˈfʌsɪ] *adj* (*person*) puntiglioso(-a), esigente; che fa le storie; (*dress*) carico(-a) di fronzoli; (*style*) elaborato(-a); **I'm not ~** (*col*) per me è lo stesso

fusty [ˈfʌstɪ] *adj* (*pej: archaic*) stantio(-a); (*: smell*) che sa di stantio

futile [ˈfjuːtaɪl] *adj* futile

futility [fjuːˈtɪlɪtɪ] *n* futilità

futon [ˈfuːtɔn] *n* futon *m inv*, letto giapponese

future [ˈfjuːtʃəʳ] *adj* futuro(-a) ■ *n* futuro, avvenire *m*; (*Ling*) futuro; **in ~** in futuro; **in the near ~** in un prossimo futuro; **in the immediate ~** nell'immediato futuro

futures [ˈfjuːtʃəz] *npl* (*Comm*) operazioni *fpl* a termine

futuristic [fjuːtʃəˈrɪstɪk] *adj* futuristico(-a)

fuze [fjuːz] *n*, *vi*, *vt* (*US*) = **fuse**

fuzzy [ˈfʌzɪ] *adj* (*Phot*) indistinto(-a), sfocato(-a); (*hair*) crespo(-a)

fwd. *abbr* = **forward**

fwy *abbr* (*US*) = **freeway**

FY *abbr* = **fiscal year**

FYI *abbr* = **for your information**

Gg

G, g [dʒiː] *n* (*letter*) G, g *for m inv*; (*Mus*): **G** sol *m*;
G for George ≈ G come Genova
G *n abbr* (*Brit Scol: mark:* = *good*) ≈ buono; (*US
Cine:* = *general audience*) per tutti
g *abbr* (= *gram, gravity*) g
G8 *n abbr* (*Pol:* = *Group of Eight*) G8 *m*
G20 *n abbr* (*Pol:* = *Group of Twenty*) G20 *m*
GA *abbr* (*US Post*) = **Georgia**
gab [gæb] *n* (*col*): **to have the gift of the ~**
avere parlantina
gabble ['gæbl] *vi* borbottare; farfugliare
gaberdine [gæbə'diːn] *n* gabardine *m inv*
gable ['geɪbl] *n* frontone *m*
Gabon [gə'bɔn] *n* Gabon *m*
gad about [gæd-] *vi* (*col*) svolazzare (qua e là)
gadget ['gædʒɪt] *n* aggeggio
Gaelic ['geɪlɪk] *adj* gaelico(-a) ■ *n* (*language*)
gaelico
gaffe [gæf] *n* gaffe *f inv*
gaffer ['gæfə^r] *n* (*Brit col*) capo
gag [gæg] *n* bavaglio; (*joke*) facezia, scherzo
■ *vt* (*prisoner etc*) imbavagliare ■ *vi* (*choke*)
soffocare
gaga ['gɑːgɑː] *adj*: **to go ~** rimbambirsi
gage [geɪdʒ] *n, vt* (*US*) = **gauge**
gaiety ['geɪɪtɪ] *n* gaiezza
gaily ['geɪlɪ] *adv* allegramente
gain [geɪn] *n* guadagno, profitto ■ *vt*
guadagnare ■ *vi* (*watch*) andare avanti;
to ~ in/by aumentare di/con; **to ~ 3lbs
(in weight)** aumentare di 3 libbre; **to ~
ground** guadagnare terreno
▶ **gain (up)on** *vt fus* accorciare le distanze da,
riprendere
gainful ['geɪnful] *adj* profittevole, lucrativo(-a)
gainfully ['geɪnfəlɪ] *adv*: **to be ~ employed**
avere un lavoro retribuito
gainsay [geɪn'seɪ] *vt* (*irreg: like* **say**)
contraddire; negare
gait [geɪt] *n* andatura
gal. *abbr* = **gallon**
gala ['gɑːlə] *n* gala; **swimming ~**
manifestazione *f* di nuoto

Galapagos Islands [gə'læpəgəs-] *npl*: **the ~**
le isole Galapagos
galaxy ['gæləksɪ] *n* galassia
gale [geɪl] *n* vento forte; burrasca; **~ force 10**
vento forza 10
gall [gɔːl] *n* (*Anat*) bile *f*; (*fig: impudence*) fegato,
faccia ■ *vt* urtare (i nervi a)
gall. *abbr* = **gallon**
gallant ['gælənt] *adj* valoroso(-a); (*towards
ladies*) galante, cortese
gallantry ['gæləntrɪ] *n* valore *m* militare;
galanteria, cortesia
gall bladder ['gɔːl-] *n* cistifellea
galleon ['gælɪən] *n* galeone *m*
gallery ['gælərɪ] *n* galleria; loggia; (*for
spectators*) tribuna; (*in theatre*) loggione *m*,
balconata; (*also:* **art gallery**: *state-owned*)
museo; (: *private*) galleria
galley ['gælɪ] *n* (*ship's kitchen*) cambusa; (*ship*)
galea; (*also:* **galley proof**) bozza in colonna
Gallic ['gælɪk] *adj* gallico(-a); (*French*) francese
galling ['gɔːlɪŋ] *adj* irritante
gallon ['gælən] *n* gallone *m* (*Brit* = 4.543 *l*;
8 pints; *US* = 3.785 *l*)
gallop ['gæləp] *n* galoppo ■ *vi* galoppare;
galloping inflation inflazione *f* galoppante
gallows ['gæləuz] *n* forca
gallstone ['gɔːlstəun] *n* calcolo biliare
Gallup Poll ['gæləp-] *n* sondaggio a campione
galore [gə'lɔː^r] *adv* a iosa, a profusione
galvanize ['gælvənaɪz] *vt* galvanizzare;
to ~ sb into action (*fig*) galvanizzare qn,
spronare qn all'azione
Gambia ['gæmbɪə] *n* Gambia *m*
gambit ['gæmbɪt] *n* (*fig*): (**opening**) **~** prima
mossa
gamble ['gæmbl] *n* azzardo, rischio calcolato
■ *vt, vi* giocare; **to ~ on** (*fig*) giocare su; **to ~
on the Stock Exchange** giocare in Borsa
gambler ['gæmblə^r] *n* giocatore(-trice)
d'azzardo
gambling ['gæmblɪŋ] *n* gioco d'azzardo
gambol ['gæmbəl] *vi* saltellare

game [geɪm] n gioco; (*event*) partita; (*Hunting*) selvaggina ■ adj coraggioso(-a); (*ready*): **to be ~ (for sth/to do)** essere pronto(-a) (a qc/a fare); **games** npl (*Scol*) attività fpl sportive; **big ~** selvaggina grossa

game bird n uccello selvatico

gamekeeper ['geɪmki:pəʳ] n guardacaccia m inv

gamely ['geɪmlɪ] adv coraggiosamente

gamer [geɪməʳ] n chi gioca con i videogame

game reserve n riserva di caccia

games console n console f inv dei videogame

gameshow ['geɪmʃəu] n gioco a premi

gamesmanship ['geɪmzmənʃɪp] n abilità

gaming ['geɪmɪŋ] n gioco d'azzardo; (*Comput*) il giocare con i videogame

gammon ['gæmən] n (*bacon*) quarto di maiale; (*ham*) prosciutto affumicato

gamut ['gæmət] n gamma

gang [gæŋ] n banda, squadra ■ vi: **to ~ up on sb** far combutta contro qn

Ganges ['gændʒi:z] n: **the ~** il Gange

gangland ['gæŋlænd] adj della malavita

gangling ['gæŋglɪŋ] adj allampanato(-a)

gangly ['gæŋglɪ] adj = **gangling**

gangplank ['gæŋplæŋk] n passerella

gangrene ['gæŋgri:n] n cancrena

gangster ['gæŋstəʳ] n gangster m inv

gangway ['gæŋweɪ] n passerella; (*Brit: of bus*) passaggio

gantry ['gæntrɪ] n (*for crane, railway signal*) cavalletto; (*for rocket*) torre f di lancio

gaol [dʒeɪl] n, vt (*Brit*) = **jail**

gap [gæp] n buco; (*in time*) intervallo; (*fig*) lacuna; vuoto

gape [geɪp] vi restare a bocca aperta

gaping ['geɪpɪŋ] adj (*hole*) squarciato(-a)

gap year n anno di pausa preso prima di iniziare l'università, per lavorare o viaggiare

garage ['gærɑ:ʒ] n garage m inv

garb [gɑ:b] n abiti mpl, veste f

garbage ['gɑ:bɪdʒ] n immondizie fpl, rifiuti mpl; (*fig: film, book*) porcheria, robaccia; (*: nonsense*) fesserie fpl

garbage can n (*US*) bidone m della spazzatura

garbage collector n (*US*) spazzino(-a)

garbage disposal unit n tritarifiuti m inv

garbage truck n (*US*) camion m inv della spazzatura

garbled ['gɑ:bld] adj deformato(-a); ingarbugliato(-a)

garden ['gɑ:dn] n giardino ■ vi lavorare nel giardino; **gardens** npl (*public*) giardini pubblici; (*private*) parco

garden centre n vivaio

garden city n (*Brit*) città f inv giardino inv

gardener ['gɑ:dnəʳ] n giardiniere(-a)

gardening ['gɑ:dnɪŋ] n giardinaggio

gargle ['gɑ:gl] vi fare gargarismi ■ n gargarismo

gargoyle ['gɑ:gɔɪl] n gargouille f inv

garish ['gɛərɪʃ] adj vistoso(-a)

garland ['gɑ:lənd] n ghirlanda; corona

garlic ['gɑ:lɪk] n aglio

garment ['gɑ:mənt] n indumento

garner ['gɑ:nəʳ] vt ammucchiare, raccogliere

garnish ['gɑ:nɪʃ] vt guarnire

garret ['gærɪt] n soffitta

garrison ['gærɪsn] n guarnigione f ■ vt guarnire

garrulous ['gærjuləs] adj ciarliero(-a), loquace

garter ['gɑ:təʳ] n giarrettiera; (*US: suspender*) gancio (di reggicalze)

garter belt n (*US*) reggicalze m inv

gas [gæs] n gas m inv; (*used as anaesthetic*) etere m; (*US: gasoline*) benzina ■ vt asfissiare con il gas; (*Mil*) gasare

gas cooker n (*Brit*) cucina a gas

gas cylinder n bombola del gas

gaseous ['gæsɪəs] adj gassoso(-a)

gas fire n (*Brit*) radiatore m a gas

gas-fired ['gæsfaɪəd] adj (alimentato(-a)) a gas

gash [gæʃ] n sfregio ■ vt sfregiare

gasket ['gæskɪt] n (*Aut*) guarnizione f

gas mask n maschera f antigas inv

gas meter n contatore m del gas

gasoline ['gæsəli:n] n (*US*) benzina

gasp [gɑ:sp] vi ansare, boccheggiare; (*in surprise*) restare senza fiato

▶ **gasp out** vt dire affannosamente

gas ring n fornello a gas

gas station n (*US*) distributore m di benzina

gas stove n cucina a gas

gassy ['gæsɪ] adj gassoso(-a)

gas tank n (*US Aut*) serbatoio (di benzina)

gas tap n (*on cooker*) manopola del gas; (*on pipe*) rubinetto del gas

gastric ['gæstrɪk] adj gastrico(-a)

gastric ulcer n ulcera gastrica

gastroenteritis ['gæstrəuɛntə'raɪtɪs] n gastroenterite f

gastronomy [gæs'trɔnəmɪ] n gastronomia

gasworks ['gæswə:ks] n, npl impianto di produzione del gas

gate [geɪt] n cancello; (*of castle, town*) porta; (*at airport*) uscita; (*at level crossing*) barriera

gâteau (*pl* **gâteaux**) ['gætəu, -z] n torta

gatecrash ['geɪtkræʃ] vt partecipare senza invito a

gatecrasher ['geɪtkræʃəʳ] n intruso(-a),

ospite *m/f* non invitato(-a)
gatehouse ['geɪthaʊs] *n* casetta del custode
(*all'entrata di un parco*)
gateway ['geɪtweɪ] *n* porta
gather ['gæðəʳ] *vt* (*flowers, fruit*) cogliere; (*pick
up*) raccogliere; (*assemble*) radunare;
raccogliere; (*understand*) capire ■ *vi* (*assemble*)
radunarsi; (*dust*) accumularsi; (*clouds*)
addensarsi; **to ~ speed** acquistare velocità;
to ~ (from/that) comprendere (da/che),
dedurre (da/che); **as far as I can ~** da quel
che ho potuto capire
gathering ['gæðərɪŋ] *n* adunanza
GATT [gæt] *n abbr* (= *General Agreement on Tariffs
and Trade*) G.A.T.T *m*
gauche [gəʊʃ] *adj* goffo(-a), maldestro(-a)
gaudy ['gɔːdɪ] *adj* vistoso(-a)
gauge [geɪdʒ] *n* (*standard measure*) calibro;
(*Rail*) scartamento; (*instrument*) indicatore *m*
■ *vt* misurare; (*fig: sb's capabilities, character*)
valutare, stimare; **to ~ the right moment**
calcolare il momento giusto; **petrol ~**, (US)
gas ~ indicatore *m or* spia della benzina
gaunt [gɔːnt] *adj* scarno(-a); (*grim, desolate*)
desolato(-a)
gauntlet ['gɔːntlɪt] *n* (*fig*): **to run the ~
through an angry crowd** passare sotto il
fuoco di una folla ostile; **to throw down
the ~** gettare il guanto
gauze [gɔːz] *n* garza
gave [geɪv] *pt of* **give**
gawky ['gɔːkɪ] *adj* goffo(-a), sgraziato(-a)
gawp [gɔːp] *vi*: **to ~ at** guardare a bocca
aperta
gay [geɪ] *adj* (*person*) gaio(-a), allegro(-a);
(*colour*) vivace, vivo(-a); (*col*) omosessuale
gaze [geɪz] *n* sguardo fisso ■ *vi*: **to ~ at**
guardare fisso
gazelle [gə'zɛl] *n* gazzella
gazette [gə'zɛt] *n* (*newspaper*) gazzetta;
(*official publication*) gazzetta ufficiale
gazetteer [gæzə'tɪəʳ] *n* (*book*) dizionario dei
nomi geografici; (*section of book*) indice *m* dei
nomi geografici
gazump [gə'zʌmp] *vt* (Brit): **to ~ sb** *nella
compravendita di immobili, venire meno all'impegno
preso con un acquirente accettando un'offerta migliore
fatta da altri*
GB *abbr* (= *Great Britain*) GB
GBH *n abbr* (Brit Law: *col*) = **grievous bodily
harm**
GC *n abbr* (Brit: = *George Cross*) *decorazione al valore*
GCE *n abbr* (Brit: = *General Certificate of Education*)
≈ diploma *m* di maturità
GCHQ *n abbr* (Brit: = *Government Communications
Headquarters*) *centro per l'intercettazione delle
telecomunicazioni straniere*

GCSE *n abbr* (Brit: = *General Certificate of Secondary
Education*) *diploma di istruzione secondaria
conseguito a 16 anni in Inghilterra e Galles*
Gdns. *abbr* = **gardens**
GDP *n abbr* = **gross domestic product**
GDR *n abbr* (Hist) = **German Democratic
Republic**
gear [gɪəʳ] *n* attrezzi *mpl*, equipaggiamento;
(*belongings*) roba; (*Tech*) ingranaggio; (*Aut*)
marcia ■ *vt* (*fig: adapt*) adattare; **top *or* high/
low/bottom ~** (US) quarta (*or* quinta)/
seconda/prima; **in ~** in marcia; **out of ~** in
folle; **our service is geared to meet the
needs of the disabled** la nostra
organizzazione risponde espressamente alle
esigenze degli handicappati
  ▶ **gear up** *vi*: **to ~ up (to do)** prepararsi (a
fare)
gear box *n* scatola del cambio
gear lever, (US) **gear shift** *n* leva del cambio
GED *n abbr* (US Scol) = **general educational
development**
geese [giːs] *npl of* **goose**
geezer ['giːzəʳ] *n* (Brit *col*) tizio
Geiger counter ['gaɪgə-] *n* geiger *m inv*
gel [dʒɛl] *n* gel *m inv*
gelatin, gelatine ['dʒɛlətiːn] *n* gelatina
gelignite ['dʒɛlɪgnaɪt] *n* nitroglicerina
gem [dʒɛm] *n* gemma
Gemini ['dʒɛmɪnaɪ] *n* Gemelli *mpl*; **to be ~**
essere dei Gemelli
gen [dʒɛn] *n* (Brit *col*): **to give sb the ~ on sth**
mettere qn al corrente di qc
Gen. *abbr* (Mil: = *General*) Gen
gen. *abbr* (= *general, generally*) gen.
gender ['dʒɛndəʳ] *n* genere *m*
gene [dʒiːn] *n* (Biol) gene *m*
genealogy [dʒiːnɪ'ælədʒɪ] *n* genealogia
general ['dʒɛnərl] *n* generale *m* ■ *adj*
generale; **in ~** in genere; **the ~ public**
il grande pubblico
general anaesthetic *n* anestesia totale
general delivery *n* (US) fermo posta *m*
general election *n* elezioni *fpl* generali
generalization ['dʒɛnrəlaɪ'zeɪʃən] *n*
generalizzazione *f*
generalize ['dʒɛnrəlaɪz] *vi* generalizzare
generally ['dʒɛnrəlɪ] *adv* generalmente
general manager *n* direttore *m* generale
general practitioner *n* medico generico
general strike *n* sciopero generale
generate ['dʒɛnəreɪt] *vt* generare
generation [dʒɛnə'reɪʃən] *n* generazione *f*;
(*of electricity etc*) produzione *f*
generator ['dʒɛnəreɪtəʳ] *n* generatore *m*
generic [dʒɪ'nɛrɪk] *adj* generico(-a)
generosity [dʒɛnə'rɔsɪtɪ] *n* generosità

g

577

generous ['dʒɛnərəs] *adj* generoso(-a); (*copious*) abbondante
genesis ['dʒɛnɪsɪs] *n* genesi *f*
genetic [dʒɪ'nɛtɪk] *adj* genetico(-a); **~ engineering** ingegneria genetica
genetically modified [dʒɪ'nɛtɪklɪ'mɔdɪfaɪd] *adj* geneticamente modificato(-a), transgenico(-a); **~ organism** organismo geneticamente modificato
genetic fingerprinting [-fɪŋɡəprɪntɪŋ] *n* rilevamento delle impronte genetiche
genetics [dʒɪ'nɛtɪks] *n* genetica
Geneva [dʒɪ'niːvə] *n* Ginevra; **Lake ~** il lago di Ginevra
genial ['dʒiːnɪəl] *adj* geniale, cordiale
genitals ['dʒɛnɪtlz] *npl* genitali *mpl*
genitive ['dʒɛnɪtɪv] *n* genitivo
genius ['dʒiːnɪəs] *n* genio
Genoa ['dʒɛnəuə] *n* Genova
genocide ['dʒɛnəusaɪd] *n* genocidio
Genoese [dʒɛnəʊ'iːz] *adj*, *n* (*pl inv*) genovese (*m/f*)
genome ['dʒiːnəum] *n* (*Biol*) genoma *m*
gent [dʒɛnt] *n abbr* (*Brit col*) = **gentleman**
genteel [dʒɛn'tiːl] *adj* raffinato(-a), distinto(-a)
gentle ['dʒɛntl] *adj* delicato(-a); (*person*) dolce
gentleman ['dʒɛntlmən] *n* signore *m*; (*well-bred man*) gentiluomo; **~'s agreement** impegno sulla parola
gentlemanly ['dʒɛntlmənlɪ] *adj* da gentiluomo
gentleness ['dʒɛntlnɪs] *n* delicatezza; dolcezza
gently ['dʒɛntlɪ] *adv* delicatamente
gentry ['dʒɛntrɪ] *n* nobiltà minore
gents [dʒɛnts] *n* W.C *m* (per signori)
genuine ['dʒɛnjuɪn] *adj* autentico(-a), sincero(-a)
genuinely ['dʒɛnjuɪnlɪ] *adv* genuinamente
geographer [dʒɪ'ɔɡrəfə^r] *n* geografo(-a)
geographic [dʒɪə'ɡræfɪk], **geographical** [dʒɪə'ɡræfɪkl] *adj* geografico(-a)
geography [dʒɪ'ɔɡrəfɪ] *n* geografia
geological [dʒɪə'lɔdʒɪkl] *adj* geologico(-a)
geologist [dʒɪ'ɔlədʒɪst] *n* geologo(-a)
geology [dʒɪ'ɔlədʒɪ] *n* geologia
geometric [dʒɪə'mɛtrɪk], **geometrical** [dʒɪə'mɛtrɪkl] *adj* geometrico(-a)
geometry [dʒɪ'ɔmətrɪ] *n* geometria
Geordie ['dʒɔːdɪ] *n* (*col*) abitante *m/f* del Tyneside; originario(-a) del Tyneside
Georgia ['dʒɔːdʒə] *n* Georgia
Georgian ['dʒɔːdʒən] *adj* georgiano(-a) ■ *n* georgiano(-a); (*Ling*) georgiano
geranium [dʒɪ'reɪnɪəm] *n* geranio
geriatric [dʒɛrɪ'ætrɪk] *adj* geriatrico(-a)

germ [dʒəːm] *n* (*Med*) microbo; (*Biol, fig*) germe *m*
German ['dʒəːmən] *adj* tedesco(-a) ■ *n* tedesco(-a); (*Ling*) tedesco
German Democratic Republic *n* Repubblica Democratica Tedesca
germane [dʒəː'meɪn] *adj* (*formal*): **to be ~ to sth** essere attinente a qc
German measles *n* rosolia
Germany ['dʒəːmənɪ] *n* Germania
germination [dʒəːmɪ'neɪʃən] *n* germinazione *f*
germ warfare *n* guerra batteriologica
gerrymandering ['dʒɛrɪmændərɪŋ] *n* manipolazione *f* dei distretti elettorali.
gestation [dʒɛs'teɪʃən] *n* gestazione *f*
gesticulate [dʒɛs'tɪkjuleɪt] *vi* gesticolare
gesture ['dʒɛstjə^r] *n* gesto; **as a ~ of friendship** in segno d'amicizia

 KEYWORD

get [ɡɛt] (*pt, pp* **got**, (*US*) *pp* **gotten**) *vi*
1 (*become, be*) diventare, farsi; **to get drunk** ubriacarsi; **to get killed** venire *or* rimanere ucciso(-a); **it's getting late** si sta facendo tardi; **to get old** invecchiare; **to get paid** venire pagato(-a); **to get ready** prepararsi; **to get shaved** farsi la barba; **to get tired** stancarsi; **to get washed** lavarsi
2 (*go*): **to get to/from** andare a/da; **to get home** arrivare *or* tornare a casa; **how did you get here?** come sei venuto?; **he got across the bridge** ha attraversato il ponte; **he got under the fence** è passato sotto il recinto
3 (*begin*) mettersi a, cominciare a; **to get to know sb** incominciare a conoscere qn; **let's get going** *or* **started** muoviamoci
4 (*modal aux vb*): **you've got to do it** devi farlo ■ *vt* **1**: **to get sth done** (*do*) fare qc; (*have done*) far fare qc; **to get sth/sb ready** preparare qc/qn; **to get one's hair cut** tagliarsi *or* farsi tagliare i capelli; **to get sb to do sth** far fare qc a qn
2 (*obtain: money, permission, results*) ottenere; (*find: job, flat*) trovare; (*fetch: person, doctor*) chiamare; (*: object*) prendere; **to get sth for sb** prendere *or* procurare qc a qn; **get me Mr Jones, please** (*Tel*) mi passi il signor Jones, per favore; **can I get you a drink?** le posso offrire da bere?
3 (*receive: present, letter, prize*) ricevere; (*acquire: reputation*) farsi; **how much did you get for the painting?** quanto le hanno dato per il quadro?
4 (*catch*) prendere; (*hit: target etc*) colpire;

to get sb by the arm/throat afferrare qn per un braccio/alla gola; **get him!** prendetelo!; **he really gets me** (*fig: annoy*) mi dà proprio sui nervi
5 (*take, move*) portare; **to get sth to sb** far avere qc a qn; **do you think we'll get it through the door?** pensi che riusciremo a farlo passare per la porta?
6 (*catch, take: plane, bus etc*) prendere; **he got the last bus** ha preso l'ultimo autobus; **she got the morning flight to Milan** ha preso il volo per Milano del mattino
7 (*understand*) afferrare; (*hear*) sentire; **I've got it!** ci sono arrivato!, ci sono!; **I'm sorry, I didn't get your name** scusi, non ho capito (or sentito) come si chiama
8 (*have, possess*): **to have got** avere; **how many have you got?** quanti ne ha?
▸ **get about** *vi* muoversi; (*news*) diffondersi
▸ **get across** *vt*: **to get across (to)** (*message, meaning*) comunicare (a)
■ *vi*: **to get across to** (*subj: speaker*) comunicare con
▸ **get along** *vi* (*agree*) andare d'accordo; (*depart*) andarsene; (*manage*) = **get by**
▸ **get at** *vt fus* (*attack*) prendersela con; (*reach*) raggiungere, arrivare a; **what are you getting at?** dove vuoi arrivare?
▸ **get away** *vi* partire, andarsene; (*escape*) scappare
▸ **get away with** *vt fus*: **he'll never get away with it!** non riuscirà a farla franca!
▸ **get back** *vi* (*return*) ritornare, tornare
■ *vt* riottenere, riavere; **to get back to** (*start again*) ritornare a; (*contact again*) rimettersi in contatto con
▸ **get back at** *vt fus* (*col*): **to get back at sb (for sth)** rendere pan per focaccia a qn (per qc)
▸ **get by** *vi* (*pass*) passare; (*manage*) farcela; **I can get by in Dutch** mi arrangio in olandese
▸ **get down** *vi, vt fus* scendere
■ *vt* far scendere; (*depress*) buttare giù
▸ **get down to** *vt fus* (*work*) mettersi a (fare); **to get down to business** venire al dunque
▸ **get in** *vi* entrare; (*train*) arrivare; (*arrive home*) ritornare, tornare
■ *vt* (*bring in: harvest*) raccogliere; (: *coal, shopping, supplies*) fare provvista di; (*insert*) far entrare, infilare
▸ **get into** *vt fus* entrare in; **to get into a rage** incavolarsi; **to get into bed** mettersi a letto
▸ **get off** *vi* (*from train etc*) scendere; (*depart: person, car*) andare via; (*escape*) cavarsela
■ *vt* (*remove: clothes, stain*) levare; (*send off*) spedire; (*have as leave: days, time*): **we got 2 days off** abbiamo avuto 2 giorni liberi

■ *vt fus* (*train, bus*) scendere da; **to get off to a good start** (*fig*) cominciare bene
▸ **get on** *vi*: **how did you get on?** com'è andata?; **he got on quite well** ha fatto bene, (gli) è andata bene; **to get on (with sb)** andare d'accordo (con qn); **how are you getting on?** come va la vita?
■ *vt fus* montare in; (*horse*) montare su
▸ **get on to** *vt fus* (*Brit col: contact: on phone etc*) contattare, rintracciare; (: *deal with*) occuparsi di
▸ **get out** *vi* uscire; (*of vehicle*) scendere
■ *vt* tirar fuori, far uscire; **to get out (of)** (*money from bank etc*) ritirare (da)
▸ **get out of** *vt fus* uscire da; (*duty etc*) evitare; **what will you get out of it?** cosa ci guadagni?
▸ **get over** *vt fus* (*illness*) riaversi da; (*communicate: idea etc*) comunicare, passare; **let's get it over (with)** togliamoci il pensiero
▸ **get round** *vt fus* aggirare; (*fig: person*) rigirare
■ *vi*: **to get round to doing sth** trovare il tempo di fare qc
▸ **get through** *vi* (*Tel*) avere la linea
■ *vt fus* (*finish: work*) sbrigare; (: *book*) finire
▸ **get through to** *vt fus* (*Tel*) parlare a
▸ **get together** *vi* riunirsi
■ *vt* raccogliere; (*people*) adunare
▸ **get up** *vi* (*rise*) alzarsi
■ *vt fus* salire su per
▸ **get up to** *vt fus* (*reach*) raggiungere; (*prank etc*) fare

getaway ['gɛtəweɪ] *n* fuga
getaway car *n* macchina per la fuga
get-together ['gɛttəgɛðəʳ] *n* (piccola) riunione *f*; (*party*) festicciola
get-up ['gɛtʌp] *n* (*col: outfit*) tenuta
get-well card [gɛt'wɛl-] *n* cartolina di auguri di pronta guarigione
geyser ['giːzəʳ] *n* scaldabagno; (*Geo*) geyser *m inv*
Ghana ['gɑːnə] *n* Ghana *m*
Ghanaian [gɑːˈneɪən] *adj, n* ganaense (*m/f*)
ghastly ['gɑːstlɪ] *adj* orribile, orrendo(-a)
gherkin ['gəːkɪn] *n* cetriolino
ghetto blaster [-'blɑːstəʳ] *n* maxistereo portatile
ghost [gəʊst] *n* fantasma *m*, spettro ■ *vt* (*book*) fare lo scrittore ombra per
ghostly ['gəʊstlɪ] *adj* spettrale
ghostwriter ['gəʊstraɪtəʳ] *n* scrittore(-trice) ombra *inv*
ghoul [guːl] *n* vampiro che si nutre di cadaveri

ghoulish ['guːlɪʃ] *adj* (*tastes etc*) macabro(-a)

GHQ *n abbr* (Mil: = *general headquarters*)
≈ comando di Stato maggiore

GI *n abbr* (*US col*: = *government issue*) G.I. *m*,
soldato americano

giant ['dʒaɪənt] *n* gigante(-essa) ■ *adj*
gigante, enorme; **~ (size) packet** confezione
f gigante

giant killer *n* (*Sport*) *piccola squadra che riesce a
batterne una importante*

gibber ['dʒɪbəʳ] *vi* (*monkey*) squittire
confusamente; (*idiot*) farfugliare

gibberish ['dʒɪbərɪʃ] *n* parole *fpl* senza senso

gibe [dʒaɪb] *n* frecciata ■ *vi*: **to ~ at** lanciare
frecciate a

giblets ['dʒɪblɪts] *npl* frattaglie *fpl*

Gibraltar [dʒɪ'brɔːltəʳ] *n* Gibilterra

giddiness ['gɪdɪnɪs] *n* vertigine *f*

giddy ['gɪdɪ] *adj* (*dizzy*): **to be ~** aver le
vertigini; (*height*) vertiginoso(-a); **I feel ~**
mi gira la testa

gift [gɪft] *n* regalo; (*donation, ability*) dono;
(*Comm: also*: **free gift**) omaggio; **to have a ~
for sth** (*talent*) avere il dono di qc

gifted ['gɪftɪd] *adj* dotato(-a)

gift token, gift voucher *n* buono (acquisto)

gig [gɪg] *n* (*col: of musician*) serata

gigabyte [gi:gəbaɪt] *n* gigabyte *m inv*

gigantic [dʒaɪ'gæntɪk] *adj* gigantesco(-a)

giggle ['gɪgl] *vi* ridere scioccamente ■ *n*
risolino (sciocco)

GIGO ['gaɪgəu] *abbr* (*Comput: col*: = *garbage in,
garbage out*) qualità di input = qualità di
output

gild [gɪld] *vt* dorare

gill [dʒɪl] *n* (*measure*) = 0.25 *pints* (Brit = 0.148 l;
US = 0.118 l)

gills [gɪlz] *npl* (*of fish*) branchie *fpl*

gilt [gɪlt] *n* doratura ■ *adj* dorato(-a)

gilt-edged ['gɪltedʒd] *adj* (*stocks, securities*)
della massima sicurezza

gimlet ['gɪmlɪt] *n* succhiello

gimmick ['gɪmɪk] *n* trucco; **sales ~** trovata
commerciale

gin [dʒɪn] *n* (*liquor*) gin *m inv*

ginger ['dʒɪndʒəʳ] *n* zenzero
▶ **ginger up** *vt* scuotere; animare

ginger ale, ginger beer *n* bibita gassosa allo
zenzero

gingerbread ['dʒɪndʒəbred] *n* pan *m* di
zenzero

ginger group *n* (*Brit*) gruppo di pressione

ginger-haired ['dʒɪndʒə'hɛəd] *adj*
rossiccio(-a)

gingerly ['dʒɪndʒəlɪ] *adv* cautamente

gingham ['gɪŋəm] *n* percalle *m* a righe
(*or* quadretti)

ginseng ['dʒɪnsɛŋ] *n* ginseng *m*

gipsy ['dʒɪpsɪ] *n* zingaro(-a) ■ *adj* degli
zingari

giraffe [dʒɪ'rɑːf] *n* giraffa

girder ['gə:dəʳ] *n* trave *f*

girdle ['gə:dl] *n* (*corset*) guaina

girl [gə:l] *n* ragazza; (*young unmarried woman*)
signorina; (*daughter*) figlia, figliola; **a little ~**
una bambina

girl band *n* *gruppo pop di sole ragazze creato per far
presa su un pubblico giovane*

girlfriend ['gə:lfrɛnd] *n* (*of girl*) amica; (*of boy*)
ragazza

girlish ['gə:lɪʃ] *adj* da ragazza

Girl Scout *n* (US) Giovane Esploratrice *f*

Giro ['dʒaɪrəu] *n*: **the National ~** (*Brit*) ≈ la *or* il
Bancoposta

giro ['dʒaɪrəu] *n* (*bank giro*) versamento
bancario; (*post office giro*) postagiro

girth [gə:θ] *n* circonferenza; (*of horse*) cinghia

gist [dʒɪst] *n* succo

give [gɪv] *n* (*of fabric*) elasticità ■ *vb* (*pt* **gave**,
pp **given**) [geɪv, 'gɪvn] *vt* dare ■ *vi* cedere; **to
~ sb sth, ~ sth to sb** dare qc a qn; **to ~ a cry/
sigh** emettere un grido/sospiro; **how much
did you ~ for it?** quanto (l')hai pagato?; **12
o'clock, ~ or take a few minutes**
mezzogiorno, minuto più minuto meno; **to
~ way** *vi* cedere; (*Brit Aut*) dare la precedenza
▶ **give away** *vt* dare via; (*give free*) fare dono
di; (*betray*) tradire; (*disclose*) rivelare; (*bride*)
condurre all'altare
▶ **give back** *vt* rendere
▶ **give in** *vi* cedere ■ *vt* consegnare
▶ **give off** *vt* emettere
▶ **give out** *vt* distribuire; annunciare ■ *vi*
(*be exhausted: supplies*) esaurirsi, venir meno;
(*fail: engine*) fermarsi; (: *strength*) mancare
▶ **give up** *vi* rinunciare ■ *vt* rinunciare a;
to ~ up smoking smettere di fumare; **to ~
o.s. up** arrendersi

give-and-take [gɪvən'teɪk] *n* (*col*) elasticità
(da ambo le parti), concessioni *fpl* reciproche

giveaway ['gɪvəweɪ] *n* (*col*): **her expression
was a ~** le si leggeva tutto in volto; **the exam
was a ~!** l'esame è stato uno scherzo! ■ *cpd*:
~ prices prezzi stracciati

given ['gɪvn] *pp of* **give** ■ *adj* (*fixed*: *time,
amount*) dato(-a), determinato(-a) ■ *conj*:
~ (that) ... dato che ...; **~ the circumstances** ...
date le circostanze ...

glacial ['gleɪsɪəl] *adj* glaciale

glacier ['glæsɪəʳ] *n* ghiacciaio

glad [glæd] *adj* lieto(-a), contento(-a); **to be ~
about sth/that** essere contento *or* lieto di qc/
che + *sub*; **I was ~ of his help** gli sono stato
grato del suo aiuto

gladden ['glædn] vt rallegrare, allietare

glade [gleɪd] n radura

gladioli [glædɪ'əʊlaɪ] npl gladioli mpl

gladly ['glædlɪ] adv volentieri

glamorous ['glæmərəs] adj (gen) favoloso(-a); (person) affascinante, seducente; (occasion) brillante, elegante

glamour ['glæməʳ] n fascino

glance [glɑːns] n occhiata, sguardo ■ vi: **to ~ at** dare un'occhiata a
  ▶ **glance off** vt fus (bullet) rimbalzare su

glancing ['glɑːnsɪŋ] adj (blow) che colpisce di striscio

gland [glænd] n ghiandola

glandular ['glændjuləʳ] adj: **~ fever** (Brit) mononucleosi f

glare [glɛəʳ] n riverbero, luce f abbagliante; (look) sguardo furioso ■ vi abbagliare; **to ~ at** guardare male

glaring ['glɛərɪŋ] adj (mistake) madornale

glasnost ['glæznɔst] n glasnost f

glass [glɑːs] n (substance) vetro; (tumbler) bicchiere m; (also: **looking glass**) specchio; see also **glasses**

glass-blowing ['glɑːsbləʊɪŋ] n soffiatura del vetro

glass ceiling n (fig) barriera invisibile

glasses ['glɑːsɪz] npl (spectacles) occhiali mpl

glass fibre n fibra di vetro

glasshouse ['glɑːshaʊs] n serra

glassware ['glɑːswɛəʳ] n vetrame m

glassy ['glɑːsɪ] adj (eyes) vitreo(-a)

Glaswegian [glæs'wiːdʒən] adj di Glasgow ■ n abitante m/f di Glasgow, originario(-a) di Glasgow

glaze [gleɪz] vt (door) fornire di vetri; (pottery) smaltare; (Culin) glassare ■ n smalto; glassa

glazed ['gleɪzd] adj (eye) vitreo(-a); (tiles, pottery) smaltato(-a)

glazier ['gleɪzɪəʳ] n vetraio

gleam [gliːm] n barlume m; raggio ■ vi luccicare; **a ~ of hope** un barlume di speranza

gleaming ['gliːmɪŋ] adj lucente

glean [gliːn] vt (information) racimolare

glee [gliː] n allegrezza, gioia

gleeful ['gliːful] adj allegro(-a), gioioso(-a)

glen [glɛn] n valletta

glib [glɪb] adj dalla parola facile; facile

glide [glaɪd] vi scivolare; (Aviat, birds) planare ■ n scivolata; planata

glider ['glaɪdəʳ] n (Aviat) aliante m

gliding ['glaɪdɪŋ] n (Aviat) volo a vela

glimmer ['glɪməʳ] vi luccicare ■ n barlume m

glimpse [glɪmps] n impressione f fugace ■ vt vedere di sfuggita; **to catch a ~ of** vedere di sfuggita

glint [glɪnt] n luccichio ■ vi luccicare

glisten ['glɪsn] vi luccicare

glitter ['glɪtəʳ] vi scintillare ■ n scintillio

glitz [glɪts] n (col) vistosità, chiassosità

gloat [gləʊt] vi: **to ~ (over)** gongolare di piacere (per)

global ['gləʊbl] adj globale; (world-wide) mondiale

globalization [gləʊbəlaɪ'zeɪʃən] n globalizzazione f

global warming n riscaldamento dell'atmosfera terrestre

globe [gləʊb] n globo, sfera

globetrotter ['gləʊbtrɔtəʳ] n giramondo m/f inv

globule ['glɔbjuːl] n (Anat) globulo; (of water etc) gocciolina

gloom [gluːm] n oscurità, buio; (sadness) tristezza, malinconia

gloomy ['gluːmɪ] adj fosco(-a), triste; **to feel ~** sentirsi giù or depresso

glorification [glɔːrɪfɪ'keɪʃən] n glorificazione f

glorify ['glɔːrɪfaɪ] vt glorificare; celebrare, esaltare

glorious ['glɔːrɪəs] adj glorioso(-a), magnifico(-a)

glory ['glɔːrɪ] n gloria; splendore m ■ vi: **to ~ in** gloriarsi di or in

glory hole n (col) ripostiglio

Glos abbr (Brit) = **Gloucestershire**

gloss [glɔs] n (shine) lucentezza; (also: **gloss paint**) vernice f a olio
  ▶ **gloss over** vt fus scivolare su

glossary ['glɔsərɪ] n glossario

glossy ['glɔsɪ] adj lucente ■ n (also: **glossy magazine**) rivista di lusso

glove [glʌv] n guanto

glove compartment n (Aut) vano portaoggetti

glow [gləʊ] vi ardere; (face) essere luminoso(-a) ■ n bagliore m; (of face) colorito acceso

glower ['glaʊəʳ] vi: **to ~ (at sb)** guardare (qn) in cagnesco

glowing ['gləʊɪŋ] adj (fire) ardente; (complexion) luminoso(-a); (fig: report, description etc) entusiasta

glow-worm ['gləʊwəːm] n lucciola

glucose ['gluːkəʊs] n glucosio

glue [gluː] n colla ■ vt incollare

glue-sniffing ['gluːsnɪfɪŋ] n sniffare m (colla)

glum [glʌm] adj abbattuto(-a)

glut [glʌt] n eccesso ■ vt saziare; (market) saturare

glutinous ['gluːtɪnəs] adj colloso(-a), appiccicoso(-a)

581

glutton ['glʌtn] n ghiottone(-a); **a ~ for work** un(-a) patito(-a) del lavoro

gluttonous ['glʌtənəs] adj ghiotto(-a), goloso(-a)

gluttony ['glʌtənɪ] n ghiottoneria; (sin) gola

glycerin, glycerine ['glɪsəriːn] n glicerina

GM adj abbr = **genetically modified**

gm abbr = **gram**

GMAT n abbr (US: = Graduate Management Admissions Test) esame di ammissione all'ultimo biennio di scuola superiore

GMB n abbr (Brit) = **General, Municipal, and Boilermakers (Union)**

GM-free [dʒiːɛmˈfriː] adj privo(-a) di OGM

GMO n abbr (= genetically modified organism) OGM m inv

GMT abbr (= Greenwich Mean Time) T.M.G

gnarled [nɑːld] adj nodoso(-a)

gnash [næʃ] vt: **to ~ one's teeth** digrignare i denti

gnat [næt] n moscerino

gnaw [nɔː] vt rodere

gnome [nəum] n gnomo

GNP n abbr = **gross national product**

go [gəu] vb (pt **went**, pp **gone**) [wɛnt, gɔn] vi andare; (depart) partire, andarsene; (work) funzionare; (break etc) cedere; (be sold): **to go for £10** essere venduto per 10 sterline; (fit, suit): **to go with** andare bene con; (become): **to go pale** diventare pallido(-a); **to go mouldy** ammuffire ■ n (pl **goes**) **to have a go (at)** provare; **to be on the go** essere in moto; **whose go is it?** a chi tocca?; **to go by car/on foot** andare in macchina/a piedi; **he's going to do** sta per fare; **to go for a walk** andare a fare una passeggiata; **to go dancing/shopping** andare a ballare/fare la spesa; **to go looking for sb/sth** andare in cerca di qn/qc; **to go to sleep** addormentarsi; **to go and see sb, to go to see sb** andare a trovare qn; **how is it going?** come va (la vita)?; **how did it go?** com'è andato?; **to go round the back/by the shop** passare da dietro/davanti al negozio; **my voice has gone** m'è andata via la voce; **the cake is all gone** il dolce è finito tutto; **I'll take whatever is going** (Brit) prendo quello che c'è; **... to go** (US: food) ... da portar via; **the money will go towards our holiday** questi soldi li mettiamo per la vacanza

▶ **go about** vi (also: **go around**) aggirarsi; (: rumour) correre, circolare ■ vt fus: **how do I go about this?** qual è la prassi per questo?; **to go about one's business** occuparsi delle proprie faccende

▶ **go after** vt fus (pursue) correr dietro a, rincorrere; (job, record etc) mirare a

▶ **go against** vt fus (be unfavourable to) essere contro; (be contrary to) andare contro

▶ **go ahead** vi andare avanti; **go ahead!** faccia pure!

▶ **go along** vi andare, avanzare ■ vt fus percorrere; **to go along with** (accompany) andare con, accompagnare; (agree with: idea) sottoscrivere, appoggiare

▶ **go away** vi partire, andarsene

▶ **go back** vi tornare, ritornare; (go again) andare di nuovo

▶ **go back on** vt fus (promise) non mantenere

▶ **go by** vi (years, time) scorrere ■ vt fus attenersi a, seguire (alla lettera); prestar fede a

▶ **go down** vi scendere; (ship) affondare; (sun) tramontare ■ vt fus scendere; **that should go down well with him** dovrebbe incontrare la sua approvazione

▶ **go for** vt fus (fetch) andare a prendere; (like) andar matto(-a) per; (attack) attaccare; saltare addosso a

▶ **go in** vi entrare

▶ **go in for** vt fus (competition) iscriversi a; (be interested in) interessarsi di

▶ **go into** vt fus entrare in; (investigate) indagare, esaminare; (embark on) lanciarsi in

▶ **go off** vi partire, andar via; (food) guastarsi; (explode) esplodere, scoppiare; (lights etc) spegnersi; (event) passare ■ vt fus: **I've gone off chocolate** la cioccolata non mi piace più; **the gun went off** il fucile si scaricò; **the party went off well** la festa è andata or è riuscita bene; **to go off to sleep** addormentarsi

▶ **go on** vi continuare; (happen) succedere; (lights) accendersi ■ vt fus (be guided by: evidence etc) basarsi su, fondarsi su; **to go on doing** continuare a fare; **what's going on here?** che succede or che sta succedendo qui?

▶ **go on at** vt fus (nag) assillare

▶ **go on with** vt fus continuare, proseguire

▶ **go out** vi uscire; (fire, light) spegnersi; (ebb: tide) calare; **to go out with sb** uscire con qn

▶ **go over** vi (ship) ribaltarsi ■ vt fus (check) esaminare; **to go over sth in one's mind** pensare bene a qc

▶ **go round** vi (circulate: news, rumour) circolare; (revolve) girare; (visit): **to go round (to sb's)** passare (da qn); (make a detour): **to go round (by)** passare (per); (suffice) bastare (per tutti)

▶ **go through** vt fus (town etc) attraversare; (search through) frugare in; (examine: list, book) leggere da capo a fondo; (perform) fare

▶ **go through with** vt fus (plan, crime) mettere in atto, eseguire; **I couldn't go through with it** non sono riuscito ad andare fino in fondo

▶ **go under** *vi* (*sink: ship*) affondare, colare a picco; (*: person*) andare sotto; (*fig: business, firm*) fallire

▶ **go up** *vi* salire ■ *vt fus* salire su per; **to go up in flames** andare in fiamme

▶ **go without** *vt fus* fare a meno di

goad [gəud] *vt* spronare

go-ahead ['gəuəhɛd] *adj* intraprendente ■ *n*: **to give sb/sth the ~** dare l'okay a qn/qc

goal [gəul] *n* (*Sport*) gol *m*, rete *f*; (*: place*) porta; (*fig: aim*) fine *m*, scopo

goal difference *n* differenza *f* reti *inv*

goalie ['gəulɪ] *n* (*col*) portiere *m*

goalkeeper ['gəulkiːpəʳ] *n* portiere *m*

goalpost ['gəulpəust] *n* palo (della porta)

goat [gəut] *n* capra

gobble ['gɔbl] *vt* (*also*: **gobble down, gobble up**) ingoiare

go-between ['gəubɪtwiːn] *n* intermediario(-a)

Gobi Desert ['gəubɪ-] *n*: **the ~** il Deserto dei Gobi

goblet ['gɔblɪt] *n* calice *m*, coppa

goblin ['gɔblɪn] *n* folletto

go-cart ['gəukɑːt] *n* go-kart *m inv* ■ *cpd*: **~ racing** *n* kartismo

god [gɔd] *n* dio; **G~** Dio

god-awful [gɔd'ɔːfəl] *adj* (*col*) di merda (*!*)

godchild ['gɔdtʃaɪld] *n* figlioccio(-a)

goddamn ['gɔddæm], **goddamned** ['gɔddæmd] (*esp US: col*) *excl*: **~!** porca miseria! ■ *adj* fottuto(-a) (*!*), maledetto(-a) ■ *adv* maledettamente

goddaughter ['gɔddɔːtəʳ] *n* figlioccia

goddess ['gɔdɪs] *n* dea

godfather ['gɔdfɑːðəʳ] *n* padrino

god-fearing ['gɔdfɪərɪŋ] *adj* timorato(-a) di Dio

god-forsaken ['gɔdfəseɪkən] *adj* desolato(-a), sperduto(-a)

godmother ['gɔdmʌðəʳ] *n* madrina

godparents ['gɔdpɛərənts] *npl*: **the ~** il padrino e la madrina

godsend ['gɔdsɛnd] *n* dono del cielo

godson ['gɔdsʌn] *n* figlioccio

goes [gəuz] *vb see* **go**

gofer ['gəufəʳ] *n* (*col*) tuttofare *m/f*, tirapiedi *m/f inv*

go-getter ['gəugɛtəʳ] *n* arrivista *m/f*

goggle ['gɔgl] *vi*: **to ~ (at)** stare con gli occhi incollati *or* appiccicati (a *or* addosso a)

goggles ['gɔglz] *npl* occhiali *mpl* (di protezione)

going ['gəuɪŋ] *n* (*conditions*) andare *m*, stato del terreno ■ *adj*: **the ~ rate** la tariffa in vigore; **a ~ concern** un'azienda avviata; **it was slow ~** si andava a rilento

going-over ['gəuɪŋ'əuvəʳ] *n* (*col*) controllata; (*violent attack*) pestaggio

goings-on ['gəuɪŋz'ɔn] *npl* (*col*) fatti *mpl* strani, cose *fpl* strane

go-kart ['gəukɑːt] *n* = **go-cart**

gold [gəuld] *n* oro ■ *adj* d'oro; (*reserves*) aureo(-a)

golden ['gəuldən] *adj* (*made of gold*) d'oro; (*gold in colour*) dorato(-a)

golden age *n* età d'oro

golden handshake *n* (*Brit*) gratifica di fine servizio

golden rule *n* regola principale

goldfish ['gəuldfɪʃ] *n* pesce *m* dorato *or* rosso

gold leaf *n* lamina d'oro

gold medal *n* (*Sport*) medaglia d'oro

goldmine ['gəuldmaɪn] *n* miniera d'oro

gold-plated ['gəuld'pleɪtɪd] *adj* placcato(-a) oro *inv*

goldsmith ['gəuldsmɪθ] *n* orefice *m*, orafo

gold standard *n* tallone *m* aureo

golf [gɔlf] *n* golf *m*

golf ball *n* pallina da golf

golf club *n* circolo di golf; (*stick*) bastone *m or* mazza da golf

golf course *n* campo di golf

golfer ['gɔlfəʳ] *n* giocatore(-trice) di golf

golfing ['gɔlfɪŋ] *n* il giocare a golf

gondola ['gɔndələ] *n* gondola

gondolier [gɔndə'lɪəʳ] *n* gondoliere *m*

gone [gɔn] *pp of* **go**

goner ['gɔnəʳ] *n* (*col*): **I thought you were a ~** pensavo che ormai fossi spacciato

gong [gɔŋ] *n* gong *m inv*

good [gud] *adj* buono(-a); (*kind*) buono(-a), gentile; (*child*) bravo(-a) ■ *n* bene *m*; **~!** bene!, ottimo!; **to be ~ at** essere bravo(-a) in; **it's ~ for you** fa bene; **it's a ~ thing you were there** meno male che c'era; **she is ~ with children/her hands** ci sa fare coi bambini/è abile nei lavori manuali; **to feel ~** sentirsi bene; **it's ~ to see you** che piacere vederla; **he's up to no ~** ne sta combinando qualcuna; **it's no ~ complaining** brontolare non serve a niente; **for the common ~** nell'interesse generale, per il bene comune; **for ~** (*for ever*) per sempre, definitivamente; **would you be ~ enough to ...?** avrebbe la gentilezza di ...?; **that's very ~ of you** è molto gentile da parte sua; **is this any ~?** (*will it do?*) va bene questo?; (*what's it like?*) com'è?; **a ~ deal (of)** molto(-a), una buona quantità (di); **a ~ many** molti(-e); **~ morning!** buon giorno!; **~ afternoon/evening!** buona sera!; **~ night!** buona notte!; *see also* **goods**

goodbye [gud'baɪ] *excl* arrivederci!; **to say ~ to** (*person*) salutare

good faith n buona fede
good-for-nothing ['gudfənʌθɪŋ] n buono(-a)
a nulla, vagabondo(-a)
Good Friday n Venerdì Santo
good-humoured [gud'hju:məd] adj (person)
di buon umore; (remark, joke) bonario(-a)
good-looking [gud'lukɪŋ] adj bello(-a)
good-natured [gud'neɪtʃəd] adj (person)
affabile; (discussion) amichevole, cordiale
goodness ['gudnɪs] n (of person) bontà; **for ~
sake!** per amor di Dio!; **~ gracious!** santo
cielo!, mamma mia!
goods [gudz] npl (Comm etc) merci fpl, articoli
mpl; **~ and chattels** beni mpl e effetti mpl
goods train n (Brit) treno m merci inv
goodwill [gud'wɪl] n amicizia, benevolenza;
(Comm) avviamento
goody-goody ['gudɪgudɪ] n (pej)
santarellino(-a)
gooey ['gu:ɪ] adj (Brit col: sticky)
appiccicoso(-a); (cake, dessert) troppo
zuccherato(-a)
Google® ['gu:gl] n Google® m ■ vt fare
ricerche in Internet su
goose (pl **geese**) [gu:s, gi:s] n oca
gooseberry ['guzbərɪ] n uva spina; **to play ~**
(Brit) tenere la candela
gooseflesh ['gu:sflɛʃ] n, **goosepimples**
['gu:spɪmplz] npl pelle f d'oca
goose step n (Mil) passo dell'oca
GOP n abbr (US Pol: col: = Grand Old Party) partito
repubblicano
gopher ['gəufəʳ] n = **gofer**
gore [gɔːʳ] vt incornare ■ n sangue m
(coagulato)
gorge [gɔːdʒ] n gola ■ vt: **to ~ o.s. (on)**
ingozzarsi (di)
gorgeous ['gɔːdʒəs] adj magnifico(-a)
gorilla [gə'rɪlə] n gorilla m inv
gormless ['gɔːmlɪs] adj (Brit col) tonto(-a);
(: stronger) deficiente
gorse [gɔːs] n ginestrone m
gory ['gɔːrɪ] adj sanguinoso(-a)
go-slow ['gəu'sləu] n (Brit) rallentamento dei
lavori (per agitazione sindacale)
gospel ['gɔspl] n vangelo
gossamer ['gɔsəməʳ] n (cobweb) fili mpl della
Madonna or di ragnatela; (light fabric) stoffa
sottilissima
gossip ['gɔsɪp] n chiacchiere fpl; pettegolezzi
mpl; (person) pettegolo(-a) ■ vi chiacchierare;
(maliciously) pettegolare; **a piece of ~** un
pettegolezzo
gossip column n cronaca mondana
got [gɔt] pt, pp of **get**
Gothic ['gɔθɪk] adj gotico(-a)
gotten ['gɔtn] (US) pp of **get**

gouge [gaudʒ] vt (also: **gouge out**: hole etc)
scavare; (: initials) scolpire; (: sb's eyes) cavare
gourd [guəd] n zucca
gourmet ['guəmeɪ] n buongustaio(-a)
gout [gaut] n gotta
govern ['gʌvən] vt governare; (Ling) reggere
governess ['gʌvənɪs] n governante f
governing ['gʌvənɪŋ] adj (Pol) al potere, al
governo; **~ body** consiglio di
amministrazione
government ['gʌvnmənt] n governo; (Brit:
ministers) ministero ■ cpd statale; **local ~**
amministrazione f locale
governmental [gʌvn'mɛntl] adj
governativo(-a)
government housing n (US) alloggi mpl
popolari
government stock n titoli mpl di stato
governor ['gʌvənəʳ] n (of state, bank)
governatore m; (of school, hospital)
amministratore m; (Brit: of prison)
direttore(-trice)
Govt abbr = **government**
gown [gaun] n vestito lungo; (of teacher, judge)
toga
GP n abbr (Med) = **general practitioner; who's
your GP?** qual è il suo medico di fiducia?
GPMU n abbr (Brit) = **Graphical, Paper and
Media Union**
GPO n abbr (Brit: old) = **General Post Office**;
(US: = Government Printing Office) ≈ Poligrafici
dello Stato
GPS n abbr (= global positioning system) GPS m
gr. abbr (Comm) = **gross**
grab [græb] vt afferrare, arraffare; (property,
power) impadronirsi di ■ vi: **to ~ at** tentare
disperatamente di afferrare
grace [greɪs] n grazia; (graciousness) garbo,
cortesia ■ vt onorare; **5 days'** ~ dilazione f
di 5 giorni; **to say ~** dire il benedicite; **with a
good/bad** ~ volentieri/malvolentieri; **his
sense of humour is his saving** ~ il suo
senso dell'umorismo è quello che lo salva
graceful ['greɪsful] adj elegante,
aggraziato(-a)
gracious ['greɪʃəs] adj grazioso(-a),
misericordioso(-a) ■ excl: **(good) ~!**
madonna (mia)!
gradation [grə'deɪʃən] n gradazione f
grade [greɪd] n (Comm) qualità f inv; classe f;
categoria; (in hierarchy) grado; (US Scol) voto;
classe; (gradient) pendenza, gradiente m ■ vt
classificare; ordinare; graduare; **to make
the ~** (fig) farcela
grade crossing n (US) passaggio a livello
grade school n (US) scuola elementare or
primaria

gradient ['greɪdɪənt] n pendenza, gradiente m
gradual ['grædjuəl] adj graduale
gradually ['grædjuəlɪ] adv man mano, a poco a poco
graduate n ['grædjuɪt] laureato(-a); (US Scol) diplomato(-a), licenziato(-a) ■ vi ['grædjueɪt] laurearsi
graduated pension ['grædjueɪtɪd-] n pensione calcolata sugli ultimi stipendi
graduation [grædju'eɪʃən] n cerimonia del conferimento della laurea; (US Scol) consegna dei diplomi
graffiti [grə'fiːtɪ] npl graffiti mpl
graft [grɑːft] n (Agr, Med) innesto ■ vt innestare; **hard ~** (col) duro lavoro
grain [greɪn] n (no pl: cereals) cereali mpl; (US: corn) grano; (of sand) granello; (of wood) venatura; **it goes against the ~** (fig) va contro la mia (or la sua etc) natura
gram [græm] n grammo
grammar ['græmə'] n grammatica
grammar school n (Brit) ≈ liceo; (US) ≈ scuola elementare
grammatical [grə'mætɪkl] adj grammaticale
gramme [græm] n = **gram**
gramophone ['græməfəun] n (Brit) grammofono
granary ['grænərɪ] n granaio
grand [grænd] adj grande, magnifico(-a); grandioso(-a) ■ n (col: thousand) mille dollari mpl (or sterline fpl)
grandchild (pl -children) ['grænt ʃaɪld, -tʃɪldrə n] n nipote m
granddad ['grændæd] n (col) nonno
granddaughter ['grændɔːtə'] n nipote f
grandeur ['grændjə'] n (of style, house) splendore m; (of occasion, scenery etc) grandiosità, maestà
grandfather ['grændfɑːðə'] n nonno
grandiose ['grændɪəus] adj grandioso(-a); (pej) pomposo(-a)
grand jury n (US) giuria (formata da 12 a 23 membri)
grandma ['grænmɑː] n (col) nonna
grandmother ['grænmʌðə'] n nonna
grandpa ['grænpɑː] n (col) = **granddad**
grandparent ['grænpɛərənt] n nonno(-a)
grand piano n pianoforte m a coda
Grand Prix ['grɑ̃ːˈpriː] n (Aut) Gran Premio, Grand Prix m inv
grandson ['grænsʌn] n nipote m
grandstand ['grændstænd] n (Sport) tribuna
grand total n somma complessiva
granite ['grænɪt] n granito
granny ['grænɪ] n (col) nonna
grant [grɑːnt] vt accordare; (a request) accogliere; (admit) ammettere, concedere ■ n (Scol) borsa; (Admin) sussidio, sovvenzione f; **to take sth for granted** dare qc per scontato
granulated ['grænjuleɪtɪd] adj: **~ sugar** zucchero cristallizzato
granule ['grænjuːl] n granello
grape [greɪp] n chicco d'uva, acino; **a bunch of grapes** un grappolo d'uva
grapefruit ['greɪpfruːt] n pompelmo
grapevine ['greɪpvaɪn] n vite f; **I heard it on the ~** (fig) me l'ha detto l'uccellino
graph [grɑːf] n grafico
graphic ['græfɪk] adj grafico(-a); (vivid) vivido(-a); see also **graphics**
graphic designer n grafico(-a)
graphic equalizer n equalizzatore m grafico
graphics ['græfɪks] n (art, process) grafica; (pl: drawings) illustrazioni fpl
graphite ['græfaɪt] n grafite f
graph paper n carta millimetrata
grapple ['græpl] vi: **to ~ with** essere alle prese con
grappling iron ['græplɪŋ-] n (Naut) grappino
grasp [grɑːsp] vt afferrare ■ n (grip) presa; (fig) potere m; comprensione f; **to have sth within one's ~** avere qc a portata di mano; **to have a good ~ of** (subject) avere una buona padronanza di
▶ **grasp at** vt fus (rope etc) afferrarsi a, aggrapparsi a; (fig: opportunity) non farsi sfuggire, approfittare di
grasping ['grɑːspɪŋ] adj avido(-a)
grass [grɑːs] n erba; (pasture) pascolo, prato; (Brit col: informer) informatore(-trice); (ex-terrorist) pentito(-a)
grasshopper ['grɑːshɔpə'] n cavalletta
grassland ['grɑːslænd] n prateria
grass roots npl (fig) base f
grass snake n natrice f
grassy ['grɑːsɪ] adj erboso(-a)
grate [greɪt] n graticola (del focolare) ■ vi cigolare, stridere ■ vt (Culin) grattugiare
grateful ['greɪtful] adj grato(-a), riconoscente
gratefully ['greɪtfulɪ] adv con gratitudine
grater ['greɪtə'] n grattugia
gratification [grætɪfɪ'keɪʃən] n soddisfazione f
gratify ['grætɪfaɪ] vt appagare; (whim) soddisfare
gratifying ['grætɪfaɪɪŋ] adj gradito(-a), soddisfacente
grating ['greɪtɪŋ] n (iron bars) grata ■ adj (noise) stridente, stridulo(-a)
gratitude ['grætɪtjuːd] n gratitudine f
gratuitous [grə'tjuːɪtəs] adj gratuito(-a)
gratuity [grə'tjuːɪtɪ] n mancia
grave [greɪv] n tomba ■ adj grave, serio(-a)

gravedigger ['greɪvdɪgə'] n becchino
gravel ['grævl] n ghiaia
gravely ['greɪvlɪ] adv gravemente,
solennemente; ~ **ill** in pericolo di vita
gravestone ['greɪvstəun] n pietra tombale
graveyard ['greɪvjɑ:d] n cimitero
gravitate ['grævɪteɪt] vi gravitare
gravity ['grævɪtɪ] n (all senses) gravità
gravy ['greɪvɪ] n intingolo della carne; salsa
gravy boat n salsiera
gravy train n: **the** ~ (col) l'albero della
cuccagna
gray [greɪ] adj (US) = **grey**
graze [greɪz] vi pascolare, pascere ■ vt (touch
lightly) sfiorare; (scrape) escoriare ■ n (Med)
escoriazione f
grazing ['greɪzɪŋ] n pascolo
grease [gri:s] n (fat) grasso; (lubricant)
lubrificante m ■ vt ingrassare; lubrificare;
to ~ the skids (US: fig) spianare la strada
grease gun n ingrassatore m
greasepaint ['gri:speɪnt] n cerone m
greaseproof paper ['gri:spru:f-] n (Brit) carta
oleata
greasy ['gri:sɪ] adj grasso(-a), untuoso(-a);
(Brit: road, surface) scivoloso(-a); (hands, clothes)
unto(-a)
great [greɪt] adj grande; (pain, heat) forte,
intenso(-a); (col) magnifico(-a),
meraviglioso(-a); **they're ~ friends** sono
grandi amici; **the ~ thing is that ...** il bello è
che ...; **it was ~!** è stato fantastico!; **we had a
~ time** ci siamo divertiti un mondo
Great Barrier Reef n: **the ~** la Grande
Barriera Corallina
Great Britain n Gran Bretagna
great-grandchild (pl **-children**)
[greɪt'græntʃaɪld, -tʃɪldrən] n pronipote m/f
great-grandfather [greɪt'grændfɑ:ðə'] n
bisnonno
great-grandmother [greɪt'grænmʌðə'] n
bisnonna
Great Lakes npl: **the ~** i Grandi Laghi
greatly ['greɪtlɪ] adv molto
greatness ['greɪtnɪs] n grandezza
Grecian ['gri:ʃən] adj greco(-a)
Greece [gri:s] n Grecia
greed [gri:d] n (also: **greediness**) avarizia;
(for food) golosità, ghiottoneria
greedily ['gri:dɪlɪ] adv avidamente;
golosamente
greedy ['gri:dɪ] adj avido(-a); goloso(-a),
ghiotto(-a)
Greek [gri:k] adj greco(-a) ■ n greco(-a);
(Ling) greco; **ancient/modern ~** greco
antico/moderno
green [gri:n] adj (also Pol) verde; (inexperienced)

inesperto(-a), ingenuo(-a) ■ n verde m;
(stretch of grass) prato; (also: **village green**)
≈ piazza del paese; (of golf course) green m inv;
greens npl (vegetables) verdura; **to have ~
fingers** or (US) **a ~ thumb** (fig) avere il pollice
verde; **the G~ Party** (Brit Pol) i Verdi
green belt n (round town) cintura di verde
green card n (Aut) carta verde
greenery ['gri:nərɪ] n verde m
greenfly ['gri:nflaɪ] n afide f
greengage ['gri:ngeɪdʒ] n susina Regina
Claudia
greengrocer ['gri:ngrəusə'] n (Brit)
fruttivendolo(-a), erbivendolo(-a)
greenhouse ['gri:nhaus] n serra
greenhouse effect n: **the ~** l'effetto serra
greenhouse gas n gas m inv responsabile
dell'effetto serra
greenish ['gri:nɪʃ] adj verdastro(-a)
Greenland ['gri:nlənd] n Groenlandia
Greenlander ['gri:nləndə'] n groenlandese m/f
green light n: **to give sb the ~** dare via libera
a qn
green pepper n peperone m verde
greet [gri:t] vt salutare
greeting ['gri:tɪŋ] n saluto; **Christmas/
birthday greetings** auguri mpl di Natale/di
compleanno; **Season's greetings** Buone Feste
greeting card, **greetings card** n cartolina
d'auguri
gregarious [grə'gɛərɪəs] adj gregario(-a),
socievole
grenade [grə'neɪd] n (also: **hand grenade**)
granata
grew [gru:] pt of **grow**
grey [greɪ] adj grigio(-a); **to go ~** diventar
grigio
greyhound ['greɪhaund] n levriere m
grid [grɪd] n grata; (Elec) rete f; (US Aut) area
d'incrocio
griddle ['grɪdl] n piastra
gridiron ['grɪdaɪən] n graticola
gridlock ['grɪdlɔk] n (traffic jam) paralisi f inv
del traffico
grief [gri:f] n dolore m; **to come to ~** (plan)
naufragare; (person) finire male
grievance ['gri:vəns] n doglianza, lagnanza;
(cause for complaint) motivo di risentimento
grieve [gri:v] vi addolorarsi, soffrire ■ vt
addolorare; **to ~ for sb** compiangere qn;
(dead person) piangere qn
grievous bodily harm ['gri:vəs-] n (Law)
aggressione f
grill [grɪl] n (on cooker) griglia ■ vt (Brit)
cuocere ai ferri; (question) interrogare senza
sosta; **grilled meat** carne f ai ferri or alla
griglia; see **grillroom**

grille [grɪl] n grata; (Aut) griglia
grillroom ['grɪlrum], **grill** ['grɪl] n rosticceria
grim [grɪm] adj sinistro(-a), brutto(-a)
grimace [grɪ'meɪs] n smorfia ■ vi fare smorfie
grime [graɪm] n sudiciume m
grimy ['graɪmɪ] adj sudicio(-a)
grin [grɪn] n sorriso smagliante ■ vi: **to ~ (at)** sorridere (a), fare un gran sorriso (a)
grind [graɪnd] vb (pt, pp **ground**) [graʊnd] vt macinare; (US: meat) tritare, macinare; (make sharp) arrotare; (polish: gem, lens) molare ■ vi (car gears) grattare ■ n (work) sgobbata; **to ~ one's teeth** digrignare i denti; **to ~ to a halt** (vehicle) arrestarsi con uno stridio di freni; (fig: talks, scheme) insabbiarsi; (: work, production) cessare del tutto; **the daily ~** (col) il trantran quotidiano
grinder ['graɪndər] n (machine: for coffee) macinino
grindstone ['graɪndstəʊn] n: **to keep one's nose to the ~** darci sotto
grip [grɪp] n presa; (holdall) borsa da viaggio ■ vt afferrare; **to come to grips with** affrontare; cercare di risolvere; **to ~ the road** (tyres) far presa sulla strada; (car) tenere bene la strada; **to lose one's ~** perdere or allentare la presa; (fig) perdere la grinta
gripe [graɪp] n (Med) colica; (col: complaint) lagna ■ vi (col) brontolare
gripping ['grɪpɪŋ] adj avvincente
grisly ['grɪzlɪ] adj macabro(-a), orrido(-a)
grist [grɪst] n (fig): **it's (all) ~ to the mill** tutto aiuta
gristle ['grɪsl] n cartilagine f
grit [grɪt] n ghiaia; (courage) fegato ■ vt (road) coprire di sabbia; **to ~ one's teeth** stringere i denti; **I've got a piece of ~ in my eye** ho un bruscolino nell'occhio
grits [grɪts] npl (US) macinato grosso (di avena etc)
grizzle ['grɪzl] vi (Brit) piagnucolare
grizzly ['grɪzlɪ] n (also: **grizzly bear**) orso grigio, grizzly m inv
groan [grəʊn] n gemito ■ vi gemere
grocer ['grəʊsər] n negoziante m di generi alimentari; **~'s (shop)** negozio di alimentari
groceries ['grəʊsərɪz] npl provviste fpl
grocery ['grəʊsərɪ] n (shop) (negozio di) alimentari
grog [grɔg] n grog m inv
groggy ['grɔgɪ] adj barcollante
groin [grɔɪn] n inguine m
groom [gruːm] n palafreniere m; (also: **bridegroom**) sposo ■ vt (horse) strigliare; (fig): **to ~ sb for** avviare qn a
groove [gruːv] n scanalatura, solco

grope [grəʊp] vi andare a tentoni; **to ~ for sth** cercare qc a tastoni
gross [grəʊs] adj grossolano(-a); (Comm) lordo(-a) ■ n (pl inv: twelve dozen) grossa ■ vt (Comm) incassare, avere un incasso lordo di
gross domestic product n prodotto interno lordo
grossly ['grəʊslɪ] adv (greatly) molto
gross national product n prodotto nazionale lordo
grotesque [grəʊ'tɛsk] adj grottesco(-a)
grotto ['grɔtəʊ] n grotta
grotty ['grɔtɪ] adj (Brit col) squallido(-a)
grouch [graʊtʃ] (col) vi brontolare ■ n (person) brontolone(-a)
ground [graʊnd] pt, pp of **grind** ■ adj (coffee etc) macinato(-a) ■ n suolo, terra; (land) terreno; (Sport) campo; (reason: gen pl) ragione f; (US: also: **ground wire**) (presa a) terra ■ vt (plane) tenere a terra; (US Elec) mettere la presa a terra a ■ vi (ship) arenarsi; **grounds** npl (of coffee etc) fondi mpl; (gardens etc) terreno, giardini mpl; **on/to the ~** per/a terra; **below ~** sotterra; **common ~** terreno comune; **to gain/lose ~** guadagnare/perdere terreno; **he covered a lot of ~ in his lecture** ha toccato molti argomenti nel corso della conferenza
ground cloth n (US) = **groundsheet**
ground control n (Aviat, Space) base f di controllo
ground floor n pianterreno
grounding ['graʊndɪŋ] n (in education) basi fpl
groundless ['graʊndlɪs] adj infondato(-a)
groundnut ['graʊndnʌt] n arachide f
ground rent n (Brit) canone m di affitto di un terreno
ground rules npl regole fpl fondamentali
groundsheet ['graʊndʃiːt] n (Brit) telone m impermeabile
groundsman ['graʊndzmən], (US)
groundskeeper ['graʊndziːpər] n (Sport) custode m (di campo sportivo)
ground staff n personale m di terra
groundswell ['graʊndswɛl] n maremoto; (fig) movimento
ground-to-air ['graʊndtuˈɛər] adj terra-aria inv
ground-to-ground ['graʊntəˈgraʊnd] adj: **~ missile** missile m terra-terra
groundwork ['graʊndwəːk] n preparazione f
group [gruːp] n gruppo; (Mus: pop group) complesso, gruppo ■ vt raggruppare ■ vi raggrupparsi
groupie ['gruːpɪ] n groupie m/f inv, fan m/f inv scatenato(-a)
group therapy n terapia di gruppo
grouse [graʊs] n (pl inv: bird) tetraone m ■ vi (complain) brontolare

587

grove [grəuv] n boschetto

grovel ['grɔvl] vi (fig): **to ~ (before)** strisciare (di fronte a)

grow (pt **grew**, pp **grown**) [grəu, gru:, grəun] vi crescere; (increase) aumentare; (become): **to ~ rich/weak** arricchirsi/indebolirsi ▪ vt coltivare, far crescere; **to ~ tired of waiting** stancarsi di aspettare
  ▸ **grow apart** vi (fig) estraniarsi
  ▸ **grow away from** vt fus (fig) allontanarsi da, staccarsi da
  ▸ **grow on** vt fus: **that painting is growing on me** quel quadro più lo guardo più mi piace
  ▸ **grow out of** vt fus (clothes) diventare troppo grande per indossare; (habit) perdere (col tempo); **he'll ~ out of it** gli passerà
  ▸ **grow up** vi farsi grande, crescere

grower ['grəuər] n coltivatore(-trice)

growing ['grəuɪŋ] adj (fear, amount) crescente; **~ pains** (also fig) problemi mpl di crescita

growl [graul] vi ringhiare

grown [grəun] pp of **grow** ▪ adj adulto(-a), maturo(-a)

grown-up [grəun'ʌp] n adulto(-a), grande m/f

growth [grəuθ] n crescita, sviluppo; (what has grown) crescita; (Med) escrescenza, tumore m

growth rate n tasso di crescita

grub [grʌb] n larva; (col: food) roba (da mangiare)

grubby ['grʌbɪ] adj sporco(-a)

grudge [grʌdʒ] n rancore m ▪ vt: **to ~ sb sth** dare qc a qn di malavoglia; invidiare qc a qn; **to bear sb a ~ (for)** serbar rancore a qn (per)

grudgingly ['grʌdʒɪŋlɪ] adv di malavoglia, di malincuore

gruelling, (US) **grueling** ['gruəlɪŋ] adj estenuante

gruesome ['gru:səm] adj orribile

gruff [grʌf] adj rozzo(-a)

grumble ['grʌmbl] vi brontolare, lagnarsi

grumpy ['grʌmpɪ] adj stizzito(-a)

grunge [grʌndʒ] n (Mus) grunge m inv; (style) moda f grunge inv

grunt [grʌnt] vi grugnire ▪ n grugnito

G-string ['dʒi:strɪŋ] n (garment) tanga m inv

GT abbr (Aut: = gran turismo) GT

GU abbr (US Post) = **Guam**

guarantee [gærən'ti:] n garanzia ▪ vt garantire; **he can't ~ (that) he'll come** non può garantire che verrà

guarantor [gærən'tɔːr] n garante m/f

guard [gɑ:d] n guardia; (protection) riparo, protezione f; (Boxing) difesa; (one man) guardia, sentinella; (Brit Rail) capotreno;

(safety device: on machine) schermo protettivo; (also: **fire guard**) parafuoco ▪ vt fare la guardia a; **to ~ (against** or **from)** proteggere (da), salvaguardare (da); **to be on one's ~** (fig) stare in guardia
  ▸ **guard against** vi: **to ~ against doing sth** guardarsi dal fare qc

guard dog n cane m da guardia

guarded ['gɑ:dɪd] adj (fig) cauto(-a), guardingo(-a)

guardian ['gɑ:dɪən] n custode m; (of minor) tutore(-trice)

guard's van n (Brit Rail) vagone m di servizio

Guatemala [gwɑ:tə'mɑ:lə] n Guatemala m

Guernsey ['gə:nzɪ] n Guernesey f

guerrilla [gə'rɪlə] n guerrigliero

guerrilla warfare n guerriglia

guess [gɛs] vi indovinare ▪ vt indovinare; (US) credere, pensare ▪ n congettura; **to take** or **have a ~** cercare di indovinare; **my ~ is that ...** suppongo che ...; **to keep sb guessing** tenere qn in sospeso or sulla corda; **I ~ you're right** mi sa che hai ragione

guesstimate ['gɛstɪmɪt] n (col) stima approssimativa

guesswork ['gɛswə:k] n: **I got the answer by ~** ho azzeccato la risposta

guest [gɛst] n ospite m/f; (in hotel) cliente m/f; **be my ~** (col) fai come (se fossi) a casa tua

guest-house ['gɛsthaus] n pensione f

guest room n camera degli ospiti

guff [gʌf] n (col) stupidaggini fpl, assurdità fpl

guffaw [gʌ'fɔ:] n risata sonora ▪ vi scoppiare di una risata sonora

guidance ['gaɪdəns] n guida, direzione f; **marriage/vocational ~** consulenza matrimoniale/per l'avviamento professionale

guide [gaɪd] n (person, book etc) guida; (also: **girl guide**) giovane esploratrice f ▪ vt guidare; **to be guided by sb/sth** farsi or lasciarsi guidare da qn/qc

guidebook ['gaɪdbuk] n guida

guided missile n missile m telecomandato

guide dog n (Brit) cane m guida inv

guidelines ['gaɪdlaɪnz] npl (fig) indicazioni fpl, linee fpl direttive

guild [gɪld] n arte f, corporazione f; associazione f

guildhall ['gɪldhɔ:l] n (Brit) palazzo municipale

guile [gaɪl] n astuzia

guileless ['gaɪllɪs] adj candido(-a)

guillotine ['gɪləti:n] n ghigliottina

guilt [gɪlt] n colpevolezza

guilty ['gɪltɪ] adj colpevole; **to feel ~ (about)**

sentirsi in colpa (per); **to plead ~/not ~** dichiararsi colpevole/innocente

Guinea ['gɪnɪ] n: **Republic of ~** Repubblica di Guinea

guinea ['gɪnɪ] n (Brit) ghinea (= 21 shillings: valuta ora fuori uso)

guinea pig n cavia

guise [gaɪz] n maschera

guitar [gɪ'tɑːʳ] n chitarra

guitarist [gɪ'tɑːrɪst] n chitarrista m/f

gulch [gʌltʃ] n (US) burrone m

gulf [gʌlf] n golfo; (abyss) abisso; **the (Persian) G~** il Golfo Persico

Gulf States npl: **the ~** i paesi del Golfo Persico

Gulf Stream n: **the ~** la corrente del Golfo

gull [gʌl] n gabbiano

gullet ['gʌlɪt] n gola

gullibility [gʌlɪ'bɪlɪtɪ] n semplicioneria

gullible ['gʌlɪbl] adj credulo(-a)

gully ['gʌlɪ] n burrone m; gola; canale m

gulp [gʌlp] vi deglutire; (from emotion) avere il nodo in gola ■ vt (also: **gulp down**) tracannare, inghiottire ■ n (of liquid) sorso; (of food) boccone m; **in** or **at one ~** in un sorso, d'un fiato

gum [gʌm] n (Anat) gengiva; (glue) colla; (sweet) gelatina di frutta; (also: **chewing-gum**) chewing-gum m ■ vt incollare
  ▶ **gum up** vt: **to ~ up the works** (col) mettere il bastone tra le ruote

gumboil ['gʌmbɔɪl] n ascesso (dentario)

gumboots ['gʌmbuːts] npl (Brit) stivali mpl di gomma

gumption ['gʌmpʃən] n buon senso, senso pratico

gun [gʌn] n fucile m; (small) pistola, rivoltella; (rifle) carabina; (shotgun) fucile da caccia; (cannon) cannone m ■ vt (also: **gun down**) abbattere a colpi di pistola or fucile; **to stick to one's guns** (fig) tener duro

gunboat ['gʌnbəut] n cannoniera

gun dog n cane m da caccia

gunfire ['gʌnfaɪəʳ] n spari mpl

gung-ho ['gʌŋ'həu] adj (col) stupidamente entusiasta

gunk [gʌŋk] n porcherie fpl

gunman ['gʌnmən] n bandito armato

gunner ['gʌnəʳ] n artigliere m

gunpoint ['gʌnpɔɪnt] n: **at ~** sotto minaccia di fucile

gunpowder ['gʌnpaudəʳ] n polvere f da sparo

gunrunner ['gʌnrʌnəʳ] n contrabbandiere d'armi

gunrunning ['gʌnrʌnɪŋ] n contrabbando d'armi

gunshot ['gʌnʃɔt] n sparo; **within ~** a portata di fucile

gunsmith ['gʌnsmɪθ] n armaiolo

gurgle ['gəːgl] n gorgoglio ■ vi gorgogliare

guru ['guruː] n guru m inv

gush [gʌʃ] n fiotto, getto ■ vi sgorgare; (fig) abbandonarsi ad effusioni

gushing ['gʌʃɪŋ] adj che fa smancerie, smorfioso(-a)

gusset ['gʌsɪt] n gherone m; (in tights, pants) rinforzo

gust [gʌst] n (of wind) raffica; (of smoke) buffata

gusto ['gʌstəu] n entusiasmo

gusty ['gʌstɪ] adj (wind) a raffiche; (day) tempestoso(-a)

gut [gʌt] n intestino, budello; (Mus etc) minugia; **guts** npl (col: innards) budella fpl; (: of animals) interiora fpl; (courage) fegato ■ vt (poultry, fish) levare le interiora a, sventrare; (building) svuotare; (: fire) divorare l'interno di; **to hate sb's guts** odiare qn a morte

gut reaction n reazione f istintiva

gutsy ['gʌtsɪ] adj (col: style) che ha mordente; (plucky) coraggioso(-a)

gutted ['gʌtɪd] adv (col: upset) scioccato(-a)

gutter ['gʌtəʳ] n (of roof) grondaia; (in street) cunetta

gutter press n: **the ~** la stampa scandalistica

guttural ['gʌtərl] adj gutturale

guy [gaɪ] n (also: **guyrope**) cavo or corda di fissaggio; (col: man) tipo, elemento; (figure) effigie di Guy Fawkes

Guyana [gaɪ'ænə] n Guayana f

Guy Fawkes Night [-'fɔːks-] n (Brit) vedi nota

◉ **GUY FAWKES NIGHT**

La sera del 5 novembre, in occasione della Guy Fawkes Night, altrimenti chiamata Bonfire Night, viene commemorato con falò e fuochi d'artificio il fallimento della Congiura delle Polveri contro Giacomo I nel 1605. La festa prende il nome dal principale congiurato della cospirazione, Guy Fawkes, la cui effigie viene bruciata durante i festeggiamenti.

guzzle ['gʌzl] vi gozzovigliare ■ vt trangugiare

gym [dʒɪm] n (also: **gymnasium**) palestra; (also: **gymnastics**) ginnastica

gymkhana [dʒɪm'kɑːnə] n gimkana

gymnasium [dʒɪm'neɪzɪəm] n palestra

gymnast ['dʒɪmnæst] n ginnasta m/f

gymnastics [dʒɪm'næstɪks] n, npl ginnastica

gym shoes *npl* scarpe *fpl* da ginnastica
gym slip *n* (*Brit*) grembiule *m* da scuola (*per ragazze*)
gynaecologist, (*US*) **gynecologist** [gaɪnɪˈkɔlədʒɪst] *n* ginecologo(-a)

gynaecology, (*US*) **gynecology** [gaɪnəˈkɔlədʒɪ] *n* ginecologia
gypsy [ˈdʒɪpsɪ] *n* = **gipsy**
gyrate [dʒaɪˈreɪt] *vi* girare
gyroscope [ˈdʒaɪərəskəup] *n* giroscopio

Hh

H, h [eɪtʃ] n (letter) H, h f or m inv; **H for Harry**, (US) **H for How** ≈ H come Hotel

habeas corpus [ˈheɪbɪəsˈkɔːpəs] n (Law) habeas corpus m inv

haberdashery [ˈhæbədæʃərɪ] n merceria

habit [ˈhæbɪt] n abitudine f; (costume) abito; (Rel) tonaca; **to get out of/into the ~ of doing sth** perdere/prendere l'abitudine di fare qc

habitable [ˈhæbɪtəbl] adj abitabile

habitat [ˈhæbɪtæt] n habitat m inv

habitation [hæbɪˈteɪʃən] n abitazione f

habitual [həˈbɪtjuəl] adj abituale; (drinker, liar) inveterato(-a)

habitually [həˈbɪtjuəlɪ] adv abitualmente, di solito

hack [hæk] vt tagliare, fare a pezzi ■ n (cut) taglio; (blow) colpo; (old horse) ronzino; (pej: writer) negro

hacker [ˈhækəʳ] n (Comput) pirata m informatico

hackles [ˈhæklz] npl: **to make sb's ~ rise** (fig) rendere qn furioso

hackney cab [ˈhæknɪ-] n carrozza a nolo

hackneyed [ˈhæknɪd] adj comune, trito(-a)

hacksaw [ˈhæksɔː] n seghetto (per metallo)

had [hæd] pt, pp of **have**

haddock [ˈhædək] n eglefino

hadn't [ˈhædnt] = **had not**

haematology, (US) **hematology** [hiːməˈtɔlədʒɪ] n ematologia

haemoglobin, (US) **hemoglobin** [hiːməʊˈgləʊbɪn] n emoglobina

haemophilia, (US) **hemophilia** [hiːməʊˈfɪlɪə] n emofilia

haemorrhage, (US) **hemorrhage** [ˈhɛmərɪdʒ] n emorragia

haemorrhoids, (US) **hemorrhoids** [ˈhɛmərɔɪdz] npl emorroidi fpl

hag [hæg] n (ugly) befana; (nasty) megera; (witch) strega

haggard [ˈhægəd] adj smunto(-a)

haggis [ˈhægɪs] n (Scottish) insaccato a base di frattaglie di pecora e avena

haggle [ˈhægl] vi: **to ~ (over)** contrattare (su); (argue) discutere (su)

haggling [ˈhæglɪŋ] n contrattazioni fpl

Hague [heɪg] n: **The ~** L'Aia

hail [heɪl] n grandine f ■ vt (call) chiamare; (greet) salutare ■ vi grandinare; **to ~ (as)** acclamare (come); **he hails from Scotland** viene dalla Scozia

hailstone [ˈheɪlstəʊn] n chicco di grandine

hailstorm [ˈheɪlstɔːm] n grandinata

hair [hɛəʳ] n capelli mpl; (single hair: on head) capello; (: on body) pelo; **to do one's ~** pettinarsi

hairbrush [ˈhɛəbrʌʃ] n spazzola per capelli

haircut [ˈhɛəkʌt] n taglio di capelli; **I need a ~** devo tagliarmi i capelli

hairdo [ˈhɛəduː] n acconciatura, pettinatura

hairdresser [ˈhɛədrɛsəʳ] n parrucchiere(-a)

hair-dryer [ˈhɛədraɪəʳ] n asciugacapelli m inv

-haired [hɛəd] suffix: **fair/long~** dai capelli biondi/lunghi

hairgrip [ˈhɛəgrɪp] n forcina

hairline [ˈhɛəlaɪn] n attaccatura dei capelli

hairline fracture n incrinatura

hairnet [ˈhɛənɛt] n retina (per capelli)

hair oil n brillantina

hairpiece [ˈhɛəpiːs] n toupet m inv

hairpin [ˈhɛəpɪn] n forcina

hairpin bend, (US) **hairpin curve** n tornante m

hair-raising [ˈhɛəreɪzɪŋ] adj orripilante

hair remover n crema depilatoria

hair spray n lacca per capelli

hairstyle [ˈhɛəstaɪl] n pettinatura, acconciatura

hairy [ˈhɛərɪ] adj irsuto(-a); peloso(-a); (col: frightening) spaventoso(-a)

Haiti [ˈheɪtɪ] n Haiti f

hake (pl ~ or **hakes**) [heɪk] n nasello

halal [həˈlɑːl] n: **~ meat** carne macellata secondo la legge mussulmana

halcyon [ˈhælsɪən] adj sereno(-a)

hale [heɪl] adj: **~ and hearty** che scoppia di salute

half [hɑːf] n (pl **halves**) [hɑːvz] mezzo, metà f inv; (Sport: of match) tempo; (: of ground) metà campo ■ adj mezzo(-a) ■ adv a mezzo, a metà; ~ **an hour** mezz'ora; ~ **a dozen** mezza dozzina; ~ **a pound** mezza libbra; **two and a** ~ due e mezzo; **a week and a** ~ una settimana e mezza; ~ **(of it)** la metà; ~ **(of)** la metà di; ~ **the amount of** la metà di; **to cut sth in** ~ tagliare qc in due; ~ **empty/closed** mezzo vuoto/chiuso, semivuoto/semichiuso; ~ **past 3** le 3 e mezza; **to go halves (with sb)** fare a metà (con qn)

half-back ['hɑːfbæk] n (Sport) mediano

half-baked ['hɑːfbeɪkt] adj (col: idea, scheme) mal combinato(-a), che non sta in piedi

half-breed ['hɑːfbriːd] n = **half-caste**

half-brother ['hɑːfbrʌðəʳ] n fratellastro

half-caste ['hɑːfkɑːst] n meticcio(-a)

half-hearted [hɑːf'hɑːtɪd] adj tiepido(-a)

half-hour [hɑːf'auəʳ] n mezz'ora

half-mast ['hɑːf'mɑːst] n: **at** ~ (flag) a mezz'asta

halfpenny ['heɪpnɪ] n mezzo penny m inv

half-price ['hɑːf'praɪs] adj a metà prezzo ■ adv (also: **at half-price**) a metà prezzo

half term n (Brit Scol) vacanza a or di metà trimestre

half-time [hɑːf'taɪm] n (Sport) intervallo

halfway [hɑːf'weɪ] adv a metà strada; **to meet sb** ~ (fig) arrivare a un compromesso con qn

halfway house n (hostel) ostello dove possono alloggiare temporaneamente ex detenuti; (fig) via di mezzo

half-wit ['hɑːfwɪt] n (col) idiota m/f

half-yearly [hɑːf'jɪəlɪ] adv semestralmente, ogni sei mesi ■ adj semestrale

halibut ['hælɪbət] n (pl inv) ippoglosso

halitosis [hælɪ'təusɪs] n alitosi f

hall [hɔːl] n sala, salone m; (entrance way) entrata; (corridor) corridoio; (mansion) grande villa, maniero; ~ **of residence** n (Brit) casa dello studente

hallmark ['hɔːlmɑːk] n marchio di garanzia; (fig) caratteristica

hallo [hə'ləu] excl = **hello**

Halloween ['hæləu'iːn] n vigilia d'Ognissanti; vedi nota

▢ **HALLOWEEN**

▢ Secondo la tradizione anglosassone,
▢ durante la notte di Halloween, il 31 di
▢ ottobre, è possibile vedere le streghe e i
▢ fantasmi. I bambini, travestiti da
▢ fantasmi, streghe, mostri o simili, vanno
▢ di porta in porta e raccolgono dolci e
▢ piccoli doni.

hallucination [həluːsɪ'neɪʃən] n allucinazione f

hallucinogenic [həluːsɪnəu'dʒɛnɪk] adj allucinogeno(-a)

hallway ['hɔːlweɪ] n ingresso; corridoio

halo ['heɪləu] n (of saint etc) aureola; (of sun) alone m

halt [hɔːlt] n fermata ■ vt fermare ■ vi fermarsi; **to call a** ~ **(to sth)** (fig) mettere or porre fine (a qc)

halter ['hɔːltəʳ] n (for horse) cavezza

halterneck ['hɔːltənɛk] adj allacciato(-a) dietro il collo

halve [hɑːv] vt (apple etc) dividere a metà; (expense) ridurre di metà

halves [hɑːvz] npl of **half**

ham [hæm] n prosciutto; (col: also: **radio ham**) radioamatore(-trice); (also: **ham actor**) attore(-trice) senza talento

Hamburg ['hæmbəːg] n Amburgo f

hamburger ['hæmbəːgəʳ] n hamburger m inv

ham-fisted ['hæm'fɪstɪd], (US) **ham-handed** ['hæm'hændɪd] adj maldestro(-a)

hamlet ['hæmlɪt] n paesetto

hammer ['hæməʳ] n martello ■ vt martellare; (fig) sconfiggere duramente ■ vi (at door) picchiare; **to** ~ **a point home to sb** cacciare un'idea in testa a qn
▶ **hammer out** vt (metal) spianare (a martellate); (fig: solution, agreement) mettere a punto

hammock ['hæmək] n amaca

hamper ['hæmpəʳ] vt impedire ■ n cesta

hamster ['hæmstəʳ] n criceto

hamstring ['hæmstrɪŋ] n (Anat) tendine m del ginocchio

hand [hænd] n mano f; (of clock) lancetta; (handwriting) scrittura; (at cards) mano; (: game) partita; (worker) operaio(-a); (measurement: of horse) ≈ dieci centimetri ■ vt dare, passare; **to give sb a** ~ dare una mano a qn; **at** ~ a portata di mano; **in** ~ a disposizione; (work) in corso; **we have the matter in** ~ ci stiamo occupando della cosa; **we have the situation in** ~ abbiamo la situazione sotto controllo; **to be on** ~ (person) essere disponibile; (emergency services) essere pronto(-a) a intervenire; **to** ~ (information etc) a portata di mano; **to force sb's** ~ forzare la mano a qn; **to have a free** ~ avere carta bianca; **to have in one's** ~ (also fig) avere in mano or in pugno; **on the one** ~ ..., **on the other** ~ da un lato ..., dall'altro
▶ **hand down** vt passare giù; (tradition, heirloom) tramandare; (US: sentence, verdict) emettere
▶ **hand in** vt consegnare

▶ **hand out** vt (*leaflets*) distribuire; (*advice*) elargire

▶ **hand over** vt passare; cedere

▶ **hand round** vt (Brit: *information, papers*) far passare; (*distribute: chocolates etc*) far girare; (*hostess*) offrire

handbag ['hændbæg] n borsetta

hand baggage n bagaglio a mano

handball ['hændbɔːl] n pallamano f

handbasin ['hændbeɪsn] n lavandino

handbook ['hændbuk] n manuale m

handbrake ['hændbreɪk] n freno a mano

hand cream n crema per le mani

handcuffs ['hændkʌfs] npl manette fpl

handful ['hændful] n manciata, pugno

hand-held ['hænd'held] adj portatile

handicap ['hændɪkæp] n handicap m inv ■ vt handicappare; **to be mentally handicapped** essere un handicappato mentale; **to be physically handicapped** essere handicappato

handicraft ['hændɪkrɑːft] n lavoro d'artigiano

handiwork ['hændɪwəːk] n lavorazione f a mano; **this looks like his ~** (pej) qui c'è il suo zampino

handkerchief ['hæŋkətʃɪf] n fazzoletto

handle ['hændl] n (of door etc) maniglia; (of cup etc) ansa; (of knife etc) impugnatura; (of saucepan) manico; (for winding) manovella ■ vt toccare, maneggiare; manovrare; (deal with) occuparsi di; (treat: people) trattare; **"~ with care"** "fragile"

handlebar ['hændlbɑːʳ] n, **handlebars** ['hændlbɑːz] npl manubrio

handling ['hændlɪŋ] n (Aut) maneggevolezza; (of issue) modo di affrontare

handling charges npl commissione f per la prestazione; (for goods) spese fpl di trasporto; (Banking) spese fpl bancarie

hand-luggage ['hændlʌgɪdʒ] n bagagli mpl a mano

handmade [hænd'meɪd] adj fatto(-a) a mano; (biscuits etc) fatto(-a) in casa

handout ['hændaut] n (leaflet) volantino; (press handout) comunicato stampa

hand-picked [hænd'pɪkt] adj (produce) scelto(-a), selezionato(-a); (staff etc) scelto(-a)

handrail ['hændreɪl] n (on staircase etc) corrimano

handset ['hændset] n (Tel) ricevitore m

hands-free ['hændzfriː] adj (telephone) con auricolare; (microphone) vivavoce

handshake ['hændʃeɪk] n stretta di mano; (Comput) colloquio

handsome ['hænsəm] adj bello(-a); (reward) generoso(-a); (profit, fortune) considerevole

hands-on ['hændz'ɔn] adj: **~ experience** esperienza diretta or pratica

handstand ['hændstænd] n: **to do a ~** fare la verticale

hand-to-mouth ['hændtə'mauθ] adj (existence) precario(-a)

handwriting ['hændraɪtɪŋ] n scrittura

handwritten ['hændrɪtn] adj scritto(-a) a mano, manoscritto(-a)

handy ['hændɪ] adj (person) bravo(-a); (close at hand) a portata di mano; (convenient) comodo(-a); (useful: machine etc) pratico(-a), utile; **to come in ~** servire

handyman ['hændɪmæn] n tuttofare m inv; **tools for the ~** arnesi per il fatelo-da-voi

hang (pt, pp **hung**) [hæŋ, hʌŋ] vt appendere; (criminal) (pt, pp **hanged**) impiccare ■ vi pendere; (hair) scendere; (drapery) cadere; **to get the ~ of (doing) sth** (col) cominiciare a capire (come si fa) qc

▶ **hang about** vi bighellonare, ciondolare

▶ **hang back** vi (hesitate): **to ~ back (from doing)** essere riluttante (a fare)

▶ **hang on** vi (wait) aspettare ■ vt fus (depend on: decision etc) dipendere da; **to ~ on to** (keep hold of) aggrapparsi a, attaccarsi a; (keep) tenere

▶ **hang out** vt (washing) stendere (fuori); (col: live) stare ■ vi penzolare, pendere

▶ **hang together** vi (argument etc) stare in piedi

▶ **hang up** vi (Tel) riattaccare ■ vt appendere; **to ~ up on sb** (Tel) metter giù il ricevitore a qn

hangar ['hæŋəʳ] n hangar m inv

hangdog ['hæŋdɔg] adj (guilty: look, expression) da cane bastonato

hanger ['hæŋəʳ] n gruccia

hanger-on [hæŋər'ɔn] n parassita m

hang-glider ['hæŋglaɪdəʳ] n deltaplano

hang-gliding ['hæŋglaɪdɪŋ] n volo col deltaplano

hanging ['hæŋɪŋ] n (execution) impiccagione f

hangman ['hæŋmən] n boia m, carnefice m

hangover ['hæŋəuvəʳ] n (after drinking) postumi mpl di sbornia

hang-up ['hæŋʌp] n complesso

hank [hæŋk] n matassa

hanker ['hæŋkəʳ] vi: **to ~ after** bramare

hankering ['hæŋkərɪŋ] n: **to have a ~ for sth/to do sth** avere una gran voglia di qc/di fare qc

hankie, hanky ['hæŋkɪ] n abbr = **handkerchief**

Hants abbr (Brit) = **Hampshire**

haphazard [hæp'hæzəd] adj a casaccio, alla carlona

hapless ['hæplɪs] adj disgraziato(-a); (unfortunate) sventurato(-a)

h

happen ['hæpən] vi accadere, succedere;
she happened to be free per caso era libera;
if anything happened to him se dovesse
succedergli qualcosa; **as it happens** guarda
caso; **what's happening?** cosa succede?,
cosa sta succedendo?
▶ **happen (up)on** vt fus capitare su
happening ['hæpnɪŋ] n avvenimento
happily ['hæpɪlɪ] adv felicemente;
fortunatamente
happiness ['hæpɪnɪs] n felicità, contentezza
happy ['hæpɪ] adj felice, contento(-a);
~ with (arrangements etc) soddisfatto(-a) di;
yes, I'd be ~ to (certo,) con piacere, (ben)
volentieri; **~ birthday!** buon compleanno!;
~ Christmas/New Year! buon Natale/anno!
happy-go-lucky ['hæpɪgəu'lʌkɪ] adj
spensierato(-a)
happy hour n orario in cui i pub hanno prezzi ridotti
harangue [hə'ræŋ] vt arringare
harass ['hærəs] vt molestare
harassed ['hærəst] adj assillato(-a)
harassment ['hærəsmənt] n molestia
harbour, (US) **harbor** ['hɑːbəʳ] n porto
■ vt dare rifugio a; (retain: grudge etc) covare,
nutrire
harbour dues, (US) **harbor dues** npl diritti
mpl portuali
harbour master, (US) **harbor master** n
capitano di porto
hard [hɑːd] adj duro(-a) ■ adv (work) sodo;
(think, try) bene; **to look ~ at** guardare
fissamente; esaminare attentamente; **to
drink ~** bere forte; **~ luck!** peccato!; **no ~
feelings!** senza rancore!; **to be ~ of hearing**
essere duro(-a) d'orecchio; **to be ~ on sb**
essere severo con qn; **to be ~ done by** essere
trattato(-a) ingiustamente; **I find it ~ to
believe that ...** stento or faccio fatica a
credere che ... + sub
hard-and-fast ['hɑːdən'fɑːst] adj ferreo(-a)
hardback ['hɑːdbæk] n libro rilegato
hardboard ['hɑːdbɔːd] n legno precompresso
hard-boiled egg ['hɑːd'bɔɪld-] n uovo sodo
hard cash n denaro in contanti
hard copy n (Comput) hard copy f inv,
terminale m di stampa
hard-core ['hɑːd'kɔːʳ] adj (pornography)
hardcore inv; (supporters) irriducibile
hard court n (Tennis) campo in terra battuta
hard disk n (Comput) hard disk m inv, disco
rigido
harden ['hɑːdn] vt indurire; (steel) temprare;
(fig: determination) rafforzare ■ vi (substance)
indurirsi
hardened ['hɑːdnd] adj (criminal) incallito(-a);
to be ~ to sth essere (diventato)

insensibile a qc
hard graft n: **by sheer ~** lavorando da matti
hard-headed ['hɑːd'hedɪd] adj pratico(-a)
hard-hearted ['hɑːd'hɑːtɪd] adj che non si
lascia commuovere, dal cuore duro
hard-hitting ['hɑːd'hɪtɪŋ] adj molto duro(-a);
a ~ documentary un documentario m verità
inv
hard labour n lavori forzati mpl
hardliner [hɑːd'laɪnəʳ] n fautore(-trice) della
linea dura
hard-luck story [hɑːd'lʌk-] n storia
lacrimosa (con un fine ben preciso)
hardly ['hɑːdlɪ] adv (scarcely) appena, a mala
pena; **it's ~ the case** non è proprio il caso; **~
anyone/anywhere** quasi nessuno/da nessuna
parte; **I can ~ believe it** stento a crederci
hardness ['hɑːdnɪs] n durezza
hard-nosed ['hɑːd'nəuzd] adj (people) con i
piedi per terra
hard-pressed ['hɑːd'prest] adj in difficoltà
hard sell n (Comm) intensa campagna
promozionale
hardship ['hɑːdʃɪp] n avversità f inv;
privazioni fpl
hard shoulder n (Brit Aut) corsia d'emergenza
hard-up [hɑːd'ʌp] adj (col) al verde
hardware ['hɑːdwεəʳ] n ferramenta fpl;
(Comput) hardware m
hardware shop n (negozio di) ferramenta fpl
hard-wearing [hɑːd'wεərɪŋ] adj resistente,
robusto(-a)
hard-won ['hɑːd'wʌn] adj sudato(-a)
hard-working [hɑːd'wəːkɪŋ] adj
lavoratore(-trice)
hardy ['hɑːdɪ] adj robusto(-a); (plant)
resistente al gelo
hare [hεəʳ] n lepre f
hare-brained ['hεəbreɪnd] adj folle;
scervellato(-a)
harelip ['hεəlɪp] n (Med) labbro leporino
harem [hɑː'riːm] n harem m inv
hark back [hɑːk-] vi: **to ~ back to** (former days)
rievocare; (earlier occasion) ritornare a or su
harm [hɑːm] n male m; (wrong) danno ■ vt
(person) fare male a; (thing) danneggiare;
to mean no ~ non avere l'intenzione
d'offendere; **out of ~'s way** al sicuro;
there's no ~ in trying tentar non nuoce
harmful ['hɑːmful] adj dannoso(-a)
harmless ['hɑːmlɪs] adj innocuo(-a);
inoffensivo(-a)
harmonic [hɑː'mɔnɪk] adj armonico(-a)
harmonica [hɑː'mɔnɪkə] n armonica
harmonics [hɑː'mɔnɪks] npl armonia
harmonious [hɑː'məunɪəs] adj
armonioso(-a)

harmonium [hɑːˈməʊnɪəm] n armonium m inv

harmonize [ˈhɑːmənaɪz] vt, vi armonizzare

harmony [ˈhɑːmənɪ] n armonia

harness [ˈhɑːnɪs] n bardatura, finimenti mpl ▪ vt (horse) bardare; (resources) sfruttare

harp [hɑːp] n arpa ▪ vi: **to ~ on about** insistere tediosamente su

harpist [ˈhɑːpɪst] n arpista m/f

harpoon [hɑːˈpuːn] n arpione m

harpsichord [ˈhɑːpsɪkɔːd] n clavicembalo

harrow [ˈhærəʊ] n (Agr) erpice m

harrowing [ˈhærəʊɪŋ] adj straziante

harry [ˈhærɪ] vt (Mil) saccheggiare; (person) assillare

harsh [hɑːʃ] adj (hard) duro(-a); (severe) severo(-a); (unpleasant: sound) rauco(-a); (: colour) chiassoso(-a); violento(-a)

harshly [ˈhɑːʃlɪ] adv duramente; severamente

harshness [ˈhɑːʃnɪs] n durezza; severità

harvest [ˈhɑːvɪst] n raccolto; (of grapes) vendemmia ▪ vt fare il raccolto di, raccogliere; vendemmiare ▪ vi fare il raccolto; vendemmiare

harvester [ˈhɑːvɪstəʳ] n (machine) mietitrice f; (also: **combine harvester**) mietitrebbia; (person) mietitore(-trice)

has [hæz] see **have**

has-been [ˈhæzbiːn] n (col: person): **he's/she's a ~** ha fatto il suo tempo

hash [hæʃ] n (Culin) specie di spezzatino fatto con carne già cotta; (fig: mess) pasticcio ▪ n abbr (col) = **hashish**

hashish [ˈhæʃɪʃ] n hascisc m

hasn't [ˈhæznt] = **has not**

hassle [ˈhæsl] n (col) sacco di problemi

haste [heɪst] n fretta

hasten [ˈheɪsn] vt affrettare ▪ vi affrettarsi; **I ~ to add that ...** mi preme di aggiungere che ...

hastily [ˈheɪstɪlɪ] adv in fretta, precipitosamente

hasty [ˈheɪstɪ] adj affrettato(-a), precipitoso(-a)

hat [hæt] n cappello

hatbox [ˈhætbɒks] n cappelliera

hatch [hætʃ] n (Naut: also: **hatchway**) boccaporto; (Brit: also: **service hatch**) portello di servizio ▪ vi schiudersi ▪ vt covare; (fig: scheme, plot) elaborare, mettere a punto

hatchback [ˈhætʃbæk] n (Aut) tre (or cinque) porte f inv

hatchet [ˈhætʃɪt] n accetta

hatchet job n (col) attacco spietato; **to do a ~ on sb** fare a pezzi qn

hatchet man n (col) tirapiedi m inv, scagnozzo

hate [heɪt] vt odiare, detestare ▪ n odio; **to ~ to do** or **doing** detestare fare; **I ~ to trouble you, but ...** mi dispiace disturbarla, ma ...

hateful [ˈheɪtful] adj odioso(-a), detestabile

hater [ˈheɪtəʳ] n: **cop-~** persona che odia i poliziotti; **woman-~** misogino(-a)

hatred [ˈheɪtrɪd] n odio

hat trick n (Brit Sport, also fig): **to get a ~** segnare tre punti consecutivi (or vincere per tre volte consecutive)

haughty [ˈhɔːtɪ] adj altero(-a), arrogante

haul [hɔːl] vt trascinare, tirare ▪ n (of fish) pescata; (of stolen goods etc) bottino

haulage [ˈhɔːlɪdʒ] n trasporto; autotrasporto

haulage contractor n (Brit: firm) impresa di trasporti; (: person) autotrasportatore m

haulier [ˈhɔːlɪəʳ], (US) **hauler** [ˈhɔːləʳ] n autotrasportatore m

haunch [hɔːntʃ] n anca; **a ~ of venison** una coscia di cervo

haunt [hɔːnt] vt (fear) pervadere; (: person) frequentare ▪ n rifugio; **a ghost haunts the house** la casa è abitata da un fantasma

haunted [ˈhɔːntɪd] adj (castle etc) abitato(-a) dai fantasmi or dagli spiriti; (look) ossessionato(-a), tormentato(-a)

haunting [ˈhɔːntɪŋ] adj (sight, music) ossessionante, che perseguita

Havana [həˈvænə] n l'Avana

 KEYWORD

have [hæv] (pt, pp **had**) aux vb **1** (gen) avere; essere; **to have arrived/gone** essere arrivato(-a)/andato(-a); **to have eaten/slept** avere mangiato/dormito; **he has been kind/promoted** è stato gentile/promosso; **having finished** or **when he had finished, he left** dopo aver finito, se n'è andato

2 (in tag questions): **you've done it, haven't you?** l'hai fatto, (non è) vero?; **he hasn't done it, has he?** non l'ha fatto, vero?

3 (in short answers and questions): **you've made a mistake - no I haven't/so I have** ha fatto un errore - ma no, niente affatto/sì, è vero; **we haven't paid - yes we have!** non abbiamo pagato - ma sì che abbiamo pagato!; **I've been there before, have you?** ci sono già stato, e lei?

▪ modal aux vb (be obliged): **to have (got) to do sth** dover fare qc; **I haven't got** or **I don't have to wear glasses** non ho bisogno di portare gli occhiali; **I had better leave** è meglio che io vada

▪ vt **1** (possess, obtain) avere; **he has (got) blue eyes/dark hair** ha gli occhi azzurri/i capelli scuri; **have you got** or **do you have a car/phone?** ha la macchina/il telefono?; **may I have your address?** potrebbe darmi il suo

595

indirizzo?; **you can have it for £5** te lo do
per 5 sterline
2 (+ *noun: take, hold etc*): **to have a bath** fare un
bagno; **to have breakfast** fare colazione;
to have a cigarette fumare una sigaretta;
to have dinner cenare; **to have a drink** bere
qualcosa; **to have lunch** pranzare; **to have
a party** dare *or* fare una festa; **to have an
operation** avere *or* subire un'operazione;
to have a swim fare una nuotata; **I'll have a
coffee** prendo un caffè; **let me have a try**
fammi *or* lasciami provare
3: **to have sth done** far fare qc; **to have
one's hair cut** tagliarsi *or* farsi tagliare i
capelli; **he had a suit made** si fece fare un
abito; **to have sb do sth** far fare qc a qn;
he had me phone his boss mi ha fatto
telefonare al suo capo
4 (*experience, suffer*) avere; **to have a cold/flu**
avere il raffreddore/l'influenza; **she had
her bag stolen** le hanno rubato la borsa
5 (*phrases*): **you've been had!** ci sei cascato!;
I won't have it! (*accept*) non mi sta affatto
bene!; *see also* **haves**
▸ **have in** *vt*: **to have it in for sb** (*col*)
avercela con qn
▸ **have on** *vt* (*garment*) avere addosso; (*be busy
with*) avere da fare; **I don't have any money
on me** non ho soldi con me; **have you
anything on tomorrow?** (*Brit*) ha qualcosa
in programma per domani?; **to have sb on**
(*Brit col*) prendere in giro qn
▸ **have out** *vt*: **to have it out with sb** (*settle a
problem etc*) mettere le cose in chiaro con qn

haven ['heɪvn] *n* porto; (*fig*) rifugio
haversack ['hævəsæk] *n* zaino
haves [hævz] *npl* (*col*): **the ~ and the have-
nots** gli abbienti e i non abbienti
havoc ['hævək] *n* confusione *f*, subbuglio;
  to play ~ with sth scombussolare qc;
  to wreak ~ on sth mettere in subbuglio qc
Hawaii [hə'waɪ:] *n* le Hawaii
Hawaiian [hə'waɪjən] *adj* hawaiano(-a)
  ■ *n* hawaiano(-a); (*Ling*) lingua hawaiana
hawk [hɔ:k] *n* falco ■ *vt* (*goods for sale*)
  vendere per strada
hawker ['hɔ:kəʳ] *n* venditore *m* ambulante
hawkish ['hɔ:kɪʃ] *adj* violento(-a)
hawthorn ['hɔ:θɔ:n] *n* biancospino
hay [heɪ] *n* fieno
hay fever *n* febbre *f* da fieno
haystack ['heɪstæk] *n* pagliaio
haywire ['heɪwaɪəʳ] *adj* (*col*): **to go ~** perdere
  la testa; impazzire
hazard ['hæzəd] *n* (*chance*) azzardo; (*risk*)
  pericolo, rischio ■ *vt* (*one's life*) rischiare,

mettere a repentaglio; (*remark*) azzardare;
  to be a health/fire ~ essere pericoloso per la
  salute/in caso d'incendio; **to ~ a guess** tirare
  a indovinare
hazardous ['hæzədəs] *adj* pericoloso(-a),
  rischioso(-a)
hazard pay *n* (*US*) indennità di rischio
hazard warning lights *npl* (*Aut*) luci *fpl* di
  emergenza
haze [heɪz] *n* foschia
hazel ['heɪzl] *n* (*tree*) nocciolo ■ *adj* (*eyes*)
  (*color*) nocciola *inv*
hazelnut ['heɪzlnʌt] *n* nocciola
hazy ['heɪzɪ] *adj* fosco(-a); (*idea*) vago(-a);
  (*photograph*) indistinto(-a)
H-bomb ['eɪtʃbɔm] *n* bomba H
HD *abbr* (= *high definition*) HD, alta definizione
HDTV *abbr* (= *high definition television*) televisore
  m HD, TV *f inv* ad alta definizione
HE *abbr* = **high explosive**; (*Rel, Diplomacy*: = *His
  (or Her) Excellency*) S.E.
he [hi:] *pron* lui, egli; **it is he who ...** è lui
  che ...; **here he is** eccolo
head [hɛd] *n* testa, capo; (*leader*) capo; (*on tape
  recorder, computer etc*) testina ■ *vt* (*list*) essere
  in testa a; (*group*) essere a capo di; **heads (or
  tails)** testa (o croce), pari (o dispari); **~ first** a
  capofitto; **~ over heels in love** pazzamente
  innamorato(-a); **£10 a** *or* **per ~** 10 sterline a
  testa; **to sit at the ~ of the table** sedersi a
  capotavola; **to have a ~ for business** essere
  tagliato per gli affari; **to have no ~ for
  heights** soffrire di vertigini; **to lose/keep
  one's ~** perdere/non perdere la testa; **to
  come to a ~** (*fig: situation etc*) precipitare; **to ~
  the ball** (*Sport*) dare di testa alla palla
  ▸ **head for** *vt fus* dirigersi verso
  ▸ **head off** *vt* (*threat, danger*) sventare
headache ['hɛdeɪk] *n* mal *m* di testa; **to have
  a ~** aver mal di testa
headband ['hɛdbænd] *n* fascia per i capelli
headboard ['hɛdbɔ:d] *n* testiera (del letto)
headdress ['hɛddrɛs] *n* (*of Indian etc*)
  copricapo; (*of bride*) acconciatura
headed notepaper ['hɛdɪd-] *n* carta intestata
header ['hɛdəʳ] *n* (*Brit col: Football*) colpo di
  testa; (: *fall*) caduta di testa
head-first ['hɛd'fə:st] *adv* a testa in giù; (*fig*)
  senza pensare
headhunt ['hɛdhʌnt] *vt*: **to be headhunted**
  avere un'offerta di lavoro da un cacciatore di
  teste
headhunter ['hɛdhʌntəʳ] *n* cacciatore *m* di teste
heading ['hɛdɪŋ] *n* titolo; intestazione *f*
headlamp ['hɛdlæmp] *n* (*Brit*) = **headlight**
headland ['hɛdlənd] *n* promontorio
headlight ['hɛdlaɪt] *n* fanale *m*

headline ['hɛdlaɪn] n titolo
headlong ['hɛdlɔŋ] adv (fall) a capofitto; (rush) precipitosamente
headmaster [hɛd'mɑːstəʳ] n preside m
headmistress [hɛd'mɪstrɪs] n preside f
head office n sede f (centrale)
head-on [hɛd'ɔn] adj (collision) frontale
headphones ['hɛdfəunz] npl cuffia
headquarters [hɛd'kwɔːtəz] npl ufficio centrale; (Mil) quartiere m generale
head-rest ['hɛdrɛst] n poggiacapo
headroom ['hɛdrum] n (in car) altezza dell'abitacolo; (under bridge) altezza limite
headscarf ['hɛdskɑːf] n foulard m inv
headset ['hɛdsɛt] n = **headphones**
headstone ['hɛdstəun] n (on grave) lapide f, pietra tombale
headstrong ['hɛdstrɔŋ] adj testardo(-a)
head waiter n capocameriere m
headway ['hɛdweɪ] n: **to make ~** fare progressi or passi avanti
headwind ['hɛdwɪnd] n controvento
heady ['hɛdɪ] adj che dà alla testa; inebriante
heal [hiːl] vt, vi guarire
health [hɛlθ] n salute f; **Department of H~** ≈ Ministero della Sanità
health care n assistenza sanitaria
health centre n (Brit) poliambulatorio
health food n, **health foods** npl alimenti mpl integrali
health hazard n pericolo per la salute
Health Service n: **the ~** (Brit) ≈ il Servizio Sanitario Statale
healthy ['hɛlθɪ] adj (person) in buona salute; (climate) salubre; (food) salutare; (attitude etc) sano(-a); (economy) florido(-a); (bank balance) solido(-a)
heap [hiːp] n mucchio ■ vt ammucchiare; **heaps (of)** (col: lots) un sacco (di), un mucchio (di); **to ~ favours/praise/gifts** etc **on sb** ricolmare qn di favori/lodi/regali etc
hear (pt, pp **heard**) [hɪəʳ, həːd] vt sentire; (news) ascoltare; (lecture) assistere a; (Law: case) esaminare ■ vi sentire; **to ~ about** sentire parlare di; (have news of) avere notizie di; **did you ~ about the move?** ha sentito del trasloco?; **to ~ from sb** ricevere notizie da qn
▶ **hear out** vt ascoltare senza interrompere
hearing ['hɪərɪŋ] n (sense) udito; (of witnesses) audizione f; (of a case) udienza; **to give sb a ~** dare ascolto a qn
hearing aid n apparecchio acustico
hearsay ['hɪəseɪ] n dicerie fpl, chiacchiere fpl; **by ~** adv per sentito dire
hearse [həːs] n carro funebre
heart [hɑːt] n cuore m; **hearts** npl (Cards)

cuori mpl; **at ~** in fondo; **by ~** (learn, know) a memoria; **to take ~** farsi coraggio or animo; **to lose ~** perdere coraggio, scoraggiarsi; **to have a weak ~** avere il cuore debole; **to set one's ~ on sth/on doing sth** tenere molto a qc/a fare qc; **the ~ of the matter** il nocciolo della questione
heartache ['hɑːteɪk] n pene fpl, dolori mpl
heart attack n attacco di cuore
heartbeat ['hɑːtbiːt] n battito del cuore
heartbreak ['hɑːtbreɪk] n immenso dolore m
heartbreaking ['hɑːtbreɪkɪŋ] adj straziante
heartbroken ['hɑːtbrəukən] adj affranto(-a); **to be ~** avere il cuore spezzato
heartburn ['hɑːtbəːn] n bruciore m di stomaco
-hearted ['hɑːtɪd] suffix: **a kind~ person** una persona molto gentile
heartening ['hɑːtnɪŋ] adj incoraggiante
heart failure n (Med) arresto cardiaco
heartfelt ['hɑːtfɛlt] adj sincero(-a)
hearth [hɑːθ] n focolare m
heartily ['hɑːtɪlɪ] adv (laugh) di cuore; (eat) di buon appetito; (agree) in pieno, completamente; **to be ~ sick of** (Brit) essere veramente stufo di, essere arcistufo di
heartland ['hɑːtlænd] n zona centrale; **Italy's industrial ~** il cuore dell'industria italiana
heartless ['hɑːtlɪs] adj senza cuore, insensibile; crudele
heartstrings ['hɑːtstrɪŋz] npl: **to tug at sb's ~** toccare il cuore a qn, toccare qn nel profondo
heart-throb ['hɑːtθrɔb] n rubacuori m inv
heart-to-heart ['hɑːttə'hɑːt] adj, adv a cuore aperto
heart transplant n trapianto del cuore
heartwarming ['hɑːtwɔːmɪŋ] adj confortante, che scalda il cuore
hearty ['hɑːtɪ] adj caloroso(-a), robusto(-a), sano(-a); vigoroso(-a)
heat [hiːt] n calore m; (fig) ardore m; fuoco; (Sport: also: **qualifying heat**) prova eliminatoria; (Zool): **in** or (Brit) **on ~** in calore ■ vt scaldare
▶ **heat up** vi (liquids) scaldarsi; (room) riscaldarsi ■ vt riscaldare
heated ['hiːtɪd] adj riscaldato(-a); (fig) appassionato(-a); acceso(-a), eccitato(-a)
heater ['hiːtəʳ] n stufa; radiatore m
heath [hiːθ] n (Brit) landa
heathen ['hiːðn] adj, n pagano(-a)
heather ['hɛðəʳ] n erica
heating ['hiːtɪŋ] n riscaldamento
heat-resistant ['hiːtrɪzɪstənt] adj termoresistente

h

597

heat-seeking ['hi:tsi:kɪŋ] *adj* che cerca fonti di calore

heatstroke ['hi:tstrəuk] *n* colpo di sole

heatwave ['hi:tweɪv] *n* ondata di caldo

heave [hi:v] *vt* sollevare (con forza) ■ *vi* sollevarsi ■ *n* (*push*) grande spinta; **to ~ a sigh** emettere *or* mandare un sospiro

▸ **heave to** (*pt, pp* **hove**) *vi* (*Naut*) mettersi in cappa

heaven ['hɛvn] *n* paradiso, cielo; **~ forbid!** Dio ce ne guardi!; **for ~'s sake!** (*pleading*) per amor del cielo!, per carità!; (*protesting*) santo cielo!, in nome del cielo!; **thank ~!** grazie al cielo!

heavenly ['hɛvnlɪ] *adj* divino(-a), celeste

heavily ['hɛvɪlɪ] *adv* pesantemente; (*drink, smoke*) molto

heavy ['hɛvɪ] *adj* pesante; (*sea*) grosso(-a); (*rain*) forte; (*drinker, smoker*) gran (*before noun*); **it's ~ going** è una gran fatica; **~ industry** industria pesante

heavy cream *n* (*US*) doppia panna

heavy-duty ['hɛvɪ'dju:tɪ] *adj* molto resistente

heavy goods vehicle *n* (*Brit*) veicolo per trasporti pesanti

heavy-handed ['hɛvɪ'hændɪd] *adj* (*clumsy, tactless*) pesante

heavy metal *n* (*Mus*) heavy metal *m*

heavy-set ['hɛvɪ'sɛt] *adj* (*esp US*) tarchiato(-a)

heavyweight ['hɛvɪweɪt] *n* (*Sport*) peso massimo

Hebrew ['hi:bru:] *adj* ebreo(-a) ■ *n* (*Ling*) ebraico

Hebrides ['hɛbrɪdi:z] *npl*: **the ~** le Ebridi

heck [hɛk] (*col*) *excl*: **oh ~!** oh no! ■ *n*: **a ~ of a lot of** un gran bel po' di

heckle ['hɛkl] *vt* interpellare e dare noia a (*un oratore*)

heckler ['hɛklər] *n* agitatore(-trice)

hectare ['hɛktɑ:ʳ] *n* (*Brit*) ettaro

hectic ['hɛktɪk] *adj* movimentato(-a); (*busy*) frenetico(-a)

hector ['hɛktəʳ] *vt* usare le maniere forti con

he'd [hi:d] = **he would; he had**

hedge [hɛdʒ] *n* siepe *f* ■ *vi* essere elusivo(-a); **as a ~ against inflation** per cautelarsi contro l'inflazione; **to ~ one's bets** (*fig*) coprirsi dai rischi

▸ **hedge in** *vt* recintare con una siepe

hedgehog ['hɛdʒhɔg] *n* riccio

hedgerow ['hɛdʒrəu] *n* siepe *f*

hedonism ['hi:dənɪzəm] *n* edonismo

heed [hi:d] *vt* (*also*: **take heed of**) badare a, far conto di ■ *n*: **to pay (no) ~ to, to take (no) ~ of** (non) ascoltare, (non) tener conto di

heedless ['hi:dlɪs] *adj* sbadato(-a)

heel [hi:l] *n* (*Anat*) calcagno; (*of shoe*) tacco ■ *vt* (*shoe*) rifare i tacchi a; **to bring to ~** addomesticare; **to take to one's heels** (*col*) darsela a gambe, alzare i tacchi

hefty ['hɛftɪ] *adj* (*person*) solido(-a); (*parcel*) pesante; (*piece, price*) grosso(-a)

heifer ['hɛfəʳ] *n* giovenca

height [haɪt] *n* altezza; (*high ground*) altura; (*fig: of glory*) apice *m*; (*: of stupidity*) colmo; **what ~ are you?** quanto sei alto?; **of average ~** di statura media; **to be afraid of heights** soffrire di vertigini; **it's the ~ of fashion** è l'ultimo grido della moda

heighten ['haɪtn] *vt* innalzare; (*fig*) accrescere

heinous ['heɪnəs] *adj* nefando(-a), atroce

heir [ɛəʳ] *n* erede *m*

heir apparent *n* erede *m/f* legittimo(-a)

heiress ['ɛərɛs] *n* erede *f*

heirloom ['ɛəlu:m] *n* mobile *m* (*or* gioiello *or* quadro) di famiglia

heist [haɪst] *n* (*US col*) rapina

held [hɛld] *pt, pp of* **hold**

helicopter ['hɛlɪkɔptəʳ] *n* elicottero

heliport ['hɛlɪpɔ:t] *n* eliporto

helium ['hi:lɪəm] *n* elio

hell [hɛl] *n* inferno; **a ~ of a ...** (*col*) un(-a) maledetto(-a) ...; **oh ~!** (*col*) porca miseria!, accidenti!

he'll [hi:l] = **he will, he shall**

hell-bent [hɛl'bɛnt] *adj* (*col*): **to be ~ on doing sth** voler fare qc a tutti i costi

hellish ['hɛlɪʃ] *adj* infernale

hello [hə'ləu] *excl* buon giorno!; ciao! (*to sb one addresses as "tu"*); (*surprise*) ma guarda!

helm [hɛlm] *n* (*Naut*) timone *m*

helmet ['hɛlmɪt] *n* casco

helmsman ['hɛlmzmən] *n* timoniere *m*

help [hɛlp] *n* aiuto; (*charwoman*) donna di servizio; (*assistant etc*) impiegato(-a) ■ *vt* aiutare; **~!** aiuto!; **with the ~ of** con l'aiuto di; **to be of ~ to sb** essere di aiuto *or* essere utile a qn; **to ~ sb (to) do sth** aiutare qn a far qc; **can I ~ you?** (*in shop*) desidera?; **~ yourself (to bread)** si serva (del pane); **I can't ~ saying** non posso evitare di dire; **he can't ~ it** non ci può far niente

helper ['hɛlpəʳ] *n* aiutante *m/f*, assistente *m/f*

helpful ['hɛlpful] *adj* di grande aiuto; (*useful*) utile

helping ['hɛlpɪŋ] *n* porzione *f*

helping hand *n*: **to give sb a ~** dare una mano a qn

helpless ['hɛlplɪs] *adj* impotente; debole; (*baby*) indifeso(-a)

helplessly ['hɛlplɪslɪ] *adv* (*watch*) senza poter fare nulla

helpline ['hɛlplaɪn] *n* ≈ telefono amico;

(*Comm*) servizio *m* informazioni *inv* (*a pagamento*)

Helsinki ['hɛlsɪŋkɪ] *n* Helsinki *f*

helter-skelter ['hɛltə'skɛltə^r] *n* (*Brit: in funfair*) scivolo (a spirale)

hem [hɛm] *n* orlo ▪ *vt* fare l'orlo a
  ▶ **hem in** *vt* cingere; **to feel hemmed in** (*fig*) sentirsi soffocare

he-man ['hi:mæn] *n* (*col*) fusto

hematology [hi:mə'tɔlədʒɪ] *n* (*US*) = **haematology**

hemisphere ['hɛmɪsfɪə^r] *n* emisfero

hemlock ['hɛmlɔk] *n* cicuta

hemoglobin [hi:məu'gləubɪn] *n* (*US*) = **haemoglobin**

hemophilia [hi:məu'fɪlɪə] *n* (*US*) = **haemophilia**

hemorrhage ['hɛmərɪdʒ] *n* (*US*) = **haemorrhage**

hemorrhoids ['hɛmərɔɪdz] *npl* (*US*) = **haemorrhoids**

hemp [hɛmp] *n* canapa

hen [hɛn] *n* gallina; (*female bird*) femmina

hence [hɛns] *adv* (*therefore*) dunque; **2 years ~** di qui a 2 anni

henceforth [hɛns'fɔ:θ] *adv* d'ora in poi

henchman ['hɛntʃmən] *n* (*pej*) caudatario

henna ['hɛnə] *n* henna

hen night *n* (*col*) addio al nubilato

hen party *n* (*col*) festa di sole donne

henpecked ['hɛnpɛkt] *adj* dominato dalla moglie

hepatitis [hɛpə'taɪtɪs] *n* epatite *f*

her [hə:^r] *pron* (*direct*) la, l' + *vowel*; (*indirect*) le; (*stressed, after prep*) lei ▪ *adj* il/la suo(-a), i/le suoi/sue; **I see ~** la vedo; **give ~ a book** le dia un libro; **after ~** dopo (di) lei

herald ['hɛrəld] *n* araldo ▪ *vt* annunciare

heraldic [hɛ'rældɪk] *adj* araldico(-a)

heraldry ['hɛrəldrɪ] *n* araldica

herb [hə:b] *n* erba; **herbs** *npl* (*Culin*) erbette *fpl*

herbaceous [hə:'beɪʃəs] *adj* erbaceo(-a)

herbal ['hə:bəl] *adj* di erbe; **~ tea** tisana

herbicide ['hə:bɪsaɪd] *n* erbicida *m*

herd [hə:d] *n* mandria; (*of wild animals, swine*) branco ▪ *vt* (*drive, gather: animals*) guidare; (*: people*) radunare; **herded together** ammassati (come bestie)

here [hɪə^r] *adv* qui, qua ▪ *excl* ehi!; **~!** (*at roll call*) presente!; **~ is, ~ are** ecco; **~'s my sister** ecco mia sorella; **~ she is** eccola; **~ she comes** eccola che viene; **come ~!** vieni qui!; **~ and there** qua e là

hereabouts ['hɪərəbauts] *adv* da queste parti

hereafter [hɪər'ɑ:ftə^r] *adv* in futuro; dopo questo ▪ *n*: **the ~** l'al di là *m*

hereby [hɪə'baɪ] *adv* (*in letter*) con la presente

hereditary [hɪ'rɛdɪtrɪ] *adj* ereditario(-a)

heredity [hɪ'rɛdɪtɪ] *n* eredità

heresy ['hɛrəsɪ] *n* eresia

heretic ['hɛrətɪk] *n* eretico(-a)

heretical [hɪ'rɛtɪkl] *adj* eretico(-a)

herewith [hɪə'wɪð] *adv* qui accluso

heritage ['hɛrɪtɪdʒ] *n* eredità; (*of country, nation*) retaggio; **our national ~** il nostro patrimonio nazionale

hermetically [hə:'mɛtɪklɪ] *adv* ermeticamente; **~ sealed** ermeticamente chiuso

hermit ['hə:mɪt] *n* eremita *m*

hernia ['hə:nɪə] *n* ernia

hero (*pl* **heroes**) ['hɪərəu] *n* eroe *m*

heroic [hɪ'rəuɪk] *adj* eroico(-a)

heroin ['hɛrəuɪn] *n* eroina (*droga*)

heroin addict *n* eroinomane *m/f*

heroine ['hɛrəuɪn] *n* eroina (*donna*)

heroism ['hɛrəuɪzəm] *n* eroismo

heron ['hɛrən] *n* airone *m*

hero worship *n* divismo

herring ['hɛrɪŋ] *n* aringa

hers [hə:z] *pron* il/la suo(-a), i/le suoi/sue; **a friend of ~** un suo amico; **this is ~** questo è (il) suo

herself [hə:'sɛlf] *pron* (*reflexive*) si; (*emphatic*) lei stessa; (*after prep*) se stessa, sé

Herts *abbr* (*Brit*) = **Hertfordshire**

he's [hi:z] = **he is; he has**

hesitant ['hɛzɪtənt] *adj* esitante, indeciso(-a); **to be ~ about doing sth** esitare a fare qc

hesitate ['hɛzɪteɪt] *vi*: **to ~ (about/to do)** esitare (su/a fare); **don't ~ to ask (me)** non aver timore *or* paura di chiedermelo

hesitation [hɛzɪ'teɪʃən] *n* esitazione *f*; **I have no ~ in saying (that)** ... non esito a dire che ...

hessian ['hɛsɪən] *n* tela di canapa

heterogeneous [hɛtərəu'dʒi:nɪəs] *adj* eterogeneo(-a)

heterosexual [hɛtərəu'sɛksjuəl] *adj*, *n* eterosessuale (*m/f*)

het up [hɛt'ʌp] *adj* agitato(-a)

HEW *n abbr* (*US*: = *Department of Health, Education, and Welfare*) ministero della sanità, della pubblica istruzione e della previdenza sociale

hew [hju:] *vt* tagliare (con l'accetta)

hex [hɛks] (*US*) *n* stregoneria ▪ *vt* stregare

hexagon ['hɛksəgən] *n* esagono

hexagonal [hɛk'sægənl] *adj* esagonale

hey [heɪ] *excl* ehi!

heyday ['heɪdeɪ] *n*: **the ~ of** i bei giorni di, l'età d'oro di

HF *n abbr* (= *high frequency*) AF

HGV *n abbr* = **heavy goods vehicle**

HI abbr (US) = **Hawaii**
hi [haɪ] excl ciao!
hiatus [haɪ'eɪtəs] n vuoto; (Ling) iato
hibernate ['haɪbəneɪt] vi ibernare
hibernation [haɪbə'neɪʃən] n letargo,
ibernazione f
hiccough, hiccup ['hɪkʌp] vi singhiozzare
■ n singhiozzo; **to have (the) hiccoughs**
avere il singhiozzo
hick [hɪk] n (US col) buzzurro(-a)
hid [hɪd] pt of **hide**
hidden ['hɪdn] pp of **hide** ■ adj nascosto(-a);
there are no ~ extras è veramente tutto
compreso nel prezzo; **~ agenda** programma
m occulto
hide [haɪd] n (skin) pelle f ■ vb (pt **hid**, pp
hidden) [hɪd, 'hɪdn] vt: **to ~ sth (from sb)**
nascondere qc (a qn) ■ vi: **to ~ (from sb)**
nascondersi (da qn)
hide-and-seek ['haɪdən'siːk] n rimpiattino
hideaway ['haɪdəweɪ] n nascondiglio
hideous ['hɪdɪəs] adj laido(-a); orribile
hide-out ['haɪdaut] n nascondiglio
hiding ['haɪdɪŋ] n (beating) bastonata; **to be
in ~** (concealed) tenersi nascosto(-a)
hiding place n nascondiglio
hierarchy ['haɪərɑːkɪ] n gerarchia
hieroglyphic [haɪərə'glɪfɪk] adj
geroglifico(-a); **hieroglyphics** npl geroglifici
mpl
hi-fi ['haɪfaɪ] adj, n abbr (= high fidelity) hi-fi (m) inv
higgledy-piggledy ['hɪgldɪ'pɪgldɪ] adv alla
rinfusa
high [haɪ] adj alto(-a); (speed, respect, number)
grande; (wind) forte; (Brit Culin: meat, game)
frollato(-a); (: spoilt) andato(-a) a male;
(col: on drugs) fatto(-a); (: on drink) su di giri
■ adv alto, in alto ■ n: **exports have
reached a new ~** le esportazioni hanno
toccato un nuovo record; **20m ~** alto(-a)
20m; **to pay a ~ price for sth** pagare (molto)
caro qc
highball ['haɪbɔːl] n (US: drink) whisky (or
brandy) e soda con ghiaccio
highboy ['haɪbɔɪ] n (US) cassettone m
highbrow ['haɪbrau] adj, n intellettuale (m/f)
highchair ['haɪtʃɛər] n seggiolone m
high-class ['haɪ'klɑːs] adj (neighbourhood)
elegante; (hotel) di prim'ordine; (person)
di gran classe; (food) raffinato(-a)
High Court n alta corte f; vedi nota

HIGH COURT

Nel sistema legale inglese e gallese,
la High Court e la "Court of Appeal"
compongono la "Supreme Court of

Judicature", e si occupa di casi più
importanti e complessi. In Scozia, invece,
la High Court è la corte che si occupa dei
reati più gravi e corrisponde alla "crown
court" inglese.

higher ['haɪər] adj (form of life, study etc)
superiore ■ adv più in alto, più in su
higher education n istruzione f superiore,
istruzione universitaria
highfalutin [haɪfə'luːtɪn] adj (col) pretenzioso(-a)
high finance n alta finanza
high-flier, high-flyer [haɪ'flaɪər] n (giovane)
promessa (fig)
high-flying [haɪ'flaɪɪŋ] adj (fig) promettente
high-handed [haɪ'hændɪd] adj prepotente
high-heeled [haɪ'hiːld] adj a tacchi alti
highjack ['haɪdʒæk] vt, n = **hijack**
high jump n (Sport) salto in alto
highlands ['haɪləndz] npl zona montuosa;
the H~ le Highlands scozzesi
high-level ['haɪlɛvl] adj (talks etc, Comput) ad
alto livello
highlight ['haɪlaɪt] n (fig: of event) momento
culminante ■ vt mettere in evidenza;
highlights npl (in hair) colpi mpl di sole
highlighter ['haɪlaɪtər] n (pen) evidenziatore m
highly ['haɪlɪ] adv molto; **~ paid** pagato molto
bene; **to speak ~ of** parlare molto bene di
highly-strung ['haɪlɪ'strʌn] adj teso(-a) di
nervi, eccitabile
High Mass n messa cantata or solenne
highness ['haɪnɪs] n altezza; **Her H~** Sua
Altezza
high-pitched [haɪ'pɪtʃt] adj acuto(-a)
high point n: **the ~** il momento più
importante
high-powered ['haɪ'pauəd] adj (engine) molto
potente, ad alta potenza; (fig: person) di
prestigio
high-pressure ['haɪprɛʃər] adj ad alta
pressione; (fig) aggressivo(-a)
high-rise block ['haɪraɪz-] n palazzone m
high school n (Brit) scuola secondaria; (US)
istituto d'istruzione secondaria; vedi nota

HIGH SCHOOL

Negli Stati Uniti la high school è un istituto
di istruzione secondaria. Si suddivide in
"junior high school" (dal settimo al nono
anno di corso) e "senior high school"
(dal decimo al dodicesimo), dove vengono
impartiti sia insegnamenti scolastici che
di formazione professionale. In Gran
Bretagna molte scuole secondarie si
chiamano high school.

high season n (Brit) alta stagione
high spirits npl buonumore m, euforia;
  to be in ~ essere euforico(-a)
high street n (Brit) strada principale
highway ['haɪweɪ] n strada maestra;
  the information ~ l'autostrada telematica
Highway Code n (Brit) codice m della strada
highwayman ['haɪweɪmən] n bandito
hijack ['haɪdʒæk] vt dirottare ▪ n
  dirottamento; (also: **hijacking**) pirateria aerea
hijacker ['haɪdʒækər] n dirottatore(-trice)
hike [haɪk] vi fare un'escursione a piedi ▪ n
  escursione f a piedi; (col: in prices etc) aumento
  ▪ vt (col) aumentare
hiker ['haɪkər] n escursionista m/f
hiking ['haɪkɪŋ] n escursioni fpl a piedi
hilarious [hɪ'lɛərɪəs] adj che fa schiantare dal
  ridere
hilarity [hɪ'lærɪtɪ] n ilarità
hill [hɪl] n collina, colle m; (fairly high)
  montagna; (on road) salita
hillbilly ['hɪlbɪlɪ] n (US) montanaro(-a) dal
  sud degli Stati Uniti; (pej) zotico(-a)
hillock ['hɪlək] n collinetta, poggio
hillside ['hɪlsaɪd] n fianco della collina
hill start n (Aut) partenza in salita
hill walking n escursioni fpl in montagna
hilly ['hɪlɪ] adj collinoso(-a), montagnoso(-a)
hilt [hɪlt] n (of sword) elsa; **to the ~** (fig: support)
  fino in fondo
him [hɪm] pron (direct) lo, l' + vowel; (indirect) gli;
  (stressed, after prep) lui; **I see ~** lo vedo; **give ~ a
  book** gli dia un libro; **after ~** dopo (di) lui
Himalayas [hɪmə'leɪəz] npl: **the ~**
  l'Himalaia m
himself [hɪm'sɛlf] pron (reflexive) si; (emphatic)
  lui stesso; (after prep) se stesso, sé
hind [haɪnd] adj posteriore ▪ n cerva
hinder ['hɪndər] vt ostacolare; (delay) tardare;
  (prevent): **to ~ sb from doing** impedire a qn di
  fare
hindquarters ['haɪndkwɔːtəz] npl (Zool)
  posteriore m
hindrance ['hɪndrəns] n ostacolo,
  impedimento
hindsight ['haɪndsaɪt] n senno di poi; **with
  the benefit of ~** con il senno di poi
Hindu ['hɪnduː] n indù m/f inv
hinge [hɪndʒ] n cardine m ▪ vi (fig): **to ~ on**
  dipendere da
hint [hɪnt] n accenno, allusione f; (advice)
  consiglio ▪ vt: **to ~ that** lasciar capire che
  ▪ vi: **to ~ at** accennare a; **to drop a ~** lasciar
  capire; **give me a ~** (clue) dammi almeno
  un'idea, dammi un'indicazione
hip [hɪp] n anca, fianco; (Bot) frutto della rosa
  canina

hip flask n fiaschetta da liquore tascabile
hip hop n hip-hop m
hippie ['hɪpɪ] n hippy m/f inv
hip pocket n tasca posteriore dei calzoni
hippopotamus (pl **hippopotamuses** or
  hippopotami) [hɪpə'pɔtəməs, -'pɔtəmaɪ] n
  ippopotamo
hippy ['hɪpɪ] n = **hippie**
hire ['haɪər] vt (Brit: car, equipment) noleggiare;
  (worker) assumere, dare lavoro a ▪ n nolo,
  noleggio; **for ~** da nolo; (taxi) libero(-a);
  on ~ a nolo
  ▸ **hire out** vt noleggiare, dare a nolo or
  noleggio, affittare
hire car, hired car n (Brit) macchina a nolo
hire purchase n (Brit) acquisto (or vendita)
  rateale; **to buy sth on ~** comprare qc a rate
his [hɪz] adj, pron il/la suo/sua, i/le suoi/sue;
  this is ~ questo è (il) suo
hiss [hɪs] vi fischiare; (cat, snake) sibilare
  ▪ n fischio; sibilo
histogram ['hɪstəgræm] n istogramma m
historian [hɪ'stɔːrɪən] n storico(-a)
historic [hɪ'stɔrɪk], **historical** [hɪ'stɔrɪkl] adj
  storico(-a)
history ['hɪstərɪ] n storia; **there's a long ~ of
  that illness in his family** ci sono molti
  precedenti (della malattia) nella sua
  famiglia
histrionics [hɪstrɪ'ɔnɪks] n istrionismo
hit [hɪt] vt (pt, pp ~) colpire, picchiare; (knock
  against) battere; (reach: target) raggiungere;
  (collide with: car) urtare contro; (fig: affect)
  colpire; (find: problem) incontrare ▪ n colpo;
  (success, song) successo; **to ~ the headlines**
  far titolo; **to ~ the road** (col) mettersi in
  cammino; **to ~ it off with sb** andare molto
  d'accordo con qn; **to get a ~/10,000 hits**
  (Comput) trovare una pagina Web/10.000
  pagine Web; **our web page had 10,000 hits
  last month** lo scorso mese il nostro sito ha
  avuto 10.000 visitatori
  ▸ **hit back** vi: **to ~ back at sb** restituire il
  colpo a qn
  ▸ **hit out at** vt fus sferrare dei colpi contro;
  (fig) attaccare
  ▸ **hit (up)on** vt fus (answer) imbroccare,
  azzeccare; (solution) trovare (per caso)
hit-and-run driver ['hɪtænd'rʌn-] n pirata m
  della strada
hitch [hɪtʃ] vt (fasten) attaccare; (also: **hitch
  up**) tirare su ▪ n (difficulty) intoppo,
  difficoltà f inv; **technical ~** difficoltà tecnica;
  to ~ a lift fare l'autostop
  ▸ **hitch up** vt (horse, cart) attaccare
hitch-hike ['hɪtʃhaɪk] vi fare l'autostop
hitch-hiker ['hɪtʃhaɪkər] n autostoppista m/f

hi-tech ['haɪ'tɛk] *adj* high-tech *inv*,
a tecnologia avanzata

hitherto ['hɪðə'tuː] *adv* finora

hit list *n* libro nero

hitman ['hɪtmæn] *n* (*col*) sicario

hit-or-miss ['hɪtə'mɪs] *adj* casuale; **it's ~
whether ...** è in dubbio se ...; **the service in
this hotel is very ~** il servizio dell'albergo
lascia a desiderare

hit parade *n* hit-parade *f*

HIV *n abbr* (= *human immunodeficiency virus*) virus
m inv di immunodeficienza; **~-negative/-
positive** sieronegativo(-a)/sieropositivo(-a)

hive [haɪv] *n* alveare *m*; **the shop was a ~ of
activity** (*fig*) c'era una grande attività nel
negozio
 ▶ **hive off** *vt* (*col*) separare

hl *abbr* (= *hectolitre*) hl

HM *abbr* (= *His* (*or Her*) *Majesty*) S.M. (= *Sua Maestà*)

HMG *abbr* (*Brit*) = **His** (*or* **Her**) **Majesty's
Government**

HMI *n abbr* (*Brit Scol*: = *His* (*or Her*) *Majesty's
Inspector*) = ispettore *m* scolastico

HMO *n abbr* (*US*: = *Health Maintenance
Organization*) *organo per la salvaguardia della salute
pubblica*

HMS *abbr* (*Brit*) = **His** (*or* **Her**) **Majesty's Ship**

HNC *n abbr* (*Brit*: = *Higher National Certificate*)
diploma di istituto tecnico o professionale

HND *n abbr* (*Brit*: = *Higher National Diploma*)
diploma in materie tecniche equivalente ad una laurea

hoard [hɔːd] *n* (*of food*) provviste *fpl*; (*of money*)
gruzzolo ■ *vt* ammassare

hoarding ['hɔːdɪŋ] *n* (*Brit*) tabellone *m* per
affissioni

hoarfrost ['hɔːfrɒst] *n* brina

hoarse [hɔːs] *adj* rauco(-a)

hoax [həuks] *n* scherzo; falso allarme

hob [hɒb] *n* piastra (con fornelli)

hobble ['hɒbl] *vi* zoppicare

hobby ['hɒbɪ] *n* hobby *m inv*, passatempo

hobby-horse ['hɒbɪhɔːs] *n* cavallo a dondolo;
(*fig*) chiodo fisso

hobnail boots ['hɒbneɪl-], **hobnailed boots**
['hɒbneɪld-] *n* scarponi *mpl* chiodati

hobnob ['hɒbnɒb] *vi*: **to ~ (with)** mescolarsi
(con)

hobo ['həubəu] *n* (*US*) vagabondo

hock [hɒk] *n* (*Brit*: *wine*) vino del Reno;
(*of animal, Culin*) garretto; (*col*): **to be in ~**
avere debiti

hockey ['hɒkɪ] *n* hockey *m*

hocus-pocus ['həukəs'pəukəs] *n* (*trickery*)
trucco; (*words: of magician*) abracadabra *m inv*;
(: *jargon*) parolone *fpl*

hod [hɒd] *n* (*Tech*) cassetta per portare
i mattoni

hodgepodge ['hɒdʒpɒdʒ] *n* = **hotchpotch**

hoe [həu] *n* zappa ■ *vt* (*ground*) zappare

hog [hɒg] *n* maiale *m* ■ *vt* (*fig*) arraffare;
to go the whole ~ farlo fino in fondo

Hogmanay [hɒgmə'neɪ] *n* (*Scottish*) ≈ San
Silvestro

hogwash ['hɒgwɒʃ] *n* (*col*) stupidaggini *fpl*

hoist [hɔɪst] *n* paranco ■ *vt* issare

hoity-toity [hɔɪtɪ'tɔɪtɪ] *adj* (*col*) altezzoso(-a)

hold [həuld] *vb* (*pt, pp* **held**) [hɛld] *vt* tenere;
(*contain*) contenere; (*keep back*) trattenere;
(*believe*) mantenere; considerare; (*possess*)
avere, possedere; detenere ■ *vi* (*withstand
pressure*) tenere; (*be valid*) essere valido(-a) ■ *n*
presa; (*fig*) potere *m*; (*Naut*) stiva; **~ the line!**
(*Tel*) resti in linea!; **to ~ office** (*Pol*) essere in
carica; **to ~ sb responsible for sth**
considerare *or* ritenere qn responsabile di qc;
to ~ one's own (*fig*) difendersi bene; **he
holds the view that ...** è del parere che ...;
to ~ firm *or* **fast** resistere bene, tenere; **to
catch** *or* **get** (**a**) **~ of** afferrare; **to get ~ of** (*fig*)
trovare; **to get ~ of o.s.** trattenersi
 ▶ **hold back** *vt* trattenere; (*secret*) tenere
celato(-a); **to ~ sb back from doing sth**
impedire a qn di fare qc
 ▶ **hold down** *vt* (*person*) tenere a terra; (*job*)
tenere
 ▶ **hold forth** *vi* fare *or* tenere una concione
 ▶ **hold off** *vt* tener lontano ■ *vi* (*rain*): **if the
rain holds off** se continua a non piovere
 ▶ **hold on** *vi* tener fermo; (*wait*) aspettare;
~ on! (*Tel*) resti in linea!
 ▶ **hold on to** *vt fus* tenersi stretto(-a) a; (*keep*)
conservare
 ▶ **hold out** *vt* offrire ■ *vi* (*resist*): **to ~ out
(against)** resistere (a)
 ▶ **hold over** *vt* (*meeting etc*) rimandare,
rinviare
 ▶ **hold up** *vt* (*raise*) alzare; (*support*) sostenere;
(*delay*) ritardare; (*traffic*) rallentare; (*rob: bank*)
assaltare

holdall ['həuldɔːl] *n* (*Brit*) borsone *m*

holder ['həuldəʳ] *n* (*of ticket, title*) possessore/
posseditrice; (*of office etc*) incaricato(-a); (*of
passport, post*) titolare; (*of record*)
detentore(-trice)

holding ['həuldɪŋ] *n* (*share*) azioni *fpl*, titoli
mpl; (*farm*) podere *m*, tenuta

holding company *n* holding *f inv*

holdup ['həuldʌp] *n* (*robbery*) rapina a mano
armata; (*delay*) ritardo; (*Brit: in traffic*) blocco

hole [həul] *n* buco, buca ■ *vt* bucare; **~ in
the heart** (*Med*) morbo blu; **to pick holes in**
(*fig*) trovare da ridire su
 ▶ **hole up** *vi* nascondersi, rifugiarsi

holiday ['hɒlədɪ] *n* vacanza; (*from work*) ferie

fpl; (day off) giorno di vacanza; (public) giorno
festivo; **to be on ~** essere in vacanza;
tomorrow is a ~ domani è festa
holiday camp n (Brit: for children) colonia
(di villeggiatura); (also: **holiday centre**)
≈ villaggio (di vacanze)
holiday home n seconda casa (per le vacanze)
holiday-maker ['hɒlədɪmeɪkəʳ] n (Brit)
villeggiante m/f
holiday pay n stipendio delle ferie
holiday resort n luogo di villeggiatura
holiday season n stagione f delle vacanze
holiness ['həulɪnɪs] n santità
holistic [həu'lɪstɪk] adj olistico(-a)
Holland ['hɒlənd] n Olanda
holler ['hɒləʳ] vi gridare, urlare
hollow ['hɒləu] adj cavo(-a), vuoto(-a); (fig)
falso(-a); vano(-a) ■ n cavità f inv; (in land)
valletta, depressione f
▶ **hollow out** vt scavare
holly ['hɒlɪ] n agrifoglio
hollyhock ['hɒlɪhɒk] n malvone m
Hollywood ['hɒlɪwud] n Hollywood f
holocaust ['hɒləkɔːst] n olocausto
hologram ['hɒləgræm] n ologramma m
hols [hɒlz] npl: **the ~** le vacanze
holster ['həulstəʳ] n fondina (di pistola)
holy ['həulɪ] adj santo(-a); (bread)
benedetto(-a), consacrato(-a); (ground)
consacrato(-a); **the H~ Father** il Santo Padre
Holy Communion n la Santa Comunione
Holy Ghost, Holy Spirit n Spirito Santo
Holy Land n: **the ~** la Terra Santa
holy orders npl ordini mpl (sacri)
homage ['hɒmɪdʒ] n omaggio; **to pay ~ to**
rendere omaggio a
home [həum] n casa; (country) patria;
(institution) casa, ricovero ■ cpd (life)
familiare; (cooking etc) casalingo(-a); (Econ,
Pol) nazionale, interno(-a); (Sport: team) di
casa; (: match, win) in casa ■ adv a casa; in
patria; (right in: nail etc) fino in fondo; **at ~**
a casa; **to go** (or **come**) **~** tornare a casa (or in
patria); **it's near my ~** è vicino a casa mia;
make yourself at ~ si metta a suo agio
▶ **home in on** vt fus (missiles) dirigersi
(automaticamente) verso
home address n indirizzo di casa
home-brew [həum'bruː] n birra or vino
fatto(-a) in casa
homecoming ['həumkʌmɪŋ] n ritorno
Home Counties npl contee fpl intorno a
Londra
home economics n economia domestica
home ground n (fig): **to be on ~** essere sul
proprio terreno
home-grown [həum'grəun] adj

nostrano(-a), di produzione locale
home help n (Brit) collaboratore familiare per
persone bisognose stipendiato dal comune
homeland ['həumlænd] n patria
homeless ['həumlɪs] adj senza tetto;
spatriato(-a); **the homeless** npl i senzatetto
home loan n prestito con garanzia
immobiliare
homely ['həumlɪ] adj semplice, alla buona;
accogliente
home-made [həum'meɪd] adj casalingo(-a)
Home Office n (Brit) ministero degli Interni
homeopathy etc [həumɪ'ɒpəθɪ] (US)
= **homoeopathy** etc
home page n (Comput) home page f inv
home rule n autogoverno
Home Secretary n (Brit) ministro degli
Interni
homesick ['həumsɪk] adj: **to be ~** avere la
nostalgia
homestead ['həumsted] n fattoria e terreni
home town n città f inv natale
home truth n: **to tell sb a few home truths**
dire a qn qualche amara verità
homeward ['həumwəd] adj (journey) di
ritorno ■ adv verso casa
homewards ['həumwədz] adv verso casa
homework ['həumwəːk] n compiti mpl
(per casa)
homicidal [hɒmɪ'saɪdl] adj omicida
homicide ['hɒmɪsaɪd] n (US) omicidio
homily ['hɒmɪlɪ] n omelia
homing ['həumɪŋ] adj (device, missile)
autocercante; **~ pigeon** piccione m
viaggiatore
homoeopath, (US) homeopath
['həumɪəupæθ] n omeopatico
homoeopathic, (US) homeopathic
['həumɪəu'pæθɪk] adj omeopatico(-a)
homoeopathy, (US) homeopathy
[həumɪ'ɒpəθɪ] n omeopatia
homogeneous [hɒməu'dʒiːnɪəs] adj
omogeneo(-a)
homogenize [hə'mɒdʒənaɪz] vt
omogeneizzare
homosexual [hɒməu'sɛksjuəl] adj, n
omosessuale (m/f)
Hon. abbr = **honourable; honorary**
Honduras [hɒn'djuərəs] n Honduras m
hone [həun] vt (sharpen) affilare; (fig)
affinare
honest ['ɒnɪst] adj onesto(-a), sincero(-a); **to be**
quite ~ with you ... se devo dirle la verità ...
honestly ['ɒnɪstlɪ] adv onestamente;
sinceramente
honesty ['ɒnɪstɪ] n onestà
honey ['hʌnɪ] n miele m; (US col) tesoro m

honeycomb ['hʌnɪkəum] n favo ■ vt (fig):
honeycombed with tunnels etc pieno(-a)
di gallerie etc

honeymoon ['hʌnɪmu:n] n luna di miele,
viaggio di nozze

honeysuckle ['hʌnɪsʌkl] n caprifoglio

Hong Kong ['hɔŋ'kɔŋ] n Hong Kong f

honk [hɔŋk] n (Aut) colpo di clacson
■ vi suonare il clacson

Honolulu [hɔnə'lu:lu:] n Honolulu f

honorary ['ɔnərərɪ] adj onorario(-a);
(duty, title) onorifico(-a)

honour, (US) **honor** ['ɔnəʳ] vt onorare
■ n onore m; **in ~ of** in onore di

honourable, (US) **honorable** ['ɔnərəbl] adj
onorevole

honour-bound, (US) **honor-bound**
['ɔnə'baund] adj: **to be hono(u)r-bound to
do** dover fare per una questione di onore

honours degree n (Scol) laurea (con corso di studi
di 4 o 5 anni); vedi nota

● **HONOURS DEGREE**

In Gran Bretagna esistono titoli
universitari di diverso livello. Gli studenti
che conseguono ottimi risultati e che
approfondiscono una o più materie
possono ottenere l'*honours degree*. Questo
titolo, abbreviato in Hons., viene posto
dopo il titolo ottenuto (ad esempio BA
Hons); vedi anche "ordinary degree".

honours list n (Brit) elenco ufficiale dei destinati al
conferimento di onorificenze; vedi nota

● **HONOURS LIST**

La *honours list* è un elenco di cittadini
britannici e del Commonwealth che si
sono distinti in campo imprenditoria/e,
militare, sportivo ecc, meritando il
conferimento di un titolo o di una
decorazione da parte del sovrano. Ogni
anno vengono redatte dal primo ministro
due *honours lists*, una a Capodanno e una in
occasione del compleanno del sovrano.

Hons. [ɔnz] abbr (Scol) = **hono(u)rs degree**

hood [hud] n cappuccio; (Brit Aut) capote f;
(US Aut) cofano; (col) malvivente m/f

hooded ['hudɪd] adj (robber) mascherato(-a)

hoodie ['hudɪ] n felpa con cappuccio

hoodlum ['hu:dləm] n malvivente m/f

hoodwink ['hudwɪŋk] vt infinocchiare

hoof (pl **hoofs** or **hooves**) [hu:f, hu:vz] n
zoccolo

hook [huk] n gancio; (for fishing) amo ■ vt
uncinare; (dress) agganciare; **to be hooked
on** (col) essere fanatico di; **hooks and eyes**
gancetti; **by ~ or by crook** in un modo o
nell'altro
  ▶ **hook up** vt (Radio, TV etc) allacciare,
  collegare

hooligan ['hu:lɪgən] n giovinastro, teppista m

hooliganism ['hu:lɪgənɪzəm] n teppismo

hoop [hu:p] n cerchio

hoot [hu:t] vi (Aut) suonare il clacson; (owl)
gufare ■ n colpo di clacson; **to ~ with
laughter** farsi una gran risata

hooter ['hu:təʳ] n (Aut) clacson m inv; (Naut,
at factory) sirena

hoover® ['hu:vəʳ] n (Brit) aspirapolvere m inv
■ vt pulire con l'aspirapolvere

hooves [hu:vz] npl of **hoof**

hop [hɔp] vi saltellare, saltare; (on one foot)
saltare su una gamba ■ n salto; **hops** npl
luppoli mpl

hope [həup] vt, vi sperare ■ n speranza;
I ~ so/not spero di sì/no

hopeful ['həupful] adj (person) pieno(-a) di
speranza; (situation) promettente; **I'm ~ that
she'll manage to come** ho buone speranze
che venga

hopefully ['həupfulɪ] adv con speranza;
~ he will recover speriamo che si riprenda

hopeless ['həuplɪs] adj senza speranza,
disperato(-a); (useless) inutile

hopelessly ['həuplɪslɪ] adv (live etc) senza
speranza; (involved, complicated)
spaventosamente; (late) disperatamente,
irrimediabilmente; **I'm ~ confused/lost**
sono completamente confuso/perso

hopper ['hɔpəʳ] n (chute) tramoggia

hops [hɔps] npl luppoli mpl

horde [hɔ:d] n orda

horizon [hə'raɪzn] n orizzonte m

horizontal [hɔrɪ'zɔntl] adj orizzontale

hormone ['hɔ:məun] n ormone m

hormone replacement therapy n terapia
ormonale (usata in menopausa)

horn [hɔ:n] n corno; (Aut) clacson m inv

horned [hɔ:nd] adj (animal) cornuto(-a)

hornet ['hɔ:nɪt] n calabrone m

horny ['hɔ:nɪ] adj corneo(-a); (hands)
calloso(-a)

horoscope ['hɔrəskəup] n oroscopo

horrendous [hə'rɛndəs] n orrendo(-a)

horrible ['hɔrɪbl] adj orribile, tremendo(-a)

horrid ['hɔrɪd] adj orrido(-a); (person)
antipatico(-a)

horrific [hɔ'rɪfɪk] adj (accident) spaventoso(-a);
(film) orripilante

horrify ['hɔrɪfaɪ] vt lasciare inorridito(-a)

horrifying ['hɔrɪfaɪɪŋ] *adj* terrificante
horror ['hɔrəᵊ] *n* orrore *m*
horror film *n* film *m* inv dell'orrore
horror-struck ['hɔrəstrʌk], **horror-stricken** ['hɔrəstrɪkn] *adj* inorridito(-a)
hors d'œuvre [ɔː'dəːvrə] *n* antipasto
horse [hɔːs] *n* cavallo
horseback ['hɔːsbæk]: **on ~** *adj, adv* a cavallo
horsebox ['hɔːsbɔks] *n* carro *or* furgone *m* per il trasporto dei cavalli
horse chestnut *n* ippocastano
horse-drawn ['hɔːsdrɔːn] *adj* tirato(-a) da cavallo
horsefly ['hɔːsflaɪ] *n* tafano, mosca cavallina
horseman ['hɔːsmən] *n* cavaliere *m*
horsemanship ['hɔːsmənʃɪp] *n* equitazione *f*
horseplay ['hɔːspleɪ] *n* giochi *mpl* scatenati
horsepower ['hɔːspauəᵊ] *n* cavallo (vapore), c/v
horse-racing ['hɔːsreɪsɪŋ] *n* ippica
horseradish ['hɔːsrædɪʃ] *n* rafano
horseshoe ['hɔːsʃuː] *n* ferro di cavallo
horse show *n* concorso ippico, gare *fpl* ippiche
horse-trading ['hɔːstreɪdɪŋ] *n* mercanteggiamento
horse trials *npl* = **horse show**
horsewhip ['hɔːswɪp] *vt* frustare
horsewoman ['hɔːswumən] *n* amazzone *f*
horsey ['hɔːsɪ] *adj* (col: person) che adora i cavalli; (appearance) cavallino(-a), da cavallo
horticulture ['hɔːtɪkʌltʃəᵊ] *n* orticoltura
hose [həuz] *n* (also: **hosepipe**) tubo; (also: **garden hose**) tubo per annaffiare
  ▶ **hose down** *vt* lavare con un getto d'acqua
hosepipe ['həuzpaɪp] *n* see **hose**
hosiery ['həuzɪərɪ] *n* (in shop) (reparto di) calze *fpl* e calzini *mpl*
hospice ['hɔspɪs] *n* ricovero, ospizio
hospitable [hɔ'spɪtəbl] *adj* ospitale
hospital ['hɔspɪtl] *n* ospedale *m*; **in ~**, (US) **in the ~** all'ospedale
hospitality [hɔspɪ'tælɪtɪ] *n* ospitalità
hospitalize ['hɔspɪtəlaɪz] *vt* ricoverare (in *or* all'ospedale)
host [həust] *n* ospite *m*; (TV, Radio) presentatore(-trice); (Rel) ostia; (large number): **a ~ of** una schiera di ■ *vt* (TV programme, games) presentare
hostage ['hɔstɪdʒ] *n* ostaggio(-a)
host country *n* paese *m* ospite, paese che ospita
hostel ['hɔstl] *n* ostello; (for students, nurses etc) pensionato; (for homeless people) ospizio, ricovero; (also: **youth hostel**) ostello della gioventù
hostelling ['hɔstəlɪŋ] *n*: **to go (youth) ~** passare le vacanze negli ostelli della gioventù
hostess ['həustɪs] *n* ospite *f*; (Aviat) hostess *f*

inv; (in nightclub) entraineuse *f* inv
hostile ['hɔstaɪl] *adj* ostile
hostility [hɔ'stɪlɪtɪ] *n* ostilità *f* inv
hot [hɔt] *adj* caldo(-a); (as opposed to only warm) molto caldo(-a); (spicy) piccante; (fig) accanito(-a); ardente; violento(-a), focoso(-a); **to be ~** (person) aver caldo; (thing) essere caldo(-a); (Meteor) far caldo
  ▶ **hot up** (Brit col) *vi* (situation) farsi più teso(-a); (party) scaldarsi ■ *vt* (pace) affrettare; (engine) truccare
hot-air balloon [hɔt'eə-] *n* mongolfiera
hotbed ['hɔtbɛd] *n* (fig) focolaio
hotchpotch ['hɔtʃpɔtʃ] *n* (Brit) pot-pourri *m*
hot dog *n* hot dog *m* inv
hotel [həu'tɛl] *n* albergo
hotelier [həu'tɛljeɪ] *n* albergatore(-trice)
hotel industry *n* industria alberghiera
hotel room *n* camera d'albergo
hot flush *n* (Brit) scalmana, caldana
hotfoot ['hɔtfut] *adv* di gran carriera
hothead ['hɔthɛd] *n* (fig) testa calda
hotheaded [hɔt'hɛdɪd] *adj* focoso(-a), eccitabile
hothouse ['hɔthaus] *n* serra
hot line *n* (Pol) telefono rosso
hotly ['hɔtlɪ] *adv* violentemente
hotplate ['hɔtpleɪt] *n* fornello; piastra riscaldante
hotpot ['hɔtpɔt] *n* (Brit Culin) stufato
hot potato *n* (Brit col) patata bollente; **to drop sb/sth like a ~** mollare subito qn/qc
hot seat *n* (fig) posto che scotta
hotspot ['hɔtspɔt] *n* (Comput: wireless hotspot) hotspot *m* inv Wi-Fi
hot spot *n* (fig) zona calda
hot spring *n* sorgente *f* termale
hot-tempered [hɔt'tɛmpəd] *adj* irascibile
hot-water bottle [hɔt'wɔːtə-] *n* borsa dell'acqua calda
hot-wire ['hɔtwaɪəᵊ] *vt* (col: car) avviare mettendo in contatto i fili dell'accensione
hound [haund] *vt* perseguitare ■ *n* segugio
hour [auəᵊ] *n* ora; **at 30 miles an ~** a 30 miglia all'ora; **lunch ~** intervallo di pranzo; **to pay sb by the ~** pagare qn a ore
hourly ['auəlɪ] *adj* (ad) ogni ora; (rate) orario(-a) ■ *adv* ogni ora; **~ paid** *adj* pagato(-a) a ore
house *n* [haus] (*pl* **houses**) ['hauzɪz] casa; (Pol) camera; (Theat) sala; pubblico; spettacolo ■ *vt* [hauz] (person) ospitare; **at** (*or* **to**) **my ~** a casa mia; **the H~ (of Commons/Lords)** (Brit) la Camera dei Comuni/Lords; **the H~ (of Representatives)** (US) ≈ la Camera dei Deputati; **on the ~** (fig) offerto(-a) dalla casa

605

house arrest n arresti mpl domiciliari
houseboat ['hausbəut] n house boat f inv
housebound ['hausbaund] adj confinato(-a) in casa
housebreaking ['hausbreikiŋ] n furto con scasso
house-broken ['hausbrəukn] adj (US) = **house-trained**
housecoat ['hauskəut] n vestaglia
household ['haushəuld] n famiglia, casa
householder ['haushəuldəʳ] n padrone(-a) di casa; (head of house) capofamiglia m/f
household name n nome m che tutti conoscono
househunting ['haushʌntiŋ] n: **to go ~** mettersi a cercar casa
housekeeper ['hauski:pəʳ] n governante f
housekeeping ['hauski:piŋ] n (work) governo della casa; (also: **housekeeping money**) soldi mpl per le spese di casa; (Comput) ausilio
houseman ['hausmən] n (Brit Med) ≈ interno
house-owner ['hausəunəʳ] n possessore m/f di casa
house plant n pianta da appartamento
house-proud ['hauspraud] adj che è maniaco(-a) della pulizia
house-to-house ['haustə'haus] adj (collection) di porta in porta; (search) casa per casa
house-train ['haustrein] vt (Brit: pet animal) addestrare a non sporcare in casa
house-trained ['haustreind] adj (Brit: animal) che non sporca in casa
house-warming party ['hauswɔ:miŋ-] n festa per inaugurare la casa nuova
housewife ['hauswaif] n massaia, casalinga
housework ['hauswə:k] n faccende fpl domestiche
housing ['hauziŋ] n alloggio ■ cpd (problem, shortage) degli alloggi
housing association n cooperativa edilizia
housing benefit n (Brit) contributo abitativo (ad affittuari e a coloro che comprano una casa)
housing conditions npl condizioni fpl di abitazione
housing development, (Brit) **housing estate** n zona residenziale con case popolari e/o private
hovel ['hɔvl] n capsuola
hover ['hɔvəʳ] vi (bird) librarsi; (helicopter) volare a punto fisso; **to ~ round sb** aggirarsi intorno a qn
hovercraft ['hɔvəkrɑ:ft] n hovercraft m inv
hoverport ['hɔvəpɔ:t] n porto per hovercraft
how [hau] adv come; **~ are you?** come sta?; **~ do you do?** piacere!, molto lieto!; **~ far is it to ...?** quanto è lontano ...?; **~ long have you been here?** da quanto tempo sta qui?;

~ lovely! che bello!; **~ many?** quanti(-e)?; **~ much?** quanto(-a)?; **~ many people/much milk?** quante persone/quanto latte?; **~ old are you?** quanti anni ha?; **~'s life?** (col) come va (la vita)?; **~ about a drink?** che ne diresti di andare a bere qualcosa?; **~ is it that ...?** com'è che ...? + sub
however [hau'evəʳ] adv in qualsiasi modo or maniera che; (+ adjective) per quanto + sub; (in questions) come ■ conj comunque, però
howitzer ['hauitsəʳ] n (Mil) obice m
howl [haul] n ululato ■ vi ululare
howler ['hauləʳ] n marronata
howling ['hauliŋ] adj: **a ~ wind** or **gale** un vento terribile
HP n abbr (Brit) = **hire purchase**
hp abbr (Aut) = **horsepower**
HQ n abbr (= headquarters) Q.G.
HR n abbr (US) = **House of Representatives**; (= human resources: department) ufficio personale; (: staff) risorse umane
hr, hrs abbr (= hour(s)) h
HRH abbr (= His (or Her) Royal Highness) S.A.R.
HRT n abbr = **hormone replacement therapy**
HS abbr (US) = **high school**
HST abbr (= Hawaiian Standard Time) fuso orario
HT abbr (= high tension) A.T.
HTML n abbr (Comput: = hypertext markup language) HTML
hub [hʌb] n (of wheel) mozzo; (fig) fulcro
hubbub ['hʌbʌb] n baccano
hubcap ['hʌbkæp] n (Aut) coprimozzo
HUD n abbr (US) = **Department of Housing and Urban Development**
huddle ['hʌdl] vi: **to ~ together** rannicchiarsi l'uno contro l'altro
hue [hju:] n tinta; **~ and cry** n clamore m
huff [hʌf] n: **in a ~** stizzito(-a); **to take the ~** mettere il broncio
huffy ['hʌfi] adj (col) stizzito(-a), indispettito(-a)
hug [hʌg] vt abbracciare; (shore, kerb) stringere ■ n abbraccio, stretta; **to give sb a ~** abbracciare qn
huge [hju:dʒ] adj enorme, immenso(-a)
hulk [hʌlk] n carcassa
hulking ['hʌlkiŋ] adj: **~ (great)** grosso(-a) e goffo(-a)
hull [hʌl] n (of ship) scafo
hullabaloo [hʌləbə'lu:] n (col: noise) fracasso
hullo [hə'ləu] excl = **hello**
hum [hʌm] vt (tune) canticchiare ■ vi canticchiare; (insect, plane, tool) ronzare ■ n (also Elec) ronzio; (of traffic, machines) rumore m; (of voices etc) mormorio, brusio
human ['hju:mən] adj umano(-a) ■ n (also: **human being**) essere m umano

humane [hjuː'meɪn] *adj* umanitario(-a)
humanism ['hjuːmənɪzəm] *n* umanesimo
humanitarian [hjuːmænɪ'tɛərɪən] *adj* umanitario(-a)
humanity [hjuː'mænɪtɪ] *n* umanità; **the humanities** gli studi umanistici
humanly ['hjuːmənlɪ] *adv* umanamente
humanoid ['hjuːmənɔɪd] *adj* che sembra umano(-a) ∎ *n* umanoide *m/f*
human rights *npl* diritti *mpl* dell'uomo
humble ['hʌmbl] *adj* umile, modesto(-a) ∎ *vt* umiliare
humbly ['hʌmblɪ] *adv* umilmente, modestamente
humbug ['hʌmbʌg] *n* inganno; sciocchezze *fpl*; (Brit: *sweet*) caramella alla menta
humdrum ['hʌmdrʌm] *adj* monotono(-a), tedioso(-a)
humid ['hjuːmɪd] *adj* umido(-a)
humidifier [hjuː'mɪdɪfaɪə'] *n* umidificatore *m*
humidity [hjuː'mɪdɪtɪ] *n* umidità
humiliate [hjuː'mɪlɪeɪt] *vt* umiliare
humiliation [hjuːmɪlɪ'eɪʃən] *n* umiliazione *f*
humility [hjuː'mɪlɪtɪ] *n* umiltà
humorist ['hjuːmərɪst] *n* umorista *m/f*
humorous ['hjuːmərəs] *adj* umoristico(-a); (*person*) buffo(-a)
humour, (US) **humor** ['hjuːmə'] *n* umore *m* ∎ *vt* (*person*) compiacere; (*sb's whims*) assecondare; **sense of ~** senso dell'umorismo; **to be in a good/bad ~** essere di buon/cattivo umore
humourless, (US) **humorless** ['hjuːməlɪs] *adj* privo(-a) di umorismo
hump [hʌmp] *n* gobba
humpback ['hʌmpbæk] *n* schiena d'asino; (Brit: *also*: **humpback bridge**) ponte *m* a schiena d'asino
humus ['hjuːməs] *n* humus *m*
hunch [hʌntʃ] *n* gobba; (*premonition*) intuizione *f*; **I have a ~ that** ho la vaga impressione che
hunchback ['hʌntʃbæk] *n* gobbo(-a)
hunched [hʌntʃt] *adj* incurvato(-a)
hundred ['hʌndrəd] *num* cento; **about a ~ people** un centinaio di persone; **hundreds of people** centinaia *fpl* di persone; **I'm a ~ per cent sure** sono sicuro al cento per cento
hundredweight ['hʌndrɪdweɪt] *n* (Brit) = 50.8 kg; = 112 lb; (US) = 45.3 kg; = 100 lb
hung [hʌŋ] *pt, pp of* **hang**
Hungarian [hʌŋ'gɛərɪən] *adj* ungherese ∎ *n* ungherese *m/f*; (Ling) ungherese *m*
Hungary ['hʌŋgərɪ] *n* Ungheria
hunger ['hʌŋgə'] *n* fame *f* ∎ *vi*: **to ~ for** desiderare ardentemente
hunger strike *n* sciopero della fame

hungover [hʌŋ'əuvə'] *adj* (col): **to be ~** avere i postumi della sbornia
hungrily ['hʌŋgrəlɪ] *adv* voracemente; (*fig*) avidamente
hungry ['hʌŋgrɪ] *adj* affamato(-a); **to be ~** aver fame; **~ for** (*fig*) assetato di
hung up *adj* (col) complessato(-a)
hunk [hʌŋk] *n* bel pezzo
hunt [hʌnt] *vt* (*seek*) cercare; (Sport) cacciare ∎ *vi* andare a caccia ∎ *n* caccia
▶ **hunt down** *vt* scovare
hunter ['hʌntə'] *n* cacciatore *m*; (Brit: *horse*) cavallo da caccia
hunting ['hʌntɪŋ] *n* caccia
hurdle ['hə:dl] *n* (Sport, *fig*) ostacolo
hurl [hə:l] *vt* lanciare con violenza
hurling ['hə:lɪŋ] *n* (Sport) hurling *m*
hurly-burly ['hə:lɪ'bə:lɪ] *n* chiasso, baccano
hurrah [hu'rɑː], **hurray** [hu'reɪ] *excl* urra!, evviva!
hurricane ['hʌrɪkən] *n* uragano
hurried ['hʌrɪd] *adj* affrettato(-a); (*work*) fatto(-a) in fretta
hurriedly ['hʌrɪdlɪ] *adv* in fretta
hurry ['hʌrɪ] *n* fretta ∎ *vi* affrettarsi ∎ *vt* (*person*) affrettare; (*work*) far in fretta; **to be in a ~** aver fretta; **to do sth in a ~** fare qc in fretta; **to ~ in/out** entrare/uscire in fretta; **to ~ back/home** affrettarsi a tornare indietro/a casa
▶ **hurry along** *vi* camminare in fretta
▶ **hurry away, hurry off** *vi* andarsene in fretta
▶ **hurry up** *vi* sbrigarsi
hurt [hə:t] *vb* (*pt, pp* ~) *vt* (*cause pain to*) far male a; (*injure, fig*) ferire; (*business, interests etc*) colpire, danneggiare ∎ *vi* far male ∎ *adj* ferito(-a); **I ~ my arm** mi sono fatto male al braccio; **where does it ~?** dove ti fa male?
hurtful ['hə:tful] *adj* (*remark*) che ferisce
hurtle ['hə:tl] *vt* scagliare ∎ *vi*: **to ~ past/down** passare/scendere a razzo
husband ['hʌzbənd] *n* marito
hush [hʌʃ] *n* silenzio, calma ∎ *vt* zittire; **~!** zitto(-a)!
▶ **hush up** *vt* (*fact*) cercare di far passare sotto silenzio
hush-hush ['hʌʃ'hʌʃ] *adj* (col) segretissimo(-a)
husk [hʌsk] *n* (*of wheat*) cartoccio; (*of rice, maize*) buccia
husky ['hʌskɪ] *adj* roco(-a) ∎ *n* cane *m* eschimese
hustings ['hʌstɪŋz] *npl* (Brit Pol) comizi *mpl* elettorali
hustle ['hʌsl] *vt* spingere, incalzare ∎ *n* pigia pigia *m inv*; **~ and bustle** trambusto
hut [hʌt] *n* rifugio; (*shed*) ripostiglio

hutch [hʌtʃ] n gabbia
hyacinth ['haɪəsɪnθ] n giacinto
hybrid ['haɪbrɪd] adj ibrido(-a) ∎ n ibrido
hydrant ['haɪdrənt] n (also: **fire hydrant**)
   idrante m
hydraulic [haɪ'drɔlɪk] adj idraulico(-a)
hydraulics [haɪ'drɔlɪks] n idraulica
hydrochloric [haɪdrə'klɔrɪk] adj: ~ **acid** acido
   cloridrico
hydroelectric [haɪdrəʊɪ'lɛktrɪk] adj
   idroelettrico(-a)
hydrofoil ['haɪdrəfɔɪl] n aliscafo
hydrogen ['haɪdrədʒən] n idrogeno
hydrogen bomb n bomba all'idrogeno
hydrophobia [haɪdrə'fəubɪə] n idrofobia
hydroplane ['haɪdrəupleɪn] n idrovolante m
hyena [haɪ'iːnə] n iena
hygiene ['haɪdʒiːn] n igiene f
hygienic [haɪ'dʒiːnɪk] adj igienico(-a)
hymn [hɪm] n inno; cantica
hype [haɪp] n (col) clamorosa pubblicità
hyperactive [haɪpər'æktɪv] adj iperattivo(-a)
hyperlink [haɪpəlɪŋk] n collegamento o link
   m inv ipertestuale
hypermarket ['haɪpəmɑːkɪt] n (Brit)
   ipermercato
hypertension [haɪpə'tɛnʃən] n (Med)
   ipertensione f
hypertext ['haɪpətɛkst] n (Comput) ipertesto

hyphen ['haɪfn] n trattino
hypnosis [hɪp'nəusɪs] n ipnosi f
hypnotic [hɪp'nɔtɪk] adj ipnotico(-a)
hypnotism ['hɪpnətɪzəm] n ipnotismo
hypnotist ['hɪpnətɪst] n ipnotizzatore(-trice)
hypnotize ['hɪpnətaɪz] vt ipnotizzare
hypoallergenic [haɪpəuæələ'dʒɛnɪk] adj
   ipoallergico(-a)
hypochondriac [haɪpə'kɔndriæk] n
   ipocondriaco(-a)
hypocrisy [hɪ'pɔkrɪsɪ] n ipocrisia
hypocrite ['hɪpəkrɪt] n ipocrita m/f
hypocritical [hɪpə'krɪtɪkl] adj ipocrita
hypodermic [haɪpə'dəːmɪk] adj
   ipodermico(-a) ∎ n (syringe) siringa
   ipodermica
hypotenuse [haɪ'pɔtɪnjuːz] n ipotenusa
hypothermia [haɪpəu'θəːmɪə] n ipotermia
hypothesis (pl **hypotheses**) [haɪ'pɔθɪsɪs, -siːz]
   n ipotesi f inv
hypothetical [haɪpəu'θɛtɪkl] adj ipotetico(-a)
hysterectomy [hɪstə'rɛktəmɪ] n
   isterectomia
hysteria [hɪ'stɪərɪə] n isteria
hysterical [hɪ'stɛrɪkl] adj isterico(-a);
   to become ~ avere una crisi isterica
hysterics [hɪ'stɛrɪks] npl accesso di isteria;
   (laughter) attacco di riso; **to have ~** avere una
   crisi isterica

I, i [aɪ] *n (letter)* I, i *f or m inv*; **I for Isaac**, *(US)*
 I for Item ≈ I come Imola
I [aɪ] *pron* io ■ *abbr (= island, isle)* Is.
IA *abbr (US)* = **Iowa**
IAEA *n abbr* = **International Atomic Energy Agency**
ib. ['ɪb] *abbr (= ibidem: from the same source)* ibid
Iberian [aɪ'bɪərɪən] *adj* iberico(-a)
Iberian Peninsula *n*: **the** ~ la Penisola iberica
IBEW *n abbr (US: = International Brotherhood of Electrical Workers)* associazione internazionale degli elettrotecnici
ibid. ['ɪbɪd] *abbr (= ibidem: from the same source)* ibid
i/c *abbr (Brit)* = **in charge**
ICBM *n abbr (= intercontinental ballistic missile)* ICBM *m inv*
ICC *n abbr (= International Chamber of Commerce)* C.C.I. *f*; *(US: = Interstate Commerce Commission)* commissione per il commercio tra gli stati degli USA
ice [aɪs] *n* ghiaccio; *(on road)* gelo ■ *vt (cake)* glassare; *(drink)* mettere in fresco ■ *vi (also:* **ice over**) ghiacciare; *(also:* **ice up**) gelare; **to keep sth on** ~ *(fig: plan, project)* mettere da parte (per il momento), accantonare
Ice Age *n* era glaciale
ice axe *n* piccozza da ghiaccio
iceberg ['aɪsbə:g] *n* iceberg *m inv*; **tip of the** ~ *(also fig)* punta dell'iceberg
icebox ['aɪsbɔks] *n (US)* frigorifero; *(Brit)* reparto ghiaccio; *(insulated box)* frigo portatile
icebreaker ['aɪsbreɪkə'] *n* rompighiaccio *m inv*
ice bucket *n* secchiello del ghiaccio
ice-cap ['aɪskæp] *n* calotta polare
ice-cold [aɪs'kəuld] *adj* gelato(-a)
ice cream *n* gelato
ice-cream soda *n* (gelato) affogato al seltz
ice cube *n* cubetto di ghiaccio
iced [aɪst] *adj (drink)* ghiacciato(-a); *(coffee, tea)* freddo(-a); *(cake)* glassato(-a)
ice hockey *n* hockey *m* su ghiaccio
Iceland ['aɪslənd] *n* Islanda
Icelander ['aɪsləndə'] *n* islandese *m/f*

Icelandic [aɪs'lændɪk] *adj* islandese
 ■ *n (Ling)* islandese *m*
ice lolly *n (Brit)* ghiacciolo
ice pick *n* piccone *m* per ghiaccio
ice rink *n* pista di pattinaggio
ice-skate ['aɪsskeɪt] *n* pattino da ghiaccio
 ■ *vi* pattinare sul ghiaccio
ice-skating ['aɪsskeɪtɪŋ] *n* pattinaggio sul ghiaccio
icicle ['aɪsɪkl] *n* ghiacciolo
icing ['aɪsɪŋ] *n (Aviat etc)* patina di ghiaccio; *(Culin)* glassa
icing sugar *n* zucchero a velo
ICJ *n abbr* = **International Court of Justice**
icon ['aɪkɔn] *n* icona; *(Comput)* immagine *f*
ICR *n abbr (US)* = **Institute for Cancer Research**
ICRC *n abbr (= International Committee of the Red Cross)* CICR *m*
ICT *n abbr (Brit: Scol: = Information and Communications Technology)* informatica
ICU *n abbr* = **intensive care unit**
icy ['aɪsɪ] *adj* ghiacciato(-a); *(weather, temperature)* gelido(-a)
ID *abbr* = **identification document**; *(US)* = **Idaho**
I'd [aɪd] = **I would**; **I had**
Ida. *abbr (US)* = **Idaho**
ID card *n* = **identity card**
IDD *n abbr (Brit Tel: = International direct dialling)* teleselezione *f* internazionale
idea [aɪ'dɪə] *n* idea; **good** ~! buon'idea!; **to have an** ~ **that ...** aver l'impressione che ...; **I haven't the least** ~ non ne ho la minima idea
ideal [aɪ'dɪəl] *adj, n* ideale *(m)*
idealist [aɪ'dɪəlɪst] *n* idealista *m/f*
ideally [aɪ'dɪəlɪ] *adv* perfettamente, assolutamente; ~ **the book should have ...** l'ideale sarebbe che il libro avesse ...
identical [aɪ'dɛntɪkl] *adj* identico(-a)
identification [aɪdɛntɪfɪ'keɪʃən] *n* identificazione *f*; **means of** ~ carta d'identità

identify [aɪ'dɛntɪfaɪ] vt identificare ■ vi:
to ~ with identificarsi con
Identikit® [aɪ'dɛntɪkɪt] n: ~ (picture)
identikit m inv
identity [aɪ'dɛntɪtɪ] n identità f inv
identity card n carta d'identità
identity parade n (Brit) confronto
all'americana
identity theft n furto d'identità
ideological [aɪdɪə'lɔdʒɪkəl] adj ideologico(-a)
ideology [aɪdɪ'ɔlədʒɪ] n ideologia
idiocy ['ɪdɪəsɪ] n idiozia
idiom ['ɪdɪəm] n idioma m; (phrase)
espressione f idiomatica
idiomatic [ɪdɪə'mætɪk] adj idiomatico(-a)
idiosyncrasy [ɪdɪəu'sɪŋkrəsɪ] n idiosincrasia
idiot ['ɪdɪət] n idiota m/f
idiotic [ɪdɪ'ɔtɪk] adj idiota
idle ['aɪdl] adj inattivo(-a); (lazy) pigro(-a),
ozioso(-a); (unemployed) disoccupato(-a);
(question, pleasures) ozioso(-a) ■ vi (engine)
girare al minimo; to lie ~ stare fermo, non
funzionare
▸ **idle away** vt (time) sprecare, buttar via
idleness ['aɪdlnɪs] n ozio; pigrizia
idler ['aɪdləʳ] n ozioso(-a), fannullone(-a)
idle time n tempi mpl morti
idol ['aɪdl] n idolo
idolize ['aɪdəlaɪz] vt idoleggiare
idyllic [ɪ'dɪlɪk] adj idillico(-a)
i.e. abbr (= id est: that is) cioè
if [ɪf] conj se ■ n: there are a lot of ifs and
buts ci sono molti se e ma; I'd be pleased if
you could do it sarei molto contento se
potesse farlo; if necessary se (è) necessario;
if only he were here se solo fosse qui; if
only to show him my gratitude se non
altro per esprimergli la mia gratitudine
iffy ['ɪfɪ] adj (col) incerto(-a)
igloo ['ɪglu:] n igloo m inv
ignite [ɪg'naɪt] vt accendere ■ vi accendersi
ignition [ɪg'nɪʃən] n (Aut) accensione f; to
switch on/off the ~ accendere/spegnere il
motore
ignition key n (Aut) chiave f dell'accensione
ignoble [ɪg'nəubl] adj ignobile
ignominious [ɪgnə'mɪnɪəs] adj
vergognoso(-a), ignominioso(-a)
ignoramus [ɪgnə'reɪməs] n ignorante m/f
ignorance ['ɪgnərəns] n ignoranza; to keep
sb in ~ of sth tenere qn all'oscuro di qc
ignorant ['ɪgnərənt] adj ignorante; to be ~ of
(subject) essere ignorante in; (events) essere
ignaro(-a) di
ignore [ɪg'nɔ:ʳ] vt non tener conto di; (person,
fact) ignorare
ikon ['aɪkɔn] n = **icon**

IL abbr (US) = **Illinois**
ILA n abbr (US: = International Longshoremen's
Association) associazione internazionale degli
scaricatori di porto
ill [ɪl] adj (sick) malato(-a); (bad) cattivo(-a)
■ n male m; to take or be taken ~
ammalarsi; to feel ~ star male; to speak/
think ~ of sb parlar/pensar male di qn
I'll [aɪl] = **I will; I shall**
Ill. abbr (US) = **Illinois**
ill-advised [ɪləd'vaɪzd] adj (decision) poco
giudizioso(-a); (person) mal consigliato(-a)
ill-at-ease [ɪlət'i:z] adj a disagio
ill-considered [ɪlkən'sɪdəd] adj (plan)
avventato(-a)
ill-disposed [ɪldɪs'pəuzd] adj: to be ~
towards sb/sth essere maldisposto(-a) verso
qn/qc or nei riguardi di qn/qc
illegal [ɪ'li:gl] adj illegale
illegally [ɪ'li:gəlɪ] adv illegalmente
illegible [ɪ'lɛdʒɪbl] adj illeggibile
illegitimate [ɪlɪ'dʒɪtɪmət] adj illegittimo(-a)
ill-fated [ɪl'feɪtɪd] adj nefasto(-a)
ill-favoured, (US) **ill-favored** [ɪl'feɪvəd] adj
sgraziato(-a), brutto(-a)
ill feeling n rancore m
ill-gotten ['ɪlgɔtn] adj: ~ gains maltolto
ill health n problemi mpl di salute
illicit [ɪ'lɪsɪt] adj illecito(-a)
ill-informed [ɪlɪn'fɔ:md] adj (judgement, speech)
pieno(-a) di inesattezze; (person) male
informato(-a)
illiterate [ɪ'lɪtərət] adj analfabeta,
illetterato(-a); (letter) scorretto(-a)
ill-mannered [ɪl'mænəd] adj maleducato(-a),
sgarbato(-a)
illness ['ɪlnɪs] n malattia
illogical [ɪ'lɔdʒɪkl] adj illogico(-a)
ill-suited [ɪl'su:tɪd] adj (couple) mal
assortito(-a); he is ~ to the job è inadatto
a quel lavoro
ill-timed [ɪl'taɪmd] adj intempestivo(-a),
inopportuno(-a)
ill-treat [ɪl'tri:t] vt maltrattare
ill-treatment [ɪl'tri:tmənt] n
maltrattamenti mpl
illuminate [ɪ'lu:mɪneɪt] vt illuminare;
illuminated sign insegna luminosa
illuminating [ɪ'lu:mɪneɪtɪŋ] adj
chiarificatore(-trice)
illumination [ɪlu:mɪ'neɪʃən] n
illuminazione f
illusion [ɪ'lu:ʒən] n illusione f; to be under
the ~ that avere l'impressione che
illusive [ɪ'lu:sɪv], **illusory** [ɪ'lu:sərɪ] adj
illusorio(-a)
illustrate ['ɪləstreɪt] vt illustrare

illustration [ɪləˈstreɪʃən] *n* illustrazione *f*
illustrator [ˈɪləstreɪtəʳ] *n* illustratore(-trice)
illustrious [ɪˈlʌstrɪəs] *adj* illustre
ill will *n* cattiva volontà
ILO *n abbr* (= *International Labour Organization*) OIL *f*
IM *n abbr* (= *instant messaging*) messaggeria istantanea
I'm [aɪm] = **I am**
image [ˈɪmɪdʒ] *n* immagine *f*; (*public face*) immagine (pubblica)
imagery [ˈɪmɪdʒərɪ] *n* immagini *fpl*
imaginable [ɪˈmædʒɪnəbl] *adj* immaginabile, che si possa immaginare
imaginary [ɪˈmædʒɪnərɪ] *adj* immaginario(-a)
imagination [ɪmædʒɪˈneɪʃən] *n* immaginazione *f*, fantasia
imaginative [ɪˈmædʒɪnətɪv] *adj* immaginoso(-a)
imagine [ɪˈmædʒɪn] *vt* immaginare
imbalance [ɪmˈbæləns] *n* squilibrio
imbecile [ˈɪmbəsiːl] *n* imbecille *m/f*
imbue [ɪmˈbjuː] *vt*: **to ~ sth with** impregnare qc di
IMF *n abbr* = **International Monetary Fund**
imitate [ˈɪmɪteɪt] *vt* imitare
imitation [ɪmɪˈteɪʃən] *n* imitazione *f*
imitator [ˈɪmɪteɪtəʳ] *n* imitatore(-trice)
immaculate [ɪˈmækjulət] *adj* immacolato(-a); (*dress, appearance*) impeccabile
immaterial [ɪməˈtɪərɪəl] *adj* immateriale, indifferente; **it is ~ whether** poco importa se *or* che + *sub*
immature [ɪməˈtjuəʳ] *adj* immaturo(-a)
immaturity [ɪməˈtjuərɪtɪ] *n* immaturità, mancanza di maturità
immeasurable [ɪˈmɛʒərəbl] *adj* incommensurabile
immediacy [ɪˈmiːdɪəsɪ] *n* immediatezza
immediate [ɪˈmiːdɪət] *adj* immediato(-a)
immediately [ɪˈmiːdɪətlɪ] *adv* (*at once*) subito, immediatamente; **~ next to** proprio accanto a
immense [ɪˈmɛns] *adj* immenso(-a); enorme
immensity [ɪˈmɛnsɪtɪ] *n* (*of size, difference*) enormità; (*of problem etc*) vastità
immerse [ɪˈməːs] *vt* immergere
immersion heater [ɪˈməːʃən-] *n* (*Brit*) scaldaacqua *m inv* a immersione
immigrant [ˈɪmɪɡrənt] *n* immigrante *m/f*; (*already established*) immigrato(-a)
immigration [ɪmɪˈɡreɪʃən] *n* immigrazione *f*
immigration authorities *npl* ufficio stranieri
immigration laws *npl* leggi *fpl* relative all'immigrazione
imminent [ˈɪmɪnənt] *adj* imminente
immobile [ɪˈməubaɪl] *adj* immobile

immobilize [ɪˈməubɪlaɪz] *vt* immobilizzare
immobilizer [ɪˈməubɪlaɪzəʳ] *n* (*Aut*) immobilizer *m inv*, dispositivo di bloccaggio del motore
immoderate [ɪˈmɔdərɪt] *adj* (*person*) smodato(-a), sregolato(-a); (*opinion, reaction, demand*) eccessivo(-a)
immodest [ɪˈmɔdɪst] *adj* (*indecent*) indecente, impudico(-a); (*boasting*) presuntuoso(-a)
immoral [ɪˈmɔrl] *adj* immorale
immorality [ɪmɔˈrælɪtɪ] *n* immoralità
immortal [ɪˈmɔːtl] *adj, n* immortale (*m/f*)
immortalize [ɪˈmɔːtəlaɪz] *vt* rendere immortale
immovable [ɪˈmuːvəbl] *adj* (*object*) non movibile; (*person*) irremovibile
immune [ɪˈmjuːn] *adj*: **~ (to)** immune (da)
immune system *n* sistema *m* immunitario
immunity [ɪˈmjuːnɪtɪ] *n* (*also fig: of diplomat*) immunità; **diplomatic ~** immunità diplomatica
immunization [ɪmjunaɪˈzeɪʃən] *n* immunizzazione *f*
immunize [ˈɪmjunaɪz] *vt* immunizzare
imp [ɪmp] *n* folletto, diavoletto; (*child*) diavoletto
impact [ˈɪmpækt] *n* impatto
impair [ɪmˈpɛəʳ] *vt* danneggiare
impaired [ɪmˈpɛəd] *adj* indebolito(-a)
-impaired [ɪmˈpɛəd] *suffix*: **visually~** videoleso(-a)
impale [ɪmˈpeɪl] *vt* impalare
impart [ɪmˈpɑːt] *vt* (*make known*) comunicare; (*bestow*) impartire
impartial [ɪmˈpɑːʃl] *adj* imparziale
impartiality [ɪmpɑːʃɪˈælɪtɪ] *n* imparzialità
impassable [ɪmˈpɑːsəbl] *adj* insuperabile; (*road*) impraticabile
impasse [æmˈpɑːs] *n* impasse *f inv*
impassioned [ɪmˈpæʃənd] *adj* appassionato(-a)
impassive [ɪmˈpæsɪv] *adj* impassibile
impatience [ɪmˈpeɪʃəns] *n* impazienza
impatient [ɪmˈpeɪʃənt] *adj* impaziente; **to get** *or* **grow ~** perdere la pazienza
impeach [ɪmˈpiːtʃ] *vt* accusare, attaccare; (*public official*) mettere sotto accusa
impeachment [ɪmˈpiːtʃmənt] *n* (*Law*) imputazione *f*
impeccable [ɪmˈpɛkəbl] *adj* impeccabile
impecunious [ɪmpɪˈkjuːnɪəs] *adj* povero(-a)
impede [ɪmˈpiːd] *vt* impedire
impediment [ɪmˈpɛdɪmənt] *n* impedimento; (*also*: **speech impediment**) difetto di pronuncia
impel [ɪmˈpɛl] *vt* (*force*): **to ~ sb (to do sth)** costringere *or* obbligare qn (a fare qc)

impending [ɪmˈpɛndɪŋ] *adj* imminente
impenetrable [ɪmˈpɛnɪtrəbl] *adj*
impenetrabile
imperative [ɪmˈpɛrətɪv] *adj* imperativo(-a);
necessario(-a), urgente; (*voice*) imperioso(-a);
■ *n* (*Ling*) imperativo
imperceptible [ɪmpəˈsɛptɪbl] *adj*
impercettibile
imperfect [ɪmˈpəːfɪkt] *adj* imperfetto(-a);
(*goods etc*) difettoso(-a) ■ *n* (*Ling: also:*
imperfect tense) imperfetto
imperfection [ɪmpəːˈfɛkʃən] *n* imperfezione
f; (*flaw*) difetto
imperial [ɪmˈpɪərɪəl] *adj* imperiale; (*measure*)
legale
imperialism [ɪmˈpɪərɪəlɪzəm] *n*
imperialismo
imperil [ɪmˈpɛrɪl] *vt* mettere in pericolo
imperious [ɪmˈpɪərɪəs] *adj* imperioso(-a)
impersonal [ɪmˈpəːsənl] *adj* impersonale
impersonate [ɪmˈpəːsəneɪt] *vt* impersonare;
(*Theat*) imitare
impersonation [ɪmpəːsəˈneɪʃən] *n* (*Law*)
usurpazione *f* d'identità; (*Theat*) imitazione *f*
impersonator [ɪmˈpəːsəneɪtər] *n* (*gen, Theat*)
imitatore(-trice)
impertinence [ɪmˈpəːtɪnəns] *n*
impertinenza
impertinent [ɪmˈpəːtɪnənt] *adj* impertinente
imperturbable [ɪmpəˈtəːbəbl] *adj*
imperturbabile
impervious [ɪmˈpəːvɪəs] *adj* impermeabile;
(*fig*): ~ **to** insensibile a; impassibile di
fronte a
impetuous [ɪmˈpɛtjuəs] *adj* impetuoso(-a),
precipitoso(-a)
impetus [ˈɪmpətəs] *n* impeto
impinge [ɪmˈpɪndʒ]: **to ~ on** *vt fus* (*person*)
colpire; (*rights*) ledere
impish [ˈɪmpɪʃ] *adj* malizioso(-a),
birichino(-a)
implacable [ɪmˈplækəbl] *adj* implacabile
implant [ɪmˈplɑːnt] *vt* (*Med*) innestare;
(*fig: idea, principle*) inculcare
implausible [ɪmˈplɔːzɪbl] *adj* non plausibile
implement *n* [ˈɪmplɪmənt] attrezzo; (*for
cooking*) utensile *m* ■ *vt* [ˈɪmplɪment]
effettuare
implicate [ˈɪmplɪkeɪt] *vt* implicare
implication [ɪmplɪˈkeɪʃən] *n* implicazione *f*;
by ~ implicitamente
implicit [ɪmˈplɪsɪt] *adj* implicito(-a);
(*complete*) completo(-a)
implicitly [ɪmˈplɪsɪtlɪ] *adv* implicitamente
implore [ɪmˈplɔːr] *vt* implorare
imply [ɪmˈplaɪ] *vt* insinuare; suggerire
impolite [ɪmpəˈlaɪt] *adj* scortese

imponderable [ɪmˈpɔndərəbl] *adj*
imponderabile
import *vt* [ɪmˈpɔːt] importare ■ *n* [ˈɪmpɔːt]
(*Comm*) importazione *f*; (*meaning*) significato,
senso ■ *cpd* (*duty, licence etc*) d'importazione
importance [ɪmˈpɔːtns] *n* importanza; **to be
of great/little ~** importare molto/poco,
essere molto/poco importante
important [ɪmˈpɔːtnt] *adj* importante;
it's not ~ non ha importanza; **it is ~ that**
è importante che + *sub*
importantly [ɪmˈpɔːtəntlɪ] *adv* (*pej*) con
(un'aria d')importanza; **but, more ~, ...** ma,
quel che più conta *or* importa, ...
importation [ɪmpɔːˈteɪʃən] *n* importazione *f*
imported [ɪmˈpɔːtɪd] *adj* importato(-a)
importer [ɪmˈpɔːtər] *n* importatore(-trice)
impose [ɪmˈpəuz] *vt* imporre ■ *vi*: **to ~ on sb**
sfruttare la bontà di qn
imposing [ɪmˈpəuzɪŋ] *adj* imponente
imposition [ɪmpəˈzɪʃən] *n* imposizione *f*;
to be an ~ on (*person*) abusare della
gentilezza di
impossibility [ɪmpɔsəˈbɪlɪtɪ] *n* impossibilità
impossible [ɪmˈpɔsɪbl] *adj* impossibile; **it is
~ for me to leave now** mi è impossibile
venir via adesso
impostor [ɪmˈpɔstər] *n* impostore(-a)
impotence [ˈɪmpɔtns] *n* impotenza
impotent [ˈɪmpətnt] *adj* impotente
impound [ɪmˈpaund] *vt* confiscare
impoverished [ɪmˈpɔvərɪʃt] *adj*
impoverito(-a)
impracticable [ɪmˈpræktɪkəbl] *adj*
impraticabile
impractical [ɪmˈpræktɪkl] *adj* non pratico(-a)
imprecise [ɪmprɪˈsaɪs] *adj* impreciso(-a)
impregnable [ɪmˈprɛgnəbl] *adj* (*fortress*)
inespugnabile; (*fig*) inoppugnabile;
irrefutabile
impregnate [ˈɪmprɛgneɪt] *vt* impregnare;
(*fertilize*) fecondare
impresario [ɪmprɪˈsɑːrɪəu] *n* impresario(-a)
impress [ɪmˈprɛs] *vt* impressionare; (*mark*)
imprimere, stampare; **to ~ sth on sb** far
capire qc a qn
impression [ɪmˈprɛʃən] *n* impressione *f*;
to be under the ~ that avere l'impressione
che; **to make a good/bad ~ on sb** fare una
buona/cattiva impressione a *or* su qn
impressionable [ɪmˈprɛʃnəbl] *adj*
impressionabile
impressionist [ɪmˈprɛʃənɪst] *n*
impressionista *m/f*
impressive [ɪmˈprɛsɪv] *adj* impressionante
imprint [ˈɪmprɪnt] *n* (*Publishing*) sigla
editoriale

imprinted [ɪmˈprɪntɪd] *adj*: ~ **on** impresso(-a) in

imprison [ɪmˈprɪzn] *vt* imprigionare

imprisonment [ɪmˈprɪznmənt] *n* imprigionamento

improbable [ɪmˈprɔbəbl] *adj* improbabile; (*excuse*) inverosimile

impromptu [ɪmˈprɔmptjuː] *adj* improvvisato(-a) ■ *adv* improvvisando, così su due piedi

improper [ɪmˈprɔpər] *adj* scorretto(-a); (*unsuitable*) inadatto(-a), improprio(-a); sconveniente, indecente

impropriety [ɪmprəˈpraɪətɪ] *n* sconvenienza; (*of expression*) improprietà

improve [ɪmˈpruːv] *vt* migliorare ■ *vi* migliorare; (*pupil etc*) fare progressi
  ▶ **improve (up)on** *vt fus* (*offer*) aumentare

improvement [ɪmˈpruːvmənt] *n* miglioramento; progresso; **to make improvements to** migliorare, apportare dei miglioramenti a

improvisation [ɪmprəvaɪˈzeɪʃən] *n* improvvisazione *f*

improvise [ˈɪmprəvaɪz] *vt, vi* improvvisare

imprudence [ɪmˈpruːdns] *n* imprudenza

imprudent [ɪmˈpruːdnt] *adj* imprudente

impudence [ˈɪmpjudns] *n* impudenza

impudent [ˈɪmpjudnt] *adj* impudente, sfacciato(-a)

impugn [ɪmˈpjuːn] *vt* impugnare

impulse [ˈɪmpʌls] *n* impulso; **to act on ~** agire d'impulso *or* impulsivamente

impulse buy *n* acquisto fatto d'impulso

impulsive [ɪmˈpʌlsɪv] *adj* impulsivo(-a)

impunity [ɪmˈpjuːnɪtɪ] *n*: **with ~** impunemente

impure [ɪmˈpjuər] *adj* impuro(-a)

impurity [ɪmˈpjuərɪtɪ] *n* impurità *f inv*

IN *abbr* (*US*) = **Indiana**

 KEYWORD

in [ɪn] *prep* **1** (*indicating place, position*) in; **in the house/garden** in casa/giardino; **in the box** nella scatola; **in the fridge** nel frigorifero; **I have it in my hand** ce l'ho in mano; **in town/the country** in città/campagna; **in school** a scuola; **in here/there** qui/lì dentro

2 (*with place names: of town, region, country*): **in London** a Londra; **in England** in Inghilterra; **in the United States** negli Stati Uniti; **in Yorkshire** nello Yorkshire

3 (*indicating time: during, in the space of*) in; **in spring/summer** in primavera/estate; **in 1988** nel 1988; **in May** in *or* a maggio;

I'll see you in July ci vediamo a luglio; **in the afternoon** nel pomeriggio; **at 4 o'clock in the afternoon** alle 4 del pomeriggio; **I did it in 3 hours/days** l'ho fatto in 3 ore/ giorni; **I'll see you in 2 weeks** *or* **in 2 weeks' time** ci vediamo tra 2 settimane; **once in a hundred years** una volta ogni cento anni

4 (*indicating manner etc*) a; **in a loud/soft voice** a voce alta/bassa; **in pencil** a matita; **in English/French** in inglese/francese; **in writing** per iscritto; **the boy in the blue shirt** il ragazzo con la camicia blu

5 (*indicating circumstances*): **in the sun** al sole; **in the shade** all'ombra; **in the rain** sotto la pioggia; **a rise in prices** un aumento dei prezzi

6 (*indicating mood, state*): **in tears** in lacrime; **in anger** per la rabbia; **in despair** disperato(-a); **in good condition** in buono stato, in buone condizioni; **to live in luxury** vivere nel lusso

7 (*with ratios, numbers*): **1 in 10** 1 su 10; **20 pence in the pound** 20 pence per sterlina; **they lined up in twos** si misero in fila per due; **in hundreds** a centinaia

8 (*referring to people, works*) in; **the disease is common in children** la malattia è comune nei bambini; **in (the works of) Dickens** in Dickens, nelle opere di Dickens

9 (*indicating profession etc*) in; **to be in teaching** fare l'insegnante, insegnare; **to be in publishing** lavorare nell'editoria

10 (*after superlative*) di; **the best in the class** il migliore della classe

11 (*with present participle*): **in saying this** dicendo questo, nel dire questo

12: **in that** *conj* poiché

■ *adv*: **to be in** (*person: at home, work*) esserci; (*train, ship, plane*) essere arrivato(-a); (*in fashion*) essere di moda; **their party is in** il loro partito è al potere; **to ask sb in** invitare qn ad entrare; **to run/limp etc in** entrare di corsa/zoppicando *etc*

■ *n*: **the ins and outs of the problem** tutti gli aspetti del problema

in., ins *abbr* = **inch(es)**

inability [ɪnəˈbɪlɪtɪ] *n* inabilità, incapacità; **~ to pay** impossibilità di pagare

inaccessible [ɪnəkˈsesɪbl] *adj* inaccessibile

inaccuracy [ɪnˈækjurəsɪ] *n* inaccuratezza; inesattezza; imprecisione *f*

inaccurate [ɪnˈækjurət] *adj* inaccurato(-a); (*figures*) inesatto(-a); (*translation*) impreciso(-a)

inaction [ɪnˈækʃən] *n* inazione *f*

inactivity [ɪnækˈtɪvɪtɪ] *n* inattività

inadequacy [ɪn'ædɪkwəsɪ] *n* insufficienza
inadequate [ɪn'ædɪkwət] *adj* insufficiente
inadmissible [ɪnəd'mɪsəbl] *adj* inammissibile
inadvertent [ɪnəd'vəːtənt] *adj* involontario(-a)
inadvertently [ɪnəd'vəːtntlɪ] *adv* senza volerlo
inadvisable [ɪnəd'vaɪzəbl] *adj* sconsigliabile
inane [ɪ'neɪn] *adj* vacuo(-a), stupido(-a)
inanimate [ɪn'ænɪmət] *adj* inanimato(-a)
inapplicable [ɪn'æplɪkəbl] *adj* inapplicabile
inappropriate [ɪnə'prəuprɪət] *adj* disadatto(-a); (*word, expression*) improprio(-a)
inapt [ɪn'æpt] *adj* maldestro(-a); fuori luogo
inaptitude [ɪn'æptɪtjuːd] *n* improprietà
inarticulate [ɪnɑː'tɪkjulət] *adj* (*person*) che si esprime male; (*speech*) inarticolato(-a)
inasmuch as [ɪnəz'mʌtʃæz] *adv* in quanto che; (*seeing that*) poiché
inattention [ɪnə'tɛnʃən] *n* mancanza di attenzione
inattentive [ɪnə'tɛntɪv] *adj* disattento(-a), distratto(-a); negligente
inaudible [ɪn'ɔːdɪbl] *adj* che non si riesce a sentire
inaugural [ɪ'nɔːgjurəl] *adj* inaugurale
inaugurate [ɪ'nɔːgjureɪt] *vt* inaugurare; (*president, official*) insediare
inauguration [ɪnɔːgju'reɪʃən] *n* inaugurazione *f*; insediamento in carica
inauspicious [ɪnɔːs'pɪʃəs] *adj* poco propizio(-a)
in-between [ɪnbɪ'twiːn] *adj* fra i (*or* le) due
inborn [ɪn'bɔːn] *adj* (*feeling*) innato(-a); (*defect*) congenito(-a)
inbred [ɪn'brɛd] *adj* innato(-a); (*family*) connaturato(-a)
inbreeding [ɪn'briːdɪŋ] *n* incrocio ripetuto di animali consanguinei; unioni *fpl* fra consanguinei
Inc. *abbr* = **incorporated**
Inca ['ɪŋkə] *adj* (*also*: **Incan**) inca *inv* ◼ *n* inca *m/f inv*
incalculable [ɪn'kælkjuləbl] *adj* incalcolabile
incapability [ɪnkeɪpə'bɪlɪtɪ] *n* incapacità
incapable [ɪn'keɪpəbl] *adj*: ~ **(of doing sth)** incapace (di fare qc)
incapacitate [ɪnkə'pæsɪteɪt] *vt*: **to ~ sb from doing** rendere qn incapace di fare
incapacitated [ɪnkə'pæsɪteɪtɪd] *adj* (*Law*) inabilitato(-a)
incapacity [ɪnkə'pæsɪtɪ] *n* incapacità
incarcerate [ɪn'kɑːsəreɪt] *vt* imprigionare
incarnate *adj* [ɪn'kɑːnɪt] incarnato(-a) ◼ *vt* ['ɪnkɑːneɪt] incarnare
incarnation [ɪnkɑː'neɪʃən] *n* incarnazione *f*

incendiary [ɪn'sɛndɪərɪ] *adj* incendiario(-a) ◼ *n* (*bomb*) bomba incendiaria
incense *n* ['ɪnsɛns] incenso ◼ *vt* [ɪn'sɛns] (*anger*) infuriare
incense burner *n* incensiere *m*
incentive [ɪn'sɛntɪv] *n* incentivo
incentive scheme *n* piano di incentivazione
inception [ɪn'sɛpʃən] *n* inizio, principio
incessant [ɪn'sɛsnt] *adj* incessante
incessantly [ɪn'sɛsntlɪ] *adv* di continuo, senza sosta
incest ['ɪnsɛst] *n* incesto
inch [ɪntʃ] *n* pollice *m* (= 25 mm; 12 in a foot); **within an ~ of** a un pelo da; **he wouldn't give an ~** (*fig*) non ha ceduto di un millimetro
  ▸ **inch forward** *vi* avanzare pian piano
inch tape *n* (*Brit*) metro a nastro (da sarto)
incidence ['ɪnsɪdns] *n* incidenza
incident ['ɪnsɪdnt] *n* incidente *m*; (*in book*) episodio
incidental [ɪnsɪ'dɛntl] *adj* accessorio(-a), d'accompagnamento; (*unplanned*) incidentale; ~ **to** marginale a; ~ **expenses** *npl* spese *fpl* accessorie
incidentally [ɪnsɪ'dɛntəlɪ] *adv* (*by the way*) a proposito
incidental music *n* sottofondo (musicale), musica di sottofondo
incident room *n* (*Police*) centrale *f* delle operazioni (*per indagini*)
incinerate [ɪn'sɪnəreɪt] *vt* incenerire
incinerator [ɪn'sɪnəreɪtə'] *n* inceneritore *m*
incipient [ɪn'sɪpɪənt] *adj* incipiente
incision [ɪn'sɪʒən] *n* incisione *f*
incisive [ɪn'saɪsɪv] *adj* incisivo(-a); tagliante; acuto(-a)
incisor [ɪn'saɪzə'] *n* incisivo
incite [ɪn'saɪt] *vt* incitare
incl. *abbr* = **including; inclusive (of)**
inclement [ɪn'klɛmənt] *adj* inclemente
inclination [ɪnklɪ'neɪʃən] *n* inclinazione *f*
incline *n* ['ɪnklaɪn] pendenza, pendio ◼ *vt* [ɪn'klaɪn] inclinare ◼ *vi*: **to ~ to** tendere a; **to be inclined to do** tendere a fare; essere propenso(-a) a fare; **to be well inclined towards sb** essere ben disposto(-a) verso qn
include [ɪn'kluːd] *vt* includere, comprendere; **the tip is/is not included** la mancia è compresa/esclusa
including [ɪn'kluːdɪŋ] *prep* compreso(-a), incluso(-a); ~ **tip** mancia compresa, compresa la mancia
inclusion [ɪn'kluːʒən] *n* inclusione *f*
inclusive [ɪn'kluːsɪv] *adj* incluso(-a), compreso(-a); **£50,** ~ **of all surcharges** 50 sterline, incluse tutte le soprattasse

inclusive terms npl (Brit) prezzo tutto compreso

incognito [ɪnkɔg'niːtəu] adv in incognito

incoherent [ɪnkəu'hɪərənt] adj incoerente

income ['ɪnkʌm] n reddito; **gross/net ~** reddito lordo/netto; **~ and expenditure account** conto entrate ed uscite

income support n (Brit) sussidio di indigenza or povertà

income tax n imposta sul reddito

income tax inspector n ispettore m delle imposte dirette

income tax return n dichiarazione f annuale dei redditi

incoming ['ɪnkʌmɪŋ] adj (passengers) in arrivo; (government, tenant) subentrante; **~ tide** marea montante

incommunicado [ɪnkəmjunɪ'kɑːdəu] adj: **to hold sb ~** tenere qn in segregazione

incomparable [ɪn'kɔmpərəbl] adj incomparabile

incompatible [ɪnkəm'pætɪbl] adj incompatibile

incompetence [ɪn'kɔmpɪtns] n incompetenza, incapacità

incompetent [ɪn'kɔmpɪtnt] adj incompetente, incapace

incomplete [ɪnkəm'pliːt] adj incompleto(-a)

incomprehensible [ɪnkɔmprɪ'hɛnsɪbl] adj incomprensibile

inconceivable [ɪnkən'siːvəbl] adj inimmaginabile

inconclusive [ɪnkən'kluːsɪv] adj improduttivo(-a); (argument) poco convincente

incongruous [ɪn'kɔŋgruəs] adj poco appropriato(-a); (remark, act) incongruo(-a)

inconsequential [ɪnkɔnsɪ'kwɛnʃl] adj senza importanza

inconsiderable [ɪnkən'sɪdərəbl] adj: **not ~** non trascurabile

inconsiderate [ɪnkən'sɪdərət] adj sconsiderato(-a)

inconsistency [ɪnkən'sɪstənsɪ] n (of actions etc) incongruenza; (of work) irregolarità; (of statement etc) contraddizione f

inconsistent [ɪnkən'sɪstnt] adj incoerente; poco logico(-a); contraddittorio(-a); **~ with** in contraddizione con

inconsolable [ɪnkən'səuləbl] adj inconsolabile

inconspicuous [ɪnkən'spɪkjuəs] adj incospicuo(-a); (colour) poco appariscente; (dress) dimesso(-a); **to make o.s. ~** cercare di passare inosservato(-a)

inconstant [ɪn'kɔnstnt] adj incostante; mutevole

incontinence [ɪn'kɔntɪnəns] n incontinenza

incontinent [ɪn'kɔntɪnənt] adj incontinente

incontrovertible [ɪnkɔntrə'vəːtəbl] adj incontrovertibile

inconvenience [ɪnkən'viːnjəns] n inconveniente m; (trouble) disturbo ■ vt disturbare; **to put sb to great ~** creare degli inconvenienti a qn; **don't ~ yourself** non si disturbi

inconvenient [ɪnkən'viːnjənt] adj scomodo(-a); **that time is very ~ for me** quell'ora mi è molto scomoda, non è un'ora adatta per me

incorporate [ɪn'kɔːpəreɪt] vt incorporare; (contain) contenere

incorporated [ɪn'kɔːpəreɪtɪd] adj: **~ company** (US) società f inv registrata

incorrect [ɪnkə'rɛkt] adj scorretto(-a); (statement) impreciso(-a)

incorrigible [ɪn'kɔrɪdʒəbl] adj incorreggibile

incorruptible [ɪnkə'rʌptɪbl] adj incorruttibile

increase n ['ɪnkriːs] aumento ■ vi [ɪn'kriːs] aumentare; **to be on the ~** essere in aumento; **an ~ of £5/10%** un aumento di 5 sterline/del 10%

increasing [ɪn'kriːsɪŋ] adj (number) crescente

increasingly [ɪn'kriːsɪŋlɪ] adv sempre più

incredible [ɪn'krɛdɪbl] adj incredibile

incredulous [ɪn'krɛdjuləs] adj incredulo(-a)

increment ['ɪnkrɪmənt] n aumento, incremento

incriminate [ɪn'krɪmɪneɪt] vt compromettere

incriminating [ɪn'krɪmɪneɪtɪŋ] adj incriminante

incubate ['ɪnkjubeɪt] vt (eggs) covare ■ vi (egg) essere in incubazione; (disease) avere un'incubazione

incubation [ɪnkju'beɪʃən] n incubazione f

incubation period n (periodo di) incubazione f

incubator ['ɪnkjubeɪtə'] n incubatrice f

inculcate ['ɪnkʌlkeɪt] vt: **to ~ sth in sb** inculcare qc a qn, instillare qc a qn

incumbent [ɪn'kʌmbənt] adj: **it is ~ on him to do ...** è suo dovere fare ... ■ n titolare m/f

incur [ɪn'kəː'] vt (expenses) incorrere; (debt) contrarre; (loss) subire; (anger, risk) esporsi a

incurable [ɪn'kjuərəbl] adj incurabile

incursion [ɪn'kəːʃən] n incursione f

Ind. abbr (US) = **Indiana**

indebted [ɪn'dɛtɪd] adj: **to be ~ to sb (for)** essere obbligato(-a) verso qn (per)

indecency [ɪn'diːsnsɪ] n indecenza

indecent [ɪn'diːsnt] adj indecente

indecent assault n (Brit) aggressione f a scopo di violenza sessuale

indecent exposure n atti mpl osceni in luogo pubblico

indecipherable [ɪndɪ'saɪfərəbl] adj indecifrabile

indecision [ɪndɪ'sɪʒən] n indecisione f

indecisive [ɪndɪ'saɪsɪv] adj indeciso(-a); (discussion) non decisivo(-a)

indeed [ɪn'diːd] adv infatti; veramente; **yes ~!** certamente!

indefatigable [ɪndɪ'fætɪgəbl] adj infaticabile, instancabile

indefensible [ɪndɪ'fɛnsəbl] adj (conduct) ingiustificabile

indefinable [ɪndɪ'faɪnəbl] adj indefinibile

indefinite [ɪn'dɛfɪnɪt] adj indefinito(-a); (answer) vago(-a); (period, number) indeterminato(-a)

indefinitely [ɪn'dɛfɪnɪtlɪ] adv (wait) indefinitamente

indelible [ɪn'dɛlɪbl] adj indelebile

indelicate [ɪn'dɛlɪkɪt] adj (tactless) indelicato(-a), privo(-a) di tatto; (not polite) sconveniente

indemnify [ɪn'dɛmnɪfaɪ] vt indennizzare

indemnity [ɪn'dɛmnɪtɪ] n (insurance) assicurazione f; (compensation) indennità, indennizzo

indent [ɪn'dɛnt] vt (Typ: text) far rientrare dal margine

indentation [ɪndɛn'teɪʃən] n dentellatura; (Typ) rientranza; (dent) tacca

indented [ɪn'dɛntɪd] adj (Typ) rientrante

indenture [ɪn'dɛntʃər] n contratto m formazione inv

independence [ɪndɪ'pɛndns] n indipendenza

Independence Day n (US) vedi nota

● **INDEPENDENCE DAY**

●
● Negli Stati Uniti il 4 luglio si festeggia
● l'Independence Day, il giorno in cui è stata
● firmata, nel 1776, la Dichiarazione di
● Indipendenza con la quale tredici colonie
● britanniche dichiaravano la propria
● indipendenza dalla Gran Bretagna e la
● propria appartenenza agli Stati Uniti
● d'America.

independent [ɪndɪ'pɛndnt] adj indipendente

independently [ɪndɪ'pɛndntlɪ] adv indipendentemente; separatamente; **~ of** indipendentemente da

in-depth ['ɪn'dɛpθ] adj approfondito(-a)

indescribable [ɪndɪ'skraɪbəbl] adj indescrivibile

indestructible [ɪndɪ'strʌktəbl] adj indistruttibile

indeterminate [ɪndɪ'təːmɪnɪt] adj indeterminato(-a)

index ['ɪndɛks] n (pl **indexes**) (in book) indice m; (in library etc) catalogo; (pl **indices**): (ratio, sign) indice m

index card n scheda

index finger n (dito) indice m

index-linked ['ɪndɛks'lɪŋkt], (US) **indexed** ['ɪndɛkst] adj legato(-a) al costo della vita

India ['ɪndɪə] n India

Indian ['ɪndɪən] adj, n indiano(-a)

Indian ink n inchiostro di china

Indian Ocean n: **the ~** l'Oceano Indiano

Indian Summer n (fig) estate f di San Martino

India paper n carta d'India, carta bibbia

India rubber n caucciù m

indicate ['ɪndɪkeɪt] vt indicare ■ vi (Brit Aut): **to ~ left/right** mettere la freccia a sinistra/a destra

indication [ɪndɪ'keɪʃən] n indicazione f segno

indicative [ɪn'dɪkətɪv] adj indicativo(-a) ■ n (Ling) indicativo; **to be ~ of sth** essere indicativo(-a) or un indice di qc

indicator ['ɪndɪkeɪtər] n (sign) segno; (Aut) indicatore m di direzione, freccia

indices ['ɪndɪsiːz] npl of **index**

indict [ɪn'daɪt] vt accusare

indictable [ɪn'daɪtəbl] adj passibile di pena; **~ offence** atto che costituisce reato

indictment [ɪn'daɪtmənt] n accusa

indifference [ɪn'dɪfrəns] n indifferenza

indifferent [ɪn'dɪfrənt] adj indifferente; (poor) mediocre

indigenous [ɪn'dɪdʒɪnəs] adj indigeno(-a)

indigestible [ɪndɪ'dʒɛstɪbl] adj indigeribile

indigestion [ɪndɪ'dʒɛstʃən] n indigestione f

indignant [ɪn'dɪgnənt] adj: **~ (at sth/with sb)** indignato(-a) (per qc/contro qn)

indignation [ɪndɪg'neɪʃən] n indignazione f

indignity [ɪn'dɪgnɪtɪ] n umiliazione f

indigo ['ɪndɪgəu] adj, n indaco (inv)

indirect [ɪndɪ'rɛkt] adj indiretto(-a)

indirectly [ɪndɪ'rɛktlɪ] adv indirettamente

indiscreet [ɪndɪ'skriːt] adj indiscreto(-a); (rash) imprudente

indiscretion [ɪndɪ'skrɛʃən] n indiscrezione f; imprudenza

indiscriminate [ɪndɪ'skrɪmɪnət] adj (person) che non sa discernere; (admiration) cieco(-a); (killings) indiscriminato(-a)

indispensable [ɪndɪ'spɛnsəbl] adj indispensabile

indisposed [ɪndɪ'spəuzd] adj (unwell) indisposto(-a)

indisposition [ɪndɪspə'zɪʃən] n (illness) indisposizione f

indisputable [ɪndɪ'spjuːtəbl] *adj* incontestabile, indiscutibile

indistinct [ɪndɪ'stɪŋkt] *adj* indistinto(-a); (*memory, noise*) vago(-a)

indistinguishable [ɪndɪ'stɪŋgwɪʃəbl] *adj* indistinguibile

individual [ɪndɪ'vɪdjuəl] *n* individuo ▪ *adj* individuale; (*characteristic*) particolare, originale

individualist [ɪndɪ'vɪdjuəlɪst] *n* individualista *m/f*

individuality [ɪndɪvɪdju'ælɪtɪ] *n* individualità

individually [ɪndɪ'vɪdjuəlɪ] *adv* singolarmente, uno(-a) per uno(-a)

indivisible [ɪndɪ'vɪzɪbl] *adj* indivisibile

Indochina ['ɪndəu'tʃaɪnə] *n* Indocina

indoctrinate [ɪn'dɔktrɪneɪt] *vt* indottrinare

indoctrination [ɪndɔktrɪ'neɪʃən] *n* indottrinamento

indolent ['ɪndələnt] *adj* indolente

Indonesia [ɪndəu'niːzɪə] *n* Indonesia

Indonesian [ɪndəu'niːzɪən] *adj, n* indonesiano(-a); (*Ling*) indonesiano

indoor ['ɪndɔːʳ] *adj* da interno; (*plant*) d'appartamento; (*swimming pool*) coperto(-a); (*sport, games*) fatto(-a) al coperto

indoors [ɪn'dɔːz] *adv* all'interno; (*at home*) in casa

indubitable [ɪn'djuːbɪtəbl] *adj* indubitabile

induce [ɪn'djuːs] *vt* persuadere; (*bring about*) provocare; **to ~ sb to do sth** persuadere qn a fare qc

inducement [ɪn'djuːsmənt] *n* incitamento; (*incentive*) stimolo, incentivo

induct [ɪn'dʌkt] *vt* insediare; (*fig*) iniziare

induction [ɪn'dʌkʃən] *n* (*Med: of birth*) parto indotto

induction course *n* (*Brit*) corso di avviamento

indulge [ɪn'dʌldʒ] *vt* (*whim*) compiacere, soddisfare; (*child*) viziare ▪ *vi*: **to ~ in sth** concedersi qc; abbandonarsi a qc

indulgence [ɪn'dʌldʒəns] *n* lusso (che uno si permette); (*leniency*) indulgenza

indulgent [ɪn'dʌldʒənt] *adj* indulgente

industrial [ɪn'dʌstrɪəl] *adj* industriale; (*injury*) sul lavoro; (*dispute*) di lavoro

industrial action *n* azione *f* rivendicativa

industrial estate *n* zona industriale

industrialist [ɪn'dʌstrɪəlɪst] *n* industriale *m*

industrialize [ɪn'dʌstrɪəlaɪz] *vt* industrializzare

industrial park *n* (*US*) zona industriale

industrial relations *npl* relazioni *fpl* industriali

industrial tribunal *n* (*Brit*) ≈ Tribunale *m* Amministrativo Regionale

industrial unrest *n* (*Brit*) agitazione *f* (sindacale)

industrious [ɪn'dʌstrɪəs] *adj* industrioso(-a), assiduo(-a)

industry ['ɪndəstrɪ] *n* industria; (*diligence*) operosità

inebriated [ɪ'niːbrɪeɪtɪd] *adj* ubriaco(-a)

inedible [ɪn'ɛdɪbl] *adj* immangiabile; non commestibile

ineffective [ɪnɪ'fɛktɪv] *adj* inefficace

ineffectual [ɪnɪ'fɛktʃuəl] *adj* inefficace; incompetente

inefficiency [ɪnɪ'fɪʃənsɪ] *n* inefficienza

inefficient [ɪnɪ'fɪʃənt] *adj* inefficiente

inelegant [ɪn'ɛlɪgənt] *adj* poco elegante

ineligible [ɪn'ɛlɪdʒɪbl] *adj* (*candidate*) ineleggibile; **to be ~ for sth** non avere il diritto a qc

inept [ɪ'nɛpt] *adj* inetto(-a)

ineptitude [ɪ'nɛptɪtjuːd] *n* inettitudine *f*, stupidità

inequality [ɪnɪ'kwɔlɪtɪ] *n* ineguaglianza

inequitable [ɪn'ɛkwɪtəbl] *adj* iniquo(-a)

ineradicable [ɪnɪ'rædɪkəbl] *adj* inestirpabile

inert [ɪ'nɜːt] *adj* inerte

inertia [ɪ'nɜːʃə] *n* inerzia

inertia-reel seat belt [ɪ'nɜːʃə'riːl-] *n* cintura di sicurezza con arrotolatore

inescapable [ɪnɪ'skeɪpəbl] *adj* inevitabile

inessential [ɪnɪ'sɛnʃl] *adj* non essenziale

inestimable [ɪn'ɛstɪməbl] *adj* inestimabile, incalcolabile

inevitable [ɪn'ɛvɪtəbl] *adj* inevitabile

inevitably [ɪn'ɛvɪtəblɪ] *adv* inevitabilmente; **as ~ happens ...** come immancabilmente succede ...

inexact [ɪnɪg'zækt] *adj* inesatto(-a)

inexcusable [ɪnɪks'kjuːzəbl] *adj* imperdonabile

inexhaustible [ɪnɪg'zɔːstɪbl] *adj* inesauribile; (*person*) instancabile

inexorable [ɪn'ɛksərəbl] *adj* inesorabile

inexpensive [ɪnɪk'spɛnsɪv] *adj* poco costoso(-a)

inexperience [ɪnɪk'spɪərɪəns] *n* inesperienza

inexperienced [ɪnɪk'spɪərɪənst] *adj* inesperto(-a), senza esperienza; **to be ~ in sth** essere poco pratico di qc

inexplicable [ɪnɪk'splɪkəbl] *adj* inesplicabile

inexpressible [ɪnɪk'sprɛsəbl] *adj* inesprimibile

inextricable [ɪnɪk'strɪkəbl] *adj* inestricabile

infallibility [ɪnfælə'bɪlɪtɪ] *n* infallibilità

infallible [ɪn'fælɪbl] *adj* infallibile

infamous ['ɪnfəməs] *adj* infame

infamy ['ɪnfəmɪ] *n* infamia

infancy ['ɪnfənsɪ] *n* infanzia

infant ['ɪnfənt] *n* bambino(-a)
infantile ['ɪnfəntaɪl] *adj* infantile
infant mortality *n* mortalità infantile
infantry ['ɪnfəntrɪ] *n* fanteria
infantryman ['ɪnfəntrɪmən] *n* fante *m*
infant school *n* (Brit) scuola elementare (*per bambini dall'età di 5 a 7 anni*)
infatuated [ɪn'fætjueɪtɪd] *adj*: ~ **with** infatuato(-a) di; **to become ~ (with sb)** infatuarsi (di qn)
infatuation [ɪnfætju'eɪʃən] *n* infatuazione *f*
infect [ɪn'fɛkt] *vt* infettare; **infected with** (*illness*) affetto(-a) da; **to become infected** (*wound*) infettarsi
infection [ɪn'fɛkʃən] *n* infezione *f*
infectious [ɪn'fɛkʃəs] *adj* (*disease*) infettivo(-a), contagioso(-a); (*person, laughter*) contagioso(-a)
infer [ɪn'fəːʳ] *vt*: **to ~ (from)** dedurre (da), concludere (da)
inference ['ɪnfərəns] *n* deduzione *f*, conclusione *f*
inferior [ɪn'fɪərɪəʳ] *adj* inferiore; (*goods*) di qualità scadente ■ *n* inferiore *m/f*; (*in rank*) subalterno(-a); **to feel ~** sentirsi inferiore
inferiority [ɪnfɪərɪ'ɔrətɪ] *n* inferiorità
inferiority complex *n* complesso di inferiorità
infernal [ɪn'fəːnl] *adj* infernale
inferno [ɪn'fəːnəʊ] *n* inferno
infertile [ɪn'fəːtaɪl] *adj* sterile
infertility [ɪnfəː'tɪlɪtɪ] *n* sterilità
infested [ɪn'fɛstɪd] *adj*: ~ **(with)** infestato(-a) (di)
infidelity [ɪnfɪ'dɛlɪtɪ] *n* infedeltà
in-fighting ['ɪnfaɪtɪŋ] *n* lotte *fpl* intestine
infiltrate ['ɪnfɪltreɪt] *vt* (*troops etc*) far penetrare; (*enemy line etc*) infiltrare ■ *vi* infiltrarsi
infinite ['ɪnfɪnɪt] *adj* infinito(-a); **an ~ amount of time/money** un'illimitata quantità di tempo/denaro
infinitely ['ɪnfɪnɪtlɪ] *adv* infinitamente
infinitesimal [ɪnfɪnɪ'tesɪməl] *adj* infinitesimale
infinitive [ɪn'fɪnɪtɪv] *n* infinito
infinity [ɪn'fɪnɪtɪ] *n* infinità; (*also Math*) infinito
infirm [ɪn'fəːm] *adj* infermo(-a)
infirmary [ɪn'fəːmərɪ] *n* ospedale *m*; (*in school, factory*) infermeria
infirmity [ɪn'fəːmɪtɪ] *n* infermità *f inv*
inflamed [ɪn'fleɪmd] *adj* infiammato(-a)
inflammable [ɪn'flæməbl] *adj* infiammabile
inflammation [ɪnflə'meɪʃən] *n* infiammazione *f*
inflammatory [ɪn'flæmətərɪ] *adj* (*speech*) incendiario(-a)

inflatable [ɪn'fleɪtəbl] *adj* gonfiabile
inflate [ɪn'fleɪt] *vt* (*tyre, balloon*) gonfiare; (*fig*) esagerare; gonfiare; **to ~ the currency** far ricorso all'inflazione
inflated [ɪn'fleɪtɪd] *adj* (*style*) gonfio(-a); (*value*) esagerato(-a)
inflation [ɪn'fleɪʃən] *n* (*Econ*) inflazione *f*
inflationary [ɪn'fleɪʃənərɪ] *adj* inflazionistico(-a)
inflexible [ɪn'flɛksɪbl] *adj* inflessibile, rigido(-a)
inflict [ɪn'flɪkt] *vt*: **to ~ on** infliggere a
infliction [ɪn'flɪkʃən] *n* inflizione *f*; afflizione *f*
in-flight ['ɪnflaɪt] *adj* a bordo
inflow ['ɪnfləʊ] *n* afflusso
influence ['ɪnfluəns] *n* influenza ■ *vt* influenzare; **under the ~ of** sotto l'influenza di; **under the ~ of drink** sotto l'influenza *or* l'effetto dell'alcool
influential [ɪnflu'ɛnʃl] *adj* influente
influenza [ɪnflu'ɛnzə] *n* (*Med*) influenza
influx ['ɪnflʌks] *n* afflusso
inform [ɪn'fɔːm] *vt*: **to ~ sb (of)** informare qn (di) ■ *vi*: **to ~ on sb** denunciare qn; **to ~ sb about** mettere qn al corrente di
informal [ɪn'fɔːml] *adj* (*person, manner*) alla buona, semplice; (*visit, discussion*) informale; (*announcement, invitation*) non ufficiale; **"dress ~"** "non è richiesto l'abito scuro"; **~ language** linguaggio colloquiale
informality [ɪnfɔː'mælɪtɪ] *n* semplicità, informalità; carattere *m* non ufficiale
informally [ɪn'fɔːməlɪ] *adv* senza cerimonie; (*invite*) in modo non ufficiale
informant [ɪn'fɔːmənt] *n* informatore(-trice)
informatics [ɪnfə'mætɪks] *n* informatica
information [ɪnfə'meɪʃən] *n* informazioni *fpl*; particolari *mpl*; **to get ~ on** informarsi su; **a piece of ~** un'informazione; **for your ~** a titolo d'informazione, per sua informazione
information bureau *n* ufficio *m* informazioni *inv*
information processing *n* elaborazione *f* delle informazioni
information retrieval *n* ricupero delle informazioni
information superhighway *n* autostrada informatica
information technology *n* informatica
informative [ɪn'fɔːmətɪv] *adj* istruttivo(-a)
informed [ɪn'fɔːmd] *adj* (*observer*) (ben) informato(-a); **an ~ guess** un'ipotesi fondata
informer [ɪn'fɔːməʳ] *n* informatore(-trice)
infra dig ['ɪnfrə'dɪg] *adj abbr* (col: = infra dignitatem: beneath one's dignity) indecoroso(-a)

infra-red [ˌɪnfrəˈrɛd] *adj* infrarosso(-a)
infrastructure [ˈɪnfrəstrʌktʃəʳ] *n* infrastruttura
infrequent [ɪnˈfriːkwənt] *adj* infrequente, raro(-a)
infringe [ɪnˈfrɪndʒ] *vt* infrangere; *vi*: **to ~ on** calpestare
infringement [ɪnˈfrɪndʒmənt] *n*: **~ (of)** infrazione *f* (di)
infuriate [ɪnˈfjuərɪeɪt] *vt* rendere furioso(-a)
infuriating [ɪnˈfjuərɪeɪtɪŋ] *adj* molto irritante
infuse [ɪnˈfjuːz] *vt* (*with courage, enthusiasm*): **to ~ sb with sth** infondere qc a qn, riempire qn di qc
infusion [ɪnˈfjuːʒən] *n* (*tea etc*) infuso, infusione *f*
ingenious [ɪnˈdʒiːnjəs] *adj* ingegnoso(-a)
ingenuity [ɪndʒɪˈnjuːɪtɪ] *n* ingegnosità
ingenuous [ɪnˈdʒɛnjuəs] *adj* ingenuo(-a)
ingot [ˈɪŋgət] *n* lingotto
ingrained [ɪnˈgreɪnd] *adj* radicato(-a)
ingratiate [ɪnˈgreɪʃɪeɪt] *vt*: **to ~ o.s. with sb** ingraziarsi qn
ingratiating [ɪnˈgreɪʃɪeɪtɪŋ] *adj* (*smile, speech*) suadente, cattivante; (*person*) compiacente
ingratitude [ɪnˈgrætɪtjuːd] *n* ingratitudine *f*
ingredient [ɪnˈgriːdɪənt] *n* ingrediente *m*; elemento
ingrowing [ˈɪngrəʊɪŋ], **ingrown** [ˈɪngrəʊn] *adj*: **~ (toe)nail** unghia incarnita
inhabit [ɪnˈhæbɪt] *vt* abitare
inhabitable [ɪnˈhæbɪtəbl] *adj* abitabile
inhabitant [ɪnˈhæbɪtnt] *n* abitante *m/f*
inhale [ɪnˈheɪl] *vt* inalare ■ *vi* (*in smoking*) aspirare
inhaler [ɪnˈheɪləʳ] *n* inalatore *m*
inherent [ɪnˈhɪərənt] *adj*: **~ (in *or* to)** inerente (a)
inherently [ɪnˈhɪərəntlɪ] *adv* (*easy, difficult*) di per sé, di per se stesso(-a); **~ lazy** pigro di natura
inherit [ɪnˈhɛrɪt] *vt* ereditare
inheritance [ɪnˈhɛrɪtəns] *n* eredità
inhibit [ɪnˈhɪbɪt] *vt* (*Psych*) inibire; **to ~ sb from doing** impedire a qn di fare
inhibited [ɪnˈhɪbɪtɪd] *adj* (*person*) inibito(-a)
inhibiting [ɪnˈhɪbɪtɪŋ] *adj* che inibisce
inhibition [ɪnhɪˈbɪʃən] *n* inibizione *f*
inhospitable [ɪnhɔsˈpɪtəbl] *adj* inospitale
in-house [ˈɪnˈhaus] *adj* effettuato(-a) da personale interno, interno(-a) ■ *adv* (*training*) all'interno dell'azienda
inhuman [ɪnˈhjuːmən] *adj* inumano(-a), disumano(-a)
inhumane [ɪnhjuːˈmeɪn] *adj* inumano(-a), disumano(-a)

inimitable [ɪˈnɪmɪtəbl] *adj* inimitabile
iniquity [ɪˈnɪkwɪtɪ] *n* iniquità *f inv*
initial [ɪˈnɪʃl] *adj* iniziale ■ *n* iniziale *f* ■ *vt* siglare; **initials** *npl* iniziali *fpl*; (*as signature*) sigla
initialize [ɪˈnɪʃəlaɪz] *vt* (*Comput*) inizializzare
initially [ɪˈnɪʃəlɪ] *adv* inizialmente, all'inizio
initiate [ɪˈnɪʃɪeɪt] *vt* (*start*) avviare; intraprendere; iniziare; (*person*) iniziare; **to ~ sb into sth** iniziare qn a qc; **to ~ proceedings against sb** (*Law*) intentare causa a *or* contro qn
initiation [ɪnɪʃɪˈeɪʃən] *n* iniziazione *f*
initiative [ɪˈnɪʃətɪv] *n* iniziativa; **to take the ~** prendere l'iniziativa
inject [ɪnˈdʒɛkt] *vt* (*liquid*) iniettare; (*person*) fare una puntura a; (*fig: money*): **to ~ into** immettere in
injection [ɪnˈdʒɛkʃən] *n* iniezione *f*, puntura; **to have an ~** farsi fare un'iniezione *or* una puntura
injudicious [ɪndʒuˈdɪʃəs] *adj* poco saggio(-a)
injunction [ɪnˈdʒʌŋkʃən] *n* (*Law*) ingiunzione *f*, intimazione *f*
injure [ˈɪndʒəʳ] *vt* ferire; (*wrong*) fare male *or* torto a; (*damage: reputation etc*) nuocere a; (*feelings*) offendere; **to ~ o.s.** farsi male
injured [ˈɪndʒəd] *adj* (*person, leg etc*) ferito(-a); (*tone, feelings*) offeso(-a); **~ party** (*Law*) parte *f* lesa
injurious [ɪnˈdʒuərɪəs] *adj*: **~ (to)** nocivo(-a) (a), pregiudizievole (per)
injury [ˈɪndʒərɪ] *n* ferita; (*wrong*) torto; **to escape without ~** rimanere illeso
injury time *n* (*Sport*) tempo di recupero
injustice [ɪnˈdʒʌstɪs] *n* ingiustizia; **you do me an ~** mi fa un torto, è ingiusto verso di me
ink [ɪŋk] *n* inchiostro
ink-jet printer [ˈɪŋkdʒɛt-] *n* stampante *f* a getto d'inchiostro
inkling [ˈɪŋklɪŋ] *n* sentore *m*, vaga idea
inkpad [ˈɪŋkpæd] *n* tampone *m*, cuscinetto per timbri
inky [ˈɪŋkɪ] *adj* macchiato(-a) *or* sporco(-a) d'inchiostro
inlaid [ˈɪnleɪd] *adj* incrostato(-a); (*table etc*) intarsiato(-a)
inland *adj* [ˈɪnlənd] interno(-a) ■ *adv* [ɪnˈlænd] all'interno; **~ waterways** canali e fiumi *mpl* navigabili
Inland Revenue *n* (*Brit*) Fisco
in-laws [ˈɪnlɔːz] *npl* suoceri *mpl*; famiglia del marito (*or* della moglie)
inlet [ˈɪnlɛt] *n* (*Geo*) insenatura, baia
inlet pipe *n* (*Tech*) tubo d'immissione
inmate [ˈɪnmeɪt] *n* (*in prison*) carcerato(-a); (*in asylum*) ricoverato(-a)

inmost ['ınməʊst] *adj* più profondo(-a), più intimo(-a)

inn [ın] *n* locanda

innards ['ınədz] *npl* (*col*) interiora *fpl*, budella *fpl*

innate [ı'neɪt] *adj* innato(-a)

inner ['ınə^r] *adj* interno(-a), interiore

inner city *n* centro di una zona urbana

innermost ['ınəməʊst] *adj* = **inmost**

inner tube *n* camera d'aria

innings ['ınıŋz] *n* (*Cricket*) turno di battuta; (*Brit fig*): **he has had a good ~** ha avuto molto dalla vita

innocence ['ınəsns] *n* innocenza

innocent ['ınəsnt] *adj* innocente

innocuous [ı'nɔkjuəs] *adj* innocuo(-a)

innovation [ınəʊ'veɪʃən] *n* innovazione *f*

innuendo [ınju'ɛndəʊ] *n* (*pl* **innuendoes**) insinuazione *f*

innumerable [ı'nju:mrəbl] *adj* innumerevole

inoculate [ı'nɔkjuleɪt] *vt*: **to ~ sb with sth/ against sth** inoculare qc a qn/qn contro qc

inoculation [ınɔkju'leɪʃən] *n* inoculazione *f*

inoffensive [ınə'fɛnsıv] *adj* inoffensivo(-a), innocuo(-a)

inopportune [ın'ɔpətju:n] *adj* inopportuno(-a)

inordinate [ı'nɔ:dınıt] *adj* eccessivo(-a)

inordinately [ı'nɔ:dınətlı] *adv* smoderatamente

inorganic [ınɔ:'gænık] *adj* inorganico(-a)

in-patient ['ınpeɪʃənt] *n* ricoverato(-a)

input ['ınput] *n* (*Elec*) energia, potenza; (*of machine*) alimentazione *f*; (*of computer*) input *m* ■ *vt* (*Comput*) inserire, introdurre

inquest ['ınkwɛst] *n* inchiesta

inquire [ın'kwaıə^r] *vi* informarsi ■ *vt* domandare, informarsi di *or* su; **to ~ about** informarsi di *or* su, chiedere informazioni su; **to ~ when/where/whether** informarsi di quando/su dove/se
   ▶ **inquire after** *vt fus* (*person*) chiedere di; (*sb's health*) informarsi di
   ▶ **inquire into** *vt fus* indagare su, fare delle indagini *or* ricerche su

inquiring [ın'kwaıərıŋ] *adj* (*mind*) inquisitivo(-a)

inquiry [ın'kwaıərı] *n* domanda; (*Law*) indagine *f*, investigazione *f*; **to hold an ~ into sth** fare un'inchiesta su qc

inquiry desk *n* (*Brit*) banco delle informazioni

inquiry office *n* (*Brit*) ufficio *m* informazioni *inv*

inquisition [ınkwı'zıʃən] *n* inquisizione *f*, inchiesta; (*Rel*): **the I~** l'Inquisizione

inquisitive [ın'kwızıtıv] *adj* curioso(-a)

inroads ['ınrəʊdz] *npl*: **to make ~ into** (*savings, supplies*) intaccare (seriamente)

insane [ın'seɪn] *adj* matto(-a), pazzo(-a); (*Med*) alienato(-a)

insanitary [ın'sænıtərı] *adj* insalubre

insanity [ın'sænıtı] *n* follia; (*Med*) alienazione *f* mentale

insatiable [ın'seɪʃəbl] *adj* insaziabile

inscribe [ın'skraɪb] *vt* iscrivere; (*book etc*): **to ~ (to sb)** dedicare (a qn)

inscription [ın'skrıpʃən] *n* iscrizione *f*; (*in book*) dedica

inscrutable [ın'skru:təbl] *adj* imperscrutabile

inseam ['ınsi:m] *n* (*US*): **~ measurement** lunghezza interna

insect ['ınsɛkt] *n* insetto

insect bite *n* puntura *or* morsicatura di insetto

insecticide [ın'sɛktısaɪd] *n* insetticida *m*

insect repellent *n* insettifugo

insecure [ınsı'kjuə^r] *adj* malsicuro(-a); (*person*) insicuro(-a)

insecurity [ınsı'kjuərıtı] *n* mancanza di sicurezza

insensible [ın'sɛnsıbl] *adj* insensibile; (*unconscious*) privo(-a) di sensi

insensitive [ın'sɛnsıtıv] *adj* insensibile

insensitivity [ınsɛnsı'tıvıtı] *n* mancanza di sensibilità

inseparable [ın'sɛprəbl] *adj* inseparabile

insert *vt* [ın'sə:t] inserire, introdurre ■ *n* ['ınsə:t] inserto

insertion [ın'sə:ʃən] *n* inserzione *f*

in-service ['ın'sə:vıs] *adj* (*course, training*) dopo l'assunzione

inshore [ın'ʃɔ:^r] *adj* costiero(-a) ■ *adv* presso la riva; verso la riva

inside ['ın'saɪd] *n* interno, parte *f* interiore; (*of road: Brit*) sinistra; (: *US, in Europe etc*) destra ■ *adj* interno(-a), interiore ■ *adv* dentro, all'interno ■ *prep* dentro, all'interno di; (*of time*): **~ 10 minutes** entro 10 minuti; **insides** *npl* (*col*) ventre *m*; **~ out** *adv* alla rovescia; **to turn sth ~ out** rivoltare qc; **to know sth ~ out** conoscere qc a fondo; **~ information** informazioni *fpl* riservate; **~ story** storia segreta

inside forward *n* (*Sport*) mezzala, interno

inside lane *n* (*Aut*) corsia di marcia

inside leg measurement *n* (*Brit*) lunghezza interna

insider [ın'saɪdə^r] *n* uno(-a) che ha le mani in pasta

insider dealing, insider trading *n* (*Stock Exchange*) insider trading *m inv*

insidious [ın'sıdıəs] *adj* insidioso(-a)

insight ['ɪnsaɪt] *n* acume *m*, perspicacia; (*glimpse, idea*) percezione *f*; **to gain** *or* **get an ~ into sth** potersi render conto di qc

insignia [ɪn'sɪgnɪə] *npl* insegne *fpl*

insignificant [ɪnsɪg'nɪfɪknt] *adj* insignificante

insincere [ɪnsɪn'sɪə^r] *adj* insincero(-a)

insincerity [ɪnsɪn'sɛrɪtɪ] *n* falsità, insincerità

insinuate [ɪn'sɪnjueɪt] *vt* insinuare

insinuation [ɪnsɪnju'eɪʃən] *n* insinuazione *f*

insipid [ɪn'sɪpɪd] *adj* insipido(-a), insulso(-a)

insist [ɪn'sɪst] *vi* insistere; **to ~ on doing** insistere per fare; **to ~ that** insistere perché +*sub*; (*claim*) sostenere che

insistence [ɪn'sɪstəns] *n* insistenza

insistent [ɪn'sɪstənt] *adj* insistente

insofar [ɪnsəu'fɑː^r] *conj*: **~ as** in quanto

insole ['ɪnsəul] *n* soletta; (*fixed part of shoe*) tramezza

insolence ['ɪnsələns] *n* insolenza

insolent ['ɪnsələnt] *adj* insolente

insoluble [ɪn'sɔljubl] *adj* insolubile

insolvency [ɪn'sɔlvənsɪ] *n* insolvenza

insolvent [ɪn'sɔlvənt] *adj* insolvente

insomnia [ɪn'sɔmnɪə] *n* insonnia

insomniac [ɪn'sɔmnɪæk] *n* chi soffre di insonnia

inspect [ɪn'spɛkt] *vt* ispezionare; (*Brit: ticket*) controllare

inspection [ɪn'spɛkʃən] *n* ispezione *f*; controllo

inspector [ɪn'spɛktə^r] *n* ispettore(-trice); controllore *m*

inspiration [ɪnspə'reɪʃən] *n* ispirazione *f*

inspire [ɪn'spaɪə^r] *vt* ispirare

inspired [ɪn'spaɪəd] *adj* (*writer, book etc*) ispirato(-a); **in an ~ moment** in un momento d'ispirazione

inspiring [ɪn'spaɪərɪŋ] *adj* stimolante

inst. [ɪnst] *abbr* (*Brit Comm*: = *instant*) c.m. (= *corrente mese*)

instability [ɪnstə'bɪlɪtɪ] *n* instabilità

install [ɪn'stɔːl] *vt* installare

installation [ɪnstə'leɪʃən] *n* installazione *f*

installment plan *n* (*US*) acquisto a rate

instalment, (*US*) **installment** [ɪn'stɔːlmənt] *n* rata; (*of TV serial etc*) puntata; **to pay in instalments** pagare a rate

instance ['ɪnstəns] *n* esempio, caso; **for ~** per *or* ad esempio; **in that ~** in quel caso; **in the first ~** in primo luogo

instant ['ɪnstənt] *n* istante *m*, attimo ▪ *adj* immediato(-a), urgente; (*coffee, food*) in polvere; **the 10th ~** il 10 corrente (mese)

instantaneous [ɪnstən'teɪnɪəs] *adj* istantaneo(-a)

instantly ['ɪnstəntlɪ] *adv* immediatamente, subito

instant messaging *n* messaggeria istantanea

instant replay *n* (*US TV*) replay *m inv*

instead [ɪn'stɛd] *adv* invece; **~ of** invece di; **~ of sb** al posto di qn

instep ['ɪnstɛp] *n* collo del piede; (*of shoe*) collo della scarpa

instigate ['ɪnstɪgeɪt] *vt* (*rebellion, strike, crime*) istigare a; (*new ideas etc*) promuovere

instigation [ɪnstɪ'geɪʃən] *n* istigazione *f*; **at sb's ~** per *or* in seguito al suggerimento di qn

instil [ɪn'stɪl] *vt*: **to ~ (into)** inculcare (in)

instinct ['ɪnstɪŋkt] *n* istinto

instinctive [ɪn'stɪŋktɪv] *adj* istintivo(-a)

instinctively [ɪn'stɪŋktɪvlɪ] *adv* per istinto

institute ['ɪnstɪtjuːt] *n* istituto ▪ *vt* istituire, stabilire; (*inquiry*) avviare; (*proceedings*) iniziare

institution [ɪnstɪ'tjuːʃən] *n* istituzione *f*; istituto (d'istruzione); istituto (psichiatrico)

institutional [ɪnstɪ'tjuːʃnl] *adj* istituzionale; **~ care** assistenza presso un istituto

instruct [ɪn'strʌkt] *vt* istruire; **to ~ sb in sth** insegnare qc a qn; **to ~ sb to do** dare ordini a qn di fare

instruction [ɪn'strʌkʃən] *n* istruzione *f*; **instructions (for use)** istruzioni per l'uso

instruction book *n* libretto di istruzioni

instructive [ɪn'strʌktɪv] *adj* istruttivo(-a)

instructor [ɪn'strʌktə^r] *n* istruttore(-trice); (*for skiing*) maestro(-a)

instrument ['ɪnstrumənt] *n* strumento

instrumental [ɪnstru'mɛntl] *adj* (*Mus*) strumentale; **to be ~ in sth/in doing sth** avere un ruolo importante in qc/nel fare qc

instrumentalist [ɪnstru'mɛntəlɪst] *n* strumentista *m/f*

instrument panel *n* quadro *m*, portastrumenti *inv*

insubordinate [ɪnsə'bɔːdənɪt] *adj* insubordinato(-a)

insubordination [ɪnsəbɔːdə'neɪʃən] *n* insubordinazione *f*

insufferable [ɪn'sʌfrəbl] *adj* insopportabile

insufficient [ɪnsə'fɪʃənt] *adj* insufficiente

insufficiently [ɪnsə'fɪʃəntlɪ] *adv* in modo insufficiente

insular ['ɪnsjulə^r] *adj* insulare; (*person*) di mente ristretta

insulate ['ɪnsjuleɪt] *vt* isolare

insulating tape ['ɪnsjuleɪtɪŋ-] *n* nastro isolante

insulation [ɪnsju'leɪʃən] *n* isolamento

insulin ['ɪnsjulɪn] *n* insulina

insult *n* ['ɪnsʌlt] insulto, affronto ▪ *vt* [ɪn'sʌlt] insultare

insulting [ɪn'sʌltɪŋ] adj offensivo(-a), ingiurioso(-a)

insuperable [ɪn'sju:prəbl] adj insormontabile, insuperabile

insurance [ɪn'ʃuərəns] n assicurazione f; **fire/life ~** assicurazione contro gli incendi/sulla vita; **to take out ~ (against)** fare un'assicurazione (contro), assicurarsi (contro)

insurance agent n agente m d'assicurazioni

insurance broker n broker m inv d'assicurazioni

insurance policy n polizza d'assicurazione

insurance premium n premio assicurativo

insure [ɪn'ʃuəʳ] vt assicurare; **to ~ sb** or **sb's life** assicurare qn sulla vita; **to be insured for £5000** essere assicurato per 5000 sterline

insured [ɪn'ʃuəd] n: **the ~** l'assicurato(-a)

insurer [ɪn'ʃuərəʳ] n assicuratore(-trice)

insurgent [ɪn'sə:dʒənt] adj ribelle ■ n insorto(-a), rivoltoso(-a)

insurmountable [ɪnsə'mauntəbl] adj insormontabile

insurrection [ɪnsə'rɛkʃən] n insurrezione f

intact [ɪn'tækt] adj intatto(-a)

intake ['ɪnteɪk] n (Tech) immissione f; (of food) consumo; (of pupils etc) afflusso

intangible [ɪn'tændʒɪbl] adj intangibile

integral ['ɪntɪgrəl] adj integrale; (part) integrante

integrate ['ɪntɪgreɪt] vt integrare

integrated circuit n (Comput) circuito integrato

integration [ɪntɪ'greɪʃən] n integrazione f; **racial ~** integrazione razziale

integrity [ɪn'tɛgrɪtɪ] n integrità

intellect ['ɪntəlɛkt] n intelletto

intellectual [ɪntə'lɛktjuəl] adj, n intellettuale (m/f)

intelligence [ɪn'tɛlɪdʒəns] n intelligenza; (Mil etc) informazioni fpl

intelligence quotient n quoziente m d'intelligenza

Intelligence Service n servizio segreto

intelligence test n test m inv d'intelligenza

intelligent [ɪn'tɛlɪdʒənt] adj intelligente

intelligible [ɪn'tɛlɪdʒɪbl] adj intelligibile

intemperate [ɪn'tɛmpərət] adj immoderato(-a); (drinking too much) intemperante nel bere

intend [ɪn'tɛnd] vt (gift etc): **to ~ sth for** destinare qc a; **to ~ to do** aver l'intenzione di fare

intended [ɪn'tɛndɪd] adj (insult) intenzionale; (effect) voluto(-a); (journey, route) progettato(-a)

intense [ɪn'tɛns] adj intenso(-a); (person) di forti sentimenti

intensely [ɪn'tɛnslɪ] adv intensamente; profondamente

intensify [ɪn'tɛnsɪfaɪ] vt intensificare

intensity [ɪn'tɛnsɪtɪ] n intensità

intensive [ɪn'tɛnsɪv] adj intensivo(-a)

intensive care n terapia intensiva; **~ unit** n, reparto terapia intensiva

intent [ɪn'tɛnt] n intenzione f ■ adj: **~ (on)** intento(-a) (a), immerso(-a) (in); **to all intents and purposes** a tutti gli effetti; **to be ~ on doing sth** essere deciso a fare qc

intention [ɪn'tɛnʃən] n intenzione f

intentional [ɪn'tɛnʃənl] adj intenzionale, deliberato(-a)

intentionally [ɪn'tɛnʃənəlɪ] adv apposta

intently [ɪn'tɛntlɪ] adv attentamente

inter [ɪn'tə:ʳ] vt sotterrare

interact [ɪntər'ækt] vi agire reciprocamente, interagire

interaction [ɪntər'ækʃən] n azione f reciproca, interazione f

interactive [ɪntər'æktɪv] adj interattivo(-a)

intercede [ɪntə'si:d] vi: **to ~ (with sb/on behalf of sb)** intercedere (presso qu/a favore di qn)

intercept [ɪntə'sɛpt] vt intercettare; (person) fermare

interception [ɪntə'sɛpʃən] n intercettamento

interchange n ['ɪntətʃeɪndʒ] (exchange) scambio; (on motorway) incrocio pluridirezionale ■ vt [ɪntə'tʃeɪndʒ] scambiare; sostituire l'uno(-a) per l'altro(-a)

interchangeable [ɪntə'tʃeɪndʒəbl] adj intercambiabile

intercity [ɪntə'sɪtɪ] adj: **~ (train)** ≈ (treno) rapido

intercom ['ɪntəkɔm] n interfono

interconnect [ɪntəkə'nɛkt] vi (rooms) essere in comunicazione

intercontinental ['ɪntəkɔntɪ'nɛntl] adj intercontinentale

intercourse ['ɪntəkɔ:s] n rapporti mpl; (sexual intercourse) rapporti sessuali

interdependent [ɪntədɪ'pɛndənt] adj interdipendente

interest ['ɪntrɪst] n interesse m; (Comm: stake, share) interessi mpl ■ vt interessare; **compound/simple ~** interesse composto/semplice; **business interests** attività fpl commerciali; **British interests in the Middle East** gli interessi (commerciali) britannici nel Medio Oriente

interested ['ɪntrɪstɪd] adj interessato(-a); **to be ~ in** interessarsi di

interest-free ['ɪntrɪst'fri:] adj senza interesse

interesting ['ɪntrɪstɪŋ] adj interessante

interest rate *n* tasso di interesse
interface ['ıntəfeıs] *n* (*Comput*) interfaccia
interfere [ıntə'fıər] *vi*: **to ~ (in)** (*quarrel, other people's business*) immischiarsi (in); **to ~ with** (*object*) toccare; (*plans*) ostacolare; (*duty*) interferire con
interference [ıntə'fıərəns] *n* interferenza
interfering [ıntə'fıərıŋ] *adj* invadente
interim ['ıntərım] *adj* provvisorio(-a) ▪ *n*: **in the ~** nel frattempo; **~ dividend** (*Comm*) acconto di dividendo
interior [ın'tıərıər] *n* interno; (*of country*) entroterra ▪ *adj* interiore, interno(-a)
interior decorator, interior designer *n* decoratore(-trice) (d'interni)
interjection [ıntə'dʒɛkʃən] *n* interiezione *f*
interlock [ıntə'lɔk] *vi* ingranarsi ▪ *vt* ingranare
interloper ['ıntələupər] *n* intruso(-a)
interlude ['ıntəlu:d] *n* intervallo; (*Theat*) intermezzo
intermarry [ıntə'mærı] *vi* imparentarsi per mezzo di matrimonio; sposarsi tra parenti
intermediary [ıntə'mi:dıərı] *n* intermediario(-a)
intermediate [ıntə'mi:dıət] *adj* intermedio(-a); (*Scol: course, level*) medio(-a)
interment [ın'tə:mənt] *n* (*formal*) inumazione *f*
interminable [ın'tə:mınəbl] *adj* interminabile
intermission [ıntə'mıʃən] *n* pausa; (*Theat, Cine*) intermissione *f*, intervallo
intermittent [ıntə'mıtnt] *adj* intermittente
intermittently [ıntə'mıtntlı] *adv* a intermittenza
intern *vt* [ın'tə:n] internare ▪ *n* ['ıntə:n] (*US*) medico interno
internal [ın'tə:nl] *adj* interno(-a); **~ injuries** lesioni *fpl* interne
internally [ın'tə:nəlı] *adv* all'interno; **"not to be taken ~"** "per uso esterno"
Internal Revenue, Internal Revenue Service *n* (*US*) Fisco
international [ıntə'næʃənl] *adj* internazionale ▪ *n* (*Brit Sport*) partita internazionale
International Atomic Energy Agency *n* Agenzia Internazionale per l'Energia Atomica
International Court of Justice *n* Corte *f* Internazionale di Giustizia
international date line *n* linea del cambiamento di data
internationally [ıntə'næʃnəlı] *adv* a livello internazionale
International Monetary Fund *n* Fondo monetario internazionale

international relations *npl* rapporti *mpl* internazionali
internecine [ıntə'ni:saın] *adj* sanguinoso(-a)
internee [ıntə:'ni:] *n* internato(-a)
internet ['ıntənɛt] *n*: **the ~** Internet *f*
internment [ın'tə:nmənt] *n* internamento
interplay ['ıntəpleı] *n* azione e reazione *f*
Interpol ['ıntəpɔl] *n* Interpol *f*
interpret [ın'tə:prıt] *vt* interpretare ▪ *vi* fare da interprete
interpretation [ıntə:prı'teıʃən] *n* interpretazione *f*
interpreter [ın'tə:prıtər] *n* interprete *m/f*
interpreting [ın'tə:prıtıŋ] *n* (*profession*) interpretariato
interrelated [ıntərı'leıtıd] *adj* correlato(-a)
interrogate [ın'tɛrəugeıt] *vt* interrogare
interrogation [ıntɛrəu'geıʃən] *n* interrogazione *f*; (*of suspect etc*) interrogatorio
interrogative [ıntə'rɔgətıv] *adj* interrogativo(-a) ▪ *n* (*Ling*) interrogativo
interrogator [ın'tɛrəgeıtər] *n* interrogante *m/f*
interrupt [ıntə'rʌpt] *vt* interrompere
interruption [ıntə'rʌpʃən] *n* interruzione *f*
intersect [ıntə'sɛkt] *vt* intersecare ▪ *vi* (*roads*) intersecarsi
intersection [ıntə'sɛkʃən] *n* intersezione *f*; (*of roads*) incrocio
intersperse [ıntə'spə:s] *vt*: **to ~ with** costellare di
intertwine [ıntə'twaın] *vt* intrecciare ▪ *vi* intrecciarsi
interval ['ıntəvl] *n* intervallo; (*Brit Scol*) ricreazione *f*, intervallo; **bright intervals** (*in weather*) schiarite *fpl*; **at intervals** a intervalli
intervene [ıntə'vi:n] *vi* (*time*) intercorrere; (*event, person*) intervenire
intervention [ıntə'vɛnʃən] *n* intervento
interview ['ıntəvju:] *n* (*Radio, TV etc*) intervista; (*for job*) colloquio ▪ *vt* intervistare; avere un colloquio con
interviewee [ıntəvju'i:] *n* (*TV*) intervistato(-a); (*for job*) chi si presenta ad un colloquio di lavoro
interviewer ['ıntəvju:ər] *n* intervistatore(-trice)
intestate [ın'tɛsteıt] *adj* intestato(-a)
intestinal [ın'tɛstınl] *adj* intestinale
intestine [ın'tɛstın] *n* intestino; **large/small ~** intestino crasso/tenue
intimacy ['ıntıməsı] *n* intimità
intimate *adj* ['ıntımət] intimo(-a); (*knowledge*) profondo(-a) ▪ *vt* ['ıntımeıt] lasciar capire
intimately ['ıntımıtlı] *adv* intimamente
intimation [ıntı'meıʃən] *n* annuncio

623

intimidate [ɪn'tɪmɪdeɪt] vt intimidire, intimorire

intimidation [ɪntɪmɪ'deɪʃən] n intimidazione f

into ['ɪntu] prep dentro, in; **come ~ the house** vieni dentro la casa; **~ pieces** a pezzi; **~ Italian** in italiano; **to change pounds ~ dollars** cambiare delle sterline in dollari

intolerable [ɪn'tɔlərəbl] adj intollerabile

intolerance [ɪn'tɔlərns] n intolleranza

intolerant [ɪn'tɔlərnt] adj: **~ (of)** intollerante (di)

intonation [ɪntəu'neɪʃən] n intonazione f

intoxicate [ɪn'tɔksɪkeɪt] vt inebriare

intoxicated [ɪn'tɔksɪkeɪtɪd] adj inebriato(-a)

intoxication [ɪntɔksɪ'keɪʃən] n ebbrezza

intractable [ɪn'træktəbl] adj intrattabile; (illness) difficile da curare; (problem) insolubile

intranet ['ɪntrənɛt] n Intranet f

intransigence [ɪn'trænsɪdʒəns] n intransigenza

intransigent [ɪn'trænsɪdʒənt] adj intransigente

intransitive [ɪn'trænsɪtɪv] adj intransitivo(-a)

intra-uterine device [ɪntrə'juːtərain-] n dispositivo intrauterino

intravenous [ɪntrə'viːnəs] adj endovenoso(-a)

in-tray ['ɪntreɪ] n raccoglitore m per le carte in arrivo

intrepid [ɪn'trɛpɪd] adj intrepido(-a)

intricacy ['ɪntrɪkəsɪ] n complessità f inv

intricate ['ɪntrɪkət] adj intricato(-a), complicato(-a)

intrigue [ɪn'triːg] n intrigo ■ vt affascinare ■ vi complottare, tramare

intriguing [ɪn'triːgɪŋ] adj affascinante

intrinsic [ɪn'trɪnsɪk] adj intrinseco(-a)

introduce [ɪntrə'djuːs] vt introdurre; **to ~ sb (to sb)** presentare qn (a qn); **to ~ sb to** (pastime, technique) iniziare qn a; **may I ~ ...?** permette che le presenti ...?

introduction [ɪntrə'dʌkʃən] n introduzione f; (of person) presentazione f; **a letter of ~** una lettera di presentazione

introductory [ɪntrə'dʌktərɪ] adj introduttivo(-a); **an ~ offer** un'offerta di lancio; **~ remarks** osservazioni fpl preliminari

introspection [ɪntrəu'spɛkʃən] n introspezione f

introspective [ɪntrəu'spɛktɪv] adj introspettivo(-a)

introvert ['ɪntrəuvəːt] adj, n introverso(-a)

intrude [ɪn'truːd] vi (person) intromettersi; **to ~ on** (person) importunare; **~ on** or **into** (conversation) intromettersi in; **am I intruding?** disturbo?

intruder [ɪn'truːdər] n intruso(-a)

intrusion [ɪn'truːʒən] n intrusione f

intrusive [ɪn'truːsɪv] adj importuno(-a)

intuition [ɪntjuː'ɪʃən] n intuizione f

intuitive [ɪn'tjuːɪtɪv] adj intuitivo(-a); dotato(-a) di intuito

inundate ['ɪnʌndeɪt] vt: **to ~ with** inondare di

inure [ɪn'juər] vt: **to ~ (to)** assuefare (a)

invade [ɪn'veɪd] vt invadere

invader [ɪn'veɪdər] n invasore m

invalid n ['ɪnvəlɪd] malato(-a); (with disability) invalido(-a) ■ adj [ɪn'vælɪd] (not valid) invalido(-a), non valido(-a)

invalidate [ɪn'vælɪdeɪt] vt invalidare

invalid chair n (Brit) sedia a rotelle

invaluable [ɪn'væljuəbl] adj prezioso(-a), inestimabile

invariable [ɪn'vɛərɪəbl] adj costante, invariabile

invariably [ɪn'vɛərɪəblɪ] adv invariabilmente; **she is ~ late** è immancabilmente in ritardo

invasion [ɪn'veɪʒən] n invasione f

invective [ɪn'vɛktɪv] n invettiva

inveigle [ɪn'viːgl] vt: **to ~ sb into (doing) sth** circuire qn per (fargli fare) qc

invent [ɪn'vɛnt] vt inventare

invention [ɪn'vɛnʃən] n invenzione f

inventive [ɪn'vɛntɪv] adj inventivo(-a)

inventiveness [ɪn'vɛntɪvnɪs] n inventiva

inventor [ɪn'vɛntər] n inventore m

inventory ['ɪnvəntrɪ] n inventario

inventory control n (Comm) controllo delle giacenze

inverse [ɪn'vəːs] adj inverso(-a) ■ n inverso, contrario; **in ~ proportion (to)** in modo inversamente proporzionale (a)

inversely [ɪn'vəːslɪ] adv inversamente

invert [ɪn'vəːt] vt invertire; (object) rovesciare

invertebrate [ɪn'vəːtɪbrɪt] n invertebrato

inverted commas [ɪn'vəːtɪd-] npl (Brit) virgolette fpl

invest [ɪn'vɛst] vt investire; (fig: time, effort) impiegare; (endow): **to ~ sb with sth** investire qn di qc ■ vi fare investimenti; **to ~ in** investire in, fare (degli) investimenti in; (acquire) comprarsi

investigate [ɪn'vɛstɪgeɪt] vt investigare, indagare; (crime) fare indagini su

investigation [ɪnvɛstɪ'geɪʃən] n investigazione f; (of crime) indagine f

investigative [ɪn'vɛstɪgətɪv] adj: **~ journalism** giornalismo investigativo

investigator [ɪn'vɛstɪgeɪtər] n investigatore(-trice); **a private ~** un investigatore privato, un detective

investiture [ɪn'vɛstɪtʃəʳ] n investitura

investment [ɪn'vɛstmənt] n investimento

investment income n reddito da investimenti

investment trust n fondo comune di investimento

investor [ɪn'vɛstəʳ] n investitore(-trice); (shareholder) azionista m/f

inveterate [ɪn'vɛtərət] adj inveterato(-a)

invidious [ɪn'vɪdɪəs] adj odioso(-a); (task) spiacevole

invigilate [ɪn'vɪdʒɪleɪt] vt, vi (Brit Scol) sorvegliare

invigilator [ɪn'vɪdʒɪleɪtəʳ] n (Brit) chi sorveglia agli esami

invigorating [ɪn'vɪgəreɪtɪŋ] adj stimolante; vivificante

invincible [ɪn'vɪnsɪbl] adj invincibile

inviolate [ɪn'vaɪələt] adj inviolato(-a)

invisible [ɪn'vɪzɪbl] adj invisibile

invisible assets npl (Brit) beni mpl immateriali

invisible ink n inchiostro simpatico

invisible mending n rammendo invisibile

invitation [ɪnvɪ'teɪʃən] n invito; **by ~ only** esclusivamente su or per invito; **at sb's ~** dietro invito di qn

invite [ɪn'vaɪt] vt invitare; (opinions etc) sollecitare; (trouble) provocare; **to ~ sb (to do)** invitare qn (a fare); **to ~ sb to dinner** invitare qn a cena
▸ **invite out** vt invitare fuori
▸ **invite over** vt invitare (a casa)

inviting [ɪn'vaɪtɪŋ] adj invitante, attraente

invoice ['ɪnvɔɪs] n fattura ■ vt fatturare; **to ~ sb for goods** inviare a qn la fattura per le or delle merci

invoke [ɪn'vəuk] vt invocare

involuntary [ɪn'vɔləntrɪ] adj involontario(-a)

involve [ɪn'vɔlv] vt (entail) richiedere, comportare; (associate): **to ~ sb (in)** implicare qn (in); coinvolgere qn (in); **to ~ o.s. in sth** (politics etc) impegnarsi in qc

involved [ɪn'vɔlvd] adj involuto(-a), complesso(-a); **to feel ~** sentirsi coinvolto(-a); **to become ~ with sb** (socially) legarsi a qn; (emotionally) legarsi sentimentalmente a qn

involvement [ɪn'vɔlvmənt] n implicazione f; coinvolgimento; impegno; partecipazione f

invulnerable [ɪn'vʌlnərəbl] adj invulnerabile

inward ['ɪnwəd] adj (movement) verso l'interno; (thought, feeling) interiore, intimo(-a) ■ adv verso l'interno

inwardly ['ɪnwədlɪ] adv (feel, think etc) nell'intimo, entro di sé

inwards ['ɪnwədz] adv verso l'interno

I/O abbr (Comput: = input/output) I/O

IOC n abbr (= International Olympic Committee) CIO m (= Comitato Internazionale Olimpico)

iodine ['aɪəudi:n] n iodio

IOM abbr (Brit) = **Isle of Man**

ion ['aɪən] n ione m

Ionian Sea [aɪ'əunɪən-] n: **the ~** il mare Ionio

ioniser ['aɪənaɪzəʳ] n ionizzatore m

iota [aɪ'əutə] n (fig) briciolo

IOU n abbr (= I owe you) pagherò m inv

IOW abbr (Brit) = **Isle of Wight**

IPA n abbr (= International Phonetic Alphabet) I.P.A. m

IP address n (Comput) indirizzo IP

iPod® ['aɪpɔd] n iPod® m inv, lettore m MP3

IQ n abbr = **intelligence quotient**

IRA n abbr (= Irish Republican Army) I.R.A. f; (US) = **individual retirement account**

Iran [ɪ'rɑːn] n Iran m

Iranian [ɪ'reɪnɪən] adj iraniano(-a) ■ n iraniano(-a); (Ling) iranico

Iraq [ɪ'rɑːk] n Iraq m

Iraqi [ɪ'rɑːkɪ] adj iracheno(-a) ■ n iracheno(-a)

irascible [ɪ'ræsɪbl] adj irascibile

irate [aɪ'reɪt] adj irato(-a)

Ireland ['aɪələnd] n Irlanda; **Republic of ~** Repubblica d'Irlanda, Eire f

iris ['aɪrɪs, -ɪz] n (pl **irises**) iride f; (Bot) giaggiolo, iride

Irish ['aɪrɪʃ] adj irlandese ■ npl: **the ~** gli Irlandesi

Irishman ['aɪrɪʃmən] n irlandese m

Irish Sea n: **the ~** il mar d'Irlanda

Irishwoman ['aɪrɪʃwumən] n irlandese f

irk [əːk] vt seccare

irksome ['əːksəm] adj seccante

IRN n abbr (= Independent Radio News) agenzia d'informazioni per la radio

IRO n abbr (= International Refugee Organization) O.I.R. f (= Organizzazione Internazionale per i Rifugiati)

iron ['aɪən] n ferro; (for clothes) ferro da stiro ■ adj di or in ferro ■ vt (clothes) stirare; see also **irons**
▸ **iron out** vt (crease) appianare; (fig) spianare; far sparire

Iron Curtain n: **the ~** la cortina di ferro

iron foundry n fonderia

ironic [aɪ'rɔnɪk], **ironical** [aɪ'rɔnɪkl] adj ironico(-a)

ironically [aɪ'rɔnɪklɪ] adv ironicamente

ironing ['aɪənɪŋ] n (act) stirare m; (clothes) roba da stirare

ironing board n asse f da stiro

iron lung n (Med) polmone m d'acciaio

ironmonger ['aɪənmʌŋgəʳ] n (Brit)
negoziante m in ferramenta; **~'s (shop)** n
negozio di ferramenta
iron ore n minerale m di ferro
irons ['aɪənz] npl (chains) catene fpl
ironworks ['aɪənwəːks] n ferriera
irony ['aɪrənɪ] n ironia
irrational [ɪ'ræʃənl] adj irrazionale;
irragionevole; illogico(-a)
irreconcilable [ɪrɛkən'saɪləbl] adj
irreconciliabile; (opinion): **~ with**
inconciliabile con
irredeemable [ɪrɪ'diːməbl] adj (Comm)
irredimibile
irrefutable [ɪrɪ'fjuːtəbl] adj irrefutabile
irregular [ɪ'rɛgjulə ʳ] adj irregolare
irregularity [ɪrɛgju'lærɪtɪ] n irregolarità f inv
irrelevance [ɪ'rɛləvəns] n inappropriatezza
irrelevant [ɪ'rɛləvənt] adj non pertinente
irreligious [ɪrɪ'lɪdʒəs] adj irreligioso(-a)
irreparable [ɪ'rɛprəbl] adj irreparabile
irreplaceable [ɪrɪ'pleɪsəbl] adj insostituibile
irrepressible [ɪrɪ'prɛsəbl] adj irrefrenabile
irreproachable [ɪrɪ'prəutʃəbl] adj
irreprensibile
irresistible [ɪrɪ'zɪstɪbl] adj irresistibile
irresolute [ɪ'rɛzəluːt] adj irresoluto(-a),
indeciso(-a)
irrespective [ɪrɪ'spɛktɪv]: **~ of** prep senza
riguardo a
irresponsible [ɪrɪ'spɒnsɪbl] adj irresponsabile
irretrievable [ɪrɪ'triːvəbl] adj (object)
irrecuperabile; (loss, damage) irreparabile
irreverent [ɪ'rɛvərnt] adj irriverente
irrevocable [ɪ'rɛvəkəbl] adj irrevocabile
irrigate ['ɪrɪgeɪt] vt irrigare
irrigation [ɪrɪ'geɪʃən] n irrigazione f
irritable ['ɪrɪtəbl] adj irritabile
irritant ['ɪrɪtənt] n sostanza irritante
irritate ['ɪrɪteɪt] vt irritare
irritation [ɪrɪ'teɪʃən] n irritazione f
IRS n abbr (US) = **Internal Revenue Service**
is [ɪz] vb see **be**
ISA ['aɪsə] n abbr (= individual savings account)
forma di investimento detassata
ISBN n abbr (= International Standard Book
Number) ISBN m
ISDN n abbr (= Integrated Services Digital Network)
ISDN m
Islam ['ɪzlɑːm] n Islam m
island ['aɪlənd] n isola; (also: **traffic island**)
salvagente m
islander ['aɪləndə ʳ] n isolano(-a)
isle [aɪl] n isola
isn't ['ɪznt] = **is not**
isolate ['aɪsəleɪt] vt isolare
isolated ['aɪsəleɪtɪd] adj isolato(-a)

isolation [aɪsə'leɪʃən] n isolamento
isolationism [aɪsə'leɪʃənɪzəm] n
isolazionismo
isotope ['aɪsəutəup] n isotopo
ISP n abbr (Comput: = internet service provider) ISP
m inv
Israel ['ɪzreɪl] n Israele m
Israeli [ɪz'reɪlɪ] adj, n israeliano(-a)
issue ['ɪʃuː] n questione f, problema m;
(outcome) esito, risultato; (of banknotes etc)
emissione f; (of newspaper etc) numero;
(offspring) discendenza ▪ vt (rations, equipment)
distribuire; (orders) dare; (book) pubblicare;
(banknotes, cheques, stamps) emettere ▪ vi: **to ~
(from)** uscire (da), venir fuori (da); **at ~** in
gioco, in discussione; **to avoid the ~** evitare
la discussione; **to take ~ with sb (over sth)**
prendere posizione contro qn (riguardo a qc);
to confuse or **obscure the ~** confondere le
cose; **to make an ~ of sth** fare un problema
di qc; **to ~ sth to sb, ~ sb with sth**
consegnare qc a qn
Istanbul [ɪstæn'buːl] n Istanbul f
isthmus ['ɪsməs] n istmo
IT n abbr = **information technology**

KEYWORD

it [ɪt] pron **1** (specific: subject) esso(-a) (mostly
omitted in Italian); (: direct object) lo/la, l';
(: indirect object) gli/le; **where's my book? —
it's on the table** dov'è il mio libro? — è sulla
tavola; **what is it?** che cos'è?; (what's the
matter?) cosa c'è?; **where is it?** dov'è?; **I can't
find it** non lo (or la) trovo; **give it to me**
dammelo (or dammela); **about/from/of it**
ne; **I spoke to him about it** gliene ho
parlato; **what did you learn from it?** quale
insegnamento ne hai tratto?; **I'm proud of
it** ne sono fiero; **in/to/at it** ci; **put the book
in it** mettici il libro; **did you go to it?** ci sei
andato?; **I wasn't at it** non c'ero; **above/
over it** sopra; **below/under it** sotto; **in
front of/behind it** lì davanti/dietro
2 (impers): **it's raining** piove; **it's Friday
tomorrow** domani è venerdì; **it's 6 o'clock**
sono le 6; **it's 2 hours on the train** sono or ci
vogliono 2 ore di treno; **who is it? — it's me**
chi è? — sono io

ITA n abbr (Brit: = initial teaching alphabet) alfabeto
fonetico semplificato per insegnare a leggere
Italian [ɪ'tæljən] adj italiano(-a) ▪ n
italiano(-a); (Ling) italiano; **the Italians** gli
Italiani
italic [ɪ'tælɪk] adj corsivo(-a); **italics** npl
corsivo

Italy ['ɪtəlɪ] n Italia
ITC n abbr (Brit: = Independent Television Commission) organo di controllo sulle reti televisive
itch [ɪtʃ] n prurito ∎ vi (person) avere il prurito; (part of body) prudere; **to be itching to do** non veder l'ora di fare
itchy ['ɪtʃɪ] adj che prude; **my back is ~** ho prurito alla schiena
it'd ['ɪtd] = **it would; it had**
item ['aɪtəm] n articolo; (on agenda) punto; (in programme) numero; (also: **news item**) notizia; **items of clothing** capi mpl di abbigliamento
itemize ['aɪtəmaɪz] vt specificare, dettagliare
itemized bill ['aɪtəmaɪzd-] n conto dettagliato
itinerant [ɪ'tɪnərənt] adj ambulante
itinerary [aɪ'tɪnərərɪ] n itinerario
it'll ['ɪtl] = **it will; it shall**
ITN n abbr (Brit: = Independent Television News) agenzia d'informazioni per la televisione
its [ɪts] adj, pron il/la suo(-a), i/le suoi/sue
it's [ɪts] = **it is; it has**
itself [ɪt'self] pron (emphatic) esso(-a) stesso(-a); (reflexive) si
ITV n abbr (Brit: = Independent Television) rete televisiva indipendente; vedi nota

● **ITV**
●
● La ITV è un'azienda televisiva privata
● che comprende una serie di emittenti
● regionali, la prima delle quali è stata
● aperta nel 1955. Si autofinanzia tramite
● la pubblicità ed è sottoposta al controllo
● di un ente ufficiale, la "Ofcom" vedi anche
● "BBC".

IUD n abbr = **intra-uterine device**
I've [aɪv] = **I have**
ivory ['aɪvərɪ] n avorio
Ivory Coast n Costa d'Avorio
ivory tower n torre f d'avorio
ivy ['aɪvɪ] n edera
Ivy League n (US) vedi nota

● **IVY LEAGUE**
●
● Ivy League è il termine usato per indicare
● le otto università più prestigiose degli
● Stati Uniti nordorientali (Brown,
● Columbia, Cornell, Dartmouth College,
● Harvard, Princeton, University of
● Pennsylvania e Yale).

i

Jj

J, j [dʒeɪ] n (letter) J, j f or m inv; **J for Jack**, (US) **J for Jig** ≃ J come Jersey
JA n abbr = **judge advocate**
J/A abbr = **joint account**
jab [dʒæb] vt: **to ~ sth into** affondare or piantare qc dentro ▪ vi: **to ~ at** dare colpi a ▪ n colpo; (Med: col) puntura
jabber ['dʒæbər] vt, vi borbottare
jack [dʒæk] n (Aut) cricco; (Bowls) boccino, pallino; (Cards) fante m
▸ **jack in** vt (col) mollare
▸ **jack up** vt sollevare sul cricco; (raise: prices etc) alzare
jackal ['dʒækl] n sciacallo
jackass ['dʒækæs] n (also fig) asino, somaro
jackdaw ['dʒækdɔː] n taccola
jacket ['dʒækɪt] n giacca; (of book) copertura; **potatoes in their jackets** (Brit) patate fpl con la buccia
jacket potato n patata cotta al forno con la buccia
jack-in-the-box ['dʒækɪnðəbɒks] n scatola a sorpresa (con pupazzo a molla)
jack-knife ['dʒæknaɪf] vi: **the lorry jack-knifed** l'autotreno si è piegato su se stesso
jack-of-all-trades [dʒækəv'ɔːltreɪdz] n uno che fa un po' di tutto
jack plug n (Brit) jack plug f inv
jackpot ['dʒækpɒt] n primo premio (in denaro)
Jacuzzi® [dʒə'kuːzɪ] n vasca per idromassaggio Jacuzzi®
jade [dʒeɪd] n (stone) giada
jaded ['dʒeɪdɪd] adj sfinito(-a), spossato(-a)
jagged ['dʒægɪd] adj sbocconcellato(-a); (cliffs etc) frastagliato(-a)
jaguar ['dʒægjuə'] n giaguaro
jail [dʒeɪl] n prigione f ▪ vt mandare in prigione
jailbird ['dʒeɪlbəːd] n avanzo di galera
jailbreak ['dʒeɪlbreɪk] n evasione f
jailer ['dʒeɪlə'] n custode m del carcere
jalopy [dʒə'lɒpɪ] n (col) macinino
jam [dʒæm] n marmellata; (of shoppers etc)

ressa; (also: **traffic jam**) ingorgo ▪ vt (passage etc) ingombrare, ostacolare; (mechanism, drawer etc) bloccare; (Radio) disturbare con interferenze ▪ vi (mechanism, sliding part) incepparsi, bloccarsi; (gun) incepparsi; **to get sb out of a ~** tirare qn fuori dai pasticci; **to ~ sth into** forzare qc dentro; infilare qc a forza dentro; **the telephone lines are jammed** le linee sono sovraccariche
Jamaica [dʒə'meɪkə] n Giamaica
Jamaican [dʒə'meɪkən] adj, n giamaicano(-a)
jamb [dʒæm] n stipite m
jam-packed [dʒæm'pækt] adj: **~ (with)** pieno(-a) zeppo(-a) (di), strapieno(-a) (di)
jam session n improvvisazione f jazzistica
Jan. abbr (= January) gen., genn.
jangle ['dʒæŋgl] vi risuonare; (bracelet) tintinnare
janitor ['dʒænɪtə'] n (caretaker) portiere m; (Scol) bidello
January ['dʒænjuərɪ] n gennaio; see also **July**
Japan [dʒə'pæn] n Giappone m
Japanese [dʒæpə'niːz] adj giapponese ▪ n (pl inv) giapponese m/f; (Ling) giapponese m
jar [dʒɑː'] n (container) barattolo, vasetto ▪ vi (sound) stridere; (colours etc) stonare ▪ vt (shake) scuotere
jargon ['dʒɑːgən] n gergo
jarring ['dʒɑːrɪŋ] adj (sound, colour) stonato(-a)
Jas. abbr = **James**
jasmin, jasmine ['dʒæzmɪn] n gelsomino
jaundice ['dʒɔːndɪs] n itterizia
jaundiced ['dʒɔːndɪst] adj (fig) invidioso(-a) e critico(-a)
jaunt [dʒɔːnt] n gita
jaunty ['dʒɔːntɪ] adj vivace; disinvolto(-a), spigliato(-a)
Java ['dʒɑːvə] n Giava
javelin ['dʒævlɪn] n giavellotto
jaw [dʒɔː] n mascella; **jaws** npl (Tech: of vice etc) morsa
jawbone ['dʒɔːbəun] n mandibola
jay [dʒeɪ] n ghiandaia

jaywalker ['dʒeɪwɔːkə^r] n pedone(-a) indisciplinato(-a)

jazz [dʒæz] n jazz m
▶**jazz up** vt rendere vivace

jazz band n banda f jazz inv

jazzy ['dʒæzɪ] adj vistoso(-a), chiassoso(-a)

JCB® n scavatrice f

JCS n abbr (US) = **Joint Chiefs of Staff**

JD n abbr (US: = Doctor of Laws) titolo di studio; (= Justice Department) ministero della Giustizia

jealous ['dʒɛləs] adj geloso(-a)

jealously ['dʒɛləslɪ] adv (enviously) con gelosia; (watchfully) gelosamente

jealousy ['dʒɛləsɪ] n gelosia

jeans [dʒiːnz] npl (blue-)jeans mpl

Jeep® [dʒiːp] n jeep m inv

jeer [dʒɪə^r] vi: **to ~ (at)** fischiare; beffeggiare; see also **jeers**

jeering ['dʒɪərɪŋ] adj (crowd) che urla e fischia ▪ n fischi mpl; parole fpl di scherno

jeers ['dʒɪəz] npl fischi mpl

jelly ['dʒɛlɪ] n gelatina

jellyfish ['dʒɛlɪfɪʃ] n medusa

jeopardize ['dʒɛpədaɪz] vt mettere in pericolo

jeopardy ['dʒɛpədɪ] n: **in ~** in pericolo

jerk [dʒəːk] n sobbalzo, scossa; sussulto; (col) povero scemo ▪ vt dare una scossa a ▪ vi (vehicles) sobbalzare

jerkin ['dʒəːkɪn] n giubbotto

jerky ['dʒəːkɪ] adj a scatti; a sobbalzi

jerry-built ['dʒɛrɪbɪlt] adj fatto(-a) di cartapesta

jerry can ['dʒɛrɪ-] n tanica

Jersey ['dʒəːzɪ] n Jersey m

jersey ['dʒəːzɪ] n maglia, jersey m

Jerusalem [dʒə'ruːsələm] n Gerusalemme f

jest [dʒɛst] n scherzo; **in ~** per scherzo

jester ['dʒɛstə^r] n (Hist) buffone m

Jesus ['dʒiːzəs] n Gesù m; **~ Christ** Gesù Cristo

jet [dʒɛt] n (of gas, liquid) getto; (Aut) spruzzatore m; (Aviat) aviogetto

jet-black ['dʒɛt'blæk] adj nero(-a) come l'ebano, corvino(-a)

jet engine n motore m a reazione

jet lag n (problemi mpl dovuti allo) sbalzo dei fusi orari

jetsam ['dʒɛtsəm] n relitti mpl di mare

jet-setter ['dʒɛtsɛtə^r] n membro del jet set

jettison ['dʒɛtɪsn] vt gettare in mare

jetty ['dʒɛtɪ] n molo

Jew [dʒuː] n ebreo

jewel ['dʒuːəl] n gioiello

jeweller, (US) **jeweler** ['dʒuːələ^r] n orefice m, gioielliere(-a); **~'s shop** n oreficeria, gioielleria

jewellery, (US) **jewelry** ['dʒuːəlrɪ] n gioielli mpl

Jewess ['dʒuːɪs] n ebrea

Jewish ['dʒuːɪʃ] adj ebreo(-a), ebraico(-a)

JFK n abbr (US) = **John Fitzgerald Kennedy International Airport**

jib [dʒɪb] n (Naut) fiocco; (of crane) braccio ▪ vi (horse) impennarsi; **to ~ at doing sth** essere restio a fare qc

jibe [dʒaɪb] n beffa

jiffy ['dʒɪfɪ] n (col): **in a ~** in un batter d'occhio

jig [dʒɪg] n (dance, tune) giga

jigsaw ['dʒɪgsɔː] n (tool) sega da traforo; (also: **jigsaw puzzle**) puzzle m inv

jilt [dʒɪlt] vt piantare in asso

jingle ['dʒɪŋgl] n (advert) sigla pubblicitaria ▪ vi tintinnare, scampanellare

jingoism ['dʒɪŋgəuɪzəm] n sciovinismo

jinx [dʒɪŋks] n (col) iettatura; (person) iettatore(-trice)

jitters ['dʒɪtəz] npl (col): **to get the ~** aver fifa

jittery ['dʒɪtərɪ] adj (col) teso(-a), agitato(-a); **to be ~** aver fifa

jiujitsu [dʒuː'dʒɪtsuː] n jujitsu m

job [dʒɔb] n lavoro; (employment) impiego, posto; **a part-time/full-time ~** un lavoro a mezza giornata/a tempo pieno; **that's not my ~** non è compito mio; **he's only doing his ~** non fa che il suo dovere; **it's a good ~ that ...** meno male che ...; **just the ~!** proprio quello che ci vuole!

jobber ['dʒɔbə^r] n (Brit Stock Exchange) intermediario tra agenti di cambio

jobbing ['dʒɔbɪŋ] adj (Brit: workman) a ore, a giornata

Jobcentre ['dʒɔbsɛntə^r] n ufficio di collocamento

job creation scheme n progetto per la creazione di nuovi posti di lavoro

job description n caratteristiche fpl (di un lavoro)

jobless ['dʒɔblɪs] adj senza lavoro, disoccupato(-a) ▪ npl: **the ~** i senza lavoro

job lot n partita di articoli disparati

job satisfaction n soddisfazione f nel lavoro

job security n sicurezza del posto di lavoro

job share vi fare un lavoro ripartito ▪ n lavoro ripartito

job specification n caratteristiche fpl (di un lavoro)

Jock [dʒɔk] n (col) termine colloquiale per chiamare uno scozzese

jockey ['dʒɔkɪ] n fantino, jockey m inv ▪ vi: **to ~ for position** manovrare per una posizione di vantaggio

jockey box n (US Aut) vano portaoggetti

jockstrap ['dʒɔkstræp] n conchiglia (per atleti)

jocular ['dʒɔkjulə^r] adj gioviale; scherzoso(-a)

jog [dʒɔg] *vt* urtare ■ *vi* (*Sport*) fare footing, fare jogging; **to ~ along** trottare; (*fig*) andare avanti pian piano; **to ~ sb's memory** stimolare la memoria di qn

jogger ['dʒɔgə^r] *n* persona che fa footing *or* jogging

jogging ['dʒɔgɪŋ] *n* footing *m*, jogging *m*

john [dʒɔn] *n* (*US col*): **the ~** il gabinetto

join [dʒɔɪn] *vt* unire, congiungere; (*become member of*) iscriversi a; (*meet*) raggiungere; riunirsi a ■ *vi* (*roads, rivers*) confluire ■ *n* giuntura; **to ~ forces (with)** allearsi (con *or* a); (*fig*) mettersi insieme (a); **will you ~ us for dinner?** viene a cena con noi?; **I'll ~ you later** vi raggiungo più tardi
  ▸**join in** *vt fus* unirsi a, prendere parte a, partecipare a ■ *vi* partecipare
  ▸**join up** *vi* arruolarsi

joiner ['dʒɔɪnə^r] *n* falegname *m*

joinery ['dʒɔɪnərɪ] *n* falegnameria

joint [dʒɔɪnt] *n* (*Tech*) giuntura; giunto; (*Anat*) articolazione *f*, giuntura; (*Brit Culin*) arrosto; (*col: place*) locale *m* ■ *adj* comune; (*responsibility*) collettivo(-a); (*committee*) misto(-a)

joint account *n* (*at bank etc*) conto in comune

jointly ['dʒɔɪntlɪ] *adv* in comune, insieme

joint ownership *n* comproprietà

joint-stock company ['dʒɔɪntstɔk-] *n* società *f inv* per azioni

joist [dʒɔɪst] *n* trave *f*

joke [dʒəuk] *n* scherzo; (*funny story*) barzelletta ■ *vi* scherzare; **to play a ~ on** fare uno scherzo a

joker ['dʒəukə^r] *n* buffone(-a), burlone(-a); (*Cards*) matta, jolly *m inv*

joking ['dʒəukɪŋ] *n* scherzi *mpl*

jollity ['dʒɔlɪtɪ] *n* allegria

jolly ['dʒɔlɪ] *adj* allegro(-a), gioioso(-a) ■ *adv* (*Brit col*) veramente, proprio ■ *vt* (*Brit*): **to ~ sb along** cercare di tenere qn su (di morale); **~ good!** (*Brit*) benissimo!

jolt [dʒəult] *n* scossa, sobbalzo ■ *vt* urtare

Jordan ['dʒɔːdən] *n* (*country*) Giordania; (*river*) Giordano

Jordanian [dʒɔː'deɪnɪən] *adj, n* giordano(-a)

joss stick ['dʒɔs-] *n* bastoncino d'incenso

jostle ['dʒɔsl] *vt* spingere coi gomiti ■ *vi* farsi spazio coi gomiti

jot [dʒɔt] *n*: **not one ~** nemmeno un po'
  ▸**jot down** *vt* annotare in fretta, buttare giù

jotter ['dʒɔtə^r] *n* (*Brit*) quaderno; blocco

journal ['dʒəːnl] *n* (*newspaper*) giornale *m*; (*periodical*) rivista; (*diary*) diario

journalese [dʒəːnə'liːz] *n* (*pej*) stile *m* giornalistico

journalism ['dʒəːnəlɪzəm] *n* giornalismo

journalist ['dʒəːnəlɪst] *n* giornalista *m/f*

journey ['dʒəːnɪ] *n* viaggio; (*distance covered*) tragitto; **a 5-hour ~** un viaggio *or* un tragitto di 5 ore

jovial ['dʒəuvɪəl] *adj* gioviale, allegro(-a)

jowl [dʒaul] *n* mandibola; guancia

joy [dʒɔɪ] *n* gioia

joyful ['dʒɔɪful], **joyous** ['dʒɔɪəs] *adj* gioioso(-a), allegro(-a)

joyride ['dʒɔɪraɪd] *n*: **to go for a ~** rubare una macchina per farsi un giro

joyrider ['dʒɔɪraɪdə^r] *n* chi ruba una macchina per andare a farsi un giro

joystick ['dʒɔɪstɪk] *n* (*Aviat*) barra di comando; (*Comput*) joystick *m inv*

JP *n abbr* = **Justice of the Peace**

Jr. *abbr* = **junior**

jubilant ['dʒuːbɪlnt] *adj* giubilante; trionfante

jubilation [dʒuːbɪ'leɪʃən] *n* giubilo

jubilee ['dʒuːbɪliː] *n* giubileo; **silver ~** venticinquesimo anniversario

judge [dʒʌdʒ] *n* giudice *m/f* ■ *vt* giudicare; (*consider*) ritenere; (*estimate: weight, size etc*) calcolare, valutare ■ *vi*: **judging** *or* **to ~ by his expression** a giudicare dalla sua espressione; **as far as I can ~** a mio giudizio; **I judged it necessary to inform him** ho ritenuto necessario informarlo

judge advocate *n* (*Mil*) magistrato militare

judgment, judgement ['dʒʌdʒmənt] *n* giudizio; (*punishment*) punizione *f*; **in my judg(e)ment** a mio giudizio; **to pass judg(e)ment (on)** (*Law*) pronunciare un giudizio (su); (*fig*) dare giudizi affrettati (su)

judicial [dʒuː'dɪʃl] *adj* giudiziale, giudiziario(-a)

judiciary [dʒuː'dɪʃɪərɪ] *n* magistratura

judicious [dʒuː'dɪʃəs] *adj* giudizioso(-a)

judo ['dʒuːdəu] *n* judo

jug [dʒʌg] *n* brocca, bricco

jugged hare [dʒʌgd-] *n* (*Brit*) lepre *f* in salmì

juggernaut ['dʒʌgənɔːt] *n* (*Brit: huge truck*) bestione *m*

juggle ['dʒʌgl] *vi* fare giochi di destrezza

juggler ['dʒʌglə^r] *n* giocoliere(-a)

Jugoslav ['juːgəu'slɑːv] *adj, n* = **Yugoslav**

jugular ['dʒʌgjulə^r] *adj*: **~ (vein)** vena giugulare

juice [dʒuːs] *n* succo; (*of meat*) sugo; **we've run out of ~** (*col: petrol*) siamo rimasti a secco

juicy ['dʒuːsɪ] *adj* succoso(-a)

jukebox ['dʒuːkbɔks] *n* juke-box *m inv*

Jul. *abbr* (= *July*) lug., lu.

July [dʒuː'laɪ] *n* luglio; **the first of ~** il primo luglio; **(on) the eleventh of ~** l'undici luglio; **in the month of ~** nel mese di luglio;

at the **beginning/end of** ~ all'inizio/alla fine di luglio; **in the middle of** ~ a metà luglio; **during** ~ durante (il mese di) luglio; **in** ~ **of** next year a luglio dell'anno prossimo; **each** or **every** ~ ogni anno a luglio; ~ **was wet this year** ha piovuto molto a luglio quest'anno

jumble ['dʒʌmbl] *n* miscuglio ■ *vt* (*also:* **jumble up, jumble together**) mischiare, mettere alla rinfusa

jumble sale *n* = vendita di beneficenza; *vedi nota*

jumbo ['dʒʌmbəu] *adj*: ~ **jet** jumbo-jet *m inv*; ~ **size** formato gigante

jump [dʒʌmp] *vi* saltare, balzare; (*start*) sobbalzare; (*increase*) rincarare ■ *vt* saltare ■ *n* salto, balzo; sobbalzo; (*Showjumping*) salto; (*fence*) ostacolo; **to** ~ **the queue** (*Brit*) passare davanti agli altri (*in una coda*)
▶ **jump about** *vi* fare salti, saltellare
▶ **jump at** *vt fus* (*fig*) cogliere or afferrare al volo; **he jumped at the offer** si affrettò ad accettare l'offerta
▶ **jump down** *vi* saltare giù
▶ **jump up** *vi* saltare in piedi

jumped-up ['dʒʌmptʌp] *adj* (*Brit pej*) presuntuoso(-a)

jumper ['dʒʌmpəʳ] *n* (*Brit: pullover*) maglia; (*US: pinafore dress*) scamiciato; (*Sport*) saltatore(-trice)

jump leads, (*US*) **jumper cables** *npl* cavi *mpl* per batteria

jump-start ['dʒʌmpstɑːt] *vt* (*car*) far partire spingendo; (*fig*) dare una spinta a, rimettere in moto

jump suit *n* tuta

jumpy ['dʒʌmpɪ] *adj* nervoso(-a), agitato(-a)

Jun. *abbr* (= June) giu.

Jun., Junr *abbr* = **junior**

junction ['dʒʌŋkʃən] *n* (*Brit: of roads*) incrocio; (*of rails*) nodo ferroviario

juncture ['dʒʌŋktʃəʳ] *n*: **at this** ~ in questa congiuntura

June [dʒuːn] *n* giugno; *see also* **July**

jungle ['dʒʌŋgl] *n* giungla

junior ['dʒuːnɪəʳ] *adj, n*: **he's** ~ **to me (by 2 years)**, **he's my** ~ **(by 2 years)** è più giovane

di me (di 2 anni); **he's** ~ **to me** (*seniority*) è al di sotto di me, ho più anzianità di lui

junior executive *n* giovane dirigente *m*

junior high school *n* (*US*) scuola media (*da 12 a 15 anni*)

junior minister *n* (*Brit Pol*) ministro che non fa parte del Cabinet

junior partner *n* socio meno anziano

junior school *n* (*Brit*) scuola elementare (*da 8 a 11 anni*)

junior sizes *npl* (*Comm*) taglie *fpl* per ragazzi

juniper ['dʒuːnɪpəʳ] *n*: ~ **berry** bacca di ginepro

junk [dʒʌŋk] *n* (*rubbish*) chincaglia; (*ship*) giunca ■ *vt* disfarsi di

junk bond *n* (*Comm*) titolo *m* spazzatura *inv*

junk dealer *n* rigattiere *m*

junket ['dʒʌŋkɪt] *n* (*Culin*) giuncata; (*Brit col*): **to go on a** ~ fare bisboccia

junk food *n* porcherie *fpl*, cibo a scarso valore nutritivo

junkie ['dʒʌŋkɪ] *n* (*col*) drogato(-a)

junk mail *n* posta *f* spazzatura *inv*

junk room *n* (*US*) ripostiglio

junk shop *n* chincaglieria

junta ['dʒʌntə] *n* giunta

Jupiter ['dʒuːpɪtəʳ] *n* (*planet*) Giove *m*

jurisdiction [dʒuərɪs'dɪkʃən] *n* giurisdizione *f*; **it falls** or **comes within/outside our** ~ è/non è di nostra competenza

jurisprudence [dʒuərɪs'pruːdəns] *n* giurisprudenza

juror ['dʒuərəʳ] *n* giurato(-a)

jury ['dʒuərɪ] *n* giuria

jury box *n* banco della giuria

juryman ['dʒuərɪmən] *n* = **juror**

just [dʒʌst] *adj* giusto(-a) ■ *adv*: **he's** ~ **done it/left** lo ha appena fatto/è appena partito; ~ **as I expected** proprio come me lo aspettavo; ~ **right** proprio giusto; ~ **2 o'clock** le 2 precise; **we were** ~ **going** stavamo uscendo; **I was** ~ **about to phone** stavo proprio per telefonare; ~ **as he was leaving** proprio mentre se ne stava andando; **it was** ~ **before/enough/here** era poco prima/ appena assai/proprio qui; **it's** ~ **me** sono solo io; **it's** ~ **a mistake** non è che uno sbaglio; ~ **missed/caught** appena perso/preso; ~ **listen to this!** senta un po' questo!; ~ **ask someone the way** basta che tu chieda la strada a qualcuno; **it's** ~ **as good** è altrettanto buono; **it's** ~ **as well you didn't go** per fortuna non ci sei andato; **not** ~ **now** non proprio adesso; ~ **a minute!**, ~ **one moment!** un attimo!

justice ['dʒʌstɪs] *n* giustizia; **Lord Chief J**~ (*Brit*) presidente *m* della Corte d'Appello;

this photo doesn't do you ~ questa foto non ti fa giustizia

Justice of the Peace n giudice m conciliatore

justifiable [dʒʌstɪ'faɪəbl] adj giustificabile

justifiably [dʒʌstɪ'faɪəblɪ] adv legittimamente, con ragione

justification [dʒʌstɪfɪ'keɪʃən] n giustificazione f; (Typ) giustezza

justify ['dʒʌstɪfaɪ] vt giustificare; (Typ etc) allineare, giustificare; **to be justified in doing sth** avere ragione di fare qc

justly ['dʒʌstlɪ] adv giustamente

justness ['dʒʌstnɪs] n giustezza

jut [dʒʌt] vi (also: **jut out**) sporgersi

jute [dʒuːt] n iuta

juvenile ['dʒuːvənaɪl] adj giovane, giovanile; (court) dei minorenni; (books) per ragazzi ▪ n giovane m/f, minorenne m/f

juvenile delinquency n delinquenza minorile

juvenile delinquent n delinquente m/f minorenne

juxtapose ['dʒʌkstəpəuz] vt giustapporre

juxtaposition [dʒʌkstəpə'zɪʃən] n giustapposizione f

Kk

K, k [keɪ] n (letter) K, k f or m inv; **K for King** ≈ K come Kursaal

K n abbr (= one thousand) mille ■ abbr (Brit: = Knight) titolo; (= kilobyte) K

kaftan ['kæftæn] n caffettano

Kalahari Desert [kælə'hɑːrɪ-] n Deserto di Calahari

kale [keɪl] n cavolo verde

kaleidoscope [kə'laɪdəskəup] n caleidoscopio

kamikaze [kæmɪ'kɑːzɪ] adj da kamikaze

Kampala [kæm'pɑːlə] n Kampala f

Kampuchea [kæmpu'tʃɪə] n Kampuchea f

kangaroo [kæŋgə'ruː] n canguro

Kans. abbr (US) = **Kansas**

kaput [kə'put] adj (col) kaputt inv

karaoke [kɑːrə'əukɪ] n karaoke m inv

karate [kə'rɑːtɪ] n karate m

Kashmir [kæʃ'mɪəʳ] n Kashmir m

Kazakhstan [kæzæk'stɑːn] n Kazakistan m

KC n abbr (Brit Law: = King's Counsel) avvocato della Corona; see also **QC**

kebab [kə'bæb] n spiedino

keel [kiːl] n chiglia; **on an even ~** (fig) in uno stato normale
▶ **keel over** vi (Naut) capovolgersi; (person) crollare

keen [kiːn] adj (interest, desire) vivo(-a); (eye, intelligence) acuto(-a); (competition) serrato(-a); (edge) affilato(-a); (eager) entusiasta; **to be ~ to do** or **on doing sth** avere una gran voglia di fare qc; **to be ~ on sth** essere appassionato(-a) di qc; **to be ~ on sb** avere un debole per qn; **I'm not ~ on going** non mi va di andare

keenly ['kiːnlɪ] adv (enthusiastically) con entusiasmo; (acutely) vivamente; in modo penetrante

keenness ['kiːnnɪs] n (eagerness) entusiasmo

keep [kiːp] vb (pt, pp kept) [kɛpt] vt tenere; (hold back) trattenere; (feed: one's family etc) mantenere, sostentare; (a promise) mantenere; (chickens, bees, pigs etc) allevare ■ vi (food) mantenersi; (remain: in a certain state or place) restare ■ n (of castle) maschio; (food etc): **enough for his ~** abbastanza per vitto e alloggio; **to ~ doing sth** continuare a fare qc; fare qc di continuo; **to ~ sb from doing/ sth from happening** impedire a qn di fare/ che qc succeda; **to ~ sb busy/a place tidy** tenere qn occupato(-a)/un luogo in ordine; **to ~ sb waiting** far aspettare qn; **to ~ an appointment** andare ad un appuntamento; **to ~ a record** or **note of sth** prendere nota di qc; **to ~ sth to o.s.** tenere qc per sé; **to ~ sth (back) from sb** celare qc a qn; **to ~ time** (clock) andar bene; **~ the change** tenga il resto; see also **keeps**

▶ **keep away** vt: **to ~ sth/sb away from sb** tenere qc/qn lontano da qn ■ vi: **to ~ away (from)** stare lontano (da)

▶ **keep back** vt (crowds, tears, money) trattenere ■ vi tenersi indietro

▶ **keep down** vt (control: prices, spending) contenere, ridurre; (retain: food) trattenere, ritenere ■ vi tenersi giù, stare giù

▶ **keep in** vt (invalid, child) tenere a casa; (Scol) trattenere a scuola ■ vi (col): **to ~ in with sb** tenersi buono qn

▶ **keep off** vt (dog, person) tenere lontano da ■ vi stare alla larga; **~ your hands off!** non toccare!, giù le mani!; **"~ off the grass"** "non calpestare l'erba"

▶ **keep on** vi continuare; **to ~ on doing** continuare a fare

▶ **keep out** vt tener fuori ■ vi restare fuori; **"~ out"** "vietato l'accesso"

▶ **keep up** vi mantenersi ■ vt continuare, mantenere; **to ~ up with** tener dietro a, andare di pari passo con; (work etc) farcela a seguire; **to ~ up with sb** (in race etc) mantenersi al passo con qn

keeper ['kiːpəʳ] n custode m/f, guardiano(-a)

keep-fit [kiːp'fɪt] n ginnastica

keeping ['kiːpɪŋ] n (care) custodia; **in ~ with** in armonia con; in accordo con

keeps [ki:ps] n: **for ~** (col) per sempre
keepsake ['ki:pseɪk] n ricordo
keg [kɛg] n barilotto
Ken. abbr (US) = **Kentucky**
kennel ['kɛnl] n canile m
Kenya ['kɛnjə] n Kenia m
Kenyan ['kɛnjən] adj, n Keniano(-a), Keniota (m/f)
kept [kɛpt] pt, pp of **keep**
kerb [kə:b] n (Brit) orlo del marciapiede
kerb crawler [-'krɔːləʳ] n chi va in macchina in cerca di una prostituta
kernel ['kə:nl] n nocciolo
kerosene ['kɛrəsi:n] n cherosene m
ketchup ['kɛtʃəp] n ketchup m inv
kettle ['kɛtl] n bollitore m
kettle drum n timpano
key [ki:] n (gen, Mus) chiave f; (of piano, typewriter) tasto; (on map) leg(g)enda ▪ cpd (vital: position, industry etc) chiave inv
  ▶ **key in** vt (text) introdurre da tastiera
keyboard ['ki:bɔːd] n tastiera ▪ vt (text) comporre su tastiera
keyboarder ['ki:bɔːdəʳ] n dattilografo(-a)
keyed up [ki:d ʌp] adj: **to be ~** essere agitato(-a)
keyhole ['ki:həʊl] n buco della serratura
keyhole surgery n chirurgia mininvasiva
keynote ['ki:nəʊt] n (Mus) tonica; (fig) nota dominante
keypad ['ki:pæd] n tastierino numerico
key ring n portachiavi m inv
keystroke ['ki:strəʊk] n battuta (di un tasto)
kg abbr (= kilogram) Kg
KGB n abbr KGB m
khaki ['kɑːkɪ] adj, n cachi (m)
kibbutz [kɪ'buts] n kibbutz m inv
kick [kɪk] vt calciare, dare calci a ▪ vi (horse) tirar calci ▪ n calcio; (of rifle) contraccolpo; (thrill): **he does it for kicks** lo fa giusto per il piacere di farlo
  ▶ **kick around** vi (col) essere in giro
  ▶ **kick off** vi (Sport) dare il primo calcio
kick-off ['kɪkɔf] n (Sport) calcio d'inizio
kick-start ['kɪkstɑːt] n (also: **kick-starter**) pedale m d'avviamento
kid [kɪd] n ragazzino(-a); (animal, leather) capretto ▪ vi (col) scherzare ▪ vt (col) prendere in giro
kid gloves npl: **to treat sb with ~** trattare qn coi guanti
kidnap ['kɪdnæp] vt rapire, sequestrare
kidnapper ['kɪdnæpəʳ] n rapitore(-trice)
kidnapping ['kɪdnæpɪŋ] n sequestro (di persona)
kidney ['kɪdnɪ] n (Anat) rene m; (Culin) rognone m

kidney bean n fagiolo borlotto
kidney machine n rene m artificiale
Kilimanjaro [kɪlɪmən'dʒɑːrəʊ] n: **Mount ~** il monte Kilimangiaro
kill [kɪl] vt uccidere, ammazzare; (fig) sopprimere; sopraffare; ammazzare ▪ n uccisione f; **to ~ time** ammazzare il tempo
  ▶ **kill off** vt sterminare; (fig) eliminare, soffocare
killer ['kɪləʳ] n uccisore m, killer m inv; assassino(-a)
killer instinct n: **to have a/the ~** essere spietato(-a)
killing ['kɪlɪŋ] n assassinio; (massacre) strage f; (col): **to make a ~** fare un bel colpo
kill-joy ['kɪldʒɔɪ] n guastafeste m/f inv
kiln [kɪln] n forno
kilo ['ki:ləʊ] n abbr (= kilogram) chilo
kilobyte ['kɪləbaɪt] n kilobyte m inv
kilogram, kilogramme ['kɪləʊgræm] n chilogrammo
kilometre, (US) **kilometer** ['kɪləmi:təʳ] n chilometro
kilowatt ['kɪləʊwɔt] n chilowatt m inv
kilt [kɪlt] n gonnellino scozzese
kilter ['kɪltəʳ] n: **out of ~** fuori fase
kimono [kɪ'məʊnəʊ] n chimono
kin [kɪn] n see **next of kin**; **kith**
kind [kaɪnd] adj gentile, buono(-a) ▪ n sorta, specie f; (species) genere m; **to be two of a ~** essere molto simili; **would you be ~ enough to ...?, would you be so ~ as to ...?** sarebbe così gentile da ...?; **it's very ~ of you (to do)** è molto gentile da parte sua (di fare); **in ~** (Comm) in natura; (fig): **to repay sb in ~** ripagare qn della stessa moneta
kindergarten ['kɪndəgɑ:tn] n giardino d'infanzia
kind-hearted [kaɪnd'hɑ:tɪd] adj di buon cuore
kindle ['kɪndl] vt accendere, infiammare
kindling ['kɪndlɪŋ] n frasche fpl, ramoscelli mpl
kindly ['kaɪndlɪ] adj pieno(-a) di bontà, benevolo(-a) ▪ adv con bontà, gentilmente; **will you ~ ...** vuole ... per favore; **he didn't take it ~** se l'è presa a male
kindness ['kaɪndnɪs] n bontà, gentilezza
kindred ['kɪndrɪd] adj imparentato(-a); **~ spirit** spirito affine
kinetic [kɪ'nɛtɪk] adj cinetico(-a)
king [kɪŋ] n re m inv
kingdom ['kɪŋdəm] n regno, reame m
kingfisher ['kɪŋfɪʃəʳ] n martin m inv pescatore
kingpin ['kɪŋpɪn] n (Tech, fig) perno
king-size ['kɪŋsaɪz], **king-sized** ['kɪŋsaɪzd] adj super inv; gigante; (cigarette) extra lungo(-a)

kink [kɪŋk] n (of rope) attorcigliamento; (in hair) ondina; (fig) aberrazione f

kinky ['kɪŋkɪ] adj (fig) eccentrico(-a); dai gusti particolari

kinship ['kɪnʃɪp] n parentela

kinsman ['kɪnzmən] n parente m

kinswoman ['kɪnzwumən] n parente f

kiosk ['kiːɔsk] n edicola, chiosco; (Brit: also: **telephone kiosk**) cabina (telefonica); (: also: **newspaper kiosk**) edicola

kipper ['kɪpəʳ] n aringa affumicata

Kirghizia [kəːˈgɪzɪə] n Kirghizistan

kiss [kɪs] n bacio ■ vt baciare; **to ~ (each other)** baciarsi; **to ~ sb goodbye** congedarsi da qn con un bacio; **~ of life** (Brit) respirazione f bocca a bocca

kissagram ['kɪsəgræm] n servizio di recapito a domicilio di messaggi e baci augurali

kit [kɪt] n equipaggiamento, corredo; (set of tools etc) attrezzi mpl; (for assembly) scatola di montaggio; **tool ~** cassetta or borsa degli attrezzi

▶ **kit out** vt (Brit) attrezzare, equipaggiare

kitbag ['kɪtbæg] n zaino; sacco militare

kitchen ['kɪtʃɪn] n cucina

kitchen garden n orto

kitchen sink n acquaio

kitchen unit n (Brit) elemento da cucina

kitchenware ['kɪtʃɪnwɛəʳ] n stoviglie fpl; utensili mpl da cucina

kite [kaɪt] n (toy) aquilone m; (Zool) nibbio

kith [kɪθ] n: **~ and kin** amici e parenti mpl

kitten ['kɪtn] n gattino(-a), micino(-a)

kitty ['kɪtɪ] n (money) fondo comune

kiwi fruit ['kiːwiː-] n kiwi m inv

KKK n abbr (US) = **Ku Klux Klan**

Kleenex® ['kliːnɛks] n fazzolettino di carta

kleptomaniac [klɛptəuˈmeɪnɪæk] n cleptomane m/f

km abbr (= kilometre) km

km/h abbr (= kilometres per hour) km/h

knack [næk] n: **to have a ~ (for doing)** avere una pratica (per fare); **to have the ~ of** avere l'abilità di; **there's a ~ to doing this** c'è un trucco per fare questo

knackered ['nækəd] adj (col) fuso(-a)

knapsack ['næpsæk] n zaino, sacco da montagna

knave [neɪv] n (Cards) fante m

knead [niːd] vt impastare

knee [niː] n ginocchio

kneecap ['niːkæp] n rotula ■ vt gambizzare

knee-deep ['niːdiːp] adj: **the water was ~** l'acqua ci arrivava alle ginocchia

kneel [niːl] vi (pt, pp **knelt**) [nɛlt] inginocchiarsi

kneepad ['niːpæd] n ginocchiera

knell [nɛl] n rintocco

knelt [nɛlt] pt, pp of **kneel**

knew [njuː] pt of **know**

knickers ['nɪkəz] npl (Brit) mutandine fpl

knick-knack ['nɪknæk] n ninnolo

knife [naɪf] n (pl **knives**) coltello ■ vt accoltellare, dare una coltellata a; **~, fork and spoon** coperto

knife edge n: **to be on a ~** (fig) essere appeso(-a) a un filo

knight [naɪt] n cavaliere m; (Chess) cavallo

knighthood ['naɪthud] n cavalleria; (title): **to get a ~** essere fatto cavaliere

knit [nɪt] vt fare a maglia; (fig): **to ~ together** unire ■ vi lavorare a maglia; (broken bones) saldarsi

knitted ['nɪtɪd] adj lavorato(-a) a maglia

knitting ['nɪtɪŋ] n lavoro a maglia

knitting machine n macchina per maglieria

knitting needle n ferro (da calza)

knitting pattern n modello (per maglia)

knitwear ['nɪtwɛəʳ] n maglieria

knives [naɪvz] npl of **knife**

knob [nɔb] n bottone m; manopola; (Brit): **a ~ of butter** una noce di burro

knobbly ['nɔblɪ], (US) **knobby** ['nɔbɪ] adj (wood, surface) nodoso(-a); (knee) ossuto(-a)

knock [nɔk] vt (strike) colpire; urtare; (fig: col) criticare ■ vi (engine) battere; (at door etc): **to ~ at/on** bussare a ■ n bussata; colpo, botta; **he knocked at the door** ha bussato alla porta; **to ~ a nail into sth** conficcare un chiodo in qc

▶ **knock down** vt abbattere; (pedestrian) investire; (price) abbassare

▶ **knock off** vi (col: finish) smettere (di lavorare) ■ vt (strike off) far cadere; (col: steal) sgraffignare, grattare; **to ~ off £10** fare uno sconto di 10 sterline

▶ **knock out** vt stendere; (Boxing) mettere K.O., mettere fuori combattimento

▶ **knock over** vt (object) far cadere; (pedestrian) investire

knockdown ['nɔkdaun] adj (price) fortemente scontato(-a)

knocker ['nɔkəʳ] n (on door) battente m

knocking ['nɔkɪŋ] n colpi mpl

knock-kneed [nɔkˈniːd] adj che ha le gambe ad x

knockout ['nɔkaut] n (Boxing) knock out m inv

knockout competition n (Brit) gara ad eliminazione

knock-up ['nɔkʌp] n (Tennis etc) palleggio; **to have a ~** palleggiare

knot [nɔt] n nodo ■ vt annodare; **to tie a ~** fare un nodo

knotty ['nɔtɪ] adj (fig) spinoso(-a)

k

know [nəu] vt (pt **knew**, pp **known**) [nju:,
nəun] sapere; (person, author, place) conoscere
■ vi sapere; **to ~ that ...** sapere che ...;
to ~ how to do sapere fare; **to get to ~ sth**
venire a sapere qc; **I ~ nothing about it** non
ne so niente; **I don't ~ him** non lo conosco;
to ~ right from wrong distinguere il bene
dal male; **as far as I ~ ...** che io sappia ...,
per quanto io ne sappia ...; **yes, I ~** sì, lo so;
I don't ~ non lo so
know-all ['nəuɔ:l] n (Brit pej) sapientone(-a)
know-how ['nəuhau] n tecnica; pratica
knowing ['nəuɪŋ] adj (look etc) d'intesa
knowingly ['nəuɪŋlɪ] adv consapevolmente;
di complicità
know-it-all ['nəuɪtɔ:l] n (US) = **know-all**
knowledge ['nɔlɪdʒ] n consapevolezza;
(learning) conoscenza, sapere m; **to have no ~
of** ignorare, non sapere; **not to my ~** che io
sappia, no; **to have a working ~ of Italian**
avere una conoscenza pratica dell'italiano;
without my ~ a mia insaputa; **it is
common ~ that ...** è risaputo che ...; **it has
come to my ~ that ...** sono venuto a sapere
che ...
knowledgeable ['nɔlɪdʒəbl] adj ben
informato(-a)
known [nəun] pp of **know** ■ adj (thief, facts)

noto(-a); (expert) riconosciuto(-a)
knuckle ['nʌkl] n nocca
▶ **knuckle down** vi (col): **to ~ down to some
hard work** mettersi sotto a lavorare
▶ **knuckle under** vi (col) cedere
knuckleduster ['nʌkldʌstəʳ] n tirapugni m inv
KO abbr (= knock out) ■ n K.O. m ■ vt mettere
K.O.
koala [kəu'ɑ:lə] n (also: **koala bear**) koala m inv
kook [ku:k] n (US col) svitato(-a)
Koran [kɔ'rɑ:n] n Corano
Korea [kə'rɪə] n Corea; **North/South ~** Corea
del Nord/Sud
Korean [kə'rɪən] adj, n coreano(-a)
kosher ['kəuʃəʳ] adj kasher inv
kowtow ['kau'tau] vi: **to ~ to sb** mostrarsi
ossequioso(-a) verso qn
Kremlin ['krɛmlɪn] n: **the ~** il Cremlino
KS abbr (US) = **Kansas**
Kt abbr (Brit: = Knight) titolo
Kuala Lumpur ['kwɑ:lə'lumpuəʳ] n Kuala
Lumpur f
kudos ['kju:dɔs] n gloria, fama
Kurd [kə:d] n curdo(-a)
Kuwait [ku'weɪt] n Kuwait m
Kuwaiti [ku'weɪtɪ] adj, n kuwaitiano(-a)
kW abbr (= kilowatt) kw
KY, Ky. abbr (US) = **Kentucky**

LI

L, I [ɛl] n (letter) L, l f or m inv; **L for Lucy**, (US) **L for Love** = L come Livorno
L abbr (= lake) l; (= large) taglia grande; (= left) sin.; (Brit Aut) = **learner**
l abbr (= litre) l
LA n abbr (US) = **Los Angeles** ■ abbr (US) = **Louisiana**
La. abbr (US) = **Louisiana**
lab [læb] n abbr (= laboratory) laboratorio
Lab. abbr (Canada) = **Labrador**
label ['leɪbl] n etichetta, cartellino; (brand: of record) casa ■ vt etichettare; classificare
labor etc ['leɪbər] (US) = **labour** etc
laboratory [lə'bɔrətərɪ] n laboratorio
Labor Day n (US) festa del lavoro; vedi nota

<hr>

● LABOR DAY

●
● Negli Stati Uniti e nel Canada il Labor Day,
● la festa del lavoro, cade il primo lunedì di
● settembre, contrariamente a quanto
● accade nella maggior parte dei paesi
● europei dove tale celebrazione ha luogo
● il primo maggio.

<hr>

laborious [lə'bɔ:rɪəs] adj laborioso(-a)
labor union n (US) sindacato
Labour ['leɪbər] n (Brit Pol: also: **the Labour Party**) il partito laburista, i laburisti
labour, (US) **labor** ['leɪbər] n (task) lavoro; (workmen) manodopera; (Med) travaglio del parto, doglie fpl ■ vi: **to ~ (at)** lavorare duro(a); **to be in ~** (Med) avere le doglie
labour camp, (US) **labor camp** n campo dei lavori forzati
labour cost, (US) **labor cost** n costo del lavoro
labour dispute, (US) **labor dispute** n conflitto tra lavoratori e datori di lavoro
laboured, (US) **labored** ['leɪbəd] adj (breathing) affaticato(-a), affannoso(-a); (style) elaborato(-a), pesante
labourer, (US) **laborer** ['leɪbərər] n manovale m; (on farm) lavoratore m agricolo

labour force, (US) **labor force** n manodopera
labour-intensive, (US) **labor-intensive** [leɪbərɪn'tɛnsɪv] adj che assorbe molta manodopera
labour market, (US) **labor market** n mercato del lavoro
labour pains, (US) **labor pains** npl doglie fpl
labour relations, (US) **labor relations** npl relazioni fpl industriali
labour-saving, (US) **labor-saving** ['leɪbə-seɪvɪŋ] adj che fa risparmiare fatica or lavoro
labour unrest, (US) **labor unrest** n agitazioni fpl degli operai
labyrinth ['læbɪrɪnθ] n labirinto
lace [leɪs] n merletto, pizzo; (of shoe etc) laccio ■ vt (shoe) allacciare; (drink: fortify with spirits) correggere
lacemaking ['leɪsmeɪkɪŋ] n fabbricazione f dei pizzi or dei merletti
laceration [læsə'reɪʃən] n lacerazione f
lace-up ['leɪsʌp] adj (shoes etc) con i lacci, con le stringhe
lack [læk] n mancanza, scarsità ■ vt mancare di; **through** or **for ~ of** per mancanza di; **to be lacking** mancare; **to be lacking in** mancare di
lackadaisical [lækə'deɪzɪkl] adj disinteressato(-a), noncurante
lackey ['lækɪ] n (also fig) lacchè m inv
lacklustre, (US) **lackluster** ['læklʌstər] adj (surface) opaco(-a); (style) scialbo(-a); (eyes) spento(-a)
laconic [lə'kɔnɪk] adj laconico(-a)
lacquer ['lækər] n lacca; **hair ~** lacca per (i) capelli
lacy ['leɪsɪ] adj (like lace) che sembra un pizzo
lad [læd] n ragazzo, giovanotto; (Brit: in stable etc) mozzo or garzone m di stalla
ladder ['lædər] n scala; (Brit: in tights) smagliatura ■ vt smagliare ■ vi smagliarsi
laden ['leɪdn] adj: **~ (with)** carico(-a) or caricato(-a) (di); **fully ~** (truck, ship) a pieno carico

ladle ['leɪdl] n mestolo
lady ['leɪdɪ] n signora; **L~ Smith** lady Smith; **the ladies' (toilets)** i gabinetti per signore; **a ~ doctor** una dottoressa
ladybird ['leɪdɪbəːd], (US) **ladybug** ['leɪdɪbʌg] n coccinella
lady-in-waiting ['leɪdɪɪn'weɪtɪŋ] n dama di compagnia
ladykiller ['leɪdɪkɪləʳ] n dongiovanni m inv
ladylike ['leɪdɪlaɪk] adj da signora, distinto(-a)
ladyship ['leɪdɪʃɪp] n: **your L~** signora contessa etc
lag [læg] n = **time lag** ■ vi (also: **lag behind**) trascinarsi ■ vt (pipes) rivestire di materiale isolante
lager ['lɑːgəʳ] n lager m inv
lager lout n (Brit col) giovinastro ubriaco
lagging ['lægɪŋ] n rivestimento di materiale isolante
lagoon [lə'guːn] n laguna
Lagos ['leɪgɔs] n Lagos f
laid [leɪd] pt, pp of **lay**
laid-back [leɪd'bæk] adj (col) rilassato(-a)
lain [leɪn] pp of **lie**
lair [lɛəʳ] n covo, tana
laissez-faire [lɛseɪ'fɛəʳ] n liberismo
laity ['leɪətɪ] n laici mpl
lake [leɪk] n lago
Lake District n: **the ~** (Brit) la regione dei laghi
lamb [læm] n agnello
lamb chop n cotoletta d'agnello
lambskin ['læmskɪn] n (pelle f d')agnello
lambswool ['læmzwul] n lamb's wool m
lame [leɪm] adj zoppo(-a); **~ duck** (fig: person) persona inetta; (: firm) azienda traballante
lamely ['leɪmlɪ] adv (fig) in modo poco convincente
lament [lə'mɛnt] n lamento ■ vt lamentare, piangere
lamentable ['læməntəbl] adj doloroso(-a); deplorevole
laminated ['læmɪneɪtɪd] adj laminato(-a)
lamp [læmp] n lampada
lamplight ['læmplaɪt] n: **by ~** a lume della lampada
lampoon [læm'puːn] n satira
lamppost ['læmppəust] n lampione m
lampshade ['læmpʃeɪd] n paralume m
lance [lɑːns] n lancia ■ vt (Med) incidere
lance corporal n (Brit) caporale m
lancet ['lɑːnsɪt] n (Med) bisturi m inv
Lancs [læŋks] abbr (Brit) = **Lancashire**
land [lænd] n (as opposed to sea) terra (ferma); (country) paese m; (soil) terreno; (estate) terreni mpl, terre fpl ■ vi (from ship) sbarcare; (Aviat) atterrare; (fig: fall) cadere ■ vt (obtain)

acchiappare; (passengers) sbarcare; (goods) scaricare; **to go/travel by ~** andare/viaggiare per via di terra; **to own ~** possedere dei terreni, avere delle proprietà (terriere); **to ~ on one's feet** cadere in piedi; (fig: to be lucky) cascar bene
▶**land up** vi andare a finire
landed gentry ['lændɪd-] n proprietari mpl terrieri
landfill site ['lændfɪl-] n discarica dove i rifiuti vengono sepolti
landing ['lændɪŋ] n (from ship) sbarco; (Aviat) atterraggio; (of staircase) pianerottolo
landing card n carta di sbarco
landing craft n mezzo da sbarco
landing gear n (Aviat) carrello d'atterraggio
landing stage n pontile m da sbarco
landing strip n pista d'atterraggio
landlady ['lændleɪdɪ] n padrona or proprietaria di casa
landlocked ['lændlɔkt] adj senza sbocco sul mare
landlord ['lændlɔːd] n padrone m or proprietario di casa; (of pub etc) oste m
landlubber ['lændlʌbəʳ] n marinaio d'acqua dolce
landmark ['lændmɑːk] n punto di riferimento; (fig) pietra miliare
landowner ['lændəunəʳ] n proprietario(-a) terriero(-a)
landscape ['lænskeɪp] n paesaggio
landscape architect, landscape gardener n paesaggista m/f
landscape painting n (Art) paesaggistica
landslide ['lændslaɪd] n (Geo) frana; (fig: Pol) valanga
lane [leɪn] n (in country) viottolo; (in town) stradetta; (Aut, in race) corsia; **shipping ~** rotta (marittima)
language ['læŋgwɪdʒ] n lingua; (way one speaks) linguaggio; **bad ~** linguaggio volgare
language laboratory n laboratorio linguistico
language school n scuola di lingue
languid ['læŋgwɪd] adj languente, languido(-a)
languish ['læŋgwɪʃ] vi languire
lank [læŋk] adj (hair) liscio(-a) e opaco(-a)
lanky ['læŋkɪ] adj allampanato(-a)
lanolin, lanoline ['lænəlɪn] n lanolina
lantern ['læntn] n lanterna
Laos [lauz] n Laos m
lap [læp] n (of track) giro; (of body): **in** or **on one's ~** in grembo ■ vt (also: **lap up**) papparsi, leccare ■ vi (waves) sciabordare
▶**lap up** vt (fig: compliments, attention) bearsi di
La Paz [læ'pæz] n La Paz f

lapdog ['læpdɔg] *n* cane *m* da grembo
lapel [lə'pɛl] *n* risvolto
Lapland ['læplænd] *n* Lapponia
Lapp [læp] *adj* lappone ■ *n* lappone *m/f*; (*Ling*) lappone *m*
lapse [læps] *n* lapsus *m inv*; (*longer*) caduta; (*fault*) mancanza; (*in behaviour*) scorrettezza ■ *vi* (*law, act*) cadere; (*ticket, passport*) scadere; **to ~ into bad habits** pigliare cattive abitudini; **~ of time** spazio di tempo; **a ~ of memory** un vuoto di memoria
laptop ['læptɔp] *n* (*also:* **laptop computer**) laptop *m inv*
larceny ['lɑːsənɪ] *n* furto
lard [lɑːd] *n* lardo
larder ['lɑːdəʳ] *n* dispensa
large [lɑːdʒ] *adj* grande; (*person, animal*) grosso(-a) ■ *adv*: **by and ~** generalmente; **at ~** (*free*) in libertà; (*generally*) in generale; nell'insieme; **to make larger** ingrandire; **a ~ number of people** molta gente; **on a ~ scale** su vasta scala
largely ['lɑːdʒlɪ] *adv* in gran parte
large-scale ['lɑːdʒ'skeɪl] *adj* (*map, drawing etc*) in grande scala; (*reforms, business activities*) su vasta scala
lark [lɑːk] *n* (*bird*) allodola; (*joke*) scherzo, gioco
▶ **lark about** *vi* fare lo stupido
larva (*pl* **larvae**) ['lɑːvə, -iː] *n* larva
laryngitis [lærɪn'dʒaɪtɪs] *n* laringite *f*
larynx ['lærɪŋks] *n* laringe *f*
lasagne [lə'zænjə] *n* lasagne *fpl*
lascivious [lə'sɪvɪəs] *adj* lascivo(-a)
laser ['leɪzəʳ] *n* laser *m*
laser beam *n* raggio *m* laser *inv*
laser printer *n* stampante *f* laser *inv*
lash [læʃ] *n* frustata; (*also:* **eyelash**) ciglio ■ *vt* frustare; (*tie*) legare
▶ **lash down** *vt* assicurare (con corde) ■ *vi* (*rain*) scrosciare
▶ **lash out** *vi*: **to ~ out (at** *or* **against sb/sth)** attaccare violentemente (qn/qc); **to ~ out (on sth)** (*col: spend*) spendere un sacco di soldi (per qc)
lashing ['læʃɪŋ] *n* (*beating*) frustata, sferzata; **lashings of** (*Brit col*) un mucchio di, una montagna di
lass [læs] *n* ragazza
lasso [læ'suː] *n* laccio ■ *vt* acchiappare con il laccio
last [lɑːst] *adj* ultimo(-a); (*week, month, year*) scorso(-a), passato(-a) ■ *adv* per ultimo ■ *vi* durare; **~ week** la settimana scorsa; **~ night** ieri sera, la notte scorsa; **at ~** finalmente, alla fine; **~ but one** penultimo(-a); **the ~ time** l'ultima volta; **it lasts (for) 2 hours** dura 2 ore

last-ditch ['lɑːst'dɪtʃ] *adj* ultimo(-a) e disperato(-a)
lasting ['lɑːstɪŋ] *adj* durevole
lastly ['lɑːstlɪ] *adv* infine, per finire, per ultimo
last-minute ['lɑːstmɪnɪt] *adj* fatto(-a) (*or* preso(-a) *etc*) all'ultimo momento
latch [lætʃ] *n* serratura a scatto
▶ **latch on to** *vt fus* (*cling to: person*) attaccarsi a, appiccicarsi a; (: *idea*) afferrare, capire
latchkey ['lætʃkiː] *n* chiave *f* di casa
late [leɪt] *adj* (*not on time*) in ritardo; (*far on in day etc*) tardi *inv*; tardo(-a); (*recent*) recente, ultimo(-a); (*former*) ex; (*dead*) defunto(-a) ■ *adv* tardi; (*behind time, schedule*) in ritardo; **to be (10 minutes) ~** essere in ritardo (di 10 minuti); **to work ~** lavorare fino a tardi; **~ in life** in età avanzata; **of ~** di recente; **in the ~ afternoon** nel tardo pomeriggio; **in ~ May** verso la fine di maggio; **the ~ Mr X** il defunto Signor X
latecomer ['leɪtkʌməʳ] *n* ritardatario(-a)
lately ['leɪtlɪ] *adv* recentemente
lateness ['leɪtnɪs] *n* (*of person*) ritardo; (*of event*) tardezza, ora tarda
latent ['leɪtnt] *adj* latente; **~ defect** vizio occulto
later ['leɪtəʳ] *adj* (*date etc*) posteriore; (*version etc*) successivo(-a) ■ *adv* più tardi; **~ on today** oggi più tardi
lateral ['lætərl] *adj* laterale
latest ['leɪtɪst] *adj* ultimo(-a), più recente; **at the ~** al più tardi; **the ~ news** le ultime notizie
latex ['leɪtɛks] *n* latice *m*
lath [læθ] *n* (*pl* **laths**) [læðz] assicella
lathe [leɪð] *n* tornio
lather ['lɑːðəʳ] *n* schiuma di sapone ■ *vt* insaponare ■ *vi* far schiuma
Latin ['lætɪn] *n* latino ■ *adj* latino(-a)
Latin America *n* America Latina
Latin American *adj* sudamericano(-a)
latitude ['lætɪtjuːd] *n* latitudine *f*; (*fig: freedom*) libertà d'azione
latrine [lə'triːn] *n* latrina
latter ['lætəʳ] *adj* secondo(-a); più recente ■ *n*: **the ~** quest'ultimo, il secondo
latterly ['lætəlɪ] *adv* recentemente, negli ultimi tempi
lattice ['lætɪs] *n* traliccio; graticolato
lattice window *n* finestra con vetrata a losanghe
Latvia ['lætvɪə] *n* Lettonia
Latvian ['lætvɪən] *adj* lettone *inv* ■ *n* lettone *m/f*; (*Ling*) lettone *m*
laudable ['lɔːdəbl] *adj* lodevole
laudatory ['lɔːdətrɪ] *adj* elogiativo(-a)

laugh [lɑːf] n risata ■ vi ridere
  ▶ **laugh at** vt fus (misfortune etc) ridere di;
  I laughed at his joke la sua barzelletta mi
  fece ridere
  ▶ **laugh off** vt prendere alla leggera
laughable ['lɑːfəbl] adj ridicolo(-a)
laughing ['lɑːfɪŋ] adj (face) ridente; **this is no
  ~ matter** non è una cosa da ridere
laughing gas n gas m esilarante
laughing stock n: **the ~ of** lo zimbello di
laughter ['lɑːftər] n riso; risate fpl
launch [lɔːntʃ] n (of rocket, product etc) lancio;
  (of new ship) varo; (boat) scialuppa; (also:
  motor launch) lancia ■ vt (rocket, product)
  lanciare; (ship, plan) varare
  ▶ **launch out** vi: **to ~ out (into)** lanciarsi (in)
launching ['lɔːntʃɪŋ] n lancio; varo
launch pad, launching pad n rampa di
  lancio
launder ['lɔːndər] vt lavare e stirare
Launderette® [lɔːn'drɛt], (US)
  Laundromat® ['lɔːndrəmæt] n lavanderia
  (automatica)
laundry ['lɔːndrɪ] n lavanderia; (clothes)
  biancheria; **to do the ~** fare il bucato
laureate ['lɔːrɪət] adj see **poet laureate**
laurel ['lɔrl] n lauro, alloro; **to rest on one's
  laurels** riposare or dormire sugli allori
Lausanne [ləu'zæn] n Losanna
lava ['lɑːvə] n lava
lavatory ['lævətərɪ] n gabinetto
lavatory paper n (Brit) carta igienica
lavender ['lævəndər] n lavanda
lavish ['lævɪʃ] adj abbondante; sontuoso(-a);
  (giving freely): **~ with** prodigo(-a) di, largo(-a)
  in ■ vt: **to ~ sth on sb/sth** profondere qc a
  qn/qc
lavishly ['lævɪʃlɪ] adv (give, spend)
  generosamente; (furnished) sontuosamente,
  lussuosamente
law [lɔː] n legge f; **against the ~** contro la
  legge; **to study ~** studiare diritto; **to go to ~**
  (Brit) ricorrere alle vie legali; **civil/criminal
  ~** diritto civile/penale
law-abiding ['lɔːəbaɪdɪŋ] adj ubbidiente alla
  legge
law and order n l'ordine m pubblico
lawbreaker ['lɔːbreɪkər] n violatore(-trice)
  della legge
law court n tribunale m, corte f di giustizia
lawful ['lɔːful] adj legale
lawfully ['lɔːfəlɪ] adv legalmente
lawless ['lɔːlɪs] adj senza legge; illegale
Law Lords npl ≈ Corte f Suprema
lawmaker ['lɔːmeɪkər] n legislatore m
lawn [lɔːn] n tappeto erboso
lawnmower ['lɔːnməuər] n tosaerba m or f inv

lawn tennis n tennis m su prato
law school n facoltà f inv di legge
law student n studente(-essa) di legge
lawsuit ['lɔːsuːt] n processo, causa; **to bring
  a ~ against** intentare causa a
lawyer ['lɔːjər] n (consultant, with company)
  giurista m/f; (for sales, wills etc) ≈ notaio;
  (partner, in court) ≈ avvocato(-essa)
lax [læks] adj (conduct) rilassato(-a); (person:
  careless) negligente; (: on discipline)
  permissivo(-a)
laxative ['læksətɪv] n lassativo
laxity ['læksɪtɪ] n rilassatezza; negligenza
lay [leɪ] pt of **lie** ■ adj laico(-a); secolare ■ vt
  (pt, pp **laid**) [leɪd] posare, mettere; (eggs) fare;
  (trap) tendere; (plans) fare, elaborare; **to ~ the
  table** apparecchiare la tavola; **to ~ the
  facts/one's proposals before sb** presentare
  i fatti/delle proposte a qn; **to get laid** (col!)
  scopare (!), essere scopato(-a) (!)
  ▶ **lay aside, lay by** vt mettere da parte
  ▶ **lay down** vt mettere giù; **to ~ down the
  law** (fig) dettar legge
  ▶ **lay in** vt fare una scorta di
  ▶ **lay into** vt fus (col: attack, scold) aggredire
  ▶ **lay off** vt (workers) licenziare
  ▶ **lay on** vt (water, gas) installare, mettere;
  (provide: meal etc) fornire; (paint) applicare
  ▶ **lay out** vt (design) progettare; (display)
  presentare; (spend) sborsare
  ▶ **lay up** vt (to store) accumulare; (ship)
  mettere in disarmo; (illness) costringere a
  letto
layabout ['leɪəbaut] n sfaccendato(-a),
  fannullone(-a)
lay-by ['leɪbaɪ] n (Brit) piazzola (di sosta)
lay days npl (Naut) stallie fpl
layer ['leɪər] n strato
layette ['leɪɛt] n corredino (per neonato)
layman ['leɪmən] n laico; profano
lay-off ['leɪɔf] n sospensione f, licenziamento
layout ['leɪaut] n lay-out m inv, disposizione f;
  (Press) impaginazione f
laze [leɪz] vi oziare
laziness ['leɪzɪnɪs] n pigrizia
lazy ['leɪzɪ] adj pigro(-a)
lb. abbr (= libra: pound) lb.
lbw abbr (Cricket: = leg before wicket) fallo dovuto al
  fatto che il giocatore ha la gamba davanti alla porta
LC n abbr (US) = **Library of Congress**
lc abbr (Typ) = **lower case**
L/C abbr = **letter of credit**
LCD n abbr = **liquid crystal display**
Ld abbr (Brit: = lord) titolo
LDS n abbr (Brit: = Licentiate in Dental Surgery)
  specializzazione dopo la laurea; (= Latter-day Saints)
  Chiesa di Gesù Cristo dei Santi dell'Ultimo Giorno

LEA n abbr (Brit: = local education authority)
≈ Provveditorato degli Studi

lead¹ [li:d] n (front position) posizione f di testa;
(distance, time ahead) vantaggio; (clue) indizio;
(Elec) filo (elettrico); (for dog) guinzaglio;
(Theat) parte f principale ■ vb (pt, pp **led**) [lɛd]
vt menare, guidare, condurre; (induce)
indurre; (be leader of) essere a capo di;
(: orchestra: Brit) essere il primo violino di;
(: US) dirigere; (Sport) essere in testa a ■ vi
condurre, essere in testa; **to be in the ~**
(Sport) essere in testa; **to take the ~** (Sport)
passare in testa; (fig) prendere l'iniziativa;
to ~ to menare a; condurre a; portare a; **to ~
astray** sviare; **to ~ sb to believe that ...** far
credere a qn che ...; **to ~ sb to do sth** portare
qn a fare qc
▶ **lead away** vt condurre via
▶ **lead back** vt riportare, ricondurre
▶ **lead off** vt portare ■ vi partire da
▶ **lead on** vt (tease) tenere sulla corda
▶ **lead on to** vt (induce) portare a
▶ **lead up to** vt fus portare a; (fig) preparare la
strada per

lead² [lɛd] (metal) piombo; (in pencil) mina

leaded ['lɛdɪd] adj (petrol) con piombo; **~
windows** vetrate fpl (artistiche)

leaden ['lɛdn] adj di piombo

leader ['li:dəʳ] n capo; leader m inv; (in
newspaper) articolo di fondo; **they are
leaders in their field** (fig) sono
all'avanguardia nel loro campo; **the L~ of
the House** (Brit) il capo della maggioranza
ministeriale

leadership ['li:dəʃɪp] n direzione f; **under
the ~ of ...** sotto la direzione or guida di ...;
qualities of ~ qualità fpl di un capo

lead-free ['lɛdfri:] adj senza piombo

leading ['li:dɪŋ] adj primo(-a), principale;
a ~ question una domanda tendenziosa;
~ role ruolo principale

leading lady n (Theat) prima attrice

leading light n (person) personaggio di primo
piano

leading man n (Theat) primo attore

lead pencil [lɛd-] n matita con la mina di
grafite

lead poisoning [lɛd-] n saturnismo

lead time [li:d-] n (Comm) tempo di consegna

lead weight [lɛd-] n piombino, piombo

leaf [li:f] n (pl **leaves**) foglia; (of table) ribalta;
to turn over a new ~ (fig) cambiar vita;
to take a ~ out of sb's book (fig) prendere
esempio da qn
▶ **leaf through** vt (book) sfogliare

leaflet ['li:flɪt] n dépliant m inv; (Pol, Rel)
volantino

leafy ['li:fɪ] adj ricco(-a) di foglie

league [li:g] n lega; (Football) campionato;
to be in ~ with essere in lega con

league table n classifica

leak [li:k] n (out) fuga; (in) infiltrazione f;
(fig: of information) fuga di notizie ■ vi (roof,
bucket) perdere; (liquid) uscire; (shoes) lasciar
passare l'acqua ■ vt (liquid) spandere;
(information) divulgare
▶ **leak out** vi uscire; (information) trapelare

leakage ['li:kɪdʒ] n (of water, gas etc) perdita

leaky ['li:kɪ] adj (pipe, bucket, roof) che perde;
(shoe) che lascia passare l'acqua; (boat) che fa
acqua

lean [li:n] adj magro(-a) ■ n (of meat) carne f
magra ■ vb (pt, pp **leaned** or **leant**) [lɛnt] vt:
to ~ sth on appoggiare qc su ■ vi (slope)
pendere; (rest): **to ~ against** appoggiarsi
contro; essere appoggiato(-a) a; **to ~ on**
appoggiarsi a
▶ **lean back** vi sporgersi indietro
▶ **lean forward** vi sporgersi in avanti
▶ **lean out** vi: **to ~ out (of)** sporgersi (da)
▶ **lean over** vi inclinarsi

leaning ['li:nɪŋ] n: **~ (towards)** propensione f
(per) ■ adj inclinato(-a), pendente; **the L~
Tower of Pisa** la torre (pendente) di Pisa

leant [lɛnt] pt, pp of **lean**

lean-to ['li:ntu:] n (roof) tettoia; (building)
edificio con tetto appoggiato ad altro edificio

leap [li:p] n salto, balzo ■ vi (pt, pp **leaped** or
leapt) [lɛpt] saltare, balzare; **to ~ at an offer**
afferrare al volo una proposta
▶ **leap up** vi (person) alzarsi d'un balzo,
balzare su

leapfrog ['li:pfrɒg] n gioco della cavallina
■ vi: **to ~ over sb/sth** saltare (alla cavallina)
qn/qc

leapt [lɛpt] pt, pp of **leap**

leap year n anno bisestile

learn (pt, pp **learned** or **learnt**) [lə:n, -t] vt, vi
imparare; **to ~ how to do sth** imparare a
fare qc; **to ~ that ...** apprendere che ...;
to ~ about sth (Scol) studiare qc; (hear)
apprendere qc; **we were sorry to ~ that it
was closing down** la notizia della chiusura
ci ha fatto dispiacere

learned ['lə:nɪd] adj erudito(-a), dotto(-a)

learner ['lə:nəʳ] n principiante m/f;
apprendista m/f; **he's a ~ (driver)** (Brit) sta
imparando a guidare

learning ['lə:nɪŋ] n erudizione f, sapienza

learnt [lə:nt] pt, pp of **learn**

lease [li:s] n contratto d'affitto ■ vt
affittare; **on ~** in affitto
▶ **lease back** vt effettuare un lease-back inv

leaseback ['li:sbæk] n lease-back m inv

leasehold ['li:shəuld] n (contract) contratto di affitto (a lungo termine con responsabilità simili a quelle di un proprietario) ■ adj in affitto

leash [li:ʃ] n guinzaglio

least [li:st] adj: **the ~** (+noun) il/la più piccolo(-a), il/la minimo(-a); (smallest amount of) il/la meno ■ adv: **the ~** (+adjective): **the ~ beautiful girl** la ragazza meno bella; **the ~ expensive** il/la meno caro(-a); **I have the ~ money** ho meno denaro di tutti; **at ~** almeno; **not in the ~** affatto, per nulla

leather ['lɛðəʳ] n (soft) pelle f; (hard) cuoio ■ cpd di or in pelle; di cuoio; **~ goods** pelletteria, pelletterie fpl

leave [li:v] vb (pt, pp **left**) [lɛft] vt lasciare; (go away from) partire da ■ vi partire, andarsene ■ n (time off) congedo; (Mil) licenza; **to be left** rimanere; **there's some milk left over** c'è rimasto del latte; **to take one's ~ of** congedarsi di; **he's already left for the airport** è già uscito per andare all'aeroporto; **to ~ school** finire la scuola; **~ it to me!** ci penso io!, lascia fare a me!; **on ~** in congedo; **on ~ of absence** in permesso; (public employee) in congedo; (Mil) in licenza
  ▶ **leave behind** vt (also fig) lasciare indietro; (forget) dimenticare
  ▶ **leave off** vt non mettere; (Brit col: stop): **to ~ off doing sth** smetterla or piantarla di fare qc
  ▶ **leave on** vt lasciare su; (light, fire, cooker) lasciare acceso(-a)
  ▶ **leave out** vt omettere, tralasciare

leaves [li:vz] npl of **leaf**

leavetaking ['li:vteɪkɪŋ] n commiato, addio

Lebanese [lɛbə'ni:z] adj, n (pl inv) libanese (m/f)

Lebanon ['lɛbənən] n Libano

lecherous ['lɛtʃərəs] adj lascivo(-a), lubrico(-a)

lectern ['lɛktə:n] n leggio

lecture ['lɛktʃəʳ] n conferenza; (Scol) lezione f ■ vi fare conferenze; fare lezioni; (reprove) rimproverare, fare una ramanzina a; **to ~ on** fare una conferenza su; **to give a ~ (on)** (Brit) fare una lezione (su); fare lezione (su)

lecture hall n aula magna

lecturer ['lɛktʃərəʳ] n (speaker) conferenziere(-a); (Brit: at university) professore(-essa), docente m/f; **assistant ~** (Brit) ≈ professore(-essa) associato(-a); **senior ~** (Brit) ≈ professore(-essa) ordinario(-a)

lecture theatre n = **lecture hall**

LED n abbr (Elec: = light-emitting diode) diodo a emissione luminosa

led [lɛd] pt, pp of **lead¹**

ledge [lɛdʒ] n (of window) davanzale m; (on wall etc) sporgenza; (of mountain) cornice f, cengia

ledger ['lɛdʒəʳ] n libro maestro, registro

lee [li:] n lato sottovento; **in the ~ of** a ridosso di, al riparo di

leech [li:tʃ] n sanguisuga

leek [li:k] n porro

leer [lɪəʳ] vi: **to ~ at sb** gettare uno sguardo voglioso (or maligno) su qn

leeward ['li:wəd] adj sottovento inv ■ n lato sottovento; **to ~** sottovento

leeway ['li:weɪ] n (fig): **to have some ~** avere una certa libertà di agire

left [lɛft] pt, pp of **leave** ■ adj sinistro(-a) ■ adv a sinistra ■ n sinistra; **on the ~**, **to the ~** a sinistra; **the L~** (Pol) la sinistra

left-click ['lɛftklɪk] vi (Comput): **to ~ on** fare clic con il pulsante sinistro del mouse su

left-hand drive ['lɛfthænd-] n (Brit) guida a sinistra

left-handed [lɛft'hændɪd] adj mancino(-a); **~ scissors** forbici fpl per mancini

left-hand side [lɛft'hænd-] n lato or fianco sinistro

leftie ['lɛftɪ] n: **a ~** (col) uno(-a) di sinistra

leftist ['lɛftɪst] adj (Pol) di sinistra

left-luggage [lɛft'lʌgɪdʒ], **left-luggage office** [lɛft'lʌgɪdʒ-] n deposito m bagagli inv

left-overs ['lɛftəuvəz] npl avanzi mpl, resti mpl

left wing n (Mil, Sport) ala sinistra; (Pol) sinistra ■ adj: **left-wing** (Pol) di sinistra

left-winger [lɛft'wɪŋəʳ] n (Pol) uno(-a) di sinistra; (Sport) ala sinistra

lefty ['lɛftɪ] n = **leftie**

leg [lɛg] n gamba; (of animal) zampa; (of furniture) piede m; (Culin: of chicken) coscia; (of journey) tappa; **1st/2nd ~** (Sport) partita di andata/ritorno; **~ of lamb** (Culin) cosciotto d'agnello; **to stretch one's legs** sgranchirsi le gambe

legacy ['lɛgəsɪ] n eredità f inv; (fig) retaggio

legal ['li:gl] adj legale; **to take ~ action** or **proceedings against sb** intentare un'azione legale contro qn, far causa a qn

legal adviser n consulente m/f legale

legality [lɪ'gælɪtɪ] n legalità

legalize ['li:gəlaɪz] vt legalizzare

legally ['li:gəlɪ] adv legalmente; **~ binding** legalmente vincolante

legal tender n moneta legale

legation [lɪ'geɪʃən] n legazione f

legend ['lɛdʒənd] n leggenda

legendary ['lɛdʒəndərɪ] adj leggendario(-a)

-legged ['lɛgɪd] suffix: **two-~** a due gambe (or zampe), bipede

leggings ['lɛgɪnz] npl ghette fpl

leggy ['lɛgɪ] adj dalle gambe lunghe

legibility [lɛdʒɪ'bɪlɪtɪ] n leggibilità

legible ['lɛdʒəbl] *adj* leggibile
legibly ['lɛdʒəblɪ] *adv* in modo leggibile
legion ['li:dʒən] *n* legione *f*
legionnaire [li:dʒə'nɛəʳ] *n* legionario;
~**'s disease** morbo del legionario
legislate ['lɛdʒɪsleɪt] *vi* legiferare
legislation [lɛdʒɪs'leɪʃən] *n* legislazione *f*;
a piece of ~ una legge
legislative ['lɛdʒɪslətɪv] *adj* legislativo(-a)
legislator ['lɛdʒɪsleɪtəʳ] *n* legislatore(-trice)
legislature ['lɛdʒɪslətʃəʳ] *n* corpo legislativo
legitimacy [lɪ'dʒɪtɪməsɪ] *n* legittimità
legitimate [lɪ'dʒɪtɪmət] *adj* legittimo(-a)
legitimize [lɪ'dʒɪtɪmaɪz] *vt* (*gen*) legalizzare,
rendere legale; (*child*) legittimare
legless ['lɛglɪs] *adj* (*Brit col*) sbronzo(-a),
fatto(-a)
leg-room ['lɛgru:m] *n* spazio per le gambe
Leics *abbr* (*Brit*) = **Leicestershire**
leisure ['lɛʒəʳ] *n* agio, tempo libero;
ricreazioni *fpl*; **at** ~ all'agio; a proprio
comodo
leisure centre *n* centro di ricreazione
leisurely ['lɛʒəlɪ] *adj* tranquillo(-a), fatto(-a)
con comodo *or* senza fretta
leisure suit *n* (*Brit*) tuta (da ginnastica)
lemon ['lɛmən] *n* limone *m*
lemonade [lɛmə'neɪd] *n* limonata
lemon cheese, lemon curd *n* crema di
limone (*che si spalma sul pane etc*)
lemon juice *n* succo di limone
lemon squeezer *n* spremiagrumi *m inv*
lemon tea *n* tè *m inv* al limone
lend (*pt, pp* lent) [lɛnd, lɛnt] *vt*: **to** ~ **sth** (**to
sb**) prestare qc (a qn); **to** ~ **a hand** dare una
mano
lender ['lɛndəʳ] *n* prestatore(-trice)
lending library ['lɛndɪŋ-] *n* biblioteca
circolante
length [lɛŋθ] *n* lunghezza; (*section: of road, pipe
etc*) pezzo, tratto; ~ **of time** periodo (di
tempo); **what** ~ **is it?** quant'è lungo?; **it is
2 metres in** ~ è lungo 2 metri; **to fall full** ~
cadere lungo disteso; **at** ~ (*at last*)
finalmente, alla fine; (*lengthily*) a lungo;
to go to any ~(**s**) **to do sth** fare qualsiasi
cosa pur di *or* per fare qc
lengthen ['lɛŋθən] *vt* allungare, prolungare
■ *vi* allungarsi
lengthways ['lɛŋθweɪz] *adv* per il lungo
lengthy ['lɛŋθɪ] *adj* molto lungo(-a)
leniency ['li:nɪənsɪ] *n* indulgenza, clemenza
lenient ['li:nɪənt] *adj* indulgente, clemente
leniently ['li:nɪəntlɪ] *adv* con indulgenza
lens [lɛnz] *n* lente *f*; (*of camera*) obiettivo
Lent [lɛnt] *n* Quaresima
lent [lɛnt] *pt, pp of* **lend**

lentil ['lɛntl] *n* lenticchia
Leo ['li:əu] *n* Leone *m*; **to be** ~ essere del Leone
leopard ['lɛpəd] *n* leopardo
leotard ['li:ətɑ:d] *n* calzamaglia
leper ['lɛpəʳ] *n* lebbroso(-a)
leper colony *n* lebbrosario
leprosy ['lɛprəsɪ] *n* lebbra
lesbian ['lɛzbɪən] *n* lesbica ■ *adj* lesbico(-a)
lesion ['li:ʒən] *n* (*Med*) lesione *f*
Lesotho [lɪ'su:tu] *n* Lesotho *m*
less [lɛs] *adj, pron, adv* meno; ~ **than you/
ever** meno di lei/che mai; ~ **than half**
meno della metà; ~ **and** ~ sempre meno;
the ~ **he works ...** meno lavora ...; ~ **than £1/
a kilo/3 metres** meno di una sterlina/
un chilo/3 metri; ~ **5%** meno il 5%
lessee [lɛ'si:] *n* affittuario(-a), locatario(-a)
lessen ['lɛsn] *vi* diminuire, attenuarsi ■ *vt*
diminuire, ridurre
lesser ['lɛsəʳ] *adj* minore, più piccolo(-a);
to a ~ **extent** *or* **degree** in grado *or* misura
minore
lesson ['lɛsn] *n* lezione *f*; **a maths** ~ una
lezione di matematica; **to give lessons in**
dare *or* impartire lezioni di; **it taught him a**
~ (*fig*) gli è servito di lezione
lessor ['lɛsɔ:ʳ, lɛ'sɔ:ʳ] *n* locatore(-trice)
lest [lɛst] *conj* per paura di + *infinitive*, per
paura che + *sub*
let (*pt, pp* ~) [lɛt] *vt* lasciare; (*Brit: lease*) dare in
affitto; **to** ~ **sb do sth** lasciar fare qc a qn,
lasciare che qn faccia qc; **to** ~ **sb know sth**
far sapere qc a qn; **to** ~ **sb have sth** dare qc a
qn; **he** ~ **me go** mi ha lasciato andare; ~ **the
water boil and ...** fate bollire l'acqua e ...;
~**'s go** andiamo; ~ **him come** lo lasci venire;
"to ~**"** "affittasi"
▶ **let down** *vt* (*lower*) abbassare; (*dress*)
allungare; (*hair*) sciogliere; (*disappoint*)
deludere; (*Brit: tyre*) sgonfiare
▶ **let go** *vi* mollare ■ *vt* mollare; (*allow to go*)
lasciare andare
▶ **let in** *vt* lasciare entrare; (*visitor etc*) far
entrare; **what have you** ~ **yourself in for?**
in che guai *or* pasticci sei andato a cacciarti?
▶ **let off** *vt* (*allow to go*) lasciare andare;
(*firework etc*) far partire; (*smell etc*) emettere;
(*taxi driver, bus driver*) far scendere; **to** ~ **off
steam** (*fig, col*) sfogarsi, scaricarsi
▶ **let on** *vi* (*col*): **to** ~ **on that ...** lasciar capire
che ...
▶ **let out** *vt* lasciare uscire; (*dress*) allargare;
(*scream*) emettere; (*rent out*) affittare, dare in
affitto
▶ **let up** *vi* diminuire
let-down ['lɛtdaun] *n* (*disappointment*)
delusione *f*

lethal ['li:θl] *adj* letale, mortale
lethargic [lɛ'θɑːdʒɪk] *adj* letargico(-a)
lethargy ['lɛθədʒɪ] *n* letargia
letter ['lɛtər] *n* lettera; **letters** *npl* (*Literature*)
lettere; **small/capital** ~ lettera minuscola/
maiuscola; ~ **of credit** lettera di credito;
documentary ~ **of credit** lettera di credito
documentaria
letter bomb *n* lettera esplosiva
letterbox ['lɛtəbɒks] *n* buca delle lettere
letterhead ['lɛtəhɛd] *n* intestazione *f*
lettering ['lɛtərɪŋ] *n* iscrizione *f*; caratteri *mpl*
letter-opener ['lɛtərəupnər] *n* tagliacarte
m inv
letterpress ['lɛtəprɛs] *n* (*method*) rilievografia
letter quality *n* (*of printer*) qualità di stampa
letters patent *npl* brevetto di invenzione
lettuce ['lɛtɪs] *n* lattuga, insalata
let-up ['lɛtʌp] *n* (*col*) interruzione *f*
leukaemia, (*US*) **leukemia** [lu:'ki:mɪə] *n*
leucemia
level ['lɛvl] *adj* piatto(-a), piano(-a);
orizzontale ■ *n* livello; (*also*: **spirit level**)
livella (a bolla d'aria) ■ *vt* livellare,
spianare; (*gun*) puntare (verso); (*accusation*):
to ~ (against) lanciare (a *or* contro) ■ *vi* (*col*):
to ~ with sb essere franco(-a) con qn; **to be ~
with** essere alla pari di; **a ~ spoonful** (*Culin*)
un cucchiaio raso; **to draw ~ with** (*team*)
mettersi alla pari di; (*runner, car*) affiancarsi
a; **A levels** *npl* (*Brit*) ≈ esami *mpl* di maturità;
O levels *npl* (*Brit: formerly*) *diploma di istruzione
secondaria conseguito a 16 anni in Inghilterra e Galles,
ora sostituito dal GCSE*; **on the ~** piatto(-a); (*fig*)
onesto(-a)
▶ **level off**, **level out** *vi* (*prices etc*)
stabilizzarsi; (*ground*) diventare
pianeggiante; (*aircraft*) volare in quota
level crossing *n* (*Brit*) passaggio a livello
level-headed [lɛvl'hɛdɪd] *adj* equilibrato(-a)
levelling, (*US*) **leveling** ['lɛvlɪŋ] *adj* (*process,
effect*) di livellamento
level playing field *n*: **to compete on a ~** (*fig*)
competere ad armi pari
lever ['li:vər] *n* leva ■ *vt*: **to ~ up/out**
sollevare/estrarre con una leva
leverage ['li:vərɪdʒ] *n*: ~ (**on** *or* **with**)
ascendente *m* (su)
levity ['lɛvɪtɪ] *n* leggerezza, frivolità
levy ['lɛvɪ] *n* tassa, imposta ■ *vt* imporre
lewd [lu:d] *adj* osceno(-a), lascivo(-a)
lexicographer [lɛksɪ'kɒgrəfər] *n*
lessicografo(-a)
lexicography [lɛksɪ'kɒgrəfɪ] *n* lessicografia
LGV *n abbr* (*Brit*: = *Large Goods Vehicle*)
automezzo pesante
LI *abbr* (*US*) = **Long Island**

liabilities [laɪə'bɪlətɪz] *npl* debiti *mpl*;
(*on balance sheet*) passivo
liability [laɪə'bɪlɪtɪ] *n* responsabilità *f inv*;
(*handicap*) peso
liable ['laɪəbl] *adj* (*subject*): ~ **to** soggetto(-a) a;
passibile di; (*responsible*): ~ (**for**) responsabile
(di); (*likely*): ~ **to do** propenso(-a) a fare; **to be
~ to a fine** essere passibile di multa
liaise [li:'eɪz] *vi*: **to ~ (with)** mantenere i
contatti (con)
liaison [li:'eɪzɔn] *n* relazione *f*; (*Mil*)
collegamento
liar ['laɪər] *n* bugiardo(-a)
libel ['laɪbl] *n* libello, diffamazione *f*
■ *vt* diffamare
libellous, (*US*) **libelous** ['laɪbləs] *adj*
diffamatorio(-a)
liberal ['lɪbərl] *adj* liberale; (*generous*):
to be ~ with distribuire liberalmente
■ *n* (*Pol*): **L~** liberale *m/f*
Liberal Democrat *n* liberaldemocratico(-a)
liberality [lɪbə'rælɪtɪ] *n* (*generosity*)
generosità, liberalità
liberalize ['lɪbərəlaɪz] *vt* liberalizzare
liberal-minded [lɪbərl'maɪndɪd] *adj* tollerante
liberate ['lɪbəreɪt] *vt* liberare
liberation [lɪbə'reɪʃən] *n* liberazione *f*
liberation theology *n* teologia della
liberazione
Liberia [laɪ'bɪərɪə] *n* Liberia
Liberian [laɪ'bɪərɪən] *adj, n* liberiano(-a)
liberty ['lɪbətɪ] *n* libertà *f inv*; **at ~ to do**
libero(-a) di fare; **to take the ~ of** prendersi
la libertà di, permettersi di
libido [lɪ'bi:dəu] *n* libido *f*
Libra ['li:brə] *n* Bilancia; **to be ~** essere della
Bilancia
librarian [laɪ'brɛərɪən] *n* bibliotecario(-a)
library ['laɪbrərɪ] *n* biblioteca
library book *n* libro della biblioteca
libretto [lɪ'brɛtəu] *n* libretto
Libya ['lɪbɪə] *n* Libia
Libyan ['lɪbɪən] *adj, n* libico(-a)
lice [laɪs] *npl of* **louse**
licence, (*US*) **license** ['laɪsns] *n*
autorizzazione *f*, permesso; (*Comm*) licenza;
(*Radio, TV*) canone *m*, abbonamento; (*also*:
driving licence, (*US*) **driver's license**) patente *f*
di guida; (*excessive freedom*) licenza; **import ~**
licenza di importazione; **produced under ~**
prodotto su licenza
licence number *n* (*Brit Aut*) numero di targa
license ['laɪsns] *n US* = **licence** ■ *vt* dare una
licenza a; (*car*) pagare la tassa di circolazione
or il bollo di
licensed ['laɪsnst] *adj* (*for alcohol*) che ha la
licenza di vendere bibite alcoliche

licensed trade n commercio di bevande alcoliche con licenza speciale

licensee [laɪsən'si:] n (Brit: of pub) detentore(-trice) di autorizzazione alla vendita di bevande alcoliche

license plate n (esp US Aut) targa (automobilistica)

licentious [laɪ'senʃəs] adj licenzioso(-a)

lichen ['laɪkən] n lichene m

lick [lɪk] vt leccare; (col: defeat) suonarle a, stracciare ■ n leccata; **a ~ of paint** una passata di vernice

licorice ['lɪkərɪs] n = **liquorice**

lid [lɪd] n coperchio; **to take the ~ off sth** (fig) smascherare qc

lido ['laɪdəu] n piscina all'aperto; (part of the beach) lido, stabilimento balneare

lie [laɪ] n bugia, menzogna ■ vi mentire, dire bugie (pt **lay**, pp **lain**) [leɪ, leɪn] (rest) giacere, star disteso(-a); (in grave) giacere, riposare; (object: be situated) trovarsi, essere; **to tell lies** raccontare or dire bugie; **to ~ low** (fig) latitare
  ▶ **lie about, lie around** vi (things) essere in giro; (person) bighellonare
  ▶ **lie back** vi stendersi
  ▶ **lie down** vi stendersi, sdraiarsi
  ▶ **lie up** vi (hide) nascondersi

Liechtenstein ['lɪktənstaɪn] n Liechtenstein m

lie detector n macchina della verità

lie-down ['laɪdaun] n (Brit): **to have a ~** sdraiarsi, riposarsi

lie-in ['laɪɪn] n (Brit): **to have a ~** rimanere a letto

lieu [lu:] n: **in ~ of** invece di, al posto di

Lieut. abbr (= lieutenant) Ten.

lieutenant [lɛf'tɛnənt, (US) lu:'tɛnənt] n tenente m

lieutenant-colonel [lɛf'tɛnənt'kə:nl, (US) lu:'tɛnənt'kə:nl] n tenente colonnello

life [laɪf] n (pl **lives**) vita ■ cpd di vita; della vita; a vita; **country/city ~** vita di campagna/di città; **to be sent to prison for ~** essere condannato all'ergastolo; **true to ~** fedele alla realtà; **to paint from ~** dipingere dal vero

life annuity n rendita vitalizia

life assurance n (Brit) = **life insurance**

lifebelt ['laɪfbɛlt] n (Brit) salvagente m

lifeblood ['laɪfblʌd] n (fig) linfa vitale

lifeboat ['laɪfbəut] n scialuppa di salvataggio

life expectancy n durata media della vita

lifeguard ['laɪfɡɑ:d] n bagnino

life imprisonment n ergastolo

life insurance n assicurazione f sulla vita

life jacket n giubbotto di salvataggio

lifeless ['laɪflɪs] adj senza vita

lifelike ['laɪflaɪk] adj che sembra vero(-a); rassomigliante

lifeline ['laɪflaɪn] n cavo di salvataggio

lifelong ['laɪflɔŋ] adj per tutta la vita

life preserver n (US) salvagente m; giubbotto di salvataggio; (Brit) sfollagente m inv

lifer ['laɪfər] n (col) ergastolano(-a)

life-raft ['laɪfrɑ:ft] n zattera di salvataggio

life-saver ['laɪfseɪvər] n bagnino

life sentence n (condanna all')ergastolo

life-sized ['laɪfsaɪzd] adj a grandezza naturale

life span n (durata della) vita

life style n stile m di vita

life support system n (Med) respiratore m automatico

lifetime ['laɪftaɪm] n: **in his ~** durante la sua vita; **in a ~** nell'arco della vita; in tutta la vita; **the chance of a ~** un'occasione unica

lift [lɪft] vt sollevare, levare; (steal) prendere, rubare ■ vi (fog) alzarsi ■ n (Brit: elevator) ascensore m; **to give sb a ~** (Brit) dare un passaggio a qn
  ▶ **lift off** vt togliere ■ vi (rocket) partire; (helicopter) decollare
  ▶ **lift out** vt tirar fuori; (troops, evacuees etc) far evacuare per mezzo di elicotteri (or aerei)
  ▶ **lift up** vt sollevare, alzare

lift-off ['lɪftɔf] n decollo

ligament ['lɪɡəmənt] n legamento

light [laɪt] n luce f, lume m; (daylight) luce, giorno; (lamp) lampada; (Aut: rear light) luce di posizione; (: headlamp) fanale m; (for cigarette etc): **have you got a ~?** ha da accendere? ■ vt (pt, pp **lighted**, pt, pp **lit**) [lɪt] (candle, cigarette, fire) accendere; (room) illuminare ■ adj (room, colour) chiaro(-a); (not heavy, also fig) leggero(-a) ■ adv (travel) con poco bagaglio; **lights** npl (Aut: traffic lights) semaforo; **in the ~ of** alla luce di; **to turn the ~ on/off** accendere/spegnere la luce; **to come to ~** venire in luce; **to cast** or **shed** or **throw ~ on** gettare luce su; **to make ~ of sth** (fig) prendere alla leggera qc, non dar peso a qc
  ▶ **light up** vi illuminarsi ■ vt illuminare

light bulb n lampadina

lighten ['laɪtn] vi schiarirsi ■ vt (give light to) illuminare; (make lighter) schiarire; (make less heavy) alleggerire

lighter ['laɪtər] n (also: **cigarette lighter**) accendino; (boat) chiatta

light-fingered [laɪt'fɪŋɡəd] adj lesto(-a) di mano

light-headed ['laɪt'hɛdɪd] adj stordito(-a)

light-hearted ['laɪt'hɑ:tɪd] adj gioioso(-a), gaio(-a)

lighthouse ['laɪthaus] n faro
lighting ['laɪtɪŋ] n illuminazione f
lighting-up time ['laɪtɪŋʌp-] n (Brit) orario per l'accensione delle luci
lightly ['laɪtlɪ] adv leggermente; **to get off ~** cavarsela a buon mercato
light meter n (Phot) esposimetro
lightness ['laɪtnɪs] n chiarezza; (in weight) leggerezza
lightning ['laɪtnɪŋ] n lampo, fulmine m; **a flash of ~** un lampo, un fulmine
lightning conductor, (US) **lightning rod** n parafulmine m
lightning strike n (Brit) sciopero m lampo inv
light pen n penna luminosa
lightship ['laɪtʃɪp] n battello m faro inv
lightweight ['laɪtweɪt] adj (suit) leggero(-a); (boxer) peso leggero inv
light year ['laɪtjɪər] n anno m luce inv
Ligurian [lɪ'gjuərɪən] adj, n ligure (m/f)
like [laɪk] vt (person) volere bene a; (activity, object, food): **I ~ swimming/that book/ chocolate** mi piace nuotare/quel libro/il cioccolato ■ prep come ■ adj simile, uguale ■ n: **the ~** uno(-a) uguale; **I would ~, I'd ~** mi piacerebbe, vorrei; **would you ~ a coffee?** gradirebbe un caffè?; **if you ~** se vuoi; **to be/ look ~ sb/sth** somigliare a qn/qc; **what's he ~?** che tipo è?, com'è?; **what's the weather ~?** che tempo fa?; **that's just ~ him** è proprio da lui; **something ~ that** qualcosa del genere; **I feel ~ a drink** avrei voglia di bere qualcosa; **there's nothing ~ ...** non c'è niente di meglio di or niente come ...; **his likes and dislikes** i suoi gusti
likeable ['laɪkəbl] adj simpatico(-a)
likelihood ['laɪklɪhud] n probabilità; **in all ~** con ogni probabilità, molto probabilmente
likely ['laɪklɪ] adj probabile; plausibile; **he's ~ to leave** probabilmente partirà, è probabile che parta; **not ~!** (col) neanche per sogno!
like-minded ['laɪk'maɪndɪd] adj che pensa allo stesso modo
liken ['laɪkən] vt: **to ~ sth to sth** paragonare qc a
likeness ['laɪknɪs] n (similarity) somiglianza
likewise ['laɪkwaɪz] adv similmente, nello stesso modo
liking ['laɪkɪŋ] n: **~ (for)** simpatia (per); debole m (per); **to be to sb's ~** essere di gusto or gradimento di qn; **to take a ~ to sb** prendere qn in simpatia
lilac ['laɪlək] n lilla m inv ■ adj lilla inv
Lilo® ['laɪləu] n materassino gonfiabile
lilt [lɪlt] n cadenza
lilting ['lɪltɪŋ] adj melodioso(-a)
lily ['lɪlɪ] n giglio; **~ of the valley** mughetto
Lima ['li:mə] n Lima

limb [lɪm] n membro; **to be out on a ~** (fig) sentirsi spaesato or tagliato fuori
limber ['lɪmbər]: **to ~ up** vi riscaldarsi i muscoli
limbo ['lɪmbəu] n: **to be in ~** (fig) essere lasciato(-a) nel dimenticatoio
lime [laɪm] n (tree) tiglio; (fruit) limetta; (Geo) calce f
lime juice n succo di limetta
limelight ['laɪmlaɪt] n: **in the ~** (fig) alla ribalta, in vista
limerick ['lɪmərɪk] n poesiola umoristica di cinque versi
limestone ['laɪmstəun] n pietra calcarea; (Geo) calcare m
limit ['lɪmɪt] n limite m ■ vt limitare; **weight/speed ~** limite di peso/di velocità; **within limits** entro certi limiti
limitation [lɪmɪ'teɪʃən] n limitazione f, limite m
limited ['lɪmɪtɪd] adj limitato(-a), ristretto(-a); **~ edition** edizione f a bassa tiratura
limited company, limited liability company n (Brit) ≈ società f inv a responsabilità limitata (S.r.l.)
limitless ['lɪmɪtlɪs] adj illimitato(-a)
limousine ['lɪməzi:n] n limousine f inv
limp [lɪmp] n: **to have a ~** zoppicare ■ vi zoppicare ■ adj floscio(-a), flaccido(-a)
limpet ['lɪmpɪt] n patella
limpid ['lɪmpɪd] adj (poet) limpido(-a)
linchpin ['lɪntʃpɪn] n acciarino, bietta; (fig) perno
Lincs abbr (Brit) = **Lincolnshire**
line [laɪn] n (gen, Comm) linea; (rope) corda; (wire) filo; (of poem) verso; (row, series) fila, riga; coda ■ vt (clothes): **to ~ (with)** foderare (di); (box): **to ~ (with)** rivestire or foderare (di); (trees, crowd) fiancheggiare; **to cut in ~** (US) passare avanti; **in his ~ of business** nel suo ramo di affari; **on the right lines** sulla buona strada; **a new ~ in cosmetics** una nuova linea di cosmetici; **hold the ~ please** (Brit Tel) resti in linea per cortesia; **to be in ~ for sth** (fig) essere in lista per qc; **in ~ with** d'accordo con, in linea con; **to bring sth into ~ with sth** mettere qc al passo con qc; **to draw the ~ at (doing) sth** (fig) rifiutarsi di fare qc; **to take the ~ that ...** essere del parere che ...
  ▶ **line up** vi allinearsi, mettersi in fila ■ vt mettere in fila; **to have sth lined up** avere qc in programma; **to have sb lined up** avere qn in mente
linear ['lɪnɪər] adj lineare
lined [laɪnd] adj (paper) a righe, rigato(-a); (face) rugoso(-a); (clothes) foderato(-a)

line feed n (Comput) avanzamento di una interlinea

linen ['lının] n biancheria, panni mpl; (cloth) tela di lino

line printer n stampante f parallela

liner ['laınə^r] n nave f di linea; **dustbin ~** sacchetto per la pattumiera

linesman ['laınzmən] n guardalinee m inv, segnalinee m inv

line-up ['laınʌp] n allineamento, fila; (also: **police line-up**) confronto all'americana; (Sport) formazione f di gioco

linger ['lıŋgə^r] vi attardarsi; indugiare; (smell, tradition) persistere

lingerie ['læn3əri:] n biancheria intima (femminile)

lingering ['lıŋgərıŋ] adj lungo(-a), persistente; (death) lento(-a)

lingo ['lıŋgəu] n (pl **lingoes**) (pej) gergo

linguist ['lıŋgwıst] n linguista m/f; poliglotta m/f

linguistic [lıŋ'gwıstık] adj linguistico(-a)

linguistics [lıŋ'gwıstıks] n linguistica

lining ['laınıŋ] n fodera; (Tech) rivestimento (interno); (of brake) guarnizione f

link [lıŋk] n (of a chain) anello; (connection) legame m, collegamento; (Comput) link, collegamento ■ vt collegare, unire, congiungere; (Comput) creare un collegamento con ■ vi (Comput): **to ~ to a site** creare un collegamento con un sitio; **rail ~** collegamento ferroviario; see also **links**
 ▶ **link up** vt collegare, unire ■ vi riunirsi; associarsi

links [lıŋks] npl pista or terreno da golf

link-up ['lıŋkʌp] n legame m; (of roads) nodo; (of spaceships) aggancio; (Radio, TV) collegamento

linoleum [lı'nəulıəm] n linoleum m inv

linseed oil ['lınsi:d-] n olio di semi di lino

lint [lınt] n garza

lintel ['lıntl] n architrave f

lion ['laıən] n leone m

lion cub n leoncino

lioness ['laıənıs] n leonessa

lip [lıp] n labbro; (of cup etc) orlo; (insolence) sfacciataggine f

liposuction ['lıpəusʌkʃən] n liposuzione f

lipread ['lıpri:d] vi leggere sulle labbra

lip salve n burro di cacao

lip service n: **to pay ~ to sth** essere favorevole a qc solo a parole

lipstick ['lıpstık] n rossetto

liquefy ['lıkwıfaı] vt liquefare ■ vi liquefarsi

liqueur [lı'kjuə^r] n liquore m

liquid ['lıkwıd] n liquido ■ adj liquido(-a)

liquid assets npl attività fpl liquide, crediti mpl liquidi

liquidate ['lıkwıdeıt] vt liquidare

liquidation [lıkwı'deıʃən] n liquidazione f; **to go into ~** andare in liquidazione

liquidator ['lıkwıdeıtə^r] n liquidatore m

liquid crystal display n visualizzazione f a cristalli liquidi

liquidity [lı'kwıdıtı] n (Comm) liquidità

liquidize ['lıkwıdaız] vt (Brit Culin) passare al frullatore

liquidizer ['lıkwıdaızə^r] n (Brit Culin) frullatore m (a brocca)

liquor ['lıkə^r] n alcool m

liquorice ['lıkərıs] n liquirizia

Lisbon ['lızbən] n Lisbona

lisp [lısp] n difetto nel pronunciare le sibilanti

lissom ['lısəm] adj leggiadro(-a)

list [lıst] n lista, elenco; (of ship) sbandamento ■ vt (write down) mettere in lista; fare una lista di; (enumerate) elencare; (Comput) stampare (un prospetto di) ■ vi (ship) sbandare; **shopping ~** lista or nota della spesa

listed building ['lıstəd-] n (Archit) edificio sotto la protezione delle Belle Arti

listed company n società quotata in Borsa

listen ['lısn] vi ascoltare; **to ~ to** ascoltare

listener ['lısnə^r] n ascoltatore(-trice)

listeria [lıs'tıərıə] n listeria

listing ['lıstıŋ] n (Comput) lista stampata

listless ['lıstlıs] adj svogliato(-a); apatico(-a)

listlessly ['lıstlıslı] adv svogliatamente; apaticamente

list price n prezzo di listino

lit [lıt] pt, pp of **light**

litany ['lıtənı] n litania

liter ['li:tə^r] n (US) = **litre**

literacy ['lıtərəsı] n il sapere leggere e scrivere

literacy campaign n lotta contro l'analfabetismo

literal ['lıtərl] adj letterale

literally ['lıtərəlı] adv alla lettera, letteralmente

literary ['lıtərərı] adj letterario(-a)

literate ['lıtərıt] adj che sa leggere e scrivere

literature ['lıtərıtʃə^r] n letteratura; (brochures etc) materiale m

lithe [laıð] adj agile, snello(-a)

lithography [lı'θɔgrəfı] n litografia

Lithuania [lıθju'eınıə] n Lituania

Lithuanian [lıθju'eınıən] adj lituano(-a) ■ n lituano(-a); (Ling) lituano

litigate ['lıtıgeıt] vt muovere causa a ■ vi litigare

litigation [lıtı'geıʃən] n causa

litmus ['lıtməs] n: **~ paper** cartina di tornasole

litre, (US) **liter** ['li:tə^r] n litro
litter ['lɪtə^r] n (rubbish) rifiuti mpl; (young animals) figliata ▪ vt sparpagliare; lasciare rifiuti in; **littered with** coperto(-a) di
litter bin n (Brit) cestino per rifiuti
litter lout, (US) **litterbug** ['lɪtəbʌg] n persona che butta per terra le cartacce o i rifiuti
little ['lɪtl] adj (small) piccolo(-a); (not much) poco(-a) ▪ adv poco; **a ~** un po' (di); **a ~ milk** un po' di latte; **with ~ difficulty** senza fatica or difficoltà; **~ by ~** a poco a poco; **as ~ as possible** il meno possibile; **for a ~ while** per un po'; **to make ~ of** dare poca importanza a; **~ finger** mignolo
little-known ['lɪtl'nəun] adj poco noto(-a)
liturgy ['lɪtədʒɪ] n liturgia
live¹ [lɪv] vi vivere; (reside) vivere, abitare; **to ~ in London** abitare a Londra; **to ~ together** vivere insieme, convivere
▶ **live down** vt far dimenticare (alla gente)
▶ **live in** vi essere interno(-a); avere vitto e alloggio
▶ **live off** vi (land, fish etc) vivere di; (pej: parents etc) vivere alle spalle or a spese di
▶ **live on** vt fus (food) vivere di ▪ vi sopravvivere, continuare a vivere; **to ~ on £50 a week** vivere con 50 sterline la settimana
▶ **live out** vi (Brit: students) essere esterno(-a) ▪ vt: **to ~ out one's days** or **life** trascorrere gli ultimi anni
▶ **live up** vt: **to ~ it up** (col) fare la bella vita
▶ **live up to** vt fus tener fede a, non venir meno a
live² [laɪv] adj (animal) vivo(-a); (issue) scottante, d'attualità; (wire) sotto tensione; (broadcast) diretto(-a); (ammunition: not blank) carico(-a); (unexploded) inesploso(-a)
live-in ['lɪvɪn] adj (col: partner) convivente; (servant) che vive in casa; **he has a ~ girlfriend** la sua ragazza vive con lui
livelihood ['laɪvlɪhud] n mezzi mpl di sostentamento
liveliness ['laɪvlɪnəs] n vivacità
lively ['laɪvlɪ] adj vivace, vivo(-a)
liven up ['laɪvn-] vt (room etc) ravvivare; (discussion, evening) animare
liver ['lɪvə^r] n fegato
liverish ['lɪvərɪʃ] adj che soffre di mal di fegato; (fig) scontroso(-a)
Liverpudlian [lɪvə'pʌdlɪən] adj di Liverpool ▪ n abitante m/f di Liverpool; originario(-a) di Liverpool
livery ['lɪvərɪ] n livrea
lives [laɪvz] npl of **life**
livestock ['laɪvstɔk] n bestiame m
live wire [laɪv-] n (col: fig): **to be a ~** essere pieno(-a) di vitalità

livid ['lɪvɪd] adj livido(-a); (furious) livido(-a) di rabbia, furibondo(-a)
living ['lɪvɪŋ] adj vivo(-a), vivente ▪ n: **to earn** or **make a ~** guadagnarsi la vita; **cost of ~** costo della vita, carovita m; **within ~ memory** a memoria d'uomo
living conditions npl condizioni fpl di vita
living expenses npl spese fpl di mantenimento
living room n soggiorno
living standards npl tenore m di vita
living wage n salario sufficiente per vivere
lizard ['lɪzəd] n lucertola
llama ['lɑːmə] n lama m inv
LLB n abbr (= Bachelor of Laws) ≈ laurea in legge
LLD n abbr (= Doctor of Laws) titolo di studio
LMT abbr (US: = Local Mean Time) tempo medio locale
load [ləud] n (weight) peso; (Elec, Tech, thing carried) carico ▪ vt: **to ~ (with)** (lorry, ship) caricare (di); (gun, camera) caricare (con); **a ~ of, loads of** (fig) un sacco di; **to ~ a program** (Comput) caricare un programma
loaded ['ləudɪd] adj (dice) falsato(-a); (question, word) capzioso(-a); (col: rich) pieno(-a) di soldi
loading bay ['ləudɪŋ-] n piazzola di carico
loaf [ləuf] n (pl **loaves**) pane m, pagnotta ▪ vi (also: **loaf about, loaf around**) bighellonare
loam [ləum] n terra di marna
loan [ləun] n prestito ▪ vt dare in prestito; **on ~** in prestito
loan account n conto dei prestiti
loan capital n capitale m di prestito
loan shark n (col: pej) strozzino(-a)
loath [ləuθ] adj: **to be ~ to do** essere restio(-a) a fare
loathe [ləuð] vt detestare, aborrire
loathing ['ləuðɪŋ] n aborrimento, disgusto
loathsome ['ləuðsəm] adj (gen) ripugnante; (person) detestabile, odioso(-a)
loaves [ləuvz] npl of **loaf**
lob [lɔb] vt (ball) lanciare
lobby ['lɔbɪ] n atrio, vestibolo; (Pol: pressure group) gruppo di pressione ▪ vt fare pressione su
lobbyist ['lɔbɪɪst] n appartenente m/f ad un gruppo di pressione
lobe [ləub] n lobo
lobster ['lɔbstə^r] n aragosta
lobster pot n nassa per aragoste
local ['ləukl] adj locale ▪ n (Brit: pub) ≈ bar m inv all'angolo; **the locals** npl la gente della zona
local anaesthetic n anestesia locale
local authority n autorità locale
local call n (Tel) telefonata urbana

local government n amministrazione f locale

locality [ləu'kælɪtɪ] n località f inv; (position) posto, luogo

localize ['ləukəlaɪz] vt localizzare

locally ['ləukəlɪ] adv da queste parti; nel vicinato

locate [ləu'keɪt] vt (find) trovare; (situate) collocare

location [ləu'keɪʃən] n posizione f; **on ~** (Cine) all'esterno

loch [lɔx] n lago

lock [lɔk] n (of door, box) serratura; (of canal) chiusa; (of hair) ciocca, riccio ■ vt (with key) chiudere a chiave; (immobilize) bloccare ■ vi (door etc) chiudersi; (wheels) bloccarsi, incepparsi; **~ stock and barrel** (fig) in blocco; **on full ~** (Brit Aut) a tutto sterzo
▶ **lock away** vt (valuables) tenere (rinchiuso(-a)) al sicuro; (criminal) metter dentro
▶ **lock out** vt chiudere fuori; **to ~ workers out** fare una serrata
▶ **lock up** vi chiudere tutto (a chiave)

locker ['lɔkər] n armadietto

locket ['lɔkɪt] n medaglione m

lockjaw ['lɔkdʒɔ:] n tetano

lockout ['lɔkaut] n (Industry) serrata

locksmith ['lɔksmɪθ] n magnano

lock-up ['lɔkʌp] n (prison) prigione f; (cell) guardina; (also: **lock-up garage**) box m inv

locomotive [ləukə'məutɪv] n locomotiva

locum ['ləukəm] n (Med) medico sostituto

locust ['ləukəst] n locusta

lodge [lɔdʒ] n casetta, portineria; (Freemasonry) loggia ■ vi (person): **to ~ (with)** essere a pensione (presso or da) ■ vt (appeal etc) presentare, fare; **to ~ a complaint** presentare un reclamo; **to ~ (itself) in/between** piantarsi dentro/fra

lodger ['lɔdʒər] n affittuario(-a); (with room and meals) pensionante m/f

lodging ['lɔdʒɪŋ] n alloggio; see also **board**; **lodgings**

lodging house n (Brit) casa con camere in affitto

lodgings ['lɔdʒɪŋz] npl camera d'affitto; camera ammobiliata

loft [lɔft] n soffitta; (Agr) granaio; (US) appartamento ricavato da solaio, granaio etc

lofty ['lɔftɪ] adj alto(-a); (haughty) altezzoso(-a); (sentiments, aims) nobile

log [lɔg] n (of wood) ceppo; (book) = **logbook** ■ n abbr = **logarithm** ■ vt registrare
▶ **log in, log on** vi (Comput) aprire una sessione (con codice di riconoscimento)
▶ **log off, log out** vi (Comput) terminare una sessione

logarithm ['lɔgərɪðm] n logaritmo

logbook ['lɔgbuk] n (Naut, Aviat) diario di bordo; (Aut) libretto di circolazione; (of lorry driver) registro di viaggio; (of events, movement of goods etc) registro

log cabin n capanna di tronchi

log fire n fuoco di legna

logger ['lɔgər] n boscaiolo, taglialegna m inv

loggerheads ['lɔgəhɛdz] npl: **at ~ (with)** ai ferri corti (con)

logic ['lɔdʒɪk] n logica

logical ['lɔdʒɪkəl] adj logico(-a)

logically ['lɔdʒɪkəlɪ] adv logicamente

login ['lɔgɪn] n (Comput) nome m utente inv

logistics [lɔ'dʒɪstɪks] n logistica

log jam ['lɔgdʒæm] n: **to break the ~** superare l'impasse

logo ['ləugəu] n logo m inv

loin [lɔɪn] n (Culin) lombata; **loins** npl reni fpl

loin cloth n perizoma m

loiter ['lɔɪtər] vi attardarsi; **to ~ (about)** indugiare, bighellonare

lol abbr (Internet, Tel: = laugh out loud) lol (morto dal ridere)

loll [lɔl] vi (also: **loll about**) essere stravaccato(-a)

lollipop ['lɔlɪpɔp] n lecca lecca m inv

lollipop man, lollipop lady n (Brit) vedi nota

LOLLIPOP MAN, LOLLIPOP LADY

In Gran Bretagna il lollipop man e la lollipop lady sono persone incaricate di regolare il traffico in prossimità delle scuole e di aiutare i bambini ad attraversare la strada usando una paletta la cui forma ricorda quella di un lecca lecca, in inglese, appunto, "lollipop".

lollop ['lɔləp] vi (Brit) camminare (or correre) goffamente

lolly ['lɔlɪ] (col) n lecca lecca m inv; (also: **ice lolly**) ghiacciolo; (money) grana

Lombardy ['lɔmbədɪ] n Lombardia

London ['lʌndən] n Londra

Londoner ['lʌndənər] n londinese m/f

lone [ləun] adj solitario(-a)

loneliness ['ləunlɪnɪs] n solitudine f, isolamento

lonely ['ləunlɪ] adj solitario(-a); (place) isolato(-a); **to feel ~** sentirsi solo(-a)

lonely hearts adj: **~ ads, ~ column** messaggi mpl personali; **~ club** club m inv dei cuori solitari

lone parent n (unmarried: mother) ragazza madre; (: father) ragazzo padre; (divorced) genitore m divorziato(-a); (widowed) genitore rimasto vedovo

loner ['ləunər] n solitario(-a)

lonesome ['ləunsəm] adj solo(-a)

long [lɔŋ] adj lungo(-a) ■ adv a lungo, per molto tempo ■ n: **the ~ and the short of it is that ...** (fig) a farla breve ... ■ vi: **to ~ for sth/to do** desiderare qc/di fare; non veder l'ora di aver qc/di fare; **he had ~ understood that ...** aveva capito da molto tempo che ...; **how ~ is this river/course?** quanto è lungo questo fiume/corso?; **6 metres ~** lungo 6 metri; **6 months ~** che dura 6 mesi, di 6 mesi; **all night ~** tutta la notte; **he no longer comes** non viene più; **~ before** molto tempo prima; **before ~** (+future) presto, fra poco; (+past) poco tempo dopo; **~ ago** molto tempo fa; **don't be ~!** faccia presto!; **I shan't be ~** non ne avrò per molto; **at ~ last** finalmente; **in the ~ run** alla fin fine; **so** or **as ~ as** sempre che +sub

long-distance [lɔŋ'dɪstəns] adj (race) di fondo; (call) interurbano(-a)

long-haired ['lɔŋ'heəd] adj (person) dai capelli lunghi; (animal) dal pelo lungo

longhand ['lɔŋhænd] n scrittura normale

longing ['lɔŋɪŋ] n desiderio, voglia, brama ■ adj di desiderio; pieno(-a) di nostalgia

longingly ['lɔŋɪŋlɪ] adv con desiderio (or nostalgia)

longitude ['lɔŋɡɪtju:d] n longitudine f

long johns [-dʒɔnz] npl mutande fpl lunghe

long jump n salto in lungo

long-lost ['lɔŋlɔst] adj perduto(-a) da tempo

long-playing ['lɔŋpleɪŋ] adj: **~ record (LP)** (disco) 33 giri m inv

long-range [lɔŋ'reɪndʒ] adj a lunga portata; (weather forecast) a lungo termine

longshoreman ['lɔŋʃɔ:mən] n (US) scaricatore m (di porto), portuale m

long-sighted [lɔŋ'saɪtɪd] adj (Brit) presbite; (fig) lungimirante

long-standing ['lɔŋstændɪŋ] adj di vecchia data

long-suffering [lɔŋ'sʌfərɪŋ] adj estremamente paziente; infinitamente tollerante

long-term ['lɔŋtə:m] adj a lungo termine

long wave n (Radio) onde fpl lunghe

long-winded [lɔŋ'wɪndɪd] adj prolisso(-a), interminabile

loo [lu:] n (Brit col) W.C. m inv, cesso

loofah ['lu:fə] n luffa

look [luk] vi guardare; (seem) sembrare, parere; (building etc): **to ~ south/on to the sea** dare a sud/sul mare ■ n sguardo; (appearance) aspetto, aria; **looks** npl aspetto; bellezza; **to ~ like** assomigliare a; **to ~ ahead** guardare avanti; **it looks about 4 metres long** sarà lungo un 4 metri; **it looks**

all right to me a me pare che vada bene; **to have a ~ at sth** dare un'occhiata a qc; **to have a ~ for sth** cercare qc

► **look after** vt fus occuparsi di, prendersi cura di; (keep an eye on) guardare, badare a

► **look around** vi guardarsi intorno

► **look at** vt fus guardare

► **look back** vi: **to ~ back at sth/sb** voltarsi a guardare qc/qn; **to ~ back on** (event, period) ripensare a

► **look down on** vt fus (fig) guardare dall'alto, disprezzare

► **look for** vt fus cercare

► **look forward to** vt fus non veder l'ora di; **I'm not looking forward to it** non ne ho nessuna voglia; **looking forward to hearing from you** (in letter) aspettando tue notizie

► **look in** vi: **to ~ in on sb** (visit) fare un salto da qn

► **look into** vt fus (matter, possibility) esaminare

► **look on** vi fare da spettatore

► **look out** vi (beware): **to ~ out (for)** stare in guardia (per)

► **look out for** vt fus cercare; (watch out for): **to ~ out for sb/sth** guardare se arriva qn/qc

► **look over** vt (essay) dare un'occhiata a, riguardare; (town, building) vedere; (person) esaminare

► **look round** vi (turn) girarsi, voltarsi; (in shops) dare un'occhiata; **to ~ round for sth** guardarsi intorno cercando qc

► **look through** vt fus (papers, book) scorrere; (telescope) guardare attraverso

► **look to** vt fus stare attento(-a) a; (rely on) contare su

► **look up** vi alzare gli occhi; (improve) migliorare ■ vt (word) cercare; (friend) andare a trovare

► **look up to** vt fus avere rispetto per

look-out ['lukaut] n posto d'osservazione; guardia; **to be on the ~ (for)** stare in guardia (per)

look-up table ['lukʌp-] n (Comput) tabella di consultazione

loom [lu:m] n telaio ■ vi sorgere; (fig) minacciare

loony ['lu:nɪ] adj, n (col) pazzo(-a)

loop [lu:p] n cappio; (Comput) anello

loophole ['lu:phəul] n via d'uscita; scappatoia

loose [lu:s] adj (knot) sciolto(-a); (screw) allentato(-a); (stone) cadente; (clothes) ampio(-a), largo(-a); (animal) in libertà, scappato(-a); (life, morals) dissoluto(-a); (discipline) allentato(-a); (thinking) poco rigoroso(-a), vago(-a) ■ vt (untie) sciogliere; (slacken) allentare; (free) liberare; (Brit: arrow) scoccare; ~ **connection** (Elec) filo che fa contatto; **to be at a ~ end** or (US) **at ~ ends** (fig) non saper che fare; **to tie up ~ ends** (fig) avere ancora qualcosa da sistemare

loose change n spiccioli mpl, moneta

loose-fitting ['lu:sfɪtɪŋ] adj ampio(-a)

loose-leaf ['lu:sli:f] adj: ~ **binder** or **folder** raccoglitore m

loose-limbed [lu:s'lɪmd] adj snodato(-a), agile

loosely ['lu:slɪ] adv lentamente; approssimativamente

loosely-knit ['lu:slɪ'nɪt] adj non rigidamente strutturato(-a)

loosen ['lu:sn] vt sciogliere
  ▶ **loosen up** vi (before game) sciogliere i muscoli, scaldarsi; (col: relax) rilassarsi

loot [lu:t] n bottino ■ vt saccheggiare

looter ['lu:tə'] n saccheggiatore(-trice)

looting ['lu:tɪŋ] n saccheggio

lop [lɔp] vt (also: **lop off**) tagliare via, recidere

lop-sided ['lɔp'saɪdɪd] adj non equilibrato(-a), asimmetrico(-a)

lord [lɔːd] n signore m; **L~ Smith** lord Smith; **the L~** (Rel) il Signore; **the (House of) Lords** (Brit) la Camera dei Lord

lordly ['lɔːdlɪ] adj nobile, maestoso(-a); (arrogant) altero(-a)

lordship ['lɔːdʃɪp] n (Brit): **your L~** Sua Eccellenza

lore [lɔː'] n tradizioni fpl

lorry ['lɔrɪ] n (Brit) camion m inv

lorry driver n (Brit) camionista m

lose (pt, pp **lost**) [lu:z, lɔst] vt perdere; (pursuers) distanziare ■ vi perdere; **to ~ (time)** (clock) ritardare; **to ~ no time (in doing sth)** non perdere tempo (a fare qc); **to get lost** (person) perdersi, smarrirsi; (object) andare perso or perduto

loser ['lu:zə'] n perdente m/f; **to be a good/bad ~** saper/non saper perdere

loss [lɔs] n perdita; **to cut one's losses** rimetterci il meno possibile; **to make a ~** subire una perdita; **to sell sth at a ~** vendere qc in perdita; **to be at a ~** essere perplesso(-a); **to be at a ~ to explain sth** non saper come fare a spiegare qc

loss adjuster n (Insurance) responsabile m/f della valutazione dei danni

loss leader n (Comm) articolo a prezzo ridottissimo per attirare la clientela

lost [lɔst] pt, pp of **lose** ■ adj perduto(-a); **~ in thought** immerso or perso nei propri pensieri; **~ and found property** n (US)

oggetti mpl smarriti; **~ and found** n (US) ufficio oggetti smarriti

lost property n (Brit) oggetti mpl smarriti; **~ office** or **department** ufficio oggetti smarriti

lot [lɔt] n (at auctions) lotto; (destiny) destino, sorte f; **the ~** tutto(-a) quanto(-a); tutti(-e) quanti(-e); **a ~** molto; **a ~ of** una gran quantità di, un sacco di; **lots of** molto(-a); **to draw lots (for sth)** tirare a sorte (per qc)

lotion ['ləʊʃən] n lozione f

lottery ['lɔtərɪ] n lotteria

loud [laud] adj forte, alto(-a); (gaudy) vistoso(-a), sgargiante ■ adv (speak etc) forte; **out ~** ad alta voce

loudhailer [laud'heɪlə'] n (Brit) portavoce m inv

loudly ['laudlɪ] adv fortemente, ad alta voce

loudspeaker [laud'spi:kə'] n altoparlante m

lounge [laundʒ] n salotto, soggiorno; (of hotel) salone m; (of airport) sala d'attesa ■ vi oziare; starsene colle mani in mano

lounge bar n bar m inv con servizio a tavolino

lounge suit n (Brit) completo da uomo

louse [laus] n (pl **lice**) pidocchio
  ▶ **louse up** vt (col) rovinare

lousy ['lauzɪ] adj (fig) orrendo(-a), schifoso(-a)

lout [laut] n zoticone m

louvre, (US) **louver** ['lu:və'] adj (door, window) con apertura a gelosia

lovable ['lʌvəbl] adj simpatico(-a), carino(-a); amabile

love [lʌv] n amore m ■ vt amare; voler bene a; **to ~ to do: I ~ to do** mi piace fare; **I'd ~ to come** mi piacerebbe molto venire; **to be in ~ with** essere innamorato(-a) di; **to fall in ~ with** innamorarsi di; **to make ~** fare l'amore; **~ at first sight** amore a prima vista, colpo di fulmine; **to send one's ~ to sb** mandare i propri saluti a qn; **~ from Anne, ~, Anne** con affetto, Anne; **"15 ~"** (Tennis) "15 a zero"

love affair n relazione f

love child n figlio(-a) dell'amore

loved ones [lʌvd-] npl: **my ~** i miei cari

love-hate relationship ['lʌv'heɪt-] n rapporto amore-odio inv

love letter n lettera d'amore

love life n vita sentimentale

lovely ['lʌvlɪ] adj bello(-a); (delicious: smell, meal) buono(-a); **we had a ~ time** ci siamo divertiti molto

lover ['lʌvə'] n amante m/f; (amateur): **a ~ of** un/un'amante di; un/un'appassionato(-a) di

lovesick ['lʌvsɪk] adj malato(-a) d'amore

lovesong ['lʌvsɔŋ] n canzone f d'amore

loving ['lʌvɪŋ] *adj* affettuoso(-a), amoroso(-a), tenero(-a)

low [ləu] *adj* basso(-a) ■ *adv* in basso ■ *n* (*Meteor*) depressione *f* ■ *vi* (*cow*) muggire; **to feel ~** sentirsi giù; **he's very ~** (*ill*) è molto debole; **to reach a new** *or* **an all-time ~** toccare il livello più basso *or* il minimo; **to turn (down) ~** *vt* abbassare

low-alcohol [ləu'ælkəhɔl] *adj* a basso contenuto alcolico

lowbrow ['ləubrau] *adj* (*person*) senza pretese intellettuali

low-calorie ['ləu'kælərı] *adj* a basso contenuto calorico

low-cut ['ləukʌt] *adj* (*dress*) scollato(-a)

low-down ['ləudaun] *adj* (*mean*) ignobile ■ *n* (*col*): **he gave me the ~ on it** mi ha messo al corrente dei fatti

lower ['ləuə^r] *adj, adv comparative of* **low** ■ *vt* (*gen*) calare; (*reduce: price*) abbassare, ridurre; (*resistance*) indebolire ■ *vi* ['lauə^r] (*person*): **to ~ (at sb)** dare un'occhiataccia (a qn); (*sky*) minacciare

lower case *n* minuscolo

low-fat ['ləu'fæt] *adj* magro(-a)

low-key ['ləu'ki:] *adj* moderato(-a); (*operation*) condotto(-a) con discrezione

lowland ['ləulənd] *n* bassopiano, pianura

low-level ['ləulɛvl] *adj* a basso livello; (*flying*) a bassa quota

low-loader ['ləuləudə^r] *n* camion *m* a pianale basso

lowly ['ləulı] *adj* umile, modesto(-a)

low-lying [ləu'laıɪŋ] *adj* a basso livello

low-paid [ləu'peɪd] *adj* mal pagato(-a)

low-rise ['ləuraız] *adj* di altezza contenuta

low-tech ['ləu'tɛk] *adj* a basso contenuto tecnologico

loyal ['lɔɪəl] *adj* fedele, leale

loyalist ['lɔɪəlɪst] *n* lealista *m/f*

loyalty ['lɔɪəltı] *n* fedeltà, lealtà

loyalty card *n* carta che offre sconti a clienti abituali

lozenge ['lɔzɪndʒ] *n* (*Med*) pastiglia; (*Geom*) losanga

LP *n abbr* (= *long-playing record*) LP *m*

LPG *n abbr* (= *liquefied petroleum gas*) GPL (= *gas di petrolio liquefatto*)

L-plate *n* ≈ contrassegno P principiante; *vedi nota*

⬤ **L-PLATE**
⬤
⬤ Le *L-plates* sono delle tabelle bianche con
⬤ una L rossa che in Gran Bretagna i
⬤ guidatori principianti, "learners", in
⬤ possesso di una "provisional licence", che

⬤ corrisponde al nostro foglio rosa, devono
⬤ applicare davanti e dietro alla loro
⬤ autovettura finché non ottengono la
⬤ patente.

LPN *n abbr* (*US*: = *Licensed Practical Nurse*) = infermiera diplomata

LRAM *n abbr* (*Brit*: = *Licentiate of the Royal Academy of Music*) specializzazione dopo la laurea

LSD *n abbr* (= *lysergic acid diethylamide*) L.S.D. *m*; (*Brit*: = *pounds, shillings and pence*) sistema monetario in vigore in Gran Bretagna fino al 1971

LSE *n abbr* = **London School of Economics**

LT *abbr* (*Elec*: = *low tension*) B.T.

Lt. *abbr* (= *lieutenant*) Ten.

Ltd *abbr* (*Comm*) = **limited**

lubricant ['lu:brɪkənt] *n* lubrificante *m*

lubricate ['lu:brɪkeɪt] *vt* lubrificare

lucid ['lu:sɪd] *adj* lucido(-a)

lucidity [lu:'sɪdɪtı] *n* lucidità

luck [lʌk] *n* fortuna, sorte *f*; **bad ~** sfortuna, mala sorte; **good ~** (buona) fortuna; **to be in ~** essere fortunato(-a); **to be out of ~** essere sfortunato(-a)

luckily ['lʌkɪlı] *adv* fortunatamente, per fortuna

luckless ['lʌklıs] *adj* sventurato(-a)

lucky ['lʌkı] *adj* fortunato(-a); (*number etc*) che porta fortuna

lucrative ['lu:krətɪv] *adj* lucrativo(-a), lucroso(-a), profittevole

ludicrous ['lu:dɪkrəs] *adj* ridicolo(-a), assurdo(-a)

ludo ['lu:dəu] *n* ≈ gioco dell'oca

lug [lʌg] *vt* trascinare

luggage ['lʌgɪdʒ] *n* bagagli *mpl*

luggage rack *n* portabagagli *m inv*

luggage van, (*US*) **luggage car** *n* (*Rail*) bagagliaio

lugubrious [lu'gu:brıəs] *adj* lugubre

lukewarm ['lu:kwɔ:m] *adj* tiepido(-a)

lull [lʌl] *n* intervallo di calma ■ *vt* (*child*) cullare; (*person, fear*) acquietare, calmare

lullaby ['lʌləbaı] *n* ninnananna

lumbago [lʌm'beɪgəu] *n* lombaggine *f*

lumber ['lʌmbə^r] *n* roba vecchia ■ *vt* (*Brit col*): **to ~ sb with sth/sb** affibbiare *or* rifilare qc/ qn a qn ■ *vi* (*also*: **lumber about, lumber along**) muoversi pesantemente

lumberjack ['lʌmbədʒæk] *n* boscaiolo

lumber room *n* (*Brit*) sgabuzzino

lumber yard *n* segheria

luminous ['lu:mɪnəs] *adj* luminoso(-a)

lump [lʌmp] *n* pezzo; (*in sauce*) grumo; (*swelling*) gonfiore *m* ■ *vt* (*also*: **lump together**) riunire, mettere insieme

lump sum *n* somma globale

lumpy ['lʌmpɪ] *adj* (*sauce*) grumoso(-a)
lunacy ['luːnəsɪ] *n* demenza, follia, pazzia
lunar ['luːnəʳ] *adj* lunare
lunatic ['luːnətɪk] *adj, n* pazzo(-a), matto(-a)
lunatic asylum *n* manicomio
lunch [lʌntʃ] *n* pranzo, colazione *f*; **to invite sb to** *or* **for ~** invitare qn a pranzo *or* a colazione
lunch break *n* intervallo del pranzo
luncheon ['lʌntʃən] *n* pranzo
luncheon meat *n* ≈ mortadella
luncheon voucher *n* buono *m* pasto *inv*
lunch hour *n* = **lunch break**
lunchtime ['lʌntʃtaɪm] *n* ora di pranzo
lung [lʌŋ] *n* polmone *m*
lung cancer *n* cancro del polmone
lunge [lʌndʒ] *vi* (*also*: **lunge forward**) fare un balzo in avanti; **to ~ at sb** balzare su qn
lupin ['luːpɪn] *n* lupino
lurch [ləːtʃ] *vi* vacillare, barcollare ■ *n* scatto improvviso; **to leave sb in the ~** piantare in asso qn
lure [luəʳ] *n* richiamo; lusinga ■ *vt* attirare (con l'inganno)
lurid ['luərɪd] *adj* sgargiante; (*details etc*) impressionante
lurk [ləːk] *vi* stare in agguato
luscious ['lʌʃəs] *adj* succulento(-a); delizioso(-a)

lush [lʌʃ] *adj* lussureggiante
lust [lʌst] *n* lussuria; cupidigia; desiderio; (*fig*): **~ for** sete *f* di
 ▶ **lust after** *vt fus* bramare, desiderare
luster ['lʌstəʳ] *n* (*US*) = **lustre**
lustful ['lʌstful] *adj* lascivo(-a), voglioso(-a)
lustre, (*US*) **luster** ['lʌstəʳ] *n* lustro, splendore *m*
lusty ['lʌstɪ] *adj* vigoroso(-a), robusto(-a)
lute [luːt] *n* liuto
Luxembourg ['lʌksəmbəːg] *n* (*state*) Lussemburgo *m*; (*city*) Lussemburgo *f*
luxuriant [lʌgˈzjuərɪənt] *adj* lussureggiante
luxurious [lʌgˈzjuərɪəs] *adj* sontuoso(-a), di lusso
luxury ['lʌkʃərɪ] *n* lusso ■ *cpd* di lusso
LV *n abbr* (*Brit*) = **luncheon voucher**
LW *abbr* (*Radio*: = *long wave*) O.L.
Lycra® ['laɪkrə] *n* lycra® *f inv*
lying ['laɪɪŋ] *n* bugie *fpl*, menzogne *fpl* ■ *adj* (*statement, story*) falso(-a); (*person*) bugiardo(-a)
lynch [lɪntʃ] *vt* linciare
lynx [lɪŋks] *n* lince *f*
Lyons ['laɪənz] *n* Lione *f*
lyre ['laɪəʳ] *n* lira
lyric ['lɪrɪk] *adj* lirico(-a); **lyrics** *npl* (*of song*) parole *fpl*
lyrical ['lɪrɪkl] *adj* lirico(-a)
lyricism ['lɪrɪsɪzəm] *n* lirismo

Mm

M, m [ɛm] *n* (*letter*) M, m *for* m *inv*; **M for Mary**, (US) **M for Mike** ≈ M come Milano

M *n abbr* (*Brit*) = **motorway**; **the M8** ≈ l'A8 ■ *abbr* (= *medium*) taglia media

m *abbr* (= *metre*) m; ≈ **mile; million**

MA *n abbr* (*Scol*) = **Master of Arts**; (US) = **military academy** ■ *abbr* (US) = **Massachusetts**

mac [mæk] *n* (*Brit*) impermeabile *m*

macabre [mə'kɑːbrə] *adj* macabro(-a)

macaroni [mækə'rəʊnɪ] *n* maccheroni *mpl*

macaroon [mækə'ruːn] *n* amaretto (*biscotto*)

mace [meɪs] *n* mazza; (*spice*) macis *m or f*

Macedonia [mæsɪ'dəʊnɪə] *n* Macedonia

Macedonian [mæsɪ'dəʊnɪən] *adj* macedone ■ *n* macedone *m/f*; (*Ling*) macedone *m*

machinations [mækɪ'neɪʃənz] *npl* macchinazioni *fpl*, intrighi *mpl*

machine [mə'ʃiːn] *n* macchina ■ *vt* (*dress etc*) cucire a macchina; (*Tech*) lavorare (a macchina)

machine code *n* (*Comput*) codice *m* di macchina, codice assoluto

machine gun *n* mitragliatrice *f*

machine language *n* (*Comput*) linguaggio *m* macchina *inv*

machine-readable [mə'ʃiːnriːdəbl] *adj* (*Comput*) leggibile dalla macchina

machinery [mə'ʃiːnərɪ] *n* macchinario, macchine *fpl*; (*fig*) macchina

machine shop *n* officina meccanica

machine tool *n* macchina utensile

machine washable *adj* lavabile in lavatrice

machinist [mə'ʃiːnɪst] *n* macchinista *m/f*

macho ['mætʃəʊ] *adj* macho *inv*

mackerel ['mækrəl] *n* (*pl inv*) sgombro

mackintosh ['mækɪntɒʃ] *n* impermeabile *m*

macro... ['mækrəʊ] *prefix* macro...

macroeconomics ['mækrəʊiːkə'nɒmɪks] *n* macroeconomia

mad [mæd] *adj* matto(-a), pazzo(-a); (*foolish*) sciocco(-a); (*angry*) furioso(-a); **to go ~** impazzire, diventar matto; **~ (at *or* with sb)** furibondo(-a) (con qn); **to be ~ (keen) about** *or* **on sth** (*col*) andar pazzo *or* matto per qc

madam ['mædəm] *n* signora; **M~ Chairman** Signora Presidentessa

madcap ['mædkæp] *adj* (*col*) senza senso, assurdo(-a)

mad cow disease *n* encefalite *f* bovina spongiforme

madden ['mædn] *vt* fare infuriare

maddening ['mædnɪŋ] *adj* esasperante

made [meɪd] *pt, pp of* **make**

Madeira [mə'dɪərə] *n* (*Geo*) Madera; (*wine*) madera *m*

made-to-measure ['meɪdtə'mɛʒər] *adj* (*Brit*) fatto(-a) su misura

madhouse ['mædhaʊs] *n* (*also fig*) manicomio

madly ['mædlɪ] *adv* follemente; (*love*) alla follia

madman ['mædmən] *n* pazzo, alienato

madness ['mædnɪs] *n* pazzia

Madrid [mə'drɪd] *n* Madrid *f*

Mafia ['mæfɪə] *n* mafia *f*

mag. [mæg] *n abbr* (*Brit col*) = **magazine** (*Press*)

magazine [mægə'ziːn] *n* (*Press*) rivista; (*Mil: store*) magazzino, deposito; (*of firearm*) caricatore *m*

maggot ['mægət] *n* baco, verme *m*

magic ['mædʒɪk] *n* magia ■ *adj* magico(-a)

magical ['mædʒɪkəl] *adj* magico(-a)

magician [mə'dʒɪʃən] *n* mago(-a)

magistrate ['mædʒɪstreɪt] *n* magistrato; giudice *m/f*

magistrates' court *n see* **crown court**

magnanimous [mæg'nænɪməs] *adj* magnanimo(-a)

magnate ['mægneɪt] *n* magnate *m*

magnesium [mæg'niːzɪəm] *n* magnesio

magnet ['mægnɪt] *n* magnete *m*, calamita

magnetic [mæg'nɛtɪk] *adj* magnetico(-a)

magnetic disk *n* (*Comput*) disco magnetico

magnetic tape *n* nastro magnetico

magnetism ['mægnɪtɪzəm] *n* magnetismo

magnification [mægnɪfɪ'keɪʃən] *n* ingrandimento

magnificence [mæg'nɪfɪsns] *n* magnificenza

magnificent [mæg'nɪfɪsnt] *adj* magnifico(-a)

magnify ['mægnɪfaɪ] *vt* ingrandire

magnifying glass ['mægnɪfaɪɪŋ-] *n* lente *f* d'ingrandimento

magnitude ['mægnɪtjuːd] *n* grandezza; importanza

magnolia [mæg'nəʊlɪə] *n* magnolia

magpie ['mægpaɪ] *n* gazza

mahogany [mə'hɔgənɪ] *n* mogano ■ *cpd* di *or* in mogano

maid [meɪd] *n* domestica; (*in hotel*) cameriera; **old ~** (*pej*) vecchia zitella

maiden ['meɪdn] *n* fanciulla ■ *adj* (*aunt etc*) nubile; (*speech, voyage*) inaugurale

maiden name *n* nome *m* nubile *or* da ragazza

mail [meɪl] *n* posta ■ *vt* spedire (per posta); **by ~** per posta

mailbox ['meɪlbɔks] *n* (*US*) cassetta delle lettere; (*Comput*) mailbox *f inv*

mailing list ['meɪlɪŋ-] *n* elenco d'indirizzi

mailman ['meɪlmæn] *n* (*US*) portalettere *m inv*, postino

mail-order ['meɪlɔːdəʳ] *n* vendita (*or* acquisto) per corrispondenza ■ *cpd*: **~ firm** *or* **house** ditta di vendita per corrispondenza

mailshot ['meɪlʃɔt] *n* mailing *m inv*

mail train *n* treno postale

mail truck *n* (*US Aut*) = **mail van**

mail van *n* (*Brit Aut*) furgone *m* postale; (: *Rail*) vagone *m* postale

maim [meɪm] *vt* mutilare

main [meɪn] *adj* principale ■ *n* (*pipe*) conduttura principale; **the mains** (*Elec*) la linea principale; **mains operated** *adj* che funziona a elettricità; **in the ~** nel complesso, nell'insieme

main course *n* (*Culin*) piatto principale, piatto forte

mainframe ['meɪnfreɪm] *n* (*also:* **mainframe computer**) mainframe *m inv*

mainland ['meɪnlənd] *n* continente *m*

mainline ['meɪnlaɪn] *adj* (*Rail*) della linea principale ■ *vb* (*drugs slang*) *vt* bucarsi di ■ *vi* bucarsi

main line *n* (*Rail*) linea principale

mainly ['meɪnlɪ] *adv* principalmente, soprattutto

main road *n* strada principale

mainstay ['meɪnsteɪ] *n* (*fig*) sostegno principale

mainstream ['meɪnstriːm] *n* (*fig*) corrente *f* principale

maintain [meɪn'teɪn] *vt* mantenere; (*affirm*) sostenere; **to ~ that** ... sostenere che ...

maintenance ['meɪntənəns] *n*

manutenzione *f*; (*alimony*) alimenti *mpl*

maintenance contract *n* contratto di manutenzione

maintenance order *n* (*Law*) obbligo degli alimenti

maisonette [meɪzə'nɛt] *n* (*Brit*) appartamento a due piani

maize [meɪz] *n* granturco, mais *m*

Maj. *abbr* (*Mil*) = **major**

majestic [mə'dʒɛstɪk] *adj* maestoso(-a)

majesty ['mædʒɪstɪ] *n* maestà *f inv*

major ['meɪdʒəʳ] *n* (*Mil*) maggiore *m* ■ *adj* (*greater, Mus*) maggiore; (*in importance*) principale, importante ■ *vi* (*US Scol*): **to ~ (in)** specializzarsi (in); **a ~ operation** (*Med*) una grossa operazione

Majorca [mə'jɔːkə] *n* Maiorca

major general *n* (*Mil*) generale *m* di divisione

majority [mə'dʒɔrɪtɪ] *n* maggioranza ■ *cpd* (*verdict*) maggioritario(-a)

majority holding *n* (*Comm*): **to have a ~** essere maggiore azionista

make [meɪk] *vt* (*pt, pp* **made**) [meɪd] fare; (*manufacture*) fare, fabbricare; (*cause to be*): **to ~ sb sad** *etc* rendere qn triste *etc*; (*force*): **to ~ sb do sth** costringere qn a fare qc, far fare qc a qn; (*equal*): **2 and 2 ~ 4** 2 più 2 fa 4 ■ *n* fabbricazione *f*; (*brand*) marca; **to ~ it** (*in time etc*) arrivare; (*succeed*) farcela; **what time do you ~ it?** che ora fai?; **to ~ good** *vi* (*succeed*) aver successo ■ *vt* (*deficit*) colmare; (*losses*) compensare; **to ~ do with** arrangiarsi con

▶ **make for** *vt fus* (*place*) avviarsi verso

▶ **make off** *vi* svignarsela

▶ **make out** *vt* (*write out*) scrivere; (*understand*) capire; (*see*) distinguere; (: *numbers*) decifrare; (*claim, imply*): **to ~ out (that)** voler far credere (che); **to ~ out a case for sth** presentare delle valide ragioni in favore di qc

▶ **make over** *vt* (*assign*): **to ~ over (to)** passare (a), trasferire (a)

▶ **make up** *vt* (*invent*) inventare; (*parcel*) fare ■ *vi* conciliarsi; (*with cosmetics*) truccarsi; **to be made up of** essere composto di *or* formato da

▶ **make up for** *vt fus* compensare; ricuperare

make-believe ['meɪkbɪliːv] *n*: **a world of ~** un mondo di favole; **it's just ~** è tutta un'invenzione

makeover ['meɪkəʊvəʳ] *n* cambio di immagine; **to give sb a ~** far cambiare immagine a qn

maker ['meɪkəʳ] *n* fabbricante *m*; creatore(-trice), autore(-trice)

makeshift ['meɪkʃɪft] *adj* improvvisato(-a)

make-up ['meɪkʌp] *n* trucco

make-up bag *n* borsa del trucco

m

make-up remover n struccatore m
making ['meɪkɪŋ] n (fig): **in the ~** in
  formazione; **he has the makings of an**
  actor ha la stoffa dell'attore
maladjusted [mælə'dʒʌstɪd] adj
  disadattato(-a)
maladroit [mælə'drɔɪt] adj maldestro(-a)
malaise [mæ'leɪz] n malessere m
malaria [mə'lɛərɪə] n malaria
Malawi [mə'lɑːwɪ] n Malawi m
Malay [mə'leɪ] adj malese ■ n malese m/f;
  (Ling) malese m
Malaya [mə'leɪə] n Malesia
Malayan [mə'leɪən] adj, n = **Malay**
Malaysia [mə'leɪzɪə] n Malaysia
Malaysian [mə'leɪzɪən] adj, n malaysiano(-a)
Maldives ['mɔːldaɪvz] npl: **the ~** le (isole)
  Maldive
male [meɪl] n (Bio, Elec) maschio ■ adj (gen, sex)
  maschile; (animal, child) maschio(-a); **~ and**
  female students studenti e studentesse
male chauvinist n maschilista m
male nurse n infermiere m
malevolence [mə'lɛvələns] n malevolenza
malevolent [mə'lɛvələnt] adj malevolo(-a)
malfunction [mæl'fʌŋkʃən] n funzione f
  difettosa
malice ['mælɪs] n malevolenza
malicious [mə'lɪʃəs] adj malevolo(-a); (Law)
  doloso(-a)
malign [mə'laɪn] vt malignare su; calunniare
malignant [mə'lɪgnənt] adj (Med) maligno(-a)
malingerer [mə'lɪŋgərəʳ] n scansafatiche
  m/f inv
mall [mɔːl] n (also: **shopping mall**) centro
  commerciale
malleable ['mælɪəbl] adj malleabile
mallet ['mælɪt] n maglio
malnutrition [mælnjuː'trɪʃən] n
  denutrizione f
malpractice [mæl'præktɪs] n prevaricazione
  f; negligenza
malt [mɔːlt] n malto ■ cpd (whisky) di malto
Malta ['mɔːltə] n Malta
Maltese [mɔːl'tiːz] adj, n (pl inv) maltese (m/f);
  (Ling) maltese m
maltreat [mæl'triːt] vt maltrattare
mammal ['mæml] n mammifero
mammoth ['mæməθ] n mammut m inv
  ■ adj enorme, gigantesco(-a)
man [mæn] n (pl **men**) uomo; (Chess) pezzo;
  (Draughts) pedina ■ vt fornire d'uomini;
  stare a; essere di servizio a
Man. abbr (Canada) = **Manitoba**
manacles ['mænəklz] npl manette fpl
manage ['mænɪdʒ] vi farcela ■ vt (be in charge
  of) occuparsi di; (shop, restaurant) gestire;

to ~ without sth/sb fare a meno di qc/qn;
to ~ to do sth riuscire a far qc
manageable ['mænɪdʒəbl] adj maneggevole;
  (task etc) fattibile
management ['mænɪdʒmənt] n
  amministrazione f, direzione f; gestione f;
  (persons: of business, firm) dirigenti mpl; (: of
  hotel, shop, theatre) direzione f; **"under new ~ "**
  "sotto nuova gestione"
management accounting n contabilità di
  gestione
management buyout n acquisto di una società
  da parte dei suoi dirigenti
management consultant n consulente m/f
  aziendale
manager ['mænɪdʒəʳ] n direttore m; (of shop,
  restaurant) gerente m; (of artist) manager m inv;
  sales ~ direttore m delle vendite
manageress [mænɪdʒə'rɛs] n direttrice f;
  gerente f
managerial [mænə'dʒɪərɪəl] adj dirigenziale
managing director ['mænɪdʒɪŋ-] n
  amministratore m delegato
Mancunian [mæŋ'kjuːnɪən] adj di
  Manchester ■ n abitante m/f di Manchester;
  originario(-a) di Manchester
mandarin ['mændərɪn] n (person, fruit)
  mandarino
mandate ['mændeɪt] n mandato
mandatory ['mændətərɪ] adj
  obbligatorio(-a); ingiuntivo(-a)
mandolin, mandoline ['mændəlɪn] n
  mandolino
mane [meɪn] n criniera
maneuver etc [mə'nuːvəʳ] (US) = **manoeuvre**
  etc
manful ['mænful] adj coraggioso(-a),
  valoroso(-a)
manfully ['mænfəlɪ] adv valorosamente
manganese [mæŋgə'niːz] n manganese m
mangetout ['mɔnʒ'tuː] n pisello dolce,
  taccola
mangle ['mæŋgl] vt straziare; mutilare
  ■ n strizzatoio
mango (pl **mangoes**) ['mæŋgəu] n mango
mangrove ['mæŋgrəuv] n mangrovia
mangy ['meɪndʒɪ] adj rognoso(-a)
manhandle ['mænhændl] vt (treat roughly)
  malmenare; (move by hand: goods) spostare a
  mano
manhole ['mænhəul] n botola stradale
manhood ['mænhud] n età virile; virilità
man-hour ['mænauəʳ] n ora di lavoro
manhunt ['mænhʌnt] n caccia all'uomo
mania ['meɪnɪə] n mania
maniac ['meɪnɪæk] n maniaco(-a)
manic ['mænɪk] adj maniacale

manic-depressive ['mænɪkdɪ'prɛsɪv] *adj*
maniaco-depressivo(-a) ▪ *n* persona affetta
da mania depressiva

manicure ['mænɪkjuə'] *n* manicure *f inv*

manicure set *n* trousse *f inv* della manicure

manifest ['mænɪfɛst] *vt* manifestare ▪ *adj*
manifesto(-a), palese ▪ *n* (*Aviat, Naut*)
manifesto

manifestation [mænɪfɛs'teɪʃən] *n*
manifestazione *f*

manifesto [mænɪ'fɛstəu] *n* manifesto

manifold ['mænɪfəuld] *adj* molteplice ▪ *n*
(*Aut etc*): **exhaust ~** collettore *m* di scarico

Manila [mə'nɪlə] *n* Manila

manila, manilla [mə'nɪlə] *adj* (*paper, envelope*)
manilla *inv*

manipulate [mə'nɪpjuleɪt] *vt* (*tool*)
maneggiare; (*controls*) azionare; (*limb, facts*)
manipolare

manipulation [mənɪpju'leɪʃən] *n*
maneggiare *m*; capacità di azionare;
manipolazione *f*

mankind [mæn'kaɪnd] *n* umanità, genere *m*
umano

manliness ['mænlɪnɪs] *n* virilità

manly ['mænlɪ] *adj* virile; coraggioso(-a)

man-made ['mæn'meɪd] *adj* sintetico(-a);
artificiale

manna ['mænə] *n* manna

mannequin ['mænɪkɪn] *n* (*dummy*)
manichino; (*fashion model*) indossatrice *f*

manner ['mænə'] *n* maniera, modo;
manners *npl* maniere *fpl*; (**good**) **manners**
buona educazione *f*, buone maniere; **bad
manners** maleducazione *f*; **all ~ of** ogni
sorta di

mannerism ['mænərɪzəm] *n* vezzo, tic *m inv*

mannerly ['mænəlɪ] *adj* educato(-a), civile

manoeuvrable, (*US*) **maneuverable**
[mə'nu:vrəbl] *adj* facile da manovrare; (*car*)
maneggevole

manoeuvre, (*US*) **maneuver** [mə'nu:və'] *vt*
manovrare ▪ *vi* far manovre ▪ *n* manovra;
to ~ sb into doing sth costringere
abilmente qn a fare qc

manor ['mænə'] *n* (*also*: **manor house**)
maniero

manpower ['mænpauə'] *n* manodopera

Manpower Services Commission *n* (*Brit*)
ente nazionale per l'occupazione

manservant (*pl* **menservants**) ['mænsə:vənt,
'mɛn-] *n* domestico

mansion ['mænʃən] *n* casa signorile

manslaughter ['mænslɔ:tə'] *n* omicidio
preterintenzionale

mantelpiece ['mæntlpi:s] *n* mensola del
caminetto

mantle ['mæntl] *n* mantello

man-to-man ['mæntə'mæn] *adj, adv* da
uomo a uomo

Mantua ['mæntjuə] *n* Mantova

manual ['mænjuəl] *adj, n* manuale (*m*)

manual worker *n* manovale *m*

manufacture [mænju'fæktʃə'] *vt* fabbricare
▪ *n* fabbricazione *f*, manifattura

manufactured goods *npl* manufatti *mpl*

manufacturer [mænju'fæktʃərə'] *n*
fabbricante *m*

manufacturing industries
[mænju'fæktʃərɪŋ-] *npl* industrie *fpl*
manifatturiere

manure [mə'njuə'] *n* concime *m*

manuscript ['mænjuskrɪpt] *n* manoscritto

many ['mɛnɪ] *adj* molti(-e) ▪ *pron* molti(-e),
un gran numero; **a great ~** moltissimi(-e),
un gran numero (di); **~ a ...** molti(-e) ..., più
di un(-a) ...; **too ~ difficulties** troppe
difficoltà; **twice as ~** due volte tanto; **how ~?**
quanti(-e)?

Maori ['maurɪ] *adj, n* maori (*m/f*) *inv*

map [mæp] *n* carta (geografica) ▪ *vt* fare
una carta di
  ▶ **map out** *vt* tracciare un piano di; (*fig:
  career, holiday, essay*) pianificare

maple ['meɪpl] *n* acero

mar [ma:'] *vt* sciupare

Mar. *abbr* (= *March*) mar.

marathon ['mærəθən] *n* maratona ▪ *adj*:
a ~ session una seduta fiume

marathon runner *n* maratoneta *m/f*

marauder [mə'rɔ:də'] *n* saccheggiatore *m*;
predatore *m*

marble ['ma:bl] *n* marmo; (*toy*) pallina, bilia;
marbles *n* (*game*) palline, bilie

March [ma:tʃ] *n* marzo; *see also* **July**

march [ma:tʃ] *vi* marciare; sfilare ▪ *n*
marcia; (*demonstration*) dimostrazione *f*;
to ~ into a room entrare a passo deciso in
una stanza

marcher ['ma:tʃə'] *n* dimostrante *m/f*

marching ['ma:tʃɪŋ] *n*: **to give sb his ~
orders** (*fig*) dare il benservito a qn

march-past ['ma:tʃpa:st] *n* sfilata

mare [mɛə'] *n* giumenta

marg [ma:dʒ] *n abbr* (*col*) = **margarine**

margarine [ma:dʒə'ri:n] *n* margarina

marge [ma:dʒ] *n abbr* (*col*) = **margarine**

margin ['ma:dʒɪn] *n* margine *m*

marginal ['ma:dʒɪnl] *adj* marginale; **~ seat**
(*Pol*) seggio elettorale ottenuto con una stretta
maggioranza

marginally ['ma:dʒɪnəlɪ] *adv* (*bigger, better*)
lievemente, di poco; (*different*) un po'

marigold ['mærɪgəuld] *n* calendola

m

657

marijuana [mærɪˈwɑːnə] n marijuana
marina [məˈriːnə] n marina
marinade n [mærɪˈneɪd] marinata ▪ vt [ˈmærɪneɪd] = **marinate**
marinate [ˈmærɪneɪt] vt marinare
marine [məˈriːn] adj (animal, plant) marino(-a); (forces, engineering) marittimo(-a) ▪ n fante m di marina; (US) marine m inv
marine insurance n assicurazione f marittima
marital [ˈmærɪtl] adj maritale, coniugale; ~ **status** stato coniugale
maritime [ˈmærɪtaɪm] adj marittimo(-a)
maritime law n diritto marittimo
marjoram [ˈmɑːdʒərəm] n maggiorana
mark [mɑːk] n segno; (stain) macchia; (of skid etc) traccia; (Brit Scol) voto; (Sport) bersaglio; (Hist: currency) marco; (Brit Tech): **M~ 2/3** 1a/2a serie f ▪ vt segnare; (stain) macchiare; (Brit Scol) dare un voto a; correggere; (Sport: player) marcare; **punctuation marks** segni di punteggiatura; **to be quick off the ~ (in doing)** (fig) non perdere tempo (per fare); **up to the ~** (in efficiency) all'altezza; **to ~ time** segnare il passo
  ▸ **mark down** vt (reduce: prices, goods) ribassare, ridurre
  ▸ **mark off** vt (tick off) spuntare, cancellare
  ▸ **mark out** vt delimitare
  ▸ **mark up** vt (price) aumentare
marked [mɑːkt] adj spiccato(-a), chiaro(-a)
markedly [ˈmɑːkɪdlɪ] adv visibilmente, notevolmente
marker [ˈmɑːkəʳ] n (sign) segno; (bookmark) segnalibro
market [ˈmɑːkɪt] n mercato ▪ vt (Comm) mettere in vendita; (promote) lanciare sul mercato; **to play the ~** giocare or speculare in borsa; **to be on the ~** essere (messo) in vendita or in commercio; **open ~** mercato libero
marketable [ˈmɑːkɪtəbl] adj commercializzabile
market analysis n analisi f di mercato
market day n giorno di mercato
market demand n domanda del mercato
market economy n economia di mercato
market forces npl forze fpl di mercato
market garden n (Brit) orto industriale
marketing [ˈmɑːkɪtɪŋ] n marketing m
marketplace [ˈmɑːkɪtpleɪs] n (piazza del) mercato; (world of trade) piazza, mercato
market price n prezzo di mercato
market research n indagine f or ricerca di mercato
market value n valore m di mercato

marking [ˈmɑːkɪŋ] n (on animal) marcatura di colore; (on road) segnaletica orizzontale
marksman [ˈmɑːksmən] n tiratore m scelto
marksmanship [ˈmɑːksmənʃɪp] n abilità nel tiro
mark-up [ˈmɑːkʌp] n (Comm: margin) margine m di vendita; (: increase) aumento
marmalade [ˈmɑːməleɪd] n marmellata d'arance
maroon [məˈruːn] vt (fig): **to be marooned (in or at)** essere abbandonato(-a) (in) ▪ adj bordeaux inv
marquee [mɑːˈkiː] n padiglione m
marquess, marquis [ˈmɑːkwɪs] n marchese m
Marrakech, Marrakesh [mærəˈkɛʃ] n Marrakesh f
marriage [ˈmærɪdʒ] n matrimonio
marriage bureau n agenzia matrimoniale
marriage certificate n certificato di matrimonio
marriage guidance, (US) **marriage counseling** n consulenza matrimoniale
marriage of convenience n matrimonio di convenienza
married [ˈmærɪd] adj sposato(-a); (life, love) coniugale, matrimoniale
marrow [ˈmærəu] n midollo; (vegetable) zucca
marry [ˈmærɪ] vt sposare, sposarsi con; (father, priest etc) dare in matrimonio ▪ vi (also: **get married**) sposarsi
Mars [mɑːz] n (planet) Marte m
Marseilles [mɑːˈseɪlz] n Marsiglia
marsh [mɑːʃ] n palude f
marshal [ˈmɑːʃl] n maresciallo; (US: fire marshal) capo; (: police marshal) capitano; (for demonstration, meeting) membro del servizio d'ordine ▪ vt adunare
marshalling yard [ˈmɑːʃlɪŋ-] n scalo smistamento
marshmallow [mɑːʃˈmæləu] n (Bot) altea; (sweet) caramella soffice e gommosa
marshy [ˈmɑːʃɪ] adj paludoso(-a)
marsupial [mɑːˈsuːpɪəl] adj, n marsupiale (m)
martial [ˈmɑːʃl] adj marziale
martial arts npl arti fpl marziali
martial law n legge f marziale
Martian [ˈmɑːʃən] n marziano(-a)
martin [ˈmɑːtɪn] n (also: **house martin**) balestruccio
martyr [ˈmɑːtəʳ] n martire m/f ▪ vt martirizzare
martyrdom [ˈmɑːtədəm] n martirio
marvel [ˈmɑːvl] n meraviglia ▪ vi: **to ~ (at)** meravigliarsi (di)

marvellous, (US) **marvelous** ['mɑːvələs] adj
meraviglioso(-a)

Marxism ['mɑːksɪzəm] n marxismo

Marxist ['mɑːksɪst] adj, n marxista (m/f)

marzipan ['mɑːzɪpæn] n marzapane m

mascara [mæs'kɑːrə] n mascara m inv

mascot ['mæskət] n mascotte f inv

masculine ['mæskjulɪn] adj maschile
■ n genere m maschile

masculinity [mæskju'lɪnɪtɪ] n mascolinità

MASH [mæʃ] n abbr (US Mil: = mobile army
surgical hospital) ospedale di campo di unità mobile
dell'esercito

mash [mæʃ] vt (Culin) passare, schiacciare

mashed [mæʃt] adj: ~ **potatoes** purè m di
patate

mask [mɑːsk] n (gen, Elec) maschera
■ vt mascherare

masochism ['mæsəkɪzəm] n masochismo

masochist ['mæsəkɪst] n masochista m/f

mason ['meɪsn] n (also: **stonemason**)
scalpellino; (also: **freemason**) massone m

masonic [mə'sɔnɪk] adj massonico(-a)

masonry ['meɪsnrɪ] n muratura

masquerade [mæskə'reɪd] n ballo in
maschera; (fig) mascherata ■ vi: **to ~ as**
farsi passare per

mass [mæs] n moltitudine f, massa; (Physics)
massa; (Rel) messa ■ vi ammassarsi; **the
masses** le masse; **to go to ~** andare a or alla
messa

Mass. abbr (US) = **Massachusetts**

massacre ['mæsəkər] n massacro
■ vt massacrare

massage ['mæsɑːʒ] n massaggio
■ vt massaggiare

masseur [mæ'səːr] n massaggiatore m

masseuse [mæ'səːz] n massaggiatrice f

massive ['mæsɪv] adj enorme, massiccio(-a)

mass market n mercato di massa

mass media npl mass media mpl

mass meeting n (of everyone concerned)
riunione f generale; (huge) adunata
popolare

mass-produce ['mæsprə'djuːs] vt produrre
in serie

mass production n produzione f in serie

mast [mɑːst] n albero; (Radio, TV) pilone m (a
traliccio)

mastectomy [mæs'tektəmɪ] n mastectomia

master ['mɑːstər] n padrone m; (Art etc,
teacher: in primary school) maestro; (: in secondary
school) professore m; (title for boys): **M~ X**
Signorino X ■ vt domare; (learn) imparare a
fondo; (understand) conoscere a fondo; **~ of
ceremonies** n maestro di cerimonie; **M~'s
degree** n vedi nota

Master's degree

Il *Master's degree* è il riconoscimento che
viene conferito a chi segue un corso di
specializzazione dopo aver conseguito un
"Bachelor's degree". Vi sono diversi tipi di
Master's Degree; i più comuni sono il
"Master of Arts (MA)" e il "Master of
Science (MSc)" che si ottengono dopo aver
seguito un corso e aver presentato una
tesi originale. Per il "Master of Letters
(MLitt)" e il "Master of Philosophy
(MPhil)" è invece sufficiente presentare
la tesi; vedi anche "doctorate".

master disk n (Comput) disco m master inv,
disco principale

masterful ['mɑːstəful] adj autoritario(-a),
imperioso(-a)

master key n chiave f maestra

masterly ['mɑːstəlɪ] adj magistrale

mastermind ['mɑːstəmaɪnd] n mente f
superiore ■ vt essere il cervello di

masterpiece ['mɑːstəpiːs] n capolavoro

master plan n piano generale

master stroke n colpo maestro

mastery ['mɑːstərɪ] n dominio; padronanza

mastiff ['mæstɪf] n mastino inglese

masturbate ['mæstəbeɪt] vi masturbare

masturbation [mæstə'beɪʃən] n
masturbazione f

mat [mæt] n stuoia; (also: **doormat**) stoino,
zerbino ■ adj = **matt**

match [mætʃ] n fiammifero; (game) partita,
incontro; (fig) uguale m/f; matrimonio;
partito ■ vt intonare; (go well with) andare
benissimo con; (equal) uguagliare ■ vi
intonarsi; **to be a good ~** andare bene
▶ **match up** vt intonare

matchbox ['mætʃbɔks] n scatola per
fiammiferi

matching ['mætʃɪŋ] adj ben assortito(-a)

matchless ['mætʃlɪs] adj senza pari

mate [meɪt] n compagno(-a) di lavoro; (
col: friend) amico(-a); (animal) compagno(-a);
(in merchant navy) secondo ■ vi accoppiarsi
■ vt accoppiare

material [mə'tɪərɪəl] n (substance) materiale
m, materia; (cloth) stoffa ■ adj materiale;
(important) essenziale; **materials** npl
(equipment etc) materiali mpl; occorrente m

materialistic [mətɪərɪə'lɪstɪk] adj
materialistico(-a)

materialize [mə'tɪərɪəlaɪz] vi
materializzarsi, realizzarsi

materially [mə'tɪərɪəlɪ] adv dal punto di vista
materiale; sostanzialmente

m

maternal [mə'tə:nl] *adj* materno(-a)
maternity [mə'tə:nɪtɪ] *n* maternità ∎ *cpd* di maternità; *(clothes)* pre-maman *inv*
maternity benefit *n* sussidio di maternità
maternity hospital *n* ≈ clinica ostetrica
matey ['meɪtɪ] *adj* (*Brit col*) amicone(-a)
math [mæθ] *n abbr* (*US*) = **mathematics**
mathematical [mæθə'mætɪkl] *adj* matematico(-a)
mathematician [mæθəmə'tɪʃən] *n* matematico(-a)
mathematics [mæθə'mætɪks] *n* matematica
maths [mæθs] *n abbr* (*Brit*) = **mathematics**
matinée ['mætɪneɪ] *n* matinée *f inv*
mating ['meɪtɪŋ] *n* accoppiamento
mating call *n* chiamata all'accoppiamento
mating season *n* stagione *f* degli amori
matriarchal [meɪtrɪ'ɑ:kl] *adj* matriarcale
matrices ['meɪtrɪsi:z] *npl of* **matrix**
matriculation [mətrɪkju'leɪʃən] *n* immatricolazione *f*
matrimonial [mætrɪ'məunɪəl] *adj* matrimoniale, coniugale
matrimony ['mætrɪmənɪ] *n* matrimonio
matrix (*pl* **matrices**) ['meɪtrɪks, 'meɪtrɪsi:z] *n* matrice *f*
matron ['meɪtrən] *n* (*in hospital*) capoinfermiera; (*in school*) infermiera
matronly ['meɪtrənlɪ] *adj* da matrona
matt [mæt] *adj* opaco(-a)
matted ['mætɪd] *adj* ingarbugliato(-a)
matter ['mætə[r]] *n* questione *f*; (*Physics*) materia, sostanza; (*content*) contenuto; (*Med*: *pus*) pus *m* ∎ *vi* importare; **it doesn't ~** non importa; (*I don't mind*) non fa niente; **what's the ~?** che cosa c'è?; **no ~ what** qualsiasi cosa accada; **that's another ~** quello è un altro affare; **as a ~ of course** come cosa naturale; **as a ~ of fact** in verità; **it's a ~ of habit** è una questione di abitudine; **printed ~** stampe *fpl*; **reading ~** (*Brit*) qualcosa da leggere
matter-of-fact [mætərəv'fækt] *adj* prosaico(-a)
matting ['mætɪŋ] *n* stuoia
mattress ['mætrɪs] *n* materasso
mature [mə'tjuə[r]] *adj* maturo(-a); (*cheese*) stagionato(-a) ∎ *vi* maturare; stagionare; (*Comm*) scadere
mature student *n* studente universitario che ha più di 25 anni
maturity [mə'tjuərɪtɪ] *n* maturità
maudlin ['mɔ:dlɪn] *adj* lacrimoso(-a)
maul [mɔ:l] *vt* lacerare
Mauritania [mɔrɪ'teɪnɪə] *n* Mauritania
Mauritius [mə'rɪʃəs] *n* Maurizio
mausoleum [mɔ:sə'lɪəm] *n* mausoleo
mauve [məuv] *adj* malva *inv*

maverick ['mævərɪk] *n* (*fig*) chi sta fuori del branco
mawkish ['mɔ:kɪʃ] *adj* sdolcinato(-a); insipido(-a)
max. *abbr* = **maximum**
maxim ['mæksɪm] *n* massima
maxima ['mæksɪmə] *npl of* **maximum**
maximize ['mæksɪmaɪz] *vt* (*profits etc*) massimizzare; (*chances*) aumentare al massimo
maximum ['mæksɪməm] *adj* massimo(-a) ∎ *n* (*pl* **maxima**) massimo
May [meɪ] *n* maggio; *see also* **July**
may [meɪ] *vi* (*conditional*: **might**) (*indicating possibility*): **he ~ come** può darsi che venga; (*be allowed to*): **~ I smoke?** posso fumare?; **~ I sit here?** le dispiace se mi siedo qua?; (*wishes*): **~ God bless you!** Dio la benedica!; **he might be there** può darsi che ci sia; **he might come** potrebbe venire, può anche darsi che venga; **I might as well go** potrei anche andarmene; **you might like to try** forse le piacerebbe provare
maybe ['meɪbi:] *adv* forse, può darsi; **~ he'll ...** può darsi che lui ... + *sub*, forse lui ...; **~ not** forse no, può darsi di no
mayday ['meɪdeɪ] *n* S.O.S. *m*, mayday *m inv*
May Day *n* il primo maggio
mayhem ['meɪhɛm] *n* cagnara
mayonnaise [meɪə'neɪz] *n* maionese *f*
mayor [mɛə[r]] *n* sindaco
mayoress ['mɛərɛs] *n* sindaco (*donna*); moglie *f* del sindaco
maypole ['meɪpəul] *n* palo ornato di fiori attorno a cui si danza durante la festa di maggio
maze [meɪz] *n* labirinto, dedalo
MB *abbr* (*Comput*) = **megabyte**; (*Canada*) = **Manitoba**
MBA *n abbr* (= *Master of Business Administration*) titolo di studio
MBE *n abbr* (*Brit*: = *Member of the Order of the British Empire*) titolo
MBO *n abbr* = **management buyout**
MC *n abbr* = **master of ceremonies**; (*US*: = *Member of Congress*) membro del Congresso
MCAT *n abbr* (*US*: = *Medical College Admissions Test*) esame di ammissione a studi superiori di medicina
MD *n abbr* (= *Doctor of Medicine*) titolo di studio; (*Comm*) = **managing director** ∎ *abbr* (*US*) = **Maryland**
Md. *abbr* (*US*) = **Maryland**
MDT *abbr* (*US*: = *Mountain Daylight Time*) ora legale delle Montagne Rocciose
ME *abbr* (*US*) = **Maine** ∎ *n abbr* (*Med*: = *myalgic encephalomyelitis*) sindrome *f* da affaticamento cronico; (*US*) = **medical examiner**

me [mi:] *pron* mi, m' + *vowel*; (*stressed, after prep*) me; **it's me** sono io; **it's for me** è per me

meadow ['mɛdəʊ] *n* prato

meagre, (*US*) **meager** ['mi:gər] *adj* magro(-a)

meal [mi:l] *n* pasto; (*flour*) farina; **to go out for a** ~ mangiare fuori

meals on wheels *n* (*Brit*) distribuzione *f* di pasti caldi a domicilio (*per persone malate o anziane*)

mealtime ['mi:ltaɪm] *n* l'ora di mangiare

mealy-mouthed ['mi:lɪmaʊðd] *adj* che parla attraverso eufemismi

mean [mi:n] *adj* (*with money*) avaro(-a), gretto(-a); (*unkind*) meschino(-a), maligno(-a); (*US: vicious: animal*) cattivo(-a); (: *person*) perfido(-a); (*average*) medio(-a) ■ *vt* (*pt, pp* **meant**) [mɛnt] (*signify*) significare, voler dire; (*intend*): **to ~ to do** aver l'intenzione di fare ■ *n* mezzo; (*Math*) media; **to be meant for** essere destinato(-a) a; **do you ~ it?** dice sul serio?; **what do you ~?** che cosa vuol dire?; *see also* **means**

meander [mɪˈændər] *vi* far meandri; (*fig*) divagare

meaning ['mi:nɪŋ] *n* significato, senso

meaningful ['mi:nɪŋful] *adj* significativo(-a); (*relationship*) valido(-a)

meaningless ['mi:nɪŋlɪs] *adj* senza senso

meanness ['mi:nnɪs] *n* avarizia; meschinità

means [mi:nz] *npl* mezzi *mpl*; **by ~ of** per mezzo di; (*person*) a mezzo di; **by all ~** ma certo, prego

means test *n* (*Admin*) accertamento dei redditi (*per una persona che ha chiesto un aiuto finanziario*)

meant [mɛnt] *pt, pp of* **mean**

meantime ['mi:ntaɪm], **meanwhile** ['mi:nwaɪl] *adv* (*also*: **in the meantime**) nel frattempo

measles ['mi:zlz] *n* morbillo

measly ['mi:zlɪ] *adj* (*col*) miserabile

measurable ['mɛʒərəbl] *adj* misurabile

measure ['mɛʒər] *vt, vi* misurare ■ *n* misura; (*ruler*) metro; **a litre** ~ una misura da un litro; **some ~ of success** un certo successo; **to take measures to do sth** prendere provvedimenti per fare qc
▶ **measure up** *vi*: **to ~ up (to)** dimostrarsi *or* essere all'altezza (di)

measured ['mɛʒəd] *adj* misurato(-a)

measurement ['mɛʒəmənt] *n* (*act*) misurazione *f*; (*measure*) misura; **chest/hip ~** giro petto/fianchi; **to take sb's measurements** prendere le misure di qn

meat [mi:t] *n* carne *f*; **cold meats** (*Brit*) affettati *mpl*; **crab ~** polpa di granchio

meatball ['mi:tbɔ:l] *n* polpetta di carne

meat pie *n* torta salata in pasta frolla con ripieno di carne

meaty ['mi:tɪ] *adj* che sa di carne; (*fig*) sostanzioso(-a); (*person*) corpulento(-a); (*part of body*) carnoso(-a); ~ **meal** pasto a base di carne

Mecca ['mɛkə] *n* La Mecca; (*fig*): **a ~ (for)** la Mecca (di)

mechanic [mɪˈkænɪk] *n* meccanico; *see also* **mechanics**

mechanical [mɪˈkænɪkəl] *adj* meccanico(-a)

mechanical engineering *n* (*science*) ingegneria meccanica; (*industry*) costruzioni *fpl* meccaniche

mechanics [məˈkænɪks] *n* meccanica ■ *npl* meccanismo

mechanism ['mɛkənɪzəm] *n* meccanismo

mechanization [mɛkənaɪˈzeɪʃən] *n* meccanizzazione *f*

MEd *n abbr* (= *Master of Education*) titolo di studio

medal ['mɛdl] *n* medaglia

medallion [mɪˈdælɪən] *n* medaglione *m*

medallist, (*US*) **medalist** ['mɛdəlɪst] *n* (*Sport*) vincitore(-trice) di medaglia

meddle ['mɛdl] *vi*: **to ~ in** immischiarsi in, mettere le mani in; **to ~ with** toccare

meddlesome ['mɛdlsəm], **meddling** ['mɛdlɪŋ] *adj* (*interfering*) che mette il naso dappertutto; (*touching things*) che tocca tutto

media ['mi:dɪə] *npl* (*Press, Radio, TV*) media *mpl*

media circus *n* carrozzone *m* dell'informazione

mediaeval [mɛdɪˈi:vl] *adj* = **medieval**

median ['mi:dɪən] *n* (*US: also*: **median strip**) banchina *f* spartitraffico *inv*

media research *n* sondaggio tra gli utenti dei mass media

mediate ['mi:dɪeɪt] *vi* interporsi; fare da mediatore(-trice)

mediation [mi:dɪˈeɪʃən] *n* mediazione *f*

mediator ['mi:dɪeɪtər] *n* mediatore(-trice)

Medicaid ['mɛdɪkeɪd] *n* (*US*) assistenza medica ai poveri

medical ['mɛdɪk] *adj* medico(-a); ~ (**examination**) visita medica

medical certificate *n* certificato medico

medical examiner *n* (*US*) medico incaricato di indagare la causa di morte in circostanze sospette

medical student *n* studente(-essa) di medicina

Medicare ['mɛdɪkɛər] *n* (*US*) assistenza medica agli anziani

medicated ['mɛdɪkeɪtɪd] *adj* medicato(-a)

medication [mɛdɪˈkeɪʃən] *n* (*drugs etc*) medicinali *mpl*, farmaci *mpl*

medicinal [mɛˈdɪsɪnl] *adj* medicinale

medicine ['mɛdsɪn] *n* medicina

medicine chest n armadietto farmaceutico
medicine man n stregone m
medieval [mɛdɪ'iːvl] adj medievale
mediocre [miːdɪ'əukər] adj mediocre
mediocrity [miːdɪ'ɔkrɪtɪ] n mediocrità
meditate ['mɛdɪteɪt] vi: **to ~ (on)** meditare (su)
meditation [mɛdɪ'teɪʃən] n meditazione f
Mediterranean [mɛdɪtə'reɪnɪən] adj mediterraneo(-a); **the ~ (Sea)** il (mare) Mediterraneo
medium ['miːdɪəm] adj medio(-a) ■ n (pl **media**) (means) mezzo (pl **mediums**) (person) medium m inv; **the happy ~** una giusta via di mezzo; see also **media**
medium-dry ['miːdɪəm'draɪ] adj demisec inv
medium-sized ['miːdɪəmsaɪzd] adj (tin etc) di grandezza media; (clothes) di taglia media
medium wave n (Radio) onde fpl medie
medley ['mɛdlɪ] n selezione f
meek [miːk] adj dolce, umile
meet (pt, pp **met**) [miːt, mɛt] vt incontrare; (for the first time) fare la conoscenza di; (fig) affrontare; far fronte a; soddisfare; raggiungere ■ vi incontrarsi; (in session) riunirsi; (join: objects) unirsi ■ n (Brit Hunting) raduno (dei partecipanti alla caccia alla volpe); (US Sport) raduno (sportivo); **I'll ~ you at the station** verrò a prenderla alla stazione; **pleased to ~ you!** lieto di conoscerla!, piacere!
▶ **meet up** vi: **to ~ up with sb** incontrare qn
▶ **meet with** vt fus incontrare; **he met with an accident** ha avuto un incidente
meeting ['miːtɪŋ] n incontro; (session: of club etc) riunione f; (interview) intervista; (formal) colloquio; (Sport: rally) raduno; **she's at a ~** (Comm) è in riunione; **to call a ~** convocare una riunione
meeting place n luogo d'incontro
megabyte ['mɛgəbaɪt] n megabyte m inv
megalomaniac [mɛgələu'meɪnɪæk] n megalomane m/f
megaphone ['mɛgəfəun] n megafono
megapixel ['mɛgəpɪksl] n megapixel m inv
megawatt ['mɛgəwɔt] n megawatt m inv
melancholy ['mɛlənkəlɪ] n malinconia ■ adj malinconico(-a)
mellow ['mɛləu] adj (wine, sound) ricco(-a); (person, light) dolce; (colour) caldo(-a); (fruit) maturo(-a) ■ vi (person) addolcirsi
melodious [mɪ'ləudɪəs] adj melodioso(-a)
melodrama ['mɛləudrɑːmə] n melodramma m
melodramatic [mɛlədrə'mætɪk] adj melodrammatico(-a)
melody ['mɛlədɪ] n melodia
melon ['mɛlən] n melone m

melt [mɛlt] vi (gen) sciogliersi, struggersi; (metals) fondersi; (fig) intenerirsi ■ vt sciogliere, struggere; fondere; (person) commuovere; **melted butter** burro fuso
▶ **melt away** vi sciogliersi completamente
▶ **melt down** vt fondere
meltdown ['mɛltdaun] n melt-down m inv
melting point ['mɛltɪŋ-] n punto di fusione
melting pot ['mɛltɪŋ-] n (fig) crogiolo; **to be in the ~** essere ancora in discussione
member ['mɛmbər] n membro; (of club) socio(-a), iscritto(-a); (of political party) iscritto(-a); **~ country/state** n paese m/stato membro; **M~ of Parliament (MP)** n (Brit) deputato; **M~ of the European Parliament** n eurodeputato; **M~ of the House of Representatives** n (US) membro della Camera dei Rappresentanti
membership ['mɛmbəʃɪp] n iscrizione f; (numero d')iscritti mpl, membri mpl
membership card n tessera (di iscrizione)
membrane ['mɛmbreɪn] n membrana
memento [mə'mɛntəu] n ricordo, souvenir m inv
memo ['mɛməu] n appunto; (Comm etc) comunicazione f di servizio
memoir ['mɛmwɑːr] n memoria; **memoirs** npl memorie fpl, ricordi mpl
memo pad n blocchetto per appunti
memorable ['mɛmərəbl] adj memorabile
memorandum (pl **memoranda**) [mɛmə'rændəm, -də] n appunto; (Comm etc) comunicazione f di servizio; (Diplomacy) memorandum m inv
memorial [mɪ'mɔːrɪəl] n monumento commemorativo ■ adj commemorativo(-a)
Memorial Day n (US) vedi nota

memorize ['mɛməraɪz] vt imparare a memoria
memory ['mɛmərɪ] n (gen, Comput) memoria; (recollection) ricordo; **in ~ of** in memoria di; **to have a good/bad ~** aver buona/cattiva memoria; **loss of ~** amnesia
memory card n (for digital camera) scheda di memoria m inv di memoria
memory stick n (Comput) stick m inv di memoria
men [mɛn] npl of **man**
menace ['mɛnɪs] n minaccia; (col: nuisance)

peste f ■ vt minacciare; **a public ~** un pericolo pubblico

menacing ['mɛnɪsɪŋ] adj minaccioso(-a)

menagerie [mɪ'nædʒərɪ] n serraglio

mend [mɛnd] vt aggiustare, riparare; (darn) rammendare ■ n rammendo; **on the ~** in via di guarigione

mending ['mɛndɪŋ] n rammendo; (items to be mended) roba da rammendare

menial ['miːnɪəl] adj da servo, domestico(-a); umile

meningitis [mɛnɪn'dʒaɪtɪs] n meningite f

menopause ['mɛnəupɔːz] n menopausa

menservants ['mɛnsə:vənts] npl of **manservant**

men's room n: **the ~** (esp US) la toilette degli uomini

menstruate ['mɛnstrueɪt] vi mestruare

menstruation [mɛnstru'eɪʃən] n mestruazione f

menswear ['mɛnzwɛəʳ] n abbigliamento maschile

mental ['mɛntl] adj mentale; **~ illness** malattia mentale

mental hospital n ospedale m psichiatrico

mentality [mɛn'tælɪtɪ] n mentalità f inv

mentally ['mɛntlɪ] adv: **to be ~ handicapped** essere minorato psichico

menthol ['mɛnθɒl] n mentolo

mention ['mɛnʃən] n menzione f ■ vt menzionare, far menzione di; **don't ~ it!** non c'è di che!, prego!; **I need hardly ~ that ...** inutile dire che ...; **not to ~, without mentioning** per non parlare di, senza contare

mentor ['mɛntɔːʳ] n mentore m

menu ['mɛnjuː] n (set menu, Comput) menù m inv; (printed) carta

menu-driven ['mɛnjuːdrɪvn] adj (Comput) guidato(-a) da menù

MEP n abbr = **Member of the European Parliament**

mercantile ['mə:kəntaɪl] adj mercantile; (law) commerciale

mercenary ['mə:sɪnərɪ] adj venale ■ n mercenario

merchandise ['mə:tʃəndaɪz] n merci fpl ■ vt commercializzare

merchandiser ['mə:tʃəndaɪzəʳ] n merchandiser m inv

merchant ['mə:tʃənt] n (trader) commerciante m; (shopkeeper) negoziante m; **timber/wine ~** negoziante di legno/vino

merchant bank n (Brit) banca d'affari

merchantman ['mə:tʃəntmən] n mercantile m

merchant navy, (US) **merchant marine** n marina mercantile

merciful ['mə:sɪful] adj pietoso(-a), clemente

mercifully ['mə:sɪflɪ] adv con clemenza; (fortunately) per fortuna

merciless ['mə:sɪlɪs] adj spietato(-a)

mercurial [mə:'kjuərɪəl] adj (unpredictable) volubile

mercury ['mə:kjurɪ] n mercurio

mercy ['mə:sɪ] n pietà; (Rel) misericordia; **to have ~ on sb** aver pietà di qn; **at the ~ of** alla mercè di

mercy killing n eutanasia

mere [mɪəʳ] adj semplice; **by a ~ chance** per mero caso

merely ['mɪəlɪ] adv semplicemente, non ... che

merge [mə:dʒ] vt unire; (Comput: files, text) fondere ■ vi fondersi, unirsi; (Comm) fondersi

merger ['mə:dʒəʳ] n (Comm) fusione f

meridian [mə'rɪdɪən] n meridiano

meringue [mə'ræŋ] n meringa

merit ['mɛrɪt] n merito, valore m ■ vt meritare

meritocracy [mɛrɪ'tɔkrəsɪ] n meritocrazia

mermaid ['mə:meɪd] n sirena

merriment ['mɛrɪmənt] n gaiezza, allegria

merry ['mɛrɪ] adj gaio(-a), allegro(-a); **M~ Christmas!** Buon Natale!

merry-go-round ['mɛrɪgəuraund] n carosello

mesh [mɛʃ] n maglia; rete f ■ vi (gears) ingranarsi; **wire ~** rete metallica

mesmerize ['mɛzməraɪz] vt ipnotizzare; affascinare

mess [mɛs] n confusione f, disordine m; (fig) pasticcio; (Mil) mensa; **to be (in) a ~** (house, room) essere in disordine (or molto sporco); (fig: marriage, life) essere un caos; **to be/get o.s. in a ~** (fig) essere/cacciarsi in un pasticcio

▶ **mess about, mess around** vi (col) trastullarsi

▶ **mess about** or **around with** vt fus (col) gingillarsi con; (plans) fare un pasticcio di

▶ **mess up** vt sporcare; fare un pasticcio di; rovinare

message ['mɛsɪdʒ] n messaggio; **to get the ~** (fig, col) capire l'antifona

message board n (Comput) bacheca elettronica

message switching n (Comput) smistamento messaggi

messenger ['mɛsɪndʒəʳ] n messaggero(-a)

Messiah [mɪ'saɪə] n Messia m

Messrs, Messrs. ['mɛsəz] abbr (on letters: = messieurs) Spett.

messy ['mɛsɪ] adj sporco(-a); disordinato(-a); (confused: situation etc) ingarbugliato(-a)

m

663

Met [mɛt] *n abbr* (US) = **Metropolitan Opera**
met [mɛt] *pt, pp of* **meet** ■ *adj abbr*
= **meteorological; the M~ Office** l'Ufficio
Meteorologico
metabolism [mɛ'tæbəlɪzəm] *n* metabolismo
metal ['mɛtl] *n* metallo ■ *vt* massicciare
metallic [mɛ'tælɪk] *adj* metallico(-a)
metallurgy [mɛ'tæləʤɪ] *n* metallurgia
metalwork ['mɛtlwəːk] *n* (*craft*) lavorazione f
del metallo
metamorphosis (*pl* **-phoses**)
[mɛtə'mɔːfəsɪs, -iːz] *n* metamorfosi f *inv*
metaphor ['mɛtəfəʳ] *n* metafora
metaphysics [mɛtə'fɪzɪks] *n* metafisica
mete [miːt]: **to ~ out** *vt fus* infliggere
meteor ['miːtɪəʳ] *n* meteora
meteoric [miːtɪ'ɔrɪk] *adj* (*fig*) fulmineo(-a)
meteorite ['miːtɪəraɪt] *n* meteorite *m*
meteorological [miːtɪərə'lɒʤɪkl] *adj*
meteorologico(-a)
meteorology [miːtɪə'rɒləʤɪ] *n* meteorologia
meter ['miːtəʳ] *n* (*instrument*) contatore *m*;
(*parking meter*) parchimetro; (US) = **metre**
methane ['miːθeɪn] *n* metano
method ['mɛθəd] *n* metodo; **~ of payment**
modo *or* modalità f *inv* di pagamento
methodical [mɪ'θɒdɪkl] *adj* metodico(-a)
Methodist ['mɛθədɪst] *adj, n* metodista (*m/f*)
methylated spirits ['mɛθɪleɪtɪd-] *n* (Brit: *also:*
meths) alcool *m* denaturato
meticulous [mɛ'tɪkjuləs] *adj* meticoloso(-a)
metre, (US) **meter** ['miːtəʳ] *n* metro
metric ['mɛtrɪk] *adj* metrico(-a); **to go ~**
adottare il sistema metrico decimale
metrical ['mɛtrɪkl] *adj* metrico(-a)
metrication [mɛtrɪ'keɪʃən] *n* conversione f al
sistema metrico
metric system *n* sistema *m* metrico
decimale
metric ton *n* tonnellata
metronome ['mɛtrənəum] *n* metronomo
metropolis [mɪ'trɒpəlɪs] *n* metropoli f *inv*
metropolitan [mɛtrə'pɒlɪtən] *adj*
metropolitano(-a)
Metropolitan Police *n* (Brit): **the ~** la polizia
di Londra
mettle ['mɛtl] *n* coraggio
mew [mjuː] *vi* (*cat*) miagolare
mews [mjuːz] *n* (Brit): **~ flat** *appartamentino*
ricavato da una vecchia scuderia
Mexican ['mɛksɪkən] *adj, n* messicano(-a)
Mexico ['mɛksɪkəu] *n* Messico
Mexico City *n* Città del Messico
mezzanine ['mɛtsəniːn] *n* mezzanino
MFA *n abbr* (US: = *Master of Fine Arts*) *titolo di*
studio
mfr *abbr* = **manufacture; manufacturer**

mg *abbr* (= *milligram*) mg
Mgr *abbr* (= *Monseigneur, Monsignor*) mons.;
(*Comm*) = **manager**
MHR *n abbr* (US) = **Member of the House of**
Representatives
MHz *abbr* (= *megahertz*) MHz
MI *abbr* (US) = **Michigan**
MI5 *n abbr* (Brit: = *Military Intelligence, section five*)
agenzia di controspionaggio
MI6 *n abbr* (Brit: = *Military Intelligence, section six*)
agenzia di spionaggio
MIA *abbr* = **missing in action**
miaow [miː'au] *vi* miagolare
mice [maɪs] *npl of* **mouse**
Mich. *abbr* (US) = **Michigan**
microbe ['maɪkrəub] *n* microbio
microbiology [maɪkrəubaɪ'ɔləʤɪ] *n*
microbiologia
microchip ['maɪkrəutʃɪp] *n* microcircuito
integrato, chip *m inv*
microcomputer [maɪkrəukəm'pjuːtəʳ] *n*
microcomputer *m inv*
microcosm ['maɪkrəukɔzəm] *n* microcosmo
microeconomics [maɪkrəui:kə'nɔmɪks] *n*
microeconomia
microfiche ['maɪkrəufiːʃ] *n* microfiche f *inv*
microfilm ['maɪkrəufɪlm] *n* microfilm *m inv*
■ *vt* microfilmare
microlight ['maɪkrəulaɪt] *n* aereo *m* biposto
inv
micrometer [maɪ'krɔmɪtəʳ] *n* micrometro,
palmer *m inv*
microphone ['maɪkrəfəun] *n* microfono
microprocessor [maɪkrəu'prəusesəʳ] *n*
microprocessore *m*
micro-scooter ['maɪkrəuskuːtəʳ] *n*
monopattino
microscope ['maɪkrəskəup] *n* microscopio;
under the ~ al microscopio
microscopic [maɪkrə'skɒpɪk] *adj*
microscopico(-a)
microwavable, microwaveable
['maɪkrəuweɪvəbl] *adj* adatto(-a) al forno a
microonde
microwave ['maɪkrəuweɪv] *n* (*also:*
microwave oven) forno a microonde
mid [mɪd] *adj:* **~ May** metà maggio;
~ afternoon metà pomeriggio; **in ~ air**
a mezz'aria; **he's in his ~ thirties** avrà circa
trentacinque anni
midday [mɪd'deɪ] *n* mezzogiorno
middle ['mɪdl] *n* mezzo; centro; (*waist*) vita
■ *adj* di mezzo; **I'm in the ~ of reading it** sto
proprio leggendolo ora; **in the ~ of the**
night nel mezzo della notte
middle age *n* mezza età
middle-aged [mɪdl'eɪʤd] *adj* di mezza età

Middle Ages *npl*: **the** ~ il Medioevo
middle class *adj* (*also*: **middle-class**)
≈ borghese ■ *n*: **the ~(es)** ≈ la borghesia
Middle East *n*: **the** ~ il Medio Oriente
middleman ['mɪdlmæn] *n* intermediario;
agente *m* rivenditore
middle management *n* quadri *mpl*
intermedi
middle name *n* secondo nome *m*
middle-of-the-road ['mɪdləvðə'rəud] *adj*
moderato(-a)
middleweight ['mɪdlweɪt] *n* (*Boxing*) peso
medio
middling ['mɪdlɪŋ] *adj* medio(-a)
midge [mɪdʒ] *n* moscerino
midget ['mɪdʒɪt] *n* nano(-a)
midi system ['mɪdɪ-] *n* (*hi-fi*) compatto
Midlands ['mɪdləndz] *npl* contee del centro
dell'Inghilterra
midnight ['mɪdnaɪt] *n* mezzanotte *f*; **at** ~
a mezzanotte
midriff ['mɪdrɪf] *n* diaframma *m*
midst [mɪdst] *n*: **in the** ~ **of** in mezzo a
midsummer [mɪd'sʌmə^r] *n* mezza *or* piena
estate *f*
midway [mɪd'weɪ] *adj, adv*: ~ **(between)**
a mezza strada (fra)
midweek [mɪd'wiːk] *adv, adj* a metà
settimana
midwife (*pl* **midwives**) ['mɪdwaɪf, -vz] *n*
levatrice *f*
midwifery ['mɪdwɪfərɪ] *n* ostetrica
midwinter [mɪd'wɪntə^r] *n* pieno inverno
miffed [mɪft] *adj* (*col*) seccato(-a), stizzito(-a)
might [maɪt] *vb see* **may** ■ *n* potere *m*, forza
mighty ['maɪtɪ] *adj* forte, potente ■ *adv* (*col*)
molto
migraine ['miːɡreɪn] *n* emicrania
migrant ['maɪɡrənt] *n* (*bird, animal*) migratore
m; (*person*) migrante *m/f*; nomade *m/f* ■ *adj*
migratore(-trice), nomade; (*worker*)
emigrato(-a)
migrate [maɪ'ɡreɪt] *vi* migrare
migration [maɪ'ɡreɪʃən] *n* migrazione *f*
mike [maɪk] *n abbr* (= *microphone*) microfono
Milan [mɪ'læn] *n* Milano *f*
mild [maɪld] *adj* mite; (*person, voice*) dolce;
(*flavour*) delicato(-a); (*illness*) leggero(-a)
■ *n* birra leggera
mildew ['mɪldjuː] *n* muffa
mildly ['maɪldlɪ] *adv* mitemente;
dolcemente; delicatamente; leggermente;
to put it ~ a dire poco
mildness ['maɪldnɪs] *n* mitezza; dolcezza;
delicatezza; non gravità
mile [maɪl] *n* miglio; **to do 20 miles per
gallon** ≈ usare 14 litri per cento chilometri

mileage ['maɪlɪdʒ] *n* distanza in miglia,
≈ chilometraggio
mileage allowance *n* rimborso per miglio
mileometer [maɪ'lɔmɪtə^r] *n* (*Brit*)
= **milometer**
milestone ['maɪlstəun] *n* pietra miliare
milieu ['miːljəː] *n* ambiente *m*
militant ['mɪlɪtnt] *adj, n* militante (*m/f*)
militarism ['mɪlɪtərɪzəm] *n* militarismo
militaristic [mɪlɪtə'rɪstɪk] *adj* militaristico(-a)
military ['mɪlɪtərɪ] *adj* militare ■ *n*: **the** ~
i militari, l'esercito
military service *n* servizio militare
militate ['mɪlɪteɪt] *vi*: **to** ~ **against** essere
d'ostacolo a
militia [mɪ'lɪʃə] *n* milizia
milk [mɪlk] *n* latte *m* ■ *vt* (*cow*) mungere; (*fig*)
sfruttare
milk chocolate *n* cioccolato al latte
milk float *n* (*Brit*) furgone *m* del lattaio
milking ['mɪlkɪŋ] *n* mungitura
milkman ['mɪlkmən] *n* lattaio
milk shake *n* frappé *m inv*
milk tooth *n* dente *m* di latte
milk truck *n* (*US*) = **milk float**
milky ['mɪlkɪ] *adj* lattiginoso(-a); (*colour*)
latteo(-a)
Milky Way *n* Via Lattea
mill [mɪl] *n* mulino; (*small: for coffee, pepper etc*)
macinino; (*factory*) fabbrica; (*spinning mill*)
filatura ■ *vt* macinare ■ *vi* (*also*: **mill about**)
formicolare
millennium (*pl* **milleniums** *or* **millennia**)
[mɪ'lɛnɪəm, -'lɛnɪə] *n* millennio
millennium bug *n* baco di fine millennio
miller ['mɪlə^r] *n* mugnaio
millet ['mɪlɪt] *n* miglio
milli... ['mɪlɪ] *prefix* milli...
milligram, milligramme ['mɪlɪɡræm] *n*
milligrammo
millilitre, (*US*) **milliliter** ['mɪlɪliːtə^r] *n* millilitro
millimetre, (*US*) **millimeter** ['mɪlɪmiːtə^r] *n*
millimetro
milliner ['mɪlɪnə^r] *n* modista
millinery ['mɪlɪnərɪ] *n* modisteria
million ['mɪljən] *n* milione *m*
millionaire [mɪljə'nɛə^r] *n* milionario,
≈ miliardario
millipede ['mɪlɪpiːd] *n* millepiedi *m inv*
millstone ['mɪlstəun] *n* macina
millwheel ['mɪlwiːl] *n* ruota di mulino
milometer [maɪ'lɔmɪtə^r] *n* ≈ contachilometri
m inv
mime [maɪm] *n* mimo ■ *vt, vi* mimare
mimic ['mɪmɪk] *n* imitatore(-trice) ■ *vt*
(*comedian*) imitare; (*animal, person*)
scimmiottare

m

665

mimicry ['mɪmɪkrɪ] n imitazioni fpl; (Zool) mimetismo

Min. abbr (Brit Pol: = ministry) Min.

min. abbr (= minute, minimum) min.

minaret [mɪnə'rɛt] n minareto

mince [mɪns] vt tritare, macinare ■ vi (in walking) camminare a passettini ■ n (Brit Culin) carne f tritata or macinata; **he does not ~ (his) words** parla chiaro e tondo

mincemeat ['mɪnsmi:t] n frutta secca tritata per uso in pasticceria

mince pie n specie di torta con frutta secca

mincer ['mɪnsəʳ] n tritacarne m inv

mincing ['mɪnsɪŋ] adj lezioso(-a)

mind [maɪnd] n mente f ■ vt (attend to, look after) badare a, occuparsi di; (be careful) fare attenzione a, stare attento(-a) a; (object to): **I don't ~ the noise** il rumore non mi dà alcun fastidio; **do you ~ if ...?** le dispiace se ...?; **I don't ~** non m'importa; **~ you, ...** sì, però va detto che ...; **never ~** non importa, non fa niente; **it is on my ~** mi preoccupa; **to change one's ~** cambiare idea; **to be in two minds about sth** essere incerto su qc; **to my ~** secondo me, a mio parere; **to be out of one's ~** essere uscito(-a) di mente; **to keep sth in ~** non dimenticare qc; **to bear sth in ~** tener presente qc; **to have sb/sth in ~** avere in mente qn/qc; **to have in ~ to do** aver l'intenzione di fare; **it went right out of my ~** mi è completamente passato di mente, me ne sono completamente dimenticato; **to bring** or **call sth to ~** riportare or richiamare qc alla mente; **to make up one's ~** decidersi; **"~ the step"** "attenzione allo scalino"

mind-boggling ['maɪndbɔglɪŋ] adj (col) sconcertante

-minded ['maɪndɪd] adj: **fair~** imparziale; **an industrially~ nation** una nazione orientata verso l'industria

minder ['maɪndəʳ] n (child minder) bambinaia; (bodyguard) guardia del corpo

mindful ['maɪndful] adj: **~ of** attento(-a) a; memore di

mindless ['maɪndlɪs] adj idiota; (violence, crime) insensato(-a)

mine¹ [maɪn] pron il/la mio(-a); (pl) i/le miei/ mie; **this book is ~** questo libro è mio

mine² [maɪn] n miniera; (explosive) mina ■ vt (coal) estrarre; (ship, beach) minare

mine detector n rivelatore m di mine

minefield ['maɪnfi:ld] n campo minato

miner ['maɪnəʳ] n minatore m

mineral ['mɪnərəl] adj minerale ■ n minerale m; **minerals** npl (Brit: soft drinks) bevande fpl gasate

mineralogy [mɪnə'rælədʒɪ] n mineralogia

mineral water n acqua minerale

minesweeper ['maɪnswi:pəʳ] n dragamine m inv

mingle ['mɪŋgl] vt mescolare, mischiare ■ vi: **to ~ with** mescolarsi a, mischiarsi con

mingy ['mɪndʒɪ] adj (col: amount) misero(-a); (: person) spilorcio(-a)

miniature ['mɪnətʃəʳ] adj in miniatura ■ n miniatura

minibus ['mɪnɪbʌs] n minibus m inv

minicab ['mɪnɪkæb] n (Brit) ≈ taxi m inv

minicomputer ['mɪnɪkəm'pju:təʳ] n minicomputer m inv

Minidisc® ['mɪnɪdɪsk] n minidisc m inv

minim ['mɪnɪm] n (Mus) minima

minima ['mɪnɪmə] npl of **minimum**

minimal ['mɪnɪml] adj minimo(-a)

minimalist ['mɪnɪməlɪst] adj, n minimalista (m/f)

minimize ['mɪnɪmaɪz] vt minimizzare

minimum ['mɪnɪməm] n (pl **minima**) minimo ■ adj minimo(-a); **to reduce to a ~** ridurre al minimo; **~ wage** salario minimo garantito

minimum lending rate n (Brit) ≈ tasso ufficiale di sconto

mining ['maɪnɪŋ] n industria mineraria ■ adj minerario(-a); di minatori

minion ['mɪnjən] n (pej) caudatario; favorito(-a)

mini-series ['mɪnɪsɪəri:z] n miniserie f inv

miniskirt ['mɪnɪskə:t] n minigonna

minister ['mɪnɪstəʳ] n (Brit Pol) ministro; (Rel) pastore m ■ vi: **to ~ to sb** assistere qn; **to ~ to sb's needs** provvedere ai bisogni di qn

ministerial [mɪnɪs'tɪərɪəl] adj (Brit Pol) ministeriale

ministry ['mɪnɪstrɪ] n (Brit Pol) ministero; (Rel): **to go into the ~** diventare pastore

mink [mɪŋk] n visone m

mink coat n pelliccia di visone

Minn. abbr (US) = **Minnesota**

minnow ['mɪnəu] n pesciolino d'acqua dolce

minor ['maɪnəʳ] adj minore, di poca importanza; (Mus) minore ■ n (Law) minorenne m/f

Minorca [mɪ'nɔ:kə] n Minorca

minority [maɪ'nɔrɪtɪ] n minoranza; **to be in a ~** essere in minoranza

minster ['mɪnstəʳ] n cattedrale f (annessa a monastero)

minstrel ['mɪnstrəl] n giullare m, menestrello

mint [mɪnt] n (plant) menta; (sweet) pasticca di menta ■ vt (coins) battere; **the (Royal) M~**, (US) **the (US) M~** la Zecca; **in ~ condition** come nuovo(-a) di zecca

mint sauce n salsa di menta

minuet [mɪnjuˈɛt] n minuetto
minus [ˈmaɪnəs] n (also: **minus sign**) segno
meno ■ prep meno
minuscule [ˈmɪnəskjuːl] adj minuscolo(-a)
minute¹ [ˈmɪnɪt] n minuto; (official record)
processo verbale, resoconto sommario;
minutes npl verbale m, verbali mpl; **it is 5
minutes past 3** sono le 3 e 5 (minuti); **wait a
~!** (aspetta) un momento!; **at the last ~**
all'ultimo momento; **up to the ~**
ultimissimo; modernissimo
minute² [maɪˈnjuːt] adj minuscolo(-a);
(detail) minuzioso(-a); **in ~ detail**
minuziosamente
minute book n libro dei verbali
minute hand n lancetta dei minuti
minutely [maɪˈnjuːtlɪ] adv (by a small amount)
di poco; (in detail) minuziosamente
minutiae [mɪˈnjuːʃiiː] npl minuzie fpl
miracle [ˈmɪrəkl] n miracolo
miraculous [mɪˈrækjuləs] adj miracoloso(-a)
mirage [ˈmɪrɑːʒ] n miraggio
mire [ˈmaɪəʳ] n pantano, melma
mirror [ˈmɪrəʳ] n specchio ■ vt rispecchiare,
riflettere
mirror image n immagine f speculare
mirth [məːθ] n gaiezza
misadventure [mɪsədˈvɛntʃəʳ] n
disavventura; **death by ~** (Brit) morte f
accidentale
misanthropist [mɪˈzænθrəpɪst] n
misantropo(-a)
misapply [mɪsəˈplaɪ] vt impiegare male
misapprehension [ˈmɪsæprɪˈhɛnʃən] n
malinteso
misappropriate [mɪsəˈprəuprɪeɪt] vt
appropriarsi indebitamente di
misappropriation [ˈmɪsəprəuprɪˈeɪʃən] n
appropriazione f indebita
misbehave [mɪsbɪˈheɪv] vi comportarsi male
misbehaviour, (US) **misbehavior**
[mɪsbɪˈheɪvjəʳ] n comportamento scorretto
misc. abbr = **miscellaneous**
miscalculate [mɪsˈkælkjuleɪt] vt calcolare
male
miscalculation [ˈmɪskælkjuˈleɪʃən] n errore
m di calcolo
miscarriage [ˈmɪskærɪdʒ] n (Med) aborto
spontaneo; **~ of justice** errore m giudiziario
miscarry [mɪsˈkærɪ] vi (Med) abortire; (fail:
plans) andare a monte, fallire
miscellaneous [mɪsɪˈleɪnɪəs] adj (items)
vario(-a); (selection) misto(-a); **~ expenses**
spese varie
miscellany [mɪˈsɛlənɪ] n raccolta
mischance [mɪsˈtʃɑːns] n: **by (some) ~** per
sfortuna

mischief [ˈmɪstʃɪf] n (naughtiness)
birichineria; (harm) male m, danno;
(maliciousness) malizia
mischievous [ˈmɪstʃɪvəs] adj (naughty)
birichino(-a); (harmful) dannoso(-a)
misconception [mɪskənˈsɛpʃən] n idea
sbagliata
misconduct [mɪsˈkɔndʌkt] n cattiva
condotta; **professional ~** reato
professionale
misconstrue [mɪskənˈstruː] vt interpretare
male
miscount [mɪsˈkaunt] vt, vi contare male
misdeed [mɪsˈdiːd] n (old) misfatto
misdemeanour, (US) **misdemeanor**
[mɪsdɪˈmiːnəʳ] n misfatto; infrazione f
misdirect [mɪsdɪˈrɛkt] vt mal indirizzare
miser [ˈmaɪzəʳ] n avaro
miserable [ˈmɪzərəbl] adj infelice; (wretched)
miserabile; (weather) deprimente; **to feel ~**
sentirsi avvilito or giù di morale
miserably [ˈmɪzərəblɪ] adv (fail, live, pay)
miseramente; (smile, answer) tristemente
miserly [ˈmaɪzəlɪ] adj avaro(-a)
misery [ˈmɪzərɪ] n (unhappiness) tristezza;
(pain) sofferenza; (wretchedness) miseria
misfire [mɪsˈfaɪəʳ] vi far cilecca; (car engine)
perdere colpi
misfit [ˈmɪsfɪt] n (person) spostato(-a)
misfortune [mɪsˈfɔːtʃən] n sfortuna
misgiving [mɪsˈɡɪvɪŋ] n, **misgivings**
[mɪsˈɡɪvɪŋz] npl dubbi mpl, sospetti mpl;
to have misgivings about sth essere
diffidente or avere dei dubbi per quanto
riguarda qc
misguided [mɪsˈɡaɪdɪd] adj sbagliato(-a);
poco giudizioso(-a)
mishandle [mɪsˈhændl] vt (treat roughly)
maltrattare; (mismanage) trattare male
mishap [ˈmɪshæp] n disgrazia
mishear [mɪsˈhɪəʳ] vt, vi irreg capire male
mishmash [ˈmɪʃmæʃ] n (col) minestrone m,
guazzabuglio
misinform [mɪsɪnˈfɔːm] vt informare male
misinterpret [mɪsɪnˈtəːprɪt] vt interpretare
male
misinterpretation [ˈmɪsɪntəːprɪˈteɪʃən] n
errata interpretazione f
misjudge [mɪsˈdʒʌdʒ] vt giudicare male
mislay [mɪsˈleɪ] vt irreg smarrire
mislead [mɪsˈliːd] vt irreg sviare
misleading [mɪsˈliːdɪŋ] adj ingannevole
misled [mɪsˈlɛd] pt, pp of **mislead**
mismanage [mɪsˈmænɪdʒ] vt gestire male;
trattare male
mismanagement [mɪsˈmænɪdʒmənt] n
cattiva amministrazione f

m

667

misnomer [mɪs'nəumə^r] n termine m sbagliato or improprio

misogynist [mɪ'sɔdʒɪnɪst] n misogino

misplace [mɪs'pleɪs] vt smarrire; collocare fuori posto; **to be misplaced** (trust etc) essere malriposto(-a)

misprint ['mɪsprɪnt] n errore m di stampa

mispronounce [mɪsprə'nauns] vt pronunziare male

misquote [mɪs'kwəut] vt citare erroneamente

misread [mɪs'ri:d] vt irreg leggere male

misrepresent [mɪsreprɪ'zɛnt] vt travisare

Miss [mɪs] n Signorina; **Dear ~ Smith** Cara Signorina; (formal) Gentile Signorina

miss [mɪs] vt (fail to get) perdere; (appointment, class) mancare a; (escape, avoid) evitare; (notice loss of: money etc) accorgersi di non avere più; (regret the absence of): **I ~ him/it** sento la sua mancanza, lui/esso mi manca ◾ vi mancare ◾ n (shot) colpo mancato; (fig): **that was a near ~** c'è mancato poco; **the bus just missed the wall** l'autobus per un pelo non è andato a finire contro il muro; **you`re missing the point** non capisce

▸ **miss out** vt (Brit) omettere

▸ **miss out on** vt fus (fun, party) perdersi; (chance, bargain) lasciarsi sfuggire

Miss. abbr (US) = **Mississippi**

missal ['mɪsl] n messale m

misshapen [mɪs'ʃeɪpən] adj deforme

missile ['mɪsaɪl] n (Aviat) missile m; (object thrown) proiettile m

missile base n base f missilistica

missile launcher n lancia-missili m inv

missing ['mɪsɪŋ] adj perso(-a), smarrito(-a); **to go ~** sparire; **~ person** scomparso(-a), disperso(-a); **~ in action** (Mil) disperso(-a)

mission ['mɪʃən] n missione f; **on a ~ to sb** in missione da qn

missionary ['mɪʃənrɪ] n missionario(-a)

misspell [mɪs'spɛl] vt (irreg: like **spell**) sbagliare l'ortografia di

misspent [mɪs'spɛnt] adj: **his ~ youth** la sua gioventù sciupata

mist [mɪst] n nebbia, foschia ◾ vi (also: **mist over, mist up**) annebbiarsi; (Brit: windows) appannarsi

mistake [mɪs'teɪk] n sbaglio, errore m ◾ vt (irreg: like **take**) sbagliarsi di; fraintendere; **to ~ for** prendere per; **by ~** per sbaglio; **to make a ~** (in writing, calculating etc) fare uno sbaglio or un errore; **to make a ~ about sb/sth** sbagliarsi sul conto di qn/su qc

mistaken [mɪs'teɪkən] pp of **mistake** ◾ adj (idea etc) sbagliato(-a); **to be ~** sbagliarsi

mistaken identity n errore m di persona

mistakenly [mɪs'teɪkənlɪ] adv per errore

mister ['mɪstə^r] n (col) signore m; see **Mr**

mistletoe ['mɪsltəu] n vischio

mistook [mɪs'tuk] pt of **mistake**

mistranslation [mɪstræns'leɪʃən] n traduzione f errata

mistreat [mɪs'tri:t] vt maltrattare

mistress ['mɪstrɪs] n padrona; (lover) amante f; (Brit Scol) insegnante f

mistrust [mɪs'trʌst] vt diffidare di ◾ n: ~ **(of)** diffidenza (nei confronti di)

mistrustful [mɪs'trʌstful] adj: ~ **(of)** diffidente (nei confronti di)

misty ['mɪstɪ] adj nebbioso(-a), brumoso(-a)

misty-eyed ['mɪstɪ'aɪd] adj trasognato(-a)

misunderstand [mɪsʌndə'stænd] vt, vi irreg capire male, fraintendere

misunderstanding [mɪsʌndə'stændɪŋ] n malinteso, equivoco

misunderstood [mɪsʌndə'stud] pt, pp of **misunderstand**

misuse n [mɪs'ju:s] cattivo uso; (of power) abuso ◾ vt [mɪs'ju:z] far cattivo uso di; abusare di

MIT n abbr (US) = **Massachusetts Institute of Technology**

mite [maɪt] n (small quantity) briciolo; (Brit: small child): **poor ~!** povera creaturina!

miter ['maɪtə^r] n (US) = **mitre**

mitigate ['mɪtɪgeɪt] vt mitigare; (suffering) alleviare; **mitigating circumstances** circostanze fpl attenuanti

mitigation [mɪtɪ'geɪʃən] n mitigazione f; alleviamento

mitre, (US) miter ['maɪtə^r] n mitra; (Carpentry) giunto ad angolo retto

mitt ['mɪt], **mitten** ['mɪtn] n mezzo guanto; manopola

mix [mɪks] vt mescolare ◾ vi mescolarsi ◾ n mescolanza; preparato; **to ~ sth with sth** mischiare qc a qc; **to ~ business with pleasure** unire l'utile al dilettevole; **cake ~** preparato per torta

▸ **mix in** vt (eggs etc) incorporare

▸ **mix up** vt mescolare; (confuse) confondere; **to be mixed up in sth** essere coinvolto in qc

mixed [mɪkst] adj misto(-a)

mixed-ability ['mɪkstə'bɪlɪtɪ] adj (class etc) con alunni di capacità diverse

mixed bag n miscuglio, accozzaglia; **it's a ~** c'è un po' di tutto

mixed blessing n: **it's a ~** ha i suoi lati positivi e negativi

mixed doubles npl (Sport) doppio misto

mixed economy n economia mista

mixed grill n (Brit) misto alla griglia

mixed marriage n matrimonio misto

mixed-up [mɪkst'ʌp] adj (confused) confuso(-a)
mixer ['mɪksə^r] n (for food: electric) frullatore m;
(: hand) frullino; (person): **he is a good ~**
è molto socievole
mixer tap n miscelatore m
mixture ['mɪkstʃə^r] n mescolanza; (blend: of
tobacco etc) miscela; (Med) sciroppo
mix-up ['mɪksʌp] n confusione f
MK abbr (Brit Tech) = **mark**
mk abbr (Hist: currency) = **mark**
mkt abbr = **market**
MLitt n abbr (= Master of Literature, Master of
Letters) titolo di studio
MLR n abbr (Brit) = **minimum lending rate**
mm abbr (= millimetre) mm
MMS n abbr (= multimedia messaging service) mms
m inv (servizio); **~ message** mms m inv
MN abbr (Brit) = **Merchant Navy**; (US)
= **Minnesota**
MO n abbr = **medical officer**; (US col: = modus
operandi) modo d'agire ■ abbr (US) = **Missouri**
m.o. abbr = **money order**
moan [məʊn] n gemito ■ vi gemere; (col:
complain): **to ~ (about)** lamentarsi (di)
moaner ['məʊnə^r] n (col) uno(-a) che si
lamenta sempre
moaning ['məʊnɪŋ] n gemiti mpl
moat [məʊt] n fossato
mob [mɔb] n folla; (disorderly) calca; (pej):
the ~ la plebaglia ■ vt accalcarsi intorno a
mobile ['məʊbaɪl] adj mobile ■ n (phone)
telefonino; (Art) mobile m inv; **applicants
must be ~** (Brit) i candidati devono essere
disposti a viaggiare
mobile home n grande roulotte f inv (utilizzata
come domicilio)
mobile phone n telefonino
mobile shop n (Brit) negozio ambulante
mobility [məʊ'bɪlɪtɪ] n mobilità; (of applicant)
disponibilità a viaggiare
mobilize ['məʊbɪlaɪz] vt mobilitare ■ vi
mobilitarsi
moccasin ['mɔkəsɪn] n mocassino
mock [mɔk] vt deridere, burlarsi di ■ adj
falso(-a)
mockery ['mɔkərɪ] n derisione f; **to make a ~
of** rendere ridicolo
mocking ['mɔkɪŋ] adj derisorio(-a)
mockingbird ['mɔkɪŋbə:d] n mimo (uccello)
mock-up ['mɔkʌp] n modello dimostrativo;
abbozzo
MOD n abbr (Brit) = **Ministry of Defence**;
see **defence**
mod cons ['mɔd'kɔnz] npl abbr (Brit)
= **modern conveniences**
mode [məʊd] n modo; (of transport) mezzo;
(Comput) modalità f inv

model ['mɔdl] n modello; (person: for fashion)
indossatore(-trice); (: for artist) modello(-a)
■ vt modellare ■ vi fare l'indossatore (or
l'indossatrice) ■ adj (small-scale: railway etc)
in miniatura; (child, factory) modello inv; **to ~
clothes** presentare degli abiti; **to ~ sb/sth
on** modellare qn/qc su
modem ['məʊdem] n modem m inv
moderate ['mɔdərɪt] adj moderato(-a)
■ n (Pol) moderato(-a) ■ vi ['mɔdəreɪt]
moderarsi, placarsi ■ vt moderare
moderately ['mɔdərɪtlɪ] adv (act) con
moderazione; (expensive, difficult) non troppo;
(pleased, happy) abbastanza, discretamente;
~ priced a prezzo modico
moderation [mɔdə'reɪʃən] n moderazione f,
misura; **in ~** in quantità moderata, con
moderazione
moderator ['mɔdəreɪtə^r] n
moderatore(-trice); (Rel) moderatore in
importanti riunioni ecclesiastiche
modern ['mɔdən] adj moderno(-a);
~ conveniences comodità fpl moderne;
~ languages lingue fpl moderne
modernization [mɔdənaɪ'zeɪʃən] n
rimodernamento, modernizzazione f
modernize ['mɔdənaɪz] vt modernizzare
modest ['mɔdɪst] adj modesto(-a)
modesty ['mɔdɪstɪ] n modestia
modicum ['mɔdɪkəm] n: **a ~ of** un minimo di
modification [mɔdɪfɪ'keɪʃən] n
modificazione f; **to make modifications**
fare or apportare delle modifiche
modify ['mɔdɪfaɪ] vt modificare
modish ['məʊdɪʃ] adj (literary) à la page inv
Mods [mɔdz] n abbr (Brit: = (Honour)
Moderations) esame all'università di Oxford
modular ['mɔdjʊlə^r] adj (filing, unit) modulare
modulate ['mɔdjʊleɪt] vt modulare
modulation [mɔdjʊ'leɪʃən] n modulazione f
module ['mɔdjuːl] n modulo
Mogadishu [mɔgə'dɪʃuː] n Mogadiscio f
mogul ['məʊgl] n (fig) magnate m, pezzo
grosso; (Ski) cunetta
MOH n abbr (Brit: = Medical Officer of Health)
= ufficiale m sanitario
mohair ['məʊhεə^r] n mohair m
Mohammed [məʊ'hæmɪd] n Maometto
moist [mɔɪst] adj umido(-a)
moisten ['mɔɪsn] vt inumidire
moisture ['mɔɪstʃə^r] n umidità; (on glass)
goccioline fpl di vapore
moisturize ['mɔɪstʃəraɪz] vt (skin) idratare
moisturizer ['mɔɪstʃəraɪzə^r] n idratante f
molar ['məʊlə^r] n molare m
molasses [məʊ'læsɪz] n molassa
mold etc [məʊld] (US) = **mould** etc

Moldavia [mɔl'deɪvɪə], **Moldova** [mɔl'dəuvə] n Moldavia

Moldavian [mɔl'deɪvɪən], **Moldovan** [mɔl'dəuvən] adj moldavo(-a)

mole [məul] n (animal) talpa; (spot) neo

molecule ['mɔlɪkjuːl] n molecola

molehill ['məulhɪl] n cumulo di terra sulla tana di una talpa

molest [məu'lɛst] vt molestare

mollusc, (US) **mollusk** ['mɔləsk] n mollusco

mollycoddle ['mɔlɪkɔdl] vt coccolare, vezzeggiare

Molotov cocktail ['mɔlətɔf-] n (bottiglia) Molotov f inv

molt [məult] vi (US) = **moult**

molten ['məultən] adj fuso(-a)

mom [mɔm] n (US) = **mum**

moment ['məumənt] n momento, istante m; importanza; **at the ~** al momento, in questo momento; **for the ~** per il momento, per ora; **in a ~** tra un momento; **"one ~ please"** (Tel) "attenda, prego"

momentarily ['məuməntərɪlɪ] adv per un momento; (US: very soon) da un momento all'altro

momentary ['məuməntərɪ] adj momentaneo(-a), passeggero(-a)

momentous [məu'mɛntəs] adj di grande importanza

momentum [məu'mɛntəm] n velocità acquisita, slancio; (Physics) momento; **to gather ~** aumentare di velocità; (fig) prendere or guadagnare terreno

mommy ['mɔmɪ] n (US) mamma

Mon. abbr (= Monday) lun.

Monaco ['mɔnəkəu] n Monaco f

monarch ['mɔnək] n monarca m

monarchist ['mɔnəkɪst] n monarchico(-a)

monarchy ['mɔnəkɪ] n monarchia

monastery ['mɔnəstərɪ] n monastero

monastic [mə'næstɪk] adj monastico(-a)

Monday ['mʌndɪ] n lunedì m inv; see also **Tuesday**

Monegasque [mɔnə'gæsk] adj, n monegasco(-a)

monetarist ['mʌnɪtərɪst] n monetarista m/f

monetary ['mʌnɪtərɪ] adj monetario(-a)

money ['mʌnɪ] n denaro, soldi mpl; **to make ~** (person) fare (i) soldi; (business) rendere; **danger ~** (Brit) indennità di rischio; **I've got no ~ left** non ho più neanche una lira

moneyed ['mʌnɪd] adj ricco(-a)

moneylender ['mʌnɪlɛndər] n prestatore m di denaro

moneymaker ['mʌnɪmeɪkər] n (Brit col: business) affare m d'oro

moneymaking ['mʌnɪmeɪkɪŋ] adj che rende (bene or molto), lucrativo(-a)

money market n mercato monetario

money order n vaglia m inv

money-spinner ['mʌnɪspɪnər] n (col) miniera d'oro (fig)

money supply n liquidità monetaria

Mongol ['mɔŋgəl] n mongolo(-a); (Ling) mongolo

mongol ['mɔŋgəl] adj, n (Med) mongoloide (m/f)

Mongolia [mɔŋ'gəulɪə] n Mongolia

Mongolian [mɔŋ'gəulɪən] adj mongolico(-a) ■ n mongolo(-a); (Ling) mongolo

mongoose ['mɔŋguːs] n mangusta

mongrel ['mʌŋgrəl] n (dog) cane m bastardo

monitor ['mɔnɪtər] n (Brit Scol) capoclasse m/f; (US Scol) chi sorveglia agli esami; (TV, Comput) monitor m inv ■ vt controllare; (foreign station) ascoltare le trasmissioni di

monk [mʌŋk] n monaco

monkey ['mʌŋkɪ] n scimmia

monkey business n (col) scherzi mpl

monkey nut n (Brit) nocciolina americana

monkey wrench n chiave f a rullino

mono ['mɔnəu] adj mono inv; (broadcast) in mono

mono... ['mɔnəu] prefix mono...

monochrome ['mɔnəkrəum] adj monocromo(-a)

monocle ['mɔnəkl] n monocolo

monogamous [mə'nɔgəməs] adj monogamo(-a)

monogamy [mə'nɔgəmɪ] n monogamia

monogram ['mɔnəgræm] n monogramma m

monolith ['mɔnəlɪθ] n monolito

monologue ['mɔnəlɔg] n monologo

monoplane ['mɔnəupleɪn] n monoplano

monopolize [mə'nɔpəlaɪz] vt monopolizzare

monopoly [mə'nɔpəlɪ] n monopolio;

Monopolies and Mergers Commission (Brit) commissione f antimonopoli

monorail ['mɔnəureɪl] n monorotaia

monosodium glutamate [mɔnə'səudɪəm-'gluːtəmeɪt] n glutammato di sodio

monosyllabic [mɔnəsɪ'læbɪk] adj monosillabico(-a); (person) che parla a monosillabi

monosyllable ['mɔnəsɪləbl] n monosillabo

monotone ['mɔnətəun] n pronunzia (or voce f monotona; **to speak in a ~** parlare con voce monotona

monotonous [mə'nɔtənəs] adj monotono(-a)

monotony [mə'nɔtənɪ] n monotonia

monoxide [mɔ'nɔksaɪd] n: **carbon ~** ossido di carbonio

monsoon [mɔn'suːn] n monsone m

monster ['mɔnstə^r] n mostro
monstrosity [mɔn'strɔsɪtɪ] n mostruosità f inv
monstrous ['mɔnstrəs] adj mostruoso(-a)
Mont. abbr (US) = **Montana**
montage [mɔn'tɑ:ʒ] n montaggio
Mont Blanc [mɔ̃blɑ̃] n Monte m Bianco
month [mʌnθ] n mese m; **300 dollars a ~** 300 dollari al mese; **every ~** (happen) tutti i mesi; (pay) mensilmente, ogni mese
monthly ['mʌnθlɪ] adj mensile ■ adv al mese; ogni mese ■ n (magazine) rivista mensile; **twice ~** due volte al mese
monument ['mɔnjumənt] n monumento
monumental [mɔnju'mɛntl] adj monumentale; (fig) colossale
monumental mason n lapidario
moo [mu:] vi muggire, mugghiare
mood [mu:d] n umore m; **to be in a good/bad ~** essere di buon/cattivo umore; **to be in the ~ for** essere disposto(-a) a, aver voglia di
moody ['mu:dɪ] adj (variable) capriccioso(-a), lunatico(-a); (sullen) imbronciato(-a)
moon [mu:n] n luna
moonbeam ['mu:nbi:m] n raggio di luna
moon landing n allunaggio
moonlight ['mu:nlaɪt] n chiaro di luna ■ vi fare del lavoro nero
moonlighting ['mu:nlaɪtɪŋ] n lavoro nero
moonlit ['mu:nlɪt] adj illuminato(-a) dalla luna; **a ~ night** una notte rischiarata dalla luna
moonshot ['mu:nʃɔt] n lancio sulla luna
moonstruck ['mu:nstrʌk] adj lunatico(-a)
moony ['mu:nɪ] adj (eyes) sognante
Moor [muə^r] n moro(-a)
moor [muə^r] n brughiera ■ vt (ship) ormeggiare ■ vi ormeggiarsi
moorings ['muərɪŋz] npl (chains) ormeggi mpl; (place) ormeggio
Moorish ['muərɪʃ] adj moresco(-a)
moorland ['muələnd] n brughiera
moose [mu:s] n (pl inv) alce m
moot [mu:t] vt sollevare ■ adj: **~ point** punto discutibile
mop [mɔp] n lavapavimenti m inv; (also: **mop of hair**) zazzera ■ vt lavare con lo straccio; **to ~ one's brow** asciugarsi la fronte
▶ **mop up** vt asciugare con uno straccio
mope [məup] vi fare il broncio
▶ **mope about, mope around** vi trascinarsi or aggirarsi con aria avvilita
moped ['məupɛd] n (Brit) ciclomotore m
MOR adj abbr (Mus) = **middle-of-the-road**; **~ music** musica leggera
moral ['mɔrəl] adj morale ■ n morale f; **morals** npl moralità
morale [mɔ'rɑ:l] n morale m

morality [mə'rælɪtɪ] n moralità
moralize ['mɔrəlaɪz] vi: **to ~ (about)** fare il (or la) moralista (riguardo), moraleggiare (riguardo)
morally ['mɔrəlɪ] adv moralmente
moral victory n vittoria morale
morass [mə'ræs] n palude f, pantano
moratorium [mɔrə'tɔ:rɪəm] n moratoria
morbid ['mɔ:bɪd] adj morboso(-a)

🄾 KEYWORD

more [mɔ:^r] adj **1** (greater in number etc) più; **more people/letters than we expected** più persone/lettere di quante ne aspettavamo; **I have more wine/money than you** ho più vino/soldi di te; **I have more wine than beer** ho più vino che birra
2 (additional) altro(-a), ancora; **do you want (some) more tea?** vuole dell'altro tè?, vuole ancora del tè?; **I have no** or **I don't have any more money** non ho più soldi
■ pron **1** (greater amount) più; **more than 10** più di 10; **it cost more than we expected** è costato più di quanto ci aspettassimo; **and what's more ...** e per di più ...
2 (further or additional amount) ancora; **is there any more?** ce n'è ancora?; **there's no more** non ce n'è più; **a little more** ancora un po'; **many/much more** molti(-e)/molto(-a) di più
■ adv: **more dangerous/easily (than)** più pericoloso/facilmente (di); **more and more** sempre di più; **more and more difficult** sempre più difficile; **more or less** più o meno; **more than ever** più che mai; **once more** ancora (una volta), un'altra volta; **no more, not any more** non ... più; **I have no more money, I haven't any more money** non ho più soldi

moreover [mɔ:'rəuvə^r] adv inoltre, di più
morgue [mɔ:g] n obitorio
MORI ['mɔ:rɪ] n abbr (Brit: = Market & Opinion Research Institute) istituto di sondaggio
moribund ['mɔrɪbʌnd] adj moribondo(-a)
morning ['mɔ:nɪŋ] n mattina, mattino; (duration) mattinata; **in the ~** la mattina; **this ~** stamattina; **7 o'clock in the ~** le 7 di or della mattina
morning-after pill ['mɔ:nɪŋ'ɑ:ftə-] n pillola del giorno dopo
morning sickness n nausee fpl mattutine
Moroccan [mə'rɔkən] adj, n marocchino(-a)
Morocco [mə'rɔkəu] n Marocco
moron ['mɔ:rɔn] n deficiente m/f
moronic [mə'rɔnɪk] adj deficiente

morose [mə'rəus] adj cupo(-a), tetro(-a)
morphine ['mɔːfiːn] n morfina
morris dancing ['mɔrɪs-] n (Brit) antica danza tradizionale inglese
Morse [mɔːs] n (also: **Morse code**) alfabeto Morse
morsel ['mɔːsl] n boccone m
mortal ['mɔːtl] adj, n mortale (m)
mortality [mɔː'tælɪtɪ] n mortalità
mortality rate n tasso di mortalità
mortar ['mɔːtəʳ] n (Constr) malta; (dish) mortaio
mortgage ['mɔːgɪdʒ] n ipoteca; (in house buying) mutuo ipotecario ■ vt ipotecare; **to take out a** ~ contrarre un mutuo (or un'ipoteca)
mortgage company n (US) società f inv immobiliare
mortgagee [mɔːgɪ'dʒiː] n creditore m ipotecario
mortgagor ['mɔːgɪdʒəʳ] n debitore m ipotecario
mortician [mɔː'tɪʃən] n (US) impresario di pompe funebri
mortified ['mɔːtɪfaɪd] adj umiliato(-a)
mortise lock ['mɔːtɪs-] n serratura incastrata
mortuary ['mɔːtjuərɪ] n camera mortuaria; obitorio
mosaic [məu'zeɪɪk] n mosaico
Moscow ['mɔskəu] n Mosca
Moslem ['mɔzləm] adj, n = **Muslim**
mosque [mɔsk] n moschea
mosquito (pl **mosquitoes**) [mɔs'kiːtəu] n zanzara
mosquito net n zanzariera
moss [mɔs] n muschio
mossy ['mɔsɪ] adj muscoso(-a)
most [məust] adj la maggior parte di; il più di ■ pron la maggior parte ■ adv più; (work, sleep etc) di più; (very) molto, estremamente; **the** ~ (also: + adjective) il/la più; ~ **fish** la maggior parte dei pesci; ~ **of** la maggior parte di; ~ **of them** quasi tutti; **I saw** ~ ho visto più io; **at the (very)** ~ al massimo; **to make the** ~ **of** trarre il massimo vantaggio da
mostly ['məustlɪ] adv per lo più
MOT n abbr (Brit) = **Ministry of Transport**; **the** ~ **(test)** revisione obbligatoria degli autoveicoli
motel [məu'tɛl] n motel m inv
moth [mɔθ] n farfalla notturna; tarma
mothball ['mɔθbɔːl] n pallina di naftalina
moth-eaten ['mɔθiːtn] adj tarmato(-a)
mother ['mʌðəʳ] n madre f ■ vt (care for) fare da madre a
mother board n (Comput) scheda madre
motherhood ['mʌðəhud] n maternità
mother-in-law ['mʌðərɪnlɔː] n suocera

mother-of-pearl [mʌðərəv'pəːl] n madreperla
mother's help n bambinaia
mother-to-be [mʌðətə'biː] n futura mamma
mother tongue n madrelingua
mothproof ['mɔθpruːf] adj antitarmico(-a)
motif [məu'tiːf] n motivo
motion ['məuʃən] n movimento, moto; (gesture) gesto; (at meeting) mozione f; (Brit: also: **bowel motion**) evacuazione f ■ vt, vi: **to** ~ **(to) sb to do** fare cenno a qn di fare; **to be in** ~ (vehicle) essere in moto; **to set in** ~ avviare; **to go through the motions of doing sth** (fig) fare qc pro forma
motionless ['məuʃənlɪs] adj immobile
motion picture n film m inv
motivate ['məutɪveɪt] vt (act, decision) dare origine a, motivare; (person) spingere
motivated ['məutɪveɪtɪd] adj motivato(-a)
motivation [məutɪ'veɪʃən] n motivazione f
motive ['məutɪv] n motivo ■ adj motore(-trice); **from the best motives** con le migliori intenzioni
motley ['mɔtlɪ] adj eterogeneo(-a), molto vario(-a)
motor ['məutəʳ] n motore m; (Brit col: vehicle) macchina ■ adj motore(-trice)
motorbike ['məutəbaɪk] n moto f inv
motorboat ['məutəbəut] n motoscafo
motorcade ['məutəkeɪd] n corteo di macchine
motorcar ['məutəkɑː] n automobile f
motorcoach ['məutəkəutʃ] n (Brit) pullman m inv
motorcycle ['məutəsaɪkl] n motocicletta
motorcyclist ['məutəsaɪklɪst] n motociclista m/f
motoring ['məutərɪŋ] n (Brit) turismo automobilistico ■ adj (accident) d'auto, automobilistico(-a); (offence) di guida; ~ **holiday** vacanza in macchina
motorist ['məutərɪst] n automobilista m/f
motorize ['məutəraɪz] vt motorizzare
motor oil n olio lubrificante
motor racing n (Brit) corse fpl automobilistiche
motor scooter n motorscooter m inv
motor vehicle n autoveicolo
motorway ['məutəweɪ] n (Brit) autostrada
mottled ['mɔtld] adj chiazzato(-a), marezzato(-a)
motto (pl **mottoes**) ['mɔtəu] n motto
mould, (US) mold [məuld] n forma, stampo; (mildew) muffa ■ vt formare; (fig) foggiare
moulder, (US) molder ['məuldəʳ] vi (decay) ammuffire
moulding, (US) molding ['məuldɪŋ] n (Archit) modanatura

mouldy, (US) **moldy** ['məuldɪ] adj ammuffito(-a)

moult, (US) **molt** [məult] vi far la muta

mound [maund] n rialzo, collinetta

mount [maunt] n monte m, montagna; (horse) cavalcatura; (for jewel etc) montatura ■ vt montare; (horse) montare a; (exhibition) organizzare; (attack) sferrare, condurre; (picture, stamp) sistemare ■ vi salire; (get on a horse) montare a cavallo; (also: **mount up**) aumentare

mountain ['mauntɪn] n montagna ■ cpd di montagna; **to make a ~ out of a molehill** fare di una mosca un elefante

mountain bike n mountain bike f inv

mountaineer [mauntɪ'nɪərʳ] n alpinista m/f

mountaineering [mauntɪ'nɪərɪŋ] n alpinismo; **to go ~** fare dell'alpinismo

mountainous ['mauntɪnəs] adj montagnoso(-a)

mountain range n catena montuosa

mountain rescue team n ≈ squadra di soccorso alpino

mountainside ['mauntɪnsaɪd] n fianco della montagna

mounted ['mauntɪd] adj a cavallo

mourn [mɔːn] vt piangere, lamentare ■ vi: **to ~ (for sb)** piangere (la morte di qn)

mourner ['mɔːnəʳ] n parente m/f (or amico(-a)) del defunto

mourning ['mɔːnɪŋ] n lutto ■ cpd (dress) da lutto; **in ~** in lutto

mouse (pl **mice**) [maus, maɪs] n topo; (Comput) mouse m inv

mousetrap ['maustræp] n trappola per i topi

moussaka [muˈsɑːkə] n moussaka

mousse [muːs] n mousse f inv

moustache [məsˈtɑːʃ] n baffi mpl

mousy ['mausɪ] adj (person) timido(-a); (hair) né chiaro(-a) né scuro(-a)

mouth (pl **mouths**) [mauθ, -ðz] n bocca; (of river) bocca, foce f; (opening) orifizio

mouthful ['mauθful] n boccata

mouth organ n armonica

mouthpiece ['mauθpiːs] n (Mus) bocchino; (Tel) microfono; (of breathing apparatus) boccaglio; (person) portavoce m/f

mouth-to-mouth ['mauθtə'mauθ] adj: **~ resuscitation** respirazione f bocca a bocca

mouthwash ['mauθwɔʃ] n collutorio

mouth-watering ['mauθwɔːtərɪŋ] adj che fa venire l'acquolina in bocca

movable ['muːvəbl] adj mobile

move [muːv] n (movement) movimento; (in game) mossa; (: turn to play) turno; (change of house) trasloco ■ vt muovere, spostare; (emotionally) commuovere; (Pol: resolution etc)

proporre ■ vi (gen) muoversi, spostarsi; (traffic) circolare; (also: **move house**) cambiar casa, traslocare; **to ~ towards** andare verso; **to ~ sb to do sth** indurre or spingere qn a fare qc; **to get a ~ on** affrettarsi, sbrigarsi; **to be moved** (emotionally) essere commosso(-a)

▶ **move about, move around** vi (fidget) agitarsi; (travel) viaggiare

▶ **move along** vi muoversi avanti

▶ **move away** vi allontanarsi, andarsene

▶ **move back** vi indietreggiare; (return) ritornare

▶ **move forward** vi avanzare ■ vt avanzare, spostare in avanti; (people) far avanzare

▶ **move in** vi (to a house) entrare (in una nuova casa)

▶ **move off** vi partire

▶ **move on** vi riprendere la strada ■ vt (onlookers) far circolare

▶ **move out** vi (of house) sgombrare

▶ **move over** vi spostarsi

▶ **move up** vi avanzare

movement ['muːvmənt] n (gen) movimento; (gesture) gesto; (of stars, water, physical) moto; **~ (of the bowels)** (Med) evacuazione f

mover ['muːvəʳ] n proponente m/f

movie ['muːvɪ] n film m inv; **the movies** il cinema

movie camera n cinepresa

moviegoer ['muːvɪgəuəʳ] n (US) frequentatore(-trice) di cinema

moving ['muːvɪŋ] adj mobile; (causing emotion) commovente; (instigating) animatore(-trice)

mow (pt **mowed**, pp **mowed** or **mown**) [məu, -n] vt falciare; (grass) tagliare

▶ **mow down** vt falciare

mower ['məuəʳ] n (also: **lawn mower**) tagliaerba m inv

mown [məun] pp of **mow**

Mozambique [məuzəm'biːk] n Mozambico

MP n abbr = **Military Police**; (Brit) = **Member of Parliament**; (Canada) = **Mounted Police**

MP3 n MP3 m inv

MP3 player n lettore m MP3

mpg n abbr = **miles per gallon** (30 mpg = 9.4 l. per 100 km)

mph n abbr = **miles per hour** (60 mph = 96 km/h)

MPhil n abbr (= Master of Philosophy) titolo di studio

MPS n abbr (Brit) = **Member of the Pharmaceutical Society**

Mr, Mr. ['mɪstəʳ] n: **Mr X** Signor X, Sig. X

MRC n abbr (Brit: = Medical Research Council) ufficio governativo per la ricerca medica in Gran Bretagna e nel Commonwealth

MRCP n abbr (Brit) = **Member of the Royal College of Physicians**

MRCS *n abbr* (*Brit*) = **Member of the Royal College of Surgeons**

MRCVS *n abbr* (*Brit*) = **Member of the Royal College of Veterinary Surgeons**

Mrs, Mrs. ['mɪsɪz] *n*: ~ **X** Signora X, Sig.ra X

MS *n abbr* (*US*: = *Master of Science*) *titolo di studio*; (= *manuscript*) ms; (*Med*) = **multiple sclerosis** ■ *abbr* (*US*) = **Mississippi**

Ms, Ms. [mɪz] *n* = **Miss** *or* **Mrs**; **Ms X** ≈ Signora X, ≈ Sig.ra X

MSA *n abbr* (*US*: = *Master of Science in Agriculture*) *titolo di studio*

MSc *n abbr* = **Master of Science**

MSG *abbr* = **monosodium glutamate**

MSP *n abbr* (*Brit*) = **Member of the Scottish Parliament**

MST *abbr* (*US*: = *Mountain Standard Time*) *ora invernale delle Montagne Rocciose*

MSW *n abbr* (*US*: = *Master of Social Work*) *titolo di studio*

MT *n abbr* = **machine translation** ■ *abbr* (*US*) = **Montana**

Mt *abbr* (*Geo*: = *mount*) M

mth *abbr* (= *month*) m

MTV *n abbr* = **music television**

🅞 **KEYWORD**

much [mʌtʃ] *adj, pron* molto(-a); **he's done so much work** ha lavorato così tanto; **I have as much money as you** ho tanti soldi quanti ne hai tu; **how much is it?** quant'è?; **it's not much** non è tanto; **it costs too much** costa troppo; **as much as you want** quanto vuoi ■ *adv* **1** (*greatly*) molto, tanto; **very much** molte grazie; **I like it very/so much** mi piace moltissimo/così tanto; **much to my amazement** con mio enorme stupore; **he's very much the gentleman** è il vero gentiluomo; **I read as much as I can** leggo quanto posso; **as much as you** tanto quanto te

2 (*by far*) molto; **it's much the biggest company in Europe** è di gran lunga la più grossa società in Europa

3 (*almost*) grossomodo, praticamente; **they're much the same** sono praticamente uguali

muck [mʌk] *n* (*mud*) fango; (*dirt*) sporcizia
▶ **muck about, muck around** *vi* (*col*) fare lo stupido; (: *waste time*) gingillarsi; (*tinker*) armeggiare
▶ **muck in** *vi* (*Brit col*) mettersi insieme
▶ **muck out** *vt* (*stable*) pulire
▶ **muck up** *vt* (*col: dirty*) sporcare; (: *spoil*) rovinare

muckraking ['mʌkreɪkɪŋ] *n* (*fig, col*) caccia agli scandali ■ *adj* scandalistico(-a)

mucky ['mʌkɪ] *adj* (*dirty*) sporco(-a), lordo(-a)

mucus ['mjuːkəs] *n* muco

mud [mʌd] *n* fango

muddle ['mʌdl] *n* confusione *f*, disordine *m*; pasticcio ■ *vt* (*also*: **muddle up**) mettere sottosopra; confondere; **to be in a ~** (*person*) non riuscire a raccapezzarsi; **to get in a ~** (*while explaining etc*) imbrogliarsi
▶ **muddle along** *vi* andare avanti a casaccio
▶ **muddle through** *vi* cavarsela alla meno peggio

muddle-headed [mʌdl'hɛdɪd] *adj* (*person*) confusionario(-a)

muddy ['mʌdɪ] *adj* fangoso(-a)

mud flats *npl* distesa fangosa

mudguard ['mʌdgɑːd] *n* parafango

mudpack ['mʌdpæk] *n* maschera di fango

mud-slinging ['mʌdslɪŋɪŋ] *n* (*fig*) infangamento

muesli ['mjuːzlɪ] *n* müsli *m inv*

muff [mʌf] *n* manicotto ■ *vt* (*shot, catch etc*) mancare, sbagliare; **to ~ it** sbagliare tutto

muffin ['mʌfɪn] *n* specie di pasticcino soffice da tè

muffle ['mʌfl] *vt* (*sound*) smorzare, attutire; (*against cold*) imbacuccare

muffled ['mʌfld] *adj* smorzato(-a), attutito(-a)

muffler ['mʌflər] *n* (*scarf*) sciarpa (pesante); (*US Aut*) marmitta; (*on motorbike*) silenziatore *m*

mufti ['mʌftɪ] *n*: **in ~** in borghese

mug [mʌg] *n* (*cup*) tazzone *m*; (*for beer*) boccale *m*; (*col: face*) muso; (: *fool*) scemo(-a) ■ *vt* (*assault*) assalire; **it's a ~'s game** (*Brit*) è proprio (una cosa) da fessi
▶ **mug up** *vt* (*Brit col: also*: **mug up on**) studiare bene

mugger ['mʌgər] *n* aggressore *m*

mugging ['mʌgɪŋ] *n* aggressione *f* (a scopo di rapina)

muggins ['mʌgɪnz] *n* (*col*) semplicione(-a), sprovveduto(-a)

muggy ['mʌgɪ] *adj* afoso(-a)

mug shot *n* (*col*) foto *f* inv segnaletica

mulatto (*pl* **mulattoes**) [mjuː'lætəu] *n* mulatto(-a)

mulberry ['mʌlbərɪ] *n* (*fruit*) mora (di gelso); (*tree*) gelso, moro

mule [mjuːl] *n* mulo

mull [mʌl]: **to ~ over** *vt* rimuginare

mulled [mʌld] *adj*: **~ wine** vino caldo

multi... ['mʌltɪ] *prefix* multi...

multi-access [mʌltɪ'ækses] *adj* (*Comput*) ad accesso multiplo

multicoloured, (*US*) **multicolored** ['mʌltɪkʌləd] *adj* multicolore, variopinto(-a)

multifarious [mʌltɪ'fɛərɪəs] *adj* molteplice, svariato(-a)

multilateral [mʌltɪ'lætərəl] *adj* (*Pol*) multilaterale

multi-level ['mʌltɪlɛvl] *adj* (*US*) = **multistorey**

multimillionaire [mʌltɪmɪljə'nɛəʳ] *n* multimiliardario(-a)

multinational [mʌltɪ'næʃənl] *adj, n* multinazionale (*f*)

multiple ['mʌltɪpl] *adj* multiplo(-a); molteplice ■ *n* multiplo; (*Brit: also:* **multiple store**) *grande magazzino che fa parte di una catena*

multiple choice *n* esercizi *mpl* a scelta multipla

multiple crash *n* serie *f inv* di incidenti a catena

multiple sclerosis *n* sclerosi *f* a placche

multiplex ['mʌltɪplɛks] *n* (*also:* **multiplex cinema**) cinema *m inv* multisale *inv*

multiplication [mʌltɪplɪ'keɪʃən] *n* moltiplicazione *f*

multiplication table *n* tavola pitagorica

multiplicity [mʌltɪ'plɪsɪtɪ] *n* molteplicità

multiply ['mʌltɪplaɪ] *vt* moltiplicare ■ *vi* moltiplicarsi

multiracial [mʌltɪ'reɪʃəl] *adj* multirazziale

multistorey ['mʌltɪ'stɔːrɪ] *adj* (*Brit: building, car park*) a più piani

multitude ['mʌltɪtjuːd] *n* moltitudine *f*

mum [mʌm] *n* (*Brit*) mamma ■ *adj*: **to keep ~** non aprire bocca; **~'s the word!** acqua in bocca!

mumble ['mʌmbl] *vt, vi* borbottare

mumbo jumbo ['mʌmbəu-] *n* (*col*) parole *fpl* incomprensibili

mummify ['mʌmɪfaɪ] *vt* mummificare

mummy ['mʌmɪ] *n* (*Brit: mother*) mamma; (*embalmed*) mummia

mumps [mʌmps] *n* orecchioni *mpl*

munch [mʌntʃ] *vt, vi* sgranocchiare

mundane [mʌn'deɪn] *adj* terra a terra *inv*

Munich ['mjuːnɪk] *n* Monaco *f* (di Baviera)

municipal [mjuː'nɪsɪpl] *adj* municipale

municipality [mjuːnɪsɪ'pælɪtɪ] *n* municipio

munitions [mjuː'nɪʃənz] *npl* munizioni *fpl*

mural ['mjuərəl] *n* dipinto murale

murder ['məːdəʳ] *n* assassinio, omicidio ■ *vt* assassinare; **to commit ~** commettere un omicidio

murderer ['məːdərəʳ] *n* omicida *m*, assassino

murderess ['məːdərɪs] *n* omicida *f*, assassina

murderous ['məːdərəs] *adj* micidiale

murk [məːk] *n* oscurità, buio

murky ['məːkɪ] *adj* tenebroso(-a), buio(-a)

murmur ['məːməʳ] *n* mormorio ■ *vt, vi* mormorare; **heart ~** (*Med*) soffio al cuore

MusB, MusBac *n abbr* (= *Bachelor of Music*) *titolo di studio*

muscle ['mʌsl] *n* muscolo
  ▸ **muscle in** *vi* immischiarsi

muscular ['mʌskjuləʳ] *adj* muscolare; (*person, arm*) muscoloso(-a)

muscular dystrophy *n* distrofia muscolare

MusD, MusDoc *n abbr* (= *Doctor of Music*) *titolo di studio*

muse [mjuːz] *vi* meditare, sognare ■ *n* musa

museum [mjuː'zɪəm] *n* museo

mush [mʌʃ] *n* pappa

mushroom ['mʌʃrum] *n* fungo ■ *vi* (*fig*) svilupparsi rapidamente

mushy ['mʌʃɪ] *adj* (*food*) spappolato(-a); (*sentimental*) sdolcinato(-a)

music ['mjuːzɪk] *n* musica

musical ['mjuːzɪkəl] *adj* musicale ■ *n* (*show*) commedia musicale

musical box *n* carillon *m inv*

musical chairs *n* gioco delle sedie (*in cui bisogna sedersi non appena cessa la musica*); (*fig*) scambio delle poltrone

musical instrument *n* strumento musicale

music box *n* carillon *m inv*

music centre *n* impianto *m* stereo *inv* monoblocco *inv*

music hall *n* teatro di varietà

musician [mjuː'zɪʃən] *n* musicista *m/f*

music stand *n* leggio

musk [mʌsk] *n* muschio

musket ['mʌskɪt] *n* moschetto

muskrat ['mʌskræt] *n* topo muschiato

musk rose *n* (*Bot*) rosa muschiata

Muslim ['mʌzlɪm] *adj, n* musulmano(-a)

muslin ['mʌzlɪn] *n* mussola

musquash ['mʌskwɒʃ] *n* (*fur*) rat musqué *m inv*

mussel ['mʌsl] *n* cozza

must [mʌst] *aux vb* (*obligation*): **I ~ do it** devo farlo; (*probability*): **he ~ be there by now** dovrebbe essere arrivato ormai; **I ~ have made a mistake** devo essermi sbagliato ■ *n*: **this programme/trip is a ~** è un programma/viaggio da non perdersi

mustache ['mʌstæʃ] *n* (*US*) = **moustache**

mustard ['mʌstəd] *n* senape *f*, mostarda

mustard gas *n* iprite *f*

muster ['mʌstəʳ] *vt* radunare; (*also:* **muster up**: *strength, courage*) fare appello a

mustiness ['mʌstɪnɪs] *n* odor di muffa *or* di stantio

mustn't ['mʌsnt] = **must not**

musty ['mʌstɪ] *adj* che sa di muffa *or* di rinchiuso

mutant ['mjuːtənt] *adj, n* mutante (*m*)

mutate [mjuː'teɪt] *vi* subire una mutazione

m

mutation [mju:'teɪʃən] n mutazione f
mute [mju:t] adj, n muto(-a)
muted ['mju:tɪd] adj (noise) attutito(-a), smorzato(-a); (criticism) attenuato(-a); (Mus) in sordina; (: trumpet) con sordina
mutilate ['mju:tɪleɪt] vt mutilare
mutilation [mju:tɪ'leɪʃən] n mutilazione f
mutinous ['mju:tɪnəs] adj (troops) ammutinato(-a); (attitude) ribelle
mutiny ['mju:tɪnɪ] n ammutinamento
  ■ vi ammutinarsi
mutter ['mʌtər] vt, vi borbottare, brontolare
mutton ['mʌtn] n carne f di montone
mutual ['mju:tʃuəl] adj mutuo(-a), reciproco(-a)
mutually ['mju:tʃuəlɪ] adv reciprocamente
Muzak® ['mju:zæk] n (often pej) musica di sottofondo
muzzle ['mʌzl] n muso; (protective device) museruola; (of gun) bocca ■ vt mettere la museruola a
MV abbr (= motor vessel) M/N, m/n
MVP n abbr (US Sport: = most valuable player) titolo ottenuto da sportivo
MW abbr (Radio: = medium wave) O.M.; = **megawatt**
my [maɪ] adj il/la mio(-a); (pl) i/le miei/mie
Myanmar ['maɪænmɑ:'] n Myanma
myopic [maɪ'ɔpɪk] adj miope
myriad ['mɪrɪəd] n miriade f
myself [maɪ'sɛlf] pron (reflexive) mi; (emphatic) io stesso(-a); (after prep) me
mysterious [mɪs'tɪərɪəs] adj misterioso(-a)
mystery ['mɪstərɪ] n mistero
mystery story n racconto del mistero
mystic ['mɪstɪk] adj, n mistico(-a)
mystical ['mɪstɪkəl] adj mistico(-a)
mystify ['mɪstɪfaɪ] vt mistificare; (puzzle) confondere
mystique [mɪs'ti:k] n fascino
myth [mɪθ] n mito
mythical ['mɪθɪkl] adj mitico(-a)
mythological [mɪθə'lɔdʒɪkl] adj mitologico(-a)
mythology [mɪ'θɔlədʒɪ] n mitologia

Nn

N, n [ɛn] *n* (*letter*) N, n *f or m inv*; **N for Nellie**, (*US*) **N for Nan** ≈ N come Napoli

N *abbr* (= *north*) N

NA *n abbr* (*US*: = *Narcotics Anonymous*) *associazione in aiuto dei tossicodipendenti*; (*US*) = **National Academy**

n/a *abbr* (= *not applicable*) non pertinente

NAACP *n abbr* (*US*) = **National Association for the Advancement of Colored People**

NAAFI ['næfɪ] *n abbr* (*Brit*: = *Navy, Army, & Air Force Institutes*) *organizzazione che gestisce negozi, mense ecc. per il personale militare*

nab [næb] *vt* (*col*) beccare, acchiappare

NACU *n abbr* (*US*) = **National Association of Colleges and Universities**

nadir ['neɪdɪə] *n* (*Astronomy*) nadir *m*; (*fig*) punto più basso

nag [næg] *n* (*pej: horse*) ronzino; (*person*) brontolone(-a) ▪ *vt* tormentare ▪ *vi* brontolare in continuazione

nagging ['nægɪŋ] *adj* (*doubt, pain*) persistente ▪ *n* brontolii *mpl*, osservazioni *fpl* continue

nail [neɪl] *n* (*human*) unghia; (*metal*) chiodo ▪ *vt* inchiodare; **to ~ sb down to a date/price** costringere qn a un appuntamento/ad accettare un prezzo; **to pay cash on the ~** (*Brit*) pagare a tamburo battente

nailbrush ['neɪlbrʌʃ] *n* spazzolino da *or* per unghie

nailfile ['neɪlfaɪl] *n* lima da *or* per unghie

nail polish *n* smalto da *or* per unghie

nail polish remover *n* acetone *m*, solvente *m*

nail scissors *npl* forbici *fpl* da *or* per unghie

nail varnish *n* (*Brit*) = **nail polish**

Nairobi [naɪ'rəʊbɪ] *n* Nairobi *f*

naïve [naɪ'iːv] *adj* ingenuo(-a)

naïveté [naːiːv'teɪ], **naivety** [naɪ'iːvtɪ] *n* ingenuità *f inv*

naked ['neɪkɪd] *adj* nudo(-a); **with the ~ eye** a occhio nudo

nakedness ['neɪkɪdnɪs] *n* nudità

NAM *n abbr* (*US*) = **National Association of Manufacturers**

name [neɪm] *n* nome *m*; (*reputation*) nome, reputazione *f* ▪ *vt* (*baby etc*) chiamare; (*person, object*) identificare; (*price, date*) fissare; **by ~** di nome; **she knows them all by ~** li conosce tutti per nome; **in the ~ of** in nome di; **what's your ~?** come si chiama?; **my ~ is Peter** mi chiamo Peter; **to take sb's ~ and address** prendere nome e indirizzo di qn; **to make a ~ for o.s.** farsi un nome; **to get (o.s.) a bad ~** farsi una cattiva fama *or* una brutta reputazione; **to call sb names** insultare qn

name dropping *n* menzionare qualcuno per fare bella figura

nameless ['neɪmlɪs] *adj* senza nome

namely ['neɪmlɪ] *adv* cioè

nameplate ['neɪmpleɪt] *n* (*on door etc*) targa

namesake ['neɪmseɪk] *n* omonimo

nan bread [naː-] *n* tipo di pane indiano poco lievitato di forma allungata

nanny ['nænɪ] *n* bambinaia

nanny goat *n* capra

nap [næp] *n* (*sleep*) pisolino; (*of cloth*) peluria ▪ *vi*: **to be caught napping** essere preso alla sprovvista; **to have a ~** schiacciare un pisolino

NAPA *n abbr* (*US*: = *National Association of Performing Artists*) *associazione nazionale degli artisti di palcoscenico*

napalm ['neɪpaːm] *n* napalm *m*

nape [neɪp] *n*: **~ of the neck** nuca

napkin ['næpkɪn] *n* tovagliolo; (*Brit: for baby*) pannolino

Naples ['neɪplz] *n* Napoli *f*

Napoleonic [nəpəʊlɪ'ɒnɪk] *adj* napoleonico(-a)

nappy ['næpɪ] *n* (*Brit*) pannolino

nappy liner *n* (*Brit*) fogliettino igienico

narcissistic [naːsɪ'sɪstɪk] *adj* narcisistico(-a)

narcissus (*pl* **narcissi**) [naː'sɪsəs, -saɪ] *n* narciso

narcotic [naː'kɒtɪk] *n* (*Med*) narcotico; **narcotics** *npl* (*drugs*) narcotici, stupefacenti *mpl*

nark [nɑːk] *vt* (*Brit col*) scocciare
narrate [nə'reɪt] *vt* raccontare, narrare
narration [nə'reɪʃən] *n* narrazione *f*
narrative ['nærətɪv] *n* narrativa ▪ *adj*
   narrativo(-a)
narrator [nə'reɪtə'] *n* narratore(-trice)
narrow ['nærəu] *adj* stretto(-a); (*resources,
   means*) limitato(-a), modesto(-a); (*fig*):
   to take a ~ view of avere una visione
   limitata di ▪ *vi* restringersi; **to have a ~
   escape** farcela per un pelo; **to ~ sth down to**
   ridurre qc a
narrow gauge *adj* (*Rail*) a scartamento
   ridotto
narrowly ['nærəulɪ] *adv*: **Maria ~ escaped
   drowning** per un pelo Maria non è affogata;
   he ~ missed hitting the cyclist per poco
   non ha investito il ciclista
narrow-minded [nærəu'maɪndɪd] *adj*
   meschino(-a)
NAS *n abbr* (*US*) = **National Academy of
   Sciences**
NASA ['næsə] *n abbr* (*US*: = *National Aeronautics
   and Space Administration*) N.A.S.A. *f*
nasal ['neɪzl] *adj* nasale
Nassau ['næsɔː] *n* Nassau *f*
nastily ['nɑːstɪlɪ] *adv* con cattiveria
nastiness ['nɑːstɪnɪs] *n* (*of person, remark*)
   cattiveria; (: *spitefulness*) malignità
nasturtium [nəs'təːʃəm] *n* cappuccina,
   nasturzio (indiano)
nasty ['nɑːstɪ] *adj* (*person, remark*) cattivo(-a);
   (: *spiteful*) maligno(-a); (*smell, wound, situation*)
   brutto(-a); **to turn ~** (*situation*) mettersi
   male; (*weather*) guastarsi; (*person*)
   incattivirsi; **it's a ~ business** è una brutta
   faccenda, è un brutto affare
NAS/UWT *n abbr* (*Brit*: = *National Association of
   Schoolmasters/Union of Women Teachers*) sindacato
   di insegnanti in Inghilterra e Galles
nation ['neɪʃən] *n* nazione *f*
national ['næʃənl] *adj* nazionale ▪ *n*
   cittadino(-a)
national anthem *n* inno nazionale
National Curriculum *n* (*Brit*) ≈ programma *m*
   scolastico ministeriale (*in Inghilterra e Galles*)
national debt *n* debito pubblico
national dress *n* costume *m* nazionale
National Guard *n* (*US*) milizia nazionale
   (*volontaria, in ogni stato*)
National Health Service *n* (*Brit*) *servizio
   nazionale di assistenza sanitaria*, ≈ S.A.U.B. *f*
National Insurance *n* (*Brit*) ≈ Previdenza
   Sociale
nationalism ['næʃnəlɪzəm] *n* nazionalismo
nationalist ['næʃnəlɪst] *adj, n* nazionalista
   (*m/f*)

nationality [næʃə'nælɪtɪ] *n* nazionalità *f inv*
nationalization [næʃnəlaɪ'zeɪʃən] *n*
   nazionalizzazione *f*
nationalize ['næʃnəlaɪz] *vt* nazionalizzare
nationally ['næʃnəlɪ] *adv* a livello nazionale
national park *n* parco nazionale
national press *n* stampa a diffusione
   nazionale
National Security Council *n* (*US*) consiglio
   nazionale di sicurezza
national service *n* (*Mil*) servizio militare
National Trust *n* sovrintendenza ai beni
   culturali e ambientali; *vedi nota*

◉ **NATIONAL TRUST**
◉
◉   Fondato nel 1895, il *National Trust* è
◉   un'organizzazione che si occupa della
◉   tutela e salvaguardia di edifici e
◉   monumenti di interesse storico e di
◉   territori di interesse ambientale nel
◉   Regno Unito.

nation-wide ['neɪʃənwaɪd] *adj* diffuso(-a) in
   tutto il paese ▪ *adv* in tutto il paese
native ['neɪtɪv] *n* abitante *m/f* del paese;
   (*in colonies*) indigeno(-a) ▪ *adj* indigeno(-a);
   (*country*) natio(-a); (*ability*) innato(-a); **a ~ of
   Russia** un nativo della Russia; **a ~ speaker
   of French** una persona di madrelingua
   francese; **~ language** madrelingua
Native American *n* discendente di tribù
   dell'America settentrionale
Nativity [nə'tɪvɪtɪ] *n* (*Rel*): **the ~** la Natività
nativity play *n* recita sulla Natività
NATO ['neɪtəu] *n abbr* (= *North Atlantic Treaty
   Organization*) N.A.T.O. *f*
natter ['nætə'] (*Brit col*) *vi* chiacchierare ▪ *n*
   chiacchierata
natural ['nætʃrəl] *adj* naturale; (*ability*)
   innato(-a); (*manner*) semplice; **death from ~
   causes** (*Law*) morte *f* per cause naturali
natural childbirth *n* parto indolore
natural gas *n* gas *m* metano
natural history *n* storia naturale
naturalist ['nætʃrəlɪst] *n* naturalista *m/f*
naturalization [nætʃrəlaɪ'zeɪʃən] *n*
   naturalizzazione *f*; acclimatazione *f*
naturalize ['nætʃrəlaɪz] *vt*: **to be
   naturalized** (*person*) naturalizzarsi;
   to become naturalized (*animal, plant*)
   acclimatarsi
naturally ['nætʃrəlɪ] *adv* naturalmente;
   (*by nature: gifted*) di natura
naturalness ['nætʃrəlnɪs] *n* naturalezza
natural resources *npl* risorse *fpl* naturali
natural selection *n* selezione *f* naturale

natural wastage n (Industry) diminuzione f di manodopera (per pensionamento decesso etc)
nature ['neɪtʃə'] n natura; (character) natura, indole f; **by ~** di natura; **documents of a confidential ~** documenti mpl di natura privata
-natured ['neɪtʃəd] suffix: **ill~** maldisposto(-a)
nature reserve n (Brit) parco naturale
nature trail n percorso tracciato in parchi nazionali ecc con scopi educativi
naturist ['neɪtʃərɪst] n naturista m/f, nudista m/f
naught [nɔ:t] n = **nought**
naughtiness ['nɔ:tɪnɪs] n cattiveria
naughty ['nɔ:tɪ] adj (child) birichino(-a), cattivello(-a); (story, film) spinto(-a)
nausea ['nɔ:sɪə] n (Med) nausea; (fig: disgust) schifo
nauseate ['nɔ:sɪeɪt] vt nauseare; far schifo a
nauseating ['nɔ:sɪeɪtɪŋ] adj nauseante; (fig) disgustoso(-a)
nauseous ['nɔ:sɪəs] adj nauseabondo(-a); (feeling sick): **to be ~** avere la nausea
nautical ['nɔ:tɪkl] adj nautico(-a)
nautical mile n miglio nautico or marino
naval ['neɪvl] adj navale
naval officer n ufficiale m di marina
nave [neɪv] n navata centrale
navel ['neɪvl] n ombelico
navigable ['nævɪgəbl] adj navigabile
navigate ['nævɪgeɪt] vt percorrere navigando ■ vi navigare; (Aut) fare da navigatore
navigation [nævɪ'geɪʃən] n navigazione f
navigator ['nævɪgeɪtə'] n (Naut, Aviat) ufficiale m di rotta; (explorer) navigatore m; (Aut) copilota m/f
navvy ['nævɪ] n manovale m
navy ['neɪvɪ] n marina; **Department of the N~** (US) Ministero della Marina ■ adj blu scuro inv
navy-blue ['neɪvɪ'blu:] adj blu scuro inv
Nazareth ['næzərɪθ] n Nazareth f
Nazi ['nɑ:tsɪ] adj, n nazista (m/f)
NB abbr (= nota bene) N.B.; (Canada) = **New Brunswick**
NBA n abbr (US: = National Basketball Association) ≈ F.I.P. f (= Federazione Italiana Pallacanestro); = **National Boxing Association**
NBC n abbr (US: = National Broadcasting Company) compagnia nazionale di radiodiffusione
NBS n abbr (US: = National Bureau of Standards) ufficio per la normalizzazione
NC abbr (Comm etc: = no charge) gratis; (US) = **North Carolina**
NCC n abbr (US) = **National Council of Churches**
NCO n abbr = **non-commissioned officer**

ND, N. Dak. abbr (US) = **North Dakota**
NE abbr (US) = **Nebraska; New England**
NEA n abbr (US) = **National Education Association**
neap [ni:p] n (also: **neaptide**) marea di quadratura
Neapolitan [nɪə'pɒlɪtən] adj, n napoletano(-a)
near [nɪə'] adj vicino(-a); (relation) prossimo(-a) ■ adv vicino ■ prep (also: **near to**) vicino a, presso; (in time) verso ■ vt avvicinarsi a; **to come ~** avvicinarsi; **~ here/ there** qui/lì vicino; **£25,000 or nearest offer** (Brit) 25.000 sterline trattabili; **in the ~ future** in un prossimo futuro; **the building is nearing completion** il palazzo è quasi terminato or ultimato
nearby [nɪə'baɪ] adj vicino(-a) ■ adv vicino
Near East n: **the ~** il Medio Oriente
nearer ['nɪərə'] adj più vicino(-a) ■ adv più vicino
nearly ['nɪəlɪ] adv quasi; **not ~** non ... affatto; **I ~ lost it** per poco non lo perdevo; **she was ~ crying** era lì lì per piangere
near miss n: **that was a ~** c'è mancato poco
nearness ['nɪənɪs] n vicinanza
nearside ['nɪəsaɪd] n (right-hand drive) lato sinistro; (left-hand drive) lato destro ■ adj sinistro(-a); destro(-a)
near-sighted [nɪə'saɪtɪd] adj miope
neat [ni:t] adj (person, room) ordinato(-a); (work) pulito(-a); (solution, plan) ben indovinato(-a), azzeccato(-a); (spirits) liscio(-a)
neatly ['ni:tlɪ] adv con ordine; (skilfully) abilmente
neatness ['ni:tnɪs] n (tidiness) ordine m; (skilfulness) abilità
Nebr. abbr (US) = **Nebraska**
nebulous ['nɛbjuləs] adj nebuloso(-a); (fig) vago(-a)
necessarily ['nɛsɪsrɪlɪ] adv necessariamente; **not ~** non è detto, non necessariamente
necessary ['nɛsɪsrɪ] adj necessario(-a); **if ~** se necessario
necessitate [nɪ'sɛsɪteɪt] vt rendere necessario(-a)
necessity [nɪ'sɛsɪtɪ] n necessità f inv; **in case of ~** in caso di necessità
neck [nɛk] n collo; (of garment) colletto ■ vi (col) pomiciare, sbaciucchiarsi; **~ and ~** testa a testa; **to stick one's ~ out** (col) rischiare (forte)
necklace ['nɛklɪs] n collana
neckline ['nɛklaɪn] n scollatura
necktie ['nɛktaɪ] n (esp US) cravatta
nectar ['nɛktə'] n nettare m

n

nectarine ['nɛktərɪn] n nocepesca

née [neɪ] adj: ~ **Scott** nata Scott

need [niːd] n bisogno ◾ vt aver bisogno di;
I ~ to do it lo devo fare, bisogna che io lo
faccia; **you don't ~ to go** non deve andare,
non c'è bisogno che lei vada; **a signature is
needed** occorre or ci vuole una firma; **to be
in ~ of, have ~ of** aver bisogno di; **£10 will
meet my immediate needs** 10 sterline mi
basteranno per le necessità più urgenti;
in case of ~ in caso di bisogno or necessità;
there's no ~ for ... non c'è bisogno or non
occorre che ...; **there's no ~ to do ...** non
occorre fare ...; **the needs of industry** le
esigenze dell'industria

needle ['niːdl] n ago; (on record player) puntina
◾ vt punzecchiare

needlecord ['niːdlkɔːd] n (Brit) velluto a coste
sottili

needless ['niːdlɪs] adj inutile; ~ **to say, ...**
inutile dire che ...

needlessly ['niːdlɪslɪ] adv inutilmente

needlework ['niːdlwəːk] n cucito

needn't ['niːdnt] = **need not**

needy ['niːdɪ] adj bisognoso(-a)

negation [nɪ'geɪʃən] n negazione f

negative ['nɛgətɪv] n (Phot) negativa,
negativo; (Elec) polo negativo; (Ling)
negazione f ◾ adj negativo(-a); **to answer
in the ~** rispondere negativamente or di no

negative equity n situazione in cui l'ammontare
del mutuo su un immobile supera il suo valore sul
mercato

neglect [nɪ'glɛkt] vt trascurare ◾ n (of person,
duty) negligenza; **state of ~** stato di
abbandono; **to ~ to do sth** trascurare or
tralasciare di fare qc

neglected [nɪ'glɛktɪd] adj trascurato(-a)

neglectful [nɪ'glɛktful] adj (gen) negligente;
to be ~ of sb/sth trascurare qn/qc

negligee ['nɛglɪʒeɪ] n négligé m inv

negligence ['nɛglɪdʒəns] n negligenza

negligent ['nɛglɪdʒənt] adj negligente

negligently ['nɛglɪdʒəntlɪ] adv con
negligenza

negligible ['nɛglɪdʒɪbl] adj insignificante,
trascurabile

negotiable [nɪ'gəuʃɪəbl] adj negoziabile;
(cheque) trasferibile; (road) transitabile

negotiate [nɪ'gəuʃɪeɪt] vi negoziare ◾ vt
(Comm) negoziare; (obstacle) superare; (bend in
road) prendere; **to ~ with sb for sth** trattare
con qn per ottenere qc

negotiating table [nɪ'gəuʃɪeɪtɪŋ-] n tavolo
delle trattative

negotiation [nɪgəuʃɪ'eɪʃən] n trattativa; (Pol)
negoziato; **to enter into negotiations with**
sb entrare in trattative (or intavolare
i negoziati) con qn

negotiator [nɪ'gəuʃɪeɪtər] n
negoziatore(-trice)

Negress ['niːgrɪs] n negra

Negro ['niːgrəu] adj, n (pl **Negroes**) negro(-a)

neigh [neɪ] vi nitrire

neighbour, (US) **neighbor** ['neɪbər] n
vicino(-a)

neighbourhood, (US) **neighborhood**
['neɪbəhud] n vicinato

neighbourhood watch n (Brit: also:
neighbourhood watch scheme) sistema di
vigilanza reciproca in un quartiere

neighbouring, (US) **neighboring** ['neɪbərɪŋ]
adj vicino(-a)

neighbourly, (US) **neighborly** ['neɪbəlɪ] adj:
he is a neighbo(u)rly person è un buon
vicino

neither ['naɪðər] adj, pron né l'uno(-a) né
l'altro(-a), nessuno(-a) dei/delle due ◾ conj
neanche, nemmeno, neppure ◾ adv: ~ **good
nor bad** né buono né cattivo; **I didn't move
and ~ did Claude** io non mi mossi e
nemmeno Claude; **... ~ did I refuse ...**, ma
non ho nemmeno rifiutato

neo... ['niːəu] prefix neo...

neolithic [niːəu'lɪθɪk] adj neolitico(-a)

neologism [nɪ'ɔlədʒɪzəm] n neologismo

neon ['niːɔn] n neon m

neon light n luce f al neon

neon sign n insegna al neon

Nepal [nɪ'pɔːl] n Nepal m

nephew ['nɛvjuː] n nipote m

nepotism ['nɛpətɪzəm] n nepotismo

nerd [nəːd] n (col) sfigato(-a), povero(-a)
fesso(-a)

nerve [nəːv] n nervo; (fig) coraggio;
(impudence) faccia tosta; **he gets on my
nerves** mi dà ai nervi, mi fa venire i nervi; **a
fit of nerves** una crisi di nervi; **to lose one's
~** (self-confidence) perdere fiducia in se stesso;
I lost my ~ (courage) mi è mancato il coraggio

nerve centre n (Anat) centro nervoso; (fig)
cervello, centro vitale

nerve gas n gas m nervino

nerve-racking ['nəːvrækɪŋ] adj che spezza i
nervi

nervous ['nəːvəs] adj nervoso(-a)

nervous breakdown n esaurimento nervoso

nervously ['nəːvəslɪ] adv nervosamente

nervousness ['nəːvəsnɪs] n nervosismo

nervous wreck n: **to be a ~** (col) essere
nevrastenico(-a)

nervy ['nəːvɪ] adj agitato(-a), nervoso(-a)

nest [nɛst] n nido; ~ **of tables** tavolini mpl
cicogna inv

nest egg n (fig) gruzzolo
nestle ['nɛsl] vi accoccolarsi
nestling ['nɛslɪŋ] n uccellino di nido
net [nɛt] n rete f; (fabric) tulle m; **the N~**
(internet) Internet f ■ adj netto(-a) ■ vt
(person) ricavare un utile netto di; (deal, sale)
dare un utile netto di; **~ of tax** netto, al netto
di tasse; **he earns £10,000 ~ per year**
guadagna 10.000 sterline nette all'anno
netball ['nɛtbɔ:l] n specie di pallacanestro
net curtains npl tende fpl di tulle
Netherlands ['nɛðələndz] npl: **the ~** i Paesi
Bassi
netiquette ['nɛtɪkɛt] n netiquette f inv
net profit n utile m netto
nett [nɛt] adj = **net**
netting ['nɛtɪŋ] n (for fence etc) reticolato;
(fabric) tulle m
nettle ['nɛtl] n ortica
network ['nɛtwə:k] n rete f
neuralgia [njuə'rældʒə] n nevralgia
neurological [njuərə'lɔdʒɪkl] adj
neurologico(-a)
neurosis (pl **neuroses**) [njuə'rəusɪs, -si:z] n
nevrosi f inv
neurotic [njuə'rɔtɪk] adj, n nevrotico(-a)
neuter ['nju:tər] adj neutro(-a) ■ n neutro
■ vt (cat etc) castrare
neutral ['nju:trəl] adj neutro(-a); (person,
nation) neutrale ■ n (Aut): **in ~** in folle
neutrality [nju:'trælɪtɪ] n neutralità
neutralize ['nju:trəlaɪz] vt neutralizzare
neutron bomb ['nju:trɔn-] n bomba al
neutrone
Nev. abbr (US) = **Nevada**
never ['nɛvər] adv (non...) mai; **~ again** mai
più; **I'll ~ go there again** non ci vado più;
~ in my life mai in vita mia; see also **mind**
never-ending [nɛvər'ɛndɪŋ] adj interminabile
nevertheless [nɛvəðə'lɛs] adv tuttavia, ciò
nonostante, ciò nondimeno
new [nju:] adj nuovo(-a); (brand new)
nuovo(-a) di zecca; **as good as ~** come nuovo
New Age adj, n New Age f inv
newbie ['nju:bɪ] n (Comput, Tech)
utilizzatore(-trice) inesperto(-a); (to a job or
group) nuovo(-a) arrivato(-a); (to a hobby or
experience) neofita m/f
newborn ['nju:bɔ:n] adj neonato(-a)
newcomer ['nju:kʌmər] n nuovo(-a) venuto(-a)
new-fangled ['nju:fæŋgld] adj (pej)
stramoderno(-a)
new-found ['nju:faund] adj nuovo(-a)
Newfoundland ['nju:fənlənd] n Terranova
New Guinea n Nuova Guinea
newly ['nju:lɪ] adv di recente
newly-weds ['nju:lɪwɛdz] npl sposini mpl,

sposi mpl novelli
new moon n luna nuova
newness ['nju:nɪs] n novità
news [nju:z] n notizie fpl; (Radio) giornale m
radio; (TV) telegiornale m; **a piece of ~** una
notizia; **good/bad ~** buone/cattive notizie;
financial ~ (Press) pagina economica e
finanziaria; (Radio, TV) notiziario economico
news agency n agenzia di stampa
newsagent ['nju:zeɪdʒənt] n (Brit) giornalaio
news bulletin n (Radio, TV) notiziario
newscaster ['nju:zka:stər] n (Radio, TV)
annunciatore(-trice)
newsdealer ['nju:zdi:lər] n (US) = **newsagent**
newsflash ['nju:zflæʃ] n notizia f lampo inv
newsletter ['nju:zlɛtər] n bollettino (di ditta,
associazione)
newspaper ['nju:zpeɪpər] n giornale m;
daily ~ quotidiano; **weekly ~** settimanale m
newsprint ['nju:zprɪnt] n carta da giornale
newsreader ['nju:zri:dər] n = **newscaster**
newsreel ['nju:zri:l] n cinegiornale m
newsroom ['nju:zrum] n (Press) redazione f;
(Radio, TV) studio
news stand n edicola
newsworthy ['nju:zwə:ðɪ] adj degno(-a) di
menzione (per radio, TV ecc); **to be ~** fare notizia
newt [nju:t] n tritone m
new town n (Brit) nuovo centro urbano creato con
fondi pubblici
New Year n Anno Nuovo; **Happy ~!** Buon
Anno!; **to wish sb a happy ~** augurare Buon
Anno a qn
New Year's Day n il Capodanno
New Year's Eve n la vigilia di Capodanno
New York [-'jɔ:k] n New York f, Nuova York f;
(also: **New York State**) stato di New York
New Zealand [-'zi:lənd] n Nuova Zelanda
■ adj neozelandese
New Zealander [-'zi:ləndər] n neozelandese
m/f
next [nɛkst] adj prossimo(-a) ■ adv accanto;
(in time) dopo; **~ to** prep accanto a; **~ to
nothing** quasi niente; **~ time** adv la
prossima volta; **~ week** la settimana
prossima; **the ~ week** la settimana dopo or
seguente; **the week after ~** fra due
settimane; **the ~ day** il giorno dopo,
l'indomani; **~ year** l'anno prossimo or
venturo; **"turn to the ~ page"** "vedi pagina
seguente"; **who's ~?** a chi tocca?; **when do
we meet ~?** quando ci rincontriamo?
next door adv accanto
next of kin n parente m/f prossimo(-a)
NF n abbr (Brit Pol: = National Front) partito di
estrema destra ■ abbr (Canada) = **Newfoundland**
NFL n abbr (US) = **National Football League**

Nfld. *abbr* (*Canada*) = **Newfoundland**

NG *abbr* (*US*) = **National Guard**

NGO *n abbr* = **non-governmental organization**

NH *abbr* (*US*) = **New Hampshire**

NHL *n abbr* (*US*: = *National Hockey League*) ≈ F.I.H.P. *f* (= *Federazione Italiana Hockey e Pattinaggio*)

NHS *n abbr* (*Brit*) = **National Health Service**

NI *abbr* = **Northern Ireland**; (*Brit*) = **National Insurance**

Niagara Falls [naɪˈægərə-] *npl*: **the** ~ le cascate del Niagara

nib [nɪb] *n* (*of pen*) pennino

nibble [ˈnɪbl] *vt* mordicchiare

Nicaragua [nɪkəˈrægjuə] *n* Nicaragua *m*

Nicaraguan [nɪkəˈrægjuən] *adj*, *n* nicaraguense (*m/f*)

Nice [niːs] *n* Nizza

nice [naɪs] *adj* (*holiday, trip*) piacevole; (*flat, picture*) bello(-a); (*person*) simpatico(-a), gentile; (*taste, smell, meal*) buono(-a); (*distinction, point*) sottile

nice-looking [ˈnaɪslukɪŋ] *adj* bello(-a)

nicely [ˈnaɪslɪ] *adv* bene; **that will do** ~ andrà benissimo

niceties [ˈnaɪsɪtɪz] *npl* finezze *fpl*

nick [nɪk] *n* tacca ◼ *vt* intaccare; tagliare; (*col: steal*) rubare; (*: Brit: arrest*) beccare; **in the ~ of time** appena in tempo; **in good** ~ (*Brit col*) decente, in buono stato; **to ~ o.s.** farsi un taglietto

nickel [ˈnɪkl] *n* nichel *m*; (*US*) *moneta da cinque centesimi di dollaro*

nickname [ˈnɪkneɪm] *n* soprannome *m* ◼ *vt* soprannominare

Nicosia [nɪkəˈsiːə] *n* Nicosia

nicotine [ˈnɪkətiːn] *n* nicotina

nicotine patch *n* cerotto antifumo (*a base di nicotina*)

niece [niːs] *n* nipote *f*

nifty [ˈnɪftɪ] *adj* (*col: car, jacket*) chic *inv*; (*: gadget, tool*) ingegnoso(-a)

Niger [ˈnaɪdʒəʳ] *n* Niger *m*

Nigeria [naɪˈdʒɪərɪə] *n* Nigeria

Nigerian [naɪˈdʒɪərɪən] *adj*, *n* nigeriano(-a)

niggardly [ˈnɪgədlɪ] *adj* (*person*) tirchio(-a), spilorcio(-a); (*allowance, amount*) misero(-a)

nigger [ˈnɪgəʳ] *n* (*col!*) negro(-a)

niggle [ˈnɪgl] *vt* assillare ◼ *vi* fare il/la pignolo(-a)

niggling [ˈnɪglɪŋ] *adj* pignolo(-a); (*detail*) insignificante; (*doubt, pain*) persistente

night [naɪt] *n* notte *f*; (*evening*) sera; **at** ~ la notte; la sera; **by** ~ di notte; **in the ~**, **during the** ~ durante la notte; **the** ~ **before last** l'altro ieri notte; l'altro ieri sera

night-bird [ˈnaɪtbəːd] *n* uccello notturno; (*fig*) nottambulo(-a)

nightcap [ˈnaɪtkæp] *n* bicchierino prima di andare a letto

night club *n* locale *m* notturno

nightdress [ˈnaɪtdres] *n* camicia da notte

nightfall [ˈnaɪtfɔːl] *n* crepuscolo

nightie [ˈnaɪtɪ] *n* camicia da notte

nightingale [ˈnaɪtɪŋgeɪl] *n* usignolo

night life *n* vita notturna

nightly [ˈnaɪtlɪ] *adj* di ogni notte *or* sera; (*by night*) notturno(-a) ◼ *adv* ogni notte *or* sera

nightmare [ˈnaɪtmɛəʳ] *n* incubo

night porter *n* portiere *m* di notte

night safe *n* cassa continua

night school *n* scuola serale

nightshade [ˈnaɪtʃeɪd] *n*: **deadly** ~ (*Bot*) belladonna

nightshift [ˈnaɪtʃɪft] *n* turno di notte

night-time [ˈnaɪttaɪm] *n* notte *f*

night watchman *n* guardiano notturno

nihilism [ˈnaɪɪlɪzəm] *n* nichilismo

nil [nɪl] *n* nulla *m*; (*Sport*) zero

Nile [naɪl] *n*: **the** ~ il Nilo

nimble [ˈnɪmbl] *adj* agile

nine [naɪn] *num* nove

9-11 *n* 11 settembre

nineteen [naɪnˈtiːn] *num* diciannove

ninety [ˈnaɪntɪ] *num* novanta

ninth [naɪnθ] *num* nono(-a)

nip [nɪp] *vt* pizzicare ◼ *vi* (*Brit col*): **to ~ out/down/up** fare un salto fuori/giù/di sopra ◼ *n* (*pinch*) pizzico; (*drink*) goccio, bicchierino

nipple [ˈnɪpl] *n* (*Anat*) capezzolo

nippy [ˈnɪpɪ] *adj* (*weather*) pungente; (*Brit: car, person*) svelto(-a)

nit [nɪt] *n* (*of louse*) lendine *m*; (*col: idiot*) cretino(-a), scemo(-a)

nit-pick [ˈnɪtpɪk] *vi* (*col*) cercare il pelo nell'uovo

nitrogen [ˈnaɪtrədʒən] *n* azoto

nitroglycerin, nitroglycerine [naɪtrəʊˈglɪsəriːn] *n* nitroglicerina

nitty-gritty [ˈnɪtɪˈgrɪtɪ] *n* (*col*): **to get down to the** ~ venire al sodo

nitwit [ˈnɪtwɪt] *n* (*col*) scemo(-a)

NJ *abbr* (*US*) = **New Jersey**

NLF *n abbr* (= *National Liberation Front*) ≈ F.L.N. *m*

NLRB *n abbr* (*US*: = *National Labor Relations Board*) *organismo per la tutela dei lavoratori*

NM, N. Mex. *abbr* (*US*) = **New Mexico**

 KEYWORD

no [nəʊ] *adv* (*opposite of "yes"*) no; **are you coming?** — **no (I'm not)** viene? — no (non vengo); **would you like some more?** — **no**

thank you ne vuole ancora un po'? — no, grazie; **I have no more wine** non ho più vino ■ *adj (not any)* nessuno(-a); **I have no money/ time/books** non ho soldi/tempo/libri; **no student would have done it** nessuno studente lo avrebbe fatto; **there is no reason to believe ...** non c'è nessuna ragione per credere ...; **"no parking"** "divieto di sosta"; **"no smoking"** "vietato fumare"; **"no entry"** "ingresso vietato"; **"no dogs"** "vietato l'accesso ai cani" ■ *n (pl* **noes)** no *m inv;* **I won't take no for an answer** non accetterò un rifiuto

no. *abbr (= number)* n.

nobble ['nɔbl] *vt (Brit col: bribe: person)* comprare, corrompere; *(: person to speak to, criminal)* bloccare, beccare; *(Racing: horse, dog)* drogare

Nobel prize [nəu'bɛl-] *n* premio Nobel

nobility [nəu'bɪlɪtɪ] *n* nobiltà

noble ['nəubl] *adj, n* nobile (*m*)

nobleman ['nəublmən] *n* nobile *m*, nobiluomo

nobly ['nəublɪ] *adv (selflessly)* generosamente

nobody ['nəubədɪ] *pron* nessuno

no-claims bonus [-'nəukleɪmz-] *n* bonus malus *m inv*

nocturnal [nɔk'təːnl] *adj* notturno(-a)

nod [nɔd] *vi* accennare col capo, fare un cenno; *(sleep)* sonnecchiare ■ *vt:* **to ~ one's head** fare di sì col capo ■ *n* cenno; **they nodded their agreement** accennarono di sì (col capo)

▸ **nod off** *vi* assopirsi

no-fly zone [nəu'flaɪ-] *n* zona di interdizione aerea

noise [nɔɪz] *n* rumore *m; (din, racket)* chiasso

noiseless ['nɔɪzlɪs] *adj* silenzioso(-a)

noisily ['nɔɪzɪlɪ] *adv* rumorosamente

noisy ['nɔɪzɪ] *adj (street, car)* rumoroso(-a); *(person)* chiassoso(-a)

nomad ['nəumæd] *n* nomade *m/f*

nomadic [nəu'mædɪk] *adj* nomade

no man's land *n* terra di nessuno

nominal ['nɔmɪnl] *adj* nominale

nominate ['nɔmɪneɪt] *vt (propose)* proporre come candidato; *(elect)* nominare

nomination [nɔmɪ'neɪʃən] *n* nomina; candidatura

nominee [nɔmɪ'niː] *n* persona nominata; candidato(-a)

non... [nɔn] *prefix* non...

non-alcoholic ['nɔnælkə'hɔlɪk] *adj* analcolico(-a)

non-breakable [nɔn'breɪkəbl] *adj* infrangibile

nonce word ['nɔns-] *n* parola coniata per l'occasione

nonchalant ['nɔnʃələnt] *adj* incurante, indifferente

non-commissioned [nɔnkə'mɪʃnd] *adj:* **~ officer** sottufficiale *m*

non-committal [nɔnkə'mɪtl] *adj* evasivo(-a)

nonconformist [nɔnkən'fɔːmɪst] *n* anticonformista *m/f; (Brit Rel)* dissidente *m/f* ■ *adj* anticonformista

non-contributory [nɔnkən'trɪbjutərɪ] *adj:* **~ pension scheme** *or (US)* **plan** sistema di pensionamento con i contributi interamente a carico del datore di lavoro

non-cooperation ['nɔnkəuɔpə'reɪʃən] *n* non cooperazione *f*, non collaborazione *f*

nondescript ['nɔndɪskrɪpt] *adj* qualunque *inv*

none [nʌn] *pron (not one thing)* niente; *(not one person)* nessuno(-a); **~ of you** nessuno(-a) di voi; **I have ~** non ne ho nemmeno uno; **I have ~ left** non ne ho più; **~ at all** proprio niente; *(not one)* nemmeno uno; **he's ~ the worse for it** non ne ha risentito

nonentity [nɔ'nɛntɪtɪ] *n* persona insignificante

non-essential [nɔnɪ'sɛnʃl] *adj* non essenziale ■ *n:* **non-essentials** superfluo, cose *fpl* superflue

nonetheless ['nʌnðə'lɛs] *adv* nondimeno

non-event [nɔnɪ'vɛnt] *n* delusione *f*

non-executive [nɔnɪg'zɛkjutɪv] *adj:* **~ director** direttore *m* senza potere esecutivo

non-existent [nɔnɪg'zɪstənt] *adj* inesistente

non-fiction [nɔn'fɪkʃən] *n* saggistica

non-flammable [nɔn'flæməbl] *adj* ininfiammabile

non-intervention ['nɔnɪntə'vɛnʃən] *n* non intervento

no-no ['nəunəu] *n:* **it's a ~!** *(undesirable)* è inaccettabile!; *(forbidden)* non si può fare!

non obst. *abbr (notwithstanding:* = *non obstante)* nonostante

no-nonsense [nəu'nɔnsəns] *adj* che va al sodo

non-payment [nɔn'peɪmənt] *n* mancato pagamento

nonplussed [nɔn'plʌst] *adj* sconcertato(-a)

non-profit-making [nɔn'prɔfɪtmeɪkɪŋ] *adj* senza scopo di lucro

nonsense ['nɔnsəns] *n* sciocchezze *fpl;* **~!** che sciocchezze!, che assurdità!; **it is ~ to say that ...** è un'assurdità *or* non ha senso dire che ...

nonsensical [nɔn'sɛnsɪkl] *adj* assurdo(-a), ridicolo(-a)

non-shrink [nɔn'ʃrɪŋk] *adj (Brit)* irrestringibile

non-skid [nɔn'skɪd] *adj* antisdrucciolo(-a)
non-smoker ['nɔn'sməukə^r] *n* non
fumatore(-trice)
non-starter [nɔn'stɑːtə^r] *n*: **it's a ~** è fallito
in partenza
non-stick ['nɔn'stɪk] *adj* antiaderente,
antiadesivo(-a)
non-stop ['nɔn'stɔp] *adj* continuo(-a); (*train,
bus*) direttissimo(-a) ■ *adv* senza sosta
non-taxable [nɔn'tæksəbl] *adj*: **~ income**
reddito non imponibile
non-U [nɔn'juː] *adj abbr* (*Brit col*) = **non-upper
class**
non-volatile [nɔn'vɔlətaɪl] *adj*: **~ memory**
(*Comput*) memoria permanente
non-voting [nɔn'vəutɪŋ] *adj*: **~ shares** azioni
fpl senza diritto di voto
non-white ['nɔn'waɪt] *adj* di colore ■ *n*
persona di colore
noodles ['nuːdlz] *npl* taglierini *mpl*
nook [nuk] *n*: **nooks and crannies** angoli
mpl
noon [nuːn] *n* mezzogiorno
no one ['nəuwʌn] *pron* = **nobody**
noose [nuːs] *n* nodo scorsoio, cappio;
(*hangman's*) cappio
nor [nɔː^r] *conj* = **neither** ■ *adv see* **neither**
norm [nɔːm] *n* norma
normal ['nɔːml] *adj* normale ■ *n*: **to return
to ~** tornare alla normalità
normality [nɔː'mælɪtɪ] *n* normalità
normally ['nɔːməlɪ] *adv* normalmente
Normandy ['nɔːməndɪ] *n* Normandia
north [nɔːθ] *n* nord *m*, settentrione *m* ■ *adj*
nord *inv*, del nord, settentrionale ■ *adv* verso
nord
North Africa *n* Africa del Nord
North African *adj, n* nordafricano(-a)
North America *n* America del Nord
North American *adj, n* nordamericano(-a)
Northants [nɔː'θænts] *abbr* (*Brit*)
= **Northamptonshire**
northbound ['nɔːθbaund] *adj* (*traffic*)
diretto(-a) a nord; (*carriageway*) nord *inv*
north-east [nɔːθ'iːst] *n* nord-est *m*
northerly ['nɔːðəlɪ] *adj* (*wind*) del nord;
(*direction*) verso nord
northern ['nɔːðən] *adj* del nord,
settentrionale
Northern Ireland *n* Irlanda del Nord
North Pole *n*: **the North** il Polo Nord
North Sea *n*: **the ~** il mare del Nord
North Sea oil *n* petrolio del mare del Nord
northward ['nɔːθwəd], **northwards**
['nɔːθwədz] *adv* verso nord
north-west [nɔːθ'wɛst] *n* nord-ovest *m*
Norway ['nɔːweɪ] *n* Norvegia

Norwegian [nɔː'wiːdʒən] *adj* norvegese
■ *n* norvegese *m/f*; (*Ling*) norvegese *m*
nos. *abbr* (= *numbers*) nn.
nose [nəuz] *n* naso; (*of animal*) muso ■ *vi*
(*also*: **nose one's way**) avanzare cautamente;
to pay through the ~ (for sth) (*col*) pagare
(qc) un occhio della testa
▶ **nose about, nose around** *vi* aggirarsi
nosebleed ['nəuzbliːd] *n* emorragia nasale
nose-dive ['nəuzdaɪv] *n* picchiata
nose drops *npl* gocce *fpl* per il naso
nosey ['nəuzɪ] *adj* curioso(-a)
nostalgia [nɔs'tældʒɪə] *n* nostalgia
nostalgic [nɔs'tældʒɪk] *adj* nostalgico(-a)
nostril ['nɔstrɪl] *n* narice *f*; (*of horse*) frogia
nosy ['nəuzɪ] *adj* = **nosey**
not [nɔt] *adv* non; **~ at all** niente affatto;
(*after thanks*) prego, s'immagini; **you must ~**
or **mustn't do this** non deve fare questo;
he isn't ... egli non è ...; **I hope ~** spero di no
notable ['nəutəbl] *adj* notevole
notably ['nəutəblɪ] *adv* notevolmente;
(*in particular*) in particolare
notary ['nəutərɪ] *n* (*also*: **notary public**)
notaio
notation [nəu'teɪʃən] *n* notazione *f*
notch [nɔtʃ] *n* tacca
▶ **notch up** *vt* (*score, victory*) marcare, segnare
note [nəut] *n* nota; (*letter, banknote*) biglietto
■ *vt* prendere nota di; **to take ~ of** prendere
nota di; **to take notes** prendere appunti;
to compare notes (*fig*) scambiarsi le
impressioni; **of ~** eminente, importante;
just a quick ~ to let you know ... ti scrivo
solo due righe per informarti ...
notebook ['nəutbuk] *n* taccuino; (*for
shorthand*) bloc-notes *m inv*
note-case ['nəutkeɪs] *n* (*Brit*) portafoglio
noted ['nəutɪd] *adj* celebre
notepad ['nəutpæd] *n* bloc-notes *m inv*,
blocchetto
notepaper ['nəutpeɪpə^r] *n* carta da lettere
noteworthy ['nəutwəːðɪ] *adj* degno(-a) di
nota, importante
nothing ['nʌθɪŋ] *n* nulla *m*, niente *m*; **he
does ~** non fa niente; **~ new** niente di nuovo;
for ~ (*free*) per niente; **~ at all** proprio niente
notice ['nəutɪs] *n* avviso; (*of leaving*)
preavviso; (*Brit: review: of play etc*) critica,
recensione *f* ■ *vt* notare, accorgersi di; **to
take ~ of** fare attenzione a; **to bring sth to
sb's ~** far notare qc a qn; **to give sb ~ of sth**
avvisare qn di qc; **to give ~, hand in one's ~**
(*employee*) licenziarsi; **without ~** senza
preavviso; **at short ~** con un breve preavviso;
until further ~ fino a nuovo avviso;
advance ~ preavviso; **to escape** *or* **avoid ~**

passare inosservato; **it has come to my ~ that** ... sono venuto a sapere che ...
noticeable ['nəutɪsəbl] *adj* evidente
notice board *n* (*Brit*) tabellone *m* per affissi
notification [nəutɪfɪ'keɪʃən] *n* annuncio; notifica; denuncia
notify ['nəutɪfaɪ] *vt*: **to ~ sth to sb** notificare qc a qn; **to ~ sb of sth** avvisare qn di qc; (*police*) denunciare qc a qn
notion ['nəuʃən] *n* idea; (*concept*) nozione *f*
notions ['nəuʃənz] *npl* (*US: haberdashery*) merceria
notoriety [nəutə'raɪətɪ] *n* notorietà
notorious [nəu'tɔ:rɪəs] *adj* famigerato(-a)
notoriously [nəu'tɔ:rɪəslɪ] *adv* notoriamente
Notts [nɔts] *abbr* (*Brit*) = **Nottinghamshire**
notwithstanding [nɔtwɪθ'stændɪŋ] *adv* nondimeno ■ *prep* nonostante, malgrado
nougat ['nu:gɑ:] *n* torrone *m*
nought [nɔ:t] *n* zero
noun [naun] *n* nome *m*, sostantivo
nourish ['nʌrɪʃ] *vt* nutrire
nourishing ['nʌrɪʃɪŋ] *adj* nutriente
nourishment ['nʌrɪʃmənt] *n* nutrimento
Nov. *abbr* (= *November*) nov.
Nova Scotia ['nəuvə'skəuʃə] *n* Nuova Scozia
novel ['nɔvl] *n* romanzo ■ *adj* nuovo(-a)
novelist ['nɔvəlɪst] *n* romanziere(-a)
novelty ['nɔvltɪ] *n* novità *f inv*
November [nəu'vɛmbəʳ] *n* novembre *m*; *see also* **July**
novice ['nɔvɪs] *n* principiante *m/f*; (*Rel*) novizio(-a)
NOW [nau] *n abbr* (*US*: = *National Organization for Women*) ≈ U.D.I. *f* (= *Unione Donne Italiane*)
now [nau] *adv* ora, adesso ■ *conj*: **~ (that)** adesso che, ora che; **right ~** subito; **by ~** ormai; **just ~**: **that's the fashion just ~** è la moda del momento; **I saw her just ~** l'ho vista proprio adesso; **I'll read it just ~** lo leggo subito; **~ and then**, **~ and again** ogni tanto; **from ~ on** da ora in poi; **in 3 days from ~** fra 3 giorni; **between ~ and Monday** da qui a lunedì, entro lunedì; **that's all for ~** per ora basta
nowadays ['nauədeɪz] *adv* oggidì
nowhere ['nəuwɛəʳ] *adv* in nessun luogo, da nessuna parte; **~ else** in nessun altro posto
no-win situation [nəu'wɪn-] *n*: **to be in a ~** aver perso in partenza
noxious ['nɔkʃəs] *adj* nocivo(-a)
nozzle ['nɔzl] *n* (*of hose etc*) boccaglio
NP *n abbr* = **notary public**
NS *abbr* (*Canada*) = **Nova Scotia**
NSC *n abbr* (*US*) = **National Security Council**
NSF *n abbr* (*US*) = **National Science Foundation**

NSPCC *n abbr* (*Brit*) = **National Society for the Prevention of Cruelty to Children**
NSW *abbr* (*Australia*) = **New South Wales**
NT *n abbr* (= *New Testament*) N.T. ■ *abbr* (*Canada*) = **Northwest Territories**
nth [ɛnθ] *adj*: **for the ~ time** (*col*) per l'ennesima volta
nuance ['nju:ã:ns] *n* sfumatura
nubile ['nju:baɪl] *adj* nubile; (*attractive*) giovane e desiderabile
nuclear ['nju:klɪəʳ] *adj* nucleare; (*warfare*) atomico(-a)
nuclear disarmament *n* disarmo nucleare
nuclear family *n* famiglia nucleare
nuclear-free zone ['nju:klɪə'fri:-] *n* zona denuclearizzata
nucleus (*pl* **nuclei**) ['nju:klɪəs, 'nju:klɪaɪ] *n* nucleo
NUCPS *n abbr* (*Brit*) = **National Union of Civil and Public Servants**
nude [nju:d] *adj* nudo(-a) ■ *n* (*Art*) nudo; **in the ~** tutto(-a) nudo(-a)
nudge [nʌdʒ] *vt* dare una gomitata a
nudist ['nju:dɪst] *n* nudista *m/f*
nudity ['nju:dɪtɪ] *n* nudità
nugget ['nʌgɪt] *n* pepita
nuisance ['nju:sns] *n*: **it's a ~** è una seccatura; **he's a ~** lui dà fastidio; **what a ~!** che seccatura!
NUJ *n abbr* (*Brit*: = *National Union of Journalists*) sindacato nazionale dei giornalisti
nuke [nju:k] *n* (*col*) bomba atomica
null [nʌl] *adj*: **~ and void** nullo(-a)
nullify ['nʌlɪfaɪ] *vt* annullare
NUM *n abbr* (*Brit*: = *National Union of Mineworkers*) sindacato nazionale dei dipendenti delle miniere
numb [nʌm] *adj* intorpidito(-a) ■ *vt* intorpidire; **~ with** (*fear*) paralizzato(-a) da; (*grief*) impietrito(-a) da; **~ with cold** intirizzito(-a) (dal freddo)
number ['nʌmbəʳ] *n* numero ■ *vt* numerare; (*include*) contare; **a ~ of** un certo numero di; **telephone ~** numero di telefono; **wrong ~** (*Tel*) numero sbagliato; **the staff numbers 20** gli impiegati sono in 20
numbered account ['nʌmbəd-] *n* (*in bank*) conto numerato
number plate *n* (*Brit Aut*) targa
Number Ten *n* (*Brit*: = *10 Downing Street*) *residenza del Primo Ministro del Regno Unito*
numbness ['nʌmnɪs] *n* intorpidimento; (*due to cold*) intirizzimento
numbskull ['nʌmskʌl] *n* (*col*) imbecille *m/f*, idiota *m/f*
numeral ['nju:mərəl] *n* numero, cifra
numerate ['nju:mərɪt] *adj* (*Brit*): **to be ~** saper far di conto

n

numerical [njuːˈmɛrɪkl] *adj* numerico(-a)
numerous [ˈnjuːmərəs] *adj* numeroso(-a)
nun [nʌn] *n* suora, monaca
nunnery [ˈnʌnərɪ] *n* convento
nuptial [ˈnʌpʃəl] *adj* nuziale
nurse [nəːs] *n* infermiere(-a); (*also:*
nursemaid) bambinaia ■ *vt* (*patient, cold*)
curare; (*baby; Brit*) cullare; (: *US*) allattare,
dare il latte a; (*hope*) nutrire
nursery [ˈnəːsərɪ] *n* (*room*) camera dei
bambini; (*institution*) asilo; (*for plants*) vivaio
nursery rhyme *n* filastrocca
nursery school *n* scuola materna
nursery slope *n* (*Brit Ski*) pista per
principianti
nursing [ˈnəːsɪŋ] *n* (*profession*) professione *f* di
infermiere (or di infermiera) ■ *adj* (*mother*)
che allatta
nursing home *n* casa di cura
nurture [ˈnəːtʃəʳ] *vt* allevare; nutrire
NUS *n abbr* (*Brit:* = *National Union of Students*)
sindacato nazionale degli studenti
NUT *n abbr* (*Brit:* = *National Union of Teachers*)
sindacato nazionale degli insegnanti
nut [nʌt] *n* (*of metal*) dado; (*fruit*) noce *f* (*or
nocciola or mandorla etc*) ■ *adj* (*chocolate etc*)

alla nocciola *etc*; **he's nuts** (*col*) è matto
nutcase [ˈnʌtkeɪs] *n* (*col*) mattarello(-a)
nutcrackers [ˈnʌtkrækəz] *npl* schiaccianoci
m inv
nutmeg [ˈnʌtmɛg] *n* noce *f* moscata
nutrient [ˈnjuːtrɪənt] *adj* nutriente ■ *n*
sostanza nutritiva
nutrition [njuːˈtrɪʃən] *n* nutrizione *f*
nutritionist [njuːˈtrɪʃənɪst] *n* nutrizionista *m/f*
nutritious [njuːˈtrɪʃəs] *adj* nutriente
nutshell [ˈnʌtʃɛl] *n* guscio di noce; **in a ~**
in poche parole
nutty [ˈnʌtɪ] *adj* di noce (*or nocciola or
mandorla etc*); (*Brit col*) tocco(-a), matto(-a)
nuzzle [ˈnʌzl] *vi:* **to ~ up to** strofinare il muso
contro
NV *abbr* (*US*) = **Nevada**
NWT *abbr* (*Canada*) = **Northwest Territories**
NY *abbr* (*US*) = **New York**
NYC *abbr* (*US*) = **New York City**
nylon [ˈnaɪlɔn] *n* nailon *m*; **nylons** *npl* calze
fpl di nailon
nymph [nɪmf] *n* ninfa
nymphomaniac [nɪmfəuˈmeɪnɪæk] *adj, n*
ninfomane (*f*)
NYSE *abbr* (*US*) = **New York Stock Exchange**

Oo

O, o [əu] *n* (*letter*) O, o *o* for *m inv*; (*US Scol*: = *outstanding*) ≈ ottimo; (*number*: *Tel etc*) zero; **O for Oliver**, (*US*) **O for Oboe** ≈ O come Otranto

oaf [əuf] *n* zoticone *m*

oak [əuk] *n* quercia ■ *cpd* di quercia

OAP *n abbr* (*Brit*) = **old-age pensioner**

oar [ɔːʳ] *n* remo; **to put** *or* **shove one's ~ in** (*fig*, *col*) intromettersi

oarsman ['ɔːzmən], **oarswoman** ['ɔːzwumən] *n* rematore(-trice)

OAS *n abbr* (= *Organization of American States*) O.S.A. *f* (= *Organizzazione degli Stati Americani*)

oasis (*pl* **oases**) [əu'eisis, əu'eisi:z] *n* oasi *f inv*

oath [əuθ] *n* giuramento; (*swear word*) bestemmia; **to take the ~** giurare; **on ~** (*Brit*) *or* **under ~** sotto giuramento

oatmeal ['əutmi:l] *n* farina d'avena

oats [əuts] *npl* avena

obdurate ['ɔbdjurit] *adj* testardo(-a); incallito(-a); ostinato(-a), irremovibile

OBE *n abbr* (*Brit*: = *Order of the British Empire*) titolo

obedience [ə'biːdɪəns] *n* ubbidienza; **in ~ to** conformemente a

obedient [ə'biːdɪənt] *adj* ubbidiente; **to be ~ to sb/sth** ubbidire a qn/qc

obelisk ['ɔbɪlɪsk] *n* obelisco

obese [əu'biːs] *adj* obeso(-a)

obesity [əu'biːsɪtɪ] *n* obesità

obey [ə'bei] *vt* ubbidire a; (*instructions, regulations*) osservare ■ *vi* ubbidire

obituary [ə'bɪtjuəri] *n* necrologia

object *n* ['ɔbdʒɪkt] oggetto; (*purpose*) scopo, intento; (*Ling*) complemento oggetto ■ *vi* [əb'dʒɛkt]: **to ~ to** (*attitude*) disapprovare; (*proposal*) protestare contro, sollevare delle obiezioni contro; **I ~!** mi oppongo!; **he objected that ...** obiettò che ...; **do you ~ to my smoking?** la disturba se fumo?; **what's the ~ of doing that?** a che serve farlo?; **expense is no ~** non si bada a spese

objection [əb'dʒɛkʃən] *n* obiezione *f*; (*drawback*) inconveniente *m*; **if you have no ~** se non ha obiezioni; **to make** *or* **raise an ~** sollevare un'obiezione

objectionable [əb'dʒɛkʃənəbl] *adj* antipatico(-a); (*smell*) sgradevole; (*language*) scostumato(-a)

objective [əb'dʒɛktɪv] *n* obiettivo ■ *adj* obiettivo(-a)

objectivity [ɔbdʒɪk'tɪvɪtɪ] *n* obiettività

object lesson *n*: **~ (in)** dimostrazione *f* (di)

objector [əb'dʒɛktəʳ] *n* oppositore(-trice)

obligation [ɔblɪ'geiʃən] *n* obbligo, dovere *m*; (*debt*) obbligo (di riconoscenza); **"without ~"** "senza impegno"; **to be under an ~ to sb/to do sth** essere in dovere verso qn/di fare qc

obligatory [ə'blɪgətəri] *adj* obbligatorio(-a)

oblige [ə'blaidʒ] *vt* (*force*): **to ~ sb to do** costringere qn a fare; (*do a favour*) fare una cortesia a; **to be obliged to sb for sth** essere grato a qn per qc; **anything to ~!** (*col*) questo e altro!

obliging [ə'blaidʒɪŋ] *adj* servizievole, compiacente

oblique [ə'bliːk] *adj* obliquo(-a); (*allusion*) indiretto(-a) ■ *n* (*Brit Typ*): **~ (stroke)** barra

obliterate [ə'blɪtəreit] *vt* cancellare

oblivion [ə'blɪvɪən] *n* oblio

oblivious [ə'blɪvɪəs] *adj*: **~ of** incurante di; inconscio(-a) di

oblong ['ɔblɔŋ] *adj* oblungo(-a) ■ *n* rettangolo

obnoxious [əb'nɔkʃəs] *adj* odioso(-a); (*smell*) disgustoso(-a), ripugnante

oboe ['əubəu] *n* oboe *m*

obscene [əb'siːn] *adj* osceno(-a)

obscenity [əb'sɛnɪtɪ] *n* oscenità *f inv*

obscure [əb'skjuəʳ] *adj* oscuro(-a) ■ *vt* oscurare; (*hide*: *sun*) nascondere

obscurity [əb'skjuəriti] *n* oscurità; (*obscure point*) punto oscuro; (*lack of fame*) anonimato

obsequious [əb'siːkwiəs] *adj* ossequioso(-a)

observable [əb'zə:vəbl] *adj* osservabile; (*appreciable*) notevole

observance [əb'zə:vns] *n* osservanza; **religious observances** pratiche *fpl* religiose

observant [əb'zə:vnt] *adj* attento(-a)
observation [ɔbzə'veɪʃən] *n* osservazione *f*;
(*by police etc*) sorveglianza
observation post *n* (*Mil*) osservatorio
observatory [əb'zə:vətrɪ] *n* osservatorio
observe [əb'zə:v] *vt* osservare
observer [əb'zə:və'] *n* osservatore(-trice)
obsess [əb'sɛs] *vt* ossessionare; **to be obsessed by** *or* **with sb/sth** essere ossessionato da qn/qc
obsession [əb'sɛʃən] *n* ossessione *f*
obsessive [əb'sɛsɪv] *adj* ossessivo(-a)
obsolescence [ɔbsə'lɛsns] *n* obsolescenza; **built-in** *or* **planned ~** (*Comm*) obsolescenza programmata
obsolescent [ɔbsə'lɛsnt] *adj* obsolescente
obsolete ['ɔbsəli:t] *adj* obsoleto(-a); (*word*) desueto(-a)
obstacle ['ɔbstəkl] *n* ostacolo
obstacle race *n* corsa agli ostacoli
obstetrician [ɔbstə'trɪʃən] *n* ostetrico(-a)
obstetrics [ɔb'stɛtrɪks] *n* ostetrica
obstinacy ['ɔbstɪnəsɪ] *n* ostinatezza
obstinate ['ɔbstɪnɪt] *adj* ostinato(-a)
obstreperous [əb'strɛpərəs] *adj* turbolento(-a)
obstruct [əb'strʌkt] *vt* (*block*) ostruire, ostacolare; (*halt*) fermare; (*hinder*) impedire
obstruction [əb'strʌkʃən] *n* ostruzione *f*; ostacolo
obstructive [əb'strʌktɪv] *adj* ostruttivo(-a); che crea impedimenti
obtain [əb'teɪn] *vt* ottenere ◼ *vi* essere in uso; **to ~ sth (for o.s.)** procurarsi qc
obtainable [əb'teɪnəbl] *adj* ottenibile
obtrusive [əb'tru:sɪv] *adj* (*person*) importuno(-a); (*smell*) invadente; (*building etc*) imponente e invadente
obtuse [əb'tju:s] *adj* ottuso(-a)
obverse ['ɔbvə:s] *n* opposto, inverso
obviate ['ɔbvɪeɪt] *vt* ovviare a, evitare
obvious ['ɔbvɪəs] *adj* ovvio(-a), evidente
obviously ['ɔbvɪəslɪ] *adv* ovviamente; **~!** certo!; **~ not!** certo che no!; **he was ~ not drunk** si vedeva che non era ubriaco; **he was not ~ drunk** non si vedeva che era ubriaco
OCAS *n abbr* = **Organization of Central American States**
occasion [ə'keɪʒən] *n* occasione *f*; (*event*) avvenimento ◼ *vt* cagionare; **on that ~** in quell'occasione, quella volta; **to rise to the ~** mostrarsi all'altezza della situazione
occasional [ə'keɪʒənl] *adj* occasionale; **I smoke an ~ cigarette** ogni tanto fumo una sigaretta
occasionally [ə'keɪʒənəlɪ] *adv* ogni tanto; **very ~** molto raramente

occasional table *n* tavolino
occult [ɔ'kʌlt] *adj* occulto(-a) ◼ *n*: **the ~** l'occulto
occupancy ['ɔkjupənsɪ] *n* occupazione *f*
occupant ['ɔkjupənt] *n* occupante *m/f*; (*of boat, car etc*) persona a bordo
occupation [ɔkju'peɪʃən] *n* occupazione *f*; (*job*) mestiere *m*, professione *f*; **unfit for ~** (*house*) inabitabile
occupational [ɔkju'peɪʃənl] *adj* (*disease*) professionale; (*hazard*) del mestiere; **~ accident** infortunio sul lavoro
occupational guidance *n* (*Brit*) orientamento professionale
occupational pension scheme *n* sistema pensionistico programmato dal datore di lavoro
occupational therapy *n* ergoterapia
occupier ['ɔkjupaɪə'] *n* occupante *m/f*
occupy ['ɔkjupaɪ] *vt* occupare; **to ~ o.s. by doing** occuparsi a fare; **to be occupied with sth/in doing sth** essere preso da qc/occupato a fare qc
occur [ə'kə:'] *vi* accadere; (*difficulty, opportunity*) capitare; (*phenomenon, error*) trovarsi; **to ~ to sb** venire in mente a qn
occurrence [ə'kʌrəns] *n* caso, fatto; presenza
ocean ['əuʃən] *n* oceano; **oceans of** (*col*) un sacco di
ocean bed *n* fondale *m* oceanico
ocean-going ['əuʃəngəuɪŋ] *adj* d'alto mare
Oceania [əuʃɪ'ɑ:nɪə] *n* Oceania
ocean liner *n* transatlantico
ochre, (*US*) **ocher** ['əukə'] *adj* ocra *inv*
o'clock [ə'klɔk] *adv*: **it is one ~** è l'una; **it is 5 ~** sono le 5
OCR *n abbr* = **optical character reader**; **optical character recognition**
Oct. *abbr* (= *October*) ott.
octagonal [ɔk'tægənl] *adj* ottagonale
octane ['ɔkteɪn] *n* ottano; **high-~ petrol** *or* (*US*) **gas** benzina ad alto numero di ottani
octave ['ɔktɪv] *n* ottavo
October [ɔk'təubə'] *n* ottobre *m*; *see also* **July**
octogenarian [ɔktəudʒɪ'nɛərɪən] *n* ottuagenario(-a)
octopus ['ɔktəpəs] *n* polpo, piovra
odd [ɔd] *adj* (*strange*) strano(-a), bizzarro(-a); (*number*) dispari *inv*; (*left over*) in più; (*not of a set*) spaiato(-a); **60-~** 60 e oltre; **at ~ times** di tanto in tanto; **the ~ one out** l'eccezione *f*
oddball ['ɔdbɔ:l] *n* (*col*) eccentrico(-a)
oddity ['ɔdɪtɪ] *n* bizzarria; (*person*) originale *m/f*
odd-job man [ɔd'dʒɔb-] *n* tuttofare *m inv*
odd jobs *npl* lavori *mpl* occasionali
oddly ['ɔdlɪ] *adv* stranamente
oddments ['ɔdmənts] *npl* (*Brit Comm*) rimanenze *fpl*

odds [ɔdz] *npl* (*in betting*) quota; **the ~ are against his coming** c'è poca probabilità che venga; **it makes no ~** non importa; **at ~** in contesa; **to succeed against all the ~** riuscire contro ogni aspettativa; **~ and ends** avanzi *mpl*
odds-on [ɔdz'ɔn] *adj* (*col*) probabile; **~ favourite** (*Racing*) favorito(-a)
ode [əud] *n* ode *f*
odious ['əudɪəs] *adj* odioso(-a), ripugnante
odometer [ɔ'dɔmɪtəʳ] *n* odometro
odour, (*US*) **odor** ['əudəʳ] *n* odore *m*
odourless, (*US*) **odorless** ['əudəlɪs] *adj* inodoro(-a)
OECD *n abbr* (= *Organization for Economic Cooperation and Development*) O.C.S.E. *f* (= *Organizzazione per la Cooperazione e lo Sviluppo Economico*)
oesophagus, (*US*) **esophagus** [iː'sɔfəgəs] *n* esofago
oestrogen, (*US*) **estrogen** ['iːstrəudʒən] *n* estrogeno

○ KEYWORD

of [ɔv, əv] *prep* 1 (*gen*) di; **a boy of 10** un ragazzo di 10 anni; **a friend of ours** un nostro amico; **that was kind of you** è stato molto gentile da parte sua
2 (*expressing quantity, amount, dates etc*) di; **a kilo of flour** un chilo di farina; **how much of this do you need?** quanto gliene serve?; **there were four of them** (*people*) erano in quattro; (*objects*) ce n'erano quattro; **three of us went** tre di noi sono andati; **the 5th of July** il 5 luglio; **a quarter of 4** (*US*) le 4 meno un quarto
3 (*from, out of*) di, in; **made of wood** (*fatto*) di *or* in legno

Ofcom ['ɔfkɔm] *n abbr* (*Brit*: = *Office of Communications*) organismo di regolamentazione delle telecomunicazioni

---

○ KEYWORD

off [ɔf] *adv* 1 (*distance, time*): **it's a long way off** è lontano; **the game is 3 days off** la partita è tra 3 giorni
2 (*departure, removal*) via; **to go off to Paris** andarsene a Parigi; **I must be off** devo andare via; **to take off one's coat** togliersi il cappotto; **the button came off** il bottone è venuto via *or* si è staccato; **10% off** con lo sconto del 10%
3 (*not at work*): **to have a day off** avere un giorno libero; **to be off sick** essere assente per malattia

■ *adj* (*engine*) spento(-a); (*tap*) chiuso(-a); (*cancelled*) sospeso(-a); (*Brit: food*) andato(-a) a male; **to be well/badly off** essere/non essere benestante; **the lid was off** non c'era il coperchio; **I'm afraid the chicken is off** (*Brit: not available*) purtroppo il pollo è finito; **on the off chance** nel caso; **to have an off day** non essere in forma; **that's a bit off, isn't it?** (*fig, col*) non è molto carino, vero?
■ *prep* 1 (*motion, removal etc*) da; (*distant from*) a poca distanza da; **a street off the square** una strada che parte dalla piazza; **5km off the road** a 5km dalla strada; **off the coast** al largo della costa; **a house off the main road** una casa che non è sulla strada principale
2: **to be off meat** non mangiare più la carne

offal ['ɔfl] *n* (*Culin*) frattaglie *fpl*
offbeat ['ɔfbiːt] *adj* eccentrico(-a)
off-centre, (*US*) **off-center** [ɔf'sɛntəʳ] *adj* storto(-a), fuori centro
off-colour ['ɔf'kʌləʳ] *adj* (*Brit: ill*) malato(-a), indisposto(-a); **to feel ~** sentirsi poco bene
offence, (*US*) **offense** [ə'fɛns] *n* (*Law*) contravvenzione *f*; (: *more serious*) reato; **to give ~ to** offendere; **to take ~ at** offendersi per; **to commit an ~** commettere un reato
offend [ə'fɛnd] *vt* (*person*) offendere ■ *vi*: **to ~ against** (*law, rule*) trasgredire
offender [ə'fɛndəʳ] *n* delinquente *m/f*; (*against regulations*) contravventore(-trice)
offending [ə'fɛndɪŋ] *adj* (*often humorous*): **the ~ word/object** la parola incriminata/l'oggetto incriminato
offense [ə'fɛns] *n* (*US*) = **offence**
offensive [ə'fɛnsɪv] *adj* offensivo(-a); (*smell etc*) sgradevole, ripugnante ■ *n* (*Mil*) offensiva
offer ['ɔfəʳ] *n* offerta, proposta ■ *vt* offrire; **"on ~"** (*Comm*) "in offerta speciale"; **make an ~ for sth** fare un'offerta per qc; **to ~ sth to sb, ~ sb sth** offrire qc a qn; **to ~ to do sth** offrirsi di fare qc
offering ['ɔfərɪŋ] *n* offerta
offhand [ɔf'hænd] *adj* disinvolto(-a), noncurante ■ *adv* all'improvvto; **I can't tell you ~** non posso dirglielo su due piedi
office ['ɔfɪs] *n* (*place*) ufficio; (*position*) carica; **doctor's ~** (*US*) ambulatorio; **to take ~** entrare in carica; **through his good offices** con il suo prezioso aiuto; **O~ of Fair Trading** (*Brit*) organismo di protezione contro le pratiche commerciali abusive
office automation *n* automazione *f* d'ufficio, burotica
office bearer *n* (*of club etc*) membro dell'amministrazione

689

office block, (US) **office building** n complesso di uffici

office boy n garzone m

office hours npl orario d'ufficio; (US Med) orario di visite

office manager n capoufficio m/f

officer ['ɔfɪsəʳ] n (Mil etc) ufficiale m; (of organization) funzionario; (also: **police officer**) agente m di polizia

office work n lavoro d'ufficio

office worker n impiegato(-a) d'ufficio

official [ə'fɪʃl] adj (authorized) ufficiale ■ n ufficiale m; (civil servant) impiegato(-a) statale; funzionario

officialdom [ə'fɪʃəldəm] n burocrazia

officially [ə'fɪʃəlɪ] adv ufficialmente

official receiver n curatore m fallimentare

officiate [ə'fɪʃɪeɪt] vi (Rel) ufficiare; **to ~ as Mayor** esplicare le funzioni di sindaco; **to ~ at a marriage** celebrare un matrimonio

officious [ə'fɪʃəs] adj invadente

offing ['ɔfɪŋ] n: **in the ~** (fig) in vista

off-key [ɔf'kiː] adj stonato(-a) ■ adv fuori tono

off-licence ['ɔflaɪsns] n (Brit) spaccio di bevande alcoliche; vedi nota

○ **OFF-LICENCE**

In Gran Bretagna e in Irlanda, gli off-licences sono esercizi pubblici specializzati nella vendita strettamente regolamentata di bevande alcoliche, per la quale è necessario avere un'apposita licenza. In genere sono aperti fino a tarda sera.

off-limits [ɔf'lɪmɪts] adj (esp US) in cui vige il divieto d'accesso

off line adj, adv (Comput) off line inv, fuori linea; (: switched off) spento(-a)

off-load ['ɔfləud] vt scaricare

off-peak ['ɔf'piːk] adj (ticket etc) a tariffa ridotta; (time) non di punta

off-putting ['ɔfputɪŋ] adj (Brit) un po' scostante

off-season ['ɔfsiːzn] adj, adv fuori stagione

offset ['ɔfsɛt] vt irreg (counteract) controbilanciare, compensare ■ n (also: **offset printing**) offset m

offshoot ['ɔfʃuːt] n (fig) diramazione f

offshore [ɔf'ʃɔːʳ] adj (breeze) di terra; (island) vicino alla costa; (fishing) costiero(-a); **~ oilfield** giacimento petrolifero in mare aperto

offside ['ɔf'saɪd] adj (Sport) fuori gioco; (Aut: with right-hand drive) destro(-a); (: with left-hand drive) sinistro(-a) ■ n destra; sinistra

offspring ['ɔfsprɪŋ] n prole f, discendenza

offstage [ɔf'steɪdʒ] adv dietro le quinte

off-the-cuff [ɔfðə'kʌf] adv improvvisando

off-the-job ['ɔfðə'dʒɔb] adj: **~ training** addestramento fuori sede

off-the-peg ['ɔfðə'pɛg], (US) **off-the-rack** ['ɔfðə'ræk] adv prêt-à-porter

off-the-record ['ɔfðə'rɛkɔːd] adj ufficioso(-a) ■ adv in via ufficiosa

off-white ['ɔfwaɪt] adj bianco sporco inv

Ofgem ['ɔfdʒɛm] n abbr (Brit: = Office of Gas and Electricity Markets) organo indipendente di controllo per la tutela dei consumatori

often ['ɔfn] adv spesso; **how ~ do you go?** quanto spesso ci va?; **as ~ as not** quasi sempre

Ofwat ['ɔfwɔt] n abbr (Brit: = Office of Water Services) in Inghilterra e Galles, organo indipendente di controllo per la tutela dei consumatori

ogle ['əugl] vt occhieggiare

ogre ['əugəʳ] n orco

OH abbr (US) = **Ohio**

oh [əu] excl oh!

OHMS abbr (Brit) = **On His (or Her) Majesty's Service**

oil [ɔɪl] n olio; (petroleum) petrolio; (for central heating) nafta ■ vt (machine) lubrificare

oilcan ['ɔɪlkæn] n oliatore m a mano; (for storing) latta da olio

oil change n cambio dell'olio

oilfield ['ɔɪlfiːld] n giacimento petrolifero

oil filter n (Aut) filtro dell'olio

oil-fired ['ɔɪlfaɪəd] adj a nafta

oil gauge n indicatore m del livello dell'olio

oil industry n industria del petrolio

oil level n livello dell'olio

oil painting n quadro a olio

oil refinery n raffineria di petrolio

oil rig n derrick m inv; (at sea) piattaforma per trivellazioni subacquee

oilskins ['ɔɪlskɪnz] npl indumenti mpl di tela cerata

oil slick n chiazza d'olio

oil tanker n petroliera

oil well n pozzo petrolifero

oily ['ɔɪlɪ] adj unto(-a), oleoso(-a); (food) untuoso(-a)

ointment ['ɔɪntmənt] n unguento

OK abbr (US) = **Oklahoma**

O.K., okay [əu'keɪ] excl d'accordo! ■ vt approvare ■ n: **to give sth one's O.K.** approvare qc ■ adj: **is it O.K.?, are you O.K.?** tutto bene?; **it's O.K. with o by me** per me va bene; **are you O.K. for money?** sei a posto coi soldi?

Okla. abbr (US) = **Oklahoma**

old [əuld] adj vecchio(-a); (ancient) antico(-a),

vecchio(-a); (*person*) vecchio(-a), anziano(-a); **how ~ are you?** quanti anni ha?; **he's 10 years ~** ha 10 anni; **older brother/sister** fratello/sorella maggiore; **any ~ thing will do** va bene qualsiasi cosa

old age *n* vecchiaia

old-age pensioner ['əʊldeɪdʒ-] *n* (*Brit*) pensionato(-a)

old-fashioned ['əʊld'fæʃnd] *adj* antiquato(-a), fuori moda; (*person*) all'antica

old maid *n* zitella

old people's home *n* ricovero per anziani

old-style ['əʊldstaɪl] *adj* (di) vecchio stampo *inv*

old-time ['əʊldtaɪm] *adj* di una volta

old-timer [əʊld'taɪməʳ] *n* veterano(-a)

old wives' tale *n* vecchia superstizione *f*

O levels *npl* (*Brit: formerly*) diploma di istruzione secondaria conseguito a 16 anni in Inghilterra e Galles, ora sostituito dal GCSE

olive ['ɒlɪv] *n* (*fruit*) oliva; (*tree*) olivo ◾ *adj* (*also*: **olive-green**) verde oliva *inv*

olive oil *n* olio d'oliva

Olympic [əʊ'lɪmpɪk] *adj* olimpico(-a); **the ~ Games, the Olympics** i giochi olimpici, le Olimpiadi

OM *n abbr* (*Brit*: = *Order of Merit*) titolo

Oman [əʊ'mɑːn] *n* Oman *m*

OMB *n abbr* (*US*: = *Office of Management and Budget*) servizio di consulenza al Presidente in materia di bilancio

omelet, omelette ['ɒmlɪt] *n* omelette *f inv*; **ham/cheese ~(te)** omelette al prosciutto/al formaggio

omen ['əʊmən] *n* presagio, augurio

ominous ['ɒmɪnəs] *adj* minaccioso(-a); (*event*) di malaugurio

omission [əʊ'mɪʃən] *n* omissione *f*

omit [əʊ'mɪt] *vt* omettere; **to ~ to do sth** tralasciare *or* trascurare di fare qc

omnivorous [ɒm'nɪvərəs] *adj* onnivoro(-a)

ON *abbr* (*Canada*) = **Ontario**

○ KEYWORD

on [ɒn] *prep* 1 (*indicating position*) su; **on the wall** sulla parete; **on the left** a *or* sulla sinistra; **I haven't any money on me** non ho soldi con me

2 (*indicating means, method, condition etc*): **on foot** a piedi; **on the train/plane** in treno/aereo; **on the telephone** al telefono; **on the radio/television** alla radio/televisione; **to be on drugs** drogarsi; **on holiday** in vacanza; **he's on £16,000 a year** guadagna 16.000 sterline all'anno; **this round's on me** questo giro lo offro io

3 (*referring to time*): **on Friday** venerdì; **on Fridays** il *or* di venerdì; **on June 20th** il 20 giugno; **on Friday, June 20th** venerdì, 20 giugno; **a week on Friday** venerdì a otto; **on his arrival** al suo arrivo; **on seeing this** vedendo ciò

4 (*about, concerning*) su, di; **information on train services** informazioni sui collegamenti ferroviari; **a book on Goldoni/physics** un libro su Goldoni/di *or* sulla fisica

◾ *adv* 1 (*referring to dress, covering*): **to have one's coat on** avere indosso il cappotto; **to put one's coat on** mettersi il cappotto; **what's she got on?** cosa indossa?; **she put her boots/gloves/hat on** si mise gli stivali/i guanti/il cappello; **screw the lid on tightly** avvita bene il coperchio

2 (*further, continuously*): **to walk on, go on** *etc* continuare, proseguire; **to read on** continuare a leggere; **on and off** ogni tanto; **from that day on** da quel giorno in poi; **it was well on in the evening** era sera inoltrata

◾ *adj* 1 (*in operation: machine, TV, light*) acceso(-a); (: *tap*) aperto(-a); (: *brake*) inserito(-a); **is the meeting still on?** (*in progress*) la riunione è ancora in corso?; (*not cancelled*) è confermato l'incontro?; **there's a good film on at the cinema** danno un buon film al cinema; **when is the film on?** quando c'è questo film?; **my father's always on at me to get a job** (*col*) mio padre mi tormenta sempre perché trovi un lavoro

2 (*col*): **that's not on!** (*not acceptable*) non si fa così!; (*not possible*) non se ne parla neanche!

once [wʌns] *adv* una volta ◾ *conj* non appena, quando; **~ he had left/it was done** dopo che se n'era andato/fu fatto; **at ~** subito; (*simultaneously*) a un tempo; **all at ~** (tutto) ad un tratto; **~ a week** una volta alla settimana; **~ more** ancora una volta; **I knew him ~** un tempo *or* in passato lo conoscevo; **~ and for all** una volta per sempre; **~ upon a time there was ...** c'era una volta ...

oncoming ['ɒnkʌmɪŋ] *adj* (*traffic*) che viene in senso opposto

○ KEYWORD

one [wʌn] *num* uno(-a); **one hundred and fifty** centocinquanta; **one day** un giorno; **it's one (o'clock)** è l'una; **to be one up on sb** essere avvantaggiato(-a) rispetto a qn; **to be at one (with sb)** andare d'accordo (con qn)

◾ *adj* 1 (*sole*) unico(-a); **the one book which** l'unico libro che; **the one man who** l'unico che

2 (*same*) stesso(-a); **they came in the one car** sono venuti nella stessa macchina ■ *pron* **1**: **this one** questo(-a); **that one** quello(-a); **which one do you want?** quale vuole?; **I've already got one/a red one** ne ho già uno/uno rosso; **one by one** uno per uno

2: **one another** l'un l'altro; **to look at one another** guardarsi; **to help one another** aiutarsi l'un l'altro *or* a vicenda

3 (*impersonal*) si; **one never knows** non si sa mai; **to cut one's finger** tagliarsi un dito; **to express one's opinion** esprimere la propria opinione; **one needs to eat** bisogna mangiare

one-armed bandit [ˈwʌnɑːmd-] *n* slot-machine *f inv*

one-day excursion [ˈwʌndeɪ-] *n* (*US*) biglietto giornaliero di andata e ritorno

One-hundred share index [ˈwʌnhʌndrəd-] *n* indice borsistico del Financial Times

one-man [ˈwʌnˈmæn] *adj* (*business*) diretto(-a) *etc* da un solo uomo

one-man band *n* suonatore ambulante con vari strumenti

one-off [wʌnˈɔf] (*Brit col*) *n* fatto eccezionale ■ *adj* eccezionale

one-parent family [ˈwʌnpɛərənt-] *n* famiglia monogenitore

one-piece [ˈwʌnpiːs] *adj* (*bathing suit*) intero(-a)

onerous [ˈɔnərəs] *adj* (*task, duty*) gravoso(-a); (*responsibility*) pesante

oneself [wʌnˈsɛlf] *pron* si; (*after prep*) sé, se stesso(-a); **to do sth (by)** fare qc da sé

one-shot [wʌnˈʃɔt] *n* (*US*) = **one-off**

one-sided [wʌnˈsaɪdɪd] *adj* (*decision, view*) unilaterale; (*judgement, account*) parziale; (*game, contest*) impari *inv*

one-time [ˈwʌntaɪm] *adj* ex *inv*

one-to-one [ˈwʌntəwʌn] *adj* (*relationship*) univoco(-a)

one-upmanship [wʌnˈʌpmənʃɪp] *n*: **the art of** ~ l'arte *f* di primeggiare

one-way [ˈwʌnweɪ] *adj* (*street, traffic*) a senso unico

ongoing [ˈɔngəʊɪŋ] *adj* in corso; in attuazione

onion [ˈʌnjən] *n* cipolla

on line *adj* (*Comput*) on line *inv*, in linea; (: *switched on*) acceso(-a)

onlooker [ˈɔnlʊkəʳ] *n* spettatore(-trice)

only [ˈəʊnlɪ] *adv* solo, soltanto ■ *adj* solo(-a), unico(-a) ■ *conj* solo che, ma; **an** ~ **child** un figlio unico; **not** ~ non solo; **I** ~ **took one** ne ho preso soltanto uno, non ne ho preso che

uno; **I saw her** ~ **yesterday** l'ho vista appena ieri; **I'd be** ~ **too pleased to help** sarei proprio felice di essere d'aiuto; **I would come,** ~ **I'm very busy** verrei volentieri, solo che sono molto occupato

ono *abbr* = **or nearest offer**; *see* **near**

onset [ˈɔnsɛt] *n* inizio; (*of winter*) arrivo

onshore [ˈɔnʃɔːʳ] *adj* (*wind*) di mare

onslaught [ˈɔnslɔːt] *n* attacco, assalto

Ont. *abbr* (*Canada*) = **Ontario**

on-the-job [ˈɔnðəˈdʒɔb] *adj*: ~ **training** addestramento in sede

onto [ˈɔntu] *prep* su, sopra

onus [ˈəʊnəs] *n* onere *m*, peso; **the** ~ **is upon him to prove it** sta a lui dimostrarlo

onward [ˈɔnwəd], **onwards** [ˈɔnwədz] *adv* (*move*) in avanti; **from this time** ~(s) d'ora in poi

onyx [ˈɔnɪks] *n* onice *f*

oops [ups] *excl* ops! (*esprime rincrescimento per un piccolo contrattempo*); ~**-a-daisy!** oplà!

ooze [uːz] *vi* stillare

opacity [əʊˈpæsɪtɪ] *n* opacità

opal [ˈəʊpl] *n* opale *m or f*

opaque [əʊˈpeɪk] *adj* opaco(-a)

OPEC [ˈəʊpɛk] *n abbr* (= *Organization of Petroleum-Exporting Countries*) O.P.E.C. *f*

open [ˈəʊpn] *adj* aperto(-a); (*road*) libero(-a); (*meeting*) pubblico(-a); (*admiration*) evidente, franco(-a); (*question*) insoluto(-a); (*enemy*) dichiarato(-a) ■ *vt* aprire ■ *vi* (*eyes, door, debate*) aprirsi; (*flower*) sbocciare; (*shop, bank, museum*) aprire; (*book etc: commence*) cominciare; **in the** ~ (**-air**) all'aperto; **the** ~ **sea** il mare aperto, l'alto mare; ~ **ground** (*among trees*) radura; (*waste ground*) terreno non edificato; **to have an** ~ **mind** (**on sth**) non avere ancora deciso (su qc)

▶ **open on to** *vt fus* (*room, door*) dare su

▶ **open out** *vt* aprire ■ *vi* aprirsi

▶ **open up** *vt* aprire; (*blocked road*) sgombrare ■ *vi* aprirsi

open-air [əʊpnˈɛəʳ] *adj* all'aperto

open-and-shut [ˈəʊpnənˈʃʌt] *adj*: ~ **case** caso indubbio

open day *n* (*Brit*) giornata di apertura al pubblico

open-ended [əʊpnˈɛndɪd] *adj* (*fig*) aperto(-a), senza limiti

opener [ˈəʊpnəʳ] *n* (*also*: **can opener, tin opener**) apriscatole *m inv*

open-heart [əʊpnˈhɑːt] *adj*: ~ **surgery** chirurgia a cuore aperto

opening [ˈəʊpnɪŋ] *n* apertura; (*opportunity*) occasione *f*, opportunità *f inv*; sbocco; (*job*) posto vacante

opening night *n* (*Theat*) prima

open learning n *sistema educativo secondo il quale lo studente ha maggior controllo e gestione delle modalità di apprendimento*

openly [ˈəʊpnlɪ] adv apertamente

open-minded [əʊpnˈmaɪndɪd] adj che ha la mente aperta

open-necked [ˈəʊpnnɛkt] adj col collo slacciato

openness [ˈəʊpnnɪs] n (frankness) franchezza, sincerità

open-plan [ˈəʊpnˈplæn] adj senza pareti divisorie

open prison n *istituto di pena dove viene data maggiore libertà ai detenuti*

open sandwich n canapè m inv

open shop n *fabbrica o ditta dove sono accolti anche operai non iscritti ai sindacati*

Open University n (Brit) vedi nota

⊙ **OPEN UNIVERSITY**

La *Open University* (OU), fondata in Gran Bretagna nel 1969, organizza corsi universitari per corrispondenza o via Internet, basati anche su lezioni che vengono trasmesse dalla BBC per radio e per televisione e su corsi estivi.

opera [ˈɔpərə] n opera

opera glasses npl binocolo da teatro

opera house n opera

opera singer n cantante m/f d'opera or lirico(-a)

operate [ˈɔpəreɪt] vt (machine) azionare, far funzionare; (system) usare ▪ vi funzionare; (drug, person) agire; **to ~ on sb (for)** (Med) operare qn (di)

operatic [ɔpəˈrætɪk] adj dell'opera, lirico(-a)

operating [ˈɔpəreɪtɪŋ] adj (Comm: costs etc) di gestione; (Med) operatorio(-a)

operating room n (US) = **operating theatre**

operating system n (Comput) sistema m operativo

operating theatre n (Med) sala operatoria

operation [ɔpəˈreɪʃən] n operazione f; **to be in ~** (machine) essere in azione or funzionamento; (system) essere in vigore; **to have an ~ (for)** (Med) essere operato(-a) (di)

operational [ɔpəˈreɪʃənl] adj operativo(-a); (Comm) di gestione, d'esercizio; (ready for use or action) in attività, in funzione; **when the service is fully ~** quando il servizio sarà completamente in funzione

operative [ˈɔpərətɪv] adj (measure) operativo(-a) ▪ n (in factory) operaio(-a); **the ~ word** la parola chiave

operator [ˈɔpəreɪtər] n (of machine)

operatore(-trice); (Tel) centralinista m/f

operetta [ɔpəˈrɛtə] n operetta

ophthalmologist [ɔfθælˈmɔlədʒɪst] n oftalmologo(-a)

opinion [əˈpɪnjən] n opinione f, parere m; **in my ~** secondo me, a mio avviso; **to seek a second ~** (Med etc) consultarsi con un altro medico etc

opinionated [əˈpɪnjəneɪtɪd] adj dogmatico(-a)

opinion poll n sondaggio di opinioni

opium [ˈəʊpɪəm] n oppio

opponent [əˈpəʊnənt] n avversario(-a)

opportune [ˈɔpətjuːn] adj opportuno(-a)

opportunist [ɔpəˈtjuːnɪst] n opportunista m/f

opportunity [ɔpəˈtjuːnɪtɪ] n opportunità f inv, occasione f; **to take the ~ to do** or **of doing** cogliere l'occasione per fare

oppose [əˈpəʊz] vt opporsi a; **opposed to** contrario(-a) a; **as opposed to** in contrasto con

opposing [əˈpəʊzɪŋ] adj opposto(-a); (team) avversario(-a)

opposite [ˈɔpəzɪt] adj opposto(-a); (house etc) di fronte ▪ adv di fronte, dirimpetto ▪ prep di fronte a ▪ n opposto, contrario; (of word) contrario; **"see ~ page"** "vedere pagina a fronte"

opposite number n controparte f, corrispondente m/f

opposite sex n: **the ~** l'altro sesso

opposition [ɔpəˈzɪʃən] n opposizione f

oppress [əˈprɛs] vt opprimere

oppression [əˈprɛʃən] n oppressione f

oppressive [əˈprɛsɪv] adj oppressivo(-a)

opprobrium [əˈprəʊbrɪəm] n (formal) obbrobrio

opt [ɔpt] vi: **to ~ for** optare per; **to ~ to do** scegliere di fare; **to ~ out of** (Brit: of NHS) scegliere di non far più parte di; (of agreement, arrangement) scegliere di non partecipare a

optical [ˈɔptɪkl] adj ottico(-a)

optical character reader n lettore m ottico

optical character recognition n lettura ottica di caratteri

optical fibre n fibra ottica

optician [ɔpˈtɪʃən] n ottico

optics [ˈɔptɪks] n ottica

optimism [ˈɔptɪmɪzəm] n ottimismo

optimist [ˈɔptɪmɪst] n ottimista m/f

optimistic [ɔptɪˈmɪstɪk] adj ottimistico(-a)

optimum [ˈɔptɪməm] adj ottimale

option [ˈɔpʃən] n scelta; (Scol) materia facoltativa; (Comm) opzione f; **to keep one's options open** (fig) non impegnarsi; **I have no ~** non ho scelta

o

optional ['ɔpʃənl] *adj* facoltativo(-a); *(Comm)* a scelta; ~ **extra** optional *m inv*
opulence ['ɔpjuləns] *n* opulenza
opulent ['ɔpjulənt] *adj* opulento(-a)
OR *abbr (US)* = **Oregon**
or [ɔ:ʳ] *conj* o, oppure; *(with negative)*: **he hasn't seen or heard anything** non ha visto né sentito niente; **or else** se no, altrimenti; oppure
oracle ['ɔrəkl] *n* oracolo
oral ['ɔ:rəl] *adj* orale ■ *n* esame *m* orale
orange ['ɔrɪndʒ] *n (fruit)* arancia ■ *adj* arancione
orangeade [ɔrɪndʒ'eɪd] *n* aranciata
oration [ɔ:'reɪʃən] *n* orazione *f*
orator ['ɔrətəʳ] *n* oratore(-trice)
oratorio [ɔrə'tɔ:rɪəu] *n* oratorio
orb [ɔ:b] *n* orbe *m*
orbit ['ɔ:bɪt] *n* orbita ■ *vt* orbitare intorno a; **to be in/go into ~ (round)** essere/entrare in orbita (attorno a)
orbital ['ɔ:bɪtl] *n (also: **orbital motorway**)* raccordo anulare
orchard ['ɔ:tʃəd] *n* frutteto; **apple ~** meleto
orchestra ['ɔ:kɪstrə] *n* orchestra; *(US: seating)* platea
orchestral [ɔ:'kɛstrəl] *adj* orchestrale; *(concert)* sinfonico(-a)
orchestrate ['ɔ:kɪstreɪt] *vt (Mus: fig)* orchestrare
orchid ['ɔ:kɪd] *n* orchidea
ordain [ɔ:'deɪn] *vt (Rel)* ordinare; *(decide)* decretare
ordeal [ɔ:'di:l] *n* prova, travaglio
order ['ɔ:dəʳ] *n* ordine *m*; *(Comm)* ordinazione *f* ■ *vt* ordinare; **to ~ sb to do** ordinare a qn di fare; **in ~** in ordine; *(document)* in regola; **in ~ of size** in ordine di grandezza; **in ~ to do** per fare; **in ~ that** affinché + *sub*; **a machine in working ~** una macchina che funziona bene; **to be out of ~** *(machine, toilets)* essere guasto(-a); *(telephone)* essere fuori servizio; **to place an ~ for sth with sb** ordinare qc a qn; **to the ~ of** *(Banking)* all'ordine di; **to be under orders to do sth** avere l'ordine di fare qc; **a point of ~** una questione di procedura; **to be on ~** essere stato ordinato; **made to ~** fatto su commissione; **the lower orders** *(pej)* i ceti inferiori
order book *n* copiacommissioni *m inv*
order form *n* modulo d'ordinazione
orderly ['ɔ:dəlɪ] *n (Mil)* attendente *m* ■ *adj (room)* in ordine; *(mind)* metodico(-a); *(person)* ordinato(-a), metodico(-a)
order number *n* numero di ordinazione
ordinal ['ɔ:dɪnl] *adj (number)* ordinale

ordinary ['ɔ:dnrɪ] *adj* normale, comune; *(pej)* mediocre ■ *n*: **out of the ~** diverso dal solito, fuori dell'ordinario
ordinary degree *n* laurea; *vedi nota*

● **ORDINARY DEGREE**
●
● Il corso universitario di studi che porta al
● conferimento del Bachelor's degree può
● avere una durata diversa, a seconda del
● profitto dello studente. Chi non è
● interessato a proseguire gli studi oltre tre
● anni di corso può optare per l'*ordinary*
● *degree*; *vedi anche* "honours degree".

ordinary seaman *n (Brit)* marinaio semplice
ordinary shares *npl* azioni *fpl* ordinarie
ordination [ɔ:dɪ'neɪʃən] *n* ordinazione *f*
ordnance ['ɔ:dnəns] *n (Mil: unit)* (reparto di) sussistenza
Ordnance Survey map *n (Brit)* ≈ carta topografica dell'IGM
ore [ɔ:ʳ] *n* minerale *m* grezzo
Ore., Oreg. *abbr (US)* = **Oregon**
organ ['ɔ:gən] *n* organo
organic [ɔ:'gænɪk] *adj* organico(-a); *(food, produce)* biologico(-a)
organism ['ɔ:gənɪzəm] *n* organismo
organist ['ɔ:gənɪst] *n* organista *m/f*
organization [ɔ:gənaɪ'zeɪʃən] *n* organizzazione *f*
organization chart *n* organigramma *m*
organize ['ɔ:gənaɪz] *vt* organizzare; **to get organized** organizzarsi
organized crime ['ɔ:gənaɪzd-] *n* criminalità organizzata
organized labour ['ɔ:gənaɪzd-] *n* manodopera organizzata
organizer ['ɔ:gənaɪzəʳ] *n* organizzatore(-trice)
orgasm ['ɔ:gæzəm] *n* orgasmo
orgy ['ɔ:dʒɪ] *n* orgia
Orient ['ɔ:rɪənt] *n*: **the ~** l'Oriente *m*
oriental [ɔ:rɪ'ɛntl] *adj, n* orientale *(m/f)*
orientate ['ɔ:rɪənteɪt] *vt* orientare
orifice ['ɔrɪfɪs] *n* orifizio
origin ['ɔrɪdʒɪn] *n* origine *f*; **country of ~** paese *m* d'origine
original [ə'rɪdʒɪnl] *adj* originale; *(earliest)* originario(-a) ■ *n* originale *m*
originality [ərɪdʒɪ'nælɪtɪ] *n* originalità
originally [ə'rɪdʒɪnəlɪ] *adv (at first)* all'inizio
originate [ə'rɪdʒɪneɪt] *vi*: **to ~ from** venire da, essere originario(-a) di; *(suggestion)* provenire da; **to ~ in** nascere in; *(custom)* avere origine in
originator [ə'rɪdʒɪneɪtəʳ] *n* iniziatore(-trice)
Orkneys ['ɔ:knɪz] *npl*: **the ~** *(also: **the Orkney Islands**)* le (isole) Orcadi

ornament ['ɔːnəmənt] n ornamento; (trinket) ninnolo

ornamental [ɔːnə'mɛntl] adj ornamentale

ornamentation [ɔːnəmɛn'teɪʃən] n decorazione f, ornamento

ornate [ɔː'neɪt] adj molto ornato(-a)

ornithologist [ɔːnɪ'θɒlədʒɪst] n ornitologo(-a)

ornithology [ɔːnɪ'θɒlədʒɪ] n ornitologia

orphan ['ɔːfn] n orfano(-a) ■ vt: **to be orphaned** diventare orfano

orphanage ['ɔːfənɪdʒ] n orfanotrofio

orthodox ['ɔːθədɒks] adj ortodosso(-a)

orthopaedic, (US) **orthopedic** [ɔːθə'piːdɪk] adj ortopedico(-a)

OS abbr (Brit: = Ordnance Survey) ≈ IGM m (= Istituto Geografico Militare); (: Naut) = **ordinary seaman**; (: Dress) = **outsize**

O.S. abbr = **out of stock**

Oscar ['ɔskəʳ] n Oscar m inv

oscillate ['ɒsɪleɪt] vi oscillare

OSHA n abbr (US: = Occupational Safety and Health Administration) amministrazione per la sicurezza e la salute sul lavoro

Oslo ['ɒzləu] n Oslo f

ostensible [ɒs'tɛnsɪbl] adj preteso(-a); apparente

ostensibly [ɒs'tɛnsɪblɪ] adv all'apparenza

ostentation [ɒstɛn'teɪʃən] n ostentazione f

ostentatious [ɒstɛn'teɪʃəs] adj pretenzioso(-a); ostentato(-a)

osteopath ['ɒstɪəpæθ] n specialista m/f di osteopatia

ostracize ['ɒstrəsaɪz] vt dare l'ostracismo a

ostrich ['ɒstrɪtʃ] n struzzo

OT abbr (= Old Testament) V.T.

OTB n abbr (US: = off-track betting) puntate effettuate fuori dagli ippodromi

OTE abbr (= on-target earnings) stipendio compreso le commissioni

other ['ʌðəʳ] adj altro(-a) ■ pron: **the ~** l'altro(-a); **the others** gli altri; **the ~ day** l'altro giorno; **some ~ people have still to arrive** (alcuni) altri devono ancora arrivare; **some actor or ~** un certo attore; **somebody or ~** qualcuno; **~ than** altro che; a parte; **the car was none ~ than Roberta's** la macchina era proprio di Roberta

otherwise ['ʌðəwaɪz] adv, conj altrimenti; **an ~ good piece of work** un lavoro comunque buono

OTT abbr (col) = **over the top**; see **top**

otter ['ɒtəʳ] n lontra

OU n abbr (Brit) = **Open University**

ouch [autʃ] excl ohi!, ahi!

ought (pt ~) [ɔːt] aux vb: **I ~ to do it** dovrei farlo; **this ~ to have been corrected** questo avrebbe dovuto essere corretto; **he ~ to win** dovrebbe vincere; **you ~ to go and see it** dovreste andare a vederlo, fareste bene ad andarlo a vedere

ounce [auns] n oncia (= 28.35 g; 16 in a pound)

our [auəʳ] adj il/la nostro(-a); (pl) i/le nostri(-e)

ours [auəz] pron il/la nostro(-a); (pl) i/le nostri(-e)

ourselves [auə'sɛlvz] pron pl (reflexive) ci; (after preposition) noi; (emphatic) noi stessi(-e); **we did it (all) by ~** l'abbiamo fatto (tutto) da soli

oust [aust] vt cacciare, espellere

 KEYWORD

out [aut] adv (gen) fuori; **out here/there** qui/là fuori; **to speak out loud** parlare forte; **to have a night out** uscire una sera; **to be out and about** or (US) **around again** essere di nuovo in piedi; **the boat was 10 km out** la barca era a 10 km dalla costa; **the journey out** l'andata; **3 days out from Plymouth** a 3 giorni da Plymouth

■ adj: **to be out** (gen) essere fuori; (unconscious) aver perso i sensi; (style, singer) essere fuori moda; **before the week was out** prima che la settimana fosse finita; **to be out to do sth** avere intenzione di fare qc; **he's out for all he can get** sta cercando di trarne il massimo profitto; **to be out in one's calculations** aver sbagliato i calcoli; **out of** prep **1** (outside, beyond) fuori di; **to go out of the house** uscire di casa; **to look out of the window** guardare fuori dalla finestra

2 (because of) per; **out of pity** per pietà; **out of boredom** per noia

3 (origin) da; **made out of wood** (fatto) di or in legno; **to drink out of a cup** bere da una tazza

4 (from among): **out of 10** su 10

5 (without) senza; **out of petrol** senza benzina; **it's out of stock** (Comm) è esaurito

outage ['autɪdʒ] n (esp US: power failure) interruzione f or mancanza di corrente elettrica

out-and-out ['autəndaut] adj vero(-a) e proprio(-a)

outback ['autbæk] n zona isolata; (in Australia) interno, entroterra

outbid (pt, pp ~) [aut'bɪd] vt fare un'offerta più alta di

outboard ['autbɔːd] n: **~ (motor)** (motore m) fuoribordo

outbound ['autbaund] adj: **~ (for or from)** in partenza (per or da)

o

695

outbreak ['autbreɪk] n scoppio; epidemia
outbuilding ['autbɪldɪŋ] n dipendenza
outburst ['autbə:st] n scoppio
outcast ['autkɑ:st] n esule m/f; (socially) paria m inv
outclass [aut'klɑ:s] vt surclassare
outcome ['autkʌm] n esito, risultato
outcrop ['autkrɔp] n affioramento
outcry ['autkraɪ] n protesta, clamore m
outdated [aut'deɪtɪd] adj (custom, clothes) fuori moda; (idea) sorpassato(-a)
outdistance [aut'dɪstəns] vt distanziare
outdo [aut'du:] vt irreg sorpassare
outdoor [aut'dɔ:ʳ] adj all'aperto
outdoors [aut'dɔ:z] adv fuori; all'aria aperta
outer ['autəʳ] adj esteriore; ~ **suburbs** estrema periferia
outer space n spazio cosmico
outfit ['autfɪt] n equipaggiamento; (clothes) abito; (col: organization) organizzazione f
outfitter ['autfɪtəʳ] n (Brit): **"(gent's) outfitters"** "confezioni da uomo"
outgoing ['autgəuɪŋ] adj (president, tenant) uscente; (means of transport) in partenza; (character) socievole
outgoings ['autgəuɪŋz] npl (Brit: expenses) spese fpl
outgrow [aut'grəu] vt irreg (clothes) diventare troppo grande per
outhouse ['authaus] n costruzione f annessa
outing ['autɪŋ] n gita; escursione f
outlandish [aut'lændɪʃ] adj strano(-a)
outlast [aut'lɑ:st] vt sopravvivere a
outlaw ['autlɔ:] n fuorilegge m/f ■ vt (person) mettere fuori della legge; (practice) proscrivere
outlay ['autleɪ] n spesa
outlet ['autlɛt] n (for liquid etc) sbocco, scarico; (for emotion) sfogo; (for goods) sbocco, mercato; (also: **retail outlet**) punto di vendita; (US Elec) presa di corrente
outline ['autlaɪn] n contorno, profilo; (summary) abbozzo, grandi linee fpl
outlive [aut'lɪv] vt sopravvivere a
outlook ['autluk] n prospettiva, vista
outlying ['autlaɪɪŋ] adj periferico(-a)
outmanoeuvre, (US) **outmaneuver** [autmə'nu:vəʳ] vt (rival etc) superare in strategia
outmoded [aut'məudɪd] adj passato(-a) di moda; antiquato(-a)
outnumber [aut'nʌmbəʳ] vt superare in numero
out-of-court [autəv'kɔ:t] adj extragiudiziale ■ adv (settle) senza ricorrere al tribunale
out-of-date [autəv'deɪt] adj (passport, ticket) scaduto(-a); (theory, idea) sorpassato(-a),

superato(-a); (custom) antiquato(-a); (clothes) fuori moda
out-of-the-way ['autəvðə'weɪ] adj (remote) fuori mano; (unusual) originale, insolito(-a)
outpatient ['autpeɪʃənt] n paziente m/f esterno(-a)
outpost ['autpəust] n avamposto
outpouring ['autpɔ:rɪŋ] n (fig) torrente m
output ['autput] n produzione f; (Comput) output m inv ■ vt emettere
outrage ['autreɪdʒ] n oltraggio; scandalo ■ vt oltraggiare
outrageous [aut'reɪdʒəs] adj oltraggioso(-a); scandaloso(-a)
outrider ['autraɪdəʳ] n (on motorcycle) battistrada m inv
outright adv [aut'raɪt] completamente; schiettamente; apertamente; sul colpo ■ adj ['autraɪt] completo(-a); schietto(-a) e netto(-a)
outrun [aut'rʌn] vt irreg superare (nella corsa)
outset ['autsɛt] n inizio
outshine [aut'ʃaɪn] vt irreg (fig) eclissare
outside [aut'saɪd] n esterno, esteriore m ■ adj esterno(-a), esteriore; (remote, unlikely): **an ~ chance** una vaga possibilità ■ adv fuori, all'esterno ■ prep fuori di, all'esterno di; **at the ~** (fig) al massimo; ~ **left/right** n (Football) ala sinistra/destra
outside broadcast n (Radio, TV) trasmissione f in esterno
outside lane n (Aut) corsia di sorpasso
outside line n (Tel) linea esterna
outsider [aut'saɪdəʳ] n (in race etc) outsider m inv; (stranger) straniero(-a)
outsize ['autsaɪz] adj enorme; (clothes) per taglie forti
outskirts ['autskə:ts] npl sobborghi mpl
outsmart [aut'smɑ:t] vt superare in astuzia
outspoken [aut'spəukən] adj molto franco(-a)
outspread ['autsprɛd] adj (wings) aperto(-a), spiegato(-a)
outstanding [aut'stændɪŋ] adj eccezionale, di rilievo; (unfinished) non completo(-a); non evaso(-a); non regolato(-a); **your account is still ~** deve ancora saldare il conto
outstay [aut'steɪ] vt: **to ~ one's welcome** diventare un ospite sgradito
outstretched [aut'strɛtʃt] adj (hand) teso(-a); (body) disteso(-a)
outstrip [aut'strɪp] vt (also fig) superare
out-tray ['auttreɪ] n raccoglitore m per le carte da spedire
outvote [aut'vəut] vt: **to ~ sb (by)** avere la maggioranza rispetto a qn (per); **to ~ sth (by)** respingere qc (per)

outward ['autwəd] *adj* (*sign, appearances*) esteriore; (*journey*) d'andata

outwardly ['autwədlɪ] *adv* esteriormente; in apparenza

outweigh [aut'weɪ] *vt* avere maggior peso di

outwit [aut'wɪt] *vt* superare in astuzia

oval ['əuvl] *adj, n* ovale (*m*)

Oval Office *n* (US) *vedi nota*

⬤ **OVAL OFFICE**

⬤ L' *Oval Office* è una grande stanza di forma
⬤ ovale nella White House, la Casa Bianca,
⬤ dove ha sede l'ufficio del Presidente degli
⬤ Stati Uniti. Spesso il termine è usato per
⬤ indicare la stessa presidenza degli Stati
⬤ Uniti.

ovarian [əu'vɛərɪən] *adj* ovarico(-a)

ovary ['əuvərɪ] *n* ovaia

ovation [əu'veɪʃən] *n* ovazione *f*

oven ['ʌvn] *n* forno

ovenproof ['ʌvnpruːf] *adj* da forno

oven-ready ['ʌvnrɛdɪ] *adj* pronto(-a) da infornare

ovenware ['ʌvnwɛəʳ] *n* vasellame *m* da mettere in forno

over ['əuvəʳ] *adv* al di sopra; (*excessively*) molto, troppo ■ *adj (or adv)* (*finished*) finito(-a), terminato(-a); (*too much*) troppo; (*remaining*) che avanza ■ *prep* su; sopra; (*above*) al di sopra di; (*on the other side of*) di là di; (*more than*) più di; (*during*) durante; **~ here** qui; **~ there** là; **all ~** (*everywhere*) dappertutto; (*finished*) tutto(-a) finito(-a); **~ and ~ (again)** più e più volte; **~ and above** oltre (a); **to ask ~** invitare qn (a passare); **now ~ to our Rome correspondent** diamo ora la linea al nostro corrispondente da Roma; **the world ~** in tutto il mondo; **she's not ~ intelligent** (Brit) non è troppo intelligente; **they fell out ~ money** litigarono per una questione di denaro

over... ['əuvəʳ] *prefix*: **overabundant** sovrabbondante

overact [əuvər'ækt] *vi* (*Theat*) esagerare *or* strafare la propria parte

overall *adj, n* ['əuvərɔːl] ■ *adj* totale ■ *n* (Brit) grembiule *m* ■ *adv* [əuvər'ɔːl] nell'insieme, complessivamente; **overalls** *npl* tuta (da lavoro)

overall majority *n* maggioranza assoluta

overanxious [əuvər'æŋkʃəs] *adj* troppo ansioso(-a)

overawe [əuvər'ɔː] *vt* intimidire

overbalance [əuvə'bæləns] *vi* perdere l'equilibrio

overbearing [əuvə'bɛərɪŋ] *adj* imperioso(-a), prepotente

overboard ['əuvəbɔːd] *adv* (Naut) fuori bordo, in acqua; **to go ~ for sth** (*fig*) impazzire per qc

overbook [əuvə'buk] *vt* sovrapprenotare

overcapitalize [əuvə'kæpɪtəlaɪz] *vt* sovraccapitalizzare

overcast ['əuvəkɑːst] *adj* coperto(-a)

overcharge [əuvə'tʃɑːdʒ] *vt*: **to ~ sb for sth** far pagare troppo caro a qn per qc

overcoat ['əuvəkəut] *n* soprabito, cappotto

overcome [əuvə'kʌm] *vt irreg* superare; sopraffare; **~ with grief** sopraffatto(-a) dal dolore

overconfident [əuvə'kɔnfɪdənt] *adj* troppo sicuro(-a) (di sé), presuntuoso(-a)

overcrowded [əuvə'kraudɪd] *adj* sovraffollato(-a)

overcrowding [əuvə'kraudɪŋ] *n* sovraffollamento; (*in bus*) calca

overdo [əuvə'duː] *vt irreg* esagerare; (*overcook*) cuocere troppo; **to ~ it, to ~ things** (*work too hard*) lavorare troppo

overdose ['əuvədəus] *n* dose *f* eccessiva

overdraft ['əuvədrɑːft] *n* scoperto (di conto)

overdrawn [əuvə'drɔːn] *adj* (*account*) scoperto(-a)

overdrive ['əuvədraɪv] *n* (Aut) overdrive *m inv*

overdue [əuvə'djuː] *adj* in ritardo; (*recognition*) tardivo(-a); (*bill*) insoluto(-a); **that change was long ~** quel cambiamento ci voleva da tempo

overemphasis [əuvər'ɛmfəsɪs] *n*: **~ on sth** importanza eccessiva data a qc

overemphasize [əuvər'ɛmfəsaɪz] *vt* dare un'importanza eccessiva a

overestimate [əuvər'ɛstɪmeɪt] *vt* sopravvalutare

overexcited [əuvərɪk'saɪtɪd] *adj* sovraeccitato(-a)

overexertion [əuvərɪg'zəːʃən] *n* logorio (fisico)

overexpose [əuvərɪk'spəuz] *vt* (Phot) sovraesporre

overflow *vi* [əuvə'fləu] traboccare ■ *n* ['əuvəfləu] eccesso; (*also*: **overflow pipe**) troppopieno

overfly [əuvə'flaɪ] *vt irreg* sorvolare

overgenerous [əuvə'dʒɛnərəs] *adj* troppo generoso(-a)

overgrown [əuvə'grəun] *adj* (*garden*) ricoperto(-a) di vegetazione; **he's just an ~ schoolboy** è proprio un bambinone

overhang [əuvə'hæŋ] *vt irreg* sporgere da ■ *vi* sporgere

overhaul *vt* [əuvə'hɔːl] revisionare ■ *n* ['əuvəhɔːl] revisione *f*

o

overhead *adv* [əuvə'hɛd] di sopra ■ *adj* ['əuvəhɛd] aereo(-a); (*lighting*) verticale ■ *n* (US) = **overheads**

overheads ['əuvəhɛdz] *npl* (*Brit*) spese *fpl* generali

overhear [əuvə'hɪəʳ] *vt irreg* sentire (per caso)

overheat [əuvə'hi:t] *vi* surriscaldarsi

overjoyed [əuvə'dʒɔɪd] *adj* pazzo(-a) di gioia

overkill ['əuvəkɪl] *n* (*fig*) strafare *m*

overland ['əuvəlænd] *adj, adv* per via di terra

overlap *vi* [əuvə'læp] sovrapporsi ■ *n* ['əuvəlæp] sovrapposizione *f*

overleaf [əuvə'li:f] *adv* a tergo

overload [əuvə'ləud] *vt* sovraccaricare

overlook [əuvə'luk] *vt* (*have view of*) dare su; (*miss*) trascurare; (*forgive*) passare sopra a

overlord ['əuvəlɔ:d] *n* capo supremo

overmanning [əuvə'mænɪŋ] *n* eccedenza di manodopera

overnight *adv* [əuvə'naɪt] (*happen*) durante la notte; (*fig*) tutto ad un tratto ■ *adj* ['əuvənaɪt] di notte; fulmineo(-a); **he stayed there ~** ci ha passato la notte; **if you travel ~ ...** se viaggia di notte ...; **he'll be away ~** passerà la notte fuori

overpass ['əuvəpɑ:s] *n* cavalcavia *m inv*

overpay [əuvə'peɪ] *vt*: **to ~ sb by £50** pagare 50 sterline in più a qn

overplay [əuvə'pleɪ] *vt* dare troppa importanza a; **to ~ one's hand** sopravvalutare la propria posizione

overpower [əuvə'pauəʳ] *vt* sopraffare

overpowering [əuvə'pauərɪŋ] *adj* irresistibile; (*heat, stench*) soffocante

overproduction ['əuvəprə'dʌkʃən] *n* sovrapproduzione *f*

overrate [əuvə'reɪt] *vt* sopravvalutare

overreach [əuvə'ri:tʃ] *vt*: **to ~ o.s.** volere strafare

overreact [əuvəri:'ækt] *vi* reagire in modo esagerato

override [əuvə'raɪd] *vt* (*irreg: like* **ride**) (*order, objection*) passar sopra a; (*decision*) annullare

overriding [əuvə'raɪdɪŋ] *adj* preponderante

overrule [əuvə'ru:l] *vt* (*decision*) annullare; (*claim*) respingere

overrun [əuvə'rʌn] *vt irreg* (*Mil: country etc*) invadere; (*time limit etc*) superare, andare al di là di ■ *vi* protrarsi; **the town is ~ with tourists** la città è invasa dai turisti

overseas [əuvə'si:z] *adv* oltremare; (*abroad*) all'estero ■ *adj* (*trade*) estero(-a); (*visitor*) straniero(-a)

oversee [əuvə'si:] *vt irreg* sorvegliare

overseer ['əuvəsɪəʳ] *n* (*in factory*) caposquadra *m*

overshadow [əuvə'ʃædəu] *vt* (*fig*) eclissare

overshoot [əuvə'ʃu:t] *vt irreg* superare

oversight ['əuvəsaɪt] *n* omissione *f*, svista; **due to an ~** per una svista

oversimplify [əuvə'sɪmplɪfaɪ] *vt* rendere troppo semplice

oversleep [əuvə'sli:p] *vi irreg* dormire troppo a lungo

overspend [əuvə'spɛnd] *vi irreg* spendere troppo; **we have overspent by 5000 dollars** abbiamo speso 5000 dollari di troppo

overspill ['əuvəspɪl] *n* eccedenza di popolazione

overstaffed [əuvə'stɑ:ft] *adj*: **to be ~** avere troppo personale

overstate [əuvə'steɪt] *vt* esagerare

overstatement [əuvə'steɪtmənt] *n* esagerazione *f*

overstay [əuvə'steɪ] *vt*: **to ~ one's welcome** trattenersi troppo a lungo (come ospite)

overstep [əuvə'stɛp] *vt*: **to ~ the mark** superare ogni limite

overstock [əuvə'stɔk] *vt* sovrapprovvigionare, sovraimmagazzinare

overstretched [əuvə'strɛtʃt] *adj* sovraccarico(-a); (*budget*) arrivato(-a) al limite

overstrike *n* ['əuvəstraɪk] (*on printer*) sovrapposizione *f* (di caratteri) ■ *vt* [əuvə'straɪk] *irreg* sovrapporre

overt [əu'və:t] *adj* palese

overtake [əuvə'teɪk] *vt irreg* sorpassare

overtaking [əuvə'teɪkɪŋ] *n* (*Aut*) sorpasso

overtax [əuvə'tæks] *vt* (*Econ*) imporre tasse eccessive a, tassare eccessivamente; (*fig: strength, patience*) mettere alla prova, abusare di; **to ~ o.s.** chiedere troppo alle proprie forze

overthrow [əuvə'θrəu] *vt irreg* (*government*) rovesciare

overtime ['əuvətaɪm] *n* (*lavoro*) straordinario; **to do** *or* **work ~** fare lo straordinario

overtime ban *n* rifiuto sindacale a fare gli straordinari

overtone ['əuvətəun] *n* (*also:* **overtones**) sfumatura

overture ['əuvətʃuəʳ] *n* (*Mus*) ouverture *f inv*; (*fig*) approccio

overturn [əuvə'tə:n] *vt* rovesciare ■ *vi* rovesciarsi

overview ['əuvəvju:] *n* visione *f* d'insieme

overweight [əuvə'weɪt] *adj* (*person*) troppo grasso(-a); (*luggage*) troppo pesante

overwhelm [əuvə'wɛlm] *vt* sopraffare; sommergere; schiacciare

overwhelming [əuvə'wɛlmɪŋ] *adj* (*victory, defeat*) schiacciante; (*desire*) irresistibile;

one's ~ **impression is of heat** l'impressione dominante è quella di caldo

overwhelmingly [əuvə'wɛlmɪŋlɪ] *adv* in massa

overwork [əuvə'wə:k] *vt* far lavorare troppo ■ *vi* lavorare troppo, strapazzarsi

overwrite [əuvə'raɪt] *vt* (*Comput*) ricoprire

overwrought [əuvə'rɔ:t] *adj* molto agitato(-a)

ovulation [ɔvju'leɪʃən] *n* ovulazione *f*

owe [əu] *vt* dovere; **to ~ sb sth, to ~ sth to sb** dovere qc a qn

owing to ['əuɪŋtu:] *prep* a causa di

owl [aul] *n* gufo

own [əun] *adj* proprio(-a) ■ *vt* possedere ■ *vi* (*Brit*): **to ~ to sth** ammettere qc; **to ~ to having done sth** ammettere di aver fatto qc; **a room of my ~** la mia propria camera; **to get one's ~ back** vendicarsi; **on one's ~** tutto(-a) solo(-a); **can I have it for my (very) ~?** posso averlo tutto per me?; **to come into one's ~** mostrare le proprie qualità
▶ **own up** *vi* confessare

own brand *n* (*Comm*) etichetta propria

owner ['əunə'] *n* proprietario(-a)

owner-occupier ['əunər'ɔkjupaɪə'] *n* proprietario/a della casa in cui abita

ownership ['əunəʃɪp] *n* possesso; **it's under new ~** ha un nuovo proprietario

own goal *n* (*also fig*) autogol *m inv*

ox (*pl* **oxen**) [ɔks, 'ɔksn] *n* bue *m*

Oxbridge ['ɔksbrɪdʒ] *n* le università di Oxford e/o Cambridge; vedi nota

● **OXBRIDGE**
●
● La parola *Oxbridge* deriva dalla fusione
● dei nomi Ox(ford) e (Cam)bridge e fa
● riferimento a queste due antiche
● università.

Oxfam ['ɔksfæm] *n abbr* (*Brit*: = *Oxford Committee for Famine Relief*) organizzazione per aiuti al terzo mondo

oxide ['ɔksaɪd] *n* ossido

Oxon. ['ɔksn] *abbr* (*Brit*: *of Oxford*) = **Oxoniensis**

oxtail ['ɔksteɪl] *n*: ~ **soup** minestra di coda di bue

oxyacetylene ['ɔksɪə'sɛtɪli:n] *adj* ossiacetilenico(-a); ~ **burner, ~ lamp** cannello ossiacetilenico

oxygen ['ɔksɪdʒən] *n* ossigeno

oxygen mask *n* maschera ad ossigeno

oxygen tent *n* tenda ad ossigeno

oyster ['ɔɪstə'] *n* ostrica

oz. *abbr* = **ounce**

ozone ['əuzəun] *n* ozono

ozone-friendly ['əuzəun'frɛndlɪ] *adj* che non danneggia lo strato d'ozono

o

Pp

P, p [pi:] n (letter) P, p f or m inv; **P for Peter** ≈ P come Padova

P abbr = **president; prince**

p abbr (= page) p; (Brit) = **penny; pence**

PA n abbr = **personal assistant; public address system** ■ abbr (US) = **Pennsylvania**

pa [pɑ:] n (col) papà m inv, babbo

p.a. abbr = **per annum**

PAC n abbr (US) = **political action committee**

pace [peɪs] n passo; (speed) passo; velocità ■ vi: **to ~ up and down** camminare su e giù; **to keep ~ with** camminare di pari passo a; (events) tenersi al corrente di; **to put sb through his paces** (fig) mettere qn alla prova; **to set the ~** (running) fare l'andatura; (fig) dare il la or il tono

pacemaker ['peɪsmeɪkə^r] n (Med) pacemaker m inv, stimolatore m cardiaco; (Sport) chi fa l'andatura

pacific [pə'sɪfɪk] adj pacifico(-a) ■ n: **the P~ (Ocean)** il Pacifico, l'Oceano Pacifico

pacification [pæsɪfɪ'keɪʃən] n pacificazione f

pacifier ['pæsɪfaɪə^r] n (US: dummy) succhiotto, ciuccio (col)

pacifist ['pæsɪfɪst] n pacifista m/f

pacify ['pæsɪfaɪ] vt pacificare; (soothe) calmare

pack [pæk] n (packet) pacco; (Comm) confezione f; (US: of cigarettes) pacchetto; (of goods) balla; (of hounds) muta; (of wolves) branco; (of thieves etc) banda; (of cards) mazzo ■ vt (goods) impaccare, imballare; (in suitcase etc) mettere; (box) riempire; (cram) stipare, pigiare; (press down) tamponare; turare; (Comput) comprimere, impaccare ■ vi: **to ~ one's bags** fare la valigia; **to send sb packing** (col) spedire via qn

▶ **pack in** (Brit col) vi (watch, car) guastarsi ■ vt mollare, piantare; **~ it in!** piantala!

▶ **pack off** vt (person) spedire

▶ **pack up** vi (Brit col: machine) guastarsi; (: person) far fagotto ■ vt (belongings, clothes) mettere in una valigia; (goods, presents) imballare

package ['pækɪdʒ] n pacco; balla; (also: **package deal**) pacchetto; forfait m inv ■ vt (goods) confezionare

package holiday n (Brit) vacanza organizzata

package tour n viaggio organizzato

packaging ['pækɪdʒɪŋ] n confezione f, imballo

packed [pækt] adj (crowded) affollato(-a); **~ lunch** (Brit) pranzo al sacco

packer ['pækə^r] n (person) imballatore(-trice)

packet ['pækɪt] n pacchetto

packet switching [-swɪtʃɪŋ] n (Comput) commutazione f di pacchetto

pack ice ['pækaɪs] n banchisa

packing ['pækɪŋ] n imballaggio

packing case n cassa da imballaggio

pact [pækt] n patto, accordo; trattato

pad [pæd] n blocco; (for inking) tampone m; (col: flat) appartamentino ■ vt imbottire ■ vi: **to ~ about/in** etc camminare/entrare etc a passi felpati

padded cell ['pædɪd-] n cella imbottita

padding ['pædɪŋ] n imbottitura; (fig) riempitivo

paddle ['pædl] n (oar) pagaia ■ vi sguazzare ■ vt (boat) fare andare a colpi di pagaia

paddle steamer n battello a ruote

paddling pool ['pædlɪŋ-] n piscina per bambini

paddock ['pædək] n recinto; paddock m inv

paddy ['pædɪ] n (also: **paddy field**) risaia

padlock ['pædlɔk] n lucchetto ■ vt chiudere con il lucchetto

padre ['pɑ:drɪ] n cappellano

Padua ['pædjuə] n Padova

paediatrician, (US) **pediatrician** [pi:dɪə'trɪʃən] n pediatra m/f

paediatrics, (US) **pediatrics** [pi:dɪ'ætrɪks] n pediatria

paedophile, (US) **pedophile** ['pi:dəufaɪl] adj, n pedofilo(-a)

pagan ['peɪɡən] adj, n pagano(-a)

page [peɪdʒ] n pagina; (also: **page boy**)

fattorino; (: *at wedding*) paggio ■ *vt* (*in hotel etc*) (far) chiamare

pageant ['pædʒənt] *n* spettacolo storico; grande cerimonia

pageantry ['pædʒəntrɪ] *n* pompa

page break *n* interruzione *f* di pagina

pager ['peɪdʒə'] *n* cicalino, cercapersone *m*

paginate ['pædʒɪneɪt] *vt* impaginare

pagination [pædʒɪ'neɪʃən] *n* impaginazione *f*

pagoda [pə'gəudə] *n* pagoda

paid [peɪd] *pt, pp of* **pay** ■ *adj* (*work, official*) rimunerato(-a); **to put ~ to** (*Brit*) mettere fine a

paid-up ['peɪdʌp], (*US*) **paid in** ['peɪdɪn] *adj* (*member*) che ha pagato la sua quota; (*share*) interamente pagato(-a); **~ capital** capitale *m* interamente versato

pail [peɪl] *n* secchio

pain [peɪn] *n* dolore *m*; **to be in ~** soffrire, aver male; **to have a ~ in** aver male *or* un dolore a; **to take pains to do** mettercela tutta per fare; **on ~ of death** sotto pena di morte

pained [peɪnd] *adj* addolorato(-a), afflitto(-a)

painful ['peɪnful] *adj* doloroso(-a), che fa male; (*difficult*) difficile, penoso(-a)

painfully ['peɪnfəlɪ] *adv* (*fig: very*) fin troppo

painkiller ['peɪnkɪlə'] *n* antalgico, antidolorifico

painstaking ['peɪnzteɪkɪŋ] *adj* sollecito(-a)

paint [peɪnt] *n* (*for house etc*) tinta, vernice *f*; (*Art*) colore *m* ■ *vt* (*Art: walls*) dipingere; (*door etc*) verniciare; **a tin of ~** un barattolo di tinta *or* vernice; **to ~ the door blue** verniciare la porta di azzurro; **to ~ in oils** dipingere a olio

paintbox ['peɪntbɔks] *n* scatola di colori

paintbrush ['peɪntbrʌʃ] *n* pennello

painter ['peɪntə'] *n* (*artist*) pittore *m*; (*decorator*) imbianchino

painting ['peɪntɪŋ] *n* (*activity: of artist*) pittura; (: *of decorator*) imbiancatura; verniciatura; (*picture*) dipinto, quadro

paint-stripper ['peɪntstrɪpə'] *n* prodotto sverniciante

paintwork ['peɪntwə:k] *n* (*Brit*) tinta; (: *of car*) vernice *f*

pair [peə'] *n* (*of shoes, gloves etc*) paio; (*of people*) coppia; duo *m inv*; **a ~ of scissors/trousers** un paio di forbici/pantaloni

▸ **pair off** *vi*: **to ~ off (with sb)** fare coppia (con qn)

pajamas [pə'dʒɑːməz] *npl* (*US*) pigiama *m*

Pakistan [pɑːkɪ'stɑːn] *n* Pakistan *m*

Pakistani [pɑːkɪ'stɑːnɪ] *adj, n* pakistano(-a)

pal [pæl] *n* (*col*) amico(-a), compagno(-a)

palace ['pæləs] *n* palazzo

palatable ['pælɪtəbl] *adj* gustoso(-a)

palate ['pælɪt] *n* palato

palatial [pə'leɪʃəl] *adj* sontuoso(-a), sfarzoso(-a)

palaver [pə'lɑːvə'] *n* chiacchiere *fpl*; storie *fpl*

pale [peɪl] *adj* pallido(-a) ■ *vi* impallidire ■ *n*: **to be beyond the ~** aver oltrepassato ogni limite; **to grow** *or* **turn ~** (*person*) diventare pallido(-a), impallidire; **to ~ into insignificance (beside)** perdere d'importanza (nei confronti di); **~ blue** azzurro *or* blu pallido *inv*

paleness ['peɪlnɪs] *n* pallore *m*

Palestine ['pælɪstaɪn] *n* Palestina

Palestinian [pælɪs'tɪnɪən] *adj, n* palestinese (*m/f*)

palette ['pælɪt] *n* tavolozza

paling ['peɪlɪŋ] *n* (*stake*) palo; (*fence*) palizzata

palisade [pælɪ'seɪd] *n* palizzata

pall [pɔːl] *n* (*of smoke*) cappa ■ *vi*: **to ~ (on)** diventare noioso(-a) (a)

pallet ['pælɪt] *n* (*for goods*) paletta

pallid ['pælɪd] *adj* pallido(-a), smorto(-a)

pallor ['pælə'] *n* pallore *m*

pally ['pælɪ] *adj* (*col*) amichevole

palm [pɑːm] *n* (*Anat*) palma, palmo; (*also:* **palm tree**) palma ■ *vt*: **to ~ sth off on sb** (*col*) rifilare qc a qn

palmist ['pɑːmɪst] *n* chiromante *m/f*

Palm Sunday *n* Domenica delle Palme

palpable ['pælpəbl] *adj* palpabile

palpitation [pælpɪ'teɪʃən] *n* palpitazione *f*; **to have palpitations** avere le palpitazioni

paltry ['pɔːltrɪ] *adj* derisorio(-a), insignificante

pamper ['pæmpə'] *vt* viziare, accarezzare

pamphlet ['pæmflət] *n* dépliant *m inv*; (*political etc*) volantino, manifestino

pan [pæn] *n* (*also:* **saucepan**) casseruola; (*also:* **frying pan**) padella ■ *vi* (*Cine*) fare una panoramica; **to ~ for gold** (lavare le sabbie aurifere per) cercare l'oro

panacea [pænə'sɪə] *n* panacea

panache [pə'næʃ] *n* stile *m*

Panama ['pænəmɑː] *n* Panama *m*

Panama Canal *n* canale *m* di Panama

Panamanian [pænə'meɪnɪən] *adj, n* panamense (*m/f*)

pancake ['pænkeɪk] *n* frittella

Pancake Day *n* (*Brit*) martedì *m* grasso

pancake roll *n* crêpe ripiena di verdure alla cinese

pancreas ['pæŋkrɪəs] *n* pancreas *m inv*

panda ['pændə] *n* panda *m inv*

panda car *n* (*Brit*) auto *f* della polizia

pandemic [pæn'dɛmɪk] *n* pandemia

pandemonium [pændɪ'məunɪəm] *n* pandemonio

p

pander ['pændə^r] vi: **to ~ to** lusingare; concedere tutto a

p & h abbr (US: = postage and handling) affrancatura e trasporto

P & L abbr (= profit and loss) P.P.

p & p abbr (Brit: = postage and packing) affrancatura ed imballaggio

pane [peɪn] n vetro

panel ['pænl] n (of wood, cloth etc) pannello; (Radio, TV) giuria

panel game n (Brit) quiz m inv a squadre

panelling, (US) **paneling** ['pænəlɪŋ] n rivestimento a pannelli

panellist, (US) **panelist** ['pænəlɪst] n partecipante m/f (al quiz, alla tavola rotonda etc)

pang [pæŋ] n: **to feel pangs of remorse** essere torturato(-a) dal rimorso; **pangs of hunger** spasimi mpl della fame; **pangs of conscience** morsi mpl di coscienza

panhandler ['pænhændlə^r] n (US col) accattone(-a)

panic ['pænɪk] n panico ■ vi perdere il sangue freddo

panic buying [-baɪɪŋ] n accaparramento (di generi alimentari etc)

panicky ['pænɪkɪ] adj (person) pauroso(-a)

panic-stricken ['pænɪkstrɪkən] adj (person) preso(-a) dal panico, in preda al panico; (look) terrorizzato(-a)

pannier ['pænɪə^r] n (on animal) bisaccia; (on bicycle) borsa

panorama [pænə'rɑːmə] n panorama m

panoramic [pænə'ræmɪk] adj panoramico(-a)

pansy ['pænzɪ] n (Bot) viola del pensiero, pensée f inv; (col) femminuccia

pant [pænt] vi ansare

pantechnicon [pæn'tɛknɪkən] n (Brit) grosso furgone m per traslochi

panther ['pænθə^r] n pantera

panties ['pæntɪz] npl slip m, mutandine fpl

pantihose ['pæntɪhəʊz] n (US) collant m inv

panto ['pæntəʊ] n (Brit col) see **pantomime**

pantomime ['pæntəmaɪm] n (at Christmas) spettacolo natalizio; (tecnica) pantomima; vedi nota

● **PANTOMIME**

In Gran Bretagna la pantomime (abbreviata in panto) è una sorta di libera interpretazione delle favole più conosciute che vengono messe in scena nei teatri durante il periodo natalizio. Gli attori principali sono la dama, dame, che è un uomo vestito da donna, il protagonista, principal boy, che è una donna travestita da uomo, e il cattivo, villain . È uno spettacolo per tutta la famiglia, che prevede la partecipazione del pubblico.

pantry ['pæntrɪ] n dispensa

pants [pænts] npl (Brit) mutande fpl, slip m; (US: trousers) pantaloni mpl

pantsuit ['pæntsuːt] n (US) completo m or tailleur m inv pantalone inv

papacy ['peɪpəsɪ] n papato

papal ['peɪpəl] adj papale, pontificio(-a)

paparazzi [pæpə'rætsiː] npl paparazzi mpl

paper ['peɪpə^r] n carta; (also: **wallpaper**) carta da parati, tappezzeria; (also: **newspaper**) giornale m; (study, article) saggio; (exam) prova scritta ■ adj di carta ■ vt tappezzare; **a piece of ~** (odd bit) un pezzo di carta; (sheet) un foglio (di carta); **to put sth down on ~** mettere qc per iscritto; see also **papers**

paper advance n (on printer) avanzamento della carta

paperback ['peɪpəbæk] n tascabile m; edizione f economica ■ adj: **~ edition** edizione f tascabile

paper bag n sacchetto di carta

paperboy ['peɪpəbɔɪ] n (selling) strillone m; (delivering) ragazzo che recapita i giornali

paper clip n graffetta, clip f inv

paper handkerchief n fazzoletto di carta

paper mill n cartiera

paper money n cartamoneta, moneta cartacea

paper profit n utile m teorico

papers ['peɪpəz] npl (also: **identity papers**) carte fpl, documenti mpl

paper shop n (Brit) giornalaio (negozio)

paperweight ['peɪpəweɪt] n fermacarte m inv

paperwork ['peɪpəwəːk] n lavoro amministrativo

papier-mâché ['pæpɪeɪ'mæʃeɪ] n cartapesta

paprika ['pæprɪkə] n paprica

Pap test, Pap smear ['pæp-] n (Med) pap-test m inv

par [pɑː^r] n parità, pari f; (Golf) norma; **on a ~ with** alla pari con; **at/above/below ~** (Comm) alla/sopra la/sotto la pari; **above/below ~** (gen, Golf) al di sopra/al di sotto della norma; **to feel below** or **under** or **not up to ~** non sentirsi in forma

parable ['pærəbl] n parabola (Rel)

parabola [pə'ræbələ] n parabola (Math)

parachute ['pærəʃuːt] n paracadute m inv ■ vi scendere col paracadute

parachute jump n lancio col paracadute

parachutist ['pærəʃuːtɪst] n paracadutista m/f

parade [pə'reɪd] n parata; (inspection) rivista, rassegna ■ vt (fig) fare sfoggio di ■ vi sfilare in parata; **a fashion ~** (Brit) una sfilata di moda
parade ground n piazza d'armi
paradise ['pærədaɪs] n paradiso
paradox ['pærədɔks] n paradosso
paradoxical [pærə'dɔksɪkl] adj paradossale
paradoxically [pærə'dɔksɪklɪ] adv paradossalmente
paraffin ['pærəfɪn] n (Brit): **~ (oil)** paraffina; **liquid ~** olio di paraffina
paraffin heater n (Brit) stufa al cherosene
paraffin lamp n (Brit) lampada al cherosene
paragon ['pærəgən] n modello di perfezione or di virtù
paragraph ['pærəgrɑːf] n paragrafo; **to begin a new ~** andare a capo
Paraguay ['pærəgwaɪ] n Paraguay m
Paraguayan [pærə'gwaɪən] adj, n paraguaiano(-a)
parallel ['pærəlɛl] adj (also Comput) parallelo(-a); (fig) analogo(-a) ■ n (line) parallela; (fig, Geo) parallelo; **~ (with or to)** parallelo(-a) (a)
paralysis (pl **paralyses**) [pə'rælɪsɪs, -siːz] n paralisi f inv
paralytic [pærə'lɪtɪk] adj paralitico(-a); (Brit col: drunk) ubriaco(-a) fradicio(-a)
paralyze ['pærəlaɪz] vt paralizzare
paramedic [pærə'mɛdɪk] n paramedico
parameter [pə'ræmɪtə*] n parametro
paramilitary [pærə'mɪlɪtərɪ] adj paramilitare
paramount ['pærəmaunt] adj: **of ~ importance** di capitale importanza
paranoia [pærə'nɔɪə] n paranoia
paranoid ['pærənɔɪd] adj paranoico(-a)
paranormal [pærə'nɔːml] adj paranormale
paraphernalia [pærəfə'neɪlɪə] n attrezzi mpl, roba
paraphrase ['pærəfreɪz] vt parafrasare
paraplegic [pærə'pliːdʒɪk] n paraplegico(-a)
parapsychology [pærəsaɪ'kɔlədʒɪ] n parapsicologia
parasite ['pærəsaɪt] n parassita m
parasol ['pærəsɔl] n parasole m inv
paratrooper ['pærətruːpə*] n paracadutista m (soldato)
parcel ['pɑːsl] n pacco, pacchetto ■ vt (also: **parcel up**) impaccare
▶**parcel out** vt spartire
parcel bomb n (Brit) pacchetto esplosivo
parcel post n servizio pacchi
parch [pɑːtʃ] vt riardere
parched ['pɑːtʃt] adj (person) assetato(-a)
parchment ['pɑːtʃmənt] n pergamena

pardon ['pɑːdn] n perdono; grazia ■ vt perdonare; (Law) graziare; **~!** scusi!; **~ me!** mi scusi!; **I beg your ~!** scusi!; (**I beg your**) **~?**, (US) **~ me?** prego?
pare [peə*] vt (Brit: nails) tagliarsi; (: fruit etc) sbucciare, pelare
parent ['peərənt] n padre m (or madre f); **parents** npl genitori mpl
parentage ['peərəntɪdʒ] n natali mpl; **of unknown ~** di genitori sconosciuti
parental [pə'rɛntl] adj dei genitori
parent company n società madre f inv
parenthesis (pl **parentheses**) [pə'rɛnθɪsɪs, -siːz] n parentesi f inv; **in parentheses** fra parentesi
parenthood ['peərənthud] n paternità or maternità
parenting ['peərəntɪŋ] n mestiere m di genitore
Paris ['pærɪs] n Parigi f
parish ['pærɪʃ] n parrocchia; (civil) ≈ municipio ■ adj parrocchiale
parish council n (Brit) ≈ consiglio comunale
parishioner [pə'rɪʃənə*] n parrocchiano(-a)
Parisian [pə'rɪzɪən] adj, n parigino(-a)
parity ['pærɪtɪ] n parità
park [pɑːk] n parco; (public) giardino pubblico ■ vt, vi parcheggiare
parka ['pɑːkə] n eskimo
parking ['pɑːkɪŋ] n parcheggio; **"no ~"** "sosta vietata"
parking lights npl luci fpl di posizione
parking lot n (US) posteggio, parcheggio
parking meter n parchimetro
parking offence n (Brit) infrazione f al divieto di sosta
parking place n posto di parcheggio
parking ticket n multa per sosta vietata
parking violation n (US) = **parking offence**
Parkinson's ['pɑːkɪnsənz] n (also: **Parkinson's disease**) morbo di Parkinson
parkway ['pɑːkweɪ] n (US) viale m
parlance ['pɑːləns] n: **in common/modern ~** nel gergo or linguaggio comune/moderno
parliament ['pɑːləmənt] n parlamento; vedi nota

◉ **PARLIAMENT**

Nel Regno Unito il Parlamento, *Parliament*, è formato da due camere: la House of Commons, e la House of Lords. Nella House of Commons siedono 650 parlamentari, chiamati MPs, eletti per votazione diretta del popolo nelle rispettive circoscrizioni elettorali, le constituencies. Le sessioni del

Parlamento sono presiedute e moderate
dal presidente della Camera, lo Speaker.
Alla House of Lords, i cui poteri sono più
limitati, in passato si accedeva per
nomina o per carica ereditaria mentre ora
le cariche ereditarie sono state ridotte e in
futuro verranno abolite.

parliamentary [pɑːləˈmɛntərɪ] *adj*
parlamentare

parlour, (US) **parlor** [ˈpɑːləʳ] *n* salotto

parlous [ˈpɑːləs] *adj* periglioso(-a)

Parmesan [pɑːmɪˈzæn] *n* (*also:* **Parmesan
cheese**) parmigiano

parochial [pəˈrəukɪəl] *adj* parrocchiale; (*pej*)
provinciale

parody [ˈpærədɪ] *n* parodia

parole [pəˈrəul] *n:* **on** ~ in libertà per buona
condotta

paroxysm [ˈpærəksɪzəm] *n* (*Med*)
parossismo; (*of anger, laughter, coughing*)
convulso; (*of grief*) attacco

parquet [ˈpɑːkeɪ] *n:* ~ **floor(ing)** parquet *m*

parrot [ˈpærət] *n* pappagallo

parrot fashion *adv* in modo pappagallesco

parry [ˈpærɪ] *vt* parare

parsimonious [pɑːsɪˈməunɪəs] *adj*
parsimonioso(-a)

parsley [ˈpɑːslɪ] *n* prezzemolo

parsnip [ˈpɑːsnɪp] *n* pastinaca

parson [ˈpɑːsn] *n* prete *m*; (*Church of England*)
parroco

part [pɑːt] *n* parte *f*; (*of machine*) pezzo; (*Theat
etc*) parte, ruolo; (*Mus*) voce *f*; parte ◼ *adj* in
parte ◼ *adv* = **partly** ◼ *vt* separare ◼ *vi* (*people*)
separarsi; (*roads*) dividersi; **to take** ~ **in**
prendere parte a; **to take sb's** ~ parteggiare
per qn, prendere le parti di qn; **on his** ~ da
parte sua; **for my** ~ per parte mia; **for the
most** ~ in generale; nella maggior parte dei
casi; **for the better** ~ **of the day** per la
maggior parte della giornata; **to be** ~ **and
parcel of** essere parte integrante di; **to take
sth in good/bad** ~ prendere bene/male qc;
~ **of speech** (*Ling*) parte del discorso
▶ **part with** *vt fus* separarsi da; rinunciare a

partake [pɑːˈteɪk] *vi irreg* (*formal*): **to** ~ **of sth**
consumare qc, prendere qc

part exchange *n* (*Brit*): **in** ~ in pagamento
parziale

partial [ˈpɑːʃl] *adj* parziale; **to be** ~ **to** avere
un debole per

partially [ˈpɑːʃəlɪ] *adv* in parte, parzialmente

participant [pɑːˈtɪsɪpənt] *n:* ~ **(in)**
partecipante *m/f* (a)

participate [pɑːˈtɪsɪpeɪt] *vi:* **to** ~ **(in)**
prendere parte (a), partecipare (a)

participation [pɑːtɪsɪˈpeɪʃən] *n*
partecipazione *f*

participle [ˈpɑːtɪsɪpl] *n* participio

particle [ˈpɑːtɪkl] *n* particella

particular [pəˈtɪkjuləʳ] *adj* particolare;
speciale; (*fussy*) difficile; meticoloso(-a);
particulars *npl* particolari *mpl*, dettagli *mpl*;
(*information*) informazioni *fpl*; **in** ~ in
particolare, particolarmente; **to be very** ~
about essere molto pignolo(-a) su; **I'm not** ~
per me va bene tutto

particularly [pəˈtɪkjuləlɪ] *adv*
particolarmente; in particolare

parting [ˈpɑːtɪŋ] *n* separazione *f*; (*Brit: in hair*)
scriminatura ◼ *adj* d'addio; ~ **shot** (*fig*)
battuta finale

partisan [pɑːtɪˈzæn] *n* partigiano(-a) ◼ *adj*
partigiano(-a); di parte

partition [pɑːˈtɪʃən] *n* (*Pol*) partizione *f*; (*wall*)
tramezzo

partly [ˈpɑːtlɪ] *adv* parzialmente; in parte

partner [ˈpɑːtnəʳ] *n* (*Comm*) socio(-a); (*Sport*)
compagno(-a); (*at dance*) cavaliere/dama

partnership [ˈpɑːtnəʃɪp] *n* associazione *f*;
(*Comm*) società *f inv*; **to go into** ~ **(with)**,
form a ~ **(with)** mettersi in società (con),
associarsi (a)

part payment *n* acconto

partridge [ˈpɑːtrɪdʒ] *n* pernice *f*

part-time [ˈpɑːtˈtaɪm] *adj, adv* a orario
ridotto, part-time (*inv*)

part-timer [ˈpɑːtˈtaɪməʳ] *n* (*also:* **part-time
worker**) lavoratore(-trice) part-time

party [ˈpɑːtɪ] *n* (*Pol*) partito; (*team*) squadra;
gruppo; (*Law*) parte *f*; (*celebration*)
ricevimento; serata; festa; **dinner** ~ cena;
to give *or* **throw a** ~ dare una festa *or* un
party; **to be a** ~ **to a crime** essere coinvolto
in un reato

party line *n* (*Pol*) linea del partito; (*Tel*)
duplex *m inv*

party piece *n:* **to do one's** ~ (*Brit col*) esibirsi nel
proprio pezzo forte a una festa, cena etc

party political broadcast *n* comunicato
radiotelevisivo di propaganda

pass [pɑːs] *vt* (*gen*) passare; (*place*) passare
davanti a; (*exam*) passare, superare;
(*candidate*) promuovere; (*overtake, surpass*)
sorpassare, superare; (*approve*) approvare
◼ *vi* passare; (*Scol*) essere promosso(-a)
◼ *n* (*permit*) lasciapassare *m inv*; permesso;
(*in mountains*) passo, gola; (*Sport*) passaggio;
(*Scol: also:* **pass mark**): **to get a** ~ prendere la
sufficienza; **to** ~ **for** passare per; **could you**
~ **the vegetables round?** potrebbe far
passare i contorni?; **to make a** ~ **at sb** (*col*)
fare delle proposte *or* delle avances a qn;

things have come to a pretty ~ (Brit) ecco a cosa siamo arrivati
▶ **pass away** vi morire
▶ **pass by** vi passare ■ vt trascurare
▶ **pass down** vt (customs, inheritance) tramandare, trasmettere
▶ **pass on** vi (die) spegnersi, mancare ■ vt (hand on): **to ~ on (to)** (news, information, object) passare (a); (cold, illness) attaccare (a); (benefits) trasmettere (a); (price rises) riversare (su)
▶ **pass out** vi svenire; (Brit Mil) uscire dall'accademia
▶ **pass over** vi (die) spirare ■ vt lasciare da parte
▶ **pass up** vt (opportunity) lasciarsi sfuggire, perdere
passable ['pɑːsəbl] adj (road) praticabile; (work) accettabile
passage ['pæsɪdʒ] n (gen) passaggio; (also: **passageway**) corridoio; (in book) brano, passo; (by boat) traversata
passenger ['pæsɪndʒəʳ] n passeggero(-a)
passer-by [pɑːsə'baɪ] n passante m/f
passing ['pɑːsɪŋ] adj (fig) fuggevole; **to mention sth in ~** accennare a qc di sfuggita
passing place n (Aut) piazzola (di sosta)
passion ['pæʃən] n passione f; amore m; **to have a ~ for sth** aver la passione di or per qc
passionate ['pæʃənɪt] adj appassionato(-a)
passion fruit n frutto della passione
passion play n rappresentazione f della Passione di Cristo
passive ['pæsɪv] adj (also Ling) passivo(-a)
passive smoking n fumo passivo
passkey ['pɑːskiː] n passe-partout m inv
Passover ['pɑːsəuvəʳ] n Pasqua ebraica
passport ['pɑːspɔːt] n passaporto
passport control n controllo m passaporti inv
passport office n ufficio m passaporti inv
password ['pɑːswəːd] n parola d'ordine
past [pɑːst] prep (further than) oltre, di là di; dopo; (later than) dopo ■ adv: **to run ~** passare di corsa; **to walk ~** passare ■ adj passato(-a); (president etc) ex inv ■ n passato; **quarter/half ~ four** le quattro e un quarto/e mezzo; **ten/twenty ~ four** le quattro e dieci/venti; **he's ~ forty** ha più di quarant'anni; **it's ~ midnight** è mezzanotte passata; **for the ~ few days** da qualche giorno; in questi ultimi giorni; **for the ~ 3 days** negli ultimi 3 giorni; **in the ~** in or nel passato; (Ling) al passato; **I'm ~ caring** non me ne importa più nulla; **to be ~ it** (Brit col: person) essere finito(-a)
pasta ['pæstə] n pasta
paste [peɪst] n (glue) colla; (Culin) pâté m inv;

pasta ■ vt collare; **tomato ~** concentrato di pomodoro
pastel ['pæstl] adj pastello inv
pasteurized ['pæstəraɪzd] adj pastorizzato(-a)
pastille ['pæstl] n pastiglia
pastime ['pɑːstaɪm] n passatempo
past master n (Brit): **to be a ~ at** essere molto esperto(-a) in
pastor ['pɑːstəʳ] n pastore m
pastoral ['pɑːstərl] adj pastorale
pastry ['peɪstrɪ] n pasta
pasture ['pɑːstʃəʳ] n pascolo
pasty n ['pæstɪ] pasticcio di carne ■ adj ['peɪstɪ] pastoso(-a); (complexion) pallido(-a)
pat [pæt] vt accarezzare, dare un colpetto (affettuoso) a ■ n: **a ~ of butter** un panetto di burro; **to give sb/o.s. a ~ on the back** (fig) congratularsi or compiacersi con qn/se stesso; **he knows it (off) ~**, (US) **he has it down** ~ lo conosce or sa a menadito
patch [pætʃ] n (of material) toppa; (spot) macchia; (of land) pezzo ■ vt (clothes) rattoppare; **a bad ~** (Brit) un brutto periodo
▶ **patch up** vt rappezzare
patchwork ['pætʃwəːk] n patchwork m
patchy ['pætʃɪ] adj irregolare
pate [peɪt] n: **a bald ~** una testa pelata
pâté ['pæteɪ] n pâté m inv
patent ['peɪtnt] n brevetto ■ vt brevettare ■ adj patente, manifesto(-a)
patent leather n cuoio verniciato
patently ['peɪtntlɪ] adv palesemente
patent medicine n specialità f inv medicinale
patent office n ufficio brevetti
paternal [pə'təːnl] adj paterno(-a)
paternity [pə'təːnɪtɪ] n paternità
paternity suit n (Law) causa di riconoscimento della paternità
path [pɑːθ] n sentiero, viottolo; viale m; (fig) via, strada; (of planet, missile) traiettoria
pathetic [pə'θetɪk] adj (pitiful) patetico(-a); (very bad) penoso(-a)
pathological [pæθə'lɔdʒɪkl] adj patologico(-a)
pathologist [pə'θɔlədʒɪst] n patologo(-a)
pathology [pə'θɔlədʒɪ] n patologia
pathos ['peɪθɔs] n pathos m
pathway ['pɑːθweɪ] n sentiero, viottolo
patience ['peɪʃns] n pazienza; (Brit Cards) solitario; **to lose one's ~** spazientirsi
patient ['peɪʃnt] n paziente m/f; malato(-a) ■ adj paziente; **to be ~ with sb** essere paziente or aver pazienza con qn
patiently ['peɪʃntlɪ] adv pazientemente
patio ['pætɪəu] n terrazza

p

patriot ['peɪtrɪət] n patriota m/f

patriotic [pætrɪ'ɔtɪk] adj patriottico(-a)

patriotism ['pætrɪətɪzəm] n patriottismo

patrol [pə'trəul] n pattuglia ■ vt pattugliare; **to be on ~** fare la ronda; essere in ricognizione; essere in perlustrazione

patrol boat n guardacoste m inv

patrol car n autoradio f inv (della polizia)

patrolman [pə'trəulmən] n (US) poliziotto

patron ['peɪtrən] n (in shop) cliente m/f; (of charity) benefattore(-trice); **~ of the arts** mecenate m/f

patronage ['pætrənɪdʒ] n patronato

patronize ['pætrənaɪz] vt essere cliente abituale di; (fig) trattare con condiscendenza

patronizing ['pætrənaɪzɪŋ] adj condiscendente

patron saint n patrono

patter ['pætər] n picchiettio; (sales talk) propaganda di vendita ■ vi picchiettare

pattern ['pætən] n modello; (Sewing etc) modello (di carta), cartamodello; (design) disegno, motivo; (sample) campione m; **behaviour patterns** tipi mpl di comportamento

patterned ['pætənd] adj a disegni, a motivi; (material) fantasia inv

paucity ['pɔːsɪtɪ] n scarsità

paunch [pɔːntʃ] n pancione m

pauper ['pɔːpər] n indigente m/f; **~'s grave** fossa comune

pause [pɔːz] n pausa ■ vi fare una pausa, arrestarsi; **to ~ for breath** fermarsi un attimo per riprender fiato

pave [peɪv] vt pavimentare; **to ~ the way for** aprire la via a

pavement ['peɪvmənt] n (Brit) marciapiede m; (US) pavimentazione f stradale

pavilion [pə'vɪlɪən] n padiglione m; tendone m; (Sport) edificio annesso ad un campo sportivo

paving ['peɪvɪŋ] n pavimentazione f

paving stone n lastra di pietra

paw [pɔː] n zampa ■ vt dare una zampata a; (person: pej) palpare

pawn [pɔːn] n pegno; (Chess) pedone m; (fig) pedina ■ vt dare in pegno

pawnbroker ['pɔːnbrəukər] n prestatore m su pegno

pawnshop ['pɔːnʃɔp] n monte m di pietà

pay [peɪ] n (gen) paga ■ vb (pt, pp **paid**) [peɪd] vt pagare; (be profitable to: also fig) convenire a ■ vi pagare; (be profitable) rendere; **to ~ attention (to)** fare attenzione (a); **I paid £5 for that record** quel disco l'ho pagato 5 sterline; **how much did you ~ for it?** quanto l'ha pagato?; **to ~ one's way** pagare la propria parte; (company) coprire le spese; **to ~ dividends** (fig) dare buoni frutti

▶ **pay back** vt rimborsare

▶ **pay for** vt fus pagare

▶ **pay in** vt versare

▶ **pay off** vt (debts) saldare; (creditor) pagare; (mortgage) estinguere; (workers) licenziare ■ vi (scheme) funzionare; (patience) dare dei frutti; **to ~ sth off in instalments** pagare qc a rate

▶ **pay out** vt (money) sborsare, tirar fuori; (rope) far allentare

▶ **pay up** vt saldare

payable ['peɪəbl] adj pagabile; **to make a cheque ~ to sb** intestare un assegno a (nome di) qn

pay-as-you-go ['peɪəzjə'gəu] adj (mobile phone) con scheda prepagata

pay award n aumento salariale

pay day n giorno di paga

PAYE n abbr (Brit: = pay as you earn) pagamento di imposte tramite ritenute alla fonte

payee [peɪ'iː] n beneficiario(-a)

pay envelope n (US) busta f paga inv

paying ['peɪɪŋ] adj: **~ guest** ospite m/f pagante, pensionante m/f

payload ['peɪləud] n carico utile

payment ['peɪmənt] n pagamento; **advance ~** (part sum) anticipo, acconto; (total sum) pagamento anticipato; **deferred ~**, **~ by instalments** pagamento dilazionato or a rate; **in ~ for**, **in ~ of** in pagamento di; **on ~ of £5** dietro pagamento di 5 sterline

pay packet n (Brit) busta f paga inv

payphone ['peɪfəun] n cabina telefonica

payroll ['peɪrəul] n ruolo (organico); **to be on a firm's ~** far parte del personale di una ditta

pay slip n (Brit) foglio m paga inv

pay station n (US) cabina telefonica

PBS n abbr (US: = Public Broadcasting Service) servizio che collabora alla realizzazione di programmi per la rete televisiva nazionale

PBX abbr (= private branch exchange) sistema telefonico con centralino

PC n abbr = **personal computer**; (Brit) = **police constable** ■ abbr (Brit) = **Privy Councillor** ■ adj abbr = **politically correct**

pc abbr = **per cent**; (= postcard) C.P.

p/c abbr = **petty cash**

PCB n abbr = **printed circuit board**

pcm abbr = **per calendar month**

PD n abbr (US) = **police department**

pd abbr = **paid**

PDA n abbr (= personal digital assistant) PDA m inv

PDQ abbr (col) = **pretty damn quick**

PDSA n abbr (Brit: = People's Dispensary for Sick Animals) assistenza veterinaria gratuita

PDT abbr (US: = Pacific Daylight Time) ora legale del Pacifico

PE *n abbr* (= *physical education*) ed. fisica ■ *abbr*
(*Canada*) = **Prince Edward Island**
pea [piː] *n* pisello
peace [piːs] *n* pace *f*; (*calm*) calma,
tranquillità; **to be at ~ with sb/sth** essere in
pace con qn/qc; **to keep the ~** (*policeman*)
mantenere l'ordine pubblico; (: *citizen*)
rispettare l'ordine pubblico
peaceable ['piːsəbl] *adj* pacifico(-a)
peaceful ['piːsful] *adj* pacifico(-a), calmo(-a)
peacekeeping ['piːskiːpɪŋ] *n* mantenimento
della pace; **~ force** forza di pace
peace offering *n* (*fig*) dono in segno di
riconciliazione
peach [piːtʃ] *n* pesca
peacock ['piːkɔk] *n* pavone *m*
peak [piːk] *n* (*of mountain*) cima, vetta;
(*mountain itself*) picco; (*fig*) massimo; (: *of
career*) acme *f*
peak-hour ['piːkauər] *adj* (*traffic etc*) delle ore
di punta
peak hours *npl* ore *fpl* di punta
peak period *n* periodo di punta
peak rate *n* tariffa massima
peaky ['piːkɪ] *adj* (*Brit col*) sbattuto(-a)
peal [piːl] *n* (*of bells*) scampanio, carillon *m inv*;
peals of laughter scoppi *mpl* di risa
peanut ['piːnʌt] *n* arachide *f*, nocciolina
americana
peanut butter *n* burro di arachidi
pear [pɛər] *n* pera
pearl [pəːl] *n* perla
peasant ['pɛznt] *n* contadino(-a)
peat [piːt] *n* torba
pebble ['pɛbl] *n* ciottolo
peck [pɛk] *vt* (*also:* **peck at**) beccare; (: *food*)
mangiucchiare ■ *n* colpo di becco; (*kiss*)
bacetto
pecking order ['pɛkɪŋ-] *n* (*fig*) ordine *m*
gerarchico
peckish ['pɛkɪʃ] *adj* (*Brit col*): **I feel ~** ho un
languorino
peculiar [pɪˈkjuːliər] *adj* strano(-a),
bizzarro(-a); (*particular: importance, qualities*)
particolare; **~ to** tipico(-a) di,
caratteristico(-a) di
peculiarity [pɪkjuːlɪˈærɪtɪ] *n* peculiarità *f inv*;
(*oddity*) bizzarria
pecuniary [pɪˈkjuːnɪərɪ] *adj* pecuniario(-a)
pedal ['pɛdl] *n* pedale *m* ■ *vi* pedalare
pedal bin *n* (*Brit*) pattumiera a pedale
pedantic [pɪˈdæntɪk] *adj* pedantesco(-a)
peddle ['pɛdl] *vt* (*goods*) andare in giro a
vendere; (*drugs*) spacciare; (*gossip*) mettere in
giro
peddler ['pɛdlər] *n* venditore *m* ambulante
pedestal ['pɛdəstl] *n* piedestallo

pedestrian [pɪˈdɛstrɪən] *n* pedone(-a) ■ *adj*
pedonale; (*fig*) prosaico(-a), pedestre
pedestrian crossing *n* (*Brit*) passaggio
pedonale
pedestrian mall *n* (*US*) zona pedonale
pedestrian precinct *n* (*Brit*) zona pedonale
pediatrics [piːdɪˈætrɪks] *n* (*US*)
= **paediatrics**
pedigree ['pɛdɪgriː] *n* stirpe *f*; (*of animal*)
pedigree *m inv* ■ *cpd* (*animal*) di razza
pedlar ['pɛdlər] *n* = **peddler**
pee [piː] *vi* (*col*) pisciare
peek [piːk] *vi* guardare furtivamente
peel [piːl] *n* buccia; (*of orange, lemon*) scorza
■ *vt* sbucciare ■ *vi* (*paint etc*) staccarsi
▶ **peel back** *vt* togliere, levare
peeler [piːlər] *n*: **potato ~** sbucciapatate *m inv*
peelings ['piːlɪŋz] *npl* bucce *fpl*
peep [piːp] *n* (*Brit: look*) sguardo furtivo,
sbirciata; (*sound*) pigolio ■ *vi* (*Brit*) guardare
furtivamente
▶ **peep out** *vi* (*Brit*) mostrarsi furtivamente
peephole ['piːphəul] *n* spioncino
peer [pɪər] *vi*: **to ~ at** scrutare ■ *n* (*noble*) pari
m inv; (*equal*) pari *m/f inv*, uguale *m/f*
peerage ['pɪərɪdʒ] *n* dignità di pari; pari *mpl*
peerless ['pɪəlɪs] *adj* impareggiabile, senza
pari
peeved [piːvd] *adj* stizzito(-a)
peevish ['piːvɪʃ] *adj* stizzoso(-a)
peg [pɛg] *n* (*tent peg*) picchetto; (*for coat etc*)
attaccapanni *m inv*; (*Brit: also:* **clothes peg**)
molletta ■ *vt* (*clothes*) appendere con le
mollette; (*Brit: groundsheet*) fissare con i
picchetti; (*fig: prices, wages*) fissare,
stabilizzare; **off the ~** confezionato(-a)
pejorative [pɪˈdʒɔrətɪv] *adj* peggiorativo(-a)
Pekin [piːˈkɪn], **Peking** [piːˈkɪŋ] *n* Pechino *f*
pekinese, pekingese [piːkɪˈniːz] *n*
pechinese *m*
pelican ['pɛlɪkən] *n* pellicano
pelican crossing *n* (*Brit Aut*) attraversamento
pedonale con semaforo a controllo manuale
pellet ['pɛlɪt] *n* pallottola, pallina
pell-mell ['pɛl'mɛl] *adv* disordinatamente,
alla rinfusa
pelmet ['pɛlmɪt] *n* mantovana; cassonetto
pelt [pɛlt] *vt*: **to ~ sb (with)** bombardare
qn (con) ■ *vi* (*rain*) piovere a dirotto
■ *n* pelle *f*
pelvis ['pɛlvɪs] *n* pelvi *f inv*, bacino
pen [pɛn] *n* penna; (*for sheep*) recinto; (*US col:
prison*) galera; **to put ~ to paper** prendere la
penna in mano
penal ['piːnl] *adj* penale
penalize ['piːnəlaɪz] *vt* punire; (*Sport*)
penalizzare; (*fig*) svantaggiare

p

penal servitude [-'sə:vɪtjuːd] n lavori mpl forzati

penalty ['pɛnltɪ] n penalità f inv; sanzione f penale; (fine) ammenda; (Sport) penalizzazione f; (Football: also: **penalty kick**) calcio di rigore

penalty area n (Brit Sport) area di rigore

penalty clause n penale f

penalty kick n (Football) calcio di rigore

penalty shoot-out [-'ʃuːtaut] n (Football) rigori mpl; **to beat a team in a ~** battere una squadra ai rigori

penance ['pɛnəns] n penitenza

pence [pɛns] npl (Brit) of **penny**

penchant ['pãːʃãːŋ] n debole m

pencil ['pɛnsl] n matita ■ vt (also: **pencil in**) scrivere a matita

pencil case n astuccio per matite

pencil sharpener n temperamatite m inv

pendant ['pɛndnt] n pendaglio

pending ['pɛndɪŋ] prep in attesa di ■ adj in sospeso

pendulum ['pɛndjuləm] n pendolo

penetrate ['pɛnɪtreɪt] vt penetrare

penetrating ['pɛnɪtreɪtɪŋ] adj penetrante

penetration [pɛnɪ'treɪʃən] n penetrazione f

penfriend ['pɛnfrɛnd] n (Brit) corrispondente m/f

penguin ['pɛŋgwɪn] n pinguino

penicillin [pɛnɪ'sɪlɪn] n penicillina

peninsula [pə'nɪnsjulə] n penisola

penis ['piːnɪs] n pene m

penitence ['pɛnɪtns] n penitenza

penitent ['pɛnɪtnt] adj penitente

penitentiary [pɛnɪ'tɛnʃərɪ] n (US) carcere m

penknife ['pɛnnaɪf] n temperino

Penn., Penna. abbr (US) = **Pennsylvania**

pen name n pseudonimo

pennant ['pɛnənt] n banderuola

penniless ['pɛnɪlɪs] adj senza un soldo

Pennines ['pɛnaɪnz] npl: **the ~** i Pennini

penny (pl **pennies** or **pence**) ['pɛnɪ, 'pɛnɪz, pɛns] n penny m (pl = pence); (US) centesimo

penpal ['pɛnpæl] n corrispondente m/f

penpusher ['pɛnpuʃə'] n (pej) scribacchino(-a)

pension ['pɛnʃən] n pensione f
▶ **pension off** vt mandare in pensione

pensionable ['pɛnʃənəbl] adj (person) che ha diritto a una pensione, pensionabile; (age) pensionabile

pensioner ['pɛnʃənə'] n (Brit) pensionato(-a)

pension fund n fondo pensioni

pensive ['pɛnsɪv] adj pensoso(-a)

pentagon ['pɛntəgən] n pentagono; **the P~** (US Pol) il Pentagono; vedi nota

Pentecost ['pɛntɪkɔst] n Pentecoste f

penthouse ['pɛnthaus] n appartamento (di lusso) nell'attico

pent-up ['pɛntʌp] adj (feelings) represso(-a)

penultimate [pɪ'nʌltɪmət] adj penultimo(-a)

penury ['pɛnjurɪ] n indigenza

people ['piːpl] npl gente f; persone fpl; (citizens) popolo ■ n (nation, race) popolo ■ vt popolare; **old ~** i vecchi; **young ~** i giovani; **~ at large** il grande pubblico; **a man of the ~** un uomo del popolo; **4/several ~ came** 4/ parecchie persone sono venute; **the room was full of ~** la stanza era piena di gente; **~ say that ...** si dice or la gente dice che ...

PEP [pɛp] n abbr = **personal equity plan**

pep [pɛp] n (col) dinamismo
▶ **pep up** vt vivacizzare; (food) rendere più gustoso(-a)

pepper ['pɛpə'] n pepe m; (vegetable) peperone m ■ vt pepare

peppermint ['pɛpəmɪnt] n (plant) menta peperita; (sweet) pasticca di menta

pepperoni [pɛpə'rəunɪ] n salsiccia piccante

pepperpot ['pɛpəpɔt] n pepaiola

peptalk ['pɛptɔːk] n (col) discorso di incoraggiamento

per [pəː'] prep per; a; **~ hour** all'ora; **~ kilo** etc il chilo etc; **~ day** al giorno; **~ week** alla settimana; **~ person** a testa, a or per persona; **as ~ your instructions** secondo le vostre istruzioni

per annum adv all'anno

per capita adj, adv pro capite

perceive [pə'siːv] vt percepire; (notice) accorgersi di

per cent adv per cento; **a 20 ~ discount** uno sconto del 20 per cento

percentage [pə'sɛntɪdʒ] n percentuale f; **on a ~ basis** a percentuale

percentage point n punto percentuale

perceptible [pə'sɛptɪbl] adj percettibile

perception [pə'sɛpʃən] n percezione f; sensibilità; perspicacia

perceptive [pə'sɛptɪv] adj percettivo(-a); perspicace

perch [pəːtʃ] n (fish) pesce m persico; (for bird) sostegno, ramo ■ vi appollaiarsi

percolate ['pə:kəleɪt] vt filtrare
percolator ['pə:kəleɪtər] n caffettiera a pressione; caffettiera elettrica
percussion [pə'kʌʃən] n percussione f; (Mus) strumenti mpl a percussione
peremptory [pə'rɛmptərɪ] adj perentorio(-a)
perennial [pə'rɛnɪəl] adj perenne ∎ n pianta perenne
perfect ['pə:fɪkt] adj perfetto(-a) ∎ n (also: **perfect tense**) perfetto, passato prossimo ∎ vt [pə'fɛkt] perfezionare; mettere a punto; **he's a ~ stranger to me** mi è completamente sconosciuto
perfection [pə'fɛkʃən] n perfezione f
perfectionist [pə'fɛkʃənɪst] n perfezionista m/f
perfectly ['pə:fɪktlɪ] adv perfettamente; **I'm ~ happy with the situation** sono completamente soddisfatta della situazione; **you know ~ well** sa benissimo
perforate ['pə:fəreɪt] vt perforare
perforated ulcer ['pə:fəreɪtɪd-] n (Med) ulcera perforata
perforation [pə:fə'reɪʃən] n perforazione f; (line of holes) dentellatura
perform [pə'fɔ:m] vt (carry out) eseguire, fare; (symphony etc) suonare; (play, ballet) dare; (opera) fare ∎ vi suonare; recitare
performance [pə'fɔ:məns] n esecuzione f; (at theatre etc) rappresentazione f, spettacolo; (of an artist) interpretazione f; (of player etc) performance f; (of car, engine) prestazione f; **the team put up a good ~** la squadra ha giocato una bella partita
performer [pə'fɔ:mər] n artista m/f
performing [pə'fɔ:mɪŋ] adj (animal) ammaestrato(-a)
performing arts npl: **the ~** le arti dello spettacolo
perfume ['pə:fju:m] n profumo ∎ vt profumare
perfunctory [pə'fʌŋktərɪ] adj superficiale, per la forma
perhaps [pə'hæps] adv forse; **~ he'll come** forse verrà, può darsi che venga; **~ so/not** forse sì/no, può darsi di sì/di no
peril ['pɛrɪl] n pericolo
perilous ['pɛrɪləs] adj pericoloso(-a)
perilously ['pɛrɪləslɪ] adv: **they came ~ close to being caught** sono stati a un pelo dall'esser presi
perimeter [pə'rɪmɪtər] n perimetro
perimeter wall n muro di cinta
period ['pɪərɪəd] n periodo; (Hist) epoca; (Scol) lezione f; (full stop) punto; (US Football) tempo; (Med) mestruazioni fpl ∎ adj (costume, furniture) d'epoca; **for a ~ of three weeks** per

un periodo di or per la durata di tre settimane; **the holiday ~** (Brit) il periodo delle vacanze
periodic [pɪərɪ'ɔdɪk] adj periodico(-a)
periodical [pɪərɪ'ɔdɪkl] adj periodico(-a) ∎ n periodico
periodically [pɪərɪ'ɔdɪklɪ] adv periodicamente
period pains npl (Brit) dolori mpl mestruali
peripatetic [pɛrɪpə'tɛtɪk] adj (salesman) ambulante; (Brit: teacher) peripatetico(-a)
peripheral [pə'rɪfərəl] adj periferico(-a) ∎ n (Comput) unità f inv periferica
periphery [pə'rɪfərɪ] n periferia
periscope ['pɛrɪskəup] n periscopio
perish ['pɛrɪʃ] vi perire, morire; (decay) deteriorarsi
perishable ['pɛrɪʃəbl] adj deperibile
perishables ['pɛrɪʃəblz] npl merci fpl deperibili
perishing ['pɛrɪʃɪŋ] adj (Brit col): **it's ~ (cold)** fa un freddo da morire
peritonitis [pɛrɪtə'naɪtɪs] n peritonite f
perjure ['pə:dʒər] vt: **to ~ o.s.** spergiurare
perjury ['pə:dʒərɪ] n (Law: in court) falso giuramento; (breach of oath) spergiuro
perk [pə:k] n vantaggio
▶ **perk up** vi (cheer up) rianimarsi
perky ['pə:kɪ] adj (cheerful) vivace, allegro(-a)
perm [pə:m] n (for hair) permanente f ∎ vt: **to have one's hair permed** farsi fare la permanente
permanence ['pə:mənəns] n permanenza
permanent ['pə:mənənt] adj permanente; (job, position) fisso(-a); (dye, ink) indelebile; **~ address** residenza fissa; **I'm not ~ here** non sono fisso qui
permanently ['pə:mənəntlɪ] adv definitivamente
permeable ['pə:mɪəbl] adj permeabile
permeate ['pə:mɪeɪt] vi penetrare ∎ vt permeare
permissible [pə'mɪsɪbl] adj permissibile, ammissibile
permission [pə'mɪʃən] n permesso; **to give sb ~ to do sth** dare a qn il permesso di fare qc
permissive [pə'mɪsɪv] adj tollerante; **the ~ society** la società permissiva
permit n ['pə:mɪt] permesso; (entrance pass) lasciapassare m ∎ vt, vi [pə'mɪt] permettere; **fishing ~** licenza di pesca; **to ~ sb to do** permettere a qn di fare, dare il permesso a qn di fare; **weather permitting** tempo permettendo
permutation [pə:mju'teɪʃən] n permutazione f
pernicious [pə:'nɪʃəs] adj pernicioso(-a), nocivo(-a)

pernickety [pə'nɪkɪtɪ] *adj (col: person)*
pignolo(-a); (: *task*) da certosino
perpendicular [pə:pən'dɪkjulə^r] *adj, n*
perpendicolare *(f)*
perpetrate ['pə:pɪtreɪt] *vt* perpetrare,
commettere
perpetual [pə'pɛtjuəl] *adj* perpetuo(-a)
perpetuate [pə'pɛtjueɪt] *vt* perpetuare
perpetuity [pə:pɪ'tjuːɪtɪ] *n*: **in** ~ in perpetuo
perplex [pə'plɛks] *vt* lasciare perplesso(-a)
perplexing [pə'plɛksɪŋ] *adj* che lascia
perplesso(-a)
perquisites ['pə:kwɪzɪts] *npl (also:* **perks**)
benefici *mpl* collaterali
persecute ['pə:sɪkjuːt] *vt* perseguitare
persecution [pə:sɪ'kjuːʃən] *n* persecuzione *f*
perseverance [pə:sɪ'vɪərəns] *n* perseveranza
persevere [pə:sɪ'vɪə^r] *vi* perseverare
Persia ['pə:ʃə] *n* Persia
Persian ['pə:ʃən] *adj* persiano(-a) ■ *n (Ling)*
persiano; **the** (~) **Gulf** il Golfo Persico
Persian cat *n* gatto persiano
persist [pə'sɪst] *vi*: **to** ~ **(in doing)** persistere
(nel fare); ostinarsi (a fare)
persistence [pə'sɪstəns] *n* persistenza;
ostinazione *f*
persistent [pə'sɪstənt] *adj* persistente;
ostinato(-a); (*lateness, rain*) continuo(-a);
~ **offender** (*Law*) delinquente *m/f* abituale
persnickety [pə'snɪkɪtɪ] *adj (US col)*
= **pernickety**
person ['pə:sn] *n* persona; **in** ~ di *or* in
persona, personalmente; **on** *or* **about one's**
~ (*weapon*) su di sé; (*money*) con sé; **a** ~ **to** ~
call (*Tel*) una chiamata con preavviso
personable ['pə:snəbl] *adj* di bell'aspetto
personal ['pə:snl] *adj* personale; individuale;
~ **belongings**, ~ **effects** oggetti *mpl* d'uso
personale; **a** ~ **interview** un incontro
privato
personal allowance *n* (*Tax*) quota del reddito
non imponibile
personal assistant *n* segretaria personale
personal call *n* (*Tel*) chiamata con preavviso
personal column *n* messaggi *mpl* personali
personal computer *n* personal computer *m inv*
personal details *npl* dati *mpl* personali
personal equity plan *n* (*Finance*) *fondo di
investimento azionario con agevolazioni fiscali
destinato al piccolo risparmiatore*
personal identification number *n* (*Comput,
Banking*) numero di codice segreto
personality [pə:sə'nælɪtɪ] *n* personalità *f inv*
personally ['pə:snəlɪ] *adv* personalmente
personal organizer *n* agenda; (*electronic*)
agenda elettronica
personal property *n* beni *mpl* personali

personal stereo *n* walkman® *m inv*
personify [pə:'sɔnɪfaɪ] *vt* personificare
personnel [pə:sə'nɛl] *n* personale *m*
personnel department *n* ufficio del
personale
personnel manager *n* direttore(-trice) del
personale
perspective [pə'spɛktɪv] *n* prospettiva;
to get sth into ~ ridimensionare qc
Perspex® ['pə:spɛks] *n* (*Brit*) *tipo di resina
termoplastica*
perspicacity [pə:spɪ'kæsɪtɪ] *n* perspicacia
perspiration [pə:spɪ'reɪʃən] *n* traspirazione *f*,
sudore *m*
perspire [pə'spaɪə^r] *vi* traspirare
persuade [pə'sweɪd] *vt*: **to** ~ **sb to do sth**
persuadere qn a fare qc; **to** ~ **sb of sth/that**
persuadere qn di qc/che
persuasion [pə'sweɪʒən] *n* persuasione *f*;
(*creed*) convinzione *f*, credo
persuasive [pə'sweɪsɪv] *adj* persuasivo(-a)
pert [pə:t] *adj* (*bold*) sfacciato(-a),
impertinente; (*hat*) spiritoso(-a)
pertaining [pə:'teɪnɪŋ]: ~ **to** *prep* che
riguarda
pertinent ['pə:tɪnənt] *adj* pertinente
perturb [pə'tə:b] *vt* turbare
perturbing [pə'tə:bɪŋ] *adj* inquietante
Peru [pə'ruː] *n* Perù *m*
perusal [pə'ruːzl] *n* attenta lettura
Peruvian [pə'ruːvjən] *adj, n* peruviano(-a)
pervade [pə'veɪd] *vt* pervadere
pervasive [pə'veɪsɪv] *adj* (*smell*) penetrante;
(*influence*) dilagante; (*gloom, feelings*)
diffuso(-a)
perverse [pə'və:s] *adj* perverso(-a)
perversion [pə'və:ʃən] *n* pervertimento,
perversione *f*
perversity [pə'və:sɪtɪ] *n* perversità
pervert *n* ['pə:və:t] pervertito(-a) ■ *vt*
[pə'və:t] pervertire
pessimism ['pɛsɪmɪzəm] *n* pessimismo
pessimist ['pɛsɪmɪst] *n* pessimista *m/f*
pessimistic [pɛsɪ'mɪstɪk] *adj* pessimistico(-a)
pest [pɛst] *n* animale *m* (*or* insetto) pestifero;
(*fig*) peste *f*
pest control *n* disinfestazione *f*
pester ['pɛstə^r] *vt* tormentare, molestare
pesticide ['pɛstɪsaɪd] *n* pesticida *m*
pestilence ['pɛstɪləns] *n* pestilenza
pestle ['pɛsl] *n* pestello
pet [pɛt] *n* animale *m* domestico; (*favourite*)
favorito(-a) ■ *vt* accarezzare ■ *vi* (*col*) fare il
petting; ~ **lion** *etc* leone *m etc* ammaestrato
petal ['pɛtl] *n* petalo
peter ['piːtə^r]: **to** ~ **out** *vi* esaurirsi;
estinguersi

petite [pə'ti:t] *adj* piccolo(-a) e aggraziato(-a)

petition [pə'tɪʃən] *n* petizione *f* ■ *vi*
richiedere; **to ~ for divorce** presentare
un'istanza di divorzio

pet name *n* (*Brit*) nomignolo

petrified ['pɛtrɪfaɪd] *adj* (*fig*) morto(-a) di
paura

petrify ['pɛtrɪfaɪ] *vt* pietrificare; (*fig*)
terrorizzare

petrochemical [pɛtrə'kɛmɪkl] *adj*
petrolchimico(-a)

petrodollars ['pɛtrəudɔləz] *npl* petrodollari
mpl

petrol ['pɛtrəl] *n* (*Brit*) benzina

petrol bomb *n* (*Brit*) (bottiglia) molotov *f inv*

petrol can *n* (*Brit*) tanica per benzina

petrol engine *n* (*Brit*) motore *m* a benzina

petroleum [pə'trəuliəm] *n* petrolio

petroleum jelly *n* vaselina

petrol pump *n* (*Brit*: *in car, at garage*) pompa di
benzina

petrol station *n* (*Brit*) stazione *f* di
rifornimento

petrol tank *n* (*Brit*) serbatoio della benzina

petticoat ['pɛtɪkəut] *n* sottana

pettifogging ['pɛtɪfɔgɪŋ] *adj* cavilloso(-a)

pettiness ['pɛtɪnɪs] *n* meschinità

petty ['pɛtɪ] *adj* (*mean*) meschino(-a);
(*unimportant*) insignificante

petty cash *n* piccola cassa

petty officer *n* sottufficiale *m* di marina

petulant ['pɛtjulənt] *adj* irritabile

pew [pju:] *n* panca (di chiesa)

pewter ['pju:təʳ] *n* peltro

Pfc *abbr* (*US Mil*) = **private first class**

PG *n abbr* (*Cine*: = *parental guidance*) *consenso dei
genitori richiesto*

PG 13 *abbr* (*US*: *Cine*: = *Parental Guidance* 13) *vietato
ai minori di 13 anni non accompagnati dai genitori*

PGA *n abbr* (= *Professional Golfers Association*)
associazione dei giocatori di golf professionisti

PH *n abbr* (*US Mil*: = *Purple Heart*) *decorazione per
ferite riportate in guerra*

PHA *n abbr* (*US*: = *Public Housing Administration*)
amministrazione per l'edilizia pubblica

phallic ['fælɪk] *adj* fallico(-a)

phantom ['fæntəm] *n* fantasma *m*

Pharaoh ['fɛərəu] *n* faraone *m*

pharmaceutical [fɑːmə'sjuːtɪkl] *adj*
farmaceutico(-a) ■ *n*: **pharmaceuticals**
prodotti *mpl* farmaceutici

pharmacist ['fɑːməsɪst] *n* farmacista *m/f*

pharmacy ['fɑːməsɪ] *n* farmacia

phase [feɪz] *n* fase *f*, periodo ■ *vt*: **to ~ sth
in/out** introdurre/eliminare qc
progressivamente

PhD *n abbr* = **Doctor of Philosophy**

pheasant ['fɛznt] *n* fagiano

phenomenon (*pl* **phenomena**)
[fə'nɔmɪnən, -nə] *n* fenomeno

phew [fju:] *excl* uff!

phial ['faɪəl] *n* fiala

philanderer [fɪ'lændərəʳ] *n* donnaiolo

philanthropic [fɪlən'θrɔpɪk] *adj*
filantropico(-a)

philanthropist [fɪ'lænθrəpɪst] *n* filantropo

philatelist [fɪ'lætəlɪst] *n* filatelico(-a)

philately [fɪ'lætəlɪ] *n* filatelia

Philippines ['fɪlɪpi:nz] *npl* (*also*: **Philippine
Islands**): **the ~** le Filippine

philosopher [fɪ'lɔsəfəʳ] *n* filosofo(-a)

philosophical [fɪlə'sɔfɪkl] *adj* filosofico(-a)

philosophy [fɪ'lɔsəfɪ] *n* filosofia

phlegm [flɛm] *n* flemma

phlegmatic [flɛg'mætɪk] *adj* flemmatico(-a)

phobia ['fəubjə] *n* fobia

phone [fəun] *n* telefono ■ *vt* telefonare a
■ *vi* telefonare; **to be on the ~** avere il
telefono; (*be calling*) essere al telefono
▶ **phone back** *vt*, *vi* richiamare

phone book *n* guida del telefono, elenco
telefonico

phone box, phone booth *n* cabina
telefonica

phone call *n* telefonata

phonecard ['fəunka:d] *n* scheda telefonica

phone-in ['fəunɪn] *n* (*Brit Radio*, *TV*)
*trasmissione radiofonica o televisiva con intervento
telefonico degli ascoltatori*

phone tapping [-tæpɪŋ] *n* intercettazioni *fpl*
telefoniche

phonetics [fə'nɛtɪks] *n* fonetica

phoney ['fəunɪ] *adj* falso(-a), fasullo(-a)
■ *n* (*person*) ciarlatano

phonograph ['fəunəgra:f] *n* (*US*) giradischi
m inv

phony ['fəunɪ] *adj*, *n* = **phoney**

phosphate ['fɔsfeɪt] *n* fosfato

phosphorus ['fɔsfərəs] *n* fosforo

photo ['fəutəu] *n* foto *f inv*

photo... ['fəutəu] *prefix* foto...

photocall ['fəutəukɔ:l] *n* *convocazione di
fotoreporter a scopo pubblicitario*

photocopier ['fəutəukɔpɪəʳ] *n* fotocopiatrice *f*

photocopy ['fəutəukɔpɪ] *n* fotocopia ■ *vt*
fotocopiare

photoelectric [fəutəuɪ'lɛktrɪk] *adj*: **~ cell**
cellula fotoelettrica

Photofit® ['fəutəufɪt] *n* photofit *m inv*

photogenic [fəutəu'dʒɛnɪk] *adj*
fotogenico(-a)

photograph ['fəutəgræf] *n* fotografia ■ *vt*
fotografare; **to take a ~ of sb** fare una
fotografia a *or* fotografare qn

P

photographer [fə'tɔgrəfər] n fotografo
photographic [fəutə'græfɪk] adj
fotografico(-a)
photography [fə'tɔgrəfɪ] n fotografia
photo opportunity n opportunità di scattare
delle foto ad un personaggio importante
Photostat® ['fəutəustæt] n fotocopia
photosynthesis [fəutəu'sɪnθəsɪs] n
fotosintesi f
phrase [freɪz] n espressione f; (Ling)
locuzione f; (Mus) frase f ■ vt esprimere;
(letter) redigere
phrasebook ['freɪzbuk] n vocabolarietto
physical ['fɪzɪkl] adj fisico(-a); ~
examination visita medica; ~ **education**
educazione f fisica; ~ **exercises** ginnastica
physically [fɪzɪklɪ] adv fisicamente
physician [fɪ'zɪʃən] n medico
physicist ['fɪzɪsɪst] n fisico
physics ['fɪzɪks] n fisica
physiological [fɪzɪə'lɔdʒɪkəl] adj fisiologico(-a)
physiology [fɪzɪ'ɔlədʒɪ] n fisiologia
physiotherapist [fɪzɪəu'θɛrəpɪst] n
fisioterapista m/f
physiotherapy [fɪzɪəu'θɛrəpɪ] n fisioterapia
physique [fɪ'ziːk] n fisico
pianist ['piːənɪst] n pianista m/f
piano [pɪ'ænəu] n pianoforte m
piano accordion n (Brit) fisarmonica (a
tastiera)
piccolo ['pɪkələu] n ottavino
pick [pɪk] n (tool: also: **pick-axe**) piccone m
■ vt scegliere; (gather) cogliere; (scab, spot)
grattarsi ■ vi: **to ~ and choose** scegliere con
cura; **take your ~** scelga; **the ~ of** il fior fiore
di; **to ~ one's nose** mettersi le dita nel naso;
to ~ one's teeth stuzzicarsi i denti; **to ~ sb's
brains** farsi dare dei suggerimenti da qn; **to
~ pockets** borseggiare; **to ~ a fight/quarrel
with sb** attaccar rissa/briga con qn; **to ~
one's way through** attraversare stando ben
attento a dove mettere i piedi
▶ **pick off** vt (kill) abbattere
▶ **pick on** vt fus (person) avercela con
▶ **pick out** vt scegliere; (distinguish)
distinguere
▶ **pick up** vi (improve) migliorarsi ■ vt
raccogliere; (collect) passare a prendere; (Aut:
give lift to) far salire; (learn) imparare; (Radio,
TV, Tel) captare; **to ~ o.s. up** rialzarsi; **to ~ up
where one left off** riprendere dal punto in
cui ci si era fermati; **to ~ up speed**
acquistare velocità
pickaxe, (US) **pickax** ['pɪkæks] n piccone m
picket ['pɪkɪt] n (in strike) scioperante m/f che
fa parte di un picchetto; picchetto ■ vt
picchettare

picket line n cordone m degli scioperanti
pickings ['pɪkɪŋz] npl (pilferings): **there are
good ~ to be had here** qui ci sono buone
possibilità di intascare qualcosa sottobanco
pickle ['pɪkl] n (also: **pickles**: as condiment)
sottaceti mpl; (fig): **in a ~** nei pasticci ■ vt
mettere sottaceto; mettere in salamoia
pick-me-up ['pɪkmiːʌp] n tiramisù m inv
pickpocket ['pɪkpɔkɪt] n borsaiolo
pickup ['pɪkʌp] n (Brit: on record player) pick-up
m inv; (small truck: also: **pickup truck, pickup
van**) camioncino
picnic ['pɪknɪk] n picnic m inv ■ vi fare un
picnic
picnicker ['pɪknɪkər] n chi partecipa a un
picnic
pictorial [pɪk'tɔːrɪəl] adj illustrato(-a)
picture ['pɪktʃər] n quadro; (painting) pittura;
(photograph) foto(grafia); (drawing) disegno;
(TV) immagine f; (film) film m inv ■ vt
raffigurarsi; **the pictures** (Brit) il cinema;
to take a ~ of sb/sth fare una foto a qn/di qc;
we get a good ~ here (TV) la ricezione qui è
buona; **the overall ~** il quadro generale;
to put sb in the ~ mettere qn al corrente
picture book n libro illustrato
picture messaging n picture messaging m,
invio di messaggini con disegni
picturesque [pɪktʃə'rɛsk] adj pittoresco(-a)
picture window n finestra panoramica
piddling ['pɪdlɪŋ] adj (col) insignificante
pidgin English ['pɪdʒɪn-] n inglese semplificato
misto ad elementi indigeni
pie [paɪ] n torta; (of meat) pasticcio
piebald ['paɪbɔːld] adj pezzato(-a)
piece [piːs] n pezzo; (of land) appezzamento;
(Draughts etc) pedina; (item): **a ~ of furniture/
advice** un mobile/consiglio ■ vt: **to ~
together** mettere insieme; **in pieces**
(broken) in pezzi; (not yet assembled)
smontato(-a); **to take to pieces** smontare;
~ by ~ poco alla volta; **a 10p ~** (Brit) una
moneta da 10 pence; **a six-~ band** un
complesso di sei strumentisti; **in one ~**
(object) intatto; **to get back all in one ~**
(person) tornare a casa incolume or sano e
salvo; **to say one's ~** dire la propria
piecemeal ['piːsmiːl] adv pezzo a pezzo, a
spizzico
piece rate n tariffa a cottimo
piecework ['piːswəːk] n (lavoro a) cottimo
pie chart n grafico a torta
Piedmont ['piːdmɔnt] n Piemonte m
pier [pɪər] n molo; (of bridge etc) pila
pierce [pɪəs] vt forare; (with arrow etc)
trafiggere; **to have one's ears pierced** farsi
fare i buchi per gli orecchini

piercing ['pɪəsɪŋ] *adj* (*cry*) acuto(-a)
piety ['paɪətɪ] *n* pietà, devozione *f*
piffling ['pɪflɪŋ] *adj* insignificante
pig [pɪg] *n* maiale *m*, porco
pigeon ['pɪdʒən] *n* piccione *m*
pigeonhole ['pɪdʒənhəul] *n* casella ■ *vt* classificare
pigeon-toed ['pɪdʒən'təud] *adj* che cammina con i piedi in dentro
piggy bank ['pɪgɪ-] *n* salvadanaio
pigheaded ['pɪg'hɛdɪd] *adj* caparbio(-a), cocciuto(-a)
piglet ['pɪglɪt] *n* porcellino
pigment ['pɪgmənt] *n* pigmento
pigmentation [pɪgmən'teɪʃən] *n* pigmentazione *f*
pigmy ['pɪgmɪ] *n* = **pygmy**
pigskin ['pɪgskɪn] *n* cinghiale *m*
pigsty ['pɪgstaɪ] *n* porcile *m*
pigtail ['pɪgteɪl] *n* treccina
pike [paɪk] *n* (*spear*) picca; (*fish*) luccio
pilchard ['pɪltʃəd] *n* specie di sardina
pile [paɪl] *n* (*pillar, of books*) pila; (*heap*) mucchio; (*of carpet*) pelo ■ *vb* (*also*: **pile up**) *vt* ammucchiare ■ *vi* ammucchiarsi; **in a ~** ammucchiato; *see also* **piles**
  ▶ **pile on** *vt*: **to ~ it on** (*col*) esagerare, drammatizzare
piles [paɪlz] *npl* (*Med*) emorroidi *fpl*
pileup ['paɪlʌp] *n* (*Aut*) tamponamento a catena
pilfer ['pɪlfə^r] *vt* rubacchiare ■ *vi* fare dei furtarelli
pilfering ['pɪlfərɪŋ] *n* rubacchiare *m*
pilgrim ['pɪlgrɪm] *n* pellegrino(-a)
pilgrimage ['pɪlgrɪmɪdʒ] *n* pellegrinaggio
pill [pɪl] *n* pillola; **to be on the ~** prendere la pillola
pillage ['pɪlɪdʒ] *vt* saccheggiare
pillar ['pɪlə^r] *n* colonna
pillar box *n* (*Brit*) cassetta delle lettere (a colonnina)
pillion ['pɪljən] *n* (*of motor cycle*) sellino posteriore; **to ride ~** viaggiare dietro
pillory ['pɪlərɪ] *n* berlina ■ *vt* mettere alla berlina
pillow ['pɪləu] *n* guanciale *m*
pillowcase ['pɪləukeɪs], **pillowslip** ['pɪləuslɪp] *n* federa
pilot ['paɪlət] *n* pilota *m/f* ■ *cpd* (*scheme etc*) pilota *inv* ■ *vt* pilotare
pilot boat *n* pilotina
pilot light *n* fiammella di sicurezza
pimento [pɪ'mɛntəu] *n* peperoncino
pimp [pɪmp] *n* mezzano
pimple ['pɪmpl] *n* foruncolo
pimply ['pɪmplɪ] *adj* foruncoloso(-a)

PIN *n abbr* = **personal identification number**
pin [pɪn] *n* spillo; (*Tech*) perno; (*Brit: drawing pin*) puntina da disegno; (*Brit Elec: of plug*) spinotto ■ *vt* attaccare con uno spillo; **pins and needles** formicolio; **to ~ sb against/to** inchiodare qn contro/a; **to ~ sth on sb** (*fig*) addossare la colpa di qc a qn
  ▶ **pin down** *vt* (*fig*): **to ~ sb down** obbligare qn a pronunziarsi; **there's something strange here but I can't quite ~ it down** c'è qualcosa di strano qua ma non riesco a capire cos'è
pinafore ['pɪnəfɔː^r] *n* grembiule *m* (senza maniche)
pinafore dress *n* scamiciato
pinball ['pɪnbɔːl] *n* flipper *m inv*
pincers ['pɪnsəz] *npl* pinzette *fpl*
pinch [pɪntʃ] *n* pizzicotto, pizzico ■ *vt* pizzicare; (*col: steal*) grattare ■ *vi* (*shoe*) stringere; **at a ~** in caso di bisogno; **to feel the ~** (*fig*) trovarsi nelle ristrettezze
pinched [pɪntʃt] *adj* (*drawn*) dai lineamenti tirati; (*short*): **~ for money/space** a corto di soldi/di spazio; **~ with cold** raggrinzito dal freddo
pincushion ['pɪnkuʃən] *n* puntaspilli *m inv*
pine [paɪn] *n* (*also*: **pine tree**) pino ■ *vi*: **to ~ for** struggersi dal desiderio di
  ▶ **pine away** *vi* languire
pineapple ['paɪnæpl] *n* ananas *m inv*
pine cone *n* pigna
pine needles *npl* aghi *mpl* di pino
ping [pɪŋ] *n* (*noise*) tintinnio
Ping-Pong® ['pɪŋpɔŋ] *n* ping-pong® *m*
pink [pɪŋk] *adj* rosa *inv* ■ *n* (*colour*) rosa *m inv*; (*Bot*) garofano
pinking shears ['pɪŋkɪŋ-] *n* forbici *fpl* a zigzag
pin money *n* (*Brit*) denaro per le piccole spese
pinnacle ['pɪnəkl] *n* pinnacolo
pinpoint ['pɪnpɔɪnt] *vt* indicare con precisione
pinstripe ['pɪnstraɪp] *n* stoffa gessata; (*also*: **pinstripe suit**) gessato
pint [paɪnt] *n* pinta (*Brit* = 0.57 l; *US* = 0.47 l); (*Brit col: of beer*) ≈ birra piccola
pinup ['pɪnʌp] *n* pin-up girl *f inv*
pioneer [paɪə'nɪə^r] *n* pioniere(-a) ■ *vt* essere un pioniere in
pious ['paɪəs] *adj* pio(-a)
pip [pɪp] *n* (*seed*) seme *m*; (*time signal on radio*) segnale *m* orario
pipe [paɪp] *n* tubo; (*for smoking*) pipa; (*Mus*) piffero ■ *vt* portare per mezzo di tubazione; **pipes** *npl* (*also*: **bagpipes**) cornamusa (scozzese)
  ▶ **pipe down** *vi* (*col*) calmarsi

p

713

pipe cleaner *n* scovolino
piped music [paɪpt-] *n* musica di sottofondo
pipe dream *n* vana speranza
pipeline ['paɪplaɪn] *n* conduttura; (*for oil*) oleodotto; (*for natural gas*) metanodotto; **it is in the ~** (*fig*) è in arrivo
piper ['paɪpəʳ] *n* piffero; suonatore(-trice) di cornamusa
pipe tobacco *n* tabacco da pipa
piping ['paɪpɪŋ] *adv*: **~ hot** bollente
piquant ['pi:kənt] *adj* (*sauce*) piccante; (*conversation*) stimolante
pique [pi:k] *n* picca
piracy ['paɪərəsɪ] *n* pirateria
pirate ['paɪərət] *n* pirata *m* ■ *vt* (*record, video, book*) riprodurre abusivamente
pirate radio *n* (*Brit*) radio pirata *f inv*
pirouette [pɪru'ɛt] *n* piroetta ■ *vi* piroettare
Pisces ['paɪsi:z] *n* Pesci *mpl*; **to be ~** essere dei Pesci
piss [pɪs] *vi* (*col!*) pisciare; **~ off!** vaffanculo! (*!*)
pissed [pɪst] *adj* (*Brit col: drunk*) ubriaco(-a) fradicio(-a)
pistol ['pɪstl] *n* pistola
piston ['pɪstən] *n* pistone *m*
pit [pɪt] *n* buca, fossa; (*also*: **coal pit**) miniera; (*also*: **orchestra pit**) orchestra ■ *vt*: **to ~ sb against sb** opporre qn a qn; **pits** *npl* (*Aut*) box *m*; **to ~ o.s. against** opporsi a
pitapat ['pɪtə'pæt] *adv* (*Brit*): **to go ~** (*heart*) palpitare, battere forte; (*rain*) picchiettare
pitch [pɪtʃ] *n* (*throw*) lancia; (*Mus*) tono; (*of voice*) altezza; (*fig: degree*) grado, punto; (*also*: **sales pitch**) discorso di vendita, imbonimento; (*Brit Sport*) campo; (*Naut*) beccheggio; (*tar*) pece *f* ■ *vt* (*throw*) lanciare ■ *vi* (*fall*) cascare; (*Naut*) beccheggiare; **to ~ a tent** piantare una tenda; **at this ~** a questo ritmo
pitch-black [pɪtʃ'blæk] *adj* nero(-a) come la pece
pitched battle [pɪtʃt-] *n* battaglia campale
pitcher ['pɪtʃəʳ] *n* brocca
pitchfork ['pɪtʃfɔ:k] *n* forcone *m*
piteous ['pɪtɪəs] *adj* pietoso(-a)
pitfall ['pɪtfɔ:l] *n* trappola
pith [pɪθ] *n* (*of plant*) midollo; (*of orange*) parte *f* interna della scorza; (*fig*) essenza, succo; vigore *m*
pithead ['pɪthɛd] *n* (*Brit*) imbocco della miniera
pithy ['pɪθɪ] *adj* conciso(-a); vigoroso(-a)
pitiable ['pɪtɪəbl] *adj* pietoso(-a)
pitiful ['pɪtɪful] *adj* (*touching*) pietoso(-a); (*contemptible*) miserabile
pitifully ['pɪtɪfəlɪ] *adv* pietosamente; **it's ~ obvious** è penosamente chiaro

pitiless ['pɪtɪlɪs] *adj* spietato(-a)
pittance ['pɪtns] *n* miseria, magro salario
pitted ['pɪtɪd] *adj*: **~ with** (*potholes*) pieno(-a) di; (*chickenpox*) butterato(-a) da
pity ['pɪtɪ] *n* pietà ■ *vt* aver pietà di, compatire, commiserare; **to have** *or* **take ~ on sb** aver pietà di qn; **it is a ~ that you can't come** è un peccato che non possa venire; **what a ~!** che peccato!
pitying ['pɪtɪɪŋ] *adj* compassionevole
pivot ['pɪvət] *n* perno ■ *vi* imperniarsi
pixel ['pɪksl] *n* (*Comput*) pixel *m inv*
pixie ['pɪksɪ] *n* folletto
pizza ['pi:tsə] *n* pizza
placard ['plækɑ:d] *n* affisso
placate [plə'keɪt] *vt* placare, calmare
placatory [plə'keɪtərɪ] *adj* conciliante
place [pleɪs] *n* posto, luogo; (*proper position, rank, seat*) posto; (*house*) casa, alloggio; (*home*): **at/to his ~** a casa sua; (*in street names*): **Laurel P~** via dei Lauri ■ *vt* (*object*) posare, mettere; (*identify*) riconoscere; individuare; (*goods*) piazzare; **to take ~** aver luogo; succedere; **out of ~** (*not suitable*) inopportuno(-a); **I feel rather out of ~ here** qui mi sento un po' fuori posto; **in the first ~** in primo luogo; **to change places with sb** scambiare il posto con qn; **to put sb in his ~** (*fig*) mettere a posto qn, mettere qn al suo posto; **from ~ to ~** da un posto all'altro; **all over the ~** dappertutto; **he's going places** (*fig, col*) si sta facendo strada; **it is not my ~ to do it** non sta a me farlo; **how are you placed next week?** com'è messo la settimana prossima?; **to ~ an order with sb (for)** (*Comm*) fare un'ordinazione a qn (di)
placebo [plə'si:bəu] *n* placebo *m inv*
place mat *n* sottopiatto; (*in linen etc*) tovaglietta
placement ['pleɪsmənt] *n* collocamento; (*job*) lavoro
place name *n* toponimo
placenta [plə'sɛntə] *n* placenta
placid ['plæsɪd] *adj* placido(-a), calmo(-a)
placidity [plə'sɪdɪtɪ] *n* placidità
plagiarism ['pleɪdʒərɪzəm] *n* plagio
plagiarist ['pleɪdʒərɪst] *n* plagiario(-a)
plagiarize ['pleɪdʒəraɪz] *vt* plagiare
plague [pleɪg] *n* peste *f* ■ *vt* tormentare; **to ~ sb with questions** assillare qn di domande
plaice [pleɪs] *n* (*pl inv*) pianuzza
plaid [plæd] *n* plaid *m inv*
plain [pleɪn] *adj* (*clear*) chiaro(-a), palese; (*simple*) semplice; (*frank*) franco(-a), aperto(-a); (*not handsome*) bruttino(-a); (*without seasoning etc*) scondito(-a); naturale; (*in one colour*) tinta unita *inv* ■ *adv* francamente, chiaramente ■ *n* pianura;

to make sth ~ to sb far capire chiaramente qc a qn; **in ~ clothes** (police) in borghese

plain chocolate n cioccolato fondente

plainly ['pleɪnlɪ] adv chiaramente; (frankly) francamente

plainness ['pleɪnnɪs] n semplicità

plain speaking n: **there has been some ~ between the two leaders** i due leader si sono parlati chiaro

plaintiff ['pleɪntɪf] n attore(-trice)

plaintive ['pleɪntɪv] adj (voice, song) lamentoso(-a); (look) struggente

plait [plæt] n treccia ■ vt intrecciare; **to ~ one's hair** farsi una treccia (or le trecce)

plan [plæn] n pianta; (scheme) progetto, piano ■ vt (think in advance) progettare; (prepare) organizzare; (intend) avere in progetto ■ vi: **to ~ (for)** far piani or progetti (per); **to ~ to do** progettare di fare, avere l'intenzione di fare; **how long do you ~ to stay?** quanto conta di restare?

plane [pleɪn] n (Aviat) aereo; (tree) platano; (tool) pialla; (Art, Math etc) piano ■ adj piano(-a), piatto(-a) ■ vt (with tool) piallare

planet ['plænɪt] n pianeta m

planetarium [plænɪ'tɛərɪəm] n planetario

plank [plæŋk] n tavola, asse f

plankton ['plæŋktən] n plancton m

planned economy [plænd-] n economia pianificata

planner ['plænəʳ] n pianificatore(-trice); (chart) calendario; **town** or (US) **city ~** urbanista m/f

planning ['plænɪŋ] n progettazione f; (Pol, Econ) pianificazione f; **family ~** pianificazione delle nascite

planning permission n (Brit) permesso di costruzione

plant [plɑːnt] n pianta; (machinery) impianto; (factory) fabbrica ■ vt piantare; (bomb) mettere

plantation [plæn'teɪʃən] n piantagione f

plant pot n (Brit) vaso (di fiori)

plaque [plæk] n placca

plasma ['plæzmə] n plasma m

plasma TV n TV f inv al plasma

plaster ['plɑːstəʳ] n intonaco; (also: **plaster of Paris**) gesso; (Brit: also: **sticking plaster**) cerotto ■ vt intonacare; ingessare; (cover): **to ~ with** coprire di; (col: mud etc) impiastricciare; **in ~** (Brit: leg etc) ingessato(-a)

plasterboard ['plɑːstəbɔːd] n lastra di cartone ingessato

plaster cast n (Med) ingessatura, gesso; (model, statue) modello in gesso

plastered ['plɑːstəd] adj (col) ubriaco(-a) fradicio(-a)

plasterer ['plɑːstərəʳ] n intonacatore m

plastic ['plæstɪk] n plastica ■ adj (made of plastic) di or in plastica; (flexible) plastico(-a), malleabile; (art) plastico(-a)

plastic bag n sacchetto di plastica

plastic bullet n pallottola di plastica

plastic explosive n esplosivo al plastico

plasticine® ['plæstɪsiːn] n plastilina®

plastic surgery n chirurgia plastica

plate [pleɪt] n (dish) piatto; (sheet of metal) lamiera; (Phot) lastra; (Typ) cliché m inv; (in book) tavola; (on door) targa, targhetta; (Aut: number plate) targa; (dishes): **gold ~** vasellame m d'oro; **silver ~** argenteria

plateau (pl **plateaus** or **plateaux**) ['plætəu, -z] n altipiano

plateful ['pleɪtful] n piatto

plate glass n vetro piano

platen ['plætən] n (on typewriter, printer) rullo

plate rack n scolapiatti m inv

platform ['plætfɔːm] n (stage, at meeting) palco; (Brit: on bus) piattaforma; (Rail) marciapiede m; **the train leaves from ~ 7** il treno parte dal binario 7

platform ticket n (Brit) biglietto d'ingresso ai binari

platinum ['plætɪnəm] n platino

platitude ['plætɪtjuːd] n luogo comune

platoon [plə'tuːn] n plotone m

platter ['plætəʳ] n piatto

plaudits ['plɔːdɪts] npl plauso

plausible ['plɔːzɪbl] adj plausibile, credibile; (person) convincente

play [pleɪ] n gioco; (Theat) commedia ■ vt (game) giocare a; (team, opponent) giocare contro; (instrument, piece of music) suonare; (play, part) interpretare ■ vi giocare; suonare; recitare; **to bring** or **call into ~** (plan) mettere in azione; (emotions) esprimere; **~ on words** gioco di parole; **to ~ a trick on sb** fare uno scherzo a qn; **they're playing at soldiers** stanno giocando ai soldati; **to ~ for time** (fig) cercare di guadagnar tempo; **to ~ into sb's hands** (fig) fare il gioco di qn

▶ **play about, play around** vi (person) divertirsi; **to ~ about** or **around with** (fiddle with) giocherellare con; (idea) accarezzare

▶ **play along** vi: **to ~ along with** (fig: person) stare al gioco di; (: plan, idea) fingere di assecondare ■ vt (fig): **to ~ sb along** tenere qn in sospeso

▶ **play back** vt riascoltare, risentire

▶ **play down** vt minimizzare

▶ **play on** vt fus (sb's feelings, credulity) giocare su; **to ~ on sb's nerves** dare sui nervi a qn

▶ **play up** vi (cause trouble) fare i capricci

playact ['pleɪækt] vi fare la commedia

P

playboy ['pleɪbɔɪ] n playboy m inv
played-out ['pleɪd'aut] adj spossato(-a)
player ['pleɪə'] n giocatore(-trice); (Theat) attore(-trice); (Mus) musicista m/f
playful ['pleɪful] adj giocoso(-a)
playgoer ['pleɪɡəuə'] n assiduo(-a) frequentatore(-a) di teatri
playground ['pleɪɡraund] n (in school) cortile m per la ricreazione; (in park) parco m giochi inv
playgroup ['pleɪɡruːp] n giardino d'infanzia
playing card ['pleɪɪŋ-] n carta da gioco
playing field ['pleɪɪŋ-] n campo sportivo
playmaker ['pleɪmeɪkə'] n (Sport) playmaker m inv
playmate ['pleɪmeɪt] n compagno(-a) di gioco
play-off ['pleɪɔf] n (Sport) bella
playpen ['pleɪpɛn] n box m inv
playroom ['pleɪruːm] n stanza dei giochi
plaything ['pleɪθɪŋ] n giocattolo
playtime ['pleɪtaɪm] n (Scol) ricreazione f
playwright ['pleɪraɪt] n drammaturgo(-a)
plc abbr (Brit) = **public limited company**
plea [pliː] n (request) preghiera, domanda; (excuse) scusa; (Law) (argomento di) difesa
plea bargaining n (Law) patteggiamento
plead [pliːd] vt patrocinare; (give as excuse) addurre a pretesto ■ vi (Law) perorare la causa; (beg): **to ~ with sb** implorare qn; **to ~ for sth** implorare qc; **to ~ guilty/not guilty** (defendant) dichiararsi colpevole/innocente
pleasant ['plɛznt] adj piacevole, gradevole
pleasantly ['plɛzntlɪ] adv piacevolmente
pleasantry ['plɛzntrɪ] n (joke) scherzo; (polite remark): **to exchange pleasantries** scambiarsi i convenevoli
please [pliːz] vt piacere a ■ vi (think fit): **do as you ~** faccia come le pare; **~!** per piacere!; **my bill, ~** il conto, per piacere; **~ yourself!** come ti (o le) pare!; **~ don't cry!** ti prego, non piangere!
pleased [pliːzd] adj (happy) felice, lieto(-a); **~ (with)** (satisfied) contento(-a) (di); **we are ~ to inform you that ...** abbiamo il piacere di informarla che ...; **~ to meet you!** piacere!
pleasing ['pliːzɪŋ] adj piacevole, che fa piacere
pleasurable ['plɛʒərəbl] adj molto piacevole, molto gradevole
pleasure ['plɛʒə'] n piacere m; **with ~** con piacere, volentieri; **"it's a ~"** "prego"; **is this trip for business or ~?** è un viaggio d'affari o di piacere?
pleasure cruise n crociera
pleat [pliːt] n piega
plebiscite ['plɛbɪsɪt] n plebiscito
plebs [plɛbz] npl (pej) plebe f

plectrum ['plɛktrəm] n plettro
pledge [plɛdʒ] n pegno; (promise) promessa ■ vt impegnare; promettere; **to ~ support for sb** impegnarsi a sostenere qn; **to ~ sb to secrecy** far promettere a qn di mantenere il segreto
plenary ['pliːnərɪ] adj plenario(-a); **in ~ session** in seduta plenaria
plentiful ['plɛntɪful] adj abbondante, copioso(-a)
plenty ['plɛntɪ] n abbondanza; **~ of** tanto(-a), molto(-a); un'abbondanza di; **we've got ~ of time to get there** abbiamo un sacco di tempo per arrivarci
pleurisy ['pluərɪsɪ] n pleurite f
Plexiglas® ['plɛksɪɡlɑːs] n (US) plexiglas® m
pliable ['plaɪəbl] adj flessibile; (person) malleabile
pliers ['plaɪəz] npl pinza
plight [plaɪt] n situazione f critica
plimsolls ['plɪmsəlz] npl (Brit) scarpe fpl da tennis
plinth [plɪnθ] n plinto; piedistallo
PLO n abbr (= Palestine Liberation Organization) O.L.P. f
plod [plɔd] vi camminare a stento; (fig) sgobbare
plodder ['plɔdə'] n sgobbone m
plodding ['plɔdɪŋ] adj lento(-a) e pesante
plonk [plɔŋk] n (col) (Brit: wine) vino da poco ■ vt: **to ~ sth down** buttare giù qc bruscamente
plot [plɔt] n congiura, cospirazione f; (of story, play) trama; (of land) lotto ■ vt (mark out) fare la pianta di; rilevare; (: diagram etc) tracciare; (conspire) congiurare, cospirare ■ vi congiurare; **a vegetable ~** (Brit) un orticello
plotter ['plɔtə'] n cospiratore(-trice); (Comput) plotter m inv, tracciatore m di curve
plough, (US) **plow** [plau] n aratro ■ vt (earth) arare
  ▸ **plough back** vt (Comm) reinvestire
  ▸ **plough through** vt fus (snow etc) procedere a fatica in
ploughing, (US) **plowing** ['plauɪŋ] n aratura
ploughman, (US) **plowman** ['plaumən] n aratore m; **~'s lunch** (Brit) semplice pasto a base di pane e formaggio
ploy [plɔɪ] n stratagemma m
pls abbr = **please**
pluck [plʌk] vt (fruit) cogliere; (musical instrument) pizzicare; (bird) spennare ■ n coraggio, fegato; **to ~ one's eyebrows** depilarsi le sopracciglia; **to ~ up courage** farsi coraggio
plucky ['plʌkɪ] adj coraggioso(-a)
plug [plʌɡ] n tappo; (Elec) spina; (Aut: also:

spark(ing) plug) candela ■ *vt* (*hole*) tappare; (*col: advertise*) spingere; **to give sb/sth a ~** fare pubblicità a qn/qc
▶ **plug in** (*Elec*) *vi* inserire la spina ■ *vt* attaccare a una presa

plughole ['plʌghəul] *n* (*Brit*) scarico

plum [plʌm] *n* (*fruit*) susina ■ *cpd*: **~ job** (*col*) impiego ottimo *or* favoloso

plumage ['plu:mɪdʒ] *n* piume *fpl*, piumaggio

plumb [plʌm] *adj* verticale ■ *n* piombo ■ *adv* (*exactly*) esattamente ■ *vt* sondare
▶ **plumb in** *vt* (*washing machine*) collegare all'impianto idraulico

plumber ['plʌmə*r*] *n* idraulico

plumbing ['plʌmɪŋ] *n* (*trade*) lavoro di idraulico; (*piping*) tubature *fpl*

plumbline ['plʌmlaɪn] *n* filo a piombo

plume [plu:m] *n* piuma, penna; (*decorative*) pennacchio

plummet ['plʌmɪt] *vi* cadere a piombo

plump [plʌmp] *adj* grassoccio(-a) ■ *vt*: **to ~ sth (down) on** lasciar cadere qc di peso su
▶ **plump for** *vt fus* (*col*) decidersi per
▶ **plump up** *vt* sprimacciare

plunder ['plʌndə*r*] *n* saccheggio ■ *vt* saccheggiare

plunge [plʌndʒ] *n* tuffo ■ *vt* immergere ■ *vi* (*dive*) tuffarsi; (*fall*) cadere, precipitare; **to take the ~** (*fig*) saltare il fosso; **to ~ a room into darkness** far piombare una stanza nel buio

plunger ['plʌndʒə*r*] *n* (*for blocked sink*) sturalavandini *m inv*

plunging ['plʌndʒɪŋ] *adj* (*neckline*) profondo(-a)

pluperfect [plu:'pə:fɪkt] *n* piuccheperfetto

plural ['pluərl] *adj, n* plurale (*m*)

plus [plʌs] *n* (*also*: **plus sign**) segno più ■ *prep* più ■ *adj* (*Math, Elec*) positivo(-a); **ten/ twenty ~** più di dieci/venti; **it's a ~** (*fig*) è un vantaggio

plus fours *npl* calzoni *mpl* alla zuava

plush [plʌʃ] *adj* lussuoso(-a) ■ *n* felpa

plutonium [plu:'təunɪəm] *n* plutonio

ply [plaɪ] *n* (*of wool*) capo; (*of wood*) strato ■ *vt* (*tool*) maneggiare; (*a trade*) esercitare ■ *vi* (*ship*) fare il servizio; **three-~ (wool)** lana a tre capi; **to ~ sb with drink** dare da bere continuamente a qn

plywood ['plaɪwud] *n* legno compensato

PM *n abbr* (*Brit*) = **prime minister**

p.m. *adv abbr* (= *post meridiem*) del pomeriggio

PMS *n abbr* (= *premenstrual syndrome*) sindrome *f* premestruale

PMT *n abbr* (= *premenstrual tension*) sindrome *f* premestruale

pneumatic [nju:'mætɪk] *adj* pneumatico(-a); **~ drill** martello pneumatico

pneumonia [nju:'məunɪə] *n* polmonite *f*

PO *n abbr* (= *Post Office*) ≈ P.T. (= *Poste e Telegrafi*) ■ *abbr* (*Naut*) = **petty officer**

po *abbr* = **postal order**

POA *n abbr* (*Brit*: = *Prison Officers' Association*) sindacato delle guardie carcerarie

poach [pəutʃ] *vt* (*cook*) affogare; (*steal*) cacciare (*or* pescare) di frodo ■ *vi* fare il bracconiere

poached [pəutʃt] *adj* (*egg*) affogato(-a)

poacher ['pəutʃə*r*] *n* bracconiere *m*

poaching ['pəutʃɪŋ] *n* caccia (*or* pesca) di frodo

PO box *n abbr* = **post office box**

pocket ['pɔkɪt] *n* tasca ■ *vt* intascare; **to be out of ~** rimetterci; **to be £5 in/out of ~** (*Brit*) trovarsi con 5 sterline in più/in meno; **air ~** vuoto d'aria

pocketbook ['pɔkɪtbuk] *n* (*wallet*) portafoglio; (*notebook*) taccuino; (*US: handbag*) busta

pocket knife *n* temperino

pocket money *n* paghetta, settimana

pockmarked ['pɔkmɑ:kt] *adj* (*face*) butterato(-a)

pod [pɔd] *n* guscio ■ *vt* sgusciare

podcast ['pɔdkɑ:st] *n* podcast *m inv*

podgy ['pɔdʒɪ] *adj* grassoccio(-a)

podiatrist [pɔ'di:ətrɪst] *n* (*US*) callista *m/f*, pedicure *m/f*

podiatry [pɔ'di:ətrɪ] *n* (*US*) mestiere *m* di callista

podium ['pəudɪəm] *n* podio

POE *n abbr* = **port of embarkation; port of entry**

poem ['pəuɪm] *n* poesia

poet ['pəuɪt] *n* poeta(-essa)

poetic [pəu'ɛtɪk] *adj* poetico(-a)

poet laureate *n* (*Brit*) poeta *m* laureato; *vedi nota*

○ **POET LAUREATE**
○
○ In Gran Bretagna il *poet laureate* è un poeta
○ che riceve un vitalizio dalla casa reale
○ britannica e che ha l'incarico di scrivere
○ delle poesie commemorative in occasione
○ delle festività ufficiali.

poetry ['pəuɪtrɪ] *n* poesia

poignant ['pɔɪnjənt] *adj* struggente

point [pɔɪnt] *n* (*gen*) punto; (*tip: of needle etc*) punta; (*Brit Elec*: *also*: **power point**) presa (di corrente); (*in time*) punto, momento; (*Scol*) voto; (*main idea, important part*) nocciolo; (*also*: **decimal point**): **2 ~ 3 (2.3)** 2 virgola 3 (2,3) ■ *vt* (*show*) indicare; (*gun etc*): **to ~ sth at** puntare qc contro ■ *vi* mostrare a dito; **points** *npl*

P

(*Aut*) puntine *fpl*; (*Rail*) scambio; **to ~ to** indicare; (*fig*) dimostrare; **to make a ~** fare un'osservazione; **to get the ~** capire; **to come to the ~** venire al fatto; **when it comes to the ~** quando si arriva al dunque; **to be on the ~ of doing sth** essere sul punto di *or* stare (proprio) per fare qc; **to be beside the ~** non entrarci; **to make a ~ of doing sth** non mancare di fare qc; **there's no ~ (in doing)** è inutile (fare); **in ~ of fact** a dire il vero; **that's the whole ~!** precisamente!, sta tutto lì!; **you've got a ~ there!** giusto!, ha ragione!; **the train stops at Carlisle and all points south** il treno ferma a Carlisle e in tutte le stazioni a sud di Carlisle; **good points** vantaggi *mpl*; (*of person*) qualità *fpl*; **~ of departure** (*also fig*) punto di partenza; **~ of order** mozione *f* d'ordine; **~ of sale** (*Comm*) punto di vendita; **~ of view** punto di vista
▶ **point out** *vt* far notare
point-blank ['pɔɪnt'blæŋk] *adv* (*also*: **at point-blank range**) a bruciapelo; (*fig*) categoricamente
point duty *n* (*Brit*): **to be on ~** dirigere il traffico
pointed ['pɔɪntɪd] *adj* (*shape*) aguzzo(-a), appuntito(-a); (*remark*) specifico(-a)
pointedly ['pɔɪntɪdlɪ] *adv* in maniera inequivocabile
pointer ['pɔɪntə'] *n* (*stick*) bacchetta; (*needle*) lancetta; (*clue*) indizio; (*advice*) consiglio; (*dog*) pointer *m*, cane *m* da punta
pointless ['pɔɪntlɪs] *adj* inutile, vano(-a)
poise [pɔɪz] *n* (*balance*) equilibrio; (*of head, body*) portamento; (*calmness*) calma ■ *vt* tenere in equilibrio; **to be poised for** (*fig*) essere pronto(-a) a
poison ['pɔɪzn] *n* veleno ■ *vt* avvelenare
poisoning ['pɔɪznɪŋ] *n* avvelenamento
poisonous ['pɔɪznəs] *adj* velenoso(-a); (*fumes*) venefico(-a), tossico(-a); (*ideas, literature*) pernicioso(-a); (*rumours, individual*) perfido(-a)
poke [pəuk] *vt* (*fire*) attizzare; (*jab with finger, stick etc*) punzecchiare; (*put*): **to ~ sth in(to)** spingere qc dentro ■ *n* (*jab*) colpetto; (*with elbow*) gomitata; **to ~ one's head out of the window** mettere la testa fuori dalla finestra; **to ~ fun at sb** prendere in giro qn
▶ **poke about** *vi* frugare
poker ['pəukə'] *n* attizzatoio; (*Cards*) poker *m*
poker-faced ['pəukə'feɪst] *adj* dal viso impassibile
poky ['pəukɪ] *adj* piccolo(-a) e stretto(-a)
Poland ['pəulənd] *n* Polonia
polar ['pəulə'] *adj* polare
polar bear *n* orso bianco

polarize ['pəuləraɪz] *vt* polarizzare
Pole [pəul] *n* polacco(-a)
pole [pəul] *n* (*of wood*) palo; (*Elec, Geo*) polo
poleaxe, (*US*) **poleax** ['pəulæks] *vt* (*fig*) stendere
pole bean *n* (*US*) fagiolino
polecat ['pəulkæt] *n* puzzola; (*US*) moffetta
Pol. Econ. ['pɔlɪkɔn] *n abbr* = **political economy**
polemic [pɔ'lɛmɪk] *n* polemica
pole star *n* stella polare
pole vault *n* salto con l'asta
police [pə'li:s] *n* polizia ■ *vt* mantenere l'ordine in; (*streets, city, frontier*) presidiare; **a large number of ~ were hurt** molti poliziotti sono rimasti feriti
police car *n* macchina della polizia
police constable *n* (*Brit*) agente *m* di polizia
police department *n* (*US*) dipartimento di polizia
police force *n* corpo di polizia, polizia
policeman [pə'li:smən] *n* poliziotto, agente *m* di polizia
police officer *n* = **police constable**
police record *n*: **to have a ~** avere precedenti penali
police state *n* stato di polizia
police station *n* posto di polizia
policewoman [pə'li:swumən] *n* donna *f* poliziotto *inv*
policy ['pɔlɪsɪ] *n* politica; (*of newspaper, company*) linea di condotta, prassi *f inv*; (*also*: **insurance policy**) polizza (d'assicurazione); **to take out a ~** (*Insurance*) stipulare una polizza di assicurazione
policy holder *n* assicurato(-a)
policy-making ['pɔlɪsɪmeɪkɪŋ] *n* messa a punto di programmi
polio ['pəulɪəu] *n* polio *f*
Polish ['pəulɪʃ] *adj* polacco(-a) ■ *n* (*Ling*) polacco
polish ['pɔlɪʃ] *n* (*for shoes*) lucido; (*for floor*) cera; (*for nails*) smalto; (*shine*) lucentezza, lustro; (*fig: refinement*) raffinatezza ■ *vt* lucidare; (*fig: improve*) raffinare
▶ **polish off** *vt* (*work*) sbrigare; (*food*) mangiarsi
polished ['pɔlɪʃt] *adj* (*fig*) raffinato(-a)
polite [pə'laɪt] *adj* cortese; **it's not ~ to do that** non è educato *or* buona educazione fare questo
politely [pə'laɪtlɪ] *adv* cortesemente
politeness [pə'laɪtnɪs] *n* cortesia
politic ['pɔlɪtɪk] *adj* diplomatico(-a)
political [pə'lɪtɪkl] *adj* politico(-a)
political asylum *n* asilo politico
politically [pə'lɪtɪklɪ] *adv* politicamente

politically correct adj politicamente corretto(-a)
politician [pɔlɪ'tɪʃən] n politico
politics ['pɔlɪtɪks] n politica ◼ npl idee fpl politiche
polka ['pɔlkə] n polca
polka dot n pois m inv
poll [pəul] n scrutinio; (votes cast) voti mpl; (also: **opinion poll**) sondaggio (d'opinioni) ◼ vt ottenere; **to go to the polls** (voters) andare alle urne; (government) indire le elezioni
pollen ['pɔlən] n polline m
pollen count n tasso di polline nell'aria
pollination [pɔlɪ'neɪʃən] n impollinazione f
polling ['pəulɪŋ] n (Brit Pol) votazione f, votazioni fpl; (Tel) interrogazione f ciclica
polling booth n (Brit) cabina elettorale
polling day n (Brit) giorno delle elezioni
polling station n (Brit) sezione f elettorale
pollster ['pəulstər] n chi esegue sondaggi d'opinione
poll tax n (Brit) imposta locale sulla persona fisica (non più in vigore)
pollutant [pə'lu:tənt] n sostanza inquinante
pollute [pə'lu:t] vt inquinare
pollution [pə'lu:ʃən] n inquinamento
polo ['pəuləu] n polo
polo neck n collo alto; (also: **polo neck sweater**) dolcevita ◼ adj a collo alto
poly ['pɔlɪ] n abbr (Brit) = **polytechnic**
poly bag n (Brit col) borsa di plastica
polyester [pɔlɪ'ɛstər] n poliestere m
polygamy [pə'lɪgəmɪ] n poligamia
polygraph ['pɔlɪgrɑːf] n macchina della verità
Polynesia [pɔlɪ'niːzɪə] n Polinesia
Polynesian [pɔlɪ'niːzɪən] adj, n polinesiano(-a)
polyp ['pɔlɪp] n (Med) polipo
polystyrene [pɔlɪ'staɪriːn] n polistirolo
polytechnic [pɔlɪ'tɛknɪk] n (college) istituto superiore ad indirizzo tecnologico
polythene ['pɔlɪθiːn] n politene m
polythene bag n borsa di plastica
polyurethane ['pɔlɪ'juərɪθeɪn] n poliuretano
pomegranate ['pɔmɪgrænɪt] n melagrana
pommel ['pɔml] n pomo ◼ vt = **pummel**
pomp [pɔmp] n pompa, fasto
pompom ['pɔmpɔm] n pompon m inv
pompous ['pɔmpəs] adj pomposo(-a); (person) pieno(-a) di boria
pond [pɔnd] n stagno; (in park) laghetto
ponder ['pɔndər] vi riflettere, meditare ◼ vt ponderare, riflettere su
ponderous ['pɔndərəs] adj ponderoso(-a), pesante
pong [pɔŋ] (Brit col) n puzzo ◼ vi puzzare
pontiff ['pɔntɪf] n pontefice m

pontificate [pɔn'tɪfɪkeɪt] vi (fig): **to ~ (about)** pontificare (su)
pontoon [pɔn'tuːn] n pontone m; (Brit Cards) ventuno
pony ['pəunɪ] n pony m inv
ponytail ['pəunɪteɪl] n coda di cavallo
pony trekking [-trɛkɪŋ] n (Brit) escursione f a cavallo
poodle ['puːdl] n barboncino, barbone m
pooh-pooh [puː'puː] vt deridere
pool [puːl] n (of rain) pozza; (pond) stagno; (artificial) vasca; (also: **swimming pool**) piscina; (sth shared) fondo comune; (Comm: consortium) pool m inv; (US: monopoly trust) trust m inv; (billiards) specie di biliardo a buca ◼ vt mettere in comune; **typing ~**, (US) **secretary ~** servizio comune di dattilografia; **to do the (football) pools** ≈ fare la schedina, ≈ giocare al totocalcio
poor [puər] adj povero(-a); (mediocre) mediocre, cattivo(-a) ◼ npl: **the ~** i poveri
poorly ['puəlɪ] adv poveramente; (badly) male ◼ adj indisposto(-a), malato(-a)
pop [pɔp] n (noise) schiocco; (Mus) musica pop; (US col: father) babbo; (col: drink) bevanda gasata ◼ vt (put) mettere (in fretta) ◼ vi scoppiare; (cork) schioccare; **she popped her head out** (of the window) sporse fuori la testa
▸ **pop in** vi passare
▸ **pop out** vi fare un salto fuori
▸ **pop up** vi apparire, sorgere
pop concert n concerto m pop inv
popcorn ['pɔpkɔːn] n pop-corn m
pope [pəup] n papa m
poplar ['pɔplər] n pioppo
poplin ['pɔplɪn] n popeline f
popper ['pɔpər] n (Brit) bottone m automatico, bottone a pressione
poppy ['pɔpɪ] n papavero
poppycock ['pɔpɪkɔk] n (col) scempiaggini fpl
Popsicle® ['pɔpsɪkl] n (US) ghiacciolo
populace ['pɔpjuləs] n popolo
popular ['pɔpjulər] adj popolare; (fashionable) in voga; **to be ~ (with)** (person) essere benvoluto(-a) or ben visto(-a) (da); (decision) essere gradito(-a) (a); **a ~ song** una canzone di successo
popularity [pɔpju'lærɪtɪ] n popolarità
popularize ['pɔpjuləraɪz] vt divulgare; (science) volgarizzare
populate ['pɔpjuleɪt] vt popolare
population [pɔpju'leɪʃən] n popolazione f
population explosion n forte espansione f demografica
populous ['pɔpjuləs] adj popolato(-a)
pop-up menu ['pɔpʌp-] n (Comput) menu m inv a comparsa

P

719

porcelain ['pɔːslɪn] n porcellana
porch [pɔːtʃ] n veranda
porcupine ['pɔːkjupaɪn] n porcospino
pore [pɔːʳ] n poro ■ vi: **to ~ over** essere
immerso(-a) in
pork [pɔːk] n carne f di maiale
pork chop n braciola or costoletta di maiale
porn [pɔːn] (col) n pornografia ■ adj porno inv
pornographic [pɔːnə'græfɪk] adj
pornografico(-a)
pornography [pɔː'nɔgrəfɪ] n pornografia
porous ['pɔːrəs] adj poroso(-a)
porpoise ['pɔːpəs] n focena
porridge ['pɔrɪdʒ] n porridge m
port[1] [pɔːt] n porto; (opening in ship) portello;
(Naut: left side) babordo; (Comput) porta; **to ~**
(Naut) a babordo; **~ of call** (porto di) scalo
port[2] [pɔːt] n (wine) porto
portable ['pɔːtəbl] adj portatile
portal ['pɔːtl] n portale m
portcullis [pɔːt'kʌlɪs] n saracinesca
portent ['pɔːtɛnt] n presagio
porter ['pɔːtəʳ] n (for luggage) facchino,
portabagagli m inv; (doorkeeper) portiere m,
portinaio; (US Rail) addetto ai vagoni letto
portfolio [pɔːt'fəuliəu] n (Pol: office; Econ)
portafoglio; (of artist) raccolta dei propri
lavori
porthole ['pɔːthəul] n oblò m inv
portico ['pɔːtɪkəu] n portico
portion ['pɔːʃən] n porzione f
portly ['pɔːtlɪ] adj corpulento(-a)
portrait ['pɔːtreɪt] n ritratto
portray [pɔː'treɪ] vt fare il ritratto di;
(character on stage) rappresentare; (in writing)
ritrarre
portrayal ['pɔːtreɪəl] n ritratto;
rappresentazione f
Portugal ['pɔːtjugl] n Portogallo
Portuguese [pɔːtju'giːz] adj portoghese ■ n
(pl inv) portoghese m/f; (Ling) portoghese m
Portuguese man-of-war [-mænəv'wɔːʳ] n
(jellyfish) medusa
pose [pəuz] n posa ■ vi posare; (pretend):
to ~ as atteggiarsi a, posare a ■ vt porre;
to strike a ~ mettersi in posa
poser ['pəuzəʳ] n domanda difficile; (person)
= **poseur**
poseur [pəu'zəːʳ] n (pej) persona affettata
posh [pɔʃ] adj (col) elegante; (family) per bene
■ adv (col): **to talk ~** parlare in modo snob
position [pə'zɪʃən] n posizione f; (job) posto
■ vt mettere in posizione, collocare; **to be in
a ~ to do sth** essere nella posizione di fare qc
positive ['pɔzɪtɪv] adj positivo(-a); (certain)
sicuro(-a), certo(-a); (definite) preciso(-a);
definitivo(-a)

posse ['pɔsɪ] n (US) drappello
possess [pə'zɛs] vt possedere; **like one
possessed** come un ossesso; **whatever can
have possessed you?** cosa ti ha preso?
possession [pə'zɛʃən] n possesso; (object)
bene m; **to take ~ of sth** impossessarsi or
impadronirsi di qc
possessive [pə'zɛsɪv] adj possessivo(-a)
possessiveness [pə'zɛsɪvnɪs] n possessività
possessor [pə'zɛsəʳ] n possessore/posseditrice
possibility [pɔsɪ'bɪlɪtɪ] n possibilità f inv; **he's
a ~ for the part** è uno dei candidati per la parte
possible ['pɔsɪbl] adj possibile; **it is ~ to do it**
è possibile farlo; **if ~** se possibile; **as big as ~**
il più grande possibile; **as far as ~** nei limiti
del possibile
possibly ['pɔsɪblɪ] adv (perhaps) forse; **if you ~
can** se le è possibile; **I cannot ~ come**
proprio non posso venire
post [pəust] n (Brit: mail, letters, delivery) posta;
(: collection) levata; (job, situation) posto; (pole)
palo; (trading post) stazione f commerciale;
(on internet forum) post m inv, commento ■ vt
(Brit: send by post) impostare; (Mil) appostare;
(notice) affiggere; (to internet: video) caricare;
(: comment) mandare; (Brit: appoint): **to ~ to**
assegnare a; **by ~** (Brit) per posta; **by return
of ~** (Brit) a giro di posta; **to keep sb posted**
tenere qn al corrente
post... [pəust] prefix post...; **post-1990** dopo il
1990
postage ['pəustɪdʒ] n affrancatura
postage stamp n francobollo
postal ['pəustəl] adj postale
postal order n vaglia m inv postale
postbag ['pəustbæg] n (Brit) sacco postale,
sacco della posta
postbox ['pəustbɔks] n cassetta delle lettere
postcard ['pəustkɑːd] n cartolina
postcode ['pəustkəud] n (Brit) codice m (di
avviamento) postale
postdate ['pəust'deɪt] vt (cheque) postdatare
poster ['pəustəʳ] n manifesto, affisso
poste restante [pəust'rɛstɑ̃ːnt] n (Brit) fermo
posta m
posterior [pɔs'tɪərɪəʳ] n (col) deretano, didietro
posterity [pɔs'tɛrɪtɪ] n posterità
poster paint n tempera
post exchange n (US Mil) spaccio militare
post-free [pəust'friː] adj, adv (Brit) franco di
porto
postgraduate ['pəust'grædjuət] n laureato/a
che continua gli studi
posthumous ['pɔstjuməs] adj postumo(-a)
posthumously ['pɔstjuməslɪ] adv dopo la
mia (or sua etc) morte
posting ['pəustɪŋ] n (Brit) incarico

postman ['pəustmən] n postino
postmark ['pəustmɑːk] n bollo or timbro postale
postmaster ['pəustmɑːstəʳ] n direttore m di un ufficio postale
Postmaster General n ≈ ministro delle Poste
postmistress ['pəustmɪstrɪs] n direttrice f di un ufficio postale
post-mortem [pəust'mɔːtəm] n autopsia; (fig) analisi f inv a posteriori
postnatal ['pəust'neɪtl] adj post-parto inv
post office n (building) ufficio postale; (organization) poste fpl
post office box n casella postale
post-paid ['pəust'peɪd] adj già affrancato(-a)
postpone [pəust'pəun] vt rinviare
postponement [pəust'pəunmənt] n rinvio
postscript ['pəustskrɪpt] n poscritto
postulate ['pɔstjuleɪt] vt postulare
posture ['pɔstʃəʳ] n portamento; (pose) posa, atteggiamento ■ vi posare
postwar ['pəust'wɔː] adj del dopoguerra
posy ['pəuzɪ] n mazzetto di fiori
pot [pɔt] n (for cooking) pentola; casseruola; (for plants, jam) vaso; (piece of pottery) ceramica; (col: marijuana) erba ■ vt (plant) piantare in vaso; **to go to ~** (col) andare in malora; **pots of** (Brit col) un sacco di
potash ['pɔtæʃ] n potassa
potassium [pə'tæsɪəm] n potassio
potato (pl **potatoes**) [pə'teɪtəu] n patata
potato crisps, (US) **potato chips** npl patatine fpl
potato flour n fecola di patate
potato peeler n sbucciapatate m inv
potbellied ['pɔtbɛlɪd] adj (from overeating) panciuto(-a); (from malnutrition) dal ventre gonfio
potency ['pəutnsɪ] n potenza; (of drink) forza
potent ['pəutnt] adj potente, forte
potentate ['pəutnteɪt] n potentato
potential [pə'tɛnʃl] adj potenziale ■ n possibilità fpl; **to have ~** essere promettente
potentially [pə'tɛnʃəlɪ] adv potenzialmente
pothole ['pɔthəul] n (in road) buca; (Brit: underground) marmitta
potholer ['pɔthəuləʳ] n (Brit) speleologo(-a)
potholing ['pɔthəulɪŋ] n (Brit): **to go ~** fare la speleologia
potion ['pəuʃən] n pozione f
potluck [pɔt'lʌk] n: **to take ~** tentare la sorte
potpourri [pəu'puriː] n (dried petals etc) miscuglio di petali essiccati profumati; (fig) pot-pourri m inv
pot roast n brasato
potshot ['pɔtʃɔt] n: **to take potshots at** tirare a casaccio contro

potted ['pɔtɪd] adj (food) in conserva; (plant) in vaso; (fig: shortened) condensato(-a)
potter ['pɔtəʳ] n vasaio ■ vi (Brit): **to ~ around**, **~ about** lavoracchiare; **to ~ round the house** sbrigare con calma le faccende di casa; **~'s wheel** tornio (da vasaio)
pottery ['pɔtərɪ] n ceramiche fpl; **a piece of ~** una ceramica
potty ['pɔtɪ] adj (Brit col: mad) tocco(-a) ■ n (child's) vasino
potty-trained ['pɔtɪtreɪnd] adj che ha imparato a farla nel vasino
pouch [pautʃ] n borsa; (Zool) marsupio
pouf, pouffe [puːf] n (stool) pouf m inv
poultice ['pəultɪs] n impiastro, cataplasma m
poultry ['pəultrɪ] n pollame m
poultry farm n azienda avicola
poultry farmer n pollicoltore(-trice)
pounce [pauns] vi: **to ~ (on)** balzare addosso (a), piombare (su) ■ n balzo
pound [paund] n (weight) libbra (= 453g, 16 ounces); (money) (lira) sterlina (= 100 pence); (for dogs) canile m municipale ■ vt (beat) battere; (crush) pestare, polverizzare ■ vi (beat) battere, martellare; **half a ~** mezza libbra; **a five-~ note** una banconota da cinque sterline
pounding ['paundɪŋ] n: **to take a ~** (fig) prendere una batosta
pound sterling n sterlina
pour [pɔːʳ] vt versare ■ vi riversarsi; (rain) piovere a dirotto
▶ **pour away, pour off** vt vuotare
▶ **pour in** vi (people) entrare in fiotto; **to come pouring in** (water) entrare a fiotti; (letters) arrivare a valanghe; (cars, people) affluire in gran quantità
▶ **pour out** vi (people) riversarsi fuori ■ vt vuotare; versare
pouring ['pɔːrɪŋ] adj: **~ rain** pioggia torrenziale
pout [paut] vi sporgere le labbra; fare il broncio
poverty ['pɔvətɪ] n povertà, miseria
poverty line n soglia di povertà
poverty-stricken ['pɔvətɪstrɪkən] adj molto povero(-a), misero(-a)
poverty trap n (Brit) circolo vizioso della povertà
POW n abbr = **prisoner of war**
powder ['paudəʳ] n polvere f ■ vt spolverizzare; (face) incipriare; **powdered milk** latte m in polvere; **to ~ one's nose** incipriarsi il naso; (euphemism) andare alla toilette
powder compact n portacipria m inv

p

powder keg n (fig: area) polveriera; (: situation) situazione f esplosiva

powder puff n piumino della cipria

powder room n toilette f inv (per signore)

powdery ['paʊdərɪ] adj polveroso(-a)

power ['paʊə'] n (strength) potenza, forza; (ability, Pol: of party, leader) potere m; (Math) potenza; (Elec) corrente f ▪ vt fornire di energia; azionare; **to be in ~** essere al potere; **to do all in one's ~ to help sb** fare tutto quello che si può per aiutare qn; **the world powers** le grandi potenze; **mental powers** capacità fpl mentali

powerboat ['paʊəbəʊt] n (Brit) motobarca, imbarcazione f a motore

power cut n (Brit) interruzione f or mancanza di corrente

powered ['paʊəd] adj: **~ by** azionato(-a) da; **nuclear-~ submarine** sottomarino a propulsione atomica

power failure n guasto alla linea elettrica

powerful ['paʊəful] adj potente, forte

powerhouse ['paʊəhaʊs] n (fig: person) persona molto dinamica; **a ~ of ideas** una miniera di idee

powerless ['paʊəlɪs] adj impotente, senza potere

power line n linea elettrica

power of attorney n procura

power point n (Brit) presa di corrente

power station n centrale f elettrica

power steering n (Aut: also: **power-assisted steering**) servosterzo

powwow ['paʊwaʊ] n riunione f

pp abbr (= pages) pp; (= per procurationem: by proxy): **pp J. Smith** per il Signor J. Smith

PPE n abbr (Brit Scol: = philosophy, politics, and economics) corso di laurea

PPS n abbr (Brit: = parliamentary private secretary) parlamentare che assiste un ministro; = **post postscriptum**

PQ abbr (Canada) = **Province of Quebec**

PR n abbr = **proportional representation**; **public relations** ▪ abbr (US) = **Puerto Rico**

Pr. abbr = **prince**

practicability [præktɪkə'bɪlɪtɪ] n praticabilità

practicable ['præktɪkəbl] adj (scheme) praticabile

practical ['præktɪkl] adj pratico(-a)

practicality [præktɪ'kælɪtɪ] n (of plan) fattibilità; (of person) senso pratico; **practicalities** npl dettagli mpl pratici

practical joke n beffa

practically ['præktɪklɪ] adv (almost) quasi, praticamente

practice ['præktɪs] n pratica; (of profession) esercizio; (at football etc) allenamento; (business) gabinetto; clientela ▪ vt, vi (US) = **practise**; **in ~** (in reality) in pratica; **out of ~** fuori esercizio; **2 hours' piano ~** 2 ore di esercizio al pianoforte; **it's common ~** è d'uso; **to put sth into ~** mettere qc in pratica; **target ~** pratica di tiro

practice match n partita di allenamento

practise, (US) **practice** ['præktɪs] vt (work at: piano, one's backhand etc) esercitarsi a; (train for: skiing, running etc) allenarsi a; (a sport, religion) praticare; (method) usare; (profession) esercitare ▪ vi esercitarsi; (train) allenarsi; **to ~ for a match** allenarsi per una partita

practised ['præktɪst] adj (Brit: person) esperto(-a); (: performance) da virtuoso(-a); (: liar) matricolato(-a); **with a ~ eye** con occhio esperto

practising ['præktɪsɪŋ] adj (Christian etc) praticante; (lawyer) che esercita la professione; (homosexual) attivo(-a)

practitioner [præk'tɪʃənə'] n professionista m/f; (Med) medico

pragmatic [præg'mætɪk] adj prammatico(-a)

Prague [prɑːg] n Praga

prairie ['prɛərɪ] n prateria

praise [preɪz] n elogio, lode f ▪ vt elogiare, lodare

praiseworthy ['preɪzwəːðɪ] adj lodevole

pram [præm] n (Brit) carrozzina

prance [prɑːns] vi (horse) impennarsi

prank [præŋk] n burla

prat [præt] n (Brit col) cretino(-a)

prattle ['prætl] vi cinguettare

prawn [prɔːn] n gamberetto

pray [preɪ] vi pregare

prayer [prɛə'] n preghiera

prayer book n libro di preghiere

pre... [priː] prefix pre...; **pre-1970** prima del 1970

preach [priːtʃ] vt, vi predicare; **to ~ at sb** fare la predica a qn

preacher ['priːtʃə'] n predicatore(-trice); (US: minister) pastore m

preamble [prɪ'æmbl] n preambolo

prearranged [priː'ə'reɪndʒd] adj organizzato(-a) in anticipo

precarious [prɪ'kɛərɪəs] adj precario(-a)

precaution [prɪ'kɔːʃən] n precauzione f

precautionary [prɪ'kɔːʃənərɪ] adj (measure) precauzionale

precede [prɪ'siːd] vt, vi precedere

precedence ['presɪdəns] n precedenza; **to take ~ over** avere la precedenza su

precedent ['presɪdənt] n precedente m; **to establish** or **set a ~** creare un precedente

preceding [prɪ'siːdɪŋ] adj precedente

precept ['pri:sɛpt] n precetto
precinct ['pri:sɪŋkt] n (round cathedral) recinto;
(US: district) circoscrizione f; **precincts** npl
(neighbourhood) dintorni mpl, vicinanze fpl;
pedestrian ~ zona pedonale; **shopping** ~
(Brit) centro commerciale
precious ['prɛʃəs] adj prezioso(-a) ▪ adv (col):
~ **little/few** ben poco/pochi; **your** ~ **dog**
(ironic) il suo amatissimo cane
precipice ['prɛsɪpɪs] n precipizio
precipitate adj [prɪ'sɪpɪtɪt] (hasty)
precipitoso(-a) ▪ vt [prɪ'sɪpɪteɪt] accelerare
precipitation [prɪsɪpɪ'teɪʃən] n
precipitazione f
precipitous [prɪ'sɪpɪtəs] adj (steep) erto(-a),
ripido(-a)
précis (pl ~) ['preɪsi:, -z] n riassunto
precise [prɪ'saɪs] adj preciso(-a)
precisely [prɪ'saɪslɪ] adv precisamente; ~!
appunto!
precision [prɪ'sɪʒən] n precisione f
preclude [prɪ'klu:d] vt precludere, impedire;
to ~ **sb from doing** impedire a qn di fare
precocious [prɪ'kəʊʃəs] adj precoce
preconceived [pri:kən'si:vd] adj (idea)
preconcetto(-a)
preconception [pri:kən'sɛpʃən] n
preconcetto
precondition [pri:kən'dɪʃən] n condizione f
necessaria
precursor [pri:'kə:sər] n precursore m
predate [pri:'deɪt] vt (precede) precedere
predator ['prɛdətər] n predatore m
predatory ['prɛdətərɪ] adj predatore(-trice)
predecessor ['pri:dɪsɛsər] n predecessore(-a)
predestination [pri:dɛstɪ'neɪʃən] n
predestinazione f
predetermine [pri:dɪ'tə:mɪn] vt
predeterminare
predicament [prɪ'dɪkəmənt] n situazione f
difficile
predicate ['prɛdɪkɪt] n (Ling) predicativo
predict [prɪ'dɪkt] vt predire
predictable [prɪ'dɪktəbl] adj prevedibile
predictably [prɪ'dɪktəblɪ] adv (behave, react) in
modo prevedibile; ~ **she didn't arrive** come
era da prevedere, non è arrivata
prediction [prɪ'dɪkʃən] n predizione f
predispose [pri:dɪs'pəʊz] vt predisporre
predominance [prɪ'dɔmɪnəns] n
predominanza
predominant [prɪ'dɔmɪnənt] adj
predominante
predominantly [prɪ'dɔmɪnəntlɪ] adv in
maggior parte; soprattutto
predominate [prɪ'dɔmɪneɪt] vi predominare
pre-eminent [pri:'ɛmɪnənt] adj preminente

pre-empt [prɪ'ɛmpt] vt acquistare per diritto
di prelazione; (fig) anticipare
pre-emptive [prɪ'ɛmptɪv] adj: ~ **strike**
azione f preventiva
preen [pri:n] vt: **to** ~ **itself** (bird) lisciarsi le
penne; **to** ~ **o.s.** agghindarsi
prefab ['pri:fæb] n casa prefabbricata
prefabricated [pri:'fæbrɪkeɪtɪd] adj
prefabbricato(-a)
preface ['prɛfəs] n prefazione f
prefect ['pri:fɛkt] n (Brit: in school) studente/essa
con funzioni disciplinari; (in Italy) prefetto
prefer [prɪ'fə:r] vt preferire; (Law: charges,
complaint) sporgere; (: action) intentare; **to** ~
coffee to tea preferire il caffè al tè
preferable ['prɛfrəbl] adj preferibile
preferably ['prɛfrəblɪ] adv preferibilmente
preference ['prɛfrəns] n preferenza; **in** ~ **to**
sth piuttosto che qc
preference shares npl (Brit) azioni fpl
privilegiate
preferential [prɛfə'rɛnʃəl] adj preferenziale;
~ **treatment** trattamento di favore
preferred stock [prɪ'fə:d-] npl (US)
= **preference shares**
prefix ['pri:fɪks] n prefisso
pregnancy ['prɛgnənsɪ] n gravidanza
pregnancy test n test m inv di gravidanza
pregnant ['prɛgnənt] adj incinta adj f;
(animal) gravido(-a); (fig: remark, pause)
significativo(-a); **3 months** ~ incinta di 3 mesi
prehistoric ['pri:hɪs'tɔrɪk] adj preistorico(-a)
prehistory [pri:'hɪstərɪ] n preistoria
prejudge [pri:'dʒʌdʒ] vt pregiudicare
prejudice ['prɛdʒudɪs] n pregiudizio; (harm)
torto, danno ▪ vt pregiudicare, ledere;
(bias): **to** ~ **sb in favour of/against** disporre
bene/male qn verso
prejudiced ['prɛdʒudɪst] adj (person) pieno(-a)
di pregiudizi; (view) prevenuto(-a); **to be** ~
against sb/sth essere prevenuto contro qn/qc
prelate ['prɛlət] n prelato
preliminaries [prɪ'lɪmɪnərɪz] npl preliminari
mpl
preliminary [prɪ'lɪmɪnərɪ] adj preliminare
prelude ['prɛlju:d] n preludio
premarital ['pri:'mærɪtl] adj
prematrimoniale
premature ['prɛmətʃuər] adj prematuro(-a);
(arrival) (molto) anticipato(-a); **you are being**
a little ~ è un po' troppo precipitoso
premeditated [pri:'mɛdɪteɪtɪd] adj
premeditato(-a)
premeditation [pri:mɛdɪ'teɪʃən] n
premeditazione f
premenstrual tension [pri:'mɛnstruəl-] n
(Med) tensione f premestruale

p

premier ['prɛmɪə^r] adj primo(-a) ■ n (Pol) primo ministro

première ['prɛmɪɛə^r] n prima

premise ['prɛmɪs] n premessa

premises ['prɛmɪsɪz] npl locale m; **on the ~** sul posto; **business ~** locali commerciali

premium ['priːmɪəm] n premio; **to be at a ~** (fig: housing etc) essere ricercatissimo; **to sell at a ~** (shares) vendere sopra la pari

premium bond n (Brit) obbligazione f a premio

premium deal n (Comm) offerta speciale

premium gasoline n (US) super f

premonition [prɛmə'nɪʃən] n premonizione f

preoccupation [priːɔkju'peɪʃən] n preoccupazione f

preoccupied [priː'ɔkjupaɪd] adj preoccupato(-a)

prep [prɛp] n abbr (Scol: = preparation) studio ■ adj abbr: **~ school** = **preparatory school**

prepackaged [priː'pækɪdʒd] adj già impacchettato(-a)

prepaid [priː'peɪd] adj pagato(-a) in anticipo; (envelope) affrancato(-a)

preparation [prɛpə'reɪʃən] n preparazione f; **preparations** npl (for trip, war) preparativi mpl; **in ~ for sth** in vista di qc

preparatory [prɪ'pærətərɪ] adj preparatorio(-a); **~ to sth/to doing sth** prima di qc/di fare qc

preparatory school n (Brit) scuola elementare privata; (US) scuola superiore privata; vedi nota

○ **PREPARATORY SCHOOL**

In Gran Bretagna, la prep(aratory) school è una scuola privata frequentata da bambini dai 7 ai 13 anni in vista dell'iscrizione alla "public school". Negli Stati Uniti, invece, è una scuola superiore privata che prepara i ragazzi che si iscriveranno al "college".

prepare [prɪ'pɛə^r] vt preparare ■ vi: **to ~ for** prepararsi

prepared [prɪ'pɛəd] adj: **~ for** preparato(-a) a; **~ to** pronto(-a) a; **to be ~ to help sb** (willing) essere disposto or pronto ad aiutare qn

preponderance [prɪ'pɔndərns] n preponderanza

preposition [prɛpə'zɪʃən] n preposizione f

prepossessing [priː'pə'zɛsɪŋ] adj simpatico(-a), attraente

preposterous [prɪ'pɔstərəs] adj assurdo(-a)

prerecord ['priːrɪ'kɔːd] vt registrare in anticipo; **prerecorded broadcast** trasmissione f registrata; **prerecorded**

cassette (musi)cassetta

prerequisite [priː'rɛkwɪzɪt] n requisito indispensabile

prerogative [prɪ'rɔgətɪv] n prerogativa

presbyterian [prɛzbɪ'tɪərɪən] adj, n presbiteriano(-a)

presbytery ['prɛzbɪtərɪ] n presbiterio

preschool ['priː'skuːl] adj (age) prescolastico(-a); (child) in età prescolastica

prescribe [prɪ'skraɪb] vt prescrivere; (Med) ordinare; **prescribed books** (Brit Scol) testi mpl in programma

prescription [prɪ'skrɪpʃən] n prescrizione f; (Med) ricetta; **to make up** or (US) **fill a ~** preparare or fare una ricetta; **"only available on ~"** "ottenibile solo dietro presentazione di ricetta medica"

prescription charges npl (Brit) ticket m inv

prescriptive [prɪ'skrɪptɪv] adj normativo(-a)

presence ['prɛzns] n presenza; **~ of mind** presenza di spirito

present ['prɛznt] adj presente; (wife, residence, job) attuale ■ n regalo; (also: **present tense**) tempo presente ■ vt [prɪ'zɛnt] presentare; (give): **to ~ sb with sth** offrire qc a qn; **to be ~ at** essere presente a; **those ~** i presenti; **at ~** al momento; **to make sb a ~ of sth** regalare qc a qn

presentable [prɪ'zɛntəbl] adj presentabile

presentation [prɛzn'teɪʃən] n presentazione f; (gift) regalo, dono; (ceremony) consegna ufficiale; **on ~ of the voucher** dietro presentazione del buono

present-day ['prɛzntdeɪ] adj attuale, d'oggigiorno

presenter [prɪ'zɛntə^r] n (Brit Radio, TV) presentatore(-trice)

presently ['prɛzntlɪ] adv (soon) fra poco, presto; (at present) al momento; (US: now) adesso, ora

preservation [prɛzə'veɪʃən] n preservazione f, conservazione f

preservative [prɪ'zə:vətɪv] n conservante m

preserve [prɪ'zə:v] vt (keep safe) preservare, proteggere; (maintain) conservare; (food) mettere in conserva ■ n (for game, fish) riserva; (often pl: jam) marmellata; (: fruit) frutta sciroppata

preshrunk [priː'ʃrʌŋk] adj irrestringibile

preside [prɪ'zaɪd] vi presiedere

presidency ['prɛzɪdənsɪ] n presidenza; (US: of company) direzione f

president ['prɛzɪdənt] n presidente m; (US: of company) direttore(-trice) generale

presidential [prɛzɪ'dɛnʃl] adj presidenziale

press [prɛs] n (tool, machine) pressa; (for wine) torchio; (newspapers) stampa; (crowd) folla

■ *vt* (*push*) premere, pigiare; (*doorbell*) suonare; (*squeeze*) spremere; (: *hand*) stringere; (*clothes: iron*) stirare; (*pursue*) incalzare; (*insist*): **to ~ sth on sb** far accettare qc da qn; (*urge, entreat*): **to ~ sb to do** *or* **into doing sth** fare pressione su qn affinché faccia qc ■ *vi* premere; accalcare; **to go to ~** (*newspaper*) andare in macchina; **to be in the ~** (*in the newspapers*) essere sui giornali; **we are pressed for time** ci manca il tempo; **to ~ for sth** insistere per avere qc; **to ~ sb for an answer** insistere perché qn risponda; **to ~ charges against sb** (*Law*) sporgere una denuncia contro qn
▶ **press ahead** *vi*: **to ~ ahead (with)** andare avanti (con)
▶ **press on** *vi* continuare
press agency *n* agenzia di stampa
press clipping *n* ritaglio di giornale
press conference *n* conferenza stampa
press cutting *n* = **press clipping**
press-gang ['prɛsgæn] *vt*: **to ~ sb into doing sth** costringere qn a viva forza a fare qc
pressing ['prɛsɪŋ] *adj* urgente ■ *n* stiratura
press officer *n* addetto(-a) stampa *inv*
press release *n* comunicato stampa
press stud *n* (*Brit*) bottone *m* a pressione
press-up ['prɛsʌp] *n* (*Brit*) flessione *f* sulle braccia
pressure ['prɛʃəʳ] *n* pressione *f* ■ *vt* = **to put pressure on**; **high/low ~** alta/bassa pressione; **to put ~ on sb** fare pressione su qn
pressure cooker *n* pentola a pressione
pressure gauge *n* manometro
pressure group *n* gruppo di pressione
pressurize ['prɛʃəraɪz] *vt* pressurizzare; (*fig*): **to ~ sb (into doing sth)** fare delle pressioni su qn (per costringerlo a fare qc)
pressurized ['prɛʃəraɪzd] *adj* pressurizzato(-a)
Prestel® ['prɛstɛl] *n* Videotel® *m inv*
prestige [prɛs'tiːʒ] *n* prestigio
prestigious [prɛs'tɪdʒəs] *adj* prestigioso(-a)
presumably [prɪ'zjuːməblɪ] *adv* presumibilmente; **~ he did it** penso *or* presumo che l'abbia fatto
presume [prɪ'zjuːm] *vt* supporre; **to ~ to do** (*dare*) permettersi di fare
presumption [prɪ'zʌmpʃən] *n* presunzione *f*; (*boldness*) audacia
presumptuous [prɪ'zʌmpʃəs] *adj* presuntuoso(-a)
presuppose [priːsə'pəuz] *vt* presupporre
pre-tax [priː'tæks] *adj* al lordo d'imposta
pretence, (*US*) **pretense** [prɪ'tɛns] *n* (*claim*) pretesa; (*pretext*) pretesto, scusa; **to make a ~**

of doing far finta di fare; **on** *or* **under the ~ of doing sth** con il pretesto *or* la scusa di fare qc; **she is devoid of all ~** non si nasconde dietro false apparenze
pretend [prɪ'tɛnd] *vt* (*feign*) fingere ■ *vi* far finta; (*claim*): **to ~ to sth** pretendere a qc; **to ~ to do** far finta di fare
pretense [prɪ'tɛns] *n* (*US*) = **pretence**
pretension [prɪ'tɛnʃən] *n* (*claim*) pretesa; **to have no pretensions to sth/to being sth** non avere la pretesa di avere qc/di essere qc
pretentious [prɪ'tɛnʃəs] *adj* pretenzioso(-a)
preterite ['prɛtərɪt] *n* preterito
pretext ['priːtɛkst] *n* pretesto; **on** *or* **under the ~ of doing sth** col pretesto di fare qc
pretty ['prɪtɪ] *adj* grazioso(-a), carino(-a) ■ *adv* abbastanza, assai
prevail [prɪ'veɪl] *vi* (*win, be usual*) prevalere; (*persuade*): **to ~ (up)on sb to do** persuadere qn a fare
prevailing [prɪ'veɪlɪŋ] *adj* dominante
prevalent ['prɛvələnt] *adj* (*belief*) predominante; (*customs*) diffuso(-a); (*fashion*) corrente; (*disease*) comune
prevarication [prɪværɪ'keɪʃən] *n* tergiversazione *f*
prevent [prɪ'vɛnt] *vt* prevenire; **to ~ sb from doing** impedire a qn di fare
preventable [prɪ'vɛntəbl] *adj* evitabile
preventative [prɪ'vɛntətɪv] *adj* preventivo(-a)
prevention [prɪ'vɛnʃən] *n* prevenzione *f*
preventive [prɪ'vɛntɪv] *adj* preventivo(-a)
preview ['priːvjuː] *n* (*of film*) anteprima
previous ['priːvɪəs] *adj* precedente; anteriore; **I have a ~ engagement** ho già (preso) un impegno; **~ to doing** prima di fare
previously ['priːvɪəslɪ] *adv* prima
prewar ['priː'wɔːʳ] *adj* anteguerra *inv*
prey [preɪ] *n* preda ■ *vi*: **to ~ on** far preda di; **it was preying on his mind** gli rodeva la mente
price [praɪs] *n* prezzo; (*Betting: odds*) quotazione *f* ■ *vt* (*goods*) fissare il prezzo di; valutare; **what is the ~ of ...?** quanto costa ...?; **to go up** *or* **rise in ~** salire *or* aumentare di prezzo; **to put a ~ on sth** valutare *or* stimare qc; **he regained his freedom, but at a ~** ha riconquistato la sua libertà, ma a caro prezzo; **what ~ his promises now?** (*Brit*) a che valgono ora le sue promesse?; **to be priced out of the market** (*article*) essere così caro da diventare invendibile; (*producer, nation*) non poter sostenere la concorrenza
price control *n* controllo dei prezzi
price-cutting ['praɪskʌtɪŋ] *n* riduzione *f* dei prezzi

P

priceless ['praɪslɪs] adj di valore
inestimabile; (col: amusing) impagabile,
spassosissimo(-a)
price list n listino (dei) prezzi
price range n gamma di prezzi; **it's within
my ~** rientra nelle mie possibilità
price tag n cartellino del prezzo
price war n guerra dei prezzi
pricey ['praɪsɪ] adj (col) caruccio(-a)
prick [prɪk] n puntura ■ vt pungere; **to ~ up
one's ears** drizzare gli orecchi
prickle ['prɪkl] n (of plant) spina; (sensation)
pizzicore m
prickly ['prɪklɪ] adj spinoso(-a); (fig: person)
permaloso(-a)
prickly heat n sudamina
prickly pear n fico d'India
pride [praɪd] n orgoglio; superbia ■ vt: **to ~
o.s. on** essere orgoglioso(-a) di; vantarsi di;
to take (a) ~ in tenere molto a; essere
orgoglioso di; **to take a ~ in doing** andare
orgoglioso di fare; **to have ~ of place** (Brit)
essere al primo posto
priest [priːst] n prete m, sacerdote m
priestess ['priːstɪs] n sacerdotessa
priesthood ['priːsthud] n sacerdozio
prig [prɪg] n: **he's a ~** è compiaciuto di se
stesso
prim [prɪm] adj pudico(-a); contegnoso(-a)
primacy ['praɪməsɪ] n primato
prima facie ['praɪmə'feɪʃɪ] adj: **to have a ~
case** (Law) presentare una causa in
apparenza fondata
primal ['praɪməl] adj primitivo(-a),
originario(-a)
primarily ['praɪmərɪlɪ] adv principalmente,
essenzialmente
primary ['praɪmərɪ] adj primario(-a); (first in
importance) primo(-a) ■ n (US: election)
primarie fpl; vedi nota

primary colour n colore m
fondamentale
primary school n (Brit) scuola elementare;
vedi nota

primate n (Rel: ['praɪmɪt], Zool: ['praɪmeɪt])
primate m
prime [praɪm] adj primario(-a),
fondamentale; (excellent) di prima qualità
■ n: **in the ~ of life** nel fiore della vita ■ vt
(gun) innescare; (pump) adescare; (fig)
mettere al corrente
prime minister n primo ministro
primer ['praɪmə'] n (book) testo elementare;
(paint) vernice f base inv
prime time n (Radio, TV) fascia di massimo
ascolto
primeval [praɪ'miːvl] adj primitivo(-a)
primitive ['prɪmɪtɪv] adj primitivo(-a)
primrose ['prɪmrəuz] n primavera
primus® ['praɪməs], **primus® stove** n (Brit)
fornello a petrolio
prince [prɪns] n principe m
prince charming n principe m azzurro
princess [prɪn'sɛs] n principessa
principal ['prɪnsɪpl] adj principale ■ n (of
school, college etc) preside m/f; (money) capitale
m; (in play) protagonista m/f
principality [prɪnsɪ'pælɪtɪ] n principato
principally ['prɪnsɪplɪ] adv principalmente
principle ['prɪnsɪpl] n principio; **in ~** in linea
di principio; **on ~** per principio
print [prɪnt] n (mark) impronta; (letters)
caratteri mpl; (fabric) tessuto stampato;
(Art, Phot) stampa ■ vt imprimere; (publish)
stampare, pubblicare; (write in capitals)
scrivere in stampatello; **out of ~** esaurito(-a)
▶ **print out** vt (Comput) stampare
printed circuit board [prɪntɪd-] n circuito
stampato
printed matter [prɪntɪd-] n stampe fpl
printer ['prɪntə'] n tipografo; (machine)
stampante m
printhead ['prɪntʰɛd] n testa di stampa
printing ['prɪntɪŋ] n stampa
printing press n macchina tipografica
print-out ['prɪntaut] n tabulato
print wheel n margherita
prior ['praɪə'] adj precedente ■ n (Rel) priore
m; **~ to doing** prima di fare; **without ~
notice** senza preavviso; **to have a ~ claim to
sth** avere un diritto di precedenza su qc
priority [praɪ'ɔrɪtɪ] n priorità f inv,

precedenza; **to have** or **take ~ over sth** avere la precedenza su qc
priory ['praɪərɪ] n monastero
prise [praɪz] vt: **to ~ open** forzare
prism ['prɪzəm] n prisma m
prison ['prɪzn] n prigione f
prison camp n campo di prigionia
prisoner ['prɪznəʳ] n prigioniero(-a); **to take sb ~** far prigioniero qn; **the ~ at the bar** l'accusato, l'imputato; **~ of war** prigioniero(-a) di guerra
prissy ['prɪsɪ] adj per benino
pristine ['prɪstiːn] adj originario(-a); intatto(-a); puro(-a)
privacy ['prɪvəsɪ] n solitudine f, intimità
private ['praɪvɪt] adj privato(-a); personale ■ n soldato semplice; **"~ "** (on envelope) "riservata"; **in ~** in privato; **in (his) ~ life** nella vita privata; **he is a very ~ person** è una persona molto riservata; **~ hearing** (Law) udienza a porte chiuse; **to be in ~ practice** essere medico non convenzionato (con la mutua)
private enterprise n iniziativa privata
private eye n investigatore m privato
private limited company n (Brit) società per azioni non quotata in Borsa
privately ['praɪvɪtlɪ] adv in privato; (within o.s.) dentro di sé
private parts npl (Anat) parti fpl intime
private property n proprietà privata
private school n scuola privata
privation [praɪ'veɪʃən] n (state) privazione f; (hardship) privazioni fpl, stenti mpl
privatize ['praɪvɪtaɪz] vt privatizzare
privet ['prɪvɪt] n ligustro
privilege ['prɪvɪlɪdʒ] n privilegio
privileged ['prɪvɪlɪdʒd] adj privilegiato(-a); **to be ~ to do sth** avere il privilegio or l'onore di fare qc
privy ['prɪvɪ] adj: **to be ~ to** essere al corrente di
Privy Council n (Brit) Consiglio della Corona; vedi nota

● **PRIVY COUNCIL**
●
● Il Privy Council, un gruppo di consiglieri del
● re, era il principale organo di governo
● durante il regno dei Tudor e degli Stuart.
● Col tempo ha perso la sua importanza e
● oggi è un organo senza potere effettivo
● formato da ministri e altre personalità
● politiche ed ecclesiastiche.

Privy Councillor n (Brit) Consigliere m della Corona

prize [praɪz] n premio ■ adj (example, idiot) perfetto(-a); (bull, novel) premiato(-a) ■ vt apprezzare, pregiare
prize-fighter ['praɪzfaɪtəʳ] n pugile m (che si batte per conquistare un premio)
prize giving n premiazione f
prize money n soldi mpl del premio
prizewinner ['praɪzwɪnəʳ] n premiato(-a)
prizewinning ['praɪzwɪnɪŋ] adj vincente; (novel, essay etc) premiato(-a)
PRO n abbr = **public relations officer**
pro [prəʊ] n (Sport) professionista m/f; **the pros and cons** il pro e il contro
pro- [prəʊ] prefix (in favour of) filo...; **~Soviet** adj filosovietico(-a)
pro-active [prəʊ'æktɪv] adj: **to be ~** agire d'iniziativa
probability [prɒbə'bɪlɪtɪ] n probabilità f inv; **in all ~** con ogni probabilità
probable ['prɒbəbl] adj probabile; **it is ~/ hardly ~ that ...** è probabile/poco probabile che ... + sub
probably ['prɒbəblɪ] adv probabilmente
probate ['prəʊbɪt] n (Law) omologazione f (di un testamento)
probation [prə'beɪʃən] n (in employment) periodo di prova; (Law) libertà vigilata; (Rel) probandato; **on ~** (employee) in prova; (Law) in libertà vigilata
probationary [prə'beɪʃənərɪ] adj: **~ period** periodo di prova
probe [prəʊb] n (Med, Space) sonda; (enquiry) indagine f, investigazione f ■ vt sondare, esplorare; indagare
probity ['prəʊbɪtɪ] n probità
problem ['prɒbləm] n problema m; **to have problems with the car** avere dei problemi con la macchina; **what's the ~?** che cosa c'è?; **I had no ~ in finding her** non mi è stato difficile trovarla; **no ~!** ma certamente!, non c'è problema!
problematic [prɒblə'mætɪk] adj problematico(-a)
problem-solving ['prɒbləmsɒlvɪŋ] n risoluzione f di problemi
procedure [prə'siːdʒəʳ] n (Admin, Law) procedura; (method) metodo, procedimento
proceed [prə'siːd] vi (go forward) avanzare, andare avanti; (go about it) procedere; (continue): **to ~ (with)** continuare; **to ~ to** andare a; passare a; **to ~ to do** mettersi a fare; **to ~ against sb** (Law) procedere contro qn; **I am not sure how to ~** non so bene come fare
proceedings [prə'siːdɪŋz] npl misure fpl; (Law) procedimento; (meeting) riunione f; (records) rendiconti mpl; atti mpl

p

proceeds ['prəusi:dz] *npl* profitto, incasso
process ['prəusɛs] *n* processo; (*method*)
metodo, sistema *m* ■ *vt* trattare;
(*information*) elaborare ■ *vi* [prə'sɛs] (*Brit
formal: go in procession*) sfilare, procedere in
corteo; **we are in the ~ of moving to ...**
stiamo per trasferirci a ...
processed cheese, (*US*) **process cheese** *n*
formaggio fuso
processing ['prəusɛsɪŋ] *n* trattamento;
elaborazione *f*
procession [prə'sɛʃən] *n* processione *f*,
corteo; **funeral ~** corteo funebre
pro-choice [prəu'tʃɔɪs] *adj* per la libertà di
scelta di gravidanza
proclaim [prə'kleɪm] *vt* proclamare,
dichiarare
proclamation [prɔklə'meɪʃən] *n*
proclamazione *f*
proclivity [prə'klɪvɪtɪ] *n* tendenza,
propensione *f*
procrastination [prəukræstɪ'neɪʃən] *n*
procrastinazione *f*
procreation [prəukrɪ'eɪʃən] *n* procreazione *f*
Procurator Fiscal ['prɔkjureɪtə-] *n* (*Scottish*)
procuratore *m*
procure [prə'kjuə^r] *vt* (*for o.s.*) procurarsi;
(*for sb*) procurare
procurement [prə'kjuəmənt] *n*
approvvigionamento
prod [prɔd] *vt* dare un colpetto a ■ *n* (*push,
jab*) colpetto
prodigal ['prɔdɪgl] *adj* prodigo(-a)
prodigious [prə'dɪdʒəs] *adj* prodigioso(-a)
prodigy ['prɔdɪdʒɪ] *n* prodigio
produce *n* ['prɔdju:s] (*Agr*) prodotto, prodotti
mpl ■ *vt* [prə'dju:s] produrre; (*show*) esibire,
mostrare; (*proof of identity*) produrre, fornire;
(*cause*) cagionare, causare; (*Theat*) mettere in
scena
producer [prə'dju:sə^r] *n* (*Theat*)
direttore(-trice); (*Agr, Cine*) produttore *m*
product ['prɔdʌkt] *n* prodotto
production [prə'dʌkʃən] *n* produzione *f*;
(*Theat*) messa in scena; **to put into ~**
mettere in produzione
production agreement *n* (*US*) accordo sui
tempi di produzione
production line *n* catena di lavorazione
production manager *n* production manager
m inv, direttore *m* della produzione
productive [prə'dʌktɪv] *adj* produttivo(-a)
productivity [prɔdʌk'tɪvɪtɪ] *n* produttività
productivity agreement *n* (*Brit*) accordo sui
tempi di produzione
productivity bonus *n* premio di produzione
Prof. *abbr* (= *professor*) Prof.

profane [prə'feɪn] *adj* profano(-a); (*language*)
empio(-a)
profess [prə'fɛs] *vt* professare; **I do not ~ to be
an expert** non pretendo di essere un esperto
professed [prə'fɛst] *adj* (*self-declared*)
dichiarato(-a)
profession [prə'fɛʃən] *n* professione *f*;
the professions le professioni liberali
professional [prə'fɛʃənl] *n* (*Sport*)
professionista *m/f* ■ *adj* professionale;
(*work*) da professionista; **he's a ~ man** è un
professionista; **to take ~ advice** consultare
un esperto
professionalism [prə'fɛʃnəlɪzəm] *n*
professionismo
professionally [prə'fɛʃnəlɪ] *adv*
professionalmente, in modo professionale;
(*Sport: play*) come professionista; **I only know
him ~** con lui ho solo rapporti di lavoro
professor [prə'fɛsə^r] *n* professore *m* (*titolare di
una cattedra*); (*US: teacher*) professore(-essa)
professorship [prə'fɛsəʃɪp] *n* cattedra
proffer ['prɔfə^r] *vt* (*remark*) profferire; (*apologies*)
porgere, presentare; (*one's hand*) porgere
proficiency [prə'fɪʃənsɪ] *n* competenza,
abilità
proficient [prə'fɪʃənt] *adj* competente, abile
profile ['prəufaɪl] *n* profilo; **to keep a low ~**
(*fig*) cercare di passare inosservato *or* di non
farsi notare troppo; **to maintain a high ~**
mettersi in mostra
profit ['prɔfɪt] *n* profitto; beneficio ■ *vi*: **to ~
(by *or* from)** approfittare (di); **~ and loss
account** conto perdite e profitti; **to make a
~** realizzare un profitto; **to sell sth at a ~**
vendere qc con un utile
profitability [prɔfɪtə'bɪlɪtɪ] *n* redditività
profitable ['prɔfɪtəbl] *adj* redditizio(-a); (*fig:
beneficial*) vantaggioso(-a); (: *meeting, visit*)
fruttuoso(-a)
profit centre *n* centro di profitto
profiteering [prɔfɪ'tɪərɪŋ] *n* (*pej*) affarismo
profit-making ['prɔfɪtmeɪkɪŋ] *adj* a scopo di
lucro
profit margin *n* margine *m* di profitto
profit-sharing ['prɔfɪtʃɛərɪŋ] *n*
compartecipazione *f* agli utili
profits tax *n* (*Brit*) imposta sugli utili
profligate ['prɔflɪgɪt] *adj* (*dissolute: behaviour*)
dissipato(-a); (: *person*) debosciato(-a);
(*extravagant*): **he's very ~ with his money** è
uno che sperpera i suoi soldi
pro forma ['prəu'fɔ:mə] *adv*: **~ invoice** fattura
proforma
profound [prə'faund] *adj* profondo(-a)
profuse [prə'fju:s] *adj* infinito(-a),
abbondante

profusely [prəˈfjuːslɪ] *adv* con grande
effusione

profusion [prəˈfjuːʒən] *n* profusione *f*,
abbondanza

progeny [ˈprɒdʒɪnɪ] *n* progenie *f*; discendenti
mpl

programme, *(US)* **program** [ˈprəʊgræm] *n*
programma *m* ■ *vt* programmare

programmer, programer [ˈprəʊgræməʳ] *n*
programmatore(-trice)

programming, programing [ˈprəʊgræmɪŋ]
n programmazione *f*

**programming language, programing
language** *n* linguaggio di programmazione

progress *n* [ˈprəʊgrɛs] progresso ■ *vi*
[prəˈgrɛs] *(go forward)* avanzare, procedere;
(in time) procedere; *(also:* **make progress)** far
progressi; **in ~** in corso

progression [prəˈgrɛʃən] *n* progressione *f*

progressive [prəˈgrɛsɪv] *adj* progressivo(-a);
(person) progressista

progressively [prəˈgrɛsɪvlɪ] *adv*
progressivamente

progress report *n* *(Med)* bollettino medico;
(Admin) rendiconto dei lavori

prohibit [prəˈhɪbɪt] *vt* proibire, vietare; **to ~
sb from doing sth** vietare *or* proibire a qn di
fare qc; **"smoking prohibited"** "vietato
fumare"

prohibition [prəʊɪˈbɪʃən] *n* *(US)*
proibizionismo

prohibitive [prəˈhɪbɪtɪv] *adj* *(price etc)*
proibitivo(-a)

project *n* [ˈprɒdʒɛkt] *(plan)* piano; *(venture)*
progetto; *(Scol)* studio, ricerca ■ *vt*
[prəˈdʒɛkt] proiettare ■ *vi* *(stick out)* sporgere

projectile [prəˈdʒɛktaɪl] *n* proiettile *m*

projection [prəˈdʒɛkʃən] *n* proiezione *f*;
sporgenza

projectionist [prəˈdʒɛkʃənɪst] *n* *(Cine)*
proiezionista *m/f*

projection room *n* *(Cine)* cabina *or* sala di
proiezione

projector [prəˈdʒɛktəʳ] *n* proiettore *m*

proletarian [prəʊlɪˈtɛərɪən] *adj, n*
proletario(-a)

proletariat [prəʊlɪˈtɛərɪət] *n* proletariato

pro-life [prəʊˈlaɪf] *adj* per il diritto alla, vita

proliferate [prəˈlɪfəreɪt] *vi* proliferare

proliferation [prəlɪfəˈreɪʃən] *n*
proliferazione *f*

prolific [prəˈlɪfɪk] *adj* prolifico(-a)

prologue, *(US)* **prolog** [ˈprəʊlɒg] *n* prologo

prolong [prəˈlɒŋ] *vt* prolungare

prom [prɒm] *n abbr* = **promenade**;
promenade concert; *(US: ball)* ballo
studentesco; *vedi nota*

promenade [prɒməˈnɑːd] *n* *(by sea)*
lungomare *m*

promenade concert *n* concerto *(con posti in
piedi)*

promenade deck *n* *(Naut)* ponte *m* di
passeggiata

prominence [ˈprɒmɪnəns] *n* prominenza;
importanza

prominent [ˈprɒmɪnənt] *adj* *(standing out)*
prominente; *(important)* importante; **he is ~
in the field of ...** è un'autorità nel campo
di ....

prominently [ˈprɒmɪnəntlɪ] *adv* *(display, set)*
ben in vista; **he figured ~ in the case** ha
avuto una parte di primo piano nella
faccenda

promiscuity [prɒmɪsˈkjuːɪtɪ] *n* *(sexual)*
rapporti *mpl* multipli

promiscuous [prəˈmɪskjuəs] *adj* *(sexually)*
di facili costumi

promise [ˈprɒmɪs] *n* promessa ■ *vt, vi*
promettere; **to make sb a ~** fare una
promessa a qn; **a young man of ~** un
giovane promettente; **to ~ (sb) to do sth**
promettere (a qn) di fare qc

promising [ˈprɒmɪsɪŋ] *adj* promettente

promissory note [ˈprɒmɪsərɪ-] *n* pagherò *m
inv*

promontory [ˈprɒməntrɪ] *n* promontorio

promote [prəˈməʊt] *vt* promuovere; *(venture,
event)* organizzare; *(product)* lanciare,
reclamizzare; **the team was promoted to
the second division** *(Brit Football)* la squadra
è stata promossa in serie B

promoter [prəˈməʊtəʳ] *n* *(of sporting event)*
organizzatore(-trice); *(of cause etc)*
sostenitore(-trice)

promotion [prəˈməʊʃən] *n* promozione *f*

prompt [prɒmpt] *adj* rapido(-a), svelto(-a);
puntuale; *(reply)* sollecito(-a) ■ *adv*
(punctually) in punto ■ *n* *(Comput)* guida ■ *vt*
incitare; provocare; *(Theat)* suggerire a; **at 8
o'clock ~** alle 8 in punto; **to be ~ to do sth**
essere sollecito nel fare qc; **to ~ sb to do**
spingere qn a fare

p

prompter ['prɔmptəʳ] n (Theat) suggeritore m
promptly ['prɔmptlɪ] adv prontamente;
puntualmente
promptness ['prɔmptnɪs] n prontezza;
puntualità
prone [prəun] adj (lying) prono(-a); ~ to
propenso(-a) a, incline a; to be ~ to illness
essere soggetto(-a) a malattie; she is ~ to
burst into tears if ... può facilmente
scoppiare in lacrime se ...
prong [prɔŋ] n rebbio, punta
pronoun ['prəunaun] n pronome m
pronounce [prə'nauns] vt pronunziare ■ vi:
to ~ (up)on pronunziare su; they
pronounced him unfit to drive lo hanno
dichiarato inabile alla guida
pronounced [prə'naunst] adj (marked)
spiccato(-a)
pronouncement [prə'naunsmənt] n
dichiarazione f
pronunciation [prənʌnsɪ'eɪʃən] n pronunzia
proof [pru:f] n prova; (of book) bozza; (Phot)
provino; (of alcohol): 70% ~ ≈ 40° in volume
■ vt (tent, anorak) impermeabilizzare ■ adj:
~ against a prova di
proofreader ['pru:fri:dəʳ] n correttore(-trice)
di bozze
prop [prɔp] n sostegno, appoggio ■ vt (also:
prop up) sostenere, appoggiare; (lean): to ~
sth against appoggiare qc contro or a
Prop. abbr (Comm) = **proprietor**
propaganda [prɔpə'gændə] n propaganda
propagation [prɔpə'geɪʃən] n propagazione f
propel [prə'pɛl] vt spingere (in avanti),
muovere
propeller [prə'pɛləʳ] n elica
propelling pencil [prə'pɛlɪŋ-] n (Brit) matita
a mina
propensity [prə'pɛnsɪtɪ] n tendenza
proper ['prɔpəʳ] adj (suited, right) adatto(-a),
appropriato(-a); (seemly) decente; (authentic)
vero(-a); (col: real) 'n' + vero(-a) e proprio(-a);
to go through the ~ channels (Admin)
seguire la regolare procedura
properly ['prɔpəlɪ] adv decentemente; (really,
thoroughly) veramente
proper noun n nome m proprio
property ['prɔpətɪ] n (things owned) beni mpl;
(land, building, Chem etc) proprietà f inv
property developer n (Brit) costruttore m
edile
property owner n proprietario(-a)
property tax n imposta patrimoniale
prophecy ['prɔfɪsɪ] n profezia
prophesy ['prɔfɪsaɪ] vt predire, profetizzare
prophet ['prɔfɪt] n profeta m
prophetic [prə'fɛtɪk] adj profetico(-a)

proportion [prə'pɔːʃən] n proporzione f;
(share) parte f ■ vt proporzionare,
commisurare; to be in/out of ~ to sth
sth essere in proporzione/sproporzionato
rispetto a qc; to see sth in ~ (fig) dare il
giusto peso a qc
proportional [prə'pɔːʃənl] adj proporzionale
proportional representation n
rappresentanza proporzionale
proportionate [prə'pɔːʃənɪt] adj
proporzionato(-a)
proposal [prə'pəuzl] n proposta; (plan)
progetto; (of marriage) proposta di
matrimonio
propose [prə'pəuz] vt proporre, suggerire
■ vi fare una proposta di matrimonio; to ~
to do proporsi di fare, aver l'intenzione di
fare
proposer [prə'pəuzəʳ] n (Brit: of motion)
proponente m/f
proposition [prɔpə'zɪʃən] n proposizione f;
(proposal) proposta; to make sb a ~ proporre
qualcosa a qn
propound [prə'paund] vt proporre,
presentare
proprietary [prə'praɪətərɪ] adj: ~ article
prodotto con marchio depositato; ~ brand
marchio di fabbrica
proprietor [prə'praɪətəʳ] n proprietario(-a)
propriety [prə'praɪətɪ] n (seemliness) decoro,
rispetto delle convenienze sociali
propulsion [prə'pʌlʃən] n propulsione f
pro rata [prəu'rɑːtə] adv in proporzione
prosaic [prəu'zeɪɪk] adj prosaico(-a)
Pros. Atty. abbr (US) = **prosecuting attorney**
proscribe [prə'skraɪb] vt proscrivere
prose [prəuz] n prosa; (Scol: translation)
traduzione f dalla madrelingua
prosecute ['prɔsɪkjuːt] vt intentare azione
contro
prosecuting attorney ['prɔsɪkjuːtɪŋ-] n (US)
≈ procuratore m
prosecution [prɔsɪ'kjuːʃən] n (Law) azione f
giudiziaria; (accusing side) accusa
prosecutor ['prɔsɪkjuːtəʳ] n (also: public
prosecutor) ≈ procuratore m della
Repubblica
prospect n ['prɔspɛkt] prospettiva; (hope)
speranza ■ vt [prə'spɛkt] esplorare ■ vi: to ~
for gold cercare l'oro; there is every ~ of an
early victory tutto lascia prevedere una
rapida vittoria; see also prospects
prospecting [prə'spɛktɪŋ] n prospezione f
prospective [prə'spɛktɪv] adj (buyer)
probabile; (legislation, son-in-law) futuro(-a)
prospector [prə'spɛktəʳ] n prospettore m;
gold ~ cercatore m d'oro

prospects [ˈprɔspɛkts] *npl (for work etc)*
prospettive *fpl*
prospectus [prəˈspɛktəs] *n* prospetto,
programma *m*
prosper [ˈprɔspəʳ] *vi* prosperare
prosperity [prɔˈspɛrɪtɪ] *n* prosperità
prosperous [ˈprɔspərəs] *adj* prospero(-a)
prostate [ˈprɔsteɪt] *n (also:* **prostate gland**)
prostata, ghiandola prostatica
prostitute [ˈprɔstɪtjuːt] *n* prostituta; **male ~**
uomo che si prostituisce
prostitution [prɔstɪˈtjuːʃən] *n* prostituzione *f*
prostrate *adj* [ˈprɔstreɪt] prostrato(-a) ▪ *vt*
[prɔˈstreɪt]: **to ~ o.s.** *(before sb)* prostrarsi
protagonist [prəˈtægənɪst] *n* protagonista *m/f*
protect [prəˈtɛkt] *vt* proteggere,
salvaguardare
protection [prəˈtɛkʃən] *n* protezione *f*; **to be
under sb's ~** essere sotto la protezione di qn
protectionism [prəˈtɛkʃənɪzəm] *n*
protezionismo
protection racket *n* racket *m inv*
protective [prəˈtɛktɪv] *adj* protettivo(-a);
~ custody *(Law)* protezione *f*
protector [prəˈtɛktəʳ] *n* protettore(-trice)
protégé [ˈprəʊtɪʒeɪ] *n* protetto
protégée [ˈprəʊtɪʒeɪ] *n* protetta
protein [ˈprəʊtiːn] *n* proteina
pro tem [prəʊˈtɛm] *adv abbr (for the time being:
= pro tempore)* pro tempore
protest *n* [ˈprəʊtɛst] protesta ▪ *vt, vi*
[prəˈtɛst] protestare; **to do sth under ~** fare
qc protestando; **to ~ against/about**
protestare contro/per
Protestant [ˈprɔtɪstənt] *adj, n* protestante
(m/f)
protester, protestor [prəˈtɛstəʳ] *n (in
demonstration)* dimostrante *m/f*
protest march *n* marcia di protesta
protocol [ˈprəʊtəkɔl] *n* protocollo
prototype [ˈprəʊtətaɪp] *n* prototipo
protracted [prəˈtræktɪd] *adj* tirato(-a) per le
lunghe
protractor [prəˈtræktəʳ] *n (Geom)* goniometro
protrude [prəˈtruːd] *vi* sporgere
protuberance [prəˈtjuːbərəns] *n* sporgenza
proud [praud] *adj* fiero(-a), orgoglioso(-a);
(pej) superbo(-a); **to be ~ to do sth** essere
onorato(-a) di fare qc; **to do sb ~** non far
mancare nulla a qn; **to do o.s. ~** trattarsi
bene
proudly [ˈpraudlɪ] *adv* con orgoglio,
fieramente
prove [pruːv] *vt* provare, dimostrare ▪ *vi*:
to ~ correct *etc* risultare vero(-a) *etc*; **to ~ o.s.**
mostrare le proprie capacità; **to ~ o.s./itself
(to be) useful** *etc* mostrarsi *or* rivelarsi utile

etc; **he was proved right in the end** alla
fine i fatti gli hanno dato ragione
Provence [prɔvɑ̃s] *n* Provenza
proverb [ˈprɔvəːb] *n* proverbio
proverbial [prəˈvəːbɪəl] *adj* proverbiale
provide [prəˈvaɪd] *vt* fornire, provvedere;
to ~ sb with sth fornire *or* provvedere qn di
qc; **to be provided with** essere dotato *or*
munito di
▸ **provide for** *vt fus* provvedere a
provided [prəˈvaɪdɪd] *conj*: **~ (that)** purché
+*sub*, a condizione che+*sub*
Providence [ˈprɔvɪdəns] *n* Provvidenza
providing [prəˈvaɪdɪŋ] *conj* purché+*sub*,
a condizione che+*sub*
province [ˈprɔvɪns] *n* provincia
provincial [prəˈvɪnʃəl] *adj* provinciale
provision [prəˈvɪʒən] *n (supply)* riserva;
(supplying) provvista; rifornimento;
(stipulation) condizione *f*; **provisions** *npl
(food)* provviste *fpl*; **to make ~ for** *(one's family,
future)* pensare a; **there's no ~ for this in the
contract** il contratto non lo prevede
provisional [prəˈvɪʒənl] *adj* provvisorio(-a)
▪ *n*: **P~** *(Irish Pol)* provisional *m inv*
provisional licence *n (Brit Aut)* ≈ foglio *m*
rosa *inv*
provisionally [prəˈvɪʒnəlɪ] *adv*
provvisoriamente; *(appoint)* a titolo
provvisorio
proviso [prəˈvaɪzəu] *n* condizione *f*; **with the
~ that** a condizione che+*sub*, a patto che+*sub*
Provo [ˈprɔvəu] *n abbr (col)* = **Provisional**
provocation [prɔvəˈkeɪʃən] *n* provocazione *f*
provocative [prəˈvɔkətɪv] *adj (aggressive)*
provocatorio(-a); *(thought-provoking)*
stimolante; *(seductive)* provocante
provoke [prəˈvəuk] *vt* provocare; incitare;
to ~ sb to sth/to do *or* **into doing sth**
spingere qn a qc/a fare qc
provoking [prəˈvəukɪŋ] *adj* irritante,
esasperante
provost [ˈprɔvəst] *n (Brit: of university)* rettore
m; *(Scottish)* sindaco
prow [prau] *n* prua
prowess [ˈprauɪs] *n* prodezza; **his ~ as a
footballer** le sue capacità di calciatore
prowl [praul] *vi (also:* **prowl about, prowl
around)** aggirarsi furtivamente ▪ *n*: **on the
~** in cerca di preda
prowler [ˈprauləʳ] *n* tipo sospetto *(che s'aggira
con l'intenzione di rubare, aggredire etc)*
proximity [prɔkˈsɪmɪtɪ] *n* prossimità
proxy [ˈprɔksɪ] *n* procura; **by ~** per procura
PRP *n abbr* (= *performance related pay*)
retribuzione *f* commensurata al
rendimento

731

prude [pruːd] *n* puritano(-a)
prudence ['pruːdns] *n* prudenza
prudent ['pruːdnt] *adj* prudente
prudish ['pruːdɪʃ] *adj* puritano(-a)
prune [pruːn] *n* prugna secca ■ *vt* potare
pry [praɪ] *vi*: **to ~ into** ficcare il naso in
PS *n abbr* (= *postscript*) P.S.
psalm [sɑːm] *n* salmo
PSAT® *n abbr* (US) = **Preliminary Scholastic Aptitude Test**
PSBR *n abbr* (Brit: = *public sector borrowing requirement*) *fabbisogno di prestiti per il settore pubblico*
pseud ['sjuːd] *n* (Brit col: *intellectually*) intellettualoide *m/f*; (: *socially*) snob *m/f inv*
pseudo- ['sjuːdəu] *prefix* pseudo...
pseudonym ['sjuːdənɪm] *n* pseudonimo
PSHE *n abbr* (Brit: Scol: = *personal, social and health education*) *formazione di formazione sociale e sanitaria*
PST *abbr* (US: = *Pacific Standard Time*) *ora invernale del Pacifico*
psyche ['saɪkɪ] *n* psiche *f*
psychedelic [saɪkɪ'dɛlɪk] *adj* psichedelico(-a)
psychiatric [saɪkɪ'ætrɪk] *adj* psichiatrico(-a)
psychiatrist [saɪ'kaɪətrɪst] *n* psichiatra *m/f*
psychiatry [saɪ'kaɪətrɪ] *n* psichiatria
psychic ['saɪkɪk] *adj* (*also*: **psychical**) psichico(-a); (*person*) dotato(-a) di qualità telepatiche
psycho ['saɪkəu] *n* (*col*) folle *m/f*, psicopatico(-a)
psychoanalyse [saɪkəu'ænəlaɪz] *vt* psicanalizzare
psychoanalysis (*pl* **-ses**) [saɪkəuə'nælɪsɪs, -siːz] *n* psicanalisi *f inv*
psychoanalyst [saɪkəu'ænəlɪst] *n* psicanalista *m/f*
psychological [saɪkə'lɔdʒɪkl] *adj* psicologico(-a)
psychologist [saɪ'kɔlədʒɪst] *n* psicologo(-a)
psychology [saɪ'kɔlədʒɪ] *n* psicologia
psychopath ['saɪkəupæθ] *n* psicopatico(-a)
psychosis (*pl* **psychoses**) [saɪ'kəusɪs, -siːz] *n* psicosi *f inv*
psychosomatic [saɪkəusə'mætɪk] *adj* psicosomatico(-a)
psychotherapy [saɪkəu'θɛrəpɪ] *n* psicoterapia
psychotic [saɪ'kɔtɪk] *adj, n* psicotico(-a)
PT *n abbr* (Brit: = *physical training*) ed. fisica
pt *abbr* (= *pint, point*) pt
Pt. *abbr* (*in place names*: = *Point*) Pt.
PTA *n abbr* (= *Parent-Teacher Association*) *associazione genitori e insegnanti*
Pte. *abbr* (Brit Mil) = **private**
PTO *abbr* (= *please turn over*) v.r. (= *vedi retro*)

PTV *n abbr* (US) = **pay television; public television**
pub [pʌb] *n abbr* (= *public house*) pub *m inv*; *vedi nota*

● **PUB**
●
● In Gran Bretagna e in Irlanda i *pubs* sono
● locali dove vengono servite bibite
● alcoliche ed analcoliche e dove è anche
● possibile mangiare. Sono punti di ritrovo
● dove spesso si può giocare a biliardo, a
● freccette o guardare la televisione. Le
● leggi che regolano la vendita degli alcolici
● sono molto severe in Gran Bretagna e
● quindi gli orari di apertura e di chiusura
● vengono osservati scrupolosamente.

pub crawl *n*: **to go on a ~** (Brit col) fare il giro dei pub
puberty ['pjuːbətɪ] *n* pubertà
pubic ['pjuːbɪk] *adj* pubico(-a), del pube
public ['pʌblɪk] *adj* pubblico(-a) ■ *n* pubblico; **in ~** in pubblico; **the general ~** il pubblico; **to make sth ~** render noto *or* di pubblico dominio qc; **to be ~ knowledge** essere di dominio pubblico; **to go ~** (Comm) emettere le azioni sul mercato
public address system *n* impianto di amplificazione
publican ['pʌblɪkən] *n* (Brit) gestore *m* (*or* proprietario) di un pub
publication [pʌblɪ'keɪʃən] *n* pubblicazione *f*
public company *n* ≈ società *f inv* per azioni (*costituita tramite pubblica sottoscrizione*)
public convenience *n* (Brit) gabinetti *mpl*
public holiday *n* (Brit) giorno festivo, festa nazionale
public house *n* (Brit) pub *m inv*
publicity [pʌb'lɪsɪtɪ] *n* pubblicità
publicize ['pʌblɪsaɪz] *vt* fare (della) pubblicità a, reclamizzare
public limited company *n* ≈ società per azioni a responsabilità limitata (*quotata in Borsa*)
publicly ['pʌblɪklɪ] *adv* pubblicamente
public opinion *n* opinione *f* pubblica
public ownership *n* proprietà pubblica *or* sociale; **to be taken into ~** essere statalizzato(-a)
public prosecutor *n* pubblico ministero; **~'s office** ufficio del pubblico ministero
public relations *n* pubbliche relazioni *fpl*
public relations officer *n* addetto(-a) alle pubbliche relazioni
public school *n* (Brit) scuola privata; (US) scuola statale; *vedi nota*

● PUBLIC SCHOOL

In Inghilterra le *public schools* sono scuole o
collegi privati di istruzione secondaria,
spesso di un certo prestigio. In Scozia e
negli Stati Uniti, invece, le *public schools*
sono scuole pubbliche gratuite
amministrate dallo stato.

public sector *n* settore *m* pubblico
public service vehicle *n* (*Brit*) mezzo
pubblico
public-spirited [pʌblɪk'spɪrɪtɪd] *adj* che ha
senso civico
public transport, (US) **public
transportation** *n* mezzi *mpl* pubblici
public utility *n* servizio pubblico
public works *npl* lavori *mpl* pubblici
publish ['pʌblɪʃ] *vt* pubblicare
publisher ['pʌblɪʃəʳ] *n* editore *m*; (*firm*) casa
editrice
publishing ['pʌblɪʃɪŋ] *n* (*industry*) editoria;
(*of a book*) pubblicazione *f*
publishing company *n* casa *or* società
editrice
pub lunch *n*: **to go for a ~** andare a mangiare
al pub
puce [pju:s] *adj* color pulce *inv*
puck [pʌk] *n* (*Ice Hockey*) disco
pucker ['pʌkəʳ] *vt* corrugare
pudding ['pudɪŋ] *n* budino; (*dessert*) dolce *m*;
black ~, (US) **blood ~** sanguinaccio; **rice ~**
budino di riso
puddle ['pʌdl] *n* pozza, pozzanghera
puerile ['pjuəraɪl] *adj* puerile
Puerto Rico ['pwəːtəu'riːkəu] *n* Portorico
puff [pʌf] *n* sbuffo; (*also*: **powder puff**)
piumino ■ *vt* (*also*: **puff out**: *sails, cheeks*)
gonfiare ■ *vi* uscire a sbuffi; (*pant*) ansare;
to ~ out smoke mandar fuori sbuffi di
fumo; **to ~ one's pipe** tirare sboccate di
fumo
puffed [pʌft] *adj* (*col*: *out of breath*) senza fiato
puffin ['pʌfɪn] *n* puffino
puff pastry, (US) **puff paste** *n* pasta sfoglia
puffy ['pʌfɪ] *adj* gonfio(-a)
pugnacious [pʌg'neɪʃəs] *adj* combattivo(-a)
pull [pul] *n* (*tug*) strattone *m*, tirata; (*of moon,
magnet, the sea etc*) attrazione *f*; (*fig*) influenza
■ *vt* tirare; (*muscle*) strappare, farsi uno
strappo a ■ *vi* tirare; **to give sth a ~** tirare
su qc; **to ~ a face** fare una smorfia; **to ~ to
pieces** fare a pezzi; **to ~ one's punches**
(*Boxing*) risparmiare l'avversario; **not to ~
one's punches** (*fig*) non avere peli sulla
lingua; **to ~ one's weight** dare il proprio
contributo; **to ~ o.s. together** ricomporsi,

riprendersi; **to ~ sb's leg** prendere in giro
qn; **to ~ strings (for sb)** muovere qualche
pedina (per qn)
▶ **pull about** *vt* (*Brit: handle roughly: object*)
strapazzare; (: *person*) malmenare
▶ **pull apart** *vt* (*break*) fare a pezzi
▶ **pull down** *vt* (*house*) demolire; (*tree*)
abbattere
▶ **pull in** *vi* (*Aut: at the kerb*) accostarsi; (*Rail*)
entrare in stazione
▶ **pull off** *vt* (*deal etc*) portare a compimento
▶ **pull out** *vi* partire; (*withdraw*) ritirarsi;
(*Aut: come out of line*) spostarsi sulla mezzeria
■ *vt* staccare; far uscire; (*withdraw*) ritirare
▶ **pull over** *vi* (*Aut*) accostare
▶ **pull round** *vi* (*unconscious person*) rinvenire;
(*sick person*) ristabilirsi
▶ **pull through** *vi* farcela
▶ **pull up** *vi* (*stop*) fermarsi ■ *vt* (*uproot*)
sradicare; (*stop*) fermare
pulley ['pulɪ] *n* puleggia, carrucola
pull-out ['pulaut] *n* inserto ■ *cpd* staccabile
pullover ['puləuvəʳ] *n* pullover *m inv*
pulp [pʌlp] *n* (*of fruit*) polpa; (*for paper*) pasta
per carta; (*magazines, books*) stampa di qualità
e di tono scadenti; **to reduce sth to ~**
spappolare qc
pulpit ['pulpɪt] *n* pulpito
pulsate [pʌl'seɪt] *vi* battere, palpitare
pulse [pʌls] *n* polso; **to feel** *or* **take sb's ~**
sentire *or* tastare il polso a qn
pulses ['pʌlsəz] *npl* (*Culin*) legumi *mpl*
pulverize ['pʌlvəraɪz] *vt* polverizzare
puma ['pju:mə] *n* puma *m inv*
pumice ['pʌmɪs], **pumice stone** ['pʌmɪs-] *n*
(pietra) pomice *f*
pummel ['pʌml] *vt* dare pugni a
pump [pʌmp] *n* pompa; (*shoe*) scarpetta ■ *vt*
pompare; (*fig: col*) far parlare; **to ~ sb for
information** cercare di strappare delle
informazioni a qn
▶ **pump up** *vt* gonfiare
pumpkin ['pʌmpkɪn] *n* zucca
pun [pʌn] *n* gioco di parole
punch [pʌntʃ] *n* (*blow*) pugno; (*fig: force*) forza;
(*tool*) punzone *m*; (*drink*) ponce *m* ■ *vt* (*hit*):
to ~ sb/sth dare un pugno a qn/qc; **to ~ a
hole (in)** fare un buco (in)
▶ **punch in** *vi* (US) timbrare il cartellino
(all'entrata)
▶ **punch out** *vi* (US) timbrare il cortellino
(all'uscita)
punch card, punched card ['pʌntʃ-] *n*
scheda perforata
punch-drunk ['pʌntʃdrʌŋk] *adj* (*Brit*)
stordito(-a)
punch line *n* (*of joke*) battuta finale

P

punch-up ['pʌntʃʌp] n (Brit col) rissa
punctual ['pʌŋktjuəl] adj puntuale
punctuality [pʌŋktju'ælɪtɪ] n puntualità
punctually [pʌŋktjuəlɪ] adv puntualmente;
 it will start ~ at 6 comincerà alle 6 precise or
 in punto
punctuate ['pʌŋktjueɪt] vt punteggiare
punctuation [pʌŋktju'eɪʃən] n
 interpunzione f, punteggiatura
punctuation mark n segno d'interpunzione
puncture ['pʌŋktʃəʳ] n (Brit) foratura ■ vt
 forare; **to have a ~** (Aut) forare (una gomma)
pundit ['pʌndɪt] n sapientone(-a)
pungent ['pʌndʒənt] adj piccante; (fig)
 mordace, caustico(-a)
punish ['pʌnɪʃ] vt punire; **to ~ sb for sth/for
 doing sth** punire qn per qc/per aver fatto qc
punishable ['pʌnɪʃəbl] adj punibile
punishing ['pʌnɪʃɪŋ] adj (fig: exhausting)
 sfiancante
punishment ['pʌnɪʃmənt] n punizione f;
 (fig, col): **to take a lot of ~** (boxer) incassare
 parecchi colpi; (car) essere messo(-a) a dura
 prova
punk [pʌŋk] n (person: also: **punk rocker**) punk
 m/f inv; (music: also: **punk rock**) musica punk,
 punk rock m; (US col: hoodlum) teppista m
punt [pʌnt] n (boat) barchino; (Football) colpo
 a volo; (Irish) sterlina irlandese ■ vi (Brit: bet)
 scommettere
punter ['pʌntəʳ] n (Brit: gambler)
 scommettitore(-trice)
puny ['pjuːnɪ] adj gracile
pup [pʌp] n cucciolo(-a)
pupil ['pjuːpl] n allievo(-a); (Anat) pupilla
puppet ['pʌpɪt] n burattino
puppet government n governo fantoccio
puppy ['pʌpɪ] n cucciolo(-a), cagnolino(-a)
purchase ['pəːtʃɪs] n acquisto, compera; (grip)
 presa ■ vt comprare; **to get a ~ on** (grip)
 trovare un appoggio su
purchase order n ordine m d'acquisto,
 ordinazione f
purchase price n prezzo d'acquisto
purchaser ['pəːtʃɪsəʳ] n compratore(-trice)
purchase tax n (Brit) tassa d'acquisto
purchasing power ['pəːtʃɪsɪŋ-] n potere m
 d'acquisto
pure [pjuəʳ] adj puro(-a); **a ~ wool jumper** un
 golf di pura lana; **it's laziness ~ and simple**
 è pura pigrizia
purebred ['pjuəbred] adj di razza pura
purée ['pjuəreɪ] n purè m inv
purely ['pjuəlɪ] adv puramente
purge [pəːdʒ] n (Med) purga; (Pol) epurazione f
 ■ vt purgare; (fig) epurare
purification [pjuərɪfɪ'keɪʃən] n purificazione f

purify ['pjuərɪfaɪ] vt purificare
purist ['pjuərɪst] n purista m/f
puritan ['pjuərɪtən] adj, n puritano(-a)
puritanical [pjuərɪ'tænɪkl] adj puritano(-a)
purity ['pjuərɪtɪ] n purità
purl [pəːl] n punto rovescio ■ vt lavorare a
 rovescio
purloin [pəː'lɔɪn] vt rubare
purple ['pəːpl] adj di porpora; viola inv
purport [pəː'pɔːt] vi: **to ~ to be/do** pretendere
 di essere/fare
purpose ['pəːpəs] n intenzione f, scopo; **on ~**
 apposta, di proposito; **for illustrative
 purposes** a titolo illustrativo; **for teaching
 purposes** per l'insegnamento; **for the
 purposes of this meeting** agli effetti di
 questa riunione; **to no ~** senza nessun
 risultato, inutilmente
purpose-built ['pəːpəs'bɪlt] adj (Brit)
 costruito(-a) allo scopo
purposeful ['pəːpəsful] adj deciso(-a),
 risoluto(-a)
purposely ['pəːpəslɪ] adv apposta
purr [pəːʳ] n fusa fpl ■ vi fare le fusa
purse [pəːs] n borsellino; (US: handbag)
 borsetta, borsa ■ vt contrarre
purser ['pəːsəʳ] n (Naut) commissario di bordo
purse snatcher [-'snætʃəʳ] n (US) scippatore m
pursue [pə'sjuː] vt inseguire; essere alla
 ricerca di; (inquiry, matter) approfondire
pursuer [pə'sjuːəʳ] n inseguitore(-trice)
pursuit [pə'sjuːt] n inseguimento;
 (occupation) occupazione f, attività f inv;
 in (the) ~ of sth alla ricerca di qc; **scientific
 pursuits** ricerche fpl scientifiche
purveyor [pə'veɪəʳ] n fornitore(-trice)
pus [pʌs] n pus m
push [puʃ] n spinta; (effort) grande sforzo;
 (drive) energia ■ vt spingere; (button)
 premere; (thrust): **to ~ sth (into)** ficcare qc
 (in); (fig) fare pubblicità a ■ vi spingere;
 premere; **to ~ a door open/shut** aprire/
 chiudere una porta con una spinta or
 spingendola; **to be pushed for time/
 money** essere a corto di tempo/soldi; **she is
 pushing 50** (col) va per i 50; **to ~ for** (better
 pay, conditions etc) fare pressione per ottenere;
 "~" (on door) "spingere"; (on bell) "suonare";
 at a ~ (Brit col) in caso di necessità
 ▶ **push aside** vt scostare
 ▶ **push in** vi introdursi a forza
 ▶ **push off** vi (col) filare
 ▶ **push on** vi (continue) continuare
 ▶ **push over** vt far cadere
 ▶ **push through** vt (measure) far approvare
 ▶ **push up** vt (total, prices) far salire
push-bike ['puʃbaɪk] n (Brit) bicicletta

push-button ['puʃbʌtn] *adj* a pulsante
pushchair ['puʃtʃeəʳ] *n* passeggino
pusher ['puʃəʳ] *n* (*also*: **drug pusher**)
spacciatore(-trice) (di droga)
pushover ['puʃəuvəʳ] *n* (*col*): **it's a ~** è un
lavoro da bambini
push-up ['puʃʌp] *n* (US) flessione *f* sulle braccia
pushy ['puʃɪ] *adj* (*pej*) troppo intraprendente
puss [pus], **pussy** ['pusɪ], **pussy-cat**
['pusɪkæt] *n* micio
put (*pt, pp* **~**) [put] *vt* mettere, porre; (*say*) dire,
esprimere; (*a question*) fare; (*estimate*) stimare
■ *adv*: **to stay ~** non muoversi; **to ~ sb to bed**
mettere qn a letto; **to ~ sb in a good/bad
mood** mettere qn di buon/cattivo umore; **to
~ sb to a lot of trouble** scomodare qn; **to ~ a
lot of time into sth** dedicare molto tempo a
qc; **to ~ money on a horse** scommettere su
un cavallo; **how shall I ~ it?** come dire?;
I ~ it to you that ... (*Brit*) io sostengo che ...
▶ **put about** *vi* (*Naut*) virare di bordo ■ *vt*
(*rumour*) diffondere
▶ **put across** *vt* (*ideas etc*) comunicare, far
capire
▶ **put aside** *vt* (*lay down: book etc*) mettere da
una parte, posare; (*save*) mettere da parte;
(*in shop*) tenere da parte
▶ **put away** *vt* (*clothes, toys etc*) mettere via
▶ **put back** *vt* (*replace*) rimettere (a posto);
(*postpone*) rinviare; (*delay*) ritardare; (*set back:
watch, clock*) mettere indietro; **this will ~ us
back 10 years** questo ci farà tornare indietro
di 10 anni
▶ **put by** *vt* (*money*) mettere da parte
▶ **put down** *vt* (*parcel etc*) posare, mettere giù;
(*pay*) versare; (*in writing*) mettere per iscritto;
(*suppress: revolt etc*) reprimere, sopprimere;
(*attribute*) attribuire
▶ **put forward** *vt* (*ideas*) avanzare, proporre;
(*date*) anticipare
▶ **put in** *vt* (*application, complaint*) presentare
▶ **put in for** *vt fus* (*job*) far domanda per;
(*promotion*) far domanda di
▶ **put off** *vt* (*postpone*) rimandare, rinviare;
(*discourage*) dissuadere
▶ **put on** *vt* (*clothes, lipstick etc*) mettere; (*light
etc*) accendere; (*play etc*) mettere in scena;
(*concert, exhibition etc*) allestire, organizzare;
(*extra bus, train etc*) mettere in servizio; (*food,
meal*) servire; (*brake*) mettere; (*assume: accent,
manner*) affettare; (*col: tease*) prendere in giro;
(*inform, indicate*): **to ~ sb on to sb/sth** indicare
qn/qc a qn; **to ~ on weight** ingrassare;
to ~ on airs darsi delle arie

▶ **put out** *vt* mettere fuori; (*one's hand*)
porgere; (*light etc*) spegnere; (*person:
inconvenience*) scomodare; (*dislocate: shoulder,
knee*) lussarsi; (*: back*) farsi uno strappo a ■ *vi*
(*Naut*): **to ~ out to sea** prendere il largo; **to ~
out from Plymouth** partire da Plymouth
▶ **put through** *vt* (*caller*) mettere in
comunicazione; (*call*) passare; **~ me
through to Miss Blair** mi passi la signorina
Blair
▶ **put together** *vt* mettere insieme, riunire;
(*assemble: furniture*) montare; (*: meal*)
improvvisare
▶ **put up** *vt* (*raise*) sollevare, alzare; (*pin up*)
affiggere; (*hang*) appendere; (*build*) costruire,
erigere; (*increase*) aumentare; (*accommodate*)
alloggiare; (*incite*): **to ~ sb up to doing sth**
istigare qn a fare qc; **to ~ sth up for sale**
mettere in vendita qc
▶ **put upon** *vt fus*: **to be ~ upon** (*imposed on*)
farsi mettere sotto i piedi
▶ **put up with** *vt fus* sopportare
putrid ['pju:trɪd] *adj* putrido(-a)
putt [pʌt] *vt* (*ball*) colpire leggermente
■ *n* colpo leggero
putter ['pʌtəʳ] *n* (*Golf*) putter *m inv* ■ *vi* (US)
= **potter**
putting green ['pʌtɪŋ-] *n* green *m inv*; campo
da putting
putty ['pʌtɪ] *n* stucco
put-up ['putʌp] *adj*: **~ job** montatura
puzzle ['pʌzl] *n* enigma *m*, mistero; (*jigsaw*)
puzzle *m* ■ *vt* confondere, rendere
perplesso(-a) ■ *vi* scervellarsi; **to be
puzzled about sth** domandarsi il perché di
qc; **to ~ over** (*sb's actions*) cercare di capire;
(*mystery, problem*) cercare di risolvere
puzzling ['pʌzlɪŋ] *adj* (*question*) poco chiaro(-a);
(*attitude, set of instructions*) incomprensibile
PVC *n abbr* (= *polyvinyl chloride*) P.V.C. *m*
Pvt. *abbr* (US Mil) = **private**
PW *n abbr* (US) = **prisoner of war**
pw *abbr* = **per week**
PX *n abbr* (US Mil) = **post exchange**
pygmy ['pɪgmɪ] *n* pigmeo(-a)
pyjamas, (US) **pajamas** [pə'dʒɑːməz] *npl*
pigiama *m*; **a pair of ~** un pigiama
pylon ['paɪlən] *n* pilone *m*
pyramid ['pɪrəmɪd] *n* piramide *f*
Pyrenean [pɪrə'niːən] *adj* pirenaico(-a)
Pyrenees [pɪrə'niːz] *npl*: **the ~** i Pirenei
Pyrex® ['paɪreks] *n* Pirex® *m inv* ■ *cpd*:
~ dish pirofila
python ['paɪθən] *n* pitone *m*

p

Qq

Q, q [kjuː] *n (letter)* Q, q *for m inv;* **Q for Queen** ≈ Q come Quarto

Qatar [kæˈtɑːʳ] *n* Qatar *m*

QC *n abbr (Brit: = Queen's Counsel)* avvocato della Corona

QED *abbr (= quod erat demonstrandum)* qed

QM *n abbr* = **quartermaster**

q.t. *n abbr (col: = quiet)* **on the q.t.** di nascosto

qty *abbr* = **quantity**

quack [kwæk] *n (of duck)* qua qua *m inv; (pej: doctor)* ciarlatano(-a)

quad [kwɔd] *n abbr* = **quadrangle; quadruple; quadruplet**

quadrangle [ˈkwɔdræŋgl] *n (Math)* quadrilatero; *(courtyard):* cortile *m*

quadruped [ˈkwɔdrupɛd] *n* quadrupede *m*

quadruple [kwɔˈdrupl] *adj* quadruplo(-a) ▪ *n* quadruplo ▪ *vt* quadruplicare ▪ *vi* quadruplicarsi

quadruplet [kwɔˈdruːplɪt] *n* uno(-a) di quattro gemelli

quagmire [ˈkwægmaɪəʳ] *n* pantano

quail [kweɪl] *n (Zool)* quaglia ▪ *vi:* **to ~ at** *or* **before** perdersi d'animo davanti a

quaint [kweɪnt] *adj* bizzarro(-a); *(old-fashioned)* antiquato(-a) e pittoresco(-a)

quake [kweɪk] *vi* tremare ▪ *n abbr* = **earthquake**

Quaker [ˈkweɪkəʳ] *n* quacchero(-a)

qualification [kwɔlɪfɪˈkeɪʃən] *n (degree etc)* qualifica, titolo; *(ability)* competenza, qualificazione *f; (limitation)* riserva, restrizione *f;* **what are your qualifications?** quali sono le sue qualifiche?

qualified [ˈkwɔlɪfaɪd] *adj* qualificato(-a); *(able)* competente, qualificato(-a); *(limited)* condizionato(-a); **~ for/to do** qualificato(-a) per/per fare; **he's not ~ for the job** non ha i requisiti necessari per questo lavoro; **it was a ~ success** è stato un successo parziale

qualify [ˈkwɔlɪfaɪ] *vt* abilitare; *(limit: statement)* modificare, precisare ▪ *vi:* **to ~ (as)** qualificarsi (come); **to ~ (for)** acquistare i requisiti necessari (per); *(Sport)* qualificarsi (per *or* a); **to ~ as an engineer** diventare un perito tecnico

qualifying [ˈkwɔlɪfaɪɪŋ] *adj (exam)* di ammissione; *(round)* eliminatorio(-a)

qualitative [ˈkwɔlɪtətɪv] *adj* qualitativo(-a)

quality [ˈkwɔlɪtɪ] *n* qualità *f inv* ▪ *cpd* di qualità; **of good ~** di buona qualità; **of poor ~** scadente; **~ of life** qualità della vita

quality control *n* controllo di qualità

quality papers *npl,* **quality press** *n (Brit):* **the ~** la stampa d'informazione; *vedi nota*

○ **QUALITY PAPERS**
○
○ Il termine *quality press* si riferisce ai
○ quotidiani o ai settimanali che offrono
○ un'informazione seria ed approfondita.
○ Questi giornali si differenziano da quelli
○ popolari, i "tabloid", per formato e
○ contenuti. Questa divisione tra tipi di
○ giornali riflette il tradizionale divario tra
○ classi sociali nella società britannica; *vedi*
○ *anche* "tabloid press".

---

qualm [kwɑːm] *n* dubbio; scrupolo; **to have qualms about sth** avere degli scrupoli per qc

quandary [ˈkwɔndrɪ] *n:* **in a ~** in un dilemma

quango [ˈkwæŋgəu] *n abbr (Brit:* = *quasi-autonomous non-governmental organization)* commissione consultiva di nomina governativa

quantifiable [ˈkwɔntɪfaɪəbl] *adj* quantificabile

quantitative [ˈkwɔntɪtətɪv] *adj* quantitativo(-a)

quantity [ˈkwɔntɪtɪ] *n* quantità *f inv;* **in ~** in grande quantità

quantity surveyor *n (Brit)* geometra *m (specializzato nel calcolare la quantità e il costo del materiale da costruzione)*

quantum leap [ˈkwɔntəm-] *n (fig)* enorme cambiamento

quarantine [ˈkwɔrntiːn] *n* quarantena

quark [kwɑːk] *n* quark *m inv*

quarrel ['kwɔrl] *n* lite *f*, disputa ■ *vi* litigare; **to have a ~ with sb** litigare con qn; **I've no ~ with him** non ho niente contro di lui; **I can't ~ with that** non ho niente da ridire su questo

quarrelsome ['kwɔrəlsəm] *adj* litigioso(-a)

quarry ['kwɔrɪ] *n (for stone)* cava; *(animal)* preda ■ *vt (marble etc)* estrarre

quart [kwɔːt] *n* due pinte *fpl*, ≈ litro

quarter ['kwɔːtə'] *n* quarto; *(of year)* trimestre *m*; *(district)* quartiere *m*; *(US, Canada: 25 cents)* quarto di dollaro, 25 centesimi ■ *vt* dividere in quattro; *(Mil)* alloggiare; **quarters** *npl* alloggio; *(Mil)* alloggi *mpl*, quadrato; **to pay by the ~** pagare trimestralmente; **a ~ of an hour** un quarto d'ora; **it's a ~ to 3**, *(US)* **it's a ~ of 3** sono le 3 meno un quarto, manca un quarto alle 3; **it's a ~ past 3**, *(US)* **it's a ~ after 3** sono le 3 e un quarto; **from all quarters** da tutte le parti *or* direzioni; **at close quarters** a distanza ravvicinata

quarterback ['kwɔːtəbæk] *n (US Football)* quarterback *m inv*

quarter-deck ['kwɔːtədɛk] *n (Naut)* cassero

quarter final *n* quarto di finale

quarterly ['kwɔːtəlɪ] *adj* trimestrale ■ *adv* trimestralmente ■ *n* periodico trimestrale

quartermaster ['kwɔːtəmɑːstə'] *n (Mil)* furiere *m*

quartet, quartette [kwɔː'tɛt] *n* quartetto

quarto ['kwɔːtəu] *adj, n* in quarto *(m) inv*

quartz [kwɔːts] *n* quarzo ■ *cpd* di quarzo; *(watch, clock)* al quarzo

quash [kwɔʃ] *vt (verdict)* annullare

quasi- ['kweɪzaɪ] *prefix* quasi + *noun*; quasi, pressoché + *adjective*

quaver ['kweɪvə'] *n (Brit Mus)* croma ■ *vi* tremolare

quay [kiː] *n (also:* **quayside***)* banchina

Que. *abbr (Canada)* = **Quebec**

queasy ['kwiːzɪ] *adj (stomach)* delicato(-a); **to feel ~** aver la nausea

Quebec [kwɪ'bɛk] *n* Quebec *m*

queen [kwiːn] *n (gen)* regina; *(Cards etc)* regina, donna

queen mother *n* regina madre

Queen's speech *n (Brit) vedi nota*

⬤ **QUEEN'S SPEECH**
⬤
⬤
⬤ Durante la sessione di apertura del
⬤ Parlamento britannico il sovrano legge
⬤ un discorso redatto dal primo ministro, il
⬤ *Queen's speech* (se si tratta della regina), che
⬤ contiene le linee generali del nuovo
⬤ programma politico.

queer [kwɪə'] *adj* strano(-a), curioso(-a); *(suspicious)* dubbio(-a), sospetto(-a); *(Brit: sick)*: **I feel ~** mi sento poco bene ■ *n (col)* finocchio

quell [kwɛl] *vt* domare

quench [kwɛntʃ] *vt (flames)* spegnere; **to ~ one's thirst** dissetarsi

querulous ['kwɛruləs] *adj* querulo(-a)

query ['kwɪərɪ] *n* domanda, questione *f*; *(doubt)* dubbio ■ *vt* mettere in questione; *(disagree with, dispute)* contestare

quest [kwɛst] *n* cerca, ricerca

question ['kwɛstʃən] *n* domanda, questione *f* ■ *vt (person)* interrogare; *(plan, idea)* mettere in questione *or* in dubbio; **to ask sb a ~**, **put a ~ to sb** fare una domanda a qn; **to bring** *or* **call sth into ~** mettere in dubbio qc; **the ~ is …** il problema è …; **it's a ~ of doing** si tratta di fare; **there's some ~ of doing** c'è chi suggerisce di fare; **beyond ~** fuori di dubbio; **out of the ~** fuori discussione, impossibile

questionable ['kwɛstʃənəbl] *adj* discutibile

questioner ['kwɛstʃənə'] *n* interrogante *m/f*

questioning ['kwɛstʃənɪŋ] *adj* interrogativo(-a) ■ *n* interrogatorio

question mark *n* punto interrogativo

questionnaire [kwɛstʃə'nɛə'] *n* questionario

queue [kjuː] *n* coda, fila ■ *vi* fare la coda; **to jump the ~** passare davanti agli altri (in una coda)

quibble ['kwɪbl] *vi* cavillare

quick [kwɪk] *adj* rapido(-a), veloce; *(reply)* pronto(-a); *(mind)* pronto(-a), acuto(-a) ■ *adv* rapidamente, presto ■ *n:* **cut to the ~** *(fig)* toccato(-a) sul vivo; **be ~!** fa presto!; **to be ~ to act** agire prontamente; **she was ~ to see that …** ha visto subito che …

quicken ['kwɪkn] *vt* accelerare, affrettare; *(rouse)* animare, stimolare ■ *vi* accelerare, affrettarsi

quick fix *n* soluzione *f* tampone *inv*

quicklime ['kwɪklaɪm] *n* calce *f* viva

quickly ['kwɪklɪ] *adv* rapidamente, velocemente; **we must act ~** dobbiamo agire tempestivamente

quickness ['kwɪknɪs] *n* rapidità; prontezza; acutezza

quicksand ['kwɪksænd] *n* sabbie *fpl* mobili

quickstep ['kwɪkstɛp] *n* tipo di ballo simile al fox-trot

quick-tempered [kwɪk'tɛmpəd] *adj* che si arrabbia facilmente

quick-witted [kwɪk'wɪtɪd] *adj* pronto(-a) d'ingegno

quid [kwɪd] *n (pl inv: Brit col)* sterlina

quid pro quo ['kwɪdprəu'kwəu] *n* contraccambio

q

quiet ['kwaɪət] *adj* tranquillo(-a), quieto(-a); (*reserved*) quieto(-a), taciturno(-a); (*ceremony*) semplice; (*not noisy: engine*) silenzioso(-a); (*not busy: day*) calmo(-a), tranquillo(-a); (*colour*) discreto(-a) ∎ *n* tranquillità, calma ∎ *vt, vi* (*US*) = **quieten**; **keep ~!** sta zitto!; **on the ~** di nascosto; **I'll have a ~ word with him** gli dirò due parole in privato; **business is ~ at this time of year** questa è la stagione morta
quieten ['kwaɪətn] (*Brit: also:* **quieten down**) *vi* calmarsi, chetarsi ∎ *vt* calmare, chetare
quietly ['kwaɪətlɪ] *adv* tranquillamente, calmamente; silenziosamente
quietness ['kwaɪətnɪs] *n* tranquillità, calma; silenzio
quill [kwɪl] *n* penna d'oca
quilt [kwɪlt] *n* trapunta; **continental ~** piumino
quin [kwɪn] *n abbr* = **quintuplet**
quince [kwɪns] *n* (mela) cotogna; (*tree*) cotogno
quinine [kwɪ'niːn] *n* chinino
quintet, quintette [kwɪn'tet] *n* quintetto
quintuplet [kwɪn'tjuːplɪt] *n* uno(-a) di cinque gemelli
quip [kwɪp] *n* battuta di spirito
quire ['kwaɪəʳ] *n* ventesima parte di una risma
quirk [kwəːk] *n* ghiribizzo; **by some ~ of fate** per un capriccio della sorte
quit (*pt, pp* ~ *or* **quitted**) [kwɪt] *vt* lasciare, partire da ∎ *vi* (*give up*) mollare; (*resign*) dimettersi; **to ~ doing** smettere di fare;

~ **stalling!** (*US col*) non tirarla per le lunghe!; **notice to ~** (*Brit*) preavviso (*dato all'inquilino*)
quite [kwaɪt] *adv* (*rather*) assai; (*entirely*) completamente, del tutto; **I ~ understand** capisco perfettamente; ~ **a few of them** non pochi di loro; ~ **(so)!** esatto!; ~ **new** proprio nuovo; **that's not ~ right** non è proprio esatto; **she's ~ pretty** è piuttosto carina
Quito ['kiːtəu] *n* Quito *m*
quits [kwɪts] *adj*: ~ **(with)** pari (con); **let's call it ~** adesso siamo pari
quiver ['kwɪvəʳ] *vi* tremare, fremere ∎ *n* (*for arrows*) faretra
quiz [kwɪz] *n* (*game*) quiz *m inv*; indovinello ∎ *vt* interrogare
quizzical ['kwɪzɪkəl] *adj* enigmatico(-a)
quoits [kwɔɪts] *npl* gioco degli anelli
quorum ['kwɔːrəm] *n* quorum *m*
quota ['kwəutə] *n* quota
quotation [kwəu'teɪʃən] *n* citazione *f*; (*of shares etc*) quotazione *f*; (*estimate*) preventivo
quotation marks *npl* virgolette *fpl*
quote [kwəut] *n* citazione *f* ∎ *vt* (*sentence*) citare; (*price*) dare, indicare, fissare; (*shares*) quotare ∎ *vi*: **to ~ from** citare; **to ~ for a job** dare un preventivo per un lavoro; **quotes** *npl* (*col*) = **quotation marks**; **in quotes** tra virgolette; ~ **... unquote** (*in dictation*) aprire le virgolette ... chiudere le virgolette
quotient ['kwəuʃənt] *n* quoziente *m*
qv *abbr* (= *quod vide: which see*) v
qwerty keyboard ['kwəːtɪ-] *n* tastiera qwerty *inv*

Rr

R, r [ɑːʳ] n (letter) R, r f or m inv; **R for Robert**, (US) **R for Roger** ≈ R come Roma
R abbr (= Réaumur (scale)) R; (= river) F; (= right) D; (US Cine: = restricted) ≈ vietato; (US Pol) = **republican**; (Brit) = **Rex; Regina**
RA n abbr (Brit) = **Royal Academy; Royal Academician** ■ abbr = **rear admiral**
RAAF n abbr = **Royal Australian Air Force**
Rabat [rə'bɑːt] n Rabat f
rabbi ['ræbaɪ] n rabbino
rabbit ['ræbɪt] n coniglio ■ vi: **to ~ (on)** (Brit) blaterare
rabbit hole n tana di coniglio
rabbit hutch n coffeeconigliera
rabble ['ræbl] n (pej) canaglia, plebaglia
rabid ['ræbɪd] adj rabbioso(-a); (fig) fanatico(-a)
rabies ['reɪbiːz] n rabbia
RAC n abbr (Brit: = Royal Automobile Club) ≈ A.C.I. m (= Automobile Club d'Italia)
raccoon [rə'kuːn] n procione m
race [reɪs] n razza; (competition, rush) corsa ■ vt (person) gareggiare (in corsa) con; (horse) far correre; (engine) imballare ■ vi correre; **the human ~** la razza umana; **he raced across the road** ha attraversato la strada di corsa; **to ~ in/out** etc precipitarsi dentro/fuori etc
race car n (US) = **racing car**
race car driver n (US) = **racing driver**
racecourse ['reɪskɔːs] n campo di corse, ippodromo
racehorse ['reɪshɔːs] n cavallo da corsa
race relations npl rapporti razziali
racetrack ['reɪstræk] n pista
racial ['reɪʃl] adj razziale
racial discrimination n discriminazione f razziale
racialism ['reɪʃəlɪzəm] n razzismo
racialist ['reɪʃəlɪst] adj, n razzista m/f
racing ['reɪsɪŋ] n corsa
racing car n (Brit) macchina da corsa
racing driver n (Brit) corridore m automobilista

racism ['reɪsɪzəm] n razzismo
racist ['reɪsɪst] adj, n (pej) razzista m/f
rack [ræk] n rastrelliera; (also: **luggage rack**) rete f portabagagli m inv; (also: **roof rack**) portabagagli ■ vt torturare, tormentare; **magazine ~** portariviste m inv; **shoe ~** scarpiera; **toast ~** portatoast m inv; **to go to ~ and ruin** (building) andare in rovina; (business) andare in malora or a catafascio; **to ~ one's brains** scervellarsi
▶ **rack up** vt accumulare
racket ['rækɪt] n (for tennis) racchetta; (noise) fracasso, baccano; (swindle) imbroglio, truffa; (organized crime) racket m inv
racketeer [rækɪ'tɪəʳ] n (US) trafficante m/f
racoon [rə'kuːn] n = **raccoon**
racquet ['rækɪt] n racchetta
racy ['reɪsɪ] adj brioso(-a); piccante
RADA ['rɑːdə] n abbr (Brit) = **Royal Academy of Dramatic Art**
radar ['reɪdɑːʳ] n radar m ■ cpd radar inv
radar trap n controllo della velocità con radar
radial ['reɪdɪəl] adj (also: **radial-ply**) radiale
radiance ['reɪdɪəns] n splendore m, radiosità
radiant ['reɪdɪənt] adj raggiante; (Physics) radiante
radiate ['reɪdɪeɪt] vt (heat) irraggiare, irradiare ■ vi (lines) irradiarsi
radiation [reɪdɪ'eɪʃən] n irradiamento; (radioactive) radiazione f
radiation sickness n malattia da radiazioni
radiator ['reɪdɪeɪtəʳ] n radiatore m
radiator cap n tappo del radiatore
radiator grill n (Aut) mascherina, calandra
radical ['rædɪkl] adj radicale
radii ['reɪdɪaɪ] npl of **radius**
radio ['reɪdɪəu] n radio f inv ■ vt (information) trasmettere per radio; (one's position) comunicare via radio; (person) chiamare via radio ■ vi: **to ~ to sb** comunicare via radio con qn; **on the ~** alla radio
radio... ['reɪdɪəu] prefix radio...
radioactive ['reɪdɪəu'æktɪv] adj radioattivo(-a)

r

radioactivity [ˈreɪdɪəuækˈtɪvɪtɪ] n radioattività
radio announcer n annunciatore/trice della radio
radio-controlled [ˈreɪdɪəukənˈtrəuld] adj radiocomandato(-a), radioguidato(-a)
radiographer [reɪdɪˈɔɡrəfəʳ] n radiologo(-a); (tecnico)
radiography [reɪdɪˈɔɡrəfɪ] n radiografia
radiologist [reɪdɪˈɔlədʒɪst] n radiologo(-a) (medico)
radiology [reɪdɪˈɔlədʒɪ] n radiologia
radio station n stazione f, radio inv
radio taxi n radiotaxi m inv
radiotelephone [ˈreɪdɪəuˈtɛlɪfəun] n radiotelefono
radiotherapist [ˈreɪdɪəuˈθɛrəpɪst] n radioterapista m/f
radiotherapy [ˈreɪdɪəuˈθɛrəpɪ] n radioterapia
radish [ˈrædɪʃ] n ravanello
radium [ˈreɪdɪəm] n radio
radius (pl **radii**) [ˈreɪdɪəs, -ɪaɪ] n raggio; (Anat) radio; **within a ~ of 50 miles** in un raggio di 50 miglia
RAF n abbr (Brit) = **Royal Air Force**
raffia [ˈræfɪə] n rafia
raffish [ˈræfɪʃ] adj dal look trasandato
raffle [ˈræfl] n lotteria ■ vt (object) mettere in palio
raft [rɑːft] n zattera
rafter [ˈrɑːftəʳ] n trave f
rag [ræg] n straccio, cencio; (pej: newspaper) giornalaccio; (for charity) iniziativa studentesca a scopo benefico ■ vt (Brit) prendere in giro; **rags** npl stracci mpl, brandelli mpl; **in rags** stracciato
rag-and-bone man [ˈrægənˈbəun-] n straccivendolo
ragbag [ˈrægbæg] n (fig) guazzabuglio
rag doll n bambola di pezza
rage [reɪdʒ] n (fury) collera, furia ■ vi (person) andare su tutte le furie; (storm) infuriare; **it's all the ~** fa furore; **to fly into a ~** andare or montare su tutte le furie
ragged [ˈrægɪd] adj (edge) irregolare; (cuff) logoro(-a); (appearance) pezzente
raging [ˈreɪdʒɪŋ] adj (all senses) furioso(-a); **in a ~ temper** su tutte le furie
rag trade n (col): **the ~** l'abbigliamento
rag week n (Brit) vedi nota

raid [reɪd] n (Mil) incursione f; (criminal) rapina; (by police) irruzione f ■ vt fare un'incursione in; rapinare; fare irruzione in
raider [ˈreɪdəʳ] n rapinatore(-trice); (plane) aeroplano da incursione
rail [reɪl] n (on stair) ringhiera; (on bridge, balcony) parapetto; (of ship) battagliola; (for train) rotaia; **rails** npl binario, rotaie fpl; **by ~** per ferrovia, in treno
railcard [ˈreɪlkɑːd] n (Brit) tessera di riduzione ferroviaria
railing [ˈreɪlɪŋ] n, **railings** [ˈreɪlɪŋz] npl ringhiere fpl
railway [ˈreɪlweɪ], (US) **railroad** [ˈreɪlrəud] n ferrovia
railway engine n (Brit) locomotiva
railway line n (Brit) linea ferroviaria
railwayman [ˈreɪlweɪmən] n (Brit) ferroviere m
railway station n (Brit) stazione f ferroviaria
rain [reɪn] n pioggia ■ vi piovere; **in the ~** sotto la pioggia; **it's raining** piove; **it's raining cats and dogs** piove a catinelle
rainbow [ˈreɪnbəu] n arcobaleno
raincoat [ˈreɪnkəut] n impermeabile m
raindrop [ˈreɪndrɔp] n goccia di pioggia
rainfall [ˈreɪnfɔːl] n pioggia; (measurement) piovosità
rainforest [ˈreɪnfɔrɪst] n foresta pluviale or equatoriale
rainproof [ˈreɪnpruːf] adj impermeabile
rainstorm [ˈreɪnstɔːm] n pioggia torrenziale
rainwater [ˈreɪnwɔːtəʳ] n acqua piovana
rainy [ˈreɪnɪ] adj piovoso(-a)
raise [reɪz] n aumento ■ vt (lift) alzare, sollevare; (build) erigere; (increase) aumentare; (a protest, doubt, question) sollevare; (cattle, family) allevare; (crop) coltivare; (army, funds) raccogliere; (loan) ottenere; (end: siege, embargo) togliere; **to ~ one's voice** alzare la voce; **to ~ sb's hopes** accendere le speranze di qn; **to ~ one's glass to sb/sth** brindare a qn/qc; **to ~ a laugh/a smile** far ridere/sorridere
raisin [ˈreɪzn] n uva secca
Raj [rɑːdʒ] n: **the ~** l'impero britannico (in India)
rajah [ˈrɑːdʒə] n ragià m inv
rake [reɪk] n (tool) rastrello; (person) libertino ■ vt (garden) rastrellare; (with machine gun) spazzare ■ vi: **to ~ through** (fig: search) frugare tra
rake-off [ˈreɪkɔf] n (col) parte f percentuale, fetta
rakish [ˈreɪkɪʃ] adj dissoluto(-a); disinvolto(-a)
rally [ˈrælɪ] n (Pol etc) riunione f; (Aut) rally m inv; (Tennis) scambio ■ vt riunire, radunare ■ vi raccogliersi, radunarsi; (sick person, Stock Exchange) riprendersi

▸**rally round** *vt fus* raggrupparsi intorno a; venire in aiuto di

rallying point ['rælɪɪŋ-] *n* (*Pol, Mil*) punto di riunione, punto di raduno

RAM [ræm] *n abbr* (*Comput*: = *random access memory*) RAM *f*

ram [ræm] *n* montone *m*, ariete *m*; (*device*) ariete ■ *vt* conficcare; (*crash into*) cozzare, sbattere contro; percuotere; speronare

ramble ['ræmbl] *n* escursione *f* ■ *vi* (*pej: also:* **ramble on**) divagare

rambler ['ræmblə^r] *n* escursionista *m/f*; (*Bot*) rosa rampicante

rambling ['ræmblɪŋ] *adj* (*speech*) sconnesso(-a); (*Bot*) rampicante; (*house*) tutto(-a) nicchie e corridoi

rambunctious [ræm'bʌŋkʃəs] *adj* (*US*) = **rumbustious**

RAMC *n abbr* (*Brit*) = **Royal Army Medical Corps**

ramification [ræmɪfɪ'keɪʃən] *n* ramificazione *f*

ramp [ræmp] *n* rampa; (*Aut*) dosso artificiale

rampage [ræm'peɪdʒ] *n:* **to go on the ~** scatenarsi in modo violento ■ *vi:* **they went rampaging through the town** si sono scatenati in modo violento per la città

rampant ['ræmpənt] *adj* (*disease etc*) che infierisce

rampart ['ræmpɑ:t] *n* bastione *m*

ram raiding [-reɪdɪŋ] *n* il rapinare un negozio sfondandone la vetrina con un veicolo rubato

ramshackle ['ræmʃækl] *adj* (*house*) cadente; (*car etc*) sgangherato(-a)

RAN *n abbr* = **Royal Australian Navy**

ran [ræn] *pt of* **run**

ranch [rɑ:ntʃ] *n* ranch *m inv*

rancher ['rɑ:ntʃə^r] *n* (*owner*) proprietario di un ranch; (*ranch hand*) cowboy *m inv*

rancid ['rænsɪd] *adj* rancido(-a)

rancour, (*US*) **rancor** ['ræŋkə^r] *n* rancore *m*

R & B *n abbr* = **rhythm and blues**

R & D *n abbr* = **research and development**

random ['rændəm] *adj* fatto(-a) *or* detto(-a) per caso; (*Comput, Math*) casuale ■ *n:* **at ~** a casaccio

random access *n* (*Comput*) accesso casuale

R & R *n abbr* (= *rest and recreation*) ricreazione *f*; (*US Mil*) permesso per militari

randy ['rændɪ] *adj* (*col*) arrapato(-a); lascivo(-a)

rang [ræŋ] *pt of* **ring**

range [reɪndʒ] *n* (*of mountains*) catena; (*of missile, voice*) portata; (*of products*) gamma; (*Mil: also:* **shooting range**) campo di tiro; (*also:* **kitchen range**) fornello, cucina economica ■ *vt* (*place*) disporre, allineare;

(*roam*) vagare per ■ *vi:* **to ~ over** coprire; **to ~ from ... to** andare da ... a; **price ~** gamma di prezzi; **do you have anything else in this price ~?** ha nient'altro su *or* di questo prezzo?; **within (firing) ~** a portata di tiro; **ranged left/right** (*text*) allineato(-a) a destra/sinistra

ranger ['reɪndʒə^r] *n* guardia forestale

Rangoon [ræŋ'gu:n] *n* Rangun *f*

rank [ræŋk] *n* fila; (*Mil*) grado; (*Brit: also:* **taxi rank**) posteggio di taxi ■ *vi:* **to ~ among** essere nel numero di ■ *adj* (*smell*) puzzolente; (*hypocrisy, injustice*) vero(-a) e proprio(-a); **the ranks** (*Mil*) la truppa; **the ~ and file** (*fig*) la gran massa; **to close ranks** (*Mil, fig*) serrare i ranghi; **I ~ him sixth** gli do il sesto posto, lo metto al sesto posto

rankle ['ræŋkl] *vi:* **to ~ with sb** bruciare (a qn)

rank outsider *n* outsider *m/f inv*

ransack ['rænsæk] *vt* rovistare; (*plunder*) saccheggiare

ransom ['rænsəm] *n* riscatto; **to hold sb to ~** (*fig*) esercitare pressione su qn

rant [rænt] *vi* vociare

ranting ['ræntɪŋ] *n* vociare *m*

rap [ræp] *n* (*noise*) colpetti *mpl*; (*at a door*) bussata ■ *vt* dare dei colpetti a; bussare a

rape [reɪp] *n* violenza carnale, stupro ■ *vt* violentare

rape oil, rapeseed oil ['reɪpsi:d-] *n* olio di ravizzone

rapid ['ræpɪd] *adj* rapido(-a)

rapidity [rə'pɪdɪtɪ] *n* rapidità

rapidly ['ræpɪdlɪ] *adv* rapidamente

rapids ['ræpɪdz] *npl* (*Geo*) rapida

rapist ['reɪpɪst] *n* violentatore *m*

rapport [ræ'pɔ:^r] *n* rapporto

rapt [ræpt] *adj* (*attention*) rapito(-a), profondo(-a); **to be ~ in contemplation** essere in estatica contemplazione

rapture ['ræptʃə^r] *n* estasi *f inv*; **to go into raptures over** andare in solluchero per

rapturous ['ræptʃərəs] *adj* estatico(-a)

rare [rεə^r] *adj* raro(-a); (*Culin: steak*) al sangue; **it is ~ to find that ...** capita di rado *or* raramente che ... + *sub*

rarebit ['rεəbɪt] *n see* **Welsh rarebit**

rarefied ['rεərɪfaɪd] *adj* (*air, atmosphere*) rarefatto(-a)

rarely ['rεəlɪ] *adv* raramente

raring ['rεərɪŋ] *adj:* **to be ~ to go** (*col*) non veder l'ora di cominciare

rarity ['rεərɪtɪ] *n* rarità *f inv*

rascal ['rɑ:skl] *n* mascalzone *m*

rash [ræʃ] *adj* imprudente, sconsiderato(-a) ■ *n* (*Med*) eruzione *f*; **to come out in a ~** avere uno sfogo

r

rasher ['ræʃəʳ] n fetta sottile (di lardo or prosciutto)

rasp [rɑːsp] n (tool) lima ■ vt (speak: also: **rasp out**) gracchiare

raspberry ['rɑːzbərɪ] n lampone m

raspberry bush n lampone m (pianta)

rasping ['rɑːspɪŋ] adj stridulo(-a)

Rastafarian [ræstə'fɛərɪən] adj, n rastafariano(-a)

rat [ræt] n ratto

ratable ['reɪtəbl] adj = **rateable**

ratchet ['rætʃɪt] n: ~ **wheel** ruota dentata

rate [reɪt] n (proportion) tasso, percentuale f; (speed) velocità f inv; (price) tariffa ■ vt valutare; stimare; **to ~ sb/sth as** valutare qn/qc come; **to ~ sb/sth among** annoverare qn/qc tra; **to ~ sb/sth highly** stimare molto qn/qc; **at a ~ of 60 kph** alla velocità di 60 km all'ora; ~ **of exchange** tasso di cambio; ~ **of flow** flusso medio; ~ **of growth** tasso di crescita; ~ **of return** tasso di rendimento; **pulse ~** frequenza delle pulsazioni; see also **rates**

rateable value ['reɪtəbl-] n (Brit) valore m imponibile (agli effetti delle imposte comunali)

ratepayer ['reɪtpeɪəʳ] n (Brit) contribuente m/f (che paga le imposte comunali)

rates [reɪts] npl (Brit) imposte fpl comunali

rather ['rɑːðəʳ] adv piuttosto; (somewhat) abbastanza; (to some extent) un po'; **it's ~ expensive** è piuttosto caro; (too much) è un po' caro; **there's ~ a lot** ce n'è parecchio; **I would** or **I'd ~ go** preferirei andare; **I had ~ go** farei meglio ad andare; **I'd ~ not leave** preferirei non partire; **or ~** (more accurately) anzi, per essere (più) precisi; **I ~ think he won't come** credo proprio che non verrà

ratification [rætɪfɪ'keɪʃən] n ratificazione f

ratify ['rætɪfaɪ] vt ratificare

rating ['reɪtɪŋ] n classificazione f; punteggio di merito; (Naut: category) classe f; (: sailor: Brit) marinaio semplice

ratings ['reɪtɪŋz] npl (Radio, TV) indice m di ascolto

ratio ['reɪʃɪəʊ] n proporzione f; **in the ~ of 2 to 1** in rapporto di 2 a 1

ration ['ræʃən] n razione f ■ vt razionare

rational ['ræʃənl] adj razionale, ragionevole; (solution, reasoning) logico(-a)

rationale [ræʃə'nɑːl] n fondamento logico; giustificazione f

rationalization [ræʃnəlaɪ'zeɪʃən] n razionalizzazione f

rationalize ['ræʃnəlaɪz] vt razionalizzare

rationally ['ræʃnəlɪ] adv razionalmente; logicamente

rationing ['ræʃnɪŋ] n razionamento

ratpack ['rætpæk] n (Brit col) stampa scandalistica

rat poison n veleno per topi

rat race n carrierismo, corsa al successo

rattan [ræ'tæn] n malacca

rattle ['rætl] n tintinnio; (louder) rumore m di ferraglia; (object: of baby) sonaglino; (: of sports fan) raganella ■ vi risuonare, tintinnare; fare un rumore di ferraglia ■ vt agitare; far tintinnare; (col: disconcert) sconcertare

rattlesnake ['rætlsneɪk] n serpente m a sonagli

ratty ['rætɪ] adj (col) incavolato(-a)

raucous ['rɔːkəs] adj sguaiato(-a)

raucously ['rɔːkəslɪ] adv sguaiatamente

raunchy ['rɔːntʃɪ] adj (col: person) allupato(-a); (: voice, song) libidinoso(-a)

ravage ['rævɪdʒ] vt devastare

ravages ['rævɪdʒɪz] npl danni mpl

rave [reɪv] vi (in anger) infuriarsi; (with enthusiasm) andare in estasi; (Med) delirare ■ n: **a ~ (party)** un rave ■ adj (scene, culture, music) del fenomeno rave ■ cpd: ~ **review** (col) critica entusiastica

raven ['reɪvən] n corvo

ravenous ['rævənəs] adj affamato(-a)

ravine [rə'viːn] n burrone m

raving ['reɪvɪŋ] adj: ~ **lunatic** pazzo(-a) furioso(-a)

ravings ['reɪvɪŋz] npl vaneggiamenti mpl

ravioli [rævɪ'əʊlɪ] n ravioli mpl

ravish ['rævɪʃ] vt (delight) estasiare

ravishing ['rævɪʃɪŋ] adj incantevole

raw [rɔː] adj (uncooked) crudo(-a); (not processed) greggio(-a); (sore) vivo(-a); (inexperienced) inesperto(-a); **to get a ~ deal** (col: bad bargain) prendere un bidone; (: harsh treatment) venire trattato ingiustamente

Rawalpindi [rɔː'lpɪndɪ] n Rawalpindi f

raw material n materia prima

ray [reɪ] n raggio

rayon ['reɪɔn] n raion m

raze [reɪz] vt radere, distruggere; (also: **raze to the ground**) radere al suolo

razor ['reɪzəʳ] n rasoio

razor blade n lama di rasoio

razzle ['ræzl], **razzle-dazzle** ['ræzl'dæzl] n (Brit col): **to be/go on the ~(-dazzle)** darsi alla pazza gioia

razzmatazz ['ræzmə'tæz] n (col) clamore m

RC abbr = **Roman Catholic**

RCAF n abbr = **Royal Canadian Air Force**

RCMP n abbr = **Royal Canadian Mounted Police**

RCN n abbr = **Royal Canadian Navy**

RD abbr (US Post) = **rural delivery**

Rd *abbr* = **road**
RDC *n abbr* (*Brit*) = **rural district council**
RE *n abbr* (*Brit Mil*: = *Royal Engineers*) ≈ G.M.
(= *Genio Militare*); (*Brit*) = **religious education**
re [ri:] *prep* con riferimento a
reach [ri:tʃ] *n* portata; (*of river etc*) tratto ■ *vt*
raggiungere; arrivare a ■ *vi* stendersi;
(*stretch out hand*: *also*: **reach down**, **reach over**,
reach across *etc*) allungare una mano; **out**
of/within ~ (*object*) fuori/a portata di mano;
within easy ~ (of) (*place*) a breve distanza
(di), vicino (a); **to ~ sb by phone** contattare
qn per telefono; **can I ~ you at your hotel?**
la posso contattare al suo albergo?
▸ **reach out** *vi*: **to ~ out for** stendere la mano
per prendere
react [ri:ækt] *vi* reagire
reaction [ri:ækʃən] *n* reazione *f*
reactionary [ri:ækʃənri] *adj*, *n*
reazionario(-a)
reactor [ri:æktəʳ] *n* reattore *m*
read (*pt*, *pp* **read**) [ri:d, rɛd] ■ *vi* leggere ■ *vt*
leggere; (*understand*) intendere, interpretare;
(*study*) studiare; **do you ~ me?** (*Tel*) mi
ricevete?; **to take sth as ~** (*fig*) dare qc per
scontato
▸ **read out** *vt* leggere ad alta voce
▸ **read over** *vt* rileggere attentamente
▸ **read through** *vt* (*quickly*) dare una scorsa a;
(*thoroughly*) leggere da cima a fondo
▸ **read up** *vt*, **read up on** *vt fus* studiare bene
readable [ri:dəbl] *adj* leggibile; che si legge
volentieri
reader [ri:dəʳ] *n* lettore(-trice); (*book*) libro di
lettura; (*Brit*: *at university*) *professore con funzioni
preminenti di ricerca*
readership [ri:dəʃɪp] *n* (*of paper etc*) numero
di lettori
readily [rɛdɪlɪ] *adv* volentieri; (*easily*)
facilmente
readiness [rɛdɪnɪs] *n* prontezza; **in ~**
(*prepared*) pronto(-a)
reading [ri:dɪŋ] *n* lettura; (*understanding*)
interpretazione *f*; (*on instrument*) indicazione *f*
reading lamp *n* lampada da studio
reading room *n* sala di lettura
readjust [ri:ədʒʌst] *vt* raggiustare ■ *vi*
(*person*): **to ~ (to)** riadattarsi (a)
ready [rɛdɪ] *adj* pronto(-a); (*willing*)
pronto(-a), disposto(-a); (*quick*) rapido(-a);
(*available*) disponibile ■ *n*: **at the ~** (*Mil*)
pronto a sparare; (*fig*) tutto(-a) pronto(-a);
~ for use pronto per l'uso; **to be ~ to do sth**
essere pronto a fare qc; **to get ~** *vi* prepararsi
■ *vt* preparare
ready cash *n* denaro in contanti
ready-cooked [rɛdɪ'kukt] *adj* già cotto(-a)

ready-made [rɛdɪ'meɪd] *adj*
prefabbricato(-a); (*clothes*) confezionato(-a)
ready reckoner [-'rɛkənəʳ] *n* (*Brit*) prontuario
di calcolo
ready-to-wear [rɛdɪtə'wɛəʳ] *adj* prêt-à-
porter *inv*
reagent [ri:eɪdʒənt] *n*: **chemical ~** reagente
m chimico
real [rɪəl] *adj* reale; vero(-a) ■ *adv* (*US col*: *very*)
veramente, proprio; **in ~ terms** in realtà; **in
~ life** nella realtà
real ale *n* birra ad effervescenza naturale
real estate *n* beni *mpl* immobili
realism [rɪəlɪzəm] *n* (*Art*) realismo
realist [rɪəlɪst] *n* realista *m/f*
realistic [rɪə'lɪstɪk] *adj* realistico(-a)
reality [ri:ælɪtɪ] *n* realtà *f inv*; **in ~** in realtà,
in effetti
reality TV *n* reality TV *f*
realization [rɪəlaɪ'zeɪʃən] *n* (*awareness*)
presa di coscienza; (*of hopes, project etc*)
realizzazione *f*
realize [rɪəlaɪz] *vt* (*understand*) rendersi conto
di; (*a project, Comm*: *asset*) realizzare; **I ~ that ...**
mi rendo conto *or* capisco che ...
really [rɪəlɪ] *adv* veramente, davvero
realm [rɛlm] *n* reame *m*
real time *n* (*Comput*) tempo reale
Realtor® [rɪəltɔːʳ] *n* (*US*) agente *m*
immobiliare
ream [ri:m] *n* risma; **reams** (*fig, col*) pagine e
pagine *fpl*
reap [ri:p] *vt* mietere; (*fig*) raccogliere
reaper [ri:pəʳ] *n* (*machine*) mietitrice *f*
reappear [ri:ə'pɪəʳ] *vi* ricomparire, riapparire
reappearance [ri:ə'pɪərəns] *n* riapparizione *f*
reapply [ri:ə'plaɪ] *vi*: **to ~ for** fare un'altra
domanda per
reappraisal [ri:ə'preɪzl] *n* riesame *m*
rear [rɪəʳ] *adj* di dietro; (*Aut*: *wheel etc*)
posteriore ■ *n* didietro, parte *f* posteriore
■ *vt* (*cattle, family*) allevare ■ *vi* (*also*: **rear up**:
animal) impennarsi
rear admiral *n* contrammiraglio
rear-engined [rɪəʳ'ɛndʒɪnd] *adj* (*Aut*) con
motore posteriore
rearguard [rɪəgɑːd] *n* retroguardia
rearm [ri:ɑːm] *vt*, *vi* riarmare
rearmament [ri:ɑːməmənt] *n* riarmo
rearrange [ri:ə'reɪndʒ] *vt* riordinare
rear-view mirror [rɪəvjuː-] *n* (*Aut*) specchio
retrovisivo
reason [ri:zn] *n* ragione *f*; (*cause, motive*)
ragione, motivo ■ *vi*: **to ~ with sb** far
ragionare qn; **to have ~ to think** avere
motivi per pensare; **it stands to ~ that**
è ovvio che; **the ~ for/why** la ragione *or*

r

il motivo di/per cui; **with good ~** a ragione;
all the more ~ why you should not sell it
ragione di più per non venderlo
reasonable ['ri:znəbl] adj ragionevole; (not
bad) accettabile
reasonably ['ri:znəblɪ] adv ragionevolmente;
one can ~ assume that ... uno può
facilmente supporre che ...
reasoned ['ri:znd] adj (argument)
ponderato(-a)
reasoning ['ri:znɪŋ] n ragionamento
reassemble [ri:ə'sɛmbl] vt riunire; (machine)
rimontare
reassert [ri:ə'sə:t] vt riaffermare
reassurance [ri:ə'ʃuərəns] n rassicurazione f
reassure [ri:ə'ʃuər] vt rassicurare; **to ~ sb of**
rassicurare qn di or su
reassuring [ri:ə'ʃuərɪŋ] adj rassicurante
reawakening [ri:ə'weɪknɪŋ] n risveglio
rebate ['ri:beɪt] n rimborso
rebel n ['rɛbl] ribelle m/f ■ vi [rɪ'bɛl] ribellarsi
rebellion [rɪ'bɛljən] n ribellione f
rebellious [rɪ'bɛljəs] adj ribelle
rebirth [ri:'bə:θ] n rinascita
rebound vi [rɪ'baund] (ball) rimbalzare ■ n
['ri:baund] rimbalzo
rebuff [rɪ'bʌf] n secco rifiuto ■ vt respingere
rebuild [ri:'bɪld] vt irreg ricostruire
rebuke [rɪ'bju:k] n rimprovero ■ vt
rimproverare
rebut [rɪ'bʌt] vt rifiutare
rebuttal [rɪ'bʌtl] n rifiuto
recalcitrant [rɪ'kælsɪtrənt] adj recalcitrante
recall [rɪ'kɔ:l] vt (gen, Comput) richiamare;
(remember) ricordare, richiamare alla mente
■ n ['ri:kɔl] richiamo; **beyond ~** irrevocabile
recant [rɪ'kænt] vi ritrattarsi; (Rel) fare
abiura
recap ['ri:kæp] n ricapitolazione f ■ vt
ricapitolare ■ vi riassumere
recapture [ri:'kæptʃər] vt riprendere;
(atmosphere) ricreare
recd. abbr = **received**
recede [rɪ'si:d] vi allontanarsi; ritirarsi; calare
receding [rɪ'si:dɪŋ] adj (forehead, chin)
sfuggente; **he's got a ~ hairline** è stempiato
receipt [rɪ'si:t] n (document) ricevuta; (act of
receiving) ricevimento; **to acknowledge ~ of**
accusare ricevuta di; **we are in ~ of ...**
abbiamo ricevuto ...
receipts [rɪ'si:ts] npl (Comm) introiti mpl
receivable [rɪ'si:vəbl] adj (Comm) esigibile;
(: owed) dovuto(-a)
receive [rɪ'si:v] vt ricevere; (guest) ricevere,
accogliere; **"received with thanks"** (Comm)
"per quietanza"
Received Pronunciation n (Brit) vedi nota

receiver [rɪ'si:vər] n (Tel) ricevitore m; (Radio)
apparecchio ricevente; (of stolen goods)
ricettatore(-trice); (Law) curatore m
fallimentare
receivership [rɪ'si:vəʃɪp] n curatela; **to go into**
~ andare in amministrazione controllata
recent ['ri:snt] adj recente; **in ~ years** negli
ultimi anni
recently ['ri:sntlɪ] adv recentemente; **as ~**
as ... soltanto ...; **until ~** fino a poco tempo fa
receptacle [rɪ'sɛptɪkl] n recipiente m
reception [rɪ'sɛpʃən] n (gen) ricevimento;
(welcome) accoglienza; (TV etc) ricezione f
reception centre n (Brit) centro di raccolta
reception desk n (in hotel) reception f inv;
(in hospital, at doctor's) accettazione f; (in large
building, offices) portineria
receptionist [rɪ'sɛpʃənɪst] n receptionist m/f inv
receptive [rɪ'sɛptɪv] adj ricettivo(-a)
recess [rɪ'sɛs] n (in room) alcova; (Pol etc:
holiday) vacanze fpl; (US Law: short break)
sospensione f; (US Scol) intervallo
recession [rɪ'sɛʃən] n (Econ) recessione f
recessionista [rɪsɛʃə'nɪstə] n recessionista m/f
recharge [ri:'tʃɑ:dʒ] vt (battery) ricaricare
rechargeable ['ri:'tʃɑ:dʒəbl] adj ricaricabile
recipe ['rɛsɪpɪ] n ricetta
recipient [rɪ'sɪpɪənt] n beneficiario(-a);
(of letter) destinatario(-a)
reciprocal [rɪ'sɪprəkl] adj reciproco(-a)
reciprocate [rɪ'sɪprəkeɪt] vt ricambiare,
contraccambiare
recital [rɪ'saɪtl] n recital m inv; concerto
(di solista)
recite [rɪ'saɪt] vt (poem) recitare
reckless ['rɛkləs] adj (driver etc) spericolato(-a);
(spender) incosciente
recklessly ['rɛkləslɪ] adv in modo spericolato;
da incosciente
reckon ['rɛkən] vt (count) calcolare; (consider)
considerare, stimare; (think): **I ~ that ...**
penso che .. ■ vi contare, calcolare; **to ~**
without sb/sth non tener conto di qn/qc;
he is somebody to be reckoned with è uno
da non sottovalutare

▶ **reckon on** *vt fus* contare su

reckoning ['rɛknɪŋ] *n* conto; stima; **the day of** ~ il giorno del giudizio

reclaim [rɪ'kleɪm] *vt* (*land*) bonificare; (*demand back*) richiedere, reclamare

reclamation [rɛklə'meɪʃən] *n* bonifica

recline [rɪ'klaɪn] *vi* stare sdraiato(-a)

reclining [rɪ'klaɪnɪŋ] *adj* (*seat*) ribaltabile

recluse [rɪ'kluːs] *n* eremita *m*, recluso(-a)

recognition [rɛkəg'nɪʃən] *n* riconoscimento; **to gain** ~ essere riconosciuto(-a); **in** ~ **of** in *or* come segno di riconoscimento per; **transformed beyond** ~ irriconoscibile

recognizable ['rɛkəgnaɪzəbl] *adj*: ~ **(by)** riconoscibile (a *or* da)

recognize ['rɛkəgnaɪz] *vt*: **to** ~ **(by/as)** riconoscere (a *or* da/come)

recoil [rɪ'kɔɪl] *vi* (*gun*) rinculare; (*spring*) balzare indietro; (*person*): **to** ~ **(from)** indietreggiare (davanti a) ■ *n* (*gun*) rinculo

recollect [rɛkə'lɛkt] *vt* ricordare

recollection [rɛkə'lɛkʃən] *n* ricordo; **to the best of my** ~ per quello che mi ricordo

recommend [rɛkə'mɛnd] *vt* raccomandare; (*advise*) consigliare; **she has a lot to** ~ **her** ha molti elementi a suo favore

recommendation [rɛkəmɛn'deɪʃən] *n* raccomandazione *f*; consiglio

recommended retail price [rɛkə'mɛndɪd-] *n* (*Brit*) prezzo raccomandato al dettaglio

recompense ['rɛkəmpɛns] *vt* ricompensare; (*compensate*) risarcire ■ *n* ricompensa; risarcimento

reconcilable ['rɛkənsaɪləbl] *adj* conciliabile

reconcile ['rɛkənsaɪl] *vt* (*two people*) riconciliare; (*two facts*) conciliare, quadrare; **to** ~ **o.s. to** rassegnarsi a

reconciliation [rɛkənsɪlɪ'eɪʃən] *n* riconciliazione *f*; conciliazione *f*

recondite [rɪ'kɒndaɪt] *adj* recondito(-a)

recondition [riːkən'dɪʃən] *vt* rimettere a nuovo; rifare

reconnaissance [rɪ'kɒnɪsns] *n* (*Mil*) ricognizione *f*

reconnoitre, (*US*) **reconnoiter** [rɛkə'nɔɪtəʳ] (*Mil*) *vt* fare una ricognizione di ■ *vi* fare una ricognizione

reconsider [riːkən'sɪdəʳ] *vt* riconsiderare

reconstitute [riː'kɒnstɪtjuːt] *vt* ricostituire

reconstruct [riːkən'strʌkt] *vt* ricostruire

reconstruction [riːkən'strʌkʃən] *n* ricostruzione *f*

reconvene [riːkən'viːn] *vt* riconvocare ■ *vi* radunarsi

record *n* ['rɛkɔːd] ricordo, documento; (*of meeting etc*) nota, verbale *m*; (*register*) registro; (*file*) pratica, dossier *m inv*; (*Comput*) record *m*

inv, registrazione *f*; (*also*: **police record**) fedina penale sporca; (*Mus*: *disc*) disco; (*Sport*) record *m inv*, primato ■ *vt* [rɪ'kɔːd] (*set down*) prendere nota di, registrare; (*relate*) raccontare; (*Comput*, *Mus*: *song etc*) registrare; **public records** archivi *mpl*; **Italy's excellent** ~ i brillanti successi italiani; **in** ~ **time** a tempo di record; **to keep a** ~ **of** tener nota di; **to set the** ~ **straight** mettere le cose in chiaro; **off the** ~ *adj* ufficioso(-a); *adv* ufficiosamente; **he is on** ~ **as saying that** ... ha dichiarato pubblicamente che ...

record card *n* (*in file*) scheda

recorded delivery letter [rɪ'kɔːdɪd-] *n* (*Brit Post*) lettera raccomandata

recorder [rɪ'kɔːdəʳ] *n* (*Law*) avvocato che funge da giudice; (*Mus*) flauto diritto

record holder *n* (*Sport*) primatista *m/f*

recording [rɪ'kɔːdɪŋ] *n* (*Mus*) registrazione *f*

recording studio *n* studio di registrazione

record library *n* discoteca

record player *n* giradischi *m inv*

recount [rɪ'kaunt] *vt* raccontare, narrare

re-count *n* ['riːkaunt] (*Pol*: *of votes*) nuovo conteggio ■ *vt* [riː'kaunt] ricontare

recoup [rɪ'kuːp] *vt* ricuperare; **to** ~ **one's losses** ricuperare le perdite, rifarsi

recourse [rɪ'kɔːs] *n*: **to have** ~ **to** ricorrere a

recover [rɪ'kʌvəʳ] *vt* ricuperare ■ *vi* (*from illness*) rimettersi (in salute), ristabilirsi; (*country*, *person*: *from shock*) riprendersi

re-cover [riː'kʌvəʳ] *vt* (*chair etc*) ricoprire

recovery [rɪ'kʌvərɪ] *n* ricupero; ristabilimento; ripresa

recreate [riːkrɪ'eɪt] *vt* ricreare

recreation [rɛkrɪ'eɪʃən] *n* ricreazione *f*; svago

recreational [rɛkrɪ'eɪʃənəl] *adj* ricreativo(-a)

recreational drug *n* droga usata saltuariamente

recreational vehicle *n* (*US*) camper *m inv*

recrimination [rɪkrɪmɪ'neɪʃən] *n* recriminazione *f*

recruit [rɪ'kruːt] *n* recluta ■ *vt* reclutare

recruiting office [rɪ'kruːtɪŋ-] *n* ufficio di reclutamento

recruitment [rɪ'kruːtmənt] *n* reclutamento

rectangle ['rɛktæŋgl] *n* rettangolo

rectangular [rɛk'tæŋgjuləʳ] *adj* rettangolare

rectify ['rɛktɪfaɪ] *vt* (*error*) rettificare; (*omission*) riparare

rector ['rɛktəʳ] *n* (*Rel*) parroco (*anglicano*); (*in Scottish universities*) personalità eletta dagli studenti per rappresentarli

rectory ['rɛktərɪ] *n* presbiterio

rectum ['rɛktəm] *n* (*Anat*) retto

recuperate [rɪ'kjuːpəreɪt] *vi* ristabilirsi

recur [rɪ'kəːʳ] *vi* riaccadere; (*idea*, *opportunity*) riapparire; (*symptoms*) ripresentarsi

r

745

recurrence [rɪ'kʌrəns] n ripresentarsi m;
riapparizione f
recurrent [rɪ'kʌrənt] adj ricorrente,
periodico(-a)
recurring [rɪ'kʌrɪŋ] adj (Math) periodico(-a)
recycle [riː'saɪkl] vt riciclare
red [rɛd] n rosso; (Pol: pej) rosso(-a) ◼ adj
rosso(-a); **in the ~** (account) scoperto;
(business) in deficit
red alert n allarme m rosso
red-blooded ['rɛd'blʌdɪd] adj (col)
gagliardo(-a)
red-brick university ['rɛdbrɪk-] n (Brit)
università di recente formazione; vedi nota

red carpet treatment n cerimonia col gran
pavese
Red Cross n Croce f Rossa
redcurrant ['rɛdkʌrənt] n ribes m inv
redden ['rɛdn] vt arrossare ◼ vi arrossire
reddish ['rɛdɪʃ] adj rossiccio(-a)
redecorate [riː'dɛkəreɪt] vt tinteggiare
(e tappezzare) di nuovo
redeem [rɪ'diːm] vt (debt) riscattare; (sth in
pawn) ritirare; (fig, also Rel) redimere
redeemable [rɪ'diːməbl] adj con diritto di
riscatto; redimibile
redeeming [rɪ'diːmɪŋ] adj (feature) che salva
redefine [riː'dɪ'faɪn] vt ridefinire
redemption [rɪ'dɛmpʃən] n (Rel) redenzione
f; (also: **past** or **beyond redemption**)
irrecuperabile
redeploy [riː'dɪ'plɔɪ] vt (Mil) riorganizzare lo
schieramento di; (resources) riorganizzare
redeployment [riː'dɪ'plɔɪmənt] n
riorganizzazione f
redevelop [riː'dɪ'vɛləp] vt ristrutturare
redevelopment [riː'dɪ'vɛləpmənt] n
ristrutturazione f
red-handed [rɛd'hændɪd] adj: **to be caught ~**
essere preso(-a) in flagrante or con le mani
nel sacco
redhead ['rɛdhɛd] n rosso(-a)
red herring n (fig) falsa pista
red-hot [rɛd'hɔt] adj arroventato(-a)
redirect [riː'daɪ'rɛkt] vt (mail) far seguire
redistribute [riː'dɪ'strɪbjuːt] vt ridistribuire

red-letter day ['rɛdlɛtə-] n giorno
memorabile
red light n: **to go through a ~** (Aut) passare
col rosso
red-light district [rɛd'laɪt-] n quartiere m
luce rossa inv
red meat n carne f rossa
redness ['rɛdnɪs] n rossore m; (of hair) rosso
redo [riː'duː] vt irreg rifare
redolent ['rɛdələnt] adj: **~ of** che sa di; (fig)
che ricorda
redouble [riː'dʌbl] vt: **to ~ one's efforts**
raddoppiare gli sforzi
redraft [riː'drɑːft] vt fare una nuova stesura di
redress [rɪ'drɛs] n riparazione f ◼ vt
riparare; **to ~ the balance** ristabilire
l'equilibrio
Red Sea n: **the ~** il mar Rosso
redskin ['rɛdskɪn] n pellerossa m/f
red tape n (fig) burocrazia
reduce [rɪ'djuːs] vt ridurre; (lower) ridurre,
abbassare; **"~ speed now"** (Aut)
"rallentare"; **to ~ sth by/to** ridurre qc di/a;
to ~ sb to silence/despair/tears ridurre qn
al silenzio/alla disperazione/in lacrime
reduced [rɪ'djuːst] adj (decreased) ridotto(-a);
at a ~ price a prezzo ribassato or ridotto;
"greatly ~ prices" "grandi ribassi"
reduction [rɪ'dʌkʃən] n riduzione f; (of price)
ribasso; (discount) sconto
redundancy [rɪ'dʌndənsɪ] n licenziamento
(per eccesso di personale); **compulsory ~**
licenziamento; **voluntary ~** forma di cassa
integrazione volontaria
redundancy payment n (Brit) indennità f inv
di licenziamento
redundant [rɪ'dʌndnt] adj (Brit: worker)
licenziato(-a); (detail, object) superfluo(-a);
to make ~ (Brit) licenziare (per eccesso di
personale)
reed [riːd] n (Bot) canna; (Mus: of clarinet etc)
ancia
re-educate [riː'ɛdjukeɪt] vt rieducare
reedy ['riːdɪ] adj (voice, instrument) acuto(-a)
reef [riːf] n (at sea) scogliera; **coral ~** barriera
corallina
reek [riːk] vi: **to ~ (of)** puzzare (di)
reel [riːl] n bobina, rocchetto; (Tech) aspo;
(Fishing) mulinello; (Cine) rotolo ◼ vt (Tech)
annaspare; (also: **reel up**) avvolgere ◼ vi
(sway) barcollare, vacillare; **my head is
reeling** mi gira la testa
▶ **reel off** vt snocciolare
re-election [riː'ɪlɛkʃən] n rielezione f
re-enter [riː'ɛntə'] vt rientrare in
re-entry [riː'ɛntrɪ] n rientro
re-export vt [riː'ɪk'spɔːt] riesportare ◼ n

[ri:'ekspɔːt] merce f riesportata, riesportazione f

ref [rɛf] n abbr (col: = referee) arbitro

ref. abbr (Comm: = with reference to) sogg

refectory [rɪ'fɛktərɪ] n refettorio

refer [rɪ'fəː'] vt: **to ~ sth to** (dispute, decision) deferire qc a; **to ~ sb to** (inquirer: for information) indirizzare qn a; (reader: to text) rimandare qn a; **he referred me to the manager** mi ha detto di rivolgermi al direttore

▶ **refer to** vt fus (allude to) accennare a; (apply to) riferire a; (consult) rivolgersi a; **referring to your letter** (Comm) in riferimento alla Vostra lettera

referee [rɛfə'riː] n arbitro; (Tennis) giudice m di gara; (Brit: for job application) referenza ▪ vt arbitrare

reference ['rɛfrəns] n riferimento; (mention) menzione f, allusione f; (for job application: letter) referenza; lettera di raccomandazione; (: person) referenza; (in book) rimando; **with ~ to** riguardo a; (Comm: in letter) in or con riferimento a; **"please quote this ~"** (Comm) "si prega di far riferimento al numero di protocollo"

reference book n libro di consultazione

reference library n biblioteca per la consultazione

reference number n (Comm) numero di riferimento

referendum (pl **referenda**) [rɛfə'rɛndəm, -də] n referendum m inv

referral [rɪ'fəːrəl] n deferimento; (Med) richiesta (di visita specialistica)

refill vt [riː'fɪl] riempire di nuovo; (pen, lighter etc) ricaricare ▪ n ['riː'fɪl] (for pen etc) ricambio

refine [rɪ'faɪn] vt raffinare

refined [rɪ'faɪnd] adj raffinato(-a)

refinement [rɪ'faɪnmənt] n (of person) raffinatezza

refinery [rɪ'faɪnərɪ] n raffineria

refit n ['riː'fɪt] (Naut) raddobbo ▪ vt [riː'fɪt] (ship) raddobbare

reflate [riː'fleɪt] vt (economy) rilanciare

reflation [riː'fleɪʃən] n rilancio

reflationary [riː'fleɪʃənərɪ] adj nuovamente inflazionario(-a)

reflect [rɪ'flɛkt] vt (light, image) riflettere; (fig) rispecchiare ▪ vi (think) riflettere, considerare

▶ **reflect on** vt fus (discredit) rispecchiarsi su

reflection [rɪ'flɛkʃən] n riflessione f; (image) riflesso; (criticism): ~ **on** giudizio su; attacco a; **on ~** pensandoci sopra

reflector [rɪ'flɛktə'] n (also Aut) catarifrangente m

reflex ['riːflɛks] adj riflesso(-a) ▪ n riflesso

reflexive [rɪ'flɛksɪv] adj (Ling) riflessivo(-a)

reform [rɪ'fɔːm] n riforma ▪ vt riformare

reformat [rɪ'fɔːmæt] vt (Comput) riformattare

Reformation [rɛfə'meɪʃən] n: **the ~** la Riforma

reformatory [rɪ'fɔːmətərɪ] n (US) riformatorio

reformed [rɪ'fɔːmd] adj cambiato(-a) (per il meglio)

reformer [rɪ'fɔːmə'] n riformatore(-trice)

refrain [rɪ'freɪn] vi: **to ~ from doing** trattenersi dal fare ▪ n ritornello

refresh [rɪ'frɛʃ] vt rinfrescare; (food, sleep) ristorare

refresher course [rɪ'frɛʃə-] n (Brit) corso di aggiornamento

refreshing [rɪ'frɛʃɪŋ] adj (drink) rinfrescante; (sleep) riposante, ristoratore(-trice); (change etc) piacevole; (idea, point of view) originale

refreshment [rɪ'frɛʃmənt] n (eating, resting etc) ristoro; **~(s)** rinfreschi mpl

refrigeration [rɪfrɪdʒə'reɪʃən] n refrigerazione f

refrigerator [rɪ'frɪdʒəreɪtə'] n frigorifero

refuel [riː'fjuəl] vt rifornire (di carburante) ▪ vi far rifornimento (di carburante)

refuge ['rɛfjuːdʒ] n rifugio; **to take ~ in** rifugiarsi in

refugee [rɛfju'dʒiː] n rifugiato(-a), profugo(-a)

refugee camp n campo (di) profughi

refund n ['riːfʌnd] rimborso ▪ vt [rɪ'fʌnd] rimborsare

refurbish [riː'fəːbɪʃ] vt rimettere a nuovo

refurnish [riː'fəːnɪʃ] vt ammobiliare di nuovo

refusal [rɪ'fjuːzəl] n rifiuto; **to have first ~ on sth** avere il diritto d'opzione su qc

refuse¹ ['rɛfjuːs] n rifiuti mpl

refuse² [rɪ'fjuːz] vt, vi rifiutare; **to ~ to do sth** rifiutare or rifiutarsi di fare qc

refuse collection n raccolta di rifiuti

refuse disposal n sistema m di scarico dei rifiuti

refusenik [rɪ'fjuːznɪk] n ebreo a cui il governo sovietico impediva di lasciare il paese

refute [rɪ'fjuːt] vt confutare

regain [rɪ'geɪn] vt riguadagnare; riacquistare, ricuperare

regal ['riːgl] adj regale

regale [rɪ'geɪl] vt: **to ~ sb with sth** intrattenere qn con qc

regalia [rɪ'geɪlɪə] n insegne fpl reali

regard [rɪ'gaːd] n riguardo, stima ▪ vt considerare, stimare; **to give one's regards to** porgere i suoi saluti a; **(kind) regards** cordiali saluti; **as regards, with ~ to** riguardo a

r

regarding [rɪˈɡɑːdɪŋ] *prep* riguardo a, per quanto riguarda

regardless [rɪˈɡɑːdlɪs] *adv* lo stesso; **~ of** a dispetto di, nonostante

regatta [rɪˈɡætə] *n* regata

regency [ˈriːdʒənsɪ] *n* reggenza

regenerate [rɪˈdʒɛnəreɪt] *vt* rigenerare; *(feelings, enthusiasm)* far rinascere ▪ *vi* rigenerarsi; rinascere

regent [ˈriːdʒənt] *n* reggente *m*

reggae [ˈrɛɡeɪ] *n* reggae *m*

régime [reɪˈʒiːm] *n* regime *m*

regiment *n* [ˈrɛdʒɪmənt] reggimento ▪ *vt* [ˈrɛdʒɪmɛnt] irreggimentare

regimental [rɛdʒɪˈmɛntl] *adj* reggimentale

regimentation [rɛdʒɪmɛnˈteɪʃən] *n* irreggimentazione *f*

region [ˈriːdʒən] *n* regione *f*; **in the ~ of** *(fig)* all'incirca di

regional [ˈriːdʒənl] *adj* regionale

regional development *n* sviluppo regionale

register [ˈrɛdʒɪstəʳ] *n* registro; *(also:* **electoral register**) lista elettorale ▪ *vt* registrare; *(vehicle)* immatricolare; *(luggage)* spedire assicurato(-a); *(letter)* assicurare; *(instrument)* segnare ▪ *vi* iscriversi; *(at hotel)* firmare il registro; *(make impression)* entrare in testa; **to ~ a protest** fare un esposto; **to ~ for a course** iscriversi a un corso

registered [ˈrɛdʒɪstəd] *adj* *(design)* depositato(-a); *(Brit: letter)* assicurato(-a); *(student, voter)* iscritto(-a)

registered company *n* società iscritta al registro

registered nurse *n* *(US)* infermiere(-a) diplomato(-a)

registered office *n* sede *f* legale

registered trademark *n* marchio depositato

registrar [ˈrɛdʒɪstrɑːʳ] *n* ufficiale *m* di stato civile; segretario

registration [rɛdʒɪsˈtreɪʃən] *n* *(act)* registrazione *f*; iscrizione *f*; *(Aut: also:* **registration number**) numero di targa

registry [ˈrɛdʒɪstrɪ] *n* ufficio del registro

registry office *n* *(Brit)* anagrafe *f*; **to get married in a ~** ≈ sposarsi in municipio

regret [rɪˈɡrɛt] *n* rimpianto, rincrescimento ▪ *vt* rimpiangere; **I ~ that I/he cannot help** mi rincresce di non poter aiutare/che lui non possa aiutare; **we ~ to inform you that ...** siamo spiacenti di informarla che ...

regretfully [rɪˈɡrɛtfəlɪ] *adv* con rincrescimento

regrettable [rɪˈɡrɛtəbl] *adj* deplorevole

regrettably [rɪˈɡrɛtəblɪ] *adv* purtroppo, sfortunatamente

regroup [riːˈɡruːp] *vt* raggruppare ▪ *vi* raggrupparsi

regt *abbr* (= **regiment**) Reg

regular [ˈrɛɡjuləʳ] *adj* regolare; *(usual)* abituale, normale; *(listener, reader)* fedele; *(soldier)* dell'esercito regolare; *(Comm: size)* normale ▪ *n* *(client etc)* cliente *m/f* abituale

regularity [rɛɡjuˈlærɪtɪ] *n* regolarità *f inv*

regularly [ˈrɛɡjuləlɪ] *adv* regolarmente

regulate [ˈrɛɡjuleɪt] *vt* regolare

regulation [rɛɡjuˈleɪʃən] *n* *(rule)* regola, regolamento; *(adjustment)* regolazione *f* ▪ *cpd* *(Mil)* di ordinanza

rehabilitate [riːəˈbɪlɪteɪt] *vt* *(criminal, drug addict, invalid)* ricuperare, reinserire

rehabilitation [ˈriːəbɪlɪˈteɪʃən] *n* *(see vb)* ricupero, reinserimento

rehash [riːˈhæʃ] *vt* *(col)* rimaneggiare

rehearsal [rɪˈhəːsəl] *n* prova; **dress ~** prova generale

rehearse [rɪˈhəːs] *vt* provare

rehouse [riːˈhauz] *vt* rialloggiare

reign [reɪn] *n* regno ▪ *vi* regnare

reigning [ˈreɪnɪŋ] *adj* *(monarch)* regnante; *(champion)* attuale

reimburse [riːɪmˈbəːs] *vt* rimborsare

rein [reɪn] *n* *(for horse)* briglia; **to give sb free ~** *(fig)* lasciare completa libertà a qn

reincarnation [riːɪnkɑːˈneɪʃən] *n* reincarnazione *f*

reindeer [ˈreɪndɪəʳ] *n pl inv* renna

reinforce [riːɪnˈfɔːs] *vt* rinforzare

reinforced concrete [riːɪnˈfɔːst-] *n* cemento armato

reinforcement [riːɪnˈfɔːsmənt] *n* *(action)* rinforzamento; **reinforcements** *npl* *(Mil)* rinforzi *mpl*

reinstate [riːɪnˈsteɪt] *vt* reintegrare

reinstatement [riːɪnˈsteɪtmənt] *n* reintegrazione *f*

reissue [riːˈɪʃjuː] *vt* *(book)* ristampare, ripubblicare; *(film)* distribuire di nuovo

reiterate [riːˈɪtəreɪt] *vt* reiterare, ripetere

reject *n* [ˈriːdʒɛkt] *(Comm)* scarto ▪ *vt* [rɪˈdʒɛkt] rifiutare, respingere; *(Comm: goods)* scartare

rejection [rɪˈdʒɛkʃən] *n* rifiuto

rejoice [rɪˈdʒɔɪs] *vi*: **to ~ (at** *or* **over)** provare diletto (in)

rejoinder [rɪˈdʒɔɪndəʳ] *n* *(retort)* replica

rejuvenate [rɪˈdʒuːvəneɪt] *vt* ringiovanire

rekindle [riːˈkɪndl] *vt* riaccendere

relapse [rɪˈlæps] *n* *(Med)* ricaduta

relate [rɪˈleɪt] *vt* *(tell)* raccontare; *(connect)* collegare ▪ *vi*: **to ~ to** *(refer to)* riferirsi a; *(get on with)* stabilire un rapporto con

related [rɪˈleɪtɪd] *adj* imparentato(-a); collegato(-a), connesso(-a); **~ to** imparentato(-a) con; collegato(-a) *or* connesso(-a) con

relating [rɪ'leɪtɪŋ]: ~ **to** *prep* che riguarda, rispetto a

relation [rɪ'leɪʃən] *n* (*person*) parente *m/f*; (*link*) rapporto, relazione *f*; **in ~ to** con riferimento a; **diplomatic/international relations** rapporti diplomatici/internazionali; **to bear a ~ to** corrispondere a

relationship [rɪ'leɪʃənʃɪp] *n* rapporto; (*personal ties*) rapporti *mpl*, relazioni *fpl*; (*also*: **family relationship**) legami *mpl* di parentela; (*affair*) relazione *f*; **they have a good ~** vanno molto d'accordo

relative ['rɛlətɪv] *n* parente *m/f* ■ *adj* relativo(-a); (*respective*) rispettivo(-a)

relatively ['rɛlətɪvlɪ] *adv* relativamente; (*fairly, rather*) abbastanza

relax [rɪ'læks] *vi* rilasciarsi; (*person: unwind*) rilassarsi ■ *vt* rilasciare; (*mind, person*) rilassare; **~!** (*calm down*) calma!

relaxation [ri:læk'seɪʃən] *n* rilasciamento; rilassamento; (*entertainment*) ricreazione *f*, svago

relaxed [rɪ'lækst] *adj* rilasciato(-a); rilassato(-a)

relaxing [rɪ'læksɪŋ] *adj* rilassante

relay ['ri:leɪ] *n* (*Sport*) corsa a staffetta ■ *vt* (*message*) trasmettere

release [rɪ'li:s] *n* (*from prison*) rilascio; (*from obligation*) liberazione *f*; (*of gas etc*) emissione *f*; (*of film etc*) distribuzione *f*; (*record*) disco; (*device*) disinnesto ■ *vt* (*prisoner*) rilasciare; (*from obligation, wreckage etc*) liberare; (*book, film*) fare uscire; (*news*) rendere pubblico(-a); (*gas etc*) emettere; (*Tech: catch, spring etc*) disinnestare; (*let go*) rilasciare; lasciar andare; sciogliere; **to ~ one's grip** mollare la presa; **to ~ the clutch** (*Aut*) staccare la frizione

relegate ['rɛləgeɪt] *vt* relegare; (*Sport*): **to be relegated** essere retrocesso(-a)

relent [rɪ'lɛnt] *vi* cedere

relentless [rɪ'lɛntlɪs] *adj* implacabile

relevance ['rɛləvəns] *n* pertinenza; **~ of sth to sth** rapporto tra qc e qc

relevant ['rɛləvənt] *adj* pertinente; (*chapter*) in questione; **~ to** pertinente a

reliability [rɪlaɪə'bɪlɪtɪ] *n* (*of person*) serietà; (*of machine*) affidabilità

reliable [rɪ'laɪəbl] *adj* (*person, firm*) fidato(-a), che dà affidamento; (*method*) sicuro(-a); (*machine*) affidabile

reliably [rɪ'laɪəblɪ] *adv*: **to be ~ informed** sapere da fonti sicure

reliance [rɪ'laɪəns] *n*: **~ (on)** dipendenza (da)

reliant [rɪ'laɪənt] *adj*: **to be ~ on sth/sb** dipendere da qc/qn

relic ['rɛlɪk] *n* (*Rel*) reliquia; (*of the past*) resto

relief [rɪ'li:f] *n* (*from pain, anxiety*) sollievo; (*help, supplies*) soccorsi *mpl*; (*of guard*) cambio; (*Art, Geo*) rilievo; **by way of light ~** come diversivo

relief map *n* carta in rilievo

relief road *n* (*Brit*) circonvallazione *f*

relieve [rɪ'li:v] *vt* (*pain, patient*) sollevare; (*bring help*) soccorrere; (*take over from: gen*) sostituire; (*: guard*) rilevare; **to ~ sb of his command** (*Mil*) esonerare qn dal comando; **to ~ o.s.** (*euphemism*) fare i propri bisogni

relieved [rɪ'li:vd] *adj* sollevato(-a); **to be ~ that ...** essere sollevato(-a) (dal fatto) che ...; **I'm ~ to hear it** mi hai tolto un peso con questa notizia

religion [rɪ'lɪdʒən] *n* religione *f*

religious [rɪ'lɪdʒəs] *adj* religioso(-a)

religious education *n* religione *f*

relinquish [rɪ'lɪŋkwɪʃ] *vt* abbandonare; (*plan, habit*) rinunziare a

relish ['rɛlɪʃ] *n* (*Culin*) condimento; (*enjoyment*) gran piacere *m* ■ *vt* (*food etc*) godere; **to ~ doing** adorare fare

relive [ri:'lɪv] *vt* rivivere

reload [ri:'ləud] *vt* ricaricare

relocate [ri:ləu'keɪt] *vt* (*business*) trasferire ■ *vi*: **to ~ in** trasferire la propria sede a

reluctance [rɪ'lʌktəns] *n* riluttanza

reluctant [rɪ'lʌktənt] *adj* riluttante, mal disposto(-a); **to be ~ to do sth** essere restio a fare qc

reluctantly [rɪ'lʌktəntlɪ] *adv* di mala voglia, a malincuore

rely [rɪ'laɪ]: **to ~ on** *vt fus* contare su; (*be dependent*) dipendere da

remain [rɪ'meɪn] *vi* restare, rimanere; **to ~ silent** restare in silenzio; **I ~, yours faithfully** (*Brit: in letters*) distinti saluti

remainder [rɪ'meɪndər] *n* resto; (*Comm*) rimanenza

remaining [rɪ'meɪnɪŋ] *adj* che rimane

remains [rɪ'meɪnz] *npl* resti *mpl*

remand [rɪ'mɑːnd] *n*: **on ~** in detenzione preventiva ■ *vt*: **to ~ in custody** rinviare in carcere; trattenere a disposizione della legge

remand home *n* (*Brit*) riformatorio, casa di correzione

remark [rɪ'mɑːk] *n* osservazione *f* ■ *vt* osservare, dire; (*notice*) notare ■ *vi*: **to ~ on sth** fare dei commenti su qc

remarkable [rɪ'mɑːkəbl] *adj* notevole; eccezionale

remarry [ri:'mærɪ] *vi* risposarsi

remedial [rɪ'miːdɪəl] *adj* (*tuition, classes*) di riparazione

remedy ['rɛmədɪ] *n*: **~ (for)** rimedio (per) ■ *vt* rimediare a

remember [rɪ'mɛmbə^r] vt ricordare, ricordarsi di; **I ~ seeing it, I ~ having seen it** (mi) ricordo di averlo visto; **she remembered to do it** si è ricordata di farlo; **~ me to your wife and children!** saluti sua moglie e i bambini da parte mia!

remembrance [rɪ'mɛmbrəns] n memoria; ricordo

Remembrance Sunday n (Brit) vedi nota

● **REMEMBRANCE SUNDAY**
●
● Nel Regno Unito, la domenica più vicina
● all'11 di novembre, data in cui fu firmato
● l'armistizio con la Germania nel 1918,
● ricorre il Remembrance Sunday, giorno in cui
● vengono commemorati i caduti in guerra.
● In questa occasione molti portano un
● papavero di carta appuntato al petto in
● segno di rispetto.

remind [rɪ'maɪnd] vt: **to ~ sb of sth** ricordare qc a qn; **to ~ sb to do** ricordare a qn di fare; **that reminds me!** a proposito!

reminder [rɪ'maɪndə^r] n richiamo; (note etc) promemoria m inv

reminisce [rɛmɪ'nɪs] vi: **to ~ (about)** abbandonarsi ai ricordi (di)

reminiscences [rɛmɪ'nɪsnsɪz] npl reminiscenze fpl, memorie fpl

reminiscent [rɛmɪ'nɪsnt] adj: **~ of** che fa pensare a, che richiama

remiss [rɪ'mɪs] adj negligente; **it was ~ of me** è stata una negligenza da parte mia

remission [rɪ'mɪʃən] n remissione f; (of fee) esonero

remit [rɪ'mɪt] vt rimettere

remittance [rɪ'mɪtəns] n rimessa

remnant ['rɛmnənt] n resto, avanzo; **remnants** npl (Comm) scampoli mpl; fine f serie

remonstrate ['rɛmənstreɪt] vi protestare; **to ~ with sb about sth** fare le proprie rimostranze a qn circa qc

remorse [rɪ'mɔːs] n rimorso

remorseful [rɪ'mɔːsful] adj pieno(-a) di rimorsi

remorseless [rɪ'mɔːslɪs] adj (fig) spietato(-a)

remote [rɪ'məut] adj remoto(-a), lontano(-a); (person) distaccato(-a); **there is a ~ possibility that ...** c'è una vaga possibilità che ... +sub

remote control n telecomando

remote-controlled [rɪ'məutkən'trəuld] adj telecomandato(-a)

remotely [rɪ'məutlɪ] adv remotamente; (slightly) vagamente

remoteness [rɪ'məutnɪs] n lontananza

remould ['riː'məuld] n (Brit: tyre) gomma rivestita

removable [rɪ'muːvəbl] adj (detachable) staccabile

removal [rɪ'muːvəl] n (taking away) rimozione f; soppressione f; (from house) trasloco; (from office: sacking) destituzione f; (Med) ablazione f

removal man n (Brit) addetto ai traslochi

removal van n (Brit) furgone m per traslochi

remove [rɪ'muːv] vt togliere, rimuovere; (employee) destituire; (stain) far sparire; (doubt, abuse) sopprimere, eliminare; **first cousin once removed** cugino di secondo grado

remover [rɪ'muːvə^r] n (for paint) prodotto sverniciante; (for varnish) solvente m; **make-up ~** struccatore m

remunerate [rɪ'mjuːnəreɪt] vt rimunerare

remuneration [rɪmjuːnə'reɪʃən] n rimunerazione f

Renaissance [rə'neɪsəns] n: **the ~** il Rinascimento

rename [riː'neɪm] vt ribattezzare

rend (pt, pp **rent**) [rɛnd, rɛnt] vt lacerare

render ['rɛndə^r] vt rendere; (Culin: fat) struggere

rendering ['rɛndərɪŋ] n (Mus etc) interpretazione f

rendez-vous ['rɒndɪvuː] n appuntamento; (place) luogo d'incontro; (meeting) incontro ■ vi ritrovarsi; (spaceship) effettuare un rendez-vous

rendition [rɛn'dɪʃən] n (Mus) interpretazione f

renegade ['rɛnɪgeɪd] n rinnegato(-a)

renew [rɪ'njuː] vt rinnovare; (negotiations) riprendere

renewable [rɪ'njuːəbl] adj riutilizzabile; (contract, energy) rinnovabile; **~ energy, renewables** fonti mpl di energia rinnovabile

renewal [rɪ'njuːəl] n rinnovamento; ripresa

renounce [rɪ'nauns] vt rinunziare a; (disown) ripudiare

renovate ['rɛnəveɪt] vt rinnovare; (art work) restaurare

renovation [rɛnə'veɪʃən] n rinnovamento; restauro

renown [rɪ'naun] n rinomanza

renowned [rɪ'naund] adj rinomato(-a)

rent [rɛnt] pt, pp of **rend** ■ n affitto ■ vt (take for rent) prendere in affitto; (car, TV) noleggiare, prendere a noleggio; (also: **rent out**) dare in affitto; (car, TV) noleggiare, dare a noleggio

rental ['rɛntl] n (cost: on TV, telephone) abbonamento; (: on car) nolo, noleggio

rent boy n (Brit col) giovane prostituto

renunciation [rɪnʌnsɪ'eɪʃən] *n*
rinnegamento; (*self-denial*) rinunzia
reopen [ri:'əupən] *vt* riaprire
reopening [ri:'əupnɪŋ] *n* riapertura
reorder [ri:'ɔ:dəʳ] *vt* ordinare di nuovo;
(*rearrange*) riorganizzare
reorganize [ri:'ɔ:gənaɪz] *vt* riorganizzare
Rep *abbr* (*US Pol*) = **representative**;
Republican
rep [rɛp] *n abbr* (*Comm*: = *representative*)
rappresentante *m/f*; (*Theat*: *repertory*) teatro
di repertorio
repair [rɪ'pɛəʳ] *n* riparazione *f* ■ *vt* riparare;
in good/bad ~ in buona/cattiva condizione;
under ~ in riparazione
repair kit *n* corredo per riparazioni
repair man *n* riparatore *m*
repair shop *n* (*Aut etc*) officina
repartee [rɛpɑ:'ti:] *n* risposta pronta
repast [rɪ'pɑ:st] *n* (*formal*) pranzo
repatriate [ri:'pætrɪeɪt] *vt* rimpatriare
repay [ri:'peɪ] *vt irreg* (*money, creditor*)
rimborsare, ripagare; (*sb's efforts*)
ricompensare
repayment [ri:'peɪmənt] *n* rimborsamento;
ricompensa
repeal [rɪ'pi:l] *n* (*of law*) abrogazione *f*;
(*of sentence*) annullamento ■ *vt* abrogare;
annullare
repeat [rɪ'pi:t] *n* (*Radio, TV*) replica ■ *vt*
ripetere; (*pattern*) riprodurre; (*promise, attack,
also Comm: order*) rinnovare ■ *vi* ripetere
repeatedly [rɪ'pi:tɪdlɪ] *adv* ripetutamente,
spesso
repeat order *n* (*Comm*): **to place a ~ (for)**
rinnovare l'ordinazione (di)
repel [rɪ'pɛl] *vt* respingere
repellent [rɪ'pɛlənt] *adj* repellente ■ *n*:
insect ~ prodotto *m* anti-insetti *inv*; **moth ~**
anti-tarmico
repent [rɪ'pɛnt] *vi*: **to ~ (of)** pentirsi (di)
repentance [rɪ'pɛntəns] *n* pentimento
repercussion [ri:pə'kʌʃən] *n* (*consequence*)
ripercussione *f*
repertoire ['rɛpətwɑ:ʳ] *n* repertorio
repertory ['rɛpətərɪ] *n* (*also*: **repertory
theatre**) teatro di repertorio
repertory company *n* compagnia di
repertorio
repetition [rɛpɪ'tɪʃən] *n* ripetizione *f*;
(*Comm: of order etc*) rinnovo
repetitious [rɛpɪ'tɪʃəs] *adj* (*speech*) pieno(-a)
di ripetizioni
repetitive [rɪ'pɛtɪtɪv] *adj* (*movement*) che si
ripete; (*work*) monotono(-a); (*speech*)
pieno(-a) di ripetizioni
replace [rɪ'pleɪs] *vt* (*put back*) rimettere a

posto; (*take the place of*) sostituire; (*Tel*):
"~ the receiver" "riattaccare"
replacement [rɪ'pleɪsmənt] *n* rimessa;
sostituzione *f*; (*person*) sostituto(-a)
replacement part *n* pezzo di ricambio
replay ['ri:pleɪ] *n* (*of match*) partita ripetuta;
(*of tape, film*) replay *m inv*
replenish [rɪ'plɛnɪʃ] *vt* (*glass*) riempire; (*stock
etc*) rifornire
replete [rɪ'pli:t] *adj*: ~ **(with)** ripieno(-a) (di);
(*well-fed*) sazio(-a) (di)
replica ['rɛplɪkə] *n* replica, copia
reply [rɪ'plaɪ] *n* risposta ■ *vi* rispondere; **in ~**
in risposta; **there's no ~** (*Tel*) non risponde
(nessuno)
reply coupon *n* buono di risposta
report [rɪ'pɔ:t] *n* rapporto; (*Press etc*) cronaca;
(*Brit: also*: **school report**) pagella ■ *vt*
riportare; (*Press etc*) fare una cronaca su;
(*bring to notice: occurrence*) segnalare; (: *person*)
denunciare ■ *vi* (*make a report*) fare un
rapporto (o una cronaca); (*present o.s.*): **to ~
(to sb)** presentarsi (a qn); **to ~ (on)** fare un
rapporto (su); **it is reported that** si dice che;
it is reported from Berlin that ... ci è stato
riferito da Berlino che ....
report card *n* (*US, Scottish*) pagella
reportedly [rɪ'pɔ:tɪdlɪ] *adv*: **she is ~ living in
Spain** si dice che vive in Spagna
reported speech [rɪ'pɔ:tɪd-] *n* (*Ling*) discorso
indiretto
reporter [rɪ'pɔ:təʳ] *n* (*Press*) cronista *m/f*,
reporter *m inv*; (*Radio*) radiocronista *m/f*; (*TV*)
telecronista *m/f*
repose [rɪ'pəuz] *n*: **in ~** in riposo
repossess [ri:pə'zɛs] *vt* rientrare in possesso
di
repossession order [ri:pə'zɛʃən-] *n* ordine *m*
di espropriazione
reprehensible [rɛprɪ'hɛnsɪbl] *adj* riprensibile
represent [rɛprɪ'zɛnt] *vt* rappresentare
representation [rɛprɪzɛn'teɪʃən] *n*
rappresentazione *f*; **representations** *npl*
(*protest*) protesta
representative [rɛprɪ'zɛntətɪv] *n*
rappresentativo(-a); (*Comm*) rappresentante
m (di commercio); (*US: Pol*) deputato(-a)
■ *adj*: ~ **(of)** rappresentativo(-a) (di)
repress [rɪ'prɛs] *vt* reprimere
repression [rɪ'prɛʃən] *n* repressione *f*
repressive [rɪ'prɛsɪv] *adj* repressivo(-a)
reprieve [rɪ'pri:v] *n* (*Law*) sospensione *f*
dell'esecuzione della condanna; (*fig*)
dilazione *f* ■ *vt* sospendere l'esecuzione
della condanna a; accordare una dilazione a
reprimand ['rɛprɪmɑ:nd] *n* rimprovero ■ *vt*
rimproverare, redarguire

r

reprint ['riːprɪnt] n ristampa ■ vt
ristampare

reprisal [rɪ'praɪzl] n rappresaglia; **to take
reprisals** fare delle rappresaglie

reproach [rɪ'prəutʃ] n rimprovero ■ vt: **to ~
sb with sth** rimproverare qn di qc; **beyond ~**
irreprensibile

reproachful [rɪ'prəutʃful] adj di rimprovero

reproduce [riːprə'djuːs] vt riprodurre ■ vi
riprodursi

reproduction [riːprə'dʌkʃən] n
riproduzione f

reproductive [riːprə'dʌktɪv] adj
riproduttore(-trice); riproduttivo(-a)

reproof [rɪ'pruːf] n riprovazione f

reprove [rɪ'pruːv] vt (action) disapprovare;
(person): **to ~ (for)** biasimare (per)

reproving [rɪ'pruːvɪŋ] adj di disapprovazione

reptile ['rɛptaɪl] n rettile m

Repub. abbr (US Pol) = **Republican**

republic [rɪ'pʌblɪk] n repubblica

republican [rɪ'pʌblɪkən] adj, n
repubblicano(-a)

repudiate [rɪ'pjuːdɪeɪt] vt ripudiare

repugnant [rɪ'pʌgnənt] adj ripugnante

repulse [rɪ'pʌls] vt respingere

repulsion [rɪ'pʌlʃən] n ripulsione f

repulsive [rɪ'pʌlsɪv] adj ripugnante,
ripulsivo(-a)

reputable ['rɛpjutəbl] adj di buona
reputazione; (occupation) rispettabile

reputation [rɛpju'teɪʃən] n reputazione f;
he has a ~ for being awkward ha la fama di
essere un tipo difficile

repute [rɪ'pjuːt] n reputazione f

reputed [rɪ'pjuːtɪd] adj reputato(-a); **to be ~
to be rich/intelligent** etc essere ritenuto(-a)
ricco(-a)/intelligente etc

reputedly [rɪ'pjuːtɪdlɪ] adv secondo quanto si
dice

request [rɪ'kwɛst] n domanda; (formal)
richiesta ■ vt: **to ~ (of** or **from sb)** chiedere
(a qn); **at the ~ of** su richiesta di; **"you are
requested not to smoke"** "si prega di non
fumare"

request stop n (Brit: for bus) fermata
facoltativa or a richiesta

requiem ['rɛkwɪəm] n requiem m or f inv

require [rɪ'kwaɪər] vt (need: person) aver
bisogno di; (: thing, situation) richiedere;
(want) volere; esigere; (order) obbligare; **to ~
sb to do sth/sth of sb** esigere che qn faccia
qc/qc da qn; **what qualifications are
required?** che requisiti ci vogliono?;
required by law prescritto dalla legge;
if required in caso di bisogno

required [rɪ'kwaɪəd] adj richiesto(-a)

requirement [rɪ'kwaɪəmənt] n (need)
esigenza; (condition) requisito; **to meet sb's
requirements** soddisfare le esigenze di qn

requisite ['rɛkwɪzɪt] n cosa necessaria ■ adj
necessario(-a); **toilet requisites** articoli mpl
da toletta

requisition [rɛkwɪ'zɪʃən] n: **~ (for)** richiesta
(di) ■ vt (Mil) requisire

reroute [riː'ruːt] vt (train etc) deviare

resale ['riːseɪl] n rivendita

resale price maintenance n prezzo minimo
di vendita imposto

rescind [rɪ'sɪnd] vt annullare; (law) abrogare;
(judgement) rescindere

rescue ['rɛskjuː] n salvataggio; (help) soccorso
■ vt salvare; **to come/go to sb's ~** venire/
andare in aiuto a or di qn

rescue party n squadra di salvataggio

rescuer ['rɛskjuər] n salvatore(-trice)

research [rɪ'səːtʃ] n ricerca, ricerche fpl ■ vt
fare ricerche su ■ vi: **to ~ (into sth)** fare
ricerca (su qc); **a piece of ~** un lavoro di
ricerca; **~ and development** ricerca e
sviluppo

researcher [rɪ'səːtʃər] n ricercatore(-trice)

research work n ricerche fpl

resell [riː'sɛl] vt irreg rivendere

resemblance [rɪ'zɛmbləns] n somiglianza;
to bear a strong ~ to somigliare
moltissimo a

resemble [rɪ'zɛmbl] vt assomigliare a

resent [rɪ'zɛnt] vt risentirsi di

resentful [rɪ'zɛntful] adj pieno(-a) di
risentimento

resentment [rɪ'zɛntmənt] n risentimento

reservation [rɛzə'veɪʃən] n (booking)
prenotazione f; (doubt) dubbio; (protected area)
riserva; (Brit Aut: also: **central reservation**)
spartitraffico m inv; **to make a ~ (in an
hotel/a restaurant/on a plane)** prenotare
(una camera/una tavola/un posto); **with
reservations** (doubts) con le dovute riserve

reservation desk n (US: in hotel) reception f
inv

reserve [rɪ'zəːv] n riserva ■ vt (seats etc)
prenotare; **reserves** npl (Mil) riserve fpl;
in ~ in serbo

reserve currency n valuta di riserva

reserved [rɪ'zəːvd] adj (shy) riservato(-a);
(seat) prenotato(-a)

reserve price n (Brit) prezzo di riserva, prezzo
m base inv

reserve team n (Brit Sport) seconda squadra

reservist [rɪ'zəːvɪst] n (Mil) riservista m

reservoir ['rɛzəvwaːr] n serbatoio; (artificial
lake) bacino idrico

reset [riː'sɛt] vt (Comput) azzerare

reshape [riːˈʃeɪp] vt (policy) ristrutturare
reshuffle [riːˈʃʌfl] n: **Cabinet ~** (Pol) rimpasto governativo
reside [rɪˈzaɪd] vi risiedere
residence [ˈrɛzɪdəns] n residenza; **to take up ~** prendere residenza; **in ~** (queen etc) in sede; (doctor) fisso
residence permit n (Brit) permesso di soggiorno
resident [ˈrɛzɪdənt] n (gen, Comput) residente m/f; (in hotel) cliente m/f fisso(-a) ■ adj residente
residential [rɛzɪˈdɛnʃəl] adj di residenza; (area) residenziale
residue [ˈrɛzɪdjuː] n resto; (Chem, Physics) residuo
resign [rɪˈzaɪn] vt (one's post) dimettersi da ■ vi: **to ~ (from)** dimettersi (da), dare le dimissioni (da); **to ~ o.s. to** rassegnarsi a
resignation [rɛzɪɡˈneɪʃən] n dimissioni fpl; rassegnazione f; **to tender one's ~** dare le dimissioni
resilience [rɪˈzɪliəns] n (of material) elasticità, resilienza; (of person) capacità di recupero
resilient [rɪˈzɪliənt] adj elastico(-a); (person) che si riprende facilmente
resin [ˈrɛzɪn] n resina
resist [rɪˈzɪst] vt resistere a
resistance [rɪˈzɪstəns] n resistenza
resistant [rɪˈzɪstənt] adj: **~ (to)** resistente (a)
resolute [ˈrɛzəluːt] adj risoluto(-a)
resolution [rɛzəˈluːʃən] n (resolve) fermo proposito, risoluzione f; (determination) risolutezza; (on screen) risoluzione f; **to make a ~** fare un proposito
resolve [rɪˈzɔlv] n risoluzione f ■ vi (decide): **to ~ to do** decidere di fare ■ vt (problem) risolvere
resolved [rɪˈzɔlvd] adj risoluto(-a)
resonance [ˈrɛzənəns] n risonanza
resonant [ˈrɛzənənt] adj risonante
resort [rɪˈzɔːt] n (town) stazione f; (place) località f inv; (recourse) ricorso ■ vi: **to ~ to** far ricorso a; **seaside/winter sports ~** stazione f balneare/di sport invernali; **as a last ~** come ultima risorsa
resound [rɪˈzaund] vi: **to ~ (with)** risonare (di)
resounding [rɪˈzaundɪŋ] adj risonante
resource [rɪˈsɔːs] n risorsa; **resources** npl risorse fpl; **natural resources** risorse naturali; **to leave sb to his** (or **her**) **own resources** (fig) lasciare che qn si arrangi (per conto suo)
resourceful [rɪˈsɔːsful] adj pieno(-a) di risorse, intraprendente
resourcefulness [rɪˈsɔːsfəlnɪs] n intraprendenza

respect [rɪsˈpɛkt] n rispetto; (point, detail): **in some respects** sotto certi aspetti ■ vt rispettare; **respects** npl ossequi mpl; **to have** or **show ~ for** aver rispetto per; **out of ~ for** per rispetto or riguardo a; **with ~ to** rispetto a, riguardo a; **in ~ of** quanto a; **in this ~** per questo riguardo; **with (all) due ~ I ...** con rispetto parlando, io ...
respectability [rɪspɛktəˈbɪlɪtɪ] n rispettabilità
respectable [rɪsˈpɛktəbl] adj rispettabile; (quite big: amount etc) considerevole; (quite good: player, result etc) niente male inv
respectful [rɪsˈpɛktful] adj rispettoso(-a)
respective [rɪsˈpɛktɪv] adj rispettivo(-a)
respectively [rɪsˈpɛktɪvlɪ] adv rispettivamente
respiration [rɛspɪˈreɪʃən] n respirazione f
respirator [ˈrɛspɪreɪtər] n respiratore m
respiratory [ˈrɛspərətərɪ] adj respiratorio(-a)
respite [ˈrɛspaɪt] n respiro, tregua
resplendent [rɪsˈplɛndənt] adj risplendente
respond [rɪsˈpɔnd] vi rispondere
respondent [rɪsˈpɔndənt] n (Law) convenuto(-a)
response [rɪsˈpɔns] n risposta; **in ~ to** in risposta a
responsibility [rɪspɔnsɪˈbɪlɪtɪ] n responsabilità f inv; **to take ~ for sth/sb** assumersi or prendersi la responsabilità di qc/per qn
responsible [rɪsˈpɔnsɪbl] adj (liable): **~ (for)** responsabile (di); (trustworthy) fidato(-a); (job) di (grande) responsabilità; **to be ~ to sb (for sth)** dover rispondere a qn (di qc)
responsibly [rɪsˈpɔnsəblɪ] adv responsabilmente
responsive [rɪsˈpɔnsɪv] adj che reagisce
rest [rɛst] n riposo; (stop) sosta, pausa; (Mus) pausa; (support) appoggio, sostegno; (remainder) resto, avanzi mpl ■ vi riposarsi; (remain) rimanere, restare; (be supported): **to ~ on** appoggiarsi su ■ vt (lean): **to ~ sth on/against** appoggiare qc su/contro; **to set sb's mind at ~** tranquillizzare qn; **the ~ of them** gli altri; **to ~ one's eyes** or **gaze on** posare lo sguardo su; **~ assured that ...** stia tranquillo che ...; **it rests with him to decide** sta a lui decidere
restart [riːˈstɑːt] vt (engine) rimettere in marcia; (work) ricominciare
restaurant [ˈrɛstərɔŋ] n ristorante m
restaurant car n (Brit) vagone m ristorante
rest cure n cura del riposo
restful [ˈrɛstful] adj riposante
rest home n casa di riposo
restitution [rɛstɪˈtjuːʃən] n (act) restituzione f; (reparation) riparazione f

r

restive ['rɛstɪv] *adj* agitato(-a), impaziente; (*horse*) restio(-a)

restless ['rɛstlɪs] *adj* agitato(-a), irrequieto(-a); **to get ~** spazientirsi

restlessly ['rɛstlɪslɪ] *adv* in preda all'agitazione

restock [riː'stɔk] *vt* rifornire

restoration [rɛstə'reɪʃən] *n* restauro; restituzione *f*

restorative [rɪ'stɔrətɪv] *adj* corroborante, ristorativo(-a) ■ *n* ricostituente *m*

restore [rɪ'stɔːʳ] *vt* (*building*) restaurare; (*sth stolen*) restituire; (*peace, health*) ristorare

restorer [rɪs'tɔːrəʳ] *n* (*Art etc*) restauratore(-trice)

restrain [rɪs'treɪn] *vt* (*feeling*) contenere, frenare; (*person*): **to ~ (from doing)** trattenere (dal fare)

restrained [rɪs'treɪnd] *adj* (*style*) contenuto(-a), sobrio(-a); (*manner*) riservato(-a)

restraint [rɪs'treɪnt] *n* (*restriction*) limitazione *f*; (*moderation*) ritegno; **wage ~** restrizioni *fpl* salariali

restrict [rɪs'trɪkt] *vt* restringere, limitare

restricted area [rɪs'trɪktɪd-] *n* (*Aut*) zona a velocità limitata

restriction [rɪs'trɪkʃən] *n* restrizione *f*, limitazione *f*

restrictive [rɪs'trɪktɪv] *adj* restrittivo(-a)

restrictive practices *npl* (*Industry*) pratiche restrittive di produzione

rest room *n* (*US*) toletta

restructure [riː'strʌktʃəʳ] *vt* ristrutturare

result [rɪ'zʌlt] *n* risultato ■ *vi*: **to ~ in** avere per risultato; **as a ~ (of)** in or di conseguenza (a), in seguito (a); **to ~ (from)** essere una conseguenza (di), essere causato(-a) (da)

resultant [rɪ'zʌltənt] *adj* risultante, conseguente

resume [rɪ'zjuːm] *vt, vi* (*work, journey*) riprendere; (*sum up*) riassumere

résumé ['reɪzjuːmeɪ] *n* riassunto; (*US: curriculum vitae*) curriculum vitae *m inv*

resumption [rɪ'zʌmpʃən] *n* ripresa

resurgence [rɪ'səːdʒəns] *n* rinascita

resurrection [rɛzə'rɛkʃən] *n* risurrezione *f*

resuscitate [rɪ'sʌsɪteɪt] *vt* (*Med*) risuscitare

resuscitation [rɪsʌsɪ'teɪʃən] *n* rianimazione *f*

retail ['riːteɪl] *n* (*vendita al*) minuto ■ *cpd* al minuto ■ *vt* vendere al minuto ■ *vi*: **to ~ at** essere in vendita al pubblico al prezzo di

retailer ['riːteɪləʳ] *n* commerciante *m/f* al minuto, dettagliante *m/f*

retail outlet *n* punto di vendita al dettaglio

retail price *n* prezzo al minuto

retail price index *n* indice *m* dei prezzi al consumo

retain [rɪ'teɪn] *vt* (*keep*) tenere, serbare

retainer [rɪ'teɪnəʳ] *n* (*servant*) servitore *m*; (*fee*) onorario

retaliate [rɪ'tælɪeɪt] *vi*: **to ~ (against)** vendicarsi (di); **to ~ on sb** fare una rappresaglia contro qn

retaliation [rɪtælɪ'eɪʃən] *n* rappresaglie *fpl*; **in ~ for** per vendicarsi di

retaliatory [rɪ'tælɪətərɪ] *adj* di rappresaglia, di ritorsione

retarded [rɪ'tɑːdɪd] *adj* ritardato(-a); (*also*: **mentally retarded**) tardo(-a) (di mente)

retch [rɛtʃ] *vi* aver conati di vomito

retentive [rɪ'tɛntɪv] *adj* ritentivo(-a)

rethink ['riː'θɪŋk] *vt* ripensare

reticence ['rɛtɪsns] *n* reticenza

reticent ['rɛtɪsnt] *adj* reticente

retina ['rɛtɪnə] *n* retina

retinue ['rɛtɪnjuː] *n* seguito, scorta

retire [rɪ'taɪəʳ] *vi* (*give up work*) andare in pensione; (*withdraw*) ritirarsi, andarsene; (*go to bed*) andare a letto, ritirarsi

retired [rɪ'taɪəd] *adj* (*person*) pensionato(-a)

retirement [rɪ'taɪəmənt] *n* pensione *f*

retirement age *n* età del pensionamento

retiring [rɪ'taɪərɪŋ] *adj* (*person*) riservato(-a); (*departing: chairman*) uscente

retort [rɪ'tɔːt] *n* (*reply*) rimbecco; (*container*) storta ■ *vi* rimbeccare

retrace [riː'treɪs] *vt* ricostruire; **to ~ one's steps** tornare sui propri passi

retract [rɪ'trækt] *vt* (*statement*) ritrattare; (*claws, undercarriage, aerial*) ritrarre, ritirare ■ *vi* ritrarsi

retractable [rɪ'træktəbl] *adj* retrattile

retrain [riː'treɪn] *vt* (*worker*) riaddestrare

retraining [rɪ'treɪnɪŋ] *n* riaddestramento

retread *vt* [riː'trɛd] (*Aut: tyre*) rigenerare ■ *n* ['riːtrɛd] gomma rigenerata

retreat [rɪ'triːt] *n* ritirata; (*place*) rifugio ■ *vi* battere in ritirata; (*flood*) ritirarsi; **to beat a hasty ~** (*fig*) battersela

retrial [riː'traɪəl] *n* nuovo processo

retribution [rɛtrɪ'bjuːʃən] *n* castigo

retrieval [rɪ'triːvəl] *n* ricupero

retrieve [rɪ'triːv] *vt* (*sth lost*) ricuperare, ritrovare; (*situation, honour*) salvare; (*Comput*) ricuperare

retriever [rɪ'triːvəʳ] *n* cane *m* da riporto

retroactive [rɛtrəu'æktɪv] *adj* retroattivo(-a)

retrograde ['rɛtrəugreɪd] *adj* retrogrado(-a)

retrospect ['rɛtrəspɛkt] *n*: **in ~** guardando indietro

retrospective [rɛtrə'spɛktɪv] *adj* retrospettivo(-a); (*law*) retroattivo(-a) ■ *n* (*Art*) retrospettiva

return [rɪ'təːn] *n* (*going or coming back*) ritorno;

(*of sth stolen etc*) restituzione f; (*Comm: from land, shares*) profitto, reddito; (: *of merchandise*) resa; (*report*) rapporto; (*reward*): **in ~ (for)** in cambio (di) ■ *cpd* (*journey, match*) di ritorno; (*Brit: ticket*) di andata e ritorno ■ *vi* tornare, ritornare ■ *vt* rendere, restituire; (*bring back*) riportare; (*send back*) mandare indietro; (*put back*) rimettere; (*Pol: candidate*) eleggere; **returns** *npl* (*Comm*) incassi *mpl*; profitti *mpl*; **by ~ of post** a stretto giro di posta; **many happy returns (of the day)!** auguri!, buon compleanno!

returnable [rɪ'tə:nəbl] *adj*: **~ bottle** vuoto a rendere

returner [rɪ'tə:nə^r] *n* donna che ritorna al lavoro dopo la maternità

returning officer [rɪ'tə:nɪŋ-] *n* (*Brit Pol*) funzionario addetto all'organizzazione delle elezioni in un distretto

return key *n* (*Comput*) tasto di ritorno

reunion [ri:'ju:nɪən] *n* riunione f

reunite [ri:ju:'naɪt] *vt* riunire

rev [rɛv] *n abbr* (= *revolution: Aut*) giro ■ *vb* (*also*: **rev up**) *vt* imballare ■ *vi* imballarsi

revaluation [ri:væljʊ'eɪʃən] *n* rivalutazione f

revamp ['ri:'væmp] *vt* rinnovare; riorganizzare

Rev., Revd. *abbr* = **reverend**

rev counter *n* contagiri *m inv*

reveal [rɪ'vi:l] *vt* (*make known*) rivelare, svelare; (*display*) rivelare, mostrare

revealing [rɪ'vi:lɪŋ] *adj* rivelatore(-trice); (*dress*) scollato(-a)

reveille [rɪ'vælɪ] *n* (*Mil*) sveglia

revel ['rɛvl] *vi*: **to ~ in sth/in doing** dilettarsi di qc/a fare

revelation [rɛvə'leɪʃən] *n* rivelazione f

reveller ['rɛvlə^r] *n* festaiolo(-a)

revelry ['rɛvlrɪ] *n* baldoria

revenge [rɪ'vɛndʒ] *n* vendetta; (*in game etc*) rivincita ■ *vt* vendicare; **to take ~** vendicarsi; **to get one's ~ (for sth)** vendicarsi (di qc)

revengeful [rɪ'vɛndʒful] *adj* vendicatore(-trice); vendicativo(-a)

revenue ['rɛvənju:] *n* reddito

reverberate [rɪ'və:bəreɪt] *vi* (*sound*) rimbombare; (*light*) riverberarsi

reverberation [rɪvə:bə'reɪʃən] *n* (*of light, sound*) riverberazione f

revere [rɪ'vɪə^r] *vt* venerare

reverence ['rɛvərəns] *n* venerazione f, riverenza

Reverend ['rɛvərənd] *adj* (*in titles*) reverendo(-a)

reverent ['rɛvərənt] *adj* riverente

reverie ['rɛvərɪ] *n* fantasticheria

reversal [rɪ'və:sl] *n* capovolgimento

reverse [rɪ'və:s] *n* contrario, opposto; (*back*) rovescio; (*Aut: also*: **reverse gear**) marcia indietro ■ *adj* (*order*) inverso(-a); (*direction*) opposto(-a) ■ *vt* (*turn*) invertire, rivoltare; (*change*) capovolgere, rovesciare; (*Law: judgement*) cassare ■ *vi* (*Brit Aut*) fare marcia indietro; **in ~ order** in ordine inverso; **to go into ~** fare marcia indietro

reverse-charge call *n* (*Brit Tel*) telefonata con addebito al ricevente

reverse video *n* reverse video *m*

reversible [rɪ'və:səbl] *adj* (*garment*) double-face *inv*; (*procedure*) reversibile

reversing lights [rɪ'və:sɪŋ-] *npl* (*Brit Aut*) luci *fpl* per la retromarcia

reversion [rɪ'və:ʃən] *n* ritorno

revert [rɪ'və:t] *vi*: **to ~ to** tornare a

review [rɪ'vju:] *n* rivista; (*of book, film*) recensione f ■ *vt* passare in rivista; fare la recensione di; **to come under ~** essere preso in esame

reviewer [rɪ'vju:ə^r] *n* recensore(-a)

revile [rɪ'vaɪl] *vt* insultare

revise [rɪ'vaɪz] *vt* (*manuscript*) rivedere, correggere; (*opinion*) emendare, modificare; (*study: subject, notes*) ripassare; **revised edition** edizione riveduta

revision [rɪ'vɪʒən] *n* revisione f; ripasso; (*revised version*) versione riveduta e corretta

revitalize [ri:'vaɪtəlaɪz] *vt* ravvivare

revival [rɪ'vaɪvəl] *n* ripresa; ristabilimento; (*of faith*) risveglio

revive [rɪ'vaɪv] *vt* (*person*) rianimare; (*custom*) far rivivere; (*hope, courage*) ravvivare; (*play, fashion*) riesumare ■ *vi* (*person*) rianimarsi; (*hope*) ravvivarsi; (*activity*) riprendersi

revoke [rɪ'vəuk] *vt* revocare; (*promise, decision*) rinvenire su

revolt [rɪ'vəult] *n* rivolta, ribellione f ■ *vi* rivoltarsi, ribellarsi; **to ~ (against sb/sth)** ribellarsi (a qn/qc)

revolting [rɪ'vəultɪŋ] *adj* ripugnante

revolution [rɛvə'lu:ʃən] *n* rivoluzione f; (*of wheel etc*) rivoluzione, giro

revolutionary [rɛvə'lu:ʃənrɪ] *adj, n* rivoluzionario(-a)

revolutionize [rɛvə'lu:ʃənaɪz] *vt* rivoluzionare

revolve [rɪ'vɔlv] *vi* girare

revolver [rɪ'vɔlvə^r] *n* rivoltella

revolving [rɪ'vɔlvɪŋ] *adj* girevole

revolving door *n* porta girevole

revue [rɪ'vju:] *n* (*Theat*) rivista

revulsion [rɪ'vʌlʃən] *n* ripugnanza

reward [rɪ'wɔ:d] *n* ricompensa, premio ■ *vt*: **to ~ (for)** ricompensare (per)

r

rewarding [rɪ'wɔ:dɪŋ] *adj* (*fig*) soddisfacente; **financially ~** conveniente dal punto di vista economico

rewind [ri:'waɪnd] *vt irreg* (*watch*) ricaricare; (*ribbon etc*) riavvolgere

rewire [ri:'waɪəʳ] *vt* (*house*) rifare l'impianto elettrico di

reword [ri:'wə:d] *vt* formulare *or* esprimere con altre parole

rewritable [ri:'raɪtəbl] *adj* (*CD, DVD*) riscrivibile

rewrite [ri:'raɪt] *vt irreg* riscrivere

Reykjavik ['reɪkjəvi:k] *n* Reykjavik *f*

RFD *abbr* (*US Post*) = **rural free delivery**

RGN *n abbr* (*Brit*: = *Registered General Nurse*) infermiera diplomata (*dopo corso triennale*)

Rh *abbr* (= *rhesus*) Rh

rhapsody ['ræpsədɪ] *n* (*Mus*) rapsodia; (*fig*) elogio stravagante

rhesus negative ['ri:səs-] *adj* (*Med*) Rh-negativo(-a)

rhesus positive *adj* (*Med*) Rh-positivo(-a)

rhetoric ['rɛtərɪk] *n* retorica

rhetorical [rɪ'tɔrɪkl] *adj* retorico(-a)

rheumatic [ru:'mætɪk] *adj* reumatico(-a)

rheumatism ['ru:mətɪzəm] *n* reumatismo

rheumatoid arthritis ['ru:mətɔɪd-] *n* artrite *f* reumatoide

Rhine [raɪn] *n*: **the ~** il Reno

rhinestone ['raɪnstəun] *n* diamante *m* falso

rhinoceros [raɪ'nɔsərəs] *n* rinoceronte *m*

Rhodes [rəudz] *n* Rodi *f*

Rhodesia [rəu'di:ʒə] *n* Rhodesia

Rhodesian [rəu'di:ʒən] *adj, n* Rhodesiano(-a)

rhododendron [rəudə'dendrn] *n* rododendro

Rhone [rəun] *n*: **the ~** il Rodano

rhubarb ['ru:bɑ:b] *n* rabarbaro

rhyme [raɪm] *n* rima; (*verse*) poesia ◼ *vi*: **to ~ (with)** fare rima (con); **without ~ or reason** senza capo né coda

rhythm ['rɪðm] *n* ritmo

rhythmic ['rɪðmɪk], **rhythmical** ['rɪðmɪkəl] *adj* ritmico(-a)

rhythmically ['rɪðmɪkəlɪ] *adv* con ritmo

rhythm method *n* metodo Ogino-Knauss

RI *abbr* (*US*) = **Rhode Island** ◼ *n abbr* (*Brit*) = **religious instruction**

rib [rɪb] *n* (*Anat*) costola ◼ *vt* (*tease*) punzecchiare

ribald ['rɪbəld] *adj* licenzioso(-a), volgare

ribbed [rɪbd] *adj* (*knitting*) a coste

ribbon ['rɪbən] *n* nastro; **in ribbons** (*torn*) a brandelli

rice [raɪs] *n* riso

ricefield ['raɪsfi:ld] *n* risaia

rice pudding *n* budino di riso

rich [rɪtʃ] *adj* ricco(-a); (*clothes*) sontuoso(-a); **the ~** *npl* i ricchi; **riches** *npl* ricchezze *fpl*;

to be ~ in sth essere ricco di qc

richly ['rɪtʃlɪ] *adv* riccamente; (*dressed*) sontuosamente; (*deserved*) pienamente

rickets ['rɪkɪts] *n* rachitismo

rickety ['rɪkɪtɪ] *adj* zoppicante

rickshaw ['rɪkʃɔ:] *n* risciò *m inv*

ricochet ['rɪkəʃeɪ] *n* rimbalzo ◼ *vi* rimbalzare

rid (*pt, pp ~*) [rɪd] *vt*: **to ~ sb of** sbarazzare *or* liberare qn di; **to get ~ of** sbarazzarsi di

riddance ['rɪdns] *n*: **good ~!** che liberazione!

ridden ['rɪdn] *pp of* **ride**

riddle ['rɪdl] *n* (*puzzle*) indovinello ◼ *vt*: **to be riddled with** essere crivellato(-a) di

ride [raɪd] *n* (*on horse*) cavalcata; (*outing*) passeggiata; (*distance covered*) cavalcata; corsa ◼ *vb* (*pt* **rode**, *pp* **ridden**) [rəud, 'rɪdn] *vi* (*as sport*) cavalcare; (*go somewhere: on horse, bicycle*) andare (a cavallo *or* in bicicletta *etc*); (*journey: on bicycle, motorcycle, bus*) andare, viaggiare ◼ *vt* (*a horse*) montare, cavalcare; **to go for a ~** andare a fare una cavalcata; andare a fare un giro; **can you ~ a bike?** sai andare in bicicletta?; **we rode all day/all the way** abbiamo cavalcato tutto il giorno/per tutto il tragitto; **to ~ a horse/bicycle/camel** montare a cavallo/in bicicletta/in groppa a un cammello; **to ~ at anchor** (*Naut*) essere alla fonda; **horse ~** cavalcata; **car ~** passeggiata in macchina; **to take sb for a ~** (*fig*) prendere in giro qn; fregare qn

▶ **ride out** *vt*: **to ~ out the storm** (*fig*) mantenersi a galla

rider ['raɪdəʳ] *n* cavalcatore(-trice); (*jockey*) fantino; (*on bicycle*) ciclista *m/f*; (*on motorcycle*) motociclista *m/f*; (*in document*) clausola addizionale, aggiunta

ridge [rɪdʒ] *n* (*of hill*) cresta; (*of roof*) colmo; (*of mountain*) giogo; (*on object*) riga (in rilievo)

ridicule ['rɪdɪkju:l] *n* ridicolo ◼ *vt* mettere in ridicolo; **to hold sb/sth up to ~** mettere in ridicolo qn/qc

ridiculous [rɪ'dɪkjuləs] *adj* ridicolo(-a)

riding ['raɪdɪŋ] *n* equitazione *f*

riding school *n* scuola d'equitazione

rife [raɪf] *adj* diffuso(-a); **to be ~ with** abbondare di

riffraff ['rɪfræf] *n* canaglia, gentaglia

rifle ['raɪfl] *n* carabina ◼ *vt* vuotare

▶ **rifle through** *vt fus* frugare

rifle range *n* campo di tiro; (*at fair*) tiro a segno

rift [rɪft] *n* fessura, crepatura; (*fig: disagreement*) incrinatura

rig [rɪg] *n* (*also*: **oil rig**: *on land*) derrick *m inv*; (: *at sea*) piattaforma di trivellazione ◼ *vt* (*election etc*) truccare

▸ **rig out** vt (Brit) attrezzare; (pej) abbigliare, agghindare

▸ **rig up** vt allestire

rigging ['rɪgɪŋ] n (Naut) attrezzatura

right [raɪt] adj giusto(-a); (suitable) appropriato(-a); (not left) destro(-a) ■ n (title, claim) diritto; (not left) destra ■ adv (answer) correttamente; (not on the left) a destra ■ vt raddrizzare; (fig) riparare ■ excl bene!; **the ~ time** l'ora esatta; **to be ~** (person) aver ragione; (answer) essere giusto(-a) or corretto(-a); **to get sth ~** far giusto qc; **you did the ~ thing** ha fatto bene; **let's get it ~ this time!** cerchiamo di farlo bene stavolta!; **to put a mistake ~** (Brit) correggere un errore; **~ now** proprio adesso; subito; **~ away** subito; **~ before/after** subito prima/dopo; **to go ~ to the end of sth** andare fino in fondo a qc; **~ against the wall** proprio contro il muro; **~ ahead** sempre diritto; proprio davanti; **~ in the middle** proprio nel mezzo; **by rights** di diritto; **on the ~, to the ~** a destra; **~ and wrong** il bene e il male; **to have a ~ to sth** aver diritto a qc; **film rights** diritti di riproduzione cinematografica; **~ of way** diritto di passaggio; (Aut) precedenza

right angle n angolo retto

right-click ['raɪtklɪk] vi (Comput): **to ~ on** fare click con il pulsante destro del mouse su

righteous ['raɪtʃəs] adj retto(-a), virtuoso(-a); (anger) giusto(-a), giustificato(-a)

righteousness ['raɪtʃəsnɪs] n rettitudine f, virtù f

rightful ['raɪtful] adj (heir) legittimo(-a)

rightfully ['raɪtfəlɪ] adv legittimamente

right-handed [raɪt'hændɪd] adj (person) che adopera la mano destra

right-hand man ['raɪthænd-] n braccio destro (fig)

right-hand side n lato destro

rightly ['raɪtlɪ] adv bene, correttamente; (with reason) a ragione; **if I remember ~** se mi ricordo bene

right-minded [raɪt'maɪndɪd] adj sensato(-a)

rights issue n (Stock Exchange) emissione f di azioni riservate agli azionisti

right wing n (Mil, Sport) ala destra; (Pol) destra ■ adj: **right-wing** (Pol) di destra

right-winger [raɪt'wɪŋə'] n (Pol) uno(-a) di destra; (Sport) ala destra

rigid ['rɪdʒɪd] adj rigido(-a); (principle) rigoroso(-a)

rigidity [rɪ'dʒɪdɪtɪ] n rigidità

rigidly ['rɪdʒɪdlɪ] adv rigidamente

rigmarole ['rɪgmərəul] n tiritera; commedia

rigor ['rɪgə'] n (US) = **rigour**

rigor mortis ['rɪgə'mɔːtɪs] n rigidità cadaverica

rigorous ['rɪgərəs] adj rigoroso(-a)

rigorously ['rɪgərəslɪ] adv rigorosamente

rigour, (US) **rigor** ['rɪgə'] n rigore m

rig-out ['rɪgaut] n (Brit col) tenuta

rile [raɪl] vt irritare, seccare

rim [rɪm] n orlo; (of spectacles) montatura; (of wheel) cerchione m

rimless ['rɪmlɪs] adj (spectacles) senza montatura

rimmed [rɪmd] adj bordato(-a); cerchiato(-a)

rind [raɪnd] n (of bacon) cotenna; (of lemon etc) scorza

ring [rɪŋ] n anello; (also: **wedding ring**) fede f; (of people, objects) cerchio; (of spies) giro; (of smoke etc) spirale f; (arena) pista, arena; (for boxing) ring m inv; (sound of bell) scampanio; (telephone call) colpo di telefono ■ vb (pt **rang**, pp **rung**) [ræŋ, rʌŋ] vi (person, bell, telephone) suonare; (also: **ring out**: voice, words) risuonare; (Tel) telefonare ■ vt (Brit Tel: also: **ring up**) telefonare a; **to give sb a ~** (Tel) dare un colpo di telefono a qn; **that has the ~ of truth about it** questo ha l'aria d'essere vero; **to ~ the bell** suonare il campanello; **the name doesn't ~ a bell (with me)** questo nome non mi dice niente

▸ **ring back** vt, vi (Brit Tel) richiamare

▸ **ring off** vi (Brit Tel) mettere giù, riattaccare

ring binder n classificatore m a anelli

ring finger n anulare m

ringing ['rɪŋɪŋ] n (of bell) scampanio; (: louder) scampanellata; (of telephone) squillo; (in ears) fischio, ronzio

ringing tone n (Brit Tel) segnale m di libero

ringleader ['rɪŋliːdə'] n (of gang) capobanda m

ringlets ['rɪŋlɪts] npl boccoli mpl

ring road n (Brit) raccordo anulare

ringtone n (Tel) suoneria

rink [rɪŋk] n (also: **ice rink**) pista di pattinaggio; (for roller-skating) pista di pattinaggio (a rotelle)

rinse [rɪns] n risciacquatura; (hair tint) cachet m inv ■ vt sciacquare

Rio ['riːəu], **Rio de Janeiro** ['riːəudədʒə'nɪərəu] n Rio de Janeiro f

riot ['raɪət] n sommossa, tumulto ■ vi tumultuare; **a ~ of colours** un'orgia di colori; **to run ~** creare disordine

rioter ['raɪətə'] n dimostrante m/f (durante dei disordini)

riot gear n: **in ~** in assetto di guerra

riotous ['raɪətəs] adj tumultuoso(-a); che fa crepare dal ridere

riotously ['raɪətəslɪ] adv: **~ funny** che fa crepare dal ridere

757

r

riot police n ≈ la Celere
RIP abbr (= requiescat or requiescant in pace) R.I.P.
rip [rɪp] n strappo ■ vt strappare ■ vi strapparsi
▸ **rip up** vt stracciare
ripcord ['rɪpkɔːd] n cavo di spiegamento
ripe [raɪp] adj (fruit) maturo(-a); (cheese) stagionato(-a)
ripen ['raɪpən] vt maturare ■ vi maturarsi; stagionarsi
ripeness ['raɪpnɪs] n maturità
rip-off ['rɪpɔf] n (col): **it's a ~!** è un furto!
riposte [rɪ'pɒst] n risposta per le rime
ripple ['rɪpl] n increspamento, ondulazione f; mormorio ■ vi incresparsi ■ vt increspare
rise [raɪz] n (slope) salita, pendio; (hill) altura; (increase: in wages) aumento; (: in prices, temperature) rialzo, aumento; (fig: to power etc) ascesa ■ vi (pt **rose**, pp **risen**) [rəuz, 'rɪzn] alzarsi, levarsi; (prices) aumentare; (waters, river) crescere; (sun, wind) levarsi; (also: **rise up**: rebel) insorgere; ribellarsi; **to give ~ to** provocare, dare origine a; **to ~ to the occasion** dimostrarsi all'altezza della situazione
rising ['raɪzɪŋ] adj (increasing: number) sempre crescente; (: prices) in aumento; (tide) montante; (sun, moon) nascente, che sorge ■ n (uprising) sommossa
rising damp n infiltrazioni fpl d'umidità
rising star n (also fig) astro nascente
risk [rɪsk] n rischio ■ vt rischiare; **to take** or **run the ~ of doing** correre il rischio di fare; **at ~** in pericolo; **at one's own ~** a proprio rischio e pericolo; **fire/health ~** rischio d'incendio/per la salute; **I'll ~ it** ci proverò lo stesso
risk capital n capitale m di rischio
risky ['rɪskɪ] adj rischioso(-a)
risqué ['riːskeɪ] adj (joke) spinto(-a)
rissole ['rɪsəul] n crocchetta
rite [raɪt] n rito; **last rites** l'estrema unzione
ritual ['rɪtjuəl] adj, n rituale m
rival ['raɪvl] n rivale m/f; (in business) concorrente m/f ■ adj rivale; che fa concorrenza ■ vt essere in concorrenza con; **to ~ sb/sth in** competere con qn/qc in
rivalry ['raɪvəlrɪ] n rivalità; concorrenza
river ['rɪvə'] n fiume m ■ cpd (port, traffic) fluviale; **up/down** ~ a monte/valle
riverbank ['rɪvəbæŋk] n argine m
riverbed ['rɪvəbed] n alveo (fluviale)
riverside ['rɪvəsaɪd] n sponda del fiume
rivet ['rɪvɪt] n ribattino, rivetto ■ vt ribadire; (fig) concentrare, fissare
riveting ['rɪvɪtɪŋ] adj (fig) avvincente
Riviera [rɪvɪ'ɛərə] n: **the (French)** ~ la Costa Azzurra; **the Italian** ~ la Riviera

Riyadh [rɪ'jɑːd] n Riad f
RMT n abbr (= National Union of Rail, Maritime and Transport Workers) sindacato dei Ferrovieri, Marittimi e Trasportatori
RN n abbr (Brit) = **Royal Navy**; (US) = **registered nurse**
RNA n abbr (= ribonucleic acid) R.N.A. m
RNLI n abbr (Brit: = Royal National Lifeboat Institution) associazione volontaria che organizza e dispone di scialuppe di salvataggio
RNZAF n abbr = **Royal New Zealand Air Force**
RNZN n abbr = **Royal New Zealand Navy**
road [rəud] n strada; (small) cammino; (in town) via; **main** ~ strada principale; **major/minor** ~ strada con/senza diritto di precedenza; **it takes 4 hours by** ~ sono 4 ore di macchina (or in camion etc); **on the ~ to success** sulla via del successo; **"~ up"** (Brit) "attenzione: lavori in corso"
road accident n incidente m stradale
roadblock ['rəudblɒk] n blocco stradale
road haulage n autotrasporti mpl
roadhog ['rəudhɒg] n pirata m della strada
road map n carta stradale
road rage n aggressività al volante
road safety n sicurezza sulle strade
roadside ['rəudsaɪd] n margine m della strada; **by the** ~ a lato della strada
roadsign ['rəudsaɪn] n cartello stradale
roadsweeper ['rəudswiːpə'] n (Brit: person) spazzino
road user n utente m/f della strada
roadway ['rəudweɪ] n carreggiata
roadworks ['rəudwəːks] npl lavori mpl stradali
roadworthy ['rəudwəːðɪ] adj in buono stato di marcia
roam [rəum] vi errare, vagabondare ■ vt vagare per
roar [rɔː'] n ruggito; (of crowd) tumulto; (of thunder, storm) muggito ■ vi ruggire; tumultuare; muggire; **to ~ with laughter** scoppiare dalle risa
roaring ['rɔːrɪŋ] adj: **a ~ fire** un bel fuoco; **to do a ~ trade** fare affari d'oro; **a ~ success** un successo strepitoso
roast [rəust] n arrosto ■ vt (meat) arrostire
roast beef n arrosto di manzo
roasting ['rəustɪŋ] n (col): **to give sb a ~** dare una lavata di capo a qn
rob [rɒb] vt (person) rubare; (bank) svaligiare; **to ~ sb of sth** derubare qn di qc; (fig: deprive) privare qn di qc
robber ['rɒbə'] n ladro; (armed) rapinatore m
robbery ['rɒbərɪ] n furto; rapina
robe [rəub] n (for ceremony etc) abito; (also: **bathrobe**) accappatoio ■ vt vestire

robin ['rɔbɪn] n pettirosso
robot ['rəubɔt] n robot m inv
robotics ['rəubɔtɪks] n robotica
robust [rəu'bʌst] adj robusto(-a); (material) solido(-a)
rock [rɔk] n (substance) roccia; (boulder) masso; roccia; (in sea) scoglio; (Brit: sweet) zucchero candito ■ vt (swing gently: cradle) dondolare; (: child) cullare; (shake) scrollare, far tremare ■ vi dondolarsi; oscillare; **on the rocks** (drink) col ghiaccio; (ship) sugli scogli; (marriage etc) in crisi; **to ~ the boat** (fig) piantare grane
rock and roll n rock and roll m
rock-bottom ['rɔk'bɔtəm] n (fig) stremo; **to reach** or **touch ~** (price) raggiungere il livello più basso; (person) toccare il fondo
rock climber n rocciatore(-trice), scalatore(-trice)
rock climbing n roccia
rockery ['rɔkərɪ] n giardino roccioso
rocket ['rɔkɪt] n razzo; (Mil) razzo, missile m ■ vi (prices) salire alle stelle
rocket launcher [-lɔ:ntʃəʳ] n lanciarazzi m inv
rock face n parete f della roccia
rock fall n caduta di massi
rocking chair ['rɔkɪŋ-] n sedia a dondolo
rocking horse n cavallo a dondolo
rocky ['rɔkɪ] adj (hill) roccioso(-a); (path) sassoso(-a); (unsteady: table) traballante
Rocky Mountains npl: **the ~** le Montagne Rocciose
rod [rɔd] n (metallic, Tech) asta; (wooden) bacchetta; (also: **fishing rod**) canna da pesca
rode [rəud] pt of **ride**
rodent ['rəudnt] n roditore m
rodeo ['rəudɪəu] n rodeo
roe [rəu] n (species: also: **roe deer**) capriolo; (of fish: also: **hard roe**) uova fpl di pesce; **soft ~** latte m di pesce
roe deer n (species) capriolo; (female deer: pl inv) capriolo femmina
rogue [rəug] n mascalzone m
roguish ['rəugɪʃ] adj birbantesco(-a)
role [rəul] n ruolo
role model n modello (di comportamento)
role-play ['rəulpleɪ], **role-playing** ['rəulpleɪɪŋ] n il recitare un ruolo, role-playing m inv
roll [rəul] n rotolo; (of banknotes) mazzo; (also: **bread roll**) panino; (register) lista; (sound: of drums etc) rullo; (movement: of ship) rullio ■ vt rotolare; (also: **roll up**: string) aggomitolare; (also: **roll out**: pastry) stendere ■ vi rotolare; (wheel) girare; **cheese ~** panino al formaggio
▶ **roll about, roll around** vi rotolare qua e là; (person) rotolarsi
▶ **roll by** vi (time) passare
▶ **roll in** vi (mail, cash) arrivare a bizzeffe

▶ **roll over** vi rivoltarsi
▶ **roll up** vi (col: arrive) arrivare ■ vt (carpet, cloth, map) arrotolare; (sleeves) rimboccare; **to ~ o.s. up into a ball** raggomitolarsi
roll call n appello
rolled gold [rəuld-] adj d'oro laminato
roller ['rəuləʳ] n rullo; (wheel) rotella
rollerblades ['rəuləbleɪdz] npl pattini mpl in linea
roller blind n (Brit) avvolgibile m
roller coaster n montagne fpl russe
roller skates npl pattini mpl a rotelle
rollicking ['rɔlɪkɪŋ] adj allegro(-a) e chiassoso(-a); **to have a ~ time** divertirsi pazzamente
rolling ['rəulɪŋ] adj (landscape) ondulato(-a)
rolling mill n fabbrica di laminati
rolling pin n matterello
rolling stock n (Rail) materiale m rotabile
roll-on-roll-off ['rəulɔn'rəulɔf] adj (Brit: ferry) roll-on roll-off inv
roly-poly ['rəulɪ'pəulɪ] n (Brit Culin) rotolo di pasta con ripieno di marmellata
ROM [rɔm] n abbr (Comput: = read-only memory) ROM f
Roman ['rəumən] adj, n romano(-a)
Roman Catholic adj, n cattolico(-a)
romance [rə'mæns] n storia (or avventura or film m inv) romantico(-a); (charm) poesia; (love affair) idillio
Romanesque [rəumə'nɛsk] adj romanico(-a)
Romania [rəu'meɪnɪə] n Romania
Romanian [rəu'meɪnɪən] adj romeno(-a) ■ n romeno(-a); (Ling) romeno
Roman numeral n numero romano
romantic [rə'mæntɪk] adj romantico(-a); sentimentale
romanticism [rə'mæntɪsɪzəm] n romanticismo
Romany ['rɔmənɪ] adj zingaresco(-a) ■ n (person) zingaro(-a); (Ling) lingua degli zingari
Rome [rəum] n Roma
romp [rɔmp] n gioco chiassoso ■ vi (also: **romp about**) giocare chiassosamente; **to ~ home** (horse) vincere senza difficoltà, stravincere
rompers ['rɔmpəz] npl pagliaccetto
rondo ['rɔndəu] n (Mus) rondò m inv
roof [ru:f] n tetto; (of tunnel, cave) volta ■ vt coprire (con un tetto); **~ of the mouth** palato
roof garden n giardino pensile
roofing ['ru:fɪŋ] n materiale m per copertura
roof rack n (Aut) portabagagli m inv
rook [ruk] n (bird) corvo nero; (Chess) torre f ■ vt (cheat) truffare, spennare

r

rookie ['rukɪ] n (col: esp Mil) pivellino(-a)
room [ruːm] n (in house) stanza, camera; (in school etc) sala; (space) posto, spazio; **rooms** npl (lodging) alloggio; **"rooms to let"**, (US) **"rooms for rent"** "si affittano camere"; **is there ~ for this?** c'è spazio per questo?, ci sta anche questo?; **to make ~ for sb** far posto a qn; **there is ~ for improvement** si potrebbe migliorare
rooming house ['ruːmɪŋ-] n (US) casa in cui si affittano camere o appartamentini ammobiliati
roommate ['ruːmmeɪt] n compagno(-a) di stanza
room service n servizio da camera
room temperature n temperatura ambiente
roomy ['ruːmɪ] adj spazioso(-a); (garment) ampio(-a)
roost [ruːst] n appollaiato ■ vi appollaiarsi
rooster ['ruːstəʳ] n gallo
root [ruːt] n radice f ■ vt (plant, belief) far radicare; **to take ~** (plant) attecchire, prendere; (idea) far presa; **the ~ of the problem is that …** il problema deriva dal fatto che …
▶ **root about** vi (fig) frugare
▶ **root for** vt fus (col) fare il tifo per
▶ **root out** vt estirpare
root beer n (US) bibita dolce a base di estratti di erbe e radici
rope [rəup] n corda, fune f; (Naut) cavo ■ vt (box) legare; (climbers) legare in cordata; **to ~ sb in** (fig) coinvolgere qn; **to know the ropes** (fig) conoscere i trucchi del mestiere
rope ladder n scala di corda
ropey ['rəupɪ] adj (col) scadente, da quattro soldi; **to feel ~** (ill) sentirsi male
rosary ['rəuzərɪ] n rosario; roseto
rose [rəuz] pt of **rise** ■ n rosa; (also: **rose bush**) rosaio; (on watering can) rosetta ■ adj rosa inv
rosé ['rəuzeɪ] n vino rosato
rosebed ['rəuzbɛd] n roseto
rosebud ['rəuzbʌd] n bocciolo di rosa
rosebush ['rəuzbʊʃ] n rosaio
rosemary ['rəuzmərɪ] n rosmarino
rosette [rəu'zɛt] n coccarda
ROSPA ['rɔspə] n abbr (Brit: = Royal Society for the Prevention of Accidents) ≈ E.N.P.I. m (= Ente Nazionale Prevenzione Infortuni)
roster ['rɔstəʳ] n: **duty ~** ruolino di servizio
rostrum ['rɔstrəm] n tribuna
rosy ['rəuzɪ] adj roseo(-a)
rot [rɔt] n (decay) putrefazione f; (col: nonsense) stupidaggini fpl ■ vt, vi imputridire, marcire; **dry/wet ~** funghi parassiti del legno; **to stop the ~** (Brit fig) salvare la situazione
rota ['rəutə] n tabella dei turni; **on a ~ basis** a turno

rotary ['rəutərɪ] adj rotante
rotate [rəu'teɪt] vt (revolve) far girare; (change round: crops) avvicendare; (: jobs) fare a turno ■ vi (revolve) girare
rotating [rəu'teɪtɪŋ] adj (movement) rotante
rotation [rəu'teɪʃən] n rotazione f; **in ~** a turno, in rotazione
rote [rəut] n: **to learn sth by ~** imparare qc a memoria
rotor ['rəutəʳ] n rotore m
rotten ['rɔtn] adj (decayed) putrido(-a), marcio(-a); (: teeth) cariato(-a); (dishonest) corrotto(-a); (col: bad) brutto(-a); (: action) vigliacco(-a); **to feel ~** (ill) sentirsi proprio male
rotting ['rɔtɪŋ] adj in putrefazione
rotund [rəu'tʌnd] adj grassoccio(-a); tondo(-a)
rouble, (US) **ruble** ['ruːbl] n rublo
rouge [ruːʒ] n belletto
rough [rʌf] adj aspro(-a); (person, manner: coarse) rozzo(-a), aspro(-a); (: violent) brutale; (district) malfamato(-a); (weather) cattivo(-a); (plan) abbozzato(-a); (guess) approssimativo(-a) ■ n (Golf) macchia; **~ estimate** approssimazione f; **to ~ it** far vita dura; **to play ~** far il gioco pesante; **to sleep ~** (Brit) dormire all'addiaccio; **to feel ~** (Brit) sentirsi male; **to have a ~ time (of it)** passare un periodaccio; **the sea is ~ today** c'è mare grosso oggi
▶ **rough out** vt (draft) abbozzare
roughage ['rʌfɪdʒ] n alimenti mpl ricchi di cellulosa
rough-and-ready ['rʌfən'rɛdɪ] adj rudimentale
rough-and-tumble ['rʌfən'tʌmbl] n zuffa
roughcast ['rʌfkɑːst] n intonaco grezzo
rough copy, rough draft n brutta copia
roughen ['rʌfn] vt (a surface) rendere ruvido(-a)
rough justice n giustizia sommaria
roughly ['rʌflɪ] adv (handle) rudemente, brutalmente; (make) grossolanamente; (approximately) approssimativamente; **~ speaking** grosso modo, ad occhio e croce
roughness ['rʌfnɪs] n asprezza; rozzezza; brutalità
roughshod ['rʌfʃɔd] adv: **to ride ~ over** (person) mettere sotto i piedi; (objection) passare sopra a
rough work n (at school etc) brutta copia
roulette [ruː'lɛt] n roulette f
Roumania etc [ruː'meɪnɪə] = **Romania** etc
round [raund] adj rotondo(-a) ■ n tondo, cerchio; (Brit: of toast) fetta; (duty: of policeman, milkman etc) giro; (: of doctor) visite fpl; (game: of

cards, in competition) partita; (Boxing) round m inv; (of talks) serie f inv ■ vt (corner) girare; (bend) prendere; (cape) doppiare ■ prep intorno a ■ adv: **right ~, all** ~ tutt'attorno; **the long way** ~ il giro più lungo; **all the year** ~ tutto l'anno; **in ~ figures** in cifra tonda; **it's just** ~ **the corner** (also fig) è dietro l'angolo; **to ask sb** ~ invitare qn (a casa propria); **I'll be** ~ **at 6 o'clock** ci sarò alle 6; **to go** ~ fare il giro; **to go** ~ **to sb's (house)** andare da qn; **to go** ~ **an obstacle** aggirare un ostacolo; **go** ~ **the back** passi da dietro; **to go** ~ **a house** visitare una casa; **enough to go** ~ abbastanza per tutti; **she arrived** ~ **(about) noon** è arrivata intorno a mezzogiorno; ~ **the clock** 24 ore su 24; **to go the rounds** (illness) diffondersi; (story) circolare, passare di bocca in bocca; **the daily** ~ (fig) la routine quotidiana; ~ **of ammunition** cartuccia; ~ **of applause** applausi mpl; ~ **of drinks** giro di bibite; ~ **of sandwiches** (Brit) sandwich m inv
▶ **round off** vt (speech etc) finire
▶ **round up** vt radunare; (criminals) fare una retata di; (prices) arrotondare
roundabout ['raundəbaut] n (Brit Aut) rotatoria; (at fair) giostra ■ adj (route, means) indiretto(-a)
rounded ['raundɪd] adj arrotondato(-a); (style) armonioso(-a)
rounders ['raundəz] npl (game) gioco simile al baseball
roundly ['raundlɪ] adv (fig) chiaro e tondo
round robin n (Sport: also: **round robin tournament**) ≈ torneo all'italiana
round-shouldered [raund'ʃəuldəd] adj dalle spalle tonde
round trip n (viaggio di) andata e ritorno
roundup ['raundʌp] n raduno; (of criminals) retata; **a** ~ **of the latest news** un sommario or riepilogo delle ultime notizie
rouse [rauz] vt (wake up) svegliare; (stir up) destare; provocare; risvegliare
rousing ['rauzɪŋ] adj (speech, applause) entusiastico(-a)
rout [raut] n (Mil) rotta ■ vt mettere in rotta
route [ru:t] n itinerario; (of bus) percorso; (of trade, shipping) rotta; **"all routes"** (Aut) "tutte le direzioni"; **the best** ~ **to London** la strada migliore per andare a Londra; **en** ~ **for** in viaggio verso; **en** ~ **from ... to** viaggiando da ... a
route map n (Brit: for journey) cartina di itinerario; (for trains etc) pianta dei collegamenti
routine [ru:'ti:n] adj (work) corrente, abituale; (procedure) solito(-a) ■ n (pej) routine f, tran tran m; (Theat) numero; (Comput)

sottoprogramma m; **daily** ~ orario quotidiano; ~ **procedure** prassi f
roving ['rəuvɪŋ] adj (life) itinerante
roving reporter n reporter m inv volante
row[1] [rəu] n (line) riga, fila; (Knitting) ferro; (behind one another: of cars, people) fila ■ vi (in boat) remare; (as sport) vogare ■ vt (boat) manovrare a remi; **in a** ~ (fig) di fila
row[2] [rau] n (noise) baccano, chiasso; (dispute) lite f ■ vi litigare; **to make a** ~ far baccano; **to have a** ~ litigare
rowboat ['rəubəut] n (US) barca a remi
rowdiness ['raudɪnɪs] n baccano; (fighting) zuffa
rowdy ['raudɪ] adj chiassoso(-a), turbolento(-a) ■ n teppista m/f
rowdyism ['raudɪɪzəm] n teppismo
rowing ['rəuɪŋ] n canottaggio
rowing boat n (Brit) barca a remi
rowlock ['rɔlək] n scalmo
royal ['rɔɪəl] adj reale
Royal Academy n (Brit) vedi nota

○ **ROYAL ACADEMY**
○
○ L'Accademia Reale d'Arte britannica,
○ Royal Academy (of the Arts), è un'istituzione
○ fondata nel 1768 al fine di incoraggiare la
○ pittura, la scultura e l'architettura. Ogni
○ anno organizza una mostra estiva d'arte
○ contemporanea.

Royal Air Force n (Brit) aeronautica militare britannica
royal blue adj blu reale inv
royalist ['rɔɪəlɪst] adj, n realista m/f
Royal Navy n (Brit) marina militare britannica
royalty ['rɔɪəltɪ] n (royal persons) (membri mpl della) famiglia reale; (payment: to author) diritti mpl d'autore; (: to inventor) diritti di brevetto
RP n abbr (Brit: = received pronunciation) pronuncia standard
RPI abbr (Brit) = **retail price index**
rpm abbr (= revolutions per minute) giri/min
RR abbr (US: = railroad) Ferr
RRP n abbr (Brit) = **recommended retail price**
RSA n abbr (Brit) = **Royal Society of Arts**; **Royal Scottish Academy**
RSI n abbr (Med: = repetitive strain injury) lesione al braccio tipica di violinisti e terminalisti
RSPB n abbr (Brit: = Royal Society for the Protection of Birds) ≈ L.I.P.U. f (= Lega Italiana Protezione Uccelli)
RSPCA n abbr (Brit: = Royal Society for the Prevention of Cruelty to Animals) ≈ E.N.P.A. m (= Ente Nazionale per la Protezione degli Animali)

r

RSVP *abbr* (= *répondez s'il vous plaît*) R.S.V.P.
RTA *n abbr* (= *road traffic accident*) incidente *m* stradale
Rt Hon. *abbr* (Brit: = *Right Honourable*) ≈ On. (= *Onorevole*)
Rt Rev. *abbr* (= *Right Reverend*) Rev
rub [rʌb] *n* (*with cloth*) fregata, strofinata; (*on person*) frizione *f*, massaggio ■ *vt* fregare, strofinare; frizionare; **to ~ sb up** *or* (*US*) **~ sb the wrong way** lisciare qn contro pelo
  ▶ **rub down** *vt* (*body*) strofinare, frizionare; (*horse*) strigliare
  ▶ **rub in** *vt* (*ointment*) far penetrare (massaggiando *or* frizionando)
  ▶ **rub off** *vi* andare via; **to ~ off on** lasciare una traccia su
  ▶ **rub out** *vt* cancellare ■ *vi* cancellarsi
rubber ['rʌbəʳ] *n* gomma
rubber band *n* elastico
rubber bullet *n* pallottola di gomma
rubber plant *n* ficus *m inv*
rubber ring *n* (*for swimming*) ciambella
rubber stamp *n* timbro di gomma
rubber-stamp [rʌbə'stæmp] *vt* (*fig*) approvare senza discussione
rubbery ['rʌbərɪ] *adj* gommoso(-a)
rubbish ['rʌbɪʃ] *n* (*from household*) immondizie *fpl*, rifiuti *mpl*; (*fig: pej*) cose *fpl* senza valore; robaccia; (*nonsense*) sciocchezze *fpl* ■ *vt* (*col*) sputtanare; **what you've just said is ~** quello che ha appena detto è una sciocchezza
rubbish bin *n* (Brit) pattumiera
rubbish dump *n* luogo di scarico
rubbishy ['rʌbɪʃɪ] *adj* (Brit col) scadente, che non vale niente
rubble ['rʌbl] *n* macerie *fpl*; (*smaller*) pietrisco
ruble ['ru:bl] *n* (US) = **rouble**
ruby ['ru:bɪ] *n* rubino
RUC *n abbr* (Brit: = *Royal Ulster Constabulary*) forza di polizia dell'Irlanda del Nord
rucksack ['rʌksæk] *n* zaino
ructions ['rʌkʃənz] *npl* putiferio, finimondo
rudder ['rʌdəʳ] *n* timone *m*
ruddy ['rʌdɪ] *adj* (*face*) fresco(-a); (*col: damned*) maledetto(-a)
rude [ru:d] *adj* (*impolite: person*) scortese, rozzo(-a); (: *word, manners*) grossolano(-a), rozzo(-a); (*shocking*) indecente; **to be ~ to sb** essere maleducato con qn
rudely ['ru:dlɪ] *adv* scortesemente; grossolanamente
rudeness ['ru:dnɪs] *n* scortesia; grossolanità
rudiment ['ru:dɪmənt] *n* rudimento
rudimentary [ru:dɪ'mɛntərɪ] *adj* rudimentale
rue [ru:] *vt* pentirsi amaramente di
rueful ['ru:ful] *adj* mesto(-a), triste

ruff [rʌf] *n* gorgiera
ruffian ['rʌfɪən] *n* briccone *m*, furfante *m*
ruffle ['rʌfl] *vt* (*hair*) scompigliare; (*clothes, water*) increspare; (*fig: person*) turbare
rug [rʌg] *n* tappeto; (Brit: *for knees*) coperta
rugby ['rʌgbɪ] *n* (*also:* **rugby football**) rugby *m*
rugged ['rʌgɪd] *adj* (*landscape*) aspro(-a); (*features, determination*) duro(-a); (*character*) brusco(-a)
rugger ['rʌgəʳ] *n* (*col*) rugby *m*
ruin ['ru:ɪn] *n* rovina ■ *vt* rovinare; (*spoil: clothes*) sciupare; **ruins** *npl* rovine *fpl*, ruderi *mpl*; **in ruins** in rovina
ruination [ru:ɪ'neɪʃən] *n* rovina
ruinous ['ru:ɪnəs] *adj* rovinoso(-a); (*expenditure*) inverosimile
rule [ru:l] *n* (*gen*) regola; (*regulation*) regolamento, regola; (*government*) governo; (*dominion etc*): **under British ~** sotto la sovranità britannica ■ *vt* (*country*) governare; (*person*) dominare; (*decide*) decidere ■ *vi* regnare; decidere; (*Law*) dichiarare; **to ~ against/in favour of/on** (*Law*) pronunciarsi a sfavore di/in favore di/su; **it's against the rules** è contro le regole *or* il regolamento; **by ~ of thumb** a lume di naso; **as a ~** normalmente, di regola
  ▶ **rule out** *vt* escludere; **murder cannot be ruled out** non si esclude che si tratti di omicidio
ruled [ru:ld] *adj* (*paper*) vergato(-a)
ruler ['ru:ləʳ] *n* (*sovereign*) sovrano(-a); (*leader*) capo (dello Stato); (*for measuring*) regolo, riga
ruling ['ru:lɪŋ] *adj* (*party*) al potere; (*class*) dirigente ■ *n* (*Law*) decisione *f*
rum [rʌm] *n* rum *m* ■ *adj* (Brit col) strano(-a)
Rumania *etc* [ru:'meɪnɪə] = **Romania** *etc*
rumble ['rʌmbl] *n* rimbombo; brontolio ■ *vi* rimbombare; (*stomach, pipe*) brontolare
rumbustious [rʌm'bʌstʃəs] *adj* (*person*): **to be ~** essere un terremoto
rummage ['rʌmɪdʒ] *vi* frugare
rumour, (US) **rumor** ['ru:məʳ] *n* voce *f* ■ *vt*: **it is rumoured that** corre voce che
rump [rʌmp] *n* (*of animal*) groppa
rumple ['rʌmpl] *vt* (*hair*) arruffare, scompigliare; (*clothes*) spiegazzare, sgualcire
rump steak *n* bistecca di girello
rumpus ['rʌmpəs] *n* (*col*) baccano; (: *quarrel*) rissa; **to kick up a ~** fare un putiferio
run [rʌn] *n* corsa; (*outing*) gita (in macchina); (*distance travelled*) percorso, tragitto; (*series*) serie *f inv*; (Theat) periodo di rappresentazione; (Ski) pista ■ *vb* (*pt* **ran**, *pp* **~**) [ræn, rʌn] *vt* (*operate: business*) gestire, dirigere; (: *competition, course*) organizzare; (: *hotel*) gestire; (: *house*) governare; (Comput:

program) eseguire; (*water, bath*) far scorrere; (*force through: rope, pipe*): **to ~ sth through** far passare qc attraverso; (*to pass: hand, finger*): **to ~ sth over** passare qc su ■ *vi* correre; (*pass: road etc*) passare; (*work: machine, factory*) funzionare, andare; (*bus, train: operate*) far servizio; (*: travel*) circolare; (*continue: play, contract*) durare; (*slide: drawer; flow: river, bath*) scorrere; (*colours, washing*) stemperarsi; (*in election*) presentarsi come candidato; **to go for a ~** andare a correre; (*in car*) fare un giro (in macchina); **to break into a ~** mettersi a correre; **a ~ of luck** un periodo di fortuna; **to have the ~ of sb's house** essere libero di andare e venire in casa di qn; **there was a ~ on ...** c'era una corsa a ...; **in the long ~** alla lunga; in fin dei conti; **in the short ~** sulle prime; **on the ~** in fuga; **to make a ~ for it** scappare, tagliare la corda; **I'll ~ you to the station** la porto alla stazione; **to ~ a risk** correre un rischio; **to ~ errands** andare a fare commissioni; **the train runs between Gatwick and Victoria** il treno collega Gatwick alla stazione Victoria; **the bus runs every 20 minutes** c'è un autobus ogni 20 minuti; **it's very cheap to ~** comporta poche spese; **to ~ on petrol** *or* (US) **gas/on diesel/off batteries** andare a benzina/a diesel/a batterie; **to ~ for the bus** fare una corsa per prendere l'autobus; **to ~ for president** presentarsi come candidato per la presidenza; **their losses ran into millions** le loro perdite hanno raggiunto i milioni; **to be ~ off one's feet** (*Brit*) doversi fare in quattro

▶ **run about** *vi* (*children*) correre qua e là
▶ **run across** *vt fus* (*find*) trovare per caso
▶ **run away** *vi* fuggire
▶ **run down** *vi* (*clock*) scaricarsi ■ *vt* (*Aut*) investire; (*criticize*) criticare; (*Brit: reduce: production*) ridurre gradualmente; (*: factory, shop*) rallentare l'attività di; **to be ~ down** (*battery*) essere scarico(-a); (*person*) essere giù (di corda)
▶ **run in** *vt* (*Brit: car*) rodare, fare il rodaggio di
▶ **run into** *vt fus* (*meet: person*) incontrare per caso; (*: trouble*) incontrare, trovare; (*collide with*) andare a sbattere contro; **to ~ into debt** trovarsi nei debiti
▶ **run off** *vi* fuggire ■ *vt* (*water*) far defluire; (*copies*) fare
▶ **run out** *vi* (*person*) uscire di corsa; (*liquid*) colare; (*lease*) scadere; (*money*) esaurirsi
▶ **run out of** *vt fus* rimanere a corto di; **I've ~ out of petrol** *or* (US) **gas** sono rimasto senza benzina
▶ **run over** *vt* (*Aut*) investire, mettere sotto ■ *vt fus* (*revise*) rivedere

▶ **run through** *vt fus* (*instructions*) dare una scorsa a
▶ **run up** *vt* (*debt*) lasciar accumulare; **to ~ up against** (*difficulties*) incontrare

runaround ['rʌnəraund] *n* (*col*): **to give sb the ~** far girare a vuoto qn
runaway ['rʌnəweɪ] *adj* (*person*) fuggiasco(-a); (*horse*) in libertà; (*truck*) fuori controllo; (*inflation*) galoppante
rundown ['rʌndaun] *n* (*Brit: of industry etc*) riduzione *f* graduale dell'attività di
rung [rʌŋ] *pp of* **ring** ■ *n* (*of ladder*) piolo
run-in ['rʌnɪn] *n* (*col*) scontro
runner ['rʌnər] *n* (*in race*) corridore *m*; (*on sledge*) pattino; (*for drawer etc, carpet*) guida
runner bean *n* (*Brit*) fagiolino
runner-up [rʌnər'ʌp] *n* secondo(-a) arrivato(-a)
running ['rʌnɪŋ] *n* corsa; direzione *f*; organizzazione *f*; funzionamento ■ *adj* (*water*) corrente; (*commentary*) simultaneo(-a); **6 days ~** 6 giorni di seguito; **to be in/out of the ~ for sth** essere/non essere più in lizza per qc
running costs *npl* (*of business*) costi *mpl* d'esercizio; (*of car*) spese *fpl* di mantenimento
running head *n* (*Typ*) testata, titolo corrente
running mate *n* (*US Pol*) candidato alla vicepresidenza
runny ['rʌnɪ] *adj* che cola
run-off ['rʌnɔf] *n* (*in contest, election*) confronto definitivo; (*extra race*) spareggio
run-of-the-mill ['rʌnəvðə'mɪl] *adj* solito(-a), banale
runt [rʌnt] *n* omuncolo; (*Zool*) animale *m* più piccolo del normale
run-through ['rʌnθruː] *n* prova
run-up ['rʌnʌp] *n* (*Brit: also:* **run-up to sth**) periodo che precede qc
runway ['rʌnweɪ] *n* (*Aviat*) pista (di decollo)
rupture ['rʌptʃər] *n* (*Med*) ernia ■ *vt*: **to ~ o.s.** farsi venire un'ernia
rural ['ruərl] *adj* rurale
rural district council *n* (*Brit*) consiglio (amministrativo) di distretto rurale
ruse [ruːz] *n* trucco
rush [rʌʃ] *n* corsa precipitosa; (*of crowd*) afflusso; (*hurry*) furia, fretta; (*current*) flusso; (*Bot*) giunco ■ *vt* mandare *or* spedire velocemente; (*attack: town etc*) prendere d'assalto ■ *vi* precipitarsi; **is there any ~ for this?** è urgente?; **we've had a ~ of orders** abbiamo avuto una valanga di ordinazioni; **I'm in a ~ (to do)** ho fretta *or* premura (di fare); **gold ~** corsa all'oro; **to ~ sth off** spedire con urgenza qc; **don't ~ me!** non farmi fretta!

r

▸ **rush through** vt (*meal*) mangiare in fretta; (*book*) dare una scorsa frettolosa a; (*town*) attraversare in fretta; (*Comm: order*) eseguire d'urgenza ■ vt fus (*work*) sbrigare frettolosamente

rush hour n ora di punta

rush job n (*urgent*) lavoro urgente

rush matting n stuoia

rusk [rʌsk] n fetta biscottata

Russia ['rʌʃə] n Russia

Russian ['rʌʃən] adj russo(-a) ■ n russo(-a); (*Ling*) russo

rust [rʌst] n ruggine f ■ vi arrugginirsi

rustic ['rʌstɪk] adj rustico(-a) ■ n (*pej*) cafone(-a)

rustle ['rʌsl] vi frusciare ■ vt (*paper*) far frusciare; (*US: cattle*) rubare

rustproof ['rʌstpruːf] adj inossidabile

rustproofing ['rʌstpruːfɪŋ] n trattamento antiruggine

rusty ['rʌstɪ] adj arrugginito(-a)

rut [rʌt] n solco; (*Zool*) fregola; **to be in a ~** (*fig*) essersi fossilizzato(-a)

rutabaga [ruːtə'beɪgə] n (*US*) rapa svedese

ruthless ['ruːθlɪs] adj spietato(-a)

ruthlessness ['ruːθlɪsnɪs] n spietatezza

RV abbr (= *revised version*) *versione riveduta della Bibbia* ■ n abbr (*US*) = **recreational vehicle**

rye [raɪ] n segale f

Ss

S, s [ɛs] n (letter) S, s f or m inv; (US Scol:
= satisfactory) ≈ sufficiente; **S for Sugar** ≈ S
come Savona
S abbr (= saint) S.; (= south) S; (on clothes) = **small**
SA abbr = **South Africa; South America**
Sabbath ['sæbəθ] n (Jewish) sabato; (Christian)
domenica
sabbatical [sə'bætɪkl] adj: **~ year** anno
sabbatico
sabotage ['sæbətɑːʒ] n sabotaggio ■ vt
sabotare
saccharin, saccharine ['sækərɪn] n
saccarina
sachet ['sæʃeɪ] n bustina
sack [sæk] n (bag) sacco ■ vt (dismiss)
licenziare, mandare a spasso; (plunder)
saccheggiare; **to get the ~** essere mandato a
spasso; **to give sb the ~** licenziare qn,
mandare qn a spasso
sackful ['sækful] n: **a ~ of** un sacco di
sacking ['sækɪŋ] n tela di sacco; (dismissal)
licenziamento
sacrament ['sækrəmənt] n sacramento
sacred ['seɪkrɪd] adj sacro(-a)
sacred cow n (fig: person) intoccabile m/f;
(: institution) caposaldo; (: idea, belief) dogma m
sacrifice ['sækrɪfaɪs] n sacrificio ■ vt
sacrificare; **to make sacrifices (for sb)** fare
(dei) sacrifici (per qn)
sacrilege ['sækrɪlɪdʒ] n sacrilegio
sacrosanct ['sækrəusæŋkt] adj
sacrosanto(-a)
sad [sæd] adj triste; (deplorable) deplorevole
sadden ['sædn] vt rattristare
saddle ['sædl] n sella ■ vt (horse) sellare;
to be saddled with sth (col) avere qc sulle
spalle
saddlebag ['sædlbæg] n bisaccia; (on bicycle)
borsa
sadism ['seɪdɪzəm] n sadismo
sadist ['seɪdɪst] n sadico(-a)
sadistic [sə'dɪstɪk] adj sadico(-a)
sadly ['sædlɪ] adv tristemente; (regrettably)

sfortunatamente; **~ lacking in**
penosamente privo di
sadness ['sædnɪs] n tristezza
sadomasochism [seɪdəu'mæsəkɪzəm] n
sadomasochismo
sae abbr (Brit) = **stamped addressed
envelope;** see **stamp**
safari [sə'fɑːrɪ] n safari m inv
safari park n zoosafari m inv
safe [seɪf] adj sicuro(-a); (out of danger)
salvo(-a), al sicuro; (cautious) prudente
■ n cassaforte f; **~ from** al sicuro da; **~ and
sound** sano(-a) e salvo(-a); **~ journey!** buon
viaggio!; **(just) to be on the ~ side** per non
correre rischi; **to play ~** giocare sul sicuro;
it is ~ to say that ... si può affermare con
sicurezza che ...
safe bet n: **it's a ~** è una cosa sicura
safe-breaker ['seɪfbreɪkəʳ] n (Brit)
scassinatore m
safe-conduct [seɪf'kɔndʌkt] n salvacondotto
safe-cracker ['seɪfkrækəʳ] n = **safe-breaker**
safe-deposit ['seɪfdɪpɔzɪt] n (vault) caveau m
inv; (box) cassetta di sicurezza
safeguard ['seɪfgɑːd] n salvaguardia ■ vt
salvaguardare
safe haven n zona sicura or protetta
safekeeping ['seɪf'kiːpɪŋ] n custodia
safely ['seɪflɪ] adv sicuramente; sano(-a)
e salvo(-a) prudentemente; prudentemente;
I can ~ say ... posso tranquillamente
asserire ...
safe passage n passaggio sicuro
safe sex n sesso sicuro
safety ['seɪftɪ] n sicurezza; **~ first!** la
prudenza innanzitutto!
safety belt n cintura di sicurezza
safety catch n sicura
safety net n rete f di protezione
safety pin n spilla di sicurezza
safety valve n valvola di sicurezza
saffron ['sæfrən] n zafferano
sag [sæg] vi incurvarsi; afflosciarsi

S

saga ['sɑːgə] n saga; (fig) odissea
sage [seɪdʒ] n (herb) salvia; (man) saggio
Sagittarius [sædʒɪ'tɛərɪəs] n Sagittario;
  to be ~ essere del Sagittario
sago ['seɪgəu] n sagù m
Sahara [sə'hɑːrə] n: **the ~ Desert** il Deserto
  del Sahara
Sahel [sæ'hɛl] n Sahel m
said [sɛd] pt, pp of **say**
Saigon [saɪ'gɔn] n Saigon f
sail [seɪl] n (on boat) vela; (trip): **to go for a ~**
  fare un giro in barca a vela ■ vt (boat)
  condurre, governare ■ vi (travel: ship)
  navigare; (: passenger) viaggiare per mare;
  (set off) salpare; (Sport) fare della vela; **they**
  sailed into Genoa entrarono nel porto di
  Genova
  ▸ **sail through** vt fus (fig) superare senza
  difficoltà ■ vi farcela senza difficoltà
sailboat ['seɪlbəut] n (US) barca a vela
sailing ['seɪlɪŋ] n (sport) vela; **to go ~** fare
  della vela
sailing boat n barca a vela
sailing ship n veliero
sailor ['seɪlər] n marinaio
saint [seɪnt] n santo(-a)
saintly ['seɪntlɪ] adj da santo(-a); santo(-a)
sake [seɪk] n: **for the ~ of** per, per amore di;
  for pity's ~ per pietà; **for the ~ of argument**
  tanto per fare un esempio; **art for art's ~**
  l'arte per l'arte
salad ['sæləd] n insalata; **tomato ~** insalata
  di pomodoro
salad bowl n insalatiera
salad cream n (Brit) (tipo di) maionese f
salad dressing n condimento per insalata
salad oil n olio da tavola
salami [sə'lɑːmɪ] n salame m
salaried ['sælərɪd] adj stipendiato(-a)
salary ['sælərɪ] n stipendio
salary scale n scala dei salari
sale [seɪl] n vendita; (at reduced prices)
  svendita, liquidazione f; **"for ~"** "in
  vendita"; **on ~** in vendita; **on ~ or return**
  da vendere o rimandare; **a closing-down** or
  (US) **liquidation ~** una liquidazione; **~ and**
  lease back n lease back m inv
saleroom ['seɪlrum] n sala delle aste
sales assistant n (Brit) commesso(-a)
sales clerk n (US) commesso(-a)
sales conference n riunione f marketing
  e vendite
sales drive n campagna di vendita, sforzo
  promozionale
sales force n personale m addetto alle vendite
salesman ['seɪlzmən] n commesso;
  (representative) rappresentante m

sales manager n direttore m commerciale
salesmanship ['seɪlzmənʃɪp] n arte f del
  vendere
sales tax n (US) imposta sulle vendite
saleswoman ['seɪlzwumən] n commessa
salient ['seɪlɪənt] adj saliente
saline ['seɪlaɪn] adj salino(-a)
saliva [sə'laɪvə] n saliva
sallow ['sæləu] adj giallastro(-a)
sally forth, sally out ['sælɪ-] vi uscire di
  gran carriera
salmon ['sæmən] n (pl inv) salmone m
salmon trout n trota (di mare)
saloon [sə'luːn] n (US) saloon m inv, bar m inv;
  (Brit Aut) berlina; (ship's lounge) salone m
SALT [sɔːlt] n abbr (= Strategic Arms Limitation
  Talks/Treaty) S.A.L.T. m
salt [sɔːlt] n sale m ■ vt salare ■ cpd di sale;
  (Culin) salato(-a); **an old ~** un lupo di mare
  ▸ **salt away** vt ammucchiare, mettere via
salt cellar n saliera
salt-free ['sɔːlt'friː] adj senza sale
saltwater ['sɔːltwɔːtər] adj (fish etc) di mare
salty ['sɔːltɪ] adj salato(-a)
salubrious [sə'luːbrɪəs] adj salubre; (fig:
  district etc) raccomandabile
salutary ['sæljutərɪ] adj salutare
salute [sə'luːt] n saluto ■ vt salutare
salvage ['sælvɪdʒ] n (saving) salvataggio;
  (things saved) beni mpl salvati or recuperati
  ■ vt salvare, mettere in salvo
salvage vessel n scialuppa di salvataggio
salvation [sæl'veɪʃən] n salvezza
Salvation Army n Esercito della Salvezza
salver ['sælvər] n vassoio
salvo, salvoes ['sælvəu] n salva
Samaritan [sə'mærɪtən] n: **the Samaritans**
  (organization) ≈ telefono amico
same [seɪm] adj stesso(-a), medesimo(-a)
  ■ pron: **the ~** lo(la) stesso(-a), gli(le) stessi(-e);
  the ~ book as lo stesso libro di (or che); **on**
  the ~ day lo stesso giorno; **at the ~ time** allo
  stesso tempo; **all** or **just the ~** tuttavia; **to**
  do the ~ fare la stessa cosa; **to do the ~ as sb**
  fare come qn; **the ~ again** (in bar etc) un altro;
  they're one and the ~ (person/thing) sono la
  stessa persona/cosa; **and the ~ to you!**
  altrettanto a lei!; **~ here!** anch'io!
sample ['sɑːmpl] n campione m ■ vt (food)
  assaggiare; (wine) degustare; **to take a ~**
  prelevare un campione; **free ~** campione
  omaggio
sanatorium (pl **sanatoria**) [sænə'tɔːrɪəm,
  -rɪə] n sanatorio
sanctify ['sæŋktɪfaɪ] vt santificare
sanctimonious [sæŋktɪ'məunɪəs] adj
  bigotto(-a), bacchettone(-a)

sanction ['sæŋkʃən] n sanzione f ■ vt sancire, sanzionare; **to impose economic sanctions on** or **against** adottare sanzioni economiche contro

sanctity ['sæŋktɪtɪ] n santità

sanctuary ['sæŋktjuərɪ] n (holy place) santuario; (refuge) rifugio; (for wildlife) riserva

sand [sænd] n sabbia ■ vt cospargere di sabbia; (also: **sand down**: wood etc) cartavetrare; see also **sands**

sandal ['sændl] n sandalo

sandbag ['sændbæg] n sacco di sabbia

sandblast ['sændblɑːst] vt sabbiare

sandbox ['sændbɔks] n (US: for children) buca di sabbia

sandcastle ['sændkɑːsl] n castello di sabbia

sand dune n duna di sabbia

sander ['sændər] n levigatrice f

sandpaper ['sændpeɪpər] n carta vetrata

sandpit ['sændpɪt] n (Brit: for children) buca di sabbia

sands [sændz] npl spiaggia

sandstone ['sændstəun] n arenaria

sandstorm ['sændstɔːm] n tempesta di sabbia

sandwich ['sændwɪtʃ] n tramezzino, panino, sandwich m inv ■ vt (also: **sandwich in**) infilare; **cheese/ham** ~ sandwich al formaggio/prosciutto; **to be sandwiched between** essere incastrato(-a) fra

sandwich board n cartello pubblicitario (portato da un uomo sandwich)

sandwich course n (Brit) corso di formazione professionale

sandwich man n uomo m sandwich inv

sandy ['sændɪ] adj sabbioso(-a); (colour) color sabbia inv, biondo(-a) rossiccio(-a)

sane [seɪn] adj (person) sano(-a) di mente; (outlook) sensato(-a)

sang [sæŋ] pt of **sing**

sanguine ['sæŋgwɪn] adj ottimista

sanitarium (pl **sanitaria**) [sænɪ'tɛərɪəm, -rɪə] n (US) = **sanatorium**

sanitary ['sænɪtərɪ] adj (system, arrangements) sanitario(-a); (clean) igienico(-a)

sanitary towel, (US) **sanitary napkin** n assorbente m (igienico)

sanitation [sænɪ'teɪʃən] n (in house) impianti mpl sanitari; (in town) fognature fpl

sanitation department n (US) nettezza urbana

sanity ['sænɪtɪ] n sanità mentale; (common sense) buon senso

sank [sæŋk] pt of **sink**

San Marino [sænmə'riːnəu] n San Marino f

Santa Claus [sæntə'klɔːz] n Babbo Natale

Santiago [sæntɪ'ɑːgəu] n (also: **Santiago de Chile**) Santiago (del Cile) f

sap [sæp] n (of plants) linfa ■ vt (strength) fiaccare

sapling ['sæplɪŋ] n alberello

sapphire ['sæfaɪər] n zaffiro

sarcasm ['sɑːkæzm] n sarcasmo

sarcastic [sɑː'kæstɪk] adj sarcastico(-a); **to be** ~ fare del sarcasmo

sarcophagus (pl **sarcophagi**) [sɑː'kɔfəgəs, -gaɪ] n sarcofago

sardine [sɑː'diːn] n sardina

Sardinia [sɑː'dɪnɪə] n Sardegna

Sardinian [sɑː'dɪnɪən] adj, n sardo(-a)

sardonic [sɑː'dɔnɪk] adj sardonico(-a)

sari ['sɑːrɪ] n sari m inv

SARS [sɑːz] n abbr (= severe acute respiratory syndrome) SARS f, polmonite atipica

sartorial [sɑː'tɔːrɪəl] adj di sartoria

SAS n abbr (Brit Mil: = Special Air Service) reparto dell'esercito britannico specializzato in operazioni clandestine

SASE n abbr (US: = self-addressed stamped envelope) busta affrancata e con indirizzo

sash [sæʃ] n fascia

sash window n finestra a ghigliottina

Sask. abbr (Canada) = **Saskatchewan**

SAT n abbr (US) = **Scholastic Aptitude Test**

sat [sæt] pt, pp of **sit**

Sat. abbr (= Saturday) sab.

Satan ['seɪtən] n Satana m

satanic [sə'tænɪk] adj satanico(-a)

satchel ['sætʃl] n cartella

sated ['seɪtɪd] adj soddisfatto(-a); sazio(-a)

satellite ['sætəlaɪt] adj, n satellite m

satellite television n televisione f via satellite

satiate ['seɪʃɪeɪt] vt saziare

satin ['sætɪn] n satin m ■ adj di or in satin; **with a** ~ **finish** satinato(-a)

satire ['sætaɪər] n satira

satirical [sə'tɪrɪkl] adj satirico(-a)

satirist ['sætərɪst] n (writer etc) scrittore(-trice) etc satirico(-a); (cartoonist) caricaturista m/f

satirize ['sætɪraɪz] vt satireggiare

satisfaction [sætɪs'fækʃən] n soddisfazione f; **has it been done to your** ~? ne è rimasto soddisfatto?

satisfactory [sætɪs'fæktərɪ] adj soddisfacente

satisfied ['sætɪsfaɪd] adj (customer) soddisfatto(-a); **to be** ~ **(with sth)** essere soddisfatto(-a) (di qc)

satisfy ['sætɪsfaɪ] vt soddisfare; (convince) convincere; **to** ~ **the requirements** rispondere ai requisiti; **to** ~ **sb (that)** convincere qn (che), persuadere qn (che); **to** ~ **o.s. of sth** accertarsi di qc

S

767

satisfying ['sætɪsfaɪɪŋ] *adj* soddisfacente

SATs *n abbr* (Brit: = *standard assessment tasks or tests*) esame di fine anno sostenuto dagli allievi delle scuole pubbliche inglesi a 7, 11 o 14 anni

satsuma [sæt'suːmə] *n agrume di provenienza giapponese*

saturate ['sætʃəreɪt] *vt*: **to ~ (with)** saturare (di)

saturated fat ['sætʃəreɪtɪd-] *n grassi mpl* saturi

saturation [sætʃə'reɪʃən] *n* saturazione *f*

Saturday ['sætədɪ] *n* sabato; *see also* **Tuesday**

sauce [sɔːs] *n* salsa; (*containing meat, fish*) sugo

saucepan ['sɔːspən] *n* casseruola

saucer ['sɔːsəʳ] *n* piattino

saucy ['sɔːsɪ] *adj* impertinente

Saudi ['saudɪ] *adj, n* saudita *m/f*

Saudi Arabia *n* Arabia Saudita

Saudi Arabian *adj, n* saudita *m/f*

sauna ['sɔːnə] *n* sauna

saunter ['sɔːntəʳ] *vi* andare a zonzo, bighellonare

sausage ['sɒsɪdʒ] *n* salsiccia; (*salami etc*) salame *m*

sausage roll *n* rotolo di pasta sfoglia ripieno di salsiccia

sauté ['səuteɪ] *adj* (*Culin: potatoes*) saltato(-a); (: *onions*) soffritto(-a) ■ *vt* far saltare; far soffriggere

savage ['sævɪdʒ] *adj* (*cruel, fierce*) selvaggio(-a), feroce; (*primitive*) primitivo(-a) ■ *n* selvaggio(-a) ■ *vt* attaccare selvaggiamente

savagery ['sævɪdʒrɪ] *n* crudeltà, ferocia

save [seɪv] *vt* (*person, belongings, Comput*) salvare; (*money*) risparmiare, mettere da parte; (*time*) risparmiare; (*food*) conservare; (*avoid: trouble*) evitare ■ *vi* (*also:* **save up**) economizzare ■ *n* (*Sport*) parata ■ *prep* salvo, a eccezione di; **it will ~ me an hour** mi farà risparmiare un'ora; **to ~ face** salvare la faccia; **God ~ the Queen!** Dio salvi la Regina!

saving ['seɪvɪŋ] *n* risparmio ■ *adj*: **the ~ grace of** l'unica cosa buona di; **savings** *npl* risparmi *mpl*; **to make savings** fare economia

savings account *n* libretto di risparmio

savings bank *n* cassa di risparmio

saviour, (*US*) **savior** ['seɪvjəʳ] *n* salvatore *m*

savour, (*US*) **savor** ['seɪvəʳ] *n* sapore *m*, gusto ■ *vt* gustare

savoury, (*US*) **savory** ['seɪvərɪ] *adj* saporito(-a); (*dish: not sweet*) salato(-a)

savvy ['sævɪ] *n* (*col*) arguzia

saw [sɔː] *pt of* **see** ■ *n* (*tool*) sega ■ *vt* (*pt* **sawed**, *pp* **sawed** *or* **sawn**) [sɔːn] segare; **to ~ sth up** fare a pezzi qc con la sega

sawdust ['sɔːdʌst] *n* segatura

sawmill ['sɔːmɪl] *n* segheria

sawn [sɔːn] *pp of* **saw**

sawn-off ['sɔːnɒf], (*US*) **sawed-off** ['sɔːdɒf] *adj*: **~ shotgun** fucile *m* a canne mozze

saxophone ['sæksəfəun] *n* sassofono

say [seɪ] *n*: **to have one's ~** fare sentire il proprio parere; **to have a** *or* **some ~** avere voce in capitolo ■ *vt* (*pt, pp* **said**) [sɛd] dire; **could you ~ that again?** potrebbe ripeterlo?; **to ~ yes/no** dire di sì/di no; **she said (that)** I **was to give you this** ha detto di darle questo; **my watch says 3 o'clock** il mio orologio fa le 3; **shall we ~ Tuesday?** facciamo martedì?; **that doesn't ~ much for him** non torna a suo credito; **when all is said and done** a conti fatti; **there is something** *or* **a lot to be said for it** ha i suoi lati positivi; **that is to ~** cioè, vale a dire; **to ~ nothing of** per non parlare di; **~ that ...** mettiamo *or* diciamo che ...; **that goes without saying** va da sé

saying ['seɪɪŋ] *n* proverbio, detto

SBA *n abbr* (*US*: = *Small Business Administration*) organismo ausiliario per piccole imprese

SC *n abbr* (*US*) = **supreme court** ■ *abbr* (*US*) = **South Carolina**

s/c *abbr* (= *self-contained*) indipendente

scab [skæb] *n* crosta; (*pej*) crumiro(-a)

scabby ['skæbɪ] *adj* crostoso(-a)

scaffold ['skæfəuld] *n* impalcatura; (*gallows*) patibolo

scaffolding ['skæfəldɪŋ] *n* impalcatura

scald [skɔːld] *n* scottatura ■ *vt* scottare

scalding ['skɔːldɪŋ] *adj* (*also*: **scalding hot**) bollente

scale [skeɪl] *n* scala; (*of fish*) squama ■ *vt* (*mountain*) scalare; **pay ~** scala dei salari; **~ of charges** tariffa; **on a large ~** su vasta scala; **to draw sth to ~** disegnare qc in scala; **small-~ model** modello in scala ridotta; *see also* **scales**

▸ **scale down** *vt* ridurre (proporzionalmente)

scaled-down [skeɪld'daun] *adj* su scala ridotta

scale drawing *n* disegno in scala

scale model *n* modello in scala

scales [skeɪlz] *npl* bilancia

scallion ['skæljən] *n* cipolla; (*US: shallot*) scalogna; (: *leek*) porro

scallop ['skɒləp] *n* pettine *m*

scalp [skælp] *n* cuoio capelluto ■ *vt* scotennare

scalpel ['skælpl] *n* bisturi *m inv*

scalper ['skælpəʳ] *n* (*US col: of tickets*) bagarino

scam [skæm] *n* (*col*) truffa

scamp [skæmp] *n* (*col: child*) peste *f*

scamper ['skæmpə'] *vi*: **to ~ away, ~ off** darsela a gambe

scampi ['skæmpɪ] *npl* scampi *mpl*

scan [skæn] *vt* scrutare; (*glance at quickly*) scorrere, dare un'occhiata a; (*poetry*) scandire; (*TV*) analizzare; (*Radar*) esplorare ■ *n* (*Med*) ecografia

scandal ['skændl] *n* scandalo; (*gossip*) pettegolezzi *mpl*

scandalize ['skændəlaɪz] *vt* scandalizzare

scandalous ['skændələs] *adj* scandaloso(-a)

Scandinavia [skændɪ'neɪvɪə] *n* Scandinavia

Scandinavian [skændɪ'neɪvɪən] *adj, n* scandinavo(-a)

scanner ['skænə'] *n* (*Radar, Med*) scanner *m inv*

scant [skænt] *adj* scarso(-a)

scantily ['skæntɪlɪ] *adv*: **~ clad** *or* **dressed** succintamente vestito(-a)

scanty ['skæntɪ] *adj* insufficiente; (*swimsuit*) ridotto(-a)

scapegoat ['skeɪpgəut] *n* capro espiatorio

scar [skɑ:'] *n* cicatrice *f* ■ *vt* sfregiare

scarce [skeəs] *adj* scarso(-a); (*copy, edition*) raro(-a)

scarcely ['skeəslɪ] *adv* appena; **~ anybody** quasi nessuno; **I can ~ believe it** faccio fatica a crederci

scarcity ['skeəsɪtɪ] *n* scarsità, mancanza

scarcity value *n* valore *m* di rarità

scare [skeə'] *n* spavento, paura ■ *vt* spaventare, atterrire; **to ~ sb stiff** spaventare a morte qn; **bomb ~** evacuazione *f* per sospetta presenza di un ordigno esplosivo

▶ **scare away, scare off** *vt* mettere in fuga

scarecrow ['skeəkrəu] *n* spaventapasseri *m inv*

scared [skeəd] *adj*: **to be ~** aver paura

scaremonger ['skeəmʌngə'] *n* allarmista *m/f*

scarf (*pl* **scarves**) [skɑ:f, skɑ:vz] *n* (*long*) sciarpa; (*square*) fazzoletto da testa, foulard *m inv*

scarlet ['skɑ:lɪt] *adj* scarlatto(-a)

scarlet fever *n* scarlattina

scarper ['skɑ:pə'] *vi* (*Brit col*) darsela a gambe

SCART socket ['skɑ:t-] *n* presa *f* SCART *inv*

scarves [skɑ:vz] *npl of* **scarf**

scary ['skeərɪ] *adj* (*col*) che fa paura

scathing ['skeɪðɪŋ] *adj* aspro(-a); **to be ~ about sth** essere molto critico rispetto a qc

scatter ['skætə'] *vt* spargere; (*crowd*) disperdere ■ *vi* disperdersi

scatterbrained ['skætəbreɪnd] *adj* scervellato(-a), sbadato(-a)

scattered ['skætəd] *adj* sparso(-a), sparpagliato(-a)

scatty ['skætɪ] *adj* (*col*) scervellato(-a), sbadato(-a)

scavenge ['skævɪndʒ] *vi* (*person*): **to ~ (for)** frugare tra i rifiuti (alla ricerca di); (*hyenas etc*) nutrirsi di carogne

scavenger ['skævəndʒə'] *n* spazzino

SCE *n abbr* = **Scottish Certificate of Education**

scenario [sɪ'nɑ:rɪəu] *n* (*Theat, Cine*) copione *m*; (*fig*) situazione *f*

scene [si:n] *n* (*Theat, fig etc*) scena; (*of crime, accident*) scena, luogo; (*sight, view*) vista, veduta; **behind the scenes** (*also fig*) dietro le quinte; **to appear** *or* **come on the ~** (*also fig*) entrare in scena; **the political ~ in Italy** il quadro politico in Italia; **to make a ~** (*col: fuss*) fare una scenata

scenery ['si:nərɪ] *n* (*Theat*) scenario; (*landscape*) panorama *m*

scenic ['si:nɪk] *adj* scenico(-a); panoramico(-a)

scent [sɛnt] *n* odore *m*, profumo; (*sense of smell*) olfatto, odorato; (*fig: track*) pista; **to put** *or* **throw sb off the ~** (*fig*) far perdere le tracce a qn, sviare qn

sceptic, (*US*) **skeptic** ['skɛptɪk] *n* scettico(-a)

sceptical, (*US*) **skeptical** ['skɛptɪkl] *adj* scettico(-a)

scepticism, (*US*) **skepticism** ['skɛptɪsɪzm] *n* scetticismo

sceptre, (*US*) **scepter** ['sɛptə'] *n* scettro

schedule ['ʃɛdju:l, (*US*) 'skɛdju:l] *n* programma *m*, piano; (*of trains*) orario; (*of prices etc*) lista, tabella ■ *vt* fissare; **as scheduled** come stabilito; **on ~** in orario; **to be ahead of/behind ~** essere in anticipo/ritardo sul previsto; **we are working to a very tight ~** il nostro programma di lavoro è molto intenso; **everything went according to ~** tutto è andato secondo i piani *or* secondo il previsto

scheduled ['ʃɛdju:ld, (*US*) 'skɛdju:ld] *adj* (*date, time*) fissato(-a); (*visit, event*) programmato(-a); (*train, bus, stop*) previsto(-a) (sull'orario); **~ flight** volo di linea

schematic [skɪ'mætɪk] *adj* schematico(-a)

scheme [ski:m] *n* piano, progetto; (*method*) sistema *m*; (*dishonest plan, plot*) intrigo, trama; (*arrangement*) disposizione *f*, sistemazione *f* ■ *vt* progettare; (*plot*) ordire ■ *vi* fare progetti; (*intrigue*) complottare; **colour ~** combinazione *f* di colori

scheming ['ski:mɪŋ] *adj* intrigante ■ *n* intrighi *mpl*, macchinazioni *fpl*

schism ['skɪzəm] *n* scisma *m*

schizophrenia [skɪtsə'fri:nɪə] *n* schizofrenia

schizophrenic [skɪtsə'frɛnɪk] *adj, n* schizofrenico(-a)

scholar ['skɔlə'] *n* erudito(-a)

scholarly ['skɔləlɪ] *adj* dotto(-a), erudito(-a)

S

769

scholarship ['skɒləʃɪp] n erudizione f; (grant) borsa di studio

school [sku:l] n scuola; (in university) scuola, facoltà f inv ■ cpd scolare, scolastico(-a) ■ vt (animal) addestrare

school age n età scolare

schoolbook ['sku:lbʊk] n libro scolastico

schoolboy ['sku:lbɔɪ] n scolaro

schoolchild (pl -children) ['sku:ltʃaɪld, -'tʃɪldrən] n scolaro(-a)

schooldays ['sku:ldeɪz] npl giorni mpl di scuola

schoolgirl ['sku:lgə:l] n scolara

schooling ['sku:lɪŋ] n istruzione f

school-leaver ['sku:lli:və⁺] n (Brit) ≈ neodiplomato(-a)

schoolmaster ['sku:lmɑ:stə⁺] n (primary) maestro; (secondary) insegnante m

schoolmistress ['sku:lmɪstrɪs] n (primary) maestra; (secondary) insegnante f

school report n (Brit) pagella

schoolroom ['sku:lru:m] n classe f, aula

schoolteacher ['sku:lti:tʃə⁺] n insegnante m/f, docente m/f; (primary) maestro(-a)

schoolyard ['sku:ljɑ:d] n (US) cortile m della scuola

schooner ['sku:nə⁺] n (ship) goletta, schooner m inv; (glass) bicchiere m alto da sherry

sciatica [saɪ'ætɪkə] n sciatica

science ['saɪəns] n scienza; the sciences le scienze; (Scol) le materie scientifiche

science fiction n fantascienza

scientific [saɪən'tɪfɪk] adj scientifico(-a)

scientist ['saɪəntɪst] n scienziato(-a)

sci-fi ['saɪfaɪ] n abbr (col) = science fiction

Scilly Isles ['sɪlɪ'aɪlz] npl, **Scillies** ['sɪlɪz] npl: the ~ le isole Scilly

scintillating ['sɪntɪleɪtɪŋ] adj scintillante; (wit, conversation, company) brillante

scissors ['sɪzəz] npl forbici fpl; a pair of ~ un paio di forbici

sclerosis [sklɪ'rəʊsɪs] n sclerosi f

scoff [skɒf] vt (Brit col: eat) tranguiare, ingozzare ■ vi: to ~ (at) (mock) farsi beffe (di)

scold [skəʊld] vt rimproverare

scolding ['skəʊldɪŋ] n lavata di capo, sgridata

scone [skɒn] n focaccina da tè

scoop [sku:p] n mestolo; (for ice cream) cucchiaio dosatore; (Press) colpo giornalistico, notizia (in) esclusiva

▶ **scoop out** vt scavare

▶ **scoop up** vt tirare su, sollevare

scooter ['sku:tə⁺] n (motorcycle) motoretta, scooter m inv; (toy) monopattino

scope [skəʊp] n (capacity: of plan, undertaking) portata; (: of person) capacità fpl; (opportunity) possibilità fpl; to be within the ~ of

rientrare nei limiti di; it's well within his ~ to ... è perfettamente in grado di ...; there is plenty of ~ for improvement (Brit) ci sono notevoli possibilità di miglioramento

scorch [skɔ:tʃ] vt (clothes) strinare, bruciacchiare; (earth, grass) seccare, bruciare

scorched earth policy [skɔ:tʃt-] n tattica della terra bruciata

scorcher ['skɔ:tʃə⁺] n (col: hot day) giornata torrida

scorching ['skɔ:tʃɪŋ] adj cocente, scottante

score [skɔ:⁺] n punti mpl, punteggio; (Mus) partitura, spartito; (twenty): a ~ venti ■ vt (goal, point) segnare, fare; (success) ottenere; (cut: leather, wood, card) incidere ■ vi segnare; (Football) fare un goal; (keep score) segnare i punti; on that ~ a questo riguardo; to have an old ~ to settle with sb (fig) avere un vecchio conto da saldare con qn; scores of people (fig) un sacco di gente; to ~ 6 out of 10 prendere 6 su 10

▶ **score out** vt cancellare con un segno

scoreboard ['skɔ:bɔ:d] n tabellone m segnapunti

scorecard ['skɔ:kɑ:d] n cartoncino segnapunti

scoreline ['skɔ:laɪn] n (Sport) risultato

scorer ['skɔ:rə⁺] n marcatore(-trice); (keeping score) segnapunti m inv

scorn [skɔ:n] n disprezzo ■ vt disprezzare

scornful ['skɔ:nful] adj sprezzante

Scorpio ['skɔ:pɪəʊ] n Scorpione m; to be ~ essere dello Scorpione

scorpion ['skɔ:pɪən] n scorpione m

Scot [skɒt] n scozzese m/f

Scotch [skɒtʃ] n whisky m scozzese, scotch m

scotch [skɒtʃ] vt (rumour etc) soffocare

Scotch tape® n scotch® m

scot-free ['skɔt'fri:] adj impunito(-a); to get off ~ (unpunished) farla franca; (unhurt) uscire illeso(-a)

Scotland ['skɒtlənd] n Scozia

Scots [skɒts] adj scozzese

Scotsman ['skɒtsmən] n scozzese m

Scotswoman ['skɒtswʊmən] n scozzese f

Scottish ['skɒtɪʃ] adj scozzese; the ~ National Party il partito nazionalista scozzese; the ~ Parliament il Parlamento scozzese

scoundrel ['skaundrl] n farabutto(-a); (child) furfantello(-a)

scour ['skauə⁺] vt (clean) pulire strofinando; raschiare via; ripulire; (search) battere, perlustrare

scourer ['skauərə⁺] n (pad) paglietta; (powder) (detersivo) abrasivo

scourge [skə:dʒ] n flagello

scout [skaut] *n* (*Mil*) esploratore *m*; (*also*:
boy scout) giovane esploratore, scout *m inv*
▶ **scout around** *vi* cercare in giro

scowl [skaul] *vi* accigliarsi, aggrottare le
sopracciglia; **to ~ at** guardare torvo

scrabble ['skræbl] *vi* (*claw*): **to ~ (at)** graffiare,
grattare; **to ~ about** *or* **around for sth**
cercare affannosamente qc ■ *n*: **S~®**
Scarabeo®

scraggy ['skrægɪ] *adj* scarno(-a), molto
magro(-a)

scram [skræm] *vi* (*col*) filare via

scramble ['skræmbl] *n* arrampicata ■ *vi*
inerpicarsi; **to ~ out** *etc* uscire *etc* in fretta;
to ~ for azzuffarsi per; **to go scrambling**
(*Sport*) fare il motocross

scrambled eggs *npl* uova *fpl* strapazzate

scrap [skræp] *n* pezzo, pezzetto; (*fight*) zuffa;
(*also*: **scrap iron**) rottami *mpl* di ferro,
ferraglia ■ *vt* demolire; (*fig*) scartare;
scraps *npl* (*waste*) scarti *mpl*; **to sell sth for ~**
vendere qc come ferro vecchio

scrapbook ['skræpbuk] *n* album *m inv* di
ritagli

scrap dealer *n* commerciante *m* di ferraglia

scrape [skreɪp] *vt, vi* raschiare, grattare ■ *n*:
to get into a ~ cacciarsi in un guaio
▶ **scrape through** *vi* (*succeed*) farcela per un
pelo, cavarsela ■ *vt fus* (*exam*) passare per
miracolo, passare per il rotto della cuffia

scraper ['skreɪpə'] *n* raschietto

scrap heap *n* mucchio di rottami; **to throw**
sth on the ~ (*fig*) mettere qc nel
dimenticatoio

scrap merchant *n* (*Brit*) commerciante *m*
di ferraglia

scrap metal *n* ferraglia

scrap paper *n* cartaccia

scrappy ['skræpɪ] *adj* frammentario(-a),
sconnesso(-a)

scrap yard *n* deposito di rottami; (*for cars*)
cimitero delle macchine

scratch [skrætʃ] *n* graffio ■ *cpd*: **~ team**
squadra raccogliticcia ■ *vt* graffiare, rigare;
(*Comput*) cancellare ■ *vi* grattare, graffiare;
to start from ~ cominciare *or* partire da
zero; **to be up to ~** essere all'altezza

scratch pad *n* (*US*) notes *m inv*, blocchetto

scrawl [skrɔ:l] *n* scarabocchio ■ *vi*
scarabocchiare

scrawny ['skrɔ:nɪ] *adj* scarno(-a), pelle e ossa
inv

scream [skri:m] *n* grido, urlo ■ *vi* urlare,
gridare; **to ~ at sb (to do sth)** gridare a qn
(di fare qc); **it was a ~** (*fig, col*) era da crepar
dal ridere; **he's a ~** (*fig, col*) è una sagoma, è
uno spasso

scree [skri:] *n* ghiaione *m*

screech [skri:tʃ] *n* strido; (*of tyres, brakes*)
stridore *m* ■ *vi* stridere

screen [skri:n] *n* schermo; (*fig*) muro,
cortina, velo ■ *vt* schermare, fare schermo a;
(*from the wind etc*) riparare; (*film*) proiettare;
(*book*) adattare per lo schermo; (*candidates etc*)
passare al vaglio; (*for illness*) sottoporre a
controlli medici

screen editing [-ɛdɪtɪŋ] *n* (*Comput*)
correzione *f* e modifica su schermo

screening ['skri:nɪŋ] *n* (*Med*) dépistage *m inv*;
(*of film*) proiezione *f*; (*for security*) controlli *mpl*
(di sicurezza)

screen memory *n* (*Comput*) memoria di
schermo

screenplay ['skri:npleɪ] *n* sceneggiatura

screensaver *n* (*Comput*) screen saver *m inv*

screen test *n* provino (cinematografico)

screw [skru:] *n* vite *f*; (*propeller*) elica ■ *vt*
avvitare; **to ~ sth to the wall** fissare qc al
muro con viti
▶ **screw up** *vt* (*paper, material*) spiegazzare;
(*col: ruin*) mandare a monte; **to ~ up one's**
face fare una smorfia

screwdriver ['skru:draɪvə'] *n* cacciavite *m*

screwed-up ['skru:d'ʌp] *adj* (*col*): **she's**
totally ~ è nel pallone

screwy ['skru:ɪ] *adj* (*col*) svitato(-a)

scribble ['skrɪbl] *vt* scarabocchiare ■ *vi*
scribacchiare ■ *vi* scarabocchiare; **to ~ sth**
down scribacchiare qc

scribe [skraɪb] *n* scriba *m*

script [skrɪpt] *n* (*Cine etc*) copione *m*; (*in exam*)
elaborato *or* compito d'esame; (*writing*)
scrittura

scripted ['skrɪptɪd] *adj* (*Radio, TV*)
preparato(-a)

Scripture ['skrɪptʃə'] *n* Sacre Scritture *fpl*

scriptwriter ['skrɪptraɪtə'] *n* soggettista *m/f*

scroll [skrəul] *n* rotolo di carta ■ *vt* (*Comput*)
scorrere

scroll bar *n* (*Comput*) barra di scorrimento

scrotum ['skrəutəm] *n* scroto

scrounge [skraundʒ] *vt* (*col*): **to ~ sth (off** *or*
from sb) scroccare qc (a qn) ■ *vi*: **to ~ on sb**
vivere alle spalle di qn

scrounger ['skraundʒə'] *n* scroccone(-a)

scrub [skrʌb] *n* (*clean*) strofinata; (*land*)
boscaglia ■ *vt* pulire strofinando; (*reject*)
annullare

scrubbing brush ['skrʌbɪŋ-] *n* spazzolone *m*

scruff [skrʌf] *n*: **by the ~ of the neck** per la
collottola

scruffy ['skrʌfɪ] *adj* sciatto(-a)

scrum ['skrʌm], **scrummage** ['skrʌmɪdʒ] *n*
mischia

S

scruple ['skru:pl] *n* scrupolo; **to have no scruples about doing sth** non avere scrupoli a fare qc

scrupulous ['skru:pjuləs] *adj* scrupoloso(-a)

scrupulously ['skru:pjuləslı] *adv* scrupolosamente; **he tries to be ~ fair/honest** cerca di essere più imparziale/onesto che può

scrutinize ['skru:tınaız] *vt* scrutare, esaminare attentamente

scrutiny ['skru:tını] *n* esame *m* accurato; **under the ~ of sb** sotto la sorveglianza di qn

scuba ['sku:bə] *n* autorespiratore *m*

scuba diving *n* immersioni *fpl* subacquee

scuff [skʌf] *vt* (*shoes*) consumare strascicando

scuffle ['skʌfl] *n* baruffa, tafferuglio

scullery ['skʌlərı] *n* retrocucina *m or f*

sculptor ['skʌlptə^r] *n* scultore *m*

sculpture ['skʌlptʃə^r] *n* scultura

scum [skʌm] *n* schiuma; (*pej: people*) feccia

scupper ['skʌpə^r] *vt* (*Brit*) autoaffondare; (*fig*) far naufragare

scurrilous ['skʌrıləs] *adj* scurrile, volgare

scurry ['skʌrı] *vi* sgambare, affrettarsi

scurvy ['skə:vı] *n* scorbuto

scuttle ['skʌtl] *n* (*Naut*) portellino; (*also*: **coal scuttle**) secchio del carbone ■ *vt* (*ship*) autoaffondare ■ *vi* (*scamper*): **to ~ away, ~ off** darsela a gambe, scappare

scythe [saıð] *n* falce *f*

SD, S. Dak. *abbr* (*US*) = **South Dakota**

SDI *n abbr* (= *Strategic Defense Initiative*) S.D.I. *f*

SDLP *n abbr* (*Brit Pol*) = **Social Democratic and Labour Party**

sea [si:] *n* mare *m* ■ *cpd* marino(-a), del mare; (*ship, port*) marittimo(-a), di mare; **on the ~** (*boat*) in mare; (*town*) di mare; **to go by ~** andare per mare; **by** *or* **beside the ~** (*holiday*) al mare; (*village*) sul mare; **to look out to ~** guardare il mare; (*out*) **at ~** al largo; **heavy** *or* **rough ~(s)** mare grosso *or* agitato; **a ~ of faces** (*fig*) una marea di gente; **to be all at ~** (*fig*) non sapere che pesci pigliare

sea bed *n* fondo marino

sea bird *n* uccello di mare

seaboard ['si:bɔ:d] *n* costa

sea breeze *n* brezza di mare

seafarer ['si:fɛərə^r] *n* navigante *m*

seafaring ['si:fɛərıŋ] *adj* (*community*) marinaro(-a); (*life*) da marinaio

seafood ['si:fu:d] *n* frutti *mpl* di mare

sea front *n* lungomare *m*

seagoing ['si:gəuıŋ] *adj* (*ship*) d'alto mare

seagull ['si:gʌl] *n* gabbiano

seal [si:l] *n* (*animal*) foca; (*stamp*) sigillo; (*impression*) impronta del sigillo ■ *vt* sigillare; (*decide: sb's fate*) segnare; (: *bargain*) concludere; **~ of approval** beneplacito

▸ **seal off** *vt* (*close*) sigillare; (*forbid entry to*) bloccare l'accesso a

sea level *n* livello del mare

sealing wax ['si:lıŋ-] *n* ceralacca

sea lion *n* leone *m* marino

sealskin ['si:lskın] *n* pelle *f* di foca

seam [si:m] *n* cucitura; (*of coal*) filone *m*; **the hall was bursting at the seams** l'aula era piena zeppa

seaman ['si:mən] *n* marinaio

seamanship ['si:mənʃıp] *n* tecnica di navigazione

seamless ['si:mlıs] *adj* senza cucitura

seamy ['si:mı] *adj* malfamato(-a); squallido(-a)

seance ['seıɔns] *n* seduta spiritica

seaplane ['si:pleın] *n* idrovolante *m*

seaport ['si:pɔ:t] *n* porto di mare

search [sə:tʃ] *n* (*for person, thing*) ricerca; (*of drawer, pockets*) esame *m* accurato; (*Law: at sb's home*) perquisizione *f* ■ *vt* perlustrare, frugare; (*scan, examine*) esaminare minuziosamente; (*Comput*) ricercare ■ *vi*: **to ~ for** ricercare; **in ~ of** alla ricerca di; **"~ and replace"** (*Comput*) "ricercare e sostituire"

▸ **search through** *vt fus* frugare

search engine *n* (*Comput*) motore *m* di ricerca

searcher ['sə:tʃə^r] *n* chi cerca

searching ['sə:tʃıŋ] *adj* minuzioso(-a); penetrante; (*question*) pressante

searchlight ['sə:tʃlaıt] *n* proiettore *m*

search party *n* squadra di soccorso

search warrant *n* mandato di perquisizione

searing ['sıərıŋ] *adj* (*heat*) rovente; (*pain*) acuto(-a)

seashore ['si:ʃɔ:^r] *n* spiaggia; **on the ~** sulla riva del mare

seasick ['si:sık] *adj* che soffre il mal di mare; **to be ~** avere il mal di mare

seaside ['si:saıd] *n* spiaggia; **to go to the ~** andare al mare

seaside resort *n* stazione *f* balneare

season ['si:zn] *n* stagione *f* ■ *vt* condire, insaporire; **to be in/out of ~** essere di/fuori stagione; **the busy ~** (*for shops*) il periodo di punta; (*for hotels etc*) l'alta stagione; **the open ~** (*Hunting*) la stagione della caccia

seasonal ['si:zənl] *adj* stagionale

seasoned ['si:znd] *adj* (*wood*) stagionato(-a); (*fig: worker, actor, troops*) con esperienza; **a ~ campaigner** un veterano

seasoning ['si:znıŋ] *n* condimento

season ticket *n* abbonamento

seat [si:t] *n* sedile *m*; (*in bus, train: place*) posto; (*Parliament*) seggio; (*centre: of government etc, of infection*) sede *f*; (*buttocks*) didietro; (*of trousers*) fondo ■ *vt* far sedere; (*have room for*) avere *or* essere fornito(-a) di posti a sedere per; **are**

there any seats left? ci sono posti?; **to take one's ~** prendere posto; **to be seated** essere seduto(-a); **please be seated** accomodatevi per favore

seat belt *n* cintura di sicurezza

seating arrangements ['siːtɪŋ-] *npl* sistemazione *f* or disposizione *f* dei posti

seating capacity *n* posti *mpl* a sedere

SEATO ['siːtəu] *n abbr* (= *Southeast Asia Treaty Organization*) SEATO *f*

sea water *n* acqua di mare

seaweed ['siːwiːd] *n* alghe *fpl*

seaworthy ['siːwəːðɪ] *adj* atto(-a) alla navigazione

SEC *n abbr* (US: = *Securities and Exchange Commission*) commissione di controllo sulle operazioni in Borsa

sec. *abbr* = **second¹**

secateurs [sɛkə'təːz] *npl* forbici *fpl* per potare

secede [sɪ'siːd] *vi*: **to ~ (from)** ritirarsi (da)

secluded [sɪ'kluːdɪd] *adj* isolato(-a), appartato(-a)

seclusion [sɪ'kluːʒən] *n* isolamento

second¹ ['sɛkənd] *num* secondo(-a) ■ *adv* (*in race etc*) al secondo posto; (*Rail*) in seconda ■ *n* (*unit of time*) secondo; (*in series, position*) secondo(-a); (*Brit Scol*) laurea con punteggio discreto; (*Aut: also:* **second gear**) seconda; (*Comm: imperfect*) scarto ■ *vt* (*motion*) appoggiare; **Charles the S~** Carlo Secondo; **just a ~!** un attimo!; **~ floor** (*Brit*) secondo piano; (*US*) primo piano; **to ask for a ~ opinion** (*Med*) chiedere un altro *or* ulteriore parere; **to have ~ thoughts (about doing sth)** avere dei ripensamenti (quanto a fare qc); **on ~ thoughts** *or* (*US*) **thought** a ripensarci, ripensandoci bene

second² [sɪ'kɔnd] *vt* (*employee*) distaccare

secondary ['sɛkəndərɪ] *adj* secondario(-a)

secondary school *n* scuola secondaria; *vedi nota*

● **SECONDARY SCHOOL**

In Gran Bretagna la *secondary school* è la scuola frequentata dai ragazzi dagli 11 ai 18 anni. Nel paese è obbligatorio andare a scuola fino a 16 anni; *vedi anche* "primary school".

second-best [sɛkənd'bɛst] *n* ripiego; **as a ~** in mancanza di meglio

second-class [sɛkənd'klɑːs] *adj* di seconda classe ■ *adv*: **to travel ~** viaggiare in seconda (classe); **to send sth ~** spedire qc per posta ordinaria; **~ citizen** cittadino di second'ordine

second cousin *n* cugino di secondo grado

seconder ['sɛkəndər] *n* sostenitore(-trice)

second-guess ['sɛkənd'gɛs] *vt* (*predict*) anticipare; (*after the event*) giudicare col senno di poi

second hand *n* (*on clock*) lancetta dei secondi

second-hand [sɛkənd'hænd] *adj* di seconda mano, usato(-a) ■ *adv* (*buy*) di seconda mano; **to hear sth ~** venire a sapere qc da terze persone

second-in-command ['sɛkəndɪnkə'mɑːnd] *n* (*Mil*) comandante *m* in seconda; (*Admin*) aggiunto

secondly ['sɛkəndlɪ] *adv* in secondo luogo

secondment [sɪ'kɔndmənt] *n* (*Brit*) distaccamento

second-rate [sɛkənd'reɪt] *adj* scadente

Second World War *n*: **the ~** la seconda guerra mondiale

secrecy ['siːkrəsɪ] *n* segretezza

secret ['siːkrɪt] *adj* segreto(-a) ■ *n* segreto; **in ~** in segreto, segretamente; **to keep sth ~ (from sb)** tenere qc segreto (a qn), tenere qc nascosto (a qn); **keep it ~** che rimanga un segreto; **to make no ~ of sth** non far mistero di qc

secret agent *n* agente *m* segreto

secretarial [sɛkrɪ'tɛərɪəl] *adj* (*work*) da segretario(-a); (*college, course*) di segretariato

secretariat [sɛkrɪ'tɛərɪət] *n* segretariato

secretary ['sɛkrətrɪ] *n* segretario(-a); **S~ of State** (*US Pol*) ≈ Ministro degli Esteri; **S~ of State (for)** (*Brit: Pol*) ministro (di)

secretary-general ['sɛkrətrɪ'dʒɛnərl] *n* segretario generale

secrete [sɪ'kriːt] *vt* (*Med, Anat, Biol*) secernere; (*hide*) nascondere

secretion [sɪ'kriːʃən] *n* secrezione *f*

secretive ['siːkrətɪv] *adj* riservato(-a)

secretly ['siːkrɪtlɪ] *adv* in segreto, segretamente

secret police *n* polizia segreta

secret service *n* servizi *mpl* segreti

sect [sɛkt] *n* setta

sectarian [sɛk'tɛərɪən] *adj* settario(-a)

section ['sɛkʃən] *n* sezione *f*; (*of document*) articolo ■ *vt* sezionare, dividere in sezioni; **the business ~** (*Press*) la pagina economica

sector ['sɛktər] *n* settore *m*

secular ['sɛkjulər] *adj* secolare

secure [sɪ'kjuər] *adj* (*free from anxiety*) sicuro(-a); (*firmly fixed*) assicurato(-a), ben fermato(-a); (*in safe place*) al sicuro ■ *vt* (*fix*) fissare, assicurare; (*get*) ottenere, assicurarsi; (*Comm: loan*) garantire; **to make sth ~** fissare bene qc; **to ~ sth for sb** procurare qc per *or* a qn

S

773

secured creditor [sɪˈkjuəd-] n creditore m privilegiato

security [sɪˈkjuərɪtɪ] n sicurezza; (for loan) garanzia; **securities** npl (Stock Exchange) titoli mpl; **to increase/tighten ~** aumentare/intensificare la sorveglianza; **~ of tenure** garanzia del posto di lavoro, garanzia di titolo or di godimento

Security Council n: **the ~** il Consiglio di Sicurezza

security forces npl forze fpl dell'ordine

security guard n guardia giurata

security risk n rischio per la sicurezza

secy. abbr = **secretary**

sedan [səˈdæn] n (US Aut) berlina

sedate [sɪˈdeɪt] adj posato(-a); calmo(-a) ■ vt calmare

sedation [sɪˈdeɪʃən] n (Med): **to be under ~** essere sotto l'azione di sedativi

sedative [ˈsɛdɪtɪv] n sedativo, calmante m

sedentary [ˈsɛdntrɪ] adj sedentario(-a)

sediment [ˈsɛdɪmənt] n sedimento

sedition [sɪˈdɪʃən] n sedizione f

seduce [sɪˈdjuːs] vt sedurre

seduction [sɪˈdʌkʃən] n seduzione f

seductive [sɪˈdʌktɪv] adj seducente

see [si:] vb (pt **saw**, pp **seen**) [sɔː, siːn] vt vedere; (accompany): **to ~ sb to the door** accompagnare qn alla porta ■ vi vedere; (understand) capire ■ n sede f vescovile; **to ~ that** (ensure) badare che + sub, fare in modo che + sub; **to go and ~ sb** andare a trovare qn; **~ you soon/later/tomorrow!** a presto/più tardi/domani!; **as far as I can ~** da quanto posso vedere; **there was nobody to be seen** non c'era anima viva; **let me ~** (show me) fammi vedere; (let me think) vediamo (un po'); **~ for yourself** vai a vedere con i tuoi occhi; **I don't know what she sees in him** non so che cosa ci trovi in lui

▶ **see about** vt fus (deal with) occuparsi di

▶ **see off** vt salutare alla partenza

▶ **see through** vt portare a termine ■ vt fus non lasciarsi ingannare da

▶ **see to** vt fus occuparsi di

seed [si:d] n seme m; (fig) germe m; (Tennis) testa di serie; **to go to ~** fare seme; (fig) scadere

seedless [ˈsiːdlɪs] adj senza semi

seedling [ˈsiːdlɪŋ] n piantina di semenzaio

seedy [ˈsiːdɪ] adj (shabby: person) sciatto(-a); (: place) cadente

seeing [ˈsiːɪŋ] conj: **~ (that)** visto che

seek [si:k] (pt, **sought**) vt cercare; **to ~ advice/help from sb** chiedere consiglio/aiuto a qn

▶ **seek out** vt (person) andare a cercare

seem [si:m] vi sembrare, parere; **there seems to be ...** sembra che ci sia ...; **it seems (that) ...** sembra or pare che ... + sub; **what seems to be the trouble?** cosa c'è che non va?

seemingly [ˈsiːmɪŋlɪ] adv apparentemente

seen [si:n] pp of **see**

seep [si:p] vi filtrare, trapelare

seer [sɪəʳ] n profeta(-essa), veggente m/f

seersucker [ˈsɪəsʌkəʳ] n cotone m indiano

seesaw [ˈsiːsɔː] n altalena a bilico

seethe [si:ð] vi ribollire; **to ~ with anger** fremere di rabbia

see-through [ˈsiːθruː] adj trasparente

segment [ˈsɛgmənt] n segmento

segregate [ˈsɛgrɪgeɪt] vt segregare, isolare

segregation [sɛgrɪˈgeɪʃən] n segregazione f

Seine [seɪn] n Senna

seismic [ˈsaɪzmɪk] adj sismico(-a)

seize [si:z] vt (grasp) afferrare; (take possession of) impadronirsi di; (Law) sequestrare

▶ **seize up** vi (Tech) grippare

▶ **seize (up)on** vt fus ricorrere a

seizure [ˈsiːʒəʳ] n (Med) attacco; (Law) confisca, sequestro

seldom [ˈsɛldəm] adv raramente

select [sɪˈlɛkt] adj scelto(-a); (hotel, restaurant) chic inv; (club) esclusivo(-a) ■ vt scegliere, selezionare; **a ~ few** pochi eletti mpl

selection [sɪˈlɛkʃən] n selezione f, scelta

selection committee n comitato di selezione

selective [sɪˈlɛktɪv] adj selettivo(-a)

selector [sɪˈlɛktəʳ] n (person) selezionatore(-trice); (Tech) selettore m

self (pl **selves**) [sɛlf, sɛlvz] n: **the ~** l'io m ■ prefix auto...

self-addressed [ˈsɛlfəˈdrɛst] adj: **~ envelope** busta col proprio nome e indirizzo

self-adhesive [sɛlfədˈhiːzɪv] adj autoadesivo(-a)

self-assertive [sɛlfəˈsəːtɪv] adj autoritario(-a)

self-assurance [sɛlfəˈʃuərəns] n sicurezza di sé

self-assured [sɛlfəˈʃuəd] adj sicuro(-a) di sé

self-catering [sɛlfˈkeɪtərɪŋ] adj (Brit) in cui si cucina da sé; **~ apartment** appartamento (per le vacanze)

self-centred, (US) **self-centered** [sɛlfˈsɛntəd] adj egocentrico(-a)

self-cleaning [sɛlfˈkliːnɪŋ] adj autopulente

self-confessed [sɛlfkənˈfɛst] adj (alcoholic etc) dichiarato(-a)

self-confidence [sɛlfˈkɔnfɪdəns] n sicurezza di sé

self-conscious [sɛlfˈkɔnʃəs] adj timido(-a)

self-contained [sɛlfkən'teɪnd] *adj* (*Brit:flat*)
indipendente
self-control [sɛlfkən'trəul] *n* autocontrollo
self-defeating [sɛlfdɪ'fiːtɪŋ] *adj* futile
self-defence, (*US*) **self-defense** [sɛlfdɪ'fɛns]
n autodifesa; (*Law*) legittima difesa
self-discipline [sɛlf'dɪsɪplɪn] *n*
autodisciplina
self-employed [sɛlfɪm'plɔɪd] *adj* che lavora
in proprio
self-esteem [sɛlfɪ'stiːm] *n* amor proprio *m*
self-evident [sɛlf'ɛvɪdənt] *adj* evidente
self-explanatory [sɛlfɪk'splænətərɪ] *adj*
ovvio(-a)
self-governing [sɛlf'gʌvənɪŋ] *adj*
autonomo(-a)
self-help ['sɛlf'hɛlp] *n* iniziativa individuale
self-importance [sɛlfɪm'pɔːtns] *n*
sufficienza
self-indulgent [sɛlfɪn'dʌldʒənt] *adj*
indulgente verso se stesso(-a)
self-inflicted [sɛlfɪn'flɪktɪd] *adj*
autoinflitto(-a)
self-interest [sɛlf'ɪntrɪst] *n* interesse *m*
personale
selfish ['sɛlfɪʃ] *adj* egoista
selfishly ['sɛlfɪʃlɪ] *adv* egoisticamente
selfishness ['sɛlfɪʃnɪs] *n* egoismo
selfless ['sɛlflɪs] *adj* altruista
selflessly ['sɛlflɪslɪ] *adv* altruisticamente
selflessness ['sɛlflɪsnɪs] *n* altruismo
self-made man ['sɛlfmeɪd-] *n* self-made
man *m inv*, uomo che si è fatto da sé
self-pity [sɛlf'pɪtɪ] *n* autocommiserazione *f*
self-portrait [sɛlf'pɔːtrɪt] *n* autoritratto
self-possessed [sɛlfpə'zɛst] *adj*
controllato(-a)
self-preservation ['sɛlfprɛzə'veɪʃən] *n*
istinto di conservazione
self-raising [sɛlf'reɪzɪŋ], (*US*) **self-rising**
[sɛlf'raɪzɪŋ] *adj*: **~ flour** miscela di farina e
lievito
self-reliant [sɛlfrɪ'laɪənt] *adj* independente
self-respect [sɛlfrɪs'pɛkt] *n* rispetto di sé,
amor proprio
self-respecting [sɛlfrɪs'pɛktɪŋ] *adj* che ha
rispetto di sé
self-righteous [sɛlf'raɪtʃəs] *adj*
soddisfatto(-a) di sé
self-rising [sɛlf'raɪzɪŋ] *adj* (*US*) = **self-raising**
self-sacrifice [sɛlf'sækrɪfaɪs] *n* abnegazione *f*
self-same ['sɛlfseɪm] *adj* stesso(-a)
self-satisfied [sɛlf'sætɪsfaɪd] *adj*
compiaciuto(-a) di sé
self-sealing [sɛlf'siːlɪŋ] *adj* autosigillante
self-service [sɛlf'sə:vɪs] *n* autoservizio, self-
service *m*

self-styled [sɛlf'staɪld] *adj* sedicente
self-sufficient [sɛlfsə'fɪʃənt] *adj*
autosufficiente
self-supporting [sɛlfsə'pɔːtɪŋ] *adj*
economicamente indipendente
self-taught [sɛlf'tɔːt] *adj* autodidatta
self-test ['sɛlftɛst] *n* (*Comput*) autoverifica
sell (*pt, pp* **sold**) [sɛl, səuld] *vt* vendere ■ *vi*
vendersi; **to ~ at** *or* **for 100 euros** essere in
vendita a 100 euro; **to ~ sb an idea** (*fig*) far
accettare un'idea a qn
  ▶ **sell off** *vt* svendere, liquidare
  ▶ **sell out** *vi*: **to ~ out (to sb/sth)** (*Comm*)
vendere (tutto) (a qn/qc) ■ *vt* esaurire;
the tickets are all sold out i biglietti sono
esauriti
  ▶ **sell up** *vi* vendere (tutto)
sell-by date ['sɛlbaɪ-] *n* scadenza
seller ['sɛlə^r] *n* venditore(-trice); **~'s market**
mercato favorevole ai venditori
selling price ['sɛlɪŋ-] *n* prezzo di vendita
Sellotape® ['sɛləuteɪp] *n* (*Brit*) nastro
adesivo, scotch® *m*
sellout ['sɛlaut] *n* (*betrayal*) tradimento; (*of
tickets*): **it was a ~** registrò un tutto esaurito
selves [sɛlvz] *npl of* **self**
semantic [sɪ'mæntɪk] *adj* semantico(-a)
semantics [sɪ'mæntɪks] *n* semantica
semaphore ['sɛməfɔː^r] *n* segnali *mpl* con
bandiere; (*Rail*) semaforo
semblance ['sɛmbləns] *n* parvenza, apparenza
semen ['siːmən] *n* sperma *m*
semester [sɪ'mɛstə^r] *n* (*US*) semestre *m*
semi... ['sɛmɪ] *prefix* semi... ■ *n*: **semi**
= **semidetached (house)**
semi-breve ['sɛmɪbriːv] *n* (*Brit*) semibreve *f*
semicircle ['sɛmɪsəːkl] *n* semicerchio
semicircular ['sɛmɪ'səːkjulə^r] *adj*
semicircolare
semicolon [sɛmɪ'kəulən] *n* punto e virgola
semiconductor [sɛmɪkən'dʌktə^r] *n*
semiconduttore *m*
semiconscious [sɛmɪ'kɔnʃəs] *adj*
parzialmente cosciente
semidetached [sɛmɪdɪ'tætʃt],
  semidetached house [sɛmɪdɪ'tætʃt-] *n*
(*Brit*) casa gemella
semifinal [sɛmɪ'faɪnl] *n* semifinale *f*
seminar ['sɛmɪnɑː^r] *n* seminario
seminary ['sɛmɪnərɪ] *n* (*Rel: for priests*)
seminario
semiprecious [sɛmɪ'prɛʃəs] *adj*
semiprezioso(-a)
semiquaver ['sɛmɪkweɪvə^r] *n* (*Brit*)
semicroma
semiskilled ['sɛmɪ'skɪld] *adj*: **~ worker**
operaio(-a) non specializzato(-a)

S

semi-skimmed ['sɛmɪ'skɪmd] *adj*
parzialmente scremato(-a)
semitone ['sɛmɪtəun] *n* (*Mus*) semitono
semolina [sɛmə'li:nə] *n* semolino
Sen., sen. *abbr* = **senator; senior**
senate ['sɛnɪt] *n* senato
senator ['sɛnɪtə^r] *n* senatore(-trice)
send [sɛnd] (*pt, pp* **sent**) *vt* mandare; **to ~ by
post** *or* (*US*) **mail** spedire per posta; **to ~ sb
for sth** mandare qn a prendere qc; **to ~ word
that …** mandare a dire che …; **she sends
(you) her love** ti saluta affettuosamente;
to ~ sb to Coventry (*Brit*) dare l'ostracismo
a qn; **to ~ sb to sleep/into fits of laughter**
far addormentare/scoppiare dal ridere qn;
to ~ sth flying far volare via qc
▸ **send away** *vt* (*letter, goods*) spedire; (*person*)
mandare via
▸ **send away for** *vt fus* richiedere per posta,
farsi spedire
▸ **send back** *vt* rimandare
▸ **send for** *vt fus* mandare a chiamare, far
venire; (*by post*) ordinare per posta
▸ **send in** *vt* (*report, application, resignation*)
presentare
▸ **send off** *vt* (*goods*) spedire; (*Brit Sport: player*)
espellere
▸ **send on** *vt* (*Brit: letter*) inoltrare;
(*luggage etc: in advance*) spedire in anticipo
▸ **send out** *vt* (*invitation*) diramare;
(*emit: light, heat*) mandare, emanare;
(*: signals*) emettere
▸ **send round** *vt* (*letter, document etc*) far
circolare
▸ **send up** *vt* (*person, price*) far salire;
(*Brit: parody*) mettere in ridicolo
sender ['sɛndə^r] *n* mittente *m/f*
send-off ['sɛndɔf] *n*: **to give sb a good ~**
festeggiare la partenza di qn
Senegal [sɛnɪ'gɔ:l] *n* Senegal *m*
Senegalese [sɛnɪgə'li:z] *adj, n* senegalese *m/f*
senile ['si:naɪl] *adj* senile
senility [sɪ'nɪlɪtɪ] *n* senilità *f*
senior ['si:nɪə^r] *adj* (*older*) più vecchio(-a);
(*of higher rank*) di grado più elevato ■ *n*
persona più anziana; (*in service*) persona con
maggiore anzianità; **P. Jones ~** P. Jones
senior, P. Jones padre
senior citizen *n* anziano(-a)
senior high school *n* (*US*) ≈ liceo
seniority [si:nɪ'ɔrɪtɪ] *n* anzianità; (*in rank*)
superiorità
sensation [sɛn'seɪʃən] *n* sensazione *f*;
to create a ~ fare scalpore
sensational [sɛn'seɪʃənl] *adj* sensazionale;
(*marvellous*) eccezionale
sense [sɛns] *n* senso; (*feeling*) sensazione *f*,

senso; (*meaning*) senso, significato; (*wisdom*)
buonsenso ■ *vt* sentire, percepire; **senses**
npl (*sanity*) ragione *f*; **it makes ~** ha senso;
there is no ~ in (doing) that non ha senso
(farlo); **~ of humour** (senso dell')umorismo;
to come to one's senses (*regain consciousness*)
riprendere i sensi; (*become reasonable*) tornare
in sé; **to take leave of one's senses** perdere
il lume *or* l'uso della ragione
senseless ['sɛnslɪs] *adj* sciocco(-a);
(*unconscious*) privo(-a) di sensi
sensibilities [sɛnsɪ'bɪlɪtɪz] *npl* sensibilità *fsg*
sensible ['sɛnsɪbl] *adj* sensato(-a),
ragionevole
sensitive ['sɛnsɪtɪv] *adj*: **~ (to)** sensibile (a);
he is very ~ about it è un tasto che è meglio
non toccare con lui
sensitivity [sɛnsɪ'tɪvɪtɪ] *n* sensibilità
sensual ['sɛnsjuəl] *adj* sensuale
sensuous ['sɛnsjuəs] *adj* sensuale
sent [sɛnt] *pt, pp* of **send**
sentence ['sɛntns] *n* (*Ling*) frase *f*; (*Law:
judgement*) sentenza; (*: punishment*) condanna
■ *vt*: **to ~ sb to death/to 5 years** condannare
qn a morte/a 5 anni; **to pass ~ on sb**
condannare qn
sentiment ['sɛntɪmənt] *n* sentimento;
(*opinion*) opinione *f*
sentimental [sɛntɪ'mɛntl] *adj* sentimentale
sentimentality [sɛntɪmen'tælɪtɪ] *n*
sentimentalità, sentimentalismo
sentry ['sɛntrɪ] *n* sentinella
sentry duty *n*: **to be on ~** essere di sentinella
Seoul [səul] *n* Seul *f*
separable ['sɛprəbl] *adj* separabile
separate *adj* ['sɛprɪt] separato(-a) ■ *vb*
['sɛpəreɪt] *vt* separare ■ *vi* separarsi; **~ from**
separato da; **under ~ cover** (*Comm*) in plico a
parte; **to ~ into** dividere in; *see also*
separates
separately ['sɛprɪtlɪ] *adv* separatamente
separates ['sɛprɪts] *npl* (*clothes*) coordinati
mpl
separation [sɛpə'reɪʃən] *n* separazione *f*
Sept. *abbr* (= *September*) sett., set.
September [sɛp'tɛmbə^r] *n* settembre *m*;
see also **July**
septic ['sɛptɪk] *adj* settico(-a); (*wound*)
infettato(-a); **to go ~** infettarsi
septicaemia, (*US*) **septicemia** [sɛptɪ'si:mɪə]
n setticemia
septic tank *n* fossa settica
sequel ['si:kwl] *n* conseguenza; (*of story*)
seguito
sequence ['si:kwəns] *n* (*series*) serie *f inv*;
(*order*) ordine *m*; **in ~** in ordine, di seguito;
~ of tenses concordanza dei tempi

sequential [sɪ'kwɛnʃəl] *adj*: ~ **access** (*Comput*) accesso sequenziale

sequin ['si:kwɪn] *n* lustrino, paillette *f inv*

Serb [səːb] *adj, n* = **Serbian**

Serbia ['səːbɪə] *n* Serbia

Serbian ['səːbɪən] *adj* serbo(-a) ■ *n* serbo(-a); (*Ling*) serbo

Serbo-Croat ['səːbəuˈkrəuæt] *n* (*Ling*) serbocroato

serenade [sɛrəˈneɪd] *n* serenata ■ *vt* fare la serenata a

serene [sɪˈriːn] *adj* sereno(-a), calmo(-a)

serenity [sɪˈrɛnɪtɪ] *n* serenità, tranquillità

sergeant ['saːdʒənt] *n* sergente *m*; (*Police*) brigadiere *m*

sergeant major *n* maresciallo

serial ['sɪərɪəl] *n* (*Press*) romanzo a puntate; (*Radio, TV*) trasmissione *f* a puntate ■ *cpd* (*number*) di serie; (*Comput*) seriale

serialize ['sɪərɪəlaɪz] *vt* pubblicare a puntate; trasmettere a puntate

serial killer *n* serial killer *m inv*

serial number *n* numero di serie

series ['sɪəriːz] *n* (*pl inv*) serie *f inv*; (*Publishing*) collana

serious ['sɪərɪəs] *adj* serio(-a), grave; **are you ~ (about it)?** parla sul serio?

seriously ['sɪərɪəslɪ] *adv* seriamente; **he's ~ rich** (*col: extremely*) ha un casino di soldi; **to take sth/sb ~** prendere qc/qn sul serio

seriousness ['sɪərɪəsnɪs] *n* serietà, gravità

sermon ['səːmən] *n* sermone *m*

serrated [sɪˈreɪtɪd] *adj* seghettato(-a)

serum ['sɪərəm] *n* siero

servant ['səːvənt] *n* domestico(-a)

serve [səːv] *vt* (*employer etc*) servire, essere a servizio di; (*purpose*) servire a; (*customer, food, meal*) servire; (*apprenticeship*) fare; (*prison term*) scontare ■ *vi* (*also Tennis*) servire; (*soldier etc*) prestare servizio; (*be useful*): **to ~ as/for/to do** servire da/per/per fare ■ *n* (*Tennis*) servizio; **are you being served?** la stanno servendo?; **to ~ on a committee/jury** far parte di un comitato/una giuria; **it serves him right** ben gli sta, se l'è meritata; **it serves my purpose** fa al caso mio, serve al mio scopo

▶ **serve out, serve up** *vt* (*food*) servire

server ['səːvəʳ] *n* (*Comput*) server *m inv*

service ['səːvɪs] *n* servizio; (*Aut: maintenance*) revisione *f*; (*Rel*) funzione *f* ■ *vt* (*car, washing machine*) revisionare; **the Services** *npl* le forze armate; **to be of ~ to sb, to do sb a ~** essere d'aiuto a qn; **to put one's car in for (a) ~** portare la macchina in officina per una revisione; **dinner ~** servizio da tavola

serviceable ['səːvɪsəbl] *adj* pratico(-a), utile; (*usable, working*) usabile

service area *n* (*on motorway*) area di servizio

service charge *n* (*Brit*) servizio

service industries *npl* settore *m* terziario

serviceman ['səːvɪsmən] *n* militare *m*

service provider *n* (*Comput*) provider *m inv*

service station *n* stazione *f* di servizio

serviette [səːvɪˈɛt] *n* (*Brit*) tovagliolo

servile ['səːvaɪl] *adj* servile

session ['sɛʃən] *n* (*sitting*) seduta, sessione *f*; (*Scol*) anno scolastico (*or* accademico); **to be in ~** essere in seduta

session musician *n* musicista *m/f* di studio

set [sɛt] *n* serie *f inv*; (*Radio, TV*) apparecchio; (*Tennis*) set *m inv*; (*group of people*) mondo, ambiente *m*; (*Cine*) scenario; (*Theat: stage*) scene *fpl*; (: *scenery*) scenario; (*Math*) insieme *m*; (*Hairdressing*) messa in piega ■ *adj* (*fixed*) stabilito(-a), determinato(-a); (*ready*) pronto(-a) ■ *vb* (*pt, pp* ~) *vt* (*place*) posare, mettere; (*fix*) fissare; (*assign: task, homework*) dare, assegnare; (*adjust*) regolare; (*decide: rules etc*) stabilire, fissare; (*Typ*) comporre ■ *vi* (*sun*) tramontare; (*jam, jelly*) rapprendersi; (*concrete*) fare presa; **to be ~ on doing** essere deciso a fare; **to be all ~ to do sth** essere pronto fare qc; **to be (dead) ~ against** essere completamente contrario a; **~ in one's ways** abitudinario; **a novel ~ in Rome** un romanzo ambientato a Roma; **to ~ to music** mettere in musica; **to ~ on fire** dare fuoco a; **to ~ free** liberare; **to ~ sth going** mettere in moto qc; **to ~ sail** prendere il mare; **a ~ phrase** una frase fatta; **a ~ of false teeth** una dentiera; **a ~ of dining-room furniture** una camera da pranzo

▶ **set about** *vt fus* (*task*) intraprendere, mettersi a; **to ~ about doing sth** mettersi a fare qc

▶ **set aside** *vt* mettere da parte

▶ **set back** *vt* (*progress*) ritardare; **to ~ back (by)** (*in time*) mettere indietro (di); **a house ~ back from the road** una casa a una certa distanza dalla strada

▶ **set in** *vi* (*infection*) svilupparsi; (*complications*) intervenire; **the rain has ~ in for the day** ormai pioverà tutto il giorno

▶ **set off** *vi* partire ■ *vt* (*bomb*) far scoppiare; (*cause to start*) mettere in moto; (*show up well*) dare risalto a

▶ **set out** *vi* partire; (*aim*): **to ~ out to do** proporsi di fare ■ *vt* (*arrange*) disporre; (*state*) esporre, presentare

▶ **set up** *vt* (*organization*) fondare, costituire; (*record*) stabilire; (*monument*) innalzare

setback ['sɛtbæk] *n* (*hitch*) contrattempo, inconveniente *m*; (*in health*) ricaduta

set menu *n* menù *m inv* fisso

S

set square n squadra

settee [sɛ'tiː] n divano, sofà m inv

setting ['sɛtɪŋ] n ambiente m; (scenery) sfondo; (of jewel) montatura

setting lotion n fissatore m

settle ['sɛtl] vt (argument, matter) appianare; (problem) risolvere; (pay: bill, account) regolare, saldare; (Med: calm) calmare; (colonize: land) colonizzare ■ vi (bird, dust etc) posarsi; (sediment) depositarsi; (also: **settle down**) sistemarsi, stabilirsi; (become calmer) calmarsi; **to ~ to sth** applicarsi a qc; **to ~ for sth** accontentarsi di qc; **to ~ on sth** decidersi per qc; **that's settled then** allora è deciso; **to ~ one's stomach** calmare il mal di stomaco
  ▶ **settle in** vi sistemarsi
  ▶ **settle up** vi: **to ~ up with sb** regolare i conti con qn

settlement ['sɛtlmənt] n (payment) pagamento, saldo; (agreement) accordo; (colony) colonia; (village etc) villaggio, comunità f inv; **in ~ of our account** (Comm) a saldo del nostro conto

settler ['sɛtlə\u1d63] n colonizzatore(-trice)

setup ['sɛtʌp] n (arrangement) sistemazione f; (situation) situazione f; (Comput) setup m inv

seven ['sɛvn] num sette

seventeen [sɛvn'tiːn] num diciassette

seventh ['sɛvnθ] num settimo(-a)

seventy ['sɛvntɪ] num settanta

sever ['sɛvə\u1d63] vt recidere, tagliare; (relations) troncare

several ['sɛvərl] adj, pron alcuni(-e), diversi(-e); **~ of us** alcuni di noi; **~ times** diverse volte

severance ['sɛvərəns] n (of relations) rottura

severance pay n indennità di licenziamento

severe [sɪ'vɪə\u1d63] adj severo(-a); (serious) serio(-a), grave; (hard) duro(-a); (plain) semplice, sobrio(-a)

severely [sɪ'vɪəlɪ] adv (gen) severamente; (wounded, ill) gravemente

severity [sɪ'vɛrɪtɪ] n severità; gravità; (of weather) rigore m

sew (pt **sewed**, pp **sewn**) [səu, səud, səun] vt, vi cucire
  ▶ **sew up** vt ricucire; **it is all sewn up** (fig) è tutto apposto

sewage ['suːɪdʒ] n acque fpl di scolo

sewage works n stabilimento per la depurazione dei liquami

sewer ['suːə\u1d63] n fogna

sewing ['səuɪŋ] n cucito

sewing machine n macchina da cucire

sewn [səun] pp of **sew**

sex [sɛks] n sesso; **to have ~ with** avere rapporti sessuali con

sex act n atto sessuale

sex appeal n sex appeal m inv

sex education n educazione f sessuale

sexism ['sɛksɪzəm] n sessismo

sexist ['sɛksɪst] adj sessista

sex life n vita sessuale

sex object n oggetto sessuale; **to be treated like a ~** (woman) essere trattata da donna oggetto

sextet [sɛks'tɛt] n sestetto

sexual ['sɛksjuəl] adj sessuale; **~ assault** violenza carnale; **~ harassment** molestie fpl sessuali; **~ intercourse** rapporti mpl sessuali

sexy ['sɛksɪ] adj provocante, sexy inv

Seychelles [seɪ'ʃɛlz] npl: **the ~** le Seicelle

SF n abbr = **science fiction**

SG n abbr (US) = **Surgeon General**

Sgt. abbr (= sergeant) serg.

shabbiness ['ʃæbɪnɪs] n trasandatezza; squallore m; meschinità

shabby ['ʃæbɪ] adj trasandato(-a); (building) squallido(-a), malandato(-a); (behaviour) meschino(-a)

shack [ʃæk] n baracca, capanna

shackles ['ʃæklz] npl ferri mpl, catene fpl

shade [ʃeɪd] n ombra; (for lamp) paralume m; (of colour) tonalità f inv; (US: window shade) veneziana; (small quantity): **a ~ of** un po' or un'ombra di ■ vt ombreggiare, fare ombra a; **shades** npl (US: sunglasses) occhiali mpl da sole; **in the ~** all'ombra; **a ~ smaller** un tantino più piccolo

shadow ['ʃædəu] n ombra ■ vt (follow) pedinare; **without** or **beyond a ~ of doubt** senz'ombra di dubbio

shadow cabinet n (Brit Pol) governo m ombra inv

shadowy ['ʃædəuɪ] adj ombreggiato(-a), ombroso(-a); (dim) vago(-a), indistinto(-a)

shady ['ʃeɪdɪ] adj ombroso(-a); (fig: dishonest) losco(-a), equivoco(-a)

shaft [ʃɑːft] n (of arrow, spear) asta; (Aut, Tech) albero; (of mine) pozzo; (of lift) tromba; (of light) raggio; **ventilator ~** condotto di ventilazione

shaggy ['ʃægɪ] adj ispido(-a)

shake [ʃeɪk] vb (pt **shook**, pp **shaken**) [ʃuk, 'ʃeɪkn] vt scuotere; (bottle, cocktail) agitare ■ vi tremare ■ n scossa; **to ~ one's head** scuotere la testa; **to ~ hands with sb** stringere or dare la mano a qn
  ▶ **shake off** vt scrollare (via); (fig) sbarazzarsi di
  ▶ **shake up** vt scuotere

shake-up ['ʃeɪkʌp] n riorganizzazione f drastica

shakily ['ʃeɪkɪlɪ] adv (reply) con voce tremante; (walk) con passo malfermo; (write) con mano tremante

shaky ['ʃeɪkɪ] adj (hand, voice) tremante; (memory) labile; (knowledge) incerto(-a); (building) traballante

shale [ʃeɪl] n roccia scistosa

shall [ʃæl] aux vb: **I ~ go** andrò

shallot [ʃə'lɔt] n (Brit) scalogna

shallow ['ʃæləʊ] adj poco profondo(-a); (fig) superficiale

sham [ʃæm] n finzione f, messinscena; (jewellery, furniture) imitazione f ▪ adj finto(-a) ▪ vt fingere, simulare

shambles ['ʃæmblz] n confusione f, baraonda, scompiglio; **the economy is (in) a complete ~** l'economia è nel caos più totale

shambolic [ʃæm'bɔlɪk] adj (col) incasinato(-a)

shame [ʃeɪm] n vergogna ▪ vt far vergognare; **it is a ~ (that/to do)** è un peccato (che + sub/fare); **what a ~!** che peccato!; **to put sb/sth to ~** (fig) far sfigurare qn/qc

shamefaced ['ʃeɪmfeɪst] adj vergognoso(-a)

shameful ['ʃeɪmful] adj vergognoso(-a)

shameless ['ʃeɪmlɪs] adj sfrontato(-a); (immodest) spudorato(-a)

shampoo [ʃæm'puː] n shampoo m inv ▪ vt fare lo shampoo a; **~ and set** shampoo e messa in piega

shamrock ['ʃæmrɔk] n trifoglio (simbolo nazionale dell'Irlanda)

shandy ['ʃændɪ] n birra con gassosa

shan't [ʃɑːnt] = **shall not**

shanty town ['ʃæntɪ-] n bidonville f inv

SHAPE [ʃeɪp] n abbr (= Supreme Headquarters Allied Powers, Europe) supremo quartier generale delle Potenze Alleate in Europa

shape [ʃeɪp] n forma ▪ vt (clay, stone) dar forma a; (fig: ideas, character) formare; (: course of events) determinare, condizionare; (statement) formulare; (sb's ideas) condizionare ▪ vi (also: **shape up**: events) andare, mettersi; (: person) cavarsela; **to take ~** prendere forma; **in the ~ of a heart** a forma di cuore; **to get o.s. into ~** rimettersi in forma; **I can't bear gardening in any ~ or form** detesto il giardinaggio d'ogni genere e specie

-shaped [ʃeɪpt] suffix: **heart~** a forma di cuore

shapeless ['ʃeɪplɪs] adj senza forma, informe

shapely ['ʃeɪplɪ] adj ben proporzionato(-a)

share [ʃeəʳ] n (thing received, contribution) parte f; (Comm) azione f ▪ vt dividere; (have in common) condividere, avere in comune; **to ~ out (among** or **between)** dividere (tra); **to ~ in** partecipare a

share capital n capitale m azionario

share certificate n certificato azionario

shareholder ['ʃeəhəʊldəʳ] n azionista m/f

share index n listino di Borsa

shark [ʃɑːk] n squalo, pescecane m

sharp [ʃɑːp] adj (razor, knife) affilato(-a); (point) acuto(-a), acuminato(-a); (nose, chin) aguzzo(-a); (outline) netto(-a); (curve, bend) stretto(-a), accentuato(-a); (cold, pain) pungente; (voice) stridulo(-a); (person: quick-witted) sveglio(-a); (: unscrupulous) disonesto(-a); (Mus): **C ~** do diesis ▪ n (Mus) diesis m inv ▪ adv: **at 2 o'clock ~** alle due in punto; **turn ~ left** giri tutto a sinistra; **to be ~ with sb** rimproverare qn; **look ~!** sbrigati!

sharpen ['ʃɑːpən] vt affilare; (pencil) fare la punta a; (fig) aguzzare

sharpener ['ʃɑːpnəʳ] n (also: **pencil sharpener**) temperamatite m inv; (also: **knife sharpener**) affilacoltelli m inv

sharp-eyed [ʃɑːp'aɪd] adj dalla vista acuta

sharpish ['ʃɑːpɪʃ] adv (Brit col: quickly) subito

sharply ['ʃɑːplɪ] adv (abruptly) bruscamente; (clearly) nettamente; (harshly) duramente, aspramente

sharp-tempered [ʃɑːp'tɛmpəd] adj irascibile

shatter ['ʃætəʳ] vt mandare in frantumi, frantumare; (fig: upset) distruggere; (: ruin) rovinare ▪ vi frantumarsi, andare in pezzi

shattered ['ʃætəd] adj (grief-stricken) sconvolto(-a); (exhausted) a pezzi, distrutto(-a)

shatterproof ['ʃætəpruːf] adj infrangibile

shave [ʃeɪv] vt radere, rasare ▪ vi radersi, farsi la barba ▪ n: **to have a ~** farsi la barba

shaven ['ʃeɪvn] adj (head) rasato(-a), tonsurato(-a)

shaver ['ʃeɪvəʳ] n (also: **electric shaver**) rasoio elettrico

shaving ['ʃeɪvɪŋ] n (action) rasatura; **shavings** npl (of wood etc) trucioli mpl

shaving brush n pennello da barba

shaving cream n crema da barba

shaving soap n sapone m da barba

shawl [ʃɔːl] n scialle m

she [ʃiː] pron ella, lei; **there ~ is** eccola; **~-bear** orsa; **~-elephant** elefantessa; for ships, countries follow the gender of your translation

sheaf (pl **sheaves**) [ʃiːf, ʃiːvz] n covone m

shear [ʃɪəʳ] vt (pt **sheared**, pp **sheared** or **shorn**) [ʃɔːn] (sheep) tosare

  ▸ **shear off** vi (break off) spezzarsi

shears ['ʃɪəz] npl (for hedge) cesoie fpl

sheath [ʃiːθ] n fodero, guaina; (contraceptive) preservativo

sheathe [ʃiːð] vt rivestire; (sword) rinfoderare

sheath knife n coltello (con fodero)

S

sheaves [ʃiːvz] *npl of* **sheaf**

shed [ʃɛd] *n* capannone *m* ▪ *vt* (*pt, pp* ~) (*leaves, fur etc*) perdere; (*tears*) versare; **to ~ light on** (*problem, mystery*) far luce su

she'd [ʃiːd] = **she had; she would**

sheen [ʃiːn] *n* lucentezza

sheep [ʃiːp] *n* (*pl inv*) pecora

sheepdog [ʃiːpdɔg] *n* cane *m* da pastore

sheep farmer *n* allevatore *m* di pecore

sheepish [ʃiːpɪʃ] *adj* vergognoso(-a), timido(-a)

sheepskin [ʃiːpskɪn] *n* pelle *f* di pecora

sheepskin jacket *n* (giacca di) montone *m*

sheer [ʃɪər] *adj* (*utter*) vero(-a) (e proprio(-a)); (*steep*) a picco, perpendicolare; (*transparent*) trasparente ▪ *adv* a picco; **by ~ chance** per puro caso

sheet [ʃiːt] *n* (*on bed*) lenzuolo; (*of paper*) foglio; (*of glass*) lastra; (*of metal*) foglio, lamina

sheet feed *n* (*on printer*) alimentazione *f* di fogli

sheet lightning *n* lampo diffuso

sheet metal *n* lamiera

sheet music *n* fogli *mpl* di musica

sheik, sheikh [ʃeɪk] *n* sceicco

shelf (*pl* **shelves**) [ʃɛlf, ʃɛlvz] *n* scaffale *m*, mensola

shelf life *n* (*Comm*) durata di conservazione

shell [ʃɛl] *n* (*on beach*) conchiglia; (*of egg, nut etc*) guscio; (*explosive*) granata; (*of building*) scheletro, struttura ▪ *vt* (*peas*) sgranare; (*Mil*) bombardare, cannoneggiare
  ▶ **shell out** *vi* (*col*): **to ~ out (for)** sganciare soldi (per)

she'll [ʃiːl] = **she will; she shall**

shellfish [ʃɛlfɪʃ] *n* (*pl inv*) (*crab etc*) crostaceo; (*scallop etc*) mollusco; (*pl: as food*) crostacei; molluschi

shellsuit [ʃɛlsuːt] *n* tuta di acetato

shelter [ʃɛltər] *n* riparo, rifugio ▪ *vt* riparare, proteggere; (*give lodging to*) dare rifugio or asilo a ▪ *vi* ripararsi, mettersi al riparo; **to take ~ (from)** mettersi al riparo (da)

sheltered [ʃɛltəd] *adj* (*life*) ritirato(-a); (*spot*) riparato(-a), protetto(-a)

shelve [ʃɛlv] *vt* (*fig*) accantonare, rimandare

shelves [ʃɛlvz] *npl of* **shelf**

shelving [ʃɛlvɪŋ] *n* scaffalature *fpl*

shepherd [ʃɛpəd] *n* pastore *m* ▪ *vt* (*guide*) guidare

shepherdess [ʃɛpədɪs] *n* pastora

shepherd's pie *n* timballo di carne macinata e purè di patate

sherbet [ʃəːbət] *n* (*Brit: powder*) polvere effervescente al gusto di frutta; (*US: water ice*) sorbetto

sheriff [ʃɛrɪf] *n* sceriffo

sherry [ʃɛrɪ] *n* sherry *m inv*

she's [ʃiːz] = **she is; she has**

Shetland [ʃɛtlənd] *n* (*also:* **the Shetlands, the Shetland Isles**) le (isole) Shetland

Shetland pony *n* pony *m inv* delle Shetland

shield [ʃiːld] *n* scudo ▪ *vt*: **to ~ (from)** riparare (da), proteggere (da *or* contro)

shift [ʃɪft] *n* (*change*) cambiamento; (*of workers*) turno ▪ *vt* spostare, muovere; (*remove*) rimuovere ▪ *vi* spostarsi, muoversi; **~ in demand** (*Comm*) variazione *f* della domanda; **the wind has shifted to the south** il vento si è girato e soffia da sud

shift key *n* (*on typewriter*) tasto delle maiuscole

shiftless [ʃɪftlɪs] *adj* fannullone(-a)

shift work *n* lavoro a squadre; **to do ~** fare i turni

shifty [ʃɪftɪ] *adj* ambiguo(-a); (*eyes*) sfuggente

Shiite [ʃiːaɪt] *adj, n* sciita *m/f*

shilling [ʃɪlɪŋ] *n* (*Brit*) scellino (12 old pence; 20 in a pound)

shilly-shally [ʃɪlɪʃælɪ] *vi* tentennare, esitare

shimmer [ʃɪmər] *vi* brillare, luccicare

shimmering [ʃɪmərɪŋ] *adj* (*gen*) luccicante, scintillante; (*haze*) tremolante; (*satin etc*) cangiante

shin [ʃɪn] *n* tibia ▪ *vi*: **to ~ up/down a tree** arrampicarsi in cima a/scivolare giù da un albero

shindig [ʃɪndɪg] *n* (*col*) festa chiassosa

shine [ʃaɪn] *n* splendore *m*, lucentezza ▪ *vb* (*pt, pp* **shone**) [ʃɔn] *vi* (ri)splendere, brillare ▪ *vt* far brillare, far risplendere; (*torch*): **to ~ sth on** puntare qc verso

shingle [ʃɪŋgl] *n* (*on beach*) ciottoli *mpl*; (*on roof*) assicella di copertura

shingles [ʃɪŋglz] *n* (*Med*) herpes zoster *m*

shining [ʃaɪnɪŋ] *adj* (*surface, hair*) lucente; (*light*) brillante

shiny [ʃaɪnɪ] *adj* lucente, lucido(-a)

ship [ʃɪp] *n* nave *f* ▪ *vt* trasportare (via mare); (*send*) spedire (via mare); (*load*) imbarcare, caricare; **on board ~** a bordo

shipbuilder [ʃɪpbɪldər] *n* costruttore *m* navale

shipbuilding [ʃɪpbɪldɪŋ] *n* costruzione *f* navale

ship chandler [-ˈtʃɑːndlər] *n* fornitore *m* marittimo

shipment [ʃɪpmənt] *n* carico

shipowner [ʃɪpəunər] *n* armatore *m*

shipper [ʃɪpər] *n* spedizioniere *m* (marittimo)

shipping [ʃɪpɪŋ] *n* (*ships*) naviglio; (*traffic*) navigazione *f*

shipping agent *n* agente *m* marittimo

shipping company *n* compagnia di navigazione

shipping lane *n* rotta (di navigazione)

shipping line *n* = **shipping company**

shipshape ['ʃɪpʃeɪp] *adj* in perfetto ordine

shipwreck ['ʃɪprɛk] *n* relitto; (*event*) naufragio ■ *vt*: **to be shipwrecked** naufragare, fare naufragio

shipyard ['ʃɪpjɑːd] *n* cantiere *m* navale

shire ['ʃaɪəʳ] *n* (*Brit*) contea

shirk [ʃəːk] *vt* sottrarsi a, evitare

shirt [ʃəːt] *n* (*man's*) camicia; **in ~ sleeves** in maniche di camicia

shirty ['ʃəːtɪ] *adj* (*Brit col*) incavolato(-a)

shit [ʃɪt] *excl* (*col!*) merda (!)

shiver ['ʃɪvəʳ] *n* brivido ■ *vi* rabbrividire, tremare

shoal [ʃəul] *n* (*of fish*) banco

shock [ʃɔk] *n* (*impact*) urto, colpo; (*Elec*) scossa; (*emotional*) colpo, shock *m inv*; (*Med*) shock ■ *vt* colpire, scioccare; scandalizzare; **to give sb a ~** far venire un colpo a qn; **to be suffering from ~** essere in stato di shock; **it came as a ~ to hear that ...** è stata una grossa sorpresa sentire che ...

shock absorber *n* ammortizzatore *m*

shocker ['ʃɔkəʳ] *n*: **it was a real ~** (*col*) è stata una vera bomba

shocking ['ʃɔkɪŋ] *adj* scioccante, traumatizzante; (*scandalous*) scandaloso(-a); (*very bad: weather, handwriting*) orribile; (: *results*) disastroso(-a)

shockproof ['ʃɔkpruːf] *adj* antiurto *inv*

shock therapy, shock treatment *n* (*Med*) shockterapia

shock wave *n* onda d'urto; (*fig: usually pl*) impatto *msg*

shod [ʃɔd] *pt, pp of* **shoe**

shoddy ['ʃɔdɪ] *adj* scadente

shoe [ʃuː] *n* scarpa; (*also:* **horseshoe**) ferro di cavallo; (*brake shoe*) ganascia (del freno) ■ *vt* (*pt, pp* **shod**) [ʃɔd] (*horse*) ferrare

shoebrush ['ʃuːbrʌʃ] *n* spazzola per le scarpe

shoehorn ['ʃuːhɔːn] *n* calzante *m*

shoelace ['ʃuːleɪs] *n* stringa

shoemaker ['ʃuːmeɪkəʳ] *n* calzolaio

shoe polish *n* lucido per scarpe

shoeshop ['ʃuːʃɔp] *n* calzoleria

shoestring ['ʃuːstrɪŋ] *n* stringa (delle scarpe); **on a ~** (*fig: do sth*) con quattro soldi

shoetree ['ʃuːtriː] *n* forma per scarpe

shone [ʃɔn] *pt, pp of* **shine**

shoo [ʃuː] *excl* sciò!, via! ■ *vt* (*also:* **shoo away, shoo off**) cacciare (via)

shook [ʃuk] *pt of* **shake**

shoot [ʃuːt] *n* (*on branch, seedling*) germoglio; (*shooting party*) partita di caccia; (*competition*) gara di tiro ■ *vb* (*pt, pp* **shot**) [ʃɔt] *vt* (*game: Brit*) cacciare, andare a caccia di; (*person*)

sparare a; (*execute*) fucilare; (*film*) girare ■ *vi* (*with gun*): **to ~ (at)** sparare (a), fare fuoco (su); (*with bow*): **to ~ (at)** tirare (su); (*Football*) sparare, tirare (forte); **to ~ past sb** passare vicino a qn come un fulmine; **to ~ in/out** entrare/uscire come una freccia

▸ **shoot down** *vt* (*plane*) abbattere

▸ **shoot up** *vi* (*fig*) salire alle stelle

shooting ['ʃuːtɪŋ] *n* (*shots*) sparatoria; (*murder*) uccisione *f* (a colpi d'arma da fuoco); (*Hunting*) caccia; (*Cine*) riprese *fpl*

shooting range *n* poligono (di tiro), tirassegno

shooting star *n* stella cadente

shop [ʃɔp] *n* negozio; (*workshop*) officina ■ *vi* (*also:* **go shopping**) fare spese; **repair ~** officina di riparazione; **to talk ~** (*fig*) parlare di lavoro

▸ **shop around** *vi* fare il giro dei negozi

shopaholic ['ʃɔpə'hɔlɪk] *n* (*col*) maniaco(-a) dello shopping

shop assistant *n* (*Brit*) commesso(-a)

shop floor *n* (*Brit: fig*) operai *mpl*, maestranze *fpl*

shopkeeper ['ʃɔpkiːpəʳ] *n* negoziante *m/f*, bottegaio(-a)

shoplift ['ʃɔplɪft] *vi* taccheggiare

shoplifter ['ʃɔplɪftəʳ] *n* taccheggiatore(-trice)

shoplifting ['ʃɔplɪftɪŋ] *n* taccheggio

shopper ['ʃɔpəʳ] *n* compratore(-trice)

shopping ['ʃɔpɪŋ] *n* (*goods*) spesa, acquisti *mpl*

shopping bag *n* borsa per la spesa

shopping centre *n* centro commerciale

shop-soiled ['ʃɔpsɔɪld] *adj* sciupato(-a) a forza di stare in vetrina

shop steward *n* (*Brit Industry*) rappresentante *m* sindacale

shop window *n* vetrina

shore [ʃɔːʳ] *n* (*of sea*) riva, spiaggia; (*of lake*) riva ■ *vt*: **to ~ (up)** puntellare; **on ~** a terra

shore leave *n* (*Naut*) franchigia

shorn [ʃɔːn] *pp of* **shear**

short [ʃɔːt] *adj* (*not long*) corto(-a); (*soon finished*) breve; (*person*) basso(-a); (*curt*) brusco(-a), secco(-a); (*insufficient*) insufficiente ■ *n* (*also:* **short film**) cortometraggio; **it is ~ for** è l'abbreviazione or il diminutivo di; **a ~ time ago** poco tempo fa; **in the ~ term** nell'immediato futuro; **to be ~ of sth** essere a corto di *or* mancare di qc; **to run ~ of sth** rimanere senza qc; **to be in ~ supply** scarseggiare; **I'm 3 ~** me ne mancano 3; **in ~** in breve; **~ of doing** a meno che non si faccia; **everything ~ of** tutto fuorché; **to cut ~** (*speech, visit*) accorciare, abbreviare; (*person*) interrompere; **to fall ~ of** venire meno a; non soddisfare; **to stop ~**

781

fermarsi di colpo; **to stop ~ of** non arrivare fino a; *see also* **shorts**

shortage ['ʃɔːtɪdʒ] *n* scarsezza, carenza

shortbread ['ʃɔːtbrɛd] *n* biscotto di pasta frolla

short-change [ʃɔːt'tʃeɪndʒ] *vt:* **to ~ sb** imbrogliare qn sul resto

short-circuit [ʃɔːt'səːkɪt] *n* cortocircuito ■ *vt* cortocircuitare ■ *vi* fare cortocircuito

shortcoming ['ʃɔːtkʌmɪŋ] *n* difetto

shortcrust pastry ['ʃɔːtkrʌst-], **short pastry** *n* (*Brit*) pasta frolla

shortcut ['ʃɔːtkʌt] *n* scorciatoia

shorten ['ʃɔːtn] *vt* accorciare, ridurre

shortening ['ʃɔːtnɪŋ] *n* grasso per pasticceria

shortfall ['ʃɔːtfɔːl] *n* deficienza

shorthand ['ʃɔːthænd] *n* (*Brit*) stenografia; **to take sth down in ~** stenografare qc

shorthand notebook *n* (*Brit*) bloc-notes *m inv* per stenografia

shorthand typist *n* (*Brit*) stenodattilografo(-a)

short list *n* (*Brit: for job*) rosa dei candidati

short-lived ['ʃɔːt'lɪvd] *adj* effimero(-a), di breve durata

shortly ['ʃɔːtlɪ] *adv* fra poco

shortness ['ʃɔːtnɪs] *n* brevità; insufficienza

shorts [ʃɔːts] *npl* (*also:* **a pair of shorts**) i calzoncini

short-sighted [ʃɔːt'saɪtɪd] *adj* (*Brit*) miope; (*fig*) poco avveduto(-a)

short-staffed [ʃɔːt'stɑːft] *adj* a corto di personale

short story *n* racconto, novella

short-tempered [ʃɔːt'tɛmpəd] *adj* irascibile

short-term ['ʃɔːttəːm] *adj* (*effect*) di or a breve durata

short time *n* (*Industry*): **to work ~, be on ~** essere *or* lavorare a orario ridotto

short wave *n* (*Radio*) onde *fpl* corte

shot [ʃɔt] *pt, pp of* **shoot** ■ *n* sparo, colpo; (*shotgun pellets*) pallottole *fpl*; (*person*) tiratore *m*; (*try*) prova; (*injection*) iniezione *f*; (*Phot*) foto *f inv*; **like a ~** come un razzo; (*very readily*) immediatamente; **to fire a ~ at sb/sth** sparare un colpo a qn/qc; **to have a ~ at sth/ doing sth** provarci con qc/a fare qc; **a big ~** (*col*) un pezzo grosso, un papavero; **to get ~ of sb/sth** (*col*) sbarazzarsi di qn/qc

shotgun ['ʃɔtgʌn] *n* fucile *m* da caccia

should [ʃud] *aux vb:* **I ~ go now** dovrei andare ora; **he ~ be there now** dovrebbe essere arrivato ora; **I ~ go if I were you** se fossi in lei andrei; **I ~ like to** mi piacerebbe; **~ he phone ...** se telefonasse ...

shoulder ['ʃəuldəʳ] *n* spalla; (*Brit: of road*): **hard ~** corsia d'emergenza ■ *vt* (*fig*)

addossarsi, prendere sulle proprie spalle; **to look over one's ~** guardarsi alle spalle; **to rub shoulders with sb** (*fig*) essere a contatto con qn; **to give sb the cold ~** (*fig*) trattare qn con freddezza

shoulder bag *n* borsa a tracolla

shoulder blade *n* scapola

shoulder strap *n* bretella, spallina

shouldn't ['ʃudnt] = **should not**

shout [ʃaut] *n* urlo, grido ■ *vt* gridare ■ *vi* urlare, gridare; **to give sb a ~** chiamare qn gridando

▶ **shout down** *vt* zittire gridando

shouting ['ʃautɪŋ] *n* urli *mpl*

shouting match *n* (*col*) vivace scambio di opinioni

shove [ʃʌv] *vt* spingere; (*col: put*): **to ~ sth in** ficcare qc in ■ *n* spintone *m*; **he shoved me out of the way** mi ha spinto da parte

▶ **shove off** *vi* (*Naut*) scostarsi

shovel ['ʃʌvl] *n* pala ■ *vt* spalare

show [ʃəu] *n* (*of emotion*) dimostrazione *f*, manifestazione *f*; (*semblance*) apparenza; (*exhibition*) mostra, esposizione *f*; (*Theat, Cine*) spettacolo; (*Comm, Tech*) salone *m*, fiera ■ *vb* (*pt* **showed**, *pp* **shown**) [ʃəun] *vt* far vedere, mostrare; (*courage etc*) dimostrare, dar prova di; (*exhibit*) esporre ■ *vi* vedersi, essere visibile; **to ~ sb to his seat/to the door** accompagnare qn al suo posto/alla porta; **to ~ a profit/loss** (*Comm*) registrare un utile/ una perdita; **it just goes to ~ that ...** il che sta a dimostrare che ...; **to ask for a ~ of hands** chiedere che si voti per alzata di mano; **to be on ~** essere esposto; **it's just for ~** è solo per far scena; **who's running the ~ here?** (*col*) chi è il padrone qui?

▶ **show in** *vt* far entrare

▶ **show off** *vi* (*pej*) esibirsi, mettersi in mostra ■ *vt* (*display*) mettere in risalto; (*pej*) mettere in mostra

▶ **show out** *vt* accompagnare alla porta

▶ **show up** *vi* (*stand out*) essere ben visibile; (*col: turn up*) farsi vedere ■ *vt* mettere in risalto; (*unmask*) smascherare

showbiz ['ʃəubɪz] *n* (*col*) = **show business**

show business *n* industria dello spettacolo

showcase ['ʃəukeɪs] *n* vetrina, bacheca

showdown ['ʃəudaun] *n* prova di forza

shower ['ʃauəʳ] *n* doccia; (*rain*) acquazzone *m*; (*of stones etc*) pioggia; (*US: party*) festa in cui si fanno regali alla persona festeggiata (*di fidanzamento etc*) ■ *vi* fare la doccia ■ *vt:* **to ~ sb with** (*gifts, abuse etc*) coprire qn di; (*missiles*) lanciare contro qn una pioggia di; **to have** *or* **take a ~** fare la doccia

shower cap *n* cuffia da doccia

showerproof ['ʃauəpruːf] *adj* impermeabile
showery ['ʃauərɪ] *adj* (*weather*) con piogge intermittenti
showground ['ʃəugraund] *n* terreno d'esposizione
showing ['ʃəuɪŋ] *n* (*of film*) proiezione *f*
show jumping *n* concorso ippico (di salto ad ostacoli)
showman ['ʃəumən] *n* (*at fair, circus*) impresario; (*fig*) attore *m*
showmanship ['ʃəumənʃɪp] *n* abilità d'impresario
shown [ʃəun] *pp of* **show**
show-off ['ʃəuɔf] *n* (*col: person*) esibizionista *m/f*
showpiece ['ʃəupiːs] *n* (*of exhibition*) pezzo forte; **that hospital is a ~** è un ospedale modello
showroom ['ʃəurum] *n* sala d'esposizione
show trial *n* processo a scopo dimostrativo (*spesso ideologico*)
showy ['ʃəuɪ] *adj* vistoso(-a), appariscente
shrank [ʃræŋk] *pt of* **shrink**
shrapnel ['ʃræpnl] *n* shrapnel *m*
shred [ʃrɛd] *n* (*gen pl*) brandello; (*fig: of truth, evidence*) briciola ■ *vt* fare a brandelli; (*Culin*) sminuzzare, tagliuzzare; (*documents*) distruggere, sminuzzare
shredder ['ʃrɛdəʳ] *n* (*for documents, papers*) distruttore *m* di documenti, sminuzzatrice *f*
shrew [ʃruː] *n* (*Zool*) toporagno; (*fig: pej: woman*) strega
shrewd [ʃruːd] *adj* astuto(-a), scaltro(-a)
shrewdness ['ʃruːdnɪs] *n* astuzia
shriek [ʃriːk] *n* strillo ■ *vt, vi* strillare
shrift [ʃrɪft] *n*: **to give sb short ~** sbrigare qn
shrill [ʃrɪl] *adj* acuto(-a), stridulo(-a), stridente
shrimp [ʃrɪmp] *n* gamberetto
shrine [ʃraɪn] *n* reliquario; (*place*) santuario
shrink [ʃrɪŋk] *vb* (*pt* **shrank**, *pp* **shrunk**) [ʃræŋk, ʃrʌŋk] *vi* restringersi; (*fig*) ridursi ■ *vt* (*wool*) far restringere ■ *n* (*col: pej*) psicanalista *m/f*; **to ~ from doing sth** rifuggire dal fare qc
shrinkage ['ʃrɪŋkɪdʒ] *n* restringimento
shrink-wrap ['ʃrɪŋkræp] *vt* confezionare con plastica sottile
shrivel ['ʃrɪvl] (*also:* **shrivel up**) *vt* raggrinzare, avvizzire ■ *vi* raggrinzirsi, avvizzire
shroud [ʃraud] *n* lenzuolo funebre ■ *vt*: **shrouded in mystery** avvolto(-a) nel mistero
Shrove Tuesday ['ʃrəuv-] *n* martedì *m* grasso
shrub [ʃrʌb] *n* arbusto
shrubbery ['ʃrʌbərɪ] *n* arbusti *mpl*

shrug [ʃrʌg] *n* scrollata di spalle ■ *vt, vi*: **to ~ (one's shoulders)** alzare le spalle, fare spallucce
▶ **shrug off** *vt* passare sopra a; (*cold, illness*) sbarazzarsi di
shrunk [ʃrʌŋk] *pp of* **shrink**
shrunken ['ʃrʌŋkən] *adj* rattrappito(-a)
shudder ['ʃʌdəʳ] *n* brivido ■ *vi* rabbrividire
shuffle ['ʃʌfl] *vt* (*cards*) mescolare; **to ~ (one's feet)** strascicare i piedi
shun [ʃʌn] *vt* sfuggire, evitare
shunt [ʃʌnt] *vt* (*Rail: direct*) smistare; (: *divert*) deviare ■ *vi*: **to ~ (to and fro)** fare la spola
shunting yard *n* fascio di smistamento
shush [ʃuʃ] *excl* zitto(-a)!
shut (*pt, pp* ~) [ʃʌt] *vt* chiudere ■ *vi* chiudersi, chiudere
▶ **shut down** *vt, vi* chiudere definitivamente
▶ **shut off** *vt* (*stop: power*) staccare; (: *water*) chiudere; (: *engine*) spegnere; (*isolate*) isolare
▶ **shut out** *vt* (*person, noise, cold*) non far entrare; (*block: view*) impedire, bloccare; (: *memory*) scacciare
▶ **shut up** *vi* (*col: keep quiet*) stare zitto(-a) ■ *vt* (*close*) chiudere; (*silence*) far tacere
shutdown ['ʃʌtdaun] *n* chiusura
shutter ['ʃʌtəʳ] *n* imposta; (*Phot*) otturatore *m*
shuttle ['ʃʌtl] *n* spola, navetta; (*also:* **shuttle service**) servizio *m* navetta *inv* ■ *vi* (*vehicle, person*) fare la spola ■ *vt* (*to and fro: passengers*) portare (avanti e indietro)
shuttlecock ['ʃʌtlkɔk] *n* volano
shuttle diplomacy *n* frequenti mediazioni *fpl* diplomatiche
shy [ʃaɪ] *adj* timido(-a) ■ *vi*: **to ~ away from doing sth** (*fig*) rifuggire dal fare qc; **to fight ~ of** tenersi alla larga da; **to be ~ of doing sth** essere restio a fare qc
shyness ['ʃaɪnɪs] *n* timidezza
Siam [saɪ'æm] *n* Siam *m*
Siamese [saɪə'miːz] *adj*: **~ cat** gatto siamese; **~ twins** fratelli *mpl* (*or* sorelle *fpl*) siamesi
Siberia [saɪ'bɪərɪə] *n* Siberia
sibling ['sɪblɪŋ] *n* (*formal*) fratello/sorella
Sicilian [sɪ'sɪlɪən] *adj, n* siciliano(-a)
Sicily ['sɪsɪlɪ] *n* Sicilia
sick [sɪk] *adj* (*ill*) malato(-a); (*vomiting*): **to be ~** vomitare; (*humour*) macabro(-a); **to feel ~** avere la nausea; **to be ~ of** (*fig*) averne abbastanza di; **a ~ person** un malato; **to be (off) ~** essere assente perché malato; **to fall** *or* **take ~** ammalarsi
sickbag ['sɪkbæg] *n* sacchetto (*da usarsi in caso di malessere*)
sick bay *n* infermeria
sick building syndrome *n* malattia causata da mancanza di ventilazione e luce naturale

S

sicken ['sɪkn] vt nauseare ■ vi: **to be sickening for sth** (cold, flu etc) covare qc
sickening ['sɪknɪŋ] adj (fig) disgustoso(-a), rivoltante
sickle ['sɪkl] n falcetto
sick leave n congedo per malattia
sickle-cell anaemia ['sɪklsɛl-] n anemia drepanocitica
sickly ['sɪklɪ] adj malaticcio(-a); (causing nausea) nauseante
sickness ['sɪknɪs] n malattia; (vomiting) vomito
sickness benefit n indennità di malattia
sick pay n sussidio per malattia
sickroom ['sɪkruːm] n stanza di malato
side [saɪd] n (gen) lato; (of person, animal) fianco; (of lake) riva; (face, surface: gen) faccia; (: of paper) facciata; (fig: aspect) aspetto, lato; (team: Sport) squadra; (: Pol etc) parte f ■ cpd (door, entrance) laterale ■ vi: **to ~ with sb** parteggiare per qn, prendere le parti di qn; **by the ~ of** a fianco di; (road) sul ciglio di; **~ by ~** fianco a fianco; **to take sides (with)** schierarsi (con); **the right/wrong ~** il dritto/rovescio; **from ~ to ~** da una parte all'altra; **~ of beef** quarto di bue
sideboard ['saɪdbɔːd] n credenza
sideboards ['saɪdbɔːdz], (Brit) **sideburns** ['saɪdbəːnz] npl (whiskers) basette fpl
sidecar ['saɪdkɑːʳ] n sidecar m inv
side dish n contorno
side drum n (Mus) piccolo tamburo
side effect n (Med) effetto collaterale
sidekick ['saɪdkɪk] n (col) compagno(-a)
sidelight ['saɪdlaɪt] n (Aut) luce f di posizione
sideline ['saɪdlaɪn] n (Sport) linea laterale; (fig) attività secondaria
sidelong ['saɪdlɒŋ] adj obliquo(-a); **to give a ~ glance at sth** guardare qc con la coda dell'occhio
side plate n piattino
side road n strada secondaria
sidesaddle ['saɪdsædl] adv all'amazzone
side show n attrazione f
sidestep ['saɪdstɛp] vt (question) eludere; (problem) scavalcare ■ vi (Boxing etc) spostarsi di lato
side street n traversa
sidetrack ['saɪdtræk] vt (fig) distrarre
sidewalk ['saɪdwɔːk] n (US) marciapiede m
sideways ['saɪdweɪz] adv (move) di lato, di fianco; (look) con la coda dell'occhio
siding ['saɪdɪŋ] n (Rail) binario di raccordo
sidle ['saɪdl] vi: **to ~ up (to)** avvicinarsi furtivamente (a)
SIDS n (= sudden infant death syndrome) = **cot death**

siege [siːdʒ] n assedio; **to lay ~ to** porre l'assedio a
siege economy n economia da stato d'assedio
Sierra Leone [sɪ'ɛrəlɪ'əun] n Sierra Leone f
sieve [sɪv] n setaccio ■ vt setacciare
sift [sɪft] vt passare al crivello; (fig) vagliare ■ vi: **to ~ through** esaminare minuziosamente
sigh [saɪ] n sospiro ■ vi sospirare
sight [saɪt] n (faculty) vista; (spectacle) spettacolo; (on gun) mira ■ vt avvistare; **in ~** in vista; **out of ~** non visibile; **at first ~** a prima vista; **to catch ~ of sth/sb** scorgere qc/qn; **to lose ~ of sb/sth** perdere di vista qn/qc; **to set one's sights on sth/on doing sth** mirare a qc/a fare qc; **at ~** a vista; **I know her by ~** la conosco di vista
sighted ['saɪtɪd] adj che ha il dono della vista; **partially ~** parzialmente cieco
sightseeing ['saɪtsiːɪŋ] n turismo; **to go ~** visitare una località
sightseer ['saɪtsiːəʳ] n turista m/f
sign [saɪn] n segno; (with hand etc) segno, gesto; (notice) insegna, cartello; (road sign) segnale m ■ vt firmare; **as a ~ of** in segno di; **it's a good/bad ~ of** è buon/brutto segno; **to show signs/no ~ of doing sth** accennare/non accennare a fare qc; **plus/minus ~** segno del più/meno; **to ~ one's name** firmare, apporre la propria firma
  ▸ **sign away** vt (rights etc) cedere (con una firma)
  ▸ **sign in** vi firmare il registro (all'arrivo)
  ▸ **sign off** vi (Radio, TV) chiudere le trasmissioni
  ▸ **sign on** vi (Mil etc: enlist) arruolarsi; (as unemployed) iscriversi sulla lista (dell'ufficio di collocamento); (begin work) prendere servizio; (enrol): **to ~ on for a course** iscriversi a un corso
  ▸ **sign out** vi firmare il registro (alla partenza)
  ▸ **sign over** vt: **to ~ sth over to sb** cedere qc con scrittura legale a qn
  ▸ **sign up** (Mil) vt arruolare ■ vi arruolarsi
signal ['sɪgnl] n segnale m ■ vt (person) fare segno a; (message) comunicare per mezzo di segnali ■ vi: **to ~ to sb (to do sth)** far segno a qn (di fare qc); **to ~ a left/right turn** (Aut) segnalare un cambiamento di direzione a sinistra/destra
signal box n (Rail) cabina di manovra
signalman ['sɪgnlmən] n (Rail) deviatore m
signatory ['sɪgnətərɪ] n firmatario(-a)
signature ['sɪgnətʃəʳ] n firma
signature tune n sigla musicale

signet ring ['sɪgnət-] *n* anello con sigillo

significance [sɪg'nɪfɪkəns] *n* (*of remark*) significato; (*of event*) importanza; **that is of no ~** ciò non ha importanza

significant [sɪg'nɪfɪkənt] *adj* (*improvement, amount*) notevole; (*discovery, event*) importante; (*evidence, smile*) significativo(-a); **it is ~ that ...** è significativo che ...

significantly [sɪg'nɪfɪkəntlɪ] *adv* (*smile*) in modo eloquente; (*improve, increase*) considerevolmente, decisamente

signify ['sɪgnɪfaɪ] *vt* significare

sign language *n* linguaggio dei muti

signpost ['saɪnpəust] *n* cartello indicatore

silage ['saɪlɪdʒ] *n* insilato

silence ['saɪlns] *n* silenzio ∎ *vt* far tacere, ridurre al silenzio

silencer ['saɪlənsəʳ] *n* (*on gun, Brit Aut*) silenziatore *m*

silent ['saɪlnt] *adj* silenzioso(-a); (*film*) muto(-a); **to keep** *or* **remain ~** tacere, stare zitto(-a)

silently ['saɪlntlɪ] *adv* silenziosamente, in silenzio

silent partner *n* (*Comm*) socio accomandante

silhouette [sɪlu:'et] *n* silhouette *f inv* ∎ *vt*: **to be silhouetted against** stagliarsi contro

silicon ['sɪlɪkən] *n* silicio

silicon chip *n* chip *m inv* al silicio

silicone ['sɪlɪkəun] *n* silicone *m*

silk [sɪlk] *n* seta ∎ *cpd* di seta

silky ['sɪlkɪ] *adj* di seta, come la seta

sill [sɪl] *n* (*windowsill*) davanzale *m*; (*Aut*) predellino

silly ['sɪlɪ] *adj* stupido(-a), sciocco(-a); **to do something ~** fare una sciocchezza

silo ['saɪləu] *n* silo

silt [sɪlt] *n* limo

silver ['sɪlvəʳ] *n* argento; (*money*) monete da 5, 10, 20 o 50 pence; (*also:* **silverware**) argenteria ∎ *cpd* d'argento

silver foil, (*Brit*) **silver paper** *n* carta argentata, (carta) stagnola

silver-plated [sɪlvə'pleɪtɪd] *adj* argentato(-a)

silversmith ['sɪlvəsmɪθ] *n* argentiere *m*

silverware ['sɪlvəwɛəʳ] *n* argenteria, argento

silvery ['sɪlvərɪ] *adj* (*colour*) argenteo(-a); (*sound*) argentino(-a)

SIM card ['sɪm-] *n* (*Tel*: = *Subscriber Identity Module card*) SIM card *f inv*

similar ['sɪmɪləʳ] *adj*: **~ (to)** simile (a)

similarity [sɪmɪ'lærɪtɪ] *n* somiglianza, rassomiglianza

similarly ['sɪmɪləlɪ] *adv* (*in a similar way*) allo stesso modo; (*as is similar*) così pure

simile ['sɪmɪlɪ] *n* similitudine *f*

simmer ['sɪməʳ] *vi* cuocere a fuoco lento
  ▸ **simmer down** *vi* (*fig, col*) calmarsi

simper ['sɪmpəʳ] *vi* fare lo(la) smorfioso(-a)

simpering ['sɪmpərɪŋ] *adj* lezioso(-a), smorfioso(-a)

simple ['sɪmpl] *adj* semplice; **the ~ truth** la pura verità

simple interest *n* (*Math, Comm*) interesse *m* semplice

simple-minded [sɪmpl'maɪndɪd] *adj* sempliciotto(-a)

simpleton ['sɪmpltən] *n* semplicione(-a), sempliciotto(-a)

simplicity [sɪm'plɪsɪtɪ] *n* semplicità

simplification [sɪmplɪfɪ'keɪʃən] *n* semplificazione *f*

simplify ['sɪmplɪfaɪ] *vt* semplificare

simply ['sɪmplɪ] *adv* semplicemente

simulate ['sɪmjuleɪt] *vt* fingere, simulare

simulation [sɪmju'leɪʃən] *n* simulazione *f*

simultaneous [sɪməl'teɪnɪəs] *adj* simultaneo(-a)

simultaneously [sɪməl'teɪnɪəslɪ] *adv* simultaneamente, contemporaneamente

sin [sɪn] *n* peccato ∎ *vi* peccare

Sinai ['saɪnaɪ] *n* Sinai *m*

since [sɪns] *adv* da allora ∎ *prep* da ∎ *conj* (*time*) da quando; (*because*) poiché, dato che; **~ then** da allora; **~ Monday** da lunedì; **(ever) ~ I arrived** (fin) da quando sono arrivato

sincere [sɪn'sɪəʳ] *adj* sincero(-a)

sincerely [sɪn'sɪəlɪ] *adv* sinceramente; **Yours ~** (*at end of letter*) distinti saluti

sincerity [sɪn'serɪtɪ] *n* sincerità

sine [saɪn] *n* (*Math*) seno

sinew ['sɪnju:] *n* tendine *m*; **sinews** *npl* (*muscles*) muscoli *mpl*

sinful ['sɪnful] *adj* peccaminoso(-a)

sing (*pt* **sang**, *pp* **sung**) [sɪŋ, sæŋ, sʌŋ] *vt*, *vi* cantare

Singapore [sɪŋgə'pɔ:ʳ] *n* Singapore *f*

singe [sɪndʒ] *vt* bruciacchiare

singer ['sɪŋəʳ] *n* cantante *m/f*

Singhalese [sɪŋə'li:z] *adj* = **Sinhalese**

singing ['sɪŋɪŋ] *n* (*of person, bird*) canto; (*of kettle, bullet, in ears*) fischio

single ['sɪŋgl] *adj* solo(-a), unico(-a); (*unmarried: man*) celibe; (: *woman*) nubile; (*not double*) semplice ∎ *n* (*Brit: also:* **single ticket**) biglietto di (sola) andata; (*record*) 45 giri *m inv*; **not a ~ one was left** non ne è rimasto nemmeno uno; **every ~ day** tutti i santi giorni; *see also* **singles**
  ▸ **single out** *vt* scegliere; (*distinguish*) distinguere

single bed *n* letto a una piazza

single-breasted ['sɪŋglbrestɪd] *adj* a un petto

Single European Market *n*: **the ~** il Mercato Unico

single file n: **in ~** in fila indiana
single-handed [sɪŋgl'hændɪd] adv senza
aiuto, da solo(-a)
single-minded [sɪŋgl'maɪndɪd] adj tenace,
risoluto(-a)
single parent n ragazzo padre/ragazza
madre; genitore m separato; **~ family**
famiglia monoparentale
single room n camera singola
singles ['sɪŋglz] npl (Tennis) singolo; (US: single
people) single m/fpl
singles bar n (esp US) bar m inv per single
single-sex school ['sɪŋgl'sɛks-] n (for boys)
scuola maschile; (for girls) scuola femminile
singlet ['sɪŋglɪt] n canottiera
singly ['sɪŋglɪ] adv separatamente
singsong ['sɪŋsɔŋ] adj (tone) cantilenante ■ n
(songs): **to have a ~** farsi una cantata
singular ['sɪŋgjulər] adj (Ling) singolare;
(unusual) strano(-a), singolare ■ n (Ling)
singolare m; **in the feminine ~** al femminile
singolare
singularly ['sɪŋgjuləlɪ] adv stranamente
Sinhalese [sɪnhə'li:z] adj singalese
sinister ['sɪnɪstər] adj sinistro(-a)
sink [sɪŋk] n lavandino, acquaio ■ vb (pt
sank, pp **sunk**) [sæŋk, sʌŋk] vt (ship) (fare)
affondare, colare a picco; (foundations)
scavare; (piles etc): **to ~ sth into** conficcare qc
in ■ vi affondare, andare a fondo; (ground
etc) cedere, avvallarsi; **he sank into a chair/
the mud** sprofondò in una poltrona/nel
fango
  ▶ **sink in** vi penetrare; **it took a long time
to ~ in** ci ho (or ha etc) messo molto a capirlo
sinking ['sɪŋkɪŋ] adj: **that ~ feeling** una
stretta allo stomaco
sinking fund n (Comm) fondo
d'ammortamento
sink unit n blocco lavello
sinner ['sɪnər] n peccatore(-trice)
Sinn Féin [ʃɪn'feɪn] n movimento separatista
irlandese
sinuous ['sɪnjuəs] adj sinuoso(-a)
sinus ['saɪnəs] n (Anat) seno
sip [sɪp] n sorso ■ vt sorseggiare
siphon ['saɪfən] n sifone m ■ vt (funds)
trasferire
  ▶ **siphon off** vt travasare (con un sifone)
sir [sər] n signore m; **S~ John Smith** Sir John
Smith; **yes ~** sì, signore; **Dear S~** (in letter)
Egregio signor (followed by name); **Dear Sirs**
Spettabile ditta
siren ['saɪərn] n sirena
sirloin ['sə:lɔɪn] n controfiletto
sirloin steak n bistecca di controfiletto
sirocco [sɪ'rɔkəu] n scirocco

sisal ['saɪsəl] n sisal f inv
sissy ['sɪsɪ] n (col) femminuccia
sister ['sɪstər] n sorella; (nun) suora; (nurse)
infermiera f caposala inv ■ cpd:
~ organization organizzazione f affine;
~ ship nave f gemella
sister-in-law ['sɪstərɪnlɔ:] n cognata
sit (pt, pp **sat**) [sɪt, sæt] vi sedere, sedersi;
(dress etc) cadere; (assembly) essere in seduta
■ vt (exam) sostenere, dare; **to ~ on a
committee** far parte di una commissione
  ▶ **sit about, sit around** vi star seduto(-a)
(senza far nulla)
  ▶ **sit back** vi (in seat) appoggiarsi allo schienale
  ▶ **sit down** vi sedersi; **to be sitting down**
essere seduto(-a)
  ▶ **sit in** vi: **to ~ in on a discussion** assistere
ad una discussione
  ▶ **sit up** vi tirarsi su a sedere; (not go to bed)
stare alzato(-a) fino a tardi
sitcom ['sɪtkɔm] n abbr (TV: = situation comedy)
sceneggiato a episodi (comico)
sit-down ['sɪtdaun] adj: **~ strike** sciopero
bianco (con occupazione della fabbrica); **a ~
meal** un pranzo
site [saɪt] n posto; (also: **building site**)
cantiere m; (Comput) sito ■ vt situare
sit-in ['sɪtɪn] n (demonstration) sit-in m inv
siting ['saɪtɪŋ] n ubicazione f
sitter ['sɪtər] n (for painter) modello(-a);
(also: **baby sitter**) babysitter m/f inv
sitting ['sɪtɪŋ] n (of assembly etc) seduta;
(in canteen) turno
sitting member n (Pol) deputato(-a) in carica
sitting room n soggiorno
sitting tenant n (Brit) attuale affittuario
situate ['sɪtjueɪt] vt collocare
situated ['sɪtjueɪtɪd] adj situato(-a)
situation [sɪtju'eɪʃən] n situazione f;
"situations vacant/wanted" (Brit) "offerte/
domande di impiego"
situation comedy n (Theat) commedia di
situazione
six [sɪks] num sei
six-pack ['sɪkspæk] n (esp US) confezione f
da sei
sixteen [sɪks'ti:n] num sedici
sixth [sɪksθ] num sesto(-a) ■ n: **the upper/
lower ~** (Brit Scol) l'ultimo/il penultimo anno
di scuola superiore
sixty ['sɪkstɪ] num sessanta
size [saɪz] n dimensioni fpl; (of clothing) taglia,
misura; (of shoes) numero; (glue) colla; **I take
~ 14 in a dress** ≈ porto la 44 di vestiti; **I'd like
the small/large ~** (of soap powder etc) vorrei la
confezione piccola/grande
  ▶ **size up** vt giudicare, farsi un'idea di

sizeable ['saɪzəbl] *adj* considerevole

sizzle ['sɪzl] *vi* sfrigolare

SK *abbr* (*Canada*) = **Saskatchewan**

skate [skeɪt] *n* pattino; (*fish: pl inv*) razza ▪ *vi* pattinare

▸ **skate over, skate around** *vt* (*problem, issue*) prendere alla leggera, prendere sotto gamba

skateboard ['skeɪtbɔːd] *n* skateboard *m inv*

skater ['skeɪtəʳ] *n* pattinatore(-trice)

skating ['skeɪtɪŋ] *n* pattinaggio

skating rink *n* pista di pattinaggio

skeleton ['skɛlɪtn] *n* scheletro

skeleton key *n* passe-partout *m inv*

skeleton staff *n* personale *m* ridotto

skeptic *etc* ['skɛptɪk] (*US*) = **sceptic** *etc*

sketch [skɛtʃ] *n* (*drawing*) schizzo, abbozzo; (*Theat etc*) scenetta comica, sketch *m inv* ▪ *vt* abbozzare, schizzare

sketch book *n* album *m inv* per schizzi

sketch pad *n* blocco per schizzi

sketchy ['skɛtʃɪ] *adj* incompleto(-a), lacunoso(-a)

skew [skjuː] *n* (*Brit*): **on the ~** di traverso

skewer ['skjuːəʳ] *n* spiedo

ski [skiː] *n* sci *m inv* ▪ *vi* sciare

ski boot *n* scarpone *m* da sci

skid [skɪd] *n* slittamento; (*sideways slip*) sbandamento ▪ *vi* slittare; sbandare; **to go into a ~** slittare; sbandare

skid mark *n* segno della frenata

skier ['skiːəʳ] *n* sciatore(-trice)

skiing ['skiːɪŋ] *n* sci *m*

ski instructor *n* maestro(-a) di sci

ski jump *n* (*ramp*) trampolino; (*event*) salto con gli sci

skilful, (*US*) **skillful** ['skɪlful] *adj* abile

skilfully, (*US*) **skillfully** ['skɪlfəlɪ] *adv* abilmente

ski lift *n* sciovia

skill [skɪl] *n* abilità *f inv*, capacità *f inv*; (*technique*) tecnica

skilled [skɪld] *adj* esperto(-a); (*worker*) qualificato(-a), specializzato(-a)

skillful ['skɪlful] *adj* (*US*) = **skilful**

skillfully ['skɪlfəlɪ] *adv* (*US*) = **skilfully**

skim [skɪm] *vt* (*milk*) scremare; (*soup*) schiumare; (*glide over*) sfiorare ▪ *vi*: **to ~ through** (*fig*) scorrere, dare una scorsa a

skimmed milk *n* latte *m* scremato

skimp [skɪmp] *vi*: **to ~ on** *vt* (*work*) fare alla carlona; (*cloth etc*) lesinare

skimpy ['skɪmpɪ] *adj* misero(-a); striminzito(-a); frugale

skin [skɪn] *n* pelle *f*; (*of fruit, vegetable*) buccia; (*on pudding, paint*) crosta ▪ *vt* (*fruit etc*) sbucciare; (*animal*) scuoiare, spellare; **wet** *or* **soaked to the ~** bagnato fino al midollo

skin cancer *n* cancro alla pelle

skin-deep [skɪn'diːp] *adj* superficiale

skin diver *n* subacqueo

skin diving *n* nuoto subacqueo

skinflint ['skɪnflɪnt] *n* taccagno(-a), tirchio(-a)

skin graft *n* innesto epidermico

skinhead ['skɪnhɛd] *n* skinhead *m/f inv*

skinny ['skɪnɪ] *adj* molto magro(-a), pelle e ossa *inv*

skin test *n* prova di reazione cutanea

skintight ['skɪntaɪt] *adj* aderente

skip [skɪp] *n* saltello, balzo; (*container*) benna ▪ *vi* saltare; (*with rope*) saltare la corda ▪ *vt* (*pass over*) saltare; **to ~ school** (*US*) marinare la scuola

ski pants *npl* pantaloni *mpl* da sci

ski pass *n* ski pass *m inv*

ski pole *n* racchetta (da sci)

skipper ['skɪpəʳ] *n* (*Naut, Sport*) capitano

skipping rope ['skɪpɪŋ-] *n* (*Brit*) corda per saltare

ski resort *n* località *f inv* sciistica

skirmish ['skəːmɪʃ] *n* scaramuccia

skirt [skəːt] *n* gonna, sottana ▪ *vt* fiancheggiare, costeggiare

skirting board ['skəːtɪŋ-] *n* (*Brit*) zoccolo

ski run *n* pista (da sci)

ski suit *n* tuta da sci

skit [skɪt] *n* parodia; scenetta satirica

ski tow *n* = **ski lift**

skittle ['skɪtl] *n* birillo; **skittles** *n* (*game*) (gioco dei) birilli *mpl*

skive [skaɪv] *vi* (*Brit col*) fare il lavativo

skulk [skʌlk] *vi* muoversi furtivamente

skull [skʌl] *n* cranio, teschio

skullcap ['skʌlkæp] *n* (*worn by Jews*) zucchetto; (*worn by Pope*) papalina

skunk [skʌŋk] *n* moffetta

sky [skaɪ] *n* cielo; **to praise sb to the skies** portare alle stelle qn

sky-blue [skaɪ'bluː] *adj* azzurro(-a), celeste

sky-diving ['skaɪdaɪvɪŋ] *n* caduta libera, paracadutismo acrobatico

sky-high [skaɪ'haɪ] *adv* (*throw*) molto in alto ▪ *adj* (*col*) esorbitante; **prices have gone ~** (*col*) i prezzi sono saliti alle stelle

skylark ['skaɪlɑːk] *n* allodola

skylight ['skaɪlaɪt] *n* lucernario

skyline ['skaɪlaɪn] *n* (*horizon*) orizzonte *m*; (*of city*) profilo

sky marshal *n* agente *m/f* a bordo

Skype® [skaɪp] (*Internet, Tel*) *n* Skype® *m* ▪ *vt*: **to skype sb** chiamare qn con Skype

skyscraper ['skaɪskreɪpəʳ] *n* grattacielo

slab [slæb] *n* lastra; (*of wood*) tavola; (*of meat, cheese*) pezzo

S

slack [slæk] *adj* (*loose*) allentato(-a); (*slow*) lento(-a); (*careless*) negligente; (*Comm: market*) stagnante; (: *demand*) scarso(-a); (*period*) morto(-a) ■ *n* (*in rope etc*) parte *f* non tesa; **business is ~** l'attività commerciale è scarsa; *see also* **slacks**

slacken ['slækn] (*also:* **slacken off**) *vi* rallentare, diminuire ■ *vt* allentare; (*pressure*) diminuire

slacks [slæks] *npl* pantaloni *mpl*

slag [slæg] *n* scorie *fpl*

slag heap *n* ammasso di scorie

slain [sleɪn] *pp of* **slay**

slake [sleɪk] *vt* (*one's thirst*) spegnere

slalom ['slɑːləm] *n* slalom *m*

slam [slæm] *vt* (*door*) sbattere; (*throw*) scaraventare; (*criticize*) stroncare ■ *vi* sbattere

slammer ['slæməʳ] *n*: **the ~** (*col*) la gattabuia

slander ['slɑːndəʳ] *n* calunnia; (*Law*) diffamazione *f* ■ *vt* calunniare; diffamare

slanderous ['slɑːndrəs] *adj* calunnioso(-a); diffamatorio(-a)

slang [slæŋ] *n* gergo, slang *m*

slanging match ['slæŋɪŋ-] *n* (*Brit col*) rissa verbale

slant [slɑːnt] *n* pendenza, inclinazione *f*; (*fig*) angolazione *f*, punto di vista

slanted ['slɑːntɪd] *adj* tendenzioso(-a)

slanting ['slɑːntɪŋ] *adj* in pendenza, inclinato(-a)

slap [slæp] *n* manata, pacca; (*on face*) schiaffo ■ *vt* dare una manata a; schiaffeggiare ■ *adv* (*directly*) in pieno; **it fell ~ in the middle** cadde proprio nel mezzo

slapdash ['slæpdæʃ] *adj* abborracciato(-a)

slaphead ['slæphɛd] *n* (*Brit col*) imbecille *m/f*

slapstick ['slæpstɪk] *n* (*comedy*) farsa grossolana

slap-up ['slæpʌp] *adj* (*Brit*): **a ~ meal** un pranzo (*or* una cena) coi fiocchi

slash [slæʃ] *vt* squarciare; (*face*) sfregiare; (*fig: prices*) ridurre drasticamente, tagliare

slat [slæt] *n* (*of wood*) stecca

slate [sleɪt] *n* ardesia ■ *vt* (*fig: criticize*) stroncare, distruggere

slaughter ['slɔːtəʳ] *n* (*of animals*) macellazione *f*; (*of people*) strage *f*, massacro ■ *vt* macellare; trucidare, massacrare

slaughterhouse ['slɔːtəhaus] *n* macello, mattatoio

Slav [slɑːv] *adj, n* slavo(-a)

slave [sleɪv] *n* schiavo(-a) ■ *vi* (*also:* **slave away**) lavorare come uno schiavo; **to ~ (away) at sth/at doing sth** ammazzarsi di fatica *or* sgobbare per qc/per fare qc

slave driver *n* (*col, pej*) schiavista *m/f*

slave labour *n* lavoro degli schiavi; (*fig*): **we're just ~ here** siamo solamente sfruttati qui dentro

slaver ['slævəʳ] *vi* (*dribble*) sbavare

slavery ['sleɪvərɪ] *n* schiavitù *f*

Slavic ['slævɪk] *adj* slavo(-a)

slavish ['sleɪvɪʃ] *adj* servile; pedissequo(-a)

slavishly ['sleɪvɪʃlɪ] *adv* (*copy*) pedissequamente

Slavonic [slə'vɔnɪk] *adj* slavo(-a)

slay (*pt* **slew**, *pp* **slain**) [sleɪ, sluː, sleɪn] *vt* (*formal*) uccidere

sleazy ['sliːzɪ] *adj* trasandato(-a)

sledge [slɛdʒ] *n* slitta

sledgehammer ['slɛdʒhæməʳ] *n* martello da fabbro

sleek [sliːk] *adj* (*hair, fur*) lucido(-a), lucente; (*car, boat*) slanciato(-a), affusolato(-a)

sleep [sliːp] *n* sonno ■ *vi* (*pt, pp* **slept**) [slɛpt] dormire ■ *vt*: **we can ~ 4** abbiamo 4 posti letto, possiamo alloggiare 4 persone; **to have a good night's ~** farsi una bella dormita; **to go to ~** addormentarsi; **to ~ lightly** avere il sonno leggero; **to put to ~** (*patient*) far addormentare; (*animal: euphemistic: kill*) abbattere; **to ~ with sb** (*euphemistic: have sex*) andare a letto con qn
  ▶ **sleep in** *vi* (*lie late*) alzarsi tardi; (*oversleep*) dormire fino a tardi

sleeper ['sliːpəʳ] *n* (*person*) dormiente *m/f*; (*Brit Rail: on track*) traversina; (: *train*) treno di vagoni letto

sleepily ['sliːpɪlɪ] *adv* con aria assonnata

sleeping ['sliːpɪŋ] *adj* addormentato(-a)

sleeping bag *n* sacco a pelo

sleeping car *n* vagone *m* letto *inv*, carrozza *f* letto *inv*

sleeping partner *n* (*Brit Comm*) = **silent partner**

sleeping pill *n* sonnifero

sleeping sickness *n* malattia del sonno

sleepless ['sliːplɪs] *adj* (*person*) insonne; **a ~ night** una notte in bianco

sleeplessness ['sliːplɪsnɪs] *n* insonnia

sleepover ['sliːpəuvəʳ] *n* *il dormire a casa di amici, usato in riferimento a bambini*

sleepwalk ['sliːpwɔːk] *vi* camminare nel sonno; (*as a habit*) essere sonnambulo(-a)

sleepwalker ['sliːpwɔːkəʳ] *n* sonnambulo(-a)

sleepy ['sliːpɪ] *adj* assonnato(-a), sonnolento(-a); (*fig*) addormentato(-a); **to be** *or* **feel ~** avere sonno

sleet [sliːt] *n* nevischio

sleeve [sliːv] *n* manica; (*of record*) copertina

sleeveless ['sliːvlɪs] *adj* (*garment*) senza maniche

sleigh [sleɪ] *n* slitta

sleight [slaɪt] *n*: ~ **of hand** gioco di destrezza

slender ['slɛndəʳ] *adj* snello(-a), sottile; (*not enough*) scarso(-a), esiguo(-a)

slept [slɛpt] *pt, pp of* **sleep**

sleuth [slu:θ] *n* (*col*) segugio

slew [slu:] *vi* (*also:* **slew round**) girare ■ *pt of* **slay**

slice [slaɪs] *n* fetta ■ *vt* affettare, tagliare a fette; **sliced bread** pane *m* a cassetta

slick [slɪk] *adj* (*clever*) brillante; (*insincere*) untuoso(-a), falso(-a) ■ *n* (*also:* **oil slick**) chiazza di petrolio

slid [slɪd] *pt, pp of* **slide**

slide [slaɪd] *n* (*in playground*) scivolo; (*Phot*) diapositiva; (*microscope slide*) vetrino; (*Brit: also:* **hair slide**) fermaglio (per capelli); (*in prices*) caduta ■ *vb* (*pt, pp* **slid**) [slɪd] *vt* far scivolare ■ *vi* scivolare; **to let things ~** (*fig*) lasciare andare tutto, trascurare tutto

slide projector *n* proiettore *m* per diapositive

slide rule *n* regolo calcolatore

sliding ['slaɪdɪŋ] *adj* (*door*) scorrevole; **~ roof** (*Aut*) capotte *f inv*

sliding scale *n* scala mobile

slight [slaɪt] *adj* (*slim*) snello(-a), sottile; (*frail*) delicato(-a), fragile; (*trivial*) insignificante; (*small*) piccolo(-a) ■ *n* offesa, affronto ■ *vt* (*offend*) offendere, fare un affronto a; **the slightest** il minimo (*or* la minima); **not in the slightest** affatto, neppure per sogno

slightly ['slaɪtlɪ] *adv* lievemente, un po'; **~ built** esile

slim [slɪm] *adj* magro(-a), snello(-a) ■ *vi* dimagrire, fare *or* seguire una dieta dimagrante

slime [slaɪm] *n* limo, melma; viscidume *m*

slimming ['slɪmɪŋ] *adj* (*diet, pills*) dimagrante

slimy ['slaɪmɪ] *adj* (*also fig: person*) viscido(-a); (*covered with mud*) melmoso(-a)

sling [slɪŋ] *n* (*Med*) benda al collo ■ *vt* (*pt, pp* **slung**) [slʌŋ] lanciare, tirare; **to have one's arm in a ~** avere un braccio al collo

slink (*pt, pp* **slunk**) [slɪŋk, slʌŋk] *vi*: **to ~ away, ~ off** svignarsela

slinky ['slɪŋkɪ] *adj* (*clothing*) aderente, attillato(-a)

slip [slɪp] *n* scivolata, scivolone *m*; (*mistake*) errore *m*, sbaglio; (*underskirt*) sottoveste *f*; (*paper*) bigliettino, talloncino ■ *vt* (*slide*) far scivolare ■ *vi* (*slide*) scivolare; (*move smoothly*): **to ~ into/out of** scivolare in/via da; (*decline*) declinare; **to give sb the ~** sfuggire qn; **a ~ of paper** un foglietto; **a ~ of the tongue** un lapsus linguae; **to ~ sth on/off** infilarsi/togliersi qc; **to let a chance ~ by** lasciarsi scappare un'occasione; **it slipped from her hand** le sfuggì di mano

▸ **slip away** *vi* svignarsela
▸ **slip in** *vt* introdurre casualmente
▸ **slip out** *vi* uscire furtivamente

slip-on ['slɪpɔn] *adj* (*gen*) comodo(-a) da mettere; (*shoes*) senza allacciatura

slipped disc ['slɪpt-] *n* spostamento delle vertebre

slipper ['slɪpəʳ] *n* pantofola

slippery ['slɪpərɪ] *adj* scivoloso(-a); **it's ~** si scivola

slip road *n* (*Brit: to motorway*) rampa di accesso

slipshod ['slɪpʃɔd] *adj* sciatto(-a), trasandato(-a)

slip-up ['slɪpʌp] *n* granchio (*fig*)

slipway ['slɪpweɪ] *n* scalo di costruzione

slit [slɪt] *n* fessura, fenditura; (*cut*) taglio; (*tear*) strappo ■ *vt* (*pt, pp* ~) tagliare; **to ~ sb's throat** tagliare la gola a qn

slither ['slɪðəʳ] *vi* scivolare, sdrucciolare

sliver ['slɪvəʳ] *n* (*of glass, wood*) scheggia; (*of cheese, sausage*) fettina

slob [slɔb] *n* (*col*) sciattone(-a)

slog [slɔg] (*Brit*) *n* faticata ■ *vi* lavorare con accanimento, sgobbare

slogan ['sləugən] *n* motto, slogan *m inv*

slop [slɔp] *vi* (*also:* **slop over**) traboccare; versarsi ■ *vt* spandere; versare ■ *npl*: **slops** acqua sporca; sbobba

slope [sləup] *n* pendio; (*side of mountain*) versante *m*; (*of roof*) pendenza; (*of floor*) inclinazione *f* ■ *vi*: **to ~ down** declinare; **to ~ up** essere in salita

sloping ['sləupɪŋ] *adj* inclinato(-a)

sloppy ['slɔpɪ] *adj* (*work*) tirato(-a) via; (*appearance*) sciatto(-a); (*film etc*) sdolcinato(-a)

slosh [slɔʃ] *vi* (*col*): **to ~ about** *or* **around** (*person*) sguazzare; (*liquid*) guazzare

sloshed [slɔʃt] *adj* (*col: drunk*) sbronzo(-a)

slot [slɔt] *n* fessura; (*fig: in timetable, Radio, TV*) spazio ■ *vt*: **to ~ into** introdurre in una fessura

sloth [sləuθ] *n* (*vice*) pigrizia, accidia; (*Zool*) bradipo

slot machine *n* (*Brit: vending machine*) distributore *m* automatico; (*for amusement*) slot-machine *f inv*

slot meter *n* contatore *m* a gettoni

slouch [slautʃ] *vi* (*when walking*) camminare dinoccolato(-a); **she was slouched in a chair** era sprofondata in una poltrona
▸ **slouch about, slouch around** *vi* (*laze*) oziare

Slovak ['sləuvæk] *adj* slovacco(-a) ■ *n* slovacco(-a); (*Ling*) slovacco; **the ~ Republic** la Repubblica Slovacca

Slovakia [sləu'vækɪə] *n* Slovacchia

Slovakian [sləʊˈvækɪən] *adj, n* = **Slovak**
Slovene [ˈsləʊviːn] *adj* sloveno(-a) ■ *n*
 sloveno(-a); (*Ling*) sloveno
Slovenia [sləʊˈviːnɪə] *n* Slovenia
Slovenian [sləʊˈviːnɪən] *adj, n* = **Slovene**
slovenly [ˈslʌvənlɪ] *adj* sciatto(-a),
 trasandato(-a)
slow [sləʊ] *adj* lento(-a); (*watch*): **to be ~**
 essere indietro ■ *adv* lentamente ■ *vt, vi*
 (*also*: **slow down, slow up**) rallentare; **"~"**
 (*road sign*) "rallentare"; **at a ~ speed** a bassa
 velocità; **to be ~ to act/decide** essere lento
 ad agire/a decidere; **my watch is 20**
 minutes ~ il mio orologio è indietro di 20
 minuti; **business is ~** (*Comm*) gli affari
 procedono a rilento; **to go ~** (*driver*) andare
 piano; (*in industrial dispute*) fare uno sciopero
 bianco
slow-acting [ˈsləʊˈæktɪŋ] *adj* che agisce
 lentamente, ad azione lenta
slowly [ˈsləʊlɪ] *adv* lentamente; **to drive ~**
 andare piano
slow motion *n*: **in ~** al rallentatore
slowness [ˈsləʊnɪs] *n* lentezza
sludge [slʌdʒ] *n* fanghiglia
slug [slʌg] *n* lumaca; (*bullet*) pallottola
sluggish [ˈslʌgɪʃ] *adj* lento(-a); (*business,*
 market, sales) stagnante, fiacco(-a)
sluice [sluːs] *n* chiusa ■ *vt*: **to ~ down** *or* **out**
 lavare (con abbondante acqua)
slum [slʌm] *n* catapecchia
slumber [ˈslʌmbəʳ] *n* sonno
slump [slʌmp] *n* crollo, caduta; (*economic*)
 depressione *f*, crisi *f inv* ■ *vi* crollare; **he was**
 slumped over the wheel era curvo sul
 volante
slung [slʌŋ] *pt, pp of* **sling**
slunk [slʌŋk] *pt, pp of* **slink**
slur [slɜːʳ] *n* pronuncia indistinta; (*stigma*)
 diffamazione *f*, calunnia; (*Mus*) legatura;
 (*smear*): **~ (on)** macchia (su) ■ *vt* pronunciare
 in modo indistinto; **to cast a ~ on sb**
 calunniare qn
slurp [slɜːp] *vt, vi* bere rumorosamente ■ *n*
 rumore fatto bevendo
slurred [slɜːd] *adj* (*pronunciation*)
 inarticolato(-a), disarticolato(-a)
slush [slʌʃ] *n* neve *f* mista a fango
slush fund *n* fondi *mpl* neri
slushy [ˈslʌʃɪ] *adj* (*snow*) che si scioglie; (*Brit:*
 fig) sdolcinato(-a)
slut [slʌt] *n* donna trasandata, sciattona
sly [slaɪ] *adj* furbo(-a), scaltro(-a); **on the ~**
 di soppiatto
SM *n abbr* (= *sadomasochism*) sadomasochismo
smack [smæk] *n* (*slap*) pacca; (*on face*) schiaffo
 ■ *vt* schiaffeggiare; (*child*) picchiare ■ *vi*:

to ~ of puzzare di; **to ~ one's lips** fare uno
 schiocco con le labbra
smacker [ˈsmækəʳ] *n* (*col: kiss*) bacio; (*: Brit:*
 pound note) sterlina; (*: US: dollar bill*) dollaro
small [smɔːl] *adj* piccolo(-a); (*in height*)
 basso(-a); (*letter*) minuscolo(-a) ■ *n*: **the ~ of**
 the back le reni; **to get** *or* **grow smaller**
 (*stain, town*) rimpicciolire; (*debt, organization,*
 numbers) ridursi; **to make smaller** (*amount,*
 income) ridurre; (*garden, object, garment*)
 rimpicciolire; **in the ~ hours** alle ore piccole;
 a ~ shopkeeper un piccolo negoziante
small ads *npl* (*Brit*) piccoli annunci *mpl*
small arms *npl* armi *fpl* portatili *or* leggere
small business *n* piccola impresa
small change *n* moneta, spiccioli *mpl*
smallholder [ˈsmɔːlhəʊldəʳ] *n* (*Brit*) piccolo
 proprietario
smallholding [ˈsmɔːlhəʊldɪŋ] *n* (*Brit*) piccola
 tenuta
smallish [ˈsmɔːlɪʃ] *adj* piccolino(-a)
small-minded [smɔːlˈmaɪndɪd] *adj*
 meschino(-a)
smallpox [ˈsmɔːlpɒks] *n* vaiolo
small print *n* caratteri *mpl* piccoli; (*on*
 document) parte scritta in piccolo
small-scale [ˈsmɔːlskeɪl] *adj* (*map, model*) in
 scala ridotta; (*business, farming*) modesto(-a)
small talk *n* chiacchiere *fpl*
small-time [ˈsmɔːltaɪm] *adj* (*col*) da poco; **a ~**
 thief un ladro di polli
small-town [ˈsmɔːltaʊn] *adj* (*pej*) provinciale,
 di paese
smarmy [ˈsmɑːmɪ] *adj* (*Brit pej*) untuoso(-a),
 strisciante
smart [smɑːt] *adj* elegante; (*also fig: clever*)
 intelligente; (*quick*) sveglio(-a) ■ *vi* bruciare;
 the ~ set il bel mondo; **to look ~** essere
 elegante; **my eyes are smarting** mi
 bruciano gli occhi
smartcard [ˈsmɑːtkɑːd] *n* smartcard *f inv*,
 carta intelligente
smarten up [ˈsmɑːtn-] *vi* farsi bello(-a) ■ *vt*
 (*people*) fare bello(-a); (*things*) abbellire
smash [smæʃ] *n* (*also*: **smash-up**) scontro,
 collisione *f*; (*sound*) fracasso ■ *vt*
 frantumare, fracassare; (*opponent*)
 annientare, schiacciare; (*hopes*) distruggere;
 (*Sport: record*) battere ■ *vi* frantumarsi,
 andare in pezzi
 ▶ **smash up** *vt* (*car*) sfasciare; (*room*)
 distruggere
smash-hit [smæʃˈhɪt] *n* successone *m*
smashing [ˈsmæʃɪŋ] *adj* (*col*) favoloso(-a),
 formidabile
smattering [ˈsmætərɪŋ] *n*: **a ~ of**
 un'infarinatura di

SME *npl abbr* (= *small and medium-sized enterprises*) PMI *fpl inv* (= *Piccole e Medie Imprese*)

smear [smɪə^r] *n* macchia; (*Med*) striscio; (*insult*) calunnia ■ *vt* ungere; (*fig*) denigrare, diffamare; **his hands were smeared with oil/ink** aveva le mani sporche di olio/inchiostro

smear campaign *n* campagna diffamatoria

smear test *n* (*Brit Med*) Pap-test *m inv*

smell [smɛl] *n* odore *m*; (*sense*) olfatto, odorato ■ *vb* (*pt, pp* **smelt** *or* **smelled**) [smɛlt, smɛld] *vt* sentire (l')odore di ■ *vi* (*food etc*): **to ~ (of)** avere odore (di); (*pej*) puzzare, avere un cattivo odore; **it smells good** ha un buon odore

smelly ['smɛlɪ] *adj* puzzolente

smelt [smɛlt] *pt, pp of* **smell** ■ *vt* (*ore*) fondere

smile [smaɪl] *n* sorriso ■ *vi* sorridere

smiling ['smaɪlɪŋ] *adj* sorridente

smirk [smə:k] *n* sorriso furbo; sorriso compiaciuto

smith [smɪθ] *n* fabbro

smithy ['smɪðɪ] *n* fucina

smitten ['smɪtn] *adj*: **~ with** colpito(-a) da

smock [smɔk] *n* grembiule *m*, camice *m*

smog [smɔg] *n* smog *m*

smoke [sməuk] *n* fumo ■ *vt, vi* fumare; **to have a ~** fumarsi una sigaretta; **do you ~?** fumi?; **to go up in ~** (*house etc*) bruciare, andare distrutto dalle fiamme; (*fig*) andare in fumo

smoked [sməukt] *adj* (*bacon, glass*) affumicato(-a)

smokeless fuel ['sməuklɪs-] *n* carburante *m* che non dà fumo

smokeless zone *n* (*Brit*) zona dove sono vietati gli scarichi di fumo

smoker ['sməukə^r] *n* (*person*) fumatore(-trice); (*Rail*) carrozza per fumatori

smoke screen *n* cortina fumogena *or* di fumo; (*fig*) copertura

smoke shop *n* (*US*) tabaccheria

smoking ['sməukɪŋ] *n* fumo; **"no ~"** (*sign*) "vietato fumare"; **he's given up ~** ha smesso di fumare

smoking compartment, (*US*) **smoking car** *n* carrozza (per) fumatori

smoky ['sməukɪ] *adj* fumoso(-a); (*surface*) affumicato(-a)

smolder ['sməuldə^r] *vi* (*US*) = **smoulder**

smoochy ['smu:tʃɪ] *adj* (*col*) romantico(-a)

smooth [smu:ð] *adj* liscio(-a); (*sauce*) omogeneo(-a); (*flavour, whisky*) amabile; (*cigarette*) leggero(-a); (*movement*) regolare; (*person*) mellifluo(-a); (*landing, takeoff, flight*) senza scosse ■ *vt* lisciare, spianare; (*also*: **smooth out**: *difficulties*) appianare

▸ **smooth over** *vt*: **to ~ things over** (*fig*) sistemare le cose

smoothly ['smu:ðlɪ] *adv* (*easily*) liscio; **everything went ~** tutto andò liscio

smother ['smʌðə^r] *vt* soffocare

smoulder, (*US*) **smolder** ['sməuldə^r] *vi* covare sotto la cenere

SMS *n abbr* (= *short message service*) SMS *m* (*servizio*)

smudge [smʌdʒ] *n* macchia; sbavatura ■ *vt* imbrattare, sporcare

smug [smʌg] *adj* soddisfatto(-a), compiaciuto(-a)

smuggle ['smʌgl] *vt* contrabbandare; **to ~ in/out** (*goods etc*) far entrare/uscire di contrabbando

smuggler ['smʌglə^r] *n* contrabbandiere(-a)

smuggling ['smʌglɪŋ] *n* contrabbando

smut [smʌt] *n* (*grain of soot*) granello di fuliggine; (*mark*) segno nero; (*in conversation etc*) sconcezze *fpl*

smutty ['smʌtɪ] *adj* (*fig*) osceno(-a), indecente

snack [snæk] *n* spuntino; **to have a ~** fare uno spuntino

snack bar *n* tavola calda, snack bar *m inv*

snag [snæg] *n* intoppo, ostacolo imprevisto

snail [sneɪl] *n* chiocciola

snake [sneɪk] *n* serpente *m*

snap [snæp] *n* (*sound*) schianto, colpo secco; (*photograph*) istantanea; (*game*) rubamazzo ■ *adj* improvviso(-a) ■ *vt* (*far*) schioccare; (*break*) spezzare di netto; (*photograph*) scattare un'istantanea di ■ *vi* spezzarsi con un rumore secco; (*fig: person*) crollare; **to ~ at sb** rivolgersi a qn con tono brusco; (*dog*) cercare di mordere qn; **to ~ open/shut** aprirsi/chiudersi di scatto; **to ~ one's fingers at** (*fig*) infischiarsi di; **a cold ~** (*of weather*) un'improvvisa ondata di freddo

▸ **snap off** *vt* (*break*) schiantare

▸ **snap up** *vt* afferrare

snap fastener *n* bottone *m* automatico

snappy ['snæpɪ] *adj* rapido(-a); **make it ~!** (*col: hurry up*) sbrigati!, svelto!

snapshot ['snæpʃɔt] *n* istantanea

snare [snɛə^r] *n* trappola

snarl [snɑ:l] *vi* ringhiare ■ *vt*: **to get snarled up** (*wool, plans*) ingarbugliarsi; (*traffic*) intasarsi

snatch [snætʃ] *n* (*fig*) furto; (*Brit: small amount*): **snatches of** frammenti *mpl* di ■ *vt* strappare (con violenza); (*steal*) rubare ■ *vi*: **don't ~!** non strappare le cose di mano!; **to ~ a sandwich** mangiarsi in fretta un panino; **to ~ some sleep** riuscire a dormire un po'

▸ **snatch up** *vt* raccogliere in fretta

snazzy ['snæzɪ] *adj* (*col: clothes*) sciccoso(-a)

sneak [sniːk] *vi*: **to ~ in/out** entrare/uscire di nascosto ■ *vt*: **to ~ a look at sth** guardare di sottecchi qc

sneakers ['sniːkəz] *npl* scarpe *fpl* da ginnastica

sneaking ['sniːkɪŋ] *adj*: **to have a ~ feeling/suspicion that ...** avere la vaga impressione/il vago sospetto che ...

sneaky ['sniːkɪ] *adj* falso(-a), disonesto(-a)

sneer [snɪəʳ] *n* ghigno, sogghigno ■ *vi* ghignare, sogghignare; **to ~ at sb/sth** farsi beffe di qn/qc

sneeze [sniːz] *n* starnuto ■ *vi* starnutire

snide [snaɪd] *adj* maligno(-a)

sniff [snɪf] *n* fiutata, annusata ■ *vi* fiutare, annusare; tirare su col naso; (*in contempt*) arricciare il naso ■ *vt* fiutare, annusare; (*glue, drug*) sniffare
▶ **sniff at** *vt fus*: **it's not to be sniffed at** non è da disprezzare

sniffer dog ['snɪfə-] *n* cane *m* poliziotto (*per stupefacenti o esplosivi*)

snigger ['snɪgəʳ] *n* riso represso ■ *vi* ridacchiare, ridere sotto i baffi

snip [snɪp] *n* pezzetto; (*bargain*) (buon) affare *m*, occasione *f* ■ *vt* tagliare

sniper ['snaɪpəʳ] *n* franco tiratore *m*, cecchino

snippet ['snɪpɪt] *n* frammento

snivelling ['snɪvlɪŋ] *adj* piagnucoloso(-a)

snob [snɔb] *n* snob *m/f inv*

snobbery ['snɔbəɪ] *n* snobismo

snobbish ['snɔbɪʃ] *adj* snob *inv*

snog [snɔg] *vi* (*col*) pomiciare

snooker ['snuːkəʳ] *n* tipo di gioco del biliardo

snoop [snuːp] *vi*: **to ~ on sb** spiare qn; **to ~ about** curiosare

snooper ['snuːpəʳ] *n* ficcanaso *m/f*

snooty ['snuːtɪ] *adj* borioso(-a), snob *inv*

snooze [snuːz] *n* sonnellino, pisolino ■ *vi* fare un sonnellino

snore [snɔːʳ] *vi* russare

snoring ['snɔːrɪŋ] *n* russare *m*

snorkel ['snɔːkl] *n* (*of swimmer*) respiratore *m* a tubo

snort [snɔːt] *n* sbuffo ■ *vi* sbuffare ■ *vt* (*drugs slang*) sniffare

snotty ['snɔtɪ] *adj* moccioso(-a)

snout [snaut] *n* muso

snow [snəu] *n* neve *f* ■ *vi* nevicare ■ *vt*: **to be snowed under with work** essere sommerso di lavoro

snowball ['snəubɔːl] *n* palla di neve

snowbound ['snəubaund] *adj* bloccato(-a) dalla neve

snow-capped ['snəukæpt] *adj* (*mountain*) con la cima coperta di neve; (*peak*) coperto(-a) di neve

snowdrift ['snəudrɪft] *n* cumulo di neve (*ammucchiato dal vento*)

snowdrop ['snəudrɔp] *n* bucaneve *m inv*

snowfall ['snəufɔːl] *n* nevicata

snowflake ['snəufleɪk] *n* fiocco di neve

snowman ['snəumæn] *n* pupazzo di neve

snowplough, (US) **snowplow** ['snəuplau] *n* spazzaneve *m inv*

snowshoe ['snəuʃuː] *n* racchetta da neve

snowstorm ['snəustɔːm] *n* tormenta

snowy ['snəuɪ] *adj* nevoso(-a)

SNP *n abbr* (Brit Pol) = **Scottish National Party**

snub [snʌb] *vt* snobbare ■ *n* offesa, affronto

snub-nosed [snʌb'nəuzd] *adj* dal naso camuso

snuff [snʌf] *n* tabacco da fiuto ■ *vt* (*also*: **snuff out**: *candle*) spegnere

snuff movie *n* (*col*) film porno dove una persona viene uccisa realmente

snug [snʌg] *adj* comodo(-a); (*room, house*) accogliente, comodo(-a); **it's a ~ fit** è attillato

snuggle ['snʌgl] *vi*: **to ~ down in bed** accovacciarsi a letto; **to ~ up to sb** stringersi a qn

snugly ['snʌglɪ] *adv* comodamente; **it fits ~** (*object in pocket etc*) entra giusto giusto; (*garment*) sta ben attillato

SO *abbr* (Banking) = **standing order**

 KEYWORD

so [səu] *adv* **1** (*thus, likewise*) così; **if so** se è così, quand'è così; **I didn't do it — you did so!** non l'ho fatto io — sì che l'hai fatto!; **so do I, so am I** anch'io; **it's 5 o'clock — so it is!** sono le 5 — davvero!; **I hope so** lo spero; **I think so** penso di sì; **quite so!** esattamente!; **even so** comunque; **so far** finora, fin qui; (*in past*) fino ad allora
2 (*in comparisons etc: to such a degree*) così; **so big (that)** così grande (che); **she's not so clever as her brother** lei non è (così) intelligente come suo fratello
3: **so much** *adj* tanto(-a)
■ *adv* tanto; **I've got so much work/money** ho tanto lavoro/tanti soldi; **I love you so much** ti amo tanto; **so many** tanti(-e)
4 (*phrases*): **10 or so** circa 10; **so long!** (*col: goodbye*) ciao!, ci vediamo!; **so to speak** per così dire; **so what?** (*col*) e allora?, e con questo?
■ *conj* **1** (*expressing purpose*): **so as to do** in modo or così da fare; **we hurried so as not to be late** ci affrettammo per non fare tardi; **so (that)** affinché + *sub*, perché + *sub*
2 (*expressing result*): **he didn't arrive so I left**

non è venuto così me ne sono andata; **so you see, I could have gone** vedi, sarei potuto andare; **so that's the reason!** allora è questo il motivo!, ecco perché!

soak [səuk] vt inzuppare; (clothes) mettere a mollo ▪ vi inzupparsi; (clothes) essere a mollo; **to be soaked through** essere fradicio
  ▶ **soak in** vi penetrare
  ▶ **soak up** vt assorbire
soaking ['səukɪŋ] adj (also: **soaking wet**) fradicio(-a)
so-and-so ['səuənsəu] n (somebody) un tale; **Mr/Mrs** ~ signor/signora tal dei tali
soap [səup] n sapone m
soapbox ['səupbɔks] n palco improvvisato (per orazioni pubbliche)
soapflakes ['səupfleɪks] npl sapone m in scaglie
soap opera n soap opera f inv
soap powder n detersivo
soapsuds ['səupsʌdz] npl saponata
soapy ['səupɪ] adj insaponato(-a)
soar [sɔːr] vi volare in alto; (price, morale, spirits) salire alle stelle
sob [sɔb] n singhiozzo ▪ vi singhiozzare
s.o.b. n abbr (US col!: = son of a bitch) figlio di puttana (!)
sober ['səubər] adj non ubriaco(-a); (sedate) serio(-a); (moderate) moderato(-a); (colour, style) sobrio(-a)
  ▶ **sober up** vt far passare la sbornia a ▪ vi farsi passare la sbornia
sobriety [səu'braɪətɪ] n (not being drunk) sobrietà; (seriousness, sedateness) sobrietà, pacatezza
sob story n (col, pej) storia lacrimosa
Soc. abbr (= society) Soc
so-called ['səu'kɔːld] adj cosiddetto(-a)
soccer ['sɔkər] n calcio
soccer pitch n campo di calcio
soccer player n calciatore m
sociable ['səuʃəbl] adj socievole
social ['səuʃl] adj sociale ▪ n festa, serata
social climber n arrampicatore(-trice) sociale, arrivista m/f
social club n club m inv sociale
Social Democrat n socialdemocratico(-a)
social insurance n (US) assicurazione f sociale
socialism ['səuʃəlɪzəm] n socialismo
socialist ['səuʃəlɪst] adj, n socialista m/f
socialite ['səuʃəlaɪt] n persona in vista nel bel mondo
socialize ['səuʃəlaɪz] vi frequentare la gente; farsi degli amici; **to ~ with** socializzare con
social life n vita sociale

social network n social network m inv, rete f sociale
social networking n il comunicare tramite social network
socially ['səuʃəlɪ] adv socialmente, in società
social science n scienze fpl sociali
social security n previdenza sociale; **Department of Social Security** (Brit) ≈ Istituto di Previdenza Sociale
social services npl servizi mpl sociali
social welfare n assistenza sociale
social work n servizio sociale
social worker n assistente m/f sociale
society [sə'saɪətɪ] n società f inv; (club) società, associazione f; (also: **high society**) alta società ▪ cpd (party, column) mondano(-a)
socioeconomic ['səusɪəui:kə'nɔmɪk] adj socio-economico(-a)
sociological [səusɪə'lɔdʒɪkl] adj sociologico(-a)
sociologist [səusɪ'ɔlədʒɪst] n sociologo(-a)
sociology [səusɪ'ɔlədʒɪ] n sociologia
sock [sɔk] n calzino ▪ vt (hit) dare un pugno a; **to pull one's socks up** (fig) darsi una regolata
socket ['sɔkɪt] n cavità f inv; (of eye) orbita; (Elec: also: **wall socket**) presa di corrente; (: for light bulb) portalampada m inv
sod [sɔd] n (of earth) zolla erbosa; (Brit col!) bastardo(-a) (!)
  ▶ **sod off** vi: ~ **off!** (Brit col!) levati dalle palle! (!)
soda ['səudə] n (Chem) soda; (also: **soda water**) acqua di seltz; (US: also: **soda pop**) gassosa
sodden ['sɔdn] adj fradicio(-a)
sodium ['səudɪəm] n sodio
sodium chloride n cloruro di sodio
sofa ['səufə] n sofà m inv
Sofia ['səufɪə] n Sofia
soft [sɔft] adj (not rough) morbido(-a); (not hard) soffice; (not loud) sommesso(-a); (kind) gentile; (: look, smile) dolce; (not strict) indulgente; (weak) debole; (stupid) stupido(-a)
soft-boiled ['sɔftbɔɪld] adj (egg) alla coque
soft drink n analcolico
soft drugs npl droghe fpl leggere
soften ['sɔfn] vt ammorbidire; addolcire; attenuare ▪ vi ammorbidirsi; addolcirsi; attenuarsi
softener ['sɔfnər] n ammorbidente m
soft furnishings npl tessuti mpl d'arredo
soft-hearted [sɔft'hɑːtɪd] adj sensibile
softly ['sɔftlɪ] adv dolcemente; morbidamente
softness ['sɔftnɪs] n dolcezza; morbidezza
soft option n soluzione f (più) facile
soft sell n persuasione f all'acquisto
soft target n obiettivo civile (e quindi facile da colpire)

S

soft touch n (col): **to be a ~** lasciarsi spillare facilmente denaro

soft toy n giocattolo di peluche

software ['sɔftwɛəʳ] n software m

software package n pacchetto di software

soft water n acqua non calcarea

soggy ['sɔgɪ] adj inzuppato(-a)

soil [sɔɪl] n (earth) terreno, suolo ▪ vt sporcare; (fig) macchiare

soiled [sɔɪld] adj sporco(-a), sudicio(-a)

sojourn ['sɔdʒəːn] n (formal) soggiorno

solace ['sɔlɪs] n consolazione f

solar ['səuləʳ] adj solare

solarium (pl **solaria**) [sə'lɛərɪəm, -rɪə] n solarium m inv

solar plexus [-'plɛksəs] n (Anat) plesso solare

solar power n energia solare

sold [səuld] pt, pp of **sell**

solder ['səuldəʳ] vt saldare ▪ n saldatura

soldier ['səuldʒəʳ] n soldato, militare m; see **to soldier on** perseverare; **toy ~** soldatino

sold out adj (Comm) esaurito(-a)

sole [səul] n (of foot) pianta (del piede); (of shoe) suola; (fish: pl inv) sogliola ▪ adj solo(-a), unico(-a); (exclusive) esclusivo(-a)

solely ['səullɪ] adv solamente, unicamente; **I will hold you ~ responsible** la considererò il solo responsabile

solemn ['sɔləm] adj solenne; grave; serio(-a)

sole trader n (Comm) commerciante m in proprio

solicit [sə'lɪsɪt] vt (request) richiedere, sollecitare ▪ vi (prostitute) adescare i passanti

solicitor [sə'lɪsɪtəʳ] n (Brit: for wills etc) ≈ notaio; (in court) ≈ avvocato; vedi nota

solid ['sɔlɪd] adj (not hollow) pieno(-a); (strong, sound, reliable, not liquid) solido(-a); (meal) sostanzioso(-a); (line) ininterrotto(-a); (vote) unanime ▪ n solido; **to be on ~ ground** essere su terraferma; (fig) muoversi su terreno sicuro; **we waited 2 ~ hours** abbiamo aspettato due ore buone

solidarity [sɔlɪ'dærɪtɪ] n solidarietà

solid fuel n combustibile m solido

solidify [sə'lɪdɪfaɪ] vi solidificarsi ▪ vt solidificare

solidity [sə'lɪdɪtɪ] n solidità

solid-state ['sɔlɪdsteɪt] adj (Elec) a transistor

soliloquy [sə'lɪləkwɪ] n soliloquio

solitaire [sɔlɪ'tɛəʳ] n (game, gem) solitario

solitary ['sɔlɪtərɪ] adj solitario(-a)

solitary confinement n (Law): **to be in ~** essere in cella d'isolamento

solitude ['sɔlɪtjuːd] n solitudine f

solo ['səuləu] n (Mus) assolo

soloist ['səuləuɪst] n solista m/f

Solomon Islands ['sɔləmən-] n: **the ~** le isole Salomone

solstice ['sɔlstɪs] n solstizio

soluble ['sɔljubl] adj solubile

solution [sə'luːʃən] n soluzione f

solve [sɔlv] vt risolvere

solvency ['sɔlvənsɪ] n (Comm) solvenza, solvibilità

solvent ['sɔlvənt] adj (Comm) solvibile ▪ n (Chem) solvente m

solvent abuse n abuso di colle e, solventi

Somali [sə'mɑːlɪ] adj somalo(-a)

Somalia [sə'mɑːlɪə] n Somalia

Somaliland [səu'mɑːlɪlænd] n paesi mpl del corno d'Africa

sombre, (US) **somber** ['sɔmbəʳ] adj scuro(-a); (mood, person) triste

 KEYWORD

some [sʌm] adj **1** (a certain amount or number of): **some tea/water/cream** del tè/dell'acqua/della panna; **there's some milk in the fridge** c'è (del) latte nel frigo; **some children/apples** dei bambini/delle mele; **after some time** dopo un po'; **at some length** a lungo

2 (certain: in contrasts) certo(-a); **some people say that ...** alcuni dicono che ..., certa gente dice che ...

3 (unspecified) un(-a) certo(-a), qualche; **some woman was asking for you** una tale chiedeva di lei; **some day** un giorno; **some day next week** un giorno della prossima settimana; **in some form or other** in una forma o nell'altra

▪ pron **1** (a certain number) alcuni(-e), certi(-e); **I've got some** (books etc) ne ho alcuni; **some (of them) have been sold** alcuni sono stati venduti

2 (a certain amount) un po'; **I've got some** (money, milk) ne ho un po'; **I've read some of the book** ho letto parte del libro; **some**

(of it) was left ne è rimasto un po'; **could I have some of that cheese?** potrei avere un po' di quel formaggio?
■ *adv*: **some 10 people** circa 10 persone

somebody ['sʌmbədɪ] *pron* qualcuno; **~ or other** qualcuno

someday ['sʌmdeɪ] *adv* uno di questi giorni, un giorno o l'altro

somehow ['sʌmhau] *adv* in un modo o nell'altro, in qualche modo; *(for some reason)* per qualche ragione

someone ['sʌmwʌn] *pron* = **somebody**

someplace ['sʌmpleɪs] *adv* (US) = **somewhere**

somersault ['sʌməsɔːlt] *n* capriola; *(in air)* salto mortale ■ *vi* fare una capriola (*or* un salto mortale); *(car)* cappottare

something ['sʌmθɪŋ] *pron* qualcosa; **~ interesting** qualcosa di interessante; **~ to do** qualcosa da fare; **he's ~ like me** mi assomiglia un po'; **it's ~ of a problem** è un bel problema

sometime ['sʌmtaɪm] *adv* (in future) una volta o l'altra; (in past): **~ last month** durante il mese scorso; **I'll finish it ~** lo finirò prima o poi

sometimes ['sʌmtaɪmz] *adv* qualche volta

somewhat ['sʌmwɔt] *adv* piuttosto

somewhere ['sʌmwɛəʳ] *adv* in *or* da qualche parte; **~ else** da qualche altra parte

son [sʌn] *n* figlio

sonar ['səunɑːʳ] *n* sonar *m*

sonata [sə'nɑːtə] *n* sonata

song [sɔŋ] *n* canzone *f*

songbook ['sɔŋbuk] *n* canzoniere *m*

songwriter ['sɔŋraɪtəʳ] *n* compositore(-trice) di canzoni

sonic ['sɔnɪk] *adj* (boom) sonico(-a)

son-in-law ['sʌnɪnlɔː] *n* genero

sonnet ['sɔnɪt] *n* sonetto

sonny ['sʌnɪ] *n* (col) ragazzo mio

soon [suːn] *adv* presto, fra poco; (early) presto; **~ afterwards** poco dopo; **very/quite ~** molto/abbastanza presto; **as ~ as possible** prima possibile; **I'll do it as ~ as I can** lo farò appena posso; **how ~ can you be ready?** fra quanto tempo sarà pronto?; **see you ~!** a presto!

sooner ['suːnəʳ] *adv* (time) prima; (preference): **I would ~ do** preferirei fare; **~ or later** prima o poi; **no ~ said than done** detto fatto; **the ~ the better** prima è meglio è; **no ~ had we left than ...** eravamo appena partiti, quando ...

soot [sut] *n* fuliggine *f*

soothe [suːð] *vt* calmare

soothing ['suːðɪŋ] *adj* (ointment etc) calmante; (tone, words etc) rassicurante

SOP *n abbr* = **standard operating procedure**

sop [sɔp] *n*: **that's only a ~** è soltanto un contentino

sophisticated [sə'fɪstɪkeɪtɪd] *adj* sofisticato(-a); raffinato(-a); (film, mind) sottile

sophistication [səfɪstɪ'keɪʃən] *n* raffinatezza; (of machine) complessità; (of argument etc) sottigliezza

sophomore ['sɔfəmɔːʳ] *n* (US) studente(-essa) del secondo anno

soporific [sɔpə'rɪfɪk] *adj* soporifero(-a)

sopping ['sɔpɪŋ] *adj* (also: **sopping wet**) bagnato(-a) fradicioa(-a)

soppy ['sɔpɪ] *adj* (pej) sentimentale

soprano [sə'prɑːnəu] *n* (voice) soprano *m*; (singer) soprano *m/f*

sorbet ['sɔːbeɪ] *n* sorbetto

sorcerer ['sɔːsərəʳ] *n* stregone *m*, mago

sordid ['sɔːdɪd] *adj* sordido(-a)

sore [sɔːʳ] *adj* (painful) dolorante; (col: offended) offeso(-a) ■ *n* piaga; **my eyes are ~, I have ~ eyes** mi fanno male gli occhi; **~ throat** mal *m* di gola; **it's a ~ point** (fig) è un punto delicato

sorely ['sɔːlɪ] *adv* (tempted) fortemente

sorrel ['sɔrəl] *n* acetosa

sorrow ['sɔrəu] *n* dolore *m*

sorrowful ['sɔrəuful] *adj* triste

sorry ['sɔrɪ] *adj* spiacente; (condition, excuse) misero(-a), pietoso(-a); (sight, failure) triste; **~!** scusa! (or scusi! or scusate!); **to feel ~ for sb** rincrescersi per qn; **I'm ~ to hear that ...** mi dispiace (sentire) che ...; **to be ~ about sth** essere dispiaciuto *or* spiacente di qc

sort [sɔːt] *n* specie *f*, genere *m*; (make: of coffee, car etc) tipo ■ *vt* (also: **sort out**: papers) classificare; ordinare; (: letters etc) smistare; (: problems) risolvere; (Comput) ordinare; **what ~ of car?** che tipo di macchina?; **I shall do nothing of the ~!** nemmeno per sogno!; **it's ~ of awkward** (col) è piuttosto difficile

sortie ['sɔːtɪ] *n* sortita

sorting office ['sɔːtɪŋ-] *n* ufficio *m* smistamento *inv*

SOS *n abbr* S.O.S. *m inv*

so-so ['səusəu] *adv* così così

soufflé ['suːfleɪ] *n* soufflé *m inv*

sought [sɔːt] *pt, pp of* **seek**

sought-after ['sɔːtɑːftəʳ] *adj* richiesto(-a)

soul [səul] *n* anima; **the poor ~ had nowhere to sleep** il poveraccio non aveva dove dormire; **I didn't see a ~** non ho visto anima viva

soul-destroying ['səuldɪ'strɔɪɪŋ] *adj* demoralizzante

s

soulful ['səʊlful] *adj* pieno(-a) di sentimento
soulless ['səʊllɪs] *adj* senz'anima, inumano(-a)
soul mate *n* anima gemella
soul-searching ['səʊlsə:tʃɪŋ] *n*: **after much ~** dopo un profondo esame di coscienza
sound [saʊnd] *adj* (*healthy*) sano(-a); (*safe, not damaged*) solido(-a), in buono stato; (*reliable, not superficial*) solido(-a); (*sensible*) giudizioso(-a), di buon senso; (*valid: argument, policy, claim*) valido(-a) ■ *adv*: **~ asleep** profondamente addormentato ■ *n* (*noise*) suono; rumore *m*; (*Geo*) stretto ■ *vt* (*alarm*) suonare; (*also:* **sound out**: *opinions*) sondare ■ *vi* suonare; (*fig: seem*) sembrare; **to be of ~ mind** essere sano di mente; **I don't like the ~ of it** (*fig: film etc*) non mi dice niente; (: *news*) è preoccupante; **it sounds as if ...** ho l'impressione che ...; **it sounds like French** somiglia al francese; **that sounds like them arriving** mi sembra di sentirli arrivare
  ▶ **sound off** *vi* (*col*): **to ~ off (about)** (*give one's opinions*) fare dei grandi discorsi (su)
sound barrier *n* muro del suono
soundbite ['saʊndbaɪt] *n* frase *f* incisiva
sound effects *npl* effetti *mpl* sonori
sound engineer *n* tecnico del suono
sounding ['saʊndɪŋ] *n* (*Naut etc*) scandagliamento
sounding board *n* (*Mus*) cassa di risonanza; (*fig*): **to use sb as a ~ for one's ideas** provare le proprie idee su qn
soundly ['saʊndlɪ] *adv* (*sleep*) profondamente; (*beat*) duramente
soundproof ['saʊndpru:f] *vt* insonorizzare, isolare acusticamente ■ *adj* insonorizzato(-a), isolato(-a) acusticamente
sound system *n* impianto *m*, audio *inv*
soundtrack ['saʊndtræk] *n* (*of film*) colonna sonora
soup [su:p] *n* minestra; (*clear*) brodo; (*thick*) zuppa; **in the ~** (*fig*) nei guai
soup course *n* minestra
soup kitchen *n* mensa per i poveri
soup plate *n* piatto fondo
soupspoon ['su:pspu:n] *n* cucchiaio da minestra
sour ['saʊəʳ] *adj* aspro(-a); (*fruit*) acerbo(-a); (*milk*) acido(-a), fermentato(-a); (*fig*) acido(-a); **to go** *or* **turn ~** (*milk, wine*) inacidirsi; (*fig: relationship, plans*) guastarsi; **it's ~ grapes** (*fig*) è soltanto invidia
source [sɔ:s] *n* fonte *f*, sorgente *f*; (*fig*) fonte; **I have it from a reliable ~ that ...** ho saputo da fonte sicura che ...
south [saʊθ] *n* sud *m*, meridione *m*,

mezzogiorno ■ *adj* del sud, sud *inv*, meridionale ■ *adv* verso sud; (**to the**) **~ of** a sud di; **the S~ of France** il sud della Francia; **to travel ~** viaggiare verso sud
South Africa *n* Sudafrica *m*
South African *adj, n* sudafricano(-a)
South America *n* Sudamerica *m*, America del Sud
South American *adj, n* sudamericano(-a)
southbound ['saʊθbaʊnd] *adj* (*gen*) diretto(-a) a sud; (*carriageway*) sud *inv*
south-east [saʊθ'i:st] *n* sud-est *m*
South-East Asia *n* Asia sudorientale
southerly ['sʌðəlɪ] *adj* del sud
southern ['sʌðən] *adj* del sud, meridionale; (*wall*) esposto(-a) a sud; **the ~ hemisphere** l'emisfero australe
South Pole *n* Polo Sud
South Sea Islands *npl*: **the ~** le isole dei Mari del Sud
South Seas *npl*: **the ~** i Mari del Sud
South Vietnam *n* Vietnam *m* del Sud
southward ['saʊθwəd], **southwards** ['saʊθwədz] *adv* verso sud
south-west [saʊθ'wɛst] *n* sud-ovest *m*
souvenir [su:və'nɪəʳ] *n* ricordo, souvenir *m inv*
sovereign ['sɔvrɪn] *adj, n* sovrano(-a)
sovereignty ['sɔvrəntɪ] *n* sovranità
soviet ['səʊvɪət] *adj* sovietico(-a)
Soviet Union *n*: **the ~** l'Unione *f* Sovietica
sow¹ [səʊ] (*pt* **sowed**, *pp* **sown**) [səʊn] *vt* seminare
sow² [saʊ] *n* scrofa
soya ['sɔɪə], (US) **soy** [sɔɪ] *n*: **~ bean** seme *m* di soia; **~ sauce** salsa di soia
sozzled ['sɔzld] *adj* (*Brit col*) sbronzo(-a)
spa [spa:] *n* (*resort*) stazione *f* termale; (*US: also:* **health spa**) centro di cure estetiche
space [speɪs] *n* spazio; (*room*) posto; spazio; (*length of time*) intervallo ■ *cpd* spaziale ■ *vt* (*also:* **space out**) distanziare; **in a confined ~** in un luogo chiuso; **to clear a ~ for sth** fare posto per qc; **in a short ~ of time** in breve tempo; **(with)in the ~ of an hour/three generations** nell'arco di un'ora/di tre generazioni
space bar *n* (*on typewriter*) barra spaziatrice
spacecraft ['speɪskrɑ:ft] *n* (*pl inv*) veicolo spaziale
spaceman ['speɪsmæn] *n* astronauta *m*, cosmonauta *m*
spaceship ['speɪsʃɪp] *n* astronave *f*, navicella spaziale
space shuttle *n* shuttle *m inv*
spacesuit ['speɪssu:t] *n* tuta spaziale
spacewoman ['speɪswʊmən] *n* astronauta *f*, cosmonauta *f*

spacing ['speɪsɪŋ] n spaziatura; **single/ double ~** (*Typ etc*) spaziatura singola/doppia

spacious ['speɪʃəs] *adj* spazioso(-a), ampio(-a)

spade [speɪd] n (*tool*) vanga; pala; (*child's*) paletta; **spades** npl (*Cards*) picche fpl

spadework ['speɪdwə:k] n (*fig*) duro lavoro preparatorio

spaghetti [spə'ɡetɪ] n spaghetti mpl

Spain [speɪn] n Spagna

spam [spæm] (*Comput*) n spamming m ∎ vt: **to ~ sb** inviare a qn messaggi pubblicitari non richiesti via email

span [spæn] n (*of bird, plane*) apertura alare; (*of arch*) campata; (*in time*) periodo; durata ∎ vt attraversare; (*fig*) abbracciare

Spaniard ['spænjəd] n spagnolo(-a)

spaniel ['spænjəl] n spaniel m inv

Spanish ['spænɪʃ] *adj* spagnolo(-a) ∎ n (*Ling*) spagnolo; **the ~** npl gli Spagnoli; **~ omelette** *frittata di cipolle, pomodori e peperoni*

spank [spæŋk] vt sculacciare

spanner ['spænəʳ] n (*Brit*) chiave f inglese

spar [spɑ:ʳ] n asta, palo ∎ vi (*Boxing*) allenarsi

spare [speəʳ] *adj* di riserva, di scorta; (*surplus*) in più, d'avanzo ∎ n (*part*) pezzo di ricambio ∎ vt (*do without*) fare a meno di; (*afford to give*) concedere; (*refrain from hurting, using*) risparmiare; **to ~** (*surplus*) d'avanzo; **there are 2 going ~** (*Brit*) ce ne sono 2 in più; **to ~ no expense** non badare a spese; **can you ~ the time?** ha tempo?; **I've a few minutes to ~** ho un attimino di tempo; **there is no time to ~** non c'è tempo da perdere; **can you ~ (me) £10?** puoi prestarmi 10 sterline?

spare part n pezzo di ricambio

spare room n stanza degli ospiti

spare time n tempo libero

spare tyre n (*Aut*) gomma di scorta

spare wheel n (*Aut*) ruota di scorta

sparing ['speərɪŋ] *adj* (*amount*) scarso(-a); (*use*) parsimonioso(-a); **to be ~ with** essere avaro(-a) di

sparingly ['speərɪŋlɪ] *adv* moderatamente

spark [spɑ:k] n scintilla

sparkle ['spɑ:kl] n scintillio, sfavillio ∎ vi scintillare, sfavillare; (*bubble*) spumeggiare, frizzare

sparkler ['spɑ:kləʳ] n fuoco d'artificio

sparkling ['spɑ:klɪŋ] *adj* scintillante, sfavillante; (*wine*) spumante

spark plug n candela

sparring partner ['spɑ:rɪŋ-] n sparring partner m inv; (*fig*) interlocutore abituale in discussioni, dibattiti, tavole rotonde ecc

sparrow ['spærəu] n passero

sparse [spɑ:s] *adj* sparso(-a), rado(-a)

spartan ['spɑ:tən] *adj* (*fig*) spartano(-a)

spasm ['spæzəm] n (*Med*) spasmo; (*fig*) accesso, attacco

spasmodic [spæz'mɔdɪk] *adj* spasmodico(-a); (*fig*) intermittente

spastic ['spæstɪk] n spastico(-a)

spat [spæt] pt, pp of **spit** ∎ n (*US*) battibecco

spate [speɪt] n (*fig*): **~ of** diluvio or fiume m di; **in ~** (*river*) in piena

spatial ['speɪʃəl] *adj* spaziale

spatter ['spætəʳ] vt, vi schizzare

spatula ['spætjulə] n spatola

spawn [spɔ:n] vt deporre; (*pej*) produrre ∎ vi deporre le uova ∎ n uova fpl

SPCA n abbr (*US*: = *Society for the Prevention of Cruelty to Animals*) ≈ E.N.P.A. m (= *Ente Nazionale per la Protezione degli Animali*)

SPCC n abbr (*US*) = **Society for the Prevention of Cruelty to Children**

speak (*pt* **spoke**, *pp* **spoken**) [spi:k, spəuk, 'spəukn] vt (*language*) parlare; (*truth*) dire ∎ vi parlare; **to ~ to sb/of** or **about sth** parlare a qn/di qc; **~ up!** parli più forte!; **to ~ at a conference/in a debate** partecipare ad una conferenza/ad un dibattito; **speaking!** (*on telephone*) sono io!; **to ~ one's mind** dire quello che si pensa; **he has no money to ~ of** non si può proprio dire che sia ricco
▸ **speak for** vt fus: **to ~ for sb** parlare a nome di qn; **that picture is already spoken for** (*in shop*) quel quadro è già stato venduto

speaker ['spi:kəʳ] n (*in public*) oratore(-trice); (*also*: **loudspeaker**) altoparlante m; (*Pol*): **the S~** *il presidente della Camera dei Comuni or* (*US*) *dei Rappresentanti*; **are you a Welsh ~?** parla gallese?

speaking ['spi:kɪŋ] *adj* parlante; **Italian-~ people** persone che parlano italiano; **to be on ~ terms** parlarsi

spear [spɪəʳ] n lancia

spearhead ['spɪəhɛd] n punta di lancia; (*Mil*) reparto d'assalto ∎ vt (*attack etc*) condurre

spearmint ['spɪəmɪnt] n (*Bot etc*) menta verde

spec [spɛk] n (*Brit col*): **on ~** sperando bene; **to buy sth on ~** comprare qc sperando di fare un affare

special ['spɛʃl] *adj* speciale ∎ n (*train*) treno supplementare; **nothing ~** niente di speciale; **take ~ care** siate particolarmente prudenti

special agent n agente m segreto

special correspondent n inviato speciale

special delivery n (*Post*): **by ~** per espresso

special effects npl (*Cine*) effetti mpl speciali

specialist ['spɛʃəlɪst] n specialista m/f; **a heart ~** (*Med*) un cardiologo

speciality [spɛʃɪ'ælɪtɪ], (*esp US*) **specialty** n specialità f inv

S

797

specialize ['spɛʃəlaɪz] vi: **to ~ (in)** specializzarsi (in)

specially ['spɛʃlɪ] adv specialmente, particolarmente

special offer n (Comm) offerta speciale

specialty ['spɛʃltɪ] n (esp US) = **speciality**

species ['spi:ʃiːz] n (pl inv) specie f inv

specific [spə'sɪfɪk] adj specifico(-a); preciso(-a); **to be ~ to** avere un legame specifico con

specifically [spə'sɪfɪklɪ] adv (explicitly: state, warn) chiaramente, esplicitamente; (especially: design, intend) appositamente

specification [spɛsɪfɪ'keɪʃən] n specificazione f; **specifications** npl (of car, machine) dati mpl caratteristici; (for building) dettagli mpl

specify ['spɛsɪfaɪ] vt specificare, precisare; **unless otherwise specified** salvo indicazioni contrarie

specimen ['spɛsɪmən] n esemplare m, modello; (Med) campione m

specimen copy n campione m

specimen signature n firma depositata

speck [spɛk] n puntino, macchiolina; (particle) granello

speckled ['spɛkld] adj macchiettato(-a)

specs [spɛks] npl (col) occhiali mpl

spectacle ['spɛktəkl] n spettacolo; see also **spectacles**

spectacle case n (Brit) fodero per gli occhiali

spectacles ['spɛktəklz] npl (Brit) occhiali mpl

spectacular [spɛk'tækjuləʳ] adj spettacolare ■ n (Cine etc) film m inv etc spettacolare

spectator [spɛk'teɪtəʳ] n spettatore(-trice)

spectator sport n sport m inv come spettacolo

spectra ['spɛktrə] npl of **spectrum**

spectre, (US) **specter** ['spɛktəʳ] n spettro

spectrum (pl **spectra**) ['spɛktrəm, -rə] n spettro; (fig) gamma

speculate ['spɛkjuleɪt] vi speculare; (try to guess): **to ~ about** fare ipotesi su

speculation [spɛkju'leɪʃən] n speculazione f; congetture fpl

speculative ['spɛkjulətɪv] adj speculativo(-a)

speculator ['spɛkjuleɪtəʳ] n speculatore(-trice)

sped [spɛd] pt, pp of **speed**

speech [spi:tʃ] n (faculty) parola; (talk) discorso; (manner of speaking) parlata; (language) linguaggio; (enunciation) elocuzione f

speech day n (Brit Scol) giorno della premiazione

speech impediment n difetto di pronuncia

speechless ['spi:tʃlɪs] adj ammutolito(-a), muto(-a)

speech therapy n cura dei disturbi del linguaggio

speed [spi:d] n velocità f inv; (promptness) prontezza; (Aut: gear) marcia ■ vi (pt, pp **sped**) [spɛd]: **to ~ along** procedere velocemente; **the years sped by** gli anni sono volati; (Aut: exceed speed limit) andare a velocità eccessiva; **at ~** (Brit) velocemente; **at full** or **top ~** a tutta velocità; **at a ~ of 70 km/h** a una velocità di 70 km l'ora; **shorthand/typing speeds** numero di parole al minuto in stenografia/dattilografia; **a five-~ gearbox** un cambio a cinque marce

▶ **speed up** (pt, pp **speeded up**) vi, vt accelerare

speedboat ['spi:dbəut] n motoscafo; fuoribordo m inv

speed dating [-deɪtɪŋ] n sistema di appuntamenti grazie al quale si possono incontrare in pochissimo tempo diverse persone e scegliere eventualmente chi frequentare

speedily ['spi:dɪlɪ] adv velocemente; prontamente

speeding ['spi:dɪŋ] n (Aut) eccesso di velocità

speed limit n limite m di velocità

speedometer [spɪ'dɔmɪtəʳ] n tachimetro

speed trap n (Aut) tratto di strada sul quale la polizia controlla la velocità dei veicoli

speedway ['spi:dweɪ] n (Sport) pista per motociclismo

speedy ['spi:dɪ] adj veloce, rapido(-a); (reply) pronto(-a)

speleologist [spɛlɪ'ɔlədʒɪst] n speleologo(-a)

spell [spɛl] n (also: **magic spell**) incantesimo; (period of time) (breve) periodo ■ vt (pt, pp **spelt** or **spelled**) [spɛlt, spɛld] (in writing) scrivere (lettera per lettera); (aloud) dire lettera per lettera; (fig) significare; **to cast a ~ on sb** fare un incantesimo a qn; **he can't ~** fa errori di ortografia; **how do you ~ your name?** come si scrive il suo nome?; **can you ~ it for me?** me lo può dettare lettera per lettera?

spellbound ['spɛlbaund] adj incantato(-a), affascinato(-a)

spelling ['spɛlɪŋ] n ortografia

spelt [spɛlt] pt, pp of **spell**

spend (pt, pp **spent**) [spɛnd, spɛnt] vt (money) spendere; (time, life) passare; **to ~ time/money/effort on sth** dedicare tempo/soldi/energie a qc

spending ['spɛndɪŋ] n: **government ~** spesa pubblica

spending money n denaro per le piccole spese

spending power n potere m d'acquisto

spendthrift ['spɛndθrɪft] n spendaccione(-a)

spent [spɛnt] *pt, pp of* **spend** ■ *adj (patience)*
esaurito(-a); *(cartridge, bullets, match)* usato(-a)

sperm [spə:m] *n* sperma *m*

sperm bank *n* banca dello sperma

sperm whale *n* capodoglio

spew [spju:] *vt* vomitare

sphere [sfɪə^r] *n* sfera

spherical ['sfɛrɪkl] *adj* sferico(-a)

sphinx [sfɪŋks] *n* sfinge *f*

spice [spaɪs] *n* spezia ■ *vt* aromatizzare

spick-and-span ['spɪkən'spæn] *adj*
impeccabile

spicy ['spaɪsɪ] *adj* piccante

spider ['spaɪdə^r] *n* ragno; **~'s web** ragnatela

spiel [spi:l] *n (col)* tiritera

spike [spaɪk] *n* punta; **spikes** *npl (Sport)*
scarpe *fpl* chiodate

spike heel *n (US)* tacco a spillo

spiky ['spaɪkɪ] *adj (bush, branch)* spinoso(-a);
(animal) ricoperto(-a) di aculei

spill *(pt, pp* **spilt** *or* **spilled)** [spɪl, -t, -d] *vt*
versare, rovesciare ■ *vi* versarsi, rovesciarsi;
to ~ the beans *(col)* vuotare il sacco
▶ **spill out** *vi* riversarsi fuori
▶ **spill over** *vi*: **to ~ over (into)** *(liquid)*
versarsi (in); *(crowd)* riversarsi (in)

spillage ['spɪlɪdʒ] *n (event)* fuoriuscita;
(substance) sostanza fuoriuscita

spin [spɪn] *n (revolution of wheel)* rotazione *f*;
(Aviat) avvitamento; *(trip in car)* giretto ■ *vb
(pt, pp* **spun)** [spʌn] *vt (wool etc)* filare; *(wheel)*
far girare; *(Brit: clothes)* mettere nella
centrifuga ■ *vi* girare; **to ~ a yarn**
raccontare una storia; **to ~ a coin** *(Brit)*
lanciare in aria una moneta
▶ **spin out** *vt* far durare

spina bifida ['spaɪnə'bɪfɪdə] *n* spina bifida

spinach ['spɪnɪtʃ] *n* spinacio; *(as food)* spinaci
mpl

spinal ['spaɪnl] *adj* spinale

spinal column *n* colonna vertebrale, spina
dorsale

spinal cord *n* midollo spinale

spindly ['spɪndlɪ] *adj* lungo(-a) e sottile,
filiforme

spin doctor *n (col) esperto di comunicazioni
responsabile dell'immagine di un partito politico*

spin-dry ['spɪn'draɪ] *vt* asciugare con la
centrifuga

spin-dryer [spɪn'draɪə^r] *n (Brit)* centrifuga

spine [spaɪn] *n* spina dorsale; *(thorn)* spina

spine-chilling ['spaɪntʃɪlɪŋ] *adj* agghiacciante

spineless ['spaɪnlɪs] *adj* invertebrato(-a),
senza spina dorsale; *(fig)* smidollato(-a)

spinner ['spɪnə^r] *n (of thread)* tessitore(-trice)

spinning ['spɪnɪŋ] *n* filatura

spinning top *n* trottola

spinning wheel *n* filatoio

spin-off ['spɪnɔf] *n* applicazione *f* secondaria

spinster ['spɪnstə^r] *n* nubile *f*; zitella

spiral ['spaɪərl] *n* spirale *f* ■ *adj* a spirale ■ *vi
(prices)* salire vertiginosamente; **the
inflationary ~** la spirale dell'inflazione

spiral staircase *n* scala a chiocciola

spire ['spaɪə^r] *n* guglia

spirit ['spɪrɪt] *n (soul)* spirito, anima; *(ghost)*
spirito, fantasma *m*; *(mood)* stato d'animo,
umore *m*; *(courage)* coraggio; **spirits** *npl
(drink)* alcolici *mpl*; **in good spirits** di buon
umore; **in low spirits** triste, abbattuto(-a);
community ~, **public ~** senso civico

spirit duplicator *n* duplicatore *m* a spirito

spirited ['spɪrɪtɪd] *adj* vivace, vigoroso(-a);
(horse) focoso(-a)

spirit level *n* livella a bolla (d'aria)

spiritual ['spɪrɪtjuəl] *adj* spirituale ■ *n (also:*
Negro spiritual) spiritual *m inv*

spiritualism ['spɪrɪtjuəlɪzəm] *n* spiritismo

spit [spɪt] *n (for roasting)* spiedo; *(spittle)* sputo;
(saliva) saliva ■ *vi (pt, pp* **spat)** [spæt] sputare;
(fire, fat) scoppiettare

spite [spaɪt] *n* dispetto ■ *vt* contrariare, far
dispetto a; **in ~ of** nonostante, malgrado

spiteful ['spaɪtful] *adj* dispettoso(-a); *(tongue,
remark)* maligno(-a), velenoso(-a)

spitroast ['spɪt'rəust] *vt* cuocere allo spiedo

spitting ['spɪtɪŋ] *n*: **"~ prohibited"** "vietato
sputare" ■ *adj*: **to be the ~ image of sb**
essere il ritratto vivente *or* sputato di qn

spittle ['spɪtl] *n* saliva; sputo

spiv [spɪv] *n (Brit col)* imbroglione *m*

splash [splæʃ] *n* spruzzo; *(sound)* tonfo;
(of colour) schizzo ■ *vt* spruzzare ■ *vi (also:*
splash about) sguazzare; **to ~ paint on the
floor** schizzare il pavimento di vernice

splashdown ['splæʃdaun] *n* ammaraggio

splay [spleɪ] *adj*: **~ footed** che ha i piedi piatti

spleen [spli:n] *n (Anat)* milza

splendid ['splendɪd] *adj* splendido(-a),
magnifico(-a)

splendour, *(US)* **splendor** ['splendə^r] *n*
splendore *m*

splice [splaɪs] *vt (rope)* impiombare; *(wood)*
calettare

splint [splɪnt] *n (Med)* stecca

splinter ['splɪntə^r] *n* scheggia ■ *vi*
scheggiarsi

splinter group *n* gruppo dissidente

split [splɪt] *n* spaccatura; *(fig: division, quarrel)*
scissione *f* ■ *vb (pt, pp* **~)** *vt* spaccare; *(party)*
dividere; *(work, profits)* spartire, ripartire ■ *vi
(divide)* dividersi; **to do the splits** fare la
spaccata; **to ~ the difference** dividersi la
differenza

S

▶ **split up** vi (couple) separarsi, rompere; (meeting) sciogliersi

split-level ['splɪtlɛvl] adj (house) a piani sfalsati

split peas npl piselli mpl secchi spaccati

split personality n doppia personalità

split second n frazione f di secondo

splitting ['splɪtɪŋ] adj: **a ~ headache** un mal di testa da impazzire

splutter ['splʌtəʳ] vi farfugliare; sputacchiare

spoil (pt, pp **spoilt** or **spoiled**) [spɔɪl, -t, -d] vt (damage) rovinare, guastare; (mar) sciupare; (child) viziare; (ballot paper) rendere nullo(-a), invalidare; **to be spoiling for a fight** morire dalla voglia di litigare

spoils [spɔɪlz] npl bottino

spoilsport ['spɔɪlspɔːt] n guastafeste m/f inv

spoilt [spɔɪlt] pt, pp of **spoil** ■ adj (child) viziato(-a); (ballot paper) nullo(-a)

spoke [spəʊk] pt of **speak** ■ n raggio

spoken ['spəʊkn] pp of **speak**

spokesman ['spəʊksmən], **spokeswoman** [-wumən] n portavoce m/f inv

spokesperson ['spəʊkspɜːsn] n portavoce m/f

sponge [spʌndʒ] n spugna; (Culin: also: **sponge cake**) pan m di Spagna ■ vt spugnare, pulire con una spugna ■ vi: **to ~ on** or (US) **off of** scroccare a

sponge bag n (Brit) nécessaire m inv

sponge cake n pan m di Spagna

sponger ['spʌndʒəʳ] n (pej) parassita m/f, scroccone(-a)

spongy ['spʌndʒɪ] adj spugnoso(-a)

sponsor ['spɔnsəʳ] n (Radio, TV, Sport etc) sponsor m inv; (of enterprise, bill, for fund-raising) promotore(-trice) ■ vt sponsorizzare; patrocinare; (Pol: bill) presentare; **I sponsored him at 3p a mile** (in fund-raising race) ho offerto in beneficenza 3 penny per ogni miglio che fa

sponsorship ['spɔnsəʃɪp] n sponsorizzazione f; patrocinio

spontaneity [spɔntə'neɪɪtɪ] n spontaneità

spontaneous [spɔn'teɪnɪəs] adj spontaneo(-a)

spoof [spuːf] n presa in giro, parodia

spooky ['spuːkɪ] adj che fa accapponare la pelle

spool [spuːl] n bobina

spoon [spuːn] n cucchiaio

spoon-feed ['spuːnfiːd] vt nutrire con il cucchiaio; (fig) imboccare

spoonful ['spuːnful] n cucchiaiata

sporadic [spə'rædɪk] adj sporadico(-a)

sport [spɔːt] n sport m inv; (person) persona di spirito; (amusement) divertimento ■ vt sfoggiare; **indoor/outdoor sports** sport mpl

al chiuso/all'aria aperta; **to say sth in ~** dire qc per scherzo

sporting ['spɔːtɪŋ] adj sportivo(-a); **to give sb a ~ chance** dare a qn una possibilità (di vincere)

sport jacket n (US) = **sports jacket**

sports car n automobile f sportiva

sports ground n campo sportivo

sports jacket n giacca sportiva

sportsman ['spɔːtsmən] n sportivo

sportsmanship ['spɔːtsmənʃɪp] n spirito sportivo

sports page n pagina sportiva

sports utility vehicle n (esp US) fuoristrada m inv

sportswear ['spɔːtswɛəʳ] n abiti mpl sportivi

sportswoman ['spɔːtswumən] n sportiva

sporty ['spɔːtɪ] adj sportivo(-a)

spot [spɔt] n punto; (mark) macchia; (dot: on pattern) pallino; (pimple) foruncolo; (place) posto; (also: **spot advertisement**) spot m inv; (small amount): **a ~ of** un po' di ■ vt (notice) individuare, distinguere; **on the ~** sul posto; **to do sth on the ~** fare qc immediatamente or lì per lì; **to put sb on the ~** mettere qn in difficoltà; **to come out in spots** coprirsi di foruncoli

spot check n controllo senza preavviso

spotless ['spɔtlɪs] adj immacolato(-a)

spotlight ['spɔtlaɪt] n proiettore m; (Aut) faro ausiliario

spot-on [spɔt'ɔn] adj (Brit) esatto(-a)

spot price n (Comm) prezzo del pronto

spotted ['spɔtɪd] adj macchiato(-a); a puntini, a pallini; **~ with** punteggiato(-a) di

spotty ['spɔtɪ] adj (face) foruncoloso(-a)

spouse [spaʊz] n sposo(-a)

spout [spaʊt] n (of jug) beccuccio; (of liquid) zampillo, getto ■ vi zampillare

sprain [spreɪn] n storta, distorsione f ■ vt: **to ~ one's ankle** storcersi una caviglia

sprang [spræŋ] pt of **spring**

sprawl [sprɔːl] vi sdraiarsi (in modo scomposto) ■ n: **urban ~** sviluppo urbanistico incontrollato; **to send sb sprawling** mandare qn a gambe all'aria

spray [spreɪ] n spruzzo; (container) nebulizzatore m, spray m inv; (of flowers) mazzetto ■ cpd (deodorant) spray inv ■ vt spruzzare; (crops) irrorare

spread [sprɛd] n diffusione f; (distribution) distribuzione f; (Press, Typ: two pages) doppia pagina; (: across columns) articolo a più colonne; (Culin) pasta (da spalmare) ■ vb (pt, pp ~) vt (cloth) stendere, distendere; (butter etc) spalmare; (disease, knowledge) propagare, diffondere ■ vi stendersi, distendersi;

spalmarsi; propagarsi, diffondersi; **middle-age** ~ pancetta; **repayments will be** ~ **over 18 months** i versamenti saranno scaglionati lungo un periodo di 18 mesi

spread-eagled ['sprɛdi:gld] *adj*: **to be** *or* **lie** ~ essere disteso(-a) a gambe e braccia aperte

spreadsheet ['sprɛdʃi:t] *n* (*Comput*) foglio elettronico

spree [spri:] *n*: **to go on a** ~ fare baldoria

sprig [sprɪg] *n* ramoscello

sprightly ['spraɪtlɪ] *adj* vivace

spring [sprɪŋ] *n* (*leap*) salto, balzo; (*bounciness*) elasticità; (*coiled metal*) molla; (*season*) primavera; (*of water*) sorgente *f* ■ *vi* (*pt* **sprang**, *pp* **sprung**) [spræŋ, sprʌŋ] saltare, balzare ■ *vt*: **to** ~ **a leak** (*pipe etc*) cominciare a perdere; **to walk with a** ~ **in one's step** camminare con passo elastico; **in** ~, **in the** ~ in primavera; **to** ~ **from** provenire da; **to** ~ **into action** entrare (rapidamente) in azione; **he sprang the news on me** mi ha sorpreso con quella notizia

▶ **spring up** *vi* (*problem*) presentarsi

springboard ['sprɪŋbɔ:d] *n* trampolino

spring-clean [sprɪŋ'kli:n] *n* (*also*: **spring-cleaning**) grandi pulizie *fpl* di primavera

spring onion *n* (*Brit*) cipollina

spring roll *n* involtino fritto di verdure o carne tipico della cucina cinese

springtime ['sprɪŋtaɪm] *n* primavera

springy ['sprɪŋɪ] *adj* elastico(-a)

sprinkle ['sprɪŋkl] *vt* spruzzare; spargere; **to** ~ **water** *etc* **on**, ~ **with water** *etc* spruzzare dell'acqua *etc* su; **to** ~ **sugar** *etc* **on**, ~ **with sugar** *etc* spolverizzare di zucchero *etc*; **sprinkled with** (*fig*) cosparso(-a) di

sprinkler ['sprɪŋklə'] *n* (*for lawn etc*) irrigatore *m*; (*for fire-fighting*) sprinkler *m inv*

sprinkling ['sprɪŋklɪŋ] *n* (*of water*) qualche goccia; (*of salt, sugar*) pizzico

sprint [sprɪnt] *n* scatto ■ *vi* scattare; **the 200-metres** ~ i 200 metri piani

sprinter ['sprɪntə'] *n* velocista *m/f*

sprite [spraɪt] *n* elfo, folletto

spritzer ['sprɪtsə'] *n* spritz *m inv*

sprocket ['sprɔkɪt] *n* (*on printer etc*) dente *m*, rocchetto

sprout [spraut] *vi* germogliare

sprouts [sprauts] *npl* (*also*: **Brussels sprouts**) cavolini *mpl* di Bruxelles

spruce [spru:s] *n* abete *m* rosso ■ *adj* lindo(-a); azzimato(-a)

▶ **spruce up** *vt* (*tidy*) mettere in ordine; (*smarten up: room etc*) abbellire; **to** ~ **o.s. up** farsi bello(-a)

sprung [sprʌŋ] *pp of* **spring**

spry [spraɪ] *adj* arzillo(-a), sveglio(-a)

SPUC *n abbr* (= *Society for the Protection of Unborn Children*) associazione anti-abortista

spun [spʌn] *pt, pp of* **spin**

spur [spə:'] *n* sperone *m*; (*fig*) sprone *m*, incentivo ■ *vt* (*also*: **spur on**) spronare; **on the** ~ **of the moment** lì per lì

spurious ['spjuərɪəs] *adj* falso(-a)

spurn [spə:n] *vt* rifiutare con disprezzo, sdegnare

spurt [spə:t] *n* getto; (*of energy*) esplosione *f* ■ *vi* sgorgare; zampillare; **to put in** *or* **on a** ~ (*runner*) fare uno scatto; (*fig: in work etc*) affrettarsi, sbrigarsi

sputter ['spʌtə'] *vi* = **splutter**

spy [spaɪ] *n* spia ■ *cpd* (*film, story*) di spionaggio ■ *vi*: **to** ~ **on** spiare ■ *vt* (*see*) scorgere

spying ['spaɪɪŋ] *n* spionaggio

Sq. *abbr* (*in address*) = **square**

sq. *abbr* (*Math etc*) = **square**

squabble ['skwɔbl] *n* battibecco ■ *vi* bisticciarsi

squad [skwɔd] *n* (*Mil*) plotone *m*; (*Police*) squadra; **flying** ~ (*Police*) volante *f*

squad car *n* (*Brit Police*) automobile *f* della polizia

squaddie ['skwɔdɪ] *n* (*Mil: col*) burba

squadron ['skwɔdrn] *n* (*Mil*) squadrone *m*; (*Aviat, Naut*) squadriglia

squalid ['skwɔlɪd] *adj* sordido(-a)

squall [skwɔ:l] *n* burrasca

squalor ['skwɔlə'] *n* squallore *m*

squander ['skwɔndə'] *vt* dissipare

square [skwɛə'] *n* quadrato; (*in town*) piazza; (*US: block of houses*) blocco, isolato; (*instrument*) squadra ■ *adj* quadrato(-a); (*honest*) onesto(-a); (*col: ideas, person*) di vecchio stampo ■ *vt* (*arrange*) regolare; (*Math*) elevare al quadrato ■ *vi* (*agree*) accordarsi; **a** ~ **meal** un pasto abbondante; **2 metres** ~ di 2 metri per 2; **1** ~ **metre** 1 metro quadrato; **we're back to** ~ **one** (*fig*) siamo al punto di partenza; **all** ~ pari; **to get one's accounts** ~ mettere in ordine i propri conti; **I'll** ~ **it with him** (*col*) sistemo io le cose con lui; **can you** ~ **it with your conscience?** (*reconcile*) puoi conciliarlo con la tua coscienza?

▶ **square up** *vi* (*Brit: settle*) saldare, pagare; **to** ~ **up with sb** regolare i conti con qn

square bracket *n* (*Typ*) parentesi *f inv* quadra

squarely ['skwɛəlɪ] *adv* (*directly*) direttamente; (*honestly, fairly*) onestamente

square root *n* radice *f* quadrata

squash [skwɔʃ] *n* (*Brit: drink*): **lemon/orange** ~ sciroppo di limone/arancia; (*vegetable*) zucca; (*Sport*) squash *m* ■ *vt* schiacciare

squat [skwɔt] *adj* tarchiato(-a), tozzo(-a) ■ *vi* accovacciarsi; (*on property*) occupare abusivamente

squatter ['skwɔtə'] *n* occupante *m/f* abusivo(-a)

squawk [skwɔ:k] *vi* emettere strida rauche

squeak [skwi:k] *vi* squittire ■ *n* (*of hinge, wheel etc*) cigolio; (*of shoes*) scricchiolio; (*of mouse etc*) squittio

squeaky ['skwi:kɪ] *adj* (*col*) cigolante; **to be ~ clean** (*fig*) avere un'immagine pulita

squeal [skwi:l] *vi* strillare

squeamish ['skwi:mɪʃ] *adj* schizzinoso(-a); disgustato(-a)

squeeze [skwi:z] *n* pressione *f*; (*also Econ*) stretta; (*credit squeeze*) stretta creditizia ■ *vt* premere; (*hand, arm*) stringere ■ *vi* (*also:* **to squeeze in**) infilarsi; **to ~ past/under sth** passare vicino/sotto a qc con difficoltà; **a ~ of lemon** una spruzzata di limone
> **squeeze out** *vt* spremere

squelch [skwɛltʃ] *vi* fare ciac; sguazzare

squib [skwɪb] *n* petardo

squid [skwɪd] *n* calamaro

squint [skwɪnt] *vi* essere strabico(-a); (*in the sunlight*) strizzare gli occhi ■ *n*: **he has a ~** è strabico; **to ~ at sth** guardare qc di traverso; (*quickly*) dare un'occhiata a qc

squire ['skwaɪə'] *n* (*Brit*) proprietario terriero

squirm [skwə:m] *vi* contorcersi

squirrel ['skwɪrəl] *n* scoiattolo

squirt [skwə:t] *n* schizzo ■ *vi* schizzare; zampillare

Sr *abbr* = **senior; sister** (*Rel*)

SRC *n abbr* (*Brit*: = *Students' Representative Council*) *comitato di rappresentanza studenti*

Sri Lanka [srɪ'læŋkə] *n* Sri Lanka *m*

SRO *abbr* (*US*: = *standing room only*) solo posti in piedi

SS *abbr* = **steamship**

SSA *n abbr* (*US*: = *Social Security Administration*) ≈ Previdenza Sociale

SST *n abbr* (*US*) = **supersonic transport**

ST *abbr* (*US*: = *Standard Time*) ora ufficiale

St *abbr* = **saint; street**

stab [stæb] *n* (*with knife etc*) pugnalata; (*col: try*): **to have a ~ at (doing) sth** provare a fare qc ■ *vt* pugnalare; **to ~ sb to death** uccidere qn a coltellate

stabbing ['stæbɪŋ] *n*: **there's been a ~** qualcuno è stato pugnalato ■ *adj* (*pain, ache*) lancinante

stability [stə'bɪlɪtɪ] *n* stabilità

stabilization [steɪbəlaɪ'zeɪʃən] *n* stabilizzazione *f*

stabilize ['steɪbəlaɪz] *vt* stabilizzare ■ *vi* stabilizzarsi

stabilizer ['steɪbəlaɪzə'] *n* (*Aviat, Naut*) stabilizzatore *m*

stable ['steɪbl] *n* (*for horses*) scuderia; (*for cattle*) stalla ■ *adj* stabile; **riding stables** maneggio

staccato [stə'kɑ:təu] *adv* in modo staccato ■ *adj* (*Mus*) staccato(-a); (*sound*) scandito(-a)

stack [stæk] *n* catasta, pila; (*col*) mucchio, sacco ■ *vt* accatastare, ammucchiare; **there's stacks of time to finish it** (*Brit col*) abbiamo un sacco di tempo per finirlo

stadium ['steɪdɪəm] *n* stadio

staff [stɑ:f] *n* (*work force: gen*) personale *m*; (: *Brit: Scol*) personale insegnante; (: *servants*) personale di servizio; (*Mil*) stato maggiore; (*stick*) bastone *m* ■ *vt* fornire di personale

staffroom ['stɑ:fru:m] *n* sala dei professori

Staffs *abbr* (*Brit*) = **Staffordshire**

stag [stæg] *n* cervo; (*Brit Stock Exchange*) rialzista *m/f* su nuove emissioni

stage [steɪdʒ] *n* (*platform*) palco; (*in theatre*) palcoscenico; (*profession*): **the ~** il teatro, la scena; (*point*) fase *f*, stadio ■ *vt* (*play*) allestire, mettere in scena; (*demonstration*) organizzare; (*fig: perform: recovery etc*) effettuare; **in stages** per gradi; a tappe; **in the early/final stages** negli stadi iniziali/finali; **to go through a difficult ~** attraversare un periodo difficile

stagecoach ['steɪdʒkəutʃ] *n* diligenza

stage door *n* ingresso degli artisti

stage fright *n* paura del pubblico

stagehand ['steɪdʒhænd] *n* macchinista *m*

stage-manage ['steɪdʒmænɪdʒ] *vt* allestire le scene per; montare

stage manager *n* direttore *m* di scena

stagger ['stægə'] *vi* barcollare ■ *vt* (*person*) sbalordire; (*hours, holidays*) scaglionare

staggering ['stægərɪŋ] *adj* (*amazing*) incredibile, sbalorditivo(-a)

staging post ['steɪdʒɪŋ-] *n* passaggio obbligato

stagnant ['stægnənt] *adj* stagnante

stagnate [stæg'neɪt] *vi* (*also fig*) stagnare

stagnation [stæg'neɪʃən] *n* stagnazione *f*, ristagno

stag night, stag party *n* festa di addio al celibato

staid [steɪd] *adj* posato(-a), serio(-a)

stain [steɪn] *n* macchia; (*colouring*) colorante *m* ■ *vt* macchiare; (*wood*) tingere

stained glass window ['steɪnd-] *n* vetrata

stainless ['steɪnlɪs] *adj* (*steel*) inossidabile

stain remover *n* smacchiatore *m*

stair [stɛə'] *n* (*step*) gradino; **stairs** *npl* (*flight of stairs*) scale *fpl*, scala

staircase ['stɛəkeɪs], **stairway** ['stɛəweɪ] n scale fpl, scala

stairwell ['stɛəwɛl] n tromba delle scale

stake [steɪk] n palo, piolo; (Betting) puntata, scommessa ■ vt (bet) scommettere; (risk) rischiare; (also: **stake out**: area) delimitare con paletti; **to be at ~** essere in gioco; **to have a ~ in sth** avere un interesse in qc; **to ~ a claim (to sth)** rivendicare (qc)

stakeout ['steɪkaut] n sorveglianza

stalactite ['stæləktaɪt] n stalattite f

stalagmite ['stæləgmaɪt] n stalagmite f

stale [steɪl] adj (bread) raffermo(-a), stantio(-a); (beer) svaporato(-a); (smell) di chiuso

stalemate ['steɪlmeɪt] n stallo; (fig) punto morto

stalk [stɔːk] n gambo, stelo ■ vt inseguire ■ vi camminare impettito(-a)

stall [stɔːl] n (Brit: in street, market etc) bancarella; (in stable) box m inv di stalla ■ vt (Aut) far spegnere ■ vi (Aut) spegnersi, fermarsi; (fig) temporeggiare; **stalls** npl (Brit: in cinema, theatre) platea; **newspaper/flower ~** chiosco del giornalaio/del fioraio

stallholder ['stɔːlhəuldəʳ] n (Brit) bancarellista m/f

stallion ['stæljən] n stallone m

stalwart ['stɔːlwət] n membro fidato

stamen ['steɪmɛn] n stame m

stamina ['stæmɪnə] n vigore m, resistenza

stammer ['stæməʳ] n balbuzie f ■ vi balbettare

stamp [stæmp] n (postage stamp) francobollo; (implement) timbro; (mark, also fig) marchio, impronta; (on document) bollo; timbro ■ vi (also: **stamp one's foot**) battere il piede ■ vt battere; (letter) affrancare; (mark with a stamp) timbrare; **stamped addressed envelope** busta affrancata per la risposta
▶ **stamp out** vt (fire) estinguere; (crime) eliminare; (opposition) soffocare

stamp album n album m inv per francobolli

stamp collecting n filatelia

stamp duty n (Brit) bollo

stampede [stæm'piːd] n fuggi fuggi m inv; (of cattle) fuga precipitosa

stamp machine n distributore m automatico di francobolli

stance [stæns] n posizione f

stand [stænd] n (position) posizione f; (Mil) resistenza; (structure) supporto, sostegno; (at exhibition) stand m inv; (at market) bancarella; (booth) chiosco; (Sport) tribuna; (also: **music stand**) leggio m ■ vb (pt, pp **stood**) [stud] vi stare in piedi; (rise) alzarsi in piedi; (be placed) trovarsi ■ vt (place) mettere, porre; (tolerate,

withstand) resistere, sopportare; **to make a ~** prendere posizione; **to take a ~ on an issue** prendere posizione su un problema; **to ~ for parliament** (Brit) presentarsi come candidato (per il parlamento); **to ~ guard** or **watch** (Mil) essere di guardia; **it stands to reason** è logico; **as things ~** stando così le cose; **to ~ sb a drink/meal** offrire da bere/un pranzo a qn; **I can't ~ him** non lo sopporto
▶ **stand aside** vi farsi da parte, scostarsi
▶ **stand by** vi (be ready) tenersi pronto(-a) ■ vt fus (opinion) sostenere
▶ **stand down** vi (withdraw) ritirarsi; (Law) lasciare il banco dei testimoni
▶ **stand for** vt fus (signify) rappresentare, significare; (tolerate) sopportare, tollerare
▶ **stand in for** vt fus sostituire
▶ **stand out** vi (be prominent) spiccare
▶ **stand up** vi (rise) alzarsi in piedi
▶ **stand up for** vt fus difendere
▶ **stand up to** vt fus tener testa a, resistere a

stand-alone ['stændələun] adj (Comput) stand-alone inv

standard ['stændəd] n modello, standard m inv; (level) livello; (flag) stendardo ■ adj (size etc) normale, standard inv; (practice) normale; (model) di serie; **standards** npl (morals) principi mpl, valori mpl; **to be** or **come up to ~** rispondere ai requisiti; **below** or **not up to ~** (work) mediocre; **to apply a double ~** usare metri diversi (nel giudicare or fare etc); **~ of living** livello di vita

standardization [stændədaɪ'zeɪʃən] n standardizzazione f

standardize ['stændədaɪz] vt normalizzare, standardizzare

standard lamp n (Brit) lampada a stelo

standard time n ora ufficiale

stand-by ['stændbaɪ] n riserva, sostituto; **to be on ~** (gen) tenersi pronto(-a); (doctor) essere di guardia; **a ~ ticket** un biglietto standby; **to fly ~** essere in lista d'attesa per un volo

stand-by generator n generatore m d'emergenza

stand-by passenger n (Aviat) passeggero(-a) in lista d'attesa

stand-by ticket n (Aviat) biglietto senza garanzia

stand-in ['stændɪn] n sostituto(-a); (Cine) controfigura

standing ['stændɪŋ] adj diritto(-a), in piedi; (permanent: committee) permanente; (: rule) fisso(-a); (: army) regolare; (grievance) continuo(-a) ■ n rango, condizione f, posizione f; (duration): **of 6 months' ~** che dura da 6 mesi; **it's a ~ joke** è diventato

S

803

proverbiale; **he was given a ~ ovation** tutti si alzarono per applaudirlo; **a man of some ~** un uomo di una certa importanza

standing committee n commissione f permanente

standing order n (Brit: at bank) ordine m di pagamento (permanente); **standing orders** npl (Mil) regolamento

standing room n posto all'impiedi

stand-off ['stændɔf] n (esp US: stalemate) situazione f di stallo

standoffish [stænd'ɔfɪʃ] adj scostante, freddo(-a)

standpat ['stændpæt] adj (US) irremovibile

standpipe ['stændpaɪp] n fontanella

standpoint ['stændpɔɪnt] n punto di vista

standstill ['stændstɪl] n: **at a ~** fermo(-a); (fig) a un punto morto; **to come to a ~** fermarsi; giungere a un punto morto

stank [stæŋk] pt of **stink**

stanza ['stænzə] n stanza (poesia)

staple ['steɪpl] n (for papers) graffetta; (chief product) prodotto principale ■ adj (food etc) di base; (crop, industry) principale ■ vt cucire

stapler ['steɪplə^r] n cucitrice f

star [stɑ:^r] n stella; (celebrity) divo(-a); (principal actor) vedette f inv ■ vi: **to ~ (in)** essere il (or la) protagonista (di) ■ vt (Cine) essere interpretato(-a) da; **four-~ hotel** ≈ albergo di prima categoria; **2-~ petrol** (Brit) ≈ benzina normale; **4-~ petrol** (Brit) ≈ super f

star attraction n numero principale

starboard ['stɑ:bəd] n dritta; **to ~** a dritta

starch [stɑ:tʃ] n amido

starched ['stɑ:tʃt] adj (collar) inamidato(-a)

starchy ['stɑ:tʃɪ] adj (food) ricco(-a) di amido

stardom ['stɑ:dəm] n celebrità

stare [stɛə^r] n sguardo fisso ■ vi: **to ~ at** fissare

starfish ['stɑ:fɪʃ] n stella di mare

stark [stɑ:k] adj (bleak) desolato(-a); (simplicity, colour) austero(-a); (reality, poverty, truth) crudo(-a) ■ adv: **~ naked** completamente nudo(-a)

starkers ['stɑ:kəz] adj: **to be ~** (Brit col) essere nudo(-a) come un verme

starlet ['stɑ:lɪt] n (Cine) stellina

starlight ['stɑ:laɪt] n: **by ~** alla luce delle stelle

starling ['stɑ:lɪŋ] n storno

starlit ['stɑ:lɪt] adj stellato(-a)

starry ['stɑ:rɪ] adj stellato(-a)

starry-eyed [stɑ:rɪ'aɪd] adj (idealistic, gullible) ingenuo(-a); (from wonder) meravigliato(-a)

Stars and Stripes npl: **the ~** la bandiera a stelle e strisce

star sign n segno zodiacale

star-studded ['stɑ:stʌdɪd] adj: **a ~ cast** un cast di attori famosi

start [stɑ:t] n inizio; (of race) partenza; (sudden movement) sobbalzo; (advantage) vantaggio ■ vt cominciare, iniziare; (found: business, newspaper) fondare, creare ■ vi cominciare; (on journey) partire, mettersi in viaggio; (jump) sobbalzare; **to ~ doing sth** (in)cominciare a fare qc; **at the ~** all'inizio; **for a ~** tanto per cominciare; **to make an early ~** partire di buon'ora; **to ~ (off) with ...** (firstly) per prima cosa ...; (at the beginning) all'inizio; **to ~ a fire** provocare un incendio
▶ **start off** vi cominciare; (leave) partire
▶ **start over** vi (US) ricominciare
▶ **start up** vi cominciare; (car) avviarsi ■ vt iniziare; (car) avviare

starter ['stɑ:tə^r] n (Aut) motorino d'avviamento; (Sport: official) starter m inv; (: runner, horse) partente m/f; (Brit Culin) primo piatto

starting handle ['stɑ:tɪŋ-] n (Brit) manovella d'avviamento

starting point n punto di partenza

starting price n prezzo m base inv

startle ['stɑ:tl] vt far trasalire

startling ['stɑ:tlɪŋ] adj sorprendente, sbalorditivo(-a)

star turn n (Brit) attrazione f principale

starvation [stɑ:'veɪʃən] n fame f, inedia; **to die of ~** morire d'inedia

starve [stɑ:v] vi morire di fame; soffrire la fame ■ vt far morire di fame, affamare; **I'm starving** muoio di fame

stash [stæʃ] vt: **to ~ sth away** (col) nascondere qc

state [steɪt] n stato; (pomp): **in ~** in pompa ■ vt dichiarare, affermare; annunciare; **to be in a ~** essere agitato(-a); **the ~ of the art** il livello di tecnologia (or cultura etc); **~ of emergency** stato di emergenza; **~ of mind** stato d'animo

state control n controllo statale

stated ['steɪtɪd] adj fissato(-a), stabilito(-a)

State Department n (US) Dipartimento di Stato, ≈ Ministero degli Esteri

state education n (Brit) istruzione f pubblica or statale

stateless ['steɪtlɪs] adj apolide

stately ['steɪtlɪ] adj maestoso(-a), imponente

stately home n residenza nobiliare (d'interesse storico o artistico spesso aperta al pubblico)

statement ['steɪtmənt] n dichiarazione f; (Law) deposizione f; (Finance) rendiconto; **official ~** comunicato ufficiale; **~ of account, bank ~** estratto conto

state-owned ['steɪt'əʊnd] *adj* statalizzato(-a)
States [steɪts] *npl*: **the ~** (*USA*) gli Stati Uniti
state school *n* scuola statale
statesman ['steɪtsmən] *n* statista *m*
statesmanship ['steɪtsmənʃɪp] *n* abilità politica
static ['stætɪk] *n* (*Radio*) scariche *fpl* ■ *adj* statico(-a); **~ electricity** elettricità statica
station ['steɪʃən] *n* stazione *f*; (*rank*) rango, condizione *f* ■ *vt* collocare, disporre; **action stations** posti *mpl* di combattimento; **to be stationed in** (*Mil*) essere di stanza in
stationary ['steɪʃənərɪ] *adj* fermo(-a), immobile
stationer ['steɪʃənəʳ] *n* cartolaio(-a); **~'s shop** cartoleria
stationery ['steɪʃənərɪ] *n* articoli *mpl* di cancelleria; (*writing paper*) carta da lettere
station master *n* (*Rail*) capostazione *m*
station wagon *n* (*US*) giardinetta
statistic [stə'tɪstɪk] *n* statistica; *see also* **statistics**
statistical [stə'tɪstɪkəl] *adj* statistico(-a)
statistics [stə'tɪstɪks] *n* (*science*) statistica
statue ['stætjuː] *n* statua
statuesque [stætju'ɛsk] *adj* statuario(-a)
statuette [stætju'ɛt] *n* statuetta
stature ['stætʃəʳ] *n* statura
status ['steɪtəs] *n* posizione *f*, condizione *f* sociale; (*prestige*) prestigio; (*legal, marital*) stato
status quo [-'kwəʊ] *n*: **the ~** lo statu quo
status symbol *n* simbolo di prestigio
statute ['stætjuːt] *n* legge *f*; **statutes** *npl* (*of club etc*) statuto
statute book *n* codice *m*
statutory ['stætjutərɪ] *adj* stabilito(-a) dalla legge, statutario(-a); **~ meeting** (*Comm*) assemblea ordinaria
staunch [stɔːntʃ] *adj* fidato(-a), leale ■ *vt* (*flow*) arrestare; (*blood*) arrestare il flusso di
stave [steɪv] *n* (*Mus*) rigo ■ *vt*: **to ~ off** (*attack*) respingere; (*threat*) evitare
stay [steɪ] *n* (*period of time*) soggiorno, permanenza ■ *vi* rimanere; (*reside*) alloggiare, stare; (*spend some time*) trattenersi, soggiornare; **~ of execution** (*Law*) sospensione *f* dell'esecuzione; **to ~ put** non muoversi; **to ~ with friends** stare presso amici; **to ~ the night** passare la notte
▸ **stay behind** *vi* restare indietro
▸ **stay in** *vi* (*at home*) stare in casa
▸ **stay on** *vi* restare, rimanere
▸ **stay out** *vi* (*of house*) rimanere fuori (di casa); (*strikers*) continuare lo sciopero
▸ **stay up** *vi* (*at night*) rimanere alzato(-a)
staying power ['steɪɪŋ-] *n* capacità di resistenza

STD *n abbr* (*Brit*: = *subscriber trunk dialling*) teleselezione *f*; (= *sexually transmitted disease*) malattia venerea
stead [stɛd] *n* (*Brit*): **in sb's ~** al posto di qn; **to stand sb in good ~** essere utile a qn
steadfast ['stɛdfɑːst] *adj* fermo(-a), risoluto(-a)
steadily ['stɛdɪlɪ] *adv* continuamente; (*walk*) con passo sicuro
steady ['stɛdɪ] *adj* stabile, solido(-a), fermo(-a); (*regular*) costante; (*boyfriend etc*) fisso(-a); (*person*) calmo(-a), tranquillo(-a) ■ *vt* stabilizzare; calmare; **to ~ o.s.** ritrovare l'equilibrio
steak [steɪk] *n* (*meat*) bistecca; (*fish*) trancia
steakhouse ['steɪkhaus] *n ristorante specializzato in bistecche*
steal (*pt* **stole**, *pp* **stolen**) [stiːl, stəʊl, 'stəʊln] *vt* rubare ■ *vi* (*thieve*) rubare
▸ **steal away, steal off** *vi* svignarsela, andarsene alla chetichella
stealth [stɛlθ] *n*: **by ~** furtivamente
stealthy ['stɛlθɪ] *adj* furtivo(-a)
steam [stiːm] *n* vapore *m* ■ *vt* trattare con vapore; (*Culin*) cuocere a vapore ■ *vi* fumare; (*ship*): **to ~ along** filare; **to let off ~** (*fig*) sfogarsi; **under one's own ~** (*fig*) da solo, con i propri mezzi; **to run out of ~** (*fig*: *person*) non farcela più
▸ **steam up** *vi* (*window*) appannarsi; **to get steamed up about sth** (*fig*) andare in bestia per qc
steam engine *n* macchina a vapore; (*Rail*) locomotiva a vapore
steamer ['stiːməʳ] *n* piroscafo, vapore *m*; (*Culin*) pentola a vapore
steam iron *n* ferro a vapore
steamroller ['stiːmrəʊləʳ] *n* rullo compressore
steamship ['stiːmʃɪp] *n* piroscafo, vapore *m*
steamy ['stiːmɪ] *adj* pieno(-a) di vapore; (*window*) appannato(-a)
steed [stiːd] *n* (*literary*) corsiero, destriero
steel [stiːl] *n* acciaio ■ *cpd* di acciaio
steel band *n* banda di strumenti a percussione (*tipica dei Caribi*)
steel industry *n* industria dell'acciaio
steel mill *n* acciaieria
steelworks ['stiːlwəːks] *n* acciaieria
steely ['stiːlɪ] *adj* (*determination*) inflessibile; (*gaze*) duro(-a); (*eyes*) freddo(-a) come l'acciaio
steep [stiːp] *adj* ripido(-a), scosceso(-a); (*price*) eccessivo(-a) ■ *vt* inzuppare; (*washing*) mettere a mollo
steeple ['stiːpl] *n* campanile *m*
steeplechase ['stiːpltʃeɪs] *n* corsa a ostacoli, steeplechase *m inv*

S

805

steeplejack ['sti:pldʒæk] n chi ripara campanili e ciminiere

steer [stɪə'] n manzo ▪ vt (ship) governare; (car) guidare ▪ vi (Naut: person) governare; (: ship) rispondere al timone; (car) guidarsi; **to ~ clear of sb/sth** (fig) tenersi alla larga da qn/qc

steering ['stɪərɪŋ] n (Aut) sterzo

steering column n piantone m dello sterzo

steering committee n comitato direttivo

steering wheel n volante m

stem [stɛm] n (of flower, plant) stelo; (of tree) fusto; (of glass) gambo; (of fruit, leaf) picciolo ▪ vt contenere, arginare
  ▸ **stem from** vt fus provenire da, derivare da

stem cell n cellula staminale

stench [stɛntʃ] n puzzo, fetore m

stencil ['stɛnsl] n (of metal, cardboard) stampino, mascherina; (in typing) matrice f

stenographer [stɛ'nɔgrəfə'] n (US) stenografo(-a)

stenography [stɛ'nɔgrəfɪ] n (US) stenografia

step [stɛp] n passo; (stair) gradino, scalino; (action) mossa, azione f ▪ vi: **to ~ forward** fare un passo avanti; **steps** npl (Brit) = **stepladder**; **~ by ~** un passo dietro l'altro; (fig) poco a poco; **to be in/out of ~ with** (also fig) stare/non stare al passo con
  ▸ **step down** vi (fig) ritirarsi
  ▸ **step in** vi fare il proprio ingresso
  ▸ **step off** vt fus scendere da
  ▸ **step over** vt fus scavalcare
  ▸ **step up** vt aumentare; intensificare

step aerobics n step m inv

stepbrother ['stɛpbrʌðə'] n fratellastro

stepchild ['stɛptʃaɪld] n figliastro(-a)

stepdaughter ['stɛpdɔ:tə'] n figliastra

stepfather ['stɛpfɑ:ðə'] n patrigno

stepladder ['stɛplædə'] n scala a libretto

stepmother ['stɛpmʌðə'] n matrigna

stepping stone ['stɛpɪŋ-] n pietra di un guado; (fig) trampolino

step Reebok® [-'ri:bɔk] n step m inv

stepsister ['stɛpsɪstə'] n sorellastra

stepson ['stɛpsʌn] n figliastro

stereo ['stɛrɪəu] n (system) sistema m stereofonico; (record player) stereo m inv ▪ adj (also: **stereophonic**) stereofonico(-a); **in ~** in stereofonia

stereotype ['stɪərɪətaɪp] n stereotipo

sterile ['stɛraɪl] adj sterile

sterility [stɛ'rɪlɪtɪ] n sterilità

sterilization [stɛrɪlaɪ'zeɪʃən] n sterilizzazione f

sterilize ['stɛrɪlaɪz] vt sterilizzare

sterling ['stə:lɪŋ] adj (gold, silver) di buona lega; (fig) autentico(-a), genuino(-a) ▪ n

(Econ) (lira) sterlina; **a pound ~** una lira sterlina

sterling area n area della sterlina

stern [stə:n] adj severo(-a) ▪ n (Naut) poppa

sternum ['stə:nəm] n sterno

steroid ['stɛrɔɪd] n steroide m

stethoscope ['stɛθəskəup] n stetoscopio

stevedore ['sti:vɪdɔ:'] n scaricatore m di porto

stew [stju:] n stufato ▪ vt, vi cuocere in umido; **stewed tea** tè lasciato troppo in infusione; **stewed fruit** frutta cotta

steward ['stju:əd] n (Aviat, Naut, Rail) steward m inv; (in club etc) dispensiere m; (shop steward) rappresentante m/f sindacale

stewardess ['stju:ədɛs] n assistente f di volo, hostess f inv

stewardship ['stju:ədʃɪp] n amministrazione f

stewing steak ['stju:ɪŋ-], (US) **stew meat** n carne f (di manzo) per stufato

St. Ex. abbr = **stock exchange**

stg abbr = **sterling**

stick [stɪk] n bastone m; (of rhubarb, celery) gambo ▪ vb (pt, pp **stuck**) [stʌk] vt (glue) attaccare; (thrust): **to ~ sth into** conficcare or piantare or infiggere qc in; (col: put) ficcare; (: tolerate) sopportare ▪ vi conficcarsi; tenere; (remain) restare, rimanere; (get jammed: door, lift) bloccarsi; **to ~ to** (one's word, promise) mantenere; (principles) tener fede a; **to get hold of the wrong end of the ~** (fig) capire male; **it stuck in my mind** mi è rimasto in mente
  ▸ **stick around** vi (col) restare, fermarsi
  ▸ **stick out, stick up** vi sporgere, spuntare ▪ vt: **to ~ it out** (col) tener duro
  ▸ **stick up for** vt fus difendere

sticker ['stɪkə'] n cartellino adesivo

sticking plaster ['stɪkɪŋ-] n cerotto adesivo

sticking point n (fig) punto di stallo, impasse f inv

stick insect n insetto m stecco inv

stickleback ['stɪklbæk] n spinarello

stickler ['stɪklə'] n: **to be a ~ for** essere pignolo(-a) su, tenere molto a

stick-on ['stɪkɔn] adj (label) adesivo(-a)

stick shift n (US Aut) cambio manuale

stick-up ['stɪkʌp] n (col) rapina a mano armata

sticky ['stɪkɪ] adj attaccaticcio(-a), vischioso(-a); (label) adesivo(-a)

stiff [stɪf] adj rigido(-a), duro(-a); (muscle) legato(-a), indolenzito(-a); (difficult) difficile, arduo(-a); (cold: manner etc) freddo(-a), formale; (strong) forte; (high: price) molto alto(-a); **to be** or **feel ~** (person) essere or sentirsi indolenzito; **to have a ~ neck/back** avere il torcicollo/mal di schiena; **to keep a**

~ **upper lip** (*Brit fig*) conservare il sangue freddo

stiffen ['stɪfn] *vt* irrigidire; rinforzare ■ *vi* irrigidirsi; indurirsi

stiffness ['stɪfnɪs] *n* rigidità; indolenzimento; difficoltà; freddezza

stifle ['staɪfl] *vt* soffocare

stifling ['staɪflɪŋ] *adj* (*heat*) soffocante

stigma *n* (*Bot, Med*) (*pl* **stigmata**) (*fig*) (*pl* **stigmas**) ['stɪgmə, stɪg'mɑːtə] ■ *n* stigma *m*

stigmata [stig'mɑːtə] *npl* (*Rel*) stigmate *fpl*

stile [staɪl] *n* cavalcasiepe *m*; cavalcasteccato

stiletto [stɪ'lɛtəu] *n* (*also:* **stiletto heel**) tacco a spillo

still [stɪl] *adj* fermo(-a); (*quiet*) silenzioso(-a); (*orange juice etc*) non gassato(-a) ■ *adv* (*up to this time, even*) ancora; (*nonetheless*) tuttavia, ciò nonostante ■ *n* (*Cine*) fotogramma *m*; **keep ~!** stai fermo!; **he ~ hasn't arrived** non è ancora arrivato

stillborn ['stɪlbɔːn] *adj* nato(-a) morto(-a)

still life *n* natura morta

stilt [stɪlt] *n* trampolo; (*pile*) palo

stilted ['stɪltɪd] *adj* freddo(-a), formale; artificiale

stimulant ['stɪmjulənt] *n* stimolante *m*

stimulate ['stɪmjuleɪt] *vt* stimolare

stimulating ['stɪmjuleɪtɪŋ] *adj* stimolante

stimulation [stɪmju'leɪʃən] *n* stimolazione *f*

stimulus (*pl* **stimuli**) ['stɪmjuləs, 'stɪmjulaɪ] *n* stimolo

sting [stɪŋ] *n* puntura; (*organ*) pungiglione *m*; (*col*) trucco ■ *vb* (*pt, pp* **stung**) [stʌŋ] *vt* pungere ■ *vi* bruciare; **my eyes are stinging** mi bruciano gli occhi

stingy ['stɪndʒɪ] *adj* spilorcio(-a), tirchio(-a)

stink [stɪŋk] *n* fetore *m*, puzzo ■ *vi* (*pt* **stank**, *pp* **stunk**) [stæŋk, stʌŋk] puzzare

stinker ['stɪŋkəʳ] *n* (*col*) porcheria; (*person*) fetente *m/f*

stinking ['stɪŋkɪŋ] *adj* (*col*): **a ~ ...** uno schifo di ..., un(-a) maledetto(-a) ...; **~ rich** ricco(-a) da far paura

stint [stɪnt] *n* lavoro, compito ■ *vi*: **to ~ on** lesinare su

stipend ['staɪpɛnd] *n* stipendio, congrua

stipendiary [staɪ'pɛndɪərɪ] *adj*: **~ magistrate** magistrato stipendiato

stipulate ['stɪpjuleɪt] *vt* stipulare

stipulation [stɪpju'leɪʃən] *n* stipulazione *f*

stir [stəːʳ] *n* agitazione *f*, clamore *m* ■ *vt* rimescolare; (*move*) smuovere, agitare ■ *vi* muoversi; **to cause a ~** fare scalpore
▶ **stir up** *vt* provocare, suscitare

stir-fry ['stəː'fraɪ] *vt* saltare in padella ■ *n* pietanza al salto

stirring ['stəːrɪŋ] *adj* eccitante; commovente

stirrup ['stɪrəp] *n* staffa

stitch [stɪtʃ] *n* (*Sewing*) punto; (*Knitting*) maglia; (*Med*) punto (di sutura); (*pain*) fitta ■ *vt* cucire, attaccare; suturare

stoat [stəut] *n* ermellino

stock [stɔk] *n* riserva, provvista; (*Comm*) giacenza, stock *m inv*; (*Agr*) bestiame *m*; (*Culin*) brodo; (*Finance*) titoli *mpl*, azioni *fpl*; (*Rail: also:* **rolling stock**) materiale *m* rotabile; (*descent, origin*) stirpe *f* ■ *adj* (*fig: reply etc*) consueto(-a), solito(-a), classico(-a); (*greeting*) usuale; (*Comm: goods, size*) standard *inv* ■ *vt* (*have in stock*) avere, vendere; **well-stocked** ben fornito(-a); **to have sth in ~** avere qc in magazzino; **out of ~** esaurito(-a); **to take ~** (*fig*) fare il punto; **stocks and shares** valori *mpl* di borsa; **government ~** titoli di Stato
▶ **stock up** *vi*: **to ~ up (with)** fare provvista (di)

stockade [stɔ'keɪd] *n* palizzata

stockbroker ['stɔkbrəukəʳ] *n* agente *m* di cambio

stock control *n* gestione *f* magazzino

stock cube *n* (*Brit Culin*) dado

stock exchange *n* Borsa (valori)

stockholder ['stɔkhəuldəʳ] *n* (*Finance*) azionista *m/f*

Stockholm ['stɔkhəum] *n* Stoccolma

stocking ['stɔkɪŋ] *n* calza

stock-in-trade ['stɔkɪn'treɪd] *n* (*fig*): **it's his ~** è la sua specialità

stockist ['stɔkɪst] *n* (*Brit*) fornitore *m*

stock market *n* (*Brit*) Borsa, mercato finanziario

stock phrase *n* cliché *m inv*

stockpile ['stɔkpaɪl] *n* riserva ■ *vt* accumulare riserve di

stockroom ['stɔkrum] *n* magazzino

stocktaking ['stɔkteɪkɪŋ] *n* (*Brit Comm*) inventario

stocky ['stɔkɪ] *adj* tarchiato(-a), tozzo(-a)

stodgy ['stɔdʒɪ] *adj* pesante, indigesto(-a)

stoic ['stəuɪk] *n* stoico(-a)

stoical ['stəuɪkəl] *adj* stoico(-a)

stoke [stəuk] *vt* alimentare

stoker ['stəukəʳ] *n* fochista *m*

stole [stəul] *pt of* **steal** ■ *n* stola

stolen ['stəuln] *pp of* **steal**

stolid ['stɔlɪd] *adj* impassibile

stomach ['stʌmək] *n* stomaco; (*abdomen*) ventre *m* ■ *vt* sopportare, digerire

stomach ache *n* mal *m* di stomaco

stomach pump *n* pompa gastrica

stomach ulcer *n* ulcera allo stomaco

stomp [stɔmp] *vi*: **to ~ in/out** *etc* entrare/ uscire *etc* con passo pesante

S

stone [stəun] n pietra; (*pebble*) sasso, ciottolo; (*in fruit*) nocciolo; (*Med*) calcolo; (*Brit: weight*) 6.348 kg., 14 libbre ■ cpd di pietra ■ vt lapidare; **within a ~'s throw of the station** a due passi dalla stazione

Stone Age n: **the ~** l'età della pietra

stone-cold [stəun'kəuld] adj gelido(-a)

stoned [stəund] adj (*col: drunk*) sbronzo(-a); (*on drugs*) fuori inv

stone-deaf [stəun'dɛf] adj sordo(-a) come una campana

stonemason ['stəunmeɪsn] n scalpellino

stonewall [stəun'wɔːl] vi fare ostruzionismo ■ vt ostacolare

stonework ['stəunwəːk] n muratura

stony ['stəunɪ] adj pietroso(-a), sassoso(-a)

stood [stud] pt, pp of **stand**

stooge [stuːdʒ] n (*col*) tirapiedi m/f inv

stool [stuːl] n sgabello

stoop [stuːp] vi (*also:* **have a stoop**) avere una curvatura; (*bend*) chinarsi, curvarsi; **to ~ to sth/doing sth** abbassarsi a qc/a fare qc

stop [stɔp] n arresto; (*stopping place*) fermata; (*in punctuation*) punto ■ vt arrestare, fermare; (*break off*) interrompere; (*also:* **put a stop to**) porre fine a; (*prevent*) impedire ■ vi fermarsi; (*rain, noise etc*) cessare, finire; **to ~ doing sth** cessare or finire di fare qc; **to ~ sb (from) doing sth** impedire a qn di fare qc; **to ~ dead** fermarsi di colpo; **~ it!** smettila!, basta!
  ▸ **stop by** vi passare, fare un salto
  ▸ **stop off** vi sostare brevemente
  ▸ **stop up** vt (*hole*) chiudere, turare

stopcock ['stɔpkɔk] n rubinetto di arresto

stopgap ['stɔpgæp] n (*person*) tappabuchi m/f inv; (*measure*) ripiego ■ cpd (*measures, solution*) di fortuna

stoplights ['stɔplaɪts] npl (*Aut*) stop mpl

stopover ['stɔpəuvə'] n breve sosta; (*Aviat*) scalo

stoppage ['stɔpɪdʒ] n arresto, fermata; (*of pay*) trattenuta; (*strike*) interruzione f del lavoro

stopper ['stɔpə'] n tappo

stop press n ultimissime fpl

stopwatch ['stɔpwɔtʃ] n cronometro

storage ['stɔːrɪdʒ] n immagazzinamento; (*Comput*) memoria

storage heater n (*Brit*) radiatore m elettrico che accumula calore

store [stɔː'] n provvista, riserva; (*depot*) deposito; (*Brit: department store*) grande magazzino; (*US: shop*) negozio ■ vt mettere da parte; conservare; (*grain, goods*) immagazzinare; (*Comput*) registrare; **to set great/little ~ by sth** dare molta/poca importanza a qc; **who knows what is in ~ for us?** chissà cosa ci riserva il futuro?

▸ **store up** vt mettere in serbo, conservare

storehouse ['stɔːhaus] n magazzino, deposito

storekeeper ['stɔːkiːpə'] n (*US*) negoziante m/f

storeroom ['stɔːrum] n dispensa

storey, (*US*) **story** ['stɔːrɪ] n piano

stork [stɔːk] n cicogna

storm [stɔːm] n tempesta; (*also:* **thunderstorm**) temporale m; (*fig*) infuriarsi ■ vt prendere d'assalto

storm cloud n nube f temporalesca

storm door n controporta

stormy ['stɔːmɪ] adj tempestoso(-a), burrascoso(-a)

story ['stɔːrɪ] n storia; racconto; (*Press*) articolo; (*US*) = **storey**

storybook ['stɔːrɪbuk] n libro di racconti

storyteller ['stɔːrɪtɛlə'] n narratore(-trice)

stout [staut] adj solido(-a), robusto(-a); (*brave*) coraggioso(-a); (*fat*) corpulento(-a), grasso(-a) ■ n birra scura

stove [stəuv] n (*for cooking*) fornello; (*small*) fornelletto; (*for heating*) stufa; **gas/electric ~** cucina a gas/elettrica

stow [stəu] vt mettere via

stowaway ['stəuəweɪ] n passeggero(-a) clandestino(-a)

straddle ['strædl] vt stare a cavalcioni di

straggle ['strægl] vi crescere (*or* estendersi) disordinatamente; trascinarsi; rimanere indietro; **straggled along the coast** disseminati(-e) lungo la costa

straggler ['stræglə'] n sbandato(-a)

straggling ['stræglɪŋ], **straggly** ['stræglɪ] adj (*hair*) in disordine

straight [streɪt] adj (*continuous, direct*) dritto(-a); (*frank*) onesto(-a), franco(-a); (*plain, uncomplicated*) semplice; (*Theat: part, play*) serio(-a); (*col: heterosexual*) eterosessuale ■ adv diritto; (*drink*) liscio ■ n: **the ~** la linea retta; (*Rail*) il rettilineo; (*Sport*) la dirittura d'arrivo; **to put** or **get ~** mettere in ordine, mettere ordine in; **to be (all) ~** (*tidy*) essere a posto, essere sistemato; (*clarified*) essere chiaro; **ten ~ wins** dieci vittorie di fila; **~ away, ~ off** (*at once*) immediatamente; **~ off, ~ out** senza esitare; **I went ~ home** sono andato direttamente a casa

straighten ['streɪtn] vt (*also:* **straighten out**) raddrizzare; **to ~ things out** mettere le cose a posto

straighteners ['streɪtnəz] npl (*for hair*) piastra f per capelli

straight-faced [streɪt'feɪst] adj impassibile, imperturbabile ■ adv con il viso serio

straightforward [streɪt'fɔːwəd] adj semplice; (*frank*) onesto(-a), franco(-a)

strain [streɪn] n (Tech) sollecitazione f;
(physical) sforzo; (mental) tensione f; (Med)
strappo; (streak, trace) tendenza; elemento;
(breed) razza; (of virus) tipo ■ vt tendere;
(muscle) slogare; (ankle) storcere; (friendship,
marriage) mettere a dura prova; (filter) colare,
filtrare ■ vi sforzarsi; **strains** npl (Mus) note
fpl; **she's under a lot of ~** è molto tesa,
è sotto pressione

strained [streɪnd] adj (laugh etc) forzato(-a);
(relations) teso(-a)

strainer ['streɪnəʳ] n passino, colino

strait [streɪt] n (Geo) stretto; **to be in dire
straits** (fig) essere nei guai

straitjacket ['streɪtdʒækɪt] n camicia di
forza

strait-laced [streɪt'leɪst] adj puritano(-a)

strand [strænd] n (of thread) filo

strange [streɪndʒ] adj (not known)
sconosciuto(-a); (odd) strano(-a), bizzarro(-a)

strangely ['streɪndʒlɪ] adv stranamente

stranger ['streɪndʒəʳ] n (unknown)
sconosciuto(-a); (from another place)
estraneo(-a); **I'm a ~ here** non sono del posto

strangle ['stræŋgl] vt strangolare

stranglehold ['stræŋglhəʊld] n (fig) stretta
(mortale)

strangulation [stræŋgjuˈleɪʃən] n
strangolamento

strap [stræp] n cinghia; (of slip, dress) spallina,
bretella ■ vt legare con una cinghia; (child
etc) punire (con una cinghia)

straphanging ['stræphæŋɪŋ] n viaggiare m
in piedi (su mezzi pubblici reggendosi a un sostegno)

strapless ['stræplɪs] adj (bra, dress) senza
spalline

strapped [stræpt] adj: ~ **for cash** a corto di
soldi; **financially ~** finanziariamente a
terra

strapping ['stræpɪŋ] adj ben piantato(-a)

Strasbourg ['stræzbəːg] n Strasburgo f

strata ['strɑːtə] npl of **stratum**

stratagem ['strætɪdʒəm] n stratagemma m

strategic [strəˈtiːdʒɪk] adj strategico(-a)

strategist ['strætɪdʒɪst] n strategia m

strategy ['strætɪdʒɪ] n strategia

stratosphere ['strætəsfɪəʳ] n stratosfera

stratum (pl **strata**) ['strɑːtəm, 'strɑːtə] n
strato

straw [strɔː] n paglia; (drinking straw)
cannuccia; **that's the last ~!** è la goccia che
fa traboccare il vaso!

strawberry ['strɔːbərɪ] n fragola

stray [streɪ] adj (animal) randagio(-a) ■ vi
perdersi; allontanarsi, staccarsi (dal
gruppo); ~ **bullet** proiettile m vagante

streak [striːk] n striscia; (fig: of madness etc):

a ~ of una vena di ■ vt striare, screziare
■ vi: **to ~ past** passare come un fulmine;
to have streaks in one's hair avere le
mèche nei capelli; **a winning/losing ~**
un periodo fortunato/sfortunato

streaker ['striːkəʳ] n streaker m/f inv

streaky ['striːkɪ] adj screziato(-a), striato(-a)

streaky bacon n (Brit) ≈ pancetta

stream [striːm] n ruscello; corrente f; (of
people) fiume m ■ vt (Scol) dividere in livelli
di rendimento ■ vi scorrere; **to ~ in/out**
entrare/uscire a fiotti; **against the ~**
controcorrente; **on ~** (new power plant etc) in
funzione, in produzione

streamer ['striːməʳ] n (of paper) stella filante

stream feed n (on photocopier etc)
alimentazione f continua

streamline ['striːmlaɪn] vt dare una linea
aerodinamica a; (fig) razionalizzare

streamlined ['striːmlaɪnd] adj
aerodinamico(-a), affusolato(-a); (fig)
razionalizzato(-a)

street [striːt] n strada, via; **the back streets**
le strade secondarie; **to be on the streets**
(homeless) essere senza tetto; (as prostitute)
battere il marciapiede

streetcar ['striːtkɑːʳ] n (US) tram m inv

street cred [-kred] n (col) credibilità presso
i giovani

street lamp n lampione m

street lighting n illuminazione f stradale

street map, street plan n pianta (di una
città)

street market n mercato all'aperto

streetwise ['striːtwaɪz] adj (col) esperto(-a)
dei bassifondi

strength [strenθ] n forza; (of girder, knot etc)
resistenza, solidità; (of chemical solution)
concentrazione f; (of wine) gradazione f
alcolica; **on the ~ of** sulla base di, in virtù di;
below/at full ~ con gli effettivi ridotti/al
completo

strengthen ['strenθən] vt rinforzare;
(muscles) irrobustire; (economy, currency)
consolidare

strenuous ['strenjuəs] adj vigoroso(-a),
energico(-a); (tiring) duro(-a), pesante

stress [stres] n (force, pressure) pressione f;
(mental strain) tensione f; (accent) accento;
(emphasis) enfasi f ■ vt insistere su,
sottolineare; **to be under ~** essere sotto
tensione; **to lay great ~ on sth** dare grande
importanza a qc

stressful ['stresful] adj (job) difficile,
stressante

stretch [stretʃ] n (of sand etc) distesa; (of time)
periodo ■ vi stirarsi; (extend): **to ~ to** or

S

as far as estendersi fino a; (be enough: money, food): **to ~ (to)** bastare (per) ■ vt tendere, allungare; (spread) distendere; (fig) spingere (al massimo); **at a ~** ininterrottamente; **to ~ a muscle** tendere un muscolo; **to ~ one's legs** sgranchirsi le gambe

▶ **stretch out** vi allungarsi, estendersi ■ vt (arm etc) allungare, tendere; (spread) distendere; **to ~ out for sth** allungare la mano per prendere qc

stretcher ['strɛtʃəʳ] n barella, lettiga

stretcher-bearer ['strɛtʃəbɛərəʳ] n barelliere m

stretch marks npl smagliature fpl

strewn [struːn] adj: **~ with** cosparso(-a) di

stricken ['strɪkən] adj provato(-a), affranto(-a); **~ with** colpito(-a) da

strict [strɪkt] adj (severe) rigido(-a), severo(-a); (: order, rule) rigoroso(-a); (: supervision) stretto(-a); (precise) preciso(-a), stretto(-a); **in ~ confidence** in assoluta confidenza

strictly ['strɪktlɪ] adv severamente; rigorosamente; strettamente; **~ confidential** strettamente confidenziale; **~ speaking** a rigor di termini; **~ between ourselves** ... detto fra noi ...

stride [straɪd] n passo lungo ■ vi (pt **strode**, pp **stridden**) [strəʊd, 'strɪdn] camminare a grandi passi; **to take in one's ~** (fig: changes etc) prendere con tranquillità

strident ['straɪdnt] adj stridente

strife [straɪf] n conflitto; litigi mpl

strike [straɪk] n sciopero; (of oil etc) scoperta; (attack) attacco ■ vb (pt, pp **struck**) [strʌk] vt colpire; (oil etc) scoprire, trovare; (produce, make: coin, medal) coniare; (: agreement, deal) concludere ■ vi far sciopero, scioperare; (attack) attaccare; (clock) suonare; **to go on** or **come out on ~** mettersi in sciopero; **to ~ a match** accendere un fiammifero; **to ~ a balance** (fig) trovare il giusto mezzo

▶ **strike back** vi (Mil) fare rappresaglie; (fig) reagire

▶ **strike down** vt (fig) atterrare

▶ **strike off** vt (from list) cancellare; (: doctor etc) radiare

▶ **strike out** vt depennare

▶ **strike up** vt (Mus) attaccare; **to ~ up a friendship** fare amicizia con

strikebreaker ['straɪkbreɪkəʳ] n crumiro(-a)

striker ['straɪkəʳ] n scioperante m/f; (Sport) attaccante m

striking ['straɪkɪŋ] adj impressionante

Strimmer® ['strɪməʳ] n tagliabordi m inv

string [strɪŋ] n spago; (row) fila; sequenza; catena; (Comput) stringa, sequenza; (Mus) corda ■ vt (pt, pp **strung**) [strʌŋ]: **to ~ out**

disporre di fianco; **to ~ together** mettere insieme; **the strings** npl (Mus) gli archi; **~ of pearls** filo di perle; **with no strings attached** (fig) senza vincoli, senza obblighi; **to get a job by pulling strings** ottenere un lavoro a forza di raccomandazioni

string bean n fagiolino

stringed instrument, string instrument n (Mus) strumento a corda

stringent ['strɪndʒənt] adj rigoroso(-a); (reasons, arguments) stringente, impellente

string quartet n quartetto d'archi

strip [strɪp] n striscia; (Sport): **wearing the Celtic ~** con la divisa del Celtic ■ vt spogliare; (also: **strip down**: machine) smontare ■ vi spogliarsi

strip cartoon n fumetto

stripe [straɪp] n striscia, riga

striped ['straɪpt] adj a strisce or righe

strip light n (Brit) tubo al neon

stripper ['strɪpəʳ] n spogliarellista

strip-search ['strɪpsəːtʃ] vt: **to ~ sb** perquisire qn facendolo(-a) spogliare ■ n perquisizione f (facendo spogliare il perquisito)

striptease ['strɪptiːz] n spogliarello

strive (pt **strove**, pp **striven**) [straɪv, strəʊv, 'strɪvn] vi: **to ~ to do** sforzarsi di fare

strobe [strəʊb] n (also: **strobe light**) luce f stroboscopica

strode [strəʊd] pt of **stride**

stroke [strəʊk] n colpo; (of piston) corsa; (Med) colpo apoplettico; (Swimming: style) nuoto; (caress) carezza ■ vt accarezzare; **at a ~** in un attimo; **on the ~ of 5** alle 5 in punto, allo scoccare delle 5; **a ~ of luck** un colpo di fortuna; **two-~ engine** motore a due tempi

stroll [strəʊl] n giretto, passeggiatina ■ vi andare a spasso; **to go for a ~, have** or **take a ~** andare a fare un giretto or due passi

stroller ['strəʊləʳ] n (US) passeggino

strong [strɒŋ] adj (gen) forte; (sturdy: table, fabric etc) solido(-a); (concentrated, intense: bleach, acid) concentrato(-a); (protest, letter, measures) energico(-a) ■ adv: **to be going ~** (company) andare a gonfie vele; (person) essere attivo(-a); **they are 50 ~** sono in 50; **~ language** (swearing) linguaggio volgare

strong-arm ['strɒŋɑːm] adj (tactics, methods) energico(-a)

strongbox ['strɒŋbɒks] n cassaforte f

stronghold ['strɒŋhəʊld] n fortezza, roccaforte f

strongly ['strɒŋlɪ] adv fortemente, con forza; solidamente; energicamente; **to feel ~ about sth** avere molto a cuore qc

strongman ['strɒŋmæn] n personaggio di spicco

strongroom ['strɔŋrum] *n* camera di sicurezza

stroppy ['strɔpɪ] *adj* (*Brit col*) scontroso(-a), indisponente

strove [strəuv] *pt of* **strive**

struck [strʌk] *pt, pp of* **strike**

structural ['strʌktʃərəl] *adj* strutturale; (*Constr*) di costruzione; di struttura

structurally ['strʌktʃrəlɪ] *adv* dal punto di vista della struttura

structure ['strʌktʃəʳ] *n* struttura; (*building*) costruzione *f*, fabbricato

struggle ['strʌgl] *n* lotta ■ *vi* lottare; **to have a ~ to do sth** avere dei problemi per fare qc

strum [strʌm] *vt* (*guitar*) strimpellare

strung [strʌŋ] *pt, pp of* **string**

strut [strʌt] *n* sostegno, supporto ■ *vi* pavoneggiarsi

strychnine ['strɪkniːn] *n* stricnina

stub [stʌb] *n* mozzicone *m*; (*of ticket etc*) matrice *f*, tallonino ■ *vt*: **to ~ one's toe (on sth)** urtare *or* sbattere il dito del piede (contro qc)

▸ **stub out** *vt*: **to ~ out a cigarette** spegnere una sigaretta

stubble ['stʌbl] *n* stoppia; (*on chin*) barba ispida

stubborn ['stʌbən] *adj* testardo(-a), ostinato(-a)

stubby ['stʌbɪ] *adj* tozzo(-a)

stucco ['stʌkəu] *n* stucco

stuck [stʌk] *pt, pp of* **stick** ■ *adj* (*jammed*) bloccato(-a); **to get ~** bloccarsi

stuck-up [stʌk'ʌp] *adj* presuntuoso(-a)

stud [stʌd] *n* bottoncino; borchia; (*of horses*) scuderia, allevamento di cavalli; (*also:* **stud horse**) stallone *m* ■ *vt* (*fig*): **studded with** tempestato(-a) di

student ['stjuːdənt] *n* studente(-essa) ■ *cpd* studentesco(-a); universitario(-a); degli studenti; **a law/medical ~** uno studente di legge/di medicina

student driver *n* (*US*) conducente *m/f* principiante

students' union *n* (*Brit: association*) circolo universitario; (: *building*) sede *f* del circolo universitario

studied ['stʌdɪd] *adj* studiato(-a), calcolato(-a)

studio ['stjuːdɪəu] *n* studio

studio flat, (*US*) **studio apartment** *n* appartamento monolocale

studious ['stjuːdɪəs] *adj* studioso(-a); (*studied*) studiato(-a), voluto(-a)

studiously ['stjuːdɪəslɪ] *adv* (*carefully*) deliberatamente, di proposito

study ['stʌdɪ] *n* studio ■ *vt* studiare; esaminare ■ *vi* studiare; **to make a ~ of sth** fare uno studio su qc; **to ~ for an exam** prepararsi a un esame

stuff [stʌf] *n* (*substance*) roba; (*belongings*) cose *fpl*, roba ■ *vt* imbottire; (*animal: for exhibition*) impagliare; (*Culin*) farcire; **my nose is stuffed up** ho il naso chiuso; **get stuffed!** (*col!*) va' a farti fottere! (*!*); **stuffed toy** giocattolo di peluche

stuffing ['stʌfɪŋ] *n* imbottitura; (*Culin*) ripieno

stuffy ['stʌfɪ] *adj* (*room*) mal ventilato(-a), senz'aria; (*ideas*) antiquato(-a)

stumble ['stʌmbl] *vi* inciampare; **to ~ across** (*fig*) imbattersi in

stumbling block ['stʌmblɪŋ-] *n* ostacolo, scoglio

stump [stʌmp] *n* ceppo; (*of limb*) moncone *m* ■ *vt*: **to be stumped for an answer** essere incapace di rispondere

stun [stʌn] *vt* stordire; (*amaze*) sbalordire

stung [stʌŋ] *pt, pp of* **sting**

stunk [stʌŋk] *pp of* **stink**

stunning ['stʌnɪŋ] *adj* (*piece of news etc*) sbalorditivo(-a); (*girl, dress*) favoloso(-a), stupendo(-a)

stunt [stʌnt] *n* bravata; trucco pubblicitario; (*Aviat*) acrobazia ■ *vt* arrestare

stunted ['stʌntɪd] *adj* stentato(-a), rachitico(-a)

stuntman ['stʌntmæn] *n* cascatore *m*

stupefaction [stjuːpɪ'fækʃən] *n* stupefazione *f*, stupore *m*

stupefy ['stjuːpɪfaɪ] *vt* stordire; intontire; (*fig*) stupire

stupendous [stjuː'pɛndəs] *adj* stupendo(-a), meraviglioso(-a)

stupid ['stjuːpɪd] *adj* stupido(-a)

stupidity [stjuː'pɪdɪtɪ] *n* stupidità

stupidly ['stjuːpɪdlɪ] *adv* stupidamente

stupor ['stjuːpəʳ] *n* torpore *m*

sturdy ['stəːdɪ] *adj* robusto(-a), vigoroso(-a), solido(-a)

sturgeon ['stəːdʒən] *n* storione *m*

stutter ['stʌtəʳ] *n* balbuzie *f* ■ *vi* balbettare

Stuttgart ['ʃtutgart] *n* Stoccarda

sty [staɪ] *n* (*of pigs*) porcile *m*

stye [staɪ] *n* (*Med*) orzaiolo

style [staɪl] *n* stile *m*; (*distinction*) eleganza, classe *f*; (*hairstyle*) pettinatura; (*of dress etc*) modello, linea; **in the latest ~** all'ultima moda

styli ['staɪlaɪ] *npl of* **stylus**

stylish ['staɪlɪʃ] *adj* elegante

stylist ['staɪlɪst] *n*: **hair ~** parrucchiere(-a)

stylized ['staɪlaɪzd] *adj* stilizzato(-a)

S

stylus (pl **styluses** or **styli**) ['staɪləs, -laɪ] n (of record player) puntina

Styrofoam® ['staɪrəfəʊm] n (US) = **polystyrene** ■ adj (cup) di polistirene

suave [swɑːv] adj untuoso(-a)

sub [sʌb] n abbr = **submarine; subscription**

sub... [sʌb] prefix sub..., sotto...

subcommittee ['sʌbkəmɪtɪ] n sottocomitato

subconscious [sʌb'kɔnʃəs] adj, n subcosciente m

subcontinent [sʌb'kɔntɪnənt] n: **the (Indian)** ~ il subcontinente (indiano)

subcontract n [sʌb'kɔntrækt] subappalto ■ vt [sʌbkən'trækt] subappaltare

subcontractor ['sʌbkən'træktəʳ] n subappaltatore(-trice)

subdivide [sʌbdɪ'vaɪd] vt suddividere

subdivision ['sʌbdɪvɪʒən] n suddivisione f

subdue [səb'djuː] vt sottomettere, soggiogare

subdued [səb'djuːd] adj pacato(-a); (light) attenuato(-a); (person) poco esuberante

sub-editor ['sʌb'ɛdɪtəʳ] n (Brit) redattore(-a) aggiunto(-a)

subject ['sʌbdʒɪkt] n soggetto; (citizen etc) cittadino(-a); (Scol) materia ■ adj (liable): ~ **to** soggetto(-a) a ■ vt [səb'dʒɛkt]: **to** ~ **to** sottomettere a; esporre a; ~ **to confirmation in writing** a condizione di ricevere conferma scritta; **to change the** ~ cambiare discorso

subjection [səb'dʒɛkʃən] n sottomissione f, soggezione f

subjective [səb'dʒɛktɪv] adj soggettivo(-a)

subject matter n argomento; contenuto

sub judice [sʌb'dʒuːdɪsɪ] adj (Law) sub iudice

subjugate ['sʌbdʒugeɪt] vt sottomettere, soggiogare

subjunctive [səb'dʒʌŋktɪv] adj congiuntivo(-a) ■ n congiuntivo

sublet [sʌb'lɛt] vt, vi irreg subaffittare

sublime [sə'blaɪm] adj sublime

subliminal [sʌb'lɪmɪnl] adj subliminale

submachine gun ['sʌbmə'ʃiːn-] n mitra m inv

submarine [sʌbmə'riːn] n sommergibile m

submerge [səb'məːdʒ] vt sommergere; immergere ■ vi immergersi

submersion [səb'məːʃən] n sommersione f; immersione f

submission [səb'mɪʃən] n sottomissione f; (to committee etc) richiesta, domanda

submissive [səb'mɪsɪv] adj remissivo(-a)

submit [səb'mɪt] vt sottomettere; (proposal, claim) presentare ■ vi sottomettersi

subnormal [sʌb'nɔːməl] adj subnormale

subordinate [sə'bɔːdɪnət] adj, n subordinato(-a)

subpoena [səb'piːnə] n (Law) citazione f,

mandato di comparizione ■ vt (Law) citare in giudizio

subroutine ['sʌbruːtiːn] n (Comput) sottoprogramma m

subscribe [səb'skraɪb] vi contribuire; **to** ~ **to** (opinion) approvare, condividere; (fund) sottoscrivere; (newspaper) abbonarsi a; essere abbonato(-a) a

subscriber [səb'skraɪbəʳ] n (to periodical, telephone) abbonato(-a)

subscript ['sʌbskrɪpt] n deponente m

subscription [səb'skrɪpʃən] n sottoscrizione f; abbonamento; **to take out a** ~ **to** abbonarsi a

subsequent ['sʌbsɪkwənt] adj (later) successivo(-a); (further) ulteriore; ~ **to** in seguito a

subsequently ['sʌbsɪkwəntlɪ] adv in seguito, successivamente

subservient [səb'səːvɪənt] adj: ~ **(to)** remissivo(-a) (a), sottomesso(-a) (a)

subside [səb'saɪd] vi cedere, abbassarsi; (flood) decrescere; (wind) calmarsi

subsidence [səb'saɪdns] n cedimento, abbassamento

subsidiarity [səbsɪdɪ'ærɪtɪ] n (Pol) principio del decentramento del potere

subsidiary [səb'sɪdɪərɪ] adj sussidiario(-a); accessorio(-a); (Brit Scol: subject) complementare ■ n filiale f

subsidize ['sʌbsɪdaɪz] vt sovvenzionare

subsidy ['sʌbsɪdɪ] n sovvenzione f

subsist [səb'sɪst] vi: **to** ~ **on sth** vivere di qc

subsistence [səb'sɪstəns] n esistenza; mezzi mpl di sostentamento

subsistence allowance n indennità f inv di trasferta

subsistence level n livello minimo di vita

substance ['sʌbstəns] n sostanza; (fig) essenza; **to lack** ~ (argument) essere debole

substance abuse n abuso di sostanze tossiche

substandard [sʌb'stændəd] adj (goods, housing) di qualità scadente

substantial [səb'stænʃl] adj solido(-a); (amount, progress etc) notevole; (meal) sostanzioso(-a)

substantially [səb'stænʃəlɪ] adv sostanzialmente; ~ **bigger** molto più grande

substantiate [səb'stænʃɪeɪt] vt comprovare

substitute ['sʌbstɪtjuːt] n (person) sostituto(-a); (thing) succedaneo, surrogato ■ vt: **to** ~ **sth/sb for** sostituire qc/qn a

substitute teacher n (US) supplente m/f

substitution [sʌbstɪ'tjuːʃən] n sostituzione f

subterfuge ['sʌbtəfjuːdʒ] n sotterfugio

subterranean [sʌbtə'reɪnɪən] adj
sotterraneo(-a)
subtitle ['sʌbtaɪtl] n (Cine) sottotitolo
subtle ['sʌtl] adj sottile; (flavour, perfume)
delicato(-a)
subtlety ['sʌtltɪ] n sottigliezza
subtly ['sʌtlɪ] adv sottilmente; delicatamente
subtotal [sʌb'təutl] n somma parziale
subtract [səb'trækt] vt sottrarre
subtraction [səb'trækʃən] n sottrazione f
suburb ['sʌbə:b] n sobborgo; **the suburbs** la
periferia
suburban [sə'bə:bən] adj suburbano(-a)
suburbia [sə'bə:bɪə] n periferia, sobborghi
mpl
subversion [səb'və:ʃən] n sovversione f
subversive [səb'və:sɪv] adj sovversivo(-a)
subway ['sʌbweɪ] n (US: underground)
metropolitana; (Brit: underpass)
sottopassaggio
subzero [sʌb'zɪərəu] adj: **~ temperatures**
temperature fpl sotto zero
succeed [sək'si:d] vi riuscire, avere successo
■ vt succedere a; **to ~ in doing** riuscire a fare
succeeding [sək'si:dɪŋ] adj (following)
successivo(-a); **~ generations** generazioni
fpl future
success [sək'sɛs] n successo
successful [sək'sɛsful] adj (venture)
coronato(-a) da successo, riuscito(-a); **to be ~
(in doing)** riuscire (a fare)
successfully [sək'sɛsfəlɪ] adv con successo
succession [sək'sɛʃən] n successione f; **in ~**
di seguito
successive [sək'sɛsɪv] adj successivo(-a);
consecutivo(-a); **on 3 ~ days** per 3 giorni
consecutivi or di seguito
successor [sək'sɛsə'] n successore m
succinct [sək'sɪŋkt] adj succinto(-a), breve
succulent ['sʌkjulənt] adj succulento(-a) ■ n
(Bot): **succulents** piante fpl grasse
succumb [sə'kʌm] vi soccombere
such [sʌtʃ] adj tale; (of that kind): **~ a book** un
tale libro, un libro del genere; **~ books** tali
libri, libri del genere; (so much): **~ courage**
tanto coraggio ■ adv: **~ a long trip** un
viaggio così lungo; **~ good books** libri così
buoni; **~ a lot of** talmente or così tanto(-a);
making ~ a noise that facendo un rumore
tale che; **~ a long time ago** tanto tempo fa;
~ as (like) come; **a noise ~ as to** un rumore
tale da; **~ books as I have** quei pochi libri
che ho; **as ~** come or in quanto tale; **I said no
~ thing** non ho detto niente del genere
such-and-such ['sʌtʃənsʌtʃ] adj tale (after
noun)
suchlike ['sʌtʃlaɪk] pron (col): **and ~** e così via

suck [sʌk] vt succhiare; (baby) poppare;
(pump, machine) aspirare
sucker ['sʌkə'] n (Zool, Tech) ventosa; (Bot)
pollone m; (col) gonzo(-a), babbeo(-a)
suckle ['sʌkl] vt allattare
sucrose ['su:krəuz] n saccarosio
suction ['sʌkʃən] n succhiamento; (Tech)
aspirazione f
suction pump n pompa aspirante
Sudan [su:'dɑ:n] n Sudan m
Sudanese [su:də'ni:z] adj, n sudanese m/f
sudden ['sʌdn] adj improvviso(-a); **all of a ~**
improvvisamente, all'improvviso
sudden-death [sʌdn'dɛθ] n (also: **sudden-
death playoff**: Sport) spareggio, bella
suddenly ['sʌdnlɪ] adv bruscamente,
improvvisamente, di colpo
sudoku [su'dəuku:] n sudoku m inv
suds [sʌdz] npl schiuma (di sapone)
sue [su:] vt citare in giudizio ■ vi: **to ~ (for)**
intentare causa (per); **to ~ for divorce**
intentare causa di divorzio; **to ~ sb for
damages** citare qn per danni
suede [sweɪd] n pelle f scamosciata ■ cpd
scamosciato(-a)
suet ['suɪt] n grasso di rognone
Suez ['su:ɪz] n: **the ~ Canal** il Canale di Suez
suffer ['sʌfə'] vt soffrire, patire; (bear)
sopportare, tollerare; (undergo: loss, setback)
subire ■ vi soffrire; **to ~ from** soffrire di;
to ~ from the effects of alcohol/a fall
risentire degli effetti dell'alcool/di una
caduta
sufferance ['sʌfərəns] n: **he was only there
on ~** era più che altro sopportato lì
sufferer ['sʌfərə'] n (Med): **~ (from)**
malato(-a) (di)
suffering ['sʌfərɪŋ] n sofferenza; (hardship,
deprivation) privazione f
suffice [sə'faɪs] vi essere sufficiente, bastare
sufficient [sə'fɪʃənt] adj sufficiente; **~ money**
abbastanza soldi
sufficiently [sə'fɪʃəntlɪ] adv
sufficientemente, abbastanza
suffix ['sʌfɪks] n suffisso
suffocate ['sʌfəkeɪt] vi (have difficulty breathing)
soffocare; (die through lack of air) asfissiare
suffocation [sʌfə'keɪʃən] n soffocamento;
(Med) asfissia
suffrage ['sʌfrɪdʒ] n suffragio
suffuse [sə'fju:z] vt: **to ~ (with)** (colour)
tingere (di); (light) soffondere (di); **her face
was suffused with joy** la gioia si dipingeva
sul suo volto
sugar ['ʃugə'] n zucchero ■ vt zuccherare
sugar beet n barbabietola da zucchero
sugar bowl n zuccheriera

S

sugar cane n canna da zucchero
sugar-coated ['ʃugəkəutɪd] adj ricoperto(-a) di zucchero
sugar lump n zolletta di zucchero
sugar refinery n raffineria di zucchero
sugary ['ʃugərɪ] adj zuccherino(-a), dolce; (fig) sdolcinato(-a)
suggest [sə'dʒɛst] vt proporre, suggerire; (indicate) indicare; **what do you ~ I do?** cosa mi suggerisce di fare?
suggestion [sə'dʒɛstʃən] n suggerimento, proposta
suggestive [sə'dʒɛstɪv] adj suggestivo(-a); (indecent) spinto(-a), indecente
suicidal [suɪ'saɪdl] adj suicida inv; (fig) fatale, disastroso(-a)
suicide ['suɪsaɪd] n (person) suicida m/f; (act) suicidio; **to commit ~** suicidarsi
suicide attempt, suicide bid n tentato suicidio
suicide bomber n attentatore(-trice) suicida
suicide bombing n attentato suicida
suit [su:t] n (man's) completo; (woman's) completo, tailleur m inv; (lawsuit) causa; (Cards) seme m, colore m ■ vt andar bene a or per; essere adatto(-a) a or per; (adapt): **to ~ sth to** adattare qc a; **to be suited to sth** (suitable for) essere adatto a qc; **well suited** (couple) fatti l'uno per l'altro; **to bring a ~ against sb** intentare causa a qn; **to follow ~** (fig) fare altrettanto
suitable ['su:təbl] adj adatto(-a); appropriato(-a); **would tomorrow be ~?** andrebbe bene domani?; **we found somebody ~** abbiamo trovato la persona adatta
suitably ['su:təblɪ] adv (dress) in modo adatto; (thank) adeguatamente
suitcase ['su:tkeɪs] n valigia
suite [swi:t] n (of rooms) appartamento; (Mus) suite f inv; (furniture): **bedroom/dining room ~** arredo or mobilia per la camera da letto/sala da pranzo; **a three-piece ~** un salotto comprendente un divano e due poltrone
suitor ['su:təʳ] n corteggiatore m, spasimante m
sulfate ['sʌlfeɪt] n (US) = **sulphate**
sulfur etc ['sʌlfəʳ] (US) = **sulphur** etc
sulk [sʌlk] vi fare il broncio
sulky ['sʌlkɪ] adj imbronciato(-a)
sullen ['sʌlən] adj scontroso(-a); cupo(-a)
sulphate, (US) sulfate ['sʌlfeɪt] n solfato; **copper ~** solfato di rame
sulphur, (US) sulfur ['sʌlfəʳ] n zolfo
sulphur dioxide n biossido di zolfo
sulphuric, (US) sulfuric [sʌl'fjuərɪk] adj: **~ acid** acido solforico

sultan ['sʌltən] n sultano
sultana [sʌl'tɑːnə] n (fruit) uva (secca) sultanina
sultry ['sʌltrɪ] adj afoso(-a)
sum [sʌm] n somma; (Scol etc) addizione f
  ▶ **sum up** vt riassumere; (evaluate rapidly) valutare, giudicare ■ vi riassumere
Sumatra [su'mɑːtrə] n Sumatra
summarize ['sʌməraɪz] vt riassumere, riepilogare
summary ['sʌmərɪ] n riassunto ■ adj (justice) sommario(-a)
summer ['sʌməʳ] n estate f ■ cpd d'estate, estivo(-a); **in (the) ~** d'estate
summer camp n (US) colonia (estiva)
summerhouse ['sʌməhaus] n (in garden) padiglione m
summertime ['sʌmətaɪm] n (season) estate f
summer time n (by clock) ora legale (estiva)
summery ['sʌmərɪ] adj estivo(-a)
summing-up [sʌmɪŋ'ʌp] n (Law) ricapitolazione f del processo
summit ['sʌmɪt] n cima, sommità; (Pol) vertice m
summit conference n conferenza al vertice
summon ['sʌmən] vt chiamare, convocare; **to ~ a witness** citare un testimone
  ▶ **summon up** vt raccogliere, fare appello a
summons n ordine m di comparizione ■ vt citare; **to serve a ~ on sb** notificare una citazione a qn
sumo ['su:məu] n (also: **sumo wrestling**) sumo
sump [sʌmp] n (Aut) coppa dell'olio
sumptuous ['sʌmptjuəs] adj sontuoso(-a)
Sun. abbr (= Sunday) dom.
sun [sʌn] n sole m; **in the ~** al sole; **to catch the ~** prendere sole; **they have everything under the ~** hanno tutto ciò che possono desiderare
sunbathe ['sʌnbeɪð] vi prendere un bagno di sole
sunbeam ['sʌnbi:m] n raggio di sole
sunbed ['sʌnbed] n lettino solare
sunblock ['sʌnblɔk] n crema solare a protezione totale
sunburn ['sʌnbə:n] n (tan) abbronzatura; (painful) scottatura
sunburnt ['sʌnbə:nt], **sunburned** ['sʌnbə:nd] adj abbronzato(-a); (painfully) scottato(-a) dal sole
sun cream n crema solare
sundae ['sʌndeɪ] n coppa di gelato guarnita
Sunday ['sʌndɪ] n domenica; see also **Tuesday**
Sunday paper n giornale m della domenica; vedi nota

Sunday papers

I *Sunday papers* sono i giornali che escono di domenica. Sono generalmente corredati da supplementi e riviste di argomento culturale, sportivo e di attualità ed hanno un'alta tiratura.

Sunday school n ≈ scuola di catechismo
sundial ['sʌndaɪəl] n meridiana
sundown ['sʌndaun] n tramonto
sundries ['sʌndrɪz] npl articoli diversi, cose diverse
sundry ['sʌndrɪ] adj vari(-e), diversi(-e); **all and ~** tutti quanti
sunflower ['sʌnflauə'] n girasole m
sung [sʌŋ] pp of **sing**
sunglasses ['sʌnglɑːsɪz] npl occhiali mpl da sole
sunk [sʌŋk] pp of **sink**
sunken ['sʌŋkən] adj sommerso(-a); (eyes, cheeks) infossato(-a); (bath) incassato(-a)
sunlamp ['sʌnlæmp] n lampada a raggi ultravioletti
sunlight ['sʌnlaɪt] n (luce f del) sole m
sunlit ['sʌnlɪt] adj assolato(-a), soleggiato(-a)
sunny ['sʌnɪ] adj assolato(-a), soleggiato(-a); (fig) allegro(-a), felice; **it is ~** c'è il sole
sunrise ['sʌnraɪz] n levata del sole, alba
sunroof ['sʌnruːf] n (on building) tetto a terrazzo; (Aut) tetto apribile
sunscreen ['sʌnskriːn] n crema solare protettiva
sunset ['sʌnsɛt] n tramonto
sunshade ['sʌnʃeɪd] n parasole m
sunshine ['sʌnʃaɪn] n (luce f del) sole m
sunspot ['sʌnspɔt] n macchia solare
sunstroke ['sʌnstrəuk] n insolazione f, colpo di sole
suntan ['sʌntæn] n abbronzatura
suntanned ['sʌntænd] adj abbronzato(-a)
suntan oil n olio solare
suntrap ['sʌntræp] n luogo molto assolato, angolo pieno di sole
super ['suːpə'] adj (col) fantastico(-a)
superannuation [suːpərænju'eɪʃən] n contributi mpl pensionistici, pensione f
superb [suː'pəːb] adj magnifico(-a)
Super Bowl n (US Sport) Super Bowl m inv
supercilious [suːpə'sɪlɪəs] adj sprezzante, sdegnoso(-a)
superconductor [suːpəkən'dʌktə'] n superconduttore m
superficial [suːpə'fɪʃəl] adj superficiale
superficially [suːpə'fɪʃəlɪ] adv superficialmente
superfluous [su'pəːfluəs] adj superfluo(-a)

superglue ['suːpəgluː] n colla a presa rapida
superhighway ['suːpəhaɪweɪ] n (US) autostrada; **the information ~** l'autostrada telematica
superhuman [suːpə'hjuːmən] adj sovrumano(-a)
superimpose ['suːpərɪm'pəuz] vt sovrapporre
superintend [suːpərɪn'tɛnd] vt dirigere, sovraintendere
superintendent [suːpərɪn'tɛndənt] n direttore(-trice); (Police) ≈ commissario (capo)
superior [su'pɪərɪə'] adj superiore; (Comm: goods, quality) di prim'ordine, superiore; (smug: person) che fa il superiore ■ n superiore m/f; **Mother S~** (Rel) Madre f Superiora, Superiora
superiority [supɪərɪ'ɔrɪtɪ] n superiorità
superlative [su'pəːlətɪv] adj superlativo(-a), supremo(-a) ■ n (Ling) superlativo
superman ['suːpəmæn] n superuomo
supermarket ['suːpəmɑːkɪt] n supermercato
supermodel ['suːpəmɔdl] n top model m/f inv
supernatural [suːpə'nætʃərəl] adj soprannaturale
supernova [suːpə'nəuvə] n supernova
superpower ['suːpəpauə'] n (Pol) superpotenza
superscript ['suːpəskrɪpt] n esponente m
supersede [suːpə'siːd] vt sostituire, soppiantare
supersonic ['suːpə'sɔnɪk] adj supersonico(-a)
superstar ['suːpəstɑː'] adj, n superstar (f) inv
superstition [suːpə'stɪʃən] n superstizione f
superstitious [suːpə'stɪʃəs] adj superstizioso(-a)
superstore ['suːpəstɔː'] n (Brit) grande supermercato
supertanker ['suːpətæŋkə'] n superpetroliera
supertax ['suːpətæks] n soprattassa
supervise ['suːpəvaɪz] vt (person etc) sorvegliare; (organization) soprintendere a
supervision [suːpə'vɪʒən] n sorveglianza, supervisione f; **under medical ~** sotto controllo medico
supervisor ['suːpəvaɪzə'] n sorvegliante m/f, soprintendente m/f; (in shop) capocommesso(-a); (at university) relatore(-trice)
supervisory ['suːpəvaɪzərɪ] adj di sorveglianza
supine ['suːpaɪn] adj supino(-a)
supper ['sʌpə'] n cena; **to have ~** cenare
supplant [sə'plɑːnt] vt soppiantare
supple ['sʌpl] adj flessibile; agile

S

815

supplement n ['sʌplɪmənt] supplemento ■ vt [sʌplɪ'mɛnt] completare, integrare
supplementary [sʌplɪ'mɛntərɪ] adj supplementare
supplementary benefit n (Brit) forma di indennità assistenziale
supplier [sə'plaɪəʳ] n fornitore m
supply [sə'plaɪ] vt (goods): **to ~ sth (to sb)** fornire qc (a qn); (people, organization): **to ~ sb (with sth)** fornire a qn (qc); (system, machine): **to ~ sth (with sth)** alimentare qc (con qc); (a need) soddisfare ■ n riserva, provvista; (supplying) approvvigionamento; (Tech) alimentazione f; **supplies** npl (food) viveri mpl; (Mil) sussistenza; **office supplies** forniture fpl per ufficio; **to be in short ~** scarseggiare, essere scarso(-a); **the electricity/water/gas ~** l'erogazione f di corrente/d'acqua/di gas; **~ and demand** la domanda e l'offerta; **the car comes supplied with a radio** l'auto viene fornita completa di radio
supply teacher n (Brit) supplente m/f
support [sə'pɔːt] n (moral, financial etc) sostegno, appoggio; (Tech) supporto ■ vt sostenere; (financially) mantenere; (uphold) sostenere, difendere; (Sport: team) fare il tifo per; **they stopped work in ~ (of)** hanno smesso di lavorare per solidarietà (con); **to ~ o.s.** (financially) mantenersi
supporter [sə'pɔːtəʳ] n (Pol etc) sostenitore(-trice), fautore(-trice); (Sport) tifoso(-a)
supporting [sə'pɔːtɪŋ] adj (wall) di sostegno
supporting actor n attore m non protagonista
supporting actress n attrice f non protagonista
supporting role n ruolo non protagonista
supportive [sə'pɔːtɪv] adj d'appoggio; **I have a ~ wife/family** mia moglie/la mia famiglia mi appoggia
suppose [sə'pəuz] vt, vi supporre; immaginare; **to be supposed to do** essere tenuto(-a) a fare; **always supposing (that) he comes** ammesso e non concesso che venga; **I don't ~ she'll come** non credo che venga; **he's supposed to be an expert** dicono che sia un esperto, passa per un esperto
supposedly [sə'pəuzɪdlɪ] adv presumibilmente; (seemingly) apparentemente
supposing [sə'pəuzɪŋ] conj se, ammesso che + sub
supposition [sʌpə'zɪʃən] n supposizione f, ipotesi f inv

suppository [sə'pɔzɪtərɪ] n supposta, suppositorio
suppress [sə'prɛs] vt reprimere; sopprimere, tenere segreto(-a)
suppression [sə'prɛʃən] n repressione f; soppressione f
suppressor [sə'prɛsəʳ] n (Elec etc) soppressore m
supremacy [su'prɛməsɪ] n supremazia
supreme [su'priːm] adj supremo(-a)
Supreme Court n (US) Corte f suprema; **~ of Judicature** corte di giudizio suprema dell'Inghilterra e del Galles
supremo [su'priːməu] n autorità f inv massima
Supt. abbr (Police) = **superintendent**
surcharge ['səːtʃɑːdʒ] n supplemento; (extra tax) soprattassa
sure [ʃuəʳ] adj sicuro(-a); (definite, convinced) sicuro(-a), certo(-a) ■ adv (col: US): **that ~ is pretty, that's ~ pretty** è veramente or davvero carino; **~!** (of course) senz'altro!, certo!; **~ enough** infatti; **to make ~ of** assicurarsi di; **to be ~ of sth** essere sicuro di qc; **to be ~ of o.s.** essere sicuro di sé; **I'm not ~ how/why/when** non so bene come/perché/quando + sub
sure-fire ['ʃuəfaɪəʳ] adj (col) infallibile
sure-footed [ʃuə'futɪd] adj dal passo sicuro
surely ['ʃuəlɪ] adv sicuramente; certamente; **~ you don't mean that!** non parlerà sul serio!
surety ['ʃuərətɪ] n garanzia; **to go** or **stand ~ for sb** farsi garante per qn
surf [səːf] n (waves) cavalloni mpl; (foam) spuma ■ vt: **to ~ the Net** navigare in Internet
surface ['səːfɪs] n superficie f ■ vt (road) asfaltare ■ vi risalire alla superficie; (fig: person) venire a galla, farsi vivo(-a); **on the ~ it seems that ...** (fig) superficialmente sembra che ...
surface area n superficie f
surface mail n posta ordinaria
surface-to-surface ['səːfɪstə'səːfɪs] adj (Mil) terra-terra inv
surfboard ['səːfbɔːd] n tavola per surfing
surfeit ['səːfɪt] n: **a ~ of** un eccesso di; un'indigestione di
surfer ['səːfəʳ] n (in sea) surfista m/f; (on the internet) navigatore(-trice)
surfing ['səːfɪŋ] n surfing m
surge [səːdʒ] n (strong movement) ondata; (of feeling) impeto; (Elec) sovracorrente f transitoria ■ vi (waves) gonfiarsi; (Elec: power) aumentare improvvisamente; **to ~ forward** buttarsi avanti
surgeon ['səːdʒən] n chirurgo

Surgeon General n (US) ≈ Ministro della Sanità

surgery ['sə:dʒərɪ] n chirurgia; (Brit Med: room) studio or gabinetto medico, ambulatorio; (: session) visita ambulatoriale; (Brit: of MP etc) incontri mpl con gli elettori; **to undergo ~** subire un intervento chirurgico

surgery hours npl (Brit) orario delle visite or di consultazione

surgical ['sə:dʒɪkl] adj chirurgico(-a)

surgical spirit n (Brit) alcool denaturato

surly ['sə:lɪ] adj scontroso(-a), burbero(-a)

surmise [sə:'maɪz] vt supporre, congetturare

surmount [sə:'maunt] vt sormontare

surname ['sə:neɪm] n cognome m

surpass [sə:'pɑ:s] vt superare

surplus ['sə:pləs] n eccedenza; (Econ) surplus m inv ■ adj eccedente, d'avanzo; **it is ~ to our requirements** eccede i nostri bisogni; **~ stock** merce f in sovrappiù

surprise [sə'praɪz] n sorpresa; (astonishment) stupore m ■ vt sorprendere; stupire; **to take by ~** (person) cogliere di sorpresa; (Mil: town, fort) attaccare di sorpresa

surprising [sə'praɪzɪŋ] adj sorprendente, stupefacente

surprisingly [se'praɪzɪŋlɪ] adv sorprendentemente; **(somewhat) ~, he agreed** cosa (alquanto) sorprendente, ha accettato

surrealism [sə'rɪəlɪzəm] n surrealismo

surrealist [sə'rɪəlɪst] adj, n surrealista m/f

surrender [sə'rendə^r] n resa, capitolazione f ■ vi arrendersi ■ vt (claim, right) rinunciare a

surrender value n (Comm) valore m di riscatto

surreptitious [sʌrəp'tɪʃəs] adj furtivo(-a)

surrogate ['sʌrəgɪt] n (Brit: substitute) surrogato ■ adj surrogato(-a)

surrogate mother n madre f sostitutiva

surround [sə'raund] vt circondare; (Mil etc) accerchiare

surrounding [sə'raundɪŋ] adj circostante

surroundings [sə'raundɪŋz] npl dintorni mpl; (fig) ambiente m

surtax ['sə:tæks] n soprattassa

surveillance [sə:'veɪləns] n sorveglianza, controllo

survey n ['sə:veɪ] (comprehensive view: of situation, development) quadro generale; (study) indagine f, studio; (in housebuying etc) perizia; (of land) rilevamento, rilievo topografico ■ vt [sə:'veɪ] osservare; esaminare; (Surveying: building) fare una perizia di; (: land) fare il rilevamento di

surveying [sə'veɪɪŋ] n (of land) agrimensura

surveyor [sə'veɪə^r] n perito; (of land) agrimensore m

survival [sə'vaɪvl] n sopravvivenza; (relic) reliquia, vestigio

survival course n corso di sopravvivenza

survival kit n equipaggiamento di prima necessità

survive [sə'vaɪv] vi sopravvivere ■ vt sopravvivere a

survivor [sə'vaɪvə^r] n superstite m/f, sopravvissuto(-a)

susceptible [sə'septəbl] adj: **~ (to)** sensibile (a); (disease) predisposto(-a) (a)

suspect ['sʌspɛkt] adj sospetto(-a) ■ n persona sospetta ■ vt [səs'pɛkt] sospettare; (think likely) supporre; (doubt) dubitare di

suspected [səs'pɛktɪd] adj presunto(-a); **to have a ~ facture** avere una sospetta frattura

suspend [səs'pɛnd] vt sospendere

suspended animation n: **in a state of ~** in stato comatoso

suspended sentence n condanna con la condizionale

suspender belt [səs'pɛndə^r-] n (Brit) reggicalze m inv

suspenders [səs'spendəz] npl (Brit) giarrettiere fpl; (US) bretelle fpl

suspense [səs'pɛns] n apprensione f; (in film etc) suspense m

suspension [səs'pɛnʃən] n (gen, Aut) sospensione f; (of driving licence) ritiro temporaneo

suspension bridge n ponte m sospeso

suspicion [səs'pɪʃən] n sospetto; **to be under ~** essere sospettato; **arrested on ~ of murder** arrestato come presunto omicida

suspicious [səs'pɪʃəs] adj (suspecting) sospettoso(-a); (causing suspicion) sospetto(-a); **to be ~ of** or **about sb/sth** nutrire sospetti nei riguardi di qn/qc

suss out vt (Brit col): **I've sussed it/him out** ho capito come stanno le cose/che tipo è

sustain [səs'teɪn] vt sostenere; sopportare; (suffer) subire

sustainable [səs'teɪnəbl] adj sostenibile

sustained [sə'steɪnd] adj (effort) prolungato(-a)

sustenance ['sʌstɪnəns] n nutrimento; mezzi mpl di sostentamento

suture ['su:tʃə^r] n sutura

SUV n abbr = **sports utility vehicle**

SW abbr (Radio: = short wave) O.C.

swab [swɔb] n (Med) tampone m ■ vt (Naut: also: **swab down**) radazzare

swagger ['swægə^r] vi pavoneggiarsi

swallow ['swɔləu] n (bird) rondine f; (of food) boccone m; (of drink) sorso ■ vt inghiottire; (fig: story) bere

▶ **swallow up** vt inghiottire

S

swam [swæm] *pt of* **swim**

swamp [swɔmp] *n* palude *f* ■ *vt* sommergere

swampy ['swɔmpɪ] *adj* palludoso(-a), pantanoso(-a)

swan [swɔn] *n* cigno

swank [swæŋk] *vi* (*col: talk boastfully*) fare lo spaccone; (*: show off*) mettersi in mostra

swan song *n* (*fig*) canto del cigno

swap [swɔp] *n* scambio ■ *vt*: **to ~ (for)** scambiare (con)

SWAPO ['swɑːpəu] *n abbr* = **South-West Africa People's Organization**

swarm [swɔːm] *n* sciame *m* ■ *vi* formicolare; (*bees*) sciamare

swarthy ['swɔːðɪ] *adj* di carnagione scura

swashbuckling ['swɔʃbʌklɪŋ] *adj* (*role, hero*) spericolato(-a)

swastika ['swɔstɪkə] *n* croce *f* uncinata, svastica

SWAT [swɔt] *n abbr* (*US*: = *Special Weapons and Tactics*) reparto speciale di polizia; (= *a SWAT team*) uno squadrone del reparto speciale (di polizia)

swat [swɔt] *vt* schiacciare ■ *n* (*Brit: also:* **fly swat**) ammazzamosche *m inv*

swathe [sweɪð] *n* fascio ■ *vt*: **to ~ in** (*bandages, blankets*) avvolgere in

swatter ['swɔtəʳ] *n* (*also:* **fly swatter**) ammazzamosche *m inv*

sway [sweɪ] *vi* (*building*) oscillare; (*tree*) ondeggiare; (*person*) barcollare ■ *vt* (*influence*) influenzare ■ *n* (*rule, power*): **~ (over)** influenza (su); **to hold ~ over sb** dominare qn

Swaziland ['swɑːzɪlænd] *n* Swaziland *m*

swear (*pt* **swore**, *pp* **sworn**) [sweəʳ, swɔːʳ, swɔːn] *vi* (*witness etc*) giurare; (*curse*) bestemmiare, imprecare ■ *vt*: **to ~ an oath** prestare giuramento; **to ~ to sth** giurare qc
  ▶ **swear in** *vt* prestare giuramento a

swearword ['sweəwəːd] *n* parolaccia

sweat [swɛt] *n* sudore *m*, traspirazione *f* ■ *vi* sudare; **in a ~** in un bagno di sudore

sweatband ['swɛtbænd] *n* (*Sport*) fascia elastica (per assorbire il sudore)

sweater ['swɛtəʳ] *n* maglione *m*

sweatshirt ['swɛtʃəːt] *n* maglione *m* in cotone felpato

sweatshop ['swɛtʃɔp] *n* azienda o fabbrica dove i dipendenti sono sfruttati

sweaty ['swɛtɪ] *adj* sudato(-a); bagnato(-a) di sudore

Swede [swiːd] *n* svedese *m/f*

swede [swiːd] *n* (*Brit*) rapa svedese

Sweden ['swiːdn] *n* Svezia

Swedish ['swiːdɪʃ] *adj* svedese ■ *n* (*Ling*) svedese *m*

sweep [swiːp] *n* spazzata; (*curve*) curva; (*expanse*) distesa; (*range*) portata; (*also:* **chimney sweep**) spazzacamino ■ *vb* (*pt, pp* **swept**) [swɛpt] *vt* spazzare, scopare; (*fashion, craze*) invadere ■ *vi* camminare maestosamente; precipitarsi, lanciarsi; (e)stendersi
  ▶ **sweep away** *vt* spazzare via; trascinare via
  ▶ **sweep past** *vi* sfrecciare accanto; passare accanto maestosamente
  ▶ **sweep up** *vt, vi* spazzare

sweeper ['swiːpəʳ] *n* (*person*) spazzino(-a); (*machine*) spazzatrice *f*; (*Football*) libero

sweeping ['swiːpɪŋ] *adj* (*gesture*) ampio(-a); (*changes, reforms*) ampio(-a), radicale; **a ~ statement** un'affermazione generica

sweepstake ['swiːpsteɪk] *n* lotteria (*spesso abbinata alle corse dei cavalli*)

sweet [swiːt] *n* (*Brit*) dolce *m*; (*candy*) caramella ■ *adj* dolce; (*fresh*) fresco(-a); (*kind*) gentile; (*cute*) carino(-a) ■ *adv*: **to smell/taste ~** avere un odore/sapore dolce; **~ and sour** *adj* agrodolce

sweetbread ['swiːtbrɛd] *n* animella

sweetcorn ['swiːtkɔːn] *n* granturco dolce

sweeten ['swiːtn] *vt* addolcire; zuccherare

sweetener ['swiːtnəʳ] *n* (*Culin*) dolcificante *m*

sweetheart ['swiːthɑːt] *n* innamorato(-a)

sweetly ['swiːtlɪ] *adv* dolcemente

sweetness ['swiːtnɪs] *n* sapore *m* dolce; dolcezza

sweet pea *n* pisello odoroso

sweet potato *n* patata americana, patata dolce

sweetshop ['swiːtʃɔp] *n* (*Brit*) ≈ pasticceria

sweet tooth *n*: **to have a ~** avere un debole per i dolci

swell [swɛl] *n* (*of sea*) mare *m* lungo ■ *adj* (*col: excellent*) favoloso(-a) ■ *vb* (*pt* **swelled**, *pp* **swollen, swelled**) ['swəulən] *vt* gonfiare, ingrossare; (*numbers, sales etc*) aumentare ■ *vi* gonfiarsi, ingrossarsi; (*sound*) crescere; (*Med*) gonfiarsi

swelling ['swɛlɪŋ] *n* (*Med*) tumefazione *f*, gonfiore *m*

sweltering ['swɛltərɪŋ] *adj* soffocante

swept [swɛpt] *pt, pp of* **sweep**

swerve [swəːv] *vi* deviare; (*driver*) sterzare; (*boxer*) scartare

swift [swɪft] *n* (*bird*) rondone *m* ■ *adj* rapido(-a), veloce

swiftly ['swɪftlɪ] *adv* rapidamente, velocemente

swiftness ['swɪftnɪs] *n* rapidità, velocità

swig [swɪg] *n* (*col: drink*) sorsata

swill [swɪl] *n* broda ▪ *vt* (*also*: **swill down**) risciacquare

swim [swɪm] *n*: **to go for a ~** andare a fare una nuotata ▪ *vb* (*pt* **swam**, *pp* **swum**) [swæm, swʌm] *vi* nuotare; (*Sport*) fare del nuoto; (*head, room*) girare ▪ *vt* (*river, channel*) attraversare *or* percorrere a nuoto; **to go swimming** andare a nuotare; **to ~ a length** fare una vasca (a nuoto)

swimmer ['swɪmə'] *n* nuotatore(-trice)

swimming ['swɪmɪŋ] *n* nuoto

swimming baths *npl* (*Brit*) piscina

swimming cap *n* cuffia

swimming costume *n* (*Brit*) costume *m* da bagno

swimmingly ['swɪmɪŋlɪ] *adv*: **to go ~** (*wonderfully*) andare a gonfie vele

swimming pool *n* piscina

swimming trunks *npl* costume *m* da bagno (per uomo)

swimsuit ['swɪmsuːt] *n* costume *m* da bagno

swindle ['swɪndl] *n* truffa ▪ *vt* truffare

swindler ['swɪndlə'] *n* truffatore(-trice)

swine [swaɪn] *n* (*pl inv*) maiale *m*, porco; (*col!*) porco (!)

swine flu *n* influenza suina

swing [swɪŋ] *n* altalena; (*movement*) oscillazione *f*; (*Mus*) ritmo; (*also*: **swing music**) swing *m* ▪ *vb* (*pt, pp* **swung**) [swʌŋ] *vt* dondolare, far oscillare; (*also*: **swing round**) far girare ▪ *vi* oscillare, dondolare; (*also*: **swing round**: *object*) roteare; (: *person*) girarsi, voltarsi; **to be in full ~** (*activity*) essere in piena attività; (*party etc*) essere nel pieno; **a ~ to the left** (*Pol*) una svolta a sinistra; **to get into the ~ of things** entrare nel pieno delle cose; **the road swings south** la strada prende la direzione sud

swing bridge *n* ponte *m* girevole

swing door *n* (*Brit*) porta battente

swingeing ['swɪndʒɪŋ] *adj* (*Brit*: *defeat*) violento(-a); (: *price increase*) enorme

swinging ['swɪŋɪŋ] *adj* (*step*) cadenzato(-a), ritmico(-a); (*rhythm, music*) trascinante; **~ door** (*US*) porta battente

swipe [swaɪp] *n* forte colpo; schiaffo ▪ *vt* (*hit*) colpire con forza; dare uno schiaffo a; (*col*: *steal*) sgraffignare; (*credit card etc*) far passare (nell'apposita macchinetta)

swirl [swəːl] *n* turbine *m*, mulinello ▪ *vi* turbinare, far mulinello

swish [swɪʃ] *adj* (*col*: *smart*) all'ultimo grido, alla moda ▪ *n* (*sound: of whip*) sibilo; (: *of skirts, grass*) fruscio ▪ *vi* sibilare

Swiss [swɪs] *adj, n* (*pl inv*) svizzero(-a)

Swiss French *adj* svizzero(-a) francese

Swiss German *adj* svizzero(-a) tedesco(-a)

switch [swɪtʃ] *n* (*for light, radio etc*) interruttore *m*; (*change*) cambiamento ▪ *vt* (*also*: **switch round, switch over**) cambiare; scambiare
 ▸ **switch off** *vt* spegnere
 ▸ **switch on** *vt* accendere; (*engine, machine*) mettere in moto, avviare; (*Aut*: *ignition*) inserire; (*Brit*: *water supply*) aprire

switchblade ['swɪtʃbleɪd] *n* (*also*: **switchblade knife**) coltello a scatto

switchboard ['swɪtʃbɔːd] *n* centralino

switchboard operator *n* centralinista *m/f*

Switzerland ['swɪtsələnd] *n* Svizzera

swivel ['swɪvl] *vi* (*also*: **swivel round**) girare

swollen ['swəulən] *pp of* **swell** ▪ *adj* (*ankle etc*) gonfio(-a)

swoon [swuːn] *vi* svenire

swoop [swuːp] *n* (*by police etc*) incursione *f*; (*of bird etc*) picchiata ▪ *vi* (*also*: **swoop down**) scendere in picchiata; (*police*): **to ~ (on)** fare un'incursione (in)

swop [swɔp] *n, vt* = **swap**

sword [sɔːd] *n* spada

swordfish ['sɔːdfɪʃ] *n* pesce *m* spada *inv*

swore [swɔː'] *pt of* **swear**

sworn [swɔːn] *pp of* **swear**

swot [swɔt] *vt* sgobbare su ▪ *vi* sgobbare

swum [swʌm] *pp of* **swim**

swung [swʌŋ] *pt, pp of* **swing**

sycamore ['sɪkəmɔː'] *n* sicomoro

sycophant ['sɪkəfənt] *n* leccapiedi *m/f*

sycophantic [sɪkə'fæntɪk] *adj* ossequioso(-a), adulatore(-trice)

Sydney ['sɪdnɪ] *n* Sydney *f*

syllable ['sɪləbl] *n* sillaba

syllabus ['sɪləbəs] *n* programma *m*; **on the ~** in programma d'esame

symbol ['sɪmbl] *n* simbolo

symbolic [sɪm'bɔlɪk], **symbolical** [sɪm'bɔlɪkl] *adj* simbolico(-a); **to be ~(al) of sth** simboleggiare qc

symbolism ['sɪmbəlɪzəm] *n* simbolismo

symbolize ['sɪmbəlaɪz] *vt* simbolizzare

symmetrical [sɪ'metrɪkl] *adj* simmetrico(-a)

symmetry ['sɪmɪtrɪ] *n* simmetria

sympathetic [sɪmpə'θetɪk] *adj* (*showing pity*) compassionevole; (*kind*) comprensivo(-a); **~ towards** ben disposto(-a) verso; **to be ~ to a cause** (*well-disposed*) simpatizzare per una causa

sympathetically [sɪmpə'θetɪklɪ] *adv* in modo compassionevole; con comprensione

sympathize ['sɪmpəθaɪz] *vi*: **to ~ with sb** compatire qn; partecipare al dolore di qn; (*understand*) capire qn

sympathizer ['sɪmpəθaɪzə'] *n* (*Pol*) simpatizzante *m/f*

S

sympathy ['sɪmpəθɪ] *n* compassione *f*; **in ~ with** d'accordo con; *(strike)* per solidarietà con; **with our deepest ~** con le nostre più sincere condoglianze

symphonic [sɪm'fɔnɪk] *adj* sinfonico(-a)

symphony ['sɪmfənɪ] *n* sinfonia

symphony orchestra *n* orchestra sinfonica

symposium [sɪm'pəuzɪəm] *n* simposio

symptom ['sɪmptəm] *n* sintomo; indizio

symptomatic [sɪmptə'mætɪk] *adj*: **~ (of)** sintomatico(-a) (di)

synagogue ['sɪnəgɔg] *n* sinagoga

sync [sɪŋk] *n* *(col)*: **in/out of ~** in/fuori sincronia; *(fig: people)*: **they are in ~** sono in sintonia

synchromesh [sɪŋkrəu'meʃ] *n* cambio sincronizzato

synchronize ['sɪŋkrənaɪz] *vt* sincronizzare ■ *vi*: **to ~ with** essere contemporaneo(-a) a

synchronized swimming *n* nuoto sincronizzato

syncopated ['sɪŋkəpeɪtɪd] *adj* sincopato(-a)

syndicate ['sɪndɪkɪt] *n* sindacato; *(Press)* agenzia di stampa

syndrome ['sɪndrəum] *n* sindrome *f*

synonym ['sɪnənɪm] *n* sinonimo

synonymous [sɪ'nɔnɪməs] *adj*: **~ (with)** sinonimo(-a) (di)

synopsis *(pl* **synopses)** [sɪ'nɔpsɪs, -siːz] *n* sommario, sinossi *f inv*

syntax ['sɪntæks] *n* sintassi *f inv*

synthesis *(pl* **syntheses)** ['sɪnθəsɪs, -siːz] *n* sintesi *f inv*

synthesizer ['sɪnθəsaɪzəʳ] *n* *(Mus)* sintetizzatore *m*

synthetic [sɪn'θetɪk] *adj* sintetico(-a) ■ *n* prodotto sintetico; *(Textiles)* fibra sintetica

syphilis ['sɪfɪlɪs] *n* sifilide *f*

syphon ['saɪfən] *n*, *vb* = **siphon**

Syria ['sɪrɪə] *n* Siria

Syrian ['sɪrɪən] *adj*, *n* siriano(-a)

syringe [sɪ'rɪndʒ] *n* siringa

syrup ['sɪrəp] *n* sciroppo; *(also:* **golden syrup)** melassa raffinata

syrupy ['sɪrəpɪ] *adj* sciropposo(-a)

system ['sɪstəm] *n* sistema *m*; *(network)* rete *f*; *(Anat)* apparato; **it was a shock to his ~** è stato uno shock per il suo organismo

systematic [sɪstə'mætɪk] *adj* sistematico(-a)

system disk *n* *(Comput)* disco del sistema

systems analyst *n* analista *m/f* di sistemi

Tt

T, t [tiː] *n* (*letter*) T, t *m or f inv*; **T for Tommy** ≈ T come Taranto

TA *n abbr* (*Brit*) = **Territorial Army**

ta [tɑː] *excl* (*Brit col*) grazie!

tab [tæb] *n abbr* = **tabulator** ■ *n* (*loop: on coat etc*) laccetto; (*label*) etichetta; **to keep tabs on**; (*fig*) tenere d'occhio

tabby ['tæbɪ] *n* (*also:* **tabby cat**) (gatto) soriano, gatto tigrato

tabernacle ['tæbənækl] *n* tabernacolo

table ['teɪbl] *n* tavolo, tavola; (*chart*) tabella ■ *vt* (*motion etc*) presentare; **to lay** *or* **set the ~** apparecchiare *or* preparare la tavola; **to clear the ~** sparecchiare; **league ~** (*Football, Rugby*) classifica; **~ of contents** indice *m*

tablecloth ['teɪblklɔθ] *n* tovaglia

table d'hôte [tɑːbl'dəut] *adj* (*meal*) a prezzo fisso

table lamp *n* lampada da tavolo

tablemat ['teɪblmæt] *n* sottopiatto

table salt *n* sale *m* fino *or* da tavola

tablespoon ['teɪblspuːn] *n* cucchiaio da tavola; (*also:* **tablespoonful:** *as measurement*) cucchiaiata

tablet ['tæblɪt] *n* (*Med*) compressa; (*: for sucking*) pastiglia; (*for writing*) blocco; (*of stone*) targa; **~ of soap** (*Brit*) saponetta

table tennis *n* tennis *m* da tavolo, ping-pong® *m*

table wine *n* vino da tavola

tabloid ['tæblɔɪd] *n* (*newspaper*) tabloid *m inv* (*giornale illustrato di formato ridotto*); **the tabloids, the ~ press** i giornali popolari; *vedi nota*

○ **TABLOID PRESS**
○
○ Il termine *tabloid press* si riferisce ai
○ quotidiani o ai settimanali popolari che,
○ rispetto ai "quality papers" hanno un
○ formato ridotto e presentario le notizie in
○ modo più sensazionalistico e meno
○ approfondito; *vedi anche* "quality press".

taboo [tə'buː] *adj, n* tabù *m inv*

tabulate ['tæbjuleɪt] *vt* (*data, figures*) tabulare, disporre in tabelle

tabulator ['tæbjuleɪtəʳ] *n* tabulatore *m*

tachograph ['tækəgrɑːf] *n* tachigrafo

tachometer [tæ'kɔmɪtəʳ] *n* tachimetro

tacit ['tæsɪt] *adj* tacito(-a)

taciturn ['tæsɪtəːn] *adj* taciturno(-a)

tack [tæk] *n* (*nail*) bulletta; (*stitch*) punto d'imbastitura; (*Naut*) bordo, bordata ■ *vt* imbullettare; imbastire ■ *vi* bordeggiare; **to change ~** virare di bordo; **on the wrong ~** (*fig*) sulla strada sbagliata; **to ~ sth on to (the end of) sth** (*of letter, book*) aggiungere qc alla fine di qc

tackle ['tækl] *n* (*equipment*) attrezzatura, equipaggiamento; (*for lifting*) paranco; (*Rugby*) placcaggio; (*Football*) contrasto ■ *vt* (*difficulty*) affrontare; (*Rugby*) placcare; (*Football*) contrastare

tacky ['tækɪ] *adj* colloso(-a), appiccicaticcio(-a); ancora bagnato(-a); (*col: shabby*) scadente

tact [tækt] *n* tatto

tactful ['tæktful] *adj* delicato(-a), discreto(-a); **to be ~** avere tatto

tactfully ['tæktfəlɪ] *adv* con tatto

tactical ['tæktɪkl] *adj* tattico(-a)

tactical voting *n* voto tattico

tactician [tæk'tɪʃən] *n* tattico(-a)

tactics ['tæktɪks] *n, npl* tattica

tactless ['tæktlɪs] *adj* che manca di tatto

tactlessly ['tæktlɪslɪ] *adv* senza tatto

tadpole ['tædpəul] *n* girino

taffy ['tæfɪ] *n* (*US*) caramella *f* mou *inv*

tag [tæg] *n* etichetta; **price/name ~** etichetta del prezzo/con il nome
  ▶ **tag along** *vi* seguire

Tahiti [tə'hiːti] *n* Tahiti *f*

tail [teɪl] *n* coda; (*of shirt*) falda ■ *vt* (*follow*) seguire, pedinare; **to turn ~** voltare la schiena; *see also* **head**
  ▶ **tail away, tail off** *vi* (*in size, quality etc*) diminuire gradatamente

t

tailback ['teɪlbæk] n (Brit) ingorgo
tail coat n marsina
tail end n (of train, procession etc) coda; (of meeting etc) fine f
tailgate ['teɪlgeɪt] n (Aut) portellone m posteriore
tail light n (Aut) fanalino di coda
tailor ['teɪləʳ] n sarto ■ vt: **to ~ sth (to)** adattare qc (alle esigenze di); **~'s (shop)** sartoria (da uomo)
tailoring ['teɪlərɪŋ] n (cut) taglio
tailor-made ['teɪlə'meɪd] adj (also fig) fatto(-a) su misura
tailwind ['teɪlwɪnd] n vento di coda
taint [teɪnt] vt (meat, food) far avariare; (fig: reputation) infangare
tainted ['teɪntɪd] adj (food) guasto(-a); (water, air) infetto(-a); (fig) corrotto(-a)
Taiwan [taɪ'wɑːn] n Taiwan m
Tajikistan [tɑːdʒɪkɪ'stɑːn] n Tagikistan m
take [teɪk] vb (pt **took**, pp **taken**) [tuk, 'teɪkn] vt prendere; (gain: prize) ottenere, vincere; (require: effort, courage) occorrere, volerci; (tolerate) accettare, sopportare; (hold: passengers etc) contenere; (accompany) accompagnare; (bring, carry) portare; (conduct: meeting) condurre; (exam) sostenere, presentarsi a ■ vi (dye, fire etc) prendere; (injection) fare effetto; (plant) attecchire ■ n (Cine) ripresa; **I ~ it that** suppongo che; **to ~ for a walk** (child, dog) portare a fare una passeggiata; **to ~ sb's hand** prendere qn per mano; **to ~ it upon o.s. to do sth** prendersi la responsabilità di fare qc; **to be taken ill** avere un malore; **to be taken with sb/sth** (attracted) essere tutto preso da qn/qc; **it won't ~ long** non ci vorrà molto tempo; **it takes a lot of time/courage** occorre or ci vuole molto tempo/coraggio; **it will ~ at least 5 litres** contiene almeno 5 litri; **the first on the left** prenda la prima a sinistra; **to ~ Russian at university** fare russo all'università; **I took him for a doctor** l'ho preso per un dottore
  ▶ **take after** vt fus assomigliare a
  ▶ **take apart** vt smontare
  ▶ **take away** vt portare via; togliere; **to ~ away (from)** sottrarre (da)
  ▶ **take back** vt (return) restituire; riportare; (one's words) ritirare
  ▶ **take down** vt (building) demolire; (dismantle: scaffolding) smontare; (letter etc) scrivere
  ▶ **take in** vt (lodger) prendere, ospitare; (orphan) accogliere; (stray dog) raccogliere; (Sewing) stringere; (deceive) imbrogliare, abbindolare; (understand) capire; (include) comprendere, includere

  ▶ **take off** vi (Aviat) decollare ■ vt (remove) togliere; (imitate) imitare
  ▶ **take on** vt (work) accettare, intraprendere; (employee) assumere; (opponent) sfidare, affrontare
  ▶ **take out** vt portare fuori; (remove) togliere; (licence) prendere, ottenere; **to ~ sth out of** tirare qc fuori da; estrarre qc da; **don't ~ it out on me!** non prendertela con me!
  ▶ **take over** vt (business) rilevare ■ vi: **to ~ over from sb** prendere le consegne or il controllo da qn
  ▶ **take to** vt fus (person) prendere in simpatia; (activity) prendere gusto a; (form habit of): **to ~ to doing sth** prendere or cominciare a fare qc
  ▶ **take up** vt (one's story) riprendere; (dress) accorciare; (absorb: liquids) assorbire; (accept: offer, challenge) accettare; (occupy: time, space) occupare; (engage in: hobby etc) mettersi a; **to ~ up with sb** fare amicizia con qn
takeaway ['teɪkəweɪ] adj (Brit: food) da portar via
take-home pay ['teɪkhəum-] n stipendio netto
taken ['teɪkn] pp of **take**
takeoff ['teɪkɔf] n (Aviat) decollo
takeout ['teɪkaut] adj (US) = **takeaway**
takeover ['teɪkəuvəʳ] n (Comm) assorbimento
takeover bid n offerta di assorbimento
takings ['teɪkɪŋz] npl (Comm) incasso
talc [tælk] n (also: **talcum powder**) talco
tale [teɪl] n racconto, storia; (pej) fandonia; **to tell tales** fare la spia
talent ['tælənt] n talento
talented ['tæləntɪd] adj di talento
talent scout n talent scout m/f inv
talisman ['tælɪzmən] n talismano
talk [tɔːk] n discorso; (gossip) chiacchiere fpl; (conversation) conversazione f; (interview) discussione f ■ vi parlare; (chatter) chiacchierare; **to give a ~** tenere una conferenza; **to ~ about** parlare di; (converse) discorrere or conversare su; **to ~ sb out of/ into doing** dissuadere qn da/convincere qn a fare; **to ~ shop** parlare del lavoro or degli affari; **talking of films, have you seen ...?** a proposito di film, ha visto ...?
  ▶ **talk over** vt discutere
talkative ['tɔːkətɪv] adj loquace, ciarliero(-a)
talking point ['tɔːkɪŋ-] n argomento di conversazione
talking-to ['tɔːkɪŋtuː] n: **to give sb a good ~** fare una bella paternale a qn
talk show n (TV, Radio) intervista (informale), talk show m inv
tall [tɔːl] adj alto(-a); **to be 6 feet ~** ≈ essere

alto 1 metro e 80; **how ~ are you?** quanto è
alto?

tallboy ['tɔːlbɔɪ] n (Brit) cassettone m alto

tallness ['tɔːlnɪs] n altezza

tall story n panzana, frottola

tally ['tælɪ] n conto, conteggio ■ vi: **to ~
(with)** corrispondere (a); **to keep a ~ of sth**
tener il conto di qc

talon ['tælən] n artiglio

tambourine [tæmbə'riːn] n tamburello

tame [teɪm] adj addomesticato(-a); (fig: story,
style) insipido(-a), scialbo(-a)

Tamil ['tæmɪl] adj tamil inv ■ n tamil m/f inv;
(Ling) tamil m

tamper ['tæmpəʳ] vi: **to ~ with** manomettere

tampon ['tæmpɔn] n tampone m

tan [tæn] n (also: **suntan**) abbronzatura ■ vt
abbronzare ■ vi abbronzarsi ■ adj (colour)
marrone rossiccio inv; **to get a ~** abbronzarsi

tandem ['tændəm] n tandem m inv

tandoori [tæn'duərɪ] adj nella cucina indiana,
detto di carni o verdure cucinate allo spiedo in
particolari forni

tang [tæŋ] n odore m penetrante; sapore m
piccante

tangent ['tændʒənt] n (Math) tangente f;
to go off at a ~ (fig) partire per la tangente

tangerine [tændʒə'riːn] n mandarino

tangible ['tændʒəbl] adj tangibile; **~ assets**
patrimonio reale

Tangier [tæn'dʒɪəʳ] n Tangeri f

tangle ['tæŋgl] n groviglio ■ vt
aggrovigliare; **to get in(to) a ~** finire in un
groviglio

tango ['tæŋgəu] n tango

tank [tæŋk] n serbatoio; (for processing) vasca;
(for fish) acquario; (Mil) carro armato

tankard ['tæŋkəd] n boccale m

tanker ['tæŋkəʳ] n (ship) nave f cisterna inv;
(for oil) petroliera; (truck) autobotte f,
autocisterna

tankini [tæn'kiːnɪ] n tankini m inv

tanned [tænd] adj abbronzato(-a)

tannin ['tænɪn] n tannino

tanning ['tænɪŋ] n (of leather) conciatura

tannoy® ['tænɔɪ] n (Brit) altoparlante m;
over the ~ per altoparlante

tantalizing ['tæntəlaɪzɪŋ] adj allettante

tantamount ['tæntəmaunt] adj: **~ to**
equivalente a

tantrum ['tæntrəm] n accesso di collera;
to throw a ~ fare le bizze

Tanzania [tænzə'nɪə] n Tanzania

Tanzanian [tænzə'nɪən] adj, n tanzaniano(-a)

tap [tæp] n (on sink etc) rubinetto; (gentle blow)
colpetto ■ vt dare un colpetto a; (resources)
sfruttare, utilizzare; (telephone conversation)

intercettare; (telephone) mettere sotto
controllo; **on ~** (beer) alla spina; (fig: resources)
a disposizione

tap-dancing ['tæpdɑːnsɪŋ] n tip tap m

tape [teɪp] n nastro; (also: **magnetic tape**)
nastro (magnetico) ■ vt (record) registrare
(su nastro); **on ~** (song etc) su nastro

tape deck n piastra di registrazione

tape measure n metro a nastro

taper ['teɪpəʳ] n candelina ■ vi
assottigliarsi

tape recorder n registratore m (a nastro)

tape recording n registrazione f

tapered ['teɪpəd], **tapering** ['teɪpərɪŋ] adj
affusolato(-a)

tapestry ['tæpɪstrɪ] n arazzo; tappezzeria

tape-worm ['teɪpwəːm] n tenia, verme m
solitario

tapioca [tæpɪ'əukə] n tapioca

tappet ['tæpɪt] n punteria

tar [tɑːʳ] n catrame m; **low-/middle-~
cigarettes** sigarette a basso/medio
contenuto di nicotina

tarantula [tə'ræntjulə] n tarantola

tardy ['tɑːdɪ] adj tardo(-a); tardivo(-a)

target ['tɑːgɪt] n bersaglio; (fig: objective)
obiettivo; **to be on ~** (project) essere nei
tempi (di lavorazione)

target practice n tiro al bersaglio

tariff ['tærɪf] n tariffa

tarmac ['tɑːmæk] n (Brit: on road) macadam m
al catrame; (Aviat) pista di decollo ■ vt (Brit)
macadamizzare

tarnish ['tɑːnɪʃ] vt offuscare, annerire; (fig)
macchiare

tarot ['tærəu] n tarocco

tarpaulin [tɑː'pɔːlɪn] n tela incatramata

tarragon ['tærəgən] n dragoncello

tart [tɑːt] n (Culin) crostata; (Brit col: pej:
woman) sgualdrina ■ adj (flavour) aspro(-a),
agro(-a)

▶ **tart up** vt (col): **to ~ o.s. up** farsi bello(-a);
(pej) agghindarsi

tartan ['tɑːtn] n tartan m inv

tartar ['tɑːtəʳ] n (on teeth) tartaro

tartar sauce n salsa tartara

task [tɑːsk] n compito; **to take to ~**
rimproverare

task force n (Mil, Police) unità operativa

taskmaster ['tɑːskmɑːstəʳ] n: **he's a hard ~**
è un vero tiranno

Tasmania [tæz'meɪnɪə] n Tasmania

tassel ['tæsl] n fiocco

taste [teɪst] n gusto; (flavour) sapore m, gusto;
(fig: glimpse, idea) idea ■ vt gustare; (sample)
assaggiare ■ vi: **to ~ of** (fish etc) sapere di,
avere sapore di; **what does it ~ like?** che

823

sapore *or* gusto ha?; **it tastes like fish** sa di pesce; **you can ~ the garlic (in it)** (ci) si sente il sapore dell'aglio; **can I have a ~ of this wine?** posso assaggiare un po' di questo vino?; **to have a ~ of sth** assaggiare qc; **to have a ~ for sth** avere un'inclinazione per qc; **to be in bad** *or* **poor ~** essere di cattivo gusto

taste bud *n* papilla gustativa

tasteful ['teɪstful] *adj* di buon gusto

tastefully ['teɪstfəlɪ] *adv* con gusto

tasteless ['teɪstlɪs] *adj (food)* insipido(-a); *(remark)* di cattivo gusto

tasty ['teɪstɪ] *adj* saporito(-a), gustoso(-a)

tattered ['tætəd] *adj see* **tatters**

tatters ['tætəz] *npl:* **in ~** *(also:* **tattered**) a brandelli, sbrindellato(-a)

tattoo [tə'tu:] *n* tatuaggio; *(spectacle)* parata militare ▪ *vt* tatuare

tatty ['tætɪ] *adj (Brit col)* malandato(-a)

taught [tɔːt] *pt, pp of* **teach**

taunt [tɔːnt] *n* scherno ▪ *vt* schernire

Taurus ['tɔːrəs] *n* Toro; **to be ~** essere del Toro

taut [tɔːt] *adj* teso(-a)

tavern ['tævən] *n* taverna

tawdry ['tɔːdrɪ] *adj* pacchiano(-a)

tawny ['tɔːnɪ] *adj* fulvo(-a)

tax [tæks] *n* imposta, tassa; *(on income)* imposte *fpl*, tasse *fpl* ▪ *vt* tassare; *(fig: strain: patience etc)* mettere alla prova; **free of ~** esentasse *inv*, esente da imposte; **before/after ~** al lordo/netto delle tasse

taxable ['tæksəbl] *adj* imponibile

tax allowance *n* detrazione *f* d'imposta

taxation [tæk'seɪʃən] *n* tassazione *f*; tasse *fpl*, imposte *fpl*; **system of ~** sistema *m* fiscale

tax avoidance *n* l'evitare legalmente il pagamento di imposte

tax collector *n* esattore *m* delle imposte

tax disc *n (Brit Aut)* ≈ bollo

tax evasion *n* evasione *f* fiscale

tax exemption *n* esenzione *f* fiscale

tax exile *n* chi ripara all'estero per evadere le imposte

tax-free [tæks'fri:] *adj* esente da imposte

tax haven *n* paradiso fiscale

taxi ['tæksɪ] *n* taxi *m inv* ▪ *vi (Aviat)* rullare

taxidermist ['tæksɪdə:mɪst] *n* tassidermista *m/f*

taxi driver *n* tassista *m/f*

tax inspector *n (Brit)* ispettore *m* delle tasse

taxi rank, *(US)* **taxi stand** *n* posteggio dei taxi

tax payer *n* contribuente *m/f*

tax rebate *n* rimborso fiscale

tax relief *n* sgravio fiscale

tax return *n* dichiarazione *f* dei redditi

tax shelter *n* paradiso fiscale

tax year *n* anno fiscale

TB *n abbr* (= *tuberculosis*) TBC *f*

tbc *abbr* (= *to be confirmed*) da confermarsi

TD *n abbr (US)* = **Treasury Department**; (*: Football*) = **touchdown**

tea [ti:] *n* tè *m inv*; *(Brit: snack: for children)* merenda; **high ~** *(Brit)* cena leggera *(presa nel tardo pomeriggio)*

tea bag *n* bustina di tè

tea break *n (Brit)* intervallo per il tè

teacake ['ti:keɪk] *n (Brit)* panino dolce all'uva

teach *(pt, pp* **taught**) [ti:tʃ, tɔːt] *vt:* **to ~ sb sth, ~ sth to sb** insegnare qc a qn ▪ *vi* insegnare; **it taught him a lesson** *(fig)* gli è servito da lezione

teacher ['ti:tʃə^r] *n (gen)* insegnante *m/f*; *(in secondary school)* professore(-essa); *(in primary school)* maestro(-a); **French ~** insegnante di francese

teacher training college *n (for primary schools)* ≈ istituto magistrale; *(for secondary schools)* scuola universitaria per l'abilitazione all'insegnamento nelle medie superiori

teaching ['ti:tʃɪŋ] *n* insegnamento

teaching aids *npl* materiali *mpl* per l'insegnamento

teaching hospital *n (Brit)* clinica universitaria

teaching staff *n (Brit)* insegnanti *mpl*, personale *m* insegnante

tea cosy *n* copriteiera *m inv*

teacup ['ti:kʌp] *n* tazza da tè

teak [ti:k] *n* teak *m*

tea leaves *npl* foglie *fpl* di tè

team [ti:m] *n* squadra; *(of animals)* tiro

▶ **team up** *vi:* **to ~ up (with)** mettersi insieme (a)

team games *npl* giochi *mpl* di squadra

teamwork ['ti:mwə:k] *n* lavoro di squadra

tea party *n* tè *m inv (ricevimento)*

teapot ['ti:pɔt] *n* teiera

tear[1] [tɪə^r] *n* lacrima; **in tears** in lacrime; **to burst into tears** scoppiare in lacrime

tear[2] [tɛə^r] *n* strappo ▪ *vb (pt* **tore**, *pp* **torn**) [tɔː^r, tɔːn] *vt* strappare ▪ *vi* strapparsi; **to ~ to pieces** *or* **to bits** *or* **to shreds** *(also fig)* fare a pezzi *or* a brandelli

▶ **tear along** *vi (rush)* correre all'impazzata

▶ **tear apart** *vt (also fig)* distruggere

▶ **tear away** *vt:* **to ~ o.s. away (from sth)** *(fig)* staccarsi (da qc)

▶ **tear out** *vt (sheet of paper, cheque)* staccare

▶ **tear up** *vt (sheet of paper etc)* strappare

tearaway ['tɛərəweɪ] *n (col)* monello(-a)

teardrop ['tɪədrɔp] *n* lacrima

tearful ['tɪəful] *adj* piangente, lacrimoso(-a)

tear gas *n* gas *m* lacrimogeno

tearoom ['ti:ru:m] *n* sala da tè
tease [ti:z] *vt* canzonare; (*unkindly*) tormentare
tea set *n* servizio da tè
teashop ['ti:ʃɒp] *n* (*Brit*) sala da tè
Teasmaid® ['ti:zmeɪd] *n* macchinetta per fare il tè
teaspoon ['ti:spu:n] *n* cucchiaino da tè; (*also:* **teaspoonful:** *as measurement*) cucchiaino
tea strainer *n* colino da tè
teat [ti:t] *n* capezzolo; (*of bottle*) tettarella
teatime ['ti:taɪm] *n* ora del tè
tea towel *n* (*Brit*) strofinaccio (per i piatti)
tea urn *n* bollitore *m* per il tè
tech [tɛk] *n abbr* (*col*) = **technical college; technology**
technical ['tɛknɪkl] *adj* tecnico(-a)
technical college *n* ≈ istituto tecnico
technicality [tɛknɪ'kælɪtɪ] *n* tecnicità; (*detail*) dettaglio tecnico; **on a legal ~** grazie a un cavillo legale
technically ['tɛknɪklɪ] *adv* dal punto di vista tecnico
technician [tɛk'nɪʃən] *n* tecnico(-a)
technique [tɛk'ni:k] *n* tecnica
techno ['tɛknəʊ] *n* (*Mus*) techno *f inv*
technocrat ['tɛknəkræt] *n* tecnocrate *m/f*
technological [tɛknə'lɒdʒɪkl] *adj* tecnologico(-a)
technologist [tɛk'nɒlədʒɪst] *n* tecnologo(-a)
technology [tɛk'nɒlədʒɪ] *n* tecnologia
teddy ['tɛdɪ], **teddy bear** ['tɛdɪ-] *n* orsacchiotto
tedious ['ti:dɪəs] *adj* noioso(-a), tedioso(-a)
tedium ['ti:dɪəm] *n* noia, tedio
tee [ti:] *n* (*Golf*) tee *m inv*
teem [ti:m] *vi* abbondare, brulicare; **to ~ with** brulicare di; **it is teeming (with rain)** piove a dirotto
teenage ['ti:neɪdʒ] *adj* (*fashions etc*) per giovani, per adolescenti
teenager ['ti:neɪdʒəʳ] *n* adolescente *m/f*
teens [ti:nz] *npl*: **to be in one's ~** essere adolescente
tee-shirt ['ti:ʃəːt] *n* = **T-shirt**
teeter ['ti:təʳ] *vi* barcollare, vacillare
teeth [ti:θ] *npl of* **tooth**
teethe [ti:ð] *vi* mettere i denti
teething ring ['ti:ðɪŋ-] *n* dentaruolo
teething troubles *npl* (*fig*) difficoltà *fpl* iniziali
teetotal ['ti:'təʊtl] *adj* astemio(-a)
teetotaller, (*US*) **teetotaler** ['ti:'təʊtləʳ] *n* astemio(-a)
TEFL ['tɛfl] *n abbr* = **Teaching of English as a Foreign Language**
Teflon® ['tɛflɒn] *n* teflon® *m*

Tehran [tɛə'rɑːn] *n* Tehran *f*
tel. *abbr* (= *telephone*) tel
Tel Aviv ['tɛlə'viːv] *n* Tel Aviv *f*
telecast ['tɛlɪkɑːst] *vt, vi* teletrasmettere
telecommunications ['tɛlɪkəmjuːnɪ'keɪʃənz] *n* telecomunicazioni *fpl*
teleconferencing ['tɛlɪkɒnfərnsɪŋ] *n* teleconferenza
telegram ['tɛlɪgræm] *n* telegramma *m*
telegraph ['tɛlɪgrɑːf] *n* telegrafo
telegraphic [tɛlɪ'græfɪk] *adj* telegrafico(-a)
telegraph pole *n* palo del telegrafo
telegraph wire *n* filo del telegrafo
telepathic [tɛlɪ'pæθɪk] *adj* telepatico(-a)
telepathy [tə'lɛpəθɪ] *n* telepatia
telephone ['tɛlɪfəʊn] *n* telefono ◼ *vt* (*person*) telefonare a; (*message*) telefonare; **to have a ~**, (*Brit*) **to be on the ~** (*subscriber*) avere il telefono; **to be on the ~** (*be speaking*) essere al telefono
telephone booth, (*Brit*) **telephone box** *n* cabina telefonica
telephone call *n* telefonata
telephone directory *n* elenco telefonico
telephone exchange *n* centralino telefonico
telephone number *n* numero di telefono
telephone operator *n* centralinista *m/f*
telephone tapping *n* intercettazione *f* telefonica
telephonist [tə'lɛfənɪst] *n* (*Brit*) telefonista *m/f*
telephoto lens ['tɛlɪfəʊtəʊ-] *n* teleobiettivo
teleprinter ['tɛlɪprɪntəʳ] *n* telescrivente *f*
Teleprompter® ['tɛlɪprɒmptəʳ] *n* (*US*) gobbo
telesales ['tɛlɪseɪlz] *n* televendita
telescope ['tɛlɪskəʊp] *n* telescopio ◼ *vi* chiudersi a telescopio; (*fig: vehicles*) accartocciarsi
telescopic [tɛlɪs'kɒpɪk] *adj* telescopico(-a); (*umbrella*) pieghevole
Teletext® ['tɛlɪtɛkst] *n* (*system*) teletext *m inv*; (*in Italy*) televideo
telethon ['tɛlɪθɒn] *n* maratona televisiva
televise ['tɛlɪvaɪz] *vt* teletrasmettere
television ['tɛlɪvɪʒən] *n* televisione *f*; **on ~** alla televisione
television licence *n* (*Brit*) abbonamento alla televisione
television programme *n* programma *m* televisivo
television set *n* televisore *m*
teleworking ['tɛlɪwəːkɪŋ] *n* telelavoro
telex ['tɛlɛks] *n* telex *m inv* ◼ *vt* trasmettere per telex ◼ *vi* mandare un telex; **to ~ sb (about sth)** informare qn via telex (di qc)
tell (*pt, pp* **told**) [tɛl, təʊld] *vt* dire; (*relate: story*) raccontare; (*distinguish*): **to ~ sth from**

t

825

distinguere qc da ■ vi (have effect) farsi
sentire, avere effetto; **to ~ sb to do** dire a qn
di fare; **to ~ sb about sth** dire a qn di qc;
raccontare qc a qn; **to ~ the time** leggere
l'ora; **can you ~ me the time?** può dirmi
l'ora?; **(I) ~ you what ...** so io che cosa fare ...;
I couldn't ~ them apart non riuscivo a
distinguerli

▸ **tell off** vt rimproverare, sgridare

▸ **tell on** vt fus (inform against) denunciare

teller ['tɛlə^r] n (in bank) cassiere(-a)

telling ['tɛlɪŋ] adj (remark, detail) rivelatore(-trice)

telltale ['tɛlteɪl] adj (sign) rivelatore(-trice)
■ n malalingua, pettegolo(-a)

telly ['tɛlɪ] n abbr (Brit col: = television) tivù f inv

temerity [tə'mɛrɪtɪ] n temerarietà

temp [tɛmp] abbr (Brit col) = **temporary** ■ n
impiegato(-a) straordinarioa(-a) ■ vi
lavorare come impiegato(-a)
straordinario(-a)

temper ['tɛmpə^r] n (nature) carattere m;
(mood) umore m; (fit of anger) collera ■ vt
(moderate) temperare, moderare; **to be in a ~**
essere in collera; **to keep one's ~** restare
calmo; **to lose one's ~** andare in collera

temperament ['tɛmprəmənt] n
temperamento

temperamental [tɛmprə'mɛntl] adj
capriccioso(-a)

temperance ['tɛmpərns] n moderazione f;
(in drinking) temperanza nel bere

temperate ['tɛmprət] adj moderato(-a);
(climate) temperato(-a)

temperature ['tɛmprətʃə^r] n temperatura;
to have or **run a ~** avere la febbre

tempered ['tɛmpəd] adj (steel) temprato(-a)

tempest ['tɛmpɪst] n tempesta

tempestuous [tɛm'pɛstjuəs] adj (relationship,
meeting) burrascoso(-a)

tempi ['tɛmpiː] npl of **tempo**

template, (US) **templet** ['tɛmplɪt] n sagoma

temple ['tɛmpl] n (building) tempio; (Anat)
tempia

templet ['tɛmplɪt] n (US) = **template**

tempo (pl **tempos, tempi**) ['tɛmpəu] n
tempo; (fig: of life etc) ritmo

temporal ['tɛmpərl] adj temporale

temporarily ['tɛmpərərɪlɪ] adv
temporaneamente

temporary ['tɛmpərərɪ] adj temporaneo(-a);
(job, worker) avventizio(-a), temporaneo(-a);
~ secretary segretaria temporanea;
~ teacher supplente m/f

temporize ['tɛmpəraɪz] vi temporeggiare

tempt [tɛmpt] vt tentare; **to ~ sb into doing**
indurre qn a fare; **to be tempted to do sth**
essere tentato di fare qc

temptation [tɛmp'teɪʃən] n tentazione f

tempting ['tɛmptɪŋ] adj allettante,
seducente

ten [tɛn] num dieci ■ n dieci; **tens of
thousands** decine di migliaia

tenable ['tɛnəbl] adj sostenibile

tenacious [tə'neɪʃəs] adj tenace

tenacity [tə'næsɪtɪ] n tenacia

tenancy ['tɛnənsɪ] n affitto; condizione f di
inquilino

tenant ['tɛnənt] n inquilino(-a)

tend [tɛnd] vt badare a, occuparsi di; (sick etc)
prendersi cura di ■ vi: **to ~ to do** tendere a
fare; (colour): **to ~ to** tendere a

tendency ['tɛndənsɪ] n tendenza

tender ['tɛndə^r] adj tenero(-a); (sore)
sensibile; (fig: subject) delicato(-a) ■ n (Comm:
offer) offerta; (money): **legal ~** valuta (a corso
legale) ■ vt offrire; **to put in a ~ (for)** fare
un'offerta (per); **to put work out to ~** (Brit)
dare lavoro in appalto; **to ~ one's
resignation** presentare le proprie
dimissioni

tenderize ['tɛndəraɪz] vt (Culin) far intenerire

tenderly ['tɛndəlɪ] adv teneramente

tenderness ['tɛndənɪs] n tenerezza;
sensibilità

tendon ['tɛndən] n tendine m

tenement ['tɛnəmənt] n casamento

Tenerife [tɛnə'riːf] n Tenerife f

tenet ['tɛnət] n principio

Tenn. abbr (US) = **Tennessee**

tenner ['tɛnə^r] n (Brit col) (banconota da) dieci
sterline fpl

tennis ['tɛnɪs] n tennis m

tennis ball n palla da tennis

tennis court n campo da tennis

tennis elbow n (Med) gomito del tennista

tennis match n partita di tennis

tennis player n tennista m/f

tennis racket n racchetta da tennis

tennis shoes npl scarpe fpl da tennis

tenor ['tɛnə^r] n (Mus, of speech etc) tenore m

tenpin bowling ['tɛnpɪn-] n (Brit) bowling m

tense [tɛns] adj teso(-a) ■ n (Ling) tempo
■ vt (tighten: muscles) tendere

tenseness ['tɛnsnɪs] n tensione f

tension ['tɛnʃən] n tensione f

tent [tɛnt] n tenda

tentacle ['tɛntəkl] n tentacolo

tentative ['tɛntətɪv] adj esitante, incerto(-a);
(conclusion) provvisorio(-a)

tenterhooks ['tɛntəhuks] npl: **on ~** sulle
spine

tenth [tɛnθ] num decimo(-a)

tent peg n picchetto da tenda

tent pole n palo da tenda, montante m

tenuous ['tɛnjʊəs] *adj* tenue

tenure ['tɛnjʊəʳ] *n* (*of property*) possesso; (*of job*) incarico; (*guaranteed employment*): **to have ~** essere di ruolo

tepid ['tɛpɪd] *adj* tiepido(-a)

Ter. *abbr* = **terrace**

term [təːm] *n* (*limit*) termine *m*; (*word*) vocabolo, termine; (*Scol*) trimestre *m*; (*Law*) sessione *f* ■ *vt* chiamare, definire; **terms** *npl* (*conditions*) condizioni *fpl*; (*Comm*) prezzi *mpl*, tariffe *fpl*; **~ of imprisonment** periodo di prigionia; **during his ~ of office** durante il suo incarico; **in the short/long ~** a breve/lunga scadenza; **"easy terms"** (*Comm*) "facilitazioni di pagamento"; **to be on good terms with** essere in buoni rapporti con; **to come to terms with** (*person*) arrivare a un accordo con; (*problem*) affrontare

terminal ['təːmɪnl] *adj* finale, terminale; (*disease*) nella fase terminale ■ *n* (*Elec, Comput*) terminale *m*; (*Aviat, for oil, ore etc*) terminal *m inv*; (*Brit: also:* **coach terminal**) capolinea *m*

terminate ['təːmɪneɪt] *vt* mettere fine a ■ *vi*: **to ~ in** finire in *or* con

termination [təːmɪ'neɪʃən] *n* fine *f*; (*of contract*) rescissione *f*; **~ of pregnancy** (*Med*) interruzione *f* della gravidanza

termini ['təːmɪnaɪ] *npl of* **terminus**

terminology [təːmɪ'nɔlədʒɪ] *n* terminologia

terminus (*pl* **termini**) ['təːmɪnəs, 'təːmɪnaɪ] *n* (*for buses*) capolinea *m*; (*for trains*) stazione *f* terminale

termite ['təːmaɪt] *n* termite *f*

term paper *n* (*US University*) saggio scritto da consegnare a fine trimestre

Terr. *abbr* = **terrace**

terrace ['tɛrəs] *n* terrazza; (*Brit: row of houses*) fila di case a schiera; **the terraces** *npl* (*Brit Sport*) le gradinate

terraced ['tɛrɪst] *adj* (*garden*) a terrazze; (*in a row: house, cottage etc*) a schiera

terrain [tɛ'reɪn] *n* terreno

terrible ['tɛrɪbl] *adj* terribile; (*weather*) bruttissimo(-a); (*performance, report*) pessimo(-a)

terribly ['tɛrəblɪ] *adv* terribilmente; (*very badly*) malissimo

terrier ['tɛrɪəʳ] *n* terrier *m inv*

terrific [tə'rɪfɪk] *adj* incredibile, fantastico(-a); (*wonderful*) formidabile, eccezionale

terrify ['tɛrɪfaɪ] *vt* terrorizzare; **to be terrified** essere atterrito(-a)

territorial [tɛrɪ'tɔːrɪəl] *adj* territoriale

territorial waters *npl* acque *fpl* territoriali

territory ['tɛrɪtərɪ] *n* territorio

terror ['tɛrəʳ] *n* terrore *m*

terror attack *n* attentato terroristico

terrorism ['tɛrərɪzəm] *n* terrorismo

terrorist ['tɛrərɪst] *n* terrorista *m/f*

terrorize ['tɛrəraɪz] *vt* terrorizzare

terse [təːs] *adj* (*style*) conciso(-a); (*reply*) laconico(-a)

tertiary ['təːʃərɪ] *adj* (*gen*) terziario(-a); **~ education** (*Brit*) educazione *f* superiore post-scolastica

Terylene® ['tɛrəliːn] *n* (*Brit*) terital® *m*, terilene® *m*

TESL ['tɛsl] *n abbr* = **Teaching of English as a Second Language**

TESSA ['tɛsə] *n abbr* (*Brit*: = *Tax Exempt Special Savings Account*) *deposito a risparmio esente da tasse*

test [tɛst] *n* (*trial, check*) prova; (*: of goods in factory*) controllo, collaudo; (*Med*) esame *m*; (*Chem*) analisi *f inv*; (*exam: of intelligence etc*) test *m inv*; (*: in school*) compito in classe; (*also:* **driving test**) esame *m* di guida ■ *vt* provare; controllare, collaudare; esaminare; analizzare; sottoporre ad esame; **to put sth to the ~** mettere qc alla prova; **to ~ sth for sth** analizzare qc alla ricerca di qc; **to ~ sb in history** esaminare qn in storia

testament ['tɛstəmənt] *n* testamento; **the Old/New T~** il Vecchio/Nuovo testamento

test ban *n* (*also:* **nuclear test ban**) divieto di esperimenti nucleari

test case *n* (*Law, fig*) caso che farà testo

testes ['tɛstiːz] *npl* testicoli *mpl*

test flight *n* volo di prova

testicle ['tɛstɪkl] *n* testicolo

testify ['tɛstɪfaɪ] *vi* (*Law*) testimoniare, deporre; **to ~ to sth** (*Law*) testimoniare qc; (*gen*) comprovare *or* dimostrare qc; (*be sign of*) essere una prova di qc

testimonial [tɛstɪ'məʊnɪəl] *n* (*Brit: reference*) benservito; (*gift*) testimonianza di stima

testimony ['tɛstɪmənɪ] *n* (*Law*) testimonianza, deposizione *f*

testing ['tɛstɪŋ] *adj* (*difficult: time*) duro(-a)

test match *n* (*Cricket, Rugby*) partita internazionale

testosterone [tɛs'tɔstərəʊn] *n* testosterone *m*

test paper *n* (*Scol*) interrogazione *f* scritta

test pilot *n* pilota *m* collaudatore

test tube *n* provetta

test-tube baby ['tɛsttjuːb-] *n* bambino(-a) concepito(-a) in provetta

testy ['tɛstɪ] *adj* irritabile

tetanus ['tɛtənəs] *n* tetano

tetchy ['tɛtʃɪ] *adj* irritabile, irascibile

tether ['tɛðəʳ] *vt* legare ■ *n*: **at the end of one's ~** al limite (della pazienza)

t

Tex. *abbr* (*US*) = **Texas**

text [tɛkst] *n* testo; (*Tel*) messaggino, sms *m inv* ▪ *vt* mandare un sms a ▪ *vi* messaggiarsi

textbook ['tɛkstbuk] *n* libro di testo

textile ['tɛkstaɪl] *n* tessile *m*; **textiles** *npl* tessuti *mpl*

texting ['tɛkstɪŋ] *n* invio di sms

text message *n* (*Tel*) messaggino, sms *m inv*

textual ['tɛkstjuəl] *adj* testuale, del testo

texture ['tɛkstʃəʳ] *n* tessitura; (*of skin, paper etc*) struttura

TGIF *abbr* (*col*) = **thank God it's Friday**

TGWU *n abbr* (*Brit*: = *Transport and General Workers' Union*) sindacato degli operai dei trasporti e non specializzati

Thai [taɪ] *adj* tailandese ▪ *n* tailandese *m/f*; (*Ling*) tailandese *m*

Thailand ['taɪlænd] *n* Tailandia

thalidomide® [θə'lɪdəmaɪd] *n* talidomide® *m*

Thames [tɛmz] *n*: **the ~** il Tamigi

than [ðæn, ðən] *conj* che; (*with numerals, pronouns, proper names*): **more ~ 10/me/Maria** più di 10/me/Maria; **you know her better ~ I do** la conosce meglio di me *or* di quanto non la conosca io; **she has more apples ~ pears** ha più mele che pere; **it is better to phone ~ to write** è meglio telefonare che scrivere; **no sooner did he leave ~ the phone rang** non appena uscì il telefono suonò

thank [θæŋk] *vt* ringraziare; **~ you (very much)** grazie (tante); **~ heavens/God!** grazie al cielo/a Dio!; *see also* **thanks**

thankful ['θæŋkful] *adj*: **~ (for)** riconoscente (per); **~ for/that** (*relieved*) sollevato(a) da/dal fatto che

thankfully ['θæŋkfəlɪ] *adv* con riconoscenza; con sollievo; **~ there were few victims** grazie al cielo ci sono state poche vittime

thankless ['θæŋklɪs] *adj* ingrato(-a)

thanks [θæŋks] *npl* ringraziamenti *mpl*, grazie *fpl* ▪ *excl* grazie!; **~ to** *prep* grazie a

Thanksgiving ['θæŋksgɪvɪŋ], **Thanksgiving Day** ['θæŋksgɪvɪŋ-] *n* (*US*) giorno del ringraziamento; *vedi nota*

 THANKSGIVING (DAY)

Negli Stati Uniti il quarto giovedì di novembre ricorre il *Thanksgiving (Day)*, festa nazionale in ricordo della celebrazione con cui i Padri Pellegrini, i puritani inglesi che fondarono la colonia di Plymouth nel Massachusetts, ringraziarono Dio del buon raccolto del 1621.

 KEYWORD

that [ðæt ʃ] (*pl* **those**) *adj* (*demonstrative*) quel(quell', quello) *m*; quella(quell') *f*; **that man/woman/book** quell'uomo/quella donna/quel libro; (*not "this"*) quell'uomo/quella donna/quel libro là; **that one** quello(-a) là

▪ *pron* **1** (*demonstrative*) ciò; (*not "this one"*) quello(-a); **who's that?** chi è quello là?; **what's that?** cos'è quello?; **is that you?** sei tu?; **I prefer this to that** preferisco questo a quello; **that's what he said** questo è ciò che ha detto; **after that** dopo; **what happened after that?** che è successo dopo?; **that is (to say)** cioè; **at** *or* **with that she ...** con ciò lei ...; **do it like that** fallo così

2 (*relative: direct*) che; (: *indirect*) cui; **the book (that) I read** il libro che ho letto; **the box (that) I put it in** la scatola in cui l'ho messo; **the people (that) I spoke to** le persone con cui *or* con le quali ho parlato; **not that I know of** non che io sappia

3 (*relative: of time*) in cui; **the day (that) he came** il giorno in cui è venuto

▪ *conj* che; **he thought that I was ill** pensava che io fossi malato

▪ *adv* (*demonstrative*) così; **I can't work that much** non posso lavorare (così) tanto; **that high** così alto; **the wall's about that high and that thick** il muro è alto circa così e spesso circa così

thatched [θætʃt] *adj* (*roof*) di paglia; **~ cottage** cottage *m inv* col tetto di paglia

Thatcherism ['θætʃərɪzəm] *n* thatcherismo

thaw [θɔː] *n* disgelo ▪ *vi* (*ice*) sciogliersi; (*food*) scongelarsi ▪ *vt* (*food*) (fare) scongelare; **it's thawing** (*weather*) sta sgelando

KEYWORD

the [ðiː, ðə] *def art* **1** (*gen*) il(lo, l') *m*, la(l') *f*, I(gli) *mpl*; le *fpl*; **the boy/girl/ink** il ragazzo/la ragazza/l'inchiostro; **the books/pencils** i libri/le matite; **the history of the world** la storia del mondo; **give it to the postman** dallo al postino; **I haven't the time/money** non ho tempo/soldi; **the rich and the poor** i ricchi e i poveri; **1.5 euros to the dollar** 1.5 euro per un dollaro; **paid by the hour** pagato a ore

2 (*in titles*): **Elizabeth the First** Elisabetta prima; **Peter the Great** Pietro il Grande

3 (*in comparisons*): **the more he works, the more he earns** più lavora più guadagna; **the sooner the better** prima è meglio è

theatre, (US) **theater** ['θɪətə^r] n teatro

theatre-goer ['θɪətəgəʊə^r] n
frequentatore(-trice) di teatri

theatrical [θɪ'ætrɪkl] adj teatrale

theft [θεft] n furto

their [ðεə^r] adj il(la) loro pl i(le) loro

theirs [ðεəz] pron il(la) loro pl i(le) loro; **it is ~**
è loro; **a friend of ~** un loro amico

them [ðεm, ðəm] pron (direct) li(le); (indirect)
gli, loro (after vb); (stressed, after prep: people)
loro; (: people, things) essi(-e); **I see ~** li vedo;
give ~ the book dà loro or dagli il libro;
give me a few of ~ dammene un po' or
qualcuno

theme [θi:m] n tema m

theme park n parco dei divertimenti a
soggetto

theme song, theme tune n tema musicale

themselves [ðəm'sεlvz] pl pron (reflexive) si;
(emphatic) loro stessi(-e); (after prep) se
stessi(-e); **between ~** tra (di) loro

then [ðεn] adv (at that time) allora; (next) poi,
dopo; (and also) e poi ■ conj (therefore) perciò,
dunque, quindi ■ adj: **the ~ president** il
presidente di allora; **from ~ on** da allora in
poi; **until ~** fino ad allora; **and ~ what?** e
poi?, e allora?; **what do you want me to do
~?** allora cosa vuole che faccia?

theologian [θɪə'ləʊdʒən] n teologo(-a)

theological [θɪə'lɔdʒɪkl] adj teologico(-a)

theology [θɪ'ɔlədʒɪ] n teologia

theorem ['θɪərəm] n teorema m

theoretical [θɪə'rεtɪkl] adj teorico(-a)

theorize ['θɪəraɪz] vi teorizzare

theory ['θɪərɪ] n teoria; **in ~** in teoria

therapeutic [θεrə'pju:tɪk], **therapeutical**
[θεrə'pju:tɪkl] adj terapeutico(-a)

therapist ['θεrəpɪst] n terapista m/f

·· py ['θεrəpɪ] n terapia

KEYWORD

there [ðεə^r] adv 1: **there is, there are** c'è, ci
sono; **there are 3 of them** (people) sono in 3;
(things) ce ne sono 3; **there is no-one here**
non c'è nessuno qui; **there has been an
accident** c'è stato un incidente

2 (referring to place) là, lì; **it's there** è là or lì;
up/in/down there lassù/là dentro/laggiù;
back there là dietro; **on there** lassù; **over
there** là; **through there** di là; **he went
there on Friday** ci è andato venerdì; **it
takes two hours to go there and back** ci
vogliono due ore per andare e tornare; **I
want that book there** voglio quel libro là or
lì; **there he is!** eccolo!

3: **there, there** (esp to child) su, su

thereabouts ['ðεərəbauts] adv (place) nei
pressi, da quelle parti; (amount) giù di lì,
all'incirca

thereafter [ðεər'ɑ:ftə^r] adv da allora in poi

thereby [ðεə'baɪ] adv con ciò

therefore ['ðεəfɔ:^r] adv perciò, quindi

there's [ðεəz] = there is; there has

thereupon [ðεərə'pɔn] adv (at that point) a
quel punto; (formal: on that subject) in merito

thermal ['θə:ml] adj (currents, spring) termale;
(underwear, printer) termico(-a); (paper)
termosensibile

thermodynamics [θə:məudaɪ'næmɪks] n
termodinamica

thermometer [θə'mɔmɪtə^r] n termometro

thermonuclear ['θə:məu'nju:klɪə^r] adj
termonucleare

Thermos® ['θə:məs] n (also: **Thermos flask**)
thermos® m inv

thermostat ['θə:məstæt] n termostato

thesaurus [θɪ'sɔ:rəs] n dizionario dei
sinonimi

these [ði:z] pl pron, adj questi(-e)

thesis (pl **theses**) ['θi:sɪs, 'θi:si:z] n tesi f inv

they [ðeɪ] pl pron essi(esse); (people only) loro; **~
say that ...** (it is said that) si dice che ...

they'd [ðeɪd] = they would; they had

they'll [ðeɪl] = they will; they shall

they're [ðεə^r] = they are

they've [ðeɪv] = they have

thick [θɪk] adj spesso(-a); (crowd)
compatto(-a); (stupid) ottuso(-a), lento(-a)
■ n: **in the ~ of** nel folto di; **it's 20 cm ~** ha
uno spessore di 20 cm

thicken ['θɪkən] vi ispessire ■ vt (sauce etc)
ispessire, rendere più denso(-a)

thicket ['θɪkɪt] n boscaglia

thickly ['θɪklɪ] adv (spread) a strati spessi; (cut)
a fette grosse; (populated) densamente

thickness ['θɪknɪs] n spessore m

thickset [θɪk'sεt] adj tarchiato(-a), tozzo(-a)

thickskinned [θɪk'skɪnd] adj (fig) insensibile

thief (pl **thieves**) [θi:f, θi:vz] n ladro(-a)

thieving ['θi:vɪŋ] n furti mpl

thigh [θaɪ] n coscia

thighbone ['θaɪbəun] n femore m

thimble ['θɪmbl] n ditale m

thin [θɪn] adj sottile; (person) magro(-a); (soup)
poco denso(-a); (hair, crowd) rado(-a); (fog)
leggero(-a) ■ vt (hair) sfoltire ■ vi (fog)
diradarsi; (also: **thin out**: crowd) disperdersi;
to ~ (down) (sauce, paint) diluire; **his hair is
thinning** sta perdendo i capelli

thing [θɪŋ] n cosa; (object) oggetto;
(contraption) aggeggio; **things** npl (belongings)
cose fpl; **for one ~** tanto per cominciare; **the
best ~ would be to** la cosa migliore sarebbe

829

di; **the ~ is ...** il fatto è che ...; **the main ~ is to ...** la cosa più importante è di ...; **first ~ (in the morning)** come *or* per prima cosa (di mattina); **last ~ (at night)** come *or* per ultima cosa (di sera); **poor ~** poveretto/(-a); **she's got a ~ about mice** è terrorizzata dai topi; **how are things?** come va?

think (*pt, pp* **thought**) [θɪŋk, θɔːt] *vi* pensare, riflettere ■ *vt* pensare, credere; (*imagine*) immaginare; **to ~ of** pensare a; **what did you ~ of them?** cosa ne ha pensato?; **to ~ about sth/sb** pensare a qc/qn; **I'll ~ about it** ci penserò; **to ~ of doing** pensare di fare; **I ~ so** penso *or* credo di sì; **to ~ well of** avere una buona opinione di; **to ~ aloud** pensare ad alta voce; **~ again!** rifletti!, pensaci su!

▶ **think out** *vt* (*plan*) elaborare; (*solution*) trovare

▶ **think over** *vt* riflettere su; **I'd like to ~ things over** vorrei pensarci su

▶ **think through** *vt* riflettere a fondo su

▶ **think up** *vt* ideare

thinking ['θɪŋkɪŋ] *n*: **to my (way of) ~** a mio parere

think tank *n* gruppo di esperti

thinly ['θɪnlɪ] *adv* (*cut*) a fette sottili; (*spread*) in uno strato sottile

thinness ['θɪnnɪs] *n* sottigliezza; magrezza

third [θəːd] *n* terzo(-a) ■ *n* terzo(-a); (*fraction*) terzo, terza parte *f*; (*Brit Scol: degree*) laurea col minimo dei voti

third-degree burns ['θəːdɪ'griː-] *npl* ustioni *fpl* di terzo grado

thirdly ['θəːdlɪ] *adv* in terzo luogo

third party insurance *n* (*Brit*) assicurazione *f* contro terzi

third-rate [θəːd'reɪt] *adj* di qualità scadente

Third World *n*: **the ~** il Terzo Mondo

thirst [θəːst] *n* sete *f*

thirsty ['θəːstɪ] *adj* (*person*) assetato(-a), che ha sete; **to be ~** aver sete

thirteen [θəː'tiːn] *num* tredici

thirtieth ['θəːtɪɪθ] *num* trentesimo(-a)

thirty ['θəːtɪ] *num* trenta

 KEYWORD

this [ðɪs] *ʃ* (*pl* **these**) *adj* (*demonstrative*) questo(-a); **this man/woman/book** quest'uomo/questa donna/questo libro; (*not "that"*) quest'uomo/questa donna/questo libro qui; **this one** questo(-a) qui; **this time** questa volta; **this time last year** l'anno scorso in questo periodo; **this way** (*in this direction*) da questa parte; (*in this fashion*) così
■ *pron* (*demonstrative*) questo(-a); (*not "that one"*) questo(-a) qui; **who/what is this?** chi è/che cos'è questo?; **I prefer this to that** preferisco questo a quello; **this is where I live** io abito qui; **this is what he said** questo è ciò che ha detto; **they were talking of this and that** stavano parlando del più e del meno; **this is Mr Brown** (*in introductions, photo*) questo è il signor Brown; (*on telephone*) sono il signor Brown
■ *adv* (*demonstrative*): **this high/long** *etc* alto/lungo *etc* così; **it's about this high** è alto circa così; **I didn't know things were this bad** non sapevo andasse così male

thistle ['θɪsl] *n* cardo

thong [θɒŋ] *n* cinghia

thorn [θɔːn] *n* spina

thorny ['θɔːnɪ] *adj* spinoso(-a)

thorough ['θʌrə] *adj* (*person*) preciso(-a), accurato(-a); (*search*) minuzioso(-a); (*knowledge, research*) approfondito(-a), profondo(-a); (*cleaning*) a fondo

thoroughbred ['θʌrəbred] *n* (*horse*) purosangue *m/f inv*

thoroughfare ['θʌrəfɛəʳ] *n* strada transitabile; **"no ~"** (*Brit*) "divieto di transito"

thoroughgoing ['θʌrəgəʊɪŋ] *adj* (*analysis*) approfondito(-a); (*reform*) totale

thoroughly ['θʌrəlɪ] *adv* accuratamente; minuziosamente, in profondità; a fondo; **he ~ agreed** fu completamente d'accordo

thoroughness ['θʌrənɪs] *n* precisione *f*

those [ðəʊz] *pl pron* quelli(-e) ■ *pl adj* quei(quegli) *mpl*; quelle *fpl*

though [ðəʊ] *conj* benché, sebbene ■ *adv* comunque, tuttavia; **even ~** anche se; **it's not so easy, ~** tuttavia non è così facile

thought [θɔːt] *pt, pp of* **think** ■ *n* pensiero; (*opinion*) opinione *f*; (*intention*) intenzione *f*; **after much ~** dopo molti ripensamenti; **I've just had a ~** mi è appena venuta un'idea; **to give sth some ~** prendere qc in considerazione, riflettere su qc

thoughtful ['θɔːtful] *adj* pensieroso(-a), pensoso(-a); ponderato(-a); (*considerate*) premuroso(-a)

thoughtfully ['θɔːtfəlɪ] *adv* (*pensively*) con aria pensierosa

thoughtless ['θɔːtlɪs] *adj* sconsiderato(-a); (*behaviour*) scortese

thoughtlessly ['θɔːtlɪslɪ] *adv* sconsideratamente; scortesemente

thought-provoking ['θɔːtprəvəʊkɪŋ] *adj* stimolante

thousand ['θaʊzənd] *num* mille; **one ~** mille; **thousands of** migliaia di

thousandth ['θaʊzəntθ] *num* millesimo(-a)

thrash [θræʃ] *vt* picchiare; bastonare; (*defeat*) battere
▸ **thrash about** *vi* dibattersi
▸ **thrash out** *vt* dibattere, sviscerare
thrashing ['θræʃɪŋ] *n*: **to give sb a ~ = to thrash sb**
thread [θrɛd] *n* filo; (*of screw*) filetto ■ *vt* (*needle*) infilare; **to ~ one's way between** infilarsi tra
threadbare ['θrɛdbɛəʳ] *adj* consumato(-a), logoro(-a)
threat [θrɛt] *n* minaccia; **to be under ~ of** (*closure, extinction*) rischiare di; (*exposure*) essere minacciato(-a) di
threaten ['θrɛtn] *vi* (*storm*) minacciare ■ *vt*: **to ~ sb with sth/to do** minacciare qn, con qc/di fare
threatening ['θrɛtnɪŋ] *adj* minaccioso(-a)
three [θri:] *num* tre
three-dimensional [θri:daɪ'mɛnʃənl] *adj* tridimensionale
three-piece ['θri:pi:s]: **~ suit** *n* completo (con gilè); **~ suite** *n* salotto comprendente un divano e due poltrone
three-ply [θri:'plaɪ] *adj* (*wood*) a tre strati; (*wool*) a tre fili
three-quarters [θri:'kwɔ:təz] *npl* tre quarti *mpl*; **~ full** pieno per tre quarti
three-wheeler [θri:'wi:ləʳ] *n* (*car*) veicolo a tre ruote
thresh [θrɛʃ] *vt* (*Agr*) trebbiare
threshing machine ['θrɛʃɪŋ-] *n* trebbiatrice *f*
threshold ['θrɛʃhəuld] *n* soglia; **to be on the ~ of** (*fig*) essere sulla soglia di
threshold agreement *n* (*Econ*) ≈ scala mobile
threw [θru:] *pt of* **throw**
thrift [θrɪft] *n* parsimonia
thrifty ['θrɪftɪ] *adj* economico(-a), parsimonioso(-a)
thrill [θrɪl] *n* brivido ■ *vi* eccitarsi, tremare ■ *vt* (*audience*) elettrizzare; **I was thrilled to get your letter** la tua lettera mi ha fatto veramente piacere
thriller ['θrɪləʳ] *n* film *m inv* (*or* dramma *m or* libro) del brivido
thrilling ['θrɪlɪŋ] *adj* (*book, play etc*) pieno(-a) di suspense; (*news, discovery*) entusiasmante
thrive (*pt* **thrived** *or* **throve**, *pp* **thrived** *or* **thriven**) [θraɪv, θrəuv, 'θrɪvn] *vi* crescere *or* svilupparsi bene; (*business*) prosperare; **he thrives on it** gli fa bene, ne gode
thriving ['θraɪvɪŋ] *adj* (*industry etc*) fiorente
throat [θrəut] *n* gola; **to have a sore ~** avere (un *or* il) mal di gola
throb [θrɔb] *n* (*of heart*) battito; (*of engine*) vibrazione *f*; (*of pain*) fitta ■ *vi* (*heart*) palpitare; (*engine*) vibrare; (*with pain*) pulsare;

my head is throbbing mi martellano le tempie
throes [θrəuz] *npl*: **in the ~ of** alle prese con; **in preda a**; **in the ~ of death** in agonia
thrombosis [θrɔm'bəusɪs] *n* trombosi *f*
throne [θrəun] *n* trono
throng [θrɔŋ] *n* moltitudine *f* ■ *vt* affollare
throttle ['θrɔtl] *n* (*Aut*) valvola a farfalla; (*on motorcycle*) (manopola del) gas ■ *vt* strangolare
through [θru:] *prep* attraverso; (*time*) per, durante; (*by means of*) per mezzo di; (*owing to*) a causa di ■ *adj* (*ticket, train, passage*) diretto(-a) ■ *adv* attraverso; (*from*) **Monday ~ Friday** (US) da lunedì a venerdì; **I am halfway ~ the book** sono a metà libro; **to let sb ~** lasciar passare qn; **to put sb ~ to sb** (*Tel*) passare qn a qn; **to be ~** (*Tel*) ottenere la comunicazione; (*have finished*) avere finito; **"no ~ traffic"** (US) "divieto d'accesso"; **"no ~ road"** (*Brit*) "strada senza sbocco"
throughout [θru:'aut] *prep* (*place*) dappertutto in; (*time*) per *or* durante tutto(-a) ■ *adv* dappertutto; sempre
throughput ['θru:put] *n* (*of goods, materials*) materiale *m* in lavorazione; (*Comput*) volume *m* di dati immessi
throve [θrəuv] *pt of* **thrive**
throw [θrəu] *n* tiro, getto; (*Sport*) lancio ■ *vt* (*pt* **threw**, *pp* **thrown**) [θru:, θrəun] tirare, gettare; (*Sport*) lanciare; (*rider*) disarcionare; (*fig*) confondere; (*pottery*) formare al tornio; **to ~ a party** dare una festa; **to ~ open** (*doors, windows*) spalancare; (*house, gardens etc*) aprire al pubblico; (*competition, race*) aprire a tutti
▸ **throw about, throw around** *vt* (*litter etc*) spargere
▸ **throw away** *vt* gettare *or* buttare via
▸ **throw off** *vt* sbarazzarsi di
▸ **throw out** *vt* buttare fuori; (*reject*) respingere
▸ **throw together** *vt* (*clothes, meal etc*) mettere insieme; (*essay*) buttar giù
▸ **throw up** *vi* vomitare
throwaway ['θrəuəweɪ] *adj* da buttare
throwback ['θrəubæk] *n*: **it's a ~ to** (*fig*) ciò risale a
throw-in ['θrəuɪn] *n* (*Sport*) rimessa in gioco
thrown [θrəun] *pp of* **throw**
thru [θru:] *prep, adj, adv* (US) = **through**
thrush [θrʌʃ] *n* (*Zool*) tordo; (*Med: esp in children*) mughetto; (: *Brit: in women*) candida
thrust [θrʌst] *n* (*Tech*) spinta ■ *vt* (*pt, pp* **~**) spingere con forza; (*push in*) conficcare
thrusting ['θrʌstɪŋ] *adj* (troppo) intraprendente
thud [θʌd] *n* tonfo

thug [θʌg] *n* delinquente *m*
thumb [θʌm] *n* (*Anat*) pollice *m* ▪ *vt* (*book*) sfogliare; **to ~ a lift** fare l'autostop; **to give sb/sth the thumbs up/down** approvare/ disapprovare qn/qc
thumb index *n* indice *m* a rubrica
thumbnail ['θʌmneɪl] *n* unghia del pollice
thumbnail sketch *n* descrizione *f* breve
thumbtack ['θʌmtæk] *n* (*US*) puntina da disegno
thump [θʌmp] *n* colpo forte; (*sound*) tonfo ▪ *vt* battere su ▪ *vi* picchiare, battere
thunder ['θʌndə'] *n* tuono ▪ *vi* tuonare; (*train etc*): **to ~ past** passare con un rombo
thunderbolt ['θʌndəbəult] *n* fulmine *m*
thunderclap ['θʌndəklæp] *n* rombo di tuono
thunderous ['θʌndərəs] *adj* fragoroso(-a)
thunderstorm ['θʌndəstɔːm] *n* temporale *m*
thunderstruck ['θʌndəstrʌk] *adj* (*fig*) sbigottito(-a)
thundery ['θʌndərɪ] *adj* temporalesco(-a)
Thur., Thurs. *abbr* (= *Thursday*) gio.
Thursday ['θəːzdɪ] *n* giovedì *m inv*; *see also* **Tuesday**
thus [ðʌs] *adv* così
thwart [θwɔːt] *vt* contrastare
thyme [taɪm] *n* timo
thyroid ['θaɪrɔɪd] *n* tiroide *f*
tiara [tɪ'ɑːrə] *n* (*woman's*) diadema *m*
Tiber ['taɪbə'] *n*: **the ~** il Tevere
Tibet [tɪ'bɛt] *n* Tibet *m*
Tibetan [tɪ'bɛtən] *adj* tibetano(-a) ▪ *n* (*person*) tibetano(-a); (*Ling*) tibetano
tibia ['tɪbɪə] *n* tibia
tic [tɪk] *n* tic *m inv*
tick [tɪk] *n* (*sound: of clock*) tic tac *m inv*; (*mark*) segno; spunta; (*Zool*) zecca; (*Brit col*): **in a ~** in un attimo; (*Brit col: credit*): **to buy sth on ~** comprare qc a credito ▪ *vi* fare tic tac ▪ *vt* spuntare; **to put a ~ against sth** fare un segno di fianco a qc
  ▸ **tick off** *vt* spuntare; (*person*) sgridare
  ▸ **tick over** *vi* (*Brit: engine*) andare al minimo
ticker tape ['tɪkə-] *n* nastro di telescrivente; (*US: in celebrations*) stelle *fpl* filanti
ticket ['tɪkɪt] *n* biglietto; (*in shop: on goods*) etichetta; (: *from cash register*) scontrino; (*for library*) scheda; (*US Pol*) lista dei candidati; **to get a (parking) ~** (*Aut*) prendere una multa (per sosta vietata)
ticket agency *n* (*Theat*) agenzia di vendita di biglietti
ticket collector *n* bigliettaio
ticket holder *n* persona munita di biglietto
ticket inspector *n* controllore *m*
ticket office *n* biglietteria

tickle ['tɪkl] *n* solletico ▪ *vt* fare il solletico a, solleticare; (*fig*) stuzzicare; piacere a; far ridere
ticklish ['tɪklɪʃ] *adj* che soffre il solletico; (*which tickles: blanket, cough*) che provoca prurito
tidal ['taɪdl] *adj* di marea
tidal wave *n* onda anomala
tidbit ['tɪdbɪt] *n* (*US*) = **titbit**
tiddlywinks ['tɪdlɪwɪŋks] *n* gioco della pulce
tide [taɪd] *n* marea; (*fig: of events*) corso ▪ *vt*: **will £20 ~ you over till Monday?** ti basteranno 20 sterline fino a lunedì?; **high/ low ~** alta/bassa marea; **the ~ of public opinion** l'orientamento dell'opinione pubblica
tidily ['taɪdɪlɪ] *adv* in modo ordinato; **to arrange ~** sistemare; **to dress ~** vestirsi per benino
tidiness ['taɪdɪnɪs] *n* ordine *m*
tidy ['taɪdɪ] *adj* (*room*) ordinato(-a), lindo(-a); (*dress, work*) curato(-a), in ordine; (*person*) ordinato(-a); (*mind*) organizzato(-a) ▪ *vt* (*also*: **tidy up**) riordinare, mettere in ordine; **to ~ o.s. up** rassettarsi
tie [taɪ] *n* (*string etc*) legaccio; (*Brit: also*: **necktie**) cravatta; (*fig: link*) legame *m*; (*Sport: draw*) pareggio; (: *match*) incontro; (*US Rail*) traversina ▪ *vt* (*parcel*) legare; (*ribbon*) annodare ▪ *vi* (*Sport*) pareggiare; **"black/ white ~"** "smoking/abito di rigore"; **family ties** legami familiari; **to ~ sth in a bow** annodare qc; **to ~ a knot in sth** fare un nodo a qc
  ▸ **tie down** *vt* fissare con una corda; (*fig*): **to ~ sb down to** costringere qn ad accettare
  ▸ **tie in** *vi*: **to ~ in (with)** (*correspond*) corrispondere (a)
  ▸ **tie on** *vt* (*Brit: label etc*) attaccare
  ▸ **tie up** *vt* (*parcel, dog*) legare; (*boat*) ormeggiare; (*arrangements*) concludere; **to be tied up** (*busy*) essere occupato *or* preso
tie-break ['taɪbreɪk], **tie-breaker** ['taɪbreɪkə'] *n* (*Tennis*) tie-break *m inv*; (*in quiz*) spareggio
tie-on ['taɪɔn] *adj* (*Brit: label*) volante
tie-pin ['taɪpɪn] *n* (*Brit*) fermacravatta *m inv*
tier [tɪə'] *n* fila; (*of cake*) piano, strato
Tierra del Fuego [tɪ'ɛrədɛl'fweɪgəu] *n* Terra del Fuoco
tie tack *n* (*US*) fermacravatta *m inv*
tiff [tɪf] *n* battibecco
tiger ['taɪgə'] *n* tigre *f*
tight [taɪt] *adj* (*rope*) teso(-a), tirato(-a); (*clothes*) stretto(-a); (*budget, programme, bend*) stretto(-a); (*control*) severo(-a), fermo(-a); (*col: drunk*) sbronzo(-a) ▪ *adv* (*squeeze*) fortemente; (*shut*) ermeticamente; **to be packed ~**

(*suitcase*) essere pieno zeppo; (*people*) essere pigiati; **everybody hold ~!** tenetevi stretti!; *see also* **tights**

tighten ['taɪtn] *vt* (*rope*) tendere; (*screw*) stringere; (*control*) rinforzare ■ *vi* tendersi; stringersi

tight-fisted [taɪt'fɪstɪd] *adj* avaro(-a)

tight-lipped ['taɪt'lɪpt] *adj*: **to be ~** essere reticente; (*angry*) tenere le labbra serrate

tightly ['taɪtlɪ] *adv* (*grasp*) bene, saldamente

tightrope ['taɪtrəʊp] *n* corda (da acrobata)

tightrope walker *n* funambolo(-a)

tights [taɪts] *npl* (*Brit*) collant *m inv*

tigress ['taɪgrɪs] *n* tigre *f* (femmina)

tilde ['tɪldə] *n* tilde *f*

tile [taɪl] *n* (*on roof*) tegola; (*on floor*) mattonella; (*on wall*) piastrella ■ *vt* (*floor, bathroom etc*) piastrellare

tiled [taɪld] *adj* rivestito(-a) di tegole; a mattonelle; a piastrelle

till [tɪl] *n* registratore *m* di cassa ■ *vt* (*land*) coltivare ■ *prep, conj* = **until**

tiller ['tɪlə'] *n* (*Naut*) barra del timone

tilt [tɪlt] *vt* inclinare, far pendere ■ *vi* inclinarsi, pendere ■ *n* (*slope*) pendio; **to wear one's hat at a ~** portare il cappello sulle ventitrè; **(at) full ~** a tutta velocità

timber ['tɪmbə'] *n* (*material*) legname *m*; (*trees*) alberi *mpl* da legname

time [taɪm] *n* tempo; (*epoch: often pl*) epoca, tempo; (*by clock*) ora; (*moment*) momento; (*occasion, also Math*) volta; (*Mus*) tempo ■ *vt* (*race*) cronometrare; (*programme*) calcolare la durata di; (*remark etc*): **to ~ sth well/badly** scegliere il momento più/meno opportuno per qc; **a long ~** molto tempo; **for the ~ being** per il momento; **from ~ to ~** ogni tanto; **~ after ~, ~ and again** mille volte; **in ~** (*soon enough*) in tempo; (*after some time*) col tempo; (*Mus*) a tempo; **at times** a volte; **to take one's ~** prenderla con calma; **in a week's ~** fra una settimana; **in no ~** in un attimo; **on ~** puntualmente; **to be 30 minutes behind/ahead of ~** avere 30 minuti di ritardo/anticipo; **by the ~ he arrived** quando è arrivato; **5 times 5** 5 volte 5, 5 per 5; **what ~ is it?** che ora è?, che ore sono?; **what ~ do you make it?** che ora fa?; **to have a good ~** divertirsi; **they had a hard ~ of it** è stato duro per loro; **~'s up!** è (l')ora!; **to be behind the times** vivere nel passato; **I've no ~ for it** (*fig*) non ho tempo da perdere con cose del genere; **he'll do it in his own (good) ~** (*without being hurried*) lo farà quando avrà (un minuto di) tempo; **he'll do it in** or (*US*) **on his own ~** (*out of working hours*) lo farà nel suo tempo libero; **the bomb was timed**

to explode 5 minutes later la bomba era stata regolata in modo da esplodere 5 minuti più tardi

time-and-motion study ['taɪmənd'məʊʃən-] *n* analisi *f inv* dei tempi e dei movimenti

time bomb *n* bomba a orologeria

time card *n* cartellino (da timbrare)

time clock *n* orologio *m* marcatempo *inv*

time-consuming ['taɪmkənsjuːmɪŋ] *adj* che richiede molto tempo

time difference *n* differenza di fuso orario

time frame *n* tempi *mpl*

time-honoured, (*US*) **time-honored** ['taɪmɔnəd] *adj* consacrato(-a) dal tempo

timekeeper ['taɪmkiːpə'] *n* (*Sport*) cronometrista *m/f*

time lag *n* intervallo, ritardo; (*in travel*) differenza di fuso orario

timeless ['taɪmlɪs] *adj* eterno(-a)

time limit *n* limite *m* di tempo

timely ['taɪmlɪ] *adj* opportuno(-a)

time off *n* tempo libero

timer ['taɪmə'] *n* (*in kitchen*) contaminuti *m inv*; (*Tech*) timer *m inv*, temporizzatore *m*

time-saving ['taɪmseɪvɪŋ] *adj* che fa risparmiare tempo

time scale *n* tempi *mpl* d'esecuzione

time-sharing ['taɪmʃɛərɪŋ] *n* (*Comput*) divisione *f* di tempo

time sheet *n* = **time card**

time signal *n* segnale *m* orario

time switch *n* interruttore *m* a tempo

timetable ['taɪmteɪbl] *n* orario; (*programme of events etc*) programma *m*

time zone *n* fuso orario

timid ['tɪmɪd] *adj* timido(-a); (*easily scared*) pauroso(-a)

timidity [tɪ'mɪdɪtɪ] *n* timidezza

timing ['taɪmɪŋ] *n* sincronizzazione *f*; (*fig*) scelta del momento opportuno, tempismo; (*Sport*) cronometraggio

timing device *n* (*on bomb*) timer *m inv*

timpani ['tɪmpənɪ] *npl* timpani *mpl*

tin [tɪn] *n* stagno; (*also*: **tin plate**) latta; (*Brit: can*) barattolo (di latta), lattina, scatola; (*for baking*) teglia; **a ~ of paint** un barattolo di tinta *or* vernice

tin foil *n* stagnola

tinge [tɪndʒ] *n* sfumatura ■ *vt*: **tinged with** tinto(-a) di

tingle ['tɪŋgl] *vi* (*cheeks, skin: from cold*) pungere, pizzicare; (: *from bad circulation*) formicolare

tinker ['tɪŋkə'] *n* stagnino ambulante; (*gipsy*) zingaro(-a)
  ▶ **tinker with** *vt fus* armeggiare intorno a; cercare di riparare

tinkle ['tɪŋkl] *vi* tintinnare ■ *n* (*col*): **to give sb a ~** dare un colpo di telefono a qn

tin mine *n* miniera di stagno

tinned [tɪnd] *adj* (*Brit*: *food*) in scatola

tinnitus [tɪ'naɪtəs] *n* (*Med*) ronzio auricolare

tinny ['tɪnɪ] *adj* metallico(-a)

tin-opener ['tɪnəupnə'] *n* (*Brit*) apriscatole *m inv*

tinsel ['tɪnsl] *n* decorazioni *fpl* natalizie (*argentate*)

tint [tɪnt] *n* tinta; (*for hair*) shampoo *m inv* colorante ■ *vt* (*hair*) fare uno shampoo colorante a

tinted ['tɪntɪd] *adj* (*hair*) tinto(-a); (*spectacles, glass*) colorato(-a)

tiny ['taɪnɪ] *adj* minuscolo(-a)

tip [tɪp] *n* (*end*) punta; (*protective*: *on umbrella etc*) puntale *m*; (*gratuity*) mancia; (*for coal*) discarica; (*for rubbish*) immondezzaio; (*advice*) suggerimento ■ *vt* (*waiter*) dare la mancia a; (*tilt*) inclinare; (*overturn*: *also*: **tip over**) capovolgere; (*empty*: *also*: **tip out**) scaricare; (*predict*: *winner*) pronosticare; (: *horse*) dare vincente; **he tipped out the contents of the box** ha rovesciato il contenuto della scatola
▶ **tip off** *vt* fare una soffiata a

tip-off ['tɪpɔf] *n* (*hint*) soffiata

tipped ['tɪpt] *adj* (*Brit*: *cigarette*) col filtro; **steel-~** con la punta d'acciaio

Tipp-Ex® ['tɪpɛks] *n* (*Brit*) liquido correttore

tipple ['tɪpl] (*Brit*) *vi* sbevazzare ■ *n*: **to have a ~** prendere un bicchierino

tipster ['tɪpstə'] *n* (*Racing*) chi vende informazioni sulle corse e altre manifestazioni oggetto di

tipsy ['tɪpsɪ] *adj* brillo(-a)

tiptoe ['tɪptəu] *n*: **on ~** in punta di piedi

tiptop ['tɪptɔp] *adj*: **in ~ condition** in ottime condizioni

tirade [taɪ'reɪd] *n* filippica

tire ['taɪə'] *vt* stancare ■ *vi* stancarsi ■ *n* (*US*) = **tyre**
▶ **tire out** *vt* sfinire, spossare

tired ['taɪəd] *adj* stanco(-a); **to be/feel/look ~** essere/sentirsi/sembrare stanco; **to be ~ of** essere stanco *or* stufo di

tiredness ['taɪədnɪs] *n* stanchezza

tireless ['taɪəlɪs] *adj* instancabile

tiresome ['taɪəsəm] *adj* noioso(-a)

tiring ['taɪərɪŋ] *adj* faticoso(-a)

tissue ['tɪʃuː] *n* tessuto; (*paper handkerchief*) fazzolettino di carta

tissue paper *n* carta velina

tit [tɪt] *n* (*bird*) cinciallegra; (*col*: *breast*) tetta; **to give ~ for tat** rendere pan per focaccia

titanium [tɪ'teɪnɪəm] *n* titanio

titbit ['tɪtbɪt], (*US*) **tidbit** ['tɪdbɪt] *n* (*food*) leccornia; (*news*) notizia, ghiotta

titillate ['tɪtɪleɪt] *vt* titillare

titivate ['tɪtɪveɪt] *vt* agghindare

title ['taɪtl] *n* titolo; (*Law*: *right*): **~ (to)** diritto (a)

title deed *n* (*Law*) titolo di proprietà

title page *n* frontespizio

title role *n* ruolo *or* parte *f* principale

titter ['tɪtə'] *vi* ridere scioccamente

tittle-tattle ['tɪtltætl] *n* chiacchiere *fpl*, pettegolezzi *mpl*

titular ['tɪtjulə'] *adj* (*in name only*) nominale

tizzy ['tɪzɪ] *n* (*col*): **to be in a ~** essere in agitazione

T-junction ['tiː'dʒʌŋkʃən] *n* incrocio a T

TM *n abbr* (= *transcendental meditation*) M.T. *f*; (*Comm*) = **trademark**

TN *abbr* (*US*) = **Tennessee**

TNT *n abbr* (= *trinitrotoluene*) T.N.T. *m*

 KEYWORD

to [tuː, tə] *prep* **1** (*direction*) a; **to go to France/ London/school** andare in Francia/a Londra/ a scuola; **to go to town** andare in città; **to go to Paul's/the doctor's** andare da Paul/ dal dottore; **the road to Edinburgh** la strada per Edimburgo; **to the left/right** a sinistra/destra

2 (*as far as*) (fino) a; **from here to London** da qui a Londra; **to count to 10** contare fino a 10; **from 40 to 50 people** da 40 a 50 persone

3 (*with expressions of time*): **a quarter to 5** le 5 meno un quarto; **it's twenty to 3** sono le 3 meno venti

4 (*for, of*): **the key to the front door** la chiave della porta d'ingresso; **a letter to his wife** una lettera per la moglie

5 (*expressing indirect object*) a; **to give sth to sb** dare qc a qn; **give it to me** dammelo; **to talk to sb** parlare a qn; **it belongs to him** gli appartiene, è suo; **to be a danger to sb/sth** rappresentare un pericolo per qn/qc

6 (*in relation to*) a; **3 goals to 2** 3 goal a 2; **30 miles to the gallon** ≈ 11 chilometri con un litro; **4 apples to the kilo** 4 mele in un chilo

7 (*purpose, result*): **to come to sb's aid** venire in aiuto a qn; **to sentence sb to death** condannare a morte qn; **to my surprise** con mia sorpresa

■ *with vb* **1** (*simple infinitive*): **to go/eat** *etc* andare/mangiare *etc*

2 (*following another vb*): **to want/try/start to do** volere/cercare di/cominciare a fare

3 (*with vb omitted*): **I don't want to** non voglio (farlo); **you ought to** devi (farlo)

4 (*purpose, result*) per; **I did it to help you** l'ho fatto per aiutarti

5 (*equivalent to relative clause*): **I have things to do** ho da fare; **the main thing is to try** la cosa più importante è provare
6 (*after adjective etc*): **ready to go** pronto(-a) a partire; **too old/young to ...** troppo vecchio(-a)/giovane per ...
■ *adv*: **to push the door to** accostare la porta; **to go to and fro** andare e tornare

toad [təʊd] *n* rospo
toadstool ['təʊdstu:l] *n* fungo (velenoso)
toady ['təʊdɪ] *vi* adulare
toast [təʊst] *n* (*Culin*) toast *m*, pane *m* abbrustolito; (*drink, speech*) brindisi *m inv* ■ *vt* (*Culin*) abbrustolire; (*drink to*) brindare a; **a piece** *or* **slice of ~** una fetta di pane abbrustolito
toaster ['təʊstə'] *n* tostapane *m inv*
toastmaster ['təʊstmɑ:stə'] *n* direttore *m* dei brindisi
toast rack *n* portatoast *m inv*
tobacco [tə'bækəʊ] *n* tabacco; **pipe ~** tabacco da pipa
tobacconist [tə'bækənɪst] *n* tabaccaio(-a); **~'s (shop)** tabaccheria
Tobago [tə'beɪgəʊ] *n see* **Trinidad and Tobago**
toboggan [tə'bɔgən] *n* toboga *m inv*; (*child's*) slitta
today [tə'deɪ] *adv, n* (*also fig*) oggi *m inv*; **what day is it ~?** che giorno è oggi?; **what date is it ~?** quanti ne abbiamo oggi?; **~ is the 4th of March** (oggi) è il 4 di marzo; **~'s paper** il giornale di oggi; **a fortnight ~** quindici giorni a oggi
toddler ['tɔdlə'] *n* bambino(-a) che impara a camminare
toddy ['tɔdɪ] *n* grog *m inv*
to-do [tə'du:] *n* (*fuss*) storie *fpl*
toe [təʊ] *n* dito del piede; (*of shoe*) punta ■ *vt*: **to ~ the line** (*fig*) stare in riga, conformarsi; **big ~** alluce *m*; **little ~** mignolino
TOEFL ['təʊfl] *n abbr* = **Test(ing) of English as a Foreign Language**
toehold ['təʊhəʊld] *n* punto d'appoggio
toenail ['təʊneɪl] *n* unghia del piede
toffee ['tɔfɪ] *n* caramella
toffee apple *n* (*Brit*) mela caramellata
tofu ['təʊfu:] *n* tofu *m* (*latte di soia non fermentato*)
toga ['təʊgə] *n* toga
together [tə'gɛðə'] *adv* insieme; (*at same time*) allo stesso tempo; **~ with** insieme a
togetherness [tə'gɛðənɪs] *n* solidarietà; intimità
toggle switch ['tɔgl-] *n* (*Comput*) tasto bistabile
Togo ['təʊgəʊ] *n* Togo

togs [tɔgz] *npl* (*col: clothes*) vestiti *mpl*
toil [tɔɪl] *n* travaglio, fatica ■ *vi* affannarsi; sgobbare
toilet ['tɔɪlət] *n* (*Brit: lavatory*) gabinetto ■ *cpd* (*soap etc*) da toletta; **to go to the ~** andare al gabinetto *or* al bagno
toilet bag *n* (*Brit*) nécessaire *m inv* da toilette
toilet bowl *n* vaso *or* tazza del gabinetto
toilet paper *n* carta igienica
toiletries ['tɔɪlɪtrɪz] *npl* articoli *mpl* da toletta
toilet roll *n* rotolo di carta igienica
toilet water *n* acqua di colonia
to-ing and fro-ing ['tu:ɪŋən'frəʊɪŋ] *n* (*Brit*) andirivieni *m inv*
token ['təʊkən] *n* (*sign*) segno; (*voucher*) buono ■ *cpd* (*fee, strike*) simbolico(-a); **book/record ~** (*Brit*) buono-libro/-disco; **by the same ~** (*fig*) per lo stesso motivo
tokenism ['təʊkənɪzəm] *n* (*Pol*) concessione *f* pro forma *inv*
Tokyo ['təʊkjəʊ] *n* Tokyo *f*
told [təʊld] *pt, pp of* **tell**
tolerable ['tɔlərəbl] *adj* (*bearable*) tollerabile; (*fairly good*) passabile
tolerably ['tɔlərəblɪ] *adv* (*good, comfortable*) abbastanza
tolerance ['tɔlərns] *n* (*also Tech*) tolleranza
tolerant ['tɔlərnt] *adj*: **~ (of)** tollerante (nei confronti di)
tolerate ['tɔləreɪt] *vt* sopportare; (*Med, Tech*) tollerare
toleration [tɔlə'reɪʃən] *n* tolleranza
toll [təʊl] *n* (*tax, charge*) pedaggio ■ *vi* (*bell*) suonare; **the accident ~ on the roads** il numero delle vittime della strada
tollbridge ['təʊlbrɪdʒ] *n* ponte *m* a pedaggio
toll call *n* (*US Tel*) (telefonata) interurbana
toll-free ['təʊl'fri:] (*US*) *adj* senza addebito, gratuito(-a) ■ *adv* gratuitamente; **~ number** = numero verde
tomato (*pl* **tomatoes**) [tə'mɑ:təʊ] *n* pomodoro
tomb [tu:m] *n* tomba
tombola [tɔm'bəʊlə] *n* tombola
tomboy ['tɔmbɔɪ] *n* maschiaccio
tombstone ['tu:mstəʊn] *n* pietra tombale
tomcat ['tɔmkæt] *n* gatto
tomorrow [tə'mɔrəʊ] *adv, n* (*also fig*) domani *m inv*; **the day after ~** dopodomani; **a week ~** domani a otto; **~ morning** domani mattina
ton [tʌn] *n* tonnellata (*Brit* = 1016 *kg*; 20 *cwt*; *US* = 907 *kg*; *metric* = 1000 *kg*); (*Naut: also*: **register ton**) tonnellata di stazza (= 2.83 *cu.m*; 100 *cu.ft*); **tons of** (*col*) un mucchio *or* sacco di
tonal ['təʊnl] *adj* tonale
tone [təʊn] *n* tono; (*of musical instrument*) timbro ■ *vi* intonarsi

t

835

▶ **tone down** vt (colour, criticism, sound) attenuare

▶ **tone up** vt (muscles) tonificare

tone-deaf [təun'dɛf] adj che non ha orecchio (musicale)

toner ['təunə'] n (for photocopier) colorante m organico, toner m

Tonga ['tɔŋgə] n isole fpl Tonga

tongs [tɔŋz] npl tenaglie fpl; (for coal) molle fpl; (for hair) arricciacapelli m inv

tongue [tʌŋ] n lingua; ~ **in cheek** (fig) ironicamente

tongue-tied ['tʌŋtaɪd] adj (fig) muto(-a)

tongue-twister ['tʌŋtwɪstə'] n scioglilingua m inv

tonic ['tɔnɪk] n (Med) ricostituente m; (skin tonic) tonico; (Mus) nota tonica; (also: **tonic water**) acqua tonica

tonight [tə'naɪt] adv stanotte; (this evening) stasera ■ n questa notte; questa sera; **I'll see you** ~ ci vediamo stasera

tonnage ['tʌnɪdʒ] n (Naut) tonnellaggio, stazza

tonne [tʌn] n (Brit: metric ton) tonnellata

tonsil ['tɔnsl] n tonsilla; **to have one's tonsils out** farsi operare di tonsille

tonsillitis [tɔnsɪ'laɪtɪs] n tonsillite f; **to have** ~ avere la tonsillite

too [tu:] adv (excessively) troppo; (also) anche; **it's** ~ **sweet** è troppo dolce; **I went** ~ ci sono andato anch'io; ~ **much** adv troppo adj troppo(-a); ~ **many** adj troppi(-e); ~ **bad!** tanto peggio!; peggio così!

took [tuk] pt of **take**

tool [tu:l] n utensile m attrezzo; (fig: person) strumento ■ vt lavorare con un attrezzo

tool box n cassetta f portautensili inv

tool kit n cassetta di attrezzi

toot [tu:t] vi suonare; (with car horn) suonare il clacson

tooth (pl **teeth**) [tu:θ, ti:θ] n (Anat, Tech) dente m; **to clean one's teeth** lavarsi i denti; **to have a** ~ **out** or (US) **pulled** farsi togliere un dente; **by the skin of one's teeth** per il rotto della cuffia

toothache ['tu:θeɪk] n mal m di denti; **to have** ~ avere il mal di denti

tooth fairy n: **the** ~ fatina che porta soldini in regalo a un bimbo quando perde un dentino di latte, ≈ topolino

toothpaste ['tu:θpeɪst] n dentifricio

toothpick ['tu:θpɪk] n stuzzicadenti m inv

tooth powder n dentifricio in polvere

top [tɔp] n (of mountain, page, ladder) cima; (of box, cupboard, table) sopra m inv, parte f superiore; (lid: of box, jar) coperchio; (: of bottle) tappo; (toy) trottola; (Dress: blouse etc) camicia (or maglietta etc); (of pyjamas) giacca ■ adj

più alto(-a); (in rank) primo(-a); (best) migliore ■ vt (exceed) superare; (be first in) essere in testa a; **on** ~ **of** sopra, in cima a; (in addition to) oltre a; **from** ~ **to toe** (Brit) dalla testa ai piedi; **at the** ~ **of the stairs/ page/street** in cima alle scale/alla pagina/ alla strada; **the** ~ **of the milk** (Brit) la panna; **at** ~ **speed** a tutta velocità; **at the** ~ **of one's voice** (fig) a squarciagola; **over the** ~ (col: behaviour etc) eccessivo(-a); **to go over the** ~ esagerare

▶ **top up**, (US) **top off** vt riempire

topaz ['təupæz] n topazio

top-class ['tɔp'klɑ:s] adj di prim'ordine

topcoat ['tɔpkəut] n soprabito

topflight ['tɔpflaɪt] adj di primaria importanza

top floor n ultimo piano

top hat n cilindro

top-heavy [tɔp'hɛvɪ] adj (object) con la parte superiore troppo pesante

topic ['tɔpɪk] n argomento

topical ['tɔpɪkəl] adj d'attualità

topless ['tɔplɪs] adj (bather etc) col seno scoperto; ~ **swimsuit** topless m inv

top-level ['tɔplɛvl] adj (talks) ad alto livello

topmost ['tɔpməust] adj il(la) più alto(-a)

top-notch ['tɔp'nɔtʃ] adj (col: player, performer) di razza; (: school, car) eccellente

topography [tə'pɔgrəfɪ] n topografia

topping ['tɔpɪŋ] n (Culin) guarnizione f

topple ['tɔpl] vt rovesciare, far cadere ■ vi cadere; traballare

top-ranking ['tɔp'ræŋkɪŋ] adj di massimo grado

top-secret ['tɔp'si:krɪt] adj segretissimo(-a)

top-security ['tɔpsɪ'kjuərɪtɪ] adj (Brit) di massima sicurezza

topsy-turvy ['tɔpsɪ'tə:vɪ] adj, adv sottosopra inv

top-up ['tɔpʌp] n (for mobile phone: also: **top-up card**) ricarica; **would you like a** ~? vuole che le riempia il bicchiere (or la tazza etc)?

top-up loan n (Brit) prestito integrativo

torch [tɔ:tʃ] n torcia; (Brit: electric) lampadina tascabile

tore [tɔ:'] pt of **tear²**

torment n ['tɔ:mɛnt] tormento ■ vt [tɔ:'mɛnt] tormentare; (fig: annoy) infastidire

torn [tɔ:n] pp of **tear²** ■ adj: ~ **between** (fig) combattuto(-a) tra

tornado (pl **tornadoes**) [tɔ:'neɪdəu] n tornado

torpedo (pl **torpedoes**) [tɔ:'pi:dəu] n siluro

torpedo boat n motosilurante f

torpor ['tɔ:pə'] n torpore m

torrent ['tɔrnt] n torrente m

torrential [tɔ'rɛnʃl] *adj* torrenziale
torrid ['tɔrɪd] *adj* torrido(-a); *(fig)* denso(-a) di passione
torso ['tɔːsəʊ] *n* torso
tortoise ['tɔːtəs] *n* tartaruga
tortoiseshell ['tɔːtəʃɛl] *adj* di tartaruga
tortuous ['tɔːtjuəs] *adj* tortuoso(-a)
torture ['tɔːtʃə'] *n* tortura ■ *vt* torturare
torturer ['tɔːtʃərə'] *n* torturatore(-trice)
Tory ['tɔːrɪ] *adj* tory *inv*, conservatore(-trice) ■ *n* tory *m/f inv*, conservatore(-trice)
toss [tɔs] *vt* gettare, lanciare; *(Brit: pancake)* far saltare; *(head)* scuotere ■ *n (movement: of head etc)* movimento brusco; *(of coin)* lancio; **to win/lose the ~** vincere/perdere a testa o croce; *(Sport)* vincere/perdere il sorteggio; **to ~ a coin** fare a testa o croce; **to ~ up for sth** fare a testa o croce per qc; **to ~ and turn** *(in bed)* girarsi e rigirarsi
tot [tɔt] *n (Brit: drink)* bicchierino; *(child)* bimbo(-a)
▶ **tot up** *vt (Brit: figures)* sommare
total ['təʊtl] *adj* totale ■ *n* totale *m* ■ *vt (add up)* sommare; *(amount to)* ammontare a; **in ~** in tutto
totalitarian [təʊtælɪ'tɛərɪən] *adj* totalitario(-a)
totality [təʊ'tælɪtɪ] *n* totalità
totally ['təʊtəlɪ] *adv* completamente
tote bag ['təʊt-] *n* sporta
totem pole ['təʊtəm-] *n* totem *m inv*
totter ['tɔtə'] *vi* barcollare; *(object, government)* vacillare
touch [tʌtʃ] *n* tocco; *(sense)* tatto; *(contact)* contatto; *(Football)* fuori gioco *m* ■ *vt* toccare; **a ~ of** *(fig)* un tocco di; un pizzico di; **to get in ~ with** mettersi in contatto con; **to lose ~** *(friends)* perdersi di vista; **I'll be in ~** mi farò sentire; **to be out of ~ with events** essere tagliato fuori; **the personal ~** una nota personale; **to put the finishing touches to sth** dare gli ultimi ritocchi a qc
▶ **touch on** *vt fus (topic)* sfiorare, accennare a
▶ **touch up** *vt (improve)* ritoccare
touch-and-go ['tʌtʃən'gəʊ] *adj* incerto(-a); **it was ~ with the sick man** il malato era tra la vita e la morte
touchdown ['tʌtʃdaʊn] *n* atterraggio; *(on sea)* ammaraggio; *(US Football)* meta
touched [tʌtʃt] *adj* commosso(-a); *(col)* tocco(-a), toccato(-a)
touching ['tʌtʃɪŋ] *adj* commovente
touchline ['tʌtʃlaɪn] *n (Sport)* linea laterale
touch screen ['tʌtʃskriːn] *n (Tech)* schermo touch screen; **touch-screen mobile** telefono touch screen; **touch-screen technology** tecnologia touch screen
touch-sensitive ['tʌtʃˈsɛnsɪtɪv] *adj* sensibile al tatto

touch-type ['tʌtʃtaɪp] *vi* dattilografare (senza guardare i tasti)
touchy ['tʌtʃɪ] *adj (person)* suscettibile
tough [tʌf] *adj* duro(-a); *(resistant)* resistente; *(meat)* duro(-a), tiglioso(-a); *(journey)* faticoso(-a), duro(-a); *(person: rough)* violento(-a), brutale ■ *n (gangster etc)* delinquente *m/f*; **~ luck!** che sfortuna!
toughen ['tʌfn] *vt* indurire, rendere più resistente
toughness ['tʌfnɪs] *n* durezza; resistenza
toupee ['tuːpeɪ] *n* parrucchino
tour [tuə'] *n* viaggio; *(also:* **package tour)** viaggio organizzato *or* tutto compreso; *(of town, museum)* visita; *(by artist)* tournée *f inv* ■ *vt* visitare; **to go on a ~ of** *(region, country)* fare il giro di; *(museum, castle)* visitare; **to go on ~** andare in tournée
tour guide *n* accompagnatore(-trice) turistico(-a)
touring ['tuərɪŋ] *n* turismo
tourism ['tuərɪzəm] *n* turismo
tourist ['tuərɪst] *n* turista *m/f* ■ *adv (travel)* in classe turistica ■ *cpd* turistico(-a); **the ~ trade** il turismo
tourist class *n (Aviat)* classe *f* turistica
tourist office *n* pro loco *f inv*
tournament ['tuənəmənt] *n* torneo
tourniquet ['tuənɪkeɪ] *n (Med)* laccio emostatico, pinza emostatica
tour operator *n (Brit)* operatore *m* turistico
tousled ['tauzld] *adj (hair)* arruffato(-a)
tout [taut] *vi:* **to ~ for** procacciare, raccogliere; cercare clienti per ■ *n (Brit: also:* **ticket tout)** bagarino; **to ~ sth (around)** *(Brit)* cercare di (ri)vendere qc
tow [təʊ] *vt* rimorchiare ■ *n* rimorchio; **"on ~"**, *(US)* **"in ~"** *(Aut)* "veicolo rimorchiato"; **to give sb a ~** rimorchiare qn
toward [tə'wɔːd], **towards** [tə'wɔːdz] *prep* verso; *(of attitude)* nei confronti di; *(of purpose)* per; **~(s) noon/the end of the year** verso mezzogiorno/la fine dell'anno; **to feel friendly ~(s) sb** provare un sentimento d'amicizia per qn
towel ['tauəl] *n* asciugamano; *(also:* **tea towel)** strofinaccio; **to throw in the ~** *(fig)* gettare la spugna
towelling ['tauəlɪŋ] *n (fabric)* spugna
towel rail, *(US)* **towel rack** *n* portasciugamano
tower ['tauə'] *n* torre *f* ■ *vi (building, mountain)* innalzarsi; **to ~ above** *or* **over sb/sth** sovrastare qn/qc
tower block *n (Brit)* palazzone *m*
towering ['tauərɪŋ] *adj* altissimo(-a), imponente

town [taun] *n* città *f inv*; **to go to** ~ andare in città; (*fig*) mettercela tutta; **in (the)** ~ in città; **to be out of** ~ essere fuori città
town centre *n* centro (città)
town clerk *n* segretario comunale
town council *n* consiglio comunale
town crier [-'kraɪəʳ] *n* (*Brit*) banditore(-trice)
town hall *n* ≈ municipio
townie ['taunɪ] *n* (*Brit col*) uno(-a) di città
town plan *n* pianta della città
town planner *n* urbanista *m/f*
town planning *n* urbanistica
township ['taunʃɪp] *n* township *f inv*
townspeople ['taunzpiːpl] *npl* cittadinanza, cittadini *mpl*
towpath ['təupɑːθ] *n* alzaia
towrope ['təurəup] *n* (cavo da) rimorchio
tow truck *n* (*US*) carro a attrezzi *inv*
toxic ['tɔksɪk] *adj* tossico(-a)
toxic asset *n* (*Econ*) titolo tossico
toxic bank *n* (*Econ*) banca cattiva (*che investe in titoli tossici*)
toxin ['tɔksɪn] *n* tossina
toy [tɔɪ] *n* giocattolo
▶ **toy with** *vt fus* giocare con; (*idea*) accarezzare, trastullarsi con
toyshop ['tɔɪʃɔp] *n* negozio di giocattoli
trace [treɪs] *n* traccia ■ *vt* (*draw*) tracciare; (*follow*) seguire; (*locate*) rintracciare; **without** ~ (*disappear*) senza lasciare traccia; **there was no** ~ **of it** non ne restava traccia
trace element *n* oligoelemento
trachea [trə'kɪə] *n* (*Anat*) trachea
tracing paper ['treɪsɪŋ-] *n* carta da ricalco
track [træk] *n* (*mark: of person, animal*) traccia; (*on tape, Sport; path: gen*) pista; (: *of suspect, animal*) pista, tracce *fpl*; (*Rail*) binario, rotaie *fpl*; (*Comput*) traccia, pista ■ *vt* seguire le tracce di; **to keep** ~ **of** seguire; **to be on the right** ~ (*fig*) essere sulla buona strada
▶ **track down** *vt* (*prey*) scovare; snidare; (*sth lost*) rintracciare
tracker dog ['trækə-] *n* (*Brit*) cane *m* poliziotto *inv*
track events *npl* (*Sport*) prove *fpl* su pista
tracking station ['trækɪŋ-] *n* (*Space*) osservatorio spaziale
track meet *n* (*US*) meeting *m inv* di atletica
track record *n*: **to have a good** ~ (*fig*) avere un buon curriculum
tracksuit ['træksuːt] *n* tuta sportiva
tract [trækt] *n* (*Geo*) tratto, estensione *f*; (*pamphlet*) opuscolo, libretto; **respiratory** ~ (*Anat*) apparato respiratorio
traction ['trækʃən] *n* trazione *f*
tractor ['træktəʳ] *n* trattore *m*
trade [treɪd] *n* commercio; (*skill, job*) mestiere *m*;

(*industry*) industria, settore *m* ■ *vi* commerciare; **to** ~ **with/in** commerciare con/in; **foreign** ~ commercio estero; **Department of T- and Industry** (*Brit*) ≈ Ministero del Commercio
▶ **trade in** *vt* (*old car etc*) dare come pagamento parziale
trade barrier *n* barriera commerciale
trade deficit *n* bilancio commerciale in deficit
Trade Descriptions Act *n* (*Brit*) legge *f* a tutela del consumatore
trade discount *n* sconto sul listino
trade fair *n* fiera campionaria
trade-in ['treɪdɪn] *n*: **to take as a** ~ accettare in permuta
trade-in price *n* prezzo di permuta
trademark ['treɪdmɑːk] *n* marchio di fabbrica
trade mission *n* missione *f* commerciale
trade name *n* marca, nome *m* depositato
trade-off ['treɪdɔf] *n* compromesso, accomodamento
trader ['treɪdəʳ] *n* commerciante *m/f*
trade secret *n* segreto di fabbricazione
tradesman ['treɪdzmən] *n* fornitore *m*; (*shopkeeper*) negoziante *m*
trade union *n* sindacato
trade unionist [-'juːnjənɪst] *n* sindacalista *m/f*
trade wind *n* aliseo
trading ['treɪdɪŋ] *n* commercio
trading estate *n* (*Brit*) zona industriale
trading stamp *n* bollo premio
tradition [trə'dɪʃən] *n* tradizione *f*; **traditions** *npl* tradizioni, usanze *fpl*
traditional [trə'dɪʃənl] *adj* tradizionale
traffic ['træfɪk] *n* traffico ■ *vi*: **to** ~ **in** (*pej: liquor, drugs*) trafficare in
traffic calming [-'kɑːmɪŋ] *n* uso di accorgimenti per rallentare il traffico in zone abitate
traffic circle *n* (*US*) isola rotatoria
traffic island *n* salvagente *m*, isola *f*, spartitraffico *inv*
traffic jam *n* ingorgo (del traffico)
trafficker ['træfɪkəʳ] *n* trafficante *m/f*
traffic lights *npl* semaforo
traffic offence *n* (*Brit*) infrazione *f* al codice stradale
traffic sign *n* cartello stradale
traffic violation *n* (*US*) = **traffic offence**
traffic warden *n* addetto(-a) al controllo del traffico e del parcheggio
tragedy ['trædʒədɪ] *n* tragedia
tragic ['trædʒɪk] *adj* tragico(-a)
trail [treɪl] *n* (*tracks*) tracce *fpl*, pista; (*path*) sentiero; (*of smoke etc*) scia ■ *vt* trascinare, strascicare; (*follow*) seguire ■ *vi* essere al traino; (*dress etc*) strusciare; (*plant*)

arrampicarsi; strusciare; **to be on sb's ~** essere sulle orme di qn
▸ **trail away, trail off** vi (sound) affievolirsi; (interest, voice) spegnersi a poco a poco
▸ **trail behind** vi essere al traino
trailer ['treɪlə^r] n (Aut) rimorchio; (US) roulotte f inv; (Cine) prossimamente m inv
trailer truck n (US) autoarticolato
train [treɪn] n treno; (of dress) coda, strascico; (Brit: series): ~ **of events** serie f di avvenimenti a catena ▪ vt (apprentice, doctor etc) formare; (sportsman) allenare; (dog) addestrare; (memory) esercitare; (point: gun etc): **to ~ sth on** puntare qc contro ▪ vi formarsi, allenarsi; (learn a skill) fare pratica, fare tirocinio; **to go by ~** andare in or col treno; **one's ~ of thought** il filo dei propri pensieri; **to ~ sb to do sth** preparare qn a fare qc
train attendant n (US) addetto(-a) ai vagoni letto
trained [treɪnd] adj qualificato(-a); allenato(-a), addestrato(-a)
trainee [treɪ'niː] n allievo(-a); (in trade) apprendista m/f; **he's a ~ teacher** sta facendo tirocinio come insegnante
trainer ['treɪnə^r] n (Sport) allenatore(-trice); (of dogs etc) addestratore(-trice); **trainers** npl (shoes) scarpe fpl da ginnastica
training ['treɪnɪŋ] n formazione f; allenamento; addestramento; **in ~** (Sport) in allenamento; (fit) in forma
training college n istituto professionale
training course n corso di formazione professionale
train wreck n (fig) persona distrutta; (: pej) rottame (m); **he's a complete ~** è completamente distrutto, è un rottame
traipse [treɪps] vi: **to ~ in/out** etc entrare/uscire etc trascinandosi
trait [treɪt] n tratto
traitor ['treɪtə^r] n traditore(-trice)
trajectory [trə'dʒɛktərɪ] n traiettoria
tram [træm] n (Brit: also: **tramcar**) tram m inv
tramline ['træmlaɪn] n linea tranviaria
tramp [træmp] n (person) vagabondo(-a); (col: pej: woman) sgualdrina ▪ vi camminare con passo pesante
trample ['træmpl] vt: **to ~ (underfoot)** calpestare
trampoline ['træmpəliːn] n trampolino
trance [trɑːns] n trance f inv; (Med) catalessi f inv; **to go into a ~** cadere in trance
tranquil ['træŋkwɪl] adj tranquillo(-a)
tranquillity, (US) **tranquility** [træŋ'kwɪlɪtɪ] n tranquillità
tranquillizer, (US) **tranquilizer** ['træŋkwɪlaɪzə^r] n (Med) tranquillante m

transact [træn'zækt] vt (business) trattare
transaction [træn'zækʃən] n transazione f; **transactions** npl (minutes) atti mpl; **cash ~** operazione f in contanti
transatlantic ['trænzət'læntɪk] adj transatlantico(-a)
transcend [træn'sɛnd] vt trascendere; (excel over) superare
transcendental [trænsɛn'dɛntl] adj: **~ meditation** meditazione f trascendentale
transcribe [træn'skraɪb] vt trascrivere
transcript ['trænskrɪpt] n trascrizione f
transcription [træn'skrɪpʃən] n trascrizione f
transept ['trænsɛpt] n transetto
transfer n ['trænsfə^r] (gen, also Sport) trasferimento; (Pol: of power) passaggio; (picture, design) decalcomania; (stick-on) autoadesivo ▪ vt [træns'fəː^r] trasferire; passare; decalcare; **by bank ~** tramite trasferimento bancario; **to ~ the charges** (Brit Tel) telefonare con addebito al ricevente
transferable [træns'fəːrəbl] adj trasferibile; **not ~** non cedibile, personale
transfix [træns'fɪks] vt trafiggere; (fig): **transfixed with fear** paralizzato dalla paura
transform [træns'fɔːm] vt trasformare
transformation [trænsfə'meɪʃən] n trasformazione f
transformer [træns'fɔːmə^r] n (Elec) trasformatore m
transfusion [træns'fjuːʒən] n trasfusione f
transgress [træns'grɛs] vt (go beyond) infrangere; (violate) trasgredire, infrangere
tranship [træn'ʃɪp] vt trasbordare
transient ['trænzɪənt] adj transitorio(-a), fugace
transistor [træn'zɪstə^r] n (Elec) transistor m inv; (also: **transistor radio**) radio f inv a transistor
transit ['trænzɪt] n: **in ~** in transito
transit camp n campo (di raccolta) profughi
transition [træn'zɪʃən] n passaggio, transizione f
transitional [træn'zɪʃənl] adj di transizione
transitive ['trænzɪtɪv] adj (Ling) transitivo(-a)
transit lounge n (Aviat) sala di transito
transitory ['trænzɪtərɪ] adj transitorio(-a)
translate [trænz'leɪt] vt tradurre; **to ~ (from/into)** tradurre (da/in)
translation [trænz'leɪʃən] n traduzione f; (Scol: as opposed to prose) versione f
translator [trænz'leɪtə^r] n traduttore(-trice)
translucent [trænz'luːsnt] adj traslucido(-a)
transmission [trænz'mɪʃən] n trasmissione f
transmit [trænz'mɪt] vt trasmettere
transmitter [trænz'mɪtə^r] n trasmettitore m
transparency [træns'pɛərnsɪ] n (Phot) diapositiva

t

transparent [træns'pærnt] *adj* trasparente

transpire [træns'paɪəʳ] *vi* (*happen*) succedere; **it finally transpired that ...** alla fine si è venuto a sapere che ...

transplant *vt* [træns'plɑːnt] trapiantare ■ *n* ['trænsplɑːnt] trapianto; **to have a heart ~** subire un trapianto cardiaco

transport *n* ['trænspɔːt] trasporto ■ *vt* [træns'pɔːt] trasportare; **public ~** mezzi *mpl* pubblici; **Department of T~** (*Brit*) Ministero dei Trasporti

transportation ['trænspɔː'teɪʃən] *n* (*mezzo di*) trasporto; (*of prisoners*) deportazione *f*; **Department of T~** (*US*) Ministero dei Trasporti

transport café *n* (*Brit*) trattoria per camionisti

transpose [træns'pəuz] *vt* trasporre

transsexual [trænz'sɛksjuəl] *adj, n* transessuale *m/f*

transverse ['trænzvəːs] *adj* trasversale

transvestite [trænz'vɛstaɪt] *n* travestito(-a)

trap [træp] *n* (*snare, trick*) trappola; (*carriage*) calesse *m* ■ *vt* prendere in trappola, intrappolare; (*immobilize*) bloccare; (*jam*) chiudere, schiacciare; **to set** or **lay a ~ (for sb)** tendere una trappola (a qn); **to ~ one's finger in the door** chiudersi il dito nella porta; **shut your ~!** (*col*) chiudi quella boccaccia!

trap door *n* botola

trapeze [trə'piːz] *n* trapezio

trapper ['træpəʳ] *n* cacciatore *m* di animali da pelliccia

trappings ['træpɪŋz] *npl* ornamenti *mpl*; indoratura, sfarzo

trash [træʃ] *n* (*pej: goods*) ciarpame *m*; (*: nonsense*) sciocchezze *fpl*; (*US: rubbish*) rifiuti *mpl*, spazzatura

trash can *n* (*US*) secchio della spazzatura

trashy ['træʃɪ] *adj* (*col*) scadente

trauma ['trɔːmə] *n* trauma *m*

traumatic [trɔː'mætɪk] *adj* (*Psych: fig*) traumatico(-a), traumatizzante

travel ['trævl] *n* viaggio; viaggi *mpl* ■ *vi* viaggiare; (*move*) andare, spostarsi ■ *vt* (*distance*) percorrere; **this wine doesn't ~ well** questo vino non resiste agli spostamenti

travel agency *n* agenzia (di) viaggi

travel agent *n* agente *m* di viaggio

travel brochure *n* dépliant *m* di viaggi

traveller, (*US*) **traveler** ['trævləʳ] *n* viaggiatore(-trice); (*Comm*) commesso viaggiatore

traveller's cheque, (*US*) **traveler's check** *n* assegno turistico

travelling, (*US*) **traveling** ['trævlɪŋ] *n* viaggi *mpl* ■ *adj* (*circus, exhibition*) itinerante ■ *cpd* (*bag, clock*) da viaggio; (*expenses*) di viaggio

travelling salesman, (*US*) **traveling salesman** *n* commesso viaggiatore

travelogue ['trævəlɔg] *n* (*book, film*) diario or documentario di viaggio; (*talk*) conferenza sui viaggi

travel sickness *n* mal *m* d'auto (*or di mare or d'aria*)

traverse ['trævəs] *vt* traversare, attraversare

travesty ['trævəstɪ] *n* parodia

trawler ['trɔːləʳ] *n* peschereccio (a strascico)

tray [treɪ] *n* (*for carrying*) vassoio; (*on desk*) vaschetta

treacherous ['trɛtʃərəs] *adj* traditore(-trice); **road conditions today are ~** oggi il fondo stradale è pericoloso

treachery ['trɛtʃərɪ] *n* tradimento

treacle ['triːkl] *n* melassa

tread [trɛd] *n* passo; (*sound*) rumore *m* di passi; (*of tyre*) battistrada *m inv* ■ *vi* (*pt* **trod**, *pp* **trodden**) [trɔd, 'trɔdn] camminare
▶ **tread on** *vt fus* calpestare

treadle ['trɛdl] *n* pedale *m*

treas. *abbr* = **treasurer**

treason ['triːzn] *n* tradimento

treasure ['trɛʒəʳ] *n* tesoro ■ *vt* (*value*) tenere in gran conto, apprezzare molto; (*store*) custodire gelosamente

treasure hunt *n* caccia al tesoro

treasurer [trɛʒərəʳ] *n* tesoriere(-a)

treasury ['trɛʒərɪ] *n* tesoreria; (*Pol*): **the T~,** (*US*) **the T~ Department** ≈ il Ministero del Tesoro

treasury bill *n* buono del tesoro

treat [triːt] *n* regalo ■ *vt* trattare; (*Med*) curare; (*consider*) considerare; **it was a ~** mi (*or ci etc*) ha fatto veramente piacere; **to ~ sb to sth** offrire qc a qn; **to ~ sth as a joke** considerare qc uno scherzo

treatise ['triːtɪz] *n* trattato

treatment ['triːtmənt] *n* trattamento; **to have ~ for sth** (*Med*) farsi curare qc

treaty ['triːtɪ] *n* patto, trattato

treble [trɛbl] *adj* triplo(-a), triplice ■ *n* (*Mus*) soprano *m/f* ■ *vt* triplicare ■ *vi* triplicarsi

treble clef *n* chiave *f* di violino

tree [triː] *n* albero

tree-lined ['triːlaɪnd] *adj* fiancheggiato(-a) da alberi

treetop ['triːtɔp] *n* cima di un albero

tree trunk *n* tronco d'albero

trek [trɛk] *n* (*hike*) spedizione *f*; (*tiring walk*) camminata sfiancante ■ *vi* (*as holiday*) fare dell'escursionismo

trellis ['trɛlɪs] *n* graticcio, pergola

tremble ['trɛmbl] vi tremare; (machine) vibrare

trembling ['trɛmblɪŋ] n tremito ■ adj tremante

tremendous [trɪ'mɛndəs] adj (enormous) enorme; (excellent) meraviglioso(-a), formidabile

tremendously [trɪ'mɛndəslɪ] adv incredibilmente; **he enjoyed it** ~ gli è piaciuto da morire

tremor [trɛmə^r] n tremore m, tremito; (also: **earth tremor**) scossa sismica

trench [trɛntʃ] n trincea

trench coat n trench m inv

trench warfare n guerra di trincea

trend [trɛnd] n (tendency) tendenza; (of events) corso; (fashion) moda; ~ **towards/away from** tendenza a/ad allontanarsi da; **to set the** ~ essere all'avanguardia; **to set a** ~ lanciare una moda

trendy ['trɛndɪ] adj (idea) di moda; (clothes) all'ultima moda

trepidation [trɛpɪ'deɪʃən] n trepidazione f, agitazione f

trespass ['trɛspəs] vi: **to** ~ **on** entrare abusivamente in; (fig) abusare di; **"no trespassing"** "proprietà privata", "vietato l'accesso"

trespasser ['trɛspəsə^r] n trasgressore m; **"trespassers will be prosecuted"** "i trasgressori saranno puniti secondo i termini di legge"

trestle ['trɛsl] n cavalletto

trestle table n tavola su cavalletti

trial ['traɪəl] n (Law) processo; (test: of machine etc) collaudo; (hardship) prova, difficoltà f inv; (worry) cruccio; **trials** npl (Athletics) prove fpl di qualificazione; **horse trials** concorso ippico; **to be on** ~ essere sotto processo; ~ **by jury** processo penale con giuria; **to be sent for** ~ essere rinviato a giudizio; **to bring sb to** ~ **(for a crime)** portare qn in giudizio (per un reato); **by** ~ **and error** a tentoni

trial balance n (Comm) bilancio di verifica

trial basis n: **on a** ~ in prova

trial run n periodo di prova

triangle ['traɪæŋgl] n (Math, Mus) triangolo

triangular [traɪ'æŋgjulə^r] adj triangolare

triathlon [traɪ'æθlən] n triathlon m inv

tribal ['traɪbəl] adj tribale

tribe [traɪb] n tribù f inv

tribesman ['traɪbzmən] n membro della tribù

tribulation [trɪbju'leɪʃən] n tribolazione f

tribunal [traɪ'bju:nl] n tribunale m

tributary ['trɪbju:tərɪ] n (river) tributario, affluente m

tribute ['trɪbju:t] n tributo, omaggio; **to pay** ~ **to** rendere omaggio a

trice [traɪs] n: **in a** ~ in un attimo

trick [trɪk] n trucco; (clever act) stratagemma m; (joke) tiro; (Cards) presa ■ vt imbrogliare, ingannare; **to play a** ~ **on sb** giocare un tiro a qn; **it's a** ~ **of the light** è un effetto ottico; **that should do the** ~ (col) vedrai che funziona; **to** ~ **sb into doing sth** convincere qn a fare qc con l'inganno; **to** ~ **sb out of sth** fregare qc a qn

trickery ['trɪkərɪ] n inganno

trickle ['trɪkl] n (of water etc) rivolo; gocciolio ■ vi gocciolare; **to** ~ **in/out** (people) entrare/uscire alla spicciolata

trick question n domanda f trabocchetto inv

trickster ['trɪkstə^r] n imbroglione(-a)

tricky ['trɪkɪ] adj difficile, delicato(-a)

tricycle ['traɪsɪkl] n triciclo

trifle ['traɪfl] n sciocchezza; (Brit Culin) ≈ zuppa inglese ■ adv: **a** ~ **long** un po' lungo ■ vi: **to** ~ **with** prendere alla leggera

trifling ['traɪflɪŋ] adj insignificante

trigger ['trɪgə^r] n (of gun) grilletto
  ▶ **trigger off** vt dare l'avvio a

trigonometry [trɪgə'nɔmətrɪ] n trigonometria

trilby ['trɪlbɪ] n (Brit: also: **trilby hat**) cappello floscio di feltro

trill [trɪl] n (of bird, Mus) trillo

trilogy ['trɪlədʒɪ] n trilogia

trim [trɪm] adj ordinato(-a); (house, garden) ben tenuto(-a); (figure) snello(-a) ■ n (haircut etc) spuntata, regolata; (embellishment) finiture fpl; (on car) guarnizioni fpl ■ vt spuntare; (decorate): **to** ~ **(with)** decorare (con); (Naut: a sail) orientare; **to keep in (good)** ~ mantenersi in forma

trimmings ['trɪmɪŋz] npl decorazioni fpl; (extras: gen Culin) guarnizione f

Trinidad and Tobago ['trɪnɪdæd-] n Trinidad e Tobago m

Trinity ['trɪnɪtɪ] n: **the** ~ la Trinità

trinket ['trɪŋkɪt] n gingillo; (piece of jewellery) ciondolo

trio ['tri:əu] n trio

trip [trɪp] n viaggio; (excursion) gita, escursione f; (stumble) passo falso ■ vi inciampare; (go lightly) camminare con passo leggero; **on a** ~ in viaggio
  ▶ **trip up** vi inciampare ■ vt fare lo sgambetto a

tripartite [traɪ'pɑ:taɪt] adj (agreement) tripartito(-a); (talks) a tre

tripe [traɪp] n (Culin) trippa; (pej: rubbish) sciocchezze fpl, fesserie fpl

triple ['trɪpl] adj triplo(-a) ■ adv: ~ **the**

t

distance/the speed tre volte più lontano/ più veloce

triple jump n triplo salto

triplets ['trɪplɪts] npl bambini(-e) trigemini(-e)

triplicate ['trɪplɪkət] n: **in ~** in triplice copia

tripod ['traɪpɔd] n treppiede m

Tripoli ['trɪpəlɪ] n Tripoli f

tripper ['trɪpəʳ] n (Brit) gitante m/f

tripwire ['trɪpwaɪəʳ] n filo in tensione che fa scattare una trappola, allarme etc

trite [traɪt] adj banale, trito(-a)

triumph ['traɪʌmf] n trionfo ■ vi: **to ~ (over)** trionfare (su)

triumphal [traɪʌmfl] adj trionfale

triumphant [traɪʌmfənt] adj trionfante

trivia ['trɪvɪə] npl banalità fpl

trivial ['trɪvɪəl] adj (matter) futile; (excuse, comment) banale; (amount) irrisorio(-a); (mistake) di poco conto

triviality [trɪvɪ'ælɪtɪ] n frivolezza; (trivial detail) futilità

trivialize ['trɪvɪəlaɪz] vt sminuire

trod [trɔd] pt of **tread**

trodden ['trɔdn] pp of **tread**

trolley ['trɔlɪ] n carrello; (in hospital) lettiga

trolley bus n filobus m inv

trollop ['trɔləp] n prostituta

trombone [trɔm'bəun] n trombone m

troop [tru:p] n gruppo; (Mil) squadrone m; **troops** npl (Mil) truppe fpl; **trooping the colour** (Brit: ceremony) sfilata della bandiera

▶ **troop in** vi entrare a frotte

▶ **troop out** vi uscire a frotte

troop carrier n (plane) aereo per il trasporto (di) truppe; (Naut: also: **troopship**) nave f per il trasporto (di) truppe

trooper ['tru:pəʳ] n (Mil) soldato di cavalleria; (US: policeman) poliziotto (della polizia di stato)

troopship ['tru:pʃɪp] n nave f per il trasporto (di) truppe

trophy ['trəufɪ] n trofeo

tropic ['trɔpɪk] n tropico; **in the tropics** ai tropici; **T~ of Cancer/Capricorn** tropico del Cancro/Capricorno

tropical ['trɔpɪkəl] adj tropicale

trot [trɔt] n trotto ■ vi trottare; **on the ~** (Brit fig) di fila, uno(-a) dopo l'altro(-a)

▶ **trot out** vt (excuse, reason) tirar fuori; (names, facts) recitare di fila

trouble ['trʌbl] n (problems) difficoltà fpl, problemi mpl; (worry) preoccupazione f; (bother, effort) sforzo; (with sth mechanical) noie fpl; (Pol) conflitti mpl, disordine m; (Med): **stomach** etc ~ disturbi mpl gastrici etc ■ vt disturbare; (worry) preoccupare ■ vi: **to ~ to do** disturbarsi a fare; **troubles** npl (Pol etc) disordini mpl; **to be in ~** avere dei problemi; (for doing wrong) essere nei guai; **to go to the ~ of doing** darsi la pena di fare; **it's no ~!** di niente!; **what's the ~?** cosa c'è che non va?; **the ~ is ...** c'è che ..., il guaio è che ...; **to have ~ doing sth** avere delle difficoltà a fare qc; **please don't ~ yourself** non si disturbi

troubled ['trʌbld] adj (person) preoccupato(-a), inquieto(-a); (epoch, life) agitato(-a), difficile

trouble-free ['trʌblfri:] adj senza problemi

troublemaker ['trʌblmeɪkəʳ] n elemento disturbatore, agitatore(-trice)

troubleshooter ['trʌblʃu:təʳ] n (in conflict) conciliatore m

troublesome ['trʌblsəm] adj fastidioso(-a), seccante

trouble spot n zona calda

troubling ['trʌblɪŋ] adj (thought) preoccupante; **these are ~ times** questi sono tempi difficili

trough [trɔf] n (also: **drinking trough**) abbeveratoio; (also: **feeding trough**) trogolo, mangiatoia; (channel) canale m; **~ of low pressure** (Meteor) depressione f

trounce [trauns] vt (defeat) sgominare

troupe [tru:p] n troupe f inv

trouser press n stirapantaloni m inv

trousers ['trauzəz] npl pantaloni mpl, calzoni mpl; **short ~** (Brit) calzoncini mpl

trouser suit n (Brit) completo m or tailleur m inv pantalone inv

trousseau (pl **trousseaux** or **trousseaus**) ['tru:səu, -z] n corredo da sposa

trout [traut] n (pl inv) trota

trowel ['trauəl] n cazzuola

truant ['truənt] n: **to play ~** (Brit) marinare la scuola

truce [tru:s] n tregua

truck [trʌk] n autocarro, camion m inv; (Rail) carro merci aperto; (for luggage) carrello m portabagagli inv

truck driver, (US) **trucker** ['trʌkəʳ] n camionista m/f

truck farm n (US) orto industriale

trucking ['trʌkɪŋ] n (esp US) autotrasporto

trucking company n (esp US) impresa di trasporti

truculent ['trʌkjulənt] adj aggressivo(-a), brutale

trudge [trʌdʒ] vi trascinarsi pesantemente

true [tru:] adj vero(-a); (accurate) accurato(-a), esatto(-a); (genuine) reale; (faithful) fedele; (wall, beam) a piombo; (wheel) centrato(-a); **to come ~** avverarsi; **~ to life** verosimile

truffle ['trʌfl] n tartufo

truly ['tru:lɪ] adv veramente; (truthfully)

sinceramente; (*faithfully*) fedelmente; **yours**
~ (*in letter-writing*) distinti saluti

trump [trʌmp] n (*Cards*) atout m inv; **to turn
up trumps** (*fig*) fare miracoli

trump card n atout m inv; (*fig*) asso nella
manica

trumped-up [trʌmpt'ʌp] adj inventato(-a)

trumpet ['trʌmpɪt] n tromba

truncated [trʌŋ'keɪtɪd] adj tronco(-a)

truncheon ['trʌntʃən] n sfollagente m inv

trundle ['trʌndl] vt, vi: **to ~ along** rotolare
rumorosamente

trunk [trʌŋk] n (*of tree, person*) tronco; (*of
elephant*) proboscide f; (*case*) baule m; (*US Aut*)
bagagliaio

trunk call n (*Brit Tel*) (telefonata) interurbana

trunk road n (*Brit*) strada principale

trunks [trʌŋks] npl (*also:* **swimming trunks**)
calzoncini mpl da bagno

truss [trʌs] n (*Med*) cinto erniario ■ vt: **to ~
(up)** (*Culin*) legare

trust [trʌst] n fiducia; (*Law*)
amministrazione f fiduciaria; (*Comm*) trust
m inv ■ vt (*have confidence in*) fidarsi di; (*rely on*)
contare su; (*entrust*): **to ~ sth to sb** affidare qc
a qn; (*hope*): **to ~ (that)** sperare (che); **you'll
have to take it on ~** deve credermi sulla
parola; **in ~** (*Law*) in amministrazione
fiduciaria

trust company n trust m inv

trusted ['trʌstɪd] adj fidato(-a)

trustee [trʌs'tiː] n (*Law*) amministratore(-a)
fiduciario(-a); (*of school etc*)
amministratore(-trice)

trustful ['trʌstful] adj fiducioso(-a)

trust fund n fondo fiduciario

trusting ['trʌstɪŋ] adj = **trustful**

trustworthy ['trʌstwə:ðɪ] adj fidato(-a),
degno(-a) di fiducia

trusty ['trʌstɪ] adj fidato(-a)

truth (*pl* **truths**) [truːθ, truːðz] n verità f inv

truthful ['truːθful] adj (*person*) sincero(-a); (*description*) veritiero(-a), esatto(-a)

truthfully ['truːθəlɪ] adv sinceramente

truthfulness ['truːθəlnɪs] n veracità

try [traɪ] n prova, tentativo; (*Rugby*) meta
■ vt (*Law*) giudicare; (*test: sth new*) provare;
(*strain: patience, person*) mettere alla prova ■ vi
provare; **to ~ to do** cercare di fare; (*seek*)
cercare di fare; **to give sth a ~** provare qc;
to ~ one's (very) best *or* **one's (very)
hardest** mettercela tutta

▶ **try on** vt (*clothes*) provare, mettere alla
prova; **to ~ it on** (*fig*) cercare di farla

▶ **try out** vt provare, mettere alla prova

trying ['traɪɪŋ] adj (*day, experience*) logorante,
pesante; (*child*) difficile, insopportabile

tsar [zɑːr] n zar m inv

T-shirt ['tiːʃəːt] n maglietta

TSO n abbr (*Brit:* = *The Stationery Office*)
≈ Poligrafici mpl dello Stato

T-square ['tiːskwɛər] n riga a T

tsunami [tsuˈnɑːmɪ] n tsunami m inv

TT adj abbr (*Brit col*) = **teetotal** ■ abbr (*US*)
= **Trust Territory**

tub [tʌb] n tinozza; mastello; (*bath*) bagno

tuba ['tjuːbə] n tuba

tubby ['tʌbɪ] adj grassoccio(-a)

tube [tjuːb] n tubo; (*Brit: underground*)
metropolitana; (*for tyre*) camera d'aria;
(*col: television*): **the ~** la tele

tubeless ['tjuːblɪs] adj (*tyre*) senza camera
d'aria

tuber ['tjuːbər] n (*Bot*) tubero

tuberculosis [tjubəːkjuˈləʊsɪs] n
tubercolosi f

tube station n (*Brit*) stazione f del metrò

tubing ['tjuːbɪŋ] n tubazione f; **a piece of ~**
un tubo

tubular ['tjuːbjulər] adj tubolare

TUC n abbr (*Brit:* = *Trades Union Congress*)
confederazione f dei sindacati britannici

tuck [tʌk] n (*Sewing*) piega ■ vt (*put*) mettere
▶ **tuck away** vt riporre
▶ **tuck in** vt mettere dentro; (*child*)
rimboccare ■ vi (*eat*) mangiare di buon
appetito; abbuffarsi
▶ **tuck up** vt (*child*) rimboccare

tuck shop n negozio di pasticceria (*in una
scuola*)

Tue., Tues. abbr (= *Tuesday*) mar.

Tuesday ['tjuːzdɪ] n martedì m inv; (**the date**)
today is ~ 23rd March oggi è martedì 23
marzo; **on ~** martedì; **on Tuesdays** di
martedì; **every ~** tutti i martedì; **every
other ~** ogni due martedì; **last/next ~**
martedì scorso/prossimo; **~ next** martedì
prossimo; **the following ~** (*in past*) il
martedì successivo; (*in future*) il martedì
dopo; **a week/fortnight on ~, ~ week/
fortnight** martedì fra una settimana/
quindici giorni; **the ~ before last** martedì di
due settimane fa; **the ~ after next** non
questo martedì ma il prossimo; **~ morning/
lunchtime/afternoon/evening** martedì
mattina/all'ora di pranzo/pomeriggio/sera;
~ night martedì sera; (*overnight*) martedì
notte; **~'s newspaper** il giornale di martedì

tuft [tʌft] n ciuffo

tug [tʌɡ] n (*ship*) rimorchiatore m ■ vt tirare
con forza

tug-of-love [tʌɡəv'lʌv] n contesa per la
custodia dei figli; **~ children** bambini mpl
coinvolti nella contesa per la custodia

843

tug-of-war [ˌtʌgəvˈwɔːʳ] n tiro alla fune
tuition [tjuːˈɪʃən] n (Brit: lessons) lezioni fpl; (US: fees) tasse fpl scolastiche (or universitarie)
tulip [ˈtjuːlɪp] n tulipano
tumble [ˈtʌmbl] n (fall) capitombolo ■ vi capitombolare, ruzzolare; (somersault) fare capriole ■ vt far cadere; **to ~ to sth** (col) realizzare qc
tumbledown [ˈtʌmbldaun] n cadente, diroccato(-a)
tumble dryer n (Brit) asciugatrice f
tumbler [ˈtʌmbləʳ] n bicchiere m senza stelo
tummy [ˈtʌmɪ] n (col) pancia
tumour, (US) **tumor** [ˈtjuːməʳ] n tumore m
tumult [ˈtjuːmʌlt] n tumulto
tumultuous [tjuːˈmʌltjuəs] adj tumultuoso(-a)
tuna [ˈtjuːnə] n (pl inv: also: **tuna fish**) tonno
tune [tjuːn] n (melody) melodia, aria ■ vt (Mus) accordare; (Radio, TV, Aut) regolare, mettere a punto; **to be in/out of ~** (instrument) essere accordato(-a)/scordato(-a); (singer) essere intonato(-a)/stonato(-a); **to the ~ of** (fig: amount) per la modesta somma di; **in ~ with** (fig) in accordo con
　▸**tune in** vi (Radio, TV): **to ~ in (to)** sintonizzarsi (su)
　▸**tune up** vi (musician) accordare lo strumento
tuneful [ˈtjuːnful] adj melodioso(-a)
tuner [ˈtjuːnəʳ] n (radio set) sintonizzatore m; **piano ~** accordatore(-trice) di pianoforte
tuner amplifier n amplificatore m di sintonia
tungsten [ˈtʌŋstn] n tungsteno
tunic [ˈtjuːnɪk] n tunica
tuning [ˈtjuːnɪŋ] n messa a punto
tuning fork n diapason m inv
Tunis [ˈtjuːnɪs] n Tunisi f
Tunisia [tjuːˈnɪzɪə] n Tunisia
Tunisian [tjuːˈnɪzɪən] adj, n tunisino(-a)
tunnel [ˈtʌnl] n galleria ■ vi scavare una galleria
tunnel vision n (Med) riduzione f del campo visivo; (fig) visuale f ristretta
tunny [ˈtʌnɪ] n tonno
turban [ˈtəːbən] n turbante m
turbid [ˈtəːbɪd] adj torbido(-a)
turbine [ˈtəːbaɪn] n turbina
turbo [ˈtəːbəu] n turbo m inv
turbojet [ˈtəːbəuˈdʒɛt] n turboreattore m
turboprop [ˈtəːbəuˈprɔp] n turboelica m inv
turbot [ˈtəːbət] n (pl inv) rombo gigante
turbulence [ˈtəːbjuləns] n turbolenza
turbulent [ˈtəːbjulənt] adj turbolento(-a); (sea) agitato(-a)

tureen [təˈriːn] n zuppiera
turf [təːf] n terreno erboso; (clod) zolla ■ vt coprire di zolle erbose; **the T-** l'ippodromo
　▸**turf out** vt (col) buttar fuori
turf accountant n (Brit) allibratore m
turgid [ˈtəːdʒɪd] adj (speech) ampolloso(-a), pomposo(-a)
Turin [tjuəˈrɪn] n Torino f
Turk [təːk] n turco(-a)
Turkey [ˈtəːkɪ] n Turchia
turkey [ˈtəːkɪ] n tacchino
Turkish [ˈtəːkɪʃ] adj turco(-a) ■ n (Ling) turco
Turkish bath n bagno turco
Turkish delight n gelatine ricoperte di zucchero a velo
turmeric [ˈtəːmərɪk] n curcuma
turmoil [ˈtəːmɔɪl] n confusione f, tumulto
turn [təːn] n giro; (in road) curva; (tendency: of mind, events) tendenza; (performance) numero; (Med) crisi f inv, attacco ■ vt girare, voltare; (milk) far andare a male; (shape: wood, metal) tornire; (change): **to ~ sth into** trasformare qc in ■ vi girare; (person: look back) girarsi, voltarsi; (reverse direction) girarsi indietro; (change) cambiare; (become) diventare; **to ~ into** trasformarsi in; **a good ~** un buon servizio; **a bad ~** un brutto tiro; **it gave me quite a ~** mi ha fatto prendere un bello spavento; **"no left ~"** (Aut) "divieto di svolta a sinistra"; **it's your ~** tocca a lei; **in ~** a sua volta; **a turno**; **to take turns (at sth)** fare (qc) a turno; **at the ~ of the year/century** alla fine dell'anno/del secolo; **to take a ~ for the worse** (situation, events) volgere al peggio; (patient, health) peggiorare; **to ~ left/right** girare a sinistra/destra
　▸**turn about** vi girarsi indietro
　▸**turn away** vi girarsi (dall'altra parte) ■ vt (reject: person) mandar via; (: business) rifiutare
　▸**turn back** vi ritornare, tornare indietro
　▸**turn down** vt (refuse) rifiutare; (reduce) abbassare; (fold) ripiegare
　▸**turn in** vi (col: go to bed) andare a letto ■ vt (fold) voltare in dentro
　▸**turn off** vi (from road) girare, voltare ■ vt (light, radio, engine etc) spegnere
　▸**turn on** vt (light, radio etc) accendere; (engine) avviare
　▸**turn out** vt (light, gas) chiudere, spegnere; (produce: goods) produrre; (: novel, good pupils) creare ■ vi (appear, attend: troops, doctor etc) presentarsi; **to ~ out to be ...** rivelarsi ..., risultare ...
　▸**turn over** vi (person) girarsi; (car etc) capovolgersi ■ vt girare
　▸**turn round** vi girare; (person) girarsi
　▸**turn up** vi (person) arrivare, presentarsi;

(*lost object*) saltar fuori ■ *vt* (*collar, sound, gas etc*) alzare

turnabout ['tə:nəbaut], **turnaround** ['tə:nəraund] *n* (*fig*) dietrofront *m inv*

turncoat ['tə:nkəut] *n* voltagabbana *m/f inv*

turned-up ['tə:ndʌp] *adj* (*nose*) all'insù

turning ['tə:nɪŋ] *n* (*in road*) curva; (*side road*) strada laterale; **the first ~ on the right** la prima a destra

turning circle *n* (*Brit*) diametro di sterzata

turning point *n* (*fig*) svolta decisiva

turning radius *n* (*US*) = **turning circle**

turnip ['tə:nɪp] *n* rapa

turnout ['tə:naut] *n* presenza, affluenza

turnover ['tə:nəuvə^r] *n* (*Comm: amount of money*) giro di affari; (*: of goods*) smercio; (*Culin*): **apple** *etc* ~ sfogliatella alle mele *etc*; **there is a rapid ~ in staff** c'è un ricambio molto rapido di personale

turnpike ['tə:npaɪk] *n* (*US*) autostrada a pedaggio

turnstile ['tə:nstaɪl] *n* tornella

turntable ['tə:nteɪbl] *n* (*on record player*) piatto

turn-up ['tə:nʌp] *n* (*Brit: on trousers*) risvolto

turpentine ['tə:pəntaɪn] *n* (*also*: **turps**) acqua ragia

turquoise [tə:kwɔɪz] *n* (*stone*) turchese *m* ■ *adj* color turchese; di turchese

turret ['tʌrɪt] *n* torretta

turtle ['tə:tl] *n* testuggine *f*

turtleneck ['tə:tlnɛk], **turtleneck sweater** ['tə:tlnɛk-] *n* maglione *m* con il collo alto

Tuscan ['tʌskən] *adj, n* toscano(-a)

Tuscany ['tʌskənɪ] *n* Toscana

tusk [tʌsk] *n* zanna

tussle ['tʌsl] *n* baruffa, mischia

tutor ['tju:tə^r] *n* (*in college*) docente *m/f* (*responsabile di un gruppo di studenti*); (*private teacher*) precettore *m*

tutorial [tju:'tɔ:rɪəl] *n* (*Scol*) lezione *f* con discussione (*a un gruppo limitato*)

tuxedo [tʌk'si:dəu] *n* (*US*) smoking *m inv*

TV [ti:'vi:] *n abbr* (= *television*) tivù *f inv*

TV dinner *n* pasto *m* pronto

twaddle ['twɔdl] *n* scemenze *fpl*

twang [twæŋ] *n* (*of instrument*) suono vibrante; (*of voice*) accento nasale ■ *vi* vibrare ■ *vt* (*guitar*) pizzicare le corde di

tweak [twi:k] *vt* (*nose*) pizzicare; (*ear, hair*) tirare

tweed [twi:d] *n* tweed *m inv*

tweezers ['twi:zəz] *npl* pinzette *fpl*

twelfth [twɛlfθ] *num* dodicesimo(-a)

Twelfth Night *n* la notte dell'Epifania

twelve [twɛlv] *num* dodici; **at ~** alle dodici, a mezzogiorno; (*midnight*) a mezzanotte

twentieth ['twɛntɪɪθ] *num* ventesimo(-a)

twenty ['twɛntɪ] *num* venti

twerp [twə:p] *n* (*col*) idiota *m/f*

twice [twaɪs] *adv* due volte; ~ **as much** due volte tanto; ~ **a week** due volte alla settimana; **she is ~ your age** ha il doppio dei suoi anni

twiddle ['twɪdl] *vt, vi*: **to ~ (with) sth** giocherellare con qc; **to ~ one's thumbs** (*fig*) girarsi i pollici

twig [twɪg] *n* ramoscello ■ *vt, vi* (*col*) capire

twilight ['twaɪlaɪt] *n* (*evening*) crepuscolo; (*morning*) alba; **in the ~** nella penombra

twin [twɪn] *adj, n* gemello(-a)

twin beds *npl* letti *mpl* gemelli

twin-bedded room ['twɪn'bɛdɪd-] *n* stanza con letti gemelli

twin-carburettor ['twɪnka:bju'rɛtə^r] *adj* a doppio carburatore

twine [twaɪn] *n* spago, cordicella ■ *vi* (*plant*) attorcigliarsi; (*road*) serpeggiare

twin-engined ['twɪn'ɛndʒɪnd] *adj* a due motori; ~ **aircraft** bimotore *m*

twinge [twɪndʒ] *n* (*of pain*) fitta; **a ~ of conscience/regret** un rimorso/rimpianto

twinkle ['twɪŋkl] *n* scintillio ■ *vi* scintillare; (*eyes*) brillare

twin room *n* stanza con letti gemelli

twin town *n* città *f inv* gemella

twirl [twə:l] *n* piroetta ■ *vt* far roteare ■ *vi* roteare

twist [twɪst] *n* torsione *f*; (*in wire, flex*) storta; (*in story*) colpo di scena; (*bend*) svolta, piega ■ *vt* attorcigliare; (*weave*) intrecciare; (*roll around*) arrotolare; (*fig*) deformare ■ *vi* attorcigliarsi; arrotolarsi; (*road*) serpeggiare; **to ~ one's ankle/wrist** (*Med*) slogarsi la caviglia/il polso

twisted ['twɪstɪd] *adj* (*wire, rope*) attorcigliato(-a); (*ankle, wrist*) slogato(-a); (*fig: logic, mind*) contorto(-a)

twit [twɪt] *n* (*col*) minchione(-a)

twitch [twɪtʃ] *n* tiratina; (*nervous*) tic *m inv* ■ *vi* contrarsi; avere un tic

Twitter® ['twɪtə^r] *n* Twitter® *m*

two [tu:] *num* due; ~ **by** ~, **in twos** a due a due; **to put ~ and ~ together** (*fig*) trarre le conclusioni

two-bit [tu:'bɪt] *adj* (*esp US: col, pej*) da quattro soldi

two-door [tu:'dɔ:^r] *adj* (*Aut*) a due porte

two-faced ['tu:'feɪst] *adj* (*pej: person*) falso(-a)

twofold ['tu:fəuld] *adv*: **to increase ~** aumentare del doppio ■ *adj* (*increase*) doppio(-a); (*reply*) in due punti

two-piece ['tu:'pi:s] *n* (*also*: **two-piece suit**) due pezzi *m inv*; (*also*: **two-piece swimsuit**) (costume *m* da bagno a) due pezzi *m inv*

t

two-seater ['tu:'si:tə^r] *n* (*plane*) biposto; (*car*) macchina a due posti

twosome ['tu:səm] *n* (*people*) coppia

two-stroke ['tu:strəuk] *n* (*engine*) due tempi *m inv* ■ *adj* a due tempi

two-tone ['tu:təun] *adj* (*colour*) bicolore

two-way ['tu:weɪ] *adj* (*traffic*) a due sensi; ~ **radio** radio *f inv* ricetrasmittente

TX *abbr* (*US*) = **Texas**

tycoon [taɪ'ku:n] *n*: (**business**) ~ magnate *m*

type [taɪp] *n* (*category*) genere *m*; (*model*) modello; (*example*) tipo; (*Typ*) tipo, carattere *m* ■ *vt* (*letter etc*) battere (a macchina), dattilografare; **what ~ do you want?** che tipo vuole?; **in bold/italic ~** in grassetto/corsivo

type-cast ['taɪpkɑ:st] *adj* (*actor*) a ruolo fisso

typeface ['taɪpfeɪs] *n* carattere *m* tipografico

typescript ['taɪpskrɪpt] *n* dattiloscritto

typeset ['taɪpsɛt] *vt* comporre

typesetter ['taɪpsɛtə^r] *n* compositore *m*

typewriter ['taɪpraɪtə^r] *n* macchina da scrivere

typewritten ['taɪprɪtn] *adj* dattiloscritto(-a), battuto(-a) a macchina

typhoid ['taɪfɔɪd] *n* tifoidea

typhoon [taɪ'fu:n] *n* tifone *m*

typhus ['taɪfəs] *n* tifo

typical ['tɪpɪkl] *adj* tipico(-a)

typify ['tɪpɪfaɪ] *vt* essere tipico(-a) di

typing ['taɪpɪŋ] *n* dattilografia

typing error *n* errore *m* di battitura

typing pool *n* ufficio *m*, dattilografia *inv*

typist ['taɪpɪst] *n* dattilografo(-a)

typo ['taɪpəu] *n abbr* (*col*: = *typographical error*) refuso

typography [taɪ'pɒgrəfɪ] *n* tipografia

tyranny ['tɪrənɪ] *n* tirannia

tyrant ['taɪərnt] *n* tiranno

tyre, (*US*) **tire** ['taɪə^r] *n* pneumatico, gomma

tyre pressure *n* pressione *f* (delle gomme)

Tyrol [tɪ'rəul] *n* Tirolo

Tyrolean [tɪrə'li:ən], **Tyrolese** [tɪrə'li:z] *adj, n* tirolese *m/f*

Tyrrhenian Sea [tɪ'ri:nɪən-] *n*: **the** ~ il mar Tirreno

Uu

U, u [ju:] *n* (*letter*) U, u *m or f inv*; **U for Uncle** ≈ U come Udine

U *n abbr* (*Brit Cine*: = *universal*) per tutti

UAW *n abbr* (*US*: = *United Automobile Workers*) sindacato degli operai automobilistici

UB40 *n abbr* (*Brit*: = *unemployment benefit form 40*) modulo per la richiesta del sussidio di disoccupazione

U-bend ['ju:bɛnd] *n* (*in pipe*) sifone *m*

ubiquitous [ju:'bɪkwɪtəs] *adj* onnipresente

UCAS ['ju:kæs] *n abbr* (*Brit*) = **Universities and Colleges Admissions Service**

UDA *n abbr* (*Brit*: = *Ulster Defence Association*) organizzazione paramilitare protestante

UDC *n abbr* (*Brit*) = **Urban District Council**

udder ['ʌdər] *n* mammella

UDI *abbr* (*Brit Pol*) = **unilateral declaration of independence**

UDR *n abbr* (*Brit*: = *Ulster Defence Regiment*) reggimento dell'esercito britannico in Irlanda del Nord

UEFA [ju:'eɪfə] *n abbr* (= *Union of European Football Associations*) U.E.F.A. *f*

UFO ['ju:fəu] *n abbr* (= *unidentified flying object*) UFO *m inv*

Uganda [ju:'gændə] *n* Uganda

Ugandan [ju:'gændən] *adj, n* ugandese *m/f*

UGC *n abbr* (*Brit*: = *University Grants Committee*) organo che autorizza sovvenzioni alle università

ugh [ə:h] *excl* puah!

ugliness ['ʌglɪnɪs] *n* bruttezza

ugly ['ʌglɪ] *adj* brutto(-a)

UHF *abbr* = **ultra-high frequency**

UHT *adj abbr* = **ultra heat treated**; **~ milk** latte *m* UHT

UK *n abbr* = **United Kingdom**

Ukraine [ju:'kreɪn] *n* Ucraina

Ukrainian [ju:'kreɪnɪən] *adj* ucraino(-a) ▪ *n* (*person*) ucraino(-a); (*Ling*) ucraino

ulcer ['ʌlsər] *n* ulcera; **mouth ~** afta

Ulster ['ʌlstər] *n* Ulster *m*

ulterior [ʌl'tɪərɪər] *adj* ulteriore; **~ motive** secondo fine *m*

ultimata [ʌltɪ'meɪtə] *npl of* **ultimatum**

ultimate ['ʌltɪmɪt] *adj* ultimo(-a), finale; (*authority*) massimo(-a), supremo(-a) ▪ *n*: **the ~ in luxury** il non plus ultra del lusso

ultimately ['ʌltɪmɪtlɪ] *adv* alla fine; in definitiva, in fin dei conti

ultimatum (*pl* **ultimatums** *or* **ultimata**) [ʌltɪ'meɪtəm, -tə] *n* ultimatum *m inv*

ultrasonic [ʌltrə'sɔnɪk] *adj* ultrasonico(-a)

ultrasound [ʌltrə'saund] *n* (*Med*) ecografia

ultraviolet ['ʌltrə'vaɪəlɪt] *adj* ultravioletto(-a)

umbilical [ʌm'bɪlɪkl] *adj*: **~ cord** cordone *m* ombelicale

umbrage ['ʌmbrɪdʒ] *n*: **to take ~** offendersi, impermalirsi

umbrella [ʌm'brɛlə] *n* ombrello; **under the ~ of** (*fig*) sotto l'egida di

umlaut ['umlaut] *n* Umlaut *m inv*

umpire ['ʌmpaɪər] *n* arbitro

umpteen [ʌmp'ti:n] *adj* non so quanti(-e); **for the umpteenth time** per l'ennesima volta

UMW *n abbr* (= *United Mineworkers of America*) unione dei minatori d'America

UN *n abbr* = **United Nations**

unabashed [ʌnə'bæʃt] *adj* imperturbato(-a)

unabated [ʌnə'beɪtɪd] *adj* non diminuito(-a)

unable [ʌn'eɪbl] *adj*: **to be ~ to** non potere, essere nell'impossibilità di; (*not to know how to*) essere incapace di, non sapere

unabridged [ʌnə'brɪdʒd] *adj* integrale

unacceptable [ʌnək'sɛptəbl] *adj* (*proposal, behaviour*) inaccettabile; (*price*) impossibile

unaccompanied [ʌnə'kʌmpənɪd] *adj* (*child, lady*) non accompagnato(-a); (*singing, song*) senza accompagnamento

unaccountably [ʌnə'kauntəblɪ] *adv* inesplicabilmente

unaccounted [ʌnə'kauntɪd] *adj*: **two passengers are ~ for** due passeggeri mancano all'appello

unaccustomed [ʌnə'kʌstəmd] *adj* insolito(-a); **to be ~ to sth** non essere abituato(-a) a qc

unacquainted [ʌnə'kweɪntɪd] *adj*: **to be ~ with** (*facts*) ignorare, non essere al corrente di

u

unadulterated [ʌnə'dʌltəreɪtɪd] *adj* (*gen*) puro(-a); (*wine*) non sofisticato(-a)

unaffected [ʌnə'fektɪd] *adj* (*person, behaviour*) naturale, spontaneo(-a); (*emotionally*): **to be ~ by** non essere toccato(-a) da

unafraid [ʌnə'freɪd] *adj*: **to be ~** non aver paura

unaided [ʌn'eɪdɪd] *adv* senza aiuto

unanimity [juːnə'nɪmɪtɪ] *n* unanimità

unanimous [juː'nænɪməs] *adj* unanime

unanimously [juː'nænɪməslɪ] *adv* all'unanimità

unanswered [ʌn'ɑːnsəd] *adj* (*question, letter*) senza risposta; (*criticism*) non confutato(-a)

unappetizing [ʌn'æpɪtaɪzɪŋ] *adj* poco appetitoso(-a)

unappreciative [ʌnə'priːʃɪətɪv] *adj* che non apprezza

unarmed [ʌn'ɑːmd] *adj* (*person*) disarmato(-a); (*combat*) senz'armi

unashamed [ʌnə'ʃeɪmd] *adj* sfacciato(-a), senza vergogna

unassisted [ʌnə'sɪstɪd] *adj, adv* senza nessun aiuto

unassuming [ʌnə'sjuːmɪŋ] *adj* modesto(-a), senza pretese

unattached [ʌnə'tætʃt] *adj* senza legami, libero(-a)

unattended [ʌnə'tendɪd] *adj* (*car, child, luggage*) incustodito(-a)

unattractive [ʌnə'træktɪv] *adj* privo(-a) di attrattiva, poco attraente

unauthorized [ʌn'ɔːθəraɪzd] *adj* non autorizzato(-a)

unavailable [ʌnə'veɪləbl] *adj* (*article, room, book*) non disponibile; (*person*) impegnato(-a)

unavoidable [ʌnə'vɔɪdəbl] *adj* inevitabile

unavoidably [ʌnə'vɔɪdəblɪ] *adv* (*detained*) per cause di forza maggiore

unaware [ʌnə'wɛər] *adj*: **to be ~ of** non sapere, ignorare

unawares [ʌnə'wɛəz] *adv* di sorpresa, alla sprovvista

unbalanced [ʌn'bælənst] *adj* squilibrato(-a)

unbearable [ʌn'bɛərəbl] *adj* insopportabile

unbeatable [ʌn'biːtəbl] *adj* imbattibile

unbeaten [ʌn'biːtn] *adj* (*team, army*) imbattuto(-a); (*record*) insuperato(-a)

unbecoming [ʌnbɪ'kʌmɪŋ] *adj* (*unseemly: language, behaviour*) sconveniente; (*unflattering: garment*) che non dona

unbeknown [ʌnbɪ'nəun], **unbeknownst** [ʌnbɪ'nəunst] *adv*: **~(st) to** all'insaputa di

unbelief [ʌnbɪ'liːf] *n* incredulità

unbelievable [ʌnbɪ'liːvəbl] *adj* incredibile

unbelievingly [ʌnbɪ'liːvɪŋlɪ] *adv* con aria incredula

unbend [ʌn'bɛnd] *vb* (*irreg*) *vi* distendersi ■ *vt* (*wire*) raddrizzare

unbending [ʌn'bɛndɪŋ] *adj* (*fig*) inflessibile, rigido(-a)

unbiased, unbiassed [ʌn'baɪəst] *adj* obiettivo(-a), imparziale

unblemished [ʌn'blɛmɪʃt] *adj* senza macchia

unblock [ʌn'blɔk] *vt* (*pipe, road*) sbloccare

unborn [ʌn'bɔːn] *adj* non ancora nato(-a)

unbounded [ʌn'baundɪd] *adj* sconfinato(-a), senza limite

unbreakable [ʌn'breɪkəbl] *adj* infrangibile

unbridled [ʌn'braɪdld] *adj* sbrigliato(-a)

unbroken [ʌn'brəukən] *adj* (*intact*) intero(-a); (*continuous*) continuo(-a); (*record*) insuperato(-a)

unbuckle [ʌn'bʌkl] *vt* slacciare

unburden [ʌn'bəːdn] *vt*: **to ~ o.s.** sfogarsi

unbutton [ʌn'bʌtn] *vt* sbottonare

uncalled-for [ʌn'kɔːldfɔːr] *adj* (*remark*) fuori luogo *inv*; (*action*) ingiustificato(-a)

uncanny [ʌn'kænɪ] *adj* misterioso(-a), strano(-a)

unceasing [ʌn'siːsɪŋ] *adj* incessante

unceremonious [ʌnsɛrɪ'məunɪəs] *adj* (*abrupt, rude*) senza tante cerimonie

uncertain [ʌn'səːtn] *adj* incerto(-a); **it's ~ whether ...** non è sicuro se ...; **in no ~ terms** chiaro e tondo, senza mezzi termini

uncertainty [ʌn'səːtntɪ] *n* incertezza

unchallenged [ʌn'tʃælɪndʒd] *adj* incontestato(-a); **to go ~** non venire contestato, non trovare opposizione

unchanged [ʌn'tʃeɪndʒd] *adj* immutato(-a)

uncharitable [ʌn'tʃærɪtəbl] *adj* duro(-a), severo(-a)

uncharted [ʌn'tʃɑːtɪd] *adj* inesplorato(-a)

unchecked [ʌn'tʃɛkt] *adj* incontrollato(-a)

uncivilized [ʌn'sɪvɪlaɪzd] *adj* (*gen*) selvaggio(-a); (*fig*) incivile, barbaro(-a)

uncle ['ʌŋkl] *n* zio

unclear [ʌn'klɪər] *adj* non chiaro(-a); **I'm still ~ about what I'm supposed to do** non ho ancora ben capito cosa dovrei fare

uncoil [ʌn'kɔɪl] *vt* srotolare ■ *vi* srotolarsi, svolgersi

uncomfortable [ʌn'kʌmfətəbl] *adj* scomodo(-a); (*uneasy*) a disagio, agitato(-a); (*situation*) sgradevole

uncomfortably [ʌn'kʌmfətəblɪ] *adv* scomodamente; (*uneasily: say*) con voce inquieta; (: *think*) con inquietudine

uncommitted [ʌnkə'mɪtɪd] *adj* (*attitude, country*) neutrale

uncommon [ʌn'kɔmən] *adj* raro(-a), insolito(-a), non comune

uncommunicative [ʌnkə'mjuːnɪkətɪv] *adj*

poco comunicativo(-a), chiuso(-a)

uncomplicated [ʌnˈkɒmplɪkeɪtɪd] *adj* semplice, poco complicato(-a)

uncompromising [ʌnˈkɒmprəmaɪzɪŋ] *adj* intransigente, inflessibile

unconcerned [ʌnkənˈsɜːnd] *adj* (*unworried*) tranquillo(-a); **to be ~ about** non darsi pensiero di, non preoccuparsi di *or* per

unconditional [ʌnkənˈdɪʃənl] *adj* incondizionato(-a), senza condizioni

uncongenial [ʌnkənˈdʒiːnɪəl] *adj* (*work, surroundings*) poco piacevole

unconnected [ʌnkəˈnɛktɪd] *adj* (*unrelated*) senza connessione, senza rapporto; **to be ~ with** essere estraneo(-a) a

unconscious [ʌnˈkɒnʃəs] *adj* privo(-a) di sensi, svenuto(-a); (*unaware*) inconsapevole, inconscio(-a) ■ *n*: **the ~** l'inconscio; **to knock sb ~** far perdere i sensi a qn con un pugno

unconsciously [ʌnˈkɒnʃəslɪ] *adv* inconsciamente

unconstitutional [ʌnkɒnstɪˈtjuːʃənl] *adj* incostituzionale

uncontested [ʌnkənˈtɛstɪd] *adj* (*champion*) incontestato(-a); (*Pol: seat*) non disputato(-a)

uncontrollable [ʌnkənˈtrəʊləbl] *adj* incontrollabile, indisciplinato(-a)

uncontrolled [ʌnkənˈtrəʊld] *adj* (*child, dog, emotion*) sfrenato(-a); (*inflation, price rises*) che sfugge al controllo

unconventional [ʌnkənˈvɛnʃənl] *adj* poco convenzionale

unconvinced [ʌnkənˈvɪnst] *adj*: **to be** *or* **remain ~** non essere convinto(-a)

unconvincing [ʌnkənˈvɪnsɪŋ] *adj* non convincente, poco persuasivo(-a)

uncork [ʌnˈkɔːk] *vt* stappare

uncorroborated [ʌnkəˈrɒbəreɪtɪd] *adj* non convalidato(-a)

uncouth [ʌnˈkuːθ] *adj* maleducato(-a), grossolano(-a)

uncover [ʌnˈkʌvəʳ] *vt* scoprire

unctuous [ˈʌŋktjuəs] *adj* untuoso(-a)

undamaged [ʌnˈdæmɪdʒd] *adj* (*goods*) in buono stato; (*fig: reputation*) intatto(-a)

undaunted [ʌnˈdɔːntɪd] *adj* intrepido(-a)

undecided [ʌndɪˈsaɪdɪd] *adj* indeciso(-a)

undelivered [ʌndɪˈlɪvəd] *adj* non recapitato(-a); **if ~ return to sender** in caso di mancato recapito rispedire al mittente

undeniable [ʌndɪˈnaɪəbl] *adj* innegabile, indiscutibile

under [ˈʌndəʳ] *prep* sotto; (*less than*) meno di; al disotto di; (*according to*) secondo, in conformità a ■ *adv* (al) disotto; **from ~ sth** da sotto a *or* dal disotto di qc; **~ there** là sotto;

in ~ 2 hours in meno di 2 ore; **~ anaesthetic** sotto anestesia; **~ discussion** in discussione; **~ repair** in riparazione; **~ the circumstances** date le circostanze

under ... [ˈʌndəʳ] *prefix* sotto..., sub...

under-age [ʌndərˈeɪdʒ] *adj* minorenne

underarm [ˈʌndərɑːm] *n* ascella ■ *adj* ascellare ■ *adv* da sotto in su

undercapitalized [ʌndəˈkæpɪtəlaɪzd] *adj* carente di capitali

undercarriage [ˈʌndəkærɪdʒ] *n* (*Brit Aviat*) carrello (d'atterraggio)

undercharge [ʌndəˈtʃɑːdʒ] *vt* far pagare di meno a

underclass [ˈʌndəklɑːs] *n* sottoproletariato

underclothes [ˈʌndəkləʊðz] *npl* biancheria (intima)

undercover [ˈʌndəkʌvəʳ] *adj* segreto(-a), clandestino(-a)

undercurrent [ˈʌndəkʌrənt] *n* corrente *f* sottomarina

undercut [ʌndəˈkʌt] *vt irreg* vendere a prezzo minore di

underdeveloped [ˈʌndədɪˈvɛləpt] *adj* sottosviluppato(-a)

underdog [ˈʌndədɒg] *n* oppresso(-a)

underdone [ʌndəˈdʌn] *adj* (*Culin*) poco cotto(-a)

under-employment [ʌndərɪmˈplɔɪmənt] *n* sottoccupazione *f*

underestimate [ʌndərˈɛstɪmeɪt] *vt* sottovalutare

underexposed [ʌndərɪksˈpəʊzd] *adj* (*Phot*) sottoesposto(-a)

underfed [ʌndəˈfɛd] *adj* denutrito(-a)

underfoot [ʌndəˈfut] *adv* sotto i piedi

under-funded [ˈʌndəˈfʌndɪd] *adj* insufficientemente sovvenzionato(-a)

undergo [ʌndəˈgəʊ] *vt irreg* subire; (*treatment*) sottoporsi a; **the car is undergoing repairs** la macchina è in riparazione

undergraduate [ʌndəˈgrædjuɪt] *n* studente(-essa) universitario(-a) ■ *cpd*: **~ courses** corsi *mpl* di laurea

underground [ˈʌndəgraund] *n* metropolitana; (*Pol*) movimento clandestino ■ *adj* sotterraneo(-a); (*fig*) clandestino(-a); (*Art, Cine*) underground *inv* ■ *adv* sottoterra; clandestinamente

undergrowth [ˈʌndəgrəʊθ] *n* sottobosco

underhand [ʌndəˈhænd], **underhanded** [ʌndəˈhændɪd] *adj* (*fig*) furtivo(-a), subdolo(-a)

underinsured [ʌndərɪnˈʃuəd] *adj* non sufficientemente assicurato(-a)

underlie [ʌndəˈlaɪ] *vt irreg* essere alla base di; **the underlying cause** il motivo di fondo

u

849

underline [ʌndə'laɪn] *vt* sottolineare

underling ['ʌndəlɪŋ] *n (pej)* subalterno(-a), tirapiedi *m/f inv*

undermanning [ʌndə'mænɪŋ] *n* carenza di personale

undermentioned [ʌndə'mɛnʃənd] *adj* (riportato(-a)) qui sotto *or* qui di seguito

undermine [ʌndə'maɪn] *vt* minare

underneath [ʌndə'niːθ] *adv* sotto, disotto ■ *prep* sotto, al di sotto di

undernourished [ʌndə'nʌrɪʃt] *adj* denutrito(-a)

underpaid [ʌndə'peɪd] *adj* mal pagato(-a)

underpants ['ʌndəpænts] *npl (Brit)* mutande *fpl*, slip *m inv*

underpass ['ʌndəpɑːs] *n (Brit)* sottopassaggio

underpin [ʌndə'pɪn] *vt* puntellare; *(argument, case)* corroborare

underplay [ʌndə'pleɪ] *vt* minimizzare

underpopulated [ʌndə'pɔpjuleɪtɪd] *adj* scarsamente popolato(-a), sottopopolato(-a)

underprice [ʌndə'praɪs] *vt* vendere a un prezzo inferiore al dovuto

underprivileged [ʌndə'prɪvɪlɪdʒd] *adj* svantaggiato(-a)

underrate [ʌndə'reɪt] *vt* sottovalutare

underscore [ʌndə'skɔːʳ] *vt* sottolineare

underseal ['ʌndəsiːl] *vt* rendere stagno il fondo di

undersecretary [ʌndə'sɛkrətrɪ] *n* sottosegretario

undersell ['ʌndəsɛl] *vt irreg (competitors)* vendere a prezzi più bassi di

undershirt ['ʌndəʃəːt] *n (US)* maglietta

undershorts ['ʌndəʃɔːts] *npl (US)* mutande *fpl*, slip *m inv*

underside ['ʌndəsaɪd] *n* disotto

undersigned ['ʌndəsaɪnd] *adj, n* sottoscritto(-a)

underskirt ['ʌndəskəːt] *n* sottoveste *f*

understaffed [ʌndə'stɑːft] *adj* a corto di personale

understand [ʌndə'stænd] *vb (irreg: like* **stand***)* *vt, vi* capire, comprendere; **I ~ that ...** sento che ...; credo di capire che ...; **to make o.s. understood** farsi capire

understandable [ʌndə'stændəbl] *adj* comprensibile

understanding [ʌndə'stændɪŋ] *adj* comprensivo(-a) ■ *n* comprensione *f*; *(agreement)* accordo; **on the ~ that ...** a patto che *or* a condizione che ...; **to come to an ~ with sb** giungere ad un accordo con qn

understate [ʌndə'steɪt] *vt* minimizzare, sminuire

understatement [ʌndə'steɪtmənt] *n*: **that's an ~!** a dire poco!

understood [ʌndə'stud] *pt, pp of* **understand** ■ *adj* inteso(-a); *(implied)* sottinteso(-a)

understudy ['ʌndəstʌdɪ] *n* sostituto(-a), attore(-trice) supplente

undertake [ʌndə'teɪk] *vt irreg* intraprendere; **to ~ to do sth** impegnarsi a fare qc

undertaker ['ʌndəteɪkəʳ] *n* impresario di pompe funebri

undertaking [ʌndə'teɪkɪŋ] *n* impresa; *(promise)* promessa

undertone ['ʌndətəun] *n (low voice)* tono sommesso; *(of criticism etc)* vena, sottofondo; **in an ~** sottovoce

undervalue [ʌndə'væljuː] *vt* svalutare, sottovalutare

underwater [ʌndə'wɔːtəʳ] *adv* sott'acqua ■ *adj* subacqueo(-a)

underwear ['ʌndəwɛəʳ] *n* biancheria (intima)

underweight [ʌndə'weɪt] *adj* al di sotto del giusto peso; *(person)* sottopeso *inv*

underworld ['ʌndəwəːld] *n (of crime)* malavita

underwrite [ʌndəraɪt] *vt (Finance)* sottoscrivere; *(Insurance)* assicurare

underwriter ['ʌndəraɪtəʳ] *n* sottoscrittore(-trice); assicuratore(-trice)

undeserving [ʌndɪ'zəːvɪŋ] *adj*: **to be ~ of** non meritare, non essere degno di

undesirable [ʌndɪ'zaɪərəbl] *adj* indesiderabile, sgradito(-a)

undeveloped [ʌndɪ'vɛləpt] *adj (land, resources)* non sfruttato(-a)

undies ['ʌndɪz] *npl (col)* robina, biancheria intima da donna

undiluted [ʌndaɪ'luːtɪd] *adj* non diluito(-a)

undiplomatic [ʌndɪplə'mætɪk] *adj* poco diplomatico(-a)

undischarged ['ʌndɪs'tʃɑːdʒd] *adj*: **~ bankrupt** fallito non riabilitato

undisciplined [ʌn'dɪsɪplɪnd] *adj* indisciplinato(-a)

undisguised [ʌndɪs'gaɪzd] *adj (dislike, amusement etc)* palese

undisputed [ʌndɪs'pjuːtɪd] *adj* indiscusso(-a)

undistinguished [ʌndɪs'tɪŋgwɪʃt] *adj* mediocre, qualunque

undisturbed [ʌndɪs'təːbd] *adj* tranquillo(-a); **to leave sth ~** lasciare qc così com'è

undivided [ʌndɪ'vaɪdɪd] *adj*: **I want your ~ attention** esigo tutta la sua attenzione

undo [ʌn'duː] *vt irreg* disfare

undoing [ʌn'duːɪŋ] *n* rovina, perdita

undone [ʌn'dʌn] *pp of* **undo**; **to come ~** slacciarsi

undoubted [ʌn'dautɪd] *adj* sicuro(-a), certo(-a)

undoubtedly [ʌn'dautɪdlɪ] *adv* senza alcun dubbio

undress [ʌn'drɛs] vi spogliarsi

undrinkable [ʌn'drɪŋkəbl] adj (unpalatable) imbevibile; (poisonous) non potabile

undue [ʌn'dju:] adj eccessivo(-a)

undulating ['ʌndjuleɪtɪŋ] adj ondeggiante, ondulato(-a)

unduly [ʌn'dju:lɪ] adv eccessivamente

undying [ʌn'daɪɪŋ] adj imperituro(-a)

unearned [ʌn'ə:nd] adj (praise, respect) immeritato(-a); ~ **income** rendita

unearth [ʌn'ə:θ] vt dissotterrare; (fig) scoprire

unearthly [ʌn'ə:θlɪ] adj soprannaturale; (hour) impossibile

uneasy [ʌn'i:zɪ] adj a disagio; (worried) preoccupato(-a); **to feel ~ about doing sth** non sentirsela di fare qc

uneconomic ['ʌni:kə'nɔmɪk], **uneconomical** ['ʌni:kə'nɔmɪkl] adj non economico(-a), antieconomico(-a)

uneducated [ʌn'ɛdjukeɪtɪd] adj senza istruzione, incolto(-a)

unemployed [ʌnɪm'plɔɪd] adj disoccupato(-a) ■ npl: **the ~** i disoccupati

unemployment [ʌnɪm'plɔɪmənt] n disoccupazione f

unemployment benefit, (US) **unemployment compensation** n sussidio di disoccupazione

unending [ʌn'ɛndɪŋ] adj senza fine

unenviable [ʌn'ɛnvɪəbl] adj poco invidiabile

unequal [ʌn'i:kwəl] adj (length, objects) disuguale; (amounts) diverso(-a); (division of labour) ineguale

unequalled, (US) **unequaled** [ʌn'i:kwəld] adj senza pari, insuperato(-a)

unequivocal [ʌnɪ'kwɪvəkəl] adj (answer) inequivocabile; (person) esplicito(-a), chiaro(-a).

unerring [ʌn'ə:rɪŋ] adj infallibile

UNESCO [ju:'nɛskəu] n abbr (= United Nations Educational, Scientific and Cultural Organization) U.N.E.S.C.O f

unethical [ʌn'ɛθɪkəl] adj (methods) poco ortodosso(-a), non moralmente accettabile; (doctor's behaviour) contrario(-a) all'etica professionale

uneven [ʌn'i:vn] adj ineguale; (ground) disuguale, accidentato(-a); (heartbeat) irregolare

uneventful [ʌnɪ'vɛntful] adj senza sorprese, tranquillo(-a)

unexceptional [ʌnɪk'sɛpʃənl] adj che non ha niente d'eccezionale

unexciting [ʌnɪk'saɪtɪŋ] adj (news) poco emozionante; (film, evening) poco interessante

unexpected [ʌnɪk'spɛktɪd] adj inatteso(-a), imprevisto(-a)

unexpectedly [ʌnɪk'spɛktɪdlɪ] adv inaspettatamente

unexplained [ʌnɪk'spleɪnd] adj inspiegato(-a)

unexploded [ʌnɪk'spləudɪd] adj inesploso(-a)

unfailing [ʌn'feɪlɪŋ] adj (supply, energy) inesauribile; (remedy) infallibile

unfair [ʌn'fɛər] adj: ~ **(to)** ingiusto(-a) (nei confronti di); **it's ~ that ...** non è giusto che ...+sub

unfair dismissal n licenziamento ingiustificato

unfairly [ʌn'fɛəlɪ] adv ingiustamente

unfaithful [ʌn'feɪθful] adj infedele

unfamiliar [ʌnfə'mɪlɪər] adj sconosciuto(-a), strano(-a); **to be ~ with sth** non essere pratico di qc, non avere familiarità con qc

unfashionable [ʌn'fæʃnəbl] adj (clothes) fuori moda inv; (district) non alla moda

unfasten [ʌn'fɑ:sn] vt slacciare; sciogliere

unfathomable [ʌn'fæðəməbl] adj insondabile

unfavourable, (US) **unfavorable** [ʌn'feɪvərəbl] adj sfavorevole

unfavourably, (US) **unfavorably** [ʌn'feɪvərəblɪ] adv: **to look ~ upon** vedere di malocchio

unfeeling [ʌn'fi:lɪŋ] adj insensibile, duro(-a)

unfinished [ʌn'fɪnɪʃt] adj incompiuto(-a)

unfit [ʌn'fɪt] adj inadatto(-a); (ill) non in forma; (incompetent): ~ **(for)** incompetente (in); (: work, Mil) inabile (a); ~ **for habitation** inabitabile

unflagging [ʌn'flægɪŋ] adj instancabile

unflappable [ʌn'flæpəbl] adj calmo(-a), composto(-a)

unflattering [ʌn'flætərɪŋ] adj (dress, hairstyle) che non dona

unflinching [ʌn'flɪntʃɪŋ] adj che non indietreggia, risoluto(-a)

unfold [ʌn'fəuld] vt spiegare; (fig) rivelare ■ vi (view) distendersi; (story) svelarsi

unforeseeable ['ʌnfɔ:'si:əbl] adj imprevedibile

unforeseen [ʌnfɔ:'si:n] adj imprevisto(-a)

unforgettable [ʌnfə'gɛtəbl] adj indimenticabile

unforgivable [ʌnfə'gɪvəbl] adj imperdonabile

unformatted [ʌn'fɔ:mætɪd] adj (disk, text) non formattato(-a)

unfortunate [ʌn'fɔ:tʃnɪt] adj sfortunato(-a); (event, remark) infelice

unfortunately [ʌn'fɔ:tʃnɪtlɪ] adv sfortunatamente, purtroppo

u

unfounded [ʌn'faʊndɪd] adj infondato(-a)

unfriendly [ʌn'frɛndlɪ] adj poco amichevole, freddo(-a)

unfulfilled [ʌnful'fɪld] adj (ambition) non realizzato(-a); (prophecy) che non si è avverato(-a); (desire) insoddisfatto(-a); (promise) non mantenuto(-a); (terms of contract) non rispettato(-a); (person) frustrato(-a)

unfurl [ʌn'fəːl] vt spiegare

unfurnished [ʌn'fəːnɪʃt] adj non ammobiliato(-a)

ungainly [ʌn'geɪnlɪ] adj goffo(-a), impacciato(-a)

ungodly [ʌn'gɔdlɪ] adj empio(-a); **at an ~ hour** a un'ora impossibile

ungrateful [ʌn'greɪtful] adj ingrato(-a)

unguarded [ʌn'gɑːdɪd] adj: **in an ~ moment** in un momento di distrazione

unhappily [ʌn'hæpɪlɪ] adv (unfortunately) purtroppo, sfortunatamente

unhappiness [ʌn'hæpɪnɪs] n infelicità

unhappy [ʌn'hæpɪ] adj infelice; **~ with** (arrangements etc) insoddisfatto(-a) di

unharmed [ʌn'hɑːmd] adj incolume, sano(-a) e salvo(-a)

UNHCR n abbr (= United Nations High Commission for Refugees) Alto Commissariato delle Nazioni Unite per Rifugiati

unhealthy [ʌn'hɛlθɪ] adj (gen) malsano(-a); (person) malaticcio(-a)

unheard-of [ʌn'həːdɔv] adj inaudito(-a), senza precedenti

unhelpful [ʌn'hɛlpful] adj poco disponibile

unhesitating [ʌn'hɛzɪteɪtɪŋ] adj (loyalty) che non vacilla; (reply, offer) pronto(-a), immediato(-a)

unholy [ʌn'həʊlɪ] adj: **an ~ alliance** un'alleanza nefasta; **he returned at an ~ hour** è tornato ad un'ora indecente

unhook [ʌn'hʊk] vt sganciare; sfibbiare

unhurt [ʌn'həːt] adj incolume, sano(-a) e salvo(-a)

unhygienic [ʌnhaɪ'dʒiːnɪk] adj non igienico(-a)

UNICEF ['juːnɪsɛf] n abbr (= United Nations International Children's Emergency Fund) U.N.I.C.E.F. m

unicorn ['juːnɪkɔːn] n unicorno

unidentified [ʌnaɪ'dɛntɪfaɪd] adj non identificato(-a)

uniform ['juːnɪfɔːm] n uniforme f, divisa ■ adj uniforme

uniformity [juːnɪ'fɔːmɪtɪ] n uniformità

unify ['juːnɪfaɪ] vt unificare

unilateral [juːnɪ'lætərəl] adj unilaterale

unimaginable [ʌnɪ'mædʒɪnəbl] adj inimmaginabile, inconcepibile

unimaginative [ʌnɪ'mædʒɪnətɪv] adj privo(-a) di fantasia, a corto di idee

unimpaired [ʌnɪm'pɛəd] adj intatto(-a), non danneggiato(-a)

unimportant [ʌnɪm'pɔːtənt] adj senza importanza, di scarsa importanza

unimpressed [ʌnɪm'prɛst] adj niente affatto impressionato(-a)

uninhabited [ʌnɪn'hæbɪtɪd] adj disabitato(-a)

uninhibited [ʌnɪn'hɪbɪtɪd] adj senza inibizioni; senza ritegno

uninjured [ʌn'ɪndʒəd] adj incolume

uninspiring [ʌnɪn'spaɪərɪŋ] adj banale

uninstall [ʌnɪn'stɔːl] vt (Comput) disinstallare

unintelligent [ʌnɪn'tɛlɪdʒənt] adj poco intelligente

unintentional [ʌnɪn'tɛnʃənəl] adj involontario(-a)

unintentionally [ʌnɪn'tɛnʃnəlɪ] adv senza volerlo, involontariamente

uninvited [ʌnɪn'vaɪtɪd] adj non invitato(-a)

uninviting [ʌnɪn'vaɪtɪŋ] adj (place, food) non invitante, poco invitante; (offer) poco allettante

union ['juːnjən] n unione f; (also: **trade union**) sindacato ■ cpd sindacale; **the U~** (US) gli stati dell'Unione

unionize ['juːnjənaɪz] vt sindacalizzare, organizzare in sindacato

Union Jack n bandiera nazionale britannica

Union of Soviet Socialist Republics n (Hist) Unione f delle Repubbliche Socialiste Sovietiche

union shop n stabilimento in cui tutti gli operai sono tenuti ad aderire ad un sindacato

unique [juː'niːk] adj unico(-a)

unisex ['juːnɪsɛks] adj unisex inv

Unison ['juːnɪsn] n (trade union) sindacato generale dei funzionari

unison ['juːnɪsn] n: **in ~** all'unisono

unit ['juːnɪt] n unità f inv; (section: of furniture etc) elemento; (team, squad) reparto, squadra; **production ~** reparto m, produzione inv; **sink ~** blocco m lavello inv

unit cost n costo unitario

unite [juː'naɪt] vt unire ■ vi unirsi

united [juː'naɪtɪd] adj unito(-a); (efforts) congiunto(-a)

United Arab Emirates npl Emirati mpl Arabi Uniti

United Kingdom n Regno Unito

United Nations, United Nations Organization n (Organizzazione f delle) Nazioni Unite

United States, United States of America n Stati mpl Uniti (d'America)

unit price n prezzo unitario
unit trust n (Brit Comm) fondo d'investimento
unity ['ju:nɪtɪ] n unità
Univ. abbr = **university**
universal [ju:nɪ'vɜ:sl] adj universale
universe ['ju:nɪvɜ:s] n universo
university [ju:nɪ'vɜ:sɪtɪ] n università f inv
■ cpd (student, professor, education)
universitario(-a); (year) accademico(-a)
university degree n laurea
unjust [ʌn'dʒʌst] adj ingiusto(-a)
unjustifiable ['ʌndʒʌstɪ'faɪəbl] adj
ingiustificabile
unjustified [ʌn'dʒʌstɪfaɪd] adj
ingiustificato(-a); (Typ) non allineato(-a)
unkempt [ʌn'kɛmpt] adj trasandato(-a);
spettinato(-a)
unkind [ʌn'kaɪnd] adj poco gentile,
villano(-a)
unkindly [ʌn'kaɪndlɪ] adv (speak) in modo
sgarbato; (treat) male
unknown [ʌn'nəun] adj sconosciuto(-a); ~ **to
me** ... a mia insaputa ...; ~ **quantity** (Math:
fig) incognita
unladen [ʌn'leɪdn] adj (ship, weight) a vuoto
unlawful [ʌn'lɔ:ful] adj illecito(-a), illegale
unleaded ['ʌn'lɛdɪd] adj senza piombo; ~
petrol benzina verde or senza piombo
unleash [ʌn'li:ʃ] vt sguinzagliare; (fig)
scatenare
unleavened [ʌn'lɛvnd] adj non lievitato(-a),
azzimo(-a)
unless [ʌn'lɛs] conj a meno che (non) + sub;
~ **otherwise stated** salvo indicazione
contraria; ~ **I am mistaken** se non mi
sbaglio
unlicensed [ʌn'laɪsənst] adj (Brit) senza
licenza per la vendita di alcolici
unlike [ʌn'laɪk] adj diverso(-a) ■ prep a
differenza di, contrariamente a
unlikelihood [ʌn'laɪklɪhud] n improbabilità
unlikely [ʌn'laɪklɪ] adj improbabile;
(explanation) inverosimile
unlimited [ʌn'lɪmɪtɪd] adj illimitato(-a)
unlisted [ʌn'lɪstɪd] adj (US Tel): **to be** ~ non
essere sull'elenco; (Stock Exchange) non
quotato(-a)
unlit [ʌn'lɪt] adj (room) senza luce; (road) non
illuminato(-a)
unload [ʌn'ləud] vt scaricare
unlock [ʌn'lɔk] vt aprire
unlucky [ʌn'lʌkɪ] adj sfortunato(-a); (object,
number) che porta sfortuna, di malaugurio;
to be ~ (person) essere sfortunato, non avere
fortuna
unmanageable [ʌn'mænɪdʒəbl] adj
(tool, vehicle) poco maneggevole;
(situation) impossibile
unmanned [ʌn'mænd] adj (spacecraft) senza
equipaggio
unmannerly [ʌn'mænəlɪ] adj maleducato(-a)
unmarked [ʌn'mɑ:kt] adj (unstained)
pulito(-a), senza macchie; ~ **police car**
civetta della polizia
unmarried [ʌn'mærɪd] adj non sposato(-a);
(man only) scapolo, celibe; (woman only) nubile
unmarried mother n ragazza f madre inv
unmask [ʌn'mɑ:sk] vt smascherare
unmatched [ʌn'mætʃt] adj senza uguali
unmentionable [ʌn'mɛnʃnəbl] adj (vice, topic)
innominabile; (word) irripetibile
unmerciful [ʌn'mə:sɪful] adj spietato(-a)
unmistakable [ʌnmɪs'teɪkəbl] adj
indubbio(-a), facilmente riconoscibile
unmitigated [ʌn'mɪtɪgeɪtɪd] adj (disaster etc)
totale, assoluto(-a)
unnamed [ʌn'neɪmd] adj (nameless) senza
nome; (anonymous) anonimo(-a)
unnatural [ʌn'nætʃrəl] adj innaturale;
contro natura
unnecessary [ʌn'nɛsəsərɪ] adj inutile,
superfluo(-a)
unnerve [ʌn'nə:v] vt (accident) sgomentare;
(hostile attitude) bloccare; (long wait, interview)
snervare
unnoticed [ʌn'nəutɪst] adj: **to go** or **pass** ~
passare inosservato(-a)
UNO ['ju:nəu] n abbr = **United Nations
Organization**
unobservant [ʌnəb'zə:vənt] adj: **to be** ~ non
avere spirito di osservazione
unobtainable [ʌnəb'teɪnəbl] adj (Tel) non
ottenibile
unobtrusive [ʌnəb'tru:sɪv] adj discreto(-a)
unoccupied [ʌn'ɔkjupaɪd] adj (house)
vuoto(-a); (seat, Mil: zone) libero(-a), non
occupato(-a)
unofficial [ʌnə'fɪʃl] adj non ufficiale; (strike)
non dichiarato(-a) dal sindacato
unopened [ʌn'əupənd] adj (letter) non
aperto(-a); (present) ancora incartato(-a)
unopposed [ʌnə'pəuzd] adj senza incontrare
opposizione
unorthodox [ʌn'ɔ:θədɔks] adj non
ortodosso(-a)
unpack [ʌn'pæk] vi disfare la valigia (or le
valigie)
unpaid [ʌn'peɪd] adj (holiday) non pagato(-a);
(work) non retribuito(-a); (bill, debt) da pagare
unpalatable [ʌn'pælətəbl] adj (food)
immangiabile; (drink) imbevibile; (truth)
sgradevole
unparalleled [ʌn'pærəlɛld] adj
incomparabile, impareggiabile

u

853

unpatriotic [ˈʌnpætrɪˈɒtɪk] *adj* (*person*) poco patriottico(-a); (*speech, attitude*) antipatriottico(-a)

unplanned [ʌnˈplænd] *adj* (*visit*) imprevisto(-a); (*baby*) non previsto(-a)

unpleasant [ʌnˈplɛznt] *adj* spiacevole; (*person, remark*) antipatico(-a); (*day, experience*) brutto(-a)

unplug [ʌnˈplʌg] *vt* staccare

unpolluted [ʌnpəˈluːtɪd] *adj* non inquinato(-a)

unpopular [ʌnˈpɒpjuləʳ] *adj* impopolare; **to make o.s. ~ (with)** rendersi antipatico (a); (*politician etc*) alienarsi le simpatie (di)

unprecedented [ʌnˈprɛsɪdəntɪd] *adj* senza precedenti

unpredictable [ʌnprɪˈdɪktəbl] *adj* imprevedibile

unprejudiced [ʌnˈprɛdʒudɪst] *adj* (*not biased*) obiettivo(-a), imparziale; (*having no prejudices*) senza pregiudizi

unprepared [ʌnprɪˈpɛəd] *adj* (*person*) impreparato(-a); (*speech*) improvvisato(-a)

unprepossessing [ʌnpriːpəˈzɛsɪŋ] *adj* insulso(-a)

unpretentious [ʌnprɪˈtɛnʃəs] *adj* senza pretese

unprincipled [ʌnˈprɪnsɪpld] *adj* senza scrupoli

unproductive [ʌnprəˈdʌktɪv] *adj* improduttivo(-a); (*discussion*) sterile

unprofessional [ˈʌnprəˈfɛʃənl] *adj*: **~ conduct** scorrettezza professionale

unprofitable [ʌnˈprɒfɪtəbl] *adj* (*financially*) non redditizio(-a); (*job, deal*) poco lucrativo(-a)

UNPROFOR [ˈʌnprəfɔːʳ] *n abbr* (= *United Nations Protection Force*) reparto di protezione dell'ONU

unprotected [ˈʌnprəˈtɛktɪd] *adj* (*sex*) non protetto(-a)

unprovoked [ʌnprəˈvəukt] *adj* non provocato(-a)

unpunished [ʌnˈpʌnɪʃt] *adj*: **to go ~** restare impunito(-a)

unqualified [ʌnˈkwɒlɪfaɪd] *adj* (*worker*) non qualificato(-a); (*in professions*) non abilitato(-a); (*success*) assoluto(-a), senza riserve

unquestionably [ʌnˈkwɛstʃənəblɪ] *adv* indiscutibilmente

unquestioning [ʌnˈkwɛstʃənɪŋ] *adj* (*obedience, acceptance*) cieco(-a)

unravel [ʌnˈrævl] *vt* dipanare, districare

unreal [ʌnˈrɪəl] *adj* irreale

unrealistic [ʌnrɪəˈlɪstɪk] *adj* (*idea*) illusorio(-a); (*estimate*) non realistico(-a)

unreasonable [ʌnˈriːznəbl] *adj* irragionevole; **to make ~ demands on sb** voler troppo da qn

unrecognizable [ʌnˈrɛkəgnaɪzəbl] *adj* irriconoscibile

unrecognized [ʌnˈrɛkəgnaɪzd] *adj* (*talent, genius*) misconosciuto(-a); (*Pol: regime*) non ufficialmente riconosciuto(-a)

unrecorded [ʌnrɪˈkɔːdɪd] *adj* non documentato(-a), non registrato(-a)

unrefined [ʌnrɪˈfaɪnd] *adj* (*sugar, petroleum*) greggio(-a); (*person*) rozzo(-a)

unrehearsed [ʌnrɪˈhəːst] *adj* (*Theat etc*) improvvisato(-a); (*spontaneous*) imprevisto(-a)

unrelated [ʌnrɪˈleɪtɪd] *adj*: **~ (to)** senza rapporto (con); (*by family*) non imparentato(-a) (con)

unrelenting [ʌnrɪˈlɛntɪŋ] *adj* implacabile; accanito(-a)

unreliable [ʌnrɪˈlaɪəbl] *adj* (*person, machine*) che non dà affidamento; (*news, source of information*) inattendibile

unrelieved [ʌnrɪˈliːvd] *adj* (*monotony*) uniforme

unremitting [ʌnrɪˈmɪtɪŋ] *adj* incessante, infaticabile

unrepeatable [ʌnrɪˈpiːtəbl] *adj* (*offer*) unico(-a)

unrepentant [ʌnrɪˈpɛntənt] *adj* impenitente

unrepresentative [ʌnrɛprɪˈzɛntətɪv] *adj* atipico(-a), poco rappresentativo(-a)

unreserved [ʌnrɪˈzəːvd] *adj* (*seat*) non prenotato(-a), non riservato(-a); (*approval, admiration*) senza riserve

unresponsive [ʌnrɪsˈpɒnsɪv] *adj* che non reagisce

unrest [ʌnˈrɛst] *n* agitazione *f*

unrestricted [ʌnrɪˈstrɪktɪd] *adj* (*power, time*) illimitato(-a); (*access*) libero(-a)

unrewarded [ʌnrɪˈwɔːdɪd] *adj* non ricompensato(-a)

unripe [ʌnˈraɪp] *adj* acerbo(-a)

unrivalled, (*US*) **unrivaled** [ʌnˈraɪvəld] *adj* senza pari

unroll [ʌnˈrəul] *vt* srotolare

unruffled [ʌnˈrʌfld] *adj* (*person*) calmo(-a) e tranquillo(-a), imperturbato(-a); (*hair*) a posto

unruly [ʌnˈruːlɪ] *adj* indisciplinato(-a)

unsafe [ʌnˈseɪf] *adj* pericoloso(-a), rischioso(-a); **~ to drink** non potabile; **~ to eat** non commestibile

unsaid [ʌnˈsɛd] *adj*: **to leave sth ~** passare qc sotto silenzio

unsaleable, (*US*) **unsalable** [ʌnˈseɪləbl] *adj* invendibile

unsatisfactory [ˈʌnsætɪsˈfæktərɪ] *adj* che lascia a desiderare, insufficiente

unsavoury, (US) **unsavory** [ʌnˈseɪvərɪ] *adj* (*fig: person*) losco(-a); (: *reputation, subject*) disgustoso(-a), ripugnante

unscathed [ʌnˈskeɪðd] *adj* incolume

unscientific [ˈʌnsaɪənˈtɪfɪk] *adj* poco scientifico(-a)

unscrew [ʌnˈskruː] *vt* svitare

unscrupulous [ʌnˈskruːpjuləs] *adj* senza scrupoli

unseat [ʌnˈsiːt] *vt* (*rider*) disarcionare; (*fig: an official*) spodestare

unsecured [ʌnsɪˈkjuəd] *adj*: **~ creditor** creditore *m* chirografario

unseeded [ʌnˈsiːdɪd] *adj* (*Sport*) che non è una testa di serie

unseemly [ʌnˈsiːmlɪ] *adj* sconveniente

unseen [ʌnˈsiːn] *adj* (*person*) inosservato(-a); (*danger*) nascosto(-a)

unselfish [ʌnˈselfɪʃ] *adj* (*person*) altruista; (*act*) disinteressato(-a)

unsettled [ʌnˈsetld] *adj* (*person, future*) incerto(-a); (*question*) non risolto(-a); (*weather, market*) instabile; **to feel ~** sentirsi disorientato(-a)

unsettling [ʌnˈsetlɪŋ] *adj* inquietante

unshakable, unshakeable [ʌnˈʃeɪkəbl] *adj* irremovibile

unshaven [ʌnˈʃeɪvn] *adj* non rasato(-a)

unsightly [ʌnˈsaɪtlɪ] *adj* brutto(-a), sgradevole a vedersi

unskilled [ʌnˈskɪld] *adj*: **~ worker** manovale *m*

unsociable [ʌnˈsəʊʃəbl] *adj* (*person*) poco socievole; (*behaviour*) antipatico(-a)

unsocial [ʌnˈsəʊʃəl] *adj*: **~ hours** orario sconveniente

unsold [ʌnˈsəʊld] *adj* invenduto(-a)

unsolicited [ʌnsəˈlɪsɪtɪd] *adj* non richiesto(-a)

unsophisticated [ʌnsəˈfɪstɪkeɪtɪd] *adj* semplice, naturale

unsound [ʌnˈsaʊnd] *adj* (*health*) debole, cagionevole; (*in construction: floor, foundations*) debole, malsicuro(-a); (*policy, advice*) poco sensato(-a); (*judgment, investment*) poco sicuro(-a)

unspeakable [ʌnˈspiːkəbl] *adj* (*bad*) abominevole

unspoken [ʌnˈspəʊkən] *adj* (*words*) non detto(-a); (*agreement, approval*) tacito(-a)

unsteady [ʌnˈstedɪ] *adj* instabile, malsicuro(-a)

unstinting [ʌnˈstɪntɪŋ] *adj* (*support*) incondizionato(-a); (*generosity*) illimitato(-a); (*praise*) senza riserve

unstuck [ʌnˈstʌk] *adj*: **to come ~** scollarsi; (*fig*) fare fiasco

unsubscribe [ʌnsʌbˈskraɪb] *vi* (*Comput*) disdire l'abbonamento

unsubstantiated [ʌnsəbˈstænʃɪeɪtɪd] *adj* (*rumour, accusation*) infondato(-a)

unsuccessful [ʌnsəkˈsesful] *adj* (*writer, proposal*) che non ha successo; (*marriage, attempt*) mal riuscito(-a), fallito(-a); **to be ~** (*in attempting sth*) non riuscire; non avere successo; (*application*) non essere considerato(-a)

unsuccessfully [ʌnsəkˈsesfəlɪ] *adv* senza successo

unsuitable [ʌnˈsuːtəbl] *adj* inadatto(-a); (*moment*) inopportuno(-a)

unsuited [ʌnˈsuːtɪd] *adj*: **to be ~ for** or **to** non essere fatto(-a) per

unsung [ˈʌnˈsʌŋ] *adj*: **an ~ hero** un eroe misconosciuto

unsupported [ʌnsəˈpɔːtɪd] *adj* (*claim*) senza fondamento; (*theory*) non dimostrato(-a)

unsure [ʌnˈʃuəʳ] *adj*: **~ (of** or **about)** incerto(-a) (su); **to be ~ of o.s.** essere insicuro(-a)

unsuspecting [ʌnsəˈspektɪŋ] *adj* che non sospetta niente

unsweetened [ʌnˈswiːtnd] *adj* senza zucchero

unswerving [ʌnˈswəːvɪŋ] *adj* fermo(-a)

unsympathetic [ˈʌnsɪmpəˈθetɪk] *adj* (*attitude*) poco incoraggiante; (*person*) antipatico(-a); **~ (to)** non solidale (verso)

untangle [ʌnˈtæŋgl] *vt* sbrogliare

untapped [ʌnˈtæpt] *adj* (*resources*) non sfruttato(-a)

untaxed [ʌnˈtækst] *adj* (*goods*) esente da imposte; (*income*) non imponibile

unthinkable [ʌnˈθɪŋkəbl] *adj* impensabile, inconcepibile

unthinkingly [ˈʌnˈθɪŋkɪŋlɪ] *adv* senza pensare

untidy [ʌnˈtaɪdɪ] *adj* (*room*) in disordine; (*appearance, work*) trascurato(-a); (*person, writing*) disordinato(-a)

untie [ʌnˈtaɪ] *vt* (*knot, parcel*) disfare; (*prisoner, dog*) slegare

until [ʌnˈtɪl] *prep* fino a; (*after negative*) prima di ◼ *conj* finché, fino a quando; (*in past, after negative*) prima che + *sub*, prima di + *infinitive*; **~ now** finora; **~ then** fino ad allora; **from morning ~ night** dalla mattina alla sera

untimely [ʌnˈtaɪmlɪ] *adj* intempestivo(-a), inopportuno(-a); (*death*) prematuro(-a)

untold [ʌnˈtəʊld] *adj* incalcolabile; indescrivibile

u

855

untouched [ʌn'tʌtʃt] *adj* (*not used etc*) non toccato(-a), intatto(-a); (*safe: person*) incolume; (*unaffected*): ~ **by** insensibile a

untoward [ʌntə'wɔːd] *adj* sfortunato(-a), sconveniente

untrained ['ʌn'treɪnd] *adj* (*worker*) privo(-a) di formazione professionale; (*troops*) privo(-a) di addestramento; **to the ~ eye** ad un occhio inesperto

untrammelled [ʌn'træmld] *adj* illimitato(-a)

untranslatable [ʌntrænz'leɪtəbl] *adj* intraducibile

untrue [ʌn'truː] *adj* (*statement*) falso(-a), non vero(-a)

untrustworthy [ʌn'trʌstwəːðɪ] *adj* di cui non ci si può fidare

unusable [ʌn'juːzəbl] *adj* inservibile, inutilizzabile

unused[1] [ʌn'juːzd] *adj* (*new*) nuovo(-a); (*not made use of*) non usato(-a), non utilizzato(-a)

unused[2] [ʌn'juːst] *adj*: **to be ~ to sth/to doing sth** non essere abituato(-a) a qc/a fare qc

unusual [ʌn'juːʒuəl] *adj* insolito(-a), eccezionale raro(-a)

unusually [ʌn'juːʒuəlɪ] *adv* insolitamente

unveil [ʌn'veɪl] *vt* scoprire, svelare

unwanted [ʌn'wɒntɪd] *adj* non desiderato(-a)

unwarranted [ʌn'wɔrəntɪd] *adj* ingiustificato(-a)

unwary [ʌn'wɛərɪ] *adj* incauto(-a)

unwavering [ʌn'weɪvərɪŋ] *adj* fermo(-a), incrollabile

unwelcome [ʌn'wɛlkəm] *adj* (*gen*) non gradito(-a); **to feel ~** sentire che la propria presenza non è gradita

unwell [ʌn'wɛl] *adj* indisposto(-a); **to feel ~** non sentirsi bene

unwieldy [ʌn'wiːldɪ] *adj* poco maneggevole

unwilling [ʌn'wɪlɪŋ] *adj*: **to be ~ to do** non voler fare

unwillingly [ʌn'wɪlɪŋlɪ] *adv* malvolentieri

unwind [ʌn'waɪnd] *vb* (*irreg*) *vt* svolgere, srotolare ■ *vi* (*relax*) rilassarsi

unwise [ʌn'waɪz] *adj* (*decision, act*) avventato(-a)

unwitting [ʌn'wɪtɪŋ] *adj* involontario(-a)

unworkable [ʌn'wəːkəbl] *adj* (*plan etc*) inattuabile

unworthy [ʌn'wəːðɪ] *adj* indegno(-a); **to be ~ of sth/to do sth** non essere degno di qc/di fare qc

unwrap [ʌn'ræp] *vt* disfare; (*present*) aprire

unwritten [ʌn'rɪtn] *adj* (*agreement*) tacito(-a)

unzip [ʌn'zɪp] *vt* aprire (la chiusura lampo di); (*Comput*) dezippare

 KEYWORD

up [ʌp] *prep* su; **he went up the stairs/the hill** è salito su per le scale/sulla collina; **the cat was up a tree** il gatto era su un albero; **they live further up the street** vivono un po' più su nella stessa strada
■ *adv* **1** (*upwards, higher*) su, in alto; **up in the sky/the mountains** su nel cielo/in montagna; **up there** lassù; **up above** su in alto; **up with Leeds United!** viva il Leeds United!
2: **to be up** (*out of bed*) essere alzato(-a); (*prices, level*) essere salito(-a); (*building*) essere terminato(-a); (*tent*) essere piantato(-a); (*curtains, shutters, wallpaper*) essere su; **"this side up"** "alto"; **to be up (by)** (*in price, value*) essere salito(-a) *or* aumentato(-a) (di); **when the year was up** (*finished*) finito l'anno; **time's up** il tempo è scaduto; **he's well up in *or* on politics** (*Brit*) è molto informato di *or* sulla politica
3: **up to** (*as far as*) fino a; **up to now** finora
4: **to be up to** (*depending on*): **it's up to you** sta a lei, dipende da lei; (*equal to*): **he's not up to it** (*job, task etc*) non ne è all'altezza; (*col: be doing*): **what is he up to?** cosa sta combinando?; **what's up?** (*col: wrong*) che c'è?; **what's up with him?** che ha?, che gli prende?
■ *n*: **ups and downs** alti e bassi *mpl*
■ *vi* (*col*): **she upped and left** improvvisamente se ne andò

up-and-coming ['ʌpənd'kʌmɪŋ] *adj* pieno(-a) di promesse, promettente

upbeat ['ʌpbiːt] *n* (*Mus*) tempo in levare; (*in economy, prosperity*) incremento ■ *adj* (*col*) ottimistico(-a)

upbraid [ʌp'breɪd] *vt* rimproverare

upbringing ['ʌpbrɪŋɪŋ] *n* educazione *f*

upcoming ['ʌpkʌmɪŋ] *adj* imminente, prossimo(-a)

update [ʌp'deɪt] *vt* aggiornare

upend [ʌp'ɛnd] *vt* rovesciare

upfront [ʌp'frʌnt] *adj* (*col*) franco(-a), aperto(-a) ■ *adv* (*pay*) subito

upgrade [ʌp'greɪd] *vt* promuovere; (*job*) rivalutare; (*Comput*) far passare a potenza superiore

upheaval [ʌp'hiːvl] *n* sconvolgimento; tumulto

uphill [ʌp'hɪl] *adj* in salita; (*fig: task*) difficile ■ *adv*: **to go ~** andare in salita, salire

uphold [ʌp'həuld] *vt irreg* approvare; sostenere

upholstery [ʌp'həulstərɪ] *n* tappezzeria

upkeep ['ʌpkiːp] n manutenzione f
up-market [ʌp'mɑːkɪt] adj (product) che si rivolge ad una fascia di mercato superiore
upon [ə'pɔn] prep su
upper ['ʌpə'] adj superiore ■ n (of shoe) tomaia; **the ~ class** ≈ l'alta borghesia
upper case n maiuscolo
upper-class [ʌpə'klɑːs] adj dell'alta borghesia; (district) signorile; (accent) aristocratico(-a); (attitude) snob inv
uppercut ['ʌpəkʌt] n uppercut m inv, montante m
upper hand n: **to have the ~** avere il coltello dalla parte del manico
Upper House n: **the ~** (in Britain) la Camera Alta, la Camera dei Lords; (in US etc) il Senato
uppermost ['ʌpəməust] adj il(la) più alto(-a); predominante; **it was ~ in my mind** è stata la mia prima preoccupazione
Upper Volta [-'vɔltə] n Alto Volta m
upright ['ʌpraɪt] adj diritto(-a); verticale; (fig) diritto(-a), onesto(-a) ■ n montante m
uprising ['ʌpraɪzɪŋ] n insurrezione f, rivolta
uproar ['ʌprɔː'] n tumulto, clamore m
uproarious [ʌp'rɔːrɪəs] adj clamoroso(-a); (hilarious) esilarante; **~ laughter** risata sonora
uproot [ʌp'ruːt] vt sradicare
upset n ['ʌpsɛt] turbamento ■ vt [ʌp'sɛt] (irreg: like **set**) (glass etc) rovesciare; (plan, stomach) scombussolare; (person: offend) contrariare; (: grieve) addolorare; sconvolgere ■ adj [ʌp'sɛt] contrariato(-a); addolorato(-a); (stomach) scombussolato(-a), disturbato(-a); **to have a stomach ~** (Brit) avere lo stomaco in disordine o scombussolato; **to get ~** contrariarsi; addolorarsi
upset price n (US, Scottish) prezzo di riserva
upsetting [ʌp'sɛtɪŋ] adj (saddening) sconvolgente; (offending) offensivo(-a); (annoying) fastidioso(-a)
upshot ['ʌpʃɔt] n risultato; **the ~ of it all was that ...** la conclusione è stata che ...
upside down ['ʌpsaɪd-] adv sottosopra; **to turn ~** capovolgere; (fig) mettere sottosopra
upstage ['ʌp'steɪdʒ] vt: **to ~ sb** rubare la scena a qn
upstairs [ʌp'stɛəz] adv, adj di sopra, al piano superiore ■ n piano di sopra
upstart ['ʌpstɑːt] n parvenu m inv
upstream [ʌp'striːm] adv a monte
upsurge ['ʌpsəːdʒ] n (of enthusiasm etc) ondata
uptake ['ʌpteɪk] n: **he is quick/slow on the ~** è pronto/lento di comprendonio
uptight [ʌp'taɪt] adj (col) teso(-a)
up-to-date ['ʌptə'deɪt] adj moderno(-a); aggiornato(-a)

upturn ['ʌptəːn] n (in luck) svolta favorevole; (in value of currency) rialzo
upturned ['ʌptəːnd] adj (nose) all'insù
upward ['ʌpwəd] adj ascendente; verso l'alto ■ adv in su, verso l'alto
upwardly-mobile ['ʌpwədlɪ'məubaɪl] adj: **to be ~** salire nella scala sociale
upwards ['ʌpwədz] adv in su, verso l'alto
URA n abbr (US: = Urban Renewal Administration) amministrazione per il rinnovamento urbano
Ural Mountains ['juərəl-] npl: **the ~** (also: **the Urals**) gli Urali, i Monti Urali
uranium [juə'reɪnɪəm] n uranio
Uranus [juə'reɪnəs] n (planet) Urano
urban ['əːbən] adj urbano(-a)
urbane [əː'beɪn] adj civile, urbano(-a), educato(-a)
urbanization [əːbənaɪ'zeɪʃən] n urbanizzazione f
urchin ['əːtʃɪn] n monello; **sea ~** riccio di mare
Urdu ['uədu:] n urdu m inv
urge [əːdʒ] n impulso, stimolo ■ vt (caution etc) raccomandare vivamente; **to ~ sb to do** esortare qn a fare, spingere qn a fare; raccomandare a qn di fare
▶ **urge on** vt spronare
urgency ['əːdʒənsɪ] n urgenza; (of tone) insistenza
urgent ['əːdʒənt] adj urgente; (earnest, persistent: plea) pressante; (: tone) insistente, incalzante
urgently ['əːdʒəntlɪ] adv d'urgenza, urgentemente; con insistenza
urinal ['juərɪnl] n (Brit: building) vespasiano; (: vessel) orinale m, pappagallo
urinate ['juərɪneɪt] vi orinare
urine ['juərɪn] n orina
URL n abbr (= uniform resource locator) URL m inv
urn [əːn] n urna; (also: **tea urn**) bollitore m per il tè
Uruguay ['juərəgwaɪ] n Uruguay m
Uruguayan [juərə'gwaɪən] adj, n uruguaiano(-a)
US n abbr = **United States**
us [ʌs] pron ci; (stressed, after prep) noi
USA n abbr (Geo) = **United States of America**; (Mil) = **United States Army**
usable ['juːzəbl] adj utilizzabile, usabile
USAF n abbr = **United States Air Force**
usage ['juːzɪdʒ] n uso
USCG n abbr = **United States Coast Guard**
USDA n abbr = **United States Department of Agriculture**
USDAW ['ʌzdɔ:] n abbr (Brit: = Union of Shop, Distributive and Allied Workers) sindacato dei dipendenti di negozi, reti di distribuzione e simili

u

USDI *n abbr* = **United States Department of the Interior**

use *n* [ju:s] uso; impiego, utilizzazione *f* ∎ *vt* [ju:z] usare, utilizzare, servirsi di; **she used to do it** lo faceva (una volta), era solita farlo; **in ~** in uso; **out of ~** fuori uso; **to be of ~** essere utile, servire; **to make ~ of sth** far uso di qc, utilizzare qc; **ready for ~** pronto per l'uso; **it's no ~** non serve, è inutile; **to have the ~ of** poter usare; **what's this used for?** a che serve?; **to be used to** avere l'abitudine di; **to get used to** abituarsi a, fare l'abitudine a ▶ **use up** *vt* finire; (*supplies*) dare fondo a; (*left-overs*) utilizzare

used [ju:zd] *adj* (*car*) d'occasione

useful ['ju:sful] *adj* utile; **to come in ~** fare comodo, tornare utile

usefulness ['ju:sfəlnɪs] *n* utilità

useless ['ju:slɪs] *adj* inutile; (*unusable: object*) inservibile

user ['ju:zə'] *n* utente *m/f*; (*of petrol, gas etc*) consumatore(-trice)

user-friendly ['ju:zə'frɛndlɪ] *adj* orientato(-a) all'utente

USES *n abbr* = **United States Employment Service**

usher ['ʌʃə'] *n* usciere *m*; (*in cinema*) maschera ∎ *vt*: **to ~ sb in** far entrare qn

usherette [ʌʃə'rɛt] *n* (*in cinema*) maschera

USIA *n abbr* = **United States Information Agency**

USM *n abbr* = **United States Mint; United States Mail**

USN *n abbr* = **United States Navy**

USP *n abbr* = **unique selling point** *or* **proposition**

USPHS *n abbr* = **United States Public Health Service**

USPO *n abbr* = **United States Post Office**

USS *abbr* = **United States Ship (**or **Steamer)**

USSR *n abbr* (*Hist*) = **Union of Soviet Socialist Republics**

usu. *abbr* = **usually**

usual ['ju:ʒuəl] *adj* solito(-a); **as ~** come al solito, come d'abitudine

usually ['ju:ʒuəlɪ] *adv* di solito

usurer ['ju:ʒərə'] *n* usuraio(-a)

usurp [ju:'zə:p] *vt* usurpare

UT *abbr* (*US*) = **Utah**

utensil [ju:'tɛnsl] *n* utensile *m*

uterus ['ju:tərəs] *n* utero

utilitarian [ju:tɪlɪ'tɛərɪən] *adj* utilitario(-a)

utility [ju:'tɪlɪtɪ] *n* utilità; (*also:* **public utility**) servizio pubblico

utility room *n* locale adibito alla stiratura dei panni etc

utilization [ju:tɪlaɪ'zeɪʃən] *n* utilizzazione *f*

utilize ['ju:tɪlaɪz] *vt* utilizzare; sfruttare

utmost ['ʌtməust] *adj* estremo(-a) ∎ *n*: **to do one's ~** fare il possibile *or* di tutto; **of the ~ importance** della massima importanza; **it is of the ~ importance that ...** è estremamente importante che ...+*sub*

utter ['ʌtə'] *adj* assoluto(-a), totale ∎ *vt* pronunciare, proferire; emettere

utterance ['ʌtərəns] *n* espressione *f*; parole *fpl*

utterly ['ʌtəlɪ] *adv* completamente, del tutto

U-turn ['ju:tə:n] *n* inversione *f* a U; (*fig*) voltafaccia *m inv*

Uzbekistan [ʌzbɛkɪ'sta:n] *n* Uzbekistan

Vv

V, v [viː] n (letter) V, v m or f inv; **V for Victor** ≈ V come Venezia

v abbr (= verse) v.; (= vide: see) v.; (= volt) V.; (= versus) contro

VA, Va. abbr (US) = **Virginia**

vac [væk] n abbr (Brit col) = **vacation**

vacancy ['veɪkənsɪ] n (job) posto libero; (room) stanza libera; **"no vacancies"** "completo"; **have you any vacancies?** (office) avete bisogno di personale?; (hotel) avete una stanza?

vacant ['veɪkənt] adj (job, seat etc) libero(-a); (expression) assente

vacant lot n terreno non occupato; (for sale) terreno in vendita

vacate [vəˈkeɪt] vt lasciare libero(-a)

vacation [vəˈkeɪʃən] n (esp US) vacanze fpl; **to take a ~** prendere una vacanza, prendere le ferie; **on ~** in vacanza, in ferie

vacation course n corso estivo

vaccinate ['væksɪneɪt] vt vaccinare

vaccination [væksɪˈneɪʃən] n vaccinazione f

vaccine ['væksiːn] n vaccino

vacuum ['vækjum] n vuoto

vacuum bottle n (US) = **vacuum flask**

vacuum cleaner n aspirapolvere m inv

vacuum flask n (Brit) thermos® m inv

vacuum-packed ['vækjum'pækt] adj confezionato(-a) sottovuoto

vagabond ['vægəbɔnd] n vagabondo(-a)

vagary ['veɪgərɪ] n capriccio

vagina [vəˈdʒaɪnə] n vagina

vagrancy ['veɪgrənsɪ] n vagabondaggio

vagrant ['veɪgrənt] n vagabondo(-a)

vague [veɪg] adj vago(-a); (blurred: photo, memory) sfocato(-a); **I haven't the vaguest idea** non ho la minima or più pallida idea

vaguely ['veɪglɪ] adv vagamente

vain [veɪn] adj (useless) inutile, vano(-a); (conceited) vanitoso(-a); **in ~** inutilmente, invano

valance ['væləns] n volant m inv, balza

valedictory [vælɪˈdɪktərɪ] adj di commiato

valentine ['væləntaɪn] n (also: **valentine card**) cartolina or biglietto di San Valentino

valet ['vælɪt] n cameriere m personale

valet parking n parcheggio effettuato da un dipendente (dell'albergo etc)

valet service n (for clothes) servizio di lavanderia; (for car) servizio completo di lavaggio

valiant ['vælɪənt] adj valoroso(-a), coraggioso(-a)

valid ['vælɪd] adj valido(-a), valevole; (excuse) valido(-a)

validate ['vælɪdeɪt] vt (contract, document) convalidare; (argument, claim) comprovare

validity [vəˈlɪdɪtɪ] n validità

valise [vəˈliːz] n borsa da viaggio

valley ['vælɪ] n valle f

valour, (US) valor ['vælər] n valore m

valuable ['væljuəbl] adj (jewel) di (grande) valore; (time) prezioso(-a); **valuables** npl oggetti mpl di valore

valuation [vælju'eɪʃən] n valutazione f, stima

value ['væljuː] n valore m ▪ vt (fix price) valutare, dare un prezzo a; (cherish) apprezzare, tenere a; **to be of great ~ to sb** avere molta importanza per qn; **to lose (in) ~** (currency) svalutarsi; (property) perdere (di) valore; **to gain (in) ~** (currency) guadagnare; (property) aumentare di valore; **you get good ~ (for money) in that shop** si compra bene in quel negozio

value added tax n (Brit) imposta sul valore aggiunto

valued ['væluːd] adj (appreciated) stimato(-a), apprezzato(-a)

valuer ['væljuər] n stimatore(-trice)

valve [vælv] n valvola

vampire ['væmpaɪər] n vampiro

van [væn] n (Aut) furgone m; (Brit Rail) vagone m

V and A n abbr (Brit) = **Victoria and Albert Museum**

V

vandal ['vændl] n vandalo(-a)
vandalism ['vændəlɪzəm] n vandalismo
vandalize ['vændəlaɪz] vt vandalizzare
vanguard ['vængɑːd] n avanguardia
vanilla [və'nɪlə] n vaniglia ■ cpd (ice cream) alla vaniglia
vanish ['vænɪʃ] vi svanire, scomparire
vanity ['vænɪtɪ] n vanità
vanity case n valigetta per cosmetici
vantage ['vɑːntɪdʒ] n: ~ **point** posizione f or punto di osservazione; (fig) posizione vantaggiosa
vaporize ['veɪpəraɪz] vt vaporizzare ■ vi vaporizzarsi
vapour, (US) **vapor** ['veɪpə'] n vapore m
variable ['veərɪəbl] adj variabile; (mood) mutevole ■ n fattore m variabile, variabile f
variance ['veərɪəns] n: **to be at ~ (with)** essere in disaccordo (con); (facts) essere in contraddizione (con)
variant ['veərɪənt] n variante f
variation [veərɪ'eɪʃən] n variazione f; (in opinion) cambiamento
varicose ['værɪkəus] adj: ~ **veins** varici fpl
varied ['veərɪd] adj vario(-a), diverso(-a)
variety [və'raɪətɪ] n varietà f inv; (quantity): **a wide ~ of** ... una vasta gamma di ...; **for a ~ of reasons** per una serie di motivi
variety show n spettacolo di varietà
various ['veərɪəs] adj vario(-a), diverso(-a); (several) parecchi(-e), molti(-e); **at ~ times** in momenti diversi; (several) diverse volte
varnish ['vɑːnɪʃ] n vernice f; (for nails) smalto ■ vt verniciare; **to ~ one's nails** mettersi lo smalto sulle unghie
vary ['veərɪ] vt, vi variare, mutare; **to ~ (with** or **according to)** variare (con or a seconda di)
varying ['veərɪɪŋ] adj variabile
vase [vɑːz] n vaso
vasectomy [væ'sektəmɪ] n vasectomia
Vaseline® ['væsɪliːn] n vaselina
vast [vɑːst] adj vasto(-a); (amount, success) enorme
vastly ['vɑːstlɪ] adv enormemente
vastness ['vɑːstnɪs] n vastità
VAT [væt] n abbr (Brit) = **value added tax**
vat [væt] n tino
Vatican ['vætɪkən] n: **the ~** il Vaticano
vatman ['vætmæn] n (Brit col): **the ~** ≈ l'ispettore m dell'IVA
vault [vɔːlt] n (of roof) volta; (tomb) tomba; (in bank) camera blindata; (jump) salto ■ vt (also: **vault over**) saltare (d'un balzo)
vaunted ['vɔːntɪd] adj: **much-~** tanto celebrato(-a)
VC n abbr (Brit: = Victoria Cross) medaglia al coraggio; = **vice-chairman**

VCR n abbr = **video cassette recorder**
VD n abbr = **venereal disease**
VDU n abbr = **visual display unit**
veal [viːl] n vitello
veer [vɪə'] vi girare; virare
veg. [vedʒ] n abbr (Brit col: = vegetable(s)) = contorno
vegan ['viːgən] n (Brit) vegetaliano(-a)
vegeburger, veggieburger ['vedʒɪbəːgə'] n hamburger m inv vegetariano
vegetable ['vedʒtəbl] n verdura, ortaggio ■ adj vegetale
vegetable garden n orto
vegetarian [vedʒɪ'teərɪən] adj, n vegetariano(-a)
vegetate ['vedʒɪteɪt] vi vegetare
vegetation [vedʒɪ'teɪʃən] n vegetazione f
vegetative ['vedʒɪtətɪv] adj (also Bot) vegetativo(-a)
vehemence ['viːɪməns] n veemenza, violenza
vehement ['viːɪmənt] adj veemente, violento(-a); profondo(-a)
vehicle ['viːɪkl] n veicolo; (fig) mezzo
vehicular [vɪ'hɪkjulə'] adj: **"no ~ traffic"** "chiuso al traffico di veicoli"
veil [veɪl] n velo ■ vt velare; **under a ~ of secrecy** (fig) protetto da una cortina di segretezza
veiled [veɪld] adj (also fig) velato(-a)
vein [veɪn] n vena; (on leaf) nervatura; (fig: mood) vena, umore m
Velcro® ['velkrəu] n velcro® m inv
vellum ['veləm] n (writing paper) carta patinata
velocity [vɪ'lɒsɪtɪ] n velocità f inv
velour [və'luə'] n velours m inv
velvet ['velvɪt] n velluto
vending machine ['vendɪŋ-] n distributore m automatico
vendor ['vendə'] n venditore(-trice); **street ~** venditore ambulante
veneer [və'nɪə'] n impiallacciatura; (fig) vernice f
venerable ['venərəbl] adj venerabile
venereal disease [vɪ'nɪərɪəl-] n malattia venerea
Venetian [vɪ'niːʃən] adj, n veneziano(-a)
Venetian blind n (tenda alla) veneziana
Venezuela [venɪ'zweɪlə] n Venezuela m
Venezuelan [venɪ'zweɪlən] adj, n venezuelano(-a)
vengeance ['vendʒəns] n vendetta; **with a ~** (fig) davvero; furiosamente
vengeful ['vendʒful] adj vendicativo(-a)
Venice ['venɪs] n Venezia
venison ['venɪsn] n carne f di cervo
venom ['venəm] n veleno

venomous ['vɛnəməs] *adj* velenoso(-a)
vent [vɛnt] *n* foro, apertura; (*in dress, jacket*) spacco ◼ *vt* (*fig: one's feelings*) sfogare, dare sfogo a
ventilate ['vɛntɪleɪt] *vt* (*room*) dare aria a, arieggiare
ventilation [vɛntɪ'leɪʃən] *n* ventilazione *f*
ventilation shaft *n* condotto di aerazione
ventilator ['vɛntɪleɪtəʳ] *n* ventilatore *m*
ventriloquist [vɛn'trɪləkwɪst] *n* ventriloquo(-a)
venture ['vɛntʃəʳ] *n* impresa (rischiosa) ◼ *vt* rischiare, azzardare ◼ *vi* arrischiarsi, azzardarsi; **a business ~** un'iniziativa commerciale; **to ~ to do sth** azzardarsi a fare qc
venture capital *n* capitale *m* di rischio
venue ['vɛnjuː] *n* luogo di incontro; (*Sport*) luogo (designato) per l'incontro
Venus ['viːnəs] *n* (*planet*) Venere *m*
veracity [və'ræsɪtɪ] *n* veridicità
veranda, verandah [və'rændə] *n* veranda
verb [vəːb] *n* verbo
verbal ['vəːbəl] *adj* verbale; (*translation*) letterale
verbally ['vəːbəlɪ] *adv* a voce
verbatim [vəː'beɪtɪm] *adv, adj* parola per parola
verbose [vəː'bəus] *adj* verboso(-a)
verdict ['vəːdɪkt] *n* verdetto; (*opinion*) giudizio, parere *m*; **~ of guilty/not guilty** verdetto di colpevolezza/non colpevolezza
verge [vəːdʒ] *n* bordo, orlo; **"soft verges"** (*Brit*) "banchina cedevole"; **on the ~ of doing** sul punto di fare
▸ **verge on** *vt fus* rasentare
verger ['vəːdʒəʳ] *n* (*Rel*) sagrestano
verification [vɛrɪfɪ'keɪʃən] *n* verifica
verify ['vɛrɪfaɪ] *vt* verificare; (*prove the truth of*) confermare
veritable ['vɛrɪtəbl] *adj* vero(-a)
vermin ['vəːmɪn] *npl* animali *mpl* nocivi; (*insects*) insetti *mpl* parassiti
vermouth ['vəːməθ] *n* vermut *m inv*
vernacular [və'nækjuləʳ] *n* vernacolo
versatile ['vəːsətaɪl] *adj* (*person*) versatile; (*machine, tool etc*) (che si presta) a molti usi
verse [vəːs] *n* (*of poem*) verso; (*stanza*) stanza, strofa; (*in bible*) versetto; (*no pl: poetry*) versi *mpl*; **in ~** in versi
versed [vəːst] *adj*: **(well-)~ in** versato(-a) in
version ['vəːʃən] *n* versione *f*
versus ['vəːsəs] *prep* contro
vertebra (*pl* **vertebrae**) ['vəːtɪbrə, -briː] *n* vertebra
vertebrate ['vəːtɪbrɪt] *n* vertebrato
vertical ['vəːtɪkl] *adj, n* verticale (*m*)

vertically ['vəːtɪklɪ] *adv* verticalmente
vertigo ['vəːtɪgəu] *n* vertigine *f*; **to suffer from ~** soffrire di vertigini
verve [vəːv] *n* brio; entusiasmo
very ['vɛrɪ] *adv* molto ◼ *adj*: **the ~ book which** proprio il libro che; **~ much** moltissimo; **~ well** molto bene; **~ little** molto poco; **at the ~ end** proprio alla fine; **the ~ last** proprio l'ultimo; **at the ~ least** almeno; **the ~ thought (of it) alarms me** il solo pensiero mi spaventa, sono spaventato solo al pensiero
vespers ['vɛspəz] *npl* vespro
vessel ['vɛsl] *n* (*Anat*) vaso; (*Naut*) nave *f*; (*container*) recipiente *m*
vest [vɛst] *n* (*Brit*) maglia; (: *sleeveless*) canottiera; (*US: waistcoat*) gilè *m inv* ◼ *vt*: **to ~ sb with sth, to ~ sth in sb** conferire qc a qn
vested interest *n*: **to have a ~ in doing** avere tutto l'interesse a fare; **vested interests** *npl* (*Comm*) diritti *mpl* acquisiti
vestibule ['vɛstɪbjuːl] *n* vestibolo
vestige ['vɛstɪdʒ] *n* vestigio
vestment ['vɛstmənt] *n* (*Rel*) paramento liturgico
vestry ['vɛstrɪ] *n* sagrestia
Vesuvius [vɪ'suːvɪəs] *n* Vesuvio
vet [vɛt] *n abbr* (= *veterinary surgeon*) veterinario; (*US: col*) = **veteran** ◼ *vt* esaminare minuziosamente; (*text*) rivedere; **to ~ sb for a job** raccogliere delle informazioni dettagliate su qn prima di offrirgli un posto
veteran ['vɛtərn] *n* veterano; (*also*: **war veteran**) reduce *m* ◼ *adj*: **she's a ~ campaigner for ...** lotta da sempre per ...
veteran car *n* auto *f inv* d'epoca (*anteriore al 1919*)
veterinarian [vɛtrɪ'nɛərɪən] *n* (*US*) = **veterinary surgeon**
veterinary ['vɛtrɪnərɪ] *adj* veterinario(-a)
veterinary surgeon *n* (*Brit*) veterinario
veto (*pl* **vetoes**) ['viːtəu] *n* veto ◼ *vt* opporre il veto a; **to put a ~ on** opporre il veto a
vetting ['vɛtɪŋ] *n*: **positive ~** *indagine per accertare l'idoneità di un aspirante ad una carica ufficiale*
vex [vɛks] *vt* irritare, contrariare
vexed [vɛkst] *adj* (*question*) controverso(-a), dibattuto(-a)
VFD *n abbr* (*US*) = **voluntary fire department**
VG *abbr* (*Brit: Scol etc*: = *very good*) ottimo
VHF *abbr* (= *very high frequency*) VHF
VI *abbr* (*US*) = **Virgin Islands**
via ['vaɪə] *prep* (*by way of*) via; (*by means of*) tramite
viability [vaɪə'bɪlɪtɪ] *n* attuabilità
viable ['vaɪəbl] *adj* attuabile; vitale

861

viaduct ['vaɪədʌkt] n viadotto
vial ['vaɪəl] n fiala
vibes [vaɪbz] npl (col): **I got good/bad ~** ho trovato simpatica/antipatica l'atmosfera
vibrant ['vaɪbrənt] adj (sound) vibrante; (colour) vivace, vivo(-a)
vibraphone ['vaɪbrəfəun] n vibrafono
vibrate [vaɪ'breɪt] vi: **to ~ (with)** vibrare (di); (resound) risonare (di)
vibration [vaɪ'breɪʃən] n vibrazione f
vibrator [vaɪ'breɪtər] n vibratore m
vicar ['vɪkər] n pastore m
vicarage ['vɪkərɪdʒ] n presbiterio
vicarious [vɪ'kɛərɪəs] adj sofferto(-a) al posto di un altro; **to get ~ pleasure out of sth** trarre piacere indirettamente da qc
vice [vaɪs] n (evil) vizio; (Tech) morsa
vice- [vaɪs] prefix vice ...
vice-chairman [vaɪs'tʃɛəmən] n vicepresidente m
vice-chancellor [vaɪs'tʃɑːnsələr] n (Brit Scol) rettore m (per elezione)
vice-president [vaɪs'prɛzɪdənt] n vicepresidente m
viceroy ['vaɪsrɔɪ] n viceré m inv
vice squad n (squadra del) buon costume f
vice versa ['vaɪsɪ'vəːsə] adv viceversa
vicinity [vɪ'sɪnɪtɪ] n vicinanze fpl
vicious ['vɪʃəs] adj (remark) maligno(-a), cattivo(-a); (blow) violento(-a); **a ~ circle** un circolo vizioso
viciousness ['vɪʃəsnɪs] n malignità, cattiveria; ferocia
vicissitudes [vɪ'sɪsɪtjuːdz] npl vicissitudini fpl
victim ['vɪktɪm] n vittima; **to be the ~ of** essere vittima di
victimization [vɪktɪmaɪ'zeɪʃən] n persecuzione f; rappresaglie fpl
victimize ['vɪktɪmaɪz] vt perseguitare; compiere delle rappresaglie contro
victor ['vɪktər] n vincitore m
Victorian [vɪk'tɔːrɪən] adj vittoriano(-a)
victorious [vɪk'tɔːrɪəs] adj vittorioso(-a)
victory ['vɪktərɪ] n vittoria; **to win a ~ over sb** riportare una vittoria su qn
video ['vɪdɪəu] cpd video... ■ n (video film) video m inv; (also: **video cassette**) videocassette; (also: **video cassette recorder**) videoregistratore m
video call n videochiamata
video camera n videocamera
video cassette n videocassetta
video cassette recorder n videoregistratore m
videodisc ['vɪdɪəudɪsk] n disco ottico
video game n videogioco

video nasty n video estremamente violento o porno
videophone ['vɪdɪəufəun] n videotelefono
video recorder n videoregistratore m
video recording n registrazione f su video
video tape n videotape m inv
vie [vaɪ] vi: **to ~ with** competere con, rivaleggiare con
Vienna [vɪ'ɛnə] n Vienna
Vietnam, Viet Nam [vjɛt'næm] n Vietnam m
Vietnamese [vjɛtnə'miːz] adj vietnamita ■ n vietnamita m/f; (Ling) vietnamita m
view [vjuː] n vista, veduta; (opinion) opinione f ■ vt (situation) considerare; (house) visitare; **on ~** (in museum etc) esposto(-a); **to be in** or **within ~ (of sth)** essere in vista (di qc); **in full ~ of sb** sotto gli occhi di qn; **an overall ~ of the situation** una visione globale della situazione; **in my ~** a mio avviso, secondo me; **in ~ of the fact that** considerato che; **to take** or **hold the ~ that** ... essere dell'opinione che ...; **with a ~ to doing sth** con l'intenzione di fare qc
viewdata ['vjuːdeɪtə] n (Brit) sistema di televideo
viewer ['vjuːər] n (viewfinder) mirino; (small projector) visore m; (TV) telespettatore(-trice)
viewfinder ['vjuːfaɪndər] n mirino
viewpoint ['vjuːpɔɪnt] n punto di vista
vigil ['vɪdʒɪl] n veglia; **to keep ~** vegliare
vigilance ['vɪdʒɪləns] n vigilanza
vigilant ['vɪdʒɪlənt] adj vigile
vigilante [vɪdʒɪ'læntɪ] n cittadino che si fa giustizia da solo
vigorous ['vɪgərəs] adj vigoroso(-a)
vigour, (US) **vigor** [vɪgər] n vigore m
vile [vaɪl] adj (action) vile; (smell) disgustoso(-a), nauseante; (temper) pessimo(-a)
vilify ['vɪlɪfaɪ] vt diffamare
villa ['vɪlə] n villa
village ['vɪlɪdʒ] n villaggio
villager ['vɪlɪdʒər] n abitante m/f di villaggio
villain ['vɪlən] n (scoundrel) canaglia; (criminal) criminale m; (in novel etc) cattivo
VIN n abbr (US) = **vehicle identification number**
vinaigrette [vɪneɪ'grɛt] n vinaigrette f inv
vindicate ['vɪndɪkeɪt] vt comprovare; giustificare
vindication [vɪndɪ'keɪʃən] n: **in ~ of** per giustificare; a discolpa di
vindictive [vɪn'dɪktɪv] adj vendicativo(-a)
vine [vaɪn] n vite f; (climbing plant) rampicante m
vinegar ['vɪnɪgər] n aceto
vine grower n viticoltore m
vine-growing ['vaɪngrəuɪŋ] adj viticolo(-a) ■ n viticoltura

vineyard ['vɪnjɑːd] *n* vigna, vigneto
vintage ['vɪntɪdʒ] *n* (*year*) annata, produzione *f*; **the 1970 ~** il vino del 1970
vintage car *n* auto *f inv* d'epoca
vintage wine *n* vino d'annata
vinyl ['vaɪnl] *n* vinile *m*
viola [vɪ'əʊlə] *n* viola
violate ['vaɪəleɪt] *vt* violare
violation [vaɪə'leɪʃən] *n* violazione *f*; **in ~ of sth** violando qc
violence ['vaɪələns] *n* violenza; (*Pol etc*) incidenti *mpl* violenti
violent [vaɪələnt] *adj* violento(-a); **a ~ dislike of sb/sth** una violenta avversione per qn/qc
violently ['vaɪələntlɪ] *adv* violentemente; (*ill, angry*) terribilmente
violet ['vaɪələt] *adj* (*colour*) viola *inv*, violetto(-a) ■ *n* (*plant*) violetta
violin [vaɪə'lɪn] *n* violino
violinist [vaɪə'lɪnɪst] *n* violinista *m/f*
VIP *n abbr* (= *very important person*) V.I.P. *m/f inv*
viper ['vaɪpəʳ] *n* vipera
viral ['vaɪərəl] *adj* virale
virgin ['vəːdʒɪn] *n* vergine *f* ■ *adj* vergine *inv*; **she is a ~** lei è vergine; **the Blessed V~** la Beatissima Vergine
virginity [vəː'dʒɪnɪtɪ] *n* verginità
Virgo ['vəːɡəʊ] *n* (*sign*) Vergine *f*; **to be ~** essere della Vergine
virile ['vɪraɪl] *adj* virile
virility [vɪ'rɪlɪtɪ] *n* virilità
virtual ['vəːtjʊəl] *adj* effettivo(-a), vero(-a); (*Comput, Physics*) virtuale; (*in effect*): **it's a ~ impossibility** è praticamente impossibile; **the ~ leader** il capo all'atto pratico
virtually ['vəːtjʊəlɪ] *adv* (*almost*) praticamente; **it is ~ impossible** è praticamente impossibile
virtual reality *n* realtà *f inv* virtuale
virtue ['vəːtjuː] *n* virtù *f inv*; (*advantage*) pregio, vantaggio; **by ~ of** grazie a
virtuosity [vəːtjʊ'ɒsɪtɪ] *n* virtuosismo
virtuoso [vəːtjʊ'əʊzəʊ] *n* virtuoso
virtuous ['vəːtjʊəs] *adj* virtuoso(-a)
virulent ['vɪrʊlənt] *adj* virulento(-a)
virus ['vaɪərəs] *n* virus *m inv*
visa ['viːzə] *n* visto
vis-à-vis [viːzə'viː] *prep* rispetto a, nei riguardi di
viscount ['vaɪkaʊnt] *n* visconte *m*
viscous ['vɪskəs] *adj* viscoso(-a)
vise [vaɪs] *n* (*US Tech*) = **vice**
visibility [vɪzɪ'bɪlɪtɪ] *n* visibilità
visible ['vɪzəbl] *adj* visibile; **~ exports/ imports** esportazioni *fpl*/importazioni *fpl* visibili
visibly ['vɪzəblɪ] *adv* visibilmente

vision ['vɪʒən] *n* (*sight*) vista; (*foresight, in dream*) visione *f*
visionary ['vɪʒənərɪ] *n* visionario(-a)
visit ['vɪzɪt] *n* visita; (*stay*) soggiorno ■ *vt* (*person*) andare a trovare; (*place*) visitare; **to pay a ~ to** (*person*) fare una visita a; (*place*) andare a visitare; **on a private/official ~ in** visita privata/ufficiale
visiting ['vɪzɪtɪŋ] *adj* (*speaker, professor, team*) ospite
visiting card *n* biglietto da visita
visiting hours *npl* orario delle visite
visitor ['vɪzɪtəʳ] *n* visitatore(-trice); (*guest*) ospite *m/f*
visitors' book *n* libro d'oro; (*in hotel*) registro
visor ['vaɪzəʳ] *n* visiera
VISTA ['vɪstə] *n abbr* (= *Volunteers in Service to America*) *volontariato in zone depresse degli Stati Uniti*
vista ['vɪstə] *n* vista, prospettiva
visual ['vɪzjʊəl] *adj* visivo(-a); visuale; ottico(-a)
visual aid *n* sussidio visivo
visual arts *npl* arti *fpl* figurative
visual display unit *n* unità *f inv* di visualizzazione
visualize ['vɪzjʊəlaɪz] *vt* immaginare, figurarsi; (*foresee*) prevedere
visually ['vɪzjʊəlɪ] *adv*: **~ appealing** piacevole a vedersi; **~ handicapped** con una menomazione della vista
vital ['vaɪtl] *adj* vitale; **of ~ importance (to sb/sth)** di vitale importanza (per qn/qc)
vitality [vaɪ'tælɪtɪ] *n* vitalità
vitally ['vaɪtəlɪ] *adv* estremamente
vital statistics *npl* (*of population*) statistica demografica; (*col: woman's*) misure *fpl*
vitamin ['vɪtəmɪn] *n* vitamina
vitiate ['vɪʃɪeɪt] *vt* viziare
vitreous ['vɪtrɪəs] *adj* (*rock*) vetroso(-a); (*china, enamel*) vetrificato(-a)
vitriolic [vɪtrɪ'ɒlɪk] *adj* (*fig*) caustico(-a)
viva ['vaɪvə] *n* (*also:* **viva voce**) (*esame m*) orale
vivacious [vɪ'veɪʃəs] *adj* vivace
vivacity [vɪ'væsɪtɪ] *n* vivacità
vivid ['vɪvɪd] *adj* vivido(-a)
vividly ['vɪvɪdlɪ] *adv* (*describe*) vividamente; (*remember*) con precisione
vivisection [vɪvɪ'sekʃən] *n* vivisezione *f*
vixen ['vɪksn] *n* volpe *f* femmina; (*pej: woman*) bisbetica
viz *abbr* (= *vide licet: namely*) cioè
VLF *abbr* (= *very low frequency*) bassissima frequenza
V-neck ['viːnek] *n* maglione *m* con lo scollo a V

V

VOA *n abbr* (= *Voice of America*) voce *f*
dell'America (*alla radio*)

vocabulary [vəuˈkæbjulərɪ] *n* vocabolario

vocal [ˈvəukl] *adj* (*Mus*) vocale; (*communication*)
verbale; (*noisy*) rumoroso(-a)

vocal cords *npl* corde *fpl* vocali

vocalist [ˈvəukəlɪst] *n* cantante *m/f* (*in un
gruppo*)

vocation [vəuˈkeɪʃən] *n* vocazione *f*

vocational [vəuˈkeɪʃənl] *adj* professionale;
~ **guidance** orientamento professionale;
~ **training** formazione *f* professionale

vociferous [vəˈsɪfərəs] *adj* rumoroso(-a)

vodka [ˈvɔdkə] *n* vodka *f inv*

vogue [vəug] *n* moda; (*popularity*) popolarità,
voga; **to be in ~, be the ~** essere di moda

voice [vɔɪs] *n* voce *f* ■ *vt* (*opinion*) esprimere;
in a loud/soft ~ a voce alta/bassa; **to give ~
to** esprimere

voice mail *n* servizio di segreteria telefonica

voice-over [ˈvɔɪsəuvəʳ] *n* voce *f* fuori campo *inv*

void [vɔɪd] *n* vuoto ■ *adj*: ~ **of** privo(-a) di

voile [vɔɪl] *n* voile *m*

vol. *abbr* (= *volume*) vol.

volatile [ˈvɔlətaɪl] *adj* volatile; (*fig*) volubile

volcanic [vɔlˈkænɪk] *adj* vulcanico(-a)

volcano (*pl* **volcanoes**) [vɔlˈkeɪnəu] *n* vulcano

volition [vəˈlɪʃən] *n*: **of one's own ~** di
propria volontà

volley [ˈvɔlɪ] *n* (*of gunfire*) salva; (*of stones etc*)
raffica, gragnola; (*Tennis etc*) volata

volleyball [ˈvɔlɪbɔːl] *n* pallavolo *f*

volt [vəult] *n* volt *m inv*

voltage [ˈvəultɪdʒ] *n* tensione *f*, voltaggio;
high/low ~ alta/bassa tensione

voluble [ˈvɔljubl] *adj* loquace, ciarliero(-a)

volume [ˈvɔljuːm] *n* volume *m*; (*of tank*)
capacità *f inv*; ~ **one/two** (*of book*) volume
primo/secondo; **his expression spoke
volumes** la sua espressione lasciava capire
tutto

volume control *n* (*Radio, TV*) regolatore *m* or
manopola del volume

volume discount *n* (*Comm*) vantaggio sul
volume di vendita

voluminous [vəˈluːmɪnəs] *adj*
voluminoso(-a); (*notes etc*) abbondante

voluntarily [ˈvɔləntrɪlɪ] *adv*

volontariamente; gratuitamente

voluntary [ˈvɔləntərɪ] *adj* volontario(-a);
(*unpaid*) gratuito(-a), non retribuito(-a)

voluntary liquidation *n* (*Comm*)
liquidazione *f* volontaria

volunteer [vɔlənˈtɪəʳ] *n* volontario(-a) ■ *vi*
(*Mil*) arruolarsi volontario; **to ~ to do** offrire
(volontariamente) di fare

voluptuous [vəˈlʌptjuəs] *adj* voluttuoso(-a)

vomit [ˈvɔmɪt] *n* vomito ■ *vt, vi* vomitare

voracious [vəˈreɪʃəs] *adj* (*appetite*)
smisurato(-a); (*reader*) avido(-a)

vote [vəut] *n* voto, suffragio; (*cast*) voto;
(*franchise*) diritto di voto ■ *vi* votare ■ *vt*
(*gen*) votare; (*sum of money etc*) votare a favore
di; **to ~ to do sth** votare a favore di fare qc;
he was voted secretary è stato eletto
segretario; **to put sth to the ~, to take a ~
on sth** mettere qc ai voti; ~ **for/against** voto
a favore/contrario; **to pass a ~ of
confidence/no confidence** dare il voto di
fiducia/sfiducia; ~ **of thanks** discorso di
ringraziamento

voter [ˈvəutəʳ] *n* elettore(-trice)

voting [ˈvəutɪŋ] *n* scrutinio

voting paper *n* (*Brit*) scheda elettorale

voting right *n* diritto di voto

vouch [vautʃ] *n*: **to ~ for** *vt fus* farsi garante di

voucher [ˈvautʃəʳ] *n* (*for meal, petrol*) buono;
(*receipt*) ricevuta; **travel ~** voucher *m inv*,
tagliando

vow [vau] *n* voto, promessa solenne ■ *vi*
giurare; **to take** *or* **make a ~ to do sth** fare
voto di fare qc

vowel [ˈvauəl] *n* vocale *f*

voyage [ˈvɔɪɪdʒ] *n* viaggio per mare,
traversata

voyeur [vwɑːˈjəːʳ] *n* guardone(-a)

VP *n abbr* (= *vice-president*) V.P.

vs *abbr* (= *versus*) contro

VSO *n abbr* (Brit: = *Voluntary Service Overseas*)
servizio volontario in paesi sottosviluppati

VT, Vt. *abbr* (*US*) = **Vermont**

vulgar [ˈvʌlgəʳ] *adj* volgare

vulgarity [vʌlˈgærɪtɪ] *n* volgarità

vulnerability [vʌlnərəˈbɪlɪtɪ] *n* vulnerabilità

vulnerable [ˈvʌlnərəbl] *adj* vulnerabile

vulture [ˈvʌltʃəʳ] *n* avvoltoio

Ww

W, w ['dʌblju:] n (letter) W, w m or f inv; **W for William** ≈ W come Washington
W abbr (= west) O; (Elec: = watt) w
WA abbr (US) = **Washington**
wad [wɔd] n (of cotton wool, paper) tampone m; (of banknotes etc) fascio
wadding ['wɔdɪŋ] n imbottitura
waddle ['wɔdl] vi camminare come una papera
wade [weɪd] vi: **to ~ through** camminare a stento in ■ vt guadare
wafer ['weɪfə'] n (Culin) cialda; (Rel) ostia; (Comput) wafer m inv
wafer-thin ['weɪfə'θɪn] adj molto sottile
waffle ['wɔfl] n (Culin) cialda; (col) ciance fpl; riempitivo ■ vi cianciare; parlare a vuoto
waffle iron n stampo per cialde
waft [wɔft] vt portare ■ vi diffondersi
wag [wæg] vt agitare, muovere ■ vi agitarsi; **the dog wagged its tail** il cane scodinzolò
wage [weɪdʒ] n (also: **wages**) salario, paga ■ vt: **to ~ war** fare la guerra; **a day's wages** un giorno di paga
wage claim n rivendicazione f salariale
wage differential n differenza di salario
wage earner n salariato(-a)
wage freeze n blocco dei salari
wage packet n (Brit) busta f paga inv
wager ['weɪdʒə'] n scommessa
waggle ['wægl] vt dimenare, agitare ■ vi dimenarsi, agitarsi
wagon, waggon ['wægən] n (horse-drawn) carro; (truck) furgone m; (Brit Rail) vagone m (merci)
wail [weɪl] n gemito; (of siren) urlo ■ vi gemere; urlare
waist [weɪst] n vita, cintola
waistcoat ['weɪskəut] n panciotto, gilè m inv
waistline ['weɪstlaɪn] n (giro di) vita
wait [weɪt] n attesa ■ vi aspettare, attendere; **to ~ for** aspettare; **to keep sb waiting** far aspettare qn; **~ a moment!** (aspetti) un momento!; **"repairs while you ~"** "riparazioni lampo"; **I can't ~ to ...**

(fig) non vedo l'ora di ...; **to lie in ~ for** stare in agguato a
▶ **wait behind** vi rimanere (ad aspettare)
▶ **wait on** vt fus servire
▶ **wait up** vi restare alzato(-a) (ad aspettare); **don't ~ up for me** non rimanere alzato per me
waiter ['weɪtə'] n cameriere m
waiting ['weɪtɪŋ] n: **"no ~"** (Brit Aut) "divieto di sosta"
waiting list n lista d'attesa
waiting room n sala d'aspetto or d'attesa
waitress ['weɪtrɪs] n cameriera
waive [weɪv] vt rinunciare a, abbandonare
waiver ['weɪvə'] n rinuncia
wake [weɪk] vb (pt **woke, waked,** pp **woken, waked**) [wəuk, 'wəukn] vt (also: **wake up**) svegliare ■ vi (also: **wake up**) svegliarsi ■ n (for dead person) veglia funebre; (Naut) scia; **to ~ up to sth** (fig) rendersi conto di qc; **in the ~ of** sulla scia di; **to follow in sb's ~** (fig) seguire le tracce di qn
waken ['weɪkn] vt, vi = **wake**
Wales [weɪlz] n Galles m
walk [wɔ:k] n passeggiata; (short) giretto; (gait) passo, andatura; (path) sentiero; (in park etc) sentiero, vialetto ■ vi camminare; (for pleasure, exercise) passeggiare ■ vt (distance) fare or percorrere a piedi; (dog) accompagnare, portare a passeggiare; **10 minutes' ~ from** 10 minuti di cammino or a piedi da; **to go for a ~** andare a fare quattro passi; andare a fare una passeggiata; **from all walks of life** di tutte le condizioni sociali; **to ~ in one's sleep** essere sonnambulo(-a); **I'll ~ you home** ti accompagno a casa
▶ **walk out** vi (go out) uscire; (as protest) uscire (in segno di protesta); (strike) scendere in sciopero; **to ~ out on sb** piantare in asso qn
walkabout ['wɔ:kəbaut] n: **to go (on a) ~** avere incontri informali col pubblico (durante una visita ufficiale)

walker ['wɔːkəʳ] n (person) camminatore(-trice)

walkie-talkie ['wɔːkɪ'tɔːkɪ] n walkie-talkie m inv

walking ['wɔːkɪŋ] n camminare m; **it's within ~ distance** ci si arriva a piedi

walking holiday n vacanza fatta di lunghe camminate

walking shoes npl scarpe fpl da passeggio

walking stick n bastone m da passeggio

Walkman® ['wɔːkmən] n walkman® m inv

walk-on ['wɔːkɔn] adj (Theat: part) da comparsa

walkout ['wɔːkaut] n (of workers) sciopero senza preavviso or a sorpresa

walkover ['wɔːkəuvəʳ] n (col) vittoria facile, gioco da ragazzi

walkway ['wɔːkweɪ] n passaggio pedonale

wall [wɔːl] n muro; (internal, of tunnel, cave) parete f; **to go to the ~** (fig: firm etc) fallire
▶ **wall in** vt (garden etc) circondare con un muro

wall cupboard n pensile m

walled [wɔːld] adj (city) fortificato(-a)

wallet ['wɔlɪt] n portafoglio

wallflower ['wɔːlflauəʳ] n violacciocca; **to be a ~** (fig) fare da tappezzeria

wall hanging n tappezzeria

wallop ['wɔləp] vt (col) pestare

wallow ['wɔləu] vi sguazzare, rotolarsi; **to ~ in one's grief** crogiolarsi nel proprio dolore

wallpaper ['wɔːlpeɪpəʳ] n carta da parati; (Comput) sfondo

wall-to-wall ['wɔːltə'wɔːl] adj: **~ carpeting** moquette f

walnut ['wɔːlnʌt] n noce f; (tree) noce m

walrus (pl **~** or **walruses**) ['wɔːlrəs] n tricheco

waltz [wɔːlts] n valzer m inv ■ vi ballare il valzer

wan [wɔn] adj pallido(-a), smorto(-a); triste

wand [wɔnd] n (also: **magic wand**) bacchetta (magica)

wander ['wɔndəʳ] vi (person) girare senza meta, girovagare; (thoughts) vagare; (river) serpeggiare

wanderer ['wɔndərəʳ] n vagabondo(-a)

wandering ['wɔndrɪŋ] adj (tribe) nomade; (minstrel, actor) girovago(-a); (path, river) tortuoso(-a); (glance, mind) distratto(-a)

wane [weɪn] vi (moon) calare; (reputation) declinare

wangle ['wæŋgl] (Brit col) vt procurare (con l'astuzia) ■ n astuzia

wanker ['wæŋkəʳ] n (col!) segaiolo (!); (as insult) coglione (!) m

want [wɔnt] vt volere; (need) aver bisogno di; (lack) mancare di ■ n (poverty) miseria, povertà; **wants** npl (needs) bisogni mpl; **for ~**

of per mancanza di; **to ~ to do** volere fare; **to ~ sb to do** volere che qn faccia; **you're wanted on the phone** la vogliono al telefono; **"cook wanted"** "cercasi cuoco"

want ads npl (US) piccoli annunci mpl

wanting ['wɔntɪŋ] adj: **to be ~ (in)** mancare (di); **to be found ~** non risultare all'altezza

wanton ['wɔntn] adj sfrenato(-a); senza motivo

war [wɔːʳ] n guerra; **to go to ~** entrare in guerra

warble ['wɔːbl] n (of bird) trillo ■ vi trillare

war cry n grido di guerra

ward [wɔːd] n (in hospital: room) corsia; (: section) reparto; (Pol) circoscrizione f; (Law: child) pupillo(-a)
▶ **ward off** vt parare, schivare

warden ['wɔːdn] n (of institution) direttore(-trice); (of park, game reserve) guardiano(-a); (Brit: also: **traffic warden**) addetto(-a) al controllo del traffico e del parcheggio

warder ['wɔːdəʳ] n (Brit) guardia carceraria

wardrobe ['wɔːdrəub] n (cupboard) guardaroba m inv, armadio; (clothes) guardaroba; (Theat) costumi mpl

warehouse ['wεəhaus] n magazzino

wares [wεəz] npl merci fpl

warfare ['wɔːfεəʳ] n guerra

war game n war game m inv

warhead ['wɔːhεd] n (Mil) testata, ogiva

warily ['wεərɪlɪ] adv cautamente, con prudenza

warlike ['wɔːlaɪk] adj guerriero(-a)

warm [wɔːm] adj caldo(-a); (welcome, applause) caloroso(-a); (person, greeting) cordiale; (heart) d'oro; (supporter) convinto(-a); **it's ~** fa caldo; **I'm ~** ho caldo; **to keep sth ~** tenere qc al caldo; **with my warmest thanks** con i miei più sentiti ringraziamenti
▶ **warm up** vi scaldarsi, riscaldarsi; (athlete, discussion) riscaldarsi ■ vt scaldare, riscaldare; (engine) far scaldare

warm-blooded ['wɔːm'blʌdɪd] adj a sangue caldo

war memorial n monumento ai caduti

warm-hearted [wɔːm'hɑːtɪd] adj affettuoso(-a)

warmly ['wɔːmlɪ] adv caldamente; calorosamente; vivamente

warmonger ['wɔːmʌŋgəʳ] n guerrafondaio

warmongering ['wɔːmʌŋgrɪŋ] n bellicismo

warmth [wɔːmθ] n calore m

warm-up ['wɔːmʌp] n (Sport) riscaldamento

warn [wɔːn] vt avvertire, avvisare; **to ~ sb not to do sth** or **against doing sth** avvertire qn di non fare qc

warning ['wɔ:nɪŋ] *n* avvertimento; (*notice*) avviso; **without (any)** ~ senza preavviso; **gale** ~ avviso di burrasca

warning light *n* spia luminosa

warning triangle *n* (*Aut*) triangolo

warp [wɔ:p] *n* (*Textiles*) ordito ■ *vi* deformarsi ■ *vt* deformare; (*fig*) corrompere

warpath ['wɔ:pɑ:θ] *n*: **to be on the** ~ (*fig*) essere sul sentiero di guerra

warped [wɔ:pt] *adj* (*wood*) curvo(-a); (*fig: character, sense of humour etc*) contorto(-a)

warrant ['wɔrnt] *n* (*Law: to arrest*) mandato di cattura; (: *to search*) mandato di perquisizione ■ *vt* (*justify, merit*) giustificare

warrant officer *n* sottufficiale *m*

warranty ['wɔrəntɪ] *n* garanzia; **under** ~ (*Comm*) in garanzia

warren ['wɔrən] *n* (*of rabbits*) tana

warring ['wɔ:rɪŋ] *adj* (*interests etc*) opposto(-a), in lotta; (*nations*) in guerra

warrior ['wɔrɪəʳ] *n* guerriero(-a)

Warsaw ['wɔ:sɔ:] *n* Varsavia

warship ['wɔ:ʃɪp] *n* nave *f* da guerra

wart [wɔ:t] *n* verruca

wartime ['wɔ:taɪm] *n*: **in** ~ in tempo di guerra

wary ['wɛərɪ] *adj* prudente; **to be** ~ **about** *or* **of doing sth** andare cauto nel fare qc

was [wɔz] *pt of* **be**

wash [wɔʃ] *vt* lavare; (*sweep, carry: sea etc*) portare, trascinare ■ *vi* lavarsi ■ *n*: **to give sth a** ~ lavare qc, dare una lavata a qc; **to have a** ~ lavarsi; **he was washed overboard** fu trascinato in mare (dalle onde)

▶ **wash away** *vt* (*stain*) togliere lavando; (*river etc*) trascinare via

▶ **wash down** *vt* lavare

▶ **wash off** *vi* andare via con il lavaggio

▶ **wash up** *vi* lavare i piatti; (*US: have a wash*) lavarsi

Wash. *abbr* (*US*) = **Washington**

washable ['wɔʃəbl] *adj* lavabile

washbasin ['wɔʃbeɪsn] *n* lavabo

washcloth ['wɔʃklɔθ] *n* (*US*) pezzuola (per lavarsi)

washer ['wɔʃəʳ] *n* (*Tech*) rondella

washing ['wɔʃɪŋ] *n* (*Brit: linen etc*) bucato; **dirty** ~ biancheria da lavare

washing line *n* (*Brit*) corda del bucato

washing machine *n* lavatrice *f*

washing powder *n* (*Brit*) detersivo (in polvere)

Washington ['wɔʃɪŋtən] *n* Washington *f*

washing-up [wɔʃɪŋʌp] *n* (*dishes*) piatti *mpl* sporchi; **to do the** ~ lavare i piatti, rigovernare

washing-up liquid *n* (*Brit*) detersivo liquido (per stoviglie)

wash-out ['wɔʃaut] *n* (*col*) disastro

washroom ['wɔʃrum] *n* gabinetto

wasn't ['wɔznt] = **was not**

Wasp, WASP [wɔsp] *n abbr* (*US*: = *White Anglo-Saxon Protestant*) W.A.S.P. *m* (*protestante bianco anglosassone*)

wasp [wɔsp] *n* vespa

waspish ['wɔspɪʃ] *adj* litigioso(-a)

wastage ['weɪstɪdʒ] *n* spreco; (*in manufacturing*) scarti *mpl*

waste [weɪst] *n* spreco; (*of time*) perdita; (*rubbish*) rifiuti *mpl* ■ *adj* (*material*) di scarto; (*food*) avanzato(-a); (*energy, heat*) sprecato(-a); (*land, ground: in city*) abbandonato(-a); (: *in country*) incolto(-a) ■ *vt* sprecare; (*time, opportunity*) perdere; **wastes** *npl* distesa desolata; **it's a** ~ **of money** sono soldi sprecati; **to go to** ~ andare sprecato; **to lay** ~ devastare

▶ **waste away** *vi* deperire

wastebasket ['weɪstbɑ:skɪt] *n* = **wastepaper basket**

waste disposal, waste disposal unit *n* (*Brit*) eliminatore *m* di rifiuti

wasteful ['weɪstful] *adj* sprecone(-a); (*process*) dispendioso(-a)

waste ground *n* (*Brit*) terreno incolto *or* abbandonato

wasteland ['weɪstlænd] *n* terra desolata

wastepaper basket ['weɪstpeɪpə-] *n* cestino per la carta straccia

waste pipe *n* tubo di scarico

waste products *npl* (*Industry*) materiali *mpl* di scarto

waster ['weɪstəʳ] *n* (*col*) buono(-a) a nulla

watch [wɔtʃ] *n* (*wristwatch*) orologio; (*act of watching*) sorveglianza; (*guard: Mil, Naut*) guardia; (*Naut: spell of duty*) quarto ■ *vt* (*look at*) osservare; (: *match, programme*) guardare; (*spy on, guard*) sorvegliare, tenere d'occhio; (*be careful of*) fare attenzione a ■ *vi* osservare, guardare; (*keep guard*) fare *or* montare la guardia; **to keep a close** ~ **on sb/sth** tener bene d'occhio qn/qc; ~ **how you drive/what you're doing** attento a come guidi/quel che fai

▶ **watch out** *vi* fare attenzione

watchband ['wɔtʃbænd] *n* (*US*) cinturino da orologio

watchdog ['wɔtʃdɔg] *n* cane *m* da guardia; (*fig*) sorvegliante *m/f*

watchful ['wɔtʃful] *adj* attento(-a), vigile

watchmaker ['wɔtʃmeɪkəʳ] *n* orologiaio(-a)

watchman ['wɔtʃmən] *n* guardiano; (*also*: **night watchman**) guardiano notturno

watch stem *n* (*US*) corona di carica

watch strap *n* cinturino da orologio

W

watchword ['wɔtʃwəːd] *n* parola d'ordine
water ['wɔːtə'] *n* acqua ■ *vt* (*plant*) annaffiare
■ *vi* (*eyes*) piangere; **in British waters** nelle
acque territoriali britanniche; **I'd like a
drink of** ~ vorrei un bicchier d'acqua; **to
pass** ~ orinare; **to make sb's mouth** ~ far
venire l'acquolina in bocca a qn
  ▶ **water down** *vt* (*milk*) diluire; (*fig: story*)
  edulcorare
water closet *n* (*Brit*) W.C. *m inv*, gabinetto
watercolour, (US) **watercolor** ['wɔːtəkʌlə']
n (*picture*) acquerello; **watercolours** *npl*
colori *mpl* per acquerelli
water-cooled ['wɔːtəkuːld] *adj*
raffreddato(-a) ad acqua
watercress ['wɔːtəkrɛs] *n* crescione *m*
waterfall ['wɔːtəfɔːl] *n* cascata
waterfront ['wɔːtəfrʌnt] *n* (*seafront*)
lungomare *m*; (*at docks*) banchina
water heater *n* scaldabagno
water hole *n* pozza d'acqua
water ice *n* (*Brit*) sorbetto
watering can ['wɔːtərɪŋ-] *n* annaffiatoio
water level *n* livello dell'acqua; (*of flood*)
livello delle acque
water lily *n* ninfea
waterline ['wɔːtəlaɪn] *n* (*Naut*) linea di
galleggiamento
waterlogged ['wɔːtəlɔgd] *adj* saturo(-a)
d'acqua; imbevuto(-a) d'acqua; (*football pitch
etc*) allagato(-a)
watermark ['wɔːtəmɑːk] *n* (*on paper*)
filigrana
watermelon ['wɔːtəmɛlən] *n* anguria,
cocomero
water polo *n* pallanuoto *f*
waterproof ['wɔːtəpruːf] *adj* impermeabile
water-repellent ['wɔːtərɪˈpɛlənt] *adj*
idrorepellente
watershed ['wɔːtəʃɛd] *n* (*Geo, fig*) spartiacque *m*
water-skiing ['wɔːtəskiːɪŋ] *n* sci *m* acquatico
water softener *n* addolcitore *m*; (*substance*)
anti-calcare *m*
water tank *n* serbatoio d'acqua
watertight ['wɔːtətaɪt] *adj* stagno(-a)
water vapour *n* vapore *m* acqueo
waterway ['wɔːtəweɪ] *n* corso d'acqua
navigabile
waterworks ['wɔːtəwəːks] *npl* impianto
idrico
watery ['wɔːtərɪ] *adj* (*colour*) slavato(-a);
(*coffee*) acquoso(-a)
watt [wɔt] *n* watt *m inv*
wattage ['wɔtɪdʒ] *n* wattaggio
wattle ['wɔtl] *n* graticcio
wave [weɪv] *n* onda; (*of hand*) gesto, segno;
(*in hair*) ondulazione *f*; (*fig: of enthusiasm, strikes*

etc) ondata ■ *vi* fare un cenno con la mano;
(*flag*) sventolare ■ *vt* (*handkerchief*)
sventolare; (*stick*) brandire; (*hair*) ondulare;
short/medium/long ~ (*Radio*) onde corte/
medie/lunghe; **the new** ~ (*Cine, Mus*) la new
wave; **to** ~ **sb goodbye, to** ~ **goodbye to sb**
fare un cenno d'addio a qn; **he waved us
over to his table** ci invitò con un cenno al
suo tavolo
  ▶ **wave aside, wave away** *vt* (*person*): **to** ~ **sb
  aside** fare cenno a qn di spostarsi; (*fig:
  suggestion, objection*) respingere, rifiutare;
  (*: doubts*) scacciare
waveband ['weɪvbænd] *n* gamma di
lunghezze d'onda
wavelength ['weɪvlɛŋθ] *n* lunghezza d'onda
waver ['weɪvə'] *vi* vacillare; (*voice*) tremolare
wavy ['weɪvɪ] *adj* ondulato(-a); ondeggiante
wax [wæks] *n* cera ■ *vt* dare la cera a; (*car*)
lucidare ■ *vi* (*moon*) crescere
waxworks ['wækswəːks] *npl* cere *fpl*; museo
delle cere
way [weɪ] *n* via, strada; (*path, access*)
passaggio; (*distance*) distanza; (*direction*) parte
f, direzione *f*; (*manner*) modo, stile *m*; (*habit*)
abitudine *f*; (*condition*) condizione *f*; **which** ~?
— **this** ~ da che parte *or* in quale direzione? —
da questa parte *or* per di qua; **to crawl one's
** ~ **to ...** raggiungere ... strisciando; **he lied
his** ~ **out of it** se l'è cavata mentendo; **to
lose one's** ~ perdere la strada; **on the** ~
(*en route*) per strada; (*expected*) in arrivo; **you
pass it on your** ~ **home** ci passi davanti
andando a casa; **to be on one's** ~ essere in
cammino *or* sulla strada; **to be in the** ~
bloccare il passaggio; (*fig*) essere tra i piedi *or*
d'impiccio; **to keep out of sb's** ~ evitare qn;
it's a long ~ **away** è molto lontano da qui;
the village is rather out of the ~ il villaggio
è abbastanza fuori mano; **to go out of one's
** ~ **to do** (*fig*) mettercela tutta *or* fare di tutto
per fare; **to be under** ~ (*work, project*) essere
in corso; **to make** ~ (**for sb/sth**) far strada (a
qn/qc); (*fig*) lasciare il posto *or* far largo (a qn/
qc); **to get one's own** ~ fare come si vuole;
put it the right ~ **up** (*Brit*) mettilo in piedi
dalla parte giusta; **to be the wrong** ~ **round**
essere al contrario; **he's in a bad** ~ è ridotto
male; **in a** ~ in un certo senso; **in some ways**
sotto certi aspetti; **in the** ~ **of** come; **by** ~ **of**
(*through*) attraverso; (*as a sort of*) come; "~ **in**"
"entrata", "ingresso"; "~ **out**" "uscita"; **the**
~ **back** la via del ritorno; **this** ~ **and that** di
qua e di là; "**give** ~" (*Brit Aut*) "dare la
precedenza"; **no** ~! (*col*) assolutamente no!
waybill ['weɪbɪl] *n* (*Comm*) bolla di
accompagnamento

waylay [weɪ'leɪ] *vt irreg* tendere un agguato a; attendere al passaggio; *(fig)*: **I got waylaid** ho avuto un contrattempo

wayside ['weɪsaɪd] *n* bordo della strada; **to fall by the ~** *(fig)* perdersi lungo la strada

way station *n* *(US Rail)* stazione *f* secondaria; *(fig)* tappa

wayward ['weɪwəd] *adj* capriccioso(-a); testardo(-a)

WC *n abbr* *(Brit: = water closet)* W.C. *m inv*, gabinetto

WCC *n abbr* *(= World Council of Churches)* Consiglio Ecumenico delle Chiese

we [wi:] *pl pron* noi; **here we are** eccoci

weak [wi:k] *adj* debole; *(health)* precario(-a); *(beam etc)* fragile; *(tea, coffee)* leggero(-a); **to grow ~(er)** indebolirsi

weaken ['wi:kən] *vi* indebolirsi ▪ *vt* indebolire

weak-kneed ['wi:k'ni:d] *adj* *(fig)* debole, codardo(-a)

weakling ['wi:klɪŋ] *n* smidollato(-a); debole *m/f*

weakly ['wi:klɪ] *adj* deboluccio(-a), gracile ▪ *adv* debolmente

weakness ['wi:knɪs] *n* debolezza; *(fault)* punto debole, difetto

wealth [wɛlθ] *n* *(money, resources)* ricchezza, ricchezze *fpl*; *(of details)* abbondanza, profusione *f*

wealth tax *n* imposta sul patrimonio

wealthy ['wɛlθɪ] *adj* ricco(-a)

wean [wi:n] *vt* svezzare

weapon ['wɛpən] *n* arma; **weapons of mass destruction** armi di distruzione di massa

wear [wɛəʳ] *n* *(use)* uso; *(deterioration through use)* logorio, usura; *(clothing)*: **sports/baby ~** abbigliamento sportivo/per neonati ▪ *vb* *(pt* **wore**, *pp* **worn**) [wɔ:ʳ, wɔ:n] *vt* *(clothes)* portare; mettersi; *(beard etc)* avere; *(damage: through use)* consumare ▪ *vi* *(last)* durare; *(rub etc through)* consumarsi; **~ and tear** usura, consumo; **town/evening ~** abiti *mpl* or tenuta da città/sera; **to ~ a hole in sth** bucare qc a furia di usarlo
- ▸ **wear away** *vt* consumare; erodere ▪ *vi* consumarsi; essere eroso(-a)
- ▸ **wear down** *vt* consumare; *(strength)* esaurire
- ▸ **wear off** *vi* sparire lentamente
- ▸ **wear on** *vi* passare
- ▸ **wear out** *vt* consumare; *(person, strength)* esaurire

wearable ['wɛərəbl] *adj* indossabile

wearily ['wɪərɪlɪ] *adv* stancamente

weariness ['wɪərɪnɪs] *n* stanchezza

wearisome ['wɪərɪsəm] *adj* *(tiring)* estenuante; *(boring)* noioso(-a)

weary ['wɪərɪ] *adj* stanco(-a); *(tiring)* faticoso(-a) ▪ *vt* stancare ▪ *vi*: **to ~ of** stancarsi di

weasel ['wi:zl] *n* *(Zool)* donnola

weather ['wɛðəʳ] *n* tempo ▪ *vt* *(wood)* stagionare; *(storm, crisis)* superare; **what's the ~ like?** che tempo fa?; **under the ~** *(fig: ill)* poco bene

weather-beaten ['wɛðəbi:tn] *adj* *(person)* segnato(-a) dalle intemperie; *(building)* logorato(-a) dalle intemperie

weather forecast *n* previsioni *fpl* del tempo, bollettino meteorologico

weatherman ['wɛðəmæn] *n* meteorologo

weatherproof ['wɛðəpru:f] *adj* *(garment)* impermeabile

weather report *n* bollettino meteorologico

weather vane *n* = **weather cock**

weave *(pt* **wove**, *pp* **woven**) [wi:v, wəuv, 'wəuvn] *vt* *(cloth)* tessere; *(basket)* intrecciare ▪ *vi* *(fig)* *(pt, pp* **weaved**) *(move in and out)* zigzagare

weaver ['wi:vəʳ] *n* tessitore(-trice)

weaving ['wi:vɪŋ] *n* tessitura

web [wɛb] *n* *(of spider)* ragnatela; *(on foot)* palma; *(fabric, also fig)* tessuto; **the (World Wide) W~** la Rete

web address *n* indirizzo Internet

webbed [wɛbd] *adj* *(foot)* palmato(-a)

webbing ['wɛbɪŋ] *n* *(on chair)* cinghie *fpl*

webcam ['wɛbkæm] *n* webcam *f inv*

web page *n* *(Comput)* pagina *f* web *inv*

website ['wɛbsaɪt] *n* *(Comput)* sito

wed [wɛd] *vt* *(pt, pp* **wedded**) sposare ▪ *n*: **the newly-weds** gli sposi novelli

Wed. *abbr* *(= Wednesday)* mer.

we'd [wi:d] = **we had**; **we would**

wedded ['wɛdɪd] *pt, pp of* **wed**

wedding ['wɛdɪŋ] *n* matrimonio; **silver/golden ~** nozze *fpl* d'argento/d'oro

wedding anniversary *n* anniversario di matrimonio

wedding day *n* giorno delle nozze or del matrimonio

wedding dress *n* abito nuziale

wedding present *n* regalo di nozze

wedding ring *n* fede *f*

wedge [wɛdʒ] *n* *(of wood etc)* cuneo; *(under door etc)* zeppa; *(of cake)* spicchio, fetta ▪ *vt* mettere una zeppa sotto *(or* in); **to ~ a door open** tenere aperta una porta con un fermo

wedge-heeled shoes ['wɛdʒhi:ld-] *npl* scarpe *fpl* con tacco a zeppa

wedlock ['wɛdlɔk] *n* vincolo matrimoniale

Wednesday ['wɛdnzdɪ] *n* mercoledì *m inv*; *see also* **Tuesday**

wee [wi:] *adj* *(Scottish)* piccolo(-a)

W

weed [wiːd] n erbaccia ▪ vt diserbare
▶ **weed out** vt fare lo spoglio di
weed-killer ['wiːdkɪləʳ] n diserbante m
weedy ['wiːdɪ] adj (man) allampanato
week [wiːk] n settimana; **once/twice a ~** una volta/due volte alla settimana; **in 2 weeks' time** fra 2 settimane, fra 15 giorni; **Tuesday ~, a ~ on Tuesday** martedì a otto
weekday ['wiːkdeɪ] n giorno feriale; (Comm) giornata lavorativa; **on weekdays** durante la settimana
weekend [wiːk'ɛnd] n fine settimana m or f inv, weekend m inv
weekend case n borsa da viaggio
weekly ['wiːklɪ] adv ogni settimana, settimanalmente ▪ adj, n settimanale (m)
weep (pt, pp **wept**) [wiːp, wɛpt] vi (person) piangere; (Med: wound etc) essudare
weeping willow ['wiːpɪŋ-] n salice m piangente
weepy ['wiːpɪ] n (col) film m inv or storia strappalacrime
weft [wɛft] n (Textiles) trama
weigh [weɪ] vt, vi pesare; **to ~ anchor** salpare or levare l'ancora; **to ~ the pros and cons** valutare i pro e i contro
▶ **weigh down** vt (branch) piegare; (fig: with worry) opprimere, caricare
▶ **weigh out** vt (goods) pesare
▶ **weigh up** vt valutare
weighbridge ['weɪbrɪdʒ] n bascula
weighing machine ['weɪɪŋ-] n pesa
weight [weɪt] n peso; **sold by ~** venduto(-a) a peso; **weights and measures** pesi e misure; **to put on/lose ~** ingrassare/dimagrire
weighting ['weɪtɪŋ] n: **~ allowance** indennità f inv speciale (per carovita etc)
weightlessness ['weɪtlɪsnɪs] n mancanza di peso
weightlifter ['weɪtlɪftəʳ] n pesista m
weight training n: **to do ~** allenarsi con i pesi
weighty ['weɪtɪ] adj pesante; (fig) importante, grave
weir [wɪəʳ] n diga
weird [wɪəd] adj strano(-a), bizzarro(-a); (eerie) soprannaturale
weirdo ['wɪədəu] n (col) tipo(-a) allucinante
welcome ['wɛlkəm] adj benvenuto(-a) ▪ n accoglienza, benvenuto ▪ vt accogliere cordialmente; (also: **bid welcome**) dare il benvenuto a; (be glad of) rallegrarsi di; **to be ~** essere il/la benvenuto(-a); **to make sb ~** accogliere bene qn; **you're ~** (after thanks) prego; **you're ~ to try** provi pure
welcoming ['wɛlkəmɪŋ] adj accogliente
weld [wɛld] n saldatura ▪ vt saldare
welder ['wɛldəʳ] n (person) saldatore m

welding ['wɛldɪŋ] n saldatura (autogena)
welfare ['wɛlfɛəʳ] n benessere m
welfare state n stato sociale
welfare work n assistenza sociale
well [wɛl] n pozzo ▪ adv bene ▪ adj: **to be ~** (person) stare bene ▪ excl allora!; ma!; ebbene!; **~ done!** bravo(-a)!; **get ~ soon!** guarisci presto!; **to do ~ in sth** riuscire in qc; **to be doing ~** stare bene; **to think ~ of sb** avere una buona opinione di qn; **I don't feel ~** non mi sento bene; **as ~** (in addition) anche; **X as ~ as Y** sia X che Y; **he did as ~ as he could** ha fatto come meglio poteva; **you might as ~ tell me** potresti anche dirmelo; **it would be as ~ to ask** sarebbe bene chiedere; **~, as I was saying ...** dunque, come stavo dicendo ...
▶ **well up** vi (tears, emotions) sgorgare
we'll [wiːl] = **we will; we shall**
well-behaved ['wɛlbɪ'heɪvd] adj ubbidiente
well-being ['wɛl'biːɪŋ] n benessere m
well-bred ['wɛl'brɛd] adj educato(-a), beneducato(-a)
well-built ['wɛl'bɪlt] adj (person) ben fatto(-a)
well-chosen ['wɛl'tʃəuzn] adj (remarks, words) ben scelto(-a), appropriato(-a)
well-developed ['wɛldɪ'vɛləpt] adj sviluppato(-a)
well-disposed ['wɛldɪs'pəuzd] adj: **~ to(wards)** bendisposto(-a) verso
well-dressed ['wɛl'drɛst] adj ben vestito(-a), vestito(-a) bene
well-earned ['wɛl'əːnd] adj (rest) meritato(-a)
well-groomed ['wɛl'gruːmd] adj curato(-a), azzimato(-a)
well-heeled ['wɛl'hiːld] adj (col: wealthy) agiato(-a), facoltoso(-a)
well-informed ['wɛlɪn'fɔːmd] adj ben informato(-a)
Wellington ['wɛlɪŋtən] n Wellington f
wellingtons ['wɛlɪŋtənz] npl (also: **wellington boots**) stivali mpl di gomma
well-kept ['wɛl'kɛpt] adj (house, grounds, secret) ben tenuto(-a); (hair, hands) ben curato(-a)
well-known ['wɛl'nəun] adj noto(-a), famoso(-a)
well-mannered ['wɛl'mænəd] adj ben educato(-a)
well-meaning ['wɛl'miːnɪŋ] adj ben intenzionato(-a)
well-nigh ['wɛl'naɪ] adv: **~ impossible** quasi impossibile
well-off ['wɛl'ɔf] adj benestante, danaroso(-a)
well-read ['wɛl'rɛd] adj colto(-a)
well-spoken ['wɛl'spəukn] adj che parla bene
well-stocked ['wɛl'stɔkt] adj (shop, larder) ben fornito(-a)

well-timed ['wɛl'taɪmd] *adj* opportuno(-a)

well-to-do ['wɛltə'du:] *adj* abbiente, benestante

well-wisher ['wɛlwɪʃəᵣ] *n* ammiratore(-trice); **letters from well-wishers** lettere *fpl* di incoraggiamento

well-woman clinic ['wɛlwumən-] *n* ≈ consultorio (familiare)

Welsh [wɛlʃ] *adj* gallese ■ *n* (*Ling*) gallese *m*; **the ~** *npl* i gallesi; **the ~ National Assembly** il Parlamento gallese

Welshman ['wɛlʃmən], **Welshwoman** ['wɛlʃwumən] *n* gallese *m/f*

Welsh rarebit *n* crostino al formaggio

welter ['wɛltəᵣ] *n* massa, mucchio

went [wɛnt] *pt of* **go**

wept [wɛpt] *pt, pp of* **weep**

were [wəːᵣ] *pt of* **be**

we're [wɪəᵣ] = **we are**

weren't [wəːnt] = **were not**

werewolf (*pl* **-wolves**) ['wɪəwulf, -wulvz] *n* licantropo, lupo mannaro (*col*)

west [wɛst] *n* ovest *m*, occidente *m*, ponente *m* ■ *adj* (a) ovest *inv*, occidentale ■ *adv* verso ovest; **the W~** l'Occidente

westbound ['wɛstbaund] *adj* (*traffic*) diretto(-a) a ovest; (*carriageway*) ovest *inv*

West Country *n*: **the ~** il sud-ovest dell'Inghilterra

westerly ['wɛstəlɪ] *adj* (*wind*) occidentale, da ovest

western ['wɛstən] *adj* occidentale, dell'ovest ■ *n* (*Cine*) western *m inv*

westerner ['wɛstənəᵣ] *n* occidentale *m/f*

westernized ['wɛstənaɪzd] *adj* occidentalizzato(-a)

West German *adj, n* (*formerly*) tedesco(-a) occidentale

West Germany *n* (*formerly*) Germania Occidentale

West Indian *adj* delle Indie Occidentali ■ *n* abitante *m/f* (*or* originario(-a)) delle Indie Occidentali

West Indies [-'ɪndɪz] *npl*: **the ~** le Indie Occidentali

Westminster ['wɛstmɪnstəᵣ] *n* il parlamento (britannico)

westward ['wɛstwəd], **westwards** ['wɛstwədz] *adv* verso ovest

wet [wɛt] *adj* umido(-a), bagnato(-a); (*soaked*) fradicio(-a); (*rainy*) piovoso(-a) ■ *vt*: **to ~ one's pants** *or* **o.s.** farsi la pipì addosso; **to get ~** bagnarsi; **"~ paint"** "vernice fresca"

wet blanket *n* (*fig*) guastafeste *m/f inv*

wetness ['wɛtnɪs] *n* umidità

wet suit *n* tuta da sub

we've [wiːv] = **we have**

whack [wæk] *vt* picchiare, battere

whacked [wækt] *adj* (*col: tired*) sfinito(-a), a pezzi

whale [weɪl] *n* (*Zool*) balena

whaler ['weɪləᵣ] *n* (*ship*) baleniera

whaling ['weɪlɪŋ] *n* caccia alla balena

wharf (*pl* **wharves**) [wɔːf, wɔːvz] *n* banchina

 KEYWORD

what [wɔt] *adj* **1** (*in direct/indirect questions*) che; quale; **what size is it?** che taglia è?; **what colour is it?** di che colore è?; **what books do you want?** quali *or* che libri vuole?; **for what reason?** per quale motivo?

2 (*in exclamations*) che; **what a mess!** che disordine!

■ *pron* **1** (*interrogative*) che cosa, cosa, che; **what's in there?** cosa c'è lì dentro?; **what is his address?** qual è il suo indirizzo?; **what will it cost?** quanto costerà?; **what are you doing?** che *or* (che) cosa fai?; **what are you talking about?** di che cosa parli?; **what's happening?** che *or* (che) cosa succede?; **what is it called?** come si chiama?; **what about me?** e io?; **what about doing ...?** e se facessimo ...?

2 (*relative*) ciò che, quello che; **I saw what you did** ho visto quello che hai fatto; **I saw what was on the table** ho visto cosa c'era sul tavolo; **what I want is a cup of tea** ciò che voglio adesso è una tazza di tè

3 (*indirect use*) (che) cosa; **he asked me what she had said** mi ha chiesto che cosa avesse detto; **tell me what you're thinking about** dimmi a cosa stai pensando; **I don't know what to do** non so cosa fare

■ *excl* (*disbelieving*) cosa!, come!

whatever [wɔt'ɛvəᵣ] *adj*: **~ book** qualunque *or* qualsiasi libro+*sub* ■ *pron*: **do ~ is necessary/you want** faccia qualunque *or* qualsiasi cosa sia necessaria/lei voglia; **~ happens** qualunque cosa accada; **no reason ~** *or* **whatsoever** nessuna ragione affatto *or* al mondo; **~ it costs** costi quello che costi

whatsoever [wɔtsəu'ɛvəᵣ] *adj, pron* = **whatever**

wheat [wiːt] *n* grano, frumento

wheatgerm ['wiːtdʒəːm] *n* germe *m* di grano

wheatmeal ['wiːtmiːl] *n* farina integrale di frumento

wheedle ['wiːdl] *vt*: **to ~ sb into doing sth** convincere qn a fare qc (con lusinghe); **to ~ sth out of sb** ottenere qc da qn (con lusinghe)

W

wheel [wi:l] *n* ruota; (*Aut: also:* **steering wheel**) volante *m*; (*Naut*) (ruota del) timone *m* ■ *vt* spingere ■ *vi* (*also:* **wheel round**) girare

wheelbarrow ['wi:lbærəu] *n* carriola

wheelbase ['wi:lbeɪs] *n* interasse *m*

wheelchair ['wi:ltʃɛəʳ] *n* sedia a rotelle

wheel clamp *n* (*Aut*) morsetto *m* bloccaruota *inv*

wheeler-dealer ['wi:lə'di:ləʳ] *n* trafficone *m*, maneggione *m*

wheelie-bin ['wi:lɪbɪn] *n* (*Brit*) bidone *m* (della spazzatura) a rotelle

wheeling ['wi:lɪŋ] *n*: ~ **and dealing** maneggi *mpl*

wheeze [wi:z] *n* respiro affannoso ■ *vi* ansimare

wheezy ['wi:zɪ] *adj* (*person*) che respira con affanno; (*breath*) sibilante

 KEYWORD

when [wɛn] *adv* quando; **when did it happen?** quando è successo?

■ *conj* **1** (*at, during, after the time that*) quando; **she was reading when I came in** quando sono entrato lei leggeva; **that was when I needed you** era allora che avevo bisogno di te

2 (*on, at which*): **on the day when I met him** il giorno in cui l'ho incontrato; **one day when it was raining** un giorno che pioveva **3** (*whereas*) quando, mentre; **you said I was wrong when in fact I was right** mi hai detto che avevo torto, quando in realtà avevo ragione

whenever [wɛn'ɛvəʳ] *adv* quando mai ■ *conj* quando; (*every time that*) ogni volta che; **I go ~ I can** ci vado ogni volta che posso

where [wɛəʳ] *adv, conj* dove; **this is ~** è qui che; **~ are you from?** di dov'è?; **~ possible** quando è possibile, se possibile

whereabouts ['wɛərəbauts] *adv* dove ■ *n*: **sb's ~** luogo dove qn si trova

whereas [wɛər'æz] *conj* mentre

whereby [wɛə'baɪ] *adv* (*formal*) per cui

whereupon [wɛərə'pɔn] *adv* al che

wherever [wɛər'ɛvəʳ] *adv* dove mai ■ *conj* dovunque + *sub*; **sit ~ you like** si sieda dove vuole

wherewithal ['wɛəwɪðɔːl] *n*: **the ~ (to do sth)** i mezzi (per fare qc)

whet [wɛt] *vt* (*tool*) affilare; (*appetite etc*) stimolare

whether ['wɛðəʳ] *conj* se; **I don't know ~ to accept or not** non so se accettare o no;

it's doubtful ~ è poco probabile che; **~ you go or not** che lei vada o no

whey [weɪ] *n* siero

 KEYWORD

which [wɪtʃ] *adj* **1** (*interrogative: direct, indirect*) quale; **which picture do you want?** quale quadro vuole?, **which one?** quale?; **which one of you did it?** chi di voi lo ha fatto?; **tell me which one you want** mi dica quale vuole

2: **in which case** nel qual caso; **by which time** e a quel punto

■ *pron* **1** (*interrogative*) quale; **which (of these) are yours?** quali di questi sono suoi?; **which of you are coming?** chi di voi viene?

2 (*relative*) che; (: *indirect*) cui, il/la quale; **the apple which you ate/which is on the table** la mela che hai mangiato/che è sul tavolo; **the chair on which you are sitting** la sedia sulla quale *or* su cui sei seduto; **the book of which we were speaking** il libro del quale stavamo parlando; **he said he knew, which is true** ha detto che lo sapeva, il che è vero; **I don't mind which** non mi importa quale; **after which** dopo di che

whichever [wɪtʃ'ɛvəʳ] *adj*: **take ~ book you prefer** prenda qualsiasi libro che preferisce; **~ book you take** qualsiasi libro prenda; **~ way you ...** in qualunque modo lei ... + *sub*

whiff [wɪf] *n* odore *m*; **to catch a ~ of sth** sentire l'odore di qc

while [waɪl] *n* momento ■ *conj* mentre; (*as long as*) finché; (*although*) sebbene + *sub*; **for a ~** per un po'; **in a ~** tra poco; **all the ~** tutto il tempo; **we'll make it worth your ~** faremo in modo che le valga la pena

▶ **while away** *vt* (*time*) far passare

whilst [waɪlst] *conj* = **while**

whim [wɪm] *n* capriccio

whimper ['wɪmpəʳ] *n* piagnucolio ■ *vi* piagnucolare

whimsical ['wɪmzɪkl] *adj* (*person*) capriccioso(-a); (*look*) strano(-a)

whine [waɪn] *n* gemito ■ *vi* gemere; uggiolare; piagnucolare

whip [wɪp] *n* frusta; (*for riding*) frustino; (*Pol: person*) capogruppo; *vedi nota* ■ *vt* frustare; (*Culin: cream etc*) sbattere; (*snatch*) sollevare (*or* estrarre) bruscamente

▶ **whip up** *vt* (*cream*) montare, sbattere; (*col: meal*) improvvisare; (: *stir up: support, feeling*) suscitare, stimolare

● **WHIP**

● Nel Parlamento britannico i *whips* sono
parlamentari incaricati di mantenere la
disciplina tra i deputati del loro partito
durante le votazioni e di verificare la loro
presenza in aula.

whiplash ['wɪplæʃ] *n* (*Med*: *also*: **whiplash
injury**) colpo di frusta
whipped cream ['wɪpt-] *n* panna montata
whipping boy ['wɪpɪŋ-] *n* (*fig*) capro espiatorio
whip-round ['wɪpraund] *n* (*Brit*) colletta
whirl [wəːl] *n* turbine *m* ■ *vt* (far) girare
rapidamente; (far) turbinare ■ *vi* turbinare;
(*dancers*) volteggiare; (*leaves, dust*) sollevarsi in
un vortice
whirlpool ['wəːlpuːl] *n* mulinello
whirlwind ['wəːlwɪnd] *n* turbine *m*
whirr [wəːr] *vi* ronzare
whisk [wɪsk] *n* (*Culin*) frusta; frullino ■ *vt*
sbattere, frullare; **to ~ sb away** *or* **off** portar
via qn a tutta velocità
whiskers ['wɪskəz] *npl* (*of animal*) baffi *mpl*;
(*of man*) favoriti *mpl*
whisky, (*Irish, US*) **whiskey** ['wɪskɪ] *n* whisky
m inv
whisper ['wɪspər] *n* bisbiglio, sussurro;
(*rumour*) voce *f* ■ *vt*, *vi* bisbigliare, sussurrare;
to ~ sth to sb bisbigliare qc a qn
whispering ['wɪspərɪŋ] *n* bisbiglio
whist [wɪst] *n* (*Brit*) whist *m*
whistle ['wɪsl] *n* (*sound*) fischio; (*object*)
fischietto ■ *vi*, *vt* fischiare; **to ~ a tune**
fischiettare un motivetto
whistle-stop ['wɪslstɔp] *adj*: **~ tour** (*Pol, fig*)
rapido giro
Whit [wɪt] *n* Pentecoste *f*
white [waɪt] *adj* bianco(-a); (*with fear*)
pallido(-a) ■ *n* bianco; (*person*) bianco(-a);
to turn *or* **go ~** (*person*) sbiancare; (*hair*)
diventare bianco; **the whites** (*washing*)
i capi bianchi; **tennis whites** completo da
tennis
whitebait ['waɪtbeɪt] *n* bianchetti *mpl*
whiteboard ['waɪtbɔːd] *n* lavagna bianca;
interactive ~ lavagna interattiva
white-collar worker ['waɪtkɔlə-] *n*
impiegato(-a)
white elephant *n* (*fig*) oggetto (*or* progetto)
costoso ma inutile
white goods *npl* (*appliances*) elettrodomestici
mpl; (*linens*) biancheria per la casa
white-hot [waɪt'hɔt] *adj* (*metal*)
incandescente
White House *n*: **the ~** la Casa Bianca; *vedi
nota*

● **WHITE HOUSE**

● La *White House* è la residenza ufficiale del
presidente degli Stati Uniti e ha sede a
Washington DC. Spesso il termine viene
usato per indicare l'esecutivo del governo
statunitense.

white lie *n* bugia pietosa
whiteness ['waɪtnɪs] *n* bianchezza
white noise *n* rumore *m* bianco
white paper *n* (*Pol*) libro bianco
whitewash ['waɪtwɔʃ] *n* (*paint*) bianco di
calce ■ *vt* imbiancare; (*fig*) coprire
whiting ['waɪtɪŋ] *n* (*pl inv*) merlango
Whit Monday *n* lunedì *m inv* di Pentecoste
Whitsun ['wɪtsn] *n* Pentecoste *f*
whittle ['wɪtl] *vt*: **to ~ away**, **~ down** ridurre,
tagliare
whizz [wɪz] *vi* passare sfrecciando
whizz kid *n* (*col*) prodigio
WHO *n abbr* (= *World Health Organization*) O.M.S.
f (= *Organizzazione mondiale della sanità*)

〇 KEYWORD

who [huː] *pron* **1** (*interrogative*) chi; **who is it?**,
who's there? chi è?
2 (*relative*) che; **the man who spoke to me**
l'uomo che ha parlato con me; **those who
can swim** quelli che sanno nuotare

whodunit [huːˈdʌnɪt] *n* (*col*) giallo
whoever [huːˈɛvər] *pron*: **~ finds it** chiunque
lo trovi; **ask ~ you like** lo chieda a chiunque
vuole; **~ told you that?** chi mai gliel'ha
detto?
whole [həul] *adj* (*complete*) tutto(-a),
completo(-a); (*not broken*) intero(-a),
intatto(-a) ■ *n* (*total*) totale *m*; (*sth not broken*)
tutto; **the ~ lot (of it)** tutto; **the ~ lot (of
them)** tutti; **the ~ of the time** tutto il
tempo; **the ~ of the town** la città intera;
on the ~, **as a ~** nel complesso, nell'insieme;
~ villages were destroyed interi paesi
furono distrutti
wholehearted [həulˈhɑːtɪd] *adj* sincero(-a)
wholemeal ['həulmiːl] *adj* (*Brit*: *flour, bread*)
integrale
whole note *n* (*US*) semibreve *f*
wholesale ['həulseɪl] *n* commercio *or* vendita
all'ingrosso ■ *adj* all'ingrosso; (*destruction*)
totale
wholesaler ['həulseɪlər] *n* grossista *m/f*
wholesome ['həulsəm] *adj* sano(-a); (*climate*)
salubre
wholewheat ['həulwiːt] *adj* = **wholemeal**

W

wholly ['həulı] adv completamente, del tutto

 KEYWORD

whom [hu:m] pron 1 (interrogative) chi; **whom did you see?** chi hai visto?; **to whom did you give it?** a chi lo hai dato?
2 (relative) che, prep + il/la quale; **the man whom I saw** l'uomo che ho visto; **the man to whom I spoke** l'uomo al or con il quale ho parlato; **those to whom I spoke** le persone alle or con le quali ho parlato

whooping cough ['hu:pɪŋ-] n pertosse f
whoops [wu:ps] excl: **~-a-daisy!** ops!
whoosh [wuʃ] n: **it came out with a ~** (sauce etc) è uscito di getto; (air) è uscito con un sibilo
whopper ['wɔpər] n (col: lie) balla; (: large thing) cosa enorme
whopping ['wɔpɪŋ] adj (col: big) enorme
whore [hɔ:r] n (pej) puttana

 KEYWORD

whose [hu:z] adj 1 (possessive: interrogative) di chi; **whose book is this?, whose is this book?** di chi è questo libro?; **whose daughter are you?** di chi sei figlia?; **whose pencil have you taken?** di chi è la matita che hai preso?
2 (possessive: relative): **the man whose son you rescued** l'uomo il cui figlio hai salvato or a cui hai salvato il figlio; **the girl whose sister you were speaking to** la ragazza alla cui sorella stavi parlando
■ pron di chi; **whose is this?** di chi è questo?; **I know whose it is** so di chi è

Who's Who ['hu:z'hu:] n elenco di personalità
why [waɪ] adv, conj perché ■ excl (surprise) ma guarda un po'!; (remonstrating) ma (via)!; (explaining) ebbene!; **~ not?** perché no?; **~ not do it now?** perché non farlo adesso?; **the reason ~** il motivo per cui
whyever [waɪ'ɛvər] adv perché mai
WI n abbr (Brit: = Women's Institute) circolo femminile ■ abbr (Geo) = **West Indies**; (US) = **Wisconsin**
wick [wɪk] n lucignolo, stoppino
wicked ['wɪkɪd] adj cattivo(-a), malvagio(-a); (mischievous) malizioso(-a)
wicker ['wɪkər] n vimine m; (also: **wickerwork**) articoli mpl di vimini
wicket ['wɪkɪt] n (Cricket) porta; area tra le due porte
wicket keeper n (Cricket) ≈ portiere m

wide [waɪd] adj largo(-a); (region, knowledge) vasto(-a); (choice) ampio(-a) ■ adv: **to open ~** spalancare; **to shoot ~** tirare a vuoto or fuori bersaglio; **it is 3 metres ~** è largo 3 metri
wide-angle lens ['waɪdæŋgl-] n grandangolare m
wide-awake [waɪdə'weɪk] adj completamente sveglio(-a)
wide-eyed [waɪd'aɪd] adj con gli occhi spalancati
widely ['waɪdlɪ] adv (different) molto, completamente; (believed) generalmente; **~ spaced** molto distanziati(-e); **to be ~ read** (author) essere molto letto; (reader) essere molto colto
widen ['waɪdn] vt allargare, ampliare
wideness ['waɪdnɪs] n larghezza; vastità; ampiezza
wide open adj spalancato(-a)
wide-ranging [waɪd'reɪndʒɪŋ] adj (survey, report) vasto(-a); (interests) svariato(-a)
widescreen ['waɪdskri:n] adj (television) a schermo panoramico
widespread ['waɪdsprɛd] adj (belief etc) molto or assai diffuso(-a)
widget ['wɪdʒɪt] n (Comput) widget m inv
widow ['wɪdəu] n vedova
widowed ['wɪdəud] adj (che è rimasto(-a)) vedovo(-a)
widower ['wɪdəuər] n vedovo
width [wɪdθ] n larghezza; **it's 7 metres in ~** è largo 7 metri
widthways ['wɪdθweɪz] adv trasversalmente
wield [wi:ld] vt (sword) maneggiare; (power) esercitare
wife (pl **wives**) [waɪf, waɪvz] n moglie f
Wi-Fi ['waɪfaɪ] n WiFi m
wig [wɪg] n parrucca
wigging ['wɪgɪŋ] n (Brit col) lavata di capo
wiggle ['wɪgl] vt dimenare, agitare ■ vi (loose screw etc) traballare; (worm) torcersi
wiggly ['wɪglɪ] adj (line) ondulato(-a), sinuoso(-a)
wild [waɪld] adj (animal, plant) selvatico(-a); (countryside, appearance) selvaggio(-a); (sea) tempestoso(-a); (idea, life) folle; (col: angry) arrabbiato(-a), furibondo(-a); (enthusiastic): **to be ~ about** andar pazzo(-a) per ■ n: **the ~** la natura; **wilds** npl regione f selvaggia
wild card n (Comput) carattere m jolly inv
wildcat ['waɪldkæt] n gatto(-a) selvatico(-a)
wildcat strike n ≈ sciopero selvaggio
wilderness ['wɪldənɪs] n deserto
wildfire ['waɪldfaɪər] n: **to spread like ~** propagarsi rapidamente
wild-goose chase [waɪld'gu:s-] n (fig) pista falsa

wildlife ['waɪldlaɪf] *n* natura
wildly ['waɪldlɪ] *adv* (*applaud*) freneticamente; (*hit, guess*) a casaccio; (*happy*) follemente
wiles [waɪlz] *npl* astuzie *fpl*
wilful, (US) **willful** ['wɪlful] *adj* (*person*) testardo(-a); ostinato(-a); (*action*) intenzionale; (*crime*) premeditato(-a)

 KEYWORD

will [wɪl] *aux vb* **1** (*forming future tense*): **I will finish it tomorrow** lo finirò domani; **I will have finished it by tomorrow** lo finirò entro domani; **will you do it?** — **yes I will/ no I won't** lo farai? — sì (lo farò)/no (non lo farò); **the car won't start** la macchina non parte
2 (*in conjectures, predictions*): **he will** or **he'll be there by now** dovrebbe essere arrivato a quest'ora; **that will be the postman** sarà il postino
3 (*in commands, requests, offers*): **will you be quiet!** vuoi stare zitto?; **will you sit down?** (*politely*) prego, si accomodi; (*angrily*) vuoi metterti seduto?; **will you come?** vieni anche tu?; **will you help me?** mi aiuti?, mi puoi aiutare?; **you won't lose it, will you?** non lo perderai, vero?; **will you have a cup of tea?** vorrebbe una tazza di tè?; **I won't put up with it!** non lo accetterò!
■ *vt* (*pt, pp* **willed**); **to will sb to do** pregare tra sé perché qn faccia; **he willed himself to go on** continuò grazie a un grande sforzo di volontà
■ *n* **1** (*desire*) volontà; **against sb's will** contro la volontà or il volere di qn; **to do sth of one's own free will** fare qc di propria volontà
2 (*Law*) testamento; **to make a/one's will** fare testamento

willful ['wɪlful] *adj* (US) = **wilful**
willing ['wɪlɪŋ] *adj* volonteroso(-a) ■ *n*: **to show ~** dare prova di buona volontà; **~ to do** disposto(-a) a fare
willingly ['wɪlɪŋlɪ] *adv* volentieri
willingness ['wɪlɪŋnɪs] *n* buona volontà
will-o'-the-wisp [wɪləðə'wɪsp] *n* (*also fig*) fuoco fatuo
willow ['wɪləu] *n* salice *m*
will power *n* forza di volontà
willy-nilly ['wɪlɪ'nɪlɪ] *adv* volente o nolente
wilt [wɪlt] *vi* appassire
Wilts [wɪlts] *abbr* (Brit) = **Wiltshire**
wily ['waɪlɪ] *adj* furbo(-a)
wimp [wɪmp] *n* (*col*) mezza calzetta
win [wɪn] *n* (*in sports etc*) vittoria ■ *vb* (*pt, pp*

won) [wʌn] *vt* (*battle, prize*) vincere; (*money*) guadagnare; (*popularity*) conquistare; (*contract*) aggiudicarsi ■ *vi* vincere
▶ **win over** (Brit), **win round** *vt* convincere
wince [wɪns] *n* trasalimento, sussulto ■ *vi* trasalire
winch [wɪntʃ] *n* verricello, argano
Winchester disk ['wɪntʃɪstə-] *n* (*Comput*) disco Winchester
wind¹ [wɪnd] *n* vento; (*Med*) flatulenza, ventosità ■ *vt* (*take breath away*) far restare senza fiato; **the ~(s)** (*Mus*) i fiati; **into** or **against the ~** controvento; **to get ~ of sth** venire a sapere qc; **to break ~** scoreggiare (*col*)
wind² (*pt, pp* **wound**) [waɪnd, waund] *vt* attorcigliare; (*wrap*) avvolgere; (*clock, toy*) caricare ■ *vi* (*road, river*) serpeggiare
▶ **wind down** *vt* (*car window*) abbassare; (*fig: production, business*) diminuire
▶ **wind up** *vt* (*clock*) caricare; (*debate*) concludere
windbreak ['wɪndbreɪk] *n* frangivento
windcheater ['wɪndtʃiːtər], (US) **windbreaker** ['wɪndbreɪkər] *n* giacca a vento
winder ['waɪndər] *n* (Brit: on watch) corona di carica
windfall ['wɪndfɔːl] *n* colpo di fortuna
wind farm *n* centrale *f* eolica
winding ['waɪndɪŋ] *adj* (*road*) serpeggiante; (*staircase*) a chiocciola
wind instrument *n* (*Mus*) strumento a fiato
windmill ['wɪndmɪl] *n* mulino a vento
window ['wɪndəu] *n* (*gen, Comput*) finestra; (*in car, train*) finestrino; (*in shop etc*) vetrina; (*also:* **window pane**) vetro
window box *n* cassetta da fiori
window cleaner *n* (*person*) pulitore *m* di finestre
window dressing *n* allestimento della vetrina
window envelope *n* busta a finestra
window frame *n* telaio di finestra
window ledge *n* davanzale *m*
window pane *n* vetro
window-shopping ['wɪndəuʃɒpɪŋ] *n*: **to go ~** andare a vedere le vetrine
windowsill ['wɪndəusɪl] *n* davanzale *m*
windpipe ['wɪndpaɪp] *n* trachea
wind power *n* energia eolica
windscreen ['wɪndskriːn], (US) **windshield** ['wɪndʃiːld] *n* parabrezza *m inv*
windscreen washer *n* lavacristallo
windscreen wiper *n* tergicristallo
windshield ['wɪndʃiːld] *n* (US) = **windscreen**
windsurfing ['wɪndsəːfɪŋ] *n* windsurf *m inv*
windswept ['wɪndswɛpt] *adj* spazzato(-a) dal vento

W

wind tunnel n galleria aerodinamica or del vento

windy ['wındı] adj ventoso(-a); **it's ~** c'è vento

wine [waın] n vino ■ vt: **to ~ and dine sb** offrire un ottimo pranzo a qn

wine bar n enoteca

wine cellar n cantina

wine glass n bicchiere m da vino

wine list n lista dei vini

wine merchant n commerciante m di vino

wine tasting n degustazione f dei vini

wine waiter n sommelier m inv

wing [wıŋ] n ala; **wings** npl (Theat) quinte fpl

winger ['wıŋər] n (Sport) ala

wing mirror n (Brit) specchietto retrovisore esterno

wing nut n galletto

wingspan ['wıŋspæn], **wingspread** ['wıŋspred] n apertura alare, apertura d'ali

wink [wıŋk] n occhiolino, strizzatina d'occhi ■ vi ammiccare, fare l'occhiolino

winkle ['wıŋkl] n litorina

winner ['wınər] n vincitore(-trice)

winning ['wınıŋ] adj (team) vincente; (goal) decisivo(-a); (charming) affascinante; see also **winnings**

winning post n traguardo

winnings ['wınıŋz] npl vincite fpl

winsome ['wınsəm] adj accattivante

winter ['wıntər] n inverno; **in ~** d'inverno, in inverno

winter sports npl sport mpl invernali

wintry ['wıntrı] adj invernale

wipe [waıp] n pulita, passata ■ vt pulire (strofinando); (dishes) asciugare; **to give sth a ~** dare una pulita or una passata a qc; **to ~ one's nose** soffiarsi il naso

▸ **wipe off** vt cancellare; (stains) togliere strofinando

▸ **wipe out** vt (debt) pagare, liquidare; (memory) cancellare; (destroy) annientare

▸ **wipe up** vt asciugare

wire ['waıər] n filo; (Elec) filo elettrico; (Tel) telegramma m ■ vt (Elec: house) fare l'impianto elettrico di; (: circuit) installare; (also: **wire up**) collegare, allacciare

wire brush n spazzola metallica

wire cutters [-kʌtəz] npl tronchese m or f

wireless ['waıəlıs] n (Brit) telegrafia senza fili; (set) (apparecchio m) radio f inv ■ adj (technology) wireless inv, senza fili

wire netting n rete f metallica

wire service n (US) = **news agency**

wire-tapping ['waıətæpıŋ] n intercettazione f telefonica

wiring ['waıərıŋ] n (Elec) impianto elettrico

wiry ['waıərı] adj magro(-a) e nerboruto(-a)

Wis., Wisc. abbr (US) = **Wisconsin**

wisdom ['wızdəm] n saggezza; (of action) prudenza

wisdom tooth n dente m del giudizio

wise [waız] adj saggio(-a); (advice, remark) prudente; **I'm none the wiser** ne so come prima

▸ **wise up** vi (col): **to ~ up to** divenire più consapevole di

...wise [waız] suffix: **timewise** per quanto riguarda il tempo, in termini di tempo

wisecrack ['waızkræk] n battuta spiritosa

wish [wıʃ] n (desire) desiderio; (specific desire) richiesta ■ vt desiderare, volere; **best wishes** (on birthday etc) i migliori auguri; **with best wishes** (in letter) cordiali saluti, con i migliori saluti; **give her my best wishes** le faccia i migliori auguri da parte mia; **to ~ sb goodbye** dire arrivederci a qn; **he wished me well** mi augurò di riuscire; **to ~ to do/sb to do** desiderare or volere fare/che qn faccia; **to ~ for** desiderare; **to ~ sth on sb** rifilare qc a qn

wishbone ['wıʃbəun] n forcella

wishful ['wıʃful] adj: **it's ~ thinking** è prendere i desideri per realtà

wishy-washy ['wıʃı'wɔʃı] adj insulso(-a)

wisp [wısp] n ciuffo, ciocca; (of smoke, straw) filo

wistful ['wıstful] adj malinconico(-a); (nostalgic) nostalgico(-a)

wit [wıt] n (gen pl) intelligenza; presenza di spirito; (wittiness) spirito, arguzia; (person) bello spirito; **to be at one's wits' end** (fig) non sapere più cosa fare; **to have** or **keep one's wits about one** avere presenza di spirito; **to ~** adv cioè

witch [wıtʃ] n strega

witchcraft ['wıtʃkrɑ:ft] n stregoneria

witch doctor n stregone m

witch-hunt ['wıtʃhʌnt] n (fig) caccia alle streghe

 KEYWORD

with [wıð, wıθ] prep **1** (in the company of) con; I was with him ero con lui; we stayed with friends siamo stati da amici; I'll be with you in a minute vengo subito

2 (descriptive) con; a room with a view una camera con vista (sul mare or sulle montagne etc); the man with the grey hat/blue eyes l'uomo con il cappello grigio/gli occhi blu

3 (indicating manner, means, cause): with tears in her eyes con le lacrime agli occhi; red

with anger rosso(-a) dalla rabbia; **to shake with fear** tremare di paura; **covered with snow** coperto(-a) di neve

4: **I'm with you** (I understand) la seguo; **I'm not really with it today** (col) oggi sono un po' fuori

withdraw [wɪθ'drɔ:] vb irreg vt ritirare; (money from bank) ritirare, prelevare ■ vi ritirarsi; **to ~ into o.s.** chiudersi in se stesso

withdrawal [wɪθ'drɔ:əl] n ritiro; prelievo; (of army) ritirata; (Med) stato di privazione

withdrawal symptoms npl crisi f di astinenza

withdrawn [wɪθ'drɔ:n] pp of **withdraw** ■ adj distaccato(-a)

wither ['wɪðə'] vi appassire

withered ['wɪðəd] adj appassito(-a); (limb) atrofizzato(-a)

withhold [wɪθ'həuld] vt irreg (money) trattenere; (permission): **to ~ (from)** rifiutare (a); (information): **to ~ (from)** nascondere (a)

within [wɪð'ɪn] prep all'interno di; (in time, distances) entro ■ adv all'interno, dentro; **~ sight of** in vista di; **~ a mile of** entro un miglio da; **~ the week** prima della fine della settimana; **~ an hour from now** da qui a un'ora; **to be ~ the law** restare nei limiti della legge

without [wɪð'aut] prep senza; **to go** or **do ~ sth** fare a meno di qc; **~ anybody knowing** senza che nessuno lo sappia

withstand [wɪθ'stænd] vt irreg resistere a

witness ['wɪtnɪs] n (person) testimone m/f ■ vt (event) essere testimone di, (document) attestare l'autenticità di ■ vi: **to ~ to sth/ having seen sth** testimoniare qc/di aver visto qc; **to bear ~ to sth** testimoniare qc; **~ for the prosecution/defence** testimone a carico/discarico

witness box, (US) **witness stand** n banco dei testimoni

witticism ['wɪtɪsɪzəm] n spiritosaggine f

witty ['wɪtɪ] adj spiritoso(-a)

wives [waɪvz] npl of **wife**

wizard ['wɪzəd] n mago

wizened ['wɪznd] adj raggrinzito(-a)

wk abbr = **week**

Wm. abbr = **William**

WMD n abbr see **weapons of mass destruction**

WO n abbr see **warrant officer**

wobble ['wɔbl] vi tremare; (chair) traballare

wobbly ['wɔblɪ] adj (hand, voice) tremante; (table, chair) traballante; (object about to fall) che oscilla pericolosamente

woe [wəu] n dolore m; disgrazia

woeful ['wəuful] adj (sad) triste; (deplorable) deplorevole

wok [wɔk] n wok m inv (padella concava usata nella cucina cinese)

woke [wəuk] pt of **wake**

woken ['wəukn] pp of **wake**

wolf (pl **wolves**) [wulf, wulvz] n lupo

woman (pl **women**) ['wumən, 'wɪmɪn] n donna ■ cpd: **~ doctor** n dottoressa; **~ friend** n amica; **~ teacher** n insegnante f; **women's page** n (Press) rubrica femminile

womanize ['wumənaɪz] vi essere un donnaiolo

womanly ['wumənlɪ] adj femminile

womb [wu:m] n (Anat) utero

women ['wɪmɪn] npl of **woman**

Women's Movement, Women's Liberation Movement n (also: **Women's Lib**) Movimento per la Liberazione della Donna

won [wʌn] pt, pp of **win**

wonder ['wʌndə'] n meraviglia ■ vi: **to ~ whether** domandarsi se; **to ~ at** essere sorpreso(-a) di; meravigliarsi di; **to ~ about** domandarsi di; pensare a; **it's no ~ that** c'è poco or non c'è da meravigliarsi che + sub

wonderful ['wʌndəful] adj meraviglioso(-a)

wonderfully ['wʌndəfəlɪ] adv (+ adjective) meravigliosamente; (+ verb) a meraviglia

wonky ['wɔŋkɪ] adj (Brit col) traballante

wont [wəunt] n: **as is his/her ~** com'è solito/ a fare

won't [wəunt] = **will not**

woo [wu:] vt (woman) fare la corte a

wood [wud] n legno; (timber) legname m; (forest) bosco ■ cpd di bosco, silvestre

wood carving n scultura in legno, intaglio

wooded ['wudɪd] adj boschivo(-a); boscoso(-a)

wooden ['wudn] adj di legno; (fig) rigido(-a); inespressivo(-a)

woodland ['wudlənd] n zona boscosa

woodpecker ['wudpɛkə'] n picchio

wood pigeon n colombaccio, palomba

woodwind ['wudwɪnd] npl (Mus): **the ~** i legni

woodwork ['wudwə:k] n parti fpl in legno; (craft, subject) falegnameria

woodworm ['wudwə:m] n tarlo del legno

woof [wuf] n (of dog) bau bau m ■ vi abbaiare; **~, ~!** bau bau!

wool [wul] n lana; **to pull the ~ over sb's eyes** (fig) fargliela a qn

woollen, (US) **woolen** ['wulən] adj di lana ■ n: **woollens** indumenti mpl di lana

woolly, (US) **wooly** ['wulɪ] adj lanoso(-a); (fig: ideas) confuso(-a)

woozy ['wu:zɪ] adj (col) stordito(-a)

W

word [wə:d] *n* parola; (*news*) notizie *fpl* ■ *vt* esprimere, formulare; **~ for ~** parola per parola, testualmente; **what's the ~ for "pen" in Italian?** come si dice "pen" in italiano?; **to put sth into words** esprimere qc a parole; **in other words** in altre parole; **to have a ~ with sb** scambiare due parole con qn; **to have words with sb** (*quarrel with*) avere un diverbio con qn; **to break/keep one's ~** non mantenere/mantenere la propria parola; **I'll take your ~ for it** la crederò sulla parola; **to send ~ of** avvisare di; **to leave ~ (with** *or* **for sb) that ...** lasciare detto (a qn) che ...

wording ['wə:dɪŋ] *n* formulazione *f*

word of mouth *n* passaparola *m*; **I learned it by** *or* **through ~** lo so per sentito dire

word-perfect ['wə:d'pəfɪkt] *adj* (*speech etc*) imparato(-a) a memoria

word processing *n* word processing *m*, elaborazione *f* testi

word processor *n* word processor *m inv*

wordwrap ['wə:dræp] *n* (*Comput*) ritorno carrello automatico

wordy ['wə:dɪ] *adj* verboso(-a), prolisso(-a)

wore [wɔ:ʳ] *pt of* **wear**

work [wə:k] *n* lavoro; (*Art, Literature*) opera ■ *vi* lavorare; (*mechanism, plan etc*) funzionare; (*medicine*) essere efficace ■ *vt* (*clay, wood etc*) lavorare; (*mine etc*) sfruttare; (*machine*) far funzionare; **to be at ~ (on sth)** lavorare (a qc); **to set to ~, to start ~** mettersi all'opera; **to go to ~** andare al lavoro; **to be out of ~** essere disoccupato(-a); **to ~ one's way through a book** riuscire a leggersi tutto un libro; **to ~ one's way through college** lavorare per pagarsi gli studi; **to ~ hard** lavorare sodo; **to ~ loose** allentarsi; *see also* **works**

▶ **work on** *vt fus* lavorare a; (*principle*) basarsi su; **he's working on the car** sta facendo dei lavori alla macchina

▶ **work out** *vi* (*plans etc*) riuscire, andare bene; (*Sport*) allenarsi ■ *vt* (*problem*) risolvere; (*plan*) elaborare; **it works out at £100** fa 100 sterline

workable ['wə:kəbl] *adj* (*solution*) realizzabile

workaholic [wə:kə'hɔlɪk] *n* stacanovista *m/f*

workbench ['wə:kbɛntʃ] *n* banco (da lavoro)

worked up *adj*: **to get ~** andare su tutte le furie; eccitarsi

worker ['wə:kəʳ] *n* lavoratore(-trice); (*esp Agr, Industry*) operaio(-a); **office ~** impiegato(-a)

work force *n* forza lavoro

work-in ['wə:kɪn] *n* (*Brit*) sciopero alla rovescia

working ['wə:kɪŋ] *adj* (*day*) feriale; (*tools, conditions*) di lavoro; (*clothes*) da lavoro; (*wife*) che lavora; (*partner*) attivo(-a); **in ~ order** funzionante; **~ knowledge** conoscenza pratica

working capital *n* (*Comm*) capitale *m* d'esercizio

working class *n* classe *f* operaia *or* lavoratrice ■ *adj*: **working-class** operaio(-a)

working man *n* lavoratore *m*

working party *n* (*Brit*) commissione *f*

working week *n* settimana lavorativa

work-in-progress ['wə:kɪn'prəugrɛs] *n* (*products*) lavoro in corso; (*value*) valore *m* del manufatto in lavorazione

workload ['wə:kləud] *n* carico di lavoro

workman ['wə:kmən] *n* operaio

workmanship ['wə:kmənʃɪp] *n* (*of worker*) abilità; (*of thing*) fattura

workmate ['wə:kmeɪt] *n* collega *m/f*

workout ['wə:kaut] *n* (*Sport*) allenamento

work permit *n* permesso di lavoro

works [wə:ks] *n* (*Brit: factory*) fabbrica ■ *npl* (*of clock, machine*) meccanismo; **road ~** opere stradali

works council *n* consiglio aziendale

work sheet *n* (*Comput*) foglio col programma di lavoro

workshop ['wə:kʃɔp] *n* officina

work station *n* stazione *f* di lavoro

work study *n* studio di organizzazione del lavoro

worktop ['wə:ktɔp] *n* piano di lavoro

work-to-rule ['wə:ktə'ru:l] *n* (*Brit*) sciopero bianco

world [wə:ld] *n* mondo ■ *cpd* (*tour*) del mondo; (*record, power, war*) mondiale; **all over the ~** in tutto il mondo; **to think the ~ of sb** pensare un gran bene di qn; **out of this ~** (*fig*) formidabile; **what in the ~ is he doing?** che cavolo sta facendo?; **to do sb a ~ of good** fare un gran bene a qn; **W~ War One/Two** la prima/seconda guerra mondiale

world champion *n* campione(-essa) mondiale

World Cup *n* (*Football*) Coppa del Mondo

world-famous [wə:ld'feɪməs] *adj* di fama mondiale

worldly ['wə:ldlɪ] *adj* di questo mondo

world music *n* musica etnica

World Series *n*: **the ~** (*US Baseball*) la finalissima di baseball

world-wide ['wə:ld'waɪd] *adj* universale

worm [wə:m] *n* verme *m*

worn [wɔ:n] *pp of* **wear** ■ *adj* usato(-a)

worn-out ['wɔ:naut] *adj* (*object*) consumato(-a), logoro(-a); (*person*) sfinito(-a)

worried ['wʌrɪd] *adj* preoccupato(-a); **to be ~ about sth** essere preoccupato per qc

worrier ['wʌrɪəʳ] *n* ansioso(-a)

worrisome ['wʌrɪsəm] *adj* preoccupante

worry ['wʌrɪ] *n* preoccupazione *f* ▪ *vt* preoccupare ▪ *vi* preoccuparsi; **to ~ about** *or* **over sth/sb** preoccuparsi di qc/per qn

worrying ['wʌrɪɪŋ] *adj* preoccupante

worse [wəːs] *adj* peggiore ▪ *adv*, *n* peggio; **a change for the ~** un peggioramento; **to get ~**, **to grow ~** peggiorare; **he is none the ~ for it** non ha avuto brutte conseguenze; **so much the ~ for you!** tanto peggio per te!

worsen ['wəːsn] *vt*, *vi* peggiorare

worse off *adj* in condizioni (economiche) peggiori; (*fig*): **you'll be ~ this way** così sarà peggio per lei; **he is now ~ than before** ora è in condizioni peggiori di prima

worship ['wəːʃɪp] *n* culto ▪ *vt* (*God*) adorare, venerare; (*person*) adorare; **Your W~** (*to mayor*) signor sindaco; (*to judge*) signor giudice

worshipper ['wəːʃɪpəʳ] *n* adoratore(-trice); (*in church*) fedele *m/f*, devoto(-a)

worst [wəːst] *adj* il/la peggiore ▪ *adv*, *n* peggio; **at ~** al peggio, per male che vada; **to come off ~** avere la peggio; **if the ~ comes to the ~** nel peggior dei casi

worst-case ['wəːstˈkeɪs] *adj*: **the ~ scenario** la peggiore delle ipotesi

worsted ['wustɪd] *n*: (**wool**) **~** lana pettinata

worth [wəːθ] *n* valore *m* ▪ *adj*: **to be ~** valere; **how much is it ~?** quanto vale?; **it's ~ it** ne vale la pena; **it's not ~ the trouble** non ne vale la pena; **50 pence ~ of apples** 50 pence di mele

worthless ['wəːθlɪs] *adj* di nessun valore

worthwhile ['wəːθ'waɪl] *adj* (*activity*) utile; (*cause*) lodevole; **a ~ book** un libro che vale la pena leggere

worthy ['wəːðɪ] *adj* (*person*) degno(-a); (*motive*) lodevole; **~ of** degno di

 KEYWORD

would [wud] *aux vb* **1** (*conditional tense*): **if you asked him he would do it** se glielo chiedesse lo farebbe; **if you had asked him he would have done it** se glielo avesse chiesto lo avrebbe fatto

2 (*in offers, invitations, requests*): **would you like a biscuit?** vorrebbe *or* vuole un biscotto?; **would you ask him to come in?** lo faccia entrare, per cortesia; **would you open the window please?** apra la finestra, per favore

3 (*in indirect speech*): **I said I would do it** ho detto che l'avrei fatto

4 (*emphatic*): **it WOULD have to snow today!** doveva proprio nevicare oggi!

5 (*insistence*): **she wouldn't do it** non ha voluto farlo

6 (*conjecture*): **it would have been midnight** sarà stata mezzanotte; **it would seem so** sembrerebbe proprio di sì

7 (*indicating habit*): **he would go there on Mondays** andava lì ogni lunedì

would-be ['wudbiː] *adj* (*pej*) sedicente

wound¹ [wuːnd] *n* ferita ▪ *vt* ferire; **wounded in the leg** ferito(-a) alla gamba

wound² [waund] *pt*, *pp* *of* **wind²**

wove [wəuv] *pt* *of* **weave**

WP *abbr* (*Brit col*: = *weather permitting*) tempo permettendo ▪ *n abbr* = **word processing**; **word processor**

WPC *n abbr* (*Brit*: = *woman police constable*) donna poliziotto

wpm *abbr* (= *words per minute*) p.p.m.

WRAC *n abbr* (*Brit*: = *Women's Royal Army Corps*) ausiliarie dell'esercito

WRAF *n abbr* (*Brit*: = *Women's Royal Air Force*) ausiliarie dell'aeronautica militare

wrangle ['ræŋgl] *n* litigio ▪ *vi* litigare

wrap [ræp] *n* (*stole*) scialle *m*; (*cape*) mantellina ▪ *vt* (*also*: **wrap up**) avvolgere; (*parcel*) incartare; **under wraps** segreto

wrapper ['ræpəʳ] *n* (*of book*) copertina; (*on chocolate*) carta

wrapping paper ['ræpɪŋ-] *n* carta da pacchi; (*for gift*) carta da regali

wrath [rɔθ] *n* collera, ira

wreak [riːk] *vt* (*destruction*) portare, causare; **to ~ vengeance on** vendicarsi su; **to ~ havoc on** portare scompiglio in

wreath (*pl* **wreaths**) [riːθ, riːðz] *n* corona

wreck [rɛk] *n* (*sea disaster*) naufragio; (*ship*) relitto; (*pej*: *person*) rottame *m* ▪ *vt* demolire; (*ship*) far naufragare; (*fig*) rovinare

wreckage ['rɛkɪdʒ] *n* rottami *mpl*; (*of building*) macerie *fpl*; (*of ship*) relitti *mpl*

wrecker ['rɛkəʳ] *n* (*US*: *breakdown van*) carro *m* attrezzi *inv*

WREN [rɛn] *n abbr* (*Brit*) membro del WRNS

wren [rɛn] *n* (*Zool*) scricciolo

wrench [rɛntʃ] *n* (*Tech*) chiave *f*; (*tug*) torsione *f* brusca; (*fig*) strazio ▪ *vt* strappare; storcere; **to ~ sth from** strappare qc a *or* da

wrest [rɛst] *vt*: **to ~ sth from sb** strappare qc a qn

wrestle ['rɛsl] *vi*: **to ~ (with sb)** lottare (con qn); **to ~ with** (*fig*) combattere *or* lottare contro

wrestler ['rɛsləʳ] *n* lottatore(-trice)

wrestling ['rɛslɪŋ] *n* lotta; (*also*: **all-in wrestling**: *Brit*) catch *m*, lotta libera

W

wrestling match n incontro di lotta (or lotta libera)
wretch [rɛtʃ] n disgraziato(-a), sciagurato(-a); **little ~!** (often humorous) birbante!
wretched ['rɛtʃɪd] adj disgraziato(-a); (col: weather, holiday) orrendo(-a), orribile; (: child, dog) pestifero(-a)
wriggle ['rɪgl] n contorsione f ▪ vi dimenarsi; (snake, worm) serpeggiare, muoversi serpeggiando
wring (pt, pp **wrung**) [rɪŋ, rʌŋ] vt torcere; (wet clothes) strizzare; (fig): **to ~ sth out of** strappare qc a
wringer ['rɪŋəʳ] n strizzatoio (manuale)
wringing ['rɪŋɪŋ] adj (also: **wringing wet**) bagnato(-a) fradicio(-a)
wrinkle ['rɪŋkl] n (on skin) ruga; (on paper etc) grinza ▪ vt corrugare; raggrinzire ▪ vi corrugarsi; raggrinzirsi
wrinkled ['rɪŋkld], **wrinkly** ['rɪŋklɪ] adj (fabric, paper) stropicciato(-a); (surface) corrugato(-a), increspato(-a); (skin) rugoso(-a)
wrist [rɪst] n polso
wristband ['rɪstbænd] n (of shirt) polsino; (of watch) cinturino
wrist watch n orologio da polso
writ [rɪt] n ordine m; mandato; **to issue a ~ against sb, serve a ~ on sb** notificare un mandato di comparizione a qn
write (pt **wrote**, pp **written**) [raɪt, rəʊt, 'rɪtn] vt, vi scrivere; **to ~ sb a letter** scrivere una lettera a qn
  ▶ **write away** vi: **to ~ away for** (information) richiedere per posta; (goods) ordinare per posta
  ▶ **write down** vt annotare; (put in writing) mettere per iscritto
  ▶ **write off** vt (debt) cancellare; (depreciate) deprezzare; (smash up: car) distruggere
  ▶ **write out** vt scrivere; (copy) ricopiare
  ▶ **write up** vt redigere
write-off ['raɪtɔf] n perdita completa; **the car is a ~** la macchina va bene per il demolitore
write-protect ['raɪtprə'tɛkt] vt (Comput) proteggere contro scrittura
writer ['raɪtəʳ] n autore(-trice), scrittore(-trice)

write-up ['raɪtʌp] n (review) recensione f
writhe [raɪð] vi contorcersi
writing ['raɪtɪŋ] n scrittura; (of author) scritto, opera; **in ~** per iscritto; **in my own ~** scritto di mio pugno
writing case n nécessaire m inv per la corrispondenza
writing desk n scrivania, scrittoio
writing paper n carta da scrivere
written ['rɪtn] pp of **write**
WRNS n abbr (Brit: = Women's Royal Naval Service) ausiliarie della marina militare
wrong [rɔŋ] adj sbagliato(-a); (not suitable) inadatto(-a); (wicked) cattivo(-a); (unfair) ingiusto(-a) ▪ adv in modo sbagliato, erroneamente ▪ n (evil) male m; (injustice) torto ▪ vt fare torto a; **to be ~** (answer) essere sbagliato; (in doing, saying) avere torto; **you are ~ to do it** ha torto a farlo; **you are ~ about that, you've got it ~** si sbaglia; **to be in the ~** avere torto; **what's ~?** cosa c'è che non va?; **there's nothing ~** va tutto bene; **what's ~ with the car?** cos'ha la macchina che non va?; **to go ~** (person) sbagliarsi; (plan) fallire, non riuscire; (machine) guastarsi; **it's ~ to steal, stealing is ~** è male rubare
wrongdoer ['rɔŋduːəʳ] n malfattore(-trice)
wrong-foot [rɔŋ'fut] vt (Sport; also fig) prendere in contropiede
wrongful ['rɔŋful] adj illegittimo(-a); ingiusto(-a); **~ dismissal** licenziamento ingiustificato
wrongly ['rɔŋlɪ] adv (accuse, dismiss) a torto; (answer, do, count) erroneamente; (treat) ingiustamente
wrong number n: **you have the ~** (Tel) ha sbagliato numero
wrong side n (of cloth) rovescio
wrote [rəʊt] pt of **write**
wrought [rɔːt] adj: **~ iron** ferro battuto
wrung [rʌŋ] pt, pp of **wring**
WRVS n abbr (Brit) = **Women's Royal Voluntary Service**
wry [raɪ] adj storto(-a)
wt. abbr = **weight**
WV, W.Va. abbr (US) = **West Virginia**
WY, Wyo. abbr (US) = **Wyoming**
WYSIWYG ['wɪzɪwɪg] abbr (Comput) = **what you see is what you get**

Xx

X, x [ɛks] *n* (*letter*) X, x *f or m inv*; (*Brit Cine: old*)
≈ film vietato ai minori di 18 anni; **X for
Xmas** ≈ X come Xeres
Xerox® ['zɪərɔks] *n* (*also:* **Xerox machine**)
fotocopiatrice *f*; (*photocopy*) fotocopia ∎ *vt*
fotocopiare
XL *abbr* = **extra large**

Xmas ['ɛksməs] *n abbr* = **Christmas**
X-rated ['ɛks'reɪtɪd] *adj* (*US: film*) ≈ vietato ai
minori di 18 anni
X-ray ['ɛks'reɪ] *n* raggio X; (*photograph*)
radiografia ∎ *vt* radiografare; **to have an ~**
farsi fare una radiografia
xylophone ['zaɪləfəun] *n* xilofono

Yy

Y, y [waɪ] n (letter) Y, y f or m inv; **Y for Yellow**, (US) **Y for Yoke** ≈ Y come Yacht
yacht [jɔt] n panfilo, yacht m inv
yachting ['jɔtɪŋ] n yachting m, sport m della vela
yachtsman ['jɔtsmən] n yachtsman m inv
yam [jæm] n igname m; (sweet potato) patata dolce
Yank [jæŋk], **Yankee** ['jæŋkɪ] n (pej) yankee m/f inv, nordamericano(-a)
yank [jæŋk] n strattone m ■ vt tirare, dare uno strattone a
yap [jæp] vi (dog) guaire
yard [ja:d] n (of house etc) cortile m; (US: garden) giardino; (measure) iarda (= 914 mm; 3 feet); **builder's** ~ deposito di materiale da costruzione
yardstick ['ja:dstɪk] n (fig) misura, criterio
yarn [ja:n] n filato; (tale) lunga storia
yawn [jɔ:n] n sbadiglio ■ vi sbadigliare
yawning ['jɔ:nɪŋ] adj (gap) spalancato(-a)
yd. abbr = **yard**
yeah [jɛə] adv (col) sì
year [jɪəʳ] n (gen, Scol) anno; (referring to harvest, wine etc) annata; **every** ~ ogni anno, tutti gli anni; **this** ~ quest'anno; ~ **in,** ~ **out** anno dopo anno; **she's three years old** ha tre anni; **a** or **per** ~ all'anno
yearbook ['jɪəbuk] n annuario
yearly ['jɪəlɪ] adj annuale ■ adv annualmente; **twice-~** semestrale
yearn [jə:n] vi: **to ~ for sth/to do** desiderare ardentemente qc/di fare
yearning ['jə:nɪŋ] n desiderio intenso
yeast [ji:st] n lievito
yell [jɛl] n urlo ■ vi urlare
yellow ['jɛləu] adj giallo(-a)
yellow fever n febbre f gialla
yellowish ['jɛləuɪʃ] adj giallastro(-a), giallognolo(-a)
Yellow Pages® npl pagine fpl gialle
Yellow Sea n: **the** ~ il mar Giallo
yelp [jɛlp] n guaito, uggiolio ■ vi guaire, uggiolare
Yemen ['jɛmən] n Yemen m
yen [jɛn] n (currency) yen m inv; (craving): ~ **for/ to do** gran voglia di/di fare
yeoman ['jəumən] n: **Y~ of the Guard** guardiano della Torre di Londra
yes [jɛs] adv, n sì (m inv); **to say ~ (to)** dire di sì (a), acconsentire (a)
yesterday ['jɛstədɪ] adv, n ieri (m inv); ~ **morning/evening** ieri mattina/sera; **the day before** ~ l'altro ieri; **all day** ~ ieri tutto il giorno
yet [jɛt] adv ancora; già ■ conj ma, tuttavia; **it is not finished** ~ non è ancora finito; **the best** ~ il migliore finora; **as** ~ finora; ~ **again** di nuovo; **must you go just** ~? deve andarsene di già?; **a few days** ~ ancora qualche giorno
yew [ju:] n tasso (albero)
Y-fronts® ['waɪfrʌnts] npl (Brit) slip m inv da uomo
YHA n abbr (Brit: = Youth Hostels Association) Y.H.A. f
Yiddish ['jɪdɪʃ] n yiddish m
yield [ji:ld] n resa; (of crops etc) raccolto ■ vt produrre, rendere; (surrender) cedere ■ vi cedere; (US Aut) dare la precedenza; **a ~ of 5%** un profitto or un interesse del 5%
YMCA n abbr (= Young Men's Christian Association) Y.M.C.A. m
yob ['jɔb], **yobbo** ['jɔbəu] n (Brit col) bullo
yodel ['jəudl] vi cantare lo jodel or alla tirolese
yoga ['jəugə] n yoga m
yogourt, yoghourt ['jəugət] n iogurt m inv
yoke [jəuk] n giogo ■ vt (also: **yoke together**: oxen) aggiogare
yolk [jəuk] n tuorlo, rosso d'uovo
yonder ['jɔndəʳ] adv là
yonks [jɔŋks] npl: **for** ~ (col) da una vita
Yorks [jɔ:ks] abbr (Brit) = **Yorkshire**

 KEYWORD

you [ju:] pron **1** (subject) tu; (: polite form) lei; (: pl) voi; (: formal) loro; **you Italians enjoy**

your food a voi italiani piace mangiare bene;
you and I will go andiamo io e te (*or* lei ed io);
if I was *or* **were you** se fossi in te (*or* lei *etc*)
2 (*object: direct*) ti; la; vi; loro (*after vb*);
(*: indirect*) ti; le; vi; loro (*after vb*); **I know you**
ti (*or* la *or* vi) conosco; **I'll see you tomorrow**
ci vediamo domani; **I gave it to you** te l'ho
dato; gliel'ho dato; ve l'ho dato; l'ho dato loro
3 (*stressed, after prep, in comparisons*) te; lei; voi;
loro; **I told YOU to do it** ho detto a TE (*or* a
LEI *etc*) di farlo; **she's younger than you** è
più giovane di te (*or* lei *etc*)
4 (*impers: one*) si; **fresh air does you good**
l'aria fresca fa bene; **you never know** non si
sa mai

you'd [juːd] = **you had; you would**
you'll [juːl] = **you will; you shall**
young [jʌŋ] *adj* giovane ■ *npl* (*of animal*)
piccoli *mpl*; (*people*): **the ~** i giovani, la
gioventù; **a ~ man** un giovanotto; **a ~ lady**
una signorina; **a ~ woman** una giovane
donna; **the younger generation** la nuova
generazione; **my younger brother** il mio
fratello minore
youngish [ˈjʌŋɪʃ] *adj* abbastanza giovane
youngster [ˈjʌŋstəʳ] *n* giovanotto(-a); (*child*)
bambino(-a)
your [jɔːʳ] *adj* il/la tuo(-a); (*pl*) i/le tuoi/tue;
(*polite form*) il/la suo(-a); (*pl*) i/le suoi/sue; (*pl*)
il/la vostro(-a); (*pl*) i/le vostri(-e); (*: formal*) il/
la loro; (*pl*) i/le loro
you're [juəʳ] = **you are**
yours [jɔːz] *pron* il/la tuo(-a); (*pl*) i/le tuoi/tue;
(*polite form*) il/la suo(-a); (*pl*) i/le suoi/sue; (*pl*)

il/la vostro(-a); (*pl*) i/le vostri(-e); (*: formal*) il/la
loro; (*pl*) i/le loro; **~ sincerely/faithfully** (*in
letter*) cordiali/distinti saluti; **a friend of ~** un
tuo (*or* suo *etc*) amico; **is it ~?** è tuo (*or* suo *etc*)?
yourself [jɔːˈsɛlf] *pron* (*reflexive*) ti; (*: polite form*)
si; (*after prep*) te; se; (*emphatic*) tu stesso(-a); lei
stesso(-a); **you ~ told me** me l'hai detto
proprio tu, tu stesso me l'hai detto
yourselves [jɔːˈsɛlvz] *pl pron* (*reflexive*) vi;
(*: polite form*) si; (*after prep*) voi; loro; (*emphatic*)
voi stessi(-e); loro stessi(-e)
youth [juːθ] *n* gioventù *f*; (*young man*):
(*pl* **youths**) [juːðz] giovane *m*, ragazzo;
in my ~ da giovane, quando ero giovane
youth club *n* centro giovanile
youthful [ˈjuːθful] *adj* giovane; da giovane;
giovanile
youthfulness [ˈjuːθfəlnɪs] *n* giovinezza
youth hostel *n* ostello della gioventù
youth movement *n* movimento giovanile
you've [juːv] = **you have**
yowl [jaul] *n* (*of dog, person*) urlo; (*of cat*)
miagolio ■ *vi* urlare; miagolare
yr *abbr* = **year**
YT *abbr* (*Canada*) = **Yukon Territory**
Yugoslav [ˈjuːɡəuslɑːv] *adj, n* (*formerly*)
jugoslavo(-a)
Yugoslavia [juːɡəuˈslɑːvɪə] *n* (*formerly*)
Jugoslavia
Yugoslavian [juːɡəuˈslɑːvɪən] *adj, n* (*formerly*)
jugoslavo(-a)
Yule log [juːl-] *n* ceppo nel caminetto a Natale
yuppie [ˈjʌpɪ] *adj, n* (*col*) yuppie (*m o f*) *inv*
YWCA *n abbr* (= *Young Women's Christian
Association*) Y.W.C.A. *m*

Zz

Z, z [zɛd, (US) zi:] n (letter) Z, z for m inv; **Z for Zebra** ≈ Z come Zara
Zaire [zɑːˈiəʳ] n Zaire m
Zambia [ˈzæmbɪə] n Zambia m
Zambian [ˈzæmbɪən] adj, n zambiano(-a)
zany [ˈzeɪnɪ] adj un po' pazzo(-a)
zap [zæp] vt (Comput) cancellare
zeal [ziːl] n zelo; entusiasmo
zealot [ˈzɛlət] n zelota m/f
zealous [ˈzɛləs] adj zelante; premuroso(-a)
zebra [ˈziːbrə] n zebra
zebra crossing n (Brit) (passaggio pedonale a) strisce fpl, zebre fpl
zenith [ˈzɛnɪθ] n zenit m inv; (fig) culmine m
zero [ˈzɪərəu] n zero; **5° below ~** 5° sotto zero
zero hour n l'ora zero
zero option n (Pol) opzione f zero
zero-rated [ˈzɪərəuˈreɪtɪd] adj (Brit) ad aliquota zero
zest [zɛst] n gusto; (Culin) buccia ▪ vt
zigzag [ˈzɪgzæg] n zigzag m inv ▪ vi zigzagare
Zimbabwe [zɪmˈbɑːbwɪ] n Zimbabwe m
Zimbabwean [zɪmˈbɑːbwɪən] adj dello Zimbabwe
Zimmer® [ˈzɪməʳ] n (also: **Zimmer frame**) deambulatore m

zinc [zɪŋk] n zinco
Zionism [ˈzaɪənɪzəm] n sionismo
Zionist [ˈzaɪənɪst] adj sionistico(-a) ▪ n sionista m/f
zip [zɪp] n (also: **zip fastener**, US **zipper**) chiusura f or cerniera f lampo inv; (energy) energia, forza ▪ vt (Comput) zippare; (also: **zip up**) chiudere con una cerniera lampo
zip code n (US) codice m di avviamento postale
zither [ˈzɪðəʳ] n cetra
zodiac [ˈzəudɪæk] n zodiaco
zombie [ˈzɔmbɪ] n (fig): **like a ~** come un morto che cammina
zone [zəun] n zona
zoo [zuː] n zoo m inv
zoological [zuəˈlɔdʒɪkl] adj zoologico(-a)
zoologist [zuːˈɔlədʒɪst] n zoologo(-a)
zoology [zuːˈɔlədʒɪ] n zoologia
zoom [zuːm] vi: **to ~ past** sfrecciare; **to ~ in (on sb/sth)** (Phot, Cine) zumare (su qn/qc)
zoom lens n zoom m inv, obiettivo a focale variabile
zucchini [zuːˈkiːnɪ] n (pl inv: US) zucchina
Zulu [ˈzuːluː] adj, n zulù (m o f) inv
Zürich [ˈzjuərɪk] n Zurigo f

Grammar
Grammatica

Using the grammar

The Grammar section deals systematically and comprehensively with all the information you will need in order to communicate accurately in Italian. The user-friendly layout explains the grammar point on a left-hand page, leaving the facing page free for illustrative examples. The numbers, → ❶ etc, direct you to the relevant example in every case.

The Grammar section also provides invaluable guidance on the danger of translating English structures by identical structures in Italian. Use of Numbers and Punctuation are important areas covered towards the end of the section. Finally, the index lists the main words and grammatical terms in both English and Italian.

Italic letters in Italian words show where stress does not follow the usual rules.

Abbreviations

fem.	*feminine*
infin.	*infinitive*
masc.	*masculine*
perf.	*perfect*
plur.	*plural*
sing.	*singular*
qc	qualcosa
qn	qualcuno
sb	somebody
sth	something

Contents

Simple Tenses: Formation

In English, tenses are either simple, which means they consist of one word, e.g. *I work*, or compound, which means they consist of more than one word, e.g. *I have worked, I have been working*. The same is true in Italian.

In Italian the simple tenses are:

Present → ❶
Imperfect → ❷
Future → ❸
Present Conditional → ❹
Past Historic → ❺
Present Subjunctive → ❻
Imperfect Subjunctive → ❼

They are formed by adding endings to a verb stem. The endings show the number and person of the subject of the verb → ❽

The stem and endings of regular verbs are totally predictable. The following sections show all the patterns for regular verbs. For irregular verbs see page 80 onwards.

Regular Verbs

There are three regular verb patterns (called conjugations), each identifiable by the ending of the infinitive:

First conjugation verbs end in **-are** e.g. **parlare** to speak

Second conjugation verbs end in **-ere** e.g. **credere** to believe

Third conjugation verbs end in **-ire** e.g. **finire** to finish

These three conjugations are treated in order on the following pages.

Examples

1 parlo

      parlo?

      I speak
      I am speaking
      do I speak?

2 parlavo

      I spoke
      I was speaking
      I used to speak

3 parlerò — I shall/will/'ll speak

4 parlerei — I should/would/'d speak

5 parlai — I spoke

6 (che) parli — that I speak

7 (che) parlassi — that I should speak

8 parlo — I speak
    parliamo — we speak
    parlerei — I'd speak
    parleremmo — we'd speak

Simple Tenses: First Conjugation

The stem is formed by taking the **-are** ending off the infinitive. The stem of **parlare** is **parl-** .

Add the following endings to the stem:

		❶ PRESENT	❷ IMPERFECT	❸ FUTURE
sing.	1st person	-o	-avo	-erò
	2nd person	-i	-avi	-erai
	3rd person	-a	-ava	-erà
plur.	1st person	-iamo	-avamo	-eremo
	2nd person	-ate	-avate	-erete
	3rd person	-ano	-avano	-eranno

		❹ PRESENT CONDITIONAL	❺ PAST HISTORIC
sing.	1st person	-erei	-ai
	2nd person	-eresti	-asti
	3rd person	-erebbe	-ò
plur.	1st person	-eremmo	-ammo
	2nd person	-ereste	-aste
	3rd person	-erebbero	-arono

		❻ PRESENT SUBJUNCTIVE	❼ IMPERFECT SUBJUNCTIVE
sing.	1st, 2nd person	-i	-assi
	3rd person	-i	-asse
plur.	1st person	-iamo	-assimmo
	2nd person	-iate	-aste
	3rd person	-ino	-assero

Examples

1 PRESENT
parlo
parli
parla
parliamo
parlate
parlano

2 IMPERFECT
parlavo
parlavi
parlava
parlavamo
parlavate
parlavano

3 FUTURE
parlerò
parlerai
parlerà
parleremo
parlerete
parleranno

4 PRESENT CONDITIONAL
parlerei
parleresti
parlerebbe
parleremmo
parlereste
parlerebbero

5 PAST HISTORIC
parlai
parlasti
parlò
parlammo
parlaste
parlarono

6 PRESENT SUBJUNCTIVE
parli
parli
parli
parliamo
parliate
parlino

7 IMPERFECT SUBJUNCTIVE
parlassi
parlassi
parlasse
parlassimo
parlaste
parlassero

Simple Tenses: Second Conjugation

The stem is formed by taking the **-ere** ending off the infinitive. The stem of **credere** is **cred-** .

Add the following endings to the stem:

		① PRESENT	② IMPERFECT	③ FUTURE
	1st person	-o	-evo	-erò
sing.	2nd person	-i	-evi	-erai
	3rd person	-e	-eva	-erà
	1st person	-iamo	-evamo	-eremo
plur.	2nd person	-ete	-evate	-erete
	3rd person	-ono	-evano	-eranno

		④ PRESENT CONDITIONAL	⑤ PAST HISTORIC
	1st person	-erei	-ei or -etti
sing.	2nd person	-eresti	-esti
	3rd person	-erebbe	-ette
	1st person	-eremmo	-emmo
plur.	2nd person	-ereste	-este
	3rd person	-erebbero	-ettero

		⑥ PRESENT SUBJUNCTIVE	⑦ IMPERFECT SUBJUNCTIVE
	1st, 2nd persons	-a	-essi
sing.	3rd person	-a	-esse
	1st person	-iamo	-essimo
plur.	2nd person	-iate	-este
	3rd person	-ano	-essero

Examples

1 PRESENT
credo
credi
crede
crediamo
credete
credono

2 IMPERFECT
credevo
credevi
credeva
credevamo
credevate
credevano

3 FUTURE
crederò
crederai
crederà
crederemo
crederete
crederanno

4 PRESENT CONDITIONAL
crederei
crederesti
crederebbe
crederemmo
credereste
crederebbero

5 PAST HISTORIC
credei *or* credetti
credesti
credette
credemmo
credeste
credettero

6 PRESENT SUBJUNCTIVE
creda
creda
creda
crediamo
crediate
credano

7 IMPERFECT SUBJUNCTIVE
credessi
credessi
credesse
credessimo
credeste
credessero

Simple Tenses: Third Conjugation

Generally, the stem is formed by taking the **-ire** ending off the infinitive. The stem for most tenses of **finire** is **fin-**.

However, in the present tense and present subjunctive, **-isc-** is added to the basic stem (except for the 1st and 2nd person plural):

EXCEPTIONS: **servire** to serve, **dormire** to sleep, **soffrire** to suffer, **coprire** to cover, **sentire** to feel, **partire** to leave, **offrire** to offer, **aprire** to offer

The present tenses of **finire** and **dormire** are as follows:

	1st person	fin**isc**o	dormo
sing.	2nd person	fin**isc**i	dormi
	3rd person	fin**isc**e	dorme
	1st person	finiamo	dormiamo
plur.	2nd person	finite	dormite
	3rd person	fin**isc**ono	dormono

Both types of verb take the following endings:

		① PRESENT	② IMPERFECT	③ FUTURE
	1st person	-o	-ivo	-irò
sing.	2nd person	-i	-ivi	-irai
	3rd person	-e	-iva	-irà
	1st person	-iamo	-ivamo	-iremo
plur.	2nd person	-ite	-ivate	-irete
	3rd person	-ono	-ivano	-iranno

		④ PRESENT CONDITIONAL	⑤ PAST HISTORIC
	1st person	-irei	-ii
sing.	2nd person	-iresti	-isti
	3rd person	-irebbe	-ì
	1st person	-iremmo	-immo
plur.	2nd person	-ireste	-iste
	3rd person	-irebbero	-irono

		⑥ PRESENT SUBJUNCTIVE	⑦ IMPERFECT SUBJUNCTIVE
sing.	1st, 2nd persons	-a	-issi
	3rd person	-a	-isse
plur.	1st person	-iamo	-issimmo
	2nd person	-iate	-iste
	3rd person	-ano	-issero

① PRESENT	② IMPERFECT	③ FUTURE
finisco	finivo	finirò
finisci	finivi	finirai
finisce	finiva	finirà
finiamo	finivamo	finiremo
finite	finivate	finirete
finiscono	finivano	finiranno

④ PRESENT SUBJUNCTIVE	⑤ PAST HISTORIC
finirei	finii
finiresti	finisti
finirebbe	finì
finiremmo	finimmo
finireste	finiste
finirebbero	finirono

⑥ PRESENT SUBJUNCTIVE	⑦ IMPERFECT SUBJUNCTIVE
finisca	finissi
finisca	finissi
finisca	finisse
finiamo	finissimo
finiate	finiste
finiscano	finissero

13

First Conjugation Spelling Irregularities

Before certain endings, the stems of some **-are** verbs may change slightly.

Verbs ending: **-care**
Change: **c** becomes **ch** before **e** or **i**
Tenses affected: Present, Future, Conditional, Present Subjunctive
Model: **cercare** to look for → ❶

Why the change occurs: **h** is added to keep the **c** sound hard *k*.

Verbs ending: **-gare**
Change: **g** becomes **gh** before **e** or **i**
Tenses affected: Present, Future, Conditional, Present Subjunctive
Model: **pagare** to pay → ❷

Why the change occurs: **h** is added to keep the **g** sound hard *g*.

Examples

1 INFINITIVE
cercare

PRESENT	FUTURE
cerco	**cercherò**
cerchi	**cercherai**
cerca	**cercherà**
cerchiamo	**cercheremo**
cercate	**cercherete**
cercano	**cercheranno**

CONDITIONAL	PRESENT SUBJUNCTIVE
cercherei	**cerchi**
cercheresti	**cerchi**
cercherebbe	**cerchi**
cercheremmo	**cerchiamo**
cerchereste	**cerchiate**
cercherebbero	**cerchino**

2 INFINITIVE
pagare

PRESENT	FUTURE
pago	**pagherò**
paghi	**pagherai**
paga	**pagherà**
paghiamo	**pagheremo**
pagate	**pagherete**
pagano	**pagheranno**

CONDITIONAL	PRESENT SUBJUNCTIVE
pagherei	**paghi**
pagheresti	**paghi**
pagherebbe	**paghi**
pagheremmo	**paghiamo**
paghereste	**paghiate**
pagherebbero	**paghino**

First Conjugation Spelling Irregularities *continued*

Verbs ending: **-ciare**
Change: **i** is dropped before **e** or **i**
Tenses affected: Present, Future, Conditional, Present Subjunctive
Model: **annunciare** to announce → ❶

Why the change occurs: the **i** of the infinitive is needed to keep **c** soft
tʃ before **a** (before **e** and **i**, **c** is soft, so the **i** is
unnecessary).

Verbs ending: **-giare**
Change: **i** is dropped before **e** or **i**
Tenses affected: Present, Future, Conditional, Present Subjunctive
Model: **mangiare** to eat → ❷

Why the change occurs: the **i** of the infinitive is needed to keep **g** soft
dʒ before **a** (before **e** and **i**, **g** is soft, so the **i** is
unnecessary).

❶ INFINITIVE
annunciare

PRESENT	FUTURE
annuncio	**annuncerò**
annunci	**annuncerai**
annuncia	**annuncerà**
annunciamo	**annunceremo**
annunciate	**annuncerete**
annunciano	**annunceranno**

CONDITIONAL	PRESENT SUBJUNCTIVE
annuncerei	**annunci**
annunceresti	**annunci**
annuncerebbe	**annunci**
annunceremmo	**annunciamo**
annuncereste	**annunciate**
annuncerebbero	**annuncino**

❷ INFINITIVE
mangiare

PRESENT	FUTURE
mangio	**mangerò**
mangi	**mangerai**
mangia	**mangerà**
mangiamo	**mangeremo**
mangiate	**mangerete**
mangiano	**mangeranno**

CONDITIONAL	PRESENT SUBJUNCTIVE
mangerei	**mangi**
mangeresti	**mangi**
mangerebbe	**mangi**
mangeremmo	**mangiamo**
mangereste	**mangiate**
mangerebbero	**mangino**

First Conjugation Spelling Irregularities *continued*

Verbs ending: **-iare**
Change: i is not dropped before another **i**, which is what usually happens
Tenses affected: Present, Present Subjunctive
Model: **inviare** to send, **sciare** to ski → ❶

Why the change occurs: The **i** has to be retained in forms where it is the stressed vowel.

Verbs ending: **-gliare**
Change: i is dropped before endings beginning with **-i**
Tenses affected: Present, Present subjunctive, Imperfect Subjunctive, Imperative
Model: **consigliare** to advise, **svegliare** to wake up → ❷

Why the change occurs: There is no need to retain the **i**.

Examples

1 INFINITIVE
inviare

PRESENT
invio
invii
invia
inviamo
inviate
inviano

2 INFINITIVE
svegliare

PRESENT
sveglio
svegli
sveglia
svegliamo
svegliate
svegliano

The Imperative

The imperative is the form of the verb used to give commands or instructions. It can be used politely, as in English 'Please take a seat'. In Italian, the polite imperative is the 3rd person form, either singular or plural. The 1st person plural (we) is used to make suggestions, as in 'Let's go'.

The imperative is formed by adding endings to the stem of the verb. The endings for the 1st and 2nd persons plural are the same as those for the present tense, the others are different. → ①

			FIRST	SECOND	THIRD
sing.	2nd	person	-a	-i	-i
	3rd	person	-i	-a	-a
plur.	1st	person	-iamo	-iamo	-iamo
	2nd	person	-ate	-ete	-ite
	3rd	person	-ino	-ano	-ano

NB Third conjugation verbs which add **isc** to the stem in the present tense also do so in the imperative → ②

The imperative of irregular verbs is given in the verb tables page 80.

Position of object and reflexive pronouns with the imperative:
- they follow imperatives in the 2nd person and the **-iamo** form, and are joined on to make one word → ③
- they precede 3rd person polite imperatives, and are not joined on to them → ④

Changes to pronouns following the imperative:
- the first letter of the pronoun is doubled when the imperative is one syllable: **mi** becomes **mmi**, **ti** becomes **tti**, **lo** becomes **llo** etc → ⑤
- When the pronouns **mi**, **ti**, **ci** and **vi** are followed by another pronoun they become **-me**, **-te**, **-ce** and **-ve**, and **gli** and **le** become **glie-** → ⑥

Negative imperatives:
- **non** precedes the imperative to make it negative (except in the 2nd person singular) → ⑦
- **non** precedes the infinitive in the 2nd person singular) → ⑧
- in 2nd person singular negative commands, **non** is used with the infinitive instead of the imperative. Pronouns may be joined onto the infinitive, or precede it → ⑧

① **Compare:**
　　Aspetti, Maria?　　　　　　　　　Are you waiting, Maria?
　　and: Aspetta Maria!　　　　　　　Wait Maria!
　　Prende l'autobus　　　　　　　　He gets the bus
　　and: Prenda l'autobus, signora!　　Get the bus, madam!

② Finisci l'esercizio, Marco!　　　　Finish the exercise, Marco!
　　Finisca tutto, signore!　　　　　　Finish it all, sir!
　　Finiamo tutto　　　　　　　　　　Let's finish it all
　　Finite i compiti, ragazzi!　　　　　Finish your homework, children!
　　Finiscano tutto signori!　　　　　　Finish it all, ladies and gentlemen!

③ Guardami, mamma!　　　　　　　Look at me, mum!
　　Aspettateli!　　　　　　　　　　Wait for them!
　　Proviamolo!　　　　　　　　　　Let's try it!

④ Mi dia un chilo d'uva, per favore　Give me a kilo of grapes please
　　Si accomodi!　　　　　　　　　　Take a seat!
　　La prenda, signore　　　　　　　Take it, sir

⑤ Dimmi!　　　　　　　　　　　　Tell me!
　　Fallo subito!　　　　　　　　　　Do it immediately!

⑥ Mandameli　　　　　　　　　　Send me them
　　Daglielo　　　　　　　　　　　Give it to him
　　Mandiamogliela!　　　　　　　Let's send it to them!

⑦ Non dimentichiamo　　　　　　Don't let's forget
　　Non si preoccupi, signore　　　　Don't worry, sir

⑧ Non dire bugie Andrea!　　　　　Don't tell lies Andrea!
　　Non dimenticare!　　　　　　　Don't forget!
　　Non toccarlo! *or* Non lo toccare!　Don't touch it!
　　Non glielo dire! *or* Non dirglielo　Don't tell him about it!
　　Non preoccuparti! *or* Non ti　　Don't worry!
　　preoccupare!

Compound Tenses

Continuous tenses

The simple tense of an Italian verb, e.g. **piove**, can have two meanings: 'it rains', or 'it's raining'; the continuous tense, **sta piovendo** is an alternative way of expressing the English present continuous (it's raining).

The Present Continuous is used less in Italian than in English. It is formed with the present tense of the verb **stare**, plus the gerund → **①**

The Past Continuous is formed with the imperfect tense of **stare,** and the gerund → **②**

For information on how to form the gerund, see page 52.

The Past Continuous is also less used in Italian than in English, as the imperfect tense can be used to express this meaning.

Examples

1 Ci sto pensando

I'm thinking about it

Stanno arrivando

They're coming

Cosa stai facendo?

What are you doing?

2 Stavo studiando

I was studying

Stava morendo

He was dying

Stavano lavorando

They were working

Compound Tenses *continued*

Formed with the past participle

These are:

Perfect → ❶
Pluperfect → ❷
Future Perfect → ❸
Perfect Conditional → ❹
Past Anterior → ❺
Perfect Subjunctive → ❻
Pluperfect Subjunctive → ❼

They consist of the past past participle and an auxiliary verb. Most verbs take the auxiliary **avere**, but some take *essere* (see page 30).

These tenses are formed in the same way for regular and irregular verbs, the only difference being that an irregular verb may have an irregular past participle.

The Past Participle

The past participle of regular verbs is formed as follows:

First conjugation: replace the **-are** of the infinitive with **-ato** → ❽

Second conjugation: replace the **-ere** of the infinitive with **-uto** → ❾

Third conjugation: replace the **-ire** of the infinitive with **-ito** → ❿

with **avere**	with **essere**

1. ho parlato I spoke, have spoken   sono andato I went, have gone

2. avevo parlato I had spoken   ero andato I had gone

3. avrò parlato I will have spoken   sarò andato I will have gone

4. avrei parlato I would have spoken   sarei andato I would have gone

5. ebbi parlato I had spoken   fui andato I had gone

6. abbia parlato I spoke, have spoken   sia andato I went, have gone

7. avessi parlato I had spoken   fossi andato I had gone

8. parlare to speak → parlato spoken

9. credere to believe → creduto believed

10. finire to finish → finito finished

Compound Tenses *continued*

Verbs taking the auxiliary avere

PERFECT TENSE
The present tense of **avere** plus the past participle → **1**

PLUPERFECT TENSE
The imperfect tense of **avere** plus the past participle → **2**

FUTURE PERFECT
The future tense of **avere** plus the past participle → **3**

PERFECT CONDITIONAL
The conditional of **avere** plus the past participle → **4**

PAST ANTERIOR
The past historic of **avere** plus the past participle → **5**

PERFECT SUBJUNCTIVE
The present subjunctive of **avere** plus the past participle → **6**

PLUPERFECT SUBJUNCTIVE
The imperfect subjunctive of **avere** plus the past participle → **7**

For how to form the past participle of regular verbs see page 24. The past participle of irregular verbs is given for each verb in the verb tables, page 80 onwards.

The past participle agrees in number and gender with a preceding direct object when it is **lo, la, li** or **le**, e.g.

Le matite? Le ho comprate ieri   The pencils? I bought them yesterday

Examples

1 PERFECT

ho parlato	abbiamo parlato
hai parlato	avete parlato
ha parlato	hanno parlato

2 PLUPERFECT

avevo parlato	avevamo parlato
avevi parlato	avevate parlato
aveva parlato	avevano parlato

3 FUTURE PERFECT

avrò parlato	avremo parlato
avrai parlato	avrete parlato
avrà parlato	avranno parlato

4 PERFECT CONDITIONAL

avrei parlato	avremmo parlato
avresti parlato	avreste parlato
avrebbe parlato	avrebbero parlato

5 PAST ANTERIOR

ebbi parlato	avemmo parlato
avesti parlato	aveste parlato
ebbe parlato	ebbero parlato

6 PERFECT SUBJUNCTIVE

abbia parlato	abbiamo parlato
abbia parlato	abbiate parlato
abbia parlato	abbiano parlato

7 PLUPERFECT SUBJUNCTIVE

avessi parlato	avessimo parlato
avessi parlato	aveste parlato
avesse parlato	avessero parlato

Compound Tenses *continued*

Verbs taking the auxiliary *essere*

PERFECT TENSE
The present tense of *essere* plus the past participle → ❶

PLUPERFECT TENSE
The imperfect tense of *essere* plus the past participle → ❷

FUTURE PERFECT
The future tense of *essere* plus the past participle → ❸

PERFECT CONDITIONAL
The conditional of *essere* plus the past participle → ❹

PAST ANTERIOR
The past historic of *essere* plus the past participle → ❺

PERFECT SUBJUNCTIVE
The present subjunctive of *essere* plus the past participle → ❻

PLUPERFECT SUBJUNCTIVE
The imperfect subjunctive of *essere* plus the past participle → ❼

For how to form the past participle of regular verbs see page 24. The past participle of irregular verbs is given for each verb in the verb tables, page 80 onwards.

For agreement of past participles see page 56.

For a list of verbs and verb types that take the auxiliary *essere*, see page 30.

1 PERFECT

sono andato(a)	siamo andati(e)
sei andato(a)	siete andati(e)
è andato(a)	sono andati(e)

2 PLUPERFECT

ero andato(a)	eravamo andati(e)
eri andato(a)	eravate andati(e)
era andato(a)	erano andati(e)

3 FUTURE PERFECT

sarò andato(a)	saremo andati(e)
sarai andato(a)	sarete andati(e)
sarà andato(a)	saranno andati(e)

4 PERFECT CONDITIONAL

sarei andato(a)	saremmo andati(e)
saresti andato(a)	sareste andati(e)
sarebbe andato(a)	sarebbero andati(e)

5 PAST ANTERIOR

fui andato(a)	fummo andati(e)
fosti andato(a)	foste andati(e)
fu andato(a)	furono andati(e)

6 PERFECT SUBJUNCTIVE

sia andato(a)	siamo andati(e)
sia andato(a)	siate andati(e)
sia andato(a)	siano andati(e)

7 PLUPERFECT SUBJUNCTIVE

fossi andato(a)	fossimo andati(e)
fossi andato(a)	foste andati(e)
fosse andato(a)	fossero andati(e)

Compound Tenses *continued*

The following verbs take the auxiliary *essere*
Reflexive verbs (see page 32) → ❶

Many intransitive verbs (i.e. verbs not taking a direct object),
including the following:

andare to go	**partire** to leave
apparire to appear	**restare** to stay
arrivare to arrive → ❷	**rimanere** to stay
bastare to be enough	**ritornare** to return → ❹
cadere to fall	**riuscire** to succeed/manage → ❺
costare to cost → ❸	**salire** to go up/get on
dipendere to depend	**scadere** to expire
divenire to become	**scappare** to get away
diventare to become	**scendere** to go down
durare to last	**scivolare** to slip
entrare to come in	**sparire** to disappear → ❻
esistere to exist	**stare** to be/stay
essere to be	**succedere** to happen
fuggire to escape	**tornare** to come back
intervenire to intervene	**venire** to come
morire to die	**uscire** to go out
nascere to be born	

The following verbs, often used in impersonal constructions:

bisognare	**occorrere**
convenire	**parere** → ❽
dispiacere	**piacere** → ❾
importare	**sembrare**
mancare → ❼	

Verbs that can be used both transitively and intransitively take the
auxiliary **essere** when intransitive and **avere** when transitive → ❿

Impersonal verbs which describe the weather are used with both **essere**
and **avere** → ⓫

ⓘ Note that the past participle agrees in gender and number with the
subject of verbs conjugated with **essere**.

1 Mi sono fatto male — I've hurt *or* I hurt myself
Si è rotta la gamba — She's broken *or* She broke her leg
Vi siete divertiti? — Did you have *or* Have you had a nice time?
Si sono addormentati — They've gone *or* They went to sleep

2 È arrivata — She's arrived *or* She arrived

3 È costato parecchio — It cost a lot *or* It has cost a lot

4 Siamo ritornati — We've returned *or* We returned

5 Sei riuscito? — Did you succeed? *or* Have you succeeded?

6 Sono spariti — They've disappeared

7 Ti sono mancata? — Did you miss me?

8 Mi è parso strano — It seemed strange to me

9 Vi è piaciuta la musica? — Did you like the music?

10 **passare**
Intransitive
Sono passati molti anni — Many years have passed
Transitive
Ho passato l'esame — I've passed the exam
saltare
Intransitive
Il gatto è saltato sul tavolo — The cat jumped on the table
Transitive
Ho saltato il pranzo — I skipped lunch

11 Ha piovuto *or*
È piovuto molto — It rained a lot
Ha nevicato! *or*
È nevicato! — It's snowed!

Reflexive Verbs

A reflexive verb is one accompanied by a reflexive pronoun, e.g. **divertirsi** to enjoy oneself; **annoiarsi** to get bored.
The reflexive pronouns are:

	SINGULAR	PLURAL
1st person	mi	ci
2nd person	ti	vi
3rd person	si	si

The Italian reflexive pronoun is often not translated in English → ❶

Plural reflexive pronouns can sometimes be translated as 'each other' → ❷

Simple tenses of reflexive verbs are conjugated in exactly the same way as other verbs, except that the reflexive pronoun is always used. Compound tenses are conjugated with the auxiliary **essere**. A sample reflexive verb is conjugated in full on pages 36 and 37.

Position of Reflexive Pronouns

The pronoun generally comes before the verb → ❸

However, in positive 2nd person commands the pronoun is joined onto the end of the imperative → ❹

In the infinitive, the final **e** is dropped and replaced by the reflexive pronoun → ❺

When the infinitive is used with **non** in negative commands, the reflexive pronoun **ti** either comes first, as a separate word, or is joined on at the end → ❻

Two alternatives also exist
- when the infinitive is used after another verb, the pronoun either goes before the main verb or joins onto the infinitive → ❼
- in continuous tenses the pronoun either goes before the main verb or joins onto the gerund → ❽

1 Mi annoio — I'm getting bored
Ti fidi di lui? — Do you trust him?
Si vergogna — He's embarrassed
Non vi preoccupate! — Don't worry!

2 Si odiano — They hate each other

3 Mi diverto — I'm enjoying myself
Ci prepariamo — We're getting ready
Si accomodi! — Take a seat!

4 Svegliati! — Wake up!
Divertitevi! — Enjoy yourselves!

5 Compare:

ordinary infinitive	reflexive infinitive
lavare to wash	lavarsi to get washed, wash oneself
divertire to amuse	divertirsi to enjoy oneself

6 Non ti bruciare! or
Non bruciarti! — Don't burn yourself!
Non ti preoccupare! or
Non preoccuparti! — Don't worry!

Mi voglio abbronzare or
Voglio abbronzarmi — I want to get a tan
Ti devi alzare or
Devi alzarti — You must get up
Vi dovreste preparare or
Dovreste prepararvi — You ought to get ready

7 Ti stai annoiando? or
Stai annoiandoti? — Are you getting bored?
Si stanno alzando? or
Stanno alzandosi? — Are they getting up?

Reflexive Verbs *continued*

Past Participle Agreement

The past participle used in compound tenses of reflexive verbs generally agrees with the subject of the verb → ❶

Here are some common reflexive verbs:

accomodarsi to sit down/take a seat
addormentarsi to go to sleep
alzarsi to get up
annoiarsi to get bored/be bored
arrabbiarsi to get angry
cambiarsi to get changed
chiamarsi to be called
chiedersi to wonder
divertirsi to enjoy oneself/have fun
farsi male to hurt oneself
fermarsi to stop
lavarsi to wash/get washed
perdersi to get lost
pettinarsi to comb one's hair
preoccuparsi to worry
prepararsi to get ready
ricordarsi to remember
sbrigarsi to hurry
sedersi to sit
svegliarsi to wake up
vestirsi to dress/get dressed

Examples

1 Si è lavato le mani   He washed his hands
Si è lavata le mani   She washed her hands
I ragazzi si sono lavati le mani   The boys washed their hands
Le ragazze si sono lavate le mani   The girls washed their hands

Reflexive Verbs *continued*

Conjugation of: **divertirsi** to enjoy oneself – SIMPLE TENSES

PRESENT

mi diverto	ci divertiamo
ti diverti	vi divertite
si diverte	si divertono

IMPERFECT

mi divertivo	ci divertivamo
ti divertivi	vi divertivate
si divertiva	si divertivano

FUTURE

mi divertirò	ci divertiremo
ti divertirai	vi divertirete
si divertirà	si divertiranno

CONDITIONAL

mi divertirei	ci divertiremmo
ti divertiresti	vi divertireste
si divertirebbe	si divertirebbero

PAST HISTORIC

mi divertii	ci divertimmo
ti divertisti	vi divertiste
si divertì	si divertirono

PRESENT SUBJUNCTIVE

mi diverta	ci divertiamo
ti diverta	vi divertiate
si diverta	si divertano

IMPERFECT SUBJUNCTIVE

mi divertissi	ci divertissimo
ti divertissi	vi divertiste
si divertisse	si divertissero

Conjugation of: **divertirsi** to enjoy oneself – COMPOUND TENSES

PRESENT CONTINUOUS

mi sto divertendo *or*	ci stiamo divertendo *or*
sto divertendomi	stiamo divertendoci
ti stai divertendo *or*	vi state divertendo *or*
stai divertendoti	state divertendovi
si sta divertendo *or*	si stanno divertendo *or*
sta divertendosi	stanno divertendosi

PERFECT

mi sono divertito(a)	ci siamo divertiti(e)
ti sei divertito(a)	vi siete divertiti(e)
si è divertito(a)	si sono divertiti(e)

PLUPERFECT

mi ero divertito(a)	ci eravamo divertiti(e)
ti eri divertito(a)	vi eravate divertiti(e)
si era divertito(a)	si erano divertiti(e)

FUTURE PERFECT

mi sarò divertito(a)	ci saremo divertiti(e)
ti sarai divertito(a)	vi sarete divertiti(e)
si sarà divertito(a)	si saranno divertiti(e)

PERFECT CONDITIONAL

mi sarei divertito(a)	ci saremmo divertiti(e)
ti saresti divertito(a)	vi sareste divertiti(e)
si sarebbe divertito(a)	si sarebbero divertiti(e)

PAST ANTERIOR

mi fui divertito(a)	ci fummo divertiti(e)
ti fosti divertito(a)	vi foste divertiti(e)
si fu divertito(a)	si furono divertiti(e)

PERFECT SUBJUNCTIVE

mi sia divertito(a)	ci siamo divertiti(e)
ti sia divertito(a)	vi siate divertiti(e)
si sia divertito(a)	si siano divertiti(e)

PLUPERFECT SUBJUNCTIVE

mi fossi divertito(a)	ci fossimo divertiti(e)
ti fossi divertito(a)	vi foste divertiti(e)
si fosse divertito(a)	si fossero divertiti(e)

The Passive

In the passive, the subject *receives* the action (e.g. I was hit) as opposed to *performing* it (e.g. I hit him). In English the passive is formed with the verb 'to be' and the past participle, and in Italian the passive is formed in exactly the same way, i.e. a tense of **essere** + *past participle*.

The past participle agrees in gender and number with the subject → ➊

A sample verb is conjugated in the passive on pages 40 and 41.

In English it is possible to make the indirect object of an active sentence into the subject of a passive sentence, e.g. Someone told me → I was told.

This is not possible in Italian; instead a 3rd person plural can be used → ➋

The passive is used less overall in Italian. The following alternatives are used:
- active constructions → ➌
- the **si passivante** (preceding an active verb with **si**, to make it passive → ➍
- an impersonal construction with **si** → ➎

1 È stato costretto a ritirarsi
dalla gara

He was forced to withdraw from
the competition

L'elettricità è stata tagliata ieri

The electricity was cut off
yesterday

La partita è stata rinviata

The match has been postponed

Siamo invitati ad una festa a
casa loro

We're invited to a party at their
house

I ladri sono stati catturati

The thieves have been caught

Le finestre saranno riparate
domani

The windows will be repaired
tomorrow

2 Mi hanno dato una chiave

I've been given a key

Gli diranno tutto

He'll be told everything

3 Due persone sono morte

Two people were killed

Mi hanno rubato la macchina la
settimana scorsa

My car was stolen last week

C'erano delle microspie nella
stanza

The room was bugged

Dicono che sia molto ambizioso

He's said to be very ambitious

4 Dove si trovano i vini migliori?

Where are the best wines to be
found?

Non si accettano assegni

Cheques are not accepted

Queste parole non si usano più

These words are no longer used

Questo vino si beve a temperatura
ambiente

This wine should be drunk at
room temperature

5 Non si fa così

That's not how it's done

Si raccomanda la massima
discrezione

The utmost discretion is called
for

The Passive *continued*

Conjugation of: **invitare** to invite

PRESENT

sono invitato(a)	siamo invitati(e)
sei invitato(a)	siete invitati(e)
è invitato(a)	sono invitati(e)

IMPERFECT

ero invitato(a)	ervamo invitati(e)
eri invitato(a)	eravate invitati(e)
era invitato(a)	erano invitati(e)

FUTURE

sarò invitato(a)	saremo invitati(e)
sarai invitato(a)	sarete invitati(e)
sarà invitato(a)	saranno invitati(e)

CONDITIONAL

sarei invitato(a)	saremmo invitati(e)
saresti invitato(a)	sareste invitati(e)
sarebbe invitato(a)	sarebbero invitati(e)

PAST HISTORIC

fui invitato(a)	fummo invitati(e)
fosti invitato(a)	foste invitati(e)
fu invitato(a)	furono invitati(e)

PRESENT SUBJUNCTIVE

sia invitato(a)	siamo invitati(e)
sia invitato(a)	siate invitati(e)
sia invitato(a)	siano invitati(e)

IMPERFECT SUBJUNCTIVE

fossi invitato(a)	fossimo invitati(e)
fossi invitato(a)	foste invitati(e)
fosse invitato(a)	fossero invitati(e)

The Passive *continued*

Conjugation of: **invitare** to invite

PERFECT
sono stato(a) invitato(a) siamo stati(e) invitati(e)
sei stato(a) invitato(a) siete stati(e) invitati(e)
è stato(a) invitato(a) sono stati(e) invitati(e)

PLUPERFECT
ero stato(a) invitato(a) eravamo stati(e) invitati(e)
eri stato(a) invitato(a) eravate stati(e) invitati(e)
era stato(a) invitato(a) erano stati(e) invitati(e)

FUTURE PERFECT
sarò stato(a) invitato(a) saremo stati(e) invitati(e)
sarai stato(a) invitato(a) sarete stati(e) invitati(e)
sarà stato(a) invitato(a) saranno stati(e) invitati(e)

PERFECT CONDITIONAL
sarei stato(a) invitato(a) saremmo stati(e) invitati(e)
saresti stato(a) invitato(a) sareste stati(e) invitati(e)
sarebbe stato(a) invitato(a) sarebbero stati(e) invitati(e)

PAST ANTERIOR
fui stato(a) invitato(a) fummo stati(e) invitati(e)
fosti stato(a) invitato(a) foste stati(e) invitati(e)
fu stato(a) invitato(a) furono stati(e) invitati(e)

PERFECT SUBJUNCTIVE
sia stato(a) invitato(a) siamo stati(e) invitati(e)
sia stato(a) invitato(a) siate stati(e) invitati(e)
sia stato(a) invitato(a) siano stati(e) invitati(e)

PLUPERFECT SUBJUNCTIVE
fossi stato(a) invitato(a) fossimo stati(e) invitati(e)
fossi stato(a) invitato(a) foste stati(e) invitati(e)
fosse stato(a) invitato(a) fossero stati(e) invitati(e)

Impersonal Verbs

Any verb can be made impersonal by the use of **si** → ❶

si is often used to make the following verbs impersonal:

dire	**si dice che** → ❷ it's said that
potere	**si può** → ❸ it's possible to/you can
trattarsi	**si tratta di** → ❹ it's about/it's a matter of

Impersonal verbs are used only in the infinitive, with a gerund and in third person singular simple tenses. No pronoun is used in Italian.

e.g.	**Ha iniziato a piovere.**	It started to rain.
	Sta piovendo?	Is it raining?
	Nevicava da due giorni.	It had been snowing for two days.
	È facile capire che…	It's easy to see that…

Common impersonal verbs are:

diluviare	diluvia	it's pouring
gelare	gela	it's freezing
grandinare	grandina	it's hailing
nevicare	nevica	it's snowing
piovere	piove	it's raining
tuonare	tuona	it's thundering

Other verbs are often used impersonally:

bastare	basta	that's enough
importare	non importa	it doesn't matter

1. In quel ristorante si mangia bene e si spende poco

   In that restaurant the food's good and it doesn't cost much

2. Si dice che sia una persona strana

   It's said that he's a strange person

3. Si può visitare il castello tutti i giorni dell'anno

   You can visit the castle every day of the year

4. Di cosa si tratta?
   Si tratta di poche ore

   What's it about?
   It's a matter of a few hours

Impersonal Verbs *continued*

The following verbs are used in impersonal constructions:

INFINITIVE	CONSTRUCTIONS
bastare	**basta** + *infinitive* → ❶ you just have to
bisognare	**bisogna** + *infinitive* → ❷ you have to
convenire	*indirect pronoun* + **conviene** + *infinitive* → ❸ it's best to
essere	**è** + *noun to do with time/season* → ❹
sono	+ *plural times of the clock* → ❺ it is **è** + *adjective* + *infinitive* → ❻ **è** + *adjective* + **che** → ❼ it is
fare	**fa** + *adjective describing weather* → ❽ it is **fa** + *noun to do with weather, time of day*
occorrere	**occorre** + *infinitive* → ❾ it would be best to
parere	**pare** + **di** + **sì/no** → ❿ it seems so/not **pare** + **che** → ⓫ it seems/apparently
sembrare	**sembra** + **che** → ⓬ it seems

1 Basta chiedere a qualcuno — You just have to ask someone

2 Bisogna prenotare? — Do you have to book?
Bisogna arrivare un'ora prima — You have to get there an hour before

3 Conviene partire presto — It's best to set off early

4 È tardi. — It's late
Era presto — It was early
Era Pasqua — It was Easter
È mezzogiorno — It's midday

5 Sono le otto — It's eight o'clock

6 È stato stupido buttarli via — It was stupid to throw them away
Sarebbe bello andarci — It would be nice to go there

7 È vero che sono stato impaziente — It's true that I've been impatient
È possibile che abbia sbagliato tu — Maybe you made a mistake

8 Fa caldo — It's hot
Fa freddo — It's cold
Faceva bel tempo — It was good weather or The weather was good

Fa sempre brutto tempo — The weather's always bad
Si sta facendo buio — It's getting dark

9 Occorre farlo subito — It would be best to do it immediately

10 Sono contenti? – Pare di sì. — Are they happy? – It seems so.
L'ha creduto? – Pare di no. — Did he believe it? – Apparently not.

11 Pare che sia stato lui — Apparently it was him

12 Sembra che tu abbia ragione — It seems you're right

The Infinitive

The infinitive is the form of the verb found in dictionary entries, e.g. **parlare** to speak; **finire** to finish. The infinitive sometimes drops its final -**e**.

All regular verbs have infinitives ending in -**are**, -**ere**, or -**ire**.

A few irregular verbs have infinitives ending in -**rre**, e.g.

comporre	to compose	**condurre**	to lead
porre	to put	**produrre**	to produce
proporre	to propose	**ridurre**	to reduce
supporre	to suppose	**tradurre**	to translate

In Italian the infinitive is used in the following ways:
- after adjectives and nouns that are followed by **di** → ❶
- after another verb → ❷
- to give instructions and orders → ❸
- in 2nd person negative imperatives → ❹

See page 20 for negative imperatives

- after prepositions → ❺

See pages 190-197 for prepositions

- as the subject or object of a sentence → ❻

There are three main types of constructions when the infinitive follows another verb:
- no linking preposition → ❼
- linking preposition **a** (see also pages 70-78) → ❽
- linking preposition **di** (see also pages 70-78) → ❾

1. Sono contento di vederti — I'm glad to see you
   Sono sorpreso di vederti qui — I'm surprised to see you here
   Sono stufo di studiare — I'm fed up of studying
   Non c'è bisogno di prenotare — There's no need to book

2. Non devi mangiare se non vuoi — You don't have to eat if you don't want to
   Posso entrare? — Can I come in?
   Cosa ti piacerebbe fare? — What would you like to do?

3. Rallentare — Slow down
   Spingere — Push

4. Non fare sciocchezze! — Don't do anything silly!
   Non toccarlo! — Don't touch it!

5. È andato via senza dire niente — He went away without saying anything

6. Camminare fa bene — Walking is good for you
   Mi piace cavalcare — I like riding

7. Devi aspettare — You must wait

8. Hanno cominciato a ridere — They started to laugh

9. Quando sono entrato hanno smesso di parlare — When I came in they stopped talking

The Infinitive *continued*

Verbs followed by the infinitive with no linking preposition

dovere, **potere**, **sapere**, **volere** (i.e. modal auxiliary verbs: page 58).

verbs of seeing and hearing, e.g. **vedere** to see; **sentire** to hear → ❶

Verbs used impersonally such as **piacere**, **dispiacere**, **occorrere** and **convenire** → ❷

fare → ❸

lasciare to let, allow → ❹

The following common verbs:

bisognare → ❺	to be necessary
detestare	to hate
desiderare → ❻	to want
odiare → ❼	to hate
preferire → ❽	to prefer

1 Ci ha visto arrivare
He saw us arriving

Ti ho sentito cantare
I heard you singing

2 Mi piace andare in bici
I like cycling

Ci dispiace andar via
We're sorry to be leaving

Occorre farlo subito
It should be done immediately

Ti conviene partire presto
You'd best set off early

3 Non mi far ridere!
Don't make me laugh!

4 Lascia fare a me
Let me do it

5 Bisogna prenotare
You need to book

6 Desiderava migliorare il suo inglese
He wanted to improve his English

7 Odio alzarmi presto al mattino
I hate getting up early in the morning

8 Preferisco non parlarne
I prefer not to talk about it

The Infinitive *continued*

Set expressions

The following are set in Italian with the meaning shown:

> **far entrare** to let in → ❶
> **far sapere** to inform/let someone know → ❷
> **far fare** to have done → ❸
> **farsi fare** to have done → ❹
> **lasciare stare** to leave alone → ❺
> **sentir dire che** to hear that → ❻
> **sentir parlare di** to hear about → ❼
> **voler dire** to mean → ❽

The Perfect Infinitive

The perfect infinitive is formed using the auxiliary verb **avere** or **essere** (as appropriate) with the past participle of the verb → ❾

The perfect infinitive is found:
- after modal verbs → ❿
- after prepositions → ⓫

Examples

1. Non mi hanno fatto entrare — They wouldn't let me in

2. Ti farò sapere prima possibile — I'll let you know as soon as possible

3. Ho fatto riparare la macchina — I had the car repaired

4. Mi sono fatta tagliare i capelli — I had my hair cut

5. Lascia stare mia sorella! — Leave my sister alone!

6. Ho sentito dire che è stato licenziato — I heard he's been sacked

7. Non ho più sentito parlare di loro — I haven't heard any more about them

8. Non so che cosa vuol dire — I don't know what it means

9. aver(e) visto — to have seen
   essere partito — to have gone
   essersi fatto male — to have hurt oneself

10. Può aver avuto un incidente — He may have had an accident
    Dev'essere successo ieri — It must have happened yesterday

11. senza aver dato un esame — without having done an exam
    dopo essere rimasto chiuso — after having been closed

The Gerund

Formation

First conjugation:

Replace the **-are** of the infinitive with **-ando** → **❶**

Second and Third conjugations:

Replace the **-ere**, or **-ire** of the infinitive with **-endo** → **❷**

Exceptions to these rules are:

fare and verbs made by adding a prefix to **fare** → **❸**
dire and verbs made by adding a prefix to **dire** → **❹**
porre and verbs made by adding a prefix to **porre** → **❺**
verbs with infinitives ending in **-durre** → **❻**

The gerund is invariable.*

*A word that is invariable never changes its ending.

❶ parlare to speak → parlando speaking
andare to go → andando going
dare to give → dando giving

❷ credere to believe → credendo believing
essere to be → essendo being
dovere to have to → dovendo having to
finire to finish → finendo finishing
dormire to sleep → dormendo sleeping

❸ fare to do → facendo doing
rifare to redo → rifacendo redoing

❹ dire to say → dicendo saying
contraddire to contradict → contraddicendo contradicting

❺ porre to put → ponendo putting
comporre to compose → componendo composing
supporre to suppose → supponendo supposing

❻ condurre to lead → conducendo leading
produrre to produce → producendo producing
ridurre to reduce → riducendo reducing

The Gerund *continued*

Uses

The gerund is used with the present tense of **stare** to make the present continuous tense → ❶

The gerund is used with the imperfect tense of **stare** to make the past continuous tense → ❷

ⓘ Note that the Italian past participle is sometimes used with the verbs **stare** or **essere** to make a continuous tense, e.g.

essere or **stare disteso**	to be lying → ❸
essere or **stare seduto**	to be sitting → ❸
essere or **stare appoggiato**	to be leaning → ❸

The gerund can used adverbially, to indicate when or why something happens → ❹

Pronouns are usually joined onto the end of the gerund → ❺

When the gerund is part of a continuous tense the pronoun can either come before **stare** or be joined onto the gerund → ❻

Examples

1   Sto lavorando   I'm working
     Cosa stai facendo?   What are you doing?

2   Il bambino stava piangendo   The little boy was crying
     Stavo lavando i piatti   I was washing the dishes

3   Era disteso sul divano   He was lying on the sofa
     Stava seduta accanto a me   She was sitting next to me
     La scala era appoggiata al muro   The ladder was leaning against the wall

4   Entrando ho sentito odore di pesce   When I came in I could smell fish
     Ripensandoci, credo che non fosse colpa sua   Thinking back on it, I reckon it wasn't his fault
     Vedendolo solo, è venuta a parlargli   Seeing that he was on his own, she came to speak to him
     Sentendomi male, sono andato a letto   Because I felt ill I went to bed
     Volendo, potremmo comprarne un altro   If we wanted to, we could buy another

5   Vedendoli è scoppiata in lacrime   When she saw them she burst into tears
     Mi sono addormentato ascoltandolo   As I listened to him I fell asleep
     Sbagliando si impara   You learn by making mistakes

6   Ti sto parlando *or*
     Sto parlandoti   I'm talking to you
     Si sta vestendo *or*
     Sta vestendosi   He's getting dressed
     Me lo stavano mostrando *or*
     Stavano mostrandomelo   They were showing me it

Past Participle Agreement

For the formation of the past participle, see page 24.

Note that many Italian verbs have irregular past participles → ❶

Past participles are sometimes like adjectives, and change their endings. For the rules of agreement, see below:

		MASCULINE	FEMININE
SING.	1ˢᵗ conj	andato	andata
SING.	2ⁿᵈ conj	caduto	caduta
SING.	3ʳᵈ conj	uscito	uscita
PLUR.	1ˢᵗ conj	andati	andate
PLUR.	2ⁿᵈ conj	caduti	cadute
PLUR.	3ʳᵈ conj	usciti	uscite

Rules of Agreement in Compound Tenses

When the auxiliary verb is **avere**:

> The past participle generally remains in the masculine singular form → ❷

> EXCEPTION: When the object of the verb is **la** (*feminine*: her/it), **li** (*masculine plural*: them) or **le** (*feminine plural*: them), the participle agrees with **la**, **li** or **le** → ❸

When the auxiliary verb is **essere**:

> The past participle agrees in number and gender with the subject → ❹

For the agreement of the past participle with reflexive verbs, see page 34.

The Past Participle as an adjective

When a past participles is used as an adjective it agrees in the normal way → ❺

Examples

1 crescere to grow   cresciuto grown
dire to say   detto said
fare to do   fatto done
porre to put   posto put

2 Mio fratello ha comprato una macchina   My brother has bought a car

Mia sorella ha comprato una macchina   My sister has bought a car

I ragazzi hanno comprato dei gelati   The children bought ice creams

3 Dov'è Marco? L'hai visto?   Where's Marco? Have you seen him?

Dov'è Silvia? L'hai vista?   Where's Silvia? Have you seen her?

Dove sono i ragazzi? Li hai visti?   Where are the boys? Have you seen them?

Dove sone le ragazze? Le hai viste?   Where are the girls? Have you seen them?

4 È andato a casa   He's gone home
È andata a casa   She's gone home
I ragazzi sono usciti   The boys have gone out
Le ragazze sono uscite   The girls have gone out
Si è fatto male?   Has he hurt himself?
Si è fatta male?   Has she hurt herself?
Vi siete fatti male, ragazzi?   Have you hurt yourselves, boys?
Vi siete fatte male, ragazze?   Have you hurt yourselves, girls?

5 È chiuso il supermercato?   Is the supermarket closed?
È chiusa la banca?   Is the bank closed?
Sono chiuse le finestre?   Are the windows closed?

Modal Auxiliary Verbs

In Italian, the modal auxiliary verbs (i verbi servili) are: **dovere, potere, sapere** and **volere**.

They are followed by the infinitive (without a connecting preposition) and have the following meanings:

dovere	to have to, must → ❶
	to be going to, to be supposed to → ❷
	in the present conditional/perfect conditional:
	should/should have, ought/ought to have → ❸
potere	to be able to, can → ❹
	to be allowed to, can, may → ❺
	indicating possibility: may/might/could → ❻
sapere	to know how to, can → ❼
volere	to want/wish to → ❽
	with negative won't/wouldn't → ❾
	in polite phrases → ❿

Compound Tenses of dovere and potere

dovere and **potere** are conjugated with **avere** if the following verb is conjugated with **avere**, e.g. **dare, risolvere** → ⑪

dovere and **potere** are generally conjugated with **essere** if the following verb is conjugated with **essere**, e.g. **andare, partire, alzarsi** → ⑫

EXCEPTION: **avere** is used in compound tenses of **dovere** and **potere** when followed by **essere**, e.g. **Avrebbe dovuto essere più freddo** It should have been colder

Examples

1 Devi farlo proprio adesso?	Do you have to do it right now?
È dovuta partire	She had to leave
Dev'essere caro	It must be expensive
2 Deve scendere qui?	Are you going to get off here?
Dovevo venire, ma poi non ho avuto tempo	I was going to come, but then I didn't have time
Dovevano arrivare ieri sera	They were supposed to arrive yesterday evening
3 Dovresti parlargli	You should speak to him
Avrei dovuto stare più attento	I should have been more careful
4 Non potrò venire domani	I won't be able to come tomorrow
Cosa posso dire?	What can I say?
5 Posso entrare?	May I come in?
Non si può parcheggiare qui	You can't park here
6 Può anche essere vero	It may/might even be true
Potrebbe piovere	It may/might/could rain
7 Sai guidare?	Can you drive?
Non so fare gli gnocchi	I don't know how to make gnocchi
8 Vuole rimanere ancora un giorno	He wants to stay another day
9 Non vuole aiutarci	She won't help us
Non voleva ascoltarmi	He wouldn't listen to me
10 Vuole bere qualcosa?	Would you like something to drink?
11 Ho dovuto darglielo	I had to give it to him
Ho potuto risolvere il problema	I was able to sort out the problem
12 È dovuta partire subito	She had to leave immediately
Siamo dovuti alzarci presto	We had to get up early
Lara è potuta venire	Lara was able to come
Non sono potuti decidersi	They couldn't decide
Si sarebbero potuti sbagliare	They could have been mistaken

Use of Tenses

The Present

The Italian simple present can be used to translate both the English simple present, e.g. I work, and the English present continuous, e.g. I'm working → ➊

The Italian present continuous tense is also used for continuous actions → ➋

Italian uses the present tense with the preposition **da** to describe an action that *has been continuing for* some time, or *has continued since* some time in the past → ➌

The Italian present is also used
  * for the immediate future → ➍
  * for offers → ➎
  * for arrangements → ➏
  * for predictions → ➐
  * when asking for suggestions → ➑

The Future

The future is generally used as in English, but note the following:

> the future tense is used after **quando**, if the verb in the main clause is in the future → ➒

The Future Perfect

It is used as in English to mean 'shall/will have done' → ➓

It is also used in time clauses relating to the future, where English uses the perfect → ⑪

1 Dove abitano? — Where do they live?
Dove abitano adesso? — Where are they living now?
Piove molto qui — It rains a lot here
Ora piove — It's raining now

2 Cosa stai facendo? *or* Cosa fai? — What are you doing?
Sta piovendo *or* Piove — It's raining

3 Studio italiano da due anni — I've been learning Italian for two years

Aspettiamo da un'ora — We've been waiting for an hour
Lavora qui da settembre — She's been working here since September

Non lo vedo da un pezzo — I haven't seen him for a while
Vivono qui dal 2006 — They've lived here since 2006

4 Prendo un espresso — I'll have an espresso
È rotto, lo butto via — It's broken, I'm going to throw it away

5 Pago io! — I'll pay!
Devo tornare a casa – Ti porto io! — I need to go home – I'll take you!

6 Parto alle due — I'm leaving at two
Domani gioco a tennis — I'm playing tennis tomorrow

7 Se fai così lo rompi — If you do that you'll break it
Se piove non viene nessuno — If it rains nobody will come

8 Dove lo metto? — Where shall I put it?
Cosa facciamo? — What shall we do?

9 Quando finirò, verrò da te *or* Quando finisco, vengo da te — When I finish I'll come to yours
Lo comprerò quando avrò abbastanza soldi — I'll buy it when I've got enough money
Quando verrà saremo già in vacanza — When he comes we'll be on holiday

10 Avrò finito fra un'ora — I'll have finished in an hour

11 Quando l'avrai letto ritornamelo — When you've read it let me have it back

Partirò quando avrò finito — I'll leave when I've finished

Use of Tenses *continued*

The Imperfect

The imperfect describes:
- an action (or state) in the past without definite time limits → **①**
- habitual action(s) in the past (often translated by 'would' or 'used to') → **②**

Italian uses the imperfect tense with the preposition **da** to describe an action that *had been continuing for* some time, or *had continued since* some time in the past → **③**

The Perfect

The Italian perfect tense corresponds to both the English perfect tense and the English simple past → **④**

The Past Historic

The past historic, used mainly in written Italian, and in the south of Italy, corresponds to the English simple past → **⑤**

The Past Anterior

This tense is used instead of the pluperfect when a verb in another part of the sentence is in the past historic → **⑥**

The Perfect Conditional

The perfect conditional, not the present conditional, is used in reported speech → **⑦**

① Avevo la febbre — I had a temperature
Non ne sapeva niente — He didn't know anything about it
Guardavo la tivù — I was watching TV

② Ti prendevano in giro, vero? — They used to tease you, didn't they?

Facevamo lunghissime passeggiate — We would go for very long walks

Mi raccontava delle belle storie — She used to tell me lovely stories

③ Studiavo italiano da due anni — I had been learning Italian for two years

Aspettavamo da molto tempo — We had been waiting for a long time

Lavorava a Roma dal 2000 — She'd been working in Rome since 2000

Non lo vedevo da un pezzo — I hadn't seen him for a while

④ Non l'ho mai visto — I've never seen it
Non l'ho visto ieri — I didn't see it yesterday
Sono stata in città — I've been to town
Stamattina sono stata in città — I went to town this morning

⑤ Dormimmo profondamente e ci svegliammo riposati — We slept soundly and awoke refreshed

⑥ Mi addormentai dopo che se ne furono andati — I went to sleep after they had gone

⑦ Ha detto che mi avrebbe aiutato — He said he would help me
Ho detto che avrei pagato la metà — I said I'd pay half
Hanno promesso che sarebbero venuti — They promised they would come

The Subjunctive

When to use it

For how to form the subjunctive see page 8 onwards.

The subjunctive follows the conjunction **che**:

- when used with verbs expressing belief or hope, such as **credere, pensare** and **sperare** → ①
- when used with verbs and expressions expressing uncertainty → ②
- when it is used with **volere**. The Italian subjunctive + **che** corresponds to the infinitive construction in English → ③
- following impersonal verbs → ④
- after impersonal constructions which express necessity, possibility etc:

è meglio che	it's better (that) → ⑤
è possibile che	it's possible (that) → ⑥
è facile che	it's likely (that) → ⑦
può darsi che	it's possible (that) → ⑧
non è che	it's not that → ⑨
sembra che	it seems (that) → ⑩

1. | | |
|---|---|
| Penso che sia giusto | I think it's fair |
| Credo che partano domani | I think they're leaving tomorrow |
| Spero che Luca arrivi in tempo | I hope Luca arrives in time |

2. | | |
|---|---|
| Non so se sia la risposta giusta | I don't know if it's the right answer |
| Non sono sicura che tu abbia ragione | I'm not sure you're right |

3. | | |
|---|---|
| Voglio che i miei ragazzi siano felici | I want my children to be happy |
| Vuole che la aiuti | She wants me to help her |
| Non voglio che mi parlino | I don't want them to speak to me |

4. Mi dispiace che non siano qui — I'm sorry they're not here

5. È meglio che tu te ne vada — You'd better leave

6. È possibile che siano stranieri — It's possible they're foreigners

7. È facile che scelgano quelli rossi — They'll probably choose those red ones

8. Può darsi che non venga — It's possible that he won't come

9. Non è che si debba sempre dire la verità — You don't always have to tell the truth

10. Sembra che abbiano vinto — It seems they've won

The Subjunctive *continued*

The subjunctive is used:

- after the following conjunctions:

prima che	before → ❶
affinché	so that → ❷
a meno che	unless → ❸
benché	although → ❹
nel caso che	in case → ❺
nonostante	even though → ❻
perché	so (that) → ❼
per quanto	however → ❽
purché	as long as → ❾
sebbene	even though → ❿

- after superlatives → ⑪
  la più grande che ci sia   the biggest there is

- after:
  chiunque whoever → ⑫
  qualunque + *noun* whatever → ⑬
  per quanto however → ⑭

Note that **che** is not always followed by the subjunctive.

The indicative follows **che** when it is used with positive uses of **sapere** to know, and with other expressions indicating certainty, such as **Sono sicuro** *I'm sure* → ⑮

Examples

1. Vuoi parlargli prima che parta?

   Do you want to speak to him before he goes?

2. Ti do venti euro affinché tu possa comprarlo

   I'll give you twenty euros so that you can buy it

3. Lo prendo io, a meno che lo voglia tu

   I'll take it, unless you want it

4. Mi aiutò a fare i compiti benché fosse molto stanca

   She helped me do my homework she was very tired

5. Vi do il mio numero di telefono

   I'll give you my phone number in case

   nel caso che veniate a Roma

   you come to Rome

6. Vuole alzarsi, nonostante sia ancora malato

   He wants to get up even though he's still ill

7. Lo metto qui perché tutti possano usarlo

   I'll put it here so everyone can use it

8. Per quanto mi sforzi non riesco a capire

   I can't understand, however hard I try

9. Vengo anch'io, purché possa pagare la mia parte

   I'll come too as long as I can pay my share

10. Mi prestò il denaro sebbene non ne avesse molto

    She lent me the money even though she hadn't got much

11. È la persona più simpatica che conosca

    He's the nicest person I know

12. Chiunque sia, digli che non ci sono

    Whoever it is, tell them I'm not here

13. qualunque cosa accada

    whatever happens

14. per quanto bello sia

    however nice it may be

15. So che non è suo
    Sai che ti piace
    Sono sicura che l'ha preso lui
    Sei sicuro che verranno?

    I know it's not hers
    You know you like it
    I'm sure he took it
    Are you sure they're coming?

The Subjunctive *continued*

The Perfect Subjunctive

The perfect subjunctive follows the conjunction **che**
- when it follows verbs such as **credere**, **pensare** and **sperare** relating to something in the past → ①
- when it follows an impersonal expression → ②
- when it follows a superlative → ③
- when it follows a conjunction ending in **che** → ④

The Imperfect Subjunctive

The imperfect subjunctive is used:
- following **che**, and other conjunctions, as above → ⑤
- with past tenses of **volere** + **che** → ⑥
- following **se** in conditional clauses describing hypothetical situations → ⑦

The Pluperfect Subjunctive

The pluperfect subjunctive is used:
- after **che**, in the same way as other tenses of the subjunctive → ⑧
- after other conjunctions → ⑨
- following **se** in conditional clauses describing past hypothetical situations → ⑩

Examples

1.   Penso che sia stata una buona idea   I think it was a good idea
   Spero che non si sia fatta male   I hope she didn't hurt herself
   Spero che *abbia* detto la verità   I hope you told the truth

2.   È possibile che *abbiano* cambiato idea   It's possible they've changed their minds
   Mi dispiace che *abbia* fatto brutto tempo   I'm sorry the weather was bad

3.   la più bella che *abbia* mai visto   the most beautiful one I've ever seen

4.   Sarà qui fra poco, a meno che *abbia* perso l'*au*tobus   He'll be here soon, unless he's missed the bus

5.   Voleva alzarsi nonostante fosse ancora malato   He wanted to get up, even though he was still ill

6.   Voleva che fossimo pronti alle otto   He wanted us to be ready at eight
   Volevano che tutto fosse in ordine   They wanted everything to be tidy
   Volevo che andasse più veloce   I wanted him to go faster
   Non volevo che mi parl*a*ssero   I didn't want them to speak to me

7.   Se tu ne avessi bisogno, te lo darei   If you needed it I'd give it to you
   Se potessi dormirei fino a tardi   If I could I'd have a lie-in
   Se lo sapesse sarebbe molto deluso   If he knew he'd be very disappointed
   Se solo avessi più denaro!   If only I had more money!

8.   Non pensavo che l'avesse fatto   I didn't think he'd done it
   Credevo che f*o*ssero partiti   I thought they had left
   Ero sicuro che avesse perso il treno   I was sure he'd missed the train
   la più bella che avessi mai visto   the most beautiful one I had ever seen

9.   Non ha detto niente nonostante si fosse fatto male   He didn't say anything even though he'd hurt himself

10.   Se avessi saputo non l'avrei mai fatto   If I had known, I'd never have done it
    Se fosse stato più furbo non avrebbe detto niente   If he'd had more sense he wouldn't have said anything
    Se l'avessi visto mi crederesti   If you'd seen, it you'd believe me
    Se solo mi avessi creduto!   If only you'd believed me!

Verbs governing a and di

The following list (pages 70 to 78) contain common verbal constructions using the prepositions **a** and **di**

Note the following abbreviations:

infin.	*infinitive*
perf. infin.	*perfect infinitive*
qc	qualcosa
qn	qualcuno
sb	somebody
sth	something

Verbs governing **a** may be followed by the stressed pronouns **me, te, lui, lei, noi, voi** and **loro** → ①

More often, however, they are preceded by an unstressed indirect pronoun, without **a** → ②

For stressed and unstressed pronouns see page 162.

abituarse qn a qc/a + *infin.*	to accustom sb to sth/to doing
abituarsi a + *infin.*	to get used to doing → ③
acconsentire a qc/a + *infin.*	to agree to sth/to do → ④
accorgersi di qc	to notice sth → ⑤
accusare qn di qc/di + *(perf.) infin.*	to accuse sb of sth/of doing, having done → ⑥
affrettarsi a + *infin.*	to hurry to do
aiutare qn a + *infin.*	to help sb to do → ⑦
andare a + *infin.*	to go to do
approfittare di qc/di + *infin.*	to take advantage of sth/of doing
aspettarsi di + *infin.*	to expect to do → ⑧
assistere a qc	to attend sth, be at sth
assomigliare a qn/qc	to look/be like sb/sth → ⑨
aver bisogno di qc /di + *infin.*	to need sth/to do sth
aver paura di qc/di + *infin.*	to be afraid to do/of doing
aver voglia di qc/di + *infin.*	to want sth/to do
avvicinarsi a qn/qc	to approach sb/sth → ⑩
badare a qc/qn	to look after sth/sb
cambiarsi di qc	to change sth → ⑪
cercare di + *infin.*	to try to do → ⑫

Examples

① Assomigli a lui, non a lei — You look like him, not like her

② Gli ho chiesto i soldi — I asked him for the money

③ Si è abituato a bere di meno — He got used to drinking less

④ Non hanno acconsentito a venderlo — They haven't agreed to sell it

⑤ Non si è accorto del mio errore — He didn't notice my mistake

⑥ Mi ha accusato d'aver mentito — He accused me of lying

⑦ Aiutatemi a portare queste valigie — Help me to carry these cases

⑧ Si aspettava di vederlo? — Was she expecting to see him?

⑨ Sara assomiglia molto a sua madre — Sara looks very like her mother

⑩ Si è avvicinata a me — She came up to me

⑪ Mi sono cambiato d'abito — I changed my clothes

⑫ Ho cercato di capirla — I tried to understand her

Verbs governing a and di *continued*

cessare di + *infin.*	to stop doing → ❶
chiedere qc a qn	to ask sb sth/for sth → ❷
chiedere a qn di + *infin.*	to ask sb to do → ❸
cominciare a + *infin.*	to begin to do, to start to do → ❹
comprare qc a qn	to buy sth from sb/for sb → ❺
consentire qc a qn	to allow sb sth
consentire a qn di + *infin.*	to allow sb to do
consigliare a qn di+ *infin.*	to advise sb to do → ❻
continuare a + *infin.*	to continue to do
convincere qn a + *infin.*	to persuade sb to do → ❼
dare la colpa a qn di qc	to blame sb for sth
decidere di + *infin.*	to decide to → ❽
decidersi a + *infin.*	to resolve to do, to make up one's mind to do
diffidare di qn	to distrust sb
dimenticare di + *infin.*	to forget to do → ❾
dire a qn di + *infin.*	to tell sb to do → ❿
discutere di qc	to discuss sth
disobbedire a qn	to disobey sb → ⓫
dispiacere a qn	to displease sb → ⓬
divertirsi a + *infin.*	to enjoy doing
domandare qc a qn	to ask sb sth/for sth
dubitare di qc	to doubt sth
esitare a + *infin.*	to hesitate to do
evitare di + *infin.*	to avoid doing → ⓭
far male a qn	to hurt sb
farcela a + *infin.*	to manage to do
fare a meno di qc	to do/go without sth → ⓮
fare finta di + *infin.*	to pretend to do → ⓯
fidarsi di qn	to trust sb → ⓰
fingere di + *infin.*	to pretend to do → ⓱
finire di + *infin.*	to finish doing → ⓲
forzare qn a + *infin.*	to force sb to do
giocare a (+ *sports, games*)	to play → ⓳
giurare di + *infin.*	to swear to do
godere di qc	to enjoy sth → ⓴

①	Ha cessato di piovere?	Has it stopped raining?
②	Ho chiesto a Paola che ora fosse	I asked Paola what time it was
③	Chiedi a Francesca di farlo	Ask Francesca to do it
④	Comincia a nevicare	It's starting to snow
⑤	Cristina ha comprato a Paolo due biglietti	Cristina bought two tickets for Paolo
⑥	Ha consigliato a Paolo di aspettare	He advised Paolo to wait
⑦	Ci ha convinto a restare	She persuaded us to stay
⑧	Cosa avete deciso di fare?	What have you decided to do?
⑨	Non dimenticarti di prendere l'ombrello	Don't forget to take your umbrella
⑩	Dì a Gigi di stare zitto	Tell Gigi to be quiet
⑪	Disobbediscono spesso ai genitori	They often disobey their parents
⑫	A me non dispiace il loro modo di fare	I quite like their attitude
⑬	Evita di parlarle	He avoids speaking to her
⑭	Ho fatto a meno dell'elettricità per diversi giorni	I did without electricity for several days
⑮	Ho fatto finta di non vederlo	I pretended not to see him
⑯	Non mi fido di quella gente	I don't trust those people
⑰	Finge di dormire	She's pretending to be asleep
⑱	Ha finito di leggere questo giornale?	Have you finished reading this newspaper?
⑲	Gioca a tennis	She plays tennis
⑳	Gode di buona salute	He enjoys good health

Verbs governing a and di *continued*

imparare a + *infin.*	to learn to do → ❶
impedire a qn di + *infin.*	to prevent sb from doing → ❷
impegnarsi a + *infin.*	to undertake to do
incaricarsi di qc/di + *infin.*	to see to sth/undertake to do
incoraggiare qn a + *infin.*	to encourage sb to do → ❸
iniziare a + *infin.*	to begin to do
insegnare qc a qn	to teach sb sth
insegnare a qn a + *infin.*	to teach sb to do → ❹
intendersi di qc	to know about sth
interessarsi a qn/qc	to be interested in sb/sth → ❺
invitare qn a + *infin.*	to invite sb to do → ❻
lagnarsi di qc	to complain about sth
lamentarsi di qc	to complain about sth
mancare a qn	to be missed by sb → ❼
mancare di qc	to lack sth
mancare di + *infin.*	to fail to do → ❽
meritare di + *infin.*	to deserve to do → ❾
mettersi a + *infin.*	to begin to do
minacciare di + *infin.*	to threaten to do → ❿
nascondere qc a qn	to hide sth from sb → ⓫
nuocere a qc	to harm sth, to damage sth → ⓬
obbligare qn a + *infin.*	to oblige/force sb to do → ⓭
occuparsi di qc/qn	to look after sth/sb → ⓮
offrirsi di + *infin.*	to offer to do → ⓯
omettere di + *infin.*	to fail to do
ordinare a qn di + *infin.*	to order sb to do → ⓰
partecipare a qc	to take part in sth
pensare a qn/qc	to think about sb/sth → ⓱
pentirsi di + *(perf.) infin.*	to regret doing, having done → ⓲
perdonare qc a qn	to forgive sb for sth
perdonare a qn di + *perf. infin.*	to forgive sb for doing → ⓳
permettere qc a qn	to allow sb sth
permettere a qn di + *infin.*	to allow sb to do → ⓴

Examples

1	Sta imparando a leggere	She's learning to read
2	Il rumore mi impedisce di lavorare	The noise is preventing me from working
3	Incoraggia i figli ad essere indipendenti	She encourages her children to be independent
4	Gli sto insegnando a nuotare	I'm teaching him to swim
5	Si interessa molto di sport	She's very interested in sport
6	Mi ha invitato a cenare da lui	He invited me for dinner at his house
7	Manchi molto ai tuoi genitori	Your parents miss you very much
8	Non mancherò di dirglielo	I'll be sure to tell him about it
9	Meritano di avere la promozione	They deserve to be promoted
10	Ha minacciato di dare le dimissioni	She threatened to resign
11	Nascondile il regalo!	Hide the present from her!
12	Il fumo nuoce alla salute di tutti	Smoking damages everybody's health
13	Li ha obbligati a farlo	He forced them to do it
14	Mi occupo di mia nipote	I'm looking after my niece
15	Marco si è offerto di venire con noi	Marco has offered to go with us
16	Ha ordinato loro di sparare	He ordered them to shoot
17	Penso spesso a te	I often think about you
18	Mi pento di averglielo detto	I'm sorry I told him
19	Hai perdonato Carlo di averti mentito?	Have you forgiven Carlo for lying to you?
20	Permettetemi di continuare, per favore	Allow me to go on, please

75

Verbs governing a and di *continued*

persuadere qn a + *infin.*	to persuade sb to do
piacere a qn	to please sb → ①
portare via qc a qn	to take sth away from sb
pregare qn a + *infin.*	to beg sb to do
prendere qc a qn	to take sth from sb → ②
prendersi gioco di qn/qc	to make fun of sb/sth
preparare qn a + *infin.*	to prepare sb to do
prepararsi a + *infin.*	to get ready to do
proibire a qn di + *infin.*	to forbid sb to do → ③
promettere qc a qn	to promise sb sth
promettere a qn di + *infin.*	to promise sb to do → ④
proporre di + *infin.*	to suggest doing → ⑤
provare a + *infin.*	to try to do
rammaricarsi di + *(perf.) infin.*	to regret doing, having done
resistere a qc	to resist sth → ⑥
ricordarsi di qn/qc/di + *(perf.) infin.*	to remember sb/sth/doing, having done → ⑦
ridere di qn/qc	to laugh at sb/sth
rifiutarsi di + *infin.*	to refuse to do → ⑧
rimpiangere di + *(perf.) infin.*	to regret doing, having done
rimproverare qc a qn	to reproach sb with/for sth → ⑨
ringraziare qn di qc/di + *(perf.) infin.*	to thank sb for sth/for doing, having done → ⑩
rinunciare a qc/a + *infin.*	to give up sth /give up doing
rischiare di + *infin.*	to risk doing → ⑪
rispondere a qn	to answer sb
riuscire a + *infin.*	to manage to do → ⑫
rivolgersi a qn	to ask sb
rubare qc a qn	to steal sth from sb
scordare di + *infin.*	to forget to do
scordarsi di + *infin.*	to forget to do
scusarsi di qc/di + *(perf.) infin.*	to apologize for sth/for doing, having done → ⑬
servire a qc/a + *infin.*	to be used for sth/for doing → ⑭
servirsi di qc	to use sth → ⑮
sforzarsi di + *infin.*	to make an effort to do
smettere di + *infin.*	to stop doing → ⑯
sognare di + *infin.*	to dream of doing

Examples

1. A lui piace questo genere di film | He likes this kind of film

2. Gli ho preso il cellulare | I took his mobile phone from him

3. Ho proibito loro di uscire | I've forbidden them to go out

4. Hanno promesso a Luca di venire | They promised Luca they would come

5. Ho proposto a mio fratello di invitarli | I suggested to my brother that he should invite them

6. Come riesci a resistere alla tentazione? | How do you manage to resist the temptation?

7. Vi ricordate di Luciana? Non si ricorda di averlo perso | Do you remember Luciana? He doesn't remember losing it

8. Si è rifiutato di cooperare | He has refused to cooperate

9. Rimproverano alla figlia la sua mancanza d'entusiasmo | They reproach their daughter for her lack of enthusiasm

10. Li abbiamo ringraziati della loro gentilezza | We thanked them for their kindness

11. Rischiate di perdere soldi | You risk losing money

12. Siete riusciti a convincermi | You've managed to convince me

13. Mi scuso del ritardo | I'm sorry I'm late

14. Questo pulsante serve a regolare il volume | This button is for adjusting the volume

15. Si è servito di un cacciavite per aprirlo | He used a screwdriver to open it

16. Smettete di fare rumore! | Stop making so much noise!

Verbs governing a and di *continued*

somigliare a qn/qc	to look/be like sb/sth
sopravvivere a qn	to outlive sb → **1**
spicciarsi a + *infin.*	to hurry to do
spingere qn **a** + *infin.*	to urge sb to do
strappare via qc **a** qn	to snatch sth from sb → **2**
stufarsi di qc/qn	to be fed up with sth/sb
stupirsi di qc	to be amazed at sth
succedere a qn	to succeed sb
tardare a + *infin.*	to delay doing → **3**
telefonare a qn	to phone sb
tendere a + *infin.*	to tend to do
tenere a + *infin.*	to be keen to do → **4**
tentare di + *infin.*	to try to do → **5**
togliere qc **a** qn	to take sth away from sb
trattare di qc	to be about sth
ubbidire a qn	to obey sb
vantarsi di qc	to boast about sth
venire a + *infin.*	to come to do
vietare a qn **di** + *infin.*	to forbid sb to do → **6**
vivere di qc	to live on sth

Verbs followed by a preposition in English but not in Italian.

ascoltare qc/qn	to listen to sth/sb → **7**
aspettare qc/qn	to wait for sth/sb → **8**
cercare qc/qn	to look for sth/sb → **9**
chiedere qc	to ask for sth → **10**
guardare qc/qn	to look at sth/sb → **11**
pagare qc/qn	to pay for sth/sb → **12**

Examples

①	È sopravvissuta a suo marito	She outlived her husband
②	Il ladro le ha strappato via la borsa	The thief snatched her bag
③	Non ha tardato a prendere una decisione	He didn't take long to make a decision
④	Ci tiene a farlo da sola	She's keen to do it by herself
⑤	Ho tentato di darlo ad Alessia	I tried to give it to Alessia
⑥	Ha vietato ai bambini di giocare con i fiammiferi	He's forbidden the children to play with matches
⑦	Mi stai ascoltando?	Are you listening to me?
⑧	Aspettami!	Wait for me!
⑨	Sto cercando la chiave	I'm looking for my key
⑩	Ha chiesto qualcosa da mangiare	He asked for something to eat
⑪	Guarda la sua faccia	Look at his face
⑫	Ho già pagato il biglietto	I've already paid for my ticket

Introduction

The Verb Tables in the following section contain tables of Italian verbs (some regular and some irregular) in alphabetical order. Each table shows you the following forms: Present, Present Subjunctive, Perfect, Imperfect, Future, Conditional, Past Historic, Pluperfect, Imperative and the Past Participle and Gerund.

In Italian there are regular verbs (their forms follow the regular patterns of **-are**, **-ere** or **-ire** verbs), and irregular verbs (their forms do not follow the normal rules). Examples of regular verbs in these tables are:

parlare (regular **-are** verb)
credere (regular **-ere** verb)
capire (regular **-ire** verb)

Some irregular verbs are irregular in most of their forms, while others may only have a couple of irregular forms.

accorgersi (to realize)

	PRESENT		IMPERFECT
io	mi accorgo	io	mi accorgevo
tu	ti accorgi	tu	ti accorgevi
lui/lei/Lei	si accorge	lui/lei/Lei	si accorgeva
noi	ci accorgiamo	noi	ci accorgevamo
voi	vi accorgete	voi	vi accorgevate
loro	si accorgono	loro	si accorgevano

	FUTURE		CONDITIONAL
io	mi accorgerò	io	mi accorgerei
tu	ti accorgerai	tu	ti accorgeresti
lui/lei/Lei	si accorgerà	lui/lei/Lei	si accorgerebbe
noi	ci accorgeremo	noi	ci accorgeremmo
voi	vi accorgerete	voi	vi accorgereste
loro	si accorgeranno	loro	si accorgerebbero

	PRESENT SUBJUNCTIVE		PAST HISTORIC
io	mi accorga	io	mi accorsi
tu	ti accorga	tu	ti accorgesti
lui/lei/Lei	si accorga	lui/lei/Lei	si accorse
noi	ci accorgiamo	noi	ci accorgemmo
voi	vi accorgiate	voi	vi accorgeste
loro	si accorgano	loro	si accorsero

PAST PARTICIPLE
accorto

IMPERATIVE
accorgiti
accorgiamoci
accorgetevi

GERUND
accorgendosi

AUXILIARY
essere

addormentarsi (to go to sleep)

	PRESENT		IMPERFECT
io	mi addormento	io	mi addormentavo
tu	ti addormenti	tu	ti addormentavi
lui/lei/Lei	si addormenta	lui/lei/Lei	si addormentava
noi	ci addormentiamo	noi	ci addormentavamo
voi	vi addormentate	voi	vi addormentavate
loro	si addormentano	loro	si addormentavano

	FUTURE		CONDITIONAL
io	mi addormenterò	io	mi addormenterei
tu	ti addormenterai	tu	ti addormenteresti
lui/lei/Lei	si addormenterà	lui/lei/Lei	si addormenterebbe
noi	ci addormenteremo	noi	ci addormenteremmo
voi	vi addormenterete	voi	vi addormentereste
loro	si addormenteranno	loro	si addormenterebbero

	PRESENT SUBJUNCTIVE		PAST HISTORIC
io	mi addormenti	io	mi addormentai
tu	ti addormenti	tu	ti addormentasti
lui/lei/Lei	si addormenti	lui/lei/Lei	si addormentò
noi	ci addormentiamo	noi	ci addormentammo
voi	vi addormentiate	voi	vi addormentaste
loro	si addormentino	loro	si addormentarono

PAST PARTICIPLE
addormentato

IMPERATIVE
addormentati
addormentiamoci
addormentatevi

GERUND
addormentandosi

AUXILIARY
essere

andare (to go)

	PRESENT		IMPERFECT
io	vado	io	andavo
tu	vai	tu	andavi
lui/lei/Lei	va	lui/lei/Lei	andava
noi	andiamo	noi	andavamo
voi	andate	voi	andavate
loro	vanno	loro	andavano

	FUTURE		CONDITIONAL
io	andrò	io	andrei
tu	andrai	tu	andresti
lui/lei/Lei	andrà	lui/lei/Lei	andrebbe
noi	andremo	noi	andremmo
voi	andrete	voi	andreste
loro	andranno	loro	andrebbero

	PRESENT SUBJUNCTIVE		PAST HISTORIC
io	vada	io	andai
tu	vada	tu	andasti
lui/lei/Lei	vada	lui/lei/Lei	andò
noi	andiamo	noi	andammo
voi	andiate	voi	andaste
loro	vadano	loro	andarono

PAST PARTICIPLE	IMPERATIVE
andato	vai
	andiamo
	andate

GERUND	AUXILIARY
andando	essere

aprire (to open)

	PRESENT		IMPERFECT
io	apro	io	aprivo
tu	apri	tu	aprivi
lui/lei/Lei	apre	lui/lei/Lei	apriva
noi	apriamo	noi	aprivamo
voi	aprite	voi	aprivate
loro	aprono	loro	aprivano

	FUTURE		CONDITIONAL
io	aprirò	io	aprirei
tu	aprirai	tu	apriresti
lui/lei/Lei	aprirà	lui/lei/Lei	aprirebbe
noi	apriremo	noi	apriremmo
voi	aprirete	voi	aprireste
loro	apriranno	loro	aprirebbero

	PRESENT SUBJUNCTIVE		PAST HISTORIC
io	apra	io	aprii
tu	apra	tu	apristi
lui/lei/Lei	apra	lui/lei/Lei	aprì
noi	apriamo	noi	aprimmo
voi	apriate	voi	apriste
loro	aprano	loro	aprirono

PAST PARTICIPLE	IMPERATIVE
aperto	apri
	apriamo
	aprite

GERUND	AUXILIARY
aprendo	avere

assumere (to take on, to employ)

	PRESENT		IMPERFECT
io	assumo	io	assumevo
tu	assumi	tu	assumevi
lui/lei/Lei	assume	lui/lei/Lei	assumeva
noi	assumiamo	noi	assumevamo
voi	assumete	voi	assumevate
loro	assumono	loro	assumevano

	FUTURE		CONDITIONAL
io	assumerò	io	assumerei
tu	assumerai	tu	assumeresti
lui/lei/Lei	assumerà	lui/lei/Lei	assumerebbe
noi	assumeremo	noi	assumeremmo
voi	assumerete	voi	assumereste
loro	assumeranno	loro	assumerebbero

	PRESENT SUBJUNCTIVE		PAST HISTORIC
io	assuma	io	assunsi
tu	assuma	tu	assumesti
lui/lei/Lei	assuma	lui/lei/Lei	assunse
noi	assumiamo	noi	assumemmo
voi	assumiate	voi	assumeste
loro	assumano	loro	assunsero

PAST PARTICIPLE	IMPERATIVE
assunto	assumi
	assumiamo
	assumete

GERUND	AUXILIARY
assumendo	avere

avere (to have)

	PRESENT		IMPERFECT
io	ho	io	avevo
tu	hai	tu	avevi
lui/lei/Lei	ha	lui/lei/Lei	aveva
noi	abbiamo	noi	avevamo
voi	avete	voi	avevate
loro	hanno	loro	avevano

	FUTURE		CONDITIONAL
io	avrò	io	avrei
tu	avrai	tu	avresti
lui/lei/Lei	avrà	lui/lei/Lei	avrebbe
noi	avremo	noi	avremmo
voi	avrete	voi	avreste
loro	avranno	loro	avrebbero

	PRESENT SUBJUNCTIVE		PAST HISTORIC
io	abbia	io	ebbi
tu	abbia	tu	avesti
lui/lei/Lei	abbia	lui/lei/Lei	ebbe
noi	abbiamo	noi	avemmo
voi	abbiate	voi	aveste
loro	abbiano	loro	ebbero

PAST PARTICIPLE	IMPERATIVE
avuto	abbi
	abbiamo
	abbiate

GERUND	AUXILIARY
avendo	avere

bere (to drink)

	PRESENT		IMPERFECT
io	bevo	io	bevevo
tu	bevi	tu	bevevi
lui/lei/Lei	beve	lui/lei/Lei	beveva
noi	beviamo	noi	bevevamo
voi	bevete	voi	bevevate
loro	bevono	loro	bevevano

	FUTURE		CONDITIONAL
io	berrò	io	berrei
tu	berrai	tu	berresti
lui/lei/Lei	berrà	lui/lei/Lei	berrebbe
noi	berremo	noi	berremmo
voi	berrete	voi	berreste
loro	berranno	loro	berrebbero

	PRESENT SUBJUNCTIVE		PAST HISTORIC
io	beva	io	bevvi
tu	beva	tu	bevesti
lui/lei/Lei	beva	lui/lei/Lei	bevve
noi	beviamo	noi	bevemmo
voi	beviate	voi	beveste
loro	bevano	loro	bevvero

PAST PARTICIPLE	IMPERATIVE
bevuto	bevi
	beviamo
	bevete

GERUND	AUXILIARY
bevendo	avere

cadere (to fall)

	PRESENT		IMPERFECT
io	cado	io	cadevo
tu	cadi	tu	cadevi
lui/lei/Lei	cade	lui/lei/Lei	cadeva
noi	cadiamo	noi	cadevamo
voi	cadete	voi	cadevate
loro	cadono	loro	cadevano

	FUTURE		CONDITIONAL
io	cadrò	io	cadrei
tu	cadrai	tu	cadresti
lui/lei/Lei	cadrà	lui/lei/Lei	cadrebbe
noi	cadremo	noi	cadremmo
voi	cadrete	voi	cadreste
loro	cadranno	loro	cadrebbero

	PRESENT SUBJUNCTIVE		PAST HISTORIC
io	cada	io	caddi
tu	cada	tu	cadesti
lui/lei/Lei	cada	lui/lei/Lei	cadde
noi	cadiamo	noi	cademmo
voi	cadiate	voi	cadeste
loro	cadano	loro	caddero

PAST PARTICIPLE	IMPERATIVE
caduto	cadi
	cadiamo
	cadete

GERUND	AUXILIARY
cadendo	essere

capire (to understand)

	PRESENT		IMPERFECT
io	capisco	io	capivo
tu	capisci	tu	capivi
lui/lei/Lei	capisce	lui/lei/Lei	capiva
noi	capiamo	noi	capivamo
voi	capite	voi	capivate
loro	capiscono	loro	capivano

	FUTURE		CONDITIONAL
io	capirò	io	capirei
tu	capirai	tu	capiresti
lui/lei/Lei	capirà	lui/lei/Lei	capirebbe
noi	capiremo	noi	capiremmo
voi	capirete	voi	capireste
loro	capiranno	loro	capirebbero

	PRESENT SUBJUNCTIVE		PAST HISTORIC
io	capisca	io	capii
tu	capisca	tu	capisti
lui/lei/Lei	capisca	lui/lei/Lei	capì
noi	capiamo	noi	capimmo
voi	capiate	voi	capiste
loro	capiscano	loro	capirono

PAST PARTICIPLE
capito

IMPERATIVE
capisci
capiamo
capite

GERUND
capendo

AUXILIARY
avere

cercare (to look for)

	PRESENT		IMPERFECT
io	cerco	io	cercavo
tu	cerchi	tu	cercavi
lui/lei/Lei	cerca	lui/lei/Lei	cercava
noi	cerchiamo	noi	cercavamo
voi	cercate	voi	cercavate
loro	cercano	loro	cercavano

	FUTURE		CONDITIONAL
io	cercherò	io	cercherei
tu	cercherai	tu	cercheresti
lui/lei/Lei	cercherà	lui/lei/Lei	cercherebbe
noi	cercheremo	noi	cercheremmo
voi	cercherete	voi	cerchereste
loro	cercheranno	loro	cercherebbero

	PRESENT SUBJUNCTIVE		PAST HISTORIC
io	cerchi	io	cercai
tu	cerchi	tu	cercasti
lui/lei/Lei	cerchi	lui/lei/Lei	cercò
noi	cerchiamo	noi	cercammo
voi	cerchiate	voi	cercaste
loro	cerchino	loro	cercarono

PAST PARTICIPLE	IMPERATIVE
cercato	cerca
	cerchiamo
	cercate

GERUND	AUXILIARY
cercando	avere

chiudere (to close)

	PRESENT		IMPERFECT
io	chiudo	io	chiudevo
tu	chiudi	tu	chiudevi
lui/lei/Lei	chiude	lui/lei/Lei	chiudeva
noi	chiudiamo	noi	chiudevamo
voi	chiudete	voi	chiudevate
loro	chiudono	loro	chiudevano

	FUTURE		CONDITIONAL
io	chiuderò	io	chiuderei
tu	chiuderai	tu	chiuderesti
lui/lei/Lei	chiuderà	lui/lei/Lei	chiuderebbe
noi	chiuderemo	noi	chiuderemmo
voi	chiuderete	voi	chiudereste
loro	chiuderanno	loro	chiuderebbero

	PRESENT SUBJUNCTIVE		PAST HISTORIC
io	chiuda	io	chiusi
tu	chiuda	tu	chiudesti
lui/lei/Lei	chiuda	lui/lei/Lei	chiuse
noi	chiudiamo	noi	chiudemmo
voi	chiudiate	voi	chiudeste
loro	chiudano	loro	chiusero

PAST PARTICIPLE	IMPERATIVE
chiuso	chiudi
	chiudiamo
	chiudete

GERUND	AUXILIARY
chiudendo	avere

correre (to run)

	PRESENT		IMPERFECT
Io	corro	io	correvo
tu	corri	tu	correvi
lui/lei/Lei	corre	lui/lei/Lei	correva
noi	corriamo	noi	correvamo
voi	correte	voi	correvate
loro	corrono	loro	correvano

	FUTURE		CONDITIONAL
io	correrò	io	correrei
tu	correrai	tu	correresti
lui/lei/Lei	correrà	lui/lei/Lei	correrebbe
noi	correremo	noi	correremmo
voi	correrete	voi	correreste
loro	correranno	loro	correrebbero

	PRESENT SUBJUNCTIVE		PAST HISTORIC
io	corra	io	corsi
tu	corra	tu	corresti
lui/lei/Lei	corra	lui/lei/Lei	corse
noi	corriamo	noi	corremmo
voi	corriate	voi	correste
loro	corrano	loro	corsero

PAST PARTICIPLE	IMPERATIVE
corso	corri
	corriamo
	correte

GERUND	AUXILIARY
correndo	avere

credere (to believe)

	PRESENT		IMPERFECT
io	credo	io	credevo
tu	credi	tu	credevi
lui/lei/Lei	crede	lui/lei/Lei	credeva
noi	crediamo	noi	credevamo
voi	credete	voi	credevate
loro	credono	loro	credevano

	FUTURE		CONDITIONAL
io	crederò	io	crederei
tu	crederai	tu	crederesti
lui/lei/Lei	crederà	lui/lei/Lei	crederebbe
noi	crederemo	noi	crederemmo
voi	crederete	voi	credereste
loro	crederanno	loro	crederebbero

	PRESENT SUBJUNCTIVE		PAST HISTORIC
io	creda	io	credetti or credei
tu	creda	tu	credesti
lui/lei/Lei	creda	lui/lei/Lei	credette
noi	crediamo	noi	credemmo
voi	crediate	voi	credeste
loro	credano	loro	credettero

PAST PARTICIPLE	IMPERATIVE
creduto	credi
	crediamo
	credete

GERUND	AUXILIARY
credendo	avere

crescere (to grow)

	PRESENT		IMPERFECT
io	cresco	io	crescevo
tu	cresci	tu	crescevi
lui/lei/Lei	cresce	lui/lei/Lei	cresceva
noi	cresciamo	noi	crescevamo
voi	crescete	voi	crescevate
loro	crescono	loro	crescevano

	FUTURE		CONDITIONAL
io	crescerò	io	crescerei
tu	crescerai	tu	cresceresti
lui/lei/Lei	crescerà	lui/lei/Lei	crescerebbe
noi	cresceremo	noi	cresceremmo
voi	crescerete	voi	crescereste
loro	cresceranno	loro	crescerebbero

	PRESENT SUBJUNCTIVE		PAST HISTORIC
io	cresca	io	crebbi
tu	cresca	tu	crescesti
lui/lei/Lei	cresca	lui/lei/Lei	crebbe
noi	cresciamo	noi	crescemmo
voi	cresciate	voi	cresceste
loro	crescano	loro	crebbero

PAST PARTICIPLE
cresciuto

IMPERATIVE
cresci
cresciamo
crescete

GERUND
crescendo

AUXILIARY
essere

dare (to give)

	PRESENT		IMPERFECT
io	do	io	davo
tu	dai	tu	davi
lui/lei/Lei	dà	lui/lei/Lei	dava
noi	diamo	noi	davamo
voi	date	voi	davate
loro	danno	loro	davano

	FUTURE		CONDITIONAL
io	darò	io	darei
tu	darai	tu	daresti
lui/lei/Lei	darà	lui/lei/Lei	darebbe
noi	daremo	noi	daremmo
voi	darete	voi	dareste
loro	daranno	loro	darebbero

	PRESENT SUBJUNCTIVE		PAST HISTORIC
io	dia	io	diedi or detti
tu	dia	tu	desti
lui/lei/Lei	dia	lui/lei/Lei	diede or detti
noi	diamo	noi	demmo
voi	diate	voi	deste
loro	diano	loro	diedero or dettero

PAST PARTICIPLE
dato

IMPERATIVE
dai or da'
diamo
date

GERUND
dando

AUXILIARY
avere

dire (to say)

	PRESENT		IMPERFECT
io	dico	io	dicevo
tu	dici	tu	dicevi
lui/lei/Lei	dice	lui/lei/Lei	diceva
noi	diciamo	noi	dicevamo
voi	dite	voi	dicevate
loro	dicono	loro	dicevano

	FUTURE		CONDITIONAL
io	dirò	io	direi
tu	dirai	tu	diresti
lui/lei/Lei	dirà	lui/lei/Lei	direbbe
noi	diremo	noi	diremmo
voi	direte	voi	direste
loro	diranno	loro	direbbero

	PRESENT SUBJUNCTIVE		PAST HISTORIC
io	dica	io	dissi
tu	dica	tu	dicesti
lui/lei/Lei	dica	lui/lei/Lei	disse
noi	diciamo	noi	dicemmo
voi	diciate	voi	diceste
loro	dicano	loro	dissero

PAST PARTICIPLE	IMPERATIVE
detto	di'
	diciamo
	dite

GERUND	AUXILIARY
dicendo	avere

dirigere (to direct)

	PRESENT		IMPERFECT
io	dirigo	io	dirigevo
tu	dirigi	tu	dirigevi
lui/lei/Lei	dirige	lui/lei/Lei	dirigeva
noi	dirigiamo	noi	dirigevamo
voi	dirigete	voi	dirigevate
loro	dirigono	loro	dirigevano

	FUTURE		CONDITIONAL
io	dirigerò	io	dirigerei
tu	dirigerai	tu	dirigeresti
lui/lei/Lei	dirigerà	lui/lei/Lei	dirigerebbe
noi	dirigeremo	noi	dirigeremmo
voi	dirigerete	voi	dirigereste
loro	dirigeranno	loro	dirigerebbero

	PRESENT SUBJUNCTIVE		PAST HISTORIC
io	diriga	io	diressi
tu	diriga	tu	dirigesti
lui/lei/Lei	diriga	lui/lei/Lei	diresse
noi	dirigiamo	noi	dirigemmo
voi	dirigiate	voi	dirigeste
loro	dirigano	loro	diressero

PAST PARTICIPLE	IMPERATIVE
diretto	dirigi
	dirigiamo
	dirigete

GERUND	AUXILIARY
dirigendo	avere

dormire (to sleep)

	PRESENT		IMPERFECT
io	dormo	io	dormivo
tu	dormi	tu	dormivi
lui/lei/Lei	dorme	lui/lei/Lei	dormiva
noi	dormiamo	noi	dormivamo
voi	dormite	voi	dormivate
loro	dormono	loro	dormivano

	FUTURE		CONDITIONAL
io	dormirò	io	dormirei
tu	dormirai	tu	dormiresti
lui/lei/Lei	dormirà	lui/lei/Lei	dormirebbe
noi	dormiremo	noi	dormiremmo
voi	dormirete	voi	dormireste
loro	dormiranno	loro	dormirebbero

	PRESENT SUBJUNCTIVE		PAST HISTORIC
io	dorma	io	dormii
tu	dorma	tu	dormisti
lui/lei/Lei	dorma	lui/lei/Lei	dormì
noi	dormiamo	noi	dormimmo
voi	dormiate	voi	dormiste
loro	dormano	loro	dormirono

PAST PARTICIPLE	IMPERATIVE
dormito	dormi
	dormiamo
	dormite

GERUND	AUXILIARY
dormendo	avere

dovere (to have to)

	PRESENT		IMPERFECT
io	devo	io	dovevo
tu	devi	tu	dovevi
lui/lei/Lei	deve	lui/lei/Lei	doveva
noi	dobbiamo	noi	dovevamo
voi	dovete	voi	dovevate
loro	devono	loro	dovevano

	FUTURE		CONDITIONAL
io	dovrò	io	dovrei
tu	dovrai	tu	dovresti
lui/lei/Lei	dovrà	lui/lei/Lei	dovrebbe
noi	dovremo	noi	dovremmo
voi	dovrete	voi	dovreste
loro	dovranno	loro	dovrebbero

	PRESENT SUBJUNCTIVE		PAST HISTORIC
io	debba	io	dovetti
tu	debba	tu	dovesti
lui/lei/Lei	debba	lui/lei/Lei	dovette
noi	dobbiamo	noi	dovemmo
voi	dobbiate	voi	doveste
loro	debbano	loro	dovettero

PAST PARTICIPLE	IMPERATIVE
dovuto	–

GERUND	AUXILIARY
dovendo	avere

essere (to be)

	PRESENT			IMPERFECT
io	sono		io	ero
tu	sei		tu	eri
lui/lei/Lei	è		lui/lei/Lei	era
noi	siamo		noi	eravamo
voi	siete		voi	eravate
loro	sono		loro	erano

	FUTURE			CONDITIONAL
io	sarò		io	sarei
tu	sarai		tu	saresti
lui/lei/Lei	sarà		lui/lei/Lei	sarebbe
noi	saremo		noi	saremmo
voi	sarete		voi	sareste
loro	saranno		loro	sarebbero

	PRESENT SUBJUNCTIVE			PAST HISTORIC
io	sia		io	fui
tu	sia		tu	fosti
lui/lei/Lei	sia		lui/lei/Lei	fu
noi	siamo		noi	fummo
voi	siate		voi	foste
loro	siano		loro	furono

PAST PARTICIPLE	IMPERATIVE
stato	sii
	siamo
	siate

GERUND	AUXILIARY
essendo	essere

fare (to do, to make)

	PRESENT		IMPERFECT
io	faccio	io	facevo
tu	fai	tu	facevi
lui/lei/Lei	fa	lui/lei/Lei	faceva
noi	facciamo	noi	facevamo
voi	fate	voi	facevate
loro	fanno	loro	facevano

	FUTURE		CONDITIONAL
io	farò	io	farei
tu	farai	tu	faresti
lui/lei/Lei	farà	lui/lei/Lei	farebbe
noi	faremo	noi	faremmo
voi	farete	voi	fareste
loro	faranno	loro	farebbero

	PRESENT SUBJUNCTIVE		PAST HISTORIC
io	faccia	io	feci
tu	faccia	tu	facesti
lui/lei/Lei	faccia	lui/lei/Lei	fece
noi	facciamo	noi	facemmo
voi	facciate	voi	faceste
loro	facciano	loro	fecero

PAST PARTICIPLE
fatto

IMPERATIVE
fai *or* fa'
facciamo
fate

GERUND
facendo

AUXILIARY
avere

leggere (to read)

	PRESENT		IMPERFECT
Io	leggo	io	leggevo
tu	leggi	tu	leggevi
lui/lei/Lei	legge	lui/lei/Lei	leggeva
noi	leggiamo	noi	leggevamo
voi	leggete	voi	leggevate
loro	leggono	loro	leggevano

	FUTURE		CONDITIONAL
io	leggerò	io	leggerei
tu	leggerai	tu	leggeresti
lui/lei/Lei	leggerà	lui/lei/Lei	leggerebbe
noi	leggeremo	noi	leggeremmo
voi	leggerete	voi	leggereste
loro	leggeranno	loro	leggerebbero

	PRESENT SUBJUNCTIVE		PAST HISTORIC
io	legga	io	lessi
tu	legga	tu	leggesti
lui/lei/Lei	legga	lui/lei/Lei	lesse
noi	leggiamo	noi	leggemmo
voi	leggiate	voi	leggeste
loro	leggano	loro	lessero

PAST PARTICIPLE
letto

IMPERATIVE
leggi
leggiamo
leggete

GERUND
leggendo

AUXILIARY
avere

mettere (to put)

	PRESENT		IMPERFECT
io	metto	io	mettevo
tu	metti	tu	mettevi
lui/lei/Lei	mette	lui/lei/Lei	metteva
noi	mettiamo	noi	mettevamo
voi	mettete	voi	mettevate
loro	mettono	loro	mettevano

	FUTURE		CONDITIONAL
io	metterò	io	metterei
tu	metterai	tu	metteresti
lui/lei/Lei	metterà	lui/lei/Lei	metterebbe
noi	metteremo	noi	metteremmo
voi	metterete	voi	mettereste
loro	metteranno	loro	metterebbero

	PRESENT SUBJUNCTIVE		PAST HISTORIC
io	metta	io	misi
tu	metta	tu	mettesti
lui/lei/Lei	metta	lui/lei/Lei	mise
noi	mettiamo	noi	mettemmo
voi	mettiate	voi	metteste
loro	mettano	loro	misero

PAST PARTICIPLE	IMPERATIVE
messo	metti
	mettiamo
	mettete

GERUND	AUXILIARY
mettendo	avere

morire (to die)

	PRESENT		IMPERFECT
io	muoio	io	morivo
tu	muori	tu	morivi
lui/lei/Lei	muore	lui/lei/Lei	moriva
noi	moriamo	noi	morivamo
voi	morite	voi	morivate
loro	muoiono	loro	morivano

	FUTURE		CONDITIONAL
io	morirò	io	morirei
tu	morirai	tu	moriresti
lui/lei/Lei	morirà	lui/lei/Lei	morirebbe
noi	moriremo	noi	moriremmo
voi	morirete	voi	morireste
loro	moriranno	loro	morirebbero

	PRESENT SUBJUNCTIVE		PAST HISTORIC
io	muoia	io	morii
tu	muoia	tu	moristi
lui/lei/Lei	muoia	lui/lei/Lei	morì
noi	moriamo	noi	morimmo
voi	moriate	voi	moriste
loro	muoiano	loro	morirono

PAST PARTICIPLE
morto

IMPERATIVE
muori
moriamo
morite

GERUND
morendo

AUXILIARY
essere

muovere (to move)

	PRESENT		IMPERFECT
io	muovo	io	muovevo
tu	muovi	tu	muovevi
lui/lei/Lei	muove	lui/lei/Lei	muoveva
noi	muoviamo	noi	muovevamo
voi	muovete	voi	muovevate
loro	muovono	loro	muovevano

	FUTURE		CONDITIONAL
io	muoverò	io	muoverei
tu	muoverai	tu	muoveresti
lui/lei/Lei	muoverà	lui/lei/Lei	muoverebbe
noi	muoveremo	noi	muoveremmo
voi	muoverete	voi	muovereste
loro	muoveranno	loro	muoverebbero

	PRESENT SUBJUNCTIVE		PAST HISTORIC
io	muova	io	mossi
tu	muova	tu	muovesti
lui/lei/Lei	muova	lui/lei/Lei	mosse
noi	muoviamo	noi	muovemmo
voi	muoviate	voi	muoveste
loro	muovano	loro	mossero

PAST PARTICIPLE	IMPERATIVE
mosso	muovi
	muoviamo
	muovete

GERUND	AUXILIARY
muovendo	avere

nascere (to be born)

	PRESENT		IMPERFECT
io	nasco	io	nascevo
tu	nasci	tu	nascevi
lui/lei/Lei	nasce	lui/lei/Lei	nasceva
noi	nasciamo	noi	nascevamo
voi	nascete	voi	nascevate
loro	nascono	loro	nascevano

	FUTURE		CONDITIONAL
io	nascerò	io	nascerei
tu	nascerai	tu	nasceresti
lui/lei/Lei	nascerà	lui/lei/Lei	nascerebbe
noi	nasceremo	noi	nasceremmo
voi	nascerete	voi	nascereste
loro	nasceranno	loro	nascerebbero

	PRESENT SUBJUNCTIVE		PAST HISTORIC
io	nasca	io	nacqui
tu	nasca	tu	nascesti
lui/lei/Lei	nasca	lui/lei/Lei	nacque
noi	nasciamo	noi	nascemmo
voi	nasciate	voi	nasceste
loro	nascano	loro	nacquero

PAST PARTICIPLE	IMPERATIVE
nato	nasci
	nasciamo
	nascete

GERUND	AUXILIARY
nascendo	essere

parlare (to speak)

	PRESENT		IMPERFECT
io	parlo	io	parlavo
tu	parli	tu	parlavi
lui/lei/Lei	parla	lui/lei/Lei	parlava
noi	parliamo	noi	parlavamo
voi	parlate	voi	parlavate
loro	parlano	loro	parlavano

	FUTURE		CONDITIONAL
io	parlerò	io	parlerei
tu	parlerai	tu	parleresti
lui/lei/Lei	parlerà	lui/lei/Lei	parlerebbe
noi	parleremo	noi	parleremmo
voi	parlerete	voi	parlereste
loro	parleranno	loro	parlerebbero

	PRESENT SUBJUNCTIVE		PAST HISTORIC
io	parli	io	parlai
tu	parli	tu	parlasti
lui/lei/Lei	parli	lui/lei/Lei	parlò
noi	parliamo	noi	parlammo
voi	parliate	voi	parlaste
loro	parlino	loro	parlarono

PAST PARTICIPLE	IMPERATIVE
parlato	parla
	parliamo
	parlate

GERUND	AUXILIARY
parlando	avere

piacere (to be pleasing)

	PRESENT		IMPERFECT
io	piaccio	io	piacevo
tu	piaci	tu	piacevi
lui/lei/Lei	piace	lui/lei/Lei	piaceva
noi	piacciamo	noi	piacevamo
voi	piacete	voi	piacevate
loro	piacciono	loro	piacevano

	FUTURE		CONDITIONAL
io	piacerò	io	piacerei
tu	piacerai	tu	piaceresti
lui/lei/Lei	piacerà	lui/lei/Lei	piacerebbe
noi	piaceremo	noi	piaceremmo
voi	piacerete	voi	piacereste
loro	piaceranno	loro	piacerebbero

	PRESENT SUBJUNCTIVE		PAST HISTORIC
io	piaccia	io	piacqui
tu	piaccia	tu	piacesti
lui/lei/Lei	piaccia	lui/lei/Lei	piacque
noi	piacciamo	noi	piacemmo
voi	piacciate	voi	piaceste
loro	piacciano	loro	piacquero

PAST PARTICIPLE	IMPERATIVE
piaciuto	piaci
	piacciamo
	piacciate

GERUND	AUXILIARY
piacendo	essere

piovere (to rain)

PRESENT
piove

IMPERFECT
pioveva

FUTURE
piover*à*

CONDITIONAL
pioverebbe

PRESENT SUBJUNCTIVE
piova

PAST HISTORIC
piovve

PAST PARTICIPLE
piovuto

IMPERATIVE
–

GERUND
piovendo

AUXILIARY
essere

potere (to be able)

	PRESENT		IMPERFECT
io	posso	io	potevo
tu	puoi	tu	potevi
lui/lei/Lei	può	lui/lei/Lei	poteva
noi	possiamo	noi	potevamo
voi	potete	voi	potevate
loro	possono	loro	potevano

	FUTURE		CONDITIONAL
io	potrò	io	potrei
tu	potrai	tu	potresti
lui/lei/Lei	potrà	lui/lei/Lei	potrebbe
noi	potremo	noi	potremmo
voi	potrete	voi	potreste
loro	potranno	loro	potrebbero

	PRESENT SUBJUNCTIVE		PAST HISTORIC
io	possa	io	potei
tu	possa	tu	potesti
lui/lei/Lei	possa	lui/lei/Lei	poté
noi	possiamo	noi	potemmo
voi	possiate	voi	poteste
loro	possano	loro	poterono

PAST PARTICIPLE	IMPERATIVE
potuto	–

GERUND	AUXILIARY
potendo	avere

prendere (to take)

	PRESENT		IMPERFECT
io	prendo	io	prendevo
tu	prendi	tu	prendevi
lui/lei/Lei	prende	lui/lei/Lei	prendeva
noi	prendiamo	noi	prendevamo
voi	prendete	voi	prendevate
loro	prendono	loro	prendevano

	FUTURE		CONDITIONAL
io	prenderò	io	prenderei
tu	prenderai	tu	prenderesti
lui/lei/Lei	prenderà	lui/lei/Lei	prenderebbe
noi	prenderemo	noi	prenderemmo
voi	prenderete	voi	prendereste
loro	prenderanno	loro	prenderebbero

	PRESENT SUBJUNCTIVE		PAST HISTORIC
io	prenda	io	presi
tu	prenda	tu	prendesti
lui/lei/Lei	prenda	lui/lei/Lei	prese
noi	prendiamo	noi	prendemmo
voi	prendiate	voi	prendeste
loro	prendano	loro	presero

PAST PARTICIPLE	IMPERATIVE
preso	prendi
	prendiamo
	prendete

GERUND	AUXILIARY
prendendo	avere

rompere (to break)

	PRESENT		IMPERFECT
io	rompo	io	rompevo
tu	rompi	tu	rompevi
lui/lei/Lei	rompe	lui/lei/Lei	rompeva
noi	rompiamo	noi	rompevamo
voi	rompete	voi	rompevate
loro	rompono	loro	rompevano

	FUTURE		CONDITIONAL
io	romperò	io	romperei
tu	romperai	tu	romperesti
lui/lei/Lei	romperà	lui/lei/Lei	romperebbe
noi	romperemo	noi	romperemmo
voi	romperete	voi	rompereste
loro	romperanno	loro	romperebbero

	PRESENT SUBJUNCTIVE		PAST HISTORIC
io	rompa	io	ruppi
tu	rompa	tu	rompesti
lui/lei/Lei	rompa	lui/lei/Lei	ruppe
noi	rompiamo	noi	rompemmo
voi	rompiate	voi	rompeste
loro	rompano	loro	ruppero

PAST PARTICIPLE	IMPERATIVE
rotto	rompi
	rompiamo
	rompete

GERUND	AUXILIARY
rompendo	avere

salire (to go up)

	PRESENT		IMPERFECT
io	salgo	io	salivo
tu	sali	tu	salivi
lui/lei/Lei	sale	lui/lei/Lei	saliva
noi	saliamo	noi	salivamo
voi	salite	voi	salivate
loro	salgono	loro	salivano

	FUTURE		CONDITIONAL
io	salirò	io	salirei
tu	salirai	tu	saliresti
lui/lei/Lei	salirà	lui/lei/Lei	salirebbe
noi	saliremo	noi	saliremmo
voi	salirete	voi	salireste
loro	saliranno	loro	salirebbero

	PRESENT SUBJUNCTIVE		PAST HISTORIC
io	salga	io	salii
tu	salga	tu	salisti
lui/lei/Lei	salga	lui/lei/Lei	salì
noi	saliamo	noi	salimmo
voi	saliate	voi	saliste
loro	salgano	loro	salirono

PAST PARTICIPLE	IMPERATIVE
salito	sali
	saliamo
	salite

GERUND	AUXILIARY
salendo	essere

sapere (to know)

	PRESENT		IMPERFECT
Io	so	io	sapevo
tu	sai	tu	sapevi
lui/lei/Lei	sa	lui/lei/Lei	sapeva
noi	sappiamo	noi	sapevamo
voi	sapete	voi	sapevate
loro	sanno	loro	sapevano

	FUTURE		CONDITIONAL
io	saprò	io	saprei
tu	saprai	tu	sapresti
lui/lei/Lei	saprà	lui/lei/Lei	saprebbe
noi	sapremo	noi	sapremmo
voi	saprete	voi	sapreste
loro	sapranno	loro	saprebbero

	PRESENT SUBJUNCTIVE		PAST HISTORIC
io	sappia	io	seppi
tu	sappia	tu	sapesti
lui/lei/Lei	sappia	lui/lei/Lei	seppe
noi	sappiamo	noi	sapemmo
voi	sappiate	voi	sapeste
loro	sappiano	loro	seppero

PAST PARTICIPLE
saputo

IMPERATIVE
sappi
sappiamo
sappiate

GERUND
sapendo

AUXILIARY
avere

scrivere (to write)

	PRESENT		IMPERFECT
io	scrivo	io	scrivevo
tu	scrivi	tu	scrivevi
lui/lei/Lei	scrive	lui/lei/Lei	scriveva
noi	scriviamo	noi	scrivevamo
voi	scrivete	voi	scrivevate
loro	scrivono	loro	scrivevano

	FUTURE		CONDITIONAL
io	scriverò	io	scriverei
tu	scriverai	tu	scriveresti
lui/lei/Lei	scriverà	lui/lei/Lei	scriverebbe
noi	scriveremo	noi	scriveremmo
voi	scriverete	voi	scrivereste
loro	scriveranno	loro	scriverebbero

	PRESENT SUBJUNCTIVE		PAST HISTORIC
io	scriva	io	scrissi
tu	scriva	tu	scrivesti
lui/lei/Lei	scriva	lui/lei/Lei	scrisse
noi	scriviamo	noi	scrivemmo
voi	scriviate	voi	scriveste
loro	scrivano	loro	scrissero

PAST PARTICIPLE
scritto

IMPERATIVE
scrivi
scriviamo
scrivete

GERUND
scrivendo

AUXILIARY
avere

sedere (to sit)

	PRESENT		IMPERFECT
io	siedo	io	sedevo
tu	siedi	tu	sedevi
lui/lei/Lei	siede	lui/lei/Lei	sedeva
noi	sediamo	noi	sedevamo
voi	sedete	voi	sedevate
loro	siedono	loro	sedevano

	FUTURE		CONDITIONAL
io	sederò	io	sederei
tu	sederai	tu	sederesti
lui/lei/Lei	sederà	lui/lei/Lei	sederebbe
noi	sederemo	noi	sederemmo
voi	sederete	voi	sedereste
loro	sederanno	loro	sederebbero

	PRESENT SUBJUNCTIVE		PAST HISTORIC
io	sieda	io	sedetti
tu	sieda	tu	sedesti
lui/lei/Lei	sieda	lui/lei/Lei	sedette
noi	sediamo	noi	sedemmo
voi	sediate	voi	sedeste
loro	siedano	loro	sedettero

PAST PARTICIPLE	IMPERATIVE
seduto	siedi
	sediamo
	sedete

GERUND	AUXILIARY
sedendo	essere

stare (to be)

	PRESENT		IMPERFECT
io	sto	io	stavo
tu	stai	tu	stavi
lui/lei/Lei	sta	lui/lei/Lei	stava
noi	stiamo	noi	stavamo
voi	state	voi	stavate
loro	stanno	loro	stavano

	FUTURE		CONDITIONAL
io	starò	io	starei
tu	starai	tu	staresti
lui/lei/Lei	starà	lui/lei/Lei	starebbe
noi	staremo	noi	staremmo
voi	starete	voi	stareste
loro	staranno	loro	starebbero

	PRESENT SUBJUNCTIVE		PAST HISTORIC
io	stia	io	stetti
tu	stia	tu	stesti
lui/lei/Lei	stia	lui/lei/Lei	stette
noi	stiamo	noi	stemmo
voi	stiate	voi	steste
loro	stiano	loro	stettero

PAST PARTICIPLE	IMPERATIVE
stato	stai
	stiamo
	state

GERUND	AUXILIARY
stando	essere

succedere (to happen)

	PRESENT			IMPERFECT
sing.	succede		sing.	succedeva
plur.	succedono		plur.	succedevano

	FUTURE			CONDITIONAL
sing.	succederà		sing.	succederebbe
plur.	succederanno		plur.	succederebbero

	PRESENT SUBJUNCTIVE			PAST HISTORIC
sing.	succeda		sing.	successe
plur.	succedano		plur.	successero

PAST PARTICIPLE	IMPERATIVE
successo	–

GERUND	AUXILIARY
succedendo	essere

tenere (to hold)

	PRESENT		IMPERFECT
io	tengo	io	tenevo
tu	tieni	tu	tenevi
lui/lei/Lei	tiene	lui/lei/Lei	teneva
noi	teniamo	noi	tenevamo
voi	tenete	voi	tenevate
loro	tengono	loro	tenevano

	FUTURE		CONDITIONAL
io	terrò	io	terrei
tu	terrai	tu	terresti
lui/lei/Lei	terrà	lui/lei/Lei	terrebbe
noi	terremo	noi	terremmo
voi	terrete	voi	terreste
loro	terranno	loro	terrebbero

	PRESENT SUBJUNCTIVE		PAST HISTORIC
io	tenga	io	tenni
tu	tenga	tu	tenesti
lui/lei/Lei	tenga	lui/lei/Lei	tenne
noi	teniamo	noi	tenemmo
voi	teniate	voi	teneste
loro	tengano	loro	tennero

PAST PARTICIPLE	IMPERATIVE
tenuto	tieni
	teniamo
	tenete

GERUND	AUXILIARY
tenendo	avere

uscire (to go out)

	PRESENT		IMPERFECT
io	esco	io	uscivo
tu	esci	tu	uscivi
lui/lei/Lei	esce	lui/lei/Lei	usciva
noi	usciamo	noi	uscivamo
voi	uscite	voi	uscivate
loro	escono	loro	uscivano

	FUTURE		CONDITIONAL
io	uscirò	io	uscirei
tu	uscirai	tu	usciresti
lui/lei/Lei	uscirà	lui/lei/Lei	uscirebbe
noi	usciremo	noi	usciremmo
voi	uscirete	voi	uscireste
loro	usciranno	loro	uscirebbero

	PRESENT SUBJUNCTIVE		PAST HISTORIC
io	esca	io	uscii
tu	esca	tu	uscisti
lui/lei/Lei	esca	lui/lei/Lei	uscì
noi	usciamo	noi	uscimmo
voi	usciate	voi	usciste
loro	escano	loro	uscirono

PAST PARTICIPLE	IMPERATIVE
uscito	esci
	usciamo
	uscite

GERUND	AUXILIARY
uscendo	essere

vedere (to see)

	PRESENT		IMPERFECT
io	vedo	io	vedevo
tu	vedi	tu	vedevi
lui/lei/Lei	vede	lui/lei/Lei	vedeva
noi	vediamo	noi	vedevamo
voi	vedete	voi	vedevate
loro	vedono	loro	vedevano

	FUTURE		CONDITIONAL
io	vedrò	io	vedrei
tu	vedrai	tu	vedresti
lui/lei/Lei	vedrà	lui/lei/Lei	vedrebbe
noi	vedremo	noi	vedremmo
voi	vedrete	voi	vedreste
loro	vedranno	loro	vedrebbero

	PRESENT SUBJUNCTIVE		PAST HISTORIC
io	veda	io	vidi
tu	veda	tu	vedesti
lui/lei/Lei	veda	lui/lei/Lei	vide
noi	vediamo	noi	vedemmo
voi	vediate	voi	vedeste
loro	vedano	loro	videro

PAST PARTICIPLE	IMPERATIVE
visto	vedi
	vediamo
	vedete

GERUND	AUXILIARY
vedendo	avere

venire (to come)

	PRESENT		IMPERFECT
io	vengo	io	venivo
tu	vieni	tu	venivi
lui/lei/Lei	viene	lui/lei/Lei	veniva
noi	veniamo	noi	venivamo
voi	venite	voi	venivate
loro	vengono	loro	venivano

	FUTURE		CONDITIONAL
io	verrò	io	verrei
tu	verrai	tu	verresti
lui/lei/Lei	verrà	lui/lei/Lei	verrebbe
noi	verremo	noi	verremmo
voi	verrete	voi	verreste
loro	verranno	loro	verrebbero

	PRESENT SUBJUNCTIVE		PAST HISTORIC
io	venga	io	venni
tu	venga	tu	venisti
lui/lei/Lei	venga	lui/lei/Lei	venne
noi	veniamo	noi	venimmo
voi	veniate	voi	veniste
loro	vengano	loro	vennero

PAST PARTICIPLE	IMPERATIVE
venuto	vieni
	veniamo
	venite

GERUND	AUXILIARY
venendo	essere

vincere (to defeat)

	PRESENT		IMPERFECT
io	vinco	io	vincevo
tu	vinci	tu	vincevi
lui/lei/Lei	vince	lui/lei/Lei	vinceva
noi	vinciamo	noi	vincevamo
voi	vincete	voi	vincevate
loro	vincono	loro	vincevano

	FUTURE		CONDITIONAL
io	vincerò	io	vincerei
tu	vincerai	tu	vinceresti
lui/lei/Lei	vincerà	lui/lei/Lei	vincerebbe
noi	vinceremo	noi	vinceremmo
voi	vincerete	voi	vincereste
loro	vinceranno	loro	vincerebbero

	PRESENT SUBJUNCTIVE		PAST HISTORIC
io	vinca	io	vinsi
tu	vinca	tu	vincesti
lui/lei/Lei	vinca	lui/lei/Lei	vinse
noi	vinciamo	noi	vincemmo
voi	vinciate	voi	vinceste
loro	vincano	loro	vinsero

PAST PARTICIPLE	IMPERATIVE
vinto	vinci
	vinciamo
	vincete

GERUND	AUXILIARY
vincendo	avere

vivere (to live)

	PRESENT		**IMPERFECT**
io	vivo	io	vivevo
tu	vivi	tu	vivevi
lui/lei/Lei	vive	lui/lei/Lei	viveva
noi	viviamo	noi	vivevamo
voi	vivete	voi	vivevate
loro	vivono	loro	vivevano

	FUTURE		**CONDITIONAL**
io	vivrò	io	vivrei
tu	vivrai	tu	vivresti
lui/lei/Lei	vivrà	lui/lei/Lei	vivrebbe
noi	vivremo	noi	vivremmo
voi	vivrete	voi	vivreste
loro	vivranno	loro	vivrebbero

	PRESENT SUBJUNCTIVE		**PAST HISTORIC**
io	viva	io	vissi
tu	viva	tu	vivesti
lui/lei/Lei	viva	lui/lei/Lei	visse
noi	viviamo	noi	vivemmo
voi	viviate	voi	viveste
loro	vivano	loro	vissero

PAST PARTICIPLE	**IMPERATIVE**
vissuto	vivi
	viviamo
	vivete

GERUND	**AUXILIARY**
vivendo	avere

volere (to want)

	PRESENT		IMPERFECT
io	voglio	io	volevo
tu	vuoi	tu	volevi
lui/lei/Lei	vuole	lui/lei/Lei	voleva
noi	vogliamo	noi	volevamo
voi	volete	voi	volevate
loro	vogliono	loro	volevano

	FUTURE		CONDITIONAL
io	vorrò	io	vorrei
tu	vorrai	tu	vorresti
lui/lei/Lei	vorrà	lui/lei/Lei	vorrebbe
noi	vorremo	noi	vorremmo
voi	vorrete	voi	vorreste
loro	vorranno	loro	vorrebbero

	PRESENT SUBJUNCTIVE		PAST HISTORIC
io	voglia	io	volli
tu	voglia	tu	volesti
lui/lei/Lei	voglia	lui/lei/Lei	volle
noi	vogliamo	noi	volemmo
voi	vogliate	voi	voleste
loro	vogliano	loro	vollero

PAST PARTICIPLE	IMPERATIVE
voluto	–

GERUND	AUXILIARY
volendo	avere

The Gender of Nouns

In Italian, all nouns are either masculine or feminine, whether they denote people, animals or things.

The gender of a noun is often indicated by its final letter. Here are some guidelines to help you determine what gender a noun is:

Nearly all nouns ending in **-o** are masculine, e.g.
il treno the train
l'uomo the man
un topo a mouse
un gatto a (tom)cat
un italiano an Italian (man)

EXCEPTIONS:
la mano the hand
una foto a photo
la radio the radio
una moto a motorbike

Very many nouns ending in **-a** are feminine, e.g.
la casa the house
una donna a woman
una gatta a (she) cat
un'italiana an Italian woman

There are, however, numerous exceptions, e.g.
il dramma the drama
il papa the pope
il problema the problem

A few nouns ending in **-a** are feminine, but can refer to a man or a woman, e.g.
una guida a guide (male or female)
una persona a person (male or female)
una vittima a victim (male or female)

Nouns ending in **-ista** denoting people, can be masculine or feminine, e.g.
un giornalista a (male) journalist
una giornalista a (female) journalist

The Gender of Nouns *continued*

un pessimista a (male) pessimist
una pessimista a (female) pessimist

Nearly all words ending in -à, -sione and -zione are feminine, e.g.
una difficoltà a difficulty
un'occasione an opportunity
una conversazione a conversation

Nouns ending in a consonant are nearly always masculine, e.g.
un film a film
un computer a computer
un box a garage

EXCEPTIONS:
una jeep a jeep
una star a star

Nouns ending in -e or -i can be masculine or feminine, e.g.
un mese a month
la mente the mind
un brindisi a toast
una crisi a crisis

The names of languages, and all months, are masculine, whether they end in -o or -e, e.g.
il tedesco German
il francese French
lo scorso febbraio last February
il prossimo dicembre next December

Suffixes that differentiate between male and female are shown on page 128.

Some words have different meanings depending on their gender, e.g.

il fine the objective	la fine the end
un posto a place	la posta the mail
il manico the handle	la manica the sleeve
un modo a way	la moda the fashion
un mostro a monster	una mostra an exhibition
il capitale capital (money)	una capitale a capital city

127

The Formation of Feminines

As in English, male and female are sometimes differentiated by the use of quite different words, e.g.

> **un fratello** a brother
> **una sorella** a sister
> **un toro** a bull
> **una mucca** a cow

More often, however, words in Italian show gender by their ending:

> Many Italian nouns ending in **-o** can be made feminine by changing the ending to **-a** → **❶**

> Some nouns ending in **-e** also change the ending to **-a** for the feminine → **❷**

> Some nouns ending in **-a** or **-e** have no change of ending for the feminine → **❸**

> Nouns ending in **-ese** that describe nationality are the same for masculine and feminine → **❹**

> Nouns ending in **-ante** are the same for masculine and feminine → **❺**

> Nouns ending in **-tore** make the the feminine by substituting the ending **-trice** → **❻**

> Some nouns ending in **-e** have feminine forms ending in **-essa** → **❼**

1

un cuoco	a (*male*) cook
una cuoca	a (*female*) cook
uno zio	an uncle
una zia	an aunt
una ragazzo	a boy
una ragazza	a girl
un italiano	an Italian (man)
un'italiana	an Italian (woman)

2

un signore	a gentleman
una signora	a lady
un infirmiere	a (*male*) nurse
un'infirmiera	a (*female*) nurse
un parrucchiere	a (*male*) hairdresser
una parrucchiere	a (*female*) hairdresser

3

un collega	a (*male*) colleague
una collega	a (*female*) colleague
il mio dentista	my dentist (*male*)
la mia dentista	my dentist (*female*)
un nipote	a grandson
una nipote	a granddaughter

4

un irlandese	an Irishman
un'irlandese	an Irishwoman
uno scozzese	a Scotsman
una scozzese	a Scotswoman

5

un cantante	a (*male*) singer
una cantante	a (*female*) singer
un amante	a (*male*) lover
un'amante	a (*female*) lover
un principiante	a (*male*) beginner
una principiante	a (*female*) beginner

6

un attore	an actor
un'attrice	a (*female*) actor
un pittore	a (*male*) painter
una pittrice	a (*female*) painter

7

il professore	the (*male*) teacher
la professoressa	the (*female*) teacher
uno studente	a (*male*) student
una studentessa	a (*female*) student

The Formation of Plurals

Masculine nouns, whether they end in **-o, -a** or **-e,** nearly always take the ending **-i** in the plural → ❶

Feminine nouns ending in **-a** take the ending **-e** in the plural → ❷

Feminine nouns ending in **-e** take the ending **-i** in the plural → ❸

Nouns that have no change of ending in the plural

Nouns ending in an accented vowel do not change the ending in the plural → ❹

Nouns ending in **-i** and **-ie** do not change in the plural → ❺

Words ending with a consonant remain unchanged in the plural → ❻

Other common words that do not change in the plural are:

il cinema cinema	**i** cinema
la radio radio	**le** radio
la moto motorbike	**le moto**
l'auto car	**le auto**
la foto photo	**le foto**

①

un anno	one year
due anni	two years
un ragazzo	a boy
i ragazzi	the boys
un ciclista	a (*male*) cyclist
due ciclisti	two cyclists
un problema	a problem
molti problemi	lots of problems
un mese	one month
due mesi	two months
un francese	a Frenchman
due francesi	two Frenchmen

②

una settimana	one week
due settimane	two weeks
una ragazza	one girl
due ragazze	two girls

③

un'inglese	an Englishwoman
due inglesi	two Englishwomen
la vite	the vine
le viti	the vines

④

la città	the city
le città	the cities
la loro università	their university
le loro università	their universities
un caffè	a coffee
due caffè	two coffees
una virtù	a virtue
le sue virtù	her virtues

⑤

un'analisi	an analysis
delle analisi	analyses
una serie	a series
due serie	two series
una specie	a sort
varie specie	various sorts

⑥

il film	the film
i film	the films
il manager	the manager
i manager	the managers
il computer	the computer
i computer	the computers
la jeep	the jeep
le jeep	the jeeps

Irregular Plural Forms

Some masculine nouns become feminine in the plural, and take the ending -a → ❶

The plural of **uomo** man is *uomini*. The plural of **la mano** hand is **le mani.**

Nouns ending in **-ca** and **-ga** add an **h** before the plural ending, to keep the sound of the **c** and **g** hard → ❷

Some nouns ending in **-co** and **-go** also add an **h** before the plural ending, to keep the sound of the **c** and **g** hard → ❸

There are numerous exceptions. You can check the plural of such nouns in the dictionary.

> EXCEPTIONS:
> **amico** friend (*plural* **amici**)
> **nemico** enemy (*plural* **nemici**)
> **psicologo** psychologist (*plural* **psicologi**)
> **geologo** geologist (*plural* **geologi**)

The plurals of compound nouns such as **pescespada** (*swordfish*), **capolavoro** (*masterpiece*), or **apriscatole** (*tin opener*) do not always follow the usual rules. You can find them in the dictionary.

❶ il dito   the finger
le dita   the fingers
un uovo   an egg
le uova   the eggs
il lenzuolo   the sheet
le lenzuola   the sheets

❷ amica   (*female*) friend
amiche   (*female*) friends
buca   hole
buche   holes
riga   line
righe   lines
casalinga   housewife
casalinghe   housewives

❸ gioco   game
giochi   games
fuoco   fire
fuochi   fires
luogo   place
luoghi   places
borgo   district
borghi   districts

The Definite Article

il (l')/lo, la(l'), i/gli;le

	MASCULINE	FEMININE
SING.	il	la
	lo	
	l'	l'
PLUR.	i	le
	gli	

The form of the Italian article depends on the gender and number of the noun it accompanies. It also depends on the letter the noun starts with.

il is used with masculine nouns starting with most consonants, except for **z**, **gn**, **pn**, **ps**, **x**, **y** and impure **s***; **lo** is used with these. **l'** is used before vowels → **①**

i is used with masculine plural nouns starting with most consonants; **gli** is used before vowels and **z**, **gn**, **pn**, **ps**, **x**, **y** and impure **s***. → **②**

la is used before feminine singular nouns beginning with a consonant, and **l'** is used before a vowel → **③**

le is used with all feminine plural nouns → **④**

if the article is separated from the noun by an adjective, the first letter of the adjective determines the choice of article → **⑤**

For uses of the definite article see page 138.

*Impure **s** means **s** + another consonant.

1

il ragazzo	the boy
il cellulare	the mobile phone
lo zio	the uncle
lo studente	the student
lo pneumatico	the tyre
lo psichiatra	the psychiatrist
lo yogurt	the yoghurt
l'ospedale	the hospital
l'albergo	the hotel

2

i fratelli	the brothers
i cellulari	the mobile phones
gli studenti	the students
gli zii	the uncles
gli gnocchi	the gnocchi
gli pneumatici	the tyres
gli yogurt	the yoghurts
gli amici	the friends
gli orari	the timetables

3

la ragazza	the girl
la macchina	the car
l'amica	the (girl) friend
l'arancia	the orange

4

le ragazze	the girls
le amiche	the (girl) friends

5

l'amico the friend	il migliore amico the best friend
lo studente the student	il migliore studente the best student
gli studenti the students	i migliori studenti the best students

The Definite Article *continued*

The prepositions **a, da, di, in** and **su** combine with the article to form one word.

a + article → ❶

SING.	a + il = al	a + la = alla
	a + l' = all'	a + l' = all'
	a + lo = allo	
PLUR.	a + i = ai	a+ le = alle
	a + gli = agli	

da + article → ❷

SING.	da + il = dal	da + la = dalla
	da + l' = dall'	da + l' = dall'
	da + lo = dallo	
PLUR.	da + i = dai	da+ le = dalle
	da + gli = dagli	

di + article → ❸

SING.	di + il = del	di + la = della
	di + l' = dell'	di + l' = dell'
	di + lo = dello	
PLUR.	di + i = dei	di+ le = delle
	di + gli = degli	

in + article → ❹

SING.	in + il = nel	in + la = nella
	in + l' = nell'	in + l' = nell'
	in + lo = nello	
PLUR.	in + i = nei	in+ le = nelle
	in + gli = negli	

su + article → ❺

SING.	su + il = sul	su + la = sulla
	su + l' = sull'	su + l' = sull'
	su + lo = sullo	
PLUR.	su + i = sui	su + le = sulle
	su + gli = sugli	

1 al cinema   to the cinema
allo stadio   at *or* to the stadium
ai concerti   at *or* to the concerts
alle partite   at *or* to the matches

2 dall'albergo   from the hotel
dalla stazione   from the station
dagli aeroporti   from the airports
della squadra   of the team
degli studenti   of the students

3 nel giardino   in the garden
nell'appartamento   in the flat

4 nei dintorni   in the surroundings

5 sullo scoglio   on the rock
sulla spiaggia   on the beach

The Definite Article *continued*

Uses of the Definite Article

The definite article is used much more in Italian than it is in English. It generally translates the English definite article, but is also used in many contexts where English has no article:

with possessive pronouns → **1**

with plurals and uncountable* nouns → **2**

in generalizations → **3**

with the names of regions and countries → **4**
EXCEPTIONS: no article with countries following the Italian preposition **in** *in/to* → **5**

with parts of the body, replacing the English possessive adjective → **6**

'Ownership' of parts of the body, and of clothes, is often indicated by an indirect object pronoun or a reflexive pronoun → **7**

with the time, dates and years → **8**

in expressions of quantity/rate/price → **9**

with titles, ranks, professions followed by a proper name, and colloquially, with female names → **10**

* An uncountable noun is one which cannot be used in the plural or with an indefinite article, e.g. *milk*.

Examples

1. la mia casa — my house
   le sue figlie — her daughters
   i vostri amici — your friends

2. I bambini soffrono — Children are suffering
   Mi piacciono gli animali — I like animals
   Le cose vanno meglio — Things are going better
   Il nuoto è il mio sport preferito — Swimming is my favourite sport
   Non mi piace il riso — I don't like rice

3. Lo zucchero non fa bene — Sugar isn't good for you
   La povertà è un grande problema — Poverty is a big problem

4. L'Australia è molto grande — Australia is very big
   La Calabria è bella — Calabria is beautiful

5. Vado in Francia a giugno — I'm going to France in June
   Lavorano in Germania — They work in Germany

6. Dammi la mano — Give me your hand
   Attento alla testa! — Mind your head!

7. Mi fa male il piede — My foot is hurting
   Soffiati il naso! — Blow your nose!
   Si è tolto il cappotto — He took off his coat
   Mettiti le scarpe — Put your shoes on

8. all'una — at one o'clock
   alle due — at two o'clock
   Era l'una — It was one o'clock
   Sono le due — It's two o'clock
   Sono nata il primo maggio 1990 — I was born on May 1, 1990
   Verranno nel 2011 — They're coming in 2011

9. Costano 3 euro al chilo — They cost 3 euro a kilo
   70 km all'ora — 70 km an hour
   50.000 dollari al mese — 50,000 dollars per month
   due volte alla settimana — twice a week

10. La signora Rossi è qui — Mrs. Rossi is here
    Il dottor Gentile — Doctor Gentile
    la regina Elisabetta — Queen Elizabeth
    Ecco la Silvia! — Here's Silvia!

The Partitive Article

The partitive article has the sense of 'some' or 'any', although the Italian is not always translated in English.

Forms of the partitive

	WITH MASC. NOUN	WITH FEM. NOUN
SING.	del	della
	dell'	dell'
	dello	
PLUR.	dei	delle
	degli	

del burro	some butter
dell'olio	some oil
della carta	some paper
dei fiammiferi	some matches
delle uova	some eggs
Hanno rotto dei bicchieri	They broke some glasses
Mi ha fatto vedere delle foto	He showed me some photos
Ci vuole del sale	It needs (some) salt
Aggiungi della farina	Add (some) flour

The Indefinite Article

MASCULINE	FEMININE
un	una
uno	un'

The form of the indefinite article depends on the gender of the noun it accompanies. It also depends on the letter the noun starts with.

un is used with masculine nouns starting with vowels and most consonants, except for **z**, **gn**, **pn**, **ps**, **x**, **y** and impure **s*** → **❶**

uno is used with these → **❷**

una is used before feminine nouns beginning with a consonant, and **un'** is used before a vowel → **❸**

If the article is separated from the noun by an adjective, the first letter of the adjective determines the choice of article → **❹**

The indefinite article is used in Italian largely as it is in English except: → **❺**

- with the words **cento** and **mille**
- when translating *a few* or *a lot*
- in exclamations with **che**

The indefinite article is not used when speaking of someone's profession – either the verb **essere** is used, with no article, or **fare** is used with the definite article → **❻**

* impure **s** means **s** + another consonant.

1 un cellulare — a mobile phone
un uomo — a man

2 uno studente — a student
uno zio — an uncle
uno psichiatra — a psychiatrist

3 una ragazza — a girl
una mela — an apple
un'ora — an hour
un'amica — a (girl) friend
un albergo — a hotel

4 uno splendido albergo — a magnificent hotel
uno scultore — a sculptor
un bravo scultore — a good sculptor

5 cento volte — a hundred times
mille sterline — a thousand pounds
qualche parola — a few words
molti soldi — a lot of money
Che sorpresa! — What a surprise!
Che peccato! — What a pity!

6 È medico — He's a doctor
Sono professori — They're teachers
Faccio l'ingegnere — I'm an engineer
Fa l'avvocato — She's a lawyer

The formation of feminines and plurals

Most adjectives agree in number and gender with the noun or pronoun.

The formation of feminines

If the masculine singular form of the adjective ends in **-o**, the feminine ends in **-a** → ①

If the adjective ends in **-e**, the ending does not change for the feminine → ②

The formation of plurals

If the masculine singular of the adjective ends in **-o**, the ending changes to **-i** for the masculine plural, and to **-e** for the feminine plural → ③

If the adjective ends in **-e**, the ending changes to **-i** for both masculine and feminine plural → ④

Invariable adjectives

Some adjectives have no change of ending either for the feminine or the plural → ⑤

① un ragazzo alto — a tall boy
una ragazza alta — a tall girl
un film italiano — an Italian film
una squadra italiana — an Italian team

② un libro inglese — an English book
una famiglia inglese — an English family
un treno veloce — a fast train
una macchina veloce — a fast car

③ un fiore rosso — a red flower
dei fiori rossi — red flowers
un computer nuovo — a new computer
dei computer nuovi — new computers
una strada pericolosa — a dangerous road
delle strade pericolose — dangerous roads
una moto nera — a black motorbike
delle moto nere — black motorbikes

④ un esercizio difficile — a difficult exercise
degli esercizi difficili — difficult exercises
un sito web interessante — an interesting website
dei siti web interessanti — interesting websites
una storia triste — a sad story
delle storie tristi — sad stories
una valigia pesante — a heavy case
delle valigie pesanti — heavy cases

⑤ un calzino rosa — a pink sock
una maglietta rosa — a pink T-shirt
un paio di guanti rosa — a pair of pink gloves

un tappeto blu — a blue rug
una macchina blu — a blue car
delle tende blu — blue curtains

un gruppo pop — a pop group
la musica pop — pop music
dei gruppi pop — pop groups

Irregular Adjectives

When **bello** *beautiful* is used in front of a masculine noun it has different forms depending on which letter follows it.

MASC. SING.	MASC. PLUR.	EXAMPLES
bel	bei	before most consonants → ①
bell'	begli	before vowels → ②
bello	begli	before z, gn, pn, ps, x and impure s* → ③

When used after a verb, **bello** has the same endings as any other adjective ending in **-o** → ④

buono *good* is becomes **buon** when used before a masculine singular noun, unless the noun starts with **z, gn, pn, ps, x** or impure **s*** → ⑤

grande *big, great* is often shortened to **gran** when it comes before a singular noun starting with a consonant → ⑥

*Impure **s** means **s** + another consonant.

Examples

1 bel tempo   beautiful weather
    bei nomi   beautiful names

2 un bell'*albero*   a beautiful tree
    dei begli *alberi*   beautiful trees

3 un bello strumento   a beautiful instrument
    dei begli strumenti   beautiful instruments

4 Il tempo era bello   The weather was beautiful
    I fiori sono belli   The flowers are beautiful

5 Buon vi*a*ggio!   Have a good journey!
    un buon uomo   a good man
    un buono studente   a good student

6 la Gran Bretagna   Great Britain
    un gran n*u*mero di m*a*cchine   a large number of cars

147

Comparatives and Superlatives

Comparatives are formed using the following constructions:

più ... (di) more ... (than) → ①
meno ... (di) less ... (than) → ②
(così) .... come as ... as → ③
(tanto) .... quanto as ... as → ④

Superlatives are formed using the following constructions:

il/la/i/le più ... (che) the most ... (that) → ⑤
il/la/i/le meno ... (che) the least ... (that) → ⑥

After a superlative the preposition **di** is often translated as 'in' → ⑦

If a clause follows a superlative the verb is in the subjunctive → ⑧

Adjectives with irregular comparatives/superlatives

ADJECTIVE	COMPARATIVE	SUPERLATIVE
buono	**migliore**	**il migliore**
good	better	the best
cattivo	**peggiore**	**il peggiore**
bad	worse	worst
grande	**maggiore**	**il maggiore**
big	bigger/older	the biggest/oldest
piccolo	**minore**	**il minore**
small	smaller/younger	the smallest/youngest
alto	**superiore**	**il superiore**
high	higher	the highest
basso	**inferiore**	**l'inferiore**
low	lower	the lowest

The above words also have regular comparatives/superlatives → ⑨

Emphatic adjectives

For added emphasis, the final vowel of an adjective can be replaced with the ending **-issimo**, or **-issima** → ⑩

Examples

1. una macchina più grande — a bigger car
   Sono più alto di te — I'm taller than you

2. un computer meno caro — a less expensive computer
   i suoi film meno interessanti — his less interesting films
   Quello verde è meno caro del nero — The green one is less expensive than the black one

3. È alta come sua sorella — She's as tall as her sister
   La mia borsa non è pesante come la tua — My bag's not as heavy as yours
   Non è così lontano come credi — It's not as far as you think

4. Sono stanca quanto te — I'm just as tired as you are
   Ha tanto lavoro quanto ne hai tu — He's got as much work as you have
   Non ho tanti soldi quanti ne hai tu — I haven't got as much money as you

5. il più alto — the tallest
   Queste sono le scarpe più comode — These shoes are the most comfortable

6. il meno interessante — the least interesting
   Gianni è il meno ambizioso — Gianni is the least ambitious

7. lo stadio più grande d'Italia — the biggest stadium in Italy
   il ristorante più caro della città — the most expensive restaurant in the town

8. la persona più pigra che conosca — the laziest person I know
   È una delle cose più belle che ci siano — It's one of the nicest things there is

9. Il libro è migliore del film — The book is better than the film
   Questo è più buono — This one's better
   la loro sorella minore — their younger sister
   il loro fratello più piccolo — their younger brother

10. Il tempo era bellissimo — The weather was really beautiful
    Anna è sempre elegantissima — Anna is always terribly smart
    Sono educatissimi — They're extremely polite

Demonstrative Adjectives

questo/questa/questi/queste → **①**

	MASCULINE	FEMININE	
SING.	questo	questa	this
PLUR.	questi	queste	these

quello has different forms, depending on the gender of the following noun, and the letter it starts with.

	MASCULINE	FEMININE	
SING.	quel	quella	that
	quello		
	quell'	quell'	
PLUR.	quei	quelle	those
	quegli		

quel is used before most consonants, except for **z**, **gn**, **pn**, **ps**, **x** and impure **s**. **quello** is used before these letters. **quell'** is used before vowels. **quei** is used before most consonants; **quegli** is used before vowels and **z**, **gn**, **pn**, **ps**, **x** and impure **s***.

quella is used before feminine singular nouns beginning with a consonant, with **quell'** used before a vowel → **②**

*Impure **s** means **s** + another consonant.

Examples

❶   Questa gonna è troppo stretta   This skirt is too tight
Questi pantaloni mi piacciono   I like these trousers
Queste scarpe sono comode   These shoes are comfortable

❷   quel ragazzo   that boy
quello zaino   that rucksack
quello studente   that student
quell'albero   that tree
quei cani   those dogs
quegli uomini   those men
quegli studenti   those students
quella ragazza   that girl
quell'amica   that friend
quelle macchine   those cars

Interrogative Adjectives

che? what?

che is invariable → ❶

quale/quali? → ❷

	MASCULINE/FEMININE	
SING.	**quale**	what?; which?
PLUR.	**quali**	what?; which?

quanto/quanta/quanti/quante? → ❸

	MASCULINE	FEMININE	
SING.	**quanto**	**quanta**	how much?
PLUR.	**quanti**	**quante**	how many?

Interrogative adjectives are often preceded by prepositions → ❹

Exclamatory Adjectives

che and **quanto** are used with nouns in exclamations → ❺

che is also used with other adjectives → ❻

1

Che giorno è oggi?	What day is it today?
Che ore sono?	What time is it?
Che gusto preferisci?	Which flavour do you like best?
Che film hai visto?	Which film did you see?
Che programmi hai?	What plans have you got?

2

| Quale tipo vuoi? | What kind do you want? |

3

Quanto pane hai comprato?	How much bread did you buy?
Quanta minestra vuoi?	How much soup do you want?
Quanti bicchieri ci sono?	How many glasses are there?
Quante uova vuoi?	How many eggs do you want?

4

A che ora ti alzi?	What time do you get up?
Di che colore è?	What colour is it?
Per quale squadra tifi?	Which team do you support?

5

Che peccato!	What a pity!
Che disordine!	What a mess!
Che bella giornata!	What a lovely day!
Che brutto tempo!	What awful weather!
Quanto tempo sprecato!	What a waste of time!
Quanta gente!	What a lot of people!
Quanti soldi!	What a lot of money!
Quante storie!	What a fuss!

6

| Che carino! | Isn't he sweet! |
| Che brutti! | They're horrible! |

Possessive Adjectives

WITH SING. NOUN		WITH PLUR. NOUN		
MASC.	FEM.	MASC.	FEM.	
il mio	la mia	i mlei	le mie	my
il tuo	la tua	i tuoi	le tue	your
il suo	la sua	i suoi	le sue	his; her; its; your
il nostro	la nostra	i nostri	le nostre	our
il vostro	la vostra	i vostri	le vostre	your
il loro	la loro	i loro	le loro	their

Possessive adjectives are generally preceded by the article → ➊

Possessive adjectives agree in number and gender with the noun they describe (i.e. the thing which is owned), not with the owner → ➋

il suo/la sua/i suoi/le sue can mean either 'his' or 'her'. To make clear which is meant, **di lui** can be used for 'his', and **di lei** for 'her' → ➌

The article is not used with any possessive adjective except loro when referring to singular family members → ➍

EXCEPTIONS: **mamma**, **babbo** and **papà**

Examples

1
Dove sono le mie chiavi?	Where are my keys?
Luca ha perso il suo portafoglio	Luca has lost his wallet
Ecco i nostri passaporti	Here are our passports
Qual è la vostra camera?	Which is your room?
Il tuo amico ti aspetta	Your friend is waiting for you

2
| Anna ha perso il suo cellulare | Anna has lost her mobile phone |
| Le ragazze hanno i loro biglietti | The girls have got their tickets |

3
| Le scarpe di lui sono eleganti | His shoes are smart |
| Le scarpe di lei non mi piacciono | I don't like her shoes |

4
con mia madre	with my mother
Dov'è tuo padre?	Where's your father?
lei e suo marito	she and her husband
È sua moglie	She's his wife
mia sorella ed io	my sister and I
Non è il loro padre	He's not their father
Maria e il suo papà	Maria and her dad

Position of Adjectives

Italian adjectives usually follow the noun → ①

Adjectives of colour or nationality *always* follow the noun → ②

As in English, demonstrative, possessive, numerical and interrogative adjectives precede the noun → ③

The adjectives **ogni**, **qualche** and **nessuno** always precede the noun → ④

The following common adjectives can precede the noun:

ottimo very good	**pessimo** very bad
bello beautiful	**brutto** bad, ugly
bravo good	**buono** good
prossimo next	*ultimo* last
povero poor	**grande** big, great
nuovo new	**vecchio** old
breve short	*piccolo* small

The meaning of the following adjectives can be affected by their position:

	AFTER NOUN	BEFORE NOUN
grande	big	great → ⑤
povero	poor	unfortunate → ⑥
vecchio	old	long-standing → ⑦

Adjectives following the noun are linked by **e** → ⑧

1 un gesto spontaneo — a spontaneous gesture
una partita importante — an important match

2 capelli biondi — blonde hair
pantaloni neri — black trousers
una parola italiana — an Italian word

3 questo cellulare — this mobile phone
la mia mamma — my mum
il primo piano — the first floor
Quale gusto? — What flavour?

4 ogni giorno — every day
qualche volta — some times
Non c'è nessun bisogno di andarci — There's no need to go

5 un uomo grande — a big man
una grande sorpresa — a great surprise

6 gente povera — poor people
Povera Anna! — Poor Anna!

7 una casa vecchia — an old house
un mio vecchio amico — an old friend of mine

8 un libro lungo e noioso — a long, boring book
ragazze antipatiche e maleducate — nasty rude girls

Personal Pronouns

	SUBJECT PRONOUNS	
	SINGULAR	PLURAL
1st person	**io** I	**noi** we
2nd person	**tu** you	**voi** you
3rd person (*masc.*)	**lui** he	**loro** they
(*fem.*)	**lei** she	
(*used as polite 'you'*)	**lei/Lei** you	

Italian verbs are frequently used without subject pronouns → ❶

tu/lei
Lei, as well as being the 3rd person singular feminine, is used when addressing someone politely. As a general rule, use **tu** only when addressing a friend, a child, a fellow student, someone you know very well, or when invited to do so. In other cases use **lei,** which is occasionally spelled with a capital when used to mean *you* ❷

loro
Loro is used only to refer to people, not to things → ❸

Loro is occasionally used as a very formal alternative to **voi** → ❹

Examples

❶ Conosci Paolo?
Parlo italiano
Costa troppo

Do you know Paul?
I speak Italian
It costs too much

❷ Tu cara, cosa prendi?

Lei, signora, cosa prende?

What are you going to have, dear?

What are you going to have, madam?

❸ Loro chi sono?
Cosa sono? – Sono noci.

Who are they?
What are they? – They're walnuts.

❹ Loro cosa prendono?

What will you have, ladies and gentlemen?

Personal Pronouns *continued*

3rd Person Pronouns

lui, **lei** and **loro** are the subject pronouns normally used in spoken Italian. In older written Italian you may find **egli** (masc. sing.), **ella** (fem. sing.), **essi** (masc. plur.) and **esse** (fem. plur.).

esso and **essa** are subject pronouns meaning *it*, but they are very rarely used. In Italian there is normally no pronoun corresponding to *it* at the start of a sentence → ①

Subject pronouns often follow the verb → ②

Subject pronouns are used:
- to add emphasis, for clarity, or to attract someone's attention → ③
- after **anche** *too*, **neanche** *neither* and **pure** *as well* → ④
- when the verb in Italian is understood → ⑤

	UNSTRESSED DIRECT OBJECT PRONOUNS	
	SINGULAR	PLURAL
1st person	**mi** me	**ci** us
2nd person	**ti** you	**vi** you
3rd person (*masc.*)	**lo (l')** him; it	**li** them
(*fem.*)	**la (l')** her; it	**le** them
(*used as polite 'you'*)	**la/La (l')** you	**le** you

mi, **ti**, **ci** and **vi** can (but do not have to) become **m'**, **t'**, **c'** and **v'** before a vowel or mute **h** → ⑥

lo and **la** change to **l'** before a vowel or mute **h** → ⑦

For information on past participle agreement see page 56.

lo/la /li/le

lo means *him*, or *it*, when the object referred to is masculine → ⑧

la means *her*, or *it*, when the object referred to is feminine → ⑨

li refers to people, or objects that are masculine → ⑩

le refers to females, or objects that are feminine → ⑪

1
Fa caldo — It's hot
Sono le tre — It's three o'clock
È tardi — It's late

2
Pago io — I'll pay
Ci pensiamo noi — We'll see to it

3
Tu cosa dici? — What do you think?
No, l'ha fatto lui — No, he did it
Lei, signore, cosa prende? — And you sir, what will you have?

4
Prendi un gelato anche tu? — Are you going to have an ice cream too?
Non so perché. – Neanch'io — I don't know why. – Neither do I
È venuto pure lui — He came as well

5
Chi è il più bravo? – Lui. — Who's the best? – He is.
Viene lui, ma lei no — He's coming, but she isn't

6
Non c'hanno visto or — They didn't see us
Non ci hanno visto

7
Non l'ho visto più — I didn't see him again
L'ho incontrata ieri — I met her yesterday

8
Gianni? Non lo vedo mai — Gianni? I never see him
Dov'è il mio cellulare? Non lo vedo — Where's my mobile phone? I can't see it

9
Chiara? Non la vedo mai — Chiara? I never see her
La birra? Non la bevo mai. — Beer? I never drink it.

10
Marco e Sara – li conosci? — Marco and Sara – do you know them?
Hai i biglietti? Sì, li ho nel portafoglio — Have you got the tickets? Yes, I've got them in my wallet

11
Le sue sorelle? Non le conosco — His sisters? I don't know them
Hai le chiavi? Sì, le ho in tasca — Have you got the keys? Yes, I've got them in my pocket

Personal Pronouns *continued*

Position of unstressed direct object pronouns

The pronoun generally comes before the verb → ❶

Unstressed direct pronouns come after the verb

- in imperatives, with the pronoun joined onto the verb → ❷

ⓘ If the verb consists of a single syllable, the initial consonant of the pronoun is doubled, except in the case of **gli** → ❸

- in infinitive constructions, when the final **-e** of the infinitive is dropped, and replaced by the pronoun → ❹

Stressed direct object pronouns

		STRESSED DIRECT OBJECT PRONOUNS	
		SINGULAR	PLURAL
1st	person	me	noi
2nd	person	te	voi
3rd	person (*masc.*)	lui	loro
	(*fem.*)	lei	loro
(*used as polite 'you'*)		lei/Lei	loro

Stressed direct object pronouns are used:
- for emphasis or contrast → ❺
- after prepositions → ❻
- in comparisons → ❼

For further information, see Order of Object Pronouns, page 166.

Reflexive Pronouns

These are dealt with under reflexive verbs, page 32.

Examples

❶ Ti amo

Lo invito alla festa

Non lo mangio

La guardava

Vi cercavo

Li conosciamo

I love you

I'm inviting him to the party

I'm not going to eat it

He was looking at her

I was looking for you

We know them

❷ Aiutami!

Lasciala stare

Help me!

Leave her alone

❸ Fallo subito!

Do it right away!

❹ Potresti venire a prendermi?

Non posso aiutarvi

Devo proprio farlo?

Could you come and get me?

I can't help you

Do I really have to do it?

❺ Amo solo te

Invito lui alla festa, ma lei no

Non guardava me, guardava lei

I love only you

I'm inviting him to the party but not her

He wasn't looking at me, he was looking at her

❻ Vengo con te

Sono arrivati dopo di noi

I'll come with you

They arrived after us

❼ Sei più alto di me

Sono più ricchi di lui

You're taller than me

They're richer than him

Personal Pronouns *continued*

		UNSTRESSED INDIRECT OBJECT PRONOUNS	
		SINGULAR	PLURAL
1ˢᵗ	person	**mi**	**ci**
2ⁿᵈ	person	**ti**	**vi**
3ʳᵈ	person *(masc.)*	**gli**	**gli** *or* **loro**
	(fem.)	**le**	**gli** *or* **loro**
(used as polite 'you')		**le**	**loro**

The pronouns in the above table replace the preposition **a** + *noun*, where the noun is a person or an animal → ❶

Indirect object pronouns are used with verbs governing **a** → ❷

Unstressed indirect pronouns are also used with impersonal verbs which govern **a** → ❸

Position of unstressed indirect object pronouns

Unstressed indirect pronouns generally come before the verb → ❹

Unstressed indirect pronouns come after the verb:
- in imperatives, with the pronoun joined onto the verb → ❺

ⓘ If the verb consists of a single syllable, the initial consonant of the pronoun is doubled, except in the case of **gli** → ❻

- in infinitive constructions. The final **-e** of the infinitive is dropped, and replaced by the pronoun → ❼

1 Ho detto la verità a Paola — I told Paola the truth
Le ho detto la verità — I told her the truth
Hai dato del latte al gatto? — Have you given the cat some milk?

Gli hai dato del latte? — Have you given him some milk?
Potresti dare qualche consiglio ai signori? — Could you give the lady and gentleman some advice?
Potresti dar loro or dargli qualche consiglio? — Could you give them some advice?

2 telefonare a qn — to phone sb
Non le ho telefonato — I didn't phone her
promettere qc a qn — to promise sb sth
Mi ha promesso un regalo — He promised me a present
consigliare a qn di fare qc — to advise sb to do sth
Ci ha consigliato di aspettare — He advised us to wait

3 Le piacciono i gatti — She likes cats
Non gli importa il prezzo, sono ricchi — They don't care about the price, they're rich
Se gli interessa può venire con me — If he's interested he can come with me

4 Mi assomiglia? — Does she look like me?
Ti piace? — Do you like it?

5 Rispondigli! — Answer him!
Mandami un SMS — Send me a text

6 Dimmi dov'è — Tell me where it is
Dacci una mano — Give us a hand

7 Dovresti scriverle — You ought to write to her
Luigi? Non voglio parlargli — Luigi? I don't want to talk to him

Personal Pronouns *continued*

Stressed Indirect Pronouns

		STRESSED INDIRECT OBJECT PRONOUNS	
		SINGULAR	PLURAL
1st	person	a me	a noi
2nd	person	a te	a voi
3rd	person (*masc.*)	a lui	a loro
	(*fem.*)	a lei	a loro
(*used as polite 'you'*)		a lei	a loro

The above forms are used for special emphasis, either before or after the verb → **①**

For further information, see Order of Object Pronouns, below.

Reflexive Pronouns

These are dealt with under reflexive verbs, page 32.

Order of Object Pronouns

If direct and indirect unstressed pronouns occur together, the indirect pronoun always comes first .

mi/ti/ci/vi when followed by a direct object pronoun become **me**, **te**, **ce** and **ve** → **②**

gli and **le** when followed by a direct object pronoun both become **glie-**, and add the pronoun to make one word: **glielo**, **gliela**, **glieli** or **gliele** → **③**

When an indirect pronoun and a direct pronoun follow an imperative, or an infinitive, they join on to it to make one word → **④**

When a stressed indirect object pronoun and an unstressed direct object pronoun occur together the above rules do not apply → **⑤**

1 Ho scritto a lei, a lui no — I wrote to her, but not to him
A me piace, ma Luca preferisce l'altro — I like it, but Luca would rather have the other one

2 Me la dai? — Will you give me it?
È mia – non te la do — It's mine, I'm not going to give it to you

Ce l'hanno promesso — They promised it to us
Ve lo mando domani — I'll send it to you tomorrow

3 Glieli hai promessi — You promised them to her
Gliel'ha spedite — He sent them to them
Carlo? Glielo dirò domani — Carlo? I'll tell him tomorrow

4 Mi piacciono, ma non vuole comprarmeli — I like them but she won't buy me them
Ecco la lettera di Rita, puoi dargliela? — Here's Rita's letter, can you give it to her?
Ecco le chiavi. Dagliele — Here are the keys. Give them to her.

Non abbiamo i biglietti – può mandarceli? — We haven't got the tickets – can you send us them?

5 Mandale a lui, non a me — Send them to him, not to me

The pronoun ne

ne replaces the preposition **di** + *noun* → ❶

There may be no preposition in the English translation of verbal constructions with **di/ne** → ❷

ne also replaces the partitive article (English = some, any) + *noun* → ❸

When used with amounts or numbers, **ne** represents the noun → ❹

Position: **ne** always follows another pronoun and comes before all verbs
except imperatives and infinitives → ❺

Pronouns which precede **ne** change their form:
mi/ti/si/ci/vi before **ne** become **me/te/se/ce/ve** → ❻

ne follows the imperative and joins onto to it to make one word → ❼

ne joins onto the infinitive, which drops the final **-e** → ❽

Pronouns which come between the imperative or infinitive and **ne** change
their form: **mi**, **ti**, **ci**, **vi** become **me**, **te**, **ce** and **ve**.
gli and **le** become **glie** → ❾

Examples

① Sono conscio del pericolo — I'm aware of the danger
Ne sono conscio — I'm aware of it
Sono sicura del fatto — I'm sure of the fact
Ne sono sicura — I'm sure of it
Ha scritto della guerra sul giornale — She's written about the war in the paper

Ne ha scritto sul giornale — She's written about it in the paper
Parliamo del futuro. – Sì, parliamone. — Let's talk about the future. – Yes, let's talk about it.

② accorgersi di qc — to realize sth
Non se ne accorge — He doesn't realize it
aver bisogno di qc — to need sth
Hai bisogno della chiave? – No, non ne ho più bisogno. — Do you need the key? – No, I don't need it any more.

③ Perché non prendi delle fragole? — Why aren't you having any strawberries?
Perché non ne prendi? — Why aren't you having any?
Vuoi del pane? — Would you like some bread?
Ne vuoi? — Would you like some?

④ Hai due figli? – No, ne ho tre. — Have you got two children? – No, I've got three.
Hai dello zucchero? – Ne ho un poco. — Have you got any sugar? – I've got a bit.

⑤ Ne hai paura? — Are you afraid of it?

⑥ Ti ricordi di quel giorno? — Do you remember that day?
Te ne ricordi? — Do you remember it?
Non si accorge degli errori — He doesn't notice mistakes
Non se ne accorge — He doesn't notice them

⑦ Assaggiane un po' — Try a bit

⑧ Non voglio parlarne — I don't want to talk about it

⑨ Dammene uno per favore — Give me one of them please
Dagliene due rossi — Give him two red ones
Non posso dartene uno — I can't give you one
Non posso dargliene due rossi — I can't give him two red ones

The pronoun ci

ci replaces the preposition **a** + *noun* → **❶**

There may be no preposition in the English translation of verbal constructions with **a/ci** → **❷**

Position: like **ne**, **ci** comes before the verb, unless it is an imperative, infinitive, or the gerund → **❸**

For **ci** as a personal pronoun see page 164.

Note that **ci** is also an adverb meaning 'there' → **❹**

Examples

1   Credi ai fantasmi?   Do you believe in ghosts?
Ci credi?   Do you believe in them?
Non pensa al futuro   She doesn't think about the future

Non ci pensa   She doesn't think about it

2   far caso a qc   to notice sth
Non ci ho fatto caso   I didn't notice it
avvicinarsi a qc   to approach sth
Ci si avvicinò   He approached it

3   Ci penso io   I'll see to it
BUT
Pensaci un po'   Think about it a bit
Non so che farci   I don't know what to do about it
Ripensandoci mi sono pentito   When I thought it over I was sorry

4   Non voglio andarci   I don't want to go there
Ci sono molti turisti   There are a lot of tourists

Indefinite Pronouns

The following are indefinite pronouns:

alcuni(e) some → ①

altro(a, i, e) the other one; another one; other people → ②

chiunque anyone → ③

ciascuno(a) each → ④

molto(a, i, e) a lot, lots → ⑤

nessuno(a) nobody, anybody; none → ⑥

niente nothing → ⑦

nulla nothing → ⑧

ognuno(a) each → ⑨

parecchio, parecchia, parecchi, parecchie quite a lot → ⑩

poco, poca, pochi, poche not much, not many → ⑪

qualcosa something, anything → ⑫

qualcuno(a) somebody; any → ⑬

tanto(a, i, e) lots, so much, so many → ⑭

troppo(a, i, e) too much, too many → ⑮

tutti(e) everybody, all → ⑯

tutto everything, all → ⑰

uno(a) somebody → ⑱

Examples

1. Ci sono posti liberi? – Sì, alcuni.

   Ci sono ancora delle fragole?
   – Sì, alcune.

   Are there any empty seats?
   – Yes, some.

   Are there any strawberries left?
   – Yes, some.

2. L'altro è meno caro
   Non m'interessa quello che
     dicono gli altri
   Prendine un altro

   The other one is cheaper
   I don't care what other people
     say
   Take another one

3. Attacca discorso con chiunque

   She'll talk to anyone

4. Ne avevamo uno per ciascuno
   Le torte costano due euro ciascuna

   We had one each
   The cakes cost two euros each

5. Ne ha molto
   molti di noi

   He's got lots
   a lot of us

6. Non è venuto nessuno
   Nessuna delle ragazze è venuta

   Nobody came
   None of the girls came

7. Cosa c'è? – Niente.

   What's wrong? – Nothing.

8. Che cos'hai comprato? – Nulla.

   What did you buy? – Nothing.

9. ognuno di voi

   each of you

10. C'e ancora del pane? – Sì,
      parecchio.
    Avete avuto problemi?
      – Sì, parecchi.

    Is there any bread left? – Yes,
      quite a lot.
    Did you have problems?
      – Yes, a lot.

11. C'è pane? – Poco.
    Ci sono turisti? – Pochi.

    Is there any bread? – Not much.
    Are there any tourists? – Not many.

12. Ho qualcosa da dirti
    Ha bisogno di qualcosa?

    I've got something to tell you
    Do you need anything?

13. Ha telefonato qualcuno
    Conosci qualcuna delle ragazze?

    Somebody phoned
    Do you know any of the girls?

14. Hai mangiato? – Sì, tanto!

    Have you eaten? – Yes, lots!

15. Ci sono errori? – Sì, troppi.

    Are there any mistakes? – Yes,
      too many.

16. Vengono tutti
    Sono arrivate tutte

    Everybody is coming
    They've all arrived

17. Va tutto bene?
    L'ho finito tutto

    Is everything okay?
    I've finished it all

18. Ho incontrato uno che ti conosce

    I met somebody who knows you

Relative Pronouns

che who; whom; which; that
che is an invariable pronoun that can be the subject or object of a relative clause, and can refer to people or things → ❶

The Italian object pronoun cannot be omitted, though it need not be translated in English → ❷

After a preposition use **cui** → ❸

il che which
This is used to refer to a fact or situation that's just been mentioned → ❹

il quale, **la quale**, **i quali**, **le quali** who; whom; which; that
These are more formal relative pronouns, which agree in number and gender with the noun → ❺

il quale, **la quale**, **i quali** and **le quali** are used most often with prepositions.
The prepositions **di**, **da**, **a**, **in** and **su** combine with the articles **il**, **la**, **i** and **le** → ❻

Article + preposition combinations are dealt with on page 136

il cui, **la cui**, **i cui**, **le cui** whose
These agree in number and gender with the thing possessed → ❼

Use **cui** instead of **che** with a preposition → ❽

quello che, **ciò che** what, the thing which

These can be used as the subject or object of a relative clause. Literally they mean 'that which' → ❾

In combination with **di**, **quello** *or* **ciò che** become **quello di cui** *or* **ciò di cui** → ❿

① quella signora che ha un piccolo cane nero — that lady who has a little black dog

una persona che detesto — a person whom I detest

l'uomo che hanno arrestato — the man that they've arrested

la squadra che ha vinto — the team which won

② la persona che ammiro di più — the person (whom) I admire most

il dolce che hai fatto — the pudding (that) you made

③ la ragazza di cui ti ho parlato — the girl that I told you about

gli amici con cui andiamo in vacanza — the friends we go on holiday with

la persona a cui si riferiva — the person he was referring to

il quartiere in cui abito — the area in which I live

④ Non pagano nulla, il che non mi sembra giusto — They don't pay anything, which doesn't seem fair to me

Dice che non è colpa sua, il che è vero — She says it's not her fault, which is true

⑤ suo padre, il quale è avvocato — his father, who is a lawyer

le sue sorelle, le quali studiano a Roma — his sisters, who study in Rome

⑥ l'albergo nel quale ci siamo fermati — the hotel that we stayed at

la borsa di studio sulla quale contava — the grant he was counting on

gli amici dai quali ho avuto questo regalo — the friends I had this present from

la medicina della quale ho bisogno — the medicine I need

⑦ una persona il cui nome me sfugge — a person whose name escapes me

la persona i cui bagagli sono qui — the person whose bags are here

⑧ È quello con cui parlavo — He's the one I was talking to

⑨ Ho visto quello or ciò che c'era sul tavolo — I saw what was on the table

Quello or ciò che mi preoccupa è che... — The thing which worries me is that...

Quello or ciò che dici non ha senso — What you say doesn't make sense

Ho fatto quello or ciò che potevo — I did what I could

⑩ Non è quello or ciò di cui si tratta — That's not what it's about

Non è quello or ciò di cui mi aspettavo — That's not what I was expecting

Interrogative Pronouns

These pronouns are used in direct questions:

chi? who? whom?
che? what?
cosa? what?
che cosa? what?

These pronouns are invariable, and can be the subject or object of the verb → ➊

che cos'è/cos'è? what is it?
This is used to ask for something to be explained or identified → ➋

Prepositions come before the interrogative pronoun, and never at the end of the question → ➌

di chi? whose → ➍

quale? which? which one? what?
quale is the singular form (**qual** before a vowel), and **quali** the plural → ➎

qual è?/quali sono? what is/what are?
These are used to ask about a particular detail, name, number etc → ➏

quanto(a)? How much? → ➐

quanti(e)? How many? → ➑

All the pronouns used in direct questions can be used in indirect questions → ➒

① Chi è? Who is it?
Chi cerca? Who(m) are you looking for?
Che vuoi? What do you want?
Cosa vuole? What does he want?
Che cosa vogliono? What do they want?

② Che cos'è? – È un regalo. What is it? – It's a present.

③ A chi l'hai dato? Who did you give it to?
Con chi parlavi? Who were you talking to?
Di che cosa hai bisogno? What do you need?
A cosa ti aspettavi? What were you expecting?

④ Di chi è questa borsa? Whose is this bag?
Di chi sono queste chiavi? Whose are these keys?

⑤ Conosco sua sorella. – Quale? I know his sister. – Which one?
Ho rotto dei bicchieri. – Quali? I broke some glasses. – Which ones?

⑥ Qual è il suo indirizzo? What's her address?
Qual è la capitale della Finlandia? What's the capital of Finland?
Quali sono i loro nomi? What are their names?

⑦ Farina? Quanta ce ne vuole? Flour? How much is needed?

⑧ Quante di loro passano la sera a leggere? How many of them spend the evening reading?

⑨ Dimmi chi è Tell me who it is
Non so cosa vuol dire I don't know what it means
Ho chiesto di chi era I asked whose it was
Può dirmi di che cosa si tratta? Can you tell me what it's about?

Possessive Pronouns

Singular:

MASCULINE	FEMININE	
il mio	la mia	mine
il tuo	la tua	yours
il suo	la sua	his; hers; its; yours
il nostro	la nostra	ours
il vostro	la vostra	yours
il loro	la loro	theirs

Plural:

MASCULINE	FEMININE	
i miei	le mie	mine
i tuoi	le tue	yours
i suoi	le sue	his; hers; its; yours
i nostri	le nostre	ours
i vostri	le vostre	yours
i loro	le loro	theirs

The pronoun agrees in number and gender with the noun it replaces, not with the owner → **1**

di/da/a/su/in + *possessive pronoun*
These prepositions combine with the article → **2**

Examples

1 Paolo, questa borsa non è la mia,
   è la tua
  La nostra casa è piccola,
   la vostra è grande
  I miei genitori e i suoi si conoscono

Paolo, this bag's not mine,
   it's yours
Our house is small, yours is big

My parents and hers know
   each other

2 La mia macchina è più vecchia
   della sua
  Preferisco il nostro giardino al loro

My car is older than his

I prefer our garden to theirs

Demonstrative Pronouns

questo/questa/questi/queste
quello/quella/quelli/quelle

	MASCULINE	FEMININE	
SING.	questo	questa	this, this one
	quello	quella	that, that one, that man/that woman
PLUR.	questi	queste	these, these ones
	quelli	quelle	those, those ones, those people

The pronoun agrees in number and gender with the noun it replaces → **❶**

quello/a used to mean that man/woman is pejorative → **❷**

quello(a, i, e) che the one(s) who/which → **❸**

quello(a, i, e) di the one(s) belonging to/the one(s) of
This use is often translated by apostrophe s ('s), or s apostrophe (s') → **❹**

questo(a, i, e) qui/qua
qui or **qua** can be used with **questo** for emphasis or to distinguish between two things → **❺**

quello(a, i, e) lì/là
lì or **là** can be used with **quello** for emphasis or to distinguish between two things → **❻**

Examples

① Questo è mio marito
This is my husband
Questa è camera mia
This is my bedroom
Questi sono i miei fratelli
These are my brothers
Quali scarpe ti metti? – Queste
Which shoes are you going to
wear? – These ones

Qual è la sua borsa? – Quella
Which bag is yours? – That one
Quelli quanto costano?
How much do those cost?

② Dice sempre bugie quello
That man is always telling lies
Quelle non sono mai contente
Those women are never happy

③ È quello che preferisco
That's the one (that) I prefer
È quella che parla di più
She's the one who talks most
Sono quelli che sono partiti senza
pagare
They're the ones who left
without paying
Queste scarpe sono quelle che ha
ordinato
These shoes are the ones (that)
you ordered

④ Questo giardino è più grande di
quello di Giulia
This garden is bigger than Giulia's
Preferisco la mia macchina a
quella di mio marito
I prefer my car to my husband's
Le mie scarpe sono più belle di
quelle di Lucia
My shoes are nicer than Lucia's
i miei genitori e quelli delle mie
amiche
my parents and those of my
friends
le montagne della Svizzera e
quelle della Scozia
the mountains of Switzerland
and those of Scotland

⑤ Non quello, questo qui
Not that one, this one here
Voglio queste qua
I want these ones here

⑥ Questa gonna non ti sta bene,
prova quella là
This skirt doesn't look good
on you, try that one
Quali prendi? – Quelli lì
Which ones are you going to
have? – Those over there

Formation

Some adverbs are formed by adding **-mente** to an adjective.

-mente is added to the feminine form, (which ends in **-a**) of an adjective ending in **-o** → ❶

-mente is added to the basic form when an adjective ends in **-e** for both masculine and feminine → ❷

Adjectives ending in **-le** and **-re** drop the final **e** → ❸

Irregular Adverbs

ADJECTIVE	ADVERB
buono good	**bene** well → ❹
cattivo bad	**male** badly → ❺
migliore better	**meglio** better → ❻
peggiore worse	**peggio** worse → ❼

Adjectives used as adverbs

Certain adjectives are used adverbially. These include: **giusto**, **vicino**, **diritto**, **certo**, **solo**, **forte**, **molto**, **poco** → ❽

Examples

1 MASC./FEM. ADJECTIVE

lento/lenta slow
fortunato/fortunata lucky

ADVERB

lentamente slowly
fortunatamente luckily

2 MASC./FEM. ADJECTIVE

veloce quick, fast
corrente fluent

ADVERB

velocemente quickly, fast
correntemente fluently

3 -le/-re ADJECTIVE

facile easy
particolare particular

ADVERB

facilmente easily
particolarmente particularly

4 Parlano bene l'italiano

They speak Italian well

5 Ho giocato male

I played badly

6 Sto meglio

I'm better

7 Mi sento peggio

I'm feeling worse

8 Ha risposto giusto
Abitano vicino
Siamo andati sempre diritto
Vieni stasera? – Certo!

She answered correctly
They live nearby
We kept straight on
Are you coming tonight?
– Of course!

L'ho incontrata solo due volte
Correva forte
Quel quadro mi piace molto
Vengo in ufficio poco spesso

I've only met her twice
He was running fast
I like that picture a lot
I don't come into the office very
often

Adverbs

Position of Adverbs

When the adverb accompanies a verb in a simple tense, it generally follows the verb → **1**

For emphasis the adverb can come at the beginning of the sentence → **2**

When adverbs such as **mai**, **sempre**, **già** and **appena** accompany a verb in a compound tense, they come between the auxilary verb and the past participle → **3**

When the adverb accompanies an adjective or another adverb it generally precedes the adjective/adverb → **4**

Comparatives of Adverbs

These are formed as follows:

  più ... (di) more ... (than) → **5**
  meno ... (di) less ... (than) → **6**

sempre più is used with the adjective to mean *more and more* → **7**

Superlatives of Adverbs

più ... and **meno ...** are also used to express the superlative → **8**
più ... di tutti/meno di tutti can be used to emphasize the superlative → **9**

1. | | |
|---|---|
| Viene sempre | He always comes |
| Parli bene l'italiano | You speak Italian well |

2. | | |
|---|---|
| Ora non posso | I can't do it just now |
| Prima non lo sapevo | I didn't know that before |

3. | | |
|---|---|
| Non sono mai stata a Milano | I've never been to Milan |
| È sempre venuto con me | He always came with me |
| L'ho già letto | I've already read it |
| Se n'è appena andato | He's just left |

4. | | |
|---|---|
| Fa troppo freddo | It's too cold |
| Vai più piano | Go more slowly |

5. | | |
|---|---|
| più spesso | more often |
| più lentamente | more slowly |
| Correva più forte di me | He was running faster than me |

6. | | |
|---|---|
| meno velocemente | less quickly |
| Costa meno | It costs less |
| Vengo meno spesso di lui | I come less often than he does |

7. | | |
|---|---|
| Le cose vanno sempre meglio | Things are going better and better |
| Mio nonno sta sempre peggio | My grandfather's getting worse and worse |
| Cammina sempre più lento | He's walking slower and slower |

8. | | |
|---|---|
| È Carlo che viene più spesso | It's Carlo who comes most often |
| Sono loro che lavorano meno volontieri | They're the ones who work least willingly |

9. | | |
|---|---|
| Cammina più piano di tutti | She walks the slowest (of all) |
| L'ha fatto meno volentieri di tutti | He did it the least willingly |

Adverbs with irregular comparatives/superlatives

ADVERB	COMPARATIVE/SUPERLATIVE
bene well	**meglio** better/best
male badly	**peggio** worse/worst
molto a lot	**più** more/most
poco not much	**meno** less/least

Emphatic Adverbs

For added emphasis the ending **-issimamente** can be used. It replaces the endings **-amente**, **-emente** or **-mente** → **1**

bene and **male** have irregular emphatic forms: **benissimo** and **malissimo** → **2**

Adverbial phrases

di più and **di meno** are used to say what you do most/least → **3**

Examples

1
lentamente	slowly
lentissimamente	very slowly
velocemente	quickly
velocissimamente	very quickly

2 Hai fatto benissimo   You did very well

3
la cosa che temeva di più	the thing she feared most
quello che mi piace di meno	the one I like least
Sono quelli che guadagnano di meno	They're the ones who earn least

Some common adverbs and their usage

Some common adverbs:

abbastanza quite; enough → ①

anche too → ②

ancora still; yet → ③

appena just; only just → ④

certo certainly; of course → ⑤

così so; like this; like that → ⑥

ecco here → ⑦

forse perhaps, maybe → ⑧

già already → ⑨

mai never; ever → ⑩

molto very; very much; much → ⑪

piuttosto quite; rather → ⑫

poco not very; not at all → ⑬

presto soon; early → ⑭

quasi nearly → ⑮

spesso often → ⑯

tanto so; so much → ⑰

troppo too; too much → ⑱

Examples

1 È abbastanza alta — She's quite tall
Non studia abbastanza — He doesn't study enough

2 È venuta anche mia sorella — My sister came too

3 Sei ancora a letto? — Are you still in bed?
Silvia non è ancora arrivata — Silvia's not here yet

4 L'ho appena fatto — I've just done it
L'indirizzo ere appena leggibile — The address was only just legible

5 Certo che puoi — Of course you can
Certo che sì — Certainly

6 È così simpatica! — She's so nice!
Si apre così — It opens like this
Non si fa così — You don't do it like that

7 Ecco l'autobus! — Here's the bus!
Dov'è Carla? – Eccola! — Where's Carla? – Here she is!

8 Forse hanno ragione — Maybe they're right

9 Te l'ho già detto — I've already told you

10 Non sono mai stato in America — I've never been to America
Sei mai stato in America? — Have you ever been to America?

11 Sono molto stanca — I'm very tired
Ti piace? – Sì, molto. — Do you like it? – Yes, very much
Ora mi sento molto meglio — I feel much better now

12 Fa piuttosto caldo oggi — It's quite warm today
È piuttosto lontano — It's rather a long way

13 Mi sento poco bene — I don't feel at all well
Mi piacciono poco — I don't like them at all

14 Arriverà presto — He'll be here soon
Mi alzo sempre presto — I always get up early

15 Sono quasi pronta — I'm nearly ready

16 Vanno spesso in centro — They often go into town

17 Questo libro è tanto noioso — This book is so boring
Mi manchi tanto — I miss you so much

18 È troppo caro — It's too expensive
Parlano troppo — They talk too much

Prepositions

On the following pages you will find some of the most frequent uses of prepositions in Italian. Particular attention is paid to cases where usage differs greatly from English. It is often difficult to give an English equivalent for Italian prepositions, since usage varies so much between the two languages.

In the list below, the broad meaning of the preposition is given on the left, with examples of usage following.

Prepositions are given in alphabetical order, except for **a**, **di**, **da** and **in**. These prepositions, shown first, combine with the definite article to make one word.

For combinations of **a**, **di**, **da**, **in** and **su** with the definite article, see page 136.

a

at	**alla porta** at the door
	a casa at home
	alla prossima fermata at the next stop
	a 50 chilometri all'ora at 50 km an hour
in	**a Londra** in London
	al sole in the sun
	Sta a letto He's in bed
on	**al terzo piano** on the third floor
	alla radio on the radio
to	**Andiamo al cinema?** Shall we go to the cinema?
	Vai a letto? Are you going to bed?
	Sei mai stato a New York? Have you ever been to New York?
	dare qc a qn to give sth to sb
	A chi l'hai dato? Who did you give it to?
	promettere qc a qn to promise sth to sb
	il primo/l'ultimo a fare qc the first/last to do sth
from	**comprare qc a qn** to buy sth from sb

Examples

	nascondere qc a qn to hide sth from sb
	prendere qc a qn to take sth from sb
	rubare qc a qn to steal sth from sb
see you	**a presto** see you soon
	a domani see you tomorrow
manner	**a piedi** on foot
	a mano by hand
	a poco a poco little by little
	all'antica in the old-fashioned way
	alla milanese in the Milanese way
(made) with	**un gelato alla fragola** a strawberry ice cream
	una torta al cioccolato a chocolate cake
	gli spaghetti al pomodoro spaghetti with tomato sauce
time: at	**alle due** at two o'clock
	a mezzanotte at midnight
	a Pasqua at Easter
with month: in	**a maggio** in May
distance	**a tre chilometri da qui** three kilometres from here
	a due ore di distanza in macchina two hours away by car
purpose	**Sono uscita a fare due passi** I went out for a little walk
	Sono andati a fare il bagno They've gone to have a swim
after certain verbs	See pages 70-79

Prepositions

di

of, belonging to	**un amico di famiglia** a friend of the family **il padre di Marco** Marco's father **la casa dei miei amici** my friends' house **Di chi è?** Whose is it? **il periodo delle vacanze** the holiday season **il professore di francese** the French teacher **il campione del mondo** the world champion
(made) by	**un quadro di Picasso** a picture by Picasso **una commedia di Shakespeare** a play by Shakespeare
from	**È di Firenze** He's from Florence **Di dove sei?** Where are you from?
comparisons	**È più alto di me** He's taller than me **È più brava di lui** She's better than him
in (*after superlative*)	**il più grande del mondo** the biggest in the world **il migliore d'Italia** the best in Italy
time	**di domenica** on Sundays **di notte** at night **d'inverno** in winter
contents, composition, material, colour	**una bottiglia di vino** a bottle of wine **un gruppo di turisti** a group of tourists **una maglietta di cotone** a cotton T-shirt **Di che colore è?** What colour is it?
manner	**di rado** rarely **di solito** usually
after certain numbers	**un milione di dollari** a million dollars **un migliaio di persone** about a thousand people **una ventina di macchine** about twenty cars

Prepositions

after certain adjectives	**Le arance sono ricche di vitamina C** Oranges are rich in vitamin C **Era pieno di gente** It was full of people
after certain verbs	see pages 70-79

da

from	**a tre chilometri da qui** three kilometres from here **Viene da Roma** He comes from Rome **da cima a fondo** from top to bottom
off, out of	**Isobel è scesa dal treno** Isobel got off the train **È scesa dalla macchina** She got out of the car
at/to the home of	**Sono da Anna** I'm at Anna's house **Andiamo da Gabriele?** Shall we go to Gabriele's house?
at/to (*shop, workplace*)	**Laura è dal parrucchiere** Laura's at the hairdresser's **È andato dal dentista** He's gone to the dentist's
for	**Vivo qui da un anno** I've been living here for a year (*note tense*)
since	**da allora** since then **Ti aspetto dalle tre** I've been waiting for you since three o'clock (*note tense*)
by (*with passive agent*)	**dipinto da un grande artista** painted by a great artist **Sono stati catturati dalla polizia** They were caught by the police
to (*with infinitive*)	**C'è molto da fare** There's lots to do **È un film da vedere** It's a film that you've got to see
as	**Da bambino avevo paura del buio** As a child I was afraid of the dark

Prepositions

descriptive	**una ragazza dagli occhi azzurri** a girl with blue eyes **un vestito da cento euro** a dress costing a hundred euros

purpose/use	**un nuovo paio di scarpe da corsa**
	  a new pair of running shoes
	Non ho il costume da bagno
	  I haven't got my swimming costume

in

to, in *(place)*	**in centro** in/to the town centre **in Italia** in/to Italy
into	**Su! Sali in macchina** Come on! get into the car
on, at *(state)*	**in vacanza** on holiday **in pace** at peace
in *(years, seasons, months)*	**nel duemilasei** in two thousand and six **in estate** in summer **in ottobre** in October
in *(time taken)*	**L'ha fatto in sei mesi** He did it in six months
transport	**in treno** by train **in bici** by bike
language	**in italiano** in Italian

con

with	**Con chi sei stata?** Who were you with?
to	**Hai parlato con lui?** Have you spoken to him?
manner	**con calma** without hurrying **con la forza** by force

Prepositions

davanti a

in front of	**Erano seduti davanti a me nell' autobus**
	They were sitting in front of me in the bus
opposite	**la casa davanti alla mia** the house opposite mine

dopo

| after | **dopo cena** after dinner |
| + *pronoun* (add **di**) | **dopo di loro** after them |

fra/tra

in (*time*)	**Torno fra** *or* **tra un'ora** I'll be back in an hour
between	**fra** *or* **tra la cucina ed il soggiorno**
	between the kitchen and the living room
+ *pronoun* (add **di**)	**fra** *or* **tra di noi** between/among us

per

for	**Questo è per te** This is for you
	È troppo difficile per lui It's too difficult for him
	L'ho comprato per trenta centesimi
	I bought it for thirty cents
	Ho guidato per trecento chilometri
	I drove for three hundred kilometres
	una camera per due notti a room for two nights
	Parte per Milano She's leaving for Milan
(going) to	**il volo per Londra** the flight to London
	il treno per Roma the train to Rome
through	**I ladri sono entrati per la finestra**
	The burglars got in through the window
	Siamo passati per Crewe We went through Crewe

Prepositions

by (means of)	**per posta** by post
	per via aerea by airmail
	per posta elettronica by email
	per ferrovia by rail
	per telefono by phone
	per errore by mistake
(so as) to	**L'ho fatto per aiutarti** I did it to help you
	Si è chinato per prenderlo He bent down to get it
out of	**Ci sono andato per abitudine** I went out of habit
	Non l'ho fatto per pigrizia
	I didn't do it out of laziness
distribution	**uno per uno** one by one
	giorno per giorno day by day
	una per volta one at a time
	due per tre two times three

prima di

before (+*noun*, *pronoun*)	**prime delle sette** before seven
	prima di me before me
+ *infin*	**prima di cominciare** before starting
until	**Non sarà pronto prima delle otto**
	It won't be ready until eight o'clock

senza

without	**Esci senza cappotto?**
	Are you going out without a coat?
+ *pronoun* (add **di**)	**senza di te** without you
+ *infinitive*	**È uscito senza dire niente**
	He went out without saying anything

Prepositions

sopra

over   **le donne sopra i sessant'anni** women over sixty

above   **cento metri sopra il livello del mare**
                       a hundred metres above sea level

on top of   **sopra l'armadio** on top of the cupboard

su*

on   **sul pavimento** on the floor
                      sulla sinistra on the left
                      un libro sugli animali a book on animals

in   **sul giornale** in the paper

out of (*ratio*)   **in tre casi su dieci** in three cases out of ten
                      due giorni su tre two days out of three

approximation   **sui cinquecento euro** around five hundred euros
                      È sulla trentina She's about thirty

* **su** combines with the definite article to make one word

verso

towards (*place*)   **Correva verso l'uscita**
                      He was running towards the exit

about   **Arriverò verso le sette** I'll arrive about seven

Conjunctions

Some conjunctions introduce a main clause, e.g. **e** (and), **ma** (but), **o** (or). Others introduce subordinate clauses, e.g. **perché** (because), **mentre** (while), **quando** (when), **se** (if). Conjunctions also link single words. Most are used in much the same way as in English, but note the following:

e and
When followed by a vowel, **e** often becomes **ed** → ❶

> Some Italian conjunctions have to be followed by the subjunctive, see page 66

> Some conjunctions are split in Italian, like 'both ... and', 'either ... or' in English.
> **o ... o** either ... or → ❷
> **né ... né** neither ... nor, either ... or → ❸
> **sia ... che** both ... and → ❹

In Italian, sentences with split conjunctions can have a singular or a plural verb → ❺

che that
- is followed by the indicative in statements → ❻
- is followed by the subjunctive after verbs expressing uncertainty, see page 64

perché because, so that
When **perché** means 'because' it is followed by the indicative → ❼
When it means 'so that', it is followed by the subjunctive → ❽

Note that **perché?** can also be used as an adverb with the meaning 'why?'

se if, whether
When used in conditional clauses **se** is followed by the subjunctive → ❾
Followed by the infinitive, **se** means 'whether to' → ❿
Followed by the indicative **se** expresses doubt → ⑪

Conjunctions are sometimes used in phrases where a verb is understood → ⑫

Examples

1 mia sorella ed io — my sister and I
È venuto qui ed è rimasto mezzora — He came here and stayed for half an hour

2 o oggi o domani — either today or tomorrow

3 Non mi hanno chiamato né Claudio né Luca — Neither Claudio nor Luca has phoned me
Non avevo né guanti né scarponi — I didn't have either gloves or boots

4 Verrano sia Luigi che suo fratello — Both Luigi and his brother are coming

5 Non vengono or Non viene né lui né sua moglie — Neither he nor his wife is coming

6 Ha detto che farà tardi — He said that he'll be late

7 Sono uscita perché faceva bel tempo — I went out because it was nice weather

8 Gliel'ho dato perché lo leggesse — I gave it him so that he could read it

9 se fosse qui — if he was here
Se avessi studiato avresti passato l'esame — If you'd worked you would have passed the exam

10 Non so se andarci o no — I don't know whether to go or not

11 Mi chiedo se avresti accettato — I wonder if you would have accepted

12 Ti dispiace? – Ma no! — Do you mind? – Of course I don't!
Ho fame. – Anch'io! — I'm hungry. – So am I!
Sì, lo so – strano però — Yes, I know – it's odd though

Sentence structure

Word Order

Word order in Italian is very flexible, but:

- unstressed object pronouns always come before the verb, except when attached to the end of an infinitive or an imperative → **1**
  For details see pages 166

- most adjectives come after the noun → **2**
  For details see pages 156

- Adverbs of frequency accompanying verbs in a simple tense usually follow the verb, and those used with a compound tense follow the auxiliary verb → **3**
  For details see pages 184

Other parts of speech, however, may be positioned to give emphasis, or make a contrast:

- the noun which is the object of a verb generally follows the verb, but for emphasis it may come first → **4**

- a question word generally comes first, but for emphasis, a noun subject or object can precede it → **5**

- adjectives generally follow the verb **essere**, but may precede it for emphasis → **6**

- unstressed object pronouns generally precede the verb, but stressed pronouns can be used instead, and these follow the verb → **7**
  For details see pages 166

- subject pronouns are not normally used, but when added for emphasis they may come before or after the verb → **8**

Examples

❶ Li vedo!   I can see them!
Me l'ha dato   He gave it to me

❷ la squadra italiana   the Italian team
un vino rosso   a red wine

❸ Ci vado spesso   I often go there
Non ci sono mai stato   I've never been there

❹ Normal order:
Non posso soffrire quel cane   I can't stand that dog
Emphatic order:
Quel cane non lo posso soffrire
note object pronoun added before the verb

❺ Normal order:
Dov'è Lidia?   Where's Lidia?
Di chi sono queste scarpe?   Whose are these shoes?
Dove metto questa borsa?   Where shall I put this bag?
Emphatic order:
Lidia, dov'è?
Queste scarpe di chi sono?
Questa borsa dove la metto?
note added object pronoun

❻ Normal order
Sono belli   They're lovely
Sei pazza   You're mad
Emphatic order:
Belli sono!   They're lovely!
Pazza sei!   You're mad!

❼ Order with unstressed pronoun:
Me l'ha dato   He gave it to me
Order with stressed pronoun:
L'ha dato a me (non a te)   He gave it to me (not to you)

❽ Unemphatic:
Cosa pensi?   What do you think?
Emphatic:
Tu cosa pensi?/Cosa pensi tu?

Negatives

In Italian, sentences are generally made negative by adding **non** before the verb → ①

di no is used after verbs such as **dire**, **credere**, **pensare** and **sperare** → ②

o no? is used to mean 'or not' → ③

noun/pronoun + **no**
no is used when making a distinction between people or things → ④

non is used in combination with other negative words such as **niente** *nothing*, **nessuno** *nobody*, **mai** *never* → ⑤

When **mai** is used with a compound tense, it usually comes between the auxiliary verb and the past participle → ⑥

When **niente** or **nessuno** are the subject of the verb they can come first, or they can follow the verb. If they come first, **non** is not used → ⑦

More than one negative word can follow a negative verb → ⑧

nessuno, nessuna no
These negative adjectives change their endings according to the letter that follows them, like the indefinite article **uno** → ⑨

non ... né .... né neither ... nor/not ... either ... or
A plural verb is required if there are two subjects → ⑩

Examples

1 Non posso venire — I can't come
Non l'ho visto — I didn't see it
Non è qui — It's not here

2 Ha detto di no — He said not
Credo di no — I don't think so
Pensa di no — He doesn't think so
Speriamo di no — Let's hope not

3 Vieni o no? — Are you coming or not?
che ti piaccia o no — whether you like it or not

4 Invito lui, lei no — I'm going to invite him, but not her
Loro hanno finito, noi no — They've finished, but we haven't
Lei è brava, io no — She's good, but I'm not
Prendo un dolce, il caffè no — I'll have a sweet, but not a coffee

5 Non ho niente — I haven't got anything/I've got nothing
Non l'ho detto a nessuno — I haven't told anyone/I've told nobody
Non ci vado mai — I never go there

6 Non l'ho mai vista — I've never seen her
Non ci siamo mai stati — We've never been there

7 Niente è cambiato — Nothing has changed
BUT
Non è cambiato niente
Nessuno vuole andarci — Nobody wants to go
BUT
Non vuole andarci nessuno

8 Non fanno mai niente — They never do anything
Non si confida mai con nessuno — He never confides in anyone
Non vendiamo più niente — We no longer sell anything

9 Nessun tipo di pianta può viverci — No type of plant can live there
Non ho nessuna voglia di farlo — I have no desire to do it
Non hanno fatto nessuno sforzo — They didn't make any effort

10 Non verranno né Anna né Maria — Neither Anna nor Maria is coming
BUT
Non invito né Anna né Maria — I'm not inviting either Anna or Maria

Question Forms

In Italian, questions differ from statements in intonation, or the use of a question mark in writing. Unlike in English, the verb forms in questions are no different from those in statements › ①

Word order

When the subject of the question is a noun, it comes either before or after the verb → ②

When the object of the question is a noun, it either comes after the verb, or comes first. In this case an object pronoun agreeing with the noun is added before the verb → ③

A subject pronoun may also be added at the end of a question, for special emphasis → ④

When answering a question, either say **sì** or **no**, or **sì** or **no** with a full statement. There is no Italian equivalent for short answers such as Yes I do, or No I don't → ⑤

Question words such as **dove?** *where?*, **chi?** *who?* **cosa?** *what?* generally come first → ⑥

However, note the following:
- a noun subject can either follow the verb, or precede the question word → ⑦
- a noun object can follow the verb, or precede the question word. In this case an object pronoun agreeing with the noun is added before the verb → ⑧
- prepositions such as **di**, **con** and **a**, must precede question words → ⑨

1 STATEMENT

Basta That's enough

Sono di qui They're from here

L'ha fatto lui He did it

Va bene That's okay

QUESTION

Basta? Is that enough?

Sono di qui? Are they from here?

L'ha fatto lui? Did he do it?

Va bene? Is that okay?

2 Tua sorella è partita? or

È partita tua sorella?

La Calabria è bella? or

È bella la Calabria?

Gli spaghetti sono buoni? or

Sono buoni gli spaghetti?

Has your sister gone?

Is Calabria beautiful?

Is the spaghetti nice?

3 Vuoi un gelato? or

Un gelato lo vuoi?

Vuoi del latte or

Un po' di latte lo vuoi?

Do you want an ice cream?

Do you want some milk?

4 Contrast

Fai il bucato?

with

Il bucato lo fai tu?

Are you doing the washing?

Will you do the washing?

5 Piove? Sì or Sì, piove

Capisci? No or No, non capisco

Is it raining? Yes or Yes, it's raining

Do you understand? No or

No, I don't

6 Dove vai?

Chi parla?

Where are you going?

Who's speaking?

7 Quanto costano queste scarpe? or

Queste scarpe, quanto costano?

Chi è quella signora? or

Quella signora, chi è?

How much are these shoes?

Who is that lady?

8 Chi pagherà il conto? or

Il conto, chi lo pagherà?

Who will pay the bill?

9 Di che colore è?

Con chi parlavi?

A cosa stai pensando?

What colour is it?

Who were you talking to?

What are you thinking about?

Question Forms *continued*

no?, vero?
no? or **vero?** is used to check that what you've said is correct, like 'isn't it?' or 'haven't you?' in English → ❶

vero is used to check a negative statement → ❷

Indirect Questions

Word order in Italian indirect questions is no different from that of statements → ❸

Tenses in indirect questions are generally the same as in English, except for the use of the perfect conditional where the present conditional is used in English → ❹

Examples

1 Hai finito, no? — You've finished, haven't you?
Questa è la tua macchina, vero? — This is your car, isn't it?

2 Non sono partiti, vero? — They haven't gone, have they?
Non fa molto male, vero? — It doesn't hurt much, does it?

3 Vorrei sapere quanto costa — I'd like to know how much it costs

Mi domando cosa pensano — I wonder what they think

4 Ha detto che non era colpa sua — He said it wasn't his fault
Ha detto che verrà — He said he'll come
Aveva detto che sarebbe venuto — He'd said he'd come

Use of numbers

Cardinal (one, two *etc*)		Ordinal (first, second *etc*)	
zero	0		
uno (una, un)	1	primo	1°
due	2	secondo	2°
tre	3	terzo	3°
quattro	4	quarto	4°
cinque	5	quinto	5°
sei	6	sesto	6°
sette	7	settimo	7°
otto	8	ottavo	8°
nove	9	nono	9°
dieci	10	decimo	10°
undici	11	undicesimo	11°
dodici	12	dodicesimo	12°
tredici	13	tredicesimo	13°
quattordici	14	quattordicesimo	14°
quindici	15	quindicesimo	15°
sedici	16	sedicesimo	16°
diciassette	17	diciassettesimo	17°
diciotto	18	diciottesimo	18°
diciannove	19	diciannovesimo	19°
venti	20	ventesimo	20°
ventuno	21	ventunesimo	21°
ventidue	22	ventiduesimo	22°
ventitré	23	ventitreesimo	23°
trenta	30	trentesimo	30°
quaranta	40	quarantesimo	40°
cinquanta	50	cinquantesimo	50°
sessanta	60	sessantesimo	60°
settanta	70	settantesimo	70°
ottanta	80	ottantesimo	80°
novanta	90	novantesimo	90°
novantanove	99	novantanovesimo	99°

Use of numbers

Cardinal

cento	100
centouno	101
(centouna, centoun)	
centodue	102
centotré	103
centodieci	110
centoquarantadue	142
duecento	200
duecentouno	201
duecentotré	203
trecento	300
quattrocento	400
cinquecento	500
seicento	600
settecento	700
ottocento	800
novecento	900
mille	1000
milleuno	1001
milleduecentodue	1202
duemila	2000
cinquemilatrecento	5300
un milione	1.000.000
due milioni	2.000.000

Ordinal

centesimo	100°
centunesimo	101°
centoduesimo	102°
centotreesimo	103°
centodecimo	110°
centoquarantaduesimo	142°
duecentesimo	200°
duecentunesimo	201°
duecentotreesimo	203°
trecentesimo	300°
quattrocentesimo	400°
cinquecentesimo	500°
seicentesimo	600°
settecentesimo	700°
ottocentesimo	800°
novecentesimo	900°
millesimo	1000°
millunesimo	1001°
milleduecentoduesimo	1202°
duemillesimo	2000°
cinquemilatrecentesimo	5300°
milionesimo	1.000.000 °
duemilionesimo	2.000.000 °

Ordinal numbers are adjectives which tell you the order in which the noun occurs (first, third, etc). They end with either **o**, or **a**, depending on whether the noun is masculine or feminine:

il 15° piano	the 15th floor	**la 24ª giornata**	the 24th day

Fractions

un mezzo	a half
un terzo	a third
due terzi	two thirds
un quarto	a quarter
tre quarti	three quarters
un quinto	a fifth
un sesto	a sixth

Other numerical expressions

zero virgola cinque (0,5)	0.5
uno virgola tre (1,3)	1.3
dieci per cento	10%
sei più due	$6 + 2$
sei meno due	$6 - 2$
due volte sei	2×6
sei diviso due	$6 \div 2$

ⓘ Note the use of commas in decimal numbers, and full stops with millions.

Other Uses

Approximate numbers
- ending in **-ina**

una ventina di DVD	about twenty DVDs
Eravamo una trentina	There were about thirty of us
È sulla quarantina	He's about forty
gente sulla cinquantina	people of around fifty

- ending in **-aio**

un centinaio di persone	about a hundred people
centinaia di volte	hundreds of times
un miglaio di casi	about a thousand cases
due miglaia di macchine	about two thousand cars

Measurements

venti metri quadri	20 square metres
venti metri cubi	20 cubic metres
un ponte lungo cento metri	a bridge 100 metres long
essere largo/alto tre metri	to be 3 metres wide/long

Miscellaneous

Abitano al numero dieci	They live at number 10
nel capitolo sei	in chapter 6
Sono a pagina tre	They're on page 3
Abitano al terzo piano	They live on the 3rd floor
Sono arrivata seconda nella gara	I came second in the competition
su una scala da uno a dieci	on a scale of one to ten

Telephone numbers

The digits in a telephone number are spoken individually:

zero zero tre nove zero sei quattro due otto uno sette sei zero due
(0039 0642817602)

tre quattro sette sette zero tre quattro nove zero cinque
(3477034905)

Use of numbers

Calendar

Che data è oggi?/ Quanti ne abbiamo oggi?	What's the date today?
È il primo maggio	It's May 1st
È il due maggio	It's May 2nd
È il ventotto febbraio	It's February 28th
Arrivano il diciannove luglio	They're arriving on July 19th

ⓘ Use cardinal numbers except for the first of the month.

Years

È nata nel 1993	She was born in 1993
il dodici febbraio duemilaotto	(on) 12th February 2008

Other expressions

negli anni sessanta	in the sixties
nel ventunesimo secolo	in the twenty-first century
in or a maggio	in May
lunedì (quindici)	on Monday (the fifteenth)
di lunedì	on Mondays
fra or tra dieci giorni	in 10 days' time
otto giorni fa	8 days ago

The time

Che ore sono?	What time is it?
È l'una	It's one o'clock
Sono le due	It's two o'clock

ⓘ Use **sono** for all times except one o'clock.

00.00	mezzanotte midnight, twelve o'clock
00.10	mezzanotte e dieci ten past midnight
00.15	mezzanotte e un quarto, mezzanotte e quindici
00.30	mezzanotte e mezza, mezzanotte e trenta
00.45	l'una meno un quarto, l'una meno quindici, mezzanotte e quarantacinque
01.00	l'una di mattina one a.m., one o'clock in the morning
01.10	l'una e dieci (di mattina)
01.15	l'una e un quarto, l'una e quindici
01.30	l'una e mezza, l'una e trenta
01.45	l'una e quarantacinque; le due meno un quarto, le due meno quindici
01.50	l'una e cinquanta, le due meno dieci
01.59	l'una e cinquantanove, le due meno un minuto
12.00	mezzogiorno, le dodici noon, twelve o'clock
12.30	mezzogiorno e mezza, mezzogiorno e trenta, le dododici e mezza
13.00	l'una (del pomeriggio), le tredici, le ore tredici
01.30	l'una e mezza/trenta (del pomeriggio), le tredici e trenta, le ore tredici e trenta
19.00	le sette (di sera), le diciannove, le ore diciannove
19.30	le sette e mezza/trenta, le diciannove e trenta, le ore diciannove e trenta

ⓘ The twenty-four hour clock is widely used in Italy.

alle diciannove *or*	at nineteen hours
alle ore diciannove	at nineteen hundred hours

A che ora venite? – Alle sette

What time are you coming?
– At seven

L'ufficio è chiuso da mezzogiorno
alle due

The office is closed from twelve
to two

alle due di notte/del
pomeriggio

at two o'clock in the morning/
afternoon; at two a.m./p.m.

alle otto di sera

at eight in the evening;
at eight p.m.

alle cinque in punto

at five o'clock sharp

verso le nove

at around nine

poco dopo mezzogiorno

shortly after noon

fra le otto e le nove

between eight and nine o'clock

Erano le tre e mezza passate

It was after half past three

Devi esserci entro le nove

You have to be there by nine

Ci vogliono tre ore

It takes three hours

Ci metto una mezz'ora

It takes me half an hour

È rimasta in bagno per un'ora

She was in the bathroom for an
hour

Li aspetto da quaranta minuti

I've been waiting for them for
forty minutes

Sono partiti qualche minuto fa

They left a few minutes ago

L'ho fatto in venti minuti

I did it in twenty minutes

Il treno arriva fra un quarto d'ora

The train arrives in a quarter of
an hour

Per quanto tempo dovremo
aspettare?

How long will we have to wait?

Beware of translating word for word. The following are examples of where Italian tends to differ from English:

> English phrasal verbs (i.e. verbs such as 'to look for'; 'to fall down') are often translated by one word in Italian → ❶

> English verbs often require a preposition where there is none in Italian, or vice versa → ❷

> Different English prepositions may be translated by the one Italian preposition → ❸

> A word which is singular in English may be plural in Italian, or vice versa → ❹

> There is no Italian equivalent for the apostrophe s and s apostrophe possessive → ❺

See also at/in/to, page 220.

The following pages look at some specific problems.

Examples

① scappare   to run away
cadere   to fall down
rendere   to give back

② pagare qc   to pay for sth
guardare qc/qn   to look at sth/sb
ascoltare qc/qn   to listen to sth/sb
dire a qn   to tell sb
ubbedire a qn   to obey sb
ricordarsi di qc/qn   to remember sth/sb

③ meravigliarsi di   to be surprised at
stufo di   fed up of/with
rubare qc a   to steal sth from
restio a   reluctant to

④ gli affari   business
i suoi capelli   his/her hair
Le lasagne sono ...   Lasagne is...
i bagagli   luggage

⑤ la macchina di mia sorella   my sister's car
       (*literally*: ... of my sister)

la camera delle ragazze   the girls' bedroom
       (*literally*... of the girls)

-ing

This is translated by the gerund in Italian:

'to be ...-ing' is sometimes translated by **stare** + *gerund*, when the verb describes something at the moment, but a simple tense is often used. A simple tense must be used when the verb refers to the future. → ❶

The past participle, not the gerund, is used for physical positions such as lying and sitting → ❷

to see/hear sb ...-ing, use an infinitive or **che** + *verb* → ❸

'-ing' can also be translated by:

- an infinitive, see page 46 → ❹
- a perfect infinitive, see page 50 → ❺
- the gerund, when used abverbially, see page 52 → ❻
- a noun → ❼

to be

'to be' is generally translated by **essere** → ❽

1. Che fai *or* stai facendo? — What are you doing?
   Che fai domani sera? — What are you doing tomorrow evening?

   Partono *or* Stanno partendo — They're leaving
   Partono alle sette — They're leaving at seven

2. Erano seduti in prima fila — They were sitting in the front row
   Era sdraiata sulla sabbia — She was lying on the sand

3. L'ho visto partire — I saw him leaving
   L'ho visto che partiva
   L'ho sentita piangere — I heard her crying
   L'ho sentita che piangeva

4. Mi piace cucinare — I like cooking
   invece di rispondere — instead of answering
   prima di partire — before leaving
   Iniziò a piovere — It started raining

5. dopo aver perso molti soldi — after losing a lot of money

6. Essendo più timida di me, non ha gli ha parlato — Being shyer than me, she didn't speak to him

7. Il fumo fa molto male — Smoking is very bad for you

8. È tardi — It's late
   Sono loro — It's them
   Siamo stanchi — We're tired

Translation problems

stare is used

- with the gerund to make continuous tenses → ①
- in perfect and pluperfect tenses of **essere**, which consist of the present/imperfect tense of **essere** + past participle of **stare** → ②
- interchangeably with **essere** when talking about locations → ③
- when talking about health → ④

In various set expressions **avere** is used (with the final **e** dropped):

aver caldo/freddo	to be hot/cold
aver fame/sete	to be hungry/thirsty
aver paura	to be afraid
aver torto/ragione	to be wrong/right

fare is used to talk about the weather → ⑤

avere is used for ages → ⑥

it is, it's

These are never translated by a pronoun in Italian → ⑦

In expressions of time, use **sono**, except for one o'clock → ⑧

To describe the weather, see above.

When 'it's' is followed by a pronoun, such as 'me', 'her' or 'them', the form of **essere** agrees with the person referred to → ⑨

can, be able

Ability is generally expressed by **potere** → ⑩

If the meaning is 'to know how to' use **sapere** → ⑪

'can' with verbs of seeing and hearing is not translated in Italian → ⑫

Examples

1. Ci sto pensando — I'm thinking about it
   Stavano chiacchierando — They were chatting

2. Non ci sono mai stata — I've never been there
   Ero stato malato — I had been ill

3. La casa sta or è sulla collina — The house is on the hill
   Sta or è fuori — It's outside

4. Sto bene, grazie — I'm fine thanks
   Sta male — He's not well

5. Che tempo fa? — What's the weather like?
   Fa caldo/freddo — It's hot/cold
   Fa bel/brutto tempo — It's nice/bad weather

6. Quanti anni hai? — How old are you?
   Ho quindici anni — I'm fifteen

7. Dammelo, è mio — Give it me, it's mine
   È molto lontano — It's a long way

8. Sono le nove — It's nine o'clock
   È l'una meno un quarto — It's a quarter to one

9. Sono io — It's me
   È lei — It's her
   Sono loro — It's them

10. Puoi venire? — Can you come?

11. Non so come spiegarlo — I can't explain it

12. Si vede il mare — You can see the sea
    Non ti sento — I can't hear you

to like

piacere, the Italian verb used to translate 'to like', means 'to be pleasing', so **Mi piace l'Italia** literally means 'Italy is pleasing to me', and **Gli animali piacciono ai bambini** means 'Animals are pleasing to children'.

Remember the following when using **piacere**:
- the thing(s) liked is/are the subject of the Italian verb → **①**
- if the thing liked is singular, the verb is singular (**piace/è piaciuto** etc): if the things liked are plural, the verb is plural (**piacciono/sono piaciuti** etc) → **②**
- **piacere** is used with **a**, or an indirect object pronoun → **③**

to

'to' is often translated by **a**, see page 190 → **④**

When telling the time, e.g. ten to six, use **meno** → **⑤**

When the meaning is 'in order to' use **per** → **⑥**

When 'to' is part of the infinitive following an adjective such as 'easy', 'difficult', 'impossible', use the Italian infinitive with **da** → **⑦**

unless the infinitive has an object → **⑧**

at/in/to

For 'in' or 'to' + a country, use the Italian preposition **in** → **⑨**

For 'in' or 'to' + a town, use the Italian preposition **a** → **⑩**

When the meaning is 'to'/'at' + someone's house/place of business use **da** → **⑪**

Examples

1. Il cane piace a mio figlio
   I cani piacciono a mio figlio

   My son likes the dog
   My son likes dogs

2. Il concerto è piaciuto a tutti
   I cioccolatini piaceranno a tutti

   Everyone liked the concert
   Everyone will like the chocolates

3. A mia madre piace molto il
   giardinaggio
   Ti piace questa canzone?
   Non gli piacciono i pomodori

   My mother likes gardening very
   much
   Do you like this song?
   He doesn't like tomatoes

4. Dallo a Patrizia

   Give it to Patrizia

5. le sei meno un quarto
   l'una meno tre minuti

   a quarter to six
   three minutes to one

6. L'ho fatto per rassicurarti
   Si è fermato per guardarlo

   I did it to reassure you
   He stopped to look at it

7. facile da capire
   impossibile da dimenticare

   easy to understand
   impossible to forget

8. È facile capirlo
   È impossibile crederci

   It's easy to understand it
   It's impossible to believe it

9. Abitano negli Stati Uniti
   Andiamo in Germania il quattro
   maggio
   una città in Cina

   They live in the United States
   We're going to Germany on
   May 4
   a city in China

10. È andato a Parigi
    Vive a Bologna

    He's gone to Paris
    He lives in Bologna

11. Andiamo da Anna
    È dal parrucchiere

    Let's go to Anna's house
    She's at the hairdresser's

General Points

Vowels and consonants are always clearly pronounced in Italian, and each syllable of a word is audible, unlike in English, where letters, and sometimes whole syllables, are often not pronounced. Compare, for example:

lettera (both **e**s are equally clear, audible **r**)
letter (2nd **e** indistinct, **r** usually not pronounced)
interessante, (5 syllables)
interesting (3 syllables)

Diphthongs

A diphthong is a glide between two vowel sounds in the same syllable. The vowels in 'say', 'go' and 'might' are diphthongs. Diphthongs are very common in English, but much less so in Italian, where most vowels are a single sound, as they are in English words such as 'top', 'back' and 'set' The diphthongs found in Italian are vowels preceded by a **y**, or a **w** sound:

ia [ja] - **chiaro**	**ua** [wa] - **sguardo**
ie [je] - **pieno**	**ue** [we] - **guerra**
io [jo] - **pioggia**	**ui** [wi] - **guidare**
iu [ju] - **chiuso**	**uo** [wo] - **fuoco**

Stress

Italian words are generally stressed on the next to the last syllable, (so two-syllable words are stressed on the first syllable, three-syllable words on the second syllable, and so on):

ca sa   set ti **ma** na
ra **gaz** zo   ge ne ral **men** te

For more details see page 180.

If the stress comes on the last vowel of a word with more than one syllable, the vowel is always written with an accent:
per **ché**
par le **rò**
un i ver si **tà**

For more details see page 180.

Pronunciation of Consonants

Most consonants are pronounced as in English, except that they are always clear, and double consonants are audible. Thus, in **sabbia** *sand*, for example, the **b** sound ending the first syllable carries on to start the second syllable: sab-bya.

Note the following:

	PRONOUNCED		EXAMPLES
c before a, o, u	[k]	like k in kiss	camera, come, cubo
c before e or i	[tʃ]	like ch in China	certo, cinese
ch	[k]	like k in kiss	chiesa
g before a, o, u	[g]	like g in good	gara, largo, gusto
g before e or i	[dʒ]	like g in rage	gelato, giro
gh	[g]	like g in good	laghi, ghiaccio
gl before i	[ʎ]	like ll in million	meglio, gli
gl before other vowels	[gl]	like gl in piglet	sigla
gn	[ɲ]	like ny in canyon	gnocchi, ragno
h is not pronounced		like h in honest	hanno
r	[r]	like r in zero	raro, rapido
sc before e or i	[ʃ]	like sh in ship	scena, sci
z	[dz]	like ds in lids	zanzarra
z	[ts]	like ts in bits	ragazzo

Pronunciation of Vowels

	PRONOUNCED		EXAMPLES
a	[a]	like a in apple	animale
e	[ɛ]	like e in set	schema
e	[e]	like ay in day	stella
i	[i]	like ee in sheep	clima
i before a vowel often	[j]	like y in yoghurt	Lidia, negozio
o	[o]	like o in pot	ora
u	[u]	like oo in soot	puro
u before a vowel often	[w]	like w in win	usuale

Stress: Cases where the normal rule does not apply

In cases where the last syllable of a word is stressed, this is shown by an accent. Most of these are:

- nouns ending in **-tà**, many of which have counterparts in English ending in -ty, such as 'reality' and 'university'

re al tà	reality	u ni ver si tà	university
fe li ci tà	happiness, felicity	fe del tà	fidelity
cu rio si tà	curiosity	fa col tà	faculty
bon tà	goodness	cit tà	city
cru del tà	cruelty	e tà	age
me tà	half		

- 1st and 3rd person singular future verbs , and 3rd person singular past historics:

sa rò	I will be
fi ni rà	it will finish
as pet te rà	she'll wait
par lò	he spoke
an dò	she went

- adverbs and conjunctions such as

perché	why
però	however
così	so

In cases where the stress is on an unexpected syllable other than the last, there is no accent to show this. In this book, such vowels are shown in italics, e.g.

macchina	car
utile	useful
portatile	laptop

Stress in present tense verb forms

All present tense forms except the 3rd person plural follow the rule, and stress the next to the last syllable, e.g. *parlo* I speak; *considera* he considers

In the 3rd person plural form the stress is not on the next to the last syllable, but matches that of the 1st person singular:

1st person singular		3rd person plural	
par lo	I speak	*par* la no	they speak
con *si* de ro	I consider	con *si* de ra no	they consider
mi al *le* no	I'm training	si al *le* na no	they're training

Stress in 2nd conjugation infinitives

Stress is regular for the infinitives of all 1st and 3rd. and many 2nd conjugation verbs, e.g. **parlare** *to speak*, **finire** *to finish*, **vedere** *to see*. However, there are also many 2nd conjugation infinitives which do not stress the 1st **e** of the **-ere** ending, eg:

essere *to be*, **vendere** *to sell*, **permettere** *to allow*, **dividere** *to divide*.

When learning 2nd conjugation verbs, note which syllable of the infinitive is stressed.

From Sounds to Spelling

Apart from the occasional problem of unexpected stress, the way Italian is spelled is a good guide to how it should be pronounced. See page 180.

It is also easy to know how to spell words, if the following points are remembered:

-care/-gare verbs

Verbs with infinitives ending -care, or -gare, for example cercare and pagare, add an h to keep the c or g hard in front of endings starting with e or i:

Vowel that follows c/g	Present of cercare		Present of pagare	
o	cerco	I look for	pago	I pay
i	cerchi	you look for	paghi	you pay
a	cerca	he/she looks for	paga	he/she pays
i	cerchiamo	we look for	paghiamo	we pay
a	cercate	you look for	pagate	you pay
a	cercano	they look for	pagano	they pay

Vowel that follows c/g	Future of cercare		Future of pagare	
e	cercherò	I'll look for	pagherò	I'll pay
e	cercherai	you'll look for	pagherai	you'll pay
e	cercherà	he/she will look for	pagherà	he/she will pay
e	cercheremo	we'll look for	pagheremo	we'll pay
e	cercherete	you'll look for	pagherete	you'll pay
e	cercheranno	they'll look for	pagheranno	they'll pay

-ca/-ga nouns and adjectives

Nouns and adjectives ending in -ca and -ga always keep the hard sound of the consonant in the plural, so h is added before the plural ending -e:

Singular		Plural	
amica	friend	**amiche**	friends
riga	line	**righe**	lines
ricca	rich	**ricche**	rich
lunga	long	**lunghe**	long

-co/-go nouns and adjectives

Some nouns and adjectives ending in **-co** and **-go** keep the hard sound of the consonant in the plural, so **h** is added before the plural ending **-i**, e.g.:

Singular		Plural	
fuoco	fire	**fuochi**	fires
albergo	hotel	**alberghi**	hotels
ricco	rich	**ricchi**	rich
lungo	long	**lunghi**	long

Other nouns nouns and adjectives ending in **-co** and **-go** change the sound of the consonant in the plural from hard [k] or [g] to soft [tʃ] or [dʒ], so no **h** is added, e.g.:

Singular		Plural	
amico	friend	**amici**	friends
astrologo	astrologer	**astrologi**	astrologers
greco	Greek	**greci**	Greek
psicologico	psychological	**psicologici**	psychological

-io nouns

The plural of nouns ending **-io** is spelled **-ii** if the **i** of the **-io** ending is a stressed vowel, e.g. **zio** *uncle* plural: **zii**, and **invio** *dispatch* plural: **invii**.

In cases where the **i** of the **-io** is not a stressed vowel, but is pronounced [j], the plural is spelled with a single **i**, e.g. **occhio** *eye* plural **occhi**; **figlio** *son* plural: **figli**.

-cia/-gia nouns

Generally, if the i of the **-cia/-gia** ending of a noun is a stressed vowel, the i is retained in the plural, eg **farmacia** *chemist* plural: **farmacie**; **bugia** *lie* plural: **bugie**. If the i of the ending serves to keep the **c/g** soft, and is not pronounced as a vowel, there is no i in the plural: **faccia** *face*, plural: **facce**; **spiaggia** *beach*, plural: **spiagge**.

Accents

Use an accent when a word is stressed on the final syllable, e.g. **città**, **cercherò**, **università**. See page 180.

Accents are also used on certain one-syllable words to distinguish them from words that are spelled the same (homophones):

da	from	**dà**	he/she gives
e	and	**è**	is
la	the/it	**là**	there
li	them	**lì**	there
ne	of it/them	**né**	neither
se	if	**sé**	himself
si	himself/herself/one	**sì**	yes
te	you	**tè**	tea

The grave accent (à, è, ì, ò ,ù) is used on most words. The acute accent is used to spell conjunctions ending in **che**, such as **benché** *although*, and **perché** *because*. It is also used on **né** and **sé** (except in the phrases **se stesso** and **se stessa** *himself; herself*).

può, **già**, **ciò**, **più** and **giù** are spelled with an accent, for no obvious reason.

Alphabet

The Alphabet

A,a	a	J,j	[i'lunga]	S,s	['ɛsse]
B,b	[bi]	K,k	['kappa]	T,t	[ti]
C,c	[tʃi]	L,l	['ɛlle]	U,u	u
D,d	[di]	M,m	['ɛmme]	V,v	[vi, vu]
E,e	e	N,n	['ɛnne]	W,w	['dɔppjovu]
F,f	['ɛffe]	O,o	[ɔ]	X,x	[iks]
G,g	[dʒi]	P,p	[pi]	Y,y	['ipsilon]
H,h	['akka]	Q,q	[ku]	Z,z	[dzɛta]
I,i	i	R,r	['ɛrre]		

Capital letters are used as in English except for the following:

adjectives of nationality
e.g. una città tedesca — a German town
una scrittrice italiana — an Italian writer

languages
e.g. Parla inglese? — Do you speak English?
Parlo francese ed italiano — I speak French and Italian

days of the week:
lunedì Monday
martedì Tuesday
mercoledì Wednesday
giovedì Thursday
venerdì Friday
sabato Saturday
domenica Sunday

months of the year:
gennaio January
febbraio February
marzo March
aprile April
maggio May
giugno June
luglio July
agosto August
settembre September
ottobre October
novembre November
dicembre December

Index

The following index lists comprehensively both grammatical terms and key words in English and Italian.

Index

index

Index

Index